LABOUR LAW

Labour Law

Fourth edition

Simon Deakin MA, PhD
Robert Monks Professor of Corporate Governance and Fellow of Peterhouse,
University of Cambridge.

Gillian S Morris LLB, PhD
Former Professor of Law, now Professor Associate, Brunel University;
Barrister, Matrix Chambers.

·HART·
PUBLISHING
HART PUBLISHING
OXFORD AND PORTLAND, OREGON
2005

Published in North America (US and Canada) by
Hart Publishing
c/o International Specialized Book Services
920 NE 58th Avenue, Suite 300
Portland, OR 97213-3786
USA
Tel: +1 503 287 3093 or toll-free: (1) 800 944 6190
Fax: +1 503 280 8832
E-mail: orders@isbs.com
Web Site: www.isbs.com

Hart Publishing, Salters Boatyard, Folly Bridge, Abingdon Rd, Oxford, OX1 4LB
Telephone: +44 (0)1865 245533 Fax: +44 (0) 1865 794882
email: mail@hartpub.co.uk
WEBSITE: http//:www.hartpub.co.uk

British Library Cataloguing in Publication Data
Data Available
ISBN-13: 978-1-84113-560-1 (paperback)
ISBN-10: 1-84113-560-7 (paperback)

Edited and typeset by Rebecca Forster, in Sabon 10/11 pt
Printed and bound in Great Britain by
Page Bros, Norwich

Preface

In writing this book we have been influenced by a tradition of labour law scholarship which, as we explain in Chapter 1, views this branch of the law as indissolubly linked to the goals of social policy. How labour law operates as a mechanism for the expression of those goals involves a consideration of many wider social, economic and philosophical issues than a book such as this can hope adequately to address. Nevertheless, an essential first step in attaining a wider understanding of labour law is to explain its internal conceptual structure. Accordingly, our foremost aim has been to produce a text which, without being encyclopædic, is broadly comprehensive in nature and so can serve as a resource in the teaching of labour law in universities. We have been pleased to find that what we have had to say in previous editions has also been of interest to practitioners of labour law in the legal and other interested professions, and we hope to continue to address this group in future.

We have sought to explain the contemporary law in a way which brings out the dynamic and continuously evolving nature of doctrine in this area, and, in particular, to show how it is shaped by the interaction between the principal sources of labour law (the common law, collective bargaining, social legislation and transnational labour standards). To that end we have attempted to locate the law in its historical context; to make selective use, where appropriate, of comparative and international material; to consider areas of labour market regulation which are closely related to labour law (such as active labour market policy and aspects of tax and social security law); and to discuss, where relevant, theories and accounts of the law's economic and social impact. At various points we have, perhaps, been able to do no more than indicate further lines of inquiry for those who may be interested in considering these dimensions of the subject; but if we are able to whet the appetite of readers in this way, we shall be content.

Our aim throughout has been to integrate our account of legal doctrine with analysis of law and policy. We have attempted to make the text more digestible by the use of numbered paragraphs and sub-headings. We also conclude our analyses of areas of the law with assessment sections, either within or at the end of chapters, whose purpose is to provide a critical evaluation of those areas.

We are grateful for all the support and encouragement we have received from our publishers.

In April 2000 one of us, Gillian Morris, was appointed a deputy chairman of the CAC. This work is written entirely in a personal capacity and its contents should not be taken to represent the views of the CAC unless indicated otherwise in the text.

For the sake of clarity we have used the nomenclature of the Civil Procedure Rules throughout, regardless of whether the case with which we are concerned was subject to these rules. Thus, 'plaintiffs' become 'claimants' and 'interlocutory' injunctions are 'interim'. We also refer to 'employment' tribunals throughout.

The law of England and Wales is stated as at 6 April 2005, although it has been possible to include some amendments since that date.

SFD
GSM
24 June 2005.

Contents

Table of statutes

List of cases

Table of abbreviations

ACAS	Advisory, Conciliation and Arbitration Service
BFOQ	Bona Fide Occupational Qualification
CA	Court of Appeal
CAC	Central Arbitration Committee
CBI	Confederation of British Industry
CIE	Committee of Independent Experts
CO	Certification Officer
CPR	Civil Procedure Rules
CRE	Commission for Racial Equality
CROTUM	Commissioner for the Rights of Trade Union Members
DEFRA	Department for Environment, Food and Rural Affairs
DfEE	Department for Education and Employment
DPP	Director of Public Prosecutions
DWP	Department of Work and Pensions
DRC	Disability Rights Commission
DTI	Department of Trade and Industry
EAT	Employment Appeal Tribunal
EC	European Community
ECHR	European Convention on Human Rights
ECtHR	European Court of Human Rights
ECJ	European Court of Justice
ECSR	European Committee of Social Rights
EDT	Effective Date of Termination
EEC	European Economic Community
EOC	Equal Opportunities Commission
ESC	European Social Charter
ESOP	Employee Share Ownership Plan
ET	Employment Tribunal
ETOR	Economic, Technical or Organisational Reason
ETS	Employment Tribunals Service
EU	European Union
EWC	European Works Council
GCHQ	Government Communications Headquarters
GMP	Guaranteed Minimum Pension
GOQ	Genuine Occupational Qualification
GOR	Genuine Occupational Requirement
HL	House of Lords
HSC	Health and Safety Commission
HSE	Health and Safety Executive
ICESCR	International Covenant on Economic, Social and Cultural Rights
ICCPR	International Covenant on Civil and Political Rights
ICP	Information and Consultation Procedure
ILO	International Labour Organisation

I and C	Information and Consultation
JCHR	Joint Committee on Human Rights
JIC	Joint Industrial Council
NEDC	National Economic Development Council
NHS	National Health Service
NI CA	Court of Appeal, Northern Ireland
NIRC	National Industrial Relations Court
OMC	Open Method of Coordination
OPB	Occupational Pensions Board
OPRA	Occupational Pensions Regulatory Authority
QIP	Qualified Independent Person
SAYE	Save as You Earn Share Options Scheme
SE	Societas Europaea (European Company)
SERPS	State Earnings-Related Pension Scheme
SDDP	Statutory Dismissal and Disciplinary Procedure
SGP	Statutory Grievance Procedure
SMP	Statutory Maternity Pay
SNB	Special Negotiating Body
SOSR	Some Other Substantial Reason
SSP	Statutory Sick Pay
TEC	Training and Enterprise Council
TUC	Trades Union Congress
ULR	Union Learning Representative

LEGISLATION

CA	Companies Act
CJPOA	Criminal Justice and Public Order Act
CPA	Civil Partnership Act
DCOA	Deregulation and Contracting Out Act
DDA	Disability Discrimination Act
DPA	Data Protection Act
DRCA	Disability Rights Commission Act
EA	Employment Act
EADRR	Employment Act 2002 (Dispute Resolution) Regulations
EE(RB)R	Employment Equality (Religion or Belief) Regulations
EE(SO)R	Employment Equality (Sexual Orientation) Regulations
EPA	Employment Protection Act
EPCA	Employment Protection (Consolidation) Act
EPLLCR	European Public Limited-Liability Company Regulations
EqPA	Equal Pay Act
ERDRA	Employment Rights (Dispute Resolution) Act
ERelA	Employment Relations Act
ETA	Employment Tribunals Act
FTER	Fixed Term Employees (Prevention of Less Favourable Treatment) Regulations
FWER	Flexible Working (Eligibility, Complaints and Remedies) Regulations
FWPR	Flexible Working (Procedural Requirements) Regulations
GRA	Gender Recognition Act

HRA	Human Rights Act
HSWA	Health and Safety at Work etc Act
IA	Insolvency Act
ICER	Information and Consultation of Employees Regulations
ICTA	Income and Corporation Taxes Act
IRA	Industrial Relations Act
LGA	Local Government Act
MHSW	Management of Health and Safety at Work Regulations
MPLR	Maternity and Parental Leave etc Regulations
NIA	National Insurance Act
NMWA	National Minimum Wage Act
NMWR	National Minimum Wage Regulations
PA	Pensions Act
PALR	Paternity and Adoption Leave Regulations
PSA	Pension Schemes Act
PTWR	Part-Time Workers (Prevention of Less Favourable Treatment) Regulations
RIPA	Regulation of Investigatory Powers Act
RR(Am)A	Race Relations (Amendment) Act
RRA	Race Relations Act
SDA	Sex Discrimination Act
SPPR	Statutory Paternity Pay and Statutory Adoption Pay (General) Regulations
SSA	Social Security Act
SSAA	Social Security Administration Act
SSCBA	Social Security Contributions and Benefits Act
SSFA	Schools Standards and Framework Act
SSPA	Statutory Sick Pay Act
TCA	Tax Credits Act
TDA	Trade Disputes Act
TICER	Transnational Information and Consultation of Employees Regulations
TUA	Trade Union Act
TULRA	Trade Union and Labour Relations Act
TULRCA	Trade Union and Labour Relations (Consolidation) Act
TUPE	Transfer of Undertakings (Protection of Employment) Regulations
TURERA	Trade Union Reform and Employment Rights Act
UCTA	Unfair Contract Terms Act
WA	Wages Act
WTR	Working Time Regulations

CHAPTER 1

Introduction

LABOUR LAW: THE SCOPE AND NATURE OF THE SUBJECT

Labour law as a discipline

1.1   The discipline of *labour law* is defined in part by its subject-matter, in part by an intellectual tradition. Its immediate subject-matter consists of the rules which govern the employment relationship. However, a broader perspective would see labour law as the normative framework for the existence and operation of all the institutions of the labour market: the business enterprise, trade unions, employers' associations and, in its capacity as regulator and as employer, the state. The starting point for analysis is the existence of the employment relationship as a distinct economic and legal category. Labour law stems from the idea of 'the subordination of the individual worker to the capitalist enterprise';[1] it is above all the law of *dependent labour*, and hence is specific to those categories of economic relationship which in some way involve the exchange of *personal service or services* for remuneration. Labour law is concerned with how these relationships are constituted, a role which in common law systems is accorded primarily to contract, and with how they are regulated, a role shared by the common law and social legislation but also by extra-legal sources such as collective bargaining and workplace custom and practice. Its scope accordingly extends from the individual to the collective, from the contract of employment to relations between the institutions of organised labour and capital, and to the conduct and resolution of conflicts between them.

The intellectual tradition to which we referred sees *labour law* as a unified discipline which has outgrown its diverse origins in the law of obligations and in the regulatory intervention of the state. As a subject with its own doctrinal unity and structure, it spans the divides between common law and legislation and between private law and public law. In Britain, as elsewhere in Europe, it has established itself as one of the principal branches of legal studies.[2] The view that labour law is more than just the sum of its parts is derived initially from the writings of German jurists in the early decades of the twentieth century, who saw the subject as the embodiment of social policy in action. This view, which at its broadest implied that labour law should embrace 'sociology, social policy and the theory of business organisation',[3] came to influence the study of labour law in Britain through the writings of Sir Otto Kahn-Freund who, having been

---

1   Hepple, 1986a: p 11.
2   We will from time to time refer to 'labour law in Britain' or 'British labour law', while being fully aware that there is no such thing as 'British law'. The case for referring to 'British labour law' is that while the common law is, of course, the common law of England and Wales, labour legislation (like that of social security) is by and large general to both the legal systems of Great Britain. We do not, however, seek to discuss the distinctive features of the Scottish legal system or those principles of Scottish law which differ from those of the law of England and Wales.
3   Sinzheimer, 1910–1911, cited in Hepple, 1986a: p 9.

1

a labour court judge in the Germany of the Weimar Republic, lived and taught in Britain from the 1930s. His conception of the subject stressed the functional inter-dependence of the positive law with extra-legal sources of regulation, in particular collective bargaining: his contribution 'revolutionised the study, the teaching and the very character of labour law in Britain'.[4] This perspective remains valid today, notwithstanding the enormous changes which have taken place in the form and content of labour law since Kahn-Freund elaborated his theory of the subject in writings of the 1950s[5] which were to have a major impact not just on scholarship but also on the courts[6] and on the formulation of public policy in this area.[7]

Although the notion of labour law as the normative framework for the institutions of the labour market has commanded increasing attention in recent years,[8] it should be borne in mind that other, closely-related areas of law are also important determinants of labour market outcomes. For reasons of space, and also because these other areas are dealt with in specialist works in the fields concerned, we do not aim to provide a comprehensive treatment of each of them in this book. However, an understanding of *social security law* is essential to an appreciation of many important aspects of the employment relationship, including the impact of social security contributions on the earnings of the individual employee and the entitlements of the unemployed and those seeking work to the receipt of social security benefits. We have included material on the relevant principles of social security law[9] where their relationship with labour law is particularly close. However, it should be remembered that social security law constitutes a body of principle which is studied in its own right,[10] since it extends far beyond the employment relationship to embrace, in a wider sense, many aspects of the relationship between the citizen and the state in the distribution of economic resources. Very much the same point applies to the *law of taxation*, which also has a major impact on the employment relationship through the incidence of income tax and also on occupational pension rights,[11] but which again extends to a far broader field of public policy issues. From a slightly different perspective, it is also evident that labour law intersects with *company law*, and that some awareness of company law principles is central to an understanding of the legal nature of the business enterprise. Again, where appropriate we highlight the significance of company law and of the increasingly important area of corporate governance, in particular in our discussion of the labour law concept of the 'employer' and its relationship to company law notions of the enterprise and of its constituent elements.[12]

The techniques of *comparative law* have provided one of the most important tools of analysis of national labour law systems, and have greatly enhanced the

---

4   Wedderburn, 1983: p 29. For further analysis of Kahn-Freund's contribution, see para 1.10 below.
5   Kahn-Freund, 1954a, 1954b, 1959.
6   *Ford Motor Co Ltd v AUEFW* [1969] 2 QB 303.
7   Most notably in the Report of the Royal Commission on Trade Unions and Employers' Associations (the 'Donovan Report'), Cmnd 3623, 1968.
8   P Davies and M Freedland, 1984; Szyszczak, 1986; H Collins, 1989; Deakin and Wilkinson, 1991; Mitchell, 1995; H Collins et al, 2000; Deakin and Wilkinson, 2005.
9   See paras 3.16–3.17 (active labour market policy); paras 4.115–4.127 (occupational pension schemes); and paras 11.86–11.88 (industrial action and social security benefits).
10 See Wikeley, 2002; N Harris, 2000.
11 See paras 3.22–3.23 and 4.118–4.120 respectively.
12 See paras 3.94–3.98 below.

theory of labour law.[13] The study of comparative labour law has increased in importance in recent years largely because of the growing tendency towards international economic integration, and the development of transnational labour standards which draw on a number of different national traditions and methods. In the case of labour law in Britain, the growing influence of European Community standards has brought with it a heightened awareness of other European systems. In this work we do not purport to offer systematic comparative analyses of the issues we examine, but we make selective use of comparative material in constructing the framework for our analysis and to indicate, where it is possible to do so, how distinctive legal solutions are possible to what are frequently common problems.

Following the tradition begun by the German *sozialjuristen*, many British labour law scholars have attempted to integrate into their work the insights of other social science disciplines. The influence of industrial sociology has been most widely felt, in large part because of the close links which have long existed between labour law and the study of industrial relations. More recently, growing use has been made of labour economics, feminist legal theory, and political theory.[14] The principal aim of this book is to analyse the conceptual and doctrinal structure of labour law and to examine its application to concrete problems of the kind which frequently arise in practice, rather than to present labour law from the viewpoint of another social science discipline. We have taken this approach in the belief that a thorough explication of labour law doctrine is essential, in order for labour law to be understood both as a *juridical* and as a *social and economic* phenomenon. At the same time, we do not believe that an effective doctrinal account of this area can be provided without close consideration being given to the influence upon the law of ideas drawn from economics and social policy, and we will therefore make reference to those influences wherever appropriate in the text that follows.

The structure of this book

1.2　Certain divisions of the legal material which forms labour law have become generally accepted. A broad division is taken to exist between 'individual labour law', the law relating in a narrow sense to the relationship of employer and employee, and 'collective labour law', or the law which is concerned with collective bargaining, trade union organisation and industrial action. In practice, the 'individual' and 'collective' aspects of the subject are closely interlinked and, we would suggest, cannot be adequately considered in isolation from one another. For example, in analysing the individual employment relationship, it is necessary to take into account the influence of norms which are derived from collective sources, in particular collective bargaining.[15] Conversely, the contract of employment plays a fundamental role in relation to the economic torts and other aspects of the law governing industrial action.[16]

This does not mean that the generally-accepted classifications are not useful for the purposes of organisation and exposition of the subject. Although other

---

13　On the advantages but also the pitfalls of comparative analysis of labour law, see Kahn-Freund, 1972.
14　For a review, see H Collins, 1997.
15　See ch 4 below, in particular paras 4.26–4.30.
16　See paras 11.10 *et seq* and 11.63 *et seq*.

sub-divisions of the subject are possible,[17] we believe that there is much to be said for retaining a framework which will be broadly familiar to labour law scholars and practitioners alike. Nevertheless, within this framework, we have attempted to integrate 'individual' and 'collective' aspects of the subject wherever possible in the treatment of particular issues.

We also take the view that an appreciation of the historical development of the labour law system is essential to an understanding of its current form and content. This is particularly so with regard to the inter-relationship between the principal *sources* of labour law, namely the common law, social legislation and non-formal sources including collective bargaining and workplace custom and practice. We therefore preface our analysis of the substantive law with two introductory chapters. The remainder of this chapter examines in historical perspective some core themes of labour law in Britain and concludes by posing the question: what is the rationale of contemporary labour law? Here we analyse two apparently competing conceptions of labour law as promoting economic efficiency, on the one hand, and as protecting fundamental social and economic rights, on the other.

Chapter 2 is concerned with sources and institutions of labour law. Here we examine in greater detail the relationship between formal sources of law, in particular the common law and legislation, and what we term 'voluntary' sources, of which collective bargaining is the most significant. This chapter also explains the nature of institutions which are particular to labour law, including the employment tribunal system and forms of administrative intervention in employment relations. We also outline the role of EC law within labour law and consider the influence of other international labour standards.

The rest of the book is devoted to the study of areas of substantive legal doctrine. Chapter 3 analyses the law governing the formation and constitution of the employment relationship. Chapters 4 and 5 then examine the contents of that relationship: chapter 4 is concerned with the law governing terms and conditions of employment, and chapter 5 with the subject of discipline and termination of employment. Chapter 6 is devoted to the analysis of equal treatment in employment. Chapter 7 provides an overview of the law relating to collective organisation by both workers and employers, and thereby provides a framework for chapters 8 to 10 which examine specific aspects of collective relationships. Chapter 8 examines the law relating to freedom of association, chapter 9 collective representation and the law, and chapter 10 the law relating to trade unions and their members. Finally, in chapter 11 we analyse the legal implications at both collective and individual levels of industrial action.

Labour law, collective bargaining and labour standards

1.3   A theme to which we will return at numerous points is the role of collective bargaining in relation to social legislation, and it may be useful to clarify at the outset our use of some key terms. By *collective bargaining* we mean the process of negotiation between an employer or group of employers on the one hand and one or more trade unions on the other, designed to produce *collective agreements* which may have a number of functions. Two functions of collective agreements are particularly important: the *procedural* or *contractual* function of regulating the relationship between the collective parties themselves; and the *normative* or

---

17   For discussion of a treatment of the subject which would see labour law more clearly as a form of regulation of the labour market, see Mitchell, 1995.

rule-making function, which consists of the establishment of terms and conditions which are applicable to the contracts of individual workers. Collective agreements may operate on a number of levels. *Sector-level bargaining* refers to a process of negotiation which takes place at the level of a particular trade or industry, normally between an employers' association and one or more trade unions. This form of bargaining, once prevalent in Britain, is now rare. It is more usual for bargaining to take place either at the level of the *company* or *enterprise*, or, within companies, at the level of the *plant* or *establishment*.

The term *social legislation* refers, broadly, to legislation in the field of employment, which may be one of two types.[18] *Regulatory legislation* directly affects employment relationships, typically by laying down statutory norms which override the parties' own agreement. Examples include minimum wage legislation and legislation limiting the power of the employer to terminate the relationship (unfair dismissal legislation). *Auxiliary legislation*, by contrast, consists of legal supports for the process of collective bargaining and other aspects of collective organisation; in this sense its impact on the employment relationship is indirect. Examples of such legislation include laws which may require employers to recognise trade unions for the purpose of collective bargaining, and laws which oblige employers to consult with or give information to representatives of the workforce.

It can be seen from this analysis that *labour standards* – the protective norms which govern the employment relationship – can derive either from legal sources (legislation or, more exceptionally, the common law) or from extra-legal sources, of which collective bargaining is one of the most significant. Moreover, the balance between regulatory and auxiliary legislation is an important determinant of the extent to which the state supports or, alternatively, displaces collective bargaining as a form of regulation.

HISTORICAL DEVELOPMENT

1.4 Our intention here is to offer a brief historical outline of the evolution of labour law which is more thematic than chronological in nature.[19] We consider in turn five central themes in the development of labour law: collective organisation, and the attitude towards it of the common law; the relationship between collective bargaining and social legislation; the evolution of the employment relationship; the impact on collective bargaining of wider forms of state intervention in and management of the economy, in particular state corporatism; and legal policies aimed at enhancing the flexibility of the labour market.

Collective organisation and the common law

1.5 The common law has traditionally been hostile to the collective self-organisation of workers, and it is only by means of statutory intervention, in

---

18 The distinction between regulatory and auxiliary legislation was developed by Kahn-Freund: see P Davies and M Freedland, 1983: ch 2.
19 The subject of labour law history is an important and growing field in its own right. On the eighteenth and nineteenth centuries, see Orth, 1991; on wartime labour law, Rubin, 1987; on the development of the contract of employment, Deakin, 1998, 2000, and Deakin and Wilkinson, 2005; on the modern period, P Davies and M Freedland, 1993; and for a brief overview, Ewing and Morris, 2000.

the form of 'immunities' from common law liability, that a space has been created within which trade unions, in particular, may operate lawfully for the purposes of collective bargaining and activities associated with it, such as the conduct of industrial action and the regulation of particular trades and occupations. The hostility of the common law to collectivist values is deep-rooted, and has been expressed in a number of different legal doctrines: these include the crime (and later the tort) of conspiracy, the doctrine of restraint of trade as a ground for the invalidation of contracts, and the economic torts which protect the trade and livelihood of individuals and businesses against direct or intentional interference. One of the most remarkable features of this aspect of the common law is that it has been maintained in one form or another practically throughout the modern period, and notwithstanding periodic changes in the attitude of the legislature.

The corporative system and its decline

1.6   As late as the middle of the eighteenth century, the labour market continued to be regulated by a 'corporative' system involving controls over prices, wages, labour mobility and training, the cornerstone of which was the Statute of Artificers of 1562.[20] Wage regulation was still formally the responsibility of the local magistrates in agriculture and of the guilds in the urban trades; related legislation governed poor relief and the right to a parish settlement. The corporative system purported to guarantee workers a certain degree of wage stability and occupational protection, but at the same time restricted labour mobility and effectively outlawed strikes and combinations of workers designed to maintain and improve terms and conditions of employment. Such combinations constituted a criminal conspiracy at common law.[21] In addition, numerous Acts of Parliament from the 1720s onwards outlawed associations of journeymen and apprentices aimed at raising wages or reducing hours. The first of these measures was an Act of 1720 'for regulating the journeymen tailors' in London, which followed the formation of the London Journeymen Tailors' Union and a strike of the preceding year. The Act made agreements for the purpose of advancing wages or reducing hours null and void, and made it an offence subject to two months' imprisonment to enter into such agreements. It was also made an offence for a journeyman tailor to leave work unfinished or to quit before the end of his agreed term of employment. Similar legislation, dealing with combinations or work discipline or both, followed for individual trades, and a more general anti-combination law was passed in 1749[22] covering several expanding manufacturing trades including cotton and iron. These laws assumed that combinations to raise wages were unlawful at common law – it was 'contrary to law' for the journeymen weavers 'to enter into combinations, and to make by-laws or orders, by which they pretend to regulate the trade and prices of their goods, and to advance their wages unreasonably'[23] – but the Acts had the advantage over the common law of providing for a summary procedure for conviction. In contrast, common law actions for criminal conspiracy were less

---

20   This Act, in turn, contained elements derived from the first formal labour statutes of the middle ages, the Ordinance of Labourers of 1349 and the Statute of Labourers of 1351. See Deakin and Wilkinson, 2005: pp 44–61.
21   *R v Journeymen-Tailors of Cambridge* (1721) 8 Mod 10.
22   22 Geo II c 27.
23   12 Geo I c 34.

straightforward to argue and more expensive to bring.[24] The Combination Acts of 1799 and 1800, which imposed a general ban on combinations, went further still by empowering justices to grant a licence to employers to take on labour contrary to the apprenticeship rules of the Statute of Artificers of 1562 and related legislation, in any case where combinations of workmen struck for higher wages or interfered with business, or where:

> ... the qualified journeymen and workmen usually employed in any manufacture, trade or business, shall refuse to work therein for reasonable wages, or to work for any particular person or persons, or to work with any particular persons, or shall, by refusing to work for any cause whatsoever, or by misconducting themselves when employed to work, in any manner impede or obstruct the ordinary course of any manufacture, trade or business, or endeavour to injure the person or persons carrying on the same.[25]

Shortly after, the protective provisions of the corporative system were formally repealed. The wage-regulation provisions of the Statute of Artificers were repealed in 1813 and the repeal of the apprenticeship regulations followed a year later. They had already been eroded by restrictive judicial interpretations,[26] and had fallen into disuse in large parts of agriculture and industry. However, they were not abandoned without a struggle: in 1812–1813 the London artisans' associations mounted a substantial but unsuccessful campaign for the preservation of the regulations, through which they had been able to control entry into the trade and regulate competition and the setting of prices. It was in part as a consequence of these reforms that major employers were prepared to acquiesce in the repeal of the Combination Acts in 1824.[27] However, when this repeal led to (or at least coincided with) a wave of strikes, a second Act was passed in 1825 which reimposed certain criminal sanctions in respect of picketing and activities designed to persuade workers not to work.[28] A further measure, the Molestation of Workmen Act 1859, slightly ameliorated the restraints thereby imposed. For the fifty years or so after 1825 the legal position was, in principle, that freedom of association was permitted, and that collective bargaining could be lawfully pursued; however, strike action remained tightly confined. In practice, there was no effective right to resist employers who refused to enter into collective bargaining since the main weapon open to trade unions, namely strike action, was regulated by the criminal law. The criminal law also imposed sanctions on individual workers who quit their employment in breach of contract, by virtue of the Master and Servant Act 1823 which was the successor to a number of eighteenth-century statutes which had a similar effect.

The decriminalisation of labour law

1.7 It was not until the 'legislative settlement' of the 1870s that legislation lifted the threat of criminal sanctions from all but violent forms of behaviour associated with industrial action. The first breach in the restrictive labour laws of the early and mid-nineteenth century was the Master and Servant Act of 1867, which was intended to make imprisonment of workers for breach of

---

24 Orth, 1991: ch 4.
25 39 & 40 Geo III c 106, s 15. For further details on this legislation, see para 7.12 below.
26 *Raynard v Chase* (1756) 1 Burr 2; *Smith v Company of Armourers* (1792) Peake 199.
27 'Such a relaxed view was consistent with them having achieved mastery in their own establishments': Moher, 1989: p 241.
28 See Orth, 1991: ch 5.

contract a measure of last resort, available only for 'aggravated' misconduct and for damage to persons or property, with a fine the more normal penalty. At the same time, other aspects of the magistrates' jurisidiction were extended, including the power to award damages for breach of contract and to order specific performance of the obligation to work. Following the 1867 Act prosecutions continued at high levels and magistrates made extensive use of their remaining powers of imprisonment. The more general case for reform of the legal position of trade unions was considered by the 1867 Royal Commission under Sir William Erle, which was set up in the aftermath of disturbances during an industrial dispute which became known as the Sheffield 'outrages'. The Royal Commission was also able to consider the implications of the decision of the Court of Queen's Bench in *Hornby v Close*,[29] which held that trade unions were unlawful associations in so far as their objects included the raising of wages and the control of labour in the trades in which their members worked; such objects and activities amounted to restraint of trade. One effect of *Hornby v Close* was that union property could not necessarily be safeguarded against appropriation.

The majority report of the 1867 Royal Commission declared in favour of placing trade union organisation on a legal footing, but only in return for the removal from union rule books of clauses providing for control of apprenticeships and the prohibition of piecework and sub-contracting; the minority argued for a more complete immunisation of trade unions from the laws of conspiracy and restraint of trade. The Trade Union Act of 1871 went part of the way to meeting the minority's recommendations. Sections 2 and 3 of the Act stipulated that the purposes of trade unions (and by extension, employers' associations) were not to be deemed unlawful in either the criminal or the civil law 'by reason merely that they are in restraint of trade'. This had the effect, among other things, of reversing *Hornby v Close*,[30] so that union funds could be protected; in addition, provision was made for unions to register with the Registrar for Friendly Societies in order to gain certain tax and administrative advantages. The aim of keeping the courts out of union affairs was further reinforced by section 4 of the Act, which provided that none of the internal rules of trade unions were to be enforceable as contracts, so as to prevent unions either suing or being sued for their breach. Although meant primarily for the protection of trade unions, these provisions of the 1871 Act also had the effect that collective agreements between trade unions and employers' associations could not be given legal force or implemented by the courts, a view later endorsed by the Royal Commission on Labour of 1891–1894. At that time, this was explained on the alternative grounds, either that unions and associations lacked legal personality under section 6, or that section 4(4) prevented agreements between them being enforced as contracts.

The second measure of 1871, the Criminal Law Amendment Act, made only minor changes to the existing statutory law on molestation and obstruction. The continuing role of the criminal law in restricting trade union action was confirmed in the following year when workers taking part in the London gas stokers' strike were imprisoned for 'aggravated' breach of contract under section 14 of the 1867 Master and Servant Act and their leaders convicted of criminal conspiracy.[31] The trial judge held that the strike leaders committed the crime of

29   (1867) 10 Cox CC 393.
30   (1867) 10 Cox CC 393.
31   *R v Bunn* (1872) 12 Cox CC 316.

conspiracy at common law in addition to conspiracy to induce the criminal act of aggravated misconduct, and imposed sentences in excess of the three months stipulated for unlawful molestation by the Criminal Law Amendment Act. The decision on common law conspiracy was seen as undermining the 1871 legislation, and a further Royal Commission was established by the incoming Conservative government in 1875.

The majority report of the 1875 Commission recommended that collective rights of association should prevail over the common law doctrine of restraint of trade and that the breach of the contract of service should not give rise to criminal liability. Two Bills introduced by the Conservative administration in 1875 reflected the recommendations of the Royal Commission; they were amended in the course of their passage as a result of Liberal pressure,[32] with the result that the magistrates' criminal jurisdiction for breach of the employment contract was removed altogether by the Employers and Workmen Act 1875, and the Criminal Law Amendment Act 1871 was repealed and replaced by the more precise criminal provisions of the Conspiracy and Protection of Property Act 1875. These were now confined to the cases of violent or intimidatory picketing, deliberate breach of contract by public utility workers (gas and water), and deliberate breach of contract involving injury to persons or property. The narrowing down of these statutory criminal provisions made the new immunity from conspiracy all the more important; this provided that common law conspiracy should have no application 'to an agreement or combination by two or more persons to do or procure to be done any act in contemplation or furtherance of a trade dispute', if the act in question would not be a crime if committed by a single person. The legislation of the 1870s had thereby laid the basic legal foundations for the voluntary collective bargaining system – the principle of the legal non-enforceability of collective agreements, which emerged from the Trade Union Act, and the *trade dispute formula* of immunity from common law liability for concerted action in protection of workers' economic interests.

The economic torts and trade dispute immunities

1.8   The process begun by the legislation of the 1870s of removing restrictive legal intervention in trade union affairs was not completed until the trade dispute formula was extended to cover tortious liability by the Trade Disputes Act 1906. In the thirty years following the adoption of the Conspiracy and Protection of Property Act 1875, the courts filled the gap left by the removal of criminal liability by expanding the economic torts in a series of innovative decisions. These established that industrial action would normally involve the organisers of strikes in committing one or more of a number of torts. Calling workers out on strike involved the tort of inducing breach of contract, first formulated in a separate context in *Lumley v Gye* in 1853.[33] The courts stopped only just short of accepting the concept of *prima facie* tort liability for the 'malicious' infliction of economic loss by one person on another, the House of Lords insisting in *Allen v Flood*[34] that independently unlawful means were needed. This principle did

---

32   Spain, 1991.
33   2 E & B 216 (see Howarth, 2005); *South Wales Miners' Federation v Glamorgan Coal Co Ltd* [1905] AC 239.
34   [1898] AC 1.

not extend to the case of concerted action, however: the tort of conspiracy was likely to apply to collective industrial action taken with the aim of persuading an employer not to make use of non-union labour, for example.[35] Most importantly, in *Taff Vale Railway Co v ASRS*[36] the House of Lords held in 1901 that the trade union itself could be sued in damages under its registered name, that is the name adopted for the purposes of registration under the Trade Union Act 1871, an effect which those who drafted the Act of 1871 had neither intended nor anticipated. This opened up union funds to the threat of depletion through actions in tort by employers and others affected by strikes, effectively returning trade unions to the position they occupied prior to 1875.

The position was restored by the Trade Disputes Act 1906, which extended the trade dispute immunity to cover certain of the economic torts, namely conspiracy and the tort of inducing breach of a contract of employment. Those organising strikes were immunised against liability in these torts if they were acting 'in contemplation or furtherance of a trade dispute'; the union had a blanket immunity from being sued for tortious liability of any kind. The Act also conferred a right to take part in peaceful picketing 'merely for the purpose of peacefully persuading or communicating information, or of peacefully persuading any person to work or abstain from working'. The Act contained a wide definition of trade dispute, which extended to 'any dispute between employers and workmen, or between workmen and workmen, which is connected with the employment or non-employment, or the terms of the employment, or with the conditions of labour, of any person'; for this purpose, 'workmen' included 'all persons employed in trade or industry, whether or not in the employment of the employer with whom a trade dispute arises'.[37]

The Act was effective in insulating collective industrial relations from judicial interference for well over half a century. Minor restrictions on the scope of the immunities were introduced in the Trade Disputes and Trade Union Act 1927, but were repealed again in 1946. Moreover, the courts themselves, at least for part of this period, accepted the underlying philosophy of the 1906 Act, namely the protection of the right to strike as a basic element of a system of voluntary collective bargaining. According to Lord Wright, the commercial interest of an employer or worker in his or her trade or livelihood was not unqualified:

> ... limitations are inevitable in organised societies, where the rights of individuals may clash. In commercial affairs, each trader's rights are qualified by the right of others to compete. Where the rights of labour are concerned, the rights of the employer are conditioned by the rights of the men to give or withhold their services. The right of workmen to strike is an essential element in the principle of collective bargaining.[38]

In *Crofter*, the common law tort of conspiracy was narrowed down by the expansion of the defence of justification, in essence enabling the collective actors to combine for their own economic self-interest, without fear of incurring liability in tort for having thereby harmed the economic interests of others. In addition to its considerable implications for legal doctrine, *Crofter* also signified an important degree of judicial acceptance of strikes aimed at enforcing the 'closed shop', or the principle of compulsory union membership in certain employments,

---

35   *Quinn v Leathem* [1901] AC 495.
36   [1901] AC 426.
37   TDA 1906, s 5. See further our discussion in ch 11 below.
38   [1942] AC 435, 463.

which in many trades was a fundamental goal of trade union organisation, and which was seen as a prerequisite for the achievement of the objectives of economic security and effective collective bargaining.[39]

However, the decision in *Crofter*, issued at the height of wartime co-operation between labour and capital in 1942, is one of the few occasions on which collective values have permeated the structure of common law liability in this way. Within a further twenty years or so, in *Rookes v Barnard*,[40] a case which was also concerned with the closed shop, the House of Lords was to throw the economic torts into turmoil once again, by giving an expansionist interpretation to the tort of intimidation at the same time as construing the statutory immunities in a highly literal and formalistic way. Although Parliament acted immediately, passing the Trade Disputes Act 1965, to restore the 1906 Act, the longer-term effect of the decision in *Rookes* was to spark off further judicial innovation which resulted in the continual 'outflanking' of the statutory immunities:[41] developments have included the suggestion that 'bare' interference with contractual relations suffices for the purposes of the torts of inducing breach of contract and interference with trade by unlawful means;[42] the possibility of a new remedy in respect of pressure amounting to 'economic duress';[43] and new nominate torts of inducing breach of statutory duty and inducing breach of fiduciary duty.[44] Since 1979 these judicial developments have been over-shadowed to a certain extent by the restrictions placed on the immunities by the legislature itself.[45] However, they serve as a reminder of the continuing presence of the common law in this area and of its powers of self-regeneration.

A second area of persistent judicial intervention and innovation is that of the internal affairs of trade unions. In its judgment in the *Osborne*[46] case in 1909, the House of Lords ruled that political donations by trade unions were unlawful on grounds again related to an unanticipated interpretation of the Trade Union Acts 1871 and 1876 which was concerned, on this occasion, with the statutory definition of a 'trade union'. Parliament responded by passing the Trade Union Act 1913 which, by making it possible for such donations to be made through the medium of a political fund, effectively saved the young Labour Party from bankruptcy.[47] The courts were also hostile to section 4 of the Trade Union Act 1871, which attempted, albeit somewhat inadequately, to exclude union rule books from the normal process of the judicial construction and enforcement of contracts. Section 4 was given a narrow interpretation which meant that 'within fifty years of the Act being passed, union autonomy was protected within only a very narrow range'.[48] Judicial intervention reached the point at which trade unions were regarded as akin to public or statutory bodies whose decision-

---

39 McCarthy, 1964.
40 [1964] AC 1129.
41 See para 11.10 *et seq* below.
42 *Torquay Hotel Co Ltd v Cousins* [1969] 2 Ch 106; *Dimbleby & Sons Ltd v NUJ* [1984] 1 WLR 427; see paras 11.12 and 11.13 below.
43 *Universe Tankships Inc of Monrovia v ITWF* [1983] 1 AC 366; see para 11.16 below.
44 *Meade v Haringey London Borough Council* [1979] ICR 494 and *Associated British Ports v TGWU* [1989] 3 All ER 796, CA, and *Prudential Assurance Co v Lorenz* (1971) 11 KIR 78, respectively; see para 11.14 below.
45 See para 11.30 *et seq* below.
46 *Amalgamated Society of Railway Servants v Osborne* [1910] AC 87.
47 See generally Ewing, 1982. The 1913 Act was extensively amended by the Trade Union Act 1984 and subsequent legislation. The relevant legislation is now contained in TULRCA 1992, Ch VI; see further para 10.18 *et seq* below.
48 Elias and Ewing, 1987: p 11.

making powers were subject to judicial control on grounds of *ultra vires*. The courts implied the right to natural justice into the union rulebook practically as a mandatory term,[49] and also, on occasion, attempted to fashion doctrines such as the 'right to work' which would once more have exposed the union rules to judicial scrutiny on substantive grounds,[50] in an attempt to outflank the immunity granted to unions by statute against the common law doctrine of restraint of trade. The scale of judicial intervention has abated in recent years primarily, it would seem, because this is another area now intensively regulated by legislation restricting the powers of trade unions in respect of their individual members.[51]

Judicial activism in labour law

1.9   How may we account for this attitude of the courts towards trade unions and their activities? If there is bias, it is not conscious, according to Scrutton LJ who wrote in the 1920s that 'the habits you are trained in, the people with whom you mix, lead to your having a certain class of ideas of such a nature that, when you have to deal with other ideas, you do not give as sound and accurate judgments as you would wish'.[52] More generally, there is no doubt that the common law's sceptical attitude towards collectivism is deeply rooted and goes beyond the issue of conflicts between labour and capital. Economic liberalism has been a consistent theme in the common law since at least the start of the seventeenth century, and many of the most influential common law judges, including Coke and Mansfield, were strong proponents of open competition and hostile to monopolies and to associations of workers and producers.[53] The sociology of the legal profession itself may be relevant here: the strong individualism of barristers (notwithstanding the fact that the Bar itself was and is a kind of monopoly or 'closed shop') and their close links with the commercial and mercantile classes may help to explain the persistence of anti-collectivist values.[54]

It is perhaps significant that the judges have chosen particular moments, such as the 1900s or the mid-1960s, to launch new developments within the common law.[55] Both periods saw high inflation, low levels of unemployment and a rapidly-growing trade union movement, within which shopfloor organisation was particularly strong; during both periods there was concern at 'abuses' by trade unions of their economic power, and claims that the statutory immunities placed them above the rule of law. The passage of the Trade Disputes Act 1906 prompted Dicey to write that 'the rule of equal law is in England now exposed to a new peril',[56] while Pollock thought that 'legal science has evidently nothing to do with this violent empirical operation on the body politic'.[57] In 1980 essentially similar comments were made by the members of the House of Lords in *Duport Steels Ltd v Sirs*[58] when reluctantly giving effect to the immunities

49   *Lee v Showmen's Guild of Great Britain* [1952] 2 QB 329; see further para 10.3 below.
50   *Edwards v SOGAT* [1971] Ch 354.
51   See ch 10 below.
52   Scrutton, 1923: p 8; see generally Wedderburn, 1986: pp 27–47 for discussion of the issue of judicial impartiality.
53   Atiyah, 1979: p 112 *et seq*.
54   Atiyah, 1979: p 112 *et seq*.
55   Cf Wedderburn, 1995: p 80, discussing *Rookes v Barnard* [1964] AC 1129 and *JT Stratford & Sons Ltd v Lindley* [1965] AC 269.
56   Dicey, [1908] 1979: p 204.
57   Pollock, 1908: p v.
58   [1980] ICR 161.

laid down in succession to the Act of 1906 by the Trade Union and Labour Relations Act 1974. Whatever the origins and legitimacy of such attitudes might be, their persistence would seem to put in doubt the effectiveness of any system of immunities, no matter how widely drafted, in protecting even the most basic collective rights of organised labour.

Collective bargaining and social legislation

The meaning of collective laissez-faire

1.10 The nature of the relationship between collective bargaining and social legislation is in many ways the key to the distinctive form of labour law which has evolved in Britain, in contrast to that which has grown up elsewhere in western Europe. This distinctiveness lies in the relatively limited role played by legislation in directly regulating employment relations, and the greater importance traditionally accorded to voluntary sources, of which collective bargaining has been the most important. In 1954 Kahn-Freund wrote that 'there is, perhaps, no major country in the world in which the law has played a less significant role in the shaping of [labour-management relations] than in Great Britain'.[59] By this he meant that not only was collective bargaining, and not legislation, the principal source of norms governing wages, working time and other terms and conditions of employment for most workers; but also that legislation played little or no role in determining the form which collective bargaining between labour and management should take. The broad statutory immunities of the Trade Disputes Act 1906 created a space within which collective bargaining could develop autonomously from the state. Collective bargaining rested on the state's support for collective institutions over those of individual contract, but the law did not prescribe either the level, the form or the contents of collective agreements, which continued to be regarded as not giving rise to enforceable obligations between employers and trade unions.

Kahn-Freund described the result as 'collective laissez-faire'.[60] However, although the approach of the law at this time has also been called 'abstentionist' or 'voluntarist', the system was not one in which the state was absent, or neutral.[61] The state supported collectivism and the recognition of trade unions for the purposes of collective bargaining, not simply through the statutory immunities for those organising industrial action, but also through various non-legal means at its disposal, including its own policies as an employer and administrative encouragement towards recognition.[62] Nor could it be said that there was only a limited amount of social legislation in place in the 1950s, when Kahn-Freund advanced his notion of collective laissez-faire: there was extensive intervention, at this time, in the form of factories legislation which governed working time and health and safety at work, together with the Wages Councils Acts which provided for statutory minimum rates of pay in certain industries. However, the role of this legislation was rightly seen by Kahn-Freund as subsidiary to that of voluntary collective bargaining: it only applied to groups of workers or to sectors of the economy in which, for various reasons, voluntary collective bargaining had failed

---

59 Kahn-Freund, 1954b: p 47.
60 Kahn-Freund, 1959.
61 See Wedderburn, 1995: ch 1.
62 See generally Fredman and Morris, 1989.

to take root; or to areas of regulation, such as health and safety, which collective bargaining between trade unions and management had failed to cover. Social legislation, at least in the field of employment relations (the same did not apply to social security), was 'an adjunct to, a gloss on, collective bargaining'.[63]

Nineteenth-century attitudes to social legislation and the origins of collective laissez-faire

1.11   The origins of collective laissez-faire are traceable to two related developments of the late nineteenth and early twentieth centuries: on the one hand, there was a failure to extend the Factories Acts model of regulation into a generalised labour code; at the same time, the state made a growing commitment to the *indirect* support of voluntary collective bargaining, expressed through the statutory immunities which were embodied in the legislative settlement of the 1870s (and then of 1906), and in measures of an extra-legal kind which were designed to promote collective bargaining through conciliation and arbitration without involving the state in direct legal compulsion. To put this development in context, we need briefly to consider the nature of the nineteenth-century Factories Acts, which constituted virtually the first industrial legislation of the modern period of any country, and provided a model of regulation which was widely adopted elsewhere in the industrialising economies of that time.[64]

Early factory legislation was concerned with the conditions of employment and working hours of children, and specifically with those of pauper apprentices.[65] The working conditions of women were first the subject of regulation in the early 1840s. The Mines Regulation Act of 1842 barred women from underground working and the Factories Act of 1844 applied to women textile workers the restrictions on working hours which governed the employment of the under-18s. The fact that early industrial regulation took a legislative rather than a voluntary form reflects the weakness of the factory-based unions during the period prior to 1870 and their inability to achieve agreements through collective bargaining; at the same time, the legislature was reluctant to countenance general interference with the freedom of contract of adult males, rejecting a number of Bills to this effect in the 1850s. Male workers indirectly benefited from the controls over the hours of women and children because the working hours of each group were closely integrated; when employers attempted to defeat this effect through the 'relay system', under which the hours children were permitted to work were spread over a number of separate 'relays' across the different shifts worked by adults, Parliament enacted further legislation in 1850 and 1853 to counter this by requiring common starting and finishing times for all workers in a given factory. However, it stopped short of extending the Acts to cover all adult males.

After the 1870s legislation ceased to be the principal means of reducing working hours. By the early 1900s collective bargaining was already beginning to improve upon the hours set by legislation, and women workers covered by factories legislation frequently worked longer hours than men who had the protection of shop floor or sector-level agreements setting a nine or nine and a half hour day.[66]

---

63   Kahn-Freund, 1959: p 248. See McCarthy, 1992; P Davies and M Freedland, 1993: ch 1; Wedderburn, 1995: ch 1, 2000; Brodie, 2003, for further discussion and evaluation of Kahn-Freund's theory of collective laissez-faire.
64   See Hepple, 1986a.
65   See Hutchins and Harrison, 1926.
66   Hutchins and Harrison, 1926: p 98; J Morris, 1985: p 79.

From this period legislation regulating non-factory employment permitted longer statutory hours than was normal either for core factory employment within the Acts or for employments regulated by collective bargaining. Social legislation of this kind had become a second-best option for groups of workers (predominantly female) unable to secure the benefits of collective bargaining: the law, wrote Hutchins and Harrison in 1903 'is still ostensibly based on the idea of "protection for those who cannot help themselves", instead of openly and avowedly adopting the more fruitful principle of raising the standard of life and health for the common good'.[67]

The rise of trade union organisation

1.12   After 1870, as the role of factory legislation diminished in importance, trade union membership grew steadily, more than doubling in the period to 1905, as the effects of lifting the legal restrictions on trade union activity came to be felt. At first growth was not continuous, and early gains were reversed with the onset of the Great Depression in 1873, and again between 1889 and 1893. After 1905 the rate of increase once more accelerated, with membership doubling by 1914 and doubling again by 1920, when membership reached the figure of 8.5 million (although this was reduced to 5.5 million by 1924 in the wake of the post-war slump). Union growth took two forms during this period: on the one hand the extension of membership to the less skilled, and to white-collar and women workers, in the already organised trades; and on the other the unionisation of hitherto unorganised industries and firms. Thus, whereas in 1897 three-quarters of union members were employed in mining, construction and manufacturing – with over half employed in the mining, engineering, cotton and construction sectors alone – by 1924 the proportion of total membership in transport, public and private services and general labouring occupations had increased from 25% to 40%.[68] An important feature of union growth during this time was also the consolidation of the Trades Union Congress as the principal confederation of trade unions. Founded in the late 1860s, by the early 1920s the TUC had effectively seen off all its rivals. The strength of the TUC was that it covered unions of different kinds; craft unions organising particular trades, general unions open to a number of trades and occupations; and unions organising particular industries.[69] Unlike in other European systems where separate trade confererations had been organised on religious or political lines, in Britain there would henceforth be a single organisation representing the union movement as a whole and with mechanisms for resolving through its own procedures the vast majority of inter-union disputes.

The issue of how far to encourage collective bargaining through legislation, or to seek to regulate it by those means, was extensively debated from the time of the Royal Commission on Labour of 1891–1894. The majority report lent its support to collective bargaining based on 'powerful trade unions on the one hand and powerful associations of employers on the other',[70] but rejected proposals to grant compulsory legal effect to the awards made by the voluntary boards of conciliation which had grown up to regulate terms and conditions of employment

---

67   Hutchins and Harrison, 1926: p 209.
68   Tarling and Wilkinson, 1982.
69   See further our discussion in ch 7 below.
70   *Report of the Royal Commission on Labour*, Parliamentary Papers (1894) XXXV.9, at para 364.

in a number of sectors. As a result the Conciliation Act 1896 simply enabled the Board of Trade to conduct inquiries into trade disputes and, on the application of the parties themselves, to arrange arbitration or conciliation. Registration of joint boards of employers and employees with the Board of Trade was voluntary and primarily for the purposes of collecting information. The Board was given the power to conduct inquiries into the establishment of new, voluntary boards in sectors and districts where joint regulation did not exist. The Labour Department of the Board of Trade, which had been established in 1893, became the administrative arm by which the government's policy of promoting joint regulation was implemented; it was the forerunner of the Ministry of Labour, which was established in 1917. Although the direct legal impact of the 1896 Act was minimal, it confirmed the support of the state for the system of joint regulation while affirming the voluntarist ethos of the legislative settlement of the 1870s, and was an essential complement to the Conspiracy and Protection of Property Act 1875 and the Trade Disputes Act of 1906. The government subsequently lent its support to the extension of collective bargaining into sectors where it was vigorously resisted by employers, including the railways and the mines.[71]

Minimum wages and the regulation of the 'sweated trades'

1.13   The selective character of regulatory legislation was not universally accepted at this time. The larger, general unions, in particular, supported the campaign for a statutory eight-hour day within the TUC and in their evidence to the Royal Commission of 1891–1894. The Commission discovered that 'reduction of the normal standard hours of labour has always been one of the leading objects of trade unions; the aim of the modern movement is the attainment of this end by legislation'.[72] The majority nevertheless rejected a standard set of regulations for all trades as not 'a proposal which bears serious examination',[73] and described an existing measure, the Railway Servants (Hours of Labour) Act of 1893 as exceptional and justified by the threat posed to public safety by the long hours worked by railway employees. The minority trade union members of the Royal Commission argued for statutory intervention and called on the Board of Trade to use its statutory powers to initiate a 48-hour week for railway workers, and for statutory reforms to set a 48-hour week in textiles and extend factories legislation 'to all classes of labour', adult males included.[74] What emerged instead was the much more limited, but potentially significant measure in section 28 of the Factories and Workshops Act 1895, which authorised 'the making of special rules or requirements prohibiting the employment of, or modifying or limiting the period of employment for, all or any classes of persons in any process or particular description of manual labour which is certified by the Secretary of State... to be dangerous or injurious to health, or dangerous to life and limb'. According to Hutchins and Harrison, 'in these apparently unimportant provisions which at first sight read only like a trifling extension of regulations already enacted, the principle is however, implicitly granted that, cause being shown, the protection of the law can be extended to men as well as to women and children'.[75] However,

---

71   Clegg, 1985.
72   Parliamentary Papers (1894) XXXV.9, at para 162.
73   Parliamentary Papers (1894) XXXV.9, at para 320.
74   *Royal Commission on Labour, Minority Report*, Parliamentary Papers (1894) XXXV.9, at p 140.
75   1926: p 203.

the section was not subsequently used as a basis for regulating general working time. It was confined in its scope to the specific effect of long hours on health and safety in certain industries.

The debate for and against comprehensive regulation culminated in the campaigns surrounding the passage of the Trade Boards Act in 1909. The House of Commons had earlier passed Fair Wages Resolutions in 1891 and 1909 which required government departments to insist that their commercial suppliers should respect the prevailing wages and terms and conditions in their trades; the obligation to do so would then take effect in the commercial contract agreed between the relevant department and the supplier. The 1909 Resolution referred to 'rates of wages and ... hours of labour not less favourable than those commonly recognised by employers and trade societies (or in the absence of such recognised wages and hours, those which in practice prevail amongst good employers) in the trade in the district where the work is carried out'. The Webbs, among others, made the argument for a more extensive implementation of a 'national minimum' standard of living through legislation, leaving collective bargaining to build a 'living wage' on this foundation.[76] However, the Trade Boards Act reflected a much less ambitious conception of setting up joint wage regulation in selected sweated trades on a statutory basis, with independent members sitting with employers' and employees' representatives in order to bring about agreement; a plan to outlaw the payment of wages in all industries below the line set by the 'national minimum' was rejected.[77]

State support for employee representation and collective bargaining

1.14   The debate over the role the state should play in encouraging and regulating collective bargaining was re-opened by the Whitley Committee Reports of 1917–1919. During the war of 1914–1918 extensive controls were put in place for the regulation and direction of labour; the Munitions Acts of 1916 and 1917 marked a formal departure from voluntarism which was, however, only intended to be temporary. Nevertheless, the Whitley Reports envisaged the establishment of joint representative committees at national, district and workplace level, 'each of the three forms of organisation being linked up with the others so as to constitute an organisation covering the whole of the trade, capable of considering and advising upon matters affecting the welfare of the industry, and giving to labour a definite and enlarged share in the discussion and settlement of industrial matters with which employers and employed are jointly concerned'.[78] The Joint Industrial Council was to form the basis for national level bargaining between employers' associations and independent trade unions in the various trades. The Committee came close to recommending legal enforcement of JIC agreements – 'it may be desirable at some later stage for the State to give the sanction of law to agreements made by the Councils, but the initiative in this direction should come from the Councils themselves'.[79] For trades already well organised, government encouragement for the adoption of a standard JIC model was thought sufficient, and for the unorganised trades, it was suggested that the trade boards system

76   Webbs, [1898] 1920: p 767.
77   J Morris, 1985: p 209.
78   Ministry of Reconstruction, *Final Report of the Committee on Relations between Employers and Employed*, Cd 9153, 1918, at p 2.
79   Reconstruction Committee, *Report of the Sub-Committee on Relations between Employers and Employed*, Cd 8606, 1918, at p 16.

should be expanded. The Trade Boards Act of 1918 incorporated many of the Whitley Committee's recommendations and a vast expansion of the trade board system then took place. The trade boards were given legal powers to set minimum rates of pay and, in due course, other terms and conditions of employment in their respective trades; criminal sanctions could be levied against employers who failed to observe the terms of orders. However, in the 1920s there was a period of retrenchment, and the principle of limiting the scope of statutory intervention to unorganised trades was subsequently strictly maintained.[80] The pattern of joint regulation outside the trade board sector in the inter-war period was one in which there was no single model for multi-employer bargaining and legislation played only a marginal role in selected industries in the enforcement of minimum terms. Within the public sector national-level bargaining was established through the Whitley Councils and similar representative institutions, but in the private sector many of the remaining JICs ceased to set national wage rates. Only 20 bodies remained in operation by 1939.[81] Large areas of industry stayed outside the JIC system altogether, including coal, rail, engineering, shipping, iron and steel, and cotton.[82]

The completion of a system of national-level collective bargaining took place as a result of the second extension of governmental powers during the 1939–45 war, and the favourable conditions for trade unionism after the war including low unemployment. National collective bargaining was actively fostered by the Conditions of Employment and National Arbitration Order of 1940 (Order 1305) which banned strikes and lock-outs and established a mechanism for compulsory unilateral arbitration; this was a means by which the terms of national level agreements could be compulsorily applied to the contracts of employment of employers who did not otherwise observe the terms of such agreements. In effect, Order 1305, while amounting to legal compulsion of the kind which had previously been rejected, nevertheless finally prevented the undercutting of established wages and conditions which unions in the inter-war period had fought largely unsuccessfully to limit, by applying the fair wages principle throughout private industry: the Order made agreements 'between organisations of employers and trade unions representative respectively of substantial proportions of the employers and workers engaged in that trade or industry in that district' binding on all such employers. The wartime government also rejected formal controls on wage increases, and concentrated instead on keeping down retail prices and the rationing of essential commodities as means of containing wage inflation. In addition, the war years saw a revival of shopfloor organisation in areas such as mining and engineering where it had earlier been rolled back as a result of the inter-war depression, and its establishment for the first time in newer industries such as aircraft and motor production.

After the war, the Wages Councils Act 1945 was the occasion both for the expansion of the trade boards sectors into the service sector, and for a more general attempt to place institutional wage determination on a secure footing. The 1945 Act facilitated the setting up of new wages councils and the scope of wage regulation orders was widened to cover all questions of wages, hours and holidays (the latter now no longer subject to the one-week limit set by the Holidays with Pay Act 1938), so making the wages councils more like collective

---

80   See *Final Report of the Committee on Industry and Trade* (Balfour Report), Cmd 3282, 1929, at p 90; para 4.41 below.
81   Fox, 1985: p 297.
82   Richardson, 1938.

bargaining institutions. The result of expansion was to widen the statutory sector to cover one in four of all employees, 3.5 million being covered by wages councils and 0.75 million by agricultural wages boards.[83] In addition to strengthening the wages councils, the 1945 Act renewed Order 1305 for the enforcement of collectively agreed terms and conditions through unilateral arbitration, and in 1946 the House of Commons passed a strengthened version of the Fair Wages Resolution for government contractors. In 1951, following an unsuccessful attempt to use Order 1305 to prosecute gas workers and dockworkers, that Order was repealed and replaced by a new measure, Order 1376, which lifted the ban on strikes and lock-outs and removed penal sanctions but retained the principle of compulsory arbitration over the extension of minimum terms and conditions laid down by sector-level collective agreements; these terms could still be imposed on employers via the contracts of employment of individual employees. Measures of this sort were to remain in place up to 1980.[84] The post-war years also saw a renewal of the voluntary Joint Industrial Councils. By 1946 56 JICs had been either reactivated or newly created, and the Ministry of Labour estimated that almost 90% of workers in industries and services were covered either by joint voluntary collective bargaining or by statutory machinery. By 1960 some 200 JICs were in existence, and union membership had increased to 9.8 million from a figure of 6.1 million in 1938.

Social legislation and the floor of rights

1.15 By the means just described, a virtually comprehensive system of minimum terms and conditions was established, but without the kind of general legal intervention through a *statutory* floor of rights which characterised other European systems at this time.[85] There was a dual aspect to the system, with the separation into voluntary and statutory sectors, which had no counterpart elsewhere. The voluntary system operated at arm's length from the state through the JICs which were not statutory bodies, but with the qualification that few employers, in practice, had the option of contracting-out of the results of collective bargaining, thanks to Order 1305, Order 1376 and their successors. Non-union firms faced the likelihood of concerted collective pressure to accept the principle of trade union recognition, depending on the economic strength of the trade unions concerned, given that the law placed few restraints on the exercise of that power; and although (at that time) individual firms might nonetheless exercise the right not to engage in collective bargaining, they would normally be bound to respect the minimum wage rates and other terms and conditions laid down at sector level. In the statutorily-regulated sectors, the rates laid down by the wages councils had the force of law and penal sanctions were available against employers; in these sectors the role of the law was more directly interventionist.

The essential distinction between Britain and other systems in western Europe in the immediate post-war period, therefore, was not that there was necessarily a smaller body of law in the British system, but that labour standards in Britain were not given the formal support of legislation which laid down minimum wage levels and maximum working hours for *all* workers. There was no

83   Bayliss, 1962: p 73.
84   Order 1376 was replaced by the Terms and Conditions of Employment Act 1959, and the procedure was further modified by the IRA 1971 and the EPA 1975, Sch 11. See P Wood, 1978 and Wedderburn, 1995: pp 9–17 for discussion of these changes.
85   On the evolution of other systems in the direction of comprehensive legislation, see A Jacobs, 1986.

equivalent, for example, to the French laws of 1946, which re-established a 40-hour basic working week, and 1950, which set a statutory minimum wage, in each case providing a universal floor of labour standards under all employments. In Britain, where broadly equivalent standards operated in practice in the voluntary sector (although the basic working week was longer than in France or Germany at this point), they did so without the same direct support of the law; although this was subject to the possibility of compulsory arbitration under Order 1305 and its successors. Moreover, as has been explained, the state offered its general support for collective bargaining through other means, not least by encouraging union membership in the public sector.

The absence of statutory codification for these standards was the result of conscious policy choices at important junctures in the period following the Royal Commission of 1891–1894. In 1894 the trade union members of the Royal Commission predicted that attempts to introduce compulsion into arbitration and conciliation procedures and enforce the terms of collective agreements against trade unions would 'provoke the most embittered resistance from the whole body of Trade Unionists'.[86] Individual trade unions also resisted legal intervention to set general minimum wage rates at the time of the Trade Boards Act 1909, on the grounds that this could be used by the Board of Trade as a pretext for the introduction of compulsory arbitration procedures which would undermine the right to strike.[87] Governments and employers were reluctant, on the whole, to go down a more interventionist route. In the inter-war period, the corporatist experiments of Lloyd George's government after 1918[88] quickly gave way to an official view, expressed in the Cave Report of 1922 on the Trade Boards and in the Report of the Balfour Committee on Trade and Industry in 1929, that extensive wage regulation would be costly and impractical. Even when in 1945, with the return of a Labour government, the Wages Councils were considerably expanded in terms of the numbers of employees and sectors covered, the principle of a binding floor to wages which they embodied was not extended to the sectors which were considered to be adequately covered by voluntary collective bargaining.

This raises the question of in what sense, if at all, it made any difference to have a dual system of labour market regulation, one part voluntary and the other part directly underpinned by legal sanctions? According to Kahn-Freund, the advantages of collective laissez-faire were the flexibility it accorded to collective agreements, which could evolve 'dynamically' to meet changing industrial and economic conditions, and the democratic value of having strong collective institutions which were autonomous from the state: the absence of legal sanctions stemmed from 'the maturity of collective industrial relations in Britain'.[89] There was also an advantage for the unions in not being directly reliant on the state, since 'what the State has not given, the State cannot take away'.[90] Hence collective laissez-faire was, in Kahn-Freund's account, at least as much prescriptive and ideological in character as it was descriptive.[91]

Less attention was paid then to the disadvantages of viewing legislative intervention as a second-best option, to be limited to under-organised areas of

---

86   Parliamentary Papers (1894) XXXV.9, at p 154.
87   J Morris, 1985.
88   See Ewing, 1988.
89   Kahn-Freund, 1954b: p 212.
90   Kahn-Freund, 1959: p 244.
91   See Wedderburn, 1995: p 27.

the economy and to areas not touched by collective bargaining, such as health and safety. How far the philosophy of collective laissez-faire gave rise to a form of direct regulation which was less than satisfactory, being partial and 'subsidiary' in nature, is difficult to gauge; but the example of trade union opposition to the introduction of a general minimum wage at the time of the Trade Boards Act and subsequently,[92] a policy which was reversed only as recently as the 1980s,[93] indicates what the effects were of accepting that the regulatory intervention of the law had to be strictly confined, in order not to upset the priority of voluntary procedures. This meant, first of all, that the standard of protection conferred by statutory bodies could not be set too high, for fear that it would undermine autonomous procedures. Throughout their history, but particularly in the inter-war years, the trade boards and wages councils consistently failed to narrow the gap in terms of earnings between the lowest paid workers and the rest;[94] and the statutory standards contained in the Factories Acts, with regard to working time, lagged behind those of voluntary collective bargaining, and stopped advancing altogether after the 1930s.[95] One aspect of collective laissez-faire was therefore a certain degree of structural inequality between the voluntary and regulated sectors, and the absence of legal guarantees of universal social and economic rights for all employees.

The employment relationship

The master-servant model and its legacy

1.16 In one sense, the modern contract of employment dates from the legislative settlement of the 1870s, which repealed the Master and Servant Acts and removed the last vestiges of the pre-modern system of labour regulation under the Statute of Artificers. Prior to these reforms, the master-servant model of the eighteenth and nineteenth centuries had embodied an extensive conception of the employer's implied powers of direction and discipline, backed up by sanctions administered by the local magistracy. The Act of 1747 gave the local magistrates the power to order payment of wages due, on the one hand, but also to punish the servant or labourer for any 'misdemeanour, miscarriage or ill behaviour' by the abatement of wages or imprisonment for up to a month; they could also discharge the servant from the contract. An Act of 1758 extended this jurisdiction to cover servants in husbandry (agriculture) hired for less than one year and that of 1766 made it an offence for the servant to quit before the end of the agreed contract term. This last provision was an attempt to bring up to date the similar prohibition in section 15 of the Statute of Artificers of 1562. The Master and Servant Act of 1823 established new crimes of absconding from work and refusing to work, and provided for imprisonment of workers for up to three months. Complementing the Master and Servant Acts were numerous measures passed specifically to deal with theft and embezzlement by servants and outworkers. The use of the criminal law to enforce contractual obligations was readily

---

92 See generally Bayliss, 1962, and C Craig *et al*, 1982, for the evolution of minimum wage policy after 1909.
93 On the recent adoption of minimum wage legislation in the form of NMWA 1998, see paras 4.43–4.56 below.
94 C Craig *et al*, 1982; see also J Morris, 1985.
95 See below, para 4.72; Deakin, 1990a.

justified: 'imprisonment may be viewed as a mode of compelling the performance of contracts', wrote JE Davis in his account of the Master and Servant Act 1867:[96] 'in some cases, damages might recompense a master for the breach of a contract by his servant, but the latter is seldom in a position to pay damages, and therefore, in the absence of any other remedy, he might set his employer at defiance'. Court procedure was streamlined and, generally, beneficial to the employer who would normally be the one to bring the complaint. In complaints of neglect of work, which took the form of proceedings for a summary conviction as opposed to an order of the court for a sum of money to be paid or work to be performed, the servant could not be a witness in his or her own defence.[97]

Following the decision in *Lowther v Earl of Radnor* in 1806,[98] the Master and Servant Acts were applied to all servants and labourers, but not to higher status employees such as managers, agents and clerks. The latter were excluded by implication from the wording of the Acts. The selective effect of the disciplinary provisions of the legislation was clarified further by the Master and Servant Act of 1867, which in section 3 stated that it was only to apply to the classes of servants and labourers. The test adopted for distinguishing between servants and independent contractors was based on the criterion of 'exclusive service'.[99] Most of the leading decisions on the extent of the application of the Acts concerned skilled artisans and intermediaries such as 'butty workers' in the mines; the Acts were also used to enforce the 'pit bond' in the mining industry, a form of long-term contracting not far removed from indentured service. In terms of numbers of prosecutions alone, the material impact of the Acts was considerable, in particular in the mining and metal trades and in certain regions of the country, such as the Potteries. In England and Wales, numbers of prosecutions never fell below 7,000 per year between 1858 and the repeal of the Acts in 1875; a peak of over 17,000 prosecutions was reached in 1872. Prosecutions played an important role in relation to the business cycle, by providing employers with a disciplinary weapon to counter the effects of a tight labour market; prosecutions for absconding or refusing to work rose at times of high levels of economic activity, as workers sought better paid or less dangerous work.[100]

For the bulk of industrial and agricultural workers in the nineteenth century, the imposition of a restrictive disciplinary code supported by legislation and by the criminal jurisdiction of the magistrates' courts makes it impossible to speak of a developed contractual theory of the employment relationship before 1875. A contractual model of employment only began to emerge in the case of middle-class, salaried workers, whose position placed them outside the scope of the Master and Servant Acts. Thus, although a modern-style contract of employment can be seen developing in the nineteenth century, the scope of its application was limited by clear notions of social and economic status. One indication of this is the terminology used by the courts; the terms 'employee' and 'servant' denoted different forms of work relationship at this time.[101]

---

96 J Davies, 1868: pp 6–7.
97 J Davies, 1868: p 10.
98 8 East 113.
99 *Lancaster v Greaves* (1829) 9 B & C 628, 631–632 (Parke J).
100 Simon, 1954; Woods, 1982; Hay and Craven, 2004.
101 Foster, 1983. To some extent, the distinction between 'servant' and 'employee' was carried on in the distinction between manual and non-manual workers in social legislation between 1880 and 1945. See our discussion of the 'control test' below, at para 3.33.

The emergence of the contract of employment

1.17 The development of a contractual model based on reciprocity and mutuality of obligation can be observed in cases concerning the rights of higher-status employees to be given work and not to be wrongfully dismissed. Contractual notions were used to limit the employer's right to give orders. The modern contract action for wrongful dismissal was synthesised in 1853 in *Emmens v Elderton*,[102] a case concerning a company solicitor. The basis of the action was the employer's duty to find work for the employee for the duration of the contract, in default of which the employee would be entitled to receive damages for breach of contract. Even in the case of commission agents and others paid on a piece-rate basis, the employer's act of wrongfully preventing the employee from earning his or her commission amounted to an unjustified repudiation of the contract.[103] The status and skills of the professional set a limit to the work he or she could be required to do; if 'hired as a buyer, he was not bound to perform services not properly appertaining to that character';[104] nor would a single act of disobedience or neglect justify the summary dismissal of a manager or a journalist.[105]

The shift which occurred in 1875 was in one sense more formal than real, however.[106] The abolition of the Master and Servant Acts removed the option of criminal sanctions against the employee for breach of contract; henceforth, only civil remedies applied on both sides. However, this apparent parity of remedies did not exclude the use of the magistrates' courts by employers seeking a summary remedy for breach of contract. Under section 3(3) of the Employers and Workmen Act 1875 the court had the power in effect to order specific performance against an employee who was in breach of contract, a right not available under the general law of contract either at that time or since.[107] Damages awards made by the courts under the 1875 Act tended to be in the nature of fines, for the reason that no attempt was usually made to quantify any precise loss flowing to the employer from breach.[108] This was a clear exception to the approach normally followed in the law of contract.

The lingering influence of the master and servant model, given a practical expression in the continuing role of the magistrates as enforcers of discipline, therefore retarded the application of general contractual principles to the service relationship. It is only in decisions of the early twentieth century that the courts can first be seen applying the contractual model, which they had developed for the middle classes, to industrial workers, agricultural labourers and domestic servants. A first step was to protect the right to payment for completed labour by holding that in the case of piece workers, wages were apportionable to work actually done, and that employers could only make deductions from wages which had accrued if they could show loss flowing from a breach of contract by the employee.[109] Similarly, it was held in *Hanley v Pease & Partners*[110] that an

---

102 (1853) 13 CB 495. See further para 4.112 below.
103 See *Turner v Goldsmith* [1891] 1 QB 544.
104 *Price v Mouat* (1862) 11 CBNS 508; Foster, 1983: p 15.
105 *Cussons v Skinner* (1843) 11 M & W 161.
106 The following analysis of the Employers and Workmen Act 1875 and the evolution of the contract of employment after 1875 is based on Deakin, 1989: ch 4.
107 *De Francesco v Barnum* (1890) 45 Ch D 430.
108 On the relationship between the 1875 Act and the Truck Acts which regulated deductions from pay at this time, see Deakin, 1992 and below, paras 4.59–4.65.
109 *Parkin v South Hetton Coal Co* (1907) 98 LT 162; *George v Davies* [1911] 2 KB 445 (a case concerning a domestic servant).
110 [1915] 1 KB 698.

employer had no implied right to suspend the contract of a workman without pay for incompetence or disobedience – in the absence of an express term providing for suspension, the employee had the right to bring a claim for damages for breach of contract – and in *Devonald v Rosser & Sons Ltd*[111] employees recovered damages equivalent to wages for the employer's failure to provide work before and during a period of notice.

The impact of collective bargaining

1.18   The rise of collective bargaining was also an important factor in the decline of the service model, although this did not, in itself, give rise to the modern form of the contract of employment as we know it today. Collective bargaining led to a shortening of the notice period for most industrial workers. Although this reduced the formal legal right of individual employees to a measure of job and income security under the contract, it also achieved the more important practical effect of nullifying the disciplinary jurisdiction of the magistrates and county courts under the Employers and Workmen Act. As Tillyard noted in 1928, the restrictive provisions of the Act were 'practically a dead letter', principally because 'contracts of service are determinable more and more by short notice, so that powers to rescind and powers to enforce performance for unexpired periods of service are in practice rarely if ever wanted'.[112] The Act continued to be used as a weapon of discipline in the mining industry, and cases arising from its use reached the higher courts as late as 1940 and 1945;[113] however, in most industries it appears to have played a gradually diminishing role, although it was repealed only in the 1970s.[114] Individual sanctions against the employee enforced by law and resting on his or her formal subordination to the employer gave way to collective procedures resting more on a formal equality between the parties: Tillyard argued that:

> ... the inferior status of the worker has disappeared. This is absolutely true as regards the administration of the law, but it is also largely true of other means of settling disputes. On Boards of Conciliation, on Trade Boards, on Courts of Referees, and on other bodies dealing with trade interests, working men and employers meet on an equality.[115]

One effect of collective laissez-faire, then, was that individual litigation over contractual rights declined in significance. As collective bargaining evolved, the individual contract of employment was not completely effaced, but the role of individual agreement became a minimal one. The principal role of the contract of employment was to provide a means by which to express the regulatory or *normative* effect of a collective agreement upon the rights and obligations of the individual parties; terms and conditions of employment contained in a collective agreement were deemed to be incorporated into individual contracts by virtue of an express or implied 'bridging term' at the level of the individual contract.[116] Terms derived from wages orders and, after 1940, from arbitration awards made under Order 1305 and its successors were incorporated into

---

111   [1906] 2 KB 728.
112   Tillyard, 1928: pp 328–329.
113   *Nokes v Doncaster Amalgamated Collieries Ltd* [1940] AC 1014; *Dorman, Long & Co Ltd v Carroll* (1945) 173 LT 141.
114   See IRA 1971, Sch 9; Statute Law (Repeals) Act 1973, Sch 1.
115   Tillyard, 1928: pp 17–18.
116   *MacLea v Essex Line Ltd* (1933) 45 Ll L 254.

individual contracts as a matter of law. However, other social legislation did not depend on the contract of employment for its effect. The large body of regulations under the Factories Acts which imposed obligations on employers was mainly enforced by criminal sanctions and policed by the factory inspectorate; it owed more to a public law model of statutory regulation than to the private law institution of the contract of employment.[117] Where individual employees sued for compensation for occupational injuries or disease, they did so not in contract but almost exclusively through actions in tort, either in negligence or, where the Factories Acts had been infringed, for breach of statutory duty.[118]

Employment protection legislation

1.19 It was only with the advent of employment protection legislation in the 1960s and 1970s that the individual contract of employment came to assume the importance which it has in the modern law. Starting with the Contracts of Employment Act 1963, a basic floor of statutory rights was put in place, granting employees certain protections against loss of income and employment. This Act provided for the first time for minimum periods of notice to be given by both employer and employee of their intention to terminate the contract of employment; it also imposed an obligation upon the employer to issue the employee with a written statement of his or her terms and conditions of employment. Although, in principle, the statement merely recorded terms which were agreed separately by the parties or incorporated into the contract on the basis of a bridging term, in practice it had a considerable influence in formalising contract terms and heightening awareness of their role in regulating employment relations. The Redundancy Payments Act 1965 introduced a right to statutory compensation for loss of employment on grounds of redundancy, and the Industrial Relations Act 1971, the right not to be unfairly dismissed. The latter was re-enacted by the Trade Union and Labour Relations Act 1974 and strengthened by the Employment Protection Act 1975, most notably by granting employment tribunals the power to order the reinstatement or re-engagement of an unfairly dismissed employee. The Act of 1975 also introduced a number of measures in the area of income security, including a right to maternity pay and a right to guaranteed minimum pay in the event of lay-off for lack of work. In addition, individual employees, together with certain self-employed workers and applicants for employment, received important protection against discrimination by virtue of the Equal Pay Act 1970, the Sex Discrimination Act 1975 and the Race Relations Act 1976. Following a period of relative stagnation, at least in terms of new legislative initiatives (other than deregulatory ones) in the 1980s and 1990s,[119] a further significant strengthening of individual employment law was achieved by the Employment Relations Act 1999, although the Employment Act 2002, in establishing statutory grievance and disciplinary procedures and limiting access to employment tribunals, arguably weakened the protection available to employees while also making the legislation more complex.[120]

---

117 See below, para 4.10, for further discussion of this point.
118 See further *Lister v Romford Ice and Cold Storage Co Ltd* [1957] AC 555, discussed below at para 4.94.
119 See below, para 1.26.
120 On the EA 2002, see Hepple and Morris, 2002. See further para 2.21 *et seq* and 5.124 *et seq*.

The employment protection legislation recognised the contract of employment as the basis for the legal regulation of the individual employment relationship, and although it displaced many common law rules, the conceptual structure of the Acts was very heavily dependent on contractual language and reasoning. In this sense it gave the contract of employment a new lease of life. This might seem a contradictory statement; after all, the legislation formally overrode the freedom of contract of the individual parties in numerous respects. On the other hand, by limiting managerial prerogative, and in particular the employer's sanction of dismissal, the legislation limited the otherwise open-ended disciplinary powers which the employer had enjoyed at common law, and which owed as much to the master-servant model of the nineteenth century as it did to general principles of contract. The legislation did not, therefore, represent a straightforward movement from contract to status; on the contrary, in mitigating some aspects of the employee's subordination, it made the relationship in some ways more closely resemble the model of a contract based on reciprocal rights and duties.[121]

Nor did the employment protection legislation, extensive as it was and still is, constitute a comprehensive statutory code governing the employment relationship. Many significant aspects of the employment relationship remain governed by the common law or, indirectly, by collective bargaining. The reforms of the 1960s and 1970s did not touch on areas such as minimum rates of pay and the control of working time, partly on the grounds that these should remain within the scope of voluntary collective bargaining. Direct statutory regulation, through the Wages Councils and Agricultural Wages Boards, was still regarded as exceptional, and covered only a minority of employees; indeed, the scope of such legislation diminished after 1960, as a number of Wages Councils were wound up in the belief that statutory intervention was holding back the emergence of voluntary arrangements.[122] It was only in the late 1990s that comprehensive national minimum wage legislation was at last enacted and that working time standards laid down in European Union law were implemented.[123]

Employment protection legislation was, then, only a partial breach of the system of collective laissez-faire. One aspect of its rationale was, nevertheless, a perception that there were limits to what could be achieved through collective bargaining, and that additional legal intervention was needed to fulfil various economic and social policy goals of the state. The Contracts of Employment Act 1963 was a harbinger of a form of labour market intervention which, in various forms, was to call into question the philosophy of collective laissez-faire.

State corporatism, incomes policies and collective bargaining

The concept of corporatism in labour law

1.20   The concept of corporatism is open to a number of interpretations, but in the present context is generally understood to represent the growth of formalised links between the state and autonomous economic groups (in particular the organisations of labour and capital), ranging from consultation to more formal negotiation over economic outcomes. On the one hand the state aims to take a

---

121 See further para 3.2 below.
122 This is prefigured in Bayliss, 1962. See generally C Craig *et al*, 1982; below, paras 4.4–4.8.
123 See below, para 1.34.

more interventionist role in economic management, limiting the autonomy of the collective parties; on the other hand, the representative institutions of labour and capital are granted access to governmental policy making. The precise forms of these arrangements have differed considerably from one period to another and, in the international context, a great variety of forms may also be found.[124] In some European systems, for example, it is common for tripartite bargaining between government, employers and trade unions to lead to framework collective agreements which are subsequently given the force of law. This has not happened in Britain. However, from the 1940s onwards incomes policies, aimed at curbing wage inflation, have at various times had a highly significant impact on the labour market and on the system of collective bargaining.

Incomes policies

1.21 Incomes policies relied on a mixture of statutory and voluntary controls. The Labour Government of 1964–1970 was the first to take statutory powers in the area of pay restraint. In 1966 a statutory wage freeze was introduced via the Prices and Incomes Act which set criminal sanctions for firms disobeying the law. Although the freeze was lifted the following year and a policy of voluntary adherence was formally resumed, certain statutory powers were retained for the purpose of referring wage settlements to the National Board for Prices and Incomes, which could delay their implementation for a period of six months. This period was later extended to a year. The Conservative Government of 1970–1974 also took statutory powers to enforce wage freezes and limits on pay during its term of office.

   In a reaction against the use of coercive powers the Labour Government of 1974–1979 left the enforcement of pay norms under the Social Contract to the TUC which in effect became responsible for 'policing' settlements on the Government's behalf. The Social Contract originated in discussions between the TUC and the Labour Party in 1973, when Labour was in opposition. In essence, the agreement committed the Labour Party to introducing a series of statutory measures (including price and rent controls, improved social welfare and employment legislation, industrial democracy legislation, public control of investment, and measures for the redistribution of income and wealth through the tax and social security system), in return for voluntary pay restraint on the part of the unions. However, at its 1977 Congress the TUC voted for a return to free collective bargaining, to take effect upon the expiry of the 12-month pay settlements which were then in force. This was, in effect, the end of the Social Contract. In its final year in office the Labour Government proposed a 5% pay norm but took no direct legal measures to enforce it. In the public sector direct government influence was brought to bear, at the cost of provoking widespread strike action by local authority and health service employees during the 'winter of discontent'.

Growing state intervention in industrial relations

1.22 From a legal point of view the impact of incomes policies was quite marginal; even when statutory powers were taken, every effort was made to

---

124 See Deakin, Michie and Wilkinson, 1992, on which this discussion is based, and P Davies and M Freedland, 1983: introduction; Deakin and Wilkinson, 2005: pp 243–264.

separate incomes policies from the normal working of collective labour law and the trade dispute immunities in particular. Thus incomes policies have left no lasting mark on the institutions of labour law. During the 1960s and 1970s it continued to be public policy to maintain and promote collective bargaining, so that 'there was between 1948 and 1979 a dichotomy in government policies: anti-wage inflation policy on the one hand, and traditional labour law, or IR [industrial relations], policy on the other'.[125]

But if the institutional effects of incomes policies were limited, the effects of other forms of state intervention in the industrial relations systems in the 1960s and 1970s proved to be more enduring. A move towards greater emphasis on plant-level bargaining in the private sector was validated by the Report of the Royal Commission on Trade Unions and Employers' Associations, which was completed in 1968 (the 'Donovan Report').[126] On the face of it, Donovan confirmed the continuing relevance of the principles of collective laissez-faire. Most significantly, the Commission rejected proposals for the legal enforcement of collective agreements containing 'peace obligations' taking the form of commitments not to strike until certain procedures were exhausted. On the other hand, the Commission marked a turning point in attitudes towards the voluntary system of collective bargaining, by criticising both employers and trade unions for 'sustaining the facade of industry-wide bargaining'.[127] It favoured the development of greater formality of procedures and processes at plant level as a means of combating what was seen as the 'disorder' of the 'informal system' of industrial relations within individual firms and establishments. Employment protection legislation was to be an important part of this. The Commission recommended the enactment of unfair dismissal legislation, to be administered through a system of 'labour tribunals', one of the functions of which would be to reduce the incidence of wildcat strikes by providing a forum within which disputes over dismissal and discipline could be resolved without resort to industrial action.[128] This proposal was later enacted as part of the Industrial Relations Act 1971, which adopted for this purpose the existing system of employment tribunals, which already had jurisdiction to resolve issues arising out of legislation on training levies and redundancy compensation.

Donovan's endorsement of abstentionism in the collective sphere was qualified not just by this specific recommendation for legislation in the individual field, but also by its more general call for reform of voluntary processes. As Lewis suggests, 'Donovan's reform strategy ... departed from traditional non-intervention by advocating a series of legislative measures and by strongly emphasising the need for managerial and economic efficiency, a strand of industrial relations policy which was closely linked with the requirements of incomes policy'. However, 'the central issue for Donovan was how to restore order, peace and efficiency to industrial relations and yet to preserve and even extend the voluntarist tradition of collective bargaining'.[129] Donovan's rejection of greater legal compulsion in the field of collective relations was itself rejected by the Conservative government of 1971–1974, whose Industrial Relations Act 1971 introduced a completely new system of

---

125 Wedderburn, 1985: p 77.
126 Cmnd 3623. For analyses see R Lewis, 1986; McCarthy, 1992; P Davies and M Freedland, 1993: ch 6.
127 Cmnd 3623, 1968: para 111.
128 See ch 5 below.
129 R Lewis, 1986: p 32.

collective labour law.[130] The traditional combination of common law liability coupled with statutory immunities for industrial action was replaced by a system of unfair labour practices loosely modelled on the American Taft-Hartley Act of 1947; provision was made for pre-strike ballots and 'cooling-off periods' in emergency disputes, with a prominent role for a new labour court, the National Industrial Relations Court. Statutory controls over the closed shop were introduced for the first time. Protection for trade unions against the large part of civil liabilities was made conditional upon them being registered under the Act, but virtually all refused in order to avoid exposing their rule books to substantive powers of legal review. The Act proved to be a failure, largely thanks to the strength of union resistance; it did nothing to reduce levels of strike activity, and the National Industrial Relations Court was faced with repeated embarrassments in attempting to enforce its orders.[131] But even this measure, which contained what were then unprecedented powers of direct legal compulsion, was not necessarily hostile to the Donovan Report's underlying goal of preserving collective bargaining by reforming it. Unions were offered a range of positive rights, in particular a right to recognition in certain circumstances, in return for submitting themselves to the controls which would stem from registration under the Act. It was a package 'to draw the unions into a regulated and regulatory system'.[132] As it was, although the unions declined this offer, the supporters of the 1971 Act 'always refused to accept that it was an anti-union measure ... it was sometimes argued to be compatible with true underlying intentions of [collective laissez-faire] – if not with its outward form'.[133]

The Labour Government of 1974–1979 repealed the Industrial Relations Act 1971 and restored the 1906 pattern of statutory immunities in a strengthened form in the Trade Union and Labour Relations Act 1974. Nonetheless, certain parts of the 1971 Act were subsequently revived. The unfair dismissal jurisdiction was re-enacted in the Act of 1974, and the Employment Protection Act 1975 contained a modified recognition procedure, under which a union with substantial support in a given workplace might obtain the right to recognition through a procedure operated by the Advisory, Conciliation and Arbitration Service.[134] This procedure, although successful in achieving advances in recognition in areas of professional and managerial employment where it had previously been resisted, was dogged by the intervention of the courts through judicial review,[135] and was repealed in 1980. However, the unfair dismissal legislation, together with the other elements of employment protection law which were significantly strengthened by the Act of 1975, has largely remained in place to this day, and has had a considerable influence in leading management to adopt more formal procedures at plant level, much as the Donovan Report intended.[136] Not all agree that this formalisation of plant-level procedures has necessarily been the principal cause of rising labour productivity and a reduction in the incidence of strikes during the 1980s;[137] but there can be little doubt that the reforms initiated

130 Wedderburn, [1971] 1995: ch 3; McCarthy, 1992: pp 18–24; P Davies and M Freedland, 1993: ch 7.
131 See Weekes *et al*, 1975
132 Wedderburn, 1991b: p 21.
133 McCarthy, 1992: p 21.
134 On ACAS, see below, paras 2.28 *et seq*
135 See Simpson, 1978.
136 For further discussion see paras 1.27–1.28 below.
137 Cf Metcalf, 1989; Nolan and Marginson, 1990.

by Donovan have had a substantial impact on personnel practice and employment relations at the level of the workplace.

Labour market flexibility and deregulation

The shift in government policy after 1979

1.23   The Labour Government of 1974–1979, in common with its immediate predecessors, failed to reconcile the tensions between the traditional forms of state support for voluntary collective bargaining and increasing intervention in the economy through incomes policies.[138] The stage was set for a revolution in economic and social policy which would see the abandonment both of collective laissez-faire and of the attempt to manage the economy through state corporatism. The 1979–1997 Conservative governments chose to adopt instead a programme of economic deregulation and liberalisation, designed to promote product-market competition and reduce the size of the public sector. Reform of industrial relations and restructuring of the labour market were central parts of this wider economic programme. Legislation limited the right to strike and subjected trade unions to an unprecedented degree of external regulation and supervision, at the same time as statutory employment rights were qualified and in some instances removed completely, in favour of a return to the common law institution of the individual contract of employment. Incomes policies for the private sector were formally rejected, although in the public sector cash limits on pay were imposed at various times. Unions in the nationalised and public employment sectors suffered demoralising defeats in a series of strikes, most notably in steel and coal. The government consistently claimed a link between these statutory changes and an improved climate in industrial relations, leading to superior economic performance:

> The Government's reforms have led to major and important changes of attitude. The atmosphere of industrial relations today is very different from what it was in the 1970s. Management has regained the freedom to manage, and the incentive and the will to do so.[139]

What was perhaps most remarkable about this programme of reform was the use of labour law not as a means of achieving distributive goals or embodying a notion of industrial justice, but as part of an economic policy designed to foster competitiveness. This is not to say that considerations of rights played no part at all in the reforms of the 1980s and 1990s. The rights of individual union members, in particular, were advanced as a rationale for legislation regulating internal trade union affairs and the obligation to hold strike ballots, and the reforms to the law governing industrial action were justified in part by the need to protect the rights of third parties adversely affected by industrial disputes (consumers, members of the general public and employers who were not party to disputes).[140] We have also seen that the linking, within governmental policy, of economic and social issues began well in advance of the election of Mrs Thatcher's first administration, being traceable at least to the Donovan Report of 1968 and earlier.[141] In the 1980s, however, the subordination of social policy

---

138   P Davies and M Freedland, 1993: p 663.
139   Department of Employment, *Employment for the 1990s*, Cm 540, 1988, at p 16.
140   See Fredman, 1992a, for a discussion and critique of these justifications.
141   See above, para 1.22; P Davies and M Freedland, 1993.

to a wider economic agenda reached a new level. Any assessment of the legislative reforms of the 1980s and 1990s needs to focus on their economic impact, since that was the *principal* justification offered for the radical changes made to the law.

The neoliberal critique of collective bargaining and social legislation

1.24 The deregulation of the labour market complemented the Conservative government's adoption of a monetarist macro-economic policy and its formal abandonment of policies of managing demand in the economy in an attempt to maintain full employment.[142] Attention switched from explanations of unemployment which stressed inadequate demand to those which focused on the role of the supply side, and in particular on perceived rigidities stemming from the role of trade unions in regulating workplace practices and setting a floor to wages and conditions through sector-level collective bargaining. This policy received its clearest expression in the 1985 White Paper, *Employment: the Challenge for the Nation*,[143] which was as much a justification and review of policies already in place as a programme for future reforms. The White Paper rejected low demand as the cause of unemployment, in favour of 'the failure of our jobs market, the weak link in our economy'. The substantial increase in unemployment between 1980–1982 appeared 'in large measure [because] the disguised unemployment of earlier years, with overmanning rife, was forced into the open'. A three-fold solution was offered: a 'sound' framework of economic policy based on the control of the money supply; the removal of obstacles to the creation of jobs in the form of labour market regulation; and, in exceptional cases, direct action in the form of training and make-work schemes for the long-term and young unemployed.

Both the arguments of the government and the means by which they sought to implement them were close to the published views of FA Hayek.[144] Although the degree of Hayek's influence over legislative change has been doubted,[145] his work is significant for the way in which it expressly linked demand-management and trade union 'control' of labour markets as the twin causes of unemployment and inflation in the 1960s and 1970s.[146] For Hayek, institutions of collective regulation prevented the price mechanism of the labour market from functioning. The cure he proposed was to limit union power by removing the statutory immunities which protected the right to strike and to organise, so creating a greater scope once again for the common law of tort and contract.[147] Related libertarian arguments focused on restriction of the closed shop as a means of limiting union monopoly power.[148] Social security benefits and employment protection legislation were also identified as sources of rigidities; unemployment benefits were thought to raise the reservation wage – that is, the lowest wage which an unemployed worker would accept – above the market-clearing rate for employment in the non-union sector, so adding to unemployment, and unfair dismissal legislation was said to increase the costs for employers of hiring the

---

142 See F Wilkinson, 1987.
143 Cmnd 9474.
144 Hayek, 1960, 1973, 1984.
145 Auerbach, 1990.
146 See, in particular, Hayek, 1980.
147 Hayek, 1973: pp 141–142. For a sustained critique of this hypothesis in the context of freedom of association, see Wedderburn, 1989.
148 Hanson *et al*, 1982.

unemployed. The solution here involved the wholesale deregulation of protective legislation and the restriction of social security payments.[149] Similar approaches to labour market reform were advocated in other countries at this time, most notably in the USA and Germany, but the degree of legislative change in these systems has proved to be nowhere near as great as in the case of Britain.[150]

Reform of the law governing industrial relations

1.25   In some ways, the particular features of the British labour law and industrial relations system at the start of the 1980s presented an opportunity but also a difficulty for a strategy of deregulation. By international standards, formal labour law regulation in Britain was comparatively weak, but extra-legal sources of regulation were correspondingly strong, part of the legacy of collective laissez-faire. On the one hand, this made the task of deregulation easier in the sense that legislative regulation, much of it dating only from the 1960s and 1970s, had scarcely had time to take root. On the other hand, the support traditionally given to autonomous collective bargaining through the system of collective laissez-faire also meant that new forms of legal intervention were necessary to address the issue of union power in the labour market, as the sources of union strength lay largely outside formal legal procedures and protections. In collective labour law, then, simple delegalisation, or even a 'return to private law', would not be effective, as the sources of trade union power did not depend on a formal statutory underpinning of positive rights. Some inroads were made by the rescission in the early 1980s of the Fair Wages Resolution and the repeal of the statutory procedure for the extension of minimum terms and conditions laid down in sector-level collective agreements. The bulk of changes in trade union law, however, took the form of expanding, rather than diminishing, the role of the law.

To this end, a series of Acts cut back the scope of the statutory immunities as Hayek had proposed, so increasing the scope of common law regulation of strike activity. After a modest beginning in the Employment Act 1980, a more radical measure was the Employment Act 1982 which removed the blanket immunity of trade unions from liability in tort, narrowed down the 'trade dispute' formula which had previously protected most forms of industrial action, and prohibited industrial action aimed at extending the closed shop and union recognition to third party employers. The immunities were further narrowed down in the 1988 and 1990 Acts, which among other things imposed a general ban on secondary industrial action (action involving employers who are not immediate parties to the trade dispute) and shut off all means of enforcing the closed shop through industrial action.

In addition, new forms of statutory regulation were introduced to complement the expanded role of the common law. The Trade Union Act 1984, whose provisions were extended in 1988 and 1993, made membership ballots compulsory prior to industrial action for which the union was legally responsible, and imposed regular balloting requirements for the election of certain union officials and for the maintenance of union political funds. The Employment Act 1988 and the Trade Union Reform and Employment Rights Act 1993 provided individual members with a further set of rights against their unions, most notably

149 Minford *et al*, 1986.
150 For comparative discussion of the impact of deregulation, see Mückenberger and Deakin, 1989; Deakin, 1991.

by limiting the power of unions to discipline those refusing to obey strike calls or similar instructions, and the Employment Act 1990 extended the range of union responsibility for 'unofficial' strikes and increased employers' powers to dismiss strikers. The 1993 Act introduced new procedural requirements, including an obligation upon the union to give employers seven days' notice of the commencement of industrial action.

Changes to employment protection law further increased the difficulties facing unions. Enforcement of the post-entry closed shop[151] through dismissals of non-union members became progressively more difficult after 1980 until, in 1988, it became automatically unfair for an employer to dismiss an employee for reasons related to their non-membership of a union. In 1990 a new statutory civil wrong was established which made it unlawful for an employer to refuse to hire an individual on the grounds of membership and non-membership, thereby hampering enforcement of the pre-entry closed shop.[152] Following the judgment of the House of Lords in the *Wilson* and *Palmer* cases[153] in 1995, the way was opened for employers to offer incentives for employees to accept 'individualised' terms and conditions of employment outside the scope of collective agreements, without falling foul of the statutory obligation not to discriminate between union members and non-members, a change which had already been reflected in somewhat narrower form by an amendment introduced in the 1993 Act as the case was proceeding through the courts.

Labour market flexibility and the employment relationship

1.26 Within individual labour law, a policy of partial or selective deregulation was adopted, on the grounds that this would promote labour market flexibility. One aspect of this was the removal of legal protections for specific groups, in particular young workers and the low paid. Protective legislation governing the employment of young workers was repealed in the Employment Act 1989.[154] The limited statutory floor to wages was withdrawn, first of all through the placing of restrictions on the regulatory powers of the wages councils in the Wages Act 1986, and later through their complete abolition in the Trade Union Reform and Employment Rights Act 1993.

At the start of the period of Conservative government, employment protection legislation contained a number of exemptions which had the effect of removing certain part-time workers and fixed-term employees from protection. These exemptions were allowed to remain in place, and further disqualifications were introduced. The minimum period of continuous employment needed to qualify for unfair dismissal protection, which had been six months in 1979, was raised in stages to two years by 1985.[155] The government held back from recommending the complete abolition of employment protection legislation.[156] Nevertheless,

---

151 The 'post-entry closed shop' refers to an arrangement whereby employees are required, as a condition of continuing in employment, to become or remain a member of a particular trade union. In a 'pre-entry closed shop', the individual must be a member of the relevant union in order to be hired in the first place.
152 On the pre-entry closed shop, see note 151 above.
153 *Associated Newspapers Ltd v Wilson, Associated British Ports v Palmer* [1995] 2 AC 454; see below, paras 7.9 and 8.17 *et seq*.
154 See Deakin, 1990.
155 See below, para 3.82.
156 See Department of Employment, *Building Businesses ... Not Barriers* Cmnd 9794, 1986, and *Wages Councils: Consultation Document*, 1988.

for those employees who did qualify for protection, statutory rights which were theoretically available were diminished in value by the imposition of procedural obstacles (including the possibility of being made to pay a pre-hearing deposit as a contribution to the employer's costs, introduced in the Employment Act 1989) and by failing to raise with inflation the statutory upper limit on dismissal compensation awards.[157]

A theoretical basis for this policy of selective deregulation was provided by accounts which were critical of labour law and social security legislation for having introduced 'rigidities' into the labour market. At the micro-level, labour flexibility was argued to be necessary if firms were to deal effectively with increasingly turbulent and competitive conditions in product markets. According to an influential model,[158] firms might seek to do this through *functional flexibility*, breaking down demarcation lines between jobs and trades and encouraging multi-skilling on the part of a 'core' workforce of secure employees, while employing a 'periphery' of less secure labour employed on part-time and/ or short-term contracts (*numerical flexibility*), or on contracts under which the fixed element of the wage or salary was reduced in favour of bonus payments and overtime premia which would enable the firm to vary its costs according to shifts in demand (*financial flexibility*). Although the research on which this model was based did not itself offer any particular policy prescription others, including the Department of Employment,[159] concluded that laws and collective agreements setting minimum terms and conditions and protecting security of employment were hostile to flexibility in the sense of restricting firms' ability to hire and fire, set variable wage rates, move workers around between tasks, vary production levels by modulations in working time, and to employ sub-contract or part-time labour.

At the macro-level, the flexibility debate was concerned with the role of labour standards in slowing down processes of economic adjustment. The idea here was that at a time of high unemployment and reduced labour demand within national economies, wages should fall in order to restore equilibrium in the labour market, and workers should be prepared to move from declining sectors to those which were expanding. It was hypothesised that collective agreements and legislative regulation which imposed a minimum floor of rights within and between sectors could hold up these processes of structural adjustment.[160] In this vein, an influential comparative study by Emerson[161] argued that even if wholesale deregulation was impractical and undesirable given the disruption it would cause to existing employment relationships, a form of partial deregulation could be used to encourage the hiring of new recruits. Job protection rules should be relaxed and the costs of hiring new recruits reduced, while leaving the acquired rights of existing job holders intact. This is not unlike the policy which emerged in the UK, at least as far as individual employment law was concerned: the large part of employment protection legislation was kept intact, even though protective laws relating to particular sections of the workforce, such as those protecting the low paid, were repealed on the grounds that employers needed to be given incentives to hire workers in these categories.

157 See below, para 5.155.
158 See Atkinson, 1985.
159 Particularly in the 1985 White Paper, Cmnd 9474 above.
160 Metcalf, 1986.
161 Emerson, 1988.

To a certain extent, these developments were counter-balanced by the growing influence of European Union law. In addition to the impact of rulings of the European Court of Justice which established that European law took priority over domestic law in the event of a conflict, and the acceptance by the British courts that individuals could enforce rights which had direct effect, directives dating from the 1970s which were concerned with equal pay and equal treatment between men and women, on the one hand, and employment protection, on the other, slowly began to take effect.[162] The principle of equal pay for work of equal value was introduced into British labour law in 1983,[163] and further changes followed to the treatment of male and female workers in relation to retirement and pension rights[164] and the rights of part-time workers.[165] One of the most influential provisions was the 1977 Acquired Rights Directive,[166] which was used to protect the rights of employees in certain situations of contracting out or where there was a change in the identity of the employer following privatisation. Nevertheless, Britain was practically alone in western Europe at this time in failing to legislate for a basic statutory floor of rights to terms and conditions,[167] while legislative interference with trade union autonomy led to repeated condemnations of government policy by various supervisory bodies of the International Labour Organisation.[168]

The impact of changes in the law on trade union membership and the coverage of collective bargaining during the 1980s and 1990s

1.27   In contrast to a period of rapid growth in the 1970s, union membership declined rapidly in the 1980s and 1990s. The proportion of union members in workplaces with more than 25 workers fell from 65% in 1980 to 47% in 1990 and 36% in 1998.[169] This still represented a high figure internationally, although care must be taken in interpreting comparative data in this area as not only do methods of calculating density differ from country to country, but membership itself is not necessarily a good indicator of union strength. Britain remained in the middle order of OECD countries, with a density in terms of the labour force as a whole which was comparable to that of Italy and Germany and far higher than in France or the USA.[170] Explanations for the decline in British trade union membership focused on the cyclical effects of high unemployment and economic recession, rather than the compositional effects associated with the decline of manufacturing industry relative to services.[171] The rapid decline of manufacturing at the start of the 1980s and the resulting loss of full-time, male-dominated jobs certainly had an impact in terms of flows out of membership. However, union

---

162 See para 2.42 below.
163 In the form of the Equal Pay (Amendment) Regulations 1983, SI 1983/1794.
164 A major stimulus to change in this area was the decision of the ECJ in Case C-262/88: *Barber v Guardian Royal Exchange Assurance Group* [1990] IRLR 240.
165 Following the decision of the House of Lords in *R v Secretary of State for Employment, ex p Equal Opportunities Commission* [1994] IRLR 176 applying the then Art 119 (now 141) of the EC Treaty and Directive 76/307 on equal treatment in employment, the 8- and 16-hour thresholds for certain employment rights were removed by SI 1995/31. See paras 3.87–3.91 below.
166 Directive 77/187. See paras 3.99–3.115 and 5.193 *et seq* below.
167 Deakin, 1990b.
168 Ewing, 1994a.
169 Cully *et al*, 1999: p 235.
170 W Brown *et al*, 1997.
171 Kelly, 1990; Disney, 1990.

density fell in all sectors and not just in manufacturing. At any given time trade unions were recruiting large numbers of members and losing others; what has to be explained is the contrast to the 1970s when density rose rapidly at a time of continuing decline in manufacturing employment and a rise in female employment. From this perspective, the critical factors since 1980 appear to have been the inhibiting effect of high unemployment and the combination of relatively low inflation and the absence of an incomes policy, which produced rising real incomes for most private sector employees, in particular in those areas of the economy where collective bargaining remained strongly embedded.

The role of legislation as a factor separate from the economic cycle and from general government hostility to trade unionism is difficult to assess. An attempt to measure the impact of legal change between 1980 and 1986 by Freeman and Pelletier concluded that 'legal changes caused density to fall by 9.4 percentage points from 1980 to 1986 – effectively the entire decline in UK density in that period'. If the Labour government's legislation of the 1970s had been in force, it is estimated that there would have been a drop of only 1 to 2 percentage points in density.[172] However, other studies have argued that union weakness caused the legislation, rather than the other way around.[173]

Density, which is usually calculated on the basis of membership, is only one measure of union strength and influence; a more meaningful measure of the influence of trade union power in regulating terms and conditions of employment is the coverage of collective bargaining agreements. The coverage of collective agreements will be greater than union membership for a number of reasons. It is normal for terms and conditions laid down in agreements at either plant or sector level to be applied to union members and non-members alike in plants where unions are recognised, while in the past it has also been common for firms not recognising unions to follow sector-level agreements informally; in addition, the impact of statutory wages orders should be considered here as a substitute for collective bargaining which affected large numbers of non-unionised employees. ACAS estimates at the start of the 1980s suggested that the terms and conditions of over two-thirds of full-time employees in employment were affected in some way by a collective agreement,[174] while the extensive influence of collective bargaining in manufacturing industry and the public sector was confirmed by the first Workplace Industrial Relations Survey.[175] More recent research suggests that there was then a considerable decline in collective bargaining coverage which by the late 1990s was only just above 40% of the employed labour force, with the fall particularly marked in the private sector.[176] Here, the difference between the UK and other systems was clear, and can be largely attributed to institutional changes which contributed to the decline in sector-level collective bargaining.[177]

Derecognition and the structure of collective bargaining

1.28   Apart from some *causes célèbres* in the docks and national newspapers, formal derecognition – the withdrawal of collective bargaining rights from

---

172 Freeman and Pelletier, 1990: p 155.
173 Disney, 1990.
174 R Lewis, 1986: p 20.
175 Daniel and Millward, 1984.
176 In workplaces of 25 or more workers, coverage was 41% in 1998: see Cully *et al*, 1999: p 243. For a historical perspective on the decline in coverage, see Milner, 1995.
177 See W. Brown *et al*, 1997.

recognised unions – was rare throughout the 1980s, despite the fact that there were very few legal obstacles to it.[178] New forms of collective agreements, such as single-union deals and no-strike agreements, were also very rare. Despite the attention which they attracted,[179] they did not cover more than a small number of establishments, almost exclusively on new, 'greenfield' sites. The repeal in 1980 of the rather weak union recognition laws of the 1970s at first appeared to have had little general impact, because most bargaining arrangements pre-dated those laws and had grown up without direct legal support or regulation. Similarly, the removal of legal support for the closed shop did not immediately lead to a substantial decline in union strength in the workplace: 'the demise of the union shops is likely to have had only a marginal impact on the levels of union density, with its effects in practice having been to "top-up" by "compulsory" means levels of membership which were already high'.[180] Pre-entry closed shops had covered a declining number of workers since the 1960s,[181] and many of them were under threat even prior to the Employment Act 1990 which formally prohibited restrictions on the hiring and employment of non-union workers.

However, in the 1990s employers in a wide range of sectors resorted to derecognition, making it clear that the legal regime posed no obstacle to employers undermining longstanding bargaining arrangements, and that trade unions were not always in a strong position to respond to such tactics.[182] Derecognition occurred in companies in printing and publishing, engineering, banking and food processing. Companies sometimes coupled derecognition with offers of enhanced pay and benefits to employees who gave up rights associated with trade union membership, such as the right to trade union representation, and in other cases made unilateral cuts in pay and conditions as part of an anti-union drive. In the Timex dispute at Dundee, tactics used by the employer included the threat of mass dismissal to be followed by the employment of a completely new workforce, the lock-out of employees who refused to accept unilateral cuts in pay and benefits and, eventually, the closure of the plant.[183]

Alongside these changes at firm level, there was the continuing decline of national or sector-level bargaining, and the weakening of union power in the labour market which came with the enforced decentralisation of bargaining levels.[184] As we have seen,[185] the decline of sector-level bargaining long pre-dated the advent of the Thatcher governments; from the mid-1960s onwards national agreements in manufacturing were increasingly confined to setting a floor of minimum wages and conditions which were only directly relevant for employees without a recognised union to negotiate for them at plant or company level.[186] In the 1980s even this floor was removed, first by the repeal in the early 1980s of 'fair wages legislation' which provided for the extension of sector-level agreements to non-union firms, and more recently by the break-up of national multi-employer bargaining in a number of sectors. The then Government's attitude to multi-employer bargaining was spelled out in the 1988 White Paper:

---

178 ACAS, *Annual Report*, 1991: pp 11–12.
179 Basset, 1986.
180 Ewing, 1990: p 644.
181 Dunn and Gennard, 1984.
182 Taylor, 1994: ch 2.
183 K Miller and C Woolfson, 1994.
184 W Brown and J Walsh, 1990; W Brown, 1993; W Brown *et al*, 2000.
185 See para 1.22 above.
186 W Brown, 1981.

> ... many existing approaches to pay bargaining, beloved of trade unions and employers alike, will need to change if we are to secure the flexibility essential to employment growth. In particular, 'the going rate', 'comparability' and 'cost of living increases', are all outmoded concepts – they take no account of differences in performance, ability to pay or difficulties of recruitment, retention or motivation. Pay structures too have to change. National agreements which affect the pay of half the workforce all too often give scant regard to differences in individual circumstances or performance.[187]

A number of means, direct and indirect, were used to undermine national bargaining. These included the ending of the statutory system of industry training boards in most sectors in 1982 and the abolition in 1993 of the powers of statutory wages councils which previously determined the pay and conditions of 2.75 million low-paid workers.[188] Changes to strike law also indirectly undermined national bargaining. In some sectors, including merchant shipping and newspapers, laws restricting picketing and secondary action limited the ability of unions to resist employer moves to break up or narrow the scope of national agreements. The 1982 Act made it difficult to conduct national disputes except as the aggregation of local disputes between employers and their own employees. This was partly responsible for the demise of the national engineering agreement in 1990, which followed a series of local settlements to the engineering unions' demands for working-time reductions. Similar moves towards decentralisation of collective bargaining occurred in the public sector, as a consequence of compulsory competitive tendering following the Local Government Act 1988 and the ban on local authorities from using contract compliance to maintain union recognition and minimum terms and conditions for the privatised workforce.[189]

Restriction of industrial action

1.29   The late 1980s and 1990s saw a considerable reduction in strike activity. In terms of working days lost per year, the average of the 1980s was 7.2 million as opposed to 12.9 million in the 1970s and 3.5 million in the 1960s.[190] The figure for the 1980s was affected by a small number of very large-scale strikes, in particular the miners' strike of 1984–1985. In terms of the number of stoppages, the 1980s showed a reduction as compared with both the 1960s and the 1970s. The incidence of industrial action in the period 1990–1996 was even lower; only 278,000 and 415,000 working days were lost in 1994 and 1995 respectively. In 1996, 1.3 million working days were lost which, although an increase on the years immediately preceding it, was still a very low figure by the standards of the previous three decades.[191] For the past decade, the incidence of industrial action has continued at what is, by historical standards, a very low level.[192]

The narrowing of the immunities and the ending of the blanket immunity of trade unions from liability in tort provided employers with many more strategic options than they had previously had for breaking strike resistance, and these

---

187   Cm 540, 1988: pp 23–24.
188   Minimum wage regulation was restored, in a new form, by NMWA 1998. See below, paras 4.43–4.56.
189   Compulsory competitive tendering has since been replaced by the system of 'best value' (see LGA 1999) and it is once again permissible to use fair wages clauses under certain specified circumstances (SI 2001/909; para 2.6, below).
190   Bird, 1991.
191   Sweeney, 1997.
192   See Monger, 2004; W Brown and S Oxenbridge, 2004; ch 11, below.

were put to effective use in particular disputes, such as the Wapping and Messenger disputes in the newspaper printing industry.[193] The imposition of controls on internal union procedures had a more ambiguous effect, at least initially, both upon strike levels and upon union government more generally: as Kelly commented, 'the balloting provisions are a classic example of unintended consequences'.[194] By making unions formally responsible for a wide range of strikes, and by requiring membership ballots in the case of all strikes which were in law the union's responsibility, the Trade Union Act 1984 strengthened the power of central union organisation over the rank and file, reversing a trend towards fragmentation which had weakened unions in some sectors. Although some strikes foundered owing to the failure of unions early on to observe the balloting requirements of the 1984 Act, where they were observed they could be put to good effect to rally support for industrial action and to put pressure on employers in advance of the strike commencing. Brown and Wadwhani suggested that 'while the new procedure may thus reduce the actual occurrence of strikes, it may not commensurately diminish the impact of the strike threat': their research, published in 1990, found that over 90% of strike ballots under the new procedures had resulted in votes for industrial action.[195] Nor was it the case, on the whole, that the provisions of the 1988 Act preventing unions from disciplining members who refused to take part in strikes greatly weakened the strike weapon, given the small numbers of such individuals.

Against the background of criticism from the new right that the 1984 balloting laws could lend a 'spurious legitimacy' to industrial action,[196] the Government introduced amendments in the 1988, 1990 and 1993 Acts which sought to diminish the effectiveness of ballots as a source of union negotiating strength; it was this legislation rather more than the original Act of 1984 which was largely responsible for creating a situation in which industrial action could not be undertaken without going through procedures of inordinate complexity.[197] Research found that union officials saw these new procedural requirements as constraining their capacity to respond quickly to changes in circumstances in the run up to a trade dispute.[198]

These legal factors were not the only influence on the reduced strike activity of the later 1980s and the 1990s. Higher unemployment and the absence of an incomes policy more clearly distinguish the 1980s from the strike-prone 1970s. Nevertheless, the decline in strike activity in Britain since the late 1970s was greater than the average for OECD countries, and this might suggest some role for factors which were particular to the British experience, one of which may have been the legislation.[199]

Labour market outcomes: employment, unemployment, wage distribution, and inequality[200]

1.30 Even though the UK economy underwent significant 'flexibilisation' in the 1980s and 1990s, the level of unemployment did not consistently fall during

193 Ewing and Napier, 1986.
194 Kelly, 1990: p 56.
195 W Brown and S Wadwhani, 1990: p 62.
196 Hanson and Mather, 1988: p 77.
197 See further para 11.32 *et seq* below.
198 Elgar and Simpson, 1996.
199 See W. Brown *et al*, 1997: p 78.
200 This part summarises Deakin and Reed, 2000b, to which the reader is referred for a more detailed account.

this period, but rather became more volatile than it had been in previous decades. Unemployment swung from 6.4% in 1980 to 12.4% in 1983, down to 6.8% in 1990, up again to 10% in 1993, and then down to below 6% by 2001[201] and below 5% by 2004.[202] During this period unemployment became increasingly concentrated among 'workless households' in which neither adult worked; these amounted to almost 20% of all households by the end of the 1990s. Employment levels rose during the 1980s and 1990s, mainly as a result of growing female participation in paid employment. In part, this was related to a significant decline in full-time, permanent employment and an increase in the use of 'flexible' forms of work since 1980. However, the link between this change and the framework of regulation governing employment is clear. The growth in part-time work began in the 1960s and 1970s, prior to the general trend towards deregulation in the 1980s. The most significant rise in 'atypical' work after 1979 was the rapid increase in male self-employment, but this was concentrated in the early 1980s. After 1990 the growth in self-employment almost ceased. During the mid-1990s there was an increase in the use of fixed-term contracts especially in public administration, health and education which appears to have been linked to the exclusion of this type of employment from dismissal protection.[203] The tax-benefit system also played a role. The growth of both self-employment and part-time work at low rates of weekly pay in the 1980s can convincingly be linked to features of income tax and social security contributions which, in effect, subsidised these forms of work.[204] However, these effects are waning thanks to more recent regulatory changes. In the mid-1990s, during the period of Conservative government, the Inland Revenue began to take steps to regularise the position of many freelancers and self-employed construction workers, in the process eliminating many of the tax advantages they had formerly enjoyed, and this policy continued following the election of a Labour government in 1997.[205]

There was a growing consensus amongst commentators that increased flexibility and the comparatively low unemployment rate in Britain had been achieved at the price of a deterioration in wages, growing insecurity, and increasing poverty.[206] After a long period of wage stability, wage inequality grew sharply in the 1980s and 1990s, resulting in higher differentials than at any other time during this century.[207] The pay gap between the lowest decile and the highest decile of workers grew consistently, and although the real earnings of workers in the lowest decile rose in real terms during the 1990s, low pay was disproportionately experienced by women in low paying industries or occupations and by members of ethnic minorities. The impact of the decline in collective bargaining on pay and terms and conditions of employment during this period is difficult to assess, because other relevant factors at this time included changes

---

201 See *Labour Market Trends*, February 2001, Table A.1. The figures quoted in the text refer to the ILO definition of unemployment which is significantly higher than the claimant count (see *Labour Market Trends*, February 2001, p S2). On the significance of different measures of unemployment, see Nickell, 1999.

202 *Labour Market Trends*, March 2005, Figure 3.

203 See Burchell *et al*, 1999. On the nature of this exclusion, and changes to the law in 1999 and 2002 which limited its impact, see paras 3.83–3.86.

204 M Harvey, 1995.

205 See para 3.61 below.

206 Marx, 1999. On the record of the New Labour government since 1997 in mitigating some of the effects of rising poverty and inequality during the preceding period of Conservative government, see IFS, 2005.

207 Machin, 1996.

in general labour market conditions and increased competition in product markets. Studies nevertheless suggest that the decline in the coverage of collective bargaining was responsible for between one-eighth and one-quarter of the increase in earnings inequality during this period.[208] The alternative explanation for inequality would place more emphasis upon falling demand for 'unskilled' labour as a result of changes in technology and in the structure of demand for goods and services. However, comparative studies suggest that these factors can only account for a part of the polarisation of earnings in systems such as Britain, the USA and New Zealand which engaged in policies of market liberalisation. These more flexible systems saw the pay of their relatively less skilled workers fall more rapidly than in systems which offered more systematic institutional support for investment in human capital, such as Germany and Sweden, casting doubt on the skills-based explanation.[209]

Employment policy and work incentives

1.31 An increasingly important form of direct labour market intervention which was used to counter the rise in unemployment in the 1980s and 1990s was employment policy. This consisted of measures aimed at making labour supply more flexible, ranging from direct subsidies paid to employers offering training and/or work experience, to changes to social security and employment law designed to cut employers' hiring costs and encourage the unemployed to enter or re-enter the labour market 'at wages which employers can afford to pay'.[210] Training policy also received a higher profile in the 1980s and 1990s than before, but for most of this time it was subordinated to the wider policy goal of labour market deregulation. As a result, the role of trade unions in the training infrastructure was marginalised, with the abolition of the statutory industrial training boards and the winding up of the Manpower Services Commission, on both of which unions had been represented. Training subsidies, including the Youth Training allowance and payments under various short-lived youth employment schemes,[211] were designed to set a low ceiling of 'more realistic levels of pay' to the wages and income of young workers.[212] To similar effect was the removal after 1988 of access to income support for the under-18s, part of the reforms to social security brought about by the Social Security Act 1986, on the assumption that all those below this age would either be in education or in employment or, failing that, would receive an offer of a training place. It was argued that these policies, by linking training and occupational development to the more general strategy of subsidising low pay, directly contradicted the government's efforts to raise awareness of the importance of training and to improve training quality.[213]

Extensive changes made in social security included the tightening of the qualifying conditions for unemployment benefits; the widening of the grounds for disqualification from benefit; the introduction of greater monitoring of the unemployed by employment officers through the *Restart* programme, a process which was carried a stage further by the introduction of the jobseeker's allowance to replace unemployment benefit with effect from 1997; changes to the system

208 Gosling and Machin, 1995.
209 Nickell, 1997: p 71.
210 Cmnd 9474, 1985. See paras 3.16–3.17 below.
211 See below, paras 3.17 and 3.49.
212 Cmnd 9474, 1985: Annex 2.
213 Keep, 1990: p 154.

of national insurance contributions, designed to lower contributions in respect of low-paid work; and the introduction of family credit as an addition to the net, after-tax earnings of low-paid employees.[214] The restriction of social security entitlements was influenced by two limited surveys of the unemployed from which the government concluded in 1988 that 'there is evidence that a significant minority of benefit claimants are not actively looking for work'.[215] The size of the fall in unemployment in the mid-1980s and its timing have been ascribed to the tightening of social security administration brought about in 1986 by the *Restart* programme, under which the long-term unemployed were subject to regular monitoring by employment service officials to assess their availability for work.[216]

The assumption that incentives for the unemployed could be improved by these means was widely criticised. Research showed that the greatest disincentive for the unemployed was often the precariousness of work and income in most of the jobs which were on offer to them.[217] Studies of local labour markets in areas of high unemployment demonstrated that over half the jobs taken up by benefit recipients involved non-standard working hours or forms of employment, and that the median level of pay on offer to the unemployed was very low, at less than half the average hourly wage.[218] Disenchantment with the prevailing policy of deregulation led policy-makers to perceive the need to combine work incentives with a basic framework of labour market regulation which would make employment more feasible and attractive for the unemployed, and this fed into the new turn in labour market regulation which accompanied the election of a Labour government in 1997.

Pragmatic reconstruction? Labour law under 'New Labour'

1.32   A number of elements characterised labour law policy following the election of a 'New Labour' government in 1997. In the first place, there was acceptance of the Conservative reforms in the law relating to industrial action, joined with a willingness, nevertheless, to use legal means to encourage trade union recognition at workplace and enterprise level, thereby offering support to collective bargaining. Second, basic labour standards were strengthened in the areas of minimum wages, working time and employment protection with the aim, in part, of achieving a better balance between working life and family life, albeit within the framework of a continuing commitment to labour market flexibility. Third, employment policy was used to promote employment opportunities, together with an increasing emphasis on the 'responsibilities' of workers and jobseekers. What links these developments is less, perhaps, an overarching philosophy of the 'third way'[219] than a deeply pragmatic but also cautious approach to modernisation and reconstruction of the labour market following two decades of neo-liberalism.

---

214 See generally Deakin and Wilkinson, 1991; P Davies and M Freedland, 1993: ch 10.
215 Cm 540, 1988: p 55.
216 Dicks and Hatch, 1989.
217 McLaughlin *et al*, 1989.
218 Marsh *et al*, 1990.
219 On the 'third way', see Blair, 1998; Giddens, 1998; and for views of its influence on labour law, see H Collins, 2001b; Novitz and Skidmore, 2001; Kilpatrick, 2004; Fredman, 2004a; P Smith and G Morton, 2002.

Collective labour law: towards 'partnership'?

1.33   The present government has insisted that there should be 'no going back' to the period, during the 1970s, when industrial action was characterised by secondary action, widespread picketing and strikes without ballots.[220] On this basis, it has declined to accept calls for the restoration of the trade-dispute immunities to the position they occupied at the end of the 1970s. The large part of the balloting and notice legislation of the 1980s and 1990s has been retained; such changes as there have been appear to have done relatively little to make it more straightforward for union officials to conduct industrial action in an effective way.[221] Nor have many changes been made to the law governing trade union organisation.

At the same time, the government has initiated a major change in the law relating to collective bargaining, by re-introducing the principle that a trade union with majority support in a bargaining unit is legally entitled, under particular circumstances, to require the employer to enter into negotiations over pay and certain conditions of employment. A law of this kind operated for most of the 1970s, without great success. For most of the modern period, trade unions have relied on a combination of organising strength, the protection of the trade-dispute immunities and the (intermittent) support of government to promote recognition; a legal duty to bargain has generally been regarded as impractical and possibly even counter-productive.[222] Nor does the new law, introduced by the Employment Relations Act 1999,[223] mark a complete break with this 'voluntarist' past. In effect, it holds statutory recognition in reserve as a threat for employers who fail to enter into voluntary recognition agreements with trade unions. The new procedure is designed principally to operate in respect of bargaining units where, prior to the law's coming into force, there was no recognition agreement, thus leaving most voluntary arrangements untouched. The procedure is designed to encourage employers and unions at any one of a number of stages to make a voluntary agreement which will avert the need for the intervention of the Central Arbitration Committee. Even if an order of statutory recognition is made, this need not lead to the making of a collective agreement, nor to the incorporation of improved terms and conditions into the contracts of workers in the relevant bargaining unit.

The apparent contradiction in legislating for union recognition while doing little or nothing to restore the collective rights formerly guaranteed by the trade-dispute formula disappears on closer inspection. Both the new recognition law and the preservation of the constraints on industrial action reflect the present government's stress on 'partnership at work' between labour and management as a means of raising productivity and improving economic performance.[224] While the idea of partnership is, in many ways, highly diffuse, in the context of collective bargaining it implies a process through which unions achieve a recognised status within the workplace as the means for expressing collective employee 'voice', in return for facilitating organisational changes which enhance performance and

---

220   *Fairness at Work*, Cmnd 3968 (1998), at 4 (Foreword by the Prime Minister). See Novitz and Skidmore, 2001: pp 6–8.
221   See ch 11 below.
222   See Simpson, 1991.
223   The relevant law, contained in Schedule A1 of TULRCA 1992, was amended further by the Employment Relations Act 2004. See below, para *9.5 et seq*.
224   See W Brown, 2000.

productivity. In some respects, this is not new; the pursuit of co-operative labour-management relations was a principal goal of the industrial relations reforms of the 1960s and 1970s. What is new, by comparison with the 1960s, is the changed economic environment within which the compromise between labour and management is being forged. Both the effectiveness of union sanctions and the scope for redistribution through collective bargaining have been limited, in part by the law but to a much greater degree by increased product market competition and growing financial pressures on corporate management.[225] Under these circumstances, the present partnership agenda is vulnerable to the objection that the role envisaged for unions is, of necessity, a highly constrained one.

Nor is the nature of the present government's commitment to the delivery of partnership through independent employee representation entirely clear.[226] The *Fairness at Work* White Paper stated:

> Collective representation can help achieve important business objectives, including good communication. It can facilitate negotiation on terms and conditions without preventing the recognition of good individual performance. Representatives who are respected by other employees can help employers to explain the company's circumstances and the need for change. Collective representation can give employees a more effective voice in discussion with employers by drawing on a wide range of expertise and experience in the company.[227]

Nevertheless, it has been suggested that 'the "partnership" which New Labour seeks to encourage within the employment relationship is not one which necessarily involves trade unions'.[228] Evidence for this view comes from the encouragement given by recent legislative reforms to employee share ownership[229] as a means of incentivising workers. Recent legislation has also significantly expanded the role of employee representatives outside the structure of trade unions. In workplaces where there is no recognised trade union or no collective agreement in force, the implementation of statutory rights in such areas as working time and parental leave may now be achieved through 'workforce agreements' between the employer and employee representatives who may have no link to a union.[230] These employee representatives may also exercise information and consultation rights in relation to redundancies, transfers of undertakings and health and safety issues (although, contrary to the position taken under legislation adopted under a Conservative government in 1995, they may no longer do so where a recognised trade union is already established).[231] Whether forms of representation of this kind can adequately represent employees' interests in such a way as to respect laws for the protection of the employee while also promoting a partnership agenda may be open to doubt. It remains open to trade unions to use information and consultation laws for their own ends, and there is growing evidence that they are capable of doing so.[232] On this

225 See W Brown *et al*, 2001; W Brown and S Oxenbridge, 2004; Stuart and Martinez-Lucio, 2005.

226 On the concept of 'independence' in this context, see paras 7.22 *et seq* below.

227 Cmnd 3968, para 4.3.

228 Novitz and Skidmore, 2001: p 14.

229 See para 4.70 below.

230 See, respectively, paras 4.74 and 6.104 below.

231 See para 9.31 below.

232 See McCarthy, 2000, for discussion of union policy on this issue, and Armour and Deakin, 2003, for case-study evidence of union use of consultation laws in the context of corporate reorganisation.

basis, the present government's equivocal attitude towards collective representation is nowhere better illustrated than in its reluctance to support European Union proposals aimed at extending information and consultation rights at work over a range of issues previously left untouched by UK legislation.[233] The relevant directive[234] only came into force in the UK in 2005, and even then the UK government took advantage of derogations to limit the impact of the new legislation.[235]

Labour standards and labour flexibility

1.34 The *Fairness at Work* White Paper committed the government to pursuing a 'flexible and efficient labour market'[236] and the Prime Minister's Foreword, warning of 'overburdensome regulation', asserted that '[e]ven after the changes we propose, Britain will have the most lightly regulated labour market of any leading economy in the world'.[237] The changes made to employment protection law by the Employment Relations Act 1999 and related measures were, nevertheless, highly significant; they included the removal of derogations from unfair dismissal protection for fixed-term contract workers, the shortening of the qualifying period for unfair dismissal from two years to one, and the raising of the upper limit on unfair dismissal compensation awards to £50,000 (from £12,000) and its indexing to price inflation for future years. Yet, within a short period the government was persuaded to enact a series of measures which sought to limit access to employment tribunals, on the grounds that rising litigation was imposing an undue burden on employers. These provisions, principally contained in the Employment Act 2002, require employees to institute an internal grievance procedure prior to bringing a tribunal claim in respect of a wide range of statutory employment rights, with provision for a substantial reduction in compensation, if the employee's claim is successful, for non-completion of that procedure.[238] In addition, employees who fail to exhaust an internal disciplinary procedure prior to bringing a tribunal claim risk a substantial reduction in their unfair dismissal compensation,[239] while at the same time the content of procedural standards in relation to unfair dismissal has been watered down.[240] Whatever their social impact turns out to be, they have already introduced considerable extra complexity into this area of the law.[241]

Two particularly important developments in the area of basic labour standards were the National Minimum Wage Act 1998, which established a comprehensive statutory minimum wage for the first time in Britain, and the Working Time Regulations 1998, which, by finally implementing the Working Time Directive of 1993, introduced comprehensive working time standards. The process by which the national minimum wage was established exemplified the government's pragmatic and consensus-building approach to labour law policy, in particular through the involvement of both trade unions and employers' organisations in

---

233 On the nature of this opposition, see Bercusson, 2001.
234 Directive 2002/14/EC establishing a general framework for informing and consulting employees within the European Community. See below, para 9.30.
235 See below, para 9.50 *et seq*.
236 Cmnd 3968, para 1.8.
237 Cmnd 3968, p 4.
238 See para 2.21 *et seq*.
239 See para 5.124 *et seq*.
240 See para 5.143.
241 See generally Hepple and Morris, 2002.

the Low Pay Commission which has responsibility, among other things, for making recommendations on the rate of the minimum wage. Subsequent rises in the minimum wage have done something to assuage criticism of the low rate at which it was initially set.[242] The process by which the Working Time Directive was adopted has proved to be a more enduring source of controversy, thanks to the very wide derogations contained in the 1998 and 1999 Regulations.[243] The exceptions contained in the Regulations exploit to the full the derogations contained in the Directive; arguably, in some respects, they go beyond them. Similarly, the manner in which the EC Directives on Part-Time Work,[244] Parental Leave[245] and Fixed-Term Work[246] were implemented prompted concerns that the government's aim of achieving a better reconciliation of family time and work time was unlikely to be realised.[247]

At the same time, these measures mark a break with the view, which was widely held during the 1980s and 1990s, that mandatory labour standards are incompatible with labour market flexibility and efficiency. The economic argument for re-regulation of basic standards, although muted in *Fairness at Work*, was more fully acknowledged in the government's Regulatory Impact Assessment of the (then) Employment Relations Bill 1999. This stated that 'employers have shown that establishing decent standards is consistent with, and can contribute to, competitive business' and noted that while 'the main reason for introducing parental leave is to help individuals to balance work and home life', there should also be 'economic benefits to the economy and to individual employers through reduced staff turnover, and improved commitment leading to improved labour productivity'.[248] Whether this is a view which can, over time, truly be reconciled with the many gaps which are currently to be found in the framework of labour standards, and which are justified by reference to arguments of the regulatory 'burden', remains to be seen.

'Rights and responsibilities' in the labour market

1.35 In so far as the present government's policy represents a departure not just from the policies of the 1980s but also from the period of the welfare state which preceded them, it may lie in the development of a distinctive language of 'rights and responsibilities' which is coupled with a role for government in terms of the 'enabling state'. The coupling of rights and responsibilities is exemplified by the 'New Deal' for the delivery of training and employment opportunities for the unemployed, which operates alongside the stringent benefit

---

242 On the law governing the national minimum wage, and the changes which have taken place in its rate over time, see paras 4.43–4.56 below; for an account of its minimal impact on poverty and the structure of employment, see R Dickens and A Manning, 2003.

243 See paras 4.74–4.78 below; Barnard *et al*, 2003.

244 See para 3.91 below.

245 See para 6.104 below.

246 See para 3.86 below.

247 For discussion, see McColgan, 2000a, 2000b; Kilpatrick, 2004; see paras 6.97–6.107 below, for discussion of the complex body of law which has taken shape in this area since the early 2000s.

248 Department of Trade and Industry, *Employment Relations Bill. Regulatory Impact Assessment*, February 1999: paras 15–16. See also para 16, referring to the 'adverse selection' argument for labour market regulation. For an overview of this and related justifications for intervention, see H Collins, 2001a, 2003; Deakin and Wilkinson, 2005. For conflicting views of the role of mandatory labour standards in promoting competitiveness, see H. Collins, 2001a, 2001b, 2003; Deakin and Wilkinson, 2005.

disqualification rules of the Jobseekers Act 1995 and related measures introduced by Conservative governments.[249] As the Chancellor of the Exchequer explained in his James Meade Memorial Lecture of May 2000, the basis of the New Deal is the notion that government measures should support not just 'new opportunities for employment' but also 'new obligations to seize them'. The government's task of building a 'strong economy and fairer society' implies a 'new, modern understanding of the duties of citizenship and the role and limits of Government'.[250]

On this basis, the provision of government aid designed to find work for the unemployed is symmetrically dependent upon regulations which require the unemployed to take up the opportunities which they are offered, on pain of losing benefit entitlements. More broadly, the idea of 'making work pay' by improving incentives is distinctly doubled-edged: the raising of the minimum wage and the subsidisation of low wages through tax credits is conditional upon increasing legal regulation of the process of transition from unemployment into work.[251] The wider implications for labour law are perhaps less clear. One possibility is a version of corporate responsibility which would counter-balance the regulation of trade union internal affairs. The Chancellor's 2000 James Meade Memorial Lecture referred fleetingly to the need for 'a responsible citizenship' whether it be 'individual or corporate responsibility'.[252] This limited notion of corporate citizenship may be contrasted, however, from the more far-reaching 'stakeholder' conception of corporate governance which the government marginalised in the context of its review of companies legislation.[253]

ASSESSMENT: THE PROSPECTS FOR LABOUR LAW

1.36 The 1979–1997 Conservative administration transformed British labour law, reversing the policies not only of its Labour predecessors but also, in its attack on the principles of collective laissez-faire, undermining the framework which, with varying degrees of enthusiasm, all governments had supported since 1918. Since 1997 the basic elements of a new structure have begun to emerge, but the final shape is not yet clear. What are the prospects for labour law at a time of rapid economic and technological change when the nature of legal intervention of the labour market is also being transformed?

The radical reform of labour law instituted by the 1979–1997 Conservative administration raised fundamental questions for labour lawyers as to the legitimate role of the law in industrial relations and, indeed, the very purpose of labour law itself. The nature of the changes introduced made it impossible to continue to see the principal rationale of labour law as the support of voluntary collective bargaining. The abandonment of the policy of collective laissez-faire

---

249 See para 3.17 below.
250 Chancellor of the Exchequer, Gordon Brown MP, *James Meade Memorial Lecture* at the London School of Economics, 8 May 2000, at p 3.
251 On this coupling of rights and responsibilities, see S White, 1999.
252 *James Meade Memorial Lecture*, 8 May 2000, at 3.
253 See Department of Trade and Industry, *Modern Company Law for a Competitive Economy. Developing the Framework*, March 2000, at para 2.24, and on the eclipse of stakeholder-related thinking in Labour party policy after the general election of 1997, see Novitz and Skidmore, 2001: 14; Deakin, 2004; Wedderburn, 2004. For an argument in favour of employee participation which combines labour law and corporate governance perspectives, see Njoya, 2004.

resolved the tension which had existed in the 1960s and 1970s between voluntary collective bargaining and the state's wider economic goals in favour of the latter. However, it inevitably raised the question: if the principal purpose of labour law is no longer the support of collective bargaining, what is it?

Davies and Freedland have identified the ever-intensifying problem for labour law as being 'how to reconcile the various demands upon governments in relation to industrial society, within a framework of reasonably acceptable, democratic, representative and humane labour law'.[254] Accordingly, the relationship between labour market regulation, economic efficiency and competitiveness is a central issue in labour law today. At the same time, the decline of collective bargaining has led to renewed interest in how far labour law could or should be used to articulate certain fundamental social and economic rights.[255] The degree to which such fundamental rights may be enshrined in law without burdening enterprises with excessive costs, or creating harmful labour-market rigidities, continues to be at the heart of debates over the future development of legislative policy both in Britain and in the European Union. In the remainder of this chapter, we indicate the nature of this debate and the issues which it raises.[256] We also draw upon the themes referred to here in later chapters.

Labour law and economic efficiency

1.37   As we have seen, the debate over labour market flexibility and the efficiency of labour law has, since the late 1970s, stressed the degree to which over-rigid labour laws and excessive social security provision in Britain have been responsible for slowing down processes of labour market adjustment. The 1994 European Commission White Paper, *European Social Policy – A Way Forward for the Union*, acknowledged the importance of this issue when it commented that 'the need to alter fundamentally, and update, the structure of incentives which influence the labour market is still not adequately recognised'.[257] At the same time, there has been a growing recognition that the problem of incentive structures will not necessarily be solved by a simple process of deregulation, if that is understood to mean the removal of protective legislation and a return to the unregulated individual contract of employment or employment relationship. As the experience of the United Kingdom in the 1980s shows, 'deregulation' is a complex process which, while it may lead to the removal of regulatory controls in some areas, is compatible with an enlarged role for legislation in others, in particular with regard to the control of collective organisation. The extreme complexity of British legislation dealing with industrial action and with internal trade union affairs is testimony to the continuing importance of the law in this area. More generally, the removal of certain labour law protections during this period did not mean that the state had effectively withdrawn: 'contrary to all appearances, the "activist" state is by no means dismissed ... far from simply rejecting all interference, the state is assigned the task of setting the elementary conditions for a functioning market'.[258]

---

254 P Davies and M Freedland, 1993: p 663.
255 For recent discussions of the theme of fundamental rights in labour law, see Wedderburn, 1991, 1995; Ewing, Gearty and Hepple (eds), 1994; Hepple, 1995, 2005a.
256 For a wide-ranging analysis of contemporary British labour law which takes up the theme of the contrast between rights-based and efficiency-based approaches, drawing on human rights theory and on the economics of law, see A Davies, 2004.
257 COM (94) 333, at p 11.
258 Simitis, 1987: p 128.

An important implication of this is that so-called deregulation did not, of itself, reverse the process of the 'juridification' of labour relations, or the increasing intervention of the state in economic and social relations.[259] Nor is it at all clear that the aim of enhancing labour market efficiency can most effectively be met by the means of deregulation, given the persistence within 'unregulated markets' of market failures of various kinds.[260]

There is an argument to the effect that the question of efficiency should be approached by seeking to strike a better balance between economic and social policy goals: in the words of the EC White Paper, 'long-run competitiveness is to be sought, not through a dilution of the European model of social protection, but through the adaptation, rationalisation and simplification of regulations, so as to establish a better balance between social protection, competitiveness and employment creation'.[261] Elsewhere, however, the White Paper referred to a view which suggests that there is no *necessary* conflict between economic and social policy: 'the pursuit of high social standards should not be seen only as a cost but also as a key element in the competitive formula. It is for these essential reasons that the Union's social policy cannot be second string to economic development or to the functioning of the internal market'.[262]

Others have also questioned whether there is an inevitable trade-off between rights and efficiency in this context. A study published by the UK Employment Department in 1995 found substantial evidence of what it took to be increased flexibility in the labour market which could be ascribed to the legal changes introduced since 1980. At the same time, the author of the study pointed out that 'it is difficult to establish precise linkages between measures of flexibility and labour market outcomes'.[263] The study found evidence of greater micro-level flexibility in the UK in the form of an increase by firms of part-time, temporary and self-employment, as well as an increase in 'functional flexibility', or the adaptability of workers within enterprises. At the macro-level, by contrast, there was still evidence of substantial wage rigidity, and in particular a lack of responsiveness of wages to changes in levels of unemployment.

The Employment Department's analysis also confirmed a finding of several earlier studies, namely that different countries achieve flexibility by different routes.[264] Thus intensively-regulated systems like Germany, Japan and the Scandinavian countries have succeeded in maintaining a high rate of productivity growth, notwithstanding their continuing commitment to a high level of social protection and respect for employment rights. In this regard, a comprehensive comparative study by Blank found that 'there is little evidence that labour market flexibility is substantially affected by the presence of these social protection programmes, nor is there strong evidence that the speed of labour market adjustment can be increased by limiting these programmes'.[265]

---

259 Simitis, 1987: p 128. For discussion of the juridification thesis in the context of British labour law see Clark and Wedderburn, 1987; and for analysis of labour law as a mechanism of 'reflexive' social and economic regulation, see Rogowski, 1994; Rogowski and Wilthagen, 1994; H Collins, 2003; De Schutter and Deakin, 2005.
260 Deakin and Wilkinson, 1994, 2000a, 2000b, 2005.
261 COM (94) 333, at p 11.
262 COM (94) 333, p 2. See also para 2.6 below.
263 M Beatson, 1995: p 64.
264 M Beatson, 1995: p 64.
265 Blank, 1994: p 181. The United Kingdom continues to have lower productivity growth than similar, developed economies, a point recognised in a book written by the former Director-General of the Confederation of British Industry (A Turner, 2001).

More generally, there may be a case to be made for the positive economic effects of labour standards. As one of us has argued elsewhere, labour standards are one aspect of the type of business environment which is needed to foster long-termism, encourage firms to invest in labour quality through training and, more generally, to underpin a high-wage, high-productivity strategy for the achievement of economic competitiveness.[266] The very nature of the change in economic competition towards greater stress on innovation, flexibility and responsiveness by firms makes it doubtful that a low-wage strategy will be sufficient: 'ultimately, innovation and dynamism are not derived from making labour resources cheaper, but from making labour more effective, productive and innovative. While enlightened firms may follow this advice independently, commonly agreed and shared standards are needed to diffuse the productive impact of good labour use on a wider scale'.[267] As we have seen, the attitude of the present government to this argument remains deeply ambivalent. Too often the rhetoric of labour market 'flexibility' appears to obscure the essentials of the debate.

Labour law and fundamental rights

1.38   A second major theme of contemporary labour law is that of the use of the law to express and make effective in practice the fundamental civil, social and economic rights of workers. There has been a long-running debate concerning the framework of the statutory immunities for collective labour law, and whether they should be replaced by a system of 'positive rights'.[268] Because any system of positive rights would inevitably have to contain within it derogations and exceptions to the right to strike or the right to freedom of association, for example, the issue of immunities against positive rights does not, in itself, decide the question of what the substance of those rights should be. Nor would the enactment of positive rights necessarily lead to a change in the attitude of the courts, or to any reduction of their role.

The only relevant recent experience in Britain of such a radical development in the law is the period of the Industrial Relations Act 1971. That legislation excluded the common law in favour of a comprehensive framework of statutory controls over unfair labour practices, combining extensive legal compulsion over industrial action and control of the rule books and constitutions of the unions which chose to register under the Act, with significant legal guarantees of collective bargaining and recognition rights for those unions. The attitude of the judges, as expressed in particular through the National Industrial Relations Court, was based not so much on the traditional aim of the defence of the common law against the incursions of legislation,[269] as on a corporatist objective of intervening to reduce the costs of strike action and enhance the effectiveness of collective procedures in the 'public interest'.[270] The Industrial Relations Act failed for a number of reasons,[271] but not least among them was that its enactment coincided with a period of union strength and militancy when unemployment was low and the unions had the option of not co-operating with the new laws. It seems unlikely that legislation would again seek in the foreseeable future to

266 Deakin and Wilkinson, 1994, 2005.
267 Sengenberger, 1994: p 10.
268 See, in particular, with regard to the right to strike, Wedderburn, 1985; Ewing, 1986.
269 See above, para 1.9.
270 Donaldson, 1975.
271 Weekes *et al*, 1975.

combine collective rights and obligations in the fashion of the 1971 Act. This route to reform would have to face up to the trade unions' justifiable suspicion of any attempt to give the courts a more powerful role in resolving collective disputes.

A wider issue is how far employment rights of both a collective and an individual nature could or should be enshrined in a basic constitutional text, thereby granting them a status superior to that of norms contained in ordinary legislation.[272] This debate, which once seemed far removed from British experience, has been stimulated by the adoption in 1998 of the Human Rights Act. As a consequence of this Act, Convention rights – that is, rights guaranteed by the European Convention on Human Rights – must be taken into account by courts and tribunals when interpreting labour legislation and, in certain contexts, when developing rules of the common law. As we shall explore at various points throughout this book, the discourse of human rights now plays a growing role within labour law. Moreover, the UK's membership of the European Union has also meant that a constitutional status is already accorded to certain rights, including the right to equal pay between men and women, by virtue of the doctrine of direct effect. The UK Equal Pay Act 1970, and related legislation, is effectively subject to Article 141 of the EC Treaty, and courts and employment tribunals are under an obligation to apply the superior norm of European Community law in the event of conflict with the UK Act. The potential impact of EC law upon domestic legislation was illustrated in *R v Secretary of State for Employment, ex p Equal Opportunities Commission*,[273] in which the House of Lords removed a central aspect of the legislative treatment of part-time workers by ruling that the exclusion of those working for fewer than 16 and (in some instances) 8 hours per week from employment protection contravened the principle of equality of treatment in European Community law. As the jurisprudence of the ECJ continues to evolve in the direction of recognition for a range of fundamental rights,[274] the impact of European Community on UK legislation seems set to continue.

The rights which are enshrined in the European Convention on Human Rights refer mainly to individual or civil rights, and not to collective or social rights of the kind which are to be found in the constitutional texts of a number of western European systems. Hence the Italian Constitution of 1947 recognises 'all citizens' right to work',[275] as well as the right to an equitable wage, the right to equal pay for equal work between men and women, the right to social assistance, the right to trade union organisation and the right to strike.[276] The Preamble to the French Constitution of 1946 also refers to the right to work, the right to strike and the principle of trade union freedom. A particularly important development in recent years has been the use by courts in other European systems of more general constitutional provisions to provide basic protections for freedom of expression and personal dignity and autonomy in the context of the employment relationship. Much of the inspiration has come from the Basic Law of the German Federal Republic, which in Article 1 guarantees the 'Protection of human dignity', and which lays down in Article 2(1) that 'Everyone shall have the right to the free development of his personality in so far as he does not violate the rights of

---

272 For critical discussion of this concept, see Ewing, 1994b.
273 [1994] IRLR 176. See below, paras 3.88 and 6.29.
274 See para 2.43 below.
275 Constitution of the Italian Republic, 22 December 1947: Art 4.
276 Constitution of the Italian Republic, 22 December 1947: Arts 35–40.

others or offend against the constitutional order'. These provisions, together with Article 4 on freedom of opinion, conscience and religion, Article 5 on freedom of expression, and Article 6 on the protection of marriage and the family, have had an extensive influence on German labour law,[277] and also influenced the Spanish Constitution of 1978 and its subsequent interpretation by the courts. In short, these systems have experienced what has been described as the 'constitutionalisation' of labour law.[278]

In considering whether the experience of these other European systems has anything of value for Britain, the long-standing issues of the legitimate role of the courts, the degree of effectiveness, in practice, of legal rights, and the proper balance to be struck between legal intervention and self-regulation in industry are once again to the fore.[279] Whatever the prospects for constitutional reform in Britain, the continuing influence of European Union law has already given rise to a situation in which the English and Scottish courts are faced with issues which are phrased in an essentially constitutional form, namely involving conflicts between rights which are expressed in broad terms, on the one hand, and instrumental or efficiency-related factors which are put forward in justification for practices limiting those rights, on the other.[280] The Human Rights Act 1998 also requires certain labour law issues to be determined within a framework of this type of discourse. At present, the discussion, at least in the courts, is somewhat uneven, because notions of what constitutes a fundamental right in legal terms are somewhat more advanced than the notions of efficiency which are set against them.[281] Indeed, it is not always obvious what the normative or legal meaning of economic efficiency might be in this context, or to what extent such a concept should be advanced at the expense of other values or interests. It seems likely that the future of labour law as a form of market intervention will increasingly turn on how successful courts and policy-makers are in finding a language in which to express and reconcile these conflicts of rights and efficiency.

---

277 Daübler, 1991: ch 5; Simitis, 1994.
278 Del Rey Guanter, 1992.
279 For such an analysis, see Deakin, 1996a.
280 See in particular *R v Secretary of State for Employment, ex p Equal Opportunities Commission* [1994] IRLR 176, discussed above; see also paras 6.29–6.31 below.
281 See Deakin, 1994a, for a discussion of this point in the context of the ruling of the House of Lords in *Ex p Equal Opportunities Commission* [1994] IRLR 176, and for contrasting analyses of the role of economic discourse in labour law, see H Collins, 2001b, 2003; Supiot, 2000, 2005; Deakin and Wilkinson, 2005.

CHAPTER 2

Sources and institutions of labour law

INTRODUCTION

2.1 Unlike some systems labour law in Britain does not take the form of a comprehensive Labour Code; rather it is derived from a multiplicity of sources, both legal and extra-legal, which may interact in complex ways. Determining the law on a particular matter, therefore, may involve examination of a range of sources. In analysing the legal liability of those organising industrial action, for example, there is a need first to decide whether any tort has been committed. This will frequently depend upon whether the industrial action in question constitutes a breach of their employment contract by those participating in it, which may in turn require reference to collective agreements or to custom and practice in the industry or workplace. It may then be necessary to decide whether the action is afforded immunity against tortious liability by statute, which itself involves entry to a legislative maze. To assess an employer's chances of successfully pursuing a legal remedy, knowledge of civil procedure becomes important, particularly where (as is generally the case) an interim injunction is being sought. Moreover, if picketing is undertaken, whether such action infringes the criminal law, and the implications of the HRA 1998, may be at issue. Finally, it is possible that an agreement made by an employer under threat of industrial action may lead to a subsequent claim in restitution based upon the doctrine of 'economic duress'. To take another example, examining the legal consequences of making employees redundant may require not only consideration of the law governing contracts of employment and the relevant statutory rights, both individual and collective, but also EC law to see if the dismissals may be discriminatory on grounds of sex or contrary to procedures for collective consultation (for example if part-time workers are chosen first), the terms of any relevant collective agreements if unfair selection is alleged, and potential remedies in public law if the decision in question falls within its reach.

It is sometimes said that labour law in Britain lacks autonomy from the common law, in the sense that the reach of common law doctrines is particularly extensive. Employment rights may be radically affected by common law precedents argued in an entirely different legal context; thus the scope of the freedom to withdraw labour may be curtailed by a decision on the scope of a common law tort in proceedings which have no connection with industrial disputes (such as a commercial dispute between two companies). Whether there should – or can – be an autonomous system of labour law insulated against developments in the common law is a fundamental issue which those who seek to change the present system radically would need to address.[1] The HRA 1998 may now modify the application of the common law in specific contexts, such as picketing, but for the reasons we explain in para 7.9 its implications for collective labour law in general are likely to be limited.

---

1   See Wedderburn, 1987a; Howarth, 1988; Wedderburn, 1991a and references therein.

In this chapter, in order to explain the existing sources of labour law and the relationship between them we have drawn a distinction between formal (legal) sources and 'voluntary' norms created by the conduct of the parties, such as collective agreements and works rules. However, it is important to emphasise at the outset that this does not mean that the formal and voluntary sources are completely separate; on the contrary, autonomous norms will frequently play a vital role in determining the parties' legal rights. Their significance is appropriately emphasised by Hepple when he states that '[t]he interaction between autonomous norms and state law is a central aspect of any study of labour law'.[2] Equally, the ordering of our discussion, which commences with the formal sources, should not be taken as indicative of a particular hierarchy of norms; indeed until the 1970s voluntary norms were by far the more important source of labour law in Britain and it could be argued that even now, despite the vast increase in legislation, it would be equally appropriate to commence with voluntary sources. What is incontrovertible is that consideration only of the formal sources would provide a dangerously misleading picture of the contemporary law.

Having outlined the formal and informal sources of domestic labour law we then examine the nature of the institutions by which it is interpreted and enforced. We begin by examining the judicial mechanisms for dispute settlement, the courts and employment tribunals. We then look at the non-judicial bodies which play a role in this area together with those which have statutory functions in relation to specific areas of labour law such as discrimination and trade union affairs. It is important to stress at this stage that the allocation of jurisdiction between the judicial and non-judicial bodies in relation to the settlement of disputes is not immutable and, indeed, is an aspect of the contemporary labour law system which has recently been subject to reform.

Our discussion of domestic sources and institutions is followed by an analysis of the role of international labour standards in UK law. European Community law is, of course, an integral part of national law and should, strictly speaking, be analysed in that context. However, the jurisdictional base and scope of EC social law is a matter of particular significance to labour lawyers, especially given the distinctive procedures which are available for enacting legislation in this field and the many questions which these raise. In view of the importance and complexity of this area we treat it as a separate section of this chapter. We then outline the role of other international labour standards which are not, unless embodied in legislation, incorporated in national law. However, this does not mean that they can thereby be ignored: where national legislation is ambiguous there is a (rebuttable) presumption that Parliament did not intend to legislate in breach of the UK's international obligations and the courts may refer to international treaties when called upon to decide upon the position at common law. Moreover, these labour standards may be relevant when a court or tribunal is interpreting 'Convention rights' under the HRA 1998, particularly where there is no jurisprudence from the Convention organs or a domestic court is being urged to take a wider view of what a right entails. Finally, the UK's obligation in international law to comply with treaties it has ratified may be a powerful influence upon the formulation of domestic legal policy although, as we shall see, its influence upon the 1979–1997 Conservative Governments was not always a significant one, nor has it weighed heavily with their Labour

2   Sweet and Maxwell, 1992, as updated: para 1-1019.

successor. Finally, we consider the question of conflicts of law between different national systems of regulation.

The purpose of this chapter is to provide a framework for the remainder of the text. Where areas are dealt with in greater detail in later chapters, we do not, at this stage, provide full references.

FORMAL SOURCES OF LABOUR LAW

The common law

2.2   Despite the volume of legislation now governing the area of labour law, the common law remains at the core of the system at both the individual and collective levels. At the individual level, with the exception of some public service workers, the employment relationship is constituted by a contract which is governed, essentially, by principles emanating from the common law. Moreover the existence, or potential existence, of a contract is the basis of access by workers to the vast majority of statutory employment protection rights. At the collective level the mere existence of trade unions, and the organisation of industrial action, are unlawful at common law, a position which continues to be of paramount importance given the fragility of the protection afforded against this liability by statute.

The dominant effect of the common law links the current system inextricably with the past. In Wedderburn's striking phrase it 'enjoys the curse of exaggerated continuity'.[3] The doctrine of precedent means that judicial decisions remain embedded within the legal culture even though social conditions may have changed radically since they were reached. Thus decisions dating back to the nineteenth century and earlier may still be influential in the contemporary courts. At the individual level the concept of the managerial prerogative, which has its origins in the early law of master and servant, remains a powerful one in several contexts. The fact that the employment relationship is constituted in a contractual form allows the courts considerable discretion to shape it by means of implied terms where a matter is not dealt with by express agreement. The implied duties of employees to obey lawful and reasonable orders of their employer and to co-operate in the running of the enterprise are among the most notable manifestations of this inherent managerial prerogative. Furthermore, as we shall see, 'the archetypal models of master and servant' have also influenced the interpretation of modern employment protection legislation.[4] Thus, in the context of unfair dismissal legislation, for example, employers' interests in restructuring the enterprise, which may necessitate significant changes to the terms and conditions of their workforce, are accorded primary importance to the extent that they may even, in practice, trump employees' contractual rights.

At the collective level the common law is also of fundamental significance. During the nineteenth century the courts found the purposes of most trade unions to be unlawful as being in restraint of trade,[5] and to this day those organising industrial action nearly always commit a common law tort.[6] The lawfulness of

---

3   Wedderburn, 1993: p 253.
4   Wedderburn, 1993: p 261, and see generally pp 238–262 for a discussion of the relationship between the common law and 'labour'.
5   *Hornby v Close* (1867) LR 2 QB 153.
6   See ch 11.

trade unions' status and the (now very limited) freedom to take industrial action depend entirely upon statutory immunities from the common law liabilities which would otherwise apply. Reliance upon a system of immunities rather than one of positive statutory rights has important practical implications: because such immunities constitute exceptions to the common law, the courts tend to construe them narrowly and the overriding discretion of the courts to grant an interim injunction where a common law right is at stake remains, in the final analysis, intact.[7] It also means that the activities of workers' organisations are always vulnerable to the extension of liabilities at common law which are outside the protection of the immunities, a prevailing theme in the context of industrial action (exemplified in the discovery by the courts of the unprotected wrong of inducing breach of a statutory duty). The language of immunities also has important rhetorical significance, enabling opponents to present unions as having unwarranted special 'privileges' which are denied to other bodies,[8] rather than seeing them as repositories of fundamental civil and social rights.

The final area where the common law remains important (although more now in theory than in practice) is the relationship between trade unions and their members.[9] A trade union is, in legal terms, an association of individuals bound together by a contract of membership (contained primarily in the union rules) which regulates the relationship between them. In the past proceedings to enforce this contract have, again, provided judges with the opportunity to mould the relationship of the parties via the mechanism of implied terms. In general the courts have inclined towards an interpretation which protects the interests of the individual union member, although the HRA 1998 has the potential to bring greater respect for trade union autonomy in those areas left untouched by legislation. In recent years, however, the conduct of trade union affairs has become subject to increasingly extensive statutory regulation, leaving only very narrow scope for the unrestricted operation of union rules. For this reason the notion of unions as autonomous bodies whose rules are based upon agreement between their members is now no more than a fiction.

Legislation

2.3   As we saw in chapter 1, legislation played an important but subsidiary role in labour law for many years; for individual workers voluntary collective bargaining was the primary source of protection, with statute being confined to the areas which collective bargaining did not reach: the protection of women and children, some aspects of health and safety, and wage-fixing machinery for particularly vulnerable workers. In relation to collective organisation, the role of legislation was largely confined to affording (limited) protection against liabilities which would otherwise arise at common law. By contrast, the past thirty years or so has witnessed an expansion in the range and scope of legislation covering most areas of labour law; while that relating to the individual employment relationship has, in general, enhanced employment protection, in the collective field the role of legislation has varied much more greatly and in the area of industrial action is now essentially restrictive in its nature.

---

7   See in the context of industrial action Lord Diplock in *NWL Ltd v Woods* [1979] ICR 867, 881–882 (as corrected [1980] ICR 167); Lord Fraser in *Duport Steels Ltd v Sirs* [1980] ICR 161, 187.
8   See, for example, Hayek, 1980: p 58: 'there can be no salvation for Britain until the special privileges granted to trade unions three-quarters of a century ago are revoked'.
9   See generally ch 10.

Perhaps surprisingly, in view of the crucial importance of legislation in guiding the conduct of both workers and employers, it can be extremely difficult to ascertain the relevant provisions governing a particular issue. Frequently they will be scattered among several statutes and possibly also statutory instruments. Even within an individual statute the law may be located in a number of different sections and multi-paragraphed schedules may contain amendments and provisos which may easily be overlooked. Moreover, such legislation is often cast in language which it is difficult for the experienced lawyer, let alone the lay person, to comprehend. In 1981 Browne-Wilkinson J described the provisions relating to maternity leave then in force as being of 'inordinate complexity exceeding the worst excesses of a taxing statute',[10] a criticism endorsed by the Court of Appeal.[11] The same comment could equally be made of many other statutory employment protection rights. It applies with even greater force to the myriad of provisions now governing trade union conduct. The opaque or ambiguous nature of statutory language makes scrutiny of Parliamentary debates a particularly important element of legal research in this area, although the interpretation offered by the relevant minister in Parliament may not ultimately be reflected in the decisions of the courts and the opportunities for invoking parliamentary material in argument are limited.[12] The difficulties of interpretation are exacerbated when major changes are introduced in the form of statutory instruments; here time for Parliamentary debate is very limited, thus precluding detailed examination of their import, and, in general, there is no opportunity for amendments to be proposed.[13] Four important provisions, the Equal Pay (Amendment) Regulations 1983,[14] the Transfer of Undertakings (Protection of Employment) Regulations 1981,[15] the Employment Equality (Religion or Belief) Regulations 2003,[16] and the Employment Equality (Sexual Orientation) Regulations 2003[17] were introduced as delegated legislation under the European Communities Act 1972.

As this brief summary indicates, even within the confines of legislation, let alone beyond it, predicting accurately the meaning of labour law in Britain can be a hazardous task. Judicial decisions as to the interpretation of particular statutory provisions may eventually provide clarification but this is of little help to those who wish to organise their affairs in order to comply with the law from the outset. Moreover, pre-existing interpretations of legislation may require

10   *Lavery v Plessey Telecommunications Ltd* [1983] IRLR 180, 182 .
11   [1983] IRLR 202, 206 (Slade LJ).
12   See *Pepper v Hart* [1993] AC 593 where the House of Lords held that, in specific circumstances, reference could be made to Hansard. Lord Browne-Wilkinson, who gave the principal opinion, concluded that, subject to the question of House of Commons' privileges, reference should be permitted as an aid to the construction of legislation which is ambiguous or obscure or whose literal meaning leads to an absurdity provided that the parliamentary material clearly discloses the mischief aimed at or the legislative intention underlying the ambiguous or obscure words. He could not foresee that a statement other than that of a minister or other promoter of the Bill was likely to satisfy those criteria. See D Oliver, 1993 for the implications of this decision, and see *R v Secretary of State for the Environment, Transport and the Regions, ex p Spath Holme Ltd* [2001] 1 All ER 195 on the doctrine applicable to the scope of a statutory power. See also *Robinson v Secretary of State for Northern Ireland* [2002] UKHL 32 and *Wilson v Secretary of State for Trade and Industry* [2004] 1 AC 816.
13   This can happen only if the parent Act so permits: W McKay, 2004: pp 676–677.
14   SI 1983/1794; see further ch 6.
15   SI 1981/1794.
16   SI 2003/1660.
17   SI 2003/1661.

reconsideration in the light of the HRA 1998.[18] In addition, many important statutory concepts are treated as questions of fact for first instance courts or tribunals to adjudicate upon, with limited scope for appeal, so that different tribunals are able legitimately to reach opposite conclusions on identical sets of facts. This situation does little to assist those who are seeking to know their basic legal rights. The decision as to whether a worker is an 'employee', the gateway to many statutory rights, is perhaps the most important casualty of this approach.[19]

The relationship between legislation and the common law may be an intricate one. Legislation will normally prevail in the sense that any agreement between the parties specifically to exclude its operation will be void but to achieve this result it has been necessary, on occasion, to state specifically that statutory norms take precedence over the common law.[20] In the area of individual rights, legislation may be given effect in a variety of ways. In rare cases statutory provisions can displace express contractual terms and are then enforceable through the contract. One example is the equality clause which is deemed by the Equal Pay Act 1970 to be included in the terms of the contract of a woman (or man) employed at an establishment in Great Britain.[21] Another is the award which may be made if an employer refuses to comply with an order to disclose information for collective bargaining purposes as required by statute.[22] More commonly statutory rights stand independent of the contract although they may be set off against contractual rights, for example in the areas of guaranteed and maternity pay.[23] The effect of this is that any contractual payment goes towards discharging statutory liability and vice versa but liability for any greater amount under either head remains. In some cases, however, a right which may appear wholly independent of the contract may not be so in practice; thus the courts have held that access to the statutory right of unfair dismissal rests upon a valid contract with the result that where the contract is tainted with illegality, because, for example, of the employee's 'collusion' in evading tax, access to that right may be lost.[24]

In the area of collective labour law the relationship between common law and statute is particularly intricate as regards industrial action where statute affords very limited immunity against specific, but not all, common law torts. By contrast, in relation to trade union government, as we indicated in para 2.2 statute now directly or in practice overrides union rules in most important areas.

Codes of Practice

2.4   The Secretary of State for Employment, ACAS and, within their respective areas of jurisidiction, the EOC, CRE, DRC and HSC, are empowered by statute

---

18   S 3.
19   See ch 3.
20   See ERA 1996, s 203(1), but note also s 203(2) which indicates when access to rights may be precluded. The prohibition on exclusion will not necessarily prevent the employment relationship being constructed in such a way that the qualifications necessary to meet a claim are not met, for example by placing the financial risks on the worker to create a self-employed relationship in circumstances where only employees are qualified to bring a claim. The relationship between Convention rights and contract is particularly controversial: see G Morris, 2001a.
21   EqPA 1970, s 1(1).
22   TULRCA 1992, s 185(5); see further para 9.24 below.
23   See paras 4.113 and 6.103 below.
24   See para 3.29 *et seq* below.

to issue Codes of Practice which provide practical guidance on conduct in particular areas.[25] These Codes are not intended merely to codify existing practices but rather actively to promote those which are viewed as desirable, and there is evidence to suggest that they are capable of having a significant impact in the workplace.[26] Breach of a Code of Practice does not of itself render an individual liable to legal proceedings.[27] However, the Codes of Practice issued by ACAS, the EOC, and CRE are admissible in evidence in proceedings before an employment tribunal;[28] those by the Secretary of State and DRC are additionally admissible in proceedings before the courts,[29] and these bodies must take into account any provisions of a Code which seem relevant to an issue before them. Thus, although Codes of Practice are not legally binding as such, compliance or non-compliance with their provisions may influence the outcome of proceedings and, indeed, in some cases their recommendations have, in practice, been elevated almost to the status of legal principles. One notorious example of this practice was the Code of Practice on Picketing which specifies that pickets and their organisers should ensure in general a maximum of six pickets at the entrance to any workplace;[30] this has been reflected in the terms of injunctions ordered by the courts to restrict the conduct of future picketing[31] and in the use of police discretion (although, as we discuss in para 11.52 *et seq*, the HRA 1998 requires reconsideration of this approach). On occasion Codes have contained recommendations which explicitly exceed the requirements of the parent legislation. The Code of Practice on Industrial Action Ballots and Notice to Employers, which we discuss in para 11.45, is a prominent example of this.[32]

25 Codes currently in force issued by the Secretary of State are the Code of Practice on Picketing (revised in 1992); the Code of Practice on Access to Workers during Recognition and Derecognition Ballots (2000); and the Code of Practice on Industrial Action Ballots and Notice to Employers (2000). ACAS has, to date, issued Codes of Practice in three areas: Disclosure of Information to Trade Unions for Collective Bargaining Purposes (revised in 1997), Time Off for Trade Union Duties and Activities (revised in 2003), and Disciplinary and Grievance Procedures (revised in 2004). ACAS Codes require the approval of the Secretary of State and Parliament to come into force; the Secretary of State must consult ACAS and also obtain parliamentary approval before issuing a Code: TULRCA 1992, ss 199–206. A Code of Practice on Age Diversity in Employment, issued by the Department for Education and Employment in 1999, has no statutory authority.
26 See L Dickens *et al*, 1985: pp 232–234 on the impact of the ACAS Code on Disciplinary Practices and Procedures in Employment initially issued in 1977. The 1980 Workplace Industrial Relations Survey showed that in nine out of ten cases disciplinary procedures contained provision for oral then written warnings as recommended in the Code: Daniel and Millward, 1983: p 165.
27 See, for example, TULRCA 1992, s 207(1).
28 TULRCA 1992, s 207(2); SDA 1975, s 56(10); RRA 1976, s 47(10). Note that those issued under by the CRE are also admissible before a county court.
29 TULRCA 1992, s 207(3); DDA 1995, s 53A. Codes of Practice issued or approved by the Health and Safety Commission are admissible in evidence in criminal proceedings: HSWA 1974, ss 16 and 17.
30 Para 5.1 of the Code; see further para 11.52 below.
31 *Thomas v NUM (South Wales Area)* [1985] IRLR 136; *News Group Newspapers Ltd v SOGAT '82 (No 2)* [1986] IRLR 337.
32 Another, less dramatic, is the provision in the Code of Practice on Time Off for Trade Union Duties and Activities which states that employers should consider making available to officials the facilities necessary to enable them to perform their duties: see further para 8.40 below.

Public law and labour law

2.5   It may appear strange that public law should be relevant to the essentially private relationship of worker and employer. In many systems, however, public employment is governed by a wholly separate legal regime from that applicable in the private sector, and in some countries, such as Germany and France, certain public employees (*Beamten* and *fonctionnaires* respectively) are governed by public administrative law. In Britain there is no such formal demarcation between the public and private sectors, although many areas of public service employment have been subject to distinctive laws and internal regulations (special disciplinary codes and restrictions on outside or political activities, for example) to meet the perceived requirements of the individual service.[33] However, public law may have implications for employment rights where the employer is a public body which is subject to the supervisory jurisdiction of the courts through the mechanism of judicial review. An application for judicial review is subject to procedural restrictions which do not apply to claims in private law: the application may be made only with the permission of the court and the time limit within which permission must be sought is short.[34] Despite these procedural obstacles judicial review has proved a popular route for public employees although the circumstances where an application may lie in the employment context are unpredictable and controversial.[35] First, it may extend to situations where there are no remedies available in private law. Thus, when the UK Conservative Government banned membership of national civil service trade unions at Government Communications Headquarters in 1984 without any prior consultation with workers or their unions, despite a long-standing practice of consultation on important issues, a public law claim based upon breach of a legitimate expectation of consultation offered the unions their only possible remedy.[36] Second, it may offer remedies for individual groups of workers who are denied access to claims in private law. For a dismissed member of a police force, who has no contract of employment or access to the statutory remedy of unfair dismissal, judicial review is the only possible avenue to pursue beyond the rights provided in the internal disciplinary procedure. Last, even if a private law action is available the remedies in public law may be superior; for example the remedy of *certiorari* can quash an employer's decision to dismiss, thus securing at least temporary reinstatement in employment, and, unlike private law proceedings, may overturn a decision relating to a group not merely an individual worker.

---

33   For a general analysis see Fredman and Morris, 1989; for a critique of the position see G Morris and S Fredman, 1993 and G Morris, 2000 and, on political activities, G Morris, 1998b.

34   A claim form for judicial review must be filed 'promptly', and in any event not later than three months after the grounds to make the claim first arose: CPR r 54.5. There is a three-month time limit for bringing claims for unfair dismissal, subject to the discretion of the employment tribunal to extend this period: ERA 1996, s 111(2). For an overview of the regime governing judicial review applications since October 2000 see Fordham, 2001; see also Cornford and Sunkin, 2001.

35   See, in particular, Fredman and Morris, 1991a, and references therein, from which much of what follows is taken; see also Fredman and Morris, 1994 and de Smith *et al*, 1995: pp 186–191, as updated 1998; T Poole, 2000.

36   *Council of Civil Service Unions v Minister for the Civil Service* [1985] AC 374. In the event the duty to consult was trumped by national security considerations.

The courts have taken a restrictive view of when judicial review may properly lie in the employment context.[37] One might have thought that the mere fact that the employer is a public body should suffice on the ground that, although impacting upon private individuals, decisions relating to employment involve the exercise of public power. However, this view has been rejected in favour of a complex (and sometimes conflicting) set of criteria by which the designation of a claim as public or private is decided.[38] None has proved to be satisfactory. Most prominent among these tests has been the existence of a contract. In the leading case of *R v East Berkshire Health Authority, ex p Walsh*[39] the Court of Appeal held that where the application concerns rights arising directly out of a contract, rather than the exercise of statutory duties or powers, then it is properly one of private law. This decision assumes that the pattern of contractual and non-contractual relations in the public services is coherent whereas in reality it is usually the product of ad hoc, historical evolution rather than of principle. In the context of civil service employment it also produced some unseemly contradictory tactical arguments by the Crown as to the existence of a contract of employment, depending upon whether a claim was brought in public or in private law.[40] A second approach to demarcation, developed primarily by Lord Woolf, is based upon the subject-matter of the decision. Taking as its starting-point the premise that the employment relationship is essentially a private one, it acknowledges that there may nevertheless be situations where judicial review may be appropriate, for example where a process of dismissal has a statutory or similar underpinning relating to procedure or a decision is one of policy affecting a group of workers and not merely a single individual.[41] This is equally unsatisfactory; the latter category, for example, immediately prompts questions as to when a sufficiently large group of workers will be deemed to be affected and overlooks the 'precedent' value of a decision which may, ostensibly, only concern a single individual. Third, an application for judicial review may be defeated, even if one of the above two tests is satisfied, if the court considers that there are alternative remedies in private law, such as the right to claim unfair dismissal or breach of contract, even though the remedies may not, in fact, be true equivalents.[42] Moreover, the courts have recently adopted a further test that asks whether 'the defendant was performing a public duty owed to the claimant in the particular circumstances under consideration'.[43]

---

37 The courts have taken the view that not only should CPR Part 54 (formerly RSC Order 53) be used for 'public law' matters pursuant to the House of Lords decision in *O'Reilly v Mackman* [1983] 2 AC 237, but have also refused to allow an applicant to use Part 54 if the claim is properly classified as 'private'. Although the decision in *Roy v Kensington and Chelsea and Westminster Family Practitioner Committee* [1992] 1 AC 624 showed signs of greater flexibility it left the divide essentially intact: see Fredman and Morris, 1994: pp 82–83; although cf *Mercury Communications Ltd v Director General of Telecommunications* [1996] 1 All ER 575, HL, noted P Craig, 1996; *Trustees of the Dennis Rye Pension Fund v Sheffield City Council* [1997] 4 All ER 747, 754–756, Lord Woolf MR; *Steed v Secretary of State for the Home Department* [2000] 3 All ER 226.
38 *O'Reilly v Mackman* [1983] 2 AC 237.
39 [1985] QB 152.
40 See Fredman and Morris, 1991b.
41 See *McLaren v Home Office* [1990] IRLR 338; *R v Derbyshire County Council, ex p Noble* [1990] IRLR 332.
42 See further para 5.47 below.
43 *R (on the Application of Tucker) v Director General of the National Crime Squad* [2003] IRLR 439, para 24 (Scott Baker LJ).

The area of public employment has proved one of the most difficult in which to implement the procedural divide between public and private law.[44] However, while some members of the higher judiciary have shown impatience with the divide's constraints,[45] at the time of writing there are no immediate prospects that it will be abandoned.[46]

As well as being potentially applicable to public employees, judicial review is also important in controlling the exercise of discretion by various statutory bodies which have jurisdiction in the field of labour law. It has been particularly significant in relation to decisions of the Central Arbitration Committee and also of the Equal Opportunities Commission and Commission for Racial Equality, whose powers of investigation have been severely constrained as a result. However, it has also been an important weapon in the hands of bodies with statutory functions. In the landmark case of *R v Secretary of State for Employment, ex p EOC*[47] the EOC successfully brought judicial review proceedings for a declaration that the (then) 16-hour qualifying threshold for redundancy and unfair dismissal rights under EPCA 1978 was contrary to Article 141 (then Article 119) of the EC Treaty and to the Equal Treatment Directive.[48] In that case the House of Lords upheld the argument, rejected by the Court of Appeal, that the EOC had standing to bring the application. As has been argued elsewhere this decision means that the EOC is now in a strong position to challenge, before the UK courts, legislation which contravenes the principle of gender equality.[49]

Finally it should be noted that, despite the procedural divide, the influence of public law concepts, in particular procedural fairness, has spread in some contexts to proceedings brought in private law although the courts have failed to adopt the suggestion that natural justice should be implied into every contract of employment.[50] We discuss this development further in para 5.53 below. As we shall see in chapter 10 public law values have also been heavily influential in the courts' treatment of the relationship between trade unions and their members and officials, to which the concepts of 'natural justice' have been applied, although in recent years statutory restrictions have rendered this area less significant in practice.

Administrative practices

2.6   In recent years the primary mechanism by which the state has sought to regulate employment practices has been by legislation. Historically, however,

---

44   See Woolf, 1995: p 64.

45   See *Roy v Kensington and Chelsea and Westminster Family Practitioner Committee* [1992] 1 AC 624, 653–655 (Lord Lowry); *Lonrho plc v Tebbit* [1992] 4 All ER 280, 288 (Sir Michael Kerr); *Chief Adjudication Officer v Foster* [1993] 1 All ER 705, 712 (Lord Bridge); *Mercury Communications Ltd v Director General of Telecommunications* [1996] 1 All ER 575.

46   The Law Commission recommended maintaining the divide, although with greater flexibility for cases to transfer between the predecessor of CPR Part 54 and the writ procedure: see *Administrative Law: Judicial Review and Statutory Appeals*, Law Com No 226, HC 669, 1994, Part III.

47   [1994] IRLR 176.

48   EC Directive 76/207; see further para 3.87 below.

49   See Deakin, 1994a.

50   See Woolf LJ in *R v Derbyshire County Council, ex p Noble* [1990] IRLR 332 at 337; Sedley, 1994; Laws, 1997. For a broader discussion of the influence of public law on labour law, see P Davies and M Freedland, 1997.

its administrative practices also played an important role. For most of the twentieth century the state perceived itself as setting an example to the private sector by virtue of its own employment practices.[51] Thus, collective bargaining was introduced into the civil service in 1919 despite misgivings as to its appropriateness because the government believed that it could not otherwise expect private employers to do the same. Another means by which the state sought to exercise its influence was by means of its extensive power as contractor with the private sector.[52] The use of a 'contract compliance' strategy in Britain dates back to 1891 when the House of Commons passed the first of three Fair Wages Resolutions (the others being in 1909 and 1946).[53] This required government departments to include a term in contracts with private sector employers that contractors should pay their workers the generally accepted rate for the job. Subsequent Resolutions extended these requirements to other conditions of employment and to freedom of association. Although not within the terms of the Resolution, from an early stage local authorities also applied fair wages policies and in later years nationalised industries were encouraged by successive governments to implement its terms. In more recent times local authorities also used contract compliance policies to further other purposes such as discouraging reliance on self-employed labour by contractors; promoting equal opportunities, training and the provision of trade union facilities; insisting upon health and safety policies; and encouraging the use of local labour on contracts whenever possible.[54]

The Conservative Government which came to office in 1979 had a very different view of its role as employer, seeking to reverse the traditional model by implementing in the public sector practices which it deemed typical of private sector employers. It perceived the Fair Wages Resolution as a damaging anachronism, impeding competitiveness and destroying jobs, and in 1982 gave notice to rescind it from 1983, a move which necessitated denouncing ILO Convention No 94 on Labour Clauses in Public Contracts which requires contracts between public authorities and employers to include a 'fair wages' clause. Later in the decade the use of contract compliance as a strategy was further undermined when the Local Government Act 1988 made it unlawful for local authorities and several other public bodies to consider 'non-commercial matters' in their choice of, and dealings with, contractors.[55] This prevented consideration of matters such as wages and conditions, employee status, freedom of association or equal opportunities (with a very limited exception for local authorities in the case of race[56]). The Local Government Act 1999 empowers the Secretary of State to provide by order that any of these matters should cease to be a 'non-commercial' matter, either generally or in a specific context, in relation to authorities, including local authorities, that operate according to the 'best value' regime the Act establishes.[57] At the time of writing the terms and conditions of

51   See generally Fredman and Morris, 1989.
52   For a useful overview, see Hepple *et al*, 2000, para 3.61–3.77 and references therein.
53   For a detailed study of the history and operation of the fair wages policy see Bercusson, 1978; see also para 1.13 above.
54   Institute of Personnel Management, 1987: ch 2.
55   LGA 1988, s 17. See further Fredman and Morris, 1989: ch 12.
56   See s 18(2). This was inserted because of the duty of local authorities under the RRA 1976, s 71 to have regard, *inter alia*, to the promotion of equality of opportunity. A duty on a broader range of bodies is imposed under s 71 as substituted by the Race Relations (Amendment) Act 2000, s 2 and Sch 1A.
57   LGA 1999, s 19. 'Best value' authorities are defined in s 1; see also s 2.

employment of workers; the composition of and opportunities afforded to the workforce; and the conduct of contractors or their workers in industrial disputes, are no longer treated as 'non-commercial', but only so far as necessary or expedient to permit or facilitate compliance with the best value requirements of the Act or where there is a transfer of staff to which TUPE may apply.[58]

Limited steps have been taken to revive contract compliance as a strategy.[59] The Race Relations (Amendment) Act 2000 obliges a wide range of public authorities to promote race equality[60] and contracts are likely to include a condition that a contractor must not discriminate unlawfully under race equality legislation.[61] The Government has indicated that 'in due course' it will introduce a duty on public bodies to promote equality of opportunity between women and men,[62] and the creation of a single Equality Commission (see para 2.39 below) may create pressures for the application of a more wide-ranging duty. In the contemporary 'contract state' contract compliance has considerable potential as a mechanism for disseminating specific employment practices, although reliance upon it now requires an eye to the restrictions imposed by EC Directives on Public Procurement.[63] As we indicate in para 2.48, the use of an analogous strategy as a mechanism for securing international labour standards is a current issue of debate.

VOLUNTARY SOURCES

2.7 As we emphasised in para 2.1 voluntary norms have been, and continue to be, a crucial source of labour law in Britain. The lack of legislation governing the employment relationship left largely unrestricted the discretion of employers and workers and/or trade unions to shape it as they chose and despite the extension of statutory regulation this is still true today in many areas. We begin this section by discussing the role of collective agreements as a source of law. As we saw in chapter 1 historically trade unions regarded collective bargaining as preferable to legislation as a means of securing workers' terms and conditions of employment. It was estimated that in 1984 71% of employees were covered by collective agreements.[64] By 1990 this figure had fallen to 54%,[65] and by 1998 to 41%,[66] but, despite this, collective agreements still remain a highly significant source of labour law, and, indeed, the growth in recognition agreements since 1998[67] may increase their coverage once again. The other voluntary sources of labour law we consider much more briefly:

---

58   The Local Government Best Value (Exclusion of Non-commercial Considerations) Order 2001, SI 2001/ 909.
59   On the position in Northern Ireland, see Fitzpatrick, 1999.
60   RRA 1976, s 71. See also DDA 2005, s 3, inserting DDA 1995, s 49A (at the time of writing not yet in force).
61   See generally Commission for Racial Equality, *Race Equality and Public Procurement: A Guide for Public Authorities and Contractors.*
62   *Fairness for All: A New Commission for Equality and Human Rights: White Paper,* Cm 6185, 2004, para 7.58. The Equality Bill 2005 contains such a duty.
63   See further Wedderburn 1995: pp 379–385; Hepple *et al,* 2000: paras 3.71–3.73; Arrowsmith, 1995: pp 248–282.
64   Millward *et al,* 1992: p 94
65   Millward *et al,* 1992: p 94
66   Cully *et al,* 1999: p 242.
67   See para 9.2.

works rules and other documents issued by employers to workers and self-regulatory codes of conduct issued by trade unions and other bodies. We conclude by reviewing briefly the relationship between the formal and informal sources of labour law.

Collective agreements

2.8 Collective agreements fulfil two major purposes.[68] First, they regulate relations between employers (and employers' associations) and trade unions (the *procedural* or *contractual* function). These arrangements are usually of a constitutional nature (and are generically called procedural agreements) and can take a variety of forms. Thus they may, for example, establish permanent joint machinery for the negotiation of terms and conditions of employment or specify the procedural stages to be followed for the resolution of disputes, possibly limiting industrial action until the procedure has been exhausted. The second function of collective agreements is to regulate the terms of individual contracts of employment (the *normative* function). These 'substantive' terms may cover pay scales, working hours, holidays, shift work and overtime, and many other areas. In practice both procedural and substantive terms may frequently be found in the same collective agreement. There may also be terms which cannot be classified in either category, such as an obligation on every employer belonging to an employers' association which is party to an agreement to provide copies of the agreement to its employees. In recent years collective agreements have been accorded a further role in legislation implementing EU standards. Provided that the trade unions party to it is 'independent',[69] a collective agreement may exclude or modify specified provisions relating to working time[70] and the successive use of fixed-term contracts,[71] and may determine the terms upon which parental leave is taken.[72] In addition, appeals under a procedure established by a collective agreement between such a union and two or more employers or an employers' association may constitute the final stage under the statutory dismissal and disciplinary procedures, and raising a grievance under such a procedure compliance with the applicable statutory grievance procedure, under legislation that came into force in October 2004.[73]

Collective agreements are an important source of labour law in many systems. Their importance as a source of labour law in Britain is particularly remarkable in view of their independence from the formal legal system.[74] As we explained in chapter 1, in general collective bargaining developed in this country on a voluntary basis, without legal regulation of either its procedures or its outcomes. Although there is now a statutory procedure enabling unions to gain statutory recognition, accompanied by an enforceable collective bargaining 'method', even now there remains no obligation to reach agreement.

---

68 See P Davies and M Freedland, 1983: ch 6.
69 See para 7.23.
70 See para 4.77.
71 See para 5.78
72 See para 6.104.
73 See paras 5.124 *et seq* and 2.21 *et seq.*
74 Bamber and Sheldon, 2004: para 11, make the point that '[i]n continental Europe the growth of collective bargaining was facilitated by the incorporation of collective agreements in the legal system of various countries as a new source of industrial relations rules', starting with the Dutch Civil Code (1907) and the Swiss Code of Obligations (1911) and followed by legislation in Norway, Germany, France and Finland.

Moreover, there is no legal requirement that collective agreements cover any specified matters,[75] include any specific terms or are of any minimum or maximum (or even specified) duration,[76] or are in any particular form.[77] There is no requirement for them to be registered with any administrative authority as is the case in some other jurisdictions. Most surprisingly, perhaps, to a student of civil law systems of labour law, their legal status is entirely a matter for the collective parties: although since 1971 the determination of this question has been subject to a statutory presumption relating to enforceability this does not restrict the parties' capacity to choose.

2.9   Before the Industrial Relations Act 1971 there was no provision specifically dealing with the enforceability of collective agreements. The Trade Union Act 1871, section 4(4) (repealed in 1971) prevented the enforcement of agreements between one trade union and another and, because the existing definition of 'trade union' probably covered many employers' associations, would thus have prevented collective agreements to which they were a party being enforced directly in the courts.[78] However, this provision did not touch agreements between individual employers and trade unions. In an influential analysis of the prevailing British system in 1954 Kahn-Freund wrote:

> ... [i]n the long history of British collective bargaining it does not ever seem to have happened that either a trade union or an employers' association attempted to prevent the violation of a collective agreement by an action for an injunction or to seek compensation by an action for damages. The reason can certainly not be found in the absence of such violations ...[79]

He concluded that the explanation lay in the intention of the parties that their agreements should be 'binding in honour' only, and enforceable through 'social ... but not through legal sanctions'. The correctness of the assumptions which lay behind this view has been doubted.[80] What is incontrovertible, however, is its influence on modern practice. It was mirrored in evidence presented to, and the findings of, the Donovan Commission,[81] which regarded the intention (and policy) that collective agreements should remain outside the law as 'deeply rooted' in the industrial relations structure.[82] This view, in turn, was also highly influential when the question finally came before the courts in 1969.

---

75   The 'method' contained in the statutory model which may be imposed under the statutory recognition procedure provides that an employer may not vary the pay, hours or holidays of workers in the bargaining unit unless it has first discussed its proposals with the union, but this does not impose a duty to provide for such matters in a collective agreement: see further para 9.18.

76   This does not mean that the terms of a collective agreement will necessarily be able to be applied, however; see, for example, SDA 1975, s 77 and SDA 1986, s 6 (discussed at para 6.69). A 'closed shop' agreement could not be lawfully enforced: see para 8.31 *et seq* below. At times of officially-imposed pay restraint incomes policies may prevent or delay the application of agreements.

77   *Burke v Royal Liverpool University Hospital NHS Trust* [1997] ICR 730 (collective agreement formed by an exchange of letters between employer and union).

78   The Royal Commission on Trade Unions and Employers' Associations 1965–1968, Cmnd 3623, 1968 (the Donovan Commission) took the view (para 470) that such bodies could have made their agreements 'indirectly' enforceable and, for example, obtain from a court a declaration concerning the meaning of an agreement.

79   Kahn-Freund, 1954: p 57.

80   See R Lewis, 1979, and references therein.

81   See note 78 above. It was the unanimous view of the Ministry of Labour, TUC and CBI.

82   Para 471.

In *Ford Motor Co Ltd v AUEFW*[83] the employer sought an injunction against the union on the ground that the union's support for industrial action was in breach of collective agreements between the union and the company. There was no indication in the agreements as to whether the parties had intended to create a contract and the court was forced therefore to ascertain their intention from the surrounding circumstances. The court referred, *inter alia*, to the writings of Kahn-Freund and to the Report of the Donovan Commission which clearly showed that the 'climate of opinion was almost unanimous to the effect that no legally enforceable contracts resulted from ... collective agreements',[84] and took the view that the parties to the Ford agreement must be credited with knowledge of these sources which also provided evidence of their state of mind at the time. The court reached the same conclusion applying an objective test, maintaining that 'the fact that the agreements *prima facie* deal with commercial relationships is outweighed by the other considerations, by the wording of the agreements, by the nature of the agreements, and by the climate of opinion voiced and evidenced by the extra-judicial authorities'.[85]

The unions in the *Ford* case argued in addition that the 'vague and aspirational' wording of the agreements provided further evidence that the parties could not have intended to create a contract, a view which was accepted by the court.

The extra-legal character of the collective bargaining process was also reflected in its dynamic nature; rather than aiming to conclude agreements which remained set in stone for any given period, much collective bargaining took place within a framework which allowed collective agreements to be modified or reinterpreted as the need arose.[86] This in turn meant that labour law in Britain, unlike that in many other jurisdictions, did not recognise a distinction between disputes of right, concerned with interpretation of an existing agreement, and disputes of interest, which concern conflicts over renegotiated terms; all such disputes were equally susceptible to resolution through the collective bargaining process.

In 1971 the Industrial Relations Act, as part of a general strategy of bringing industrial relations within a legal framework, imposed a statutory presumption that collective agreements were intended to be legally enforceable unless they contained a statement to the contrary. In practice nearly all agreements concluded during the currency of the Act contained such a statement; the decision to insert it seems not to have been an issue between the parties,[87] thus demonstrating the strength of the consensus that this was not an appropriate area for legal regulation. Since 1974 the reverse statutory presumption has applied – a 'collective agreement'[88] will only be regarded as legally enforceable at collective level if it is in writing and there is a clear statement indicating the intention that it should be.[89] Evidence suggests that this hardly ever happens (although notable exceptions

---

83 [1969] 2 All ER 481.
84 At 494.
85 At 496.
86 See further 4.36 below for the effect of modifying a collective agreement upon the individual contract.
87 Weekes *et al*, 1975: pp 156–161.
88 Defined by TULRCA 1992, s 178(2); see further para 9.26 below. Note that agreements outside this definition will be governed by the common law.
89 The notion of making collective agreements enforceable by law was floated and rejected on at least two occasions subsequent to the IRA 1971: see the Green Papers *Trade Union Immunities*, Cmnd 8128, 1981, para 243 and *Industrial Relations in the 1990s* Cm 1602, 1991: ch 8. Proposals to remove the immunities from industrial action in breach of procedure agreements in essential services, contained in the 1983 Conservative Party election manifesto, were also shelved.

are the collective agreement negotiated in 1997 to ensure staff relations are conducted peacefully and without disruption to operations at GCHQ, and a 2001 and subsequent agreement designed to prevent disruption in the prison service: see further paras 7.10 and 11.14). This may on occasion be a mixed blessing for unions; although until recently debate about enforceability revolved around unions reneging on obligations not to take industrial action before exhausting agreed dispute resolution procedures, in more recent years employers, too, have been more ready to flout agreements.

2.10   The general non-enforceability of collective agreements in Britain stands in marked contrast to the position in many other systems. A further contrast is the lack of any automatic or compulsory integration of the norms generated by these agreements into individual employment contracts, even where they result from statutory recognition.[90] The perception of collective agreements as non-enforceable between the collective parties has not prevented them being an important source of terms governing the relationship between individual employers and workers where their wording is sufficiently clear and precise.[91] On the contrary, it has been common practice for workers' individual contracts expressly to incorporate such agreements; where they do not but collectively-agreed terms have been applied in practice incorporation has been readily implied.[92] However, unlike in other systems, whether such a practice is observed has been a matter entirely for the individual parties, even where collective bargaining follows statutory recognition. In France, for example, the Labour Code provides that where an employer is bound by the terms of a collective agreement those terms apply to its employment contracts, replaceable only by terms more favourable to the employee.[93] This approach is reflected in ILO Recommendation No 91 concerning Collective Agreements, which stipulates that employers and workers bound by collective agreements should not be able to include in contracts of employment terms contrary to those collectively agreed and, moreover, that the terms of the collective agreement should apply to all workers of the relevant descriptions employed by such employers. In Britain, employers cannot be obliged as a matter of law to apply the terms of collective agreements, even those to which they are directly party, to their workers, although where they have so chosen they have generally applied them to all workers within the scope of the agreement irrespective of their union membership. *A fortiori* there is no mechanism by which non-parties to collective agreements can be required to abide by them. In a number of countries, including Belgium, France and Germany, there is a legal power for the public authorities, after a

---

90   For an analysis of the variety of ways in which collective agreements can bind the parties to the employment relationship (and a salutary warning against over-simplification), see Wedderburn, 1992c; 1993: p 225 *et seq*.

91   However, the courts have sometimes confused the relationship between the two: see *Loman and Henderson v Merseyside Transport Services Ltd* (1968) 3 ITR 108; *Gascol Conversions Ltd v Mercer* [1974] ICR 420. See now, however, *Marley v Forward Trust Group Ltd* [1986] ICR 891, CA; see further para 4.26 below.

92   The written statement of employment terms which employers are now obliged to give their new employees (or existing employees on request) must contain particulars of any collective agreements which directly affect the terms and conditions of the employment including, where the employer is not a party, the persons by whom they were made: ERA 1996, s 1(4)(j); see further para 4.16 below.

93   Article L 135-2. For a comparative survey of the relationship between collective agreements and individual contracts of employment, see Sewerynski, 2003.

variety of complex procedures, to extend the application of a collective agreement to additional employers and their workers by order. This prevents any downward flexibility in the application of sectoral agreements and any consequent competitive advantage to employers who may otherwise be tempted to reward their workers below the collectively-agreed rate. Again this concept of 'extension' is enshrined in ILO Recommendation No 91.[94] Between 1940 and 1980 English law contained a form of extension mechanism which unions or employers within a particular trade or industry could invoke but this was repealed on the ground of its allegedly inflationary effect.[95]

A final consequence of the lack of legal regulation of collective bargaining is that where bargaining takes place at different levels there is no procedure for determining which of two (or possibly more) collective agreements, containing different provisions, should apply. As William Brown explains:

> Any one bargaining unit may be influenced by bargaining at more than one level. An employer on a building site, for example, might augment an industry agreement with a site agreement. Furthermore, any one bargaining level may deal with more than one bargaining unit. A chemicals refinery, for example, might have separate site agreements for the process workers, the maintenance workers and the staff. Finally, an employee may be included in different bargaining units for different aspects of his or her terms and conditions of employment. For example, there may be a company-wide training agreement. a divisional redundancy agreement, and a workplace performance-related pay agreement.[96]

The decision as to which agreement should apply in case of conflict has been treated, in our system, as a question for the courts, unlike in systems which prescribe a specific hierarchy of norms.[97] Few, if any, coherent principles have developed in this area.[98] However, this presents less of a practical problem now that single-employer bargaining has superseded the pattern of earlier years, when national industry-wide agreements set basic rates, supplemented by bargaining at company or plant level.[99]

In summary, therefore, to invoke the language of Kahn-Freund, in Britain the collective agreement is neither a contract nor a Code.[100] This has implications at European Community, as well as at domestic, level. Collective agreements are potentially capable of having a multiple role in Community law; first as a source of legal obligations under the terms of the 'social dialogue'; second, as a method of implementing Community obligations derived from other sources (such as directives); and third, as a mechanism, under controlled circumstances, for derogating from standards laid down in directives.[101] The absence of any mechanism for securing compliance with terms that have been collectively agreed means that, in Britain, the second of these roles is not currently an option.

---

94 Para 5.
95 See paras 1.25 above and 7.15 below.
96 W Brown, 1992: p 297.
97 See further para 4.26 below.
98 See *Clift v West Riding County Council* (1964) Times, 10 April; *Loman and Henderson v Merseyside Transport Services Ltd* (1968) 3 ITR 108; *Gascol Conversions Ltd v Mercer* [1974] IRLR 155 (criticised Hepple, 1974). In *South Tyneside Metropolitan Borough Council v Graham* UKEAT/0107/03/DA the tribunal was required to decide whether there was a 'local agreement' in existence.
99 W Brown 1992, 1993.
100 See, for example, P Davies and M Freedland, 1983: ch 6.
101 See Bercusson, 1994d; Bercusson, 1996: ch 35; and para 2.8 above.

Workforce agreements

2.11   We referred in para 2.8 above to the novel role accorded to collective agreements in modifying or excluding standards in the area of working time and use of successive fixed-term contracts, and in determining the terms on which parental leave is taken, provided that the trade unions party to the agreement are independent. The legislation in these areas also permits this function to be performed by a 'workforce agreement', an innovative statutory vehicle designed to implement the flexibility in the application of standards permitted by the respective EC Directives where the employer does not recognise a union.[102] We discuss the definition of a 'workforce agreement' in para 4.74, but essentially it means an agreement made either with elected representatives of the workforce or, in certain circumstances, a majority of the workers themselves. Notably, there is no requirement that such representatives meet the criteria of 'independence' required of trade unions, a cause for concern given the significance of their powers.

Works rules, notices and other documents issued by management to employees

2.12   Documents issued by management to their employees take a wide variety of forms, ranging from general rule books and handbooks governing conduct at the workplace to notices on specific matters. Whether these will take effect as terms of the individual contract, or are merely emanations of the managerial prerogative which can be changed at will, depends upon the application of tests which we discuss in detail in chapter 4. In the past internal disciplinary and grievance procedures have generally been viewed as giving rise to contractual terms, particularly in the light of the employer's obligation to issue a written statement of terms and conditions of employment, although, in *obiter* remarks in *Johnson v Unisys Ltd*, Lord Hoffman cast doubt on this approach.[103] Irrespective of whether such procedures are contractually binding, they are relevant in unfair dismissal proceedings, although, since 1 October 2004, failure to abide by disciplinary procedures beyond those specified as statutory minima does not of itself make a dismissal unfair if the employer shows it would have dismissed the employee even if it had followed those procedures.[104] As well as formal documents, informal arrangements in the workplace or particular industry, commonly designated 'custom and practice' or 'trade usage', may eventually take effect as terms of the contract if they are deemed 'reasonable, certain and notorious'.[105] However, as we indicate in para 4.32 below, the greater formalisation of contract terms and conditions, and in particular the statutory provision for employees to receive a written statement of their employment terms, is likely to make it much more difficult than in the past to establish that practices which are solely a matter of custom and practice have contractual force.

Self-regulatory codes of conduct

2.13   In paragraph 2.4 we outlined Codes of Practice which are issued under statutory authority and whose effect is governed by statute. Private organisations

---

102 See further paras 4.77, 6.104 and 5.78 .
103 [2001] IRLR 279, paras 63–66; see further para 5.35. At the time of writing EA 2002, s 30 has not been brought into force.
104 ERA 1996, s 98A(2); see further para 5.143.
105 *Sagar v H Ridehalgh & Son Ltd* [1930] 2 Ch 117.

may also issue codes of conduct to govern practices within their sphere of operation. The most prominent example is the TUC 'Bridlington' Principles, first promulgated by the TUC[106] in 1939 and most recently revised in 2000.[107] These principles were designed to minimise disputes between unions over membership questions. Although not intended to constitute a legally enforceable contract, they are 'accepted by all affiliated organisations as a binding commitment for their continued affiliation to the TUC'.[108] The primary aim of these procedures is to promote voluntary settlement of disputes between unions but if this avenue fails the matter may be referred to an internal Disputes Committee. Failure to comply with an award of that Committee attracts a variety of sanctions including, ultimately, exclusion from the TUC.

The TUC has also issued other guidance to its members on occasion. Thus in 1984 it issued a 'statement of guidance on political fund arrangements' designed to ensure that union members are informed about and able to exercise their right to contract out from contributing if their union has a 'political fund'. In 1979, during the 'winter of discontent' disputes which preceded the General Election of that year, it issued a Guide to Affiliated Unions on the Conduct of Industrial Disputes, designed to ensure that essential services were maintained. This formalised a practice followed by many unions with members in these services. Observance of such codes was generally conditional on employers exercising reciprocal self-restraint by not seeking to undermine the action in ways considered unacceptable by unions.[109] In the light of a greater willingness on the part of employers to invoke legal sanctions during disputes (and the 'statutory' right of action for consumers created by TURERA 1993) unions may be less likely to follow this course in the future.[110]

Relationship between the formal and informal sources

2.14 The interplay between the formal and the informal sources of labour law is complex. First, as we have seen, collective agreements, while not themselves constituting legally-binding contracts, may be accorded legal force if incorporated into individual contracts of employment. Second, such agreements,[111] together with 'workforce agreements' discussed in para 2.11, may modify or exclude standards in the area of working time and the use of successive fixed-term contracts, and may determine the terms of parental leave. Third, in assessing the rights of trade union officials and members to time off for union duties and activities during working hours, the terms of the agreement between the collective parties will be an important guide to what is 'reasonable'.[112] Finally, internal disciplinary procedures, even if not incorporated directly into the individual contract, may influence a tribunal in assessing whether an employer has acted fairly in deciding to dismiss.[113] The procedural terms of collective agreements may also have indirect

---

106 The TUC, formed in 1868, is a permanent federation of trade unions to which nearly all major unions are affiliated. For its history, see RM Martin, 1980; Taylor, 2000.
107 *TUC Disputes Principles and Procedures*, TUC, 2000. For an evaluation of the operation of the principles before revision see Elgar and Simpson, 1994, and references therein. See further para 10.11 below.
108 *TUC Disputes Principles and Procedures*, Preface.
109 See generally G Morris, 1986a: chs 5 and 6.
110 See further chs 11 and 12; G Morris, 1991 and 1993.
111 Provided that the trade union party to the agreement is 'independent': see para 2.8.
112 See further para 8.36 below.
113 Although note ERA 1996, s 98A(2), discussed at para 5.143.

legal effect in relation to the granting of injunctions to halt industrial disputes; the Code of Practice issued by the Secretary of State recommends that a ballot should not take place until any agreed procedures which might lead to a resolution of the dispute without the need for industrial action have been completed.[114] Compliance with the terms of a procedural agreement on the part of an employer is also relevant in determining whether the period for which it is automatically unfair to dismiss an employee for taking 'protected industrial action' extends beyond twelve weeks.[115] In many areas, therefore, it is crucial to have regard to standards derived from voluntary sources in order to ascertain individual or collective rights.

THE ROLE OF COURTS AND EMPLOYMENT TRIBUNALS

2.15   Just as there is no Labour Code in England, equally there is no separate labour court system for dealing with all labour law disputes.[116] Rather the judicial determination of labour law matters is divided between tripartite employment tribunals, which, broadly speaking, hear claims involving statutory employment rights as well as certain common law claims, and the common law courts. Issues before the common law courts are most likely to involve matters of contract and tort and, for specific groups of workers, public law. The appropriate forum for a common law claim depends upon its value; claims for more than £15,000 can be brought in the High Court (other than for personal injuries, where the minimum is £50,000), those for less than that normally in a locally-based county court.[117] Thus many contractual or minor personal injuries claims will be heard in the county court; employers' claims in tort against trade unions in relation to industrial action are heard in the High Court, together with claims for interim injunctions to halt the action. Claims in public law are always heard in the Administrative Court, subject, as we indicated in para 2.5, to the need for permission. We discuss the procedural aspects of bringing common law claims in greater detail in those contexts, such as dismissal and industrial action, where they have particularly significant implications.

The bifurcation between courts and tribunals means that an employee generally needs to bring separate proceedings in each where both contractual and statutory rights are at issue. One exception to this principle, introduced in 1994, allows employment tribunals to hear claims for money due under the contract, or damages for breach of contract, of up to £25,000 if the claim arises or is outstanding on termination of an employee's employment.[118] This means that

---

114   See further para 11.45 below.

115   See para 11.80.

116   There is a considerable literature on the issues which the introduction of a Labour Court would raise: see, for example, Wedderburn, 1991a, and references therein. For a brief comparative overview, see Gladstone, 2004.

117   High Court and County Courts Jurisdiction (Amendment) Order 1991, as amended; CPR Part 7 Practice Direction paras 2.1–2.4.

118   Employment Tribunals Extension of Jurisdiction (England and Wales) Order 1994, SI 1994/1623; ETA 1996, ss 2, 3. Certain claims are excluded, including damages for personal injuries. There is no jurisdiction if the complaint is presented before the effective date of termination of the contract: *Capek v Lincolnshire County Council* [2000] IRLR 590. The claim must be immediately enforceable at that date: *Peninsula Business Services Ltd v Sweeney* [2004] IRLR 49; see also *Miller Bros and F P Butler Ltd v Johnston* [2002] IRLR 386. It is notable that the Donovan Commission envisaged that the 'labour tribunals' they proposed should cover all cases arising from the contract of employment as well as statutory claims: see Royal Commission on Trade Unions and Employers' Associations 1965–1968: *Report*, Cmnd 3623, 1968, ch X.

an employee who is dismissed with less than the contractually-agreed period of notice, for example, may be able to sue for damages and claim unfair dismissal compensation in the same set of proceedings.[119] However, tribunals may not award an injunction to restrain the termination of a contract; an employee who seeks this remedy will still have to bring an action under common law. The upper limit of £25,000 on common law claims in tribunals appears anomalous given that there is no limit on the compensation which tribunals may award in a variety of contexts, including discrimination cases[120] and those involving unauthorised deductions from pay contrary to ERA 1996, ss 13–27.[121]

Termination of employment apart, all other contractual claims must be brought in the common law courts.[122] This does not mean that common law concepts are irrelevant in tribunal hearings, however. On the contrary, there is a variety of contexts in which the scope and terms of the contract of employment are material to a statutory claim – whether an employee has been 'constructively dismissed' due to the employer's repudiatory breach, for example – and the status of employee, which is crucial to access to many employment rights, is based entirely upon common law tests.[123]

As the discussion which follows makes clear, there are important differences between courts and employment tribunals which make the choice of forum significant for the parties. For example, in employment tribunals applicants can be represented by the person of their choice, such as a union official, whereas in the courts the only alternative to legal representation is self-representation. State-funded legal aid is not available for employment tribunals, unlike for courts[124] and, whereas courts may award costs against the unsuccessful party at their discretion, costs in tribunals have to date been awarded only in exceptional circumstances.[125] Where the applicant is free to make a choice as to where to initiate a claim these may be material considerations. However, the differences between the systems become less apparent if the right to appeal is exercised. Appeals can be made from employment tribunals to another tripartite body, the Employment Appeal Tribunal (EAT).[126] Although the right to the representative of one's choice remains, legal aid is available for EAT proceedings. Subsequent appeals may be made, with leave, to the Court of Appeal and thence to the House of Lords. At that point proceedings are subject to the procedural rules which normally apply and in that sense the statutory and common law jurisdictions can be said to converge. It is perhaps ironic that ultimately the

---

119 If the employee takes this course it is then open to an employer to bring a counterclaim in contract if grounds for doing so exist.

120 See further para 6.67 below.

121 See further para 4.69 below.

122 Note, however, that claims under ERA 1996, ss 13–27 may, in practice, involve the determination of contractual matters: see para 4.69 below.

123 See further Anderman, 2000.

124 It is arguable that the failure to make legal aid available for complex cases may contravene Art 6 of the ECHR: see *Airey v Ireland* judgment of 9 October 1979, (1979–80) 2 EHRR 305, paras 20–28; *Steel v UK* judgment of 15 February 2005. Legal aid for representation in employment tribunals where specified criteria are satisfied has been available in Scotland since January 2001: see now the Advice and Assistance (Assistance by way of Representation) (Scotland) Regulations 2003, Scottish SI 2003/179.

125 In 2003–2004 they were awarded in 976 cases disposed of at hearings (332 to applicants and 644 to respondents): Employment Tribunals Service, *Annual Report and Accounts 2003–2004*, HC 714, 2004, App 1, Table 8.

126 Note that appeals from the decisions of employment tribunals in their 'non-employment' jurisdiction, such as health and safety at work, lie to the High Court under the provisions of the Tribunals and Inquiries Act 1992, s 11.

most authoritative interpretations of the law come from the non-specialist, appellate courts; for this reason the system of labour courts lacks genuine autonomy unlike that in Germany, for example, where the Federal Labour Court has the final word on issues of interpretation. The general principles of *stare decisis* apply within this area. Thus the employment tribunals are bound by decisions of the EAT which itself is bound by decisions of the higher courts. For the EAT its own previous decisions are of persuasive value. Employment tribunal decisions have no precedent value for other tribunals although in the absence of any other authority they may be regarded as persuasive.

In the following paragraphs we outline the constitution and operation of employment tribunals and the EAT. We then consider the implications of reforms that have recently been made to the tribunal system and to its relationship with other means of dispute settlement, including, as from 1 October 2004, the obligation on employees (exceptional circumstances apart) to exhaust a statutory grievance procedure prior to presenting a complaint to an employment tribunal.

Employment tribunals

2.16 Employment tribunals, until ERDRA 1998 called 'industrial tribunals', were established in 1964, initially to deal with appeals by employers against industrial training levies imposed under the Industrial Training Act. In 1965 their jurisdiction was extended to cover claims for the newly-introduced statutory redundancy payments. They were accorded a more central role in labour law disputes with the introduction of protection against unfair dismissal in the Industrial Relations Act 1971 and since then their jurisdiction has been progressively extended to a wide range of employment-related matters.[127] Most of their work involves unfair dismissal complaints (33% of applications in 2003–2004) but the volume of complaints relating to unauthorised deductions from pay is also very significant (around 18% of applications in 2003–2004).[128] Employment tribunals also have jurisdiction over statutory rights which may be exercised against trade unions in relation to discipline or exclusion or expulsion from membership. A further area of their jurisdiction (which lies largely beyond the scope of this work) is in the field of health and safety. Tribunals have no jurisdiction to award injunctions. They can order re-instatement or re-engagement of an employee found to have been unfairly dismissed but these orders cannot be enforced; the sanction against an employer who refuses to comply with such an order is additional financial compensation to the claimant.[129] Moreover, they have no power to enforce their money judgments; if an award is not paid the applicant has to seek the assistance of the county court. In 2003–2004 over 115,000 applications were made to employment tribunals, although some 68% did not reach a hearing because they were resolved either through ACAS conciliation or withdrawn, for example, as a result of a private settlement.[130]

---

127 The returns of the Employment Tribunals Service ('ETS') provide statistical information relating to employment tribunals.
128 Employment Tribunals Service, *Annual Report and Accounts 2003–2004*, HC 714, 2004, p 4; App 1, Table 1. The percentage of cases relating to unfair dismissal has fallen dramatically from 1994–1995, when it stood at 59%: *Labour Market Trends*, September 1999: p 493.
129 ERA 1996, s 117.
130 Employment Tribunals Service, *Annual Report and Accounts 2003–2004*, HC 714, 2004, p 4; App 1, Table 2. See further para 2.17.

The constitution and procedures of employment tribunals are governed by ETA 1996 and statutory regulations.[131] In England and Wales there are 21 employment tribunal offices. Hearings may also sometimes be arranged in temporary locations.[132] Since 1 April 1997 administrative support for employment tribunals and the EAT has been provided by the Employment Tribunals Service (ETS), an executive agency of the Department of Trade and Industry. At the time of writing it is proposed that the ETS will transfer to a unified Tribunal Service in 2006.[133]

Unlike the ordinary courts, employment tribunals are tripartite in their composition. Each tribunal is chaired by a barrister or solicitor who has been qualified as such for at least seven years, appointed by the Lord Chancellor.[134] He or she normally sits with two lay members drawn from separate panels of employer and employee representatives who are appointed by the Secretary of State.[135] For cases involving sex discrimination, an attempt is made to include at least one woman on the tribunal, and in race discrimination cases a member with experience and training in race cases in the area of employment. The purpose of the lay members is to lend to the proceedings their practical knowledge and experience of industrial relations. Although the chairman controls the conduct of proceedings the lay members can also intervene and their vote is equal to the chairman's on all matters. However, they do not sit as representatives of their respective organisations and should make an independent judgement. In practice a high proportion of decisions are unanimous.[136] Employment tribunals have sometimes been dubbed by the higher courts 'industrial juries',[137] a description criticised by Wedderburn because, unlike the standard jury system, in this case the legal chair retires with the jury.[138]

Before 1993 chairmen could sit without the lay members only for very limited purposes such as interlocutory matters. TURERA 1993 extended this power to include, for example, cases on unauthorised deductions from pay, rights on the insolvency of the employer, breach of contract proceedings (where permitted) and those where the parties agree to this course.[139] ERDRA 1998 empowered a chairman

---

131 The Employment Tribunals (Constitution and Rules of Procedure) Regulations 2004, SI 2004/1861. For a description of tribunal practice and procedure, see Harvey, 1972, as updated, Division T.

132 The number of tribunals to be established is determined by the President of the Employment Tribunals (England and Wales), who is appointed by the Lord Chancellor. The Lord Chancellor has the power to appoint Regional Chairmen each of whom is then responsible for the administration of justice by tribunals in the area specified by the President: SI 2004/1861, regs 4–6.

133 Employment Tribunals Service, *Annual Report and Accounts 2003–2004*, HC 714, 2004, p 2.

134 ETA 1996, s 4(1); SI 2004/1861, regs 8, 9. Special provisions apply in national security cases: regs 10–12.

135 In *Smith v Secretary of State for Trade and Industry* [2000] IRLR 6, 9 Morrison P opined that there was a 'real and troubling question' as to whether an employment tribunal therefore constituted an 'independent and impartial tribunal' for the purposes of Art 6 of the ECHR in claims against the Secretary of State. Subsequently an element of open competition was introduced for appointments together with greater safeguards against non-renewal or withdrawal and in *Scanfuture UK Ltd v Secretary of State for Trade and Industry* [2001] IRLR 416 the EAT concluded that these safeguards were sufficient to comply with Art 6.

136 Harvey, 1972 as updated, Division T, para 30.

137 See, for example, Lord Donaldson MR in *British Telecommunications plc v Sheridan* [1990] IRLR 27, 30.

138 Wedderburn, 1991a: p 40.

139 ETA 1996, s 4. Where jurisdiction is based upon the parties' consent, there is no requirement for either party to have received independent advice before agreeing to this course.

to sit alone on a yet wider range of matters, including unauthorised deduction of union subscriptions by employers,[140] non-payment of a guarantee payment or protective award in the context of redundancies,[141] disputes over entitlement to a redundancy payment[142] and, most controversially, complaints relating to the written statement of employment particulars.[143] The practice of chairmen sitting alone saves money,[144] but runs counter to the philosophy which underlies the tribunal system, and the EAT has on occasion expressed disquiet as to its use in circumstances where the experience of lay members could be significant.[145]

2.17   The Donovan Commission expressed the view that 'labour tribunals' should provide 'an easily accessible, speedy, informal and inexpensive procedure' for the settlement of disputes.[146] This yardstick continues to be applied to the assessment of their operation[147] although it may be questioned whether, in view of the complexity of the law, it is now a realisable aim. However it provides a convenient framework within which to discuss the tribunals' distinctive features. We discuss more major reforms, designed to assist employment tribunals to deal with the increasing number of applications being made to them and to encourage parties to attempt to resolve problems internally first, in para 2.20 *et seq*. Since April 2001 tribunals have had an overriding statutory objective to deal with cases 'justly', which includes, so far as practicable, ensuring that the parties are on an equal footing; saving expense; dealing with a case in ways that are proportionate to the complexity or importance of the issues; and ensuring that it is dealt with expeditiously and fairly.[148]

In terms of accessibility a claimant who believes that he or she has a claim completes a claim form which requires his or her name and address; that of the person against whom the claim is made; details of the claim; and whether or not the claimant has raised the subject matter of the claim with the respondent at least 28 days before presenting the claim and if not, why not.[149] Once accepted by the Secretary of employment tribunals a copy of the claim is sent to the employer who has 28 days to enter a response stating whether it intends to resist the claim and, if so, on what grounds. These forms are then copied to the Advisory Conciliation and Arbitration Service (ACAS) whose conciliation officers have a duty for most types of claim[150] to attempt to promote a settlement between

---

140   See para 8.41 below.
141   See paras 4.113 and 9.40 below. Non-payment of an award for failure to consult on a transfer of the undertaking is also included in the power: see para 9.45 below.
142   See para 5.173 *et seq* below.
143   See para 4.14 *et seq* below.
144   At 1 April 2005 and at the time of writing lay members were paid £157.50 for a whole day's sitting and £78.75 for half a day.
145   See, for example, *Southwark London Borough Council v O'Brien* [1996] IRLR 420; *Sutcliffe v Big C's Marine* [1998] IRLR 428 at 430–431. On the exercise of the discretion to sit alone, see *Sogbetun v London Borough of Hackney* [1998] IRLR 676; cf. *Post Office v Howell* [2000] IRLR 224; *Morgan v Brith Gof Cyf* [2001] ICR 978.
146   *Royal Commission on Trade Unions and Employers' Associations 1965–1968: Report*, Cmnd 3623, 1968, para 578.
147   Employment Tribunals Service, *Annual Report and Accounts 2003–2004*, HC 714, 2004, p 4 (although the term 'inexpensive' is omitted here, it appears in SI 2004/1861, reg 3(2)(d)).
148   SI 2004/1861, reg 3.
149   See generally on rules of procedure SI 2004/1861, reg 16 and Sch 1. See further para 2.21 *et seq* on the statutory grievance procedure that must generally be followed by an employee prior to presenting a claim.
150   ETA 1996, s 18.

the parties without the need for a tribunal hearing.[151] As we indicated earlier, a high proportion of cases are settled by ACAS conciliation or withdrawn. Settlements reached under the auspices of a conciliation officer and recorded on the appropriate form may not then proceed to a tribunal hearing.[152] TURERA 1993 also introduced the 'compromise agreement' as a further mechanism by which binding settlements could be reached.[153] To be effective the applicant must have received 'independent' advice as to the meaning of and effect of the agreement from a qualified lawyer[154] insured for loss arising from any subsequent claim on the advice.[155] ERDRA 1998 extended this provision to 'advice from a relevant independent adviser', a category which includes, as well as lawyers, officers, officials, employees or members of an independent trade union[156] whom the union has certified in writing as competent to give advice and has authorised to do so, and those who work at advice centres (whether as employees or volunteers) whom the centre has so certified and authorised.[157] However, any such persons are excluded if they are employed by or acting *in the matter* (our italics) for the employer or an associated employer;[158] if the union or centre giving advice is itself the employer or an associated employer; or, in the case of advice centres, if the worker pays for the advice. The compromise agreement must state that the statutory conditions have been satisfied.[159]

The tribunal itself may screen out claims at a 'pre-hearing review', an 'interim hearing' conducted by a chairman alone unless a party otherwise requests not less than ten days before the scheduled date and the chairman considers that a substantive issue of fact is likely to be determined and that a full tribunal would be desirable.[160] Oral or written representations or evidence, as well as the claim form and response, may be considered.[161] Preliminary issues, such as whether the tribunal has jurisdiction to hear a case – for example whether the employee had the requisite period of service – may be determined at a pre-hearing review and, if appropriate, the claim may be struck out at this stage. In addition, if it appears the contentions put forward by a party in relation to a particular matter

---

151 SI 2004/1861, Sch 1, rr 21–24. For most types of claims there is now a fixed period for conciliation (a 'standard' period of 13 weeks, or a 'short' period of seven weeks, depending on the nature of the claim) but this fixed period does not apply to discrimination claims or claims relating to a 'protected disclosure': r 22(1). There is provision for limited extension of these periods in specified circumstances: r 22(7), (8).

152 ETA 1996, s 18; ERA 1996, s 203(1)(e). There are provisions equivalent to s 203(1)(e) in other relevant statutes: see for example SDA 1975, s 77(4)(a).

153 ERA 1996, s 203(2)(f), (3), (4). A compromise agreement will only cover claims which the parties could not have had in contemplation (for example, claims that as a matter of law did not exist) if they use language that unambiguously indicates that it does so: *BCCI SA (in Compulsory Liquidation) v Ali* [2001] IRLR 292. See also *Hinton v University of East London* [2005] IRLR 552.

154 A barrister or solicitor who holds a practising certificate: ERA 1996, s 203(4)(a). 'Independent' advice means that it was given by a lawyer who was not acting in the matter for an employer or an associated employer: s 203(4).

155 ERA 1996, s 203(3)(d).

156 See para 7.23 below.

157 The Secretary of State may extend this category by order; see, for example, SI 2004/754. All 'relevant legal advisers' must be covered by a contract of insurance or an indemnity provided for members of a profession or professional body.

158 See para 3.98 below for the definition of an 'associated employer'.

159 ERA 1996, s 203(3)(f). A compromise agreement that fails to comply with the statutory conditions may still be valid in respect of non-statutory claims: see *Sutherland v Network Appliance Ltd* [2001] IRLR 12.

160 SI 2004/1861, Sch 1, r 18(1), (3), (4).

161 SI 2004/1861, Sch 1, r 18(2).

have 'little reasonable prospect of success' that party may be ordered to pay a deposit of up to £500 as a condition of being permitted to continue to take part in the proceedings relating to that matter.[162] In determining whether a deposit should be ordered, and the amount, the tribunal must take account of the party's means.[163] The tribunal should also give a warning that the party will be liable for the other party's costs or preparation time if they subsequently lose the case and could lose their deposit[164] (which is set off against a costs or preparation time award).[165] If the required deposit is not paid within 21 days, and no extension of this period has been requested and granted, the claim or response, as appropriate, will be struck out.[166]

Where a deposit is required and the party giving it loses at the tribunal, the tribunal retains its discretion to award costs according to the general test that the party has in bringing or conducting the proceedings[167] acted 'vexatiously, abusively, disruptively or otherwise unreasonably' or the bringing or conducting of the proceedings was 'misconceived'[168] (which includes 'having no reasonable prospect of success').[169] Costs orders may be awarded only to a legally-represented party;[170] when making an order, the tribunal may (but is not required to) have regard to a party's ability to pay.[171] Under the 2004 Regulations there is now provision, in similar circumstances, for 'preparation time' orders to be made in favour of non-legally represented parties (including time spent by employees and advisers up to but not including at any hearing),[172] subject to a current maximum of £25 per hour and a total of £10,000.[173] In addition, 'wasted costs' orders may be made against a representative, unless he or she is not acting in pursuit of profit with regard to those proceedings, as a result of any 'improper, unreasonable or negligent act or omission' by the representative or which, in the light of any such act or omission occurring after the costs were incurred, the tribunal considers it 'unreasonable' to expect a party to pay.[174]

This 'move to strengthen ... [employment] ... tribunal procedures to deter and weed out cases at an early stage'[175] replaced a procedure of 'pre-hearing assessments' introduced in 1980, which did not include a deposit system and which was not, in later years, widely used.[176] The deposit system has the clear

---

162   SI 2004/1861, Sch 1, r 20(1).
163   SI 2004/1861, Sch 1, r 20(2).
164   SI 2004/1861, Sch 1, r 20(3).
165   SI 2004/1861, Sch 1, r 47(2). Note, however, that in *Gee v Shell UK Ltd* [2003] IRLR 82 the Court of Appeal held that in the circumstances the costs warning constituted unfair pressure on the claimant to withdraw her claim.
166   SI 2004/1861, Sch 1, r 20(4).
167   Or his or her representative in conducting them.
168   SI 2004/1861, Sch 1, r 40(2), (3). Costs orders may also be made against a party who has not complied with an order or practice direction or where on the application of a party the tribunal or chairman has postponed the day or time fixed for or adjourned a hearing or pre-hearing review: Sch 1, r 40(1), (4).
169   SI 2004/1861, Sch 1, r 2. See *Scott v Commissioners of Inland Revenue* [2004] IRLR 713.
170   SI 2004/1861, Sch 1, r 38(2).
171   SI 2004/1861, Sch 1, r 41(2), overturning the effect of *Kovacs v Queen Mary and Westfield College* [2002] IRLR 414.
172   SI 2004/1861, Sch 1, r 42(3).
173   SI 2004/1861, Sch 1, r 43–45.
174   SI 2004/1861, Sch 1, r 48. Regard must be had to the representative's ability to pay: r 48(6).
175   *Employment Gazette*, October 1994: p 367.
176   In 1992–1993 and 1993–1994 there were 196 and 185 pre-hearing assessments respectively: *Employment Gazette*, October 1994, table 7A. In the year ending September 1984 there were 3,000: Hepple and Fredman, 1992: para 85.

potential to discourage applicants with limited means, particularly if unrepresented, from proceeding with a case whose merits may not be apparent without evidence from witnesses or the opportunity to cross-examine those of the other party (there is no requirement on a chairman to hear evidence before ordering a deposit to be paid).[177] Moreover, the very cases which may appear unarguable to tribunal chairmen may be those which radically change the law.[178] Prior to the 2004 Regulations, a deposit could be required only if there was 'no reasonable prospect of success'; the change to 'little reasonable prospect of success' is a lower hurdle and may encourage deposits to be ordered in a greater range of cases. As we have seen, the powers of tribunals to award costs have to date been rarely used, and the perception that the system of being used by unmeritorious claimants is based on anecdote rather than research.[179]

As far as the speed of the tribunal process is concerned, the time limit for presenting claims is specified under each head of statutory jurisdiction. It varies between claims but is commonly within three months of the act complained of.[180] If this deadline is not met the tribunal usually has jurisdiction to grant such further period as it considers reasonable if satisfied that it was not 'reasonably practicable' for the complaint to be presented in time.[181] The onus is on the applicant to show this.[182] There is considerable case law on what is meant by 'reasonably practicable', which has been interpreted as 'reasonably feasible',[183] although this is largely a question of fact for the tribunal. In the light of this, previous cases are of limited value but afford some general guidance. To show that it was not 'reasonably practicable' to present a claim in time is now a difficult test to satisfy, particularly if the applicant has engaged 'skilled advisers' which include in this context solicitors,[184] trade union officers,[185] and a Citizens Advice Bureau[186] (but not

---

177 SI 2004/1861, Sch 1, r 18(2)(c).

178 See, for example, the *Marshall* litigation, discussed in para 6.53 below.

179 A 1998 Survey of Employment Tribunal Applications found that fewer than 4% of cases were 'vexatious' in the sense that the claimant had been advised by a professional adviser that they were likely to lose, and in seven of the 35 cases so classified the applicant went on to win at a tribunal hearing: *Findings from the 1998 Survey of Employment Tribunal Applications*, Employment Relations Research Series 13, DTI, 2002: p 28.

180 The statutory language varies as to whether the date of the act itself counts for the purposes of computation. There is provision for extension in specified circumstances where the statutory dismissal or disciplinary procedures, or greivance procedures, apply: EADRR 2004, reg 15.

181 See, for example, ERA 1996, s 111(2). Note that under the discrimination legislation a tribunal may consider a claim which is out of time if in all the circumstances it considers that it is just and equitable to do so (see, for example, SDA 1975, s 76(5)). This discretion is broader than in the context of the unfair dismissal provisions: see *Hawkins v Ball and Barclays Bank plc* [1996] IRLR 258; *British Coal Corpn v Keeble* [1997] IRLR 336.

182 *Porter v Bandridge Ltd* [1978] IRLR 271.

183 *Palmer and Saunders v Southend-on-Sea Borough Council* [1984] IRLR 119. In *Schultz v Esso Petroleum Co Ltd* [1999] 3 All ER 338 the Court of Appeal held that attention would normally focus on the closing rather than the early stages of the period in assessing whether something should have been done. In *Marley (UK) Ltd v Anderson* [1996] IRLR 163 the Court of Appeal held (surprisingly) that although an employee's complaint on the initial ground put forward was time-barred, it had jurisdiction to consider the complaint on a different ground which had subsequently come to light and which the employee had raised, by amendment to his existing claim, within a reasonable period after acquiring the relevant knowledge.

184 *Dedman v British Building and Engineering Appliances Ltd* [1973] IRLR 379.

185 *Union Cartage Co Ltd v Blunden* [1977] IRLR 139.

186 *Riley v Tesco Stores Ltd* [1980] IRLR 103, cf, however, *Marks and Spencer plc v Williams-Ryan* [2005] IRLR 562, Lord Phillips MR at para 32.

an employee of an employment tribunal).[187] However, tribunals have been warned against treating recourse to a skilled adviser as an absolute bar to extension of the time limit regardless of the circumstances.[188] Because the time limit goes to the tribunal's jurisdiction the employer cannot unilaterally agree to waive it. Once in the system, the aim is to bring 75% of cases to a first hearing within 26 weeks, a target that the ETS exceeded in 2003–2004.[189] Although any delay is highly undesirable, particularly in cases of dismissal, the speed with which cases are now heard by tribunals compares favourably with the ordinary courts.

2.18   Full hearings of tribunals must normally take place in public.[190] However, a government minister may direct that a tribunal should sit in private in the interests of national security for all or part of particular Crown proceedings, and the tribunal itself may decide to do so on this ground[191] or where evidence is likely to consist of information whose disclosure would be contrary to statute, which has been communicated in confidence, or which would cause substantial injury to the employer's undertaking other than any effects it may have on collective bargaining.[192] The tribunal chairman may give directions on any matter arising in connection with the proceedings, including requiring a party to give additional information, the provision and exchange of witness statements, and the provision of written answers to questions put by the tribunal. They may also grant orders for the disclosure and inspection of documents and require the attendance of witnesses and production of documents.[193] A failure to comply with a direction or requirement may result in the claim or response being struck out, or the respondent debarred from defending the claim altogether.[194]

The form of employment tribunal proceedings remains adversarial rather than investigatory; each party has to present and prove its case and may cross-examine the witnesses of the other. However, the chairman or tribunal shall ' [s]o far as it appears appropriate ..., seek to avoid formality in his or its proceedings and shall not be bound by any enactment or rule of law relating to the admissibility of evidence in proceedings before the courts'.[195] This means that the hearsay rule of evidence, for example, does not apply. Moreover, the chairman or tribunal 'shall make such enquiries of persons appearing before him or it and witnesses as he or it considers appropriate and shall otherwise conduct the hearing in such manner as he or it considers most appropriate for the clarification of the issues and generally for the just handling of the proceedings'.[196]

Despite the emphasis on informality, appearing at an employment tribunal is likely to be a stressful experience for the non-represented litigant,

---

187   *Jean Sorelle Ltd v Rybak* [1991] IRLR 153.
188   *London International College Ltd v Sen* [1993] IRLR 333, 336 (Bingham MR).
189   Employment Tribunals Service, *Annual Report and Accounts 2003–2004*, HC 714, 2004: p 8.
190   SI 2004/1861, Sch 1, r 26(3). In *Storer v British Gas Plc* [2000] IRLR 495 the Court of Appeal quashed a tribunal decision where the public had not been afforded unimpeded access to the hearing.
191   SI 2004/1861, Sch 1, r 54.
192   SI 2004/1861, Sch 1, r 16. See also r 50 and ETA 1996, ss 11, 12 for provisions relating to restricted reporting orders in cases involving allegations of sexual misconduct or complaints relating to disability discrimination and *Chief Constable of West Yorkshire Police v A* [2000] IRLR 465 and *X v Stevens* [2003] IRLR 411.
193   SI 2004/1861, Sch 1, r 10. This may be done either at the request of one of the parties or at the Chairman's own initiative.
194   SI 2004/1861, Sch 1, r 13.
195   SI 2004/1861, Sch 1, r 14(2).
196   SI 2004/1861, Sch 1, r 14(3).

particularly in the light of the technical nature of much of the contemporary law. As we indicated earlier, parties to tribunal hearings can be represented by the person of their choice. In practice, despite the lack of legal aid and rarity of costs orders, a significant proportion of those appearing in tribunals obtain legal representation. A survey of cases completed between March 2002 and March 2003 showed that 51% of claimants and 54% of respondents were represented by a solicitor at a full tribunal hearing.[197] It is significant that the representation gap between employers and employees should have narrowed over time. In 1987 the Justice Report on Employment Tribunals could comment:

> In the case of individual disputes arising out of the employment relationship, the employee is usually in an inferior position to the employer. A corporate employer will normally have a personnel department and possibly an in-house lawyer, and they may have considerable experience of tribunal proceedings. The employer is more likely than the employee to be able to deal with communications from the tribunal office and the other side. The employer will usually find it easier to call witnesses and to produce documentary evidence. Where an external legal representative is thought to be desirable, it is the employer who is more likely to be able [to] afford this.[198]

Research has indicated that where employers are legally represented and applicants are not the success rate of the latter is lower than where both have legal representation. The disparity in success rates is unlikely to be accounted for solely by the strength of the initial case.[199] With the growth in tribunal claims and the large number of smaller employers now appearing as respondents without legal representation, the lack of representation for such employers may be almost as serious a cause for concern as it is in relation to employees.

Finally, reasons must be given for all tribunal judgments.[200] These need only be given orally unless a party requests written reasons,[201] or if written reasons are requested by the EAT.[202] Written reasons must contain the issues the tribunal or chairman identified as being relevant to the claim; if some identified issues were not determined, what these were and why they were not determined; findings of fact; a concise statement of the applicable law; how the relevant findings and applicable law have been applied to determine the issues; and where there is provision for compensation or other payment, how this was calculated.[203] Normally a party who wishes to lodge an appeal with the EAT must do so within 42 days of the date on which written reasons were sent to the parties or, where none were requested and written reasons were not reserved, 42 days from the date on which the written record of the judgment was sent to the parties.[204] We consider the implications of this course further below.

---

197 Hayward *et al*, 2004: pp 32, 105. The survey refers specifically to solicitors and does not refer to a separate category of representation by a barrister. 15% of applicants used a union representative and 17% a Citizens' Advice Bureau: pp 32–33, 105.

198 Justice, 1987: para 2.7.

199 L Dickens *et al*, 1985: p 105; Leonard, 1986; Genn and Genn, 1989; Hepple, 1992a: p 81. See para 2.15 for the argument that lack of legal aid for representation in complex cases may breach Art 6 of the ECHR.

200 SI 2004/1861, Sch 1, r 30(1).

201 This must be done orally at the hearing, if judgment is issued there, or in writing within 14 days of the judgment being sent to the parties: SI 2004/1861, Sch 1, r 30(3),(5).

202 SI 2004/1861, Sch 1, r 30(3).

203 SI 2004/1981, Sch 1, r 30(6).

204 The Employment Appeal Tribunal Rules 1993, SI 1993/2854, as amended r 3(3).

Employment Appeal Tribunal (EAT)

2.19   Appeals from employment tribunals on points of law are heard by the EAT.[205] The EAT was established by the Employment Protection Act 1975[206] and replaced the National Industrial Relations Court (NIRC) created by the Industrial Relations Act 1971. It also hears appeals from decisions of the Certification Officer relating to trade union matters and from the CAC on information and consultation, again on points of law. It has a limited original jurisdiction under TICER 1999 and EPLLCR 2004. The EAT has the same powers as the High Court with regard to the attendance and examination of witnesses, production and inspection of documents and other matters incidental to its jurisdiction. In disposing of an appeal the EAT may either determine the issue itself or remit the case to the same or a differently-constituted employment tribunal to be decided in the light of its ruling on the law.

The EAT has premises in London although it can also sit elsewhere.[207] Like the employment tribunals it has a tripartite composition, consisting of a judge and non-lawyer members who have special knowledge or experience of industrial relations, either as representatives of employers or of workers.[208] The lay members are appointed by the Queen on the joint recommendation of the Secretary of State and Lord Chancellor. An appeal is normally heard by a judge and two lay members who, even though the question is one of law, may outvote the judge, although this very rarely happens.[209] The judge may sit alone to deal with interim matters and can normally hear the appeal alone where the original decision was made by a tribunal chairman in the absence of lay members.

In contrast to the position with employment tribunals, legal aid is available for EAT hearings, although the parties may still have non-lawyer representation. As in the case of employment tribunals costs are not generally awarded for EAT proceedings, but the court has power to award them if it considers that the proceedings were unnecessary, improper, vexatious or misconceived or that that there has been unreasonable delay or other unreasonable conduct of proceedings by a party.[210] Since 2004, it may also make costs orders in other specified situations (for non-compliance with an order, for example) and can make wasted costs orders against representatives, subject in all cases to a discretion to consider a party's or a representative's ability to pay. There is also now provision for costs to be awarded in favour of a litigant in person.

In 2003–2004, 1,235 appeals were registered by the EAT; in 2002–2003, 1,170.[211] Of the 840 appeals disposed of at a full hearing in 2003–2004, 421 were dismissed at the hearing, and 419 allowed or remitted to a

---

205 See para 2.16 for the 'non-employment' jurisdiction of employment tribunals.
206 See now ETA 1996, s 20 *et seq.*
207 The EAT has jurisdiction to hear appeals from employment tribunals in Scotland, as well as England and Wales, and tribunals in England are bound by decisions of a Scottish division: see Morison P in *Davidson v City Electrical Factors Ltd* [1998] IRLR 435.
208 ETA 1996, s 22.
209 Unless the parties otherwise consent there should be an equal number of employer and worker representatives on any hearing. Exceptionally, the judge may sit with four lay members: see, for example, *GCSF v Certification Officer* [1993] IRLR 260. See ETA 1996, Part II for the provisions as to the membership, sittings, proceedings and powers of the EAT. The EAT's procedure is governed by Rules (Employment Appeal Tribunal Rules 1993, SI 1993/2854, as amended) and Practice Directions.
210 On costs in the EAT, see EAT Rules 1993, SI 1993/2854, rules 34 and 34A–34D, inserted by SI 2004/2526.
211 Employment Tribunals Service, *Annual Report and Accounts 2003–2004*, HC 714, 2004: p 5.

tribunal.[212] All appeals are sifted by a judge or the Registrar (with an appeal to a judge) to determine the most effective management of the case. Cases are divided into one of four tracks: those rejected on the basis that there are no reasonable grounds for bringing the appeal, that they are an abuse of process, or otherwise likely to obstruct the just disposal of proceedings; those listed for a Preliminary Hearing to determine whether there is a point of law which gives the appeal a reasonable prospect of success or some other reason the appeal should be heard; cases proceeding immediately to a full hearing; and fast track full hearing cases. For appeals on points of law fresh evidence which was not before the tribunal will be admitted only in exceptional circumstances.

The distinction between questions of law and of fact, crucial to whether an appeal will lie, is a notoriously difficult one to apply. To succeed in an appeal on a point of law an appellant must establish that the tribunal misdirected itself in law, or misunderstood the law, or misapplied the law; or that there was no evidence to support a particular conclusion or finding of fact; or that the decision was 'perverse' in that it was one which no reasonable tribunal, directing itself properly on the law, could have reached, or alternatively, was one which was obviously wrong.[213] In practice, it will be very difficult to classify as 'perverse' a decision which did not fall within one of the previous two categories.[214]

These criteria do not, in many cases, lend very much assistance. It is clear that, on the one hand, construction of a statute will be a question of law. Conversely, where witnesses' accounts of events conflict, which version is preferred will be a question of fact. However, in many situations the position is much less clear-cut. When does the 'reasonableness' of an employer's action in dismissing an employee become a question of law, for example? What of the definition of an 'employee' and the application of that definition to a given set of circumstances? As we shall see the answers to these questions have not always been consistent over time. On occasion the higher courts have made no secret of their desire to restrict appeals, sometimes in the guise of discouraging undue 'legalism' in employment matters. However, the effect of designating a matter a question of fact is that employment tribunals are then free to make their own decisions which may be at variance with those of others; that different tribunals have reached differing conclusions on the same or similar facts does not necessarily mean that one of them has made an error of law. When such decisions concern an issue fundamental to an individual's access to the right in question, such as, for many jurisdictions, the definitions of 'employee' and, for the purposes of unfair dismissal, of 'industrial action', this may have very serious consequences.[215]

Reforming the tribunal system

2.20   In 1994 the Employment Department published proposals for reform of the tribunal system 'with a view to identifying any changes which would help

212 Employment Tribunals Service, *Annual Report and Accounts 2003–2004*, HC 714, 2004: p 27, table 10.
213 *British Telecommunications plc v Sheridan* [1990] IRLR 27, 30 (Lord Donaldson MR); *Melon v Hector Powe Ltd* [1980] IRLR 477, 479 (Lord Fraser); *Hereford and Worcester County Council v Neale* [1986] IRLR 168, 174 (May LJ); *Piggott Bros & Co Ltd v Jackson* [1991] IRLR 309, 312 (Lord Donaldson MR); *Watling v William Bird & Son (Contractors) Ltd* (1976) 11 ITR 70, 71.
214 See *Yeboah v Crofton* [2002] IRLR 634.
215 For views of the successive Presidents of the EAT as to its role see Phillips, 1978; Browne-Wilkinson, 1982; Waite, 1986; Popplewell, 1987; Sir John Wood, 1990.

... to cope with an increasing volume and complexity of cases with reduced delays, while containing demands on public expenditure'.[216] It pointed to the pressures on the system resulting from the increased workload of tribunals, which had more than doubled from 34,697 applications in 1989–1990 to 71,661 in 1993–1994[217] (figures which now seem modest compared with the 115,000 plus in 2003–2004 described in para 2.16 above). The Conservative Government was removed from office before its draft Bill could be enacted; reforms were eventually introduced by the Labour Government in the shape of ERDRA 1998 and EA 2002 and amendments to the rules of procedure governing tribunals.

These reforms have had a variety of aims which space does not permit us to discuss in full.[218] Here, we focus on the primary policy aim; that of reducing the number of cases going to tribunals by encouraging parties to resolve disputes by alternative means. ERDRA 1998 began this process.[219] First, the Act empowered ACAS to prepare a scheme, for approval by the Secretary of State, for the resolution of unfair dismissal disputes by arbitration.[220] After some delay, this scheme came into effect in May 2001.[221] ACAS appoints the arbitrator from a panel of individuals chosen for their practical knowledge and experience of workplace discipline and dismissal. Recourse to arbitration is voluntary but precludes recourse to an employment tribunal on the matter,[222] and the outcome is binding on the parties. The arbitration is confined to the question of whether the dismissal was fair or unfair, and the parties are required to confirm, as a condition of admission to the scheme, that there is no dispute between them on any jurisdictional issue, such as whether the worker is an 'employee' or was 'dismissed'. The procedures to be followed are intended to be non-legalistic and more informal than tribunals,[223] and as far as possible general principles of fairness and good conduct, rather than legal precedent, are expected to be

---

216 See *Resolving Employment Rights Disputes – Options for Reform*, Employment Department, Cm 2707, 1994: para 1.1. For a commentary on these proposals, see Cockburn, 1995. For earlier recommendations as to how the system could be reformed, see Justice, 1987.

217 *Resolving Employment Rights Disputes – Options for Reform*, Employment Department, Cm 2707, 1994: table 3.1. This was attributed partly to an expansion in tribunals' jurisdiction.

218 Note in particular the recommendations of the Employment Tribunals System Taskforce, DTI, 2002. The Taskforce was established to make recommendations on how services could be made more efficient and cost effective for users, against a background of rising caseloads.

219 For an overview of ERDRA 1998, which also contained provisions relating to tribunal procedures and staffing issues, see R Lewis. 1998; see also MacMillan, 1999.

220 On unfair dismissal generally see ch 5. For the case in support of arbitration in this context see R Lewis and J Clark, 1993; see also J Clark, 1999. There is provision for this scheme to be extended to other statutory rights by statutory instrument approved by a resolution of both Houses of Parliament, and in April 2003 it was extended to cover claims under the flexible working legislation.

221 For the principles of the arbitration scheme, see SI 2004/753, revoking and replacing SI 2001/1185. ACAS has also produced guidance on the operation of the scheme. See Earnshaw and Hardy, 2001.

222 Entry to the scheme may be through a settlement reached with the assistance of an ACAS conciliation officer, or through a valid 'compromise agreement': see paras 2.17. The agreement must be accompanied by a specified 'Waiver Form'. In the event that different aspects of the same dispute (a claim for unpaid wages, for example) are being heard in the employment tribunal, the arbitrator may decide to postpone the arbitration proceedings pending the tribunal's determination.

223 Notably, cross-examination of witnesses is prohibited. The parties may, if they choose, be represented by a person of their choice.

followed. However the arbitrator may request the assistance of an ACAS-appointed legal adviser if a question of EC law or the HRA 1998 is relevant to the matter. The parties are expected to co-operate fully with the arbitration process, including complying without delay with any determination of the arbitrator on procedural or evidential matters such as the provision of documents or attendance of witnesses, and whilst the arbitrator has no power to compel compliance with these requirements, adverse inferences may be drawn from a failure to comply. The process is designed to achieve finality: there is no provision for appeal from the arbitrator's award on a point of law other than EC law and the application of the HRA 1998;[224] otherwise, awards may be challenged only on the grounds of substantive jurisdiction or specified forms of irregularity affecting the tribunal, the proceedings or the award which the court considers has caused or will cause substantial injustice to the claimant.[225] Arbitrations are conducted in private and awards are confidential to the parties, although ACAS may publish general summary information without identifying individual cases. Up to March 2004 use of the scheme has been modest; a total of 44 cases have been accepted for resolution by this means.[226] Other provisions in ERDRA 1998 designed to encourage alternative dispute resolution included extending the range of persons who may conclude 'compromise agreements', which we discussed in para 2.17, and provisions designed to encourage internal appeal procedures in unfair dismissal cases.

The reforms in ERDRA now appear modest in comparison with those introduced by EA 2002; the requirements for claimants in most cases to institute a statutory grievance procedure prior to presenting a tribunal claim and for employers to commence, and both parties to participate in, a statutory disciplinary and dismissal procedure in relation to 'direct' dismissal cases. The strength of the Government's case for these reforms, and the nature of the reforms themselves, was highly controversial.[227] We discuss the statutory grievance procedures in the paragraphs below; the statutory dismissal and disciplinary procedures in the context of our analysis of unfair dismissal protection in chapter 5.

The statutory grievance procedures

2.21 EA 2002 establishes two forms of statutory grievance procedures ('SGP'), a 'standard' procedure, applicable in the majority of cases, and a 'modified' procedure, applicable in limited circumstances.[228] There are also specified situations where neither procedure applies or where the relevant procedure is

---

224 Arbitration Act 1996, s 69, as modified by the ACAS Arbitration Scheme, above, note 221, para 164.

225 Arbitration Act 1996, ss 67 and 68, as modified by the ACAS Arbitration Scheme, above, paras 162 and 163. Applications may be made to the High Court or the Central London County Court.

226 *ACAS Annual Report and Resource Accounts 2003/04*, HC 651, 2004: p 22. Research has shown that there is low awareness of the Scheme among employees, employers and representatives: see *The ACAS Arbitration Scheme: An evaluation of parties' views*, ACAS, 2004.

227 See generally Hepple and Morris, 2002; *Routes to Resolution*, DTI, 2001; G Morris, 2005.

228 The detailed application of the procedures is laid down in EADRR 2004. In relation to grievances, the procedures apply where the action about which the employee complains occurred or continued after 1 October 2004 unless the employee had raised a grievance about the action prior to that: EADRR 2004, reg 18.

treated as complied with. A grievance is defined as 'a complaint by an employee about action which the employer has taken or is contemplating against him'.[229] This definition also covers the actions of a third party (eg a fellow employee) in situations where the employer could be vicariously liable for their actions.[230] The procedures apply in relation to any grievance about action by the employer that could form the basis of a claim by an employee to an employment tribunal under specified jurisdictions, or which could do so if the action took place.[231] These include claims about equal pay or discrimination; detriment in relation to union membership or activities, union recognition rights, matters specified in ERA 1996[232] or in relation to the national minimum wage; unauthorised deductions from pay; unfair dismissal and redundancy payments where the claim is based on constructive dismissal;[233] claims of breach of contract on termination of employment; and claims under the WTR 1998.[234] However the procedures apply to 'protected disclosures' under the 'whistleblowing provisions'[235] only if the information relates to a matter that could be raised as a grievance and the employee intended 'that the disclosure should constitute the raising of the matter with his employer as a grievance'.[236] This is intended to give the employee the right to choose whether to raise an issue as a grievance or a protected disclosure.[237]

2.22   The first step of the three-step 'standard' SGP requires the employee to set out the grievance in writing and to send the statement or a copy of it to the employer.[238] The employer must then invite the employee to attend a meeting to discuss the grievance (the second step).[239] The meeting must not take place unless the employee has informed the employer what the 'basis' for the grievance was when he or she made the statement and the employer has had a reasonable opportunity to consider his or her response to the information.[240] The employee must take all 'reasonable steps' to attend the meeting, following which the employer must inform the employee of his or her decision and of the right to appeal against it.[241] If the employee wishes to appeal (the third step) he or she

---

229 EADRR 2004, reg 2.
230 *Guidance on the Employment Act 2002 (Dispute Resolution) Regulations 2004 and associated provisions in the Employment Act 2002*, DTI, 2004, para 56.
231 EADRR 2004, reg 6(1).
232 See ERA 1996, s 48.
233 Situations where the employer has dismissed, or is contemplating dismissing, the employee or is contemplating 'relevant disciplinary action' are covered by the statutory dismissal and disciplinary procedures: EADRR 2004, reg 6(5),(6). These apply to dismissals that take the form of termination by the employer or termination of a limited-term contract by virtue of the limiting event without renewal: EADRR 2004, regs 3, 2; unfair constructive dismissal complaints must be preceded by use of the appropriate grievance procedure. As we discuss in para 5.71 the dividing-line between termination by the employer and constructive dismissal is not always clear-cut.
234 See EA 2002, Schs 3 and 4, as amended.
235 See para 4.103.
236 EA 2002, Sch 2, para 15(2).
237 *Guidance on the Employment Act 2002 (Dispute Resolution) Regulations 2004 and associated provisions in the Employment Act 2002*, DTI, 2004, para 57.
238 EA 2002, Sch 2, para 6. Issuing a questionnaire under the discrimination legislation (see para 6.18) does not of itself constitute a statement for these purposes: EADRR 2004, reg 14.
239 EA 2002, Sch 2, para 7(1).
240 EA 2002, Sch 2, para 7(2). It is unclear how the 'basis' of the grievance and the grievance itself are to be distinguished.
241 EA 2002, Sch 2, para 7(3),(4).

must inform the employer, whereupon the employer must invite him or her to attend a further meeting which the employee must take all reasonable steps to attend, following which the employer must inform the employee of his or her final decision.[242] So far as reasonably practicable, the employer should be represented at the appeal by a more senior manager than attended the first meeting, unless the most senior manager attended the first meeting.[243] Each step and action under both the 'standard' and the 'modified' procedures must be taken without unreasonable delay; the timing and location of meetings must be reasonable; and meetings must be conducted in a manner that enables both employer and employee to explain their cases.[244] In addition, meetings under both procedures constitute 'hearings' for the purposes of the statutory right to be accompanied by a union official or fellow worker that we discuss in chapter 5.[245] If it is not reasonably practicable for the employee (or if he or she is exercising the statutory right to be accompanied, his or her companion) or the employer to attend a meeting organised in accordance with the applicable statutory procedure for a reason which was not foreseeable when the meeting was arranged, the employer or the employee, as to the case may be, will not be treated as having failed to comply with the procedure.[246] It is then for the employer to invite the employee to attend another meeting.[247] If that second meeting fails to occur for an unforeseeable reason, the parties are then treated as having complied with the applicable procedure.[248]

The two-step 'modified' procedure applies where the employee has ceased to be employed by the employer and either the employer was unaware of the grievance before the employment ended or was so aware but the standard procedure was not commenced or completed before the last day of the employee's employment. In addition the parties must have agreed in writing in relation to the grievance after the employer became aware of it that the modified procedure should apply.[249] It is thus designed to cover situations 'where there is no ongoing employment relationship and the parties have no interest in following the standard procedures, and where they are in mutual agreement on this point'.[250] The need for the employer to be aware of the specific grievance means that there cannot be a general agreement (in a contract of employment, for example) that any grievance unresolved at the termination of employment should be subject to the modified procedure. The modified procedure requires as a first step that the employee must set out in writing the grievance and the basis for it and send the statement or a copy of it to the employer.[251] The second step is for the employer to set out his or her response in writing and send the statement or a copy of it to the employee.[252]

---

242 EA 2002, Sch 2, para 8.
243 EA 2002, Sch 2, paras 11, 13(3).
244 EA 2002, Sch 2, paras 11, 12, 13(1), (2).
245 EA 2002, Sch 2 para 14; see further para 5.132 *et seq*. The hearing must constitute a 'grievance hearing' for the purposes of that right but the definition of a 'grievance hearing' is likely to cover most, if not all, cases covered by the SGPs.
246 EADRR 2004, reg 13(1).
247 EADRR 2004, reg 13(2). Where the employee is exercising his or her rights under ERelA 1999, s 10 and the employee proposes an alternative time under s 10(4) the employer has a duty to invite the employee to attend a meeting at that time.
248 EADRR 2004, reg 13(3), (4).
249 EADRR 2004, reg 6(3).
250 *Guidance on the Employment Act 2002 (Dispute Resolution) Regulations 2004 and associated provisions in the Employment Act 2002*, DTI, 2004, para 64.
251 EA 2002, Sch 2, para 9(1).
252 EA 2002, Sch 2, para 10.

2.23   The consequences for an employee who fails to follow the applicable SGP are severe. First, an employee is debarred from presenting a complaint covered by an SGP to an employment tribunal if he or she has failed to send a copy of the grievance to the employer in accordance with the first step of the procedure.[253] Having sent a copy of the grievance, the employee must then wait for a minimum of 28 days before presenting the complaint in order to allow the employer time to respond to it.[254] Second, where the employee begins proceedings prior to completion of the SGP, and non-completion was wholly or mainly attributable to failure by the employee to comply with a requirement of the procedure or to exercise a right of appeal under it, tribunals must (unless there are exceptional circumstances which would make such a reduction 'unjust or inequitable') reduce any award they make to the employee by 10% and have a discretion to reduce it by up to 50%.[255] An employer's failure to complete the applicable procedure also has legal consequences; tribunals must (exceptional circumstances apart) increase the award to the employee by 10% and have a discretion to increase it by 50%.[256] If either party fails to comply with a requirement of an applicable SGP, neither party has any obligation to comply with any further requirement of that procedure.[257]

Where the SGPs apply, the normal time limit for presenting a complaint to an employment tribunal is extended for a period of three months beginning with the day after that on which it would otherwise have expired in specified circumstances.[258] The first is where an employee presents a complaint to a tribunal within the normal time period but without having complied with the first step of the applicable procedure or before 28 days have passed since a copy of the grievance was sent to the employer.[259] The extended time period affords the employee the opportunity to comply with the first step, and there is a duty on the Secretary of employment tribunals to notify the claimant of the time limit and the consequences of not complying with that first step.[260] However the

253   EA 2002, s 32(1), (2).
254   EA 2002, s 32(3).
255   EA 2002, s 31(2), (4). As discussed in Hepple and Morris, 2002: p 256 the Joint Committee on Human Rights found that these penalties could be compatible with Art 6(1) and Art 1 of Protocol No 1 of the ECHR on the basis that tribunals would be required to construe 'exceptional circumstances' in the light of Convention rights, which may require these words to be given an 'extended meaning'. The JCHR also adopted a broad brush approach to proportionality instead of applying the test to each of the statutory rights affected, an approach which may be open to challenge in relation to deductions from amounts already legally vested in the employee. It is also possible that the courts will find that a penalty imposed for a reason unrelated to the unlawful conduct which gave rise to the right to compensation is a breach of Convention rights, and, where a breach of Community rights is at issue (unlawful discrimination for example), that this is incompatible with the requirement under EC law of effective and adequate reparation: *Marshall v Southampton and South West Hampshire Area Health Authority (No 2)* Case C-271/91 [1993] ECR I-4367.
256   EA 2002, s 31(3), (4). In the case of unfair dismissal compensation, the reduction or increase applies only to the compensatory award: ERA 1996, s 124A.
257   EADRR 2004, reg 12(1).
258   EADRR reg 15(1). 'Normal time limit' is defined in terms that exclude the discretion to extend that period: reg 15(5). The discretion of tribunals to extend a time limit for presenting a claim (see para 2.17) is unaffected by these changes: *Guidance on the Employment Act 2002 (Dispute Resolution) Regulations 2004 and associated provisions in the Employment Act 2002*, DTI, 2004, para 125.
259   EADRR reg 15(1), (3)(a). This wording is anomalous, given that EA 2002, s 32(2) and (3) state that an employee 'shall not present a complaint' to a tribunal in such circumstances.
260   SI 2004/1861, Sch 1, r 3(6).

employee will be debarred from presenting the complaint if the day on which the first step was complied with was more than one month after the end of the original time limit for making the complaint.[261] The second situation where the time limit is extended is where the employee complied with the first step within the normal time period but presented his or her complaint after the expiry of the normal time period.[262]

2.24   There are a number of situations where neither of the SGPs applies. The normal time limits apply to such claims. The first is where the employee has ceased to be employed by the employer; neither procedure has been commenced; and since the employee ceased to be employed it has ceased to be reasonably practicable for him or her to comply with the first step of either procedure.[263] The second is where the employer has dismissed or is contemplating dismissing the employee or the employer has taken or contemplates taking disciplinary action on the basis of conduct or capability; these situations are covered instead by the statutory dismissal and disciplinary procedures.[264] However, the need to comply with the appropriate grievance procedure will still apply if the employer has taken or contemplates taking conduct or capability-related disciplinary action and the employee considers that this action amounted to or, if it took place, would amount to unlawful discrimination[265] or that the employer is, in fact, taking the action on grounds unrelated to those it claims to be relying upon.[266] However it is sufficient to constitute compliance here for the employee to send a written copy of the grievance to the employer prior to an appeal under the relevant disciplinary procedure, if this is being followed, or if it is not being followed, before presenting a complaint arising out of the grievance to an employment tribunal.[267] If the disciplinary procedure has been completed, however, the employee will need to comply with the applicable SGP in the normal way.

In addition to these specific exceptions the application of the SGPs is subject to two general exclusions. The first covers circumstances where the procedure is not commenced because a party has reasonable grounds to believe that this would result in a significant threat to himself or another person, or to his or her property; the party has been subjected to harassment and has reasonable grounds to believe that this would result in further harassment; or it is not practicable for the party to commence the procedure within a reasonable period.[268] However where the procedure is not commenced because of a threat or harassment resulting from the behaviour of either the employer or the employee, that party is treated

---

261   EA 2002, s 32(4).
262   EADRR 2004, reg 15(1), (3)(b)
263   EADRR 2004, reg 6(4).
264   EADRR 2004, reg 6(5), (6). Note, however, the restricted definition of 'dismissal' in this context; see para 5.124.
265   An act or omission in respect of which a complaint would lie under the EqPA 1970, SDA 1975, RRA 1976, DDA 1995, EE(RB)R 2003 or EE(SO)R 2003; see further ch 6.
266   EADRR 2004, reg 7(1).
267   EADRR 2004, reg 7(2).
268   EADRR 2004, regs 6(7), 11(1), (3). 'Harassment' is defined in reg 11(4). It means conduct which has the purpose or effect of '(a) violating the person's dignity' or (b) creating an intimidating, hostile, degrading, humiliating or offensive environment for him' or her but conduct is only to be regarded as having that purpose or effect if 'having regard to all the circumstances, including in particular the perception of the person who was the subject of the conduct, it should reasonably be considered as having that purpose or effect'.

as if the procedure had applied and he, she or it had failed to comply with it.[269] The second exclusion is where it would not be possible to comply with an applicable SGP without disclosing information whose disclosure would be contrary to the interests of national security.[270]

2.25   In addition to these exceptions, there are five sets of circumstances in which the parties are treated as having complied with the relevant SGP even though the procedure has not been completed. Unlike situations where the SGPs do not apply at all, the employee may benefit from the provision for an extended time limit to apply to the tribunal described in para 2.23 above. The first is where the standard procedure applies; the employee has ceased to be employed by the employer; the employee has complied with the 'first step' of the procedure; and since the end of the employment it has ceased to be reasonably practicable for the employee, or the employer, to comply with the second or third steps.[271] Where, however, there has already been a 'second step' meeting between employer and employee the employer is required to inform the employee in writing of its decision in response to the grievance.[272] The second is designed to deal with collective grievances. The parties are treated as complying with the applicable SGP if a person who is an 'appropriate representative' of the employee with the grievance has written to the employer setting out the grievance and has specified in writing the names of at least two employees, of whom one is the employee with the grievance, as being the employees on behalf of whom he or she is raising the grievance.[273] A person is an 'appropriate representative' for this purpose if, at the time of writing to the employer, he or she is either (a) an official[274] of an independent trade union[275] recognised by the employer for the purposes of collective bargaining[276] in respect of a description of employees that includes the employee with the grievance, or (b) an employee of the employer who is an employee representative elected or appointed by employees consisting of or including employees of the same description as the employee with the grievance and who, having regard to the purposes for which and method by which he or she was elected or appointed, has the authority to represent employees of that description under an established procedure for resolving grievances agreed between employer representatives and the employer.[277] The third situation is designed to allow dispute resolution procedures developed by groups of employers and unions to continue to operate. The parties are treated as complying with the SGP if at the time the employee raises the grievance there is a procedure in operation, under a collective agreement made between two or more employers or an employers' association[278] and one or more independent unions, that provides for employees of the employer to raise grievances and have them considered; and the employee is entitled to raise the grievance under that procedure and does so.[279] The fourth is where the employer

---

269 EADRR 2004, reg 12(3).
270 EADRR 2004, reg 16.
271 EADRR 2004, reg 8(1).
272 EADRR 2004, reg 8(2).
273 EADRR 2004, reg 9(1).
274 See TULRCA 1992, s 119; EADRR 2004, reg 9(3).
275 See TULRCA 1992, s 5, discussed para 7.23; EADRR 2004, reg 2(1).
276 See TULRCA 1992, s 178, discussed para 7.27; EADRR 2004, reg 9(3).
277 EADRR 2004, reg 9(2). See further para 9.34.
278 See TULRCA 1992, s 122, discussed para 7.21; EADRR 2004, reg 2(1).
279 EADRR 2004, reg 10.

has invited the employee to a meeting which has subsequently been re-arranged and both meetings have needed to be cancelled because of an unforeseeable reason.[280] The fifth is where the procedure has been started but a party does not comply with a subsequent requirement on the grounds relating to threats, harassment or impracticality specified in para 2.24 above.[281] However, if the requirement is not complied with because of a threat or harassment resulting from the behaviour of the employer or employee, non-compliance is treated as a failure, attributable to that party, to comply with the procedure.[282]

2.26   The Government has predicted that the introduction of the statutory grievance and dismissal and disciplinary procedures will, in the long term, prevent an estimated 35,000–40,000 claims a year being presented to employment tribunals.[283] It remains to be seen whether this aim will be realised and, if so, whether any reduction in claims will be due to employees' grievances being satisfactorily resolved at workplace level. It also remains to be seen whether the provisions governing the application of the procedures, which as the above account makes clear are complex, themselves generate additional litigation. There is obvious potential for factual disputes as to whether the procedures themselves have been complied with; for example, although the ACAS Code of Practice on Disciplinary and Grievance Procedures recommends that employers respond in writing to grievances,[284] this is not a mandatory requirement. Whether an exception applies – for instance, whether there has been harassment or a party has reasonable grounds to believe that commencing the procedure would result in a 'significant threat' – may be further areas of dispute. The question whether a worker is an 'employee', which may not be relevant to a substantive claim, such as one of discrimination, may also need to be determined as a preliminary issue to decide if an SGP, if not followed, should have been. Whether or not a procedure applies or has been completed and, if it does apply and was not completed, which party was at fault can have very significant financial implications, particularly in relation to discrimination cases where there is no statutory limit on the amount of compensation that can be awarded and hearings may be lengthened considerably by the need to resolve such issues. Moreover, an employee's rights are in danger of being prejudiced by ignorance of what the legislation obliges him or her to do.[285] Although employers are required to include information about grievance (and disciplinary) procedures in the written statement of employment terms, this statement need not be issued until two months after the commencement of employment and there is no requirement for employees to be notified specifically of the consequences of not abiding by the statutory procedures, either in the written statement or elsewhere.[286] The financial consequences if an employer fails to comply with its minimal statutory

---

280   EADRR 2004, reg 13(3), (4).
281   EADRR 2004, reg 11(2)–(4).
282   EADRR 2004, reg 12(4).
283   *Amendment of Employment Tribunal Regulations: Full Regulatory Impact Assessment*, DTI, 2004: para 14. See also *Statutory Dispute Resolution Procedures: Full Regulatory Impact Assessment*, DTI, 2004.
284   Para 81.
285   See Hepple and Morris, 2002: pp 262–263, on which the remainder of this paragraph draws heavily.
286   ERA 1996, s 1, 3; see further para 4.14 *et seq*.

obligations are derisory,[287] particularly when contrasted with the drastic consequences for employees if they do not complete an applicable SGP. Finally, even though the standard procedure requires an employee to be told of a 'right' to appeal against an employer's decision following an initial meeting, there is no requirement to say what the consequences are of failing to exercise that 'right'. All these points raise serious questions as to whether these new procedures will further or obstruct what should be the overriding objective of the just resolution of disputes.[288]

GOVERNMENTAL INSTITUTIONS RELEVANT TO LABOUR LAW

2.27   In this section we outline the activities of a range of institutions which, although funded by government, operate at a day-to-day level independently from it. They are a heterogeneous collection. The Advisory, Conciliation and Arbitration Service (ACAS) has a broad range of functions across the field of industrial relations. The Central Arbitration Committee (CAC) has an adjudicatory jurisdiction in the field of collective labour law, including statutory recognition and information and consultation, and can also serve as a voluntary arbitral body. The Certification Officer has a wide range of functions in relation to trade unions. Finally, the Equal Opportunities Commission (EOC), Commission for Racial Equality (CRE) and Disability Rights Commission (DRC) are charged with the elimination of discrimination and promotion of equal opportunities in their respective jurisdictions. As in the case of statutory bodies generally the decisions of the majority of these bodies are subject to judicial review, a remedy that has placed considerable constraints on some investigatory activities of the EOC and CRE and has also been significant in relation to the decisions of the CAC. Decisions of the Certification Officer may be appealed against in the EAT, as may those of the CAC in relation to information and consultation.

The Advisory, Conciliation and Arbitration Service (ACAS)

2.28   State involvement in the processes of conciliation and arbitration dates back to the Conciliation Act 1896.[289] However, for many decades this function was performed by the government department charged with responsibility for employment matters. By the time the Labour Party came into office in 1974 'the conciliation and arbitration services of the Department [of Employment] had become tainted, in the eyes of the labour movement, by the Department's involvement first with prices and incomes policy and then with the operation of the Industrial Relations Act'.[290] There was perceived to be an urgent need to

---

287 Between two and four weeks' pay can be awarded for failure to provide an initial statement of particulars or to notify the employee of changes, but only where the employee has been successful in relation to other specified proceedings: EA 2002, s 38, Sch 5. A 'week's pay is subject to the statutory maximum in ERA 1996, s 227, which as of 1 February 2005 and at the time of writing is £280.

288 See Hepple and Morris, 2002: pp 268–269 for discussion of possible alternatives to these procedures.

289 For a summary of the background to the performance of these functions before the establishment of ACAS see Sir John Wood, 1992; Mumford, 1996.

290 Freedland, 1992: p 282.

establish an independent body for these purposes and ACAS was set up soon after the Government took office and placed on a statutory basis by the Employment Protection Act 1975.[291] The Service is directed by a tripartite council consisting of a chairman and nine 'ordinary' members, three nominated by the TUC, three by the CBI and three independent members (although it is also open to the Secretary of State to appoint a further two ordinary members and up to three deputy chairmen).[292] In 2003–2004 it employed an average staff of 878.[293] Its independence from ministerial direction as to the performance of its functions is specifically enshrined in statute[294] although it submits an annual report to the Secretary of State on its activities each year.[295] It is charged with the general duty of promoting 'the improvement of industrial relations'.[296] Originally its statutory remit also included the extension, development and, where necessary, reform of collective bargaining machinery. However, this aspect of its duties was removed by TURERA 1993, an important symbol of the abandonment of support for collective bargaining by the Conservative Government. Despite a more hospitable environment for collective bargaining under its Labour successor, the specific duty has not been reinstated, but activities relating to collective bargaining are almost certainly permissible under its general duty.[297]

Although the industrial relations climate in which ACAS operates has altered radically since its inception it has always worked within a voluntary framework; there is no compulsion on the industrial relations actors to use its services. As the list which follows indicates, the functions it performs range widely.

(i) Conciliation in individual cases

2.29   The process of conciliation involves assisting the parties to clarify their points of disagreement and attempting to promote a settlement, but the terms of any settlement remain the responsibility of the parties. As we saw in para 2.17 the conciliation stage is provided for by statute in relation to the majority of types of claim which are presented to employment tribunals. The Secretary of employment tribunals forwards to ACAS a copy of the claim form, response and any other relevant documents.[298] It will then be for an ACAS conciliation officer to contact the parties to see whether a conciliated settlement is possible, either at the request of one of the parties or on his or her own initiative.[299] In most cases ACAS has a duty to conciliate only during the 'standard' 13 week or 'short' seven week conciliation period, following which it has a power to do so.[300] Either party can decline to co-operate with the conciliation process. All discussions with the conciliation officer are confidential and nothing said by or

---

291   It was initially established on a non-statutory basis in September 1974. For the argument that the removal of the conciliation and arbitration function from the Department of Employment had major implications for its perception of future policy formation see Freedland, 1992. See Towers and Brown, 2000 for reflections on the first 25 years of ACAS.
292   TULRCA 1992, s 248.
293   *Annual Report 2003–2004*: p 74. This number does not take account of staff who work in the Certification Office or CAC, who are also employed by ACAS.
294   TULRCA 1992, s 247(3).
295   TULRCA 1992, s 253(1). These reports are published and constitute a useful source of information for researchers.
296   TULRCA 1992, s 209.
297   Hepple, 2000a: p 153.
298   SI 2004/1861, Sch 1, para 22.
299   ETA 1996, s 18(2).
300   ETA 1996, s 18(2A); SI 2004/1861, paras 22–24; see para 2.17 above.

to him or her is admissible if the process fails and the matter goes forward to a hearing. This service is free of charge to the parties.[301]

As we saw in para 2.16, a high proportion of cases are either settled or withdrawn at the conciliation stage.[302] There are considerable savings to the Exchequer if a claim is dealt with in this way.[303] Additional benefits of this form of resolution are avoidance of the stress of a tribunal hearing, savings to the parties, confidentiality, ability of the parties to determine the terms of settlement, and benefits in dismissal cases of speedy re-employment if this can be arranged.[304] However, the fact that ACAS does not give advice on the merits of proposed settlements has led to concerns being voiced that the relative inequalities of the parties may be perpetuated by this process.[305] In 1987 the Justice report proposed that advice agencies such as Citizens' Advice Bureaux and Law Centres should be funded to provide advice to applicants at the conciliation stage but this has not been followed up.[306] As the level of applications to tribunals has increased so has the workload of ACAS; in 2003–2004 it dealt with more than 102,000 applications.[307] As we discuss in para 2.20, only a very modest number of cases have so far been received under the ACAS Arbitration Scheme for unfair dismissal claims and flexible working.

(ii) Conciliation in collective disputes

2.30   ACAS provides facilities for settling existing or apprehended 'trade disputes'[308] by conciliation, either at the request of one of the parties or on its own initiative.[309] However, regardless of how the process starts it remains entirely voluntary and any of the parties is free to withdraw at any stage. As in the area of individual disputes ACAS, when acting as conciliator, does not recommend the terms of settlement. Before offering its services ACAS must have regard to the desirability of encouraging the parties to use their agreed procedures for the negotiation or settlement of disputes, although reference to ACAS may be incorporated in the procedural terms of collective agreements. In recent years an annual average of 1,300 requests for collective conciliation have been made, around 40% consisting of joint requests by management and trade unions, and close to 90% of completed cases result in a settlement or progress towards a settlement.[310] Sir John Wood offers an interesting comparison between the 'success rates' of collective and individual conciliation in this respect. 'The parties seeking collective conciliation realise that the alternative

---

301   Curiously the provision of individual conciliation does not fall within ACAS's statutory functions. This is material in that the power to direct it to charge for its statutory functions to which we refer below does not extend to this area.

302   See generally L Dickens, 2000; Dix, 2000.

303   In 2002/3 it was estimated that it cost an average £910 to process a tribunal claim: *Statutory Dispute Resolution Procedures: Full Regulatory Impact Assessment*, DTI, 2004: para 34.

304   It may also lead to shortcomings in the employer's procedures or communication systems being corrected, so having wider implications than the instant claim: *ACAS Annual Report 2003–2004*; p 22.

305   See L Dickens *et al*, 1985: p 180; L Dickens, 2000: pp 75–78.

306   Justice, 1987: para 2.28.

307   *ACAS Annual Report 2003–2004*: p 22.

308   These are defined in TULRCA 1992, s 218 and have a wider meaning than in the context of the industrial action immunities: see s 244(1), analysed in para 11.25 *et seq* below.

309   TULRCA 1992, s 210. See generally Dix and Oxenbridge, 2004.

310   J Goodman, 2000: pp 37–47.

is costly strife, whereas the individual still has the opportunity to shun conciliation and seek his remedy before the tribunal'.[311]

(iii) References to mediation and arbitration in collective disputes

2.31   If agreed procedures have been exhausted and conciliation has failed or seems unlikely to succeed, ACAS may appoint a mediator to attempt to settle the dispute. However, this can be done only at the request of one or more of the parties and they must all consent to this. Mediation differs from conciliation in that a mediator may make positive recommendations, although the parties themselves retain the responsibility to resolve the details of any settlement. ACAS considers that this process is most suited to dealing with complex issues 'where the parties have to weigh for themselves the impact of the options that may be available'.[312] In practice it is used much less commonly than arbitration,[313] which may be conducted provided that the same conditions are met (as with conciliation this may be incorporated as the final stage of the parties' own procedures). The arbitration may be conducted by a person appointed by ACAS, although independent of the service, or by the CAC.[314] The parties agree on the form of arbitration and the arbitrator's terms of reference. Although the award is not legally binding ACAS makes it clear in advance to the parties that there is a long-established principle that both sides must accept the arbitrator's decision.[315] The cost of conducting the arbitration is borne by ACAS but the parties pay their own expenses and there is no power to award the payment of costs against an 'unsuccessful' party. For that reason legal representation is rare and would normally, in any case, require the consent of the arbitrator. The award may be published if ACAS so decides and all parties consent to this.[316]

The arbitration caseload has declined sharply from nearly 350 cases in 1979 to an average of below 200 in the early 1980s; in 2003–2004 there were 63 cases.[317] By far the most popular method of third party intervention in disputes is reference to a single arbitrator; in 2003–2004, 62 cases were referred for settlement in this way.[318]

(iv) Advisory and information services

2.32   ACAS provides advice on a wide range of industrial relations matters to employers and their associations, workers and trade unions, either by telephone, letter or personal visit.[319] In the year 2003–2004 ACAS received more than 796,000 calls at its enquiry points and held over 1,900 advisory meetings.[320] Wherever possible it attempts to involve both sides of industry in a joint examination of their problems. All advice is given on an impartial and

---

311 Sir John Wood, 1992: p 250.
312 *Annual Report* 1994: p 49.
313 There were six requests for dispute mediation in 2003–2004: ACAS *Annual Report 2003–2004*: p 50.
314 TULRCA 1992, s 212(1).
315 ACAS brochure *Using ACAS in Industrial Disputes*.
316 TULRCA 1992, s 212(4)(b).
317 *ACAS Annual Report 2003–2004*: p 50. During the period 1997–2000 the caseload averaged only 55: J Goodman, 2000: pp 56–57; *ACAS Annual Report 1999–2000*: p 52. For an assessment of ACAS's arbitration work in a historical perspective, see Mumford, 1996.
318 J Goodman, 2000: pp 56–57; *ACAS Annual Report 2003–2004*: p 50.
319 TULRCA 1992, s 213.
320 *ACAS Annual Report 2003–2004*: p 52.

confidential basis. Until recently all aspects of this service, like other ACAS services, were free. Since TURERA 1993 it has been empowered to charge a fee for exercising its statutory functions, subject to directions from the Secretary of State, although the latter cannot direct this course without consulting ACAS.[321] ACAS now charges for some of its training activities and advisory publications.[322]

(v) Inquiry

2.33   ACAS has the statutory power, as it thinks fit, to hold inquiries on 'any question relating to industrial relations generally or in a particular industry or undertaking or part thereof'.[323] The findings may be published. This power appears not to have been used since 1983.[324]

(vi) Codes of practice

2.34   ACAS has a general power to issue codes of practice containing practical guidance to promote the improvement of industrial relations, subject to approval by the Secretary of State and Parliament.[325] As we indicated in para 2.4, these Codes are admissible in evidence before employment tribunals and the CAC but not (unlike those issued by the Secretary of State) in courts.[326] ACAS has issued three codes to date: on Disclosure of Information to Trade Unions for Collective Bargaining Purposes (revised in 1997); on Time Off for Trade Union Duties and Activities (revised in 2003); and on Disciplinary and Grievance Procedures (revised in 2004).[327] ACAS has also issued good practice guidance on the regulations relating to discrimination on grounds of sexual orientation and religion and belief, and a number of advisory booklets on particular matters such as the handling of redundancies.

(vii) Equal pay

2.35   ACAS has the responsibility of designating independent experts to report on claims for equal pay for work of equal value when required to do so by an employment tribunal. It maintains a list of such experts of which, as of March 2004, there were 17.[328]

(viii) Disclosure of information and information and consultation

2.36   ACAS has specific functions in relation to these procedures which we discuss in paras 9.24 and 9.50 below.

The Central Arbitration Committee

2.37   The Central Arbitration Committee (CAC) was established by the Employment Protection Act 1975 as a permanent and independent industrial

---

321 TULRCA 1992, s 251A.
322 See *ACAS Annual Report 2003–2004*: p 53.
323 TULRCA 1992, s 214(1). See also ss 215–216 for provision for the Secretary of State to appoint a court of inquiry in relation to a particular dispute.
324 Information supplied by ACAS. See Sir John Wood, 1992: pp 262–267 for the use which has been made historically of the inquiry process.
325 TULRCA 1992, ss 199–202.
326 TULRCA 1992, s 207(2).
327 The first two of these were issued pursuant to specific duties: TULRCA 1992, s 199(2).
328 *ACAS Annual Report 2003–2004*: p 25.

relations arbitration body.[329] As such it constitutes a direct descendant to the Industrial Court which was established in 1919 to provide a national government-funded facility for this purpose. It is composed of a chairman, deputy chairmen, and other members appointed by the Secretary of State.[330] All are 'persons experienced in industrial relations', some of whom have experience as representatives of employers, some as representatives of workers.[331] The chairman is currently a High Court judge. The CAC is charged with operating the statutory recognition and derecognition procedures; adjudicating on complaints relating to a failure by employers to disclose information for collective bargaining purposes; and adjudicating on specified matters under TICER 1999, ICER 2004 and EPLLCR 2004.[332] It can also serve as a voluntary arbitration body on a reference from ACAS, as described above,[333] but last performed this role in 1989.

In all areas of its jurisdiction the CAC seeks to adopt a flexible and problem-solving approach. On receiving a complaint in relation to a failure to disclose information, it is standard practice for the chairman or a deputy, together with an ACAS conciliation officer, to meet the parties and to attempt to encourage a joint, rather than an adversarial, approach to the problem in preference to 'passing judgment on them and leaving aside the question of their continuing relationship'.[334] It has had considerable success in this approach; from 1 February 1977, when the disclosure provisions came into force, until the end of 2004 the Committee had received 518 complaints of which only 13.13% resulted in a formal decision.[335] As Davies and Freedland have remarked, in this area of its jurisdiction the CAC has developed 'a genuinely novel approach to the process of adjudication which may serve as a model in any future proposals for reform'.[336] In performing its functions generally, the CAC is composed of the chairman, or a deputy, and such other members as the chairman may direct; there is also a discretion to call in one or more assessors to assist it.[337] For the purposes of the recognition and derecognition procedures, however, the CAC is required to consist only of a tripartite panel chaired by the chairman or a deputy chairman; a member whose experience is as a representative of employers; and a member whose experience is as a representative of workers.[338] Decisions are reached by a majority; if there is no majority, the chairman of the panel decides.[339] Subject to this, each panel is formally free to regulate its own procedure,[340] although

---

329 See now TULRCA 1992, s 259. For a discussion of CAC activities up to 2001, see Rideout, 2002.

330 TULRCA 1992, s 260. Members are appointed by the Secretary of State after consultation with ACAS.

331 TULRCA 1992, s 260(3). As of March 2004 there were 11 deputy chairmen and 45 employer and worker members: *CAC Annual Report 2003–2004*: p 23.

332 See further ch 9. For the CAC's other areas of jurisdiction during the period 1975–1980 (now abolished) see P Davies and M Freedland 1993: pp 394–396.

333 The parties may, subject to the agreement of the CAC, nominate a representative from the panel of members and these together with the independent chairman, will form the arbitration committee. Its procedures are entirely flexible, and there is a moral, but not a legal, obligation, to honour the award.

334 *Annual Report* 1993: para 2.1.

335 Information supplied by the CAC.

336 P Davies and M Freedland, 1993: p 396.

337 TULRCA 1992, s 263.

338 TULRCA 1992, s 263A.

339 TULRCA 1992, s 263A(5),(6).

340 TULRCA 1992, s 263A(7).

in practice there is a measure of consistency between panels.[341] The CAC is generally required to consider evidence put to it by the union and employer when deciding particular questions, and each side has the opportunity to comment on the other's case and evidence material to it. An application must be supported by such documents as the CAC requires,[342] but beyond that there is no power to order documents to be disclosed. If a hearing is needed to decide a particular matter, it will be conducted in as informal a manner as is consistent with clarity and fairness; the parties may appoint representatives, but there is no obligation to use lawyers and no power to award costs. It is notable that once an application for recognition (and, in some cases, derecognition) has been accepted by the CAC, it is accorded the role both of conciliator and of adjudicator. However, in trying to help the parties the CAC may suggest that they seek assistance from ACAS, a course that may be preferable where a party wishes to communicate confidential information; while the CAC panel would maintain confidentiality at the conciliation stage, if the case goes to a hearing that information may need to be revealed at the other party to enable it to check or challenge it. The caseload of applications to the CAC under these procedures, and their outcomes, are discussed at para 9.18. At the time of writing there have been only three applications under TICER 1999 and none under ICER 2004 or EPLLCR 2004.

The Certification Officer

2.38   The Certification Officer is an independent officer with statutory responsibility for an extensive range of functions relating to trade unions and employers' associations.[343] He or she is appointed by the Secretary of State after consultation with ACAS. The first Certification Officer was appointed in 1975 and took over the role previously performed by the former Registrar of Friendly Societies under earlier trade union legislation. The functions of the Certification Officer now include maintaining lists of unions and employers' associations and ensuring that they comply with their accounting obligations; determining whether unions meet the statutory test of 'independence'; dealing with complaints relating to trade union elections; ensuring observance of the procedures concerning trade union political funds; and supervising union mergers. In 1993 the Certification Officer was also granted controversial powers of investigation in relation to unions' financial affairs. Prior to the Employment Relations Act 1999 the Certification Officer's jurisdiction was confined to breaches of specified statutory obligations. However, as we discuss in para 10.5, it has now been extended to cover alleged breaches of union rules in specific areas, giving union members an alternative to seeking redress from the High Court.[344] The procedure for applying to the Certification Officer is relatively simple; details of the application are forwarded by the Office to the union for comment and any comments are then copied to the applicant for observation. The Certification Officer makes such inquiries as he or she thinks fit in relation to

---

341   The procedures that panels can be expected to follow are detailed in *Statutory Recognition – A Guide for the Parties*, obtainable from the CAC.
342   See TULRCA 1992, Sch A1, para 33, for example.
343   TULRCA 1992, s 254; see further ch 10.
344   These avenues of complaint are now mutually exclusive. The Certification Officer's jurisdiction was extended following the abolition of the Commissioner for the Rights of Trade Union Members: see para 7.18.

an application and is required to give the applicant and union an opportunity to present their case at a hearing. The Certification Office pays expenses by applicants and their witnesses in attending hearings, but does not pay legal costs. If the Certification Officer upholds an application, he or she must grant a declaration and, unless this is considered inappropriate, an 'enforcement order' which requires the union to take specified steps to remedy the declared failure and/or to abstain from specified acts in the future. Enforcement orders may be enforced as if they were orders of the court, so rendering the union liable for contempt in the event of non-compliance. Either party may appeal against a decision of the Certification Officer to the EAT.

The Equal Opportunities Commission (EOC), Commission for Racial Equality (CRE) and Disability Rights Commission (DRC)

2.39 These Commissions were established by the Sex Discrimination Act 1975, Race Relations Act 1976, and Disability Rights Commission Act 1999 respectively and have the general duty to work towards the elimination of discrimination, the promotion of equality of opportunity between men and women, persons of different racial groups, and disabled persons, as appropriate, and to review the operation of the anti-discrimination legislation.[345] Each consists of up to 15 members appointed by the Secretary of State. Further details of the activities of each Commission are given in chapter 6. At the time of writing the Government is proposing to establish a single Commission to take over the responsibilities of the EOC, CRE and DRC, together with the enforcement and promotion of legislation on age, religion or belief, and sexual orientation, and human rights.[346]

EUROPEAN UNION LAW

2.40 European Union law has become a major source of UK labour law.[347] As we shall see in subsequent chapters of this book, many of the most significant legislative initiatives of the past decade, including new legislation in relation to working time, the work-life balance, equality of treatment, the treatment of part-time and fixed-term contract workers, and information and consultation of worker representatives, are derived from European directives.[348] EU law in the area of social policy mostly takes the form of Treaty provisions and directives.[349] Directives are in most cases

---

345 SDA 1975, s 53; RRA 1976, s 43; DRCA 1999, s 2.
346 *Fairness for All: A New Commission for Equality and Human Rights: White Paper*, Cm 6185, 2004; Equality Bill, 2005.
347 On European Union law relating to social policy, see Bercusson, 1996; P Davies *et al*, 1996; Nielsen and Szyszczak, 1997; Hervey, 1998; Barnard, 2000a; Shaw, 2000; Hervey and Kenner, 2003; De Schutter and Deakin, 2005. Although it is strictly accurate to refer in this regard to 'European Community law' in certain contexts, including that of social policy, the term 'European Union law' is increasingly used, and we shall follow that practice here. If the Treaty establishing a Constitution for Europe, agreed by the Member States in 2004 (see OJ C310, vol. 47, 16.12.2004), comes into force (see below, para 2.43), the separate legal entity of the European Community will cease to exist.
348 On working time, see para 4.74 *et seq* below; on work-life balance issues, para 6.97 *et seq*; on part-time and fixed-term working, para 3.83 *et seq*; on information and consultation, para 9.29 *et seq*.
349 The relevant Treaty provisions are outlined below, para 2.42; relevant directives and other instruments, such as regulations and opinions, are referred to at various points in the detailed account of the law in this book.

given effect in UK law through delegated legislation derived from powers conferred by the European Communities Act 1972.[350] As we have already noted,[351] this mode of implementation has given rise to a certain number of stand-alone provisions in such areas as transfers of undertakings and equality of treatment, which are not well integrated into the wider body of legislation governing those matters.[352] In certain other cases, amending legislation has taken the form of changes to Acts of Parliament, and where this has been done – as, for example, in the recent case of major alterations to the law governing sex, race and disability discrimination[353] – the fragmentation of the law which often results from the implementation of directives has been alleviated, if not necessarily avoided altogether.

2.41   The European Court of Justice has also had a pivotal influence on the development of UK labour law in areas which include transfers of undertakings, sex discrimination and occupational pensions, both through references from national courts for preliminary rulings on points of EU law, and through decisions in infringement proceedings brought against the United Kingdom by the Commission.[354] Moreover, the principle of the direct effect of certain Treaty provisions and directives has enabled both the ECJ and UK courts, where appropriate, to apply certain principles of EU law even where they conflict with domestic legislation. This principle has had a major impact, in particular, on the development of the law governing equality of pay between men and women.[355] The principle that UK courts should, as far as possible, interpret UK legislation purporting to implement EU directives in line with the provision of those directives (so-called 'indirect effect'), has also played a highly significant role in shaping UK labour law on certain issues, as recent decisions on sex discrimination law[356] and transfers of undertakings[357] illustrate.

350 ECA 1972, s 2(2). Occasionally, a power is taken to adopt legislation in a field governed by EU law which goes beyond the powers conferred by s 2(2); see, eg, ERelA 1999, s 38, which is likely to be relied on in the near future in the context of amendments to the law governing transfers of undertakings (see DTI, *TUPE Draft Revised Regulations Public Consultation Document* (2005), para 11).

351 See para 2.3 above.

352 For example, the failure to integrate the law governing transfers of undertakings into the general provisions governing employment protection, contained in ERA 1996 and its precedessor statutes, has caused considerable difficulty and confusion over the link between the different categories of potentially fair reasons in TUPE 1981 and the 1996 Act. See DTI, *TUPE Draft Revised Regulations Public Consultation Document* (2005), paras 52–53.

353 Thus major changes were made to sex discrimination legislation by SI 2001/2660, to race discrimination legislation by SI 2003/1626, and to disability discrimination by SI 2003/ 1673, in each case using powers under ECA 1972, s 2(2). See generally ch 6, below, for analysis of these provisions and their impact on anti-discrimination law.

354 For the purposes of this book we assume a basic knowledge of the relationship between EU Treaty provisions, directives, regulations and other legal acts, and UK domestic law. A full account of the meaning of the concepts of direct effect and indirect effect, and the process of preliminary references and infringement proceedings, is also beyond the scope of this work. For the background to these concepts, the reader is referred to the relevant standard works on EU law and UK constitutional law.

355 Landmark judgments of the ECJ in this area include Case 43/73 *Defrenne v Sabena* [1976] ECR 455, on the direct effect of Art 119 of the EEC Treaty (now Art 141 of the EC Treaty), and Case C-262/88 *Barber v Guardian Royal Exchange Assurance Group* [1990] IRLR 240, applying that principle to occupational pension schemes. See generally para 6.5 below.

356 See, in particular, the decision of the HL in *Rhys-Harper v Relaxion Group plc* [2003] IRLR 484.

357 See the decision of the Court of Appeal in *ADI (UK) Ltd v Willer* [2001] IRLR 542, in particular the judgment of Dyson LJ.

2.42 It is deeply paradoxical, then, that, to begin with, social policy provisions occupied only a marginal and contentious place in the developing European legal order. Article 117 of the Treaty of Rome of 1957 (now, heavily amended, Article 136 of the Treaty Establishing the European Community ('EC')),[358] provided that 'Member States agree upon the need to promote improved working conditions and an improved standard of living for workers, so as to make possible their harmonisation while the improvement is being maintained'. However, this provision did not create any jurisdiction to implement social policy through directives or regulations. Similarly, under Article 118 (now Article 140 EC), the European Commission was confined to promoting co-operation between the Member States on a number of matters relating to social policy (including working conditions, social security, occupational health and safety, the right of association and collective bargaining), while under Article 122 (now Article 145 EC) it simply had an obligation to make annual reports on social policy to the Parliament. Articles 119 and 120 (now respectively Articles 141 and 142 EC) alone placed specific substantive obligations on Member States in relation to labour law. Article 119 laid down the principle of equal pay for equal work between men and women which, as we have just noted, was to form the basis for many of the later interventions of the European Court of Justice; Article 120, which required the Member States to 'endeavour to maintain the existing equivalence between paid holiday schemes', by contrast proved to be completely insignificant. These two Articles were included in the original treaty on the insistence of the French government which raised the threat of unfair competition from states with less extensive legal protections. Overall, however, 'the social provisions of the Treaty ... turned out to be pretty meagre',[359] and the period of the implementation of the first phase of the common market up to the late 1960s was one of 'benign neglect' as far as social policy was concerned.[360]

This changed with the enlargement of the Community to nine states in 1971. The first Social Action Programme was adopted in 1974 and this led eventually to the adoption by the Council of a series of directives relating to equal pay and equality of treatment between the sexes in relation to employment and social security.[361] Less extensive but nevertheless significant measures were also adopted in relation to employment protection, with directives laying down minimum standards of redundancy consultation and protection of employee rights in the event of business transfers and the insolvency of companies.[362] These measures could be adopted without amendment of the Treaty; general provisions empowering the Council to adopt measures for the implementation of the common market and related purposes were used as a jurisdiction base.[363] The difficulty was that these provisions required the Council to be unanimous. The Single European Act of 1986 introduced a new Article 118a (this is now, in an amended form, Article 137 EC), allowing qualified majority voting (in this context,

---

358 The Treaty of Amsterdam led to a renumbering of articles of the Treaty establishing the European Community (EC) as from 1 May 1999.
359 P Davies, 1992: p 325.
360 Mosley, 1990.
361 Directive 75/117 on equal pay; Directive 77/207 on equal treatment in employment; Directive 79/7 on equal treatment in social security; Directive 86/378 on equal treatment in occupational social security.
362 Directive 75/129 on collective redundancies; Directive 77/187 on acquired rights on transfers of undertakings; Directive 80/987 on protection of employee rights in the event of insolvency.
363 Arts 100 and 235 of the Treaty (now Arts 94 and 308 EC).

overriding the veto of a single Member State) in the area of health and safety. The so-called Social Charter adopted by eleven of the (then twelve) Member States at the Strasbourg summit in November 1989 (the United Kingdom was the exception) did not, however, mark a significant legal advance, being simply a declaration of principle. Continuing dissatisfaction with the lack of progress on social policy led to a number of Treaty amendments being proposed as part of the inter-governmental conference on economic union leading up to the Maastricht summit in November 1991. Treaty amendments require unanimity, and the United Kingdom duly used its veto to block what would have been the 'Social Chapter' of the new Treaty. Under a last-minute political compromise, the other Member States agreed to a procedure for the implementation of the social dimension separately from the United Kingdom, contained in a separate Protocol and Agreement on Social Policy.

The Agreement on Social Policy had three main purposes: to confirm and clarify the legal competence of the Community in regard to social policy; to extend qualified majority voting in the social area; and to give greater institutional priority to the social dialogue between management and labour at transnational level.[364] The Agreement provided for qualified majority voting on matters including health and safety, working conditions, information and consultation of workers, equality between the sexes and integration of excluded groups. For certain other areas, including social security, protection of workers in relation to the termination of employment, 'representation and collective defence' of workers (including co-determination), rights of third-country nationals, and financial measures for the promotion of employment, unanimity was required. Finally, some matters were excluded from the Agreement altogether: these were 'pay, the right of association, the right to strike [and] the right to impose lock-outs'. But the most innovative aspect of the Agreement on Social Policy was the introduction of a mechanism by which European-level legislation could be produced through a process of *social dialogue* between the social partners, that is, the transnational federations of the ETUC (representing trade unions), UNICE and CEEP (representing private-sector and public-sector employers respectively).[365] In particular, the social partners were given the option of concluding framework agreements which could be implemented either according to the procedures and practices of each Member State or by way of a Council 'decision', a term which was taken to include directives.

Following a change of government in 1997, the United Kingdom indicated that it wished to 'opt in' to the Agreement on Social Policy. In part as a consequence of this, the Treaty of Amsterdam made a series of further amendments to the social policy provisions of the EC Treaty. In effect, most of the terms of the Agreement were incorporated into a revised Social Chapter in the main body of the EC Treaty (Articles 136–145 EC). The substance of the Agreement was not greatly affected.[366] The solution to the United Kingdom's need to 'opt in' was for the Council to re-adopt a number of directives agreed between 1994 and 1998 under the Agreement, with the United Kingdom now fully bound by

---

364 The Agreement also reproduced in a slightly modified form the equal pay provisions of Art 119 of the old Treaty, with a new provision for limited forms of positive discrimination in favour of women (Art 6(3)).

365 In Case T-135/96 *UEAPME v Council of the European Union* [1998] IRLR 602 an unsuccessful challenge was made to the parental leave directive on grounds of the lack of representativity of the social partners, by a European association representing the interests of small and medium-sized undertakings.

366 See Barnard, 1997a for an account of the changes made at Amsterdam.

their provisions.[367] Since then the social dialogue procedure has produced a further agreement and directive, on fixed-term work,[368] and an agreement on teleworking.[369] However, the social partners failed to agree on the text of an agreement concerning information and consultation, and a directive was eventually adopted on this issue by agreement of the Council and European Parliament.[370]

Another important step taken at Amsterdam was the adoption of an Employment Title, heralded by the inclusion in Article 2 of a new task for the Community of promoting 'a high level of employment and of social protection', which has had the effect of placing Community action in the area of active labour market policy on a clearer legal footing.[371] In addition, a new legal basis was given for prohibiting discrimination on the grounds of sex, racial or ethnic origin, religion or belief, disability, age or sexual orientation (Article 13 EC).[372] The Council of Ministers went on to agree two particularly significant directives under this provision, the so-called Framework Directive providing a general framework for equal treatment in employment and occupation in relation to religion or belief, disability, age, and sexual orientation,[373] and the Race Directive on equal treatment irrespective of racial or ethnic origin.[374] These have had a considerable influence in reshaping UK anti-discrimination law.[375]

2.43   The area of fundamental social rights has increasingly become the focus of developments in European Law. The Treaty of European Union committed the EU to respect fundamental rights, as guaranteed by the ECHR and 'as they result from the constitutional traditions common to the Member States, as general principles of Community law'.[376] In December 2000 a Charter of Fundamental Rights of the European Union, drafted by a Convention,[377] was proclaimed by the President of the European Parliament, the president of the European Commission, and the President of the Council of Ministers after approval by Member States.[378] The Charter is divided into six chapters: dignity, freedoms, equality, solidarity, citizens' rights and justice. Most of the classic fundamental

367   Directives on European Works Councils (94/45/EC) and Parental Leave (96/34/EC) were readopted in this way in December 1997 (by Directives 97/74/EC and 97/75/EC, respectively); the Part-time Work Directive (97/81/EC) in April 1998 (by Directive 98/23/EC); and the Burden of Proof Directive (97/80/EC) in July 1998 (98/52/EC).
368   Directive 99/70/EC; see further para 3.86 below.
369   See below, para 3.63.
370   Directive 2002/14/EC; see further para 9.30, below.
371   On the history of active labour market policy in the Community, see Freedland, 1996a. The development of a distinctive method of regulation, the 'open method of coordination' or OMC, began in the context of the European employment strategy which grew out of the Employment Title. For a recent review of developments in respect of the OMC, see De Schutter and Deakin, 2005.
372   See L Waddington, 1999.
373   Directive 2000/78 EC.
374   Directive 2000/43 EC.
375   See generally ch 6, below.
376   Art 6. Note, however, that from an early stage of the Community, fundamental rights were regarded by the ECJ as general principles of Community law: Case 11/70 *Internationale Handelsgesellschaft v Einfuhr- und Vorratsstelle fur Getreide* [1970] ECR 1125, 1134; Case 4/73 *Nold v Commission* [1974] ECR 491, para 13.
377   This was the body entrusted by the Council with drafting the Charter. It was composed of 15 representatives of heads of state or government, 16 members of the European Parliament, 30 members of national parliaments and a Commissioner representing the President of the Commission.
378   See further Lenaerts, 2000; de Burca, 2001; Lenaerts and de Smijter, 2001.

rights, such as the right to life, the prohibition of slavery and forced labour, the right to respect for private life, and freedom of expression, are based on the provisions of the ECHR and were uncontroversial (although some have been amplified or updated to take account of more recent societal developments). The inclusion of social rights was more contentious, with some Member States maintaining that these were not fundamental in nature, or that they remained a matter for individual states.[379] Eventually it was agreed that fundamental social rights could be included under the banner of 'solidarity'. Those of particular relevance to labour lawyers include the right of workers and their representatives, at appropriate levels, to information and consultation within the undertaking; the right of workers and employers, or their organisations, to negotiate and conclude collective agreements and, in cases of conflicts of interest, to take collective action, including strike action; and the right of every worker to protection against 'unjustified dismissal'.[380] All of these rights are exercisable only 'in accordance with Community law and national laws and practices'. Notably, however, there is an unqualified right for every worker 'to working conditions which respect his or her health, safety and dignity' as well as a right to 'limitation of maximum working hours, to daily and weekly rest periods and to an annual period of paid leave'.[381]

The Charter itself is not legally binding, nor does it establish any new power or task for the Community. However it has been used by the ECJ as a source of general principles of European Union law.[382] More generally, the ECJ is playing an increasingly important role in interpreting fundamental rights which have a bearing on the social policy field. In *Albany*, where the relationship between collective agreements and social policy measures, on the one hand, and EC competition law, on the other, was at issue, the Court emphasised that under Article 3(1)(g) and (j) EC:

> ... the activities of the Community are to include not only a 'system ensuring that competition in the internal market is not distorted' but also 'a policy in the social sphere'. Article 2 ... [EC] provides that a particular task of the Community is 'to promote throughout the Community a harmonious and balanced[383] development of economic activities' and 'a high level of employment and of social protection.[384]

The Court has also recognised freedom of association as a fundamental right,[385] and in *Albany* Advocate General Jacobs considered that the collective right of workers to take action, in addition to the right to form and join a union, had been also been confirmed as such a right.[386]

---

379 See Hepple, 2001b for the concerns raised by the UK Government. For an analysis of the Charter, see Hervey and Kenner, 2003.
380 Art 27, 28 and 30; see now, Treaty establishing a Constitution for Europe, Arts II-87, II-88 and II-90.
381 Art 31; see now, Treaty establishing a Constitution for Europe, Art II-91.
382 See, in particular, Case C-173/99 *BECTU v Secretary of State for Trade and Industry* [2001] ECR I-4881.
383 This is the wording of the judgment. Art 2 refers to 'harmonious, balanced and sustainable development ...'.
384 Case C-67/96 *Albany International BV v Stichting Bedrijfspensioenfonds Textielindustrie* [1999] ECR I-5751, para 54. See further para 7.11.
385 Case C-415/93 *Union Royale Belge des Societes de Football Association ASBL v Jean-Marc Bosman* [1995] ECR I-4921, paras 79 and 80.
386 Case C-67/96 above, Opinion of 28 January 1999, para 139 [1999] ECR I-5751.

Two events have recently reshaped the institutions of the European Union, with potentially profound implications for social policy. The first has been the expansion of the Union, with effect from 2004, to take in ten new Member States from central and eastern Europe. It remains to be seen whether the expansion of the Union makes it more difficult for agreement to be reached on new measures in the social policy sphere, but there are already signs that the new Member States share some of the scepticism demonstrated by successive UK governments towards social policy initiatives.[387] The second major development was the adoption by the Member States in 2004 of a new Treaty establishing a Constitution for Europe, which would replace the existing treaties. The adoption of the Treaty would mark a significant step in clarifying the relationship between the Union and the Member States, and in placing on a more systematic legal basis the exercise of various powers by the Union's different organs. In relation to social policy, the Treaty represents a consolidation of existing provisions; the Employment Title and Social Chapter are reproduced without significant amendment.[388] The Charter of Fundamental Rights appears as Part II of the Treaty.[389] At the time of writing, however, it is not clear whether the Treaty will come into force in its current form, or indeed at all.[390]

INTERNATIONAL LABOUR STANDARDS

2.44   As well as its obligations deriving from membership of the European Community the United Kingdom is subject to a wide range of other international labour standards which, although not part of domestic law, it is obliged under international law to secure. By far the most numerous and specific standards emanate from the International Labour Organisation (ILO), established in 1919 and based upon a tripartite structure of governments and of employers' and workers' representatives.[391] The constitution of the ILO, revised in 1946, affirms that 'labour is not a commodity', that 'freedom of expression and of association are essential to sustained progress', that 'poverty anywhere constitutes a danger to prosperity everywhere' and that 'all human beings, irrespective of race, creed or sex, have the right to pursue both their material well-being and their spiritual development in conditions of freedom and dignity, of economic security and equal opportunity'.[392] The ILO comprises three main bodies.[393] First is the International Labour Conference which normally meets once a year. It consists

---

387 This is the case, for example, with regard to the Commission's plans to revise the Working Time Directive (2003/88/EC), on which, see para 4.74 *et seq* below.

388 See, respectively, Part III, Chapter III, Sections 1 and 2 of the Treaty.

389 For a discussion of the background to the incorporation of the Charter into the Treaty, with specific regard to those of its provisions relating to social rights, see Bercusson, 2004.

390 Under Art IV-447 of the Treaty, the earliest it can come into force is November 2006, if all Member States have ratified it by that point. Otherwise it will come into force 'on the first day of the second month following the deposit of the instrument of ratification of the last signatory State to take this step'. At the time of writing referenda in France and The Netherlands have produced a majority against ratification.

391 For the history of the ILO see Alcock, 1971; and, for a more recent overview, Ewing, 1994a.

392 Taken from the Declaration of Philadelphia adopted by the International Labour Conference in 1944 and subsequently incorporated into the ILO's Constitution.

393 See generally; Valticos and von Potobsky, 1995; Bartolemei, von Potobsky and Swepston, 1996; Swepston, 1997; Swepston, 2004; Creighton, 2004b.

of delegations from Member States containing two government delegates and one employers' and workers' delegate, each nominated in agreement with the most representative organisations of employers and workers within that state. The second is the Governing Body which consists of 56 members, 28 representing governments, the remainder an equal number of employer and worker representatives. Its members are elected every third year at the Conference by their respective groups.[394] The third is the International Labour Office, the permanent secretariat of the Organisation, whose Director-General is appointed by the Governing Body.

The Constitution of the ILO lays down a number of principles, such as freedom of association and non-discrimination, which are regarded as a direct source of law. Other standards are laid down in Conventions and Recommendations. A state which ratifies a Convention is then obliged to 'take such action as may be necessary to make effective' its provisions,[395] although, at certain intervals, it is open to states to denounce a previously ratified Convention. Recommendations aim at providing guidance to policy, legislation and practice and currently are 'used mainly to supplement Conventions, in order to indicate in greater detail the manner of giving effect to their provisions or to advocate the establishment of higher standards'.[396] The adoption of a new Convention or Recommendation requires approval by a two-thirds majority of the delegates at the International Labour Conference, normally after discussion at two successive sessions. Adoption is preceded by what can be a lengthy process[397] which includes the preparation of a preliminary report by the International Labour Office setting out existing law and practice on the question in different countries which is then circulated for comment by governments which in turn are expected to consult the most representative organisations of unions and employers in their respective countries.[398] As of February 2005 the ILO had adopted more 185 Conventions and 195 Recommendations.[399] Eight Conventions (relating to freedom of association and the right to organise; the abolition of forced labour; equality; and the elimination of child labour)[400] are regarded as fundamental, in the dual senses of being applicable irrespective of the level of development of an individual state and of being a precondition for the application of other labour standards.

2.45   The ILO Constitution prescribes that any question or dispute relating to the interpretation of the Constitution or a Convention shall be submitted to the International Court of Justice. This has happened only once, in 1932. However, the International Labour Office is frequently consulted as to the interpretation of Conventions. These opinions are communicated to the Governing Body and

---

394 Ten of the government seats are reserved for states of chief industrial importance, of which the UK is one.

395 ILO Constitution, Art 19(5)(d).

396 Swepston, 2004: para 15. They may also be used to deal with subjects that are not yet ripe for a Convention or do not lend themselves to the adoption of Conventions entailing international obligations: Swepston, 2004: para 15.

397 See Ewing, 1994a: paras 3.5–3.6.

398 For countries which have ratified the Tripartite Consultation (International Labour Standards) Convention 1976 (No 144) such consultation is mandatory.

399 See the ILO web site www.ilo.org for the text of these Conventions. For an overview see Swepston, 2004: paras 32–67. Some Conventions are confined to particular industries, such as coal mining, or particular groups of workers, such as seafarers. For a critique of the number and quality of standards, see Creighton, 2004b: pp 257–259.

400 Conventions Nos. 87, 98, 29, 105, 111, 100, 138 and 182. See Bellace, 2001.

published in the *Official Bulletin*. In addition, the various supervisory bodies have built up a body of case law relating to the scope and meaning of various Conventions. Each state is required by the ILO Constitution to supply reports at regular intervals (the period depending on the Convention in question)[401] on the measures taken to implement the Conventions it has ratified. These are examined by an independent Committee of Experts whose reports are submitted to a tripartite Committee on the Application of Conventions and Recommendations, established at each session of the International Labour Conference, before which Government representatives may appear. In its report the Committee may draw attention to the most serious violations of ratified Conventions in a 'special paragraph', one of the strongest sanctions which may be taken against a Member State.

As well as these monitoring procedures (which are vulnerable to states failing to meet their reporting obligations)[402] there are also those instigated by complaints. These may be made either by one Member State against another co-signatory to a Convention, or by the Governing Body of its own motion or at the instigation of a delegate to the Conference. In addition employers' or workers' organisations may make representations that a state is not securing the application of a ratified Convention; such representations are considered initially by a three-member committee of the Governing Body and then by the Governing Body itself. The significance of respect for the principles of freedom of association for the effective functioning of the ILO is reflected in the special procedures which have been developed to deal with alleged failures of compliance in this area.[403] Two bodies are concerned with this. First, there is a tripartite Committee on Freedom of Association, composed of nine members appointed by the Governing Body, which has dealt with a large number of individual cases, based mainly on written submissions but sometimes involving oral hearings or visits to the states concerned.[404] In addition there is a Fact-finding and Conciliation Commission, composed of independent persons, which may undertake more extensive investigations, similar to a commission of inquiry, provided that the Member State consents. These procedures can be invoked against governments which have not ratified all or any of the freedom of association Conventions because it is assumed that the very fact of ILO membership carries with it an obligation to respect these principles.[405]

2.46 As of February 2005, the UK had ratified a total of 85 ILO Conventions.[406] Although this is a higher number than many countries, many significant Conventions were omitted;[407] those which have never been ratified include the

---

401 In the case of fundamental and 'priority' Conventions (the latter covering tripartite consultation (No 144) labour inspection (Nos 81 and 129) and employment policy (No 122)) alternate years; in the case of other Conventions, every five years.

402 In 2000, the compliance rate with reporting requirements was only 61.4%, with 39 states failing to submit any or the majority of reports due: Ewing and Sibley, 2000: p 37.

403 Creighton, 1994: p 2.

404 See ILO, 1996, for a digest of its decisions to that date.

405 Creighton, 1993: p 2. See now the ILO Declaration on Fundamental Principles and Rights at Work, 1998. Governments that have ratified a freedom of association Convention are also subject to the normal supervisory procedures relating to ratified Conventions.

406 For recent accounts of the relationship between Britain and the ILO see Ewing, 1994a; Creighton, 1993; D Brown and A McColgan, 1992; Mills, 1997; Novitz, 1998, 2000; for an earlier account see Stewart, 1969.

407 Ewing, 1994a: paras 4.8–4.12.

Hours of Work (Industry) Convention 1919 (No 1); the Holidays with Pay Convention, 1936 (No 52); and the Occupational Safety and Health Convention, 1981 (No 155). Moreover, in furtherance of its deregulatory strategy the UK Conservative administration of 1979–1997 denounced a number of Conventions, including the Minimum Wage-Fixing Machinery Convention, 1928 (No 26), the Labour Clauses (Public Contracts) Convention 1949 (No 94) and the Protection of Wages Convention 1949 (No 95); indeed, as of February 2005, 17 Conventions previously ratified had been denounced (although in six cases this was as a result of ratification of later Conventions instead). It is notable that, despite the traditional policy of ratifying ILO Conventions only when domestic law and practice were in compliance with their specifications, the Conservative Government introduced and maintained legislation which breached Conventions Nos 87 and 98 on freedom of association despite 'unprecedented levels of criticism'[408] from ILO supervisory bodies. We discuss the specific nature of these breaches later in this work. The intransigence of the UK Government in the light of the condemnation of its actions demonstrated the limits of a system which relies ultimately upon goodwill and persuasion. As our discussion shows, many of these breaches have not been remedied by its Labour successor.[409]

2.47 Standards relevant to labour law are also present in a number of instruments which deal with a wider range of human, civil and political or socio-economic rights. These include the Universal Declaration of Human Rights, adopted by the United Nations General Assembly in 1948, to which effect was given in international law by the International Covenant on Economic Social and Cultural Rights (ICESCR) and International Covenant on Civil and Political Rights (ICCPR), both of 1966. In the case of the UK, compliance with both covenants is monitored by means of reports from signatory states.[410] At European level the European Convention on Human Rights (ECHR) and its economic and social counterpart, the European Social Charter (ESC) both include provisions relating to labour law. The ECHR is enforced by means of state and (more commonly) individual applications;[411] in the field of labour law the provision most relevant to the UK has been Article 11, which guarantees freedom of association, including the right to form and join trade unions. The HRA 1998 enabled the ECHR to be relied upon in domestic courts and tribunals in a much wider range of situations than heretofore, and Convention rights other than Article 11, which we examine in appropriate sections of this book, are also likely to be significant in future. The ESC contains a much larger number of provisions which are relevant to labour law than the ECHR.[412] Part II of the

---

408 Creighton, 1994: p 4.
409 See Novitz 1998, 2000, 2003.
410 In the case of the ICCPR there is an optional inter-state procedure and an individual communications procedure to the Human Rights Committee which the UK has not accepted. On the ICESCR see Craven, 1998; Joint Committee on Human Rights, 21st Report, Session 2003/2004.
411 On the procedure for bringing a case before the European Court of Human Rights see Clements *et al*, 1999; see also N Rowe and V Schlette, 1998.
412 A revised ESC was opened for signature on 3 May 1996. The changes made include widening the non-discrimination principle and adding new rights such as the right to protection in cases of termination of employment, the worker's right to dignity and the right of workers with family responsibilities to equal opportunities and equal treatment. The UK signed the revised charter in November 1997, but at the time of writing has not ratified it. See generally Blanpain, 2001.

Charter contains 19 articles, including the right to work (Article 1), the right to just conditions of work (Article 2), the right to safe and healthy working conditions (Article 3), the right to a fair remuneration (Article 4), the right to organise (Article 5), the right to bargain collectively and the right to strike (Article 6); the right of children and young persons to protection (Article 7) and the right of employed women to protection (Article 8). However, signatory states may choose to be bound by only ten of these articles (or 45 numbered paragraphs).[413] Moreover, unlike the ECHR, there is no avenue for enforcing the Charter open to individuals although in 1995 a Protocol providing for a system of collective complaints by management, labour and non-governmental organisations was introduced.[414] However the general mechanism for enforcement is scrutiny by a committee of nine independent experts, assisted by an ILO representative in a consultative capacity, of reports on law and practice within each signatory state supplied by the respective governments, although unions and employers' organisations have a chance to comment on them. This Committee, now known as the European Committee of Social Rights,[415] draws up a report which is sent to the organs of the Council of Europe. In the last resort the Committee of Ministers can make any necessary recommendations to an individual state. This procedure is open to a number of criticisms, including the fact that evidence of compliance with Charter obligations is produced solely by governments, unless some other body chooses gratuitously to furnish evidence, and that ultimately the role of the Committee of Ministers means that the parties are judges in their own cause.[416]

We shall refer to the relevant provisions of the instruments referred to above as they relate to the particular areas dealt with in this work. Here we confine ourselves to emphasising that the standards they prescribe are, in general, considerably less detailed than those formulated by the ILO. Moreover, they are not rooted in a labour relations framework, a consequence which, as we shall see, has produced significant differences in the interpretation of the freedoms which they guarantee from the standards developed by the ILO. The dangers of such discrepancies are amply demonstrated by the differential treatment of the UK Government's ban on membership of national civil service trade unions in 1984 which we discuss in para 7.10.[417]

2.48 In the UK, international obligations are not, as such, part of domestic law unless enshrined in legislation. This does not mean that they should thereby be ignored, however. Apart from their importance as a benchmark of accepted standards, in interpreting ambiguous legislation the courts act on a (rebuttable) presumption that Parliament intended to legislate in accordance with international

---

413 Art 20. Ironically, because the ESC allows contracting states some discretion as to the articles they accept it has been used by the ECtHR to bolster a narrow interpretation of Art 11 of the ECHR: see further *National Union of Belgian Police v Belgium* judgment of 27 October 1975, (1975) 1 EHRR 578 at para 38 and para 7.9 below. The revised Charter also allows a measure of discretion in this respect: see Arts A and B.

414 See Brillat, 1996; Cullen, 2000; Evju, 2001a; Churchill and Khaliq, 2004.

415 Formerly the Committee of Independent Experts. For a useful overview of the Committee's jurisprudence, see Samuel, 1997. Recent ECSR Conclusions are on the ESC web site: www.coe.int.

416 See D Harris, 1984; O'Higgins, 1991.

417 For a more detailed critique of the relationship between standards formulated by the ILO and those of other bodies in the area of freedom of association see G Morris, 1994a. For a broader discussion, see O'Higgins, 2002.

obligations. In addition when interpreting the common law the courts may be persuaded to take cognisance of international standards,[418] and they may look beyond decisions of the ECtHR in interpreting the scope of 'Convention rights' pursuant to the HRA 1998. It is also possible that standards drawn from other instruments may enter UK domestic law via EC obligations; the principle of equal pay for work of equal value, incorporated in ILO Convention No 100 on Equal Remuneration, being one prominent example.[419] Moreover, it is conceivable that ILO principles may inform the decisions of the ECJ in interpreting existing community law, as has the ECHR.[420] However, unless specifically enshrined in EC legislation, it could not be argued that the principles contained in ILO Conventions constituted free-standing, enforceable rights under EC law.[421]

A common feature of institutionalised international labour standards generally is the weakness in the mechanisms for enforcing them. An additional mechanism, of potentially great significance, is to make compliance with such standards a condition of international trade agreements, a strategy analogous to that of contract compliance outlined in para 2.6. There are a number of recent examples of 'social clauses' being inserted into trade agreements, although to date a social clause has yet to be adopted by the World Trade Organisation, and opponents have suggested (disingenuously or otherwise) that clauses of this nature may act as a form of protectionism in preserving jobs in rich countries that have the resources to meet such standards rather than promoting economic progress in poorer ones.[422] A further development in recent years has been the adoption of codes by transnational corporations keen to advertise themselves as upholders of ethical business practices, so 'privatising' labour standards, although research has shown that the content of these codes may be highly selective (with few addressing freedom of association, for example), and compliance with them inadequately monitored and enforced.[423] It is unlikely that the economic power of these corporations alone can be relied upon to secure core labour standards in the absence of independent supervision.

LABOUR STANDARDS AND PRIVATE INTERNATIONAL LAW

2.49   With increasing transnational mobility of labour and, in particular, of capital, the issue of conflicts of law between different labour law regimes is a very live one.[424] The issues here include the question of which law governs employment relationships, and what the relationship is between a formal choice of law clause in a contract and the potentially overriding rules of employment protection law.

---

418 See Laws, 1993; Hunt, 1997. For the dangers of exposing ILO instruments to (mis)interpretation by the UK courts see *R v Secretary of State for Foreign and Commonwealth Affairs, ex p Council of Civil Service Unions* [1984] IRLR 353, CA and the trenchant critique by Ewing, 1994a: paras 8.10–8.13.
419 For an assessment of the (limited) opportunities for incorporating ILO standards further into EC law see Ewing, 1994a: paras 8.14–8.18.
420 See Grief, 1991.
421 Ewing, 1994a: p 49.
422 See generally Hepple, 1997a: pp 360–362; Ewing and Sibley, 2000; Tsogas, 2000; Cullen, 2000b; Murray, 2001; Gibbons, 2004; Hepple, 2005b.
423 Hepple, 1999a; Arthurs, 2002; Gibbons, 2004; Hepple, 2005b: ch 3.
424 For a fuller treatment of this complex subject, see L Collins *et al*, 2000 and supplements: paras 33-048–33-084.

The proper law of the contract of employment

2.50   The starting point for analysis is the rules of conflict of laws applied by English and Scottish courts for ascertaining the proper law of the contract of employment. Where the parties have made a formal choice of law the courts will generally respect this, although it is thought that they would disregard a choice of law clause which established as the proper law one with which the contract had no real connection, and which was manifestly to the employee's disadvantage.[425] In the absence of an express or implied choice, the test of 'closest and most real connection' applies. This has been applied flexibly to cover the differing situations of employees. For senior employees, the proper law is usually held to be that of the state in which the undertaking is based or from which it is controlled.[426] For lower level employees, the proper law will normally be the state in which they reside or in which they normally work.[427] The justification for this different treatment is that high-level employees are more closely associated with the central control of the organisation and hence with its base. The place in which the contract is made may also be a relevant factor.

The territorial scope of employment protection legislation

2.51   A choice of law clause in a contract of employment does not exclude protective standards in UK labour and social security legislation if enforcement of the standard would otherwise fall within the jurisdiction of the UK courts.[428] While this sometimes poses a problem for transnational employers with employees working in a number of different jurisdictions, any other approach would run the risk of contracts being framed so as to evade local employment protection, social security and tax laws, in favour of regulation by the weaker laws of another state.

Until recently many significant employment protection rights were denied to employees who ordinarily worked outside Great Britain.[429] This restriction was abolished by ERelA 1999 in relation to rights protected by ERA 1996.[430] However, the Court of Appeal has since confirmed, in *Lawson v Serco Ltd*,[431] that the Act is confined to employment in Great Britain except where there is express provision to the contrary.[432] The basis for this ruling is a general presumption that regulatory statutes such as ERA 1996 have a limited territorial scope: it is a 'governing principle' that 'all legislation is prima facie territorial'.[433] In addition, section 244 of ERA 1996 states, 'This Act extends to England and Wales, and Scotland but not to Northern Ireland'; according to the Court of Appeal in *Serco* this limited its application

---

425 See Kahn-Freund, 1978a; Hepple, 1978; Morse, 1982.
426 *Re Anglo-Austrian Bank* [1920] 1 Ch 69.
427 *South African Breweries v King* [1899] 2 Ch 173.
428 See, for example, the EqPA 1970, s 1(11); TULRCA 1992, s 289; ERA 1996, s 204.
429 ERA 1996, s 196 (now repealed). The terms of the exclusion varied with the right in question. On the application of the Act to offshore employments in the territorial waters of the UK and on the continental shelf, a category which includes employment on North Sea oil platforms, see ERA 1996, s 201; the Employment Protection (Offshore Employment) Order 1976, SI 1976/766, as amended.
430 S 32(3).
431 [2004] IRLR 206. At the time of writing permission has been given to appeal to the House of Lords.
432 [2004] IRLR 206, para 22 (Pill LJ).
433 *Ex p Blain* (1879) 12 Ch. D. 522, 528 (James LJ), cited with approval in *Lawson v Serco Ltd* [2004] IRLR 206, para 11 (Pill LJ).

to Great Britain. It further followed that the Act did not extend to claims against an employer simply because it carried on business in Great Britain. In the instant case, this approach excluded a claim arising out of employment which took place entirely on Ascension Island, where the employer was a company registered in England and Wales with a head office in Middlesex.[434] The Court emphasised that in deciding whether employment is in Great Britain there may be a need for a degree of flexibility; thus, a dismissal during a short absence from Great Britain would not normally exclude the protection of the Act.[435] Express geographical restrictions remain in place in relation to certain other important statutory rights. The discrimination legislation is limited in its scope to employment 'at an establishment in Great Britain'[436] (although the EAT has held that this restriction in the RRA 1976 conflicts with an individual's directly effective right under Article 48 of the EC Treaty to work anywhere within the EC[437]). The NMWA 1998 requires the individual to work, or ordinarily work, in the UK under his or her contract in order to qualify for the national minimum wage.[438] Specified rights under TULRCA 1992 – the right not to be denied access to employment, or to suffer a detriment in employment, on grounds relating to trade union membership and activities, and the right to time off for union duties and activities – are excluded where under his or her contract of employment 'an employee works, or in the case of a prospective employee, would ordinarily work, outside Great Britain'.[439] In addition, in deciding whether a valid request for recognition may be made against an employer, it may be necessary to determine whether workers employed by an associated employer ordinarily worked in Great Britain during a particular period.[440]

As the examples given above make clear, where express 'place of work' restrictions remain in place, they are not framed in a uniform fashion. However, they commonly refer to where an individual 'ordinarily' works. This concept formerly applied to the application of unfair dismissal protection, and the considerable body of case law derived from that context remains of relevance. The courts have held that the test of where work is 'ordinarily' done is principally regulated by the contract terms themselves rather than the practice, if that differs from the contract.[441] However, in cases of doubt – such as contracts which accord the employer a discretion as to where the work is to be done – it has been suggested that the location of the employee's 'base' or centre of control may determine in which country he or she ordinarily works.[442] This means that

---

434 *Lawson v Serco Ltd* [2004] IRLR 206.
435 [2004] IRLR 206, para 28. See also *Crofts v Cathay Pacific Airways Ltd* [2005] EWCA Civ 599.
436 EqPA 1970, s 1(1); SDA 1975, s 6; RRA 1976, s 4; DDA 1995, s 4(6); EE(SO)R 2003, reg 6; EE(RB)R 2003, reg 9. On when employment is treated as being at an establishment in Great Britain see SDA 1975, s 10(1); RRA 1976, s 8(1); DDA 1995, s 68(2); EE(SO)R 2003, reg 9; EE(RB)R 2003, reg 9.
437 *Bossa v Nordstress Ltd* [1998] IRLR 284 (Italian national could complain under the RRA 1976 of a failure to accord him an interview in Britain for a job in Italy).
438 S 1(2).
439 S 285. The duty to notify the Secretary of State of collective redundancies is also excluded in relation to such employees. TULRCA 1992, ss 145A–151 do not apply to employment where under his or her contract personally to do work or perform services a worker who is not an employee works outside Great Britain: s 285(1A).
440 TULRCA 1992, Sch A1, paras 7(3), (4).
441 *Wilson v Maynard Shipbuilding Consultants AB* [1978] ICR 376, 385 (Megaw LJ).
442 *Wilson v Maynard Shipbuilding Consultants AB* [1978] ICR 376, 387; see also *Janata Bank v Ahmed* [1981] IRLR 457; *Weston v Vega Space Systems Engineering Ltd* [1989] IRLR 429; *Carver v Saudi Arabian Airlines* [1999] IRLR 370; *Crofts v Cathay Pacific Airways Ltd* [2005] EWCA Civ 599; cf *Todd v British Midland Airways Ltd* [1978] ICR 959.

an airline pilot or long-distance lorry driver who works from a base within Great Britain is likely to be protected even though he or she may spend the majority of their working time outside the country. In identifying the base, account should be taken of such contract terms 'as expressly define his (sic) headquarters, or which indicate where the travels involved in his employment begin and end; where his private residence – his home – is, or is expected to be; where, and perhaps in what currency, he is expected to be paid; [and] whether he is to be subject to pay national insurance contributions in Great Britain'.[443] A person ordinarily works either in or outside Great Britain; the argument that he or she could simultaneously work in both has been rejected.[444]

European Community standards

2.52   The EC Convention on the Law Applicable to Contractual Obligations 1980 (the 'Rome Convention') was signed by the UK in 1981, and was incorporated into UK law by the Contracts (Applicable Law) Act 1990.[445] The aim of the Convention is to harmonise different national rules of the conflict of laws, but it may make a major difference to British practice at least as far as the contract of employment is concerned, by limiting the effectiveness of a choice of law clause in such a contract. Under Article 6(1), 'in a contract of employment a choice of law made by the parties shall not have the result of depriving the employee of the protection afforded to him by the mandatory rules of the law which would be applicable ... in the absence of choice', while under Article 6(2), in the absence of choice, a contract of employment is to be governed:

(a)   by the law of the country in which the employee habitually carries out his work in performance of the contract, even if he is temporarily employed in another country; or

(b)   if the employee does not habitually carry out his work in any one country, by the law of the country in which the place of business through which he was engaged is situated;

unless it appears from the circumstances as a whole that the contract is more closely connected with another country, in which case the contract shall be governed by the law of that country.

These provisions may only apply for the benefit of the employee. Article 6(1) seems to open up the possibility of the employee suing in the English courts (for example) for the application of a foreign employment protection statute, which marks a departure from the strict principle of national territoriality, although the practical difficulties involved in mounting such a claim (in particular, providing requisite proof of the relevant rule of law in the other jurisdiction) are considerable.[446]

   The issue of jurisdiction is important because an exclusive jurisdiction clause may purport to require a worker to pursue any claim before the courts of the state where the employer is based; that court might take a different view of the applicable law. This is meant to happen less with the harmonisation of rules of private international law under the Rome Convention. Even so it could be inconvenient (to say the least) to deprive the employee of the right to sue his or

---

443   *Wilson v Maynard Shipbuilding Consultants AB* [1978] ICR 376, 387.
444   *Wilson v Maynard Shipbuilding Consultants AB* [1978] ICR 376, 384.
445   R Smith and V Cromack, 1993.
446   For the impact of EC Directive 96/71 on the posting of workers, see below.

her employer in the courts of his or her country of residence. As far as rights under ERA 1996 are concerned, a contract term purporting to oust the jurisdiction of the employment tribunal is invalid.[447] Other cases normally fall under the Brussels Convention of 1968 which is transposed into UK law by the Civil Jurisdiction and Judgments Acts 1982 and 1991. Initially, an exclusive jurisdiction clause would be given effect by the courts, even if it was contained in an employment contract.[448] In the absence of an exclusive jurisdiction clause, the normal rule would be that the employer could be sued in the jurisdiction where the employee had to perform his or her duties (the 'characteristic' obligation of the contract).[449] In 1989, however, the Brussels Convention was amended.[450] The basic rule for employment contracts now is to grant jurisdiction to the country in which the employee habitually carries out his or her work, or, if there is no such country, in the place where the business which engaged the employee is or was situated; and an exclusive jurisdiction clause in a contract of employment can only have effect broadly speaking, in the employee's favour or in a case where the agreement conferring jurisdiction was entered into after the dispute arose. In *Rutten v Cross Medical Ltd*[451] the ECJ held that where a contract of employment is performed in more than one Contracting State, the 'place where the employee habitually carried out his work' is the place where the employee has established the effective centre of his or her working activities and where, or from which, they in fact perform the essential part of their duties vis-à-vis the employer. In reaching this decision the court was concerned to protect the employee as the weaker party to the contract and to identify the place where it was least expensive for him or her to bring or defend proceedings. In *Weber v Universal Ogden Services Ltd* the ECJ held that where an employee performs for his or her employer the same activities in more than one Contracting State, the place where he or she 'habitually works' will be the place where the employee has worked the longest unless, on the facts, the subject-matter of the dispute is more closely connected with a different place of work.[452] If these criteria do not enable the national court to identify the habitual place of work, the employee will have the choice of suing the employer either in the courts of the place where the business which engaged him or her is situated, or in the courts of the Contracting State in whose territory the employer is domiciled.[453]

2.53 Directive 96/71 concerning the posting of workers in the framework of the provision of services, adopted by the Community in December 1996, ousts the normal rules as laid down in the Rome Convention in the situation where workers are temporarily posted by their employer to work in a Member State (the 'host state') other than that in which they are normally employed (the 'home state'). The Directive provides that such workers must receive the protection of certain minimum labour standards which apply to employment in the *host state,* for the period in question. It was required to be implemented by Member States by 16 December 1999.

---

447 See ERA 1996, s 203.
448 Case C-25/79: *Sanicentral v Collin* [1979] ECR 3423, ECJ.
449 Case C-32/88: *Six Constructions v Humbert* [1989] ECR 341.
450 By the San Sebastian Convention. For the issues raised by the Brussels Convention see Kidner, 1998.
451 Case C-383/95 [1997] IRLR 249. See also *Harada Ltd t/a Chequepoint UK v Turner* 2 November 1999, EAT 516/99, IRLB No 634, February 2000.
452 Case C-37/00 [2002] IRLR 365, para 58.
453 Case C-37/00 [2002] IRLR 365, para 58.

The Directive applies in the following three situations: where undertakings in the home state and host state agree a contract for the supply of labour services between them; where the posting takes place through administrative arrangements made within a single group of companies (for example, where an employee of a group company based in the home state is seconded to a group company in the host state); and, where the posting takes place in the course of the supply of labour by an employment business/agency in the home state to an employer or agency in the host state.

The host state must then ensure that the workers concerned are covered by basic standards contained in laws, regulations and administrative provisions governing the following matters which are listed in Article 3(1): working hours, holidays, minimum pay, regulation of conditions of supply of labour by agencies, health and safety, protection of pregnancy and maternity, and equal treatment of men and women and 'other provisions on discrimination'.[454] In respect of the building and construction trades only,[455] the host state must also apply standards derived from collective agreements 'which have been declared universally applicable',[456] ie, those agreements or awards which must be observed by all undertakings in the geographical area and in the profession or industry concerned'.[457] In the absence of a system for declaring agreements or awards to be of universal application Member States may, if they so decide, adopt for this purpose agreements or awards 'which are generally applicable to all similar undertakings' in the area and sector and/or collective agreements which have been concluded by the 'most representative' employers' and labour organisations at national level and which are applicable throughout national territory.[458]

The Directive goes on to state that host states *may* enlarge their regulatory competence in two ways:[459] first, by applying norms derived from collective agreements (as defined above) to posted workers other than those in the building and construction industries; and second, by applying to posted workers norms from laws, regulations and administrative provisions other than those contained in the list of compulsory items in Article 3(1) (such as unfair dismissal laws and laws relating to employee representation).

A proposal to exempt from the Directive all postings for less than three months, which had been included in an earlier draft, was removed from the final, agreed version. Three broad categories of exemptions remain.[460] First, a host state *must* exempt from the minimum pay and paid annual holiday provisions workers involved in cross-border provision of initial assembly and/or installation of goods where this is an integral part of a contract for the supply of goods, necessary for taking the goods supplied into use and carried out by skilled and/or specialist

---

454 An obligation is also imposed upon the home state: its courts will be required to apply the minimum standards of the law of the host state for the period of the posting even if, in other respects, the contract is governed by the law of the home state. However, it is arguable that the relevant minimum standards here are cumulative, so that an employee cannot be made worse off by the application of the laws of the host state. See generally P Davies, 1997. The Directive gives workers the right to have proceedings instituted in the Member State to which they have been posted without prejudice, where applicable, to the right, under existing international conventions on jurisdiction, to institute proceedings in another State: Art 6.

455 The relevant sectors are defined in the Annex to the Directive.

456 Art 3(1).

457 Art 3(8).

458 Art 3(8).

459 Art 3(10).

460 Art 3(2)–(6).

workers of the supplying undertaking, and the posting does not exceed eight days.[461] Second, in the case of postings for less than one month, the host state, after consulting the social partners, may exempt workers from the provisions of minimum pay provisions, but this does not apply to agency-supplied labour. Third, in the case of postings where 'the amount of work to be done is not significant', exemption from minimum pay and paid leave provisions is allowed, but again this does not apply to agency-supplied labour.

The Directive can be seen as a vindication of the interests of the predominantly northern host states, which are net importers of labour, in limiting low-cost competition from elsewhere in the Union. However, Article 57 (now Article 47 EC), which constitutes the Directive's 'treaty base', authorises the Council by qualified majority voting to adopt harmonising directives not for protective purposes, but 'in order to make it easier for persons to take up and pursue activities as self-employed persons', and Article 66 (now Article 55 EC) duplicates this with regard to the freedom to provide services. The protective intentions of the Directive may nevertheless be seen as compatible with the goal of regularising the position of posted workers and, hence, with encouragement for the trans-border supply of services: 'as a means of protecting both the established workforce in the higher paying country and the migrant worker, who is ignorant about the general level of costs in the new country, one could argue that the ... full integration of workers from other Member States into the domestic labour regulation of the importing state is the correct policy'.[462] However, this may not prevent legal challenges to certain aspects of the Directive, in particular in so far as it involves the application of its provisions to posted workers 'from day one'.[463]

Collective aspects

2.54   The determination of the proper law may also affect the enforceability and application of collective agreements and the incidence of liability for industrial action. As far as collective agreements are concerned, in the absence of an express choice the test of 'closest and most real connection' applies again. In *Monterosso Shipping Co Ltd v ITWF*[464] this led the Court of Appeal to conclude that an agreement entered into in Spain and regulating the recruitment of Spanish seamen was governed by Spanish law, with the effect that the shipowners could sue for damages for its breach; had English law been the proper law, the action would have been barred by the statutory presumption that collective agreements are not legally binding as contracts between parties to them.[465] In cases of

---

461   As P Davies, 1997 points out at p 583 this appears to be an exemption from the *obligation* on the host state to apply its national provisions to posted workers, but does not state whether the host state is *prohibited* from imposing these provisions. However, it seems that the exemption must have this effect in order to distinguish this provision from those which give host states a choice. Note that this exemption does not apply to the building trades listed in the Annex to the Directive.

462   P Davies, 1997: p 600.

463   P Davies, 1997: p 600. Note also Case C-165/98 *Belgium v Mazzoleni* [2001] ECR I-2189.

464   [1982] ICR 675.

465   TULRCA 1992, s 179; see para 9.26 below. See also *Dimskal Shipping Co SA v ITWF* [1992] IRLR 78, in which the determination of the proper law of a contract as English law meant that the union was held liable to make restitution for economic duress, when under the law of Sweden, where the industrial action took place, no liability would have been incurred.

industrial action, there may be a 'trade dispute' with regard to matters occurring outside the UK only so long as the persons acting in contemplation or furtherance of that dispute are likely to be affected by its outcome in respect of one or more of the matters which may otherwise provide the basis for lawful industrial action by them.[466] This is a severe restriction upon the ability of British workers to participate in transnational trade disputes.

466 TULRCA 1992, s 244(3).

CHAPTER 3

The employment relationship

INTRODUCTION

3.1 This chapter is concerned with the law governing the definition and formation of the individual employment relationship. Contractual concepts are central here, a role recognised in Kahn-Freund's striking description of the contract of employment as the 'cornerstone' of the modern labour law system.[1] The existence of the legal relationship of employment presupposes the voluntary consent of the parties to its creation, expressed through the process of hiring. The hiring process itself is the subject of only limited statutory intervention: there are few controls over the form it may take, and the protection of applicants for employment against exclusion by reason of discrimination of various kinds is far from comprehensive. In this area, at least, the common law of contract, and more specifically the principle of freedom of contract, retains much of its force.

The role of freedom of contract is, however, more limited in relation to the contents of the employment relationship and the means by which the relationship may be terminated. Subsequent chapters examine in greater detail the specific norms, deriving from statute, the common law and (indirectly) from collective bargaining, which apply in these areas.[2] In order to delimit the scope of these regulatory norms, it has been necessary for the law to develop criteria by which the subject-matter of labour law regulation, *dependent labour*, may be identified. These criteria have largely been borrowed from the common law, with the result that the category of dependent labour coincides largely, although not completely, with the common law concept of the contract of employment. Only an *employee* who is employed under a contract of employment is capable of qualifying for the vast majority of the protective rights contained in ERA 1996 and TULRCA 1992; the self-employed worker and independent contractor, whether or not they have a business of their own or employ others, are for the most part excluded from this legislation. Given that the process of identifying the contract of employment is, accordingly, crucial to determining the scope of this legislation, it is both surprising and unfortunate that the statutes themselves have had little or nothing to say about the criteria to be applied, leaving it to the courts to decide this issue according to common law tests which have become notorious for their complexity. Nevertheless, the development by the courts of these notions of employment status in the context of social legislation serves as a reminder that, as the 'cornerstone' of the labour law system, the concept of the contract of employment has a dual function: while underpinning the managerial power of the employer, it also serves as the gateway to social protection for the employee.[3]

---

1   Kahn-Freund, 1954b: p 47.
2   See, in particular, chs 4 and 5 below.
3   See Deakin, 1998.

The contract of employment is not the only concept deployed to these ends. In certain areas, which include equal treatment and health and safety legislation, the legislature has extended the normal definition of dependent labour beyond the contract of employment, to include certain categories of the self-employed and individuals whose employment status would otherwise be doubtful. These extensions are an important reminder that self-employment is not altogether excluded from the scope of labour law and, moreover, that statutory intervention can be used to overcome some of the limitations of the common law concept of the employee. It is significant, in this context, that the broader concept of the *worker* forms the basis for the application of the minimum wage, controls over working time, and other statutory labour standards which were introduced in the late 1990s. In addition, section 23 of the Employment Relations Act 1999 introduced a power, as yet unexercised, under which a statutory instrument can be used to extend the scope of employment rights to individuals who would not otherwise be protected by legislation.

Legislation contains additional bases for classifying and sub-dividing employment relationships. Once an individual has achieved employee status, to gain statutory protection it will often be necessary to show that he or she has also crossed certain minimum *qualifying thresholds* relating, in particular, to the length and regularity of their employment. These thresholds are expressed in the statutory concept of *continuity of employment* which is found in ERA 1996 and, in a slightly different form, in parts of SSCBA 1992. Between them, the requirements of employee status and continuity of employment potentially exclude from protection many individuals who either do not work a standard, full-time working week; who are employed on fixed-term contracts or for a short duration; who are employed as trainees or on government-funded employment schemes; who are employed to work at or from home; or who work on the basis that their labour is supplied to an employer by an employment agency or business. As the numbers of those in such 'flexible' or 'atypical' forms of employment have grown as a proportion of the labour force, so have the difficulties of applying to them a conceptual framework for labour law which, for the most part, is still wedded to the notion that the full-time, 'permanent' and regular employment relationship is the norm.

Just as it is essential to determine the legal status of a worker in relation to protective rights, so it is also vital to ascertain the nature and identity of the *employer* upon whom, or which, obligations may be imposed. While only an individual person can be an employee, the employer may in principle be either an individual or a legal entity in the form of a partnership, a limited company, or a public authority or similar body. Courts and tribunals may then be faced with the question of which one of several different but related legal entities constitutes the employer for legal purposes. While in general there are few controls over the corporate form in which the owners of a business may choose to constitute it, employees may in some cases be able to shift liability from the employer with whom they are in direct contractual privity to another company within the same corporate group, using the statutory concept of 'associated employers', or to a successor or purchaser company or other entity, to which the business in which they are or were employed has been transferred (a 'transfer of employment'). Situations also arise in which the normal functions of the employer are divided between different entities. This is the case with agency work, for example. Here, the law has a role to play in determining which obligations will normally attach to the agency or 'employment business', and which are assumed by the 'user' or direct recipient of the worker's services. The principles according to which liability can be redistributed in these various ways are considered in later sections of this chapter. We also analyse concepts which are used, in particular contexts, to determine the form and scope of the *unit of employment*. The most important of these is the *establishment*, a term which is not limited to the physical location of work but which may for some purposes also embrace a managerial, financial or administrative unit.

CONTRACT OR STATUS?

3.2 Although the basic conceptual framework for the individual employment relationship is provided by contract, many have questioned whether it is useful to think of the employment relationship in this way. Kahn-Freund wrote of the employment relationship that '[i]n its inception it is an act of submission, in its operation it is a condition of subordination, no matter how much the submission and the subordination may be concealed by that indispensable figment of the legal mind known as the contract of employment'.[4] Prior to the hiring, there is rarely any parity in the relative bargaining power of employer and worker. This is not just because of the size of many modern employing organisations; few individuals have the independent means to enable them not to work. Thus Adam Smith, for example, recognised that:

> It is not ... difficult to see which of the two parties must, upon all occasions, have the advantage in the dispute and force the other into compliance with their terms ... Many workmen could not subsist a week, few could subsist a month, and scarce any a year, without employment. In the long run, the workman may be as necessary to his master as his master is to him; but the necessity is not so immediate.[5]

Social security law, while providing an alternative source of income to waged labour, also contains disciplinary mechanisms which may, for example, penalise the unemployed (or 'jobseekers') for not 'actively seeking work' or for refusing offers of employment,[6] and so can only be said partially to mitigate the pre-contractual inequality of employer and worker.

3.3 A second sense in which the employment relationship seems to lack the normal features of a contract is that agreement between the parties plays a relatively minor role in determining the substance of their reciprocal obligations. In part this is because of the inherent power of command which vests in the employer. As Fox has shown, this 'managerial prerogative' does not simply result from the employer's superior bargaining power prior to the agreement; it is also underpinned by certain legal norms, which today tend to take the form of the common law implied terms of the contract of employment. These implied obligations of fidelity, obedience and care which fill in the 'empty boxes of the contract'[7] can be traced back in many cases to the master and servant legislation of the nineteenth century and before: the needs of employers 'were met by infusing the employment contract with the traditional law of master and servant, thereby granting them a legal basis for the prerogative they demanded'.[8] The contract

4   P Davies and M Freedland, 1983: p 8.
5   A Smith [1776] 1886: pp 27–28.
6   See para 3.17 below.
7   Fox, 1974: p 183.
8   Fox, 1974: p 184.

may be said to create a form of *status* which, as a source of the norms which govern the relationship of the parties, is separate from their express agreement.

Legal support for managerial powers is only one aspect of status in the modern employment relationship, however. The asymmetrical qualities of the employment relationship have been offset by a second form of status, derived from employment protection legislation and collective bargaining. Employment protection, working time and minimum wage statutes, among others, formally limit freedom of contract by providing rights which in most cases are 'inderogable', in the sense that they cannot be contracted away or made the subject of waiver.[9] This type of legislation has created new forms of status-based classifications, dividing workers, as we shall see, not simply according to whether they are employees or self-employed, but also, within the category of employees, according to the degree of length and regularity of employment, the duration of the normal working week and the normal weekly wage or salary. These forms of protective regulation are sometimes said to have reversed what Maine described as the movement of 'progressive societies' from status to contract.[10] The application of this description to modern labour law is not straightforward, however. Kahn-Freund pointed out that Maine used the term 'status' to refer to relationships in which rights and obligations were imposed upon a person completely independently of his or her own volition, for example by virtue of their place of birth, nationality, or familial origin; in contrast, the modern usage of the term 'status' refers to relationships such as employment or marriage which although regulated by law are voluntarily entered into by the parties concerned. Although protective labour legislation frequently provides for 'inderogable rights', it also assumes the prior existence of a contract of employment (or, less usually, of another contract of some kind, such as a contract for personal services) which has been voluntarily entered into by the parties.[11] Contract and status (in the modern sense of that term) can be seen as interdependent: the capacity to contract is itself a form of status recognised by law, and the more specific status which attaches to the employment relationship 'operates on an existing contractual relation'.[12]

3.4   However, a wider point is at issue in neo-liberal critiques of labour law which echo Maine by suggesting that modern employment legislation represents a regression to status relations. These see protective regulation as illegitimate on the twin grounds of compromising the autonomy of the contracting parties and of creating unnecessary rigidities, and hence inefficiencies, in the labour market.[13] The contract-status debate persists in large part because it reflects this deeper concern about the legitimacy of statutory regulation of contract. The central issue is whether contract and status are opposites, as the neoliberal critiques imply, or whether, as historical and institutional accounts suggest, they are better viewed as *interdependent* 'layers of regulation'.[14] Some points have already been made about this wider debate within economic and legal theory.[15] For immediate purposes, it may be useful to supplement our earlier

---

9   On the notion of 'inderogability' in this sense, see Wedderburn, 1992b.

10   Maine, [1861] 1927: p 174.

11   Kahn-Freund, 1967: p 640; cf the definition of an employee in ERA 1996, s 230(1), as 'an individual who has entered into or works under ... a contract of employment'.

12   Kahn-Freund, 1967: p 640.

13   See Epstein, 1983, 1984.

14   Mückenberger and Deakin, 1989: p 192.

15   See our analysis in ch 1 at paras 1.16–1.19 above.

analysis by considering some instances of the way in which tensions between contract and social legislation have been managed within the modern law of the employment relationship.

3.5 Summers, writing about the relationship between collective agreements and contract in US labour law, has suggested that the most important question is not whether these agreements are contracts since (in this, US, context) 'no one doubts' that they are:

> ... but how much they are unlike other contracts and whether this makes them somehow less contractual in character. More specifically, in what particular respects are [they] unique, and how does their uniqueness affect their contractual character?[16]

Certain of the distinctive features of US collective agreements, as identified by Summers, apply also to contracts of employment; in particular, they are characterised by a high degree of incompleteness and uncertainty in the way the contract terms are defined. Individual bargaining provides, at most, only a general framework of express terms to govern the performance of the contract, which is partly why other sources of contract terms are also important: these range from implicit assumptions of the parties, the parties' own conduct subsequent to the formation of the contract and custom and practice in the workplace concerned, to formal external sources of regulation, including collective agreements and legislation. Extending Summers's analysis, then, it could be argued that these distinctive features – the incompleteness of the contract and the role of sources subsequent or external to the agreement in completing it – make it inappropriate to apply to the contract of employment those principles of contract law which are designed to govern specific commercial transactions of a *different kind*, such as the sale of goods. As Lord Steyn has recently put it, whatever the position may have been in the past, '[i]t is no longer right to equate a contract of employment with commercial contracts. One possible way of describing a contract of employment in modern terms is as a relational contract'.[17] This does not necessarily mean that all of the general principles of contract law are irrelevant to the employment relationship. The question is whether these general principles of contract law are sufficiently flexible to be applied to the employment relationship without producing artificial reasoning and unsatisfactory results.

3.6 One area of employment law in which the principles of the common law of contract have undergone a substantial modification concerns the relationship between the collective agreement and the individual contract of employment. Terms from the collective agreement which are designed to regulate individual contracts take legal effect by virtue of the contractual doctrine of incorporation; the terms are incorporated by a 'bridging term' which may be express or implied into the contract of employment.[18] In this way, a principle of the common law achieves the same end as legislation performs in more highly regulated systems. Whether it does so in a fully effective way is perhaps doubtful. The courts have failed to deal consistently, for example, with the problem of conflicts between separate levels of bargaining, which is approached more systematically in systems

16 Summers, 1969: p 528.
17 *Johnson v Unisys Ltd* [2001] IRLR 279, para 20.
18 See ch 4, below, at para 4.28.

which recognise a hierarchical relationship between separate sources of norms.[19] But in general it seems a reasonable assessment to say that 'in this country, the individual contract has been skilfully refashioned by the courts to take collective bargaining into account while leaving the individual free to negotiate and enforce his own contract, which may be either more or less advantageous to him than the terms of the collective agreement'.[20]

3.7   The relationship between the common law of contract and social legislation is also a complex one.[21] The description given to the systems of law and equity in the decades following the Judicature Acts, namely that 'the two streams of jurisdiction, though they run in the same channel, run side by side, and do not mingle their waters',[22] is to some extent applicable to the relationship between common law and legislation within modern labour law. Statutory rights, for example, are rarely given the form of terms of the contract of employment.[23] Instead they more normally take the form of extra-contractual impositions,[24] which are often administered outside the regular system of the civil courts: the criminal courts were the principal mechanism for the enforcement of the nineteenth century Factory Acts and Truck Acts, as are employment tribunals in the case of modern employment protection legislation.[25] Some of the most difficult and persistent doctrinal questions in labour law have arisen at the point where the two bodies of principle come into contact with each other. There are rules for dealing with *conflicts* between them: it is a basic constitutional principle that legislation prevails over the common law. The precise scope of the statutory norm may not be readily ascertainable, however. A central question here is how far the application of statutory rules can be defeated by the contrary contractual intent of the parties. In part because of the extra-contractual form taken by most statutory rights, courts have in the past allowed parties to derogate from or 'contract out' of statutory rights, arguing that common law rights can only be ousted by clear wording in the statute.[26] In response, statutes have had to be drafted increasingly precisely, so that contractual terms which purport to remove statutory protection are *explicitly* prohibited and the limits of any permissible derogations are set by the legislation itself.[27] A further set of questions concerns what might be called the capacity of the two bodies of principle for *mutual recognition*. An enormous amount of litigation has been devoted to the question of how far regulatory legislation carrying criminal responsibility also creates implied civil obligations in contract and tort. This concerns issues such

19   See Supiot, 1994: p 30.
20   Hepple, 1981b: p 56.
21   Hepple, 2005a: lecture 3; J Beatson, 1997.
22   Ashburner, 1933: p 18; cf the more modern view of fusion which is that expressed by Lord Diplock in *United Scientific Holdings Ltd v Burnley Borough Council* [1978] AC 904, 925; and see Freedland, 2003: pp 3–4.
23   Rare examples are the implication into contracts of employment and certain contracts for personal services of an 'equality clause' under EqPA 1970, s 1 (see para 6.91 below) and the insertion into contracts of employment of statutory grievance and disciplinary procedures under EA 2002, s 30, which at the time of writing has not been brought into force (see ch 2 at paras 2.21–2.26 and ch 5 at paras 5.124–5.131).
24   Hepple, 1981b: p 57.
25   The difference is less marked with the extension of the jurisdiction of employment tribunals by SI 1994/1623: see para 2.15 above.
26   For a clear statement of this, see *Valentine v Hyde* [1919] 2 Ch 129, 153 (Astbury J).
27   Cf ERA 1996, s 203 (on which, see para 3.93 below), and TULRCA 1992, s 288.

as whether minimum wage legislation can be invoked to enable an employee to sue the employer in contract for the wages set by statute,[28] and whether the employer's failure to meet standards set by health and safety legislation can found an action for breach of statutory duty in tort.[29]

In the modern law, we can identify three principal ways in which the relationship between contractual and statutory rights has come to be defined. In the first place, there are areas in which legislation plays no direct regulatory role. Legislation says little or nothing about the formation of the contract of employment, for example, or about the conditions under which wages and salaries are payable by the employer in return for the employee's performance of the contract. In a second set of cases, legislation supplies a *floor of rights*[30] upon which contractual practice, and the common law, have built. In the areas of income and employment security covered by ERA 1996, NMWA 1998 and other statutes, as we have seen, derogation from the statutory norms is generally prohibited, but improvement on the standards set by statute is not prohibited, and is implicitly encouraged. This has created an additional role for contract. Terms may be improved by collective bargaining or by internal company rules, the relevant parts of which may then be incorporated into individual contracts of employment; in addition, contractual terms can be implied at common law, for example in relation to sick pay or lay off, for the protection of the employee.[31] In a third set of cases, legislation has established a further role for contract by explicitly allowing for contractual derogation from the norms it lays down. Thus under Part II of ERA 1996 (formerly the Wages Act 1986), express agreement by the parties to the contract of employment may displace and override statutory standards which would otherwise regulate deductions from wages.[32] Here, the derogation is 'controlled' in the sense of being subject to written formalities. Thus the legislation creates a space within which agreement can operate to make the application of protective standards more flexible, and to some extent moulds the form which that agreement will take.

Even in the areas where it is now accepted that statute has ousted contrary rules of the common law, extensive statutory intervention has, paradoxically, enhanced the importance of contractual principles by borrowing concepts and language from the common law. As Elias has put it, 'far from being cowed by [the] statutory assault, the contract of employment has emerged more resilient, and has proved to be infinitely more relevant than could possibly have been foreseen', largely because 'the statutory rights have been built upon the common law contractual framework, so that whilst the contract is of diminishing importance as a direct independent source of rights, it remains central to the operation of these statutory provisions'.[33]

Statutory borrowing of the common law tests of employee status, the courts' use of the doctrine of illegal contracts of employment and the influence of contractual reasoning on the statutory notion of continuity of employment, each

---

28   *Gutsell v Reeve* [1936] 1 KB 272 and *Cooner v PS Doal & Sons* [1988] IRLR 338 suggested that the employee can bring a civil claim of this kind even where the statute is silent or unclear. For the position under the National Minimum Wage Act 1998, see ch 4, below, at para 4.55.
29   See G Williams, 1960, and our discussion below, ch 4, para 4.82.
30   Wedderburn, 1986: p 6; see below, paras 4.9–4.12.
31   See below, paras 4.3–4.8.
32   ERA 1996, s 13.
33   Elias, 1982: p 95.

of which is considered later in this chapter,[34] illustrate this process, as do many other examples which are examined in this book. One which may briefly be considered here concerns the statutory definition of 'constructive dismissal' in section 95(1)(c) of ERA 1996. This provides that a dismissal takes place (*inter alia*) in a situation where 'the employee terminates ... [the contract of employment] ... (with or without notice), in circumstances in which he is entitled to terminate it without notice by reason of the employer's conduct'.[35] In *Western Excavating (ECC) Ltd v Sharp*[36] the Court of Appeal held that the question of when the employee was entitled to terminate the contract was to be settled by reference to principles of the common law of contract, namely the law relating to the right of an innocent party (the employee) to elect to terminate a contract for repudiatory breach by the other (the employer). The decision in *Western Excavating* has been criticised as setting up an unduly complex and restrictive test.[37] Just as important as the decision itself, however, are the developments which it subsequently prompted within the common law: faced with the task of defining the meaning of the employer's repudiatory breach for the purposes of section 95(1)(c) of ERA 1996, courts and tribunals extended the notion of the reciprocal duty of co-operation, in the process imposing certain obligations upon the employer to respect the personal dignity and autonomy of the employee.[38] This is one area in which the common law of contract has evolved in new directions as a consequence of its encounter with social legislation.[39]

3.8   There is no doubt that in the absence of a comprehensive labour code, the uncodified nature of the common law and the fragmented quality of much modern legislation have contributed to a sharpening of the contract-status divide in British labour law. But, as we have just seen, these conflicts between sources may be thought to mask a deeper, functional interdependence between contract and status as modes of governing the employment relationship. Not only does the common law contain within it elements of status derived in part from the legacy of 'master and servant'; modern legislation, in addition to using contractual concepts, preserves for contract the important functions of building on the statutory 'floor of rights' and providing a method of 'controlled derogation' from certain standards. It is increasingly difficult to view the common law of contract and social legislation as separate streams whose waters 'do not mingle'.

---

34   See below, paras 3.33–3.46 and 3.92 respectively. Freedland, 2003: pp 10–11 draws an important distinction between 'statutory contractual formulae' which borrow straightforwardly from the common law, such as the definition of dismissal in ERA 1996, s 95(1)(c), and 'statutory para-contractual formulae', such as the notion of continuity of employment under ERA 1996, ss 210–219, which adapt or modify common law concepts.
35   See below, paras 5.72–5.75
36   [1978] QB 761.
37   Kerr, 1984.
38   Hepple, 1981b: ch 9; see below, paras 4.91–4.93
39   See Deakin, 1997; Anderman, 2000; Freedland, 2003: ch 1; Hepple, 2005a: lecture 3. On the relationship between contract and HRA 1998, G Morris, 2001a. The decision of the majority of the House of Lords in *Johnson v Unisys Ltd* [2001] IRLR 279 suggested that there might be limits to how far the courts were prepared to allow the common law to evolve in this way, and that the presence of social legislation might, paradoxically, provide a reason for limiting the further development of the common law; see also *Eastwood v Magnox Electric plc; McCabe v Cornwall Council* [2004] IRLR 733. The view we express in the text accords more closely, however, with Lord Steyn's dissent in *Johnson*, which saw the common law as advancing in response to changes in social legislation. See generally our discussion of these cases at paras 5.44–5.46 below.

THE HIRING PROCESS

3.9   There are relatively few formal procedures governing the hiring process, and few rights are conferred on applicants for employment as opposed to those who are employed, as employees or otherwise. An important issue, however, is that of access to the national labour market of the United Kingdom, which is governed by the Immigration Rules and by the principle of freedom of movement of labour within the European Economic Area. A full treatment of this subject lies outside the scope of this book, but the central principles will be briefly outlined here. Access to a particular employment is subject for the most part to the principle of freedom of contract, but with protection against discrimination on a number of grounds including sex, sexual orientation, race, religion, disability, and membership or non-membership of a trade union. A further area of state intervention in the hiring process is that formed by *active labour market policy*, which in addition to providing direct employment subsidies of various kinds also extends to certain legal measures which have been designed with a view to their impact on workers' and employers' incentives. Rules concerning eligibility for social security benefits, for example, have an influence on the individual's decisions to search for work and to accept particular job offers; conversely, a range of measures in the form of taxation, social security benefits, and direct state subsidies aim to provide incentives to employers to hire workers.

Access to the labour market

3.10   Rights of access to the labour market for non-UK citizens are governed by the relevant rules of European Union law for states within the European Economic Area,[40] and by the Immigration Act 1971 and the Immigration Rules for nationals of other countries. The Immigration Rules are not delegated legislation as such but are promulgated and applied under the authority of the Home Office as an aspect of the prerogative power, although under the Immigration Act 1971 they must be laid before both Houses of Parliament for their approval.[41] If a resolution of either House is passed within forty days disapproving the proposed Rules, the Home Secretary is required to make such changes as he or she thinks fit and to re-submit them to Parliament.

Non-EEA nationals

3.11   The general effect of the Immigration Rules governing employment is to regulate very strictly the supply of foreign labour into the UK.[42] Most non-EEA nationals require a work permit to work in the UK. Those exempted from this rule fall under a number of miscellaneous categories. In addition to certain seasonal farm workers, exchange teachers, Commonwealth citizens with the right of abode in the UK, and certain trainees, a number of occupations qualify for 'non-work permit employment'. These include overseas broadcasters and

---

40   The European Economic Area (EEA) consists of the Member States of the European Union and of the European Free Trade Area (EFTA).

41   The current rules are based on HC Vol 395, Sess 1993–1994, 23 May 1994, as amended. A consolidated text is available on the web site of the Home Office: http://www.ind.homeoffice.gov.uk/content/ind/en/home.html.

42   See generally, on immigration and asylum law, Jackson and Warr, 2001; N Blake and R Hussain, 2003; Clayton, 2004.

journalists, sole representatives of foreign-based companies, private servants of diplomatic staff, domestic servants, foreign government employees, and ministers of religion. With the exception of domestic servants, those qualifying for non-work permit employment are able, under the Immigration Rules, to move around between jobs, as long as they remain within the general category of employment for which they were given permission to enter. Leave to enter is normally given for an initial period of twelve months, with a subsequent extension for three years; after four years, the individual concerned can apply for indefinite leave to remain.

All other non-EEA nationals seeking employment in the UK require, in principle, a work permit. The general principle behind the granting of a work permit is that the employer must demonstrate that the work in question needs skills which are in acutely short supply within the UK. Moreover, work permits are tied to particular jobs. An employee who needs a work permit cannot change jobs unless the work permit is varied. If he or she loses their job with the initial employer for whatever reason, and either has no other job to go to or is denied permission to change jobs, they also forfeit their rights of residence in the UK. Again, as with non-work permit employment, the individual only qualifies to apply for indefinite leave to remain after four years of employment.[43]

Citizens of EEA states

3.12   By contrast, for citizens of EEA states – that is to say nationals of EU Member States and of other states which are party to the Agreement on the European Economic Area of 1992 – the rights of free movement of labour, as guaranteed by EU law, apply.[44] Article 18(1) of the EC Treaty states that 'every citizen of the Union shall have the right to move and reside freely within the territory of the Member States subject to the limitations and conditions laid down in this Treaty and by the measures adopted to give it effect'.[45] Under Articles 39 and 40 of the Treaty, three rights are established in relation to the free movement of workers: these are the *right to enter* another Member State for the purposes of employment, which includes the right to enter to look for work; a *right to reside* in the Member State where the worker has found work or (for a limited period) is seeking work, which may be lost once employment ends, except in certain cases of retirement and incapacity for work; and *a right to work on equal terms* with the nationals of the Member State concerned.[46] There are a number of general derogations to these rights on the grounds of public policy, public security and public health, which are strictly construed.[47]

---

43   Immigration Rules, rule 134; the employer must certify that the individual is still required for the work in question. However, once indefinite leave is granted, the individual may take up another employment (see Clayton, 2004: p 161).

44   See the Immigration (European Economic Area) Regulations 2000, SI 2000/2326, as amended.

45   It is unclear whether this and related provisions provide rights of free movement which go beyond the prevailing conception of 'market citizenship' which ties mobility to participation in the labour market: see Case C085/96 *Martínez Sala* [1998] ECR I-2691; Douglas Scott, 1998: 62–64; Szyszczak, 2000a: 55–57.

46   Arts 39 and 40 have direct effect in national law, following the opinion of the ECJ in Case 41/74 *Van Duyn v Home Office* [1974] ECR 1337. The importance of equal treatment in this context was strongly emphasised by the ECJ in Case C-415/93 *Bosman* [1995] ECR I-4921.

47   Case 41/74 *Van Duyn v Home Office* [1974] ECR 1337. Art 39(4) contains an exception for public employment which has also been strictly construed: Case 152/73 *Sotgiu v Deutsche Bundespost* [1974] ECR 153; Case 149/79 *Commission v Belgium* [1980] ECR 3881.

In relation to access, UK law is currently based on EC Directive 68/360 which requires Member States to grant workers who are nationals of another Member State access to their territory on the production of a valid identity card or passport, without demanding additional documents in the form of entry visas, and to facilitate entry by other family members.[48] The Directive, together with other Community instruments in this area, covers 'workers', a term broadly defined by the ECJ to include persons engaged in part-time or low-paid work; moreover, the ECJ has said that the term must be given a uniform meaning in the context of freedom of movement, and should not be independently defined by the different laws of the Member States.[49] In addition, social security Regulations at European Union level give migrant workers the right, under certain circumstances, to receive unemployment benefit for up to three months after entering another Member State.[50] In *R v Immigration Appeal Tribunal, ex p Antonissen*[51] the ECJ held that a right to enter a Member State to search for work was implicit in Article 39 of the EC Treaty and in Article 3 of Directive 68/360, and upheld the UK practice of allowing six months to find a job. The Court ruled that it was lawful to deport a national of another Member State who could neither find work nor show that they had a genuine chance of finding it within, or shortly after, six months of entry.[52]

With regard to residence, Directive 68/360 requires the issue of a residence permit to workers entering a Member State who already have a confirmation of employment from an employer in that territory in relation to a job expected to last at least twelve months, and residence rights extend to members of the worker's immediate family. UK law, following the 1968 Directive,[53] requires the residence permit to be valid for five years, to cover the whole territory of the Member State and to be automatically renewable for a further five years. As a result of this provision, citizens of EEA states enjoy superior rights to those applying to other foreign workers within the UK. A citizen of an EEA state may take any work once he or she is in the territory of the UK, and has automatic rights to the extension of their residence permit as long as they are in employment. If such a worker becomes *involuntarily* unemployed, he or she does not necessarily lose their rights of residence, but upon the first renewal of the residence permit a time limit of a further twelve months may be placed upon their right to reside.[54] The position of a person who becomes voluntarily unemployed is not spelled out but by implication he or she could presumably be regarded as a new entrant, and hence required to find another job according to the principles outlined above. It is implicit in the 1968 Directive that the right of residence will also be lost by an absence of longer than six months, since it is stated that the right may not be lost for an absence of less than six months.[55] Special provisions apply for the issue of temporary residence permits issued to fixed-term contract and seasonal workers, and to the case of frontier workers and short-term workers employed for less than three months, for

---

48 Directive 68/360, Art 3. The regime set out in Directive 68/360 is set to be replaced by that contained in Directive 2004/38/EC by April 2006.
49 Case 53/81 *Levin v Staatssecretaris van Justitie* [1982] ECR 1035.
50 Regulation 1408/71, Art 69(1)(c).
51 Case C-292/89: [1991] ECR I-745.
52 The right to enter may, in practice, be substantially qualified by the need to comply with frontier controls which seek to establish whether a person has the right which he or she is claiming. The UK is not a party to the Schengen Agreement of 14 June 1985 which was later incorporated into the framework of the EC Treaty. See Langrish, 1998.
53 SI 2000/2326, reg 18; Directive 68/360, Arts 4, 6 and 7.
54 Directive 68/360, Art 7. See also SI 2000/2326, reg 19.
55 Art 6.

whom the normal requirement of a residence permit may be dispensed with.[56] The access and residence rules for citizens of EEA states are due to be further liberalised and considerably simplified by virtue of the adoption of Directive 2004/38/EC, which must be implemented in the UK by April 2006.

The right of a citizen of an EEA state to work on equal terms with the indigenous workers of the Member State is enshrined by Article 39(2) of the EC Treaty and by Regulation 1612/68 (as amended by Directive 2004/38). In addition to providing for equal treatment for workers' families, these provisions are concerned with ensuring equality of access to jobs and equality of treatment within jobs. They provide freedom of access in the sense that other nationals of other Member States must be free to receive and to take up offers of employment without discrimination, and must receive the same support from the state employment services as indigenous workers. In addition, equality of treatment requires the removal of all laws attaching different terms to the contracts of overseas workers, and provision for equal access to training, trade union membership and representation rights, and social security benefits and fiscal subsidies.[57]

Obligations of employers under immigration and asylum legislation

3.13   The regulatory effect of immigration controls was further reinforced by the passage of the Asylum and Immigration Act 1996, which makes it an offence[58] punishable by a fine[59] for an employer to employ a person who has not been granted leave to enter or remain in the United Kingdom, or in the case of one who has been granted leave, whose leave is no longer subsisting or whose right to take up employment is subject to a condition which he or she does not satisfy. The employer has a defence in a number of situations, including where, prior to the employment beginning, 'there was produced to the employer a document which appeared to him to relate to the employee and to be of a description specified in an order by the Secretary of State', and the employer retained the document or a copy of it.[60] However, this defence is not available where the employer (in practice the relevant senior employee[61]) knew that the employment was in breach of immigration law.[62]

56   Arts 6 and 7.
57   For a full account (prior to the changes made by the 2004 Dirctive), see Barnard, 2000a: 120–154, and, in relation to the rules governing co-ordination of social security for migrant workers, see Wikeley, 2002: ch 3. The right to remain in residence after retirement or in the case of incapacity arising from employment is governed by Council Regulation 1251/70.
58   Asylum and Immigration Act 1996, s 8. For further discussion of the implications of this provision see Ryan, 1997.
59   This was initially set at a level not exceeding level 5 on the standard scale, but by virtue of the Asylum and Immigration (Treatment of Claimants, Etc) Act 2004, it has become possible to try offences under s 8 of the 1996 Act on indictment (as opposed to summarily as before) and without any upper limit to the fine which may be imposed.
60   Asylum and Immigration Act 1996, s 8(2), as amended. See SI 2004/755, Schedule, where the documents specified under this provision are listed.
61   The normal principles of vicarious liability for the acts of senior managers apply here; in addition, the Act (s 8(5)) stipulates that where an offence is proved to be committed by 'any director, manager, secretary or other similar officer of the body corporate' or 'any person who was purporting to act in any such capacity', they too shall be guilty of an offence. See also s 8(6).
62   Asylum and Immigration Act 1996, s 8(3). Regardless of whether this defence applies, the contract of employment of a worker who knowingly misleads his or her employer in circumstances where s 8 applies will almost certainly be void for illegality, with the result that common law claims along with claims which would otherwise arise under employment protection and/or equal treatment legislation will be barred: *Vakante v Addey and Stanhope School* [2004] EWCA Civ 1065; see below, para 3.31.

This part of the Act had a controversial passage, for two reasons. First, it places an onerous obligation upon employers who may not always be in a good position to ascertain the significance of documents which are offered to them as proof of an individual's right to work in the United Kingdom. In the case of certain individuals who are exempt from the need for a work permit, the only proof of the right to work may be their passport,[63] but the effect of this may be apparent 'only by applying a detailed knowledge of the Immigration Rules and law'.[64] The relevant rules of immigration law are subject to periodic changes, making the position of the potential employer even more problematic.

Second, the Act can be seen as imposing a set of obligations upon employers which will make them more reluctant to employ individuals who *appear* not to have United Kingdom citizenship, and to that extent, will have an adverse impact upon particular racial groups. Arguably, then, it may encourage behaviour by employers which is racially discriminatory. However, it is not clear that an employer who refuses to employ an individual because of doubts over his or her right to work thereby commits an act of racial discrimination. In *Dhatt v McDonald's Hamburgers Ltd*,[65] a case decided prior to the passage of the 1996 Act, the Court of Appeal held that no breach of the Race Relations Act 1976 had occurred in a case where an employee, who was born in India and held Indian citizenship, was dismissed for failing to convince his employer that he had the right to take up employment in the UK. The evidence offered by the employee, namely his passport stamped with the words 'Given leave to enter the United Kingdom for an indefinite period', should have been adequate to establish his right to work, had the employer been aware of the relevant principles of immigration law. However, the Court held that the complainant had not been the subject of direct discrimination against him on the grounds of his *race*. It was also suggested that if the case were to be viewed as one of indirect discrimination, the steps taken by the employer would provide a defence of justification.[66] This second aspect of the judgment seems particularly questionable. It could be said that the employer in this case did not take adequate steps to ascertain the correct legal position.

If a similar case to *Dhatt* were to arise again after the 1996 Act, an employer would have a defence against criminal liability where the employee had presented, prior to the beginning of the employment, a document of the type, specified by order, which established his or her right to take up the employment in question. Given the existence of this defence, it is arguable that an employer would not be justified in dismissing or refusing to hire an individual on the grounds of their ethnic origin or nationality when they were, *objectively*, entitled to work. However, a more difficult question is whether an employee from a minority ethnic group can claim to have been the victim of racial discrimination where he or she is required, by a potential employer, to take steps to establish their right to work. It is conceivable that an employer could claim that such steps were justified by the combined effect of the immigration rules and the threat of prosecution under the 1996 Act. Nevertheless, it would be stretching this principle a long way to allow the employer to impose such requirements

---

63   Such individuals include those who have been granted indefinite leave to enter and remain in the UK, EEA nationals, and individuals in the categories of non-work permit employment as outlined in the text.

64   See Macdonald and Blake, 1995: p 288.

65   [1991] IRLR 130. See also below, para 6.16.

66   On the difference between direct and indirect discrimination, and the role of the justification defence, see below, para 6.11.

upon an employee who could show that he or she held UK citizenship (*Dhatt*, it must be remembered, was not such a case).

Access to employment: non-discrimination

3.14   The traditional approach of the common law to the hiring process was based on freedom of contract: the employer was free to refuse to hire a person for any reason, no matter how capricious, or for no reason at all.[67] However, discrimination in hiring is now prohibited by statute in relation to a number of specified criteria. In particular, decisions may not be based on the sex, sexual orientation, race, religion or belief, or disability of the applicant.[68] A wide range of regulations which formerly excluded women workers from certain jobs on health and safety grounds were repealed in the 1980s,[69] leaving only a few such exclusions in place; a large body of regulations restricting the employment of children below the school leaving age remains in force. These provisions are considered in more detail in later chapters.[70] Legislation also forbids employers to hire or to refuse to hire an individual on the basis of their current membership or non-membership of a trade union. The principal aim behind the introduction of this legislation was to restrict the operation of the pre-entry closed shop.[71]

3.15   Additionally, an employer may not refuse to hire an individual on the basis of a 'spent conviction' as that is defined by the Rehabilitation of Offenders Act 1974.[72] The Act does not provide any explicit civil remedy for such discriminatory action by an employer; there is no provision for damages to be awarded to a disappointed job applicant, nor for the employer to be required to hire him or her. The Act does provide, however, that the individual is permitted to conceal a spent conviction in answer to a question put to them by a prospective employer, and that 'the person questioned shall not be subjected to any liability or otherwise prejudiced in law by reason of any failure to acknowledge or disclose a spent conviction'.[73] In effect, then, those who go on to become employees are protected by the general law relating to dismissal: the employer may not later lawfully dismiss them if it should emerge that they lied about the spent conviction prior to being hired. Such a dismissal would be both a breach of contract at common law and equivalent to being an automatically unfair dismissal for statutory purposes. However, if an individual gives a misleading answer in relation to a conviction which is not spent, he or she commits a misrepresentation which renders the contract voidable at common law. It is also unlikely that an employer who finds out about such a conviction would be regarded as committing an unfair dismissal if it decided to terminate the employment.[74]

---

67   As restated in *Allen v Flood* [1898] 1 AC 1, 173 (Lord Davey).
68   See generally our analysis in ch 6 below, in particular at paras 6.34–6.40
69   By virtue of SDA 1986 and EA 1989. See Deakin, 1990a.
70   See ch 4, para 4.79 below.
71   TULRCA 1992, ss 137-143; see below, ch 8, at paras 8.27–8.32
72   Rehabilitation of Offenders Act 1974, s 4(3). There are numerous derogations from this principle for particular occupations (see the Rehabilitation of Offenders 1974 (Exceptions) Order 1975, SI 1975/1023, as amended) and the notion of a 'spent conviction' is only applicable to certain offences.
73   Rehabilitation of Offenders Act 1974, s 4(2).
74   *Torr v British Railways Board* [1977] IRLR 184; and, more generally on pre-contract misrepresentations and dismissal law, see *O'Brien v Prudential Assurance Co Ltd* [1979] IRLR 140, discussed below, para 5.147.

Active employment policy

3.16   In the modern period, state direction of labour to particular employments has been implemented only as a temporary measure during periods of national emergency during the two world wars. Regulations providing particular groups with a monopoly in the supply of labour for certain employments, such as the monopoly at one time enjoyed by Registered Dock Workers under the National Dock Labour Scheme, have been repealed.[75] A more persistent form of state intervention, however, is constituted by active employment policy, which consists of measures designed to promote employment opportunities and facilitate the hiring process in various ways.

Employment subsidies and welfare to work transitions

3.17   Numerous subsidy schemes from the 1970s onwards have sought to protect or to promote employment through the payment of direct or indirect subsidies to employers.[76] From a juridical point of view, the impact of active employment policy has turned out to be negligible. The statutes which authorised government departments and other bodies to operate these schemes did so in extremely broad terms,[77] and the detailed rules determining eligibility for the various subsidies took the form not of statutory instruments, but of administrative guidance or circulars which are subject to frequent changes. While this 'leaflet law' is of considerable interest in its own right and may give rise to protected legitimate expectations in public law, it has almost completely escaped close judicial scrutiny.[78]

From an economic viewpoint, there are difficulties inherent in the process of active labour market policy which go part of the way, at least, to explaining the brief life of most schemes. In the first place, they form a direct and highly visible charge on public expenditure. They also suffer from two related effects which may substantially detract from their effectiveness. One is the 'deadweight effect', or the tendency for subsidies to support jobs which employers would have created anyway. Then there is the 'displacement effect', according to which the creation of jobs in the form intended by the subsidy detracts from the creation of other, possibly more permanent forms of employment.

The framework for employment subsidies currently takes the form of the *New Deal* programme, which started to come into effect from April 1998. The general aim of the New Deal is to ease the process of transition of unemployed individuals from 'welfare to work'.[79] The scheme for young unemployed people offers 18–24 year olds a range of options for training and work experience, which include employment with an employer, an Environmental Task Force or a voluntary organisation, in each case leading to a recognised qualification, or full-time education for a year, leading to qualification at NVQ level 2 or above. The New Deal for those aged 25 or over offers broadly similar help to those in this age group who have been unemployed for two years or more. Other schemes have been put in place for lone parents in receipt of state benefits, disabled

---

75   The National Dock Labour Scheme was repealed by the Docks Work Act 1989.
76   See generally Freedland, 1980, 1983; Lindley, 1983; Syszczak, 1990.
77   Employment and Training Act 1973, s 2; Employment Subsidies Act 1978, s 1.
78   See Freedland, 1983.
79   For an assessment of the New Deal in the wider context of the Labour government's welfare policy, see Puttick, 1999.

persons claiming incapacity and disability benefits, and those aged between 50 and 59. Employers who take on the long-term unemployed under these programmes qualify for a range of wage subsidies.

The hiring process is also implicitly encouraged by social security benefits which are targeted on to lower paid employment. This is currently done through the system of tax credits which, while in some respects building on initiatives of the 1970s and 1980s, assumed its current form in 1999 with the introduction of the *working family tax credit*. This benefit was 'designed to make work pay for families, guaranteeing them a minimum income, above and beyond the minimum wage'; the government hoped that 'its clear link with employment [would] demonstrate the rewards of work over welfare and help ensure that people move off welfare into work'.[80] In 2003 a new *working tax credit*, covering both households and single earners on low incomes, was introduced.[81]

The rules governing eligibility for unemployment benefits are another important aspect of state intervention in the hiring process. Social security legislation has contained an element of work discipline from its inception, although the rigour of the tests involved has fluctuated over time. In the 1920s the unemployed had to show that they were 'genuinely seeking whole-time employment' in order to retain benefit, and in the 1980s, when unemployment again reached historically-high levels, a number of similar initiatives were taken with the aim of 'sharpening' work incentives.[82]

This process was taken a step further by the Jobseekers Act 1995. Disqualification for voluntary unemployment was retained, as were requirements that the individual should be available for work and actively seeking work; the penalties for failure were strengthened to the extent that entitlement could now be completely lost for a period of up to 26 weeks.[83] One of the most significant new provisions was the inclusion of a novel condition for receipt of benefits, namely that the claimant agrees to enter into a 'jobseeker's agreement' which lays out the steps that must be taken to find work. Loss of benefit may follow if the claimant fails to observe the agreement or to comply with directions issued by a local benefits officer.

The European Employment Strategy

3.18   A general framework for the conduct of active employment policy is now provided by the European Employment Strategy. The main legal source for this is the Employment Title of the EC Treaty, which was inserted by the Treaty of Amsterdam in 1997. Article 125 of the EC Treaty specifies that 'Member States and the Community shall ... work towards developing a co-ordinated strategy for employment and particularly for promoting a skilled, trained and adaptable workforce and labour markets responsive to economic change'. Article 126 outlines the more detailed obligations of the Member States. They are called on to co-ordinate their policies for the promotion of employment (which is to be regarded as an issue of 'common concern') within the Council, although, with

---

80   HM Treasury, *The Modernisation of Britain's Tax and Benefits System: Number Three. The Working Families Tax Credit and Work Incentives*, April 1998. The principal legislation governing the WFTC was the Tax Credits Act 1999.
81   The relevant legislation here is the Tax Credits Act 2002. See Wikeley, 2002: ch 10.
82   See Wikeley, 1989b; Deakin and Wilkinson, 1991.
83   Jobseekers Act 1995, s 19; see also the Jobseeker's Allowance Regulations, SI 1996/207 (as amended).

an eye to social policy, they are also to have regard to 'national practices related to the responsibilities of management and labour', a significant reference to the role of the social partners.[84] At the same time, the Member States are required act within the framework of the set of policies aimed at economic and monetary union (EMU) and in particular the broad economic guidelines which are issued annually by the Council as part of the process of ensuring economic stability and convergence.[85]

Article 127 calls on the Community to contribute to a high level of employment by encouraging and supporting the action of the Member States, and by *complementing* their action only 'if necessary' and after respecting 'the competences of the Member States'. The subsidiarity principle thereby carefully circumscribes the Community's role. Under Article 129 the Council can act to 'adopt incentive measures designed to encourage co-operation between Member States and to support their action in the field of employment through initiatives aimed at developing exchanges of information and best practices, providing comparative analysis and advice as well as promoting innovative approaches and evaluative experiences, in particular by recourse to pilot projects'. However, these limited measures 'shall not include harmonisation of the laws and regulations of the Member States'.

The framework put in place by the Employment Title is therefore facilitative rather than prescriptive; in that respect, it is an illustration (and arguably the principal one) of the novel technique of EU-level governance known as the 'open method of coordination'. Member States continue to have immediate control over their own employment policies, which may well be highly diverse in terms of their approach and effects. However, the Commission has been given the task of issuing employment guidelines to the Member States which in turn must formulate and report on their respective National Action Plans (NAPs). The first sets of guidelines have centred on four main 'pillars'. The first pillar is *employability*, which focuses on the prevention of long-term and youth unemployment by the means of vocational education and training and active labour market policies through work experience schemes and subsidies to employers offering training. Secondly, the *entrepreneurship* pillar attempts to make the process of business start-ups more straightforward, and incorporates steps to revise regulations affecting small businesses. The *adaptability* pillar has provided the main focus for functional flexibility and measures aimed at negotiation over the improvement of productivity through the reorganisation of working practices and production processes. The reduction and re-negotiation of working time, the flexible implementation of labour standards, and information and consultation over training issues have also come under this heading. Finally, the *equal opportunities* pillar has been concerned with raising awareness of issues relating to gender equality in terms of equal access to work, family friendly policies, and the needs of people with disabilities. It remains to be seen what impact the Employment Strategy will have on the convergence of active labour market policies of the different Member States.[86]

---

84   EC Treaty, Art 126(2).
85   EC Treaty, Art 126(1).
86   For assessments of the Employment Strategy and related aspects of the open method of coordination, see Biagi, 1998; Kenner, 1999a; Szyszczak, 2000b; Ashiagbor, 2000; Deakin and Reed, 2000a; De Schutter and Deakin, 2005; and on the wider context and history of active labour market policy at EC level, see Freedland, 1996.

IDENTIFYING DEPENDENT LABOUR

Classifying labour as 'dependent' or 'independent'

3.19   All systems of labour law draw a fundamental distinction between employment which is categorised as 'dependent' or 'subordinate' and that which is 'independent' or 'autonomous'.[87] In Britain this distinction principally takes the form of the classification of workers as either *employees*, on the one hand, or *self-employed* or *independent contractors* on the other. Employees are subject to the employer's common law powers of direction and control which, if they do not take the form of express contract terms, tend to be read into the contract as implied terms.[88] In return, employees come under the scope of employment protection and social security legislation: they may benefit from statutory rights to wage protection, limits on working time, income maintenance, and compensation for loss of employment.[89] By contrast, few of the burdens or benefits of dependent status apply to a relationship in which the worker is self-employed.

This basic picture must, however, be qualified in a number of respects. In the first place there is lack of consensus on the appropriate criteria for identifying dependence or subordination. The English courts have had occasion to use many different and potentially contradictory tests for this purpose, including 'control', 'integration', 'economic reality' and 'mutuality of obligation'.[90] However, this problem is unique neither to English law nor to the common law in general.[91] In most systems there is a conflict or tension between the use of criteria of *formal or personal subordination*, on the one hand, and those of *economic subordination*, on the other, as the principal tests of dependence.[92] The use of 'economic' criteria tends to result in a widening of the scope of statutory protection, encompassing relationships in which the worker retains extensive discretion over the manner and timing of performance of the work but is nevertheless bound to the employer through dependence on wages or salary for subsistence. In English law a move towards the adoption of 'economic' criteria occurred when the courts used the integration test to extend employee status to certain professionals, such as doctors or accountants, who were employed within large organisations,[93] and also when they invoked the 'economic reality' test to extend the scope of protective legislation to include certain part-time workers and homeworkers.[94] But in

---

87   Barbagelata, 1986; Hepple, 1986b: p 74; Burchell *et al*, 1999; P Davies and M Freedland, 2000, 2004. See also *Hall v Lorimer* [1994] IRLR 171, 174, in which Nolan LJ refers to 'the extent to which the individual is dependent or independent of a particular paymaster for the financial exploitation of his talents'.

88   See, for example, *Sim v Rotherham Metropolitan Borough Council* [1987] Ch 216, discussed in ch 4, below, at para 4.63.

89   See generally chs 4 and 5, below.

90   See below, paras 3.33–3.46

91   Couturier, 1988: p 87 refers to a 'long-running debate' in France on the distinguishing features of the contract of employment. See, for comparative perspectives, Pedrazzoli, 1988. On the use of the term 'subordination' to define the scope of the principle of equal pay in EU law, see Case C-256/01 *Allonby v Accrington and Rossendale College* [2004] IRLR 224, Judgment of the Court, at para 68, discussed below, para 3.55.

92   The contrast is clearly expressed in the decision of the US Supreme Court in *United States v Silk* 331 US 704 (1946) and in the judgment of Cooke J in *Market Investigations Ltd v Minister of Social Security* [1969] 2 QB 173. See also Deakin, 1986.

93   *Stevenson, Jordan and Harrison Ltd v Macdonald and Evans* [1952] 1 TLR 101; *Beloff v Pressdram Ltd* [1973] 1 All ER 241.

94   *Market Investigations Ltd v Minister of Social Security* [1969] 2 QB 173; *Airfix Footwear Ltd v Cope* [1978] ICR 1210.

general it cannot be said that economic criteria have successfully displaced rival tests: although control 'can no longer be regarded as the sole determining factor'[95] it must still be taken into account, and the more modern test of mutuality of obligation has led to a renewed emphasis on formality of commitment between the parties which has placed the status of many casual workers in doubt.[96]

A second problem is that the boundary between dependent and independent labour shifts according to the statutory context which is being considered. There is no universal dividing-line of general application between employees, who are protected by legislation, and the rest who are not. Thus while it is the case that only employees may qualify for most rights under ERA 1996, other statutes explicitly cover certain categories of the self-employed. In particular, protective legislation may be applicable to individuals who are independent contractors without having an identifiable business of their own. Some provisions of health and safety legislation apply to this group, as do equal pay and anti-discrimination legislation and legislation for basic labour standards in relation to minimum wages and working time. Moreover, although the self-employed have no protection against dismissal in the context of industrial action, a dispute between self-employed workers and their employer may form the basis for a legitimate trade dispute which may enable the individual organisers of industrial action and their trade union to avoid liability in tort. The precise scope of these statutes in relation to the self-employed is examined in greater detail below;[97] for the moment, it is sufficient to point out that the self-employed are very far from being excluded completely from labour law regulation.[98]

The process of classification is complicated by the lack of a uniform terminology in the different Acts of Parliament which regulate the employment relationship. In ERA 1996 the term 'employee' is used to describe dependent labour but the equivalent term for most of the benefits provided by SSCBA 1992 is 'employed earner'. In older statutes and judgments the terms 'servant' and 'workman' were used, but these expressions are not necessarily synonymous with the modern 'employee'. The terms 'employment', which is used in discrimination legislation, and 'worker', which is used in parts of ERA 1996 (such as Part II, consolidating provisions derived from the Wages Act 1986) and more generally under TULRCA 1992, NMWA 1998 and WTR 1998, offer yet another set of definitions, being wider in scope than 'employee' and therefore encompassing certain of the self-employed. Finally, specific provisions regulate the status of civil servants and certain others employed in the public sector.

Employees and employed earners

3.20   Under ERA 1996, an 'employee' is defined as an 'individual who has entered into or works under ... a contract of employment', and 'contract of employment' is defined, in turn, to mean 'a contract of service or apprenticeship,

---

95   *Market Investigations Ltd v Minister of Social Security* [1969] 2 QB 173, 185 (Cooke J).
96   The leading modern judgment is *O'Kelly v Trusthouse Forte plc* [1983] IRLR 369, discussed below, paras 3.37 and 3.45.
97   See paras 3.51–3.61.
98   The growing inclusion within protective labour statutes of certain categories of the self-employed, together with the difficulties faced by the courts in applying the distinction between employment and self-employment, led Freedland (2003) to argue for a unified concept of the 'personal employment contract' in place of the existing scheme of classification of employment relationships.

whether express or implied, and (if it is express) whether oral or in writing'.[99] No further definition is offered: the scope of the legislation, in effect, rests upon the common law tests as developed and applied over time by the courts. The principal rights which are thereby confined to employees concern unfair dismissal protection, redundancy compensation, minimum notice upon termination, guaranteed pay, the right to maternity, paternity and parental leave, and the right to return to work after taking such leave.

3.21   Certain European Union directives are stated to apply to employees: these include Directive 2001/23 on the protection of acquired rights in relation to transfers of undertakings and Directive 91/533 on information concerning terms and conditions of employment.[100] The European Court of Justice has decided that national courts are entitled to apply their own national definitions of employment status when applying these employment protection directives, even if this results in some inconsistency in the implementation of directives in the different Member States. In this vein, the Directive of 1991 on information concerning terms and conditions of employment applies to 'every paid employee having a contract or employment relationship defined *by the law in force in a Member State and/or governed by the law in force in a Member State*' (emphasis added),[101] and is stated to be 'without prejudice to national law and practice concerning: the form of the contract or employment relationship, proof as regards the existence and content of a contract or employment relationship, [and] the relevant procedural rules'.[102] By contrast, the Court has insisted on wide definitions and greater conformity to a single standard throughout the Member States for the term 'worker' set by European Union law in cases concerning freedom of movement and equal opportunities, on the grounds that these two areas are concerned with 'fundamental rights' contained in the EC Treaty and recognised as such by the jurisprudence of the Court.[103]

3.22   Income taxation and social security legislation also divide the labour force into the two principal groups of employees and the self-employed. Income from employment under a contract of service is taxable under Schedule E which means, among other things, that the employer is responsible for making the relevant deduction at source and paying the amounts over to the Inland Revenue under the PAYE system.[104] Under social security legislation, an 'employed earner' is liable to pay primary Class 1 national insurance contributions on his or her earnings up to the upper earnings limits and their employer, in addition to being under a legal duty to deduct these sums at source, must also pay secondary

---

99   ERA 1996, s 230(1), (2).

100   By contrast, Directive 98/59 on Collective Redundancies uses the term 'worker'; the implications of this, if any, are unclear.

101   Directive 91/533, Art 1.

102   Directive 91/533, Art 6. See also Directive 94/33 on the protection of young people at work, which applies (subject to derogations) to 'any person under 18 years of age having an employment contract or an employment relationship defined by the law in force in a Member State and/or governed by the law in force in a Member State' (Article 2(1)).

103   In the context of free movement see the ruling in Case 53/81 *Levin v Staatssecretaris van Justitie* [1982] ECR 1035, discussed at para 3.12, above, and in relation to equality of opportunity, see Case C-256/01 *Allonby v Accrington and Rossendale College* [2004] IRLR 224, discussed further, below, para 3.55. It should be noted that the term 'worker' does not necessarily bear the *same* wide meaning in these two different contexts: see *Allonby*, Judgment of the Court, at para 63.

104   Income Tax (Earnings and Pensions) Act 2003, Part 11.

Class 1 national insurance contributions on the employee's earnings, for the purpose of which no upper limit applies. Under SSCBA 1992, an 'employed earner' is defined as an individual who is 'gainfully employed under a contract of service'.[105] By contrast, workers who are self-employed arrange their own payments of income tax under Schedule D, with the opportunity to set their tax off against a range of expenses, and pay Class 2 and/or Class 4 national insurance contributions without involving their employer in any additional liability to contribute. The adoption of self-employment by the worker may therefore bring significant tax and contribution savings to both parties to the contract.[106] On the other hand, only an employed earner who has paid Class 1 contributions can qualify for the jobseeker's allowance[107] and rights to statutory maternity pay and statutory sick pay are also confined to 'employed earners' in this sense.[108]

3.23 It might be thought that since the same concept of the contract of employment or service underlies the definitions used in employment, social security and tax legislation, a common test should be applied which would result in an individual having a single status for these different purposes. This would also seem to accord with the philosophy underlying the division between employees and the self-employed. Employment protection and social security legislation are both forms of regulation designed to protect the employee against risks arising from loss of income and/or employment. They are appropriate for relationships characterised by a high degree of personal and economic dependence between employer and worker, but much less so in cases of self-employment in which the worker is by definition not so highly dependent upon a single employer over a substantial period of time. Moreover, in determining employee status, courts and tribunals frequently have recourse to precedents deriving from legislation of a different kind from that which is immediately at issue, as well as from the cases concerning the vicarious liability of the employer at common law.[109]

However, it cannot be assumed as a general rule that a decision from one area of law will necessarily determine the outcome in another, and, indeed, the recent practice of the courts tends to suggest that they will not pay much regard to the tax or social security law status of the worker when deciding on their status for employment law purposes. There may be good reasons for treating each area of law separately. For example, it is arguable that in cases of tax and

---

105 SSCBA 1992, ss 1(2)(a)(i), 2(1)(a); in addition, primary Class 1 contributions are also payable by individuals employed in an office with emoluments subject to income tax under Schedule E. Under SSCBA 1992, s 122(1), a 'contract of service' is defined as 'any contract of service or apprenticeship whether written or oral and whether express or implied'. On the meaning of 'gainfully employed', see *Vandyk v Minister of Pensions and National Insurance* [1955] 1 QB 29.

106 For example, in *Hall v Lorimer* [1994] IRLR 171, the respondent had over a period of time received fees of £32,875 in respect of his employment, against which he had incurred expenses of £9,250. It was only by establishing that he was self-employed that he was able to set the latter sum off against the former, so reducing the net sum on which he was liable to pay income tax. See below, para 3.46.

107 Jobseekers Act 1995, s 2.

108 See SSCBA 1992, ss 164(1), 171(1) (statutory maternity pay), and ss 151 and 163(1) (statutory sick pay), and see further below, paras 6.103 and 4.111, respectively, on the more detailed qualifying conditions for these benefits.

109 See, eg, the important tax case of *Hall v Lorimer* [1994] IRLR 171, in which the judgment of Nolan LJ refers to cases in social security law (*Market Investigations Ltd v Minister of Social Security* [1969] 2 QB 173) and employment law (*O'Kelly v Trusthouse Forte plc* [1983] IRLR 369 and *Lee Ting Sang v Chung Chi-Keung* [1990] IRLR 236).

national insurance, the public interest in ensuring the efficient collection of revenue should weigh strongly against any attempts by the parties to adopt the form of self-employment in order simply to avoid paying the normal incidence of tax. In cases involving vicarious liability, the interests of third parties – tort victims – are at stake. Where, on the other hand, no third party is directly affected by the parties' own determination of the worker's status, as will tend to be the case with regard to employment protection, the courts might be justified in paying greater regard to the parties' expressed wish to adopt self-employment. But to take this view would be to assume that the worker has made a conscious choice to weigh up the costs and benefits of employee status, when, in practice, it may well be the case that he or she has been presented by the employer with a standard form agreement which there has been no effective opportunity to modify. Moreover, fragmenting the status of the worker across different areas of law can produce real hardship. This is the case, for example, where casual workers, who are often treated as dependent labour for tax purposes, and therefore have their income tax deducted at source, fail to qualify as employees for labour law purposes.[110] It can also result in serious conceptual confusion of the kind which arises when workers who are regarded as self-employed in respect of employment law are treated as 'servants' or employees for the purposes of triggering the vicarious liability of their employer in tort.[111] But for the time being at least, it seems that there is no prospect of a unified approach emerging.

Fact or law?

3.24   The lack of a unified approach has arisen partly because consistency in the application of the statutory tests has been sacrificed to a perceived need to defer to the decisions of lower-level tribunals whenever possible. In *O'Kelly v Trusthouse Forte plc*[112] the Court of Appeal decided by a majority (Ackner LJ dissenting) that the application of the legal criteria for identifying a contract of employment was a 'question of mixed law and fact' to which several correct answers are possible. Because appeals may only lie from employment tribunals on a point of law,[113] this means that the appellate courts have no power to interfere with the finding of an employment tribunal unless the tribunal adopts the wrong test, states the law incorrectly, or applies the law in a perverse way, in the sense of reaching a decision which 'no reasonable tribunal would make'. Although in principle it is open to the EAT or Court of Appeal to substitute their own decision for that of the tribunal if they decide that the tribunal made an error of law,[114] this will not happen as a matter of course. Under this approach, it is not possible to lay down anything other than the most general of guidelines for tribunals, with the result that the position of casual workers such as the applicants in *O'Kelly* is at best uncertain, at worst one of exclusion from the scope of statutory protection. It also means that tribunals may legitimately decide essentially similar cases in different ways, thereby undermining the regulatory impact of employment protection legislation.

---

110 This is by no means unusual in practice. See the cases discussed in Burchell *et al*, 1999.
111 On this point, see the judgment of Sedley LJ in *Dacas v Brook Street Bureau (UK) Ltd* [2004] IRLR 358.
112 [1983] ICR 728.
113 ETA 1996, s 21. See further para 2.19, above.
114 This occurred, for example, in *Hellyer Bros v McLeod* [1987] ICR 526, in favour of the employer, and in *Lee Ting Sang v Chung Chi-Keung* [1990] IRLR 236, in favour of the employee.

Prior to *O'Kelly* there were numerous decisions in which it was either expressly stated or implicitly assumed that the question of whether a particular contract is a contract of employment or some other kind of contract was a question of law to which there was a right and a wrong answer,[115] and after *O'Kelly* the House of Lords held in *Davies v Presbyterian Church of Wales*[116] that the employment status of a church minister was also a question of law. In *Hellyer Bros v McLeod*,[117] however, the Court of Appeal distinguished *Davies* and preserved the status of *O'Kelly* on the grounds that the former was a decision concerning the construction of a written contract, whereas the latter, involving an arrangement based partly on conduct and partly on writing, fell to be decided as a question of mixed fact and law. In principle there seems to be no good reason for drawing such a distinction, nor can it be inferred from the relevant provisions of the employment protection legislation. On the contrary, the legislation implicitly negates such a distinction, defining a contract of employment as 'a contract of service ... *whether express or implied, and (if it is express) whether oral or in writing*' (emphasis added).[118] However, in *Carmichael v National Power plc*[119] the House of Lords reaffirmed the view laid out in *O'Kelly*. According to the majority opinion of Lord Irvine of Lairg LC, the construction of an employment contract could only be question of pure law if the parties had intended the written documents passing between them to be the exclusive source of their agreement. In the view of Lord Hoffmann, who gave a concurring opinion, whether the parties had such an intention in a given case was itself a question of fact. In the construction of employment contracts, it would normally be open to a tribunal to take into account the behaviour of the parties after entering into the relationship of employment as well as their subsequent understanding of what the contract required them to do. Cases of completely written contracts of employment would therefore be 'untypical'.[120]

While the flexible approach to construction advanced by Lord Hoffman has much to commend it in the context of employment contracts, it remains highly undesirable that crucial questions concerning the applicability of employment protection legislation cannot be settled according to a clearer framework of principle. In this context, what is of paramount importance is not the artificial and unsatisfactory distinction between completely written and partly oral or implicit agreements, which entered employment law after *Davies* and *Hellyer*, but the need for consistency in the application of the law if the aims of protective legislation are not be frustrated. Notwithstanding *Carmichael*, the appellate tribunal or court is still entitled to intervene in a case where the employment tribunal misconstrues the meaning of contractual documents or fails to apply the correct test for the implication of a contract term, since these amount to errors of law. In the end, then, it is for the appellate court itself to define what

---

115 See *Young & Woods Ltd v West* [1980] IRLR 201; *Addison v London Philharmonic Orchestra Ltd* [1981] ICR 261; *WHPT Housing Association Ltd v Secretary of State for Social Services* [1981] ICR 737; *President of the Methodist Conference v Parfitt* [1984] IRLR 141.
116 [1986] ICR 280. On the status of ministers of religion, see below, para 3.70.
117 [1987] ICR 526, 537.
118 ERA 1996, s 230(1), (2).
119 [2000] IRLR 43; see also the Privy Council case of *Lee Ting Sang v Chung Chi-Keung* [1990] IRLR 236, 239 (Lord Griffiths), referring to 'the threat of the appellate courts being crushed by the weight of appeals if the many borderline cases were considered to be questions of law'.
120 [2000] IRLR 43, 46.

amounts, in a given case, to an error of law *within* the wider process of determining employment status. Given that this is so, it is far from clear that the decision in *Carmichael* will reduce the volume of cases going to the courts on appeal. It seems more likely that *Carmichael*, by preventing appellate courts laying down general guidelines for tribunals to follow, will engender greater uncertainty in the operation of the law and provide further opportunities for litigation.

Parties' own choice: waiving employee status

3.25   There are two parts to the process by which the courts identify dependent labour: 'in order to enter the magic circle of employees, the worker has to solve not only the riddle of "contract" but also that of "employment"'.[121] We shall begin our analysis by considering the role of contract before looking in more detail at the principal tests of employment, which to an increasing degree, particularly in the case of the test of 'mutuality of obligation', have become imbued with a contractual logic.

An issue which arises at the outset, given the contractual foundations of the employment relationship, is how far the parties can make their own explicit designation of employment status, in the contract or otherwise. On one view, the status of the worker is a question which only the court can resolve, by looking at all the evidence. If the 'reality' is one of employee status, the parties cannot override this by 'choosing' to adopt self-employment in order to avoid the impact of tax and protective legislation or for any other purpose: a 'statement that ... [a worker] supplies [services] as a self-employed worker is not conclusive of his status, since it has been said many times that whether someone is an employee is a matter of analysing all the rights and obligations created by the contract'.[122] Similarly, in the final analysis it is for the court and not for the parties to determine whether a contractual nexus can be inferred from the regular practice of work being carried out in return for payment.

It is possible to go further, and argue that an attempted waiver of this kind should be ignored on public policy grounds. In *Ferguson v John Dawson & Partners (Contractors) Ltd*[123] Megaw LJ said that 'a declaration by the parties, even if it were incorporated in the contract, that the workman was to be, or was to be deemed to be, self-employed, an independent contractor, ought to be wholly disregarded – not merely treated as not being conclusive – if the remainder of the contractual terms, governing the realities of the relationship, showed the relationship of employer and employee'. One reason for taking this view is that any other will fail to accord adequate recognition to the power of statutory regulation to override the common law: hence it should not be open to the parties themselves 'by their own whim, by the use of a verbal formula, unrelated to the reality of the relationship, [to] influence the decision on whom the responsibility for the safety of workmen, as imposed by statutory regulations, should rest'.[124] The full application of health and safety legislation may be

---

121   Hepple, 1986b: p 71.
122   *McMeechan v Secretary of State for Employment* [1995] IRLR 461, 463 (Mummery J). See also the judgments of the Court of Appeal, [1997] IRLR 353.
123   [1976] 1 WLR 1213, 1223. The statement in the text is, on one view, *obiter*, since Megaw LJ decided the case on a separate ground.
124   [1976] 1 WLR 1213, 1223. See also *Lane v Shire Roofing Co (Oxford) Ltd* [1995] IRLR 493, 496 (Henry LJ).

thought to be of paramount importance from a public policy perspective. However, similar arguments could also be made in the context of the rights contained in employment legislation, much of which explicitly limits the contractual power of the employer in the interests of protecting the employee, and to tax and national insurance regulations, one purpose of which is to ensure the efficient collection of revenue.[125]

Nevertheless, arguments based on public policy have not won universal approval. In *Calder v H Kitson Vickers & Sons (Engineers) Ltd*[126] Ralph Gibson LJ said that 'a man is without question free under the law to contract to carry out certain work for another without entering into a contract of service. Public policy has nothing to say either way'. This does not mean that the courts will simply validate whatever status the parties choose to confer on themselves, if all the evidence points the other way; but in a finely balanced case, the parties' own view of their relationship may tip the scales in one direction or another: 'since the law looks to substance and not to form, the fact that the parties honestly intend that between themselves the contract shall be a contract for services and not a contract of service is not conclusive but it is a relevant fact, and when parties do deliberately agree for the man [sic] to be self-employed it may afford strong evidence that that is their real relationship'.[127]

Substitution clauses

3.26 More subtle forms of contracting out may be available to the parties. One route is for the parties to enter into a formal agreement containing a term which is incompatible with employee status. This could be a term denying that the employer has any obligation to provide work on a continuing basis, a provision which may lead a court to conclude that the relationship lacks the necessary 'mutuality of obligation' to be a contract of employment.[128] Another example is a term according to which the worker is not required to provide his or her personal service, but can nominate a substitute. In *Express and Echo Publications Ltd v Tanton*[129] the presence of such a term persuaded the Court of Appeal that the applicant was not an employee. The applicant argued in vain that this term was not observed in practice and did not reflect the way in which the parties' relationship had been conducted. *Tanton* has since been followed in a line of cases in which courts have held that the presence of a 'substitution

---

125 See, eg, *Rennison v Minister of Social Security* (1970) 10 KIR 65.
126 [1988] ICR 232, 251.
127 [1988] ICR 232, 251. For further illustrations of this approach see *Massey v Crown Life Assurance Co Ltd* [1978] ICR 590, 596 and *WHPT Housing Association Ltd v Secretary of State for Social Services* [1981] ICR 737, and, in the context of the definition of 'worker' under WTR 1998, *Redrow Homes (Yorkshire) Ltd v Wright* [2004] IRLR 720, at para 21 (Pill LJ); by contrast, clauses providing for workers to be self-employed were ignored in *Young & Woods Ltd v West* [1980] IRLR 201; and in *Catamaran Cruisers Ltd v Williams* [1994] IRLR 386, where other factors pointed strongly to employee status. See also *Thames TV Ltd v Wallis* [1979] IRLR 136 in which the court expressly disapproved attempts to contract out of unfair dismissal legislation by this route, and Case C-256/01 *Allonby v Accrington and Rossendale College* [2004] IRLR 224 for an argument that, in the context of the right to equal pay for equal work under Art 141 of the EC Treaty, a worker with a merely 'notional' independence should fall under the scope of protection (Judgment of the Court, at para 71).
128 See below, para 3.36. For an empirical study providing evidence of the use of such terms, see Burchell *et al*, 1999: ch 6.
129 [1999] IRLR 367.

clause' is enough to deflect not only employee status,[130] but also the possibility that the applicant might qualify for certain rights as a self-employed 'worker' under a contract to supply personal services.[131] This is because the substitution clause is said to negative the 'irreducible minimum of obligation' which must be present in any contract, whether for employment or self-employment, which involves the provision of personal service.

If *Tanton* were to be regularly followed, workers would have little or no protection against the insertion, by employers, of status-denying clauses into standard sets of terms and conditions which are very rarely if ever the subject of individual negotiation. According to Peter Gibson LJ's judgment in that case, the first task of a court or tribunal is to identify the contract terms. If it appears that a term is present which is incompatible with employee status, there is no need to go further and consider the range of factors discussed above. This approach elevates the role of the formal contract term in determining issues of status, at the expense of a more fully-rounded view of the bargain entered into by the parties. In this context, the post-*Tanton* case law arguably pays insufficient regard to the need to interpret employment contracts flexibly according to the approach laid down by the House of Lords in *Carmichael v National Power plc*,[132] which gives the courts some leeway to interpret the terms of the contract in the light of the behaviour of the parties during its performance. While, in principle, it is not possible to ignore an express term if it is clear and unambiguous, a substitution clause which is uncertain in its scope or meaning might carry little weight if the parties never relied upon it in practice, or if it is contradicted by other factors within the overall 'factual matrix' being considered by the court.[133] It is also open to a court, following entirely orthodox rules of construction, to find that an unusual term in a standard-form agreement does not form part of the contract if the party seeking to rely on it did not bring to the other's attention prior to the contract being made,[134] although this argument may require the term in question to have been contained in a separate document from the main part of the agreement,[135] which may not often be the case in the context which we are currently considering. Finally, some courts have suggested that even a clearly-worded 'substitution clause' will not necessarily defeat employee status, for the reason that a *limited* or *partial* right to substitute another to do part of the agreed work may not be incompatible with the existence of a contract of employment.[136] For these various reasons, it is by no means certain that a would-be 'substitution clause' will, without more, have the effect of avoiding 'employee' or 'worker' status.

130 *Staffordshire Sentinel Newspapers Ltd v Potter* [2004] IRLR 752; *Lanksford v Business Post Ltd* [2004] EWCA Civ 1448.
131 *Tanton* was used in this way in *Commissioners of Inland Revenue v Post Office Ltd* [2003] IRLR 199.
132 [2000] IRLR 43, in particular the opinion of Lord Hoffmann.
133 See, for discussion of *Tanton* along these lines, *MacFarlane v Glasgow City Council* [2001] IRLR 7; *Byrne Bros. (Formwork) Ltd v Baird* [2002] IRLR 96; and *Redrow Homes (Yorkshire) Ltd v Wright* [2004] IRLR 720.
134 See Spencer, 1974.
135 See *Interfoto Picture Library Ltd v Stiletto Visual Pictures Ltd* [1989] QB 433.
136 See *MacFarlane v Glasgow City Council* [2001] IRLR 7, in which the EAT held that a limited power to delegate was not necessarily incompatible with the contract of employment; *Byrne Bros (Formwork) Ltd v Baird* [2002] IRLR 96, discussing the judgment of McKenna J. on this point in *Ready Mixed Concrete (South East) Ltd v Minister for Pensions and National Insurance* [1968] 2 QB 497; and the IR35 case of *Usetech Ltd v Young* [2004] EWHC 2248 (Ch), discussing the Privy Council decision in *Narich Pty Ltd v Commissioner of Pay-Roll Tax* [1984] ICR 286, to similar effect.

3.27   In addition, legislation provides that a formal agreement by an individual to waive protective rights under ERA 1996 or TULRCA 1992 is void[137] (subject to exceptions explicitly provided for in the Acts). These prohibitions on contracting out could, conceivably, be invoked to nullify a contract term which purports to derogate from an individual's status as an employee. However, there is an element of circularity here. Unless the individual can establish, on independent grounds, that they are employed as an employee, they cannot invoke the statutory prohibitions on contracting out. If they can establish this, however, the statutory provisions concerning derogations will probably be unnecessary, since any term which is merely a 'sham', as opposed to one which alters the substance of the relationship, will most likely be ignored by the courts when applying the common law tests of employee status.

The use of personal service companies and other intermediaries

3.28   A further route which the parties may adopt in order to deflect employee status is for the worker to contract to supply his or her services through a 'personal service company' set up for this purpose. There may, as a result, be no contract between the worker and the end user of his or her services. There is nothing unlawful, per se, in contracting for labour to be supplied in this way, and from the worker's point of view it was once advantageous to do so for tax reasons, since it was possible, by this route, to avoid paying income tax on the relevant earnings, and pay a much lower rate of corporation tax instead. That route has now been blocked off by reforms to tax law which introduced the so-called 'IR35' status for subcontractors operating through personal service companies.[138] In the employment law context, there are examples of the courts 'lifting the corporate veil' to find that, notwithstanding the use of the personal service company, there was a contractual nexus between the two principal parties to the transaction. This is more likely where, prior to entering into this type of arrangement, the worker concerned was previously directly employed as an employee by the same employer,[139] although there are decisions where even this was not enough to persuade the court to lift the veil.[140]

Agency work is another situation in which an intermediary – here, the agency or 'employment business' – comes between the worker and the end 'user'. Again, there are cases in which the courts have held that the user assumes the duties of an employer, either because the user exercises managerial powers in relation to the worker in such a way as to satisfy the common law test of 'control',[141] or because

---

137   ERA 1996, s 203; TULRCA 1992, s 288.

138   The IR35 legislation is contained in the Income Tax (Earnings and Pensions) Act 2003, Part II, ch 8 (for income tax) and SSCBA 1992, s 4A, inserted by the Welfare Reform and Pensions Act 1999 (for national insurance). See *R (on the application of the Professional Contractors Group Ltd) v IRC* 2002 STC 165 (in which a challenge to the legislation on human rights grounds was rejected); *Synaptek Ltd v Young* [2003] ICR 1149; and *Usetech Ltd v Young* [2004] EWHC 2248 (Ch).

139   This was the case in *Catamaran Cruisers Ltd v Williams* [1994] IRLR 386. On intermediary companies and 'lifting the corporate veil' more generally, see below, paras 3.68 and 3.96.

140   See *Hewlett Packard v O'Murphy* [2002] IRLR 4; *Lanksford v Business Post Ltd* [2004] EWCA Civ 1448.

141   *Motorola Ltd v Davidson* [2001] IRLR 4; although a different outcome was reached in *Hewlett Packard v O'Murphy* [2002] IRLR 4 and *Stephenson v Delphi Diesel Systems Ltd* [2003] ICR 471. The leading case on agency work is now *Dacas v Brook Street Bureau (UK) Ltd* [2004] IRLR 358. See below, paras 3.64–3.68.

a particular statutory provision allows the user to be treated as if it were the employer for certain purposes.[142] We consider agency work in more detail below.[143]

The effects of illegality on the contract of employment

3.29   If an employee is party to an agreement unlawfully to evade tax or national insurance contributions, or to commit some other unlawful act, the contract may be void on the grounds of illegality. This will have the effect of depriving the employee of any statutory employment rights, since he or she will be unable to show that they were employed 'under a contract of employment' or other contract at the relevant time. The scope of this principle is unclear, however, and its application, in such a way as to defeat otherwise valid claims for employment protection, is highly controversial.

3.30   Most cases concerning illegality have arisen out of attempts to defraud the Inland Revenue, for example by agreeing to a certain payment being made without any deduction of income tax or national insurance contributions. Such an agreement will be void *ab initio* regardless of whether either party was unaware that the arrangement in question was illegal.[144] Where, by contrast, it is the employer who takes the initiative in the non-payment of tax, the outcome will depend on the employee's state of mind. If he or she did not know that his or her wages were being paid without tax being deducted, or that the employer was attempting to defraud the Revenue, the employee may be able to enforce the contract which is said to be 'tainted by illegality', as opposed to being void *ab initio*. The test of knowledge is subjective – what did the employee actually know or understand? – but a tribunal may be justified in inferring that the employee was, at least, familiar with the normal arrangements for deduction of tax and was put on notice that something was amiss if the normal deductions did not appear in the wage slip or other statement of pay.[145] In a case where both employer and employee were 'in it up to the neck', the employee was held to have forfeited the right to statutory employment protection.[146]

The ground for denying efficacy to the contract of employment in this situation is public policy, and in particular the need to ensure the effectiveness of the revenue collection system. An employee who attempts to cheat the system should not, it is said, be in a position to benefit from the protection provided by employment law. However, in most cases it is the employer who presses for arrangements of this kind to be made, and who benefits most clearly from them. Research has shown that wages of workers in the 'shadow economy' tend to be paid below the level of normal wages, the difference representing the tax and national insurance contributions which the employer is able to avoid paying.[147] It is odd that an employee who does not object to such an arrangement, and who perhaps may be in no position to do so while still retaining that

---

142 *Abbey Life Assurance Co. Ltd v Tansell* [2000] IRLR 387; see below, para 3.68.
143 See para 3.64 *et seq.*
144 *Miller v Karlinski* (1945) 62 TLR 85; *Salvesen v Simons* [1994] IRLR 52. A similar result follows if legislation forbids the formation of a particular contract, as is the case with child protection laws: Mogridge, 1981: p 24.
145 See *Davidson v Pillay* [1979] IRLR 275; *Corby v Morrison* [1980] IRLR 218; *Colen v Cebrian (UK) Ltd* [2004] IRLR 210; *Soteriou v Ultrachem Ltd* [2004] IRLR 870 (HC), [2004] EWCA Civ 1520, CA.
146 *Tomlinson v Dick Evans 'U' Drive Ltd* [1978] ICR 639.
147 S Smith, 1986.

employment, should then be punished by the loss of employment protection rights. The suggestion has therefore been made that tribunals should have regard to the importance, when weighing public policy considerations, of ensuring that statutory employment protection rights are not evaded, and should either enforce employment rights regardless of illegality affecting the contract or pay closer attention to the relative blameworthiness of employer and employee.[148]

Moreover, the line drawn between a case of defrauding the Revenue and one in which the parties legitimately but unsuccessfully attempt to arrange their affairs so as to as to limit tax liability is often so fine as to be virtually invisible.[149] In *Rennison v Minister of Social Security*[150] Bridge J saw through a scheme to describe weekly paid secretarial workers as self-employed for tax and national insurance purposes, holding that they were employees and liable to pay Class 1 national insurance contributions. There was no suggestion that the contracts they entered into were illegal as such, however. Similarly, in *Young & Woods Ltd v West*[151] the Court of Appeal held that the applicant was entitled to claim unfair dismissal on the grounds that 'in reality' he had a contract of employment, and that an attempt to present him as self-employed was a sham. It could easily, however, have held the arrangement to have been illegal, in which case the employee would have been unable to pursue his unfair dismissal claim. These cases are 'not readily distinguishable'[152] from others in which statutory rights have been forfeited on the public policy grounds mentioned above.

3.31 The principle of nullity may also apply in cases where overseas workers are employed under circumstances where they do not have the right to work in the United Kingdom. In *Vakante v Addey and Stanhope School*[153] the applicant, a Croatian national who had earlier entered the UK as an asylum seeker, falsely told his employer that he had the right to take up paid employment. He was subsequently dismissed for other reasons, and brought a claim alleging racial discrimination. The EAT and Court of Appeal ruled that the contract, having been entered into in contravention of immigration legislation and on the basis of a fraudulent representation by the applicant, was void from the outset, with the effect that the claim was barred.

3.32 Other recent decisions demonstrate a reluctance to exclude employment claims on illegality grounds. In *Leighton v Michael*[154] the EAT, under Mummery J, drew a distinction between a claim for unfair dismissal or redundancy compensation under ERA 1996, which 'is directly founded upon, relies upon and seeks to enforce the contract of employment', and a claim of sex discrimination under SDA 1975, which although it 'involves a reference to the contract to determine whether the person is "employed" within the meaning of the statute', is not a claim founded upon contract since it does not require the complainant to show that he or she was dismissed or otherwise deprived of contractual rights.[155] Attractive as this idea might

---

148 Mogridge, 1981: p 33.
149 See, eg, *Lightfoot v D & J Sporting Ltd* [1996] IRLR 64.
150 (1970) 10 KIR 65.
151 [1980] IRLR 201.
152 Mogridge, 1981: p 33.
153 [2004] EWCA Civ 1065. On the EAT judgment ([2004] ICR 279), see Forshaw and Pilgerstorfer, 2005.
154 [1996] IRLR 67.
155 [1996] IRLR 67, 69.

be, as a way of preventing unmeritorious attempts by employers to avoid protective obligations to employees, it seems to be based on a false distinction. Like ERA 1996, the SDA 1975 defines 'employment' exclusively in contractual terms.[156]

A sounder basis for the outcome in *Leighton* may be inferred from the later decision of the Court of Appeal in *Hall v Woolston Hall Leisure Ltd*.[157] The Court of Appeal reasserted the view that employment contracts which incorporated an unlawful method of payment, as opposed to an unlawful purpose, were unlikely to be void, at least where it was the employer who instigated the arrangement in question and the employee did not actively participate in the illegality. Mere knowledge of the illegality on the part of the employee would not be enough.[158] This argument would be equally applicable to employment protection cases. The *Hall* judgment is principally significant for the purposive approach taken to the interpretation of employment legislation. The case turned on the interpretation to be given to the Sex Discrimination Act 1975 by reference to the Equal Treatment Directive, 76/207. Mance LJ said: 'construing the 1975 Act in the light of the Directive, I doubt whether it is appropriate ... to treat the statutory requirement of a contract as subject to domestic conceptions of public policy which would prevent an employee from enforcing it in the English courts if she had sued upon it. The Directive contains no such reservation'.[159] It is possible that this approach could also be applied to purely domestic legislation, as a matter of statutory interpretation: even in the absence of a Directive, it is arguably inappropriate to operate the illegality doctrine in a rigid way where the effect of doing so is to deflect the intended application of protective legislation.

It does not follow that the doctrine of illegality would then be irrelevant in every case, but its scope would be limited and, possibly, clarified. It would remain open to a court to disqualify a claim arising under employment or equal treatment legislation where the claim in question was 'inextricably bound up' with the relevant illegality.[160] This would almost certainly be the case where the employment was entered into with a clearly illegal purpose which was known to the employee from the outset. A clearer focus on the issue of the causal link between the illegality and the claim in question would be preferable, in this context, to the somewhat artificial idea that claims arising from illegal employment contracts necessarily fall outside the scope of protective legislation.

---

156 SDA 1975, s 82(1); see below, para 3.55. This aspect of *Leighton* was upheld by the Court of Appeal in *Hall v Woolston Hall Leisure Ltd* [2000] IRLR 578, in part on the grounds that since sex discrimination is a form of 'statutory tort', a clear causal link between the illegality and the loss which forms the basis of the complaint would have to be shown before the doctrine can apply. While this is entirely correct, it still does not get round the problem that if the contract is void for illegality, the complaint falls at the outset since the complainant does not fall under the personal scope of the statute (see the judgment of the EAT in *Hall*, cited at [2000] IRLR 578, 584). *Hall* was approved but distinguished on its facts by the Court of Appeal in *Vakante v Addey and Stanhope School* [2004] EWCA Civ 1065.

157 [2000] IRLR 578.

158 See [2000] IRLR 578, 583 (Peter Gibson LJ), 588 (Mance LJ).

159 [2000] IRLR 578, 589.

160 On the 'inextricability' test, see the judgment of Peter Gibson LJ in *Hall* ([2000] IRLR 578, at para 42), and for an argument that, contrary to *Hall*, even this test should not apply in the context of EU Directives in the area of equality of treatment, see Forshaw and Pilgerstorfer, 2005.

Control

3.33 Having considered the role of 'contract' in the contract of employment, we now turn to examine in more detail the tests used by the courts in determining 'employment' or 'service'. A test which has been applied in some form or another since at least the last quarter of the nineteenth century and which retains a certain force today is that of 'control'. The best known expression of the test is that of Bramwell LJ in *Yewens v Noakes*:[161] a 'servant is a person who is subject to the command of his master as to the manner in which he shall do his work'. This dictum needs to be treated with a good deal of care, however. There is a sense in which 'the "control test" has been misapplied almost from the moment of its emergence'.[162] This is because the concept of 'servant' which Bramwell LJ was addressing was not the same as the modern day notion of 'employee'. The term 'servant' in the middle and late nineteenth century did not simply denote a worker who was wage-dependent as opposed to being self-employed; it was used to draw a distinction *within* the category of wage-dependent workers, namely between mainly manual workers who were classified as 'servants' or 'workmen' on the one hand, and higher-status employees such as professionals and managers on the other. The former group, but not the latter, were subject to the Master and Servant Acts and, after the repeal of those Acts, to the Employers and Workmen Act 1875 under which the magistrates retained a civil law jurisdiction to deal with employment disputes; similarly, early social legislation, such as the Workmen's Compensation Acts and National Insurance Acts, drew distinctions between manual and non-manual labour in terms of the scope of statutory coverage.[163] It was in the context of *this* distinction, and not that between dependent and independent labour in the modern sense, that the control test evolved.

Yewens v Noakes itself was a tax case, in which the court decided that a clerk, earning a substantial yearly salary, was not a servant, any more than were 'the manager of a bank, a foreman with high wages, persons almost in the position of gentlemen'.[164] The leading cases which later established Bramwell's dictum as a principal test of status were concerned with the scope of workmen's compensation[165] and national insurance legislation.[166] In this context, control was used to exclude from the scope of regulation those higher-status employees for whom the court considered protective legislation inappropriate,[167] as well as workers who were not in a direct employment relationship with the ultimate

---

161 (1880) 6 QBD 530, 532, 533.
162 Merritt, 1982: p 113
163 See the definitions of 'workman' and associated concepts in the Employers and Workmen Act 1875, s 10; the Employers Liability Act 1880, s 8; the Workmen's Compensation Act 1897, s 7(2); and the Truck (Amendment) Act 1887, s 2. The National Insurance Act 1911, s 1 and Sch 1, excluded from its provisions non-manual workers earning over £160 a year. The emergence of the 'employee' concept during the first half of the twentieth century is discussed by Deakin, 1998, 2000, and Deakin and Wilkinson, 2005: ch 2; on the same development in Australia, see Howe and Mitchell, 1999.
164 *Yewens v Noakes* (1880) 6 QBD 530, 538 (Thesiger LJ).
165 *Simmons v Heath Laundry Co* [1910] 1 KB 543. Cases of vicarious liability appear not to have played a major role in the development of the control test since at this time actions in vicarious liability were very rare as a consequence of the doctrine of common employment and the operation of the *volenti* defence.
166 *Scottish Insurance Comrs v Edinburgh Royal Infirmary* 1913 SC 751; *Hill v Beckett* [1915] 1 KB 578.
167 *Simpson v Ebbw Vale Steel, Iron & Coal Co* [1905] 1 KB 453.

employer. This was at a time when the internal contracting system was common in mining, shipbuilding, construction, textiles and iron and steel; foremen or 'butty workers' would be responsible for hiring gangs of workmen and for supplying their services to the employer. The foreman or butty was likely to be classified in law as an independent contractor,[168] while those directly under his command might not, for this reason, be regarded as under the control of the ultimate employer, who was thereby relieved of the legal responsibilities imposed by social legislation.[169]

The notion that a dependent worker is one whose mode of performance is closely monitored and controlled by a superior embodies a strong version of personal or formal subordination, which is not appropriate for many workers whom the modern law regards as employees. Bramwell's test would not classify as 'dependent' those workers who have a high level of occupational or professional training, or who have a substantial degree of discretion as to their hours of work and mode of performance. However, many doctors, lawyers, managers and others who work in large, bureaucratic organisations are self-evidently employed as employees and not as independent contractors. Moreover, the legal distinction between manual and clerical workers now has little or no place in the law; as far as workmen's compensation and social insurance are concerned it was replaced, after 1945, by the more clear-cut division between employees and the self-employed which we are familiar with in the modern law,[170] and which as we have seen was subsequently incorporated into employment protection legislation. For these various reasons, the control test as formulated by Bramwell has fallen into disuse.

If control is understood as the employer's right to dictate the precise way in which work is done, the test is anachronistic as Kahn-Freund argued: 'the control test postulates a combination of managerial and technical functions in the person of the employer, ie what to modern eyes appears as an imperfect division of labour'.[171] In a wider sense, however, the idea that an employee is one who agrees to *serve*, as opposed to producing finished goods or supplying a specified service, is still retained as one of the tests of employee status, and if control is understood as the employer's right to give orders and direct the general nature of the employee's work it is far from irrelevant in a modern context. According to MacKenna J in *Ready Mixed Concrete (South East) Ltd v Minister for Pensions and National Insurance*,[172] 'control includes the power of deciding the thing to be done, the means to be employed in doing it, the time when and the place where it shall be done. All these aspects of control must be considered in deciding whether the right exists in a sufficient degree to make one party the master and the other his servant'. Similarly, in *McMeechan v Secretary of State for Employment*[173] an agreement under which an agency worker agreed 'to fulfil the normal common law duties which an employee would owe to an employer so far as they are applicable', including

---

168 See, eg, *Vanplew v Parkgate Iron & Steel Co* [1903] 1 KB 851.
169 See, eg, *Littlejohn v Brown & Co Ltd* 1909 SC 169.
170 The National Insurance Act 1946, s 1(2), established two main classes of contributors, 'employed earners' (akin to employees) and others, in place of the multiplicity of categories which had operated under the 1911 Act and its successors.
171 Kahn-Freund, 1951: p 505.
172 [1968] 2 QB 497, 515.
173 [1995] IRLR 461, EAT; affd [1997] IRLR 353, CA; cf *Montgomery v Johnson Underwood Ltd* [2001] IRLR 269.

duties of fidelity, confidentiality and obedience to instructions, was for that reason held more likely to give rise to a contract of employment between himself and the agency. Control has also recently been invoked to support a finding that the user of an agency worker's labour may assume the status of his employer,[174] although this will not be the case unless a contractual nexus can also be implied between these two parties, assuming that one has not been expressed.[175] These cases demonstrate that while the control which exists under modern labour market conditions may be less personal and more bureaucratic in nature than that identified by the nineteenth century judges,[176] it is arguably no less important as a feature which separates the employment relationship from other forms of the provision of labour.

Integration

3.34 An alternative to control which sees the essence of employment as the employee's subjection to the rules and procedures of an organisation, rather than as subjection to personal command, is the integration test: 'one feature which seems to me to run through the instances is that, under a contract of service, a man is employed as part of the business and his work is done as an integral part of the business; whereas under a contract for services his work, although done for the business, is not integrated into it but is only accessory to it'.[177] When it was formulated this test was a response to the difficulties, referred to above, in applying Bramwell's test to professional employees, and adequately explains, for example, why a journalist working on a newspaper or nurses and doctors employed by a hospital will normally have contracts of employment. Thus in *Beloff v Pressdram Ltd* a highly-paid journalist was unable to argue that, given her high status, she could not be regarded as having a contract of employment, even though she worked full-time for the newspaper and was treated as an employee for tax and national insurance purposes. According to Ungoed-Thomas J, 'the greater the skill required for an employee's work, the less significant is control in determining whether the employee is under a contract of service'.[178]

The notion of which work is 'integral' to a business is not easily applied, however. The integration test may be useful for explaining the employee status of managerial and professional workers, but it is less effective in explaining the position of outworkers or workers employed by a sub-contractor of the ultimate user of labour: their work may frequently be 'integral' to the user business, without them necessarily being its employees. With the increasing tendency of employers to make use of 'outsourcing' of various kinds and to employ workers with a peripheral or 'marginal' attachment to the firm in order to reduce direct labour costs, the focus of the modern case law has shifted to two tests which often provide divergent answers, namely 'economic reality' and 'mutuality of obligation'.

---

174 *Motorola Ltd v Davidson* [2001] IRLR 4.
175 *Dacas v Brook Street Bureau (UK) Ltd* [2004] IRLR 358. See further below, para 3.67.
176 Cf H Collins, 1986.
177 *Stevenson, Jordan & Harrison v MacDonald & Evans* [1952] 1 TLR 101, 111 (Denning LJ).
178 [1973] 1 All ER 241, 250; see also *Cassidy v Minister of Health* [1951] 2 KB 343.

Economic reality

3.35   The test of business or 'economic' reality essentially asks whether the worker is in business on his or her own account, as an entrepreneur, or works for another who takes the ultimate risk of loss or chance of profit. Casual or irregular workers and others who may have a high degree of personal autonomy in their working arrangements may nevertheless be classified as employees under this test if they are economically dependent on one principal employer. In *Market Investigations Ltd v Minister of Social Security*[179] it was held that a part-time market researcher could be an employee for this reason, notwithstanding that she had 'a limited discretion as to when she should do the work'.

The same approach may be applied to skilled and professional workers who organise their own working schedules and do not come under close personal supervision. They will probably still be employees if the ownership of the relevant tools or equipment vests principally in the employer and if it is the latter who takes the residual risk of the business failing. The method of payment may give some indication as to who bears the residual risk, but this should not be taken too far. If the worker receives a regular salary or a wage based on time rates, there would normally be little doubt that he or she is an employee. Even if, on the other hand, he or she is paid on a piece-rate basis or receives either all of part of the wage in the form of profit-related pay, they may still be an employee. An employer's decision to link pay to performance or profits does not, in itself, imply that the worker undertakes responsibility for the management and profitability of the business in the sense used here.

As Lord Griffiths put it in *Lee Ting Sang v Chung Chi-Keung*,[180] there is a difference between 'a skilled artisan earning his living by working for more than one employer as an employee and ... a small businessman venturing into business on his own account as an independent contractor with all its attendant risks'. In this case, an appeal from Hong Kong, the Privy Council held that a skilled construction worker was employed as an employee, so as to come within the scope of health and safety regulations. The applicant neither hired his own helpers nor provided his own equipment; moreover, 'he had no responsibility for investment in, or management of, the work on the construction site, he simply turned up for work and chipped off concrete to the required depth upon the beams indicated to him on a plan by the [employer]... It is true that he was not supervised in his work, but this is not surprising, he was a skilled man and he had been told the beams upon which he was to work and the depth to which they were to be cut and the work was measured to see that he achieved that result'.[181]

This does not mean, however, that either a professional or a casual worker *must* be an employee so long as he or she does not have an identifiable business of his own. On the contrary, there is a category of workers who are self-employed without necessarily being entrepreneurs, for the reason that they lack dependence on any particular employer. This was the case in *Hall v Lorimer*,[182] where the

---

179 [1969] 2 QB 173, applying the US case of *United States v Silk* 331 US 704 (1946), where the term 'economic reality' originated; see also *Airfix Footwear Ltd v Cope* [1978] ICR 1210.
180 [1990] ICR 409, 414; see also *Ferguson v John Dawson & Partners (Contractors) Ltd* [1976] 1 WLR 1213.
181 Lord Griffiths, [1990] ICR 409, 413–414.
182 [1994] IRLR 171.

respondent was a skilled television technician who worked for around 20 separate companies on a series of short-term engagements. He was held to be self-employed, and therefore chargeable to income tax under Schedule D. According to Nolan LJ:

> ... the question, whether the individual is in business on his own account, though often helpful, may be of little assistance in the case of one carrying on a profession or vocation. A self-employed author working from home or an actor or a singer may earn his living without any of the normal trappings of a business ... the most outstanding feature to my mind is that Mr Lorimer customarily worked for 20 or more production companies and that the vast majority of his assignments ... lasted only for a single day.[183]

This approach makes sense given the context of the decision, namely the assessment of income over an extended period (here, a year) for the purpose of determining the incidence of tax. However, it leaves open the question of how the court should approach the designation of status in a case where it is required to consider the position of a worker during a short-term hiring for a particular employer. In *Lane v Shire Roofing Co (Oxford) Ltd*,[184] the claimant was a building worker who was hired by the defendant employer to carry out a re-roofing job for which he was to be paid according to a daily rate. The defendant 'considered it prudent and advantageous to hire for individual jobs'.[185] While carrying out the work, the claimant fell and was injured. It was held that he was an employee for the purposes of the job, and so was owed the common law duty of care with regard to his health and safety. According to Henry LJ, applying the test of economic reality, the 'business' involved in the work was that of the defendant, not the claimant. The health and safety context of *Lane* cannot be ignored; the courts appear to take a strict approach to claims that a worker is self-employed in this type of case. Nevertheless, it indicates that there may well be circumstances under which a pattern of successive short-term hirings with different employers is compatible with employee status.

Mutuality of obligation

3.36 Notwithstanding the clarity of the test of 'economic reality', recent decisions of the courts have placed a fresh emphasis on a form of personal control in the form of 'mutuality of obligation'. Mutuality is a necessary feature of all bilateral contracts: without reciprocal promises, the basic element of consideration will be lacking and the arrangement will have no contractual force.[186] In this fundamental sense, mutuality of obligation is a feature not just

---

183 [1994] IRLR 171, 175. Cf also *Wickens v Champion Employment* [1984] ICR 365, 371: the common law 'does not include as a necessary element the question whether the individual carries on a separate business. If it did, then it would follow that a casual worker must always be employed under a contract of service unless he has his own business and that, plainly [sic], cannot be the law'.
184 [1995] IRLR 493.
185 [1995] IRLR 493, 496 (Henry LJ).
186 A difficult question is whether a 'unilateral' contract – one involving the performance of an act in return for a promise – can constitute a 'contract of employment' or a 'contract for personal services' within the meaning of those terms in modern employment legislation. Recent decisions interpreting the 'worker' concept can be read as indicating that a unilateral contract is outside the scope of this legislation. See our analysis, below, at para 3.56, and the discussion of unilateral employment contracts by Freedland, 2003: p 89–90.

of contracts of employment, but also of contracts for the supply of personal services;[187] it cannot therefore function as an indicator of employee status.

However, a separate meaning of 'mutuality of obligation' entered employment law in the late 1970s:[188] with specific reference to the contract of employment, this referred to the presence of mutual commitments to maintain the employment relationship in being over a period of time. This was an adaptation of the idea that the contract of employment is more than just a contract to serve in return for wages; in addition, there is a *second tier of obligation* consisting of mutual promises of future performance. Mark Freedland's treatise, *The Contract of Employment*, published in 1976, contained this passage:

> At the first level there is an exchange of work for remuneration. At the second level there is an exchange of mutual promises of future performance. The second level – the promises to employ and to be employed – provides the arrangement with its stability and with its continuity as a contract. The promises to employ and to be employed may be of short duration or may be terminable at short notice; but they still form an integral and most important part of the contract. They are the mutual undertakings to maintain the employment relationship in being which are inherent in any contract of employment so called.[189]

One interpretation of Freedland's analysis is that the second tier of obligation, if not the subject of an express term, should normally be implied into the contract as a necessary incident of the employment relationship. However, a different interpretation is that work relationships in which the second tier of obligation is lacking for some reason do not constitute contracts of employment for the purposes of statutory employment protection. The second interpretation has only a tenuous connection, at best, to the first, and is, moreover, contradicted by a large number of older cases in which courts had no difficulty accepting the presence of an express right, on the part of the employer, to suspend work or terminate the employment relationship without notice (or on minimal notice), within the framework of a contract of service or employment.[190] Nor was the duration of the hiring, at this point, regarded as a significant factor pointing away from employee status.[191] But be that as it may, the mutuality test was put forward with increasing frequency from the mid-1980s onwards in cases involving workers hired on a casual, short-term or intermittent basis. Often the result was that work relationships of this kind were classified as falling outside the scope of

187 This is recognised in the growing case law concerning the 'worker' concept under NMWA 1998 and WTR 1998, and the concept of 'employment' under equal treatment legislation. See the decision of the Court of Appeal in *Mingeley v Pennock* [2004] IRLR 373, and our discussion at para 3.56 below.

188 There is an extensive if recent case law on the 'mutuality of obligation' test which dates back to *Airfix Footwear Ltd v Cope* [1978] ICR 1210 (although the EAT, in that case, found that there was sufficient evidence of mutuality to establish a contract of employment in a case concerning an outworker). The test received the approval of the Court of Appeal in *O'Kelly v Trusthouse Forte plc* [1983] ICR 728 and *Nethermere (St Neots) Ltd v Taverna and Gardiner* [1984] IRLR 240 and of the House of Lords in *Carmichael v National Power plc* [2000] IRLR 43.

189 Freedland, 1976b: pp 21–22. In his 2003 treatise, The *Personal Employment Contract*, which both updates and extends his earlier analysis, Freedland discusses this passage in the light of the intervening case law and the growing use by legislation of the 'worker' concept. See Freedland, 2003: pp 91-92.

190 See, in particular, *Marshall v English Electric Co Ltd* [1945] 1 All ER 653, discussed in the context of lay-off below, ch 4, at para 4.112.

191 On this point, see the discussion of Leighton, 1984.

protective employment legislation. This could be for one of two reasons: either there was no 'global' or 'umbrella' contract of employment linking separate hirings, with the result that applicants lacked the necessary continuity of employment to bring statutory claims for which a minimum period of service was required; or the individual hirings themselves, because of the absence of a commitment to make work available in future (on the part of the employer) and to be available for work (on the part of the worker), could not be classified as contracts of employment.

3.37 In the leading case of *O'Kelly v Trusthouse Forte plc*[192] the applicants, who were wine waiters, were employed by a hotel chain as so-called 'regular casuals'. This meant that they were hired periodically to work on a particular catering job and could be relied upon to offer their services at regular intervals; the employer kept a list of their names and gave them preferential treatment in the allocation of any available work. They had no other regular employment and, if they refused work offered to them by the employer, they would be taken off the preferential list. They claimed that they had been dismissed on the grounds of their membership of an independent trade union, a claim which does not depend upon continuity of employment but simply requires employee status at the time of dismissal.[193] There were two possible ways of construing the arrangements so as to find employee status: by interpreting each separate engagement as a contract of employment, or by finding a continuing or 'global' contract of employment which spanned the separate engagements. The employment tribunal held that they had neither a global contract of employment nor a series of separate ones. The EAT reversed on the second of these two points but the Court of Appeal restored the employment tribunal's decision.

The employment tribunal found against the applicants on the grounds that they were under no *obligation* to offer their services on a regular basis:

> The applicants entered into their relationship with the company in the expectation that they would be provided with any work which was currently available. It was a purely commercial transaction for the supply and purchase of services for specific events, because there was no obligation for the company to provide work and no obligation for the applicants to offer their further services.[194]

They were therefore in the position of independent contractors who simply chose to work for a single client. The tribunal refused to imply a term into the contract on the grounds of 'business efficacy' requiring the employer to provide work, on the basis that the arrangement could work perfectly well without one. This view was confirmed by the Court of Appeal: the judgment of the EAT 'must involve a misdirection of law or every independent contractor who is content or able only to attract one client would be held to work under a contract of employment'. Nor was there clear evidence of a global contract: 'what happened could equally well be attributed to market forces'.[195]

3.38 In other decisions, courts have been able to construe working practices in such a way as to discover a legal obligation on the part of the employer to find

192 [1983] ICR 728.
193 The relevant law is now contained in TULRCA 1992, s 152. Note that since 1 October 2004 protection against subjection to a detriment for this reason has applied to the wider category of workers: see para 8.5 below.
194 Cited at [1983] ICR 730, 744.
195 [1983] 730, 763 (Sir John Donaldson MR).

work for the employee, indicating that there there is some leeway in the application of the mutuality test. In *Airfix Footwear Ltd v Cope*[196] and *Nethermere (St Neots) Ltd v Taverna and Gardiner*,[197] cases concerning homeworkers, the courts declined to accept that arrangements for the regular placing of work with the applicants lacked all legal force. In *Nethermere* Dillon LJ found it 'unreal to suppose that the work in fact done by the applicants for the company over the not inconsiderable periods ... was done merely as a result of the pressures of market forces on the applicants and the company and under no contract at all',[198] and Stephenson LJ could not see 'why well-founded expectations of continuing homework should not be hardened or refined into enforceable contracts by regular giving and taking of work over periods of a year or more, and why outworkers should not thereby become employees under contracts of service, like those doing similar work in the factory'.[199] Stephenson LJ also invoked the long-standing authority of *Devonald v Rosser & Sons Ltd*[200] to hold that the obligation on the employee's part to accept work could be used to imply an obligation on the part of the employer to offer it, by way of reciprocity.[201]

By contrast, in *Clark v Oxfordshire Health Authority*[202] the Court of Appeal held that there was no evidence of a global contract of employment in the case of a nurse who, under an arrangement with the health authority, was offered work as and when the need arose, but who otherwise had no regular working hours. Similarly, in *Carmichael v National Power plc*,[203] the House of Lords ruled that tour guides who worked on a 'casual as required basis' had been correctly classified as being employed under arrangements which lacked the mutuality of obligation needed to establish a global contract. These cases suggest that it may be difficult to establish a continuing legal nexus in cases of so-called 'zero hours contracts', where the employer unequivocally refuses to commit itself in advance to make any given quantum of work available.[204] Nevertheless, a vital aspect of *Carmichael* was that, in the view of the tribunal, the applicants were free to refuse to work even when invited to by the employer. A different outcome is possible in a case where the employee contracts to be on call, that is, to be available to work whenever the employer calls upon him or her to do so. It is then open to a court to infer the existence of the reciprocal obligation on the employer's part to offer work when it becomes available. Where that is the case, there could be sufficient mutuality to establish a global contract of employment.

3.39   It is also completely consistent with *Carmichael* for workers who are employed on a 'zero-hours' basis to be employees during the period when they are at work or in respect of particular engagements or hirings. One possible interpretation of *O'Kelly* and the cases which followed it is that very short-term hirings are incompatible with employee status; unless there is a global contract of employment spanning the gaps between jobs, the individual hirings must also take the form of contracts for services. But the better view is that there is no

196 [1978] ICR 1210; although cf *Mailway (Southern) Ltd v Willsher* [1978] ICR 511.
197 [1984] IRLR 240.
198 [1984] IRLR 240, 246.
199 [1984] IRLR 240.
200 [1906] 2 KB 728; see below, ch 4, at para 4.112.
201 [1984] IRLR 240, 246.
202 [1998] IRLR 125.
203 [2000] IRLR 43. See H Collins, 2000b.
204 In 1998, approximately 200,000 individuals were employed on zero hours contracts. See DTI, *Fairness at Work*, Cm 3968, 1998, at para 3.14.

reason why a particular hiring should not take the form of a contract of employment; duration is not a decisive factor. This was the conclusion of the Court of Appeal in *McMeechan v Secretary of State for Employment*:[205] under his terms and conditions, the agency worker in that case might have been employed by the agency as either an employee or as self-employed for the purposes of a particular assignment or 'single engagement'. As we have noted, it will often be necessary for an employee to establish a global contract in order to show that he or she has the necessary continuity of employment to claim certain statutory rights which depend upon length and regularity of service.[206] However, there are numerous employment protection rights which do not depend upon extensive continuity of service, and for the purposes of these provisions, the decision in *McMeechan* is potentially highly significant.[207]

3.40   The emergence of the mutuality test at a particular point in the evolution of modern employment law suggests that it should be seen as an attempt to refute the criterion of 'economic reality' and to reassert formal subordination as the basis of employment: workers who do not make a formal, long-term commitment to the firm are viewed as having no claim to employment protection from it.[208] For example, it was on this ground that temporary workers employed by an agency were said 'wholly to lack the elements of continuity, and care of the employer for the employee, that one associates with the contract of service'.[209] Yet it may be argued that the strict application of the mutuality test, by making the *duration* of the hiring a central factor in deciding employment status, produces some odd results.[210] If one of the waiters in *O'Kelly* had spilled the contents of a bottle of wine on one of Trusthouse Forte's customers, would a court have denied the customer an action against the company on the grounds that it was not vicariously liable for the negligence of independent contractors?[211] One way out of this difficulty would be to decide that the individual, although not an employee for the purposes of employment protection legislation, could be regarded as such for the different purposes of the employer's vicarious liability

---

205 [1997] IRLR 353; see also *Clark v Oxfordshire Health Authority* [1998] IRLR 125 and *Carmichael v National Power plc* [2000] IRLR 43.
206 See our analysis at para 3.92 below.
207 For example, of the cases discussed in the text, *McMeechan* concerned employees' rights in the event of the employer's insolvency (ERA 1996, Part XII), and *O'Kelly* was about the right of an employee not to be dismissed for trade-union related reasons (TULRCA 1992, s 152). *Carmichael v National Power plc* concerned the right to a written statement of terms and conditions of employment (ERA 1996, s 1) for which one month's continuity is required; on this aspect of the case, see Collins, 2000b. It should also be noted that the Court of Appeal in *Clark v Oxfordshire Health Authority* did not decide that there could not be individual contracts of employment in respect of the periods when the applicant was employed to work; this point was remitted to the tribunal.
208 For discussion of the values underlying the mutuality test, see Leighton, 1984; Deakin, 2003. In recent cases, 'mutuality' and 'control' have often been considered alongside each other, as overlapping criteria for identifying employment status. See, eg, *Stephenson v Delphi Diesel Systems Ltd.* [2003] ICR 471; *Bridges v Industrial Rubber plc*, EAT, 21 September 2004, Appeal No UKEAT/0150/04/DM.
209 *Wickens v Champion Employment* [1984] ICR 365, 371; see also *Ironmonger v Movefield Ltd* [1988] IRLR 461.
210 The courts' stress on this particular factor also differs from the emphasis given by Freedland in his formulation of the test, in which 'the promises to employ and to be employed may be of short duration or may be terminable at short notice' (see above).
211 See the discussion of this point by Sedley LJ in *Dacas v Brook Street Bureau (UK) Ltd* [2004] IRLR 358.

in tort.[212] It is arguable that the individual should be bound by the arrangement he or she chooses to make with the employer when it comes to defining the scope of their mutual rights and obligations, but that a third party should not be deprived of the right to sue the employer in tort by a contract to which he or she is not privy. But this is surely to place too much emphasis on an arrangement which was offered to the worker on a 'take it or leave it basis' and was the result of the casualisation of the trade in question, rather than a measured weighing by the workers concerned of the costs and benefits of independent contractor status.

3.41   Although there are serious implications for the effectiveness of employment protection legislation of the use by the courts of a test whose origins are contentious and whose effects are potentially highly confusing, the importance of the mutuality test has if anything increased over time. There is now a considerable body of case law on the correct approach to the interpretation of standard-form employment agreements which refer to the mutuality issue. A 'no mutuality' clause, under which the parties agree that the employer shall be under no obligation to offer work beyond a given hiring, and that the worker is free to refuse future offers of work, may have the effect of excluding employee status for the reasons discussed above.[213] It may also be read as denying the existence of a bilateral contract of any kind, thereby excluding rights which depend on the application of the concept of the 'worker' or 'employed person'. Such clauses, then, give rise to similar issues of construction to those arising in the context of the 'substitution clauses' which we considered in the light of the Court of Appeal decision in *Express & Echo Publications Ltd v Tanton*.[214]

3.42   Thus the agreements in question nearly always take the form of standard contract terms which are in effect imposed by the employer. A 'no mutuality' clause which was never observed in practice could arguably be avoided, using entirely conventional approaches to the construction of contracts of adhesion, if it was not explicitly brought to the worker's attention prior to contracting.[215] A court can also look beyond a 'no mutuality' clause if it is convinced that it is a 'sham', in the sense that it 'does not represent the real intentions of the parties objectively ascertained',[216] or if it can find evidence that the parties, notwithstanding the formal agreement they initially made, subsequently entered into a new employment contract by conduct.[217] Mutual obligations may be implied from a repeated course of dealing. Even if no global contract can be implied, a single hiring is highly likely to be regarded as a bilateral legal arrangement, either a contract for the supply of personal services or a contract of employment, for as

212 See McKendrick, 1990.
213 See *Stevedoring and Haulage Services Ltd v Fuller* [2001] IRLR 627 for a clear illustration of this point.
214 [1999] IRLR 367.
215 *Interfoto Picture Library Ltd v Stiletto Visual Pictures Ltd* [1989] QB 433; see para 3.26 above.
216 *Accounttax Marketing Ltd v Halstead*, EAT, 6 November 2003, Appeal No UKEAT/0313/03/ZT, at para 18.
217 For a recent reminder that a contract of employment can be entered into *entirely* on the basis of conduct, where that is sufficient to imply an exchange of promises, see *Newnham Farms Ltd v Powell*, EAT, 7 March 2003, Appeal No EAT/0711/01/MAA.
218 *McMeechan v Secretary of State for Employment* [1997] IRLR 353; *Stevedoring & Haulage Services Ltd v Fuller* [2001] IRLR 627; *Stephenson v Delphi Diesel Systems Ltd* [2003] ICR 471.

long as work is continuing.[218] But for a court or tribunal to imply a contract on the basis of conduct, it must have evidence that the parties had the relevant contractual intention, and it must be also able to spell out what the relevant terms of the contract are.[219] For some tribunals and courts, these requirements have proved to be a substantial barrier to a finding of employee status.[220]

A 'multi-factor test'?

3.43 None of the tests considered so far will necessarily be decisive on its own. According to Lord Wright in *Montreal v Montreal Locomotive Works*, 'in many cases the question can only be settled by examining the whole of the various elements which constitute the relationship between the parties'.[221] This open-ended approach is exemplified by the 'multi-factor' or 'multiple' test as stated by MacKenna J in *Ready Mixed Concrete (South East) Ltd v Minister for Pensions and National Insurance*:[222]

> A contract of service exists [when] three conditions are fulfilled. (i) The servant agrees that, in consideration of a wage or other remuneration, he will provide his own work and skill in the performance of some service for his master. (ii) He agrees, expressly or impliedly, that in the performance of that service he will be subject to the other's control in a sufficient degree to make that other master. (iii) The other provisions of the contract are consistent with its being a contract of service.

Although this test has since been cited with approval on numerous occasions, in its first two stages it represents little more than a repetition of the test of personal control. The third stage adds nothing, since it neither indicates what the core features of the contract of service (or employment) are, nor which features are necessarily inconsistent with it. It invites the courts to engage in a balancing act, the outcome of which may be almost impossible to predict in advance. This adds to the uncertainty created by the decision in *O'Kelly v Trusthouse Forte plc*,[223] limiting the scope for appellate guidance and review of tribunals' decisions. In particular, it makes it difficult for the parties to rely on earlier decisions in similar cases; it has been said that 'the process involves painting a picture in each individual case',[224] and that it is 'quite impossible in a field where a very large number of factors have to be weighed, to gain any real assistance by looking at the facts of another case and comparing them one by one to see what facts are common, what are different and what particular weight is given by another Tribunal to the common facts'.[225] As a result, courts and advisers often

---

219 *Accounttax Marketing Ltd v Halstead*, EAT, 6 November 2003, Appeal No UKEAT/ 0313/03/ZT, at paras 35, 39.
220 See *Bunce v Postworth Ltd t/a Skyblue* [2005] IRLR 557 (no contract of employment, an agency worker and employment agency); *Hewlett Packard Ltd v O'Murphy* [2002] IRLR 4; *Stephenson v Delphi Diesel Systems Ltd* [2003] ICR 471 (no contract of employment, agency worker and user); *PA News Ltd t/a The Press Association v Loveridge*, EAT, 1 September 2003, Appeal No EAT 0135/03/MAA (no contract of employment, freelance sports reporters); *Bridges v Industrial Rubber plc*, EAT, 21 September 2004, Appeal No UKEAT/0150/04/DM (no contract of employment, homeworkers).
221 [1947] 1 DLR 161, 169.
222 [1968] 497, 515.
223 [1983] ICR 728.
224 *Hall v Lorimer* [1992] 1 WLR 939, 944 (Mummery J); see also the Court of Appeal judgments ([1994] IRLR 171).
225 *Walls v Sinnett* (1987) 60 TC 150, 164 (Vinelott J).

have to have resort to what Wedderburn has termed the 'elephant test': the contract of employment has become 'an animal too difficult to define, but easy to recognise when you see it'.[226] Some of the uncertainties to which this gives rise can be illustrated by considering in turn the leading cases of *Ready Mixed Concrete*, *O'Kelly* and *Hall v Lorimer*.

3.44   *Ready Mixed Concrete* concerned the status, for national insurance contribution purposes, of a lorry driver who delivered cement for the applicants. He was in the process of buying the lorry from them on hire purchase terms and had to paint it in the company's colours, to drive it on the company's business for a certain number of hours per week and to wear the company's uniform when doing so. He was paid according to a rate per mile for a given quantity of delivered cement. If he was unable to work he had to hire a replacement. The contract described him as self-employed but also required him to obey all reasonable orders of the company. MacKenna J held that he was self-employed, because 'these are obligations more consistent, I think, with a contract of carriage than with one of service. The ownership of the assets, the chance of profit and the risk of loss in the business of carriage are his and not the company's'.[227]

The decision is surprising, given the duty to obey orders and the clear identification of the work to be done with the company's own business. It is perhaps begging the question to talk of the 'business of carriage' being the business in relation to which the worker took the risk of loss and the chance of profit; arguably, the relevant business here was the company's cement business. Whatever arguments might be put for or against the outcome, however, *Ready Mixed Concrete* is a good example of the balancing act which courts and tribunals must engage in when applying the 'multiple test' without any clear guidance from the legislation itself or from the appellate courts as to which factors are more important than others.

3.45   In *O'Kelly v Trusthouse Forte*[228] the employment tribunal produced a list of no fewer than 18 different relevant factors, some of which were considered consistent with the existence of a contract of employment. These included the lack of any financial investment by the applicants in the company's business; the payment by the company of holiday pay and an incentive bonus based on past service; the presence of control by the company when the waiters were at work; and the fact that they were paid weekly in arrears with tax and national insurance deducted at source. A second category contained factors which were regarded as *not inconsistent* with a contract of employment. The applicants were only paid for work actually performed, but 'the method of calculating entitlement to remuneration is not an essential aspect of the employment relationship'; similarly, it was not fatal that there were no regular weekly working hours, nor that the applicants were not members of the company's sick pay and pension schemes. Finally, the tribunal recognised a category of factors which were inconsistent with employee status. These were: the contracts were terminable without notice on either side; the applicants had the right to refuse work; the company was under no obligation to provide it; the parties themselves took the view that the applicants, as casual workers, were independent contractors;

226 Wedderburn, 1986: p 116.
227 [1968] 2 QB 497, 526.
228 [1983] ICR 728.

and it was also the recognised custom and practice in the industry to treat casual workers as employed under contracts for services. The tribunal considered that while none of these factors was decisive in its own right, on balance 'it would be irresponsible lightly to disregard the clear evidence of the parties derived from an engagement under custom and practice, because this would have widespread and damaging repercussions throughout the whole industry';[229] this was therefore a case in which the parties' own designation of status tipped the balance.

3.46 Self-employment was also the outcome in the leading tax case of *Hall v Lorimer*.[230] Mr Lorimer was a skilled television technician (a 'vision mixer') who had previously worked as an employee for one particular company, but had then become a freelance worker, building up a clientele of around twenty different production companies. He did not supply or own his own equipment and worked on the premises of the companies concerned; on the other hand, he was paid on a fee basis for each separate engagement and occasionally hired a substitute when he could not carry out certain work. In any one year he had over 100 separate engagements, most of which lasted no more than one day, and had no continuing or 'global' contract with any one company. The Court of Appeal, dismissing an appeal by the Inland Revenue, found that Mr Lorimer was self-employed.

3.47 In both *Ready Mixed Concrete* and *O'Kelly* there was clear evidence of both personal and economic dependence between worker and employer. In each case the worker consistently contracted with the same employer, was required to obey certain orders and was dependent on that employer for continuing work and income. *Lorimer*, by contrast, seems a much clearer case of self-employment. Like the applicants in *O'Kelly*, Lorimer had no business of his own, but this is not necessarily a crucial factor, as we have seen.[231] An essential difference in his case, though, was that he was 'independent of a particular paymaster for the financial exploitation of his talents':[232] he worked for a large number of different businesses without being economically dependent on any one of them. An emphasis on economic dependence, so defined, would arguably produce greater predictability than the open-ended multiple test, in which any one of a number of factors could turn out to be essential in tipping the balance on one side or the other.

QUASI-DEPENDENT LABOUR

3.48 The uncertainty created by the common law tests for defining employee status has led to a number of extensions of the scope of protective legislation. Those affected include apprentices and trainees; self-employed workers who are economically dependent on the business of another; homeworkers; and agency workers. These individuals are *employed* – they do not have their own businesses – without necessarily being *subordinated* workers according to the criteria

---

229 [1983] ICR 728, 745 (Ackner LJ, summarising the decision of the employment tribunal).
230 [1994] IRLR 171.
231 See para 3.37 above.
232 [1994] IRLR 171, 175.

examined above. Because of this, and because they are treated as being equivalent to employees only for certain purposes, the term 'quasi-dependent labour' may be used to refer to this group.

Apprentices and trainees

3.49   Apprentices come within the scope of employment protection legislation, the contract of apprenticeship being included within the broad definition of the contract of employment for this purpose.[233] The essence of apprenticeship is that the employer undertakes formally to train and instruct the apprentice in a particular trade or skill; the apprentice, in turn, contracts to serve the employer[234] and to learn from those from whom he or she receives instruction. According to Widgery LJ in *Dunk v George Waller & Son Ltd,*[235] 'a contract of apprenticeship secures three things for the apprentice; it secures him, first, a money payment during the period of apprenticeship; secondly, that he shall be instructed and trained and thereby acquire skills which will be of value to him for the rest of his life; and thirdly it gives him status, because ... once a young man, as here, completes his apprenticeship and can show by certificate that he has completed his time with a well-known employer, this gets him off to a good start in the labour market and gives him a status the loss of which may be of considerable damage to him'. The contract is normally one for a fixed term and cannot be terminated by either party, by the giving of notice, before the term has expired. The grounds on which the employer may dismiss the apprentice for misconduct are also more limited than they would be in the case of an employee. Hence, in *Dunk*[236] the employer was not entitled to end the apprenticeship when the apprentice failed a certain examination, and had to pay damages representing not just lost wages but the prospective loss of skills and enhanced earning capacity. Nor can the apprentice normally be dismissed for redundancy during the term of the contract; such a dismissal is only permitted in extreme circumstances, such as the total closure of the employment unit.[237] However, once the agreed period of training comes to an end there is no obligation on the part of the employer to continue employing the now-qualified apprentice, nor does the latter qualify for a redundancy payment if he or she is not re-employed.[238] There is no legal maximum age limit for beginning an apprenticeship; traditionally, industrial apprenticeships were invariably begun immediately upon leaving school, but this is no longer an inflexible practice.

The number of apprenticeships has declined considerably since the late 1970s, partly as a consequence of increased government funding for alternative forms of work-related training. The element of state subsidy in supporting the wages of trainees, together with the predominant role played by governmental bodies in setting the framework for the training process, are among the factors distinguishing these forms of training from the traditional apprenticeship. A

---

233 ERA 1996, s 230(1), (2).
234 If the individual does not undertake to serve, the relationship cannot be one of apprenticeship: *Edmonds v Lawson QC* [2000] IRLR 391 (a pupil barrister was not employed under a contract of apprenticeship for the purposes of NMWA 1998).
235 [1970] 2 QB 163, 169.
236 [1970] 2 QB 163.
237 *Wallace v C A Roofing Services Ltd* [1996] IRLR 435.
238 *North East Coast Shiprepairers v Secretary of State for Employment* [1978] ICR 755; *Ryan v Shipboard Maintenance* [1980] ICR 88.

majority of the EAT in *Daley v Allied Suppliers Ltd*[239] concluded that a trainee under the Youth Training Scheme which was then in force had no contract of any kind. The principal reason given was that the terms of the trainee's placement were set by the rules laid down by a state agency which was responsible for administering the training programme (at that time the Manpower Services Commission) and not by the parties themselves. As was said in the similar case of *Hawley v Fieldcastle & Co Ltd*,[240] 'because of the intervention of the [Manpower Services Commission] by agreement between both the applicant and the respondent and the limitations which that intervention imposes upon the freedom of action of both the parties, the relationship between the parties in [this] case is not that of employer/employee'. This is not a very convincing argument, however; many contracts of employment are subject to regulation by an external source of norms, such as a collective agreement, without losing their character as contracts. A second line of argument in *Daley* was that the applicant had a *contract for training* which was juridically distinct from a contract of employment or apprenticeship, and therefore outside the scope of the relevant legislation: 'the underlying purpose of any contract between [the parties] was not to establish a relationship of an employer and an employee but to enable Miss Daley to acquire certain skills and experience',[241] without the parties having entered into the more specific obligations characteristic of an apprenticeship. So-called 'modern apprenticeships', notwithstanding the terminology used, are in certain respects the successors to the scheme considered in *Daley*, and for that reason may not necessarily be classified as giving rise to an apprenticeship relation.[242]

3.50   Since the decision in *Daley*, the legislature has acted to grant a partially protected status to trainees who are not accorded employee or apprentice status by their employers: as a result, they are covered by legislation in the areas of health and safety, working time, and equal treatment discrimination,[243] while remaining excluded from most of the protective rights contained in ERA 1996. Apprentices below the age of 19, and apprentices below the age of 26 during their first year of training, are excluded from the coverage of the national minimum wage. All workers below the age of 16 are excluded; those between 16-17 and 18-21 receive lower minimum rates. A number of more specific exclusions also apply to particular training schemes.[244]

The Employment Act 1988[245] conferred a power on the Secretary of State to designate the status of trainees on youth training programmes by order for

239 [1983] IRLR 14.
240 [1982] IRLR 223.
241 *Daley v Allied Suppliers Ltd* [1983] IRLR 14, 17; see also *Wiltshire Police Authority v Wynn* [1980] ICR 649.
242 For two contrasting EAT decisions on this point see *Whitely v Marton Electrical Ltd* [2003] IRLR 197, and *Thorpe v Dul*, EAT, 1 July 2003, Appeal No EAT/0630/02/TM.
243 See, for health and safety, SI 1983/1919; for working time, WTR 1998, reg 42; for sex discrimination, SDA 1975, s 14 and for racial discrimination, RRA 1976, s 13 both as amended by EA 1989, s 7; for disability discrimination, DDA 1995, ss 4, 68(1); for sexual orientation discrimination, EE(SO)R 2003, reg 17; and for discrimination on the grounds of religion or belief, EE(RB)R 2003, reg 17.
244 See paras 4.44-4.46 below.
245 S 26. The power was extended by the Learning and Skills Act 2000; see the discussion of this provision in *Thorpe v Dul*, EAT, 1 July 2003, Appeal No EAT/0630/02/TM, at para 42.

particular purposes. An order may state that such persons are to be treated as employed, or not, and that their status may be that of trainees or employees; the legal nature of the payments they receive by way of the training allowance may also be determined by this means. Powers under this section have been exercised on a number of occasions.

'Workers', the self-employed, and those supplying personal services

3.51   The self-employed are currently thought to represent around 12% of the active labour force. The legal notion of self-employment is, however, not easy to pin down, and the 12% figure given in official statistics represents a highly heterogeneous category.[246] The legal nature of self-employment has achieved a new importance as a result of growing reliance on the 'worker' concept, in preference to the more normal 'employee'. The following definition is the one now widely in use:

> '... "worker"... means an individual who has entered into or works under (or, where the employment has ceased, worked under) -
>
> (a)   a contract of employment, or
>
> (b)   any other contract, whether express or implied and (if it is express) whether oral or in writing, whereby the individual undertakes to do or perform personally any work or services for another party to the contract whose status is not by virtue of the contract that of a client or customer of any profession or undertaking carried on by the individual;
>
> and any reference to a worker's contract shall be construed accordingly.'[247]

3.52   The reason for using this extended definition of dependent status is to be found in the purpose of the particular statutory provisions to which it applies. A first set of such provisions is concerned with the application of basic labour standards in relation to minimum wages, protection against arbitrary deductions from pay, and protection from excessive working hours. Here, through its use of the worker definition, the legislature has in essence taken the view that casual workers who would not necessarily fall within 'employee' status should not, for that reason, be denied basic protections which do not depend, for their effective functioning, upon the employment relationship in question being regular or long-term.

3.53   Health and safety law has long operated according to a similar principle. The Health and Safety at Work Act 1974 imposes a general duty on employers 'to ensure, so far as is reasonably practicable, the health, safety and welfare at work of all [their] employees', as well as more specific duties including the maintenance of a safe plant and system of work and a safe workplace, the

---

246   See Burchell *et al*, 1999, for a discussion of the statistical definitions of the self-employed used by government, and historical background on the rise of self-employment in the 1980s and 1990s, and Lindsay and Macauley, 2004 for a more recent review of different usages.

247   ERA 1996, s 230(3) (this definition is used in ERA in the context of the right not to have arbitrary deductions made from wages under Part II of the Act (formerly Part I of the Wages Act 1986)). See also similar provisions in NMWA 1998, s 54 (minimum wage); WTR 1998, reg 2 (working time); TULRCA, 1992, s 296(1) (various collective rights); ERelA 1999, s 13 (right to be accompanied in disciplinary hearings).

provision of information and training and the maintenance of an adequate working environment as regards facilities and arrangements for welfare.[248] As elsewhere, an 'employee' is defined here as a person employed under a contract of employment or apprenticeship.[249] In addition, the employer is under a duty to conduct his undertaking in such a way as to ensure that, as far as reasonably practicable, 'persons not in his employment who may be affected thereby are not thereby exposed to risks to their health or safety', a phrase which would certainly cover self-employed workers employed on or about the employer's premises.[250]

3.54 A second category relates to collective rights, including the provision of immunity from liability in tort for those who organise industrial action and provisions governing the formation and constitution of trade unions. Here, the widened definition of 'worker' means that there may be a lawful trade dispute (a prerequisite of immunity for the organisation of industrial action) in defence of the interests of self-employed 'workers' in the sense described above, and not merely to defend the interests of employees. The legislature also recognises that trade unions recruit and represent the interests of many individuals who are not employees in the legal sense of that term, either because they are seeking employment (this particular definition applies to those looking for employment as either employees or workers) or because their status is in doubt on account of a lack of regular employment or a high degree of autonomy in the way they do their work (while, at the same time, excluding associations of professionals, such as the Law Society, from this definition[251]). Following this logic, the right of the individual not to be dismissed or otherwise discriminated against within employment on grounds related to the statutory trade union recognition procedure applies to workers as well as to employees, as do other aspects of that procedure.[252] In addition, the right to be protected against discrimination on grounds of membership of an independent trade union has recently been extended to workers.[253] However the right to protection against discrimination for taking part in industrial action continues to apply only to employees.[254]

3.55 A third category relates to the principle of equal treatment. Equal treatment legislation extends to employment 'under a contract of service or of apprenticeship or a contract personally to execute any work or labour'[255] as

---

248 HSWA 1974, s 2(1)–(2).

249 HSWA 1974, s 53(1).

250 HSWA 1974, s 3. The phrase 'persons not in his employment' can be read as meaning all those who are not his employees: under s 53(1), '"employee" means an individual who works under a contract of employment, and *related expressions shall be construed accordingly*' (emphasis added). See also the Framework Directive on Health and Safety, Directive 89/391, Art 3(a)–(b).

251 *Carter v Law Society* [1973] ICR 113. The definition of 'trade union' is contained in TULRCA 1992, s 1; see para 7.20 below.

252 For example, under TULRCA 1992, Sch A1, para 1, the union may seek recognition in respect of a 'group or groups of workers'; see *R (on the application of the BBC) v CAC* [2003] IRLR 460. The anti-discrimination provisions are to be found in Sch A1, paras 156–165.

253 TULRCA 1992, s 146, as amended by ERelA 2004, s 30.

254 TULRCA 1992, s 237–238A.

255 EqPA 1970, s 1(6)(a); SDA 1975, s 82; RRA 1976, s 78. See also DDA 1995, s 68(1); EE(RB)R 2003, reg 2; EE(SO)R 2003, reg 2 (employment means 'employment under a contract of service or of apprenticeship or a contract personally to do any work').

well as to applicants for employment, so defined.[256] In relation to equality of pay between men and women, this wide definition is now underpinned by European Union law. In *Allonby v Accrington and Rossendale College*[257] the ECJ held that the term 'worker', in the context of the right to equal pay for equal work in Article 141 EC, 'cannot be defined by reference to the legislation of the Member States but has a Community meaning'.[258] Moreover, because the right to equal pay 'forms part of the foundations of the Community',[259] the worker concept 'cannot be interpreted restrictively'.[260] For this purpose, 'there must be considered as a worker a person who, for a certain period of time, performs services for and under the direction of another person in return for which he receives remuneration',[261] although 'independent providers of services who are not in a relationship of subordination with the person who receives the services'[262] are excluded. Thus the principle of equality of pay must extend beyond the narrow category, in UK labour law, of the 'employee'. Exactly how far this extension has to go, however, is not clear, in part because the civil law category of 'subordination' to which the ECJ referred does not map neatly on to the concepts used by the English courts. One possible reading of the ECJ's judgment is that it used the term 'subordination' to refer to the concept of one who acts 'under the direction of another', a notion broadly analogous to the 'control' test in UK labour law.[263]

The Court's wide reading of the term 'worker' could also extend to other aspects of anti-discrimination law which are underpinned by EU law, which recognises the equality principle as a fundamental social right. Since that is now, or will soon be, the case with regard to discrimination on the grounds of sex, race (in the sense of race and national or ethnic origin), sexual orientation, religion or belief, disability and age,[264] the principle enunciated in *Allonby* could have a wide application. This possibility is reinforced by a subsequent ruling of the Court, *Wippel*, in which it held that a part-time worker employed under a 'framework' contract which did not specify set working hours (in the manner of a 'zero-hours' contract) had to be regarded as a worker covered by the Equal Treatment Directive.[265]

The precise issue before the Court in *Allonby* was whether the exclusion of the applicant from a public sector pension scheme governed by legislation, the Teachers' Superannuation Scheme, on the grounds that she was not an employee – she was an agency worker employed by the agency under a contract for services, and had no contract of any kind with the user to whom she supplied her services – amounted to an infringement of the equal pay principle. The Court held that, in the absence of justification, Mrs Allonby's exclusion from the TSS could amount to indirect discrimination under Article 141, if it could be shown that the relevant rules of the scheme disproportionately affected more

256 SDA 1975, s 6; RRA 1976, s 4; DDA 1995, s 4; EE(RB)R 2003, reg 6; EE(SO)R 2003, reg 6.
257 Case C-256/01, [2004] IRLR 224.
258 Case C-256/01, [2004] IRLR 224, Judgment of the Court, at para 66.
259 Case C-256/01, [2004] IRLR 224, para 65.
260 Case C-256/01, [2004] IRLR 224, para 66.
261 Case C-256/01, [2004] IRLR 224, para 67.
262 Case C-256/01, [2004] IRLR 224, para 68.
263 This expression appears in para 67 of the Judgment. On the control test, see para 3.33, above.
264 See generally our analysis of the principle of equal treatment in ch 6 below, particularly at paras 6.34–6.40 (prohibited grounds of discrimination – the prohibition on age discrimination is due to come into force in the autumn of 2006).
265 Case C-313/02 *Wippel v Peek & Coppenburg GmbH & Co KG* [2005] IRLR 211.

female than male workers, and that this could not be justified.[266] As it currently stands, UK equal treatment legislation most likely satisfies the *Allonby* test, given the inclusion in that legislation not just of employees but of workers with contracts for personal services; however, *Allonby* may well be of assistance in future to applicants in borderline cases.

3.56 Not all forms of the provision of labour services are covered by the definitions of 'worker' and 'employment' just referred to. There must, in addition, be a contractual nexus of some kind between the worker and employer. It is for this reason that, in a number of recent decisions, tribunals and courts applying the 'worker' concept have insisted on the need for 'mutuality of obligation'.[267] The use of the term 'mutuality' appears to refer here to the basic elements of consideration which must be present in any contract, rather than to the specific sense of 'mutuality' which has been used, in a separate context, to draw a distinction between contracts of employment and contracts giving rise to self-employment.[268] It is, to say the least, confusing to see the phrase 'mutuality of obligation' used in these two distinct senses. When the phrase is used in relation to the 'worker' concept, it is not clear what, if anything, is being added to the requirement of consideration. One possibility is that, for the 'worker' concept to apply, labour services must be provided under a 'bilateral' contract, that it to say, one in which the parties undertake mutual commitments in advance of performance. A 'unilateral' contract, under which the employer's obligations are triggered only at the point when the work is completed, would be excluded. But there is much to be said for the courts operating according to a presumption in favour of implying a bilateral contract, all other things being equal, when work is carried out in return for remuneration.[269]

3.57 A further limitation on the 'worker' and 'employment' concepts relates to those who do not contract to supply *personal* services. One possibility here is that the 'dominant purpose' of an arrangement is for a person to supply an end product or service without necessarily contracting to supply their *own* work and labour. It is partly for this reason that in a series of cases, courts have held that postmasters and postmistresses fall outside the scope of equal treatment and minimum wage legislation.[270] By contrast, in *Loughran and Kelly v Northern Ireland Housing Executive*[271] the House of Lords held that individual solicitors

---

266 On the concepts of adverse impact and group disadvantage under the test for indirect discrimination, see our analysis in ch 6 below, at paras 6.22–6.29.
267 See, in particular, *Byrne Brothers (Formwork) Ltd v Baird* [2002] IRLR 96; *Stephenson v Delphi Diesel Systems Ltd* [2003] ICR 471.
268 See paras 3.36–3.42, above.
269 See *Stephenson v Delphi Diesel Systems Ltd* [2003] ICR 471, at para 13: [t]he question of mutuality of obligation ... poses no difficulties during the period when the individual is actually working. For the period of such employment a contract must, in our view, clearly exist' (Elias, J.); see also, on the tendency of the courts to construe employment relations as giving rise to bilateral and relational contracts, Freedland, 2003: 89–90.
270 *Tanna v Post Office* [1981] ICR 374; *Mirror Group v Gunning* [1986] ICR 145; *Sheehan v Post Office Counters Ltd* [1999] ICR 73; *Commissioners of Inland Revenue v Post Office Ltd* [2003] IRLR 199. See also *Mingeley v Pennock* [2004] IRLR 373 (a private hire taxi driver did not have a personal work contract with the vehicle operator).
271 [1998] IRLR 593. This action was brought under the Fair Employment (Northern Ireland) Act 1976 which contains in s 57 a particularly wide definition of 'employment'. In other contexts, the existence of a partnership between individuals has been held to provide evidence that they do not contract as 'workers' in their individual capacity with the end user of their services: see *Firthglow Ltd t/a Protectacoat v Descombes*, EAT, 19 January 2004, Appeal No UKEAT/0916/03/ILB.

could bring an action for unlawful discrimination against the respondent even though they had applied for employment not in their personal capacity but through the firms through which they worked. This decision turns on the nature of a solicitors' partnership; the partnership or 'firm' is not an entity in its own right which can be regarded as separate from the individual partners. The decision is questionable since, as Lord Clyde commented in his dissent, the correct construction of the terms of appointment in question was surely that the solicitors in question would arrange for the work to be done by one of the members of their respective firms, rather than undertaking to supply their own services. Lords Slynn and Steyn considered that the Act could also confer rights upon the partnership as such as well as upon individuals, but this view was rejected by Lords Griffiths, Lloyd and Clyde.[272]

3.58   In respect of both the need for 'mutuality' and the requirement of 'personal services', employers may try to avoid the application of protective statutes through the insertion of standard-form terms and conditions which are designed to exclude the obligation to provide personal services. The decision of the Court of Appeal in *Express & Echo Publications Ltd v Tanton*[273] is just as much in point here as it is in the context of the definition of 'employee' status, and similar arguments will apply. Thus it is open to an applicant to argue that a 'substitution' clause has not been effectively incorporated into the relevant contract,[274] or that the term in question, if it is ambiguous, should be read in the light of the way in which the work was carried out.[275]

However, in a case where a contract cannot be implied because of the presence of a 'substitution' or similar clause, it can be argued, following the judgment of the ECJ in the *Allonby* case, that, in respect of statutory obligations which are underpinned by European Union law on equality of treatment,[276] the precise legal nature of the work relationship should not matter, as long as services are being provided to another under conditions of 'subordination'. This is because of the Court's ruling that '[p]rovided that a person is a worker within the meaning of Article 141(1) EC, the nature of his legal relationship with the other party to the employment relationship is of no consequence in regard to the application of that article'. The Court went on to indicate that '[t]he formal classification of a self-employed worker under national law does not exclude the possibility that a person must be classified as a worker within the meaning of Article 141(1) EC if his independence is merely notional, thereby disguising an employment relationship within the meaning of that Article'.[277] It also stated that, in determining whether agency workers in the position of Mrs. Allonby fell under Article 141, it would be necessary to consider 'the extent of any limitation on

---

272   It should be noted that specific rules operate to provide limited protection to individuals who do not clearly benefit from the protection of the 'worker' concept, such as EC Directive 86/653 concerning commercial agents. For a recent case in which the Directive and the implementing UK regulations were applied, see *King v T Tunnock Ltd* [2000] IRLR 569.

273   See *Express & Echo Publications Ltd v Tanton* [1999] IRLR 367, discussed above at para 3.26.

274   See *Morris Homes (North) Ltd v Batty*, EAT, 16 June 2004, Appeal No UKEAT/0691/03/DM.

275   *Redrow Homes (Yorkshire) Ltd v Wright* [2004] IRLR 720.

276   On this point, see our discussion above, para 3.55.

277   *Allonby*, Judgment of the Court, at paras 70 and 71.

their freedom to choose their timetable, and the place and content of their work', while 'the fact that no obligation is imposed on them to accept an assignment is of no consequence in that context'.[278] The Court appears, here, to be leaning towards a test of *factual* rather than purely *legal* subordination, that is to say, one in which the presence of the substantive indicia of the employment relationship – in particular, the provision of personal services in return for remuneration, and an element of subordination to the direction of another – outweighs the absence of a formal, juridical nexus between the parties of the kind required under the 'mutuality of obligation' test. It remains to be seen how the UK courts interpret the ruling of the ECJ when they reconsider the *Allonby* case.

3.59 A further distinction which must be drawn under the 'worker' category is between independent contractors who have a business of their own, and who in that sense can be said to be entrepreneurs who take the risk of losses and the chance of profits, and those, such as the taxpayer in *Hall v Lorimer*,[279] who do not have an identifiable business but who work as professionals or otherwise for a large number of separate employers or clients. An entrepreneur, if the business is incorporated, will most likely be an employee of *that* business; there is nothing to prevent the individual owner and controller of a business being the employee of the corporate entity which is the formal legal mechanism through which the business operates.[280] This means that for the purposes of labour law, the most important group of self-employed workers consists of those who do not have a business of their own (or, at least, do not choose to incorporate it), but who are not in a position of subordination or dependence to another such as to make them employees.

3.60 What the legislature appears to have in mind, then, is a category of self-employed workers who have neither a regular profession to protect them, nor a business of their own. This group is sometimes referred to as the 'dependent self-employed'[281] or those with a 'semi-dependent worker's contract'.[282] The logic of this distinction reflects the notion of 'economic dependence' which forms part of the tests for employee status, but seeks to extend protection to those with irregular or intermittent work falling outside the 'employee' concept.[283] This was recognised by the EAT in *Byrne Brothers (Formwork) Ltd v Baird*,[284] a case arising under the Working Time Regulations 1998:

> The reason why employees are thought to need [working time] protection is that they are in a subordinate and dependent position vis-à-vis their employers:

---

278 *Allonby*, Judgment of the Court, at para 72.
279 [1994] IRLR 171.
280 *Lee v Lee's Air Farming Ltd* [1961] AC 12; *Secretary of State for Trade and Industry v Bottrill* [1998] IRLR 120; *Sellars Arenascene Ltd v Connolly* [2001] IRLR 222; see para 3.96 below.
281 See Burchell *et al*, 1999.
282 Freedland, 2003: p 30.
283 The notion of 'economic dependence' may also be relevant in determining whether the individual is a member of a regular 'profession' which can be understood as offering protection and support. See *R (on the application of the BBC) v CAC* [2003] IRLR 460.
284 [2002] IRLR 96, at para 17; although for a different view of the value of a policy perspective, see the judgment of Pill LJ in *Redrow Homes (Yorkshire) Ltd v Wright* [2004] IRLR 720, at para 21.

the purpose of the Regulations is to extend protection to workers who are, substantively and economically, in the same position. Thus the essence of the intended distinction must be between, on the one hand, workers whose degree of dependence is essentially the same as that of employees and, on the other, contractors who have a sufficiently arm's-length and independent position to be treated as being able to look after themselves in the relevant respects.

A similarly purposive approach has been adopted in equal treatment legislation as a means of overcoming the problem of 'feigned' self-employment. In *Quinnen v Hovells*[285] the EAT held that the Equal Pay and Sex Discrimination Acts applied to the employment of a temporary sales assistant who had been taken on by his employer as self-employed in order to avoid 'the relationship of employer and employee and the complications that accompany that relationship'. The EAT held that although self-employed, the applicant came within the scope of the Acts: 'a contract for the personal execution of work or labour was intended, in our judgment, on a proper reading of the legislative purpose of the two Acts to enlarge upon (as opposed merely to supplying an instance of) the ordinary connotation of employment, so as to include persons outside the master-servant relationship'.[286]

3.61   A different type of solution has been adopted to deal with the widespread use of self-employment in the construction industry. In the early 1990s a new scheme for the collection of income tax was instituted in this sector, as part of which tax was to be deducted at source under Schedule E *whether or not the worker was an employee*. The only workers who were allowed an exemption from this rule were those who had acquired from the Inland Revenue a certificate stating that they are genuinely carrying on their own business.[287] This is one of a number of instances of workers being treated as employees for the purposes of tax and national insurance legislation, even where they do not clearly have the benefit of employment protection law.[288] Such workers do at least now have the possibility of protection of minimum wage and working time legislation; a large proportion of the case law generated by the 'worker' concept refers to self-employed construction workers who pay a proportion of their tax at source under the Inland Revenue rules referred to above. For the most part, tribunals and courts have held that the 'worker' concept does apply in this type of situation, but in the absence of a certification mechanism which could definitively establish the status of the individual for employment law purposes in the manner of the Inland Revenue scheme, cases continue to go both ways.[289]

---

285 [1984] IRLR 227. See also the discussion of this point by the ECJ in Case C-256/01 *Allonby v Accrington and Rossendale College* [2004] IRLR 224, at para 71.

286 [1984] IRLR 227, 229.

287 See M. Harvey, 1995.

288 For discussion of this issue, see Burchell *et al*, 1999, in particular chs 6 and 7. The IR35 procedure (see above, para 3.28) for dealing with personal service companies is another indication of the radical solutions which operate in fiscal law and which have no true equivalent in employment law.

289 In addition to the *Byrne, Redrow* and *Morris* cases noted above, contrast *JNJ Bricklaying Ltd v Stacey*, EAT, 8 July 2003, Appeal No EAT/0088/03/ILB, in which members of a construction gang were classified as 'workers' with *Bamford v Persimmon Homes NW Ltd*, EAT, 16 June 2004, Appeal No UKEAT/0049/04/DM, reaching the opposite result. In *Staddon v Dent*, EAT, 17 March 2003, Appeal No EAT/0945/02/SM and *McCarthy v Blue Sword Construction Ltd*, EAT, 14 July 2003, Appeal No EAT/0223/03/DM, casual construction workers were found to be employees.

Homeworkers

3.62   Homeworking is a form of work which also grew rapidly in the 1970s and 1980s, when it doubled to reach about 3% of the active labour force.[290] Those who work *at home* tend to be women workers; 'freelances' and others who work *from home* tend to be male, and probably should not be considered in the same category although for statistical purposes the two groups are difficult to separate. Homeworking is associated in many cases with low pay, poor working conditions and lack of access to fringe benefits.[291] While a great deal of attention has been devoted to new technology homeworking and 'teleworking', this form of work still accounts for only a few thousand people; the majority of homeworkers are employed in more traditional occupations.[292]

Homeworkers do not have a clear employment status. The precariousness of their work and in particular the lack of clear mutual commitments to make work available and to be available to do it make it difficult for a court or tribunal to infer the existence of a contract of employment, although the case law has not consistently come down against employee status.[293] However, any homeworker who is able to establish employee status may be unable to go on to prove that he or she has the necessary continuity of employment to claim rights such as statutory sick pay and protection from unfair dismissal.[294]

3.63   The difficulty of classifying homeworkers led to attempts in the past to extend protective legislation beyond the categories of 'employee' and 'worker'.[295] There is now a specific definition of 'homeworker' for the purposes of the national minimum wage, according to which a homeworker is one who 'contracts with a person, for the purposes of that person's business, for the execution of work to be done in a place not under the control or management of that person'.[296] This definition, like the 'worker' concept, therefore stresses the criterion of economic dependence (hence the need to show that the homeworker is employed for the purposes of the other contracting party's business, rather than his or her own[297]), at the expense of control (the absence of which, as we have just seen, is explicitly stated to be irrelevant to protected status in this context). Although specific protection for homeworkers remains exceptional, the establishment of standards of good practice for certain categories of homeworkers may also be assisted by the adoption in 2004 of *Telework Guidance*[298] by the CBI, TUC and the UK branch of the European public employers' federation, CEEP. The *Guidance*, which is voluntary, follows on from a non-binding framework agreement on teleworking agreed by UNICE, CEEP and the ETUC under the EU social dialogue process.

---

290   Hakim, 1985. For a more recent estimate, see Felstead and Jewson, 1995.
291   Rubery and Wilkinson, 1981.
292   Stanworth and Stanworth, 1989.
293   For differing outcomes, see *Airfix Footwear Ltd v Cope* [1978] ICR 1210; *Nethermere (St Neots) Ltd v Taverna and Gardiner* [1984] ICR 612; *Bridges v Industrial Rubber plc*, EAT, 21 September 2004, Appeal No UKEAT/0150/04/DM.
294   See below, para 3.92.
295   See National Insurance Act 1911, Sch 1, Part 1; SRO 1912/880; SRO 1913/33; Wages Act 1986, s 26(1).
296   NMWA 1998, s 35
297   In *Commissioners of Inland Revenue v Post Office Ltd* [2003] IRLR 199, postmasters and postmistresses were held to fall outside the definition of 'homeworker' for this reason.
298   *Telework Guidance*, as agreed by the CBI, TUC and CEEP (2004), available on the DTI website (http://www.dti.gov.uk/er/individual/telework.pdf).

Agency employment and other employment through intermediaries

3.64   Estimates of the number of temporary agency workers vary widely but all surveys reveal a substantial increase in their numbers over the past ten years or so. The DTI estimates that about 600,000 people are working as temporary agency workers at any particular time in the UK.[299] The supply of labour by employment agencies and employment businesses is governed by the Employment Agencies Act 1973[300] and the Conduct of Employment Agencies and Employment Businesses Regulations 2003.[301] However, this legislation says little or nothing about the nature of the contractual relationships to which agency work gives rise, which is one of the most difficult and controversial in contemporary employment law. The difficulty arises, in large part, because the worker has two separate, overlapping relations: one with the 'agency', which normally arranges work assignments and is responsible for ensuring payment; and the other the 'user', which normally assumes the power to give orders and takes the direct benefit of the services which are being provided.

3.65   Workers hired out by an agency for use by a third party have been held to have a unique '*sui generis*' status, being neither employees nor self-employed.[302] There is an unsatisfactory, ad hoc air to this decision, suggesting as it does that the courts can invent new categories of employment status at will. A better view is that agency workers will almost certainly have a contract of some kind with the agency; depending on the terms upon which they make themselves available for work, this can either be a contract of employment or a contract providing for self-employment. In addition, it is possible, but less likely, that the worker will have a contractual relationship with the user. Whether or not there is a contract in either case, legislation imposes certain obligations on both agencies and users.

3.66   The 2003 Regulations (like their predecessors of 1976) do not specify what the status of temporary workers should be for the purposes of employment legislation, leaving the matter to be decided under the common law tests of status. This is in contrast to income tax and national insurance legislation, each of which treats temporary workers as if they were the employees of the agency for the purposes of determining liability for income tax under Schedule E and

---

299   See DTI, *Proposal for a Directive of the European Parliament and of the Council on Working Conditions for Temporary Agency Workers – Regulatory Impact Assessment*, p 7. This figure contrasts with the figures of 275,000 given in the Labour Force Survey and 1.3 million given by the Recruitment and Employment Confederation, both of which are regarded by the DTI as unreliable for reasons explained in the assessment.

300   As amended. For the purposes of these provisions, a distinction is drawn between recruitment agencies which aim to find employment for workers with another employer (these are referred to as 'employment agencies') and suppliers of agency labour (these are referred to as 'employment businesses'). In practice, the term 'employment agency' is commonly used in other contexts (including the case law on the employment status of agency workers) to refer to organisations which would most likely be classified as employment businesses for the 1973 Act, and we therefore retain this general usage in the text. See also the Gangmasters (Licensing) Act 2004 which applies specific requirements in relation to agricultural work, gathering shellfish, and related activities.

301   SI 2003/3319, replacing SI 1976/715. On regulations governing agency work, see generally G Morris, 2004b, and for a comparative survey, Blanpain and Graham (eds), 2004.

302   *Construction Industry Training Board v Labour Force Ltd* [1970] 3 All ER 220.

Class 1 national insurance contributions.[303] Precisely because it is imposed by statute, the courts tend to take the view that the tax and national insurance treatment of agency workers has no bearing on their employment status for other purposes.[304] The 1976 regulations merely require the agency to issue its temporary workers with a written statement of terms and conditions, which must indicate whether the agency regards them as its employees or as self-employed.[305] This statement will not necessarily determine their status in law: even in cases where temporary workers have been designated as employees in the written statement, courts have disregarded this to hold that they were self-employed, on the grounds that the arrangement between them and the agency lacked the mutuality of obligation needed for a contract of employment.[306] But although a 'global' contract may be ruled out by the intermittent nature of most agency work, this may not prevent the courts from finding on occasion either a contract of employment or a contract for personal services in respect of specific hirings or periods of employment.[307] Whether or not they are employees, the agency is under an obligation not to discriminate against agency workers on grounds related to their sex, sexual orientation, race, and religion or belief.[308]

3.67 It is possible that the user will be regarded as the employer under circumstances where it assumes managerial authority over the performance of the work for a substantial period of time. The leading case is *Dacas v Brook Street Bureau (UK) Ltd.*[309] Here, the applicant had worked for the user for several years before she was subject to an allegation of misconduct. Her agency was then informed that her services were no longer required. The employment tribunal found that she has no contract of employment with the agency, following the well-established case law on this issue. The EAT reversed on this point but the Court of Appeal restored the original tribunal decision. However, the Court of Appeal held by a majority (Munby J dissenting) that the tribunal had made an error of law in not giving adequate consideration to the possibility that there was an implied contract of employment between the applicant and the user. Both Mummery and Sedley LJJ also thought that a triangular employment contract, with both the agency and the user sharing the responsibilities of the employer, was, in principle, a possible way of analysing agency relations.

Mrs Dacas's claim failed on a procedural point – by the time her case reached the Court of Appeal, the user of her services had ceased to be a party to the litigation. We therefore do not know whether the user could, finally, have been fixed with liability. Although a contract of employment may be implied from conduct, it is not straightforward to do so. It is necessary for there to be not

---

303 See Income Tax (Earnings and Pensions) Act 2003, Part 2, Ch 7 (and for case law interpreting earlier, analogous provisions, *Brady v Hart (trading as Jaclyn Model Agency)* [1985] STC 498; *Bhadra v Ellan* [1988] STC 239); Social Security (Categorisation of Earners) Regulations, SI 1978/1689.
304 *McMeechan v Secretary of State for Employment* [1997] IRLR 353, 358 (Waite LJ).
305 SI 2003/3319, reg 15(a).
306 *Wickens v Champion Employment* [1984] ICR 365; *Ironmonger v Movefield Ltd* [1988] IRLR 461. Later decisions have taken a similar line on the need for mutuality and control: see *Montgomery v Johnson Underwood Ltd* [2001] IRLR 269.
307 See, in particular, *McMeechan v Secretary of State for Employment* [1997] IRLR 353, in which a contract of employment for a specific hiring was found.
308 SDA 1975, s 15; EE(SO)R 2003, reg 18; RRA 1976, s 14; EE(RB)R 2003, reg 18.
309 [2004] IRLR 358; to similar effect is another Court of Appeal decision, *Franks v Reuters Ltd* [2003] IRLR 423. See also *Bunce v Postworth Ltd t/a Skyblue* [2005] IRLR 557 (agency worker an employee of neither the agency nor the user).

simply control over the manner in which the work is carried out, but a contractual nexus between the two parties. This may be difficult to demonstrate in a situation in which the user is not responsible for arranging the payment of remuneration to the worker (this is normally done by the agency).[310] It is possible to infer a contract with the user in a case where the supplier or agency was only acting as a go-between or recruitment agency, and had no continuing relation with the worker, but, by definition, this is not the paradigm case of agency employment.

A contract of employment was implied between the user and agency in *Motorola Ltd v Davidson*.[311] However, the EAT in *Davidson* did not address (because it was not called on to do so) the possibility that the applicant had a separate contract with the agency or supplier of his labour. If such a contract exists, and it is construed as a contract of employment as opposed to a contract for services, it is not altogether easy to see how the worker can also have a contract of employment, in respect of the work in question, with the user. Although the notion of a trilateral employment contract has now been given the approval, in obiter dicta, of the Court of Appeal in *Dacas*, unanswered questions remain concerning the precise division of powers and responsibilities between agency and user. However, it is more likely, as we have seen, that the relation between the agency and the worker does not give rise to a contract of employment, in which case these difficulties no longer pose an obstacle.

3.68   In addition, it is entirely possible, indeed likely, that the user will be fixed with certain duties of an employer with regard to the worker, whether or not there is a contractual nexus between them. In particular, it will be subject to the requirements of the equal treatment legislation.[312] The user, described here as the 'principal', must not discriminate on these grounds against 'contract workers'. A 'principal' is one who makes work available for doing by individuals who are employed by another person who supplies them under a contract; a 'contract worker' is an individual supplied to the principal under such a contract.[313]

A growing body of case law illustrates that this type of provision applies to a number of situations where employment is arranged through an intermediary or where the normal duties of the employer are divided between separate entities. *Harrods Ltd v Remick*[314] concerned the complex set of commercial and employment arrangements which can arise as a result of franchising arrangements. Employees of companies which were concessionaires (similar to franchisees) of the Harrods department store alleged that they had been subjected to discrimination by Harrods on the grounds of their race. Harrods had withdrawn from the employees, or in one case had refused to grant, 'store approval', as a result of which they were dismissed by their employers (or, in

---

310 For cases denying, on various grounds, the existence of a contract between the worker and the user, see *Hewlett Packard Ltd v O'Murphy* [2002] IRLR 4 and *Stephenson v Delphi Diesel Systems Ltd* [2003] ICR 471, and see the dissenting judgment of Munby J in *Dacas v Brook Street Bureau (UK) Ltd* [2004] IRLR 358.

311 [2001] IRLR 4.

312 SDA 1975, s 9; EE(SO)R 2003, reg 8; RRA 1976, s 7; EE(RB)R 2003, reg 8; DDA 1995, s 12.

313 There is a slightly different definition of 'agency worker' for the purposes of the national minimum wage: NMWA 1998, s 34.

314 [1997] IRLR 9, EAT; affd [1997] IRLR 583, CA. See also, for slightly more straightforward applications of the anti-discrimination Acts to end users of labour, *BP Chemicals Ltd v Gillick* [1995] IRLR 128 and *Patefield v Belfast City Council* [2000] IRLR 664; in *Secretary of State for Education and Employment v Bearman* [1998] IRLR 431, by contrast, a similar type of claim failed. For further discussion of these cases, see Deakin, 2001a.

the one case, not employed when they otherwise would have been). Under the contractual arrangements made between Harrods and the concessionaires, the latter undertook to market the goods in question (which were the property of Harrods) and to promote their sale, and to ensure that the relevant department was adequately staffed. The Court of Appeal held that the arrangement fell under the provision in the Act aimed at protecting 'contract workers'. This was so, notwithstanding that the main purpose of the contract in each case was, arguably, for the concessionaire to promote the sale of the goods, and not to supply labour as such; nor was it considered relevant that Harrods did not have immediate powers of direction and control over the staff.[315]

This is a highly significant decision, but some potential limits must be borne in mind. In particular, it is not clear how far the non-discrimination principle, when applied to contract workers, allows the applicant to compare his or her position to that of a comparable worker in the user's 'regular' employment or simply to that of a fellow contract worker. If the former were the case, the requirement of equal treatment would impose a strict limit on the employer's use of agency work to differentiate between categories of workers in terms of their benefits and treatment. While this could legitimately be taken to have been the intention of the legislature, given the purpose of the Acts in question, such a conclusion has so far been resisted by the courts. This is the effect of the ruling of the ECJ in the *Allonby* case, in which the Court ruled that under Article 141 of the EC Treaty, it was not possible for the applicant, who was an agency worker, to compare her employment with that of a comparator who was employed by the user, even though the applicant had previously been directly employed by the user in question, and had only recently been dismissed by it with the aim of limiting its employment law obligations to her.[316]

The second significant case is *Abbey Life Assurance Co Ltd v Tansell*,[317] a decision under the Disability Discrimination Act for the purposes of which the need to identify a comparator, in the sense just described, does not arise.[318] The applicant had set up his own personal service company for the supply of his services as a computer consultant. His personal service company (Intelligents) contracted with an employment agency (MHC) to supply his services to the end user, Abbey Life. The contract between Intelligents and MHC had the effect of placing the complainant 'under the control of Abbey Life'[319] as part of a team working on the impact of the 'millennium bug' on Abbey Life's computer systems. About five months into this arrangement, Abbey Life terminated its use of the complainant's services, shortly after he had been diagnosed as suffering from diabetes. He brought claims against both MHC and Abbey Life for disability discrimination. The EAT and the Court of Appeal held that Abbey Life, but not MHC, owed the complainant obligations of

---

315 See [1997] IRLR 583, 585–586.
316 Case C-256/01 *Allonby v Accrington and Rossendale College* [2004] IRLR 224, discussed further in ch 6, below, at paras 6.41 and 6.75. The question of equal treatment between agency workers and 'permanent' workers of the user is one of the core issues currently considered in the context of a proposal for an EU directive on agency work. See *Amended Proposal for a Directive of the European Parliament and the Council on Working Conditions for Temporary Workers* COM/2002/701 final 28 November 2002. It should also be noted that agency workers are specifically excluded from the scope of the requirement of equal treatment between fixed-term and permanent employees under FTER 2002 (see reg 19).
317 [2000] IRLR 387; see also the judgment of the EAT sub nom *MHC Consulting Ltd v Tansell* [1999] IRLR 677.
318 On the reasons for this, see para 6.110 below.
319 [2000] IRLR 387, 388.

non-discrimination under section 12 of the Disability Discrimination Act, even though there was no contract between Abbey Life (the alleged 'principal') and Intelligents. According to Mummery LJ, 'the statutory definition only requires the supply of the individual to be "under a contract made with [the principal]". It does not expressly stipulate who is to be the party who contracts with [the principal]'.[320]

The user is also under a responsibility to ensure the health and safety of temporary workers while they are working on its premises. As an employer, the user will owe a duty under the Health and Safety at Work Act 1974 to persons who are not in his employment 'who may be affected thereby',[321] a category which would appear to cover any temporary workers. It is less clear whether the user will incur obligations to the temporary workers working on his premises by virtue of the employer's common law duty of care in respect of the health and safety of its employees. There is some authority to suggest that this duty is only owed to those employed under a contract of employment, a lower standard being imposed with regard to independent contractors and others.[322] On the other hand, it has been held that the common law duty of care can extend from a main contractor to cover the employees of one of its sub-contractors working on the same site.[323] Temporary workers working on the user's premises are arguably in an analogous position. If they are not, the United Kingdom is potentially in breach of Directive 91/383. This Directive, which is concerned with the health and safety both of fixed-term contract workers and agency workers, requires Member States to ensure that 'without prejudice to the responsibility of the temporary employment business as laid down in national legislation, the user undertaking and/or establishment is/are responsible, for the duration of the assignment, for the conditions governing performance of the work'.[324] In requiring the user to be responsible for the 'conditions governing performance', the Directive appears to envisage that it could be liable for any breach of health and safety law with regard to the workers assigned to its use. A decision which is highly questionable in the context of the Directive is *Costain Building and Civil Engineering Ltd v Smith*,[325] in which it was held that an agency worker who was elected to be a health and safety representative on the site where he was working did not have the protection of legislation designed to prevent the unlawful dismissal of such representatives, since he was not an employee of the user.

3.69   The legislation which we have been considering so far uses the technique of attaching particular obligations to the user and others to the agency. The problem with this approach is that some of the responsibilities which are normally assumed by the employer may fall upon neither of them. Labour standards legislation attempts to deal with this issue by stipulating that the national minimum wage and working time controls must be observed by 'whichever of the agent and the principal [or user] is responsible for paying the agency worker in respect of the work', or, failing that, whichever of them actually pays the agency worker in respect of the work.[326]

---

320   [2000] IRLR 387, 390.
321   HSWA 1974, s 3(1).
322   *Jones v Minton Construction Ltd* (1973) 15 KIR 309.
323   *McArdle v Andmac Roofing Co* [1967] 1 All ER 583; but cf Hepple and Napier, 1978.
324   Directive 91/383, Art 8(1).
325   [2000] ICR 215.
326   NMWA 1998, s 34; WTR 1998, reg 36; see generally Deakin, 2001a. See also ERelA 1999, s 13(2)(c), stipulating that in the context of a worker's right to be accompanied at a disciplinary or grievance hearing, either the agency or the user may be designated the employer of an agency worker.

Ministers of religion

3.70   The courts have consistently held that persons holding religious office do not normally have a contract of any kind, let alone a contract of employment. A number of reasons have been given for this approach; few, if any of them, can be said to be convincing. It has been argued that the spiritual nature of a religious office makes it incompatible with the undertaking of contractual obligations,[327] but there seems no reason why spiritual and temporal authority should not exist alongside each other for this purpose.[328] Alternatively, it has been said that in these cases, there is no intention to create legal relations. This, however, contradicts the normal approach of the courts to the construction of the contract of employment, which is to infer the existence of a contractual nexus from the regular exchange of service or services for payment.[329] A more specific ground for rejecting this normal approach is that the status of certain holders of religious office is regulated by public law or by a particular ecclesiastical status. Hence, in the case of a Church of England curate:

> The legal effect of the ordination of a person admitted to the order of priesthood is that he [sic] is called to an office, recognised by law and charged with functions designated by law in the ordinal, as set out in the Book of Common Prayer ... The legal implications of the appointment of an assistant curate must be considered in the context of that historic and special pre-existing legal framework of a church, of an ecclesiastical hierarchy established by law, of spiritual duties defined by public law rather than by private contract, and of ecclesiastical courts with jurisdiction over the discipline of clergy. In that context, the law requires clear evidence of an intention to create a contractual relationship in addition to the pre-existing legal framework.[330]

If this is the correct basis for the court's approach, it presumably has little or no application outside the context of the established Church. Nor is it particularly convincing to argue that the presence either of pre-existing regulation, or of an element of public law, requires the court to find against the existence of a contract of employment. In other contexts, the courts have rejected the idea that an office holder is barred, for that reason, from being an employee.[331]

Voluntary workers

3.71   The position of 'volunteers' or 'voluntary workers' has given rise to a growing body of litigation. In principle, it is open to the parties to a work relationship to make a voluntary arrangement which excludes the possibility of a contract of employment or contract for personal services. A volunteer who carries out work for charitable bodies may be entitled, by agreement with the organisation concerned, to receive work-related expenses. However, this arrangement, without more, will most likely lack the mutuality of obligation

---

327 *Re Employment of Church of England Curates* [1912] 2 Ch 563; *President of the Methodist Conference v Parfitt* [1984] ICR 176; *Davies v Presbyterian Church of Wales* [1986] IRLR 194.
328 See Brodin, 1996, for a comprehensive analysis which argues that 'religious or spiritual duties are not incompatible with a contract of employment'.
329 See, eg, the modern approach of the courts to the finding of a contract of employment in the case of civil servants: *R v Lord Chancellor's Department, ex p Nangle* [1991] IRLR 343, discussed below, para 3.73.
330 *Diocese of Southwark v Coker* [1998] ICR 140,147, per Mummery LJ.
331 *102 Social Club v Bickerton* [1977] ICR 911.

needed to imply either a contract of employment or a contract for personal services, unless the individual in question also undertakes an obligation to make himself or herself available for work over a given period of time.[332] Alternatively, the parties to a voluntary arrangement could be described as lacking the intention to create legal relations. It is arguable, nevertheless, that tribunals and courts should be slow to reach such a conclusion. Clear evidence should be required of a joint intention to create a voluntary work relationship. The case law suggests that it is not unknown for employers to present wages as expenses in an attempt to avoid the coverage of protective legislation.[333]

Moreover, there is an argument to the effect that genuine volunteers, even if (by definition) they should not have the right to the minimum wage or to the rights to income and job security which are conferred by employment protection legislation, should be entitled to certain other protections which relate to the way in which work is organised. This argument could extend, for example, to health and safety legislation, as well as to legislation ensuring equality of treatment within employment on the grounds of sex, sexual orientation, race, religion or belief, or disability. However, volunteers will not be 'employed persons' within the meaning of equal treatment legislation unless they can establish that they are employed under, at the very least, a contract to provide personal services, and this, for the reasons discussed above, is unlikely to be the case. Specific legislative provision may therefore be required to ensure that voluntary workers receive this basic level of protection in the workplace.

The power to confer employment rights on other categories of individuals

3.72   Section 23(1) of the Employment Relations Act 1999 empowers the Secretary of State by order to confer upon 'individuals who are of a specified description' any 'right conferred on an individual against an employer (however defined)' under one of the following provisions: TULRCA 1992, ERA 1996, the 1999 Act itself, and instruments made under section 2(2) of the European Communities Act 1972 (this last category includes TUPE 1981 and WTR 1998). Thus statutory employment rights under these provisions can be extended, by order, to cover individuals who are not currently protected by them. The order can take effect either as a free-standing statutory instrument or as an amendment to primary legislation.[334] The power of extension applies even if the exclusion results from an express provision in the statute in question. One type of case which the Act seems to have in mind, but which is not explicitly mentioned in section 23, is one in which the exclusion arises from a contract term, or from judicial construction of working or commercial arrangements. This is implicit in section 23(4), which states that an order under this section may '(a) provide

---

332 See *South East Sheffield CAB v Grayson* [2004] IRLR 353; *Bruce v Dial House Chester*, 20 August 2004, Appeal No UKEAT/0555/04/SM; *Melhuish v Redbridge Citizens' Advice Bureau* [2005] IRLR 419.

333 See D Morris, 1999, discussing case law in which tribunals and courts concluded, on the one hand, that the payment of 'expenses' was a sham and, on the other, in which 'employment' was distinguished from 'membership' of a voluntary organisation.

334 S 23 was amended by ERelA 2004, s 39 explicitly to allow an order to extend employment rights either by the use of a free-standing provision or by amending the legislation conferring the right.

that individuals are to be treated as parties to workers' contracts or contracts of employment', and '(b) make provision as to who are to be regarded as the employers of individuals'. Under section 23(5), the order can operate in such a way as to modify the application of the right in question. Section 41 NMWA 1998 contains a broadly analogous power to extend the application of the national minimum wage.

The origins of section 23 lie in the *Fairness at Work* White Paper of 1998, which noting that the national minimum wage and working time controls would apply to 'all those who work for another person, not just those employed under a contract of employment', advanced 'the idea of legislation enabling [the government] similarly to extend the coverage of some or all existing employment rights by regulation'.[335] The reference to the minimum wage and working time link what is now section 23 to the 'worker' concept. One possible use of section 23, then, would be to extend protection to those who are not 'employees' but who are 'workers'. However, this does not mean that the 'worker' concept sets limits to the power contained in section 23. On the face of it, the Secretary of State has the power to confer employment rights on individuals who would otherwise be neither employees nor workers, and, for statutory purposes, to deem them to be employed under the relevant contract. An Opposition motion to amend section 23, so as to make it clear that it should only apply to 'an individual who is a worker within the meaning of section [13]' of the Act, together with related changes, was debated and rejected during the House of Commons Committee stage. The minister concerned rejected the motion on the grounds that 'it would place too great a restriction on the flexibility of the new rule-making power', and made specific reference to 'members of the clergy, registration officers, share fisherman, merchant seamen, members of the armed forces, and police officers' as categories of individuals who could benefit from the exercise of the new power.[336]

The suggestion that section 23 can be used to extend rights to police officers or registration officials suggests that something in the nature of a tidying up operation is intended. If, because of a statutory oversight or an adverse court decision, an individual in one of these categories falls within neither the 'employee' nor the 'worker' category, they can be brought within protection by means of the new power.[337] The power can also be used to specify which one of several possible parties is the employer of the individual concerned.[338] With the exception of share fishermen (an almost vanished category in any event), all the other groups listed by the minister in his reply consist of employments which largely satisfy the criteria of both formal and economic dependence.[339] For various reasons, however, most of which are ad hoc or the result of historical accident

---

335 Cm 3968 (1998), at para 3.18.

336 Mr Willis MP, *Hansard*, House of Commons Standing Committee E, 2 March 1999, col 237.

337 For examples of the types of problem which can arise, see *Commissioner of Police of the Metropolis v Lowrey-Nesbitt* [1999] ICR 401, in which the EAT held that a police officer in the Metropolitan Police was not a 'worker' for the purposes of the law governing deductions from wages; *Johnson v Ryan* [2000] ICR 236, in which it held that a rent officer was not an employee of either the chief rent officer or the Secretary of State, but of the relevant local authority; and *Perceval-Price v Department of Economic Development* [2000] IRLR 380, in which the Northern Ireland Court of Appeal held that employment tribunal chairmen were 'workers' for the purposes of European Union sex discrimination law.

338 See *Johnson v Ryan* [2000] ICR 236.

339 See above, para 3.19 and below, paras 3.59–3.60.

as much as anything, they are not regarded as being employed under a contract of employment. Although there may well be compelling practical considerations for ministers to consider for extending full employment rights to these groups, such extensions would not mark a radical departure from current practice; rather, they would signify the final extension of the predominant legal model of employment to a set of anomalous cases.

A more radical use of section 23 would be to extend further the application of certain labour law rights to the self-employed. References were made during the relevant Parliamentary debates to the need to deal with 'feigned' self-employment,[340] but there is a wider case to be made for extending labour legislation with a human rights dimension (such as rights of expression) and rights which do not depend upon regularity of employment to certain of the self-employed and to agency workers.[341]

PUBLIC SECTOR EMPLOYMENT

3.73 For statistical purposes, the government defines the public sector as covering employment in central government, which includes the civil service, armed forces, and the National Health Service; local government; the police; maintained educational establishments;[342] and the 'public corporations' such as Royal Mail and British Nuclear Fuels plc.[343] On this basis, around 5.45 million workers were employed in the UK public sector in 2003.[344] However, these categories do not form a homogeneous group for legal purposes: 'there is no clear legal test for determining what makes employment public'.[345]

In recent years the boundaries of state employment have been further blurred by the introduction of compulsory competitive tendering, market testing and internal contracting in large parts of central and local government. This means that identical jobs may be performed either by those directly employed in the public service, or by those who work for private sector employers which have a contractual relationship with the public body in question. Even before these reforms, however, there was no hard dividing line between the law of public-sector employment and that of private-sector employment, as exists in some other European countries. Public-sector employees are subject, for the most part, to the same basic principles of labour law as apply more generally.[346] There are some specific restrictions in relation to freedom of association for

---

340 See Lord Simon of Highbury, HL Debs, 10 May 1999, cols. 968–969: s 23 will 'empower the Secretary of State to rationalise and update the coverage of the existing body of employment rights by conferring, by order, some or all of those rights on specified categories of individuals who may not or clearly cannot benefit from them at present but who are not genuinely self-employed'; and Mr Phil Hope MP, House of Commons Standing Committee E, 2 March 1999, col 235: 'It is intended that the new powers will not be extended to the genuinely self-employed. The clause deals with the grey zone that has grown up over the past 20 years'.

341 See Deakin, 2001b. For a suggestion that s 23 should be invoked in the case of agency workers, see *Montgomery v Johnson Underwood Ltd* [2001] IRLR 269, at para 43.

342 Note that universities, and higher and further education, and sixth-form colleges are now treated as part of the private sector.

343 Black, Richardson and Herbert, 2004.

344 Black, Richardson and Herbert, 2004: p 277.

345 G Morris and S Fredman, 1993: p 120.

346 See S Fredman and G Morris, 1989; G Morris and S Fredman, 1993.

particular groups of public sector workers.[347] In general, however, public and private sector employment share the same conceptual framework.[348]

Civil servants

3.74 Although public sector employment is largely assimilated to the model of the contract of employment, doubts remain about the status of civil servants, who are in the distinct position of having the Crown as their employer.[349] It was thought at one stage that since the Crown could not fetter its own discretion by contract,[350] it could not be contractually bound by any undertakings it made to those in its employment. In *R v Civil Service Appeal Board, ex p Bruce*,[351] however, the Divisional Court concluded that it was constitutionally possible for civil servants to have a contract of employment, but that there was no contractual nexus in the case before it for the quite separate reason that the parties did not intend to create legal relations. This was the consequence of paragraph 14 of the Civil Service Pay and Conditions Code then in force which stated that 'a civil servant does not have a contract of employment enforceable in the courts'. This last part of the analysis was rejected, however, by the Court of Appeal in *R v Lord Chancellor's Department, ex p Nangle*,[352] on the grounds that paragraph 14 was merely descriptive of the state of affairs which the parties believed to exist. The test of intention to create legal relations was objective and depended on the view the court took of the terms of the relationship. According to Stuart-Smith LJ, 'the relationship of employer and employee, master and servant, which plainly exists here must of its very nature be one that involves an intention to create legal relations, unless such intention is clearly excluded expressly or by necessary implication'.[353]

The decision in *Nangle* can be criticised on the grounds that the notion of 'contractual intention' is a judicial construct, which is capable of being manipulated to suit the particular circumstances of individual cases. The discovery of a contractual nexus in that case, for example, ruled out the possibility of civil

---

347 See para 8.2 below.
348 It should nevertheless be noted that HRA 1998 gives a free standing right of action to those who work for certain public authorities to enforce Convention rights against their employer, which is not available to other workers: see G Morris, 1998c: pp 299–303. For a critique of the assimilation of public-sector employment to the wider labour law model, see G Morris, 2000.
349 The power to determine the pay and conditions of civil servants apparently derives from the royal prerogative, which for this purpose is delegated to the Minister for the Civil Service by the Civil Service Order in Council 1995 (as amended). Pursuant to the Civil Service (Management Functions) Act 1992, the Minister for the Civil Service has in turn made delegations to Ministers and office holders in charge of departments to determine certain terms and conditions (who may in turn delegate further, in respect of executive agencies, to Agency Chief Executives); the rules and principles to which they must adhere are set out in the Civil Service Management Code 1996. For a discussion of the constitutional implications of this, see Freedland, 1996; G Morris, 1999a. At the time of writing the Government is consulting about whether there should be a Civil Service Act: *A Draft Civil Service Bill: A Consultation Document*, Cm 6373, 2004.
350 *Rederiaktiebolaget Amphitrite v R* [1921] 3 KB 500.
351 [1988] ICR 649.
352 [1991] IRLR 343.
353 [1991] ICR 743, 752. Note that in 1994 the Conservative Government resolved that its relationship with Senior Civil Servants should become explicitly contractual: *The Civil Service: Continuity and Change*, Cm 2627, 1994. See Freedland, 1995 for a discussion of the issues raised by this.

servants using judicial review to challenge an exercise of disciplinary power. There are other reasons for thinking that this remedy will not normally be available to them anyway, however.[354] In other contexts, too, the precise status of the civil servant has little practical significance. Although at common law civil servants can be dismissed at will, notwithstanding any agreement to the contrary such as an undertaking to employ them for a fixed term or to operate procedures governing discipline and dismissal,[355] the effect of this rule has been mitigated by the extension to civil servants of most of the protective provisions of TULRCA 1992 and ERA 1996,[356] together with those of the anti-discrimination legislation[357] and basic labour standards regulation.[358] Conversely, TULRCA 1992 deems civil servants to have a contract of employment for the purpose of ensuring that the normal incidents of liability in tort attach to those who organise industrial action in the civil service.[359] Moreover, the courts have held that principles of contract law are applicable for other purposes, even if the precise status of the civil servant remains unclear: thus a civil servant necessarily comes under an implied duty to serve the employer faithfully and with reasonable care and skill and, conversely, has the right to sue for arrears of pay.[360] One area where the absence of a contract of employment might harm civil servants is in relation to the variation of terms: here there is little effective statutory intervention and the protection of terms and conditions depends, as a result, on the application of principles drawn from the common law of contract, which may not be applicable to civil servants if their relationship of employment is not formally classified as contractual in nature.[361] That being said, once it is accepted that the concept of dismissal at will is not incompatible with the existence of a contract of employment, it is conceivable that variation at will may also be viewed in this way, on the basis that it constitutes the exercise of power to terminate a contract followed by the offer of another contract on different terms.[362]

Members of the armed forces

3.75   Members of the armed forces, like civil servants, are subject to the authority of the Crown exercised through the royal prerogative, but unlike civil servants there have been few suggestions that they either have or should have contracts of employment. Long-standing precedents clearly indicate that they cannot claim damages for breach of agreements concerning security of employment.[363] However, in recent years there have been moves to bring their statutory rights

---

354   S Fredman and G Morris, 1991b; see below, paras 5.46–5.52.
355   *Dunn v R* [1896] 1 QB 116; *Rodwell v Thomas* [1944] KB 596; *Riordan v War Office* [1959] 1 WLR 1046.
356   TULRCA 1992, ss 273–276; ERA 1996, ss 191–193. The main exceptions are the right to a minimum notice period and the right to a statutory redundancy payment. Provision for compensation on dismissal for redundancy is made in the Civil Service Compensation Scheme.
357   EqPA 1970, s 1(8); SDA 1975, s 85; EE(SO)R 2003, reg 36; RRA 1976, s 75; EE(RB)R 2003, reg 36; DDA 1995, s 64.
358   See NMWA 1998, s 36; WTR 1998, reg 37.
359   TULRCA 1992, s 245.
360   *Reilly v R* [1934] AC 176; *Riordan v War Office* [1959] 1 WLR 1046.
361   See below, paras 4.34–4.39.
362   See Freedland, 1995: p 230.
363   See *De Dohse v R* (1886) 3 TLR 114; *Grant v Secretary of State for India* (1877) 2 CPD 445.

more closely into line with civilian workers. They are now protected, with minor modifications,[364] by legislation on equal pay[365] and by legislation concerning discrimination on the grounds of sex,[366] racial discrimination,[367] sexual orientation, and religion or belief.[368] However, they are not covered by the DDA 1995.[369] They are outside the scope of the national minimum wage[370] but, with some modifications, they are protected by working time legislation.[371] At the time of writing they are also excluded from the ERA 1996 but there is provision for certain rights, including protection against unfair dismissal, to be brought into force by order.[372] However, they remain excluded from statutory collective rights:[373] they have no right, as a result, to legal protection against discrimination on the grounds of trade union membership, nor do they have the right to collective representation in respect of the matters over which employers are normally required to inform and consult representatives of their employees.

Parliamentary staff

3.76 Parliamentary staff are in a distinct position thanks to the doctrine of Parliamentary privilege. Matters internal to the Houses of Parliament are excluded from the jurisdiction of the courts, as a consequence of which it is thought that parliamentary staff do not have contracts of employment;[374] but as in the case of civil servants, not much turns on this.[375] Procedures for the appointment of House of Commons staff and for the establishment of their terms and conditions of employment, which are broadly comparable to those of civil servants, are governed by the House of Commons (Administration) Act

364 In all cases they are required to make use of the armed forces internal redress procedures before applying to an employment tribunal: see EqPA 1970, s 7A; SDA 1975, s 85; EE(SO)R 2003, reg 36(7)–(10); RRA 1976, s 75; and EE(RB)R 2003, reg 36(7)–(10) (in each case the legislation follows the model set out initially in the Armed Forces Act 1996). The period for bringing complaints of discrimination on these grounds was extended to six months to allow the internal procedures to be carried out.
365 EqPA 1970, s 1(9), excluding the armed forces from the equal pay provisions, was repealed by the Armed Forces Act 1996, s 24, which introduced a new s 7A into the 1970 Act. The armed forces, like other workers in both the public and the private sectors, were in any case protected by the principle of equal pay laid down in Art 141 (ex 119) of the EC Treaty and because of their relationship with the state could also invoke the protection of Directive 75/117 on Equal Pay: see further para 2.41 above on the 'horizontal' direct effect of Art 141 and the 'vertical' direct effect of the equality directives.
366 SDA 1975, s 85(2)(c). There is an exception for acts done to ensure 'combat effectiveness': SDA 1975, s 85(4), as amended by the Sex Discrimination Act 1975 (Application to Armed Forces etc.) Regulations 1994, SI 1994/3276. EC Directive 76/207 on Equality of Treatment in Employment applies to the armed forces: see further *Ministry of Defence v Cannock* [1994] IRLR 509; *R v Ministry of Defence, ex p Smith and Grady* [1996] IRLR 100. This exclusion appears to be compatible with Art 2(2) of Directive 76/207, subject to the normal tests of proportionality: Case C-273/97 *Sirdar v Army Board and Secretary of State for Defence* [2000] IRLR 47.
367 RRA 1976, s 75(2)(c).
368 EE(SO)R 2003, reg 36(2)(c); EE(RB)R 2003, reg 36(2)(c).
369 DDA 1995, s 64(7).
370 NMWA 1998, s 37.
371 WTR 1998, reg 38; but note also the effect of reg 18(c), discussed below, para 4.75.
372 ERA 1996, s 192(1), (2). At the time of writing ERA 1996, Sch 2, para 16 applies.
373 TULRCA 1992, s 274.
374 See Lock, 1983; Fredman and Morris, 1989: pp 73–74.
375 Note, in particular, TULRCA 1992, ss 277(2) and 278(2A) and ERA 1996, ss 194(4) and 195(4).

1978. House of Commons staff and House of Lords staff are also covered by anti-discrimination legislation and by most of the provisions of TULRCA 1992 and ERA 1996,[376] and by labour standards legislation.[377]

Police officers

3.77   The balance of judicial opinion is that police officers do not have contracts of employment.[378] In constitutional terms, police constables are regarded as 'independent officers' capable of exercising legal powers derived from the nature of their office. This is why it has been held that for the purpose of vicarious liability in tort they were not the employees of the relevant police authority.[379] In practice, police officers are subject to the managerial control of their superiors, and their scope for individual action is limited by the powers of the chief constable as well as by the Police Regulations. The chief constable exercises powers of promotion, discipline and dismissal and is vicariously liable in respect of any unlawful conduct by constables under his direction or control in the performance or purported performance of their functions.[380] Wages and salaries, on the other hand, are the responsibility of the local police authority. It has been argued that police officers should be regarded as employees of the local police authority;[381] although this would have some attractions, not least the reduction of litigation relating to their employment status, it would represent a fundamental change in their constitutional position.

Police officers are explicitly excluded from most of the protective provisions of ERA 1996.[382] The courts have taken the view that, given the absence of a contractual nexus between a police constable and any putative employer, the police are implicitly excluded from those other rights on which ERA 1996 is silent.[383] Formal exclusions also apply to collective rights: police officers cannot be 'employees' or 'workers' for the purposes of TULRCA 1992, nor can they invoke rights in relation to trade union membership.[384] For these and other reasons, they have no right to take part in industrial action, nor to form or join a trade union.[385] However, all police officers below the rank of superintendent

---

376   EqPA 1970 s 1(10A), (10B); SDA 1975, ss 85A, 85B; EE(SO)R 2003, regs 37–38; RRA 1976, ss 75A, 75B; EE(RB)R 2003, regs 37–38; TULRCA 1992, ss 277, 278; DDA 1995, s 65; ERA 1996, ss 194, 195.

377   NMWA 1998, ss 38, 39; WTR 1998, regs 39, 40.

378   The cases were recently reviewed and reaffirmed by the EAT in *Commissioner of Police of the Metropolis v Lowrey-Nesbit* [1999] ICR 401.

379   *Fisher v Oldham Corpn* [1930] 2 KB 364.

380   Police Act 1996, ss 10 and 88, as amended by the Police Reform Act 2002. See *White v Chief Constable of South Yorkshire Police* [1999] IRLR 110, where for the purposes of a negligence claim against the Chief Constable, police officers were regarded as being analogous to employees; *Waters v Commissioner of Police of the Metropolis* [2000] IRLR 720; *Lennon v Commissioner of Police of the Metropolis* [2004] IRLR 385.

381   Lustgarten, 1986:p 31; S Fredman and G Morris, 1989: pp 71–73. Possession of the powers of a constable has not been regarded as incompatible with employee status in relation to members of the British Transport Police: *Spence v British Railways Board* [2001] ICR 232. On the status of members of the 'extended police family' see G Morris, 2002b.

382   ERA 1996, s 200. Note, however, the Police (Health and Safety) Act 1997 which provides, *inter alia*, that police constables and cadets have the right not to be unfairly dismissed, or subjected to any detriment, in health and safety cases.

383   See *Commissioner of Police of the Metropolis v Lowery-Nesbit* [1999] ICR 401, discussing the meaning, in this context, of ERA 1996, s 200.

384   TULRCA 1992, s 280(1).

385   See further paras 7.13 and 11.60, respectively.

automatically belong to the Police Federation, a body established by legislation whose membership is confined to the police service.[386]

Although outside the scope of statutory employment protection, police officers are nevertheless covered by the anti-discrimination legislation; these provisions impose obligations on the chief constable or, in an appropriate case, on the local police authority.[387] Moreover, the police are explicitly covered by working time legislation.[388] Legislation governing the national minimum wage is silent on the matter of police service. As a general rule the right of police officers to invoke judicial review to cure a breach of natural justice or other *ultra vires* act is well recognised and extends to all ranks, including trainee officers;[389] this is so by virtue not simply of the office they occupy but also because of the clear absence of any alternative contractual or statutory remedies for the protection of their employment. However the courts have recently qualified this position by holding that whether judicial review will lie depends upon whether 'the defendant was performing a public duty owed to the claimant in the particular circumstances under consideration',[390] a development we discuss further in para 5.50.

Prison officers

3.78 Prison officers, who were at one time held to be 'in police service' for the purposes of unfair dismissal legislation,[391] had their position clarified by the Criminal Justice and Public Order Act 1994 and are not to be treated as being in police service for the purposes of TULRCA 1992 and ERA 1996;[392] as a result, they may claim employment protection rights and form a trade union. They have no right to take part in industrial action, however, thanks to the establishment by the 1994 Act of a statutory duty not to induce a prison officer to withhold his duties or to commit a breach of discipline.[393] At the time of writing the Home Secretary has announced that this restriction on prison officers will be withdrawn in the light of a new legally-enforceable collective agreement governing the Prison Service, but it will remain in force for private sector 'prisoner custody officers' and 'custody officers' until a similar agreement is reached in relation to these groups.[394]

Employment in public corporations, local government, education and the NHS

3.79 Those employed in public corporations, local government, the education service and the National Health Service work under normal contracts of

---

386 The Police Federation was initially established by the Police Act 1919; the relevant provision is now the Police Act 1996.
387 SDA 1975, s 17(1); RRA 1976, s 16(1); EE(RB)R 2003, reg 11; EE(SO)R 2003, reg 11; DDA 1995, s 64A. Although not expressly excluded, the police would seem not to fall within any of the categories covered by the EqPA 1970. However, in practical terms the former exclusion matters little as they are covered by Art 141 (ex 119) of the EC Treaty and Directive 75/117 on Equal Pay.
388 WTR 1998, reg 41.
389 *Chief Constable of North Wales Police v Evans* [1982] 1 WLR 1155.
390 *R (on the application of Tucker) v Director General of the National Crime Squad* [2003] IRLR 439, para 24 (Scott Baker LJ).
391 *Home Office v Robinson* [1982] ICR 31.
392 CJPOA 1994, s 126(1)–(2); ERA 1996, s 200(2)(a).
393 CJPOA 1994, s 127(1)–(2); see generally, G Morris, 1994b.
394 See further para 11.14 below.

employment. Their employers are bodies created by statute, so the uncertainties which attach to the status of civil servants who are employed by the Crown do not apply here. The identity of the employer is not always straightforward, however. In the case of a nationalised corporation it is the relevant corporate body established by statute. Local government workers are employed by the relevant local authority, which means the council and not the councillors who are elected to it.[395] Local councils are empowered by statute to employ such officers as they consider necessary for the discharge of their functions,[396] although no councillor of the authority may serve as an officer[397] and certain posts are 'politically restricted' which means that their holders may not be members, *inter alia*, of any local authority.[398] The discretion of local authorities to employ labour directly was for some years limited by legislation which required certain classes of work to be subjected to periodic competitive tendering and, under some circumstances, contracted-out to external suppliers of services.[399] This has now been replaced by an obligation to obtain 'best value', measured by reference to economy, efficiency and effectiveness, whether from the public or the private sector.[400]

Teachers in the public sector are employed by the local education authority (LEA),[401] with the exception of those who work in voluntary aided and foundation schools, which employ their staff directly.[402] However, as part of a process of devolving powers and responsibilities to individual schools, most of the powers usually exercised by an employer are accorded to the governing body of the school, to the extent that governing bodies have been described as 'employers in practice, even where the formal contract is with the ... [LEA]'.[403] Thus the LEA cannot normally refuse to appoint staff recommended by the governing body,[404] and must terminate the contract of any staff the governing body dismisses (or attempt to redeploy them if their employment is not solely at that school).[405] Moreover, the governing body is the respondent in specified statutory (but not contractual) proceedings brought by staff consequent upon the exercise of its employment powers.[406] However, the LEA retains the burdens of being the

---

395 A council can be vicariously liable for an act of a councillor which undermines the obligation of trust and confidence in the employment relationship; for discussion of when, precisely, vicarious liability of this kind may arise, see *Moores v Bude-Stratton Town Council* [2000] IRLR 676.

396 Local Government Act 1972, s 112.

397 Local Government Act, ss 80(1), 116.

398 Local Government and Housing Act 1989, ss 1, 2. The Act, and the Local Government Officers (Political Restrictions) Regulations 1990, SI 1990/851 made thereunder, prohibit a wide range of political activities: see further G Morris, 1998a, 1998b. In *Ahmed v UK* [1999] IRLR 188, the European Court of Human Rights ruled that these restrictions did not violate Arts 10 or 11, or Art 3 of Protocol 1, of the ECHR; see G Morris, 1999b.

399 Local Government Acts of 1988 and 1992.

400 Local Government Act 1999.

401 Education Act 2002, s 35.

402 Education Act 2002, s 36; School Staffing (England) Regulations 2003, SI 2003/1963, as amended.

403 *Teachers: Meeting the challenge of change*, DfEE, 1998, para 172. This process was begun by the 1979–1997 Conservative Government and extended by the Labour Government which took office in 1997. See generally G Morris, 1999d.

404 SI 2003/1963, reg 14.

405 SI 2003/1963, reg 17. See *Askew v Governing Body of Clifton Middle School* [1999] IRLR 708.

406 Education (Modification of Enactments Relating to Employment) Order 2003, SI 2003/1964, reg 6. The Order covers specified sections of SDA 1975, RRA 1976, TULRCA 1992, DDA 1995, ERA 1996, and EA 2002.

employer in the sense that it must meet any legal costs and statutory compensation payable to an employee,[407] and will only in exceptional circumstances be able to shift all or part of these costs to the governing body.[408]

Like the education service, the National Health Service has been subject to extensive statutory changes designed to encourage the devolution of budgetary controls and the management of personnel and resources. The majority of hospital staff are now employed in self-governing trusts which have the status of autonomous entities for this purpose.[409]

Office holders

3.80   The category of 'office holder' which applies to certain high-ranking public-sector employees confers few if any special privileges or protections. The traditional definition of an office is 'a subsisting, permanent, substantive position which had an existence independent from the person who filled it, which went on and was filled in succession by successive holders ...'[410] This definition adequately describes many posts in the public services, some created explicitly by statute,[411] whose holders almost certainly have contracts of employment and will therefore benefit from the protections conferred upon employees by labour legislation.[412] Even if a court takes the view that the holder of a statutory public office may not, as such, be regarded as having a contract of employment, it may nevertheless regard the relationship as 'analogous to contract' and apply contract law principles to determine the common law rights of the parties. This occurred, for example, in *Miles v Wakefield Metropolitan District Council*,[413] a case concerning a claim for payment of salary by a Registrar of Births, Deaths and Marriages. It should also be noted that office holders who are not employees will nevertheless be liable to pay income tax under Schedule E[414] as well as primary Class 1 national insurance contributions.[415] In short, the category of officer holder, like that of civil servant, is gradually losing any distinctive character it once had in relation to the contract of employment,[416] although serious anomalies remain in relation to the statutory employment protection afforded to particular groups.[417]

407 Education (Modification of Enactments Relating to Employment) Order 2003, SI 2003/ 1964, reg 6(3).
408 Education Act 2002, s 37.
409 See the National Health Service and Community Care Act 1990, Sch 2, para 16(1)(d); G Morris, 1999a: pp 73–76.
410 *Great Western Rly Co v Bater* [1920] 3 KB 266, 274.
411 S Fredman and G Morris, 1989: pp 74–75.
412 See, however, *Lincolnshire County Council v Hopper* EAT/819/01, 24 May 2002, where the EAT was 'reluctantly driven' to conclude that a Registrar of Births, Marriages and Deaths, along with other substantial groups, was not an employee.
413 [1987] ICR 368.
414 Income Tax (Pensions and Earnings) Act 2003, s 5.
415 SSCBA 1992, s 2(1)(a).
416 See *Johnson v Ryan* [2000] ICR 236 (a local authority rent officer could be both an employee and an office holder) and *Perceval-Price v Department of Economic Development* [2000] IRLR 380 (tribunal chairmen were within employment for the purposes of the EC Equal Treatment Directive (76/207; see now also Directive 2000/78 and Directive 2002/73). It should be noted that the category of 'office-holder' no longer seems to be relevant to the availability of the remedy of judicial review if, indeed, it ever truly was.
417 See *Lincolnshire County Council v Hopper* EAT/819/01, 24 May 2002. The EAT was highly critical of the position and sent a copy of the judgment to the Minister for the Office for National Statistics.

CONTINUITY OF EMPLOYMENT, QUALIFYING THRESHOLDS, AND EQUALITY OF TREATMENT FOR FIXED-TERM AND PART-TIME WORKERS

3.81   The category of 'employee' contains within it further sub-divisions of employment status. Distinctions which used to exist between manual and non-manual employees have now almost completely disappeared from the law.[418] However, more modern legislation has drawn distinctions between employees according to such criteria as length of service, regularity of employment, the duration of the working week and the amount of weekly pay. These have had the effect of excluding some part-time and temporary workers who have the status of employees but who lack the necessary continuity of employment to earn employment protection under ERA 1996. It is only in respect of certain rights, such as the employee's right not to be dismissed or discriminated against for taking leave for family reasons, that an employee is exempt from qualifying thresholds of this kind.

The statutory concept of *continuity of employment* is therefore an important filter for employment protection. The two dimensions of continuity are *length* and *regularity* of employment. As far as length is concerned, one year's continuous employment is currently needed for protection against unfair dismissal and two years in respect of the right to redundancy compensation: many temporary and fixed-term employees are thereby placed outside the scope of protection. The need for regularity means that employees who are employed on a periodic basis, with frequent spells of non-employment in between periods of work, may also be excluded from protection.

It is not just 'flexible' or 'atypical' employment forms which are affected by the need for continuity. Because continuity must be maintained intact up to the event triggering the legal claim (such as a dismissal),[419] employees of many years' seniority may lose statutory rights by virtue of working on a periodic or irregular basis near the end of their period of service. Continuity is also important for determining the extent as well as the basic entitlement of employees to protection; for example, the length of continuous employment will determine the amount of redundancy compensation to which an employee is entitled.

Qualifying periods of continuous employment

3.82   Continuity is computed in weeks, so that *regularity* of employment must be established from one working week to the next;[420] *length* of employment is calculated in years and months.[421] The present qualifying period of one year's continuous employment for unfair dismissal was established in 1999, after a period of almost fifteen years during which a two-year period applied.[422] The one-year qualifying period does not apply to 'automatically unfair' reasons for dismissal.[423] The qualifying period for redundancy compensation remains two years.[424]

---

418 See our discussion in the context of the right to wages, ch 4, at para 4.58 *et seq* below.
419 On the 'effective date of termination' in the law of unfair dismissal, see below, paras 5.83–5.87
420 ERA 1996, ss 210–219.
421 ERA 1996, s 210. A 'year' is, for these purposes, twelve calendar months: s 210(1), (2).
422 ERA 1996, s 108(1); see SI 1999/1436.
423 See generally paras 5.95–5.114 below.
424 ERA 1996, s 155.

For guarantee payments and payments during suspension on medical grounds the specified period of continuity is one month.[425] The right to receive a minimum period of notice of dismissal is also dependent upon continuous employment of one month. This gives the employee the right to receive one week's notice. After two years of continuous employment this rises to two weeks, and so on for each year of extra service up to a maximum of 12.[426]

In the cases of statutory sick pay (SSP) and statutory maternity pay (SMP), the qualifying conditions reflect the history of these two benefits, which straddle the boundary between social insurance and employment protection.[427] The social insurance origins of SSP can be seen in the rule that employees whose normal weekly earnings fall below the lower earnings limit do not qualify for protection.[428] The intention of this is to exclude employees who do not regularly pay primary Class 1 national insurance contributions, even though the payment of these contributions is no longer, *as such*, a precondition of qualifying.

SMP is available to an employee who has been continuously employed in employed earners' employment for a period of 26 weeks up to the qualifying week, that is to say, the fifteenth week before the expected week of confinement. In addition she must show that she had average weekly earnings above the lower earnings limit for contributions for the period of eight weeks prior to the qualifying week.[429] Following the implementation of Directive 92/85 in TURERA 1993, the qualifying period of two years for claims for unfair dismissal on the grounds of pregnancy was abolished,[430] and the introduction of a general right to 14 weeks' maternity leave, not dependent upon any continuity of employment, was introduced. This has now been extended to 26 weeks.[431] However, continuous employment of 26 weeks is still required if the employee wishes to exercise the right to return to work after taking 'additional maternity leave' which can extend to a further 26 weeks.[432]

Certain other employment protection rights, while not dependent upon continuity of employment in the sense required by Part XIV of ERA 1996, are nevertheless dependent upon service of a certain length. Thus the employer must issue a written statement of terms and conditions to all employees whose employment continues for one month and the statement must be issued within two months of the employment beginning.[433]

As we have already noted, employment protection legislation does not simply require employees to have minimum periods of continuous service; where continuity is required, it must be maintained for the specified period of time ending with the particular event which triggers the legal claim. In the case of SMP, for example, this is the fifteenth week before the expected week of confinement as explained above;[434] for the exercise of the right to return to work

---

425 See, respectively, ERA 1996, ss 29, 65.
426 ERA 1996, s 86.
427 See below, paras 4.111, 6.103, respectively.
428 SSCBA 1992, Sch 11, para 2(c).
429 SSCBA 1992, s 164(1)–(2). Parallel provisions apply in the case of statutory paternity pay. See SSCBA 1992, s 171ZA(2)(b)–(c).
430 See now ERA 1996, s 99(1)–(3).
431 Maternity and Parental Leave (Amendment) Regulations 2002, SI 2002/2789.
432 SI 1999/3312, reg 5(b). 26 weeks of continuous employment are required for statutory paternity leave and adoption leave following, respectively, the birth or adoption of a child: see PALR 2002, regs 4(2)(a), 8(2)(a) and 15(2)(b). Entitlement to parental leave for the purposes of caring for a child requires one year's continuous employment: MPLR 1999, reg 13(1)(a).
433 ERA 1996, ss 1(1), (2), 2(6) and 5(1).
434 SSCBA 1992, s 164(2)(a).

after 'additional' maternity leave, it is the beginning of the fourteenth week before the expected week of childbirth.[435] For unfair dismissal, continuity of one year up to the 'effective date of termination'[436] is needed, and for redundancy compensation the same notion is expressed in the concept of the 'relevant date', prior to which two years of continuity are needed.[437] Thus it is only partially true that the continuity requirement is a function of the need for an employee to have accrued a certain degree of seniority before being allowed a claim against his or her employer. In practice, seniority or length of service is only one factor; because of the stress on regularity of employment, employees with years of service may forfeit employment protection benefits in a somewhat arbitrary way by virtue of the operation of the continuity rule.[438]

Temporary and fixed-term employment, qualifying service and equality of treatment

3.83   As we have just seen, the qualifying thresholds referred to above have the potential to affect all employees, but they are particularly significant in the case of those employed on fixed-term or temporary contracts.[439] A large proportion of temporary jobs are low paid and there is substantial overlap with part-time work and self-employment.[440] Sectors where this form of work is common include hotel and catering and general services, and the public sector where cuts in funding have increased the pressure on employers to hire temporary staff.[441]

Individuals employed on a fixed-term contract are usually classed as employees for legal purposes. From 1999 they could no longer be required by their employers to waive their rights to unfair dismissal protection upon the expiry of the fixed term,[442] and from 2002 the possibility of them waiving claims to redundancy compensation was also removed.[443]

Challenges to qualifying periods

3.84   The two-year qualifying period for unfair dismissal which operated from 1985 to 1999 was challenged on the grounds of its incompatibility with Article 119 (now Article 141) of the EC Treaty[444] and with the Equal Treatment Directive[445]

---

435   SI 1999/3312, reg 5(b).
436   ERA 1996, s 97(1).
437   ERA 1996, s 155.
438   See, eg, *Hellyer Bros Ltd v McLeod* [1987] ICR 526, discussed below.
439   The numbers employed on temporary work of various kinds is reported to be around 7% of the active labour force (Sly and Stilwell, 1997) but this figure does not count a further category, perhaps as much as 10% of the active labour force, of employees who regard themselves as being in 'permanent' work but are employed under fixed-term contracts. See Burchell *et al*, 1999: ch 5, where the difficulties which arise in arriving at a reliable figure for those employed on fixed-term contracts are discussed. For accounts of employers' reasons for using temporary labour, see Heather *et al*, 1996; Casey *et al*, 1997.
440   See Sly and Stilwell, 1997.
441   Sly and Stilwell, 1997: pp 351–352.
442   ERelA 1999, s 18, amending ERA 1996, s 197.
443   By virtue of FTER 2002. See further below.
444   This part of the claim was added at the stage of the Court of Appeal hearing. See [1995] IRLR 464, 467.
445   Directive 76/107, now replaced by Directive 2000/78.

in *R v Secretary of State, ex p Seymour-Smith and Perez*.[446] Evidence was led which indicated that between 1985 (when the two-year qualifying period was introduced) and 1991, between 72% and 77.4% of male employees working 16 hours or more per week had two years' or more service, compared to between 63.8% and 68.9% of women. On average, the number of women qualifying was around 90% of the number of men. After lengthy litigation, during which a number of questions were referred to the ECJ for a preliminary ruling, the House of Lords concluded (by a bare majority) that a case of adverse impact was made out, but went on to hold that the government was able to show that the qualifying period was capable of being justified on the grounds that it fell within 'the broad margin of discretion afforded to governments when adopting measures of this type'.[447] This decision illustrates the substantial leeway given to governments to make exceptions to the equal treatment principle on grounds related to more general labour market considerations, in this case, 'to encourage recruitment by employers'.[448]

Directive 91/383 on protection of the health and safety of temporary workers

3.85 Temporary work has been the subject of several attempts to introduce directives providing for parity of treatment of different forms of employment relationships.[449] Only one of the measures put forward has achieved agreement in the Council. Directive 91/383 provides that employees with a fixed-term contract of employment or with a temporary employment relationship with an agency or employment business, as part of which they are assigned to work with a third party user, are entitled to 'the same level of protection as that of other workers in the user undertaking and/or establishment'.[450] More specific obligations concern the provision of information and training to temporary workers (and to certain third parties) and medical surveillance of their activities. These provisions were incorporated into UK law by the Management of Health and Safety Regulations 1992.[451]

Directive 99/70/EC concerning the Framework Agreement on Fixed-Term Work concluded by ETUC, UNICE, and CEEP, and the Fixed-Term Employees (Prevention of Less Favourable Treatment) Regulations 2002

3.86 This Directive implemented a framework agreement made by the social partners under the social dialogue procedure put in place by the Maastricht Treaty.[452] The Agreement is premised on the view that 'contracts of an indefinite duration are, and will continue to be, the general form of employment relationship between employers and workers'.[453] While there is recognition that 'fixed-term employment contracts respond, in certain circumstances, to the needs of both

---

446 [1994] IRLR 448, DC (see Freedland, 1994), [1995] IRLR 464, CA; [1997] IRLR 315, HL; Case C-167/97 [1999] IRLR 253 (ECJ); [2000] IRLR 263 (HL) (see Barnard and Hepple, 2000).
447 [2000] IRLR 263, 271 (Lord Nicholls).
448 [2000] IRLR 263, 270 (Lord Nicholls). The adverse impact and justification aspects of this decision are considered in greater detail in ch 6, below.
449 See generally, Hepple, 1990a.
450 Directive 91/383, Art 2(1).
451 SI 1992/2051, regs 10 and 13.
452 See para 2.42 above.
453 Directive 99/70, Annex (Framework Agreement on Fixed-Term Work concluded by ETUC, UNICE and CEEP), recital 2.

employers and workers',[454] the Agreement aims to control what it regards as abuse by employers of the fixed-term contract option, and, by imposing a requirement of equal treatment between fixed-term and permanent workers, arguably reinforces the sense in which the indeterminate-duration contract of employment is to be regarded as the norm.[455]

The Agreement firstly establishes a general principle of equal treatment, according to which 'fixed-term workers shall not be treated in a less favourable manner than comparable permanent workers solely because they have a fixed-term contract or relation unless different treatment is justified on objective grounds'.[456] Equality here means equal treatment 'pro rata temporis', that is, taking into account differences in actual length of service, but the agreement prohibits laws which count continuity of employment differently according to whether employment is fixed term or permanent.[457] Beyond this, the precise meaning of objective justification is left open.

The second principal advance taken by the Agreement is to require Member States to take measures to 'prevent abuse arising from the use of successive fixed-term contracts or relationships'.[458] Member States are called on to 'introduce in a manner which takes account of the needs of specific sectors and/or categories of workers, one or more of the following measures: (a) objective reasons justifying the renewal of such contracts or relationships; (b) the maximum total duration of successive fixed-term employment contracts or relationships; c) the number of renewals of such contracts or relationships'. This provision signifies a radical departure from the traditional position in UK law, which was to impose no restrictions upon the rights of the parties to agree successive fixed-term employment contracts.

The Directive was implemented in the UK by the Fixed-Term Employees (Prevention of Less Favourable Treatment) Regulations which came into effect in 2002.[459] These Regulations have several notable features. Their scope is limited to *employees*;[460] thus they do not confer any protection on fixed-term workers who are unable to establish employee status, for example because of the absence of mutuality of obligation. On the other hand, the relevant definition of 'fixed-term contract' is wider than that used in the context of 'dismissal' for the purposes of unfair dismissal and statutory redundancy payments (which itself was extended by the Regulations to cover non-renewal of a 'limited-term contract').[461] For the

---

454 Directive 99/70, Annex (Framework Agreement on Fixed-Term Work concluded by ETUC, UNICE and CEEP), recital 2.

455 For assessments of the Agreement which discuss its policy orientation, see Murray, 1999; Tiraboschi, 1999; P Lorber, 1999.

456 Framework Agreement on Fixed-Term Work, cl 4(1). Definitions of 'fixed-term worker' and 'comparable permanent worker' are contained in cl 3. Note that the comparison must normally be with a permanent worker in the same establishment but if none is available, a comparison can be made by reference to relevant collective agreements (which could presumably be agreements at employer, industry or national level) or to national law or practice.

457 The Agreement refers to 'period-of-service qualifications'. UK law on continuity of employment arguably complies with the Agreement in this respect: see *Kingston upon Hull City Council v Mountain* [1999] ICR 715, 720.

458 Framework Agreement on Fixed-Term Work, cl 5.

459 FTER 2002, SI 2002/2034. The Regulations came into force on 1 October 2002, but it should be noted that they were subject to a number of transitional provisions, in particular affecting the use of waivers to exclude liability for redundancy compensation. See Sch 2, Part 2.

460 FTER 2002, reg 1(2).

461 See ERA 1995, ss 95(1)(b), 136(1)(b), 235(2A), (2B); see further paras 5.78–5.79.

purposes of the Regulations, 'fixed-term contract' includes contracts which are intended to terminate on the expiry of a 'fixed term' (for the purposes of which, a contract which also contains a notice clause is not, for that reason, excluded from the scope of the Regulations[462]), and it also covers task contracts and contracts which are intended to terminate 'on the occurrence or non-occurrence of any other specific event' except the attainment by the employee of any normal and bona fide normal retiring age in the establishment for the position which he or she holds. By contrast, the notion of the 'comparable permanent employee' is narrowly specified: the two employees must be employed by the same employer, engaged in broadly similar work and must normally be based at the same establishment. No comparison can be made if the permanent employee has ceased to be employed by the employer.[463] This definition of 'comparable permanent worker' does not appear adequate to comply with the Directive.

The right to equality consists of the right to be treated no less favourably in relation to the terms of the contract of employment and the right not to be subjected to any detriment by the employer; this includes a right to equal treatment in relation to any relevant period of qualifying service, opportunities for training, and opportunities to secure a permanent position in the establishment.[464] The pro-rata principle applies: this means that 'where a comparable permanent employee receives or is entitled to pay or any other benefit, a fixed-term employee is to receive or be entitled to such proportion of that pay or other benefit as is reasonable in the circumstances having regard to the length of his contract or employment and to the terms on which the pay or other benefit is offered'.[465] However, the right to equality is only infringed if the ground for unequal treatment was the fixed-term status of the applicant; and the right is in any event subject to an open-ended defence of objective justification.[466] Justification will be made out if the employer can show that the 'the terms of the fixed-term employee's contract of employment, taken as a whole, are at least as favourable as the terms of the comparable permanent employee's contract of employment'.[467] It is open to question whether this 'package' approach to justification complies with the Directive. The principal remedy for breach of these provisions is a complaint to an employment tribunal which may make a recommendation to the employer and award compensation to the employee.[468]

The most far-reaching change to UK law is brought about by regulation 8. Where an employee is employed under successive fixed-term contracts and has continuity of employment of four years or more from 10 July 2002 (the transposition date of the Directive), the term limiting the duration of the contract of employment is to be of no effect from the date on which the four years of continuous employment were acquired, or from the date on which the contract was most recently renewed, if later. This provision is subject to the possibility

---

462 *Allen v National Australia Group Europe Ltd* [2004] IRLR 847.
463 FTER 2002, reg 2. Comparison beyond the establishment is only possible if there is no comparable permanent employee in the establishment in question (FTER 2002, reg 2).
464 FTWR 2002, reg 3. Refusal to renew or extend a fixed-term contract does not constitute less favourable treatment for the purposes of reg 3: *Department of Work and Pensions v Webley* [2005] IRLR 288.
465 FTER 2002, reg 1(2).
466 FTER 2002, reg 3(3).
467 FTER 2002, reg 4.
468 FTER 2002, reg 7. In addition, there is a right to receive from the employer a written statement of the reasons for less favourable treatment (reg 5), and dismissal is automatically unfair if it is for the reason that the employee has, in one or more of a number of ways, asserted his or her rights under the Regulations (reg 6).

of the employer showing that the use of a fixed term is 'justified on objective grounds'. These are not specified, and it remains to be seen how far the courts will be persuaded that objective grounds include factors of the kind which have proved relevant in the context of the law of unfair dismissal, such as the ending of an external grant or commercial contract to which the employment in question was linked.[469] In addition, it is open to the employer to vary the effect of regulation 8 through a collective or workforce agreement. This may specify the maximum total period for which an employee may be employed on fixed-term contracts before they are deemed to be permanent; the maximum number of renewals of fixed-term contracts which may be made; and more detailed objective grounds justifying fixed-term employment.[470] We discuss this provision further in para 5.78.

Part-time work and weekly hours thresholds

3.87   There is no legal definition of part-time work *as such*. For statistical purposes the UK authorities count those working 30 hours or less as employed part-time: the numbers so employed have grown rapidly in the past 25 years, mainly in services, and currently constitute around 25% of the employed labour force, an increase from 19% in 1990 and 16% in 1979.[471] The 30-hour threshold does not carry any legal significance. However, until 1995, the relevant employment protection legislation contained qualifying thresholds which had the effect of potentially excluding certain part-time employees from the scope of employment protection legislation. The basic rule was that an employee had to be regularly employed for at least 16 hours per week for that week to count towards continuity. An exception was made for employees with five years' continuous employment with their employer, for whom an 8-hour threshold applied. The effect, then, was that an employee had to have worked for at least 16 hours per week for two years or for at least 8 hours for five years prior to dismissal in order to have protection against unfair dismissal and redundancy.

A number of different justifications were put forward for the existence of weekly hours thresholds of this kind. Their use goes back to the Contracts of Employment Act 1963, the first modern employment protection statute, which introduced the rights to notice of termination and to receive a written statement of terms and conditions. That Act laid down a 21-hour weekly threshold which was later carried over into the Redundancy Payments Act 1965 and the unfair dismissal provisions of the Industrial Relations Act 1971. In 1963 the threshold was explained as being intended to exclude 'people with spare-time occupations and those who do weekend jobs' and cases where 'the employment relationship is not of substantial importance to the parties concerned' such as twilight shift workers who were 'nearly all women with domestic responsibilities'.[472] In 1975 the main threshold was lowered from 21 to 16 hours, but further reductions were resisted, in the 1980s, by the government's insistence that an extension of employment protection rights would have a harmful impact on labour demand and hence on employment opportunities for those who wished to work part-time.

---

469   *Terry v East Sussex County Council* [1976] ICR 536; see below, para 5.183.
470   See our discussion in ch 5, below, at paras 5.78–5.79. The relevant definitions of 'collective' and 'workforce' agreements are contained in Sch 1.
471   Labour Force Survey figures, reported in Deakin and Reed, 2001b, Table 4.
472   William Whitelaw MP, HC Debs, 5th Series, Vol 676, col 1154, 1 May 1963. See Deakin, 1994; Kilpatrick, 2003.

In the 1980s there was an increase in the numbers of employees excluded from protection by these thresholds, in particular in those employed for less than 16 hours per week. While part-time work as a whole, defined as work for less than 30 hours per week, grew by 30% between 1979 and 1987, employment for 16 hours or less per week increased by 66%, to reach 11% of the employed labour force.[473] The increase was particularly pronounced in certain sectors, such as retailing.[474] Overall, in 1994 it was estimated that 38% of women part-time workers, or 1.9 million employees, were employed for less than 16 hours per week.[475] However, both the 8-hour and 16-hour thresholds were abolished in 1995,[476] following the decision of the House of Lords in *R v Secretary of State for Employment, ex p Equal Opportunities Commission*[477] that they contravened European Union law concerning equal treatment between male and female employees.

Another significant threshold operated in social security law, by virtue of the lower earnings limit for national insurance contributions; it was estimated in the early 1990s that as many as 2.5 million part-time workers, or just over 10% of the employed labour force, received weekly earnings below this lower threshold, with the consequence that they were unable to build up the contributions record needed to claim social insurance benefits (including the contribution-based jobseeker's allowance and the state retirement pension).[478] To some extent the problem of part-time earnings outside the social insurance system has been addressed by changes to the structure of national insurance contributions introduced from the late 1990s, which mitigate the effect on net income of earnings rising above the lower earnings level.[479]

Hourly thresholds and sex discrimination

3.88 The vast majority of part-time workers in Britain are women with domestic and family responsibilities, although the numbers of young, single men and women working part-time have increased in recent years. The clear link between part-time work and women's employment is legally significant, since it raises issues of sex discrimination under both domestic and European law. Unequal treatment of part-time workers may constitute indirect sex discrimination by virtue of the fact that any exclusion of part-timers is likely to affect far more women than men within the relevant group. This has been recognised by English courts and by the ECJ.[480] Following the *Barber* judgment of the ECJ which extended the concept of 'pay' under Article 119 (now Article 141) to include

---

473 Deakin and Wilkinson, 1991.
474 See L Dickens, 1992: between 1972 and 1987 the proportion of retail sales assistants employed for less than 16 hours per week increased from 26% to 46% of the total, and the proportion of checkout operatives employed in this way more than doubled.
475 Hakim, 1993.
476 SI 1995/31.
477 [1994] IRLR 176.
478 See L Dickens, 1992: p 27; and, for a more recent discussion, Fredman, 2004b.
479 Because contributions became payable on all earnings including those below the threshold (although at a lower rate) once the lower earnings level was reached, there was a disincentive to raise earnings to that point. From 1999, a new system of national insurance contributions came into force under which contributions were payable only on earnings above the threshold. See Deakin and Wilkinson, 2005: p 189.
480 See, in particular, Case 96/80 *Jenkins v Kingsgate (Clothing Productions) Ltd* [1981] ICR 592, ECJ; *Clarke v Eley (IMI) Kynoch Ltd* [1983] ICR 165, EAT; Case 170/84 *Bilka-Kaufhaus GmbH v Weber von Hartz* [1986] IRLR 317; Case 171/88 *Rinner-Kühn v FWW Spezial Gebäudereinigung GmbH & Co KG* [1989] ECR 2743.

certain statutory payments made by employers,[481] a challenge to the 8- and 16-hours thresholds under employment protection legislation became possible. The central question was whether the thresholds could be supported by a justification defence of some kind, such a defence in principle being available in claims of indirect discrimination.

In *R v Secretary of State for Employment, ex p Equal Opportunities Commission* [482] the Equal Opportunities Commission launched a challenge to the legislation by way of proceedings for judicial review against the Secretary of State for Employment, and this eventually succeeded in the House of Lords. A declaration was granted to the effect that the thresholds for redundancy were contrary both to Article 119 and to the Equal Treatment Directive (76/207), and that those for unfair dismissal were contrary to the Directive.[483] Both sides in *Ex p EOC* accepted that a *prima facie* case of indirect discrimination arose, by virtue of the fact that the overwhelming proportion of part-time workers in the UK are female. On the issue of justification, Lord Keith accepted that the promotion of job opportunities was an appropriate goal for employment legislation, but concluded that an affidavit from a Department of Employment official did not contain 'anything capable of being regarded as factual evidence' in support of the Department's contentions. Nor had the Secretary of State attempted to argue that the 16-hour threshold was justified by the administrative burden involved with providing protection for part-timers on very short hours. In the light of subsequent decisions of the ECJ and House of Lords,[484] it is possible that *ex parte EOC* would not now be decided the same way. This is because a wide of margin of discretion has been allowed to governments to make exceptions to employment protection laws with the aim of reducing employers' hiring costs.[485] As it is, this decision marked a turning point in the treatment of part-time workers in the sense that it stimulated statutory reforms which did much to remove the legislative discrimination which previously affected part-time work. On 20 December 1994 the then Secretary of State for Employment, Mr Portillo, announced that 'having taken very careful account of the policy options and their legal implications, the Government has been advised that the judgment [of the House of Lords] requires the removal of all existing distinctions based on the number of hours worked per week'.[486] A statutory instrument subsequently repealed all the relevant hours thresholds contained in the Employment Protection (Consolidation) Act 1978 (the predecessor of ERA 1996) and in TULRCA 1992.[487] However, the lower earnings limit for national insurance purposes was unaffected by this process, and it is still the case that qualification for statutory sick pay and statutory maternity pay depends on the employee having had regular weekly earnings at or above this level. As a result, part-time employment continues to be excluded from certain forms of protective legislation.

---

481 Case C-262/88 *Barber v Guardian Royal Exchange Assurance Group plc* [1990] ECR I-1889.
482 [1991] IRLR 493, DC; affd [1993] IRLR 10, CA; on appeal [1994] IRLR 176, HL; Deakin, 1994a.
483 In his judgment in *Ex p EOC*, Lord Keith considered that it was not necessary to decide whether the unfair dismissal threshold infringed Art 119 as well as Directive 76/307, but once the general question of justification was resolved in favour of the EOC his reasoning could be read as extending to Art 119 as well (see *Mediguard Services Ltd v Thame* [1994] IRLR 504).
484 In particular the decisions in *Ex p Seymour Smith and Perez* Case 167/97 [1999] IRLR 253 (ECJ), [2000] IRLR 263 (HL), discussed above, para 3.84.
485 See para 6.30 below.
486 HC Debs, 6th series, Vol 251, Written Answers, 20 December 1994, cols 1100–1101.
487 SI 1995/31.

Access to occupational pension schemes

3.89 Inequality between part-time work and full-time work is not confined to the issue of statutory hours thresholds; similar thresholds may operate at the level of occupational benefits provided by employers. Benefits provided by occupational pension schemes fall under the definition of 'pay' in Article 141 (formerly Article 119) of the EC Treaty,[488] and the exclusion of part-time workers from access to these schemes may, as a consequence, amount to unlawful sex discrimination. In its judgment in *Vroege*,[489] the ECJ ruled that the bar on 'retrospective' claims under the *Barber* judgment did not apply to rights of access to schemes (as opposed to rights to equality in respect of benefits paid out). However, separate time limits applied in *domestic* law by virtue of the Equal Pay Act 1970 and the question of whether these time limits placed a bar on actions being brought in respect of exclusions dating back more than two years gave rise to a highly complex body of case law.[490] In *Magorrian and Cunningham v Eastern Health and Social Services Board*,[491] the ECJ, on a reference from Northern Ireland, held that such a limitation would be contrary to EC law, on the ground that it would render ineffective, in practice, the exercise of Community law rights under Article 141. Since the Northern Irish legislation was very similar to the equivalent statute governing the rest of the United Kingdom, it was open to the British courts to declare the domestic time limits invalid at that point; however, in *Preston v Wolverhampton Healthcare NHS Trust*[492] the House of Lords decided instead to refer a number of outstanding questions to the ECJ by way of a preliminary ruling. The ECJ again confirmed that the two-year limitation was contrary to the principle that rights under Article 141 should be effective, but noted that workers applying to join pension schemes with retrospective effect would not have the right to avoid paying contributions for the periods in question.[493]

Further applications of the principle of non-discrimination on the grounds of sex: equality of pay; seniority; the right to work part-time

3.90 Part-time work is linked with lower than average levels of hourly pay: there is a clear differential across the whole economy between part-time and full-time earnings, even allowing for the existence of a gap between female and male earnings in general.[494] Inequality of pay also arises from the limited access of part-time workers to fringe benefits and from their lack of entitlement to overtime premia, shift rates and paid leave (all of which tend to be calculated on the basis that a full-time working week of between 35 and 40 hours is the norm).[495] To some extent, these forms of differential treatment can be challenged through the means provided by the Equal Pay Act 1970, which enables a female

---

488 Case C-262/88 *Barber v Guardian Royal Exchange Assurance Group plc* [1990] ECR I-1889.
489 Case C-57/93 *Vroege v NCIV Instituut voor Volkshuisvesting BV* [1994] IRLR 651. See also Case C-435/93 *Dietz v Stichting Thuiszorg Rotterdam* [1996] IRLR 692.
490 See *Vroege*, where the relevant cases are discussed.
491 Case C-246/96 [1998] IRLR 86.
492 [1998] IRLR 197. See further paras 6.92 and 6.94 below.
493 Case C-78/98 [2000] IRLR 506, applied by the HL in *Preston v Wolverhampton Healthcare NHS Trust (No 2)* [2001] IRLR 237. See now EqPA 1970, ss 2ZA–2ZC; discussed at paras 6.92–6.94 below.
494 See generally Equal Opportunities Commission, *Facts about Women and Men in Britain* (2005).
495 See L Dickens, 1992a; Horrell, Rubery and Burchell, 1989.

part-time worker to claim equality of hourly pay with a male worker, whether full-time or part-time, if they are employed in the same employment and she can show that he is employed either on like work, work rated as equivalent, or work of equal value to hers.[496] That she works part-time and he works full-time is unlikely, in itself, to provide grounds for a finding that they are not employed on like work or work of equal value; nor will such a difference in itself provide an employer with the defence of material difference or material factor.[497] However, the limitations on claims under the EqPA 1970 should also be borne in mind (particularly the need for an applicant to find a male comparator who is employed by her employer at the same establishment or at an establishment covered by common terms and conditions of employment[498]).

In the context of redundancy, the EAT has held that the selection of part-timers for dismissal ahead of full-timers gave rise to a prima facie case of indirect sex discrimination, which in the circumstances could not be justified.[499] A more difficult question concerns the principle of 'last in, first out' (LIFO) in redundancy selection. This could give rise to adverse impact against women, on the grounds that because women workers are more likely than men to take career breaks for family or related reasons, they may not have comparable seniority to men and so are more likely to be selected for redundancy where LIFO is applied. The EAT left open the possibility that LIFO or a similar seniority principle might provide the basis for a justification defence in these circumstances.[500]

In other respects, the ECJ has strictly applied the equality principle to claims that part-time workers should not be granted equal seniority rights to those working full time. The effect of its rulings in *Kording*[501] and *Gerster*[502] are that periods of part-time employment should be counted equally with periods of full-time employment when computing length of service for the purposes of access to promotion or occupational qualification, unless objective reasons can be found for doing otherwise. *Gerster* concerned civil service regulations which stated that for promotion purposes, periods of employment under half normal working hours were not to be counted at all; hours between a half and two-thirds of normal time were to be counted at the rate of two-thirds; and hours which were two thirds or more of the norm were to be counted in the same way as full-time hours. In *Kording*, the applicant, who was employed for half normal working hours, was required to have fifteen years of service in order to be exempt from an examination in order to qualify as a tax consultant; the employer argued that her periods of employment should only be counted *pro rata* according to the hours she actually worked. In each case, the Court held that because of the association of part-time employment with female work, there was a prima facie case of indirect discrimination, and that the seniority rules could only be defended if the employer was able to show that they were objectively justified. This meant, for example, that the employer would have to demonstrate 'that part-time employees are generally slower than full-time employees in acquiring job-related abilities and skills'.[503]

---

496 EqPA 1970, s 1.
497 Case 96/80 *Jenkins v Kingsgate (Clothing Productions) Ltd* [1981] ICR 592, ECJ.
498 See paras 6.75–6.97 below.
499 *Clarke v Eley (IMI) Kynoch Ltd* [1983] ICR 165.
500 *Clarke v Eley (IMI) Kynoch Ltd* [1983] ICR 165.
501 Case C-100/95 *Kording v Senator für Finanzen* [1997] IRLR 710.
502 Case C-1/95 *Gerster v Freistaat Bayern* [1997] IRLR 699.
503 Case C-1/95 *Gerster v Freistaat Bayern* [1997] IRLR 699, 709; see also Case C-77/02 *Steinicke v Bundesanstalt für Arbeit* [2003] IRLR 892.

This effects-orientated approach can be contrasted with the Court's earlier decision in *Stadt Lengerich v Helmig*,[504] where the court rejected an argument to the effect that it was discriminatory for an employer to confine overtime premia to employees working a full-time week. Although such a practice arguably disadvantages part-timers in the same way as the seniority rules in *Kording* and *Gerster*, the Court concluded that 'part-time employees do receive the same overall pay as full-time employees for the same number of hours worked'.[505] By contrast, in *Elsner-Lakeberg v Land Nordrhein-Westfalen*[506] the ECJ held that a practice under which teachers received additional remuneration for extra hours worked above a minimum threshold of three hours per month discriminated against part-time workers, since the threshold was more difficult for them to surmount.

A further question is whether an employee who normally works full-time has the *right* to work part-time if, for reasons related to family or domestic responsibilities or for some other reason, it is impractical for them to work full-time for a period. In general the individual employee has no right to have his or her contract terms varied to suit their changing circumstances, but an issue of sex discrimination can be seen to be involved if women employees, who are more likely than men to have family responsibilities, are not provided with a degree of flexibility in their working time arrangements. A series of decisions which are considered in greater detail in chapter 6 illustrate that it is not necessarily a straightforward matter to establish adverse impact or a *prima facie* finding of indirect discrimination, and that even if this can be shown there is still the possibility of the employer invoking a justification defence.[507] To some extent, however, the issue has been resolved in favour of the employee, by the enactment of a statutory right to request flexible working to look after a child for which he or she is responsible.[508]

Directive 97/81EC Concerning the Framework Agreement on Part-Time Work concluded by ETUC, UNICE and CEEP and the Part-Time Workers (Prevention of Less Favourable Treatment) Regulations 2000

3.91 Numerous proposals have been advanced by the European Commission since the early 1980s for the adoption of measures to ensure greater parity of treatment between part-time and full-time workers. The principle of equal treatment in respect of terms and conditions of employment and the application of statutory employment protection is recognised in most other European systems.[509] However, the embodiment of this principle in an EC directive was for many years prevented by the consistent opposition of the British government, on the grounds that regulation of this kind would add to costs and inhibit job creation.[510]

In 1997 a Directive on part-time work was finally agreed.[511] The Directive incorporates a Framework Agreement between the social partners which was

504 Cases C-399, 409, 425/92, 34, 50, 78/93 [1995] IRLR 216.
505 [1995] IRLR 216, 223.
506 Case C-285/02, [2005] IRLR 209.
507 *Home Office v Holmes* [1984] IRLR 299; *Kidd v DRG (UK) Ltd* [1985] ICR 405; *Clymo v Wandsworth London Borough Council* [1989] IRLR 241; see below, para 6.23.
508 ERA 1996, s 80F; see ch 6, below, at para 6.104.
509 Eg, French *Code du Travail*, Article L 212-4-2.
510 See the statement of Secretary of State for Employment, Michael Portillo MP, HC Debs, 6th series, Vol 251, Written Answers, 20 December 1994, at cols 1100–1101. An account of the various draft directives in this area is contained in Hepple, 1990a.
511 Directive 97/81 on part-time work. See OJ 1998 L14/9.

made under the social dialogue procedure of the Maastricht Agreement on Social Policy. The Agreement, while formally adopting a principle of equal treatment between part-time and full-time workers, also allows for some significant exceptions, and by no means bars the way to the use of deregulation to encourage part-time work.

Under clause 2(1) of the Framework Agreement, the agreement applies to part-time workers with an employment contract or employment relationship as defined by the relevant law, collective agreement or practice of the Member State; in addition, the Member State is permitted under clause 2(2) to exclude certain casual workers from the coverage of the Agreement, 'for objective reasons' and after consulting the social partners and acting in accordance with national law, collective agreements or practice. In *Wippel* the ECJ held that, under these provisions, a part-time worker employed under a 'framework contract' with no set hours (akin to a 'zero-hours contract') was covered by the Agreement if she satisfied the requirement of national law for the existence of an employment contract or relationship, and did not fall under any derogation by the Member State under clause 2(2).[512]

Clause 1 of the Framework Agreement states that it aims 'to provide for the removal of discrimination against part-time workers and to improve the quality of part-time work', and 'to facilitate the development of part-time work on a voluntary basis and to contribute to the flexible organisation of working time in a manner which takes into account the needs of employers and workers'.[513] To achieve these ends, it stipulates in clause 4 that 'in respect of employment conditions, part-time workers shall not be treated in a less favourable manner than comparable full-time workers solely because they work part time unless different treatment is justified on objective grounds'.[514]

For this purpose, a part-time worker is defined as 'an employee whose normal hours of work, calculated on a weekly basis or on average over a period of employment of up to one year, are less than the normal hours of work of a comparable full-time worker', while a comparable full-time worker is 'a full-time worker in the same establishment having the same type of employment contract or relationship, who is engaged in the same or similar work/ occupation, due regard being given to other considerations which may include seniority and qualifications/skills'. Where there is no comparable full-time worker in the establishment, comparison may be made by reference to an applicable collective agreement or, if there is no such agreement, in accordance with national law, collective agreements or practice.[515]

The Agreement goes on to state that in judging whether there is less favourable treatment, 'where appropriate, the principle of *pro rata temporis* shall apply'.[516] As we have just seen in our discussion of the seniority cases, the application of the pro rata principle, in this context, could be seen as having an indirectly discriminatory effect. The Framework Agreement also permits Member States and/or the social partners in appropriate cases to 'make access to particular conditions of employment subject to a period of service, time worked or earnings qualification'.[517] This is conditional upon the exemption being justified by objective grounds.

---

512 Case C-313/02 *Wippel v Peek & Cloppenburg GmbH & Co KG* [2005] IRLR 211.
513 Directive 97/81, Framework Agreement on Part Time Work, cl 1.
514 Directive 97/81, Framework Agreement on Part Time Work, cl 4(1).
515 Directive 97/81, Framework Agreement on Part Time Work, cl 3.
516 Directive 97/81, Framework Agreement on Part Time Work, cl 4(2).
517 Directive 97/81, Framework Agreement on Part Time Work, cl 4(4).

In *Wippel*[518] the ECJ held that clause 4 of the Agreement did not invalidate national legislation which set a maximum working week for full-timers 'which is by definition greater than that for part-time work',[519] nor did it invalidate an open-ended 'framework' or zero-hours contract which the applicant had entered into with her employer. The main obstacle facing the applicant in this case, according to the Court, was that there was no full-time worker, either in or beyond the establishment, whose position was comparable to hers,[520] a ruling which illustrates the limited scope of the Agreement.

The other main substantive provision of the Framework Agreement is concerned with promoting opportunities for part-time work. Clause 5(1) calls on Member States and the social partners to identify and review potential obstacles to part-time work and, where appropriate, to eliminate them. On the face of it, this measure could be used to justify a degree of deregulation, and this is also hinted at by a further provision which states:

> Implementation of the provisions of this Agreement shall not constitute valid grounds for reducing the general level of protection afforded to workers in the field of this agreement. This does not prejudice the right of Member States and/or social partners to develop different legislative, regulatory or contractual provisions, in the light of changing circumstances, and does not prejudice the application of clause 5.1 as long as the principle of non-discrimination in clause 4.1 is complied with.[521]

Much turns, then, on how clauses 5(1) and 4(1) are to be reconciled by the Member States.

The Agreement also provides that a worker's refusal to transfer from full-time to part-time work or vice versa is not in itself to constitute a valid ground for dismissal (although without prejudice to 'other reasons such as may arise from the operational requirements of the establishment concerned');[522] conversely, employers are required to give consideration to a number of matters including requests for such transfers by workers, the provision of information on the availability of part-time and full-time positions in the establishment, facilitating access to part-time work at all levels of the enterprise 'including skilled and managerial positions' where appropriate; facilitating access of part-time workers to 'vocational training to enhance career prospects and occupational mobility'; and providing information about part-time working to workforce representatives.[523]

The Agreement was brought into effect in UK law by the Part-Time Workers (Prevention of Less Favourable Treatment) Regulations 2000.[524] The Regulations address the central issue of comparability between part-time and full-time workers in a highly detailed and complex way.[525] A full-time worker is defined as one who 'is paid wholly or in part by reference to the time he works and, having regard to the custom and practice of the employer in relation to workers employed

---

518 Case C-313/02 *Wippel v Peek & Cloppenburg GmbH & Co KG* [2005] IRLR 211.
519 *Wippel*, Judgment, at para 49.
520 *Wippel*, Judgment, at para 66 (and reaching the same conclusion with regard to a claim under Art 5 of the Equal Treatment Directive).
521 Directive 97/81, Framework Agreement on Part Time Work, clause 6(2). Note also clause 6(1) which states that Member States and/or the social partners 'may maintain or introduce more favourable provisions than set out in this agreement'.
522 Directive 97/81, Framework Agreement on Part Time Work, cl 5(2).
523 Directive 97/81, Framework Agreement on Part Time Work, cl 5(3).
524 PTWR 2000: SI 2000/1551. See McColgan, 2000a.
525 PTWR, 2000 reg 2.

by the worker's employer under the same type of contract, is identifiable as a full-time worker'. A part-time worker is one who is not identifiable as a 'full-time worker' in the same way.[526] For a part-time worker to be able to compare his or her position with that of a full-time worker, it must be shown that both workers are employed by the same employer under the same 'type of contract'; that they are engaged 'in the same or broadly similar work having regard, where relevant, to whether they have a similar level of qualification, skills and experience'; and that they work at the same establishment, unless there are no comparable full-time workers employed at the applicant's establishment, in which case employment at another establishment of the employer will suffice. The expression 'type of contract' is defined by reference to a number of determinants which include whether or not the contract is a contract for services, a contract of employment or a contract of apprenticeship, with a final residual category referring to 'any other description of worker that it is reasonable for the employer to treat differently from other workers on the ground that workers of that description have a different type of contract'. This last provision was given a narrow reading by the Court of Appeal in *Mathews v Kent and Medway Towns Fire Authority*:[527] 'to enable an employer to remove an employee from [one of the principal categories] because it is reasonable to treat him differently on the grounds that alleged comparators have a different type of contract would severely limit the scope of the protection provided by the Regulations'.

The applicant can compare their position to that of a *hypothetical* comparator in only two situations: first, where he or she has moved from full-time to part-time work and, second, where he or she returns to part-time work after absence from work of less than one year. Then, the claim can be made 'as if there were a comparable full-time worker' employed under the terms that applied to the applicant before his or her contract was varied or, in the case of returning to work, the terms of the contract they had before the period of absence commenced.[528]

The content of the right to equal treatment is described in regulation 5. A part-time worker must not be treated less equally either 'as regards the terms of his contract' or 'by being subjected to any other detriment by any act, or deliberate failure to act, of his employer'. The treatment must be 'on the ground that the worker is a part-time worker' and must not be justified on objective grounds. The pro-rata principle is to be applied 'unless it is inappropriate'. It is also made clear that part-time workers are not be entitled to receive overtime premia unless they have worked full-time, normal hours.

A part-time worker has the right to receive from the employer a statement of reasons for being treated less favourably. The main remedy for breach of the Regulations is a complaint to an employment tribunal that the worker has suffered a detriment.[529] Workers who are also employees can bring a claim for unfair dismissal under specified circumstances of victimisation, for which no qualifying period is needed.[530]

---

526 For these purposes, the term 'worker' bears the same meaning as it does under the more general labour law provisions discussed in para 3.51 *et seq* above. See PTWR 2000, reg 1.

527 [2004] IRLR 697, at para 12 (Maurice Kay LJ). However, the CA confirmed the view of the EAT and ET in this case that 'retained firefighters' could not compare their position with that of full-time firefighters, given significant differences in the nature of the jobs in question.

528 PTWR 2000, regs 3 and 4.

529 If the claim is upheld, the employment tribunal may make a declaration of rights, order compensation, or issue a recommendation to the employer: PTWR 2000, reg 8(7).

530 PTWR 2000, reg 7.

The requirement of an actual comparator (for all but a few cases) is at odds with the approach under equal treatment law more generally. Both SDA 1975 and RRA 1976, in common with other areas of anti-discrimination law, allow a hypothetical comparator.[531] McColgan suggests that 'the comparator problem is so overwhelming as to render the [Regulations] largely irrelevant to the vast majority of part-time workers'.[532] Figures produced by the government during the consultation process indicate that only one sixth of the 6 million part-time workers in the UK would find a comparator within the meaning of the Regulations, and that only around 400,000 individuals would be likely to benefit directly from the equal treatment principle.[533] Unlike the relevant principles of UK and EC sex discrimination law, the Regulations do not protect applicants for employment. Nor do they confer any rights on full-time workers, so missing the opportunity to provide for a more extensive right to transfer from full-time to part-time work. For these reasons, and because of limitations in the remedial structure of the Regulations, it seems likely that claims will continue to be brought under the general provisions of sex discrimination law.[534]

Establishing continuity: the significance of the contract

3.92 Continuity is defined for the purposes of ERA 1996 by Part XIV, Chapter I of that Act, and broadly analogous (although not identical) provisions are contained in other relevant regulations.[535] At least formally, these texts override the contract of employment as the source of continuity.[536] Thus continuity may be maintained across a number of separate contracts, as long as the requirements of the Act are met: 'even though a man may change his job from, say, manual work to clerical work, even though he may change the site of his work from one place to another, even though he may change the terms of his contract of employment and enter into a new contract of employment, as long as he is with the same employer all the way through, then it is continuous employment'.[537] The accumulation of continuity is not a matter for bargaining for employer and employee,[538] and any agreement to waive continuity would be void under section 203 of ERA 1996. There is also a presumption that employment 'during any period' is continuous unless the contrary is shown;[539] in effect the employer has the onus of disproving continuity.

Nevertheless, the Act defines continuity in such a way that it *is* dependent in practice on the express and implied terms of the contract of employment, and only in exceptional cases can it be acquired and maintained without reference to the contract terms. Under Chapter I of Part XIV, the basic unit of continuous

---

531 See ch 6 below.
532 McColgan, 2000a: p 266.
533 McColgan, 2000a: p 263.
534 McColgan, 2000a: p 267.
535 See, eg, those governing SMP (SI 1986/1960, regs 11–16) and SPP (SI 2002/2822, regs 33–38).
536 *Collison v BBC* [1998] IRLR 238; *Carrington v Harwich Dock Co Ltd* [1998] IRLR 567; *Sweeney v J & S Henderson (Concessions) Ltd* [1999] IRLR 306 (casting doubt on *Roach v CSB (Moulds) Ltd* [1991] IRLR 200); see Anderman, 2000: pp 235–237.
537 *Wood v York County Council* [1978] IRLR 228, 229 (Lord Denning MR).
538 *Hanson v Fashion Industries (Hartlepool) Ltd* [1980] IRLR 393; *Jennings v Salford Community Service Agency* [1981] IRLR 76; *Morris v Walsh Western UK Ltd* [1997] IRLR 562; *Bradford Metropolitan District Council v Dawson* [1999] ICR 312.
539 ERA 1996, s 210(5).

employment is the working week. With one major exception,[540] any week which does not count towards a qualifying period also breaks continuity,[541] so cancelling out accrued periods of continuous employment. In *Booth v United States of America*,[542] the employer sought to avoid the accrual of an employee's continuity of employment by following a practice of inserting regular two-week gaps in between successive fixed-term contracts. The EAT found that continuity had indeed been broken.

As a result of the amendments introduced in 1995 following the judgment of the House of Lords in *Ex p EOC*,[543] the basic rule is that 'any week during the whole or part of which an employee's relations with his employer are governed by a contract of employment counts in computing the employee's period of employment'.[544] This replaces a complex set of provisions which previously required the employee to show that he or she was either actually employed for 16 hours or more in a given week, or employed for any part of it under a contract of employment which normally involved employment for 16 or more hours per week. The courts are no longer required to explore the question of whether a period of work was part of an employee's normal contractual hours.[545]

Pre-1995 case law may still be relevant, however, in a second type of situation which arises where there are periodic gaps in the provision of work by the employer to the employee. Where the work is discontinuous, it may be possible to discover, through construction, a global or umbrella contract of employment. Alternatively, it could be that each separate period of work is carried out under a separate contract of employment, which, following the 1995 amendments, will enable the week in question to be counted. However, it could also be the case that all or some of the separate hirings are for contracts for services, in which case continuity cannot be established.

In *Hellyer Bros Ltd v McLeod*[546] claims for redundancy compensation were made by a number of deep sea trawlermen whose employers had withdrawn their fleets from service following a decline in fishing stocks. In each case the applicant had worked exclusively for the employer over periods amounting to several decades. They were employed on a series of crew agreements which lasted for the duration of each voyage; in between voyages, the men claimed unemployment benefit. They regarded themselves as bound to their respective employers and did not miss a voyage without their permission; the employers also provided equipment and operated holiday pay and pension schemes. As fishing stocks declined the gaps between voyages grew longer until the employers decided not to fish any further.

The employment tribunal found that the men had each been employed under a global contract of employment and that they therefore had sufficient continuity to bring a claim in redundancy, but the EAT reversed this ruling, and its judgment was upheld by the Court of Appeal. The Court found insufficient evidence of

540 This concerns weeks lost through strikes and lock-outs. Such weeks do not count towards the qualifying period but do not cancel out accrued periods of continuity either: ERA 1996, s 216. Other exceptions are contained in ss 215 and 217.
541 ERA 1996, s 210(4).
542 [1999] IRLR 16.
543 [1994] IRLR 176; SI 1995/31. See above, para 3.88.
544 ERA 1996, s 212(1).
545 *Parkes Classic Confectionery v Ashcroft* (1973) 8 ITR 43; *Dean v Eastbourne Fishermen's Society* [1977] ICR 556; *Lake v Essex County Council* [1979] ICR 577; *Letheby & Christopher Ltd v Bond* [1988] ICR 480.
546 [1987] ICR 526.

mutual commitments to offer work and to accept it: 'we do not see how it is possible to infer from the parties' conduct the existence in between crew agreements of a trawlerman's obligation *to serve*, which is part of the "irreducible minimum of obligation" on the part of the employee required to support the existence of a contract of service'.[547]

The decision in *Hellyer* turns on its own rather distinctive facts, but it is unsatisfactory that the issue of redundancy entitlement under statute should have turned on such a narrow and debatable construction of the particular contractual arrangements in that case, not least because mutual obligations were implied by other courts in cases with not dissimilar facts.[548] However, the 1995 amendments at least overcame the situation which arose in *Surrey County Council v Lewis*,[549] whereby an employee with a series of separate but overlapping contracts of employment with the same employer failed to establish continuity for the reason that she could not aggregate the hours worked under the separate arrangements. With the abolition of the hours threshold, it is simply necessary to show that the employee was employed under a contract of employment for any *part* of the week in question.

Establishing continuity outside the contract

3.93 Section 212(3) of ERA 1996 provides for continuity to be preserved in certain limited circumstances where no contract of employment is in force between the parties.[550] These are periods of incapability through sickness or injury, up to a maximum of 26 weeks;[551] absence 'on account of a temporary cessation of work';[552] and absence in circumstances such that the worker is regarded as a matter of custom or arrangement as continuing in employment.[553]

Section 212 has no application to a week in which there *is* a contract of employment in force. Until 1995 this posed a problem in cases of job-sharing

---

547 [1987] ICR 526, 549 (Slade LJ).
548 *Boyd Line Ltd v Pitts* [1986] ICR 244 (trawler captain); *Nethermere (St Neots) Ltd v Taverna and Gardiner* [1983] ICR 319 (homeworkers).
549 [1987] 3 All ER 641.
550 This is the effect of the heading to the paragraph, 'periods in which there is no contract of employment', as interpreted by Lord Diplock in *Ford v Warwickshire County Council* [1983] IRLR 126. Cf Lord Upjohn in *Fitzgerald v Hall, Russell & Co* [1970] AC 984, 1000: 'Counsel on neither side was able to give it any sensible meaning ... I propose for the purpose of construing the [Act] to ignore that cross-heading'.
551 ERA 1996, s 212(3)(a), (4). Incapability for work is defined by reference to the work which the employee was employed to do before the period of absence began and, if it is different, to the work which he is employed to do subsequently: *Pearson v Kent County Council* [1993] IRLR 165; *Donnelly v Kelvin International Services* [1992] IRLR 496.
552 ERA 1996, s 212(3)(b); see below.
553 ERA 1996, s 212(3)(c). This may apply to situations of lay-off for lack of work (*Puttick v John Wright & Sons (Blackwall) Ltd* [1972] ICR 457) and to the lending or secondment of an employee to another employer (*Wishart v National Coal Board* [1974] ICR 460), but its scope is limited; it is not clear whether it could have had any application in *Hellyer Bros Ltd v McLeod* [1987] ICR 526, where it was not argued. In *Booth v United States of America* [1999] IRLR 16 the EAT rejected a suggestion that it could be invoked to deal with regular fortnightly gaps between fixed-term contracts which were adopted by the employer in order to avoid the accrual of continuity of employment and in *Curr v Marks & Spencer plc* [2003] IRLR 74 it was held not to cover a situation of a 'child break scheme' lasting several years (but cf the opposite outcome in *Unwin v Barclays Bank plc*, EAT, 26 February 2003, Appeal No EAT/0273/02). Quaere whether an 'arrangement' needs to be in place before the gap: see *London Probation Board v Kirkpatrick* [2005] IRLR 443.

where two employees would work alternate weeks; the employee's week off would break continuity under the Act since it would prevent him or her from reaching the weekly hours threshold of 8 or 16 as the case might be, but nor could the week be counted under the predecessor of section 212 since the contract of employment had not come to an end.[554] However, with the removal of the 8- and 16-hour thresholds, this problem has been solved: the week off will now count under section 212(1) of ERA 1996, since it is a week in which the employee is employed under a contract of employment.

In the cases where section 212 does apply, it can be read as giving statutory recognition to certain extra-contractual expectations of the employee. Continuity, the foundation of statutory rights, may remain in force notwithstanding the employer's termination of the contract of employment. One effect, as Lord Upjohn put it in *Fitzgerald v Hall, Russell & Co*,[555] is that 'a previous contract of employment which has been terminated may be relevant in computing the period of employment', while in *Ford v Warwickshire County Council*[556] Lord Diplock said that it was among the provisions which take 'the relationship between employer and employee out of the field of contract and into that of status'. It follows that the question of whether there is a 'temporary cessation of work' or a 'customary absence' should not be decided primarily by reference to the contract.

Ford illustrates this principle. The employee was employed as a lecturer on a series of fixed-term contracts spanning the academic year from September to July; for the summer months in between contracts she was not employed by the Council. The House of Lords held that the gaps between work could be counted under the forerunner to section 212(3)(b) on the grounds that the employee's absence was caused by a temporary cessation of work. It was irrelevant that the contracts themselves provided for the absence by setting a fixed term for their duration or that the applicant's expectations of a renewal of her contract 'had never hardened into an enforceable obligation':[557] what mattered was the *substantive reason* for the break, and not the *form* it was given in the contract.

The court had to examine the substantive reason for the absence, in Lord Diplock's view, since the termination of the fixed-term contract amounted to a dismissal[558] for which the employer would normally have to show a potentially fair reason if he was to avoid a finding of unfair dismissal. This is not a very good argument since there may be cases in which an employee does not, at the time of the dismissal, have the necessary qualifying service to bring an unfair dismissal claim. The better view is probably that there can be a 'cessation of work' within the meaning of section 212(3)(b) whether or not the employer contemplated it at the time of contracting. But whatever the precise reason, it is clear that the form of the contract – whether it is fixed-term or for an indefinite duration – is irrelevant in this context.[559]

It is the *cessation of work* and not the *absence* which must be temporary; this means that continuity will be maintained until such time as the cessation becomes

---

554   The decision to the contrary in *Lloyds Bank Ltd v Secretary of State for Employment* [1979] ICR 258, applying the provision which is now contained in ERA s 212(3)(c), appeared to be wrong in the light of Lord Diplock's judgment in *Ford v Warwickshire County Council* [1983] IRLR 126; see also *Corton House Ltd v Skipper* [1981] IRLR 78, anticipating *Ford*.

555   [1970] AC 984, 1001.

556   [1983] IRLR 126, 128.

557   The phrase used by Stephenson LJ in the Court of Appeal: [1982] ICR 520.

558   Under ERA 1996, s 95(1)(b). See below, ch 5, para 5.78.

559   See Lord Brightman in *Ford*, [1983] IRLR 126, 130.

permanent, even if the employment does not resume. Where work is resumed, the question of whether the cessation is temporary or not is to be determined in the first instance by comparing the length of the break to the periods of work on either side of it, as in *Ford*.[560] However, this is only one possible approach, and it may be appropriate in a given case to take a much broader view, looking at the length and number of the breaks in relation to the period of employment as a whole.[561] The application of the test is inevitably somewhat impressionistic.

However, although *Ford* clearly ruled that the terms of the contract are not central to establishing whether there is a *temporary cessation*, the same cannot be said with confidence of the approach the courts will take to the question of whether *work* has temporarily ceased or not. A number of decisions have appeared to 'recontractualise' section 212(3)(b) at this stage of the test.

In *Byrne v Birmingham City District Council*[562] the applicant was employed as a street cleaner under a contract which allowed the employer to allocate work to him as it became available on a 'pool' basis with other employees. The Court of Appeal took the view that there was no global contract of employment in this case as the arrangement lacked the necessary mutuality of obligation; nor could the applicant rely on the predecessor of section 212(3)(b) to bridge the gaps between periods of work. This was because the employer had work available, but, in accordance with the arrangements agreed between the parties, had exercised the right to allocate it to others for the periods in question. According to Purchas LJ, 'the expression "cessation of work" must denote that some "quantum of work" had for the time being ceased to exist, and, therefore, was no longer available for the employer to give to the employee'.[563]

Byrne is a problematic decision since it ignores the limitations which section 212(3)(b) implicitly places on the employer's powers to determine continuity under the Act. It also goes against *dicta* in the earlier House of Lords decision of *Fitzgerald v Hall, Russell & Co*, in which Lord Upjohn held that the correct test was whether work is made available by the employer *to that individual employee*, and not whether there was a wider 'quantum' of work to be shared amongst employees as a group.[564]

Independently of section 212, there may be instances in which a contract term which apparently has the effect of removing accrued continuity of employment will be denied that effect by section 203 of ERA, which (subject to certain exceptions) renders void any contract term to the extent that it purports to 'exclude or limit the operation of any provision of this Act'. In *Secretary of State for Employment v Deary*,[565] section 203 (previously section 140 of EPCA 1978) was applied to a term reducing employees' hours below the statutory threshold for continuity after they had previously acquired the necessary qualifying service, thereby enabling continuity to be preserved. In effect, the term only had validity at common law for the purpose of defining the mutual rights and obligations of the parties under the contract. No distinction was drawn in *Deary* between terms introduced for the purpose of undermining the Act, and terms simply having that effect: in both cases, the court thought that section 203 could

560 [1983] IRLR 126, 130 (Lord Diplock); *Sillars v Charrington Fuels Ltd* [1988] IRLR 180.
561 *Flack v Kodak Ltd* [1986] IRLR 255, applying *Fitzgerald v Hall, Russell & Co* [1970] AC 984.
562 [1987] ICR 519.
563 [1987] ICR 519, 525. To similar effect is *Letheby and Christopher v Bond* [1988] ICR 480.
564 [1970] AC 984.
565 [1984] ICR 413.

be invoked. By contrast, in *Surrey County Council v Lewis*[566] the House of
Lords held that contractual documents would be taken at face value unless they
were clearly a sham. The predecessor of section 203 was apparently not cited to
the courts in *Lewis*; had it been, the outcome might have been different. *Deary*
nevertheless remains a somewhat isolated authority as far as the application of
section 203 to the concept of continuity is concerned.

IDENTIFYING THE EMPLOYER[567]

3.94   In the vast majority of cases the employer will not be an individual but
will instead be a legal entity, that is to say a partnership or company, a statutory
body such as a local authority or, in the case of civil servants, the Crown.[568]
Freedom of contract means that the employer's identity is essentially a matter
for the parties themselves, and one employer cannot normally be substituted for
another without the consent of the parties to the original contract and of the
third-party employer. However, consent may not be needed for certain statutory
responsibilities to be shared amongst or shifted between 'associated employers',
where, for example, one company controls the other or both are controlled by a
third party. These occasions are rare; on the whole, labour law respects the
'corporate veil' which separates the legal entity of the limited liability company
from its owners and controllers.

Employer, undertaking and establishment

3.95   It is important to separate these concepts. The 'employer' is not the business
or undertaking itself, but, in general, the *owner* of the undertaking. The concept
of the 'undertaking', in turn, represents the notion of the business as a *going
concern*. It is therefore not constituted simply by the business assets of the
employer (machinery, land, intellectual property, and so on); it embraces business
goodwill and other non-tangible assets, although not the right to the future
services of the employees: their contracts of employment may not be transferred
to another employment if they refuse to give consent.[569] As we shall see shortly,[570]
for the purposes of the TUPE (Transfer of Undertakings (Protection of
Employment)) Regulations 1981 and of the Acquired Rights Directive (77/187;
now 2001/23) which it aims to implement, an undertaking must be an 'economic
entity' in its own right, and not merely a particular 'activity' of that employer.

Employee rights may also be defined by reference to the establishment, rather
than to the employer or undertaking: this concept is used to delimit the scope of
comparisons between male and female employees in equal pay legislation and

---

566   [1987] 3 All ER 641; see also *Booth v United States of America* [1999] IRLR 16.
567   See Collins, 1990a; Deakin, 2001a; Freedland 2003: ch 1.
568   Freedland, 2003: p 36 argues that the 'personal' conception of the employment relationship
      is a legacy of nineteenth century legal attitudes which 'imposes a strongly defined and
      prescriptive view of the institutional organization of work which is outdated and artificial'
      and suggests that (at p 39) 'because it is so important to keep it in mind that the
      employing party is not normally a single (male) human being trading as such, we [should]
      use the terminology of the "employing entity" instead of that of the "employer" to refer
      to the human or corporate persons who may constitute the employing party'.
569   *Nokes v Doncaster Amalgamated Collieries Ltd* [1940] AC 1014; see below, para 3.100.
570   See below, para 3.99 *et seq*.

also for the purposes of defining the employer's obligation to consult over proposals for redundancy, although in neither case is the term 'establishment' actually defined in the legislation itself.[571] It seems that the concept refers not to the business as defined above, but to a sub-unit of the business such as the place of work of an employee or group of employees. However, it may also cover a number of separate sites if they are linked by a common managerial structure or if they form part of a single unit for accounting or financial purposes. Thus a series of building sites owned by single employer could, for this purpose, form a single 'establishment'.[572]

Employer and company

3.96   The employer need not be, but may well be, a legal entity such as a partnership or company. Whereas equity partners remain personally liable, on a joint and several basis, for the debts of the business, the shareholders of a limited liability company are sheltered from personal responsibility for its debts and normally stand to lose only the nominal value of their shares if the business fails.[573] Thus 'among the principal reasons which induce persons to form private companies ... are the desire to avoid the risk of bankruptcy, and the increased facility for borrowing money. By means of a private company ... a trade can be carried on with limited liability, and without exposing the persons interested in it in the event of failure to the harsh provisions of company law. A company, too, can raise money on debentures, which an ordinary trader cannot do'.[574] Although Parliament has sought to 'lift the corporate veil' for various purposes, chiefly in the field of taxation law, the courts themselves are more reluctant to do so. The fact that one company (a 'subsidiary') is owned or controlled by another company (its 'parent'), or by a certain individual, is not in itself grounds for ignoring the separate legal personality of that company.[575] It has been said that 'where the character of a company, or the nature of the persons who control it, is a relevant feature the court will go behind the mere status of the company as a legal entity, and will consider who are the persons as shareholders or even as agents who direct and control the actitivies of a company which is incapable of doing anything without human assistance'.[576] But this begs the question of what precisely in the character of a company or its shareholders will suffice for this purpose. A clear case of corporate personality being used in an attempt to deflect a pre-existing legal liability might be enough.[577] But otherwise, the mere presence of cross-shareholdings between companies in a company 'group' will not suffice to confer corporate personality on that 'group' as a separate entity, nor to enable the court to ignore the separate legal personalities of the companies within it. In particular, the court will not lift the corporate veil:

---

571   EqPA 1970, s 1(1), (6), and TULRCA 1992, s 188(2). See also TULRCA 1992, s 228 which, in the context of strike ballots, refers to a 'workplace' (see s 228(4) for a definition).
572   *Barratt Developments (Bradford) v UCATT* [1978] ICR 319; see further para 9.31 below.
573   Insolvency Act 1986, s 74(2).
574   *Salomon v A Salomon & Co Ltd* [1897] AC 22, 52 (Lord Macnaghten).
575   The suggestions of Lord Denning that it should be (*Littlewoods Mail Order Stores Ltd v IRC* [1969] 1 WLR 1241, 1254; *Wallersteiner v Moir* [1974] 1 WLR 991, 1013) have not been followed.
576   *Merchandise Transport Ltd v British Transport Commission* [1962] 2 QB 173 (Danckwerts LJ).
577   *Jones v Lipman* [1962] 1 WLR 832.

> ... merely because the corporate structure has been used so as to ensure that
> the legal liability (if any) in respect of particular future activities of the group
> (and correspondingly the risk of enforcement of that liability) will fall on
> another member of the group rather than the defendant company. Whether
> or not this is desirable, the right to use a corporate structure in this manner is
> inherent in our corporate law.[578]

This principle was applied in a labour law context in *Michael Peters Ltd v
Farnfield.*[579] Mr Farnfield was chief executive of MPG plc, which was the parent
company in a group containing twenty-five subsidiary companies. The parent
and its subsidiaries were put into receivership and Mr Farnfield was dismissed
for redundancy; four of the subsidiaries were subsequently sold to buyers. For
the purposes of the TUPE Regulations 1981,[580] Mr Farnfield argued that he was
an employee of one of those subsidiaries, and therefore entitled to continuing
employment with that company. The EAT held that the companies concerned
did not form a 'single economic unit' and that it would therefore be wrong to
lift the corporate veil on this occasion: Mr Farnfield was not an employee of the
subsidiary company.

   Nonetheless, the EAT went on to say that it might be appropriate in a given
case to treat a 'single economic unit' of companies as a single employer for
employment purposes, where the subsidiaries 'do not have discretion to determine
their continued membership of their parent company'.[581] If this were done on a
regular basis, it might considerably limit the potential of separate corporate
personality as a mechanism for delimiting the impact of employment law upon
a given business. The scope of the principle adverted to by the EAT is wider
than that previously applied, and there is doubt as to whether it could be
compatible with the general approach of the courts in this area. However, there
is some authority[582] for a more extensive use of the notion of the 'economic unit'
in interpreting provisions of European Union law and the provisions of UK law
derived from it, of which the TUPE Regulations 1981 are one instance.

Company directors, partners and employees

3.97   One consequence of separate corporate personality is that a company
director may be, but need not necessarily be, an employee of that company.
If he or she is a managing or executive director with a service contract of
some kind, they will be employed by the company, most likely in the capacity
of employee according to the tests considered earlier in this chapter. The
concept of 'employee' is not in any way restricted to personnel of a particular
rank, so that high-level managers may be employees just as much as those
below them in the company hierarchy. Nor does holding a directorship,
which is an 'office' for the purposes of company law, in any way prevent the
person who holds it from also being an employee. A company director who
is also the principal shareholder or *de facto* controller of the company is

---

578 *Adams v Cape Industries plc* [1990] Ch 433, 544 (Slade LJ), on which, see the discussion
     of P Davies and M Freedland, 2004. See also *Bank of Tokyo Ltd v Karoon* [1987] AC
     45n, 64 (Robert Goff LJ).
579 [1995] IRLR 190. See also *Sunley Turriff Holdings Ltd v Thomson* [1995] IRLR 184;
     Colt Group v Couchman [2000] ICR 327.
580 See below, para 3.99 *et seq.*
581 [1995] IRLR 190, 192.
582 See [1995] IRLR 190, 192.

not, for that reason, prevented from being its employee as opposed to the employer. Once the owner has taken the decision to incorporate the business as a limited liability company with a separate legal personality, the company normally becomes the employer. The right to take advantage of incorporation under the Companies Acts in this way is not easily lost and the courts will only rarely lift the corporate veil to impose a personal liability upon the shareholders or controller of the company, or otherwise disregard the company's separate legal personality.[583]

It is not uncommon for some individuals to offer their services via companies which they have set up for the purpose, with themselves and another person as directors. Normally, as we have just seen, the individual will be the employee of the company which they have set up in this way, and not the employee of the company or other entity which is the end user of their services. However, in a case of a 'sham' arrangement it is open to the courts to disregard the presence of the intermediary, and find that the true employer is indeed the end user. This occurred in *Catamaran Cruisers Ltd v Williams*.[584] Mr Williams was initially employed as an employee with the appellant and then, when he moved to work of a different kind, was told that he would have to offer his services as an independent contractor. This he agreed to do; however, the Inland Revenue persisted in regarding him as an employee for tax purposes. Mr Williams then set up a company, Unicorn Enterprises, with himself and his mother as directors. Unicorn next contracted to supply Mr Williams' services to the appellant, for which it received a fee paid without deduction of income tax. Subsequently, these services were no longer needed and the question arose of Mr Williams' entitlement to compensation for unfair dismissal. The employment tribunal found that apart from the change in the form of payment, 'there was no factual change whatsoever in the terms of Mr Williams' employment',[585] and concluded that he was still an employee of the appellants. This judgment was upheld by the EAT, which considered that 'there is no rule of law that the importation of a limited company into a relationship such as existed in this case prevents the continuation of a contract of employment. If the true relationship is that of employer and employee, it cannot be changed by putting a different label upon it'.[586]

Unlike a director, an equity partner in a partnership such as a firm of solicitors or accountants cannot be an employee of that firm, for the reason that the firm has no legal personality separate from its partners who are, collectively, the employers.[587] Since a person cannot be simultaneously the employer and an employee in relation to the same business, it also follows that the owner of an unincorporated business will be the employer of those who work for him or her, and not one of the employees of that business.

The employees of a partnership are employed by *all* the partners at any given time. According to Scott LJ in *Briggs v Oates*,[588] in large partnerships 'common sense' dictates that the contracts of employment of the employees

583 *Lee v Lee's Air Farming* [1961] AC 12; *Secretary of State for Trade and Industry v Bottrill* [1998] IRLR 120, [1999] IRLR 326, doubting *Buchan v Secretary of State for Employment* [1997] IRLR 80; see also *Fleming v Secretary of State for Trade and Industry* [1997] IRLR 682; *Sellars Arenascene Ltd v Connolly* [2001] IRLR 222.
584 [1994] IRLR 386.
585 [1994] IRLR 386, 388.
586 [1994] IRLR 386. See also *Abbey Life Assurance Co Ltd v Tansell* [2000] IRLR 387, discussed above, paras 3.67–3.68; Deakin, 2001a.
587 *Cowell v Quilter Goodison & Co Ltd* [1989] IRLR 392.
588 [1990] IRLR 472.

continue in force as partners come and go.[589] The process can be seen as the novation of the contracts concerned which operates on the implicit consent of all the parties concerned. However, if an employee raises an objection to a particular partner, it is difficult to see how the contract of the employee concerned can then be said to have been novated. There is authority to suggest that under these circumstances the contract is automatically terminated, at least where the change in the identity of the partners affects the nature of the business or the employee's role in it.[590]

Non-executive directors of a company who are not contracted to provide their labour or services to the business will not be employees merely by virtue of their director's office.[591] However, under the Companies Acts and under the principles of fiduciary obligation, all directors necessarily incur duties to the company and, more exceptionally, to the shareholders, whether or not they are employed by the company. As part of their duties to the company, directors are required to have regard to the interests of 'the company's employees in general' as well as to those of its members (the shareholders).[592] However, the Companies Act 1985 'appears to make it clear that shareholders' (and creditors') interests prevail in any crunch situation'.[593] One clear exception is the cessation or transfer of the business, whereupon the company is granted a power by statute to make provision for the benefit of employees and ex-employees, 'notwithstanding that [this power's] exercise is not in the best interests of the company'.[594] This provision can be read as implying, however, that in other situations the company does not have power to rank employees' interests over those of creditors and shareholders.

A number of reporting requirements are imposed on directors in companies of a certain type and size. These include an obligation on companies normally employing more than 250 persons to indicate in the directors' annual report the measures taken in that year to provide information to the workforce on 'matters of concern to them as employees'; to consult employees or their representatives on a regular basis 'so that the views of employees can be taken into account in making decisions which are likely to affect their interests'; to encourage employee participation in company performance, through share schemes or otherwise; and to achieve 'a common awareness on the part of all employees of the financial and economic factors affecting the performance of the company'.[595]

589 This result was achieved in the context of an unincorporated association in *Affleck v Newcastle Mind* [1999] IRLR 405: the employer consisted of the management committee and its members as constituted at any given time.
590 *Brace v Calder* [1895] 2 QB 253; see further para 3.100 below.
591 See, eg, *Parsons v Albert J Parsons Ltd* [1979] ICR 271; cf *Folami v Nigerline (UK) Ltd* [1978] ICR 277. In practice a non-executive director may receive written terms of appointment but these will rarely be intended to have the result of making him or her an employee of the company.
592 CA 1985, s 309, described as 'obscure and ambiguous' by the Company Law Review Steering Committee (*Modern Company Law for a Competitive Economy: Final Report Volume 1* (2001), at p. 352), which argued for its repeal (*Modern Company Law for a Competitive Economy: The Strategic Framework* (1999), at para 5.1.20). For discussion of this and related aspects of corporate governance reform, see Wedderburn, 2004.
593 Wedderburn, 1986: p 102; although cf Prentice, 1981.
594 CA 1985, s 719.
595 CA 1985, Sch 7, Part V (employee involvement) and Sch 7 Part III (disclosure of information concerning disabled persons). On statutory consultation requirements under ICER see para 9.50 *et seq.*

Associated employers

3.98 Statute provides for what is in effect a limited lifting of the corporate veil in a number of specified instances. For these purposes, two employers are to be treated as associated if '(a) one is a company of which the other (directly or indirectly) has control, or (b) both are companies of which a third person (directly or indirectly) has control'.[596] In practice the most important occasion on which this provision may be invoked relates to continuity of employment. If an employee moves his or her employment from one associated employer to another, their continuity is unbroken and their service from the previous employment is counted towards it.[597]

Other occasions on which the principle of associated employers may be invoked are few in number; nor do they *always* favour the employee, although most do. Certain employment rights only apply if the number of employees employed by the employer is greater than a specified number; for this purpose, employees of an associated employer can normally be added to the total.[598] For the purposes of a claim for equal pay the applicant may choose as a comparator an employee of the same employer or of an associated employer, if they fulfil the other necessary conditions of being employed at the same establishment or in an establishment to which common terms and conditions apply.[599] An employment tribunal may, in the event of unfair dismissal, order re-engagement against an associated employer.[600] But an associated employer may, conversely, make an offer of re-engagement to an employee who has been made redundant, which, if the employee unreasonably refuses, will lead to him or her losing any entitlement to redundancy compensation,[601] and an employee will lose the right to a guarantee payment if he or she is laid off on account of an industrial dispute involving an employee of his employer or an associated employer.[602] The position of an associated employer is also relevant in relation to the right of an employee to return to work after pregnancy. The failure to permit the employee to return to work is regarded as an automatically unfair dismissal, unless it is not reasonably practicable for her employer to permit her to return or for her employer or an associated employer to make her a suitable offer of alternative employment.[603] Nor will there be an automatically unfair dismissal if an associated employer makes an offer of suitable alternative employment and this offer is either accepted or unreasonably refused.[604] Finally, in the collective sphere, the obligation to disclose information to a recognised trade union for the purposes of collective bargaining extends to certain information in the possession of either the employer or an associated employer. The employer must disclose information the absence of which would seriously impede collective bargaining between itself and the trade union; however, it is not required to disclose information relevant to collective bargaining between the union and the associated employer.[605] This leaves something of a gap in a situation where

596 ERA 1996, s 231; TULRCA 1992, s 297.
597 ERA 1996, s 218(6).
598 See, for example, TULRCA 1992, Sch A1, para 7.
599 EqPA 1970, s 1(6).
600 ERA 1996, s 115.
601 ERA 1996, s 146(1).
602 ERA 1996, s 29(3).
603 See SI 1999/3312, reg 20(6)(b). The right to return is also lost if, at the relevant time, the numbers employed by the employer or an associated employer are five or less: SI 1999/3312, reg 20(6)(a).
604 SI 1999/3312, reg 20(7).
605 TULRCA 1992, s 181(2).

the associated employer does not recognise the trade union for collective bargaining purposes and so cannot itself be made subject to the disclosure requirement.

The notion of associated employers provides a useful means of closing off some of the more obvious routes by which the application of statutory rights could be avoided by the adoption of separate corporate personality for different parts of an undertaking. By no means all the possible escape routes are covered, however, and some have been opened up again by legislation. Thus it used to be the case that a shop steward was entitled to paid time off for duties connected with industrial relations not just between his or her employer and its employees, but also for those between an associated employer and its employees. This reference to associated employers was deleted, along with other changes, in the Employment Act 1989.[606]

Moreover, the courts sometimes take the view that by extending the effects of employment legislation to associated employers in certain specific instances, Parliament implicitly rules out action by the courts to lift the corporate veil in other, closely related situations. In *Dimbleby & Sons Ltd v National Union of Journalists*[607] Lord Diplock would not 'wholly exclude the possibility even in the absence of express words stating that one company, although separately incorporated, is to be treated as sharing the same legal personality of another'; such a conclusion could be justified by a purposive interpretation. However, statutory phrases should not be interpreted in this way if, in the same legislation, specific but more limited provision had been made to lift the corporate veil: the more specific provision would then become 'entirely otiose'.[608]

The term 'control' is, however, capable of being interpreted in a flexible way, and is potentially broader than tests based exclusively on the presence of a majority shareholding, which are 'both too narrow, as a majority shareholding need not confer control due to weighted voting, and too wide, as control may be obtained without a majority shareholding'.[609] As a result, the definition of associated employers in terms of control of one company by another, or of the two of them by a third party, is capable of embracing the concept of corporate group liability. A company group can be identified as consisting of inter-linked associated employers, as in *Pinkney v Sandpiper Drilling Co*.[610] Here, companies which had been formed into a 'partnership of companies' were found to be associated employers, so that each one was responsible as employer to the employees of the various different entities. This is a somewhat unusual case, however, and there would seem to be ample scope for more complex corporate arrangements to be put in place which could avoid this outcome.

In some cases the employment law test has shown itself incapable of recognising the realities of control. Although the 'person' who controls two associated employers need not be an individual but could be a group of individuals acting together,[611] it has been held that they must be the *same*

---

606 The old law was contained in EPCA 1978, s 27, and was amended by EA 1989, s 14 (see Deakin, 1990a: p 16). The relevant provision is now TULRCA 1992, s 168.
607 [1984] ICR 386, 410.
608 The case concerned the definition of secondary industrial action, which now makes no reference to associated employers since the relevant provision (EA 1980, s 17(4)) has been repealed (by EA 1990, s 4). See TULRCA 1992, s 224.
609 Bercusson, 1986: p 149.
610 [1989] IRLR 425.
611 *Zarb and Samuels v British and Brazilian Produce Co (Sales) Ltd* [1978] IRLR 78.

individuals in the case of both companies. In *Poparm Ltd v Weekes*[612] the applicant, prior to her dismissal, had previously been employed by Bamfords International Ltd and claimed that this was an associated employer of Poparm. Poparm was owned 50% by Mr Zabadne and 20% by his wife, the remainder of the shares being owned by a third party. Bamfords was a wholly owned subsidiary of a company, Euranglo Trading Ltd, whose shares were owned 35% by Mr Zabadne, 25% each by two of his brothers and 15% by a third brother. The EAT held that Bamfords and Poparm were not associated employers. Although Mr Zabadne was in a position to control Poparm by acting in concert with his wife and to control Euranglo by acting in concert with his brothers, it could not be said that any one person was in control of both companies. By contrast, control was established in *Payne v Secretary of State for Employment*[613] where a husband and wife together held shares in a company, and the wife was shown to be a nominee of the husband.

It was held in *Gardiner v Merton London Borough Council*[614] that the term 'company' meant a limited company, and did not refer to other forms of body corporate such as a local authority.[615] However, the company in question need not necessarily be incorporated in the United Kingdom; it suffices that it is a company which, in its essentials, may be likened to a limited company incorporated under the UK Companies Acts.[616] In this way, the notion of associated employers may extend to a transnational corporate group, consisting of companies incorporated in different jurisdictions.

Notwithstanding the notion of associated employers, it remains the case that labour law lacks sufficiently flexible conceptual devices for dealing with the liability of groups of interrelated economic entities. Corporate entities can be bound together not just by cross-shareholdings but also through contractual arrangements such as franchises, joint ventures and subcontracting. Collins[617] has suggested that the law 'should continue to respect the general principle that one person should not be held responsible for the actions of another, whilst recognising that the formal separation of legal identities in complex economic organisations may conceal what in reality constitutes a single set of productive relations which should be treated as a united group for the purpose of the ascription of legal responsibility'.

In the light of this suggestion, it is interesting to consider again the decision of the Court of Appeal in *Harrods Ltd v Remick*.[618] The Court accepted that Harrods could (if allegations were proved) be responsible for acts of racial discrimination which arose from the dismissal of the complainants by companies which were, themselves, concessionaires or franchisees of Harrods. The terms of the commercial contracts between Harrods and the franchisees placed Harrods in the perhaps unexpected position of being the 'principal' to whom 'contract workers' were supplied for the purposes of section 7 of the Race Relations Act 1976. One effect of these contractual arrangements was that Harrods had the

---

612 [1984] IRLR 388.
613 [1989] IRLR 352.
614 [1980] IRLR 472.
615 The decision was reversed on its specific facts by SI 1983/1160, providing for continuity of employment to be preserved on a change of employment from one local authority to another.
616 *Hancill v Marcon Engineering Ltd* [1990] IRLR 51.
617 H Collins, 1990a: p 744.
618 [1997] IRLR 583; see para 3.68 above.

final word over who worked in its department store, even in respect of persons who were not its own employees. Here, then, the court can be seen as having identified the true source of the economic power to which the complainants were subject. A similar outcome was achieved in *Abbey Life Assurance Co Ltd v Tansell*,[619] under the parallel provisions of section 12 of the Disability Discrimination Act 1995: here, the end user of the applicant's services, Abbey Life, was bound to respect the principle of equal treatment, even though it had no direct contractual relationship with Mr. Tansell, who was not only contracting through his own personal service company but, in addition, through an employment agency who arranged for his services to be supplied to Abbey Life.

TRANSFERS OF EMPLOYMENT

3.99   The TUPE Regulations 1981 constitute a major limitation on both the principle of freedom of contract and the power of employers to arrange their commercial and corporate affairs in such a way as to minimise or fragment their employment law liabilities. The main effect of the Regulations is to enable the contract of employment of an employee to be transferred over to the buyer of a business in the event of its sale from one employer to another. The Regulations are also capable of applying where work is first contracted out from a central organisation to sub-contractors, or possibly when one sub-contractor subsequently succeeds another. Since the effect of the Regulations is not only to preserve the employment relationship but also the pre-existing terms and conditions of the employees affected, it has a direct and potentially substantial impact on the employment liabilities and costs of both the transferor and the transferee.

The Regulations touch on a number of substantive issues which are considered in more detail in later chapters: these include the consequences of a relevant transfer in terms of statutory dismissal rights,[620] the preservation of collective agreements and of union recognition,[621] and the scope of the duty to inform and consult representatives of the workforce.[622] At this point, some of the more salient features of the Regulations will be noted as they relate to the concepts of employer and undertaking and to the effects of a relevant transfer on the employment relationship.

At the time of writing the government has issued a public consultation document setting out proposals for the amendment of the Regulations, partly by way of implementation of revisions made to the Directive in 1998, and partly in order to extend and clarify their scope in the interests of creating a '"level playing field" for contractors bidding for service contracts, so that tendering decisions are taken on commercial merit rather than on differing views as to the employment rights of employees, and so that transaction risks and costs are reduced'.[623] Although draft revised Regulations were issued at the same time, their final, definitive form is not yet known, so our account below is based on the law as it stood at the beginning of April 2005, with references where appropriate to the proposed changes.

---

619 [2000] IRLR 387.
620 See below, para 5.193 *et seq.*
621 See below, para 9.26.
622 See below, paras 9.42–9.44.
623 DTI, *TUPE Draft Revised Regulations Public Consultation Document* (2005), para 18.

Novation of the contract of employment

3.100   At common law, the sale or transfer of a business or undertaking by one employer (the transferor) to another (the transferee) has the effect of terminating the contracts of employment of the employees of the transferor. The effect is normally thought to be that of a wrongful dismissal,[624] although another possibility is that the contract is determined automatically, that is to say, without a breach.[625] The transferee cannot be substituted as a party to any contract of employment without both its consent and the consent of the employee concerned. This need for mutual consent is a clear consequence of the contractual basis of the employment relationship. On the one hand, it preserves the employee's freedom to refuse to serve a new employer, a right which Lord Atkin in *Nokes v Doncaster Amalgamated Collieries Ltd* considered to be 'ingrained in the personal status of a citizen under our laws'.[626] The contracts of employment, being personal to the employees concerned, cannot be treated in the same way as other business assets of the employer.

On the other hand, *Nokes* denies the employee any right to continuing employment, and frees the transferee to employ a new workforce. The resulting lack of security for employees is addressed by legislation in the form of TUPE 1981,[627] which implements EC Directive 2001/23 (the 'Acquired Rights Directive').[628] The initial Regulations, which were introduced with a 'lack of enthusiasm' by the Conservative Government of Mrs Thatcher, failed to implement the Directive effectively in a number of respects,[629] but they were significantly strengthened by amendments made by TURERA 1993. These amendments were themselves the product of the threat of a hostile ruling by the ECJ in infringement proceedings brought against the UK by the European Commission.[630]

The TUPE Regulations oust the common law rule by providing that 'a relevant transfer shall not operate so as to terminate the contract of employment of any person employed by the transferor in the undertaking or part transferred but any such contract which would otherwise have been terminated by the transfer shall have effect after the transfer as if originally made between the person so employed and the transferee'.[631] Unlike a common law novation, the statutory

---

624 *Brace v Calder* [1895] 2 QB 253; *Nokes v Doncaster Amalgamated Collieries Ltd* [1940] AC 1014, 1019 (Viscount Simon LC).

625 A winding up order leading to a company's liquidation was thought to lead to an automatic discharge of the employees' contracts in *Re General Rolling Stock Co, Chapman's Case* (1866) LR 1 Eq 346. See further paras 5.190–5.192 below.

626 [1940] AC 1014, 1026. For discussion of the appropriateness of this 'personified' view of the employment relationship, see Freedland, 2003: pp 38–39, and for a recent application of the same principle outside the context of TUPE, see *Bolwell v Redcliffe Homes Ltd and O'Connor* [1999] IRLR 485.

627 SI 1981/1794.

628 The Directive dates back to 1977 (77/187), was amended in 1998 (Directive 98/50), and consolidated in 2001. The 1998 amendments were required to be brought into effect in the UK by July 2001, but the most important changes made in 1998 relate to the definition of 'relevant transfer' (see below paras 3.102–3.106), which were arguably assimilated into the relevant case law in any event, and to the possibility of derogations from the general principle of the transfer of employees' rights (see below, para 3.115), which were optional. See now the amendments proposed in DTI, *TUPE Draft Revised Regulations Public Consultation Document* (2005).

629 Hepple, 1982.

630 The infringement proceedings eventually resulted in the rulings in Cases C-382/92 and C-383/92: *EC Commission v United Kingdom* [1994] IRLR 392, 412.

631 TUPE 1981, reg 5(1).

novation is automatic in that it does not depend upon the employee receiving notice of the transfer itself, nor of the identity of the transferee.[632] Nor does it depend in any way upon the transferee accepting the transfer.[633]

The Regulations go on to state that 'on the completion of a relevant transfer, (a) all the transferor's rights, powers duties and liabilities under or in connection with any such contract shall be transferred ... to the transferee; and (b) anything done before the transfer is completed by or in relation to the transferor in respect of that contract or a person employed in that undertaking or part shall be deemed to have been done by or in relation to the transferee'.[634] This is subject, initially, to the employee's right to inform either party that he or she objects to becoming employed by the transferee. In its judgment in *Katsikas v Konstandinidis*,[635] the ECJ said that the Directive did not require Member States to make provision for compulsion against the employee: 'such an obligation would undermine the fundamental rights of the employee who must be free to choose his employer and cannot be obliged to work for an employer that he has not freely chosen'.[636]

Following this ruling, an amendment was made to the Regulations by TURERA 1993.[637] This provides, first, that if the employee objects to being employed by the transferee,[638] the contract of employment will not be novated as it would otherwise be (regulation 5(4A)); and, second, that under these circumstances the transfer will be regarded as terminating the contract of employment, but without the employee being regarded as dismissed by the transferor for any purpose (regulation 5(4B). This, then, would appear to prevent the employee bringing any claim for unfair dismissal or redundancy against either the transferor or, since the contract of employment has not been novated, the transferee.[639] However, regulation 5(4A) is then stated to be 'without prejudice to any right of an employee arising apart from these Regulations to terminate his contract of employment without notice if a substantial change is made in his working conditions to his detriment; but no such right shall arise by reason only that, under [reg 5(1)], the identity of his employer changes unless the employee shows that, in all the circumstances, the change is a significant change and is to his detriment'.[640] In other words, the employee is entitled to terminate the contract of employment without giving notice, if the proposed change of employment would result in a significant and disadvantageous change in his or her terms and conditions of employment.

What is not precisely clear is whether an employee who takes this step is then entitled to claim for statutory purposes that he or she was constructively dismissed, in which case an action for unfair dismissal and/or redundancy

---

632 *Secretary of State for Trade and Industry v Cook* [1997] IRLR 150, EAT, rejecting the conclusion reached by differently constituted EAT in *Photostatic Copiers (Southern) Ltd v Okuda* [1995] IRLR 11.

633 Case C-305/94 *Rotsart de Hertaing v J Benoidt (in liquidation) and IGC Housing Service SA* [1997] IRLR 127, ECJ.

634 TUPE 1981, reg 5(2).

635 Case C-132/91 [1993] IRLR 179. See also Case C-171/94 *Merckx v Ford Motor Co. (Belgium)* [1996] IRLR 467.

636 [1993] IRLR 179, 183.

637 TURERA 1993, s 33(1), (4)(b).

638 On the meaning of 'objects', see *Hay v George Hanson (Building Contractors) Ltd* [1996] IRLR 427; *Senior Heat Treatment Ltd v Bell* [1997] IRLR 614. On the use of this as a device in the NHS Retention of Employment Model see R Davies, 2004.

639 TUPE 1981, reg 5(4A)–(4B).

640 TUPE 1981, reg 5(5). See below, paras 5.196–5.198 for further discussion of this point.

compensation might be available, as well as a common law claim for wrongful dismissal. Since a finding of constructive dismissal is a consequence of the right of an employee to terminate his contract of employment in the circumstances described in regulation 5(5), it is arguable that such claims could be made. The issue was addressed by the Court of Appeal in *University of Oxford v Humphreys and Associated Examining Board*.[641] Here, the employee objected in advance to the transfer and, when it went ahead, lodged a claim for wrongful dismissal against the transferor. The Court held that regulation 5(5) took priority over not just regulation 5(4A), as clearly indicated by the Regulations, but also over regulation 5(4B), an interpretation which was supported by a close reading of these two provisions as well as by a desire to give to the Regulations a purposive interpretation in line with Article 4 of the Directive and the case law of the ECJ. The Court made two further important rulings: first, that regulation 5(5) covered the situation where the employee raised an objection in anticipation of the transfer and not simply the case where the substantial detriment, post-transfer, had actually occurred; second, that in a case such as the present, liability would rest with the transferor alone. The transferee cannot be liable because an employee who invokes paragraph (4A) thereby prevents the novation of his or her contract of employment from taking place; under these circumstances, there is no means by which liability could be shifted to the transferee.[642]

Scope of the Regulations: 'undertaking' and 'relevant transfer'

'Undertaking'

3.101 In order for the Regulations to apply a number of conditions must be satisfied. This involves consideration of the meaning of the terms 'undertaking' and 'relevant transfer'. The Regulations define an 'undertaking' as including 'any trade or business'.[643] This definition used to contain the additional words 'but does not include any undertaking or part of an undertaking which is not in the nature of a commercial venture' but these were removed by TURERA 1993, following the ruling of the ECJ in *Dr Sophie Redmond Stichting v Bartol*.[644] This held that the Acquired Rights Directive *may*, in principle, apply to transfers of public sector undertakings into the private sector, whether through privatisation involving a change of legal identity and status, or through a process of contracting out work which was previously done in-house. In *Henke*[645] the Court ruled that the Directive has no application to transfers concerned exclusively with 'activities involving the exercise of public authority',[646] such as the transfer of administrative functions from one public authority to another. This is because 'the Directive sets out to protect workers against the potentially unfavourable consequences for them of changes in the structure of undertakings resulting from economic trends at national and Community level'.[647] However, the Court has since ruled

641 [2000] IRLR 183; see also *Rossiter v Pendragon plc* [2002] IRLR 483 and our discussion of these cases in the wider context of unfair dismissal in ch 5 below (paras. 5.196–5.198).
642 [2000] IRLR 183, 189.
643 TUPE 1981, reg 2(1).
644 Case C-29/91 [1992] IRLR 366.
645 Case C-298/94 *Henke v Gemeinde Schierke and Verwaltungsgemeinschaft 'Brocken'* [1996] IRLR 701.
646 [1996] IRLR 701, 710.
647 [1996] IRLR 701.

that the Directive does apply to the transfer of an entity from a non-profit making association governed by private law to a public law organisation.[648] It has also reaffirmed that the transfer of industrial undertakings from state ownership into private ownership will normally be caught by the Directive.[649] Within the UK context, a *Statement of Practice on Staff Transfers in the Public Sector*, issued by the Cabinet Office on 7 January 2000, provides that, as a general rule, the provisions of TUPE should be applied to the transfer of functions within the public sector as well as to transfers (in either direction) between the public and private sectors, even where to do so might go beyond the strict terms of the Regulations.[650]

'Relevant transfer': the 'economic entity' test

3.102   The principal test under the Directive and, by extension, the Regulations is whether there has been a transfer of an 'economic entity which retains its identity, meaning an organised grouping of resources which has the objective of pursuing an economic activity, whether or not that activity is central or ancillary'.[651] This is the formula contained in the revised version of the Directive which was agreed in 1998.[652] The consultation document issued by the DTI in March 2005 proposes to incorporate a reference to this test into the revised Regulations.[653] Since this definition largely follows the pre-existing case law of the ECJ,[654] it is doubtful that such a change would make much difference to the approach to this issue taken by the British courts.

In its ruling in the *Süzen* case, the ECJ held that '[t]he term entity… refers to an organised grouping of persons and assets facilitating the exercise of an economic activity which pursues a specific objective'.[655] In the case of sale of a business, the notion of an economic entity means that there must be a transfer of the undertaking or part of it as a 'going concern'; it is not sufficient merely to transfer certain assets or property (such as machinery, buildings, stock or intellectual property rights) from one employer to another; there must normally be a transfer of business goodwill as well.[656]

The application of the 'economic entity' test to situations involving privatisation, sub-contracting and other forms of outsourcing has been particularly problematic. The transfer of staff within the public sector, as a

---

648   Case C-175/99 *Mayeur v APIM* [2000] IRLR 783. See also Case C-234/98 *Allen v Amalgamated Construction Co Ltd* [2000] IRLR 119 in which the Court held that the Directive could apply to a transfer between two companies in the same corporate group.

649   Case C-343/98 *Collino and Chiappero v Telecom Italia SpA* [2000] IRLR 788.

650   This will continue to be the case notwithstanding the proposed revisions to the Regulations: see DTI, *TUPE Draft Revised Regulations Public Consultation Document* (2005), at para 16; the Cabinet Office statement is published online at: http://www.civilservice.gov.uk/publications/staff_transfers/publications_and_forms/pdf/stafftransfers.pdf.

651   Directive 77/187, Art 1(1)(b), as amended by Directive 98/50. See now Directive 2001/23, Art 1(1)(b).

652   On the background to the amendments made by the 1998 Directive, see Hunt, 1999, and for assessments of the changes, see P Davies, 1998; Hardy and Painter, 1999.

653   *TUPE Draft Revised Regulations Public Consultation Document* (2005), at p 39.

654   Case 24/85 *Spijkers v Gebroeders* [1986] ECR 1119; Case C-29/91 *Dr Sophie Redmond Stichting v Bartol* [1992] 366; Case C-48/94 *Rygaard v Dansk Arbejdsgiverforening, acting for Strø Mølle Akustik A/S* [1996] IRLR 51.

655   Case C-13/95 *Süzen v Zehnacker Gebäudereinigung GmbH Krankenhausservice* [1997] IRLR 255, 259.

656   *Melon v Hector Powe Ltd* [1981] ICR 43, a case decided under the parallel provisions of EPCA 1978, Sch 13, para 17 (these provisions are now contained in ERA 1996, s 218).

result of the introduction of internal quasi-markets, frequently involves a change of employment; specific legislation provides for contracts of employment to be continued in such cases, but it may also be the case that the Acquired Rights Directive applies to these transfers, in which case superior rights may be established, particularly at the level of collective labour relations.[657] Under legislation beginning with the Local Government Act 1988, local authorities were required to submit large parts of their services to a process of periodic compulsory competitive tendering (CCT), which enables outside suppliers to bid against the direct labour organisation or internal workforce of the authority for the right to carry out the work. A major feature of the 1988 Act was that it ruled out the stipulation by the local authority of 'non-commercial matters' such as 'fair wages' policies which used to be common in dealings between councils and their suppliers; it became unlawful to insist, as a precondition of a supplier winning the contract, that they should respect generally-applicable terms and conditions of employment, or maintain recognition of an independent trade union. However, if the Directive and Regulations could be shown to apply, there was the chance of reintroducing a degree of fair wages control through this route, since the supplier would then have to respect the pre-existing terms and conditions of the internal workforce, as well as offering employment to those employees. The Labour government elected in 1997 has replaced CCT with a duty to obtain 'Best Value', and the Secretary of State is empowered to provide, by order, that a matter should be excluded from the list of 'non-commercial matters'.[658] At the time of writing one such order has been made.[659]

Whether the court can identify an 'economic entity which retains its identity' depends on a variety of factors: a 'relevant transfer' is more likely where some employees are taken on by the transferee, some of the work is carried on at the same premises as before, and there is a sale or lease of equipment. However, none of these factors is conclusive in itself, nor is the absence of any one of them necessarily fatal to there being a relevant transfer.[660] The ECJ has held that neither the absence of a sale of assets[661] nor the failure to transfer assets of any kind will necessarily prevent the Directive (and, by extension, the Regulations) applying.[662] Nor need there necessarily be any agreement by the transferee to take on all or part of the workforce of the transferor.[663] The Regulations themselves specify that there may be a relevant transfer notwithstanding that it is effected through more than one transaction.[664]

---

657 See Napier, 1993: p 9. Examples of specific legislation are the Further and Higher Education Act 1992, s 26 and the National Health Service and Community Care Act 1990, s 6.
658 See Local Government Act 1999, s 19; Department of the Environment, Transport and the Regions, Consultation Paper, *Modernising Local Government: Improving Local Services through Best Value*, 1997.
659 SI 2001/909; see para 2.6 above.
660 See generally Case C-171/94 *Merckx and Neuhuys v Ford Motors Co Belgium SA* [1996] IRLR 467.
661 Case 324/86 *Foreningen v Daddy's Dance Hall* [1988] IRLR 315; Case 101/87: *P Bork International v Foreningen* [1989] IRLR 41 (both cases of the lease of property).
662 Case C-209/91 *Rask v ISS Kantineservice* [1993] IRLR 133 at para 15; TUPE 1981, reg 3(4)(b); although this principle sits uneasily with the Court's suggestion that, in the context of undertakings which are not 'based essentially on manpower' (sic), there must be a transfer of tangible assets for the Directive to apply: Case C-172/99 *Oy Liikenne Ab v Liskojärvi* [2001] IRLR 171; cf *P & O Trans European Ltd v Initial Transport Services Ltd* [2003] IRLR 128.
663 Case C-392/92 *Schmidt v Spar- und Leihkasse der früheren Ämter Bordesholm, Kiel und Cronshagen* [1994] IRLR 302.
664 TUPE 1981, reg 3(4)(a).

According to the EJC in *Spijkers v Gebroeders Benedik Abbattoir CV*:[665]

> ... it is necessary to consider whether the business was disposed of as a going concern, as would be indicated, *inter alia*, by the fact that its operation was actually continued or resumed by the new employer, with the same or similar activities. In order to determine whether these conditions are met, it is necessary to consider all the facts characterising the transaction in question, including the type of undertaking or business, whether or not the business's tangible assets, such as building and moveable property, are transferred, the value of its intangible assets at the time of the transfer, whether or not the majority of its employees are taken over by the new employer, whether or not its customers are transferred and the degree of similarity between the activities carried on before and after the transfer and the period, if any, for which those activities were suspended.

This test was repeated virtually word for word by the ECJ in the later case of *Süzen v Zehnacker Gebäudereinigung GmbH Krankenhausservice*.[666] The *Süzen* case was widely regarded at the time it was decided as having narrowed the test of 'relevant transfer' by drawing a distinction between an 'economic entity' and an 'activity', particularly where the 'activity' consists only of supplying services under a specific contract. This suggestion closely followed a proposal of the European Commission to the effect that the Directive should be amended, so that a 'transfer only of an activity of an undertaking, business or part of a business, whether or not it was previously carried out directly, does not in itself constitute a transfer within the meaning of the Directive'.[667] In the event, this form of words did not find its way into the amendments of 1998. Moreover, the better view is that the *Süzen* test merely clarified a tendency which was present in the pre-existing case law of the Court. For this reason, the Court's pre-*Süzen* case law cannot be disregarded. More recent decisions of the ECJ suggest that *Süzen* was less of a turning point than some assumed,[668] and the British courts, likewise, have been reluctant to see established approaches overturned.[669]

There are four central issues in the post-*Süzen* case law: these relate to transfers involving single-contract entities; transfers to a second subcontractor; transfers in which the transferee declines to take on any of the employees; and transfers not involving the sale of any tangible assets.

TRANSFERS INVOLVING SINGLE-CONTRACT ENTITIES

3.103   In *Schmidt v Spar- und Leihkasse der früheren Ämter Bordesholm, Kiel und Cronshagen*[670] the employee worked in a bank as a cleaner and was dismissed when her employer wished to contract out the work to a company which was already responsible for cleaning the bank's other branches. She was offered a job with the cleaning company for less pay. The ECJ, on an application for a

---

665 Case 24/85 [1986] 2 CMLR 296, at para 13.

666 Case C-13/95 [1997] IRLR 255, 259, at para 14; see also the emphasis on a broad, multi-factor test by the EAT in *Cheesman v R Brewer Contracts Ltd* [2001] IRLR 144 and the more recent decision of the ECJ in Case C-340/01 *Abler v Sodexho* [2004] IRLR 168.

667 COM(94) 300 final, 8.9.94.

668 See, in particular, Joined Cases C-127/96, C-229/96 and C-74/97 *Francisco Hernández Vidal SA v Gomez Pérez* [1999] IRLR 132.

669 The most significant such judgment is *ECM (Vehicle Delivery Service) Ltd v Cox* [1999] IRLR 559. The Cox line was confirmed by the Court of Appeal, notwithstanding a strong dissent, in *ADI (UK) Ltd v Willer* [2001] IRLR 542 and in *RCO Support Services Ltd v Unison* [2002] IRLR 401.

670 Case C-392/92 [1994] IRLR 302; John McMullen, 1994.

preliminary ruling, held that the employee's position could constitute 'part of an undertaking' for the purposes of the Directive: 'when an undertaking entrusts by contract the responsibility for operating one of its services, such as cleaning, to another undertaking which thereby assumes the obligations of an employer towards employees assigned to those duties, that operation may come within the scope of the Directive'.[671] The idea that a single employee could constitute a relevant undertaking perhaps sits uneasily with the entity test put forward in *Süzen* and in the new form of the Directive. However, it is not out of the question that a single employee, or, for that matter, several employees working on a 'single-contract' arrangement for a particular client, could amount to an economic entity for this purpose, if other aspects of the test are satisfied. Hence in *Argyll Training Ltd v Sinclair and Argyll and the Islands Enterprise Ltd*[672] the EAT held that the transfer of a training contract under which a single employee had been employed by the transferor could, in principle, be caught by the Regulations, in the process giving a narrow interpretation to the ECJ's suggestion, in the *Rygaard* case,[673] that a transfer must relate 'to a stable economic entity whose activity is not limited to one specific works contract'.

TRANSFERS FROM ONE SUBCONTRACTOR TO ANOTHER ('SECOND GENERATION' TRANSFERS)

3.104   In principle, the Regulations may apply both to a situation in which work is contracted out for the first time[674] and to a situation in which one subcontractor succeeds another (a so-called 'second-generation transfer'). *Süzen* contains statements which suggest that it is less likely that a court will find that there is a transfer in the *second* of these two situations. The Court held that:

> ... the mere fact that the service provided by the old and the new awardees of a contract is similar does not ... support the conclusion that an economic entity has been transferred. An entity cannot be reduced to the activity entrusted to it. Its identity also emerges from other factors, such as its workforce, its management staff, the way in which its work is organised, its operating methods or indeed, where appropriate, the operational resources available to it.

> The mere loss of a service contract to a competitor cannot therefore by itself indicate the existence of a transfer within the meaning of the Directive. In those circumstances, the service undertaking previously entrusted with the contract does not, on losing a customer, thereby cease fully to exist, and a business belonging to it cannot be considered to have been transferred to the new awardee of the contract.[675]

In *Betts v Brintel Helicopters Ltd and KLM Era Helicopters (UK) Ltd*,[676] a case decided by the Court of Appeal shortly after *Süzen*, Brintel had provided helicopter services for North Sea oil rigs under three separate contracts with Shell (UK) Ltd. When the contracts expired, Shell awarded Brintel two of the contracts, but awarded the third to KLM. KLM did not re-hire any of the employees previously employed by Brintel, and used its own helicopters and infrastructure; it also

671 [1994] IRLR 302, 304.
672 [2000] IRLR 630; *Dudley Bower Building Services Ltd v Lowe* [2003] IRLR 260.
673 Case C-48/94 [1996] IRLR 51.
674 See *Kenny v South Manchester College* [1993] IRLR 265; *BSG Property Services v Tuck* [1996] IRLR 134.
675 [1997] IRLR 255, 259.
676 [1997] IRLR 361.

flew out of a different base. The Court of Appeal decided that there had been no transfer. By contrast, in the pre-*Süzen* case of *Dines v Initial Health Care Services Ltd*,[677] a transfer was established where the new contractor took on most of the employees (at lower rates of pay) of the company which it had just defeated in the process of competitive tendering. However, *Dines* is not necessarily bad law following *Süzen*. Where the large majority of the pre-existing workforce is retained, this factor weighs significantly in favour of there being a transfer.[678]

TRANSACTIONS IN WHICH THE TRANSFEREE FAILS TO TAKE ON ANY OF THE EMPLOYEES IN THE UNDERTAKING

3.105   In the *ECM* case,[679] the Court of Appeal declined to interpret *Süzen* as deciding that transfers in which the new employer takes on none of the pre-existing employees necessarily fall outside the Directive and Regulations. This led the EAT in *RCO Support Services and Aintree Hospital Trust v UNISON*[680] formally to reject the claim that 'the absence of movement both of significant assets and of a major part of the workforce must necessarily deny the existence of a relevant transfer',[681] a view later confirmed by the Court of Appeal in the same case[682] and its majority ruling in *ADI (UK) Ltd v Willer*.[683] Likewise, in *Lightways (Contractors) Ltd v Associated Holdings Ltd*[684] the Court of Session ruled that a tribunal was entitled to inquire into the motive of the transferee in declining to take on the employees, and to scrutinise with particular care a transaction deliberately structured with a view to avoiding TUPE altogether. These decisions are in line with certain recent judgments of the ECJ which, by stressing the importance of the presence of 'an organised grouping of persons and assets' prior to the transfer, implicitly makes it more difficult for the transferee to avoid the Directive by such means.[685]

TRANSFERS NOT INVOLVING THE MOVEMENT OF TANGIBLE ASSETS

3.106   By contrast to the purposive approach above, in *Oy Liikenne Ab v Liskojärvi*,[686] the ECJ enunciated the novel principle that, in certain cases, a transfer which did not involve the sale of significant tangible assets of the undertaking could not fall within the Directive: 'in a sector such as scheduled public transport by bus, where the tangible assets contribute significantly to the

---

677 [1994] IRLR 336.
678 *Betts v Brintel Helicopters Ltd* [1997] IRLR 361, 366 (Kennedy LJ); *Süzen* [1997] IRLR 255, 259, at para 21. See also the decision of the EFTA Court of Justice in Case E-2/95 *Eidesund v Stavanger Catering A/S* [1996] IRLR 684.
679 [1999] IRLR 559.
680 [2000] IRLR 624.
681 [2000] IRLR 624, 629.
682 [2002] IRLR 401.
683 [2001] IRLR 542. See also the decision of the EAT in *Astle v Cheshire County Council* [2005] IRLR 12, laying out the steps which tribunals should follow in applying the *ECM* case.
684 [2000] IRLR 247; although for a case in which the outcome went the other way, see *Whitewater Leisure Management Ltd v Barnes* [2000] IRLR 456.
685 Joined Cases C-127/96, C-229/96 and C-74/97 *Francisco Hernández Vidal SA v Gomez Pérez*, etc [1999] IRLR 132; Joined Cases C-173/96 and C-247/96 *Sánchez Hidalgo v Asociación de Servicios ASER*, etc [1999] IRLR 136; Case C-340/01 *Abler v Sodexho MM Catering GmbH* [2004] IRLR 168; see Hardy and Painter, 1999; for a different view of the earlier of these cases, suggesting that they reinforce *Süzen*, see John McMullen, 1999.
686 Case C-172/99 [2001] IRLR 171, 175. See P Davies, 2001.

performance of the activity, the absence of a transfer to a significant extent from the old to the new contractor of such assets, which are necessary for the proper functioning of the entity, must lead to the conclusion that the entity does not retain its identity'. The peculiar feature of this case is that, in a reversal of the situation just discussed, most of the employees were taken by the new contractor, but none of the vehicles and other 'tangible assets' were transferred. The Court sought to draw a distinction between activities which were 'based mainly on manpower', in which a transfer of employees alone could suffice, and those in which physical plant and other non-human or 'tangible' assets were essential to the entity prior to the transfer. By dividing human and non-human assets of the entity in this way, this judgment once more raises the spectre of employers framing commercial transactions so as to avoid the protective purpose of the Directive; it remains to be seen whether it will be interpreted as having this effect.[687]

The upshot of these decisions is that the application of the Directive and Regulations to cases of outsourcing remains unclear. The precise commercial nature of the transaction between the supplier of labour and the end user is not the crucial test; what matters is whether there is sufficient continuity of personnel, resources and function before and after the reorganisation takes place. The practical application of this test will inevitably turn to a large extent on the weighting of the various factors made by first instance courts and tribunals. At the same time, the courts increasingly accept that TUPE should be given a purposive reading which has regard to its protective purpose; in the words of the EAT, 'the basic principle of [TUPE] is that employees should be protected where the undertaking in which they work is transferred "over their heads"... if both tenderers bid on a level playing field, that is, one where the terms and conditions of the staff are the same in either case, this provides the necessary protection for the employees, who can have no influence over whether or not the undertaking in which they work changes hands'.[688]

'SERVICE PROVISION CHANGES' BEYOND THE SCOPE OF THE DIRECTIVE

3.107 Doubts concerning the scope of the Directive led the UK government, in its March 2005 consultation document, to propose extending the scope of TUPE to cover additional categories of 'service provision changes', in the interests of introducing greater certainty into the law and ensuring employee protection in all appropriate cases. A 'service provision change' would occur where 'there is an organised grouping of employees situated immediately before the change in the United Kingdom which has as its principal purpose the carrying out of the activities concerned on behalf of the client' and 'the client intends that the activities will, following the service provision change, be carried out by the transferee...'.[689] The concept would cover the situation of a first-time contracting

---

687 It is relevant, in this context, that the UK courts, in recent decisions, appear to be taking a more flexible view of the scope of the Regulations than the Court is taking with regard to the Directive: see *Cheesman v R Brewer Contracts Ltd* [2001] IRLR 144; *P & O Trans European Ltd v Initial Transport Services Ltd* [2003] IRLR 128.

688 *Securicor Guarding Ltd v Fraser Security Services Ltd* [1996] IRLR 552, 556 (Judge Clark); although a rather different view of the implications of the Directive for competition in the supply of services is implied by the remarks of the Advocate General in C-13/95 *Süzen* [1997] IRLR 255, 257.

689 See *TUPE Draft Revised Regulations Public Consultation Document* (2005), at p 39 (outlining the draft reg 3 of the new version of the Regulations).

out of activities from a client to a contractor; a second-generation change from one contractor to another; and the reabsorption of the activities into the organisation of the client.[690] However, it would also be subject to a number of exceptions: it would not apply to the 'one-off buying in of services', where no continuing relationship with a contractor is created; it would not apply to a situation in which the purpose of the subcontract was the 'procurement or supply of goods for the client's use' as opposed to the carrying out of service activities; it would not apply to so-called 'innovative bids' which involve the introduction of a completely new technology or work process; and, most controversially, it would have no application to 'professional business services' provided by white collar workers who by virtue of having skills that are generally highly sought-after by employers are 'less in need of additional legal protection than those who provide services that entail, in the main, routine manual work'.[691] It is important to stress that these exceptions do not relate to the core concept of a relevant transfer under the Directive, only to the *additional* notion of a service provision change. At the time of writing it was unclear whether the professional services exception, on which substantive consultation was being sought, would be enacted in the form suggested in the consultation document.

Transfer of the part of the undertaking to which the employee is assigned

3.108   A difficult question is how to apply the Regulations in a case where only part of an undertaking is transferred, in circumstances where an employee's duties prior to the transfer related both to that part which was transferred and partly also to other aspects of the work of the transferor which are not the subject of the transfer. In *Botzen v Rotterdamsche Droogdok Maatschappij BV*[692] the ECJ rejected an argument that the relevant test was whether the employee worked full-time in the department or sector which was transferred, 'to the exclusion of those engaged in partial tasks in various businesses or parts of businsses and those who, although working for several businesses or parts of businsses, form part of the remaining staff'. Instead, the relevant test was whether 'a transfer takes place of the department to which they were assigned and which formed the organisational framework within which their employment relationship took effect'.

The basis on which it should be determined whether or not an employee has been assigned to a department for this purpose is not entirely clear. In *Duncan Web Offset (Maidstone) Ltd v Cooper*[693] the EAT declined to give guidance to employment tribunals on this issue because it considered that the facts of cases could vary markedly. The Appeal Tribunal accepted that all of the following factors could be relevant: the amount of time spent on one part of the business or other; the amount of value given to each part by the employee; the terms of the contract showing what the employee could be required to do; and how the cost to the employer of the employee's services had been allocated between the different parts of the business. However, it also held that this was not an exhaustive list. In practice, the application of the test will often be finely balanced; it is perhaps unfortunate that the test of the requisite connection could not be

690 See *TUPE Draft Revised Regulations Public Consultation Document* (2005), at p 39.
691 See generally *TUPE Draft Revised Regulations Public Consultation Document* (2005), at paras 17–36.
692 Case 186/83 [1986] 2 CMLR 50.
693 [1995] IRLR 633.

more clearly specified. In *Sunley Turriff Holdings Ltd v Thomson*[694] the EAT applied *Botzen* to a case of a company secretary who was employed by one company but was also company secretary of a subsidiary company in the group and worked part of the time on the subsidiary's affairs. Both companies went into receivership and the subsidiary was sold together with a part of the parent company's undertaking. The EAT held that the employee's employment had been transferred over to the transferees, since his employment related to that part of the parent company which was subject to the transfer.

The solution proposed by the draft Regulations published in March 2005 is to clarify the scope of the principle of novation, so that it only covers those employees who are 'assigned to the organised grouping of resources or employees that is subject to the relevant transfer'.[695] 'Assignment' here means assigned 'other than on a temporary basis'.[696] Whether this will greatly help matters remains to be seen; according to the consultation document issued by the DTI, '[a]ssignment is a question of fact in each case'.[697]

Change of control through share purchase

3.109   A particularly important limitation on the scope of the Regulations is the exclusion of changes of control in a company through share purchase.[698] The rationale for this exclusion is that, in this case, the identity of the employer does not change: the employer is the same company as before, even though there has been a change of controlling interest. Nor, as we have just seen,[699] will the courts normally be prepared to lift the corporate veil to the extent of disregarding the separate legal personality of the company and treating the controller (whether it be an individual or a parent company) as the 'real' employer. This means, on the one hand, that an employee cannot decline to work for the company on account of the change of control; on the other hand, although statutory intervention is not strictly necessary to ensure that the contractual nexus between employer and employee is maintained, nor can a recognised trade union (or other relevant body) invoke the provisions of the Regulations concerning the employer's duty to inform and consult with the representatives of the workforce.

The point is not a new one and was raised in the slightly different context of a company reconstruction and amalgamation in *Nokes v Doncaster Amalgamated Collieries Ltd.*[700] There Lord Romer, in a dissenting judgment, argued that it was artificial to suggest that the personal liberty of the employees was at stake in a case where a reconstruction led to a formal change in the identity of the employer, but not in a case where there was a change in control through share transfer:

> … in truth it is an exaggeration to use the word injustice in such a connection as the present. If all or the large majority of the shares in one company are acquired

694   [1995] IRLR 184. See also *Securicor Guarding Ltd v Fraser Security Services Ltd* [1996] IRLR 552.
695   DTI, *TUPE Draft Revised Regulations Public Consultation Document* (2005), at para 40.
696   DTI, *TUPE Draft Revised Regulations Public Consultation Document* (2005), at para 40.
697   DTI, *TUPE Draft Revised Regulations Public Consultation Document* (2005), at para 39.
698   *SI (Systems and Instrumentation) Ltd v Grist* [1983] IRLR 391; *Brookes v Borough Care Services Ltd and CLS Care Services* [1998] IRLR 636. The only occasion on which the purchase of shares representing a controlling interest in a company is contained within the definition of a transfer relates to the situation of 'hiving down' in the sale of an insolvent company, as envisaged by TUPE 1981, reg 4. See below, paras 5.199–5.201.
699   Para 3.98 above.
700   [1940] AC 1014. The relevant legislation was CA 1939, s 129.

by another, the first company will almost certainly come under the control of new directors and managers carrying out a policy that may differ widely from that of their predecessors. Yet no one could possibly say without gross exaggeration that the landlord, the contractors, or the servants of the first company had suffered an injustice. Their position nevertheless would differ little for any practical purpose from the position they would be in had the first company been amalgamated with the second company by means of [a reconstruction].[701]

The Acquired Rights Directive and the TUPE Regulations, conversely, take the view that there *is* a potential injustice to employees in the event of a change of ownership, but if this is so there is a fundamental flaw in their approach: they do not apply to the most common method by which control of a business, as distinct from its formal ownership, is transferred, that is to say by the sale of a controlling shareholding.

The transfer of contractual and statutory rights

Transfer and preservation of contractual rights

3.110   Once a relevant transfer is identified, the Regulations have effect in relation to the contract of employment of 'a person employed in the undertaking ... immediately before the transfer'.[702] The transfer is deemed to take place, for this purpose, at a given moment in time when the relevant transaction or transactions are effected.[703] Under regulation 5(2), the effect of a transfer is to assign to the transferee 'all the transferor's rights, powers, duties and liabilities under or in connection with [the contract of employment]'.

The ECJ has said that the effect of the equivalent provision in the Directive is mandatory, in the sense that it may not be the subject of derogation through bargaining between the employer and the employee.[704] In principle, then, the transferee comes under a duty not just to re-employ the employees, but also to maintain their pre-transfer terms and conditions of employment.[705] However, in many instances the transferee will wish to make changes to terms and conditions of employment, in order to bring the employment contracts of the transferred employees into line with those of other employees. The following question then arises: what impact do the Regulations have on the power of the transferee to effect a variation of this kind?

One way of approaching this issue is by putting it in the context of the overall purpose of the Directive and Regulations, which is to transfer and preserve *existing* rights; they are not intended to confer *additional* rights to those which the employees would have had against the transferor had they stayed in its employment.[706] On

---

701 [1940] AC 1014, 1046–1047.
702 TUPE 1981, reg 5(3).
703 *Secretary of State for Employment v Spence* [1986] IRLR 248; although cf the more flexible approach of the CA in *Astley v Celtec Ltd* [2002] IRLR 969. The House of Lords gave leave to appeal in *Astley* for the purpose of making a reference to the ECJ: [2003] ICR 999. However, the ECJ ruled that the transfer should be deemed to take place at a particular point in time, and could not be altered at the will of the transferor or transferee (Case C-478/03 *Celtec Ltd v Astley*, Judgment of 26 May 2005).
704 Case 324/86 *Foreningen af Arbejdsledere i Danmark v Daddy's Dance Hall A/S* [1988] IRLR 315; Case C-209/91 *Rask v ISS Kantineservice A/S* [1993] IRLR 133; Case C-305/94 *Rotsart de Hertaing v J Benoidt SA* [1997] IRLR 127.
705 TUPE 1981, reg 5(2)(a).
706 This view is inherent in Lord Slynn's judgment in *Wilson v St Helen's Borough Council/British Fuels Ltd v Baxendale and Meade* [1998] IRLR 408; see also Upex, 1999 and the decision of the EAT in *Ralton v Havering College of Further & Higher Education* [2001] IRLR 738.

this basis, the answer to the question just posed is reasonably straightforward: the transferee can bring about a valid variation of the contract terms in just the same way as any other employer can. In other words, the variation will be effective if it is individually agreed with the relevant employee. Alternatively, in the event of the contract terms being governed by a 'bridging term' which allows for incorporation from a collective agreement, the transferee can seek to make an amending agreement with the relevant trade union.[707] Such changes will not be rendered ineffective by the anti-waiver provisions of the Directive and Regulations; because the legislation cannot confer any greater rights upon the employees than they had before, what would have a valid variation pre-transfer will also be effective post-transfer.

This view has much to commend it in terms of logic and clarity, but there are several decisions of the ECJ and of the British courts standing in the way of this conclusion. The most important barrier is a dictum of the ECJ in *Daddy's Dance Hall*,[708] according to which:

> ... employees are not entitled to waive the rights conferred on them by the Directive and ... those rights cannot be restricted even with their consent. This interpretation is not affected by the fact that... the employee obtains new benefits in compensation for the disadvantages resulting from an amendment to his contract of employment, so that, taking the matter as a whole, he is not placed in a worse position than before.[709]

This statement could be read as saying no more than that the employee cannot agree to waive the right to have his or her pre-transfer terms carried over into the new employment. However, the Court went on to formulate a broader principle, according to which any subsequent variation would be ineffective if the reason for it was the transfer itself:

> ... in so far as national law allows the employment relationship to be altered in a manner unfavourable to employees in situations other than the transfer of an undertaking, in particular as regards their protection against dismissal, such an alternative is not precluded merely because the undertaking has been transferred in the meantime and the agreement has therefore been made with the new employer. Since by virtue of Article 3(1) of the Directive the transferee is subrogated to the transferor's rights and obligations under the employment relationship, that relationship may be altered with regard to the transferee to same extent as it could have been with regard to the transferor, *provided that the transfer of the undertaking itself may never constitute the reason for that amendment.*[710] [emphasis added]

The scope of this principle is unclear. At one time, it seemed that it was linked, in the UK context at least, to the rules concerning dismissal in the event of a transfer. Under regulation 8(1) of TUPE, any dismissal for a reason connected with the transfer is automatically unfair, subject only to the possibility of fair dismissal under regulation 8(2) for an 'economic, technical or organisational reason entailing changes in the workforce'. The matter was considered by the House of Lords *Wilson v St Helen's Borough Council/British Fuels Ltd v Baxendale and Meade*,[711] two cases in which employees who were

---

707 For a general overview of the principles governing variation of the contract of employment, see below, paras 4.34–4.39.
708 Case 324/86 [1988] IRLR 315, at paras 14–17. See also *Wilson v St Helen's Borough Council* [1996] IRLR 320, EAT, [1997] IRLR 505, CA, [1998] IRLR 706, 715–16 (dictum of Lord Slynn); *Crédit Suisse First Boston (Europe) Ltd v Lister* [1998] IRLR 700.
709 *Daddy's Dance Hall*, at para 15.
710 *Daddy's Dance Hall*, at para 17.
711 [1998] IRLR 706.

dismissed by a transferor prior to a TUPE transfer were then re-employed by the transferee on inferior terms and conditions of employment. The Court of Appeal[712] (reversing, in each case, a ruling of the EAT[713]) had held that the employees in *Wilson* had been dismissed for a potentially fair reason under regulation 8(2) (redundancy), and that the subsequent variation to their terms and conditions of employment was therefore effective. In *Baxendale and Meade*, by contrast, there was no potentially fair reason for the dismissal. The Court concluded that under regulation 8(1) the purported dismissal was a nullity, that the former contract of employment should be regarded as remaining in force, and that the pre-existing terms and conditions of employment would apply even after the transfer of employment took place. The House of Lords, reversing the result in *Baxendale and Meade*, held that a dismissal which contravened regulation 8(1) was not, for that reason, ineffective. Although an employee dismissed contrary to regulation 8(1) could assert claims for compensation for wrongful and unfair dismissal against the transferee,[714] English law did not accept the idea that such a dismissal was a nullity. Nor was such a conclusion required by the Directive since, as Lord Slynn explained, 'neither the Regulations nor the Directive nor the jurisprudence of the Court create a Community law right to continue in employment which does not exist under national law'.[715]

Lord Slynn's opinion strives to separate the issue of variation from that of dismissal. A clear implication of his approach is that a validly agreed variation should now have precisely the same effect in a transfer situation as it would in any other context. However, the dictum of the ECJ in *Daddy's Dance Hall* apparently prevents this. Because the *Wilson* and *Baxendale and Meade* cases all arose from dismissals, Lord Slynn was not required directly to address the question of what happens if there is a variation of the contract terms by consent. He nevertheless commented that, for the purposes of such a variation, 'there must, or at least may, come a time when the link with the transfer is broken or can be treated as no longer effective', and said that if this issue had been raised on the facts of the cases then before him, he would have referred the question to the ECJ.[716]

It appears, then, that the pre-transfer contract terms are entrenched against even a consensual variation for a certain period of time following the transfer, unless the variation can be understood to take place for a reason other than the transfer itself.[717] Neither the length of time for which this period of preservation

---

712 [1997] IRLR 505.
713 [1996] IRLR 320 (*Wilson*) and 541 (*Meade*).
714 This is the effect of the decision of the House of Lords in *Litster v Forth Dry Dock & Engineering Co. Ltd* [1989] IRLR 161, discussed at para 5.196 *et seq* below.
715 [1998] IRLR 706, 714.
716 [1998] IRLR 708, 715. The issue did not arise because, on the facts, Lord Slynn found that there had been valid variations in each of the cases.
717 For an application of this, see *Crédit Suisse First Boston (Europe) Ltd v Lister* [1998] IRLR 700. However, another possibility is that employees who are subject to a transfer can enter into valid 'compromise agreements' with the transferee: see *Solectron Scotland Ltd v Roper* [2004] IRLR 4. A variation may also be effected by a post-transfer change in the collective agreement governing the employment, depending on the scope of the relevant bridging term: see *Whent v T Cartledge Ltd* [1997] IRLR 153; *Ackinclose v Gateshead Metropolitan Borough Council* [2005] IRLR 79. Finally, if the transfer takes place from the private to the public sector, the equivalent of a post-transfer variation may be possible according to the ECJ in Case C-425/02 *Boor v Ministre de la Fonction Publique et de la Réforme Administrative* [2005] IRLR 61: here, an exception to the principle of the non-derogability of terms following a transfer arose on the grounds of the mandatory principles of public law of the Member State concerned.

might last, nor the test to be applied when determining whether the transfer itself is the reason for the variation, is clear. The law therefore provides little or no guidance to employers or employees (or their representatives) in determining the period for which a contractual variation will be ineffective. Article 3(3) of the Directive (as amended) offers a possible solution to this problem, by allowing Member States to limit the period for which the transferee could be required to observe terms and conditions laid down under a collective agreement which was previously applicable to the employment in question, as long as the period is at least a year in length. However, this option was not taken up in the TUPE Regulations; nor in any case, would it be effective in cases where the terms and conditions in question did not derive from a collective agreement.

It has been suggested that an employer might try to get round the preservation of pre-transfer terms by dismissing the employee and offering a new contract of employment.[718] One difficulty with this route is that the dismissal, if found to be by reason of the transfer, will be automatically unfair (under regulation 8(1)) unless the employer can show that it was for an 'economic, technical or organisational reason' or ETOR (under regulation 8(2)). Although the dismissal will not be treated as if it were a nullity, following Lord Slynn's judgment in *Wilson*, the employer might incur very substantial liabilities by way of compensation for unfair dismissal and/or redundancy.[719] It is also possible that the employee could be reinstated as a result of a tribunal decision in his or her favour,[720] and, indeed, that he or she could carry on working while still maintaining an unfair dismissal claim which leads to reinstatement.[721] But even if these difficulties are overcome, it is still not clear that the variation would be effective, since there is nothing in the ECJ's ruling in *Daddy's Dance Hall* to suggest that the principle stated in that case can be evaded by these means.

The consultation document issued by the DTI in March 2005 attempts to deal with the problem by drawing a distinction between purported variations 'for which the sole or principal reason is the transfer itself or a reason connected with the transfer which is not an ETO reason', and variations for which there is an ETOR. Those falling into the first category are to be 'void – ie ineffective' – while those in the second 'are to be potentially effective – ie effective, subject to being agreed between the parties (or their representatives)'.[722] According to the consultation document, this change is consistent with the Directive; without an ETOR exception for variations, given the possibility of a fair dismissal based upon an ETOR, there would be 'a perverse incentive for employers to dismiss employees and then offer to re-engage them (with loss of continuity), or recruit new staff, on different terms and conditions, contrary to the employment protection aims of the legislation'.[723]

3.111 Another problem arising in connection with regulation 5 is that of determining whether certain contractual liabilities are, on their true construction, capable of being transferred from one employer to another. In *Unicorn Consultancy Services Ltd v Westbrook*,[724] the transferor operated a profit-related pay scheme

---

718 See John McMullen, 1999a: 81.
719 *Cornwall County Care Ltd v Brightman* [1998] IRLR 228; and see below, para 5.164 *et seq.*
720 See below, para 5.149.
721 See below, para 4.39.
722 *TUPE Draft Revised Regulations Public Consultation Document* (2005), at para 44.
723 *TUPE Draft Revised Regulations Public Consultation Document* (2005), at para 45.
724 [2000] IRLR 80.

according to which the pay of employees was linked to the profits of the corporate group of which it formed part. Following the transfer, the employees claimed that the new employer, which had no contact of any kind with the corporate group of their former employer, was nevertheless obliged to continue to observe the terms of the profit-related pay scheme. This was not simply a claim for any amounts still outstanding under the scheme at the time the transfer took place; the employees' argument was that the terms of the profit-related pay scheme had been incorporated into their contracts of employment prior to the transfer, and continued to apply to them once the transfer had taken place. An employment tribunal allowed the employees' claims and its decision was upheld on appeal. The EAT held that, on a proper construction of the rules of the scheme, the employees were still within its provisions post-transfer; regulation 5 of TUPE, under which all contractual liabilities were transferred to the transferee, did the rest. The EAT's decision, taken with full awareness of the practical difficulties of operating the scheme once the transferred undertaking was no longer part of the transferor's group, illustrates the potentially very far-reaching effects of regulation 5.[725]

Transfer and preservation of statutory rights

3.112   The Regulations do not expressly indicate whether accrued statutory rights under ERA 1996 are also transferred over under regulation 5(2)(a). These rights normally do not take the form of contractual terms and conditions, but it is arguable that they nevertheless arise 'under or in connection with' the contract of employment since, as we have seen,[726] they depend upon the prior existence of such a contract. If this interpretation is correct, accrued continuity of employment would be maintained from one employment to another.[727]

To this extent, the TUPE regulations overlap closely[728] with the continuity provisions of ERA 1996. Under section 218(2), 'if a trade or business or an undertaking ... is transferred from one person to another – (a) the period of employment of an employee in the trade or business or undertaking at the time of the transfer counts as a period of employment with the transferee, and (b) the transfer does not break the continuity of the period of employment'. This provision pre-dated the 1981 Regulations; unlike them, it did not override the common law rule that the sale of the business terminated the contracts of employment of the employees, and so would only apply if both the transferee and the employee concerned agreed to the latter entering the employment of the former. With the 1981 Regulations in force, section 218 may now usefully be regarded as spelling out what regulation 5(2)(a) fails to make completely clear, namely that continuity rights are preserved along with the assignment to the transferee of rights and obligations arising directly under the contract. The scope of section 218 largely coincides with that of regulation 5 of TUPE. Thus the employee must be employed by the transferor at the time of the transfer; this has led to problems where there is a gap of a week or more between the end of the employee's employment and

---

725 For a contrasting approach, however, see *Mitie Managed Services Ltd v French* [2002] IRLR 512, EAT.

726 See above, para 3.2 *et seq.*

727 Support for this proposition may be found in *Secretary of State for Trade and Industry v Lassmann* [2000] IRLR 411, where the employees' claim was lost on other grounds.

728 The two provisions are not integrated because the decision was taken in 1981 to implement the Acquired Rights Directive in the form of regulations under the European Communities Act 1972, rather than by way of primary legislation amending EPCA 1978.

the date of the transfer, not least because under the continuity provisions of ERA 1996 the loss of one week normally breaks the employee's continuity.[729] For this purpose it is arguable that the purposive interpretation given to regulation 5 by the House of Lords in the *Litster* case could be applied to section 218, to bridge any such gap;[730] if it could not, direct reliance would have to be placed on regulation 5 in order to ensure that continuity rights were carried over to the new employment, but there are potential problems in this. For one thing, it is not clear that *Litster* has any application to a case where the employee does not have the necessary continuity of employment (now one year) to claim unfair dismissal at the time of the transfer.[731] But in practice it seems that the courts are capable of giving a broad interpretation to section 218 in any event, and that its effect is unlikely to diverge much from that of regulation 5 of TUPE.[732]

Transfer of other liabilities

3.113 In addition, the Regulations provide that 'anything done before the transfer is completed by or in relation to the transferor in respect of that contract [of employment] or a person employed in that undertaking or part shall be deemed to have been done by or in relation to the transferee'.[733] This reinforces the point that it is not just contractual obligations which may be transferred; liabilities arising out of other acts done by the transferor in relation to the employee, such as (for example) conduct amounting to sex discrimination[734] and liabilities in tort,[735] may also be carried over. The same principle also applies to liabilities which an employer may incur for failure to comply with statutory information and consultation requirements.[736]

Exclusion of rights of access to occupational pension schemes

3.114 It is provided by regulation 7 of TUPE that regulation 5 should not apply to 'so much of a contract of employment ... as relates to' an occupational pension scheme which is contracted-out of the state pension

---

729 ERA 1996, s 210(4); see *Teesside Times Ltd v Drury* [1980] ICR 338; *Brook Line Finance Co Ltd v Bradley* [1988] IRLR 283.

730 *Macer v Abafast Ltd* [1990] ICR 234. The purposive interpretation given to reg 5 could be extended to ERA 1996, s 218(2), notwithstanding the fact that the predecessors of s 218(2) preceded the adoption of the Acquired Rights Directive, by invoking the broad principle of 'indirect effect' in Case C-106/89 *Marleasing SA v La Comercial Internacional de Alimentación SA* [1990] ECR I-4135.

731 See below, paras 5.196–5.198.

732 This has been done by holding that the notion of the 'time of a transfer' can under certain circumstances, for the purposes of s 218(2), span a gap of more than a week during which work is not done. *A & G Tuck Ltd v Bartlett* [1994] IRLR 162; *Justfern Ltd v D'Ingerthorpe* [1994] IRLR 164; *Clark & Tokeley Ltd v Oakes* [1997] IRLR 564, [1998] IRLR 577.

733 TUPE 1981, reg 5(2)(b).

734 *DJM International Ltd v Nicholas* [1996] IRLR 76.

735 *Bernadone v Pall Mall Services Group/Martin v Lancashire County Council* [2000] IRLR 487. In a highly purposive judgment, the Court of Appeal also held that the transferee received the benefit of the transferor employer's liability insurance policy, since without this, the employee might be significantly disadvantaged by the transfer (for example, if the transferee became insolvent).

736 *Kerry Foods Ltd v Creber* [2000] IRLR 10; *Alamo Group (Europe) Ltd v Tucker* [2003] IRLR 266; cf *TGWU v James McKinnon* [2001] IRLR 597; see further para 9.45, where we also discuss the proposals made in the *TUPE Draft Revised Regulations Public Consultation Document* (2005) in relation to this area.

scheme under the provisions of what is now the Pensions Act 2004.[737] While this is clear enough, there is a question of its compatibility with the Directive. Article 3(4)(a) of the Directive (as amended) allows a Member State to exclude from the scope of regulation 'employees' rights to old-age, invalidity or survivors' benefits under supplementary company or inter-company pension schemes outside the statutory social security schemes in Member States'.[738] It could be argued that a contracted-out, defined benefit scheme under the 2004 Act *is* part of the statutory social security scheme operating in the United Kingdom, since it operates in partial substitution for the state retirement pension and is intensively regulated by statute. However, this argument was rejected by the EAT (in relation to the predecessors of the 2004 Act) in *Walden Engineering Co Ltd v Warrener*[739] on the grounds that schemes of this kind, because they fall under the scope of Article 119 (now Article 141) of the EC Treaty for the purposes of equal pay, are for that reason also 'outside the statutory social security schemes in Member States' for the purposes of the Acquired Rights Directive.[740]

Article 3(4)(b) of the Directive provides that if Member States take advantage of the derogation in Article 3(4((a), they 'shall adopt the measures necessary to protect the interests of employees and of persons no longer employed in the transferor's business at the time of the transfer in respect of rights conferring on them immediate or prospective entitlement to old-age benefits, including survivors' benefits' under occupational pension schemes. In *Adams v Lancashire County Council*[741] the Court of Appeal concluded that this provision did not have the effect of requiring a Member State to put in place laws requiring transferees to maintain an occupational pension scheme, to which employees transferred under TUPE could have access on terms equivalent to those they enjoyed when employed by the transferor. Rather, the effect of limb b was to require Member States to take steps to protect only those rights of employees which had already *accrued* by virtue of their earlier service.[742] Under the Pensions Act 2004, provision is now made, in a case where the employee was a member of an occupational pension scheme run by the transferor at the time of the transfer,[743] for the transferee

---

737 TUPE 1981, reg 7. On the Pensions Act 2004, see ch 4, below, at para 4.116 *et seq.*

738 This formula does no cover benefits paid in the event of premature retirement on grounds of redundancy: Case C-164/00 *Beckmann v Dynamco Whicheloe MacFarlane Ltd* [2000] IRLR 578; Case C-4/01 *Martin v South Bank University* [2004] IRLR 74; Pollard, 2005.

739 [1993] IRLR 420. See also Case E-2/95 *Eidesund v Stavanger Catering A/S* [1996] IRLR 684.

740 See also *Perry v Intec Colleges Ltd* [1993] IRLR 56, where an employment tribunal argued for a purposive interpretation to be given to regulation 5 which would have the effect of transferring over pension rights to the extent necessary to comply with the second limb of Art 3(4)(b) of the Directive.

741 [1997] IRLR 436.

742 This obligation was arguably met by the provisions of occupational pensions legislation: see *Adams v Lancashire County Council* [1997] IRLR 436, 438 (discussing the provisions of Part IV of the Pension Schemes Act 1993 which are now contained in the Pensions Act 2004. See also Hepple and Mumgaard, 1998, for discussion of Article 3(4) and some of the problems which would be encountered if TUPE, reg 5 were to include provision for the transfer of occupational pension rights.

743 More precisely, the employee must have been either an active member, eligible to become one, or eligible to become one upon completing a further period of service: Pensions Act 2004, s 257(1)–(4). See, generally, Pollard, 2005.

to assume one of two obligations: either to provide the employee with membership of another occupational pension scheme, or to provide, and to contribute towards, a 'stakeholder' pension.[744]

Derogations in the event of insolvency and/or situations of severe economic crisis

3.115 The 1998 amendments to the Acquired Rights Directive allow Member States to put in place derogations from the normal transfer rules for insolvent undertakings, whether or not they are subject to proceedings aimed at the liquidation of the transferor.[745] The 2005 consultation document published by the DTI sets out a series of proposals for taking advantage of certain of these derogations. We discuss these proposals in our analysis of TUPE and unfair dismissal in chapter 5, below.[746]

ASSESSMENT

3.116 Labour law has tended to privilege a particular form of the employment relationship, namely employment based on an open-ended or 'permanent' contract, combined with regular and full-time working hours. Other, so-called 'flexible' or 'non-standard' forms of employment have tended to fall outside the core of protection as a result. This problem has been associated with a narrow approach to defining the 'threshold' concepts through which the law filters access to employment protection rights, namely, the common law concept of the contract of employment and the statutory concept of continuity of employment. To a certain extent, this problem has been addressed by legislative changes which began, in the mid-1990s, by liberalising the rules on continuity. The initial basis for this change was the impact of equal treatment principle, and, above all, the perception that the exclusion of part-time workers from employment protection was contrary to EC law rules prohibiting discrimination on the grounds of sex, following the judgment of the House of Lords in the *Ex p EOC* case.[747] More recently, the legislature has addressed the issue of the basic definition of the employment relationship, through greater use of the 'worker' concept and by enacting the power to extend employment rights to individuals in section 23 of the Employment Relations Act 1999.

This last development builds on a proposal made by Hepple in the mid-1980s, to the effect that 'the contract of service should be replaced by a broad definition of an "employment relationship" between the worker and the

---

744 Pensions Act 2004, s 258; SI 2005/649. On occupational and stakeholder pensions, see below, ch 4, at paras 4.116–4.121. The obligation to contribute to a stakeholder pension is significant in this context, since normally the employer is only obliged to make such a scheme available to the employee – it is not obliged to contribute to it. However, it may be noted that the Pensions Act 2004, s 258(6) states that it is open to the employer and employee, after the transfer, to make a contract varying or nullifying the transfer of pension obligations. As it goes against the principle of the non-derogability of contract terms following a transfer (see para 3.110 above), this provision presumably reflects the view that the Directive does not require this form of pension protection.

745 Directive 2001/23, reg 5. For discussion, see P Davies, 1998; Hardy and Painter, 1999; Armour and Deakin, 2000, 2003.

746 See paras 5.193–5.203

747 [1994] IRLR 176; para 3.88 above.

undertaking by which he is employed'.[748] Hepple's proposal involved extending the notion of service or employment to embrace 'both the intermittent exchange of work for remuneration, and the single continuous contract'. This was intended to address the issue of 'mutuality of obligation'; legislation would still exclude the independent contractor who was in business on his or her own account, but would seek to cover economically dependent contractors without a business of their own. In essence, this is the direction in which the law has moved since 1997. Nevertheless, some deep ambiguities remain in the use of the 'worker' concept.[749] It can be seen as essentially clarifying the notion of dependent labour, by in effect displacing the mutuality of obligation test with the rival test of economic dependence which is inherent in the test of 'economic reality'. A more radical interpretation, though, would see in the worker concept the increasing encroachment of labour law regulation on the category of self-employment. This implies that the 'binary divide'[750] between employees and the self-employed, on which the modern forms of employment regulation and taxation have been based, is itself breaking down, in favour of a much more complex and variegated form of regulation of the different types of employment relationship.[751]

The other element of Hepple's proposal addressed the notion of the 'employer'. He suggested redefining the employer as 'the company or other person or persons who has control of the undertaking in which the employee is employed ... An implication of this definition would be that the worker would retain rights on a change of control, eg a change in the share ownership of the controlling company'.[752] Reform in this area has been much slower to arrive. The test for the identification of the employer remains predominantly contractual. The TUPE regulations mark a significant exception to this, but other qualifications to the employer's right of incorporation, such as the statutory concept of 'associated employers', remain under-developed. Nevertheless, the imaginative use of the 'agency labour' provisions of the discrimination legislation is one sign that statutory solutions may be available to deal with the fragmentation of the traditional functions of the enterprise among several different entities.[753] One implication of decisions such as *Dacas*[754] and *Tansell*[755] is that concepts in this area of law are sufficiently flexible to deal with contractual devices, such as agency work and the supply of labour through intermediaries, which would otherwise have the effect of fragmenting the legal notion of the enterprise in such a way as to deny workers employment protection. In particular, these judgments point the way to a legal analysis of intermediary work which will respect the need for a clear division of legal responsibilities between the end user of labour and the supplier of workers to be established.

A wider issue is how far labour law should aim to legitimise forms of work other than the open-ended, full-time employment relationship. In principle there

---

748 Hepple, 1986: p 74.
749 See P Davies and M Freedland, 2000, 2004; Deakin, 2001b; Freedland, 2003: chs 1 and 2 (proposing the integration of the contract of employment and the 'semi-dependent worker's contract' within a single category of 'personal employment contracts'); Deakin and Wilkinson, 2005: ch 5.
750 See Freedland, 1995.
751 For further discussion of the prospects for conceptual 'mutations' through which labour law can adapt to changing conditions of work and employment, see Supiot (ed), 1999; Deakin, 2001c.
752 Hepple, 1986: p 74.
753 See Deakin, 2001a.
754 *Dacas v Brook Street Bureau (UK) Ltd* [2004] IRLR 358.
755 *Abbey Life Assurance Co Ltd v Tansell* [2000] IRLR 387.

is widespread agreement that, as the European Commission has put it, 'in no circumstances can the need for these specific forms of employment relationship be called into question ... What is required is to define a number of basic rules which [have] regard on the one hand to firms' need for flexibility and on the other, the aspirations of a number of workers'.[756] There is less consensus on how such a compromise might be achieved. The need for flexibility can be invoked as an argument for avoiding regulation of part-time and temporary or fixed-term work. However, this option is intrinsically undesirable: the economic benefits to both employers and employees of part-time work appear to be such as to outweigh any disadvantages which might follow from the extension of general principles of employment law to that form of work. Moreover, as a practical possibility the option of discrimination is restricted by Article 141 of the EC Treaty and by related provisions in the law of equal treatment, including the provisions recently introduced with the aim of specifically protecting part-time and fixed-term workers. The aim of integrating non-standard forms of work into the existing framework of labour law is not straightforward, however. It is not enough simply to extend the concept of dependent labour, on the one hand, and to reduce the impact of qualifying thresholds, on the other; changes are also required to the substance of many regulations which are designed with the model of the full-time, indefinite-duration contract in mind. Legislation governing income protection – sick pay and lay-off – is one such example. Many other rights in labour law and social security are based on seniority and will inherently favour those who work on a regular, full-time basis over an extended period of time. This is not to suggest that regulations of this kind do not fulfil important functions of income and employment protection. It is important to recognise here that the model of regular employment, although no longer so clearly the 'norm' in the labour market, still represents the best prospect for most individuals of access to a secure and reliable source of income. Part-time and fixed-term contract jobs are very often thought of as transitory, or as appropriate for particular points in the life-cycle; trainees and workers employed on fixed-term contracts often hope or expect to get a 'permanent' job in due course and women workers tend to be employed part-time during periods when family responsibilities are most demanding. One implication of this is that the legal framework should not necessarily seek to undermine full-time employment as such, but should seek to avoid penalising individuals for making particular choices at points in the life-cycle when full-time work or a 'permanent' contract of employment may not be a viable option, and by striking a better overall balance between working time and family time.

---

756 European Commission, *Explanatory Memorandum* COM (90) 228 final: para 4.

CHAPTER 4

Terms of employment and working conditions

INTRODUCTION

4.1   This chapter examines the law concerning the contents of the individual employment relationship. Although the basic conceptual framework of that relationship is derived from the common law of contract, in practice very few of the parties' rights and obligations are based on express agreement between them. The contract of employment is above all a mechanism for expressing the impact upon the individual relationship of one or more of a number of external sources of governance or regulation. These sources are external to the individual relationship in the sense that they derive not from the parties' own agreement but, for example, from agreements involving third parties, as in the case of collective agreements, or from sources of legal regulation to which, in whole or in part, the relationship is understood to be subject, such as the applicable rules of the common law of employment and those of legislation. The employer's own rule-making power can also be thought of as an external source in this sense, since it goes beyond the scope of the express contract terms agreed with the individual employee. The central legal issues here are how these external forms of regulation are given contractual expression at the level of the individual relationship, and how conflicts between different sources are resolved.

The role of the common law is particularly important. Terms implied at common law loosely define the employee's open-ended obligations of obedience, co-operation and care, and thereby underwrite important aspects of the employer's rule-making power. Conversely, the employer may also be bound without formal consent to maintain the contract during interruptions caused, for example, by the employee's illness or by a lack of available work. These implied 'default' terms normally apply only in the absence of any express agreement to the contrary. To what extent there are certain irreducible obligations which apply regardless of the content of the express terms, such as an obligation to maintain the 'mutual trust and confidence' on which the employment relationship is said to rest, is unclear in the present state of the law. In relation to collective bargaining, the 'normative' or regulatory function of collective agreements takes effect within the individual contract through the common law doctrine of the incorporation of terms; rules derived from managerial prerogative may also be incorporated in this way. Social legislation has imposed a further set of obligations on the employer with regard to protection of income and employment. These statutory interventions tend to be seen as external impositions which formally constrain freedom of contract, but without necessarily taking the form of contract terms themselves. They are nevertheless an important source of rights and obligations of the parties. Moreover, rather than restricting contractual autonomy they can be seen as restoring a degree of contractual reciprocity to the employment relationship, by virtue of the limits which they place on managerial prerogative.

The chapter begins by outlining the means by which the contract gives expression to the different sources of regulation and how conflicts between them are resolved. The employer's statutory obligation to issue the employee with a written statement of terms and the common law processes of the construction, incorporation and variation of terms are considered next. The remainder of the chapter is concerned with particular substantive aspects of the employment relationship: the basic terms of the wage-work bargain, governing wages and working time; terms and conditions relating to health and safety and the working environment; the implied obligations of obedience, co-operation and care; employee fidelity, the enforcement of non-competition clauses and the protection of confidential information; protection of income security in the event of interruptions to work; and the law governing occupational employee benefits, in particular those under defined-benefit pension schemes.

SOURCES OF CONTRACTUAL TERMS AND CONDITIONS

4.2   Before examining the substance of the employment relationship in detail, it is necessary to consider the nature of the sources of contractual terms and conditions. An important issue here is how far the law recognises the normative effect of the different sources, and how it deals with conflicts between them. We shall consider, in turn, managerial prerogative; common law implied terms; and regulation through social legislation and collective bargaining.

Express terms and managerial prerogative

4.3   The express terms of the contract of employment are only capable of playing a limited role in defining the agreement made by the parties. The precise degree of effort which the employee must devote to the work in order to earn the agreed wages cannot be stated in advance: 'the contract of employment hardly ever specifies exactly what the employee undertakes to do during each hour or day of his employment'.[1] The contract may lay down formal rules and procedures, such as those governing discipline and dismissal, as well as terms and conditions of employment such as wage or salary rates, working hours, holidays, sick pay and pension rights. Whether these express terms are agreed individually or, as is more usual, incorporated by reference to a collective agreement or other external source, they give rise to legally-binding, reciprocal obligations between the two parties. But 'a vital part of the contract, the content of the work to be done and the quality, intensity and pace of work effort, can neither be specified, nor enforced in the same way'.[2]

One reason for this which is suggested by transaction cost economics is that to specify the precise contents of performance in advance would be too costly. All long-term contracts contain this element of incompleteness, in the sense that limited information prevents the parties from anticipating all future contingencies and specifying the form which performance is to take under those conditions.[3] What is distinctive about the contract of employment is that the problem of incompleteness is addressed by granting one party, the employer, unilateral rights of direction over the other, the employee. The employee agrees to *serve*

---

1   Lupton and Bowey, 1974: p 72.
2   Pankhurst, 1988: p 5.
3   O Hart, 1989.

in return for wages, rather than undertaking to provide a particular service or product within which his or her labour is embodied; hence what the employer buys '*is not an agreed amount of labour, but the power to labour over an agreed period of time*'.[4] The employee undertakes to accept, within limits which are not always clearly defined, the authority of the employer to determine the mode of performance.

The idea that the employer possesses a prerogative power which lies beyond the express terms of the contract, just as the employee owes the employer a 'diffuse obligation of obedience',[5] is recognised by the common law of the contract of employment. The employer has the implied power to lay down certain norms for the performance of work which do not take the form of contract terms; they do not need to be agreed in advance with the employees on an individual or collective basis (through their representatives), and they can be changed unilaterally. This can be seen from cases involving the practice of 'working to rule' as part of industrial action against the employer. The employees may adhere precisely and literally to the work rules, but if these rules are simply an expression of the employer's prerogative power they cannot claim to have exhausted their contractual obligations by doing so. On the contrary, since the aim of the work to rule is to impair the effectiveness of the employer's business or service, the individual employees will be in breach of contract by virtue of not fulfilling their 'duty of co-operation' which, if unstated, is nevertheless regarded by the courts as fundamental to the contract.[6]

There is a lack of clarity about precisely where the express contract terms end and managerial prerogative begins. The employer has no power to vary unilaterally the wage rates, hours of work and other conditions of employment which constitute contract terms.[7] Thus an employee's working hours may not normally be altered without his or her agreement. The precise form taken by a weekly timetable of lessons taught by a schoolteacher has been held, on the other hand, to be subject to the employer's right to specify the mode of performance, subject only to the need for the orders given to be lawful and reasonable in the circumstances.[8] This doctrine, while undoubtedly an important source of flexibility from the employer's point of view, can only be taken so far without undermining the contractual nature of the employment relationship. Obligations which are *specific* in nature will normally be construed as express terms which limit the employee's more open-ended duties of obedience and co-operation.[9] Moreover, although its open-endedness makes it seem to lie 'beyond contract',[10] the employer's residual prerogative power is nevertheless clothed in the form of various implied terms which may be limited in their scope not just by formal agreement between the parties but also by terms incorporated from sources external to the relationship, in particular collective bargaining.

4   Braverman, 1974: p 54 (emphasis in original). Braverman's analysis is an elaboration of Marx's distinction in Volume 1, chapter 7 of *Capital* between labour and labour power.
5   Gouldner, 1954: p 152.
6   *Secretary of State for Employment v ASLEF (No 2)* [1972] 2 QB 455; *Cresswell v Board of Inland Revenue* [1984] ICR 508; *Sim v Rotherham Metropolitan Borough Council* [1987] Ch 216.
7   *Robertson v British Gas Corpn* [1983] ICR 351.
8   *Sim v Rotherham Metropolitan Borough Council* [1987] Ch 216.
9   See below, para 4.7.
10 Cf Fox, 1974.

Terms implied at common law

4.4   The common law is a highly significant source of regulation of contractual terms and conditions. The 'bridging' term, through which the normative contents of collective agreements are given effect in the contract of employment, is one of the most important examples of a common law implied term.[11] Terms implied at common law underpin managerial prerogative by expressing the employee's duties of obedience, fidelity and care,[12] but also protect certain of the employee's expectations of continuing work and employment. Thus the employer may come under an obligation to compensate the employee for lay-off or suspension of work caused by lack of demand, and to pay sick pay if the employee falls ill.[13] The reciprocal duty of co-operation places both sides under a residual obligation to take steps to ensure that the contract can be made to work effectively. The scope of this obligation is notoriously unclear. Sometimes it amounts to little more than saying that the employee's first responsibility is to the business, even at the possible cost of their own job security;[14] but it is also capable of generating an obligation on the employer's side to respect the dignity and person of the employee. To permit or acquiesce in the sexual harassment of an employee, for example, would amount to a breach by the employer of the duty of co-operation.[15]

4.5   The obligations created by implied terms are, by their nature, diffuse and open-ended. They epitomise the merging of contract and status within the contract of employment: 'to the employee, the arrangement is much more like the all-encompassing status agreement than the express limited regime of contract'.[16] Merritt has traced their presence in the modern contract back to nineteenth century master and servant legislation: 'the status-based incidents of the old master-servant relationship, appropriate to domestic and agricultural service, were grafted on to the relationship of principal and independent contractor, producing, by the end of the nineteenth century, the concepts of employer and employee'.[17] Her analysis relates to the employment law of New South Wales, but other studies have found evidence that a similar process took place in other common law jurisdictions in North America and England: 'the merger of master-servant law and contract meant that the law never treated the employment contract as the result of free bargaining and mutual consent, despite dogma that this was indeed the case. Instead, the contract was deemed to include "implied" terms which reserved to the employer the full authority and direction of employees'.[18]

An important finding of Merritt's study is that the concept of the contract of employment developed comparatively recently; until the last quarter of the nineteenth century it was not possible to speak of a contract of employment applying to all categories of wage-dependent labour. Instead, there were separate

---

11   See below, para 4.28.
12   See below, para 4.96 *et seq.*
13   See below, para 4.109 *et seq.*
14   Cf *Cresswell v Board of Inland Revenue* [1984] ICR 508, discussed below, para 4.90.
15   *Wood v Freeloader Ltd* [1977] IRLR 455.
16   Atleson, 1983: p 8.
17   Merritt, 1982b: p 56; also on the development of the contract of employment in Australia, see Howe and Mitchell, 1999.
18   Atleson, 1983: p 8; also on the US, see Tomlins, 1993; on Britain, Foster, 1983; Deakin, 1998, 2001; Steinfeld, 2003; Deakin and Wilkinson, 2005.

categories of *service* and *employment*.[19] In England the notion of service, with its implications of hierarchy and command, applied to relationships coming under the scope of the Master and Servant Acts and, after their repeal, the Employers and Workmen Act 1875. It was only in the case of higher-status workers such as managers and clerks, who were outside the scope of this legislation, that employment was recognisably contractual in the sense of being based on reciprocal obligations. This is not to say that *none* of the features of the service relationship was defined by contract. The doctrine of common employment, whereby the servant bore the risk of negligence by a worker in the same employment, operated through an implied contract term.[20] However, in the case of those classified as servants, contract played little or no role in defining the limits to managerial prerogative or in providing any degree of income security.

In so far as there was a contractual model of employment in the nineteenth century its application was limited to employees in the professional and managerial classes. The extension of this model to all categories of wage-dependent workers took place alongside the extension of social legislation and of collective bargaining, which regulated the exercise of managerial prerogative.[21] During this time many incidents of the employment relationship were still not conceptualised in contractual terms, but were thought of as duties imposed by the law of tort. The employer's duty to take reasonable care with regard to the health and safety of its employees was formulated as a duty of care in tort in *Wilsons & Clyde Coal Co v English*, decided in 1937.[22] When in 1957 the House of Lords considered the employee's obligation of care and attention in *Lister v Romford Ice and Cold Storage Co Ltd*, Lord Radcliffe commented that 'there is no real distinction between the two sources of obligation. But it is certainly, I think, as much contractual as tortious. Since in modern times the relationship between master and servant, between employer and employed, is inherently one of contract, it seems to me entirely correct to attribute the duties which arise from that relationship to implied contract'.[23]

Today, even though the implied incidents of the employment relationship are generally understood to be contractual in nature, it is only with some difficulty that they can be made to fit into a contractual framework, and they bear evident signs of their origins in statutory regulation and the law of tort. The normal tests for implying a contract term, the 'officious bystander' and 'business efficacy' tests,[24] seek to discover the unstated intentions of the parties; consent remains the rationale for the presence of the term. Implied terms in the contract of employment, on the other hand, are sometimes said to arise as 'legal incidents' of the relationship; they do not necessarily arise from the presumed intention of the parties but by virtue of the nature of the underlying transaction. In a similar context, Lord Denning has said of this technique, 'these obligations are not

---

19 Foster, 1983.
20 Napier, 1986: p 329.
21 Deakin, 1989: ch 4, 1998, 2000; Howe and Mitchell, 1999; Merritt, 1982b: pp 79–82.
22 [1938] AC 57.
23 [1957] AC 555, 587. Lord Simonds referred to *Harmer v Cornelius* (1858) 5 CBNS 236 as authority of the existence of the employee's *contractual* duty to exercise care and attention, but as Merritt points out (1982b: p 59) this case concerned an independent contractor, not a servant or employee.
24 *Shirlaw v Southern Foundries (1926) Ltd* [1939] 2 KB 206 and *The Moorcock* (1889) 14 PD 64, respectively.

founded on the intention of the parties, actual or presumed, but on more general considerations ... the obligation is a legal incident of the relationship which is attached by the law itself and not by reason of any implied term'.[25]

4.6   The incidents which are implied into the contract of employment are, characteristically, those which reflect the continuing nature of the employment relationship and the mutual dependence to which it gives rise. In *Mears v Safecar Security Ltd*[26] Stephenson LJ referred to obligations which 'the general law will impose and imply, not as satisfying the business efficacy or officious bystander tests applicable to commercial contracts where there is no such relationship, but as legal incidents of those other kinds of contractual relationship'. In this case the Court of Appeal was prepared to imply a term for the payment of sick pay: '[w]e can treat as an agreed term a term which would not have been assented to by both parties at the time when they made the contract'.[27] Similarly, a court may imply into a contract of employment the 'bridging term' necessary to give effect to a collective agreement which is applicable to that contract, on the grounds that this aligns the legal contents of the contract with the circumstances governing its operation in practice.[28]

The House of Lords has said that an 'incident' of the relationship must be 'necessary' to give effect to the transaction, and not simply 'reasonable' in the eyes of the court.[29] This is because, in principle, the courts have no power to insert a term at common law on the grounds of 'reasonableness', having the power only to strike out agreed terms on the limited grounds allowed by the doctrine of public policy. The common law courts do not formally draw what Kahn-Freund referred to as 'the distinction between *ius cogens* and *ius dispositivum*, between "imperative" and "optional" norms of the law of contract, [which] is familiar to every practising lawyer in any Continental legal system'.[30] The scope given to the intention of the contracting parties apparently means that common law implied terms can only ever be 'dispositive' or optional, that is to say, terms which the parties are free to depart from if they wish to. An express term should therefore prevail over a potential implied term relating to the same matter.[31] In this vein, the EAT has said that 'if it is not necessary to make the contract work there is no room for such a further implied term. Certainly the court cannot intervene [simply] because it appears reasonable or equitable to do so'.[32]

However, the common law implied terms are not as fragile as the priority of express terms would tend to suggest. This is partly because, being by nature residual, the implied terms occupy the space which the express terms, because of their incompleteness, inevitably leave behind. The implied terms of obedience and care are used to resolve issues of the precise definition of work effort and the scope of the employee's commitment which, as we saw above, cannot be completely specified in advance, since to do so would be too costly. Where, however, an

---

25   *Shell UK Ltd v Lostock Garage Ltd* [1977] 1 All ER 481, 487.
26   [1982] ICR 626, 650.
27   [1982] ICR 626, 651.
28   *Tadd v Eastwood and the Daily Telegraph Ltd* [1983] IRLR 320.
29   *Liverpool County Council v Irwin* [1977] AC 239; although see *Crossley v Faithful and Gould Holdings Ltd* [2004] IRLR 377 in which Dyson LJ describes the 'necessity' test as 'protean' and 'elusive', and discusses an alternative test based on 'reasonableness, fairness and the balancing of competing policy considerations' (at paras 34–36).
30   Kahn-Freund, 1967: p 641.
31   For a recent application of this principle, see *Reda v Flag Ltd* [2002] IRLR 747.
32   *Express Lift Co Ltd v Bowles* [1977] ICR 474, 477 (Kilner Brown J).

express term has been agreed which deals with the issues in question, it may be regarded as narrowing down or limiting the effect of the relevant implied term: 'if there is a term of the contract which is in general terms (eg a duty to take reasonable care not to injure the employee's health) and another term which is precise and detailed (eg an obligation to work on particular tasks notwithstanding that they involve an obvious health risk expressly referred to in the contract) the ambit of the employer's duty of care for the employee's health will be narrower than it would be if there were no such express term'.[33] Similarly, a job description accorded to a particular employee or an express mobility clause will serve to identify the limits to his or her implied obligation of obedience.[34]

4.7 To what extent is it possible to go further and state that certain implied terms constitute an irreducible core of obligation in the contract of employment, which cannot be removed by express agreement? It is difficult, for example, to envisage a contract of employment which did not contain *some* implied obligation of co-operation and obedience on the employee's part. How far does the contract contain an equivalent implied obligation on the part of the employer to treat the employee with dignity and respect? The courts have found a way of limiting the effect of express terms by requiring the employer to *act reasonably* in exercising the option to invoke the powers such terms confer. An express mobility clause will necessarily prevail over the limits which might have been set by an implied term;[35] but an employer must give the employee reasonable notice of the move to a new place of work.[36] In *Imperial Group Pension Trust Ltd v Imperial Tobacco Ltd* Browne-Wilkinson VC held that the discretion given to an employer, under the terms of an occupational pension scheme, to agree to increases in pensions, was not unqualified: the employer was not obliged to agree to an increase, but it *was* obliged to exercise its powers in good faith and avoid an arbitrary or capricious result.[37]

4.8 The notion that express terms are qualified by an implied obligation to exercise the powers they create in a reasonable way is not without its difficulties, however. It may amount to the same thing as imposing a qualification on the scope of the term itself: 'are not all contractual obligations optional in that they may or may not be exercised by the promisee and compulsory only in that they bind the promisor when they are exercised?'[38] This approach, then, arguably does little to clarify the essential questions of which qualifications might be justifiably imposed, and on what grounds. The issues were considered by the Court of Appeal in *Johnstone v Bloomsbury Health Authority*.[39]

The employee, a junior hospital doctor, sought damages for ill health brought on by working excessive hours, and a declaration that his contract of employment did not require him to work hours beyond the point where his health was put in

---

33   *Johnstone v Bloomsbury Health Authority* [1992] QB 333, 350 (Browne-Wilkinson VC); see also *Johnson v Unisys Ltd* [2001] IRLR 279, at para 24 (Lord Steyn); *Reda v Flag Ltd* [2002] IRLR 747 (express power to dismiss without notice qualified implied term).

34   See below, paras 4.85, 4.95.

35   *Express Lift Co Ltd v Bowles* [1977] ICR 474.

36   *United Bank Ltd v Akhtar* [1989] IRLR 507.

37   [1991] IRLR 66. See also *Scally v Southern Health and Social Services Board* [1991] IRLR 522; *Clark v Nomura International Ltd* [2000] IRLR 766; *Mallone v BPB Industries Ltd* [2002] IRLR 452; see para 4.91 *et seq* below.

38   McLean, 1992: p 25.

39   [1992] QB 333.

danger. His contract required him to work a basic 40-hour working week and to be available for a further 48 hours overtime per week. Leggatt LJ, who would have struck out the claim as disclosing no cause of action, took the view that the express agreement to be available for up to 88 hours a week prevailed over any implied term for the protection of the employee's safety and health.

The two other judges refused to strike out the claim but gave different reasons for their decisions. Stuart-Smith LJ said that the contract terms did not override the duty of the employer in both contract and tort to take reasonable care to ensure the employee's safety and health. Browne-Wilkinson VC, reiterating his analysis in the *Imperial Tobacco* case,[40] argued that the 'express and implied terms of the contract have to be capable of co-existence without conflict'[41] and that the effect of the express term, in this case, was to narrow down the implied obligation of care owed by the employer to the employee. However, the agreement to work overtime simply gave the employer the *option* to call on the employee to perform, and this option had to be exercised reasonably, with regard to the consequences of doing so for the employee's health.

There are a number of reasons for thinking that the judgment of Stuart-Smith LJ is correct in principle, notwithstanding that he found himself in a minority of one in believing that the express term governing working hours was limited by the employer's implied obligations with regard to health and safety. First, it would be odd if the employer's obligation, which is both an implied term in the contract and also a duty of care in tort, could be limited by an express contract term which did not take the form of a formal disclaimer or exclusion clause of the kind which would normally be needed to oust a tort duty of this kind.[42] Second, if the contract term does limit the employer's duty of care in tort, since that duty relates to the physical health and safety of the employee the term would be nullified by section 2(1) of the Unfair Contract Terms Act 1977. Third, it is arguable in this case that the ambit of the express term was limited by public policy,[43] although this was not accepted by any member of the Court of Appeal in *Johnstone*.

However, none of the arguments advanced so far is of general application to the relationship between implied and express terms. The first argument rests on the rather fortuitous factor that, in this case, the contract term in question was replicated by a duty of care in tort. This will not always be so. In relation to the second argument, the application of the Unfair Contract Terms Act 1977 to employment contracts is not completely assured. Arguably, section 2 and section 3 of the Act should apply to contracts of employment since the employer could be said to be contracting in the course of its business, and will frequently do so on its written standard terms of employment; alternatively, for the purposes of section 3, the employee could be said to be contracting as a 'consumer', since he or she is not contracting in the course of their own business,[44] although this

---

40 [1991] IRLR 66.
41 [1992] QB 333, 350.
42 Deakin, Johnston and Markesinis, 2003: pp 765–766.
43 Weir, 1991: p 399.
44 See *Micklefield v SAC Technology Ltd* [1990] IRLR 218l; *Brigden v American Express Bank Ltd* [2000] IRLR 94; *Peninsula Business Services Ltd v Sweeney* [2004] IRLR 49; Watson, 1995; para 4.70 below. The provisions of UCTA 1977 which apply in Scotland make it clear that they do not extend to contracts of employment (see *Chapman v Aberdeen Construction Group plc* [1991] IRLR 505); nor would it be easy to demonstrate that employment contracts fall under the Unfair Terms in Consumer Contracts Regulations, SI 1999/2083, which implement Directive 91/13, since those regulations only apply to a contract between a consumer and a 'seller or supplier' (reg 4(1)). See generally Brodie, 1998b: pp 83–86.

reading of the word 'consumer' seems strongly counter-intuitive. Public policy will only be of assistance, in this context, if the term in question relates to an issue of life and limb.

There is authority, however, for a broader principle which could be invoked to explain the result in *Johnstone* if not the reasoning used in that case. This is that the contract does indeed contain an irreducible obligation on the part of the employer 'not to destroy the mutual trust and confidence on which co-operation rests'.[45] This is not necessarily equivalent to a duty to act reasonably, but it does imply an obligation not unreasonably to prevent the other party from performing the contract, in particular by avoiding action which is completely capricious and arbitrary.[46] In his opinion in the leading case of *Malik v BCCI*,[47] Lord Steyn referred to the implied term of trust and co-operation as a default rule, suggesting that it only applies in the absence of an express agreement on the point in question. This use of the expression 'default term', however, opens up a potentially important discussion on the different types of default which may operate in the context of the employment relationship. The *Malik* term of good faith or trust and co-operation could be described as a 'strong' default which can only be qualified by an express term of a very clear and precise nature, in contrast to other types of default term which are more easily waivable.[48] This formulation respects the central place occupied by the *Malik* term within the modern employment contract,[49] without infringing the orthodox view of the relationship between express and implied terms at common law.[50]

Regulation by statute and collective bargaining[51]

4.9 Statutory norms of income and employment protection do not, on the whole, take the form of implied terms of the contract of employment. Minimum wage legislation provides for automatic incorporation into contracts of employment of the rates of pay laid down by statute.[52] The EqPA 1970 provides that 'if the terms of a contract under which a woman is employed at an establishment in Great Britain do not include (directly or by reference to a

---

45 Hepple, 1981: p 134. The leading judicial decision on the duty of mutual trust and co-operation is now the ruling of the House of Lords in *Malik v BCCI SA* [1997] IRLR 462; see Brodie, 1998b. This aspect of *Malik* is discussed below, para 4.92.

46 *Woods v WM Car Services (Peterborough) Ltd* [1982] ICR 693; *White v Reflecting Roadstuds Ltd* [1991] IRLR 331; McLean, 1992.

47 [1997] IRLR 462, 468; see Brodie, 1998b: pp 82–83.

48 This is a well-known distinction in the theoretical literature on implied terms and other default rules in contract and company law. See the seminal paper by Ayres and Gertner, 1989, and for an application to part of UK company law, see Deakin and Hughes, 1999.

49 On this, see Brodie, 1998b.

50 See also *Johnson v Unisys Ltd* [2001] IRLR 279, at paras 24 (Lord Steyn) and 37 (Lord Hoffmann). All the opinions in this case concluded that the common law implied term of a duty to act fairly (the term preferred, in the context of termination, to 'mutual trust and confidence') could, in principle, be applied to termination of employment notwithstanding the presence of an express notice clause; there was no necessary conflict between the express and implied terms. However, the majority (Lord Steyn dissenting) ruled that the common law should not be developed in a way which would undermine the separate, statutory jurisdiction of unfair dismissal. See below paras 5.25 and 5.44 for further discussion of *Johnson*.

51 See generally, Anderman, 2000.

52 For an authority under the now-repealed wages councils legislation, see *Cooner v PS Doal & Sons* [1988] IRLR 338; and on the position under NMWA 1998, see *WA Armstrong & Sons Ltd v Borrill* [2000] ICR 367; *Paggetti v Cobb* [2002] IRLR 861; para 4.55 below.

collective agreement or otherwise) an equality clause they shall be deemed to include one'.[53] The equality clause is a device for modifying existing express terms of the contract and including others, and it is these other terms rather than the equality clause itself which will be relied on to give effect to a claim to equal treatment. This is a rare instance of legislation explicitly altering the substance of the terms of the contract, as opposed to attaching to it statutory obligations which override contrary agreement. The effect is not completely synonymous with a statutory variation of the contract: the effective period of limitation under the statute is not the same as would apply to a common law claim for arrears of pay.[54]

A similar approach is taken with regard to minimum periods of notice imposed by statute upon employers and employees. The legislation states that notice 'is not less' than a specified period and lays down that 'any provision for shorter notice ... has effect subject to' these periods.[55] The statute provides that either side retains the right to waive the right to notice or to accept payment in lieu of notice, thereby replicating the common law rules which would apply to a contract term.[56] It also states that failure by the employer to give the requisite notice 'shall be taken into account in assessing his liability for breach of the contract'.[57] Nothing is said explicitly about the *employee's* liability for failing to give minimum statutory notice, but it is probably the case that an employer would have an action for damages for breach of contract in this event.[58]

4.10   The courts traditionally regarded 'protective legislation, such as that imposing standards of health, safety or welfare in factories, mines, etc, or maximum hours of work ... not as operating on a contract but as imposing extra-contractual obligations, enforceable through criminal prosecutions and actions in tort'.[59] The Truck Acts were viewed, for example, as giving rise to a statutory right to sue for the agreed wage and not a right under the contract, so that statutory limitation periods applied.[60] One reason for the failure to achieve a better fit between statute and contract was that, during the period when most of this legislation was passed, the contract of employment as we know it today did not exist; as we have seen, few incidents of the service relationship were clearly rationalised in contractual terms.[61]

As the role of the contract of employment has grown, so it has become more common for the courts to assume that protective rights originating in statute can take effect as contract terms. Hence in *Barber v RJB Mining*[62] it was held

---

53   EqPA 1970, s 1(1). The meaning of the 'equality clause' is explained in EqPA 1970, s 1(2). These provisions are analysed in para 6.71 *et seq* below.

54   The normal limitation period for claims of arrears of pay in contract is six years from the accrual of the cause of action (Limitation Act 1980, s 5). Special rules apply to claims under the EqPA 1970. See below, paras 6.92–6.94.

55   ERA 1996, s 86(1), (3).

56   ERA 1996, s 86(3). See para 5.14 below.

57   ERA 1996, s 91(5). The Court of Appeal recognised the contractual nature of the employee's action for damages by imposing a mitigation requirement in *Westwood v Secretary of State for Employment* [1985] ICR 209.

58   See also EA 2002, s 30, providing for the implication into contracts of employment of statutory disciplinary and grievance procedures. This part of the reforms introduced by the 2002 Act has yet to be brought into effect. See our analysis, below, para 5.124 *et seq*.

59   Kahn-Freund, 1967: p 641.

60   *Pratt v Cook, Son & Co (St Pauls) Ltd* [1940] AC 437.

61   See above, para 4.5.

62   [1999] IRLR 308.

that the 48-hour weekly limit to working time in WTR 1998, regulation 4(1), operated as a contract term, enabling the applicants to obtain a declaration of their rights under the relevant standard. The decision is particularly striking since the Working Time Regulations are silent on the question of private enforcement through the contract of employment, and it might have been supposed that, by providing for other remedies, they had implicitly closed this route off. *Barber*, then, suggests that protective rights of this kind should be regarded as having contractual force, unless there is clear provision to the contrary in the legislation itself.

Contract plays a central role in defining the scope of modern employment protection legislation since, as we have seen, that legislation adopts the common law concept of the contract of employment for a number of purposes including the classification of employment relationships.[63] However, the employee's claims are still seen as being statutory in nature. Adjudication is undertaken by statutory bodies, mainly the employment tribunals, which until 1994 had no jurisdiction to hear common law claims for damages for breach of contract.[64] As far as terms and conditions of employment other than those relating to dismissal are concerned,[65] the principal statutory rights are the right to receive the agreed wage or salary without certain deductions by the employer, the right to security of income in the event of lay-off, sickness or maternity, and rights in respect of working time limits. Failure to pay the agreed wage gives rise to what is in effect a statutory claim for restitution before an employment tribunal,[66] as does non-payment of statutory guaranteed pay in the event of lay-off.[67] The effective limitation periods for these statutory rights are much shorter than is the case for breach of contract claims.[68]

4.11 As we saw earlier,[69] employment protection legislation mostly forms a 'floor of rights', setting minimum standards from which derogation is not permitted. Contracting out from rights contained in ERA 1996 and TULRCA 1992 is formally prohibited by statutory rules to the effect that 'any provision in an agreement (whether a contract of employment or not) is void in so far as it purports – (a) to exclude or limit the operation of any provision of this Act or (b) to preclude a person from bringing any proceedings under this Act before an employment tribunal'.[70] Similar provisions apply to the rights to SSP and SMP under SSCBA 1992.[71] This means that the employee cannot

---

63 See above, para 3.19 *et seq.*

64 Their jurisdiction was extended by SI 1994/1623; D Brown, 1994. See para 2.15 *et seq* above.

65 Dismissal is considered in ch 5 below.

66 ERA 1996, ss 23, 24.

67 ERA 1996, s 34. Note that claims for statutory sick pay and statutory maternity pay, which were formerly made before social security adjudication officers (or the Secretary of State in respect of certain issues), under the Social Security Contributions (Transfer of Functions etc.) Act 1999 are now made to officers of the Board of Inland Revenue, from whom there may be an appeal to the tax commissioners. See Wikeley, 2002: pp 531, 564.

68 In contrast to the six-year period for breach of contract claims, claims for the statutory rights referred to in the text must be lodged within three months of the relevant event. See eg ERA 1996, s 23.

69 See para 1.15 above.

70 ERA 1996, s 203(1); TULRCA 1992, s 288. For discussion of whether contract can be used to exclude Convention rights under HRA 1998, see G Morris, 2001a.

71 SSCBA 1992, s 151(2) and s 164(6), respectively.

validly contract to receive *inferior* rights and/or benefits to those stipulated by legislation. The few exceptions to this principle are strictly limited by legislation itself.[72]

In principle, the purpose of the statutory floor of rights is to provide a platform on which individual agreement or, more likely, collective bargaining can build to provide more advantageous terms and conditions of employment. This has not been the sole aim of the legislation providing rights to security of income, however. The imposition on employers of the obligations to pay statutory sick pay and guaranteed pay were designed to shift responsibility away from the social security system, which had previously borne the cost of meeting these payments through sickness benefit and unemployment benefit.[73] The shift to payment by the employer resulted in employees being, if anything, worse off. Previously, employees would often receive social security sickness benefit in addition to any contractual entitlement to sick pay under occupational schemes which many employers operated. When statutory sick pay was introduced after 1982, however, provision was made for statutory and contractual rights to be set-off against each other.[74]

Floor of rights legislation in Britain has, historically, lacked the comprehensive character of its equivalents in mainland European systems. Instead of entrenching minimum wage rates and maximum working hours which applied throughout the labour force, the practice in Britain was for many decades to legislate only in the case of specific groups of workers, who tended to be those who were not protected by collective agreements of any kind. This was the case, for example, with the working time provisions of the Factories Acts, which did not apply to adult male workers, and with the Trade Boards Acts and Wages Councils Acts, whose application was confined to particular, low-paying sectors of the economy.[75] As long as an effective system of sector-level collective bargaining was in place for most of the labour force, this policy of selective statutory regulation had limited consequences. However, during the 1980s the effectiveness of sector level collective agreements declined rapidly, with the result that the coverage of collective bargaining narrowed from some three-quarters of the labour force to less than half.[76] At the same time, deregulatory legislation removed the remaining controls on minimum wages in the Wages Councils sectors and the working time provisions of the Factories Acts, leaving only the Agricultural Wages Boards as bodies capable of setting legally-binding minimum terms and conditions of employment.[77] As a result, a situation came into existence in which a large segment of the employed labour force was without statutory or collective protection of any kind in respect of minimum wage levels and maximum hours of work. However, the absence of effective, general regulation has been

---

72   Collective exemptions are possible from the guaranteed pay and unfair dismissal provisions of ERA 1996: see below, paras 4.113 and 5.64. The Working Time Directive makes extensive provision for both collective and individual derogation which is reflected in the provisions adopted to bring it into force in the UK: see below, paras 4.73–4.78.
73   See below, para 4.73 *et seq*.
74   SSCBA 1992, Sch 12, para 2(2); see also Sch 13, para 3(2) (SMP). The introduction of guaranteed pay also led to employees being worse off, since at that time unemployment benefit (the forerunner to the jobseeker's allowance) had provided for a higher level of compensation: see below, paras 4.112–4.113.
75   See above, para 1.11.
76   See above, para 1.27.
77   See below, para 4.41.

addressed, in part at least, by the enactment of the National Minimum Wage Act 1998[78] and by the translation into UK law of relevant provisions of the EC Directives on Working Time and Young People at Work.[79]

4.12 Sector level collective bargaining continues in some industries, and collective bargaining at the level of the company or establishment also remains a significant source of regulation of terms and conditions for many employees. Its legal impact on the individual contract of employment is determined by the common law doctrine of incorporation. Incorporation is neither compulsory nor automatic,[80] but rests instead on the presence of an express or implied 'bridging term' in the contract of employment.[81] While the common law is quite effective for most purposes in translating the normative terms of the collective agreement into the individual contract, it has difficulty in resolving conflicts between different external sources of norms, in particular different levels of collective agreements. Nor has the law succeeded in entrenching the normative terms of the collective agreement against attempts by employers to derogate from or vary them. Although the employer cannot unilaterally alter the contract terms, it may destroy their effect by dismissing the employees and offering them new terms. This route is not entirely risk-free: if large numbers of employees are involved, the employer *may* face potentially extensive liability in the form of unfair dismissal or redundancy compensation payments to those who have been dismissed.[82] This may act as something of a disincentive. However, dismissal in breach of contract is not automatically unfair, and is likely to be fair if the employer can demonstrate that it was in the interests of the business. In short, British labour law has no equivalent to the compulsory effect which is accorded to the normative terms of collective agreement by the civil law systems.[83]

WRITTEN NOTIFICATION OF TERMS

4.13 No formalities attach to the formation of the contract of employment at common law.[84] This is reflected in the definition of the contract of employment for statutory purposes, which makes it clear that it may be either express or implied and, if it is express, either oral or in writing.[85] However, legislation has superimposed a duty upon the employer to provide the employee with written information concerning particulars of employment, including certain terms of the contract and certain statutory rights.[86]

---

78 See below, para 4.41 *et seq*.
79 See below, para 4.71 *et seq*.
80 Legislation providing for a form of compulsory incorporation (the EPA 1975, Sch 11) was repealed by the EA 1980, and the Fair Wages Resolution of the House of Commons, which had a broadly similar effect in relation to work performed under public contracts, was rescinded with effect from 1983.
81 See below, para 4.28.
82 See below, para 4.39.
83 See below, para 4.39.
84 For a recent example, stressing the potential informality of the hiring process, see *Stransky v Bristol Rugby Ltd* 2002 WL31914196, High Court, 11 December 2002.
85 ERA 1996, s 230(2).
86 ERA 1996, s 1.

The scope of the statutory written statement

4.14   The right to the written statement was (along with the right to mimimum periods of notice) the first of the modern employment protection rights to be enacted, in the Contracts of Employment Act 1963. Its immediate aims included the reduction of disputes over contract terms and the formalisation of procedures at the level of the individual company or establishment; in these respects it anticipated later developments in the area of employment protection, in particular the unfair dismissal and income protection legislation of the 1970s, into which it was subsumed.[87] The scope of the employer's duty, initially confined to the most basic of the contract terms, was widened by the IRA 1971 and the EPA 1975 to include reference to job title and to disciplinary and grievance procedures. Further modifications were introduced by TURERA 1993, implementing Directive 91/533. The Directive is 'designed to provide employees with improved protection against possible infringements of their rights and to create greater transparency on the labour market'.[88] The TURERA amendments liberalised the relevant qualifying conditions, replacing the 16-hour weekly threshold with one of 8 hours (although this was subsequently repealed in its turn) and shortening the period within which the statement must be issued from 13 weeks to the present two months. They also imposed for the first time the obligation to give details of collective agreements affecting the employment relationship, and strictly limited the option of referring the employee to another 'reference document'. Under the old section 2(3) of EPCA 1978, the employer could discharge its obligations by reference in the written statement to 'some document which the employee has reasonable opportunities of reading in the course of his employment or which is made reasonably accessible to him in some other way'. The right to invoke a reference document is now limited to certain specific particulars, namely those concerning illness or incapacity for work, pension rights, length of notice and disciplinary procedures. TURERA 1993 also significantly tightened the obligation to notify the employee of changes to the particulars. Previously, under the old section 4 of EPCA 1978, changes could be notified via the reference document within one month of them taking effect. Now, the changes must be notified in an additional written statement provided to each employee. This has created fears of an excess of paperwork.[89] The emphasis on greater certainty and transparency in the employment relationship was, on the other hand, welcomed by several employers' organisations and by the TUC at the time of the adoption of the Directive.[90]

---

87   R Lewis, 1986: pp 13, 32; P Davies and M Freedland, 1993: p 145.
88   Directive 91/533, Recital, para 2. On the Directive, see generally Clark and Hall, 1992; Wedderburn, 1995: pp 4–6; and Joined Cases C-253/96 to C-258/96: *Kampelmann v Landschaftsverband Westfalen-Lippe* [1998] IRLR 333 (discussed by Kenner, 1999), in which the ECJ held that the provisions of Article 2(2)(c) of the Directive, under which the employer is obliged to notify the employee of his or her job title or to provide a brief description of their duties, are sufficiently unconditional and precise to have direct effect in national law. See also Case C-350/99 *Lange v Georg Schünemann GmbH* [2001] IRLR 244, where the ECJ emphasised that Art 2(2) of the Directive did not reduce the scope of the general requirement under Art 2(1) for the employer to notify employees of the essential aspects of the contract or employment relationship (in that case the obligation to work overtime on request).
89   See the account of the Parliamentary debates on these provisions in Ewing, 1993a: p 169.
90   Clark and Hall, 1992: p 114.

Information which must be contained in a single document

4.15 Under ERA 1996, s 1 the employer must issue a 'written statement of particulars of employment' as a single document containing, first, basic information about the employment relationship, that is to say the names of the parties, the date on which employment began and the date on which the employee's continuous employment began, taking into account employment with a previous employer which counts towards that period.[91] Second, the same document must also contain information about certain terms and particulars of employment.[92] These are: the scale or rate of remuneration or the method of calculating it;[93] the intervals at which it is paid (weekly, monthly or other specified interval); any terms relating to hours of work and normal working hours; any terms relating to holidays (including public holidays and holiday pay); the job title;[94] and the employee's place of work or, failing that, the employer's name and address.

Information which may be contained in a separate document issued to the employee

4.16 A third category of information may be provided in a separate document issued to the employee. This is information concerning the period for which the contract is expected to continue or the date fixed for it to come to an end, in cases where it is not intended to be 'permanent' or indefinite; any collective agreements 'which directly affect the terms and conditions of the employment including, where the employer is not a party, the persons by whom they were made'; and, where the employee is required to work outside the United Kingdom for more than one month, details of the time to be spent working abroad, the currency in which he or she will be paid, any additional payment due for working abroad, and any terms and conditions relating to his or her return to the UK.[95]

Information which may be contained either in a written statement or in another reasonably accessible document

4.17 A fourth category relates to information which may be notified to the employee either in a written statement or in another document which the employee has a reasonable opportunity to read in the course of employment or which is made reasonably accessible in some way.[96] The relevant particulars are those

---

91   ERA 1996, ss 1(3), 2(3).
92   ERA 1996, s 1(4).
93   This includes any minimum rate of remuneration to which the employee becomes entitled by virtue of NMWA 1998. The itemised pay statement which must be issued under ERA 1996, s 8, must also make reference to the details of the wages paid to the employee (see para 4.66 below). NMWA 1998, s 12, confers a power on the Secretary of State to make provision for a minimum wage statement to be issued to all workers (a wider group than the 'employees' covered by ERA 1996, ss 1 and 8), but this power has not yet been exercised. See further para 4.56 below.
94   More precisely, 'the title of the job which the employee is employed to do or a brief description of the work for which he is employed' (ERA 1996, s 1(4)(f)). In interpreting the equivalent provision of Directive 91/533 (Art 2(2)(c)(ii)), the ECJ held that 'the mere designation of an activity cannot in every case amount to even a brief specification or description of the work done by an employee' so as to comply with the Directive: Joined Cases C-253/96 to C-258/96: *Kampelmann v Landschaftsverband Westfalen-Lippe* [1998] IRLR 333, 342; Kenner, 1999b.
95   ERA 1996, s 1(4)(g), (j), (k).
96   ERA 1996, s 6.

relating to incapacity for work (including entitlement to sick pay),[97] and occupational pension schemes and benefits (unless the scheme takes effect by or under an Act of Parliament which, independently of ERA 1996, requires such information to be given to the employee).[98] Details of the length of notice which the employee is entitled to receive and which he or she is required to give may be provided by way of reference to the relevant law (contained in sections 86 *et seq* of ERA 1996) or to any relevant collective agreement, which must be accessible to the employee in the sense used above.[99]

Disciplinary and grievance procedures

4.18   A fifth category concerns disciplinary and grievance procedures (other than those relating to health and safety at work). Any such procedures must be specified to the employee in the written statement; disciplinary procedures may alternatively be specified in another, reasonably accessible document.[100] Details of a person to whom an employee may apply to seek redress of a grievance must also be notified in writing.[101]

Timing of notification

4.19   The relevant information must be notified to all employees whose employment continues for one month or more,[102] and the statement must be issued within two months of the employment beginning,[103] even if the employment ends at some point in the second month.[104] If the statement is issued in the form of more than one document – that is, the 'written statement' followed by additional 'instalments' – then they must all be issued within this two-month period.[105] The particulars must be those which were in effect on a specified date not more than seven days before the date on which the statement was issued. If there are no particulars in effect in respect of one of the categories listed above (with the exception of disciplinary procedures), that fact must itself be stated.[106]

Changes to the particulars

4.20   If there is a change to any of the relevant particulars, section 4 provides that the employer must issue a further written statement 'at the earliest

---

97   ERA 1996, ss 1(4)(d)(ii), 2(2).
98   ERA 1996, ss 1(4)(d)(iii), 1(5) and 2(2).
99   ERA 1996, ss 1(4)(e) and 2(3).
100 ERA 1996, s 3. This category includes, in addition to procedures laid down in the contract of employment, the statutory dispute resolution procedures which were introduced by EA 2002 (see s 3(1)(aa)). The 2002 Act also repealed provisions excluding the duty to provide a written statement of disciplinary procedures in a case where the employer, together with an associated employer, employed fewer than twenty employees (formerly ERA 1996, s 3(3)–(4)). On dispute resolution, see above, paras 2.21–2.26, and below, paras 5.124–5.131.
101 ERA 1996, s 3(1)(b)(ii). On grievance procedures and implied terms, see *WA Goold (Pearmak) Ltd v McConnell* [1995] IRLR 516, discussed below, para 4.91; and on the statutory right of a worker to be accompanied at a grievance hearing, see paras 5.132–5.135 below.
102 ERA 1996, s 198, previously s 5(1) of EPCA 1978 as amended by SI 1995/31, removing the 8-hour threshold. See paras 3.87 and 3.88 above.
103 ERA 1996, ss 1(2).
104 ERA 1996, s 2(6).
105 ERA 1996, s 1(2). This states that '[t]he statement may (subject to s 2(4)) be given in instalments and (whether or not given in instalments) shall be given not later than two months after the beginning of the employment'.
106 ERA 1996, s 2(1).

opportunity' and at any event not later than one month after the change took place.[107] This section 4 statement need only detail the relevant changes; it does not need to lay out all the relevant particulars in full, as under section 1. The section 4 statement may, as under section 1, make reference to other documents. A section 4 statement is sufficient if the only change is to the name but not to the identity of the employer, or if the employer's identity changes without the employee losing continuity of employment or any other relevant particulars being affected.[108]

Remedies

4.21   The remedy for the employer's failure to comply with its obligations under section 1 is by way of a reference to an employment tribunal under section 11, which may 'amend those particulars, or substitute other particulars for them, as [it] may determine to be appropriate'.[109] The tribunal has no general power to award compensation to the employee; nor is the employer's failure to comply with the Act a criminal offence.[110] However, since 1 October 2004 where the employee has been successful in relation to other specified statutory proceedings, between two and four weeks' pay can be awarded for failure to provide an initial statement of particulars or to notify the employee of changes.[111]

Limited normative effect of sections 1–4

4.22   The Act has been interpreted as requiring the employer to notify the employee only of those particulars which have independent contractual force (in addition to the statutory rights to notice and continuity of employment which are also specifically mentioned).[112] This is despite the fact that it is not stated clearly that the 'terms and conditions' which must be notified are those which are *contractual* in nature. It is conceivable that certain particulars could take the form of the work rules considered by the Court of Appeal in *Secretary of State for Employment v ASLEF (No 2)* to be 'in no way terms of the contract of employment'.[113] Whether, if they did, this would affect the employer's obligations under the Act is unclear. The answer is probably that as a matter of construction, any rules concerning the matters listed in sections 1 and 3 are presumed to be contractual in nature, unless the contrary is shown; and that, as such, they trigger the employer's statutory obligations in respect of the written statement. In the unlikely event that it could be shown that certain rules of this kind did not have contractual force, no obligation of notification under the Act would arise (except to say that no relevant particulars existed); nor would it arise if there were neither contract terms nor particulars of any other kind.

---

107   ERA 1996, s 4(1), (3). If the change relates to the employee working abroad, the new statement must be issued no later than the time of departure from the United Kingdom: ERA 1996, s 4(3)(b). The equivalent provisions of Directive 91/533 are contained in Art 5.

108   ERA 1996, s 4(5)–(8).

109   ERA 1996, s 12(2).

110   The Contracts of Employment Act 1963 made provision for breach by the employer to be an offence, punishable by fine, but this was repealed in 1965: Wedderburn, 1986: p 139.

111   EA 2002, s 38; Sch 5. A week's pay is subject to the statutory maximum in ERA 1996, s 227, which as of 1 February 2005 stood at £280.

112   *Eagland v British Telecommunications plc* [1992] IRLR 323; *Morley v Heritage plc* [1993] IRLR 400.

113   [1972] 2 QB 455, 490 (Lord Denning MR); see above, para 4.3.

This seems to be the effect, in the first place, of section 2(1), which states that '[i]f, in the case of a statement under section 1, there are no particulars to be entered under any of the heads of paragraph (d) or (k) of subsection (4) of that section, or under any of the other paragraphs of subsection (3) or (4) of that section, that fact shall be stated'. This implies that if there are no agreed terms (or other particulars) relating to a certain matter, there is nothing to notify to the employee, except the fact of their absence.[114] Presumably for the avoidance of doubt, some (but not all) of the paragraphs and heads of section 1 require notification of '*any* terms and conditions' on the matters listed there (emphasis added).[115] Under section 3(1)(a) and (aa), the employer is only required to notify the employee of 'any disciplinary rules' and 'any procedure applicable to the taking of disciplinary decisions'; again, if there are no such rules, or procedure, there is nothing on which the statute can bite.[116] However, section 3(1)(b) does not contain the normal qualification, and apparently *requires* the employer to identify a person to whom a complaint may be made if the employee is dissatisfied with a disciplinary decision relating to him or her and the name of a person to whom he or she may present a grievance.[117] In these two cases only does the Act clearly have an effect which is independent of the contract terms.

Apart from this, the Act would not prevent there being, for example, a 'zero hours' contract of employment, under which no fixed hours are laid down and employees are called in to work on demand by the employer; nor, at a less extreme level, does the contract necessarily have to contain terms relating to holidays, incapacity or to pension benefits. This absence of any general normative effect would seem at first sight to defeat the purpose of the Act: an employer can avoid the statutory obligation to formalise and record the contract terms by declining to agree to them in the first place. However, this interpretation has been put beyond doubt by two decisions of the Court of Appeal.

In *Eagland v British Telecommunications plc*[118] the Court held that a written statement which contained no reference to holiday pay, sick pay, pension entitlements and disciplinary rules was an accurate record of the employee's contractual entitlements and had therefore not been issued in breach of section 1. According to Parker LJ, although an employment tribunal considering an application to amend the statutory statement would have the power to conclude that 'because the contract turned out to be a contract of employment, it was a necessary legal incident of that contract that the ordinary requirement of such a relationship be included', these requirements 'do not include disciplinary rules, pension, sick pay or holiday pay and in my judgment they have no power to impose upon an employer any such terms if it be the fact... that either it had been agreed that there should be no pension, sick pay, holiday pay or disciplinary rules, or the matter had not been agreed at all. The wording of the section makes it perfectly plain, as indeed must be the case at common law, that there

---

114 *Eagland v British Telecommunications plc* [1992] IRLR 323, 327 (Leggatt LJ).
115 ERA 1996, s 1(4)(c), (d), (j) and (k)(iv).
116 S 3(1)(aa) was inserted by EA 2002, s 35, and reflects the role of the statutory disciplinary procedures provided for by that Act (on which, see below, paras 5.124 *et seq*). Although provision has been made under the 2002 Act (s 30) for those procedures to take effect as terms in all contracts of employment, this has not yet been brought into force, and perhaps may never be: see para 5.19 below.
117 See *WA Goold (Pearmak) Ltd v McConnell* [1995] IRLR 516, 517 (Morison J).
118 [1992] IRLR 323.

may be no such terms and there is nothing in any section of the Act which empowers or requires the Tribunal to impose upon the parties terms which had not been agreed ...'[119]

In *Morley v Heritage plc*[120] the Court considered the requirement that particulars concerning holidays should be 'sufficient to enable the employee's entitlement, including any entitlement to accrued holiday pay on the termination of employment, to be precisely calculated'.[121] It was held that this did not mean that a term providing for either holidays or holiday pay had to be implied: on the contrary, section 1 'so far from requiring that a contract of employment must give entitlement to pay in lieu of holiday not taken, does no more than recognise that a contract can include such a provision'.[122]

In *Eagland*[123] Parker LJ referred to a distinction between 'mandatory' and 'non-mandatory' terms of the contract of employment in the following terms:

> So far as mandatory terms are concerned... [t]here may be a case where there is, for example, no provision as to the length of notice. In such a case the Tribunal would in my view have power to conclude that there must be reasonable notice. It may also have power to decide, as would a court of law, the length of such notice, which would be a question of fact. But I do not consider that even in mandatory cases the Tribunal have power to impose on parties terms which have not been agreed.

The meaning of the phrase 'mandatory term' is not immediately obvious. The only terms which the Act requires the statement to contain are, as we have just seen, those relating to certain aspects of disciplinary and grievance procedures under section 3(1)(b). If it is meant to refer to the statutory minimum period of notice which is imposed upon the parties by statute,[124] this should arguably be notified to the employee by virtue of section 1(3)(e) of the Act, regardless of agreement. One possible interpretation of Parker LJ's remarks is that the employment tribunal has the duty, under a section 11 application, to seek to clarify the nature of those implied terms which are 'necessary legal incidents' of the contract. But what these might be – other than the inevitably diffuse implied obligations such as those of obedience, co-operation and care – is unclear. They could be said to include matters such as the identity of the parties and the rate or method of calculating pay, since it is difficult to envisage there being a contract of employment which did not contain *some* terms on these matters.

4.23   The failure of the Act to impose any general normative effect is easier to understand, if not necessarily to justify, by bearing in mind that the regulatory framework for terms and conditions of employment was far more comprehensive at the time of the Act's inception than it is today. When the Contracts of Employment Act 1963 was enacted, the vast majority of employees were protected either by the minimum terms set by sector-level collective agreements or by the

---

119 [1992] IRLR 323, 326. The statement made by Stephenson LJ in *Mears v Safecar Security Ltd* [1982] IRLR 183, 191, to the effect that s 11 requires the tribunal to 'find the specified terms, and in the last resort invent them for the purposes of literally writing them into the contract', was expressly disapproved.
120 [1993] IRLR 400.
121 ERA 1996, s 1(4)(d)(i).
122 [1993] IRLR 400, 402 (Rose LJ). On the right to paid annual leave under WTR 1998, see para 4.76.
123 [1992] IRLR 323, 326.
124 ERA 1996, s 86.

legally-binding provisions of statutory wages orders, in each case incorporated into individual contracts of employment. The statutory notification requirements were therefore underpinned by substantive rights in the case of most employees and they, in turn, contributed to the effectiveness of those rights in practice. Research carried out in the 1970s showed that the practice of issuing written statements became widespread following the passage of the 1963 Act, and that although there was in many cases some confusion between the statements issued by employers and the normative terms laid down by collective agreements, there was also a greater awareness on the part of individual employees of their contractual rights than there had been prior to the passage of the 1963 Act.[125]

Since this research was undertaken, the obligations upon employers to adopt the minimum terms of sector-level collective agreements have been abolished and the coverage of collective bargaining has been reduced to less than 40% of the employed labour force.[126] It is possible, then, that in respect of employment which is no longer protected by a floor of rights, there will *not* be any terms relating to such issues as hours of work, holidays, incapacity, pension benefits and disciplinary procedures, since these are not necessarily matters which the contract of employment is obliged by statute to provide for, either directly or by reference to a collective agreement.[127] This lack of an effective floor of minimum terms and conditions considerably limits the scope, in practice, of the employer's obligations under section 1, although to some extent the situation has now been ameliorated by the enactment of basic labour standards legislation in relation to minimum wages and maximum working hours.[128] There may also be an irreducible minimum of information concerning the 'necessarily legal incidents' of the contract, in the sense identified above.[129] But there is evidence to suggest that in workplaces without an effective trade union presence, employees are less likely to receive written statements or may receive documents whose status (contract or statement) is highly ambiguous, thanks in part to employers' ignorance of the law but also to the lack of an effective sanction for its breach.[130]

EC Directive 91/533 is differently worded from the equivalent provisions of ERA 1996. Article 2 of the Directive states that 'an employer shall be obliged to notify an employee to whom this Directive applies ... of the essential aspects of the contract or employment relationship'. These 'essential aspects' are then stated to 'cover at least' a number of listed matters which include, for example, 'the amount of paid leave to which the employee is entitled or, where this cannot be indicated when the information is given, the procedures for allocating and determining such leave',[131] and 'the length of the employee's normal working

---

125 Leighton and Dunville, 1977.
126 See generally W Brown *et al*, 2000.
127 Moreover, EA 2002, s 30, stipulating that the statutory disciplinary procedures provided for by that Act should take effect as terms in all contracts of employment, is not yet in force, and perhaps may never be (for the reasons discussed in paras 5.19 and 5.143 below).
128 See paras 4.41–4.47, on the minimum wage, and 4.71–4.79, on working time. It would seem to follow from the decision of the High Court in *Barber v RJB Mining Ltd* [1999] IRLR 308, holding that working time limits laid down in WTR 1998, reg 4(1) formed part of the contracts of employment of workers covered by the Regulations, that the employer is obliged to include details of these working time limits in the written statement issued under ERA 1996, s 1.
129 See above, para 4.7.
130 Empirical studies addressing the recent operation of the written statement law include NACAB, 1990 (see Clark and Hall, 1992: p 116); Deakin, 1999; W Brown *et al*, 2000.
131 Directive 91/533, Art 2(2)(f).

day or week'.[132] Since the language used here is unqualified, and there is no reference to an obligation to inform the employee of the *absence* of particulars on any point, the Directive could be read as requiring the employer to provide for particulars on the matters which make up the 'essential aspects' of the employment relationship. This interpretation is strengthened by the sixth recital to the Directive, which refers to point 9 of the Community Charter of Fundamental Social Rights for Workers under which '[t]he conditions of employment of every worker of the European Community shall be stipulated in laws, a collective agreement or a contract of employment, according to arrangements applying in each country'. On the other hand, Article 6 of the Directive states that '[t]his Directive shall be without prejudice to national law and practice concerning the form of the contract or employment relationship, proof as regards the existence and content of a contract or employment relationship, [and] the relevant procedural rules'. This can be read as preserving the pre-existing position of British labour law, namely that sections 1 to 4 of the Act do not create an obligation to inform the employee of particulars which have no independent contractual (or other) existence, although the point is far from clear.

Distinguishing contract and statement

4.24   Even if, in principle, contract and statement are conceptually discrete, in practice one or both of the parties may regard the statement as being equivalent to a contract in both form and effect. Particular difficulty arises from the practice of employers of issuing statements which either purport to be contracts in their own right or which depart in some respect or other from the entitlements which are meant to vest in employees by virtue of incorporation from a collective agreement or some other external source.[133] Since the written statement is merely *declaratory* of the contract terms, it cannot prevail over terms which are expressly or impliedly agreed by the parties, including those which are incorporated from a collective agreement. On the face of it, the statement is only the employer's view of the contract's contents. Although it may be *evidence* of what the parties have agreed, and to this extent may need to be considered alongside other factors, such as their conduct, in construing the agreement, there is a presumption that it cannot be relied on by the employer to derogate from what would otherwise be clear contractual entitlements of the employee: this can only be done if there is clear evidence that the statement represents the contractual intentions of both parties.

An early decision which suggested that the statement might readily be accorded normative effect as an offer of contract terms was *Gascol Conversions Ltd v Mercer*.[134] The employer sent each of its existing employees a document which purported to discharge its obligations to issue a written statement under the IRA 1971 (a predecessor of ERA 1996, section 1), but which was headed 'contract of employment'. The applicant signed and returned to the employer a form which stated: 'I confirm receipt of a new contract of employment ... which sets out as required under the Industrial Relations Act 1971 the terms and conditions of my employment'. The Court of Appeal held that the document constituted an offer of a new contract, which the employee accepted by returning the signed form.

---

132 Directive 91/533, Art 2(2)(i).
133 Empirical research suggests that both of these have been widespread practices since the enactment of the legislation. See Leighton and Dunville, 1977; W Brown *et al*, 1998; Deakin, 1999.
134 [1974] ICR 420.

Since the contract was in writing, there was a presumption against according contractual force to any other terms which might have been expressed orally or implied by conduct. The employee's acceptance of the statement had amounted to a variation of the original contract terms.

The difficulty in the reasoning in *Mercer* is that a document which purports to discharge the employer's statutory obligations is meant to be a statement of the *existing* contract terms; it cannot, logically, be at the same time an offer of *new* terms. This means that 'in the absence of an acknowledgement by the parties that the statement is itself a contract and that the terms are correct, such as that contained in the *Mercer* case, the statutory statement does not itself constitute a contract in writing'.[135] Short of such acknowledgement, the employee cannot be taken to have agreed to a contractual variation; merely carrying on working will not suffice. Moreover, in attempting to introduce new or different terms by means of the written statement the employer will be in breach of its statutory obligations under section 1, and this makes it difficult to argue that the employee is estopped from denying that the contract has been varied: the employer will not be allowed to set up his own legal wrong as the basis for such an estoppel.[136]

Although later decisions have distinguished *Mercer* without actually overruling it, the present position is that an employer will not easily be able to present the statement as evidence of those terms which derogate from the terms which would otherwise apply. Far from being equivalent to the contract, under these circumstances the statement is 'not even conclusive evidence of the contract'.[137]

Where, conversely, the statement favours the employee, it has been held to represent 'strong prima facie evidence' of the contract terms. The written particulars 'place a heavy burden on the employer to show that the actual terms of contract are different from those which he has set out in the statutory statement'.[138] This 'heavy burden' does not apply to the employee who wishes to show that the contract terms are different from those in the statement.[139]

In effect, then, the statement is strong evidence in the employee's favour, but weak evidence in favour of the employer. This is appropriate, given that statute has placed the duty of clarifying the contract terms clearly on the employer, without, however, seeking to undermine the effectiveness of terms incorporated from collective agreements or other external sources for the protection and regulation of terms and conditions of employment.[140] Nevertheless, what has just been said does not amount to saying that the employer is conclusively bound by the contents of the written statement; nor does it have the effect of reversing the burden of proof which would normally fall on the employee as applicant or claimant if he or she is seeking to establish the existence of a

---

135 *System Floors Ltd v Daniel* [1982] ICR 54, 58. See also *Glendale Managed Services v Graham* [2003] IRLR 465, at para 5: 'written particulars of employment supplied by an employer in performance of its statutory duty do not normally constitute the contract of employment itself, but are simply evidence of the terms of the contract and not conclusive evidence' (Keene LJ).

136 *Robertson v British Gas Corpn* [1983] ICR 351, 355 (Ackner LJ). On variation generally, see below, paras 4.34–4.39.

137 *Turiff Construction Ltd v Bryant* (1967) 2 KIR 659.

138 *System Floors (UK) Ltd v Daniel* [1982] ICR 54, 58 (Browne-Wilkinson J).

139 The Court of Appeal has rejected an argument that 'an equally heavy burden rests on the employee': *Robertson v British Gas Corpn* [1983] ICR 351, 355 (Ackner LJ).

140 What has been said in the text about the effect of s 1 statements also applies to statements of changes to particulars under s 4: this is discussed in the context of the variation of contract terms at para 4.35 below.

contract term on a particular matter. Hence, in interpreting the equivalent provisions of Directive 91/533, the ECJ has held that:

> ... the notification referred to in Article 2(1) of the Directive, in so far as it informs an employee of the essential aspects of the contract or employment relationship and, in particular, of the points listed in Article 2(2)(c), enjoys the same presumption as to its correctness as would attach, in domestic law, to any similar document drawn up by the employer and communicated to the employee. The employer must none the less be allowed to bring any evidence to the contrary, by showing that the information in the notification is either inherently incorrect or has been shown to be so in fact.[141]

CONSTRUCTION, INCORPORATION AND VARIATION OF TERMS

4.25 Subject to what has just been said about the very slight normative effect of sections 1–4 of ERA 1996,[142] the terms of the contract will be determined by techniques of construction derived from the common law. Construing an employment contract is not necessarily straightforward, however, and the approach taken to construing commercial agreements may be of little help or even positively misleading.[143] There may be a formal offer of employment contained in a written document to which the employee is invited to assent, but even then it would be unusual for the document to constitute an *exhaustive* account of the contract terms. It would be usual for some terms, at least, to be implied or incorporated by reference to one of a number of external sources, such as a collective agreement or company handbook. The manner in which the contract is performed is also an important guide to its contents. In principle, the substance of a contract, once made, cannot be modified merely by the parties' subsequent behaviour; contractual obligations can only be varied by mutual agreement. This is to assume, however, that the substance of the original agreement is completely clear; and this will rarely be the case with contracts of employment. Two forms of practice, in particular, will be important in construing the agreement: the 'custom and practice' of the plant or establishment, which the parties may (not must) be assumed to have had in mind when they contracted; and their own conduct subsequent to the agreement, which may be taken to be a guide to what they initially intended.[144]

Incorporation of terms from collective agreements

4.26 Labour law has played a negligible role in regulating and enforcing collective agreements between trade unions and employers. Section 4 of the Trade Union Act 1871, which denied contractual force to agreements between trade unions, also had this effect with relation to sector-level collective

---

141 Joined Cases C-253/96 to C-258/96: *Kampelmann v Landschaftsverband Westfalen-Lippe* [1998] IRLR 333, 342 (see also the opinion of Tesauro AG, [1998] IRLR 333, 337); see also Case C-350/99 *Lange v Georg Schünemann GmbH* [2001] IRLR 244 making, in this respect, much the same point.

142 See para 4.22 above.

143 On the need for a flexible approach to the construction of employment contracts, see the judgment of Lord Hoffmann in *Carmichael v National Power plc* [2000] IRLR 43.

144 See *Dunlop Tyres Ltd v Blows* [2001] IRLR 629.

agreements, since an employers' association was deemed to be a 'trade union' for the purpose of that Act.[145] At common law, agreements between a trade union and a single employer were thought to lack contractual force on the twin grounds of uncertainty and the absence of any intention to create legal relations.[146] There is now a statutory presumption that a collective agreement is 'not to have been intended by the parties to be a legally enforceable contract'. This presumption is displaced if the agreement is in writing and contains a provision stating that the parties do intend it to have legal effect, whereupon it is conclusively presumed to be a legally binding contract. Agreements made binding in this way are very rare.[147] However, the non-enforceability of the vast majority of agreements at the collective level does not affect their enforceability as terms of the individual contract of employment.[148] This 'normative' or term-setting function of the collective agreement, as distinct from its 'contractual' function of regulating the relationship of the collective parties, finds legal expression through the incorporation of terms into individual contracts.

In most mainland European systems, legislation lays down rules for the circumstances in which the normative terms of collective agreements take effect, regulating the sectoral scope and level of their application, the extent to which they apply to non-union members and their temporal effect in the case of the lapse or termination of relations between the collective parties. Where the employer is a member of the relevant employers' association for the industry, the effect of a sector-level agreement is generally both *automatic*, in the sense that the terms apply immediately to all contracts of employment whether or not previously agreed by the individual parties, and *compulsory*, in the sense of laying down minimum rights which cannot be derogated from by individual contract. In France, Article L 135-2 of the Labour Code provides that 'where an employer is bound by the terms of a [relevant collective agreement], these terms take effect in the contracts of employment to which he is a party, unless more advantageous terms apply'.[149] The employee cannot waive his or her minimum entitlements under the terms of the collective agreement, and the collective terms are substituted for the individual ones where the latter provide inferior benefits. The effect of the collective agreement does not depend upon incorporation via the individual contract, but upon its own 'regulatory nature', which is similar to that of legislation.[150] Nor is the trade-union status of the employee relevant: the normative terms apply whether or not he or she is a member of any or a particular trade union. A broadly similar approach is taken in Germany, under the terms of the Collective Agreements Act.[151] In both systems, provision is made for the *extension* of sectoral agreements to cover non-associated employers, in this way ensuring that minimum norms are respected throughout a given industry.[152]

---

145 TUA 1871, s 4(4). The Act was repealed by the IRA 1971.
146 Kahn-Freund, 1959; *Ford Motor Co Ltd v AUEFW* [1969] 2 QB 303.
147 TULRCA 1992, s 179(1)–(2). See below, para 9.26.
148 *Marley v Forward Trust Group* [1986] ICR 891.
149 'Lorsqu'un employeur est lié par les clauses d'une convention ou d'un accord collectif du travail, ces clauses s'appliquent aux contrats conclus avec lui, sauf dispositions plus favorables'.
150 See Pelissier, Supiot and Jeammaud, 2004: p 917 *et seq.*
151 German Collective Agreements Act 1949, Art 2. Non-union members are not automatically covered by all normative terms; see Weiss, 1992: p 9; Wedderburn, 1992c: p 246.
152 French Labour Code, Art L 133-8; German Collective Agreements Act, Art 5. See Weiss, 1992: p 23.

The civil law technique of according collective bargaining regulatory effect over the contract of employment may be contrasted with the approach taken in the North American systems, where plant or company-level collective agreements come close to displacing the individual contract of employment altogether. In the United States, where an employer comes under a duty to bargain with a certified bargaining agent of the workforce, the resulting collective agreement is seen as exhaustively defining the mutual rights and obligations of the parties with regard to terms and conditions of employment. Neither derogation from nor improvement upon terms is allowed, since 'the very purpose of providing by statute for the collective agreement is to supersede the terms of separate agreements by employees with terms which reflect the strength and bargaining power and welfare of the group'.[153] In Canada it has been said that 'the common law as it applies to individual contracts of employment is no longer relevant to employer-employee relationships governed by a collective agreement which ... deals with discharge, termination of employment, severance pay and a host of other matters that have been negotiated between union and company as the principal parties thereto'.[154]

At no point has general legislation in the United Kingdom provided for automatic and compulsory effect to be granted to the normative terms of sector-level collective agreements.[155] The closest British labour law has come to this is the Conditions of Employment and National Arbitration Order of 1940 (Order 1305), which established compulsory unilateral arbitration on terms and conditions as a *quid pro quo* for banning strikes and lock-outs. This made 'recognised terms and conditions', defined as terms deriving from agreements 'between organisations of employers and trade unions representative respectively of substantial proportions of the employers and workers engaged in that trade or industry in that district', generally binding, in the sense that 'all employers in the trade or industry in that district shall observe the recognised terms and conditions or such terms and conditions of employment as are not less favourable than the recognised terms and conditions'.[156] Failure to observe the recognised terms was a criminal offence and the trade union or employers' association in question had the standing to seek arbitration before the National Arbitration Tribunal, which had the power to make an award implying the relevant terms and conditions into the individual contracts of the employees affected. This procedure was continued in force after the end of World War Two, although, from 1951, without criminal sanctions,[157] and was later merged with the principle of enforcement of the 'general level' of terms and conditions in a given trade, in Schedule 11 of the EPA 1975.[158]

Order 1305 and its successors differed from the mainland European pattern of regulation in two important respects. First, its effect was not automatic. The making of an agreement did not, in itself, confer rights on employees; they acquired the protection of the minimum terms only after an arbitral award had

---

153 *JI Case Co v NLRB* 321 US 332, 338 (1943) (Jackson J).
154 *McGavin Toastmasters Inc v Ainscough* [1976] 1 SC 718, 725 (Laskin CJ).
155 This was done, exceptionally, for certain categories of public sector employment (National Health Service Act 1977, Sch 5, para 10(1) and SI 1974/296).
156 SR & O 1940/1305, reg 5(1); Wages Councils Act 1945, s 19 and Sch 3, para 1(1).
157 Cf the Industrial Disputes Order, SI 1951/1376; Terms and Conditions of Employment Act 1959, s 8.
158 The 'general level' principle referred to the level observed in practice, as distinct from that laid down by agreement. See P Davies and M Freedland, 1984: pp 159–163.

been made by the relevant tribunal.[159] Nor did employees have standing to seek such an award. Second, it did not take the form of an *extension* procedure which was specific to the non-federated firms. The same arbitration procedure applied to *all* employers in the trade, whether they were federated or not. Schedule 11 of the EPA 1975 was repealed in 1980 on the grounds that it had an inflationary effect on pay claims, as well as being part of the Conservative government's rolling programme of labour market deregulation.[160]

In the absence of statutory regulation the issue of incorporation is dealt with by the common law, which knows no principle of automatic and compulsory effect.[161] The legal basis for the normative effect of the collective agreement must rest at the level of the individual contract of employment, because the collective agreement lacks the 'regulatory effect' or force of law accorded to it in other systems. A number of conceptual explanations for incorporation have been offered.

Agency

4.27 One possibility is that the trade union, through one or more of its officials, negotiates with the employer as agent for each individual union member as principal, with the resulting terms forming part of the contract of employment without the need for further agreement. This has been put forward as the most likely explanation in a small number of cases.[162] As a general explanation, though, it is unconvincing. It is unable to account for the incorporation of terms into the contracts of employment of non-members, for example; nor does it deal with the position of employees who either join the employment or, conceivably, the union, after the collective agreement has been concluded. It would also suggest that an individual member can unilaterally revoke his or her authority to the union to negotiate on their behalf, and in this way avoid the normative effect of the collective agreement completely. This is unlikely to reflect the intention of either the trade union or the employer. From the union's point of view, it would be undesirable to allow the effect of the collective agreement to be fragmented by enabling non-unionists to opt out. For the employer, collective bargaining is a way of avoiding the high transaction costs involved in treating union members and non-members differently and being required to negotiate individually with those who are outside the union. In *practice*, terms and conditions of employment are normally applied uniformly, to members and non-members alike. To differentiate between these two groups may, depending on the employer's purpose, give rise to a breach of the anti-discrimination provisions of TULRCA 1992.[163]

These points notwithstanding, there is no reason in principle why an agency agreement should not be made between a trade union and an individual member (or, for that matter, between an individual employee and another organisation which undertakes to negotiate on his or her behalf), nor is there any obstacle to an employer negotiating with a trade union on the basis that the final terms will

---

159 *Hulland v William Saunders & Son* [1945] KB 78.
160 See above, para 1.24.
161 *Dudfield v Ministry of Works* (1964) 108 Sol Jo 118.
162 *Holland v London Society of Compositors* (1924) 40 TLR 440; *Edwards v Skyways* [1964] 1 WLR 349; *Singh v British Steel Corpn* [1974] IRLR 131; *Harris v Richard Lawson Autologistics Ltd* [2002] IRLR 476.
163 See further, para 8.13 *et seq*.

take effect in individual contracts of employment via such agency. However, there would have to be clear evidence that these were the intentions of the parties concerned. The mere existence of the contract of membership between union and member does not authorise the former to act as agent for the latter;[164] something more specific is needed.[165]

The 'bridge' term

4.28 The most generally accepted basis for incorporation is that it takes place through a 'bridging term' in the contract of employment.[166] The principal function of the 'bridge' is to identify the external source from which the terms of the contract are to be drawn, but it may also perform other functions: it may determine which terms are appropriate for incorporation and resolve conflicts between different sources. Once it is present, incorporation may take effect automatically in the senses that no further authorisation or agreement by either party to the contract of employment is needed, although this will depend to a large degree on practice in the workplace in question.[167]

A bridging term could be expressly agreed by the parties.[168] It is more likely that any express reference will today be found in the written statement of terms and conditions.[169] The written statement is not, as we have seen, the same thing as the contract, but it is evidence of it; hence, a reference to the normative effect of a collective agreement can be regarded as significant evidence of a term which was either previously expressed by the parties or tacitly accepted by them. The chances of finding such a reference have strengthened as a result of the amendments made to section 1 of EPCA 1978 (now section 1 of ERA 1996) in 1993, introducing for the first time the obligation to include details of 'any collective agreements which directly affect the terms and conditions of the employment'.[170]

If there is no express bridging term one may be implied by using the normal common law tests, but its existence cannot be assumed simply from the presence of the collective agreement. A term may be implied on the basis of custom and practice, if it is the regular practice in the plant or establishment in question to observe the terms of a particular agreement.[171] A more modern way of achieving this result is to use the 'incidents of employment' test. A bridging term may be 'imposed by law as a necessary incident of the contract, without which that contract would be inefficacious, absurd or futile'.[172] If this approach is taken, it may not matter that the employee had no specific knowledge of the collective

---

164 *Boxfoldia Ltd v NGA (1982)* [1988] ICR 752: a union has no implied authority to terminate the employment contracts of its members by giving strike notice to their employer.
165 See *Burton Group v Smith* [1977] IRLR 351; *Lee v GEC Plessey Telecommunications Ltd* [1993] IRLR 383, 391. It is not clear what this more specific element might have been in *Harris v Richard Lawson Autologistics Ltd* [2002] IRLR 476.
166 Hepple, 1983: p 402.
167 See *Glendale Managed Services v Graham* [2003] IRLR 465.
168 *National Coal Board v Galley* [1958] 1 WLR 16.
169 For an example, see *Edinburgh Council v Brown* [1999] IRLR 208.
170 EPCA 1978, s 1(3)(j), now contained in ERA 1996, s 1(4)(j).
171 *MacLea v Essex Line Ltd* (1933) 45 Ll L Rep 254; *Henry v London General Transport Services Ltd* [2002] IRLR 472; *Tees and Hartlepool Port Authority v Bosomworth*, EAT, 10 July 2003, Appeal No EAT/0728/02/SM.
172 *Tadd v Eastwood and the Daily Telegraph Ltd* [1983] IRLR 320, 327.

agreement in question:[173] the implication is based not so much on his or her tacit consent and understanding, as on the need for the contract to reflect the reality of the parties' relationship. The 'legal incidents' test therefore brings the common law closer to the civilian model of regulation and further away from a consensual model of contract.

This approach may be applied not simply to a plant or company-level agreement but also to one at sector level. In *Howman & Son Ltd v Blyth*[174] the EAT implied a right to sick pay on the basis that 'the relationship between the parties requires that there should be some agreed term which has not in fact been agreed but both parties would have agreed what that term would be if they had been asked'. The fact that sick pay was regularly paid in the *industry* in question was thought to be relevant: 'in an industry where the normal practice is to provide sick pay for a limited period only, the reasonable term to imply is the term normally applicable in that industry'.[175] Here, a term was implied from industry-wide practice without the need even for a 'bridge' as such. This is to stretch the language of contract to the limit: 'the latitude which is asserted is ... a latitude to engage in judicial legislation about the terms of the contract of employment'.[176] In effect, the EAT found a common law route to the insertion into contracts of the 'general level' of protection in an industry, to replace the statutory mechanism which previously had this effect under Schedule 11 of the EPA 1975. This case illustrates the inherent flexibility and wide applicability of these common law techniques.

Appropriateness of terms for incorporation

4.29   A major limitation on the normative effect of collective agreements is the doctrine of the *appropriateness* of terms for incorporation.[177] Terms intended to regulate the employment of one group of employees will not be incorporated into the contracts of others.[178] It may also be that certain terms are intended to be part of the 'contractual' function of the agreement which governs the collective relationship between employer and trade union, as opposed to regulating the terms and conditions of employees. This question could be dealt with expressly, either in the individual contract or in the collective agreement. Express terms in the collective agreement can take effect in the individual contract via the bridging term. More often, the bridging term will be silent on the matter. Difficulty arises, in particular, if a term which is collective in nature is also capable of conferring rights or imposing obligations upon an individual employee.

One possible basis for addressing the issue of appropriateness is to distinguish between terms which are procedural in nature and those which are substantive. Substantive terms, laying down entitlements in relation to pay, working time and other benefits, are normally incorporated into contracts of employment without difficulty. The terms of a collective agreement concerning employees' entitlements to severance pay would be incorporated into their individual contracts, for example.[179] By extension, an employment opportunities policy,

---

173   Cf the discussion of Hepple, 1981b: p 128.
174   [1983] ICR 416.
175   [1983] ICR 416, 420 (Browne-Wilkinson J).
176   P Davies and M Freedland, 1984: p 306.
177   *Young v Canadian Northern Rly Co* [1931] AC 83; *Burroughs Machines Ltd v Timmoney* [1977] IRLR 404.
178   Hepple, 1981b: p 129.
179   *Lee v GEC Plessey Telecommunications Ltd* [1993] IRLR 383.

stating that employees were not to be discriminated against on a number of grounds including age, was held to be suitable for incorporation by the House of Lords in *Taylor v Secretary of State for Scotland*.[180] By contrast, a 'no compulsory redundancy' agreement was held by the Court of Appeal to be inappropriate for incorporation in *Kaur v MG Rover Group Ltd*, on the grounds that it reflected 'an aspiration rather than a binding contractual term'.[181] While all these decisions turn, in the end, on their own facts, *Kaur* is difficult to reconcile with the previous case law on the incorporation of substantive terms.

Procedural clauses have often been regarded as inappropriate for incorporation. In *British Leyland (UK) Ltd v McQuilken*[182] a collective agreement provided that the employer would interview employees in order to establish whether they wished to take up an option of retraining or accept redundancy. This was held to be 'a long-term plan, dealing with policy rather than the rights of individual employees under their contracts of employment'.[183] In *Alexander v Standard Telephones and Cables Ltd (No 2)*[184] a last-in, first-out agreement, according to which employees would be selected for redundancy according to their length of service with the employer, was also deemed inappropriate for incorporation. As a general guide, this would seem to be highly questionable: the seniority acquired by an individual employee can be seen as an important feature of his or her overall contractual package. In *Alexander v Standard Telephones and Cables Ltd*,[185] Aldous J, considering an application for an injunction which he rejected on separate grounds, was prepared to incorporate the last-in, first-out agreement on the basis that it was 'designed and intended to benefit' individual employees in proportion to their length of service. This approach seems to be preferable to that of drawing a sharp distinction between procedural and substantive terms. In general, 'it may be a mistake to assume that a provision which is procedural in nature necessarily has no impact on the position of individual employees, and therefore wrong to assume that all such provision should be excluded from incorporation'.[186] Many apparently 'procedural' terms are capable of benefiting employees, and there is no reason in principle why terms relating to disciplinary procedures, for example, should not be incorporated into individual contracts since they are capable of conferring important protections upon employees.[187] Similarly, in *Adams v British Airways plc*[188] the Court of Appeal seems to have had little difficulty in accepting that provisions governing seniority rights were appropriate for incorporation into individual contracts of employment.

The decision of the Court of Appeal in *Camden Exhibition and Display Ltd v Lynott*[189] illustrates the problems which may arise from deciding the issue of

---

180 [2000] IRLR 502.
181 [2005] IRLR 40, at para 32 (Keene LJ).
182 [1978] IRLR 245.
183 [1978] IRLR 245, 246 (Lord McDonald).
184 [1991] IRLR 286.
185 [1990] ICR 291, 303; to similar effect is *Anderson v Pringle of Scotland Ltd* [1998] IRLR 64, in which the Outer House of the Court of Session not only held that a 'first-in, last-out' clause was incorporated into the employee's contract of employment, but granted an interim interdict to restrain his dismissal in breach of that provision. See further para 5.61.
186 Auerbach, 1993: p 18.
187 Much of the recent case law of the effect of disciplinary procedures on contractual rights and remedies assumes that they are capable of being incorporated in this way. See below, paras 5.53–5.60
188 [1996] IRLR 574.
189 [1966] 1 QB 555.

incorporation according to whether a term is procedural or substantive in nature. The Court held by a majority that the following term of a national level collective agreement was incorporated into individual contracts of employment: 'overtime required to ensure the due and proper performance of contracts shall not be subject to restriction, but may be worked by mutual agreement and direct arrangement between the employer and the operatives concerned'. The majority construed this as imposing a substantive obligation on the individual employees not to take any action to restrict overtime, such as an overtime ban.[190] This appears to have been a misreading of a term whose intention was to regulate the relationship between the national collective agreement and agreements at company or plant level: the amount of overtime was to be agreed at plant level, without restriction by the national agreement.[191] The essential point, however, was not so much that the term was procedural, as that it was intended to regulate the collective relationship and not that of the individual parties, which was to be free from any national-level 'restriction'.

'No legal effect' clauses

4.30   Related to the issue of appropriateness is the question of how far the employer can avoid incorporation by denying that the norms in question were intended to have legal effect at the individual level. A statement in a collective agreement that the terms are intended to be 'binding in honour only' is likely to be interpreted as referring only to the collective relationship. It was common in the early 1970s to place TINALEA clauses in collective agreements ('this is not a legally enforceable agreement'), since at that time it was necessary to do so in order to avoid giving them legal effect as contracts under the provisions of the IRA 1971. Now the presumption is reversed, and clear words are necessary to create, rather than to exclude, legal effect.[192] It is conceivable that collective agreements may still contain TINALEA clauses, however, either through inertia or to make the parties' intentions completely clear. There is no reason to infer from such a clause that the collective parties did not intend the normative terms to have effect in individual contracts of employment.[193]

Conflicts between levels of bargaining

4.31   An issue which the courts have not addressed satisfactorily is that of conflicts between different levels of collective bargaining. If the floor of rights character of regulation is taken into account, resolving these conflicts should not be too problematic: sectoral agreements would be regarded as providing the basic floor on which company or plant-level agreements are permitted to build, but from which they may not derogate.[194] Unfortunately, the matter cannot be approached so straightforwardly. There is no legislative guidance on the issue of derogation from sectoral agreements, following the repeal of Schedule 11 of the EPA 1975. The question falls to be decided at common law as usual,

---

190   As such, it would now be subject to the specific rules governing the incorporation of no-strike clauses into contracts of employment under TULRCA 1992, s 180: see below, para 11.66.

191   [1966] 1 QB 555, per Russell LJ, dissenting.

192   TULRCA 1992, s 179; see below, para 9.26.

193   *Marley v Forward Trust Group* [1986] ICR 891. See also the discussion of 'no legal effect' clauses in the context of employer handbooks in para 4.33 below.

194   Cf French Labour Code, Art L 132-13.

and will be determined by the scope of any express or implied bridging term. If an express term deals clearly with the conflict of levels, there is no difficulty; such a term might be incorporated by reference to one of the relevant collective agreements.[195] If the court, on the other hand, has to operate on the basis of an implied bridging term or one which is silent on this question, the matter is much less clear. No obvious principle emerges from the few cases in which it has been addressed, except to say that the courts have evidently not been guided by the argument that sectoral agreements should be viewed, at least presumptively, as providing a non-derogable floor of rights. In one case, a local agreement providing for inferior benefits was given priority, apparently because it was agreed later in time than the sectoral agreement.[196] In other cases, sectoral agreements setting lower basic working hours prevailed over local agreements providing for longer hours (and hence higher levels of weekly pay).[197] The courts appear to have been worried about the fragmentation of national level agreements,[198] but this is to misunderstand the function of the local agreement in building on the basic floor set nationally. With the decline of national level bargaining in many sectors, the issue has lost some of its urgency.

Custom and practice

4.32 Collective agreements are a relatively formal, documentary source of norms governing pay, working hours and similar incidents of employment. Terms may also be incorporated by reference to the less formal 'custom and practice' of the plant or workplace or to a 'trade usage'. This will only be the case, however, if it can be shown that the parties implicitly contracted on the assumption that these informal norms would apply. Custom and practice has been defined as 'those transactional rules of job regulation which arise, not from any explicit and formal negotiation, but from a process whereby managerial error or omission establishes a practice which workers see as legitimate to defend'.[199] Examples are as numerous as the practices of particular plants, but a typical illustration from a period when managements were weaker than they are now was the right of engineering piece workers to boycott jobs which could not earn them a satisfactory wage.[200] Custom and practice may also take a form which favours management, such as an alleged implied right of lay off.[201] Whether unwritten practices of this sort should be accorded contractual recognition is doubtful. The importance of custom and practice is less than it was, thanks in part to the very formalisation of contract terms and conditions which employment protection legislation, and in particular the introduction of the statutory written statement, has encouraged.

In principle, a custom can only be incorporated into a contract of employment if it is 'reasonable, certain and notorious'.[202] That this is a more

---

195 Eg, *Barrett v National Coal Board* [1978] ICR 1101.
196 *Clift v West Riding County Council* (1964) Times, 10 April.
197 *Loman and Henderson v Merseyside Transport Services Ltd* (1968) 3 ITR 108; *Gascol Conversions Ltd v Mercer* [1974] ICR 420.
198 *Loman and Henderson v Merseyside Transport Services Ltd* (1968) 3 ITR 108, 112 (Lord Denning).
199 W Brown, 1972: p 61.
200 W Brown, 1973.
201 Cf *Bond and Neads v CAV Ltd* [1983] IRLR 360.
202 *Devonald v Rosser & Sons* [1906] 2 KB 728, 743 (Farwell LJ); *Sagar v H Ridehalgh & Son Ltd* [1930] 2 Ch 117, 133 (Farwell J); *Henry v London General Transport Services Ltd* [2002] IRLR 472.

restrictive test than normally applies to the implication of contract terms is justified by the informal nature of custom and practice. A court would not normally decline to imply a term simply on the grounds that it is not 'reasonable' to do so.[203] Certainty, in this context, means that the court can distil a clear and specific term from the practice in question, and notoriety means that the practice is widely known and observed in the plant or trade. It is not, apparently, necessary for the individual employee to know of the custom or practice, however. In *Sagar v H Ridehalgh & Son Ltd*[204] the employer claimed the benefit of a custom of 'making deductions for careless work [which] had been in existence for many years' in its mill. It was also argued that a majority of mills in the district observed a similar practice. The employee 'stated that at the time of his engagement he knew nothing of the system of fines or deductions, and that until much later he did not become aware that there was a system in vogue at the defendants' mill'. He claimed to be entitled to payment according to a list of prices agreed between his trade union and the employers' association of which the employer was a member, and which was posted up as a notice in the mill. Farwell J held against incorporation on the grounds that the usage was not sufficiently general (15% of the Lancashire mills did not observe it) and that 'the practice was not reasonable or certain, because it was precarious, depending on the will of the master'.[205] His decision was reversed by the Court of Appeal. Lawrence LJ, citing the employer's evidence that the practice had been in operation at the mill for over 30 years, held that 'it is clear that the claimant accepted employment in the defendants' mill on the same terms as the other weavers employed at that mill ... it is immaterial whether he knew of it or not, as I am satisfied that he accepted his employment on the same terms as to deductions for bad work as the other weavers at the mill'.[206] Nor was the usage either insufficiently general within the trade or unreasonable in the circumstances: 'the deductions are not arbitrary deductions at the will and pleasure of the employers; they are limited to cases where there has been bad work, and they are limited to an amount which does not exceed the actual or estimated damage or loss occasioned to the employer by the act or omission of the workman'.[207]

The same result would not necessarily be achieved today, thanks to the degree of formalisation now imposed upon the employment relationship by legislation. Contract terms of this kind, concerning the method of calculation of pay, should be included in the section 1 written statement.[208] The failure to refer to a term of this kind in the written statement does not have the effect of nullifying that term at common law. However, the absence of any reference to a particular custom or practice in the written statement may well be strong evidence that the parties did not regard it as having normative effect, at least in a case where the alleged term favours the employer.[209] For this reason, it may be said that the existence of the employer's duty to issue the written statement makes it more difficult to invoke custom and practice as a source of contract terms.

---

203 See above, para 4.6.
204 [1930] 2 Ch 117; revsd [1931] 1 Ch 310.
205 [1930] 2 Ch 117, 133.
206 [1931] 1 Ch 310, 336.
207 [1931] 1 Ch 310, 338.
208 ERA 1996, s 1(4)(a).
209 *System Floors (UK) Ltd v Daniel* [1982] ICR 54, discussed above, at para 4.24.

The greater formality of collective agreements has also had this effect. In *Bond v CAV Ltd*[210] an alleged implied right to lay off employees without pay was rejected on the grounds that the custom had been overtaken (and implicitly limited) by a national level collective agreement on guaranteed pay.

Works rules and company handbooks

4.33   As we saw above, works rules may not constitute terms of the contract if they are simply a codified form of instructions from the employer, which can be altered unilaterally as part of managerial prerogative.[211] Certain rules are too precise in their effect to be classified in this way, however; in particular, rules concerning discipline, hours of work or the method of calculating pay would normally be contract terms. The mere existence of such rules in a notice or handbook does not, however, confer upon them contractual effect. Their effect depends upon the same principles as we have just been examining: they must either be incorporated through a bridging term in the individual contract, or by way of analogy to custom and practice. A number of old authorities suggest that a notice posted in the workplace can form part of the contract, on the basis that the parties impliedly contracted subject to the general rules of the plant. It was considered irrelevant that the employee might be illiterate or never have read the notice, or even never have had it brought to his or her attention.[212] But these decisions must, again, be read subject to the statutory notification requirements of ERA 1996, section 1, in particular following the 1993 amendments. These limit the use which the employer may make of notices and other 'reference documents' in discharging the duty to issue the statutory written statement. Subject to only a few exceptions, the substance of any notice, and not just a reference to that notice, must be reproduced in the written statement which is issued to the employee.[213] If the statutory statement does not refer to the contents of the notice, this does not in itself deny them contractual effect; but it raises a rebuttable presumption against the employer that the parties did not intend them to form part of the contract of employment. To rebut such a presumption the employer would probably have to produce evidence that the employee was made aware both of the notice and of its contractual force, or alternatively that employees generally were aware of its existence and significance.

A company handbook which is given to individual employees on their appointment may serve as the written statement which the employer is required to issue under section 1 as well as a source of contractual terms and conditions in its own right. To satisfy section 1, however, it would have to be adapted to contain certain information which was specific to each employee, such as the date on which their employment began. If a company handbook is general in nature, the employer will not have satisfied section 1 by merely issuing that handbook together with a written statement which refers the employee to its

---

210   *Bond and Neads v CAV Ltd* [1983] IRLR 360.
211   See above, para 4.3; *Secretary of State for Employment v ASLEF (No 2)* [1972] 2 QB 455. See also *Wandsworth London Borough Council v D'Silva* [1998] IRLR 193: provisions in an employer's code of practice on staff sickness relating to the level at which absence would be reviewed were not contractually binding on the employer.
212   *Carus v Eastwood* (1875) 32 LT 855; *Petrie v MacFisheries Ltd* [1940] 1 KB 258.
213   See above, para 4.14.

contents. The written statement must itself contain the substance of those particulars which the Act requires to be issued in a 'single document'.[214]

An increasingly important issue with regard to handbooks is the legal meaning of statements denying that particular benefits or provisions are legally binding on the employer. It may be open to a court to regard the terms in question as non-enforceable on the grounds of a lack of intention to create legal relations.[215] If, however, the terms in practice constitute the normative basis for the parties' relationship in the sense of being regularly observed and understood to be binding, a court may treat as irrelevant a statement by the employer that they are not, and conclude that they have contractual effect. This is because it is for the court, and not for the parties alone, to construe the arrangements in question; and the test of whether contractual effect exists is an objective one.[216] In addition, as we have seen,[217] the employer will find it difficult in practice to contradict the contents of the section 1 written statement; thus if reference is made to a particular benefit in the written statement, there would be a strong presumption that the employer intended to be contractually bound by that provision.

It is also open to an employee to argue that a 'no legal effect' clause of this type is caught by section 3 of the Unfair Contract Terms Act 1977. After some hesitation, the courts are coming round to the view that this Act does apply to employment contracts. This is because the employee can, however artificially, be regarded as contracting as a 'consumer' within the meaning of section 12 of the Act.[218] However, even if UCTA applies to employment contracts, its usefulness as a device for regulating 'no legal effect' clauses is limited. This is because UCTA does not regulate unfair contract terms in general, but only exclusion or limitation clauses in the particular sense prescribed by that Act. For the purposes of section 3, this means terms which enable the employer either: 'when himself in breach of contract, [to] exclude or restrict any liability of his in respect of the breach'; to 'render a contractual performance substantially different from that which was reasonably expected of him'; or to render no performance at all.[219] In *Brigden v American Express Bank Ltd*[220] the High Court ruled that a clause under which the employer's disciplinary procedure did not apply to dismissals in the first two years of employment was not an exclusion clause within the meaning of the Act: the clause 'although expressed in negative terms, is a clause setting out the claimant's entitlement and the limits of his rights'.[221]

The short discussion of this issue in *Brigden* does not do justice to some of the complexities involved. Section 13 of the Act makes it clear that an exclusion

---

214 Cf ERA 1996, s 1(3)–(4), 2(4).
215 *Cadoux v Central Regional Council* [1986] IRLR 131; *Quinn v Calder Industrial Materials Ltd* [1996] IRLR 126.
216 See, in a different context, the judgment of Stuart-Smith LJ in *R v Lord Chancellor's Department, ex p Nangle* [1991] IRLR 343. Several decisions have arisen in which the courts have had to construe the terms of employer handbooks in connection with sickness and disability schemes: see *Briscoe v Lubrizol Ltd* [2002] IRLR 607; *Pioneer Technology (UK) Ltd v Jowitt* [2002] IRLR 190, [2003] IRLR 356; *Scottish Courage Ltd v Guthrie*, 5 February 2004, Appeal No UKEAT/0788/03/MAA.
217 See para 4.24 above.
218 See *Brigden v American Express Bank Ltd* [2000] IRLR 94, 95–96. The judge doubted whether the employer's standard terms and conditions of employment counted as 'written standard terms of business' under UCTA 1977 s 12 since their 'business was banking, not that of an employment agency'.
219 UCTA 1977, s 3(2).
220 [2000] IRLR 94.
221 [2000] IRLR 94, 96. See also *Peninsula Business Services Ltd v Sweeney* [2004] IRLR 49.

clause can include a term the effect of which is to narrow down 'primary' contractual obligations which, but for that term, would have arisen. The relevant clause in *Brigden,* which made a special exception for employees of less than two years' standing from the normal rule for the operation of disciplinary procedures, arguably falls into this category. The question of what an 'exclusion clause' is in this context cannot be answered by formal construction of the contract terms; it must also be undertaken by reference to the 'reasonable expectations' of both parties, in particular given the reference in section 3 to the performance which was 'reasonably expected' of the employer.[222] Now that the courts seem disposed to apply UCTA to employment contracts, this is one of the issues which could generate a significant body of case law on the principles to be applied by employers when drafting standard-form terms and conditions.

Variation of contract terms

4.34   The employer has no implied right unilaterally to vary the contract terms. This is so notwithstanding the existence of a category of 'prerogative' powers to determine the manner in which performance takes place through works rules and instructions which do not have contractual status. The express terms of the contract, by defining the scope of the employee's implied obligations of obedience, co-operation and care, also limit managerial prerogative; although every contract of employment must contain a certain irreducible element of co-operation, including an obligation not to obstruct the introduction of new technology or forms of work organisation,[223] this cannot be invoked to override terms and conditions on such matters as pay, hours and employee benefits which were clearly understood to be mutually binding.

An employer may nevertheless attempt to reserve for itself an express power to vary a particular term of the contract unilaterally. In *Wandsworth London Borough Council v D'Silva* the Court of Appeal stated, *obiter,* that 'clear language' would be required 'to reserve to one party an unusual power of this sort'.[224] The Court distinguished between 'contractual provisions with which [a] party was required to comply and those giving rights to employees';[225] only in the former case would a court be likely to favour a power of unilateral variation. However, the dividing-line between these categories of terms is obscure; the employer's obligation is the obverse of the employee's right.

An employer may also attempt to reserve to itself a wide power to insist on flexibility by including a wide mobility clause or job-classification clause in the employee's conditions of employment. Such a clause may overcome the absence of a general implied power to change the terms and conditions, but it should also be read subject to the implied, reciprocal duty of co-operation. Courts have been prepared to hold that certain rights under express mobility clauses must be exercised in good faith and in such a way not to undermine mutual trust and

---

222 See E Macdonald, 1992, discussing this point in the wider context of UCTA case law.
223 *Cresswell v Board of Inland Revenue* [1984] ICR 508; discussed below, para 4.90.
224 [1998] IRLR 193, 197, Lord Woolf MR. *Securities and Facilities Division v Hayes* [2001] IRLR 81 also stresses the need for an express term to justify variation of a contractual bonus scheme. From this perspective, *Airlie v City of Edinburgh District Council* [1996] IRLR 516, in which the EAT held that despite the lack of an express power for the employer to alter a bonus scheme in a wholesale and comprehensive way, the scheme as a whole could be construed to afford such a power, seems anomalous.
225 [1998] IRLR 193, 197.

confidence, so that, for example, an employee must be given adequate notice of a change of his or her place of work.[226] Although there is no implied requirement that an employer should always act reasonably, a court or tribunal 'may nevertheless be persuaded to intervene where the employer is exercising a discretionary right to impose change in a situation where the implications for the employee are particularly oppressive'.[227]

However, nearly all the terms of the contract of employment may be varied at any time by agreement between the individual parties, just like any other contract.[228] Legislation is capable of creating non-derogable rights (such as the right to statutory sick pay or the right to unfair dismissal) but until recently it did so, by and large, through non-contractual 'statutory impositions'. Minimum rates of pay, maximum hours of work, overtime and holiday entitlements now form part of a statutory floor of rights under NMWA 1998 and WTR 1998. However, above this floor, standards are provided by collective bargaining which has no statutory effect. We consider here how far terms which are not supported by legislation are vulnerable to employer pressure or to concessions via collective bargaining itself with which the individual employee may not agree.

Variation through the written statement of particulars of employment

4.35   A *first* possibility is that an employer attempts to vary agreed or incorporated contract terms by reference to the written statutory statement of terms. As we have already seen,[229] the written statement normally cannot be used in this way to derogate from the agreed terms. It has no contractual force in its own right and will not be regarded as strong evidence of the contract if its effect is to deprive the employee of vested contractual rights. Because it purports to be declaratory of the *existing* contract terms, a written statement will not normally be capable of being construed as an offer of *new* terms. This applies both to initial section 1 statements and to statements of changes issued under section 4. A section 4 statement which alters the particulars, without further oral discussion between the parties, 'cannot be compelling evidence of an express oral variation'.[230] Nor will an employee who continues to work without objection necessarily be taken to have consented to the variation. According to the EAT in *Jones v Associated Tunnelling Co Ltd*[231] a court should find a variation only 'with great caution', at least if the term has no 'immediate practical effect'. This is because 'it would be unrealistic of the law to require him to risk a confrontation with his employer on a matter which has no immediate practical

---

226 *United Bank Ltd v Akhtar* [1989] IRLR 507; on the implied duty of co-operation, see further para 4.86 below.

227 Auerbach, 1993: p 14. See also *Selectron Scotland Ltd v Roper* [2004] IRLR 4 where at para 27 Elias J doubted that a custom could ever vary existing contractual rights, and said that even if it could, it would require a very long established practice before it could be concluded that a party had accepted less favourable rights on this basis.

228 The one apparent exception to this principle arises in the case of certain variations carried out in connection with a transfer of an undertaking: see *Wilson v St. Helens BC/ British Fuels v Baxendale and Meade* [1998] IRLR 706, 715–716 (dictum of Lord Slynn); *Crédit Suisse First Boston (Europe) Ltd v Lister* [1998] IRLR 700.

229 Para 4.24 above.

230 *Jones v Associated Tunnelling Co Ltd* [1981] IRLR 477, 481 (Browne-Wilkinson J).

231 *Jones v Associated Tunnelling Co Ltd* [1981] IRLR 477; see also *Hogg v Dover College* [1990] ICR 39.

impact on the employee'. Nor will an estoppel easily be implied in the employer's favour, given that it has acted in breach of section 1 by issuing a statement which is incorrect: this would be to enable the employer to benefit from its own legal wrong.[232]

Improvements negotiated through a collective agreement

4.36 A *second* situation to consider is that in which a collective agreement improves upon the terms and conditions which are applicable to a given category of employment, as the result, for example, of annual negotiations between the employer and the trade union. If an employee's contract contains an express or implied bridging term, its effect may be to incorporate the new terms without the need for any further agreement.[233] The outcome may depend on how the bridging term is phrased; if, for example, it states that the employee's terms and conditions will be such as are 'laid down from time to time' in a given collective agreement, that is likely to suffice to incorporate the new terms without the need for anything further from the individual parties. Additional consideration would not then be needed, at this point, for the improved terms to be binding on the employer. Consideration may alternatively be inferred from the avoidance of any dispute over pay: by continuing to work, the employees abandon 'any argument that the increase should have been even greater and [remove] a potential area of dispute between employer and employee'.[234]

More generally, 'if in each individual contract of employment there were incorporated the provisions of relevant collective agreements agreed from time to time, as well as general instructions and notices, the contention that each improvement in the employee's terms requires fresh consideration fails to give proper recognition to the value to be attributed by the employer to the continuation of the same workforce in his employ and/or to the possibility of making adjustments from time to time to the detail of the contracts of employment without having to issue new contracts whenever adjustments are put into effect'.[235] This amounts to saying that in virtually all circumstances involving a bridging term, consideration for the improved terms can easily be implied. But in principle, there is reason to think that the question of consideration is irrelevant, at least if the bridging term expressly or impliedly refers not just to the present agreement of the collective parties but to future agreements between them. As long as the bridge itself is supported by the consideration at the time the initial contract was made, incorporation of the new terms would effectively be automatic. Thus in *Robertson v British Gas Corpn*[236] Ackner LJ thought that when 'from time to time the collective scheme modified the bonus which was payable ... that variation became a part of the employer's obligation to pay and the employee's obligation to accept in satisfaction'; similarly, Kerr LJ accepted a submission of counsel that 'when the terms of the collective agreements were varied by consent between the two [collective] sides, then the new terms clearly became incorporated into the individual contracts of employment'.[237] Neither Lord Justice appears to have thought that consideration was an issue here.

232 *Robertson v British Gas Corpn* [1983] ICR 351, 357 (Ackner LJ).
233 *Glendale Managed Services v Graham* [2003] IRLR 465.
234 *Lee v GEC Plessey Telecommunications Ltd* [1993] IRLR 383, 389.
235 *Lee v GEC Plessey Telecommunications Ltd* [1993] IRLR 383, 389.
236 [1983] ICR 351, 356.
237 [1983] ICR 351, 358.

Derogations negotiated through a collective agreement

4.37   A *third* possible scenario arises where a collective agreement introduces changes which are detrimental to particular employees, as a result, for example, of 'concession bargaining' over pay and conditions. In *Lee v GEC Plessey Telecommunications Ltd*[238] the employer attempted to revoke an agreement it had made with the union in 1985 concerning severance pay, in favour of less generous compensation arrangements. In the 1991 pay round an agreement was reached with recognised trade unions that the 1985 terms would apply up to 31 May 1991; thereafter, terms would be subject to negotiation. At the same time, a pay increase of 4.25% was agreed. Employees sought declarations that their contracts of employment included a term entitling them to severance pay at the original, higher rate, in the event of their being made redundant. The employers argued that the new terms had been incorporated by agreement at the time of the 1991 pay round, but this was rejected by Connell J who granted the declarations sought. The agreement to negotiate over severance pay in respect of redundancies after 1991 was, he held, too uncertain to be enforceable and was not appropriate for incorporation, since it related to collective negotiations between the employer and the trade union. The terms of the 1985 agreement, having previously been incorporated into contracts, remained in force at the individual level.

Although, in this case, incorporation of a concession was not achieved, the judgment does not rule out the possibility that it might have been had the employer taken a different approach. Had the employer communicated to the employees at the time of the 1991 pay round that it was ending the 1985 agreement *and* that acceptance of the 1991 pay increase amounted to consent to the change to the terms reducing entitlement to severance pay, that, in the view of the judge, would have been sufficient.[239]

This case suggests therefore that in the event of concession bargaining, an employer may succeed in varying the contract terms if it offers the employees a *quid pro quo*, in the form of a pay increase or some other new benefit, in return for the loss of rights elsewhere. It would be up to each individual employee to decide whether to accept or reject the new offer.

The result could be a fragmentation of contractual terms and conditions as different employees respond in different ways, an outcome which collective bargaining is designed to avoid. There is a case for saying that just as any improvement may be automatically incorporated into contracts by virtue of the bridging term, so will any derogation as long as it is contained in a collective agreement of the kind referred to, implicitly or expressly, by the bridge. This would maintain the uniform application of the agreement. There is some authority for this view.[240] In so far as this matter remains unresolved, it is perhaps because of a reluctance on the part of the courts to subordinate individual consent so completely to the normative effect of the collective agreement. The individual contract of employment remains the legal source of the agreement's effectiveness, unlike the position in other systems where the collective has in varying degrees displaced the individual level of bargaining. Although certain civilian systems allow collective agreements, on occasion, to derogate not just from pre-existing

238 [1993] IRLR 383; see also *Whent v T Cartledge Ltd* [1997] IRLR 153.
239 [1993] IRLR 383, 392.
240 *Miller v Hamworthy Engineering Ltd* [1986] IRLR 461; *MacBeth v United Counties Omnibuses Ltd* (1988) 350 IRLIB 9. Dicta of Ackner and Kerr LJJ in *Robertson v British Gas Corpn* [1983] ICR 351, 356, 358 can also be seen as lending support to this view.

terms but also from certain statutory standards, the circumstances in which this is permitted are strictly controlled, and only unions which achieve a certain level of representation among the workforce are granted this power.[241] These safeguards are lacking in the British system.

Abrogation by the employer of the collective agreement

4.38   A *fourth* situation is that in which an employer either abrogates all or part of a collective agreement or gives notice, under the terms of that agreement, to terminate it. This may happen if the employer is unsuccessful in achieving concessions, or simply wishes to end the union's collective negotiating rights. Unless recognition has been attained as a result of a request made under the statutory recognition procedure,[242] the employer is under no duty to bargain with any trade union and has the legal right to withdraw recognition. In doing so, it will almost certainly not be liable to the union for breach of contract, since nearly all collective agreements are non-enforceable within the terms of section 179 of TULRCA 1992.[243] However, the lack of collective enforcement does not affect the individual contract. In principle, terms and conditions which have previously been incorporated via the bridging term will remain in force until such time as the individual employee consents to vary them.

In *Robertson v British Gas Corpn*[244] a collective agreement provided for a bonus incentive scheme, the results of which were incorporated into the contracts of individual employees. The employer gave notice to the trade union that it was terminating the scheme. No new scheme was agreed and the employer ceased paying bonus payments. The employees brought a claim for arrears of pay based on the old scheme, to which they were held to be entitled. Kerr LJ said that once incorporation has taken place, 'it is only if and when those terms are varied collectively by agreement that the individual contracts of employment will also be varied. If the collective scheme is not varied by agreement, but by some unilateral abrogation or withdrawal or variation to which the other side does not agree, then it seems to me that the individual contracts of employment remain unaffected'. This view was reinforced by the high degree of interdependence between the different terms of the contract: the bonus scheme constituted 'an integrated and general framework for a very large number of the mutual rights and obligations of the parties. Indeed, it becomes virtually impossible to determine what the full terms of these individual contracts of employment are if you once take away the agreed collective scheme for an incentive bonus as an integral part of these contracts'.[245]

The employer's refusal to abide by the agreed contract terms is, then, almost invariably a repudiatory breach of contract, which the employee has the option to accept, bringing the contract to an end; or he or she may, alternatively, affirm the contract by remaining in employment. This, in itself, does not amount to agreement to vary the contract terms in the employer's favour. In particular, if the employee makes his or her disagreement clear, there can be no possibility of variation. The employee can remain in employment and claim wages or salary at the rate provided for in the contract; a claim in debt, for accrued

241 See Wedderburn, 1992c.
242 See further para 9.5 *et seq* below.
243 See above, para 4.26.
244 [1983] ICR 351; see also *Ackinclose v Gateshead Metropolitan Borough Council* [2005] IRLR 79.
245 [1983] ICR 351, 358.

wages, or in damages for the employer's breach of contract, can be made, and a declaration granted with respect to the future performance of the contract.[246] If, on the other hand, the contract of employment has been brought to an end, the employee's rights under the contract will not be kept in force merely because the collective agreement from which they initially derived is still in existence.[247]

Dismissal and re-engagement on new terms

4.39   *Robertson's* case appears to make the terms incorporated from a collective agreement mandatory on the employer. This appearance is deceptive, however, as a *fifth* option exists for the employer, namely to dismiss the employees in question and offer them employment on new terms and conditions. At common law, this may be done without breach of contract by giving the employees notice; if they are summarily dismissed, that would normally amount to a breach of the duty to give notice, but damages would most likely be limited to net wages or salary for the notice period.[248] Such action amounts to a dismissal, whether or not the employees accept the offer of new terms, and it is possible that the employees may be able to bring claims for redundancy compensation and/or compensation for unfair dismissal.[249] If this is the case, the employer may face liabilities which outweigh any savings to be made from abrogating the collective agreement. Formally, incorporated terms are not entrenched against the superior bargaining power of the employer: they can be changed through the route of dismissal and re-employment. They may be entrenched *de facto*, however, if statutory remedies for termination of employment defeat the employer's aim of cutting costs.

However, it is possible that dismissal in these circumstances will be held to be neither for reasons of redundancy, nor unfair. The issue is perhaps sufficiently unclear to deter an employer, but the statutory remedies cannot necessarily be relied on by the employees. At the outset, the employee will need to have been continuously employed for the requisite period prior to the dismissal.[250] Moreover, if the employer can show that there is a good business reason for seeking to change the contract terms, such as the need to enhance flexibility or efficiency of work organisation or even, simply, to make savings in response to a fall in external funding or in demand for its products, any dismissal flowing from the refusal of the employee to accept the new terms is likely to be potentially fair. It could be for reasons of redundancy, in which case the employee is automatically entitled to receive a statutory redundancy payment.[251] It is more likely, however, that the tribunal will find that it falls into the residual category of 'some other substantial reason',[252] in which case the employee may receive

---

246   *Morris v CH Bailey Ltd* [1969] 2 Lloyd's Rep 215; *Burdett-Coutts v Hertfordshire County Council* [1984] IRLR 91; *Gibbons v Associated British Ports* [1985] IRLR 376; *Rigby v Ferodo Ltd* [1988] ICR 29; *Lee v GEC Plessey Telecommunications Ltd* [1993] IRLR 383.

247   *City and Hackney Health Authority v NUPE* [1985] IRLR 252.

248   See generally, para 5.20 below.

249   On the relationship between dismissal and re-engagement on new terms, and the statutory grievance and dismissal procedures introduced by EA 2002, see paras 5.124–5.131.

250   ERA 1996, s 108(1); see above, para 3.82.

251   ERA 1996, s 135; see below, para 5.173 *et seq.*

252   ERA 1996, s 98(1)(b); *Hollister v National Farmers' Union* [1979] ICR 542. If the dismissal is found to be in connection with a transfer of an undertaking, however, it may be more difficult to show that the dismissal is potentially fair under TUPE 1981, reg 8(2): see para 5.194 below.

additional compensation for unfair dismissal but may, alternatively, receive nothing if the tribunal finds that the dismissal was fair in the circumstances.[253] This will be determined not simply according to whether the offer of new terms was reasonable from the point of view of the employee, but according to whether a *reasonable employer* would have dismissed the employee for refusing the new terms.[254] This is essentially a question for the tribunal, and tribunals are entitled to reach findings on a case-by-case basis with similar cases resulting in different outcomes.[255] In assessing reasonableness, however, it is largely irrelevant that the employer is seeking unilaterally to alter the agreed contract terms; what matters is the nature of the economic pressure which the business is facing and the reasonableness of the employer's response to it. Only in rather extreme circumstances have employees succeeded in winning unfair dismissal claims of this kind, as in a case where the new terms gave the employer an apparently unqualified right to call on the employee to work unlimited overtime hours on demand.[256]

The authorities were reviewed by the EAT in *Catamaran Cruisers Ltd v Williams*.[257] A business which had been in financial difficulties was taken over by a new owner, which then negotiated changes to terms and conditions of employment with the recognised trade union. The new terms, which departed from those laid down by a federation of employers for the trade in question, were offered to the employees, most of whom accepted. Those who did not were dismissed. The employment tribunal found that the dismissals were unfair, on the basis of a two-stage test under which they first considered whether the employer had a sound business reason and second, 'whether, in refusing to accept the new terms and conditions, the employees are acting unreasonably, having regard to the necessity which the employer has for proposing the new terms': with regard to the second stage, the tribunal considered that if the new terms are 'much less favourable to the employee than were the old terms, then unless the business reasons are so pressing that it is absolutely vital for the survival of the employer's business that the terms be accepted, then the employee is not ... unreasonable in refusing to accept those terms and, consequently, any dismissal of him for a refusal to accept is unfair'. This view of the law was held to be incorrect by the EAT, which remitted the case for rehearing. Specifically, it was incorrect to say that the employer could only propose less or much less favourable terms if the existence of the business depended on it. The tribunal had to consider the benefit or potential benefit to the employer in balancing the two interests and should also, in a case such as this, consider the relevance of the large majority of employees accepting the new terms.

Catamaran Cruisers tilts the balance in the employer's favour: the tribunal's error was not to have failed to consider the employer's motives and position, but to have apparently accorded this equal weight to the employees' interests in avoiding a serious deterioration in their pay and conditions. The lay members of the EAT in that case felt it necessary to state that 'much of recent employment

---

253 This can present employers and their advisers with a dilemma when considering the implications of forcing through a variation to terms and conditions of employment. See *Port of Sheerness Ltd v Brachers* [1997] IRLR 214.
254 *St John of God (Care Services) Ltd v Brooks* [1992] IRLR 546; *Farrant v Woodroffe School* [1998] IRLR 176.
255 *Kent County Council v Gilham* [1985] ICR 227.
256 *Evans v Elemeta Holdings Ltd* [1982] IRLR 143.
257 [1994] IRLR 386.

law has been to protect employees against arbitrary changes of their terms and conditions of employment and ... this, as a principle, must stand'.[258] But the hurdle which the employer must overcome, in demonstrating a business reason for altering terms and conditions, is not a high one after this decision.

Some qualifications should nevertheless be borne in mind. Even though dismissals of this kind may not amount to redundancies for individual purposes, they will almost certainly fall under the expanded definition of redundancy for the purposes of collective consultation rights, namely a dismissal 'for a reason not related to the individual concerned'.[259] An employer's failure adequately to comply with the collective consultation rights would, under this provision, result in liability to pay a protective award to the employees concerned. Another factor which may increase the risk of liability for the employer is the nature of the response from the workforce as a whole. If a large majority of employees opposes the change, it may be more difficult for a tribunal to conclude that their dismissal was fair.

In *Catamaran Cruisers*, not only did most of the employees accept the new contracts, but the terms being offered were the result of negotiation with the recognised trade union. This was a very different case, then, from one in which an employer presents its workforce with terms on a 'take-it-or-leave-it basis', or chooses to go down the route of a mass dismissal. The constraints imposed by unfair dismissal law, although they do not provide automatic protection for the agreed contract terms, 'may in practice provide the union more opportunities to engage in the process of negotiation of new terms and conditions'.[260]

PAYMENT OF WAGES AND SALARIES

4.40   Legislative regulation of wages and salaries may perform one or both of two related functions. First, *minimum wage legislation* may regulate basic rates of pay in order to ensure that employees receive a certain minimum level of income in return for their labour. This can be done directly by inserting a stated minimum level of hourly, weekly or monthly pay into contracts of employment, or indirectly by providing for wage-fixing machinery which will then be used to set legally-enforceable basic rates.[261] In Britain, regulation has, traditionally, been indirect in the sense of supplying statutory force to certain wage-fixing machinery. This type of intervention, which was associated with the Wages Councils which operated in a number of forms between 1909 and 1993, was confined to particular sectors or industries. However, with the passage of the National Minimum Wage Act 1998, a single, statutory minimum wage covering the labour force as a whole is now in force in the UK for the first time.[262]

258 [1994] IRLR 386, 389.
259 TULRCA 1992, s 195. This expanded definition was inserted by the TURERA 1993, s 34(1), implementing Directive 75/129, Art 1(a). See para 9.32 below.
260 Auerbach, 1993: p 26. The use of mass dismissal notices as a means of bringing about a change in employment conditions is rare in practice. It was used by Rolls Royce plc in 1991 but the company eventually withdrew the notices and resumed negotiations with the recognised trade union. The case is discussed by Jeremy McMullen and Philippa Kaufman, 1991.
261 ILO instruments lay down standards for regulation by the latter, indirect route: Convention concerning the Creation of Minimum Wage-Fixing Machinery, No 26, 1928; Convention concerning Minimum Wage-Fixing in Agriculture, No 99, 1951. The UK was a signatory to these Conventions but denounced them in the 1980s.
262 See below, para 4.43 *et seq.*

A second form of regulation is that constituted by *wage protection legislation*. This aims to ensure, among other things, that the employee is paid on a regular basis and receives his or her mandated or agreed wage in full, that is to say, free from arbitrary or excessive deductions by the employer.[263] The employer's power of deduction may be limited by *substantive* controls, such as a requirement that any deduction should be related to an identifiable breach of discipline and should be reasonable in the circumstances, or by controls of a *procedural* kind, such as an obligation to agree relevant rules with a recognised trade union (or equivalent representative body) and to notify employees of their existence. Legislation governing deductions from pay has a long history. The Truck Acts of the nineteenth century, which extended the scope of regulations which had previously applied at the level of individual trades, required wages to be paid in full in the coin of the realm (thereby outlawing 'truck' or payment in kind)[264] and regulated disciplinary 'fines' and deductions from pay.[265] However, this legislation was complex and difficult to apply and was never accorded a clear priority over the common law, which continued to determine the scope of the employer's obligation to pay wages in return for service rendered. The Wages Act 1986 (now consolidated in Part II of ERA 1996) repealed the Truck Acts and replaced them with a looser form of statutory regulation, under which substantive limits on deductions are imposed only in relation to cash shortages and stock deficiencies occurring in the course of retail employment. Otherwise, this legislation permits deductions from agreed wages, as long as they are authorised by statute or by a term of the individual's contract; in the latter case, the deduction will be valid if the individual has given his or her prior consent in writing, or if the employer has provided them with written notification of the deduction before it takes place (not necessarily before the event giving rise to it). Outside the retail sector, then, the employer's obligation is at present confined to a procedural one of providing information to an individual whose pay is subjected to a deduction.

Collective bargaining has traditionally been the primary source of regulation of basic rates of pay, the intervals between payment and methods of calculating pay. Payment systems are mostly specific to particular occupations and industries. Industrial workers tend to be paid either on a piece-work basis, that is to say by reference to particular items or quantities of completed work, or on a time-rate, normally by the hour or by the day, or by some combination of the two, with weekly or monthly intervals between payment. Professional, managerial and clerical workers, whether or not they are covered by collective bargaining, normally receive salaries calculated without reference to particular items of completed work or to hours spent in employment, and are normally paid at monthly intervals. With the relative decline in the scope and influence of collective bargaining, payment systems have become less standardised, and in many cases a larger element of an employee's pay is now determined by reference to an individual's performance or to the profitability of the company or group as a whole. The law offers encouragement to the use of profit-related pay by a variety of tax reliefs, but it has so far failed to provide effective protection for employees who may lose valuable share option rights if they are wrongfully dismissed.[266]

---

263 ILO Convention concerning the Protection of Wages, No 95, 1949. This Convention was denounced by the UK in 1985.
264 Truck Act 1831; see below, para 4.41.
265 Truck Acts 1887 and 1896; see below, para 4.41.
266 McLean, 1994; see below, para 4.70.

Given the decreasing importance of both legislation and collective bargaining in the regulation of pay, the common law has come to assume a pre-eminent role as a source of norms in this area. A number of presumptions have grown up which the courts rely on to interpret the 'wage-work bargain' made by the parties. One issue here is the determination of precisely what the employee must do in order to earn his or her wages: is it the completion of a given quantum of work or labour, or is it being ready and willing to work? The answer depends largely on how the employee's pay is calculated: piece work and hourly-paid workers are less likely to succeed in showing that they are paid for being ready to work than salaried workers are.

A related question concerns the scope of the employer's power to make deductions from the agreed wage. At common law, once the employee has shown that he or she has performed the contractual obligation which triggers the employer's obligation of payment, any deduction from or retention of wages or salary must be justified by contractual authority of some kind, such as an express or implied term or an implied right of set-off for breach of contract. It must, in addition, satisfy the obligations imposed by Part II of ERA 1996. The employee's rights in relation to payment can be asserted by way of an application to an employment tribunal if they arise under Part II[267] or, if the claim is related to the termination of the employment, at common law.[268]

Statutory minimum rates of pay

Evolution of minimum wage legislation

4.41 A number of different objectives have, at various times, influenced legislative policy in Britain towards minimum wages. The first modern legislation was part of a broader attempt at the end of the nineteenth and start of the twentieth century to curb the insanitary labour conditions and exploitation in the form of very low pay which were associated with 'sweated labour'. The sweated trades were seen as 'parasitic', on the basis that employers who paid wages below what was needed for subsistence were receiving a subsidy from the rest of the community. Hence, 'the enforcement of a common standard throughout the trade not only stops the degradation, but in every sense conduces to efficiency'.[269] State regulation of wages was undertaken in response to this in the form of the Fair Wages Resolutions of 1891, 1909 and 1946, and in the Trade Boards Act 1909 which introduced statutory regulation for the first time but only covered a selected number of very low paying industries. The subsequent history of the wages councils (as the trade boards became) reflects a tension between the original aim of controlling 'sweating' and a second objective, namely that of using legal enforcement of minimum rates to support the wider system of collective bargaining. The Wages Councils Act 1945 'amounted to the use of State power to keep collective bargaining going when economic circumstances tended to destroy it, and was quite different from the simpler, ameliorative purpose of abolishing sweating'.[270] The wages councils system did little to address a third objective, namely the reduction of poverty. The minimum rates set by wages regulation orders tended to follow those separately set by collective

267 ERA 1996, s 23.
268 SI 1994/1623; D Brown, 1994.
269 Webb and Webb, [1898] 1920: p 767.
270 Bayliss, 1962: p 56.

agreements, and were not used for the purpose of ensuring a levelling-up of the position of the lower paying sectors relative to the rest.

Between 1960 and 1980 a major retrenchment of the wages council system took place, as 27 councils covering half a million workers were abolished. The pressure for reform came from a perception, shared by trade unions and government, that wages councils were stifling the development of voluntary collective bargaining. In the 1980s a further reduction in the scope of statutory regulation took place, but not with the aim of enhancing voluntary collective bargaining. On the contrary, both wages councils and collective bargaining were now seen as contributing to unemployment by setting minimum wages above the market clearing rate. The Wages Act 1986[271] took the first steps towards complete abolition by excluding workers under the age of 21 from the scope of coverage; restricting the powers of wages councils to setting single minimum wage rates for each sector as a whole (as opposed to a range of rates for workers of different grades within each sector as previously); abolishing their power to regulate paid holidays and other terms and conditions of employment; and requiring wages councils to consider 'the effect that that rate will have on the level of employment among the workers to whom it will apply, and in particular in those areas where the remuneration received by such workers is generally less than the national average for such workers'.[272] The remaining powers of the wages councils were abolished completely in 1993.[273] This move affected around 2.5 million workers, or 10% of the employed labour force, who were covered by wages orders prior to 1993.[274]

International labour standards and comparative perspectives on minimum wages

4.42 Most of EC Member States either legislate directly for a minimum wage or provide legal support for wage-fixing machinery which secures an effective floor of rights.[275] France, the Netherlands, Luxembourg, Spain and Portugal each have minimum wages whose levels are set directly by statute. In France, the SMIC (*salaire minimum interprofessionel de croissance*) applies to all sectors and occupations and may not be the subject of derogation by either individual or collective bargaining.[276] It is expressed as a minimum hourly rate, and further provision is made for workers employed for at least the basic working week to receive a monthly minimum based on this rate. The relevant law contains a mechanism linking the statutory minimum to increases in both wages and prices. The rate must be raised automatically with every 2% increase in the official consumer price index, and must maintain an annual rate of growth of at least 50% of the growth in the purchasing power of the average wage. In other systems with a statutory minimum, provisions for indexation are weaker and exemptions for younger workers tend to be more extensive. An alternative method of regulating minimum pay is through collective agreements at national or sectoral level. In Belgium, for example, national-level collective agreements

271 WA 1986, Pt II.
272 WA 1986, s 14(6)(a).
273 TURERA 1993, s 35.
274 For the policy background to this repeal and assessment of its effects, see Deakin and Wilkinson, 1992; R Dickens *et al*, 1993.
275 See Deakin, 1990b.
276 French Labour Code, Art R 141-1 *et seq.*

are concluded annually by representatives of trade unions and employers' associations; the minimum rates thereby established apply to the small minority of employments which are not covered by a separate industry-level agreement. In Germany, on the other hand, basic rates are supplied by sector-level agreements whose terms can be given general legal effect through extension procedures. The vast majority of employees receives a basic legal entitlement by this means. Denmark achieves general protection through a combination of sectoral and company-level collective bargaining, and Ireland has a system of selective statutory regulation, similar to the former wages council model, for sectors lacking voluntary collective bargaining.[277]

Prior to the Wages Act 1986, the then Conservative government took the opportunity to denounce ILO Convention No 26 of 1928 on Machinery for Minimum Wage-Fixing, which had been modelled on the British Trade Boards Acts. A number of other international instruments remain relevant to the question of minimum wages. Article 4(1) of the Council of Europe's Social Charter of 1961 provides that Member States should recognise 'the right of workers to a remuneration such as will give them and their families a decent standard of living'.[278] There is no right of individual petition under the Social Charter;[279] instead, periodic reports of the European Committee on Social Rights are made to see how far Member States are complying with their obligations. In interpreting Article 4(1), the Committee of Experts has developed the notion of a 'decency threshold' of 68% of average (mean) earnings as a benchmark level for legal minimum wages.

Article 5 of the European Community Charter of Fundamental Social Rights, adopted by all the Member States except the UK in 1989, states that 'all employment shall be fairly remunerated ... in accordance with the arrangements applying in each country' and goes on to provide, inter alia, that 'workers shall be assured of an equitable wage, ie a wage sufficient to enable them to have a decent standard of living'. The Charter has no legal force in its own right, and there is no prospect of the European Union adopting a legally-binding measure on minimum wages which might give effect to Article 5 in the near future. 'Pay' was one of the issues stated to be outside the scope of the Maastricht Agreement on Social Policy,[280] the text of which has since been incorporated into the EC Treaty.[281] In September 1993 the European Commission agreed a non-binding Opinion on an Equitable Wage. It noted that 'the persistence of very low wage levels raises problems of equity and social cohesion, which could be harmful to the effectiveness of the economy in the long term', but reiterated the view taken

---

277 Italy lacks a formal minimum wage. However, in contrast to the UK, Italian sector-level collective bargaining is an effective mode of regulation in larger firms, and terms and conditions may be extended to non-federated firms using a judicial procedure derived from an activist interpretation of Art 36 of the Italian Constitution. See Deakin, 1990b.

278 This is reiterated in the 1996 Charter which the UK has signed but not ratified. See also UN Universal Declaration of Human Rights, Art 23(3): the right of every worker 'to just and favourable remuneration ensuring for himself and his family an existence worthy of human dignity'. The International Covenant on Economic, Social and Cultural Rights refers to the right of every person to the enjoyment of just and favourable conditions of work (Art 7) and a decent living for workers and their families (Art 7(a)(1)).

279 A 1995 Protocol makes provision for collective complaints, but this has not been signed by the UK.

280 Agreement on Social Policy, Art 2(6), now EC Treaty, Art 137(6). No reference to minimum wages is made in the final text of the Charter of Fundamental Rights of the European Union agreed at the Nice summit in 2001.

281 See para 2.42.

by the Commission in the Social Action Programme of 1989 that 'wage setting is a matter for the Member States and the social partners'.[282] Member States were called on, *inter alia*, to improve the collection and dissemination of information and to consider legislation 'to ensure that the right to an equitable wage is protected' with particular reference to discrimination, the treatment of homeworkers and 'mechanisms for the establishment of negotiated minima and the strengthening of collective bargaining arrangements'.[283] However, the Opinion, by its nature, does not impose any legal obligation upon Member States; it is advisory only.

The National Minimum Wage Act 1998[284]

4.43 The introduction of a national statutory minimum wage was a commitment in the Labour Party manifestos of 1992 and 1997, and after the General Election of 1997 the new government made it the first priority of employment law reform. The National Minimum Wage Act 1998 provides for a minimum basic hourly rate of pay for workers of 26 or over, with the possibility of a lower rate (or rates) for younger workers, some of whom may also be completely excluded. The Act has many features of a framework provision, with more detailed aspects of the regulation of the minimum wage being left to the National Minimum Wage Regulations 1999. The Low Pay Commission, a tripartite body, offers advice to the Secretary of State on matters of setting and implementing the minimum wage. This advice has, in some instances, been reflected in the terms of the National Minimum Wage Regulations.[285]

SCOPE

4.44 The Act applies initially to any 'worker' who 'is working, or ordinarily works, in the United Kingdom under his contract', and who is above compulsory school leaving age.[286] A 'worker', for this purpose, means an individual who has entered into or works under either a contract of employment or a contract whereby he or she 'undertakes to do or perform personally any work or services for another party to the contract whose status is not by virtue of the contract that of a client or customer of any profession or business undertaking carried on by the individual'.[287] The Act thereby adopts the wide definition of 'worker'

---

282 Commission Opinion on an Equitable Wage, COM (93) 388 final, OJ 1993 C 248/7, recitals 5 and 7 respectively.
283 Agreement on Social Policy, Art 3.
284 For a comprehensive account of the legal issues arising from this Act, see Simpson, 1999a, 1999b and for a later assessment, Simpson 2004.
285 The Low Pay Commission (LPC) was initially set up in a non-statutory form in July 1997. Its members comprise representatives of employers' bodies and trade unions and a number of academics. The Act provided for this 'non-statutory Low Pay Commission' to be put on a more permanent, statutory footing (NMWA 1998, s 8). The Secretary of State was required to consult the LPC when first setting the rate of the minimum wage (see s 5) and has the power to refer other matters concerning the minimum wage to it (ss 6–7). The Commission's first report, *The National Minimum Wage. First Report of the Low Pay Commission*, was published in June 1998, and a number of further reports have since been published. For an account of the work of the LPC by one of its members, see Metcalf, 1999.
286 NMWA 1998, s 1(2).
287 NMWA 1998, s 54(3); see *Edmonds v Lawson* QC [2000] IRLR 391, in which the Court of Appeal held that a pupil barrister was neither an apprentice nor, more generally, a worker within the meaning of this provision, essentially because of the apparent absence of a commitment to serve.

which was previously used under the wages councils legislation and is currently used in a number of other statutory contexts.[288]

Agency workers and homeworkers are also the subject of special treatment. The Act recognises that an 'agency worker' (defined as one who is 'supplied by a person (the 'agent') to do work for another (the 'principal') under a contract or other arrangements made between the agent and the principal') might not be a 'worker' as just defined, because of the absence of the necessary contractual nexus between the individual and either the agency (the 'agent') who supplies them or the client for whom they work (the 'principal'). Under these circumstances, the Act applies as if there were a worker's contract between the agency worker, and whichever one of the agency or client is responsible for paying the individual or, failing that, whichever one actually makes the payment.[289]

Under the Act, a 'homeworker' means an individual who 'contracts with a person, for the purposes of that person's business, for the execution of work to be done in a place not under the control or management of that person'. A homeworker, so defined, is capable of coming under the definition of a 'worker' even if he or she does not undertake personally to supply the work or services in question.[290]

The Act applies (with only minor modifications) to Crown employees (but not members of the armed forces), House of Lords and House of Commons staff, and certain workers on board ships registered in the United Kingdom.[291] Additionally, the Secretary of State has a sweeping reserve power to make regulations for the application of the Act to 'any individual of a prescribed description who would not otherwise be a worker', and to identify, for this purpose, their employer.[292]

The scope of the Act is considerably broader, then, than that of employment protection legislation, which is mostly confined to employees employed under a contract of employment.[293] This makes it necessary for the Act to confer certain rights which are normally granted only to employees – such as the right to protection against being subjected to a detriment by the employer – upon workers as well.[294] However, the Act stops short of granting a worker the right not to be unfairly dismissed for asserting his or her rights in respect of the national minimum wage – this form of protection remains confined to employees.[295]

4.45   This extensive coverage of the Act is subject to a number of exceptions. Share fishermen, voluntary workers and prisoners are specifically exempted.[296] More broadly, sections 3 and 4 confer specific powers of exclusion and

---

288 See paras 3.51–3.61 above. NMWA 1998 has no application to postmasters and postmistresses: *Commissioners of Inland Revenue v Post Office Ltd* [2003] IRLR 199.
289 NMWA 1998, s 34. On agency workers, see paras 3.64–3.69 above.
290 NMWA 1998, s 35; *Commissioners of Inland Revenue v Post Office Ltd* [2003] IRLR 199. On homeworkers, see paras 3.62–3.63 above.
291 NMWA 1998, ss 36–40.
292 NMWA 1998, s 41.
293 See ch 3, above.
294 NMWA 1998, ss 23–24. In addition, s 12 empowers the Secretary of State to adopt regulations providing for workers to receive a written statement of their minimum wage entitlements from their employer; however, this power has not been exercised.
295 NMWA 1998, s 25.
296 NMWA 1998, ss 43–45. Note also ss 44A and 45A. On voluntary workers, see Simpson, 1999a: pp 6–7; D Morris, 1999.

modification on the Secretary of State; certain groups may, by regulation, be excluded from the application of the national minimum wage, and/or made subject to a different minimum rate from that generally in force. However, the Secretary of State may not adopt regulations which provide for different treatment by reference to different areas, sectors of employment, undertakings of different sizes, or different occupations.[297] Under the 1999 Regulations, as amended, the following categories of workers are completely excluded from the minimum wage: workers under compulsory school age;[298] apprentices under the age of 26, during the first year of their apprenticeship; apprentices under the age of 19; certain workers participating in designated government-run training schemes; and certain workers receiving training at a higher education institution.[299] In addition, the 1999 Regulations added *au pairs* and family workers to the list of those outside the protection of the Act.[300] A further series of groups receives the minimum wage at a lower rate than the adult rate. Those aged 18 or over but less than 22 years receive the minimum wage at a lower 'development rate' which was set £4.10 from October 2004 and is due to rise to £4.25 in October 2005. The development rate is also paid to workers aged 22 or over who are in the first six months of their employment with a new employer, and who have agreed to take part in an accredited training course for at least 26 days during that 6-month period.[301] The rate is £3.00 an hour (with effect from 1 October 2004) for 16 and 17-year olds.

DETERMINATION OF THE MINIMUM HOURLY RATE

4.46 The power to set the rate is vested in the Secretary of State for Trade and Industry who, when setting the rate for the *first* time, was required to consult the Low Pay Commission.[302] The Act makes no provision for the automatic uprating of the minimum hourly rate, as is the case with certain social security benefits.[303] Whether it is raised in subsequent years is, therefore, a matter for the discretion of the Secretary of State, who *may* make a reference on this question to the Low Pay Commission,[304] but is not obliged to do so. In June 1998 the Government announced that the rate for those aged 22 or over would be £3.60 an hour from April 1999. By 1 October 2004 it had risen to £4.85 per hour and from 1 October 2005 it is due to rise further to £5.05.

APPLICATION OF THE MINIMUM HOURLY RATE

4.47 After the minimum rate is set, it is necessary to determine how the rate is to be applied to different types of contractual arrangements governing pay and

---

297 See ss 3(3) and 4(2).
298 See NMWA 1998, s 1(2)(c). The previous restriction of the NMW to workers over the age of 18 was removed by SI 2004/1930.
299 NMWR 1999, reg 12, as amended (see SI 2004/1930 for the most recent updating amendments). The term 'apprentice' here has a special meaning which refers to arrangements under various government-run schemes (see SI 2000/1989 for an updating amendment to reg 12 on this point).
300 NMWR 1999, reg 2(2)–(4). Family workers are those who work for a 'family business' as a member of the family in question and reside in the family home of the employer. For discussion, see Simpson, 1999b: pp 174–175.
301 Ibid, reg 13. See Simpson 2004: pp 25–28 for a critique of these provisions.
302 NMWA 1998, s 5.
303 On the uprating of social security benefits, see Wikeley, 2002: pp 265–267.
304 NMWA 1998, s 6.

working time. The Act says relatively little about how this is to be done, instead delegating the power to make regulations on these questions to the Secretary of State who, on the adoption of the first regulations, was required to consult the Low Pay Commission (and who *may* consult the LPC when adopting further regulations).

4.48   The Act and the Regulations address these issues through three core legal concepts.[305] The first of these is the *pay reference period*.[306] Payments made during this period must, when averaged out, be such as to ensure that the worker receives the statutory minimum rate in respect of the relevant hours worked. The pay reference period is defined as the interval between the payments normally received by the worker, up to a maximum of one month.[307] For certain purposes, a payment made in one pay reference period can be counted towards satisfying the employer's obligation in respect of the immediately preceding one.[308]

4.49   The next step is to determine which payments count towards the *wage* or 'remuneration' of the worker for the purposes of satisfying the employer's obligation to observe the minimum rate.[309] The starting point is the gross wage or salary paid to the worker during the pay reference period. Included in total gross pay for this purpose are incentive pay, bonuses, and tips paid through the payroll.[310] Certain deductions made by the employer from gross pay also 'count' towards the wage for this purpose. These are: deductions for income tax and national insurance purposes; deductions made under the worker's contract in relation, for example, of a breach of discipline;[311] deductions in respect of an advance of wages; deductions to pay for shares or securities; deductions to recover accidental overpayments of wages; and deductions not made for the employer's benefit, such as the worker's pension contribution or union membership dues. Certain payments are outside the scope of statutory remuneration. These include overtime and shift premia, geographical and other allowances,[312] exceptional payments for bad weather, and payments in kind

---

305 See Simpson, 1999a: p 11. See generally DTI, *A Detailed Guide to the National Minimum Wage* (regularly updated: references here are to the October 2004 edition), for the background to the Regulations.

306 NMWA 1998, s 1(4). The 'payment reference period' is the 'unit of account' by reference to which the wage or salary is paid, in contrast to the 'time' spent working which is 'the amount of time spent on the work (or deemed work)' under the Regulations: see the judgment of Arden LJ in *Walton v Independent Living Organisation Ltd* [2003] IRLR 469, at para 37.

307 NMWR 1999, reg 10.

308 NMWR 1999, reg 30(b). See Simpson, 1999a: pp 12–13. The pay reference period can also be adjusted to take into account situations where workers submit worksheets some time after the relevant period: see reg 30(c); *Detailed Guide to the National Minimum Wage*, paras 58–62.

309 NMWR 1999, regs 30–37; *Detailed Guide to the National Minimum Wage*, paras 67–87.

310 In a case decided under wages councils legislation, it was held that tips paid by credit card or cheque were the property of the employer, so that when the employer passed them on to the worker through the payroll, it thereby discharged part of the obligation to pay the minimum wage: *Nerva v RL & G Ltd* [1996] IRLR 461. In *Nerva v United Kingdom* [2002] IRLR 815 the ECtHR held that this practice did not contravene the worker's property rights under Art 1 of Protocol 1 of the European Convention on Human Rights and Freedoms.

311 See reg 33(a). This regulation makes no reference to the lawfulness of the deduction under ERA 1996, Part II (see below, para 4.69). See Simpson, 1999a: p 15.

312 Thus attendance allowances fall outside the definition of remuneration for this purpose: see *Laird v AK Stoddart Ltd* [2001] IRLR 591.

(with an exception made for the provision of accommodation subject to an upper weekly limit).[313]

4.50   The third key concept is that of the *working time* for which the national minimum rate must be paid.[314] Four employment types are identified for this purpose: time work, salaried-hours work, output work, and unmeasured work. These four categories are exhaustive in the sense that between them, they cover all types of employment falling under the Act and Regulations, and also mutually exclusive in the sense that only one of them can apply to a given period of working time; however, it is possible that within a single employment or work relationship, more than one could be relevant for different periods.

4.51   Under regulation 3, *time work* is work that is paid by reference to a set or varying period of time, typically an hour or number of hours.[315] In *British Nursing Association v Inland Revenue (National Minimum Wage Compliance Team)*[316] the Court of Appeal held that duty nurses who worked at home during the night, responding to telephone requests for nursing help, were engaged in 'time work' throughout the period of their shift, and not simply when they were answering the telephone. On similar grounds, a night watchman was able to argue that the entire period of his shift during counted as time work.[317] Under regulation 15(1), the definition of time work is extended to cover 'time when a worker is available at or near a place of work for the purpose of doing time work' and is required by their contract to be so available. As Buxton LJ put it in the *British Nursing Association* case, this extension 'relates to workers who are, in colloquial terms, "on call"'.[318] It is subject to two exceptions: the first applies where the worker in question under their contract spends time on call at home, and their home is at or near their place of work;[319] the second relates to a period when the worker, 'by arrangement', spends part of the on-call time sleeping, using facilities provided by the employer.[320] However, these exceptions only apply to the 'on-call' provisions set out in regulation 15(1) and not to the core definition of time work under regulation 3.[321] Regulation 15 also provides that periods of training and certain periods spent travelling in connection with work (but not travelling to and from home) are within the definition of time work. Various periods of absence from work on account of rest and meal breaks,

---

313 The Regulations set this initially at £19.95. From October 2004, it stood at £26.25.
314 NMWR 1999, regs 15–29A; Simpson, 1999a: pp 16–20, 1999b: pp 176–180; *Detailed Guide to the National Minimum* Wage, paras 114–196. As the EAT pointed out in *South Holland District Council v Stamp*, 3 June 2003, EAT/1097/02 RN, the phrase 'working time' does not appear in the NMWA 1998 and NMWR 1999, and the concept of 'working time' under WTR 1998 is, on the face of it, an entirely separate one. We nevertheless suggest that it is appropriate to use the expression 'working time' in the context of the NMW to refer to a composite notion of the four concepts of 'time work', 'salaried work', 'output work' and 'unmeasured work' referred to in the text. It is certainly arguable that, in the interests of consistency and clarity in the application of labour legislation, the NMW legislation should *as far as possible* be interpreted in line with the WTR, but this question is one on which the courts have yet to give a reasoned view.
315 See also reg 15; Simpson 2004: pp 29–32.
316 [2002] IRLR 480. See also *Walton v Independent Living Organisation* [2003] IRLR 469.
317 *Scottbridge Construction Ltd v Wright* [2001] IRLR 589, [2003] IRLR 21.
318 [2002] IRLR 480, para 17.
319 NMWR 1999, reg 15(1)(a)–(b).
320 NMWR 1999, reg 15(1A).
321 *Scottbridge Construction Ltd v Wright* [2003] IRLR 21.

holidays, maternity or parental leave, industrial action, and periods of sickness or ill health are excluded.

4.52   *Salaried work* exists where the worker is paid in relation to a set basic number of hours per year, is entitled to an annual salary, and is paid in equal instalments (for example, 12 monthly or 52 weekly payments).[322] The definition of working time is essentially the same as for a time worker, except that certain periods of absence which are normally remunerated now count as working time. It is customary for salaried workers to be paid in respect of 'absences' such as meal breaks, sick leave, and holidays;[323] in a given case, the definition of working time for this purpose will turn on the relevant terms of the worker's contract. Detailed rules govern the situation in which a salaried worker works annual hours in excess of those set out in the contract.[324]

4.53   *Output work* refers to work in respect of which the payment is linked to the number of items or products produced by the worker, as in the case of piece work or commission work, without reference to a given period of time.[325] The Regulations initially made provision for the employer and worker to make a 'fair estimate' agreement setting out the number of hours which the worker was expected to work during the relevant pay reference period. This had to be not be less than four fifths of the time an average worker would take to do the same amount of work in the same conditions. The employer was then under an obligation to pay the statutory minimum for the 'fair estimate' hours. With effect from 1 October 2004, this system was replaced by one based on 'fair piece rates'.[326] Now, the employer must either pay the minimum rate for each hour actually worked, or put in place a system for determining the 'mean hourly output rate' for a particular piece or task. This can be done either by measuring the performance of all the workers concerned or of a representative sample. The 'fair piece rate' in a given case must be such as to enable a worker achieving the 'mean hourly output rate' to earn the minimum wage in respect of that hour. From 6 April 2005 the fair piece rate is calculated by reference to 120% of the time which an average worker would take to earn the minimum wage, in effect increasing its value by a fifth.[327]

4.54   *Unmeasured work* is work which does not fall into one of the other three categories.[328] This would be the case, for example, with a task contract which does not specify times or periods during the work is to be done. The employer must either pay the minimum rate for each hour worked, or come to an agreement in writing with the worker which specifies a 'daily average' of hours to be worked.[329]

---

322 NMWR 1999, reg 4.
323 See below, para 4.58.
324 NMWR 1999, reg 22; *Detailed Guide to the National Minimum Wage*, paras 154–172.
325 NMWR 1999, reg 5.
326 NMWR 1999, regs 24–26A, as amended by SI 2004/1161, reg 2; *Detailed Guide to the National Minimum Wage*, paras 173–183.
327 See NMWR reg 26, as amended by SI 2004/1161, reg 3.
328 NMWR 1999, reg 6.
329 NMWR 1999, regs 18, 27–29; *Detailed Guide to the National Minimum Wage*, paras 184–196; for an example of a 'daily average' agreement under reg 28, see *Walton v Independent Living Organisation Ltd* [2003] IRLR 469.

EFFECT AND ENFORCEMENT[330]

4.55   The right to receive the national minimum wage takes effect as a term in the worker's contract. The Act provides that '[I]f a worker who qualifies for the national minimum wage is remunerated for any pay reference period by his employer at a rate which is less than the national minimum wage, the worker shall be taken to be entitled under his contract to be paid, as additional remuneration in respect of that period, the amount'[331] which is the difference between what he actually received and what he 'would have received for that period had he been remunerated by the employer at a rate equal to the national minimum wage'.[332] Aside from the possibility of a claim for wages due under the common law or Part II of ERA 1996[333] which this provision creates, the Act provides for an extensive array of additional mechanisms of enforcement. In particular, an enforcement notice may be issued by a government officer[334] against an employer who is failing or who has failed to comply with the law, requiring the employer to make the necessary payments to one or more workers.[335] The employer has the right to appeal against the issuing of the notice to an employment tribunal. If an enforcement notice is not complied with, the officer may present a complaint on behalf of the worker concerned to an employment tribunal under Part II of ERA 1996 or commence proceedings for breach of contract and may, additionally, require the employer to pay a fine equivalent to twice the amount of the underpayment.[336] In addition, an employer who wilfully neglects to pay the national minimum wage is guilty of an offence punishable by a fine not exceeding level 5 on the standard scale.[337] In the case of corporate entities, both the employer and a corporate officer may be convicted of an offence.[338]

RELATED OBLIGATIONS OF EMPLOYERS

4.56   In addition to the obligation to pay the national minimum wage, employers must also meet a number of requirements which are designed to facilitate enforcement and to protect workers who assert their rights to the minimum wage. Particularly relevant are the obligations to keep wages records[339] and to

---

330   See Simpson, 1999a: pp 24–28, and 1999b: pp 180–181, and 2004: pp 35–39 for commentary on these provisions; Skidmore, 1999.

331   NMWA 1998, s 17(1).

332   NMWA 1998, s 17(2).

333   See below, para 4.69.

334   NMWA 1998, s 13 provides for the Secretary of State to appoint officers for the purposes of performing this and various related functions under the Act, or to arrange for these functions to be carried out by a government department or other body performing functions on behalf of the Crown.

335   Note also NMWA 1998, ss 19(2A) and (2B), overruling the effect of *Inland Revenue Wales v Bebb Travel plc* [2003] ICR 1271.

336   NMWA 1998, ss 20, 21. Under s 21(4) the Secretary of State may amend this 'multiplier' by regulation. The employer may appeal to an employment tribunal against the fine (or 'penalty notice'): NMWA 1998, s 22.

337   NMWA 1998, s 31.

338   NMWA 1998, s 32; on the definition of a corporate officer, see s 32(3). See also s 48 dealing with 'superior employers'.

339   NMWA 1998, s 9. The power, under s 12, to make regulations requiring employers to issue a minimum wage statement to all workers entitled to receive the statutory minimum (as opposed to employees who will in any event receive an itemised pay statement under ERA 1996, s 8) has not yet been exercised; although a draft was prepared at an early stage of the process of producing the 1999 Regulations, this did not survive into the final version of the Regulations. See Simpson, 1999b: pp 180–181 on the background to this issue.

allow workers and their representatives to have access to them.[340] As we have already noted, a worker who suffers detriment as a result of asserting his or her rights in relation to the minimum wage may present a complaint to that effect to an employment tribunal,[341] and an employee who is dismissed in such circumstances may make a claim of unfair dismissal which, if upheld, will be regarded as automatically unfair.[342] Also important from the point of view of enforcement is a general provision to the effect that in proceedings in respect of the minimum wage, the employer has the burden of showing either that an individual is not covered by the Act or that he or she did receive the required minimum payment.[343]

Minimum wage protection for agricultural workers

4.57   An estimated 155,000[344] agricultural workers are protected by statutory orders made by the Agricultural Wages Boards for England and Wales and for Scotland under legislation which has been in force, in various forms, since the 1920s.[345] The Agricultural Wages Boards have the power to regulate minimum rates of pay together with holiday entitlements and other terms and conditions of employment. These minimum terms take effect automatically and compulsorily in the contracts of the workers affected, so that an individual may bring a civil claim in debt or damages for the difference between the wages paid to him or her by their employer and those due to them under the relevant statutory order.[346] They may also apply to an employment tribunal to recover arrears of pay.

The Agricultural Wages Board remains in operation after the passage of the National Minimum Wage Act 1998. However, that Act amends the Agricultural Wages Act,[347] so as to ensure that the rate set by the Agricultural Wages Board is not less than the relevant rate set for the national minimum wage. If at any time after the Board sets a rate, it is overtaken by the national minimum wage rate, the latter prevails. The enforcement provisions of the 1998 Act are also applicable (with some minor modifications) to the rates set for agricultural workers.

The common law of the wage-work bargain

4.58   The principal mechanism by which an individual may claim his or her wages is by a civil action in debt (or an 'action for the price'); hence, the employee's right to payment depends upon performance of the contractual obligation which corresponds to the employer's obligation to pay. For this purpose, the court seeks to discover, through a process of construction, whether wages are payable in return for finished work, services actually rendered over a period of time, or readiness to work. Where the contract stipulates that wages are to be paid on a piece-work basis, it is self-evident that the right to payment

---

340 NMWA 1998, ss 10–11. Under s 10(4)(b), the worker may be accompanied, for the purposes of inspection, by 'such other person as the worker may think fit'.
341 NMWA 1998, ss 23–24.
342 NMWA 1998, s 25, inserting a new s 104A into ERA 1996; see para 5.103 below.
343 NMWA 1998, s 28. Note also the formal ban on contracting out (s 49).
344 Figures supplied by DEFRA, January 2005.
345 Now the Agricultural Wages Act 1948; Agricultural Wages (Scotland) Act 1949.
346 *Gutsell v Reeve* [1936] 1 KB 272.
347 NMWA, 1998, ss 46–47 and Sch 2.

depends upon the relevant work being finished.[348] In relation to time rates of payment, there was at one stage a presumption that hourly-paid employees – that is to say, those paid by reference to an hourly rate of pay – had to complete each hour of work in order to be entitled to their wages.[349] In their case, no work meant no pay: 'the consideration for work is wages, and the consideration for wages is work'.[350] By contrast, salaried employees were regarded as receiving payment in return for a more general commitment of loyalty and 'faithful service' over time.[351] As a result, merely being ready and willing to work sufficed for them to claim payment. What this meant in practice was that salaried employees were entitled to payment in the event of being unable to work for reasons beyond their control, such as illness or lay-off caused by a lack of work,[352] whereas hourly-paid employees were not.[353]

At the time this distinction was most clearly articulated, in the late 1930s,[354] it appears to have been influenced by social insurance legislation, which drew a similar distinction between manual and non-manual employees. It was reasonable to argue at that point that because manual employees were covered by the state social insurance system in relation to loss of income caused by illness and unemployment, they should not also be covered by the contract; but this was not so for salaried employees, most of whom were outside state social insurance at this point.[355] Modern social security legislation no longer draws this distinction. Moreover, many manual or hourly-paid employees benefit from long notice periods and other features of stable, long-term employment relationships such as occupational sick pay and pension rights, to the extent that that they are in a similar position to salaried staff of being paid in return for a general commitment of faithful service. The formal harmonisation of the terms and conditions of manual and non-manual staff is well advanced in some sectors and companies, but is by no means complete.

It is arguable, then, that the approach to construction, whatever it is, should be the same for both groups. This view was taken by the House of Lords in *Miles v Wakefield Metropolitan District Council*,[356] which concerned a claim for salary arising in the context of limited industrial action. According to Lord Templeman, in this context 'there is no logical distinction between a superintendent registrar who is paid a weekly salary for a 37-hour week and a municipal dustman who is paid a weekly wage for a 37-hour week'.[357] In both cases, the employee would have to show that he was at least willing to work as a *necessary condition* of claiming payment;[358] *Miles* does not clearly decide whether, in other contexts such as involuntary illness or lay-off, readiness to

---

348 Eg, *Devonald v Rosser & Sons* [1906] 2 KB 728.
349 This was apparently also the case if the term governing the rate of pay was not agreed but was imposed by statute, as in *Gutsell v Reeve* [1936] 1 KB 272.
350 *Browning v Crumlin Valley Collieries Ltd* [1926] 1 KB 522, 528 (Greer LJ); see also *Automatic Fire Sprinklers Pty Ltd v Watson* (1946) 72 CLR 435, 465 (Dixon CJ).
351 Denning, 1939: p 354.
352 Eg, *Orman v Saville Sportswear Ltd* [1960] 1 WLR 1055.
353 *Hancock v BSA Tools Ltd* [1939] 4 All ER 538, *Petrie v Macfisheries Ltd* [1940] 1 KB 258 (both sick pay cases), *Marshall v English Electric Co Ltd* [1945] 1 All ER 653 (suspension).
354 See in particular, Denning, 1939, and the sick pay cases cited above.
355 Denning, 1939: pp 356–357 made this point.
356 [1987] AC 539. See below, para 4.64.
357 [1987] AC 539, 556–557. This statement may now have to be read in the light of NMWR 1999, which, as we have seen (paras 4.51–4.52), draws a distinction between time work and salaried work similar to that made by Denning, 1939.
358 See *Beveridge v KLM (UK) Ltd* [2000] IRLR 765.

work is a *sufficient* condition for such a claim.

The construction of the wage-work bargain, although essential in determining the scope of any claim by the employee in *debt,* is only one aspect of the employer's obligations under the contract. The employer may alternatively be liable for a breach of contract resulting in an award of *damages,* which in some circumstances will offer an alternative form of income protection to the employee. In *Devonald v Rosser & Sons*[359] piece-workers who were laid off without pay were able to claim by way of damages an amount equivalent to their net wages for the contractual period of notice, through an implied term that the employer would ensure that work was made available to them for this period. Similarly, an implied or express term may be the basis for a claim in damages for sick pay, as an alternative to a claim for the agreed wages in debt.[360]

There are some important differences between debt claims and damages claims however. The claim in debt is for a liquidated sum (that is, a sum set by the contract itself) and no duty to mitigate arises on the part of the employee. Damages, by contrast, represent the claimant's loss and are paid as an unliquidated sum assessed by the court. They may be subject to reductions for the employee's failure to mitigate or in respect of their receipt of offsetting gains (such as unemployment compensation). Thus the employee will normally choose the action in debt to enforce the employer's promise to pay a sum of money in return for performance.

The failure to pay wages at the agreed time is, in itself, a breach of contract by the employer giving rise to a claim in damages,[361] although the employee will not be compensated twice over in respect of the same quantum of wages or salary. The principal significance of the employer's failure to pay being a breach of contract is that if the breach is repudiatory at common law, which it may be depending on the circumstances, the employee will be entitled to terminate the contract without notice and bring actions for wrongful and/or unfair dismissal.[362]

Deduction and retention at common law

4.59 The circumstances under which an employer can withhold all or part of the agreed wage are determined, in the first instance, by the common law. The first issue to consider here is the point at which the employee's contractual right to payment accrues. Where payment is governed by a time rate of some kind, an employee who has performed the contract as required becomes entitled to payment in respect of *that* period. There is a distinction to be drawn here between the point at which the right to payment accrues, which is when the performance is completed, and the point at which the wage becomes payable, which may be later. It is standard practice in many employments, for example, to pay wages and salaries a week or month in arrears; there is nothing unlawful about this practice, although it would be normal for it to be supported either by an express

359 [1906] 2 KB 728; see below, para 4.112.

360 *Mears v Safecar Security Ltd* [1982] ICR 626 is a case of an implied term; the earlier sick pay cases, such as *Marrison v Bell* [1939] 2 KB 187 and *Petrie v Macfisheries Ltd* [1940] 1 KB 258 appear to have been argued solely in debt. See *New Century Cleaning Co Ltd v Church* [2000] IRLR 27 for a refusal to imply a term preventing the employer from implementing a unilateral pay cut in response to a fall in profits. The scope of the implied terms relating to income security is considered later in this chapter, at paras 4.110 and 4.112 below.

361 See, eg, *Rigby v Ferodo Ltd* [1988] ICR 29.

362 See *Cantor Fitzgerald International v Callaghan* [1999] IRLR 234 on the circumstances under which a failure to pay wages or salary amounts to a repudiatory breach.

contract term or by one implied from a collective agreement or from custom and practice. Notwithstanding this possibility of an interval between accrual and actual payment of the wage, once the right has accrued it cannot be forfeited by anything which the employee does between that point and the time at which payment falls due,[363] except to the extent that the employee may commit a subsequent breach of contract which gives rise to a counterclaim or set-off in damages.

It follows that the right to payment of an hourly-paid worker accrues hour by hour, as the work is carried out (subject to the possibility of an employee showing that mere readiness to work suffices). In the case of a salaried employee for whom no time rate as such is set, the interval between payments – normally a month – becomes important in establishing the point at which the right to payment is earned.[364] In principle, performance must be rendered in full for each month before *any part* of the salary for that month (or other period) becomes due. This was established in a number of nineteenth-century cases concerning employees who either quit or who were dismissed for breach of contract before the expiry of their fixed term of employment: the courts held that they had no claim for work done either in contract or in quantum meruit.[365] The outcome is sometimes seen as an aspect of the common law doctrine of 'entire obligations': the debt, or price, cannot be apportioned except to the extent that the contract itself provides for this. The courts do not normally imply a term allowing for pro rata payment where to do so would contradict an express agreement.[366]

4.60   It is possible, however, that an employee may invoke, in this context, section 2 of the Apportionment Act 1870, which provides that 'all rents, annuities, dividends, and other periodical payments in the nature of income [shall] be considered as accruing from day to day, and shall be apportionable in respect of time accordingly'; for this purpose, the term 'annuities' is expressed to include 'salaries'. Although there is evidence that it was not the intention at the time this Act was passed to apply this part of it to contracts of employment in general,[367] in *Sim v Rotherham Metropolitan Borough Council*[368] Scott J thought that it did apply to the salaries of monthly-paid schoolteachers which 'may be regarded as accruing day by day'.[369] The term 'wages' is not mentioned in the 1870 Act and it is unclear whether the Act could apply to non-salaried employees. However, the recent tendency of the courts has been to give the Act a general application to contracts of employment.[370]

4.61   The harshness of the common law doctrine of entire performance is also mitigated by the principle that *substantial* performance is sufficient to discharge

363 *George v Davies* [1911] 2 KB 445.
364 *Sim v Rotherham Metropolitan Borough Council* [1987] Ch 216, 255 (Scott J).
365 *Turner v Robinson* (1833) 5 B & Ad 789; *Ridgway v Hungerford Market Co* (1835) 3 Ad & El 171; *Saunders v Whittle* (1876) 33 LT 816; *Boston Deep Sea Fishing & Ice Co v Ansell* (1888) 39 Ch D 339.
366 G Williams, 1941.
367 Matthews, 1982.
368 [1987] Ch 216, 255.
369 See also, for more recent applications of this Act, *Thames Water Utilities v Reynolds* [1996] IRLR 186; *Taylor v East Midlands Offender Employment* [2000] IRLR 760.
370 The Divisional Court held that it applied to a case of directors' fees in *Moriarty v Regent's Garage Co Ltd* [1921] 2 KB 766; its decision was reversed on different grounds. In *Item Software (UK) Ltd v Fassihi* [2004] IRLR 928, the Court of Appeal held that the Act applied in a case of a salaried director.

a contractual obligation, and gives rise to the equivalent obligation on the part of the payor. In the context of employment this has been taken to mean that an employee cannot be prevented from claiming payment in respect of a particular period of employment merely because he or she has committed a minor breach of contract which falls short of being repudiatory.[371] For example, an hourly-paid employee who completes a basic 39-hour week is, *prima facie*, entitled to the normal weekly wage based on the applicable hourly rate; if he or she has, at some point in that week, committed a minor breach of discipline, this would not, *in itself*, entitle the employer to withhold all or part of the payment for that week.[372] Under these circumstances, a deduction would be lawful only if the employer could point either to an express term authorising the deduction, or to an implied right of abatement or set-off.[373]

4.62   Any express term has to have been incorporated into the contract according to the tests considered earlier in this chapter.[374] Even then, the effect of the term is not guaranteed, since it could be struck down in equity as a penalty clause[375] if the court considers that it was inserted *in terrorem* and not by way of a genuine attempt at a pre-estimate of the cost of breach to the employer. The implied right of set-off, conversely, depends upon the employer showing that the employee committed a breach of contract which caused him loss of some kind; that loss can be abated or set off against the wages which are due to the employee.

4.63   In *Sim v Rotherham Metropolitan Borough Council*[376] schoolteachers who were taking part in industrial action refused to cover the classes of absent colleagues as they would normally have done. Their employers deducted a small percentage of their monthly salaries in respect of the hours when they refused to work normally. The teachers' action was held to have been a breach of their contractual duty of trust and co-operation, resulting in damage to the employer which was at least the equivalent of the deductions made from their monthly salaries. According to Scott J:

> ... the correct approach in cases like the present is to start with the teachers' contractual monthly salary entitlement. If in the course of the month there has been a breach of contract by a teacher, it is necessary to consider what, if any, damages can be claimed by the employer by reason of that breach of contract. If the breach of contract has not given rise to any recoverable loss to the education authority, then ... there is no deduction that can properly be made from the salary on account of the breach. If recoverable loss has been caused to the education authority, it is necessary to consider whether the law allows, by way of abatement or by way of set-off, the deduction of the damages from the monthly salary ...[377]

---

371   G Williams, 1941. On repudiatory breach of the contract of employment, see paras 5.18–5.19 below.
372   Freedland, 1976: p 229.
373   On the need for the employer to be able to point to a contract term authorising deduction once the employee has established that the wages or salary are due in return for performance, see *Davies v MJ Wyatt (Decorators) Ltd* [2000] IRLR 759; *Beveridge v KLM (UK) Ltd* [2000] IRLR 765.
374   See para 4.25 *et seq* above.
375   According to the principle in *Dunlop Pneumatic Tyre Co Ltd v New Garage & Motor Co Ltd* [1915] AC 79; for a more recent application see *Giraud (UK) Ltd v Smith* [2000] IRLR 763.
376   [1987] Ch 216.
377   [1987] Ch 216, 255.

The principal argument against allowing an *implied* right of set-off in contracts of employment is that it may undermine explicit procedures for dealing with breach of discipline. However, Scott J held that there was no distinction, for this purpose, between contracts of employment and other contracts to which set-off applied; accordingly, the deductions made were lawful.[378]

If the approach in *Sim* is adopted, the employer must prove both breach and damage before any deduction may be made. The result may be described as 'part work, part pay': the partial failure of performance is reflected in the amount deducted by way of set-off. In cases of industrial action involving a deliberate refusal to perform the contract as intended, however, cases decided after *Sim* suggest that the employer may be able to rely on a wider principle to withhold payment completely.

4.64   In *Miles v Wakefield Metropolitan District Council*,[379] as part of industrial action, a local government registrar of births, deaths and marriages refused to conduct weddings on Saturday mornings. He normally worked a 37-hour week. On the Saturdays in question he attended his office for the normal three hours and carried out other duties related to his work. His employer made a deduction of 3/37ths of his salary for the period of the industrial action; his action for the recovery of the full salary was rejected in the House of Lords.

According to Lord Templeman, 'when a worker in breach of contract declines to work in accordance with the contract, but claims payment for his wages, it is unnecessary for the employer to rely on the defences of abatement or equitable set-off. The employer may or may not sustain and be able to prove and recover damages by reason of the breach of contract of each worker. But so far as wages are concerned, the worker can only claim them if he is willing to work'.[380] The employee's claim fails at the outset, then, on the grounds of failure to perform the contract as required; and even though the employer may receive certain benefits from part performance, it does not have to pay for them if it informs the employees that it declines to accept partial performance as equivalent to the whole.

This left open the possibility of an action in restitution for the value of the partial services rendered by the employee. Lords Brightman and Templeman were prepared to entertain this possibility, but Lord Bridge thought it 'contrary to the realities of the situation'[381] and Lords Brandon and Oliver expressly reserved their opinion on the question.

4.65   The full implications of *Miles* became clear in *Wiluszynski v London Borough of Tower Hamlets*.[382] Local government officers taking part in industrial action refused over a period of several weeks to deal with queries from the constituents of councillors. During this period they carried out other duties as

---

378   Abatement was a doctrine of the common law, set-off one of equity. In the context of employment, *Sim* decides that there is no difference between them. There is some authority, notwithstanding the judgment of Scott J, to suggest that nineteenth-century courts did not accept the application of the doctrines of set-off and abatement to salaries: *Le Loir v Bristow* (1815) 4 Camp 134; *Stimson v Hall* (1857) 1 H & N 831; see Deakin, 1992: p 850.
379   [1987] AC 539.
380   [1987] AC 539, 561. See also *British Telecommunications plc v Ticehurst* [1992] ICR 383, discussed further below at para 11.70.
381   [1987] AC 539, 552.
382   [1989] IRLR 259.

normal. After the industrial action was over they were able to deal with the backlog of queries in a matter of a few hours. The employer withheld payment in full for the period of the industrial action and was held to have acted lawfully in doing so.

A deliberate refusal in advance of performance to work under the contract as normal therefore *completely* defeats the employee's contractual claim to wages or salary. This continues for as long as the refusal fully to perform goes on (in practice, the duration of the industrial action) and the employer can defeat any claim to *part* payment by making it clear that it declines to waive its right to receive performance in full. The effect is 'part work, *no pay*'.[383] Nor is the alternative quantum meruit route to partial compensation a particularly feasible one. In principle, if the employer's refusal to waive the right to full performance is regarded as effective in contract, it should operate for the restitutionary claim too. The contract has not been discharged, and so should continue to govern the parties' relationship either way.[384]

It is not clear that the decisions in *Miles* and *Wiluszynski* can readily be justified by contract law doctrine, however. It is odd that the employer can apparently suspend the obligation of payment while other aspects of the contract remain in force. At common law, the employer in these cases could have dismissed the employees for committing repudiatory breaches of contract. That it did not do so suggests that it may have been concerned about legal consequences in the form of actions for unfair dismissal,[385] but also that it did not wish to lose completely the services of valued staff. In either case, the issue is whether the employer should go on receiving the substantial benefit of performance in return for nothing, simply by virtue of a unilateral declaration to the effect that it was not 'accepting' part performance.

Lord Templeman in *Miles* thought that some protection for the employer was necessary in order to avoid a situation in which a worker was protected against 'losing both his job and his wages' in the event of taking industrial action. However, it is not clear that this situation would have arisen. First, it was not then the case that, as his Lordship put it, 'an individual worker is unfairly dismissed if the only reason for his dismissal is that he has taken part in industrial action unless all workers who take part are also dismissed'.[386] Even now, employees are deemed to be unfairly dismissed for taking industrial action only in a relatively restricted range of circumstances.[387]

Second, if *Miles* had been decided differently, the employee would not necessarily have received payment in full; some deduction would have been permissible by way of set-off or abatement, to reflect the employee's breach of contract. As *Sim* shows, in the context of industrial action such a breach can justifiably be seen as causing damage to the employer in the form of the loss of a certain proportion of the services of the employee in question. The latter may admittedly be difficult to quantify in a given case. In *Miles* and *Sim* the deductions were calculated by reference to the hours in a given month when less than full performance was rendered. Similarly, in *British Telecommunications plc v Ticehurst*[388] deductions from monthly pay were made in proportion to particular

383 G Smith, 1989.
384 Although, for a different point of view on this, see G Mead, 1991.
385 See *Miles v Wakefield Metropolitan District Council* [1987] AC 539, 559.
386 [1987] AC 539, 559.
387 TULRCA 1992, s 237–238A; see below, para 11.72 *et seq*.
388 [1992] ICR 383.

days during which no work was carried out, following a withdrawal of goodwill by the employees. In *Royle v Trafford Borough Council*[389] rather greater artificiality was employed to make a deduction according to the number of pupils excluded from classes by teachers' industrial action concerning maximum class size.

More generally, in so far as *Miles* represents a gloss on the common law notions of what constitutes contractual performance, its effects are probably confined to the specific situation of industrial action involving a deliberate refusal to perform the contract as intended. For the reasons given above, it should have no application to a situation of inadvertent or non-premeditated breach of the duties of care or obedience.[390]

Recovery of overpayments

4.66   If an employee is overpaid on one or more occasions, the employer may be able to recover the overpayment by an action for money had and received. Until recently the courts drew a distinction between payments made under a mistake of fact and those made under a mistake of law, but after the House of Lords decision in *Kleinwort Benson Ltd v Lincoln City Council*[391] there is a general right to recover money paid under a mistake subject to a number of possible defences including change of position. The nature of this defence is illustrated by *Avon County Council v Howlett*,[392] which was brought as a test case following a number of overpayments which arose in the aftermath of local government reorganisations in the 1970s. The employee, who was on leave of absence through illness, was paid at the full rate of pay for the whole of this period. Under his contract he should have received only half his normal pay after six months of leave had elapsed. When the mistake was discovered his employers initiated an action to recover the overpayment of £1,007, which the employee had already spent. The employee was able, however, to invoke the defence of change of position. In general, this will be possible if the employee can show: first, that the employer made a representation of fact leading them to believe that the money was theirs; second, that they changed their position, in good faith, in reliance on the representation; and third, that the overpayment was not caused by their own fault. In *Avon County Council v Hewlett*[393] these conditions were satisfied, and the employee kept the entire amount by which he had been overpaid. The Court of Appeal rejected an argument that the principle of estoppel should only apply to that proportion of the overpayment which could clearly be shown to have been spent in reliance on the employer's representation: this would be to impose an excessive burden on the employee of showing precisely when and how the sums in question were spent.

Statutory wage protection

4.67   The practice of making deductions from pay is a disciplinary device of long standing, which legislation has not been particularly effective in controlling. The

---

389   [1984] IRLR 184.
390   This was the view in *Miles* itself of Lord Brightman ([1987] AC 539, 552) and Lord Templeman ([1987] AC 539, 561).
391   [1998] 4 All ER 513.
392   [1983] IRLR 171.
393   [1983] IRLR 171.

Truck Act of 1831, which consolidated and generalised a series of earlier enactments, restricted the payment of wages in kind and was interpreted as also regulating deductions, since 'the truck system, against which the statute was confessedly levelled, was itself a system of stoppage or deduction. Deduct so much for supplies and pay the balance of cash, constituted the evil the statute was passed to remedy; nor is it easy to perceive how there could be a part payment of goods, or otherwise than in the current coin of the realm, without a stoppage or deduction'.[394] Section 3 of the 1831 Act required the payment of 'the entire amount of the wages earned by or payable to' the worker to be made in the current coin of the realm. The courts, however, succeeded in reserving to the common law the question of whether wages were 'earned by or payable to' an individual under their contract. Thus agreed deductions for the 'rent' of the employer's equipment or a part of the cost of heating and lighting the factory were not caught by the Act. These were 'the mode of calculating the amount of wages, and nothing more', so that the wages 'payable to' the worker were the net, and not the gross amount.[395]

The Truck Act 1896 attempted to clarify workers' rights in respect of works rules authorising the abatement of wages for acts of negligence and disobedience, but encountered similar difficulties of statutory interpretation. The Act required any power to levy a disciplinary 'fine' or a deduction for bad workmanship to be notified in advance to the worker in a fixed notice or written contract; to be proportionate to the loss caused to the employer; to be 'fair and reasonable, having regard to all the circumstances of the case'; and, in the case of a fine, to specify the amount to be deducted and the acts and omissions in respect of which the deduction could take place.[396] The courts nevertheless held that these provisions did not regulate contractual terms for the disciplinary suspension without pay of employees, because 'you cannot deduct something from nothing'; 'such a contract is not a contract for any deduction from the sum contracted to be paid since no sum was ever contracted to be paid during a period of suspension'.[397] The aims of the 1896 Act were given clearer effect in *Bristow v City Petroleum*,[398] decided only after the Act had already been repealed.

The Truck Acts were once described as 'suffering from an incurable logical disease'[399] and certainly left a great deal to be desired from the point of view of legal clarity. They have now been replaced by Part II of ERA 1996 (formerly Part I of the Wages Act 1986), a measure which on the whole imposes a somewhat looser regime of controls over the practice of disciplinary deductions or fines and payments to the employer.

4.68   Section 13 of ERA permits deductions to be made without limit in two situations: where the employee has given his or her prior written agreement to

---

394   *Archer v James* (1862) 2 B & S 67, 78 (Keating J). In support of this construction, ss 23 and 24 of the 1831 Act specified that certain deductions were to be lawful, a provision which would have been unnecessary if ss 1–3 had been confined to payments in kind.

395   *Chawner v Cummings* (1846) 8 QB 311, 323 (Denman CJ); *Archer v James*, above (in which the Court of Exchequer Chamber divided equally on the question); *Redgrave v Kelly* (1889) 5 TLR 477.

396   Truck Act 1896, ss 1–2. S 1 applied to both manual workers and shop assistants; s 2, like the Truck Act 1831, applied only to manual workers ('workmen': see also the Truck (Amendment) Act 1887, s 2). The Lancashire cotton trades sought and won exemption from the Act of 1896: cf *Sagar v H Ridehalgh & Son Ltd* [1931] 1 Ch 310.

397   *Bird v British Celanese Ltd* [1945] 1 All ER 488, 491 (Scott LJ) and 492–493 (Lawrence LJ).

398   [1988] ICR 165.

399   Kahn-Freund, 1949: p 2.

the deduction; and where the employer has some statutory or contractual authority to make it.[400] In the first case, the written agreement must precede the event or conduct of the employee which triggers the deduction.[401] In the second case, however, the employer is simply obliged to pre-notify the employee in writing that he has the required authority before he exercises it – not necessarily before the event occurs which gives him the occasion to do so.[402] If the employer is relying on a written contract term, he must give the employee a copy of it before making the deduction.[403] If he is relying on the 'effect' of a term or upon an implied or oral term, he must give the worker written notification prior to making the deduction.[404] This last provision enables the employer to continue to rely on any common law rights of implied abatement or set-off, as long as it satisfies the pre-notification requirements of the Act as explained above.[405] Only if a contract term is varied after the commencement of employment is there an obligation to notify the employee of the effect of its terms in advance of the conduct or event in question occurring.[406] There is no specific time limit for making deductions under this part of the Act, other than that implied by the general six-year limitation period for actions in contract. Section 15 of the Act applies parallel provisions to the case of payments made to the employer.

4.69 Part II of ERA 1996 applies to all employees, both manual and non-manual, and to some self-employed workers who fall under the definition of 'worker'.[407] The right to protection against deductions is, however, subject to some exceptions: under sections 14 and 16, these are deductions in respect of overpayments of wages; recovery of sums due in consequence of a statutory disciplinary procedure; sums required by statute to be paid to a public authority (such as income tax under Schedule E); sums which the individual has agreed should be paid over to third parties (such as union dues or pension contributions); deductions made or payments received in respect of participation in a strike or industrial action; and sums payable in satisfaction of an order of a court or tribunal.[408]

The provisions of Part II of the Act cut somewhat awkwardly across the employer's separate statutory duty to issue a written statement of terms under section 1 of ERA 1996, for which the primary remedy is the amendment of the

---

400 ERA 1996, s 13(1). The question of what is a relevant statutory authorisation was discussed in *McCree v London Borough of Tower Hamlets* [1992] IRLR 56.
401 ERA 1996, s 13(6).
402 ERA 1996, s 13(1).
403 ERA 1996, s 13(2)(a).
404 ERA 1996, s 13(2)(b), which was overlooked in *Pename Ltd v Paterson* [1989] IRLR 195. According to *Potter v Hunt Contracts Ltd* [1992] IRLR 108, 109, the notification must take the form of a 'document in writing'. In *Kerr v Sweater Shop Ltd* [1996] IRLR 424 the EAT held that the display of a notice in a factory did not constitute adequate notification under the Act. On the relationship between notification under s 13 and the requirements of working-time legislation for deductions in respect of 'excess' holiday pay, see *Hill v Chapell* [2003] IRLR 19.
405 In *Chiltern House v Chambers* [1990] IRLR 88, 90 the EAT confirmed, *obiter*, that an employer would not be able to avoid the formal requirements of the provision which is now s 13 of the Act by claiming that a deduction was made to meet a future damages claim. For discussion of whether the Act adequately meets the need formally to override common law rights, see Deakin, 1992: p 856.
406 S 13(5); *York and City District Travel v Smith* [1990] IRLR 213; *Discount Tobacco and Confectionery Ltd v Williamson* [1993] IRLR 327.
407 See ERA 1996, s 230(3).
408 ERA 1996, ss 14 and 16.

statutory statement by the tribunal.[409] The employer is also under an obligation to give details of any deductions in the itemised pay statement required by section 8 of ERA 1996, on pain of being required to repay the amounts in question,[410] but this statement may be issued on the pay day itself and so does not give the employee any greater protection than Part II of ERA 1996.[411]

The only substantive controls contained in the Act relate to the employment of retail workers.[412] The Act places an upper limit on deductions for cash shortages and stock deficiencies of 10% of a retail worker's gross weekly earnings on a given pay day, and sets a time limit of twelve months from the date on which the shortage could reasonably have been discovered for the deduction (or the first of a series) to be made. The full amount of any shortage can be deducted on the final pay day of the worker's employment.

The remedy for breach of Part II is an application to an employment tribunal for the restitution of the amounts in question; the employer is then precluded from suing for the sums by any other legal means such as a civil action in contract.[413] The employee must lodge an application within three months of the date of the pay day when the deduction took effect.[414]

As we have just seen, section 13 of the Act makes reference to the common law rules on the construction of the contract. The tribunal must consider first whether the employer has contractual authority to make a deduction, and second whether it has complied with the formalities imposed by the Act; moreover, the Act applies to a case of complete non-payment as well as to a partial deduction.[415] The Act can be invoked, therefore, to challenge a failure to pay agreed wages in full, in situations where an employer's attempt to effect a unilateral variation of contract terms is ineffective, on the ground that the wages remain due at common law.[416] However, section 13 does not apply to sums payable by way of damages for breach of contract, such as a failure to give the employee due notice of termination. This is the effect of the House of Lords' decision in *Delaney v Staples*.[417] The applicant was summarily dismissed from a recruitment agency, and claimed payment of outstanding commission of £18 and accrued holiday pay at the date of dismissal of £37.50. She also claimed recovery of £82 as wages in lieu of

---

409   See above, para 4.21. Note, however, EA 2002, s 38, Sch 5, which came into force on 1 October 2004; see further para 4.21.

410   ERA 1996, s 12(4). This jurisdiction was preserved by the WA 1986 (s 6(2)), now contained in ERA 1996, s 26. The applicant may therefore proceed under both Acts, but the total he or she can recover in respect of any one deduction may not be more than the amount of that particular deduction (ERA 1996, s 26). EA 2002, s 38 does not apply to ERA 1996, s 12: see EA 2002, Sch 5.

411   The European Committee on Social Rights has formed the view that the limited nature of substantive controls over deductions places the UK in breach of Art 4(5) of the European Social Charter (Conclusions XIV, 2, 1999).

412   ERA 1996, ss 17–21.

413   ERA 1996, s 25(4); *Potter v Hunt Contracts Ltd* [1992] IRLR 108.

414   ERA 1996, s 23(2); see *Taylorplan Services Ltd v Jackson* [1996] IRLR 184; *Group 4 Nightspeed Ltd v Gilbert* [1997] IRLR 398.

415   *Delaney v Staples* [1991] IRLR 112; *Fairfield Ltd v Skinner* [1993] IRLR 4.

416   *Yemm v British Steel plc* [1994] IRLR 117 (a refusal to pay wages as due was not an error of computation under s 13(4)); *Bruce v Wiggins Teape (Stationery) Ltd* [1994] IRLR 536; *Davies v Hotpoint Ltd* [1994] IRLR 538; *International Packaging Corpn (UK) Ltd v Balfour* [2003] IRLR 11. Conversely, in *Ali v Christian Salvesen Food Services Ltd* [1997] IRLR 17 (overturning [1995] IRLR 624), *Hussman Manufacturing Ltd v Weir* [1998] IRLR 288 and *New Century Cleaning Co Ltd v Church* [2000] IRLR 27 (see Freedland, 1999) claims for unauthorised deduction failed because variations in payments were found to be contractually permissible.

417   [1992] ICR 483.

notice, which her employer had refused to pay on the ground that she had broken the contract by removing confidential information. Both her claims failed in the EAT; the Court of Appeal allowed an appeal in relation to the outstanding sums but not the payment in lieu of notice and an appeal on the latter point was rejected by the House of Lords. The Act itself is unclear on the question of notice, although it contains a broad definition of 'wages' which covers 'any sums payable to the worker by his employer in connection with his employment, including (a) any fee, bonus, commission, holiday pay or other emolument referable to his employment, whether payable under his contract or otherwise'.[418] According to Lord Browne-Wilkinson, however, 'the provisions of the Act cannot be made to work if payments in lieu were included in the word "wages"'. Because notice payments take the form of damages for breach of contract there is no fixed date upon which they fall due, thereby making it impossible to calculate the 'occasion' when wages became payable under section 13(3) and the date from which the three-month time limit for bringing an action starts to run under section 23(2).

Thus, apart from payments specifically mentioned in section 27(1), the term 'wages' is confined to payments in respect of work done, or to be done, under a subsisting contract of employment.[419] A lump sum paid to the employee at the start of 'garden leave' would probably be 'wages', even though paid in advance, because the contract is still subsisting, but sums paid or payable in respect of termination are outside the Act whether they are the result of a contract term providing for payment in lieu, a special agreement to that effect or simply damages for breach of contract by the employer. Although not subject to the pre-notification requirements of ERA 1996, from 1994 contractual claims in respect of notice pay could be brought before employment tribunals in their own right.[420]

The scope of the exemptions listed in section 14 has given rise to difficulties of interpretation. In *Home Office v Ayres*[421] the EAT expressed the view that deductions made to recover an overpayment of wages fell within the Act, notwithstanding section 14(1) (formerly section 1(5)(e) of the Wages Act 1986), if the employer could not show that it had lawful authority, contractual or otherwise, to make the deduction. However, the better view is probably that the tribunal has no jurisdiction if, for example, an overpayment, or the employee's participation in industrial action, is the reason for the deduction, whether or not the deduction was permitted at common law.[422] The employment tribunal must nonetheless still satisfy itself that there has in fact been, for example, an overpayment or industrial action, and not simply rely on the employer's assertion to that effect.[423] This issue is less pressing than it was now that the employment tribunals have jurisdiction over common law claims for payment in addition to their jurisdiction under Part II of ERA 1996; however, they only have this jurisdiction in respect of common law claims arising out of termination of employment.

418 ERA 1998, s 27(1). On bonuses see *Farrell Matthews and Weir v Hansen* [2005] IRLR 160. Applications to enforce entitlement to holiday pay under WTR 1998 must be made under WTR 1998, reg 30: *Commissioners of Inland Revenue v Ainsworth* [2005] IRLR 465. Among the matters excluded from the definition of 'wages' under s 27(2) are work-related expenses: see *Southwark London Borough v O'Brien* [1996] IRLR 420.

419 In *Robertson v Blackstone Franks Investment Management Ltd* [1998] IRLR 376 the Court of Appeal held that wages for work done before termination may be payable and paid after termination without thereby losing their character as wages.

420 As a result of SI 1994/1623; D Brown, 1994.

421 [1992] IRLR 59.

422 *Sunderland Polytechnic v Evans* [1993] IRLR 196; *SIP (Industrial Products) Ltd v Swinn* [1994] IRLR 323; see also *Scott v Strathclyde Fire Board* EATS/0050/03 26 April 2004.

423 *Gill v Ford Motor Co* [2004] IRLR 840.

Two significant aspects of wage protection which are not regulated in any way by Part II of ERA 1996 are payments in kind (which were formerly regulated by the Truck Acts[424]) and the length of intervals between payment. These matters are therefore subject only to the terms agreed by the parties or implied into the contract of employment by reference to a collective agreement, custom and practice or some other external source. In relation to intervals, the present state of the law contrasts unfavourably with Article 12(1) of ILO Convention No 95 on the Protection of Wages (1949) which states: '[w]ages shall be paid regularly. Except where other appropriate arrangements exist which ensure the payment of wages at regular intervals, the intervals for the payment of wages shall be prescribed by national laws or regulations or fixed by collective agreement or arbitration award'. The UK government denounced this Convention in anticipation of the passage of the Wages Act 1986.

More generally, Part II of ERA 1996 might well be thought to be an inadequate response to the problems of deductions as a mechanism of discipline. The Act poses few substantive restraints on the power to make deductions and does not limit this power to situations where the individual employee was clearly at fault. Nor does it require the employer to observe minimum procedures before making a deduction. In this way, the failure to regulate deductions undermines the more general protection provided against arbitrary discipline by the law of unfair dismissal and in particular by the ACAS Code of Practice on Disciplinary and Grievance Procedures.[425]

Share options and related forms of financial participation

4.70   Since the early 1980s, in parallel with the reduction in the extent of institutional regulation of pay through legislation and sector-level collective bargaining, there has been a rise in the use of discretionary or flexible payment systems at company level which are designed to motivate individual employees. This was a change encouraged by the policy of the Conservative governments of that period. According to the Department of Employment in 1988, 'the "going rate", "comparability" and "cost of living increases", are all outmoded concepts – they take no account of differences in performance, ability to pay or difficulties of recruitment, retention or motivation. Pay structures too have to change. National agreements which affect the pay of half the workforce all too often give scant regard to differences in individual circumstances or performance'.[426]

Many organisations in both the public and private sector have introduced appraisal systems as part of which an individual's pay is linked to their assessed performance. In legal terms, the effect is to reduce the scope of the contractually-guaranteed wage or salary. In principle, the individual parties are free to agree to a discretionary element in the pay package. Although the contract of employment may then incorporate rules or principles derived from a company handbook or some other document issued by the employer, these normally reserve the final decision on appraisal to management, thereby limiting the degree of wage security enjoyed by the employee.

---

424 The Truck Acts required payment in cash but they did not apply to salaried employees, for whom payment by cheque or bank transfer was and is normal. The Payment of Wages Act 1960 set up a scheme whose main feature was to enable workers covered by the Truck Acts to opt into payment by way of cheque, bank transfer or postal order by giving written notice to their employer.
425 See further para 5.136 *et seq* below.
426 Department of Employment, *Employment for the 1990s*, Cm 540, 1988, at pp 23–24.

Profit-related pay seeks to link all or part of an employee's pay not to their individual performance but to the profitability of the company, or a part of it, in which they are employed. Together with share ownership schemes of various kinds which offer employees the chance to buy shares in their companies at discounted or subsidised prices, the practice of linking pay to profits constitutes a form of employee involvement in the enterprise which is referred to as 'financial participation', to distinguish it from more direct forms of participation in management decision-making. Financial participation was actively encouraged from the mid-1980s by a series of tax reliefs and related fiscal measures. Some of these have since been removed. For example, relief on profit-related pay, established by the Finance Act 1987, had been phased out by the start of 2000; too many employers had 'used profit-related pay as a method of cutting wage bills through tax relief'.[427]

Tax reliefs on employee share ownership come in a number of forms, some of which allow the company to give its employees financial assistance for the purchase of shares. In certain cases, tax relief is available when share options are exercised, thereby enabling employees to profit from increases in share values without paying capital gains tax. However, tax legislation provides only limited protection for an employee who loses what may be highly valuable share options as a consequence of loss of employment,[428] thereby leaving open the question of whether, at common law, the employer may be liable in damages for a wrongful dismissal or other act which deprives the employee of valuable options. Employers often attempt to protect themselves from this possibility by including exemption clauses in the scheme rules.

In *Thompson v ASDA-MFI Group plc*[429] the claimant was employed by Wades Departmental Stores Ltd which was a wholly-owned subsidiary of the defendant company. Under the rules of an ASDA group employee share option scheme, the claimant was granted a number of options to buy ASDA group shares. ASDA then sold its shares in Wades and wrote to the claimant informing him that the options had automatically lapsed, under the rules of the scheme set up by ASDA, once Wades ceased to be an ASDA subsidiary. Rule 5 of the scheme provided that 'no option shall be exercised at any time when the person seeking to exercise it is excluded from such exercise' by the relevant legislation. Scott J held that at common law, this term validly excluded any contractual rights of the claimant, and he rejected an argument that a term should be implied to the effect that the company would not sell its shares in Wades if the effect was to frustrate the employee's rights.[430]

A similar clause was considered in *Micklefield v SAC Technology Ltd*, a case of wrongful dismissal.[431] The clause was again upheld at common law but

---

427 McLean, 1994: p 8.
428 The relevant legislation is currently contained in a number of statutes including ICTA 1988 and the Income Tax (Earnings and Pensions) Act 2003. For an account of the relevant principles behind its introduction, see McLean, 1994: ch 3.
429 [1988] IRLR 340; H Collins, 1989a; Watson, 1995. Where share options rights have vested prior to dismissal, the termination of the employment will not (all other things being equal) affect their exercise: *Mallone v BPB Industries plc* [2002] IRLR 452.
430 By contrast, in *Tesco Stores Ltd v Pook* [2004] IRLR 618 a term was implied to the effect that an employee who had acted in breach of fiduciary duties owed to the employer could not validly exercise certain share options.
431 [1990] IRLR 218. See also *Levett v Biotrace Ltd* [1999] IRLR 375 and *Peninsula Business Services Ltd v Sweeney* [2004] IRLR 49, on the construction of such clauses, and *Brigden v American Express Bank Ltd* [2000] IRLR 94, on the application of UCTA 1977 to employment contracts.

on this occasion a challenge was also made to its validity under the Unfair Contract Terms Act 1977. Deputy Judge Mowbray held that even if a contract of employment could be held to come within the scope of UCTA section 3, this was a case concerning 'the creation or transfer of securities' to which the Act had no application by virtue of Schedule 1, paragraph 1(e).

Different provisions of UCTA 1977 apply in Scotland which make it less likely that the Act can be disapplied for this reason.[432] As far as English law is concerned, it seems likely that the courts will continue to uphold such exemption clauses at common law. The problem could best be addressed by extending the limited protection already accorded to employees by the taxation regulations, rather than relying on contract law or UCTA 1977.[433]

It would be premature to suggest that financial participation along the lines considered here represents a move towards more complete 'economic democracy' within companies. Forms of direct participation, such as co-determination and statutory information and consultation, enable the employees to present a collective voice to management on issues affecting the organisation of the enterprise. Financial participation, on the other hand, is essentially individual in nature, and in so far as it extends employee ownership it does so by merging employees into the larger mass of shareholders: there is no recognition that the workforce may have interests distinct from those of the managers and owners of the business. A related issue is whether financial participation results in superior employee performance. The evidence here is equivocal: companies which operate profit-related pay and employee share ownership schemes are, on the whole, more productive and profitable than those which do not, but a clear causal link between the success of these companies and the schemes concerned has not been established.[434]

On the other hand, a negative feature of both performance-related and profit-related pay is the degree of wage insecurity which they may induce. Linking all or part of pay to individual performance is nothing new, as the long tradition of piece-work contracting in many industries indicates. Where the measurement of performance is not straightforward, however, the possibility of abuse of such payment systems arises. In the past this has been addressed by collective bargaining and through shop-floor custom and practice, as well as by legislation in some exceptional instances. Few of these regulatory constraints now remain in place. As far as profit-related pay and employee share options are concerned, an element of insecurity may be derived to the extent that these variable forms of remuneration displace the previously fixed obligation of the employer to pay for performance rendered by the employee. Share ownership schemes have been termed a modern form of 'truck' or payment in kind,[435] which may turn out to offer illusory gains in so far as the employer retains unilateral powers to limit employee options.

Some of these tensions are reflected in the advisory EC Recommendation concerning the promotion of participation of employed persons in profits and enterprise results (including equity participation) of 1992.[436] The Recommendation notes that financial participation 'may be seen as achieving a wider distribution

432 *Chapman v Aberdeen Construction Group plc* [1991] IRLR 505.
433 McLean, 1994: p 17.
434 There is a large and growing literature addressing these questions. See, in particular, Pendleton, Wilson and Wright, 1998.
435 H Collins, 1989a: p 56.
436 OJ 1992 L245/92.

of the wealth generated by enterprises which the employed persons have helped to produce'.[437] On the other hand, among the points which Member States are invited to consider are the need to frame financial participation schemes so as to ensure that they do not 'stand in the way of normal negotiations dealing with wages and conditions of employment',[438] a very different emphasis from that of the UK government of the 1980s and early 1990s. Schemes should also recognise that 'apart from the risks of income fluctuation inherent in participation schemes, employed persons may be exposed to additional risk if their participation takes the form of investments that are relatively undiversified; in this context, the possibility of providing for mechanisms to protect against the risk of depreciation in the value of assets merits consideration'.[439]

WORKING TIME

4.71   The regulation of working time is designed to set maximum limits to the 'basic' or 'normal' working day and week. These may be exceeded in return for the employer paying a premium for overtime working; regulation may also set a ceiling to overtime itself, thereby imposing a maximum limit on actual hours worked in a given period. It may also recognise the notion of 'unsocial hours working' by limiting and/or setting premia for nightwork and shift working, and place limits on annual working time by providing for minimum periods of annual paid leave.

The placing of limits on working time is one of the most essential objectives of labour law and collective bargaining; it was the goal of the first modern industrial legislation, the British factories legislation of the nineteenth century, and of the first ILO Convention in 1919, which embodied the principle of the 8-hour normal working day. In France, legislation of 1919 established a basic 8-hour day and in 1936 a 40-hour basic working week. In Germany, legislation of 1938 set a basic working day of 8 hours and a basic week of 48 hours. In Britain, however, statutory working time standards of this kind were slow to develop. This was in part a result of the tradition of voluntarism: as with regulation of minimum rates of pay, the state's preference for support for collective bargaining over direct legal regulation meant that statutory intervention was confined to sectors of the economy which were characterised by lack of voluntary organisation, or to particular groups of workers (mostly young workers and women in industrial employment). In the 1980s, however, policies of deregulation began which brought about not simply the removal of the limited statutory protections which used to exist in this area, but also a restriction of the coverage of the sector-level collective agreements which were formerly the principal mechanism of regulation of basic hours of work, overtime and shiftwork premia and annual paid holidays. The balance has recently been redressed by recent EC Directives in the areas of working time and the protection of young workers. These impose certain basic standards in respect of the length of the working day and week and annual holidays, subject, however, to numerous and extensive derogations which are amply reflected in the terms of the Working Time Regulations 1998.

437 OJ 1992 L245/92, Preamble, para 3.
438 OJ 1992 L245/92, Annex, point 3.
439 OJ 1992 L245/92, Annex, point 7.

The traditional model: factories legislation and sectoral collective bargaining

4.72 The factories legislation of the nineteenth century was confined to regulating the employment of women, young persons and children in factories and workshops, and failed to develop into a comprehensive code of working time controls as occurred in other European countries. The minority report of the Royal Commission on Labour of 1894 commented that 'for the mass of workers an eight hour day with the effective suppression of overtime can be secured only by further legislative enactment' and rejected the pattern of regulating on a trade by trade basis on the grounds that this 'would not only consume much valuable time, but would, in our judgment, result at best in a lopsided regulation of industry'.[440] The majority, however, rejected the principle of general statutory regulation, and apart from a few exceptional instances of intervention[441] the hours of adult male workers remained outside the scope of legislative controls. The pattern of selective and partial regulation was firmly enough established to lead to British refusal to ratify the first ILO Convention, the Hours of Work Industry Convention of 1919, which embodied a standard 8-hour basic working day and 48-hour basic working week.[442]

Statutory restrictions upon nightwork and Sunday work by women and the limitations upon their weekly hours, together with related controls on breaks, shift work and overtime, were repealed by the Sex Discrimination Act 1986, and the controls on the hours of young persons were repealed by the Employment Act 1989.[443] This left regulations in place only for children under the minimum school leaving age.[444]

The Shops Act 1950, which consolidated a number of earlier statutes, restricted Sunday and evening opening by shops and regulated the working time of retail employees by establishing the right to a weekly half-day holiday for shop assistants, limiting Sunday working hours and specifying minimum breaks for meals. The hours of young workers in shops were also the subject of specific controls. The Act was repealed in 1993;[445] weekday and Saturday opening is now completely deregulated, while Sunday opening is subject to a more liberal regime than before under which larger shops may open for a maximum of six consecutive hours between 10 am and 6 pm. Under certain circumstances it is automatically unfair to dismiss retail employees for refusing to work on Sundays.[446] Other statutory controls repealed as a consequence of deregulatory policies includes those governing the number of hours spent underground by mineworkers[447] and nightwork by bakery workers.[448]

---

440 *Royal Commission on Labour, Minority Report*, Parliamentary Papers (1894) XXXV.9, at pp 140–141.
441 These included the Railway Servants (Hours of Labour) Act 1893 and the Coal Mines Regulation Act 1908.
442 Ewing, 1994a: p 20.
443 Deakin, 1990a. The repeals of controls specific to women workers were the consequence of EC Directive 76/207.
444 See generally Deakin, 1990a.
445 The restrictions on Sunday opening were replaced by those of the Sunday Trading Act 1994, and weekday restrictions were completely repealed by DCOA 1994.
446 Sunday Trading Act 1994 and ERA 1996, Part IV and s 101; Deakin, 1994b; see para 5.105 below.
447 By virtue of the Coal Industry Act 1991.
448 SDA 1986, s 8, repealing the Banking Industry (Hours of Work) Act 1954.

National-level collective agreements for separate industries or sectors were the principal mechanism for the regulation of the basic working week for manual workers from the 1920s, when the 48-hour week was generally established in the engineering industry, to the end of the 1980s, when structures for national-level bargaining began to break up. The national engineering agreement achieved further reductions in the basic working week to 44 hours in 1947, 42 hours in 1960, 40 hours in 1965 and 39 hours in 1979. Reductions in most other sectors of the economy tended to follow on those achieved in the national engineering agreement. Sector-level collective bargaining also achieved gradual improvement to holiday and leave rights. In the early 1970s a basic entitlement to 8 days of paid public holidays and 3 weeks' paid leave per employee was established more or less throughout the economy by this route. A general 4-week entitlement was achieved in the early 1980s, and some sector agreements subsequently achieved a 5-week entitlement. It is largely thanks to collective bargaining that the tradition of respecting 'bank holidays' has been widely followed, since the legislation itself simply prohibits certain financial dealings on the days in question and says nothing about a general right to leave, paid or otherwise.[449]

However, in many respects sector-level bargaining in Britain was less effective than the equivalent forms of statutory control of working time elsewhere in Western Europe. For one thing, British agreements have never sought to impose absolute upper limits on overtime working; nor have they laid down the precise form and limits of shift work. Instead, sector-level agreements have been confined to setting overtime and shift premium payments. In themselves these premia do not provide employers with much of a disincentive to limit overtime working, in particular since they have normally been multiples (such as time-and-a-half or double time) of the national basic wage rate, and not of the higher basic rate which might be set by plant- or company-level agreements. This is one reason why overtime and shift working in Britain has been particularly prevalent for full-time workers, compared to practice on the continent. Actual hours worked in manufacturing regularly exceed the basic working week of 37–39 hours.[450]

In 1989 national negotiations in the engineering industry for a phased reduction to a basic 37½-hour and then a 35-hour week broke down. Reduced hours were eventually agreed at plant and company level following a series of local strikes, but no new national agreement could be reached and the 1989 dispute marked the effective end, at least for the time being, of national-level bargaining in engineering. Sector-level bargaining, for reasons examined earlier,[451] has undergone a more general decline, with a corresponding loss of effectiveness in working-time regulation. The abolition of the wages councils in 1993 also contributed to this decline. Thanks in large part to the tradition of loose regulation, British employment patterns have displayed a wide variety of non-standard working time arrangements.[452]

The new model: regulating the duration and organisation of working time

4.73 The main premise of the Working Time Directive of 1993 was that 'in order to ensure the safety and health of Community workers, the latter must be

---

449 Banking and Financial Dealings Act 1971, s 1, Sch 1.
450 See Rubery *et al*, 1994.
451 See above, para 1.27.
452 See Wareing, 1992.

granted minimum daily, weekly and annual periods of rest and adequate breaks', and that 'it is necessary in this context to place a maximum limit on weekly working hours'.[453] The European Commission argued prior to the adoption of the Directive that reductions in working time were not incompatible with the maintenance of flexibility in *operating times*, citing evidence that many industrial and service establishments made increasing use of shiftworking and other flexible arrangements to ensure extended daily and weekly continuity of production and services.[454] The legal authority for the Directive was Article 118a (now consolidated in Article 137) of the EC Treaty, which confers powers to adopt instruments, by qualified majority voting, designed to improve the working environment, with regard to health and safety. In *UK v EU Council (Working Time)*[455] the ECJ rejected the United Kingdom's challenge to the validity of the Directive, holding that it could be justified as a health and safety measure, in the process giving a broad definition to Article 118a.[456] Following amendments made in 2000, a consolidated version of the Directive came into force in 2004.[457]

The process of implementing the Working Time Directive only began to take shape following the judgment of the ECJ in the *Working Time* case,[458] which confirmed that the Directives had been validly adopted. Proposals put forward by the Conservative government in 1996 were subjected to further revision following the election of the Labour government in May 1997. In April 1998 the Department of Trade and Industry published a consultation paper and draft regulations[459] for bringing the Working Time Directive and relevant provisions of the Young Workers' Directive (94/33) into force; the Regulations were adopted in 1998[460] and amended in 1999[461] and on a number of subsequent occasions.

The Working Time Directive and the Working Time Regulations 1998[462]

SOURCES OF REGULATION: THE RESPECTIVE ROLES OF LEGISLATION AND AGREEMENT

4.74   The implementation of the Working Time Directive marked a turning point in the regulation of basic terms and conditions of employment in the UK. For the first time, working time controls were put in place which, in principle, could cover the working population in general, subject only to specific derogations. This reversed the previous approach whereby statutory regulations

---

453 Directive 93/104, Preamble, para 8.
454 See *Explanatory Memorandum on the Draft Directive concerning Working Time* COM (90) 317. An earlier Regulation (3820/85) governing the hours of lorry drivers had already sets a normal daily limit of nine hours driving which can be extended to ten but with a two-weekly limit of 90 hours and breaks every four and a half hours. See *Prime v Hosking* [1995] IRLR 143; Case C-394/92: *Criminal Proceedings against Michielsen & Geybels Transport Service NV* [1995] IRLR 171; Case C-193/99 *Criminal Proceedings against Hume* [2001] IRLR 103.
455 Case C-84/94: [1996] ECR I-5755.
456 See para 2.6 above; Fitzpatrick, 1997.
457 See Directives 2000/34/EC and 2003/88/EC respectively.
458 Case C-84/94 [1996] ECR I-5755.
459 *Measures to Implement Provisions of the EC Directives on the Organisation of Working Time ('The Working Time Directive') and the Protection of Young People at Work ('The Young Workers Directive')*, April 1998.
460 SI 1998/1833 (henceforth WTR 1998); see Barnard, 1999.
461 SI 1999/3372; see Barnard, 2000b.
462 The Regulations should be read together with the regulatory guidance issued by the DTI by reference to WTR 1998, reg 35A. The guidance is reproduced on the DTI web site and is regularly updated; see http://www.dti.gov.uk/er/work_time_regs/wtr0.htm.

applied only to certain specified sectors and/or occupations, or to particular groups of workers, leaving the unregulated areas untouched. The Working Time Regulations of 1998 made a second important change in the mode of application of standards. Using the scope for derogations allowed for in the original Directive, the Regulations devolve much of the responsibility for arriving at precise standards to agreement at lower levels, including not just collective agreements but also individual agreements. This form of devolution of law-making authority from statute to collective bargaining (and, beyond that, to individual contract) is unusual in the UK context, although it has a longer history in continental systems.[463]

A central concept under the Regulations is that of a 'relevant agreement'. This is an agreement which is capable of varying or in some cases complementing the statutory standards laid down in the Regulations. A relevant agreement, 'in relation to a worker, means a workforce agreement which applies to him, any provision of a collective agreement which forms part of a contract between him and his employer,[464] or any other agreement in writing which is legally enforceable as between the worker and his employer'.[465] A 'workforce agreement' is, essentially, one made either with specified representatives of the workforce or, in certain circumstances, with a majority of the workers themselves.[466] More precisely, a workforce agreement may not be made in respect of any part of the workforce which is already covered by terms and conditions of employment which derive from a collective agreement between an employer and an independent trade union.[467] It must either cover all members of the employer's workforce whose terms and conditions are not regulated by such a collective agreement, or, alternatively, all such members (known as 'relevant members') who 'belong to a particular group'. A 'particular group' is defined as 'a group of the relevant members of a workforce who undertake a particular function, work at a particular workplace or belong to a particular department or unit within their employer's business'.[468] The agreement must be signed either by representatives of the workforce or, if the agreement only covers a 'particular group', by representatives of that group. 'Representatives' here means workers duly elected to represent either the workforce or the group as the case may be.[469] The number of representatives is set by the employer. The candidates must be members of the workforce or group in question. The employer may not unreasonably exclude any member of the workforce who, on this basis, is eligible to stand, from doing so. Arrangements for the election must ensure that the vote is taken in secret, that there is a fair and accurate count, and that the workers

---

463 The technique of regulating through a generally-applicable standard from which limited derogations are then carved out is more a feature of continental labour law than it is of British labour law, although there are some British precedents; for example, the health and safety inspectorate had powers to make exemptions from the (now repealed) nightwork provisions of the Factories Acts, but with the right to attach conditions for the protection of the workforce. See Deakin, 1990.

464 For this purpose, the definition of collective agreement in TULRCA 1992, s 178, is relevant, with the qualification that the agreement must be made by an independent trade union (see the definition of collective agreement in WTR 1998, reg 2(1)), and the common law rules for the incorporation of terms into collective agreements are implicitly adopted (see para 4.26 *et seq* above).

465 WTR 1998, reg 2(1).

466 See generally WTR 1998, Sch 1.

467 WTR 1998, Sch 1, para 2.

468 WTR 1998, Sch 1, para 2.

469 WTR 1998, Sch 1, para 2.

are entitled to vote for as many candidates as there representatives to be elected.[470] The agreement must normally be signed by the relevant representatives who must, for this purpose, be employed by the employer on the date when the agreement is made available for signature;[471] if, on that date, the employer employs 20 or fewer workers, the agreement may be signed by a majority of the workers in employment at that time.[472] Other conditions for the validity of a workplace agreement are that it must be in writing;[473] it must take effect for a specified period not exceeding five years;[474] and, before the agreement is signed, all workers affected by it must be sent a written copy of its contents by the employer and must be given guidance by the employer as to its effect.[475]

In the words of the consultation document which presaged the 1998 Regulations, '[t]he use of workplace agreements may be particularly apt for small and medium size enterprises, perhaps where there are no union members among their workforce. Agreement by signature from the majority of relevant members of the workforce may be appropriate and practical for very small businesses, with election arrangements being confined only to relatively larger ones'.[476] This is an acknowledgement of the need to have a mechanism for achieving flexibility in the application of standards in certain workplaces. However, this aspect of the Regulations raises wider questions concerning the effectiveness and legitimacy of agreements made without the support of an independent union.[477] The Regulations preserve the priority of agreements made through the normal channel of the recognised trade union, but only where arrangements for collective bargaining are in place; otherwise, the employer is free to make a workforce agreement with representatives who may not be 'independent' in the sense used to refer to an independent union. Even more controversial is the third type of relevant agreement, that is, a legally enforceable agreement made between the employer and an individual worker. As we shall see below, by no means all of the standards laid down in the Regulation can be modulated using either workforce agreements or individual agreements. However, among the rights which can be affected in these ways is the core right of workers not be required to work more than 48 hours on average per week.

SCOPE

4.75   The 1993 Directive was stated to apply to all areas of economic activity as defined by the Framework Directive on Health and Safety,[478] but then went on to exclude 'air, rail, road, sea, inland waterway and lake transport, sea fishing, other work at sea and the activities of doctors in training'.[479] These

470 WTR 1998, Sch 1, para 3.
471 WTR 1998, Sch 1, para 1(d)(i).
472 WTR 1998, Sch 1, para 1(d)(ii).
473 WTR 1998, Sch 1, para 1(a).
474 WTR 1998, Sch 1, para 1(b).
475 WTR 1998, Sch 1, para 1(e).
476 *Measures to Implement Provisions of the EC Directives on the Organisation of Working Time ('The Working Time Directive') and the Protection of Young People at Work ('The Young Workers Directive')*, April 1998, at p 2.
477 The issue of the legitimacy of workers' representatives is addressed under WTR 1998 Sch 1, para 3, which, as we have just seen, lays down rules governing the process of election; however, this is in principle subject to the test of representativity laid down by the Court of First Instance in Case T-135/96 *UEAPME v Council* [1998] IRLR 602; see Barnard, 1999: p 69.
478 Directive 89/391, Art 2; see below, para 4.83.
479 Art 1(3).

exclusions were subsequently narrowed, or in some cases removed altogether, by the Horizontal Amending Directive of 2000,[480] and additional Directives were put in place for specific sectors.[481] As a result, special rules now apply to mobile workers in sea, road and air transport.[482] With effect from 1 August 2003, non-mobile workers in these sectors, in addition to all workers in rail transport and all workers in other forms of work at sea (such as offshore oil and gas workers), gained the full protection of the 1998 Regulations, and mobile workers in road transport received the benefit of the provisions governing paid annual leave and health assessment for nightwork.[483]

The reference in the 1993 Directive to 'doctors in training' excluded British junior hospital doctors from the scope of protection and left them dependent upon any claim which might have been framed for breach of the employer's common law duty to protect the safety and health of its employees.[484] However, the Horizontal Amending Directive of 2000 improved their position,[485] and from 1 August 2004 the 1998 Regulations were applied to their situation, with two exceptions. Firstly, it was provided that the 48-hour weekly limit for working time would not come into effect in their case until 1 August 2009; a limit of 58 hours would apply from 1 August 2004 to 31 July 2007, and one of 56 hours between 1 August 2007 and 31 July 2009. Secondly, specific rules were put in place for calculating reference periods, based on a normal period of 26 weeks.[486]

Otherwise, the Regulations apply to 'workers',[487] and they also extend to Crown employees, House of Lords and House of Commons staff, the police, and members of the armed forces.[488] However, the Regulations do not apply to situations 'where characteristics peculiar to certain specified services such as the armed forces or the police or to certain specific activities in the civil protection services, inevitably conflict with the provisions of these Regulations'.[489] This exclusion, which is referable to Article 2(2) of the Framework Directive on Health and Safety,[490] 'seems to envisage a distinction between desk jobs (which are not covered by the exception) and other, frontline jobs'.[491] The Regulations also contain a wide set of exemptions with regard to domestic servants.[492] Finally,

---

480 Directive 2000/34/EC.
481 See COM (98) 662 final, laying out a series of proposals for amendments to the 1993 Directive and the adoption of new Directives in relation to mobile workers in the road transport sector, self-employed drivers, and the maritime sector. In May 2000 the Council agreed to amend the 1993 Directive so as to include non-mobile workers in the transport sector, who, it was subsequently confirmed, were outside its scope (Case C-133/00 *Bowden v Tuffnells Parcels Express Ltd* [2001] IRLR 838).
482 See, respectively, the Seafarers' Directive (1999/63/EC), the Road Transport Directive (2002/15/EC) and the Aviation Directive (2000/79/EC).
483 This was the effect of changes made to WTR 1998 by a number of amending regulations, principally SI 2003/1684.
484 *Johnstone v Bloomsbury Health Authority* [1992] QB 333; see above, para 4.8 and below, para 4.81. It is possible that they may be able to invoke Art 4(2) of the ECHR: see *Van der Musselle v Belgium* Judgment of 23 November 1983 (1984) 6 EHRR 163, at para. 37.
485 Directive 2000/34/EC, Art 1(6), inserting a new para 2.4 in Art 17 of the 1993 Directive; see now Directive 2003/88, Art 17(5).
486 See WTR 1998, reg 25A.
487 WTR 1998, reg 2; on the 'worker' concept, see paras 3.51–3.61 above.
488 WTR 1998, regs 36–43.
489 WTR 1998, reg 18(c).
490 Directive 89/391/EEC, Art 2(2).
491 Barnard, 1999: 63.
492 See WTR 1998, reg 19 (the exemptions relate to the rules concerning the weekly limit on working time, night work, and the pattern of work).

the Regulations were held in *Addison v Ashby*[493] to have no application to children below the minimum school age, thereby excluding a paper boy's claim for holiday pay. The EAT held that since the Regulations contain specific provisions governing 'young workers' between the minimum school age and 18[494] and are silent on the position of children below school leaving age, the latter are implicitly excluded.

LIMITS AND ENTITLEMENTS IN RELATION TO WORKING TIME

4.76 Under the Directive, Member States are required to take 'measures necessary to ensure that, in keeping with the need to protect the health and safety of workers ... the period of weekly working time is limited by means of laws, regulations or administrative provisions or by collective agreements or agreements between the two sides of industry', and to ensure that 'the average working time for each seven-day period, including overtime, does not exceed 48 hours'.[495] The Regulations, likewise, impose a duty upon the employer to 'take all reasonable steps, in keeping with the need to protect the health and safety of workers', to ensure that the 48-hour limit is 'complied with in the case of each worker employed by him'.[496]

The Directive and Regulations also lay down standards with regard to night work and unsocial hours working.[497] The first of these is a limit to normal average night work of eight hours in any 24-hour period, and an absolute limit of eight hours in any 24 if the work involves special hazards, or heavy physical or mental strain. Nightworkers must be provided with periodic, free health assessments, and those found to be suffering health problems as a result of night work following an assessment by a registered medical practitioner must be transferred, where possible, to suitable day work. The Directive stipulates that in organising working patterns of shifts, employers must also take into account 'the general principle of adapting work to the worker, with a view, in particular, to alleviating monotonous work and work at a predetermined work-rate, depending on the type of activity, and of safety and health requirements, especially as regards breaks during working time'.[498] This is based on the important principle of the 'humanisation of work' which is borrowed from German labour law.[499]

Nightwork is defined by the Directive as a period of not less than seven hours including at least the period from midnight to 5 am.[500] Under the Regulations, the period between 11 p.m. and 6 a.m. is used for this purpose, unless a relevant agreement specifies a different seven-hour period between the hours of 10 p.m. and 7 a.m. A broad definition of 'nightworker' is used which includes workers who work at night for a least three hours on the majority of days they work or for such number of days as is agreed by a relevant agreement, or, as a residual category, to such extent that they can be said to normally work on a night work basis.[501] In *R v A-G for Northern Ireland, ex p Burns*[502] this

---

493 [2003] IRLR 211.
494 See below, para 4.79 for legislation specifically governing the position of children below school leaving age.
495 Directive 2003/88, Art 6.
496 WTR 1998, reg 4(2).
497 Directive 2003/88, Arts 8–13; WTR 1998, regs 4, 6–7.
498 Directive 2003/88, Art 13.
499 Däubler, 1990: p 321.
500 Directive 2003/88, Art 2(3).
501 See WTR 1998, reg 2(1); Barnard, 1999: p 73.
502 [1999] IRLR 315.

definition was held to be wide enough to cover a worker who worked between the hours of 9 p.m. and 7 a.m. in one week in three.

The limits on working time are subject to the concept of the 'reference period' over which actual working hours may be averaged out.[503] The Directive lays down a default reference period of four months in respect of the maximum working week of 48 hours, which in the Regulations is stated as 17 weeks. The starting point of the 17-week period may be set by a 'relevant agreement' but if no such agreement is made, it is any period of 17 weeks of the worker's employment.

The Directive defines 'working time' as 'any period during which the worker is working, at the employer's disposal and carrying out his activity or duties, in accordance with national laws and/or practice', and a rest period is 'any period which is not working time'.[504] In the *SIMAP* case,[505] the ECJ took the view that time spent on call by doctors could be 'working time' if they were required to be present at their place of work during this period, but not otherwise. The Court implicitly viewed the three elements of the 'working time' definition as cumulative rather than alternative, since it took the view that even if the doctors were 'at the disposal of their employer' while away from the workplace, they failed to satisfy the other elements of the definition since in that case they 'may manage their own time with fewer constraints and pursue their own interests'.[506]

The Regulations establish a complex formula for calculating weekly average working time and time spent on night work.[507] The problem addressed here is the one of calculating time spent at work in such a way as to take into account days spent on leave for various reasons, known as 'excluded days'. Essentially, the average figure is arrived at by adding the aggregate hours worked by the worker during the reference period to an additional number of hours in respect of days worked in the *next* reference period which make up for the 'excluded days'. The combined figure is then divided by the number of weeks in the reference period.

The Directive and Regulations also lay down a minimum daily rest period of eleven consecutive hours out of every 24;[508] rest breaks of twenty minutes (unless a different period is set by a collective or workforce agreement) every six hours during the working day;[509] and a period of weekly rest. In the Directive, the weekly rest period is specified to be a period of 35 consecutive hours per week (24 hours plus the eleven hours of minimum daily rest), which may be reduced to 24 hours in total where 'objective, technical or work organisation conditions so justify'.[510] In the Regulations, reference is made to the 24-hour rest period being taken as either two uninterrupted rest periods of 24 hours or one uninterrupted rest period of 48 hours in a 14-day period.[511] The Directive

---

503 Directive 2003/88, Art 16.
504 Directive 2003/88, Art 2(1), 2(2).
505 Case C-303/98 *SIMAP v Conselleria de Sanidad y Consumo de la Generalidad Valenciana* [2000] IRLR 845; to broadly similar effect is Case C-151/02 *Landeshaupstadt Kiel v Jaeger* [2003] IRLR 804. The European Commission has proposed to modify the Directive to provide that on-call time spent at the place of work should not be classed as 'working time': see COM (2004) 607 final.
506 *SIMAP*, Judgment of the Court, at para 50.
507 See regs 4(6) and 6(5).
508 Directive 2003/88, Art 3; WTR 1998, reg 10.
509 Directive 2003/88, Art 4; WTR 1998, reg 12. A 'rest break' must be fixed in advance of its commencement: see *Gallagher v Alpha Catering Services Ltd* [2005] IRLR 102, at para 50 (Peter Gibson LJ).
510 Directive 2003/88, Art 5.
511 Directive 2003/88, reg 11.

originally provided that the period of weekly rest 'shall in principle include Sunday', but this provision, alone of the terms of the Directive, was struck down by the ECJ in the *Working Time* case.[512]

Finally, provision is made for minimum annual paid leave of four weeks.[513] The Regulations originally provided for a minimum qualifying period of thirteen weeks continuous employment to apply,[514] but this restriction, which is not to be found in the Directive, was successfully challenged before the ECJ[515] and subsequently removed.[516] The Directive provides that the right may not be commuted into a payment in lieu, except where the employment is terminated.[517] It is unclear whether the practice of 'rolled up' holiday pay – whereby a premium is added to wages paid in respect of periods of completed work, to represent holiday pay, and no extra payment is made in respect of the period of leave itself – is compatible with the Directive. This question has given rise to extensive litigation, culminating in a reference to the ECJ.[518] Even if the extra element in respect of holiday pay can be clearly identified, it is arguable that the practice falls outside the Directive in so far as it discourages workers from taking the leave to which they are entitled.[519] The Court of Appeal has recently held that workers who are on prolonged leave of absence by virtue of illness, who have exhausted their entitlement to sick pay, are not entitled to paid annual leave or a payment in lieu if the employment is terminated.[520]

DEROGATIONS

4.77   Article 17 of the Directive permits Member States to make derogations in five broadly defined areas. The first relates to what may be thought of as workers with a degree of control over their own working time: 'managing executives or others with autonomous decision-making powers', 'family workers'

---

512 [1996] ECR I-5755.
513 Directive 2003/88, Art 7; WTR 1998, regs 13–16. Prior to November 1999, the period of leave provided for by the Regulations was three weeks, under a derogation allowed by the 1993 Directive (Art 18).
514 WTR 1998, reg 13(2).
515 Case C-173/99 *BECTU v Secretary of State for Trade and Industry* [2001] ECR I-4881. See also *Gibson v East Riding of Yorkshire Council* [2000] IRLR 598 in which the Court of Appeal held that the right contained in the Directive was not sufficiently precise to be capable of having direct effect, since, in any given case, the worker's right to leave could only be ascertained once their working time was known; in the Court's view, the Directive itself did not contain a clear or precise enough definition of 'working time' for the nature of the right to leave to be deduced from this source alone. It is arguable that this approach is not reconcilable with that of the ECJ in the *SIMAP* and *BECTU* cases.
516 SI 2001/3256.
517 In the event of termination, the employer must make a payment in lieu if worker has used up a lesser proportion of their leave entitlement than that represented by their service for the year in question (WTR 1998, reg. 14) but there is no equivalent entitlement to make a deduction from wages due if the worker has taken a higher proportion of their leave entitlement (*Hill v Chapell* [2003] IRLR 19).
518 See *Witley & District Men's Club v Mackay* [2001] IRLR 595; *Blackburn v Gridquest Ltd* [2002] IRLR 604; *MPB Structures v Munro* [2004] 2 CMLR 44, [2003] IRLR 350; *Caulfield v Marshalls Clay Products Ltd* [2004 IRLR 564 (following which a reference to the ECJ was made); *Smith v AJ Morrisroes and Sons Ltd* [2005] IRLR 72.
519 See, in particular, the judgment of the Inner House of the Court of Session in *MPB Structures v Munro* [2003] IRLR 350; *Bamsey v Albon Engineering and Manufacturing plc* [2004] IRLR 457.
520 *Commissioners of Inland Revenue v Ainsworth* [2005] IRLR 465.

and those 'officiating at religious ceremonies in churches and religious communities',[521] and applies to the provisions governing the working week, nightwork, weekly and daily rest, but not to the rights to annual paid leave and to free health assessments. For this group, no required method of derogation is specified. Under the Regulations,[522] this category is referred to in terms of 'unmeasured working time', which means a situation where 'on account of the specific characteristics of the activity in which [the worker] is engaged, the duration of his working time is not measured or predetermined or can be determined by the worker himself'. In an amendment made by the 1999 Regulations,[523] this derogation also covers workers part of whose activities fall into this category; for this purpose, the limits on working time and night work apply only to those activities which are not measured or predetermined by the worker.[524]

A second category is a miscellaneous group of workers for whom rigid controls may be inappropriate. These are:[525] those employed a long distance from their residence; security workers; workers employed in activities requiring continuity of service and production (particularly, health workers, residential care workers, and prison officers; dock or airport workers; media workers; emergency service workers; workers in the utilities sectors; workers employed in continuous process industries ('industries in which work cannot be interrupted on technical grounds');[526] research and development workers; and agricultural workers); workers subject to a 'foreseeable surge in activity' (in particular in agriculture, tourism, and postal services); and those working in emergency or accident situations. Under the Directive, derogations here must take the form of laws, regulations or collective agreements and must involve compensatory rest periods for the workers concerned or, in exceptional circumstances, other appropriate protection; they do not apply to the right to annual paid leave or to the limit upon weekly working time. The Regulations spell out in detail the excluded categories under this heading.[527]

A third set of derogations concerns certain shift workers. Again, these derogations must take the form of laws, regulations or collective agreements (the level of which is not specified) and must involve compensatory rest periods for the workers concerned; they apply only to the daily rest and weekly rest provisions.[528]

Fourth, the Directive permits derogations to be made without reference to the type of work being carried out, if they take the form of collective agreements at national or regional level, or of lower-level collective agreements made in accordance with the rules laid down by national or regional agreements.[529]

---

521 Directive 2003/88, Art 17(1); WTR 1998, reg 20.
522 WTR 1998, reg 20.
523 SI 1999/3372, reg 4.
524 For discussion, see Barnard, 2000b: pp 169–171.
525 See Directive 2003/88, Art 17(3).
526 See *Gallagher v Alpha Catering Services) t/a Alpha Flight Services* [2005] IRLR 102 and Joined Cases C-397/01–C403/01 *Pfeiffer v Deutsches Rotes Kreutz, Kreizverband Waldshut eV* [2005] IRLR 137.
527 WTR 1998, reg 21. As Barnard (1999) points out, these derogations apply to workers employed in activities of a particular kind, and not to all workers in the occupations in question.
528 See WTR 1998, reg 22 (although note also reg 24(6)).
529 Directive 2003/88, Art 18.

Derogating agreements may modify the rules relating to night work, daily and weekly rest periods, and rest breaks; if so, they must provide for equivalent rest periods or, in an exceptional case where this is not possible, 'appropriate protection' for workers concerned and such agreements may be extended to cover workers outside their express scope. No derogations may be made under this category with respect to annual paid leave, nor to the length of the maximum working week. However, the default reference period for the calculation of the maximum working week can be extended from four months to up to one year.[530]

This potentially very wide derogating power has been implemented in the Regulations. These allow collective agreements or workforce agreements to make the allowable modifications to the statutory standards which would otherwise apply. These agreements can also extend the reference period for calculating maximum weekly working hours from 17 to 52 weeks where objective or technical reasons, or reasons related to the organisation of work, require this.[531] The Regulations implement the principle that compensatory rest should be provided in return for the derogation.[532]

In addition, Article 22 of the Directive allows Member States to permit individual derogations to be made from the 48-hour maximum working week. This may be done on condition that the power of the employer to ask a worker to work more than 48 hours per week may only be exercised where 'he has obtained the worker's agreement' to do so[533] and also on condition that regular records are kept of workers' employed hours over this limit. This provision was set to operate for a period of seven years after the Directive came into force on 23 November 1996. At the end of 2003 the Commission initiated a review process, which at the time of writing is still continuing.[534]

Under the 1998 Regulations, individual derogations were subject to a number of strict conditions; they had to be in writing and allow for termination by the worker by seven days' notice in writing, or such longer period, up to a maximum of three months, as the parties agreed. The 1998 Regulations also imposed upon employers extensive record-keeping requirements, including an obligation to specify those workers agreeing to work in excess of 48 hours, the terms on which they did so, and the hours worked by these workers in each reference period since the agreement came into effect. These provisions were amended in 1999. Now there is a simple requirement for the agreement to be in writing and for the employer to record those workers who had made an agreement of this kind.[535]

---

530 Directive 2003/88, Art 19.
531 WTR 1998, reg 23.
532 WTR 1998, reg 24.
533 Art 22(1)(a). According to the ECJ in Case C-303/98 *SIMAP* [2000] IRLR 845, this does not include the situation in which a trade union representing the worker makes the agreement on his or her behalf. See Joined Cases C-397/01–C-403/01 *Pfeiffer v Deutsches Rotes Kreutz, Kreizverband Waldshut eV* [2005] IRLR 137 for more general guidance on the conditions that must be met including the need for genuine consent on the part of the worker.
534 For an account of the background to the Commission's review, together with an overview and assessment of empirical evidence relating to the individual opt out, see Barnard *et al*, 2004. In the course of 2004 the Commission produced a consultation paper directed to the Member States (COM (2003) 843 final) and initiated a consultation process with the social partners (SEC (2004) 610) before making a proposal to amend the Directive (COM (2004) 607 final). This would retain the possibility of an individual opt-out from the 48 hour week but only in those workplaces or sectors where there was no applicable collective agreement. It would also impose more stringent record-keeping requirements and stricter formalities as conditions of the individual opt-out, and set a new upper limit of 65 hours per week, which could only be varied by collective agreement.
535 WTR 1998, reg 4(1), as amended.

At first sight, the standards in the Directive and Regulations are severely qualified by the scope of these various derogations and exceptions. However, it would be misleading to conclude that, for this reason, the Directive has not had a substantial impact on British labour law. It effectively requires a complete change of approach from the tradition of piecemeal regulation, specific to individual sectors, in favour of a general floor of rights. For the most part, the Directive imposes strict conditions on derogations, requiring them to take the form of laws or of collective agreements and sometimes requiring compensation for the individual workers affected by them. The need to construe the derogations narrowly has also been emphasised by the ECJ in the *SIMAP* and *Pfeiffer* cases.[536] This casts some doubt on some of the wide derogations allowed for in the Regulations, particularly those introduced in 1999.

ENFORCEMENT

4.78   The Directive permits Member States to comply with its terms either by legislation or by ensuring that the two sides of industry establish the necessary measures by agreement. In the latter case, the Member State is obliged to take any necessary steps to enable them to guarantee at all times that the provisions laid down by this Directive are fulfilled.[537] The Regulations make provision for a range of criminal and civil enforcement methods.[538] The scheme laid down in the Regulations envisages that 'working time limits' – the 48-hour weekly limits, and limits on night work – would be enforced through criminal prosecutions and administrative action by the Health and Safety Executive, which would also have responsibility for monitoring record keeping.[539] By contrast, 'working time entitlements' – the rights to rest periods and annual leave – would be enforceable by individual workers before employment tribunals.[540] This scheme was upset, however, by the judgment of the High Court in *Barber v RJB Mining Ltd*,[541] in which it was held that the right not to be required to work in excess of 48 hours per week formed part of the individual contracts of workers covered by the Regulations. This judgment demonstrates a more flexible approach to the relationship between statutory standards and contractual rights than has often hitherto been the case.[542] On this basis, the 'limits' specified by the Directive and Regulations are capable of giving rise to rights which are enforceable by individual workers.

The Young Workers Directive and implementing Regulations

4.79   A further EC instrument, the Directive on the Protection of Young Persons at Work,[543] contains provisions regulating the working hours of children and young persons as well as more general measures of a health and safety nature.[544]

---

536 Case C-303/98 *SIMAP* [2000] IRLR 845; Joined Cases C-397/01–C403/01 *Pfeiffer v Deutsches Rotes Kreutz, Kreizverband Waldshut eV* [2005] IRLR 137.
537 Art 18(1).
538 WTR 1998, regs 28–34.
539 WTR 1998, regs 28 and 29. Note that local authorities also have an enforcement role in specific circumstances: reg 28(3)–(5).
540 WTR 1998, reg 30. Rights not to be dismissed or subject to a detriment are provided by reg 31.
541 [1999] IRLR 308; A Edwards, 2000.
542 See above 4.10.
543 Directive 94/33.
544 On the latter, see footnote 552 below.

The employment of children, defined here as persons below the minimum school leaving age or 15 years, whichever is higher, is prohibited. There are exceptions only for work in theatres and films, work experience and/or training, and light work, with strict conditions attached in each case.[545] In particular, children falling within one of these exceptions must not work for more than two hours on any school day or for more than 12 hours a week during term time.[546] Night work by children is prohibited between 8 pm and 6 am.[547] Persons aged between 15 (or the minimum school leaving age) and 18, classified in Britain as 'young persons' for health and safety purposes and termed 'adolescents' in the Directive, are limited to a maximum working day of 8 hours and a maximum working week of 40 hours.[548] Night work by this group is prohibited between the hours of 10 pm and 6 am or 11 pm and 7 am.[549] Minimum daily and weekly rest periods are also laid down for children and adolescents;[550] in addition, there are provisions for derogation from certain of the working-time standards which are similar to those contained in the Working Time Directive.

The UK was granted the benefit of a provision entitling it (but no other Member State) to delay the implementation of most of the Directive for a further four years from the date when the Directive came into force (which was 22 June 1996).[551] Much of the Directive was implemented in the form of regulations adopted in 1997 and 1998.[552] The Working Time Regulations 1998 implement those parts of the Directive which relate to what the 1994 Directive calls 'adolescents' and the Regulations call 'young workers' between the minimum school leaving age and the age of 18.[553]

HEALTH AND SAFETY AND THE WORKING ENVIRONMENT

4.80   The subject of occupational health and safety is a substantial one in its own right. Much of health and safety law operates by imposing regulatory duties upon employers which are enforced through the powers of the health and safety inspectorate and, ultimately, the sanctions of the criminal courts; the detailed provisions of these public-regulatory statutes and their mechanisms of enforcement lie outside the scope of this work.[554] Instead, this section will briefly consider the impact of health and safety standards on the individual employment relationship. In some cases of a breach of a criminal statute, an individual

---

545 Directive 94/33, Arts 4, 5.
546 Directive 94/33, Art 8(1)(a)–(b).
547 Directive 94/33, Art 9.
548 Directive 94/33, Art 8.
549 Directive 94/33, Art 9.
550 Directive 94/33, Arts 10–12.
551 Directive 94/33, Art 17.
552 The Health and Safety (Young Persons) Regulations, SI 1997/135, implemented Arts 6 and 7 of the Directive which relate to the general obligations of employers with regard to the health and safety of young persons and the prohibition of certain types of employment of young persons. These were then revoked by the Management of Health and Safety at Work Regulations 1999 (SI 1999/3242), reg 19 of which deals with the employment of young persons. The Children (Protection at Work) Regulations, SI 1998/276, implement those parts of the Directive which concern the employment of children (that is, those below the compulsory school leaving age). See generally the Children and Young Persons Act 1933 as amended.
553 WTR 1998, regs 5A and 6A, as inserted by SI 2002/3128.
554 See Ford and Brown, 2003.

worker may bring an action for damages *via* the tort of breach of statutory duty; this is an action developed by the courts at common law. In the absence of a specific statute, the employer may be held liable in negligence for its breach of the general common law duty to provide safe working conditions, or may find itself vicariously liable for the tort of an employee. The Health and Safety at Work Act 1974 also imposes a general responsibility on the employer to ensure 'so far as is reasonably practicable' the health, safety and welfare of employees, as well as aiming to incorporate aspects of health and safety observance into managerial practice. Finally, European-level regulation has come to have a major influence in this area, mainly through the 1989 Framework Directive[555] and the daughter directives designed to implement its general objectives in the areas of workplace safety, protection against hazardous substances and specific industries.

Common law duties of the employer

4.81 Employees' actions for damages for personal injury suffered at work were stymied for most of the nineteenth century by the doctrine of common employment. This operated through an implied term in the contract of service, the effect of which was that the employee or servant took the risk of injury or damage caused by a fellow servant's negligence. The employer was thereby absolved of any vicarious liability for a tort committed by one fellow worker against another.[556] If the injury was caused by the employee of another employer, it was highly possible that the victim's claim would be defeated by contributory negligence or *volenti non fit injuria*.[557] The doctrine of common employment was abolished by statute in 1948;[558] around the same time, contributory negligence was made a partial as opposed to a complete defence,[559] and the courts began to take a much more restrictive view than previously of the scope of *volenti*.[560] Even before these changes, developments within the common law had enabled the courts to outflank the broad, pro-employer defences. The defences of *volenti* and common employment were held to be inapplicable to claims based on the civil action for breach of statutory duty, which was widely applied to factories legislation following the decision of the Court of Appeal in *Groves v Lord Wimborne* in 1898.[561] Then in *Wilsons & Clyde Coal Co v English*, decided in 1937,[562] the House of Lords confirmed the existence of an employer's *general* duty of care in tort with regard to the safety of its employees. The duty was affirmative in nature and could not be discharged merely by delegation to an appropriate employee or agent of the employer; the doctrine of common employment, which focused on the negligence of the *employee*, was therefore irrelevant to this claim.

---

555 Directive 89/391.
556 *Priestley v Fowler* (1837) 3 M & W 1; *Farwell v Boston and Worcester Railroad Corpn* 4 Metcalf 49 (1842) (Supreme Court of Massachusetts); *Bartonshill Coal Co v Reid* (1858) 3 Macq 266.
557 See, eg, *Woodley v Metropolitan District Rly Co* (1877) 2 Ex D 384.
558 Law Reform (Personal Injuries) Act 1948, s 1.
559 Law Reform (Contributory Negligence) Act 1945.
560 The restriction of *volenti* began with *Smith v Charles Baker & Sons Ltd* [1891] AC 325, so that by the time contributory negligence had been made a partial defence, *volenti* had also ceased to be a major obstacle to employees' claims. Since 1945 it has only been applied in somewhat exceptional cases such as *ICI Ltd v Shatwell* [1965] AC 656.
561 [1898] 2 QB 402. On *volenti* in this context, see *Wheeler v New Merton Board Mills Ltd* [1933] 2 KB 669.
562 [1938] AC 57.

The *Wilsons* case lays down what is, in effect, a four-fold duty of care. Lord Wright said that the employer's responsibilities related to the provision of competent fellow workers, safe materials and a proper system of work; in addition, there is the category of a safe place of work. More generally, it may be said that 'convenient as these categories are, they are only aspects of the broad duty to see that reasonable care is taken'.[563] Thus an employer is required to take care in choosing staff and will be liable for exposing an employee to injury caused by his or her colleagues' practical jokes.[564] Equally, the employer may be liable to failing to take steps to ensure that an employee is not subjected to harassment and victimisation which results in physical and/or mental harm.[565] The duty to provide safe equipment is now strict, as a result of the Employer's Liability (Defective Equipment) Act 1969. This effectively overrules the decision of the House of Lords in *Davie v New Merton Board Mills Ltd*,[566] according to which an employer cannot be held liable for undiscoverable defects in materials or equipment supplied to it by a third party. The Act imposes liability on the employer if the defect was caused by the fault of the manufacturer or supplier. By contrast, the common law duty to provide a safe place of work and safe working system is still based on fault, and an employer may avoid liability if it can show that, in the circumstances, it took all reasonable steps to ensure the safety of its employees. For example, in determining what is reasonable, the court may take into account the possible costs to the employer of closing down all or part of its operations, if no other means of avoiding the risk of injury was available.[567]

The expression of the employer's common law obligations in terms of a common law duty of care in tort as opposed to an implied contract term is, in many ways, a product of historical accident as much as anything else. As long as the doctrine of common employment operated through an implied contract term, the scope for a contractual solution to the employee's interest in health and safety protection was limited. Moreover, when the *Wilsons* case was decided few aspects of the individual employment relationship were given contractual form; the expression of extensive reciprocal duties through the individual contract of employment is largely a post-1945 development.[568]

In *Lister v Romford Ice and Cold Storeage Co*,[569] decided in 1955, Lord Radcliffe thought that the employer's implied obligations could be equally well expressed in either contract or tort. In terms of the substance of the obligation it seems that it does not matter whether tort or contract is used, but the distinction is not without significance. In particular, the limitation period for actions in tort begins later than that in contract, namely at the point when the injury or damage is sustained as opposed to the point at which the breach of duty takes place.[570] Moreover, the damages which are recoverable in a tort claim will incorporate

---

563 Deakin, Johnston and Markesinis, 2003: p 563. For recent decisions on the common law duty of care to avoid physical harm to the employee which discuss issues arising from repetitive strain injury, see *Pickford v ICI* [1998] IRLR 435; *Alexander v Midland Bank* [1999] IRLR 723; Larkin, 2000.
564 *Hudson v Ridge Manufacturing Co Ltd* [1957] 2 QB 348.
565 *Waters v Commissioner of Police of the Metropolis* [2000] IRLR 720.
566 [1959] AC 604.
567 *Latimer v AEC Ltd* [1953] AC 643.
568 See above, para 4.4 *et seq*.
569 [1957] AC 555.
570 See Deakin, Johnston and Markesinis, 2003: pp 772–781 for an account of the relevant principles.

an element for loss of earning capacity and loss of future earnings which will not normally be recoverable in contract.[571] On the other hand, it may be useful to an employee to be able to show that the employer has acted in breach of contract by disregarding their health and safety; this is the case, for example, where the employee resigns and claims constructive dismissal.[572] In *Waltons & Morse v Dorrington*[573] the applicant, a non-smoker who worked as a secretary for a firm of solicitors, left her employment in protest at her employer's failure to deal adequately with her complaints about being exposed to the cigarette smoke of fellow employees. The EAT, upholding a finding of constructive dismissal, held that 'the correct implied term to deal with the complaint in this case is that the employer will provide and monitor for his employees, so far as is reasonably practicable, a working environment which is reasonably suitable for the performance by them of their contractual duties'.[574] The employment tribunal had been entitled to find, in this case, that it would have been reasonably practicable for the employer to have prohibited employees from smoking inside the building which it occupied.

The employer's common law duty of care extends to an obligation to ensure that the employee is not placed in a position, through overwork or otherwise, of undue exposure to mental stress. This is so notwithstanding that the employee may have express contractual commitments to work a certain number of daily or weekly hours or to carry out certain supervisory or managerial tasks. *Johnstone v Bloomsbury Health Authority*[575] is authority for the proposition that where an individual employee foreseeably contracts illness or disease through working excessive hours, the employer cannot avoid liability simply by arguing that the working hours in question were those laid down in the contract. The basis for this ruling is not altogether clear, however, since the majority judges did not offer the same set of reasons.[576] Browne-Wilkinson VC thought that the employer had the right to call on the employee to work hours up to the limit set by the contract (88 per week in total); however, in respect of overtime hours (above 40) this right was qualified by the duty to act in such a way as to maintain the trust and co-operation which was essential to the employment relationship, which in this context meant avoiding placing the employee's health and safety in danger. Stuart-Smith LJ, by contrast, thought that such a contract term was ineffective to oust the common law duty of care. Stuart-Smith LJ's view seems preferable: at the very least, clear words should be needed to override the employer's implied duty with regard to health and safety. It is possible to go further and to suggest that public policy would strike down any contract term purporting to provide for working arrangements

571 On the reasons for the limited extent of damages for breach of contract at common law, see paras 5.21–5.29 below.

572 On constructive dismissal, see below, paras 5.72–5.75.

573 [1997] IRLR 488.

574 [1997] IRLR 488, 490.

575 [1992] QB 333. The remedies sought in *Johnstone* included a declaration of the parties' rights and an injunction preventing future breaches of contract by the employer. The judgments in that case were pursuant to a striking out application, which was rejected; the case did not subsequently go to trial. In *Barber v RJB Mining Ltd* [1999] IRLR 308 a declaration was granted to support employees' claims that their employer was acting in breach of WTR 1998, reg 4(1), which imposes a statutory obligation requiring employers to observe the 48-hour weekly limit to working time. If this approach is widely followed, enforcement of health and safety standards would be significantly strengthened. See A Edwards, 2000: pp 285–287.

576 See para 4.8 above.

which foreseeably endanger an employee's health,[577] but none of the judges in *Johnstone* expressed support for this view.

Johnstone was a case of alleged physical injury; in other cases, employers have been held liable for the negligent infliction of psychiatric harm. In *Walker v Northumberland County Council*[578] the court held an employer liable for psychiatric disease caused by exposure to a stressful working situation. The employee worked as a senior social services manager. Over a period of years his workload increased considerably, as a large number of child abuse cases were referred to the division which he managed, but without any increase in staff. He complained of overwork but was told that he would have to make do with his existing resources. He suffered a nervous breakdown and, after a short interval, returned to his previous post. Extra staff help was provided for a short period but then withdrawn; he subsequently suffered a second nervous breakdown, following which he was incapable of work and was dismissed on the grounds of ill health. The court held that the *second* nervous breakdown had been foreseeable, and that the employer's response had not been appropriate: the seriousness of the potential risk to the employee, coupled with the high likelihood of further injury following the initial breakdown, made the employer's response unreasonable.

This decision does not mean that employers will always be liable for the effects of working conditions which induce stress in their employees. The relevant standard is that of the reasonable employer, and as usual in negligence cases the court will balance the risk of harm and the likelihood of it occurring against the cost and practicability of preventive measures. In *Walker* the employer argued that the allocation of employees between different parts of its organisation was a matter for it to decide, but the court held that while this had to be weighed in the balance against the risk to the employee, it was not decisive on its own. However, it is significant that in *Walker* there were clear warning signs, based not just on the employee's complaints but also on his earlier illness. Employees in positions of managerial responsibility, in particular, may inevitably be exposed to a degree of stress as part of their work, and an employer probably would not be acting unreasonably merely by placing substantial demands upon them.[579]

The question of when an employer is liable for post-traumatic stress disorder suffered by an employee in response to witnessing an accident caused by the employer was discussed by the House of Lords in *White v Chief Constable of South Yorkshire Police*.[580] Here, police officers suffered post-traumatic stress disorder as a result of tending victims of the Hillsborough disaster. The deaths and injuries of the victims were caused by the negligence of a fellow police

---

577 Weir, 1993. Such a term might also be struck out by virtue of UCTA 1977; see above, para 4.8.

578 [1995] IRLR 35.

579 In *Barber v Somerset County Council* [2004] IRLR 475 the House of Lords affirmed that the overall test is still the conduct of the reasonable and prudent employer taking positive thought for the safety of its workers in the light of what it knows or ought to know, a test proposed by Swanwick J in *Stokes v Guest Keen and Nettleford (Bolts and Nuts) Ltd* [1968] 1WLR 1776. See also *Petch v Customs and Excise Comrs* [1993] ICR 789. *Sutherland v Hatton* [2002] IRLR 263; *Marshall Specialist Vehicles Ltd v Osborne* [2003] IRLR 672; *Pratley v Surrey County Council* [2003] IRLR 794; *Bonser v RJB Mining Co (UK) Ltd* [2004] IRLR 164; *Hartman v South Essex Mental Health and Community Care NHS Trust* [2005] IRLR 293; Barrett, 1995, 1996, 1999, 2001, 2004.

580 [1999] IRLR 110.

officer for which their employer was vicariously liable. The House of Lords rejected the claim, on the basis that the claimants were 'secondary victims' who fell outside the normal categories of those who could recover. An employee who is neither a rescuer nor a particularly close relative or possibly friend of the victim is now in no better position than a bystander.[581] However, the post-traumatic stress disorder cases are arguably distinguishable from *Walker* and other cases in which the employee is more closely analogous to a 'primary' victim of the employer's negligence or breach of contract.[582] This is confirmed by the more recent decision of the House of Lords in *Waters v Commissioner of Police of the Metropolis*,[583] in which it was held that the employer could be liable for exposing the claimant to psychological harm as a result of a failure to treat seriously a claim that she had been sexually assaulted by a fellow officer, and by preventing her from being victimised and harassed by other police officers once she made her initial complaint.

Statutory duties

4.82 The imposition on employers of specific statutory duties to ensure a safe place of work and system of working can be traced back to the earliest Factories Acts of the nineteenth century; as industrialisation developed, successive waves of legislation extended the scope of employers' duties without, however, achieving a general framework of health and safety for all workplaces.[584] Instead, regulation developed in a piecemeal fashion, in response to the needs or demands of particular industries. These measures were eventually collected in a series of separate Acts governing factories, mines and quarries and offices, shops and railway premises.[585] The Factories Act 1961, which consolidated earlier measures, laid down in Part I a series of provisions governing cleanliness, overcrowding, temperature, ventilation, lighting, drainage and sanitation. Part II of the Act was concerned with safety and contained measures relating to, *inter alia*, the construction, fencing and maintenance of machinery; the maintenance of floors, passages, stairs and means of access; the supply of drinking water and washing facilities; and seating facilities. Many of these provisions were regarded, through a process of judicial inference, as giving rise to civil actions for breach of statutory duty.[586]

Unlike the regulation of working time, which was largely confined to women workers and young workers, health and safety legislation was applied also to adult males, although many regulations set differential standards of protection for male and female employees. Women workers were, on the whole, subject to lower limits of exposure to dangerous substances and were excluded from a wide range of jobs which were considered at the time to pose a particular risk to the female physiognomy and reproductive capacity. The scientific basis for most of these distinctions now appears to have been dubious, since many of the

---

581 On this, see *McFarlane v EE Caledonia Ltd* [1994] 2 All ER 1.
582 See Deakin, Johnston and Markesinis, 2003: p 564.
583 [2000] IRLR 720; see also, on psychiatric damage in the context of the duty of mutual and confidence, *Gogay v Hertfordshire County Council* [2000] IRLR 703; para 4.91 below. On harassment in the context of health and safety law, see generally Barrett, 2000.
584 See generally Hutchins and Harrison, 1926.
585 The Factories Act 1961; the Mines and Quarries Act 1954; and the Offices, Shops and Railway Premises Acts 1963, respectively.
586 See Deakin, Johnston and Markesinis, 2003: p 358 *et seq.*

substances in question (such as lead and ionising radiation) have been shown to be equally dangerous to men.[587] The vast majority of those regulations which were specific to women were abolished by the Employment Act 1989, as part of the UK's implementation of the EC Directive on Equal Treatment.[588]

The passage of the Health and Safety at Work Act 1974 marked a change of direction in statutory policy. The Robens report which preceded the Act[589] recommended the enactment of general duties extending to all workplaces and to the self-employed. It also proposed greater encouragement of self-regulation through, amongst other things, the involvement in health and safety issues of workforce representatives. The main achievements of the Act were the imposition of a general statutory duty of care upon all employers; the extension of this duty in some instances to the self-employed; the establishment of a unified inspection and enforcement process, under the Health and Safety Executive; the setting-up of a tripartite Health and Safety Commission with the responsibility for drafting regulations and Codes of Practice and overseeing the work of the inspectorate; and the making of provision for the election of safety representatives in workplaces with recognised trade unions, with various responsibilities including membership of joint labour-management safety committees.[590]

The aims of the Act include 'securing the health, safety and welfare of persons at work', protecting other persons against risks to health and safety arising from work-related activities, and controlling the use of dangerous substances.[591] The category of 'persons at work' includes employees and the self-employed.[592] The Act imposes a duty on 'every employer to ensure, so far as is reasonably practicable, the health, safety and welfare at work of all his employees';[593] more specifically, the employer must ensure so far as reasonably practicable that safe plant and systems of work are maintained; arrangements are made for the minimisation of risks from dangerous articles and substances; information, instruction, training and supervision in health and safety matters are made available to employees; the workplace and the means of access to it are kept in a safe condition; and a 'working environment' for employees is provided which is 'safe, without risks to health, and adequate as regards facilities and arrangements for [employees'] welfare at work'.[594] The employer must also prepare a written health and safety policy.[595]

In addition, both employers and the self-employed must ensure so far as reasonably practicable that persons other than employees who may be affected by their activities are not thereby exposed to risks to their health and safety;[596] similar duties with regard to non-employees are also imposed on persons in control of non-domestic premises.[597] Employees themselves must take reasonable

---

587 See generally Deakin, 1990a.
588 Directive 76/207/EC.
589 *Report of the Committee on Health and Safety at Work*, Cmnd 5034, 1972.
590 On the 1974 Act in general, see James and Lewis, 1986, and on the current provisions relating to safety representatives and safety committees (which were amended in 1996), see paras 9.46–9.47 below.
591 HSWA 1974, s 1(1).
592 HSWA 1974, s 51.
593 HSWA 1974, s 2(1).
594 HSWA 1974, s 2(2).
595 HSWA 1974, s 2(3).
596 HSWA 1974, s 3; see *R v Associated Octel Co Ltd* [1997] IRLR 123 (discussed by Barrett, 1997); *R v Nelson Group Services (Maintenance) Ltd* [1999] IRLR 646. The Act does not apply to domestic employment, however: HSWA 1974, s 51.
597 HSWA 1974, s 4. S 6 imposes duties on manufacturers with regard to articles and substances for use at work.

care for their own health and safety and, in respect to duties imposed on their employer, must 'co-operate with him so far as is necessary to enable that duty or requirement to be performed or complied with'.[598]

The Act provides for enforcement of the duties referred to above by way of powers of inspection (including the use of 'improvement' and 'prohibition' notices) and by criminal sanctions;[599] no civil action by an employee or self-employed person is possible in respect of these general duties.[600] However, the more specific regulations made under the Act are assumed to give rise to a civil action for damages unless the contrary is stated.[601] This provision preserves the civil action for breach of statutory duty in respect of regulations made under the Act which replace earlier provisions made under the Factories Acts and legislation governing mines and non-factory premises.

At the time of its passage it was intended that the 1974 Act would provide a framework for the modernisation and integration of the many industry-specific regulations made under earlier statutes. This process has led to some significant strengthening of regulation, in the area, for example, of the control of dangerous substances.[602] However, many areas of pre-1974 regulation remain untouched, and the process of gradually bringing these up to date has been counter-balanced by the enactment of a general power to repeal pre-1974 health and safety legislation in the Deregulation and Contracting Out Act 1994.

Protection of the working environment

4.83 While domestic policy was turning towards deregulation in health and safety in the 1980s, a new minimum floor of rights was provided by the EC Framework Directive of 1989 and its 'daughter directives'.[603] The authority for these measures derives from Article 118a of the EC Treaty, which was inserted by the Single European Act of 1986 and is now consolidated in Article 137 of the Treaty. Prior to this, the Community had adopted only a small number of measures in the field of health and safety: a series of measures concerning safety signs,[604] exposure to certain hazardous agents[605] and exposure to noise at work.[606] Article 118a called on Member States to 'pay particular attention to encouraging improvements, especially in the working environment, as regards the health and safety of workers', and provides for the adoption of directives on the basis of qualified majority voting. The concept of the working environment originated in the Nordic systems of labour law, and as Nielson and Szyszczak explain, refers not simply to health and safety in the traditional sense but more generally to 'the arrangement of the workplace, the physical and socio-psychological conditions under which work is performed, the use of work equipment by workers at work, and the exposure of workers to toxic and other dangerous substances at work'.[607] The notion of the 'working environment' in

598 HSWA 1974, s 7.
599 HSWA 1974, ss 18–42.
600 HSWA 1974, s 47(1).
601 HSWA 1974, s 47(2).
602 The principal measure here is the Control of Substances Hazardous to Health Regulations, SI 2002/2677. For a general assessment of the progress made in relation to health and safety practice under the Act of 1974, see James, 1993.
603 For overviews of EC health and safety law, see Neal, 1998; Barnard, 2000a: ch 6.
604 Directive 77/556.
605 Directives 78/610, 88/1107, 82/605 and 83/477.
606 Directive 86/188.
607 Nielson and Szyszczak, 1997: p 331. See also Hydén, 1992.

the EC Treaty is evidently more extensive than the concept of 'health and safety', to which the Article also refers; however, the precise scope of the Article remains somewhat unclear. It cannot be construed as embracing all aspects of the individual employee's well-being; however, in *United Kingdom v EU Council (Working Time)* the ECJ ruled that it has a broad scope which, in that case, extended to cover the regulation of working time under Directive 93/104.[608]

The 1989 Framework Directive for the introduction of measures to encourage improvements in the safety and health of workers[609] is intended to provide a generally-applicable set of guidelines and principles for the promotion of health and safety. It does not, however, preclude more specific regulation, being 'without prejudice to more stringent present or future Community provisions',[610] a large number of which have subsequently been adopted. The purposes of the Directive include the economic goal of harmonisation designed to avoid 'competition at the expense of safety and health', but it is also stated that 'the improvement of workers' safety, hygiene and health at work is an objective which should not be "subordinated to purely economic considerations"'.[611] The standards contained in the Directive are minimum levels of protection, upon which Member States may improve.[612]

The Directive applies to 'all sectors of activity, both public and private',[613] and imposes a general duty on employers 'to ensure the safety and health of workers in every aspect related to the work'.[614] The obligations imposed on the employer are effectively six-fold:[615] a duty of awareness, which embraces a duty to be aware of risks, of developments in scientific and technological understanding and an awareness of the capabilities of workers; a duty to ensure safety and health by minimising avoidable risks; a duty to develop a 'coherent overall prevention policy'[616] with regard to risks; a duty to provide health and safety training for the workforce; a duty of information and consultation with regard to health and safety matters;[617] and a duty to maintain the required records and reports to enable national authorities to carry out their responsibilities of monitoring and enforcement. Article 6(2) lists a number of 'general principles of prevention' which employers should observe in implementing health and safety protection: these include the 'principle of substitution',[618] whereby the employer shall '[replace] the dangerous by the non-dangerous or the less dangerous',[619] and the principle of the

---

608 Case C-84/94 [1996] ECR I-5755; Fitzpatrick, 1997.
609 Directive 89/391.
610 Directive 89/391, Preamble, para 15.
611 Directive 89/391, Preamble, paras 9 and 13 respectively.
612 Directive 89/391, Preamble, para 2, and Art 1(3); Case C-84/94 *United Kingdom v EU Council (Working Time)* [1996] ECR-I 5755; Case C-2/97 *Società Italiana Petroli SpA v Borsana Srl* [1998] ECR I-8597; Szyszczak, 1999. In this respect the health and safety directives differ from those designed to harmonise technical standards relating to packaging and labelling of dangerous substances under Art 100a(3); Member States may not impose more rigorous standards than those laid down by these latter provisions. See Case 278/85: *EC Commission v Denmark* [1985] ECR 4069; Directive 89/178, Art 13; James, 1993: p 7; Nielson and Szyszczak, 1997: p 354.
613 Directive 89/391, Art 2(1).
614 Directive 89/391, Art 5(1).
615 See Neal, 1990.
616 Directive 89/391, Art 6(2)(g).
617 Directive 89/391, Art 10. See below, para 9.46.
618 Nielson and Szyszczak, 1997: p 340.
619 Directive 89/391, Art 6(2)(f). For an application of this principle in the context of one of the daughter directives, see Case C-2/97 *Società Italiana Petroli SpA v Borsana Srl*, [1998] ECR I-8597, discussed by Szyszczak, 1999.

'humanisation of work',[620] according to which it must '[adapt] the work to the individual, especially as regards the design of workplaces, the choice of work equipment and the choice of working and production methods, with a view, in particular, to alleviating monotonous work and work at a pre-determined work rate and to reducing their effect on health'.[621] The Directive also imposes a less extensive set of obligations upon workers, who must 'take care as far as possible' for their own safety and health in accordance with their training and with the employer's instructions.[622]

The Framework Directive, while similar in its aims to the Health and Safety at Work Act 1974, is at the same time more specific in terms of the detailed obligations it imposes on employers. Accordingly, new regulations were thought necessary in order to transpose the Directive into UK law: these are the Management of Health and Safety at Work Regulations 1999.[623]

The MHSW Regulations, breach of which can give rise to a civil cause of action in relation to persons in the employer's employment but not to any other persons,[624] establish a number of additional requirements for employers. In particular, both employers and the self-employed must undertake risk assessments in relation to their employees and to other persons who may be exposed to health and safety risks by their activities. Employers must also put in place health and safety arrangements 'for the effective planning, organisation, control, monitoring and review of the preventive and protective measures' which they must undertake. Further obligations refer to health surveillance, health and safety assistance, procedures for dealing with serious and imminent danger and danger areas within the workplace, the provision of information to employees and co-operation between employers sharing the same workplace.

The MSHW Regulations also implement certain provisions of one of the daughter directives, namely Directive 91/383 on the safety and health of temporary workers.[625] These impose obligations on employers and self-employed persons to ensure the provision of health and safety information to employees of another employer who are temporarily working in their undertaking, and to their own fixed-term contract employees.[626]

In the period since the adoption of the Framework Directive, numerous 'daughter directives' have been agreed, and in some cases their provisions have already been transposed in UK law by regulations which are gradually replacing the parallel provisions of the Factories Act 1961 and other pre-1974 legislation. These measures fall roughly into three categories: the protection of health and safety in the workplace; protection against exposure to certain substances and agents; and industry-specific regulations. Detailed accounts of their provisions may be found in specialist works on health and safety.[627]

---

620 See above, in the context of working time, at para 4.76.
621 Directive 89/391, Art 6(2)(d).
622 Directive 89/391, Art 13.
623 SI 1999/3542, replacing SI 1992/2051. See James 1993: pp 25 *et seq* for discussion of the 1992 Regulations.
624 SI 1999/3542, reg 22, as amended by SI 2003/2457. The amendment has been drafted in such a way as to create the anomalous result that *employees* may be liable for breach of statutory duty to third parties such as consumers if they breach the duty to inform under reg 14(2) although employers could not be sued for the failure to perform their duties: see *Speak Up or Pay Up*, Public Concern at Work, 2004.
625 See above, para 3.85.
626 Arts 10 and 13 respectively. Oddly, different requirements are imposed for these two groups: for discussion, see James, 1993: pp 27–29.
627 See, eg, Ford and Brown, 2003.

DUTIES OF OBEDIENCE, CO-OPERATION AND CARE

4.84   The employee's obligations of obedience, co-operation and care take the form of terms implied into the contract by the common law. The potential scope of these duties is very wide, but in practice they will tend to be limited by the express terms of the contract and by those implied from custom and practice or collective agreements. The principal role of the common law is therefore to fill in the gaps. This would once have been largely a question of granting legal expression to managerial prerogative, but the duty of co-operation, in particular, is now acknowledged to be reciprocal in nature, and to impose certain obligations upon the employer.

The duty of obedience

4.85   The employee owes an implied obligation to obey lawful and reasonable orders of the employer: this is a 'condition essential to the contract of service'.[628] What is reasonable depends in part upon the substance of the other terms of the contract, and the employee's job title and description, rank and professional status may also be relevant factors. The law has moved on a certain way from *Turner v Mason* (1845),[629] in which the Court of Exchequer Chamber found that a domestic servant had been lawfully dismissed for paying a visit to her mother, who was seriously ill, against her master's wishes. The mother's illness was thought not 'sufficient to justify her in disobedience to his order; there is not any imperative obligation on a daughter to visit her mother under such circumstances, although it may be unkind and uncharitable not to permit her'.[630] The Court considered that only an unlawful order could be deliberately disobeyed.[631] This near-blanket duty of obedience may have been seen as an aspect of the status of a servant, at a time when the law drew a distinction between the categories of 'servant' and 'employee'. In respect of the latter, even nineteenth-century courts recognised contractual limits to the employer's power: as far as an employee hired to buy lace was concerned, 'if he was hired as a buyer, he was not bound to perform services not properly appertaining to that character'.[632] Similarly, isolated acts of disobedience or neglect would not necessarily justify the dismissal of a manager or a journalist.[633]

   Today this approach is more generally applied to all employees: 'one act of disobedience can justify dismissal only if it is of a nature which goes to show (in effect) that the servant is repudiating the contract'.[634] But something of old attitudes still remains. In 1978 the EAT decided that an employer was entitled to dismiss an employee who had taken time off work without permission to look after her young son who had just been diagnosed as suffering from diabetes and was having difficulty administering the necessary treatment of insulin.[635]

---

628   *Laws v London Chronicle (Indicator Newspapers) Ltd* [1959] 1 WLR 698, 700 (Lord Evershed MR).
629   14 M & W 112.
630   14 M & W 112, 117 (Parke B).
631   14 M & W 112 (Rolfe B).
632   *Price v Mouat* (1862) 11 CBNS 508 (Erle CJ).
633   *Cussons v Skinner* (1843) 11 M & W 161 and *Edwards v Levy* (1860) 2 F & F 94, respectively.
634   *Laws v London Chronicle (Indicator Newspapers) Ltd* [1959] 1 WLR 698, 701 (Lord Evershed MR).
635   *Warner v Barbers Stores Ltd* [1978] IRLR 109. The employer's power to give orders in this type of situation would now be subject to the statutory right of an employee to take time off for urgent family-related reasons. See below, para 6.105.

An employee is always entitled to disobey an unlawful order.[636] In the context of threats to health and safety, the courts have accepted that this would include an order 'to direct a servant to continue where she is in danger of violence to her person, or of infectious disease',[637] but for this purpose the Privy Council has said that there must be 'an immediately threatening danger by violence or disease to the person of the servant before an order to remain in the zone of danger can be held to be unlawful'.[638] It is not clear why the danger should be 'immediately threatening', and this decision may no longer be particularly persuasive. In principle, there would seem to be no reason why, if very long working hours could be shown to be likely to induce a stress-related illness, the employee should not be entitled to disobey an order to carry on working beyond the point of danger, even if the impact upon their health was cumulative rather than immediate.[639] In this context, the courts have increasingly come to accept that statutory health and safety standards may circumscribe the employer's common law right to give orders which may have the effect of endangering the employee. Hence in *Barber v RJB Mining Ltd*[640] the High Court issued a declaration to the effect that employees protected by the statutory right not to work more than 48 hours per week over a specified reference period were entitled to refuse to work excessive hours which would have taken their working time over the threshold. It is also arguable that the duty of obedience is now circumscribed by Convention rights under HRA 1998; hence, if the employer issued an instruction which amounted to breach of such a right, such as the right to respect for private life under ECHR Article 8, special justification would be needed.

While *Barber* confirms that an employee is entitled to refuse to obey an unlawful order, in the sense of an order which would result in the breach of a statutory obligation imposed upon the employer for the protection of the employee, *Macari v Celtic Football and Athletic Co Ltd*[641] rules that this principle does not extend so far as to allow the employee to withhold performance under the contract of employment in circumstances where the employer is acting in breach of the *Malik* term of good faith. Although there are dicta suggesting that an employee might be entitled to refuse to obey a *specific* order made in bad faith by his or her employer[642] – in the sense of an order which would have the effect of harming the employee in a significant way – the Court ruled that an employee who refuses to obey an order which is, in itself, both reasonable and lawful, thereby commits a repudiatory breach of contract, even if the employer is in breach of the duty to maintain trust and confidence in some *other* respect.

The effect of these decisions, then, is that if the employer commits a generalised breach of the implied duty of co-operation, the employee has the option of terminating the contract and claiming appropriate relief, or of maintaining the

---

636 *Gregory v Ford* [1951] 1 All ER 121; *Lister v Romford Ice and Cold Storage Co Ltd* [1957] AC 555 (Viscount Simonds); *Morrish v Henlys (Folkestone) Ltd* [1973] ICR 482.
637 *Turner v Mason* (1845) 14 M & W 112.
638 *Bouzourou v Ottoman Bank* [1930] AC 271, 276; cf *Ottoman Bank v Chakarion* [1930] AC 277.
639 The issue of long working hours was considered by the Court of Appeal in *Johnstone v Bloomsbury Health Authority* [1992] 1 QB 333. See also the discussion of this issue in the context of ERA 1996, s 100, discussed below at para 5.104.
640 [1999] IRLR 308; A Edwards, 2000.
641 [1999] IRLR 787.
642 See [1999] IRLR 787, 798 (Lord Caplan); however, this suggestion was not accepted by the Lord President ([1999] IRLR 787, 791–792).

contract. If the latter route is chosen, the employee is not entitled to withhold all performance from the employer. The right to withhold performance arises only in respect of those obligations of the employee which correspond to the employer's own breach. Thus it is only if the employer issues a specific order which would result in unlawfulness or would significantly harm the employee that the employee has the right to maintain the employment relationship while also refusing to obey the order in question.

The reciprocal duty of co-operation

4.86   The term 'duty of co-operation' is sometimes used to refer to an obligation which is implied into a contract to require each party to avoid taking steps to obstruct the other's performance.[643] In the context of the contract of employment, it has been transformed into an affirmative obligation on the part of the employee to use his or her best efforts to ensure the efficient running of the enterprise. To a less certain extent, it also involves an obligation on the part of the employer not to break the 'trust and confidence' on which the relationship rests.

Obligations of the employee

4.87   The idea of the employee's affirmative duty of co-operation is illustrated by *Secretary of State for Employment v ASLEF (No 2)*.[644] The issue was whether limited industrial action taken by the rail unions involved employees in committing breaches of contract. The unions argued that the employees were performing the contract by sticking to the letter of the work rules book issued by the employer (examples included guards ensuring that a train was safe to leave the station by opening and then closing all its carriage doors, a process which ensured a substantial delay in the train's departure). In the Court of Appeal it was held that breaches of contract had taken place. Lord Denning MR argued that the lack of good faith with which performance was carried out rendered it a breach of contract, and added that '[t]here are many branches of our law when an act which would otherwise be lawful is rendered unlawful by the motive or object with which it is done. So here it is the wilful disruption which is the breach'.[645] Roskill LJ, by contrast, thought that 'questions of intent are usually irrelevant in determining whether or not there has been a breach of contract'. Instead Roskill LJ referred to the presence of an implied term that the employee would not seek so to interpret and act upon the rules as to disrupt the railway system; Buckley LJ spoke of an implied term 'that within the terms of the contract the employee must serve the employer faithfully with a view to promoting those commercial interests for which he is employed'.[646]

A crucial step in *ASLEF (No 2)* was, as we have seen,[647] the classification of the rule book: it did not establish contract terms, but simply reflected managerial prerogative. Although this creates a space within which the employer can dispense with contractual consent in setting or altering the form in which performance shall take place, the Court was also at pains to point out that this power is limited by the express contract terms: '[i]t does not mean that the

---

643   *Shirlaw v Southern Foundries (1926) Ltd* [1939] 2 KB 206.
644   [1972] 2 QB 455; Napier, 1972.
645   [1972] 2 QB 455, 492.
646   [1972] 2 QB 455, 506, 508, 498, respectively.
647   See paras 4.3 and 4.22 above.

employer could require a man to do anything which lay outside his obligations under the contract, such as to work excess hours of work or to work an unsafe system of work'.[648]

4.88   Nonetheless, the gap-filling function of the implied terms will grow in importance if the express terms are narrowly construed. In *Sim v Rotherham Metropolitan Borough Council*[649] it was held that schoolteachers who withdrew co-operation in the course of industrial action by refusing to cover for sick and absent colleagues were acting in breach of contract. Their terms and conditions of employment were laid down in a national-level collective agreement whose terms were embodied in the 'Burgundy Book'. However, Scott J held 'these provisions, although in many respects detailed and comprehensive, do not attempt to detail the obligations imposed on teachers by their respective contracts of service'. The contracts were 'silent as to the extent of the teachers' obligations as teachers'; in this case it was appropriate for the court to imply a term on the basis of professional standards 'set both by the profession itself and by public expectation'.[650]

4.89   Similarly, in *Ticehurst v British Telecommunications plc*[651] a managerial employee was held to be subject to the duty of co-operation to exercise 'her judgement and discretion in giving instructions to others and in supervising their work ... faithfully in the interests of the employers'. Her failure to sign an undertaking to work 'normally' was held to amount to a breach of contract: a breach is committed 'when the employee does an act, or omits to do an act, which it would be within her contract and the discretion allowed to her not to do, or to do, as the case may be, and the employee so acts or omits to do the act, not in honest exercise of choice or discretion for the faithful performance of her work but in order to disrupt the employer's business'. The most significant aspect of this case is that the only source of the breach was the employee's refusal to sign the undertaking. The decision effectively adopts Lord Denning's view in *ASLEF (No 2)* that motive can, *in itself,* transform an act from being the lawful exercise of a right into being a breach of contract. This is contrary to a 'general principle of English law that the exercise of a right ... will not be rendered unlawful only because of the bad motives of the person exercising that right'.[652]

4.90   A decision which also imposes an extensive affirmative obligation on the employee is *Cresswell v Board of Inland Revenue,*[653] in which Walton J held that employees were acting in breach of contract by refusing to co-operate with the introduction of new, computer-based technology: 'an employee is expected to adapt himself to new methods and techniques introduced in the course of his employment', subject only to an obligation on the part of the employer to offer retraining where 'esoteric skills' were involved which it would not otherwise be reasonable to expect the employee to acquire.[654] If this decision were widely followed, it might be used to justify unilateral alteration of job gradings and

---

648   [1972] 2 QB 455, 498 (Buckley LJ). See also *Burgess v Stevedoring Services Ltd* [2002] IRLR 810, discussed para 11.65 below.
649   [1987] Ch 216.
650   [1987] Ch 216, 244–245, 252.
651   [1992] IRLR 219, 225.
652   Hepple, 1981b: p 97, citing Lord Davey in *Allen v Flood* [1898] AC 1, 173.
653   [1984] IRLR 190.
654   [1984] IRLR 190, 195.

other forms of job classification. If the integrity of the contract terms is not to be seriously eroded by this route, Walton J's dictum should perhaps be qualified by the observation that the implied duty of co-operation cannot, in itself, be invoked to override express terms or those derived from collective agreements.

Obligations of the employer: the duty of mutual trust and confidence

4.91   The imposition of a general duty of co-operation upon the employer is a comparatively recent development.[655] Its evolution, according to Lord Steyn in *Malik v BCCI SA*,[656] 'is part of the history of the development of employment law in this century. The notion of a "master and servant" relationship became obsolete'. In particular, this shift in the common law has been prompted by the development of the unfair dismissal jurisdiction and above all by the statutory concept of 'constructive dismissal', according to which an employee (with the requisite period of qualifying service) has the right to quit and claim unfair dismissal in response to a repudiatory breach of contract by the employer.[657] This statutory jurisdiction has greatly increased the frequency with which questions of employer breach of contract have come before courts and employment tribunals. An employer who permits an employee to be the victim of persistent verbal abuse[658] or of sexual harassment[659] will on the face of it have committed a breach of the duty of mutual trust and confidence; other examples are failing to investigate a legitimate complaint about health and safety,[660] making an unsubstantiated allegation of theft,[661] unjustifiably insisting that the employee should undergo psychiatric examination,[662] providing a 'misleading and potentially destructive reference' to a prospective employer,[663] and suspending the employee as an automatic response to unsubstantiated allegations of child abuse.[664] The courts have gone so far as to suggest that an employer who 'arbitrarily, capriciously and inequitably' singled out an employee for an inferior pay rise to that granted to her colleagues might thereby have committed a repudiatory breach of contract.[665] At the same time, they have also held that employers have *not* been under implied duties to offer an annual pay rise, or, in general, to treat comparable employees equally for the purpose of pay increases.[666] A further development in this unfolding jurisprudence is the passage of HRA 1998, which raises the possibility (as yet untested) that conduct of the employer which amounts to a breach of a Convention right might be classified as a breach of the duty of co-operation.[667]

---

655 For overviews of this development, see Brodie, 2001b; Freedland, 2003: pp 154–170.
656 [1997] IRLR 462, 468.
657 ERA 1996, s 95(1)(c); *Western Excavating (ECC) Ltd v Sharp* [1978] QB 761.
658 *Palmanor Ltd v Cedron* [1978] ICR 1008. For more recent discussion see *Horkulak v Cantor Fitzgerald International* [2003] IRLR 756.
659 *Wood v Freeloader Ltd* [1977] IRLR 455.
660 *British Aircraft Corpn v Austin* [1978] IRLR 332.
661 *Robinson v Crompton Parkinson Ltd* [1978] ICR 401.
662 *Bliss v South-East Thames Regional Health Authority* [1985] IRLR 308.
663 *TSB Bank v Harris* [2000] IRLR 157.
664 *Gogay v Hertfordshire County Council* [2000] IRLR 703.
665 *FC Gardner Ltd v Beresford* [1978] IRLR 63; to similar effect is *Transco v O'Brien* [2002] IRLR 444 in which the Court of Appeal held that the arbitrary refusal to offer the claimant, alone of a group of employees, a new contract of employment with enhanced redundancy terms was a breach of the duty of mutual trust and confidence.
666 *Bridgen v Lancashire County Council* [1987] IRLR 58; *Murco Petroleum Ltd v Forge* [1987] IRLR 50.
667 See Hepple, 1998b.

The implied term has been described as an obligation that the employer shall not 'without reasonable and proper cause, conduct [itself] in a manner calculated to or likely to destroy or seriously damage the relationship of confidence and trust between employer and employee'.[668] In its most far-reaching form, this development could be said to mark an extension of the duty of co-operation 'from the restricted obligation not to prevent or hinder the occurrence of an express condition upon which performance of the contract depends to a positive obligation to take all those steps which are necessary to achieve the purposes of the employment relationship ... this broader, functional view – which rests essentially on a tribunal's view of "good industrial relations practice" – embraces not only the material conditions of employment such as pay and safety, but also those psychological conditions which are essential to the performance by an employee of his part of the bargain'.[669] This seems to be the most appropriate basis for the decision of the EAT in *WA Goold (Pearmak) Ltd v McConnell*,[670] to the effect that a contract of employment contained an implied term requiring the employer to provide a grievance procedure.

4.92 Likewise, in *Malik v BCCI SA*,[671] Lord Steyn gave a broad interpretation to the meaning of the term by holding that in order for there to be a breach, it was necessary neither for the employer's conduct to be directed at the employee as an individual, nor for the employee to have been aware of the breach while it was taking place. This broad interpretation was important in the context of the *Malik* case, which arose out a claim for damages based on the loss of reputation caused by employees' unwitting association with a series of frauds perpetrated by the employer.[672] The post-*Malik* case law has sought to clarify where the limits to the concept may lie.[673] In *BCCI v Ali*[674] and *University of Nottingham v Eyett*[675] the courts substantially qualified the idea that the employer has an affirmative obligation to provide information to the employee which is relevant to the continuing relationship of employment. In *Ali*, this meant that the employer was not in breach of contract for failing to inform its employees about fraudulent activities being undertaken by management; in *Eyett*, the employer was under no obligation to advise and inform employees of the most financially advantageous way in which complex pension rights could be

---

668 *Woods v WM Car Services (Peterborough) Ltd* [1981] IRLR 347, 350 (Browne-Wilkinson J), approved in *Lewis v Motorworld Garages Ltd* [1985] IRLR 465; *Imperial Group Pension Trust Ltd v Imperial Tobacco Ltd* [1991] IRLR 66; *Malik v BCCI SA* [1997] IRLR 462, 468 (Lord Steyn); *Brown v Merchant Ferries Ltd* [1998] IRLR 682 (NICA adopting Lord Steyn's test).

669 Hepple, 1981b: p 135.

670 [1995] IRLR 516; see also *Waltons & Morse v Dorrington* [1997] IRLR 488. On statutory disciplinary and grievance procedures, see paras 5.122–5.131 and 2.21–2.26

671 [1997] IRLR 462, 468–469; see Brodie, 1996, 1998a, 1998b, 1999a, 1999b, 2001a, 2001b; Lindsay, 2001.

672 On the admissibility of the damages claim, see para 5.27 below.

673 In addition to the cases cited in the text, see also *Johnson v Unisys Ltd* [2001] IRLR 279 in which the House of Lords held that the obligation of mutual trust and confidence had limited application in the area of termination of employment by the employer. See also *Eastwood v Magnox Electric/McCabe v Cornwall County Council* [2004] IRLR 733. These cases are discussed in the context of wrongful dismissal at paras 5.44–5.45 below.

674 [1999] IRLR 226.

675 [1999] IRLR 87. See also *Ibekwe v London General Transport Services Ltd* [2003] IRLR 697.

exercised. At one level these decisions seem to be incompatible with the idea of mutual trust and confidence as the core obligation at the heart of the employment relationship. However, they also involve an acknowledgement of the contractual autonomy of the parties. One potentially negative consequence of an over-extensive duty of co-operation would be the imposition upon *employees* of a wide-ranging duty to provide information to the employer; the mutual nature of the *Malik* term means that decisions in these cases cut both ways.[676]

4.93   It is also the case that the employer's obligations may be limited by the express terms of the contract, just as the employee's are. This makes it difficult to rely on the duty of co-operation as a general guarantor of employee protection: its content is not fixed, but will differ from one case to the next depending on how the express terms are framed. Nevertheless, there is authority to suggest that express contractual powers of the employer may be limited by a requirement that these powers be exercised 'in good faith' (again, in parallel with the notion that employees must exercise discretionary contract powers so as not to defeat the interests of the business). In *Imperial Group Pension Trust Ltd v Imperial Tobacco Ltd*[677] the employer had the power, under the rules of an occupational pension scheme, to refuse consent to certain increases in pension benefits proposed by the trustees of the fund. Browne-Wilkinson VC held that the scheme had to be construed against the background of the contract of employment and the implied 'obligation of good faith' which it contained. The employer's powers under the trust deed had to be exercised in accordance with this implied obligation. This did not mean that the employer had to act 'reasonably', but it was required to exercise its rights with regard to the efficient running of the scheme and to consider requests for increases on their merits; it could not give a blanket refusal to consider increases, nor could it refuse them in order to persuade employees to give up their rights under that scheme and transfer to a different one.

But a difficulty here is in knowing when a contractual right or power should be construed so as to be unqualified, and when it is subject to the requirement of good faith. As part of this approach some problematic distinctions have had to be drawn between, for example, an employee's obligation to work basic weekly hours, which was said in *Johnstone v Bloomsbury Health Authority*[678] to be unqualified, and a contractual obligation to work overtime, which was said in the same case to be subject to the implied obligation of the employer not to undermine the relationship by subjecting the employee to excessive hours. In *Hussman Manufacturing Ltd v Weir*[679] the EAT expressed 'very great reservations as to the extent to which [the implied duty of trust and confidence] can bear upon management decisions legitimately taken in terms of agreements between the employer and the employees'.

---

676   An employee is not obliged at common law to disclose to the employer that he or she has earned sums from third parties from outside employment: *Bell v Lever Bros Ltd* [1932] AC 161; *Nottingham University v Fishel* [2000] IRLR 471, 480–481; unless the employee is also a fiduciary: *Neary v Dean of Westminster* [1999] IRLR 288; see below, para 4.98.

677   [1991] IRLR 66. See also *Clark v BET plc* [1997] IRLR 348, discussed below, para 5.21 and *Mallone v BPB Industries Ltd* [2002] IRLR 452.

678   [1992] QB 333 (Browne-Wilkinson VC). See above, para 4.7.

679   [1998] IRLR 288, 290; see *Ali v Christian Salveson Food Services Ltd* [1997] IRLR 17; *Hill v General Accident Fire and Life Assurance Corpn plc* [1998] IRLR 641; *Reda v Flag Ltd* [2002] IRLR 747.

In principle, it is clear that the *Malik* term, as an implied obligation, can be excluded by an express term which is sufficiently clearly and precisely expressed. The 'default'[680] nature of the *Malik* term, however, does not mean that it has no practical effect. The onus is clearly on the employer of formulating an express term which is capable of overriding the implied obligation. The very imprecision of the *Malik* term works in the employee's favour here; drafting a watertight exclusion may not always be straightforward.

Mutual obligations of care

4.94   The employee impliedly contracts to use the normal degree of skill and care in the performance of his or her work, and will be liable in damages for breach of contract for loss caused to the employer by virtue of their negligence. The employer is not obliged by the contract of employment to take out insurance to cover this loss nor to cover the employee against possible liability to third parties. These principles follow from the controversial decision of the House of Lords in *Lister v Romford Ice & Cold Storage Co Ltd*.[681] The respondent caused the injury of a fellow worker, who happened to be his father, by his negligent driving, and the employer paid damages to the father on the basis of its vicarious liability for the respondent's negligence. It then sued the respondent for damages for breach of the implied contractual duty to exercise care and skill in the course of employment (the action was brought in the employer's name by its insurers, exercising their rights of subrogation). The action succeeded and appeals to the Court of Appeal and House of Lords were rejected. The House unanimously found that there had been a breach of contract by the employee, but a bare majority held against the implication of a term requiring the employer to indemnify the employee against third party or similar claims. According to Viscount Simonds, such a term could not be formulated with the 'necessary precision'.

Following *Lister*, insurers have observed a practice of not taking up rights of subrogation against employees in this type of situation, but this practice rests upon a 'gentlemen's agreement' and not upon a legally-binding waiver of rights. Aside from its implications from the point of view of insurance,[682] *Lister* is of considerable importance for the employment relationship. An employee may face a claim for a substantial sum either from his or her employer or from a third party. Even if such claims are not often pursued by reason of an employee's limited resources, deductions from wages to reflect employers' losses are common. The relevant duty is not just imposed on highly-skilled employees: 'even in so-called unskilled operations an exercise of care is necessary to the proper performance of duty'.[683]

Since *Lister* was decided, the notion of the employer's duty to maintain the 'trust and confidence' of the employee has been greatly extended,[684] and an

---

680   See [1997] IRLR 462, 468 (Lord Steyn).
681   [1957] AC 555. For a recent decision stressing the need to ensure, in the employment context, that the substance of the employer's duty of care in tort and that of the employer's implied obligation to maintain trust and confidence largely coincide, see *Outram v Academy Plastics Ltd* [2000] IRLR 499.
682   See *Morris v Ford Motor Co Ltd* [1973] QB 792; Deakin, Johnston and Markesinis, 2003: pp 496–497.
683   *Lister v Romford Ice and Cold Storage Co Ltd* [1957] AC 555, 573 (Viscount Simonds).
684   See above, para 4.91.

argument can be made that, on this basis, an employer is under a responsibility to indemnify the employee against third party claims.[685]Otherwise, an employee who committed an isolated act of negligence could end up facing personal bankruptcy. It is difficult to see how this could be compatible with the employer's obligation to 'take all those steps which are necessary to achieve the purposes of the employment relationship'.[686]

More recent decisions have indeed taken a broader view of the employer's responsibilities for the economic welfare of the employee.[687] In *Scally v Southern Health and Social Services Board*[688] an employer was found to have acted in breach of contract by failing to bring information to employees' attention concerning the exercise of options under their occupational pension scheme, and in *Spring v Guardian Assurance plc*[689] the House of Lords held that an employer owed a duty to take due care when writing a reference in respect of former or present employees, the duty being owed to the employee both in tort and by way of an implied term in the contract of employment. According to Lord Woolf in *Spring*,[690] the principle in that case and in *Scally* 'recognises that, just as in the earlier authorities the courts were prepared to imply by necessary implication a term imposing a duty on an employer to exercise due care for the physical well being of his employees, so in the appropriate circumstances would the court imply a like duty as to his economic well-being'. In *Scally* the information in question could not easily have been discovered by the employees, whereas the employer could have disclosed it at little cost; in *Spring*, it was recognised that 'it must often be very difficult for an employee to obtain fresh employment without the benefit of a reference from his present or a previous employer ... it is plain that the employee relies on him to exercise due skill and care in the preparation of the reference before making it available to the third party'.[691] The scope of the employer's obligation to provide a reference has been clarified in subsequent case law, the essence of which is that the reference must be 'true, accurate and fair' in the sense of not giving a misleading overall impression through the unfairly selective use of information or the misleading use of information which is in itself accurate; however, there is no obligation upon the employer to report all material aspects of the employee's work record.[692]

---

685   It may also be argued that the employer has such a responsibility if it was under a separate statutory duty to take out liability insurance in respect of such claims, on the authority of *Gregory v Ford* [1951] 1 All ER 121; or that if the employer is insured against the relevant loss or liability, it cannot take action against the employee because it suffers no loss (Hepple, 1981b: p 140), although this would not prevent the insurance company bringing an action by way of subrogation.

686   Hepple, 1981b: p 135. Statute (the Employers' Liability (Compulsory Insurance) Act 1969) imposes a duty on an employer to carry liability insurance to cover claims by third parties against itself, not against its employees.

687   See Freedland, 2003: pp 140–154 for discussion of this case law.

688   [1992] 1 AC 294; however, this decision must be read in the light of later decisions limiting the employer's obligation to provide such information (see above, para 4.92.

689   [1994] 3 All ER 129.

690   [1994] 3 All ER 129, 178.

691   [1994] 3 All ER 129, 146 (Lord Goff).

692   See *Bartholomew v London Borough of Hackney* [1999] IRLR 246; *Kidd v Axa Equity & Law Life Assurance Society Ltd* [2000] IRLR 301; *TSB Bank v Harris* [2000] IRLR 157; *Cox v Sun Alliance Ltd* [2001] IRLR 448; Middlemiss, 2004. At the same time, the courts have limited the potential liability in tort of insurers and experts who give advice to employers which has economic consequences for those employers' employees: *Kapfunde v Abbey National plc and Daniel* [1998] IRLR 583; *Briscoe v Lubrizol Ltd* [2000] ICR 694.

Spring and *Scally* might be thought to have opened the way to an extension of the employer's responsibility to have regard for the economic well being of the employee. However, in subsequent judgments the courts have resisted the imposition of a general duty of care in tort with regard to economic interests, and have also narrowly construed the parallel contractual obligation which arises out of the duty of mutual trust and confidence.[693] In particular, the post-*Scally* case law suggests that an employer will only rarely come under an implied duty to bring information about pension scheme arrangements to the attention of the employee.[694] By contrast, an *express* undertaking by an employer to provide information to an employee about pension or other benefits in the context of a transfer of undertaking or similar corporate reorganisation is highly likely to give rise to a duty of care.[695]

Employee mobility

4.95 Contracts of employment frequently contain clauses under which the employer reserves the power to transfer the employee to another place of work or to work of a different kind within the organisation. There is no power at common law to limit or strike down an express mobility or flexibility clause of this kind on the grounds of 'unreasonableness'; instead the court must give priority to the express term over any term which it might have implied in the same circumstances.[696] However, the clause, like any other contained in a standard form contract, will be construed *contra proferentem* which in this instance means that any ambiguity will be resolved in favour of the employee. Moreover, the manner in which a mobility clause is invoked can be made subject to the implied duty of co-operation. In particular, an employer is required to give the employee adequate notice of any move.[697] However, it has been held that this is not the same thing as implying a term into the contract to require the employer to 'act reasonably'. In *White v Reflecting Roadstuds Ltd*[698] the EAT held that the obligation is merely to avoid exercising a discretionary power in such a way as to prevent the employee carrying out his or her side of the contract. To insert a general common law obligation to act 'reasonably' into all contracts of employment would not only create uncertainty in the interpretation of contract terms, but could also be seen as an illegitimate judicial usurpation of the statutory jurisdiction of unfair dismissal.[699] But the test formulated in *White*'s case is, in its turn, weaker than the version of the duty of co-operation which has been applied in numerous other cases, namely that the employer is under a duty to maintain 'mutual trust and confidence' on which the relationship rests.[700] The EAT seems to have ignored the possibility of applying this

---

693   See the review of this area by the CA in *Crossley v Faithful and Gould Holdings Ltd* [2004] IRLR 377.
694   *Outram v Academy Plastics Ltd* [2000] IRLR 499
695   *Hagen v ICI Chemicals and Polymers Ltd* [2002] IRLR 31; *Lennon v Commissioner of Police of the Metropolis* [2004] IRLR 385.
696   *Express Lifts Co Ltd v Bowles* [1977] ICR 474.
697   *United Bank Ltd v Akhtar* [1989] IRLR 507.
698   [1991] IRLR 331, applying *Rank Xerox (UK) Ltd v Churchill* [1988] IRLR 280; McLean, 1992.
699   In *White* [1991] IRLR 331 it was said that to imply a general duty to act reasonably would go against the decision of the Court of Appeal in *Western Excavating (ECC) Ltd v Sharp* [1978] ICR 221, on which see below, para 5.72.
700   *Lewis v Motorworld Garages Ltd* [1985] IRLR 465; *Imperial Group Pension Trust Ltd v Imperial Tobacco Ltd* [1991] IRLR 66.

'intermediate' form of the duty of co-operation, in between the negative duty not to obstruct the contract at one extreme and the blanket duty to act reasonably at the other. *White* may be contrasted with *French v Barclays Bank plc.*[701] Here, the defendant bank changed the terms of a bridging loan which it had agreed to make available to the employee in order to assist him in relocating from one office to another. The Court of Appeal held that the employer was not entitled to exercise its discretion in such a way as to impose a significant financial detriment on the employee.

A term requiring mobility may also be implied into the contract; this is an application of the employee's duty of co-operation, considered above.[702] However, since the contract will in most cases indicate the employee's normal place of work by way of an express term or one implied from a collective agreement or custom and practice, the scope for implying a duty to move to another place of work must be limited.[703] The scope of any implied mobility clause will also be restricted by the employer's duty not to undermine 'mutual trust and confidence'. On this basis it could be argued, for example, that any implied right to transfer the employee to another place of work should take account of the latter's family commitments and practical ability to comply with the request, although clear authority on this point is lacking.[704]

An unusual case of implication was *Courtaulds Northern Spinning Ltd v Sibson.*[705] The employee, who had been a union member, resigned over a dispute concerning the use of union funds; this led the other employees to ostracise him. He refused a request from the employer to transfer to another depot a mile away. It was held in the Court of Appeal that the employer had been entitled to make the request and that the employee should have acceded to it (so there was no constructive dismissal). There was no express term governing mobility; however, partly because the employee was employed as a lorry driver, the Court felt that a term could be implied giving the employer the power to direct him to any place of work which was within reasonable travelling distance of his home. Slade LJ thought it likely that the parties would have agreed this term if asked; but in the absence of an express term an equally plausible interpretation was, arguably, that the employee's normal place of work was the depot at which he had worked for over ten years, and no other.

DUTIES OF FIDELITY, CONFIDENTIALITY AND PRIVACY

4.96 Among the most important obligations of the employee is the duty of fidelity or loyalty which is implied into the contract at common law; there is now growing recognition of corresponding duties of the employer to respect the private life and dignity of the employee.[706] As long as the contract is in force, the employee is bound not to compete with the employer or to work for a competitor without permission. Express terms, so-called 'restrictive covenants', are frequently inserted into contracts for the purposes of clarifying the scope of

---

701 [1998] IRLR 646.
702 See para 4.87 above.
703 See *Aparau v Iceland Frozen Foods plc* [1996] IRLR 119.
704 See below, para 6.23, for further discussion of this point in the context of indirect sex discrimination; note also the potential implications of the HRA 1998.
705 [1988] ICR 451; Holland and Chandler, 1988.
706 See Hepple, 1999a.

the employee's duty of fidelity and extending the period during which certain forms of competition are restricted to beyond the life of the contract itself. 'Post-contractual' restraints of the latter kind can only take effect by express agreement; they will not be implied. Post-contractual restraints are also subject to the common law doctrine of illegality, as part of which the courts can strike down terms which are in restraint of trade. However, the court will uphold a particular restraint if the employer shows that it protects a legitimate interest of the business and that its scope is reasonable in the circumstances.

An exceptional feature of the employee's duties of fidelity is that the employer can normally enforce them by way of an injunction; elsewhere, the role of specific relief in the contract of employment is a limited one, damages being the normal remedy for breach of contract.[707] Specific relief may also be available to prevent the use by employees, both during the performance of the contract and for a limited period after it, of confidential information acquired in the course of their employment. There is no general right of the employee to release information which is of a wider public interest, and few protections for 'whistleblowers'; on the contrary, many contracts of employment contain confidentiality clauses designed to prevent employees speaking out about work practices, and these will normally be upheld by the courts. However, the balance has been redressed to some extent by the Public Interest Disclosure Act 1998 and by the enactment of HRA 1998, which makes reference to the Convention right of freedom of expression.[708]

In comparison to the extensive protection granted to employers' interests, there were traditionally few controls over the collection, storage and use by an employer of information of a personal nature concerning individual employees. However, the Data Protection Act 1998 (which replaces a less extensive Act of 1984) provides significant protections in relation to the use of information which is collected and held by the employer, and as this body of law comes to be interpreted in the light of the HRA, its influence over employment relations is being increasingly felt.

The employee's duty of fidelity

The content of the implied duty of fidelity

4.97 An employee is not, in general, prohibited from doing another job during his or her spare time; however, he or she must not work for a rival employer if the effect of this will be seriously to damage the principal employer's business. In *Hivac Ltd v Park Royal Scientific Instruments Ltd*[709] highly skilled employees of the claimant worked for the defendants, who manufactured precisely the same product, in their spare time. This was sufficient for the court to grant an injunction restraining the defendant from taking on the employees, since to do so amounted to inducement to breach their contracts of employment with the claimant. According to Lord Greene MR, 'the obligation of fidelity, which is an implied term of the contract, may extend very much further in the case of one class of employee than it does in others'; the court would be reluctant to impose restraints on manual workers whose obligation of fidelity 'may be one the

---

707 See paras 5.20 and 5.53 below.
708 ECHR, Art 10.
709 [1946] Ch 169; *Adamson v B & L Cleaning Services Ltd* [1995] IRLR 193.

operation of which will have a comparatively limited scope'.[710] However, 'it would be deplorable if it were laid down that a workman could, consistently with his duty to his employer, knowingly, deliberately and secretly set himself to do in his spare time something which would inflict great harm on his employer's business'.[711]

Employees as fiduciaries

4.98   The implied duty of fidelity operates as a term of the contract of employment, which arises as an incident of the employment relationship; it must therefore be distinguished from the separate notion of a fiduciary obligation which may incurred by an employee to his or her employer. Only employees who undertake particular duties and responsibilities, normally associated with a senior position, will become fiduciaries and thereby assume the wide-ranging legal duties which are attached to that status. In particular, fiduciaries come under an open-ended, affirmative duty of disclosure which is not part of the employee's general duty of fidelity under the contract of employment. Failure to comply with a fiduciary duty of disclosure will generally be grounds for dismissal by the employer, regardless of whether the employee was aware that he or she was under this obligation. The far-reaching effect of such a rule is evident in *Neary v Dean of Westminster*,[712] in which the employee was held to have acted in breach of the duty of mutual trust and confidence in failing to disclose profits which he had made from recording contracts and related arrangements which he entered into by virtue of his position as an organist at Westminster Abbey.

The other relevant feature of fiduciary status for present purposes is that a breach of fiduciary duty may enable the employer to mount a claim for an account of profits or a similar claim in restitution. In a normal breach of contract claim, the employer has to show loss in order to recover damages;[713] the possibility of a claim for breach of fiduciary duty may therefore be highly significant. It was on this basis that a claim for profits made by a university researcher in relation to work undertaken for third parties was mounted in *Nottingham University v Fishel*.[714]

The crucial issue arising from *Neary* and *Fishel* concerns the circumstances in which it is appropriate for a court to imply fiduciary status. A company director necessarily owes fiduciary obligations to the company so that he or she must, among other things, disclose secret profits made in that capacity;[715] but what of employees who are not directors? According to the analysis of Elias J in *Fishel*,[716] while fiduciary obligations may be incurred by a wide range of employees in a variety of circumstances, the employment relationship is not, in itself, a fiduciary relationship. Before fiduciary obligations can be implied, therefore, it is necessary to find specific evidence to support a claim that the employee has undertaken to act for or on behalf of the employer. Moreover, an

---

710 [1946] Ch 169, 174.
711 [1946] 1 Ch 169, 178.
712 [1999] IRLR 288.
713 See *A-G v Blake* [1998] Ch. 439, [2001] IRLR 36 for discussion of the circumstances in which a claim for restitutionary damages may lie in contract.
714 [2000] IRLR 471.
715 *Regal (Hastings) Ltd v Gulliver* [1967] 2 AC 134n; see *Horcal Ltd v Gatland* [1983] IRLR 459.
716 [2000] IRLR 471, 482–484; Sims, 2001.

employee who incurs fiduciary obligations does so only in relation to specific undertakings or commitments of this kind; thus an employee who is entrusted with company property or with confidential information may act as a fiduciary for those purposes, without incurring similar obligations with regard to other aspects of the employment relationship.

Part of the difficulty in determining when the notion of fiduciary responsibility is applicable to employment derives from the similar language used to describe, on the one hand, the position of the fiduciary and, on the other, the status of the employee under the contract of employment. Hence a leading modern definition of a fiduciary refers to 'someone who has undertaken to act for or on behalf of another in a particular matter in circumstances which give rise to a relationship of trust and confidence. The distinguishing obligation of a fiduciary is the obligation of loyalty'.[717] The main obstacle to the imposition of a fiduciary duty upon employees other than company directors is *Bell v Lever Bros*.[718] However, it has been suggested that 'the development of the specifically fiduciary obligations of directors, on the one hand, and of the obligations of fidelity and loyalty under the contract of employment, on the other, have been congruent with each other, to the point where *Bell v Lever Bros* is quite isolated in so far as it suggests a sharp contrast between the two sets of obligations'.[719] Moreover, the terms 'acting for another', 'duty of loyalty' and 'relationship of trust and confidence' can be read as linked to aspects of the implied obligations of the employee under the 'core' *Malik* term of mutual co-operation.[720] However, it was argued in *Fishel* that 'these concepts are... used in the employment context to describe situations where a party merely has to take into consideration the interests of another, but does not have to act in the interests of that other.'[721] In so far as this may be taken to mean that the employee is not required to subordinate his or her interests to those of the employer except to the extent determined by contract, this is an important reminder of the need for employment law to recognise the contractual autonomy of the parties to the employment relationship.

If this analysis is correct, it would be inappropriate to attach fiduciary duties of a general kind to an employee *solely* on the grounds that he or she owes duties of trust and confidence to the employer.[722] The issue becomes instead one of determining when 'within a particular contractual relationship there are specific contractual obligations which the employee has undertaken which have placed him in a situation where equity imposes [on him] these rigorous [fiduciary] duties'.[723] The introduction of a fiduciary element into the relationship is not dependent on the seniority of the employee concerned, since the most junior of employees can be entrusted with the employer's property in such a way as to give rise to a specific obligation to restore it (together with any secret profits that may have been made through its use).[724] Nevertheless, very senior employees

717 *Bristol and West Building Society v Mothew* [1998] 1 Ch 1, 18 (Millett LJ).
718 [1932] AC 161.
719 Freedland, 1984: p 35.
720 See Brodie, 1998a, 2001; Clarke, 1999; cf Sims, 2001.
721 [2000] IRLR 471, 483.
722 In so far as this was the basis for *Neary*, that decision would seem to be irreconcilable with *Fishel*, but *Neary* can be seen as turning on the distinctive position occupied by the employee in an institution of particular national and religious significance.
723 Elias J in *Fishel*: [2000] IRLR 471, 483.
724 [2000] IRLR 471, 482.

who are in a position of special trust and responsibility with regard to the management of the employer's organisation and assets will almost necessarily incur extensive fiduciary duties to the employer.

Thus in *Sybron Corpn v Rochem Ltd*[725] a group of managers in the claimant company set up the defendant company, along with several others, and then diverted to those companies a series of contracts which had come to them in the course of their work for the claimant. One of the managers, Mr Roques, took early retirement with a pension before the fraud was discovered. The claimant sued for the return of the pension. On the authority of *Bell v Lever Bros Ltd*[726] it was held that Mr Roques could not be held to have acted unlawfully by failing to disclose his own misconduct, but he could be held in breach of contract for failing to disclose the misconduct of his subordinates. On this basis, he was required to make restitution of the pension on the grounds that the money was paid over under a mistake of fact. An alternative and probably preferable ground for the decision would have been that Mr Roques had committed a breach of fiduciary duty, for which he could have been liable both to make an account of the profits he received and to pay damages to the employer for its losses. In *Fishel*,[727] Elias J. held that the defendant was not in a position of being a fiduciary merely by virtue of the research post which he held, since while this was a reasonably senior position, this could not fairly be equated with that of an executive director of a company. He went on to hold that no specific undertaking had been made of the kind which could have given rise to a more limited fiduciary duty. However, the defendant was found to be under a duty to account for income received in respect of work done by other university employees for whom he had been responsible.

The extent of the obligation of a director or employee to disclose their own wrongdoings – in effect, a duty of confession – is an aspect of *Bell* that many courts and commentators have found puzzling. Although in some cases it may make no difference whether the employee has this 'superadded' duty or not,[728] it may have a considerable impact on the adjustment of their respective claims in situations if, as in *Bell* or *Sybron*, the employer can argue that a failure to disclose constitutes grounds for avoiding a severance payment or pension claim. *Bell* may turn on the jury's finding that the finding that the appellants did not fraudulently conceal their earlier wrongdoings at the time they entered into the severance agreement which was the subject of the action. The decision is also explicable on the grounds that the appellants were not directors of the respondent company. In *Item Software (UK) Ltd v Fassihi*[729] the Court of Appeal held that a director was under a duty to disclose his own wrongdoing; according to Arden LJ, this could be understood as an integral part of the duty of loyalty which a director owes to the company by virtue of being a fiduciary. Moreover, 'the duties of a director are in general higher than those imposed by law on an employee. This is because a director is not simply a senior manager of the

---

725 [1983] ICR 801; Freedland, 1984.
726 [1932] AC 161.
727 [2000] IRLR 471, 484–487.
728 This was the case in *Fishel*.
729 [2004] IRLR 928. See also, on the distinction between the director's fiduciary duty of loyalty and the employee's contractual duty of fidelity, the judgment of Deputy Judge Strauss QC at first instance in *Fassihi* ([2003] IRLR 769) and that of Hart J in *British Midland Tool Ltd v Midland International Tooling Ltd* [2003] EWHC 466, at paras 77–95. See also *Tesco Stores Ltd v Pook* [2004] IRLR 618; Wynn-Evans, 2005.

company. He is a fiduciary and with his fellow directors he is responsible for the success of the company's business'.[730] As we have seen, a senior employee may also be a fiduciary under certain circumstances. How far a 'duty of confession' then arises remains unclear. It may be that care should be taken to avoid the assimilation of even senior employees to a fiduciary model developed initially for the distinctive legal position of the company director.

Specific enforcement of the duty of fidelity

4.99   If the employee breaks the duty of fidelity, he or she may be dismissed for repudiatory breach of contract if the breach is serious enough.[731] The court may also grant an injunction to prevent an employee from breaking either the implied duty of fidelity or an express agreement not to compete during the period of the contract.[732] This equitable remedy is discretionary, and may be refused if its effect is equivalent to ordering the employee to work for a particular employer. Courts of equity traditionally would not grant specific performance to enforce the contractual obligation to work, and this practice is now embodied in a statutory rule.[733] However, the granting of a negative injunction preventing the employee from working for a competitor is thought not to infringe the rule against specific performance, as long as the employee is not thereby faced with a choice of 'work or starve' which would drive him or her back to their original employer. 'Work or starve' is not an issue if the individual, finding one line of work closed off by the injunction, is considered to be sufficiently resourceful to find a viable alternative which would enable them to earn a reasonable living.[734] However, it is also open to a court to find that, in a given situation, an alternative career is not a realistic option, in which case an injunction may be refused and the employer limited to a claim in damages and/or restitution.[735]

One means of avoiding the rule against specific performance is for the employer to pay the employee his or her wages or salary for the remainder of the contract period, without requiring them to come into work. During this period of 'garden leave' the employee is financially secure without needing to work for the employer; there is no choice of 'work or starve', and so a court is not prevented from issuing an injunction preventing the employee from working for a competitor. Such clauses are very commonly found in the contracts of professional and managerial employees; employers regard them as essential means of preventing rival businesses from exploiting the specialised knowledge of senior staff. However, garden leave does little to serve the employee's interests: not only is he or she deprived of the chance to get a better paid job, but by being out of employment for a lengthy period their value to any future employer may be greatly reduced.

The possibility of abuse is heightened if the period during which the contract remains formally in force is particularly long. In *Evening Standard Co Ltd v Henderson*[736] a contract of employment contained a clause requiring the employee

---

730 [2004] IRLR 928, at para 34.

731 Eg, *Boston Deep Sea Fishing Co Ltd v Ansell* (1888) 39 Ch D 339.

732 An express term may well be necessary to clarify or extend the scope of the implied duty of fidelity: see *Symbian Ltd v Christensen* [2001] IRLR 77.

733 TULRCA 1992, s 236.

734 *Warner Bros Pictures Inc v Nelson* [1937] 1 KB 209; cf *Page One Records Ltd v Britton* [1968] 1 WLR 159.

735 *Warren v Mendy* [1989] 1 WLR 853.

736 [1987] ICR 588.

to give a year's notice of termination, together with an express agreement not to work for a competitor while the contract was in force. He quit to work for a rival firm on only a month's notice. An injunction was granted and was upheld by the Court of Appeal. The employee's action was a repudiatory breach of contract, but the employer had not accepted it and the contract was therefore still in force. Because the employer undertook to pay the employee's normal salary and to allow him to work during his notice period, 'work or starve' was not an issue.

A more problematic case is where the employer does not allow the employee to return to work. In *Euro Brokers Ltd v Rabey*[737] it was held that it was not necessary for the employer to offer continuing employment to the employee, a money broker, in order to obtain an injunction against him. In *GFI Group Inc v Eaglestone*[738] an injunction was also issued to prevent a foreign exchange dealer starting work for a competitor before his contractual notice period had expired, although the court exercised its discretion to shorten the period of the restraint from that specified in the notice clause. This was because other employees had been allowed to work for the same competitor after a shorter period of time than the employee's notice clause provided for. By contrast, in *William Hill Organisation Ltd v Tucker*[739] the Court of Appeal declined to grant an injunction to enforce garden leave, on the grounds that the employer was contractually obligated to provide work for the employee during the notice period. In part, this was because of the 'specific and unique post' which the employee held within the organisation.[740] However, Morritt LJ considered that 'as social conditions have changed, the courts have increasingly recognised the importance to the employee of the work, not just the pay';[741] on this basis, there seems to be no reason why the courts not should be willing to imply an obligation to provide work, where it is available, into most contracts of employment.

In a case such as *Henderson* the long notice period could also be attacked on a separate ground, via the doctrine of restraint of trade. This doctrine is normally applied to *post-contractual* restraints but if the contract is for a long, fixed term or contains a provision for a long notice period, there is no reason why it should not apply to restraints which operate during the period when the contract is still subsisting. The doctrine has been applied in this way to recording and agency contracts lasting several years.[742] In *William Hill Organisation Ltd v Tucker*[743] Morritt LJ deprecated the 'trend towards increasing reliance on garden leave provisions in preference to conventional restrictive covenants', and suggested that:

> ... if injunctive relief is sought, then it has to be justified on similar grounds to those necessary to the validity of an employee's covenant in restraint of trade. It seems to me that the court should be careful not to grant [interim] relief to enforce a garden leave clause to any greater extent than would be covered by a justifiable covenant in restraint of trade previously entered into by an employee.

---

737 [1995] IRLR 206.
738 [1994] IRLR 119.
739 [1998] IRLR 313.
740 [1998] IRLR 313, 317 (Morritt LJ).
741 [1998] IRLR 313, 317 (Morritt LJ).
742 See eg *A Schroeder Music Publishing Co Ltd v Macaulay* [1974] 1 WLR 1308.
743 [1998] IRLR 313, 318. See also *Crédit Suisse Asset Management Ltd v Armstrong* [1996] IRLR 450; *Symbian Ltd v Christensen* [2001] IRLR 77.

Post-contractual restraints on competition and protection of confidential information

4.100   An express agreement not to compete after the contract has come to an end may be highly significant for both parties, since the implied duty of fidelity will not, *in itself*, extend to this period.[744] But as we have just seen, a post-contractual restraint of this sort faces an additional obstacle, namely the doctrine of restraint of trade. This holds that a contract term which purports to restrict competition is *prima facie* void, but can be justified according to a test of 'reasonableness'. As far as employment contracts are concerned, an agreement by the employee not to compete after the contract is over will be struck down unless the employer can point to a more specific 'proprietary interest' which the agreement is designed to protect.[745] This will normally have to be in the form of confidential information or the protection of its existing base of customers, or possibly its employees. Thus in *Herbert Morris Ltd v Saxelby*[746] a term under which the employee agreed not to compete in the relevant trade for a period of seven years after leaving his employer's employment was struck down: according to Lord Parker, there had been no case in which such a restraint against post-contractual competition:

> ... has, as such, ever been upheld by the Court. Wherever such covenants have been upheld it has been on the ground, not that the servant or apprentice would, by reason of his employment or training, obtain the skill or knowledge necessary to equip him as a possible competitor in the trade, but that he might obtain such personal knowledge of or influence over the customers of his employer, or such an acquaintance with his employer's trade secrets, as would enable him, if competition were allowed, to take advantage of his employer's trade connection or utilise information confidentially obtained.

Where an employee has acquired specialist knowledge of customers through his or her contacts with them, the employer may legitimately restrain the employee from soliciting them for business after he or she has left the employment.[747] This principle has been applied to solicitors and others working in law offices,[748] and even to a hairdressers' assistant.[749] However, this principle would not justify placing a restraint on an employee who never came into contact with the employer's clients, such as a shop-floor employee. The employer's interest in protecting the client-base it has built up could also arguably extend to its own workforce; an agreement not to recruit former fellow-employees would probably be upheld on this basis.[750]

As far as confidential information is concerned, the courts have traditionally drawn a distinction between specific trade secrets, such as secret designs or recipes, and general know-how: the employer can restrain the use of the former after the employment has ended, but not the latter. It has been suggested that the

---

744 *Faccenda Chicken Ltd v Fowler* [1986] IRLR 69; *Wallace Bogan & Co v Cove* [1997] IRLR 453.

745 See, for example, *Scully (UK) Ltd v Lee* [1998] IRLR 259.

746 [1916] 1 AC 688, 709.

747 For an application of this principle see *International Consulting Services (UK) Ltd v Hart* [2000] IRLR 227.

748 Eg, *Fitch v Dewes* [1921] 2 AC 158; *Fellowes & Son v Fisher* [1976] QB 122.

749 *Marion White Ltd v Francis* [1972] 1 WLR 1423.

750 Sales, 1990; *Office Angels Ltd v Rainer-Thomas* [1991] IRLR 214; *Dawnay, Day & Co Ltd v De Braconier d'Alphen* [1997] IRLR 442.

essence of the distinction is between 'objective knowledge' which is the employer's property and 'subjective knowledge' which relates to the way in which a trade or profession is carried on, and which remains the property of the employee.[751] An express term may help to clarify the categories of information which are sufficiently precise to fall into the category of trade secrets; in addition, the implied duty of fidelity may assist the employer. An employee who copies lists of customers while he or she is still employed and seeks to use them later may be restrained from doing so, whether or not there was an express term not to compete.[752] However, if the information is too vague to be classified as a trade secret, it may be that neither an express nor an implied term will help the employer.

Hence in *Faccenda Chicken Ltd v Fowler*[753] the defendant employee resigned as a sales manager of the claimant and set up in competition against it, taking on many of his former colleagues. His contract did not contain any express terms governing the use of confidential information, nor any express agreement not to compete post-contract. The judge refused to grant an injunction and his view was upheld in the Court of Appeal. The information being used by the defendant was in the nature of general know-how about the nature of the work which he had picked up in the course of his employment and did not rank as a trade secret. Even if there had been an express non-competition clause, it would not have led to the granting of an injunction. According to Neill LJ, 'a restrictive convenant will not be enforced unless the protection sought is reasonably necessary to protect a trade secret or to prevent some personal influence over customers being abused in order to entice them away'.[754]

By contrast, in *Roger Bullivant Ltd v Ellis*[755] an employee, while still employed, acquired a company for the purpose of competing with his employer, and on leaving his employment took with him a card index of customers' names. His contract contained an express term under which he undertook not to enter into similar employment for a period of one year after his employment ended, and this was enforced by an injunction. The information concerning customers was precise in nature and had been illicitly acquired for the purpose of setting up as a competitor.

Most confidential information will not be protected indefinitely. In *Bullivant* the purpose of the injunction was to prevent the ex-employee making unfair use of the information he had acquired, but after a period had elapsed competition would be permitted. This is an application of the 'springboard doctrine': the person entrusted with information while still employed 'should not get a start over others by using the information he received in confidence. At any rate, he should not get a start without paying for it. It may not be a case for an injunction or even an account [of profits], but only for damages, depending on the worth of the confidential information in saving him time and trouble'.[756] But there are also some categories of information whose disclosure will be restrained

---

751 *SBJ Stephenson Ltd v Mandy* [2000] IRLR 233.
752 *Robb v Green* [1895] 2 QB 315. This decision was recently applied in *British Midland Tool Ltd v Midland International Tooling Ltd* [2003] EWHC 466.
753 [1986] IRLR 69; *Lancashire Fires Ltd v SA Lyons & Co Ltd* [1997] IRLR 113.
754 [1986] IRLR 69, 75.
755 [1987] ICR 464.
756 *Seager v Copydex Ltd* [1967] 1 WLR 923, 931–932 (Lord Denning MR). See also *Universal Thermosensors Ltd v Hibben* [1992] 1 WLR 840.

indefinitely. Secret processes and formulae may fall into this category,[757] and so may details of the personal life of an employer or another, stipulated individual.[758]

The scope of restraints on competition

4.101   The employer will not succeed in enforcing an agreement not to compete merely by showing that it protects a 'proprietary interest'; the restraint must also be shown to be reasonable in its scope. Thus in *Mason v Provident Clothing and Supply Co*[759] the defendant had been employed to canvass business and collect payments from customers in a part of Islington; however, a clause in his contract barred him from entering into similar work within 25 miles of London for a period of three years after his employment came to an end. The clause was struck down as bearing no relation to the protection of the employer's legitimate interest, which was confined to the area in which the employee had previously worked.[760]

In addition to the area of the restraint, its duration will be taken into account. In *Fitch v Dewes*[761] a covenant not to practise as a solicitor's clerk within seven miles of Tamworth Town Hall after leaving the employer's employment was upheld: the clients of the practice tended to stay with it throughout their lives, and so imposing a lifelong restraint on the employee was necessary to protect the practice's business.

This was a somewhat unusual case. In *Fellowes & Son v Fisher*[762] Lord Denning thought that a one-year non-solicitation clause would be appropriate for an articled clerk, and in *Bridge v Deacons*[763] the Privy Council upheld a five-year period in the case of a partner in a solicitors' practice. However, more recent decisions have confirmed that an indefinite restraint may be reasonable in certain circumstances as a means of protecting the employer's interests.[764]

What matters here is the balance between the proper interests of the promisee and the interests of the public in the maintenance of healthy competition; the employee's interests appear not to be relevant as such. The courts have, for example, rejected the proposition that the restraint should not be upheld if it confers only a minor benefit on the promisee but a major detriment on the promisor.[765] It is only if the consideration received by the promisor for the restrictive term is completely inadequate that considerations of injustice to the employee are said to come into play. [766]

A clause which is over-wide in its scope may be saved if the court can 'sever' the offending words, but this may only be done if two conditions are satisfied:

---

757 *Printers and Finshers Ltd v Holloway* [1965] 1 WLR 1; *Thomas Marshall (Exports) Ltd v Guinle* [1978] ICR 905.
758 *A-G v Barker* [1990] 3 All ER 257.
759 [1913] AC 724; on area restraints, see also *Fellowes & Son v Fisher* [1976] QB 122.
760 This principle also applies to limit the legitimate scope of restraints to those aspects of a business in which the employee concerned was directly employed, and not all aspects of the business of the employer in question: *Turner v Commonwealth & British Minerals Ltd* [2000] IRLR 114.
761 [1921] 2 AC 158.
762 [1976] QB 122.
763 [1984] AC 705.
764 *Office Angels Ltd v Rainer-Thomas* [1991] IRLR 214; *Dentmaster (UK) Ltd v Kent* [1997] IRLR 636.
765 *Allied Dunbar (Frank Weisinger) Ltd v Weisinger* [1988] IRLR 60.
766 *A Schroeder Music Publishing Co Ltd v Macaulay* [1974] 1 WLR 1308.

the remaining words must make some grammatical sense;[767] and the effect must not be to alter the meaning and nature of the contract.[768] The courts try to resist severance of restraints in contracts of employment, for the reason that to allow it on a regular basis would encourage employers to widen the scope of clauses, safe in the knowledge that they could always fall back on the court-supplied term.[769]

In *Attwood v Lamont*[770] the head of the tailoring department in an outfitter's business contracted not to work for a period after leaving the employment in the 'trade or business of a tailor, dressmaker, general draper, milliner, hatter, haberdasher, gentlemen's, ladies', or children's outfitter' within ten miles of the town in which the business was situated. The court rejected an attempt to sever all the parts of the clause not referring to tailoring; it was found that the employer's intention had been to prevent competition across the range of trades mentioned, and not just in respect of the particular work undertaken by the employee; the covenant was held to be void on the grounds that it was wider than necessary for the protection of the employer's interests.

A more recent case which illustrates a questionably liberal attitude to construing restraints is *Littlewoods Organisation Ltd v Harris*,[771] in which the Court of Appeal, by a majority, felt able to construe the broad words of a clause by reference to the protectable interest of the employer: a restriction on the ex-employee working in any similar 'trade or business' was interpreted as referring to any trade or business in which he might use the confidential information he had acquired when working for the company. Browne LJ dissented on the grounds that 'this is re-rewriting the clause, and rewriting it so as to make enforceable what would otherwise be unenforceable ... I think that is something which the court cannot do'.[772]

It was thought, following the judgment of Scott J in *Briggs v Oates*,[773] that covenants which were expressed to apply to any termination of the contract 'howsoever arising' or 'howsoever caused' would necessarily be struck down on the grounds that '[a] restrictive covenant, having effect after the termination of a contract of service or for services, which on its face applies to the employer's benefit even where the termination has been induced by his own breach is necessarily unreasonable'.[774] However, in *Rock Refrigeration Ltd v Jones*[775] the Court of Appeal took a different view. In part, the judgment rests on the conceptual point that it is neither necessary nor possible to invoke the restraint of trade doctrine to strike down a restrictive covenant if the employer has wrongfully repudiated the contract. This is because, under the principle in *General Billposting Co Ltd v Atkinson*,[776] the effect of the employer's

---

767 See *T Lucas & Co Ltd v Mitchell* [1974] Ch 129.
768 See *Goldsoll v Goldman* [1915] 1 Ch 292.
769 *Mason v Provident Clothing and Supply Co Ltd* [1913] AC 724.
770 [1920] 3 KB 571.
771 [1977] 1 WLR 1472; see also *Hollis & Co v Stocks* [2000] IRLR 712; but cf *Wincanton Ltd v Cranny and SDM European Transport Ltd* [2000] IRLR 716.
772 [1977] 1 WLR 1472, 1493.
773 [1990] IRLR 472; see *Living Design (Home Improvements) Ltd v Davidson* [1994] IRLR 69; *PR Consultants Scotland Ltd v Mann* [1996] IRLR 188; *D v M* [1996] IRLR 192.
774 *D v M* [1996] IRLR 192, 198 (Laws J).
775 [1996] IRLR 675.
776 [1909] AC 118. This decision is open to question in the light of the House of Lords decision in *Photo Production Ltd v Securicor Transport Ltd* [1980] AC 827 (see [1996] IRLR 675, 678 (Philips LJ)), but it has not been overruled and for the time being at least remains good law.

repudiation is automatically to release the employee from his contractual obligations, including any restrictive covenants. It follows that there is no justification for holding such a covenant to be invalid in *other* situations, namely where the contract is brought to an end lawfully, or where it is wrongfully terminated by the employee.

Disclosure of confidential information in the public interest and protection of 'whistleblowers'

4.102   At common law, the disclosure of confidential information by 'whistleblowers' has only very rarely been allowed on the grounds of an overriding public interest. One clear category is the revelation of criminal acts: 'there is no confidence as to the disclosure of iniquity'.[777] In *Initial Services Ltd v Putterill*[778] the Court of Appeal thought that the employee's implied duty of fidelity would not prevent disclosure of documents relating to his employer's attempts to rig the market in laundry services, contrary to the Restrictive Trade Practices Act 1956. The Court discussed, without clearly deciding, the question of whether disclosure in such a case must be made to the relevant authorities, as opposed to the press.

This common-law defence of public interest is quite limited in scope, and provides little protection for 'whistleblowers' who seek to bring unethical behaviour to the attention of the wider public. Doctors and nurses in the National Health Service, for example, are formally required both by their conditions of service and by the codes of their professional associations to maintain patient confidentiality.[779] This raises the possibility of a conflict between contractual confidentiality and the wider professional obligations of the employee; the courts have not clearly stated, however, that a professional obligation overrides a contract term for the purposes of authorising disclosure of information.[780]

If the information is revealed while the employee is still employed, he or she may face the prospect of discipline or dismissal. Prior to the passage of the Public Interest Disclosure Act in 1998, there were only isolated statutory provisions allowing for (or in some cases, requiring) disclosure of wrongs committed by the employer.[781] The position of the common law was that whistleblowing would normally be a breach of the employee's obligation of trust and confidence.[782] The employee's duty of fidelity has been a relevant consideration in the application of tests for determining the scope of the public interest in protecting the identity of whistleblowers. In *Camelot Group plc v*

---

777 *Gartside v Outram* (1856) 3 Jur NS 39.
778 [1968] 1 QB 396.
779 McHale, 1992, 1993; D Lewis, 1995; Vickers, 1995, 2002.
780 See generally Cripps, 1995.
781 Under the Pensions Act 1995, s 48, actuaries and auditors of occupational pension schemes came under a *duty* to inform the Occupational Pensions Regulatory Authority of certain breaches of duty by managers and/or trustees of such schemes. Other persons, including trustees or managers of schemes, *might* make such information available to the Authority. In both cases, the Act specified that no duty to which the person was subject should be regarded as contravened merely because of any information or opinion contained in a report submitted to the Authority. The 1995 Act has been repealed by Pensions Act 2004, s 320, Sch 13 as from a date to be appointed: see now Pensions Act 2004, ss 69 and 70.
782 *Thornley v Aircraft Research Association Ltd* (11 May 1977, unreported); Cripps, 1995: pp 315–317.

Centaur Communications Ltd[783] Camelot, the operators of the national lottery, sought a court order for the return of documents containing the company's draft accounts, which had been leaked to a journalist employed by Centaur. Camelot alleged that the documents had been leaked by a disloyal employee, and that it was necessary for this individual to be identified and dismissed if its operations were not to be disrupted. Centaur invoked section 10 of the Contempt of Court Act, under which '[n]o court may require a person to disclose ... the source of information contained in a publication for which he is responsible, unless it be established to the satisfaction of the court that disclosure is necessary in the interests of justice or national security or for the prevention of disorder or crime'. The judge granted the order requested by Camelot and his ruling was upheld by the Court of Appeal. According to Mummery LJ, 'an employer in the position of Camelot Group has a legitimate and continuing interest in enforcing an obligation of loyalty and confidentiality against an employee who has made unauthorised disclosure and use of documents acquired by him in his employment'. It was also relevant (if rather surprising) that the judges in this case did not consider that any relevant public interest was served by the disclosure of the information in question, which related to the payment of increased salaries to the directors of Camelot. Hence, Mummery LJ thought that '[r]ather than serving a public interest, it appears that the prior and premature disclosure and publication of the draft accounts served a private purpose of the source or a private purpose of Centaur Communications in securing a scoop, ahead of other publications, of information which would have become legitimately available to the public five days later.'[784] Similarly, Schiemann LJ thought that '[t]his is not a case of disclosing iniquity; it is not a whistleblowing case'.[785]

4.103   Specific legal protection of whistleblowers was provided by the Public Interest Disclosure Act 1998, the relevant parts of which have been incorporated into ERA 1996.[786] Protection is provided in respect of a 'protected disclosure'.[787] To be protected, a disclosure must concern subject matter of a certain kind and must be made in a particular way.[788] With regard, first, to subject matter, a 'qualifying disclosure' must be one which, in the reasonable belief of the worker concerned, tends to show that one or more of the following has occurred or is likely to occur: the commission of a criminal offence; the failure of a person to comply with a legal obligation;[789] the occurrence of a miscarriage of justice; the endangering of a person's health and safety; damage to the environment; or the deliberate concealment of information concerning any of the above. However,

---

783 [1998] IRLR 80. See also the opinions of the House of Lords in *X Ltd v Morgan Grampian (Publishers) Ltd* [1991] 1 AC 1 and *Ashworth Hospital Authority v MGN Ltd* [2002] 1 WLR 2033, and , under Art 10 of the European Convention on Human Rights, that of the European Court of Human Rights in *Goodwin v United Kingdom* (1996) 22 EHRR 123.

784 [1998] IRLR 80, 85.

785 [1998] IRLR 80, 84.

786 See Gobert and Punch, 2000; D Lewis, 1998, 2001; Bowers *et al*, 1999; Cripps, 2000. The provisions of the then Bill (which was introduced as a private members bill with government support) are explained in *Consultation Paper on Mr Richard Shepherd's Public Interest Disclosure Bill*, Public Concern at Work, 1997.

787 ERA 1996, s 43A.

788 ERA 1996, ss 43B–43H.

789 This has been widely construed to include a breach by the employer of a contract of employment, including the applicant's own: *Parkins v Sodexho Ltd* [2002] IRLR 109. See also *Kraus v Penna plc* [2004] IRLR 260.

a disclosure which involves the commission, by the person making it, of a criminal offence,[790] cannot be a 'qualifying disclosure'.[791]

With regard to the mode of disclosure, a 'qualifying disclosure' is most likely to be 'protected' if it is made internally, that is to say, to the worker's employer or a person to whom the employer has authorised this type of disclosure, or, where the worker reasonably believes the failure relates solely or mainly to the conduct of another person, that person.[792] Other potentially protected disclosures are those made to a legal adviser, a Minister of the Crown, or (in essence) a regulatory person or body.[793] 'External' disclosures will only be protected under a very limited range of conditions. These are, first, where the worker can show that he or she reasonably believed that the information disclosed was substantially true;[794] second, that the disclosure was not made for personal gain; third, where the information concerns conduct of 'an exceptionally serious nature'; and fourth, where, in all the circumstances of the case, it is reasonable for the worker to make the disclosure. The worker must also make the disclosure in good faith.[795] Where the conduct is not exceptionally serious, the worker must show, in addition, that he or she believed at the time of the disclosure that they would be subjected to a detriment by the employer if they raised the matter internally; that (in a case where there is no relevant regulatory person or body) the worker reasonably believed that internal disclosure would lead to the concealment of evidence by the employer; that the worker had previously made disclosure of substantially the same information to their employer or to a regulatory person or body; and that in all the circumstances, it was reasonable to make the disclosure. The legislation then goes on to stipulate that 'reasonableness' here depends on factors which include the identity of the person to whom the disclosure is made; the seriousness of the conduct or failure in question; the likelihood of that failure continuing; whether the disclosure is made in breach of a duty of confidentiality owed by the employer to another person; action previously taken by the workers' employer or a regulatory person or body in response to the initial disclosure of the information to them; and whether, in making the initial disclosure, the worker had complied with any procedure for disclosure which was laid down by the employer.

The remedies available under the Act include the right of a worker[796] to complain to an employment tribunal that he or she has been subjected to a detriment by reason of having made the disclosure;[797] employees also have the

---

790 Particularly relevant here would be offences under the Official Secrets Act 1989. See McColgan, 2000d.

791 ERA 1996, s 43B.

792 ERA 1996, s 43C.

793 ERA 1996, ss 43D–43H; the Public Interest Disclosure (Prescribed Persons) Order 1999, SI 1999/1549, as amended by SI 2003/1993.

794 The belief must be *reasonable*, not correct: see *Darnton v University of Surrey* [2003] IRLR 133.

795 See *Street v Derbyshire Unemployed Workers' Centre* [2004] IRLR 687.

796 ERA 1996, s 47B; on the meaning of the term 'worker', see paras 3.51–3.61 above, and see also 43K, which contains a particularly wide extension of the term to include a situation in which an individual is introduced or supplied to work for another by a third person under circumstances where the terms on which he works are determined 'not by him but by the person for whom he works or worked, by the third person or by both of them'. In *Douglas v Birmingham City Council*, EAT, 17 March 2003, Appeal No EAT/0518/02 ILB this provision was used to bring within the Act a disclosure made by the applicant to members of the Governing Body of the school for which she worked, when her contract was with the relevant local authority.

797 On compensation, see *Virgo Fidelis Senior School v Boyle* [2004] IRLR 268.

right to complain of unfair dismissal (dismissal in relation to a protected disclosure being categorised as an automatically unfair dismissal under Part X of ERA 1996, for which, unusally, there is no statutory limit on compensation[798]). The Act also renders void any contract term purporting to preclude a worker from making a protected disclosure.[799]

The changes made by the Public Interest Disclosure Act now need to be considered alongside the possible impact of the Human Rights Act 1998, under which domestic legislation must now be interpreted, so far as possible, in such a way as to give effect to Convention rights,[800] and courts and tribunals must have regard to the jurisprudence on those rights developed by the European Court of Human Rights and other specified bodies of the Council of Europe.[801] In addition, the Act creates a new cause of action for breach of Convention rights by public authorities,[802] and opens up the possibility that the common law itself may be open to reinterpretation in the light of the Convention's provisions.[803]

The Human Rights Act came into force in England and Wales in October 2000. If the case law of the European Court of Human Rights is any guide, the impact of the Act on freedom of expression in employment may be limited. This is because of the qualifications placed on the right to freedom of expression in Article 10(2) of the Convention, which legitimises 'such formalities, conditions, restrictions or penalties as are prescribed by law and are necessary in a democratic society, in the interests of national security, territorial integrity or public safety, for the prevention of disorder or crime, for the protection of health or morals, for the protection of the reputation or rights of others, for preventing the disclosure of information received in confidence, or for maintaining the authority and impartiality of the judiciary'. It is possible that the rights contained in Article 10 go no further than those provided for by the Public Interest Disclosure Act, particularly since a failure to go through the internal procedures specified for 'protected disclosures' could justify any subsequent interference by the employer with freedom of expression rights.[804]

Protection of employee dignity and privacy

The common law

4.104   So far we have considered the remedies available to an employer to restrain an employee's use of confidential information; however, the employer itself may also collect information of a confidential and/or personal kind about its employees. The English common law has been reluctant to recognise a general right to the protection of privacy,[805] with the result that the employer has not to date been prevented from requiring the employee to provide information of a personal kind at the hiring stage.[806] An employee is entitled not to reveal a spent conviction as defined by the Rehabilitation of Offenders Act 1974,[807] but this is

---

798 ERA 1996, s 103A. On automatically unfair reasons for dismissal, see below, para *5.95 et seq.*
799 ERA 1996, s 43J.
800 HRA 1998, s 3.
801 HRA 1998, s 2.
802 HRA 1998, s 6.
803 S 6(3).
804 For discussion, see McColgan, 2000d: pp 70–72.
805 Most recently, in *Wainwright v Home Office* [2004] 2 AC 406.
806 For discussion of the implications of HRA 1998 in this area, see G Morris, 2001a.
807 See above, para 3.15.

the only occasion on which false information may be given without giving rise to the normal legal consequences for misrepresentation. Once the employment has begun, an employer's request for private information could amount to a breach of the duty of mutual trust and confidence.[808] However, the difficulty here lies in knowing how far the courts would balance the employee's interests against what, in an appropriate case, the employer would seek to describe as its business needs.

Convention rights

4.105 As we have seen, the passage of the Human Rights Act 1998 makes it possible for human rights issues to be presented directly to UK courts which may be called upon to apply the Convention directly and/or as an aid to interpretation.[809] Article 8 of the European Convention on Human Rights states that:

> Everyone has the right to respect for his private and family life, his home and his correspondence.

> There shall be no interference by a public authority with the exercise of this right except such as is in accordance with the law and is necessary in a democratic society in the interests of national security, public safety or the economic well being of the country, for the prevention of disorder or crime, for the protection of health or morals, or for the protection of the rights and freedoms of others.

In *Halford v United Kingdom*,[810] the European Court of Human Rights held that Article 8 had been breached where the applicant's employer had intercepted telephone calls which she had made from her place of work, for purposes which allegedly included collecting evidence against her in connection with a claim which she was making for sex discrimination. The Court held that the calls made from her place of work were capable of falling under Article 8, and rejected the United Kingdom government's submission that 'an employer should, in principle, without the prior knowledge of the employee, be able to monitor calls made by the latter on telephones provided by the employer'.[811] The applicant's case was assisted by the fact that she had not been given any prior warning of the interference, that she had been given sole use of a private phone in her office, and that she had been informed in writing that she could use this phone for the purpose of the sex discrimination proceedings. It is unclear whether the employer's conduct would have fallen under Article 8 if these special features of the case had not been present. *Halford* could provide a basis for the use of Article 8 to restrict the use by employers of surveillance and other devices which interfere with employee privacy, although the scope of any such principle is as yet comparatively untested in this context. In *McGowan v Scottish Water*[812] the EAT thought that Article 8 would be engaged in a case of covert surveillance of the employee's home, but that its application was subject to the principle of proportionality; in the instant case, the employer was justified in making videotapes of the employee's comings and goings where these established that he had been falsifying time sheets.

---

808 See para 4.91 above.
809 On privacy and the ECHR in employment, see Ford, 2000; G Morris, 2001a: pp 61–65; Hendrickx, 2001; Ford 2002; H Oliver, 2002.
810 [1997] IRLR 471, 475; see Craig and Oliver, 1998.
811 See [1997] IRLR 471, 475.
812 [2005] IRLR 167.

The interaction of data protection and human rights law

4.106 Highly relevant in this context is the role played by data protection law. Once personal information has been collected and stored, its disclosure by the employer to a third party would be subject to the normal rules of breach of confidence, but these rules will not in themselves prevent this information being used by the employer for legitimate purposes internal to the organisation. Certain restrictions are however imposed on the storage and use of employee data by employers under the Data Protection Act 1998, which implements Directive 95/46 and significantly strengthens an earlier Act of 1984.[813]

For the purposes of the 1998 Act, the term 'data' is defined as information which is either 'being processed by means of equipment operating automatically in response to instructions given for that purpose', is recorded with the intention of being processed by such means, or 'is recorded as part of a relevant filing system or with the intention that it should form part of a relevant filing system'.[814] Those, including employers, who process data on individuals within the terms of the Act come under statutory obligations as 'data controllers'. 'Personal data' under the Act means data which relate to a living individual who can be identified from those data or from those data together with other information in the possession of the data controller, including 'any expression of opinion about the individual and any indication of the intentions of the data controller or any other person in respect of the individual'.[815] In *Durant v Financial Services Authority*[816] this definition was clarified by the Court of Appeal. Precisely because the purpose of the Act is to protect the privacy of the individual, 'it is not an automatic key to any information, readily accessible or not, of matters in which he may be named or involved'. In particular, 'mere mention of the data subject in a document held by a data controller does not necessarily amount to his personal data'.[817] Auld LJ went on:

> It seems to me that there are two notions that may be of assistance. The first is whether the information is biographical in a significant sense, that is, going beyond the recording of the putative data subject's involvement in a matter or an event that has no personal connotations, a life event in respect of which his privacy could not be said to be compromised. The second is one of focus. The information should have the putative data subject as its focus rather than some other person with whom he may have been involved or some transaction or event in which he may have figured or have had an interest, for example, as in this case, an investigation into some other person's or body's conduct that he may have instigated. In short, it is information that affects his privacy, whether in his personal or family life, business or professional capacity.[818]

It followed that the claimant was unable to obtain disclosure of information relating to the treatment by the Authority of a complaint which he had made against his bank.

813　See Ford, 1998b; 1999; and on the evolution of EC rules in this area, Simitis, 1998. See Jay and Hamilton, 2003 on UK data protection law and practice.
814　A 'relevant filing system' must be one which enables 'identification of relevant information with a minimum of time and costs, through clear referencing mechanisms': *Durant v Financial Services Authority* [2004] FSR 28, at para 45.
815　DPA 1998, s 1(1).
816　[2004] FSR 28. See S Lorber, 2004.
817　[2004] FSR 28, at para 27.
818　[2004] FSR 28, at para 28.

The 'processing' of data is widely defined in the Act to refer to 'obtaining, recording or holding the information or data or carrying out any operation or set of operations on the information or data'. Included in this definition are 'adaptation', 'retrieval', 'consultation', 'use', 'disclosure', 'alignment', 'combination', 'blocking', 'erasure' or 'destruction' of data.[819] Personal data can only be processed if the individual concerned has given his or her consent, or if one of a number of other specific conditions has been met.[820] More generally, all processing of data must respect the 'data protection principles'[821] which are derived from the Council of Europe Convention on Data Protection and from Directive 95/46.[822] These require, *inter alia*, that personal data is held only for one or more specified and lawful purposes, that data shall not be disclosed in a manner incompatible with those purposes, and that data shall not be retained for any longer than necessary. The individual is entitled to be informed of the fact that data concerning him or her is held, to have access to that data and to have it corrected or erased in appropriate cases. Failure to comply with the data protection principles does not automatically give rise to criminal liability but it may lead to the Information Commissioner issuing an enforcement notice (with which the data user must comply, on pain of criminal liability).

Particularly stringent controls are imposed on the processing of 'sensitive personal data', a category which includes information relating to the race or ethnic origin of the data subject, his or her political opinions, religious or other beliefs, membership or non-membership of a trade union, physical or mental health or condition, sexual life, and the commission or alleged commission of any offence and any proceedings relating to an offence.[823] At least one of a narrowly-defined set of conditions has to be satisfied: these include the 'explicit consent' of the individual concerned, and processing which is 'necessary for the purposes of exercising or performing any right or obligation which is conferred or imposed by law on the data controller in connection with employment'.[824] These various statutory obligations are complemented by Codes of Practice issued by the Information Commissioner; they may be referred to in enforcement proceedings under the Act. They include an *Employment Practices Data Code*,[825] and a *CCTV Data Protection Code of Practice*.

The core individual rights under the Act are the right of access to personal data, the right to know the purposes for which that data will be used, the right to prevent processing which is likely to cause damage or distress, and the right not to be subjected to certain categories of decisions based solely on the automatic processing of personal data. With respect to the latter, the Act provides:

> An individual is entitled at any time, by notice in writing to any data controller, to require the data controller to ensure that no decision taken by or on behalf

---

819 DPA 1998, s. 1(1).
820 DPA 1998, s 4, Sch 1 para 1, and Sch 2.
821 See DPA 1998, Sch 1, Part I.
822 DPA 1998, s 4 and Sch 1, Part I.
823 The definition of 'sensitive personal data' is contained in s 2 of the Act; Sch 3 outlines the restrictions which relate to the processing of such data for the purposes of the interpretation of the data protection principles under Sch 1.
824 DPA 1998, Sch 3, paras 1, 2(1). For discussion of the relevance of this provision in one particular context, see Joseph Rowntree Foundation, *Report of Independent Inquiry into Drug Testing at Work* (2004), ch 1.4.
825 See generally the Information Commissioner's website: http://www.information commissioner.gov.uk/.

of the data controller which significantly affects that individual is based solely on the processing by automatic means of personal data in respect of which that individual is the data subject for the purpose of evaluating matters relating to him such as, for example, his performance at work ...[826]

The Act provides a general right to compensation for damage incurred by wrongful processing of data.[827] However, confidential references are not covered by the right of access,[828] nor is a data controller such as an employer obliged to provide information about its stance during negotiations.[829]

Appeals from determinations of the Information Commissioner lie to the Information Tribunal. In addition, specific criminal offences are created in relation to the holding, use, obtaining, disclosure or transfer of personal data which is unauthorised in the sense of going beyond the purposes stated in the entry on the data register. It is also a criminal offence for an employer to require an employee or job applicant to supply it with a 'relevant record' of (among other things) his or her criminal record.[830]

4.107   Additional statutory recognition of the employee's right to control over personal data regardless of whether it is automatically processed is provided by the Access to Medical Records Act 1988. An employer or prospective employer who wishes to gain access to a medical report made on an individual for employment purposes[831] must notify the individual concerned, who is then entitled to see the report before it is supplied to the employer and to request that any errors be corrected. The medical practitioner who made the report may refuse to correct the alleged errors, but must then, at the individual's request, attach a statement of the individual's views to his report. The court has power to grant a specific order to require compliance with the Act.

4.108   The obligations to respect employee privacy which derive from data protection legislation cut across recent legislation which is designed to enable employers and others to intercept electronic communications for business purposes. The Telecommunications Data Protection Directive,[832] which was implemented in the UK by the Regulation of Investigatory Powers Act 2000, requires the confidentiality of electronic communications to be respected, but allows for certain derogations of which interceptions for business purposes is one. To this end, the Telecommunications (Lawful Business Practice) (Interception of Communications) Regulations 2000[833] legitimise interceptions made for various purposes including establishing compliance with regulatory or self-regulatory practices or procedures, investigating or detecting unauthorised use of telecommunication systems, and monitoring communications to see if they are

---

826   DPA 1998, s 12(1).
827   DPA 1998, s 13.
828   DPA 1998, s 37 and Sch 7, para 1.
829   See DPA 1998, s 37 and Sch 7, paras 5 and 7.
830   DPA 1998, s 56.
831   These are defined as 'the purposes in relation to the individual of any person by whom he is or has been, or is seeking to be, employed (whether under a contract of service or otherwise)': Access to Medical Records Act 1988, s 1(1). Note also that under the Data Protection Act 1998, Sch 3, para 8, processing of health records may only be undertaken by a health professional or by a person who owes a duty of confidentiality equivalent to that which would be owed by a health professional. See also DPA 1998, s 57.
832   Directive 97/66.
833   SI 2000/2699.

of a business nature. Such conduct is lawful only if the person making the interception 'has made all reasonable efforts to inform every person who may use the telecommunications system in question that communications transmitted by means thereof may be intercepted'.[834] The Department of Trade and Industry has taken the view that the employer's obligation extends to its own workers and to others making use of the system, but not to those calling, or receiving calls, from outside.[835] Interceptions made with the consent of the persons making and receiving the communications are outside the scope of the primary legislation. The Act and the Regulations, then, permit employers to monitor e-mail communications between employees (and, more generally, between employees and third parties) under a wide range of circumstances. However, any data collected by an employer under this provision would remain subject to the requirements of the Data Protection Act 1998, as outlined above, and of the HRA 1998.[836]

INCOME SECURITY: SICK PAY AND LAY-OFF

4.109 The common law offers some residual protection to employees against loss of income through no fault of their own in the cases of sickness or suspension of employment on account of lack of work ('lay-off'). A common law claim may be brought in the form of wages due as earned, but only if the employee can show that being ready and willing to work is sufficient 'consideration' for payment, and this is normally only the case for salaried employees.[837] If actual performance of work is required for suing in debt, the employee may nevertheless be able to benefit from an implied term that the employer will pay sick pay in the event of illness or, in the case of lay-off, ensure that work is available; if the payments are not made, a claim in damages will ensue. However, at common law such claims will only last for a limited period of time. Moreover, if the contract explicitly places the risk of such losses on the employee, or if it is a 'contract at will', containing neither a notice clause nor a term requiring the employer to show good cause for dismissal or suspension, the common law is completely unable to protect the employee's expectations of continuing payment.

These common law rules have been supplemented by collective bargaining and, more recently, by statutory regulation in the form of statutory sick pay and guaranteed pay. These statutory interventions were not principally guided by the aim of ensuring security of income, however. In each case their goal was to shift obligations which had previously been borne by the state social insurance system, in the form of unemployment and sickness benefits, on to individual employers; rather than building on social security entitlements, they replaced them, while in general providing lower levels of payment. The statutory entitlements to which they give rise may also in most cases be set off against the employee's contractual rights.[838]

---

834 SI 2000/2699, reg 3.
835 See G Morris, 2002a.
836 In this respect, the Information Commissioner's *Employment Practices Data Code*, referred to above, provides extensive guidance on, among other things, the monitoring of emails.
837 See above, para 4.58.
838 See generally Szyszczak, 1986.

The right to sick pay at common law

4.110   The question of whether the employee is entitled to receive payments during periods of illness was for a long time treated from the point of view of the construction of the basic wage-work bargain. If the consideration was faithful service as opposed to the completion of work, wages would continue throughout the period of absence, until such time as the employer terminated the contract by giving notice. This principle applied to more senior and salaried employees, such as the production manager employed in a textiles factory in *Orman v Saville Sportswear Ltd*.[839] But in each case, the question was whether the contract of employment was based on an agreement to the effect that the employee would be paid when ready and willing to work, or only for time spent actually working. The employer could resolve the question by posting a notice or otherwise making it clear that wages were not paid during sickness.[840] In the absence of an express term or one implied by custom and practice, most hourly-paid workers and piece workers were regarded as receiving wages only for work done, and so had no inherent right to sick pay. The only clear decision to the contrary, *Marrison v Bell*,[841] was subsequently distinguished in a string of cases,[842] and has had little influence on the subsequent development of the law.

The more modern tendency has been to regard the issue not in terms of the 'consideration' for payment, but to see whether a term can be implied to provide the right to sick pay independently of whether the principle of 'no work, no pay' applies to other situations. In *Howman & Son Ltd v Blyth*[843] a term was implied based on the custom in the *industry* of which the firm was a part, and in *Mears v Safecar Security Ltd*[844] the Court of Appeal was prepared to imply a term as a 'necessary incident' of the employment relationship. This can be done on the basis that the payment of sick pay is necessary to the long-term maintenance of the relationship between the parties. However, there is no presumption either in favour or against such a term and it can easily be excluded by evidence of a contrary intention on the part of the employer, which is what happened in *Mears* itself.

The terms of any express provision made by an employer for sick pay or disability benefits will normally be incorporated into the contracts of employment of individual employees, according to the normal tests. Once incorporation has taken place, the employer is bound to follow the provisions of the scheme, the terms of which fall to be interpreted by the principle that the employer should as far as possible act in good faith and avoid perverse or irrational decisions, thereby aligning the express terms with the implied duty of mutual trust and confidence.[845] Nor can the employer avoid such contractual obligations by purporting to dismiss the employee through the exercise of any general power to terminate the contract by giving notice. This result can be understood by reference to an implied term to the effect that the employer will not give notice under these circumstances. The basis for implying such a term is that neither

---

839 [1960] 1 WLR 1055.
840 *Petrie v MacFisheries Ltd* [1940] 1 KB 258.
841 [1939] 2 KB 187.
842 *Hancock v BSA Tools Ltd* [1939] 4 All ER 538 (engineering worker); *Petrie v MacFisheries Ltd* [1940] 1 KB 258 (fish packer); *O'Grady v M Saper Ltd* [1940] 2 KB 469 (commissionaire).
843 [1983] ICR 416.
844 [1982] ICR 626.
845 See *Scottish Courage Ltd v Guthrie*, 5 February 2004, Appeal No UKEAT/0788/03/MAA.

party could have intended the notice clause to operate in such a case; otherwise, there would have been no point in making provision for sickness benefits in the first place.[846] Alternatively, it is open to the court to decide that, on the true construction of the *express* terms of the contract, the notice clause has been limited by the clause relating to sickness benefits.[847]

Statutory sick pay

4.111 The payment of a short-term benefit in respect of loss of income through illness was for a long period the preserve of social security. A social insurance benefit, sickness benefit, was available to those employees (technically, 'employed earners') with an adequate contribution record;[848] and many employers made payments of occupational sick pay on top of employees' social security entitlements. In 1980 a White Paper[849] proposed to shift the responsibility for the administration of short-term sickness payments from the state to employers, on the grounds that over 80% of employers already had schemes in place for dealing with this problem and could deal with it more effectively than the state could. Accordingly, the Social Security and Housing Benefits Act 1982 introduced statutory sick pay (SSP), which was to be payable by employers for the first eight weeks of illness at one of a number of rates set by the Act. SSP payments were directly set off against employees' contractual entitlements, so ending the 'double compensation' which had operated, *de facto*, under the previous system. The 1982 Act provided for the costs of SSP payments to be recovered in full by employers, in the form of rebates on their own national insurance contributions. Since then the scheme has gradually been amended so that it now covers the first twenty-eight weeks of illness, after which the employee transfers to one of a number of social security benefits.[850] The direct cost to employers was also increased by the withdrawal of the national insurance rebate for all but smaller firms.[851]

The category of employees capable of qualifying for SSP was considered in chapter 3 above:[852] essentially, the individual must be an employed earner with normal weekly wages at or above the lower earnings level for national insurance contributions purposes,

A claim is made in relation to a 'day of incapacity' which is defined as a day 'in relation to a contract of service ... [when] the employee concerned is, or is deemed in accordance with regulations to be, incapable by reason of some specific disease or bodily or mental disablement of doing work which he can reasonably be expected to do under that contract'.[853]

A number of further conditions must then be met for the 'day of incapacity' to count. First, it must fall within a 'period of incapacity' which is a period of at

846 *Aspden v Webbs Poultry & Meat Group (Holdings) Ltd* [1996] IRLR 521, 524 (Sedley J); *Villella v MFI Furniture Centres Ltd* [1999] IRLR 468; *Briscoe v Lubrizol Ltd* [2002] IRLR 607; cf. *Hill v General Accident Fire and Life Assurance Corpn plc* [1998] IRLR 641.

847 *Adin v Sedco Forex International Resources Ltd* [1997] IRLR 280.

848 On the meaning of the term 'employed earner' and the conditions for making social security contributions, see above, para 3.22.

849 DHSS, *Income During Sickness: A New Strategy* (1980, Cmnd 7684).

850 Wikeley, 2002: ch 15.

851 By the SSPA 1994. Another significant reform was the transfer of adjudication of SSP matters from the social security system to the Inland Revenue, by the Social Security Contributions (Transfer of Functions etc) Act 1999. See Wikeley, 2002: p 531.

852 See para 3.22 above; *Brown v Chief Adjudication Officer* [1997] IRLR 110.

853 SSCBA 1992, s 151(4); SI 1982/894, reg 2(2).

least four consecutive days of incapacity, including days of the week when the employee does not normally work, or holidays.[854] Second, it must fall within a 'period of entitlement'[855] which roughly follows the period of incapacity but which only begins when the employee's contract of employment first takes effect and ends after twenty-eight weeks or when the contract of employment ends, if that is sooner; however, the employer may not terminate the contract for the purposes of avoiding SSP liability.[856] Third, it must fall on a 'qualifying day' which is to be agreed between the employer and employee involved (which could be via a term incorporated from a collective agreement between the employer and a trade union representing the employee). If no such day is agreed, the Statutory Sick Pay (General) Regulations[857] provide that it shall be the normal agreed working days in the week in question or, if there are no such days, the Wednesday of that week. Finally, no SSP is payable for the first three qualifying days in any period of entitlement (the 'waiting days'). However, if there are less than eight weeks between two periods of incapacity then they are treated as one linked period for this purpose, so that the employee does not have to endure three 'waiting days' at the start of the second period.[858]

SSP is paid at a weekly rate which was set at £68.20 from April 2005.[859] SSP payments reduce any contractual entitlement to sick pay by an equivalent amount.[860] The employee's entitlement is exhausted once he or she is paid the equivalent of 28 weeks of sick pay during any one period of entitlement, the maximum length of which is three years.[861] Once SSP entitlement ceases for this reason, the individual's entitlement is transferred to the long-term social security incapacity benefit.[862]

The employee or somebody acting on his or her behalf must notify the employer of their incapacity for work; the Act and Regulations allow the employer to set the time limit and form in which notification is to take place, as long as it takes reasonable steps to make this known to the employee.[863] The employer is entitled to set a time limit by reference to the first qualifying day. If notification is late, the employer may refuse to pay SSP in respect of that day. The employee must also notify the employer of a day of incapacity even if it is one of the waiting days in respect of which no SSP is payable; if notification is late, the employer is entitled to refuse to pay SSP in respect of the first day when he would otherwise have to do so, but not in respect of any further qualifying days.[864]

Suspension and lay-off at common law

4.112   The employer has no *inherent* or automatic right of lay-off at common law, which starts from the principle that 'there should be either employment or

---

854 SSCBA 1992, s 152.
855 SSCBA 1992, s 153; SI 1982/894, reg 3.
856 SSCBA 1992, s 153(10); SI 1982/894, reg 4.
857 SI 1982/894.
858 SSCBA 1992, s 152(3).
859 SSCBA 1992, s 157(1), as amended. The daily rate is the weekly rate divided by the number of qualifying days in respect of any claim: SSCBA 1992, s 157(3).
860 SSCBA 1992, Sch 12, para 2.
861 SI 1982/894, reg 3(3).
862 Wikeley, 2002: ch 15.
863 SSCBA 1992, s 156; SI 1982/894, reg 7.
864 This at least *appears* to be the effect of SSCBA 1992, s 156(2)(b).

non-employment and that suspension is an uneasy and uncertain limbo'.[865] If work is suspended then the employee is *prima facie* entitled to wages for this period and for any period of notice which the employer would need to have given to terminate the contract lawfully. These basic principles were established in two landmark cases in the development of modern employment law.

In *Devonald v Rosser & Sons Ltd*[866] the employer, which owned a tinplate works, closed the works for lack of business during a depression in the trade, and two weeks later gave notice of one month to terminate the contracts of the manual workforce. During this six-week period the employees, who were piece workers, received no pay. They could not bring a claim in debt, since they were paid for each completed piece of work, and none had been done during the period in question. However, a claim in damages succeeded on the basis of an implied term that the employer would find them work for the period during which they remained in employment. Lord Alverstone CJ said that:

> ... the necessary implication to be drawn from this contract is at least that the master will find a reasonable amount of work up to the expiration of a notice given in accordance with the contract ... it would be no excuse to the master, for non-performance of his implied obligation to provide the workman with work, that he could no longer make his plates at a profit for orders or for stock. It is to be observed that the question of how the works are to be carried on, whether they are to work short or full time, is a matter which rests entirely in the hands of the [employer]...[867]

Gorrell Barnes P also thought that the lack of work 'is not a matter which is not in any sense within the knowledge or control of the workman; it rests entirely with the employer, who can anticipate in respect of such matters ... It seems to me that it is not reasonable to imply that the risk of that was in the contemplation of both sides as being taken by the workman'.[868]

In the second case, *Hanley v Pease & Partners Ltd*[869] the employee was a mineworker who overslept one morning and missed a shift. The employer had a rule that anyone who was more than ten minutes late for a shift would not be allowed to work on that day. On the next day the employee turned up for work on time but he was suspended for that day. He successfully sued for damages for wrongful dismissal. The court held that the contract contained no express right of suspension in respect of the second day, and that no such right could be implied either: 'after declining to dismiss the workman – after electing to treat the contract as a continuing one – the employers took upon themselves to suspend him for one day; in other words to deprive the workman of his wages for one day, thereby assessing their own damages for the servant's misconduct at the sum which would be represented by one day's wages. They have no possible right to do that'.[870]

The effect of these two cases is that in relation to piece workers and others whose right to payment is correlative with their completion of work, the employer is under a certain duty to find work in order to enable the employee to earn his or her wages. If, on the other hand, the employee is salaried, the right to

---

865 McCallum, 1989: p 233.
866 [1906] 2 KB 728.
867 [1906] 2 KB 728, 740.
868 [1906] 2 KB 728, 743.
869 [1915] 1 KB 698.
870 [1915] 1 KB 698, 705 (Lush J).

continuing payment arises on the employee simply showing that he or she was ready to work.[871]

The extent of the obligation to find work may be limited, however, if the employer can point to factors beyond his control. In *Minnevitch v Café de Paris (Londres) Ltd*[872] the owner of a cabaret closed his business for six days following the death of King George V. His musicians, who were paid according to performance, received nothing while the club was closed for mourning in this way. The court held that a closure of two days would have been reasonable, but that the employees were entitled to payment for the extra four days. This case could be seen as one of an express contractual right of lay-off, since employment was expressly on the basis of 'no work, no pay'.[873] However, in this respect *Minnevitch* is no different from *Devonald*, in which the employees were expressly to be paid by the piece for work completed; but that did not prevent them from claiming wages for the whole period during which the works was closed. The difference between the two cases is that in *Minnevitch* the employer had an implied right to suspend employment without pay in circumstances where the reason for the suspension was something he could do nothing about, whereas in *Devonald*'s case the lack of work was seen to be the employer's responsibility.

A more problematic case is *Browning v Crumlin Valley Collieries Ltd*.[874] Here, mineworkers were laid off without pay while their mine was closed by reason of flooding. The judge simply applied 'no work, no pay' to decide the case, which is not satisfactory since it does not take into account the possibility of an implied term of the kind found by the court in *Devonald v Rosser & Son Ltd*. As Freedland has argued, to say that the risk was shared between employer and employee in this case is to ignore the point that the responsibility for ensuring that the mine was safe to work in was, in law and in practice, that of the employer. Courts have declined to follow *Browning* in a number of subsequent decisions,[875] while *Devonald* has been expressly approved.[876]

If the employer wishes to have a right to suspend work without pay, it must contract for it explicitly, and such a term, like any other imposed in a standard form contract, will be construed *contra proferentem*. A contract at will or 'minute contract' under which the employer retains the right to dismiss by giving summary notice effectively achieves the same end: there is no difference here between dismissal and suspension.[877] What might look like suspension is simply dismissal and re-employment; nor will any damages be payable for wrongful dismissal, since the employer is, by definition, entitled to dispense with notice. However, a contract of this kind is now unusual in Britain. This is partly because since the Contracts of Employment Act 1963, statute has implied minimum notice periods into most contracts of employment.[878]

It might be thought, on the authority of *Turner v Sawdon & Co*,[879] that an employer is not obliged to provide work for the employee to do as long as he pays his or her wages for the period of employment. The issue here is whether

---

871 See above, para 4.58.
872 [1936] 1 All ER 884.
873 McCallum, 1989: p 215.
874 [1926] 1 KB 522.
875 *Jones v Harry Sherman Ltd* (1969) 4 ITR 63; *Johnson v Cross* [1977] ICR 872.
876 In *Bauman v Hulton Press Ltd* [1952] 2 All ER 1121, 1123; *Bond v CAV Ltd* [1983] IRLR 360, 366; Freedland, 1976b: p 89; McCallum, 1989: pp 216–217.
877 See *Marshall v English Electric Co Ltd* [1945] 1 All ER 653, discussed below, para 4.112.
878 See below, para 5.15.
879 [1901] 2 KB 653.

the employee can quit and claim damages for wrongful and/or unfair dismissal, on the basis that the employer, in failing to provide him or her with work, has committed a repudiatory breach of contract. An employee who needs to work in order to retain the skills necessary to practise his or her chosen trade, or who needs to display their work to a wider audience, could well have a claim of this sort. In *Turner v Sawdon*[880] it was said that 'in the case of an actor who accepts an engagement, it may be an important consideration with him to have an opportunity of displaying his abilities before the public, and it may be that there is an implied obligation on the part of the master to afford such an opportunity'. It is therefore 'necessary to look at the background to the contract to see how it should be construed',[881] and it would be unusual if, given the expansion of the reciprocal duty of co-operation, denying the employee the opportunity to work did not amount to a breach of the obligation of 'mutual trust and confidence' between the two parties.[882]

The implication of a duty to provide work significantly affects the practice of employers insisting on employees taking 'garden leave' before their term of employment may be terminated.[883] If an employee is forced into idleness while waiting to sit out his or her notice, this can be seen as an employer's breach of the obligation to enable a skilled employee to maintain their ability to work in his or her chosen trade or livelihood. To avoid a finding of breach by the employer in such a case, it is arguable that 'garden leave' clauses would have to be drafted in such a way as to give the employer an express power to exclude the employee from work for the period of notice.[884] However, this would greatly increase the chances of such clauses being struck down for restraint of trade.[885]

Statutory guaranteed pay

4.113 The statutory right to guaranteed pay was introduced by the EPA 1975 and is now consolidated in Part III of ERA 1996. Prior to 1977 when the relevant provisions were brought into effect, income maintenance for employees who were laid off might come from one of three sources: the individual contract of employment, guaranteed-week collective agreements between employers and trade unions, and unemployment benefit. The immediate purpose of the new statutory provision was to provide a 'floor of rights' within the employment relationship, thereby granting a measure of protection to workers who were not covered by a guaranteed week agreement; but at the same time it was also intended to shift the burden of compensation for short-term unemployment away from the state national insurance system onto individual employers.[886]

Employees with continuous employment of at least one month ending with the day before the payment is claimed qualify for protection. The right to the statutory payment arises in relation to each particular day without work, referred to as a 'workless day'.[887] The employee must show that throughout the day in

---

880 [1901] 2 KB 653, 659 (Stirling LJ).
881 *Breach v Epsylon Industries Ltd* [1976] ICR 316, 321.
882 On the mutual duty of trust and confidence, see para 4.91 above.
883 *William Hill Organisation Ltd v Tucker* [1998] IRLR 313.
884 See the discussion of this point by Morritt LJ in *William Hill Organisation v Tucker* [1998] IRLR 313, 317–318.
885 See para 4.99 above.
886 See Hepple *et al*, 1977; Szyszczak, 1990: ch 5.
887 ERA 1996, s 28(1), (3)(a).

question, he or she was not provided with work by his employer by reason of either 'a diminution in the requirements of the employer's business for work of the kind which the employee is employed to do',[888] or 'any other occurrence affecting the normal working of the employer's business'[889] in relation to such work. The employee must also show that the day is one in respect of any part of which 'he would normally be required to work in accordance with his contract of employment'.[890] No claim may be made in any day when the lack of work is caused by lock-out, strike or other industrial action involving an employee of the employer or an associated employer;[891] and a claim is also excluded if the employee refuses an offer from the employer of alternative work for that day which is 'suitable in all the circumstances, (whether or not it is work which the employee is under his contract employed to perform)'.[892]

The amount of the statutory 'guarantee payment' is calculated by reference to the normal working hours of the employee in question and the minimum 'guaranteed hourly rate'. This is derived by taking the employee's normal weekly pay[893] and dividing it by his or her normal working hours in that week or, if normal working hours differ from week to week, taking a twelve-week average.[894] However, the statutory payment is subject to an upper limit in respect of each day (£18.40 from 1 February 2005), and in any three-month period the employee is restricted to receiving statutory payments for a maximum of five days or the number of days he or she normally works in a week, whichever is less. The statutory payment is claimed by way of complaint to an employment tribunal which must normally be brought within three months of the day in respect of which the claim is made.[895] The statutory payment goes to discharge, by an equivalent amount, any contractual obligation of the employer.[896]

Many of the difficulties associated with these provisions stem from their central premise that normal daily and weekly working hours can be identified in a given case. It is clear that if the employee is not required to work on a particular day, because it falls on a holiday or a weekly break, no claim can be made in respect of *that* day,[897] even if it does arise in respect of other days without work. However, a claim could be defeated completely if the employer can show that the employee had no contractual right to work on *any* particular day. This will be the case if the employee is employed on a casual basis to the degree that there are no normal hours, so that the concept of a 'workless day' becomes meaningless.[898]

Hours may also be varied by agreement, in response, for example, to reduced demand for labour. Where this happens, it is open to an employer to argue that

---

888 The same phrase is used to define 'redundancy' for the purposes of dismissal under ERA 1996, s 139: on its meaning, see below, paras 5.164–5.172.

889 This apparently does not cover a voluntary closure by the employer, for example to observe a Jewish holiday (*North v Pavleigh* [1977] IRLR 461), but it seems highly likely that the employee would have a contractual claim in these circumstances (cf *Minnevitch v Café de Paris (Londres) Ltd* [1936] 1 All ER 884).

890 ERA 1996, s 28(1).

891 ERA 1996, s 29(3).

892 ERA 1996, s 29(4)(a). The employee must also comply with 'reasonable requirements imposed by his employer with a view to ensuring that his services are available' (s 29(5)). On the case law under these provisions, see Szyszczak, 1990: pp 107–111.

893 This is as defined by ERA 1996, ss 220–224. See below, para 5.124.

894 ERA 1996, s 30.

895 ERA 1996, s 34. On time limits in general, see para 2.17 above.

896 ERA 1996, s 32.

897 Cf ERA 1996, s 30(1); *York and Reynolds v Colledge Hosiery Co Ltd* [1978] IRLR 53.

898 *Mailway (Southern) Ltd v Willsher* [1978] ICR 511; cf *Miller v Harry Thornton (Lollies) Ltd* [1978] IRLR 430; Szyszczak, 1990: p 103.

on the days when no work is done, the employee is no longer 'normally ... required to work in accordance with his contract of employment'[899] on those days, and so again they do not count as 'workless days'.[900] This would seem to defeat the purposes of the Act, but the fault appears to lie in the way it was drafted. When calculating the amount of the statutory payment in a case where the contract has been varied for the purposes of short-time working, section 30(5) expressly requires the tribunal to take into account the terms of the original contract before it was varied;[901] but no such provision is made in section 28 which governs the initial determination of the employee's entitlement. It could be argued section 28 should nevertheless be interpreted by reference to section 30(5), on the grounds that if this were not done, the latter would make no sense.[902]

A further difficulty with the Act is illustrated by the facts of *Trevethan v Sterling Metals Ltd*.[903] The employee was employed as a night-shift worker and worked four ten-hour shifts per week. Employees on the day-shift worked five eight-hour shifts. The factory was closed for a week. The day-shift workers received statutory guarantee payments in respect of five workless days, but the tribunal held that the employee was entitled only to four, since his normal hours were spread over four working days as opposed to five.

A night-shift worker whose working hours span midnight is deemed to be employed on either one of the two days in question, but not both.[904] However, the wider problem is that the Act measures lack of work in units of days, as opposed to looking simply at the reduction in working hours over the week or month in question. By assuming a normal working week of five days, it indirectly penalises those employees whose normal working week is concentrated into a shorter period.

The upper limit on the amount of statutory payments means that the 'floor of rights' set by the Act is not high in relation to average provision.[905] The Act also permits the Secretary of State to issue an exemption order, excluding employees already covered by guaranteed week collective agreements from the application of the Act. An agreement does not necessarily have to provide equivalent benefits to those guaranteed by the Act, although it must provide for a dispute-resolution procedure.[906] A number of orders have been issued from time to time, mainly giving priority to agreements which have been designed with the requirements of particular industries in mind.[907]

Payment on suspension from work on medical grounds

4.114 ERA 1996 also provides for a right of payment where an employee is suspended from work on medical grounds as a result of a requirement imposed by statute or a recommendation contained in a code of practice issued under the Health and Safety at Work Act 1974, if it is also related to one of a number of matters listed in the Act, which are mainly concerned with exposure to lead,

899 ERA 1996, s 28(1).
900 *Clemens v Peter Richards Ltd* [1977] IRLR 332; *Daley v Strathclyde Regional Council* [1977] IRLR 414.
901 Specifically, under s 30(5) the tribunal must take the last day on which the original contract was in force as the equivalent of the day on which the statutory payment is payable.
902 See Szyszczak, 1990: p 102.
903 [1977] IRLR 416.
904 ERA 1996, s 28(5).
905 See Szyszczak, 1990: p 98.
906 ERA 1996, s 35(4).
907 For an account of the position up to the late 1980s, see Szyszczak, 1990: pp 112–114.

radiation and certain chemical processes.[908] The employee is entitled to receive a week's pay for each week of suspension, for a period of up to 26 weeks. The qualifying conditions with regard to continuity of employment are basically the same as for statutory guaranteed pay,[909] and there are similar exclusions for cases in which the employee refuses an offer of suitable alternative work or does not comply with reasonable requirements to ensure that his or her services are available to the employer.[910] No claim may be made in respect of any period when the employee is incapable of work by reason of disease or disablement.[911] Statutory payments under these provisions discharge any contractual obligations of the employer by an equivalent amount.[912]

OCCUPATIONAL PENSION SCHEMES[913]

4.115   An employee's interest in the receipt of an occupational pension from his or her employer following retirement through age or ill health is likely to be among his or her most valuable financial assets. Employment law plays a surprisingly marginal role in identifying and protecting this interest. In part this is because the state has sought to regulate pension provision through other means, principally through social security law and tax law. However, the goal of providing comprehensive provision through state social security is currently in retreat,[914] and this is responsible, in part, for refocusing the interest of policy-makers on to employer-based schemes. Another factor has been growing evidence that occupational schemes are vulnerable to predatory employer behaviour. The most dramatic example of this, the fraudulent depletion of the Mirror Group pension funds, is nevertheless atypical. More common and in some ways more problematic from the point of view of legal regulation are practices which, without involving fraud in any way, may enable employers to release pension scheme surpluses to fund merger and takeover activity and other activities of the business, at a potential cost in terms of reduced benefits for future and existing pensioners. The past few years have seen a rapid rise in litigation designed to establish the respective rights of employers, pension fund trustees and beneficiaries in this type of situation,[915] and the beginnings of a more systematic approach to statutory pension protection.[916]

908 ERA 1996, ss 64–65, 69–70.
909 ERA 1996, s 65(1)–(2).
910 ERA 1996, s 65(4).
911 ERA 1996, s 65(3).
912 ERA 1996, s 69(3).
913 In this section, we focus on those aspects of pensions law which relate closely to the employment relationship; we do not seek to provide a full treatment of the tax and social security aspects of the subject. For fuller detail, specialist works may be consulted. See Wikeley, 2002: ch 17.
914 On the reasons for this, see Wikeley, 2002: ch 17. The election of a Labour government in 1997 did not signal a reversal of this particular aspect of pensions policy.
915 The possibilities of litigation were greatly increased by the decision of the Court of Appeal in *McDonald v Horn* [1994] OPLR 281, allowing the costs of beneficiaries in an action for breach of trust against pension fund trustees to be met out of the assets of the fund. The establishment of the office of the Pensions Ombudsman by the Social Security Act 1990 (see Wikeley, 2002: pp 650–651) has also assisted the growth of pensions litigation. See Nobles, 2000b, for a critical assessment of the courts' response to the Ombudsman's exercise of the powers conferred upon him.
916 The principle of equal treatment has also exerted a growing influence. See below, para 6.94.

Types of pension scheme

4.116 Pension schemes come in a variety of different forms. A basic division may be drawn between state schemes; employer-based or occupational schemes; and personal or individual schemes.

State pension schemes

4.117 The state retirement pension is a contributory social insurance benefit consisting of two main components. The 'basic pension' is a flat-rate benefit payable to an individual who has reached pensionable age.[917] There is no longer a retirement condition attached to the receipt of the pension, nor is there any deduction for earnings from employment after reaching pensionable age,[918] so that the receipt of the pension may be combined with either full- or part-time employment at the option of the individual concerned. Pensionable age is currently 65 for men and 60 for women,[919] but measures introduced by the Pensions Act 1995[920] will give effect to a gradual equalisation, raising the pensionable age of women to 65 over 10 years starting from April 2010. The right to the benefit is based on the individual's national insurance contributions while in employment, or, in some cases, the contributions of his or her spouse; there are also rights to additional payments for dependants and in the case of invalidity, and to a small age-addition for those who have reached the age of 80. The level of the basic pension has undergone a gradual decline since the early 1980s when it began to be up-rated with prices, rather than with whichever of earnings and prices was rising more quickly.[921] By the early 1990s it represented less than 15% of average earnings.[922] The present Labour government has repeatedly rejected calls to restore the link with earnings.

State social security also provides for an additional, earnings-related pension, through the state earnings-related pension scheme (SERPS).[923] When introduced in the Social Security Act 1975, SERPS was intended to provide a pension equivalent to around one-quarter of the employee's average pre-retirement earnings between the lower and upper earnings limits for national insurance contributions.[924] The Social Security Act 1986 changed the pension formula with the effect that those reaching pensionable age after April 1999 would receive reduced benefits. Over a ten-year transitional period the rate of accrual was reduced so as to produce a pension based on one-fifth as opposed to one-quarter of average earnings; moreover, these were to be based on an average of earnings in all years of an individual's working life as opposed to the 'best twenty years' as initially provided for.[925] Further changes were made by the Child Support, Pensions and Social Security Act 2001. This restructured SERPS and renamed it the 'state second pension' (or 'S2P').[926] In a 'first phase' of these reforms, the S2P focuses benefits on to lower earners, replacing the uniform SERPS accrual rate

---

917 See generally Wikeley, 2002: pp 222–240.
918 The retirement condition and earnings rule were abolished for most purposes by the SSA 1989, s 7 and Sch 1.
919 SSCBA 1992, s 122.
920 PA 1995, s 126 and Sch 4.
921 SSA 1980, s 1.
922 Hills, 1993.
923 SSCBA 1992, ss 44, 45.
924 On the lower and upper earnings limits, see above, para 3.22.
925 See Wikeley, 2002: p 595.
926 See generally Wikeley, 2002 pp 620–625.

of 20% with three separate rates according to earnings. In the second phase of S2P, which has not yet been brought into force, the earnings-related element would disappear altogether to be replaced by a flat-rate pension.

Occupational pension schemes: final salary or defined benefit schemes

4.118   If an employer chooses to operate an occupational pension scheme, it may do so in substitution for making contributions to the additional state earnings-related pension scheme, as long as its own scheme satisfies certain minimum requirements. Occupational schemes which do this are 'contracted out' of the second-tier state pension: this means that a certain proportion of the national insurance contributions of the employer and employee are, in effect, diverted from the state scheme into the employer's own.[927] Occupational schemes have enjoyed some form of a rebate on national insurance contributions since the late 1950s.[928]

The majority of occupational schemes are 'defined-benefit' or 'salary-related' schemes which guarantee the employee benefits based on his or her average or final salary and number of years' service with the employer. Tax regulations place implicit limits on the size of the pension payments which such schemes may provide. In the case of schemes which are 'approved' by the Inland Revenue, the fund's investments are free from income tax and capital gains tax, and various tax reliefs operate on the employer's and employees' contributions. Pension payments to former employees attract income tax in the normal way but lump sums paid on retirement are not taxed.[929]

Under the 1975 Social Security Pensions Act, the principal requirement which the contracted-out scheme had to meet was to provide its employees with a guaranteed minimum pension, or GMP, which was meant to be roughly the equivalent of the benefits to which they would have been entitled under SERPS. This requirement, apparently designed to safeguard the interests of the employees, was also intended to prevent too great a burden being placed on the state scheme; the individual employee retained a residual right to receive his or her SERPS entitlement from the state, notwithstanding having been in contracted-out employment, if the occupational scheme failed. The Pensions Act 1995 instituted a new set of rules for contracting-out which replaced the GMP arrangements over a period of five years from 6 April 1997.[930] With the replacement of SERPS by S2P following the Child Support, Pensions and Social Security Act 2001, a new 'reference scheme test' comes into effect, which essentially defines a minimum required level of pension accrual.

Occupational pension schemes: money purchase or defined contribution schemes

4.119   Prior to the Social Security Act 1986, only those occupational schemes which offered defined benefits based on the employee's salary could be contracted out of SERPS. Under the 1986 Act it also became possible for employers to contract out by offering employees benefits under a 'money purchase' or 'defined contribution'

927 The employer and employee pay a 'contracted out' rate of national insurance contributions into the National Insurance Fund: see SSCBA 1992, s 8(1); PSA 1993, s 41.
928 The first such measure was the National Insurance Act 1959.
929 See generally Nobles, 1993, for an account of the interaction of tax and social security legislation and trust law in the construction of the legal concepts governing occupational pension schemes.
930 The exceptionally complex rules on the GMP and its successors are set out by Wikeley, 2002: pp 631–634.

scheme.[931] Under this arrangement, certain minimum contributions must be paid in but the scheme need not guarantee a pension based on any particular formula. The pension may simply be based, then, on the returns from investments made, and not on the salary and service record of the individual employee. Money purchase schemes do not need to guarantee a certain minimum level of income to the employee in order to qualify for contracting out. In place of a guaranteed income floor, the employee is indirectly protected by regulations governing the form in which the investment may be made. Notwithstanding these protections, the essence of a money-purchase scheme is the transfer of risk from employer to employee. In the past decade, increasing numbers of defined-benefit schemes have been closed to new members and replaced by money-purchase schemes.[932]

Personal pension schemes

4.120 The Social Security Act 1986 also introduced a number of measures designed to extend individual choice in relation to pension provision. In particular, it allowed individual employees the option of leaving either SERPS or their employer's occupational scheme and setting up personal pension schemes of their own, in which the contracted-out portion of their national insurance contributions and those of their employer would then be invested.[933] These are individual money-purchase schemes which, like their occupational counterparts, do not in themselves guarantee a particular level of final benefit; nor are they required by legislation to match the benefits which SERPS would have provided to a given employee.[934] As a consequence of the widening of individual choice, an employer may no longer insist on its employees becoming members of an occupational pension scheme;[935] however, the employer is not obliged to make additional contributions to an employee's individual scheme, beyond its national insurance contribution liability. In practice only a small minority of employers makes such additional contributions.[936] The tax treatment of individual schemes is more favourable than that governing occupational defined-benefit and money-purchase schemes, but this effect is generally confined to higher earners.[937]

The principal effect of the 1986 Act was to shift the balance of pension provision in favour of personal schemes at the expense of SERPS; occupational scheme membership was not affected to the same degree. Between 1988 and 1995 over five million individuals chose to set up personal schemes, of whom several hundred thousand had previously been in an occupational scheme. Few personal schemes are likely to match the level of benefits provided by most occupational schemes, in particular since the employer is not obliged to continue funding an employee's personal scheme at the same level of contributions as it previously paid into the occupational scheme of which the employee was a member. The changes made by the 1986 Act have had a substantial impact on the *form* of occupational pension provision; a growing number of employers, particularly in the private sector, are adopting money-purchase schemes in

---

931 See PSA 1993, ss 9(3), 10, 26–33.
932 See Deakin, 2004.
933 See Wikeley, 2002: p 249.
934 See Wikeley, 2002: pp 257–259.
935 PSA 1993, s 160.
936 In 1991, of full-time male employees with personal pension schemes, fewer than one in five had schemes to which the employer made additional contributions: see Wikeley, 2002: pp 257–258.
937 See Dilnot and Disney, 1989.

preference to the more traditional type of salary-related scheme.[938] Successive statutory interventions from the mid-1990s onwards, by imposing a substantial regulatory burden on final salary schemes but leaving money-purchase schemes less intensively regulated, may have accelerated this process.

Stakeholder pensions

4.121   The Welfare Reform and Pensions Act 1999[939] introduced a requirement that all employers employing more than five employees, and not already providing either an occupational scheme or a personal pension scheme to which the employer makes a specific minimum contribution, must offer employees with more than three months continuous employment access to a 'stakeholder pension'. This requirement came into effect from 1 April 2001. A stakeholder pension may be (and in practice often will be) provided not by the employer, but by a commercial provider. The employer is not under an obligation to make any contribution; its obligation is to choose a designated scheme, make the necessary deductions of employees' contributions, and arrange for the payment of contributions to the pension provider.

The 'balance of power' in occupational schemes

4.122   Occupational pension schemes are almost invariably constituted in the form of a trust. The immediate reason is that a scheme must be set up in this form if it is to benefit from the tax advantages just referred to. More generally, the great advantage of the trust form from the employer's point of view is its flexibility. The employer can set the 'balance of power'[940] in its favour at the outset when it drafts the terms of the trust deed laying down the rules of the scheme; because of this, the formal separation of the trust fund from the employer's business assets need not imply a loss of control. Trust deeds may be drafted in such a way as 'to ensure that the employer can use the scheme for its own commercial purposes and keep control of its financial commitments to the scheme'.[941] However, these powers of the employer are now subject to the provisions of the Pensions Acts of 1995 and 2004,[942] as well as to a growing body of case law applying the principles of fiduciary obligation and the contractual notion of good faith.

Member-nominated trustees

4.123   In the past it was not unknown for the employer itself or a wholly-owned subsidiary to be constituted the sole trustee of the fund. This is now no longer possible for those types of funds (in practice, the vast majority of significant occupational pension funds) in which scheme members have the statutory right to nominate trustees.[943] This provision, going back to the Pensions Act 1995, implemented one of the central recommendations of the Pension Law Review Committee (the 'Goode Committee') which reported in 1993.[944] This Act also

938 IFS, 1995.
939 Part I; SI 2000/1403.
940 Cf Nobles, 1993: p 28; Mesher, 1993.
941 Mesher, 1993: p 105.
942 On the 1995 Act, see Nobles, 1996.
943 See PA 1995, s 16, repealed by PA 2004 s 320 and Sch 13 as from a date to be appointed; PA 2004, ss 241–243.
944 See *Pension Law Reform, Report of the Pension Law Review Committee* (1993, Cd 2342-I). See also see also the DSS White Paper, *Security, Equality, Choice: the Future for Pensions* (1994, Cm 2594-I, II).

made provision for the protection of trustees. A trustee who is also an employee (who may not necessarily be a statutory member-nominated trustee) has the right to paid time off for the performance of duties and for training;[945] there are also provisions governing the right of employee trustees not to suffer detriment in employment and to be protected against unfair dismissal for having performed (or having proposed to perform) any of the functions of a trustee.[946]

In addition, trustees are given certain powers, but also duties, in relation to investments. Trustees must observe the general 'prudential standard' as part of the fiduciary principle when taking investment decisions,[947] and may not exclude or restrict this duty (although this does not rule out provision for insurance or indemnification).[948] The trustees must prepare and from time to time review a written statement of their investment principles; neither the terms of the trust scheme nor the statement may make their investment decisions subject to the veto of the employer.[949] The trustees are required to seek expert advice on their investment strategy and may delegate its implementation to a fund manager, but they will face potential personal liability if they were careless in selecting that person.[950]

The Act also makes provision in relation to the role of the trustees in the administration of the scheme. The trustees are required to obtain periodic audits of the scheme accounts and to maintain separation between certain bank accounts.[951] Certain rigid rules of trust law are modified to make it possible for employee and pensioner trustees to act in the context of an occupational fund: hence trustees may act by a majority unless the trust scheme provides otherwise,[952] contrary to the normal rules of trust law requiring unanimity, and the fiduciary principle to the effect that a trustee may not allow there to be a conflict between his or her personal interest and their duty to the beneficiaries is modified so as not to prevent 'a trustee of a trust scheme, who is also a member of the scheme, exercising the powers vested in him in any manner, merely because their exercise in that manner benefits, or may benefit, him as a member of that scheme'.[953] In some cases prior to the Act, the fiduciary principle had been strictly applied to the extent of placing individual trustees who were also members of a scheme in a difficult position if they made recommendations for amendment of the scheme rules from which the membership as a whole made a gain.[954]

The fiduciary relationship

4.124   Both the employer and the trustees will necessarily come under certain implied duties by virtue of the general law of contract and trusts respectively,

---

945   PA 1995, ss 42–45, now consolidated in ERA 1996, ss 58–60.
946   PA 1995, s 46, now consolidated in ERA 1996, ss 46 and 102.
947   One aspect of this is the rule that their investment decisions should be made with the aim of maximising financial returns to the fund, which may appear to limit the extent to which investments may be directed on ethical or environmental grounds. The question has not, however, received the attention of courts above first-instance level (see *Cowan v Scargill* [1984] IRLR 260).
948   PA 1995, s 33(1).
949   PA 1995, s 35.
950   PA 1995, s 34.
951   PA 1995, s 49.
952   PA 1995, s 32.
953   PA 1995, s 39.
954   *Manning v Drexel Burnham Lambert Holdings Ltd* [1994] OPLR 71: trustees recommending changes to the scheme rules had to seek the permission of the court to participate in any resulting benefits to the members; cf *Re William Makin & Sons Ltd* [1993] OPLR 171.

which now interact with the provisions of the 1995 and 2004 Acts in a number of ways. Two parallel sets of relationships need to be considered here: the *fiduciary* relationship between the trustees on the one hand and the employees and pensioners as future and present beneficiaries on the other; and the *contractual* relationship between the employer and the members of the scheme, both as employee-contributors and benefit recipients.

The trustees owe implied fiduciary duties to the beneficiaries of the trust; this is normally taken to mean that they must not exercise their discretion contrary to the interests of the beneficiaries and, in particular, must not benefit personally from their position.[955] Within these general constraints, the trustees have a wide discretion to balance the interests of present beneficiaries (pension recipients) against future ones (employees).[956] Member-nominated trustees owe the same general duties as other trustees.

The same principle may prevent the employer from exercising certain powers in its capacity as trustee for its own benefit. This principle emerges from *Mettoy Pensions Trustees v Evans*[957] where, following the employer's insolvency, the liquidator sought guidance on how to exercise a power of the employer, under the trust deed, to increase benefits to the members of the pension scheme in the event of a winding up. Warner J held that the liquidator owed a fiduciary duty to the members at the same time as owing a duty to the creditors of the company to advance their interests; since these duties were in irreconcilable conflict, the power had to be exercised by the court. However, there is room for flexibility in the application of this test; courts have on occasion diluted the test of fiduciary duty to the point of simply requiring trustees to act in good faith. In *Icarus (Hertford) Ltd v Driscoll*[958] this resulted in a finding that a receiver exercising a power originally granted to the employer under the trust deed was entitled, in her discretion, to decline to increase benefits for members on a winding up, so ensuring that the scheme surplus went to discharge the company's debts to its creditors. The receiver's fiduciary obligation to the members was, in this case, no more than a procedural one.[959]

The contractual relationship

4.125   In *Mettoy* and *Icarus* the powers concerned had been granted to or were exercised by the employer in its capacity as trustee. However, as we have just noted, the trust deed may grant significant powers to the employer without it being a trustee; in this case, there is no necessary presumption that the power in question is a fiduciary one. The employer may nevertheless be subject to the *contractual* duty of good faith, which imposes a lesser, but not insignificant, degree of control than the trust law concept of fiduciary obligation.

In *Imperial Group Pension Trust Ltd v Imperial Tobacco Ltd*[960] the rules of a trust deed provided that pension benefits were to be increased annually by an amount equivalent to retail price inflation or 5%, whichever was less. The

---

955 *Regal (Hastings) Ltd v Gulliver* [1967] 2 AC 134n, 137 (Note).
956 *Edge v Pensions Ombudsman* [2000] ICR 748.
957 [1990] 1 PLR 9.
958 [1990] 1 PLR 1.
959 See Nobles, 1993: p 88.
960 [1991] IRLR 66; *Engineering Training Authority v Pensions Ombudsman* [1996] OPLR 167; *Hillsdown Holdings plc v Pensions Ombudsman* [1996] OPLR 291; *Wheeler v NBC Pension Trustee Ltd* [1996] OPLR 337; *National Grid Co plc v Laws* [1997] OPLR 247 (Pensions Ombudsman) [1997] PLR 157 (Ch D), *National Grid Co. plc v Mayes* [2000] ICR 174 (CA), [2001] IRLR 394 (HL).

trustees of the fund also had the power to grant a greater increase by altering the rules of the scheme, but this required the consent of the company. Browne-Wilkinson VC held that the power of the company to give its consent was not a fiduciary one; the company was entitled to take its own interests into account, in particular the increased funding burden it would face if higher benefits were to be paid out. However, he went on to hold that the trust deed had to be 'construed against the background of the contract of employment', which meant that 'the pension trust deed and rules themselves are to be taken as being impliedly subject to the limitation that the rights and powers of the company can only be exercised in accordance with the implied obligation of good faith'.[961] In particular, 'the company's right to give or withhold its consent to an amendment ... is subject to the implied limitation that the right shall not be exercised so as to destroy or seriously damage the relationship of confidence and trust between the company and its employees and former employees'.[962]

The background to *Imperial Tobacco* was that a hostile takeover bid for the company had been mounted a few years before the action came to trial by Hanson plc. When Hanson's bid was pending, the management of Imperial Tobacco together with the trustees and committee of management of the Imperial Tobacco scheme had amended the trust deed of the scheme, introducing a rule that the scheme would close to new members in the event of the ownership of the company changing hands. The provision for automatic minimum annual increases in pensions of up to 5% was also inserted at that point. The aim had been to make Hanson swallow a 'poison pill' which would make the takeover of Imperial Tobacco less attractive. After the takeover had been concluded, Hanson opened a separate pension scheme for new employees, under which it offered to make provision for annual increases in pension benefits of up to 15%; at the same time it refused to agree to any increase beyond 5% under the Imperial Tobacco scheme. It then invited members of the Imperial Tobacco scheme to transfer over to the new scheme. If all of them had done so, under the arrangements offered by Hanson the surplus in the Imperial Tobacco scheme would have been transferred over to the new scheme, whereupon it would have come under Hanson's control. It is not clear whether this was Hanson's purpose in refusing its consent to the 5% increase suggested by the trustees of the Imperial Tobacco scheme. However, the Vice Chancellor held that 'if the sole purpose of withholding consent to increase benefits out of the fund is to force its present and past employees to give up their accrued rights in an existing fund so as to confer on the company benefits that it cannot enjoy unless the members give up such rights, in my judgment this conflicts with the company's duty to act fairly and in good faith to its employees'.[963]

A similar conclusion on the scope of a power of amendment was reached in *British Coal Corpn v British Coal Staff Superannuation Scheme Trustees Ltd.*[964] Here, the employer was prevented from amending the rules so as to enable a scheme surplus to be used to meet its obligations to make additional payments to members who had opted for early retirement.

961 [1991] IRLR 66, 70.
962 [1991] IRLR 66, 71.
963 [1991] IRLR 66, 71.
964 [1994] OPLR 51; see also the ruling of the Pensions Ombudsman in *Laws v National Grid Co plc* [1997] OPLR 73, reversed on appeal to the High Court, *National Grid Co plc v Laws* [1997] PLR 157, reversed in the Court of Appeal, *National Grid plc v Mayes* [2000] ICR 174, and finally reversed again in the House of Lords [2001] IRLR 394; see Nobles, 1998, 2000b.

In general, the principle derived from *Imperial Tobacco* may be regarded as an important and innovative development, which is in line with a general movement in favour of the implication of reciprocal obligations of good faith in the contract of employment.[965] However, in the context of occupational pension rights, it is not without its problems.[966] As a matter of construction, because the trustees *must* exercise their discretion in the interests of the beneficiaries, it might be thought that separate powers conferred on the employer do *not* have to be exercised in the same way. In particular, the employer should be able to take into account certain commercial interests of its own. What precisely is permissible here is not clear. This point is a general problem with the use of open-ended implied terms, but it is particularly acute when such terms are applied in the context of tightly-drafted commercial documents such as pension trust deeds. A further difficulty concerns the category of persons whose interests must be taken into account. Is the employer bound to take into consideration the interests of former employees, for example, or those of employees' dependants who may have claims on the fund?

The notion of the implied contractual duty of good faith has also been deployed to assist individual employees in their assertion of rights under pension schemes which form parts of their contracts of employment. At one stage it was thought that the employer was under no contractual duty to individual employees to oversee the effective running of the pension scheme or to ensure the delivery of the intended benefits upon retirement; at most, it was simply required to pay its own, promised pension contributions into the fund.[967] This view is now no longer tenable. The turning point was *Milhenstedt v Barclays Bank International Ltd*[968] in which the Court of Appeal held that an employer's power to grant a pension upon an employee's early retirement for ill health implied a contractual obligation to do so if the necessary conditions were satisfied; the employer was contractually bound to consider the employee's claim, take medical advice and form a reasoned opinion of her entitlement. Similarly, in *Scally v Southern Health and Social Services Board*,[969] the House of Lords held that the employer was under an implied contractual duty to inform employees of their rights to take up certain options under the highly technical terms of a statutory occupational pension scheme.

These decisions make it clear that the establishment of the trust and the appointment of trustees who owe duties of various kinds to the beneficiaries do not exhaust the employer's *contractual* duty to scheme members in their capacity as employees. In particular, the contents of the trust deed are capable of being construed so as to impose contractual entitlements on employees which employers must neither deliberately obstruct nor render ineffective.[970] The judgment in *Milhenstedt* is based on the assumption that certain terms of the pension trust are appropriate for incorporation into individual contracts of employment. In

---

965 Brodie, 1996, 1998, 2001; see para 4.91 above.
966 See Mesher, 1993: pp 106–108.
967 See Moffat and Ward, 1986: p 395.
968 [1989] IRLR 522; *Aspden v Webbs Poultry & Meat Group (Holdings) Ltd* [1996] IRLR 521; *Brompton v AOC International Ltd* [1997] IRLR 639.
969 [1991] IRLR 522; but see also later cases qualifying the employer's duty to provide information concerning occupational pension schemes, in particular *Nottingham University v Eyett* [1999] IRLR 87 and *Outram v Academy Plastics Ltd* [2000] IRLR 499.
970 For discussion, suggesting that the courts are adopting 'circular' reasoning in these cases, see Nobles, 1993: p 58.

principle there is no reason why those terms which are capable of conferring valuable benefits on employees should not be incorporated.[971] However, many schemes contain statements indicating that the rules they contain are not intended to have any contractual effect.[972] The value of a unilateral declaration by the employer of this kind may nevertheless be doubted, in the light of decisions to the effect that it is for the courts to judge, taking into account the available evidence, whether particular arrangements have contractual force, and that they may not treat unilateral statements by one side or the other as conclusive.[973]

A number of central substantive issues remain unclear, however. For example, it is undoubtedly the obligation of the trustees to ensure that pension benefits are paid promptly and in full to the current beneficiaries of the trust; but does the employer owe an additional contractual duty to ensure that former employees receive the pension payments which are referable to their past service? In principle, such an obligation could be implied as an aspect of the duty of good faith. It could also survive the ending of the employment relationship by retirement, by analogy with other obligations such as the employee's duty of confidentiality.[974]

The winding-up of a scheme, or the limitation of restriction of the rights of an individual or of a class of employees, could be seen as a breach of contract by the employer. Even if a scheme contains an express clause allowing the employer to terminate its contributions and wind the scheme up, it is arguable that these powers would be read as subject to the implied duty of good faith, as discussed by Browne-Wilkinson VC in *Imperial Tobacco*.[975] On the other hand, in *Air Jamaica v Charlton*[976] the Privy Council took the view that the entitlements of the members of an occupational pension scheme derive from trust law, not contract law; although 'pensions are earned by [the members'] services under their contracts of employment as well as by their contributions', and hence 'are often not inappropriately described as deferred pay', this did not mean, according to Lord Millett, that they had 'contractual rights to their pensions'. His Lordship considered that the employer's contractual duties were limited to deducting the employee members' contributions from their salaries and paying them over to the trustees, and paying over its own contributions. Whether this view is sustainable may be doubted. From an employment law perspective, it completely fails to integrate the occupational pension scheme into the wider framework of the employer's implied and express contractual obligations.

Pension benefits as deferred pay

4.126 Contrary to *Air Jamaica*, decisions to the effect that the rules of occupational schemes might give rise to contractual entitlements offer support

---

971 See above, para 4.29.
972 See Nobles, 1993: p 54.
973 *R v Lord Chancellor's Department, ex p Nangle* [1991] IRLR 343.
974 See Elias, 1982: p 97.
975 It should also be noted that if the power to change the scheme rules is vested in trustees, they will not normally have a free hand but will have to act in compliance with their fiduciary duties to the beneficiaries of the scheme as explained in the text; for some of the implications of this, see *Lloyds Bank Pension Trust Corpn Ltd v Lloyds Bank plc* [1996] OPLR 181.
976 [1999] 1 WLR 1399.

for the notion of pension benefits as deferred pay, in other words as an element of the employee's remuneration which is earned by service. Particularly important is the recognition by the courts that pension trusts cannot be analysed in the same way as the standard family trust, in which the beneficiaries are volunteers. This is because the members of a pension trust contribute to their own benefits, either by way of their own periodic contributions or, if the scheme is non-contributory, in the form of their service as employees;[977] this, in turn, may make it more difficult for both the employer and the trustees to exercise contractual and fiduciary powers, as the case may be, in such a way as to harm the members' interests.

However, the growing judicial acceptance of the notion of deferred pay does not mean that the members' interests will necessarily prevail over those of other parties, such as the employer or its creditors in the event of insolvency. A central issue here is the nature of claims over pension fund surpluses. Many schemes built up surpluses in the 1980s when investment returns were high. As a result, it was common for employers to institute 'contribution holidays', reducing or eliminating their own contributions on the grounds that the scheme was already capable of meeting its accrued liabilities. This practice will normally be lawful, according to Vinelott J in *Taylor v Lucas Pensions Trust*:

> The pension fund, to the extent that it is in surplus (that is, that the funds are more than are needed to meet accrued liabilities under the scheme), does not in any intelligent sense belong to anyone. Members and pensioners (present and future) have an interest if and in so far as the fund is capable of being applied in improving benefits or adding new benefits. They also have an interest in ensuring that the fund is retained intact, in that it represents additional security for payment of benefits and may have to be applied for improving benefits for members and pensioners on a winding-up. However, an employer has an interest in so far as a surplus in the fund can be used to relieve him of his obligation to contribute to the fund.[978]

In practice, decisions on whether to allow a surplus to be returned to the employer tend to turn on the precise construction of the terms of the trust deed, with the general principles of contractual and fiduciary liability playing only a residual role.[979] In addition, the Pensions Act 1995 provides that any power under the scheme rules to return all or part of the surplus to the employer must be exercised by the trustees, and may only be so exercised if a number of conditions are met.[980]

Pension scheme protection

4.127   A number of statutory measures for the protection of pension fund assets were introduced following the 1989 report of the Occupational Pensions Board, *Protecting Pensions*,[981] and again following the report of the Pensions Law Review Committee in 1993. These aimed to protect members' expectations that the real

---

977 *Mettoy Pension Trustees v Evans* [1990] 1 PLR 9; *Imperial Group Pension Trust Ltd v Imperial Tobacco Ltd* [1991] IRLR 66; *Taylor v Lucas Pensions Trust* [1994] OPLR 29.
978 [1994] OPLR 29, 31.
979 Compare *British Coal Corpn v British Coal Staff Superannuation Scheme Trustees* [1994] OPLR 51 with the litigation which culminated in *National Grid Co plc v Mayes* [2001] IRLR 394.
980 PA 1995, s 37 (as amended by PA 2004, s 250).
981 1989, Cm 573.

value of benefits will be maintained over time and to limit the use by employers of scheme assets for their own commercial purposes. The principal reform was the introduction by the Pensions Act 1995 of a 'minimum funding requirement' under which the trustees were required to ensure that the value of the scheme's assets exceeded its liabilities. If assets fell below 90% of liabilities, the employer came under a duty to make up the difference. This approach engendered substantial criticism on the grounds that, while stopping short of providing a guarantee that members' rights would be met in full in the event of employer insolvency, it could also distort investment decisions. In September 2000 the Department of Social Security and HM Treasury issued a consultation document laying out a series of options for reform[982] and after a further consultation process[983] the requirement was repealed by the Pensions Act 2004. It was replaced by a new 'statutory funding objective' which was intended to provide trustees and employers with greater flexibility to take into account scheme-specific factors, including the scheme's investment policy, the age profile of members, staff turnover and likely future salary increases, when determining the scheme's funding strategy.

The 2004 Act also introduced new mechanisms for the protection of members against scheme failure. With effect from April 2005 a Pension Protection Fund was set up, funded from levies charged on defined benefit and certain 'hybrid' schemes, with the aim of providing compensation to members of schemes which fail by reason of the insolvency of the employer. The Fund essentially incorporates and extends an earlier scheme of compensation, set up by the 1995 Act, which was however confined to cases of misappropriation involving the commission of a criminal offence. In addition, the 2004 Act established a Financial Assistance Scheme to deal with other cases of underfunding involving schemes which have been wound up. This mechanism depends on a grant of £400 million over twenty years from public funds.[984]

ASSESSMENT

4.128 This chapter has illustrated the continuing importance of the contract of employment as a means of giving expression to the rights and obligations of the parties to the employment relationship. The basic contractual framework of the relationship remains intact, notwithstanding the influence of social legislation and collective bargaining. The body of legislation providing a floor of rights in the employment relationship, while far from negligible, is incomplete in many respects. Fundamental issues concerning the nature of the wage-work bargain, the employee's right to payment and the organisation of working time have until recently been left relatively untouched by statute. The common law is also pre-eminent in relation to the employee's obligations of obedience, co-operation and fidelity and in the treatment of non-competition clauses. In the areas of income security legislation has had a certain impact, but the main purpose of

---

982 See DSS/HM Treasury, *Security for Occupational Pensions. A Consultation Document,* September 2000.

983 See DWP, *Simplicity, Security and Choice: Working and Saving for Retirement. Action on Occupational Pensions,* Cm 5835, June 2003. See also the first report of the Pensions Commission, *Pensions: Challenges and Choices* (2004).

984 See *Action on Occupational Pensions,* Cm 5835, June 2003, for an explanation of the background to these and related changes made by the 2004 Act.

intervention in the form of statutory guaranteed pay and statutory sick pay was to shift the burden of payments away from social insurance and onto individual employers, rather than seeking to establish a floor of rights for collective bargaining.

The contract of employment has become increasingly important as a device for protecting collectively-agreed terms and conditions of employment against unilateral changes by employers. During the period up to 1983 when the Fair Wages Resolution was still in place and provided a basic floor of rights at sector-level, the role of the contract of employment in this regard appears to have been negligible. After the rescission of the Fair Wages Resolution this constraint was lifted, at the same time as encouragement was given to employers to bargain for more flexible terms and conditions at plant and company level. However, as we have seen the courts, in numerous judgments, affirmed that the abrogation of all or part of a collective agreement, while completely lawful in most cases at the level of management-union relations, did not necessarily entail the abrogation of those terms at the individual level; on the contrary, individual agreement to a variation of contract terms would not lightly be inferred. Another area in which the notion of employees' vested contractual rights has proved to be important is that of occupational pension benefits: an employer may be bound by express obligations incurred as part of its funding and payment responsibilities under the pension trust, and by the residual duty to exercise its powers in good faith.

There are, at the same time, limits to how far the common law can be used to protect employee expectations. In the absence of mandatory regulation, employers can adopt the tactic of describing conditions of employment relating to such matters as occupational benefit schemes and disciplinary procedures as non-contractual. The courts have the final responsibility for determining whether any particular arrangement has legal effect, and disclaimers issued by employers will not necessarily be effective either at common law or under the Unfair Contract Terms Act 1977. However, it is not possible to state as a general rule that conditions of this kind *must* have legal effect, or that such terms are necessarily incorporated into individual contracts of employment: it will be a question of the construction of the contract in each case.

British labour law traditionally lacked a comprehensive labour code of the kind found in some civil law systems. Collective bargaining was supplemented by direct statutory regulation in areas where joint regulation had failed to develop. More recently, the policy of deregulation saw the removal of direct statutory regulation of this kind, but without any legal encouragement for voluntary collective bargaining to take its place. However, the passage of the National Minimum Wage Act 1998 signifies a new turn in the debate over labour standards. The importance of this measure also lies in the justifications given for it: the case for the national minimum wage was put not just in terms of equity, but also by reference to economic criteria such as the need to raise labour productivity and to ensure the adequate operation of work incentives. The primary legislation left open the level at which the wage is set, and the procedure for up-rating it in future years. In these respects, the 1998 Act lacks the comprehensiveness of similar legislation in mainland European systems, in particular the French *SMIC* or minimum growth wage, which is intended to maintain the link between the lowest paid and increases in purchasing power among the working population as a whole. However, the 1998 Act provides a model for possible extensions of the floor of rights to other areas of the employment relationship.

The cause of basic labour standards has been further advanced by the implementation of the Working Time Directive in the Working Time Regulations 1998. The Directive and Regulations together mark a different approach to regulation to that which has traditionally prevailed in relation to working time. First, the new standards have a more or less general application, as opposed to the former practice of industry- or group-specific regulation. Second, the new model makes extensive provision for flexibility in implementation, by way of 'bargained derogations', envisaging, from one perspective, a new role for collective agreements as mechanisms for implementing and varying statutory standards, in particular at plant and company level. Bargaining takes place within the broad framework set by legal standards, and is to some extent directed by them;[985] by contrast, the previous British practice had been to preserve a more formal autonomy of collective bargaining from the state, so that in most sectors pay and working-time issues were dealt with without reference to legally-binding minimum standards of any kind.

It is nevertheless arguable that from the point of view of advancing collective bargaining as a mechanism for the application of labour standards, the Working Time Regulations represent a lost opportunity. By providing for extensive derogations from a wide range of basic standards to be brought about through 'workforce agreeements' which are not concluded by an independent trade union and which offer few, if any, guarantees of equitable treatment for the individuals or groups of workers who sign them, the Regulations deny to independent employee representation the role which was arguably envisaged for it under the Directive. Moreover, in allowing individual derogations to be implemented by employers in a relatively cost-free way, the 1999 amendments open up the possibility for widespread abuse of the right to qualify the core statutory right to a 48-hour limit on weekly working time. The amendments to the Directive which were proposed by the European Commission in 2004 arguably do little to address this problem.[986]

The effectiveness of the basic contractual model of the employment relationship has been extensively debated. The 'primacy' of contractual reasoning is a principal feature of the British system,[987] in contrast to the civilian systems in which 'contract' is only one aspect of a broader employment 'relationship'. The common law model of contract is, it is suggested, inadequate to the task of expressing the nature of the employment relationship, at least in larger, bureaucratic organisations. Collins has argued that this is because 'the ordinary relations of authority found in employment cannot be reduced to a simple contractual formulation'; the result of attempting to do so is 'a series of artificial and unpersuasive explanations of the content and structure of the employment relation'.[988] The explanatory force of contract is limited to the hiring process or 'port of entry' to the organisation, after which the rules of the workplace, which are better thought of as a private bureaucratic code, govern the relationship. This approach would permit the courts to make greater use of concepts drawn from public law, such as notions of legitimate expectation, whose function is to control the exercise of power.

---

985 Bercusson, 1994a, 1994b, refers to this is an instance of 'bargaining in the shadow of the law'.
986 For discussion, see Hobbs and Njoya, 2005.
987 Honeyball, 1988.
988 H Collins, 1986: pp 2–3.

This analysis has been criticised for placing proceduralism above the protection of substantive rights,[989] and it arguably also contradicts one of the most important developments of the modern law governing the employment relationship, namely the identification of commitments entered into by employers with regard to pay, hours and working conditions as contractual in nature and hence legally binding upon them. This process, which has involved a considerable limitation of unilateral managerial decision-making, began in regard to the employment of managerial and clerical workers and was extended to the greater body of employees following the passage of the Contracts of Employment Act 1963 and later employment protection legislation. It is still going on today, as we can see from the continuing debate over the extent of the contractual and fiduciary responsibilities of employers with regard to pension fund schemes. Collins suggests that as a matter of 'industrial reality ... the code governing the employment relation, whether or not it is produced by joint regulation, does not create a set of contractual entitlements but provides a set of administrative rules which create expectations which deserve a measure of protection'.[990] However, this might be thought to do less than justice to the achievements of the doctrine of the incorporation of terms. Not only does this doctrine illustrate the flexibility and adaptability of contract law; given the particular nature of the British system, these contractual entitlements perform, however incompletely, the essential function of providing a floor to employment conditions which in other systems is achieved through statute or collective agreements which have a direct regulatory effect.

In certain other respects it could be argued that Collins's aim of requiring managerial power to be exercised in such a way as to respect the legitimate expectations of the individual employee has been achieved within the framework provided by contractual reasoning. The extension of the implied duty of co-operation has reached the point where employers have been required to act 'in good faith' and to avoid arbitrary reasoning and collateral purposes. This principle is open to the criticism that its scope is unclear, its practical application is capable of varying from one case to the next and it only offers a residual protection against the employer's superior contractual power. These are, of course, criticisms which can and have been levelled against the public-law model of governance too.[991] It is not entirely clear what the legitimate expectations of the employees might be under this approach, although it is suggested that they would not be able 'to frustrate changes in tasks performed and work patterns and to inhibit the introduction of new technology by providing a blanket defence of existing styles of work under the guise of the enforcement of terms of the contract'.[992] The same outcome is achieved under the contract model by way of the employee's open-ended duty of co-operation.[993]

Despite their superficial similarity, however, the bases of the contractual duty of co-operation and of the review of powers in public law are not identical. The contractual concept is based on an extended notion of private bargain, but this does not necessarily detract from the goal of controlling the employer's superior power: on the contrary, it emphasises that mutual respect and reciprocity are essential means of ensuring that both parties realise their expected gains

---

989 Fredman and Lee, 1987.
990 H Collins, 1986: p 8.
991 Fredman and Lee, 1987.
992 H Collins, 1986: p 9.
993 *Cresswell v Board of Inland Revenue* [1984] IRLR 190.

from the relationship.[994] It represents, in other words, legal recognition of the economic need for co-operation in complex, long-term economic relationships such as employment. The advanced pace of technical change and the increased product-market pressure facing many firms make it more essential than ever to put in place arrangements for eliciting and maintaining workforce co-operation;[995] from this point of view, the emergence within legal doctrine of the extended duty of contractual co-operation is appropriate and timely. However, it may be questioned how far such developments in the common law, or in the area of basic statutory labour standards, can be made effective in the absence of adequate procedures for ensuring independent and comprehensive collective representation of employees.[996]

994 See Brodie, 1998b, 1999a, 2001b; Freedland, 2003.
995 Deakin and Wilkinson, 1996.
996 See Ewing, 1998; W Brown *et al*, 2000.

CHAPTER 5

Discipline and termination of employment

INTRODUCTION

5.1 The law governing termination of employment occupies a central place in modern labour law. The overwhelming number of litigated disputes arise out of terminations of the employment relationship. In 2003–2004, out of 93,973 registered cases disposed of by employment tribunals, 37,901 concerned unfair dismissal and 4,059 redundancy pay.[1] From a doctrinal point of view, the legislation on unfair dismissal represents a major incursion into the common law, limiting the employer's otherwise open-ended power to bring the contract of employment to an end without the need for substantive justification, and imposing general standards of procedural fairness upon the process of dismissal. Redundancy payments legislation, the other major area of statutory intervention, grants the employee the right to compensation, based loosely on the principle of seniority, for the loss of a job on economic grounds.

At the same time, the law relating to unfair dismissal and redundancy is about much more than the process of termination and its results; it affects the entire structure of the employment relationship. Just as the power of dismissal is 'the fiercest sanction which backs up managerial authority to direct the workforce', so dismissal law has become the 'tail [wagging] the whole dog of the employment relation'.[2] The norms which govern the circumstances in which dismissal is legitimate indirectly set the limits to the employer's power to operate lesser disciplinary sanctions, such as suspension or demotion; accordingly this chapter is also concerned with the law relating to disciplinary procedures and the extent of the employer's power to impose sanctions short of dismissal.[3] Statutory intervention has also qualified the employer's common law rights to insist on unilateral changes to terms and conditions of employment. As long as the employer could terminate the contract of employment at will (or on short notice), it effectively had the right to dismiss and re-employ on those terms which it deemed acceptable. Now that this power of the employer is limited by the principles of unfair dismissal law, dismissal legislation does not simply underpin the accrued contractual rights of the employees; the framework of implied and express terms through which the parties' reciprocal rights and obligations are expressed rests upon the capacity of dismissal law to stabilise the employment relationship (although we shall see below that this is far from unqualified). Dismissal protection is also an essential bulwark of those fundamental employment rights which are currently recognised by British legislation: these include rights in relation to trade union membership, health

---

1 *Employment Tribunals Service: Annual Report and Accounts 2003-2004*, DTI, App 1, Table 2. Applications may cover more than one jurisdiction, eg unfair dismissal and sex discrimination. These figures refer to the principal type of claim identified by ETS staff on receipt of the application.
2 H Collins, 1993: pp 1, 270 respectively.
3 See also the discussion in ch 4 above of the scope of the employee's duties of obedience and care, and the legality of deductions from wages for breaches of discipline.

and safety protection, the protection of pregnancy and maternity and, by extension from the anti-discrimination legislation, rights to equal treatment on the grounds of sex, race, disability, religion or belief and sexual orientation.

The structure of this chapter is as follows. The next section considers the aims, forms and impact of dismissal legislation. We then analyse the doctrinal framework of the law governing termination, beginning with an analysis of the common law of wrongful dismissal and the scope and effects of contractual disciplinary procedures and job security clauses. The statutory concept of dismissal is considered next, followed by an analysis of the principles governing fairness of dismissal, with emphasis on the extent of procedural and substantive protections. This is followed by an integrated account of the principles governing economic dismissals, covering the right to redundancy compensation; unfair dismissal in the context of redundancies and reorganisations; the rights of employees in situations of employer insolvency; and dismissals related to business transfers.

DISMISSAL LEGISLATION: FORMS, AIMS AND IMPACT

(i) Forms of dismissal legislation

5.2 Dismissal legislation in Britain takes the form of rights conferred on the individual employee against his or her employer, and administered by the specialised system of labour courts, the employment tribunals, charged with the task of interpreting and enforcing employment protection legislation.[4] In this respect, the UK follows a pattern well established in the systems of mainland Europe.[5] In France and Germany the movement of regulation began in the inter-war period with the imposition of minimum notice periods and of restrictions on the exercise of the right of summary dismissal; in the post-war period, the requirement of good cause as a condition for termination of employment became more widely embodied in legislation.[6] The UK was relatively late to adopt this form of intervention. Notice periods were introduced in the Contracts of Employment Act 1963 and redundancy compensation in the Redundancy Payments Act 1965; unfair dismissal law was introduced as part of the Industrial Relations Act 1971. The relevant provisions of the 1971 Act were re-enacted in 1974, extended in 1975 and currently constitute Parts IX and X of ERA 1996. Part XI of that Act is the successor to the Redundancy Payments Act of 1965. These statutory schemes are now subject to changes introduced by the Employment Act 2002 to encourage the establishment and use of internal dispute resolution procedures before claims are brought to tribunals.

The regulation of dismissal may take a collective as opposed to an individual form. In the United States regulation exists in the form of arbitration under the umbrella of collective bargaining agreements (although these now cover only a small proportion of the total workforce). In the UK, the law accords collective relations an important role in the regulation of economic dismissals, where workforce representatives have the right to be consulted over planned

---

4　In May 2001 a scheme for the resolution of unfair dismissal disputes by arbitration as an alternative to proceedings in the employment tribunal came into force: see further para 2.20 above.

5　For an analysis of European provisions on dismissal law, see Hepple, 1997b.

6　See Vogel-Polskey, 1986; Deakin, 1990b.

redundancies.[7] Collective arbitration over dismissals also exists, but for the most part alongside and not by way of substitution for unfair dismissal protection.[8] One advantage of arbitration, in addition to the possible reduction of legalism in procedures, is that the arbitrator is closer to the parties concerned than a labour court can be, and may as a result be in a better position to award reinstatement. However, there is disagreement on the question of whether north American arbitration is any more effective than the individual model in protecting employees against the exercise of managerial prerogative;[9] it also suffers from the weakness of providing protection only in those workplaces (a small minority in the USA) where unions are established as representative bargaining agents and have established collective agreements containing job security provisions.

(ii) Aims and influences

5.3 The apparent goal of dismissal legislation, namely the achievement of greater employment security, is neither straightforward in itself, nor the only or even principal objective of statutory intervention. At the outset it is important to clarify the various meanings which might be ascribed to the term 'employment security'.[10] The notion of 'job security', for example, can be taken to imply that a worker is protected in the *particular job* which he or she holds; this in turn presupposes the existence of quite rigid job classifications and, from a regulatory perspective, the placing of limits on the employer's right to change those classifications at will. At the opposite extreme, 'employment security' in its widest sense could be taken to refer to the availability of employment opportunities in a given economy; if this is the goal, economic and regulatory policy should be concerned to maximise the chances of employees finding a job and being able to move between jobs throughout their career, rather than being protected in relation to a given job which they might hold at any one time.[11] Dismissal legislation does not neatly fit either of these definitions. It rarely goes to the lengths of granting a worker absolute protection in relation to a specific job classification; but nor is it concerned simply with individuals' opportunities in the labour market. It focuses instead on employees' positions within employing organisations, and operates on the disciplinary and managerial powers of employers in relation to those who are employees, and not in relation to those who are job seekers or applicants for employment. Moreover, as Büchtemann has pointed out, the term employment security should be distinguished from *de facto* employment stability. The latter describes a situation in which stable, long-term employment relationships are the norm, which may occur even in systems, such as that of the USA, where there are few legal or other controls over managerial prerogative.[12] This situation may persist, thanks to economic circumstances or to shared expectations of the contracting parties, but it cannot

---

7   TULRCA 1992, ss 188 *et seq*; see para 9.32 *et seq* below. See also ICER 2004, reg 20, discussed at para 9.54 *et seq* below.
8   ERA 1996, s 110 (as amended by ERDRA 1998, s 12 and EA 2002, s 44) provides a power to exempt employees from the scope of the unfair dismissal provisions of the Act where a collective 'dismissal procedures agreement', designated by order of the Secretary of State, is in place. See para 5.64 below.
9   For differing views, see H Collins, 1982; Glasbeek, 1984.
10   See Büchtemann, 1993.
11   Lindbeck and Snower, 1989.
12   See Addison and Castro, 1987.

be said that the worker in such a situation enjoys security as opposed to the bare expectation that employment will continue. Employment security properly understood, by contrast, refers to the existence of 'explicit or implicit rules and provisions putting a restraint on the ability of firms to dismiss workers "at will"',[13] that is to say, without the need to show good cause or to respect certain procedures. In other words, the key to the meaning of employment security is the existence of some form of regulatory intervention designed to protect workers against *arbitrary* managerial decision-making.

5.4   Employment security is sometimes said to confer a form of *job property* or 'ownership of jobs' on workers.[14] The idea should not be taken too literally; an employee is unlikely to be in a position where he or she can sell (or otherwise alienate) their job rights to another, so that any analogy between this form of property and the legally-recognised forms of property rights over tangible and intangible assets is inevitably incomplete. Although legislation or collective agreements may confer on employees the right to be compensated *ex post* for the loss of employment arising from redundancy, it is not clear that anything is gained by describing this as a right to compensation for the expropriation of a property right; a core feature of property is the ability of the right-holder to enjoin, *ex ante*, any interference with his or her enjoyment of it, and not simply to receive compensation after the interference has taken place. Nevertheless the notion of job property could be thought of, less formalistically, as implying a recognition not simply of the dependence of workers on their jobs for economic subsistence but, more broadly, of the need for 'job satisfaction' in the sense of personal self-expression and the fulfilment of career-related and occupational goals. This notion also coincided, for a time, with the practice in large organisations of offering, in effect, lifetime employment to their employees. The expectation was that employment would continue in the absence of good cause justifying dismissal, and that the employee's salary and employment benefits, including occupational pension rights, would be linked to their seniority or length of service with the organisation; job mobility, training and occupational development and career progress would take place largely within the *internal labour market* of the firm itself. While the practice of 'lifetime employment' was most strongly entrenched from a cultural and social point of view in countries such as Japan,[15] it also formed a part of the expectations of many workers in both the private and public sectors in north America and western Europe. Today, it is widely thought that the idea of the 'job for life' is becoming defunct in western industrialised countries, and it is also under pressure, if not to the same degree, in Japan. But even during the period, roughly from the 1950s to the mid-1970s, when the aim of permanent employment had greater resonance, the expectation of a job for life was rarely translated into a legal guarantee. A few workers, such as civil servants in some European systems, enjoyed *de jure* job security in the sense of being dismissible only for cause.[16] For the most part, however, neither collective bargaining nor employment protection legislation guaranteed workers against the loss of employment by reason of technical change,

---

13   See Büchtemann, 1993: p 8.
14   See Meyers, 1964, for discussion.
15   Dore, 1987.
16   This was not the case in the UK where, thanks to the long-standing view that civil servants did not have contracts of employment (see para 3.74 above), their legal position was somewhat precarious, even if they enjoyed considerable *de facto* job security.

changing skills requirements, or shifts in the nature of the demand for labour. It is doubtful if such guarantees can be made legally effective in a market economy: in such an economy, 'employment security can for the vast majority of workers mean security only from ungrounded or arbitrary job terminations'.[17]

5.5 The limitations of the job property model has led to a search for principles which can more legitimately be said to underlie the legal control of managerial power. Collins has suggested in this vein that instead of seeing the individual rights of employees in terms of property rights over jobs, 'the employee's interest in job security is better conceived as a right to dignity combined with the establishment of conditions for autonomy and freedom'.[18] The *right to dignity and autonomy* involves a recognition of the employee's rights to be treated with respect for his or her person and individuality. At the same time, it is to accept the legitimacy of those dismissals which are motivated by rational considerations and which are implemented with regard for due process or procedural fairness. Hence the dismissal of an employee on the grounds that there is no longer any demand for his or her services (redundancy) or that he or she is unable to perform the tasks required of them (incapability) does not involve any infringement of the right of personal dignity, nor are such dismissals 'irrational'; 'where, however, the dismissal is based upon irrelevant considerations, such as conduct wholly unconnected to the employee's performance at work, or the employee's characteristics such as sex or race which the employer views as reasons for treating the employee with less than equal respect, then the dismissal does involve a violation of the right to dignity and so justice requires that it should be prohibited or penalised'.[19] Similarly, the goal of personal autonomy – allowing the individual employee the necessary conditions for self-expression and personal development through his or her work – provides a justification for norms which impose certain procedural obligations upon employers. This requires not just that the employer should put explicit disciplinary rules in place, but also that those rules should be themselves judged by reference to external standards. The set of disciplinary rules should be one which 'satisfies the demands of autonomy ... yet which remains compatible with the demands of an efficient and competitive business organisation'.[20]

In this approach there is an explicit borrowing of public law techniques for the regulation of administrative discretion. Here, 'public law properly refers to a function, a kind of activity, and not to an institution'.[21] Hence the norms of public law which require decisions to be based on relevant considerations and which seek to minimise the element of arbitrariness in decision-making may be, up to a point, transmissible to the large private-sector bureaucracies which are found within employing organisations: this involves an acknowledgement that 'the internal management of the firm [is] a form of bureaucratic organisation'.[22]

5.6 The fundamental notion that managerial power should be exercised so as to be compatible with notions of formal rationality is reflected in ILO Recommendation No 119 of 1963, which was influential in the development of the unfair dismissal

---

17   Büchtemann, 1993: p 8.
18   H Collins, 1993: p 28.
19   H Collins, 1993: p 17.
20   H Collins, 1993: p 20.
21   Selznick, 1980: p 273.
22   H Collins, 1993: p 23. See also P Davies and M Freedland, 1997, especially pp 323–327.

laws of many systems including that of the UK.[23] The Recommendation prescribes that '[t]ermination of employment should not take place unless there is a valid reason for such termination connected with the capacity or conduct of the worker or based on the operational requirements of the undertaking, establishment or service'.[24] The idea that certain employee rights should be protected regardless of the costs to the employer or, more widely, to society, of doing so finds its practical application in the creation of a category of reasons for dismissal which 'should not constitute valid reasons for termination of employment': the Recommendation identifies these as reasons related to trade union membership or participation in trade union activities; seeking to become or acting in the capacity of a workers' representative; making, in good faith, a complaint against the employer of alleged violation of laws or regulations; or discriminatory dismissal, defined broadly to include 'race, colour, sex, marital status, religion, political opinion, national extraction or social origin'.[25] As we shall see,[26] the British legislation recognises the principle of 'automatically unfair' reasons, without, however, applying this concept as broadly as the ILO Recommendation suggests.

The ILO Recommendation also lays down procedural guidelines for employers to follow in cases where dismissal is for what, in the language used in our own system, are referred to as 'potentially fair reasons'.[27] In particular, dismissal without notice should not take place except for 'serious misconduct' and where the employer could not 'in good faith be expected to take any other course'. If the employer does not take action within a reasonable time of discovering serious misconduct, it is taken to have waived the right to dismiss on those grounds; and '[b]efore a decision to dismiss a worker for serious misconduct becomes finally effective, the worker should be given an opportunity to state his case promptly, with the assistance where appropriate of a person representing him'.[28] The principle of rational behaviour also extends to economic dismissals. Even though the right of the employer to terminate employment on this ground is recognised, '[p]ositive steps should be taken by all parties concerned to avert or minimise as far as possible reductions of the work force by the adoption of appropriate measures, without prejudice to the efficient operation of the undertaking, establishment or service'.[29] In addition to consultation with the workers' representatives, the employer must observe the principle of rationality in the process of selection for redundancy: this should be done on the basis of precise criteria, notified in advance, and which may take into account the following factors: the 'need for the efficient operation of the undertaking, establishment or service'; the 'ability, experience, skill and occupational qualifications of individual workers'; length of service; age; family situation; or 'such other criteria as may be appropriate under national conditions'.[30]

---

23   Note also the later ILO Convention No 158 (1982) concerning termination of employment at the initiative of the employer and the accompanying Recommendation No 166. Convention No 158 defines with greater precision than the 1963 Recommendation certain invalid reasons for dismissal (eg 'family responsibilities' and 'pregnancy'); Recommendation No 166 adds new grounds of invalid dismissal such as age. See further Hepple, 1997b: pp 216–218. To date only a minority of EC Member States have ratified the Convention.
24   ILO Recommendation No 119, Art 2(1).
25   ILO Recommendation No 119, Art 2(3).
26   See para 5.95 below.
27   See para 5.115 below.
28   ILO Recommendation No 119, Art 10(5).
29   ILO Recommendation No 119, Art 12.
30   ILO Recommendation No 119, Art 15.

5.7   If the promotion of formal rationality in managerial decision-making can be seen to be the basis for the protection of the fundamental individual right to dignity and autonomy at work, it can also be viewed as the foundation for the enhancement of *managerial efficiency* within the enterprise. This was the view of the Donovan Report of 1968 which supported the adoption of unfair dismissal legislation in the UK, partly by way of implementing ILO Recommendation No 119, which the UK had earlier adopted,[31] but also as part of the wider programme of industrial relations reform put forward by the Royal Commission in its Report. An essential aspect of that programme was the strengthening and formalisation of plant-level procedures. Prior to Donovan, procedures for dealing with disputes over discipline and dismissal operated at sector-level in a number of industries;[32] this resulted in long delays in processing disputes, making their outcome of little relevance for the employees concerned who would have found other work in the meantime, and encouraged resort to unofficial strikes at plant level as the most effective means, for many, of ensuring *de facto* job security. The Royal Commission was concerned both to limit the number and extent of unofficial strikes and to end the division between the two systems of industrial relations, the 'formal system' at the level of the sector and the 'informal system' of plant-level relations. Unfair dismissal legislation, since it took the individual employer and not the multi-employer sector as the focus of regulation, was seen as a means of achieving these goals; even though the introduction of legislation marked a departure from the tradition of voluntarism, it was a central part of Donovan's wider purpose of supporting collective bargaining procedures by deepening and reforming them: 'the central issue for Donovan was how to restore order, peace and efficiency to industrial relations and yet preserve and even extend the voluntarist tradition of collective bargaining'.[33] The result was that the legislation was only partially influenced by considerations of employee rights: the legislation had at the very least a 'dual purpose of ... managerial efficiency and employment protection'.[34]

The legislation was also influenced by a broader efficiency-related theme, that of *labour market flexibility*. Although this aspect came more to the fore in the 1980s, it was implicit in the legislation from the start. The exclusion of protection for part-time workers (removed in 1995[35]) and the potential to exclude protection from workers employed on fixed-term contracts (removed for unfair dismissal in 1999[36] and statutory redundancy payments in 2002[37]) was incorporated into the Redundancy Payments Act 1965 and the first legislation on unfair dismissal in the Industrial Relations Act 1971. More generally, the main aim of the Redundancy Payments Act was not, as it might seem, to recognise a kind of property right in jobs, but to ensure that employees displaced from declining industries were given incentives to abandon resistance to technical change, and to enhance job mobility by granting displaced workers a form of compensation which would assist them in job search. Since the 1965 Act did not seek to place any restraints on managerial decision-making, it has been suggested that 'to claim that the provisions of the statute amount to an improvement in

---

31   On the relationship between UK law and the various Conventions and Recommendations of the ILO in this field, see Napier, 1983.
32   See Meyers, 1964.
33   R Lewis, 1986: p 32.
34   Anderman, 1986: p 416.
35   By SI 1995/31; see para 3.87 above.
36   By ERelA 1999, s 18; see para 5.78 below.
37   By FTER 2002, Sch 2 para 3(15); see para 5.175 below.

employment security is akin to arguing that legislating for insurance cover for a proportion of road users would be about road safety'.[38]

5.8   The concern that excessive regulation impairs the responsiveness of firms to changes in the external market environment was a major influence on the reforms of dismissal legislation undertaken by successive Conservative Governments after 1979. The Employment Act 1980 introduced changes to the statutory test of fairness, removing a provision placing the burden of showing fairness on the employer, and allowing for the standard of reasonableness to be modified to take into account the limited size and resources of smaller firms. A more significant change made at around the same time was the lengthening of the qualifying period of service for unfair dismissal from six months to one year in 1979 and eventually to two years for all firms in 1985. From 1989 employees in firms employing fewer than 20 employees ceased to have the right to receive written statements of disciplinary procedures (an exclusion removed in 2004).[39] But in other respects, few substantive changes were made to dismissal law during this period; the bulk of it remained intact. When a Labour Government was returned to office in 1997, it reduced the normal period of qualifying service for unfair dismissal to one year and removed the exemptions from protection for employees employed on fixed-term contracts.[40] In 2002, however, it introduced more radical changes to the structure of unfair dismissal law as part of a wider policy of attempting to reduce the number of cases going to tribunals.[41] These amendments, which came into force on 1 October 2004, are designed to provide incentives to employers to establish, and both parties to exhaust, workplace dismissal and disciplinary procedures prescribed by statute before a complaint goes to a tribunal.[42] However they also have the effect of downgrading the importance of procedural standards beyond the statutory minima.[43]

(iii) The effects of the legislation

5.9   The impact of the legislation on personnel practice has been considerable. The Warwick survey of unfair dismissal law and practice, carried out in the mid-1980s, found that the legislation had led to considerable formalisation of plant-level procedures, as well as to changes in their content, and had strengthened the role of central management. Personnel processes had become more highly bureaucratic and there had been a reduction in the discretion accorded to lower levels of management. At the same time, the role of unions in negotiating disciplinary rules was limited, although their participation in the operation of disciplinary procedures was more extensive.[44] A number of studies looked into the issue of recruitment and the question of possible disincentives arising out of regulation.[45] The consensus here has been that the legislation has had an impact in making employers more careful about whom they hire, and in this sense

38   Fryer, 1973: p 3. For a legal and economic assessment of UK law relating to redundancy compensation, see Deakin and Wilkinson, 1999.
39   See now ERA 1996, s 3 as amended by EA 2002 and para 4.18 above.
40   See *Fairness at Work*, 1998, Cm 3968, at paras 3.9–3.13, and paras 5.63 and 5.78 below.
41   See Hepple and Morris, 2002.
42   ERA 1996, s 98A(1); EA 2002, s 31.
43   ERA 1996, s 98A(2).
44   L Dickens *et al*, 1985.
45   Daniel and Stilgoe, 1978; W Brown *et al*, 1981; Evans *et al*, 1985.

contributed both to greater efficiency in the screening of applicants and to a reduction in the overall rate of dismissals. Nor did employers place much stress on any disincentive effects, at least in larger firms; but this was partly because 'managers in all sized establishments [attributed] little effect to the unfair dismissal provisions in terms of inhibiting dismissal'.[46] The impact of the law on unofficial strikes has been difficult to judge, because of the general decline in strike activity since the late 1960s and even more so since the early 1990s. Throughout the 1980s they remained virtually constant at between 10% and 15% of the total.[47] Recent surveys of strike activity do not break down statistics on this basis.[48]

By promoting developments within plant-level procedures the law contributed to greater security and stability of employment for many workers, but this effect varies according to how far procedures have been formalised and how far trade unions have become involved in them.[49] Formalisation is not necessarily identical with an increase in the level of job security; in respect of individual misconduct and lack of capability, formal procedures may become 'conveyor belts' for dismissal, a more effective means of legitimating managerial decisions.[50] There is, in effect, a dual system in place: employees in workplaces with a trade union presence benefit from joint procedures which are underpinned by the legislation, but they do not need to rely on that legislation directly except in rare instances. By contrast, the large majority of those who make direct use of the tribunal system are non-union members or employees in non-unionised workplaces, who have to rely on the tribunals for protection. Since tribunals rarely award reinstatement or re-engagement and the average level of compensation is low (in 2003/04 the median award was £3,375),[51] the level of job security which these workers enjoy is not greatly increased, although it still represents a substantial advance on the common law. Empirical research suggests that employers who comply with the requirements of procedural fairness very rarely lose in employment tribunals.[52] At the time of writing it remains to be seen whether the amendments to the unfair dismissal legislation which came into force on 1 October 2004 will have the desired effect of encouraging those organisations that previously lacked workplace procedures[53] to establish and to use them, and whether, if so, this will lead to greater job security.[54]

5.10   Collective agreements concerning the right of management to make workers redundant have been rare. From time to time, agreements have incorporated a commitment by management of 'no compulsory redundancies', but these are unusual.[55] By far the most common form of

---

46   L Dickens *et al*, 1985: p 257.
47   See Hepple, 1992: p 87.
48   In 2003 'redundancy issues' accounted for six per cent of stoppages, 'staffing issues' seven per cent: Monger, 2004: pp 244–245.
49   See Earnshaw *et al*, 1998; Knight and Latreille, 2000.
50   L Dickens *et al*, 1985: p 257.
51   *Employment Tribunals Service: Annual Report and Accounts 2003-2004*, DTI, App 1, Table 3.
52   See Earnshaw *et al*, 1998.
53   It was part of the Government's case for requiring only basic procedural standards to be followed that 48% of employers going before tribunals lacked internal procedures: Alan Johnson, HC Standing Committee F, col 140, 13 December 2001.
54   See *Statutory Dispute Resolution Procedures: Full Regulatory Impact Assessment*, DTI, January 2004.
55   See Deakin and Wilkinson, 1999.

collective agreement on redundancies concerns the procedures for their implementation and the levels of compensation above the statutory maximum. The introduction of the Redundancy Payments Act 1965 led to a rapid growth in agreements of this kind,[56] as well as in practices of redundancy management at establishment level. In particular, larger firms were encouraged to make provision for voluntary redundancies, through schemes whose rules were designed to attract older workers to accept generous redundancy terms. Compulsory redundancies were more common in smaller firms and in non-unionised establishments; where redundancies were compulsory, the last-in, first-out principle was widely observed.[57] The Act also encouraged the growth of collective bargaining on redundancy; this was nearly all at establishment or company, rather than at multi-employer level, a practice that accords with the more general trend towards the decentralisation of collective bargaining arrangements in the UK since the late 1960s. In general collective agreements improved on the level set by the Act: survey evidence suggests that in 1984 over 90% did so, with a majority providing for twice the statutory level of payment or better,[58] although patterns varied with the size of firm, with the more generous agreements in larger firms and the manufacturing and public employment sectors.[59] Many schemes were designed to be attractive to older workers and to encourage them to accept voluntary redundancies in the event of business reorganisations. Later, the state followed the same pattern by enacting special statutory schemes to provide additional benefits in government-controlled industries undergoing structural change (in particular coal, steel and shipbuilding).

The effect of these developments was to facilitate the use of *voluntary* redundancy as a mechanism of workforce reduction and to limit the degree to which trade unions could effectively adopt a policy of resisting redundancies as such, which had been the strategy of many unions prior to 1965. Instead their role was largely one of ensuring that where redundancies took place they were voluntary rather than compulsory, and that the resulting payments were as generous as possible: 'whatever their initial feelings might have been, trade unions soon found themselves to be powerless in the face of the growth of voluntary redundancy schemes. If they tried to challenge and oppose the need for redundancies, they were undermined by individual members eager to accept voluntary redundancy terms'.[60] Moreover, the fact that strike action in opposition to redundancies could disqualify the strikers from any entitlement to compensation appears to have limited the willingness of employees to support strategies of opposition. Management also made use of the flexibility provided by their own non-statutory schemes to provide various additional inducements to employees, such as giving them only a short period of time to accept an offer of compensation before it was withdrawn. The combination of widespread provisions for redundancy compensation together with the loose controls on managerial prerogative in the area of dismissal combined in the 1980s to make

---

56   Prior to the Act around 17% of employees were covered by redundancy arrangements derived from collective agreements or unilateral practices of employers: S Parker *et al*, 1971.
57   Daniel and Stilgoe, 1978; Daniel, 1985 and, for data drawn from the 1990 Workplace Industrial Relations Survey, Millward *et al*, 1992: p 325.
58   Gordon, 1984: p 27.
59   Levie *et al*, 1984; Daniel, 1985.
60   Daniel, 1985: p 74.

redundancy the normal mechanism of workforce reduction in circumstances of periodic economic recession and substantial restructuring. Between 1977 and 1983 alone over 3.3 million employees received statutory redundancy payments. The extent of labour shedding during this period has been ascribed to a 'snowball effect' as increasing numbers of employers abandoned practices of labour hoarding: 'there is a threshold level in job loss expectations beyond which employing organisations can shed labour without attracting significant attention to themselves. For some employers there were no better reasons for making labour redundant in 1981 than there had been in 1978 or 1975 or 1972. But because other large employers were announcing job losses, and because of a generally gloomy economic outlook, this has been seized upon as an opportunity to de-man'.[61]

5.11 The collective information and consultation requirements of the 1975 Directive,[62] initially transposed into UK law by the EPA 1975,[63] are more clearly concerned to stabilise and protect the jobs of employees threatened with redundancy. In contrast to the legislation on redundancy payments, however, these provisions have had little influence on the development of management practice. Daniel[64] explains this by the fact that prior to 1975 the practices leading to the acceptance of voluntary redundancy by management, workers and unions alike had already been put in place, under the influence of the earlier 1965 Act. The successful use of dismissal law to prevent employers forcing through unilateral cuts in pay and conditions is rare, largely because it is not conclusively established whether such action amounts to unfair dismissal or whether an injunction can be obtained to restrain breach of the normative terms of collective agreements. Nevertheless, employers who go down this road face potentially high costs in doing so. In 1991 the possibility of legal action is reported to have helped to persuade Rolls Royce to withdraw dismissal notices issued to several thousand of its workers as a prelude to the imposition of new contracts, but this also depended on a strong trade union presence within that company.[65] It is notable that situations where an employer dismisses all the employees within a particular 'description' or 'category' and then offers re-engagement on different terms and conditions are excluded from the statutory dismissal and disciplinary procedures, failure to comply with which, on the part of the employer, renders a dismissal automatically unfair.[66] This means that failure by an employer to follow any procedure prior to dismissing employees in this context will not render the dismissal unfair if it shows it would have decided to dismiss the employee in any event.[67]

61 Gordon, 1984: p 72. For redundancy rates between 1995 and winter 2003/2004 see Heap, 2004.
62 Council Directive 75/129 of 17 February 1975 on the approximation of the laws of the Member States relating to collective redundancies; see now Directive 98/59. See also Directive 2002/14/EC on Information and Consultation, implemented in Britain by ICER 2004 on 6 April 2005.
63 See now TULRCA 1992, s 188. See further para 9.32 *et seq* below.
64 Daniel, 1985: p 78.
65 Jeremy McMullen and Philippa Kaufman, 1991.
66 EADRR 2004, reg 4(1)(a), ERA 1996, s 98A(1); see further para 5.124 *et seq*.
67 ERA 1996, s 98A(2). There may be a duty to consult representatives of the employees under TULRCA 1992, s 188 but the remedies for a failure to consult are limited: see further para 9.40.

WRONGFUL DISMISSAL

5.12   We begin our more detailed consideration of the law relating to termination of employment with an analysis of the common law of *wrongful dismissal*. Damages for wrongful dismissal compensate the employee for losses suffered as a result of the wrongful termination of the contract of employment by the employer. In principle, the level of compensation payable by these means could be substantial, but all depends on the terms of the contract (both express and implied) and on the application of the general rules by which contract damages are calculated. In practice, damages for wrongful dismissal are very rarely substantial, essentially for two reasons. The first is that either as a result of express agreement or by way of an implied term, the employer will almost invariably possess the right at common law to terminate the contract simply by giving notice, without needing to have a good reason, or any reason, for doing so (the 'notice rule'). Second, any damages payable to the employee for the employer's failure to give notice will be limited by the principle of mitigation as well as by the principle that the victim of breach of contract may only claim, by way of compensation, damages for those losses which he or she can show derive from a clear contractual entitlement, as opposed to a 'bare' or unprotected expectation. Since, in most cases, the employee is not *entitled* to remain in employment for longer than the minimum period of notice contained in the contract, damages will be limited to a sum representing net salary for the notice period only, and will not normally include an amount for harm done to reputation or for loss of earning capacity.[68] These rules explain why, for most employees, the protection offered by the common law of dismissal is inadequate, and why it was felt necessary for the legislature to intervene by introducing the principle of statutory *unfair dismissal*.

The experience of other legal systems, however, suggests that this restrictive approach to the protection of the employee's interests in job security is not an inevitable feature of the common law. In some states of the USA, courts have implied terms into contracts of employment which require employers to act in good faith or subject to a requirement of reasonableness when taking decisions relating to discipline or dismissal.[69] In Australia the focus has been on the terms of disciplinary procedures incorporated into individual contracts from collective arbitration awards; the courts have required employers to observe these procedures and have made substantial awards of damages where they have failed to do so.[70] The award of substantial damages is far from being automatic in these jurisdictions, however, and in the United States many states continue to apply a version of the traditional American rule of 'employment at will', which allows either party to terminate the contract at short notice or without any notice at all.[71] Nevertheless, the diversity of approaches to be found elsewhere

---

68   For further discussion of this point see *Malik v BCCI SA* [1997] IRLR 462, *Johnson v Unisys Ltd* [2001] IRLR 279, *Eastwood v Magnox Electric plc* [2004] IRLR 733, and paras 5.26 and 5.27 below.

69   See Pitt, 1989.

70   *Gregory v Philip Morris Ltd* (1988) 80 ALR 455; see Ewing, 1989. However in *Byrne and Frew v Australian Airlines Ltd* (1995) 131 ALR 422 the High Court of Australia held that this principle was limited to cases where there was an express agreement between employer and employee to incorporate the terms of the award into the employment contract: see further John McMullen, 1996.

71   See Estlund, 2002: pp 205-209.

in the common law world suggests that the English-law rule of minimal compensation for wrongful dismissal is not immutable.

Two relatively recent developments in the English common law also indicate that some reassessment of the traditional rule is needed here. In the first place, the courts have granted more extensive damages in cases where employers have failed to observe contractual disciplinary procedures;[72] in the second, they have shown themselves to be prepared to grant specific relief in equity in order to restrain certain breaches of contract by the employer.[73] In both instances, the normal 'notice rule' is effectively undermined: as a result of the court's intervention, the employer can no longer rely on the power of the notice term to dispense with the need for procedural fairness or for adequate substantive grounds for an act of discipline or dismissal. At the same time, these new lines of authority are somewhat fragile: they have not received the clear endorsement of the House of Lords and a number of doctrinal issues concerning the relationship between the notice term and other terms of the contract, and the remedies available to the employee, remain unresolved. It is also doubtful whether these rights and remedies will be available to more than a minority of high-status employees.

Notice and duration

5.13 Where a contract of employment is silent on the question of termination it will normally be construed as being of an indeterminate duration. If so, a term will normally be implied at common law to make provision for notice. The principal function of this 'notice rule' is to give both sides the option of escaping from the arrangement at low cost. However, the length of notice may be set so as to grant one or both of the parties some degree of warning of, and monetary compensation for, the ending of the relationship.

(i) The development of the common law notice rule

5.14 The development of the notice rule at common law is linked, historically, to changes in the typical duration of contracts of employment. When it became normal for contracts to have an *indefinite or indeterminate* duration – as opposed to a duration for a *fixed term* – it became necessary for the parties, or for the courts through the technique of implied terms, to make provision for termination by notice. During the industrial revolution there was a legal presumption that servants in agriculture were hired for a fixed term of a year. This rule was originally based on the Statute of Artificers of 1562 and on the poor laws of the seventeenth century which conferred a parish settlement (or right to relief) on servants with a yearly hiring, but survived the abolition of this legislation to become a presumption of the common law.[74] It was formally removed from the law by the Court of Appeal in 1969,[75] but had fallen into disuse long before

---

72   *Gunton v Richmond-upon-Thames London Borough Council* [1981] Ch 448; *Dietman v Brent London Borough Council* [1987] ICR 737; *Boyo v Lambeth London Borough Council* [1995] IRLR 50.

73   See, in particular, *Powell v Brent London Borough Council* [1987] IRLR 466; *Jones v Gwent County Council* [1992] IRLR 521; see further para 5.54 *et seq* below.

74   Settlement by hiring was abolished by the Poor Law Amendment Act 1834, s 64, and the provisions of the Statute of Artificers 1563 requiring yearly hirings in agriculture were repealed in 1875. On the survival of the presumption into the middle of the nineteenth century, see Jacoby, 1982.

75   *Richardson v Koefod* [1969] 1 WLR 1812.

then. By the middle of the nineteenth century indefinite hirings were becoming common, and the modern notice rule began to emerge: either party could terminate the contract by giving the other reasonable notice.[76] In the absence of an express clause, what was 'reasonable' tended to be determined by one of two rival criteria, namely the period by which the wage or salary was calculated, and the custom in the relevant trade. An employee whose wage was calculated by the week might, for that reason, be entitled to receive at least a week's notice of termination;[77] otherwise, 'general usages are tacitly annexed to all contracts relating to the business with reference to which they are made, unless the terms of such contracts expressly or impliedly exclude them'.[78] For domestic servants, a month's notice was customary; for professional or managerial employees, periods of minimum notice ranged from a month to a quarter or, less usually, a year.[79] In other cases, employers made use of express notice clauses to prevent workers quitting on short notice; the contracts of many industrial workers contained long notice clauses which bound them to their employer for a certain period and also had the effect of triggering the application of the Master and Servant Acts, which imposed criminal sanctions for certain breaches of contract.[80]

The English judges of the nineteenth century did not develop a legal presumption that employment contracts were terminable 'at will', or on summary notice, as the American courts did during the last quarter of the nineteenth century.[81] However, the use of contractual presumptions in the English common law could often produce a similar result: in England, so-called 'minute contracts' were common during this period in industries such as the docks, construction and engineering where short-term engagements and sub-contracting were widespread. The contracts of employment of the workers in *Allen v Flood*,[82] for example, the leading case on the law of tortious interference with trade and livelihood, were all terminable at short notice by either side, which was one reason why the organiser of strike activity in that case incurred no liability in tort. In later cases, too, the courts construed the contracts of hourly-paid industrial workers (that is to say, workers who were paid on the basis of an hourly rate for work done) as terminable by an hour's notice on either side. One effect of this was to reduce the contractual security of the hourly-paid worker practically to nothing. In *Marshall v English Electric Co Ltd*[83] the Court of Appeal considered whether the employer had the implied right under such a contract to impose a disciplinary suspension on the employee. They concluded that it had, on the basis that 'what is called suspension is in truth dismissal with an intimation that at the end of so many days, or it may be hours, the man will be re-employed if

---

76   See *Baxter v Nurse* (1844) 6 Man & G 935; and for modern restatements of the rule, Lord Oaksey in *McClelland v Northern Ireland General Health Service Board* [1957] 1 WLR 594, 599 and Lord Millett in *Reda v Flag Ltd* [2002] IRLR 747, para 57 (emphasising that the rule is confined to contracts that contain no provision for determination and does not apply to fixed term contracts).

77   *Baxter v Nurse* (1844) 6 Man & G 935 (Coltman J).

78   *Metzner v Bolton* (1854) 9 Exch 518, 521 (Parke B).

79   See Jacoby, 1982.

80   Industrial workers came under the master and servant regime if they had an agreement for 'exclusive service' with an employer for a certain period; long notice clauses were regarded as important evidence of this. See, eg, *Whittle v Frankland* (1862) 2 B & S 49.

81   *Payne v Western & Atlantic Railroad* 81 Tenn 507 (1884); see Jacoby, 1982, for discussion of the reasons for the divergence between the English and American systems.

82   [1898] AC 1. See para 11.10 below.

83   [1945] 1 All ER 653.

he chooses to apply for reinstatement'.[84] Because the minimum period of notice was so short, the employer's power to terminate the contract effectively embraced an unconditional power of suspension too. This approach was not followed for all employees: as a matter of construction, salaried employees, who were paid by the month or longer period, enjoyed superior rights to minimum notice. In *Nokes v Doncaster Amalgamated Collieries Ltd*[85] Lord Atkin contrasted the position of manual workers, at best 'confined to weekly or fortnightly contracts', with 'the longer-term contracts of accountants, managers, salesmen, doctors, and ... managing directors employed for a term of years'.

(ii) Statutory minimum notice periods

5.15 Minimum periods of notice are now inserted into the contracts of employment of all employees with continuity of employment of at least one month. The relevant legislation, which was first enacted as part of the Contracts of Employment Act 1963, is now contained in sections 86 *et seq* of ERA 1996. The employee is entitled, after one month's continuous employment, to receive a minimum of one week's notice of dismissal; after two years this rises to two weeks, and goes on rising by one week for each additional year of continuous employment up to a limit of twelve weeks' minimum notice.[86] In the event of breach by the employer, the employee has available the common law action for damages for breach of contract. For this purpose the Act provides that its provisions prevail over any shorter period of notice in the contract[87] and that the employer's failure to comply with these provisions is to be taken into account in assessing its liability for breach of contract.[88] The effect is that damages will be based, at least, on the minimum notice period provided for by statute. The courts have also inferred that in claiming damages for breach of the statutory provisions, the employee must mitigate his or her loss according to normal contract law principles.[89] Conversely, after one month of continuous employment the employee is obliged to give the employer at least one week's notice of termination of the contract.[90] The Act is silent on the question of the employee's liability for breach of contract for failure to give the minimum statutory notice. The Act does not rule out the parties themselves agreeing to longer minimum periods on either side,[91] nor does it prevent either party from waiving their right to notice on any occasion or from accepting a payment in lieu of notice.[92]

---

84 [1945] 1 All ER 653, 655.
85 [1940] AC 1014, 1028.
86 Where an employee has been continuously employed for three months or more under a 'contract for a term certain of one month or less' the contract has effect as if it were for an indefinite period and the statutory minimum periods of notice of termination apply: ERA 1996, s 86(4); for the application of this provision in relation to entitlement to statutory sick pay see *Brown v Chief Adjudication Officer* [1997] IRLR 110. See also s 86(5).
87 ERA 1996, s 86(3). Note, however, that they do not affect the right of either party to terminate the contract without notice by reason of the conduct of the other: s 86(6).
88 ERA 1996, s 91(5).
89 *Secretary of State for Employment v Wilson* [1978] ICR 200, 203–204 (Phillips J); *Westwood v Secretary of State for Employment* [1985] ICR 209, 218–219 (Lord Bridge).
90 ERA 1996, s 86(2).
91 At common law, where a notice term was implied it normally provided for the same length of minimum notice to be given by both sides: *Creen v Wright* (1876) 1 CPD 591. The Act departs from this principle of strict reciprocity by providing for longer minimum periods in the case where notice is given by the employer.
92 ERA 1996, s 86(3).

Once either party gives notice, sections 87–91 of the Act govern the rights and liabilities of the parties during the period of notice.[93] In particular, the employee is entitled to receive wages based on his or her normal working hours even if no work is done by reason of lay-off, incapability through sickness or injury, absence by virtue of pregnancy, childbirth, adoption, parental or paternity leave, or absence on holiday; although if the employee receives any other contractual or statutory payments from the employer in respect of their absence, such as statutory sick pay or contractual holiday pay, these will go to discharge this liability.[94]

(iii) The implications of the notice rule

5.16   Notwithstanding the minimum periods imposed by the Act, the reciprocal right to give notice to terminate the contract means that the employer has only a limited right to the future services of the employee. The employee normally has an unfettered right to resign by giving the notice required by the contract. In giving notice, the employee is exercising a contractual power to bring the contract to an end; it follows that the employee cannot unilaterally revoke the notice once it is given.[95]

The converse to this is, however, that the employee has only a limited right to job security, at least at common law. The employee 'has no right to any particular employment if it depends on the will of another'.[96] The Privy Council has recently held that where a contract expressly gives the employer the power to dismiss the employee without cause this power cannot be made subject to any implied qualification, such as the implied term of trust and confidence.[97] However, there are cases where the contract itself expressly or impliedly places restrictions on the employer's right to give notice, such as those which may be inferred from the existence of disciplinary procedures. We return to this issue in the context of our discussion of contractual job security clauses below.[98]

(iv) The implications of no provision for notice

5.17   Contracts containing neither an express nor an implied notice term are, by their nature, rare. In a contract of fixed-term duration, the absence of an express notice clause might not be surprising: both parties might expect the contract to be worked out for the period agreed.[99] Where, on the other hand, the contract is 'permanent' or for an indeterminate duration, there is a presumption

---

93   Note that these provisions do not apply if the contractual notice to be given by the employer to terminate the contract is at least one week more than the statutory minimum: ERA 1996 s 87(4) as interpreted in *Scotts Company (UK) Ltd v Budd* [2003] IRLR 145 where the EAT accepted that this was a 'curious result'.

94   ERA 1996, s 88. Section 89 deals with the situation in which the employee has no normal working hours.

95   *Riordan v War Office* [1959] 1 WLR 1046; *a fortiori* if the employee resigns in breach of contract, whereupon the employer has the right to accept the repudiation and will not easily be taken to have waived the right to do so. The employee may be liable for damages for breach of contract in this situation, assuming that the employer can show loss, which may be difficult.

96   *Allen v Flood* [1898] AC 1, 172 (Lord Davey).

97   *Reda v Flag Ltd* [2002] IRLR 747.

98   See para 5.31 *et seq*.

99   The presence of a notice clause will not, on the other hand, prevent a fixed-term contract being defined as such for the purposes of ERA 1996, s 235(2B)(a) or FTER 2002: see paras 3.86 and 5.78.

that a notice clause will be implied according to the normal common law tests,[100] with the Act now prescribing its minimum length. It would be normal to imply a notice term for the benefit of the employee, who would otherwise be bound to serve a particular employer indefinitely. However, there may be certain cases in which the implication of a clause granting the *employer* the right to give notice is not appropriate. This occurred in *McClelland v Northern Ireland General Health Services Board*,[101] where the House of Lords concluded that the omission of such a clause from the contract of a senior health service employee in the public sector was deliberate, since it reflected the high level of job security which was part of the contractual package agreed by the parties. The employee's contract incorporated an extensive procedure, known as the 'September Conditions', governing dismissal for misconduct, inefficiency and unfitness; no mention was made of any express right to dismiss for redundancy. The effect of this was that the employee had a contractual right to remain in the employment until she reached the retirement age, subject only to the possibility of dismissal for good cause which on the facts was not made out (she was dismissed for having married). She was granted a declaration to the effect that her contract of employment was still subsisting, in effect nullifying the purported dismissal.[102]

It must be said that while the principle behind *McClelland* is clear, not many employees are in a position to benefit from it. It was always unlikely that a court would assume that the parties intended to create such a stable employment environment in anything other than the public sector, and it is difficult to think of any major group of workers that would now fall within this protected category.[103]

Summary dismissal

5.18 The employer is entitled to dispense with contractual notice, or with the minimum notice prescribed by statute,[104] and summarily dismiss an employee who has committed a repudiatory breach of contract. This is an application of the general rule of contract law that following repudiatory breach, the innocent party has the option to terminate or to affirm the contract.[105] The nature of the conduct which is considered to constitute repudiation by the employee has to some degree changed over time, to reflect changing social values.[106] It is no longer sufficient for the employee to have committed an isolated and minor act of disobedience or negligence. For an isolated breach to suffice it must be such 'as to show the servant to have disregarded the essential conditions of the contract of service',[107] or to be 'inconsistent with the continuance of confidence' between employer and employee.[108] The wilful disobedience of a reasonable and lawful order, or the unauthorised taking of the employer's property, will almost certainly

---

100 See para 4.4 *et seq*.
101 [1957] 1 WLR 594.
102 See further para 5.41 *et seq* below.
103 *McClelland* has never been available to civil servants, who, as employees of the Crown, are regarded as dismissible at will: see para 3.74. On the position of university teachers, see Farrington 1998.
104 Cf ERA 1996, s 86(6).
105 *White and Carter (Councils) Ltd v McGregor* [1962] AC 413.
106 See the discussion of Edmund Davies LJ in *Wilson v Racher* [1974] ICR 428.
107 *Laws v London Chronicle (Indicator Newspapers) Ltd* [1959] 1 WLR 698, 700 (Lord Evershed MR).
108 *Sinclair v Neighbour* [1967] 2 QB 279, 289 (Sachs LJ).

justify summary dismissal at common law.[109] If, however, it is the employer who provokes, by its own conduct, the breakdown of relations of trust and confidence, summary dismissal will not be justified, and the employer itself will be liable for wrongful dismissal.[110]

5.19 At common law the right to summary dismissal applies even though, at the time of the dismissal, the employer was not aware of the breach in question or of its seriousness. In *Boston Deep Sea Fishing and Ice Co v Ansell*[111] the claimant, the manager of the defendant's business, was dismissed for reasons which Kekewich J found to be groundless. However, after the dismissal had taken place the defendant discovered that the claimant had, several years earlier, accepted a secret commission which should have been directed to the business. This misconduct would have justified summary dismissal, had the employer been aware of it. The Court of Appeal found that the dismissal had not been wrongful, 'even though [the employer] did not discover the fraud until after [it] had actually pronounced the sentence of dismissal'.

In effect, this is saying that the employee did not lose anything of value by virtue of his dismissal: by virtue of his earlier fraud, he had no right to continuing employment.[112] A different outcome will occur if the employer, knowing of the breach, expressly waives the right to terminate the contract in response to it. If, alternatively, it takes no action, then after a reasonable period has elapsed it will again be taken to have waived the right of dismissal.[113]

These aspects of the common law of summary dismissal must now be read subject to the requirements imposed by unfair dismissal law in cases which fall within the scope of ERA 1996. Importantly, in contrast to the common law, the statutory regime does not permit an employer to the employer to advance as a reason for dismissal one which it did not actually rely upon at the time.[114] The common law principles must also now be considered subject to the statutory dismissal and disciplinary procedures which came into force on 1 October 2004; an employer's failure to complete the requisite procedure renders a dismissal that falls within the scope of ERA 1996 automatically unfair.[115] Under these procedures an employer may not dismiss an employee prior to inviting an employee to a meeting to discuss the employee's conduct other than in exceptional circumstances, which are not coterminous with those in which summary dismissal is permissible at common law.[116] There is provision in EA 2002 for the requirements of the statutory procedures to take effect as terms of an employee's contract of employment.[117] However this provision has not yet been brought into force, and may never be; the Government has indicated that the need for

---

109 See the cases cited in the two notes above and for more recent examples *Macari v Celtic Football and Athletic Club* [1999] IRLR 787 (discussed at para 4.85) and *Briscoe v Lubrizol Ltd* [2002] IRLR 607. On the scope of the duty of obedience see para 4.85 *et seq* above, and on aspects of the duty of fidelity which are relevant in this context, see para 4.97 *et seq*.
110 *Wilson v Racher* [1974] ICR 428.
111 (1888) 39 Ch D 339.
112 *Quaere* whether the same principle would apply if the employee committed a repudiatory breach *after* the employer's breach; cf *Ridgway v Hungerford Market Co* (1835) 3 Ad & El 171, discussed by Hepple, 1981a: pp 253–254.
113 Cf, in a different context, *Peyman v Lanjani* [1985] Ch 457.
114 See para 5.89 below.
115 ERA 1996, s 98A(1). See further paras 5.124 *et seq*.
116 EADRR 2004, reg 3.
117 EA 2002, s 30.

such a provision will be considered in the light of a general evaluation of the impact of the procedures in 2006.[118]

Damages for wrongful dismissal

5.20 An employer's failure to give notice as due under the contract of employment gives rise to a distinctive type of damages claim which has come to be known as an action for 'wrongful dismissal'.[119] As a basis for an action for wages or salary, claims for damages are clearly inferior to claims in debt: in debt, the employee has no general duty to mitigate loss and can claim the liquidated sum set by the contract itself, as opposed to the unliquidated damages which are ascertained by the court and subject to deductions of various kinds.[120] However, as we shall see, the employee is only able in exceptional circumstances to maintain the contract in force after a summary dismissal has taken place, and even then any claim in debt for wages due will only operate for a limited period.[121] In the vast majority of cases, the ending of the employment relationship by the employer, even where it is a wrongful act, has the effect of confining the employee to a claim in damages.

(i) The measure of damages: general principles

5.21 Consistently with general principles of contract law:

> ... where a servant is wrongfully dismissed, he is entitled, subject to mitigation, to damages equivalent to the wages he would have earned under the contract from the date of dismissal to the end of the contract. The date when the contract would have come to an end, however, must be ascertained on the assumption that the employer would have exercised any power he may have had to bring the contract to an end in the way most beneficial to himself; that is to say, that he would have determined the contract at the earliest date at which he could properly do so.[122]

---

118 *Guidance on the Employment Act 2002 (Dispute Resolution) Regulations 2004 and Associated Provisions in the Employment Act 2002*, DTI, 2004, para 146.

119 For discussion of the circumstances in which other kinds of claim may lie in respect of wrongful termination, see paras 5.31 *et seq* below.

120 Note that even where an employee has been dismissed without notice, if the contract provides for payment in these circumstances the claim may be brought in debt. See *Abrahams v Performing Rights Society* [1995] IRLR 486 where the employer had the right to terminate the employee's contract by giving two years' notice or an equivalent payment in lieu; the Court of Appeal held that the effect of this agreement was that the claimant was entitled to payment in lieu as a contractual debt when his contract was terminated without notice. The agreement in that case was distinguished by the Court of Appeal in *Gregory v Wallace* [1998] IRLR 387 where the employee's contract was not terminated in accordance with the procedure specified in that contract and the claim was held to lie in damages. However, because the employee's contract specifically permitted him to take other employment during the notice period, he was entitled to damages undiminished by earnings in his new employment, this being the appropriate measure of his loss. See also *Cerberus Software Ltd v Rowley* [1999] IRLR 690, [2001] IRLR 160, and Fodder and Freer, 2001. Failure to give the period of notice prescribed by ERA 1996, s 86 gives rise to a claim in damages, not debt: *Hardy v Polk (Leeds) Ltd* [2004] IRLR 420.

121 See paras 5.36 *et seq* and 5.54 *et seq* below.

122 *Gunton v Richmond-upon-Thames London Borough Council* [1980] ICR 755, 772 (Buckley LJ). See also *Abrahams v Herbert Reiach Ltd* [1922] 1 KB 477, 482 (Scrutton LJ); *Lavarack v Woods of Colchester Ltd* [1967] 1 QB 278, 294 (Diplock LJ); *Janciuk v Winerite Ltd* [1998] IRLR 63, 64; *Morran v Glasgow Council of Tenants' Associations* [1998] IRLR 67.

It follows from this and from the notice rule that in the case of an indefinite hiring, damages for wrongful dismissal will normally be restricted to net salary for the notice period. An employee who is employed under a fixed-term contract which does *not* contain a notice clause is on the face of it entitled to receive net salary for the unexpired period of the contract. 'Net salary' here means the employee's normal weekly or monthly wage or salary, after making deductions for the normal incidence of income tax.[123] The impact of income tax on the earnings which the employee would have had in the notice period is 'something which the law does not regard as too remote';[124] if, conversely, the employee has to pay income tax on the damages which the court then awards, the damages will be grossed up to ensure that he or she is fully compensated for his or her loss.[125] This will occur where the damages exceed £30,000.[126] It is also common for deductions to be made in respect of the employee's national insurance contributions and contributions, if any, to an occupational pension or similar employee benefit scheme,[127] but there is some authority to suggest that these deductions should not be made unless the employee also receives some compensation for loss of the insurance-related benefits to which his or her previous contributions were directed.[128]

(ii) Claims for lost opportunities to earn financial benefits

5.22   Whether the employee can recover for the loss of benefits other than salary depends on whether these benefits are ones to which the employee is entitled under the terms of the contract. In *Lavarack v Woods of Colchester Ltd*[129] the dismissed employee was unable to claim damages for the lost opportunity to earn bonuses which had been made available by the directors at their discretion in the past, but which the company was under no contractual obligation to maintain. This decision may be contrasted to those in which the employer was under a contractual obligation to pay commission in return for performance, and where damages for wrongful dismissal included an amount for the normal commission or bonus which the employee could have expected to earn in the notice period (or the unexpired period of the contract term).[130] In the light of recent case law, recovery may be possible even if a benefit is expressed

---

123 This may involve consideration of whether the employee would have received an increase during the unexpired period of the contract. In *Clark v BET plc* [1997] IRLR 348, the employee's service agreement provided for a basic salary 'which shall be reviewed annually and be increased by such amount if any as the board shall in its absolute discretion decide'. The Court held that it would have been a breach of contract for the board to have exercised its discretion capriciously or in bad faith to award a nil increase, and on the basis of the evidence the claimant would have been entitled to an annual increase of 10%. See also *Clark v Nomura International plc* [2000] IRLR 766; *Horkulak v Cantor Fitzgerald International* [2004] IRLR 942.
124 *Shove v Downs Surgical plc* [1984] ICR 532, 537 (Sheen J).
125 [1984] ICR 532, 537.
126 ICTA 1988, s 148. For criticism of the court's approach to taxation in the measurement of damages, see Bishop and Kay, 1987.
127 See *Shove v Downs Surgical plc* [1984] ICR 532, 538–539.
128 *Gothard v Mirror Group Newspapers Ltd* [1988] ICR 729, 734 (Lord Donaldson MR).
129 [1967] 1 QB 278.
130 *Turner v Goldsmith* [1891] 1 QB 544; *Addis v Gramophone Co Ltd* [1909] AC 488; *Clark v BET plc* [1997] IRLR 348; *Clark v Nomura International plc* [2000] IRLR 766, *Horkulak v Cantor Fitzgerald International* [2004] IRLR 942. The same principle would apply to a contract under which the employee was paid according to a piece rate for work completed.

to be discretionary. In *Horkulak v Cantor Fitzgerald International* the Court of Appeal held that *Laverack* had no application to cases where there was a contractual entitlement to a bona fide and rational exercise by the employer of its discretion as to whether the employee should receive a bonus and, if so, how much.[131] In such circumstances the court should put itself in the shoes of those making the decision and decide what figure would have been arrived at had the discretion been exercised in accordance with these principles.[132] It may also be necessary to consider whether entitlement to benefits is dependent upon the maintenance of the employment relationship. In *Micklefield v SAC Technology Ltd*,[133] for example, the effect of the employee's dismissal was that certain share options which would otherwise have been available to him automatically lapsed under the rules of the company scheme in question. As a result he was not entitled to any compensation in respect of this head of loss.

Ultimately, in any given case the outcome depends on whether the benefit can be construed as one to which the employee is contractually or otherwise legally entitled. For example in *Shove v Downs Surgical plc*[134] damages included amounts in respect of the employee's exclusion from the employer's life insurance scheme, the loss of his subscription to a private health care scheme and his loss of the use of a company car. An employee will also normally recover damages for loss of accrued holiday pay: in other words, he or she will receive a sum in respect of days of paid leave to which they were entitled on the basis of past service, but had not yet taken at the time of the dismissal.[135] The Court of Appeal has recently held that an employee who is wrongfully dismissed before he or she has acquired the necessary period of service to bring an unfair dismissal claim cannot claim damages for the loss of opportunity to bring such a claim; to permit this would subvert the statutory provision that in effect extends the period of employment of a summarily dismissed employee for this purpose by the *statutory minimum*, not the contractual, period of notice to which the employee is entitled.[136]

(iii) The duty to mitigate loss

5.23   The employee's duty to mitigate his or her loss normally requires them to claim the jobseeker's allowance[137] and to look for alternative work; failure to do so will reduce their damages. For this purpose the employee is not normally required to accept a job entailing a lower rate of pay or an inferior position to the one he or she previously occupied;[138] nor is it normally unreasonable to refuse an offer of re-employment from the employer who has just committed a

---

131 [2004] IRLR 942, para 46 (Potter LJ).
132 Above, para 72.
133 [1990] IRLR 218. See also *Thompson v ASDA-MFI Group plc* [1988] IRLR 340, but cf *Mallone v BPB Industries plc* [2002] IRLR 452. The validity of these exclusion clauses is more doubtful in Scotland: cf *Chapman v Aberdeen Construction Group plc* [1991] IRLR 505 (on which see Watson, 1995) and see para 4.70 above.
134 [1984] ICR 532.
135 See, eg, *Shove v Downs Surgical plc* [1984] ICR 532, 542.
136 *Harper v Virgin Net Ltd* [2004] EWCA Civ 271, [2004] IRLR 390, applying the reasoning in *Johnson v Unisys Ltd* [2001] IRLR 279, discussed in paras 5.44 and 5.45 below. For discussion of the relevant statutory provision – ERA 1996, s 97(2) – see para 5.84 below.
137 See para 3.17 above.
138 *Yetton v Eastwoods Froy Ltd* [1967] 1 WLR 104. To this extent, the common law is considerably less disciplinary in its effects on the unemployed worker than the law of social security: see para 3.17 above.

wrongful dismissal.[139] If the employee is successful in mitigation and earns salary or fees from work found after the dismissal, these sums will go to reduce the employer's obligation to pay damages.[140]

(iv) Other deductions

5.24   Where the employee receives the jobseeker's allowance following dismissal, this will be deducted from damages on the grounds that it is a direct replacement for the claimant's lost earnings.[141] However, in certain circumstances it is possible that the full amount received will not be subject to deduction. As we discussed in para 3.17 the jobseeker's allowance is composed of a contribution-based allowance, available for six months, and an income-based allowance, which is subject to a household means test. The failure to allow the employee to work out his or her notice may deprive them of time during which they could have found alternative work and postponed a claim for the jobseeker's allowance; if, as a result, their entitlement to the contribution-based allowance runs out sooner than it would otherwise have done they have suffered a loss attributable to the employer's breach of contract. In *Westwood v Secretary of State for Employment*[142] the House of Lords, dealing with a situation where an employee's entitlement to unemployment benefit expired and he qualified only for the lower 'supplementary benefit' then available, dealt with the loss constituted by the 'premature expiry of the unemployment benefit'[143] by deducting from the sum based on the employee's net wages for the notice period not the actual (unemployment) benefit he had received during that period but the lesser sum received as supplementary benefit after the unemployment benefit had prematurely expired. This sum properly represented the net gain for which he was bound to give account by way of mitigation. It seems likely that the same approach would be followed, *mutatis mutandis*, in relation to the respective elements of the jobseeker's allowance.

5.25   What other deductions may be made from a wrongfully dismissed employee's award of damages? The compensatory award for unfair dismissal, as its name implies, is designed to replace earnings lost after the dismissal.[144] Where an employee has been awarded unfair dismissal compensation, the 'best view is that those elements of the compensatory award which are capable of being allocated to any of the heads of damages for wrongful dismissal should be deducted from the award of damages, but only to the extent that they are capable of being so allocated'.[145] By contrast, statutory redundancy payments are not normally set off against damages in this way. This is said to be because they represent 'compensation for loss of an established job, not for loss of future earnings'.[146] The basis of calculation is the past service of the employee not the

139 *Shindler v Northern Raincoat Co Ltd* [1960] 1 WLR 1038.
140 For example *Shove v Downs Surgical plc* [1984] ICR 532, 542–543.
141 *Parsons v BNM Laboratories Ltd* [1964] 1 QB 95. Unemployment benefit, at issue in this case, was the precursor of the jobseeker's allowance.
142 [1985] ICR 209.
143 [1985] ICR 209, 221 (Lord Bridge).
144 See further para 5.155 below.
145 Upex, 2001: para 10.68. Cf *O'Laoire v Jackson International Ltd (No 2)* [1991] IRLR 170 at 175–176, where the defendants could not show that the claimant would be obtaining compensation under two heads for the same loss.
146 *Wilson v National Coal Board* [1981] SLT 67, 72 (Lord Keith of Kinkel).

effect of dismissal on his or her future earning capacity, as a result of which the statutory payment is 'payable even though the dismissed employee at once finds work elsewhere at higher wages'.[147] On the face of it, then, the employee is entitled to be given notice of dismissal for redundancy and then to receive the statutory payment in addition.[148] Similarly, common law damages will not be affected either by the receipt of the basic award for unfair dismissal,[149] nor, by analogy, by the receipt of an additional award, since neither of these is regarded as compensatory in nature; nor is any deduction made in respect of the receipt of long-term occupational sickness or pension benefits paid under contributory schemes.[150] The total award of damages will suffer a further reduction to reflect the fact that the payment is an accelerated single receipt of entitlements covering the whole unexpired term, and the fact that the 'vicissitudes of life' might shorten the period of salary entitlement.[151]

(v) Damages for lost reputation or lost earning capacity?

5.26   A controversial issue in this area has been whether an employee should be able to claim damages for lost reputation or for lost earning capacity arising from a wrongful dismissal. For many years the leading authority on this point was the decision of the House of Lords in *Addis v Gramophone Co Ltd*.[152] The employee, who managed the employer's business in Calcutta, was employed under a contract which entitled him to receive six months' notice of dismissal. He was summarily dismissed and prevented from working out his notice; in compensation he received six months' salary from his employer. A jury awarded him a substantial sum for lost salary extending beyond the period of notice, as well as a sum representing lost commission for the period when he was not allowed to work. In the House of Lords his damages were confined to salary and commission for the notice period only. According to Lord Loreburn LC, damages for wrongful dismissal 'cannot include compensation either for the injured feelings of the servant, or for the loss he may sustain from the fact that his having been dismissed of itself makes it more difficult for him to obtain fresh employment'.[153]

5.27   Until relatively recently both aspects of this rule were applied in an unquestioning way[154] and, indeed, the first limb reflects the limited nature of

---

147   [1981] SLT 67, 72.
148   There are exceptions to this in personal injury cases where it can be shown that the employee would not have been made redundant but for the injury: *Wilson v National Coal Board* [1981] SLT 67; *Colledge v Bass Mitchells & Butlers Ltd* [1988] ICR 125; or, in a case of wrongful dismissal, where the right to the statutory redundancy payment only arose because the employee was summarily dismissed, thereby ensuring that he was made redundant before a special scheme offering favourable terms expired: *Baldwin v British Coal Corpn* [1995] IRLR 139.
149   *Shove v Downs Surgical plc* [1984] ICR 532, 543. On the basic and additional awards, see paras 5.154 and 5.150 respectively.
150   *Hopkins v Norcross plc* [1994] ICR 11, applying *Parry v Cleaver* [1970] AC 1; see Deakin, Johnston and Markesinis, 2003: pp 797-99.
151   See Upex, 2001: para 10.74.
152   [1909] AC 488.
153   [1909] AC 488, 491.
154   *Cox v Philips Industries Ltd* [1976] 1 WLR 638; *Shove v Downs Surgical plc* [1984] ICR 532; *Bliss v South East Thames Regional Health Authority* [1985] IRLR 308; *Malik v BCCI SA (in compulsory liquidation)* [1995] IRLR 375.

this head of recovery in the common law in general for injury to feelings.[155] However, in *Malik v BCCI SA*[156] the House of Lords held, in relation to the second limb, that an employee might be able to recover damages where a breach by the employer of the implied term of trust and confidence harmed his or her reputation in such a way as to limit opportunities for alternative employment. In this case the claimants lost their jobs with the defendant bank when it collapsed. The claimants argued that, because the bank had operated its business dishonestly and corruptly, they, although personally innocent, were stigmatised by reason of their employment by it, and consequently disadvantaged in the labour market. The House of Lords held that on the assumption that the conduct of the bank had been as pleaded, the bank had breached the trust and confidence owed to its employees and the claimants were not barred from recovering loss flowing from that breach by reason of discovering the conduct only after termination of their employment. The court distinguished *Addis* on the basis that it had been decided before the implied term of mutual trust and confidence had been developed.[157] However, in the later decision of *Johnson v Unisys Ltd*[158] the majority of the House of Lords held that *Malik* could not be invoked to support a cause of action for lost reputation as a result of a wrongful dismissal. *Addis* itself was not regarded as an insuperable obstacle to reliance on *Malik*[159] in these circumstances; rather, the difficulty lay, in the view of the majority, in the argument that implying a duty to act fairly (the term preferred in this context to trust and confidence)[160] in relation to the employer's power of dismissal would go contrary to the will of Parliament in establishing a statutory unfair dismissal scheme which was limited in its application.[161]

In essence, two issues arise here: a narrow issue, of the damages properly awardable for an employer's failure to give notice under the contract; and a wider issue of the relationship between express notice clauses and the implied term of mutual trust and confidence. The opinions in *Johnson* address the second, wider issue, and we will return to this below.[162] The narrower issue turns on whether the employee can show that the employer's failure to give notice, assuming this is a breach of contract, caused him or her loss over and above net wages or salary for the notice period. At one level, the question can simply be approached as one of causation. If this is done, it is far from obvious that an employer should escape liability for causing unwarranted harm to an employee's reputation by the manner of dismissal. If notice is dispensed with, the implication is that the employer has grounds for doing so. If there are no such grounds, the

---

155 See Deakin, Johnston and Markesinis, 2003: pp 96 *et seq.* For the argument that the implied duty of trust and confidence is relevant to recovery of damages for distress see John McMullen, 1997.

156 [1997] IRLR 462; see Brodie, 1998b; para 4.91 *et seq* above.

157 [1997] IRLR 462, 465–466 (Lord Nicholls, with whom Lord Goff and Lord MacKay concurred). Lord Steyn (referring to Enonchong, 1996: p 596) held that *Addis* was irrelevant because it merely decided that the loss of reputation there was not caused by a breach of contract: 470. The claimants in *Malik* failed at trial on the issue of causation: *BCCI SA v Ali (No 3)* [2002] IRLR 460.

158 [2001] IRLR 279.

159 See Lord Hoffman at para 44, Lord Millett at para 77. Lord Bingham agreed with both these opinions.

160 For the view that this term should be preferred in relation to the power of dismissal: see Lord Hoffman at para 46, Lord Millett at paras 78-79.

161 See also *Eastwood v Magnox Electric plc, McCabe v Cornwall County Council* [2004] IRLR 733, discussed in para 5.45 below.

162 See paras 5.44 and 5.45.

employee can argue that the stigma which attaches to him or her as a result is the direct consequence of the employer's breach of contract. The failure to allow the employee to serve out the notice period may also make it more difficult than it would otherwise have been to find alternative work; in general it is more costly and time consuming for an unemployed person to find suitable work than it is for an employed person to find a similar job with a different employer. It may be that an employee faces a high evidentiary burden in demonstrating losses of this kind, and that as a result claims of this kind will rarely succeed,[163] but this is not the same thing as saying that the cause of action, as a matter of law, cannot be sustained.

In *Johnson*, the point discussed above was only indirectly addressed; the case was pleaded in terms of the employer's breach of the implied duty of mutual trust and confidence,[164] and it was in this context that the majority of the House (Lord Steyn dissenting on this point) ruled that the employee's claim should be struck out as disclosing no cause of action. This leaves *Addis* itself as the major obstacle to the success of a claim for reputational losses. In *Johnson*, Lord Steyn argued that this aspect of Lord Loreburn's judgment in *Addis* did not clearly command the consent of a majority of the judges in that case, and that, in any event, it was contrary to basic principles of contract law which allow recovery of financial losses flowing from breach as long as a causal link can be established. In his opinion, Lord Hoffmann (with whom Lords Bingham and Millett agreed) concluded that in the light of the express terms of the contract in *Johnson*, '[t]he action for wrongful dismissal could ... yield no more than the salary which should have been paid during the contractual period of notice'.[165] However, this conclusion rested not simply on the express notice clause in Mr Johnson's contract, but also on a provision under which the company reserved the right to make a payment in lieu of notice (or 'PILON') in the event of dismissal, a right which they exercised. On this basis, Mr Johnson's contract contained a PILON clause which Lord Hoffmann appears to have construed as permitting the company to dismiss him summarily without thereby committing any breach, as long as they paid a sum equivalent to net wages for the notice period.[166] On the basis of this interpretation of *Johnson*, it would remain open to courts in future cases not involving a similar PILON clause to reconsider the issue of precisely what was decided in *Addis* and whether that decision is consistent with basic principles governing the award of damages for breach of contract.

(vi) The effect of the payment of wages in lieu of notice

5.28   It is often the case in practice that an employer will summarily dismiss an employee and, at the same time, pay him or her the net wages which they would have received during the period of minimum notice to which they were entitled (a 'payment of wages in lieu of notice' or 'PILON'). This may or may

---

163 This was the basis on which Lord Steyn ruled that the claim in *Johnson* should be struck out ([2001] IRLR 279, para 29).

164 This was also the case in *Eastwood v Magnox Electric plc* and *McCabe v Cornwall County Council* [2004] IRLR 733.

165 [2001] IRLR 279, para 41.

166 See para 5.28 below for further discussion of PILON clauses. It is not entirely clear that Mr Johnson's contained a true PILON clause; if it did, he would not have had a wrongful dismissal claim for net wages, as Lord Hoffmann appears to imply, but, for reasons we explain below, no action for wrongful dismissal at all.

not be a wrongful dismissal, depending on the circumstances. An employee is entitled to waive the right to receive notice, just as with any other contractual right, whereupon the dismissal will not be wrongful.[167] However, for a waiver of contractual rights to be effective it must be given in return for consideration of some kind, or be subject to an estoppel. If an employee voluntarily accepts a payment of wages in lieu of notice, this would normally be seen as discharging his or her contractual rights against the employer. It is also possible for an employee to give up the rights both to notice and to receive wages in lieu, in return for receiving some other benefit. In *Baldwin v British Coal Corpn*[168] the employee's contract was terminated without him receiving the twelve weeks' notice to which he was entitled. This was done in order to enable him to receive a redundancy payment of £5,000 under a statutory scheme, the terms of which would have been inapplicable had he been dismissed at a later date. It was held that he had thereby waived any right to receive, in addition, net salary for the contractual notice period.

Conversely, where the employment relationship is ended consensually on the basis that the employee will receive wages in lieu of notice, this arrangement could be construed as involving a promise by the employer to pay a sum equivalent to *gross* salary for the period in question. Because the contract is discharged by agreement there is no question of there being a wrongful dismissal, and no presumption that the sum payable by the employer in return for ending the relationship should be the same as the sum normally awarded by a court by way of damages for failure to give notice. Thus in *Gothard v Mirror Group Newspapers Ltd*[169] the Court of Appeal thought that the most natural construction of an agreement for voluntary early retirement was that the payment of wages in lieu of notice would be made gross. The same principle may apply to a PILON clause, that is to say, a clause in the contract which provides that the employer has a choice of either giving notice or making a payment in lieu. If the employer fails to give notice, the payment in lieu may be characterised as a contractual debt rather than as a payment of damages. Where the payment in lieu can be characterised in this way (an issue which turns on the construction of the contract terms) the effect (among other things) is that the employee has no duty of mitigation, and no deduction may be made to take account of the accelerated receipt of wages or salary.[170]

(vii) A 'right to work'?

5.29   What happens where the employee does not agree to waive the right to notice? Under these circumstances, it is far from clear that he or she has any enforceable right to work out the period of notice. A payment of wages in lieu of notice will normally be seen as discharging in full the employer's liability to

---

167   *Trotter v Forth Ports Authority* [1991] IRLR 419; *Baldwin v British Coal Corpn* [1995] IRLR 139. This rule is preserved in the context of the statutory minimum notice periods by ERA 1996, s 86(3).

168   [1995] IRLR 139.

169   [1988] ICR 729.

170   See *Cerberus Software Ltd v Rowley* [1999] IRLR 690, which was overturned on the basis of a different construction of the contract by the Court of Appeal [2001] IRLR 160; see also *EMI Group Electronics Ltd v Coldicott (Inspector of Taxes)* [1999] IRLR 630 (where the contract makes provision for a payment in lieu of notice, the amount is taxable as an emolument from employment, which will not be the case if the payment is made as damages for breach of contract).

pay damages for breach of contract. This follows from *Addis v Gramophone Co Ltd*.[171] It is only in exceptional cases that an employer may be liable for an additional breach of contract in refusing to allow the employee to work. In cases involving actors and others whose work is displayed to the public at large, the employer's failure to permit the employee to perform as contractually agreed has been held to give rise to claims for harm to reputation, which the courts have been prepared to quantify.[172] However, in other contexts quantification may be more difficult. The courts are unlikely to grant an order for specific performance of a contract of employment[173] and, in practice, the issue is likely to arise most frequently in relation to situations where the employer wishes the employee to remain on 'garden leave', but employees, to preserve their skills, wish to start working for another employer.[174]

The position with regard to the protection of skills and earning capacity is more clearly defined in the case of a contract of apprenticeship, which will normally be for a fixed term without provision for the employer to terminate the contract by giving notice. The apprentice is entitled not simply to be employed, but also to receive training and instruction. The employer has no general power to dismiss without giving a reason, and the range of conduct for which the apprentice may be summarily dismissed is highly restricted: in *Dunk v George Waller & Son Ltd*[175] it was not enough that the apprentice had failed certain examinations. If the apprentice is wrongfully dismissed, he or she is entitled to damages not just for lost wages but also for the loss of training opportunities and the consequent harm done to their chances of eventually obtaining a good job.

The right to training is an integral part of the contract of apprenticeship. It is not necessarily a part, integral or otherwise, of the contract of employment. However, a contract of employment may contain a term providing a right to training or to retraining, either by way of incorporation from a collective agreement or other external source, or by way of an implied term.[176] Under these circumstances, there seems to be no reason why an employee who is wrongfully dismissed should not receive an award of damages to reflect the loss of these rights, by way of analogy with the apprenticeship cases.

(viii) Clauses providing for dismissal 'with immediate effect'

5.30 Contracts of employment sometimes contain clauses specifying that the employer shall have the right to bring the employment to an end 'with immediate effect' in the event of a breach of contract of a certain kind by the employee. In

---

171 [1909] AC 488. See also *Dixon v Stenor* [1973] ICR 157, 158 (Sir John Donaldson P); *Gothard v Mirror Group Newspapers Ltd* [1988] ICR 729, 733 (Lord Donaldson MR).
172 See *Herbert Clayton and Jack Waller Ltd v Oliver* [1930] AC 209; para 4.112 above.
173 See Brodie, 1998. On injunctions and declarations to maintain the contract of employment, see para 5.54 *et seq* below.
174 See *William Hill Organisation Ltd v Tucker* [1998] IRLR 313 in which the Court of Appeal held, somewhat unusually, that the employer was under a contractual obligation to supply the employee with work and, as it was in breach of this term during the notice period, was not entitled to an injunction restraining him from working for a competitor during the notice period.
175 [1970] 2 QB 163. See also *Wallace v CA Roofing Services Ltd* [1996] IRLR 435; *Whitely v Marton Electrical Ltd* [2003] IRLR 197 (employment under a 'modern apprenticeship pact').
176 See *Cresswell v Board of Inland Revenue* [1984] IRLR 190; para 4.90 above.

T & K Home Improvements Ltd v Skilton[177] the Court of Appeal held that such a clause was effective in allowing the employer to end the contract without notice, and that the employee was not entitled to work or to be on the employer's premises after that point. However, the Court found that, on the construction of the particular contract before it, the 'immediate effect' clause did not override another clause in the contract under which the employee was entitled to receive three month's written notice of termination.[178] The employee was therefore entitled to receive a payment of wages in lieu of notice for this period. In other words, the Court construed the 'immediate effect' clause as qualifying the employee's right to work during the notice period, but not his right to receive a payment in lieu.

Contractual job security

5.31   Contracts of employment may contain express terms, or terms incorporated from external sources, which purport to provide guarantees of job security going beyond that provided by the right to minimum notice. It is possible, for example, for a contract to incorporate a guarantee that the employer will not make the employee compulsorily redundant, although such terms are rare and may even, in respect of some public-sector employments, be open to legal challenge as illegitimately fettering the employer's discretion.[179] It is more common, but still rare, for a contract to omit the normal provision allowing the employer to terminate the contract by simply giving notice: this may have the same effect as preventing compulsory redundancy.[180] Alternatively, a contract could incorporate a term making compulsory redundancy conditional upon a particular selection procedure being followed.[181] Contracts may also incorporate the terms relating to the exercise by the employer of powers of discipline and dismissal. These frequently provide superior protection to that which is available under unfair dismissal legislation, in terms of such procedural issues as the employee's rights to be represented (rather than merely accompanied)[182] at a hearing of the issues and more specific rights in relation to the conduct of the hearing, such as an express right to put his or her side of the case.[183] Terms of this kind normally

---

177   [2000] IRLR 595.

178   Here, the notice term was express, but it is also possible that similar notice clauses (of varying lengths) could take effect in contracts by virtue of ERA 1996, ss 86 *et seq* (see para 5.15 above). It would arguably be contrary to principle (and, more specifically, contrary to ERA 1996, s 203) to allow the employer to contract out of the obligation to give notice which arises by virtue of this legislation.

179   See Ewing, 1989: p 217.

180   On notice clauses, see *McClelland v Northern Ireland General Health Services Board* [1957] 1 WLR 594 and the discussion in para 5.17 above. Cf *Kaur v MG Rover Group Ltd* [2005] IRLR 40.

181   *Anderson v Pringle of Scotland* [1998] IRLR 64; *Peace v City of Edinburgh Council* [1999] IRLR 417; cf *Alexander v Standard Telephones and Cables (No 2)* [1991] IRLR 286. A further possibility is that the contract incorporates an equal opportunities policy which qualifies the employer's powers of dismissal: see *Taylor v Secretary of State for Scotland* [2000] IRLR 502, discussed at para 5.65 below.

182   ERA 1999, ss 10–15 gives a right to be accompanied; see further para 5.132.

183   Cf rights under the statutory dismissal and disciplinary procedures contained in EA 2002, Sch 2, discussed in para 5.124 *et seq*. The ACAS Code of Practice on Disciplinary and Grievance Procedures, 2004, para 15, provides, *inter alia*, that employees should be allowed to set out their case and to answer any allegations made and employment tribunals must take the Code into account, but failure to follow a procedure beyond the statutory minima will not of itself make a dismissal unfair if the employer shows that it would have decided to dismiss the employee had it followed the procedure: ERA 1996, s 98A(2); see further para 5.143.

require the employer to follow a particular procedure as a pre-condition of exercising the power, under the contract, to discipline or dismiss an employee who has been found guilty of misconduct. They can be read, then, as doing one or both of two things: they impose a procedure which the employer must observe when exercising a disciplinary power; and they impliedly restrict the right of the employer to circumvent this procedure by dismissing an employee for no reason at all by simply invoking the right to give notice under the contract. In other words, the effect of these clauses could be both procedural and substantive: if the protection against arbitrary discipline is to mean anything, the employer must have impliedly given up the right, which the notice rule otherwise confers, to end the contract without needing to have a reason for doing so.[184]

5.32   In addition to the higher standards which they frequently embody, contractual job security clauses have other advantages over statutory protection against unfair dismissal. As we shall see,[185] an employee may under certain circumstances be able to enforce his or her contractual rights by way of an injunction or declaration. This remedy – effectively enabling a dismissal to be nullified and the employment relationship maintained – is not normally available under unfair dismissal legislation. This legislation is only triggered once dismissal has already taken place,[186] and although re-employment is in principle the primary remedy for unfair dismissal,[187] it is very rarely awarded in practice.[188]

Nor does unfair dismissal law provide fully adequate protection to an employee who suffers disciplinary action short of dismissal. Unless the action in question falls into one of a number of specific cases in which a worker or employee can bring a claim based on being subjected to a detriment without necessarily being dismissed,[189] the employee's only option under the Act is to accept that the contract has come to an end and claim unfair dismissal. This need not always lead to the employee resigning; in some cases the courts have accepted that the employee can bring a claim for unfair dismissal while continuing to work for the employer under a new contract.[190] But even if a tribunal finds that there was an unfair dismissal in these circumstances, the employee is unlikely to get the previous contract terms reinstated: financial compensation is the much more likely outcome.[191] Where it would be preferable from the employee's point of view to have the wrongful disciplinary action *nullified* as opposed to being compensated for its effects, this can only be effectively achieved by way of an injunction or declaration under the common law.

Finally, in a case where a specific order of injunction or declaration is not available, the employee may nevertheless be able to obtain substantial damages

---

184 See further para 5.41–5.43 below.
185 See para 5.54 *et seq* below.
186 Note, however, that under the standard dismissal and disciplinary procedure, in force since 1 October 2004, an employee must not be dismissed before an initial meeting with the employer to discuss the circumstances leading the employer to contemplate dismissal: EA 2002, Sch 2, para 2(1); see further para 5.125 below.
187 ERA 1996, ss 112 and 113.
188 See para 5.152 below.
189 These apply to the situations listed in TULRCA 1992, s 146 and Sch A1, para 156; ERA 1996, ss 43M–47E; NMWA 1998 s 23; ERelA 1999, s 12; TICER 1999, reg 31; PTWR 2000, reg 7; FTER 2002, reg 6; FWPR 2002, reg 16; ICER 2004, reg 32; and EPLLCR 2004, reg 44.
190 *Hogg v Dover College* [1990] ICR 39; *Joseph v British Railways Board* (2 September 1993, IT, unreported) noted by Curran, 1994; *Alcan Extrusions v Yates* [1996] IRLR 327.
191 See para 5.152 below.

for breach of a contractual job security clause. This will be important in cases where unfair dismissal compensation falls short of meeting the employee's losses in full, thanks to the upper limits on compensation which apply to claims under the Act.[192]

A further possibility is that a degree of contractual job security may be provided by implied terms, and, in particular, by the implied duty of mutual trust and confidence.[193] Where this is the case, it may be open to an employee to argue that substantial damages should be awarded, going beyond the net wages and salary for the notice period which is the usual measure of damages for a 'direct' wrongful dismissal claim. However, the application of the implied obligation of trust and confidence in relation to termination of employment raises complex and difficult questions, which we discuss in paras 5.44 and 5.45 below.

(i) The legal effect of express job security clauses

5.33   We begin our analysis with a closer examination of the legal status of express job security clauses. It is necessary to examine a number of arguments which have been made against granting normative effect to such clauses.

IS THE TERM INCORPORATED INTO THE CONTRACT?

5.34   In the first place, it may be that the clause is not effectively incorporated into the individual contract of employment. There should be no difficulty, in principle, on the grounds of the term's *appropriateness* for incorporation:[194] such clauses can be seen as intended to regulate the individual relationship, and are not normally a matter for collective relations only. In *Alexander v Standard Telephone and Cables Ltd (No 2)*[195] Hobhouse J held that a clause in a collective agreement laying down a 'last-in, first-out' procedure for redundancy selection was not intended to give rise to individual rights and was not incorporated at the level of the individual contract. However, this was a somewhat exceptional outcome[196] and goes against the tide of numerous other decisions in which contractual job security clauses have been regarded as incorporated into individual contracts, almost as a matter of course.[197]

It may nevertheless be open to an employer to deny normative force to the clause by stating that it is not intended to have legal effect. Against this, the courts have insisted that they, and not the parties, are the final arbiters of whether an agreement is a legally-binding contract or not.[198] If, in all other respects, a clause of this kind possesses the necessary attributes of a binding contract term, the courts should arguably be reluctant to rubber-stamp a bare statement by the employer to the effect that the clause is binding in honour only.

---

192 See para 5.155 *et seq* below. A contract clause which requires the employer to observe the substance of unfair dismissal protection might be one means of seeking to combine the strengths of unfair dismissal with those of the common law, while seeking to avoid their respective weaknesses. See Ewing, 1989.

193 On the implied term of mutual trust and confidence, see para 4.91 *et seq* above.

194 See para 4.29 above.

195 [1991] IRLR 286; see para 4.29 above.

196 Cf, in the context of redundancy, the Court of Session decision in *Anderson v Pringle of Scotland* [1998] IRLR 64, discussed further in para 5.61. In *Kaur v MG Rover Group Ltd* [2005] IRLR 40, however, a clause in a collective agreement stating [t]here will be no compulsory redundancy' was found in the circumstances not to be apt for incorporation.

197 This is so in virtually all the cases discussed in this and the following paragraph.

198 *R v Lord Chancellor's Department, ex p Nangle* [1991] IRLR 343.

5.35 A further difficulty is raised by the opinion of Lord Hoffmann in *Johnson v Unisys Ltd.* [199] Here, Mr. Johnson sought unsuccessfully to maintain that he had a cause of action based on the employer's breach of the implied duty of trust and confidence in respect of the psychological illness which he alleged had been caused by his summary dismissal without a fair hearing and in breach of the company's disciplinary procedure. He did not argue that the provisions of the disciplinary procedure constituted express terms of his contract of employment. Lord Hoffmann, with whose opinion Lords Bingham and Millett agreed, nevertheless decided that it would be useful to 'examine the matter in a little more detail'.[200] In lengthy *obiter* remarks, he stated that the employee handbook 'has to be construed against the relevant background and the background which fairly looms over the disciplinary procedure is Part X of the [Employment Rights Act]', that is, the legislation conferring on employees the right to claim compensation and/or re-employment for unfair dismissal.[201] From this perspective, in Lord Hoffmann's view, the main purpose of the disciplinary procedure was to ensure that an employee was not unfairly dismissed. Procedures of this kind were, he argued, included in employee handbooks out of concern for the provisions of ERA 1996, Part X and the Code of Practice on Disciplinary and Grievance Procedures (as it now is) issued by ACAS, and in order to comply with the obligation in section 3 of ERA 1996 to notify employees in writing of disciplinary procedures governing their employment. Lord Hoffmann then went on to say:

> ... given this background to the disciplinary procedures, I find it impossible to believe that Parliament, when it provided in section 3(1) of the 1996 Act that the statement of particulars of employment was to contain a note of any applicable disciplinary rules, or the parties themselves, intended that the inclusion of those rules should give rise to a common law action in damages which would create the means of circumventing the restrictions and limits which Parliament had imposed on compensation for unfair dismissal ... It is, I suppose, possible that they may have contractual effect in determining whether the employer can dismiss summarily in the sense of not having to give four weeks' notice or payment in lieu. But I do not think they can have been intended to qualify the employer's common law power to dismiss without cause on giving such notice, or to create contractual duties which are independently actionable.[202]

This statement is capable of being read in a number of ways. It could be construed as meaning that the existence of Part X of the 1996 Act must be interpreted as preventing courts giving effect to contractual disciplinary procedures which provide rights over and above those supplied by statute. An

199 [2001] IRLR 279.
200 [2001] IRLR 279, para 60.
201 [2001] IRLR 279, para 63.
202 [2001] UKHL 13, [2001] IRLR 279, para 66. Lord Hoffmann's reference to the role of the written statement of disciplinary procedures in this context is difficult to understand. As we have seen (para 4.22), the courts have held that the employer is only obliged to record in the statement those terms and conditions (including disciplinary procedures) which have contractual effect. A disciplinary procedure which, applying Lord Hoffmann's reasoning in *Johnson*, had no contractual effect, would not need to be referred to in a written statement. On this basis, it is arguable that the enactment of ERA 1996, s 3 is evidence that Parliament intended disciplinary procedures to have contractual effect unless there was clear intention to the contrary.

alternative reading is that there is merely a strong presumption against giving contractual effect to disciplinary procedures adopted by employers in order to comply with their statutory obligations. In either case, this would be a highly novel approach to the interpretation of protective employment legislation and of its relationship to contract. It is normal for such legislation to limit the degree to which the parties to the employment relationship can contract out of provisions designed for the protection of the employee.[203] However, far from preventing the parties from contracting for superior or complementary protections, one of the aims of such legislation is precisely to induce improvements at this kind, hence its characterisation as a *'floor* of rights'.[204] If Lord Hoffmann's analysis were to be widely followed, statutory standards of this kind would in future act as a 'ceiling' rather than as a 'floor' for contractual rights and obligations. This would create the anomalous situation that employees may be better protected in areas in which Parliament has failed or chosen not to legislate than those in which it has. In particular, there is now a danger that the relatively rudimentary statutory dismissal and disciplinary procedures contained in the Employment Act 2002 will be regarded as setting the limits of fair procedures unless it is clearly evident that procedures that go beyond them are intended to have contractual effect.[205]

THE 'ELECTIVE' AND 'AUTOMATIC' THEORIES OF CONTRACT TERMINATION

5.36   A second argument against granting legal effect to job security clauses concerns the effect of a wrongful summary dismissal on the future contractual obligations of the parties. According to the 'automatic' or 'unilateral' theory of contract termination, the act of summary dismissal of itself brings the contract to an end, as would the employee's abrupt walk-out or resignation; the employer's obligations under the job security clause are discharged along with the rest of the contract. This theory seeks to draw distinctions between different kinds of repudiatory breach. A repudiatory breach which is not aimed at bringing the relationship to an end, such as an employer's failure to pay wages or salary as agreed, does not, it is said, terminate the contract.[206] However, it is also said that the *contract* cannot be maintained in force once the *relationship* of employment has come to an end by virtue of the deliberate act of either party.[207] The result would be that following summary dismissal, the employee could not rely on a contractual job security clause to protect his or her expectations of continuing employment. This argument has, however, been discredited in the

---

203 See, eg, ERA 1996, s 203; and see our discussion of the relationship between statutory standards and the contract of employment at para 4.11 above.
204 See our discussion at para 4.11 above, and, for an empirical analysis of this effect in practice, see W Brown *et al*, 2000, cited by Lord Steyn in his dissenting judgment in *Johnson* [2001] UKHL 13, para 23, [2001] IRLR 279, 284.
205 Note that the provision in EA 2002, s 30 for the requirements of the statutory procedures themselves to have contractual effect has not yet been brought into force: see para 5.19 above.
206 *Rigby v Ferodo Ltd* [1988] ICR 29; *Boyo v Lambeth London Borough Council* [1995] IRLR 50, 59 (Ralph Gibson LJ).
207 *Sanders v Ernest A Neale Ltd* [1974] IRLR 236 (Sir John Donaldson P); *Gunton v Richmond-upon-Thames London Borough Council* [1980] ICR 755, 762 (Shaw LJ, dissenting); *London Transport Executive v Clarke* [1981] ICR 355 (Lord Denning MR, dissenting); *R v East Berkshire Area Health Authority, ex p Walsh* [1984] ICR 743, 756 (May LJ); *Boyo v Lambeth London Borough Council* [1995] IRLR 50, 57 (Ralph Gibson LJ), 49 (Staughton LJ), 60 (Sir Francis Purchas).

context of the law of contract more generally, where an unaccepted repudiation is regarded as 'a thing writ in water':[208] the contract is only brought to an end if the innocent party chooses to terminate it in response to the repudiatory breach.[209] This 'bilateral' or 'elective' theory of termination is also supported by decisions specific to the contract of employment. The elective theory explains, for example, why an employer may be able to obtain an injunction against a former employee, restraining him or her from making use of confidential information or for working for a competitor for a certain period.[210] For this purpose, the contract term in question must have survived the employee's wrongful repudiation of the contract. If this principle works in favour of the employer, contractual reciprocity requires that it should work in favour of the employee too.[211]

5.37 It is nevertheless maintained by some that the application of the bilateral theory to the ending of the contract of employment is impractical, and that these practical considerations should outweigh more abstract arguments in favour of aligning contracts of employment with the rule which applies to other contracts.[212] For example, it has been suggested that the effect of the elective theory is to allow the employee, following a refusal to accept that the contract has been brought to an end by the summary dismissal, to 'sit in the sun' and claim his or her wages indefinitely, without needing to do any work for them. This is because no duty to mitigate loss arises in the context of a debt claim, to which the employee might, under these circumstances, be entitled.[213] However, this would only be the case if the employee were entitled to wages for being ready and available for work, as opposed to receiving wages for work actually done.[214]

Even then, it is an established principle of contract law that the innocent party is not entitled to uphold the contract in all circumstances. He or she only has the right to do so if they have a 'legitimate interest' in maintaining that contract in force as opposed to any other. The unavailability of alternative work might be such an interest.[215] Where the innocent party has no 'legitimate interest', however, he or she may be taken to have accepted the other's repudiatory breach, and is then left only with a claim for damages. This would seem to deal fully with the point at issue here. In the context of employment, an employee would have a legitimate interest in maintaining the contract if he or she were genuinely seeking to keep the relationship intact by asserting their rights to a

---

208 *Howard v Pickford Tool Co Ltd* [1951] 1 KB 417, 421 (Asquith LJ), itself an employment case.
209 *White and Carter (Councils) Ltd v McGregor* [1962] AC 413.
210 *Thomas Marshall (Exports) Ltd v Guinle* [1979] Ch 227; *Evening Standard Co Ltd v Henderson* [1987] ICR 588.
211 It accordingly seems beside the point that the employer cannot obtain an order of *specific performance* against the employee (cf *Boyo v Lambeth London Borough Council* [1995] IRLR 50, 60, per Sir Francis Purchas). If the employer can obtain prohibitory injunctions against the employee after the relationship of employment has come to an end, why should not the employee have the reciprocal right? There is a distinction here between specific performance, which is generally not available to either party, and a prohibitory injunction, which may be. See further para 5.54 below.
212 For discussion, see John McMullen, 1982 and 1995.
213 *White and Carter (Councils) Ltd v McGregor* [1962] AC 413; *Sanders v Ernest A Neale Ltd* [1974] IRLR 236; *Boyo v Lambeth London Borough Council* [1995] IRLR 50, 57, 59.
214 On this, see para 4.58 above.
215 *White and Carter (Councils) Ltd v McGregor* [1962] AC 413, *per* Lord Reid.

fair hearing under the contract, but in few other cases.[216] Moreover, acceptance is easily implied by, for example, the act of seeking alternative employment.[217] The danger of an employee 'sitting in the sun' and claiming wages indefinitely is also simply enough avoided, in these circumstances, by the employer agreeing to operate the procedure as required by the contract.

5.38   A related objection is that the elective theory does not work very well in the context of unfair dismissal, which adopts the common law notion of dismissal for a number of purposes.[218] Without a dismissal, the employment tribunal has no jurisdiction to hear the employee's complaint. Section 95(1) of ERA 1996 defines dismissal as including the case where the contract is 'terminated by the employer (whether with or without notice)'. If the elective theory were correct, this section would have no application to the case of a wrongful summary dismissal in which the contract was brought to an end not by the employer's breach, but by the employee's acceptance of that breach. This point is easily enough dealt with, however, by the provision made for constructive dismissal in section 95(1)(c), which states that there is a dismissal for the purposes of the Act where the 'employee terminates the contract under which he is employed (with or without notice) in circumstances in which he is entitled to terminate it without notice by reason of the employer's conduct'. This provision extends the jurisdiction of the tribunal to cover the case where the employee accepts the repudiatory breach of the employer.

However, where the contract is terminated by the employee's acceptance in this way, it may be difficult to establish precisely when the contract was brought to an end, in particular in a case where the employee is *taken* to have waived the right to affirm the contract by virtue of having no legitimate interest in keeping it alive. In *Robert Cort & Son Ltd v Charman*[219] the EAT concluded that in a case of summary dismissal, the 'effective date of termination' for statutory purposes should be set by reference to the date of that summary dismissal, even if the elective view was correct and the contract would be determined only where the employee accepted the repudiation. Because the jurisdiction of the tribunal rests, in part, on identifying the effective date of termination, there is a need for certainty in this area.[220] But even if, for reasons of certainty, the unilateral theory has to be adopted for this purpose, this is no reason for applying the same rule in the common law, where its effect would be to deny all normative force to contractual job security clauses: that would surely be a case of the tail wagging the dog.

---

216   Another possibility might be an interest in keeping the contract on foot in order to acquire the necessary continuity of employment to claim unfair dismissal. This is discussed further at para 5.83 *et seq* below.

217   *Dietman v Brent London Borough Council* [1987] ICR 737. The judgments of the Court of Appeal in *Boyo v Lambeth London Borough Council* [1995] IRLR 50 express doubt on this point (see eg [1995] IRLR 50, 59, per Ralph Gibson LJ) but it seems well enough established by authority and by principle. In *Soares v Beazer Investments Ltd* [2004] EWCA Civ 482, however, the Court of Appeal held that if there is an evidential lacuna about acceptance it should benefit the employee not the employer (para 26, Maurice Kay LJ).

218   See *London Transport Executive v Clarke* [1981] ICR 355, discussed at para 5.76 below.

219   [1981] IRLR 437. See also *Octavius Atkinson and Sons Ltd v Morris* [1989] ICR 431. See Freedland, 2003: pp 382–384 for a critique of these decisions, which allow the employing entity 'to take advantage of its own breach of contract' (p 383).

220   See para 5.83 *et seq* below.

5.39 In terms of contract principle, there would seem to be no good reason to depart from the general rule in favour of giving the innocent party the option to keep the contract on foot for the pursuit of a 'legitimate interest'. The alternative can be seen as unjust, in the sense that it would allow the party in breach to profit from its own wrong.[221] A number of judges have also questioned the idea that the subjective intention of the guilty party to end the relationship should determine the extent of the other's contractual rights.[222] The application of the elective theory to the contract of employment is, in effect, one further aspect of the courts' recognition that terms incorporated from collective agreements and other external sources have normative force at the level of the individual relationship. To deny the application of the elective theory would be to deny the fundamentally reciprocal nature of the parties' obligations under the individual contract of employment, and to return to a more hierarchical, master-servant model of the employment relationship.

5.40 There is also support for the elective theory from the point of view of authority. It was accepted by a majority of the Court of Appeal in *Gunton v Richmond-upon-Thames London Borough Council*[223] and was approved after extensive analyses at first instance in *Thomas Marshall (Exports) Ltd v Guinle*[224] and *Dietman v Brent London Borough Council*.[225] Numerous decisions in which employees have been granted declarations or injunctions to prevent employers acting in breach of disciplinary procedures also depend on the application of the elective theory, including the decision of the House of Lords in *McClelland v Northern Ireland General Health Services Board*;[226] it is not clear if or how far these decisions constitute some kind of exceptional category.[227] In *Rigby v Ferodo Ltd*[228] the House of Lords declined to decide the matter, in a case not directly concerned with dismissal but with a cut in wages imposed, in breach of contract, by the employer. However, Lord Oliver said:

> I entirely fail to see how the continuance of the primary contractual obligation can be made to depend on the subjective desire of the contract-breaker and I do not understand what is meant by the injured party having no alternative but to accept the breach ... I can see no reason in law or in logic why, leaving aside for the moment the extreme case of outright dismissal or walk-out, a contract of employment should be on any different footing from any other contract ....[229]

Despite this the application of the elective theory continues to be controversial, and it is unfortunate that the House of Lords did not choose to clarify the law when it could arguably have done so in *Rigby v Ferodo Ltd*.[230] More recently, in *Boyo v Lambeth London Borough Council*[231] a unanimous Court of Appeal

---

221 *Thomas Marshall (Exports) Ltd v Guinle* [1979] Ch 227, 240 (Sir Robert Megarry, VC).
222 [1979] Ch 227. See also *Rigby v Ferodo Ltd* [1988] ICR 29, 35 (Lord Oliver).
223 Shaw LJ dissented.
224 By Sir Robert Megarry VC.
225 By Hodgson J.
226 [1957] 1 WLR 594. See also *Vine v National Dock Labour Board* [1957] AC 488; *Hill v CA Parsons & Co Ltd* [1972] Ch 305.
227 See para *5.54 et seq* below.
228 [1988] ICR 29.
229 [1988] ICR 29, 35.
230 [1988] ICR 29, 35.
231 [1995] IRLR 50.

took the opportunity to cast fresh doubt on the elective theory, while at the same time feeling bound to apply the majority ruling in an earlier judgment of the Court of Appeal, *Gunton v Richmond-upon-Thames London Borough Council.*[232] *Gunton*, according to the Court in *Boyo*, had produced law 'distinctly lacking in rhyme and reason',[233] and was not to be preferred, in principle, to the judgment of Sir John Donaldson P in *Sanders v Ernest A Neale Ltd* laying out the case for the automatic theory.[234] Although, at present, the elective theory has prevailed,[235] in the light of powerful *dicta* casting doubt on it, its future can hardly be regarded as assured.[236]

(ii) The relationship between contractual job security clauses and the notice rule

5.41   Even if the application of the elective theory would remove an important obstacle to the effectiveness of contractual job security clauses, it would not settle the question of the legal meaning of such clauses. This is because their relationship to the notice rule has not been properly resolved. Arguably, job security clauses of this kind can only be truly effective if they limit the notice rule. One possible construction of contracts containing these clauses is that they limit the employer's normal right to dismiss by giving notice: in the absence of an express clause empowering the employer to dismiss for redundancy, for example, it may only terminate the contract for good cause as laid down in the contractual procedure. If this is seen as a far-reaching and possibly unintended restriction upon the employer's powers, a second possibility is that where the employer seeks to dismiss for misconduct or breach of discipline, it may only do so after adhering to the contractual procedures laid down for *these* situations; but that otherwise, it remains free to dismiss for no reason at all, simply by giving notice.[237] If this were the case, however, the employer could easily evade the job security clause by relying on its general power of dismissal. The employee would be back at square one. As Shaw LJ put it in his judgment in *Gunton* (which, on this point, departed from the majority view):

> How is the [procedural] code as to dismissal for breaches of discipline to be reconciled with the express provision for the termination of the [claimant's] contract of service by one month's notice on either side? A possible solution is that the code extends or varies that express provision where the council purports to dismiss on disciplinary grounds, but that in any other circumstances the contract of service may be determined by reference to the express provision. This, however, would produce a grotesque result, for it would mean that the council could, without assigning any reason, terminate the [claimant's] employment by a month's notice, but could not, if they complained of misconduct on his part, determine that employment save by what might prove a long protracted process.[238]

232   [1980] ICR 755.
233   [1995] IRLR 50, 50 (Staughton LJ).
234   [1995] IRLR 50, 57 (Ralph Gibson LJ), 60 (Sir Francis Purchas).
235   *Soares v Beazer Investments Ltd* [2004] EWCA Civ 482, para 17 (Maurice Kay LJ).
236   See also the discussion of this point by Sedley LJ in *Cerberus Software Ltd v Rowley* [2001] IRLR 160, 164–165.
237   This analysis was suggested by the Court of Appeal in *Kaur v MG Rover Ltd* [2005] IRLR 40, para 27 (in that context, on the hypothesis that a 'no compulsory redundancy' provision in a collective agreement had been incorporated into an employee's contract of employment).
238   [1980] ICR 755, 760.

5.42　In *Gunton* the employee was dismissed for misconduct without the benefit of a hearing to which he was contractually entitled. The majority of the Court concluded that the contractual procedure was binding on the employer, and awarded the employee damages representing net salary for the period during which the procedure should have been operated, plus damages for the notice period laid down under his contract.[239] The majority appears to have assumed that the employer was under an obligation to operate the procedure, but was not bound to reach a particular result; and, moreover, that after the hearing, it could have exercised its right to dismiss the employee without needing to offer a reason, by giving the minimum period of contractual notice to terminate the contract. In that case, however, why could not the employer have given notice at the outset?

The notion of extended damages representing salary for the period of the disciplinary period was also applied, but with evident reluctance, in the later Court of Appeal judgment in *Boyo v Lambeth London Borough Council*.[240] In this case the claimant was suspended from work on full pay after he was charged with an alleged fraud against the council. Later he was prevented, as a condition of his bail, from having contact with certain of his colleagues. At that stage the council attempted to argue that the contract had been frustrated, and that Mr Boyo's employment was at an end. It was later accepted that the council's conduct amounted to a repudiation of Mr Boyo's contract, which had not been frustrated. Mr Boyo was acquitted of fraud and brought an action for his salary on the basis that his contract of employment was still in force. The trial judge held that once Mr Boyo agreed to go ahead with a contested hearing of this action, his employment was at an end, but that he was entitled to damages representing net salary for the period of his contractual notice plus five months, which was deemed a reasonable length of time for the carrying out of disciplinary proceedings against him. The Court of Appeal, regarding itself as bound by *Gunton*, upheld the order of the judge, in the process rejecting a claim for damages based on the assumption that the claimant would have stayed with the council for most of the rest of his working life – 'a claim of this magnitude offends against common sense and reason, when it is to be remembered that the whole engagement could be brought to a conclusion by one month's notice on either side'.[241]

5.43　Although the solution arrived at in *Gunton* and *Boyo* has a certain practical value – the employee is given something by way of damages to represent the loss of his or her procedural rights – it does not otherwise have much to commend it. It would have been more consistent, on the one hand, to have confined the employee to net salary for the notice period (the traditional rule), on the basis that the notice rule was effective in limiting the employee's right to continuing employment, or, on the other, to have awarded him more substantial damages for the loss of his employment, on the basis that the job security clause placed a substantive restriction on the employer's right to terminate the contract by giving notice.[242]

239　See also *Dietman v Brent London Borough Council* [1987] ICR 737, for a similar decision on the measure of damages to be awarded in such a case.
240　[1995] IRLR 50.
241　[1995] IRLR 50, 59 (Sir Francis Purchas).
242　A further possible solution is the idea of damages for loss of a chance (cf *Chaplin v Hicks* [1911] 2 KB 786) although this was rejected by the EAT in *Janciuk v Winerite Ltd* [1998] IRLR 63. For discussion see Ford, 1998a.

The first of these alternatives was, in essence, the conclusion reached by Hobhouse J in *Alexander v Standard Telephones and Cables (No 2):*[243] where the contract contains a notice clause, his Lordship considered that:

> ... it is always open to an employer, as a matter of contract, to say to his employee that after the expiry of the contractual notice period the employer will only continue the contract of employment on different terms ... The employer's right to vary the contract is effectively equivalent to his right to terminate the contract.

The second alternative, the award of extended damages on the basis that contractual job security clauses can place substantive limits on the notice rule,[244] has some authority to support it, although the impression given by the decisions of the Court of Appeal and House of Lords in *R v Lord President of the Privy Council, ex p Page*[245] was that the courts are unwilling to construe contracts of employment in such a way as to achieve this end. Mr Page was employed as a university lecturer from October 1966, under terms in his letter of appointment which provided for his employment to be terminated 'by either party on giving three months' notice in writing expiring at the end of a term or of the long vacation'. No fixed term was set for the contract's duration, but the contract incorporated a term from the University's statutes stating that the employee would retire not later than the September following his 67th birthday. The contract also incorporated from the University statutes a term whereby employees 'holding their appointments until the age of retirement may be removed by the Council for good cause', as well an extensive disciplinary procedure to be operated in a case where good cause was alleged. In 1988 Mr Page was given three months' notice of dismissal on the grounds of redundancy. He complained to the Visitor that the University was not entitled to dismiss him except for good cause. The Visitor (the Lord President) rejected his petition and proceedings for judicial review followed.

The Divisional Court found that the Visitor had made an error of law and quashed his decision. This ruling was overturned by the Court of Appeal on the merits, but in the House of Lords the Visitor succeeded in showing that his decision, even if it were based on an error of law, was outside the scope of judicial review.[246] Lords Slynn and Mustill dissented from this part of the ruling, and Lord Slynn (with whom Lord Mustill agreed) went on to find that, on the merits, no error of law had been committed. Lord Browne-Wilkinson, who gave the principal judgment of the majority, found it 'unnecessary to express any view on the proper construction of the charter and statutes beyond saying that I

243　[1991] IRLR 286, 296.

244　*Aspden v Webbs Poultry and Meat Group (Holdings) Ltd* [1996] IRLR 521 (employer's contractual power to give notice to terminate the contract should not be exercised to frustrate the employee's entitlement to benefit under the permanent health insurance scheme); *Adin v Sedco Forex International Resources Ltd* [1997] IRLR 280 (employee's contractual rights under a disability benefit scheme could not be defeated by the employer's decision to dismiss him under a notice provision in the contract). See Ford, 1998a. See also *Jenvey v Australian Broadcasting Corporation* [2002] IRLR 520; *Briscoe v Lubrizol Ltd* [2002] IRLR 607; and *Kaur v MG Rover Ltd* [2005] IRLR 40, para 27 (*obiter*).

245　[1993] ICR 114, HL, in the Court of Appeal *sub nom R v Hull University Visitor, ex p Page* [1992] ICR 67.

246　A fuller consideration of this question lies outside the scope of this book. See H Wade, 1993.

have heard nothing which persuades me that the views of [the Visitor] and the Court of Appeal were wrong'.[247]

The views on the merits of the majority were *obiter* since they were unnecessary for the decision in *Page*, which was that judicial review would not lie against the Visitor; nor is the minority view of Lords Slynn and Mustill strictly binding on lower courts. However, these statements are evidently an important indication of judicial thinking in this area. According to Lord Slynn, the provision in Mr Page's contract for compulsory retirement at the age of 67 did not mean that he was entitled to stay in post until he reached that age:

> ... whether members of staff can so continue depends on the other terms and conditions of the employment. Those terms in this case include provision for termination for good cause ... and on three months' notice as one of the terms of the appointment ... This result could have been spelled out more clearly in the statutes but it seems to me to follow from the provisions of the statutes as they stand and, contrary to the argument of Mr Page, no more curious than the alternative for which he contends.[248]

The judgments on the merits of the Court of Appeal were not *obiter*, and can be seen as direct authority for the view that the notice rule will prevail unless it is explicitly limited by the contract itself, notwithstanding the presence of a procedural clause dealing with the case of good-cause dismissal. However, their weight is somewhat weakened by their failure to mention *Gunton* or, apparently, to appreciate the significance of that case for the issue of construction addressed in *Page*. Moreover, in *Kaur v MG Rover Ltd* the Court of Appeal has recently expressed the view that *Page* did not establish a general principle of law to the effect that notice clauses are to prevail over other express terms concerned with termination; rather '[i]t will in all cases be a matter of construing the individual contract of employment'.[249]

In *Page* the courts were faced with a situation which was also essentially the situation which arose in *Gunton* and *Boyo*, namely that of a contract of employment containing two clauses, one dealing with a power to dismiss with notice and the other with dismissal via a complex disciplinary procedure, whose legal effects were apparently irreconcilable. The outcome arrived at by the courts in *Page*, while apparently containing 'nothing improbable',[250] nevertheless suffers from the major weakness that it deprives the procedure clause of virtually all legal force.[251] At no point in the judgments in *Page* did the courts explain why the procedure clause, as opposed to the notice clause, should be the one to be denied legal force in this way. One possible construction which would have reconciled the two would have been to regard the procedure clause as limiting the employer's general power to dismiss, and the notice clause as applying in the event of good cause being established; in other words, the employee could only be dismissed for good cause, as defined by the statutes, *and* with the minimum notice required by Mr Page's conditions of appointment. But this construction was explicitly rejected by the Court of Appeal and by Lord Slynn.

---

247 [1993] ICR 114, 129.
248 [1993] ICR 114, 137.
249 [2004] EWCA Civ 1507, [2005] IRLR 40, para 26 (*obiter*).
250 [1992] ICR 67, 81 (Staughton LJ).
251 *Quaere*, however, whether it could be argued that it would be an abuse of power under public law for the University to rely upon the notice clause in circumstances falling within the definition of 'good cause'. See also Ford, 1998a.

Despite more recent indications that the courts may be prepared to constrain an employer's reliance on a notice clause in specific circumstances,[252] the point has yet to be established by higher appellate authority in England.[253]

(iii) The role of the implied duty of mutual trust and confidence

5.44 Many of the same issues of conflicts between notice clauses and other terms of the contract of employment arise in the context of discussion of the effect upon termination of the implied duty of mutual trust and confidence. As we have seen, the centrality of the term to the modern analysis of the contract of employment was affirmed by the House of Lords in *Malik v BCCI SA*.[254] In *Johnson v Unisys Ltd*,[255] however, the House of Lords concluded that the implied term could not have the effect of restricting the employer's common law power to end the contract without the need to show good cause. The judgments in *Malik* confirmed that the implied duty operates as a default term, which can be ousted by a clear, express term to the contrary.[256] However, this was not the central issue on which the decision in *Johnson* turned. Lord Hoffmann, while noting that, in the light of the express term governing dismissal with notice (or by way of a payment of wages in lieu of notice), it was 'very difficult to imply a term that the company should not do so except for some good cause and after giving [Mr Johnson] a reasonable opportunity to demonstrate that no such cause existed',[257] was nevertheless prepared to accept the existence within the contract of 'a separate term that the power of dismissal will be exercised fairly and in good faith'.[258] Such a term, he felt, would not have contradicted the express term that the employer had the power to dismiss without cause. Lord Millett, likewise, was prepared to countenance a common law term imposing upon the employer a 'general obligation ... to treat his employee fairly even in the manner of his dismissal'.[259]

What, instead, proved decisive in turning the outcome in *Johnson* against the application of the implied term was concern that to develop the common law in this way would frustrate the intention of Parliament in enacting unfair dismissal legislation. As Lord Hoffmann put it, '[f]or the judiciary to construct a general common law remedy for unfair circumstances attending dismissal would be to go contrary to the evident intention of Parliament that there should be such a remedy but that it should be limited in application and extent'.[260] The statutory limits to which Lord Hoffmann referred here include the necessity for a minimum qualifying period of service prior to dismissal and the upper limit on

252 See the cases referred to in note 244 above.
253 *Adin v Sedko Forex International Resources Ltd* [1997] IRLR 280 was a decision of the Court of Session; in *Briscoe v Lubrizol Ltd* [2002] EWCA Civ 508, [2002] IRLR 607 it was not disputed that the employer would not terminate employment save for a cause other than ill health as a means of removing an employee's entitlement to benefit under a long-term disability scheme (see para 21).
254 [1997] IRLR 462.
255 [2001] IRLR 279; see paras 5.27 and 5.35 above for other aspects of the case. See H Collins, 2001c; Brodie 2001b; Freedland, 2003: pp 162–167, 303–305, 342–345; Barmes, 2004.
256 See generally para 4.91 *et seq* above, and see also *Reda v Flag Ltd* [2002] IRLR 747, para 45.
257 [2001] IRLR 279, para 42.
258 [2001] IRLR 279, para 46.
259 [2001] IRLR 279, para 79. See also Lord Nicholls, [2001] IRLR 279, para 2, and the judgment of McLachlin J in *Wallace v United Grain Growers Ltd* (1997) 152 DLR (4th) 1, discussed by Lord Hoffmann in *Johnson*.
260 *Johnson*, above, para 58.

compensation for unfair dismissal.[261] Lord Millett adverted to the possibility of overlapping systems of statutory and common law jurisdiction as a 'recipe for chaos'.[262] More specifically, it was suggested that Parliament adopted the unfair dismissal legislation on the assumption that the House of Lords decision in *Addis v Gramophone Co Ltd*,[263] apparently limiting a claim for damages for wrongful dismissal to net wages for the notice period, was correctly decided.[264]

5.45 The argument that Parliament had intended to exclude the development of the common law by creating a statutory remedy for unfair dismissal was a highly contentious one; the absence of any reference to the common law in the legislation may have occurred because Parliament was content to let the courts develop it in the usual way.[265] Indeed, it would be open to the courts to reason by analogy that a requirement for employers to follow a fair procedure is not regarded by Parliament as unduly onerous.[266] Moreover the majority's reasoning created the anomalous position that, although the courts had accepted that lesser powers, including the power to suspend an employee,[267] must be exercised with due regard to trust and confidence, the 'more drastic power of dismissal was free from any equivalent constraint'.[268] In *Eastwood v Magnox Electric plc, McCabe v Cornwall County Council*,[269] however, the majority of the House of Lords reaffirmed the '*Johnson* exclusion area', whereby claims for loss resulting from dismissal fell within that area whereas a cause of action acquired prior to dismissal, which by definition existed independently of the dismissal, did not.[270] Their Lordships recognised that this 'boundary line' produced 'strange results', such as rendering it potentially cheaper for an employer to dismiss an employee than to suspend him or her.[271] They also acknowledged that the boundary line could be difficult to apply, particularly in cases concerning financial loss flowing from psychiatric illnesses. In some cases a continuing course of conduct, typically a disciplinary process followed by dismissal, 'may have to be chopped artificially into separate pieces',[272] and the division of remedial jurisdiction between courts and tribunals would lead to a duplication of proceedings. Moreover,

---

261 See generally paras 5.63 and 5.155 below.
262 *Johnson* [2001] IRLR 279, para 80; see also Lord Nicholls, at para 2.
263 See paras 5.26–5.27 above.
264 Cf the dissenting opinion of Lord Steyn on this point, who argued that '[I]t cannot be said that the unfair dismissal legislation would be unworkable if the House departs from *Addis's* case' (*Johnson* above, note 194, para 22) and suggested that '[I]f Parliament is deemed to have been aware of the *Addis* decision, one must also deem Parliament to have been aware that the system it was creating was only capable of dealing effectively and justly with less serious cases where the threshold of a breach of contract was not necessarily established' (para 23).
265 H Collins, 2001c: p 306. See also Freedland, 2003: p 304: 'As an account of the intention of Parliament ... that was more than slightly artificial. It was really an assertion of their Lordships' '*own underlying view* that the law concerning the termination of personal work or employment contracts now had two distinct context-specific aspects ... and that developments in one sphere should not necessarily be replicated in the other sphere.'
266 Cf J Beatson, 1997: 310.
267 *Gogay v Hertfordshire County Council* [2000] IRLR 703. See also *King v University Court of the University of St Andrews* [2002] IRLR 252, discussed by Brodie, 2002.
268 Hepple and Morris, 2002: p 254.
269 [2004] IRLR 733. See Barratt, 2004; Brodie, 2004.
270 [2004] IRLR 733, para 27 (Lord Nicholls, with whom Lords Hoffman, Rodger and Brown agreed).
271 [2004] IRLR 733, para 32.
272 [2004] IRLR 733, paras 30 and 31.

In cases of constructive dismissal a distinction will have to be drawn between loss flowing from antecedent breaches of the trust and confidence term and loss flowing from the employee's acceptance of these breaches as a repudiation of the contract.[273] The loss flowing from the impugned conduct taking place before actual or constructive dismissal lies outside the *Johnson* exclusion area, the loss flowing from the dismissal itself is within that area. In some cases this legalistic distinction may give rise to difficult questions of causation in cases such as those now before the House, where financial loss is claimed as the consequence of psychiatric illness said to have been brought on by the employer's conduct before the employee was dismissed.[274] Judges and tribunals, faced perhaps with conflicting medical evidence, may have to decide whether the fact of dismissal was really the last straw which proved too much for the employee, or whether the onset of the illness occurred even before he was dismissed.[275]

The majority did not, however, conclude that 'an inter-relation between the common law and statute having these awkward and unfortunate consequences' should lead to *Johnson* being reconsidered;[276] rather, it attributed the difficulties to the statutory cap on the compensatory award for unfair dismissal, which precluded tribunals from awarding full compensation for a dismissed employee's financial loss, so leading employees to attempt to construct a claim at common law. This situation 'merit[ed] urgent attention by the government and the legislature'.[277]

The majority in *Eastwood* reiterated the argument in *Johnson* that Parliament had 'occupied the field' relating to unfair dismissal and that it would be wrong for the courts 'to expand a common law principle into the same field and produce an inconsistent outcome'.[278] As we noted at the beginning of this paragraph, however, this is not the only sustainable analysis of the position. Moreover this argument, would, if more generally applied, have already prevented the application of the implied term of mutual trust and confidence to many other aspects of the employment relationship.[279] It may be argued that just as employment legislation normally acts as a 'floor of rights' in relation to the contract of employment, implicitly encouraging the parties to improve on the

---

273 See para 5.72 *et seq* below. There was room for doubt as to whether *Johnson* applied to constructive dismissal: see Freedland, 2001. *Eastwood* assumes that it does. This means that an employee who affirms the contract and continues working may be in a better position than one who purports to accept the repudiation: see Barmes, 2004. Moreover, '[t]he more outrageous the breach the less likely it is that the employee can affirm the contract': *Eastwood*, above, para 40 (Lord Steyn).

274 In *Eastwood* the claimants alleged that they had suffered psychiatric illnesses caused by a deliberate course of conduct by certain individuals using the machinery of the disciplinary process; in *McCabe* the claimant alleged that he had sustained psychiatric illness as a result of his suspension and the employer's failure properly to investigate allegations against him or to inform him of those allegations.

275 *Eastwood*, above note 269, para 31 (Lord Nicholls).

276 [2004] IRLR 733, para 33. Cf Lord Steyn, who acknowledged that oral argument had not been heard from counsel on the correctness of *Johnson* but sought to provide 'some focus for a future re-examination of the position' (para 36) in the light, *inter alia*, of critical academic commentary of the majority opinions.

277 [2004] IRLR 733, para 33.

278 *Eastwood*, above note 269, para 14 (Lord Nicholls).

279 Thus there has been extensive statutory intervention in the areas of health and safety at work, grievance procedures, and the exercise of employer discretion in relation to occupational pension schemes, all of which have been the subject of judicial innovation in respect of the duty of mutual trust and confidence and which were accepted as legitimate in both *Malik* and *Johnson*. See generally para 4.91 *et seq* above.

basic standards supplied by statute, so the courts should be willing, in appropriate cases, to use the enactment of protective legislation as a basis for extending, rather than limiting, recognition of the legitimate common law interests of the employee.[280]

(iv) Contractual job security: the way ahead?

5.46   Many of the fears expressed at the possible extension of the wrongful dismissal action to include financial losses going above and beyond net wages for the notice period are arguably misplaced. There seems no reason in principle why substantial, extended damages for lost earnings capacity should not be awarded in a case where a job security clause can be shown to be effective in limiting the notice rule. This has been done not simply in a number of US and Australian cases,[281] but also, in a slightly different British context, in cases involving dismissals in breach of discrimination law.[282] The result need not and should not involve the employee receiving salary for the rest of his or her working life. As explained above, a debt claim is ruled out here; the claim can only be in damages, and while these can extend to a period going beyond both the notice period and the period envisaged for any procedure, the relevant period would not be that from dismissal to retirement: the relevant period would be the expected time out of employment, which would have to be calculated in such a way as to take into account the possibility of the employee finding alternative work. The court would also reduce the period in respect of which damages were payable by the chance that the employee's working life would be shortened by injury or illness, as is routinely done in cases involving compensation for work-related injuries.[283] If it still remains to be seen precisely how the general principles of the law of damages could be adapted to the extended action for wrongful dismissal, there seems to be less doubt that they *could* be effectively applied in some way or other, if the law in this area were to continue to evolve in the direction of stronger employment protection.

As we have just seen, the main obstacle to the further development of the common law in this area is the concern that the unfair dismissal jurisdiction would thereby be undermined. However, as Lord Steyn opined in *Eastwood*, if the statutory cap on unfair dismissal awards 'is allowed to constrain the development of the common law it may come at too high a price in the failure of corrective justice'.[284] The coherence of employment law in this area is also greatly diminished by the failure in *Johnson*, as confirmed in *Eastwood*, to apply the implied term of mutual trust and confidence to issues of termination, when its application to most other aspects of the employment

---

280 This is arguably what happened prior to *Johnson*; the enactment of unfair dismissal legislation in the early 1970s was a catalyst for the development of the implied term of trust and confidence, so making the protection offered by that legislation more effective. See Hepple, 1981: pp 134–135; Deakin, 1997; Brodie, 2001; and Lord Steyn in *Johnson* [2001] UKHL 13, [2001] IRLR 279, paras 18 and 21. For a wider discussion see the third of Professor Sir Bob Hepple's 2004 Hamlyn Lectures (Hepple, 2005a).

281 See para 5.12 above; Pitt, 1989; Ewing, 1989, 1993, discussing *Gregory v Philip Morris Ltd* (1988) 80 ALR 455; although cf *Byrne and Frew v Australian Airlines Ltd* (1995) 131 ALR 422 (High Court of Australia), discussed John McMullen, 1996.

282 See para 6.67 below.

283 See Deakin, Johnston and Markesinis, 2003: pp 820–826.

284 *Eastwood v Magnox Electric plc, McCabe v Cornwall County Council* [2004] IRLR 733, para 51.

relationship (including the disciplinary process prior to, and short of, dismissal)[285] has been generally accepted.[286]

Specific remedies in public law

5.47   The most effective remedy for an employee who seeks to resist dismissal is an order of the court which prevents the dismissal taking effect. Public employees may be able to bring proceedings for judicial review against their employer, challenging the decision on the grounds of illegality, '*Wednesbury* unreasonableness' or procedural impropriety.[287] If successful this can lead to the decision being quashed.[288] In the case of dismissal it is thus akin to the statutory remedy of reinstatement following unfair dismissal, with the difference that the dismissal is deemed never to have taken place. Moreover, it does not depend upon the applicant having met the general requirements of a minimum period of continuous employment or, indeed, being an 'employee'. Judicial review may also afford a remedy in cases of disciplinary action short of dismissal which in private law could, until recently, only be remedied by an action for damages for breach of contract, for which quantifiable loss would have to be shown.[289] This is now subject to the possibility, analysed below,[290] that a court may grant an injunction or declaration in equity to prevent dismissal or disciplinary action by the employer in breach of contract; but this private law remedy is by no means generally available and, as we have seen, it suffers from the difficulty that the legal status of contractual job security clauses is not altogether clear. Alternatively, an employee who is subject to disciplinary action which breaches the contract may seek to show that this amounts to constructive dismissal, and then bring a statutory claim for unfair dismissal; but, once again, this requires the necessary conditions to be met. Judicial review has other potential advantages over private law routes to employee protection. In particular, judicial review may be used to overturn a decision relating to a group of employees; although an action in private law may, in practice, be treated as a 'test case', in strict terms it only binds the parties to the particular action.[291]

---

285   This was expressly recognised in *Eastwood*: see above, paras 15 and 32 (Lord Nicholls).
286   See paras 4.4 *et seq* and 4.91 *et seq* above.
287   This is the classification adopted by Lord Diplock in *Council of Civil Service Unions v Minister for the Civil Service* [1985] AC 374. It continues to survive, although *Wednesbury* unreasonableness has become a concept of 'variable intensity' depending on the context: see Le Sueur, 2005
288   This is done by way of the public law remedy of a quashing order (formerly known as *certiorari*). An order to require the employer to perform a duty may also be sought by means of the remedy of a mandatory order (formerly known as *mandamus*). For a detailed account of the remedies available in public law see H Wade and C Forsyth, 2004: Part VII; C Lewis, 2004; de Smith, Woolf and Jowell, 1995 and supplement, Part IV.
289   However, see the limitation in *R (on the application of Tucker) v Director General of the National Crime Squad* [2003] IRLR 439, discussed in para 5.50 below.
290   See para 5.54 *et seq.*
291   See, for example, *R v Liverpool City Council, ex p Ferguson* (1985) Times, 20 November (noted by G Morris, 1986), where the court found that dismissal notices issued by the council to its employees terminating their employment from a specified date on the ground that the Council would thereafter be unable to pay their wages, and offering them re-employment one month later, were *ultra vires* and void because the decision to dismiss arose out of the setting of an illegal rate, and a consequent failure by the Council to balance its budget. Here, a remedy was granted even though there was no breach of contract on the part of the employer.

(i) When is judicial review available?

5.48 For all the reasons indicated above judicial review has proved a popular route for public employees who have been subject to dismissal or to other disciplinary action short of dismissal.[292] However, it is not available as of right to public employees, merely because their employer is a public body; rather, it requires showing that the claim falls on the 'public side' of the procedural divide erected between public and private law.[293]

In deciding whether judicial review should be available in the employment context, the courts have formulated a series of (sometimes conflicting) tests. In broad terms these relate to the existence of a contract between the parties; the subject-matter of the claim; and the availability of alternative remedies. We consider here the application of each of these criteria as they relate specifically to dismissal and other disciplinary action.[294]

5.49 The use of contract as a line of demarcation stems from the decision of the Court of Appeal in *R v East Berkshire Area Health Authority, ex p Walsh*.[295] Mr Walsh, a senior nursing officer in the National Health Service, was dismissed for misconduct. He sought to have the decision quashed by way of proceedings for judicial review, on the grounds that the decision had been taken in breach of natural justice and contrary to the disciplinary procedure which formed part of his conditions of service under the relevant Whitley Council collective agreement. The Court of Appeal, overruling Hodgson J, held that an application for judicial review was inappropriate, since the issue raised by the applicant was one of 'private law' only. Sir John Donaldson MR affirmed that 'employment by a public authority does not *per se* inject any element of public law. Nor does the fact that the employee is in a "higher grade" or is an "officer"'.[296] The applicant's employment was founded on a contract of employment, and was no less contractual simply because the terms of the Whitley Council collective agreement were incorporated into it by a statutory instrument.[297] Similarly, Purchas LJ held that:

> ... the rules of natural justice may well be imported into a private contractual relationship ... but in such circumstances they would go solely to the question of rights and duties involved in the performance of the contract of employment itself. The manner in which the authority terminated, or purported to terminate, the applicant's contract of employment related to their conduct as employers in a pure master and servant context and not the performance of their duties, or exercise of their powers as an authority providing a health service for the public at large.[298]

On the basis of *Walsh* the only circumstances in which an individual could invoke judicial review to challenge a decision of his or her employer would be where the employment relationship is not expressed in contractual terms (as in the case of the police) or where, despite the existence of a contract, the

---

292 See para 5.72 *et seq* below, on constructive dismissal.
293 *O'Reilly v Mackman* [1983] 2 AC 237; see para 2.5 above.
294 For a general critique of these tests, see Fredman and Morris, 1991a, 1994; see also T Poole, 2000.
295 [1984] ICR 743.
296 [1984] ICR 743, 751.
297 SI 1974/296; see [1984] ICR 743, 752.
298 [1984] ICR 743, 768.

matter in dispute does not concern the exercise of contractual rights. On the latter point it was accepted in *Walsh* that had the relevant terms of the Whitley Council collective agreement not been incorporated into the applicant's contract of employment as required by statute, that would have provided a basis for judicial review to order the employer to comply with its duty to include it.[299] As an illustration of the former category of cases, in *R v Secretary of State for the Home Department, ex p Benwell*[300] Hodgson J was able to allow an application for judicial review to proceed in a case concerning disciplinary action against a prison officer, notwithstanding *Walsh*. The critical factors here were the absence of a contractual nexus between the parties[301] and the fact that the power of the employer to take disciplinary action had a specific statutory source. Also material was the fact that, at this stage, prison officers were excluded from the scope of unfair dismissal legislation (they are now included).[302]

5.50 In *Benwell* the court was clearly influenced by the fact that to have denied the applicant access to judicial review would have left him without any legal means of redress.[303] The converse view has also been applied; the courts have consistently regarded the possibility of a remedy in private law as a justification for denying judicial review. Thus in *Walsh*[304] May LJ thought that in 'the great majority of cases involving disputes about the dismissal of an employee by his employer, the most appropriate forum for their resolution is an [employment] tribunal', and in *R v Civil Service Appeal Board, ex p Bruce*[305] the Court of Appeal rejected a civil servant's application for judicial review of the board's decision largely on these grounds. Since then, civil servants have lost further ground as a result of the Divisional Court's decision in *R v Civil Service Appeal Board, ex p Nangle*,[306] to the effect that their relationship with the Crown is based on contract and not on a distinctive public law status.[307] Since *Benwell* the status of prison officers has been altered by legislation in such a way as to bring them within the scope of ERA 1996.[308] This could mean that the courts will henceforth exercise their discretion to exclude them from judicial review in relation to dismissal on the ground that an alternative remedy exists. However, in their case it is possible that statutory underpinning in the

---

299 [1984] ICR 743, 752 (Sir John Donaldson MR).
300 [1985] IRLR 6; cf *McClaren v Home Office* [1990] IRLR 338, in which a prison officer's action which had been begun by writ was allowed by the Court of Appeal to proceed. See Fredman and Morris, 1991b: p 307.
301 This decision preceded *R v Lord Chancellor's Department, ex p Nangle* [1991] IRLR 343.
302 See para 3.78 above.
303 Although Dillon LJ in *R v Derbyshire County Council, ex p Noble* [1990] IRLR 332, 337 refused to regard the non-availability of an alternative remedy as a reason for granting judicial review; see also Stuart-Smith LJ in *Nangle* [1991] IRLR 343, 348.
304 [1984] ICR 743, 757.
305 [1989] ICR 171. For an example of circumstances where judicial review was permitted despite the availability of an alternative, internal remedy, see *R v Chief Constable of the Merseyside Police, ex p Calveley* [1986] 1 All ER 257.
306 [1991] IRLR 343; see para 3.74 above.
307 Fredman and Morris, 1991b. Note that some aspects of civil servants' employment remain susceptible to review, however: see, for example, *Council of Civil Service Unions v Minister for the Civil Service* [1985] AC 374; *R v Civil Service Appeal Board, ex p Cunningham* [1991] IRLR 297 (although note also *R v Secretary of State for the Home Department, ex p Moore* [1994] COD 67).
308 See para 3.78 above.

form of the Code of Discipline governing the service[309] may, for reasons we consider below, persuade the courts to continue to allow judicial review to lie.

The idea that by comparison with judicial review an unfair dismissal claim is adequate protection for the employee is, to say the least, debatable, since the statutory jurisdiction contains no mechanism for nullifying an abuse of power by the employer, as opposed to granting the employee redress after the event, and re-instatement is rarely granted.[310] Nor, in relation to the protection of contractual rights, is an equivalent remedy commonly granted. From a wider perspective, to deny judicial review on the grounds of the availability of an alternative remedy for the individual is to ignore the fact that the remedy of judicial review is concerned with the exercise of public power, scrutiny of which should not be obstructed by a co-existent remedy concerned only with private rights. The two jurisdictions could more usefully be seen as complementary and not as alternatives. As matters stand, only members of a public sector group which has no possibility of an action in private law for individual claims arising out of disciplinary action, most notably the police,[311] could feel moderately confident of a potential remedy in judicial review. Even then, however, a claimant may now have to surmount a recently-created additional obstacle that asks not only whether the function performed by the public body is public or private in nature but further whether 'the defendant was performing a public duty owed to the claimant in the particular circumstances under consideration'.[312] On this basis the Court of Appeal concluded that the decision to send a detective inspector of police seconded to the National Crime Squad back to his local force because of perceived deficiencies in his skills and conduct was a 'decision tailor-made' to him and of an 'operational nature' and for these reasons did not involve the performance of a public duty,[313] even though it is likely to have had repercussions for his reputation and career prospects.[314]

5.51 The *Walsh* principle had the potential to exclude large areas of public employment from the purview of judicial review, regardless of the context, scope, and nature of the employer's conduct. In the event the courts shied away from a consistently rigorous application of *Walsh* by indicating that the availability of judicial review may also be influenced by the subject-matter of the claim. The emphasis on subject-matter was developed by Lord Woolf in a

---

309 The Code is made under the Prison Rules (SI 1999/728), which are made under the Prison Act 1952, s 47.

310 See para 5.152 below. See also *R (on the application of Dunbar) v Hampshire Fire and Rescue Service* [2003] EHWC 431 (Admin), [2004] ACD 148.

311 The capacity to seek judicial review seems to be well established for officers of all ranks, including probationary officers. See *Chief Constable of the North Wales Police v Evans* [1982] 1 WLR 1155; and on the nature of the employment relationship in the context of the police, see para 3.77 above.

312 *R (on the application of Tucker) v Director General of the National Crime Squad* [2003] IRLR 439, para 24 (Scott Baker LJ).

313 [2003] IRLR 439, para 25. The line between the operation of formal disciplinary proceedings, which the court acknowledged remained amenable to review, and 'operational and management decisions, where the police are entitled to run their own affairs without the interference of the courts' (para 35) may not be as clear cut as this judgment suggests.

314 See also *R (On the Application of Morgan) v Chief Constable of South Wales* [2001] EWHC Admin 262, para 19, where Scott Baker LJ opined that the courts should only in the most exceptional circumstances, if ever, interfere with a decision to remove the claimant from a pool awaiting promotion due to an operational incident that resulted in admonishment.

series of judgments and extra-judicial writings.[315] Lord Woolf has taken as his starting point the proposition that the employment relationship is an essentially private one, enforceable by ordinary action and not appropriate for judicial review.[316] This demarcation is based upon the fact that it is the 'public as a whole ... who are the beneficiaries of what is protected by public law and it is the individuals or the bodies entitled to the rights who are the beneficiaries of the protection provided by private law'.[317] However, he has also accepted that there may be situations in which judicial review may be appropriate. The first is where the employee 'contends that he is adversely affected by a decision of general application by his employer' which is argued to be flawed on the grounds of *Wednesbury* unreasonableness.[318] In *R v Derbyshire County Council, ex p Noble*[319] this question was reduced to a numerical measure – if the decision affected only one individual it was a private law issue, whereas if it affected many it could become one of public law. Lord Woolf viewed the availability of a remedy in the case of the ban on membership of national civil service trade unions at GCHQ as an example of this exception.[320] This is a welcome recognition of the public dimension to employers' decisions in this context; however, it is difficult to see why a decision affecting a single individual, rather than a group, is, from this point of view, any less worthy of supervision by the courts.

Another situation in which judicial review may lie on the basis of the subject-matter of a dispute concerns the exercise of a statutory discretion in such a way as to interfere with an individual's exercise of his or her trade or livelihood. In *R v Broxtowe Borough Council, ex p Bradford*,[321] the Court of Appeal granted judicial review of the Council's decision to exclude the applicant from coaching young children on its tennis courts on the grounds that allegations of child abuse had been made against him in respect of previous employments, without giving him the right to respond to these allegations. According to Lord Woolf, the council 'have a responsibility not to use their position as a local authority to interfere with an individual's right to earn his living without proper cause and without extending to the individual concerned the basic requirements of fairness'.[322] This was not a case in which the council was the applicant's employer; rather, he was applying for employment with the council, and the effect of its decision would also be to restrict his existing employment with a tennis club which used the council's courts. Thus it is not clear how far this decision can be read as providing protection to employees. However, it is arguable that the principle enunciated by Lord Woolf in this case could equally well apply to decisions taken by statutory authorities with regard to their employees, as it did to the applicant in this case.

The second major situation where Lord Woolf has taken the view that judicial review may be appropriate is 'where there exists some disciplinary or other body established under the prerogative or by statute [which has] a sufficient

---

315 Lord Woolf has more recently acknowledged that his attempts to find 'indicators that would penetrate the gloom' in clarifying a distinction between public and private in the realm of public employment have not been wholly successful: Woolf, 1995: p 64.
316 Woolf, 1986: p 223; and see also Woolf J in *R v BBC, ex p Lavelle* [1983] ICR 99.
317 Woolf, 1986: p 222.
318 *McClaren v Home Office* [1990] IRLR 338, 342. See *R v Sunderland City Council, ex p Baumber* [1996] COD 211.
319 [1990] IRLR 332.
320 *Council of Civil Service Unions v Minister for the Civil Service* [1985] AC 374.
321 [2000] IRLR 329.
322 [2000] IRLR 329, 330.

public law element, which it almost invariably will have if the employer is the Crown, and it is not domestic or wholly informal'.[323] The public law element arises from a statutory or similar underpinning which must relate to the procedure for dismissal.[324] This is one of the bases on which *Benwell* was decided, and it may mean that the courts continue to grant judicial review to prison officers despite their now having access to unfair dismissal protection. It has also been invoked to explain pre-*O'Reilly v Mackman* decisions such as those in *Ridge v Baldwin*[325] and *Malloch v Aberdeen Corpn*,[326] to which we refer below. But even in this category of case, it may be that other factors weigh against judicial review in a purely individual case, as the decisions of the Court of Appeal in *Bruce* and *Nangle* demonstrate.

5.52   The circumstances in which the courts will grant employees access to judicial review remain unpredictable,[327] and the courts have recently shown a willingness to construct new obstacles to such access.[328] Whether the procedural divide between public law and private law should be maintained is a larger issue upon which opinions sharply differ.[329] In the area of public employment one of the most undesirable consequences of its existence has been the opportunistic litigation which it has encouraged. Employees and their advisers have been unable to predict with confidence whether a particular dispute should be litigated under the 'public' CPR Part 54 (formerly RSC Order 53) procedure or by way of an action begun in private law, while employers have not lost the chance to argue that judicial review was inappropriate and that, whichever forum was chosen, it was the wrong one. Thus in *Benwell* the Home Department attempted to argue that judicial review was inappropriate and that the application should have been begun by writ, only to argue the opposite in *McClaren v Home Office* even though that case also concerned the employment of a prison officer. More fundamentally, the dividing line formulated in *Walsh* is based on the assumption that the private can easily be disentangled from the public. However, as has been argued elsewhere, the distinctive nature of public employment, in which public and private realms are closely interconnected, would be more effectively recognised if both dimensions could be considered in the same forum simultaneously.[330] Such a course, as well as allowing appropriate supervision of the exercise of public powers, would also minimise the risk of costly preliminary litigation designed to establish jurisdictional boundaries.[331]

---

323 [1990] IRLR 338, 342.
324 *R v Derbyshire County Council, ex p Noble* [1990] IRLR 332.
325 [1964] AC 40.
326 [1971] 1 WLR 1578.
327 In *R v CPS, ex p Hogg* [1994] 6 Admin LR 778 the Court of Appeal suggested that if a case arose where the independence of a Crown Prosecutor was at stake, the necessary public law element for judicial review might be present. It is also possible to argue that an infringement of an individual's 'Convention right' under HRA 1998 may afford the requisite 'public element': see G Morris, 1998c: pp 299–303.
328 *R (on the application of Tucker) v Director General of the National Crime Squad* [2003] IRLR 439, discussed in para 5.50 above.
329 In 1994 the Law Commission recommended maintaining it, although with greater flexibility for cases to transfer between the public law route and the claim form procedure: *Administrative Law: Judicial Review and Statutory Appeals*, Law Com No 226, HC 669, 1994, Part III.
330 Fredman and Morris, 1991a: p 305; see also Sedley, 1994.
331 Fredman and Morris, 1991a: pp 314–315.

(ii) Public law standards in private law claims

5.53   A further method of dealing with the dual dimension, which also has much wider implications, is to introduce public law standards into the employment relationship as implied terms in the contract of employment. In *Ridge v Baldwin*,[332] an action begun by writ, the House of Lords indicated that there could be an implied right to a hearing in special cases, such as those of 'office holders', although not in relation to the 'pure master and servant relationship' or in the case of those employed 'at the pleasure' of their employer and hence subject to an open-ended power of dismissal by the giving of notice. A classic office-holder was an individual, such as the Chief Constable in *Ridge*, who not only held a high-status position but who also had the express protection of certain procedural guarantees in the event of being subjected to suspension or exclusion from the office in question.

In *Malloch v Aberdeen Corpn*[333] this notion was extended to cover a school-teacher who, under the relevant Scottish legislation, was stated to 'hold office' under statutorily-constituted local school boards and to be dismissible only after 'due deliberation', in particular after three weeks' notice had been given of any motion for dismissal. The intervention of the court rested, here, partly upon the public nature of the employment and partly upon the existence of statutory rules underpinning both the employment in general and the power to dismiss in particular. According to Lord Reid:

> An elected public body [such as the school board] is in a very different position from a private employer. Many of its servants in the lower grades are in the same position as servants of a private employer. But many in the higher grades or 'offices' are given special statutory status or protection. The right of a man to be heard in his own defence is the most elementary protection of all and, where a statutory form of protection would be less effective if it did not carry with it a right to be heard, I would not find it difficult to imply this right.[334]

Similarly, Lord Wilberforce defined the scope of the principle in these terms:

> One may accept that if there are relationships in which all requirements of the observance of rules of natural justice are excluded (and I do not wish to assume that this is inevitably so), these must be confined to what have been called 'pure master and servant cases', which I take to mean cases in which there is no element of public employment or service, no support by statute, nothing in the nature of an office or a status which is capable of protection. If any of these elements exist then, in my opinion, whatever the terminology used, and even though in some inter partes aspects the relationship may be called that of master and servant, there may be essential procedural requirements to be observed, and failure to observe them may result in dismissal being declared to be void.[335]

The principle was extended still further in *Stevenson v United Road Transport Union*,[336] a decision concerning a trade union official who, as an employee of the union, was neither in public employment nor in an office underpinned by statutory rules. The Court of Appeal nevertheless granted the employee a declaration to the effect that a decision to dismiss him made by the union's

---

332 [1964] AC 40, 65.
333 [1971] 1 WLR 1578.
334 [1971] 1 WLR 1578, 1586.
335 [1971] 1 WLR 1578, 1595–1596.
336 [1971] 1 WLR 1578, 1595–1596.

executive committee was void on the grounds of *ultra vires* and Buckley LJ formulated the following broad test:

> Where one party has a discretionary power to terminate the tenure or enjoyment by another of an employment ..., is that power conditional upon the party invested with the power being first satisfied upon a particular point which involves investigating some matter upon which the other party ought in fairness to be heard or to be allowed to give his explanation or put his case? If the answer to the question is 'Yes', then unless, before the power purports to have been exercised, the condition has been satisfied after the other party has been given a fair opportunity of being heard or of giving his explanation or putting his case, the power will not have been well exercised.[337]

If the notion of office-holder is defined so widely as to cover any employee who has a legal right to protection against arbitrary dismissal, then it could be argued that it should extend at least to all employees with the benefit of a contractual disciplinary procedure, and possibly even further to all those qualifying for statutory unfair dismissal protection.[338] Indeed, it has been suggested that the time has come to consider the implication of public law doctrines of procedural fairness, at the very least, into all contracts of employment.[339] At present, however, the law is some way off recognising the existence of such a generally-applicable implied term, and, indeed, the House of Lords decision in *Johnson v Unisys Ltd*[340] constitutes a formidable obstacle to a development of this nature in the context of dismissal.

Specific remedies and contractual rights

5.54   The failure of public law to develop a fully-fledged system of employment protection has proved to be less significant than it might have seemed, thanks to 'breathtaking developments' in the remedies available under the common law of contract: 'in appropriate cases injunctive relief may be available to restrain not only an attempt by an employer unilaterally to vary the contract, but also dismissal of an employee in breach of its terms'.[341] The basis for the court's intervention here is its equitable jurisdiction to grant injunctions or declarations in support of the parties' private rights, in this case their rights under the contract of employment. Only a short time ago, it seemed unlikely that specific relief would be available in these situations, thanks to the rule against specific performance of contracts of employment. This long-standing rule is based on a number of considerations: the assumed adequacy of damages in most cases; the difficulty facing the court in supervising the performance of either party;[342] the potential oppression of either party, but in particular the employee, in being required to maintain a contract involving the supply of personal services;[343] and

---

337   [1977] ICR 893, 902.

338   This extension of the notion of office-holder was considered by Woolf J in *R v BBC, ex p Lavelle* [1983] ICR 99, although he refused to allow an application for judicial review in that case on the grounds that only contractual rights were at stake: see Ewing and Grubb, 1987: pp 146, 156–157.

339   *R v Derbyshire County Council, ex p Noble* [1990] IRLR 332, 337; Sedley, 1994; Laws, 1997.

340   [2001] IRLR 279; see further paras 5.44 and 5.45 above.

341   Ewing, 1993b: p 406. See also John Hendy and Jeremy McMullen, 1987; John McMullen, 1995.

342   *Ryan v Mutual Tontine Westminster Chambers Association* [1893] 1 Ch 116.

343   *De Francesco v Barnum* (1890) 45 Ch D 430, 438.

the need for the parties to maintain 'mutual trust and confidence' in one another for the order to have any purpose.[344] Nonetheless, the courts have always accepted some exceptions to the rule: in *CH Giles & Co Ltd v Morris*[345] Sir Robert Megarry VC did 'not think that it should be assumed that as soon as any element of personal service or continuous services can be discerned in a contract the court will, without more, refuse specific performance'. Legislation prohibits orders for specific performance against employees on one of the grounds also recognised by the common law, namely the need to protect the individual against direct legal compulsion to work.[346] Reciprocity between employer and employee would seem to demand that the employer should be equally free from specific enforcement, but the matter is not so straightforward. Employers are able to obtain negative injunctions against employees preventing them from working for competitors in breach of contract, as long as the circumstances do not constitute the equivalent of requiring the employee to work for the employer against their will. An injunction will normally be issued in a case where the employee is not faced with a direct choice of 'work or starve', which is tantamount to making him or her perform the contract.[347] By extension, it should be and is possible for negative injunctions to be issued in certain circumstances against the employer, to prevent a disciplinary action or the dismissal of the employee being carried out in breach of contract. Again, the courts must respect the principle that no injunction should be granted in an employment case if its effects are equivalent to specific performance. But recent decisions have shown the traditional objections to specific orders to have lost much of their force.

The principal situation to be considered is that in which an employer purports to dismiss the employee without granting him or her the benefit of a contractual procedure, or without having established a good substantive reason when required to do so by the contract. The employee may then refuse to accept that the employer's repudiatory breach has brought the contract to an end,[348] and seek an injunction or declaration to restrain the employer from treating the employee as dismissed until the correct procedure is operated and/or a good reason established.[349] A specific order may also be sought to prevent a unilateral variation of the contract terms,[350] or unauthorised disciplinary action short of dismissal.[351] These actions are begun by claim form in the High Court, separately from the special procedure for judicial review under CPR Part 54. Any injunction will normally be interim, pending a full trial or the completion of the agreed

---

344 For a summary of the traditional reasons for denying specific performance, see *Chappell v Times Newspapers Ltd* [1975] 1 WLR 482. For a critique of the traditional view, see Brodie, 1998a.

345 [1972] 1 WLR 307, 324.

346 TULRCA 1992, s 236.

347 *Warner Bros Pictures Inc v Nelson* [1937] 1 KB 209; see para 4.99 above.

348 See paras 5.36–5.40 above, for discussion of the competing 'elective' and 'automatic' theories of contract termination.

349 *Jones v Lee* [1980] ICR 310; *Irani v Southampton and South West Hampshire Health Authority* [1985] IRLR 203; *Robb v Hammersmith and Fulham London Borough Council* [1991] IRLR 72; *Ali v Southwark London Borough Council* [1988] ICR 567; *Jones v Gwent County Council* [1992] IRLR 521.

350 *Burdett-Coutts v Hertfordshire County Council* [1984] IRLR 91; *Keir and Williams v County Council of Hereford and Worcester* [1985] IRLR 505; *Hughes v Southwark London Borough Council* [1988] IRLR 55; *Rigby v Ferodo Ltd* [1988] ICR 29; *Powell v Brent London Borough Council* [1988] ICR 176; *McLaren v Home Office* [1990] IRLR 338.

351 *Honeyford v Bradford Metropolitan City Council* [1986] IRLR 32.

procedure, but it may alternatively be permanent in form.[352] The effect of an injunction is to require the employer to refrain from undertaking the action enjoined, on pain of being found to be in contempt of court. A declaration may also be issued, normally if the court is satisfied that the parties will act on this statement of their rights and obligations without the need to invoke the threat of contempt of court proceedings.

(i) The need to retain mutual trust and confidence

5.55 A key issue is whether the employer can be said to retain trust and confidence in the capacity of the employee to carry out his or her work. In *Hill v CA Parsons & Co Ltd*[353] an injunction was granted in rather unusual circumstances: the employee, who had refused to join a trade union which operated a closed shop in the establishment where he worked, had been dismissed as a result of pressure from the union. The aim of the injunction was to prevent the dismissal from taking effect until after the expiry of the period of notice to which the employee was entitled, by which time the Industrial Relations Act 1971 would have come into force and rendered the employee's dismissal on grounds related to his non-membership of the union unlawful. In this case, because the only reason for dismissal was the pressure exercised by a third party and there was no loss of mutual confidence between the two parties to the contract, an injunction was deemed appropriate.

Although the facts of *Hill* were exceptional and unlikely to be repeated, the principle it enunciated was not exceptional: in an appropriate case, an injunction could be issued to maintain the employment relationship if there was still mutual trust and confidence between the parties. The application of this principle to a broader category of cases of discipline and dismissal was achieved, to striking effect, in *Irani v Southampton and South West Hampshire Health Authority*.[354] In this case the employee, an ophthalmologist, was dismissed after he fell out with a senior consultant at the hospital where he worked. The health authority made no complaint about the employee's own work. His dismissal had taken place in breach of procedures incorporated into his contract of employment from the 'blue book' of NHS terms and conditions. Warner J granted a declaration that the purported dismissal had been in breach of contract and issued an interim injunction to prevent the employer acting on the dismissal until he had operated the contractual disciplinary procedure, 'the effect of which [was] to compel the defendant authority to continue to employ Mr Irani until the trial or at all events until it had in the meantime completed the procedure'.[355] In the judge's view, 'it remains the fact that the defendant authority has perfect faith in the honesty, integrity and loyalty of Mr Irani';[356] as in *Hill*, an injunction could be issued where the dismissal was not caused by any lack of confidence in the employee.

---

352 As in *Jones v Gwent County Council* [1992] IRLR 521.
353 [1972] Ch 305.
354 [1985] IRLR 203. *Irani* is not quite the first case of this kind; there is a long line of case law concerning the grant of injunctions or declarations to protect the position of schoolteachers which do not appear to rest on any principle of public law (see *Young v Cuthbert* [1906] 1 Ch 451; *Crisp v Holden* (1910) 54 Sol Jo 784; *Smith v McNally* [1912] 1 Ch 816; *Jones v Lee* [1980] ICR 310). See John Hendy and Jeremy McMullen, 1988: p 28.
355 [1985] IRLR 203, 206.
356 [1985] IRLR 203, 209.

5.56   More problematic are cases where an employer insists before the court that the reinstatement of the employee would be impractical, notwithstanding the absence of fault on the employee's part, because of irreconcilable personal differences between that individual and other members of the organisation, in particular close colleagues or immediate superiors in the managerial hierarchy. Case law nevertheless suggests that this is not an insuperable obstacle to the issue of a specific order. In *Powell v Brent London Borough Council*[357] the Council attempted to revoke Mrs Powell's promotion to a more senior post within the organisation, for reasons relating to an alleged procedural impropriety concerning her appointment (these were found by the court to be groundless). No complaint was made concerning Mrs Powell's ability to do the job to which she had been appointed, and which she was carrying out at the time of the legal proceedings. Mrs Powell sought an interim injunction to prevent the Council re-advertising the post and to require them to treat her as employed in that capacity. Knox J refused to grant the order on the grounds that mutual trust and confidence were lacking, but the Court of Appeal allowed an appeal. The relevant test of confidence was, in the view of Ralph Gibson LJ, to 'be judged by reference to the circumstances of the case, including the nature of the work, the people with whom the work must be done and the likely effect upon the employer and the employer's operations if the employer is required by injunction to suffer the [claimant] to continue in the work'.[358] In this case, it was relevant that 'Brent Council is a large organisation employing many people in different departments';[359] in an organisation of such size, the clearest evidence of a breakdown of personal relations would be required, particularly where there was no rational reason for the claimant's competence to be questioned.

5.57   *Jones v Gwent County Council*[360] is an even stronger case. Mrs Jones, who was employed by the Council as a lecturer, was accused of misconduct on a number of grounds and her case was considered twice by an internal disciplinary committee of the college at which she worked, in accordance with her contractual disciplinary procedure. She was cleared on each occasion, but the governors of the college nevertheless decided to continue to suspend her from work on full pay and then to dismiss her since they believed that 'your return to the college would cause an irrevocable breakdown in the relationships between staff and between management and staff based on your past behaviour'. The judge assumed this view to be 'sincerely held' but based on a perception of the claimant's past conduct which had not been substantiated. He issued a declaration under Rules of the Supreme Court, Order 14A, rule 1, to the effect that the continuing suspension of the claimant was in breach of contract; an interim injunction preventing the claimant from being dismissed in breach of the procedure laid down in her contract; and a permanent injunction preventing the Council acting on the governors' previous decision to dismiss her.

CPR Part 24 permits the court to give summary judgment against a claimant or defendant if (a) it considers that the claimant has no real prospect of succeeding on the claim or issue, or the defendant has no real prospect of successfully defending the claim or issue and (b) there is no other compelling reason why the case or issue should be disposed of at a trial. CPR Part 24

357 [1987] IRLR 466; see Ewing and Grubb, 1987.
358 [1987] IRLR 466, 473.
359 [1987] IRLR 466.
360 [1992] IRLR 521.

permits summary disposal in three types of cases which were previously dealt with by separate provisions, one of which – RSC Order 14A – allowed summary disposal of a case on a point of law or construction of a document.[361] In *Jones v Gwent County Council*, Chadwick J thought that so far as Order 14A was concerned, the issue of mutual trust and confidence between the parties was not relevant: to argue otherwise was 'to misunderstand the nature of the power conferred by that Order', which was to determine issues of construction which do not depend on trust and confidence. His judgment can be seen as having 'elided completely the requirement of continuing confidence as a condition of injunctive relief'.[362] A court acting under CPR Part 24 may take a more restrictive view. However, *Jones v Gwent County Council* remains significant in suggesting that mutual confidence cannot be denied simply by the subjective assertion of the contract-breaker, where, on objective grounds, there is no good reason to believe that the employee cannot carry out his or her work effectively.

On the same grounds, it can be argued more generally that where an employee is seeking to enforce the terms of a disciplinary procedure, mutual confidence should hardly ever be an issue, for the reason that until the procedure is properly carried out the employer is not justified in regarding the employee as unfit to continue in employment.[363] To regard it as a relevant consideration can be said to be allowing the employer to take advantage of its own wrong. Nor should it be an issue in cases where the employee is attempting to resist a unilateral change in terms and conditions of employment which is unrelated to any question of his or her personal misconduct. Thus in *Keir and Williams v County Council of Hereford and Worcester*[364] an injunction was granted to prevent an employer removing car expense allowances in breach of terms incorporated into contracts from national and local-level collective agreements, while in *Hughes v Southwark London Borough Council*[365] an injunction was granted to prevent an employer implementing an order, made in breach of contract, purporting to change the claimant social worker's place of work and to alter her job description.[366]

(ii) The balance of convenience

5.58 Under the general principles laid down by the House of Lords in *American Cyanamid Co v Ethicon Ltd*[367] the claimant seeking an interim injunction or declaration is not necessarily required to show a *prima facie* case that they will succeed at full trial, but rather that there is a serious issue to be tried and that damages would not be adequate, whereupon the court will decide whether to issue the order by weighing up the 'balance of convenience' between the parties.

---

361 Of the other provisions, RSC Order 14 dealt with summary judgment; RSC Order 18, r 19 with striking out proceedings.

362 Ewing, 1993b: p 435. Order 14A was used more generally as a means of acquiring a declaration of rights in cases concerning, for example, transfers of employment: *Kenny v South Manchester College* [1993] IRLR 265.

363 Ewing, 1989; *Robb v Hammersmith and Fulham London Borough Council* [1991] IRLR 72; *Barros D'Sa v University Hospital Coventry and Warwickshire NHS Trust* [2001] EWCA Civ 983, [2001] IRLR 691, although cf the decision apparently to the contrary in *Ali v Southwark London Borough Council* [1988] IRLR 100.

364 [1985] IRLR 505.

365 [1988] IRLR 55.

366 Declarations have also been granted in cases concerning attempts by employers to implement unilateral wage cuts: *Burdett-Coutts v Hertfordshire County Council* [1984] IRLR 91; *Miller v Hamworthy Engineering Ltd* [1986] ICR 846; *Rigby v Ferodo Ltd* [1988] ICR 29.

367 [1975] AC 396; see further para 11.49.

This test, because it favours the status quo, inherently favours the employee who is seeking to defend the position he or she occupied prior to the allegedly unlawful act of the employer. Damages rarely will be adequate, since the employee is unlikely to be entitled to receive substantial compensation for wrongful dismissal at common law;[368] nor will unfair dismissal normally be a viable alternative, since, for reasons examined below,[369] it is unlikely to lead to reinstatement. It nevertheless remains open to the court, in its discretion, to refuse to grant an equitable order on the grounds that damages would be sufficient in the circumstances,[370] or to refuse to do so because it finds that the claimant's own conduct has not been above reproach.[371] The right to seek equitable relief may also be lost if the employee has, at some stage, accepted the employer's repudiatory breach of contract, for example by looking for or taking work elsewhere;[372] he or she will then be limited to a claim for damages, or to an action for unfair dismissal.

(iii) The effect of an injunction or declaration

5.59   The practical effect of an injunction or declaration is to reinstate the employee into his or her employment, or to re-establish the agreed terms of the contract of employment; but this may depend both on the nature of the contract terms which the employee is seeking to uphold and on the way in which the court chooses to exercise its equitable discretion. In a situation where the employment relationship is continuing and the employer is not seeking to dismiss the employee, equitable relief would normally have the desired effect of realigning the relationship with the agreed contract terms, as well as confirming the employee's right to bring an action in debt or damages for the preceding breach of contract and for any continuing breach.[373] What happens where, following the issue of an injunction, the employer then seeks to dismiss the employee by properly operating the disciplinary procedure in question? One effect of the court's intervention may be to ensure that the employee receives his or her normal salary while the procedure is continuing,[374] but the wider question is whether it will result in the employee keeping their job once the process is exhausted. We suggested above[375] that contractual job security clauses of the kind which are now frequently found in practice have an effect which is both procedural and substantive: they do not simply require a certain procedure to be observed, they also limit the employer's power of arbitrary dismissal. It should follow from this that the employer does not meet its contractual obligations by simply going through the motions of a given procedure; there must also be good objective grounds, at the end of the procedure, for arriving at a decision to discipline or dismiss the employee. Accordingly, there is no reason why an injunction should not be granted to restrain a *substantive* breach of contract in an appropriate case. For example, in *Jones v Gwent County Council*[376] the

---

368   *Powell v Brent London Borough Council* [1987] IRLR 466, 474; *Hughes v Southwark London Borough Council* [1988] IRLR 55; although cf *Marsh v National Autistic Society* [1993] ICR 453.

369   See para 5.148 *et seq* below, and *Robb v Hammersmith and Fulham London Borough Council* [1991] IRLR 72.

370   *Marsh v National Autistic Society* [1993] ICR 453.

371   *Wadcock v Brent London Borough Council* [1990] IRLR 223.

372   *Dietman v Brent London Borough Council* [1987] ICR 737.

373   See, eg, *Rigby v Ferodo Ltd* [1987] ICR 457; affd [1988] ICR 29.

374   *Robb v Hammersmith and Fulham London Borough Council* [1991] IRLR 72.

375   See para 5.31 *et seq.*

376   [1992] IRLR 521, 527.

interim injunction granted by Chadwick J restrained the defendant from 'dismissing [the claimant] unless proper grounds exist and until after a proper procedure has been carried out, both in accordance with the [claimant's] contract of employment'. Since the intervention of the court derives from its equitable jurisdiction and is designed to protect the private rights of the parties, it would seem appropriate for it to have the power to protect the *substance* of those rights and not simply the procedural aspects of the contract. Judicial review is more clearly limited to providing procedural protection for the party whose legitimate expectations are affected by the relevant determination; but there would seem to be no reason, in principle, for extending the public law distinction between substance and procedure to actions begun by claim form.

(iv) The significance of the notice rule

5.60 One remaining barrier to this result could be the notice rule which, as we saw earlier,[377] may provide the employer with a residual right to bring the contract to an end without needing to invoke any given procedure or to offer a reason for doing so. Implicitly, the cases which we have just been considering make little or no sense unless they are seen as limiting the notice rule: what is the point of the court intervening to uphold a given procedure if the employer can outflank it by simply giving notice of termination to the employee? Here, as in relation to the question of damages,[378] the issue remains unclear. It was briefly considered in *Powell v Brent London Borough Council* where Ralph Gibson LJ said:

> The length of the security of tenure in the post which the [claimant] might enjoy is very short. The defendants say three weeks. The [claimant] says 10, because of continuing service with other local authorities. The period of notice does not seem to me to delimit the legitimate interests of the [claimant] in retaining her alleged right to the post ... It is not probable that the Borough of Brent will treat the [claimant] unfairly or contrary to their normal policy. If the [claimant] can prove her right to the post, even if it causes disappointment to the legal department, she will probably keep it until she secures further promotion or, if things go ill, she is removed under the disciplinary procedures or however else Brent Council may lawfully proceed.[379]

This does not quite answer the point: could the Council 'lawfully proceed' to dismiss Mrs Powell by giving notice, or would they be obliged to operate the disciplinary procedure and find good cause for dismissal? It is one thing to talk of the *expectation* that Mrs Powell would keep her job, another to consider whether she had the *right* to do so indefinitely. Where the contract contains no notice clause (either express or implied), *McClelland v Northern Ireland General Health Services Board*[380] indicates that a declaration may be issued to prevent the employer treating the employee as dismissed. It seems from the dissenting opinion of Lord Keith of Avonholm that the purpose of the declaration in this case was to establish the claimant's right to substantial damages for breach of contract, although the point does not emerge clearly from the report.[381] If a declaration could be granted for this purpose, it is only a short step to granting

---

377 See paras 5.41–5.43 above.
378 See para 5.20 *et seq.*
379 [1987] IRLR 466, 475.
380 [1957] 1 WLR 594.
381 See Ewing, 1993b: pp 425–426.

an injunction, which would be as good as reinstatement as the employer would then be threatened with contempt of court proceedings for non-compliance. The same result could follow even in cases where the contract contains an express notice clause, if the court is able to construe a contractual job security clause as impliedly limiting the employer's right to give notice. This point does not seem to have been expressly considered in *Jones v Gwent County Council*,[382] but Chadwick J nevertheless granted the injunction sought 'expressly on the basis that the seriousness of being in breach of a court order, if the council continues on the course that it has so far adopted, may perhaps concentrate the minds of those responsible for its affairs'.[383]

(v) *The employment relationships covered by the principle*

5.61   There remains, as a final question, the issue of how far the principle enunciated in these decisions extends to different varieties of employment relationship. There is no reason why the equitable intervention of the courts should be limited to public sector employment relationships, nor to employees of a particular status. In practice, however, employees in insecure employment are unlikely to benefit from this form of intervention, if only because their own contractual terms and conditions will probably lack the kind of job security clauses which courts have intervened to protect. Nor have the courts taken any further the suggestion of Woolf J in *Lavelle*,[384] that office-holder status be extended to all employees benefiting from the protection of unfair dismissal legislation,[385] and, indeed, *Johnson v Unisys Ltd*[386] constitutes a formidable obstacle to this. Is it just coincidence that virtually all the cases in which injunctions or declarations have been issued to prevent dismissal have concerned employees in secure jobs in the public sector? The new line of case law appears not to have shaken off entirely the traditional notion of an office holder as one occupying a post which has 'a subsisting, permanent, substantive position',[387] a description which can only with difficulty be applied to any private-sector employment, no matter how elevated. Where private-sector employees have sought specific relief to retain their jobs they have, until recently, failed to do so, although the reasons given by the courts do not formally discriminate between employment in the public and private sectors.

Thus in *Marsh v National Autistic Society*[388] an injunction was refused on the grounds that damages would be an adequate remedy. An injunction was also refused in *Alexander v Standard Telephones and Cables Ltd*[389] where it was sought to enforce the terms of a 'last-in, first-out' redundancy selection procedure by nullifying the dismissals of employees who had been dismissed

---

382   The claimant's contract provided for her to be dismissed on notice of not less than two months, but to have the right even then to make representations to the effect that the dismissal was not for good cause. See [1992] IRLR 521, 525. This could be read as qualifying the employer's residual power of arbitrary dismissal.

383   [1992] IRLR 521, 527.

384   [1983] ICR 99. See para 5.53 above.

385   The substantial costs of High Court litigation will also be a practical bar to most employees who are not supported financially by their trade unions and even, perhaps, to many who are: Ewing, 1993b: p 436.

386   [2001] IRLR 279; see paras 5.44 and 5.45 above.

387   *Great Western Rly Co v Bater* [1920] 3 KB 266, 273–274. On the notion of 'office holder', see para 3.80 above.

388   [1993] ICR 453.

389   [1990] IRLR 55.

when fellow workers with less seniority had been kept on. According to Aldous J, 'it cannot be said that the defendant has complete confidence in the [claimants], as it has less confidence that they can do the work than the other members of the workforce that have been retained. The relationship of employer and employee has in fact broken down'.[390] In *Anderson v Pringle of Scotland Ltd*,[391] however, where the facts were in material respects identical to those of *Alexander,* the Court of Session, Outer House dismissed such an argument. Lord Prosser was 'not persuaded' that there was 'any true analogy between the respondents' preference for other employees and the need for confidence which is inherent in the employer/employee relationship'.[392] Moreover, while it may be 'very inconvenient or difficult for the respondents to abide by the priorities' they had agreed to, 'they can hardly call it unfair to be held to their own bargain'.[393] The court therefore granted interim relief to prevent the employer selecting employees for redundancy on any basis other than the agreed procedure.

We would suggest that *Anderson* shows a much more appropriate approach to the enforcement of redundancy selection procedures than *Alexander*. It also demonstrates that there is no reason why a court should not grant an injunction or declaration to a private-sector employee in an appropriate case. It remains to be seen whether it will mark the beginning of a trend towards the more extensive protection of the contractual rights of private, as well as public, sector employees.

THE STATUTORY CONCEPT OF DISMISSAL

5.62   We now turn to the legislation governing the employer's liability for unfair dismissal. For the unfair dismissal jurisdiction to be invoked the employee must first satisfy a number of qualifying conditions, the most important of which, for present purposes, is that he or she has been *dismissed*.[394] This is also a pre-requisite for a claim to statutory redundancy compensation.[395] The statutory concept of dismissal builds on the common law of the contract of employment.[396] Under section 95(1) of ERA 1996:

> ... an employee is treated as dismissed by his employer if (and ... only if)-
>
> (a) the contract under which he is employed is terminated by the employer, (whether with or without notice),
>
> (b) he is employed under a limited-term contract and that contract terminates by virtue of the limiting event without being renewed under the same contract,[397] or

---

390 [1990] IRLR 55, 61.
391 [1998] IRLR 64. Anderson was applied in a public-sector context in *Peace v City of Edinburgh Council* [1999] IRLR 417.
392 [1998] IRLR 64, 67.
393 [1998] IRLR 64. The court in *Anderson* considered that, for the purposes of the interim application before it, there was sufficient evidence that the terms of the collective agreement had been incorporated into individual contracts. It is notable that the question as to whether the terms were appropriate for incorporation did not arise: cf *Alexander v Standard Telephones and Cables Ltd (No 2)* [1991] IRLR 286 and *Kaur v MG Rover Group Ltd* [2005] IRLR 40; see further para 4.29 above.
394 Elias, 1978.
395 On this, see para 5.165 *et seq* below.
396 *Western Excavating (ECC) Ltd v Sharp* [1978] QB 761.
397 As amended by FTER 2002, Sch 2, Part 1. See ERA 1996, s 235(2A), (2B) for the definition of 'limited-term contract' and 'limiting event'.

(c) the employee terminates the contract under which he is employed (with or without notice) in circumstances in which he is entitled to terminate it without notice by reason of the employer's conduct.[398]

Partly through its reliance on the common law of contract and partly as a consequence of derogations contained elsewhere in the Act, this statutory concept is not completely comprehensive, and certain important cases of non-consensual termination of employment fall outside its scope. The principal statutory derogations involve retirement[399] and, in a case where the employee has signed a valid waiver prior to 25 October 1999, the expiry of certain fixed-term contracts;[400] employees protected by a collective agreement governing dismissal procedures may also be excluded.[401] To these the courts have added a number of situations which, in their view, fall outside the scope of section 95(1): these include the discharge of the contract by way of frustration.[402] All of these derogations or exclusions go to the employment tribunal's jurisdiction, so that where they apply the tribunal is unable to decide the applicant's claim on the merits. Where an employee is claiming to have been constructively dismissed (ie a dismissal as defined in section 95(1)(c) above) he or she must usually institute the appropriate grievance procedure before a complaint can be presented to an employment tribunal.[403] Dismissals as defined in section 95(1)(a) and (b) must generally be preceded by recourse on the employer's part to the applicable statutory dismissal and disciplinary procedure in order not to be automatically unfair.[404]

Initial qualifying conditions

5.63 The applicant must have been employed as an employee[405] and must normally have had continuity of employment of not less than one year[406] at the time of the dismissal, the 'effective date of termination'.[407] Continuity of employment is only unnecessary in respect of a limited category of dismissals for automatically unfair reasons, which are considered in more detail below.[408] The employment must also have fallen within the territorial scope of UK labour legislation.[409]

---

398 This is subject to s 95(2) (employee who has been given notice of termination who then himself or herself gives notice to expire at an earlier date still treated as dismissed). S 95(1) and s 136(1) (redundancy) are in substantially similar terms. Those respects in which the definition of dismissal for the purposes of redundancy compensation differs from that for unfair dismissal are considered at para 5.173 below.
399 ERA 1996, s 109(1); see para 5.65 *et seq* below.
400 ERA 1996, s 197, now repealed; see para 5.78 below.
401 ERA 1996, s 110; see para 5.64 below.
402 See para 5.80 *et seq* below.
403 EA 2002, s 32; see generally para 2.21 *et seq*.
404 ERA 1996, s 98A(1); see para 5.124 *et seq*
405 ERA 1996, ss 95(1), 230(1); see para 3.19 *et seq* above. On the position of civil servants and members of the armed forces, see above, paras 3.74 and 3.75.
406 ERA 1996, s 108(1). On changes to the qualifying period for unfair dismissal since the inception of this legislation in 1971, see para 3.84 above.
407 On this, see para 5.83 *et seq* below.
408 See para 5.95 *et seq* below.
409 See *Lawson v Serco Ltd* [2004] IRLR 206. ERA 1996, s 196, under which an unfair dismissal claim was excluded if 'under the employee's contract of employment he ordinarily works outside Great Britain', was repealed in 1999 (ERelA 1999, s 32). On jurisdictional scope in general, see para 2.51 above.

Derogation for collective dismissal procedures

5.64   A special derogation for certain collective agreements establishing dismissal procedures is allowed for under the Act.[410] This provision, a concession to the wish of collective parties to disputes procedures to avoid recourse to law, has to date only been exercised in one case, concerning the Joint Industry Board for the Electrical Contracting Industry, although the order granting exemption was revoked on 1 June 2001 on the ground that the agreement no longer satisfied the relevant statutory conditions.[411] The Secretary of State may by order exempt from the scope of the legislation those employees covered by a collective 'dismissal procedure agreement'. The agreement then displaces the legislation, excluding the right of the employees concerned to bring complaints of unfair dismissal before employment tribunals.[412] To be valid, the agreement must be agreed by or on behalf of one or more independent trade unions and one or more employers or employers' associations,[413] and must also meet certain conditions to the satisfaction of the Secretary of State. These are, among other things, that the agreement lays down procedures which apply to all employees within the scope of the agreement without discrimination; that the agreement either makes general provision for arbitration or, alternatively, allows arbitration where an initial decision cannot be reached and on a point of law; and that 'the remedies provided ... in respect of unfair dismissal are on the whole as beneficial as (but not necessarily identical with) those provided in respect of unfair dismissal' by the Act.[414] The legislation itself provides that an award made under a 'designated dismissal procedure agreement' (that is to say, one approved by the Secretary of State) may be enforceable in the same way as a judgment of the County Court.[415]

Retirement

5.65   Under section 109(1) of the Act, the right to protection against unfair dismissal does not apply to the dismissal of an employee if on or before the effective date of termination[416] he or she has attained:

(a)   in a case where – (i) in the undertaking in which the employee was employed there was a normal retiring age for an employee holding the position held by the employee, and (ii) the age was the same whether the employee holding that position was a man or a woman, that normal retiring age; and

(b)   in any other case, the age of sixty-five.

The effect of this is that the employee is excluded if he or she has attained the normal retiring age, whether that is above or below the age of 65; it is only if there is no normal retiring age in the undertaking in question that the age limit of 65 years applies. This principle was established in *Nothman v Barnet London Borough Council*.[417] Miss Nothman was employed as a schoolteacher under a

---

410   ERA 1996, s 110.
411   SI 2001/1752.
412   Prior to 1 August 1998, s 110(2) excluded dismissals relating to pregnancy or maternity or the assertion of a statutory right. ERDRA 1998, s 12 amended the section to exclude only those descriptions of dismissal excluded by the agreement itself, with the aim of making dismissal procedure agreements more flexible.
413   ERA 1996, s 235(1).
414   ERA 1996, s 110(3).
415   ERA 1996, s 110(6), as inserted by ERDRA 1998, s 12.
416   See para 5.83, below.
417   [1979] ICR 111.

contract of employment which provided for her to retire at the age of 65. She was dismissed for alleged inability to perform her duties when she was aged 61 and brought proceedings for unfair dismissal. At that point, the relevant provision excluded from the scope of the Act dismissals where the employee had attained the normal retiring age 'or, if a man, attained the age of 65, or, if a woman, attained the age of 60'. The House of Lords held that Miss Nothman was entitled to proceed with her claim: since she had a normal retiring age of 65, the exception in the case of women who had reached the age of 60 did not apply to her. According to Lord Salmon, the Act

> ... sets up only one barrier to be overcome by the class of employee whose conditions of employment specify a normal retiring age, and another and entirely different barrier to be overcome by the class of employee whose conditions of employment specify no retiring age. The first class of employee preserves the right to claims in respect of unfair dismissal only if it is established that that dismissal took effect before the normal retiring age specified in the conditions of employment had been reached. The second class of employee preserves the right to claim in respect of unfair dismissal only if he or she establishes that that dismissal took effect before the employee, if a man, had reached the age of 65 years or, if a women 60 years.[418]

This opinion must now be read in the light of the common age of 65 for both men and women which is currently prescribed in the Act, and which was introduced by the Sex Discrimination Act 1986 in order to comply with the principle of equal treatment contained in Directive 76/307.[419] The interpretation arrived at in *Nothman* was not the only, or even the most obvious, one of the provision then in force. A strong dissent by Lord Fraser, with which Lord Diplock agreed, argued that the legislature had intended to use the pensionable age in the state retirement pension to set an upper age-limit to unfair dismissal rights.[420] It is still the case, for example, that those aged 65 or over have no right to receive redundancy compensation or the basic award for unfair dismissal following loss of employment.[421] However, the amendments to the predecessor of ERA 1996, section 109(1) made in 1986 in effect confirmed *Nothman* by making it clear that for unfair dismissal purposes, the 65-year age-limit only applies 'in any other case', in other words where there is no normal retiring age. In long-running litigation, this 65-year age-limit was challenged unsuccessfully as being indirectly discriminatory against men, the Court of Appeal holding that the tribunal had erred in finding that it had a disparate impact on men.[422] However this and other age limits are currently under review in the light of the provisions on age discrimination contained in Directive 2000/78/EC. We discuss these further in chapter 6.

---

418 [1979] ICR 111, 116.

419 SDA 1986, s 3. The catalyst for this reform was the judgment of the ECJ in Case 152/84 *Marshall v Southampton and South West Hampshire Area Health Authority (Teaching)* [1986] ECR 723.

420 [1979] ICR 111, 120 (Lord Fraser of Tullybelton).

421 ERA 1996, s 156(1) (redundancy compensation: the upper limit is either 65 or the normal retiring age if that is *lower*); s 119(4)–(5)(basic award).

422 *Secretary of State for Trade and Industry v Rutherford (No 2)* [2004] IRLR 892: see further para 6.24. In *Taylor v Secretary of State for Scotland* [2000] IRLR 502 the House of Lords held that an equal opportunities policy under which the employer undertook not to discriminate on grounds including age and sex, while incorporated into the applicant's contract, did not qualify a separate contract term under which the employer had a right to terminate the contract when the applicant reached the minimum retirement age of 55, after which any continuing employment was at the employer's discretion.

5.66 In many cases the normal retiring age for the purposes of the Act will be well below the age of 65, leaving employees vulnerable to enforced early retirement. In the 1980s early retirement was more actively encouraged as a means of reducing the size of the active labour force at a time of high unemployment, and many employers, particularly in the public sector, attempted to force the issue by unilaterally introducing a lower automatic retirement age. This produced extensive litigation around the issue of precisely what was meant by the phrase 'normal retiring age'.

The Court of Appeal in *Nothman* concluded that 'normal retiring age' meant the age specified in the employee's contract of employment: Lawton LJ construed the word 'retiring' in the phrase 'the normal retiring age' as having 'gerundial' qualities so as to give it the sense of 'must' or 'should'.[423] It follows that the normal retiring age of teachers employed by the council is the age at which they would have to retire unless their service was extended by mutual agreement'. However, this strict contract view was qualified by the House of Lords in *Waite v Government Communications Headquarters*.[424] Lieutenant Colonel Waite was employed as a higher executive officer at the Government Communications Headquarters from 1961 when aged 44. At first he was employed on a temporary contract which specified his retirement age as 65; when his employment was confirmed in 1966 it was made subject to the Civil Service Pay and Conditions Code, which establishes a retirement age of 60. To qualify for a pension he needed to have twenty years' service; in 1978, when he was 60, he was compulsorily retired from his executive post and redeployed to work as a clerical officer in order to enable him to achieve the minimum service requirement for his pension. Redeployment of staff over the age of 60 in this way was a departmental policy at the time. He made a claim for unfair dismissal in relation to the decision to require him to retire from the more senior post.

Lord Fraser, with whom the other law lords agreed, held that the contractual retirement age was 60, but that this did not necessarily settle the matter of the normal age. Nor was that simply the 'usual' age, as determined by a statistical count of the age at which similar employees took their retirement. It was necessary instead to 'ascertain what would be the reasonable expectation or understanding of the employees holding that position at the relevant time. The contractual retiring age will prima facie be the normal [age], but it may be displaced by evidence that it is regularly departed from in practice. The evidence may show that the contractual retirement age has been superseded by some definite higher age, and, if so, that will have become the normal retiring age'.[425] Because there was no evidence in this case of a regular practice of employees retiring after the age of 60 – only around a quarter were kept on for one reason or another, which fell 'far short of showing that the contractual retiring age had been abandoned'[426] – the contractual age applied, and the tribunal had no jurisdiction to hear the claim.

---

423 [1978] ICR 336, 346.

424 [1983] ICR 653.

425 [1983] ICR 653, 662–663. Cf *Wall v British Compressed Air Society* [2004] IRLR 147, where the Court of Appeal held that an employee whose position was not comparable to any other employee in the undertaking could still have a 'normal retiring age' provided that he or she had a contractual retiring age, which would represent the age at which he or she could reasonably expect to retire.

426 [1983] ICR 653, 663. Cf *Whittle v Manpower Services Commission* [1987] IRLR 441, where, in the relevant group of employees, over 90% stayed on beyond the contractual retiring age of 60, which as a result could not be regarded as the normal retiring age for the purposes of the Act.

One reason for modifying the strict contract test is that it might otherwise offer employers an unintended means of derogating from the Act by, for example, inserting a clause into contracts for compulsory retirement at a low age, and then keeping employees on subsequently only as a matter of discretion. As it is, the Act, as interpreted, still allows an employer to operate a retirement age below 65 years but only if 'he clearly publishes a genuine retiring age – not a sham – abides by it and treats each category of employee even-handedly and within his policy'.[427] The contractual retiring age, in the sense of the age identified by the contract as the automatic retiring age, is the starting point for analysis, but may be departed from if there is a 'policy retirement age' established by a stated declaration of the employer.[428] This is not necessarily decisive, however, since the tribunal may also look to statistical evidence to see what is done in practice within the 'undertaking' for 'positions' of the kind occupied by the employee. For this purpose, the 'undertaking' will be determined by regard to a test of managerial control, so that there may be several different 'undertakings' within a single company or government body if, for example, district or regional bodies possess a degree of managerial autonomy.[429]

5.67   The notion of a 'position' in relation to an employee 'means the following matters taken as a whole – (a) his status as an employee, (b) the nature of his work, and (c) his terms and conditions of employment'.[430] The application of this phrase is largely a matter for the employment tribunal; in *Brooks v British Telecommunications plc*[431] the tribunal was considered to have committed no error of law when it decided to define the position of the applicant by reference to the nature of his job and not exclusively to the grade he occupied within the structure established by the employer. Finally, the *Waite* test requires the tribunal to establish what similarly-placed employees reasonably considered was the age at which they could be compelled to retire. The test is objective,[432] and the reasonable opinion of the group is to be assessed at the time of the effective date of termination in the case before the tribunal.[433]

The departure from the strict contract approach has meant that the test is more flexible but also undoubtedly more complex in its application. The employer also has a very broad discretion to set and to change the normal retiring age by reference to policy practices and guidance. In *Hughes v Department of Health and Social Security*[434] a number of civil servants who had transferred from local to central government employment in the 1940s had been told that while subject to the Civil Service Pay and Conditions of Service Code, which stipulated 60 as

---

427 *Brooks v British Telecommunications plc* [1991] IRLR 4, 16 (Wood J). This should be read subject to the decision in *Wall v British Compressed Air Society*, note 425 above, that a 'unique' employee may have a normal retiring age.

428 In *Bratko v Beloit Walmsley Ltd* [1995] IRLR 629 the EAT affirmed that in *Waite v Government Communications Headquarters* [1983] ICR 653 the House of Lords contemplated only the possibility of a normal retiring age higher than the contractual retiring age and not one lower; see also *Wall v British Compressed Air Society*, above, note 425, at para 14 (Simon Brown LJ).

429 *Brooks v British Telecommunications plc* [1991] IRLR 4.

430 ERA 1996, s 235.

431 [1991] IRLR 4.

432 *Hughes v Department of Health and Social Security* [1984] IRLR 360, 370· (Sir John Donaldson MR).

433 *Hughes v Department of Health and Social Security* [1985] ICR 419, 429–30 (Lord Diplock).

434 [1985] ICR 419; see also *Whittle v Manpower Services Commission* [1987] IRLR 441.

the retirement age, they would normally be allowed to stay on until 65 subject to continued efficiency. However, in the early 1980s their departments announced a unilateral change of policy, requiring employees in their grades to retire at 60. The House of Lords held that the contractual age of the applicants was 60 and that while they may once have had reasonable expectations of continuing until 65, these were ended once the policy change was announced.

It follows from the above decisions that an employee may have a normal retiring age which is above his or her contractual retiring age. However, where the employee has reached the compulsory contractual retiring age in his or her employment but is able to show that the retiring age in practice is higher and that section 109(1) therefore has no application to their case, it does not necessarily follow that the termination of their employment will be unfair. An employer might still claim that the dismissal[435] was for a potentially fair reason and was reasonable in the circumstances:[436] it is conceivable that the dismissal could be presented as having been for 'some other substantial reason',[437] and that the employer could be said to have acted reasonably in operating an age-related bar on continuing employment where this was in the interests of the business. This might be difficult to do, however, in a case where an employee was made to retire at a contractual retiring age which, *ex hypothesi*, was not the normal retiring age for his or her position, since this would mean that he or she had not been treated in the same way as other employees in that position.

Dismissal by the employer

5.68 The first of the three categories of dismissal listed in section 95(1)(a) of ERA 1996 consists of the termination of contract under which the employee is employed, either with or without notice. For this, no formalities are required: the act of dismissal may be carried out in writing or by words or conduct. Whether words and/or conduct amount to a dismissal in a given case depends in part upon the intentions of the employer and in part upon the reasonable understanding of the employee:

> ... the test which has to be applied in cases of this kind is along these lines. Were the words spoken those of dismissal, that is to say, were they intended to bring the contract of employment to an end? What was the employer's intention? In answering that a relevant, and perhaps the most important, question is how would a reasonable employee, in all the circumstances, have understood what the employer intended by what he said and did?[438]

---

435 ERA 1996, s 95(1)(b) includes within the definition of dismissal termination of a 'limited-term contract' by virtue of the limiting event without being renewed under the same contract. A limiting event, in the case of a contract which provides for its termination on the occurrence of an event, means the occurrence of the event: ERA 1996, s 235. Unlike the definition of 'fixed-term contract' in FTER 2002, reg 2 the attainment of a 'normal and bona fide retiring age' is not excluded from this definition of a limiting event. A contract is a 'limited-term contract' if it is not intended to be 'permanent' and 'provision is accordingly made in the contract for it to terminate by virtue of a limiting event'. There is no definition of 'permanent' in this context; in particular, employment does not become 'permanent' after a specified period. In FTER 2002, reg 2 permanent employment is anything other than 'fixed-term'.

436 On potentially fair reasons and reasonableness, see paras 5.115 *et seq* and 5.118 *et seq* below.

437 Cf ERA 1996, s 98(1)(b), discussed at paras 5.115 and 5.117 below.

438 *Tanner v DT Kean Ltd* [1978] IRLR 110, 111.

This test is equally applicable to words and conduct of the employee which might be taken as indicating an intention to resign. Again, no formalities are required by law for an employee to resign his or her employment. Unless it can be construed as a 'constructive dismissal', which, as we shall see, requires the employee to resign in response to a repudiatory breach of contract by the employer,[439] resignation is outside the scope of section 95(1). Leaving the case of constructive dismissal to one side for the moment,[440] the question becomes whether the employer or the employee was the one to bring the contract to an end. Some basic principles of contract law for ascertaining the intentions of the parties are relevant here: one party cannot rely on an undisclosed intention which the other party could not reasonably have ascertained; but if both parties subjectively understand the contract to have been terminated, the reasonableness of their views is irrelevant.[441] The court may also construe the words used by reference to their accepted or customary meaning in the trade in question.[442]

Where words are uttered in the heat of the moment, the tribunal 'ought to be careful to ensure that what has taken place really is a dismissal' or, conversely, a resignation, 'and not merely some words uttered for particular reasons which everybody quite understood were little more than abuse or something of that sort'.[443] However, some words are sufficiently unambiguous as to leave nobody in any doubt as to their meaning, even when they are spoken in anger. If the employee says 'I am resigning', these words are not ambiguous, according to the Court of Appeal: they signify a present intention to resign, with immediate effect, and if the employer understands them in this way that is the end of the matter. Otherwise it would be difficult for mere words ever to effect a valid resignation.[444] Where there is ambiguity, however, 'if one is concerned with an immature employee, or decisions taken in the heat of the moment, then what might otherwise appear to be a clear resignation, should not be so construed'.[445] In these 'special circumstances', although it would be going too far to say that the employer is necessarily under a responsibility to take steps to ascertain the true intention of the employee, nevertheless 'a reasonable period of time should be allowed to lapse and if circumstances arise during that period which put the employer on notice that further inquiry is desirable to see whether the resignation was really intended and can properly be assumed, then such inquiry is ignored at the employer's risk'.[446] Now that termination by the employer without recourse to one of the statutory dismissal and disciplinary procedures is generally unfair,[447] employers will have to be particularly careful to ensure that the termination can be attributed to the employee's action and not to their own.

5.69   The employer will be deemed to have dismissed the employee if it prompts or induces the latter to resign by way of a threat of dismissal: 'if an employee is

439   ERA 1996, s 95(1)(c).
440   It is discussed in para 5.72 *et seq* below.
441   *Sothern v Frank Charlesly & Co* [1981] IRLR 278.
442   *Futty v D and D Brekkes Ltd* [1974] IRLR 130.
443   *Chesham Shipping Ltd v Rowe* [1977] IRLR 391, 392.
444   *Sothern v Franks Charlesly & Co* [1981] IRLR 278; *BG Gale Ltd v Gilbert* [1978] ICR 1149 ('I am leaving, I want my cards').
445   *Sovereign House Security Services Ltd v Savage* [1989] IRLR 115, 116 (the employee said he was 'jacking the job in': held, no resignation); *Barclay v City of Glasgow District Council* [1983] IRLR 313 ('mentally defective employee'); *Futty v D and D Brekkes Ltd* [1974] IRLR 130 (no dismissal intended when manager and employee had an altercation).
446   *Kwik-Fit (GB) Ltd v Lineham* [1992] ICR 183, 191.
447   ERA 1996, s 98A(1).

told that she is no longer required in her employment and is expressly invited to resign, a court of law is entitled to come to the conclusion that, as a matter of common sense, the employee was dismissed'.[448] The question is seen as one of causation. If it can be shown that the employee agreed to go because, for example, of the severance terms which he or she is offered, a tribunal may find that the generosity of the severance terms and not the initial threat of dismissal was the operative cause of the contract coming to an end, in which case there will have been no dismissal.[449] This doctrine can place employees in a dilemma where they are offered incentives for voluntary redundancy or early retirement. In *Birch v University of Liverpool*[450] the University, faced with the need to make cuts in staff, introduced a scheme under which employees taking early retirement would receive a pension and lump sum from the University's pension fund. Mr Birch made an application under the scheme which the University accepted; he later lodged a separate claim for a statutory redundancy payment. The University claimed that he had not been dismissed, and this contention was upheld. There had been no threat of compulsory early retirement and no other pressure on Mr Birch to resign, and the contract had therefore been terminated by mutual consent.[451] By contrast, in *Scotch Premier Meat Ltd v Burns*[452] the EAT took the robust view that 'where the whole background to the departure was determination by the employer to close a factory and make the employees inevitably redundant, the fact that some employees accepted a package as the means of effecting that decision does not in our opinion preclude a finding that there was a dismissal'.[453] This decision turned on the meaning of the term 'dismissal' in the context of an employee's entitlement to remuneration under a protective award granted in respect of the employer's failure to consult and inform employee representatives of proposed redundancies,[454] but it would be just as appropriate for it to be applied to individual applications in relation to unfair dismissal and/or redundancy compensation.

Employees also need to avoid resigning prematurely, before a threat of dismissal becomes operative. In *Logan Salton v Durham County Council*[455] the employee was the subject of disciplinary proceedings which reached the stage of the Council recommending that he be summarily dismissed. Before this recommendation could be considered by the internal committee convened to deal with the matter, the employee decided to resign and agreed severance terms with the Council. It was held that his employment had been terminated by agreement. In *Roberts v West Coast Trains Ltd*[456] a further potential trap for employees was exposed. The applicant was dismissed following a disciplinary

---

448 *East Sussex County Council v Walker* (1972) 7 ITR 280, 281 (Sir John Brightman).
449 *Sheffield v Oxford Controls Co Ltd* [1979] ICR 396; see also *Catherall v Michelin Tyre plc* [2003] IRLR 61 (case remitted to tribunal to determine whether, where an employee was given the choice between redundancy and retirement through ill health, the absence of choice was the cause of the termination or whether the situation provided the opportunity for satisfactory terms to be negotiated for the termination of employment).
450 [1985] ICR 470.
451 See also, in the context of provisions of a pension scheme, *AGCO Ltd v Massey Ferguson Works Pension Trust Ltd* [2003] IRLR 793 (voluntary redundancy was 'retirement at the request of the employer' and in reality 'consensual dismissal' (sic); compulsory redundancy was not).
452 [2000] IRLR 639.
453 [2000] IRLR 639, 642.
454 See generally para 9.33 below.
455 [1989] IRLR 99.
456 [2004] IRLR 788.

hearing. He launched an internal appeal against that decision but before the outcome of that appeal was known he started proceedings in the employment tribunal claiming unfair dismissal. Following the internal appeal he was informed that his punishment had been reduced from dismissal to demotion. The sanctions of demotion and suspension without pay were specified in the contractual disciplinary procedure. When the applicant pursued his unfair dismissal claim the Court of Appeal affirmed the decisions of the tribunal and EAT that he had not been dismissed. The terms of the employment contract permitted the employer to demote the employee in place of the earlier decision to dismiss, so that they could retrospectively achieve a position where he was not dismissed for the purposes of bringing an unfair dismissal claim. In this case, which preceded the new statutory dismissal and disciplinary procedures, the court emphasised that the initial dismissal would have stood if the applicant had never instituted an appeal and/or if he had withdrawn his appeal before a decision was made. Under the new procedures, however, a dismissed employee who failed to exhaust the appeal procedure would risk a significant reduction in the compensatory award.[457] The issue of whether an employee who is initially dismissed but subject to a lesser sanction on appeal should be treated as a dismissed employee who has been offered re-instatement or re-engagement, or not dismissed at all, may become increasingly important in future litigation.[458]

5.70   Where the employer has given notice to the employee to terminate the contract, the courts are reluctant to conclude that any subsequent agreement to end the employment before the notice expires amounts to termination by consent. The initial decision to dismiss will be regarded as the operative one, particularly if there is any evidence of the employee being pressurised into leaving.[459] If, having been given notice by the employer, the employee then gives notice of his or her resignation to take effect before the employer's notice has expired, section 95(2) provides that the employee is nevertheless to be taken to have been dismissed by the employer, for the reasons which the employer had at the time the initial notice was given. There is no specified minimum period of notice which the employee must comply with in order for this provision to apply.[460] However, if the employee fails to give the minimum notice required by their contract, it is possible that the employer will thereby acquire a claim against them for damages for breach of contract, which is not precluded in any way by section 95(2). Where the employee gives notice of his or her intention to resign and subsequently receives shorter notice of termination from the employer, the employer will be taken to have terminated the contract and there is a dismissal.[461] An employer in that situation will need to have regard to its obligations under the statutory dismissal and disciplinary procedures.[462]

5.71   Dismissal under section 95(1)(a) normally involves the ending of the employment relationship, but this is not inevitable as *Hogg v Dover College*[463]

---

457 See para 5.124 *et seq*
458 An employee who is subject to a disciplinary sanction which he or she considers to be a repudiatory breach of contract could claim to have been constructively dismissed. Constructive dismissal was not argued in *Roberts*.
459 *Lees v Arthur Greaves (Lees) Ltd* [1974] ICR 501.
460 *Cardinal Vaughan Memorial School Governors v Alie* [1987] ICR 406.
461 *British Midland Airways Ltd v Lewis* [1978] ICR 782.
462 See para 5.124 *et seq*
463 [1990] ICR 39.

shows. Mr Hogg was employed full-time as a teacher and head of department at the College. Then, following an illness, he received a letter from the headmaster of the College offering him teaching on a part-time basis with a reduced salary. In response he lodged a claim for unfair dismissal while continuing to work under the new arrangement, making it clear that this was done under protest. The employment tribunal found that the headmaster's letter did not amount to a dismissal under section 95(1)(a), and that Mr Hogg could not claim constructive dismissal either under section 95(1)(c) as he had waived the employer's repudiatory breach of contract. The EAT overturned this ruling in both respects. The headmaster's letter amounted to a termination of Mr Hogg's *contract*, as required by section 95(1)(a), regardless of whether he carried on in employment: 'he was being told that his former contract was from that moment gone'.[464] Alternatively there was a constructive dismissal since his employment continued under a *new* contract, Mr Hogg having terminated the old one by accepting the employer's repudiation.

The application of the principle in *Hogg* was upheld in *Alcan Extrusions v Yates*.[465] Here the employers had imposed a continuous rolling shift system, which had knock-on effects for pay and holidays, in place of the shift system prescribed in their employees' contracts of employment. The EAT affirmed that in this case the departure from the terms of the existing contract was sufficiently substantial to constitute withdrawal of the contract.

Hogg and *Alcan* are potentially far-reaching decisions which make it possible for employees to use unfair dismissal legislation to challenge unilateral variations or impositions of contract terms, and disciplinary action short of dismissal,[466] without the need to resign from their employment and find another job.[467] The possible weak link in the reasoning of the EAT in these cases is the argument that there were two different contracts of employment here, one before and one after the change in working hours took place. While it is true that for there to be a dismissal under section 95(1) it is enough for the *contract* and not the *relationship* of employment to be brought to an end, it may be a matter of fine judgement whether, in a given case, a unilateral change in working conditions leads to a new contract being created or simply amounts to a purported variation of the old one. There is authority to suggest that where the employer seeks to change an important element of a contractual package, 'if an employee goes on working, having made his protest about the exclusion of the important element, the true position in law is that he has been dismissed but re-engaged on a fresh contract'.[468] However the dictum by the EAT in *Alcan* that whether the departure from the original contract is sufficiently radical to amount to the termination of that contract and its replacement by a different one is a question of fact for the employment tribunal to decide[469] can only be a recipe for uncertainty in the law

464 [1990] ICR 39, 42.
465 [1996] IRLR 327.
466 *Joseph v British Railways Board*, IT (2 September 1993, unreported) noted by Curran, 1994; cf *Hunt v British Railways Board* [1979] IRLR 379.
467 Curran, 1994; R White, 1997. *Waite v Government Communications Headquarters* [1983] ICR 653, discussed at para 5.66 above, is another case in which the employee brought a claim for unfair dismissal while still working for the employer. The case was decided for the employer on the grounds of the age-related exclusion contained in ERA 1996, s 109(1), but at no point does it seem to have been argued that Lieutenant Colonel Waite had not been dismissed.
468 *Land v West Yorkshire Metropolitan County Council* [1979] ICR 452 (Kilner Brown J); cf *Marriott v Oxford and District Co-operative Society Ltd (No 2)* [1970] 1 QB 186.
469 [1996] IRLR 327, 329. See R White, 1997 for a critique of this decision.

in this area. The implications of this uncertainty for the application of the statutory dismissal and disciplinary procedures, on the one hand, and the statutory grievance procedures, on the other, are discussed in para 5.131 below.

Constructive dismissal

5.72   There is a dismissal where the employee terminates the contract, either with or without notice, 'in circumstances in which he is entitled to terminate it without notice by reason of the employer's conduct'.[470] On general principles, it is not necessary for the employee to inform the employer, at the time of the termination, of his or her reason for leaving the employment; the test is simply one of causation, that is to say, was the employee's departure caused by the employer's conduct?[471] However since 1 October 2004 an employee who wishes to present a complaint to an employment tribunal of unfair constructive dismissal must usually first institute one of the statutory grievance procedures, under which the grievance must be set out in writing and the basis for it explained.[472] The test of employer misconduct in the context of constructive dismissal implicitly incorporates the common law of contract relating to the employee's right to resign in the face of a repudiatory breach of contract by the employer.[473] For a time, tribunals applied a more general test of whether the employer had acted 'unreasonably' in prompting the employee to quit the employment.[474] However, in *Western Excavating (ECC) Ltd v Sharp*[475] the Court of Appeal, in a judgment subsequently regarded as authoritative,[476] imposed a contract test. This was done in large part in order to avoid duplicating within the concept of dismissal the test of reasonableness provided for separately by what is now section 98(4) of ERA 1996.[477] Although the effect of this ruling might have been to limit the scope of the Act by reference to the highly technical law of repudiatory breach of contract, this has not happened largely because of the expansion of the implied duty of co-operation within the contract of employment. In this way, the law of unfair dismissal has been indirectly responsible for one of the most important recent developments within the common law of employment.[478]

---

470 ERA 1996, s 95(1)(c).
471 *Weathersfield Ltd (t/a Van & Truck Rentals) v Sargent* [1999] IRLR 94, CA, overruling *Holland v Glendale Industries Ltd* [1998] ICR 493, EAT. The employee must communicate to the employer the intention to terminate the employment: *Edwards v Surrey Police* [1999] IRLR 456. In *Rai v Somerfield Stores Ltd* [2004] IRLR 124 the EAT held that presentation of an originating application to the tribunal did not constitute the requisite communication.
472 EA 2002, s 32; see further para 2.21 *et seq*. Under the general law, an alleged failure by an employee to follow a grievance procedure is irrelevant: *Tolson v Governing Body of Mixenden Community School* [2003] IRLR 842.
473 The employee must leave because of the breach (*Walker v Josiah Wedgwood & Sons Ltd* [1978] IRLR 105) but the breach need not be the sole cause as long as it is the 'effective cause': *Jones v F Sirl & Son (Furnishers) Ltd* [1997] IRLR 493, 495. Thus the fact that an employee has another job to go to may not prevent a finding of constructive dismissal if the employer's breach was the main operative cause of his or her resignation: [1978] IRLR 105.
474 *Gilbert v Goldstone Ltd* [1977] ICR 36; *Turner v London Transport Executive* [1977] ICR 952.
475 [1978] QB 761.
476 For an argument that the courts might have chosen to follow the prior Court of Appeal judgment in *Turner v London Transport Executive* [1977] ICR 952, see Elias *et al*, 1980: p 563.
477 [1978] QB 761, 770 (Lord Denning MR); on s 98(4), see para 5.118 *et seq* below.
478 See para 4.91 *et seq* above.

5.73 In *Western Excavating*[479] Lawton LJ found it neither 'necessary [nor] advisable to express any opinion as to what principles of law operate to bring a contract of employment to an end by reason of an employer's conduct' and suggested that it would be a 'waste of legal learning' for tribunals to expend much time and effort examining the law of repudiatory breach. The voluminous case law which has developed around section 95(1)(c) simply indicates that the circumstances giving rise to a constructive dismissal are as varied as those of employment itself. A breach by the employer of the duty to maintain mutual trust and confidence, which is part of the reciprocal duty of co-operation, will be regarded as sufficient.[480] Conduct falling into this category has included subjecting the employee to abusive and insulting language;[481] refusing to investigate a justified complaint relating to health and safety;[482] making an unsubstantiated allegation of theft against the employee;[483] issuing a final written warning in respect of a relatively minor incident;[484] insisting without good cause that the employee should undergo a psychiatric examination;[485] 'arbitrarily, capriciously and inequitably' singling out an employee for an inferior pay rise to that received by other employees;[486] unjustifiably demoting the employee for a minor disciplinary offence;[487] denying the employee access to the company's premises by changing the locks, and telling customers that the employee no longer worked for the company;[488] failing to support the employee, who was a supervisor, in his relations with shop-floor workers;[489] failing reasonably and promptly to afford a reasonable opportunity to obtain redress of grievances;[490] instructing the employee to change her place of work in the absence of a term authorising this;[491] allowing an employee to be subjected to sexual harassment;[492] giving the employee an instruction which amounted to discrimination on racial grounds;[493] writing a misleading reference for a prospective employer;[494] failing to inform an employee on maternity leave about a vacancy for which she would have applied had she known about it;[495] and suspending the employee in response to unsubstantiated allegations of child abuse.[496] However, the notion of reciprocal co-operation has so far stopped short of imposing an obligation on an employer to offer an annual pay rise or an offer

---

479 [1978] QB 761, 772.
480 In *Morrow v Safeway Stores plc* [2002] IRLR 9 the EAT held that a breach of the implied term of trust and confidence would always be repudiatory; there is no room for assessing the seriousness of the breach. See also *London Borough of Waltham Forest v Omilaju* [2005] IRLR 35, para 14 (Dyson LJ).
481 *Palmanor Ltd v Cedron* [1978] ICR 1008.
482 *British Aircraft Corpn v Austin* [1978] IRLR 332. Note, however, *Marshall Specialist Vehicles Ltd v Osborne* [2003] IRLR 672 (need to apply approach in *Sutherland v Hatton* [2002] IRLR 263 discussed in para 4.81 in examining whether breach of implied term to take reasonable care for the safety of employees in context of alleged overwork).
483 *Robinson v Crompton Parkinson Ltd* [1978] ICR 401.
484 *Stanley Cole (Wainfleet) Ltd v Sheridan* [2003] IRLR 52.
485 *Bliss v South East Thames Regional Health Authority* [1985] IRLR 308.
486 *FC Gardner Ltd v Beresford* [1978] IRLR 63.
487 *BBC v Beckett* [1983] IRLR 43.
488 *Brown v JBD Engineering Ltd* [1993] IRLR 568.
489 *Industrial Rubber Products v Gillon* [1977] IRLR 389.
490 *WA Goold (Pearmak) Ltd v McConnell* [1995] IRLR 516.
491 *Aparau v Iceland Frozen Foods plc* [1996] IRLR 119.
492 *Wood v Freeloader Ltd* [1977] IRLR 455; *Western Excavating (ECC) Ltd v Sharp* [1978] QB 761, 772 (Lawton LJ).
493 *Weathersfield Ltd (t/a Van & Truck Rental) v Sargent* [1999] IRLR 94.
494 *TSB Bank plc v Harris* [2000] IRLR 157.
495 *Visa International Service Association v Paul* [2004] IRLR 42.
496 *Gogay v Hertfordshire County Council* [2000] IRLR 703.

of regrading.[497] On the other hand, an attempt by the employer unilaterally to vary the express contract terms, by, for example, cutting pay,[498] reducing hours,[499] or requiring the employee to relinquish his principal job in favour of another role,[500] will almost certainly be regarded as a repudiation.[501]

A series of separate acts, taken together, may amount to good grounds for repudiation.[502] It is not necessary for the 'final straw' itself to be a breach of contract to result in a breach of the implied term of trust and confidence, but:

> ... the quality that the final straw must have is that it should be an act in a series whose cumulative effect is to amount to a breach of the implied term ... The act does not have to be of the same character as the earlier acts. Its essential quality is that, when taken in conjunction with the earlier acts on which the employee relies, it amounts to a breach of the implied term of trust and confidence. It must contribute something to that breach, although what it adds may be relatively insignificant.[503]

The tribunal may need to investigate closely whether the conduct of the employee is such as to disentitle him or her to rely upon acts that may have preceded the 'final straw' by some time.[504]

5.74   The concept of constructive dismissal has not entirely escaped the more specific, technical aspects of the law of repudiatory breach. There must, for example, be an immediate threat to the express contract terms for the employer to have committed a repudiation; it may not be enough for the employer merely to voice a difference of opinion about the contract terms, even if it should subsequently turn out that the employee was right. This is an application of the principle, enunciated by the House of Lords in *Woodar Investment Development Ltd v Wimpey Construction UK Ltd*,[505] that an assertion of a contractual right, unless it is made in bad faith, does not amount to a repudiation merely because it 'has proved to be wrong in law'. For the assertion to amount to a repudiation, the guilty party must '[evince] an intention not to be bound by the contract'.[506] Similarly, '[t]he mere fact that an employer is of the opinion, albeit mistakenly, that there is something to be discussed with his employee about the contract is a very long way from the employer taking up the attitude that he is not under any circumstances at all going to be bound by it'.[507]

This doctrine could place an employee in a difficult position where the employer fails to respect contractual rights to which the employee believes,

---

497 *Murco Petroleum Ltd v Forge* [1987] IRLR 50 and *Bridgen v Lancashire County Council* [1987] IRLR 58 respectively. On whether HRA 1998 may lead to a widening of the employer's duties of co-operation and good faith, see Hepple, 1998b; 2001a.

498 *Industrial Rubber Products v Gillon* [1977] IRLR 389; *Cantor Fitzgerald International v Callaghan* [1999] IRLR 234.

499 *Hogg v Dover College* [1990] ICR 39.

500 *Hilton v Shiner Ltd – Builders Merchants* [2001] IRLR 727.

501 A wholly exceptional case is *Adams v Charles Zub Associates Ltd* [1978] IRLR 551, where an employer's failure to pay on time was excused on the grounds of unanticipated cash-flow difficulties.

502 *Lewis v Motorworld Garages Ltd* [1985] IRLR 465.

503 *London Borough of Waltham Forest v Omilaju* [2005] IRLR 35, para 19 (Dyson LJ).

504 *Logan v Commissioners of Customs and Excise* [2004] IRLR 63, paras 30-33 (Ward LJ).

505 [1980] 1 WLR 277, 280 (Lord Wilberforce).

506 [1980] 1 WLR 277, 299 (Lord Scarman).

507 *Financial Techniques (Planning Services) Ltd v Hughes* [1981] IRLR 32, 35 (Lawton LJ); see also *Frank Wright & Co (Holdings) Ltd v Punch* [1980] IRLR 217.

with reason, he or she is entitled. However, it should not be taken as exempting employers from the consequences of actual, as opposed to anticipatory, breaches of the express contract terms relating to pay and hours; nor does it prevent the operation of the implied obligation to maintain trust and confidence in an appropriate situation. The best view would seem to be that the assertion of a genuine but mistaken view of the contract *might* give rise to a repudiation in a given case, where other factors also point in that direction; at least as far as employment contracts are concerned, there is no rule to the effect that the good faith nature of an erroneous assertion of rights, by itself, prevents there being a repudiation.[508] In *BBC v Beckett*[509] the employee was at first dismissed for committing an act of negligence which led to the injury of a fellow worker and then, on appeal, offered a job at a lower grade and in a different department. He refused to accept this and resigned. The employment tribunal found that the punishment inflicted on the employee was out of proportion to his offence, and that the employer's conduct amounted to a repudiation. On appeal it was argued that the employer had purported to exercise an express power in good faith and therefore could not be said to have committed a repudiatory breach, but the EAT held that the principle in *Woodar v Wimpey*[510] did not 'derogate from the general proposition that a party to a contract may so act that his conduct viewed objectively amounts to a fundamental breach of his contractual obligations':[511] accordingly, there had been a constructive dismissal.

As we have seen, the decisions of the EAT in *Hogg v Dover College*[512] and *Alcan Extrusions v Yates*[513] indicate that an employee faced with a repudiatory breach short of dismissal may not necessarily have to resign in order to force the issue of constructive dismissal; he or she may have the right to accept the repudiation and bring the original contract to an end, while then remaining in employment under a new contract. This is because '[t]he question is not whether the relationship between the parties has ceased; the question is not whether there was any contract between the parties; the question is whether the particular contract under which the employee was employed by the employer at the relevant time was terminated by the employer'.[514] If the employee makes it clear that he or she is working under protest, they are not taken to have waived the right to terminate the original contract.[515] If this doctrine is correct it would mean, for example, that Mr Beckett could have accepted the inferior post offered to him by the BBC and then brought an action for unfair dismissal, without needing to quit; the employment tribunal, on finding that he was unfairly dismissed, would then have had the power to order his reinstatement into the job which he previously occupied.[516] Reinstatement is very rarely awarded, and financial

---

508 *Financial Techniques (Planning Services) Ltd v Hughes* [1981] IRLR 32, 36–37 (Templeman LJ); see also *Brown v JBD Engineering Ltd* [1993] IRLR 568. See also Reynold and Palmer, 2005.
509 [1983] IRLR 43.
510 [1980] 1 WLR 277.
511 [1983] IRLR 43, 46 (Neill J).
512 [1990] ICR 39.
513 [1996] IRLR 327.
514 [1990] ICR 39, 43.
515 Cf [1990] ICR 39, 44: 'the applicant accepted the employer's conduct as repudiatory and cannot, by his subsequent conduct, be said to have affirmed the original contract or any original contract as varied' (Garland J). See also *WE Cox Toner (International) Ltd v Crook* [1981] IRLR 443, *Henry v London General Transport Services* [2002] IRLR 472.
516 ERA 1996, ss 113–114.

compensation is a much more likely outcome;[517] nonetheless, *Hogg* and *Alcan* place the employee in a far better position than decisions which suggest that the employee has no choice but to resign if he or she wishes to claim unfair dismissal in response to unjustified disciplinary action or a unilateral change in terms and conditions.[518]

More generally, there will be no ready assumption of waiver or estoppel in a case where the employee's hesitation is due to ignorance of his or her rights,[519] nor where the employer's breach of contract also amounts to a statutory wrong which the employee has no power to waive.[520]

5.75   Although a constructive dismissal necessarily entails a repudiatory breach of contract by an employer, this does not mean that the dismissal is automatically unfair. The tribunal may find that the dismissal was for a potentially fair reason and that the employer acted reasonably in the circumstances; a unilateral cut in pay could, for example, be justified by external cuts in the funding received by the employer.[521] This means that while unfair dismissal law goes part of the way to entrenching the existing contract terms against unilateral variation, it also grants overriding priority to certain interests of the employer, in particular its claims to have the right to reorganise production processes in the interests of efficiency.[522]

'Self-dismissal' and resignation

5.76   Where the employee commits a repudiatory breach of contract, the elective theory holds that the contract is only terminated once the employer, as the innocent party, has accepted the breach. Since the contract is ended by the employer, there is a dismissal for the purposes of section 95(1)(a). Because, *ex hypothesi*, the employee has committed a serious contractual breach, the employer may not find it difficult to establish that there was a potentially fair reason for the dismissal and that it acted reasonably in the circumstances, but this does not inevitably follow. A more effective way of protecting the employer in these circumstances is the idea of 'self-dismissal', but this doctrine is of doubtful validity. In *Gannon v JC Firth Ltd*[523] it was suggested that employees who walked out of their employment in the course of a wildcat strike had thereby 'dismissed themselves', and in *London Transport Executive v Clarke*[524] Lord Denning MR argued that the same reasoning should apply in a case where the employee took seven weeks' leave of absence without permission. The majority of the Court of Appeal found, however, that there had been a dismissal in this case, and applied the elective theory to section 95(1). According to Templeman LJ, 'the acceptance by an employer of repudiation by a worker who wishes to continue his employment notwithstanding his repudiatory conduct constitutes the determination of the contract of employment by the employer ...'[525] However,

---

517   See para 5.152 below.
518   *Hunt v British Railways Board* [1979] IRLR 379, distinguished in *Hogg* [1990] ICR 39, 44.
519   *Peyman v Lanjani* [1985] Ch 457.
520   *Reid v Camphill Engravers Ltd* [1990] IRLR 268.
521   Eg *Kent County Council v Gilham* [1985] ICR 227. See paras 5.117 and 5.183 *et seq* below.
522   See para 5.183 *et seq* below.
523   [1976] IRLR 415; not followed in *Rasool v Hepworth Pipe Co Ltd* [1980] IRLR 88.
524   [1981] ICR 355.
525   [1981] ICR 355, 368.

his Lordship distinguished the situation where the employee walked out *without* wishing to continue the relationship of employment; here, the employer accepted the repudiation by taking no action to affirm the contract and the unfair dismissal legislation could apply only if there was a constructive dismissal, in the sense that the employee was responding to a repudiatory breach by the employer.[526] The latter part of this dictum amounts to saying that in such a situation the elective theory will not, in fact, apply.

It is already the case that the application of the elective theory to section 95 causes a certain blurring of the categories of termination by the employer, on the one hand, and constructive dismissal, on the other.[527] Prior to October 2004 the classification was primarily relevant to the questions of the employee's common law rights[528] and the effective date of termination;[529] it made little or no difference to the outcome of an unfair dismissal complaint whether the dismissal fell into one category or the other. However, in the light of the new statutory procedures, in force since 1 October 2004, the issue becomes a crucial one; unfair constructive dismissal complaints must usually be preceded by the use of the appropriate statutory grievance procedure in order for the tribunal to consider the complaint;[530] termination by the employer without completing the applicable statutory dismissal and disciplinary procedure will be an automatically unfair dismissal.[531] A further complication is that, if the elective theory is strictly applied to the case of the employee who quits employment without good reason, what looks at first sight like resignation could turn out to be dismissal by the employer: if the employee's departure is analysed as a repudiatory breach, the contract is only brought to an end by the employer's acceptance, which would bring the situation within section 95(1)(a). This would leave very little room for an effective concept of employee resignation, and may explain why in *Clarke* Templeman LJ was reluctant to apply the elective theory to this kind of case.

As the law currently stands, then, the notion of self-dismissal is not completely discredited: conduct of the employee which evinces an intention not to carry on with the relationship of employment may be regarded as terminating the contract of employment, according to the automatic theory. Such conduct may be regarded, in effect, as a form of resignation; but the conditions for drawing such an inference are strict. In principle it should not be appropriate to do so, for example, in the context of industrial action, since it is very rarely the intention of striking employees

---

526 [1981] ICR 355, 368.
527 See, eg, *Hogg v Dover College* [1990] ICR 39, where the employer's repudiation was analysed alternately as a dismissal under s 95(1)(a) and as a constructive dismissal under s 95(1)(c), and *Shook v Ealing London Borough Council* [1986] ICR 314 where it was suggested that in a case where the employer gave notice in breach of contract, this was best analysed as a constructive dismissal. Curran, 1994, argues that employer repudiation is best analysed as a dismissal under paragraph (a); cf R White, 1997.
528 For the employee to gain a specific remedy to prevent the employer acting on a wrongful dismissal, he or she must show that they have refused to accept the employer's repudiatory breach and are seeking to keep the contract on foot (see para 5.54 *et seq* above). If this common law action fails, an action for unfair dismissal may subsequently be brought on the basis that the dismissal was constructive; for these purposes, a provisional claim may be lodged with the employment tribunal: *R v East Berkshire Health Authority, ex p Walsh* [1984] ICR 743, 749 (Sir John Donaldson MR); *Shook v Ealing London Borough Council* [1986] ICR 314, 325.
529 See para 5.83 *et seq* below.
530 EA 2002, s 32; see para 2.21 *et seq*
531 ERA 1996, s 98A(1); see para 5.124 *et seq*.

to give up the employment in question and seek another; by definition, they are normally seeking improvement to the terms and conditions contained in their *existing* contracts of employment. This is not to say that conduct of this sort is not *repudiatory*, simply that it is not, in itself, the equivalent of resignation.

5.77   An agreement by the employee that he or she will be taken to have resigned in the event of committing a particular breach of discipline or some other act is likely to be struck down for statutory purposes by section 203(1) of ERA 1996, which, subject to some stated exceptions, renders void any contract or contract term purporting to exclude the operation of the Act. In *Igbo v Johnson Matthey Chemicals Ltd*[532] the employee was granted extended holiday leave, as a condition of which she signed a document stating that if she failed to return to work on an agreed date, 'your contract of employment will automatically terminate on that date'. When she came back from her holiday she was ill, sent her employer a medical certificate and reported for work after the date agreed for her return. She was told that her employment had come to an end. In the Court of Appeal it was held that Mrs Igbo had been dismissed, the agreement for self-dismissal being void under section 203(1) (previously section 140 of EPCA 1978): otherwise 'the whole object of the Act can be easily defeated by the inclusion of a term in a contract of employment that if the employee is late for work on the first Monday in any month, or indeed on any day, no matter for what reason, the contract shall automatically terminate'.[533]

On the other hand, section 203(1) will not be read as invalidating a genuinely consensual termination of employment. Where it can be shown that the employee agreed to resign by virtue of the severance terms offered by the employer, the resignation will probably not, as we have seen, constitute a dismissal;[534] nor will the severance agreement necessarily be struck down under section 203. This is because 'in the resolution of industrial disputes it is in the best interests of all concerned that a contract made without duress, for good consideration, preferably after proper and sufficient advice, and which has the effect of terminating a contract of employment by mutual agreement (whether at once or on some future date) should be effective between the contracting parties'.[535]

Expiry of limited-term contract

5.78   Section 95(1)(b) provides that there is a dismissal for the purposes of the Act where an employee is employed under a limited-term contract and that contract terminates by virtue of the limiting event without being renewed under the same contract.[536] A 'limited-term contract' is one where '(a) the employment

---

532 [1986] IRLR 215, overruling *British Leyland (UK) Ltd v Ashraf* [1978] IRLR 330; see also *Midland Electric Manufacturing Co Ltd v Kanji* [1980] IRLR 185; *Tracey v Zest Equipment Co Ltd* [1982] IRLR 268. See the useful discussion of this decision in Freedland, 2003: pp 432–439.
533 [1986] IRLR 215, 217 (Parker LJ).
534 *Logan Salton v Durham County Council* [1989] IRLR 99.
535 [1989] IRLR 99, 103.
536 This provision was substituted by FTER 2002, reg 11, Sch 2, para 3(1),(7). Prior to 25 October 1999 s 197(1) of ERA 1996 provided that, if the employment was in the form of a fixed term of at least one year and the dismissal took the form of the non-renewal of the contract under s 95(1)(b), the employee lost the right to claim unfair dismissal if he or she agreed in writing, before the expiry of the term, to exclude this right. This provision was repealed by ERelA 1999 and only valid waivers agreed before 25 October 1999 remain effective.

under the contract is not intended to be permanent, and (b) provision is accordingly made in the contract for it to terminate by virtue of a limiting event'.[537] A 'limiting event means:

(a) in the case of a contract for a fixed-term,[538] the expiry of the term,
(b) in the case of a contract made in contemplation of the performance of a specific task, the performance of that task, and
(c) in the case of a contract which provides for its termination on the occurrence of an event (or the failure of an event to occur), the occurrence of the event (or the failure of the event to occur).[539]

Prior to 1 October 2002 the legislation was confined to expiry of a fixed-term contract without renewal, a provision which excluded 'task contracts' to carry out a particular job unless they contained a set date when they were due to terminate.[540] In addition the legislation did not restrict the use of fixed-term contracts, unlike many continental systems which provided that if there was no good reason for the use of a fixed-term contract, or if a contract was renewed more that the minimum number of times allowed for by legislation, the employee was treated as if he or she was employed on a contract of indefinite duration, with the full protection of dismissal law.[541] Since 1 October 2002 protection against non-renewal of the more widely-defined 'limited-term contract' has applied, and restrictions have been introduced on the use of successive fixed-term contracts by FTER 2002 in order to comply with Directive 99/70/EC.[542] A provision that restricts the duration of a contract, where that contract (referred to here as the 'subsequent contract') has previously been renewed[543] or the employee has previously been employed on a fixed-term contract, will be of no effect and the employee will be deemed to be a permanent employee, provided that:

(a) the employee has been continuously employed under the subsequent contract, or under that contract taken with a previous fixed-term contract, for a period of four years or more (disregarding any period of employment before 10 July 2002)[544] and
(b) the employment of the employee under a fixed-term contract was not justified on objective grounds –

---

537 ERA 1996, s 235(2A).
538 A provision for earlier termination by notice does not prevent a contract being for a 'fixed term': *Allen v National Australia Group Europe Ltd* [2004] IRLR 847.
539 ERA 1996, s 235(2B).
540 *Wiltshire County Council v NATFHE* [1980] ICR 455.
541 On Spain, see Auvergnon and Gil y Gil, 1994; on Germany, Daübler and Le Friant, 1985; on France, Pélissier, Supiot and Jeammaud, 2004: pp 371–388.
542 See further para 3.86. Clause 5.1 of the Framework Agreement required Member States to introduce one or more of the following measures: (a) objective reasons justifying the renewal of such contracts or relationships; (b) the maximum total duration of successive fixed-term contracts; and (c) the number of renewals of such contracts or relationships. Clause 5.2 required Member States to determine under what conditions fixed-term employment contracts or relationships are to be regarded as 'successive' and deemed to be contracts or relationships of indefinite duration.
543 Renewal includes extension: FTER 2002, reg 1(2).
544 The date by which the Directive should have been transposed. The UK Government took the view that giving any retrospective effect to the restrictions on renewal would place unnecessary burdens on business: *Government Response to the Final Consultation on the Draft Fixed Term Employees (Prevention of Less Favourable Treatment) Regulations 2002*, DTI, 2002.

(i)   where the subsequent contract has been renewed, at the time when it was last renewed;

(ii) where the subsequent contract has not been renewed, at the time when it was entered into.[545]

The employee is deemed to be permanently employed as from the date on which he or she acquired four years' continuous employment or the date on which the subsequent contract was last entered into or renewed, whichever is the later. The 'objective grounds' that may justify continued employment under a fixed-term contract are not defined in the Regulations. The application of these measures may be modified in relation to a particular employee or description of employees by means of a 'collective agreement'[546] or 'workforce agreement'. [547]

5.79   The requirement for employment to be 'continuous' in order for the measures against abuse to apply is a considerable restriction on their effectiveness, given the ease with which continuity can be broken by employers.[548] Unless British courts can be persuaded to adopt a different version of the continuity rules in this context on the ground that the purpose of the Directive can be too easily circumvented, employees can be employed on successive fixed-term contracts of less than four years' duration indefinitely, provided that the employer ensures that there is a two-week gap between them to break continuity.

The Government declined to make it automatically unfair under FTER 2002 to dismiss an employee to prevent him or her acquiring permanent status,[549] concluding that it was unnecessary to do so because it is unlawful to dismiss a fixed-term employee for enforcing or seeking to enforce their rights.[550] However it is far from clear that it was unnecessary. An employee who is dismissed prior to acquiring permanent status never acquires a right to permanence and it is difficult, under these circumstances, to identify any other right that has been infringed.[551] If this view is correct, such a dismissal would need to be judged on ordinary unfair dismissal principles.

Frustration

5.80   At common law a contract discharged by frustration is terminated automatically, regardless of the 'opinions, or even knowledge' of the parties concerned;[552] accordingly, a contract of employment discharged in this way cannot be said to have been terminated by a dismissal within the meaning of

---

545   Reg 8.

546   See para 2.8 above.

547   See para 2.11 above.

548   *Booth v United States of America* [1999] IRLR 16; see generally para 3.92 *et seq.*

549   *Government Response to the Final Consultation on the Draft Fixed Term Employees' (Prevention of Less Favourable Treatment) Regulations 2002*, DTI, 2002, regulation 6. Cf the proposal by the TUC: *The Fixed-Term Employees (Prevention of Less Favourable Treatment) Regulations 2002*, TUC.

550   FTER 2002, reg 6.

551   Unless the employee has refused or proposed to refuse to forego the right to acquire permanent status, so bringing him or her within Regulation 6(3)(a)(vi). In *Department for Work and Pensions v Webley* [2005] IRLR 288 the Court of Appeal held that the termination of a fixed-term contract by effluxion of time could not, of itself, constitute less favourable treatment by comparison with a permanent employee nor could it represent a 'detriment'.

552   *Hirji Mulji v Cheong Yue SS Co Ltd* [1926] AC 497, 509; *GF Sharp & Co Ltd v McMillan* [1998] IRLR 632.

section 95(1)(a) or (c), each of which relies on one of the parties taking steps to bring the contract to an end. There is no doubt that the doctrine of frustration can apply to a contract of employment, as to most other kinds of contract. Supervening events which could, potentially, give rise to frustration include the death of either party[553] (although, for the purposes of redundancy compensation only, the death of the employer is deemed by the Act to be a dismissal[554]); an illness or injury of the employee which is either immediately disabling or, over a longer term, leads to prolonged absences;[555] and the imprisonment of the employee.[556] However, it is also an established principle that a contract will not be frustrated merely by a supervening event or *force majeure* if the parties have made provision for that event in their contract, and have expressly allocated the risk of its occurring; nor if the frustrating event is brought about by the fault of one of the parties. The application of these principles to the contract of employment has been far from straightforward.

5.81   There is much to be said for the view that in the normal contract of employment which is terminable by either party on short notice, the risk of a supervening event is already dealt with in the contract; if, for example, the employee is incapable of working by virtue of injury or illness, the employer has the option of terminating the contract by giving notice. Similarly, if the employee is imprisoned as a consequence of committing a criminal offence, it might be thought that he or she has thereby committed a repudiatory breach of contract, for which the employer may summarily dismiss them. In these cases, the doctrine of frustration is simply not needed to protect the employer's position at common law. The doctrine is invoked only because the employer wishes to avoid dismissing the employee under section 95(1)(a) and thereby triggering the unfair dismissal jurisdiction.

In *Harman v Flexible Lamps Ltd*[557] this prompted Bristow J to observe that 'in the field of employment the concept of discharge by operation of law, that is frustration, is normally only in play where the contract of employment is for a long term which cannot be determined by notice. Where the contract is terminable by notice, there is really no need to consider the question of frustration'. This sensible approach was, nevertheless, disapproved by the Court of Appeal in *Notcutt v Universal Equipment Co (London) Ltd*.[558] Dillon LJ gave two reasons for his view that frustration could apply to a contract terminable by short notice: such a contract 'may none the less be intended in many cases by both parties to last for many years'; and 'the power of the employer to terminate the contract by notice is subject to the provisions for the protection of employees against unfair dismissal'. Neither reason is very convincing. The bare expectation of the parties that the contract will continue indefinitely in no way detracts from the employer's right, at common law, to terminate it by giving notice;[559] while

---

553 Eg, *Cutter v Powell* (1795) 6 Term Rep 320, which would now be classified as a case of frustration.
554 ERA 1996, s 136(5). Other events which in accordance with any statute or rule of law operate to terminate the contract are also treated as dismissal by the employer for the purposes of statutory redundancy payments: s 136(5).
555 *Egg Stores (Stamford Hill) Ltd v Leibovici* [1977] ICR 260; *GF Sharp & Co Ltd v McMillan* [1998] IRLR 632.
556 *FC Shepherd & Co Ltd v Jerrom* [1986] IRLR 358.
557 [1980] IRLR 418, 419.
558 [1986] IRLR 218, 220–221.
559 See para 5.12 *et seq* above; there may be an exception if the contract contains a job security clause, see para 5.31 *et seq*.

Dillon LJ's second observation is the very reason normally given for limiting the doctrine of frustration, namely that it could defeat the aim of the Act in providing a degree of job security for the employee. In the case of long-term illness, for example, unfair dismissal law normally imposes certain minimum procedural requirements on the employer, in relation to the need to establish the nature of the illness, investigate the possibility of the employee being found alternative work and consider the feasibility of hiring a temporary replacement.[560] In addition statute now requires employers to comply with a basic dismissal and disciplinary procedure other than where the dismissal is constructive.[561] These procedural obligations are avoided at a stroke if the illness is regarded as frustrating the contract, thereby bringing it to an end without any dismissal.

Nor does a finding of dismissal necessarily decide the issue of fairness in the employee's favour; on the contrary, the tribunal may go on to find that the employer acted reasonably in the circumstances under section 98(4) of the Act, particularly since the advent of the 'no difference' rule in October 2004.[562] It would be difficult to envisage the tribunal reaching any other conclusion in a case, for example, where the employee's criminal conduct, whether in or out of work, had resulted in his imprisonment for a substantial period of time. The event which is alleged to give rise to frustration will normally constitute a potentially fair reason for dismissal,[563] but there is a difference between using the notion of a supervening event to find that dismissal was fair, and invoking the doctrine of frustration to decide that no dismissal even took place: the former route allows the tribunal to consider the merits of the case, the latter does not. The effects of frustration, in terms of wiping out statutory entitlements, may be far reaching. An employee whose contract is frustrated cannot qualify for a statutory redundancy payment, nor for the statutory right to receive notice prior to the termination of employment, since both these sets of rights depend on upon there being a dismissal.[564] Moreover, where the contract is discharged by frustration, the parties may have great difficulty in determining precisely when the contract came to an end.

Notwithstanding *Notcutt*, the EAT stressed in *Williams v Watsons Luxury Coaches Ltd*[565] that cases of frustration of employment contracts will be 'rare occurrences' and that 'the court must guard against too easy an application of the doctrine'; the lay members in this case also thought that 'the doctrine of frustration when applied to employment contracts is one which, unless severely limited in its scope, can do harm to good industrial relations as it provides an easy escape from the obligations of investigation which should be carried out by a conscientious employer',[566] but this is not a view which had the support of Wood J.

5.82   In deciding whether a particular contract of employment is frustrated, the essential question is whether it can be said that the future performance of the employee had become impossible at the time in question. For this purpose a distinction should be drawn between, on the one hand, 'an event (eg a crippling

---

560 *Lynock v Cereal Packaging Ltd* [1988] IRLR 510; see para 5.145 below.
561 ERA 1996, s 98A(1); EA 2002, Sch 2, Part 1.
562 ERA 1996, s 98A(2); see further para 5.143.
563 See para 5.115 below.
564 See generally *GF Sharp & Co Ltd v McMillan* [1998] IRLR 632.
565 [1990] IRLR 164, 166.
566 [1990] IRLR 164, 167.

accident) so dramatic and shattering that everyone concerned will realise immediately that to all intents and purposes the contract must be regarded as at an end' and, on the other, 'an event, such as illness or accident, the course and outcome of which is uncertain'.[567] For example, in the case of illness the court will look both at the nature of the disabling event (the length of the illness, its likely future duration, its effect on the employee's ability to work) and at the contract terms to see whether the provision made for termination and for payment of wages or sick pay in the event of illness impliedly exclude the doctrine. In *Egg Stores (Stamford Hill) Ltd v Leibovici*[568] the EAT listed a number of other factors to be considered, including the length of the employee's previous employment, the parties' expectations of continuing employment, the availability of a replacement, the risk to the employer of incurring statutory or other obligations by retaining the employee in employment, and 'whether in all the circumstances a reasonable employer could be expected to wait any longer'. This type of inquiry is very wide-ranging, and seems to be inviting the tribunal to consider issues which should, more properly, be considered under the heading of the test of fairness under section 98(4). In *Notcutt v Universal Equipment* Co *(London) Ltd*[569] the Court of Appeal took a somewhat simpler approach in concluding that once the employee's doctor had told him that he would probably never work again following a heart attack, the contract was frustrated.

The Court of Appeal has also held that the imprisonment of the employee may give rise to frustration on the grounds of his or her resulting inability to perform the contract, notwithstanding that, at common law, 'self-induced frustration' of this kind would not normally suffice to discharge the primary obligations of the party at fault.[570] This seems nothing more than an opportunistic use of the doctrine to avoid the application of the Act,[571] and although the result may well have been the right one, the same end could have been achieved more consistently with principle by a finding that the dismissal was fair in the circumstances.

Effective date of termination

5.83   The date of dismissal, known as the 'effective date of termination' (or EDT), is important for a number of purposes under the Act and can affect the employee's claim for unfair dismissal in two particularly significant ways. The first concerns the length of the employee's continuous employment: leaving aside the few cases where no qualifying service is needed, the employee must have been continuously employed for a period of one year 'ending with the effective date of termination'.[572] The second relates to what is, in effect, the limitation period for unfair claims: the employment tribunal shall not

---

567 *Egg Stores (Stamford Hill) Ltd v Leibovici* [1977] ICR 260, 265.
568 [1977] ICR 260, 265. See also *Marshall v Harland and Wolff Ltd* [1972] IRLR 90.
569 [1986] IRLR 218.
570 *FC Shepherd & Co Ltd v Jerrom* [1986] IRLR 358; cf *Hare v Murphy Bros Ltd* [1974] IRLR 342; *Four Seasons Healthcare Ltd v Maughan* [2005] IRLR 324.
571 The Court of Appeal in *Shepherd* was influenced by the argument that it was the *applicant* who was attempting to rely on his own fault to exclude frustration in what was regarded as a mirror image of the usual context in which frustration is pleaded: Lawton LJ at 362, Mustill LJ at 364; see also *Ananwu v London South Bank Students Union* ULEAT 0280/ 03, EAT 20 November 2003. However this is not an answer to the wider policy objections to the operation of the doctrine in this context.
572 ERA 1996, s 108(1). On continuity of employment, see para 3.92 *et seq* above.

consider the applicant's complaint unless it is presented before the end of a period of three months beginning with the EDT, subject to a limited power of the tribunal to extend this period where the employee can show that it was not reasonably practicable to present the complaint within the time limit.[573] Since 1 October 2004 this time limit may be extended in specified circumstances where the statutory dismissal and disciplinary procedures apply;[574] we discuss this further in para 5.124 below. The EDT is a 'statutory construct which depends on what has happened between the parties over time and not on what they may agree to treat as having happened'.[575] It cannot, therefore, be fixed by agreement between the parties.[576]

5.84   Under section 97(1) of the Act, the 'effective date of termination':

(a)   in relation to an employee whose contract of employment is terminated by notice, whether given by his employer or by the employee, means the date on which the notice expires;

(b)   in relation to an employee whose contract of employment is terminated without notice, means the date on which the termination takes effect; and

(c)   in relation to an employee who is employed under a limited-term contract which terminates by virtue of the limiting event without being renewed under the same contract, means the date on which the termination takes effect.[577]

The principal issue which this provision leaves open is the effect on the EDT of a breach of contract by the employer. If, for example, the employer fails to give sufficient notice of termination, is the EDT the date on which the notice expires, or the date when it should have expired? The courts have opted for the first of these possibilities,[578] which is apparently in line with the reference to 'the notice', read as the notice actually given, in section 97(1)(a). However, the EAT has held that the EDT cannot be earlier than the date on which the applicant knows he or she is being dismissed.[579] Section 97(2) provides that where the employee does not receive the minimum *statutory* notice to which he or she was entitled,

---

573   ERA 1996, s 111(2). Where a dismissal is with notice, the tribunal can consider a complaint after the notice is given but before the EDT: s 111(3). In *Rai v Somerfield Stores Ltd* [2004] IRLR 124 the EAT held that a notice which enables the employer to terminate the contract of employment only if the employee does or does not perform a particular act specified in the notice, which only the employee can choose whether or not to perform, is not a 'notice' for the purpose of s 111(3).

574   EADRR 2004, reg 15.

575   *Fitzgerald v University of Kent at Canterbury* [2004] IRLR 300, para 20 (Sedley LJ).

576   In addition, any such agreement would be void under ERA 1996, s 203: *Fitzgerald*, above, para 22 (Sedley LJ).

577   Substantially the same provision applies in the context of redundancy compensation (the 'relevant date': ERA 1996, s 145) but with some further qualifications: see para 5.173 below. On the meaning of 'limited-term contract' and 'limiting event' see para 5.78 above.

578   *TBA Industrial Products Ltd v Morland* [1982] IRLR 331. On the difficult questions of construction which may arise in this context, see *Dedman v British Building and Engineering Appliances Ltd* [1974] ICR 53; *Chapman v Letherby and Christopher Ltd* [1981] IRLR 440.

579   *McMaster v Manchester Airport plc* [1998] IRLR 112. The EAT declined to allow an argument based upon constructive or presumed knowledge. It follows that, in a case of constructive dismissal, the EDT will normally be the date on which the employee communicates to the employer his or her decision to leave the employment: *Edwards v Surrey Police* [1999] IRLR 456.

the EDT shall be extended for certain purposes[580] to the date on which the statutory notice, had it been given, would have expired; the existence of this provision can be read as impliedly supporting the proposition that *contractual* notice cannot be taken into account under section 97(1)(a), if it is not actually given. If, having received notice from the employer, the employee exercises the statutory right to give a shorter counter-notice under section 95(2), the EDT will be the date on which the counter-notice expires.[581] Where the employer's notice is deemed still to be the operative cause of the termination of employment but the employee accepts the employer's invitation to leave early, the position is more complex; for clarity's sake employers would be best advised to withdraw the original notice and substitute a second notice which contains the earlier date.[582]

5.85   A second situation to consider is that in which the employer summarily dismisses the employee without good cause: is the contract terminated forthwith, or at some later date when the employee has accepted the employer's repudiatory breach? The elective theory would give the employee the right to delay acceptance where he or she has a 'legitimate interest' in doing so, and it would not perhaps be stretching the notion of 'legitimate interest' too far to include a case where the employee sought to delay the EDT in order to ensure that he or she acquires the necessary continuity of employment. This argument could be applied for example, to the situation in which the employer dismisses the employee a few days or weeks short of the completion of the qualifying period, for the sole purpose of ensuring that the employee does not acquire the protection of the Act. However, in general the attitude of the courts has been that in the interests of certainty, the automatic theory should determine the EDT under section 97(1)(b), so that the termination 'takes effect' when the act of summary dismissal takes place.[583] In *Stapp v Shaftesbury Society*[584] the Court of Appeal expressly ruled out the possibility of using the elective theory to extend the period of continuous employment by holding that 'the effect of ... summary dismissal in fixing the effective date of termination' cannot be questioned, although this was not a case where the employer was found to have ended the contract for the sole purpose of avoiding the application of the Act.

---

580 These include the establishment of the period of continuity of employment for the purposes of s 108(1) and the calculation of the basic award for unfair dismissal (s 119(1)) but not the period of three months for the claim in time under s 111(2). See *Fox Maintenance Ltd v Jackson* [1977] IRLR 306. In *Harper v Virgin Net Ltd* [2004] IRLR 390, s 97(2)(b) was invoked to preclude a claim for damages for loss of a chance of recovering compensation for unfair dismissal in circumstances where the employee had not been given the three months' notice to which she was entitled under her contract; see further para 5.22 above.

581 *Thompson v GEC Avionics Ltd* [1991] IRLR 488. The effect of s 95(2) is that the employee is still regarded as having been dismissed in this situation.

582 *TBA Industrial Products Ltd v Morland* [1982] IRLR 331. In *Palfrey v Transco plc* [2004] IRLR 916 the EAT found on the facts that the employers had done this, but also opined that there should be scope for variation even if they had not and that *TBA Industrial Products Ltd* was *per incuriam*.

583 The leading judgment is that of Browne-Wilkinson J in *Robert Cort & Son Ltd v Charman* [1981] IRLR 437; see also *Dedman v British Building and Engineering Appliances Ltd* [1973] IRLR 379; *Stapp v Shaftesbury Society* [1982] IRLR 326; *Batchelor v British Railways Board* [1987] IRLR 136; *BMK Ltd v Logue* [1993] IRLR 477; although cf *Shook v Ealing London Borough Council* [1986] ICR 314.

584 [1982] IRLR 326, 330.

5.86   A third situation is that in which the employer, this time in accordance with the contract, operates a disciplinary procedure which results in the confirmation of an earlier decision to summarily dismiss the employee: is the EDT the date upon which an initial decision to dismiss is taken, or is the employee dismissed only once his or her internal rights of appeal are exhausted? The courts have taken the view that the EDT is normally the earlier of these two dates, unless the contract itself provides for the employee to be suspended from employment, but continuing to receive wages or salary, during the period of any appeal (as opposed to being dismissed with the possibility of reinstatement), in which case the EDT is the date on which the employer informs the employee of the outcome of the appeal.[585] Prior to October 2004 the only course open to employees who failed to comply with the three-month time limit for presenting an unfair dismissal complaint because they were awaiting the outcome of an internal appeal was to invoke section 111(2) of the Act, whereby the normal three-month period may be extended where the tribunal 'is satisfied that it was not reasonably practicable for the complaint to be presented before the end' of this period. Whether or not an extension is granted is a matter for the discretion of the individual tribunal.[586] Since 1 October 2004 the time limit for presenting an unfair dismissal complaint may be extended in specified circumstances where the statutory dismissal and disciplinary procedures (SDDPs) apply.[587] If a dismissed employee presents a complaint after the three-month period has expired, the time limit is extended for a further three months beginning with the day after that on which it would otherwise have expired, provided that the employee had reasonable grounds for believing, when the initial time limit expired, that a dismissal or disciplinary procedure, *whether statutory or otherwise*, was being followed in respect of matters that consisted of or included the substance of the complaint to the tribunal.[588] If, however, the SDDPs do not apply (for example, because the dismissal falls within one of the exempted categories) the employee will not be covered by this provision and will need to rely on the general discretion to extend even if he or she has delayed presenting the complaint in order to pursue an internal appeal. It is notable that, to qualify for the three-month extension, the employee must believe that the procedure is being followed

---

585   *Drage v Governors of Greenford High School* [2000] IRLR 314, CA, reviewing earlier case law including *Savage v J Sainsbury Ltd* [1981] ICR 1. On the use of the time limit provisions in ERA 1996 s 111 to overcome restrictive readings of the EDT, see para 2.17 above.

586   *Bodha v Hampshire Area Health Authority* [1982] ICR 200, not following *Crown Agents for Overseas Governments and Administration v Lawal* [1979] ICR 103, where it was suggested that an extension would regularly be granted where an application was delayed by reason of an internal procedure; see further para 2.17. In *Marley (UK) Ltd v Anderson* [1996] IRLR 163 the Court of Appeal held (surprisingly) that although an employee's complaint on the initial ground put forward was time-barred, the tribunal did have jurisdiction to consider the complaint on a different ground which had subsequently come to light and which the employee had raised, by amendment to his existing claim, within a reasonable period after acquiring the relevant knowledge.

587   See further para 5.124. Note that the SDDPs apply only to s 95(1)(a) and (b) dismissals; complaints of unfair constructive dismissal must usually be preceded by instituting one of the statutory grievance procedures. On the extension provisions that apply in relation to the grievance procedures, see para 2.23 above.

588   EADRR 2004, reg 15(1),(2). The drafting of reg 15 is curious. The term 'dismissal and disciplinary procedures' is defined in reg 2(1) of EADRR 2004 as the statutory procedures. However reg 15(2) refers to a dismissal or disciplinary procedure, whether statutory or otherwise and seems, therefore, to envisage provision for extension in relation to any such procedure.

when the initial time limit expired. If the employer concludes the procedure very shortly before that time the employee will need to rely on the tribunal's general discretion. It is also possible that disputes will arise as to whether it was reasonable to believe that a procedure which had in fact lapsed was still being actively followed.

Section 111(3)–(4) of ERA 1996 makes explicit provision for a complaint to be made after notice of dismissal has been given but while the employee is still in employment, and in a case where the employee seeks to keep the contract on foot by applying to the High Court for a declaration or injunction it has been normal for him or her to make an application to an employment tribunal at the same time, pending the outcome of the other action.[589] This course now presents dangers for employees, however; an employee who fails to complete a statutory procedure, including an appeal, 'before the proceedings were begun' risks losing between 10% and 50% of the compensatory award unless he or she can convince the tribunal that there are 'exceptional circumstances' which would make such a reduction inequitable.[590]

5.87   The three-month period for bringing claims is extremely short in comparison to the normal six-year limitation period for actions in breach of contract,[591] but the justification for this is the less formal procedure which operates in employment tribunals.[592] Under the early unfair dismissal legislation a 28-day period applied; when this was extended to the current three months, Lord Denning thought that as a result there was even 'less reason for granting an indulgence to the complainant'.[593] The circumstances when it will be regarded as not 'reasonably practicable' to make a claim in time are limited.[594] It is not normally acceptable to delay a claim pending the outcome of other legal proceedings, such as criminal proceedings relating to an alleged offence or a claim for the jobseeker's allowance.[595] In the past it has normally been relevant that the employee was hoping to avoid litigation by seeking alternative remedies,[596] but where the specific provision for the extension of time in EADRR 2004 applies this may make the courts more reluctant to grant a further extension in addition to that provided by those Regulations, where the alternative remedy in question consists of the pursuit of a dismissal or disciplinary procedure.

FAIRNESS OF DISMISSAL

5.88   Section 98 of ERA 1996 sets up a two-stage test of fairness which separates the *reasons for dismissal* from the *reasonableness of the employer's conduct.* At the first stage the employer is required to show that the dismissal took place for reasons which were 'potentially fair', that is to say capable of providing a

---

589 This course was recommended in *R v East Berkshire Health Authority, ex p Walsh* [1984] ICR 743, 753 and *Shook v Ealing London Borough Council* [1986] ICR 314, 325.
590 EA 2002, s 31; ERA 1996, s 124A; see further para 5.161.
591 Limitation Act 1980, s 5.
592 This point was discussed by the Donovan Commission, which recommended a maximum period of five working days from the dismissal: Cmnd 3623, 1968: p 147.
593 *Wall's Meat Co Ltd v Kho* 1979] ICR 52, 59.
594 See para 2.17 above.
595 *Wall's Meat Co I* 338 c 79] ICR 52.
596 See *Schultz v* (\ [1999] IRLR 488.

legitimate basis for the termination of employment. Although the burden of proof is placed on the employer at this stage, the statutory categories of potentially fair reasons are very broadly defined, and only a completely unreasoned or arbitrary dismissal is likely to fall outside their scope. However, the employee may nevertheless win the case at this point if the tribunal finds that the dismissal took place for one of a strictly-defined set of automatically unfair reasons which are deemed to be illegitimate *per se* or (for dismissals contemplated on or after 1 October 2004) that the employer failed to complete the appropriate statutory dismissal and disciplinary procedure. Conversely, the employer may be able to show that the dismissal took place in circumstances where it enjoys an immunity (these are also narrowly defined). Otherwise, the tribunal proceeds to the second stage, at which it assesses whether the employer 'acted reasonably or unreasonably' in treating the reason relied upon as a sufficient reason, in the circumstances, for dismissing the employee. The Act's explicit reference to the employer's conduct stresses that the standard here is more procedural than substantive, that is to say, concerned less with the fairness of the outcome than with the fairness of the process by which it was arrived at. However the emphasis on procedural justice has been somewhat reduced since October 2004 by the provision that failure to follow a procedure beyond the statutory minimum does not of itself make the employer's action unreasonable if it shows that it would still have decided to dismiss the employee had that procedure been followed. In other respects the standard of 'reasonableness' is variable, in the sense that the tribunal must take into account the 'size and administrative resources of the employer's undertaking', and embodies a strong element of discretion: the tribunal must decide whether the employer acted reasonably 'in accordance with equity and the substantial merits of the case' in question.

Discretion also affects the question of remedies. The grant of the remedies of reinstatement and re-engagement is discretionary, and an employer may be able to resist one or the other on the grounds of its impracticability. Even if an order involving re-employment is made, it cannot be specifically enforced; at best the employee will obtain additional compensation. Compensation may be awarded under a wider range of heads of loss than allowed at common law, but the tribunal may reduce the award for, among other things, the employee's non-completion of the appropriate statutory procedure or contributory fault.

Relevant reasons

5.89   Under section 98(1) of ERA 1996, the employer is required to show 'the reason (or, if more than one, the principal reason) for the dismissal' and to show that it comes within one or other of the 'gateways' of potentially fair reasons.[597] The only relevant 'reason' or 'principal reason', for this purpose, is one which the employer had at the time of the dismissal;[598] and it is in relation to *this* reason that the employer's conduct is to be judged. Under section 98(4), whether a dismissal is fair depends on whether 'the employer acted reasonably or unreasonably in treating *it* as a sufficient reason' (emphasis added); the 'it' is the reason actually relied on.[599] As a result 'what must be shown to be reasonable and sufficient is the employer's action in treating the reason shown by him (the

---

597 ERA 1996, s 98(1).
598 See the discussion below for what constitutes the ▲ f dismissal in this context.
599 *W Devis & Sons Ltd v Atkins* [1977] IRLR 314 ▲ iscount Dilhorne).

employer) as the reason for dismissing the employee'.[600] The distinction between the two stages of inquiry – the first, at which the reason or reasons for dismissal are established and classified as potentially fair or otherwise, and the second, at which the reasonableness of the employer's conduct is assessed – is fundamental to the approach of the Act to evaluating fairness in dismissal.[601] On the face of it, the first stage begins with a purely factual inquiry – what was the reason actually relied on by the employer? – while the question of whether that reason was objectively justifiable in the circumstances is one for the second stage.

5.90 The main issue facing the tribunal under section 98(1), properly understood, is the identification of the reason which motivated the dismissal. Some leeway is allowed to the employer by the principle that in an appropriate case the tribunal may infer, from the evidence offered, that the employer was motivated by a reason which was not clearly expressed as such at the relevant time. In *Abernethy v Mott, Hay and Anderson*[602] Cairns LJ said:

> A reason for the dismissal of an employee is a set of facts known to the employer, or it may be of beliefs held by him, which cause him to dismiss the employee. If at the time of his dismissal the employer gives a reason for it, that is no doubt evidence, at any rate as against him, as to the real reason, but it does not necessarily constitute the real reason.

Cairns LJ gave three examples of situations in which the given reason might not be the 'real reason': where a false reason is given out of kindness; where the employer 'might have difficulty in proving the facts that actually led him to dismiss'; and where he 'may describe his reason wrongly through some mistake of language or of law'. In the first case, where a false reason is deliberately given, the burden on the employer of showing that he had a different reason to that given at the time may be particularly heavy, but is not insurmountable. In the second case, where the employer did not have good grounds at the time for taking the decision to dismiss, the reason may well be potentially fair but it is doubtful that the employer will be held to have acted reasonably under section 98(4). For the tribunal 'to accept as a reasonably sufficient reason for dismissal a reason which, at least, in respect of an important part was neither established in fact nor believed to be true on reasonable grounds is ... an error of law'.[603] This is because, as we shall see, the requirements of procedural fairness normally impose an obligation upon the employer at the very least to formulate the charges against an employee; if the employer is not even clear, at the time of dismissal, what the reason for it was, a breach of procedural fairness is likely to be made out. By extension, if the tribunal finds that the employer could have dismissed the employee fairly for one reason which was backed up by evidence, but that the employer was in fact motivated by a different reason for which there was no adequate evidence, the dismissal will most likely be held to be unfair on procedural grounds: the tribunal cannot impute to the employer a reason which it did not have at the time.[604]

---

600 *W Devis & Sons Ltd v Atkins* [1977] IRLR 314, 320 (Lord Simon of Glaisdale).
601 *Beedell v West Ferry Printers Ltd* [2000] IRLR 650, 655; *Post Office v Foley; HSBC Bank plc v Madden* [2000] IRLR 827; cf *Midland Bank plc v Madden* [2000] IRLR 288, 291–292, which undermined this distinction.
602 [1974] IRLR 213, 215.
603 *Smith v Glasgow City District Council* [1987] ICR 796, 804.
604 *Smith v Glasgow City District Council* [1987] ICR 796, 804.

Cairns LJ's third category, that of misdescription, is the one most likely to assist the employer. The employer does not necessarily have to have used the same words as those used in the statutory definition of the potentially fair reasons, such as 'misconduct' or 'incapability', when dismissing the employee. The *Abernethy* principle can even extend to a case of constructive dismissal, where the employer may not realise at the time that a dismissal is taking place. In *Ely v YKK Fasteners (UK) Ltd*[605] Waite LJ said that 'if resort can be had to a state of facts known to and relied on by the employer at the time, for the purpose of substituting a valid reason for any invalid or misdescribed reason given by the employer through misapprehension or mistake, there seems to me to be every justification for extending that principle to enable resort to be had to a state of facts known to and relied on by the employer, for the purposes of supplying him with a reason for dismissal which, as a consequence of his misapprehension of the true nature of the circumstances, he was disabled as treating as such at the time'.

In this case, the employee led his employer to believe that he was about to resign, but changed his mind before a formal resignation was submitted. The employer treated the employment at an end; this was found to be a constructive dismissal. It was held that the employer was entitled to argue that the dismissal was for 'some other substantial reason' under section 98(1)(b) of the Act. In effect, the employer can treat as the reason for dismissal the reason it had for the *conduct which gave rise to the dismissal*, in other words the conduct which amounted to a repudiatory breach; or, as Lord Browne-Wilkinson has put it, 'the only way in which the statutory requirements of the Act of ... [1996] ... can be made to fit a case of constructive dismissal is to read section ... [98(1)] as requiring the employers to show the reasons for their conduct which entitled the employee to terminate the contract thereby giving rise to a deemed dismissal'.[606] This might seem to be a considerable enlargement of the *Abernethy* principle, but it needs to be remembered that a constructive dismissal is not automatically unfair.[607] It therefore seems unavoidable that an employer can seek to show that its reasons for acting as it did are also the reasons for the dismissal for statutory purposes; otherwise it would be impossible to find that a constructive dismissal was ever fair. *Ely* does not formally seek to disturb the principle that the tribunal cannot substitute for the reason given a reason which the employer did not actually rely on.

5.91   The statutory dismissal and disciplinary procedures introduced by EA 2002 require the employer to set out in writing the employee's alleged conduct or characteristics, or other circumstances, which lead it to contemplate dismissal.[608] In addition the employer is under a separate statutory obligation, contained in section 92 of ERA 1996, to give a written statement of the reasons for dismissal within 14 days of the employee requesting such a statement,[609] except where the dismissal was constructive.[610] The statement is admissible in any proceedings,

---

605 [1993] IRLR 500, 503.
606 *Berriman v Delabole Slate Ltd* [1985] ICR 546, 555–556.
607 See para 5.75 above.
608 See further para 5.124 *et seq*.
609 ERA 1996, s 92(2). An employee who is dismissed while pregnant or during a period of ordinary or additional maternity or adoption leave is entitled to a statement without having to request one: ERA 1996, 92(4), (4A).
610 ERA 1996, s 92(1).

and it seems that the main justification for the right to such a statement is to assist the employee in relation to legal claims arising out of the dismissal.[611] However, in general[612] the right vests only in employees with at least one year's continuity of employment at the time of dismissal.[613] The requirement for a lengthy period of continuous employment to enjoy the right was introduced by the Employment Act 1989, which set a period of two years;[614] before that only six months' continuity was needed. At the time it was argued that the qualifying period for this purpose should be the same as that applying to unfair dismissal generally,[615] and this remains the case even though the period for both rights has now been reduced to one year.[616] This is not a very convincing reason since numerous legal rights arising out of dismissal are not dependent on continuity in this sense. These include claims for the jobseeker's allowance, for the purposes of which it may be important to establish that the claimant was not dismissed for good cause, in which case he or she faces disqualification for being 'voluntarily unemployed'. The employee may also wish to show that dismissal took place for an automatically unfair reason, for which in most cases no period of continuity is needed, or to bring a claim for damages for wrongful dismissal.

The employer is required to provide a statement as a distinct document which must 'be of such a kind that the employee, or anyone to whom he may wish to show it, can know from reading the document itself why the employee has been dismissed'; the document may refer to other materials but must in itself 'contain a simple statement of the essential reasons for the dismissal'.[617] If the employer unreasonably fails to provide a written statement, or provides one whose particulars are inadequate or untrue, the employee may complain to an employment tribunal, which has the power to declare what it considers to have been the real reasons for dismissal and to award the employee a sum equal to two weeks' pay.[618]

It does not follow, however, that the reasons given by the employer in this written statement will necessarily be those found to be the relevant ones for the purposes of an unfair dismissal claim. Under the *Abernethy* principle, the employer may apparently still seek to show that the reasons given at the time were misdescribed, and that the real reasons were otherwise. But the result is unfortunate, since the penalty against the employer for misleading the employee in this way is the relatively insignificant award of two weeks' pay. It is arguable that the courts should invoke in this context the principle of estoppel, to restrict the right of the employer to seek to go back on its statement to the employee.

5.92 The principle that the employer cannot rely on a reason which it did not have at the time of dismissal but only *might* have had means that facts emerging

---

611 ERA 1996, s 92(5).
612 No minimum period of employment is required if an employee is dismissed while pregnant or during a period of ordinary or additional maternity or adoption leave: ERA 1996, s 92(4), (4A).
613 ERA 1996, s 92(3).
614 EA 1989, ss 15(1) and 29(6) and Sch 9, amending EPCA 1978, s 53(2), now ERA 1996, s 92(3).
615 Mr Patrick Nicholls, HC Official Report, Standing Committee A, col 374, 28 February 1989.
616 On the reasoning behind this change, see *Fairness at Work*, Cm 3968, para 3.9.
617 *Horsley Smith and Sherry Ltd v Dutton* [1977] ICR 594, 597.
618 ERA 1996, s 93. The complaint must be presented within the same time limits as a claim for unfair dismissal in respect of that dismissal: s 93(3). The statutory grievance procedures, described in para 2.21 *et seq* above, do not apply to such complaints.

after the dismissal cannot be taken into account in the employer's favour in establishing what the relevant reason was or (subject to section 98A(2))[619] in showing that it acted reasonably in treating as sufficient.[620] It follows that the time of dismissal needs to be pinpointed with some degree of precision for this rule to operate. On one view of the statute the date of 'dismissal' is defined by reference to the 'effective date of termination'. In other words, when the termination is by notice, this is the date upon which that notice expires.[621] However, this creates the risk of undermining procedural fairness in potentially allowing the employer to find a reason, or justification, for dismissal subsequent to having given the employee notice (although equally it means that a change in circumstances after notice but before the EDT may make an otherwise fair dismissal unfair[622]). It also runs counter to the statutory dismissal procedure which, in its standard form, requires the employer to inform the employee of the circumstances which lead it to contemplate dismissal and to invite the employee to a meeting to discuss the matter prior to dismissal.[623] In *Parkinson v March Consulting Ltd*[624] the Court of Appeal held that where the employment was terminated by notice, the employer's reason should be determined both by reference to the reason for giving the prior notice to terminate and the reason at the time the dismissal occurred. This decision was applied in the later Court of Appeal decision in *Alboni v Ind Coope Retail Ltd*.[625] The approach in these cases has been criticised as confusing the point at which a dismissal takes place with the reason for dismissal, which should be identified by reference to the date when 'the reason has crystallised by the employer giving notice of dismissal to the employee'.[626] There is considerable substance in this criticism. However, in terms of the language, if not the purpose, of the statute it is defensible to say that 'dismissal' means the termination of the employee's actual employment.[627]

5.93   A further problem has been created by the insistence of the courts that where there are internal disciplinary proceedings which result in summary dismissal, the EDT is the date of any initial decision to dismiss and not the later date upon which the dismissal is confirmed by a higher tribunal or authority within the internal process.[628] This principle has been only partially qualified by the more recent view that the EDT can be extended to the end of the appeal in a case where the employee was suspended pending the hearing of the appeal.[629] While this qualification is helpful, it does not address the situation of an employee who is excluded from employment altogether during the hearing of the appeal and therefore only has the hope of 'reinstatement' if the appeal goes in his or her favour. In such a case, if the rule against taking into account irrelevant reasons is taken literally, reasons which emerge *after* the initial decision is

---

619   See para 5.143 below.
620   *W Devis & Sons Ltd v Atkins* [1977] IRLR 314.
621   ERA 1996, s 97(1).
622   See *Stacey v Babcock Power Ltd* [1986] ICR 221 (failure to offer employee given notice of redundancy fresh employment when it became available before his notice expired); *White v South London Transport Ltd* [1998] ICR 293.
623   See further para 5.125 below.
624   [1997] IRLR 308, 312 (Evans LJ).
625   [1998] IRLR 131.
626   [1998] IRLR 107: editorial commentary on *Alboni*.
627   *Parkinson v March Consulting Ltd* [1997] IRLR 308, 312 (Evans LJ).
628   *J Sainsbury Ltd v Savage* [1981] ICR 1.
629   *Drage v Governors of Greenford High School* [2000] IRLR 314.

made cannot help the employer; nor can conduct based on those reasons. In *West Midlands Co-operative Society Ltd v Tipton*[630] the House of Lords modified the effect of the rule just stated by deciding that the appeal process should be taken as one with the rest of the internal procedure for the purposes of assessing whether the employer acted reasonably. However, the House of Lords held in the same decision that evidence emerging during the appeal could only be used to support the original reason given, and not a separate and better reason which had not been relied on at the time. An employer faced with a newly-emerging reason would, it seems, have to rescind the dismissal and start the internal process all over again, whether or not this was objectively necessary to safeguard the employee's right to procedural fairness. The result is artificial since it denies the natural meaning of the EDT in this context. However, the extended time limit for complaining to an employment tribunal of unfair dismissal where an employee had reasonable grounds for believing, when the normal three month period expired, that a dismissal or disciplinary procedure was still in train should avoid, in most cases, the need for employees to present what may be an otiose complaint of unfair dismissal in order to avoid being out of time.[631] Indeed, employees who present a complaint prior to completing the procedure run the risk of having their compensatory award radically reduced if the failure to complete the procedure can be attributed to them.

Employer's immunity

5.94 The employer is effectively immune from unfair dismissal liability in two situations. The first situation of immunity is in relation to complaints where 'it is shown that the action complained of was taken for the purpose of safeguarding national security'; thereupon, 'the tribunal shall dismiss the complaint'.[632] The second situation arises where, at the time of dismissal, the employee was taking part in a strike or other industrial action in the circumstances defined by sections 237 and 238 of TULRCA 1992. Section 237 covers situations where there is an unofficial strike or industrial action. Section 238 refers to situations of 'non-unofficial' strikes or industrial action where all those taking part at the relevant time at the applicant's establishment are dismissed and none of them is re-employed by the same employer or an associated employer for a period of three months. The immunity provided to the employer by section 238, however, has no application where the employee is dismissed for taking 'protected industrial action' within the meaning of the Act.[633] Neither do the immunities provided by either section apply where the employee is dismissed, or selected for redundancy,[634] for one of a number of specified reasons, as defined in the Act.[635] The reasons specified relate to leave for family reasons; health and safety; acting as a representative of the workforce for the purpose of the Working Time Regulations or as a candidate for such a position; acting as an employee representative or as a candidate for such a position; the taking of time off for

630 [1986] AC 536.
631 EADRR 2004, reg 15(1), (2), (5); see further para 5.124.
632 ETA 1996, s 10(1).
633 TULRCA 1992, s 238A. See para 11.78 *et seq* below. The statutory dismissal and disciplinary procedures do not apply to dismissals for taking protected industrial action that, as such, would be regarded as unfair: EADRR 2004, reg 4(1)(d).
634 Within the meaning of ERA 1996, s 105(1), (9).
635 TULRCA 1992, ss 237(1A), 238(2A); see para 11.12 below.

dependants; flexible working; jury service; and (in the case of section 237 only) making a protected disclosure. The rationale for this list is not immediately clear. The first five categories arise out of the requirements of EC Directives on the matters concerned, but this is not true of the others. If compliance with EC law is not the issue here, there seems no reason for not extending the same approach to all cases of automatically unfair dismissal.[636] Nor is it at all clear (unless it is simply the result of a drafting mistake) why the immunity should be lifted in the case of a protected disclosure for cases of unofficial industrial action under section 237, but not under section 238. It should also be noted in this context that neither section 237 nor section 238 prevent an employee who was the victim of unlawful discrimination in dismissal from bringing a claim to an employment tribunal under the relevant statute (such as the SDA 1975 or RRA 1976, for example).[637]

Automatically unfair reasons

5.95   The following reasons for dismissal, or for selection on grounds of redundancy,[638] are automatically unfair:[639] reasons related to the employee's membership or non-membership of an independent trade union, participation in the activities, or use of services, of such a union at the appropriate time, or failure to accept an employer's offer that is designed to move workers away from collectively-agreed terms of employment;[640] reasons related to leave for family reasons or flexible working;[641] the employee's assertion of certain statutory rights against the employer;[642] the exercise of rights relating to the protection of part-time workers and employees on fixed-term contracts;[643] reasons relating to statutory working time standards,[644] the enforcement of the national minimum wage,[645] and claims for employment-related tax credits;[646] certain reasons concerned with health and safety at work;[647] in the case of certain retail employees, the employee's refusal to work on Sundays;[648] the making by an employee of a 'protected disclosure';[649] jury service;[650] taking part in specified circumstances in protected industrial action;[651] performing the functions of an employee representative or candidate for such position;[652] fulfilling specified representative roles, or being a candidate for such positions, in relation to the

636 On the automatically unfair reasons, see para 5.95 below.
637 See further ch 6.
638 In these cases it must be shown that the circumstances constituting the redundancy applied equally to one or more other employees in the same undertaking who held positions similar to that held by the employee and who have not been dismissed: ERA 1996, s 105(1)(b).
639 The term 'automatically unfair' is not used in the Acts, but has entered general usage.
640 TULRCA 1992, ss 152(1), 153. See further para 8.5 below.
641 ERA 1996, ss 99, MPLR 1999, reg 20; ERA 1996, ss 104C, 105(1).
642 ERA 1996, ss 104, 105(1), (7).
643 PTWR 2000, reg 7; FTER 2002, reg 6; ERA 1996, s 105(1), (7E), (7F).
644 ERA 1996, ss 101A, 105(1), (4A).
645 ERA 1996, ss 104A, 105(1), (7A).
646 ERA 1996, ss 104B, 105(1), (7B).
647 ERA 1996, ss 100, 105(1), (3).
648 ERA 1996, ss 101, 105(1), (4).
649 ERA 1996, ss 103A, 105(1), (6A).
650 ERA 1996, ss 98B, 105(1), (2A).
651 TULRCA 1992, s 238A; ERA 1996, s 105(1), (7C).
652 ERA 1996, ss 103, 105(1), (6).

establishment or operation of a European Works Council or information or consultation procedure;[653] fulfilling specified representative roles, or being a candidate for such positions, or engaging in specified activities in relation to information and consultation at national level[654] or in relation to a European Public Limited-Liability Company;[655] performing the functions of a trustee of an occupational pension scheme;[656] and specified acts relating to the statutory recognition and derecognition procedures.[657] It is also automatically unfair to dismiss an employee[658] for the exercise of the right to be accompanied, or to accompany, at a grievance or disciplinary hearing or hearing relating to flexible working[659] or in connection with a transfer of an undertaking, unless it is for an 'economic, technical or organisational reason entailing changes in the workforce of either the transferor or transferee'.[660] In addition a 'spent conviction' under the Rehabilitation of Offenders Act 1974 is not a proper ground for dismissal.[661]

5.96 The principal advantage of these provisions is that where they apply, they close off any possibility of the conduct being shown to be reasonable under section 98(4): the second stage of inquiry is short-circuited and the tribunal makes an immediate finding of unfair dismissal. This prevents the employer from seeking to justify the dismissal by showing that the needs of the business or some other instrumental consideration made it reasonable to dismiss the employee; nor is it a defence that the employer acted reasonably in the sense of following a course of action which a reasonable employer, in the same circumstances, might have followed; nor is it enough for the dismissal to have complied with the requirements of procedural fairness. The categories of automatically unfair reasons therefore represent substantive rights of employees which may not, on the whole, be weighed in the balance against the managerial or business-related interests of the employer. In addition, no qualifying period of employment is needed to assert these rights (with the exceptions of dismissal in connection with a transfer of the undertaking[662] and a remedy for dismissal for a 'spent conviction'[663]). However, with the exception of dismissals for taking part in protected industrial action, the statutory dismissal and disciplinary procedures apply to dismissals for these reasons. This creates the anomalous result that an employee's compensation may be reduced by up to 50% if he or she failed to comply with a requirement of the procedure or exercise a right of appeal under it even in circumstances where, but for the reason being automatically unfair, the tribunal would have no jurisdiction to hear the complaint and the employer's non-compliance with the procedure would have no legal consequences.[664]

653 TICER 1999, reg 28; ERA 1996, s 105(1), (7D).
654 ICER 2004, reg 30; ERA 1996, s 105(1), (7H).
655 EPLLCR 2004, reg 42; ERA 1996, s 105(1), (7G).
656 ERA 1996, ss 102, 105(1), (5).
657 TULRCA 1992, Sch A1, paras 161, 162.
658 But not to select an employee for redundancy. In relation to the right to accompany or to be accompanied the reasons for this omission are obscure.
659 ERelA 1999, s 12; FWPR, reg 16.
660 TUPE 1981, reg 8(1), (2).
661 S 4(3)(b).
662 TUPE 1981, reg 8(5).
663 The Rehabilitation of Offenders Act 1974 does not provide a remedy for breach of s 4(3)(b); employees need to rely on the general unfair dismissal law: see *Property Guards Ltd v Taylor* [1982] IRLR 175.
664 See further paras 5.124 *et seq.*

5.97   The main disadvantage of the concept of automatically unfair reasons is that the burden of proof in establishing the reason for dismissal rests with the employee, at least in a case where the employee does not have the requisite period of continuous employment. Where continuity is established, section 98(1) places the burden of identifying the reason on the employer, whether or not the employee is seeking to argue that the reason is automatically unfair.[665] However, in any other case the employee has the burden of proof because, in the absence of continuity of employment, the categorisation of the reason as automatically unfair is a point which goes to the jurisdiction of the tribunal, and, as such, must be established by the applicant (the employee) on the balance of probabilities. This was the ruling of the Court of Appeal (Lord Denning MR dissenting) in the trade union membership case of *Smith v Hayle Town Council.*[666] Eveleigh LJ considered that the statutory provision for automatically unfair dismissal had to be construed narrowly as an exception to the general rule requiring an employee to show continuity of employment:

> ... when one considers that [TULRCA 1992, section 152] is in fact introducing an exception, one bears in mind the principle that it is for the person relying upon the exception to bring himself within it. Once the employer has established ... that the employee has not been employed for ... [the requisite period], the employer has, as it were, put up an obstacle to the employee obtaining advantage under ... [ERA 1996, s 98]. So [TULRCA 1992, s 152], in my view, is worded to the intent that, and by the nature of its being an exceptions paragraph, the burden of proof must be upon the employee.[667]

According to Sir David Cairns, clearer words than those used in what is now section 152 would be necessary to reverse the burden of proof which normally rests on the applicant or claimant in civil cases: 'the appropriate language, if the burden was put the other way [ie on the employer], would be in some such form as "unless it is shown that the reason or the principal reason was not"' an automatically unfair reason.[668] However, placing the burden on the employee in this way negates much of the benefit he or she derives from not needing to show continuity; it will inevitably be difficult to contradict the employer's own assertion of the reason which motivated it.

5.98   The content of the present categories of automatically unfair reasons owes as much to historical accident and ad hoc concerns of the legislature as anything else; it can hardly be regarded as an attempt to make a comprehensive statement of employees' civil or personal rights at work.[669]

(i) Reasons related to trade union membership and non-membership

5.99   The category of dismissals related to trade union membership and non-membership and trade union activities is largely a legacy of the legislation of the 1970s concerning freedom of association and the closed shop. Here, it seems that unfair dismissal law has simply been the mechanism through which policy

---

665 *Maund v Penwith District Council* [1984] ICR 143. Dismissal for taking part in 'protected industrial action' is an exception to this principle since, in that case, the employee must establish that this is the reason for dismissal in order for the tribunal to have jurisdiction. See para 11.78 below.
666 [1978] ICR 996.
667 [1978] ICR 996, 1002.
668 [1978] ICR 996, 1003.
669 Deakin, 1996.

towards the exercise of collective power has been implemented; if Parliament had intended to protect employees' expressions of opinion as such, it is odd that it should have done so only in relation to trade union membership and not more broadly, extending to the expression of political opinions, for example. ERelA 2004 added protection against dismissal for failing to accept an offer by an employer that is designed to move workers away from terms of employment that are collectively agreed. The details of these statutory provisions are considered at greater length in our discussion of freedom of association and collective rights in chapter 8 below.

(ii) Reasons related to leave for family reasons or flexible working

5.100   Although pregnancy was established as an automatically unfair reason for dismissal with the introduction of this category in the EPA 1975, it was only in 1993 that the two-year qualifying period was removed, together with certain defences which had been available to employers.[670] Further changes were introduced partly as a consequence of decisions of the ECJ interpreting Directive 76/307 on Equal Treatment, and partly by virtue of Directive 92/85 on the Protection of Pregnant Workers. With the enactment of the Employment Relations Act 1999, further provision was made for protection in relation to maternity leave and, more generally, parental leave (following the adoption of EC Directive 96/34 on Parental Leave), and for protection with respect to time off for dependants.[671] The Employment Act 2002 introduced specific rights to paternity and adoption leave, and a right to request flexible working, with protection against dismissal in relation to the exercise of these rights.[672] The protection given to employees in relation both to pregnancy and to these other aspects of leave for family reasons is considered in chapter 6, below.

(iii) Assertion of a statutory right

5.101   Section 104 of the Act protects the employee against dismissal for the assertion of a 'relevant statutory right', either by initiating proceedings against the employer or by alleging an infringement of that right. This right, introduced initially by TURERA 1993, closed what had previously been an obvious gap in the law. Although it is immaterial whether the employee actually had the right, or whether it had been infringed, he or she must have made the claim in question 'in good faith',[673] and it is sufficient that he or she made it 'reasonably clear' to the employer what the right was, without specifying it exactly.[674] The provision applies to any right contained in ERA 1996 which is enforced by way of a complaint to an employment tribunal; the statutory right to minimum notice of termination of employment;[675] rights conferred by WTR 1998;[676] and certain of the rights contained in TULRCA 1992, namely the right not to have union dues deducted from pay without consent, the right not to be subjected to a detriment on specified trade union or collective bargaining grounds, and the right to time

---

670 TURERA 1993, s 24(1).
671 See ERelA 1999, ss 7–8 and Sch 4. The relevant law is now contained in ERA 1996, ss 57A–57B, Part VIII and s 99, and in SI 1999/3312.
672 See EA 2002, ss 1, 3, 47 and SI 2002/2788; SI 2002/3207 and SI 2002/3236.
673 ERA 1996, s 104(2).
674 ERA 1996, s 104(3).
675 ERA 1996, s 86.
676 Together with legislation applicable to merchant shipping and fishing vessels.

off for carrying out trade union duties or activities of a learning representative.[677] It does not, however, apply to infringements of contractual rights.[678]

(iv) The exercise of rights relating to the protection of part-time workers and employees on fixed-term contracts

5.102   The right of a part-time worker to be treated no less favourably than a comparable full-time worker unless that treatment can be justified objectively came into force in 2000; [679] that of a fixed-term employee to be treated no less favourably than a comparable permanent employee in 2002.[680] Both these rights were introduced as a result of EC Directives (Directive 98/23 and Directive 99/70 respectively). There is protection against dismissal for a wide range of activities: bringing proceedings against the employer; giving evidence or information in connection with proceedings brought by another worker or otherwise doing anything under the respective Regulations in relation to the employer or any other worker; alleging that the employer had infringed the Regulations (unless the allegation is false and not made in good faith); requesting a written statement of reasons for less favourable treatment (or, in the case of the Regulations relating to fixed-term employees, a statement of variation); or refusing or proposing to forego a right conferred by the Regulations.[681] In the case of the Regulations covering fixed-term employees there is also protection against dismissal for refusal to sign a workforce agreement which can modify the statutory standards designed to prevent abuse of successive fixed-term contracts (the maximum total period for which employees may be employed on a fixed-term contract, the maximum number of successive fixed term contracts, and the objective grounds justifying the renewal of fixed-term contracts or engagement under successive fixed-term contracts) and for performing the functions or activities of a workforce representative or candidate for such a position.[682] However there is no express provision making it automatically unfair to dismiss a fixed-term employee to prevent him or her acquiring permanent status and it is open to doubt whether this is covered by the protection for enforcing or seeking to enforce a right under the Regulations.[683]

(v) Enforcement of statutory rights in relation to working time, the national minimum wage and tax credits

5.103   In addition to the general right contained in section 104, specific provisions make it automatically unfair for the employer to dismiss the employee

---

677   TULRCA 1992, ss 68, 86, 145A, 145B, 146, 168, 168A, 169 and 170 respectively.
678   In *Mennell v Newell & Wright (Transport Contractors) Ltd* [1997] IRLR 519 the applicant argued unsuccessfully that he was asserting a right relating to deductions from his wages under ERA 1996, ss 13–27 when he refused to sign a new contract, one term of which related to deduction of training costs from final salary; he could not show that he had ever alleged that the employer was in breach of a statutory right as required by s 104. A complaint about alleged unlawful deductions from wages and for threatening to commence tribunal proceedings is capable of amounting to asserting a statutory right: *Pearce v Dyer* UKEAT/0465/04/LA, 20 October 2004.
679   ERelA 1999, s 19, SI 2000/1551.
680   EA 2002, ss 45, 51(1); SI 2002/2034.
681   SI 2000/1551, reg 7; SI 2002/2034, reg 6. Employees are also protected against dismissal on the ground that the employer believes or suspects that the employee has done or intends to do any of these things.
682   See further para 2.11 and 3.86 for the role of such agreements and representatives.
683   This point is discussed further in para 5.79 above.

for reasons related to statutory standards in relation to working time, the national minimum wage, and employment-related tax credits (the working family tax credit and associated benefits). Dismissal of an employee for asserting rights under WTR 1998 is already covered by section 104.[684] In addition, it is automatically unfair to dismiss an employee for refusing, or proposing to refuse, to comply with a requirement imposed by the employer in contravention of a requirement contained in WTR 1998; for refusing, or proposing to refuse, to forego a right conferred by those Regulations; and for failing to sign a workforce agreement or refusing to enter into, or to agree to vary or extend, any other agreement with the employer which may vary working time standards under those Regulations. Specific protection is also accorded against dismissal for performing the functions or activities of a workforce representative or candidate for such a position.[685] The provisions relating to the national minimum wage and tax credits also closely follow the model of section 104. Hence dismissal in respect of any action taken or proposed to be taken by or on behalf of the employee with a view to enforcing or otherwise securing the benefit of these rights, or in respect of action leading to the prosecution of the employer under the relevant legislation, is automatically unfair,[686] as is any dismissal taken for the reason that the employee either qualifies, or will or might qualify, for these rights. In relation to dismissals in relation to actions taken by or on behalf of the employee, it is not necessary that the employee should actually have had the right in question or that it should have been infringed by the employer, as long as the claim to that effect is made in good faith.[687]

(vi) Health and safety

5.104   Section 100 of the 1996 Act, which governs dismissals on grounds related to health and safety, derives from European Community law, in this case Framework Directive 89/391 on Health and Safety.[688] Dismissal is deemed to be unfair if the reason or principal reason is that the employee was carrying out activities relating to his or her duties as a health and safety representative, or in connection with their membership of a health and safety committee, either in accordance with arrangements established pursuant to legislation or having been acknowledged as such a representative or member by the employer. Provision is also made for protection for employees who are designated by the employer to carry out activities in connection with the prevention or reduction of health and safety risks at work.[689]

Section 100 also provides that in a workplace where there is neither a health and safety committee nor health and safety representatives,[690] an employee who brings 'to his employer's attention, by reasonable means, circumstances connected

---

684 ERA 1996, s 104(4)(d).
685 ERA 1996, s 101A.
686 See ERA 1996, ss 104A(1) (minimum wage) and 104B (tax credit). The precise rights under NMWA 1998 and TCA 2002 in respect of which these provisions apply are spelled out in ss 104A(3) and 104B(1).
687 ERA 1996, ss 104A(2), 104B(2).
688 See para 4.83 above. See also ERA 1996, s 44, which provides protection against detrimental action short of dismissal in cases involving health and safety representatives.
689 ERA 1996, s 100(1)(a), (b). In *Goodwin v Cabletel UK Ltd* [1997] IRLR 665, the EAT held that the way in which a designated employee carries out health and safety activities, as well as the actual doing of them, can fall within the protection.
690 Or if there is such a representative or committee but it was not reasonably practicable for the employee to raise the matter by those means.

with his work which he reasonably believed were harmful or potentially harmful to health and safety', may not be dismissed for doing so.[691] Employees are also protected against dismissal for taking part in consultations with their employer pursuant to the Health and Safety (Consultation) Regulations 1996[692] or in the election of representatives of employee safety.[693] Finally, in all workplaces, where an employee reasonably apprehends a 'serious and imminent' danger which he could not reasonably be expected to avert, he or she may not be dismissed for leaving the place of work or the dangerous part of it or, while the danger persists, refusing to return to it;[694] and in the same circumstances, an employee may not be dismissed for taking 'appropriate steps to protect himself or other persons from the danger',[695] these steps to be assessed by reference to circumstances including the employee's own knowledge and the facilities and advice available to him at the time.[696] In this last case only, the dismissal will not be automatically unfair if the employer can show that the steps taken were so negligent that a reasonable employer would have dismissed the employee.[697]

A number of points arise for discussion here. First, it should be noted that section 100 confers greater protection on individual employees to make complaints in workplaces where there is no statutory or other representation,[698] out of recognition of the necessarily greater role played by the individual in these circumstances. Second, the protection conferred on employees who take steps to avert a danger to themselves or to 'other persons' complements the protection otherwise provided for 'whistleblowers' who alert third parties to dangers arising at the workplace.[699] However, the legislation contains the important qualification allowing the employer a defence where the 'reasonable employer' would have dismissed the employee for negligence. The notion of the 'reasonable employer' is derived from the extensive case law applying the test of reasonableness under section 98(4); its appearance here reintroduces into section 100 the kind of balancing act between employee rights, on the one hand, and the business needs of the employer, on the other, which is more characteristic of the general test of fairness in dismissal than it is of cases of automatically unfair dismissal. Finally the EAT has held that industrial action does not constitute 'reasonable means' of bringing an employer's attention to

---

691 ERA 1996, s 100(1)(c). See *Balfour Kilpatrick Ltd v Acheson* [2003] IRLR 683. This provision is not limited to harm at the employee's place of work or to employees: *Von Goetz v St George's Healthcare NHS Trust* EAT 1395/97.

692 SI 1996/1513.

693 ERA 1996, s 100(1)(ba); see further para 9.46.

694 The source of the danger may be the behaviour of a fellow employee: *Harvest Press Ltd v McCaffrey* [1999] IRLR 778.

695 The category of 'other persons' extends to protection of members of the public and is not confined to fellow employees of the applicant: *Masiak v City Restaurants (UK) Ltd* [1999] IRLR 780; *Von Goetz v St George's Healthcare NHS Trust* EAT 1395/97. In *Balfour Kilpatrick Ltd v Acheson* [2003] IRLR 683 the EAT suggested that the words 'or to communicate these circumstances by any appropriate means to the employer' be added to give effect to Art 13 of the Directive.

696 ERA 1996, ss 100(1)(d), (e), 100(2). In *Kerr v Nathan's Wastesavers Ltd* EAT 91/95, discussed IRLB 564, March 1997: p 9 the EAT warned against placing 'an onerous duty of enquiry' on an employee in a case such as this.

697 ERA 1996, s 100(3).

698 S 100(1)(c).

699 On the wide scope of the phrase 'other persons' in this context see *Masiak v City Restaurants (UK) Ltd* [1999] IRLR 780 and *Von Goetz v St George's Healthcare NHS Trust* EAT 1395/97, and on protection for whistleblowers who make 'protected disclosures' see para 4.103 above.

health and safety concerns, although an employee who leaves a workplace where he or she reasonably apprehends a 'serious and imminent' danger they cannot reasonably be expected to avert, and refuses to return to it while the danger persists, may not be dismissed.[700] Employees who leave the workplace when the terms of protection are not met may risk dismissal without redress if they are regarded as taking unofficial industrial action.[701] The line between the two may not be an easy one to draw.

(vii) Sunday work

5.105 The explicit right to protection against dismissal in relation to Sunday work only applies to retail workers.[702] The reason for their particular treatment is that until relatively recently, legislation prevented most shops from opening on Sunday, thereby indirectly protecting retail workers from being required to work on that day of the week.[703] When it was proposed that the legislation governing opening hours was liberalised, it was accepted by a number of employers' groups and by the government that this should be done on condition that new protections were introduced for employees in these sectors.[704] This compromise was subsequently embodied in the Sunday Trading Act 1994 and is now consolidated in ERA 1996.

There are two broad categories of shop workers who potentially fall within the scope of protection. The first consists of 'protected shop workers', those employed as shop workers at the commencement of the 1994 Act (but not to work only on Sunday) and subsequently continuously employed in that capacity, and those who work under contracts such that they may not be required to work on Sunday even if the provisions of ERA 1996 were disregarded.[705] It is automatically unfair for an employer to dismiss a protected shop worker for refusing or proposing to refuse to do shop work on Sundays in general or on a particular Sunday.[706] However, a protected shop worker may lose this protected status at any time on or after the commencement date by agreeing to carry out Sunday work *and* giving the employer an 'opting-in notice' in the prescribed form: the notice must be in writing, must be dated and signed by the employee and must state that he or she wishes to work on Sunday and has no objection to working on Sunday.[707] The employer is also required to issue a written explanatory statement detailing these statutory rights.[708]

The second protected status created by the Act is that of 'opted-out shop worker'. This refers to workers who are not 'protected' and may therefore be required to work on Sundays, either because they were not employed as a shop worker by their current employer when the Act came into force or because, having been protected, they gave the employer an opting-in notice. Such a worker may give the employer an opting-out notice to the effect that he or she

---

700 *Balfour Kilpatrick Ltd v Acheson* [2003] IRLR 683.
701 See para 11.84 below.
702 For discussion of discrimination on grounds of religion see para 6.40.
703 See para 4.72 above.
704 For the background to the campaign to reform the Sunday trading laws, see Diamond, 1991, and on the controls over opening introduced in 1994, see Deakin, 1994b.
705 ERA 1996, s 36.
706 ERA 1996, s 101. Such workers are also protected against being subjected to any detriment for this reason: s 45.
707 ERA 1996, s 36(5), (6).
708 ERA 1996, s 42.

objects to Sunday working (and which must also be in writing, signed and dated). There is then a three-month gap before automatic unfair dismissal protection is acquired, but during which the employee may not be dismissed for having given the opting-out notice.[709] Two groups are not protected by ERA 1996 at all: these are shop workers who are 'opted-in'; and those employed to work only on Sundays.[710] These groups must rely on any protection they might have under general unfair dismissal law.

(viii) Protected disclosures

5.106   An employee who is dismissed for making a 'protected disclosure'[711] is regarded as automatically unfairly dismissed for the purposes of ERA Part X.[712] The law relating to protected disclosures is analysed in more detail in our discussion of protection of 'whistleblowers'.[713]

(ix) Jury service

5.107   It is automatically unfair to dismiss an employee for having been summoned for jury service, or for having been absent from work because he or she attended for jury service.[714] However this will not be the case if the employer can show that the circumstances were such that the employee's absence in pursuance of being so summoned was likely to cause substantial injury to the employer's undertaking; that the employer brought those circumstances to the attention of the employee; that the employee refused or failed to apply to the appropriate officer for excusal from or a deferral of the obligation to attend in pursuance of being so summoned; and that the refusal or failure was not reasonable.[715] This right was introduced by ERelA 2004[716] and came into force on April 6 2005.

(x) Participation in protected industrial action

5.108   It is automatically unfair to dismiss an employee for taking part in protected industrial action, that is to say, action which is not actionable in tort by virtue of the statutory immunities contained in TULRCA 1992, section 219, during the first twelve weeks of the employee's participation in that action. (If the employee is locked-out by the employer at any time during this twelveweek period the period of protection is extended by the number of days for which this occurs.) After the twelve-week period (extended if appropriate for lock-out days), dismissal for this reason is automatically unfair only if the employee had stopped

---

709 ERA 1996, ss 40–42, 101(2), (3). Parallel provisions apply to detrimental action short of dismissal: s 45.
710 ERA 1996, s 40(3)(b).
711 'Protected disclosures' are defined in detail in ERA 1996, ss 43A–43L. All the requirements of these provisions must be satisfied on the evidence: *Alm Medical Services Ltd v Bladon* [2002] IRLR 807. It is immaterial whether the disclosure took place prior to the protection against dismissal coming into force (2 July 1999) provided that the dismissal occurred after that date: *Miklaszewicz v Stolt Offshore Ltd* [2002] IRLR 344; *Meteorological Office v Edgar* [2002] ICR 149.
712 ERA 1996, s 103A.
713 See para 4.103.
714 ERA 1996, s 98B(1). Parallel provisions apply to detrimental action short of dismissal: s 43M.
715 ERA 1996, s 98B(2). 'Appropriate officer' is defined in s 98B(3).
716 S 40.

taking protected industrial action before the end of that period or if the employer had not taken all reasonable procedural steps to resolve the dispute.[717] We consider these provisions, and their relationship to other provisions bearing upon industrial action and dismissal, in our discussion of industrial action, below.[718]

(xi) Activities of employee representatives and other representative roles

5.109   There is an automatically unfair dismissal if the employee was an employee representative for the purposes of information and consultation relating to collective redundancies or transfers of undertakings, or was a candidate for election to such a position, and was dismissed for performing or proposing to perform the activities of such a representative.[719] In addition, it is automatically unfair to dismiss an employee for taking part in the election of employee representatives under these provisions.[720] There are analogous protections for those acting, or standing as candidates for, representative positions in relation to the establishment or operation of a European Works Council or information or consultation procedure; information and consultation at national level; and in relation to a European Public Limited-Liability Company, and for employees exercising specified rights in relation to these procedures.[721] We examine the status and functions of employee representatives and the rights of employees in relation to these various provisions in our discussion of employee representation.[722]

(xii) Functions of pension fund trustees

5.110   It is automatically unfair to dismiss an employee for carrying out the functions of the trustee of a relevant occupational pensions scheme.[723]

(xiii) Protection of workers for acts relating to the statutory recognition and derecognition procedures

5.111   It is automatically unfair for an employer to dismiss a worker (not just an employee) if the reason or main reason is one of a number of specified acts relating to the statutory procedures for the recognition and derecognition of a trade union, under Schedule A1 of TULRCA 1992.[724] These provisions are considered in chapter 9, below.

(xiv) The right to be accompanied, and to accompany, for the purposes of a grievance or disciplinary hearing or a hearing relating to a request for flexible working[725]

5.112   Under ERelA 1999, section 10, as amended by ERelA 2004, a worker has the right to be accompanied at a grievance or disciplinary hearing by another

---

717 TULRCA 1992, s 238A, as inserted by ERelA 1999, s 16 and Sch 5 and amended by ERelA 2004, ss 26-28.
718 See para 11.78 *et seq.*
719 ERA 1996, s 103(1).
720 ERA 1996, s 103(2).
721 TICER 1999, reg 28; ICER 2004, reg 30; EPLLCR 2004, reg 42.
722 See ch 9 below.
723 ERA 1996, s 102. On pension fund trustees, see para 4.123 above.
724 TULRCA 1992, Sch A1, para 161.
725 Note that in relation to categories (xiv)–(xvi), unlike (i)–(xiii) above, selection for redundancy on the specified ground is not automatically unfair.

person of his choice who may either be an official employed by a union, any other union official whom the union has reasonably certified in writing as having experience of, or having received training in, accompanying workers at disciplinary or grievance hearings, or any other worker of the employer in question. A worker who is unfairly dismissed for exercising the right to be accompanied, or for seeking to accompany another worker (not necessarily employed by the same employer) for this purpose, will be regarded as automatically unfairly dismissed.[726] The right to be accompanied is examined in more detail below, in our discussion of the law relating to disciplinary procedures.[727] The same protections are accorded to employees in relation to the right to be accompanied at meetings to request flexible working or to appeal against an employer's decision to refuse an employee's application.[728]

(xv) Transfer of the undertaking

5.113   Dismissal in connection with a transfer of an undertaking falling within the scope of TUPE 1981 is automatically unfair, unless it is for an 'economic, technical or organisational reason' in which case it is potentially fair. These provisions are analysed in our discussion of redundancies and business reorganisations.[729]

(xvi) Spent convictions

5.114   A further category of automatically unfair reasons is that of dismissal for a spent conviction. Under the Rehabilitation of Offenders Act 1974, the possession of a spent conviction or the failure to disclose it 'shall not be a proper ground for dismissing or excluding a person from any office, profession, occupation or employment, or for prejudicing him in any way in any occupation or employment'.[730] This is broadly equivalent to categorising such action as an automatically unfair reason for dismissal. A conviction cannot become spent if, *inter alia*, it results in a sentence of imprisonment exceeding thirty months.[731] Otherwise, various rehabilitation periods apply, ranging from three to ten years, in order for the conviction to become spent. There are numerous exemptions in relation to public employment, the professions and occupations involving trust and confidence, such as those in the medical and financial service sectors.[732] Dismissal for a conviction which, for one reason or another, is not spent in the sense laid out in the Act, will almost certainly be for a potentially fair reason.[733]

---

726 ERelA 1999, s 12. This provision refers to the dismissal of a 'worker' which, as defined in s 13, includes not just 'workers' in the sense of ERA 1996, s 230(3), but also 'agency workers' and 'home workers' along the same lines as NMWA 1998 (see para 4.44 above). The unfair dismissal provisions of ERA 1996 are deemed to apply to 'workers' as so defined, and not just employees, for this purpose: see ERelA 1999, s 12(6). Parallel provisions apply to detrimental action short of dismissal: s 12(1), (2).

727 See para 5.132.

728 SI 2002/3207, reg 16.

729 See para 5.193 *et seq* below.

730 Rehabilitation of Offenders Act 1974, s 4(3)(b); *Property Guards Ltd v Taylor* [1982] IRLR 175.

731 Rehabilitation of Offenders Act 1974, s 5(1)(b).

732 SI 1975/1023 as amended. On the interpretation of the exception in the case of the provision of social services to persons over 65 see *Wood v Coverage Care Ltd* [1996] IRLR 264.

733 Cf *Torr v British Railways Board* [1977] IRLR 184.

Potentially fair reasons

5.115 The Act lists five categories of potentially fair reasons: reasons related to the individual's capability or qualifications for performing work of the kind he or she was employed to do; reasons related to the employee's conduct; redundancy; a statutory prohibition upon the employee continuing to work in the position he or she holds; and 'some other substantial reason of a kind such as to justify the dismissal of an employee holding the position which the employee held'.[734] Capability and qualifications are defined to mean, respectively, 'capability assessed by reference to skill, aptitude, health or any other physical or mental quality', and 'any degree, diploma or other academic, technical or professional qualification relevant to the position' which the employee held.[735] Redundancy bears the same meaning here as in the context of the right to statutory redundancy compensation, namely a situation in which the business where the employee works ceases, or in which there is a diminution in the business' requirements for employees to do work of a particular kind.[736]

These potentially fair reasons are simply the 'gateways' through which the employer has to pass if it is to demonstrate that the dismissal was fair. The employer only has to show, at this stage, that the dismissal was motivated by reasons which fall within one of these gateways; it does not have to show that the facts justify the dismissal in question.[737] A potentially fair reason is 'one which can justify the dismissal, not which *does* justify the dismissal'.[738] Even when it comes to the second stage, the Act does not lay down in detail the circumstances under which, for example, a dismissal by reason of misconduct or lack of capability is deemed to be fair or unfair. The test of fairness under section 98(4) is essentially procedural and, as we shall see, an employer may escape liability if it can show that the procedure it adopted was fair in the circumstances, even if the substantive outcome was one with which the tribunal might have disagreed.[739]

It does not greatly matter, in most cases, which of the potentially fair reasons under section 98(1)–(2) is being relied on by the employer.[740] Nevertheless, case law, together with the ACAS Code of Practice on Disciplinary and Grievance Procedures, has given rise to specific guidelines to be followed in relation to dismissals of different types; in this sense, it may make a difference that the employer is relying, for example, on redundancy as opposed to misconduct.[741] It should be borne in mind, though, that the norms thereby established are no more than applications of the general test of reasonableness in dismissal, and that there is considerable overlap in the guidelines which apply to dismissals of different types. In addition the case law must now be considered in the light of the new statutory dismissal and disciplinary procedures, discussed in para 5.124 *et seq* below.

734 ERA 1996, s 98(1)–(2).
735 ERA 1996, s 98(3).
736 ERA 1996, s 139(1), (2).
737 See para 5.89 above.
738 *Mercia Rubber Mouldings Ltd v Lingwood* [1974] ICR 256, 257 (Sir John Donaldson P).
739 See para 5.122 *et seq* below. Note, however, the possible implications of HRA 1998 in this context.
740 Except where the dismissal falls into a category to which the statutory dismissal and disciplinary procedures do not apply, such as dismissal due to a statutory prohibition on continued working: see para 5.128 below.
741 For an example of a case where this made a difference see *Wilson v Post Office* [2000] IRLR 834, where the employer successfully sought to argue that the case was one of misconduct, not incapability.

5.116   The four specific categories contained in section 98(2) are, in themselves, broadly defined. The reason must in each case be 'substantial',[742] so that if the reason relied on by the employer was completely trivial, the dismissal is not capable of being justified. On the other hand, the reference to a reason which 'relates to' capability, qualifications and misconduct means that these categories are even wider than they might otherwise be;[743] the Act does not say that the reason must relate 'wholly or mainly to' the category in question, for example (although, in terms of the second-stage test of fairness, the reason will have to be a 'sufficient' one in the circumstances for dismissal to be actually fair). The category of misconduct has broadly been defined to include, for example, a refusal to obey an order to carry out extra-contractual duties. In *Redbridge London Borough Council v Fishman*[744] a dismissal was held to be potentially fair on these grounds where the employee, who had been employed at a school in an essentially managerial capacity, was asked to undertake some teaching. She refused and was dismissed. The tribunal made a finding of unfair dismissal which was upheld, in part, on the grounds that the order was one she was not contractually obliged to obey. However, the point for present purposes is that the dismissal was for a reason which could have been justified in slightly different circumstances; elsewhere, tribunals and courts have made findings of fair dismissal in cases where employees were dismissed for resisting unilateral changes to their existing terms and conditions of employment.[745] In a similarly broad interpretation, it has been held that the potentially fair reason of lack of capability does not have to be established in relation to each and every aspect of an employee's contractual duties.[746]

Dismissal by reason of a statutory contravention under section 98(2)(d) applies where the employee could not continue to work 'in the position which he held' without contravening, or causing the employer to contravene, a 'duty or restriction' imposed by legislation. This is only a potentially fair reason. The employer may be found to have acted unreasonably in failing to allow an employee time to acquire a necessary licence or permit,[747] or in failing to look into the possibility of suitable alternative employment.[748] Notably, however, the statutory dismissal and disciplinary procedures are not applicable to such dismissals.[749]

The definition of redundancy is particularly important since in addition to opening the gateway to a fair dismissal, it also grants the employee an entitlement to receive a statutory redundancy payment, if he or she is otherwise qualified to do so.[750] A dismissal for economic reasons which falls outside the scope of

---

742 This follows from the reference to 'some other substantial reason' in ERA 1996, s 98(1)(b).
743 *Shook v Ealing London Borough Council* [1986] ICR 314, 326.
744 [1978] ICR 569.
745 Eg, *Industrial Rubber Products v Gillon* [1977] IRLR 389; and see generally *Gilham v Kent County Council (No 3)* [1986] IRLR 56. In *Farrant v Woodroffe School* [1998] IRLR 176, the EAT upheld a finding that the employers had acted reasonably in dismissing the employee because of their genuine, if mistaken, view that they were contractually entitled to require him to work to a new job description and that he was guilty of gross misconduct in refusing to do so.
746 *Shook v Ealing London Borough Council* [1986] ICR 314.
747 *Sutcliffe and Eaton Ltd v Pinney* [1977] IRLR 349.
748 *Appleyard v FM Smith (Hull) Ltd* [1972] IRLR 19.
749 EADRR 2004, reg 4(1)(f).
750 Note that in the context of an unfair dismissal complaint it will be for the employer to show redundancy as a 'fair' reason (s 98(1)) whereas for the purposes of a statutory redundancy payment a dismissal is presumed to be for redundancy unless otherwise shown: ERA 1996, s 163(2).

redundancy may be potentially fair on the separate grounds that it falls within the category of 'some other substantial reason' in section 98(1)(b); the employee will not then receive statutory redundancy compensation. The extensive case law in this area is examined later in this chapter in the discussion of redundancies and business reorganisations.[751]

5.117   If a dismissal does not come under any of the four specific gateways in section 98(2), it is more than likely that it will qualify under the heading of the residual category of 'some other substantial reason of a kind such as to justify the dismissal of an employee holding the position which the employee held' (or SOSR).[752] In addition to greatly expanding the scope of legitimate economic reasons for dismissal, as we have just noted, the concept of SOSR also blurs the edges of the other specific reasons listed by the Act. If an employer dismisses an employee whom he mistakenly thinks lacks the necessary work permit, when in fact the employee had the permission needed, the dismissal may fail to be justifiable by reference to a statutory prohibition within the meaning of section 98(2)(d), but may, instead, qualify as an SOSR.[753] Dismissals for reasons which could only with difficulty be classified as related to conduct or incapability have also come under the SOSR category. Such cases include the dismissal of an employee for failure to reveal a history of mental illness when asked about this at the job interview,[754] and a dismissal brought about by pressure from a major customer of the employer.[755]

The scope of SOSR is not, however, limited to reasons similar to those cited in section 98(2). This has been the view of the courts since the early decision of Brightman J in *RS Components Ltd v Irwin*.[756] The employment tribunal had proceeded on the basis that 'a reason for dismissal is not capable of being "some other substantial reason" unless it is a reason *ejusdem generis* with the reasons specified in subsection (2)'. This was rejected on appeal, on the basis that:

> ... there are not only legal, but also practical objections to a narrow construction of 'some other substantial reason'. Parliament may well have intended to set out in section [98(2)] the common reasons for a dismissal, but can hardly have hoped to produce an exhaustive catalogue of all the circumstances in which an employer would be justified in terminating the services of an employee.[757]

---

751 See para 5.183 *et seq*.

752 See Bowers and Clarke, 1981. The requirement that the reason justifies the dismissal of an employee 'holding the position which the employee held' may, on occasion, be significant: see *Cobley v Forward Technology Industries plc* [2003] IRLR 706, para 21 (in deciding whether there was a substantial reason to dismiss a chief executive after a hostile takeover, different considerations would apply to him than to a case of a secretary or storeman: *per* Mummery LJ).

753 *Bouchaala v Trusthouse Forte Hotels Ltd* [1980] ICR 721. Note, however, that such a dismissal would now be automatically unfair if a consequence of this mistake was that the employer failed to utilise the statutory dismissal and disciplinary procedure, thinking that it did not apply to the dismissal: see further para 5.124 *et seq*.

754 *O'Brien v Prudential Assurance Co Ltd* [1979] IRLR 140. Note now the DDA 1995 in relation to disability discrimination: see further para 6.109 *et seq*.

755 *Scott Packaging and Warehousing Ltd v Patterson* [1978] IRLR 166.

756 [1973] ICR 535.

757 [1973] ICR 535, 540. See, more recently, *Cobley v Forward Technology Industries plc* [2003] IRLR 706, para 22 (Mummery LJ).

This assertion, for which no grounds were offered, is in any case beside the point; Parliament might well have intended to give employers some flexibility via the notion of SOSR, while still linking that concept to the specific categories listed in section 98(2), so that it should be construed *ejusdem generis* with them. The residual category would then have operated as a safety valve, allowing a potentially fair dismissal in situations closely analogous to those listed. If, by contrast, the category of SOSR is capable of extending to *any* substantial reason, what was the point of enacting section 98(2)? The principal concern of the NIRC in *RS Components* was apparently to preserve free of legal control the power of the employer to initiate changes beneficial to the 'development of industry',[758] without incurring the costs of unfair dismissal or of redundancy compensation. This has led to an important narrowing of the concept of redundancy. It has also had a more general effect, practically removing the check on employers apparently imposed by section 98(1)–(2): 'in very few reported cases have employers not reached the threshold of "substantiality"'.[759] It remains to be seen whether this definition of 'substantiality' will be affected by the enactment of the Human Rights Act 1998; to date consideration of the impact of the Act on unfair dismissal law has focussed on the application of the reasonableness test, to which we turn below, rather than on whether the reason itself should be regarded as potentially fair.

Reasonableness: issues of fact and law

5.118   Under section 98(4), 'the determination of the question whether the dismissal is fair or unfair (having regard to the reason shown by the employer) – (a) depends on whether in the circumstances (including the size and administrative resources of the employer's undertaking) the employer acted reasonably or unreasonably in treating it as a sufficient reason for dismissing the employee and (b) shall be determined in accordance with equity and the substantial merits of the case'. The Employment Act 1980[760] inserted the reference to the size and resources of the employer's undertaking and removed a provision which had previously placed the burden of proof on the employer under this subsection; the burden of proof is now neutral as between the two parties.

The appellate courts have, through various self-denying ordinances, consistently preserved a broad area of autonomy for individual tribunals in determining the question set out in section 98(4). The statute signals the discretionary nature of the tribunal's task by its reference to 'equity and the substantial merits of the case'. 'Equity' here means 'common fairness': the result is that the tribunal 'has to look at the question in the round and without regard to lawyers' technicalities. It has to look at it in an industrial relations context'.[761] However this is now subject to provisions relating to procedural fairness introduced by the Employment Act 2002. These amendments to ERA 1996 render a dismissal automatically unfair if one of the statutory dismissal and disciplinary procedures applies to the dismissal; the procedure has not been completed; and non-completion is wholly or mainly attributable to the failure by the employer to comply with its requirements.[762] However subject to this a failure by an

758 [1973] ICR 535.
759 Bowers and Clarke, 1981: p 35.
760 S 6.
761 *Union of Construction Allied Trades and Technicians v Brain* [1981] ICR 542, 550 (Donaldson LJ).
762 ERA 1996, s 98A(1); see further para 5.124 *et seq.*

employer to follow a procedure in relation to an employee's dismissal is not to be regarded as of itself making the employer's action unreasonable if it shows that it would have decided to dismiss the employee had it followed the procedure.[763] This introduces an important constraint on tribunals' discretion.

An appeal only lies to the EAT (and further to the Court of Appeal and House of Lords) on a point of law,[764] and a tribunal will only commit an error of law if it either misdirected itself on the relevant legal test or misunderstood or misapplied the law; made a finding of fact for which there was no evidence; or the decision was 'perverse' in that it was one which no reasonable tribunal, directing itself properly on the law, could have reached or, alternatively, was one which was obviously wrong.[765] In practice it will be very difficult to classify as 'perverse' a decision which did not fall within one of these categories.

In the context of unfair dismissal it has been held that decisions applying the fairness test in section 98(4) to particular situations do not create precedents which are strictly binding on future tribunals or courts.[766] Nor are tribunals required rigidly to follow guidelines for the interpretation of section 98(4) which are laid down by the EAT.[767] So although the EAT has given guidance of a general kind in relation, for example, to the procedures to be followed in cases of dismissal for misconduct,[768] incapability[769] and redundancy,[770] it is not necessarily an error of law for a tribunal to decline to follow these guidelines (which should in any event now be read in the light of the amendments made by EA 2002 and the revised ACAS Code of Practice on Disciplinary and Grievance Procedures, discussed below). In general, 'it should ... be very rare for any decision of an ... [employment] ... tribunal under this section to give rise to any question of law'.[771]

Although the intention here was to limit the number of legal citations made before tribunals, to respect the comparative informality of tribunal proceedings and preserve their autonomy of decision-making, the effect has also been to deny a degree of certainty and consistency in the application of the law. It is quite possible that different tribunals may reach different decisions on essentially similar facts, as occurred in *Kent County Council v Gilham*.[772] The Court of Appeal considered a number of appeals from determinations of tribunals (and of the EAT) in cases where dinner ladies employed by various local government authorities had been dismissed for refusing to accept a cut in pay. In each case the employers argued that cuts in their budgets, imposed by central government,

---

763 ERA 1996, s 98A(2); see further para 5.143.
764 ETA 1996, s 21.
765 *British Telecommunications plc v Sheridan* [1990] IRLR 27, 30 (Lord Donaldson MR); *Neale v Hereford and Worcester County Council* [1986] ICR 471, 483 (May LJ); *Piggott Bros & Co Ltd v Jackson* [1991] IRLR 309, 312 (Lord Donaldson MR); *Watling v William Bird & Son (Contractor) Ltd* (1976) 11 ITR 70, 71.
766 *Jowett v Earl of Bradford (No 2)* [1978] ICR 431.
767 *Bailey v BP Oil (Kent Refinery) Ltd* [1980] ICR 642; *Union of Construction Allied Trades and Technicians v Brain* [1981] ICR 542.
768 *ILEA v Gravett* [1988] IRLR 497.
769 *Lynock v Cereal Packaging Ltd* [1988] IRLR 510.
770 *Williams v Compair Maxam Ltd* [1982] IRLR 83.
771 *Union of Construction Allied Trades and Technicians v Brain* [1981] ICR 542, 550 (Donaldson LJ). Note, however, that it is highly likely that a tribunal that found that an employer who had violated an employee's Convention rights in dismissing him or her had acted 'reasonably' would be regarded as having misapplied the law: see *Pay v Lancashire Probation* Service [2004] IRLR 129, paras 32, 33; *X v Y* [2004] IRLR 625, CA.
772 [1985] ICR 227.

had forced them to make savings on wage costs. Most tribunals accepted that this constituted a potentially fair reason for dismissal; some tribunals, the majority, then went on to find the dismissals to be fair in the circumstances, others that the dismissals had been unfair. The Court of Appeal held that it was permissible for the tribunals concerned to disagree, and that the decisions made by one tribunal did not bind the others.

Reasonableness test: the band of reasonable responses

5.119   The tribunal must determine whether the employer 'acted reasonably' in treating as sufficient the reason which was the basis for the dismissal. This emphasis on the employer's conduct means that the substantive justice of the dispute is, by and large, a secondary consideration. As Viscount Dilhorne said in *W Devis & Sons Ltd v Atkins*,[773] section 98(4) directs the tribunal 'to focus on the conduct of the employer and not on whether the employee in fact suffered any injustice'. Moreover, (infringement of Convention rights apart) the employer's conduct is judged not by reference to the nature of the right of the employee which might have been infringed, but by reference to the standard set by a notional 'reasonable employer'. The relevant principles were summarised by Browne-Wilkinson J on behalf of the EAT in *Iceland Frozen Foods Ltd v Jones*:[774]

> ... in judging the reasonableness of the employer's conduct an ... [employment] ... tribunal must not substitute its decision as to what was the right course to adopt for that of the employer – in many, though not all, cases there is a band of reasonable responses to the employee's conduct within which one employer might reasonably take one view, another may quite reasonably take another; ... the function of the ... [employment] ... tribunal, as an industrial jury, is to determine whether in the particular circumstances of each case the decision to dismiss the employee fell within the band of reasonable responses which a reasonable employer might have adopted.

5.120   The fundamental difficulty with this test, as Collins has written, is that 'the idea of a range of reasonable conduct broadens the scope for legitimate disciplinary action by denying implicitly that a fixed standard of reasonableness should be applied'.[775] In *Haddon v Van den Bergh Foods*[776] the EAT, under the presidency of Morison J, took the view that the band of reasonable responses test was an unjustifiable gloss on the statute and that the basic test of fairness in section 98(4) should be applied 'without embellishment'.[777] The reasonable responses test was illegitimate because it 'led tribunals to adopt a perversity test of reasonableness',[778] that is to say, one in which an employer's decision could not be disturbed unless it was one which no reasonable employer could have arrived at. However, decisions coming after *Haddon* saw a reversion to the traditional approach. In *Midland Bank plc v Madden*[779] and *Beedell v West Ferry Printers Ltd*[780] the EAT accepted that the reasonable responses test, having

773 [1977] IRLR 314, 317.
774 [1983] ICR 17, 24–25. See also Lord Denning in *British Leyland (UK) Ltd v Swift* [1981] IRLR 91, referring to a 'band of reasonableness'.
775 H Collins, 1993: p 38. See also H Collins, 2004: ch 5 for a more recent critique of this test.
776 [1999] IRLR 672; see also *Wilson v Ethicon Ltd* [2000] IRLR 4; H Collins, 2000c; Freedland, 2000.
777 [1999] IRLR 672, 676.
778 [1999] IRLR 672, 676.
779 [2000] IRLR 288.
780 [2000] IRLR 650.

been approved by the Court of Appeal, could not be overturned by a decision of the Appeal Tribunal. At the same time, while it was agreed that a 'perversity test' was not compatible with the language of section 98(4), it was also asserted in *Madden* that 'the band test has always been intended not to lead to one of perversity'.[781] In *Beedell* the EAT went further in stressing that the tribunal was not entitled to substitute its judgment for that of the employer at any point in the application of section 98(4): 'the employment tribunal should not put themselves in the place of management to decide whether they, the employment tribunal members, would have dismissed the applicant or not'; equally, 'it is not for the employment tribunal to re-try the factual issues before the employer at the dismissal (including appeal) stage'.[782] In *Post Office v Foley; HSBC Bank v Madden*[783] the Court of Appeal did its utmost to restore the pre-*Haddon* position, by asserting that the EAT in that case had made 'an unwarranted departure from binding authority'.[784] The Court took the view that an authority which had 'been followed almost every day in almost every employment tribunal and on appeals for nearly 20 years [should] remain binding' until such time as Parliament chose to change the basic statutory text underpinning the test.[785] In 2002, even more controversially, the Court of Appeal held that the third element of this test – whether investigation into suspected misconduct was reasonable in the circumstances – was subject to the 'band of reasonable responses' test.[786] We discuss the implications of this further in para 5.144 below.

5.121 The courts may be thought of as having adapted to the employment context an approach of the common law of tort and contract to the assessment of the standard of care expected of professionals in negligence cases: the same notion of a range of legitimate responses is used there to create a space for professional discretion and judgment.[787] Adopting this suggestion in *Beedell*, the EAT commented: '[j]ust as the question of a doctor's negligence will depend upon whether a reasonable body of medical practitioners would have accepted the practice which he followed, even if another body of equally reasonable practitioners would have acted differently (a band of reasonable responses), so it may be said that the question of whether an employer has acted reasonably in dismissing his employee will depend upon the range of responses of reasonable employers'.[788]

However, this is not the only conceivable approach to the setting of the relevant standards in the common law, and if the courts wish to draw inspiration from the analogy with *Bolam* they should also look to decisions which have qualified the traditional test by making reference to the *reasonable expectations of treatment of the claimant* (or, here, the employee).[789] It remains the case that there is nothing in section 98 to indicate that Parliament intended a 'band of

---

781 [2000] IRLR 288, 295. See also *Beedell v West Ferry Printers* [2000] IRLR 650, 656.
782 [2000] IRLR 650, 656.
783 [2000] IRLR 827.
784 [2000] IRLR 827, 829 (Mummery LJ).
785 [2000] IRLR 827, 830 (Mummery LJ). Cf Anderman, 2004: p 127, who states that '[t]he inability of judges to see that the current interpretation of section 98(4) *is* a form of judicial legislation is evidence of their underlying assumptions about exclusive employer property rights in the contract of employment'.
786 *Sainsbury's Supermarkets Ltd v Hitt* [2003] IRLR 23.
787 *Bolam v Friern Hospital Management Committee* [1957] 1 WLR 582.
788 [2000] IRLR 650, 656.
789 For discussion, see Deakin, Johnston and Markesinis 2003: pp 174–177.

reasonableness' test to be applied by employment tribunals, in contrast to the clear authority in the statutory scheme for the separation of reasons and reasonableness, which the Court of Appeal also (and correctly) reasserted in *Madden*.[790] In the final analysis, there remains a strong case for reviewing the band of reasonableness test given that it is essentially a judicial addition to the statutory formula, and, arguably, one which has done much to limit the effectiveness of the statutory protection provided to employees, no matter how hallowed it has become with the passage of time.

Procedural fairness

(i) An overview

5.122   As we discussed above, the statute directs attention to the employer's conduct rather than to the overall fairness of the outcome. In assessing whether an employer has acted reasonably a crucial source of the employer's obligations has been the ACAS Code of Practice on Disciplinary and Grievance Procedures, originally issued in 1977 and revised in 1997, 2000, and, most recently, in 2004. Like other Codes issued by virtue of powers now contained in the TULRCA 1992, the Disciplinary Code must be taken into account by employment tribunals where it appears to be relevant to any matter arising in the course of the proceedings,[791] and the House of Lords has confirmed that it should be regularly consulted in cases of disciplinary dismissal.[792] Despite the status of the Code, however, the importance accorded by courts and tribunals to procedural fairness has oscillated since the unfair dismissal protection came into being.[793] Initially the courts 'demanded scrupulous attention to detailed procedural guidelines' and maintained that an unfair procedure alone could render a dismissal unfair.[794] This was replaced by an approach that allowed substantive standards to prevail. According to the test expressed in *British Labour Pump v Byrne*[795] a dismissal which had not been preceded by the appropriate procedural steps could nevertheless be fair if an employment tribunal was satisfied, on the balance of probabilities, that the result would have been the same had the proper procedure been followed and the employer could show that, in the light of the information it would thereby have acquired, it would have been behaving reasonably in deciding to dismiss. In 1987, in *Polkey v AE Dayton Services Ltd*,[796] this approach, which had been subject to considerable criticism, was overruled by the House of Lords as inconsistent with the statutory language. Lord Mackay said:

> Where there is no [automatically unfair dismissal] the subject matter for the tribunal's consideration is the employer's action in treating the reason as a sufficient reason for dismissing the employee. It is that action and that action only that the tribunal is required to characterise as reasonable or unreasonable. That leaves no scope for the tribunal considering whether, if the employer had acted differently, he might have dismissed the employee. It is what the employer

---

790 See para 5.120 above.
791 TULRCA 1992, s 207; see *Lock v Cardiff Rly Co Ltd* [1998] IRLR 358.
792 *West Midlands Co-operative Society Ltd v Tipton* [1986] AC 536.
793 See H Collins, 1992: pp 111–120.
794 H Collins, 1992: p 112.
795 [1979] IRLR 94, affirmed by the Court of Appeal in *W and J Wass Ltd v Binns* [1982] IRLR 283.
796 [1987] IRLR 503.

did that is to be judged, not what he might have done. On the other hand, in judging whether what the employer did was reasonable it is right to consider what a reasonable employer would have had in mind at the time he decided to dismiss as the consequence of not consulting or not warning.[797]

The result of *Polkey* was to reaffirm the significance of adherence to procedures, although it did not mark a return to the initial strict approach. Under this test an employer could dispense with procedure in a case where a reasonable employer would have decided to dismiss the employee summarily: 'there may be cases where the offence is so heinous and the facts so manifestly clear that a reasonable employer could take the view that whatever explanation the employee advanced it would make no difference'.[798] Similarly, an employer might legitimately dispense with a disciplinary procedure 'where, on the undisputed facts, dismissal was inevitable, as for example where a trusted employee, before dismissal, was charged with, and pleaded guilty to, a serious offence of dishonesty committed in the course of his employment'.[799] As Collins explained, this allowed an element of flexibility in exceptional cases albeit at the expense of the principle of respect for the dignity of the individual worker that a stricter adherence to procedural fairness embodies.[800]

5.123   The principles laid down in *Polkey* governed the position prior to the entry into force on 1 October 2004 of fundamental changes to unfair dismissal law introduced by EA 2002. The 2002 Act eroded the *Polkey* principle from two directions. First, it introduced statutory dismissal and disciplinary procedures which, other than in limited circumstances, must be followed by all employers.[801] A dismissal will be automatically unfair if the relevant statutory procedure has not been completed and non-completion was 'wholly or mainly attributable to failure by the employer to comply with its requirements'.[802] The dismissed employee will be entitled to a minimum of four week's pay (unless the tribunal considers that it would result in 'injustice' to the employer)[803] and the compensatory award must be increased by 10% (unless there are exceptional circumstances which would make such an increase 'unjust or inequitable') and can be increased by up to 50%.[804] An employee's failure to complete the applicable procedure also has legal consequences; tribunals must (exceptional circumstances apart) reduce the compensatory award for unfair dismissal by 10%, and have a discretion to reduce it by up to 50%.[805] (The provision for percentage increases and reductions also applies to a failure to complete the relevant statutory grievance procedure in cases of constructive dismissal.) Secondly, EA 2002 provides that, subject to the requirement, where applicable, to follow the statutory minimum, 'failure by an employer to follow a procedure in relation to the dismissal of an employee shall not be regarded ... as by itself making the employer's action unreasonable if he shows that he would have decided to dismiss

797 [1988] ICR 142, 153.
798 *Sillifant v Powell Duffryn Timber Ltd* [1983] IRLR 91, 97 (Browne-Wilkinson J), an analysis approved by Lord MacKay in *Polkey* [1988] ICR 142, 157.
799 *West Midlands Co-operative Society Ltd v Tipton* [1986] AC 536, 548 (Lord Bridge of Harwich).
800 H Collins, 1992: pp 118–126.
801 EA 2002, s 98A; Sch 2, Part 1.
802 ERA 1996, s 98A(1).
803 ERA 1996, s 120(1A), (1B).
804 EA 2002, s 31(3); ERA 1996, s 124A.
805 EA 2002, s 31(2); ERA 1996, s 124A.

the employee if he had followed the procedure'.[806] This provision, in effect, reinstates the 'no difference' rule removed by *Polkey* for procedures beyond the statutory minima, including those that are enshrined in the current version of the ACAS Code.[807] It does not mean that adherence to the statutory minimum procedure will, of itself, mean that the employer has acted reasonably (and, indeed, a dismissal may be unfair as falling outside the band of reasonable responses, discussed above). However where an employer can show that following a procedure beyond the statutory minimum would not have changed the decision to dismiss, its failure to follow that procedure will not, of itself, make the dismissal unfair. As a result of these important statutory changes, the extensive case law on the meaning of fairness in cases of disciplinary dismissal, which has provided useful illustrations of the kinds of approach that tribunals may take to the question of reasonableness, must now be treated with considerable caution.

In the following paragraphs we analyse the scope of the new statutory dismissal and disciplinary procedures and their relationship with the statutory right to be accompanied at disciplinary hearings, introduced by ERelA 1999. We then examine the broader standards of procedural fairness that are laid down in the ACAS Code and have been developed by tribunals; compare them with the statutory procedures; and assess the likely implications of non-adherence to those broader standards in the light of EA 2002.

(ii) The statutory dismissal and disciplinary procedures

5.124   EA 2002 establishes two forms of statutory dismissal and disciplinary procedure ('SDDP'), a 'standard' procedure, applicable in the majority of cases, and a 'modified' procedure, applicable in limited circumstances. There are also specified situations where neither procedure applies or where the relevant procedure is treated as having been complied with. These situations apart, the procedures apply regardless of the reason for the dismissal, including compulsory retirement.[808] The procedures cover dismissals within the meaning of section 95(1)(a) and (b) of ERA 1996, ie, where the employee's contract is terminated by the employer or where the employee is employed under a limited-term contract and that contract terminates by virtue of the limiting event without being renewed.[809] Where an employee is claiming to have been constructively dismissed he or she must usually institute the appropriate statutory grievance procedure before an unfair dismissal complaint can be presented to a tribunal.[810]

An employee will be regarded as unfairly dismissed if one of the SDDPs applies to the dismissal; the procedure has not been completed; and the non-completion of the procedure (which includes non-commencement)[811] is 'wholly or mainly attributable to failure by the employer to comply with its

---

806   EA 2002, s 98A(2).

807   Hepple and Morris, 2002: p 264.

808   *Guidance on the Employment Act 2002 (Dispute Resolution) Regulations 2004 and associated provisions in the Employment Act 2002*, DTI, 2004, para 12 suggests that the procedures need not be followed if the employee has reached the normal retiring age or, if none, 65 and would thus be barred from presenting an unfair dismissal complaint. (See further para *5.65 et seq.*) However, given that the upper age limit does not apply to a range of automatically unfair dismissals, employers may be best advised to follow the procedures in any event in case the employee was able successfully to argue that one such reason was, in fact, the principal reason for the dismissal.

809   EADRR 2004, reg 3, 2(1).

810   See further para 2.21 *et seq*, although see also para 5.131 below.

811   ERA 1996, s 98A(3), EADRR 2004 reg 2(1).

requirements'.[812] However, unlike most automatically unfair dismissals, an employee is still required to have the necessary qualifying period of service to complain that a dismissal is unfair because the SDDPs have not been followed;[813] thus, unless the dismissal is for an automatically unfair reason for which no qualifying period of service is required,[814] an employee who lacks the requisite one year's continuous employment on the EDT will not receive any compensation in respect of the employer's failure in this regard. If either party fails to comply with a requirement of an applicable SDDP neither party has any obligation to comply with any further requirement of that procedure.[815]

The time limit for presenting an unfair dismissal complaint to an employment tribunal may be extended in specified circumstances where the SDDPs apply. If a dismissed employee presents a complaint after the three-month time limit has expired, the time limit is extended for a further three months beginning with the day after that on which it would otherwise have expired, provided that the employee had reasonable grounds for believing, when the initial time limit expired, that a dismissal or disciplinary procedure, whether statutory or otherwise, was being followed in respect of matters that consisted of or included the substance of the complaint to the tribunal.[816] The principles governing the application of the respective SDDPs are laid down in the Employment Act 2002 (Dispute Resolution) Regulations ('EADRR') 2004.

5.125   The three-step 'standard' SDDP applies where an employer contemplates dismissing or taking 'relevant disciplinary action' against an employee.[817] 'Relevant disciplinary action' means 'action, short of dismissal, which the employer asserts to be based wholly or mainly on the employee's conduct or capability, other than suspension on full pay or the issuing of warnings (whether oral or written)'.[818] This definition is designed to exclude 'actions which are themselves part of a workplace procedure'.[819] The exclusion of suspension on full pay, which is rarely a sanction in itself, is consistent with that objective; that of warnings is less obvious given the significance that a warning on an employee's record can have (as recognised by its inclusion in the right to be accompanied, discussed below[820]). In the event that an employee considered that suspension on full pay or a warning infringed some other statutory right, such as rights relating to discrimination, or wished to complain that it gave rise to unfair constructive dismissal, he or she would need to institute the statutory grievance procedure.

812 ERA 1996, s 98A(1).
813 See para 5.63 above.
814 See para 5.95 above.
815 EADRR 2004, reg 12(1).
816 EADRR 2004, reg 15(1),(2). The provision for extension does not apply to s 95(1)(a) or (b) dismissals where the SDDPs do not apply. The drafting of reg 15 is curious. The term 'dismissal and disciplinary procedures' is defined in reg 2(1) of EADRR 2004 as the statutory procedures. However reg 15(2) refers to a dismissal or disciplinary procedure, whether statutory or otherwise and seems, therefore, to envisage provision for extension in relation to any such procedure. See further para 5.83 for the principles governing the time limit.
817 EADRR 2004, reg 3(1).
818 EADRR 2004, reg 2(1). 'Action' includes omission: reg 2(1). Thus a failure to award a pay increase on grounds of capability or conduct would be covered, for example.
819 *Guidance on the Employment Act 2002 (Dispute Resolution) Regulations 2004 and associated provisions in the Employment Act 2002*, DTI, 2004, para 7.
820 See para 5.132.

The first step of the standard SDDP requires the employer to set out in writing the employee's alleged conduct or characteristics, or other circumstances, which lead it to contemplate dismissing or taking disciplinary action against the employee. The employer must send the statement or a copy of it to the employee and invite the employee to attend a meeting to discuss the matter.[821] The meeting (the second step) must not take place unless the employer has informed the employee what the 'basis' was for including in the statement the specified grounds and the employee has had a reasonable opportunity to consider his or her response to that information. The employee must take all 'reasonable steps' to attend the meeting, following which the employer must inform the employee of its decision and of the right to appeal against it.[822] If the employee wishes to appeal (the third step) he or she must inform the employer, whereupon the employer must invite him or her to attend a further meeting which the employee must take all reasonable steps to attend, following which the employer must inform the employee of its final decision.[823] Failure to appeal constitutes non-completion of the procedure on an employee's part and can give rise to a reduction in the compensatory award.[824]

So far as reasonably practicable, the employer should be represented at the appeal by a more senior manager than attended the first meeting, unless the most senior manager attended the first meeting.[825] The initial meeting must take place before disciplinary action is taken, except where that action takes the form of disciplinary suspension,[826] but the appeal need not.[827] Each step and action under both the 'standard' and the 'modified' procedures must be taken without unreasonable delay; the timing and location of meetings must be reasonable; and meetings must be conducted in a manner that enables both employer and employee to explain their cases.[828] In addition, meetings under both procedures constitute 'hearings' for the purposes of the right to be accompanied by a union official or fellow worker,[829] although the right applies only where the 'hearing' falls within the definition of either a 'disciplinary hearing' or a 'grievance hearing'.[830] We discuss the right to be accompanied, and its relationship with the SDDPs, in para 5.132 *et seq* below. However it should be noted at this stage that breach of the right to be accompanied does not of itself constitute a failure to comply with a SDDP; whether there was such a failure would depend upon whether some specific aspect of the relevant procedure, such as a provision relating to arranging meetings, had been breached.

If it is not reasonably practicable for the employee (or, if he or she is exercising the statutory right to be accompanied, his or her companion) or the employer to

821 EA 2002, Sch 2, para 1.
822 EA 2002, Sch 2, para 2.
823 EA 2002, Sch 2, para 3.
824 EA 2002, s 31(2)(c)(ii); ERA 1996, s 124A.
825 EA 2002, Sch 2, para 13(3).
826 Suspension on full pay is outside the definition of 'relevant disciplinary action': see above.
827 EA 2002, Sch 2, para 2(1). If an employee is dismissed but then re-instated or re-employed on appeal continuity of employment is preserved and the period between the date of dismissal and reinstatement counts in computing the employee's period of employment: SI 1996/3147, reg 2, as amended by SI 2004/752, reg 17(e). This provision also applies where the employee is reinstated or re-employed after appeal under the 'modified' procedure.
828 EA 2002, Sch 2, paras 12, 13(1), (2).
829 EA 2002, Sch 2, para 14.
830 See ERelA 1999, s 13(4), (5) and para 5.134 below.

attend a meeting organised in accordance with the applicable statutory procedure for a reason which was not foreseeable when the meeting was arranged, the employee or employer, as the case may be, will not be treated as having failed to comply with the procedure.[831] It is then for the employer to invite the employee to attend another meeting.[832] If that second meeting fails to occur for an unforeseeable reason the parties are then treated as having complied with the applicable procedure.[833]

5.126 The two-step 'modified' procedure, applicable where the employee has already been dismissed, requires as a first step that the employer sets out in writing the employee's alleged misconduct which led to the dismissal, the basis for thinking at the time of the dismissal that the employee was guilty of the alleged misconduct, and the employee's right to appeal against dismissal. The employer must send the statement or a copy of it to the employee.[834] If the employee wishes to appeal (the second step) he or she must inform the employer, whereupon the employer must invite him or her to attend a meeting which the employee must take all reasonable steps to attend, following which the employer must inform the employee of its final decision.[835] There are four conditions which must be satisfied in order for an employer to be justified in using the 'modified', rather than the 'standard', procedure. These are that employer dismissed the employee by reason of his or her conduct without notice; the dismissal occurred at the time the employer became aware of the conduct or immediately thereafter; the employer was entitled, in the circumstances, to dismiss the employee by reason of his conduct without notice or any payment in lieu of notice; and it was reasonable for the employer, in the circumstances, to dismiss the employee before enquiring into the circumstances in which the conduct took place.[836] However neither of the SDDPs applies in relation to such a dismissal where the employee presents a complaint relating to the dismissal to an employment tribunal at a time when the employer has not complied with step 1 of the modified procedure.[837] The DTI guidance on the procedures explains that this provision is included 'because it would be unfair to leave open the possibility that the employee might be held at fault for failure to complete the statutory procedure if he presented a tribunal complaint before the employer had so written, given that the employer might delay writing for some considerable time, or might ultimately fail to write at all.'[838] In these circumstances, and others where the SDDPs do not apply, the employee must comply with the normal three-month time limit for presenting the unfair dismissal complaint.[839]

5.127 Both the standard and the modified procedures fall considerably short of the requirements imposed by the ACAS Code of Practice on Disciplinary

---

831 EADRR 2004, reg 13(1).
832 EADRR 2004, reg 13(2). Where the employee is exercising his or her rights under ERelA 1999, s 10 and the employee proposes an alternative time under s 10(4) the employer has a duty to invite the employee to attend a meeting at that time.
833 EADRR 2004, reg 13(3),(4).
834 EA 2002, Sch 2, para 4.
835 EA 2002, Sch 2, para 5.
836 EADRR 2004, reg 3(2).
837 EADRR 2004, reg 3(2).
838 *Guidance on the Employment Act 2002 (Dispute Resolution) Regulations 2004 and associated provisions in the Employment Act 2002*, DTI, 2004, para 48.
839 Three months beginning with the EDT: see further para 5.83 *et seq*.

and Grievance Procedures 2004 (the current version of which itself represents a dilution of the standards contained in its predecessor).[840] The Government defended this position at the time of EA 2002's parliamentary passage by claiming that it would be unduly onerous to oblige employers that lacked internal procedures (according to official figures 48% of those going before tribunals) to proceed immediately to best practice.[841] However it also emphasised that a dismissal that complied merely with the SDDPs would not necessarily be fair.[842] To that extent the SDDPs have the potential to mislead employers, as well as to prejudice the interests of employees; an employer may justifiably feel aggrieved if it has followed the SDDP to the letter but the dismissal is nevertheless found to be unfair. Most surprisingly, the SDDPs do not oblige the employer to investigate the facts prior to dismissal, a requirement of the Code (usually) for gross, as well as less serious, misconduct.[843] The Government maintained that the requirement to state the 'basis' for relying on the specified ground would act as a 'strong incentive' to investigate.[844] However the strength of this argument is lessened by statutory incorporation of the 'no difference' principle, whereby failure to follow a procedure does not render a dismissal unfair if the employer can show that it would still have decided to dismiss the employee if the procedure had been followed.[845] In addition there is no provision for graded sanctions related, for example, to the seriousness of the offence and whether any prior warning has been issued,[846] nor need the employer keep records of, or even put in writing, the nature of any disciplinary action taken,[847] although clearly it would be prudent to do so. The absence of an obligation on the part of employers to warn employees of the consequences of failing to comply with the SDDP, in particular of non-exercise of the right to appeal, is another significant weakness of the legislation.

The 'modified' procedure, which dispenses with the requirement for an initial hearing altogether, constitutes a particularly striking erosion of procedural justice; it is strongly arguable that cases of alleged gross misconduct are precisely those where the need to ensure that employers have reasonable grounds for their belief and have afforded employees the opportunity to state their case is especially strong. In practice employers that rely on the modified procedure may be taking a significant risk in doing so. The circumstances in which summary dismissal can be justified are not always self-evident.[848] Moreover, it is difficult to envisage many situations in which it will be reasonable for an employer to dismiss the employee 'before enquiring into the circumstances in which the conduct took place' rather than imposing a temporary suspension to investigate the facts;[849] even a case of fighting in the workplace or other ostensible gross misconduct may require consideration of an employee's record and the extent of any

---

840 A number of the points made in this paragraph derive from Hepple and Morris, 2002: pp 259–260. See also G Morris, 2005. Cf H Collins, 2004: ch 6, especially p 51, where it is stated that the criticisms made by Hepple and Morris may be 'too harsh'.

841 Alan Johnson, HC Standing Committee F, col 140, 13 December 2001.

842 Alan Johnson, above, col 143.

843 ACAS Code of Practice on Disciplinary and Grievance Procedures 2004, paras 8, 35.

844 Lord Falconer of Thoroton, HL Debs col 150, 11 June 2002.

845 EA 2002, s 98A(2).

846 Cf ACAS Code paras 17 *et seq.*

847 Cf ACAS Code para 49.

848 See para 5.18 *et seq.*

849 Cf ACAS Code para 35.

provocation or other mitigating factors.[850] For this reason the potential of the 'modified' procedure to give employers a false sense of security is particularly great.

5.128 There are a number of situations where neither of the SDDPs applies. Such dismissals will still be subject to the general principles of fairness, but the 'no difference' principle described in para 5.123 above will mean that failure to abide by any procedure, even the rudimentary SDDPs, will not of itself render the dismissal unfair if the employer shows it would have decided to dismiss had it followed the procedure. The normal time limits apply to such dismissals.

The first situation is where all the employees of a description or in a category to which the employee belongs are dismissed, provided that the employer offers to re-engage all the employees so dismissed either before or upon the termination of their contracts.[851] This would cover reorganisations, for example, where an employer dismisses employees and then offers re-engagement on different terms and conditions. The terms 'description' and 'category' are not defined; this will probably be a question of fact for the tribunal to determine. There seems no reason why a single employee should not be covered where he or she is the only member of the 'category'. The second is where the dismissal is one of a number of collective redundancies in respect of which the duty to consult in TULRCA 1992, s 188 applies.[852] We discuss this duty in Chapter 9. As our discussion there reveals, it is not always easy to determine when it applies; this exception could create the curious result that an employer which commences collective consultation in circumstances where the duty does not, in fact, apply and does not institute the standard SDDP could thereby be liable to a finding of automatically unfair dismissal. The third situation is where at the time of the employee's dismissal he or she is taking part in an unofficial strike or other unofficial industrial action, or any other strike or industrial action (except protected industrial action) unless the employer dismisses employees or offers re-engagement on a selective basis so that its immunity from unfair dismissal complaints is removed.[853] The fourth is where the reason for dismissal is that the employee took protected industrial action and the dismissal would be regarded as automatically unfair.[854] The fifth is where 'the employer's business suddenly ceases to function, because of an event unforeseen by the employer, with the result that it is impractical for him to employ any employees'.[855] The sixth is where the employee could not continue to work in the position which he or she held without either the employee or the employer contravening a statutory duty or restriction.[856] As we saw in para 5.116, a dismissal on this ground is only potentially unfair and the reason for excluding this category of dismissal is not immediately apparent. Seventh, the SDDPs are excluded where the employee is

---

850 See, for example, *Taylor v Parsons Peebles Nei Bruce Peebles Ltd* [1981] IRLR 119; *Ladbroke Racing Ltd v Arnott* [1983] IRLR 154; *Strouthos v London Underground Ltd* [2004] IRLR 636.
851 EADRR 2004, reg 4(1)(a). An employer is regarded as offering to re-engage an employee if that employer, a successor of that employer or an associated employer of that employer offers to re-engage the employee, either in the job which he held immediately before the date of dismissal or in a different job which would be suitable in his case: reg 4(2).
852 EADRR 2004, reg 4(1)(b).
853 EADRR 2004, reg 4(1)(c), (2). See further paras 11.75 *et seq*.
854 EADRR 2004, reg 4(1)(d), (2). See further paras 11.78 *et seq*.
855 EADRR 2004, reg 4(1)(e).
856 EADRR 2004, reg 4(1)(f).

covered by a 'dismissal procedures agreement'.[857] Such agreements are discussed in para 5.64 above.

In addition to these specific exceptions the application of the SDDPs is subject to two general exclusions, applicable to both the disciplinary and the grievance procedures. The first covers circumstances where the procedure is not commenced because a party has reasonable grounds to believe that this would result in a significant threat to himself or another person, or to his or her property; the party has been subjected to harassment and has reasonable grounds to believe that this would result in further harassment; or it is not practicable for the party to commence the procedure within a reasonable period.[858] However, where the procedure is not commenced because of a threat or harassment resulting from the behaviour of either the employer or the employee, that party is treated as if the procedure had applied and he, she or it had failed to comply with it.[859] The second exclusion is where it would not be possible to comply with an applicable SDDP without disclosing information whose disclosure would be contrary to the interests of national security.[860]

5.129   In addition to these exceptions, there are two sets of circumstances in which the parties are treated as having complied with the relevant SDDP even though they have not complied with the provisions relating to appeal (step 3 of the standard procedure, step 2 of the modified). Unlike situations where the SDDPs do not apply at all, the employee may benefit from the provision for an extended time limit to apply to the tribunal described in para 5.124 above. The first is where the employee applies for interim relief, a remedy that empowers the employment tribunal to maintain the applicant in his or her employment pending the hearing of an unfair dismissal claim.[861] This remedy, which can be sought only in limited situations, requires an application to the tribunal within seven days of the EDT. Provided that steps 1 and 2 of the standard procedure, or step 1 of the modified procedure, have been complied with, the parties are treated as having complied with steps 3 or 2 respectively.[862] The second is designed to allow dispute resolution procedures developed by groups of employers and unions to continue to operate; the parties are treated as having complied with steps 3 or 2 as appropriate where at the time of dismissal (or other relevant disciplinary action) an 'appropriate procedure' exists and the employee has appealed under that procedure.[863] A procedure is 'appropriate' if it gives the employee an effective right of appeal against dismissal or disciplinary action and operates by virtue of a collective agreement made between two or more employers or an employers' association and one or more independent trade unions.[864]

5.130   There are two further situations, applicable to both the disciplinary and grievance procedures, where the parties are treated as having complied with

---

857 EADRR 2004, reg 4(1)(g).
858 EADRR 2004, reg 11(1),(3),(4).
859 EADRR 2004, reg 12(3).
860 EADRR 2004, reg 16.
861 See further para 5.163 below.
862 EADRR 2004, reg 5(1).
863 EADRR 2004, reg 5(2).
864 EADRR 2004, reg 5(3), 2(1). See para 9.26 for the definition of 'collective agreement' and paras 7.20 and 7.23, and 7.21, for the definition of 'independent trade union' and 'employers' association' respectively.

the applicable procedure regardless of the stage which has been reached. The first is where the employer has invited the employee to a meeting which has subsequently been re-arranged and both meetings have needed to be cancelled because of an unforeseeable reason.[865] The second is where the procedure has been started but a party does not comply with a subsequent requirement on the grounds relating to threats, harassment or impracticability specified in para 5.128 above.[866] Once again, if the requirement is not complied with because of a threat or harassment resulting from the behaviour of the employer or employee, non-compliance is treated as a failure, attributable to that party, to comply with the procedure.[867]

5.131   EADRR aims to avoid overlap between situations where the SDDPs and the statutory grievance procedures respectively apply. Thus, there is no requirement for an employee to follow a grievance procedure if the employer has dismissed or is contemplating dismissing him or her, nor if the employer has taken or is contemplating 'relevant disciplinary action' based on conduct or capability; these are covered by the SDDP.[868] However, as we stated in para 5.124 above, the SDDPs apply only where the dismissal takes the form of termination by the employer or termination of a limited-term contract by virtue of the limiting event without renewal; unfair constructive dismissal complaints must be preceded by use of the appropriate statutory grievance procedure.[869] The difficulty here is that, as we saw in para 5.71, the dividing line between termination by the employer and constructive dismissal is not always clear cut and, indeed, the same situation may be capable of being analysed as falling into either category. Whilst in the past this has mattered little, a complaint presented to an employment tribunal may now be sent back to the applicant at the outset because it has appeared, on paper, to constitute constructive rather than 'direct' dismissal. It may be argued that the consequent requirement to institute the grievance procedure will merely delay the presentation of the applicant's complaint rather than causing any material disadvantage even if the evidence shows that the dismissal could, indeed, properly be classified (additionally or alternatively) as 'direct'. However, as well as the inconvenience of being required, possibly incorrectly, to comply with a procedure unnecessarily, employees in this situation are likely to have been deprived of the benefits of the

---

865 EADRR 2004, reg 13(4).
866 EADRR 2004, reg 11(2), (3), (4).
867 EADRR 2004, reg 12(4).
868 EADRR 2004, reg 6(5),(6). Under reg 7 there is an exception if the grievance takes the form that the employer has taken or is contemplating relevant disciplinary action against the employee and one reason for the grievance is either: (a) that the action amounted to, or, if it took place, would amount to, unlawful discrimination on grounds of sex, race, disability, religion or belief or sexual orientation or (b) that the grounds on which the employer took, or is contemplating taking, the action were or are unrelated to the grounds asserted (eg, a personality clash rather than the employee's conduct). In those circumstances the standard or modified grievance procedure, depending on the circumstances, will apply but the parties are treated as having complied with that procedure if the employee sets out the grievance in a written statement and sends the statement or a copy of it to the employer prior to the appeal meeting, if either SDDP is being followed, or, where neither is being followed, prior to presenting a complaint arising out of the grievance to an employment tribunal.
869 *Quaere* whether this is so where the constructive dismissal complaint is based upon the taking of 'relevant disciplinary action' which itself is excluded from the requirement to follow a grievance procedure. Here the question of whether the standard SDDP was followed will be relevant to the issue of compensation.

SDDPs that they should properly have enjoyed. Given that the financial consequences of non-completion of a statutory procedure by a party can be significant, tribunals may be faced with difficult issues in this area. As we saw in para 5.69, the dividing line between termination by mutual consent and dismissal can also be contentious. Employers may be best advised to institute the SDDP in all cases where they are aware that an employee's contract is being terminated.

(iii) The right to be accompanied

5.132   We referred in para 5.125 to the right of employees to be accompanied at 'disciplinary' meetings called for the purposes of the SDDPs. This right also applies to meetings within the statutory grievance procedures and therefore covers complaints of unfair constructive dismissal, for example.[870] The right to be accompanied was introduced by ERelA 1999[871] and therefore pre-dates, and is independent of, the new statutory procedures, although provision is made in the context of those procedures to cater for the availability of an employee's chosen companion. The right to be accompanied also extends to disciplinary and grievance hearings called for purposes outside the scope of the statutory procedures, such as disciplinary warnings, for example. The ACAS Code states that employers should advise workers who are invited to a meeting of their right to be accompanied[872] but this is not a statutory obligation.

ERelA 1999 provides that where a worker is 'required or invited by his employer to attend a disciplinary or grievance hearing' and 'reasonably requests to be accompanied' at that hearing, the employer must allow him or her to be accompanied by any one of the following: a trade union official employed by the union itself; any official of a trade union (including a lay official or shop steward) whom the union has reasonably certified as either having experience of, or having received training in, acting as a worker's companion for these purposes; or, any other worker of the employer.[873] It is not clear on what if any grounds the courts could decide that a request to be accompanied was not 'reasonable'; since section 98(4) is not in point here, there would seem to be no adequate basis for invoking the 'band of reasonableness' test, described in para 5.119, in this context. The ACAS Code suggests that it would not be reasonable to insist on being accompanied by a colleague whose presence would prejudice the hearing or who might have a conflict of interest, nor would it be reasonable for a worker to select a colleague from a geographically remote location when someone suitably qualified was on site.[874] It is not clear that this accords with the statutory language, however; the statute refers to the reasonableness of the request *to be accompanied* not to the choice of companion, which appears to be for the worker himself or herself to decide. If a union official is chosen, he or she can be an official of any union; the worker does not have to be a member of that union, nor need that union be recognised by the employer for the purposes of collective bargaining. There is no requirement that the union is independent.[875]

---

870 EA 2002, Sch 2 para 14 expressly provides that a meeting held for the purposes of the statutory procedures is a 'hearing' for the purposes of ERelA 1999, s 13.
871 ERelA 1999, ss 10–15. See generally Clancy and Seifert, 2000, for an account of the law relating to disciplinary and grievance hearings and the operation of the statutory right to be accompanied in ERelA 1999, ss 10–15 prior to the amendments made by ERelA 2004.
872 ACAS Code on Disciplinary and Grievance Procedures 2004, paras 13 and 77.
873 ERelA 1999, s 10 as amended by ERelA 2004, s 37.
874 ACAS Code on Disciplinary and Grievance Procedures 2004, para 103.
875 See para 7.23 for the meaning of this term.

Equally, the Act imposes no *duty* upon the chosen companion to act if he or she does not wish to do so. Where a group of workers invited to a disciplinary or grievance hearing each may choose a different companion or they may select a single companion to support them all.[876]

If the chosen companion is not available at the time set by the employer for the hearing, the employer must agree to a postponement of the hearing to an alternative time proposed by the worker which must be 'reasonable' and within five working days beginning with the first working day after the day proposed by the employer.[877] If a meeting has been organised in accordance with one of the statutory procedures and it is not reasonably practicable for an employee's companion to attend that meeting for a reason which was not foreseeable when the meeting was arranged, the employer has a duty to invite the employee to attend a meeting at a different time which, once again, may be subject to postponement on the same basis as the original meeting if the companion is not available at the time proposed by the employer.[878] If it is not reasonably practicable for the companion to attend that meeting the parties are treated as having complied with the applicable statutory procedure.[879]

5.133   The right to be accompanied is a free-standing statutory right which is separate from the right to claim unfair dismissal, although denial of the right may, depending on the circumstances, render a dismissal unfair if it breaches a requirement of an applicable SDDP or on general principles under the reasonableness test.[880] It may be claimed by a 'worker', a term which, in particular in this context, is considerably wider than the category of 'employee' which is relevant for the purposes of unfair dismissal law. Not only does it cover, for example, home workers and agency workers, but in relation to agency workers it is specified that the employer can be either the user (or 'principal') or the agency, in a appropriate case.[881] Breach by the employer can give rise to a claim for up to two weeks' pay (subject to the normal upper limits on compensation) by the worker, in addition to any compensation that may be awarded in relation to any other complaint that may be brought at the same time, such as unfair dismissal.[882] A worker and/or his or her companion who is subjected to a detriment or dismissal in connection with the exercise of rights under this provision may also bring a complaint to an employment tribunal.[883] The companion has a statutory right to paid time off during working hours to fulfil his or her responsibilities, but only if employed by the same employer as the worker.[884]

5.134   A key issue is when the right to be accompanied arises. The Act defines a disciplinary hearing as one which could result in either the administration by the employer of a formal warning; the taking of some other action by the employer with regard to the worker (such as dismissal or some lesser penalty);

---

876 This interpretation was confirmed by Lord Triesman, HL Debs col GC 163, 15 June 2004.
877 ERelA 1999, s 10(4),(5).
878 EADRR 2004, reg 13(1),(2).
879 EADRR 2004, reg 13(3),(4).
880 See further paras 5.124 *et seq* and 5.136.
881 See ERelA 1999, s 13(2).
882 ERelA 1999, s 11.
883 ERelA 1999, s 12.
884 This is the effect of ERelA 1999, s 10(6)–(7); see the ACAS Code of Practice on Disciplinary and Grievance Procedures 2004, para 109.

or the confirmation of a previously issued warning or of some other action taken by the employer.[885] The Code seeks to draw a distinction between informal discussions or counselling sessions and investigations, on the one hand, and formal disciplinary hearings on the other.[886] However whether there has been a 'hearing' for the purposes of the right may not be self-evident; the courts have declined to specify criteria and held that this is a matter for the tribunal to decide on the facts.[887] Moreover, whether a warning is 'formal' may also involve looking beyond the terminology used by the employer; thus a hearing that results in what is described as a 'informal oral warning' may, in practice, attract the right to be accompanied if that warning has a degree of formality attached to it and becomes part of the employee's disciplinary record.[888] Meetings called for the purposes of the statutory procedures are expressly stated to be 'hearings'.[889]

Grievance procedures are defined by the Act as hearings which concern 'the performance of a duty by an employer in relation to a worker'.[890] The ACAS Code explains that this duty may arise from statute or from common law; thus whether an individual's request for a pay rise, for example, is covered may depend upon whether there is a contractual right to such an increase or an issue about equal pay is raised.[891] Once again meetings called for the purposes of the statutory grievance procedures are expressly deemed to be 'hearings'.[892]

5.135   A further crucial issue is the role of the companion at the relevant hearing. The activities the companion may undertake were spelt out in more detail in ERelA 2004 in an attempt to deal with uncertainties arising from the original definition. It is now made clear that the companion must be permitted by the employer to address the hearing to put the worker's case, sum up that case, and respond on the worker's behalf to any view expressed at the hearing. The companion may also confer with the worker during the hearing.[893] In addition the Code of Practice recommends that the companion be permitted 'participate as fully as possible in the hearing, including asking witnesses questions'.[894] However, importantly, the employer is not required to permit the companion to answer questions on behalf of the worker;[895] the Government rejected calls from unions to change the right to be accompanied to a right to be represented.[896] Nor need the companion be permitted by the employer to use the statutory powers in a way that prevents the employer from explaining its case or any

---

885   ERelA 1999, s 13(4). In *London Underground Ltd v Ferenc-Batchelor* [2003] IRLR 252 the EAT held that 'some action' in this context meant some form of disciplinary sanction and would not, therefore, normally cover imposed training, coaching or counselling. See also *Skiggs v South West Trains Ltd* [2005] IRLR 459. In *Heathmill Multimedia ASP Ltd v Jones* [2003] IRLR 856 the EAT held that a meeting at which the applicants were dismissed on grounds of redundancy was not a 'disciplinary hearing'.

886   ACAS Code of Practice on Disciplinary and Grievance Procedures 2004, para 99.

887   *London Underground Ltd v Ferenc-Batchelor* [2003] IRLR 252.

888   [2003] IRLR 252.

889   EA 2002, Sch 2, para 14.

890   ERelA 1999, s 13(5).

891   Code of Practice, paras 101–102.

892   EA 2002, Sch 2, para 14.

893   ERelA 1999, s 10(2B).

894   Code of Practice, para 114.

895   ERelA 1999, s 10(2C)(a).

896   *Review of the Employment Relations Act 1999: Government Response to the Public Consultation*, DTI, December 2003, para 3.47. The Government disputed the argument that a right to be represented was required by the ECtHR: *Wilson and Palmer v UK* [2002] IRLR 568; see further para 7.9 below.

other person at the hearing from contributing to it, nor to address the hearing if the worker indicates at it that he or she does not wish the companion so to do.[897] This latter provision is designed to ensure that the worker remains in control of how the proceedings are conducted on his or her behalf.

(iv) General standards of procedural fairness

5.136 The right to be accompanied, described above, is important in the context of dismissal and other disciplinary action, although, as we have indicated, it extends to many situations beyond those. Having analysed the statutory procedures and rights that are relevant in the context of dismissal, we now consider the broader principles that apply in considering the fairness of a dismissal, regardless of whether it is one to which the SDDPs apply. As we indicated in para 5.122 above, the ACAS Code of Practice on Disciplinary and Grievance Procedures is a crucial source of employer's obligations, and we examine the contents of that Code, and the principles developed by courts and tribunals, in the paragraphs that follow. However, as we have warned already, case law prior to the statutory amendments to unfair dismissal law, and the 2004 version of the Code, that came into effect on 1 October 2004 should be treated with some caution; in particular, the implications of the 'no difference' rule,[898] discussed in para 5.123 above and 5.143 below, should be borne in mind. It should also be remembered at this stage that tribunals are required to have regard to the size and administrative resources of an employer's undertaking in deciding whether it has acted reasonably,[899] and the Code makes clear that in small organisations it may not be practicable to adopt all the detailed good practice guidance set out in the Code.[900]

FORMALISATION OF RULES AND PROCEDURES

5.137 The Code emphasises that '[m]anagement is responsible for maintaining and setting standards of performance in an organisation and for ensuring that disciplinary rules and procedures are in place'.[901] Such rules and procedures 'help to promote orderly employment relations as well as fairness and consistency in the treatment of individuals'[902] The rules should be specific about the nature of the offences which may give rise to disciplinary action: 'the aim should be to specify those that are necessary for ensuring a safe and efficient workplace and for maintaining good employment relations'.[903] The Code recommends that employees (and, where appropriate, their representatives) should be involved in making or changing rules and procedures, and that these rules should be readily available to employees, for example on a noticeboard or, in larger organisations, in a staff handbook or on the intranet.[904] Management should do all they can to ensure that every employee knows and understands the rules and should inform

---

897 ERelA 1999, s 10(2), (2C)(b), (c).
898 ERA 1996, s 98A(2).
899 ERA 1996, s 98(4).
900 Code of Practice, para 7.
901 Code of Practice, para 52.
902 Code of Practice, para 1.
903 Code of Practice, para 53.
904 See para 4.18 for the information required to be included in the written statement of employment terms issued to employees. Note that there is no requirement for an employer to distinguish between what is and what is not required by the SDDPs, nor to notify employees of the consequences of failing to abide by those procedures.

employees of the likely consequences of breaking them; in particular they should list examples of acts of gross misconduct that may warrant summary dismissal.[905] New or additional rules should only be introduced after reasonable notice has been given to all employees and any employee representatives have been consulted.[906]

The Code recommends that disciplinary procedures should be seen primarily as a way of encouraging improvement among employees whose conduct or performance is unsatisfactory rather than as a means of imposing sanctions.[907] Good procedures should be in writing; be non-discriminatory; provide for matters to be dealt with without undue delay; allow for matters to be kept confidential; indicate the nature of the disciplinary action which may be taken, against whom and by which level of management; provide for individuals to be informed of the complaints against them, and supporting evidence, before a meeting and to be given an opportunity to state their case before a decision is reached; give individuals the right to be accompanied;[908] provide that, except for a case of gross misconduct, no individual may be dismissed for a first offence; require management to investigate fully before any disciplinary action is taken; ensure that any penalty is explained; and provide for an appeal procedure.[909] As we saw in para 5.127, these recommendations exceed what is required by the SDDPs, most notably in emphasising the need for full investigation prior to dismissal.

5.138   Courts and tribunals have held that the non-existence of formalised rules, or the failure to communicate them to employees, does not necessarily prevent the employer from taking disciplinary action in a case of a clear breach of acceptable behaviour, such as theft or fighting at work,[910] or even a serious criminal offence committed outside work.[911] Nor does the mere existence of a rule make a dismissal automatically fair, since a tribunal may conclude that either the rule itself or its application in this case was arbitrary or otherwise unfair.[912] If the rules are incorporated into the employee's contract of employment this may be a factor weighing in the employer's favour,[913] but it is still open to the tribunal to find that while a dismissal was contractually justified, it was unfair under the Act, or vice versa. The contract terms are not in themselves decisive, for example, in determining whether dismissal for a refusal to obey orders was justified. Although it would not be normal for dismissal to be fair where the employee insists on doing only what he or she is required to do by the contract,[914] in exceptional circumstances the employer may be able to argue

---

905   Code of Practice, paras 53, 55, 56.
906   Code of Practice, para 62.
907   Code of Practice, para 58.
908   See para 5.132 for the statutory right to be accompanied.
909   Code of Practice, para 60; see also para 59.
910   *Pringle (RA) v Lucas Industrial Equipment Ltd* [1975] IRLR 266.
911   *Mathewson v RB Wilson Dental Laboratory Ltd* [1988] IRLR 512: an employee arrested and, later, convicted for possession of cannabis, had committed a serious offence since the crime was deliberate and he was in a position of trust.
912   *Greenslade v Hoveringham Gravels Ltd* [1975] IRLR 114; *Taylor v Parsons Peebles Nei Bruce Peebles Ltd* [1981] IRLR 119; *Ladbroke Racing Ltd v Arnott* [1983] IRLR 154.
913   Note that the classification of the conduct may be material where the contract provides for differing procedures to deal with different forms of misconduct: *Skidmore v Dartford and Gravesham NHS Trust* [2003] IRLR 445.
914   As in *Redbridge London Borough Council v Fishman* [1978] ICR 569 but cf *Farrant v Woodroffe School* [1998] IRLR 176.

that the order was reasonable in the light of the need for flexibility.[915] In so far as the employee's implied duty of obedience is concerned, there may well be a high degree of overlap between reasonableness at common law and under the Act, since in each case the tribunal or court will take into account the nature of the work the employee is employed to do as well as the wider needs of the business. Dismissal for refusal to obey an unlawful order is very unlikely to be fair.[916]

WARNINGS, INVESTIGATIONS AND SUSPENSION PRIOR TO A DISCIPLINARY HEARING

5.139 The Code suggests that cases of minor misconduct or unsatisfactory performance are usually best dealt with informally; a 'quiet word' may be all that is required.[917] If the offence is more serious, or informal action does not bring about an improvement, a formal written warning, setting out the nature of the misconduct, and the consequences of a failure to change behaviour, and making clear that it is part of the formal disciplinary process, should be given.[918] Similarly, an employee who is found to be performing unsatisfactorily should be given a written note setting out the performance problem; the improvement that is required; the timescale for achieving this improvement; a review date; and any support the employer will provide to help the employee.[919] In the event of repeated misconduct or unsatisfactory performance, or a sufficiently serious first offence, a final written warning may be necessary.[920] In cases of gross misconduct the employer may decide to dismiss even though the employee has not previously received a warning for misconduct.[921] In this event the Code suggests that a short period of suspension with full pay may be helpful or necessary in order to establish the facts, although it is recognised (and reflected in the modified statutory procedure) that there may be rare occasions where the dismissal will be fair even though an employer has dismissed an employee immediately without a meeting.[922] A note of warnings should be kept but should be disregarded for disciplinary purposes after a specified period; six months is suggested for a first formal warning, twelve for a final written warning.[923]

5.140 Particular guidance is given in the Code on dealing with criminal charges or convictions. The Code states that where an employee is charged with, or convicted of, a criminal offence not related to work, this is not in itself reason for disciplinary action. The employer should establish the facts of the case and consider whether the matter is serious enough to warrant starting the disciplinary procedure: 'the main consideration should be whether the offence, or alleged offence, is one that makes the employee unsuitable for their type of work'.[924] Where a charge is pending, the Code advises that the employee should not be

---

915 For example, *Simmonds v Dowty Seals Ltd* [1978] IRLR 211.
916 *Morrish v Henlys (Folkestone) Ltd* [1973] ICR 482.
917 Code of Practice, para 11.
918 Code of Practice, paras 21 and 22.
919 Code of Practice, para 19.
920 Code of Practice, para 24.
921 Code of Practice, para 18; see also *Retarded Children's Aid Society Ltd v Day* [1978] IRLR 128; *Mathewson v RB Wilson Dental Laboratory Ltd* [1988] IRLR 512.
922 Code of Practice, paras 35–36; see also para 5.126 above.
923 Code of Practice, paras 20, 22, 24.
924 Code of Practice, para 43. See, for example, *X v Y* [2004] IRLR 625.

dismissed solely because they are absent from work as a result of being remanded in custody.[925] However the courts have found that where an employee admits to having committed an offence outside work, summary dismissal may be justified depending on the circumstances. In *Mathewson v RB Wilson Dental Laboratory Ltd*[926] a skilled and senior employee who was arrested for possession of cannabis during his lunch break was summarily dismissed on returning to work an hour late and explaining the circumstances to his employer. The dismissal was found to be fair, taking into account 'involvement in the use of prohibited drugs; the intervention of the police; the admission by the appellant ...; the possible influence on other members of staff; and the suitability of continuing to employ the appellant in the job for which he was employed'. In respect of allegations of criminal behaviour which are work related, the EAT has suggested that the employer should initiate an investigation if it has not already done so, although being careful 'not to trap the employee into making any sort of admission against his interests'.[927] It would only be in an exceptional case in which 'the circumstances may be so blatant, and the circumstances sufficiently brought to the attention of the employer to warrant a reasonable belief as to guilt', that further investigation may be dispensed with. In *A v B*[928] the EAT emphasised that an investigator should 'focus no less on any potential evidence that may exculpate or at least point towards the innocence of the employee as he should on the evidence directed towards proving the charges against him' particularly where the employee in question is suspended and denied the opportunity of contacting potentially relevant witnesses. These dicta must now be considered in the light of the decision of the Court of Appeal to the effect that the issue of whether investigation into suspected misconduct was reasonable in the circumstances is subject to the 'band of reasonable responses' test.[929] We discuss the implications of this further in para 5.144 below.

DISCIPLINARY HEARINGS

5.141   Hearings (or 'meetings') are integral to the SDDPs, described in para 5.124 *et seq* above, and the Code of Practice is based on the statutory provisions. However, like other provisions of the Code, those covering meetings apply regardless of whether an SDDP applies to the action in question. The Code also amplifies the statutory provisions in some respects. It states that, where possible, the timing and location of the meeting should be agreed with the employee[930] and that the length of time between the written notification of the alleged conduct or other circumstances which lead the employer to contemplate dismissal or other disciplinary action should be long enough to allow the employee to prepare but not so long that memories fade. The employer should hold the meeting in a private location and ensure that there will be no interruptions.[931] The employee should be informed of his or her right to be accompanied at the meeting and

---

925 Code of Practice, para 43.
926 [1988] IRLR 512, 513–514.
927 *Lovie Ltd v Anderson* [1999] IRLR 164, 165.
928 [2003] IRLR 405, 409.
929 *Sainsbury's Supermarkets Ltd v Hitt* [2003] IRLR 23.
930 Code of Practice, para 14. Cf the SDDPs, which state that the timing and location of meetings must be 'reasonable' and that the employee must take 'all reasonable steps to attend the meeting': EA 2002, Sch 2, paras 2, 3, 5, and 13. Special provisions apply in relation to the right to be accompanied: see para 5.132 above.
931 Code of Practice, para 14.

given copies of any documents that should be produced at it.[932] At the meeting the employer should explain the complaint against the employee and go through the evidence that has been gathered. The employee should be allowed to set out their case; to answer any allegations made; and to ask questions, present evidence, call witnesses and be given an opportunity to raise points about any information provided by witnesses.[933]

Beyond the limits of these statutory requirements and of the Code, only a general standard of fairness applies to the conduct of hearings. Thus in *Hussain v Elonex plc*[934] the Court of Appeal rejected a plea by the applicant that his employer's failure to disclose the existence of witness statements to him during the hearing invalidated the procedure. According to Mummery LJ, '[I]t is a matter of what is fair and reasonable in each case', so that, in the absence of a contractual disciplinary procedure, 'there are no hard and fast rigid rules' beyond the basic requirement that the employee should be informed of the case against him or her and given a chance to respond to it.[935] However it 'is a basic proposition ... that the charge against ... the employee facing dismissal should be precisely framed, and that evidence should be confined to the particulars given in the charge'.[936] The 'circumstances in which it is permissible to go beyond that charge in a decision to take disciplinary action are very limited'.[937] There is no rule of law requiring an employer to give an employee the opportunity to cross-examine a person making a complaint; this will depend upon the circumstances.[938] It may be even be reasonable in certain situations to dismiss an employee on the basis of written statements from fellow employees whose identities remained anonymous to the investigating and the dismissing officer, as well as to the dismissed employee, on the ground that, in a close-knit community, they feared retaliation in the event that their identities were disclosed.[939]

PENALTIES, SANCTIONS AND THE RIGHT TO APPEAL

5.142 The Code emphasises that before making any decision of disciplinary action the employer 'should take account of the employee's disciplinary and general record, length of service, actions taken in any previous similar case, the explanations given by the employee and – most important of all – whether the intended disciplinary action is reasonable under the circumstances'.[940] The 'final stage' in the disciplinary process might be dismissal or (if the employee's contract allows it or it is mutually agreed) some other penalty such as demotion, disciplinary transfer, or loss of seniority/pay. In general, the penalty should be proportionate to the nature of the offence; the position and seniority of the employee; and the degree of wilfulness with which it was committed.[941] It should also be reasonably consistent with the employer's previous practice in similar cases.[942] If an employee is dismissed he or she should be informed as soon as

932 Code of Practice, para 13.
933 Code of Practice, para 15.
934 [1999] IRLR 420.
935 [1999] IRLR 420, 423. Cf *A v B* [2004] IRLR 405.
936 *Strouthos v London Underground Ltd* [2004] IRLR 636, para 12 (Pill LJ).
937 *Strouthos v London Underground Ltd* [2004] IRLR 636, para 41.
938 *Santamera v Express Cargo Forwarding t/a IEC Ltd* [2003] IRLR 273.
939 *Ramsey v Walkers Snack Foods Ltd* [2004] IRLR 754.
940 Code of Practice, para 17.
941 *Ladbroke Racing Ltd v Arnott* [1983] IRLR 154.
942 *Cain v Leeds Western Health Authority* [1990] IRLR 168, although note *Hadjioannou v Coral Casinos* [1981] IRLR 352.

possible of the reasons for the dismissal, the date on which the employment contract will terminate, the appropriate period of notice, and their right of appeal.[943]

As we saw in paras 5.125 and 5.126, the granting and exercise of the right to appeal is integral to the SDDPs. Even where the SDDPs do not apply, failure to allow an appeal may result in a finding of unfairness, particularly where the right to appeal forms part of a contractual disciplinary procedure.[944] Before 1 October 2004 whether a procedural defect could be cured on appeal depended on the extent of unfairness at the initial hearing; in a case of a serious breach, then according to the EAT 'if there is a rehearing de novo at first instance, the omission may be corrected, but it seems to us that if there is to be a correction by the appeal then such an appeal must be of a comprehensive nature, in essence a rehearing and not a mere review'.[945] This approach is now subject to the 'no difference' principle, discussed below.

(v) The effect of a failure to comply with procedural requirements

5.143   As we saw in para 5.122, failure to comply with the minimum procedural requirements described above would generally have led to a finding of unfair dismissal under the law as it stood prior to 1 October 2004. It was not open to the employer to argue that, notwithstanding a breach of procedure, the dismissal was fair on substantive grounds, either because of facts which emerged later[946] or because, viewed objectively, the failure to operate the procedure would have made no difference to the outcome[947] (although should facts have emerged later that showed that a disciplinary dismissal could have been justified, or that a failure to consult over redundancy would have made no difference, the compensation payable to the employee could have been reduced, possibly to nothing[948]).

Since 1 October 2004, a dismissal is automatically unfair if the relevant statutory procedure has not been completed and non-completion was 'wholly or mainly attributable to failure by the employer to comply with its requirements'.[949] Subject to this, however, it is now provided that 'failure by an employer to follow a procedure in relation to the dismissal of an employee shall not be regarded for the purposes of section 98(4)(a) as by itself making the employer's action unreasonable if he shows that he would have decided to dismiss the employee if he had followed the procedure'.[950] This means that if an employer can show that following a procedure beyond the statutory minimum would not have changed its decision to dismiss, its failure to follow that procedure will not, of itself, make the dismissal unfair. Tribunals will thus have the unenviable task of embarking upon a hypothetical inquiry of what an employer would

---

943   Code of Practice, para 25.
944   *West Midlands Co-operative Society Ltd v Tipton* [1986] AC 536, although failure to observe the contractual procedure in every respect does not inevitably make the dismissal unfair: *Westminster City Council v Cabaj* [1996] IRLR 399 (appeal panel composed of two members instead of three).
945   *Whitbread & Co plc v Mills* [1988] IRLR 501, 509; *Whitbread plc (t/a Whitbread Medway Inns) v Hall* [2001] IRLR 275.
946   *W Devis & Sons Ltd v Atkins* [1977] IRLR 314.
947   *Polkey v AE Dayton Services Ltd* [1987] IRLR 503.
948   *Sillifant v Powell Duffryn Timber Ltd* [1983] IRLR 91, 97 (Browne-Wilkinson J).
949   ERA 1996, s 98A(1). The procedures apply to dismissal or relevant disciplinary action first contemplated by an employer after 1 October 2004.
950   ERA 1996, s 98A(2).

have done had it followed that procedure, presupposing that a realistic assessment can be made of this.[951] This rule also creates incoherence in the law. As we saw in para 5.118 *et seq* the test established in section 98(4) is whether the employer acted reasonably in treating the reason *it relied on* as a sufficient reason for dismissal. This means the reason it relied on at the time of dismissal.[952] However the 'no difference' test does not ask whether the employer *acted reasonably* in assuming at the time of dismissal that following a procedure would have made no difference; the employer may, indeed, have acted entirely unreasonably in doing so: all that is involved is a retrospective assessment of whether compliance with procedures would probably have affected the result. Thus, the emphasis shifts to asking whether the employee received his or her 'just desserts',[953] an issue that should properly be dealt with at the remedies stage, rather than whether the employer has acted fairly.

The Government justified the re-instatement of the 'no difference' principle removed by *Polkey* on the basis that employers would be discouraged from adopting more extensive procedures if a dismissal that breached them would thereby be unfair.[954] However there is little point in having such procedures if they can be regarded with relative impunity in the context of unfair dismissal,[955] even if they are contractual in their nature;[956] indeed, employers have every incentive to withdraw procedures that improve on the rudimentary statutory procedures in order to avoid the risk of employees invoking a contractual remedy.[957] Such a consequence does nothing to promote the 'orderly employment relations as well as fairness and consistency in the treatment of individuals' that disciplinary rules and procedures are intended to promote.[958]

It should be noted that dismissals effected by employers who have complied with the requirements of the Code of Practice are likely to be fair, even if it later appears that the employee was innocent of the disciplinary charges brought against him or her, or if a more thorough investigation would have revealed this to be the case. This is because the procedural obligation imposed on the employer is far from absolute; the employer's internal procedures do not have to resemble those of a court or tribunal, nor do they have to comply with the strict requirements of natural justice – such as the rule against personal bias or the employer being judge in his own cause – in so far as they go further than the Code.[959] Moreover the requirement for tribunals to consider the size and administrative resources of the undertaking in deciding reasonableness[960] means

---

951 See Elias 1981: p 215.
952 *W Devis & Sons Ltd v Atkins* [1977] IRLR 314.
953 Elias, 1981: p 215.
954 Alan Johnson, HC Standing Committee F, 13 December 2001, cols 142–143.
955 Hepple and Morris, 2002: p 265.
956 Cf *West Midlands Co-operative Society Ltd v Tipton* [1986] AC 536; *Tower Hamlets Health Authority v Anthony* [1988] ICR 499; *Whitbread & Co plc v Mills* [1988] IRLR 501; *Stoker v Lancashire County Council* [1992] IRLR 75; although see also *Westminster City Council v Cabaj* [1996] IRLR 399.
957 EA 2002, s 30 makes it a term of a contract of employment that the employer and employee shall comply with the requirements of an applicable statutory procedure. This section has not yet been brought into force. The Government intends to evaluate the need to bring it into force in the light of a review of the impact of the statutory procedures which is scheduled for 2006: *Guidance on the Employment Act 2002 (Dispute Resolution) Regulations 2004 and associated provisions in the Employment Act 2002*, DTI, 2004, para 146.
958 Code of Practice, para 1.
959 *Slater v Leicestershire Health Authority* [1989] IRLR 16.
960 ERA 1996, s 98(4)(a).

that less stringent standards may be demanded where the business is relatively small. It is strongly arguable that this provision should have been relied upon to safeguard the position of businesses which may have found it unduly difficult to develop procedures beyond the statutory minimum overnight rather than reducing the incentive for managers in larger enterprises to follow the broader principles of fairness stated in the Code.

(vi) Misconduct: particular features

5.144   In a case of dismissal for a serious disciplinary offence, such as theft or fighting, the courts applied for many years a three-fold test, requiring an employer to show first, that it honestly believed that the employee had committed the offence in question; second, that it had reasonable grounds upon which to sustain that belief; and third, that the employer had at the stage at which the belief was formed carried out as much investigation into the matter as was reasonable in the circumstances of the case.[961] On this the EAT suggested that there was, in effect, a sliding scale of responsibility:

> ... at one extreme there will be cases where the employee is virtually caught in the act and at the other there will be situations where the issue is one of pure inference. As the scale moves towards the latter end, so the amount of inquiry and investigation, including questioning of the employee, which may be required is likely to increase. The sufficiency of the relevant evidence and the reasonableness of the conclusion seem to us to be inextricably intertwined.[962]

In 2002, however, the Court of Appeal held that the third element of this test – whether investigation into suspected misconduct was reasonable in the circumstances – was subject to the 'band of reasonable responses' test discussed in para 5.119 *et seq*.[963] Thus, tribunals should not substitute their own view as to what was a reasonable and adequate investigation; rather they should apply 'the objective standard of the reasonable employer as to what was a reasonable investigation'.[964] The general criticisms that we made of the 'band of reasonable responses' test in our discussion above apply with even greater strength in this context; the idea that a very basic principle of procedural justice should itself be subject to the broad and highly speculative test of whether a reasonable employer might have considered what was done to be reasonable is particularly troubling in the light of the severe consequences for an employee's reputation of dismissal for theft or other acts of serious misconduct.[965]

Moreover, the requirement to conduct an investigation is itself now subject to the 'no difference' principle discussed in para 5.143. As we stated above, this, again, marks an especially radical weakening of procedural justice in this context. It has never been the case that employers have been required to conduct inquiries

---

961   *British Home Stores Ltd v Burchell* [1978] IRLR 379; *W Weddell & Co Ltd v Tepper* [1980] ICR 286. In *Boys and Girls Welfare Society v McDonald* [1996] IRLR 129 the EAT held that a 'simplistic application' (at 132) of the *Burchell* test, promulgated when the onus lay on employers to show that they had acted reasonably, could lead tribunals into error. In practice, however, it is difficult to see how an employer who did not act in accordance with its terms could nevertheless have acted reasonably, a view affirmed by the Court of Session in *Scottish Daily Record and Sunday Mail (1986) Ltd v Laird* [1996] IRLR 665.

962   *ILEA v Gravett* [1988] IRLR 497, 499.

963   *Sainsbury's Supermarkets Ltd v Hitt* [2003] IRLR 23.

964   *Sainsbury's Supermarkets Ltd v Hitt* [2003] IRLR 23, para 28 (Mummery LJ).

965   Cf *A v B* [2003] IRLR 405, paras 58 *et seq*.

that would establish, to the standards applied in a criminal court, whether an employee is guilty of misconduct, and the question of what is reasonable does not depend on the outcome of a criminal trial that takes place later. Now, however, instead of focussing purely on the reasonableness of the employer's conduct at the time of dismissal, tribunals may have the added complication of assessing the credibility of an employer's argument that, although it failed to investigate the facts prior to dismissal, it would nevertheless have decided to dismiss had it done so.[966]

A further issue that may arise in the context of misconduct dismissals is whether it is fair to dismiss more than one employee if it is not possible to identify which of them was responsible for offences being committed. Since the employer is normally required to take into account not simply the circumstances surrounding the alleged offence but also the seniority and past record of the individual employee concerned, it would be difficult to justify a group dismissal which takes no account of such individual circumstances. Nonetheless, in an exceptional case a group dismissal may be possible, where, for example, an employer reasonably concludes, following an investigation, that a number of employees could have committed the act in question, that each member of the group in question was capable of having done so and that 'as between members of the group the employer could not reasonably identify the individual perpetrator; then, provided that the beliefs were held on solid and sensible grounds at the date of dismissal, an employer is entitled to dismiss each member of the group'.[967] In this context it would seem harder for an employer who dismisses without investigation successfully to argue that following a procedure beyond the statutory minimum would have made no difference to the outcome.

(vii) Capability: particular features

5.145   Broadly the same principles concerning procedural fairness apply by extension to cases of dismissal for incapability on the grounds of lack of competence or illness.[968] According to the EAT, where illness causes intermittent absences from work, 'it is important to realise that these cases are not cases of disciplinary situations; what is important is that the employers should treat each case individually where there is genuine illness and with sympathy, understanding and compassion'. The purpose of a warning in this context is not to get the individual to change his or her behaviour, but 'to give a caution that the stage has been reached where with the best will in the world, it becomes impossible to continue with the employment'.[969] The employee need not necessarily be absent from work at the time of dismissal, nor need the employer require firm medical evidence that the absences will continue, if there has been a regular pattern in the past; factors to be taken into account in considering whether to dismiss include the nature of the illness; the likelihood of its recurring; the length of the absences in relation to the periods of good health; the employer's dependence on the work done by the employee; the effect of their absence on fellow workers; the ease with which the employee's work could be redeployed during their absence; and 'the extent to which the difficulty of the situation and

---

966   Cf *Panama v London Borough of Hackney* [2003] IRLR 278.
967   *Parr v Whitbread and Co plc* [1990] ICR 427, 432 (Wood J); *Monie v Coral Racing Ltd* [1981] ICR 109.
968   For the suggestion that employers may, in certain circumstances, have a duty to dismiss employees on health grounds for their own good, see *Coxall v Goodyear Great Britain Ltd* [2002] IRLR 742, para 29 (Simon Brown LJ), discussed by Elvin, 2003.
969   *Lynock v Cereal Packaging Ltd* [1988] IRLR 510, 511.

the position of the employer has [sic] been made clear to the employee so that the employee realises that the point of no return, the moment when the decision was ultimately being made may be approaching'.[970] The ACAS Code also advises consideration of whether alternative work is available and how similar situations have been handled in the past,[971] and indicates that smaller organisations may be entitled to act at an earlier stage than large in the case of long-term absences, because the impact of such absences on them is likely to be greater.[972] The EAT has held that an employer's treatment of an employee which causes ill health, which in turn causes the incapacity that the employer treats as a reason for dismissal, can be taken into account in considering the fairness of a capability dismissal, but that it does not necessarily make that dismissal unfair.[973]

Substantive fairness

5.146   To what extent, if at all, does section 98 of the Act embody a notion of substantive fairness in dismissal, which can be related to the result and not simply to the process or procedure leading up to it? Whether the individual's interest in job security is viewed as akin to a 'property right' in the job[974] or, more justifiably, as a right to the recognition of their personal dignity and autonomy,[975] the protection accorded by section 98 is highly qualified. To date, limitations placed on the free speech or self-expression of employees have generally been permitted if the employer could show that they were loosely justified on business-related grounds. What the tribunal aims for 'is the striking of a balance between the need of the employer to control the business for which he is responsible, in the interests of the business itself – and after all, it is upon its continued prosperity that everybody's interests depend – a balance between that need, on the one hand, and the reasonable freedom of the employee, on the other'.[976] The employer has accordingly been accorded a wide discretion to impose rules relating, for example, to dress codes, or guidelines governing the personal appearance of employees;[977] conversely, the employer has been given a discretion 'to instruct an employee not to wear some sign or symbol that could be offensive to fellow-employees and customers'.[978] Moreover the 'band of reasonable responses' test discussed in para 5.119 *et seq*, in embodying a reactive standard that incorporates not the best employer practice but an ill-defined 'middle ground', also diminishes standards of substantive fairness.[979]

---

970 [1988] IRLR 510, 512. See also the earlier case of *Spencer v Paragon Wallpapers Ltd* [1977] ICR 301, and on warnings in the context of incompetence, *James v Waltham Holy Cross UDC* [1973] ICR 398.

971 Code of Practice, para 38.

972 Code of Practice, para 39.

973 *Edwards v Governors of Hanson School* [2001] IRLR 733; *Frewin v Consignia plc* EAT/0981/ 02/LA, 18 July 2003, cf *London Fire and Civil Defence Authority v Betty* [1994] IRLR 384.

974 Cf Meyers, 1964.

975 H Collins, 1993: p 28; see para 5.5 above.

976 *Boychuk v HJ Symons Holdings Ltd* [1977] IRLR 395, 396.

977 *Schmidt v Austicks Bookshops Ltd* [1978] ICR 85; *Department for Work and Pensions v Thompson* [2004] IRLR 348.

978 *Boychuk v HJ Symons Holdings Ltd* [1977] IRLR 395, 396.

979 Its most controversial application was the decision of the EAT in *Saunders v Scottish National Camps Association* [1980] IRLR 174, where the dismissal of an attendant in a boys' camp on the grounds solely of his homosexuality was found to be fair, even though he regarded his sexuality as an entirely private matter and there was no evidence of its affecting the way he performed his job. This would now be contrary to EE(SO)R 2003, but the court's approach to the band of reasonable responses in this case may still apply in other contexts.

These decisions may now require reconsideration in the light of the Human Rights Act 1998; more generally, it is strongly arguable that the 'band of reasonable responses' test should not be applied in its existing form where an employee's Convention rights have been violated, although to date judicial comments to this effect have been *obiter*.[980] The courts have attempted to give some general guidance on how tribunals should consider HRA points in the context of unfair dismissal cases. The Court of Appeal has confirmed that section 3 of the HRA requires tribunals to read and give effect to the unfair dismissal legislation in a way that is compatible with Convention rights so far as it is possible to do so regardless of the legal identity of the employer.[981] However according to Mummery LJ, in general section 3 can be ignored; 'the reasonable expectation is that a decision that a dismissal was fair under s 98 would not be incompatible with Article 8 or Article 14 of the Convention'[982] (an assertion for which, unfortunately, no clear authority or justification was provided). He proposed that in cases between private litigants, tribunals should ask first whether the circumstances of the dismissal fall within the ambit of a Convention right; second, if so, whether the state has a positive obligation to secure enjoyment of that right between private persons (since, if not, the right is unlikely to affect the outcome of the claim);[983] and third, if the state does have such an obligation, whether the interference with the right in question is justified. If the interference is not justified, the tribunal should then ask whether there is a permissible reason for the dismissal which does not involve unjustified interference with a Convention right: if not the dismissal would be unfair. If there is justification for the interference, the tribunal should then ask whether the dismissal was fair, reading and giving effect to section 98 of ERA 1996 under section 3 of the HRA so as to be compatible with the Convention right.[984] Beyond general guidance of this nature, there is little indication to date of how the courts and tribunals will respond to the new possibilities for a human rights jurisprudence which the HRA creates.

5.147 It should be noted that, discrimination law aside, the employer can make the out-of-work activities of the employee a relevant matter from the point of view of employment by raising them prior to the formation of the contract of employment. The lack of effective controls over the hiring stage is also significant here.[985] An employee who conceals his past or his out-of-work activities is open to dismissal on the ground of misrepresentation, however irrelevant the matter might be to the subsequent performance of his or her job. In *O'Brien v Prudential Assurance Co Ltd*[986] a prospective employee made no mention in his application form of his history of mental illness, despite a specific question about this matter on the application form. He was employed by the company and later applied for life assurance with it, at which point a more thorough medical examination led to his previous condition being revealed. He was then dismissed. The dismissal was held to have been within the SOSR

---

980 *Pay v Lancashire Probation Service* [2004] IRLR 129, paras 33–34.
981 *X v Y* [2004] IRLR 625.
982 *X v Y* [2004] IRLR 625, para 58(5). Arts 8 and 14 were the Convention rights at issue in that case.
983 In practice, this is highly likely to be the case.
984 [2004] IRLR 625, para 63.
985 See paras 3.14 and 3.15 above; on the HRA 1998 and hiring, see generally G Morris, 2001a.
986 [1979] IRLR 140. For the provisions of the DDA 1995 in relation to mental illness see para 6.109 *et seq.*

category and to have been fair in the circumstances, given the employee's history of illness and his misleading the employer at the time of his appointment.

O'Brien may be contrasted with the special category of cases established by the Rehabilitation of Offenders Act 1974: an employee is entitled to mislead a prospective employer at the point of hiring by not revealing the existence of a spent conviction, and grounds related to the conviction cannot constitute a proper ground for dismissal thus rendering a dismissal for this reason, in effect, automatically unfair. More generally, the categories of automatically unfair reasons creates a space in which the 'balancing act' between substantive rights and the employer's business interests is, by and large, avoided; however, these categories are, as we have seen, an essentially arbitrary grouping and, since they are seen as exceptions to the more general rule of section 98, their scope is narrowly construed.[987]

REMEDIES FOR UNFAIR DISMISSAL

Re-employment

5.148   ERA 1996 provides[988] that if, on a finding of unfair dismissal, the employee indicates a wish to be re-employed, the tribunal may make an order of either reinstatement or re-engagement under sections 114 and 115; if no order is made under this section, it must make an award of compensation calculated in accordance with sections 118 to 126. Accordingly, 'the preferred remedies for unfair dismissal are reinstatement, re-engagement and monetary compensation in that order'.[989] The term 're-employment', while not appearing in the Act, is used here as a genus term covering both reinstatement and re-engagement. Where an order for re-employment is made in respect of a dismissal that was automatically unfair because the appropriate SDDP was not followed, the tribunal must award the employee a minimum of four weeks' pay (subject to the statutory maximum limit)[990] unless it considers that such an award would result in injustice to the employer.[991]

5.149   An order for reinstatement requires the employer to 'treat the complainant in all respects as if he had not been dismissed', and must specify any amount payable by the employer in respect of the period during which the employee should have been, but was not, in employment, including back pay, and also any rights and privileges, including seniority and pension rights, which should be restored to the employee.[992] In effect, then, the employee is put back into the job which he or she occupied, restored to the benefits they enjoyed and compensated for those lost in the interim. Re-engagement, by contrast, involves re-employment by the employer or an associated employer in employment

---

987 *Smith v Hayle Town Council* [1978] ICR 996, 1003 (Sir David Cairns); para 5.97 above.
988 S 116(1), (2).
989 *O'Laoire v Jackel International Ltd* [1990] ICR 197, 200 (Lord Donaldson MR).
990 As of 1 February 2005 and at the time of writing £280 per week: ERA 1996, s 227.
991 ERA 1996, s 112(5),(6).
992 ERA 1996, s 114(1), (2). If the employee would have benefited from a further improvement in terms and conditions during the period in question, that must also be taken into account from the date when such improvement would have come into effect: s 114(3). Note also the provision for adjustment of the amount payable to the employee where he or she has been in receipt of certain payments: s 114(4).

'comparable to that from which he was dismissed or other suitable employment'.[993] The order for re-engagement must specify the identity of the employer, the nature of the employment, the remuneration to be paid, an amount payable for lost benefit in the period following dismissal, and rights and benefits to be restored to the employee.[994] Orders for reinstatement and re-engagement must also indicate the date by which they must be complied with.

In each case the award is discretionary. In deciding upon reinstatement, the tribunal must consider not simply whether the complainant wishes to be reinstated, but also 'whether it is practicable for the employer to comply with an order for reinstatement' and, in a case where the employee contributed to the dismissal, whether reinstatement would be 'just'.[995] If reinstatement is not deemed appropriate the tribunal will go on to consider re-engagement, whereupon it will take the same factors into account.[996] Except in a case where the employee contributed to his or her own dismissal, an order for re-engagement must be on terms 'which are, so far as reasonably practicable, as favourable as an order for reinstatement'.[997] In exercising its discretion to make either order, the tribunal may not take into account the fact that the employer has hired a permanent replacement for the complainant unless the employer can show that it was not practicable to do otherwise or that it engaged the replacement after a reasonable period had elapsed without the complainant indicating that he or she wished to be re-employed.[998]

5.150 The statutory order for re-employment is unlike an equitable order restraining dismissal by way of an injunction or declaration in two important respects. First, the statutory order necessarily assumes that there has been a dismissal and, as a result, that not just the employment but also the contractual nexus itself has been broken. This is one reason why reinstatement, although the 'primary' remedy for unfair dismissal, is 'something of a rarity... [It] may be that by the time that the complaint reaches the ... [employment] ... tribunal, relations between the complainant and his employer have usually reached a stage at which reinstatement has ceased to be a realistic option'.[999] It seems that it is formally or perhaps psychologically more difficult to put the employee back into a job which he or she has 'lost' than it is to enable them to retain it; for the employment tribunal, the status quo is the dismissal which the statutory order must reverse, whereas for the High Court the status quo is the position prior to the employer's alleged breach of contract, so that in the latter case the 'balance of convenience' inherently favours the employee.[1]

The second major difference is that the employer will not incur contempt of court proceedings for refusing to implement a statutory order for re-employment. The statutory order does not have the power to 'concentrate the mind'[2] in the way that the equitable order can. Under section 117 of the Act, in a case where

---

993 ERA 1996, s 115(1).
994 ERA 1996, s 115(2).
995 ERA 1996, s 116(1).
996 ERA 1996, s 116(2)
997 ERA 1996, s 116(4). In *Rank Xerox (UK) Ltd v Stryczek* [1995] IRLR 568 the EAT held that re-engagement could not be on *more* favourable terms than reinstatement.
998 ERA 1996, s 116(5), (6).
999 *O'Laoire v Jackel International Ltd* [1990] ICR 197, 201 (Lord Donaldson MR).
1   See para 5.58 above.
2   *Jones v Gwent County Council* [1992] IRLR 521, 527. Cf also the provisions of the Reserve Forces (Safeguard of Employment) Act 1985.

an order for reinstatement or re-engagement is not fully complied with, the only option is for the tribunal to make one or more of a number of compensatory awards to the employee. Two situations need to be considered. The first is where the employee is taken back into employment, but the terms of the order are not fully complied with. Here the tribunal can make an award of compensation of such amount as it thinks fit, having regard to the employee's loss. This sum is calculated according to the principles laid down for the computation of the compensatory award in section 124 of the Act, except that the statutory maximum for such an award (as of 1 February 2005 and at the time of writing £56,800)[3] may be exceeded to the extent necessary to enable the award fully to reflect the amount specified in the reinstatement or re-engagement order as payable for the period between termination of employment and the date of re-employment.[4] A more highly-paid employee might therefore receive substantial compensation under this head.

The second situation is where the employee is not reinstated or, in an appropriate case, re-engaged. Here the tribunal makes a basic award, a compensatory award and a further 'additional award' to reflect the employer's failure to comply with that order.[5] The additional award is an amount equivalent to between 26 and 52 weeks' pay.[6] Once again the statute allows the limits on the compensatory award to be exceeded, in this context to enable the aggregate of the compensatory and additional awards to reflect the amount specified as payable in the re-instatement and re-engagement order.[7] However the courts have held that the arrears of pay that would have been payable had reinstatement or re-engagement taken place are subsumed in the compensatory award, so where those arrears do not themselves exceed the statutory limit on the compensatory award, the total award is subject to the statutory cap.[8]

5.151   The employer may avoid the additional award by showing that it was not practicable to comply with the order.[9] This means that the employer gets two chances to argue for the impracticability of re-employment. According to the EAT, 'one process looks forward, the other looks back and although it may be that a cherry that is rejected at the first bite will be likely to be regarded as indigestible at the second, there is in our view no doubt at all that two bites are allowed'.[10] The determination of practicability at the first stage does not raise an estoppel against the employer putting a different point of view at the second stage.[11] At the first stage, the tribunal is simply required to 'take into account' the question of practicability, but must nevertheless make a determination that the remedy would be practicable and so must give due consideration to arguments that it is not.[12] At the second stage, the burden is clearly placed on the employer to satisfy the tribunal that re-employment was not practicable.[13]

3   ERA 1996, s 124(1), as amended; see para 5.155 below.
4   ERA 1996, s 124(3). Any award under s 112(5) is deducted from this award.
5   ERA 1996, s 117(3).
6   ERA 1996, s 117(3). Again this is subject to the statutory maximum limit, which stands £280 at 1 February 2005 and at the time of writing: ERA 1996, s 227(1).
7   S 124(4).
8   *Parry v National Westminster Bank plc* [2005] IRLR 193; see also *Selfridges Ltd v Malik* [1997] IRLR 577.
9   ERA 1996, s 117(4)(a).
10   *Mabrizi v National Hospital for Nervous Diseases* [1990] IRLR 133, 135 (Knox J).
11   *Timex Corpn v Thomson* [1981] IRLR 522; *Port of London Authority v Payne* [1994] IRLR 9.
12   *Port of London Authority v Payne* [1994] IRLR 9, 14; Bennett, 1994.
13   ERA 1996, s 117(4)(a); see also *Port of London Authority v Payne* above.

At both stages, the courts have made it clear that what is practicable should not be equated with what is possible. The tribunal should not award re-engagement, it has been said, where 'the evidence points overwhelmingly to the conclusion that the consequence of any attempt to re-engage the employee will result in serious industrial strife'.[14] Nor would it be appropriate where the parties had been in a 'close personal relationship' which has irretrievably broken down,[15] or where the employer, no matter how unreasonably, remains convinced of the employee's wrongdoing.[16] To this extent, the exercise of the tribunal's statutory discretion follows the approach of the courts at common law: factors of the kind to be taken into account are 'the fact that the atmosphere in the factory is poisoned ... the fact that the employee has displayed her distrust and lack of confidence in her employers and would not be a satisfactory employee on reinstatement ... insufficient employment for the employee'.[17]

The Court of Appeal has also said that the tribunal must avoid substituting its commercial judgment for that of the employer. In *Port of London Authority v Payne*[18] a decision that re-engagement was not impracticable on the grounds that the employer could have considered offering voluntary redundancy to existing staff in order to make way for the applicant was held to have been incorrect. The tribunal:

> ... should give due weight to the commercial judgment of the management unless of course the witnesses are disbelieved. The standard must not be set too high. The employer cannot be expected to explore every possible avenue which ingenuity might suggest. The employer does not have to show that reinstatement or re-engagement was *impossible*. It is a matter of what is practicable in the circumstances of the employer's business at the relevant time.

One difficulty with this approach is that it creates a further stage at which the employee's rights can be defeated by the invocation of business-related factors which, by their nature, are exceptionally difficult for a tribunal to challenge or to second-guess; the 'band of reasonableness' test is carried over to the stage of remedies.

5.152 Orders of re-engagement and reinstatement have amounted on average to around only 5% of successful unfair dismissal claims and 1% of all claims proceeding to a hearing since the introduction of the present remedy in 1975. The Warwick survey of the employment tribunal system which was carried out by the Industrial Relations Research Unit in the early 1980s reported a figure of 7.6% of cases in a survey sample resulting in re-employment, and there is some evidence that the Department of Employment figures might underestimate the true extent of re-employment by not counting cases in which it is brought about by agreement between the parties rather than being ordered by the tribunal.[19] In

---

14 *Bateman v British Leyland UK Ltd* [1974] ICR 403, 406; *Coleman and Stephenson v Magnet Joinery Ltd* [1975] ICR 46.
15 *Ennesy Co SA (t/a Tulchan Estate) v Minoprio* [1978] IRLR 489.
16 *Wood Group Heavy Industrial Turbines Ltd v Crossan* [1998] IRLR 680; D Lewis,1999.
17 *Rao v Civil Aviation Authority* [1992] IRLR 203, 207.
18 [1994] IRLR 9, 16. This was a case concerning entitlement to enhanced compensation as part of the special award for trade-union related dismissals under what is now TULRCA 1992, s 158, where the same test of practicability applies. See also *Cold Drawn Tubes Ltd v Middleton* [1992] IRLR 160; and see further, para 8.5 below.
19 L Dickens *et al*, 1985: p 110; and see the discussion in para 2.16 *et seq* above.

2003/4 only 11 cases out of 4,363 upheld resulted in orders of reinstatement or re-employment.[20]

Research in this area has shown several reasons for the low rate of re-employment. One is that applicants may not ask to be reinstated; this is especially likely to be the case in smaller firms, where employees in this position are unlikely to benefit from a protective union environment and where they will come into personal contact with the manager or owner who was responsible for their dismissal.[21] But another factor is the reluctance of tribunals to make this order in all but the most exceptional cases. The Warwick survey concluded that:

> ... the [employment] tribunals pay a lot of attention to the employers' views regarding the acceptability and practicability of re-employment and rarely award the remedy in the face of employer opposition. This is partly because of a view that re-employment which has to be imposed will not work.[22]

This perception may not be justified; there is evidence that re-employment rarely produces disruption to relations within the undertaking concerned and that most reinstated or re-engaged employees stay with the employer for a reasonable length of time after the order is made.[23]

Compensation

5.153   In a case where no order of re-employment is made, the Act envisages an award of compensation which comes in two parts, a basic and a compensatory award.[24]

(i) The basic award

5.154   The basic award is meant to reflect the loss of accrued continuity of employment following the dismissal: on finding new employment, the employee will have to begin again to acquire the continuity needed for the purposes of entitlement to a statutory redundancy payment. Under the original unfair dismissal jurisdiction conferred by the Industrial Relations Act 1971, the courts would include within damages a sum representing the discounted value of lost unfair dismissal and redundancy rights;[25] the present basic award was introduced by the EPA 1975 in order to put this practice on a firmer statutory basis as far as redundancy is concerned. Accordingly, the basic award is calculated in precisely the same way as a statutory redundancy payment, so that it is a function of the employee's age, length of service and normal weekly pay at the time of dismissal;[26] it is also reduced by the amount of any statutory redundancy payment actually received by the employee in respect of the dismissal.[27] From 1 February

---

20   *Employment Tribunals Service Annual Report and Accounts 2003–2004*, DTI, App 3, p 25.
21   L Dickens *et al*, 1985: pp 114–119; K Williams, 1983.
22   L Dickens *et al*, 1985: p 138.
23   K Williams and D Lewis, 1981. To date only a small number of cases have been determined under the ACAS arbitration scheme, discussed in para 2.20.
24   ERA 1996, s 118.
25   *Norton Tool Co Ltd v Tewson* [1972] ICR 501 (Sir John Donaldson P).
26   ERA 1996, s 119; on the calculation of the statutory redundancy payments, see para 5.174 below.
27   ERA 1996, s 122(4). However, this applies only where the dismissal was, in fact, by reason of redundancy; thus, no deduction should be made under s 122(4) for the element of an *ex gratia* payment expressed as incorporating the employee's statutory redundancy entitlement: *Boorman v Allmakers Ltd* [1995] IRLR 553.

2005 and at the time of writing, the maximum amount which may be awarded under this head is £8,400 as a result of the present upper limit of £280 applicable to an employee's normal weekly pay for these purposes.[28] If, however, the employee is made redundant in circumstances such that he or she is unfairly dismissed but does not qualify for a redundancy payment, either because they refuse to accept a suitable offer of re-employment[29] or because their contract is renewed or they are re-engaged within four weeks of the dismissal,[30] the Act provides that they should receive a basic award equivalent to two weeks' pay.[31] Because the basic award covers only redundancy compensation and not unfair dismissal rights, a sum representing the loss of the latter may be included in the compensatory award; it is common to award an amount of around a few hundred pounds under this head.

A minimum basic award of £3,800 is payable if the employee was dismissed or selected for redundancy on grounds related to trade-union membership or activities, or on grounds of activities as a health and safety representative, employee representative (including representation for the purposes of working time), or trustee of an occupational pension scheme.[32] In addition, where an employee is regarded as unfairly dismissed because the appropriate SDDP has not been followed by the employer, a minimum award of four weeks' pay is to be made, unless the tribunal considers that this would result in injustice to the employer.[33] In general, reductions in the basic award may be made for the employee's contributory fault[34] and for the employee's refusal to accept an offer of reinstatement; both of these may also go to reduce the minimum amount of payable in the special cases stated above.[35] A reduction may also be made in respect of the employee's misconduct prior to the dismissal,[36] and for any redundancy payment awarded in respect of the same dismissal or other payment by the employer on the ground that the dismissal was by reason of redundancy.[37]

(ii) The compensatory award

5.155   The compensatory award payable under section 123 is 'such amount as the tribunal considers just and equitable in all the circumstances having regard to the loss sustained by the complainant in consequence of the dismissal in so far as that loss is attributable to action taken by the employer'.[38] Awards under this head are currently subject to an upper limit which since 1 February 2005

28   ERA 1996, s 227. The calculation of a week's pay in this context (and the loss of earnings for the compensatory award) is subject to the national minimum wage: *Paggetti v Cobb* [2002] IRLR 861.
29   ERA 1996, s 141(2)–(4).
30   ERA 1996, s 138(1).
31   ERA 1996, s 121.
32   TULRCA 1992, s 156(1); ERA 1996, s 120(1).
33   ERA 1996, s 120(1A), (1B). This provision applies where the amount of the award, prior to any reduction for an award under a designated dismissal procedures agreement or payment made in respect of redundancy, is less than four weeks' pay.
34   This does not apply in a redundancy case unless the reason for selecting the employee for dismissal was one of those in respect of which a minimum award is payable under section 120(1); in that case s 122(2) applies only to so much of the basic award as is payable because of s 120(1): s 122(3).
35   ERA 1996, s 122(1)–(3); the parallel provision in trade union cases is TULRCA 1992, s 156.
36   ERA 1996, s 122(2)–(3); see below.
37   ERA 1996, s 122(4). See also s 122(3A) in respect of awards under a designated dismissal procedures agreement.
38   ERA 1996, s 123(1).

and at the time of writing stands at £56,800.[39] The *Fairness at Work* White Paper proposed the abolition of the maximum limit to the compensatory award, on the grounds that this would both enable individuals to be fully compensated for their losses and encourage employers to establish more effective voluntary systems.[40] This proposal followed a decades-long decline in the value of the upper limit relative to average earnings since it was first set in the Industrial Relations Act 1971. The Secretary of State had power to raise this sum by order[41] but, in contrast with the regulations governing the up-rating of most social security benefits, he or she had no obligation to make an annual increase, nor need any increase be linked to inflation. ERelA 1999 substituted a new requirement on the Secretary of State to adjust (upwards or downwards) the upper limit once a year in line with any changes in the retail prices index 'as soon as practicable' following the publication of the September year-on-year figures.[42] The upper limit does not apply to dismissal (or, subject to specified conditions, selection for redundancy) on health and safety grounds, nor to dismissal for making a 'protected disclosure'.[43] More generally, no upper compensation limits apply to the principal anti-discrimination statutes. The upper limit was removed for cases involving sex discrimination on the grounds of its incompatibility with Directive 76/307,[44] and a parallel change was later made in relation to cases of racial discrimination[45] and applied to disability discrimination and discrimination on grounds of religion or belief and sexual orientation.[46] The cap on the compensatory award, which may preclude tribunals from awarding full compensation for a dismissed employee's financial loss, has recently been blamed by the House of Lords as the principal cause of the 'awkward and unfortunate consequences' flowing from the unsatisfactory inter-relation between the common law and statute in the context of dismissal,[47] discussed in para 5.45 above.

5.156   The object of the compensatory award 'is to compensate, and to compensate fully, but not to award a bonus'.[48] At the same time, the common law categories of loss are not directly relevant: the statutory claim is 'an entirely new cause of action'.[49] The limited common law right of the employee to continued employment – the consequence of the notice rule[50] – no longer poses an automatic barrier to substantial compensation claims. In a creative gloss on the statute the NIRC suggested that 'in the context of unfair dismissal … it is appropriate and in accordance with the intentions of Parliament that

---

39   ERA 1996, s 124(1) (as amended by SI 2004/2989).
40   *Fairness at Work*, Cm 3968, 1968, para 3.5.
41   ERA 1996, ss 124(2), 236(3), now repealed.
42   ERelA 1999, s 34.
43   ERA 1996, s 124(1A).
44   *Marshall v Southampton and South West Hampshire Area Health Authority (No 2)* Case C-271/91 [1993] IRLR 445; SI 1993/2798; see para 6.67 below.
45   Race Relations (Remedies) Act 1994.
46   On the relevant provisions of the DDA 1995, EE(RB)R 2003 and EE(SO)R 2003, see further para 6.67 below. The CA has held that where an employee has been subject to discrimination, unfair dismissal does not break the chain of causation for the purposes of assessing loss: *HM Prison Service v Beart (No 2)* [2005] IRLR 568.
47   *Eastwood v Magnox Electric plc* [2004] IRLR 733, para 33 (Lord Nicholls).
48   *Norton Tool Co Ltd v Tewson* [1972] ICR 501, 504 (Sir John Donaldson P).
49   [1972] ICR 501.
50   See para 5.13 *et seq*.

we should treat an employee as having suffered a loss in so far as he receives less than he would have received in accordance with good industrial practice'.[51] The principal application of this idea was in a series of cases ruling that an employee should be entitled to receive compensation representing wages in lieu of notice, regardless of actual earnings he or she may have had from alternative employment during the notice period. At common law, such earnings would automatically reduce the damages payable by the employer, but under the Act the NIRC considered that it was 'good industrial practice' for an employer to pay wages in lieu as a matter of course, and that there should accordingly be no deduction from this payment in respect of the employee's earnings.[52] This was a surprising interpretation in the light of an express statutory instruction to the effect that 'the tribunal shall apply the same rule concerning the duty of a person to mitigate his loss as applies to damages recoverable under the common law',[53] and produced the anomalous result that a failure to mitigate by looking for work counted against the employee when actual mitigation did not. In *Hardy v Polk (Leeds) Ltd*[54] the EAT declined to follow the earlier case law and held that earnings during the notice period should be taken into account in assessing the loss that the employee had suffered, although a differently-constituted EAT has since affirmed the previous position and held that they should not be taken into account.[55]

The emphasis on the compensatory function of the compensatory award is also reflected in the principle, established by the Court of Appeal in 1987, that where the employer has made a payment in lieu of notice this will be deducted from the employee's compensation for lost earnings even if the employee fails to get another job during the notice period.[56] The argument that entitlement to wages in lieu of notice was an 'independent right' of the employee, for which he should be compensated *in addition to* lost wages for the period spent out of, or in less well paid, employment was rejected. In Ralph Gibson LJ's words, 'if the employer has paid the wages due in lieu of notice at the time of dismissal, the employer has complied with good industrial practice. If the employee does not get employment during the period of notice, no principle of good industrial practice can secure to the employee any further payment by way of lost wages in respect of the period of notice; he has received the wages for that period and if he is to recover the same amount again it must be by reference to some rule of law outside the provisions of the ... [1996 Act] ... and in my view no such rule exists'.[57]

51 *Norton Tool Co Ltd v Tewson* [1972] IRLR 86, 88 (Sir John Donaldson P).
52 [1972] IRLR 86. This was followed by the EAT in *TBA Industrial Products Ltd v Locke* [1984] IRLR 48 and approved in *Babcock Fata Ltd v Addison* [1987] IRLR 173, although cf an earlier EAT judgment, *Tradewinds Airways Ltd v Fletcher* [1981] IRLR 272.
53 ERA 1996, s 123(4). For this purpose, no account is taken of job offers received before the dismissal took place: *Savoia v Chiltern Herb Farms Ltd* [1981] IRLR 65; *McAndrew v Prestwick Circuits Ltd* [1988] IRLR 514. On the principles to be applied in determining whether a dismissed employee who has refused an offer of re-employment has failed in his duty to mitigate his loss, see *Wilding v British Telecommunications plc* [2002] IRLR 524.
54 [2004] IRLR 420. The EAT relied on *Cerberus Software Ltd v Rowley* [2001] IRLR 160, discussed in para 5.28 above, in construing the statutory provisions.
55 *Voith Turbo Ltd v Stowe* [2005] IRLR 228.
56 *Babcock FATA Ltd v Addison* [1987] IRLR 173.
57 [1987] IRLR 173, 178. Cf the different approach taken by the Scottish Division of the EAT in *Finnie v Top Hat Frozen Foods* [1985] ICR 433.

A sum paid *ex gratia* by the employer to the employee will also normally be taken into account in reducing the employer's liability,[58] and if the employer makes a statutory or contractual redundancy payment to the employee which is in excess of the basic award, the difference will also go to reduce the amount of any compensatory award for unfair dismissal.[59]

5.157   Jobseeker's allowance or income support received by the applicant while unemployed, which at common law would be deducted from damages representing lost earnings, is dealt with by special recoupment regulations as far as the statutory claim is concerned.[60] In respect of lost earnings up to the tribunal hearing, the tribunal must make an award of compensation in full against the employer, taking no account of any receipt of jobseeker's allowance or income support by the applicant up to that point. The Secretary of State may then serve a recoupment notice on the employer, claiming back an amount equivalent to the benefit paid out to the applicant for the period in question. As a result, the employee only *receives* compensation based on his or her *net* loss, but the employer must pay out in full, the difference going to the state. In effect the state is subrogated to the employee's claim against the employer, to the extent needed to reimburse it for the costs of paying out the benefit. The recoupment regulations do not apply to payments of unfair dismissal compensation made by way of a settlement between the parties; this is a strong incentive, then, to settle out of the tribunal.

Different rules apply to the period after the tribunal hearing, that is to say for *future* lost earnings. The tribunal may award compensation under this head without making any deduction for any jobseeker's allowance which might be received; however, this amount is then treated as earnings for the purposes of calculating entitlement to jobseeker's allowance.[61] The recoupment regulations do not apply to other social security benefits, and it has been held that any invalidity benefit received (or at least a proportion of it) should be deducted from the compensatory award.[62]

In calculating lost earnings, the court will have regard to evidence of actual loss up to the hearing or, if the employee has found a permanent better-paid job, up to the point where he ceased to be unemployed[63] or, in an exceptional case,

---

58   *Finnie v Top Hat Frozen Foods Ltd* [1985] ICR 433; *Horizon Holidays Ltd v Grassi* [1987] IRLR 371.

59   ERA 1996, s 123(7). In *Digital Equipment Co Ltd v Clements (No 2)* [1998] IRLR 134 the Court of Appeal held that the full amount of any payment should be deducted from the compensatory award after it had been subject to a percentage reduction to reflect the chance of the employee remaining in employment if the dismissal had not been procedurally unfair.

60   Employment Protection (Recoupment of Jobseeker's Allowance and Income Support) Regulations, 1996, SI 1996/2349.

61   Jobseeker's Act 1995, ss 2–4; Jobseeker's Allowance Regulations 1996, SI 1996/207, reg 98.

62   In *Puglia v C James and Sons* [1996] ICR 301 the EAT held that the whole amount should be deducted, a view recently endorsed in *Morgans v Alpha Plus Security Ltd* [2005] IRLR 234; cf *Rubenstein and Roskin (t/a McGuffies Dispensing Chemists) v McGloughlin* [1996] IRLR 557 where a differently constituted EAT held that one-half should be deducted. In *Savage v Saxena* [1998] IRLR 182 the EAT held that no deduction should be made in respect of housing benefit.

63   *Fentiman v Fluid Engineering Products Ltd* [1991] IRLR 150; *Whelan (t/a Cheers Off Licence) v Richardson* [1998] IRLR 114. The former employer cannot rely on the employee's increased earnings to reduce the loss sustained prior to the new employment being taken up.

beyond that point, if the employee is dismissed by the new employer under circumstances where a causal link with the original dismissal can be established.[64] If the applicant is unemployed at the time of the hearing the tribunal may also allow a claim for losses in the future, depending on the circumstances. The employee is most unlikely to recover a sum approaching net salary for the rest of his or her working life. This is not just because of the statutory upper limit; even if that were removed, future earnings would be discounted to take into account the chance that illness or redundancy would have brought an end to the employment lawfully, or that the employee would in any case have moved on from that job to another, as well as the chances of the employee finding work following the dismissal.[65] Nor have the courts taken the chance to escape completely certain other limitations of the common law. No sum is recoverable, for example, for any form of non-economic loss, such as hurt feelings or distress arising from the manner of the dismissal,[66] or for lost job satisfaction.[67] A claim for damages for lost reputation arising from an unjustified summary dismissal may only be made 'if there is cogent evidence that the manner of the dismissal caused financial loss, as, for example, by making it more difficult to find future employment';[68] nor were damages awarded in a case where a failure to provide a written reference in good time was alleged to have affected the employee's chances of getting alternative work.[69] Nevertheless, some courts remain true to the flexibility shown by the NIRC in the Norton case. In *Leonard v Strathclyde Buses Ltd*[70] the Court of Session stressed that an employment tribunal was required 'to apply the statutory test as a whole and assess what is just and equitable having regard to the loss so far as attributable to the employer'; this meant that it was inappropriate 'to introduce principles of foreseeability or remoteness in the technical sense in which those concepts apply in other legal contexts'. Such flexibility was demonstrated in *Ignarski v BBC*, in which the EAT indicated that, in principle, compensation might be awarded for the additional child care costs of an applicant who had been unfairly dismissed from a night-work job which she had taken so that she and her husband, who worked a day-shift, could share child care responsibilities, if it could be shown that she could not find an alternative night-work employment.[71]

---

64   *Dench v Flynn & Partners* [1998] IRLR 653.
65   In *Kingston upon Hull City Council v Dunnachie (No 3)* [2003] IRLR 843 the EAT held that tribunals should consider the use of the 'Ogdon tables' ('actuarial tables with explanatory notes for use in personal injury and fatal accident tables') in calculating compensation for future loss of earnings only where it is established that there is a prima facie career-long loss.
66   *Dunnachie v Kingston upon Hull City Council* [2004] IRLR 727, affirming *Norton Tool Co Ltd v Tewson* [1972] ICR 501. See Brodie, 2004: pp 352–354. For the difficulties of distinguishing between acts constituting detriment short of dismissal, for which non-economic loss is recoverable, and dismissal, see Bowers and Lewis, 2005: pp 87–89.
67   *Robert Normansell (Birmingham) Ltd v Barfield* (1973) 8 ITR 171.
68   *Vaughan v Weighpack Ltd* [1974] ICR 261, 265–266. On the common law position see now *Malik v BCCI SA* [1997] IRLR 462 and *Johnson v Unisys Ltd* [2001] IRLR 279, discussed at paras 4.91 *et seq* and 5.44–5.45 above.
69   *Lewis Shops Group v Wiggins* [1973] ICR 335.
70   [1998] IRLR 693, 696. In this case, the flexible approach adopted by the court to the calculation of damages for loss of share options may be contrasted with the more rigid approach adopted at common law in *Micklefield v SAC Technology Ltd* [1990] IRLR 218; see para 4.70 above.
71   Unreported, discussed by L Blake, 1991; see further our discussion of work-life balance issues in ch 6 below, at para 6.97 *et seq*.

5.158 Where an employee has suffered no loss as a result of the dismissal the compensatory award may be nil. If, for example, a dismissal for redundancy is unfair because the SDDP has not been followed but the employer can show that redundancy was imminent in any event, the compensatory award may be reduced to virtually nothing.[72] Prior to 1 October 2004, if the employer could show that a failure to consult an employee before dismissal would have made no difference since no work could have been found even if the correct procedure had been followed, this would reflected in reduced compensation payable to the employee, even though the dismissal itself was unfair.[73] For dismissals contemplated from 1 October 2004 onwards the 'no difference' rule that we discussed in para 5.143 will mean that a failure to follow a procedure beyond the statutory minimum will not of itself render that dismissal unfair,[74] so that the case for reducing the compensatory award on that ground is unlikely to arise. However if the tribunal thinks that there is some doubt about whether following the procedure would have made a difference, the dismissal will still be unfair but may be subject to a percentage reduction to reflect the chance that the employee would still have lost his or her employment.

5.159 By virtue of section 123(2), the compensatory award may include amounts in respect of expenses reasonably incurred by the employee as a consequence of the dismissal and 'loss of any benefit which he might reasonably be expected to have had but for the dismissal'. The first of these rules essentially follows the common law; expenses incurred in search of alternative employment would normally be taken into account in relation to mitigation, for example. The second category would seem to be broad enough to capture some benefits which the employee would have normally expected to receive, even though they contain a discretionary element and so may not be recoverable at common law. The point has not been clearly settled. Employees have recovered sums in respect of such perks as a company car and share options,[75] although there seems to be no hard and fast rule that such losses will be recoverable in every case.

Often the most important prospective benefit is the retirement pension which the employee would have expected to receive under an occupational pension scheme; but the difficulties in calculating this loss are considerable. The government has issued guidelines, *Compensation for Loss of Pension Rights: Employment Tribunals*, which are not strictly binding on tribunals but which may be taken into account,[76] and regularly are in practice. The calculation depends upon what type of occupational scheme is being considered.[77] If it is a money-purchase scheme,

---

72 This follows from cases preceding the coming into force of EADRR 2004 such as *British United Shoe Machinery Co Ltd v Clarke* [1978] ICR 70.

73 *Polkey v AE Dayton Services Ltd* [1987] IRLR 503. Reductions of between 50% and 75% of compensation were known: *Hough v Leyland DAF Ltd* [1991] IRLR 194; *Campbell v Dunoon and Cowal Housing Association Ltd* [1992] IRLR 528. 100% deductions were possible in the case of misconduct dismissals: *Fisher v California Cake & Cookie Ltd* [1997] IRLR 212.

74 ERA 1996, s 98A(2).

75 *Crompton v Dacorum Motors Ltd* [1975] IRLR 168; *Bradshaw v Rugby Portland Cement Ltd* [1972] IRLR 46.

76 *Bingham v Hobourn Engineering Ltd* [1992] IRLR 298. However, in *Port of Tilbury (London) Ltd v Birch* [2005] IRLR 92, the EAT emphasised that there is no duty on tribunals to follow these guidelines and it is an error of law for a tribunal to reject a party's submissions on the basis that they do not reflect an assessment suggested in them.

77 On the distinctions between money purchase and defined benefit or salary-related schemes, see paras 4.118 and 4.119 above.

the employee's loss will normally be the value of the employer's future contributions to the pension. In a defined-benefit scheme, it will be the difference between the deferred pension which the employee is entitled to receive, upon retirement, on the basis of service prior to the dismissal,[78] and the pension which he or she would have received had they stayed in the employment in question. This means taking the value of the deferred pension and applying to it a multiplier which is a function of the service thought to be necessary to earn the full pension. The tribunal must also take into account the likelihood that the employee might have withdrawn from the scheme in any event, by virtue of ill health or resignation, or that he or she might have been fairly dismissed.[79] These factors may lead to very considerable reductions in the amount awarded under this head.

5.160   Under section 123(6), 'where the tribunal finds that the dismissal was to any extent caused or contributed to by any action of the complainant, it shall reduce the amount of the compensatory award by such proportion as it considers just and equitable having regard to that finding'.[80] Misconduct may qualify as contributory fault if it is found to have prompted the employer's action, and where section 123(6) may be invoked the courts have held that a 100% deduction, while unlikely, is not ruled out by the Act.[81] Mere incompetence of the employee, on the other hand, is unlikely to be enough.[82] Participation in trade union activities, or the employee's being or not being a member of an independent trade union, may not constitute contributory fault;[83] nor, the House of Lords has held, may taking part in industrial action in the absence of individually blameworthy conduct additional to or separate from the mere act of participation.[84] A similar but not quite identical provision applies in the case of the basic award; here, the tribunal may make a deduction by reason of 'any conduct of the complainant before the dismissal'.[85] The difference is that with the basic award, there need not be any causal link between the dismissal and the conduct of the employee.

5.161   Since 1 October 2004 the compensatory award can be significantly decreased if the tribunal finds that one of the statutory disciplinary or grievance procedures applied to the dismissal in question; that procedure was not completed before the proceedings began; and the non-completion was wholly or mainly attributable to failure by the employee to comply with a requirement of the procedure or to exercise a right of appeal under it.[86] In these circumstances the

---

78   An 'early leaver' has certain rights to have the deferred pension preserved and revalued in line with price inflation. See Wikeley, 2002: pp 647–687.
79   *TBA Industrial Products Ltd v Locke* [1984] ICR 228.
80   The deduction can only be made in respect of the award made by the tribunal and not in respect of any payment of wages in lieu of notice which the employer may make to the employee: *Heggie v Uniroyal Englebert Tyres Ltd* [1999] IRLR 802.
81   *W Devis & Sons Ltd v Atkins* [1977] IRLR 314. Cf the *obiter dictum* of Chadwick LJ in *Friend v Civil Aviation Authority* [2001] IRLR 819, para 37 that a 100% reduction should be appropriate only in exceptional circumstances as it requires the tribunal to satisfy itself that, although some part of the loss sustained is attributable to the employer for the purposes of s 123(1), the complainant's contribution to the dismissal makes it just and equitable that he or she should receive no compensatory award.
82   *Kraft Foods Ltd v Fox* [1977] IRLR 431.
83   TULRCA 1992, s 155.
84   *Crosville Wales Ltd v Tracey (No 2)* [1997] IRLR 691.
85   ERA 1996, s 122(2). Note also s 122(3).
86   EA 2002, s 31(2). An employee who complains of unfair constructive dismissal is required to complete the applicable grievance procedure: see further paras 5.124 and 2.21 *et seq.*

tribunal must reduce any award by 10% unless there are 'exceptional circumstances' which would make this 'unjust or inequitable', and may, if it considers it 'just and equitable in all the circumstances to do so' reduce it by a further amount up to 50%.[87] Conversely, if the tribunal finds that non-completion was wholly or mainly due to failure by the employer it must, exceptional circumstances apart, increase the award by 10% and may increase it by up to 50%.[88] In addition, if the employer has breached its duty to give the employee a written statement of initial employment particulars or to notify the employee of changes in those particulars,[89] the tribunal must (exceptional circumstances apart) award the employee a minimum of two weeks' pay and may award four weeks' pay if it considers this 'just and equitable in all the circumstances'.[90] These reductions and increases respectively are to be applied immediately before any reduction for an employee's contribution to the dismissal.[91] As Collins remarks, '[t]his means the tribunal could increase the award by 50% for an employer's blatant disregard of procedural fairness, but then, at the end of the assessment, reduce it to nil in the light of the employee's contributory fault.'[92]

The 10% minimum apart, tribunals are given a wide discretion in assessing the extent of the percentage reduction or uplift. In applying the uplift, there is no requirement to have regard to an employee's loss, which will in any event have been taken into account under section 123(1). By analogy with the remedies for detriment short of dismissal,[93] there seems no reason to exclude injury to feelings due, for example, to the suddenness of a decision to dismiss or a failure to permit the employee to respond to the employer's statement. Tribunals may then be faced with the difficult task of separating injury resulting from breach of the procedure, which may be compensated, from injury resulting from the dismissal itself, which is not.[94]

(iii) The level of awards

5.162   In practice, the average award of compensation in unfair dismissal cases is much less than the various statutory maxima allow. In 2003/4 the median award was £3,375; in 1990/91 it was £1,773 and in 1986/87 it was £1,676.[95] The rate of awards is low, in part, because many of the applicants for unfair dismissal protection are comparatively low earners with short service, but also because of the manner in which the employee's loss is calculated by the tribunal and the possibility of deductions for contributory fault and failure to mitigate. According to research published by Dickens and her colleagues in 1985:

> ... the explanation [lies] in the statutory principles underlying the calculation of compensation and in the way in which tribunals exercise the discretion granted to them by statute in determining what would be just and equitable. Only certain kinds of loss are compensatable. There is no intention that the

---

87   EA 2002, s 31(2), (4).
88   EA 2002, s 31(3),(4).
89   ERA 1996, ss 1,4. See para 4.14 *et seq.*
90   EA 2002, s 38. A 'week's pay' is subject to the statutory maximum, which at 1 February 2005 and at the time of writing stands at £280.
91   ERA 1996, s 124A.
92   H Collins, 2004: p 50.
93   See, for example, para 8.16.
94   See generally Bowers and Lewis, 2005: pp 92–95.
95   *Employment Tribunals Service Annual Report and Accounts 2003-2004*, DTI, App 3, p 25. *Labour Market* Trends, September 1999, 494; HC Debs col 542, 30 June 1992 (written answers).

employer should be penalised for dismissing unfairly. A deterrent-regulatory view of money awards is not taken and to adopt anything other than *restitutio in integrum* (that is, putting the applicant in the position in which he or she would have been if the wrong had not been sustained) would be seen by the courts to represent 'punishment' of the employer ... Taken together, the limited use of the re-employment remedy and the way in which compensation is assessed serve typically to set a low price on the unfair deprivation of a job and can have little deterrent value for most employers.[96]

Interim relief

5.163   Exceptionally, the employment tribunal has the power to maintain the applicant in his or her employment pending the hearing of an unfair dismissal claim, if the applicant is claiming that the reason for the dismissal is one which relates to trade union membership or activities; their position as a health and safety or employee representative (including representatives for working time purposes); their position as a trustee of an occupational pension scheme; the making of a protected disclosure; the exercise of rights relating to trade union recognition and derecognition procedures; and the exercise of the right to be accompanied (or the accompaniment of another worker) at a grievance or disciplinary hearing.[97] The claim must be lodged within seven days of the EDT.[98] The tribunal must be satisfied that at the full hearing it is likely to accept the employee's claim of automatically unfair dismissal under one or other of the above heads.[99] The tribunal may then make an interim order of either reinstatement or, in an appropriate case, re-engagement, but only if the employer states that it is willing to accept re-employment.[100] If the employer either does not attend the hearing or refuses to re-employ the employee, the tribunal must make an order for the interim continuation of the contract of employment: this is an order to the effect that the contract of employment is still in force for the purposes of the employee's pay and benefits under the contract, and for the purposes of the computation of statutory continuity of employment.[101] An order for the continuation of the contract may also be made, along with an order of compensation, if the employer fails to comply with an order of interim reinstatement or re-engagement.[102]

This power, remarkable as it is, is confined to the instances cited above, where protection against victimisation of employee representatives and those making protected disclosures was thought particularly important. Were interim relief available more widely, the effectiveness of the unfair dismissal jurisdiction in preserving employment could be much greater than it currently is, and tribunals might be more willing to order reinstatement as the primary remedy for unfair dismissal. The extension of interim relief to support the right to be accompanied at a grievance or disciplinary hearing is a significant step in this regard.

---

96   L Dickens *et al*, 1985: pp 138–139.
97   ERA 1996, ss 128–132; TULRCA 1992, ss 161–166; ERelA 1999, s 12(5); see also para 8.5 below.
98   ERA 1996, s 128(1), (2). See para 5.129 above for the relationship between this remedy and the SDDPs.
99   ERA 1996, s 129. On the approach to the question of whether the employee is 'likely' to win at the full hearing, see *Taplin v C Shippam Ltd* [1978] ICR 1068.
100 ERA 1996, s 129.
101 ERA 1996, s 129(9), 130.
102 ERA 1996, s 132.

ECONOMIC DISMISSALS

5.164   Economic dismissals – dismissals involving redundancy, reorganisation and business transfers – form a distinct category within the law governing termination of employment. They touch on the key area of managerial prerogatives in the organisation of work and raise countervailing claims of job ownership by employees. Distributional conflicts of interest are particularly sharp: 'economic dismissals pose the question of how should the social costs resulting from economic dislocation be distributed between the workers and their employer'.[103] Where termination arises out of the failure or economic difficulty of the business concerned, third parties are directly affected by decisions on the extent of the employer's liability; these include potential purchasers of the business, who may inherit these liabilities as a result of a transfer of employment, and creditors of the insolvent company, who may find their claims ranked behind those of the employees. The state also has an interest, since it retains a residual responsibility to meet certain liabilities of insolvent or bankrupt employers.

We begin our analysis by examining the concept of redundancy. Where a dismissal is for redundancy, a statutory redundancy payment is available to employees who have met the qualifying conditions, and a complaint for unfair dismissal is also possible.[104] Where, on the other hand, dismissal falls into the SOSR category, no statutory redundancy payment is due, and the dismissal may well be fair, leaving the employee with nothing. We then consider employees' claims in insolvency against their former employer and against the state. Finally, we examine the extent to which the TUPE Regulations 1981 apply to sales and transfers of businesses, and their impact on the rights of the parties involved in these transactions.

The scope of redundancy

5.165   A finding of redundancy means that a dismissal is potentially fair,[105] but it also makes the employer liable to pay a redundancy payment to the employee, calculated by reference to the employee's seniority, normal weekly pay and age.[106] This dual purpose of the definition has led to some difficulty in its interpretation by the courts.

A curious result follows from the rule that, for a redundancy payment, a dismissal is presumed to be by reason of redundancy,[107] whereas for the purposes of defending an unfair dismissal claim the employer must demonstrate what the reason was.[108] In finely-balanced circumstances this means that a dismissal can be found to be for redundancy for the former purpose but not the latter.[109]

Under section 139(1) of ERA 1996, a dismissal of an employee is taken to be by reason of redundancy if it is attributable wholly or mainly to one of two circumstances:

---

103   H Collins, 1993: p 65.
104   Note that the standard statutory dismissal and disciplinary procedure applies to dismissals for redundancy on the same basis as it applies to dismissals for other reasons except where the duty to consult under TULRCA 1992, s 188 applies: see para 5.128 *et seq* above and para 5.183 *et seq* below.
105   ERA 1996, s 98(2)(c).
106   ERA 1996, s 162.
107   ERA 1996, s 163(2).
108   ERA 1996, s 98(1), (2).
109   *Midland Foot Comfort Centre Ltd v Moppett* [1973] ICR 219.

(a) the fact that his employer has ceased, or intends to cease –
  (i) to carry on the business for the purposes of which the employee was employed by him, or
  (ii) to carry on that business in the place where the employee was so employed, or
(b) the fact that the requirements of that business –
  (i) for employees to carry out work of a particular kind, or
  (ii) for employees to carry out work of a particular kind in the place where the employee was employed by the employer,
have ceased or diminished or are expected to cease or diminish.

These two criteria are referred to respectively as 'cessation of business' and 'diminishing requirements'. 'Cease' and 'diminish' mean 'cease and diminish either permanently or temporarily and for whatever reason'.[110]

(i) The relevance of the employer's motives

5.166 In their interpretation of section 139(1) the courts have, on the whole, respected the employer's right to decide matters concerning the size, scope and direction of the enterprise. In particular, the test of whether there is a 'cessation of business' is not concerned with the wider purposes of the employer in making decisions of this kind. In *Moon v Homeworthy Furniture (Northern) Ltd*[111] the EAT held that it was not the tribunal's task to inquire into management's motives for the closure of a factory (it had been alleged that the factory was closed out of retaliation for union activism). The mere fact of closure was sufficient for there to be a redundancy in law. According to Kilner Brown J there 'cannot be any investigation into the rights and wrongs of the declared redundancy'.

This case indicates that it is essentially for the employer to decide if and when to close down a business, and that the law regards a clear cessation of business as a redundancy situation. However, it is also important to be clear what *Moon* does not decide. It does not decide that the subjective opinion of the employer is decisive in classifying the dismissal as potentially fair or otherwise. The employer must show evidence that it had the relevant motive at the time of the dismissal.[112] In *Moon* the tribunal found that there were good objective grounds for a finding of redundancy, and when the EAT agreed with this finding only one outcome was possible. It seems unlikely that a decision to shut down a whole business could ever be anything but redundancy, but this begs the question of whether the business has indeed ceased to be carried on at the place of work in question, and in a case of a sham closure there is no reason, in principle, why a tribunal should not find that no redundancy has occurred, or that the dismissals, although potentially fair, were not fair in the circumstances under section 98(4) of the Act.

(ii) 'Place where the employee was so employed'

5.167 The reference in section 139(1) to the 'place where the employee was so employed' has given rise to a considerable body of case law concerning contractual mobility clauses. Where part of a business is shut down, the contents of the employee's contract may determine if there is a redundancy or not. If the

---

110 ERA 1996, s 139(6).
111 [1977] ICR 117, 121.
112 See also *Hindle v Percival Boats Ltd* [1969] 1 WLR 174; *Baxter v Limb Group of Companies* [1994] IRLR 572.

contract of employment contains an express or implied mobility clause, the employee may be required by the contract to move to a new location, which may prevent there being a redundancy under section 139(1)(a).[113] If there is an express clause the court cannot formally limit its scope by reference to the concepts of good faith or reasonableness,[114] but it can invoke the principle of construction *contra proferentem* or require the employer to give the employee a reasonable period of notice of the move.[115] A mobility clause favouring the employer may also be implied into the contract.[116] However, an implied term will not normally require the employee to move beyond a reasonable travelling distance from home.[117]

In recent years the courts have taken the view that the contract should not be the exclusive test of the employee's place of work for the purpose of determining whether the employee is redundant, in particular where the employer has inserted a mobility or flexibility clause which is particularly broad or which has not, in practice, been invoked. In *High Table Ltd v Horst*[118] the applicants were employed as silver-service waitresses by a company which provided catering services for companies in the City of London and elsewhere. The employer's staff handbook, which formed part of their terms of employment, provided that '[y]our place of work is as stated in your letter of appointment which acts as part of your terms and conditions. However, given the nature of our business, it is sometimes necessary to transfer staff on a temporary or permanent basis to another location. Whenever possible, this will be within reasonable daily travelling distance of your existing place of work'. In practice the applicants had all worked for one particular client, Hill Samuel, from 10am to 4pm on weekdays for a number of years. In 1993 cuts in Hill Samuel's catering budget necessitated a reorganisation of the services provided by the employers which resulted in a need for fewer waitresses working longer hours, and the applicants were dismissed. The Court of Appeal upheld the employer's claim (in defence of a complaint of unfair dismissal) that the applicants were redundant, rejecting the argument that 'the place where the employee was so employed' extended to every place where the employee could be required to work. Peter Gibson LJ, giving the judgment of the court, stated that the question of where the employee was employed:

> ... is one to be answered primarily by a consideration of the factual circumstances which obtained until the dismissal. If an employee has worked in only one location under his contract of employment for the purposes of the employer's business, it defies common sense to widen the extent of the place where he was so employed, merely because of the existence of a mobility clause. Of course, the refusal by the employee to obey a lawful requirement under the contract of employment for the employee to move may constitute a valid reason for dismissal, but the issues of dismissal, redundancy and reasonableness in the actions of an employer should be kept distinct. It would be unfortunate if the law were to encourage the inclusion of mobility clauses in contracts of employment to defeat genuine redundancy claims ... If the work of the employee for his employer has involved a change of location ... then the contract of employment may be helpful to determine the extent of the

---

113 *Sutcliffe v Hawker Siddley Aviation Ltd* [1973] ICR 560; *United Kingdom Atomic Energy Authority v Claydon* [1974] ICR 128.
114 *Express Lifts Co Ltd v Bowles* [1977] ICR 474.
115 *United Bank Ltd v Akhtar* [1989] IRLR 507.
116 See para 4.95 above.
117 *O'Brien v Associated Fire Alarms Ltd* [1969] 1 All ER 93.
118 [1997] IRLR 513. See also *Bass Leisure Ltd v Thomas* [1994] IRLR 104.

place where the employee was employed. But it cannot be right to let the contract be the sole determinant, regardless of where the employee actually worked for the employer.[119]

(iii) Diminished requirements for 'work of a particular kind'

5.168 On the face of it, the test of 'diminishing requirements' under section 139(1)(b) of the Act is sufficiently wide to cover both the situation in which reduced demand for labour is the result of business difficulties, and the situation in which it is the result of technological change or workforce reorganisation. However, its application to the second situation is unclear. This is not simply the fault of the courts. The definition contained in ERA 1996, section 139(1) is significantly narrower, for example, than the definition of redundancy used for the purposes of defining the collective consultation and information rights of trade union representatives, 'dismissal for a reason not related to the individual concerned'.[120] This wider definition was introduced to comply with Directive 75/129; no plans have been announced to extend it to section 139(1) of the 1996 Act.

5.169 In interpreting the concept of 'work of a particular kind' in section 139(1)(b) the courts have traditionally drawn a distinction between the employer's 'requirement' for employees to perform a particular quantum of work and its needs for that quantum of work to be performed in a particular way or on specific terms and conditions. The demand for employees to perform the quantum may remain the same even though the interests of the business demand that the work should in future be performed according to a different working schedule, or even through the use of different technology. In *Chapman v Goonvean and Rastowrack China Clay Co Ltd*[121] the employer withdrew free transport from a group of employees on the grounds of cost and employed local workers in their stead. It was found that there had been no redundancy. According to Lord Denning MR, 'it is very desirable, in the interests of efficiency, that employers should be able to propose changes in the terms of a man's employment for such reasons as these: so as to get rid of restrictive practices: or to induce higher output by piece work or to cease to provide free transport at an excessive cost'.[122] Buckley LJ thought that while 'the employer must ... justify his expectation by reference to objective circumstances relating to the commercial situation of his business and those commercial and economic conditions which exist generally, at the relevant time or which could then reasonably be anticipated in the future', there was 'nothing in the language of the section to suggest that the employer should be treated as bound or likely to carry on his business in all, or indeed in any, respects in precisely the way in which he was carrying it on at the time when the facts have to be considered'.[123]

For similar reasons, it seems that a redundancy will not normally arise in cases where the employer rearranges working-time schedules in the interests of greater efficiency, such as might be involved in adopting a different pattern of shift work.[124] The courts have been explicit in the reasoning behind these

---

119 [1997] IRLR 513, 518.
120 TULRCA 1992, s 195, as amended by TURERA 1993, s 34. See para 9.32 below.
121 [1973] ICR 310.
122 [1973] ICR 310, 315.
123 [1973] ICR 310, 318.
124 In *MacFisheries Ltd v Findley* [1985] ICR 160, however, the EAT upheld the finding of the employment tribunal that on the facts night work (as compared to day work) was 'work of a particular kind'.

decisions, namely to cut the potential costs to the employer of business reorganisation: 'an employer is entitled to reorganise his business in order to improve its efficiency and in doing so to propose to his staff a change in the terms and conditions of employment; and to dispense with their services if they do not agree';[125] similarly, it is said that 'nothing should be done to impair the ability of employers to reorganise their workforce and their terms and conditions of work so as to improve efficiency'.[126]

Other decisions have denied employees the right to redundancy compensation where they were unable to adapt to changing methods of working, on the grounds that the change in the nature of their work was not sufficient. In *North Riding Garages Ltd v Butterwick*[127] the employee, who was manager of a garage, was dismissed following the introduction by new owners of different methods of working, which involved him in more paperwork and less engineering work than previously. He claimed redundancy compensation but this was rejected. Widgery J held that for these purposes, 'an employee who remains in the same kind of work is expected to adapt himself to new methods and techniques and cannot complain if his employer insists on higher standards of efficiency than those previously required; but if new methods alter the nature of the work required to be done it may follow that no requirement remains for employees to do work of the particular kind which has been superseded and that they are truly redundant'. In this case, the work for which the employee was employed remained essentially the same, since the vehicle workshop remained, as did the requirement for a workshop manager.[128]

5.170   These decisions, dating from the early 1970s and never formally overruled, nevertheless run counter to one of the principal aims of the redundancy compensation scheme at its inception in 1965. By ensuring that employees who were displaced from employment by technological change would receive compensation, it was hoped to encourage firms to embark on necessary economic restructuring and at the same time to provide displaced workers with financial assistance for mobility and job-search in the labour market.[129] Moreover, for the early part of its life (including the period during which this case law developed) the redundancy payments scheme subsidised the costs of these payments to individual employers, by refunding varying proportions of redundancy payments through the rebate system (this was repealed in 1989).[130]

---

125 *Johnson v Nottinghamshire Combined Police Authority* [1974] ICR 170, 184. However, an employer cannot escape a finding of redundancy by arguing that it still has a need for certain work to be done, but because of funding cuts can no longer afford to pay for the work done by the employee: *Association of University Teachers v University of Newcastle-upon-Tyne* [1988] IRLR 10.
126 *Lesney Products & Co Ltd v Nolan* [1977] ICR 235, 238.
127 [1967] 2 QB 56, 63; cf *Robinson v British Island Airways Ltd* [1977] IRLR 477.
128 See also *Cresswell v Board of Inland Revenue* [1984] IRLR 190, discussed in para 4.90 above. However, some changes will be so complete as to amount to a redundancy, as in a case where the introduction of new heating equipment meant that the employer needed a heating engineer rather than a plumber with the result that the applicant was made redundant: *Murphy v Epsom College* [1985] ICR 80.
129 See para 5.7 above.
130 EA 1989, s 17. Under the initial scheme the rebate represented between 66% and 78% of compensation, with the higher rebate paid in respect of older employees. In 1969 a general rebate of 50% was introduced and in 1977 this became 41%. In 1986 it was confined to firms employing fewer than ten employees and reduced to 35% before being abolished completely in 1989. At the same time the redundancy contribution was abolished and in 1990 the Redundancy Fund was merged into the National Insurance Fund: EA 1990, s 16.

Since all employers contributed to the Redundancy Payments Fund through a supplementary levy to their national insurance (social security) contributions, the costs of redundancy were spread beyond the individual business. Even during the period the rebate scheme was in force the 'cost-spreading' aspect was ignored by the courts, who seem to have thought that managerial prerogatives were somehow under threat when redundancies were alleged to exist.

5.171 The test put forward in this line of case law has been described as the 'job function' test since, as we have just seen, it attempts to identify a redundancy in terms of the economic requirement for employees to perform a particular quantum of work. A rival approach, the 'contract test', suggests on the contrary that in order to determine whether there is a redundancy it is necessary to ascertain whether there is a diminished requirement by reference to the whole range of contractual duties which the employee could be required to perform, not merely those which he had been performing. This latter test is exemplified by *Cowen v Haden Ltd*,[131] where the EAT felt itself bound by the earlier decision of the Court of Appeal in *Nelson v BBC*[132] to hold that 'it is not sufficient in order to establish redundancy to show merely that the requirements of the employers for employees to carry out work of the kind on which the employee was actually engaged had ceased or diminished; it is necessary to show that such diminution or cessation was in relation to any work that he could have been asked to do'.[133] In this case the contract of employment contained a broad flexibility clause, under which the employee could have been called on to perform 'any and all duties which reasonably fall within the scope of his capabilities'; he attempted to argue (for the purposes of an unfair dismissal claim) that he had not been made redundant, since his contractual duties were sufficiently extensive for him to have been redeployed to do new work without entering into a new contract. The Court of Appeal reversed the EAT's finding of no redundancy on the facts, holding that the employee had been employed to carry out the particular kind of work of a divisional contracts surveyor, but did not disturb the wider legal principle relied upon.

In *Nelson* and *Cowen* the contract test was invoked by employees in order to show that their employers, by failing to redeploy them on other duties which they could be contractually required to perform, would be unable to show redundancy as a potentially fair reason for dismissal.[134] In other cases, the principle in *Nelson* was deployed by employers to avoid a finding of unfair dismissal by extending the notion of redundancy to embrace a wider range of functions than those actually performed by the employee and thus create a test which, in certain situations, may be easier to satisfy.[135] The confusion between the 'job function' and 'contract' tests arose, then, largely because the statutory

---

131 [1983] ICR 1.
132 [1977] ICR 649; *Nelson v BBC (No 2)* [1980] ICR 110: the employee was employed as a managerial producer and editor grade 3 who could be required to work in any country or capacity which the BBC decided. When the Caribbean Service, in which he worked, closed down he was held not to be redundant because there was no diminution in the work of producers and editors grade 3.
133 [1983] ICR 1, 7.
134 For a further example see *Johnson v Peabody Trust* [1996] IRLR 387.
135 *Pink v White* [1985] IRLR 489: the employee under his contract was a making and finishing room operative, although his actual work was sole layer/pre-sole fitter; as there was a diminished requirement for the former (although not the latter) the employee was redundant.

definition of redundancy serves the two different purposes referred to earlier; it is the gateway to automatic statutory compensation, but also to a potentially fair dismissal.

5.172 In the second half of the 1990s the EAT showed impatience with both the 'function' and the 'contract' tests, regarding both as distorting the statutory language. In *Safeway Stores v Burrell* the court considered that in examining whether the requirements of the business for employees to carry out work of a particular kind have diminished, employees' contractual terms are irrelevant; they become relevant only when asking whether the dismissal was attributable to redundancy, as compared, for example, to a refusal to transfer to another job where the employee's contract requires this.[136] In *Church v West Lancashire NHS Trust*[137] a differently-constituted EAT affirmed that 'the proper test is neither contractual nor functional but a sensible blend of the two', as exemplified by the approach in *High Table Ltd v Horst*,[138] discussed in para 5.167 above. This more flexible approach subsequently received the support of the House of Lords. In *Murray v Foyle Meats Ltd*[139] Lord Irvine LC commented that 'both the contract test and the function test miss the point. The key work in the statute is "attributable" and there is no reason in law why the dismissal of an employee should not be attributable to a diminution in the employer's need for employees irrespective of the terms of his contract or the function which he performed'.[140] The suggestion, then, is that a test of factual causation should be applied; the correct approach is to treat the question as 'a factual inquiry, without any artificial subtlety'.[141] Stated in this way, the test has the merit of potentially bringing within the scope of redundancy so-called 'bumping' cases in which an employee is dismissed to make way for another employee who would otherwise have been made redundant. To treat this part of the definition of redundancy as turning on a predominantly factual inquiry, however, is to invite inconsistency in the application of the law by tribunals.

Redundancy compensation

5.173 In order to claim a redundancy payment, the employee must have been dismissed; for this purpose, the same basic definition of dismissal applies as for unfair dismissal.[142] There are some slight differences which are specific to the issue of redundancy compensation. First, under certain circumstances, there will be no dismissal if the employer offers the employee suitable alternative employment.[143] This is explored in more detail below. Second, if the employee, having received notice of dismissal, then gives a counter-notice to terminate the contract at an earlier date, the employer may require the employee to withdraw the counter-notice on pain of losing any right to a redundancy payment. However,

---

136 *Safeway Stores plc v Burrell* [1997] IRLR 200, 206–207 (Judge Peter Clark).
137 [1998] IRLR 4, 9 (Morison J).
138 [1997] IRLR 513.
139 [1999] IRLR 562.
140 [1999] IRLR 562, 564.
141 [1999] IRLR 562, 565 (Lord Clyde). See also *Shawkat v Nottingham City Hospital NHS Trust* [2001] IRLR 555.
142 ERA 1996, s 136(1). Many of the same problems arise, particularly with reference to resignation. See *Morton Sundour Fabrics Ltd v Shaw* (1966) 2 ITR 84; *Maher v Fram Gerrard Ltd* [1974] ICR 31; *Birch v University of Liverpool* [1985] ICR 470.
143 ERA 1996, s 138; see para 5.178 below.

the employee may still receive some payment if an employment tribunal concludes that 'having regard to – (a) the reasons for which the employee seeks to leave the employment, and (b) the reasons for which the employer requires him to continue in it' it is 'just and equitable' that he or she should receive the whole or a part of the redundancy payment to which he or she would otherwise have been entitled.[144] Third, the definition of dismissal is given a special extension, for the purposes of redundancy compensation only, to cover cases of 'implied or constructive termination of contract'. This means that there is a dismissal where '(a) an act on the part of an employer, or (b) any event affecting an employer (including, in the case of an individual, his death) operates to terminate' the contract of employment.[145] The dismissal, so defined, will be deemed to be for redundancy if the employee is not then re-employed for a reason which falls under section 139(1).[146]

To be eligible for a statutory redundancy payment, the employee must have had two years' continuity of employment up to the 'relevant date'.[147] For this purpose, only continuity over the age of 18 is counted.[148]

5.174 The statutory redundancy payment is calculated as a function of the age, weekly pay and seniority of the employee.[149] The employee receives one-and-a-half week's gross pay for each year of employment in which he was not below the age of 41; one week's pay for each year he was 22 and over (but below 41); and half a week's pay for each year he was over 18 (but below 22).[150] A maximum of 20 years' employment can be taken into account.[151] There is a statutory ceiling on the gross weekly wage which can be used in this calculation, which as of 1 February 2005 and at the time of writing stands at £280,[152] making the maximum sum which may currently be awarded £8,400. The redundancy payment therefore incorporates some elements of a reward for seniority, but in other respects it does not resemble a seniority payment. It is not available as of right in return for service in the manner of a retirement pension, but only in the event of a redundancy dismissal. Since it is meant to assist the individual employee in his or her search for alternative employment, the right does not currently apply where the employee has reached the age of 65 or, where lower, the normal retiring age for those holding his or her position,[153] and those over the age of 64

144 ERA 1996, s 142.
145 ERA 1996, s 136(5).
146 ERA 1996, s 139(4).
147 ERA 1996, s 155. The notion of the 'relevant date' under ERA 1996, s 145, broadly corresponds to that of the EDT under s 97(1), adapted to the particular variations on the concept of dismissal which are discussed in the text.
148 ERA 1996, s 211(2).
149 ERA 1996, s 162. Normal weekly pay is in accordance with ss 221–227.
150 Service here refers to the employee's continuous employment over the age of 18: ERA 1996, s 211(2).
151 ERA 1996, s 162(3).
152 ERA 1996, s 227(1); SI 2004/2989. The concept of a week's pay is based on the employee's 'normal working hours', a phrase which normally excludes consideration of overtime hours: *Tarmac Roadstone Holdings Ltd v Peacock* [1973] ICR 273. On bonuses, see *British Coal Corpn v Cheesebrough* [1990] ICR 317.
153 ERA 1996, s 156(1). The normal retiring age must be the same for men and women. Note the difference from the age exclusion for unfair dismissal, where the normal retiring age applies whether or not it is less than 65: see para 5.65 above. In *Secretary of State for Trade and Industry v Rutherford (No 2)* [2004] IRLR 892 the Court of Appeal held that the tribunal had erred in finding that this age limit had a disparate impact on men. These age limits are currently under review in the light of the provisions on age discrimination contained in Directive 2000/78/EC see further para 6.38.

have their entitlement progressively reduced the nearer they are to 65.[154] The policy of promoting job search is also reflected in the enactment of a statutory right of employees under notice of redundancy to take time off to look for alternative work.[155]

Either party may refer to an employment tribunal the issue of entitlement to a redundancy payment or the appropriate quantum.[156] Since 1 October 2004 redundancy dismissals have been subject to the statutory dismissal and grievance procedures.[157] This means that where an employee has been constructively dismissed, he or she will need to have instituted the appropriate statutory grievance procedure prior to referring the issue of entitlement to a redundancy payment to a tribunal.[158] In cases of termination of the employee's contract by the employer, or non-renewal of a limited-term contract, the employer must institute the 'standard' dismissal and disciplinary procedure on the usual basis unless the dismissal is one of a number in respect of which the duty to consult under TULRCA 1992, section 188 applies.[159] Non-completion of the relevant procedure can result in the payment being increased or reduced depending on whether this failure is attributable to the employer or the employee.[160] The provision for reduction for this reason is particularly anomalous given that there is no equivalent provision in relation to the basic award for unfair dismissal.

5.175   The employee's statutory rights may be waived collectively if there is an exemption order in force, granting effect to a collective agreement. An order shall not be made under this provision unless the Secretary of State is satisfied that the parties are willing to submit questions of an individual's entitlement to an employment tribunal.[161] Prior to 1 October 2002, an employee employed under a contract of employment for a fixed term of two years or more could agree in writing to exclude any right to a redundancy payment in the event of the expiry of that term without renewal.[162] This provision was repealed in order to comply with Directive 99/70/EC on Fixed-Term Work.

5.176   The employer may avoid the obligation to make a redundancy payment in one of a number of situations.[163]

---

154   ERA 1996, s 162(4), (5).
155   ERA 1996, ss 52–54.
156   ERA 1996, s 163(1). See s 164 for time limits in relation to this matter.
157   EA 2002, Schs 2–4. See generally paras 5.124 *et seq* and 2.21 *et seq*.
158   See para 2.23 for discussion of the compatibility of this requirement with Convention rights.
159   EADRR 2004, para 4(1)(b).
160   EA 2002, s 31. Note also s 38 and Sch 5 relating to a breach of an employer's duty under ERA 1996, s 1(1) or s 4(1); see further para 4.14 *et seq*.
161   ERA 1996, s 157; Redundancy Payments (Exemption) Order 1980, SI 1980/1052 (covering certain employees of Lancashire County Council).
162   ERA 1996, s 197, repealed by FTER 2002, SI 2002/2034, Sch 2, Part 1, para 3: see *Wiltshire County Council v NATFHE* [1980] ICR 455; *Housing Services Agency v Cragg* [1997] IRLR 380; *BBC v Kelly-Phillips* [1998] IRLR 294. Agreements entered into and taking effect before 1 October 2002 that comply with the conditions of the repealed s 197 remain effective only where the contract was entered into before 1 October 2002 or, where there have been one or more renewals, the only or most recent renewal was agreed before that date: SI 2002/2034, Sch 2, Part 2, para 5.
163   See generally Upex, 2001: pp 149–152 and pp 260–266.

(i) An offer of renewed or alternative employment

5.177   An offer of renewed or alternative employment by the employer, or an associated employer,[164] may prevent an employee being entitled to a redundancy payment.[165] The provisions governing this situation are complex and operate in two separate ways: either they result in the employee not being treated as having been dismissed for the purposes of claiming a redundancy payment,[166] or they disentitle an employee who is treated as dismissed from receiving a redundancy payment which would otherwise be payable.

5.178   Section 138(1) provides that employees who have been given notice of dismissal for redundancy (or have been constructively dismissed) *will not be regarded as dismissed* if (a) their contract of employment is renewed, or they are re-engaged under a new contract in pursuance of an offer made before the end of the employment under the previous contract[167] and (b) the renewal or re-engagement takes effect either immediately on, or after an interval of not more than four weeks after, the end of that employment. Where the provisions of the contract as renewed, or the new contract, differ from those of the previous contract a four-week 'trial period' operates.[168] If the employee leaves or is dismissed during the trial period (for a reason connected with or arising out of any difference between the renewed or new contract and the previous one), he or she is treated as having been dismissed on the date on which his or her employment under the previous contract ended, for the reason for which he or she would have been dismissed had the offer of re-employment not been made.[169] Once the employee is treated as dismissed, he or she may still be disentitled from receiving a redundancy payment for the reasons provided in section 141, discussed below.

The timing of the four-week trial period has been considered in the context of the employee's broader rights to refuse to accept a repudiatory breach of contract by the employer which amounts to a dismissal. Where the employer commits such a breach, the employee is entitled at common law to carry on working under protest without being taken to have waived the rights under the original terms and conditions, at least for a certain period. For statutory purposes, the employee may wish to try out the new conditions and, if they prove unacceptable, resign and claim constructive dismissal. The courts have held that for the purposes of redundancy compensation, the employee may resign in this way even after the end of the four-week trial period envisaged by section 138: this provision does not take away the more general rights of the employee. The result is somewhat arbitrary: the employee who is dismissed by the employer and then

164 ERA 1996, s 146(1). See para 3.98 for the definition of 'associated employer'.
165 ERA 1996, ss 138, 141.
166 Note that these provisions apply only for the purposes of Part XI of the Act: see *Jones v Governing Body of Burdett Coutts School* [1997] ICR 390.
167 'Renewal' includes 'extension': ERA 1996, s 235(1). In *SI (Systems and Instrumentation) Ltd v Grist* [1983] ICR 788 the EAT opined that it is only in cases of re-engagement that the offer needs to be made before termination of the contract of employment, but cf the terms of s 141(1) where it is clear that this condition applies to both.
168 S 138(2), (3). The period begins at the end of the employee's employment under the previous contract and ends with the period of four weeks beginning with the date on which the employee starts work under the renewed or new contract. The parties may agree a longer trial period but only where this is for the purpose of retraining: see s 138(3)(b)(ii), (6).
169 ERA 1996, s 138(2)(b), (4).

offered a new contract is subject to the four-week trial period, and will be taken not to have been dismissed if he or she stays in the new job after the end of that period.[170] If, on the other hand, the employer simply announces that the old employment is at an end and offers new terms, the effect is that of a repudiation and the employee may well have the benefit of a common law trial period extending well beyond the four weeks provided for by the Act.[171]

5.179   Section 141 deals with the position of the employee *who is treated as dismissed for redundancy but disentitled from receiving a redundancy payment.* This occurs if the employee unreasonably refuses an offer of alternative employment under a renewed contract or a new contract.[172] Where the provisions of the renewed or new contract differ from the corresponding provisions of the previous contract, the right to a payment will be lost only if the employment also satisfies the condition of being 'suitable'. (This question does not arise if the provisions of the new contract do not differ from those of the old.) If the employee embarks upon a trial period pursuant to section 138 and then leaves during it, entitlement to a payment will be lost if the new employment was suitable and the termination of the employment during the trial period was unreasonable.[173]

The essential questions under these provisions, then, are whether an alternative job offer is suitable and whether an employee's refusal to accept the new job is unreasonable. In *Taylor v Kent County Council*[174] Lord Parker CJ thought that suitability should be assessed by reference to the individual concerned, and that 'suitability means something substantially equivalent to the employment which has ceased'. A significant change in salary or status – such as, in *Taylor*, the demotion of a headmaster to a position which was effectively that of a supply teacher – would be likely to render the alternative job unsuitable. In *Thomas Wragg & Sons Ltd v Wood*[175] factors which the EAT held could be taken into account included the fact that the offer was made very late in the day; the employee's acceptance, by that date, of other work; and his fear of continuing to work in a declining industry.

(ii) Misconduct

5.180   Where the employee has committed a repudiatory breach of contract which would entitle the employer to dismiss him or her summarily, the employer may avoid any liability for redundancy which it would otherwise have had by either dismissing the employee without notice; dismissing him or her by giving shorter notice than, but for the employee's breach, would have been required; or by giving the employee the normal contractual or statutory notice to which

---

170   Eg, *Meek v J Allen Rubber Co Ltd* [1980] IRLR 21.
171   *Shields Furniture Ltd v Goff* [1973] ICR 187; *Sheet Metal Components Ltd v Plumridge* [1974] ICR 373; *Air Canada v Lee* [1978] ICR 1202. In an appropriate case the statutory four-week trial period may only begin once the common law trial period has come to an end: *Turvey v CW Cheney & Son Ltd* [1979] ICR 341. See also *East Suffolk Local Health Services NHS Trust v Palmer* [1997] ICR 425.
172   ERA 1996, s 141(1). The offer must have been made before the end of the employment, with renewal or re-engagement to take effect either immediately on, or after an interval of not more than four weeks after, the end of the employment.
173   ERA 1996, s 141(4).
174   [1969] 2 QB 560; for a more recent illustration, see *Cambridge & District Co-operative Society Ltd v Ruse* [1993] IRLR 156.
175   [1976] ICR 313.

he or she was entitled, but including with that a written statement to the effect that the employer would have been entitled to dismiss the employee without notice.[176] At first sight it is not easy to see the point of this provision since if dismissal was for misconduct, there would be no redundancy in the first place; however, section 140(1) pre-dates the introduction of unfair dismissal legislation, which may account for its existence and rather convoluted form. As it is, the provision could apply in a situation where the employee was first dismissed for redundancy, but then, in the period of notice, committed an act which justified summary dismissal.[177] Even where section 140(1) applies, if the employee is dismissed during the 'obligatory period of notice', which means the minimum period of notice to which the employee is entitled, the tribunal has the power to award the employee all or part of the redundancy payment to which, in the absence of section 140(1), they would have been entitled.[178]

(iii) Participation in a strike

5.181 In some circumstances the employee may not lose his or her entitlement by virtue of taking part in a strike. This provision forms an exception to the general disqualification for misconduct,[179] which would otherwise apply since the act of going on strike is a repudiatory breach of contract by the employee which entitles the employer to terminate the contract without notice.[180] Section 140(2) provides that the misconduct disqualification has no application in a case where the employee has been given notice of dismissal by the employer and who then takes part in a strike during the 'obligatory period of notice' and is dismissed for so doing. This exception was designed to give employees some protection in the case of a strike called to protest against redundancy. However, the protection is not very effective since it does not apply to the interval between an employer's announcement of impending redundancies and the issue of notices to individual workers. If a strike starts during this interval, the employees concerned will forfeit any rights to redundancy compensation.[181] Even where the strike begins after notices have been sent out, the employer may still require the employee to work the extra period of days lost by virtue of the strike in order to receive the redundancy payment.[182] Industrial action short of a strike which constitutes a repudiatory breach of contract will be dealt with under section 140(1); see further para 11.85 below.

(iv) Lay-off or short-time working

5.182 A fourth exclusion relates to a situation of temporary lay-off or short-time working. The Act attempts, in an exceptionally complicated fashion, to

---

176 ERA 1996, s 140(1).
177 Elias *et al*, 1980: p 698. In *Simmons v Hoover Ltd* [1977] ICR 61 the EAT affirmed that s 140(1) applies both where there is a 'single' dismissal (ie, a dismissal for redundancy and not explicitly for misconduct) as well as a 'double' dismissal (ie, a dismissal for redundancy followed by a dismissal for misconduct).
178 ERA 1996, ss 140(3)–(5), 136(4).
179 Cf s 140(1).
180 *Simmons v Hoover Ltd* [1977] ICR 61.
181 *Simmons v Hoover Ltd* [1977] ICR 61. Note also s 136(2) which provides that if an employee terminates his or her contract of employment without notice in response to a lock-out which constitutes a repudiatory breach of contract, this is excluded from the definition of 'constructive dismissal', so denying the employee any form of statutory redundancy payment.
182 ERA 1996, s 143. See further para 11.85.

deal with the overlap between the right to redundancy compensation and the guaranteed pay provisions of the ERA 1996.[183] Where an employee is 'laid off or kept on short time' there may be no right to a redundancy payment, even if there would otherwise have been a redundancy. For these purposes, lay-off describes a situation in which the employee does not receive work under the contract of employment and, as a result, receives no pay;[184] short-time is a situation in which, by reason of a diminution in the employee's work, the remuneration received is less than half a week's pay.[185] Under these circumstances, there is only a redundancy if the employee has been laid off or kept on short time for four or more consecutive weeks, or has been laid off or kept on short time for six or more weeks (of which not more than three were consecutive) in any period of thirteen weeks.[186] To be entitled to claim redundancy compensation, the employee must then give the employer a notice of intention to claim a redundancy payment, which must be issued within four weeks of the last of the four or six weeks of lay-off and/or short-time, as just described.[187] This notice will be of no effect if, on the date it was served, it was reasonably expected that within four further weeks the employee's employment would return to normal and that he or she would then enter into a period of uninterrupted employment lasting at least thirteen weeks,[188] and the employer also gives the employee a counter-notice that it will contest liability for redundancy compensation.[189] Assuming the notice of claim is effective, the employee must finally give the employer a further notice of termination of the contract of employment, which must be notice of at least a week, and must be more if the terms of the employee's contract of employment provide for that; and this notice of termination must be given within a period which, for most purposes, is four weeks from the date upon which the initial notice of claim was given.[190]

Unfair dismissal in cases of redundancy and reorganisation

5.183 Both redundancy and some other substantial reason (SOSR) are potentially fair reasons for an economic dismissal. Whereas the statutory definition of a 'redundancy' has been narrowly confined by case law, the residual SOSR category has been greatly expanded to cover most economic dismissals which do not fall into the category of redundancy. The effect is that an economic dismissal will not be unfair just because it cannot be classified as a redundancy; it will most likely fall into the SOSR category and so be potentially fair. On the other hand, if a dismissal is categorised as falling into the SOSR category, there is no automatic compensation for loss of employment as there is in the case of redundancy.

183 ERA 1996, ss 147–152; on guaranteed pay see ERA 1996, ss 28–35; see para 4.113 above.
184 ERA 1996, s 147(1).
185 ERA 1996, s 147(2).
186 ERA 1996, s 148(2).
187 ERA 1996, s 148(1), (2).
188 This means uninterrupted in the sense of there being neither lay-off nor short-time for any week in this period: ERA 1996, s 152(1). However, this exception in the employer's favour does not apply if, in the four weeks after the employee issues the notice of claim, he or she is laid off or kept on short time for each of those four weeks: ERA 1996, s 152(2), 154.
189 ERA 1996, ss 149, 152(1)(b).
190 See ERA 1996, s 150(3), (4) for further details dealing with the various situations which may exist with regard to the employer's counter-notice.

The category of SOSR has been held to cover, for example, cases in which employees have been dismissed for refusing to accept changes in working hours and shift arrangements made in the business interests of the employer.[191] This is so even where the employer attempts to make unilateral changes to contract terms and conditions, and the employee resigns in response to the employer's repudiatory breach of contract.[192] SOSR has also applied where temporary workers employed on a succession of fixed-term contracts were dismissed upon the expiry of the final agreement.[193] The type of reason which the employer needs to put forward has been described simply as a 'sound, good business reason'.[194] The burden of proof on the employer is easily met: 'it is not an onus which it is at all difficult to discharge'.[195] Although the tribunal has the right to disregard the reason put forward by the employer and conclude that, objectively speaking, no good business reason existed,[196] it may not substitute its judgment of what is in the commercial interests of the business for that of the employer. Although a finding of SOSR does not necessarily lead to a finding that the dismissal was fair in the circumstances – SOSR is only a potentially fair reason, and the employer must not make demands on the employee which are wholly excessive – it has to date tended to do so in all but the most exceptional of cases,[197] although an employer's failure to complete the statutory dismissal and disciplinary procedure may, from 1 October 2004, render an otherwise fair dismissal automatically unfair.[198]

5.184 It remains axiomatic that under section 98(4) there is an area of economic decision-making which is beyond the legitimate scope of tribunal review: in one redundancy case the Court of Appeal reiterated the view that 'it was not open to the court to investigate the commercial and economic reasons which prompted the closure. It may be that the court should have this power, but it does not have [it] at present'.[199] This does not mean that either redundancy or SOSR is an *automatically* fair reason for dismissal. There is a world of difference between saying that a dismissal is for a potentially fair reason, and concluding that the employer acted reasonably as treating that reason as sufficient in the particular circumstances of the case. Thus even if the decision is motivated by economic considerations, the employer must still show that there were grounds upon which a reasonable employer could conclude that there was a need for

---

191 *Ellis v Brighton Co-operative Society* [1976] IRLR 419. Note that the statutory dismissal and disciplinary procedures do not apply where all the employees of a description or in a category to which the employee belongs are dismissed, provided that the employer offers to re-engage all the employees so dismissed either before or on the termination of their contracts: EADRR 2004, reg 4(1)(a). This would apply to reorganisations, where the employer dismisses employees and offers re-engagement on different terms and conditions.

192 *Knighton (RG) v Henry Rhodes Ltd* [1974] IRLR 71; *Bumpus (JF) v Standard Life Assurance Ltd* [1974] IRLR 232; Bowers and Clarke, 1981: p 40.

193 *North Yorkshire County Council v Fay* [1985] IRLR 247; *Terry v East Sussex County Council* [1976] ICR 536. Note now the limitation on successive fixed-term contracts in FTER 2002, SI 2002/2034, reg 8, discussed at paras 5.78–5.79.

194 *Hollister v National Farmers' Union* [1979] ICR 542, 551 (Lord Denning MR).

195 *Banerjee v City and East London Area Health Authority* [1979] IRLR 147, 150 (Arnold J).

196 *Orr v Vaughan* [1981] IRLR 63; *Ladbroke Courage Holidays Ltd v Asten* [1981] IRLR 59.

197 See below.

198 ERA 1996, s 98A. Note, however, EADRR 2004, reg 4(1)(a): see note 191 above.

199 *James W Cook & Co (Wivenhoe) Ltd v Tipper* [1990] IRLR 386.

changes leading to redundancy or re-organisation.[200] If the employer fails to offer any convincing evidence of business pressures leading to change, the tribunal may legitimately find the dismissal to have been unfair.[201]

Nonetheless, in SOSR cases courts have found that an employer may be acting reasonably in forcing through changes which amount to a unilateral abrogation of existing collective agreements and, by extension, of terms incorporated from those agreements into individual contracts of employment. There is nothing in the Act to say that either a constructive dismissal or any other dismissal in which the employer acts in repudiatory breach of contract must be unfair; and it is also important to bear in mind that the contract terms have no greater stability, for much of the time, under the common law than they do under statute, since the common law normally allows the employer to end the contract by giving notice. However, there is a good case for saying that 'since the statute was arguably enacted to enhance employee rights, it would have been perfectly proper to treat the contract and collective agreement as establishing minimum rights for employees to be improved upon by the statute'.[202] Instead, redundancy or reorganisation in breach of contract is a potentially fair reason, which the employer can show was fair in the circumstances by producing evidence of business necessity in some form or other.

Even if the employer can produce evidence of cost savings or enhanced efficiency, however, dismissal may be unfair if the new demands being placed on the employee are excessive. In *Evans v Elemeta Holdings Ltd*[203] the employee was offered new terms, as part of a reorganisation, which would have required him to work overtime, unpaid, up to an unspecified number of hours per week. He resigned and claimed constructive dismissal. The EAT, reversing the tribunal, found that the unreasonableness of the terms offered made the dismissal unfair. However, the unreasonableness of the terms offered may not, in itself, be enough to justify such a finding. In *St John of God (Care Services) Ltd v Brooks*[204] a hospital funded by the NHS, faced with substantial cuts in its funding, offered its employees new contracts involving lower rates of pay, the abolition of holiday entitlements and the abolition of overtime premia for weekend and holiday work. The tribunal found that the resulting dismissals were unfair because no reasonable employer could have expected the employees to agree to such terms. By a majority the EAT overruled this decision, holding that the tribunal had applied the wrong test: it was wrong to focus on the offer, to the exclusion of other factors; and the tribunal's approach 'tends to lead to giving undue importance to the factor that the employee is acting reasonably in refusing the offer'.[205]

5.185   If the law of unfair dismissal places few restraints on the employer's right to direct the business and organise the workforce as it sees fit, it places more effective restraints on the manner in which the employer conducts the process of redundancy and in particular its selection of the employees to be

---

200   *Orr v Vaughan* [1981] IRLR 63. On the band of reasonableness test in this context, see *Richmond Precision Engineering Ltd v Pearce* [1985] IRLR 179, *Cobley v Forward Technology Industries plc* [2003] IRLR 706.
201   *Ladbroke Courage Holidays Ltd v Asten* [1981] IRLR 59.
202   Anderman, 1986: p 428.
203   [1982] IRLR 143.
204   [1992] ICR 715. See also *Catamaran Cruisers Ltd v Williams* [1994] IRLR 386, discussed at para 4.39 above.
205   [1992] ICR 715, 722.

dismissed. It used to be the case that two forms of redundancy selection were automatically unfair: selection for reasons related to trade union activities and membership or non-membership, and selection contrary to an agreed or customary procedure. The latter provision, which applied to procedures such as 'last-in, first-out' (LIFO), was repealed in 1994.[206] The former is still retained and the model it embodies has been extended to cover a number of other automatically unfair reasons.[207] The normal qualifying period of service does not apply in these cases.[208]

Although selection contrary to an agreed or customary procedure is no longer automatically unfair, the process of selecting an employee must still comply with section 98(4) of ERA 1996. As Millett LJ explained:

> Criticism of the fairness of the process of selection for redundancy may take either or both of two forms. It may take the form of a challenge to the fairness of the system of selection which the employer adopted, including the criteria for redundancy, safeguards against bias and extent of consultation; or it may take the form of a challenge to the fairness of the manner in which the system was applied in practice.[209]

5.186 In order successfully to challenge the operation of selection criteria it will often be important to know the points awarded or assessments given to those who were not selected for redundancy. In *British Aerospace plc v Green*[210] the Court of Appeal took a restrictive approach to this question, holding that the 530 employees selected for redundancy out of a workforce of 7,000 were not entitled to discovery of the assessment forms of those who had not been selected. Millett LJ indicated that an applicant who sought an order for discovery 'must specify the respect in which he claims that the process was unfairly applied with sufficient particularity to demonstrate the relevance of the material the discovery of which is sought'.[211] In many cases, however, this will place an impossible burden on an employee. This point was recognised by the EAT in a decision reached shortly after *British Aerospace* where the employee was selected for redundancy from a group of eight, despite the fact that length of service was one of the criteria for selection; he had longer service than one of those retained; and there had never been any complaints about his performance. The EAT dismissed the employer's appeal against an order for discovery; only by knowing the applicant's markings and how they compared with those of the other seven employees was it possible to know whether the selection criteria had been applied fairly and reasonably to him.[212] In *John Brown Engineering Ltd v Brown* the

206 DCOA 1994, s 36(1).
207 See para 5.95 above.
208 ERA 1996, s 108(3).
209 *British Aerospace plc v Green* [1995] IRLR 433, 437. *Quaere* whether s 98A(2), which provides that failure by an employer to follow 'a procedure in relation to the dismissal of an employee' shall not be regarded as making the employer's action unreasonable if it shows that it would have decided to dismiss the employee if it had followed the procedure, applies to redundancy selection procedures. In practice where the system of selection, or application of that system, is successfully challenged the employer would be unlikely to be able to show that it would have decided to dismiss the employee if the procedure had been followed.
210 [1995] IRLR 433.
211 [1995] IRLR 433, 438.
212 *FDR Ltd v Holloway* [1995] IRLR 400, 402. Although it could be argued that the applicant in this case met the test set out by Millett LJ in *British Aerospace*, the decision in *FDR* was regarded by the Court of Session in *King v Eaton Ltd* [1996] IRLR 199, 201 as 'irreconcilable' with *British Aerospace*, which was affirmed to be correct.

EAT went further in holding that 'a policy decision to withhold all markings in a particular selection process may result in individual unfairness if no opportunity is thereafter given to the individual to know how he has been assessed. We recognise it may be invidious to publish the whole identified "league tables", but in choosing not to do so the employer must run the risk that he is not acting fairly in respect of individual employees'.[213] Adoption of a more transparent approach of this nature also avoids protracted litigation over the boundaries of appropriate discovery orders in this context.

5.187   The process of redundancy may also be unfair by reason of a general breach of procedural fairness under section 98(4) of ERA 1996. The employer may come under an obligation, depending on the circumstances, to give prior warnings to the employees; to enter into consultations with their trade union; to investigate the possibility of alternative employment; to consider the timing of the redundancies and their financial implications; and to allow for an appeal.[214] A lower standard of procedural propriety is set in the case of smaller firms,[215] consonant with the reference in the subsection to the need to take into account the 'size and administrative resources of the employer's undertaking'. Generally, however, these provisions require the employer to produce some objective justification of the process adopted.[216] The obligations imposed by section 98(4) do not replicate precisely the obligations placed upon the employer to consult at a collective level with employee or union representatives.[217] However in *Rowell v Hubbard Group Services Ltd*[218] the EAT thought that it would be normal for a tribunal to follow the approach suggested for collective consultation by Glidewell LJ in *R v British Coal Corpn and Secretary of State for Trade and Industry, ex p Price:*[219] in particular, there should be consultation at an early stage of the formulation of the proposals; there should be adequate provision of information to the employees or, where appropriate, their representatives; they should be given adequate time to respond; and their response should be conscientiously considered by the employer.

5.188   From 1 October 2004, redundancy dismissals have been subject to the standard statutory dismissal and disciplinary procedure except where the dismissal is one of a number of collective redundancies in respect of which the duty to consult under TULRCA 1992, s 188 applies.[220] An employer's failure to complete the procedure where applicable will render the dismissal automatically

---

213   [1997] IRLR 90, 91 (Lord Johnston).
214   See generally the judgment of the EAT in *Williams v Compair Maxam Ltd* [1982] IRLR 83; see also *Langston v Cranfield University* [1998] IRLR 172; *Lloyd v Taylor Woodrow Construction* [1999] IRLR 782.
215   *Gray v Shetland Norse Preserving Co* [1985] IRLR 53.
216   *Williams v Compair Maxam Ltd* [1982] IRLR 83; *NC Watling & Co Ltd v Richardson* [1978] ICR 1049; *Thomas and Betts Manufacturing v Harding* [1978] IRLR 213.
217   TULRCA 1992, ss 188 *et seq*; see para 9.32 *et seq* below. Nor does consultation with the union over selection criteria release the employer from consulting with the individual employee: see *Mugford v Midland Bank plc* [1997] IRLR 208.
218   [1995] IRLR 195, 197.
219   [1994] IRLR 72. See also *King v Eaton Ltd* [1996] IRLR 199.
220   EA 2002, Sch 2, Part 1; EADRR 2004, reg 4(1)(b); see further para 5.124 *et seq*. Note that an employee who complains of constructive dismissal must institute the relevant statutory grievance procedure. There is no exception for situations where the duty under TULRCA 1992, s 188 applies but it is likely that in such circumstances an 'appropriate representative' will raise the grievance on behalf of the group: EADRR 2004, reg 9.

unfair.[221] However, failure by an employer to follow a procedure other than the statutory minimum will not of itself render the employer's action unreasonable if it shows that it would have decided to dismiss the employee if it had followed that procedure.[222] This is clearly capable of applying to a failure to consult or warn an employee prior to dismissal, for example. The employer's obligations under TULRCA 1992, s 188 are not affected by this provision.

5.189 Finally, selection must comply with the general requirements of legislation outlawing discrimination on the grounds of race, sex, disability, religion or belief or sexual orientation.[223] In *Clarke v Eley (IMI) Kynoch Ltd*[224] the EAT held that a practice of dismissing all the part-time workers at the establishment, before any full-time workers were dismissed, amounted to indirect sex discrimination since the large majority of the part-time staff were female. The prior selection of the part-time staff amounted to the imposition of a requirement which the women in the establishment were proportionally less able to meet than the men. The employer failed in a defence of justification. The EAT also discussed the possibility that LIFO itself might contravene the Sex Discrimination Act 1975, on the grounds that women were, as a consequence of breaks in service for childcare and other purposes, less likely to have long service than men. The question was left open; it is possible that an employer might successfully invoke the justification defence to support LIFO.

Employer insolvency

5.190 Legislation provides certain guarantees to employees in the event of their employer's insolvency.[225] It may be possible for the employees to claim, first of all, against the insolvent employer in their capacity as preferred creditors. Accrued wages for four months up to a limit of £800, together with accrued holiday pay and certain other payments, are protected in this way.[226] In practice, even the employees' preferred claims against the estate of the insolvent employer will be defeated in most cases by the prior claims of any creditor holding a fixed charge over the company's assets, and will in any event only be ranked *pari passu* with those of other preferred creditors. Where wages in excess of £800 are owed, employees rank *pari passu* with other unsecured creditors.

More useful in practice is the second possibility, which is that the employees can make a claim for certain payments against the National Insurance Fund.[227]

---

221 ERA 1996, s 98A(1).
222 ERA 1996, s 98A(2). See further para 5.143.
223 See ch 6.
224 [1983] ICR 165. See generally paras 3.83 *et seq* and 3.90 above. The application of the Part-Time Workers (Prevention of Less Favourable Treatment) Regulations 2000, SI 2000/1551 would now need to be considered: see para 3.91.
225 For a more detailed examination of the complex area of corporate rescue and insolvency see Belcher, 1997.
226 IA 1986, ss 386–387 and Sch 6, para 9; SI 1986/1996.
227 ERA 1996, ss 166–170 and 182–190, which are intended to implement the UK's commitments under EC Council Directive 80/987. In some respects, UK law goes beyond the Directive, for example by protecting employees in the case of administrative receiverships triggered by a debenture holder, which do not fall under the definition of insolvency in Directive 80/987: *Mann v Secretary of State for Employment* [1999] IRLR 566. On the definition of insolvency for this purpose under ERA 1996, s 183, see *Secretary of State for Trade and Industry v Walden* [2000] IRLR 168. Amendments to Directive 80/987 in Directive 2002/74/EC are due to be transposed into national law by 8 October 2005: see Sargeant, 2003.

The Fund is then statutorily subrogated to the employees' claims, in respect of these sums, against the insolvent employer. The claims met by the Fund include certain arrears of wages for up to eight weeks (and subject to a ceiling which from 1 February 2005 and at the time of writing stands at £280 per week);[228] statutory guaranteed pay; the protective award; holiday pay; wages for the statutory notice period; any basic award of unfair dismissal compensation (but not the compensatory award or any further additional award); and any statutory redundancy payment.[229] Where the Secretary of State fails to make a payment, or pays too little, the employee may complain to an employment tribunal, which may declare the amount of payment due.[230]

The statutory scheme, then, provides only limited protection for employees in a direct claim against the remaining assets of the insolvent employer, and envisages that in most cases the state will have to meet the employer's residual liabilities. However, this compromise is capable of being upset in situations where administrators are appointed to run insolvent companies with a view to saving the businesses concerned, as opposed to simply realising their assets as quickly as possible.[231] Before examining the reasons for this, it is necessary briefly to consider the types of insolvency which may arise and their impact on the employees of the company.

5.191   Traditionally, a receiver (referred to as an 'administrative receiver' by modern insolvency legislation) was appointed by a secured creditor, typically a debenture-holder with a fixed and/or floating charge over the company's assets, in order to realise that creditor's security interest in the event of default.[232] The Insolvency Act 1986 then made provision for an administrator to be appointed by order of the court, on a petition from one of the company's creditors, to run a company which could not meet its debts as they fell due, with the purpose of effecting a rescue. In the interests of further promoting the 'rescue culture', the Enterprise Act 2002 substantially limited the right of a floating charge holder to appoint a receiver; this possibility is now restricted to cases where the charge was

228 In *Potter v Secretary of State for Employment* [1997] IRLR 21 the Court of Appeal left open the question whether the statutory ceiling on the total amount payable by the Secretary of State was in accordance with the social objective of the Insolvency Directive. A reference to the ECJ on this point was not necessary to dispose of the case. The EAT has held that the statutory ceiling should be applied before making any deductions for national insurance contributions and any relevant benefits to be recouped: *Titchener v Secretary of State for Trade and Industry* [2002] IRLR 195. Art 4(3) of the amended Directive, to be transposed by 8 October 2005, states that ceilings set 'must not fall below a level which is socially compatible with the social objectives' of the Directive. In *Mann v Secretary of State for Employment* [1999] IRLR 566 Lord Hoffmann suggested that employees can choose the eight weeks they regard as most favourable to them for the purposes of the claim against the Secretary of State.

229 ERA 1996, s 184. The EAT has held that the list of payments in s 184 is exhaustive and that payments under contractual guarantee pay provisions in respect of lay-offs that exceed the statutory entitlement, or payments in respect of absence through sickness or maternity due under the contract, are not recoverable: *Benson v Secretary of State for Trade and Industry* [2003] IRLR 748.

230 ERA 1996, ss 182–188. The ECJ has held that if the employer discharges part of the debt owed to an employee, this goes to reduce the employer's liability *outside* the three-month protected 'reference' period under the Directive, leaving the residual liability of the 'guarantee institution' (in the UK, the National Insurance Fund) within the reference period unaffected: Case C-125/97 *Regeling v Bestuur van de Bedrijfsvereniging Voor de Metaalnijverheid* [1999] IRLR 379.

231 P Davies, 1994a.

232 On receivership, see Armour and Frisby, 2001.

created before the 2002 Act came into force, and certain special cases (including certain complex capital market transactions and public-private partnerships). Thus the case of receivership is now of diminishing relevance. The 2002 Act also made it possible for an administrator to be appointed by the company itself, its directors or a floating-charge holder, without a court order. A further possibility is that a liquidator is appointed by the creditors following a voluntary liquidation; rather than aiming to save the company, the liquidator's principal role is to sell its assets, with a view to maximising returns to the creditors.

An administrator is deemed to act as the agent of the company and is thereby empowered to make contracts on its behalf.[233] Case law from before the passage of the 1986 and 2002 Acts indicates that where an administrator (or liquidator) acts as the company's agent, their appointment does not, of itself, terminate the contracts of employment of the company's employees.[234] This law also suggests that if an administrator enters into new contracts with the employees (or some of them) after being appointed, he or she might then become personally liable to those employees for debts arising out of their employment or for any claims in damages for wrongful dismissal which might arise.[235] Under insolvency legislation, the administrator has a right to be indemnified out of the company's assets in respect of any such personal liabilities, and expenses and debts incurred in this way are a first charge on the assets of the company.[236] Thus if the employees can establish a personal claim against the administrator, the effect is to gain a 'super-priority' placing them above all other creditors, since their claims would reduce the sums available to meet the company's other debts.[237] Perhaps this does not greatly matter, since giving the employees a first charge on the company's assets could be thought to be protecting those who are most sharply affected by the company's collapse. But even if the point about the vulnerability of the employees is right, there is a problem in short-circuiting the intended statutory ranking of creditors in this way; and, from a more practical point of view, it could give administrators a strong disincentive to keep the employees in employment while attempting to salvage the fortunes of the business. Faced with the prospect of open-ended liability to the employees, they might be more likely to seek a quick sale of assets in order to meet the claims of the charge-holder and other commercial creditors.

5.192 The Insolvency Act 1986 attempted to strike a balance between these conflicting considerations by providing that administrators were to be personally liable on contracts entered into in the course of carrying out their functions, as well as any contracts of employment adopted by them; but that, on the other hand, they should not be taken to have adopted a contract of employment in respect of anything done within 14 days of their appointment.[238]

233 IA 1986, Sch B1, para 69, as inserted by the Enterprise Act 2002.
234 *Reigate v Union Manufacturing Co (Ramsbottom) Ltd* [1918] 1 KB 592 (liquidator). By contrast, an appointment made by the court was thought to terminate contracts of employment, on the grounds that an agency relationship was lacking in that case: *Reid v Explosives Co Ltd* (1887) 19 QBD 264. This would no longer be so in the case of an administrator appointed by the court, thanks to the statutory deeming provision in IA 1986, referred to above.
235 *Re Mack Trucks (Britain) Ltd* [1967] 1 All ER 977; cf *Nicoll v Cutts* [1985] BCLC 322, where the Court of Appeal drew a distinction between continuing and adopting contracts of employment. The matter is now dealt with by IA 1994 and consequent amendments to IA 1986 (see below, this paragraph).
236 IA 1986, Sch B1, para 99(3).
237 P Davies, 1994a.

Subsequently, in *Re Specialised Mouldings*[239] Harman J held that an insolvency practitioner could avoid liability under these provisions even if he or she continued with the contracts of employees beyond 14 days, merely by writing to the employees concerned informing them that they would not be adopting their contracts and would not be personally liable on them. There was nothing in the Act to justify such an exclusion clause in itself, and the decision in *Re Specialised Mouldings* also appeared to elide the distinction between adopting and continuing a contract of employment in such a way to undermine the apparent aim of the 1986 amendments. Nevertheless, the judgment was widely relied on as providing insolvency practitioners with a means of keeping on the core employees of the business without incurring extensive liability to them. However, in *Re Paramount Airways (No 3), Powdrill v Watson*[240] Harman J's interpretation of the Act was rejected as unfounded, first in the Court of Appeal and then in the House of Lords.

Following the Court of Appeal's ruling, Parliament enacted the Insolvency Act 1994 which amended the 1986 Act in such a way as to restrict the impact of the *Paramount Airways* judgment. For claims arising after 15 March 1994, the administrator could only be liable for 'qualifying liabilities', that is to say wages (including contractual holiday and sickness payments) and occupational pension contributions arising in respect of service after the point at which the contract was adopted. This formula was retained in the changes made by the Enterprise Act 2002.[241] Thus claims for wrongful dismissal, as well as any claims for wages in respect of previous service, now rank simply as unsecured debts and are subject to the general rules concerning the priority of such debts.

Dismissal and transfers of employment

5.193   At common law, the transfer of a business from one employer (the 'transferor') to another (the 'transferee') often precipitates the dismissal of the employees who work in that business. They may be dismissed by the transferor, for redundancy or for some other business-related reason, at some point before the transfer takes place; alternatively, if they are still employed when the business is sold, the sale constitutes a repudiatory breach of contract by the employer which, at common law, the employees are entitled to treat as a wrongful dismissal.[242] If the business is insolvent, the appointment of an administrator or liquidator does not normally, as we have seen, automatically terminate the employee's contracts;[243] if the business is subsequently sold, however, there is normally a dismissal at that point.

The concept of a 'relevant transfer' of an 'undertaking' under the Transfer of Undertakings (Protection of Employment) Regulations 1981 and the effect of

238 IA 1986, s 19(5) (now repealed).
239 (13 February 1987, unreported.)
240 [1994] IRLR 295; affd [1995] 2 AC 394.
241 See now IA 1986, Sch B1, para 99(4)–(6).
242 See *Nokes v Doncaster Amalgamated Collieries Ltd* [1940] AC 1014, 1019 (Viscount Simon); *Litster v Forth Dry Dock and Engineering Co Ltd* [1989] IRLR 161, 169 (Lord Oliver). It is doubtful that the employees have a sufficient 'legitimate interest' at common law to keep the contract alive against the transferor, if it no longer owns the business, nor can the common law (as opposed to TUPE) grant the employees automatic rights of continuing employment against the transferee.
243 See para 5.191 above. The same reasoning may not apply, however, if the liquidator or administrator is appointed by the court.

the Regulations on the contract of employment and the rights and liabilities of the parties were considered in chapter 3 above.[244] By virtue of regulation 8(1) of TUPE, it is automatically unfair to dismiss an employee of either the transferor or the transferee where the reason or principal reason for the dismissal is 'the transfer or a reason connected with it'. This is so whether the dismissal takes effect before or after the transfer. Unlike other categories of automatically unfair dismissal, the employee is required to satisfy the normal one-year qualifying period to claim unfair dismissal.[245]

5.194 Regulation 8(2) immediately qualifies the principle of automatically unfair dismissal in regulation 8(1) by providing that a dismissal shall be for a potentially fair reason where it is for 'an economic, technical or organisational reason entailing changes in the workforce of either the transferor or the transferee before or after a relevant transfer'. The scope of this 'ETOR' exception is therefore central to the question of determining the effect of regulation 8 as a whole. The concept of ETOR has been interpreted as being in some ways wider and in some ways narrower than the notion of SOSR which is its rough counterpart under ERA 1996. It is wider in the sense that ETOR embraces a dismissal by reason of redundancy;[246] otherwise, redundancy, although generally a potentially fair reason for dismissal, would cease to be so for the purposes of business transfers, which can hardly have been the intention here. However, it is also significantly narrower in that it does not cover a range of economic dismissals which would, under the Act of 1996, fall into the SOSR category and hence be potentially fair; in the context of a transfer these dismissals are automatically unfair under regulation 8(1). This occurs largely because regulation 8(2) covers only those economic reasons 'entailing changes in the workforce' of either employer; as a result, dismissals which would almost certainly have been classed as SOSR reorganisations, because of their aim of job flexibility or cost-cutting, fail to qualify here as potentially fair.[247]

5.195 In evaluating the impact of regulation 8 on transfer situations, it must be considered together with regulation 5, which provides for automatic novation of the contracts of employment of the transferor which would otherwise have been terminated by the transfer, unless the individual employees concerned object,[248] and for the transmission to the transferee of all rights and liabilities

---

244 SI 1981/1794; see para 3.99 *et seq* above.
245 TUPE, reg 8(5)(b), inserted by the Collective Redundancies and Transfer of Undertakings (Protection of Employment)(Amendment) Regulations 1995, SI 1995/2587, overruling *Milligan v Securicor Cleaning Ltd* [1995] IRLR 288.
246 *Anderson and McAlonie v Dalkeith Engineering Ltd* [1985] ICR 66; *Gorictree Ltd v Jenkinson* [1985] ICR 51; *Warner v Adnet Ltd* [1998] IRLR 394; although, for a different view, cf *Canning v Niaz and McLoughlin* [1983] IRLR 431. It can be argued that reg 8(2) does not deem an ETOR to be synonymous with SOSR under the 1996 Act; it merely deems ETOR to be a substantial reason for the purposes of s 98(1)(b) of the Act. This means that ETOR could, in some circumstances, be an SOSR, but it could also be, in the words of s 98(1)(b), 'a reason falling within subsection (2)', in other words one of the other potentially fair reasons, including redundancy. However, the Government has felt it necessary to propose an amendment to TUPE which will put beyond doubt the inclusion of redundancy within the ETOR category: DTI, *TUPE Draft Revised Regulations Public Consultation Document*, March 2005, at para 52.
247 *Berriman v Delabole Slate Ltd* [1985] ICR 546; *Crawford v Swinton Insurance Brokers Ltd* [1990] ICR 85.
248 TUPE 1981, reg 5(4A), (4B); see para 3.100 above.

arising in or under these contracts. Particularly where the transferor is insolvent or, more generally, where its business is in difficulty, the price paid for a business by the transferee may well be affected by whether or not it inherits the pre-existing liabilities of the transferor to its employees; these might take the form of common law obligations to pay accrued wages or damages for wrongful dismissal, or statutory obligations with regard to unfair dismissal and redundancy. Equally, the price might be higher if the transferee has a free hand, after the transfer, to employ whom it wishes, or to offer whatever terms it thinks fit. The prospective imposition of these various obligations may mean that the sale does not go ahead. Where that is so, the employees of the transferor will lose their chance of continuing employment; this raises the possibility that the level of protection conferred by the TUPE Regulations might be counter-productive from the point of view ensuring *de facto* security of employment. This is a question which cannot be answered except by way of empirical research;[249] it is not a factor which the courts have taken into account, at least formally, in their interpretation of the Regulations. Whether, from a legal point of view, the Regulations strictly apply in all situations of restructuring which accompany a transfer is, in itself, unclear. Four particular problems need to be considered: the application of the Regulations to pre-transfer dismissals; the significance, if any, of the transferor's insolvency; the effect of post-transfer dismissals; and the issue of the joint liability of transferor and transferee.[250]

(i) Pre-transfer dismissals

5.196   The decision of the House of Lords in *Litster v Forth Dry Dock and Engineering Co Ltd*[251] has made it difficult for the Regulations to be avoided by collusion between the two employers designed to ensure that, at the point of transfer, the employees of the transferor have already been dismissed. This did seem a possibility for a while when the Court of Appeal, in *Secretary of State for Employment v Spence*,[252] overruled a number of earlier decisions[253] to hold that the completion of a transfer takes place at a single point in time, and cannot be deemed to be spread over a number of hours or days. In *Spence* this meant that employees dismissed by the transferor for redundancy at 11.00am, some three hours before an agreement was completed for the sale of the business, did not thereby become employees of the transferee: the time of the transfer was 2.00pm, and not the day as a whole. Because it is only the contracts of those employees who are employed 'immediately before the transfer' which are subject to regulation 5, this meant that, as the EAT had noted in an earlier decision, 'it would be very easy for a transferor without funds to agree with a transferee, for reasons convenient to them both, that employees should be dismissed a short time before transfer, thus leaving them with a worthless remedy and so defeating the protection afforded by the Regulations'.[254]

---

249   On this, see Frisby, 2000; Armour and Deakin, 2000, 2003.
250   Issues of dismissal law may also arise in the context of an employee's refusal to enter the employment of the transferee; these are discussed at para 3.100 above.
251   [1989] IRLR 161.
252   [1986] IRLR 248. See also Case C-478/03 *Celtec v Astley*, ECJ.
253   *Apex Leisure Hire v Barratt* [1984] ICR 452; *Secretary of State for Employment v Anchor Hotel (Kippford) Ltd* [1985] IRLR 452.
254   *Apex Leisure Hire v Barratt* [1984] ICR 452, 457 (Tudor Evans J).

In *Litster* this scenario was realised. The transferor (Forth Dry Dock), which was in receivership, dismissed its workforce one hour before the completion of a transfer of business assets to the transferee (Forth Estuary), which also took a lease of the business premises concerned (together these were found to constitute a relevant transfer). Forth Estuary declined to take on any of the workforce of the insolvent company, since it had hired employees who were willing to work for lower pay. Forth Dry Dock's receivers were unable to meet its liabilities to its employees by way of holiday pay and damages for wrongful and unfair dismissal, since there were no assets left after the debenture holder had realised its security. The employees made claims for compensation instead against Forth Estuary, which was solvent. The Court of Session, applying *Spence*, ruled that none of the employees had been employed by Forth Dry Dock immediately before the transfer, and so had no claim against Forth Estuary. The House of Lords allowed an appeal.

Lord Oliver thought that under Article 4 of the Directive, as construed by the European Court of Justice, a dismissal effected before the transfer and solely because of the transfer of the business is, in effect, prohibited and is, for the purpose of considering the application of Article 3(1), required to be treated as ineffective.[255] This interpretation could legitimately be extended to regulation 5 notwithstanding the difference between its wording and that of the Directive, since the aim of both the Directive and the Regulations was to safeguard the rights of the employees on a transfer and to provide effective remedies to this end. The remedies provided 'in the case of an insolvent transferor are largely illusory unless they can be exerted against the transferee'.[256] Accordingly, Article 5(3) should be read as applying both to an employee actually employed immediately before the transfer and to one who 'would have been so employed if he had not been unfairly dismissed in the circumstances described in regulation 8(1)'.

It follows that *Spence* is still correct on the question of the timing of the transfer. *Spence* is also correctly decided on its facts, since the dismissals in that case were genuinely for redundancy and were not connected to the transfer.[257] Where, however, a dismissal which took place prior to the transfer is automatically unfair under regulation 8(1), *Litster* decides that the transferee will inherit the pre-existing liabilities of the transferor towards its employees. The employees may therefore bring any outstanding claims for compensation against the transferee. However, if a dismissal falls under regulation 8(2), the transfer, although the reason for the dismissal,[258] is not the reason for that dismissal being *unfair*, in contrast to the position under regulation 8(1). As a

255 [1989] IRLR 161, 172. The judgments of the ECJ which Lord Oliver relied on directly were Case 19/83 *Wendelboe v LJ Music ApS* [1985] ECR 457; Case 324/86 *Foreningen af Arbejdsledere i Danmark v Daddy's Dance Hall* [1988] IRLR 315; and Case 101/87 *P Bork International A/S v Foreningen af Arbejdsledere i Danmark* [1989] IRLR 41.
256 [1989] IRLR 161, 172.
257 See Lord Oliver in *Litster* [1989] IRLR 161, 171, and also *Porter and Nanyakkara v Queen's Medical Centre (Nottingham University Hospital)* [1993] IRLR 486.
258 *Warner v Adnet Ltd* [1998] IRLR 393, cf *Whitehouse v Charles A Blatchford & Sons Ltd* [1999] IRLR 492. The Government has indicated that it intends to make it clear in revised TUPE Regulations that ETOR constitutes a subset of reasons *connected with* the transfer: *Transfer of Undertakings (Protection of Employment) Regulations 1981: Government Proposals for reform*, DTI, September 2001, para 75; DTI, *TUPE Draft Revised Regulations Public Consultation Document*, March 2005, paras 49–51.

result, only automatically unfair dismissals under regulation 8(1) trigger the principle enunciated in *Litster*.[259]

5.197 In assessing the impact of the *Litster* principle, it is significant that a broad reading has been given to regulation 8(1). In *Morris v John Grose Group Ltd*[260] the EAT held that the 'the words "the transfer" towards the end of regulation 8(1) do not by necessary construction have to refer to the relevant particular transfer which has actually taken place'; they could refer to the possibility of a transfer on different terms, perhaps to another transferee, which was in the mind of the employer at the time of the dismissal.

Equally, a narrow reading has been given to regulation 8(2). Where a prospective purchaser puts pressure on the vendor to make a number of dismissals as a precondition of the sale going ahead, or as a precondition of a higher price, it could be argued that the dismissals fall into the ETOR category. However, in *Wheeler v Patel*[261] the EAT ruled that in these circumstances, where the dismissals were motivated by purely financial considerations, the dismissals were not 'economic' within the meaning of regulation 8(2); the term 'economic' should, for this purpose, be construed *ejusdem generis* with 'technical and organisational', so as to require there to have been good business-related reasons for re-structuring the workforce. While this closes the door to a case of open collusion, it does allow dismissals to take place where the prospective purchaser had good business reasons for pressing for certain dismissals, or where the transferor would have carried out the dismissals for such reasons in any event.[262]

5.198 It was unclear following *Litster* whether that judgment had an application beyond the issue of whether employees could claim compensation for unfair dismissal from the transferee. In *P Bork International A/S v Foreningen af Arbejdsledere i Danmark* the ECJ said that 'workers employed by the undertaking whose contract of employment or employment relationship has been terminated on a date before that of the transfer, in breach of Article 4(1) of the Directive, must be considered as still employed in the undertaking on the date of the transfer with the consequence, in particular, that the obligations of an employer towards them are fully transferred from the transferor to the transferee, in accordance with Article 3(1)'.[263] This could be read as meaning that the dismissals in question were to be regarded as a nullity. In *Litster* Lord Oliver spoke of such a dismissal being 'prohibited' and, for the purposes of applying the Directive, 'required to be treated as ineffective'; as a result the employment was 'statutorily continued'.[264] The notion of a dismissal being nullified in this way is not,

---

259 See *Kerry Food Ltd v Creber* [2000] IRLR 10, 12; *Thompson v SCS Consulting Ltd* [2001] IRLR 801; DTI, *TUPE Draft Revised Regulations Public Consultation Document*, March 2005, para 43 (proposing a statutory codification of *Litster* which would make this clear). See also *BSG Property Services v Tuck* [1996] IRLR 134, where the EAT held that where notice was given by the transferor which expired after the date of transfer, it was the transferor's reason for dismissing which was material, even though liability in connection with the dismissal was transferred to the transferee.
260 [1998] IRLR 499, 503.
261 [1987] IRLR 211.
262 See, for example, *Whitehouse v Charles A Blatchford & Sons Ltd* [1999] IRLR 492; *Thompson v SCS Consulting Ltd* [2001] IRLR 801.
263 [1989] IRLR 41, 44.
264 [1989] IRLR 161, 172.

however, one which is found elsewhere in the law of unfair dismissal, and there was authority to suggest that the English and Scottish courts would not be obliged to adopt a remedy which did not already have a place in national law: in *Wendelboe v LJ Music ApS*[265] Advocate-General Slynn thought that 'whether the remedy for such unlawful dismissal consists in a court order declaring that dismissal to be a nullity or the award of damages or some other effective remedy is for member states to determine'. In *Wilson v St Helens Borough Council/ British Fuels Ltd v Baxendale and Meade*,[266] Lord Slynn repeated this view: 'the overriding emphasis in the European Court's judgment is that the existing rights of employees are to be safeguarded if there is a transfer ... But neither the Regulations nor the Directive nor the jurisprudence of the Court create a Community law right to continue in employment which does not exist under national law'. Because UK labour law has no general concept of the nullity of a dismissal, then, *Litster* is confined to providing dismissed employees with a right to compensation from the transferee.

That this is the effect of *Litster* would be further confirmed if a proposed amendment to TUPE, put forward by the government for consultation in March 2005, were to be adopted. This would codify the *Litster* ruling in the following terms by extending the coverage of the Regulations to the transfer of any person 'employed immediately before the transfer, or who would have been so employed if he had not been unfairly dismissed in the circumstances described in regulation 7(1)' – regulation 7(1) being the equivalent to regulation 8(1) in the draft revised Regulations.[267] Elsewhere, the Consultation Document refers to a regulation 7(1) dismissal being *unfair*, not *void*.[268] But this attempt at clarification may not be the last word on the matter. As we have just seen, the crucial step in Lord Slynn's judgment in *Wilson* was the argument that the concept of nullity has no place in UK labour law. The government's proposed amendments would, however, introduce the notion of nullity in the context of variations by reason of the transfer or a reason connected with the transfer which is not an ETOR.[269] If the concept of nullity can be applied to variations, its application to dismissals, as intended by the ECJ in the *Bork* case, may have been facilitated.

(ii) The application of the Regulations to a situation of insolvency

5.199 On the face of it, the TUPE Regulations apply to situations of employer insolvency just as they do to any other situation in which a transfer may arise. However, the original draft of the Directive only applied to *certain* situations of insolvency. As a result of the jurisprudence of the ECJ, it was understood to be compulsorily applicable to insolvency proceedings whose object was, broadly speaking, to effect a corporate rescue with a view to keeping the business intact where possible, but not to insolvency proceedings whose purpose was to liquidate

---

265 [1985] ECR 457, 460.
266 [1998] IRLR 706, 713–714, overturning the judgment of the Court of Appeal ([1997] IRLR 505). See also the similar emphasis of the ECJ on the relationship between national law and the Directive in Case C-343/98 *Collino and Chiappero v Telecom Italia Spa* [2000] IRLR 788, and see para 3.110 above for discussion of the implications of the *British Fuels* decision for post-transfer variation of contract terms.
267 DTI, *TUPE Draft Revised Regulations Public Consultation Document*, March 2005, draft reg 4(3).
268 DTI, *TUPE Draft Revised Regulations Public Consultation Document*, March 2005, paras 50–51.
269 This proposal is contained in draft reg 4(4): see also DTI, *TUPE Draft Revised Regulations Public Consultation Document*, March 2005, paras 44–45.

the assets of the transferor. Member States were free to apply the provisions of the Directive in the second set of situations,[270] but were not obliged to do so. The basis of this distinction was Article 1(1) of the Directive, which limited its scope to transfers made 'as a result of a legal transfer or merger'; this expression was held not to cover certain insolvency proceedings in the national legal systems of Member States. In *Abels v Bedrijfsvereniging Voor de Metaalindustrie en de Electrotechnische Industrie*[271] the ECJ held that there was no 'legal transfer' within the meaning of the Directive in a case where a transfer took place 'in the context of insolvency proceedings instituted with a view to the liquidation of the assets of the transferor under the supervision of the competent judicial authority'. Two reasons were given. The principal reason relied on was the fear that the application of the Directive in this situation would be counter-productive; the employees' interests in job security would best be met by enabling the sale of assets to go ahead as quickly as possible, without being restricted by the imposition of the insolvent company's liabilities on any prospective purchaser.

The second reason was the 'specificity of insolvency law', or the principle that the ranking of creditors in insolvency law should not easily be upset by contrary principles of employment law. As Advocate General Van Gerven put it in the later case of *d'Urso v Ercole Marelli Elettromeccanica Generale SpA*,[272] 'insolvency law is characterised by special procedures intended to weigh up the various interests involved, in particular those of the various classes of creditors, which implies that in all the Member States there are specific rules which may derogate, at least partially, from other provisions, of a general nature, including provisions of social law'. This is the problem of the employees' 'super-priority' which we also encountered in the context of the personal liability of administrators.[273] If, in a case such as *Litster*, the transferee necessarily inherits the pre-existing employment law liabilities of the transferor, the employees alone of all the creditors get the benefit of a direct claim for their loss against the solvent transferee; all the other creditors have is a claim against the assets of the insolvent transferor. Because the price paid by the transferee is likely (other things being equal) to be reduced to the extent that it has to meet in full the claims of the workforce, the employees' gain is the other creditors' loss: the value of the insolvent company and the proceeds of the sale of the business are that much less. The problem of 'super-priority' is therefore two-fold: not only are the employees ranked above all other creditors, but their claims are met in full when those of the others (with the possible exception of the debenture holder) will almost certainly be met only in part.[274] Since, in the British context, legislation guarantees that part (although not all) of the employee's claims against an insolvent transferor will be met by the National Insurance Fund in any event,[275] there may be even less reason to give the employees claims in full against the solvent transferee.

5.200 In *Abels* and in *d'Urso* the ECJ ruled that these considerations also applied to the case of proceedings whose function is not the liquidation of assets as such but rather the preservation or 'rescue' of the undertaking as a going

---

270 Directive 77/187, Art 7.
271 Case 135/83 [1985] ECR 469.
272 Case C-362/89 [1992] IRLR 136, 142.
273 See para 5.191 above, and see Pollard, 1996.
274 See H Collins, 1989b; P Davies, 1989; Schumacher, 1994.
275 See para 5.190 above.

concern, such as the Dutch procedure of 'judicial suspension of debts'.[276] This procedure is akin to administration in the British system. The basis for distinguishing between liquidation and administration is that the purpose of the latter is to see if the business can be kept intact and to postpone or avoid the situation in which it has to be broken up.[277] Advocate General Slynn argued in *Abels* that this is just as much a situation in which the jobs of the employees may be at risk if a buyer for the business is not found, and the same factors concerning the 'specificity' of insolvency procedures could also be said to apply, at least in the British context where an administrator has not just the power to run the business with a view to saving it, but also the power to sell it with a view to paying off the creditors.[278]

These arguments might seem to be irrelevant to the interpretation of TUPE, since the Directive enables a Member State to apply the protections of the Directive even in those situations, such as insolvency by liquidation, where their application is optional.[279] However, it could be argued that TUPE does attempt, in a rather indirect way, to exclude certain insolvency situations from its scope, by virtue of regulation 4 which purports to permit the practice of 'hiving down'. This is a process whereby an administrator or other insolvency practitioner transfers the business of an insolvent company to a specially-created subsidiary, while retaining the employees in the employment of the insolvent parent. The parent then lends the use of the employees' labour to the subsidiary. The subsidiary is sold to a third party which takes the business without being required to take the employees as well. Regulation 4 deems the transfer of the parent's undertaking to the subsidiary to take place no sooner than the moment immediately before the subsidiary's business is sold to the transferee, or the transferee takes a controlling shareholding in the subsidiary. What this appears to mean is that the administrator may dismiss the employees, who remain employed by the parent, before the point at which the Regulations bite, so that they never enter the subsidiary's employment and so cannot be transferred to the ultimate purchaser of the business.

After *Litster*, however, the validity of regulation 4 was plainly in doubt, since it could be argued that at the point when the administrator, at the purchaser's behest, dismissed the employees, the dismissal should be disregarded and their employment 'statutorily continued', first with the subsidiary and then with the transferee, at the point when it either bought the subsidiary's business or took a

---

276 See also Case C-319/94 *Jules Dethier Equipement SA v Dassy and Sovram SPRL* [1998] IRLR 266 where the ECJ affirmed that in deciding whether the Directive applied to a transfer subject to an administrative or judicial procedure the determining factor was the purpose of the procedure, and also its form, in particular in so far as it means that the undertaking continues or ceases trading.

277 The ECJ's judgments in *Abels* and *d'Urso* also suggest that there is an important distinction here between 'consensual' legal transfers, which are within the mandatory scope of the Directive, and those which are subject to close judicial control, which for that reason may not be.

278 It does not follow, however, that protective regulation will necessarily chill the sale of a business in financial distress, since there may still be scope for 'bargaining in the shadow' of the Regulations which will be aided by the information and consultation requirements of TUPE (regs 10–11A): see generally Armour and Deakin, 2000, 2003, and on the duty of the receiver to begin consultation with the representatives of the employees if contemplating the sale of business, see *Kerry Foods Ltd v Creber* [2000] IRLR 10.

279 Directive 2001/23, Art 5, formerly Directive 77/187, Art 7.

controlling interest in its shares.[280] Following the later judgment of the House of Lords in *Wilson v St. Helens Borough Council/British Fuels v Baxendale and Meade*,[281] the rights of the employees would be limited to a claim for compensation against the transferee, rather than a right to continuing employment; nevertheless, a claim for compensation could be highly significant in practice in terms of imposing liabilities on the transferee.

5.201   The Directive was amended in 1998 in such a way as to encourage greater flexibility in its application to insolvency. Article 5(2) now provides for two derogations which apply to 'insolvency proceedings which have been opened in relation to a transferor (whether or not those proceedings have been instituted with a view to the liquidation of the assets of the transferor) and provided that such proceedings are under the supervision of a competent public authority (which may be an insolvency practitioner determined by national law)'.[282] The first derogation[283] allows the Member State to specify that debts of the transferor which arise from contracts of employment or employment relationships do not get transferred to the transferee, as long the employees have protection (in respect of their claims against the transferor) equivalent to that laid down in the Insolvency Directive.[284] The second derogation permits a Member State to make a provision according to which 'the transferee, transferor, or person or persons exercising the transferor's functions, on the one hand, and the representatives of the employees on the other hand may agree alterations, insofar as current law or practice permits, to the employees' terms and conditions of employment designed to safeguard employment opportunities by ensuring the survival of the undertaking, business or part of the undertaking or business'.[285]

In 2001 the Government indicated an intention to take advantage of these derogations in revising TUPE,[286] and in March 2005 published draft regulations to this effect.[287] The derogations would apply to administration, company and individual voluntary arrangements, and creditors' voluntary winding-up, but

---

280 For a clear application of this principle, see *In the matter of Maxwell Fleet and Facilities Management Ltd (No 2), Re* [2000] IRLR 368. The Government has proposed removing reg 4: *Transfer of Undertakings (Protection of Employment) Regulations 1981: Government Proposals for reform*, DTI, September 2001, para 103, and *TUPE Draft Revised Regulations Public Consultation Document*, March 2005, para 74.

281 [1998] IRLR 706; see para 5.198 above.

282 Directive 2001/23, Art 5(2).

283 Directive 2001/23, Art 5(2)(a).

284 Directive 80/987; see para 5.190 above.

285 Directive 2001/23, Art 5(2)(b). It is also specified that a Member State may take advantage of this particular derogation in the case of 'any transfers where the transferor is in a situation of serious economic crisis, as defined by national law, provided that the situation is declared by a competent national authority and open to judicial supervision, on condition that such provisions already existed in national law by 17 July 1998' (Art 5(3)); this would seem to have no application to the UK, and has not been relied on by the UK Government in putting forward proposals for the reform of TUPE (see below).

286 See generally *Transfer of Undertakings (Protection of Employment) Regulations 1981: Government Proposals for reform*, DTI, September 2001, paras 84–97. A DTI Press Release of 14 February 2003 stated only that the Government intended to 'introduce new flexibility into the Regulations' application in relation to the transfer of insolvent businesses, giving a significant boost to our promotion of the "rescue culture"'. For discussion of the potential implications of these derogations for the UK see P Davies, 1998; Frisby, 2000; Armour and Deakin, 2000, 2003.

287 DTI, *TUPE Draft Revised Regulations Public Consultation Document*, March 2005, paras 54–72.

not to administrative receivership or members' voluntary winding up. The first derogation would cover any employees who had passed from the transferor to the transferee by virtue of a relevant transfer, or would have done but for a *Litster*-type dismissal. Payments covered by the statutory insolvency payments provisions,[288] together with statutory redundancy payments,[289] could be claimed against the Secretary of State under the insolvency scheme.[290] The second derogation would create a category of 'permitted variations' to terms and conditions of employment, negotiated by 'appropriate representatives' of the employees assigned to the organised grouping involved in the relevant transfer. 'Permitted variations' would be those designed to safeguard employment opportunities by ensuring the survival of the organised grouping involved in the transfer. The 'appropriate representatives' would be defined in essentially the same way as they are for the purposes of information and consultation requirements arising under TUPE.[291]

(iii) Post-transfer dismissals

5.202   If, following the transfer, the transferee takes into its employment the employees of the business concerned, it may not immediately seek unilaterally to change their terms and conditions of employment. Any such change would be not simply a constructive dismissal, but could be automatically unfair by virtue of regulation 8(1): the employee concerned could argue that the dismissal arose in connection with the transfer and was not potentially fair under regulation 8(2). This is because, as noted earlier, the concept of ETOR is significantly narrower than that of SOSR under section 98(1) of the Act of 1996. In *Berriman v Delabole Slate Ltd*[292] the transferee attempted, after the transfer had taken place, to harmonise the terms and conditions of employment of staff previously employed by the transferor, by cutting their entitlement to a guaranteed basic wage. Mr Berriman resigned and claimed constructive dismissal. The tribunal found that he had been constructively dismissed and that the reason was an ETOR. The EAT and Court of Appeal both took a different view, namely that the reason for the dismissal was the employer's wish to alter the terms and conditions of the transferred staff. Here, 'the reason itself (ie to produce standardisation of pay) does not involve any change either in the number or the functions of the workforce. The most that can be said is that such organisational reason *may* (not must) lead to the dismissal of those employees who do not fall into line'.

However, there does not necessarily need to be a net drop in the number of employees employed by the transferee for there to be an ETOR. In *Crawford v Swinton Insurance Brokers Ltd*[293] a transferred employee, who had been employed as a clerk, was offered different work as an insurance salesman, which he refused. It was held that his resulting dismissal was for an ETOR since the aim was to bring about a 'change in the workforce', substituting a worker doing one job for one doing another.

---

288 See para 5.190 above.
289 See para 5.174 above.
290 DTI, *TUPE Draft Revised Regulations Public Consultation Document*, March 2005, paras 57–65.
291 DTI, *TUPE Draft Revised Regulations Public Consultation Document*, March 2005, paras 66–72.
292 [1985] ICR 546, 551.
293 [1990] ICR 85.

The effect of *Berriman* is that a transferred employee is, for a while, in a better position than those who worked for the transferee throughout, who cannot protect their terms and conditions of employment against a re-organisation on efficiency grounds which constitutes an SOSR. The question is how long this period of protection lasts in the case of the transferred employees: at what point would their dismissal for refusing new terms cease to be for a reason connected with the transfer?[294] The Regulations provide no answer. Interestingly, the Directive provides that following the transfer, the transferee should observe the terms of any applicable collective agreement of the transferor for a period which Member States may limit to one year.[295] This provision does not fit easily into the context of British labour law, where the collective agreement is not in any case normally binding between employer and trade union, and was not transposed into the Regulations. Nor is the issue of post-transfer dismissals confined to the effect of collective agreements. However, the clear implication of this provision is that after one year the transferee is entitled to insist on harmonising the terms and conditions of the transferred employees with those of its own staff; whether it could be relied on by employment tribunals applying the Regulations is an open question.

In *Berriman*, the court found that the attempt by the transferee to impose new terms and conditions of employment amounted to a constructive dismissal; however, this will not always be the case. In *Rossiter v Pendragon plc*[296] a dispute over commission payments was held not to give rise to a breach of contract by the employer. In the alternative, the employee was held to have affirmed any such breach. In *Air Foyle Ltd. v Crosby-Clarke*[297] the transferee's decision to alter the employee's working hours was held to be contractually justified, since it was done to comply with mandatory legislation setting limits to the working time of pilots. The Court of Appeal held that, in each case, there had been no constructive dismissal, rejecting an argument that under regulation 5(5) of TUPE a substantial change in working conditions was enough to trigger the protection of the Regulations, whether or not it amounted to a repudiatory breach by the employer. The Government has now proposed to amend TUPE so that 'where a relevant transfer involved or would involve a substantial change in working conditions to the detriment of a person whose contract of employment was or would be transferred ... such an employee may treat the contract of employment as having been terminated, and the employee shall be treated for any purpose as having been dismissed with notice by the employer'.[298]

(iv) Joint liability

5.203   A final question to consider here is whether the transfer of employment from one employer to another puts an end to all liabilities of the transferor. In the context of insolvency this question is quite often irrelevant, but it has considerable importance where work is contracted out from one employer to

---

294 See also discussion of this issue in relation to consensual variations in para 3.110 above.
295 Directive 2001/23, Art 3(3).
296 [2002] IRLR 483.
297 [2002] IRLR 483.
298 DTI, *TUPE Draft Revised Regulations Public Consultation Document*, March 2005, draft reg 4(9). The justification for this change is stated to be the need to comply with Art 4(2) of the Directive. The reference to dismissal 'with notice' reflects the Government's view that 'it would not ... be right for an employer to be penalised for failing to give notice of termination in ... [these] circumstances': see Consultation Document, para 46.

another, and both remain solvent. The Directive expressly permits, but does not require, Member States to maintain the liability of the transferor after the transfer.[299] After some hesitation the British courts have held that clear provision would be required in order for the transferor's liability to be maintained, and that not only is there no such provision in TUPE, but regulation 5 of TUPE, which provides for all the transferor's liabilities to be transferred to the transferee, prevents any such interpretation.[300]

ASSESSMENT

5.204 As this chapter has shown, the law governing termination of employment is of pivotal importance in contemporary labour law. It has also exhibited a degree of stability which was surprising at a time when deregulation became the predominant tendency in other areas. Unfair dismissal law was not left untouched by the reforms of the 1980s and 1990s, not least of which was the extension of the qualifying period from six months in 1979 to two years (now reduced to one). Recent amendments have sought to encourage recourse to basic workplace dismissal procedures whilst allowing greater latitude in adherence to procedures going beyond these. Nonetheless, the preservation of the basic structure of unfair dismissal protection much as it was when it was enacted in the 1970s is, perhaps, testimony to a general acceptance of the principle that there should continue to be legal regulation of employment terminations. In this respect, Hepple has suggested that unfair dismissal law has survived thanks to its 'chameleon-like qualities both of protecting individuals against arbitrary management, and simultaneously of strengthening managerial legitimacy and control'.[301] Three aspects of dismissal law will be considered in the light of this statement: the extent to which the law has led to greater control of managerial prerogative; the impact of legal procedures and processes on the resolution of individual disputes; and the wider social and economic implications of job security.

(i) Controlling managerial prerogative

5.205 A key issue here is how far the present body of law is effective in imposing controls on management decision-making. Collins has argued that dismissal legislation sees the employment relationship not as an individualised transaction (the model he associates with contract), but instead as embedded in the structure of bureaucratic rules which characterise the business enterprise. If the enterprise is viewed as a bureaucratic organisation, it can be said that managerial decisions

---

299 Directive 2001/23, Art 3(1).

300 *Stirling District Council v Allan* [1995] IRLR 301; see also *Thompson v Walon Car Delivery and BRS Automotive Ltd* [1997] IRLR 343. The Government has proposed that the transferor and transferee should, exceptionally, be jointly and severally liable for liabilities to employees for injury or disease arising from their pre-transfer employment in those cases where the transferor is a public sector employer not subject to, or exempted from, the requirement to effect insurance under the Employers' Liability (Compulsory Insurance) Act 1969: DTI, *TUPE Draft Revised Regulations Public Consultation Document*, March 2005, paras 86–90. The same proposals suggest that there should be joint and several liability for a failure to comply with the information and consultation requirements of the regulations (see paras 81–85); we discuss these below at para 9.45.

301 Hepple, 1993: p 95.

are most effective where they comply with notions of formal rationality which are similar to those which are found in the public law model of control of discretionary powers. 'Rationality' here means that employers should exercise disciplinary powers for a rational purpose, which means 'one which avoids substantial harm to the business', and in a rational manner, or in 'a way which is conducive to efficient decisions'.[302] It also means respecting certain fundamental rights of employees. The law is entitled to intervene to require this of employers because managerial prerogative, in common with other examples of discretionary power, 'can only be legitimate if exercised for rational business purposes and without infringement of individual rights'.[303] Legal regulation is necessary, then, both to protect individuals from potential injustice, but also to underpin good practice by employers which, in the long run, is conducive to the more efficient operation of organisations.

Collins's formulation of the aims of dismissal protection is valuable not least because it helps to explain why dismissal legislation in Britain falls a long way short of providing absolute protection against loss of a job, or a 'job property' right on the part of the employee. Except in the relatively few cases of automatically unfair dismissals (and subject to the potential impact of the Human Rights Act 1998), the essence of the obligation imposed by the law on the employer is procedural. Fundamental principles applied by the courts under section 98(4), such as the principle that the tribunal must not substitute its judgment for that of the employer and that it must apply a 'band of reasonableness' test when judging the employer's conduct, testify to the peripheral place occupied by notions of substantive fairness in this area of the law; the focus is above all on the *process* of dismissal or discipline, and only second on the *outcome*.[304] But this does not mean that the law is necessarily failing in the task which it was set. It should be borne in mind that the Donovan Commission placed little emphasis on the goal of substantive justice for individual employees when making the case for what became unfair dismissal legislation. The Commission regarded dismissal legislation as a means of streamlining and formalising plant-level procedures, with a view to strengthening managerial decision-making at this level; the subsequent experience of the legislation could be seen as largely fulfilling this aim.

Whether the law goes far enough in imposing procedural requirements over the exercise of disciplinary powers is much more open to debate. Prior to 1 October 2004 the courts allowed procedural requirements to be waived where a 'reasonable employer' would have dispensed with them.[305] The legislation now provides that (certain situations apart) a dismissal will be automatically unfair if the relevant statutory dismissal and disciplinary procedure has not been completed and this non-completion was mainly attributable to failure by the employer to comply with its requirements. At first sight this enhances the importance of procedure. However, this is counterbalanced by the rudimentary nature of the statutory procedures, which fall significantly short of accepted standards of procedural fairness, and the provision that failure to follow a procedure beyond the statutory minimum will not render the dismissal unfair if the employer shows that it would have decided to dismiss even if that procedure

---

302 H Collins, 1993: p 272.
303 H Collins, 1993: p 273.
304 For the argument that the interpretation of the unfair dismissal legislation has been distorted by judicial defence of employers' property rights see Anderman, 2004.
305 *Polkey v AE Dayton Services Ltd* [1987] IRLR 503.

had been followed (the 'no difference' principle). This represents a significant downgrading of procedural fairness and gives little incentive to employers to adopt procedures that go beyond the minimum.[306] Another major weakness of the current law is that the protection of employees against unfair disciplinary action short of dismissal is limited. In most cases, an employee who is subjected to such action has the option to resign and claim constructive dismissal, but making a complaint while still remaining in employment is much more difficult to do.[307] More generally, remedies associated with unfair dismissal are widely regarded as being too weak. Although the statutory ceiling on the compensatory award has been raised substantially, the ease with which the employer can resist re-employment continues to pose a major obstacle to effective employment protection.

The limited nature of statutory protection in the case of individual dismissals for misconduct or lack of capability is one reason for the growth of interest in alternative routes to protection which utilise either public law or the common law of contract. Both judicial review and the equitable remedies of injunction and declaration can, in principle, be deployed to counter disciplinary action short of dismissal, and can also have an effect which is essentially that of nullifying a purported dismissal, a power denied to the employment tribunals in their statutory jurisdiction. The use of the common law to uphold contractual job security clauses also illustrates how the law can confer protection which is substantive and not simply procedural in nature. However, the difficulty here continues to be that only a small group of employees, mainly in the public sector, has succeeded in deploying these legal mechanisms, while the courts retain a wide discretion in granting specific remedies of this kind. Continuing doubt over the correctness of the 'bilateral' theory of contract termination also qualifies the advantages offered by these routes to protection. Finally, the refusal of the courts to subject the contractual power of dismissal to a duty to act fairly on the ground that such a term would subvert the statutory unfair dismissal scheme has left the law in a regrettably incoherent and unsatisfactory state.

In the area of economic dismissals, the extent of the employer's duty is, in most cases, to act with regard to the rational business needs of the enterprise; there may be procedural restrictions, in the form of a duty to inform and consult at collective level, but requirements at the individual level are limited. Compensation for loss of employment may then be left up to the system of social security, on the grounds that the costs of displacing employees from their jobs are best met collectively through national insurance and the taxation system. In practice, this is what the redundancy payment scheme did for much of its life, via the system of redundancy rebates which operated until 1990. As the value of redundancy rebates was reduced prior to their complete abolition, the potential costs of restructuring to individual employers were increased, whilst amendments made to comply with EC obligations significantly added to the content of the employer's collective obligations of consultation and information.[308] In these ways, the law now imposes firmer procedural obstacles to the implementation of redundancies than it has at any point since the introduction of redundancy compensation in 1965, but their value for workers might have been greater during the period of large-scale job losses in industry in the 1980s. In general,

---

306 See generally Hepple and Morris, 2002.
307 See, however, *Hogg v Dover College* [1990] ICR 39 and *Alcan Extrusions v Yates* [1996] IRLR 327, discussed at paras 5.71 and 5.74.
308 See para 9.30 *et seq* below.

as we saw in our earlier discussion,[309] there can be little doubt that the overall effect of legal intervention in this area since 1965 has been to facilitate job restructuring through redundancy or reorganisation, sometimes at the expense of agreed contract terms, and not to support job security as such.

The law has also been weak in the area of civil liberties or 'public rights' dismissals. While the goal of protecting individual dignity and autonomy at work is recognised to be an important objective of dismissal law[310] (and, indeed, of labour law more generally),[311] it is a different matter to argue that this objective is even close to being fulfilled in the current law. The technique of making certain reasons for dismissal automatically unfair provides a potentially useful model for entrenching certain rights against instrumental arguments based on considerations of efficiency or business rationality. However, as Pitt suggests with regard to the existing categories of automatically unfair dismissal, 'no coherent philosophy such as protection for public rights or civil liberties underpins their special status; rather, there are separate reasons for each category'.[312] This is so notwithstanding the continuing growth of new categories of automatically unfair reasons. There is no good reason, it would seem, for the inclusion within the legislation of discrimination on grounds related to trade union membership or activities, on the one hand, and the absence, on the other, of any reference to political opinions, to give but one example. For the most part, the merits of 'public rights dismissals', just like any others, fall to be determined under section 98(4). Here, considerations of 'efficiency' or business rationality, very loosely defined, regularly prevail over employees' claims to rights-based protection.[313] There is an instructive contrast here with the approach under equal treatment legislation, where the test of proportionality in indirect discrimination requires arguments about efficiency to be much more precisely formulated than is possible under the 'band of reasonableness' test, and where the weighing exercise must be undertaken with a view to limiting, as far as possible, any infringement of the fundamental right whose application is at stake.[314] At the time of writing it still remains uncertain what impact the Human Rights Act 1998 will have on the core test of fairness in section 98(4), but it is strongly arguable that a different analysis of the 'band of reasonable responses' test will be required in cases of dismissal involving interference with a Convention right.

In short, as a result of unfair dismissal legislation, the law no longer permits the employer to act wholly arbitrarily in the area of discipline and dismissal, and an element of the rule of law has been injected into relations within the firm. However, the relevant statutory standards are set at too low a level, and the remedies established by statute, in their existing form, arguably do little to persuade employers who are bent on dismissal to take a contrary course of action. Nor has the common law evolved to the point of providing a satisfactory alternative. The common law has stopped well short of implying into all contracts of employment an obligation upon the employer to observe natural justice, or, less specifically, to act fairly, when exercising a contractual power to discipline or dismiss; nor have doubts about the availability of specific remedies in equity, or by way of judicial review, been satisfactorily resolved. Under these

---

309 See in particular paras 5.10, 5.163 and 5.183 above.
310 See H Collins, 1993: pp 16–21.
311 See Hepple, 1995
312 Pitt, 1993: p 264.
313 See para 5.183 *et seq* above.
314 See Deakin, 1996; para 6.29 below.

circumstances, it may be premature to speak of a 'new paradigm' of the employment relationship based around the control of bureaucratic power; at the very least, as Collins accepts, this paradigm is still 'struggling to the surface of popular and legal consciousness'.[315]

(ii) The role of the law and 'legalism' in dispute resolution

5.206   Dismissal legislation is one of the clearest examples of the process of the 'juridification' of employment relations. Juridification does not simply signify an increase in legal regulation; more specifically it involves the displacement of contractual autonomy of the parties by legislative rules which are designed to bring about certain goals of public policy.[316] A potentially negative feature of juridification is the possibility of 'regulatory failure', which may be the result of regulation which fails to take into account the role of autonomous social and economic processes governing the object of regulation. As we have seen,[317] there is some uncertainty as to whether this has been true of the impact of dismissal legislation in Britain. Although it has fallen short of providing strong guarantees of job protection, it is arguable that this was never a clear aim of the legislation. Moreover, in stimulating the growth of more formal procedures at plant level, the legislation may be said to have a considerable *indirect* impact which is consonant with the goals set out by the Donovan Commission. At any rate, the apparent inability of the legislation to provide an effective right against being unfairly dismissed does not necessarily mean that, in this case, the process of intervention can be said to have been subject to 'regulatory failure' in the sense referred to above.

There has been a substantial debate since the inception of unfair dismissal legislation concerning the desirability of introducing formal legal processes into individual employment disputes, and in particular into the role played by the employment tribunal system. Although employment tribunals were meant to provide an informal setting for the resolution of disputes and to avoid recourse to over-extensive legal argument, this has proved difficult to achieve. Proceedings before employment tribunals are inevitably adversarial, with cross-examination of witnesses and opposing arguments being presented by the two sides, and frequently involve discussion of highly technical points of law (such as the definition of the terms 'employee' or 'dismissal'). The formality, cost and 'excessive legalism' of tribunal proceedings have been unfavourably compared with voluntary arbitration; the latter is said to be 'cheaper, speedier, more informal, and more accessible, it avoids the legalism and publicity associated with the tribunals, and offers the possibility of a more flexible range of remedies, including a greater likelihood of reinstatement and re-engagement'.[318]

Two points may be made in the context of this long-running debate. The first is that it was probably unavoidable that the employment tribunals would come to operate in a judicial fashion, given that their jurisdiction involves adjudication on questions of legal rights which have a wider significance than the particular disputes which come before them.[319] The second is that while 'legalism' may have certain unattractive features, it is a necessary part of the process by which certain clear legal limits are set to managerial prerogative. If, for example,

315 H Collins, 1993: p 273.
316 Simitis, 1987.
317 See para 5.9 *et seq* above.
318 R Lewis and J Clark, 1993: p 33; see also L Dickens, 1988, and our discussion at para 2.20
      above.
319 See Munday, 1981.

dismissal law is to play a more extensive role in future in protecting employees in the context of public-rights dismissals,[320] a clearer statutory articulation of those rights will have to be made, and their enforcement entrusted to adjudicatory bodies to which the employee has access whether or not the employer agrees. This is not to deny that alternative dispute resolution does not have a valuable role to play in processing individual disputes, merely to point out that this is unlikely to be at the expense of a continuing role for more formal mechanisms of legal enforcement. To date little use has been made of the scheme by ACAS for the resolution of unfair dismissal disputes by arbitration, discussed in para 2.20 above.[321] It remains to be seen whether the new statutory workplace dismissal and disciplinary procedures will have the desired effect of finding 'flexible solutions ... before the breakdown of the employment relationship'[322] and thus prevent disputes reaching the tribunals.

(iii) The social and economic implications of job security

5.207   An assessment of dismissal legislation must also take into account the degree to which developments in the forms of employment and in the labour market more generally have undermined the goal of job security, or have confined its achievement to a minority of workers in the 'core'. Legislation has encouraged this development, in the United Kingdom and elsewhere in western Europe, by exempting certain categories of temporary employment from dismissal protection; there has also been a rise in forms of casual employment which involve only minimal guarantees, on the part of the employer, of work and payment.[323] In addition there has been a direct challenge to the legitimacy of dismissal protection from accounts which argue that the model of the contract at will is, after all, an efficient basis for constituting the employment relationship. It is said that the advantage of the contract at will is that both parties can exercise at low cost the option of quitting the relationship and re-entering the market in search of another contract. An employer who acts arbitrarily in its treatment of an employee will be punished not by the law but by the market; the employee will leave to get better employment and the employer will pay a price for its behaviour in terms of its diminished reputation for fair treatment, which will make it more difficult to attract and retain high-quality employees.[324] This argument correctly points to the existence of non-legal sanctions for breach of contract, which its proponents claim also explains why the common law traditionally provided so little in the way of formal employment protection; however, its weakness is its failure to deal with the point that market failures of various kinds will frequently make it impossible for these non-legal sanctions to be effectively deployed.[325] Nor does it answer the objection that the market cannot provide a remedy, after the event, for injustices which may have been suffered by individual employees; the employer who acts arbitrarily may suffer from a diminished reputation, without the employee necessarily receiving adequate compensation for the psychic and financial costs arising from job loss.

---

320 Cf Pitt, 1993.
321 Between May 2001, when the scheme came into force, and the end of March 2004 43 cases had been accepted.
322 *Statutory Dispute Resolution Procedures: Full Regulatory Impact Assessment* DTI, 2004: p 4, para 2.
323 See paras 3.81 *et seq* and 3.36 *et seq* above.
324 Epstein, 1984.
325 Mückenberger and Deakin, 1989: pp 187 *et seq.*

As we have seen, security of employment is not necessarily the same thing as the right not to be dismissed from a particular job;[326] it may be that the interests of society as a whole and of individual employees would be better served by a system which ensured that all individuals had a wide choice of jobs in the labour market, rather than allowing a minority the privilege of absolute job protection at the cost, perhaps, of limiting opportunities for the rest. To the extent that dismissal legislation has this effect (which is not consistently borne out by empirical studies),[327] the answer may lie not so much in deregulation as in the development of mechanisms which might secure individual economic security at the level of the labour market as a whole, rather than at the level of the individual business enterprise.[328] Nor should it be assumed from this that the goal of job security is necessarily outmoded. Although 'atypical' or 'non-standard' jobs take up a significant number of new hirings, the majority of employees in the United Kingdom continue to work in jobs which take the form of contracts for an indefinite duration,[329] and a secure job is still an essential aspect, for most individuals, of their long-term economic security. This suggests that dismissal protection will remain an important aspect of labour market regulation, even if other forms of intervention based on active labour market policy and social security transfers may come to play a more important role in future than they have in the past.

326 See our discussion in para 5.3 above.
327 See Büchtemann, 1993.
328 See Deakin and Wilkinson, 1991, for a discussion of the form which might be taken by labour-market rights in this context.
329 Coutts and Rowthorn, 1995; findings from the Working in Britain in 2000 survey, discussed Taylor, (no date given); see para 1.30 above.

CHAPTER 6

Equality of treatment

INTRODUCTION

6.1   The law recognises the right of an individual worker not to be discriminated against on a number of specified grounds, which include sex, sexual orientation, race, religion and belief, disability and, from 2006, age. This area of law subjects employers' decisions in all aspects of the employment relationship, from hiring through to termination, to a distinct form of legal scrutiny which operates on two levels. At the first level, it means that 'like must be treated alike' in the sense that access to benefits (or, conversely, the imposition of detriments) must not be based on one of the prohibited grounds referred to above. At the second level, it entails a legal examination of the effects of policies, practices and requirements which, while facially neutral, may result in institutionalised disadvantage to the members of a group which is defined by reference to one of those grounds, such as sex or race. These two types of inequality are known, respectively, as 'direct' and 'indirect' discrimination, and as the basis for legal intervention they together form the conceptual basis of the *principle of equal treatment* as it has come to be embodied in British labour law.

The common law, with its emphasis on freedom of contract, sees nothing inherently wrong with discrimination in the sense just described, as long as no pre-existing contract or property right is infringed. Statutory intervention in this area, as critics are quick to point out, therefore represents a further erosion of contractual autonomy.[1] Three potential justifications, which are not necessarily complementary, may be offered for this. One stresses the role of labour law in protecting the dignity of the individual worker in a situation where he or she is in a relationship of economic subordination; the second emphasises the role of the law in correcting for systematic disadvantage suffered by particular groups; and the third sees equality law as a means of overcoming certain market failures, in particular barriers to market access on the part of excluded groups, in such a way as to make the labour market more transparent. As we shall see, each of these elements may be found within the present body of law, and the tensions between them help to account for the dynamic nature of this area of doctrine.

Given the wider, constitutional importance of the principles involved and the large amount of case law which they have generated, it is in many ways surprising that legislation in this area is such a relatively recent addition to the body of labour law in this country. The first race relations legislation dates only from 1965, legislation governing equal pay for equal work from 1970, and more general anti-discrimination legislation in respect of both sex and race from 1975 and 1976 respectively. The Equal Pay Act 1970 and the Sex Discrimination Act 1975 have since been much amended, largely as a consequence of the influence of European Community law. The Race Relations Act 1976 has seen fewer changes, in part because the European Community has been less of a direct influence. It was only in 2000 that an EC Directive prohibiting racial

---

1   See Epstein, 2002, and the rejoinder by Deakin, 2002.

discrimination was adopted. Legislation concerning disability discrimination, the Disability Discrimination Act, was introduced in the UK in 1995. In 2000 the European Community adopted a Framework Directive prohibiting discrimination in employment on grounds including religion or belief, and sexual orientation; these parts of the Directive were implemented in 2003. Amendments to disability discrimination legislation required to comply with the Directive came into force in 2004. Provisions relating to age discrimination are due to be implemented in 2006. A further significant event for UK discrimination law was the enactment of the Human Rights Act 1998 which, while not conferring a free-standing right to equal treatment, is nevertheless likely to have an impact on litigation strategies and judicial interpretations in the coming years.

The explanation for the UK's failure to legislate before the 1960s and 1970s may lie in the persistence of the tradition of voluntarism or, more precisely, of 'collective laissez-faire'. If this is the case, it seems that the traditional concerns may have been misplaced: the system of collective laissez-faire was arguably able to assimilate anti-discrimination legislation without too much difficulty, since the latter was not directly concerned with setting the level and substance of terms and conditions of employment: it operated on a framework of labour standards which was brought into being by other means. If the premises of collective laissez-faire have ceased to operate in the British system of labour law, it is for quite separate reasons to do with the neo-liberal reform agenda of the 1980s.[2]

This chapter continues with an account of the background to the principal anti-discrimination statutes and then briefly examines the nature of their aims and impact. This is followed by an account of the legal concept of discrimination, by an examination of the scope of the general protection against employment discrimination, and by studies of two areas requiring specific analysis, namely equal pay and family-related rights. We conclude with an analysis of the law governing disability discrimination for which, because it is to some extent *sui generis*, a separate treatment is needed.

THE ORIGINS, RATIONALES AND IMPACT OF EQUAL TREATMENT LEGISLATION

Historical development and influences

6.2   The present legislation on equal treatment in employment has been influenced by diverse social and political forces; these include the pressure exercised by campaigning groups and also, to a degree not matched elsewhere in labour law, the models established in other jurisdictions and also given expression in transnational labour standards, in particular those contained in European Community law. The statutory form taken by the principle of equal treatment in this country is heavily reliant on the model first established by the US Civil Rights Act of 1964, while European Community law, which had a marginal effect initially, has become increasingly important in shaping the form and substance of the law of equal pay and sex discrimination and has thereby indirectly also influenced race relations law. In recent years it has been crucial to the introduction of legislation prohibiting discrimination on grounds of sexual orientation and religion or belief.

---

2   See ch 1 above.

Early campaigns for sexual and racial equality

6.3   The campaign for equal pay and equal access of men and women to employment goes back well into the nineteenth century, when it was linked to the causes of factory reform and the extension of the right to vote in public elections. The first government inquiry was undertaken at the end of the 1914–1918 war,[3] and in the following year Parliament passed the Sex Disqualification (Removal) Act 1919 which abolished formal restrictions on women entering certain professions (including the solicitors' profession), the civil service and the universities. Section 1 provided that 'a person shall not be disqualified by sex or marriage from the exercise of any public function, or from being appointed to or holding any judicial office or post or from entering or assuming or carrying on any profession or vocation'. Many trade union campaigns for equal pay had at this time a dual rationale of advancing women's rights while also maintaining the model of the male worker's 'breadwinner wage'; 'support among trade unionists for equal pay was, in effect, a demand for protection of male employment',[4] since it was expected that increases in women's pay would neutralise their value to employers as a source of 'cheap labour'. There was also a strong lobby among trade unionists at the time of the Trade Boards Act 1909 which 'wanted more protective legislation to restrict the extent of female labour' on the grounds that 'women should not have to engage in waged work'.[5] Both world wars saw a great influx of female labour into industrial occupations where they carried out jobs which had previously been restricted to men. The response of the industrial unions during the second world war was to support the campaign for the phased introduction of equal pay, which began in the public sector, and to couple this with demands for nurseries and a right to maternity pay. After the war the TUC echoed the call for the introduction of equal pay in public-sector employment, but it was not until 1961 that it called on the government to take measures to implement ILO Convention No 100 of 1951 on Remuneration for Men and Women Workers, and only in 1963 did it make its first clear recommendation of legislation.[6]

A number of local authorities introduced the principle of equal pay for equal work for men and women in their employment in the 1920s. However, in *Roberts v Hopwood*[7] this practice was successfully challenged as being *ultra vires*, with Lord Atkinson describing as unlawful payment systems which were movitated by 'eccentric principles of socialistic philanthropy, or by a feminist ambition to secure the equality of the sexes'.[8] The inter-war period also saw judicial confirmation of the marriage bar, or the practice of dismissing women upon marriage which was common in the case of schoolteachers employed by local authorities, notwithstanding the apparently clear words of the Sex Disqualification (Removal) Act 1919.[9] Further progress in this area had to wait until after 1945. In 1955 the government accepted the principle of equal pay in

3   *Report on the War Cabinet Committee on Women in Industry*, Cmd 135, 1918.
4   Meehan, 1985: p 37.
5   J Morris, 1986: p 221. Nor was it impossible for this attitude to be expressed in public relatively recently: Meehan, 1985: p 41, reports that in 1973 a trade union official 'told the Select Committee on Expenditure that he did not believe in women working'.
6   Meehan, 1985: pp 37–38.
7   [1925] AC 578.
8   [1925] AC 578, 594.
9   *Price v Rhondda Urban District Council* [1923] 2 Ch 372; *Short v Poole Corpn* [1926] Ch 66. A major weakness of the Act was its failure to provide an aggrieved individual with a remedy for its breach.

the civil service and, shortly afterwards, in other areas of public-sector employment including education and local government.[10] When a Labour government was elected in 1964 there was at first a reluctance to legislate, but a series of strikes over equal pay helped force the government's hand and a commitment to introduce statutory mechanisms was made in 1968 by the Secretary of State for Employment and Productivity, Barbara Castle.[11] The result was the Equal Pay Act 1970, which embodied a limited version of equal pay for equal work: the right to equality was confined to situations where a female worker could point to a male worker in the same employment who was employed on 'like work' or 'work rated as equivalent' by a job evaluation scheme instituted by the employer. Since there was no means of requiring an employer to adopt job evaluation or of challenging the results of a particular job evaluation scheme, this was something less than the principle of 'equal pay for work of equal value' contained in ILO Recommendation No 90.[12] This stipulated that:

> ... where appropriate for the purpose of facilitating the determination of rates or remuneration in accordance with the principle of equal remuneration for men and women workers for work of equal value, each Member should, in agreement with the employers' and workers' organisations concerned, establish or encourage the establishment of methods for objective appraisal of the work to be performed, whether by job analysis or by other procedures, with a view to providing a classification of jobs without regard to sex ...[13]

Moreover, the implementation of the 1970 Act was to be delayed for five years, in order to give employers time to adjust, as well as encouraging voluntary compliance through collective bargaining. When the Act was finally brought into force, Parliament enacted, at the same time, the Sex Discrimination Act 1975 which embodied a more general principle of equal treatment in employment, proscribing discrimination against applicants, employees and other employed persons on the grounds of sex.

The common law took the view that race discrimination, like sex discrimination, was a legitimate exercise of the employer's right to freedom of contract.[14] In the absence of any equivalent to the Sex Disqualification (Removal) Act 1919 for acts of racial discrimination,[15] no precise legal means were available to prise open access to particular occupations and employments until the 1960s. The catalyst for reform was provided by the large-scale entry into the United Kingdom of immigrants from the 'new commonwealth' during the post-war boom. The Race Relations Acts of 1965 and 1968 were part of a cross-party consensus 'that there was a need to control the numbers of immigrants and a requirement to eradicate the discrimination that was increasingly being directed at those already settled in Britain. Thus a twin strategy – inherently contradictory – was adopted',[16] which saw the enactment of anti-discrimination legislation on the one hand and the introduction of curbs over entry into the United Kingdom

---

10   Meehan, 1985: p 43. See Fredman and Morris, 1989: ch 9.
11   Meehan, 1985: p 38.
12   The Recommendation is more precise, in this respect, than ILO Convention No 100, which was adopted in the same year (1951).
13   Art 5. Cf Convention No 100, Art 2.
14   This was a consequence of Lord Davey's often-cited dictum in *Allen v Flood* [1898] AC 1, 172, that an 'employer may refuse to employ [an individual] for the most mistaken, capricious, malicious or morally reprehensible motives that can be conceived, but the workman has no right of action against him'. See also *Nagle v Feilden* [1966] 2 QB 633.
15   See *Weinberger v Inglis (No 2)* [1919] AC 606.
16   Mirza, 1995: p 1; see Hepple, 1968; Sooben, 1990.

by immigration legislation on the other. The Race Relations Act 1965 prohibited racial segregation and discrimination in public places such as hotels, restaurants, dance halls and sports grounds; it did not touch on employment, or on the question of access to housing. Awareness of the legal issues surrounding racial discrimination in employment was raised by the Street Report which was published in 1967 by Political and Economic Planning (the forerunner of the Policy Studies Institute);[17] however, the Race Relations Act 1968 stopped short of establishing a fully effective set of measures for combating discrimination. This was in part because of 'concerted action by the TUC and the CBI who both argued against legal intervention, preferring to maintain the tradition of voluntarism'.[18] Although the Act introduced the right to equal treatment on the grounds of race for both applicants and individuals in employment, it contained a rather complex dispute resolution procedure, as part of which individuals had to complain to the Secretary of State who could then refer the matter to voluntary arbitration or to the Race Relations Board.

The influence of US civil rights legislation

6.4 The strengthening of anti-discrimination legislation which took place in the 1970s borrowed directly from the model established in Title VII of the US Civil Rights Act 1964. The Civil Rights Act was the federal legislature's response to the civil rights movement and its campaign for equality of access to facilities and jobs and for equal treatment within employment. The main target of the Act was discrimination based on race and colour; a prohibition on sex discrimination was added at a late stage, initially by opponents of the measure who thought it might discredit it. In other respects, though, the addition of sex discrimination was a natural extension of an earlier measure, the federal Equal Pay Act of 1963, and of a number of equal treatment statutes at state level.[19] In addition to prohibiting 'disparate treatment' based on an individual's race or sex, the 1964 Act was interpreted as applying also to 'disparate impact' or measures which, while facially neutral, disproportionately affected one racial group, or the members of one sex, as opposed to the other. A classic example of this was the use of aptitude tests which tended to exclude members of racial minorities from access to particular grades or occupations. The concept of disparate impact, arrived at by the Supreme Court in *Griggs v Duke Power Co*,[20] greatly extended the reach of the law. The Sex Discrimination Act 1975 incorporated a version of disparate impact which, in the British context, has come to be termed 'indirect discrimination' to distinguish it from 'direct discrimination' or disparate treatment.[21] The Act of 1975, like the Equal Pay Act 1970, provided for an individual right of recourse to an employment tribunal; this right was extended to cases of racial discrimination in the Race Relations Act 1976, which also embodied the concept of indirect discrimination. A further important feature of this legislation was the establishment of bodies, outside the departmental structure of central government, charged with the task of monitoring the new law, supporting litigation financially and with advice, and themselves having powers to enforce certain of its provisions: these bodies were

17   Street *et al*, 1967.
18   Mirza, 1995: p 3.
19   See generally Meehan, 1985: ch 2.
20   401 US 424 (1971).
21   See below, paras 6.20–6.31.

the Equal Opportunities Commission and the Commission for Racial Equality.[22]

American influence was also important in the adoption of the Disability Discrimination Act 1995.[23] Two federal US statutes, the Rehabilitation Act 1973 and the Americans with Disabilities Act 1990, provided a conceptual basis for legislation aimed at combating disability discrimination, in particular through the notion of the employer's duty to make reasonable accommodation for the known physical or mental incapacities of an otherwise qualified applicant or employee. Legislation embodying the US approach was adopted in Canada, Australia and New Zealand in the 1970s and 1980s. Private members' bills were unsuccessfully introduced in the UK Parliament every year from 1982 and a number of extra-Parliamentary organisations maintained a campaign for reform under the umbrella group Voluntary Organisations for Anti-Discrimination Legislation (later renamed the Right Now Campaign). The then Conservative government brought forward the 1995 Act apparently in order to forestall a more far-reaching private members' bill, the Civil Rights (Disabled Persons) Bill. The 1995 Act reflected this rather lukewarm support of the government of the day, since it was by far the weakest of the principal anti-discrimination statutes, although it has been strengthened considerably by important amendments, introduced to comply with European Union law, which came into force in 2004.

The influence of European Community law

6.5   The United Kingdom's membership of the European Community appears to have had little or no influence on the form and substance of the Sex Discrimination Act 1975. Lord Lester, who in the mid-1970s was a special adviser on discrimination law to the Home Secretary, has explained that the Act was drafted without regard to the draft of the Equal Treatment Directive, which was being prepared at around the same time and which was adopted in 1976.[24] The full significance of European Community law as a source of UK law in this area only began to become clear following the ruling of the ECJ in the second *Defrenne* case,[25] to the effect that the principle of equal pay for equal work in Article 119 (now 141) of the EC Treaty had direct effect in national law.

Article 119 owed its presence in the Treaty of Rome to a compromise on the issue of social policy harmonisation which was made at the time of the Treaty's adoption. Article 119, together with Article 120 concerning annual paid leave, represented limited concessions to the possibility that economic integration could be impeded by distortions of competition arising from social policy differences between Member States. The Community essentially adopted the position taken by a group of experts chaired by the Swedish economist Bertil Ohlin, whose 1956 Report for the ILO looked into the question of labour costs and economic integration. Ohlin rejected pleas for general harmonisation of social policy, on

---

22   Further significant amendments were made to RRA 1976 by the Race Relations (Amendment) Act 2000, which (among other things) imposed a general duty on specified public authorities, when carrying out their functions, to have regard to the need to 'eliminate unlawful racial discrimination' and 'to promote equality of opportunity and good relations between persons of different racial groups' (RRA 1976, s 71, as amended by RR(A)A 2000, s 2). See O'Cinneide, 2001.

23   See Doyle, 1995, 1996; Gooding, 1996; Stacey and Short, 2000.

24   See Lester, 1994.

25   Case 43/75 *Defrenne v SA Belge de Navigation Aérienne* [1976] ECR 455.

the grounds that differences in costs *between* Member States were a reflection, by and large, of differences in the relative productivity of labour. However, Ohlin also accepted that in some instances, transnational harmonisation of social policy was needed to eliminate 'such discrepancies within each country as would substantially distort international trade'. The problem arose not because the general level of wages in a given country might be low in comparison to that in another, but because, instead, an industry might enjoy an advantage in terms of wage levels and/or social charges which were exceptionally low in relation to the general level of costs in *that country*. If this advantage was unrelated to productivity, 'the whole situation is economically unsound' and workers and employers in other countries could justifiably complain about 'unfair competition'. The low-cost producer would obtain the benefit of what was in effect a subsidy, since differences in national exchange rates, which reflect general prices and productivity within states, would not cancel out the advantage enjoyed by just one industry. In particular:

> ... a certain distortion of international competition arises from differences in the extent to which the principle of equal pay for men and women applies in different countries. Countries in which there are large wage differentials by sex will pay relatively low wages in industries employing a large proportion of female labour and these industries will enjoy what might be considered a special advantage over their competitors abroad where differentials according to sex are smaller or non-existent.[26]

In *Defrenne v SA Belge de Navigation Aérienne* the ECJ affirmed the economic origins of Article 119 by stating that it had a 'double aim, which is at once economic and social'.[27] Its economic purpose was to 'avoid a situation in which undertakings established in States which have actually implemented the principle of equal pay suffer a competitive disadvantage in intra-Community competition as compared with undertakings established in States which have not yet eliminated discrimination against women workers as regards pay'.[28] But at the same time, Article 119 was 'part of the social objectives of the Community, which is not merely an economic union, but is at the same time intended, by common action, to ensure social progress and to seek the constant improvement of the living and working conditions of their peoples'.[29] As we shall examine further below,[30] the Court has since given Article 141 (as it has become) a broad interpretation at the same time as ensuring that its direct effect, which here is both horizontal and vertical, means that individuals have the benefit of its protection, regardless of the position adopted in national legislation.

In addition to Article 141, the Equal Pay Directive of 1975[31] and the Equal Treatment Directive of 1976[32] have also had a substantial impact on domestic law. The 1975 Directive led to the amendment in 1983 of the Equal Pay Act 1970, introducing the principle of equal pay for work of equal value, after the ECJ had held in favour of the Commission in infringement proceedings brought against the UK under Article 189 (now consolidated in Articles 226–228) of the

---

26 ILO, 1956: p 107.
27 Case 43/75 [1976] ECR 455, at para 12.
28 Case 43/75 [1976] ECR 455, at para 9.
29 Case 43/75 [1976] ECR 455, at para 10.
30 See para 6.74 below.
31 Directive 75/117.
32 Directive 76/207.

Treaty.[33] The impact of the Equal Treatment Directive has been felt in a number of areas including the removal of protective legislation limiting women's working hours and access to particular kinds of employment,[34] the imposition of equal retirement ages for men and women[35] and the extension of the rights of pregnant workers.[36] The ECJ's broad interpretation of Article 141 caused upheaval in the law of occupational pensions following its decision in 1990 in *Barber v Guardian Royal Exchange Assurance Group*,[37] and also contributed to the removal in 1995 of legislation discriminating against part-time workers by excluding those working for fewer than 8 or, in some cases, 16 hours, from employment protection rights. In *R v Secretary of State for Employment, ex p EOC*[38] the House of Lords, applying principles of European Community law which had been fashioned by the ECJ, decided that these qualifying thresholds amounted to indirect sex discrimination on the grounds that they significantly affected women more than men and could not be justified by reference to wider considerations of social and economic policy.

If the impact of European Community law on the law of sex discrimination and equal pay has been immense, it has also had an important if indirect impact on the law of racial discrimination. This is because, in practice, it proved politically impossible to introduce certain improvements to sex discrimination law without also extending them to the Race Relations Act: thus when the statutory upper limit on compensation for acts of sex discrimination was removed following the ruling of the ECJ in *Marshall v Southampton and South West Hampshire Health Authority (No 2)*,[39] it was felt both desirable and necessary to take the same step under the Race Relations Act.[40]

European Community law has also provided the context for attempts to extend the principle of equal treatment into new areas. The open-ended quality of Article 141 and the various directives relating to equal treatment has provided opportunities for innovative interpretations which are not available under the more rigidly-confined terms of domestic legislation. In *P v S and Cornwall County Council*[41] the ECJ accepted that discrimination against a transsexual was an infringement of the Equal Treatment Directive; however, in *Grant v South West Trains Ltd*[42] it held that discrimination on the grounds of an

---

33   Case 61/81 *EC Commission v United Kingdom of Great Britain and Northern Ireland* [1982] ICR 578.

34   In the SDA 1986 and the EA 1989. See Deakin, 1990a; below, para 6.55.

35   SDA 1986, introduced following the decision of the ECJ in Case 152/84 *Marshall v Southampton and South West Hampshire Health Authority* [1986] IRLR 140.

36   See generally paras 6.97–6.103 below.

37   Case C-262/88 [1990] IRLR 240; see below, para 6.96.

38   [1994] IRLR 176; see below, paras 6.24 and 6.30. The EOC's case was argued under Art 119 and the Equal Treatment Directive. Although the House of Lords was content to decide the case solely by reference to the Directive, other courts subsequently decided that Art 119 was also applicable here, so as to give the norm of European Community law both horizontal and vertical direct effect in this context.

39   Case C-271/91 [1993] IRLR 445; SI 1993/2798.

40   Race Relations (Remedies) Act 1994.

41   Case C-13/94 [1996] IRLR 347. Following this judgment, the relevant UK law was amended by the Sex Discrimination (Gender Reassignment) Regulations 1999, SI 1999/1102. On discrimination against transsexuals, see para 6.35 below.

42   Case C-249/96 [1998] IRLR 206. The conceptual approach of the ECJ in *Grant* was broadly followed by the House of Lords in *MacDonald v Advocate General for Scotland, Pearce v Governing Body of Mayfield School* [2003] IRLR 512. On discrimination on the grounds of sexual orientation, see below, para 6.37.

individual's sexual orientation did not contravene Article 141, using reasoning which appeared to cast doubt on the broad application of the equality principle which it had made in *P v S*. The Court has also given an important but qualified recognition to the possibility of affirmative action under EC law.[43]

The continuing importance of EC law in the legislative field was confirmed by the adoption through the Treaty of Amsterdam in 1997 of what is now Article 13 of the EC Treaty. This provided a new power to the Community to legislate across the whole range of discrimination issues including sex, sexual orientation, racial or ethnic origin, religion and belief, disability, and age. Two Directives were adopted in 2000 under this provision. The Race Directive[44] prohibits discrimination on the grounds of race and ethnic or national origin in respect of a range of matters relating to employment, social protection, social advantages, and access to goods and services. Implementation took place in 2003.[45] The so-called Framework Directive[46] prohibits discrimination in relation to employment and occupation on the grounds of religion or belief, disability, age, and sexual orientation. The provisions on religion, belief and sexual orientation were implemented in 2003; those relating to disability in 2004.[47] Those relating to age must be implemented by 2 December 2006.[48] Other recent EC measures include the Burden of Proof Directive of 1997,[49] which altered the meaning of the concept of discrimination in the context of sex discrimination law,[50] and a Directive of 2002[51] which amends the 1976 Directive on equal treatment for men and women in employment.

Conceptions of the principle of equality

6.6 As a consequence of these developments, the legal principle of equal treatment in employment, at least with regard to sex and race discrimination, is now firmly established. However, the rapid pace of legal change has tended to obscure some underlying uncertainties concerning the nature and rationale of this body of legislation. Within the law as it currently stands there are several different, competing conceptions of the equality principle.

---

43 Case C-409/95 *Marschall v Land Nordrhein-Westfalen* [1998] IRLR 39; cf Case C-450/93 *Kalanke v Freie Hansestadt Bremen* [1995] IRLR 660; see below, para 6.32.
44 Directive 2000/43/EC. See further para 6.39 below.
45 By virtue of the Race Relations Act 1976 (Amendment) Regulations 2003, SI 2003/1626.
46 Directive 2000/78/EC.
47 By virtue of the Employment Equality (Sexual Orientation) Regulations, SI 2003/1661 (henceforth referred to as EE(SO)R); the Employment Equality (Religion or Belief) Regulations, SI 2003/1660 (henceforth referred to as EE(RB)R); and the Disability Discrimination Act 1995 (Amendment) Regulations 2003, SI 2003/1673. The provisions relating to disability were not required to be implemented until 2 December 2006.
48 It should also be noted that the European Convention on Human Rights, in Art 14, contains a prohibition of discrimination on grounds of 'sex, race, colour, language, religion, political or other opinion, national or social origin, association with a national minority, property, birth or other status', but this only covers discriminatory treatment in relation to the 'enjoyment of the rights and freedoms set forth in this Convention'. It is therefore necessary to find that the discriminatory treatment falls within the ambit of one of the other Convention rights.
49 Directive 97/80/EC.
50 See in particular para 6.18 below.
51 Directive 2002/73/EC. The provisions of this measure must be implemented by October 2005.

Protection of the dignity and autonomy of the individual

6.7   The principal conception is that of equal treatment as part of the individual worker's right to respect for their *personal dignity*: each person has the right to be treated on the basis of their individual characteristics, merits and achievements, and not on the basis of stereotypical assumptions about them which are based solely on their sex or race. This was clearly recognised in the White Paper, *Equality for Women*, which preceded the Sex Discrimination Act 1975: 'the variations of character and ability within each sex are greater and more significant than the differences between the sexes'.[52] Feminist social and legal theory has shown that many of the assumed differences between men and women in terms of their capacity for particular kinds of tasks are not the product of differences between the biological sexes, but are based on assumptions originating in social practices which are nationally and historically contingent and, in many cases, backed up by legal rules either requiring or condoning segregation and discrimination.[53]

Remedying group disadvantage

6.8   The notion of the right to equal treatment as the *individual's* right to personal dignity is most clearly reflected in the concept of direct discrimination, which is the legal form of the principle that 'like should be treated alike'.[54] But there is an immediate tension with a second conception of the equality principle, which sees its rationale as remedying the social and economic disadvantage suffered by particular *groups*.[55] From the point of view of direct discrimination, the unequal treatment of men on the grounds of their sex or of white individuals on the basis of their colour is inherently wrong, and a breach of the personal rights of the individuals concerned, as the unequal treatment of women and of blacks is for the same reasons; if, however, remedying collective disadvantage is the aim of anti-discrimination legislation, space should be created for measures designed to enhance the standing and opportunities of those groups who were previously the victims of unequal treatment, if necessary through affirmative action which may involve an element of 'reverse discrimination'. Title VII of the US Civil Rights Act incorporated a compromise between these two ideas: the prohibition on disparate treatment was broadly worded and came to be interpreted in such a way as to permit certain limited forms of affirmative action on the basis of past disadvantages suffered by particular groups.[56] In addition, it was coupled with the enactment of Federal Executive Order 11246 which instituted a wide-ranging programme of contract compliance, aimed at

52   Cmnd 5724, 1974, at para 16.
53   See Pannick, 1985: pp 14 *et seq*; Fredman, 1997c: ch 1. There is a potentially important analytical distinction here between practices which are based on *gender*, that is to say on the *assumed or attributed characteristics* of men and women, and those based on the biological differences between the sexes (see Oakley, 1972); the vast majority of acts of 'sex discrimination', as the law describes it, fall into the former category. The term 'sex discrimination' is the term given by the law to what may more accurately be referred to as 'gender discrimination'; in this book we use the phrase 'sex discrimination' because of the legal meaning which it has come to acquire, but this is not to assume that the practices which constitute sex discrimination in the eyes of the law are based on biological factors.
54   See below, paras 6.12–6.19.
55   Lacey, 1992; and on the relationship between discrimination law and social inclusion, see H Collins, 2003.
56   *United Steelworkers of America v Weber* 443 US 193 (1979); see below, para 6.32.

requiring government contractors to promote affirmative action in their own personnel policies. More recently, the practices made possible by these legal means have come under substantial attack, both politically and in the federal courts.

In Britain, the issue of affirmative action was dealt with differently from the start. The definition of direct discrimination in the Acts of 1975 and 1976 was much more precisely formulated than its counterpart in the Civil Rights Act 1964, in such a way as clearly to rule out reverse discrimination; this was a conscious policy choice to which only one formal concession was made, in the case of training designed to benefit members of a particular sexual or racial group which was under-represented in an area of employment or in a particular organisation.[57]

There is a more general difficulty in attempting to use the legislative model established in the Civil Rights Act and in the UK anti-discrimination statutes to promote greater sexual and racial equality. The notion that 'like should be treated alike' requires comparisons to be made on the basis of a 'white male norm' which may be inappropriate: 'the doctrine inherently assumed that the goal is assimilation to an existing standard without questioning the desirability of that standard'.[58] A strict comparison of 'like with like' is capable of being counter-productive where the rights of (female) part-time workers are compared to those of (male) full-timers,[59] or where the position of pregnant women is compared to that of men who are absent from work on account of illness.[60] In both these cases, notwithstanding the use of the equality principle to bring about far-reaching improvements, there is a case for saying that improvements in the position of the disadvantaged group would best be brought about by regulation which deals with the specific situation in question, such as legislation outlawing the adverse treatment of part-timers and pregnant workers as such, and not by always attempting to fit these cases into the framework provided by anti-discrimination legislation.[61]

Equality and the market order

6.9 A third conception of equality sees its role differently again, namely in terms of the promotion of *equality within a market order*:[62] here the principal aim is to do what is necessary to ensure free and equal competition in the labour market, but to regulate outcomes in terms of the distribution of economic and social resources as little as possible. The view of equality legislation which sees it in terms of opening access and extending competition is hostile to equal value legislation, on the grounds that this is an unwarranted interference with the outcomes of private bargaining; on the other hand, it might be favourably disposed to certain affirmative action policies designed to break down women's entry into previously closed occupations and professions.[63] However, many

---

57 SDA 1975, ss 47–48; RRA 1976, ss 37–38.
58 Finley, 1986: p 1143; see also Fredman, 1992b, 1997c: ch 1.
59 Case C-399/92 *Stadt Lengerich v Helmig* [1995] IRLR 216, discussed below at paras 6.88, 6.91 and 6.121.
60 *Webb v EMO Air Cargo Ltd* [1993] IRLR 27, HL; refd [1994] IRLR 482, ECJ; *(No 2)* [1995] IRLR 645, HL; see below, at para 6.96.
61 See Finley, 1986; Hepple, 1990a; Fredman, 1994b.
62 See the discussions of Deakin, 1990a; Fredman, 1992b, 1997c: ch 9, part III; McColgan, 1997.
63 Fischel and Lazear, 1986.

neoliberal accounts are simply against anti-discrimination legislation in principle, on the grounds that the free market is capable of arriving at the necessary economic equilibrium unaided and that the interference with freedom of contract which all such legislation entails is illegitimate. According to Becker's influential economic theory of discrimination, discrimination on grounds of sex or race arises from employers' subjective preferences or 'tastes'; if certain employers behave irrationally, for example hiring men when women would work more productively, the market will require them to pay a price in the form of competition from employers who have no such predelictions.[64] Where there is job segregation, it is often explicable, according to Becker, on the basis of individual choice: women, by preferring domestic responsibilities over continuous participation in the labour market, thereby 'choose' to diminish their own human capital, and to reduce their value to employers.[65] This point of view has been challenged by labour market segmentation theory, which stresses the institutional forces shaping labour supply decisions and the role of customary assumptions about relative worth which tend to undervalue the labour of particular groups. From this point of view, the 'unregulated' labour market is one in which social norms serve to reinforce racial and sexual stereotypes, thereby opening up the possibility of institutionalised discrimination and providing an economic basis for more extensive legal intervention.[66]

There are elements in the law of equal treatment which support both of these approaches. Equal value legislation, for example, openly challenges the assumption that rankings arrived at by job evaluation systems are necessarily objective. On the other hand, there is a sense in which anti-discrimination legislation can also be used to justify the removal, as part of a policy of deregulation, of practices whose aim is principally protective. One of the results of the Equal Treatment Directive, for example, has been the removal from domestic law of protective legislation regulating nightwork by women and limiting their exposure to certain dangerous substances; when the relevant legislation was repealed by the Sex Discrimination Act 1986 and the Employment Act 1989, nothing was put in its place, although the alternative would have been to enact a general measure providing protection for *all* workers.[67] The point is that there is nothing in Article 141 or in the Equality Directives which specifically requires what may be called 'levelling up' of the disadvantaged group to the level of the advantaged group.[68] An example of the problems this creates is provided by the occupational pension case, *Smith v Avdel Systems Ltd*,[69] in which the ECJ condoned employers' practice of raising the pensionable age of women from 60 to 65, in order to achieve formal equality with male employees. In short, in certain of its guises the equality principle is only capable of dealing with the issue of 'horizontal equality' between comparable individuals or groups; it may have nothing to say about 'vertical equality', or the redistribution of social and economic resources between groups in the labour market hierarchy. In so far as equality legislation achieves such a redistribution,

---

64   Becker, 1971.
65   Becker, 1975. See Mayhew and Addison, 1983.
66   See Rubery, 1988; Rubery, *et al*, 1989; Deakin and Wilkinson, 1992; Humphries and Rubery, 1995.
67   See Deakin, 1990a. A similar debate took place in France in regard to Art L 213-1 *et seq* of the French *Code du Travail*, which were declared incompatible with Directive 76/307 by the ECJ (Case C-345/89 *Re Stoeckel* [1991] ECR I-4047).
68   Deakin, 1995a.
69   Case C-408/92 [1994] IRLR 602.

it only does so in conjunction with other forms of social protection, including collective bargaining and regulatory legislation, which set a floor of minimum standards upon which any 'equalisation' of rights must build, and in conjunction with more results-orientated forms of affirmative action in support of disadvantaged groups.

The impact of anti-discrimination legislation

6.10 This last point highlights some of the reasons for the limited impact, in certain respects, of equal treatment legislation in Britain: UK legislation tends to be characterised by an emphasis on horizontal as opposed to vertical equality and accepts only a marginal role for affirmative action, and is heavily dependent on other regulatory instruments, in particular collective bargaining, for its effective implementation. Following the passage of the Equal Pay Act in 1970 there was a substantial narrowing of the pay gap between men and women. Average hourly wages for women, which had been below 60% of men's in 1970, rose to over 70% by 1980. Although incomes policies, which at this time embodied a strong tendency to favour the lower paid, may also have contributed to the narrowing of the pay gap, it has been argued that neither incomes policies nor changes in the industrial structure would have been decisive on their own; instead, the Act itself was chiefly responsible for the change, in combination with the use of centralised pay bargaining to achieve equalisation.[70] Thus the improvement began in the early 1970s, before the Act came into force, as sector-level collective agreements were voluntarily amended in anticipation of the law becoming formally operative.[71] As originally enacted, the Act contained a mechanism by which payment structures of this kind could be amended by an award of the Central Arbitration Committee,[72] and the threat of this legal sanction appears to have directly influenced collective bargaining behaviour. What this finding suggests is that the Act was successful because it was combined with an effective collective procedure for enhancing pay and conditions. There is ample evidence, by contrast, that individual actions for pay equality are extremely costly and difficult to mount, are diffuse in their effects and often unsatisfactory for the workers concerned, who may face subsequent victimisation.[73] Since 1986, however, when the CAC's jurisdiction over equal pay issues was repealed,[74] the individual route is effectively all that remains. It is not clear whether the introduction of equal value legislation in 1983 has been responsible for the small but steady improvement in the relative position of women's pay since then: for example, the proportion of female to male full-time hourly earnings rose from 75% in 1988 to 79% in 1992 and 82% in 2000, where it has remained since.[75] One possible cause of the improvement in the 1990s was the combination of a decline in the degree of occupational segregation and a rise in women's full-time working.[76] More generally, the decline of sector-level collective

---

70 Zabalza and Tsannatos, 1985.
71 Zabalza and Tsannatos, 1985.
72 EqPA 1970, s 3, repealed by the SDA 1986; see below, para 6.95. Prior to 1975 the relevant body was the Industrial Arbitration Board.
73 See Leonard, 1987; Fredman 1997c: pp 251 *et seq*.
74 See below, para 6.95.
75 For recent figures, see Equal Opportunities Commission, *Facts about Women and Men in Great Britain* (2005). For part-time workers, the gender pay gap is much higher at 40%.
76 Hakim, 1993: p 107.

bargaining in Britain poses a major problem for the full implementation of the principle of equal pay for work of equal value: a comparative study of gender inequality in OECD countries concluded that 'a centralised industrial relations system, high levels of public employment relative to total employment and sustained expenditure on active labour market programmes are most likely to deliver relatively high earnings for women', and that as a result 'the emancipatory potential of legislative moves will be best enhanced within a "collective" framework'.[77]

For similar reasons, the failure of the Race Relations Act 1976 to counter increasing levels of relative poverty and unemployment among ethnic minority groups needs to be put in the context not simply of the limits to the role of the law in economic and social regulation, but also of the clear shortcomings of that particular legislation.[78] The unemployment rate for all ethnic minorities is over twice that for whites, although it should be noted that there are significant variations in the activity rates of different ethnic groups.[79] There is evidence of institutionalised racial discrimination both in recruitment and in the selection of workers for redundancy. Weaknesses in the Act of 1976 included difficulties inherent in the burden of proof in discrimination cases; the lack of a class action procedure; the complexity of the statutory definition of indirect discrimination; the large range of exemptions contained in the Act; and the failure to entrench the Act against other legislative measures which may contradict its aims. Research in the mid-1990s showed that success rates in race discrimination cases before employment tribunals were about 20%, which was about half the rate for sex discrimination and unfair dismissal cases, and that race discrimination cases were the most likely to be withdrawn and the least likely to be settled without a hearing.[80] These and other difficulties were raised by the CRE in two reviews of the legislation in the 1980s and 1990s[81] as well as by independent research.[82] Since that time, as we shall see in more detail in the following sections of this chapter, the 1976 Act has been substantially amended, and many of the structural weaknesses referred to above have been addressed. It remains to be seen what the impact these relatively recent changes will have.

THE CONCEPT OF DISCRIMINATION

6.11   The principal UK anti-discrimination statutes, the SDA 1975 and the RRA 1976, contain a two-fold definition of discrimination. *Direct discrimination* denotes unequal treatment based on the relevant prohibited grounds, while *indirect discrimination* describes inequality resulting from the application of a provision or practice which is neutral on its face, but which has a disadvantageous effect upon the members of one group (for example, the members of one sex, or a particular racial group) as opposed to another. The distinction between the two

---

77   Whitehouse, 1992: p 63; see also McColgan, 1997.
78   See Hepple, 1991, and D Bell, 1992 for an assessment of the limited impact of civil rights legislation in the USA.
79   For data from the 1980s and 1990s, see R Jenkins, 1988: pp 314–315 and McCrudden *et al*, 1991; for more recent governmental figures on ethnic minority employment and unemployment, see *Labour Market Trends*, December 2003, p 599.
80   Mirza, 1995: p 14.
81   *Review of the Race Relations Act 1976: Proposals for Change*, CRE 1985; *Second Review of the Race Relations Act 1976*, CRE 1992.
82   McCrudden *et al*, 1991; Hepple *et al*, 2000.

categories is important principally because in the case of indirect discrimination, the legislation grants the employer (or other respondent) the benefit of a potentially broad defence of justification. It is not quite true to say that adverse treatment of the kind involved in direct discrimination can never be justified; such justification is, in effect, the function of the statutory genuine occupational qualifications[83] and of certain exceptions to the equality principle which are expressly laid down in the legislation itself.[84] The point, though, is that in the case of direct discrimination, the circumstances in which these qualifications and exceptions apply are exhaustively defined by the legislation and may not be added to by the courts, whereas with indirect discrimination the circumstances in which the defence of justification can apply are left open-ended.[85]

If the distinction between the two forms of discrimination is a central issue, its precise basis is elusive.[86] Both the UK courts and the ECJ, in interpreting the relevant provisions of European Community law, have rejected the proposition that direct discrimination is based on the intention or motive of the employer. This has led to emphasis being placed, instead, on the mere existence of a causal link between the adverse treatment suffered by the victim and the illegitimate ground in question. To see the gist of discrimination in terms of the impact on the victim is an important strengthening of the equality principle; as Ellis stresses, 'it is at the very heart of the notion of discrimination that it is the *effect* on its victims with which the law is truly concerned, not the precise nature of the conduct of its perpetrators'.[87] At the same time, by minimising the importance of the employer's intention the courts have, perhaps unavoidably, blurred the boundary between direct and indirect discrimination, leading to suggestions, so far rejected by the ECJ, that, at the level of European Community law, the open-ended justification defence should be extended to cases of direct discrimination.[88]

The division between direct and indirect discrimination is also relevant in the context of the EqPA 1970. It has long been accepted that, as far as possible, the Act of 1970 should be interpreted in tandem with the provisions of the SDA 1975.[89] However, the EqPA 1970 makes no explicit reference to the distinction between direct and indirect discrimination and, although it allows for defences of material difference and 'material factor' which operate in a

---

83 SDA 1975, s 7; RRA 1976, s 5. In the case of discrimination on the grounds of sexual orientation and of religion or belief, these are referred to as 'genuine occupational requirements': see para 6.51 below.

84 See, in particular, SDA 1975, Part V; RRA 1976, Part VI.

85 However, it should be noted that in cases of discrimination falling under the new, widened definition set out in the Framework and Race Directives, the concept of a genuine occupational *requirement*, which provides a defence to claims of both direct and indirect discrimination, is defined in an open-ended way, by contrast to the more narrowly prescribed concept of the genuine occupational *qualification* which dates back to the SDA 1975 and RRA 1976. The effect is arguably to efface part of the distinction which formerly existed between direct and indirect discrimination. On genuine occupational requirements, see RRA 1976, s 4A, EE(SO)R 2003, reg 7 and EE(RB)R 2003, reg 7, and our discussion below, at para 6.51.

86 See Case C-132/92 *Birds Eye Walls Ltd v Roberts* [1994] IRLR 29, 35 (Advocate General Van Gerven).

87 Ellis, 1994: pp 564–565; for discussion, see Watt, 1998.

88 Most notably from Advocate General Van Gerven in his opinions in Case C-152/91 *Neath v Hugh Steeper Ltd* [1994] IRLR 91, Case C-132/92 *Birds Eye Walls Ltd v Roberts* [1994] IRLR 29 and Case C-32/93 *Webb v EMO Air Cargo Ltd* [1994] IRLR 482. See also Bowers and Moran, 2002; Gillard Monaghan, 2003; Bowers, Moran and Honeyball, 2003.

89 *Shields v E Coomes (Holdings) Ltd* [1978] 1 WLR 1408.

manner akin to the defence of justification in indirect discrimination, it does not clearly state that a finding of adverse impact must be made before the employer is required to justify the difference in pay. In *Strathclyde Regional Council v Wallace*[90] Lord Browne-Wilkinson argued that the EqPA 1970 nevertheless had to be considered in the light of the jurisprudence of the ECJ, which, in relation to Article 119 (now 141) of the EC Treaty, had accepted the existence of the distinction between direct and indirect discrimination.[91] This meant that 'in considering section 1(3) of the Equal Pay Act 1970, the only circumstances in which questions of "justification" can arise are those in which the employer is relying on a factor which is sexually discriminatory. There is no question of the employer having to "justify"... all disparities of pay'. This approach broadly aligns the 1970 Act with the general conceptual framework of the principle of equal treatment, although, thanks to the particular way in which the Act is drafted, presumptions of sex discrimination may arise in circumstances where they would not otherwise do so, in which case the employer may, exceptionally, have the burden of demonstrating the absence of adverse impact.[92]

But legislative changes made in the early 2000s have fragmented the previously unified concept of discrimination. This first occurred with a modification of the definition contained in the SDA 1975, which was necessitated by the need to comply with the Burden of Proof Directive of 1997.[93] The Framework Directive and Race Directive of 2000 contained a definition of discrimination which seemed, on the face of it, to be significantly wider than that set out in UK law as it then stood, in particular as it related to indirect discrimination.[94] This widened definition of indirect discrimination has now been incorporated into the RRA 1976,[95] but only to the extent necessary to comply with EC law. The result is that the concept of indirect discrimination appears to have a wider meaning when it is applied to the grounds of race or national or ethnic origins, which are covered by the Race Directive, than it does when applied to the grounds of colour or nationality, which are outside that Directive. This wider definition also applies to discrimination on the grounds of sexual orientation and those of religion or belief,[96] under the provisions of the legislation implementing the relevant parts of the Framework Directive. Although the courts may be able to re-impose a degree of conceptual unity through interpretation of these various provisions, it may be assumed, for the time being at least, that the meaning of the concept of indirect discrimination shifts according to the precise context being considered.[97]

---

90   [1998] 1 WLR 259, 265. Cf. the contrary view of Lord Slynn in *North Yorkshire County Council v Ratcliffe* [1995] ICR 833, 839.

91   In particular, in Case 170/84 *Bilka-Kaufhaus GmbH v Weber von Hartz* [1986] IRLR 317.

92   See our discussion below, at para 6.73.

93   See SDA 1975 s 1(2), as substituted by SI 2001/2660.

94   In each case, this definition is contained in Art 2(2)(b) of the Directive.

95   RRA 1976, s 1A, as inserted by SI 2003/1626.

96   See EE(SO)R 2003, reg 3, and EE(RB)R 2003, reg 3.

97   It should be borne in mind here that the definition of discrimination for sex discrimination purposes will be more or less realigned with the widened definition originating in the Framework and Race Directives by virtue of the changes made to the Equal Treatment Directive by Directive 2002/73/EC: see Directive 76/207/EC, Art. 2, as amended. These must be brought into force in the UK by 5 October 2005. The wider definition is already in place for discrimination against married persons and persons in civil partnerships (SDA 1975, s 3, as amended by the Civil Partnership Act 2004, s 251), although at the time of writing it is not yet in force.

The DDA 1995, in its turn, adopts a further, distinctive concept of discrimination.[98] This test is effectively *sui generis* and is considered in greater detail in the context of our discussion of disability legislation.[99]

Direct discrimination

6.12   Under section 1(2)(a) of the SDA 1975, a person is taken to discriminate against a woman if 'on the ground of her sex he treats her less favourably than he treats or would treat a man'. This provision applies equally to discrimination against a man on the grounds of his sex.[100] Discrimination against a married person on the ground of marital status is also prohibited by the Act.[101] The parallel provision of the RRA 1976 states that a person discriminates against another where 'on racial grounds he treats that other less favourably than he treats or would treat other persons'.[102] Here, the expression 'on racial grounds' means that the scope of the Act is significantly wider than it would have been had it simply relied upon the notion of discrimination on the ground of the *victim's* race; thus under the RRA, the victim of discrimination is entitled to the protection of the law if he or she is victimised on grounds related to the race *of another person* or, more generally, because of the attitude which they take towards racism against others.[103] This is also the case under the regulations governing discrimination on the grounds of sexual orientation and religion or belief. Here, direct discrimination is defined as a situation in which, on the relevant grounds, one person treats another 'less favourably than he treats or would treat other persons'.[104] Thus the sexual orientation or religion or belief in question need not be that of the applicant. It also follows that protection extends to a case in which the respondent acts on a *mistaken* belief concerning, the sexual orientation, or religion or belief, of the applicant or another person.[105] However, the characteristics of the person committing the discriminatory act or omission in question are irrelevant. The Regulations governing religious belief, exceptionally, spell this out: they provide that the reference to 'religion or belief' as prohibited grounds of direct discrimination, does not refer to the religion or belief of the discriminator.[106]

Direct discrimination rests on what in the US law is known as 'disparate treatment': this involves comparing the treatment received by the victim with the treatment which either is or would have been received by persons of a

---

98   DDA 1995, s 3A (as inserted by SI 2003/1673).
99   See paras 6.109–6.112 below.
100 SDA 1975, s 2(1).
101 SDA 1975, s 3.
102 RRA 1976, s 1(1)(a).
103 *Showboat Entertainment Centre Ltd v Owens* [1984] IRLR 7; *Weathersfield Ltd v Sargent* [1998] IRLR 14, [1999] IRLR 94; *MacDonald v A-G for Scotland, Pearce v Governing Body of Mayfield School* [2003] IRLR 512, paras 80–82 (Lord Hope).
104 See, respectively, EE(SO)R 2003, reg 3(1)(a); EE(RB)R 2003, reg 3(1)(a). By contrast, in relation to discrimination on the grounds of gender reassignment, it is the transsexuality of the applicant alone which counts: SDA 1975, s 2A(1).
105 For discussion of this point (on which direct authority is scarce) see DTI, *Explanatory Notes for the Employment Equality (Sexual Orientation) Regulations 2003 and the Employment Equality (Religion or Belief) Regulations 2003* (2003), at para 25.
106 EE(RB)R 2003, reg 3(2); see DTI, *Explanatory Notes for the Employment Equality (Sexual Orientation) Regulations 2003 and the Employment Equality (Religion or Belief) Regulations 2003* (2003), at paras 28–30.

different group. Adapting this notion, the UK legislation provides that the treatment of a person of one sex is to be compared with that of a person of the opposite sex[107] and the treatment of a married person with that of a person of the same sex who is unmarried.[108] In the case of the other prohibited grounds, the comparison is between the treatment of a member of a group defined by reference to the relevant characteristic of the applicant – that is, his or her race, sexual orientation, religion or belief, or transsexuality – with that of all 'other persons'.[109] The comparison of persons must be such that 'the relevant circumstances in the one case are the same, or not materially different, in the other'.[110] This is therefore the principal statutory recognition of the idea that like persons should be treated alike.[111] 'Direct discrimination involves that an individual is not treated on his merits but receives unfavourable treatment because he is a member of a group';[112] by prohibiting it, the law upholds the right of each individual to be treated 'by reference to their own qualities and defects, and not by reference to characteristics commonly associated with persons of their own sex or race'.[113]

'Trivial' forms of differential treatment

6.13   In the first case under the Act of 1975 to reach the higher courts, *Peake v Automotive Products Ltd*,[114] Mr Peake challenged his employer's practice of allowing female shop floor workers to leave five minutes earlier than their male colleagues at the end of a shift. The employer claimed that this was done on the grounds of safety. The EAT, allowing an appeal, held that he had been unlawfully discriminated against; according to Phillips J, section 1(1)(a) 'requires one to look to see what in fact is done amounting to less favourable treatment, and whether it is done to the man or the woman because he [sic] *is* a man or a woman'.[115] However, the Court of Appeal allowed an appeal. Lord Denning MR thought that 'it is not discrimination for mankind to treat womankind with the courtesy and chivalry which we have been taught to believe is right conduct in our society', while Shaw LJ considered that unequal treatment 'involves an element of something which is inherently adverse or hostile to the interests of the persons of the sex which is said to be discriminated against'.[116]

These dicta have not stood the test of time, and *Peake* is now probably best regarded as based on a misreading of the Act. Some of its effects were undone in *Ministry of Defence v Jeremiah*,[117] in which Lord Denning repudiated his earlier comments about chivalry, and attempted to justify the outcome in *Peake* on *de minimis* grounds. This is not a very convincing argument, since the five minutes

---

107 SDA 1975, s 1(2)(a), 2(1).
108 SDA 1975, s 3(1)(a).
109 See, respectively, RRA 1976, s 1(1)(a); EE(SO)R 2003, reg 3(1)(a); EE(RB)R 2003, reg 3(1)(a); SDA, s 2A(1).
110 SDA 1975, s 5(3); RRA 1976, s 3(4); EE(SO)R 2003, reg 3(2); EE(RB)R 2003, reg 3(2). However, there is no equivalent provision in the case of gender reassignment: on this point, see para 6.17 below.
111 Pannick, 1985: pp 19, 26.
112 *West Midlands Passenger Transport Executive v Singh* [1988] ICR 614, 619 (Balcombe LJ).
113 Pannick, 1985, p 37.
114 [1977] QB 780; revsd [1978] QB 233.
115 [1977] QB 780, 787.
116 [1978] QB 233, 238, 240 respectively.
117 [1980] ICR 13.

extra working time per day which the men had to complete takes on a different aspect when it is translated into an extra half-hour or so of work each week. In *Jeremiah* male employees in an ordnance factory were obliged, as a condition of doing overtime, to undertake dirty and uncomfortable work in the factory's colour bursting shop. This condition was not imposed on their female colleagues, partly because they objected to undertaking such work. The Court of Appeal upheld a complaint of sex discrimination and implicitly accepted the view of Phillips J in *Peake*, namely that motive was irrelevant and that a simple test of causation should apply.

Subsequent decisions have limited the application of any *de minimis* principle. In an important case under the provisions of SDA 1975 relating to access to goods and services, *Gill v El Vino Co Ltd*,[118] a female journalist challenged the practice of the well-known Fleet Street wine bar in insisting that women should sit at a table if they wished to be served; men could be served either at the bar or at a table. The practice was held to be discriminatory. On one view, this was because access to service at El Vino's might have been of importance to a journalist in his or her profession,[119] but it is likely that there would have been unlawful discrimination even if this had not been so; the differential treatment of customers could not, in this case, have been thought of as negligible.[120] Similarly, in *Greig v Community Industry*[121] the EAT rejected any suggestion that the refusal of a place on a work experience scheme could be excused on *de minimis* grounds.

Irrelevance of motive: the 'but for' test

6.14   The irrelevance of motive was established in two decisions of the House of Lords, *R v Birmingham County Council, ex p EOC*[122] and *James v Eastleigh Borough Council*.[123] In the former, the Council operated a number of single-sex grammar schools to which entry was by competitive examination; as there were fewer schools for girls than for boys, the pass mark for girls was set at a higher level. This practice was ruled unlawful. According to Lord Goff:

> There is discrimination under the statute if there is less favourable treatment on the ground of sex, in other words if the relevant girl or girls would have received the same treatment as the boys but for their sex. The intention or motive of the defendant to discriminate ... is not a necessary condition to liability; it is perfectly possible to envisage cases where the defendant had no such motive, and yet did in fact discriminate on the ground of sex.[124]

In *James* the issue was whether the Council was entitled to offer free entry to its swimming pool to individuals who had reached the state pensionable age of 65 for men and 60 for women. Mr James, who was 61, complained that he had to pay to gain admission when his wife, who was the same age, did not. The Court of Appeal concluded that this was not a case of direct discrimination, since 'one is looking not to the causative link between the defendant's behaviour and the

---

118 [1983] QB 425.
119 [1983] QB 425, 432 (Griffiths LJ).
120 [1983] QB 425, 431 (Eveleigh LJ).
121 [1979] ICR 356.
122 [1989] IRLR 173.
123 [1990] IRLR 288; see also *Chief Constable of Greater Manchester Police v Hope* [1999] ICR 338.
124 [1989] IRLR 173, 175.

detriment to the plaintiff but to the reason why the defendant treated the plaintiff less favourably'.[125] The House of Lords reversed this ruling by a bare majority. According to Lord Bridge, the criterion of pensionable age was 'no more than a convenient shorthand expression which refers to the age of 60 in a woman and to the age of 65 in a man'; in this context, 'it cannot possibly make any difference whether the alleged discriminator uses the shorthand expression or spells out its full meaning'.[126] Although the Council had no intention to discriminate in favour of women and had acted from the laudable motive of providing a concession to those it assumed were retired and no longer in receipt of income from full-time employment, in adopting the criterion of state pensionable age it relied on a ground which was formally based on the sex of individuals, and so contravened the Act.

It is arguable that the Council could have acted lawfully by making the offer of free admission to those who were *actually* retired from full-time employment, since this group would not necessarily have been coterminous with those who had reached state pensionable age; thanks mainly to early retirements, such a classification would arguably not have been one which was formally based on sex.[127] Had this been the case, the Council's actions could have given rise to a prima facie finding of indirect discrimination, but its reasons for acting would have been relevant to the justification defence. As it was, arguments in favour of the Council's practice could not be weighed in the balance as potentially justifying factors once it had been decided that the discrimination was direct as opposed to indirect.

The effect of *James* is that neither the lack of an intention to discriminate, nor (which is a different thing) a superior motive, will deprive treatment which is substantially connected to an individual's sex or race of its character as direct discrimination.[128] In principle, the applicant must still show that the respondent *treated* him or her less favourably, and in so far as this entails deliberate conduct of some kind it could be said to necessitate the intentional commission of an act constituting the unequal treatment. It has not so far been suggested, in this context, that the anti-discrimination Acts do not prohibit a mere *omission* to extend to one individual a benefit extended to another. The act-omission distinction is without merit here, since treating one person differently from another is both an act and an omission.[129]

'Stereotyping'

6.15   An important principle is that the anti-discrimination legislation catches disparate treatment caused by stereotypical assumptions about the members of

---

125 [1989] IRLR 318, 321 (Browne-Wilkinson VC).

126 [1990] IRLR 288, 291.

127 See G Mead, 1990.

128 The converse is true: the views or beliefs of the respondent do not matter if the objective basis for the treatment in question is non-discriminatory. This is clarified in the context of discrimination based on the grounds of religion or belief, where, seemingly for the avoidance of doubt, it is stated that the reference to religion or belief does not include discrimination based on the religion or belief of the discriminator: EE(RB)R 2003, reg 3(2); DTI, *Explanatory Notes for the Employment Equality (Sexual Orientation) Regulations 2003 and the Employment Equality (Religion or Belief) Regulations 2003* (2003), at paras 28–30.

129 Moreover, anti-discrimination legislation specifies that 'act' includes 'omission': SDA 1975, s 82(1); RRA 1976, s 78(1); EE(SO)R 2003, reg 2(3) and EE(RB)R 2003, reg 2(3) ('deliberate omission').

one group, as opposed to a belief which is specific to a particular individual. In *Horsey v Dyfed County Council*[130] Browne-Wilkinson J thought that the words 'on the grounds of' in the definition of direct discrimination in the SDA 1975 were wide enough to cover 'cases where the alleged discriminator acts on generalised assumptions as to the characteristics of women or married or coloured persons' and not just those cases where 'the sole factor influencing the decision of the alleged discriminator is the sex, marital status or race of the complainant'. In this case, Mrs Horsey lived in Aberystwyth; her husband got a job in London and she applied for secondment to a social service course in Maidstone so that she could live with him near his place of work. This was denied on the basis that she was unlikely to return; this view, in turn, was found to be based on a 'generalised assumption that married women follow their husband's jobs'. The EAT found that Mrs Horsey had been the victim of discrimination on the ground of her sex: she would have been treated differently had she been a comparable man.[131]

In *R (on the application of European Roma Rights Centre and others) v Immigration Officer at Prague Airport*[132] it was found that UK immigration officers in Prague who were operating a pre-clearance scheme for asylum seekers were subjecting Czech Roma to longer and more intrusive questioning than was the case with non-Roma. This was because 'Roma alone as a group suffer discrimination (whether or not amounting to persecution) in the Czech Republic and so in general have a much greater incentive than others to seek asylum and therefore, when being questioned at Prague airport, to lie about their intentions in visiting the United Kingdom'; as a result, the immigration officers 'are inevitably more sceptical of a Roma applicant's true intentions than those of a non-Roma, and are less easily persuaded that the Roma is genuinely intending to come only for a limited purpose'.[133] The majority of the Court of Appeal considered that this practice was not discriminatory on the grounds of race; the immigration officers had not departed from the principle that each case had to be treated on its individual merits. According to Simon Brown LJ, an employer would be entitled to take sex or race into account to the extent of questioning individual applicants for employment more intensively if this was relevant to the job in question: an employer 'interviewing for a job involving heavy lifting' was entitled 'to question a female applicant for the job more sceptically and rigorously than her male counterpart'.[134] By contrast, in his dissent (on this point), Laws LJ regarded the practice of the immigration officers as an 'inescapable' case of stereotyping.[135] On appeal to the House of Lords this view of the facts of the case was accepted, and the majority decision of the Court of Appeal overturned. As Baroness Hale put it, 'the object of the legislation is to ensure that each person is treated as an individual and not assumed to be like other members of the group'.[136]

Difficult questions of causation: some illustrations

6.16 As we shall examine in greater detail below,[137] it has proved difficult to assimilate specific protection for pregnant workers with the general principles

130 [1982] IRLR 395, 397. See also *Hurley v Mustoe* [1981] IRLR 208.
131 See also *Skyrail Oceanic Ltd v Coleman* [1980] IRLR 226.
132 [2003] IRLR 577 (CA), [2005] IRLR 115, HL.
133 [2003] IRLR 577, at para 67.
134 [2003] IRLR 577, at para 81.
135 [2003] IRLR 577, at para 109.
136 [2005] IRLR 115, at para 82.
137 See para 6.98.

of discrimination law. Special treatment in favour of pregnant workers was exempted from the scope of the equality principle when the latter was first introduced at both a domestic and a European level, on the grounds that such protection might otherwise be classified as a form of unlawful positive discrimination in favour of women.[138] Although this put beyond doubt the legitimacy of specific protections for the protection of pregnant workers, it left open the possibility that the equality principle, far from prohibiting pregnancy protection, might instead be construed as *requiring* it. This question was clarified in *Dekker v VJV Centrum*,[139] where the ECJ held that an employer's refusal to employ a worker on the ground of her pregnancy was a form of *direct* discrimination which was contrary to the 1976 Directive: 'as employment can only be refused because of pregnancy to a woman, such a refusal is direct discrimination on the grounds of sex'. Moreover, 'a refusal to employ because of the financial consequences of absence connected with pregnancy must be deemed to be based principally on the fact of the pregnancy. Such discrimination cannot be justified by the financial detriment in the case of recruitment of a pregnant woman suffered by the employer during her maternity leave'.[140]

This can be seen as the same approach as that adopted by the House of Lords in *James*: direct discrimination occurs where the ground relied on by the employer for its action – in *Dekker* the employee's impending absence on account of pregnancy, and in *James* the fact that the complainant had not reached pensionable age – is itself an immediate consequence of the sex of the victim, so that 'but for' the victim's sex they would not have been subjected to the unequal treatment in question.[141]

The same principle was applied by the ECJ in the later case of *Webb v EMO Air Cargo Ltd*,[142] which concerned the dismissal of a pregnant employee who, by reason of her pregnancy, would have been absent from work for the same period of time as the employee she was hired to replace. The House of Lords had initially held that although dismissal for reasons of pregnancy would normally constitute direct discrimination, being based on the sex of the victim, this was not the case here: 'the appellant was not dismissed simply because she was pregnant but because her pregnancy had the consequence that she would not be available for work at the critical period'. According to Lord Keith, for the purposes of the comparison required to be made by section 5(3) of the Act, her case was not 'materially different' from that of a man who might have been absent on account of an illness which could only affect males (such as to require, for example, a prostate operation). In this context:

> The question is whether they are materially different, and the answer must be that they are not, because both sets of circumstances have the result that the person concerned is not going to be available at the critical time. Then it has to be considered whether there is something special about pregnancy which ought to lead to the conclusion that the case of a woman due to be unavailable for that reason is materially different from the case of a man due to be unavailable because of an unexpected prostate operation. In logic, there would not appear to be any valid reason for that conclusion.[143]

---

138 See SDA 1975, s 2(1); Directive 76/307, Art 2(3).
139 Case 177/88, [1991] IRLR 27; see also Case C-207/98 *Mahlburg v Land Mecklenburg-Vorpommern* [2000] IRLR 277.
140 [1991] IRLR 27, 29–30.
141 Ellis, 1994: p 567.
142 Case C-32/93 [1994] IRLR 482; see also, on this point, Case C-320/01 *Busch v Klinikum Neustadt GmbH & Co. Betriebs-KG* [2003] IRLR 625.
143 [1993] IRLR 27, 30.

His Lordship went on to hold that a situation of *indirect* discrimination had been established, on the grounds that the employer had applied a condition of continuous availability for work which women, on account of the possibility of pregnancy, were in general less capable of meeting than men, but that the employer had succeeded in showing the condition to be justifiable in the circumstances. However, when the case was referred to the ECJ for a preliminary reference, the Court held that the comparison made by the House of Lords was unacceptable: 'there can be no question of comparing the situation of a woman who finds herself incapable, by reason of pregnancy ... of performing the task for which she was recruited with that of a man similarly incapable for medical or other reasons ... pregnancy is not in any way comparable with a pathological condition'.[144] The Court classed Mrs Webb's dismissal as direct discrimination.

Although the ECJ's judgment in *Webb* is an important recognition of the importance of pregnancy protection and is consonant with the approach taken in the same area by Directive 92/85,[145] it is not without its problems from the point of view of the concept of direct discrimination.[146] In particular, *Webb* does not resolve the difficulty of identifying precisely when the grounds relied on by the respondent are gender-based. An absence caused by pregnancy is, it seems, directly linked to the sex of the employee, since only women can become pregnant. On the other hand, in *Hertz v Aldi Marked K/S*[147] the Court ruled that dismissal on the grounds of absence caused by a pregnancy-related illness which appeared after maternity leave did not amount to direct sex discrimination; the causal link here was too tenuous. As Ellis suggests, 'at one level of abstraction, a "pregnancy-related illness" can be said to be something from which a person cannot suffer *but for* her female sex; at another level of abstraction, it can be said that "illness" can be suffered alike by either sex'.[148] In practice, the certainty offered by the 'but-for' test is more apparent than real, since the court is still left with the task of identifying a *sufficient* causal link between the differential treatment received by the victim, on the one hand, and his or her sex or race on the other. When *Webb* returned to the House of Lords, Lord Keith interpreted the Court's ruling as meaning that 'in a case where a woman is engaged for an indefinite period, the fact that the reason why she will be temporarily unavailable for work at a time when to her knowledge her services will be particularly required is pregnancy is a circumstance relevant to her case, being a circumstance which could not be present in the case of the hypothetical man'; he thought, however, that dismissal on grounds of pregnancy would not necessarily be for a sex-related reason if the employee had been hired on a fixed-term contract.[149]

The complexity inherent in the task of identifying an adequate causal link for the purposes of direct discrimination is also illustrated by immigration cases. In *Dhatt v McDonald's Hamburgers Ltd*[150] the complainant, who was Indian by

---

144 [1994] IRLR 482, 494.
145 See below, para 6.98.
146 See Wintemute, 1998; Watt, 1998.
147 Case C-179/88 [1991] IRLR 31. On pregnancy-related illness prior to the ending of maternity leave, see Case C-394/96 *Brown v Rentokil Ltd* [1998] IRLR 445.
148 Ellis, 1994: p 567.
149 *Webb v EMO Air Cargo Ltd (No 2)* [1995] IRLR 645, 647–648; see also Case C-109/00 *Tele Danmark A/S v Handels-Og Kontorfunktionaerernes Forbund I Danmark (HK), acting on behalf of Brandt-Nielsen* [2001] IRLR 853 and our discussion in paras 6.98–6.99 below.
150 [1991] IRLR 130; see para 3.13 above for discussion of the importance of this case in the context of access to the labour market. See also *Bullock v Alice Ottley School* [1992] IRLR 564; *Barclays Bank plc v Kapur (No 2)* [1995] IRLR 87.

birth and nationality but who had acquired the right to live and work in the UK, was asked on an application form to provide evidence of his right to do so. The employer would not have made the same request of a British citizen or other EC national. The complainant produced his passport, which was stamped 'Given leave to enter the United Kingdom for an indefinite period' and hence, properly understood, gave him the right to work; however, the employer did not accept this as adequate evidence and he was dismissed. The Court of Appeal held that there had been no infringement of the RRA 1976. According to Neill LJ, the treatment accorded to Mr Dhatt was not based on his nationality as such, but on the statutory rules, deriving from immigration legislation, that required non-UK and non-EC nationals to have the necessary authority in order to enter into employment. Stocker LJ thought that the 'vital distinction' between this case and *James* was that whereas the Council adopted the criterion of state pensionable age out of convenience, in this case the employer 'had no alternative but to enquire whether or not an applicant was lawfully entitled to accept employment'.[151]

The need for a comparator and the 'relevant circumstances' test

6.17 In *Zafar v Glasgow City Council*[152] the House of Lords, upholding a ruling of the Court of Session,[153] ruled that the question in a racial discrimination case is not whether the employer has acted unreasonably, but whether it has treated the complainant less favourably than it would have treated an otherwise similarly situated employee belonging to another racial group. This crucial principle has been reasserted in several more recent cases.[154] For this purpose, it may be not simply appropriate to choose a hypothetical comparator; in a case where no actual comparator can be found, it will be essential.[155] The identification of the comparator turns on the principle already referred to, namely that 'a comparison of the cases ... must be such that the relevant circumstances in the one case are the same, or not materially different, in the other'.[156] Where a hypothetical comparator is invoked, the court or tribunal inevitably has some discretion in identifying which circumstances are relevant and whether the comparator's position is, for this purpose, the same or not materially different. The point emerges most clearly in decisions concerning the application of the equal treatment principle to discrimination based on an individual's sexual orientation. Where an individual is discriminated against on the grounds that he or she has a partner of the same sex, both the domestic courts[157] and the

---

151 [1991] IRLR 130, 134.
152 [1998] IRLR 36; see Watt, 1998.
153 [1997] IRLR 299.
154 *Martins v Marks & Spencer plc* [1998] IRLR 326; *Chief Constable of West Yorkshire v Vento* [2001] IRLR 124; *Shamoon v Chief Constable of the Royal Ulster Constabulary* [2003] IRLR 285; *Bahl v Law Society* [2004] IRLR 799. See also the opinion of Lord Keith of Kinkel in *Webb v EMO (Air Cargo) Ltd. (No. 2)* [1995] IRLR 645, 647–648, insisting on the need in UK law for a male comparator in cases of sex discrimination based on pregnancy, whatever the case might be under EC law as a result of the judgments of the ECJ in *Dekker* and *Webb*.
155 *Chief Constable of West Yorkshire v Vento* [2001] IRLR 124.
156 SDA 1975, s 5(3); the same principle applies to the other prohibited grounds of discrimination, with the exception of discrimination on the grounds of gender reassignment (see para 6.12 above).
157 Most recently the House of Lords in *MacDonald v A-G for Scotland, Pearce v Governing Body of Mayfield School* [2003] IRLR 512.

ECJ[158] (applying Article 141) have held that the appropriate comparator is a homosexual person of the opposite sex; on this basis, the complainant cannot be said to have suffered any discrimination on the grounds of their *sex*. By contrast, in *P v S*[159] the ECJ, applying the Equal Treatment Directive which for this purpose is not materially different from either the SDA 1975 nor from Article 141, held that the appropriate comparator in the case of a transsexual is a person 'of the sex to which he or she was deemed to belong before undergoing gender reassignment'; on this basis, discrimination against an individual on the grounds of their decision to undergo gender reassignment was categorised as sex discrimination. There is no clear conceptual distinction between these two sets of cases.[160]

Proof of direct discrimination

6.18   It has been accepted since the early days of the legislation that a finding of discrimination depends on the court or tribunal drawing an inference from the primary facts. In *Chattopadhyay v Headmaster of Holloway School*,[161] Browne-Wilkinson J went so far as to say that 'if an applicant shows that he has been treated less favourably than others in circumstances which are consistent with that treatment being based on racial grounds, the employment tribunal should draw an inference that such treatment was on racial grounds, unless the respondent can satisfy the employment tribunal that there is an innocent explanation'. On the other hand, according to Neill LJ in *King v Great Britain-China Centre*, given that it is 'unusual to find direct evidence of racial discrimination', the tribunal was entitled to draw an inference from the primary facts and to reach a conclusion 'bearing in mind both the difficulties which face a person who complains of unlawful discrimination and the fact that it is for the complainant to prove his or her case'.[162] Until recently, the tribunal was not *bound* to draw an inference of discrimination merely because no clear explanation was offered by the employer. However, the position has now been altered in respect of those grounds of discrimination which are covered by the requirements of EC law. The model here is section 63A of the SDA 1975, inserted by way of compliance with the Burden of Proof Directive of 1997. This provides that where the complainant 'proves facts from which the tribunal could ... conclude in the absence of an adequate explanation that the respondent ... has committed an act of discrimination ... the tribunal shall uphold the complaint unless the respondent proves that he did not commit ... that act'.[163] The complainant must still show, on the balance of probabilities, that there are facts from which an inference of discrimination could be drawn. Only then will the burden shift. At

---

158 Case C-249/96 *Grant v South West Trains Ltd* [1998] IRLR 206; see para 6.36 below.
159 Case C-13/94 [1996] IRLR 347, 354; see also Case C-117/01 *KB v National Health Service Pensions Agency* [2004] IRLR 240 and our analysis in para 6.35 below.
160 Notwithstanding the approach taken in *P v S*, the legislation giving effect to that decision, SDA 1975, s 2A, must be read in the light of the 'relevant circumstances' test (see SDA 1975, s 5(3), as amended).
161 [1981] IRLR 487, 490. See also *Khanna v Ministry of Defence* [1981] IRLR 331; *North West Thames Regional Health Authority v Noone.* [1988] ICR 813, 822 (May LJ); *King v Great Britain-China Centre* [1991] IRLR 513.
162 [1991] IRLR 513, 518. This test was expressly approved by the House of Lords in *Zafar v Glasgow City Council* [1998] IRLR 36, 38.
163 To similar effect are RRA 1976, s 54A (which however does not apply to discrimination on the grounds of colour or nationality), EE(SO)R 2003, reg 29 and EE(RB)R 2003, reg 29.

this point, the respondent 'must prove, on the balance of probabilities, that the treatment was in no sense whatsoever on the grounds of sex, since "no discrimination whatsoever" is compatible with the Burden of Proof Directive'.[164] To this end, the tribunal should require 'cogent evidence' from the employer.[165] However, it remains the case that the tribunal should *not* draw an inference of discrimination merely because it considers that the complainant has been treated unreasonably or unfairly.[166]

The burden on the complainant is also eased by the provision made for the tribunal to admit in evidence the respondent's response to a questionnaire which the complainant is entitled to send it, requiring the respondent to explain its conduct.[167] The form of the questionnaire is laid down by statutory instrument.[168] The respondent is called on to explain, among other things, why it disputes the claim of unlawful discrimination; why the complainant received the treatment accorded to him or her; and how far their sex, marital status, race, sexual orientation or religion or belief affected the treatment they received. If the respondent 'deliberately, and without reasonable excuse' fails to reply to the questionnaire within a reasonable period of time,[169] or makes a reply which the tribunal considers 'evasive or equivocal', the tribunal is then entitled to 'draw any inference from that fact that it considers it just and equitable to draw, including an inference that [the respondent] committed an unlawful act'.[170] In the case of questionnaires relating to alleged discrimination on grounds of sexual orientation; religion or belief; or race, or ethnic or national origin; or harassment on any of these grounds, the tribunal may draw such an inference if the respondent fails to reply within eight weeks of being served with the questionnaire.[171]

In *King v Great Britain-China Centre*[172] the complainant was Chinese by origin and had lived most of her life in the UK. She made an application for the

---

164   *Barton v Investec Henderson Crosthwaite Securities Ltd.* [2003] IRLR 332, at para 25, approved, in amended form, by the Court of Appeal in *Igen Ltd (formerly Leeds Careers Guidance) v Wong* [2005] IRLR 258, para 76. The reference is to Art 2(1) of the Burden of Proof Directive, 97/80/EC. See also *University of Huddersfield v Wolff* [2004] IRLR 534. Evidence of bias on the part of a selection panel may give rise to a finding of discrimination even in a case where it was only one factor in the employer's decision: *O'Donoghue v Redcar and Cleveland BC* [2001] IRLR 615.

165   *Barton v Investec Henderson Crosthwaite Securities Ltd.* [2003] IRLR 332, at para 25; *Igen Ltd (formerly Leeds Careers Guidance) v Wong* [2005] IRLR 258, at para 76.

166   *Zafar v Glasgow City Council* [1997] IRLR 229, Ct of Sess; affd [1998] IRLR 36, HL; *Martins v Marks & Spencer plc* [1998] IRLR 326; *Madden v Preferred Technical Group Cha Ltd.* [2005] IRLR 46. The employer is *not* required to prove on the balance of probabilities, in the event of unreasonable treatment of the complainant, that a similarly situated comparator of the complainant would have been treated just as unreasonably (see *Anya v University of Oxford* [2001] IRLR 377, at para 14, discussed in *Bahl v Law Society* [2003] IRLR 640, at para 97, [2004] IRLR 799, at para 101). Thus the respondent does not have the burden of disproving a race discrimination claim (*Parliamentary Commissioner for Administration v Fernandez* [2004] IRLR 22) and an employment tribunal must set out the facts from which it has drawn an inference of discrimination in looking to the respondent to explain the conduct in question (*Sinclair, Roche and Temperley v Heard* [2004] IRLR 763). See also *Dresdner Kleinwort Wasserstein v Adebayo* [2005] IRLR 514.

167   SDA 1975, s 74; RRA 1976, s 65; EE(SO)R 2003, reg 33; EE(RB)R 2003, reg 33.

168   The Sex Discrimination (Questions and Replies) Order, SI 1975/2048, and the Race Relations (Question and Replies) Order, SI 1977/842; EE(SO)R 2003, Sch 2; EE(RB)R 2003, Sch 2.

169   SDA 1975, s 74(2)(b); RRA 1976, s 65(2)(b).

170   SDA 1975, s 74(2)(b); RRA 1976, s 65(2)(b); EE(SO)R 2003, reg 33(2)(b); EE(RB)R, reg 33(2)(b).

171   EE(SO)R 2003, reg 33(2)(b); EE(RB)R, reg 33(2)(b); RRA 1976, s 65(2)(b).

172   [1991] IRLR 513.

post of deputy director of the Centre but was not shortlisted for interview despite being very well qualified on paper. The majority of the employment tribunal held that she had been treated less favourably than certain other candidates who, while in a similar position, had been interviewed; they also considered that the employer, who had been sent a statutory questionnaire, had failed to give an adequate explanation of its conduct. A finding of racial discrimination was accordingly made, and was upheld on appeal.

Statistical evidence of a racial or sexual imbalance between different job grades or groups within the employer's workforce may also be used to draw an inference of direct discrimination. This was accepted by the Court of Appeal in *West Midlands Passenger Transport Executive v Singh*.[173] According to Balcombe LJ:

> Statistics obtained through monitoring are not conclusive in themselves, but if they show racial or ethnic imbalance or disparities, then they may indicate areas of racial discrimination. If a practice is being operated against a group then, in the absence of a satisfactory explanation in a particular case, it is reasonable to infer that the complainant, as a member of the group, has himself been treated less favourably on grounds of race. Indeed, evidence of discriminatory conduct against the group in relation to promotion may be more persuasive of discrimination in the particular case than previous treatment of the applicant, which may be indicative of personal factors peculiar to the applicant and not necessarily racially motivated.

In particular, statistical evidence may assist an applicant first in showing that racial or sexual discrimination was an effective cause of the treatment he or she received, and second, in rebutting an employer's argument that it was operating an effective equal opportunities policy.[174] The importance of statistical evidence is reinforced by the Codes of Practice issued by the CRE and EOC, both of which recommend that employers should regularly carry out monitoring exercises as part of equal opportunities policies, in order to measure the effects of employment and promotion decisions and to see how far racial and sexual imbalances between jobs or departments exist.[175] What is not so clear, in the present state of the case law, is the precise degree of imbalance which a court or tribunal is justified in regarding as strong *prima facie* evidence of discriminatory practices; at present, this is still seen as largely a question for individual employment tribunals to decide, with only loose guidance from the higher courts.

The employment tribunal has the power to order disclosure of documents by the respondent on the application of the complainant or of its own motion,[176] and this may help him or her to overcome the burden of proof. In exercising this power, however, the tribunal must balance the importance of the documents or information in question for the conduct of the proceedings with the need to preserve confidentiality.[177] Confidentiality is very likely to be an issue where the complainant seeks disclosure of documents relating to an employment or

---

173 [1988] ICR 614, 619, effectively overruling, on this point, *Jalota v Imperial Metal Industry (Kynoch) Ltd* [1979] IRLR 313.
174 [1988] ICR 614, 621; *Home Office v Coyne* [2000] IRLR 838.
175 CRE, *Code of Practice for the Elimination of Racial Discrimination and the Promotion of Equality of Opportunity in Employment* (1983), paras 1.33–1.43; EOC, *Code of Practice for the Elimination of Discrimination on the Grounds of Sex and Marriage and the Promotion of Equality of Opportunity in Employment* (1985), paras 37–40. See also *West Midlands Passenger Transport Executive v Singh* [1988] ICR 614 (Balcombe LJ).
176 See SI 2004/1861, Sch 1, para 10.
177 *Science Research Council v Nassé* [1978] ICR 1124; affd [1979] ICR 921.

promotion which he or she failed to secure. Another possibility is that the complainant will seek disclosure of statistical evidence concerning the sexual or racial composition of parts of the employer's workforce; as we have just seen, although the Court of Appeal accepted in *West Midlands Passenger Transport Executive v Singh*[178] that this could in principle form evidence of a discriminatory practice which operated to the detriment of a particular individual, it also warned against 'oppressive disclosure', which would include the provision of information which is only available at great expense or which would add unreasonably to the cost and length of the hearing.

Justification for direct discrimination?

6.19   The issue underlying many of the direct discrimination cases is whether the law should prohibit unequal treatment which is sex-based or based on racial grounds, but which is either motivated by potentially legitimate intentions or which might otherwise be justifiable. In principle, this should not be possible: if the courts were to accept the possibility of an open-ended justification defence in cases of disparate treatment, they would in effect be eliminating the distinction between direct and indirect discrimination. Were this to happen, the application of the equality principle would become highly contingent, being dependent, in effect, on courts' assessment of the justification defence in individual cases.

The SDA 1975 provides no general defence of justification to direct discrimination. Discrimination, whether direct or indirect, is permissible where the sex of the applicant or person in employment is a 'genuine occupational qualification' for a particular job, but this concept applies 'only where' a given case falls within the particular situations which are laid out in detail in the Act itself.[179] When first enacted, the Act also contained extensive exceptions from the equality principle in relation to the question of retirement,[180] but, again, these derogations were expressly created by the legislation and were narrowly construed. In the current state of the law, there would have to be an amendment to the Acts of 1975 and 1976 if the scope for justification was to be increased.

Under the EC Treaty and the various equality directives the matter is less clear. In relation to the Equal Pay and Equal Treatment Directives, the ECJ rejected, in both *Dekker*[181] and *Webb*,[182] arguments that direct discrimination in the context of pregnancy could be justified by reference to such factors as the financial expenses incurred by the employer or the practical difficulties caused by the employee's absence. The issue also arose in *Birds Eye Walls Ltd v Roberts*.[183] This case concerned an employer's practice of paying 'bridging pensions' to employees who took early retirement, the aim of which was, in general terms, to bring their income up to the level which would have been provided by the state retirement pension. The bridging payments ceased when employees reached pensionable age under the rules of the state scheme; since this was 60 for women and 65 for men, the bridging pension paid to women ceased when they reached the age of 60.

On a preliminary reference to the ECJ, Advocate General Van Gerven suggested that the Court could decide the issue by holding that although there

---

178 [1988] ICR 614.
179 SDA 1975, s 7; see below, para 6.50.
180 SDA 1975, s 6(3)–(4) (as amended by SDA 1986).
181 Case 177/88, [1991] IRLR 27.
182 Case C-32/93 [1994] IRLR 482.
183 Case C-132/92 [1994] IRLR 29.

had been differential treatment based on sex, the practice was justified in the circumstances. He gave two reasons for not restricting the possibility of justification to cases of indirect discrimination: first, that 'direct and indirect discrimination cannot in all cases be distinguished from another with the same degree of clarity', and secondly that in the interests of flexibility of approach it was not 'desirable to arrive at the categorical conclusion that discrimination directly based on sex cannot be justified'.[184] However, the Court declined to follow this advice and found a different ground for ruling that no discrimination had taken place, namely that the positions of male and female employees over the age of 60 were not comparable because only the female employees were in principle entitled to receive the state pension from that age. In the view of the Court, then, this was not a case of comparing like with like.

The Court's view on the issue of comparison is questionable here, since if the 'but-for' test is applied as it was in *Dekker*[185] (or, for that matter, in the House of Lords in *James*[186]), it would seem that the *only* material reason for the women receiving a state pension five years earlier than the men was their sex. However, its reluctance to extend the open-ended justification defence to cases of direct discrimination is significant, given the potential breadth of this defence and the broad discretion exercised by the courts in applying it.[187]

Indirect discrimination

6.20   The concept of indirect discrimination or, as it is known in US law, 'disparate impact', originates in the case law of the US Supreme Court in interpreting Title VII of the Civil Rights Act 1964.[188] Section 703(a) of that measure provides that:

> It shall be an unlawful employment practice for an employer -
>
> (1) to fail or refuse to hire or to discharge any individual, or otherwise to discriminate against any individual with respect to his compensation, terms, conditions, or privileges or employment, because of such individual's race, color, religion, sex, or national origin ...[189]

At first sight, this provision might appear to stretch no further than the notion of direct discrimination in UK law. However, in *Griggs v Duke Power Co*[190] the Supreme Court held that it also applied to a situation of institutional or structural discrimination arising from the common application of a rule or practice which was, *in itself*, free of racial bias. Prior to the coming into force of the Civil Rights Act, the employer in this case had discriminated against black employees by offering jobs in grades with a higher level of pay and conditions only to whites. After the Act came into effect, this practice was ended, but the employer made it a condition of transfer to the jobs in the higher grades that an employee should pass a standardised educational test. It was found that the employer had not introduced this test with any intention of perpetuating its discrimination

---

184 [1994] IRLR 29, 35.
185 Case 177/88, [1991] IRLR 27.
186 [1990] IRLR 288.
187 See also Case C-152/91 *Neath v Hugh Steeper Ltd* [1994] IRLR 91; Ellis, 1994: pp 568–569; Bowers and Moran, 2002; Gill and Monaghan, 2003; Bowers, Moran and Honeyball, 2003.
188 See McCrudden, 1985.
189 42 USC s 2000e-2(a).
190 401 US 424 (1971).

against blacks, but, in addition, that the test was unrelated to the requirements of the jobs in question and, at the same time, tended to disqualify black applicants at a significantly higher rate than white applicants. The Court held that the use of such a test by the employer was prohibited. According to Burger CJ, 'the Act proscribes not only overt discrimination but also practices that are fair in form, but discriminatory in operation. The touchstone is business necessity. If an employment practice which operates to exclude [members of one racial group] cannot be shown to be related to job performance, the practice is prohibited'.[191]

The concept of indirect discrimination which was originally enacted in the SDA 1975 and the RRA 1976 was based on *Griggs*.[192] That definition provided that sex discrimination (for example) occurred where a person:

> ... applies to [a woman] a requirement or condition which he applies or would apply equally to a man but -
> (i)   which is such that the proportion of women who can comply with it is considerably smaller than the proportion of men who can comply with it, and
> (ii) which he cannot show to be justified irrespective of the sex of the person to whom it is applied, and
> (iii) which is to her detriment because she cannot comply with it.[193]

This definition has been referred to by leading authorities on discrimination law as 'technical and crabbed'[194] and 'so vague ... that the effective use of the concept still depends on sympathetic judicial interpretation'.[195] In relation to discrimination on the grounds of sex, a series of changes were made with effect from October 2001, as part of the process of implementing the Burden of Proof Directive.[196] The words 'requirement or condition' were replaced by the expression 'provision, criterion or practice', sub-paragraph (i) was modified to refer to an adverse impact which was 'to the detriment of a considerably larger proportion of women than of men', the term 'justifiable' replaced 'justified' in sub-paragraph (ii), and the words 'because she cannot comply with it' in sub-paragraph (iii) were removed.

Then, under the EU Framework Directive on Discrimination of 2000, a completely different definition was provided. This referred to a situation where:

> ... an apparently neutral provision, criterion or practice would put persons having a particular religion or belief, a particular disability, a particular age, or a particular sexual orientation at a particular disadvantage compared with other persons, unless (i) that provision, criterion or practice is objectively justified by a legitimate aim and the means of achieving that aim are appropriate and necessary...[197]

---

191 401 US 424, 431.
192 See Lester, 1994: p 227; *Steel v Union of Post Office Workers* [1978] ICR 181, 188; *Clarke v Eley (IMI) Kynoch Ltd* [1983] ICR 165, 171. It should be noted that later US case law on the meaning of disparate impact has qualified *Griggs* (see *Wards Cove Packing Co v Atonio* 460 US 642 (1989)) and that a number of amendments have been made to the definition of discrimination under Title VII of the Civil Rights Act 1964.
193 SDA 1975, s 3(1)(b); RRA 1976, s 1(1)(b).
194 Lester, 1994: p 227.
195 Pannick, 1985: p 40.
196 This change took effect by virtue of the insertion of a new s 1(2) into the Act and by amending s 3 in relation to discrimination against married persons (see SI 2001/2660, reg 3).
197 Directive 2000/78, Art 2(2)(b). Sub-paragraph (ii) of Art 2(2)(b) refers to aspects of the definition which are specific to disability discrimination, on which, see paras 6.109–6.112 below.

This test, a version of which was also adopted in the context of the Race Directive,[198] appears to be significantly wider both than the original test and the modified version introduced for sex discrimination in 2001. It has now been incorporated into UK law for those parts of the Race Relations Act which cover discrimination on the grounds of race and national or ethnic origin, as well as in respect of the new headings of discrimination on the grounds of sexual orientation and religion or belief. Racial discrimination on the grounds of nationality or colour, which falls outside the scope of the Race Directive, is still governed by the original definition, while the definition of sex discrimination remains as it stood after the reforms, just referred to, which implemented the Burden of Proof Directive. However, a version of the wider definition for sex discrimination is due to come into force in October 2005.[199] At the time of writing the Government is consulting on the form that the amending regulations should take.[200]

Under the original definition of indirect discrimination, four separate elements to the concept could be identified: the application by the employer or other respondent of a requirement or condition; the adverse impact of this requirement or condition on members of one particular sexual or racial group; the impact of the condition upon the individual complainant, who had to suffer a 'detriment' as a result of his or her inability to 'comply' with it; and the defence of justification. The new definition would appear to be less complex than this and, at important points, significantly broader in its scope, than the original. For example, the version set out in the RRA 1976, as amended, now provides:

> A person ... discriminates against another if ... he applies to that other a provision, criterion or practice which he applies or would apply equally to persons not of the same race or ethnic or national origins as that other, but –
> (a) which puts or would put persons of the same race or ethnic or national origins as that other at a particular disadvantage when compared with other persons,
> (b) which puts that other at that disadvantage, and
> (c) which he cannot show to be a proportionate means of achieving a legitimate aim.[201]

Because of the absence of case law on the new definition at the time of writing, and the continuing (if diminishing) significance of the original one, our analysis will follow the structure originally laid down in the SDA 1975 and RRA 1976, while referring to the new, wider concept at appropriate points.

From 'requirement or condition' to 'provision, criterion or practice'

6.21   A key aspect of the original test was that the complainant should be able to point to a specific requirement which imposed an 'absolute bar' upon compliance. In *Perera v Civil Service Commission (No 2)*[202] Mr Perera, a Sri

---

198 Directive 2000/43, Art 2(2)(b).

199 This is the effect of the amendments made to Directive 76/207 by Directive 2002/73. The new definition of indirect discrimination in contained in Art 2(2) of the revised Directive. The widened definition is also applied to cases of discrimination against married persons and persons in a civil partnership by virtue of the Civil Partnership Act 2004, s 251 (which at the time of writing is not yet in force); see below, para 6.36.

200 DTI, *Equality and Diversity: Updating the Sex Discrimination Act* (2005).

201 RRA 1976, s 1(1A), as inserted by SI 2003/1626, reg 3. See also EE(SO)R 2003, reg 3(1)(b) and EE(RB)R 2003, reg 3(1)(b).

202 [1983] ICR 428; see also *Meer v Tower Hamlets London Borough Council* [1988] IRLR 399.

Lankan by birth who had lived in Britain since 1973, claimed that he had been denied the post of legal assistant in the civil service, for which he had the necessary professional qualifications, on racially motivated grounds. He argued that other criteria taken into account by the selection board, including the candidate's age, his or her command of the English language, their experience in the UK and whether they were, or had applied to become, British citizens, had an adverse impact on him on the grounds of his race. His claim failed on the grounds that 'none of those factors could possibly be regarded as a requirement or a condition in the sense that the lack of it, whether of British nationality or even of the ability to communicate well in English, would be an absolute bar. The whole of the evidence suggests that a brilliant man whose personal qualities made him suitable as a legal assistant might well have been sent forward on a short list by the interview board in spite of being, perhaps, below standard on his knowledge of English and his ability to communicate in that language'.[203]

This test set an exceptionally high hurdle. By contrast, the test formulated by the US Supreme Court in *Griggs v Duke Power Co*[204] focused on 'employment practices', and this was relied on by the EAT to give a broad interpretation to the notion of 'requirement or condition' in a number of decisions which preceded *Perera*.[205] In its later decision in *Wards Cove*[206] the Supreme Court held that the plaintiff had to point to a specific employment practice as the source of adverse treatment and could not simply rely on statistical evidence of a racial or sexual imbalance between different employment categories; however, the Court did not go as far as the Court of Appeal in *Perera* in insisting on an *absolute* barrier to employment, promotion or some other benefit. The US Civil Rights Act 1991, which partially reversed *Wards Cove*, also retained the expression 'employment practice', and enabled a number of separate practices to be taken as one for the purposes of defining their adverse impact if the 'decision-making process' was not sufficiently clear for them to be analysed individually.

Even prior to the 2000 Framework Directive, European Community law took a more flexible line on the definition of indirect discrimination. In *Enderby v Frenchay Health Authority*[207] it was held that a prima facie case of discrimination arose where there was an 'appreciable difference in pay between two jobs of equal value, one of which is carried out almost exclusively by women and the other predominantly by men'.[208] Hence statistical evidence of a significant disparity was sufficient to shift the burden of proof on to the employer by requiring it to justify the differential in pay, even though no precise 'requirement' or 'condition' could be established. According to Advocate General Van Gerven, 'attention should be directed less to the existence of a requirement or a hurdle by means of which women suffer a disadvantage, and more to the discriminatory result'.[209] By adopting this test, the ECJ went significantly further than the Supreme Court, which in *Wards Cove* rejected precisely this proposition: the majority in that case held that 'racial imbalance in one segment of an employer's work force does not, without more, establish a *prima facie* case of

---

203 [1983] ICR 428, 437–438 (Stephenson LJ).
204 401 US 424 (1971).
205 *Price v Civil Service Commission* [1978] ICR 27; *Clarke v Eley (IMI) Kynoch Ltd* [1983] ICR 165; *Watches of Switzerland Ltd v Savell* [1983] IRLR 141; see Pannick, 1985: p 42.
206 460 US 642 (1989).
207 [1991] IRLR 44; on appeal [1992] IRLR 15; refd Case C-127/92 [1993] IRLR 591.
208 [1993] IRLR 591, 595.
209 [1993] IRLR 591, 601.

disparate impact with respect to the selection of workers'.[210] Even the US Civil Rights Act 1991 did not go as far as *Enderby* since it retained the need to show that adverse impact arose from a specific employment practice. The liberal line taken in *Enderby* was repeated in the Burden of Proof, Framework and Race Directives, each of which, as we have seen, refers to a 'provision, criterion or practice' in its definition of indirect discrimination. The incorporation of this formulation into UK law may therefore be expected to overcome the rigid *Perera* test. Courts were already leaning in that direction. In *Bhudi v IMI Refiners Ltd*[211] the EAT held that an employment tribunal had erred in deciding that the employer had not imposed a requirement under section 1(1)(b) of the SDA 1975, in a case where it dismissed part-time workers for redundancy ahead of full-timers. This is consistent with a number of earlier decisions in which tribunals and courts have taken the view that such practices constitute an implicit requirement that employees should be employed on a full-time contract or its equivalent in order to retain their employment or to gain access to a particular employment-related benefit.[212] In *Falkirk Council v Whyte*[213] the EAT refused to follow *Perera*, holding that the term 'requirement' in the Act of 1975 should be given a 'liberal' interpretation with the result that it applied to a statement by the prospective employer that a certain level of training and supervisory experience was 'desirable'.[214]

Adverse impact

6.22 The second element in the original test was that the requirement or condition, although applied equally to members of the two groups in question, should result in the members of one of those groups being significantly disadvantaged. It is through this concept that challenges have been mounted to social or organisational practices which perpetuate group disadvantage, such as maximum age or full-time working requirements which tend to operate against women workers, for the reason that they are more likely than men to have spent time out of the labour market or to be unable to work a full-time schedule on account of family responsibilities.

ABILITY TO COMPLY

6.23 The anti-discrimination Acts require the complainant to show that the members of one group are proportionately less able to comply with the requirement than those of another. The phrase 'can comply' has, on the whole, been flexibly interpreted. In *Mandla v Dowell Lee*[215] a school refused to allow

---

210 490 US 642, 653 (1989).

211 [1994] IRLR 204.

212 See *Clarke v Eley (IMI) Kynoch Ltd* [1983] ICR 165 and *Allonby v Accrington and Rossendale College* [2001] IRLR 364 (stressing that for this purpose, it is of no relevance that the employer might be able to point to an alternative, unobjectionable requirement); cf *Kidd v DRG (UK) Ltd* [1985] ICR 405; *Clymo v Wandsworth London Borough Council* [1989] ICR 250.

213 [1997] IRLR 560.

214 The reasons given by the EAT in the *Whyte* case included the existence of allegedly conflicting authority in the Court of Appeal (*Meer v Tower Hamlets London Borough Council* [1988] IRLR 399) and the need to construe the SDA 1975 in the light of Directive 76/207 (which had not then been amended). See the discussion of Connolly, 1998.

215 [1983] ICR 385, 394; *JH Walker Ltd v Hussain* [1996] IRLR 11.

Sikh students to wear turbans, on the grounds that this was not an acceptable part of the school uniform. The House of Lords held that this amounted to indirect discrimination. According to Lord Fraser, the phrase 'can comply', in the context of the concept of indirect discrimniation, should be read 'not as meaning "can physically", so as to indicate a theoretical possibility, but as meaning "can in practice" or "can consistently with the customs and cultural traditions of the racial group"'.

Similarly, in *Price v Civil Service Commission*[216] the EAT thought that it 'should not be said that a person "can" do something merely because it is theoretically possible for him to do so; it is necessary to see whether he can do so in practice'. This case concerned a maximum age bar for a particular employment which Mrs Price claimed was indirectly discriminatory on the grounds of sex. The EAT held that 'it is relevant in determining whether women can comply with the condition to take into account the current usual behaviour of women in this respect, as observed in practice, putting on one side behaviour and responses which are unusual or extreme'. In this respect, 'knowledge and experience suggest that a considerable number of women between the mid-twenties and the mid-thirties are engaged in bearing children and in minding children, and that while many find it possible to take up employment many others, while desiring to do so, find it impossible, and that many of the latter as their children get older find that they can follow their wish and seek employment'.

Evidence of social practices which lead to adverse impact may be of some value, but may not be sufficient unless combined with more precise statistical evidence. Thus in *Price v Civil Service Commission*[217] the EAT declined to make a finding of adverse impact on this impressionistic evidence alone, preferring to weigh its effect together with that of statistical evidence of female employment participation rates for the population as a whole, which showed a marked decline in employment of women between the ages of 23 and 33. Even then, the evidence was deemed insufficient to support a finding that a considerably smaller proportion of women could comply with the requirement, and the case was remitted to the employment tribunal for a further hearing, at which the complainant succeeded.

A number of decisions have considered the application of the indirect discrimination concept under the SDA 1975 to the question of working schedules and the differential treatment of part-time and full-time workers. In *Meeks v NUAAW*,[218] a case arising out of an employer's practice of paying part-time workers a lower hourly rate than full-time workers, evidence produced by the complainant included 'her own unchallenged statement that married women like herself generally have to work part-time because of family commitments'. This was accepted as evidence of adverse impact when combined with statistical details of numbers of men and women working full-time in the particular occupation in question and in the working population as a whole. By contrast, in *Kidd v DRG (UK) Ltd*[219] an employment tribunal rejected a claim that women's domestic responsibilities made it more difficult for them to work full-time, out of recognition of 'the fact ... that mothers of young children in the modern community are no longer conforming universally to the traditional notion that their place is in the home; and that there are plenty of couples (married and

216 [1978] ICR 27, 31.
217 [1978] ICR 27.
218 [1976] IRLR 198.
219 [1985] ICR 405.

unmarried) today with young children, where the male partner stays at home
for all or part of the time to release his female partner to undertake full-time
work'.[220] The EAT declined to overturn this aspect of the Tribunal's ruling,
commenting that 'although it is an entirely permissible exercise of a Tribunal's
function to proceed in a suitable case upon what they regard as safe assumptions
about the social and working patterns of behaviour in particular sections of the
community, that is by no means the same thing as saying that any tribunal
which declines to act on generalised assumptions which they regard as too
unsafe for acceptance is acting unreasonably'.[221] But in *Home Office v Holmes*[222]
the EAT offered no criticism of an employment tribunal which 'unhesitatingly'
accepted that the proportion of women who could comply with a full-time
working requirement was considerably smaller than the proportion of men, on
the grounds that 'despite the changes in the role of women in modern society, it
is still a fact that the raising of children tends to place a greater burden upon
them than it does upon men'. Similarly, in *Clarke v Eley (IMI) Kynoch Ltd*[223]
the EAT held that it was unlawful sex discrimination for an employer to operate
a practice of making all part-time workers compulsorily redundant before
dismissing any full-time workers, refusing to interfere with the employment
tribunal's decision that such a practice was by its nature sure to affect women
more than men. In *Meade-Hill v British Council*[224] the complainant argued that
the inclusion of a mobility clause in her contract of employment was indirectly
discriminatory on the grounds of sex; the court accepted that 'because a higher
proportion of women than men are secondary earners, it is more difficult for
them to move house and therefore a considerably greater proportion of women
than men could not in practice comply with a direction to move house'.

In *Holmes* the complainant succeeded in arguing that her employer's failure
to offer her part-time working after she gave birth to her child and had difficulty
in working full-time raised a prima facie finding of adverse impact. However,
the notion of indirect discrimination is too open-ended and subject to tribunal
discretion in its application for one to be confident of this finding being repeated
in other cases. A similar argument failed in *Clymo v Wandsworth London
Borough Council*.[225] The applicant was a librarian employed in a senior position
by a local authority, who, following the birth of her child, asked to be allowed
to work part-time, sharing her job with her husband who was also a qualified
librarian. The employer refused on the ground that job-sharing was not
appropriate for the managerial position which the applicant held. She claimed
that she had been subjected to unlawful sex discrimination. The tribunal
considered that the relevant pool here consisted of librarians occupying the
senior position of the applicant and who had dependent children. The tribunal
then held that 'at this level of income, and most particularly in the London
area, with child minding facilities readily available ... people of these
qualifications and this combined income and with a professional career both
behind and ahead of them could certainly conduct their family arrangements
on less old fashioned bases than the less qualified and more lowly paid' [sic].[226]

220 [1985] ICR 405, 414.
221 [1985] ICR 405, 415–416.
222 [1984] ICR 678, 681.
223 [1983] ICR 165. See also *Bhudi v IMI Refiners Ltd* [1994] IRLR 204.
224 [1995] IRLR 478, 481.
225 [1989] ICR 250.
226 [1989] ICR 250, 261.

This finding was not upset on appeal. It is reported[227] that detailed statistical evidence was presented to the tribunal to show that a significantly larger proportion of men than women worked full-time and stayed in employment after the birth of a child, but the tribunal dismissed this as insufficiently 'firm' and the EAT thought that this evidence 'can be used, as so often with statistics, to support arguments being advanced although directly opposed to each other'.[228]

BASIS FOR COMPARISON: THE 'POOL'

6.24   In deciding whether there is an adverse impact, the courts have held that it is necessary to identify a 'pool' or population of those to whom the condition is applied. The pool consists of those who, apart from being of the opposite sex or from different racial groups, are in a comparable position: this is the effect, for example, of section 5(3) of the SDA 1975, which provides that 'a comparison of the cases of persons of different sex or marital status ... must be such that the relevant circumstances in the one case are the same, or not materially different, in the other'. Section 3(4) of the RRA 1976 – which applies to the new definition of race discrimination as well as to the original one which covers discrimination on the grounds of colour or nationality – is to the same effect.[229] As Ralph Gibson LJ put it in *Jones v University of Manchester*:[230]

> In order to compare the proportion of women who can comply with the requirement with the proportion of men who can comply with it, it is necessary to determine the relevant total. In my judgment, the relevant total is the number of men and women referred to in the subsection; ie those men and women to whom the person, ie the employer in this case, applies or would apply the requirement.

In *Jones*, the University advertised for a career officer who had to be 'a graduate, preferably aged 27–35 years with a record of successful experience in an industrial, commercial or public service setting'. Miss Jones, who was aged 46 when she applied for the post but was otherwise well qualified for it, was not shortlisted, apparently on the grounds of her age. She had attended university as a mature student and had obtained her degree when aged 38. The employment tribunal found that she had been the victim of unlawful sex discrimination. For this purpose, the relevant pool was taken to consist of all mature students graduating after the age of 25. Of this group, the proportion of women who took their degrees after the age of 30 was considerably larger than the proportion of men; on this basis, the tribunal concluded that the proportion of women able to comply with the age condition in the advertisement was considerably smaller than the proportion of men. The EAT reversed this aspect of the tribunal's decision on the grounds that the wrong pool had been used, and their view was upheld on appeal. The Court of Appeal held that the correct total in this case was *all graduates*, and not just those who graduated as mature students. This was because the job was open to all those with a degree and not just those who had been mature students. As a result, the proportion of women capable of meeting the requirement was greater than it would otherwise have been and considerably closer to the relevant proportion of men.

227 [1989] ICR 250, 262–263.
228 [1989] ICR 250, 262–263.
229 See also the equivalent provision in EE(SO)R 2003, reg 3(2) and EE(RB)R 2003, reg 3(3).
230 [1993] IRLR 218, 226.

The test formulated by Ralph Gibson LJ in *Jones* holds out the possibility that some much-needed precision can be introduced into the process of defining the pool. However, the question 'to whom was the condition applied?' can obviously be answered at different levels of generality. If an age requirement or a requirement of full-time working is made a condition of a particular job, is this being imposed on all qualified applicants in the working population; on all those in a particular profession; or those employed in a particular organisation? The EAT has held that the definition of the pool is a question of fact for the tribunal to decide,[231] and if this is maintained the scope for appellate control is very limited. However, in *London Underground Ltd v Edwards*[232] the EAT overturned a ruling of an employment tribunal which, in a case concerning the impact of flexible work rosters, had held that the appropriate comparison was between all female employees of the respondent who were single parents, and all male employees who were single parents. The Appeal Tribunal held that the appropriate basis for comparison consisted of *all* those female employees to whom the requirement to work flexibly was being applied, and all such male employees.

Clymo v Wandsworth London Borough Council,[233] which was considered above, is an example of case where the outcome turned to a certain extent on how the relevant pool was defined. The restriction of the pool to employees occupying the particular job and grade of the applicant, as opposed to male and female employees more generally, made it more difficult to establish adverse impact. By contrast, in *R v Secretary of State, ex p EOC*,[234] in which the EOC successfully invoked the Equal Treatment Directive to challenge the 8- and 16-hour qualifying thresholds for employment protection rights contained in the ERA 1996, the relevant pool was taken to be the working population as a whole, and it was accepted on both sides that a prima facie case of adverse impact was made out: it was 'common ground that a very large majority of part-time employees are women and a majority of full-time employees are men, and it is common ground also that the main reason why women seek part-time employment is their responsibility as carers for children or elderly relatives'.[235] In *Rutherford v Secretary of State for Trade and Industry (No 2)*[236] a similarly wide pool was used in the context of legislation excluding employees over the age of 65 from entitlement to a redundancy payment. According to the Court of Appeal, it was necessary to focus on the adult workforce as a whole rather than a group consisting of older employees approaching, or past, the age of 65. This widening of the pool undermined the applicants' claim, because while there were significantly more men than women in the category of older employees, the respective proportions of the two sexes in the workforce as a whole were almost identical.

These decisions may be compared with *Staffordshire County Council v Black*.[237] This case concerned an employer's decision, under the terms of its

231 In *Kidd v DRG (UK) Ltd* [1985] ICR 405.
232 [1995] IRLR 355.
233 [1989] ICR 250.
234 [1991] IRLR 493; affd [1993] IRLR 10; on appeal [1994] IRLR 176; see para 3.88 above. See also, on this point, Case C-167/97 *R v Secretary of State for Employment, ex p Seymour-Smith* [1999] IRLR 253.
235 [1993] IRLR 10, 13 (Dillon LJ); cf the sceptical comments of Nolan LJ in the Divisional Court [1991] IRLR 493, 500.
236 [2004] IRLR 892.
237 [1995] IRLR 234.

pension scheme, to credit full-time workers with additional contributions on the basis of past service, but to credit additional contributions to part-time workers only in respect of their past service under their regular contracts of employment, without regard for additional duties carried out under supply contracts and temporary contracts of employment. The tribunal took as the relevant pool those employees of the council who were aged 50 or more at the time Mrs Black was made redundant, on the grounds that only this group had been eligible for the additional contributions in question. It found that of this group, 89.5% of women worked full-time (and so qualified for the higher rate of additional contribution), compared to 97% of men. On this basis it concluded that the proportion of women capable of complying with the full-time requirement was not considerably smaller than the proportion of men, and the EAT agreed that this difference was 'very small'.[238]

In *Black*, the choice of a pool which was confined to a particular category of employees in a particular organisation limited the complainant's chances of success, because she happened to work in a profession and for an organisation where an unusually large proportion of women worked full-time. In *Ex p EOC* and *Rutherford* the courts were considering the impact of legislation affecting all employees working in Great Britain: this made the broad scale of the comparison appropriate. But more generally, it is arguable that to narrow the size of the relevant pool, as occurred in *Clymo* and in *Black*, is to undermine the purpose of indirect discrimination: Pannick, for example, suggests that 'section 1(1)(b) and the principle of disparate impact do not intend to make one's rights dependent on the arbitrary factors of where one works, and the number of men and women who do particular jobs there'.[239] Similarly, in *R v Secretary of State for Education, ex p Schaffter*[240] Schiemann J commented that with the choice of a very small pool, there is a 'real risk that you have incorporated an act of discrimination into your definition'.

A further difficulty in the concept of the pool is illustrated by *Lord Chancellor v Coker*.[241] The complainants alleged, respectively, sex and race discrimination arising from the Lord Chancellor's decision to appoint a close acquaintance, who happened to be male, to be his special adviser, without advertising the post. The employment tribunal and the EAT accepted that a 'requirement' had been imposed as result of this method of recruitment, namely that the successful candidate had to be personally known to the Lord Chancellor. The employment tribunal went to hold, in a rather impressionistic way, that the proportion of women who could comply with this requirement was substantially smaller than the proportion of men; likewise with regard to members of ethnic minority groups by comparison to whites. The EAT, in a majority judgment, reversed on the grounds that 'the Lord Chancellor determined upon only one person and thus can be said to discriminate against *everybody else* ... be they men or women, and accordingly there is no relevant pool'.[242] The point was put slightly differently and perhaps more accurately in the Court of Appeal: there was a pool of potential applicants, but because nearly everyone in it was disqualified, there could not be said to have been discrimination. As a result, 'making an appointment from within a circle of family, friends and personal acquaintances

238 [1995] IRLR 234, 238.
239 Pannick, 1985: p 47.
240 [1987] IRLR 53, 56.
241 [1999] IRLR 396, ET; [2001] IRLR 116 EAT, [2002] IRLR 80, CA.
242 [2001] IRLR 116, 121.

is seldom likely to constitute indirect discrimination. Those known to the employer are likely to represent a minute proportion of those who would otherwise be qualified to fill the post.'[243]

DEGREE OF IMPACT

6.25 The original statutory formula requires the complainant to show that a 'considerably smaller proportion' of the allegedly disadvantaged group can comply with the condition. The essential issue here is what degree of adverse impact is sufficient to trigger the application of the paragraph. In *R v Secretary of State for Employment, ex p Seymour-Smith*,[244] it was found that the proportion of women meeting the then two-year qualifying period for unfair dismissal protection was approximately 90% of the proportion of men who met this requirement; put differently, about 77% of all male employees in the United Kingdom at the relevant time were capable of qualifying under this rule, compared to 69% of all female employees. The House of Lords, applying a ruling of the ECJ, held that although this was not in itself a sufficiently large gap, a finding of adverse impact was justified because the disparity persisted at a more or less constant level over many years.

In *London Underground Ltd v Edwards (No 2)*[245] the Court of Appeal held that in a case where 100% of male employees could comply with a requirement for flexible hours working, but only 95% of women could comply, there was again a sufficient difference in treatment for a finding of adverse impact. This case suggests that there is more to the test than a purely mechanical application of statistical differences. In *Edwards*, the complainant (who was a single parent) was the only woman out of 21 female train drivers who was unable to comply with the requirement; but there were over 2,000 male train drivers, all of whom could comply with it. The Court held that it was not appropriate to apply any rule of thumb defining the threshold level below which a difference in the impact of the requirement could not be regarded as sufficient, and that, in this case, the tribunal had been entitled to have regard to the very large disparity between the number of male and female train drivers employed by the respondent. It was also relevant in this case that, among the working population as a whole, women were much more likely than men to be single parents and hence unable to comply with an employer's requirement for flexible working.

Under US anti-discrimination law some courts have applied a presumption that the success rate of those in the disadvantaged group should not be more than 80% of the success rate for the other group.[246] This standard is derived from the Uniform Guidelines of the US Equal Employment Opportunities Commission, but it is not strictly binding and many courts apply instead a more

---

243 [2002] IRLR 80, at para 39.
244 [1994] IRLR 448, DC; varied [1995] IRLR 464, CA; refd [1997] IRLR 315, HL; Case C-167/97 [1999] IRLR 253, ECJ; [2000] IRLR 263, HL; Freedland, 1994; Barnard and Hepple, 1999, 2000; Townshend-Smith, 2000. See also para 3.84 above.
245 [1998] IRLR 364. Other recent cases on the issue of the relative proportions of those able to comply with a requirement include *Whiffen v Milham Ford Girls' School* [2001] IRLR 468 and *Chief Constable of Bedfordshire Constabulary v Graham* [2002] IRLR 239.
246 See, eg, *United States v City of Chicago* 648 F 2d 531 (1982); and see *McCausland v Dungannon District Council* [1993] IRLR 583, a case under the Fair Employment (Northern Ireland) Act 1989, in which 1.5% of all Catholics and 2.1% of all Protestants were able to meet a qualifying condition for a post. As the one figure was calculated as 71% of the other, the Northern Ireland Court of Appeal held that a 'considerably smaller proportion' of Catholics could comply.

open-ended test of what amounts to 'substantial' or 'significant' impact.[247] More generally, there is a good argument that in principle it should be 'inappropriate to deny the character of [indirect] discrimination to any disparity which is more than *de minimis*',[248] although the courts are currently a long way from accepting this.[249]

ALTERNATIVE APPROACHES: FOCUSING ON COMPARATIVE FAILURE RATES OR THE COMPOSITION OF THE DISADVANTAGED AND ADVANTAGED GROUPS

6.26   The approach to adverse impact incorporated in the original form of the SDA 1975 and RRA 1976 appears to rule out alternative bases of comparison, such as a focus on relative failure rates. If failure rates had been considered in *Black*, for example, the result there could have been expressed as a finding that the proportion of women failing to meet the requirement was three times as great as it was for men (10% as opposed to 3%). This is not to suggest that relative failure rates are, in principle, a better guide to the extent of adverse impact than relative success rates; simply that the difference may be made to appear greater or smaller depending on which criterion is chosen, and this seems to be a largely arbitrary matter. In *R v Secretary of State for Employment, ex p Seymour-Smith*[250] it was suggested by the Divisional Court, at an early stage of the litigation, that the use of comparative failure rates would only be appropriate if success rates in each case were very low; the House of Lords left the matter open when applying the ruling of the ECJ on this issue.[251]

In *Rutherford v Secretary of State for Trade and Industry (No 2)* the Court of Appeal held that a focus on the disadvantaged group was not required by the Burden of Proof Directive: that Directive did not prescribe a particular methodology for assessing the statistical evidence, thereby leaving it up to national courts to 'work out from case to case a satisfactory method … applying considerations of logic, relevance and common sense'.[252] Section 1(2) SDA 1975, as amended in the light of the Directive, directs attention to a provision, criterion or practice 'which is such that it would be to the detriment of a considerably larger proportion of women than of men'; by contrast, the original formula under section 1(1)(b) of the Act referred to a requirement 'which is such that the proportion of women who can comply with it is considerably smaller than the proportion of men who can comply with it'. The implication of the Court of Appeal judgment in *Rutherford* is that this change has made no difference to the law, but if this is so, given the change in the relevant wording, it is surprising. At the very least, it can be argued that the change made by virtue of the Directive gives the courts increased leeway to focus on the disadvantaged group if it regards this as appropriate. As we have just seen, there are cases in which this will make a difference to the outcome.

Another alternative approach to the measurement of adverse impact is not to compare the relative success rates of the two groups (for example, women and men) but to compare instead the sexual or racial composition of the group of

247   See *Moore v South Western Bell Telephone Co* 593 F 2d 607 (1982).
248   Freedland, 1994: p 340.
249   See, eg, *Nelson v Carillion Services Ltd* [2003] IRLR 428, in which the Court of Appeal held that it was possible to ignore a statistical disparity based on a small pool which the court considered to be 'fortuitous' rather than 'significant'.
250   [1994] IRLR 448; Freedland, 1994.
251   See Case C-167/97, [1999] IRLR 253, ECJ; [2000] IRLR 263, HL.
252   [2004] IRLR 892, at para 35 (Mummery LJ).

those who are able to comply with the composition of the group consisting of those who cannot. For example, it may be that in a given case, women and men make up roughly 50% each of the relevant pool. We would then expect roughly the same proportion of women and men to be found in the two groups of those able and those not able to comply with the requirement. Where there is a significant disparity, there may be the basis for a finding of adverse impact. What is being compared here is not the relative success rate of women and men, but the sexual composition of the failed group and the successful group; and the picture presented may be completely different as a result.

Hence in *Black*, the pool consisted of 1,772 teachers who were over the age of 50. Of these, 1,141 were women (64% of the total) and 631 were men (36%). One hundred and thirty-nine persons out of the group as a whole could not comply with the full-time requirement imposed by the employer; of these, 120 were women (86%) and 19 were men (14%). So whereas women made up 86% of the failed group, they represented only 64% of the pool as a whole, arguably a substantial difference, and certainly a more substantial adverse impact than appears from the measurement of comparative success rates.

Again, the point is not that this 'compositional' approach is necessarily a better way of assessing adverse impact than the comparison of success rates; but it is not clear that it is any worse, in principle. In particular, it may be appropriate to use the compositional approach in situations where, as in the example just given, numbers in the disadvantaged group are small in relation to the pool as a whole. This is because '[t]he smaller the disadvantaged group in proportionate terms, the narrower will be the differential' in terms of comparative success rates.[253] As far as cases brought under the UK anti-discrimination Acts are concerned, the original formula in section 1(1)(b), because it expressly directs the attention of the tribunal to relative success rates, could be read as ruling out the 'compositional' approach. However, under European Community sex discrimination law it would seem to be a viable option. Such a test seems implicit, for example, in the concept of indirect discrimination adopted by ECJ in *Enderby v Frenchay Health Authority*: 'if the pay of speech therapists is significantly lower than that of pharmacists and if the former are almost exclusively women while the latter are predominantly men, there is a prima facie case of sex discrimination, at least where the two jobs are of equal value'.[254] This would benefit complainants who were in a position to invoke the doctrine of direct effect to claim rights under Article 141 and the Equal Treatment Directive. It is also arguable that the compositional approach could be encouraged by the amendments made to the SDA 1975 by way of implementation of the Burden of Proof Directive. The UK courts have maintained that the Directive, in this context, merely codifies the relevant case law rather than altering the

---

253 *Barry v Midland Bank plc* [1999] IRLR 581, 586 (Lord Nicholls of Birkenhead). Although Lord Nicholls concurred in the result in this case, the reasoning he offered on the point of adverse impact was not that of the majority, so the validity of his approach remains open to further argument. See Thomas, 2000.

254 Case C-127/92, [1993] IRLR 591, 595; the same approach was recommended by the ECJ in Case C-236/98 *Jämställdhetsombudsmannen v Örebro Läns Landsting* [2000] IRLR 421. The so-called compositional approach was also adopted by Mustill LJ in *Jones v Chief Adjudication Officer* [1990] IRLR 533, a decision on the meaning of Directive 79/7 on equality in state social security, and approved by Ralph Gibson LJ and Evans LJ in *Jones v University of Manchester* [1993] IRLR 218, although neither judge seems to have considered the argument that this might not be compatible with the formula in SDA 1975, s 1(1)(b) which was being applied in the *Jones* case.

pre-existing position, and that the burden of proof rests on the complainant throughout.[255]However, if the changes made by the Directive are to have any impact all, it is arguably in the direction of permitting courts to use a wider range of methods when applying the test of adverse impact.

THE NEW TEST: GROUP DISADVANTAGE

6.27   The new test for indirect discrimination which applies to the prohibited grounds of race, national or ethnic origin, sexual orientation, and religion or belief, goes much further than the Burden of Proof Directive: it no longer refers to a requirement or condition which has an adverse or disparate impact, but instead to a provision, criterion or practice which puts a person of one race (for example) 'at a particular disadvantage when compared with other persons'.[256] One possible reading of this provision is that the court is no longer required to identify a particular level of statistical discrepancy in the treatment of the two groups. However, the test, as drafted, does not do away with the need for the identification of advantaged and disadvantaged groups whose cases are, in relevant respects, 'not materially different'.[257] Thus it would seem to be necessary to identify a pool from which these groups can, in turn, be constructed. Nor would it seem to be enough for the complainant simply to point to a credible suggestion of indirect discrimination, any more than it is at present. The approach taken by the courts may in future be less rigid than it has been in the past, but it is unlikely that the old case law on adverse impact will lose all significance.

Detriment and disadvantage suffered by the complainant

6.28   The original indirect discrimination test stipulated that the requirement or condition had be to the 'detriment' of the complainant because he or she 'cannot comply with it'.[258] This provision was meant to make it clear that the individual complainant must have been disadvantaged by the requirement in question.[259] The meaning of 'detriment' is examined in greater detail in our discussion of the substantive scope of the employment discrimination legislation.[260] The new definition of indirect discrimination refers to a provision, criterion or practice which, in addition to putting members of the group at a particular disadvantage compared to others, also 'puts [the complainant] at that disadvantage',[261] thereby capturing essentially the same idea. The old case law established that individual detriment had to be assessed at the time at which the condition or requirement was to be fulfilled, and not at some future hypothetical time;[262] the same principle would seem to be applicable under the new test.

The phrase 'cannot comply' was intended to be the equivalent for the individual complainant of the notion of group compliance which, as we have just seen, is an important aspect of adverse impact. In principle, the phrase should have had a flexible meaning in both contexts, but this was not always the case, as *Clymo*

---

255 See, in particular, *Rutherford v Secretary of State for Trade and Industry (No 2)* [2004] IRLR 892.
256 RRA 1976, s 1(1A)(b); EE(SO)R 2003, reg 3(1)(b)(i); EE(RB)R 2003, reg 3(1)(b)(i).
257 RRA 1976, s 3(4); EE(SO)R 2003, reg 3(2); EE(RB)R 2003, reg 3(3).
258 SDA 1975, s 1(1)(b)(iii); RRA 1976, s 1(1)(b)(iii).
259 See Pannick, 1985: pp 54–55, for an account of the legislative history of this provision in the SDA 1975.
260 See paras 6.42–6.44 below.
261 RRA 1976, s 1(1A)(b), EE(SO)R 2003, reg 3(1)(b)(ii), EE(RB)R 2003, reg 3(1)(b)(ii).
262 *Steel v Union of Post Office Workers* [1978] ICR 181, 186.

v Wandsworth London Borough Council[263] shows. Here the employment tribunal thought that Mrs Clymo would have been able to comply with a full-time working requirement by paying for child care, on grounds which included her apparent ability to meet the costs of doing so. Following the changes made to the SDA 1975 by virtue of the Burden of Proof Directive, the issue of individual 'compliance' is no longer relevant to claims of sex discrimination, but it remains relevant to discrimination on the grounds of nationality or colour under RRA 1976. Even under the SDA, it is arguably open to the courts to retain the essence of the old 'compliance' test by insisting that the complainant must show that he or she is truly at a 'disadvantage'.

Justification

6.29 The respondent could escape liability under the original definition contained in the SDA 1975 if it could show the requirement or condition to be justifiable 'irrespective of the sex of the person to whom it is applied' or, in the case of the original formula of the RRA 1976, to be justifiable irrespective of their 'colour, race, nationality or ethnic or national origins'.[264] The same formula is used in the revised definition for sex discrimination.[265] The new definition which applies to cases of discrimination on the grounds of race, national or ethnic origin, sexual orientation and religion or belief allows a defence where the respondent cannot show the provision, criterion or practice 'to be a proportionate means of achieving a legitimate aim'.[266] It is arguable that the new test will not be significantly different from the old one in this respect, since the concepts of proportionality and legitimacy had already been read into the statutory formula by virtue of the influence of EU law, in particular the relevant case law of the ECJ.

The justification defence is a constituent element of the concept of indirect discrimination; no discrimination has taken place, in the eyes of the law, if the defence is available, and so it is not a question of any *discrimination*, as such, being justifiable. The point is not so clear in the case law of the ECJ, where, as Advocate General Van Gerven has remarked, 'the terms "unequal treatment" and "discrimination" are used interchangeably' in this context,[267] although it does not seem that any point of substance turns on the precise terminology used.

The justification defence, which at one stage was exceptionally loose, has been tightened very largely as a consequence of the growing influence of European Community law, which adopts a much stricter test incorporating the concept of proportionality. The low point was *Ojutiku v Manpower Services Commission*[268] in which the Court of Appeal thought that 'if a person produces reasons for doing something, which would be acceptable to right-thinking people as sound and tolerable reasons for so doing, then he has justified his conduct'.[269] Moreover, this implied 'a lower standard than the word "necessary"'.[270] By

---

263 [1989] ICR 250, 264.
264 SDA 1975, s 1(1)(b)(ii); RRA 1976, s 1(1)(b)(ii).
265 SDA 1975. s 1(2)(b)(ii).
266 RRA 1976, s 1(1A)(c); EE(SO)R 2003, reg 3(1)(b)(iii); EE(RB)R 2003, reg 3(1)(b)(iii). Note that by virtue of EE(RB)R 2003, reg 26, the application to a Sikh of a provision, criterion or practice requiring him to wear a safety helmet on a construction site cannot be a proportionate means of achieving a legitimate aim under reg 3(1)(b)(iii).
267 Case C-132/92 *Birds Eye Walls Ltd v Roberts* [1994] IRLR 29, 37.
268 [1982] ICR 661.
269 [1982] ICR 661, 668 (Eveleigh LJ).
270 [1982] ICR 661, 670 (Kerr LJ).

contrast, the proportionality test developed by the ECJ requires,[271] first of all, that the practice be capable of justification by reference to an objective which is, in itself, legitimate; second, that it employs means which are appropriate and necessary to the achievement of that end; and third that, on balance, the means chosen do not unduly interfere with the principle of equality. This is a much stricter test since it enables the tribunal not just to judge the value of the objective being put forward by the alleged perpetrator, but also the legitimacy of the means chosen to implement it and their relationship to the end in question. In particular, it strikes at discriminatory practices in cases where alternative means were available which could have achieved the objective sought without interfering to the same extent with the principle of equality.[272]

It was established even prior to recent legislative changes that a version of this test would be applied in domestic legislation under both the SDA 1975 and the RRA 1976, as well as in the application of the equal pay defences of material difference and material factor which correspond, in general terms, to the defence of justification.[273] In *Rainey v Greater Glasgow Health Board*[274] the House of Lords applied the proportionality test laid down by the ECJ in its decision in *Bilka-Kaufhaus*[275] in the context of an equal pay claim; subsequently, the *Ojutiku* test was challenged in the context of the RRA 1976 in *Hampson v Department of Education and Science*.[276] Here, Balcombe LJ suggested that the justifiability test 'requires an objective balance between the discriminatory effect of the condition and the reasonable needs of the party who applies the condition',[277] a formulation derived from *Rainey* and hence from *Bilka-Kaufhaus*. In *Webb v EMO Air Cargo Ltd*[278] Lord Keith said that Balcombe LJ's analysis 'must now be regarded as the appropriate one and as superseding that of Eveleigh LJ in *Ojutiku*'. Since Balcombe LJ also said that 'it is obviously desirable that the tests of justifiability applied in all these closely related fields should be consistent with each other',[279] meaning the areas of equal pay and sex and race discrimination in employment, there would seem to be little if any scope to exploit differences in terminology between the EqPA 1970 and the two principal anti-discrimination Acts; it also follows that the strict European Union law test sets the limits to what is permissible for the RRA 1976.

In *R v Secretary of State for Employment, ex p EOC*[280] the House of Lords, applying the proportionality test, struck down the 8- and 16-hour qualifying thresholds which were at that time contained in Schedule 13 of EPCA 1978, on the grounds that they were incompatible with the Equal Treatment Directive. The *EOC* case indicates, firstly, that the burden of demonstrating justification is clearly on the respondent once a prima facie finding of adverse impact is made, and, secondly, that a strict standard of proof will be applied to claims of

---

271 See in particular Case 170/84 *Bilka-Kaufhaus GmbH v Weber von Hartz* [1986] IRLR 317; Case 171/88 *Rinner-Kühn v FWW Spezial-Gebäudereinigung Gmbh* [1989] IRLR 493; Case C-1/95 *Gerster v Freistaat Bayern* [1997] IRLR 699; Case C-100/95 *Kording v Senator für Finanzen* [1997] IRLR 710.

272 A similar approach has been adopted by some US courts under Title VII: see eg *Robinson v Lorillard Corpn* 444 F 2d 791 (1971).

273 On the equal pay defences, see paras 6.82–6.83 and 6.86–6.90 below.

274 [1987] IRLR 26.

275 Case 170/84 *Bilka-Kaufhaus GmbH v Weber von Hartz* [1986] IRLR 317.

276 [1989] ICR 179.

277 [1989] ICR 179, 191.

278 [1993] IRLR 27, 30.

279 [1989] ICR 179, 192.

280 [1994] IRLR 176.

the effectiveness of the means chosen to meet the end being aimed at. The defence offered by the Secretary of State was that the hours thresholds, by excluding certain part-time workers from statutory employment protection rights, encouraged employers to hire more workers than they would otherwise have done to work on a part-time basis. Although the promotion of jobs was accepted to be a legitimate goal of social policy, the House of Lords held that the Secretary of State had failed to show that the means chosen were appropriate to this end. There was, said Lord Keith, no 'factual evidence'[281] to support the argument being offered.

This strict test has been put in doubt as a result of the litigation which took place over the lawfulness of the two-year qualifying period for unfair dismissal in *R v Secretary of State for Employment, ex p Seymour-Smith*.[282] In contrast to the rather brief discussion in *ex p EOC*, on this occasion there was an extended analysis by the courts of the statistical and other evidence offered by the government. The Divisional Court and Court of Appeal considered the evidence to be inadequate, with some critical comments being passed on the value of the surveys which the Department of Employment had carried out in the mid-1980s in support of the policy of labour market deregulation.[283] When, however, the case reached the ECJ on a preliminary reference from the House of Lords, the Court enunciated a more flexible test which, when applied by the House, resulted in a finding in favour of the government. On balance, the best reading of *Seymour-Smith* is probably that it has liberalised the basic test for cases of legislative policy only,[284] with the result that it is necessary to consider this category separately from cases involving employers.

LEGITIMATE JUSTIFICATIONS: STATE POLICY

6.30 Having said all that, the range of potentially legitimate justifying factors is extensive. At the level of state policy, it not only covers the goals of increasing labour market participation and job creation which were defended in *ex p EOC* and *ex p Seymour-Smith*, but also measures taken to promote the growth of smaller firms. Thus in *Kirshammer-Hack v Sidal*[285] the ECJ considered, from this point of view, the validity of a German law which excluded from dismissal protection undertakings employing five or fewer employees, and for this purpose did not count employees working less than ten hours per week or 45 hours per month. The German government argued that this legislation was 'intended to alleviate the constraints on small businesses, which play an essential role in economic development and job-creation within the Community'. The Court held that even if there was a prima facie case of indirect discrimination in this instance (which it doubted), the grounds put forward in defence of the legislation were potentially legitimate: Article 118a (now Article 137) of the EC Treaty, which qualified the power to adopt directives in the area of health and safety by reference to the need to avoid 'imposing administrative, financial and legal constraints in a way which would hold back the creation and development of

---

281 [1994] IRLR 176, 182; see also paras 3.87–3.88 above, and Deakin, 1994a.
282 [1994] IRLR 448, DC; varied [1995] IRLR 464, CA; refd [1997] IRLR 315, HL; Case C-167/97 [1999] IRLR 253, ECJ; [2000] IRLR 263, HL.
283 For discussion of this point see Freedland, 1994: p 341.
284 Although see the judgment of the EAT in *Lord Chancellor v Coker* [2001] IRLR 116, 122, assuming the opposite point of view; but the specific context of the *Seymour-Smith* decision was apparently not considered in that case.
285 Case C-189/91 [1994] IRLR 185.

small and medium-sized undertakings', meant that under Community law 'these undertakings can be the object of special economic measures'.[286]

In other decisions under EC sex discrimination law, the ECJ has held that Member States have a wide 'margin of discretion' in determining the range of relevant factors which may be weighed in the balance against the principle of equal treatment.[287] In *Seymour-Smith* it stated that the relevant test was whether 'the ... rule reflects a legitimate aim of [the government's] social policy, that that aim is unrelated to any discrimination based on sex, and that it could reasonably consider that the means chosen were suitable for attaining that aim'.[288] It was in applying this test that the House of Lords ruled in favour of the government.[289]

EMPLOYERS' JUSTIFICATIONS

6.31   At the level of practices undertaken by individual employers, numerous justifying factors are also possible. On the whole, even though, under the test enunciated by the House of Lords in *Rainey*,[290] objective grounds of an economic, technical or administrative nature must be advanced, this category has been widely defined. In *Clymo v Wandsworth London Borough Council*[291] the employer was found to be justified in refusing to allow a job-sharing arrangement for what it claimed were reasons of managerial efficiency. In *Mandla v Dowell Lee*[292] the House of Lords could find no objective justification in a rule that forbade pupils from wearing a turban at a school, but in *Board of Governors of St Matthias Church of England School v Crizzle*[293] a school was held to be justified in requiring that its headteacher should be a communicant Christian (thereby causing a situation of adverse impact against the complainant, who was an Asian), since this was thought necessary to sustain the particular religious nature of the school as defined by its governors.[294] Much of the relevant case law in this area has arisen in the context of the equal pay defences, and is considered later in this chapter.[295] The important decision of the ECJ in *Enderby v Frenchay Health Authority*[296] establishes that factors such as individual seniority and scarcity of particular categories of labour can be relied upon to justify differences in pay for work of equal value under Article 141 and the

---

286   [1994] IRLR 185, 188.
287   Case C-317/93 *Nolte v Landesversicherungsanstalt Hannover* [1996] IRLR 225; Case C-444/93 *Megner and Scheffel v Innungskrankenkasse Vorderpfalz* [1996] IRLR 236; but see also the limits to the margin of discretion laid down in Case C-226/98 *Jorgensen v Foreningen Af Speciallæger and Synesikringens Forhandlingsudvalg* [2000] IRLR 726.
288   Case C-167/97 [1999] IRLR 253, Judgment, at para 77.
289   [2000] IRLR 263. Cf *Hockenjos v Secretary of State for Social Security* [2005] IRLR, 471. In *Rutherford v Secretary of State for Trade and Industry (No 2)* [2004] IRLR 892 a number of policy-related grounds were put forward for justifying the denial of redundancy compensation to employees over the age of 65; in the event, the case was decided on other grounds. See below, para 6.38, for a discussion of possible justifications for age discrimination of this kind.
290   [1987] IRLR 26.
291   [1989] ICR 250.
292   [1983] IRLR 209.
293   [1993] IRLR 472.
294   This legislation must now be read in the light of Art 9, ECHR. Special provisions apply to the appointment of a head teacher of a 'foundation' or 'voluntary' school which has a religious character: School Standards and Framework Act 1998, s 60(4). See also EE(RB)R 2003, reg 7.
295   See paras 6.86–6.90 below.
296   Case 127/92 [1993] IRLR 591.

Equal Pay Directive, but that the mere existence of separate collective bargaining arrangements for different groups is unlikely to be enough. Nor is *Enderby* properly regarded as any authority for the proposition that market forces of supply and demand *in themselves* – or the willingness of individuals to work for low pay – can justify unequal pay for equal work.[297] In relation to the differential treatment of part-time work, an employer may be able to justify lower rates of pay and benefits by arguing that these are intended to *discourage* part-time employment, on the grounds of the higher proportionate overhead costs which it involves.[298] However, since employers more usually often hire part-timers in preference to full-timers and see advantages in their employment in terms of flexibility and high productivity for those working shorter periods of time, it would seem that such arguments should not often be valid. On the other hand, the practice of not paying overtime premia to part-time workers until their hours exceed the normal weekly limit for a full-time worker, as opposed to their own normal weekly limit, may be justified by reference to 'the additional physical effort and the restriction on the use of free time entailed in working overtime' in the case of full-timers.[299] In general, the range of justifying factors in employers' cases remains tightly circumscribed, and is narrower than the margin of discretion granted to states.[300]

Affirmative action

6.32   As we have seen,[301] 'positive' or 'reverse' discrimination, in so far as that is understood to mean preferential treatment of an individual on the grounds of his or her sex, or racial group, is ruled out by the concept of direct discrimination contained as set out in the SDA 1975 and the RRA 1976.[302] This exclusion is made all the more clear by the House of Lords' decision in *James v Eastleigh Borough Council*, determining that motive is irrelevant in the application of the concept of direct discrimination.[303] The principal anti-discrimination Acts contain

---

297 See the discussion in para 6.89 below, and on the approach that should be taken to employers' arguments based on the need to cut costs or impose tighter budgetary controls, see the judgment of Sedley LJ in *Allonby v Accrington and Rossendale College* [2001] IRLR 364.
298 See Case 170/84 *Bilka-Kaufhaus v Weber von Hartz* [1986] IRLR 317.
299 Case C-399/92 *Stadt Lengerich v Helmig* [1995] IRLR 216, 219 (Advocate General Van Gerven). In that case, the ECJ held that practice referred to did not even raise a prima facie finding of adverse impact, but it reached a different outcome on the adverse impact point in Case C-285/02 *Elsner-Lakeberg v Land Nordrhein-Westfalen* [2005] IRLR 290. See paras 6.88 and 6.91 below.
300 See Case C-281/97 *Krüger v Kreiskrankenhaus Ebersberg* [1999] IRLR 808.
301 See para 6.12 above.
302 For an argument that employers' 'diversity' policies, aimed at promoting the participation of women and ethnic minority workers in employment, might be facilitated by a looser definition of the direct discrimination concept, see Barmes, 2003.
303 For an application of the equal treatment principle under SDA 1975, s 13 which ruled out positive action in relation to the activities of a body with the power to grant access to a trade or profession (which in this case was held to extend to the position of Members of Parliament) see *Jepson and Dyas-Elliot v The Labour Party* [1996] IRLR 116. This was in effect reversed by the Sex Discrimination (Election Candidates) Act 2002, s 1, inserting s 42A SDA 1975. This disapplies the equal treatment principle to the selection of party candidates if they are 'adopted for the purpose of reducing inequality in the numbers of men and women elected, as candidates of the party, to be members' of a relevant body. But see also *Triesman v Ali* [2002] IRLR 489, holding that the Labour Party is not a qualifying body under RRA 1976, s 12.

a sole derogation which is designed to permit preferential treatment as such, relating to arrangements for training and the encouragement of employment opportunities. Under section 47 of the SDA 1975, access to training facilities may be made available to women only or to men only, or the employer can encourage women only or men only to take up opportunities for doing certain work, where it reasonably appears to the provider that in the preceding twelve months there were no persons of that sex doing work of that kind in Great Britain, or that the number of such persons was comparatively small. Similarly, an employer is entitled by section 48 of the Act to make similar access available to training in relation to work in its employment, again where there were either no members of that sex doing such work or a comparatively small number within the preceding twelve months. The same provisions apply to training facilities for particular racial groups by virtue of sections 37 and 38 of the RRA 1976.

The genuine occupational qualifications for employment under both the SDA 1975 and the RRA 1976 may be of some use to employers wishing to pursue affirmative action. Section 5(2)(d) of the RRA 1976 allows a GOQ on grounds of race where 'the holder of the job provides persons of that racial group with personal services promoting their welfare, and those services can most effectively be provided by a person of that racial group'. However, this was given a narrow construction in *Lambeth London Borough Council v Commission for Racial Equality*,[304] where the Council attempted to restrict two housing managers' posts to Afro-Caribbean and Asian applicants on the grounds that they wished to make the delivery of their housing services more sensitive to the needs of these racial groups. The employment tribunal held that the jobs in question did not involve personal services, a ruling which is highly debatable but which was not upset on appeal. Balcombe LJ was 'wholly unpersuaded that one of the two main purposes of the Act is to promote positive action to benefit racial groups'.[305] As Pitt points out, a more acceptable route to the same end in a case of this sort may be for an employer to require applicants to have a particular language qualification or direct experience of contact with particular racial groups, as a condition of the job; under the test for indirect discrimination laid down in *Perera v Civil Service Commission (No 2)*,[306] this might not constitute the necessary 'absolute bar'; therefore there would be some scope for lawful affirmative action (although this argument will no longer work for the widened definition of indirect discrimination which applies to discrimination on the grounds of race, national or ethnic origin, sexual orientation, and religion or belief[307]). Moreover, with indirect discrimination, even if there is a prima facie finding of adverse impact, the possibility of justification remains.

The ban on preferential treatment in the sense defined above does not mean, however, that the law prohibits *all* forms of what may loosely be termed affirmative action, or measures taken to assist disadvantaged groups. Hiring quotas are not lawful, for example, in the UK, but as part of an equal opportunities policy it is arguable than an employer may legitimately decide to employ or promote a woman, for example, who is found to be *equally well qualified* with a male applicant or colleague, with the aim of improving the balance of women and men in particular parts of its workforce.[308] This point has not yet been

---

304 [1990] ICR 768.
305 [1990] ICR 768, 774.
306 [1983] ICR 428; see para 6.21 above; Pitt, 1992: p 297.
307 See paras 6.20–6.21 above.
308 Pitt, 1992: p 283.

clearly tested in the UK courts, and it is not impossible that an appointment made to improve the sexual or racial balance of a workforce would be regarded as based on the sex or race of the successful candidate and hence as illegitimate. The EOC Code of Practice notes that while 'selection for recruitment or promotion must be on merit, irrespective of sex', employers may, consistently with section 47 of the SDA, take such measures as 'positive encouragement to women to apply for management posts' and 'advertisements which encourage application from the minority sex but make it clear that selection will be on merit without reference to sex'.[309]

In the USA, private-sector voluntary affirmative action programmes designed to remedy conspicuous racial imbalances in an employer's workforce, which are designed to be temporary in nature and which do not unnecessarily interfere with the interests of white employees (particularly in the sense of preserving accrued seniority rights) were declared lawful under Title VII by the Supreme Court in *United Steelworkers of America v Weber*.[310] In addition to this permissive interpretation of the Civil Rights Act, Executive Order 11246, adopted in 1965, required federal government contractors to take 'affirmative action' to recruit, hire and promote women and racial minorities where they had previously been 'under-utilised' in the employer's workforce. The legality of this type of practice has increasingly been called into question, in the employment field and more widely, both under Title VII and under the Fourteenth Amendment to the US Constitution.[311]

The legality of affirmative action under EC law was first considered in *Kalanke v Freie Hansestadt Bremen*.[312] In this case the rule in question 'automatically gave priority to women in sectors where they are underrepresented, underrepresentation being deemed to exist when women do not make up at least half of the staff in the individual pay brackets in the relevant personnel group'.[313] The Court considered that a rule which meant that 'where women and men who are candidates for the same promotion are equally qualified, women are automatically to be given priority in sectors where they are underrepresented, involves discrimination on grounds of sex'[314] and so was contrary to the Equal Treatment Directive. It also refused to bring this type of practice within the derogation provided by Article 2(4) of the Directive, which, at that point, permitted 'measures to promote equal opportunity for men and women, in particular by removing existing inequalities which affect women's opportunities', ruling that the derogation had to be narrowly construed. By contrast, in *Marschall v Land Nordrhein Westfalen*[315] the Court held that a form of affirmative action under which, in a situation of underrepresentation of female employees, an equally well qualified female applicant would be given preference over a male, did not contravene the Equal Treatment Directive, as long as the following conditions were met: first, the employer made provision

---

309 Paras 41, 42. See also CRE Code of Practice, paras 1.44 and 1.45.
310 443 US 193 (1979).
311 See *Johnson v Santa Clara County* 480 US 616 (1987); *Richmond v JA Croson* 488 US 469 (1989); *Podbersky v Kirwan* 38 F 3d 147 (1994); *Gratz v Bollinger* 539 US 244 (2003).
312 Case C-450/93 [1995] IRLR 660. See Schiek, 1996, 2000; Prechal, 1996; Fredman, 1997a; Barnard, 1998; Betten and Shrubshall, 1998; Barnard and Hepple, 2000.
313 [1995] IRLR 660, 667.
314 [1995] IRLR 660, 667.
315 Case C-409/95 [1998] IRLR 39. See, to similar effect, Case C-158/97 *Application by Badeck and others* [2000] IRLR 432.

for a 'saving clause' under which it could take into account objective factors which were specific to an individual male; and, second, the criteria involved in such a process were not such as to discriminate against the female candidates. The basis for the ruling was that the derogation in Article 2(4) could be triggered, subject to the need for the saving clause, where affirmative action was aimed at counteracting 'the prejudicial effects on female candidates' of stereotypical attitudes and behaviour relating to the roles and capacities of women in working life.[316] A substantial case law has built up applying this test, the effect of which is that measures to promote the underrepresented sex are in principle permitted, but will be strictly scrutinised to see if they pass the test of proportionality under Art. 2(4). Thus hiring rules which did not permit sufficient flexibility in their application, to take into account the objective merits of the candidates, have been struck down as going beyond the scope of Art. 2(4),[317] as have rules which indiscriminately favour all widows over all widowers, regardless of individual circumstances,[318] whereas the restriction of child care places to female employees was held to be permissible as long as their benefit was also extended to male employees with child-care responsibilities.[319]

The legality of affirmative action was also confirmed by the amendments to the EC Treaty which were agreed in the Treaty of Amsterdam. In relation to equal treatment between men and women, Article 141(4) now contains a wide derogation intended to permit Member States to maintain or adopt 'measures providing for specific advantages in order to make it easier for the under-represented sex to pursue a vocational activity or to prevent or compensate for disadvantages in professional careers'. This was a wider provision than that contained in Article 2(4) of the Equal Treatment Directive at that point, and it was also wider than the equivalent measure under Article 6 of the Agreement on Social Policy from which the revised Article 141 was derived, since it was stated that the derogation applied to the 'principle of equal treatment' and not simply to issues relating to equal pay. The amended Article 141(4) also implied an extension of the scope of this part of EC law, which was be aimed at 'ensuring full equality in practice between men and women in working life', a phrase which could be interpreted as going beyond the restricted notion of equality of opportunity which the ECJ relied on in *Kalanke*. This phrase has since been incorporated into the revised version of the Equal Treatment Directive.[320] In addition, the Framework Directive on Discrimination and the Race Directive[321] both contain a provision according to which '[w]ith a view to ensuring full equality in practice, the principle of equal treatment shall not prevent any Member State from maintaining or adopting specific measures to prevent or compensate for disadvantages linked to' the ground of discrimination in question. In line with this provision, UK legislation permits positive action to be taken to afford persons of a particular religion or belief, or sexual orientation, access to facilities for training that would help fit them for particular work, or to encourage such persons to take advantage of opportunities

---

316 [1998] IRLR 39, 48.
317 Case C-407/98 *Abrahamsson and Anderson v Fogelqvist* [2000] IRLR 732; Case E-1/02 *EFTA Surveillance Authority v Kingdom of Norway* [2003] IRLR 318.
318 Case C-319/03 *Brihèche v Ministre de l'Intérieure* [2005] 1 CMLR 4.
319 Case C-476/99 *Lommars v Minster van Landbouw, Natuurbeheer en Visserij* [2002] ECR-I 2891; see also Case C-366/00 *Griesmar v Ministre de l'Économie, des Finances et de l'Industrie* [2001] ECR-I 9383.
320 Directive 76/207, Art 2(8), as inserted by Directive 2002/73, which permits, but does not require, Member States to adopt measures aimed at this objective.
321 Directive 2000/78, Art 7 and Directive 2000/42, Art 5, respectively.

for doing particular work, to compensate them for disadvantages linked to their religion or belief or sexual orientation.[322] These are nevertheless limited provisions, which are similar in form to those which have long been in force in respect of sex and race discrimination.[323]

DISCRIMINATION IN EMPLOYMENT

6.33   Having examined the meaning of the concept of discrimination, we now turn to a consideration of the substance of protection contained in anti-discrimination legislation. Important issues here include the precise scope of the prohibited grounds; the extent of the employment-related issues covered by the equality principle; the exceptions allowed by the legislation; and the remedies available for breach of the law.

Prohibited grounds

6.34   Sex, marital and civil status,[324] sexual orientation, race (broadly defined), religion and belief and disability are the grounds upon which employment discrimination is explicitly prohibited under the law of Great Britain.[325] By contrast, ILO Convention No 111 of 1958 on Discrimination in respect of Employment and Occupation refers to 'any distinction, exclusion or preference made on the basis of race, colour, sex, religion, political opinion, national extraction or social origin'[326] (although omitting disability, age, and sexual orientation). Article 13 of the EC Treaty, which was inserted by the Treaty of Amsterdam, provided the Community with the power to legislate across a range of matters relating to discrimination on grounds of sex, racial or ethnic origin, religion or belief, disability, age or sexual orientation.[327] This paved the way for the Framework Directive on Discrimination which was adopted in November 2000.[328] Under its terms, Member States had to implement prohibitions on discrimination on the grounds of religion or belief and sexual orientation by 2 December 2003, and prohibitions on discrimination on the grounds of age and disability by 2 December 2006. The relevant implementing measures, so far, are the Employment Equality (Religion or Belief) Regulations 2003,[329] the Employment Equality (Sexual Orientation) Regulations 2003[330] and the Disability Discrimination Act 1995 (Amendment) Regulations 2003.[331] The Race

---

322   EE(SO)R 2003, reg 26 and EE(RB)R 2003, reg 25, respectively. See DTI, *Explanatory Notes on the Employment Equality (Sexual Orientation) Regulations 2003 and the Employment Equality (Religion and Belief) Regulations 2003* (2003), paras 155–157.
323   SDA 1975, s 47 and RRA 1976, s 37; see above.
324   Civil status refers here to the status of civil partnership, created by the Civil Partnership Act 2004. See para 6.36 below.
325   Other grounds which are the subject of partial prohibitions are an individual's trade union membership or non-membership (see ch 8, below), and his or her having a criminal conviction which is now spent under the Rehabilitation of Offenders Act 1974 (see paras 3.15 and 5.95 above). In addition, other kinds of discrimination may violate specific Convention rights contrary to HRA 1998.
326   Art 1(1)(a).
327   See L Waddington, 1999, 2000; M Bell, 2000.
328   Directive 2000/78.
329   SI 2003/1660 ('EE(RB)R 2003').
330   SI 2003/1661 ('EE(SO)R 2003').
331   SI 2003/1673, amending DDA 1995.

Directive,[332] adopted in July 2000, was implemented by the Race Relations Act 1976 (Amendment) Regulations 2003,[333] with effect from 19 July 2003.

Sex

6.35   The terms 'sex' is not defined in the SDA 1975. In the absence of any specific statutory guidance in this context, the UK courts first took the view that the criteria for determining the sex of an individual were biological and not, for example, psychological or social. This was the approach taken by the courts in other contexts at this time,[334] and it was followed at tribunal level under the SDA 1975,[335] with the result that transsexuals were regarded for these purposes as retaining the sex with which they were born; the effect was to exclude discrimination by employers against transsexuals from the scope of the Act. However, the ECJ in *P v S and Cornwall County Council*[336] reversed this line of reasoning, holding that discrimination against an individual on the grounds that they are proposing to undergo or have undergone gender reassignment was contrary to the Equal Treatment Directive. The Court's ruling was based on the argument that such discrimination 'is based, essentially if not exclusively, on the sex of the person concerned. Where a person is dismissed on the ground that he or she intends to undergo, or has undergone, gender reassignment, he or she is treated unfavourably by comparison with persons of the sex to which he or she was deemed to belong before undergoing gender reassignment'.[337] Thus the Court assumed that the effect of gender reassignment was to alter the sex of the individual concerned for the purposes of the principle of equal treatment. It also made a crucial choice of hypothetical comparator, namely, a person of the sex to which the individual belonged prior to the reassignment. Underlying the Court's approach was a broad view of the Equal Treatment Directive as protecting 'the dignity and freedom to which [an individual] is entitled',[338] for the purposes of which it was necessary to assert, in the words of Advocate General Tesauro, 'the irrelevance of a person's sex with regard to the rules regulating relations in society'.[339]

---

332   Directive 2000/43.
333   SI 2003/1626, amending RRA 1976.
334   Eg, *Corbett v Corbett* [1970] 2 All ER 33 (marriage); *R(P) 1/75, R(P) 1/80* (social security). See Earnshaw and Pace, 1991: p 243.
335   *Calvin v Standard Telephone and Cables plc* London (North) Employment tribunal 16.1.86, COIT 1835/37; *White v British Sugar Corpn Ltd* [1977] IRLR 121, both discussed by Earnshaw and Pace, 1991: p 249. See also the same approach under Title VII of the US Civil Rights Act in *Holloway v Arthur Anderson & Co* 566 F 2d 659 (1977).
336   Case C-13/94 [1996] IRLR 347.
337   [1996] IRLR 347, 354.
338   [1996] IRLR 347, 354.
339   [1996] IRLR 347, 352. *P v S* was used by the EAT as an aid to the interpretation of the SDA 1975 in *Chessington World of Adventures v Reed* [1997] IRLR 556, prior to its amendment by SI 1999/1102 (see below). In *Bavin v NHS Trust Pensions Agency* [1999] ICR 1192, the EAT held that this aspect of the principle of equal treatment did not extend to a rule of an occupational pension scheme which confined rights to surviving spouses of scheme members, thereby excluding the long-term unmarried partner of a transsexual, but in Case C-117/01 *KB v National Health Service Pensions Agency* [2004] IRLR 240 the ECJ took a contrary view, ruling that legislation preventing transsexuals from marrying a member of their former sex and so from fulfilling a marriage requirement which was required to be met for one of them to benefit from a survivor's pension, was contrary to Art 141, but allowing some discretion to national courts in determining the precise circumstances in which this principle was infringed. This issue is now governed by the Gender Recognition Act 2004, which in Sch 5 makes a number of changes to the law relating to state benefits and occupational pension schemes; see below.

Following the ruling in *P v S*, the Sex Discrimination Act was amended[340] to reflect the prohibition on discrimination on grounds related to gender reassignment. Thus it is unlawful for an employer (or other relevant respondent) to treat the complainant less favourably than it treats or would treat other persons on the ground that the complainant is intending to undergo, is undergoing or has undergone gender reassignment.[341] The effect, then, is to make unlawful direct discrimination on grounds related to gender reassignment. The Act also states that it is unlawful for the employer to apply rules concerning absence which are less favourable than those which would apply either to a worker absent on the grounds of sickness or injury, or which are less favourable than those which would apply 'if the absence was due to some other cause and, having regard to the circumstances of the case, it is reasonable for [the complainant] to be treated no less favourably'.[342] For these purposes, 'gender reassignment' means 'a process which is undertaken under medical supervision for the purpose of reassigning a person's sex by changing physiological or other characteristics of sex, and includes any part of such a process'.[343]

A number of exceptions apply in addition to the normal genuine occupational qualifications[344] on grounds of sex. These 'supplementary' GOQs arise in the following situations:[345] where the job holder is likely to be called on to perform 'intimate physical searches pursuant to statutory powers'; where the job involves access to an individual in his or her private home and reasonable objection might be taken to the work being done by a person undergoing gender reassignment on the grounds of the degree of physical or social contact with a person living in the home or because of knowledge of the intimate details of such a person's life; where the job involves living on premises provided by the employer under circumstances where reasonable objection could be taken, on the grounds of preserving privacy and decency, to the job holder sharing facilities with members of either sex while undergoing gender reassignment and it is not reasonable to expect the employer to make alternative arrangements; and, most sweepingly, where the holder of the job 'provides vulnerable individuals with personal services promoting their welfare, or similar personal services, and in the reasonable view of the employer those services cannot be effectively provided by a person whilst that person is undergoing gender reassignment'. The last two of these exceptions only apply where the complainant either intends to undergo or is still undergoing gender reassignment.

---

340 By SI 1999/1102. See also *Consultation Paper: Legislation Regarding Discrimination on Grounds of Transsexualism* (DfEE, 1998).
341 SDA 1975, s 2A(1).
342 SDA 1975, s 2A(3).
343 SDA 1975, s 82(1). In *Croft v Royal Mail Group plc* [2003] IRLR 592 the Court of Appeal ruled that, in relation to these provisions, an individual undergoing gender reassignment did not have the right to be treated, with immediate effect, as a member of their reassigned sex, but that, conversely, an employer was not entitled to insist on treating them as a member of their biological sex until the point at which the reassignment process was completed. According to Pill LJ, in determining whether there was unequal treatment, 'the tribunal has to make a judgment as to when the employee becomes a woman and entitled to other facilities as other women though that judgment must have regard to the applicant's self-definition and cannot be determined by the views of other employees' (para 47). This decision must now be read in the light of the Gender Recognition Act 2004, under which the responsibility of determining the gender of the applicant rests with a Gender Recognition Panel and not an employment tribunal; see below.
344 SDA 1975, s 7A.
345 SDA 1975, s 7B. Further exceptions arise in relation to employment as a minister of religion: SDA 1975, s 19(3)–(4).

In *A v Chief Constable of West Yorkshire Police*[346] the applicant, a post-operative male to female transsexual, was denied the right to apply for employment as a police constable, on the grounds she would be unable to carry out in full the duties of that post. In particular, it would be contrary to section 54(9) of the Police and Criminal Evidence Act 1984 ('PACE') to allow her carry out intimate searches of women, since, under the terms of that provision, she would not be 'of the same sex as the person searched'. The applicant argued that she had been discriminated against on the grounds of sex; the claim arose before the amendments to the SDA 1975 introducing the supplementary GOQs had been brought into force. The Chief Constable argued that her case fell within section 7(2)(b)(i) of the SDA, under which sex was a GOQ in cases where the members of one sex might reasonably object to physical contact being carried out by a member of the opposite sex. In the House of Lords, the Chief Constable's defence was rejected on the grounds that by virtue of *P v S*, the applicant was entitled to be treated as having the gender to which she had been reassigned. Accordingly, section 54(9) of PACE had to be read as applying to the applicant in her reassigned gender unless there were strong public policy reasons to the contrary.

The supplementary GOQs contained in s 7B of the SDA, in particular the exception relating to 'intimate physical searches pursuant to statutory powers', must now be read not just in the light of the decision in *A*, but also by reference to the terms of the Gender Recognition Act 2004, which came into force on 1 July of that year. This Act was passed in order to implement the ruling of the European Court of Human Rights in *Goodwin v United Kingdom*,[347] to the effect that the denial of legal recognition of gender reassignment, including the right to marry as a member of the reassigned gender and to acquire a new birth certificate, infringed Articles 8 and 12 of the European Convention on Fundamental Rights and Freedoms. Under the 2004 Act, to obtain recognition of gender reassignment, an applicant must demonstrate to a Gender Recognition Panel that they have, or have had, the condition of gender dysphoria;[348] that they have lived in their new gender for two years prior to the application; and that they intend to do so permanently.[349] Once these conditions are met, the Panel must grant a certificate of gender recognition; the applicant's gender thereupon becomes the 'acquired gender' for legal purposes. This means, among other things, that the supplementary GOQs set out in section 7B of the 1975 Act are disapplied in a case where a certificate of gender recognition has been granted.[350] The Act goes significantly further than the pre-existing law, since it does not draw a formal distinction between pre- and post-operative transsexuals.

Marital and civil status

6.36   The prohibition on discrimination against married persons on the grounds of marital status was principally introduced to outlaw the 'marriage bar' which

---

346   [2004] IRLR 573.

347   [2002] IRLR 664.

348   The Act (s 25) simply defines 'gender dysphoria' as 'the disorder variously referred to as gender dysphoria, gender identity disorder and transsexualism'. There is a more helpful account of the medical background to the concept in the judgment of Lord Nicholls in *Bellinger v Bellinger* [2003] 2 AC 467.

349   Gender Recognition Act 2004, s 2.

350   The relevant changes to the SDA 1975 are contained in Sch 6 of the Gender Recognition Act 2004. Sch 5 makes related changes to the law governing social security benefits and occupational pension schemes.

operated in a highly public way in a number of occupations, including public sector employment, as late as the 1950s. Because the marriage bar only operated, in practice, against married *women*, its application would probably amount to unlawful sex discrimination even without the reference to marital status in section 3 of the SDA 1975.[351] As it is, section 3 put the matter beyond doubt. It is also due to be extended to cover cases of civil partnership.[352]

In the early case of *Skyrail Oceanic Ltd v Coleman*[353] section 3 was invoked in a case where a female employee was dismissed following marriage, on the grounds that her husband worked for a rival employer. This was direct discrimination on the grounds prohibited by section 3, and so no justification was allowed. However, section 3 has no application where action is taken against an individual on the basis of his or her impending marriage (or, now, civil partnership).[354] Here it would be necessary to argue the case as one of discrimination on the grounds of sex, for the purposes of which the complainant would have to show that a comparable member of the opposite sex would not have been treated in the same way.[355] It may also be possible to argue that dismissal in these circumstances violates the Convention right to respect for private life.[356]

Sexual orientation

6.37 Although discrimination on the grounds of a person's sexual orientation was not prohibited in so many words by the SDA 1975, attempts were made to bring it within the scope of the Act. One such argument was based on the application of what in US law was known as 'sex plus' discrimination, in other words discrimination based on the victim's sex plus some other characteristic which was related to it. This idea is also recognised in the UK case law: an example is *Hurley v Mustoe*,[357] in which the complainant was dismissed on the grounds that she was a mother with a young family, which her employer considered made her unreliable as a worker. The difficulty with using this idea to counter discrimination on the grounds of an individual's sexual orientation, however, is that the complainant must show that a comparable individual of the opposite sex would have been treated less favourably or, in the case of indirect discrimination, subjected to the same condition.[358] It is highly likely that an employer who refuses to employ a homosexual male on the grounds of his sexual orientation but who does not or would not object to employing a lesbian, or vice versa, will thereby contravene the SDA 1975. On the other hand, an employer who objects to individuals on the grounds of their homosexuality regardless of their sex may escape the effects of the Act. The argument turns on the effect of section 5(3), which requires the comparison of

351 *McLean v Paris Travel Service Ltd* [1976] IRLR 202, IT.
352 By virtue of the Civil Partnership Act 2004, s 251, which at the time of writing is not yet in force. This provision also modifies the definition of discrimination in this context to include the 'extended' definition of indirect discrimination set out in the revised form of the Equal Treatment Directive (76/207): see above, para 6.20.
353 [1981] ICR 864; see also *Horsey v Dyfed County Council* [1982] IRLR 395; *Chief Constable of the Bedfordshire Constabulary v Graham* [2002] IRLR 239.
354 *Bick v Royal West of England Residential School for the Deaf* [1976] IRLR 326.
355 This is the effect of SDA 1975, s 5(3). See also in this context *Horsey v Dyfed County Council* [1982] IRLR 395.
356 Under Art 8, ECHR.
357 [1981] ICR 490.
358 SDA 1975, s 5(3).

the cases of persons of different sex to be 'such that the relevant circumstances in the one case are the same, or not materially different, in the other'. As Earnshaw and Pace point out, it is open to a tribunal to conclude that an individual's sexuality is *not* a relevant circumstance for this purpose, so that the adverse treatment of a homosexual male would be compared, for this purpose, to the treatment which would have been accorded to persons generally of the opposite sex.[359]

This argument has generally been rejected, however, both by the domestic courts and by the ECJ, applying Article 141 and the Equal Treatment Directive. In *Grant v South West Trains*[360] the ECJ, considering a case in which only employees who were married or who had a partners of the opposite sex could qualify for cheap rail fares for their spouse or partner, ruled that '[t]hat condition, the effect of which is that the worker must live in a stable relationship with a person of the opposite sex in order to benefit from the travel concessions, is, like the other alternative conditions prescribed in the [employer's] regulations, applied regardless of the sex of the worker concerned. Thus travel concessions are refused to a male worker if he is living with a person of the same sex, just as they are to a female worker if she is living with a person of the same sex'. However, at no point did either the Divisional Court or the ECJ explain its choice of comparator. The failure to do so means that the conceptual basis on which these decisions rest is not clear. In particular, there is a striking contrast with *P v S*, in which the ECJ compared the position of a male to female transsexual not with that of a female to male transsexual, but with the position of a male employee who was not undergoing gender reassignment; in other words, the transsexuality of the complainant was not, in this case, a 'relevant' circumstance, to use the language of section 5(3) of the SDA 1975.

In *Smith and Grady v United Kingdom*[361] the European Court of Human Rights held that the policy of conducting investigations into the alleged homosexuality of members of the armed forces and discharging from service those found to be of homosexual orientation contravened the right to respect for private life in Article 8 of the Convention. The Court ruled that the UK government had not offered sufficient justification for these practices. In particular, no evidence had been presented to support the government's argument that the morale and effectiveness of the armed forces would otherwise be undermined, except for indications of 'a predisposed bias on the part of a heterosexual majority against a homosexual minority'.[362] The Court noted that 'these negative attitudes cannot, of themselves, be considered by the Court to amount to sufficient justification for the interferences with the applicants' rights [under Article 8] any more than similar negative attitudes towards those of a different race, origin or colour'.[363] Together with the Human Rights Act, *Smith* made it possible to argue that the SDA 1975 should be interpreted in such a way as to bring discrimination on the grounds of sexual orientation within the scope of the equality principle. However, this argument was rejected by the House of

---

359 Earnshaw and Pace, 1991: p 248. See also Bamforth, 1994, 1998 and Wintemute, 1997a, 1997b, for general analyses of discrimination law relating to sexual orientation.
360 Case C-249/96 [1998] IRLR 206, 218; Barnard, 1998; Bamforth, 2000.
361 [1999] IRLR 734.
362 [1999] IRLR 734, 748.
363 [1999] IRLR 734, 748. The Court also found a breach of Art 13 of the Convention (lack of access to a legal remedy) but rejected claims under Art 3 (degrading treatment) and did not consider a claim under Art 10 (freedom of expression).

Lords in two cases heard together, *MacDonald v A-G for Scotland* and *Pearce v Governing Body of Mayfield Secondary School*,[364] essentially on the grounds, as in *Grant v South West Trains*,[365] that the sexual orientation of the applicant constituted 'relevant circumstances' for the purposes of the SDA 1975.

The reform of UK law had to await the implementation of the Framework Directive on Discrimination, which outlaws both direct and indirect discrimination on the grounds of sexual orientation.[366] This part of the Directive was brought into effect from 1 December 2003 by the Employment Equality (Sexual Orientation) Regulations ('EE(SO)R') 2003.[367] The Regulations do not define the term 'sexual orientation' except to indicate that it refers to 'a sexual orientation towards – (a) persons of the same sex; (b) persons of the opposite sex; or (c) persons of the same sex and of the opposite sex'.[368] The Regulations follow broadly the same structure as the principal anti-discrimination Acts, as they have been (or will be) amended in the light of EU legislation:[369] thus they outlaw both direct and indirect discrimination,[370] as well as creating specific wrongs of harassment and victimisation,[371] and make provision for a number of exceptions to the equal treatment principle, including a defence based on the concept of a genuine occupational requirement for the post in question.[372]

Age

6.38 Discrimination on the grounds of age may be impliedly covered by the SDA 1975. As we have seen,[373] maximum age bars for recruitment or promotion potentially constitute a form of indirect discrimination against women, on the basis that women are on the whole more likely to have spent time out of the labour market looking after children and relatives, and hence to have had less of the necessary training or experience than comparable men of the same age are likely to have had. However, much depends in any given case on how the relevant total population or pool is determined and on whether the tribunal considers the resulting difference in the proportionate treatment of men and women to be sufficiently large to trigger the Act, and this is still the case

---

364 [2003] IRLR 512.

365 Case C-249/96 [1998] IRLR 206.

366 For the background to this aspect of the Framework Directive, see *Proposal for a Council Directive Establishing a General Framework for Equal Treatment in Employment and Occupation*, COM (1999) 565 final, which notes that 'employment is an area in which people may hide their sexual orientation for fear of discrimination and harassment' (p 4).

367 SI 2003/1661. See DTI, *Explanatory Notes for the Employment Equality (Sexual Orientation) Regulations 2003 and the Employment Equality (Religion or Belief) Regulations 2003* (2003), and ACAS, *Sexual Orientation in the Workplace. A Guide for Employers and Employees* (2003).

368 Reg 2(1). 'Sexual orientation' is not defined in the Directive either, but the Commission Proposal states, 'a clear dividing line should be drawn between sexual orientation, which is covered by this proposal, and sexual behaviour, which is not' (COM (1999) 565 final, at p 8).

369 Thus the structure of the 2003 Regulations broadly follows that now set out in the RRA 1976 as amended in the light of the Race Directive (2000/43). The revised version of the Equal Treatment Directive (76/207, as amended by Directive 2002/73), which follows broadly similar lines, must be implemented by 5 October 2005, entailing consequent changes to the SDA 1975.

370 See above, paras 6.12 and 6.20.

371 See below, paras 6.45 and 6.65.

372 See below, para 6.51, and H Oliver, 2004.

373 *Price v Civil Service Commission* [1978] ICR 27; *Jones v University of Manchester* [1993] IRLR 218; see generally para 6.24 above.

notwithstanding the recent changes which have taken place to the definition of indirect discrimination.[374] Moreover, with indirect discrimination there is always the possibility of justification. Here, tribunals and courts have an extensive discretion in weighing the various factors involved, which makes a successful outcome for the complainant far from certain even if a prima facie finding of adverse impact is made.

For example, in *Jones v University of Manchester*,[375] a maximum age bar was imposed by the employer in order, as it saw it, to achieve a better balance of ages in the relevant department, and because it considered that the post of careers officer should be occupied by a younger person capable of relating more effectively to the students whom he or she would be advising. The employment tribunal considered that these factors did not weigh heavily when set against the negative impact of an age requirement of that kind upon the 'thousands of women enrolled as mature students in English universities who will not obtain their degree until they are aged 30 or more'.[376] However, the EAT and Court of Appeal took a different view, holding that the impact of the age requirement could not be considered in such a broad fashion and that the tribunal should have considered the more limited impact of the inclusion of the age bar as a condition of appointment to the particular posts advertised. The complainant's claim failed.

Unequal retirement and pensionable ages for men and women are regarded as giving rise to direct sex discrimination, and are only lawful by virtue of specific statutory derogations from the equality principle whose scope is considered in greater detail below and which have largely now disappeared from the law.[377] However, legislation implementing the principle of equal treatment in this area took the form of harmonising compulsory retirement ages rather than outlawing compulsion as such. In *Nash v Mash/Roe Group Ltd*[378] an employment tribunal accepted the argument that legislation which provides employers with, in effect, an immunity from unfair dismissal where they apply a common retirement age of 65 to men and women alike,[379] was *indirectly* discriminatory on grounds of sex, since significantly more men are employed at that age than women. However, this argument was rejected by the Court of Appeal in the context of similar legislation governing redundancy payments[380] in *Rutherford v Secretary of State for Trade and Industry (No 2)*,[381] on the grounds that the relevant pool, for the purposes of comparison, consisted not of those in employment at or near the age of 65, but the whole adult workforce. On that basis, there was no significant disparity between the treatment of male and female workers. A number of possible justifications for age discrimination were also put forward by the government in *Rutherford*:[382] these were 'enabling employers to meet the expectations of younger employees for advancement; assisting employers to identify their future recruitment needs; and enabling employers to dismiss an older and less capable employee without the need to justify the dismissal'. Because of its ruling on the disparate impact point, the court did not have to consider the validity of these justifications.

---

374 See above, paras 6.20–6.27.
375 [1993] IRLR 218.
376 [1993] IRLR 218, 223.
377 See below, paras 6.38 and 6.96.
378 [1998] IRLR 168.
379 The relevant legislation is now contained in ERA 1996, s 109.
380 ERA 1996, s 156.
381 [2004] IRLR 892.
382 See [2004] IRLR 892, at para 45.

The EC Framework Directive[383] contains a prohibition on age discrimination which must be implemented by 2 December 2006. The 25th recital to the Directive states that while the prohibition of age discrimination should be 'an essential part' of the European employment strategy and a basis for diversity in the workforce, differences in treatment on the grounds of age may nevertheless be justified. Article 6 of the Directive accordingly states that Member States may provide that 'differences of treatment on grounds of age shall not constitute discrimination, if, within the context of national law, they are objectively and reasonably justified by a legitimate aim, including legitimate employment policy, labour market and vocational training objectives, and if the means of achieving that aim are appropriate and necessary'. This derogation is intended to apply to both direct and indirect forms of discrimination.[384] Article 6 goes on to state that such legitimate differences of treatment may *include* the setting of age-related conditions on access to employment and vocational training which are designed to promote vocational integration or to protect the workers concerned; the fixing of minimum conditions of age, professional experience or seniority for access to employment or employment-related benefits; and the fixing of maximum ages for recruitment where this is based on training requirements or on the need for a 'reasonable period of employment before retirement'.[385]

These derogations are likely to play a prominent role in legislation implementing the Directive in the UK. Following a consultation process which began in 2003,[386] the Secretary of State for Trade and Industry announced in December 2004 that such legislation should set a 'default retirement age' of 65, with employees being restricted to a right to request working beyond that age, a request which employers would be bound to consider, but not to accede to. Employers would also be able to justify a retirement age below 65 if they could show that it was appropriate and necessary.[387]

Race, national and ethnic origin, nationality and colour

6.39 The RRA 1976 contains an extended definition of 'racial grounds' which covers race, colour, nationality, and national or ethnic origins.[388] However, the extended definition of indirect discrimination which is derived from the Race Directive does not apply to the grounds of nationality or colour, which are outside the scope of that Directive and are therefore still covered by the original and somewhat more rigid concept of indirect discrimination which is set out in

---

383 Directive 2000/78.
384 This appears to be the significance of the cross-reference to Art 2(2) in Art 6(1); see also COM (1999) 565 final, at pp 10–11. These derogations are additional to the genuine occupational requirements referred to in Art 4.
385 See also Art 6(2) which allows Member States to provide for differential pensionable ages in occupational (employer-run) social security schemes; state-run social security schemes and employment subsidies are stated to be outside the scope of the Directive (see Art 3(3)). Member States may also provide that the armed forces are exempt from the age discrimination requirements of the Directive (Art 3(4)).
386 See DTI, *Equality and Diversity: Age Matters. Age Consultation 2003* (2003). A number of extra-legal initiatives had previously been adopted, including a non-statutory Code of Practice drawn up by the DfEE in 1999. See generally Sergeant, 1999; Desmond, 2000, 2003; Fredman and Spencer (eds), 2003.
387 Statement of the Secretary of State for Trade and Industry (Patricia Hewitt MP), 14 December 2004, reproduced on the DTI web site (http://www.dti.gov.uk/er/equality/statement.htm).
388 RRA 1976, s 3(1).

section 1(1) of the Act.[389] It will therefore be necessary for the courts to arrive at working definitions of the various different grounds set out in the Act.

The leading case under the 1976 Act to date is *Mandla v Dowell Lee*,[390] in which the House of Lords held that Sikhs constituted an identifiable ethnic group. Lord Fraser said:

> For a group to constitute an ethnic group in the sense of the Act of 1976, it must, in my opinion, regard itself, and be regarded by others, as a distinct community by virtue of certain characteristics. Some of these characteristics are essential: others are not essential but one or more of them will commonly be found and will help to distinguish the group from the surrounding community. The conditions which appear to me to be essential are these: (1) a long shared history, of which the group is conscious as distinguishing it from other groups, and the memory of which it keeps alive; (2) a cultural tradition of its own, including family and social customs and manners, often but not necessarily associated with religious observance. In addition, to those two essential characteristics the following characteristics are, in my opinion, relevant: (3) either a common geographical origin, or descent from a small number of common ancestors; (4) a common language, not necessarily peculiar to the group; (5) a common literature peculiar to the group; (6) a common religion different from that of neighbouring groups or from the general community surrounding it; (7) being a minority or being an oppressed or a dominant group within a larger community ...[391]

On this basis, although Sikhs are not (as the courts decided in this case) distinguishable in a biological sense from other inhabitants of the Punjab, their distinctive history and tradition and their own religion and written language mean that they are protected by the Act. The Act has also been held to extend to discrimination against Jews[392] and gypsies.[393] However, in *Dawkins v Department of the Environment*[394] it was held that Rastafarians were not an ethnic group, in part on the grounds that they had only been an identifiable group, separate from other Jamaicans, for around sixty years.

Religion and belief

6.40   The RRA 1976 does not protect individuals against discrimination on the grounds of their religion, except in so far as that forms one aspect of discrimination on racial grounds as that is defined in the Act: as we have just seen, an ethnic group may be defined by its religion, amongst other factors. Religious discrimination may also constitute indirect discrimination on racial grounds where, for example, employers' practices of denying Muslim employees time off to attend the mosque can be seen as imposing a condition which black individuals are less able to comply with than white individuals.[395] The

---

389   On this aspect of the definition of indirect discrimination, see above, paras 6.20–6.21.
390   [1983] IRLR 209.
391   [1983] IRLR 209, 211.
392   *Seide v Gillette Industries Ltd* [1980] IRLR 427.
393   *Commission for Racial Equality v Dutton* [1989] IRLR 8.
394   [1993] IRLR 284. In *Northern Joint Police Board v Evans* [1997] IRLR 610 the EAT held that the Scots and the English were separate racial groups defined by reference to 'national origins', although they did not have separate 'ethnic origins'; see also *BBC Scotland v Souster* [2001] IRLR 150.
395   *Yassin v North-West Homecare Ltd* (1994) 19 *EOR Case Law Digest*; see Mirza, 1995: p 20; *JH Walker Ltd v Hussain* [1996] IRLR 11.

Fair Employment (Northern Ireland) Act 1976 which, as amended in 1989, prohibits both direct and indirect discrimination on the grounds of religion and of political belief, has no application in the rest of the United Kingdom. However, the Framework Directive on Discrimination introduced a general prohibition on discrimination on the grounds of 'religion or belief' which has now been implemented in the Employment Equality (Religion or Belief) Regulations 2003. These follow the same model as the Sexual Orientation Regulations: thus they provide for an extended definition of discrimination and for specific wrongs of harassment and victimisation, while also setting out a number of derogations including the concept of a genuine occupational requirement.[396]

The relevant prohibited grounds are briefly described as 'any religion, religious belief, or similar philosophical belief'.[397] The DTI's *Explanatory Notes* on the Regulations suggest that the term religion, if it is to be interpreted in line with the case law of the European Court of Human Rights interpreting Article 9 of the Convention, would cover all religions widely recognised in the UK, and that the term also covers sects within a religion, such as the Catholic and Protestant branches of the Christian Church.[398] The European Court's case law, which requires a religion to have a clear structure and belief system,[399] thereby incorporates such belief systems as those of Druidism and the Church of Scientology. The term 'religious belief', the Notes indicate, would also include 'beliefs founded in a religion, if they attain a certain level of cogency, seriousness, cohesion and importance, provided the beliefs are worthy of respect in a democratic society and are not incompatible with human dignity'.[400] The third category, 'philosophical belief', only covers those philosophical and political beliefs which are similar to religious beliefs, as just defined. The Notes suggest that 'the belief should occupy a place in the person's life parallel to that filled by the God/Gods of those holding a particular religious belief'.[401] The European Court's case law indicates that discrimination on the grounds of a belief structure which involves the absence of certain beliefs is within the scope of the Regulations: 'if a Christian employer refuses an individual a job, because he is not Christian, regardless of whether he is Muslim, Hindu, atheist (etc.), that would be direct discrimination on the grounds of that individual's religious belief, which can be described as "non-Christian"'.[402]

The Notes suggest that a distinction should be drawn between a 'manifestation' of religious belief, for example in the form of clothing or the expression of certain views, and the belief itself. If this approach is followed, dress codes, or rules governing breaks for prayers, are unlikely to constitute direct discrimination under the Regulations, but they might amount to indirect discrimination, in which case they can be justified by the employer.[403]

---

396 On genuine occupational requirements, see below, paras 6.51; more generally, on the 2003 Regulations, see Vickers, 2003.
397 EE(RB)R 2003, reg 2(1).
398 *Explanatory Notes for the Employment Equality (Sexual Orientation) Regulations 2003 and the Employment Equality (Religion or Belief) Regulations 2003* (2003), at para 11.
399 *X v UK* (1977) 11 DR 55.
400 *Explanatory Notes*, at para 12, referring to *Campbell and Cousans v UK* (1982) 4 EHRR 293.
401 *Explanatory Notes*, at para 13.
402 *Explanatory Notes*, at para 14, referring to *Kokkanikis v Greece* (1994) 17 EHRR 397.
403 *Explanatory Notes*, at para 15.

The scope of protection

Personal scope

6.41   Anti-discrimination legislation applies the equality principle to all aspects of the employment relationship, from hiring through to (and in some cases beyond) termination. A first point to note is that the legislation applies both to employees and to those who are employed under contracts for services, where these give rise to an obligation personally to execute work or labour.[404] Agency workers have the benefit of the protection of the legislation in their relationships with both the agency and with the end user.[405] These are useful extensions to the coverage of the law. However, they by no means solve all the problems of classification which may arise. For example, the courts have recently asserted that, under the test for identifying the meaning of employment under the RRA 1976, not only is mutuality of obligation required for there to be a contract for services,[406] but that a clear personal commitment to provide work or labour, on the part of the complainant, is essential.[407] In relation to agency work, the fragmentation of the normal responsibilities of the employer between two distinct entities – the agency and the user or 'principal' – gives rise to problems which are not fully addressed by the present law. Although the issue is not free from doubt, the legislation can be read as imposing upon the user an obligation to treat agency workers equally with comparable 'permanent' workers in relation, for example, to the general working environment in the employment in question. But in so far as the user is not directly responsible for setting terms and conditions of employment, which are normally determined by the agency, it is arguable that, for this purpose, there can be no comparison of, for example, the pay and hours of agency staff and those of the 'permanent' workers in the same employment.[408]

---

404   This is the effect of the definition of 'employment': SDA 1975, s 82(1), RRA 1976, s 78(1), DDA 1995, s 68(1); EE(SO)R 2003, reg 2(3); EE(RB)R 2003, reg 2(3). See our discussion in ch 3, above, at paras 3.51–3.61. Note that the provisions of the anti-discrimination legislation on territorial scope (see SDA 1975, ss 6(1), 10; RRA 1976, ss 4(1), 8; DDA 1995, s 68(2), (2A), (4); EE(SO)R 2003, reg 9; EE(RB)R 2003, reg 9) are discussed in ch 2 above; see para 2.50.

405   Users or 'principals' are covered by SDA 1975, s 9; RRA 1976, s 7; DDA 1995, s 4B; EE(SO)R 2003, reg 8; and EE(RB)R 2003, reg 8; employment agencies and businesses by SDA 1975, s 15; RRA 1976, s 14; DDA 1995, reg 21A; EE(SO)R 2003, reg 18; and EE(RB)R 2003, reg 18. See generally para 3.68 above. Office-holders who do not otherwise fall under the relevant definitions are also covered, with certain specified exceptions: RRA 1976, s 76ZA; DDA 1995, ss 4C–4F; EE(SO)R 2003, reg 10; EE(RB)R 2003, reg 10.

406   *Mingeley v Pennock* [2004] IRLR 373.

407   See, for various applications of this test, *Loughran and Kelly v Northern Ireland Housing Executive* [1998] IRLR 593; *Perceval-Price v Department of Economic Development* [2000] IRLR 380; *Patterson v Legal Services Commission* [2004] IRLR 153.

408   See the judgment of the Court of Appeal in the sex discrimination case of *Allonby v Accrington and Rossendale College* [2001] IRLR 364, at paras 34–36 (Sedley LJ). These matters were remitted to the employment tribunal for further consideration. In this case the claim for parity of treatment in relation to contractual terms and conditions fell under the EqPA 1970 and not the SDA 1975 (for the reasons for this, see below, para 6.71) and the Court of Appeal referred questions relating to the scope of comparison under the EqPA to the ECJ, which decided on a narrow reading of Art 141 of the EC Treaty, under which comparisons across undertakings are generally not possible (Case C-256/01 *Allonby v Accrington and Rossendale College* [2004] IRLR 224). See further our analysis at para 6.76 below. DDA 1995, s 4B, is also worthy of note in this context. It states that the duty to make reasonable adjustments under s 4A of that Act is applicable to the principal as if it were a contract worker's employer, and the contract worker its employee, except that 'a principal is not required to take a step in relation to a disabled contract worker if under [s 4A] the disabled contract worker's employer is required to take the step in relation to him' (DDA 1995, s 4B(6)–(7)).

Discrimination against partners and applicants for partnerships falls under the Framework and Race Directives and hence under those parts of UK law derived from these provisions.[409] This currently produces the result that racial discrimination on the grounds of nationality or colour is only prohibited in the case of firms consisting of six or more partners,[410] while the SDA 1975 makes no reference to discrimination within partnerships.[411]

Trade unions, employers' associations and trade associations fall under the anti-discrimination legislation in respect of their treatment of applicants and members,[412] and 'qualifying' or 'qualification' bodies which are responsible for conferring authorisations or qualifications for professional purposes are also covered,[413] as are providers of vocational training.[414] Nor may a local authority or the Secretary of State for Employment commit discrimination in the provision of training services or facilities under the Employment and Training Act 1973.[415]

The anti-discrimination Acts mostly apply to the Crown and to Parliamentary staff,[416] to the police,[417] and to the armed forces.[418] In the case of the SDA 1975 the inclusion of the armed forces was achieved by an amendment made necessary by the Equal Treatment Directive but only implemented in 1994,[419] following litigation which established the right of servicewomen dismissed on the grounds of pregnancy to bring actions for compensation under the Directive.[420] By virtue of section 85(4) of the Act as amended, however, an act shall not constitute unlawful sex discrimination where it is done 'for the purpose of ensuring the combat effectiveness' of the armed forces.[421]

---

409 RRA 1976, s 10 (as amended by SI 2003/1626, reg 12); DDA 1995, ss 6A–6C; EE(SO)R 2003, reg 14; EE(RB)R 2003, reg 14. On discrimination against barristers and advocates, see SDA 1975, ss. 35A, 35B; RRA 1976, ss. 26A, 26B; DDA 1995, s 7A–7D; EE(SO)R 2003, regs 12–13; EE(RB)R 2003, regs 12–13.

410 RRA 1976, s 10.

411 The revised Equal Treatment Directive, which must be brought into force by 5 October 2005, provides for the inclusion of partnerships (Directive 76/207, Art 3(1)(d)).

412 SDA 1975, s 12; RRA 1976, s 11; DDA 1995, ss. 13–14; EE(SO)R 2003, reg 15; EE(RB)R 2003, reg 15.

413 SDA 1975, s 13; RRA 1976, s 12; DDA 1995, ss 14A, 14B; EE(SO)R 2003, reg 16; EE(RB)R 2003, reg 16. In *Arthur v A-G* [1999] ICR 631 it was held that the position of justice of the peace is not a 'profession' or 'occupation'. In *Triesman v Ali* [2002] IRLR 489 the Court of Appeal held that the Labour Party was not a 'qualifying body' for the position of local government councillor, holding that *Sawyer v Ashan* [1999] IRLR 609 was wrongly decided (but going on to hold that, in this regard, the Labour Party fell under a separate provision, s 25 of the RRA 1976, governing discrimination by associations not within s 11 of the Act). Under SDA 1975, s 42A, Parts II and IV (governing, respectively, discrimination in employment and other unlawful acts) do not apply to selection of party candidates in a relevant election if they are 'adopted for the purpose of reducing inequality in the numbers of men and women elected, as candidates of the party, to be members' of a relevant body.

414 SDA 1975, s 14; RRA 1976, s 13; DDA 1995, 14C, 14D (referring, more narrowly, to the provision of 'practical work experience'); EE(SO)R 2003, reg 17; EE(RB)R 2003, reg 17.

415 SDA 1975, ss 15(2), 16; RRA 1976, ss 14(2), 15; EE(SO)R 2003, reg 19; EE(RB)R 2003, reg 19. This prohibition does not apply in the context of the DDA 1995.

416 SDA 1975, ss 85, 85A, 85B; RRA 1976, ss 75, 75A, 75B; DDA 1995, ss. 64, 65; EE(SO)R 2003, regs 36–38; EE(RB)R 2003, regs 36–38.

417 SDA 1975, s 17; RRA 1976, ss 76A–76B; DDA 1995, s 64A; EE(SO)R 2003, reg 11; EE(RB)R 2003, reg 11.

418 See SDA 1975, s 85; RRA 1976, s 75; EE(SO)R 2003, reg 36; EE(RB)R 2003, reg 36. The armed forces are outside the DDA 1995. The Framework Directive allows a derogation for the armed forces in respect of disability and age discrimination.

419 SI 1994/3276, amending SDA 1975, s 85(4).

420 *Ministry of Defence v Cannock* [1994] IRLR 509.

421 See Case C-273/97 *Sirdar v Army Board and Secretary of State for Defence* [2000] IRLR 47.

Hiring

6.42   At the hiring stage, it is unlawful for an employer to discriminate against a person on the relevant grounds '(a) in the arrangements he makes for the purpose of determining who should be offered that employment, or (b) in the terms on which he offers her that employment, or (c) by refusing or deliberately omitting to offer her that employment'.[422] In addition to being able to show that the employer contravened the equality principle by refusing or omitting to hire him or her on grounds which were discriminatory, the applicant may also challenge the arrangements made by the employer for determining who is appointed, including the composition of the shortlist and the form of the interview,[423] as well as the terms on which the job is offered. Although difficulties of proof are substantial here, they may be eased, as we have seen,[424] by the use of the statutory questionnaires to elicit from the respondent the reasons for its decision,[425] as well as by the willingness of the courts, following *West Midlands Passenger Transport Executive v Singh*,[426] to countenance the use of statistical evidence concerning the composition of the workforce and patterns of previous hirings as evidence of discriminatory practices. The changes made to the definition of discrimination as a result of the implementation of the Burden of Proof Directive, together with similar provisions in the Framework and Race Directives, have also helped in this regard.[427] The remedies available to a disappointed applicant may also be significant; because damages for injury to feelings may be awarded[428] and because the upper limit on compensation formerly applicable in cases of sex and race discrimination no longer applies,[429] damages may well be more than nominal, and there is also the possibility (albeit not a very strong one) that the tribunal could make a recommendation that the complainant be hired on the next occasion of a vacancy arising.[430]

It is unlawful to publish or cause to be published an advertisement which indicates or might reasonably be understood as indicating an intention to commit an unlawful act of sex, race or disability discrimination in relation to employment;[431] for this purpose, the relevant intention is established if the advertisement contains a 'job description with a sexual connotation (such as "waiter", "salesgirl", "postman" or "stewardess")'.[432] However, only the EOC, CRE or DRC, as the case may be, has the power to enforce this provision.[433]

---

422 SDA 1975, s 6(1); see also RRA 1976, s 4(1); DDA 1995, s 4(1); EE(SO)R 2003, reg 6(1); EE(RB)R 2003, reg 6(1).
423 See *Roadburg v Lothian RC* [1976] IRLR 283; *Saunders v Richmond-upon-Thames London Borough Council* [1978] ICR 75.
424 See para 6.18 above.
425 See *King v Great Britain-China Centre* [1991] IRLR 513, discussed in para 6.18 above.
426 [1988] ICR 614.
427 See para 6.18 above.
428 SDA 1975, s 66(4); RRA 1976, s 57(4); DDA 1995, s 17A(4); EE(SO)R 2003, reg 31(3); EE(RB)R 2003, reg 31(3) .
429 See below, para 6.67.
430 See *North West Thames Regional Health Authority v Noone* [1988] ICR 813, discussed below.
431 SDA 1975, s 38; RRA 1976, s 29; DDA 1995, s 16B.
432 SDA 1975, s 38(3).
433 *Cardiff Women's Aid v Hartup* [1994] IRLR 390. For an example of an action brought by the CRE, see *Lambeth London Borough Council v Commission for Racial Equality* [1990] ICR 768.

Treatment of employed persons: general issues

6.43 It is unlawful for an employer to discriminate against an employed person under the SDA '(a) in the way he affords her access to opportunities for promotion, transfer or training, or to any other benefits, facilities or services, or by refusing or deliberately omitting to afford her access to them, or (b) by dismissing her, or subjecting her to any other detriment', and broadly similar formulae are used in the case of the other anti-discrimination statutes.[434] Some special features of the regulation of employment need to be noted.

At the outset, the scope of the SDA 1975 is artificially restricted in order to ensure that it does not trespass on the ground covered by the EqPA 1970. The EqPA is more limited as an anti-discrimination measure in significant respects; unlike the SDA, which enables a comparison to be made between the complainant and a hypothetical comparator, the EqPA requires an actual comparator who also falls into one of the three situations specified in the Act, namely like work, work rated as equivalent and work of equal value with that of the applicant. Nor does the EqPA 1970 apply to discrimination on the grounds of marital status.[435] Notwithstanding these limits, section 6 of the SDA 1975 has no application 'to benefits consisting of the payment of money when the provision of those benefits is regulated by the woman's contract of employment'.[436] The effect of this is that once the employment has begun, differences in contractual terms and conditions affecting pay must be judged under the EqPA 1970 and cannot be challenged by means of the SDA 1975.[437]

The definition of employment discrimination is also wider under the RRA 1976 than under the SDA 1975 in two further and highly significant respects. First, section 1(2) of the RRA 1976 provides that 'segregating a person from other persons on racial grounds is treating him less favourably than they are treated'. No similar provision operates under the SDA 1975, with the result that sex segregation is not unlawful unless it can clearly be shown that those in one group are being treated less favourably than, and not just differently from, those in the other. Second, the RRA 1976 prohibits discrimination against another 'on racial grounds' and not on the grounds of *his or her race*, as the SDA 1975 does with regard to the complainant's own sex. This means, for example, that it is a contravention of the RRA 1976 for an employer to dismiss a white employee on the grounds that he or she refuses to implement an instruction not to serve black customers.[438] This wider approach to the definition of discrimination has been followed in the Regulations governing equal treatment in relation to sexual orientation and religion or belief.[439]

---

434 SDA 1975, s 6(2); RRA 1976, s 4(2); DDA 1995, s 4(2); EE(SO)R 2003, reg 6(2); EE(RB)R 2003, reg 6(2).
435 See below, para 6.71.
436 SDA 1975, s 6(6); see, eg *Meeks v NUAAW* [1976] IRLR 198.
437 It is not clear whether Art 141 of the EC Treaty and the Equal Treatment Directive are mutually exclusive in the same way. For a view that the Equal Treatment Directive, prior to its amendment, was applicable to certain issues of contractual terms and conditions and employment-related benefits which might also fall under Art 141, see the Opinion of Advocate General Van Gerven in Case C-262/88 *Barber v Guardian Royal Exchange Assurance Group* [1990] IRLR 240 (and see Ellis, 1991: p 136); for a decision suggesting the opposite, see the Judgment of the ECJ in Case C-77/02 *Steinicke v Bundesanstalt für Arbeit* [2003] IRLR 892. Art 3(1)(c) of the revised Directive, inserted by Directive 2002/73, refers to pay, but Recital 16 of Directive 2002/73 can be read as implying the preservation of the pre-existing law on this point.
438 *Showboat Entertainment Centre Ltd v Owens* [1984] IRLR 7; *Weathersfield v Sargent* [1999] IRLR 94.
439 EE(SO)R 2003, reg 3; EE(RB)R 2003, reg 3.

The term 'detriment' in limb (b) of the definition of employment discrimination has been broadly defined. The approach in *Peake v Automotive Products Ltd*[440] in which the Court of Appeal held that the employer's practice of allowing women workers to leave the factory floor five minutes earlier than their male colleague was held to be, in Lord Denning's words, 'perfectly harmless',[441] has not been followed. In the more representative decision of *Ministry of Defence v Jeremiah*[442] the requirement that men, but not women, should agree to undertake dirty and unpleasant work in order to be eligible for overtime, was held to be a detriment. In this case there was a 'deprivation of choice', and it was irrelevant that Jeremiah received financial compensation for doing the work in question. In *Kirby v Manpower Services Commission*[443] the transfer of the employee to a less interesting job was held to be a 'detriment' for this purpose. In *Shamoon v Chief Constable of the Royal Ulster Constabulary*[444] the House of Lords stressed that it is not necessary for an applicant to demonstrate some physical or economic consequence, but the tribunal must find that by reason of the act complained of a reasonable worker might take the view that he or she had thereby been disadvantaged in the circumstances in which they had thereafter to work. A detriment can arise from psychological illness or stress but transient hurt feelings may not suffice.[445]

Areas of particular controversy in which the courts have tested the limits of the equality principle with regard to the treatment of employees are the imposition by employers of rules concerning dress and appearance and the definition of harassment.

Dress and appearance

6.44   At the level of the contract of employment, it is clear that the employer has an inherent power to lay down rules governing dress and appearance at work ('dress codes'). Such rules are unlikely, in themselves, to be terms of the contract; it is more likely that they are akin to the rule book issued in *ASLEF (No 2)*,[446] which was no more than an emanation of the employer's managerial prerogative. Like other rules of this kind, dress codes are subject to the common law notion of the reciprocal duty of co-operation; if an employer were to impose rules which were clearly oppressive to individuals in the sense of undermining their personal dignity,[447] or which not were reasonably related to the jobs which they carried out, it is arguable that *to that extent* the rules could not be enforced, in the sense that to do so would be a breach of contract by the employer. However, it must be said that this common law constraint on the employer's power is residual, at best, and unlikely to provide a firm foundation for a challenge mounted by an employee. More concrete support may be provided by HRA 1998; dress codes may constitute an interference with respect for private life or

---

440 [1978] QB 233.
441 [1978] QB 233, 239.
442 [1980] ICR 13.
443 [1980] IRLR 229. See also *Gloucester Working Men's Club & Institute v James* [1986] ICR 603, 606 (threatening a person with dismissal may be a 'detriment' even though that threat is not carried out).
444 [2003] IRLR 285.
445 *Jiad v Byford* [2003] IRLR 232.
446 *Secretary of State for Employment v ASLEF (No 2)* [1972] 2 QB 455.
447 An example of this might be a rule requiring an employee to wear a uniform which was sexually provocative and which exposed him or her to sexual harassment: see, eg, the US case of *EEOC v Sage Realty Corpn* 507 F Supp 599 (1981), in which a rule of this kind was found to violate Title VII of the Civil Rights Act.

freedom of expression unless they can be justified, although they likely to be easier to justify if confined to the workplace than if they also intrude on conduct outside work.[448]

However, the contractual position on dress codes is necessarily subject to the principle of equal treatment: the employer must not apply rules governing dress and appearance which discriminate between different individuals on the grounds of their sex or race, or which have an adverse impact which cannot be justified. In practice the greatest difficulty here is caused by rules which formally differentiate between the sexes: if such rules amount to direct discrimination there is no possibility of the open-ended justification defence being invoked, so that managerial prerogative in an important area would then be significantly qualified. Whatever the business justifications for dress codes, there is an argument to the effect that dress codes, at least in certain forms, reinforce sex-based stereotypes of the kind which it is the purpose of the Act to undermine.[449] The courts have struggled to find a clear line which might successfully reconcile these two positions.

In *Schmidt v Austick Bookshops Ltd*[450] the EAT was faced with a complaint about a rule that female employees were not allowed to wear trousers at work. A variety of grounds were offered for concluding that no breach of the Act of 1975 had taken place. One was that male and female employees were not being treated unequally: 'there were in force rules restricting wearing apparel and governing appearance which applied to men and also applied to women, although obviously, women and men being different, the rules in the two cases were not the same'.[451] In *Smith v Safeway plc*[452] the EAT interpreted *Schmidt* as establishing the principle that 'the law permits different rules to be applied to men and women provided they enforce a common principle of smartness if read as a whole'. The difficulty with this view, plausible as it might seem, is that it strikes at the core of the concept of direct discrimination: as Cunningham points out, 'the whole purpose of the Act is to limit the extent to which women and men, different as they are, can be differently treated'. To say that the undeniable difference between men and women is a sufficient reason for applying different rules to women than to men is 'to demolish it in its entirety'.[453] This aspect of *Schmidt* is even more difficult to defend in the light of the 'but-for' test applied by the House of Lords in the *Birmingham County Council*[454] and *James*[455] cases: clearly, Miss Schmidt would not have been treated in the same way had she been a man.

A more coherent (if, nonetheless, debatable) ground offered in *Schmidt* was that the complainant in that case suffered no 'detriment' by being required to wear a skirt or dress when at work. Similarly, in *Burrett v West Birmingham Health Authority*[456] the EAT and Court of Appeal decided that a female nurse who was required to wear a cap as part of her uniform, when male nurses were not required to do so as part of theirs, had not thereby been sufficiently disadvantaged for a detriment to arise, despite the complainant arguing that it

448 *Kara v UK*, Application No 36528/97; see G Morris, 2001a.
449 See generally Flynn, 1995, and for a review of the issue of legal regulation of dress and appearance, Skidmore, 1999.
450 [1977] IRLR 360.
451 [1977] IRLR 360, 361.
452 [1995] IRLR 132, 133.
453 Cunningham, 1995: p 178.
454 [1989] IRLR 173.
455 [1990] IRLR 288.
456 [1994] IRLR 7, EAT; (3 March 1994, unreported), CA, discussed by Cunningham, 1995.

was demeaning. The Court of Appeal went on to hold that while the complainant had later suffered a detriment when she was disciplined for refusing to wear the cap, this was not an act of sex discrimination since a man in the same position, who had refused to wear part of his uniform, would also have been subjected to a disciplinary sanction.

In *Smith v Safeway plc*[457] the Court of Appeal, overturning a ruling of the EAT, held that a male shop assistant in a supermarket delicatessen who was dismissed for having a pony-tail had not thereby been discriminated against on the grounds of his sex. Safeway operated two different rules, one for men and one for women. Men were required to have 'tidy hair not below shirt collar length', for women, 'shoulder-length hair must be clipped back'. The majority of the EAT (Pill J dissented) distinguished *Schmidt* on the grounds that that case was concerned with the issue of dress and appearance while at work; *Smith*, on the other hand, addressed 'the issues of appearance which extend beyond working hours and thereby affect individual choice detrimentally at all times'. The majority also thought that it was unnecessary for the employer to have imposed differential rules on hair-length for men and women: 'the need to present a conventional appearance at work is already met by the standards laid down as to hairstyle which, in the case of a pony-tail, is specifically capable of being treated the same for both men and women'.[458] In the Court of Appeal, by contrast, Peter Gibson LJ considered that an employer would not be acting unlawfully by adopting a 'code which applies conventional standards' to both sexes.[459]

The concept of detriment arguably needs to be given a broad meaning if the legislation is not to be stymied, and should be concerned solely with the question of whether the complainant has suffered a tangible disadvantage and not with the quite separate issue of whether the disadvantage was *justifiable*, since that would be to undermine the distinction between direct and indirect discrimination.[460] Of the cases just considered, *Burrett* is particularly worrying, in so far as it suggests that the courts could indeed limit the scope of the equality principle under the Acts of 1975 and 1976 by defining 'detriment' narrowly and by drawing a distinction between the effect of the rule itself, which may be discriminatory but not a detriment, and the effect of the disciplinary action designed to enforce the rule, which may be a detriment but not discriminatory. But perhaps it is the case that 'a reading of the Act which has the result that employers may not in general enforce different dress codes on their male and female employees suggests a more radical contempt for social *mores* than can have been intended when the Act was drafted'.[461]

Harassment

6.45   Harassment may be unlawful under the general tests for discrimination in employment.[462] Key issues here are whether the treatment received by the

---

457 [1996] IRLR 456.

458 [1995] IRLR 132, 134.

459 [1996] IRLR 456, 459. To similar effect is the decision of the EAT in *Department for Work and Pensions v Thompson* [2004] IRLR 348.

460 Cunningham, 1995.

461 Cunningham, 1995: p 179.

462 However, for an argument that harassment is best regarded as an employment-related wrong in itself, without reference to the element of discrimination, see Dine and Watt, 1995, discussing the seminal work of McKinnon, 1979; on this question, see also Conaghan, 1996; Hepple, 2000: p 180. In this context it is noteworthy that the Protection from Harassment Act 1997 creates both criminal and civil liability where a person pursues a

employee amounts to a 'detriment' and whether he or she was disadvantaged by virtue of the relevant prohibited ground. The term 'detriment' is, as elsewhere, broadly applied here; a single act of verbal sexual harassment may be sufficient, as in *Insitu Cleaning Co Ltd v Heads*.[463] Here the employee, who occupied a managerial position, was subjected to a gratuitously insulting sexual remark by another manager who was the son of two of the company's directors. The EAT rejected an argument that verbal harassment was only caught by the Act when it was repeated over a period of time. This is a rather more forthright application of section 6(2)(b) of the SDA 1975 (and by extension of section 4(2)(c) of the RRA 1976) than the statement of the Court of Appeal in *De Souza v Automobile Association*,[464] to the effect that 'racially to insult a coloured employee is not enough by itself even if that insult caused him or her distress; before the employee can be said to have been subjected to some "other detriment" the court or Tribunal must find that by reason of the act or acts complained of a reasonable worker would or might take the view that he had thereby been disadvantaged in the circumstances in which he had thereafter to work'. This seems to be out of line with the broad approach normally taken to the interpretation of 'detriment'. In *Thomas v Robinson* the EAT said that the *De Souza* case 'must now be treated with some reserve' and ruled that while 'a single instance of racial abuse does not necessarily amount to harassment', a single act of verbal racial or sexual harassment would be enough.[465] 'Harassment' was to be distinguished from 'abuse' by the presence of two elements: 'the first is the targeting of the person being harassed' while the second 'is the causing of distress to the target'.[466]

Whether the harassment is sexual or racial depends on how far the victim can show that he or she would have been treated differently but for their sex or race. In *Porcelli v Strathclyde Regional Council*[467] the applicant worked as a laboratory technician in the same department as two male colleagues who were found to have 'pursued a policy of vindictive unpleasantness towards the applicant for the deliberate purpose of making her apply for a transfer'. This included sexual insults and physical intimidation. The employer argued that the two employees would have behaved in the same way towards a male colleague whom they had disliked, but the Court of Session rejected this analysis: their treatment of her 'was a particular kind of weapon, based upon the sex of the victim, which, as the employment tribunal recognised would not have been used against an equally disliked man'.[468]

This decision may be contrasted with *Stewart v Cleveland Guest (Engineering) Ltd*.[469] Miss Stewart, who was employed as an inspector in an engineering

---

course of conduct which he or she knows or ought to know amounts to the harassment of another; in *Majrowski v Guy's and St Thomas's NHS Trust* [2005] IRLR 340 the Court of Appeal held that an employer could be vicariously liable for an employee's breach of the Act, committed in the course of employment.

463 [1995] IRLR 4; see also *Bracebridge Engineering Ltd v Darby* [1990] IRLR 3; *Mecca Leisure Group plc v Chatprachong* [1993] IRLR 531.
464 [1986] IRLR 103, 107.
465 [2003] IRLR 7, at paras 24, 25.
466 [2003] IRLR 7, at para 25.
467 [1986] IRLR 134.
468 [1986] IRLR 134, 137; see also, on this point, *Pearce v Governing Body of Mayfield School* [2003] IRLR 512, at paras 90–94 (Lord Hope).
469 [1994] IRLR 440; a similarly restrictive decision is *Brumfit v Ministry of Defence* [2005] IRLR 4.

company, was required as part of her responsibilities to visit the factory floor where a large number of calendars displaying nude women were on view. She complained to the works manager and asked for the calendars to be removed; at first he refused on the grounds that the complaint was trivial, but when Miss Stewart raised the matter with her trade union the works manager changed his mind and ordered the calendars to be removed. It became known that Miss Stewart had made the initial complaint and, when a deputation of women employees informed management that they did not share her view, she resigned on the grounds that the employer was unable to protect her from embarassment and distress. An employment tribunal found that she had been constructively dismissed on the grounds that the employer was in breach of the duty of mutual trust and confidence, and found her dismissal unfair, but it also concluded that there had been no sex discrimination: 'the display itself was neutral. A man might well find this sort of display as offensive as the applicant did'.[470] The EAT refused to overturn this ruling on the narrow ground that the tribunal's decision was not perverse.

Stewart illustrates the inherent difficulty in using the principle of equal treatment to combat harassment where the conduct in question could be offensive to members of both sexes or regardless of the race of the person concerned.[471] Under the anti-discrimination Acts, the employer may seek to argue that a comparator of the opposite sex (or another race) would have been just as badly treated as the complainant.[472] However, the key issue here is whether the conduct in question is *equally* offensive. In *Stewart* it was argued that sexually explicit imagery was *particularly* offensive to women employees and that the psychological detriment to which they were subjected should not have been *equated with* the offence felt by men. The argument for Miss Stewart was that

> ... a man's objection to such a display would be based on other grounds (eg moral grounds) not on the ground of his sex. As the pictures depicted women, and not men, a man, even one who objected to the pictures, would not have found the pictures offensive *in the same way* as Miss Stewart did ... this treatment was unfavourable to a woman because she was *more vulnerable* to it than a man was.[473]

In *Driskel v Peninsula Business Services*[474] it was accepted that 'sexual badinage' of a woman by a male fellow employee should not be equated with similar words and behaviour between two men, while in *Burton v De Vere Hotels Ltd*[475] a racially hostile environment was found to be particularly humiliating

---

470   [1994] IRLR 440, 442.
471   Dine and Watt, 1995.
472   This was confirmed by the judgment of the House of Lords in *Pearce v Governing Body of Mayfield School* [2003] IRLR 512. As a result, the suggestion in *Sidhu v Aerospace Composite Technology Ltd* [2000] IRLR 602, 606 that the position of the comparator is not relevant in a case where 'the very action complained of is in itself less favourable treatment on sexual or racial grounds' cannot stand under the general provisions of the SDA. However, the introduction of a specific wrong of harassment in the context of the RRA, DDA, EE(SO)R and EE(RB)R goes some way to remedying this point; see the text in this paragraph, below. It should also be noted that the revisions to the Equal Treatment Directive (see Directive 76/206/EC, as amended by Directive 2002/73/EC) require the introduction of a specific wrong of sexual harassment by October 2005, and that the Government is currently consulting on appropriate implementing legislation: DTI, *Equality and Diversity. Updating the Sex Discrimination Act* (2005).
473   [1994] IRLR 440, 443.
474   [2000] IRLR 151; *Moonsar v Fiveways Express Transport Ltd.* [2005] IRLR 9.
475   [1996] IRLR 596.

to black employees. But in *Pearce v Governing Body of Mayfield School*[476] the House of Lords held that *Burton* was wrongly decided on this point, since white waitresses might have been just as insulted as the complainants were. This approach fails to take into account the argument, just made, for the particular vulnerability of the members of one group as opposed to another.

A more effective approach would be to reduce as far as possible the importance of the hypothetical comparator. In this vein, the Framework Directive and Race Directive define harassment as a form of discrimination which occurs when 'unwanted conduct related to [a prohibited ground] takes place with the purpose or effect of violating the dignity of a person and of creating an intimidating, hostile, degrading, humiliating or offensive environment'.[477] This more open-ended formula has now been incorporated into those parts of UK law which are derived from the Framework and Race Directives. The formula is taken more or less word for word from the Directives, except that the conduct in question must give rise to an environment which is intimidating, and so on, for the complainant specifically, and if, in all the circumstances, including in particular the perception of the complainant, the conduct 'can reasonably be considered' as having the effect contended for.[478]

The Framework Directive's definition of harassment indicates that it is to be understood as a 'form of discrimination' and hence refers back to the definitions of direct and indirect discrimination set out in the Directive.[479] The definition of direct discrimination refers, in turn, to the treatment of another in a 'comparable situation', while the definition of indirect discrimination refers to the disadvantage suffered by the complainant 'compared with other persons'. The formulae adopted in the UK legislation make no such references back to the concepts of direct and indirect discrimination. To that extent, these new forms of harassment appear to be free-standing wrongs, operating separately from and in addition to the wrong of unlawful discrimination.[480] However, it must still be shown that the harassment takes place on the relevant prohibited ground. Thus the best interpretation of these new provisions is not that the element of comparison is completely absent, but rather that it is open to the courts to approach the process of comparison more flexibly in future. In particular, the requirement that there should be a hypothetical comparator whose position was in all material respects similar to that of the complainant can no longer be regarded as relevant in this context, not least because there is no reference in the definition of 'harassment' to the 'relevant circumstances' test which applies in cases of direct and indirect discrimination.[481]

---

476 [2003] IRLR 512, at para 30 (Lord Nicholls). The process of comparison was much less rigidly applied in *Scott v Commissioners of Inland Revenue* [2004] IRLR 713 to find that a male employee wrongly accused of sexual harassment was discriminated against on the grounds of his sex, on the grounds that a female employee would not have been so treated. See also *Moonsar v Fiveways Express Transport Ltd.* [2005] IRLR 9 for a more flexible approach than that adopted in *Pearce*.

477 Directive 2000/78, Art 2(3); Directive 2000/42, Art 2(3).

478 RRA 1976, s 3A (applying only to discrimination on the grounds of race and national or ethnic origin); DDA 1995, s 3B; EE(SO)R 2003, reg 5; EE(RB)R 2003, reg 5.

479 See Directive 2000/78, Art 2(2)(a).

480 Cf. RRA 1976, s 4(2A); DDA 1995, s 4(3); EE(SO)R 2003, reg 6(3); EE(RB)R 2003, reg 6(3).

481 If that approach were to be adopted, it is difficult to see how *Stewart v Cleveland Guest (Engineering) Ltd* [1994] IRLR 440 could now be decided the same way. *Pearce v Governing Body of Mayfield School* [2003] IRLR 512 would now be decided differently, on this point, even under the strict comparator test, since in that case it was clear that a heterosexual employee in the position of the complainant would not have been submitted to the same treatment.

Dismissal

6.46   Dismissal is one of the specific employment-related wrongs covered by the anti-discrimination legislation. The definition of dismissal is stated in certain contexts to include the termination of a fixed-term contract ('the termination of [a] person's employment by the expiration of any period (including a period expiring by reference to an event or circumstance), not being a termination immediately after which the employment is renewed on the same terms') and a constructive dismissal ('the termination of that person's employment by any act of his (including the giving of notice) in circumstances such that he is entitled to terminate it without notice by reason of the conduct of the employer').[482] It is arguable that the definition of dismissal extended to these categories in any event, and that it has a general application throughout anti-discrimination legislation.[483]

Discriminatory dismissal is almost bound to be unfair under ERA 1996, although it is not automatically unfair in the sense that certain other categories of reasons are.[484] In practice, where the complainant can choose between these statutory claims, resort to anti-discrimination legislation is more likely. In contrast to most unfair dismissal claims, no qualifying period is required under the anti-discrimination legislation. Nor are there any statutory upper limits on compensation. The changes made to the law governing the burden of proof[485] have made a discrimination claim more attractive, by comparison to an unfair dismissal claim, than used to be the case. In addition, the right to claim unfair dismissal under ERA 1996 is confined to employees, whereas the anti-discrimination legislation extends to a wider category of employed persons.[486]

Post-contractual and post-relationship discrimination

6.47   In *Rhys-Harper v Relaxion Group plc*[487] the House of Lords held that certain discriminatory acts occurring after the termination of the complainant's contract of employment were within the coverage of the anti-discrimination legislation. This issue initially arose in the context of employees who, following an initial decision to dismiss, lodged an appeal under the employer's internal disciplinary procedures. According to the Court of Appeal in *Post Office v Adekeye (No 2)*,[488] any discrimination occurring at this later stage applied to a period when the complainant was no longer 'employed'. In *Coote v Granada Hospitality Ltd.*[489] the ECJ held that, under the Equal Treatment Directive (prior to its amendment[490]), a remedy had to be provided for ex-employees who were the subject of victimisation by their employer. The EAT and Court of Appeal in *Rhys-Harper* held that this decision had no application beyond victimisation

---

482 SDA 1975, s 82(1A); RRA 1976 s 4(4A) (applying only to race and national or ethnic origins); DDA 1995, s 4(5); EE(SO)R 2003, reg 6(5); EE(RB)R 2003, reg 6(5).
483 See *Derby Specialist Fabrication Ltd v Burton* [2001] IRLR 69.
484 See para 5.95 above.
485 See above, paras 6.18 and 6.22.
486 See para 6.41 above.
487 *Rhys-Harper v Relaxion Group plc, D'Souza v London Borough of Lambeth, Jones v 3M Healthcare Ltd., Kirker v British Sugar plc, Angel v New Possibilities NHS Trust, Bond v Hackney Citizens Advice Bureau* [2003] IRLR 484.
488 [1997] IRLR 105. See also *Nagarajan v Agnew* [1994] IRLR 61.
489 Case C-185/97 *Coote v Granada Hospitality Ltd* [1998] IRLR 656, applied in *Coote v Granada Hospitality Ltd (No 2)* [1999] IRLR 452.
490 By Directive 2002/73.

cases.[491] When the case reached the House of Lords, the majority concluded that the reference to an 'employed' person was, after all, sufficiently wide to cover ex-employees as long as certain elements of the employment relationship remained in place notwithstanding the termination of the complainant's contract. In Lord Nicholls's view:

> ... the natural and proper interpretation of s 6(2) of the Sex Discrimination Act and the corresponding provisions of the [Race Relations Act and Disability Discrimination Act] in this context is that once two persons enter into the relationship of employer and employee, the employee is intended to be protected against discrimination by the employer in respect of all the benefits arising from that relationship ... This being the purpose, it would make no sense to draw an arbitrary line at the precise moment when the contract of employment ends, protecting the employee against discrimination in respect of all benefits up to that point but in respect of none thereafter.[492]

According to Lord Rodger, the Acts applied where 'there is a substantive connection between the discriminatory conduct and the employment relationship',[493] while Lord Hobhouse pointed to the need to show that a given dispute fell within the 'employment field'[494] in order for an employment tribunal to have jurisdiction. Lord Hope, drawing more explicitly on the ECJ judgment in *Coote*, argued that 'the relationship between the employer and the employee does not necessarily come to an end at the precise moment when their contract terminates'. Under section 6(2) of the SDA as interpreted by reference to the Directive, a former employee was protected as 'long as the transactions that remain to be completed are attributable to a continuation of [the] relationship of employer and employee', and there was, in his view, no reason not to extend this meaning to the similar expressions used in the RRA and DDA.[495] Lord Scott took a more restricted view of the reach both of the Acts and of the Directive and confined his judgment to ruling that, on its proper interpretation, the legislation could apply to cases of internal appeal procedures, but not to other instances of post-employment discrimination beyond a limited range of scenarios.[496]

The effect of the ruling in *Rhys-Harper* and a series of other cases decided at the same time is that a failure of the employer to apply an internal disciplinary procedure, to respond to a reasonable request for a reference or to return property to the employee, in so far as they involve a breach of the equal treatment principle, are all capable of coming under the anti-discrimination statutes, although an employer's refusal to comply with a reinstatement or re-engagement order issued by an employment tribunal is not.[497] The issue has also received the attention of the legislature. By virtue of amendments made while the *Rhys-Harper* case was still being decided, where a 'relevant relationship' has 'come to an end' it is unlawful for the respondent to discriminate against the other party on one of the prohibited grounds by subjecting them to a detriment, or to

---

491 [2000] IRLR 810; [2001] IRLR 460.
492 [2003] IRLR 484, at para 37.
493 [2003] IRLR 484, at para 215.
494 [2003] IRLR 484, at para 150, referring to SDA 1975, s 63(1), RRA 1976, s 54(1) and DDA 1995, s 8(1).
495 [2003] IRLR 484, at paras 114–115.
496 [2003] IRLR 484, at para 200.
497 This was the effect of the ruling in *D'Souza v London Borough of Lambeth* [2003] IRLR 484.

subject them to harassment, 'where the discrimination or harassment arises out of and is closely connected to that relationship'. A 'relevant relationship' is, in essence, one of employment within the meaning of the relevant anti-discrimination provision.[498] This provision does more than clarify the meaning of *Rhys-Harper*. The judgments of the House of Lords refer to discrimination which is post-contractual but within the period when the 'relationship' of employment is still subsisting. By referring to a 'post-relationship' period, the recent amendments to the legislation potentially extend still further the reach of the equal treatment principle.

The personal and vicarious liability of the employer

6.48   Employers may be liable under the anti-discrimination legislation either personally or vicariously. The legislation contains important extensions of the primary liability which employers and others may bear. In effect they set up a statutory system of secondary civil liability,[499] by in each case providing that '[a] person who knowingly aids another person to do an act made unlawful by this Act shall be treated for the purposes of this Act as himself doing an unlawful act of the like description'. Those liable as accessories in this way may include employees or agents for whose acts employers or principals are deemed to be liable.[500]

Vicarious liability is also specifically provided for: '[a]nything done by a person in the course of his employment shall be treated for the purposes of this Act as done by his employer as well as by him, whether or not it was done with the employer's knowledge or approval', and the same applies to anything done by an agent with the authority, express or implied, of his or her principal. This is subject to the employer (but not the principal) being able to show that 'he took such steps as were reasonably practicable to prevent the employee from doing that act, or from doing in the course of his employment acts of that description'.[501] Employers have less leeway here than under the common law of vicarious liability. In *Jones v Tower Boot Co Ltd*[502] the complainant was subjected to racial taunts and acts of violence by his fellow employees, of a kind which were sufficiently extreme to fall outside the course of those employees' course of employment as defined by the common law. The Court ruled that, for this purpose, the phrase 'course of employment' in the context of the RRA 1976 had

---

498   See SDA 1975, s 20A; RRA 1976, s 27A (which has no application to discrimination on the grounds of nationality and colour); DDA 1995, s 16A; EE(SO)R 2003, reg 21; EE(RB)R 2003, reg 21.

499   This is an important but 'theoretically under-developed' area of the common law of obligations: Deakin, Johnston and Markesinis, 2003: pp 856–858.

500   SDA 1975, s 42; RRA 1976, s 33; DDA 1995, s 57; EE(SO)R 2003, reg 23; EE(RB)R 2003, reg 23. Hence the complainant can sue a fellow employee for aiding and abetting an act of discrimination by the employer: *AM v WC and SPV* [1999] IRLR 410. The notion of 'aiding and abetting' has received a narrow interpretation in this context which excludes acts which merely enable or facilitate, as opposed to assisting, unlawful acts: see *Anyanwu v South Bank Students' Union* [2001] IRLR 305; *Hallam v Avery* [2001] IRLR 312. Also potentially liable for sex, race or disability discrimination are those who 'induce, or attempt to induce, a person to do any act which contravenes' the substantive parts of the Act: SDA 1975, s 40; RRA 1976, s 31; DDA 1995, s 16C(2)–(3) ('pressure to discriminate'). See also SDA 1975, s 39, RRA 1976, s 30, DDA 1995, s 16C(1) ('instructions to discriminate'). These provisions may only be enforced by the EOC, CRE or DRC, respectively.

501   SDA 1975, s 41; RRA 1976, s 32; DDA 1995, s 58; EE(SO)R 2003, reg 22; EE(RB)R 2003, reg 22.

502   [1997] IRLR 168, reversing the EAT ([1995] IRLR 529).

to be given a purposive interpretation, precisely in order to avoid the conclusion that 'the more heinous the act of discrimination, the less likely it will be that the employer would be liable'. To apply the traditional common law test would, thought Waite LJ, 'seriously undermine the statutory scheme of the Discrimination Acts and flout the purposes which they were passed to achieve'.[503]

It can be argued that an employer which fails to put in place a policy of discouraging sexual or racial harassment, which may be inferred if it lacks a procedure for dealing with complaints, may for that reason be *personally* liable under the anti-discrimination Acts for subjecting employees for example, to a working environment in which sexual or racial harassment is possible. This is consistent with the European Commission's Recommendation of 27 November 1991 on the protection of the dignity of women and men at work.[504] The Recommendation calls on Member States to take action to promote awareness that sexual harassment, or 'conduct of a sexual nature, or other conduct based on sex affecting the dignity of women and men at work' is unacceptable, which will be the case where it is 'unwanted, unreasonable and offensive to the recipient'; leads to the victim being adversely treated in his or her employment; and/or 'creates an intimidating, hostile or humiliating work environment'.[505] The Commission's Code of Practice, which is appended to the Recommendation, lays out a number of suggestions to be followed by employers and by trade unions. It notes that 'as sexual harassment is often a function of women's status in the employment hierarchy, policies to deal with sexual harassment are likely to be most effective where they are linked to a broader policy to promote equal opportunities and improve the position of women'.[506] It is suggested that employers should have a clear policy stating that sexual harassment at work will not be permitted and should put in place procedures for dealing with complaints, including provision for investigations and disciplinary offences. In *Wadman v Carpenter Farrer Partnership*[507] the EAT said that this definition of sexual harassment 'may ... be of some assistance' to employment tribunals; this seems seriously to underestimate the importance of the Recommendation, both as an instrument which courts should take into account in its own right[508] but also as expressing in extended form the requirements which are in any event probably imposed upon employers by Articles 3–5 of the Equal Treatment Directive[509] as well as by the SDA 1975. Since that judgment the Directive has been amended to impose a clear obligation on Member States to legislate to make sexual harassment a free-standing wrong,[510] and this provision is due to be implemented by October 2005.[511]

---

503 [1997] IRLR 168, 172; a similarly broad construction was given to the term 'course of employment' in a different context in *Chief Constable of the Lincolnshire Police v Stubbs* [1999] IRLR 81. But even though the courts accept the need to go beyond the common law test, they continue to recognise limits to the employer's responsibility for incidents, such as assaults, occurring away from the place of employment: see *Sidhu v Aerospace Composite Technology Ltd.* [2000] IRLR 602. On the development of the common law test, see *Lister v Hesley Hall Ltd.* [2001] IRLR 472.
504 The Recommendation built on an expert report carried out by Rubinstein, 1988.
505 Art 1.
506 Code of Practice, para 3.
507 [1993] IRLR 374, 377.
508 On the status of recommendations, see Case C-322/88 *Grimaldi v Fonds de Maladies Professionelles* [1990] IRLR 400.
509 For discussion of this point see Ellis, 1991: pp 148 *et seq.*
510 Directive 76/207/EC, Art 2(3) (as inserted by Directive 2000/73/EC).
511 See DTI, *Equality and Diversity. Updating the Sex Discrimination Act* (2005), at pp 15–18

A robust approach to the issue of harassment was taken in the racial discrimination case of *Burton v De Vere Hotels*.[512] Here, two black women who were employed as waitresses alleged that they had suffered racial harassment as a result of racial remarks made by a stand-up comedian and by customers during a dinner at which they were serving. The employment tribunal found that they had been subjected to a detriment, but that the employer was not responsible for it. The EAT reversed on the basis that the employer had itself 'subjected' the complainants to a 'detriment' under section 4(2)(c) of the Act, by failing to take steps to prevent the harassment occurring when it could have done so. According to Smith J, '... an employer subjects an employee to the detriment of racial harassment if he causes or permits the racial harassment to occur in circumstances in which he can control whether it happens or not'.[513] However, in *Pearce v Governing Body of Mayfield School*[514] the House of Lords held that *Burton* had been wrongly decided: the harassment in question was carried out by a third party for whose conduct the employer could not have been vicariously liable. The 'control' test suggested in *Burton* was explicitly rejected.[515] The coming into force of a free-standing statutory wrong of harassment does not necessarily reverse *Pearce* on this point: it is still necessary to establish that the employer or other respondent is either personally or vicariously liable for the conduct which amounts to the harassment.[516]

Genuine occupational qualifications and requirements

6.49   The concept of a 'genuine occupational qualification' or 'genuine occupational requirement' refers to a feature of a particular job or position which potentially justifies the exclusion of an individual from that employment on grounds which would otherwise be prohibited. These concepts draw on the notion of 'bona fide occupational qualifications' (or BFOQs) in the US Civil Rights Act 1964. Under that legislation, a BFOQ arises where 'religion, sex, or national origin is a bona fide occupational qualification reasonably necessary to the normal operation of that particular business or enterprise'.[517] Guidelines issued by the US Equal Employment Opportunity Commission provide more specific indications of what is permitted and what is not, in particular by prohibiting refusals to hire based on:

> ... stereotyped characterisations of the sexes. Such stereotypes include, for example, that men are less capable of assembling intricate equipment; that women are less capable of aggressive salesmanship [sic]. The principle of non-discrimination requires that individuals be considered on the basis of individual capacities and not on the basis of any characteristics generally attributed to the group.[518]

The SDA 1975 and the RRA 1976, as initially drafted, made reference to a number of specific genuine occupational qualifications (or 'GOQ's). The list

---

512 [1996] IRLR 596.
513 [1996] IRLR 596, 600.
514 [2003] IRLR 512.
515 [2003] IRLR 512, at paras 31–35 (Lord Nicholls), 100 (Lord Hope), 204 (Lord Rodger).
516 RRA 1976, s 4(2A); DDA 1995, s 4(3); EE(SO)R 2003, reg 6(3); EE(RB)R 2003, reg 6(3).
517 Civil Rights Act 1964, s 703(e); 42 USC 2000e-2(e).
518 EEOC Guidelines on Discrimination Because of Sex, s 1604.2(a); 29 CFR s 1604.2(a).

was exhaustive: a GOQ could *only* arise where the case fell under one of the situations outlined in section 7 of the SDA 1975 or section 5 of the RRA 1976. The concept of the genuine occupational requirement (or 'GOR') was introduced with reference to UK law by the Framework and Race Directives of 2000:[519]

> Member States may provide that a difference of treatment which is based on a characteristic related to [one or more of the prohibited] grounds ... shall not constitute discrimination where, by reason of the nature of the particular occupational activities concerned or of the context in which they are carried out, such a characteristic constitutes a genuine and determining occupational requirement, provided that the objective is legitimate and the requirement is proportionate.

This provision, with some modifications, has now been translated into UK law with regard to discrimination on the grounds of race and national or ethnic origin, sexual orientation, and religion or belief.[520] The effect is to introduce an open-ended defence based on occupational requirements, akin to the US concept of the BFOQ. The GOQs set out under the SDA and RRA remain in force, so that, in these cases, the effect is to extend the existing, specific defences, although just how far this extension may be taken remains unclear.

Genuine occupational qualifications

6.50 The specific GOQs contained in the SDA and RRA are designed as a form of statutory justification, permitting direct discrimination to take place in strictly limited circumstances. They only apply to the question of access to a particular employment, either at the hiring stage or via promotion or transfer from one post to another; they do not excuse discrimination in the terms and conditions offered.[521] Nor do they have any application to the free-standing wrongs of harassment[522] and victimisation.[523]

Section 7 of the SDA 1975 lists the situations in which being a member of one sex is a genuine occupational qualification for a job. It is phrased so as to refer to situations in which discrimination against women is lawful, but section 2 of the Act ensures that it also applies to situations of sex discrimination against men.[524] The first category consists of cases where being a man or woman is essential for the purposes of authenticity. These are, first, situations in which 'the essential nature of the job calls for a man [or woman] for reasons of physiology (excluding physical strength or stamina)'.[525] This rather delicately phrased provision is also arguably less than successful in its aim; the term 'physiognomy' might have been more accurate if the intention was to refer to jobs, such as an artist's model, for which the male or female physical form would be considered a prerequisite.[526] The second exception refers to situations

---

519 Art. 4(1) of the Framework Directive (2000/78) and Art 4 of the Race Directive (2000/43).

520 RRA 1976, s 4A; EE(SO)R 2003, reg 7; EE(RB)R 2003, reg 7. Art 2(6) of the revised Equal Treatment Directive (76/207/EC) provides for the introduction of a genuine occupational requirement defence into UK sex discrimination law.

521 SDA 1975, s 7(1); RRA 1976, s 5(1). This is also true of GORs: see below, para 6.51.

522 See above, para 6.45.

523 Se below, para 6.65.

524 These GOQs also apply to cases of discrimination on the grounds of gender reassignment, by virtue of SDA 1975, s 7A, although note also s 7A(1)(b).

525 SDA 1975, s 7(2)(a).

526 Pannick, 1985: p 237.

of 'dramatic performances or other entertainment', where being a man or a woman is essential for 'reasons of authenticity'.[527] These exceptions are sufficiently narrow to rule out the possibility of basing a GOQ on the basis of the 'ability to perform' certain jobs of one sex or the other. The drafter avoided opening the door here to discrimination based on stereotypical assumptions about male strength and stamina by stating clearly that the criterion of 'physical strength' cannot constitute a GOQ. By contrast, under Title VII there has been a large amount of case law on this point, although the courts have interpreted the scope of the BFOQ exception restrictively, requiring the employer to show that 'all or substantially all women' cannot perform a particular job before it can be restricted to male applicants on the grounds of physical strength.[528]

There is, secondly, a set of situations in which privacy is the main rationale for the exceptions. This is the case, first, for jobs which involve physical contact with men (for example) such that they would object to the work being carried out by a woman, or where they would object on the grounds that 'they are in a state of undress or are using sanitary facilities';[529] and, second, jobs in which the person employed is expected to live in a private home, in circumstances such that objection might be taken to the employment of a man (for example) on the grounds of '(i) the degree of physical or social contact with a person living in the home, or (ii) the knowledge of intimate details of such a person's life' which the job entails.[530] This exception was introduced by the SDA 1986 and replaces an earlier provision completely excluding the application of the Act in cases of employment in a private household, which the ECJ had declared contrary to the Equal Treatment Directive.[531] A further exception arises where the nature or location of the establishment makes it impracticable for the holder of the job to live elsewhere than in premises provided by the employer; the premises are normally occupied by the members of one sex; these premises do not provide separate sleeping and sanitary facilities for members of the opposite sex; and it is not reasonable to expect the employer to provide such facilities or to provide other premises for members of the opposite sex.[532] In addition, an exception arises where the job is part of a hospital, prison or other establishment for persons requiring 'special care, supervision or attention'; such persons are all men (for example), disregarding the exceptional presence of any women; and the exclusion of women is reasonable 'having regard to the essential nature of the establishment' or a part of it.[533]

A potentially very broad GOQ arises where 'the holder of the job provides individuals with personal services promoting their welfare or education, or similar personal services, and those services can most effectively be provided by a man' or woman as the case may be.[534] However, in *Lambeth London Borough Council v Commission for Racial Equality*[535] the term 'personal services'

---

527 SDA 1975, s 7(2)(a).
528 *Weekes v Southern Bell Telephone & Telegraph Co* 408 F 2d 228, 235 (1969).
529 SDA 1975, s 7(2)(b)(i)–(ii); *Lasertop Ltd v Webster* [1997] IRLR 498.
530 SDA 1975, s 7(2)(ba).
531 Case 165/82 *EC Commission v United Kingdom* [1984] ICR 192.
532 SDA 1975, s 7(2)(c). See *Timex Corpn v Thompson* [1981] IRLR 522; *Sisley v Britannia Security Systems Ltd* [1983] IRLR 404.
533 SDA 1975, s 7(2)(d); cf *Dothard v Rawlinson* 433 US 321 (1977), in which the Supreme Court held that a BFOQ was established under Title VII in a case where a woman applied for a job as a guard in an all-male prison.
534 SDA 1975, s 7(2)(e).
535 [1990] ICR 768.

was given a narrow reading under the parallel provision of the RRA 1976, so as to exclude the post of manager in a local government housing department.

Finally, there are two situations which are essentially concerned with the impracticability of employing a man or a woman in particular situations: these are where a job involves work outside the United Kingdom in a country 'whose laws or customs are such that the duties could not, or could not effectively, be performed by a woman',[536] and where 'the job is one of two to be held by a married couple'.[537]

A series of supplementary' GOQs apply to discrimination on the grounds of gender reassignment.[538] As we have seen,[539] these apply where the job holder is likely to be called on to perform 'intimate physical searches pursuant to statutory powers'; where the job involves access to an individual in his or her private home and reasonable objection might be taken to the work being done by a person undergoing gender reassignment on the grounds of the degree of physical or social contact with a person living in the home or because of knowledge of the intimate details of such a person's life; where the job involves living on premises provided by the employer under circumstances where reasonable objection could be taken, on the grounds of preserving privacy and decency, to the job holder sharing facilities with members of either sex while undergoing gender reassignment and it is not reasonable to expect the employer to make alternative arrangements; and, most sweepingly, where the holder of the job 'provides vulnerable individuals with personal services promoting their welfare, or similar personal services, and in the reasonable view of the employer those services cannot be effectively provided by a person whilst that person is undergoing gender reassignment'. The last two of these only apply where the complainant is intending to undergo, or still undergoing, the gender reassignment in question. More generally, none of them has any application where the complainant has been granted a certificate of gender recognition.[540]

The RRA 1976 contains a shorter list of GOQs. Three of these relate to jobs for which membership of a particular racial group is important from the point of view of authenticity: these are jobs involving dramatic performance or other entertainment, 'participation as an artist's or photographic model in the production of a work of art, visual image or sequence of visual images', and the provision of food and drink to members of the public in a particular setting (such as, presumably, a Chinese or Indian restaurant).[541] In addition, an exception is allowed for jobs providing persons of a racial group 'with personal services promoting their welfare, and those services can most effectively be provided by a person of that racial group'.[542] This is slightly narrower in scope than the equivalent provision under the SDA 1975 which refers to personal services

---

536 SDA 1975, s 7(2)(g).
537 SDA 1975, s 7(2)(h).
538 SDA 1975, s 7B. Further exceptions arise in relation to employment as a minister of religion: SDA 1975, s 19(3)–(4).
539 See para 6.35, above, discussing the interaction between these provisions and the decision of the House of Lords in *A v Chief Constable of West Yorkshire Police* [2004] IRLR 573, applying general sex discrimination law as interpreted by the ECJ in Case C-13/94 *P v S* [1996] IRLR 347.
540 By virtue of the changes made to s 7B by the Gender Recognition Act 2004. See above, para 6.35.
541 RRA 1976, s 5(2)(a)–(c); *Tottenham Green Under Five's Centre v Marshall* [1989] IRLR 147.
542 RRA 1976, s 5(2)(d).

promoting welfare *or education*. As we have seen, in *Lambeth London Borough Council v Commission for Racial Equality*[543] the Court of Appeal refused to interfere with a tribunal finding that managerial positions did not fall into the definition of 'personal services': according to Balcombe LJ, 'the Act appears to contemplate direct contact between the giver and the recipient – mainly face-to-face or where there could be susceptibility in personal, physical contact. Where language or a knowledge and understanding of cultural and religious background are of importance, then those services may be most effectively provided by a person of a particular racial group'.[544]

The relevant legislation provides that a GOQ is established even if 'some only of the duties of the job fall within [the stated exceptions] as well as where all of them do'.[545] The tribunal will examine carefully claims that a particular job necessarily contains duties of this kind: thus in *Wylie v Dee & Co (Menswear) Ltd*[546] it was held that the exclusion of a woman from working as a shop assistant in a menswear shop did not fall within a GOQ, since she would not necessarily have been required to come into physical contact with male customers when taking the measurement of an inside leg, in part because there were male shop assistants in the same employment who could have performed this task if need be.

Genuine occupational requirements

6.51   The concept of a GOR differs from that of a GOQ in providing an open-ended defence to claims of discrimination,[547] based on the concept of occupational requirement. Thus the Sexual Orientation Regulations, for example, provide the employer with a defence if, 'having regard to the nature of the employment or the context in which it is carried out ... (a) being of a particular sexual orientation is a genuine and determining occupational requirement, (b) it is proportionate to apply that requirement in the particular case, and (c) either – (i) the person to whom that requirement is applied does not meet it, or (ii) the employer is not satisfied, and in all the circumstances it is reasonable for him not to be satisfied, that the person meets it'.[548] Identically-worded provisions apply to discrimination on the grounds of race and national or ethnic origin, and religion or belief.[549] Several features of this definition are worthy of note. The condition in question must be a 'requirement', which the DTI *Explanatory Notes* suggests 'is something which is essential for the person to be able to perform the functions of the job'. It must also be 'genuine', so that the employer ' cannot simply create a requirement on a whim' and 'determining' in the sense that 'the requirement must be crucial to the post, and not merely one of several important factors'.[550] The requirement is met not simply where the complainant, objectively speaking, does not satisfy the relevant condition but where the

---

543 [1990] ICR 768; see above, para 6.32.
544 [1990] ICR 768, 775.
545 SDA 1975, s 7(3); RRA 1976, s 5(3). See also SDA 1975, s 7(4); RRA 1976, s 5(4).
546 [1978] IRLR 103.
547 The GOR defence, like that of the GOQ, does not apply to harassment (see para 6.45 above) or victimisation (see para 6.65 below).
548 EE(SO)R 2003, reg 7(2).
549 RRA 1976, s 4A(2); EE(RB)R 2003, reg 7(2).
550 DTI, *Explanatory Notes for the Employment Equality (Sexual Orientation) Regulations 2003 and the Employment Equality (Religion or Belief) Regulations 2003* (2003), at para 73.

employer reasonably thinks that they do not. The reason for this, according to the *Explanatory Notes*, is that 'the sexual orientation / religion or belief of the employee is usually something which would be in her exclusive knowledge';[551] however, '[t]his does not mean that the employer could refuse to offer an applicant a job, merely because he suspects that the applicant is not of the specified sexual orientation / religion or belief'.[552] The provision was unsuccessfully challenged as being contrary to the Framework Directive in *R (on the application of Amicus – MSF Section) v Secretary of State for Trade and Industry*.[553] According to Richards J, the formula used in the Regulations fell within the scope of the phrase 'based on a characteristic related to' sexual orientation in the Directive,[554] and, moreover, met the need to protect employers in cases where they would otherwise be required to take at face value an assertion by the complainant that they met the requirement in question.

Two further definitions of the GOR concept arise under the Sexual Orientation and Religion or Belief Regulations. The first permits discrimination on the grounds of sexual orientation in relation to certain religious employments.[555] Where employment is for the purposes of an organised religion, the employer can apply a requirement 'related to sexual orientation' in order either to 'comply with the doctrines of the religion' or 'because of the nature of the employment and the context in which it is carried out, so as to avoid conflicting with the strongly held religious convictions of a significant number of the religion's followers'.[556] This GOR applies if either the person to whom it applies cannot meet it, or the employer is reasonably satisfied that they do not. A key aspect of this provision is that it refers to a requirement related to sexual orientation, rather than the complainant being of a particular sexual orientation. This means that 'a requirement not to engage in sex with a same-sex partner would be a requirement related to sexual orientation'.[557]

The second additional GOR applies in the context of the Religion or Belief Regulations.[558] A defence is made out if the employer can show that it has a particular 'ethos based on religion or belief', and that 'having regard to that ethos and to the nature of the employment or the context in which it is carried out... being of a particular religion or belief is a genuine requirement for the job', if the application of the requirement satisfies the normal test of proportionality. Again, it is enough to show either that the complainant does not comply with the requirement or that the employer is reasonably satisfied that they do not. In this context, the GOR need not be a 'determining' one, which, according to the DTI's *Explanatory Notes*[559] means that 'the employer is not required to show that religion or belief is a determining (ie, decisive) factor in selection for the post in question'.

---

551 DTI, *Explanatory Notes*, at para 80.
552 DTI, *Explanatory Notes*, at para 81.
553 [2004] IRLR 430.
554 Directive 2000/78, Art 4.
555 EE(SO)R 2003, reg 7(3).
556 In *R (on the application of Amicus – MSF Section) v Secretary of State for Trade and Industry* [2004] IRLR 430, Richards J, in upholding this derogation under the terms of the Framework Directive, suggested that this aspect of it was 'very narrow' in scope and had to be objectively interpreted. He also held that this and other derogations contained in 2003 Regulations were not incompatible with Arts 8 and 14 of the ECHR.
557 DTI, *Explanatory Notes*, at para 93.
558 EE(RB)R 2003, reg 7(3).
559 At para 86.

Other exceptions

6.52   Each of the principal anti-discrimination measures recognises several broadly-defined exceptions from the equality principle in addition to the GOQs and GORs.

Death and retirement

6.53   As originally drafted, section 6(4) of the SDA 1975 excluded 'provision in relation to death or retirement' from the scope of matters covered by the prohibition upon discrimination against applicants and employed persons'. This was part of an interlocking set of provisions in the SDA 1975 and the EqPA 1970 which were designed to preserve the differential treatment of men and women in terms of retirement and pensionable age. The principle of different pensionable ages for men and women was also preserved by the relevant European Community provisions on social security, the Directives on Equality in State Social Security[560] and Occupational Social Security respectively.[561] However, in 1986 the ECJ decided in *Marshall v Southampton and South West Hampshire Area Health Authority*[562] that the compulsory retirement of women at the age of 60, in circumstances where comparable male workers were allowed to carry on working until 65, was contrary to the Equal Treatment Directive, which contains no derogation in respect of retirement. The Court also held that Article 5 of the Directive had vertical direct effect in national law, thereby conferring rights immediately on those employed in the public sector. The main plank of the Court's decision in *Marshall* was its ruling that the issue of compulsory retirement was separate from the issue of minimum pensionable age. As a result, the derogations contained in the social security directives were irrelevant to the issue before it: 'the question of interpretation ... does not concern access to a statutory or occupational retirement scheme, that is to say the conditions for payment of an old-age or retirement pension, but the fixing of an age limit with regard to the termination of employment pursuant to general policy concerning dismissal. The question therefore relates to the conditions governing dismissal and falls to be considered under Directive No 76/207'.[563] The Court also broadly interpreted the notion of dismissal under Article 5 of the Directive: 'an age limit for the compulsory dismissal of workers pursuant to an employer's general policy concerning retirement falls within the term "dismissal" construed in that manner, even if the dismissal involves the grant of a retirement pension'.[564]

Following *Marshall*, the SDA 1986 prohibited employers from setting different compulsory retirement ages for men and for women. Section 6 of the SDA 1975 was amended so that sex discrimination in relation to retirement is not permitted in respect of an individual's access to opportunities for promotion, transfer or training or to an individual's dismissal or demotion, or in relation to such terms and conditions of employment as make provision for any of these matters.[565] The EPCA 1978 was also amended to remove the employer's immunity from unfair dismissal arising from retirement in cases where different retirement ages were set for men and for women.[566]

560 Directive 79/7, Art 7(1)(a).
561 Directive 86/378, Art 9(a).
562 Case 152/84 [1986] IRLR 140.
563 Case 152/84 [1986] IRLR 140, para 32.
564 Case 152/84 [1986] IRLR 140, para 34.
565 SDA 1986, s 2, amending SDA 1975, s 6(4).
566 SDA 1986, s 3, amending EPCA 1978, s 64(1)(b), now ERA 1996, s 109(1).

The question of unequal pensionable ages was dealt with by the ECJ in a series of decisions beginning with its landmark decision in *Barber v Guardian Royal Exchange Assurance Group*[567] which ruled that occupational benefits fell under Article 119 (now 141) of the EC Treaty. This meant that unequal pensionable ages were contrary to the principle of equal pay for work in Article 141, but the Court limited the effects of its decision to prospective benefits, that is to say those arising on or after the date of the *Barber* judgment in 1990.[568] Shortly before *Barber* was decided, Parliament enacted Schedule 5 of the SSA 1989 which would have extended the principle of equal treatment to occupational pension schemes and other employment benefits schemes in line with the Directive on Equality in Occupational Social Security, and to that end provided for further amendments to be made to section 6 of the SDA 1975.[569] The relevant part of Schedule 5 was then repealed by the Pensions Act 1995 in favour of a different scheme for implementing equality in occupational pension provisions.[570]

Marital status

6.54   The Sexual Orientation Regulations exclude from the scope of the equal treatment principle in that context 'anything which prevents or restricts access to a benefit by reference to marital status'.[571] This derogation was challenged in *R (on the application of Amicus – MSF Section) v Secretary of State for Trade and Industry*.[572] The Framework Directive, which the Regulations purport to implement, applies to 'employment and working conditions, including dismissals and pay', a category which includes occupational benefits.[573] No exception is made in the main body of the Directive in respect of marital benefits; however, the 22nd Recital to the Directive states that it is 'without prejudice to national laws on marital status and the benefits dependent thereon'. The challenge mounted in the *Amicus* case was rejected on a variety of grounds related to the alleged cost and impracticability of extending marital benefits to unmarried couples.[574] The Civil Partnership Act 2004 has since amended the Sex Discrimination Act to extend the rights of married persons under that Act to those in civil partnerships between same-sex couples.[575]

Health and safety

6.55   The original section 51 of the SDA 1975 provided an exemption in respect of acts done under the authority of statutory requirements pre-dating the Act of 1975. The main purpose of this was to enable access to certain jobs by women to be restricted on the grounds of health and safety, and the point was reinforced by section 7(2)(f) which made it a GOQ to discriminate against a woman on the

---

567   Case C-262/88 [1990] IRLR 240. See below, para 6.96.
568   The full implications of *Barber* for occupational pension rights are considered in para 6.96 below.
569   SSA 1989, Sch 5, Part II, para 14(2)–(3).
570   See PA 1995, ss 62–66 and Sch 7, Part I; see also para 6.96 below.
571   EE(SO)R 2003, reg 25.
572   [2004] IRLR 430.
573   This is because of the inclusion within the term 'pay' of pension and other occupational benefits under the equal pay jurisprudence of the ECJ, stemming from its decision in Case C-262/88 *Barber v Guardian Royal Exchange Assurance Group* [1990] IRLR 240.
574   [2004] IRLR 430, at paras 166–171.
575   Civil Partnership Act 2004, s 251, amending SDA 1975, s 3. At the time of writing this provision has not yet been brought into force.

grounds that 'the job needs to be held by a man because of restrictions imposed by the laws regulating the employment of women'. By contrast, Title VII of the US Civil Rights Act 1964 provided that the principle of equal treatment should prevail over contrary state law which 'purports to require or permit' the doing of acts contrary to Title VII.[576] Similarly, the Equal Treatment Directive, in its original form, called on Member States to revise discriminatory protective statutes 'when the concern for protection which originally inspired them is no longer well founded',[577] with the exception of regulations concerning pregnancy and maternity;[578] a four-year timetable for review of such regulations by the individual Member States was laid down.[579] The derogation for regulations concerning pregnancy and maternity was given a narrow interpretation by the ECJ in its 1986 decision in *Johnston v Chief Constable of the Royal Ulster Constabulary*,[580] and in 1987 the European Commission issued a communication to Member States suggesting that they should implement the Equal Treatment Directive by a combination of measures removing restrictions on women's access to certain employments and 'levelling up' where appropriate by extending similar rights to men. The Commission also suggested that sex-specific regulations should only be retained where they could be justified by the 'separate biological condition' of one sex.[581]

The United Kingdom chose to implement this aspect of the Equal Treatment Directive in a series of steps. First, certain protective legislation affecting women was repealed entirely. The SDA 1986 removed controls on nightworking by women and the EA 1989 repealed restrictions on women working underground in mines and quarries, as well as certain restrictions on employment in textiles and in jute, pottery and cement manufacture.[582] Second, the EA 1989 provided that any remaining statutes which required sex discrimination contrary to the SDA 1975 were to that extent overridden,[583] and as a sweeping-up measure the Secretary of State for Employment was given the power to repeal such legislation by order.[584] Third, the EA 1989 amended section 51 of the SDA 1975 to provide for a more limited defence than previously: this was confined to cases where action in relation to a woman was necessary in order to comply with a statute concerning the protection of women with regard to '(i) pregnancy or maternity, or (ii) other circumstances giving rise to risks specifically affecting women', or necessary to comply with general health and safety legislation.[585] Fourth, for the avoidance of doubt, certain legislation restricting access to employment on grounds of a woman's pregnancy was specifically preserved.[586] The effect of the changes made by the SDA 1986 and the EA 1989 was, first, to preserve substantial scope for unequal treatment with regard to restrictions apparently justified by

---

576 Civil Rights Act 1964, s 708; *Rosenfeld v Southern Pacific Co* 444 F 2d 1219 (1971).
577 Directive 76/207, Arts 3(2)(c), 5(2)(c).
578 Directive 76/207, Art 2(3).
579 Directive 76/207, Art 9(1).
580 Case 222/84 [1986] IRLR 263.
581 *Protective Legislation for Women in the Member States of the European Community*, Communication of 20 March 1987, COM (87) 105 final.
582 See generally Deakin, 1990a.
583 EA 1989, s 1.
584 EA 1989, s 2. He or she also has the power to disapply the override: EA 1989, s 6. On the statutory override generally, see Deakin, 1990a: pp 8–9.
585 In particular, s 2(1) of the HSWA 1974: see *Page v Freight Hire (Tank Haulage) Ltd* [1981] IRLR 13.
586 EA 1989, s 5.

reference to pregnancy and maternity, many of which are open to question;[587] and, second, to have achieved compliance with the Equal Treatment Directive by levelling down, contrary to the advice given by the European Commission in its 1987 Communication. Whether levelling down is contrary to the Equal Treatment Directive is more doubtful; the Directive itself is silent on the matter, and although Article 136 (formerly 117) of the EC Treaty would appear to rule out this form of equalisation, case law of the ECJ suggests that Article 136 is not decisive in this context.[588]

Statutory authority

6.56 Unlike the SDA 1975, the RRA 1976 and the DDA 1995 contain certain generally-phrased exclusions with regard to acts of discrimination done in pursuance of statutory authority.[589]

Pregnancy and maternity

6.57 As we have seen, the SDA 1975 excludes from the definition of sex discrimination any 'special treatment accorded to women in connection with pregnancy or childbirth'.[590]

Domestic employment

6.58 Discrimination on racial grounds related to colour or nationality, other than in cases of victimisation,[591] is permitted in relation to 'employment for the purposes of a private household'.[592] The equivalent exclusion in the case of the SDA 1975 was removed by the SDA 1986[593] following the judgment of the ECJ in *Commission v United Kingdom*,[594] which held that it was contrary to the Equal Treatment Directive. The SDA now contains instead the more narrow GOQ analysed above, which exempts acts of sex discrimination in cases where the employment in question is in a private home and involves either physical contact with a person living in the house or knowledge of intimate details of his or her life.

National security

6.59 Acts done for the purpose of safeguarding national security are outside the scope of the anti-discrimination provisions if they can be justified by that purpose.[595]

Charities and educational bodies

6.60 Charitable instruments may lawfully restrict the provision of benefits to members of one sex,[596] a provision which, amongst other things, permits sex

---

587 See Deakin, 1990a.
588 Case C-408/92 *Smith v Avdel Systems Ltd* [1994] IRLR 602.
589 RRA 1976, s 41, as amended by SI 2003/1626, reg 35; see also DDA 1995, s 59(1).
590 SDA 1975, s 2(3); see para 6.96 below.
591 On victimisation in this context, see para 6.65 below.
592 RRA 1976, s 4(3).
593 SDA 1975, s 1.
594 Case 165/82 [1984] IRLR 29.
595 SDA 1975, s 52; RRA 1976, s 42; DDA 1995, s 59(2A); EE(SO)R 2003, reg 24; EE(RB)R 2003, reg 24.
596 SDA 1975, s 43; RRA 1976, s 34.

discrimination in the allocation of research fellowships by Oxford and Cambridge colleges.[597] Certain other specified educational appointments are outside the scope of the SDA 1975.[598] Charitable benefits may also be restricted on the grounds of nationality.[599]

Ministers of religion etc

6.61   The SDA 1975 does not prohibit sex discrimination in employment for the purposes of an organised religion where the employment is limited to one sex so as to comply with the doctrines of the religion, or in order to 'avoid offending the religious susceptibilities of a significant number of its followers'.[600]

Police, prison officers and members of the armed forces

6.62   The SDA 1975 does not extend to sex discrimination within the police in respect of requirements relating to height; rules governing uniform and equipment, and allowances in lieu of uniform and equipment; special treatment of women in connection with childbirth and pregnancy; and in relation to pensions of special constables and police cadets.[601] Discrimination between male and female prison officers on the ground of height is permitted,[602] and discrimination between male and female members of the armed forces is permitted 'for the purpose of ensuring the combat effectiveness' of the armed forces.[603]

Sport

6.63   The SDA 1975 permits the separate organisation of sporting events for men and women by virtue of a provision which, in relation to 'any sport, game or other activity of a competitive nature where the physical strength, stamina or physique of the average woman puts her at a disadvantage to the average man', declares lawful for this purpose 'any act related to the participation of a person as a competitor in events involving that activity which are confined to competitors of one sex'.[604]

The RRA 1976 also contains a provision relating to sport: this allows discrimination on the basis of a person's nationality, place of birth or period of residence in a particular area or place if done, first, as part of the selection of a representative of a given country, place or area to take part in a sport or game or, second, in pursuance of the rules of a sport or game governing eligibility to compete.[605]

---

597   *Hugh-Jones v St John's College, Cambridge* [1979] ICR 848.
598   EA 1989, s 5.
599   RRA 1976, s 34, which has always outlawed discrimination in this respect on the basis of colour, was amended by SI 2003/1626 reg 33 to exclude discrimination on the grounds of race and national or ethnic origin, in line with the Race Directive (2000/43).
600   SDA 1975, s 19(1). To similar effect is EE(SO)R 2003, reg 7(3), which was unsuccessfully challenged in *R (on the application of Amicus – MSF Section) v Secretary of State for Trade and Industry* [2004] IRLR 430. The position of priests in the Church of England, following the admission of women to the priesthood in that Church, is systematically analysed by Brodin, 1998.
601   SDA 1975, s 17(2), (3).
602   SDA 1975, s 18.
603   SDA 1975, s 85(4); Case C-273/97 *Sirdar v Army Board and Secretary of State for Defence* [2000] IRLR 47.
604   SDA 1975, s 44.
605   RRA 1976, s 39.

Employment on a ship

6.64 The RRA 1976 does not prohibit discrimination on the grounds of nationality and relating to pay where a person is recruited abroad to work on a ship, unless this is in connection with exploration of the seabed or subsoil of the continental shelf or the exploitation of their natural resources.[606]

Victimisation

6.65 The anti-discrimination provisions each provide for a free-standing wrong of victimisation. This arises where the 'discriminator' treats the 'person victimised' less favourably than it treats or would treat other persons by reason of one of the following 'protected acts': the person victimised has brought proceedings against the discriminator or another under the relevant provision or provisions; he or she has given evidence or information in connection with such proceedings; 'otherwise done anything under or by reference to [the relevant legislation] in relation to the discriminator or any other person'; or alleged that the discriminator or any other person has committed a breach of the relevant provision. There is also victimisation where the discriminator knows or suspects that the victim intends to do or has done any of these things. The protection does not apply where the person victimised makes a false allegation, unless it was made in good faith.[607]

The complainant does not have to show that the respondent acted with a conscious intention to victimise; it is enough that the respondent had carried out a 'protected act' and that this acted as an 'important cause' of or 'significant influence' on the decision.[608] The leading case on the elements of the claim is *Chief Constable of West Yorkshire Police v Khan.*[609] Mr. Khan made a complaint of racial discrimination against the Chief Constable in respect of his failure to gain promotion. He then applied for a post in another police force, and asked the Chief Constable to write a reference on his behalf. The Chief Constable refused on the grounds that to comment on Mr. Khan's application would prejudice the Chief Constable's case in the proceedings brought by Mr. Khan against him. This refusal formed the basis of Mr. Khan's claim for victimisation. According to Lord Nicholls, who gave the leading opinion in the House of Lords, Mr. Khan had suffered less favourable treatment within the meaning of the Act: the relevant comparator group in this context was, simply, 'other employees who have not done the protected act',[610] which in this case was the act of making the initial complaint of racial discrimination. However, Lord Nicholls went on to hold that the Chief Constable's refusal to give Mr. Khan a reference was not 'by reason that' Mr. Khan had made the first complaint of discrimination: as long as he was acting 'honestly and reasonably' he was entitled to protect his position in respect of the pending proceedings.

---

606 RRA 1976, s 9, as amended by SI 2003/1651.
607 SDA 1975, s 4; RRA 1976, s 2; DDA 1995, s 55; EE(SO)R 2003, reg 4; EE(RB)R 2003, reg 4. See also the Framework Directive on Discrimination, Directive 2000/78, Art 11, and the Race Directive, Directive 2000/43, Art 9.
608 *Nagarajan v London Regional Transport* [1999] IRLR 572; *Coote v Granada Hospitality Ltd (No 2)* [1999] IRLR 452.
609 [2001] IRLR 830.
610 [2001] IRLR 830, at para 27. For earlier, varying approaches to this issue, see *Kirby v Manpower Services Commission* [1980] IRLR 229; *Aziz v Trinity Street Taxis Ltd.* [1988] IRLR 204; *Nagarajan v London Regional Transport* [1998] IRLR 73; *Brown v TNT Express Worldwide (UK) Ltd* [2001] ICR 182. See Connolly, 2000.

The outcome in *Khan* illustrates the difficulty which complainants face in establishing victimisation where more than one ground can be imputed to the employer's conduct. To similar effect is *Aziz v Trinity Street Taxis Ltd*.[611] Here, a claim failed where the complainant was expelled from an association of taxi owners for having made secret tape recordings with a view to obtaining proof of discriminatory practices. The employer successfully argued that the reasons for the dismissal was the complainant's breach of confidentiality. By contrast, in *Visa International Service Association v Paul*[612] the EAT refused to interfere with a tribunal finding that the employer had committed victimisation against the complainant in seeking the recoupment of enhanced maternity pay in response to her claim of sex discrimination, when it would not have taken this step against other female employees who returned to work following childbirth.

Remedies

Complaint to an employment tribunal

6.66   The three remedies which are potentially available to employment tribunals in respect of discrimination are a declaration of rights, an award of compensation and a recommendation.[613] The complainant must make their application to an employment tribunal[614] within three months of the occurrence of the 'act complained of',[615] although the tribunal also has the power to hear a complaint which is out of time 'if, in all the circumstances of the case, it considers that it is just and equitable to do so'.[616] These provisions have on the whole been flexibly applied, in contrast to the rather more restrictive approach taken under the claim-in-time provisions of ERA 1996.[617] Complainants may also be helped in this regard by the notion of 'continuing discrimination'. The legislation provides that 'any act extending over a period shall be treated as done at the end of that period'.[618] This provision was applied by the House of Lords in *Barclays Bank plc v Kapur*,[619] for example, to hold that a failure by the employer

---

611   [1988] ICR 534.

612   [2004] IRLR 42.

613   SDA 1975, s 65(1); RRA 1976, s 56(1); DDA 1995, s 17A(2); EE(SO)R 2003, reg 30(1); EE(RB)R 2003, reg 30(1).

614   SDA 1975, s 63(1); RRA 1976, s 54(1); DDA 1995, s 17A(1); EE(SO)R 2003, reg 28(1); EE(RB)R 2003, reg 28(1).

615   SDA 1975, s 76(1); RRA 1976, s 68(1); DDA 1995, Sch 3, para 3(1); EE(SO)R 2003, reg 34(1)(a); EE(RB)R 2003, reg 34(1)(a). See para 2.23 above for the implications of the statutory grievance procedures for time limits. In all cases members of the armed forces are required to make use of internal redress procedures before applying to an employment tribunal and the period for bringing complaints is extended to six months to allow these procedures to be completed: SDA 1975, s 85; RRA 1976, s 75; EE(SO)R 2003, reg 36(7)–(10); EE(RB)R 2003 reg 36(7)–(10).

616   SDA 1975, s 76(5); RRA 1976, s 68(6); DDA 1995, Sch 3, para 3(2); EE(SO)R 2003, reg 34(3); EE(RB)R 2003, reg 34(3).

617   See *Hutchinson v Westward Television Ltd* [1977] IRLR 69; *Lupetti v Wrens Old House Ltd* [1984] ICR 348; and on claim in time under ERA 1996, see para 2.17 above.

618   SDA 1975, s 76(6)(b); RRA 1976, s 68(7)(b); DDA 1995, Sch 3, para 3(3); EE(SO)R reg 34(4)(b); EE(RB)R, reg 34(4)(b).

619   [1991] IRLR 136; see also *Sougrin v Haringey Health Authority* [1992] IRLR 416; *Owusu v London Fire and Civil Defence Authority* [1995] IRLR 574; *Rovenska v General Medical Council* [1997] IRLR 367; *Cast v Croydon College* [1998] IRLR 318; *Tyagi v BBC World Service* [2001] IRLR 465; *Hendricks v Commissioner of Police of the Metropolis* [2003] IRLR 96.

to count a period of previous service towards an employee's pension rights continued up to the point at which the complaint was lodged.

Compensation

6.67 An employment tribunal may award compensation for a breach of one of the anti-discrimination provisions if it considers it just and equitable to do so.[620] In the case of disability discrimination, this remedy does not depend either upon the intention of the employer or the type of discrimination which was committed. However, in other cases, the remedy of compensation is not available in a case of *indirect* discrimination if the respondent proves that the relevant criterion, provision or practice was not applied with the intention of treating the claimant unfavourably on the relevant prohibited ground, unless (in the cases of discrimination on the grounds of sex, sexual orientation, and religion or belief) a tribunal grants a declaration and/or makes a recommendation, and considers that it would be just and equitable to award compensation in addition.[621]

Compensation is payable according to the principles which would apply to a civil claim in tort,[622] and for this purpose it is declared for 'the avoidance of doubt' that 'damages in respect of an unlawful act of discrimination may include compensation for injury to feelings'.[623] This marks an important distinction between awards under the anti-discrimination Acts and those under ERA 1996 for unfair dismissal;[624] another difference is that the anti-discrimination legislation makes no provision for a reduction in damages for the complainant's contributory fault. Although an award for injury to feelings is not automatic, substantial damages may be awarded under this head; in 1992 it was thought that an award of £500 would be around the minimum which tribunals should award.[625] In *Deane v Ealing London Borough Council*,[626] where there was detailed evidence of the complainant's hurt feelings on being denied promotion on grounds of his race, an award of £1,000 was made, and in *Noone v North West Thames Regional Health Authority*[627] the Court of Appeal ordered £3,000 damages under this head for 'the affront and distress caused to Dr Noone by having her legitimate and honourable ambition to become a consultant microbiologist thwarted'. In *Doshoki v Draeger Ltd*[628] £4,000 was awarded by the EAT in respect of persistent racial taunts and insults, overturning an award of £750 by the employment tribunal. In *Armitage v Johnson*[629] the

---

620 SDA 1975, ss 65(1)(b); RRA 1976, ss 56(1)(b); DDA 1995, 17A(2)(b); EE(SO) 2003, reg 30(1)(b); EE(RB)R 2003, reg 30(1)(b).

621 SDA 1975, ss 65(1A), (1B), 66(3), (3A); RRA 1976, ss 56(1)(b), 57(3); EE(SO)R 2003, reg 30(2); EE(RB)R 2003, reg 30(2).

622 See SDA 1975, ss 65(1)(b), RRA 1976, ss 56(1)(b), DDA 1995, s 17A(3); EE(SO)R 2003, reg 30(1)(b); EE(RB)R 2003, reg 30(1)(b). On the tort-based nature of damages, see *Ministry of Defence v Cannock* [1994] IRLR 509; *Sheriff v Klyne Tugs (Lowestoft) Ltd* [1999] IRLR 481 *ICTS (UK) Ltd v Tchoula* [2000] IRLR 643; *Essa v Laing Ltd* [2004] IRLR 313 (holding that losses could be recovered if they flowed naturally and directly from the wrong, thereby rejecting a test based on foreseeability).

623 SDA 1975, s 66(4); RRA 1976, s 57(4); DDA 1995, s 17A(4); EE(SO)R 2003, reg 31(3); EE(RB)R 2003, reg 31(3) .

624 See para 5.167 above.

625 *Sharifi v Strathclyde Regional Council* [1992] IRLR 259.

626 [1993] IRLR 209; cf *Alexander v Home Office* [1988] IRLR 190; *Owusu v London Fire and Civil Defence Authority* [1995] IRLR 574.

627 [1988] IRLR 195, 204.

628 [2002] IRLR 340.

629 [1997] IRLR 163; *ICTS (UK) Ltd v Tchoula* [2000] IRLR 643; *British Telecommuncations plc v Reid* [2004] IRLR 327.

complainant was awarded £21,000 under this head for the effects of a systematic campaign of racial harassment, although in *Vento v Chief Constable of West Yorkshire Police (No 2)*[630] the tribunal's award of £50,000 for injury to feelings was reduced to £18,000.

The courts have held that exemplary or punitive damages, which are not compensatory in nature but are designed purely as a deterrent, may not normally be awarded under the anti-discrimination Acts[631] on the basis of what was understood at one time to be the general position in tort law.[632] However, aggravated damages, understood as damages payable in respect of intentional or malicious damage inflicted on the claimant or complainant, are properly regarded as compensatory in nature, and so may be awarded in an appropriate discrimination case. In *Armitage v Johnson*[633] the EAT made an award of aggravated damages on top of damages to injury to feelings, an approach followed in later case law.[634] The Law Commission has suggested that exemplary or punitive damages should be available on a more general basis in anti-discrimination cases.[635]

Until 1993 the legislation applied an upper limit to the amount of compensation which an employment tribunal could award, which was equivalent to the limit to the compensatory award for unfair dismissal.[636] However, the application of an upper limit in sex discrimination cases was successfully challenged before the ECJ on the grounds of its incompatability with the Equal Treatment Directive, in *Marshall v Southampton and South West Hampshire Area Health Authority (No 2)*.[637] The Court ruled that 'the fixing of an upper limit of the kind at issue … cannot, by definition, constitute proper implementation of Article 6 of the Directive, since it limits the amount of compensation *a priori* to a level which is not necessarily consistent with the requirement of ensuring real equality of opportunity through adequate reparation for the loss and damage sustained as a result of discriminatory dismissal.'[638] The Court also held that Article 6 required that an award of interest be made on compensation, and that in both these respects the Article had vertical direct effect in national law, so conferring immediate rights on employees in claims against organs of the state. Following *Marshall (No 2)*, the upper limits under both the SDA 1975 and the RRA 1976 were abolished and employment tribunals were granted the right to award interest on compensatory awards.[639]

The correct approach to the awards of compensation under the amended provisions can be seen from *Ministry of Defence v Cannock*,[640] a set of test cases arising from dismissals of members of the armed forces on the grounds of pregnancy. In relation

---

630 [2003] IRLR 102.
631 *Deane v Ealing London Borough Council* [1993] IRLR 209; *Ministry of Defence v Cannock* [1994] IRLR 509.
632 *AB v South West Water Services Ltd* [1993] 1 All ER 609. This decision has since been overruled by *Kuddus v Chief Constable of Leicestershire Constabulary* [2002] 2 AC 122.
633 [1997] IRLR 163.
634 See *Vento v Chief Constable of West Yorkshire Police (No 2)* [2003] IRLR 102; *Scott v Commissioners of Inland Revenue* [2004] IRLR 713.
635 Law Commission Report No 247, *Aggravated, Exemplary and Restitutionary Damages* (1997).
636 See para 5.155 above.
637 Case C-271/91 [1993] IRLR 445.
638 [1993] IRLR 445, 449.
639 SI 1993/2798; Race Relations (Remedies) Act 1994.
640 [1994] IRLR 509; *Ministry of Defence v Meredith* [1995] IRLR 539; *Ministry of Defence v Hunt* [1996] IRLR 139; see also *Ministry of Defence v Wheeler* [1998] IRLR 23 on the correct approach to deductions for loss of a chance, and *Vento v Chief Constable of West Yorkshire Police (No 2)* [2003] IRLR 102 and *Orthet Ltd v Vince-Cain* [2004] IRLR 857 on claims for lost earnings.

to the extent of compensation, the EAT held that the relevant principles of tort law should apply to claims under the Directive, as they would to claims under the SDA 1975 (or the RRA 1976). This meant that the award of compensation should be designed so as to put the complainants in the position which they would have occupied had the Ministry of Defence not dismissed them unlawfully on the grounds of pregnancy. In this respect, the EAT held that there was an important difference between a situation of unlawful dismissal such as the present one, where the career prospects of the complainant would be harmed but without her necessarily being thereby disabled from finding another employment at some point, and a situation of personal injury of the kind more normally litigated through a claim in tort, where a claimant's claim for loss of earning capacity might well be much more extensive: 'to this extent, [the complainants'] compensation for loss of earnings is not likely to be different from the thousands of cases of unfair dismissal with which the Employment tribunals are having to deal each year, albeit that there is no cap on the award'.[641] The EAT also took a different view from that of a number of the employment tribunals on the question of how to calculate the likelihood of the complainants having left the armed forces of their own free will or having been required to do so by possible future contingencies. As we have seen, it also rejected any element of exemplary damages: it was 'a misreading of *Marshall (No 2)* to suggest that the deterrent effect has any part to play in the award ... Full compensation is the deterrent; deterrence is never a factor in itself'.[642] As a result, some of the very large awards of compensation, running into tens of thousands of pounds, were reduced, although they mostly remained substantially above the amounts which unfair dismissal claimants might normally expect to receive.

Recommendations

6.68   The remedy of a recommendation enables the tribunal to call upon the respondent to take 'action appearing to the tribunal to be practicable for the purpose of obviating or reducing the adverse effect on the complainant of any act of discrimination to which the complaint relates'.[643] If the respondent fails to comply with the recommendation 'without reasonable justification', the tribunal may, if it thinks it just and equitable, order compensation to be paid or increase the amount of compensation it has already ordered to be paid.[644]

The potential of the remedy of a recommendation for correcting individual acts of discrimination remains, as yet, largely unexploited, since the courts have given it a highly restrictive application. In *Noone v North West Thames Regional Health Authority (No 2)*,[645] where the complainant was not appointed as a consultant microbiologist on grounds which were found to be racially motivated, the Court of Appeal declined to approve a recommendation that the next time a vacancy came up within the organisation for the post in question, it should not be advertised, the aim being to ensure that the complainant would be appointed. This was because the failure to advertise the post would have set at nought the statutory procedure for making the appointment.

---

641   [1994] IRLR 509, 525.
642   [1994] IRLR 509, 524; on exemplary damages in tort law generally, see *Kuddus v Chief Constable of Leicestershire Constabulary* [2002] 2 AC 122.
643   SDA 1975, s 65(1)(c); RRA 1976 s 56(1)(c); DDA 1995, s 17A(2)(c); EE(SO)R 2003, reg 30(1)(c); EE(RB)R 2003, reg 30(1)(c).
644   SDA 1975, s 65(3); RRA 1976, s 56(4); DDA 1995, s 17A(5); EE(SO)R 2003, reg 30(3); EE(RB)R 2003, reg 30(3).
645   [1988] IRLR 530.

However, a more general objection to this type of recommendation was raised in *British Gas plc v Sharma*.[646] Here the tribunal had recommended that the complainant be promoted to the post from which she had been wrongfully excluded the next time a suitable vacancy arose; this, said the EAT, was akin to positive or reverse discrimination in favour of a person on racial grounds. This is a peculiar argument; it would seem more sensible to regard such a recommendation as remedying a previous, discriminatory wrong. However, there is arguably more weight in a second point made by the EAT, namely that under the Act the recommendation must indicate the action to be taken 'within a specified period'; since it was not known when a vacancy might arise in the future, the recommendation made in this case was invalid.

Removal or modification of contract terms

6.69   In addition to the remedies outlined above, any individual 'interested in a contract' may apply to the county court for an order removing or modifying any term whose inclusion in the contract renders the making of the contract unlawful under the legislation in question, whose inclusion is done in furtherance of an act contrary to the legislation, or which provides for an act contrary to the legislation to be carried out.[647] Separate provisions govern the situation where the complaint relates to a discriminatory rule which is contained in a collective agreement (regardless of whether it is legally enforceable); to a rule made by an employer for application to persons employed by him or those applying for employment; or to a rule made by a trade organisation or qualifications body which applies to its members, prospective members or those upon it whom it has conferred, or has the power to confer, professional or trade qualifications. Here the aggrieved individual may make an application to an employment tribunal for a declaration that the rule or term in question is void.[648]

Administrative enforcement

6.70   The responsibility for enforcing certain provisions of the anti-discrimination legislation is devolved, in the case of the SDA 1975, to the Equal Opportunities Commission (EOC) in the case of the RRA 1976,[649] to the Commission for Racial Equality (CRE), and in the case of the DDA 1995, to the Disability Rights Commission ('DRC').[650] In certain specified situations the

---

646   [1991] IRLR 101. See also *Irvine v Prestcold Ltd* [1981] IRLR 281.

647   SDA 1975, s 77; RRA 1976, s 72(1); DDA 1995, s 17C and Sch 3A; EE(SO)R 2003, reg 35 and Sch 4; EE(RB)R 2003, reg 35 and Sch 4. See *Meade-Hill v British Council* [1995] IRLR 478.

648   SDA 1986, s 6(4A), (4C), (4D); RRA 1976, s 72A; DDA 1995, Sch 3A, Part 2; EE(SO)R 2003, Sch 4, Part 2; EE(RB)R 2003, Sch 4, Part 2.

649   It is noteworthy that the Race Directive, Directive 2000/43, Art 13, provides that 'Member States shall designate a body or bodies for the promotion of equal treatment of all persons without discrimination on the grounds of racial or ethnic origin'. Minimum functions of such bodies are laid down in Art 13(2).

650   With the establishment of the additional prohibited grounds of discrimination, relating to sexual orientation, religion or belief, and age, the case for the integration of the different bodies with responsibilities for enforcing and overseeing anti-discrimination law was raised. In October 2003 the government announced that it was in favour of an integrated body, and in May 2004 published a White Paper, *Fairness for All: A New Commission for Equality and Human Rights: White Paper* Cm 6185, 2004, setting out its proposals. At the time of writing the Equality Bill 2005, which will establish a new Commission for Equality and Human Rights, is before Parliament. See para 2.39 above.

relevant Commission has the exclusive right to seek a ruling of an employment tribunal to the effect that a contravention of the Act has taken place and then, if it appears to the Commission that the acts are likely to be repeated, to apply to the county court for an injunction to restrain the person in question from so acting.[651] These situations concern, first, the publication of discriminatory advertisements indicating an intention to do an act contrary to the principle of equal treatment;[652] second, the issuing of instructions to discriminate issued by a person 'who has authority over another person' or 'in accordance with whose wishes that other person is accustomed to act;[653] and, thirdly, the exercise of pressure to discriminate, where a person induces or attempts to induce another to contravene the principle of equal treatment by providing or offering to provide him or her with a benefit or subjecting or threatening to subject him or her to a detriment.[654]

More generally, each of the Commissions is given the three-fold statutory duty of working towards the elimination of discrimination; promoting equality of opportunity; and monitoring the working of the legislation.[655] Commissioners are appointed by the Secretary of State, and may hold office for up to five years; in each case, at least eight and no more than fifteen commissioners may hold office at any one time. The legislation also provides for the appointment of a 'chairman and deputy chairman'.[656] The Commissions are also vested with certain specific powers, among the most important of which is the power to grant assistance and advice to participants in legal proceedings, which they may exercise where 'the case raises a question of principle' or 'it is unreasonable, having regard to the complexity of the case or the applicant's position ... to expect the applicant to deal with the case unaided'.[657] They have powers to undertake and/or assist research and education[658] and to issue codes of practice;[659] and the Commission for Racial Equality has the power to grant financial or other assistance to any organisation appearing to it to be concerned with the promotion of equality of opportunity and good relations between persons of different racial groups.[660]

Each Commission has the power to undertake a formal investigation for any purpose connected with the performance of their three-fold statutory duty (as outlined above), and must do if required to do so by the Secretary of State.[661] The formal investigation could have been an important mechanism for challenging discriminatory practices, but it has been so hedged about with

651 SDA 1975 s 72; RRA 1976, s 63; DDA 1995, s17B.
652 SDA 1975, s 38; RRA 1976, s 29; DDA 1995, s 16B.
653 SDA 1975, s 39; RRA 1976, s 30; DDA 1995, s 16C(1).
654 SDA 1975, s 40; RRA 1976, s 31; DDA 1995, s 16C(2)–(3).
655 SDA 1975, s 53; RRA 1976, s 43; DRCA 1999, s 2 (under which the Disability Rights Commission is also given the task of taking steps with a view to encouraging good practice in the treatment of disabled persons).
656 See generally SDA 1975, s 53 and Sch 3; RRA 1976, s 43 and Sch 1; DRCA 1999, Sch 1, paras 2–6 (specifying that between 10 and 15 commissioners should serve at any one time).
657 SDA 1975, s 75(1); RRA 1976, s 66(1); see also DRCA 1999, s 7(2).
658 SDA 1975, s 54; RRA 1976, s 45; DRCA 1999, s 2(2)(c).
659 SDA 1975, s 56A; RRA 1976, s 47; DDA 1995, s 53A. Codes require the approval of the Secretary of State: SDA 1975, s 56A(4); RRA 1976, s 47(4); DDA 1995, s 53A(4).
660 RRA 1976, s 44, which specifies that no financial assistance may be given out of money provided by Parliament without the approval of the Secretary of State, given with the consent of the Treasury.
661 SDA 1975, s 57; RRA 1976, s 48; DRCA 1999, s 3.

procedural requirements that its value in this regard is highly limited. It is, first, a precondition of embarking on a formal investigation that the Commission should draw up terms of reference. Where these confine the investigation to the activities of a named person who the Commission believes may have committed acts which contravene the legislation, the Commission must inform him or her of its belief and of the proposal to investigate the acts in question; it must then offer him or her an opportunity to make oral or written representations. For this purpose the person concerned has the right to be legally represented or represented by another person of their choice whom the Commission does not regard as unsuitable.[662] Extensive powers are conferred on the Commission to obtain information during the course of formal investigations.[663]

The courts have interpreted the relevant statutory provisions with a scrupulous regard for the rights of persons subjected to investigation, but with little concern for the wider strategic role envisaged for this form of administrative enforcement in the legislation. In *Hillingdon London Borough Council v Commission for Racial Equality*[664] the House of Lords held that the Commission had to have formed a belief that an unlawful act had taken place prior to commencing an investigation against a named person, and that the investigation, once underway, could not exceed the parameters laid down in the stated terms of reference. The courts have also implied an obligation upon the Commissions to observe the rules of natural justice in the exercise of powers with regard to formal investigations.[665]

Either during or upon completion of a formal investigation the Commission may issue recommendations 'to any persons, with a view to promoting equality of opportunity ... for changes in their policies or procedures, or as to any other matters'; or, in the case of an investigation ordered by the Secretary of State, recommendations to him or her for changes in the law or otherwise.[666] In addition, if the Commission becomes satisfied in the course of a formal investigation that an unlawful discriminatory act as defined by the legislation has been committed, it may issue to the person concerned a 'non-discrimination notice' requiring him or her not to commit such acts and where this involves changes to its practices or other arrangements, to inform the Commission that such changes have been effected and what they are.[667] Prior to issuing a non-discrimination notice the Commission must give the person concerned notice of its intention to do so and the opportunity to make oral or written representations within a specified period of not less than 28 days, and then take those representations into account. The subject of such a notice may also appeal, within six weeks of it being served, to an employment tribunal or (as appropriate) the county court, which has the power to quash any requirement of the notice which it considers to be unreasonable 'because it is based on an incorrect finding of fact or for any other reason', and, if it so wishes, to substitute a new requirement in its place.[668]

---

662   SDA 1975, s 58; RRA 1976, s 49; DRCA 1999, Sch 3, Part I.
663   SDA 1975, s 59 and SI 1975/1993; RRA 1976, s 50 and SI 1977/841; DRCA 1999, Sch 3, Part I.
664   [1982] AC 779; see also *Re Prestige Group plc* [1984] IRLR 166.
665   *R v Commission for Racial Equality, ex p Hillingdon London Borough Council* [1982] QB 276, 287 (Lord Denning MR).
666   SDA 1975, s 60; RRA 1976, s 51; DRCA 1999, Sch 3, para 6.
667   SDA 1975, s 67; RRA 1976, s 58. On the differently structured provisions governing non-discrimination notices in relation to disability, see DRCA 1999, Sch 3, Part II.
668   SDA 1975, s 68; RRA 1976, s 59; DRCA 1999, Sch 3, para 10 (which, again, is differently worded from the parallel provisions under the SDA 1975 and RRA 1976).

In something of a gloss on the statute, the courts have held that in such an appeal, all findings of fact made by the Commission in the course of its investigation are open to scrutiny.[669]

The immediate effect of the issue of a non-discrimination notice is advisory only (although in practice it may be highly embarrassing for the recipient). If the discrimination persists, however, then within five years of the issue of the notice the Commission has the right to apply to the county court for an injunction to restrain the person in question from committing an unlawful discriminatory act. In a case where the original notice was not appealed, however, the Commission must first obtain a ruling from an employment tribunal to the effect that a breach of the relevant provision of the Act has in fact taken place. The Commission may also seek an injunction against a person who was previously found to have contravened one of the relevant provisions of the relevant Act (or, in the case of the EOC, the EqPA 1970) in an action brought by an individual complainant, again within a period of five years of the finding being made.[670]

EQUAL PAY

6.71 The principle of equal treatment takes a distinctive form in the context of sex discrimination over pay. At the level of domestic legislation, the SDA 1975 has no application to issues of pay; instead these are resolved under the EqPA 1970, an Act which has a different conceptual framework from the other anti-discrimination legislation and which also provides for separate procedures for the resolution of claims. At European Community level, the issue of equal pay is particularly important as a result of the presence in the EC Treaty of Article 141 (ex 119) and of the case law of the ECJ, which has not only given Article 141 a broad interpretation but has also ensured that for most purposes it confers rights directly on individuals in national law, through the doctrine of direct effect. The influence of the Equal Pay Directive[671] has also been felt, not least in bringing about the amendment of the EqPA 1970 in 1983 with the introduction of the principle of equal pay for work of equal value. We shall begin by outlining the framework provided by these different levels of regulation before examining in greater detail the substance of the law in terms of the scope and bases of comparison of pay and conditions; the defences available to employers; and the mode of implementation of awards. Our analysis will conclude with a study of the application of the principle of equal treatment to occupational pension schemes and to collective agreements.

The relationship between the Equal Pay Act and the principle of equal treatment

6.72 As we have seen,[672] the principle of equal treatment on the grounds of sex which is contained in the SDA 1975 has no application to 'benefits consisting of

---

669 *Commission for Racial Equality v Amari Plastics Ltd* [1982] IRLR 252.

670 SDA 1975, ss 71, 73; RRA 1976, ss 62, 64. The broadly parallel provision in DRCA 1999, Sch 3, para 12 relates only to non-discrimination notices (see also the provisions of Sch 3, Part III, concerning 'action plans').

671 Directive 75/117.

672 See para 6.43 above.

the payment of money when the provision of those benefits is regulated by the woman's contract of employment'.[673] Where inequality of pay exists, therefore, the complaint must be brought under the EqPA 1970, which implies into the contract of the complainant an 'equality clause'.[674] This has the effect of modifying the terms of the complainant's contract so as to ensure that they are no less favourable than those of a comparable person of the opposite sex in the same employment (the 'comparator').[675] The equality clause affects *all* contract terms and not simply those governing pay;[676] in this sense, the scope of the EqPA 1970 is wider than it strictly needs to be to fill the gap left by the exclusion of the issue of pay from the SDA 1975. However, for the purpose of identifying a comparator, only certain individuals may be chosen:[677] a female worker (for example) is only permitted to compare her pay and conditions with those of a man who is employed on either 'like work', on work 'rated as equivalent' under a job evaluation scheme, or on work of 'equal value' to hers. The result of this is that the basis of comparison under the EqPA 1970 is much more restricted than it would be if the principle of equal treatment, as laid down in the SDA 1975, were to be applied here. In effect, then, the EqPA 1970 constitutes a derogation from the broader principle of equal treatment.[678]

The role of the concept of discrimination in equal pay claims

6.73   Despite that derogation, the regime set up by the EqPA would appear, in certain respects, to be more flexible than that operating for other sex discrimination claims. In particular, it is arguable that once the complainant has identified a relevant comparator on one of the three grounds just referred to, she is not required to go on to show, in addition, that the elements of either direct or indirect sex discrimination are also met on the facts of the case. In particular, she should not have to show that there is a situation of 'adverse impact' in the sense required by the test for indirect discrimination. This suggestion is derived from the structure of section 1 of the Act. Section 1(2) sets out the grounds of comparison, and section 1(3) then allows the employer a defence if it can show that the variation is 'genuinely due to a material factor which is not the difference of sex'. As Waller LJ put it in *Home Office v Bailey*,[679] 'if a woman can point to a job being performed by a man on a higher rate of pay, which is the same job as she is performing or its equivalent in value, the subsection seems simply to place the onus on the employer of proving that "genuinely" there is a material factor explaining the difference which has nothing to do with the difference in sex ... I do not read the subsection at least at first blush, as imposing a two-stage process in which the woman having pointed to a higher paid man has some burden of

673 SDA 1975, s 6(6).
674 EqPA 1970, s 1.
675 On the meaning, in this context, of the phrase 'in the same employment', see paras 6.75–6.77 below.
676 Cf EqPA 1970, s 1(2)(a)–(c).
677 See para 6.78 below.
678 For an example of a claim which might have succeeded had it fallen under the SDA 1975 but failed under the EqPA 1970, see *Meeks v National Union of Agricultural and Allied Workers* [1976] IRLR 198. An important but so far unresolved question is whether the implementation of the revisions to the Equal Treatment Directive (76/207), contained in Directove 2002/73, necessitate a change to UK equal pay law. See para 6.43 above, at note 437.
679 [2005] IRLR 369, at para 34

establishing a prima facie case that there is discrimination, which then imposes an evidential burden on the employer to justify the factor'.

This is not to say that the concept of discrimination is *irrelevant* to the construction of the Act; rather, sex discrimination is *presumed* once the complainant brings her case under one of the grounds of comparison in section 1(2). Authority for the suggestion that the EqPA can be read as impliedly incorporating broadly similar notions of direct and indirect discrimination to those contained in the SDA 1975 goes back to the early case of *Shields v E Coomes (Holdings) Ltd*, in which Bridge LJ suggested that the Acts 'should be construed and applied as a harmonious whole and in such a way that the broad principles which underlie the whole scheme of legislation are not frustrated by a narrow interpretation or restrictive application of particular provisions'.[680] In this regard, it is relevant that although the substantive provisions of the EqPA make no reference to the concept of discrimination, the preamble to the Act states that its purpose is 'to prevent discrimination, as regards terms and conditions of employment between men and women'. For this reason, among others, Lord Browne-Wilkinson commented in *Strathclyde Regional Council v Wallace*[681] that '[t]he purpose of section 1 of the Equal Pay Act 1970 is to eliminate sex discrimination in pay not to achieve fair wages'.

The difficulty lies in identifying precisely what the role of the discrimination concept is in section 1. In *Glasgow City Council v Marshall* Lord Nicholls gave this explanation:[682]

> The scheme of the Act is that a rebuttable presumption of sex discrimination arises once the gender-based comparison shows that a woman, doing like work or work rated as equivalent or work of equal value to that of a man, is being paid or treated less favourably than the man. The variation between her contract and the man's contract is presumed to be due to the difference of sex. The burden passes to the employer to show that the explanation for the variation is not tainted with sex. In order to discharge this burden, the employer must satisfy the tribunal on several matters. First, that the proffered explanation, or reason, is genuine, and not a sham or pretence. Second, that the less favourable treatment is due to this reason ... Third, that the reason is not the 'difference of sex'. This phrase is apt to embrace any form of sex discrimination, whether direct or indirect. Fourth, that the factor relied upon is or, in a case within section 1(2)(c), may be a 'material' difference, that is, a significant and relevant difference, between the woman's case and the man's case.
>
> When section 1 is thus analysed, it is apparent that an employer who satisfies the third of these requirements is under no obligation to prove a 'good' reason for the pay disparity. In order to fulfil the third requirement he must prove the absence of sex discrimination, direct or indirect. If there is any evidence of sex discrimination, such as evidence that the difference in pay has disparately adverse impact on women, the employer will be called upon to satisfy the tribunal that the difference is pay is objectively justifiable. But if the employer proves the absence of sex discrimination he is not obliged to justify the pay disparity.

In other words, the discrimination concept is embedded in the 'material factor' defence. But even if this is so, it can be argued, that, precisely because it is part

---

680 [1978] ICR 1159, 1178 (Bridge LJ).
681 [1998] 1 WLR 259, 267. Lord Browne-Wilkinson also thought that the view of Lord Slynn in *Ratcliffe v North Yorkshire County Council* [1995] IRLR 439, 442, refusing to accept that the definition of indirect discrimination in the SDA 1975 should be read into the EqPA 1970, s 1, 'must not be carried too far': [1998] 1 WLR 259, 265.
682 [2000] IRLR 272, at paras 18–19.

of a defence, the burden of showing that there is no adverse impact in equal pay claims should normally rest on the employer. *Marshall* is an unusual case in this respect: the complainants conceded that there was no adverse impact. For this reason, *Marshall* is not a strong authority for the suggestion, made in *Nelson v Carrillion Services Ltd*,[683] that the complainant should in all cases have the burden of showing adverse impact.[684]

Whether or not the above argument on the burden of proof is accepted, there is a case for applying a more flexible test of discrimination in equal pay cases than in other sex discrimination claims. In *Enderby v Frenchay Health Authority*[685] the ECJ held that as far as equal pay claims under Article 141 and the Equal Pay Directive[686] were concerned, a broader notion of indirect discrimination than that in the SDA 1975 (as it then stood) had to be applied.[687] Thus one possible view of the combined effect of the *Marshall* and *Enderby* cases is that the concepts of direct and indirect discrimination should be read into the structure of the 1970 Act, but that some of the more rigid aspects of the definition of indirect discrimination in the 1975 Act can be overcome in equal pay cases.[688] It should also be noted that the SDA itself, having already been amended, in the light of the Burden of Proof Directive[689] to incorporate an apparently more flexible definition of indirect discrimination,[690] will shortly undergo a further redefinition of indirect discrimination by October 2005 under the terms of the revised Equal Treatment Directive.[691]

The interaction of domestic legislation and European Union law

6.74   The influence of European Union law upon the law of equal pay is of wider significance. Article 141 of the EC Treaty requires Member States to 'ensure that the principle of equal pay for male and female workers for equal work or work of equal value is applied'; for this purpose it defines pay as 'the ordinary basic or minimum wage or salary and any other consideration, whether in cash or in kind, which the worker receives, directly or indirectly, in respect of his employment from his employer.'[692] Article 1 of the Equal Pay Directive specifies, in turn, that:

683 [2003] IRLR 428. It should nevertheless be noted that *Marshall* was not the only HL authority relied on in this case; the Court of Appeal also referred to *Barry v Midland Bank plc* [1999] IRLR 581 in which the House of Lords adopted a strict test of indirect discrimination (see the discussion of Thomas, 2000).

684 See *Home Office v Bailey* [2005] IRLR 369, at para 37 (Waller LJ).

685 Case C-127/92 [1993] IRLR 591.

686 Directive 75/117; see below.

687 On the definition of indirect discrimination, see para 6.20 above.

688 In particular, it is arguably easier to establish a prima facie case of discrimination on the basis of adverse impact under *Enderby* than under the SDA 1975; see Case C-400/93 *Specialarbejderforbundet i Danmark v Dansk Industri, acting for Royal Copenhagen* [1995] IRLR 648; *British Road Services Ltd v Loughran* [1997] IRLR 92. *Ministry of Defence v Armstrong* [2004] IRLR 672 can be understood in this light.

689 Directive 97/80.

690 Now contained in SDA 1975, s 1(2), as amended by SI 2001/2660. The Burden of Proof Directive applies to equal pay cases and not just to those arising under other aspects of sex discrimination law, but did not lead to a revision of the EqPA.

691 See Directive 76/207, Art 2(2), as amended by Directive 2002/73. On this 'wider' definition of indirect discrimination, see paras 6.20–6.21 above.

692 See para 6.5 above for an account of the origins of Art 141. For an account of the general development of EC equality law which examines in detail the case law under Art 141, see Hepple, 1997.

The principle of equal pay for men and women outlined in Article [141] of the Treaty ... means, for the same work or for work to which equal value is attributed, the elimination of all discrimination on grounds of sex with regard to all aspects and conditions of remuneration.

In particular, where a job classification system is used for determining pay it must be based on the same criteria for both men and women and so drawn up as to exclude any discrimination on grounds of sex.

The ECJ has held that Article 1 of the Directive is 'principally designed to facilitate the practical application of the principle of equal pay outlined in Article [141] of the Treaty', and 'in no way alters the content or scope of that principle as defined in the Treaty'.[693] As Ellis comments, 'if the Directive therefore merely spells out the detail of Article 119 [now 141], without in any way undermining its scope, it follows that its chief practical effect today is to shed light on the more obscure objects of Article 119'.[694] This was highly significant at a time when Article 119, as it then was, made no reference to the principle of equal value; that reference was inserted through the revisions to the EC Treaty following the Treaty of Amsterdam in 1997. The ECJ had already held, on a number of occasions, that Article 119 incorporated the principle of equal value.[695] As it is, there is now no doubt that the principle of equal value has horizontal, and not simply vertical, direct effect in UK law. In addition, because the Equal Pay Directive is the immediate source of the 1983 amendments to the EqPA 1970 which introduced the principle of equal pay for work of equal value into the Act, the Act itself is to be purposively interpreted by reference to the Directive and its objectives.[696]

Although it is neither necessary nor permissible for a domestic court to consider Article 141 if the EqPA 1970 provides a fully adequate remedy,[697] in cases where European Community law provides rights over and above domestic legislation the courts have held that employment tribunals should apply Article 141 directly.[698] The ECJ has given a broad interpretation both to the substance of Article 141 and to the circumstances in which it has direct effect in national law. After some initial uncertainty, the Court has confirmed that Article 141 has direct effect in situations of indirect as well as direct discrimination, and regardless of whether the discrimination is intentional.[699] Of particular importance is the wide definition which it has accorded to the concept of 'pay'. In *Barber v Guardian Royal Exchange Assurance Group*[700] it held that the formula contained in Article 141 was sufficiently broad to extend to payments made by an employer under an occupational pension scheme, even though this was a contracted-out scheme which, under domestic UK law, operated in partial substitution for benefits

---

693 Case 96/80 *Jenkins v Kingsgate (Clothing Productions) Ltd* [1981] IRLR 228, 234.
694 Ellis, 1991: p 97.
695 Case 69/80 *Worringham v Lloyd's Bank Ltd* [1981] IRLR 178; Case 96/80 *Jenkins v Kingsgate (Clothing Productions) Ltd* [1981] IRLR 228; Case 157/86 *Murphy v Bord Telecom Eireann* [1988] ECR 673.
696 *Pickstone v Freemans plc* [1988] IRLR 357. In *Webb v EMO Air Cargo Ltd* [1993] IRLR 27, 32, Lord Keith accepted the principle of the 'indirect effect' of directives regardless of whether the domestic legislation in question was enacted before or after the adoption of the Community measure.
697 *Blaik v Post Office* [1994] IRLR 280.
698 *McKechnie v UBM Building Supplies (Southern) Ltd* [1991] IRLR 283.
699 Case 170/84 *Bilka-Kaufhaus GmbH v Weber von Hartz* [1986] IRLR 317.
700 Case 262/88 [1990] IRLR 240; see also Case C-243/95 *Hill and Stapleton v Revenue Commissioners* [1998] IRLR 466.

under the state social security system.[701] The most important division is now between employer-based payments, which in principle fall under Article 141 and the Equal Pay Directive, and social security payments which fall under the Directive on Equality in State Social Security.[702] Unemployment benefits, for example, and payments made through the basic state pension and state earnings-related pension schemes are governed by the latter; but this leaves a large category of payments within Article 141, including occupational sick pay and maternity pay;[703] rules governing access to pay increments based on seniority;[704] ex gratia payments made to employees on termination of employment;[705] redundancy compensation;[706] unfair dismissal compensation[707] and payments made in respect of time off to take part in training courses for the purposes of employee representation.[708] It is irrelevant for this purpose that the making of the particular payment is mandated by legislation (as it would be in the case of unfair dismissal and redundancy compensation). This extension of the concept of 'pay' has proved to be highly significant as a means of calling into question derogations from the principle of equal treatment under domestic law which had previously seemed safe from review. *Barber* itself has prompted the equalisation of pensionable ages in occupational pension schemes, thereby rendering ineffective a derogation inserted into the EqPA 1970;[709] it also prompted litigation which eventually led to the removal of the 8- and 16-hour weekly qualifying thresholds from the law of redundancy and unfair dismissal.[710] On the other hand, the Court has also held that the concept of pay does not extend to the contributions made by an employer into an occupational pension scheme, thereby allowing differential payments to be made in respect of male and female employees according to sex-based actuarial calculations.[711]

A further respect in which Article 141 goes further than domestic legislation concerns the concept of discrimination which it embodies. As we have just seen,[712] the EqPA 1970 only allows a limited scope for the comparison of the position of workers for the purpose of identifying inequality. Article 141, by contrast, is free of some of these limitations. For example, it allows a comparison to be made between the pay of a female complainant and a male *predecessor*[713]

701 To a large extent the benefit of this ruling was limited by the Court's ruling that it should only apply to benefits vesting on or after the date of its ruling, 17 May 1990: see below, para 6.96.

702 Directive 79/7.

703 Case 171/88 *Rinner-Kühn v FWW Spezial Gebäudereinigung GmbH* [1989] IRLR 493; C-342/93 *Gillespie v Northern Health and Social Services Board* [1996] IRLR 214; Case C-147/02 *Alabaster v Woolwich plc* [2004] IRLR 486.

704 Case C-184/89 *Nimz v Freie und Hansestadt Hamburg* [1991] IRLR 222.

705 Case 262/88 *Barber v Guardian Royal Exchange Assurance Group* [1990] IRLR 240.

706 Ibid.

707 Case C-167/97 *R v Secretary of State for Employment, ex p Seymour-Smith and Perez* [1999] IRLR 253.

708 Case C-457/93 *Kuratorium für Dialyse und Nierentransplantation eV v Lewark* [1996] IRLR 637; *Davies v Neath Port Talbot County Borough Council* [1999] IRLR 769, holding that *Manor Bakeries Ltd v Nazir* [1996] IRLR 604 was incorrectly decided on this point.

709 EqPA 1970, s 6(1A)(b). See below, para 6.96.

710 *R v Secretary of State for Employment, ex p EOC* [1994] IRLR 176; see above, para 3.88.

711 C-152/91 *Neath v Hugh Steeper Ltd* Case [1994] IRLR 91; Case C-200/91 *Coloroll Pension Trustees Ltd v Russell* [1994] IRLR 586; see below, para 6.96.

712 See above.

713 Case 129/79 *Macarthys Ltd v Smith* [1980] IRLR 210.

or successor[714] in the employment in question, and between a female complainant and a male employed on work of *less than equal value* with hers.[715] The extent of the employer's justification or 'material factor' defence to an equal pay claim may also be narrower under Article 141 than under the Act.[716]

The scope of comparison

'Same employment'

6.75   Under the EqPA 1970, a female complainant (for example) is allowed to compare her terms and conditions with those of 'a man in the same employment' who is employed either on like work, work rated as equivalent or work of equal value to hers.[717] Subject to the need to bring the case within one of these categories, whose meaning is examined below,[718] the complainant may choose any person so employed as her 'comparator', but she may not compare her treatment to that which a comparable man would *hypothetically* have received, as is possible under the SDA 1975.[719]

The concept of 'same employment' in this context has two dimensions: the complainant must show, first, that she and her comparator share the same employer (which for this purpose can be an associated employer), and, second, that they are employed at the same establishment or at different establishments covered by common terms and conditions.

Employer

6.76   The term 'same employment' which appears in the definition of the three grounds of comparison in section 1(2) of the Act means, in the first case, that the complainant and her comparator must be employed by the same employer or by an associated employer.[720] Associated employers, here as elsewhere in labour legislation, are defined according to a test of control borrowed from company law: 'two employers are to be treated as associated if one is a company of which the other (directly or indirectly) has control or if both are companies of which a third person (directly or indirectly) has control'.[721] In *Scullard v Knowles*[722] the EAT considered that 'the class of comparators defined in section 1(6) is more restricted than that available on the application of Article [141] ... Article [141] is not, for example, confined to employment in undertakings which have a particular legal form, such as a limited company'. In this case, the complainant was employed as a manager in a training unit which was part of a charitable organisation consisting of several such units across the country. The employer objected to her attempting to use, as a comparator, male employees who worked at other units. The employment tribunal held that the 'associated employer'

---

714   *Diocese of Hallam Trustee v Connaughton* [1996] IRLR 505.
715   Case 157/86 *Murphy v Board Telecom Eirrean* [1988] ECR 673.
716   See Case C-127/92 *Enderby v Frenchay Health Authority* [1993] IRLR 591, discussed below at para 6.89.
717   S 1(1)–(2).
718   See paras 6.79–6.85.
719   S 5(3).
720   This is the effect of s 1(6).
721   EqPA 1970, s 1(6)(c). For discussion of the phrase 'associated employer', see above, para 3.98.
722   [1996] IRLR 344, 345. See also *Halsey v Fair Employment Agency* [1989] IRLR 106; *South Ayrshire Council v Morton* [2001] IRLR 28, [2002] IRLR 256.

exception in section 1(6) of the Act had no application here since the different units were not limited companies within the terms of that provision. The EAT held that the wider provisions of EC law covered the complainant's case, and had to be taken into account by the tribunal by virtue of the doctrine of direct effect.

By contrast, in *Lawrence v Regent Office Care Ltd*[723] the ECJ ruled that, under Article 141 and the Equal Pay Directive, dinner ladies whose employment had been transferred from a local authority to private contractors could not claim equal pay with employees of the council for which they used to work, and whose work had been rated of equal value to theirs prior to the employment transfer. The basis for this ruling was that Article 141 required the identification of a 'single source' which was responsible for the discrimination and could put it right. Thus the Article:

> ... is addressed to those who may be held responsible for the unauthorised difference in terms and conditions of employment ... these are the legislature, the parties to a collective works agreement and the management of a corporate group. They may be held accountable in this regard. On the other hand, if differences in pay arise as between undertakings or establishments in which the respective employers are separately responsible for the terms and conditions of employment within their own undertaking or establishment, they cannot possibly be held individually accountable for any differences in the terms and conditions of employment between those undertakings.[724]

The ECJ proved equally unreceptive to arguments for allowing a broad scope of comparison in *Allonby v Accrington and Rossendale College*.[725] The complainant, a part-time lecturer in a further education college, was dismissed and re-employed, to carry out the same work on a lower rate of pay, via an employment agency. She claimed equal pay with a comparator who was a full-time, directly employed employee of the college. Her claim failed under UK law on the grounds that the agency and the college were not associated employers under section 1(6) of the Act. The ECJ ruled that 'the fact that the level of pay received by Ms Allonby is influenced by the amount which the College pays the [agency] is not a sufficient basis for concluding that the College and [the agency] constitute a single source to which can be attributed the differences identified in Ms. Allonby's conditions of pay and those of the male worker paid by the College'.[726]

Ellis had earlier argued[727] that since job content, measured objectively, was taken to be the principal criterion of equal work under the Equal Pay Directive of 1975 and hence, by extension, under Article 141, comparisons should be confined neither to individual establishments nor even to individual employers. Some authority for her argument was to be found in the early case of *Defrenne v Sabena*[728] in which the ECJ referred to the principle of equal pay for equal work as applying broadly to men and women 'in the same establishment or service', and to a later suggestion from Advocate General Van Themaat that the comparison should not be confined to individual establishments.[729] However,

---

723 Case C-320/00, [2002] IRLR 822.
724 Case C-320/00 *Lawrence v Regent Office Care* [2002] IRLR 822, Opinion of Advocate General Geelhoed, at para 52. See also the Judgment of the Court, at para 18.
725 Case 256/01, [2004] IRLR 224. See Fredman, 2004c.
726 Case 256/01 *Allonby v Accrington and Rossendale College* [2004] IRLR 224, at para 48.
727 Ellis, 1991: p 62.
728 Case 43/75 [1976] ECR 455, at para 22.
729 Case 143/83 *EC Commission v Denmark* [1985] ECR 427.

if the employment unit is not to set the limits to comparison, another acceptable basis must be found. It is not clear that job evaluation techniques, without more, are capable of providing objective guidance on such a scale.[730] Where, on the other hand, a number of employers come under the scope of a common institutional framework for regulating pay and conditions, such as a sector-level collective agreement or a single job evaluation exercise, this objection would have less force. In *Lawrence* itself the ECJ agreed that there was 'nothing in the wording of Article 141(1) EC to suggest that the applicability of that provision is limited to situations in which men and women work for the same employer' and accepted that its earlier case law had established that the principle could be invoked 'in cases of discrimination arising directly from legislative provisions or collective labour agreements'.[731]

There are several problematic aspects to the *Lawrence* and *Allonby* decisions. Article 141 makes no reference to the employment unit as the sole basis for comparison; the 'single source' concept is a gloss on the Article which the Court chose to add. Although it was claimed, in both cases, that there would be practical difficulties in allowing comparisons across employment boundaries, these did not arise in the cases before the Court: as we have seen, *Lawrence* was a case of a unified job evaluation exercise and *Allonby* involved work in a single establishment, while in both cases comparisons were being made with former co-employees. It is also a matter of concern that the supposedly fundamental right contained in Article 141 can so easily be evaded by employer action of the kinds seen in these cases.

Notwithstanding these difficulties, the concept of the 'single source' is also of relevance to comparisons made *within* employment units, following the decision of the Court of Appeal in *Robertson v DEFRA*.[732] Here, civil servants employed by one government department tried to compare their pay to more highly-paid civil servants in another. They were not employed at the same establishment and their employment was not governed by common terms and conditions, as a result of the delegation of the power to set the terms and conditions of employment of civil servants to individual departments which occurred in the early 1990s.[733] Thus they could not bring their case under section 1(6) of the Act.[734] The Court of Appeal held that, under Article 141, the Crown was not a 'single source' by virtue of its retaining a residual power to determine civil servants' pay, and that neither the Treasury nor the Ministry for the Civil Service could be said to exercise sufficient de facto control to qualify. Accordingly, the claim failed.

Establishment

6.77 The second aspect of the phrase 'same employment' refers to the idea that the complainant and comparator are either employed at the same 'establishment' in Great Britain,[735] or at different establishments 'at which common terms and conditions of employment are observed either generally or

---

730 On job evaluation, see below, para 6.83.
731 Case Case C-320/00 *Lawrence v Regent Office Care* [2002] IRLR 822, at para 17.
732 [2005] IRLR 363.
733 See [2005] IRLR 363, para 35.
734 See above, this paragraph
735 On the concept of establishment, see para 3.95, and on the territorial effect of the restriction to Great Britain, see para 2.50 above.

for employees of the relevant classes'.[736] In *Leverton v Clwyd County Council*[737] Lord Bridge said that 'the concept of common terms and conditions of employment observed generally at different establishments necessarily contemplates terms and conditions applicable to a wide range of employees whose individual terms will vary greatly *inter se*. Terms and conditions of employment governed by the same collective agreement seem to me to represent the paradigm, though not necessarily the only example, of the common terms and conditions of employment contemplated' by the Act. The application of the Act is, to that extent, dependent on the types of arrangement which happen to be in place for a particular employment; in so far as bargaining is decentralised as part of company strategies to that effect, and as sector-level collective bargaining is further weakened,[738] the range of opportunities for comparison under the Act is necessarily reduced.

In *Leverton*, a single collective agreement which formed the basis for the 'Purple Book' of terms and conditions governed the pay of the complainant and her chosen comparator. In contrast, in *British Coal Corpn v Smith*[739] three separate sets of agreements governed the terms and conditions of, respectively, canteen workers, clerical workers and surface mineworkers employed by British Coal. However, at the relevant time all of the employees had their pay and conditions set through centralised, industry-level agreements; and although the surface mineworkers enjoyed production bonuses which were calculated at local level, the tribunal considered that these could be seen in each case as 'a locally varied fulfilment of the same universally accepted central terms'. This decision was overturned in the Court of Appeal, which applied the following test:

> ... section 1(6) ... requires and permits the choice of a male comparator from a separate establishment, if he has the same employer or an associated employer, and if the terms and conditions of employment for men of the relevant class at his establishment are common with, meaning the same as, those of men of the relevant class employed at the woman's establishment, or which would be available for male employees for that work at her establishment. It is necessary that the selected male comparator should be representative of the class, or group, of male employees from whom he is selected, as regards the relevant terms etc of his contract of employment.[740]

The ruling that the relevant terms and conditions should be *the same as* those applying in the comparator's establishment seems a somewhat restrictive reading of the concept of '*common* terms and conditions'; in addition, the requirement that the male comparator be 'representative' of a group of men sharing the same terms as men employed at the complainant's establishment is arguably an unjustifiable gloss on the statute. The House of Lords allowed an appeal; according to Lord Slynn, 'the terms and conditions do not have to be identical'; it was enough if they were 'substantially comparable'.[741]

Choice of comparator

6.78   One respect in which European Community law clearly sets a more flexible standard concerns the choice of a predecessor or successor as a

736   EqPA 1970, s 1(6).
737   [1989] IRLR 28, 31.
738   On this, see paras 1.27–1.28 above.
739   [1994] IRLR 342; revsd [1996] IRLR 404.
740   [1994] IRLR 342, 358 (Balcombe LJ).
741   [1996] IRLR 404, 410.

comparator. This is not allowed under the EqPA 1970; the male comparator must be employed, or have been employed, at the same time as the complainant. In *Macarthys Ltd v Smith*[742] the female complainant was taken on as a factory manager at a wage of £50 per week; the previous holder of the job, a man, had earned £60 per week. The ECJ held on a preliminary reference that the scope of the concept of equal work, 'which is entirely qualitative in character in that it is exclusively concerned with the nature of the services in question, may not be restricted by the introduction of a requirement of contemporaneity'. The Court nevertheless declined to interpret Article 119 (now 141) as extending to cases of hypothetical comparisons.[743]

Like work

6.79   The first of the situations in which a comparison may be made is 'where the woman is employed on like work with a man in the same employment,[744] and this is the case only if 'her work and [his] is of the same or a broadly similar nature, and the differences (if any) between the things she does and the things [he does] are not of practical importance in relation to terms and conditions of employment'. For this purpose the Act requires the tribunal to take into account 'the frequency or otherwise with which any such differences occur in practice as well as to the nature and extent of the differences'.[745] This means that the employer cannot circumvent the Act by creating purely notional additional obligations. In the first case decided under the Act, *Capper Pass Ltd v Lawton*,[746] the EAT held that 'the work need not be of the *same* nature in order to be like work. It is enough if it is of similar nature. Indeed, it need only be broadly similar'; and 'trivial differences, or differences not likely in the real world to be reflected in the terms and conditions of employment, ought to be disregarded'.

The test has been applied in a fairly broad brush manner since then. One particular area of contention has been working-time arrangements, but courts and tribunals have been reluctant to classify otherwise identical jobs as dissimilar simply on the basis that one was part-time and the other full-time, or that one involves shift-working. In *Dugdale v Kraft Foods Ltd*[747] women quality control inspectors who were employed on day shifts compared their pay to those of men doing the same job on a regular night shift. The men received a higher basic rate of pay. All employees received shift premia of some kind, but the women were restricted from working nights by legislation which was in force at that time. The EAT held that 'the mere time at which the work is performed should be disregarded when considering the differences between the things which the woman does and the things which the man does'. Nor was this unjust, since 'where the work done is the same, and the only difference is the time at which it is done, the men will be compensated for the extra burden of working at night or on Sundays by the shift payment or premium. There seems no reason why the women should not have equality of treatment in respect of the basic wage'.

---

742 Case 129/79 [1980] ECR 1275, at para 11; *Diocese of Hallam Trustee v Connaughton* [1996] IRLR 505.
743 Case 129/79, at paras 14–15.
744 EqPA 1970, s 1(2)(a).
745 EqPA 1970, s 1(4).
746 [1976] IRLR 366, 367–368.
747 [1976] IRLR 368, 370, 371; see also *Electrolux Ltd v Hutchinson* [1976] IRLR 410; *Thomas v National Coal Board* [1987] IRLR 451.

The payment of premia for shifts potentially constitutes a material difference for the purposes of the employer's defences under section 1(3), and so differential payments for workers on separate shifts will be justifiable as far as the EqPA 1970 is concerned as long as the difference is not so great as to be disproportionate.[748]

Where one employee has extra responsibilities or extra duties, it is a question of fact in each case whether these are so substantial as to merit a finding that the jobs are dissimilar;[749] and even if the tribunal rules in favour of the complainant at this point, it remains open to the employer to argue that the difference is a justifiable or 'genuine material difference' under section 1(3). In *Shields v E Coomes Holdings Ltd*[750] the employer, which ran a chain of betting shops, paid a higher hourly rate to male counterhands than to female counterhands, on the basis that men were employed in shops where there was a risk of trouble from customers. Lord Denning, deciding that the jobs were similar, held that the time rate paid should be the same and that any extra duties undertaken by the men should be reflected in additional payments which would have to be justified under section 1(3).

Work rated as equivalent

6.80   The second basis upon which a claim for equal pay may be mounted occurs where the complainant and her comparator are employed on 'work rated as equivalent' by a job evaluation scheme. The assumption is that the employer has carried out a voluntary job evaluation, either of its own accord or at the behest of some other party such as a trade union, which has either resulted in an equal ranking for the two jobs, or would have done but for sex discrimination in the way the scheme was set up. More precisely, this part of the Act applies where the two jobs in question:

> ... have been given an equal value, in terms of the demand made on a worker under various headings (for instance effort, skill, decision), on a study undertaken with a view to evaluating in those terms the jobs to be done by all or any of the employees in an undertaking or group of undertakings, or would have been given an equal value but for the evaluation being made on a system setting different values for men and women on the same demand under any heading.[751]

What this provision does not do is require the employer to undertake a job evaluation scheme if it does not wish to. Moreover, the grounds on which an existing classification may be relied on are extremely difficult to meet. First, the employee has no basis for a claim if the scheme is not 'analytical'. The employee may, ironically, lose out at this point on the grounds of the study's inadequacy. An 'analytical' study is one which is 'thorough in analysis and capable of impartial application'; this will not be the case if the study 'requires the management to make a subjective judgment concerning the nature of the work before the employee can be fitted into the appropriate place in the

---

748   It also seems that employees with different professional qualifications and career structures will have difficulty demonstrating like work: see Case C-309/97 *Angestelltenbetriebsrat der Wiener Gebietskrankenkasse v Wiener Gebietskrankenkasse* [1999] IRLR 804.

749   See *Waddington v Leicester Council for Voluntary Services* [1977] IRLR 32; *Eaton Ltd v Nuttall* [1977] IRLR 71.

750   [1978] IRLR 263.

751   EqPA 1970, s 1(5).

appropriate salary grade'.[752] The study must also have been accepted as legitimate by the parties who commissioned it (usually the employer and possibly also the trade union concerned); it is not enough for consultants to have completed an analysis which is then rejected as inadequate by the employer, since it is no part of the purpose of the Act to force job evaluation schemes on those who do not want them.[753]

The second substantial hurdle which the complainant has to cross is the need to show, in a case where the study has ranked the jobs unequally, that the study was based on clear discrimination in the values set for the work of men and women respectively. This involves something akin to 'a plain error on the face of the record'.[754] In essence the contention is that the study would have resulted in a finding of equality if 'purged of some discriminatory element'; but what the complainant is unable to do 'is to base his claim on the footing that if the evaluation study had been carried out differently from the way in which it has in fact been carried out he would be entitled to the relief claimed. The claimant must take the study as it is'.[755] As a result, the chances of a successful claim being made under this head are remote.

Work of equal value

6.81   This third head was introduced in 1983 following the ruling of the ECJ in *EC Commission v United Kingdom*[756] to the effect that the Act, which as it then stood only contained the two bases of comparison referred to above, failed to comply with the standards set by the Equal Pay Directive. The Court noted that 'British legislation does not permit the introduction of a job classification system without the employer's consent. Workers in the United Kingdom are therefore unable to have their work rated as being of equal value with comparable work if their employer refuses to introduce a classification system'.[757] The Court did not hold that the Directive required the general introduction of job evaluation techniques into employing organisations, but rather that it required Member States to put in place the means by which equal value could be attributed to particular work 'notwithstanding the employer's wishes, if necessary in the context of adversarial proceedings';[758] the United Kingdom's argument that 'the criterion of work of equal value is too abstract to be applied by the courts' was brushed aside.[759]

The 1983 Equal Pay (Amendment) Regulations,[760] amending the EqPA 1970, set up a complex procedure for the adjudication of equal value claims, part of which is now to be found in the Employment Tribunal (Constitution and Rules of Procedure) Regulations 2004.[761]

---

752 *Eaton Ltd v Nuttall* [1977] IRLR 71, 74.
753 *Arnold v Beecham Group Ltd* [1982] IRLR 307; cf *O'Brien v Sim-Chem Ltd* [1980] IRLR 373. Note, however, that the EOC's Code of Practice on Equal Pay (most recently revised in 2003) recommends pay systems reviews as the 'most appropriate method of ensuring that a pay system delivers equal pay free from sex bias' (para 72).
754 *Green v Broxtowe District Council* [1977] ICR 241, 243.
755 *England v Bromley London Borough Council* [1978] ICR 1, 5.
756 Case 61/81 [1982] ICR 578.
757 Case 61/81 [1982] ICR 578, para 5.
758 Case 61/81 [1982] ICR 578, para 13.
759 Case 61/81 [1982] ICR 578, para 12.
760 SI 1983/1794.
761 SI 2004/1861, as amended by SI 2004/2351.

The 'token man' defence

6.82   An artificial obstacle faced by early complainants arose from the peculiar drafting of the amending Regulations, which were introduced under the European Communities Act 1972 and so were not subject to any amendment in the course of their parliamentary passage. In order for work to be of equal value under section 1(2)(c) of the Act, it must not be 'work in relation to which paragraph (a) or (b) above applies', paragraphs (a) and (b) referring to the 'like work' and 'work rated as equivalent' provisions of the Act. The intention here was to require complainants first of all to exhaust any rights they might have under paragraphs (a) and (b) before mounting an equal value claim, on the basis that the latter is a costly process often involving, as we shall see shortly, the appointment of an independent expert to evaluate the jobs which are the subject of the comparison. But this is not quite what paragraph (c) says: it appears to rule out a claim for equal value where, for example, there is a male individual doing the same job as the complainant ('like work'). This could be read as being 'work in relation to which paragraph (a) ... applies'. The problem with this literal interpretation of the amendments made in 1983 is that the purpose of the Regulations would have been completely defeated at the outset. The procedure envisaged for equal value claims would be easily averted by, for example, the simple device of employing a 'token male' in an otherwise female job grade; this would have rendered the procedure useless in what was arguably its most important area of application, namely breaking down inequalities caused by occupational segregation of men and women into different grades and classifications which were outside the scope of the 'like work' category. With these considerations in mind, the House of Lords held in *Pickstone v Freemans plc*[762] that the Regulations should be given a purposive interpretation which was consonant with the Directive which they were intended to implement and with Parliament's intentions, namely that 'paragraph (c) will only apply if paragraphs (a) and (b) are first held by the Tribunal not to apply in respect of the work of the woman and the work of the man with whom she seeks parity of pay'.[763]

Pre-existing job evaluation scheme

6.83   Before proceeding to determine whether the work of the complainant and her comparator are of equal value, the tribunal must consider whether there is evidence to the effect that a job evaluation scheme has already ranked the jobs unequally.[764] For this purpose, a 'stage 1 equal value hearing' must be conducted.[765] For the defence to apply, the work of the complainant and her comparator must 'have been given different values' by a job evaluation study within the meaning of section 1(5) of the Act.[766] The tribunal must reject the claim unless it has 'reasonable grounds for suspecting that the evaluation

---

762   [1988] IRLR 357.

763   [1988] IRLR 357, 363; for this purpose, their Lordships consulted Hansard to see what was said by ministers during the parliamentary debates on the draft regulations.

764   EqPA 1970, s 2A(2), (2A), as inserted by SI 2004/2352, which came into force on 1 October 2004. The 2004 Regulations removed a wider defence which had previously been available to the employer, namely that there were 'no reasonable grounds' for determining that the jobs were of equal value.

765   SI 2004/1861 Sch 6, para 4.

766   EqPA 1970, s 2A(2)(b).

contained in the study was ... made on a system which discriminates on grounds of sex'.[767] For this purpose there is sex discrimination where 'a difference, or coincidence, between values set by that system on different demands under the same or different headings is not justifiable irrespective of the sex of the person on whom those demands are made'.[768] In addition, the tribunal may decline to accept the study on the grounds that it is 'otherwise unsuitable to be relied upon'.[769]

There are, then, three requirements of this defence: the two jobs in question must have been ranked unequally; the study carried out must be an 'analytical' one within the meaning of the case law interpreting section 1(5); and it must not be tainted by sex discrimination or be otherwise unsuitable. The first of these is self-explanatory. The second necessitates some consideration of the kinds of job evaluation techniques which are acceptable for this purpose and of the extent to which the courts are prepared to scrutinise the findings of studies which have been carried out. ACAS Guide No 1 on job evaluation, which was judicially noted by the EAT in *Eaton Ltd v Nuttall*[770] identified five possible techniques: *job ranking*, where the jobs are individually assessed, then ranked in order and finally grouped into grades which form the basis of pay rates; *paired comparison*, which involves the comparison of particular pairs of jobs in turn, leading again to a ranking order; *job classification*, where 'benchmark' or typical jobs are assigned places in a pre-set grading structure and other jobs slotted in around them; *points assessment*, whereby jobs are broken down into a number of factors such as skill, responsibility, working conditions and physical and mental requirements to which points are awarded according to a predetermined scale, on the basis of which each job is given a points total which determines its place in the ranking; and *factor comparison*, whereby, for a number of 'key' jobs which serve as benchmarks, the proportion of pay which is determined by particular factors is identified, thereby producing a rate for these factors from which a composite wage can be deduced for each job. As we saw above,[771] the EAT in *Eaton* held that section 1(5) is only satisfied by a study, of whatever sort, which is capable of impartial application and does not require management to make a subjective judgment.

The degree of precision and of 'objectivity' needed was considered further by the Court of Appeal in *Bromley v H & J Quick Ltd*.[772] The employer had adopted a job evaluation study as part of which benchmark jobs were ranked on the basis of paired comparison, separate factors identified and their contribution weighted using multiple regression analysis, and grade boundaries established around the jobs. The resulting rankings were then discussed by a joint panel of management and employees on a 'felt fair' basis. Once the rankings were agreed, other jobs, for which there was no written job descriptions, were slotted into the structure on the basis of a general assessment of their worth by management, without a more specific factor-based analysis. The Court of Appeal held that this last stage of the process did not meet the requirements of section 1(5). According to Dillon LJ, the scheme must be analytical in the sense that 'the jobs of each worker covered by the study must have been valued in terms of

---

767 EqPA 1970, s 2A(2A)(a).
768 EqPA 1970, s 2A(3).
769 EqPA 1970, s 2A(2A)(b).
770 [1977] IRLR 71, 74.
771 See above, this paragraph.
772 [1988] IRLR 249.

the demands made on the worker under various headings',[773] and this was not the case here.

Quick suggests that it is expecting too much of schemes to avoid subjective judgments entirely, but that if the scheme is to be valid under section 1(5) these judgments must be placed within the framework of a 'transparent' or objectively justifiable *process* of evaluation. Dillon LJ accepted that 'there are no universally accepted external criteria for measuring how much of a factor or quality is involved in a particular job or for measuring what relative weights ought to be attached to different factors or qualities involved, to differing extents, in various jobs'. Hence, there could be 'subjective elements' but only 'in an objective process', and 'where there are such subjective elements, care has to be taken to see that discrimination is not, inadvertently, let in'.[774]

The third element in the defence, the test of discrimination, involves an examination of the criteria or weightings used in the process of evaluation to see whether they give rise to either direct or indirect discrimination and, if the latter, whether they are justifiable. The Act must be interpreted here by reference to the standards applicable under Article 141 and the Equal Pay Directive.[775]

In *Rummler v Dato-Druck GmbH*[776] the ECJ was called on to consider the position, under the Directive, of a job evaluation process under which high weightings were attached to the factor of muscular effort involved in particular jobs. The Court ruled that under the Directive a job evaluation process has to operate 'objectively' and 'must not be organised, as a whole, in such a manner that it has the practical effect of discriminating generally against workers of one sex'.[777] It held that the use of a criterion, such as muscular effort, which tended to favour men was not ruled out as such but that any discriminatory effect should be measured by reference to the job classification system as a whole, and that in comparing jobs the classification system should take into account 'other criteria in relation to which women workers may have a particular aptitude'.[778] The use of a criterion favouring one sex was also justifiable by reference to 'the nature of the job when such a difference is necessary in order to ensure a level of pay appropriate to the effort required by the work and thus corresponds to a real need on the part of the undertaking'.[779]

Rummler, together with the similar decision of the ECJ in *Danfoss*,[780] which concerned the criteria established by a collective agreement for determining pay increments, lay down a requirement of 'transparency' in pay classification systems, which means in this context that the burden is on the employer under the Act to account for the process used and to rebut suggestions of discriminatory bias: 'it is for the employer to explain how any job evaluation study worked and what was taken into account at each stage',[781] and to show that any subjective adjustments to the placings of jobs in a ranking scheme were not the result of ingrained attitudes of discrimination.

---

773 [1988] IRLR 249, 253–254.
774 [1988] IRLR 249, 253–254.
775 *Bromley v H & J Quick Ltd* [1988] IRLR 249.
776 Case 237/85 [1986] ECR 2101.
777 Case 237/85 [1986] ECR 2101, at para 13.
778 Case 237/85 [1986] ECR 2101, at para 15.
779 Case 237/85 [1986] ECR 2101, at para 24.
780 Case 109/88 *Handels-og Kontorfunktionaerernes Forbund i Danmark v Dansk Arbejdsgiver-forening (acting for Danfoss)* [1989] IRLR 532; Case C-400/93 *Royal Copenhagen* [1995] IRLR 648 (applying the principle to piecework payment systems).
781 *Bromley v H & J Quick Ltd* [1988] IRLR 249, 254 (Dillon LJ).

As we have seen, the tribunal may also reject a study, even if it passes the test of acceptable criteria and weightings, if it is 'otherwise unsuitable'. This change took effect from 1 October 2004.[782] At the time of writing it remains to be seen how this open-ended formula is used in practice, but it clearly extends to some degree the range of grounds on which a study may be set aside in this context.

Establishing equal value: the roles of the tribunal and the independent expert

6.84 If the tribunal does not reject the claim on the basis of the pre-existing job evaluation scheme defence, it must make a number of orders at the stage 1 hearing, the purpose of which is to put in place a procedure for establishing the relevant facts of the case.[783] By these means, the claimant can be required to disclose to the employer the name of the chosen comparator or such information as will enable the comparator to be identified. If it has been supplied with sufficient detail to do so, the employer must respond by providing the claimant with the comparator's name. The parties then have to provide written job descriptions for the claimant and comparator, and identify to each other the facts which they consider relevant to the question of equal value.

The tribunal must also decide at the stage 1 hearing whether to require a report to be prepared by a member of the panel of independent experts which is constituted for this purpose by ACAS.[784] In deciding whether or not to require a report, it may, on the application of a party, take into account representations of both of the parties on the availability to the employer of the defence of genuine material factor.[785] If no independent expert is appointed, the tribunal must set a date for the main hearing according to an indicative timetable set out in the Regulations, at which it must resolve the issue of equal value. If, on the other hand, an independent expert is appointed, the tribunal must first conduct a 'stage 2 equal value hearing' at which it determines the facts on which the expert must, exclusively, base his or her report. The role of determining the relevant facts, in so far as they are not agreed by the parties themselves, rests with the tribunal and not the independent expert,[786] but the tribunal may call on the independent expert to assist it in fact finding under certain specified circumstances.[787] The independent expert may apply for some or all of the facts, as determined by the tribunal, to be amended, supplemented or omitted.[788]

Once appointed, the independent expert has a number of duties, the most important one of which is to prepare a report and send it to the tribunal and the parties.[789] The tribunal has powers to manage proceedings during this process, including the power to order the parties to provide relevant information and documents to the independent expert.[790] The employer may be required to grant access to its premises and to allow the independent expert to carry out interviews with relevant persons.[791]

The tribunal may withdraw the requirement to prepare the report and order the independent expert to provide it with documentation and to accede to any

---

782 SI 2004/2352, inserting EqPA 1970 s 2A(2A)(b).
783 SI 2004/1861, Sch 6, reg 5.
784 EqPA 1970, s 2A(1)(b), 2A(4); SI 2004/1861, Sch 6, reg 4(3)(b).
785 SI 2004/1861, Sch 6, reg 4(5). On the material factor defence, see para 6.86 below.
786 This is the effect of SI 2004/1861, Sch 6, regs 7(3) and 8(1)(b).
787 SI 2004/1861, Sch 6, reg 6.
788 SI 2004/1861, Sch 6, reg 7(6).
789 SI 2004/1861, Sch 6, reg 10(2)(f).
790 SI 2004/1861, Sch 6, reg 3(1)(d).
791 SI 2004/1861, Sch 6, reg 5(1)(c).

other request related to the withdrawal of the requirement.[792] If it does not withdraw the requirement, the tribunal must not determine the issue of equal value without receiving the report[793] and admitting it at the final hearing.[794] The scope for argument at the full hearing is tightly circumscribed: the tribunal may refuse to hear evidence or argument on issues which were not properly disclosed in advance under the rules set out above, unless it was not reasonably practicable for the party concerned to have done so.[795] However, the purpose of the hearing is not simply to rubber-stamp the report. If the tribunal decides that the report is not based on the relevant facts, it may decide the issue of equal value without reference to the report, or commission another one.[796] This last provision could be read as implying that the tribunal must, in all other cases, accept the independent expert's conclusions. However, the Regulations also provide that the parties may, with the tribunal's permission, submit an expert report of their own and/or call such an expert to give evidence at the hearing.[797] In addition, they may challenge the report of the independent expert, or that of a rival expert, by putting questions to them in writing prior to the hearing.[798] Because the independent expert's report can be challenged in this way, case law under pre-2004 Regulations which suggested that it was open to the tribunal, having admitted the report, to disagree with its conclusions, without needing to commission a new one,[799] is probably still valid.

Limits to the equal value principle: no right to proportionate pay

6.85   The Act provides a right to equal treatment only where the work of the complainant and her comparator are 'equal'; it does not provide a right to 'proportionate' pay in a case where, for example, it is shown by job evaluation or by some other means that the complainant's work is worth 95% of the comparator's but she receives only 70%.[800] Nor does it apparently provide a right to equal pay in a case where the work done by the complainant is *more valuable* than the comparator's.[801] In the former situation, Article 141 and the Equal Pay Directive may provide a solution but only if they are clearly seen to extend to the situation of the 'hypothetical' male comparator, in other words to the situation which the complainant would have been in had she been male.[802] The latter situation is clearly covered by Article 141 as a consequence of the ECJ's ruling on a preliminary reference in *Murphy v Bord Telecom Eireann*:[803] 'a contrary interpretation would be tantamount to rendering the principle of equal pay ineffective and negatory'.[804]

792 EqPA 1970, s 2A(1B).
793 EqPA 1970, s 2A(1C).
794 SI 2004/1861, Sch 6, para 9(1).
795 SI 2004/1861, Sch 6, reg 9(3).
796 SI 2004/1861, Sch 6, reg 9(2).
797 SI 2004/1861, Sch 6, reg 11.
798 SI 2004/1861, Sch 6, reg 12.
799 *Tennants Textile Colours Ltd v Todd* [1989] IRLR 3; *Aldridge v British Telecommunications plc* [1990] IRLR 10.
800 As in the US case, *County of Washington v Gunther* 452 US 161 (1981); McCrudden, 1983: p 209.
801 At least, this may be inferred from the like work case of *Waddington v Leicester Council for Voluntary Services* [1977] IRLR 32, where it was concluded in such circumstances that s 1(1)(a) of the Act was not satisfied.
802 See Szyszczak, 1985: p 151.
803 Case 157/86 [1988] IRLR 267.
804 [1988] IRLR 267, 269.

Material factor

6.86 Under section 1(3) of the EqPA 1970, the equality clause has no application in relation to a variation in terms and conditions between the complainant and her comparator where 'the variation is genuinely due to a material factor which is not the difference of sex'. In the case of claims in respect of like work and work rated as equivalent, this factor must also be a 'material difference'.[805] The distinction between a 'material factor' and a 'material difference' seems intended to allow for a wider defence in respect of equal value claims, but whether this is permissible under Article 141 and the Equal Treatment Directive seems doubtful; at any rate, there is no clear authorisation for it in European Union law.

The concept of 'material factor' is a variant on the justification defence in indirect discrimination and the general characteristics of that defence are relevant here.[806] However, there is some doubt as to the circumstances under which the employer has the burden of demonstrating an objective justification for a disparity in pay. The decision of the House of Lords in *Strathclyde Regional Council v Wallace*[807] is authority for the proposition that in a case where the complainant is unable to show that the difference in pay is due to a practice which has an adverse impact on the members of one sex as opposed to the other, there is no need for the difference to be objectively justified; it is sufficient if the employer points to a 'material factor' in a wider sense of that term, that is to say, a factor which explains the difference in pay and which is not tainted by sex discrimination. In *Wallace*[808] the complaint related to the employer's refusal to promote a particular group of teachers; the House of Lords held that this practice had nothing to do with the sex of any particular teacher, and so did not need to be objectively justified. However, a central finding of fact was that of the unpromoted group, most were men.[809] Had a significant majority of the unpromoted group been women, it is difficult to see how the courts could have avoided the conclusion that the burden of proving objective justification lay on the employer, applying the ECJ decisions in *Danfoss* and *Enderby*.[810]

Three broad areas of potentially justifiable factors may be identified in the case law of the domestic courts and of the ECJ: these refer to personal factors; factors arising out of the internal organisation of the enterprise; and factors operating at the level of the labour market.

Personal factors

6.87 The early case law of the domestic courts confined the defence of material factor and/or material difference to factors specific to the individual complainant and her comparator. In *Clay Cross (Quarry Services) Ltd v Fletcher*[811] the Court

---

805 EqPA 1970, s 1(3)(a).
806 See paras 6.29–6.31 above.
807 [1998] 1 WLR 259. See also *Tyldesley v TML Plastics* [1996] IRLR 395; *Glasgow City Council v Marshall* [2000] IRLR 272; *Home Office v Bailey* [2004] IRLR 921, [2005] IRLR 369; see above, para 6.80.
808 [1998] 1 WLR 259.
809 See Lord Browne-Wilkinson's opinion, [1998] 1 WLR 259, 263.
810 Case 109/88 *Handels-og Kontorfunktionaerernes Forbund i Danmark v Dansk Arbejdsgiver-forening (acting for Danfoss)* [1989] IRLR 532; Case C-127/92 *Enderby v Frenchay Health Authority* [1993] IRLR 591. See also, for a restatement of the need for objective justification and for the application of a proportionality test, Case C-381/99 *Brunnhofer v Bank der Österreichischen Postsparkasse AG* [2001] IRLR 571 applied in *Barton v Investec Henderson Crosthwaite Securities Ltd* [2003] IRLR 332.
811 [1978] IRLR 361.

of Appeal held that in applying section 1(3), the tribunal 'is to have regard to...
the personal equation of the woman as compared to that of the man B irrespective
of any extrinsic forces which led to the variation in pay'.[812] The kind of factors
permissible here include the greater seniority of a given individual; his or her
superior qualifications for the job; their greater productivity; or the difference
between permanently-established workers and secondees.[813] Also covered are
cases of so-called 'red circling'. This occurs where it is 'necessary to protect the
wages of an employee, or a group of employees, moved from a better paid type
of work to a worse paid type of work, perhaps because the first is no longer
being undertaken'.[814] In judging whether the red circling is legitimate in a given
case, the tribunal should take into account such factors as whether the differential
treatment was intended to be temporary or permanent; whether the class of
those protected in this way was open or closed; whether it had been the subject
of collective negotiation; whether it originated in an act of sex discrimination;
and whether movement between the grades in question was equally possible for
men and women.[815]

In *Snoxell v Vauxhall Motors Ltd* the employers red circled a group of male
inspectors who, before 1970, had been in a high grade for male inspectors only;
there were two other grades, a lower grade for male inspectors and a grade
exclusively for women inspectors. When the Act was passed all the male and
female grades were merged but those employees who had been in the higher
male grade kept their higher rate of pay. The EAT held that the employer had
failed to make out a section 1(3) defence since 'past sex discrimination has
contributed to the variation'.[816]

An arguably illegitimate extension of the category of 'personal factors' is the
acceptance by some courts of an employer 'error' as the basis for a material
factor defence.[817] Where, for example, an employee is placed in the wrong job
category by mistake and thereafter retains his or her advantage through red
circling, it is arguable that this is not a 'material' factor.[818]

Organisational factors

6.88 In *Rainey v Greater Glasgow Health Board*[819] the House of Lords held
that the scope of the defence of material factor cannot be confined to the 'personal
equation' as suggested in *Clay Cross*;[820] at least in a case where there was no
intention to discriminate, 'a difference which is connected with economic factors
affecting the efficient carrying on of the employer's business or other activity may
well be relevant'.[821] The ECJ referred, in *Bilka-Kaufhaus*, to measures which
'correspond to a real need on the part of the undertaking, are appropriate with a

---

812 [1978] IRLR 361, 363 (Lord Denning MR).
813 On this last point see *Wakeman v Quick Corporation* [1999] IRLR 424, a race
      discrimination claim.
814 *Snoxell v Vauxhall Motors Ltd* [1977] IRLR 123, 125 (Phillips J).
815 [1977] IRLR 123, 126.
816 [1977] IRLR 123, 128 ; see also *United Biscuits Ltd v Young* [1978] IRLR 15; *Outlook
      Supplies Ltd v Parry* [1978] ICR 388.
817 *Yorkshire Blood Transfusion Service v Plaskitt* [1994] ICR 74; cf the decision of the
      NICA in *McPherson v Rathgael Centre for Children and Young People* [1991] IRLR 206.
818 Kilpatrick, 1994: p 325.
819 [1987] IRLR 26.
820 [1978] IRLR 361.
821 [1987] IRLR 26, 29.

view to achieving the objectives pursued and are necessary to that end'.[822] This is a precise test, in which the Court broadly accepted the argument put forward by the European Commission in that case, namely that 'it is not sufficient to show that in adopting a pay practice which discriminates against women workers the employers sought to achieve objectives other than discrimination against women ... It is also necessary to ascertain whether the pay practice in question is necessary and in proportion to the objectives pursued by the employer'.[823]

The Court also held in the *Danfoss*[824] case that once a *prima facie* finding of adverse impact has been made, the burden of proof lies on the employer. Here, the effect of a pay classification system operated by the employer under a collective agreement was that in each grade the pay of women was around 7% lower than that of men. The Court ruled that 'where an undertaking applies a system of pay which is characterised by a total lack of transparency, the burden of proof is on the employer to show that his pay practice is not discriminatory, where a female worker establishes, by comparison with a relatively large number of employees, that the average pay of female workers is lower than that of male workers.'[825]

The issue in many of the cases which have arisen in this area concerns how far institutional rules or practices governing working time arrangements, seniority, labour flexibility and access to benefits can be justified. In *Bilka- Kaufhaus*[826] the Court accepted that the differential treatment of part-time workers (in this case, exclusion from an occupational pension scheme) could in principle be justified by reference to the needs of the business if it was the aim of the employer to *reduce* the numbers of part-timers employed, for example because of high overhead and training costs. However, in *Steinicke*[827] the Court held that, in such a case, it was insufficient for an employer to make generalised observations concerning the need to encourage the recruitment of full-time workers, in the absence of evidence which could enable a court to judge whether the means chosen were proportionate to that aim. Moreover, it was not open to an employer to justify an otherwise discriminatory practice simply on the grounds that it reduced its costs.[828]

Payment systems favouring 'labour flexibility', in the sense of the 'adaptability of the worker to variable work schedules and places of work', which could disadvantage female workers on account of their greater household and family duties, have to be justified by reference to 'the performance of the specific duties entrusted to the worker concerned', as do requirements of vocational training which may also have an adverse impact.[829] Rules incorporating the principle

---

822 Case 170/84 *Bilka-Kaufhaus v Weber von Hartz* [1986] IRLR 317, 320.

823 Case 170/84 *Bilka-Kaufhaus v Weber von Hartz* [1986] IRLR 317, 320; for a more recent reassertion of this principle, see Case C-243/95 *Hill and Stapleton v Revenue Commissioners* [1998] IRLR 466.

824 Case 109/88 [1989] IRLR 532.

825 [1989] IRLR 532, 537.

826 Case 170/84 *Bilka-Kaufhaus v Weber von Hartz* [1986] IRLR 317, 320; see also Case C-33/89 *Kowalska v Freie und Hansestadt Hamburg* [1990] IRLR 447.

827 Case C-77/02 *Steinicke v Bundesanstalt für Arbeit* [2003] IRLR 892.

828 To similar effect, on this last point, are the judgment of the Court of Appeal in *Allonby v Accrington and Rossendale College* [2001] IRLR 364 and the ECJ's judgments in Case C-187/00 *Kütz-Bauer v Freie und Hansestadt Hamburg* [2003] IRLR 368 and Joined Cases C-4/02 and C-5/02 *Schönheit v Staft Frankfurt am Main, Becker v Land Hessen* [2004] IRLR 983.

829 Case 109/88 *Danfoss* [1989] IRLR 532, 536–537.

that benefits accrue with seniority do not, on the other hand, need to be justified by reference to *specific duties* in this way, since 'seniority goes hand in hand with experience which generally places a worker in a better position to carry out his [sic] duties'.[830] However, this does not mean that seniority rules which have an adverse impact do not need to be justified *at all*, as, for example, in a context where only a limited proportion of part-timers' accrued service was recognised for seniority purposes.[831]

Although the extensive case law at both domestic and European Community level concerning the impact of the principle of equal treatment on working-time arrangements has established that it is not, in general, permissible to differentiate between part-time and full-time workers in terms of the basic rate of their wage or salary, a much more contentious area is that of fringe benefits including overtime and premium payments for shifts. In *Stadt Lengerich v Helmig* Advocate General Van Gerven considered that where overtime premia were restricted to employees who worked more than the normal *full-time* working week, 'the additional physical effort and the restriction on the use of free time entailed in working overtime constitute objective reasons to be appraised by the national courts, which may justify a difference in treatment as between part-time and full-time employees'.[832] Similarly, in *Calder v Rowntree Mackintosh Confectionery Ltd*[833] the Court of Appeal refused to upset a finding of an employment tribunal to the effect that a defence of justification was made out where the employer paid shift premia to full-time employees (mainly men) working on rotating daytime and night-time shifts which was not available to part-time employees (mainly women) who worked a regular twilight shift, partly because of the 'inconvenience of rotation, which we understand can cause physical problems, eg disturbance of sleeping patterns [and] is disruptive of family life'.[834] However, in *Krüger v Kreiskrankenhaus Ebersberg*[835] a collective agreement which excluded part-time workers from eligibility from a Christmas bonus simply on the grounds that to do so mirrored a rule in the state social security system was held not be justified.

Labour market factors

6.89   In *Clay Cross*[836] the Court of Appeal held that the defence of material difference did not cover a case where, thanks to external market forces, the employer found it necessary to hire an individual at a higher rate than those already employed. Under these circumstances, the employer came under a duty to raise the pay of the latter group:

---

830   Case 109/88 *Danfoss* [1989] IRLR 532, 536–537.

831   Case C-184/89 *Nimz v Freie und Hansestadt Hamburg* [1991] IRLR 222. In *Cadman v Health and Safety Executive* [2004] IRLR 971 the Court of Appeal made a reference to the ECJ in an attempt to clarify the relationship between the *Danfoss* and *Nimz* judgments.

832   Case C-399/92 [1995] IRLR 216, 219. The Court reached the same conclusion in this case but on a different ground: see para 6.89 below. In Case C-285/02 *Elsner-Lakeberg v Land Nordrhein Westfalen* [2005] IRLR 209 the ECJ ruled that the application to part-time and full-time workers of different rules for calculating overtime work required justification, but did not consider the precise grounds for such justification.

833   [1993] IRLR 212.

834   [1993] IRLR 212, 217.

835   Case C-281/97 [1999] IRLR 808. It is surprising that a similar argument should have succeeded in the context of pension benefits in *Trustees of Uppingham School Retirement Benefits Scheme for Non-Teaching Staff v Shillcock* [2002] IRLR 702.

836   [1978] IRLR 361, 363.

... the Tribunal is not to have regard to any extrinsic forces which have led to the man being paid more. An employer cannot avoid his obligations under the Act by saying: 'I paid him more because he asked for more', or 'I paid her less because she was willing to work for less'. If any such excuse were permitted, the Act would be a dead letter. Those are the very reasons why there was unequal pay before the Statute. They are the very circumstances in which the Statute was intended to operate.

This statement is not necessarily an inaccurate one in the context of the circumstances which the Court had to deal with in *Clay Cross*, despite the later overruling of the Court's decision that comparisons could never extend to 'extrinsic factors'. Although *Rainey v Greater Glasgow Health Board*[837] opened up the possibility of external market forces constituting a defence, the House of Lords did not, in that case, accept that *any* form of this argument would succeed.

In *Rainey* a disparity in pay arose between a group of medical professionals, prosthetists, who were hired to join the NHS from the private sector when a prosthetic service was set up for the first time in Scotland, and their colleagues who were either hired from other regions within the NHS or joined after the service was established. The former group had been paid at a higher rate which matched their private-sector salaries because of the difficulties experienced in recruiting entirely from within the NHS. The House of Lords held that the difference in pay was justified under section 1(3).

Rainey can be explained quite adequately on the basis that the higher paid group were 'red circled'; moreover, there was specific evidence of a labour shortage causing the difficulty in recruitment. Arguably it would not affect the outcome in *Clay Cross*, where the employer was basically doing little more than asserting that because Mrs Fletcher had been prepared to work for less than her male comparator, the difference between their pay was caused by 'market forces' in the sense of supply and demand.

The view that differential pay rates are legitimate *solely* because they are the outcome of an agreement between the parties which may be assumed to have been influenced to some degree by supply and demand, although apparently acceptable to some US courts in the context of the Federal Equal Pay Act 1963 and Civil Rights Act 1964,[838] has not been accepted at any point either by the domestic UK courts or by the ECJ: on the contrary, they have insisted on specific evidence of labour scarcity or geographical factors causing differential pay rates. In the leading case under Article 141, *Enderby v Frenchay Health Authority*,[839] the ECJ held that 'the state of the employment market, which may lead an employer to increase the pay of a particular job in order to attract candidates, may constitute an objectively justified economic ground'; but it was also necessary 'for the national court to determine, if necessary by applying the principle of proportionality, whether and to what extent the shortage of candidates for a job and the need to attract them by higher pay constitutes an objectively justified economic ground for the difference in pay between the jobs in question'.[840] This suggests that the employer must do considerably more than merely assert that a given pay differential is the outcome of 'supply and demand'. In particular, objective evidence must be provided of the basis for retention

837 [1987] IRLR 26.
838 *Christiansen v Iowa* 563 F 2d 706 (1980); *American Nurses Association v State of Illinois* 783 F 2d 716 (1986).
839 Case C-127/92 [1993] IRLR 591; Fredman, 1994a.
840 [1993] IRLR 591, 595.

bonuses and other incentive payments which are offered to individuals on a selective basis.[841] The ECJ in *Enderby* also rejected an argument that the mere existence of separate collective bargaining processes for given grades of workers can amount to justification.[842]

A further decision which limits the 'market forces' defence is *Ratcliffe v North Yorkshire County Council*.[843] Here the Council's direct service organisation cut the pay of a group of employees in order to enable it to place a low bid to carry out work which was being put out to competitive tender under the Local Government Act 1988. The Court of Appeal accepted a view that 'the "material factor" which led to the lower rates of pay ... was the operation of market forces resulting from the statutory requirement in the 1988 Act that [the employer's] tender could not succeed unless it took full account of those forces'.[844] However, the House of Lords took a different view. According to Lord Slynn the employer was not entitled to make cuts in pay simply in order to compete with an external contractor, which was apparently able to set wages at rates below those set by national collective bargaining by employing only women to do the work in question: 'though conscious of the difficult problem facing the employers in seeking to compete with a rival tenderer,' to reduce the women's wages below those of their male comparators was 'the very kind of discrimination in relation to pay which the [1970] Act sought to remove'.[845]

The proportionality test

6.90   To some extent the width of the grounds which may be put forward in defence of pay inequality is balanced by the precision required of respondents by the proportionality test. Under European Union law, this requires both that the aim being pursued by the employer is legitimate in itself and that the means chosen are necessary to achieve it, while also interfering with the principle of equal treatment as little as possible.[846] One important aspect of the ECJ's decision in *Enderby*[847] is that although a discriminatory practice may *to some extent* justify a differential in pay, it may not be capable of explaining all of it: where 'the national court has been able to determine precisely what proportion of the increase in pay is attributable to market forces, it must necessarily accept that the pay differential is objectively justified to the extent of that proportion'.[848] Arguably, the defence of material factor under section 1(3) is not made out where *all* of the variation in pay cannot be justified by the factor in question.[849]

---

841   *Barton v Investec Henderson Crosthwaite Securities Ltd.* [2003] IRLR 332.
842   Case C-127/92 [1993] IRLR 591; see also *Barber v NCR (Manufacturing) Ltd* [1993] IRLR 95; *British Coal Corpn v Smith* [1994] IRLR 342, 362; *British Road Services v Loughran* [1997] IRLR 92. In Case C-243/95 *Hill and Stapleton v Revenue Comrs and Department of Finance* [1998] IRLR 466 the ECJ affirmed that an employer could not justify discrimination arising from a jobsharing scheme solely on the ground that avoidance of such discrimination would involve increased costs.
843   [1994] IRLR 342; revsd [1995] IRLR 439; H Collins, 1994.
844   [1994] IRLR 342, 363.
845   [1995] IRLR 439, 443.
846   See paras 6.29–6.31 above.
847   Case C-127/92 [1993] IRLR 591; Fredman, 1994a.
848   Case C-127/92 [1993] IRLR 591, para 27.
849   See Kilpatrick, 1994, discussing the divergent approaches of the domestic courts on this point in *National Coal Board v Sherwin* [1978] IRLR 122 and *Calder v Rowntree Mackintosh Confectionery Ltd* [1993] IRLR 212.

Implementation of the equality clause

6.91 The effect of the equality clause is that where 'any term of the woman's contract is or becomes less favourable to the woman than a term of a similar kind in the contract under which [her comparator] is employed, that term of the woman's contract shall be treated as so modified as to be not less favourable';[850] and any term benefiting the comparator which is not included in the complainant's contract shall henceforth be included.[851] This process involves identifying the precise source of the inequality of treatment, and remedying it accordingly. Following the decisions of the House of Lords in *Hayward v Cammell Laird Shipbuilders Ltd*[852] and of the ECJ in *Barber v Guardian Royal Exchange Assurance Group*[853] it was established that the correct approach is to take each significant term of the contract separately; the employer is not entitled to argue that inequality with regard to one term is outweighed by an advantage elsewhere in the terms and conditions of the complainant and his or her comparator. It may not be argued, for example, that differences in the basic rate of pay should be offset by differences in working hours or in fringe benefits such as free meals;[854] this, according to the ECJ, is because 'if the national courts were under an obligation to make an assessment and a comparison of all the various types of consideration granted, according to the circumstances to men and women, judicial review would be difficult and the effectiveness of Article [141] diminished as a result'.[855] The employer is not, in any case, prevented from raising any relevant differences between the two cases in the separate context of the material factor defence.[856]

It may nevertheless be the case that at the level of an individual 'element' of the pay package, no inequality is found to exist. This may be a far from straightforward issue, as the judgment of the ECJ in *Stadt Lengerich v Helmig*[857] illustrates. The Court ruled that the employer's failure to pay overtime premia to part-time employees when they exceeded their normal *part-time* working week, on the grounds that premia were only payable to employees working in excess of the normal *full-time* week, did not give rise to unequal treatment:

> There is unequal treatment wherever the overall pay of full-time employees is higher than that of part-time employees for the same number of hours worked on the basis of an employment relationship. In the circumstances considered in these proceedings, part-time employees do receive the same overall pay as full-time employees for the same number of hours worked. A part-time employee whose contractual working hours are 18 receives, if he works 19 hours, the same overall pay as a full-time employee who works 19 hours.[858]

---

850 EqPA 1970, s 1(1)(a)(i), (b)(i) and (c)(i).
851 EqPA 1970, s 1(1)(a)(ii), (b)(ii), (c)(ii). This can involve a very precise identification of the applicant's new position within the employer's pay scale and grading structure: see *Evesham v North Hertfordshire HA and Secretary of State for Health* [2000] IRLR 257.
852 [1988] ICR 464.
853 Case C-262/88 [1990] IRLR 240; but cf. the race discrimination case of *Wakeman v Quick Corporation* [1999] IRLR 425, adopting a more impressionistic approach, and *Redcar and Cleveland Borough Council v Degnan* [2005] IRLR 179, in which the EAT in effect amalgamated, for this purpose, a number of different bonus schemes into a single significant contract term. This approach was upheld by the CA: [2005] EWCA Civ 726.
854 As in *Hayward* [1988] ICR 464.
855 Case C-262–88 *Barber*, at para 34.
856 See above, para 6.86.
857 Case C-399/92 [1995] IRLR 216.
858 [1995] IRLR 216, 223.

It is arguable, however, that the treatment received here was differential, in that part-time employees would have had to work greatly in excess of *their* normal working hours in order to qualify for the premium; while such a difference could, perhaps, have been justified, the burden of doing so should have rested on the employer. This was the view subsequently taken in by the ECJ in *Elsner-Lakeberg v Land Nordrhein Westfalen*.[859]

Limitation periods and claims for arrears

6.92   A claim for equal pay must be brought within six months of the end of the complainant's employment, which is flexibly defined for this purpose, and, if the claim is successful, an award, in addition to its prospective effect, may allow for arrears of pay for a period of up to six years before the relevant legal proceedings were instituted.[860] These rules, which are now to be found, respectively, in sections 2ZA and 2ZB of the 1970 Act, were inserted with effect from July 2003, as a result of amendments made to bring the law into line with a number of rulings of the ECJ and UK courts applying Article 141 EC. The trigger for change was the ECJ's decision in *Barber v Guardian Royal Exchange Assurance Group*[861] to the effect that benefits paid under occupational pension schemes fell under the equal pay principle, coupled with its ruling that Article 141 prohibited indirect discrimination in the terms of access to occupational pension schemes.[862] This seemed to open the way for compensation to be claimed by part-time workers excluded from schemes all the way back to 1976, the point at which the ECJ decided the issue of the direct effect of Article 141 in *Defrenne v Sabena*.[863] Over 60,000 such claims were made before employment tribunals in the mid-1990s. However, in the case of domestic legislation applying the principle of equal treatment to occupational pension schemes which was introduced in 1995 in the aftermath of *Barber*, there was in force at this point a two-year limit on any claim to backdated membership.[864] Employers also resisted claims brought directly under Article 141 on the grounds that section 2(5) of the Equal Pay Act then set a two-year limit on arrears, and section 2(4) required proceedings to be instituted within six months of the end of employment.

In *Magorrian and Cunningham v Eastern Health and Social Services Board*,[865] a claim made under Northern Ireland legislation, the ECJ ruled on a preliminary reference that the two-year limit on arrears was contrary to Article 141, on the

---

859 Case C-285/02 [2005] IRLR 209.
860 EqPA 1970, s 2(5) as originally enacted imposed a two-year limitation period, but in Case C-326/96 *Levez v TH Jennings (Harlow Pools) Ltd* [1999] IRLR 36 the ECJ held that this was contrary to Art 141 of the EC Treaty and to Directive 76/207; when the case returned to the EAT, the six-year limitation period was applied (*Levez v TH Jennings (Harlow Pools) Ltd (No 2)* [1999] IRLR 764). See also *National Power plc v Young* [2001] IRLR 32.
861 Case C-262/88 [1990] IRLR 240.
862 Case C-262/88 [1990] IRLR 240. See Tether, 1995.
863 Case 43/75 [1976] ECR 445.
864 At this point PA 1995, ss 62–65 deemed an occupational pension scheme to contain an 'equal treatment rule' which operated in a manner akin to the equality clause under EqPA 1970, and SI 1995/3183 provided for remedies in relation to sex discrimination in occupational schemes which included the power of a court or tribunal to declare a right of admission to a scheme and to require the employer to provide additional resources to the scheme in connection with the right of access only in respect of a period of two years preceding the institution of the claim.
865 Case C-246/96 [1998] IRLR 86.

grounds that the limitation struck 'at the very essence of the rights conferred by the Community legal order' and was 'such as to render any action by individuals relying on Community law impossible in practice'.[866] In *Preston v Wolverhampton Healthcare NHS Trust*[867] the House of Lords ruled that *Magorrian* had not settled a number of complex issues which arose in the context of the English litigation, and referred several questions to the ECJ for further consideration; the ECJ, however, basically affirmed its earlier rulings in holding that the two-year limitation period in section 2(5) of the EqPA 1970 was contrary to Article 141.

The ECJ also held in the *Preston* case that the six-month time limit for bringing claims in section 2(4) was potentially compatible with Article 141 in so far as it satisfied the principle of equivalence between remedies. However, when the case returned to the House of Lords in *Preston (No 2)*[868] it was held that, where an employee was employed on a series of short-term contracts, it was contrary to the principle of the effectiveness of remedies to require the complainant to lodge a claim within six months of the end of *each* contract, so long as there was evidence of a 'stable employment relationship' spanning different contracts. This, along with related rulings of the ECJ and the House of Lords on time limits, led to further changes to the 1970 Act.

Time limits

6.93 The 2003 amendments[869] introduced a more flexible approach to time limits. Proceedings must be instituted on or before the 'qualifying date',[870] which is defined in section 2ZA. In a so-called 'standard case', the qualifying date is the date falling six months after the last day on which the complainant was employed in the employment.[871] A 'standard case' is any case which is not one of four other cases set out in section 2ZA. The first of these is a 'stable employment case'. This refers to the situation which was the focus of the House of Lords decision in *Preston (No 2)*, and which is here defined as a case where the 'proceedings relate to a period during which a stable employment relationship subsists between the woman and the employer, notwithstanding that the period includes any time after the ending of a contract of employment when no further contract of employment is in force'.[872] The qualifying date is six months after the last day on which the stable employment relationship ended.[873] This is a significant extension to the legislation, whose scope is nevertheless unclear. It would have the effect of enabling a complainant to ignore gaps between contracts, and choose the end of the last

---

866 [1998] IRLR 86, 100; here the Court in effect distinguished its earlier judgments on time limits in Case C-410/92 *Johnson v Chief Adjudication Officer (No 2)* [1995] IRLR 157 and Case C-338/91 *Steenhorst-Neerings v Bestuur van de Bedrijfsvereniging voor Detailhandel, Ambachten en Huisvroouwen* [1994] IRLR 244.

867 [1998] IRLR 197. In addition to the basic issue of the time limits in domestic law which *Magorrian* seemed to have settled (since the limits in *Preston* and *Magorrian* were, in essence, identical), the House of Lords also referred a number of questions concerning the relevance of the timing of the UK's accession to the EC (in 1972, after the passage of EqPA 1970) and the treatment of fixed-term contract employees.

868 *Preston v Wolverhampton Healthcare NHS Trust (No 2)* [2001] IRLR 237.

869 SI 2003/1656.

870 EqPA 1970, s 2(4), as amended.

871 EqPA 1970, s 2ZA(3). It should be noted that a nine-month time limit applies to service personnel in the armed forces (EqPA 1970, s 7AA(3), as inserted by SI 2003/1656) and that there is no special provision in their case for 'stable employment relationships'.

872 EqPA 1970, s 2ZA(2).

873 EqPA 1970, s 2ZA(4).

contract as the point from which time begins to run. It may also be possible to invoke it after that point if some elements of the employment relationship remain. This is therefore a provision which could potentially be applied to cover situations of extra-contractual family or educational leave, although whether this turns out to be the case remains to be seen.

A 'concealment' case is a situation in which the employer deliberately concealed from the complainant a 'qualifying fact' which was relevant to the complaint and without knowledge of which the complainant could not reasonably have been expected to institute proceedings.[874] If the complainant did not discover the qualifying fact until after the last day of her employment or of a 'stable employment relationship' as the case may be, the 'qualifying date' is six months after the day on which she did discover it or could with reasonable diligence have done so.[875] A 'disability case' occurs where the complainant was under a disability at any time during the six months after the end of the employment or stable employment relationship, as the case may be; here the time begins to run six months from the date on which the complainant ceased to be under a disability.[876] If the case is one of both concealment and disability, the qualifying date is whichever of the two relevant dates is later.[877]

Arrears

6.94   Section 2ZB provides that the normal period for which arrears may be awarded, in a 'standard case', is set by reference to an 'arrears date' which is six years before the day on which proceedings were instituted.[878] The arrears date is altered in a 'concealment' or 'disability' case. For this purpose, a 'concealment' case is defined as one in which the complainant instituted the proceedings within six years of the day on which she either discovered or could have with reasonable diligence have discovered a fact relevant to the contravention, and a 'disability case' is one in which she instituted proceedings within six years of the day on which she ceased to be under a disability which affected her at the time of the contravention.[879] Under these circumstances, the arrears date is, simply, the date of the contravention itself.[880] The effect is the same, namely that arrears of up to six years' wages can be claimed, from the relevant date.

Collective agreements

6.95   Prior to 1986 it was possible to obtain a remedy which would lead to the amendment of an entire payment structure, such as a collective agreement or wages order, to comply with the principle of equal treatment in matters of pay; this took the form of unilateral arbitration before the Central Arbitration

---

874   EqPA 1970, s 2ZA(2).
875   EqPA 1970, s 2ZA(5).
876   EqPA 1970, s 2ZA(6).
877   EqPA 1970, s 2ZA(7). For this purpose, a 'disability case' includes one in which the complainant was under a disability at any time during the six months after the day on which she either discovered or could with reasonable diligence have discovered the 'qualifying' fact deliberately concealed from her by the employer: EqPA 1970, s 2ZA(2).
878   EqPA 1970, ss 2(5), as amended, s 2ZB(3). In the case of service personnel in the armed forces, the arrears date is set by reference to the date on which a relevant complaint under the service redress procedures was made: EqPA 1970, s 7AB, inserted by SI 2003/1656. On the service redress procedures, see above, para 3.75.
879   EqPA 1970, s 2ZB(2).
880   EqPA 1970, s 2ZB(4).

Committee.[881] However, the effectiveness of this route for the ending of discrimination based on segregation was restricted by the Court of Appeal's decision in *R v Central Arbitration Committee, ex p Hy-Mac Ltd*,[882] limiting the jurisdiction of the Committee under the Act to situations of *direct discrimination*. This meant that only those provisions of a collective agreement which set differential rates for men and women as such could be challenged using this route.

Rather than extending the jurisdiction of the Central Arbitration Committee to cover indirect discrimination, the Sex Discrimination Act 1986 abolished it completely and replaced it with a provision which extends the effect of section 77 of the SDA 1975 to collective agreements.[883] The effect is to render 'void' any term of a collective agreement which has the effect of providing for the inclusion, within a contract, of a term which would render necessary the application of the equality clause under section 1 of the EqPA 1970. The county court has the power to make an order 'removing or modifying any term made unenforceable' by this provision.[884] This is considerably less helpful than the previous remedy of unilateral arbitration before the Central Arbitration Committee. The latter enabled the Committee to make a positive amendment to the terms of collective agreements which could, if necessary, be inserted into the individual contracts of the employees and others whose contracts were governed by it, thereby ensuring the levelling-up of the disadvantaged group. The new provision merely enables a discriminatory term to be removed from the collective agreement, without specifying a means by which this might lead to the improvement of individual terms and conditions of employment.[885]

The amendment made by the 1986 Act is, strangely, the product of a decision of the ECJ in infringement proceedings brought against the United Kingdom, to the effect that the EqPA 1970 did not comply with Article 4(b) of the Equal Treatment Directive.[886] Since Article 4(b) provides that 'any provisions contrary to the principle of equal treatment which are included in collective agreements ... shall be, or may be declared, null and void *or may be amended*' (emphasis added),[887] it is not at all obvious that the abolition of the Central Arbitration Committee's jurisdiction is compatible with the Directive. Nor would British domestic law appear to have an effective means, in this context, of complying with Article 141, which according to the ECJ has the effect that 'where there is indirect discrimination in a provision of a collective agreement, the members of the group which is disadvantaged because of that discrimination must be treated in the same way and have the same system applied to them as the other workers, in proportion to their hours of work'.[888]

Occupational pensions

6.96 When the ECJ decided, in *Barber v Guardian Royal Exchange Assurance Group*,[889] that benefits under occupational pension schemes fell under Article

---

881 EqPA 1970, s 3, as amended by the EPA 1975.
882 [1979] IRLR 461.
883 SDA 1986, s 6. On SDA 1975, s 77, see para 6.67 above.
884 SDA 1975, s 77(5).
885 The issue of incorporation is particularly important since the collective agreement is most unlikely to be binding between the parties to it, by virtue of TULRCA 1992, s 179.
886 Case 165/82 *EC Commission v United Kingdom* [1984] IRLR 29.
887 Directive 75/117, Art 4 is in substantially the same terms.
888 Case 33/89 *Kowalska v Freie und Hansestadt Hamburg* [1990] IRLR 447, at para 20.
889 Case C-262/88 [1990] IRLR 240.

119 (now 141) of the EC Treaty,[890] the effect was to override a number of derogations contained in the Directive on Equality in Occupational Social Security[891] which would have permitted, among other things, the maintenance of unequal pensionable ages and the use of actuarial factors to set different benefit and contribution rates for male and female employees. For this reason, the Court limited the effect of *Barber* to claims already instituted[892] and, in other cases, to 'acquisition of entitlement to a pension as from the date of this judgment' (17 May 1990). This was because the Member States, in common with many employers, had assumed, by virtue of the Directive on Occupational Social Security, that Article 141 was irrelevant to the question of pensions equality; under these circumstances 'overriding considerations of legal certainty preclude legal situations which have exhausted all their effects in the past from being called in question where that might upset retroactively the financial balance' of schemes constructed on this assumption.[893] The implementation of *Barber* was, in effect, suspended while a number of further references were made to the Court to establish precisely what was meant by its ruling on non-retroactivity.

In *Ten Oever v Stichting Bedrijfspensioenfonds voor het Glazenwassers-en Schoonmaakbedrijf*[894] the Court decided that Article 141 only applied to occupational pension benefits which were payable in respect of periods of service after the date of the *Barber* judgment, thereby fortuitously finding common cause with Protocol No 2 to the Treaty on European Union which provided that '[f]or the purposes of Article [141] of this Treaty benefits under occupational social security schemes shall not be considered as remuneration if and so far as they as they are attributable to periods of employment prior to 17 May 1990'. According to Advocate General Van Gerven, in the case of a defined-benefit pension scheme there is 'a distinction between the coming into being of pension rights, namely as a result of the *accrual* of the pension on the basis of completed periods of service, and those rights becoming exercisable, namely when the pension *falls to be paid for the first time*'.[895] This meant that a male employee in a scheme setting a lower pensionable age for women (say, 60) could become entitled to a part of his pension at that age, the part-pension being referable to his service after 17 May 1990.[896]

The effects of *Barber* were also limited by two further preliminary rulings of the ECJ. First, in *Neath v Hugh Steeper Ltd*[897] the Court held that Article 141

---

890 The following fall within Art 141: survivors' pensions (both widows' and widowers'); and benefits under occupational pension schemes which are 'supplementary' or additional to state retirement pensions (as well as benefits under those which are 'contracted-out', that is, operate in partial substitution for the state pension, as in *Barber* itself). See Case C-109/91 *Ten Oever v Stichting Bedrijfspensioenfonds voor het Glazenwassers-en Schoonmaakbedrijf* [1993] IRLR 601; Case C-110/91 *Moroni v Firma Collo GmbH* [1994] IRLR 130; Case C-152/91 *Neath v Hugh Steeper Ltd* [1994] IRLR 91.
891 Directive 86/378.
892 For an application of this aspect of the *Barber* ruling, see *Howard v Ministry of Defence* [1995] IRLR 570.
893 *Barber*, Case C-262/88, at para 44.
894 Case C-109/91 [1993] IRLR 601; Fitzpatrick, 1994.
895 Case C-109/91 *Ten Oever*, Opinion of Advocate General Van Gerven, at para 17.
896 On the Barber Protocol, see *Quirk v Burton Hospitals NHS Trust* [2001] IRLR 198, [2002] IRLR 353; Joined Cases C-4/02 and C-5/02 *Schönheit v Staft Frankfurt am Main, Becker v Land Hessen* [2004] IRLR 983.
897 Case C-152/91 [1994] IRLR 91.

did not prohibit sex-based inequalities in employers' contributions in defined-benefit or final-salary schemes where these are justified by actuarial factors. Although employees' contributions were 'pay', at least where they were deducted from salary or wages,[898] the Court concluded that Article 141 'does not necessarily have to do with the funding arrangements chosen to secure the periodic payment of the pension, which thus remain outside the scope of application of Article [141]'.[899]

Second, the ECJ ruled in *Smith v Avdel Systems Ltd*[900] that Article 141 'does not preclude measures which achieve equal treatment by reducing the advantages of the persons previously favoured'. The Court drew what was arguably an artificial distinction between the immediate period following a court's ruling that a particular practice contravenes Article 141, during which time there had to be levelling-up, and the period after which the employer (or the Member State, as the case may be) took formal steps to purge the discriminatory practice and establish equality. With regard to the first of these two periods, the Court reasoned that levelling-up was obligatory since at this time, the 'only valid point of reference' was the level of advantage enjoyed 'by the persons in the favoured class'.[901] However, once the discrimination was purged, the Court held, there was nothing in Article 141 to prevent levelling-down from then on. An employer might therefore implement the requirement of equality of pensionable ages in occupational schemes by raising the relevant age for women employees from 60 to 65, rather than by lowering the age for men from 65 to 60.

The outcome was complicated by *Barber*'s non-retroactive effect as interpreted in *Ten Oever*. The result in a case such as *Avdel Systems* was, first, that no rights accruing prior to 17 May 1990 were affected by *Barber*, so that women retained a right to a pension at 60 in respect of service up to that point; second, that men and women alike could claim a pension at the age of 60 in respect of service from 17 May 1990 to the point at which the common pensionable age of 65 was introduced, which in *Advel Systems* itself was 1 July 1991; but, finally, that service from that date would only earn a pension at 65 for men and women alike.

A distinctive feature of the ECJ's decision in *Avdel Systems* is that in most respects, domestic British legislation prevents levelling-down of the kind approved by the Court in this context. Under the EqPA 1970, the equality clause requires levelling-up: the contract of the complainant 'shall be treated as so modified as not to be less favourable' than that of the comparator.[902] Specific provisions now govern the application to occupational pension schemes of the 'equal treatment' rule.[903] Schedule 5 of the Social Security Act 1989, which is based on the Directive on Equality of Treatment in Occupational Social Security, contains a derogation in respect of pensionable ages for women and men.[904]

---

898 Case 69/80 *Worringham v Lloyds Bank Ltd* [1981] ECR 767.
899 Case C-152/91 *Neath*, at para 30.
900 Case C-408/92 [1994] IRLR 602, at para 21; see also Case C-28/93 *Van den Akker v Stichting Shell Pensioenfonds* [1994] IRLR 616, at para 19; Case C-200/91 *Coloroll Pension Trustees Ltd v Russell* [1994] IRLR 586, at para 33; Deakin, 1995a; Tether, 1995.
901 Case C-408/92 *Avdel Systems*, at paras 16–17.
902 EqPA 1970, s 1(2)(a)(i).
903 See PA 1995, ss 62–66.
904 See SSA 1989, Sch 5, para 2(4)(d).

PROTECTION OF PREGNANCY, MATERNITY AND FAMILY TIME

6.97   Legislation protecting employees from dismissal on the grounds of pregnancy and/or maternity and providing a right to maternity leave was first introduced in the EPA 1975, together with a statutory right to receive maternity pay from the employer. In each case there were extensive qualifying requirements and restrictions on the scope of substantive rights. The impetus for the removal of most of these restrictions came initially from Directive 92/85 on measures to encourage improvements in the safety and health of pregnant workers and workers who have recently given birth (the 'Pregnant Workers Directive'). This directive was derived not from the principle of equal treatment as expressed in Article 141 or in the Directives on Equal Pay and Equal Treatment, but instead from Article 118a of the EC Treaty (now contained in Article 137) which is concerned with the promotion of improvements in the working environment. The Employment Relations Act 1999 marked another important turning point. In addition to a further streamlining of maternity protection, this legislation introduced rights to parental leave and to take time off work to look after dependants as part of the 'family friendly' policies being pursued by the Labour Government elected in 1997. The Employment Act 2002 took this process several steps further by enacting rights to statutory paternity pay and leave and adoption pay and leave, as well as a right to request flexible working. We begin our analysis by examining the relationship between pregnancy and the principle of equal treatment before turning to the substance of the various statutory provisions which now operate in this area.

Pregnancy and the principle of equal treatment

6.98   As we have seen in earlier sections of this chapter, the protection of pregnancy and maternity has not consistently been seen as assimilable to the principle of equal treatment. The EqPA 1970, the SDA 1975 and the Equal Treatment Directive all contain derogations designed to ensure that protective provisions in respect of maternity and pregnancy do not constitute sex discrimination against men.[905] A similar debate has been conducted in US discrimination law: courts initially held that employers' practices excluding pregnancy from disability protection schemes did not contravene Title VII of the Civil Rights Act 1964,[906] before the federal Congress passed the Pregnancy Discrimination Act in 1978. This amended Title VII to provide that discrimination on the grounds of sex includes discrimination on the grounds of pregnancy, and specifically states that 'women affected by pregnancy, childbirth, or related medical conditions shall be treated the same for all employment-related purposes, including receipt of benefits under fringe benefit programs, as other persons not so affected but similar in their ability or inability to work.'[907] The Supreme Court has also held that state-level laws providing for minimum maternity leave do not thereby contravene the principle of equal treatment in Title VII.[908]

---

905   EqPA 1970, s 6(1)(b); SDA 1975, s 2(2); Directive 76/207, Art 2(7) (as amended by Directive 2002/73).
906   *Geduldig v Aiello* 417 US 484 (1974); *General Electric Co v Gilbert* 429 US 125 (1976).
907   Civil Rights Act 1964, Title VII, s 701(k); 42 USC s 2000e-2(k).
908   *California Savings & Loan Association v Guerra* 479 US 272 (1987); see Deakin, 1990a: p 11.

Thanks to these various qualifications, the equal treatment principle does not *prohibit* legislation protecting pregnancy and maternity. Turning the question round the other way, does the equal treatment principle *require* a certain degree of protection for pregnant workers? The decisions of the ECJ in *Dekker v VJV-Centrum*[909] and *Webb v EMO Air Cargo Ltd*[910] establish that, in principle, the adverse treatment of an employee on pregnancy-related grounds amounts to *direct* sex discrimination contrary to the Equal Treatment Directive, and cannot be justified. As we saw in our earlier discussion of the concept of sex discrimination,[911] there is some doubt as to how far the principle first enunciated in *Dekker* extends: as a consequence of the Court's ruling in *Hertz*,[912] it appears not to cover, for example, a case of dismissal on the grounds of a pregnancy-related illness after the period of maternity leave comes to an end, although it is hard to see why this should be so since the employee in such a case could argue that the substantial cause of her dismissal was her pregnancy. In *Brown v Rentokil Ltd*[913] the ECJ affirmed that dismissal on the grounds of a pregnancy-related illness during pregnancy, as well as during maternity leave, constituted direct sex discrimination.[914]

The ECJ's judgment in *Brown* is consistent with its earlier decision in *Habermann-Beltermann*[915] where the Court held that it was a breach of the Directive for an employer to dismiss a pregnant worker who was employed as a night attendant in a residential home, solely on the grounds of a statutory prohibition upon employees working at night while pregnant. The Court concluded that 'the termination of a contract without a fixed term on account of the woman's pregnancy, whether by annulment or avoidance, cannot be justified on the ground that a statutory prohibition, imposed because of pregnancy, temporarily prevents the employee from performing night-time work'.[916] An important aspect of this decision was the use made of the pregnancy derogation in Article 2(3) of the Directive, which provides that the Directive 'shall be without prejudice to provisions concerning the protection of women, particularly as regards pregnancy and maternity'. According to the Court, this provision 'recognises the legitimacy, in terms of the principle of equal treatment, of protecting, first, a woman's biological condition during and after pregnancy, and secondly, the special relationship between a woman and her child over the period which follows pregnancy and childbirth'. In other words, Article 2(3) is not a denial of the principle of equal treatment but marks an extension of it to take into account the *particular* position of women with regard to pregnancy and maternity and the potential discrimination which may result from that, in particular 'the disadvantages which women, by comparison with men, suffer with regard to the retention of employment'.[917]

---

909 Case C-177/88 [1991] IRLR 27; see also Case C-207/98 *Mahlburg v Land Mecklenburg-Vorpommern* [2000] IRLR 277.
910 Case C-32/93 [1994] IRLR 482.
911 See para 6.19 above.
912 Case C-179/88 *Hertz v Aldi Marked K/S* [1991] IRLR 31.
913 Case C-394/96 [1998] IRLR 445; *Abbey National plc v Formoso* [1999] IRLR 222. See Wynn, 1999.
914 In so deciding, the ECJ did not follow its earlier decision in Case C-400/95 *Handels-OG Kontorfunktionaerernesforbund, acting on behalf of Larsson v Dansk Handel & Service, acting on behalf of Føxted Supermarked A/S* [1997] IRLR 643.
915 Case C-421/92 *Habermann-Beltermann v Arbeiterwohlfahrt, Bezirksverband Ndb/pf eV* [1994] IRLR 364.
916 [1994] IRLR 364, 367.
917 [1994] IRLR 364, 367.

The position under the SDA 1975 was determined by the House of Lords when it reconsidered *Webb* in the light of the ECJ's ruling in that case. In *Webb (No 2)*[918] their Lordships ruled that in a case where a female employee is employed under a contract for an indeterminate period, her dismissal for a pregnancy-related reason is for a reason relating to her sex. However, the same reasoning would not necessarily apply to a case where the employment was for a limited term which would have expired by the time the employee was ready to return to work after her period of maternity leave.[919] The basis for Lord Keith's opinion is obscure. He seems to have regarded himself as bound to accept the ruling of the ECJ in *Webb*, and conclude that, at least in the case of an open-ended contract of employment, dismissal for pregnancy amounts to *direct* sex discrimination. In *Jiménez-Melgar v Ayuntamiento de los Barrios* the ECJ took a similar view, holding that the non-renewal of a pregnant worker's fixed-term contract (which the Court treated as a refusal of employment) on the grounds of her pregnancy was directly discriminatory under the Equal Treatment Directive.[920]

A solution which is arguably more consistent with a proper construction of the 1975 Act is that the adverse treatment of a worker on pregnancy-related grounds is potentially a form of *indirect* sex discrimination which may therefore be justified by business necessity or some similar criterion.[921] The reasoning here is that the dismissal, for example, of a pregnant worker, amounts to the imposition of a 'provision, criterion or practice' within the meaning of section 1(2)(a) of the Act of 1975 – in this case, a practice to the effect that the worker should be continuously available for employment – with which women, as a group, are proportionately less able to comply than men. If a man affected by illness, and therefore obliged to spend time away from work, would have been treated differently to a pregnant woman, a prima facie case of adverse impact is made out. If a sick man would have been treated in the *same* way, there is no adverse impact. Even if adverse impact is found, the employer may seek to argue justification on the basis of the impracticability or cost of continuing to employ an employee during and after her pregnancy and confinement. This was the analysis adopted by the House of Lords in *Webb (No 1)*,[922] and although the ECJ took a different view, it could be argued that the relevant provisions of the SDA 1975 are not sufficiently ambiguous to allow for the application of the principle of the 'indirect effect' of directives in this case.[923]

More recent decisions of the ECJ have focused on the provision of maternity pay and related benefits both before and during the period of maternity leave, and on the relationship between the equal treatment principle and the Pregnant

---

918 [1995] IRLR 645. This decision has since been applied in *British Telecommunications v Roberts* [1996] IRLR 601 and in *Iske v P & O European Ferries (Dover) Ltd* [1997] IRLR 401 (on which, see the Suspension from Work on Maternity Grounds (Merchant Shipping and Fishing Vessels) Order 1998, SI 1998/587).

919 In *Caruana v Manchester Airport plc* [1996] IRLR 378 the EAT held that any possible special rule for fixed-term contracts was limited to cases where the employee would not be available for any part of the term.

920 Case C-438/99, [2001] IRLR 848.

921 See generally Wintemute, 1998; cf the discussion of Honeyball, 2000.

922 [1993] IRLR 27. See also *Turley v Allders Stores Ltd* [1980] ICR 66; *Hayes v Malleable Working Men's Club and Institute* [1985] IRLR 367; Lacey, 1986; S Bailey, 1989; Hare, 1992.

923 See the post-*Webb (No 1)* decisions in *Dixon v Rees* [1993] IRLR 468 and *Brown v Rentokil Ltd* [1995] IRLR 211.

Workers Directive. The Court has sought to draw a line between the adverse treatment of pregnant workers prior to and following maternity leave – which can in principle amount to sex discrimination – and the position during maternity leave itself, which, in some respects, is now beyond the reach of the equal treatment principle. The basis for this distinction is the insistence of the Court that it is inappropriate to compare the position of a pregnant worker with that of a male employee who is absent from work on the grounds of sickness.[924] More prosaically, the Court appears to take the view that the Pregnant Workers Directive, rather than the Equal Treatment and Equal Pay Directives, should be the focus for rights to maternity leave and maternity pay. Arguably, though, the approach of the Court has been inconsistent, since in relation to rights *outside* the leave period (and indeed, as we shall see below, in relation to certain rights within it), the Pregnant Workers Directive has been read in a way which incorporates and builds on the equal treatment principle.[925] The Court's jurisprudence has also been criticised for its assumption of 'a stereotyped idea of motherhood', according to which care of newly-born children is undertaken mainly by the mother rather than being shared by both parents.[926]

Dismissal on the grounds of pregnancy and maternity

6.99 Under ERA 1996, section 99, it is automatically unfair to dismiss an employee for taking 'leave for family reasons' which includes a reason relating to pregnancy, childbirth or maternity, or to 'ordinary, compulsory or additional maternity leave'.[927] For this purpose, 'ordinary' leave refers to the basic statutory right to leave of 26 weeks; 'compulsory leave' is the period of two weeks' absence following childbirth which is mandated by law; and additional leave is the extra period following ordinary leave which employees with 26 weeks of continuous employment may qualify for.[928] As Bailey has explained, 'the protection afforded by the Sex Discrimination Act is based on women receiving the same protection as male employees, while [ERA 1996, section 99] embodies the idea of pregnant women being treated as privileged employees because of their pregnancies and accorded special rights'.[929] Nevertheless, when the forerunner of section 99 was introduced in the EPA 1975, the rights it contained were so hedged about with restrictions as to put its effectiveness in doubt. The

---

924 See, in particular, Case C-411/96 *Boyle v Equal Opportunities Commission* [1998] IRLR 717; Case C-66/96 *Handels-og Kontorfunktionærernes Forbund i Danmark (acting for Høj Pedersen) v Fællesforeningen For Danmarks Brugsforeninger* [1999] IRLR 55; Case C-218/98 *Abdoulaye v Régie Nationale des Usines Renault* [1999] IRLR 811; Case C-147/02 *Alabaster v Woolwich plc and Secretary of State for Social Security* [2004] IRLR 486.

925 See, in addition to the cases cited above, Case C-320/01 *Busch v Klinikum Neustadt GmbH & Co Betriebs-KG* [2003] IRLR 625 (refusal to allow a worker to return to work before the end of her parental leave, on the grounds of her pregnancy, was contrary to the Equal Treatment Directive and the Pregnant Workers' Directive), and Case C-342/02 *Merino Gómez v Continental Industries del Caucho SA* [2004] IRLR 407 (a pregnant worker had the right to take her annual leave entitlement in addition to her maternity leave). The UK courts have also taken the view that the SDA 1975 should be read in the light of the Pregnant Workers Directive: see *Hardman v Mallon* [2002] IRLR 516 (failure to provide a health and safety risk assessment to a pregnant worker was sex discrimination).

926 See generally Caraciollo di Torella, 1999.

927 ERA 1996, s 99(1), (2). Other aspects of 'family leave' under s 99 are considered in para 6.104 *et seq* below.

928 See generally para 6.100 below.

929 S Bailey, 1989: p 86.

provision which, following consolidation, is now ERA 1996, section 99, was first introduced by TURERA 1993 in order to comply with the requirements of the Pregnant Workers Directive, and was amended further by the Employment Relations Act 1999. The substance of this legislation is no longer to be found in the body of the Act itself, but instead in the Maternity and Parental Leave etc. Regulations 1999 (MPLR), as amended.[930] No qualifying period of service is now required. The complainant can complain of dismissal on the grounds of maternity in a number of cases. These include situations in which dismissal occurs by reason of the 'pregnancy of the employee';[931] where the employee gives birth, with dismissal ending the period of ordinary or additional maternity leave; where the employee is dismissed because she is suspended from work on maternity grounds for reasons relating to health and safety;[932] and where the employee takes or seeks to take ordinary or additional maternity leave.[933] It is also automatically unfair to select an employee for redundancy on one of the above grounds (where others in the same position were not dismissed),[934] and unlawful for the employer to subject the employee to a detriment for one of these reasons.[935]

These provisions fall to be interpreted in the light of the Pregnant Workers Directive. Article 10 states that Member States must take steps to 'prohibit the dismissal of workers ... during the period from the beginning of their pregnancy to the end of the maternity leave [period] save in exceptional cases not connected with their condition which are permitted under national legislation and/or practice.'[936] In *Caledonia Bureau Investment & Property Ltd v Caffrey*[937] the EAT held that the forerunner of the general right not to be dismissed on the grounds of pregnancy extended to a situation in which the employee was dismissed after her period of maternity leave had come to an end; dismissal for a pregnancy-related illness, in this case post-natal depression, was for a reason connected with pregnancy. The Appeal Tribunal also held that the dismissal amounted to unlawful sex discrimination.

The right to claim automatically unfair dismissal is qualified in two sets of circumstances. The first situation occurs where it is not reasonably practicable either for the employer to permit the employee to return to a job which is suitable and appropriate for her or for an associated employer to offer her a job of that kind, and the employer and any associated employer between them employ five or fewer employees.[938] The second situation occurs where, again, it

---

930   SI 1999/3312, as amended by SI 2002/2789.
931   On the meaning of this phrase, see *Brown v Stockton-on-Tees Borough Council* [1989] AC 20.
932   On suspension from work on maternity grounds, see para 6.101 below.
933   MPLR 1999, reg 20(3).
934   MPLR 1999, reg 20(2)(3).
935   MPLR 1999, reg 19; ERA 1996, ss 47C, 48–49 (providing for a right to bring a complaint to an employment tribunal).
936   Directive 92/85, Art 10(1). Where dismissal takes place within the scope of the exception allowed by Art 10(1), Art 10(2) requires the employer to cite 'duly substantiated grounds' for this. Art 10 is sufficiently clear, precise and unconditional to have direct effect in national law: Case C-438/99 *Jiménez Melgar v Ayuntamiento de los Barrios* [2001] IRLR 848, and applies in a case where the worker was employed on a fixed-term contract and did not tell her employer prior to the hiring that she pregnant, even though she was aware of this: Case C-109/00 *Tele Danmark A/S v Handels-Og Kontorfunktionaererernes Forbund I Danmark (HK), acting on behalf of Brandt-Nielsen* [2001] IRLR 853.
937   [1998] IRLR 110.
938   MPLR 1999, reg 20(6).

is not reasonably practicable for the employer to allow the employee to return to work for a reason other than redundancy; an associated employer makes an offer of alternative employment which is appropriate and suitable; and the employee either unreasonably refuses or accepts that offer.[939]

Maternity leave

6.100 The right not to be dismissed for pregnancy-related reasons would be of limited use in itself were no provision also made for a minimum period of maternity leave and for the maintenance of employment-related rights and benefits during that period. Accordingly the Pregnant Workers Directive provides for a continuous minimum period of maternity leave of 14 weeks.[940] ERA 1996 and MPLR 1999 now provide for a period of 26 weeks' leave (increased from 18 weeks in 2003), known as 'ordinary maternity leave'. There is no minimum qualifying period of service. The leave begins on the date indicated by the employee, which may not be earlier than the eleventh week before the expected week of childbirth,[941] or, alternatively, the first day after the beginning of the fourth week before the expected week of childbirth on which she is absent from work wholly or partly because of pregnancy, whichever of these two dates is the earlier.[942] The latest day on which the leave can begin is the day following that on which the birth occurs.[943] During this period of leave, the employee is entitled to all the normal terms and conditions of her employment and benefits which would have applied if she had not been absent, with the exception of any right to remuneration.[944] In the absence of a contractual right to pay, minimum income maintenance during pregnancy takes the form, as we shall see,[945] of the right to statutory maternity pay. However, the latter is unavailable to employees with less than 26 weeks' continuous employment; there is therefore a category of employees with minimal service who have the right to ordinary maternity leave, but not the right to income maintenance to go with it.

The right to ordinary maternity leave is conditional upon the employee meeting certain notification requirements which are laid down in the Act. She must inform the employer (in writing if the employer so requests) that she is pregnant no later than the end of the fifteenth week before her expected week of childbirth or, if that is not reasonably practicable, as soon as it is reasonably practicable. She must at the same time indicate to the employer the expected week of childbirth and the date on which she intends her ordinary maternity leave to start. She must also, if requested by the employer to do so, provide it with a certificate from a registered doctor or midwife stating the expected week of childbirth.[946] She may vary the commencement of the maternity leave by

---

939 MPLR 1999, reg 20(7).
940 Directive 92/85, Art 8.
941 This is the effect of the written notification requirement contained in MPLR 1999, reg 4(2).
942 MPLR 1999, reg 6(1).
943 MPLR 1999, reg 6(2).
944 ERA 1996, s 71(4)–(5). In addition, SSA 1989, Sch 5, provides that seniority for the purposes of employment benefits (such as occupational pension benefits) should continue to accrue as normal during periods of maternity and family leave. This part of the Schedule was brought into force by SI 1994/1661.
945 See below, para 6.103.
946 MPLR 1999, reg 4(1).

doing so at least 28 days before either the varied date or the new date.[947] If she wishes to return to work before the end of the maternity leave period she must give 28 days' notice of her intention to do so: otherwise the employer is entitled to postpone her return to work for such time until the 28 days' notice is given (although not beyond the end of the maternity leave period), and is under no obligation to pay her during the period she is away from work for this reason.[948]

At the end of the leave period, the employee has the right to return to work to the job in which she was employed before her absence; this means that her seniority, pension rights and similar rights must be the same as they would have been if she had not been absent, and that the terms and conditions on which she returns must be not less favourable.[949] If, however, during the leave period it becomes no longer practicable to continue to employ the employee by reason of redundancy, she is entitled to be offered suitable alternative employment.[950] If an employee has a contractual right to leave in addition to the statutory right, she may not accumulate the two rights, but she may exercise a 'composite' right which means that she can rely on whichever of the two rights is more favourable in relation to a particular aspect of her leave entitlements.[951]

In addition to providing this basic and universal right to leave, legislation provides for 'compulsory' maternity leave of two weeks commencing on the day of childbirth. The employer must not permit the employee to work during this period, subject to the possibility of criminal conviction and a fine not exceeding level 2 on the standard scale.[952]

Legislation also provides for the right to take 'additional maternity leave'.[953] The equivalent of this right originated in the Employment Protection Act 1975; the relevant provisions have since been much amended, in particular by the Trade Union Reform and Employment Rights Act 1993, the Employment Relations Act 1999, and the Employment Act 2002, along with relevant regulations. The principle of a full year's leave, taking the 'ordinary' and 'additional' periods together, only came in by virtue of the 2002 changes. Twenty-six weeks of qualifying service are required at the beginning of the fourteenth week before the expected week of childbirth.[954] The employee has the right to leave of 26 weeks beginning from the day after her ordinary maternity leave comes to an end.[955] Broadly similar notification requirements and conditions attaching to the right to return to work apply as in respect of ordinary maternity leave.[956]

---

947 MPLR 1999, reg 4(1A).
948 MPLR 1999, reg 11.
949 ERA 1996, S 71(4)(c), (7). The preservation of seniority follows the principles laid down in SSA 1989, Sch 5, but also subject to exceptions contained in that provision (see ERA 1999, s 71(7)(a)).
950 ERA 1996, s 74; MPLR 1999, reg 10.
951 MPLR 1999, reg 21.
952 See ERA 1996, s 72 and MPLR 1999, reg 8.
953 ERA 1999, s 73.
954 MPLR 1999, reg 5.
955 MPLR 1999, regs 6, 7.
956 MPLR 1999, regs 17 and 18A. There are some differences in approach in respect of additional maternity leave such as the statutory requirement that both sides observe the implied contract term of trust and confidence during the period of leave (reg 17), specific notification requirements concerning return to work after additional maternity leave (reg 12) and greater flexibility for the employer in substituting for the employee's original job a different one which is suitable and appropriate for her (reg 18(2)).

Until December 1999, legislation provided that an employer who did not allow the employee to return to work after she had exercised her right to do so in the manner prescribed by the Act was to be treated as having dismissed her.[957] This provision was extremely complex, and, arguably, was not even necessary, on the ground that the contract continued in force during the period of the employee's absence; if the employer refused to take the employee back, it would be committing a repudiatory breach of contract which would amount to a constructive dismissal. It is now stated that an employee who exercises her right to ordinary and/or additional maternity leave is, during the period of leave, 'entitled to the benefit of the terms and conditions of employment which would have applied if she had not been absent', and, in turn, 'is bound by any obligations arising under those terms and conditions' except in so far as they might qualify the statutory right to leave itself.[958] One possible reading of this is that the contract of employment remains in force for a number of purposes during the period of leave; this can also be inferred from Articles 8 (concerning leave) and 10 (concerning dismissal) of the Pregnant Workers Directive. What happens if the employee does not exercise the right to leave in the normal way, or does not notify her employer of her wish to return to work within the terms of the Act, is less clear. Under the now-repealed legislation, the courts failed to reach a consensus on this question, but there seems no reason in principle why it should not be open to them to find that an employer who excludes an employee from employment when she wishes to return thereby dismisses her, even if the precise statutory requirements for notification were not complied with.[959]

Suspension from work on grounds of maternity

6.101   As a result of a further amendment made in 1993, where the employee is suspended from work on maternity grounds by virtue of a statutory prohibition or of a recommendation contained in a code of practice issued under the HSWA 1974, she is entitled to be offered any available suitable alternative work or, failing that, to be paid during her period of suspension. If she is suspended without an offer of suitable alternative work when that was available, she has the right to complain to an employment tribunal which may make an award of compensation.[960] No qualifying period applies here.

Right to paid time off for ante-natal care

6.102   The employee has the right to paid time off during working hours in order to keep an appointment for the purpose of receiving ante-natal care. There is no qualifying period, and the remedy is by way of a complaint to an employment tribunal.[961]

---

957 ERA 1996, s 96, now repealed. See *Halfpenny v IGE Medical Services Ltd* [2001] IRLR 96 for a decision under the old law which amply illustrates its byzantine complexity.

958 ERA 1996, ss 71(4), 73(4).

959 See *Lewis Woolf Griptight Ltd v Corfield* [1997] IRLR 432; *Caledonia Bureau Investment & Property v Caffrey* [1998] IRLR 110. In *Curr v Marks and Spencer plc* [2003] IRLR 74 the Court of Appeal held that the contract of employment was not in force during a period of extended childcare leave (which is not the same as a period of statutory maternity leave).

960 ERA 1996, ss 66–70.

961 ERA 1996, ss 55–57.

Statutory maternity pay

6.103   Although the statutory right to maternity pay was introduced in the EPA 1975, the present form of SMP derives essentially from the SSA 1986, which modelled the right on the form taken by statutory sick pay: the employer is primarily responsible for making the relevant payments, but recovers the cost of doing so by way of a rebate on national insurance contributions, the extent of which varies according to the size of the employer.[962]

The 1992 Directive requires the 'maintenance of a payment to, and/or entitlement to an adequate allowance' for the pregnant worker during the period of maternity leave;[963] it also stipulates that this payment must be 'at least equivalent to that which the worker concerned would receive in the event of a break in her activities on grounds connected with her state of health, subject to any ceiling laid down under national legislation'.[964] In response to the Directive, the Department of Social Security proposed aligning the level of SMP with the standard rate for SSP, and at one stage also considered abolishing entirely the qualifying period for SMP,[965] a move which would have integrated income maintenance under this head with the introduction of the right to 14 weeks' maternity leave at this time. However, in the event the amending legislation for SMP retained a 26-week qualifying period, and it was only from December 1999 that the basic period of 'ordinary maternity leave' was harmonised with the then 18 weeks of SMP entitlement. By virtue of changes made by the Employment Act 2002, this period was extended to 26 weeks for both pay and leave purposes.

SMP is available to an employee who has been continuously employed in employed earner's employment[966] for 26 weeks up to the fifteenth week before the expected week of confinement, and whose average weekly earnings in the eight weeks up to the qualifying week are at least equal to the lower earnings limit for national insurance contributions.[967] Self-employed workers, and others unable to meet this qualifying condition, may nevertheless qualify for the state maternity allowance on the basis of having paid Class 1 or Class 2 national insurance contributions in any 26 weeks in the 66 weeks ending with the qualifying week.[968] In order to receive SMP, the employee must still be pregnant at the eleventh week before the expected week of confinement or have been confined by that time.[969] She must also have ceased to work. A set of notification requirements must again be complied with. The employee must give the employer at least 28 days' notice of her intended absence for reasons of pregnancy or confinement, unless it is not reasonably practicable to do so; if the employer insists, this notice must be in writing.[970]

---

962 See SSCBA 1992, s 167.
963 Directive 92/85, Art 11(1).
964 Directive 92/85, Art 11(3).
965 Department of Social Security, *Changes in Maternity Pay: Proposals for Implementing the EC Pregnant Workers Directive* (1993).
966 This expression, used in social security law, effectively reproduces the requirement that an individual be employed as an employee. See ch 3, above, at para 3.22.
967 SSCBA 1992, s 164(2)(a), (b). A claim by a part-time worker that her exclusion from statutory maternity pay on the grounds that she earned less than the lower earning limit contravened Art 119 (now 141) failed in *Banks v Tesco Stores and (2) Secretary of State for Employment* (3 June 1997, unreported), case no 18985/95/C.
968 See SSCBA 1992, s 35.
969 SSCBA 1992, s 164(2)(c).
970 SSCBA 1992, s 164(4), (5); SI 1986/1960, reg 23.

SMP is payable at 90% of the employee's normal average weekly earnings for a period of six weeks (the 'earnings-related rate') and at a rate set by statute for a further twenty weeks.[971] The payment period will normally begin in the week when the employee has either ceased to work in conformity with the notice given by her to the employer, which may not be earlier than the start of the eleventh week before the expected week of confinement, or is confined.[972]

The principal statutory remedy for a failure to pay SMP is an application to an officer of the Board of Inland Revenue, from whom an appeal may lie to the tax comissioners.[973] If, once the employer's liability is established, it fails to comply with the ruling, it commits an offence.[974] Alternatively, an employee may argue that a failure to pay statutory maternity pay amounts to an unlawful deduction from wages due under Part II of ERA 1996.[975]

Laws and practices relating to maternity pay and leave have been analysed by the ECJ in a series of recent cases. In *Gillespie v Northern Health and Social Services Board*[976] the Court held that although statutory maternity pay fell within the definition of 'pay' in Article 119 (now 141) of the EC Treaty, it was not a breach of Article 141 for the amount of SMP to be set at a level below the earnings which an individual was receiving while she was in employment, since this did not give rise to a case of unequal treatment on the grounds of sex. In further litigation, the Northern Ireland Court of Appeal held that statutory maternity pay which was set at a higher level than statutory sick pay under the relevant legislation could not, for this reason, be categorised as 'inadequate' under Article 11(3) of the Pregnant Workers Directive.[977]

The principle in *Gillespie* has since been interpreted as turning on a distinction between the period of maternity leave, on the one hand, and the period of employment prior to and after the leave, on the other. During the leave period, according to the Court, it is illegitimate to compare the position of a pregnant woman with either that of a sick man or with that of a woman in regular employment. In effect, the equal treatment principle is suspended while the leave period is in effect, and the Pregnant Workers Directive is the sole source of protection. This principle has been interpreted as meaning that it is not unlawful for an employer to operate a rule requiring pregnant employees who do not return to work after their leave has ended to repay the difference between their contractual maternity pay and their basic SMP entitlement, even though such a rule would not be applied to employees who were in receipt of sick pay or some other contractual payment while absent from work.[978] Nor, for the same reason, is it a breach of the equal treatment principle for an employer to pay a maternity bonus to women on maternity leave, thereby engaging in what might otherwise

971 SSCBA 1992, s 166; SI 1986/1960, regs 20–21. The rate was set at £106 from April 2005.
972 SSCBA 1992, s 165; SI 1986/1960, regs 2 and 8–9 as amended.
973 See the Social Security Contributions (Transfer of Functions) Act 1999.
974 SI 1986/1960, regs 29, 32. Note that by virtue of SI 1986/1960, regs 7 and 30, as amended by the Social Security Contributions (Transfer of Functions etc) Act 1999, when an employer is in default, a claim may be made by the employee against the Inland Revenue.
975 This is the combined effect of ERA 1996, ss 13(3), 23 and 27(1)(c); see *Alabaster v Woolwich plc* [2000] IRLR 754.
976 Case C-342/93 [1996] IRLR 214.
977 *Gillespie v Northern Health and Social Services Board (No 2)* [1997] IRLR 410. The same principle was applied in *Edwards v Derby City Council* [1999] ICR 115 and *British Airways (European Operations at Gatwick) v Moore and Botterill* [2000] IRLR 296, although cf *P & O European Ferries (Dover) Ltd v Iverson* [1999] ICR 1088.
978 Case C-411/96 *Boyle v Equal Opportunities Commission* [1998] IRLR 717.

have been a form of positive discrimination in favour of women.[979] By contrast, it is unlawful for an employer to make a deduction from the pay of a pregnant worker who is absent from work on the grounds of illness *before* the start of her maternity leave, if the same deduction would not be made from the pay of a sick man;[980] and it is unlawful to deny to a worker a performance appraisal which could result in her later promotion simply because, at the relevant time, she was absent from work, since this affects her employment after the leave period comes to an end.[981] It is far from obvious that the distinction drawn by the Court in this context between the leave period and other periods is justifiable, in particular given the assumption contained in the Pregnant Workers Directive[982] (and, as we have seen, now translated into UK law) that the employment relationship continues during maternity leave.[983]

Parental leave

6.104   Parents have the right to take unpaid parental leave for the purposes of caring for a child under legislation introduced as part of the Employment Relations Act 1999. The legislation implements a Directive which, in its turn, refers to a Framework Agreement made by the social partners under the process of European social dialogue.[984] The implementing legislation is distinctive, in the British context, in leaving much of the application of the law to workplace- or enterprise-level agreements between employers and employees (or their representatives), subject only to a 'default' or 'fallback' scheme if the parties fail to agree.

The statutory framework is provided by ERA 1996, sections 76-80, and the details of the right are contained in MPLR 1999.[985] The Regulations provide for an employee with continuous employment of not less than one year to take

979 Case C-218/98 *Abdoulaye v Régie Nationale des Usines Renault* [1999] IRLR 811.
980 Case C-66/96 *Handesl-Og Kontorfunktionærernes Forbund i Danmark, acting on behalf of Hoj Pedersen v Fællesforeningen for Danmarks Brugsforeninger, acting on behalf of Kvickly Skive* [1999] IRLR 55.
981 Case C-136/95 *Thibault v Caisse Nationale D'Assuarance Vieillesse des Travailleurs Salariés* [1999] ICR 160; applied in *Gus Home Shopping Ltd v Green* [2001] IRLR 74. In *Halfpenny v IGE Medical Systems Ltd* [2001] IRLR 96 the HL rejected a claim of sex discrimination on the grounds that the applicant, when attempting to return to work following maternity leave, was not at that point in employment within the meaning of SDA 1975. This decision, which was questionable as a matter of contractual construction, also looks highly suspect in the light of *Thibault*.
982 In particular, Arts 8 (maternity leave) and 10 (dismissal).
983 See *Gus Home Shopping Ltd v Green* [2001] IRLR 74; cf the decision of the Court in Case C-333/97 *Lewen v Denda* [2000] IRLR 67, applying Art 119 (now 141) to a situation in which a pregnant worker absent from work during *parental* leave (as opposed to maternity leave) was denied a pay-related benefit (a Christmas bonus) in a discriminatory fashion. It is far from clear on what basis the equal treatment principle should be applicable to a period of parental leave but not to a period of maternity leave. For discussion of the inconsistencies of the ECJ's approach in these cases, see P Lewis, 2000. Even more confusingly, in Case C-147/02 *Alabaster v Woolwich plc and Secretary of State for Social Security* [2004] IRLR 486, the ECJ held that under Art 141, maternity pay paid during the period of maternity leave had to take into account a relevant pay rise occurring after the leave began, rejecting the advice of the Advocate General that, to be consistent with the post-*Gillespie* case law, this issue fell to be decided by reference to the Directive and not Art 141. The ruling in *Alabaster* has been given effect by the Statutory Maternity Pay (General) (Amendment) Regulations 2005 , SI 2005/729, with effect from 6 April 2005. See also *Alabaster v Barclays Bank plc and Secretary of State for Social Security (No 2)* [2005] IRLR 576.
984 Directive 96/34 on the framework agreement on parental leave concluded by UNICE, CEEP and the ETUC, extended to the UK by Directive 97/75.
985 MPLR 1999, regs 13–16.

parental leave of up to thirteen weeks in respect of any individual child for whom he or she has responsibility.[986] The thirteen weeks' leave may be taken at various points up to the child's fifth birthday or, if the child is disabled and entitled to disability living allowance, his or her eighteenth birthday. In the case of an adopted child, the leave may be taken up to the fifth anniversary of the date on which the placement of the child began, or his or her eighteenth birthday, whichever is the earlier. The meaning of a 'week' of leave for this purpose is calculated by reference to the normal working time of the employee; if his or her weekly working time varies, an annualised average is used.[987]

In relation to protection against detriment and dismissal and the right to return to work after the leave has ended, broadly similar provisions apply as in the case of maternity leave.[988] This essentially means that the employee's employment continues during the period of leave and that he or she is allowed to resume their normal employment when they return to work.[989] If the period of leave is four weeks or less, the employee has the right to return to the same job as before; if the leave is longer than four weeks, the employer may offer alternative employment if it is not reasonably practicable to reinstate the employee to the old job. The new employment must, however, be suitable and appropriate for the employee, and must offer terms and conditions which are not less favourable than those which applied before. Seniority rights must be preserved during the period of leave according to the same principle that applies for maternity rights.[990] An employee whose employer unreasonably postpones a requested period of parental leave or who prevents or attempts to prevent the employee from taking parental leave may make a claim to an employment tribunal which has the power to award compensation as well as issuing a declaration.[991]

The Regulations provide for the detail of the operation of parental leave schemes to be worked out by agreement between employers and employees. If no agreement is made, a default scheme operates.[992] This appears to provide for

---

986 As originally drafted, the right to parental leave was confined to parents of children born after 15 December 1999. In *R v Secretary of State for Trade and Industry, ex p TUC* [2000] IRLR 565 the TUC argued that, under the Directive, the right to leave should have been provided in respect of all children under the age of five at the date the Regulations came into force, and not those born on or after that date. The Divisional Court referred the question to the ECJ and declined to grant an interim order for the protection of parents affected by the alleged failure to transpose the Directive correctly, even though it considered the TUC's argument likely to prevail before the ECJ. The Regulations were subsequently amended (by SI 2001/4010) to provide that parents of children born before between 15 December 1994 and 15 December 1999 had until 31 March 2005 to exercise the right to leave, and may include service with a previous employer for the purposes of computing their continuity of employment, provided that this is notified to the current employer. See now MPLR 1999, regs 13(1A), 15(2) and Sch 2, para 2A.

987 MPLR 1999, reg 14.

988 A 'detriment' includes subjecting the employee to a disciplinary hearing and a warning in respect of an otherwise unauthorised period of absence; however, a successful claim can only be made under the Act only if the employee can show that they were entitled to the statutory right: *South Central Trains Ltd v Rodway* [2004] IRLR 777, [2005] IRLR 583.

989 ERA 1996, s 77; MPLR 1999, reg 18.

990 MPLR 1999, reg 18A.

991 ERA 1996, s 80.

992 MPLR 1999, reg 16 and Sch 2. In this context, it should be noted that an employee who makes an individual agreement with his or her employer on the matter of parental leave is able to exercise a 'composite right' along the same lines as that which applies to cases of maternity leave, enabling him or her to claim the advantage of whichever scheme (the contractual scheme or the statutory 'default' scheme) provides superior benefits with regard to a particular aspect of the leave (MPLR 1999, reg 21).

leave to be taken in blocks or multiples of one week.[993] In *South Central Trains Ltd. v Rodway*[994] it was held that, as a result, there was no right to take leave for a period of less than a week, rejecting an argument that such an absence was to be treated as exhausting a week's entitlement. The default scheme also sets an upper limit of four weeks' leave in any one year. The employee must give notice of 21 days before taking leave. The employer has the right to postpone the taking of leave for up to six months if it 'considers that the operation of his business would be unduly disrupted if the employee took leave during the period identified in [his or her] notice'; the employer must agree alternative dates on which the leave is to be taken within the six-month period.[995]

In order to displace the provisions of the default scheme, the employer must make either a collective agreement or a workforce agreement governing the operation of parental leave, and ensure that the relevant terms of the agreement are incorporated into the contracts of employment of the employees.[996] A 'collective agreement', for this purpose, must be one which is made with an independent trade union.[997] A workforce agreement[998] may only be made if there is no collective agreement (in the sense just defined) governing the terms and conditions of the employees in question. A workforce agreement must be made in writing, have effect for a specified period not exceeding five years, and be concluded with representatives of the workforce in question[999] or the relevant part of it; if, however, the employer employs fewer than 21 employees on the date the agreement was first made available for signature, the agreement may be made with the workforce representatives or with a majority of the employer's employees. In addition, prior to making the agreement available for signature, the employer must send written copies of it, together with appropriate guidance, to the employees whom it will affect.

Rights arising in connection with paternity and adoption

6.105   Rights to statutory paternity leave and pay and to statutory adoption leave and pay were introduced with effect from April 2003 by virtue of the Employment Act 2002[1] and associated regulations.[2] The structure of the law

---

993 Sch 2, para 7, except in the case of a parent of a child in receipt of disability living allowance. In *South Central Trains v Rodway* [2004] IRLR 777 the EAT held that reg 14(4), which appears to envisage periods of leave for less than one week, only applies to the disability living allowance case. However, the relevant DTI Guidance assumes that reg 14(4) applies more generally: *Parental Leave (PL 509 rev 1): A Guide for Employers and Employees* (2004), at para 2.3. The EAT's interpretation of reg 14(4) was doubted by the CA: see [2005] IRLR 583, para 24 (Keane LJ).

994 [2004] IRLR 777, [2005] IRLR 5833.

995 MPLR 1999, Sch 2, para 6.

996 MPLR 1999, reg 16 (under which it is also sufficient if the contract of employment otherwise 'operates by reference to' the collective or workforce agreement).

997 MPLR 1999, reg 2(1).

998 See generally MPLR 1999, Sch 1.

999 Rules governing the election or appointment of workforce representatives are laid down in MPLR 1999, Sch 2, para 3.

1   The relevant parts of the 2002 Act (ss 1–16) took effect through amendments to other legislation. For statutory paternity and adoption leave, see ERA 1996, ss. 80A–80E and 75A–75D respectively, and for statutory paternity and adoption pay, SSCBA 1992, ss. 171ZA–171ZK and 171ZL–171ZT, respectively. These statutory provisions set out the framework for the relevant rights; the substantive details are contained in regulations (see next footnote).

2   The most important of these are the Paternity and Adoption Leave Regulations (henceforth 'PALR'), SI 2002/2788, and the Statutory Paternity Pay and Statutory Adoption Pay (General) Regulations (henceforth 'SPPR'), SI 2002/2822.

governing these rights is essentially the same as that for statutory maternity leave and pay.

To qualify for statutory paternity leave, an individual must be an employee with 26 weeks' continuous employment up to the fifteenth week before the expected week of the child's birth, and must be either the father of the child or, if not the father, married to or the partner of the child's mother.[3] A 'partner' is 'a person (whether of a different sex or the same sex) who lives with the mother ... and the child in an enduring family relationship but is not a relative of the mother'.[4] Thus despite its name, 'paternity' leave is confined neither to fathers, nor to male partners. In addition, the complainant must have or expect to have, if he is the father, 'responsibility for the upbringing of the child', and, in any other case, 'the main responsibility (apart from any responsibility of the mother) for the upbringing of the child'.[5] The leave must be taken for the purpose of 'caring for a child or supporting the child's mother'.[6] The entitlement consists of two weeks' leave which either be taken as a single block, or in two blocks of a week each, and it must be taken within 56 days of the birth or, if earlier, the expected week of childbirth.[7] The leave entitlement is not increased if more than one child is born from the relevant pregnancy.[8] The employee must give notice to the employer specifying the expected week of childbirth, the intended period of leave and the date on which he or she has chosen to start the leave. The notice must be given in or before the fifteenth week before the expected week of childbirth or, if that is not possible, as soon as reasonably practicable; if the employer requires, the employee must provide a written declaration that he or she is taking leave for the relevant purpose, and that they have met the conditions of entitlement.[9] The continuation of certain terms and conditions of employment during the paternity leave, and the provisions governing the employee's right to return to work after the completion of leave, mirror those for ordinary maternity leave.[10]

To qualify for statutory paternity pay, the employee must meet the conditions for paternity leave which have just been outlined, and must, in addition, be in employed earner's employment for 26 weeks ending with the fifteenth week before the expected week of childbirth, and have had earnings at or above the lower earnings limit for national insurance contributions for the last eight weeks of that period.[11] A number of notification requirements have to be met which, essentially, are the same as those which apply to paternity leave. The amount of paternity pay is 90% of the employee's average weekly earnings, up to a ceiling set by statute.[12]

The right to statutory adoption leave vests in an employee with 26 weeks' continuous employment ending with the week in which they are notified by

---

3   PALR 2002, reg 4(2)(a)–(b). On continuity if the child is born before the expected week of childbirth, see reg 4(3).
4   PALR 2002, reg 1(1).
5   PALR 2002, reg 4(2)(c).
6   PALR 2002, reg 4(1).
7   PALR 2002, reg 5.
8   PALR 2002, reg 4(6).
9   PALR 2002, reg 6 (which also provides for the date on which leave commences to be varied by notice of 28 days prior to the relevant date); on the corresponding provisons governing maternity leave, see above, para 6.100.
10   PALR 2002, regs 12–14.
11   SSCBA 1992, s 171ZA(2)(b)–(d).
12   SI 2002/2818, reg 2. The ceiling was set at £106 with effect from April 2005.

a UK adoption agency that they have been matched with a child for the purposes of adoption.[13] They must inform the employer of their intention to take adoption leave within seven days of receiving the notice of matching from the adoption agency.[14] The leave may begin either on the date on which the child is placed with the employee for adoption or up to 14 days before the expected date of placement.[15] The employee is then entitled to take 'ordinary' adoption leave of 26 weeks[16] and 'additional' leave of a further 26 weeks,[17] unless the ordinary leave is disrupted (by, for example, the death of the child or the return of the child to the adoption agency) or the employee is dismissed prior to its completion.[18] At the end of the leave the employee is entitled to return to their previous employment, if they took ordinary leave; if they took additional leave as well, they are entitled either to return to their previous employment or, if that is not reasonably practicable, to one which is 'both suitable for him and appropriate for him to do in the circumstances'.[19]

To qualify for statutory adoption pay, an employee must show that, in addition to meeting the qualifying conditions for leave, they were in employed earner's employment for 26 weeks up to the week in which they were notified that they had been matched with the child, and had earnings at or above the lower earnings limit for national insurance contributions for the last eight weeks of that period.[20] Adoption pay is payable at 90% of the employee's average weekly earnings up to a ceiling set by statute,[21] for a period of 26 weeks.[22]

A child may be adopted by one member of a couple, or by both of them. Until the coming into force in 2004 of the Adoption and Children Act 2002, joint adoption was only possible if the coupled were married, but this possibility now also extends to unmarried couples who are partners living in an enduring family relationship, and to members of a civil partnership, which is the quasi-marital status created for members of same-sex relationships.[23] Where joint adoption occurs, only one member of the couple may opt to take the relevant statutory adoption leave and/or pay.[24] The other member of the couple – whether or not they jointly adopted the child – may then be entitled to statutory paternity leave of two weeks for the purposes of supporting the adopter or caring for the newly adopted child, and to statutory paternity pay for the same period, if in all other respects they meet the relevant qualifying conditions. The provisions governing statutory paternity leave and pay in relation to birth apply, *mutatis mutandis*, to these rights in relation to adoption.[25]

---

13   PALR 2002, reg 15.
14   PALR 2002, reg 17(2).
15   PALR 2002, reg 16.
16   PALR 2002, reg 18.
17   PALR 2002, reg 20.
18   PALR 2002, regs 22, 24.
19   PALR 2002, reg 26.
20   SSCBA 1992, s 171ZL(2)(b)–(d).
21   SI 2002/2818, reg 3.
22   SSCBA 1992, reg 171ZN(2); the more detailed rules governing statutory adoption pay are set out in SPPR 2002, regs 21–30.
23   For this purpose the definition of 'couple' is that contained in the Adoption and Children Act 2002, s 144(4), as amended by the Civil Partnership Act 2004, s 79.
24   See PALR 2002, reg 2(1) (defining 'adopter') and SSCBA 1992, ss 171ZB(2)(e) and 171ZL(2)(e) (governing election to receive statutory paternity pay and statutory adoption pay respectively).
25   See PALR 2002, regs 8–14 and SPPR 2002, regs 11–16.

An employee may not be subjected to a detriment or be dismissed for taking or seeking to take paternity or adoption leave.[26] An employer's failure to make a payment of statutory paternity or adoption pay may be referred to the Inland Revenue for adjudication,[27] or the employee may make an application for the payment of wages due under Part II of ERA 1996.[28]

The right to time off to provide urgent assistance to dependants

6.106 By way of implementation of the Parental Leave Directive,[29] the Employment Relations Act 1999[30] established a new right for employees[31] to take a reasonable amount of time off during working hours to provide urgent assistance to dependants. The right is principally set out in section 57A of ERA 1996. There is no qualifying period of continuous employment for this right. Specifically, an employee has the right to time off to provide assistance if a dependant falls ill, gives birth, or is injured or assaulted; to make arrangements for the care of a dependant who is ill or injured; in consequence of the death of a dependant; because of unexpected disruption or termination of arrangements for care of a dependant; or to deal with an incident involving the employee's child during a time when an educational establishment would normally be responsible for that child.[32] The employee must notify the employer as soon as reasonably practicable of his or her intention to take time off, and how long he or she expects to be absent (unless it was not possible to tell the employer in advance).[33] The category of dependants includes not just a spouse, child or parent, but also a person living in the same household (other than a tenant, lodger or boarder) and, for relevant purposes, any person who reasonably relies on the employee for assistance when that person falls ill or is injured or assaulted, or for the making of arrangements for care.[34] An employee who is unreasonably refused time off may make a complaint to an employment tribunal which has the power to issue a declaration and to order compensation in an appropriate case,[35] and dismissal of the employee for seeking to exercise this right is automatically unfair.[36]

The right is one 'to be permitted to take a reasonable amount of time off work during working hours in order to deal with a variety of unexpected or

---

26   See ERA 1996, s 47 (detriment) and 99 (dismissal), and PALR 2002, regs 28 (detriment) and 29 (dismissal).
27   SI 2002/2820, reg 12. If the employer does not pay, the Inland Revenue may become responsible under certain circumstances for making the payment to the employee: see SPPR 2002, reg 43.
28   Statutory paternity pay and statutory adoption pay fall under the definition of 'wages' for this purpose: ERA 1996, s 27(1)(ca), (cb).
29   Directive 96/34, Framework Agreement, cl 3, referring to 'time off from work on grounds of force majeure ... for urgent family reasons in cases of sickness or accident making the immediate presence of the worker indispensable'.
30   ERelA 1999, s 8 and Sch 4, Part II, inserting ERA 1996, ss 57, 57A.
31   The police and members of the armed forces may also qualify for statutory paternity pay and adoption pay, but not for paternity leave and adoption leave. See above at paras 3.77 and 3.75, respectively.
32   ERA 1996, s 57A(1).
33   ERA 1996, s 57A(2). However, this does not give rise to an obligation to keep the employer informed of the situation on a daily basis: *Qua v John Ford Morrison Solicitors* [2003] IRLR 184, at para 28.
34   ERA 1996, s 57A(3)–(5).
35   ERA 1996, s 57B.
36   ERA 1996, s 99(3)(d); see *Qua v John Ford Morrison Solicitors* [2003] IRLR 184.

sudden events affecting their dependants, as defined, and in order to make any necessary longer-term arrangements for their care'.[37] It follows that it does not cover leave of an extended duration to care for a sick dependant. Even if the employee gives notice to the employer and takes only a reasonable amount of time off on each occasion, although time off may be taken for the purposes of organising long-term care, any right to further leave on the part of employee himself or herself must be brought under the parental leave provisions of the Act and Regulations.[38] Nor does section 57A provide a right to compassionate leave following a bereavement, although it may well cover 'many other matters' consequent upon the death of a dependant, such as registering the death and dealing with the administration of the deceased's estate.[39] However, 'what is reasonable time off in the particular situation which has arisen will depend on what has occurred and the individual employee's own circumstances'; in this context, 'the operational needs of the employer cannot be relevant to a consideration of the amount of time an employee reasonably needs to deal with emergency circumstances of the kind specified'.[40]

The right to request flexible working in relation to childcare responsibilities

6.107   With effect from April 2003,[41] an employee[42] can apply to his or her employer for a change in their terms and conditions of employment for the purposes of enabling them to carry out childcare responsibilities. Specifically, the change must relate to the hours which the employee is required to work, the times at which he or she is required to work, and 'where, as between his home and a place of business of his employer, he is required to work'.[43] It must be made in order to enable the employee to care for a child[44] who is below the age of six or, in the case of a disabled child, eighteen.[45] The employee must have had 26 weeks of continuous employment with the employer at the time of making the request.[46] In addition, the employee must be either the mother, father, adopter, guardian or foster parent of the child, or married to or the partner of one of the above.[47] For this purpose the normal definition of a partner is used, namely a person who lives with the child and their mother, father etc. 'in an enduring family relationship' without being a relative of that other person.[48] The employee

---

37   [2003] IRLR 184, at para 15.
38   [2003] IRLR 184, at para 21.
39   *Forster v Cartwright Black* [2004] IRLR 781, at para 17 (EAT).
40   *Qua v John Ford Morrison Solicitors* [2003] IRLR 184, at para 22.
41   The right was introduced by the Employment Act 2002, s 47, and is now to be found in ERA 1996, ss 80F–80I, the Flexible Working (Procedural Requirements) Regulations (henceforth 'FWPR'), SI 2002/3207, and the Flexible Working (Eligibility, Complaints and Remedies) (henceforth 'FWER'), SI 2002/3236.
42   This right does not apply to members of the armed forces. See para 3.75 above. There is a specific exclusion for agency workers, defined as those 'supplied by a person ("the agent") to do work for another ("the principal") under a contract or other arrangement made between the agent and the principal' (ERA 1996, s 80F(8)(b)).
43   ERA 1996, s 80F(1)(a).
44   ERA 1996, s 80F(1)(b).
45   ERA 1996, s 80F(3).
46   FWER 2002, reg 3(1)(a).
47   FWER 2002, reg 3(1)(b).
48   FWER 2002, reg 2(1).

must also have or expect to have 'responsibility for the upbringing of the child'.[49] The application must be made in writing to the employer[50] and must state, among other things, the change being requested and 'what effect, if any, the employee thinks making the change applied for would have on his employer and how, in his opinion, any such effect might be dealt with'.[51] If a previous application was made, the employee must wait twelve months before making another one.[52]

The employer is under no obligation to accede to the request, no matter how reasonable it might be. However, the employer may only refuse an application on one of a number of specified grounds. These are listed as: a 'burden of additional costs'; a 'detrimental effect' on the employer's 'ability to meet customer demand; its 'inability to re-organise work among existing staff' or to 'recruit additional staff', a 'detrimental impact on quality' or 'on performance'; 'insufficiency of work during the periods the employee proposes to work; and 'planned structural changes'.[53] The Secretary of State is empowered to add to this list by regulation.[54] Regulations set out the procedure which should be followed when an application is made; among other things, these provide for the employee to have the right to be accompanied at relevant meetings.[55] An employee may not be subjected to a detriment or dismissed in connection with the rights created by these provisions,[56] and may make a complaint to an employment tribunal if the employer fails to comply with the requirement to deal with the request according to the Act or makes a decision on the basis of incorrect facts.[57] The tribunal has power to order the application to be reconsidered, and/or to award such sum of compensation as it considers just and equitable in the circumstances, [58] up to a maximum of two weeks' pay.[59]

DISABILITY DISCRIMINATION

North American and European antecedents

6.108   The issue of disability discrimination has been the subject of repeated attempts at legislative reform since the early 1980s. The Disabled Persons (Employment) Act 1944 established a quota scheme for the employment of disabled persons which was widely considered to have been ineffective.[60] In the United States, the civil rights model of anti-discrimination law was extended to cover disability discrimination as a result of two federal statutes, the Federal Rehabilitation Act 1973 and the Americans with Disabilities Act 1990. Title V of the 1973 Act imposed an obligation upon the federal government in its capacity as employer to adopt

49   FWER 2002, reg 3(1)(c).
50   FWER 2002, reg 4.
51   ERA 1996, s 80F(2).
52   FWER 2002, reg 80F(4).
53   ERA 1996, s 80G(1)(b).
54   ERA 1996, s 80G(1)(b)(ix).
55   See FWPR 2002, in particular reg 14.
56   FWPR 2002, reg 16.
57   ERA 1996, s 80H(1); FWER 2002, reg 6.
58   FWER 2002, reg 80I.
59   SI 2002/3207, reg 15. This is subject to the statutory maximum in ERA 1996, s 227(1), which at 1 February 2005 and at the time of writing stands at £280 per week.
60   See Doyle, 1995: ch 2.

affirmative action programmes for the hiring, promotion and advancement of disabled persons, and put in place a federal contract compliance programme covering the employment practices of government contractors. The 1990 Act prohibited discrimination on the grounds of disability in both the private and public sectors, and covered not just employment but also housing, education, recreation and health services, as well as a number of other areas.

In 1986 a European Community Recommendation on the Employment of Disabled People was adopted which called upon Member States to eliminate discrimination by, amongst other things, 'limiting exceptions to the principle of equal treatment in access to training or employment to the cases justified on the ground of a specific incompatibility between a particular activity forming part of a job or course of training and a particular disability; if necessary, it should be possible to have this incompatibility confirmed by a medical certificate'.[61] The Recommendation also contained a guideline framework for positive action to be taken by employers, workers' organisations and the state.

In 1990 the British government responded to the growing pressure for reform of domestic legislation by issuing a consultative document which rejected the extension of anti-discrimination legislation to disability, on grounds which included the observation that 'a major difficulty is that disability, unlike sex or race, can be relevant to job performance and what might seem like discrimination may in reality be recruitment based on legitimate preferences and likely performance'.[62] As Doyle comments, this argument 'does not withstand close scrutiny ... If a disabled person is refused an employment opportunity because he or she cannot perform the work or is ill-suited to the job, that is not unlawful discrimination and it is not proposed that it should be so'.[63] By January 1995 there had been a change in the official line, and a White Paper was published accepting the principle of legislative intervention.[64] A government measure, the Disability Discrimination Bill, was published early in 1995; a more far-reaching private members' bill, the Civil Rights (Disabled Persons) Bill was introduced at about the same time but was pre-empted by the government's intervention.

The DDA 1995 repealed the quota system which operated under the Disabled Persons (Employment) Act 1944 (although it retained the system of 'supported employment' in organisations providing work specifically designed for disabled persons[65]) and introduced a new framework of rights introduced, loosely based on the model of equal treatment. At the same time, the 1995 Act's conceptual and remedial structure was distinct from that of the principal anti-discrimination Acts, and in many respects marked a new departure in the law of equal treatment in employment. It provided inspiration for the incorporation of a prohibition on disability discrimination into the EC Framework Directive on Discrimination in Employment which was adopted in December 2000,[66] and this led, in its turn, to further amendments to the UK legislation, significantly strengthening and clarifying the law.[67] The Disability Discrimination Act 2005 has recently made additional amendments to the legislation.

---

61   Recommendation 86/379, Art 2(a)(iii).
62   Department of Employment, *Employment and Training for People with Disabilities: Consultative Document*, 1990, at para 5.14.
63   Doyle, 1995: p 47.
64   *Ending Discrimination against Disabled People*, Cm 2729, 1995.
65   13,000 persons were employed in such organisations in 1996. See Gooding, 1996: p 29.
66   Directive 2000/78. The prohibition on disability discrimination must be implemented by Member States by 2 December 2006.
67   See in particular SI 2003/1673.

The concept of discrimination under the Disability Discrimination Act

Forms of discrimination

6.109   The original version of the DDA contained a distinctive definition of discrimination under which 'an employer discriminates against a disabled person if (a) for a reason which relates to the disabled person's disability, he treats him less favourably than he treats or would treat others to whom that reason does not or would not apply; and (b) he cannot show that the treatment in question is justified'.[68] In effect, the definition was a 'hybrid, incorporating elements of direct and elements of indirect discrimination'.[69] Its most unusual feature was that direct discrimination could be justified. For a justification defence to be made out, the employer had to show that the justifying factor was 'both material to the circumstances of the particular case and substantial'. The Act also introduced the separate concept of the employer's duty to make reasonable adjustments to the arrangements on the basis of which employment was offered, and to 'any physical feature of premises' which placed the disabled person 'at a substantial disadvantage in comparison with persons who are not disabled'.[70] The Act allowed the employer to invoke a justifying factor as a defence even if it had failed to make a reasonable adjustment, although the scope for applying the justification defence in these circumstances was said by the Court of Appeal to be 'heavily restricted'.[71]

A new definition of discrimination came into force with effect from 1 October 2004.[72] The principal changes were the creation of a new wrong of direct discrimination on the grounds of disability with no justification defence allowed, and the removal of the 'restricted' justification defence in cases where the employer fails to show that it has made a reasonable adjustment. As a result, there are now three forms of discrimination under the Act: direct discrimination; discrimination arising from a failure to make reasonable adjustments; and a residual category of disability-related discrimination.

Direct discrimination

6.110   Direct discrimination is discrimination against a disabled person where 'on the ground of the person's disability, [the respondent] treats the disabled person less favourably than he treats or would treat a person not having that particular disability whose relevant circumstances, including his abilities, are the same as, or not materially different from, those of the disabled person.'[73] As just noted, the justification defence is not available here.[74] This, then, is the requirement that 'like should be treated alike',

---

68   DDA 1995, s 5(1), as originally enacted.
69   *O'Neill v Symm & Co Ltd* [1998] IRLR 233, 235, reporting a submission of counsel. The EAT did not comment on this submission, except to say that it regarded the complaint in that case as one of direct discrimination ([1998] IRLR 233, 236).
70   DDA 1995, s 6(1), as originally enacted.
71   *Collins v Royal National Theatre Board Ltd* [2004] IRLR 395, at para 36 (Sedley LJ).
72   See now DDA 1995, s 3A. On the background to this reform, which was anticipated by the report of a ministerial task force in 1999 and then prompted by the adoption of the Framework Directive, see the judgment of Sedley LJ in *Collins v Royal National Theatre Board Ltd* [2004] IRLR 395, paras 6–9.
73   DDA 1995, s 3A(5).
74   DDA 1995, s 3A(4).

applied to disability.[75] The concept involves a comparison of the treatment of the complainant with that accorded to a person whose circumstances were in all relevant respects similar to that of the complainant, with the exception that they did not have the particular disability in question. The comparator can be either hypothetical or real. The *Code of Practice: Employment and Occupation* issued by the Disability Rights Commission gives this example:

> A blind woman is not short-listed for a job involving computers because the employer wrongly assumes that blind people cannot use them. The employer makes no attempt to look at the individual circumstances. The employer has treated the woman less favourably than other people by not short-listing her for the job. The treatment was on the ground of woman's disability (because assumptions would not have been made about a non-disabled person).[76]

Although the statutory formula used here is similar to that adopted elsewhere in anti-discrimination legislation, it differs in one fundamental respect: it only confers rights on disabled persons, not on the non-disabled. This is generally the case in relation to rights created by the DDA. Thus there is greater scope, in this context, for reconciling positive action for disadvantaged groups with the prohibition on direct discrimination.[77]

The duty to make reasonable adjustments

6.111   An employer commits discrimination under the Act if it 'fails to comply with a duty to make reasonable adjustments imposed on [it] in relation to the disabled person'.[78] The duty arises 'where (a) a provision, criterion or practice applied by or on behalf of an employer, or (b) any physical feature of premises occupied by the employer, places the disabled person at a substantial disadvantage in comparison with persons who are not disabled'. It is then the duty of the employer 'to take such steps as it is reasonable, in all the circumstances of the case, for [it] to have to take in order to prevent the provision, criterion or practice, or feature, having that effect'.[79] The duty arises in respect of both applicants for employment and employed persons, although, in the case of the former, it only applies to arrangements for determining to whom employment is offered if the disabled person has notified the employer that he or she is an applicant for the employment in question.[80] More generally, the employer is under no duty if it does not know, or could not be reasonably expected to know, that the disabled person is an applicant or, if already employed, has a disability which places him or her at a substantial disadvantage.[81] Thus in the pre-2004

---

75   Thus case law defining the role of motive and intention in relation to direct discrimination, in particular the judgment of the House of Lords in *James v Eastleigh Borough Council* [1990] IRLR 288, is relevant here.

76   Disability Rights Commission, *Code of Practice: Employment and Occupation* (2004), at para 4.8. Failure to comply with the Code does not, of itself, make a person liable to proceedings but its provisions must be taken into account in legal proceedings (DDA 1995, s 53A(7)(8)).

77   Cf. our discussion of this point in the wider context of the concept of direct discrimination at paras 6.12–6.19 above. It should also be noted that although the Act thereby permits positive action in favour of disabled persons, it does not require it, except in so far as this is the effect of the duty to make reasonable adjustments (see DDA 1995, s 18D(1)).

78   DDA 1995, s 3A(2).

79   DDA 1995, s 4A(1).

80   DDA 1995, s 4A(2)(a).

81   DDA 1995, s 4A(3).

case of *O'Neill v Symm & Co Ltd*[82] the EAT held that the employer was not under an obligation under this provision to seek a medical opinion or prognosis on the condition of the applicant, when it had been given no reason to believe that she was suffering from a condition sufficiently serious to amount to a disability within the meaning of the Act.

The reference in the statutory formula to a 'provision, criterion or practice' which places the applicant at a substantial disadvantage provides a link to the notion of indirect discrimination which operates in other parts of anti-discrimination law, and the concept of reasonableness, in this context, plays a functionally similar role to the justification defence which is also an integral part of the indirect discrimination concept.[83] In part for this reason, no additional defence of justification is available if the employer fails to make out a case of reasonable adjustment.[84] But in other respects, the duty to make reasonable adjustments goes beyond the scope of the indirect discrimination concept. In particular, the need to consider how a real or hypothetical comparator would have been treated is not relevant here. Thus the Act may require the employer to take steps which constitute more favourable treatment of the disabled person. As Baroness Hale put it in *Archibald v Fife Council*,[85] the 1995 Act:

> ... is different from the Sex Discrimination Act 1975 and the Race Relations Act 1976. In the latter two, men and women or black and white, as the case may be, are opposite sides of the same coin. Each is to be treated in the same way. Treating men more favourably than women discriminates against women. Treating women more favourably than men discriminates against men. Pregnancy apart, the differences between the genders are generally regarded as irrelevant. The 1995 Act, however, does not regard the differences between disabled people and others as irrelevant. It does not expect each to be treated in the same way. It expects reasonable adjustments to be made to cater for the special needs of disabled people. It necessarily entails an element of more favourable treatment.

The point is clarified further by the Act which provides that while, in general, its provisions do not require more favourable treatment of disabled persons, this is subject to the employer's duty to make reasonable adjustments.[86]

Other provisions of the Act amplify the notion of reasonable adjustments. Thus regard must be had to a number of factors including 'the extent to which taking the step would prevent the effect in relation to which the duty is imposed', the practicability of the step in question, the financial and other costs which would fall on the employer and the disruption to its activities, the extent of the employer's financial and other resources, the availability of financial or other assistance, and the nature of the employer's activities and the size of its undertaking. If the employer is a private household, the court must take into account the extent to which taking the step would 'disrupt that household' or 'disturb any person residing there'.[87] The Act also specifies that adjustments

---

82   [1998] IRLR 233, 237; *Ridout v TC Group* [1998] IRLR 628; *Fu v London Borough of Camden* [2001] IRLR 186.
83   See generally, paras 6.29–6.31 above.
84   As we have already noted, this marks a major change from the pre-2004 position: see the discussion of Sedley LJ in *Collins v Royal National Theatre Board Ltd* [2004] IRLR 395.
85   [2004] IRLR 651, at para 47.
86   DDA 1995, s 18D.
87   DDA 1995, s 18B(1)(a). See the *Code of Practice: Employment and Occupation*, at paras 5.27–5.42.

may include making adjustments to premises; allocating some of the disabled person's duties to another person; transferring the disabled person to fill a vacancy; altering his or her working hours; assigning them to a different place of work; allowing them to be absent during working hours for rehabilitation, assessment or treatment; providing them with training; acquiring or modifying equipment; modifying instructions or reference manuals; modifying procedures for testing or assessment; providing a reader or interpreter; and providing supervision or other support.[88]

The leading case on the meaning of the duty is the decision of the House of Lords in *Archibald v Fife Council*.[89] The complainant, who was employed in a manual occuaption, had a spinal anaesthetic for a minor operation, after which she was unable to walk without considerable pain. She received retraining for other jobs including non-manual work, but was unable to obtain a new position with the Council despite applying for over 100 posts. About two years after the operation, she was dismissed on the grounds that all efforts to redeploy her had failed. She claimed that, rather than being required to apply for a new post on the basis of competitive interviews, she should have been reallocated to a suitable alternative post once it became available. The employment tribunal held that the employers had not failed to comply with the duty to make reasonable adjustments. The House of Lords, remitting the case for a new hearing, held that the tribunal in this case had erred in rejecting her contention that it would have been a reasonable adjustment not to require her to go through competitive interviews if she could show that she was qualified and suitable for an existing vacancy. The duty to make adjustments may require the employer to treat a disabled person more favourably to remove the disadvantage that is attributable to the disability. The substantive outcome in this case was not necessarily wrong; the employer had taken certain steps, including offering retraining, to assist the complainant. However, as the judgments in *Archibald* indicate, the reference in the legislation itself to the transfer of the disabled person to fill a vacancy for another position,[90] in addition to similar suggestions in the Code of Practice,[91] suggest that in a case such as this, the employer cannot necessarily fall back on an argument that appointments or transfers should be made exclusively on merit.

Disability-related discrimination

6.112   The third form of discrimination under the Act occurs where 'for a reason which relates to the disabled person's disability, [the respondent] treats him less favourably than he treats or would treat others to whom that reason does not or would not apply' and 'he cannot show that the treatment in question is justified.'[92] The formula used here does not rely on the like-for-like

---

88   DDA 1995, s 18B(2); *Code of Practice: Employment and Occupation*, at paras 5.18–5.22.

89   [2004] IRLR 651, at para 47. For other relevant decisions under the pre-2004 law (some of which are complicated by the presence of the additional justification defence which now no longer applies to the duty to make reasonable adjustments) see *Fu v London Borough of Camden* [2001] IRLR 186; *London Clubs Management Ltd. v Hood* [2001] IRLR 719; *Mid-Staffordshire General Hospitals NHS Trust v Cambridge* [2003] IRLR 566; *Paul v National Probation Service* [2004] IRLR 190; and *Nottinghamshire County Council v Meikle* [2004] IRLR 703.

90   See now DDA 1995, s 18B(2)(c).

91   *Code of Practice: Employment and Occupation*, para 5.18.

92   DDA 1995, s 3A(1).

comparison which applies to cases of direct discrimination falling under the Act. This does not mean that the concept of the comparator is entirely irrelevant; however it is different from the one adopted in indirect discrimination cases under the SDA 1975 and the RRA 1976. The relevant benchmark is simply the treatment of others to whom the relevant reason does not or would not apply. In *Clark v Novacold*[93] the Court of Appeal, applying the pre-2004 law which was not materially different on this point, held that the phrase 'that reason' referred to the reason for the employer's treatment of the applicant. On this basis, the correct comparison was with a person to whom the reason for the unfavourable treatment did not apply; in deciding that the correct comparator was someone off work for a reason *other than disability*, the EAT in that case had erroneously applied what is now (under the post-2004 law) the test for direct discrimination. The Code of Practice[94] explains the point by reference to this example:

> A disabled woman is refused an administrative job because she cannot type. She cannot type because she has arthritis. A non-disabled person who was unable to type would also have been turned down. The disability-related reason for the less favourable treatment is the women's inability to type, and the correct comparator is the person to whom that reason does not apply – that is, someone who can type. Such a person would not have been refused the job. Nevertheless, the disabled woman has been treated less favourably for a disability-related reason and this will be unlawful unless it can be justified. There is no direct discrimination, however, because the comparator for direct discrimination is a person who does not have arthritis, but who is also unable to type.

The effect of the *Novacold* decision, now implicitly confirmed by the statutory changes which came into force in 2004, is that once a sufficient causal link between the complainant's disability and his or her treatment has been established, an initial case of discrimination has been made out and the focus shifts to the issue of justification. The Act indicates that justification must be 'both material to the circumstances of the particular case and substantial'.[95] The Code[96] suggests that where 'a man who has severe back pain and is unable to bend is rejected for a job as a carpet fitter as he cannot carry out the essential requirement of the job, which is to fit carpets', this rejection would be lawful 'as the reason he is rejected is a substantial one and is clearly material to the circumstances.' The Act also indicates that in determining if justification has been made out, if the employer is under a duty to make reasonable adjustments in relation to the applicant, the tribunal must consider whether the treatment of the applicant would have been justified if the duty to make reasonable adjustments had been complied with.[97] This principle is illustrated in the following way by the Code of Practice:

> An applicant for an administrative job appears not to be the best person for the job, but only because her typing speed is too slow as a result of arthritis in her hands. If a reasonable adjustment – perhaps an adapted keyboard – would overcome this, her typing speed would not in itself be a substantial

---

93   [1999] IRLR 318, reversing the EAT ([1998] IRLR 420; see also *British Sugar plc v Kirker* [1998] IRLR 624.
94   *Code of Practice: Employment and Occupation*, at para 4.30.
95   DDA 1995, s 3A(3).
96   *Code of Practice: Employment and Occupation*, at para 6.3.
97   DDA 1995, s 3A(6).

reason for not employing her. Therefore the employer would be unlawfully discriminating if, on account of her typing speed, he did not employ her or provide that adjustment.[98]

The correct approach to assessing justification under the Act was considered by the Court of Appeal in *Jones v Post Office*.[99] The complainant, who was employed as a mail delivery driver, was diagnosed with diabetes for which, following a heart attack, he received insulin. The employer operated under a rule which excluded all insulin-dependent employees from driving. After reviewing the complainant's case, it offered him limited driving duties. The complainant claimed that this limited offer amounted to disability discrimination. The employer relied on the medical examination and risk assessment of the complainant which it had carried out, but this was challenged by medical evidence led by the complainant. The employment tribunal ruled in his favour but this finding was overturned by the EAT and Court of Appeal. According to Pill LJ, 'where a properly conducted risk assessment provides a reason which is on its face both material and substantial, and is not irrational, the tribunal cannot substitute its own appraisal'.[100] The tribunal's role was comparable to that undertaken in the context of unfair dismissal law when assessing the reasonableness of the employer's decision to dismiss an employee:

> Under [the ERA 1996], the tribunal's task is to consider the reasonableness of the employer's response, and under [the DDA 1995] it is to consider the materiality and substantiality of his reason. In both cases, the members of the tribunal might themselves have come to a different conclusion on the evidence, but they must respect the opinion of the employer, in the one case if it is within the range of reasonable responses and in the other if the reason given is material and substantial.[101]

This would appear to imply, then, a low threshold for employers to meet, and one which is below the benchmark which applies to the justification defence in sex and race discrimination claims.[102]

The concept of disability

6.113 Only disabled persons may bring complaints of discriminatory treatment under the Act. For this purpose, a 'disabled person' is a person with a 'disability'[103] at the material time, which means the point at which the allegedly discriminatory act occurs.[104] 'Disability' means 'a physical or mental impairment which has a substantial and long-term adverse effect on [the

---

98 *Code of Practice: Employment and Occupation*, at para 6.5.
99 [2001] IRLR 384. See also *Murray v Newham Citizens Advice Bureau Ltd.* [2003] IRLR 340; *Mid-Staffordshire General Hospitals NHS Trust v Cambridge* [2003] IRLR 566.
100 [2001] IRLR 384, at para 25.
101 [2001] IRLR 384, at para 28. See also *Williams v J Walter Thompson Group Ltd* [2005] IRLR 376. However, this does not necessarily mean that the tribunal can never take into account medical evidence not available to the employer: *Surrey Police v Marshall* [2002] IRLR 843; nor does the tribunal have to defer to the employer's view if a full medical risk assessment has not been carried out and the medical evidence upon which the employer relied is contested: *Paul v National Probation Service* [2004] IRLR 190.
102 Cf. [2001] IRLR 384, at para 43 (Arden LJ).
103 DDA 1995, s 1(2).
104 *Goodwin v Patent Office* [1999] IRLR 4; *Greenwood v British Airways plc* [1999] IRLR 600; *Cruickshank v VAW Motorcast Ltd* [2002] IRLR 24.

complainant's] ability to carry out normal day-to-day activities'.[105] In *Goodwin v Patent Office*[106] the EAT analysed this definition into four parts: the impairment condition, the adverse effect condition, the substantial condition and the long-term condition.

The impairment condition

6.114 The term 'physical impairment' is not defined in the Act; the *Disability Guidance* 1996 states that it includes 'sensory impairments, such as those affecting sight or hearing'.[107] Mental impairment was defined in the 1995 Act to refer to a mental illness which was 'clinically well-recognised';[108] at the time of writing provision has been made for this requirement to be repealed.[109] In *McNicol v Balfour Beatty Rail Maintenance Ltd*[110] the Court of Appeal declined to overturn a tribunal ruling rejecting a claim of impairment on the basis of back pain which could not be shown to have been caused by a medical condition of either a physical or mental kind.

An impairment affects a person's ability to carry out 'normal day-to-day activities' only if it affects one of the following: mobility; manual dexterity; physical co-ordination; continence; ability to lift, carry or otherwise move everyday objects; speech, hearing or eyesight; memory or ability to concentrate, learn or understand; and perception of the risk of physical danger. There is a power to add a factor to or remove one from this list by regulation.[111] Regulations currently exclude a number of conditions from the definition of impairment: these are addictions to alcohol, nicotine or any other substance; pyromania, kleptomania, a tendency to physical or sexual abuse, exhibitionism and voyeurism; and seasonal allergic rhinitis.[112]

The adverse effect condition

6.115 In relation to the requirement of an 'adverse effect', the EAT has suggested that '[w]hat the Act is concerned with is an impairment on the person's *ability* to carry out activities. The fact that a person can carry out such activities does not mean that his ability to carry them out has not been impaired'. It has also noted that 'disabled persons often adjust their lives and circumstances to enable them to cope for themselves' without ceasing to have a disability within the

---

105 DDA 1995, s 1(1).
106 [1999] IRLR 4.
107 *Guidance on Matters to be Taken into Account in Determining Questions Relating to the Definition of Disability*, 1996 (henceforth, '*Disability Guidance*'), Part I, para 12. Under DDA 1995, s 3, such guidance must be taken into account by a court or tribunal where it appears to it to be relevant. On the need for a flexible approach in applying the notion of impairment, given the absence of a statutory definition, see *College of Ripon and York St. John v Hobbs* [2002] IRLR 185.
108 DDA 1995, Sch 1, para 1(1); see *Disability Guidance*, Part I, paras 13–15; *Goodwin v Patent Office* [1999] IRLR 4; *Morgan v Staffordshire University* [2002] IRLR 190 (medical notes referring in general terms to 'anxiety', 'stress' and 'depression' did not establish mental impairment).
109 See DDA 2005, s 18(2), not in force at the time of writing.
110 [2002] IRLR 711.
111 DDA 1995, Sch 1, para 4; *Disability Guidance*, Part II, paras C1–C23.
112 SI 1996/1455, regs 3–5. It should be noted, in relation to this list of exceptions, that a recognised condition, such as depression, is not outside the Act merely because it was induced in part by alcoholism: *Power v Panasonic UK Ltd.* [2003] IRLR 151.

meaning of the Act, and that the effect of a disability might be cumulative in the sense of impairing more than one capacity.[113]

The substantial condition

6.116   The term 'substantial' is not defined in the Act.[114] According to the EAT, following the *Disability Guidance*, it means 'more than minor or trivial'. In applying this part of the test, the employment tribunal must consider both the 'deduced' effects of the applicant's condition, that is to say, the impact it would have but for the medication which may be taken to counter it,[115] as well as the 'actual' effects after medication. The question then for the tribunal is 'whether the actual and deduced effect on the applicant's abilities to carry out normal and day-to-day activities is *clearly more than trivial*' (emphasis in original).[116]

The long-term condition

6.117   A 'long-term' effect is defined in the Act as one which has either lasted twelve months or is expected to last for twelve months or (if less) for the rest of the person's life.[117] In applying this part of the test, tribunals should take into account the likelihood of a condition or effect recurring.[118]

Extending the concept of disability

6.118   There are several problematic aspects of the basic statutory definition of disability. Unlike the relevant US definition, it does not formally extend to *perceived* impairments; nor does it cover numerous cases of characteristics which commonly give rise to prejudicial behaviour. Certain extensions of the definition have however been made which partially rectify these omissions. First, individuals who have suffered disabilities in the past are protected against discrimination, even if they have recovered from the condition or if the effect of the impairment has become less than substantial.[119] Second, individuals with recurring disabilities are brought under the Act by a provision to the effect that '[w]here an impairment ceases to have a substantial adverse effect on a person's ability to carry out normal day-to-day activities, it is to be treated as continuing to have that effect if that effect is likely to recur'.[120] Third, a severe disfigurement is to be treated as being a relevant impairment for the purposes of the Act.[121]

---

113   *Goodwin v Patent Office* [1999] IRLR 4, 7. See also *Leonard v Southern Derbyshire Chamber of Commerce* [2001] IRLR 19, suggesting that employment tribunals should focus on what applicants cannot do, or cannot do easily, rather than on what they can do, in determining whether the adverse effect condition is satisfied.

114   Paras A1–A10 of the *Disability Guidance*, Part II, outline factors which may have a bearing on the meaning of 'substantial': these include the time taken to carry out an activity, the way in which an activity is carried out, the cumulative effects of an impairment, the modification by the person of his or her behaviour, and the effects of the working environment.

115   See *Kapadia v London Borough of Lambeth* [2000] IRLR 699.

116   *Goodwin v Patent Office* [1999] IRLR 4, 9; *Ekpe v Commissioner of Police of the Metropolis* [2001] IRLR 605; *Law Hospital NHS Trust v Rush* [2001] IRLR 611.

117   DDA 1995, Sch 1, para 2(1); *Disability Guidance*, Part II, paras B1–B5.

118   *Greenwood v British Airways plc* [1999] IRLR 600.

119   DDA 1995, s 2 and Sch 2; *Disability Guidance*, Part II, para B9.

120   DDA 1995, Sch 1, para 2(2); *Disability Guidance*, Part II, paras B3–B5; *Swift v Chief Constable of Wiltshire Constabulary* [2004] IRLR 540.

121   DDA 1995, Sch 1, para 3; SI 1996/1455 (excluding tattoos and piercings); *Disability Guidance*, Part II, paras A16–A17.

Fourth, an impairment which would be likely to have a substantial effect on day-to-day activities but for medical treatment of various kinds is also deemed to have that effect for the purposes of the Act.[122] Fifth, persons with certain 'progressive conditions' which have an effect (but not one which is a substantial adverse effect) on their ability to carry out day-to-day activities are deemed to be covered by the Act if the condition in question is likely to result in a substantial adverse effect at some point. As examples of progressive conditions, the Act lists cancer, multiple sclerosis, muscular distrophy, and infection by HIV.[123] Finally, as a failsafe measure, persons whose names were on the register of disabled persons set up under the 1944 Act in 1995 and on the date of the commencement of the DDA 1995 are also deemed to be disabled for the purposes of the latter Act.[124] The DDA 2005 provides that certain conditions necessarily give rise to a disability; these are named as cancer, HIV infection, and multiple sclerosis.[125] Once this provision is brought into force it will avoid some of the uncertainty which was considered to attach to the provision governing 'progressive conditions'.

The concept of disability has been held to extend to cases of, among other things, chronic fatigue syndrome or ME;[126] severe abdominal pains of a kind associated with uteric colic, but for which there was no precise diagnosis;[127] paranoid schizophrenia;[128] an upper arm condition;[129] autism;[130] and depression.[131]

Scope

6.119 The 1995 Act has many of the same features determining the scope of its application as the principal anti-discrimination Acts. Thus it applies to employees and certain self-employed workers who contract to supply personal services[132] and to Crown employees.[133] The only significant exclusion, following the amendments to the law which came into force in October 2004, relates to members of the armed forces.[134] Agency workers ('contract workers') who are supplied by or through an employment agency are protected against discrimination by the client or 'principal' who uses their labour.[135] The Act applies to all employers no matter how many persons they employ.[136]

---

122 DDA 1995, Sch 1, para 6; *Disability Guidance*, Part II, paras A11–A14, B6; *Abadeh v British Telecommunications* plc [2001] IRLR 23; *Woodrup v London Borough of Southwark* [2003] IRLR 111.
123 DDA 1995, Sch 1, para 8.
124 DDA 1995, Sch 1, para 7. The register itself was wound up by the 1995 Act.
125 DDA 2005, s 18, inserting DDA 1995, Sch 1, para 6A.
126 *O'Neill v Symm & Co Ltd* [1998] IRLR 233.
127 *Howden v Capital Copiers Ltd*, 30.7.97, Edinburgh Employment tribunal, case no 400005/97, DCLD No 33, reported in IRLIB 586 (February 1998).
128 *Goodwin v Patent Office* [1999] IRLR 4.
129 *Vicary v British Telecommunications plc* [1999] IRLR 680.
130 *Hewett v Motorola Ltd.* [2004] IRLR 545.
131 *Kapadia v London Borough of Lambeth* [2000] IRLR 699; *Greenwood v British Airways plc* [1999] IRLR 600.
132 DDA 1995, s 68(1).
133 DDA 1995, s 64.
134 DDA 1995, s 64(7).
135 DDA 1995, s 4B; *Abbey Life Assurance Co Ltd v Tansell* [2000] IRLR 387, discussed above, para 3.68. The employment agency itself is covered by s 21A of the Act.
136 DDA 1995, s 7, as originally enacted, excluded employers with fewer than fifteen employees; this was repealed with effect from October 2004.

The matters in respect of which discrimination is prohibited include, with regard to applicants, arrangements for appointment, the terms on which employment is offered, and a refusal to offer employment;[137] with regard to employed persons, they include terms and conditions of employment, opportunities offered for training, promotion, transfer or 'any other benefit', and the dismissal of the individual or 'any other detriment' to which he or she is subjected.[138] Similar provisions to those contained in general anti-discrimination law concerning the vicarious liability of employers,[139] assistance for unlawful acts,[140] victimisation,[141] harassment,[142] and the obligations of trade unions and professional associations,[143] qualification bodies[144] and providers of vocational training apply.[145] The Act also covers discrimination against office holders,[146] partners[147] and barristers and advocates.[148]

Enforcement

6.120   The principal remedy laid down by the Act is a complaint to an employment tribunal which has broadly the same powers to grant awards of compensation (with no upper limit[149]) and to make recommendations as under the other anti-discrimination legislation.[150] Similar provisions apply in relation to time limits[151] and the burden of proof including the use of questionnaires to elicit evidence of the employer's reasons for taking a particular decision.[152] Administrative enforcement and a range of related measures are undertaken by the Disability Rights Commission which was established in April 2000.[153]

ASSESSMENT

6.121   In a relatively brief period, the principle of equal treatment has come to permeate many areas of labour law and of industrial relations practice. In numerous respects, the anti-discrimination legislation marks a radical departure from more traditional forms of labour law regulation. It provides a useful model for a type of labour legislation which extends beyond a narrow focus on the relationship of employer and employee. By regulating the hiring stage as well as aspects of the continuing employment relationship and by protecting certain

---

137 DDA 1995, s 4(1).
138 DDA 1995, s 4(2). 'Dismissal' includes constructive dismissal: *Nottinghamshire County Council v Meikle* [2004] IRLR 703.
139 DDA 1995, s 58; see Code of Practice: Employment and Occupation, at para 3.23.
140 DDA 1995, s 57.
141 DDA 1995, s 55.
142 DDA 1995, s 3B; see above, para 6.63.
143 DDA 1995, ss 13–14; *Sadek v Medical Protection Society* [2005] IRLR 57.
144 DDA 1995, ss 14A, 14B.
145 DDA 1995, ss 14C–14D.
146 DDA 1995, ss 4C–4F.
147 DDA 1995, ss 6A–6C.
148 DDA 1995, ss 7A–7D.
149 As a result, it has been suggested that 'careful judicial management' of claims is needed: *Buxton v Equinox Design Ltd* [1999] IRLR 158.
150 DDA 1995, s 8.
151 DDA 1995, Sch 3, para 3.
152 DDA 1995, s 56.
153 The DRC was set up by the Disability Rights Commission Act 1999.

economically dependent workers who are not 'employees' in the sense required by most of employment protection and social security legislation, they express the growing importance of rights operating at the level of the labour market and not simply at the level of the individual business enterprise. Anti-discrimination legislation also explicitly recognises the individual's right to occupational training and development, both in the 'negative' sense of requiring equal access to professional and other associations but also through sanctioning positive action in favour of minorities with regard to training and also embracing access to promotion and employment opportunities within employment.

In other ways, it is clear that the substantive scope of the legislation has until recently been restricted. If the goal of equal treatment legislation was a deeper recognition of the values of individual dignity and autonomy at work, it made no sense to limit the intervention of the law to discrimination on the grounds of sex, race and disability. Although 'racial grounds' were quite widely defined in the initial form of the RRA 1976, it is clear from the case law which grew up around the interpretation of that Act that they only marginally protected, for example, freedom of religious expression.[154] Similarly, attempts to stretch the SDA 1975 to cover discrimination on the grounds of an individual's sexual orientation were only occasionally successful. The limited scope of the two principal Acts was even more difficult to defend when the principle of protection for expression of religious and political expression is accepted, however inadequately, in the Fair Employment (Northern Ireland) Act 1989; there is also the model provided by Title VII of the US Civil Rights Act 1964 as far as religious discrimination is concerned. More tangible progress has resulted from the adoption of Article 13 of the EC Treaty in 1997 and the subsequent Race and Framework Directives of November 2000. It is the implementation of the Directives which has led to the adoption of equal treatment regulations governing sexual orientation and religion or belief, to the strengthening of race, disability and (prospectively) sex discrimination laws, and to the impending adoption of age discrimination legislation.

Turning from substance to form, it is important not to underestimate the importance of legislation which enshrines, in the concept of direct discrimination, the principle that like should be treated alike. But at the same time, there are obvious limits to the usefulness of this concept for the purpose of remedying collective injustice. In this respect, British legislation makes very few concessions to the goals of affirmative or positive action, and certainly far fewer than the US Civil Rights Act 1964. This is not just a question of sanctioning preferential treatment or reverse discrimination. That may be an important aspect of positive action programmes, but it is far from being the only one, and a strong argument can be made that what affirmative action is concerned with is not reverse discrimination as such but rather a notion of equality which fully recognises the role played by institutional forces and by stereotyped assumptions in reproducing the conditions for social disadvantage and injustice. In US practice, for example, affirmative action programmes were permitted by the Supreme Court precisely because in many cases they were put in place to overcome the historical legacy of institutionalised discrimination; this was not a denial of the principle of equal treatment but rather a means of strengthening it. The Court could do this in part because the definition of adverse treatment in Title VII is relatively loose. By contrast, the specific wording of section 1 of the SDA 1975 and of the

---

154 Cf *Mandla v Dowell Lee* [1983] ICR 385; para 6.39 above.

RRA 1976 provides little scope for even the temporary and limited kind of affirmative action programme which the Supreme Court upheld in *United Steelworkers of America v Weber*.[155] It seems clear that the drafter was instructed to restrict affirmative action from the fact that obvious derogations from section 1 were made in the case of discrimination in favour of minority groups in the provision of vocational training.[156] Only marginally greater leeway has been allowed, through the case law of the ECJ, under the terms of the Equal Treatment Directive,[157] although the amendments made to Article 141 (ex 119) at the time of the Treaty of Amsterdam hold out the prospect of a more liberal approach as do the more recent references to positive action in the Framework and Race Directives of 2000. The Disability Discrimination Act 1995 is an important exception to this approach; by confining rights to disabled persons, it preserves a space for affirmative action programmes of various kinds.

The lack of a firm commitment in the legislation to a concept of equality more clearly focused on remedying 'group disadvantage' is also evident in the structure of enforcement mechanisms which is provided for. There is no formal provision for class actions of the kind which may be deployed under Title VII, nor for exemplary damages to provide an effective incentive for employers to unravel institutional discrimination (although, as we have seen, exemplary or punitive damages are the subject of a Law Commission report recommending a change to the law). Over time the role of collective enforcement under the British legislation has, if anything, diminished, thanks to the abolition of collective arbitration of equal pay claims before the Central Arbitration Committee, and the courts' restrictive interpretations of the powers of the EOC and CRE.[158] The risks and costs of individual litigation have been worsened by the enormous complexity, for example, of the procedures put in place for the adjudication of equal value claims.[159] A strong case exists for amendment of the legislation so as to enhance the strategic role of the EOC, DRC and the CRE in the enforcement of the law, through, for example, action to follow up successful individual claims.[160] The House of Lords' acceptance of the right of the EOC to challenge the failure of domestic legislation to match up to the standards set by European Community law was a welcome recognition of the Commissions' wider role.[161] Other infrastructural reforms which could be considered here include a revived and extended role for contract compliance[162] and the introduction of a broader affirmative obligation upon employers to put in place mechanisms for ensuring pay equity.[163]

An important issue in the evolution in the principle of equal treatment, above all in the area of pay determination, is the scope permitted to employers' defences based on 'business necessity' or a similar criterion. Much of the recent case law of the ECJ and of the domestic courts has been concerned with

---

155 443 US 193 (1979).
156 SDA 1975, s 47; RRA 1976, s 37. See para 6.32 above.
157 See para 6.32 above.
158 See para 6.70 above.
159 See para 6.84 above.
160 See Mirza, 1995. The proposed Commission for Equality and Human Rights, which will replace the EOC, DRC and CRE, will have a range of powers to monitor the effectiveness of equality and human rights legislation, under the Equality Bill 2005 before Parliament at the time of writing.
161 *R v Secretary of State for Employment, ex p EOC* [1994] IRLR 176.
162 Bourn, 1995: p 47.
163 McColgan, 1994, 1997. See also the EOC's Code of Practice on Equal Pay, para 9 *et seq.*

issues arising from the tension between the economic, efficiency-related goals of the legislation and the aim of eradicating institutional discrimination. The 'economic goal' of regulating labour market competition is one of the two bases of Article 141 EC (ex 119) and of its subsequent development by the ECJ.[164] As the technique of identifying adverse impact in apparently sex-neutral practices has advanced, so has the range of arguments placed against it by way of justification; whereas these were at one time confined, in the context of equal pay, to the 'personal equation' of the applicant and his or her comparator, they have now broken the bounds set by the organisational limits of the business enterprise to embrace a variety of factors operating at the level of the labour market, including labour scarcity or simply, and more crudely, 'market forces'. One vital issue here is how far the courts will be prepared to take arguments concerning efficiency at their face value. In *R v Secretary of State for Employment, ex p EOC*[165] the House of Lords refused to do so, insisting that the respondent had not met the high burden of proof imposed on the respondent in adverse impact cases. But it is not at all difficult to find illustrations of a much more lax attitude on the part of the courts,[166] declining to scrutinise employer practices closely or to require employers to adopt the *least harmful* means of achieving a non-equality related goal, as the test of proportionality insists they should. This is not to suggest that factors of labour market efficiency should not play a role in this area. However, much more care needs to be taken in identifying precisely what aspect of, for example, allocative or productive efficiency is being pursued by a particular policy,[167] whether at the level of the state's own social policy or within individual enterprises. The courts would be right to insist on a high degree of precision in the economic and other evidence put forward in this type of claim. At a more abstract level, too, it seems doubtful that the courts have a clear conception at present of the kind of efficiency-related arguments which *should* be accepted, and which should not. This involves a closer consideration of what, precisely, 'economic efficiency' is meant to serve, of how far it can be thought of as a neutral or value-free principle in its own right, and when it should be 'trumped' by human-rights arguments. Finally, more effective progress would be made in this area if legislation placed employers under a clearer, affirmative responsibility to justify persistent inequalities and to take steps to remedy them. To this end, a range of 'procedural' solutions can be envisaged within a general framework of 'default' legal provisions which would apply in the absence of enterprise- or workplace-level implementation.[168] In this context, the duty placed on specified public authorities by the Race Relations (Amendment) Act 2000, to have regard to the need to eliminate unlawful racial discrimination and promote equality of opportunity between persons of different racial groups in the performance of their functions, is an important

164 Case 43/75 *Defrenne v Sabena* [1976] ECR 455.
165 [1994] IRLR 176.
166 In particular the decision of the House of Lords *in R v Secretary of State for Employment, ex p Seymour-Smith and Perez (No 2)* [2000] IRLR 263, and the discussion of this case by Barnard and Hepple, 2000. For an important analysis of the question of justification in equal pay cases, see Kilpatrick, 1994.
167 See Deakin and Wilkinson, 1994.
168 See, in the context of sex discrimination and equal pay, McColgan, 1997; EOC, *Sex Equality in the 21st Century* (2001); and the report of the EOC-sponsored Equal Pay Task Force, *Just Wages* (2001); and in the context of race discrimination, Monaghan, 2000; Hepple *et al*, 2000.

step forward and is likely to constitute a model for developments in other areas of discrimination.[169]

In all this it will also be important to appreciate the limits of what may legitimately be expected from the principle of equal treatment. Its potential to transform, even to destabilise long-standing and apparently secure practices of a discriminatory kind is evident from such judicial *causes célèbres* as *ex p EOC*[170] and *Barber*[171] (although the ECJ rapidly drew back from the full implications of pensions equality when faced with a vociferous campaign against its ruling in the latter case). There are other areas in which the principle of equal treatment has been bent beyond the point where it retains its conceptual integrity to achieve the goal of reducing disadvantage; pregnancy discrimination is one such example.[172] The ECJ's decision in *Stadt Lengerich v Helmig*,[173] declining to rule that a fringe benefit system favouring full-timers even raised an issue of unequal treatment, indicates the limits to how far the principle of equality may go in the area of part-time workers' rights. While a fuller notion of equality, based on the concept of group difference, is one way forward here, one may question how coherent arguments based on horizontal comparison can be made in this area. To persist with the notion of horizontal equality may even be to risk a large degree of levelling-down of the kind approved by the ECJ in its decision in *Smith v Avdel Systems Ltd.*[174] Another reason for questioning the usefulness of the equality principle in contexts such as parental rights is the use of the male norm as the basis for comparison; as a result, 'the traditional values are so deeply embedded in the concept of equality that it is difficult to prevent the continued use of the concept from reinforcing those values';[175] as a result, it may be argued that 'the traditional equality-difference conceptual framework is not capable of providing a satisfactory theoretical basis for legal intervention in respect of pregnancy and parenthood'.[176] It is significant, in the light of this comment, that the improvement in the employment protection rights of pregnant workers should have come about principally through the adoption and implementation of a European Community directive based not on the principle of equal treatment but instead on the protection of the working environment and of the individual worker's place within it.[177] Equally, the adoption of legislation aimed specifically at the protection of family time marks a step forward in a more even division of labour between the sexes.[178]

---

169 See O'Cinneide, 2001; Fredman, 2001. Note, in this regard, DDA 2005, s 3, inserting DDA 1995, s 49A (at the time of writing, not yet in force). See also the Equality Bill 2005 in relation to gender.

170 [1994] IRLR 176.

171 Case C-262/88 [1990] IRLR 240.

172 See para 6.98 above, for the conceptual difficulties stemming from the decision of the ECJ in Case 177/88 *Dekker v VJV-Centrum* [1991] IRLR 27.

173 Case C-399/92 [1995] IRLR 216; this decision looks increasingly isolated in the light of later judgments including Case C-285/02 *Elsner-Lakeberg v Land Nordrhein Westfalen* [2005] IRLR 209.

174 Case C-408/92 [1994] IRLR 602.

175 Fredman, 1994b: p 122.

176 Fredman, 1994b: p 121. For a general development of this argument, see Fredman, 1997.

177 Directive 92/85, discussed above, at para 6.98; see Honeyball, 2000.

178 See McColgan, 2000b; L Anderson, 2003.

CHAPTER 7

Collective organisation: trade unions and employers' associations

INTRODUCTION

7.1 We have described in earlier chapters the central role which collective bargaining has played as a source of norms in labour law in Britain. In this chapter we examine from a broader perspective the nature and functions of collective organisations in the employment context and the relationship between such organisations and the law. In doing so we provide a framework for the more detailed analysis of the substantive law which follows in chapters 8 to 10. We discuss the development of the law relating to industrial action in chapter 11.

This chapter begins by outlining the rationale for, and role of, collective organisation on the part of workers and employers respectively. We do not attempt to describe exhaustively here how these organisations have developed, the variety of structures which they may assume and the disparate range of functions which they may perform; these are areas upon which many library shelves can be filled. Our focus is to explain in basic terms the factors which stimulate the formation of such organisations and the ways in which they may attempt to influence decisions both in the workplace and beyond. We then discuss the various international standards relevant to this area. There follows an overview of the history of legal policy in this country towards collective organisation, with particular reference to the ideology which has shaped the current law. We then analyse some basic legal concepts in this area: the definition of a 'trade union', of an 'employers' association', and of trade union 'independence' and 'recognition', terms which are crucial in discussing the application of a series of statutory provisions dealt with in later chapters and which also embody some important assumptions about the legitimate functions of such organisations. We conclude the chapter by commenting briefly upon the influence which trade unions now exercise in contemporary employment relations and the challenges which they face in a changing labour market.

THE RATIONALE AND ROLE OF COLLECTIVE ORGANISATION

7.2 On the workers' side there are compelling reasons for collective action. In advanced industrial societies the employer almost always has greater economic and social power than any individual worker. Occasionally a worker may be in a stronger bargaining position if he or she possesses skills or experience which are much in demand although even then entry into a contract of employment may, as we explain in chapter 3, entail subordination to the commands of the employer. However, for workers in general to have any effective power in the employment relationship they must join together to further their demands on a collective basis; only then can they stand any chance of counterbalancing the power of the employer.[1]

The means by which workers' organisations have sought to exercise this function has varied over time and between countries. In analysing the development of British unions Turner's distinction between 'open' and 'closed' unions is a helpful one.[2] 'Closed' unions were those whose primary interest consisted of regulating the supply of labour to particular occupations and which maintained an exclusive claim to employment within those occupations. As a result these organisations had little interest in increasing their numerical strength; indeed their interest lay rather in the opposite direction. By contrast the larger 'open' unions were 'content to recruit all workers in those occupations whom the employers themselves engage[d]'. Being usually unable to bring pressure on employers through controlling labour supply they relied instead upon strength of numbers for their bargaining power.

7.3   Since the nineteenth century British trade unions have, in general, perceived their primary role as the improvement of their members' terms and conditions of employment through the mechanism of collective bargaining. As we have seen already this is not merely the functional equivalent of individual bargaining on a collective scale; rather it is more accurately described as a process of joint regulation which prescribes not only the terms upon which individual contracts should draw but may also extend to broader aspects of job regulation and the working environment, such as disciplinary and grievance procedures and training.[3] As such it is capable of serving as a conduit for wider democratic participation on the part of workers in the operation of the enterprise although clearly the extent to which it performs this function will depend upon a variety of different factors.

A further benefit of effective collective organisation is that it may assist workers to enforce their legal rights. The provision of statutory rights is sometimes seen as antipathetic to collective organisation which, it is argued, can be rendered otiose if workers can enforce their rights directly through the legal system or by complaint to an administrative agency. Kahn-Freund, for one, would have given short shrift to such an argument. Evidence relating to compliance with nineteenth-century legislation regulating deductions from workers' wages led him to conclude that:

> Where labour is weak ... Acts of Parliament, however well intentioned and well designed, can do something, but cannot do much to modify the power relation between labour and management. The law has important functions in labour relations but they are secondary if compared with the impact of the labour market ... and ... with the spontaneous creation of a social power on the workers' side to balance that of management. Even the most efficient inspectors can do but little if the workers dare not complain to them about infringements of the legislation they are seeking to enforce ...[4]

Although there is now statutory protection in some areas for workers who are discriminated against for attempting to enforce certain statutory rights[5] the

---

1   See P Davies and M Freedland, 1983: ch 1.
2   See H Turner, 1962: pp 241–242.
3   See generally Flanders, 1970.
4   P Davies and M Freedland, 1983: p 19
5   ERA 1996, s 104; see para 5.101 above. For the protection afforded by the anti-discrimination legislation see ch 6.

protection which the law can provide in this respect is ultimately limited and it seems likely that Kahn-Freund's argument is no less applicable today. Polls have shown that many workers join unions because of the access which this gives to legal representation.[6] Representation by an organisation which has the knowledge to recognise the potential of test cases is additionally beneficial in putting pressure on employers to comply with their legal obligations. It can also mean that cases are more likely to be brought which clarify the law in workers' interests; where, for example, it is necessary to test compliance with European Community obligations. Nevertheless, although the provision of this and other benefits to members, such as welfare and financial benefits, has been a traditional part of union activity it has generally been regarded as secondary to collective bargaining. This focus is, indeed, reflected in the statutory definition of a 'trade union' which requires such an organisation to have as among its principal purposes the regulation of relations between workers and employers.[7] This definition, which we explore in greater detail in para 7.20, has been interpreted to mean that the organisation must at least have sought recognition from an employer for the purposes of collective bargaining to constitute a 'trade union'.[8] Although other forms of representation, such as assistance in disciplinary and grievance proceedings,[9] are also important, collective bargaining remains fundamental to trade union purposes.

7.4 The commitment to collective bargaining has also been important in shaping unions' activities beyond the workplace. As we discussed in chapter 1, unions in this country, unlike some of their European counterparts, achieved industrial power before they achieved political power through the extension of the franchise, and reliance upon collective bargaining rather than legislation as the preferred method of securing the best possible terms and conditions of employment remained even after they obtained greater access to political influence. This is not to say that the union movement stayed wholly aloof from the political process; for any interest group it is essential to ensure that the legal and economic environment is hospitable to its goals and operation and that the views of its members are adequately represented in the political process by lobbying and other means. Indeed the TUC – the first permanent federation on a multi-union basis – was formed in 1868 as an annual meeting of unions to discuss matters of common interest, with a 'parliamentary committee' which directed union campaigns between such meetings to influence the political parties to support pro-union legislation. Moreover, the Labour Party in its inception was a product of the trade union movement; a number of TUC-affiliates combined with the Marxist Social-Democratic Federation, the Independent Labour Party and the Fabian Society to establish a Labour Representation Committee from which emerged the modern Labour Party. It is notable, however, that it was the landmark case of *Taff Vale Rly Co v ASRS*,[10] where the House of Lords decided that trade unions, although not corporate bodies, could be sued for the torts of

---

6   Mr John Monks, General Secretary TUC, Evidence to the House of Commons Employment Committee, Session 1993–1994, Third Report, The Future of Trade Unions, Volume II, p 20, Q 31.
7   TULRCA 1992, s 1(a).
8   See *Midland Cold Storage Ltd v Turner* [1972] ICR 230, NIRC, discussed at para 7.20 below.
9   This may become more significant in the light of the statutory right to be accompanied introduced by ERelA 1999, ss 10–15; see further para 5.132 *et seq*.
10 [1901] AC 426.

their officials,[11] which inspired the TUC to participate in this project; once unions had obtained as much as they thought possible in the Trade Disputes Act 1906 they returned to industrial activity.[12] The law has explicitly recognised the legitimacy of trade unions pursuing political objects since the Trade Union Act 1913 although subject to approval of the establishment of a separate political fund for expenditure on such objects from which members must be able to claim exemption from contributing.[13] This provision thus assumes and incorporates a distinction between the industrial and the political realms. Although it may be argued that this is an impossible line to draw, particularly at times when legislation in the labour field is central to the programmes of the major political parties, it nevertheless remained undisturbed even during periods when the Labour Party was in power and has continued to this day.

7.5   As well as being affiliated to a political party or acting as a pressure group trade unions may also be more closely integrated into the political process. Again the extent to which this occurs varies widely between countries and within individual countries at particular times. In France, Belgium, the Netherlands, Portugal and Luxembourg, for example, there has been an obligation to consult national tripartite or bipartite bodies before new labour legislation is introduced.[14] In a number of European countries the concept of unions and employers' organisations as 'social partners' is much more developed than in Britain, a concept which, as we saw in chapter 2, has been reflected in European Community law. In some states tripartite agreements between unions, employers and government have been concluded to attempt to reconcile collective bargaining with the government's economic objectives, agreements which may also embrace aims such as increasing employment, combating price rises and helping the low-paid.[15] In addition, tripartite bargaining may be used as a basis for introducing labour market reforms particularly in the areas of flexibility of working time and new technology.[16] In this country the role of unions has been subject to considerable variation. During the two World Wars trade union leaders were appointed to ministerial office in order to ensure co-operation of the labour movement in promoting the war effort. During the 1945–1951, 1964–1970 and 1974–1979 Labour Governments unions were brought into the political process through attempts to constitute arrangements whereby they would exercise restraint in pursuing pay demands in return for legislative and administrative policies which were perceived to further the interests of union members. The legislation of the 'Social Contract' period of the 1974–1979 Labour Government was a striking illustration of this process. Even under Conservative governments before 1979 trade unions exercised a measure of influence, such as participation in the National Economic Development Council, a (tripartite) body established in 1962 with policy functions in relation to economic planning and in the organisation of industrial training.[17] The NEDC was abolished in 1992 and, indeed, from 1979 until 1997 unions were progressively marginalised in relation

11   Between 1906 and 1982 trade unions could not, with specified exceptions, be sued in tort. The Employment Act 1982 removed this immunity.
12   Hepple, 1986a: p 25.
13   See further para 10.18 *et seq.*
14   Deakin *et al*, 1992: p 21.
15   Bamber and Sheldon, 2004: paras 89–92.
16   Deakin *et al*, 1992: p 21.
17   See P Davies and M Freedland, 1993: pp 333–345 for the activities of the Heath Conservative Government in this area and see paras 1.20 and 1.21 above.

to the political process, an element in the broader strategy of undermining their role as socially legitimate organisations. The election of a Labour Government in 1997 produced a more hospitable environment, with a greater emphasis on 'social partnership' and enhanced institutionalised participation in specific areas, such as training.[18] However, the government was keen from the outset to avoid the appearance that the union movement would enjoy any favoured status; 'indeed, one commentator has observed that 'the prime minister appeared to give more of his time to wooing big business tycoons like Rupert Murdoch of News International' than to union leaders.[19]

In addition to their marginalisation by government during the 1979–1997 Conservative administration, the collective bargaining role of unions was also subject to severe challenge and trade unions were left fighting a difficult struggle to maintain their role as bargaining partners and to retain their membership. We shall see in para 7.30 and later chapters the variety of attempts which they made to counteract these trends by, *inter alia*, becoming publicly more open to other forms of representative structures, such as consultative bodies, and broadening the range of services which they offer their members. There have been signs of a reduction in the rate of decline in union membership in recent years,[20] and factors such as enhanced (but complex) employment protection legislation, the new statutory disciplinary and grievance procedures, and the right for individuals to be accompanied by a union representative during disciplinary and grievance hearings, as well as the statutory recognition and information and consultation procedures, may encourage more workers to join.[21] Moreover, the concept of 'social dialogue' at European level has the potential to offer the union movement a broader participative function in the political process. The range of roles that unions may play in the rapidly changing political and economic environment should not disguise the quintessential rationale for the existence of trade unions, however: in Kahn-Freund's ringing phrase, on the side of labour the (only) power is collective power.[22]

7.6   On the employers' side the rationale for collective organisation is different from that of workers. Although employers do form associations both at sectoral and national multi-industry level these are not the functional equivalent of trade unions in that the individual employer is already a 'collective power' in being a holder of capital. In Europe the reasons historically which led to associations being formed vary from the desire to oppose the labour movement (Denmark and Germany) to exerting an influence upon legislators (the Netherlands and Italy).[23] In Britain 'it was the realisation by employers in industries such as building, engineering and printing that they could be defeated one by one by the craft unions that led them to associate, as in the Engineering Employers' Federation (1897)'.[24] After the First World War employers' associations became

---

18   See W Brown, 2000, who notes the importance for the legitimacy of recommendations made by the Low Pay Commission that three of its members were, in practice, from union backgrounds: see further para 4.43.

19   Taylor, 2000: p 265. See also J Waddington, 2003a.

20   See para 7.30.

21   Aggressive anti-union tactics by employers may also be significant, however, together with a range of other variables: see generally Charlwood 2003, 2004a; Freeman and Diamond, 2003.

22   P Davies and M Freedland, 1983: p 17.

23   A Jacobs, 1986: pp 222–223.

24   A Jacobs, 1986: p 223.

more significant negotiators in collective bargaining. In industries where firms were small the knowledge and experience of the association could be particularly advantageous. Since the Second World War the significance of employers' associations in that area has declined in tandem with the decline in sectoral bargaining, a trend which accelerated further during the 1980s.[25] Their other major traditional role, as a source of information and advice to employers, has also diminished,[26] although this varies between sectors.[27] The main national employers' organisation, the Confederation of British Industry, was formed in 1965 by the merger of three earlier bodies; its membership is largely drawn from the manufacturing sector. As in the case of unions the 'social dialogue' has afforded the CBI the opportunity of a wider role.

INTERNATIONAL STANDARDS RELATING TO COLLECTIVE ORGANISATION

Overview

7.7   Freedom of association is regarded as a fundamental right under international human rights conventions. An important element of this right is the freedom of workers to associate in order to further and defend their interests.[28] The fundamental importance of freedom of association in this context is emphasised by its presence in treaties dealing both with civil and political rights, on the one hand, and economic, social and cultural rights on the other. The Universal Declaration of Human Rights, adopted by the United Nations General Assembly in 1948, proclaims that '[e]veryone has the right to form and to join trade unions for the protection of his interests', a right which was given effect in international law by the International Covenant on Economic, Social and Cultural Rights (ICESCR) and the International Covenant on Civil and Political Rights (ICCPR) of 1966.[29] Freedom of association has been a fundamental principle of the ILO since its inception in 1919; the ingredients of the freedom are spelt out in a number of instruments, the most important being the Freedom of Association and the Right to Organise Convention 1948 (No 87) and the Right to Organise and Collective Bargaining Convention 1949 (No 98).[30] However, it is assumed that the very fact of membership of the ILO carries with

25   Roderick Martin, 1992: p 83. In contrast to the demise of multi-employer bargaining over pay in Britain, this structure continues to prevail in many other Western European countries: W Brown *et al*, 2003: p 209. The *Annual Report of the Certification Officer for 2003–2004* gives returns for 172 employers' associations: para 4.17, App 6. However, in many sectors membership fails to reach 50% of the eligible companies: P Edwards *et al*, 1998: p 19; see also Millward *et al*, 2000: p 75.
26   Millward *et al*, 2000: pp 73, 75.
27   The Engineering Employers' Federation, for example, claims a membership of 6,000 manufacturing, engineering and technology-based businesses: see www.eef.org.uk.
28   The freedom of employers to associate is also affirmed in ILO Conventions and the European Social Charter and is implicit in general guarantees.
29   On the background to the right in the ICESCR, see Craven, 1998.
30   Other ILO Conventions which seek to ensure respect for the principles of freedom of association are: Right of Association (Agriculture) 1921 (No 11); Right of Association (Non-Metropolitan Territories) 1947 (No 84); Workers' Representatives, 1971 (No 135); Rural Workers' Organisations 1975 (No 141); Labour Relations (Public Service) 1978 (No 151); Collective Bargaining 1981 (No 154); and Private Employment Agencies 1997 (No 181). On ILO standards in this area see generally Creighton, 2004a.

it a constitutional obligation to respect these principles.[31] The right is also expressed in treaties agreed at a regional level including the European Convention on Human Rights (ECHR) and the European Social Charter (ESC), and, most recently, the Charter of Fundamental Rights of the European Union.[32] In addition, as we discuss in para 7.11, there is authority for its recognition as a 'fundamental right' within the EC legal order, albeit that it is excluded from the Social Policy provisions of the current EC Treaty.[33]

There is, therefore, wide agreement upon the importance of the right of workers to associate both as the hallmark of a democratic society and more specifically in their role as economic actors. There is less consensus, however, about the scope of this right in practice, beyond the basic right to form and to join trade unions.[34] Does it, for example, include the right to form or join a union of one's choice regardless of the impact upon industrial relations? Does it include the right not to join a union? Does it include a right to organise? Does it include a right for trade unions to engage in collective bargaining? Does it imply a right to strike? What level of interference, if any, by the state in the affairs of unions should be permitted?

7.8 The most detailed elaboration is contained in the relevant ILO Conventions, supplemented by the jurisprudence of the Governing Body's Committee on Freedom of Association[35] and reports of the Committee of Experts on the Application of Conventions and Recommendations.[36] Convention No 87 provides that all workers 'without distinction whatsoever, shall have the right to establish and, subject to the rules of the organisation concerned, to join organisations of their own choosing without previous authorisation'.[37] Such organisations also have the right to establish and join federations and confederations and to affiliate with international organisations of workers.[38] In addition there are guarantees relating to the free functioning of organisations.[39] Member States undertake to take 'all necessary and appropriate measures' to ensure that workers may exercise freely the right to organise, and the law of the land shall not impair guarantees in the Convention.[40] Convention No 98 provides that workers should enjoy adequate protection against acts of anti-union discrimination in respect of their employment and their organisations should enjoy adequate protection against interference by other organisations and by employers in their establishment, functioning and administration.[41] The Convention also states that measures appropriate to national conditions should be taken, where necessary, to encourage

---

31 See now the *ILO Declaration on Fundamental Principles and Rights at Work and its Follow-Up*, ILO, 1998, and on the special machinery to deal with alleged failures of compliance in this area see para 2.45 above.

32 See further para 2.43 for the status of the Charter. For further regional instruments in other areas of the world see Creighton, 2004a: para 11.

33 Art 137(6) EC.

34 See generally Wedderburn 1987b; Christian and Ewing, 1988; Leader, 1992; Betten, 1993; Bercusson 2000: pp 416–420; Novitz, 2003. See also G Morris, 1994a, from which much of the discussion which follows is taken.

35 The key features of this jurisprudence are digested in ILO, 1996.

36 For a general survey of reports to the date of publication, see ILO, 1983.

37 Art 2.

38 Art 5.

39 Art 3.

40 Arts 11 and 8(2). See generally Gernigon *et al*, 2000.

41 Art 1 and 2. Again there is an obligation to establish 'machinery appropriate to national conditions', where necessary, to ensure respect for the right to organise: Art 3.

and promote collective bargaining machinery.[42] There is no express reference in either of these Conventions to the right to strike. However, ILO supervisory bodies have derived this right from them on the basis that it is one of the essential and legitimate means by which workers and their organisations may promote and defend their economic and social interests and is therefore integral to the free exercise of the rights they guarantee (with the proviso that in the case of public officials recognition of the freedom to associate does not necessarily imply the right to strike).[43] Although less detailed than the ILO Conventions the ICESCR also obliges signatory states to ensure the right of everyone to join the union of their choice, subject to the union's rules; the right of unions to join federations, confederations and international union organisations; and the right of unions to function freely.[44] In addition it explicitly guarantees the right to strike, although subject to the proviso that 'it is exercised in conformity with the laws of the particular country'.[45]

7.9   The ICCPR and ECHR both articulate trade union freedom as a manifestation of a broader freedom to associate. Article 11 of the ECHR provides that 'Everyone ... has the right to freedom of association with others, including the right to form and to join trade unions for the protection of his interests'. The jurisprudence relating to the scope of this right is relatively sparse and undeveloped by comparison with that relating to ILO Conventions, the ICESCR and the ESC.[46] However, in such case law as there is the European Court of Human Rights (ECtHR) has, until recently, adopted a narrow interpretation of this right which has failed to take account of its function in the employment context.[47] Thus it has held that the Article does not give union members a right that their union should be able to engage in collective bargaining nor even that it should be consulted by their employer. The Court denied that this rendered otiose the words 'for the protection of his interests' in Article 11. The words showed that:

> ... the Convention safeguards freedom to protect the occupational interests of trade union members by trade union action, the conduct and development of which the Contracting States must both permit and make possible ... It follows that the members of a trade union have a right, in order to protect their interests, that the trade union should be heard. [However the article] leaves each State a free choice of the means to be used towards this end. While consultation is one of these means, there are others. What the Convention

---

42   Art 4. See also Convention 154 Concerning the Promotion of Collective Bargaining (1981) (not ratified by the UK) and Recommendations 92 on Voluntary Conciliation and Arbitration (1951), 130 on Examination of Grievances (1967) and 163 on Collective Bargaining (1981).

43   ILO, 1996: paras 531 *et seq*. See also Hodges-Aeberhard and Odero de Dios, 1987; Ben-Israel, 1988; Gernigon *et al*, 1998; Novitz, 2003: ch 8. For discussion of the permissible restrictions on this right, and of the scope of the right to strike under other international treaties, see paras 11.3 and 11.4 below.

44   Art 8. See Craven 1998: ch 7.

45   Art 8(1)(d).

46   For an overview, see Novitz, 2003: pp 224 *et seq*. We discuss the implications of specific aspects of this jurisprudence in greater detail at appropriate points in the text.

47   See also *Collymore v A-G of Trinidad and Tobago* [1970] AC 538, where the Privy Council held that constitutional protection of freedom of association does not extend to collective bargaining and the right to strike, and case law on the application of the Canadian Charter of Rights and Freedoms 1982. Cf the discussion by Hendy and Walton, 1997.

requires is that under national law trade unions should be enabled, in conditions not at variance with Article 11, to strive for the protection of their members' interests.[48]

The Court has also indicated that:

> In view of the sensitive character of the social and political issues involved in achieving a proper balance between the competing interests and, in particular, in assessing the appropriateness of State intervention to restrict union action aimed at extending a system of collective bargaining, and the wide degree of divergence between the domestic systems in the particular area under consideration, the Contracting States should enjoy a wide margin of appreciation in the choice of the means to be employed.[49]

In its 2002 decision in *Wilson and NUJ v UK; Palmer, Wyeth and RMT v UK* and *Doolan v UK*,[50] however, the Court showed greater appreciation of the rationale of freedom of association in the context of employment. In these cases the employers had each refused a pay rise to employees who refused to transfer to personal contracts in place of collectively agreed terms and conditions of employment. These contracts also required those who signed them to forgo the entitlement to be represented by a union in some or all of their dealings with the employer. While continuing to state that collective bargaining was 'not indispensable for the effective enjoyment of trade union freedom' the Court affirmed that '[t]he union and its members must, however, be free, in one way or another, to seek to persuade the employer to listen to what it has to say on behalf of its members'.[51] Moreover,

> ... it is of the essence of the right to join a trade union for the protection of their interests that employees should be free to instruct or permit the union to make representations to their employer or to take action in support of their interests on their behalf. If workers are prevented from so doing, their freedom to belong to a trade union, for the protection of their interests, becomes illusory. It is the role of the State to ensure that trade union members are not prevented or restrained from using their union to represent them in attempts to regulate their relations with their employers.[52]

Here, UK law had permitted employers to treat less favourably employees who were not prepared to renounce a freedom that was an essential feature of union membership, so allowing an employer 'effectively to undermine or frustrate a trade union's ability to strive for the protection of its members' interests'.[53] By permitting employers to use financial incentives to induce employees to surrender important union rights, the State had failed in its positive obligation to secure the enjoyment of the rights under Article 11 of the Convention, a violation as regards both the applicant unions and the individual applicants.[54]

---

48 *National Union of Belgian Police v Belgium* judgment of 27 October 1975, (1979–80) 1 EHRR 578 at para 39; *Swedish Engine Drivers Union v Sweden* judgment of 6 February 1976, (1979–80) 1 EHRR 617, para 40.
49 *Gustafsson v Sweden* judgment of 28 March 1996, (1996) 22 EHRR 409, para 45. In this case (noted Novitz, 1997) the Court affirmed that the Convention did not guarantee a right not to enter a collective agreement.
50 Judgment of 2 July 2002, [2002] IRLR 568.
51 Para 44.
52 Para 46.
53 Para 48.
54 Para 48.

This decision has been seen as representing 'a significant break with the past'.[55] Opinions differ as to its implications.[56] However it seems that, at the very least, as well as requiring the State to secure the right of individuals not to be restrained from using their union to represent them in their relations with their employer, it also requires the State positively to ensure that there is an available mechanism by which a union can be 'heard' in the private, as well as the public, sector, although the choice of mechanism remains with the State and there remains, as 'yet',[57] no specific right to recognition or consultation.[58]

The Court has, to date, taken a similarly cautious approach in relation to the right to strike. Unlike the supervisory organs of the ILO, it has not been prepared to derive the right from the general principle of freedom of association; while it is 'one of the most important' of the means by which the occupational interests of trade union members may be protected by trade union action, 'there are others'.[59] However in *UNISON v UK*, where it was argued that the right to strike, and thereby freedom of association, was unjustifiably restricted under UK law, the Court was prepared to acknowledge that the strike in question concerned 'the occupational interests of the applicant's members' and therefore fell within the scope of Article 11, although it concluded that the prohibition on the strike could be justified under Article 11(2) on the grounds that it protected the rights of the employer, including its ability to contract with other bodies.[60] As Ewing remarks, this decision accords the right to strike ' a curious twilight status'; although not formally protected, the Court regarded restrictions on the right as falling within Article 11(1).[61] The ESC, the economic and social counterpart to the ECHR, protects trade union rights more extensively, and expressly includes, in Article 6, obligations to promote joint consultation between workers and employers and, where necessary and appropriate, collective bargaining machinery and the right to strike.[62] Ironically, however, because the ESC allows contracting states some discretion as to the articles they accept, it has been invoked

---

55 Ewing, 2003: p 5.
56 See Ewing, 2003; cf. *Review of the Employment Relations Act 1999: Government Response*, DTI, 2003, ch 3. See also paras 8.17 *et seq* below.
57 The term interestingly, used by the ECtHR in *Wilson* and *Palmer* above, note 50, at para 44.
58 This argument would seem to apply even if there is a channel for receiving the views of other unions; in *Swedish Engine Drivers Union v Sweden* judgment of 6 February 1976, (1979–80) 1 EHRR 617 it was material that the applicant union was still able to make representations to the government for the protection of its members' interests. A requirement to ensure that relevant organisations can be 'heard' does not entail according them *equal* status as negotiating or consultative partners, and differences in treatment are unlikely to violate Arts 11 and 14 together provided that a legitimate aim, such as the desire to avoid a large number of such partners, can be demonstrated and the action is proportionate to that aim: *Swedish Engine Drivers*, paras 44–48. See also *National Union of Belgian Police v Belgium* judgment of 27 October 1975, (1979–80) 1 EHRR 578, paras 43–49 and *Schettini v Italy* admissibility decision of 9 November 2000.
59 *Schmidt and Dahlstrom v Sweden* judgment of 6 February 1976, (1979–80) 1 EHRR 632 at para 36. See also *X v Germany* Application No 10365/83,(1985) 7 EHRR 461. Ben-Israel, 1988: pp 28–29, however, considers that the Court provided 'powerful support' for the argument that freedom to strike is essential to freedom of association. Hendy, 1998, argues that if a union has no other means of conveying its members' interests a right to strike could be implied, an argument that may carry greater weight in the light of the ECtHR decision in *Wilson* and *Palmer*.
60 Admissibility decision of 10 January 2002, [2002] IRLR 497. See further para 11.26 for discussion of this case.
61 Ewing, 2003: p 18.
62 A revised ESC, which accords additional rights in the field of employment, was open for signature in May 1996: see para 2.47. The UK signed the revised Charter in November 1997, but at the time of writing has not ratified it. Arts 5 and 6, and the terms of Art 31, remain the same in both versions of the Charter; Art 31 is Art G in the new Charter.

by the ECtHR to bolster a narrow interpretation of Article 11. Thus the Court took the view that, given that a state may not have accepted Article 6 of the ESC, to conclude that a right to joint consultation derived directly from Article 11 would 'amount to admitting that the 1961 Charter took a retrograde step in this direction'.[63] The Court's restrictive approach towards collective rights is of particular concern in the light of the Human Rights Act 1998; although there will be little to be lost in raising arguments derived from ILO and other jurisprudence before UK courts it is difficult to predict with confidence that they will be regarded as heavily persuasive. This may matter less if the right to strike is accepted as a fundamental right in EC law; as we discuss in para 7.11, there is some authority in favour of this development. However, at the time of writing the content of any such putative right remains unclear.

7.10 The discrepancies between the texts of these various international treaties are also disturbing at a broader level, especially in the light of the different procedures for supervising compliance with them which we outlined in chapter 2. We explore the implications of these discrepancies in greater detail in specific contexts. In our present discussion we confine ourselves to one dramatic example which highlights the dangers of these disparities: the permissible exceptions to the freedom to associate. All the treaties which guarantee the right exempt specific groups from its application, leaving their position to be regulated entirely by national law; some also allow restrictions to meet specified objectives.[64] For most treaties the armed forces and the police are the only categories specifically exempted; however, the ECHR and the ICESCR also allow 'lawful restrictions' on the exercise of this right by 'members ... of the administration of the state'. In 1984 the UK Conservative Government peremptorily banned membership of national civil service unions by workers at Government Communications Headquarters (GCHQ), which safeguards the security of the UK's military and official communications and provides signals intelligence for the government.[65] This ban was found to breach ILO principles of freedom of association.[66] However a complaint that it infringed Article 11 of the ECHR was ruled inadmissible by the (now defunct) European Commission on Human Rights on the ground that workers at GCHQ were 'members ... of the administration of the state'.[67] This

63   *Belgian Police v Belgium*, above, note 58, para 38.
64   For a detailed examination of the scope of these exemptions, see G Morris, 1994a. In relation to restrictions to meet specified objectives the ECHR, for example, provides that 'No restrictions shall be placed on the exercise of these rights other than such as are prescribed by law and are necessary in a democratic society in the interests of national security or public safety, for the prevention of disorder or crime, for the protection of health or morals or for the protection of the rights and freedoms of others'. (Article 11(2).)
65   See G Morris, 1985b for the background to this ban.
66   Freedom of Association Committee, Case 1261, whose recommendation was adopted by the governing body of the ILO in June 1984. The ILO regularly and repeatedly exhorted the UK government to reach an agreement with the unions which would reconcile the government's wish for continuity of operations with the application of freedom of association principles and welcomed the decision by the Labour Government to do this: see the Provisional Record of the International Labour Conference, Eighty-Fifth Session, Geneva, 1997, Report of the Committee on the Application of Standards, 19/100–19/101.
67   *CCSU v UK* Application No 11603/85 (1987) 10 EHRR 269. The Commission also rejected the applicants' argument that 'restrictions' in Art 11(2) did not extend to a complete ban. See further Fredman and Morris, 1988. Note that the ECtHR has since held that the concept of members of the administration of the state should be interpreted 'narrowly, in the light of the post held by the official concerned': *Vogt v Germany* judgment of 26 September 1995, (1996) 21 EHRR 205, para 67; *Grande Oriente D'Italia di Palazzo Giustiniani v Italy* judgment of 2 August 2001, para 31.

latter finding was invoked by the Conservative Government to add weight to its refusal to accept the finding by the ILO, the conclusions of whose supervisory bodies it found easier, across a range of contexts, to ignore than those of the ECHR.[68] The differential treatment of this case under different treaties[69] substantiates the broader argument that adjudication of the scope of labour rights, at least in the collective realm, should be vested exclusively in the ILO whose tripartite and specialist nature and depth of experience gives it the greatest claim to legitimacy in this area.

Freedom of Association in EC Law and EC Competition Law

7.11   As we indicated in para 7.7 above, the Social Policy provisions of the EC Treaty expressly exclude the right of association and the right to strike.[70] However, despite this barrier to future legislation on these matters, there is authority in ECJ jurisprudence which supports their recognition as 'fundamental rights' within Community law.[71] As we saw in para 2.43, the Treaty on European Union explicitly bound the EU to respect as general principles of Community law fundamental rights as guaranteed by the ECHR, and as they result from the constitutional traditions common to the Member States.[72] However, even before this provision was introduced, the ECJ had held that fundamental rights were integral to Community law,[73] so obliging both Community institutions and Member States when acting in the field of Community law to respect them. The status of freedom of association as a fundamental right was affirmed by the ECJ in *Bosman*.[74] Notably, however, the ECJ has not felt bound to follow the restrictive interpretation of the right to join trade unions adopted by the European Court of Human Rights in relation to Article 11 of the ECHR, which we describe in para 7.9 above. Rather, the ECJ has affirmed, in the context of considering the ambit of the right to union membership enshrined in EU Staff Regulations, that this right entails that staff associations are 'free to do anything lawful to protect the interests of their members as employees',[75] and that Community institutions may not penalise their staff from participating in union activities.[76] In *Albany* Advocate General Jacobs considered, on the basis of these authorities, that the collective right of workers to take action, in addition to the right to form and join a union, had thereby been confirmed as

---

68   See Report of the ILO Committee of Experts on the Application of Conventions and Recommendations, Report III (Part 4A), 1992: pp 242–243 and see generally Creighton, 1994; Ewing, 1994a and Mills, 1997.

69   See further G Morris, 1994a. The ban on union membership at GCHQ was also found not to infringe the ESC (see ESC Committee of Independent Experts Conclusions X-1 (1989), 80) although the reasons for this were not spelt out.

70   Art 137(6) EC.

71   See Novitz, 2003: ch 10.

72   Art 6(2) EU.

73   Case 11/70 *Internationale Handelsgesellschaft mbH v Einfuhr und Vorratsstelle fur Getreide und Futtermitte* [1970] ECR 1125, 1134; Case 4/73 *Nold v Commission* [1974] ECR 491, para 13.

74   Case C-415/93 *Union Royale Belge des Societes de Football Association ASBL v Jean-Marc Bosman* [1995] ECR I-4921, paras 79 and 80.

75   Case 175/73 *Union Syndicale, Massa and Kortner v Commission* [1974] ECR 917, para 14.

76   Joined Cases C-193/87 and C-194/87 *Maurissen and European Public Service Union v Court of Auditors of the European Communities* [1990] ECR I-95, paras 11–16 and 21.

a fundamental right in EC law.[77] Further support for the right to strike being accorded such a status is given by Council Regulation 2679/98, which, in establishing an intervention mechanism to safeguard free trade in the single market, affirmed that the Regulation 'may not be interpreted as affecting in any way the exercise of fundamental rights as recognised in Member States, *including the right or freedom to strike*' (our italics).[78] The recognition of the right (or freedom) to strike as fundamental is highly significant, although it leaves unresolved issues as to its proper scope,[79] which we discuss in para 11.4.

In *Albany*, Advocate General Jacobs considered whether collective bargaining could be considered a fundamental right.[80] He concluded that it could not, despite the emphasis placed upon the concept of 'social dialogue' and collective agreements within the Community legal order. In his view, national legal systems and international instruments did not sufficiently converge in recognising such a right: the guarantee of the right to bargain collectively in Article 6 of the European Social Charter did not accord it fundamental status, given that acceptance of Article 6 was optional on the part of signatory states;[81] ILO Convention 98 merely imposed an obligation to 'encourage and promote' collective bargaining, and no such right could be derived from Article 11 of the ECHR. He also opined that the collective bargaining process, like any other negotiation between economic actors, was sufficiently protected by the general principle of freedom of contract, so obviating the need for more specific protection.[82] In so reasoning, Advocate General Jacobs overlooked the fact that, as we have emphasised in earlier chapters, collective bargaining is not merely the functional equivalent of individual negotiation.

The issue of the status of collective bargaining arose in *Albany* because the ECJ was required to consider for the first time the crucial question of the relationship between collective agreements and social policy measures, on the one hand, and EC competition law on the other. Article 81 EC (formerly Article 85) prohibits agreements between undertakings, decisions by associations of undertakings and concerted practices which may affect trade between Member States and which have as their object or effect the prevention, restriction or distortion of competition within the common market, and renders such agreements void. In *Albany*, the Court was required to consider whether a sector-level collective agreement establishing a pension fund, which had been given compulsory legal effect, was contrary to Article 81. Advocate General Jacobs rejected the argument of the pension funds that social policy was outside the ambit of the competition rules altogether; there was no provision authorising

---

77   Case C-67/96 *Albany International BV v Stichting Bedrijfspensioenfonds Textielindustrie* Opinion of 28 January 1999, [1999] ECR I-5751, para 139.

78   Art 2.

79   Note, however, that Advocate General Jacobs' Opinion suggests that any impairment of the substance of the right to strike, even if imposed in the 'public interest', might be unlawful: see paras 133, 162. By contrast, the judgment of the ECtHR in *UNISON v United Kingdom* [2002] IRLR 497 (see para 7.9 above) would allow a wide-ranging derogation from the right to strike in order to protect the 'rights of others' including the right of the employer to contract freely with third parties.

80   For discussion of *Albany*, see Barnard and Deakin, 2000; Barnard, 2000: pp 554–555 and 567–72; Vousden, 2000; Evju, 2001b. For a comparison between the *Albany* test and 'EFTA Guidelines', see Johansen, 2004.

81   Advocate General Jacobs also, controversially, classified the rights in the ESC as mere 'policy goals', given that they were not 'enforceable rights': Opinion, para 146.

82   Opinion, paras 131–161.

such exemption in the Treaty.[83] He also rejected the Commission's view that collective agreements should be excluded; even if, contrary to his view, collective bargaining was a fundamental right, this would not suffice to shield it from competition law.[84] However, he recognised that there were provisions of the Treaty and the then Agreement on Social Policy (now incorporated in the Social Policy provisions of the Treaty) that encouraged collective bargaining, and which thereby assumed that collective agreements were in principle lawful. On this basis, he proposed that a collective agreement should have immunity from review under competition rules if it complied with three conditions: first, it had been made 'within the formal framework of collective bargaining between both sides of industry'; second, it was made 'in good faith', and third, it dealt with 'core subjects of collective bargaining such as wages and working conditions which do not directly affect third markets and third parties'.[85] The third of these conditions was particularly restrictive, and would have opened up many multi-employer agreements to the review of competition policy authorities.[86] By contrast, the Court, which emphasised the general social policy objectives of the Treaty[87] in addition to the provisions encouraging social dialogue, adopted a much broader view of the exemption. It affirmed that it was

> ....[b]eyond question that certain restrictions of competition are inherent in collective agreements between organisations representing employers and workers. However, the social policy objectives pursued by such agreements would be seriously undermined if management and labour were subject to ... [Article 81 EC] ... when seeking jointly to adopt measures to improve conditions of work and employment. It therefore follows from an interpretation of the provisions of the Treaty as a whole which is both effective and consistent that agreements concluded in the context of collective negotiations between management and labour in pursuit of such objectives must, by virtue of their nature and purpose, be regarded as falling outside the scope of ... [Article 81][88]

This test, which focuses upon the aims the social partners are pursuing in negotiations, accords much greater respect to the autonomy of the social partners than the criteria propounded by the Advocate General.[89] Nevertheless it is not free from difficulty. Collective bargaining may take place on a range of matters whose relationship with the improvement of conditions of work and employment may be tangential, such as those relating to family life, for example.[90] It remains to be seen whether *Albany* will mark the beginning of a tide of litigation relating to the application of the boundary it establishes, but there seems much to be said in favour of amending the Treaty specifically to exclude social policy measures from the application of competition rules.

---

83   Opinion, paras 120–130. Art 81(3) allows the provisions of Art 81(1) to be declared inapplicable in specified circumstances, but none relate to social policy objectives.
84   Opinion, para 163.
85   Opinion, paras 165–194.
86   Barnard and Deakin, 2000: p 335.
87   Now Arts 2 and 3(1)(j) EC.
88   [1999] ECR I-5751, paras 59 and 60.
89   See also Case C-222/98 *Van der Woude v Stichting Breatrixoord* [2000] ECR I-7111, where the Advocate General considered that the scope of the exception from Art 85 is not 'limited to matters that the parties to the agreement are capable of carrying out themselves'. The Court did not expound on this view. See generally Evju, 2001b.
90   See further Vousden, 2000.

LEGAL POLICY RELATING TO COLLECTIVE ORGANISATION[91]

7.12 Legal policy relating to collective organisation in this country has passed through a series of radical changes. In common with the rest of Western Europe, the initial response to the growth of trade unionism was to attempt to suppress it by means of the criminal law.[92] As we saw in chapter 1, during the eighteenth century a number of Acts of Parliament forbade combinations in specific trades and places (clothing and London respectively in particular)[93] and combining workers could also be prosecuted for conspiracy at common law. At the turn of the century a new and more comprehensive statutory offence was created by the famous Combination Acts of 1799 and 1800 which made all combinations of workmen unlawful.[94] These Acts applied also to employers who combined for specified purposes but there appears to be no record of employers being convicted under them, possibly because 'the justices [who heard proceedings] were from the employers' class and would likely be their close neighbours or personal acquaintances'.[95] In practice the Acts were enforced only infrequently even against unions, perhaps because there was no shortage of other legal weapons available, including the Master and Servant Acts which made it a criminal offence to break a contract of employment.

In 1824/25 Britain became the first country in Western Europe to remove criminal sanctions from trade unions when the Combination Acts and other legislation forbidding combinations were repealed. Interestingly the leading campaigner for their repeal, Francis Place, was not a champion of trade union organisation; rather he believed that recruits were attracted to joining associations because of their illegal status and that once the prohibitions were repealed they would wither away. This did not happen; indeed, the newly-legalised organisations[96] demanded higher wages, and furthered these demands by strikes. This led to amending legislation in 1825 which modified the 1824 Act in two important ways. First, whilst confirming the repeal of the previous statutory restrictions, it excluded the application of common law conspiracy only for combinations (both of workmen and, *mutatis mutandis*, of employers) concerned with wages, prices and hours of work. Secondly, it severely restricted the freedom to strike by creating criminal offences involving vague and indeterminate terms such as violence to the person or property, intimidation and molestation.

The repeal of the statutory prohibitions on combinations, whilst removing the fear of prosecution, did not accord any specific legal status to workers' organisations and their position was, in fact, problematic. As unincorporated associations they were prey to officials embezzling their funds who, because the

---

91 The account which follows is intended merely to highlight in broad terms the strategies which have lain behind the development of the law and to provide a backcloth for the more detailed analysis of the contemporary law which follows in subsequent chapters. For recent histories of this area see Orth, 1991; P Davies and M Freedland, 1993; Rubin, 2000.

92 See A Jacobs, 1986.

93 See Orth, 1991: ch 2.

94 The Acts appear to have been inspired partly by fears of the potentially revolutionary nature of trade unionism and partly because industrial action was obstructing trade: Elias and Ewing, 1987: p 1.

95 Elias and Ewing, 1987: p 1.

96 Sidney and Beatrice Webb found no instance of the use of the term 'trade union' in the first third of the nineteenth century: Webb and Webb, 1920: p 113.

property was owned jointly by all the members, were merely taking their own property in so doing. The Friendly Societies Act 1855 enabled the officials of societies with benefit functions to be prosecuted in case of fraud and it was assumed that the Act applied to trade unions provided they complied with specified formalities. However, in *Hornby v Close*[97] the court declared that because the purposes of trade unions were in restraint of trade they were 'illegal' and thereby fell outside the scope of this Act. In 1867 a Royal Commission was established to investigate the whole question of trade unionism. This produced a majority report which proposed that unions should be governed by a highly restrictive regime, and a minority report, drafted by union sympathisers, which recommended that unions be accorded the legal protections which they required in order to function but otherwise should be free from legal supervision. The minority approach prevailed with the Liberal government which accepted the principle of non-intervention in union affairs. This led to the Trade Union Act 1871 which provided that the purposes of trade unions should not, by reason of being in restraint of trade, be deemed unlawful so as to render any member liable to criminal prosecution (section 2) and stipulated that the restraint of trade doctrine should not render trade union agreements or trusts void or voidable (section 3). A further provision (section 4) which precluded any of their agreements from being directly enforceable or subject to damages for breach was designed to exclude union rules from the purview of the courts although, due to tortuous drafting, it achieved only partial success in this endeavour.[98] The Act also introduced a system of voluntary registration, carrying some small advantages, and most unions did, indeed, register under it.[99]

7.13   The Trade Union Act 1871 provided the legal basis for trade union freedom for about a century. It also initiated a strategy which was to be replicated in the area of industrial action; that of according statutory immunity against common law liability but without bestowing any positive rights. As we described in chapter 2 this approach left unions vulnerable to the resurgence of common law doctrines; thus in *Edwards v SOGAT*,[100] for example, it was suggested that a rule which enabled unions to act in a 'capricious and despotic' manner was not proper to the purposes of a union and therefore unprotected by section 3.[101] It also meant that, although individuals were free to join unions in so far as this was not specifically forbidden,[102] workers have been left unprotected against any curtailment of this freedom by the state. In 1919 the police were forbidden by statute from joining trade unions on the ground that this was incompatible with their law enforcement role and since that time they have been restricted to membership of bodies confined to the service. The lower ranks are automatically members of the Police Federation whose constitution and activities are tightly

---

97   (1867) LR 2 QB 153. See also *Hilton v Eckersley* (1855) 6 E & B 47, where an agreement between a group of employers to adopt a common policy on matters such as wages and hours was held to be unenforceable as being in restraint of trade.

98   See Elias and Ewing, 1987: pp 6–12.

99   TUA 1871, s 6.

100   [1971] Ch 354.

101   Per Sachs LJ at 382. Protection against the restraint of trade doctrine was extended to trade union rules in TULRA 1974 and this has continued ever since: see now TULRCA 1992, s 11.

102   Thus members of the armed forces, for example, may join trade unions, given that there is no legislation to the contrary, provided that this does not involve them in activities which would conflict with their military duties.

defined by statute.[103] In 1984, as we discussed in para 7.10, a ban on membership of national civil service unions at GCHQ was imposed (and remained in force until the advent of a Labour Government in 1997). Here the decision was the subject of an application for judicial review in which the House of Lords accepted the unions' argument that they had a public law right to be consulted before their members' terms and conditions were varied although in the circumstances this right was outweighed by the interests of the state in national security.[104] However, this right of consultation was not specifically related to the nature of the freedom being curtailed. Finally, the lack of any independent right to freedom of association has meant that workers may be discriminated against with impunity by employers on the grounds of their union membership and activities unless they fall within the relatively limited statutory protection against such action which has been in force in various forms since the Industrial Relations Act 1971. This 'negative' approach stands in marked contrast to systems where freedom of association is a fundamental, sometimes even a constitutional, right. Whether such a right serves as an adequate guarantee of collective organisation depends upon the way in which it is drafted and interpreted and any qualifications to which it is made subject; it is not, of itself, a panacea. Nevertheless it is undoubtedly the case that, in legal terms, reliance purely upon a system of immunities left trade unions and their members in a fragile situation. The Human Rights Act 1998, in giving 'further effect' in UK law to rights and freedoms guaranteed under the ECHR, grants for the first time a positive right to join trade unions. This is particularly significant because the right applies to '[e]veryone', not only 'workers' who alone at present are covered by the statutory protections against detriment on grounds of union membership and activities. However, there is a free-standing right of action only against public authorities (or, possibly, 'pure' public authorities); those who are discriminated against by other employers will have to invoke an existing common law right of action or defence, or a statutory right, in order to rely upon the general principle of freedom of association in proceedings. Moreover, as we noted in para 7.9, the ECtHR has, in general, adopted a restrictive approach to the interpretation of the right, and there are specified groups, including the police, which do not enjoy its full protection. Nevertheless there are areas in which it may extend greater protection to unions and their members than has been accorded to them to date. The extent to which the Act has the potential to influence the interpretation of existing legislation, or the development of the common law, is discussed in greater detail in specific contexts.

7.14 The 'negative' legal strategy adopted towards collective organisation by the 1871 Act did not mean that governments remained wholly indifferent to trade unions. In parallel to their attitude towards collective bargaining, which we describe below, government policy shifted from one of tolerance towards more positive encouragement. However, this was expressed not through legislation but by the government's own conduct as an employer by which it hoped to set an example to be followed by the private sector.[105] Initially union activity in the civil service, which began on a regular basis in the 1880s and

---

103 Police Act 1996, s 59; Police Federation Regulations 1969, SI 1969/1789, as amended; Fredman and Morris, 1989: pp 95–98.
104 For a critique of this decision see Fredman, 1985.
105 See generally Fredman and Morris, 1989: ch 4, from which the material which follows is taken.

1890s, was met by considerable opposition. In 1898, however, the Secretary of the Treasury confirmed that Post Office workers were free to enter combinations[106] and in 1906 the Postmaster-General in the new Liberal Government affirmed the value of their doing so.[107] The final seal of approval on public service trade unionism came in 1919 when the government adopted collective bargaining in the civil service.[108] It then became official practice to encourage civil servants to join an appropriate trade union on the grounds that fully representative organisations promoted good staff relations and contributed to greater efficiency, as well as benefiting the individual,[109] a policy reflected in later years in local government and the National Health Service. The impact of this policy was amply demonstrated by the high level of trade union membership in the public as compared with the private sector: in 1948, when overall union density was 45.2%, density in central government was 52.9%, in local government and education 69.4% and in posts and telecommunications (then a government department) 87.3%.[110] By 1974 the disparity was even greater; trade union density in the public sector as a whole was estimated at 83% as compared with 38.6% in the private sector.[111] This pattern has continued; in 2003 union density in the public sector stood at 59.1% as compared with 18.2% in the private sector.[112]

The first step towards more direct encouragement of union membership in the private sector came in 1946 when the House of Commons Fair Wages Resolution of that year, unlike its predecessors, included a clause that government contracts with private employers should require contractors to recognise the freedom of their workers to be members of trade unions.[113] Although not covered by the Resolution, many local authorities followed this example and inserted such clauses in their contracts for works, supplies and services.[114] Due to inadequate monitoring and enforcement the efficacy of the Fair Wages Resolution in upholding freedom of association in practice has been doubted.[115] Nevertheless it constituted important symbolic support for the principle of trade unionism although, as we discuss further in para 8.2, not all employers were persuaded to follow the example set.

7.15   The approach of the government towards trade union organisation needs to be viewed in tandem with its attitude towards collective bargaining. From the last years of the nineteenth century and more actively from the end of the First World War it became government policy to support collective bargaining as the preferred method of determining terms and conditions of employment. Again this was furthered in the main by example rather than by statute. The

---

106   Hans (4th Ser) vol LIII col 1136 (18 February 1898).
107   Hans (4th Ser) vol CLIX col 396 (21 June 1906).
108   See below.
109   Civil servants' freedom of association was temporarily restricted by the Trade Disputes and Trade Unions Act 1927. Passed in the wake of the General Strike, the Act prohibited established civil servants from joining unions which, *inter alia*, were not confined to Crown servants. The Act was repealed by the Labour Government in 1946.
110   Bain and Price, 1983: tables 1.1 and 1.5.
111   Price and Bain, 1976: table 2, p 342.
112   T Palmer *et al*, 2004: p 1.
113   See para 2.6 for the status of the Resolution and the sanction for non-compliance with its terms.
114   Hepple and O'Higgins, 1971: p 60.
115   Bercusson, 1978: ch 17.

government resolved actively to promote collective bargaining in the wake of a landmark report by the Whitley Committee, established in 1916, a time of considerable industrial unrest, to make recommendations 'for securing a permanent improvement in the relations between employers and workmen'.[116] The Committee recommended that henceforth rates of pay and major terms of employment should be jointly determined by management and labour through a system of joint (national) industrial councils, district councils and works committees. The Ministry of Labour endorsed these proposals and drew up a model Joint Industrial Council constitution for industry to follow. It also encouraged the formation of employers' associations. The government demonstrated its own commitment to collective bargaining by establishing a system of 'Whitley Councils' for the civil service, despite reservations as to the appropriateness of this model in this context.[117] By 1921, 74 Joint Industrial Councils had been established in the private sector. Although the active promotion of collective bargaining ceased during that year with the advent of the post-war depression, the Whitley model was sufficiently well established to survive in many industries until national-level bargaining itself went into decline in the 1960s.

Although the prevailing theme in relation to collective bargaining was one of state abstentionism, there were a number of measures which lent it auxiliary support.[118] First, in a scheme dating back originally to 1909, provision was made for trade boards (later called wages councils) to be established in any industry in which there was no effective collective bargaining machinery. These bodies, composed of union and employer representatives and independent members, were empowered to determine binding terms and conditions of employment for individual sectors. Once embodied in a ministerial order, these terms took automatic effect in the contracts of employment of those working in the industry and could be enforced in the same way as any other contractual terms.[119] It was also a criminal offence for an employer to breach an order. By the end of 1921 there were 63 trade boards in existence; by the early 1950s, 12% of the workforce was covered by them. Their success in extending voluntary collective bargaining has been doubted (although it seems that the threat of establishing a board was a useful lever in persuading employers to establish joint industrial councils in the period after the First World War).[120] However, in formal terms at least, they endorsed the view that vulnerable groups of workers should be protected against exploitation.

The next layer of support was constituted by the House of Commons Fair Wages Resolutions. The first Resolution, passed in 1891, required the government,

---

116 For a summary of the Committee's recommendations, and references to interim reports, see Ministry of Reconstruction: Committee on Relations between Employers and Employed: *Final Report*, Cd 9153 (1918).

117 The ultimate power of government and Parliament to decide upon terms and conditions of employment was constantly affirmed. For an analysis of collective bargaining, and other methods of determining terms and conditions of employment in the public services, such as the role of 'Review Bodies', see Fredman and Morris, 1989: ch 5.

118 See P Davies and M Freedland, 1993: ch 1, for the argument that these measures taken collectively made considerable inroads into the doctrine of collective laissez-faire, and that had they had greater impact the collective bargaining system may have been much more dependent upon statutory support than the traditional view suggests.

119 See para 4.41 above.

120 See P Davies and M Freedland 1993: 29–30, 40. On the wages councils in general see Bayliss, 1962; Deakin and Wilkinson, 2005: 226–243.

in concluding contracts, to 'make every effort to secure the payment of the rate of wages generally accepted as current for a competent workman in his trade'. This was designed to combat sweated labour by removing government support for employers who paid low wages and in 1909 was extended to hours of work. The further Resolution passed in 1946 made explicit reference to collective agreements as a yardstick for determining appropriate conditions, thus enshrining a commitment to secure observance of collectively-agreed terms in sectors where it could be applied. Express support was also accorded in the post-war statutes which nationalised a number of important industries and services (denationalised during the 1980s), such as coal, iron and steel, electricity and transport; these placed a legal obligation on the new public corporations to seek or enter into consultation with appropriate organisations with a view to establishing joint bargaining and consultative machinery. Last, a procedure introduced during the Second World War for enforcing recognised terms and conditions of employment determined in collective bargaining as the *quid pro quo* for a prohibition on strikes,[121] was continued after the war (although the ban on strikes was removed in 1951[122]) and then re-enacted in 1959.[123] Although used only infrequently it again provided an important demonstration of commitment to the collective bargaining process. Moreover, as one of us has commented elsewhere, its existence, together with that of the Fair Wages Resolution, may have served as an disincentive to denying collective bargaining rights: '[a]s long as a sector-level agreement could be made legally binding, through arbitration, on all employers in a certain trade, any cost advantages which might accrue to employers from non-recognition or the withdrawal of collective bargaining rights were limited'.[124]

7.16   This structure remained in place until the Conservative Government led by Mr (now Sir) Edward Heath introduced the Industrial Relations Act 1971. As we indicated in chapter 1, this Act was a bold but ultimately unsuccessful attempt to bring British industrial relations within a framework of legal regulation at one stroke. The causes of its failure have been analysed in detail elsewhere.[125] In this context, and from our present day perspective, it is important merely to note that, whilst the Act sought to transform the legal culture within which collective bargaining was conducted, unlike later Conservative legislation it was clearly grounded in a continuing belief in the value of collective organisation and collective bargaining, albeit coupled with a greater degree of intervention in internal union affairs. Thus, for the first time, a statutory right to join a trade union, and participate in its activities, was created (although a right not to join a union was also introduced). Moreover, a trade union (or group of unions) which had been denied recognition could seek, through a statutory procedure, designation as the sole bargaining agent for a specified bargaining unit, whereupon the employer would be legally obliged to bargain with it. An employer could be required to disclose to union representatives information required for collective bargaining purposes.[126]

---

121 SR&O 1940, No 1305; see further para 4.26 above.
122 Industrial Disputes Order, SI 1951/1376.
123 Terms and Conditions of Employment Act 1959, s 8.
124 Deakin *et al*, 1992: p 12.
125 Weekes *et al*, 1975. For a more recent analysis of its provisions see P Davies and M Freedland, 1993: ch 7.
126 This provision was never brought into force.

In the event these rights had very little practical impact because they could be invoked only by unions, and members of such unions, which were registered under the Act, and TUC policy opposed such registration. However, they heralded what turned out to be a lasting departure from the abstentionist tradition in the area of collective labour law.[127] Although the Act itself was repealed by the Trade Union and Labour Relations Act 1974 when the Labour Party was returned to power, what has come to be known as the 'Social Contract' legislation incorporated statutory rights which promoted a much more extensive and coherent role for the law than heretofore in supporting trade unions and collective bargaining. Thus employees were accorded a statutory right not to be dismissed or otherwise discriminated against for joining or participating in the activities of an independent trade union. Moreover, although closed shop agreements remained voluntary on the part both of unions and employers, where they had been agreed it was, as from 1976, (with a very limited exception) automatically fair to dismiss an employee who refused to join a specified union or unions. The terms of reference of the newly-constituted ACAS explicitly referred to encouraging the extension of collective bargaining and independent unions could apply, under a statutory procedure, for recognition or extended recognition from employers. Where recognised such unions had rights to information from employers for collective bargaining purposes and the results of collective bargaining could be extended by law to other employers who did not pay the going rate.[128] Recognised unions also had rights to be consulted by employers in the areas of health and safety, dismissals for redundancy and occupational pensions, and their officials had the right to time off with pay during working hours for the performance of duties connected with the conduct of industrial relations, with members having a similar right (unpaid) for union activities. As Davies and Freedland have emphasised, this programme, although superficially ambitious, was characterised by a considerable degree of tentativeness about harnessing the law to promote collective bargaining, as manifested, for example, in the weakness of the sanctions for breach of these provisions.[129] Thus in relation to the recognition procedure, the 'linchpin' of the system, an employer could not legally be forced to give the requisite information to ascertain the views of the workforce on a recognition claim, nor could it be required ultimately to bargain with a union if such a claim were successful; refusal met only with compulsory unilateral arbitration of the terms and conditions of employment of employees covered by the recommendation. This approach was echoed in the provisions relating to disclosure of information. Despite these limitations, however, the legislation was significant in marking another step away from the abstentionist tradition.

7.17 The advent of a Conservative Government in 1979 under Mrs Thatcher, elected in the wake of a period of strikes dubbed the 'winter of discontent', quickly brought a reversal of this strategy. Her government viewed the free market as the most efficient economic principle. The reform of collective labour law was seen as integral to the government's broader economic agenda and, in particular, to the restructuring of the labour market.[130] Trade unions were

---

127 As we point out in ch 1, incomes policies and some employment protection legislation had also modified the tradition of state abstentionism.

128 See Bercusson, 1976.

129 P Davies and M Freedland, 1993: p 385 *et seq*; see also L Dickens and G Bain, 1986.

130 See P Davies and M Freedland, 1993: ch 9 *et seq*; W Brown *et al*, 1997; and para 1.26 above.

characterised as legally-overprivileged bodies which, by their very nature obstructed the operation of market forces and threatened individual freedoms. Collective bargaining was also seen as an undesirable constraint upon a market which required the individualisation of the employment relationship in order to function properly. The 'unique' character of trade unions was said to justify an unprecedented degree of statutory intervention in their internal affairs and individuals were accorded rights against them ostensibly to secure union democracy and prevent the abuse of union power but with the effect in practice of prejudicing their ability to function as effective organisations. It is immediately apparent therefore that the policies of this Government marked a reversal not only of those of its immediate Labour predecessor but also of the approach to industrial relations which had prevailed for most of the century. They were further marked by a series of measures which imposed increasingly complex and restrictive requirements upon the organisation of industrial action and reduced the already limited protections available to those participating in it.

On this occasion, unlike 1971, the Conservative Government did not attempt to achieve its goals (which in any case evolved rather than being precisely formulated at the outset) in a single piece of legislation; rather they introduced reforms on an incremental basis. They began by dismantling major supports to collective bargaining; the (admittedly defective) recognition procedure and the extension procedure were repealed without replacement by the Employment Act 1980. This Act also made inroads into the closed shop by extending the categories of employee exempted from non-membership and requiring a high majority of the workforce to be in favour before new closed shops could be established. The 1982 Employment Act extended further these exempted categories and also required a ballot for a closed shop to continue with protection from the law. This Act also brought a more direct attack upon collective organisation by making it unlawful for persons awarding contracts for the supply of goods or services to make decisions by reference to whether the contractor used union (or non-union) labour or recognised a union (and made void any contractual specification of these matters). A major focus of the 1984 Trade Union Act was the regulation of trade unions' internal affairs; its provisions included a novel requirement for members of the principal executive committee to undergo periodic elections, the extension of the 'political objects' for which a separate political fund was needed and an obligation to approve the continued existence of such a fund in a ballot held at least once every ten years. This process was continued by the Employment Act 1988 which imposed further restrictions upon trade unions in relation to elections and gave a broad range of additional rights to union members, including the right not to be 'unjustifiably disciplined' by their union, the right to inspect union accounting records and the right to prevent the unlawful use of union property. Another radical development was the creation of a Commissioner for the Rights of Trade Union Members, with power to grant assistance, including financial assistance, to individuals contemplating High Court proceedings against their union. In the light of the unavailability of legal aid for proceedings in employment tribunals this move sent another clear message as to where government priorities lay. This Act also removed the remaining legal protection from employers who dismissed or otherwise discriminated against employees for non-membership of a union, thus preventing altogether the enforcement of closed shops. This was followed in 1990 by legislation which, for the first time since the Industrial Relations Act, extended protection to those refused employment for non-membership (or membership) of a trade union. The final major statute in this area, the Trade Union Reform and Employment Rights Act 1993, made further major inroads into trade union autonomy by providing that unions could only lawfully exclude or expel individuals from membership on grounds specified in the legislation. It also required them to comply with more onerous reporting requirements and gave the Certification Officer extensive powers to investigate their affairs. The pursuit of individualism was further facilitated by a provision intended to remove any obstacle to employers offering employees inducements to move from collectively-agreed terms and conditions of employment to personal contracts. Finally, and significantly from a symbolic point of view, the goal of encouraging the extension of collective bargaining was removed from the terms of reference of ACAS.

Hostility to collective organisation was also manifested in the Conservative Government's role as contractor and as employer.[131] In 1982 it gave notice of its intention to rescind the Fair Wages Resolution, a step which necessitated denouncing an ILO Convention in whose formulation British practice had been highly influential. Despite having been in force in various forms since 1891 it was perceived by the government as a damaging anachronism which impeded competitiveness, destroyed jobs and undermined established pay structures. The ban on national civil service unions at GCHQ, discussed in para 7.10, was a particularly dramatic demonstration of its new role as employer; other less direct attacks included threats to trade unionists' freedom of expression and withdrawal of check-off facilities for union subscriptions during official industrial action. This hostility to collective organisation was mirrored in the treatment of collective bargaining in public services where government sought to undermine national bargaining structures by encouraging more local bargaining, and the introduction of individualised reward structures, most notably performance-related pay. Collective bargaining machinery was withdrawn altogether for schoolteachers, to be replaced by unilateral determination of terms and conditions, after following only limited advisory and consultation procedures, by the Secretary of State.[132] Union influence was further reduced by programmes of compulsory competitive tendering in local government and the National Health Service reinforced, in the case of local government, by restrictions in the Local Government Act 1988 which made it unlawful for local authorities and other specified public bodies to have regard to 'non-commercial matters', including, *inter alia*, the payment of fair wages, when awarding and operating contracts.[133]

As even this short summary makes clear, at the time the Conservative administration left office in 1997, the law relating to collective organisation was extremely complex and, in general, restrictive. This is not to say that some remnants of earlier strategies did not remain; it was still unlawful for employers to discriminate against trade union members, for example, although the scope of this protection was radically reduced, and obligations under European Community law necessitated the provision of some specific collective rights of information and consultation. However, the predominant aim was to undermine the capacity of trade unions to act as effective organisations. In this respect legal policy in Britain towards collective organisation came almost full circle; from state abstentionism to positive support returning to hostility, although this was manifested in a rather more sophisticated form than at the beginning of the

131 See generally Fredman and Morris, 1989.
132 See the Teachers' Pay and Conditions Act 1987, itself replaced by the School Teachers' Pay and Conditions Act 1991, discussed Fredman and Morris, 1992.
133 LGA 1988, s 17.

nineteenth century. It was notable that a number of those changes brought the UK into conflict with international standards, particularly those formulated by the ILO,[134] a development which was particularly poignant given the leading role which the UK took initially in their formulation.[135] We consider these conflicts in greater detail when we discuss individual provisions.

7.18   The election of a Labour Government in May 1997 heralded a less hostile environment for trade unions, with emphasis upon a culture of 'partnership' in the conduct of industrial relations.[136] There were two immediate changes of considerable symbolic significance to collective labour law: the restoration of the freedom of workers at GCHQ to join national civil service unions, and at EU level, a commitment to adopt the Agreement on Social Policy (which has become the new Social Chapter of the revised EC Treaty) and the European Works Council Directive adopted under it. The most comprehensive development at a collective level was the enactment of the Employment Relations Act 1999, the 'industrial relations settlement' for the duration of the government's first term of office.[137] The Act significantly extended the protection for union members against discrimination by employers. However, its most controversial aspect was the re-introduction of a procedure for the mandatory recognition of trade unions by employers. This procedure shows that lessons had been learnt from its 1975 predecessor in that it specifies the criteria for designating a bargaining unit and imposes a duty on employers to co-operate with the balloting process.[138] However, in some ways it is less far-reaching: the scope of mandatory recognition is confined to 'pay, hours and holidays'; if the employer fails to comply with the collective bargaining method imposed by the Central Arbitration Committee (CAC) which is charged with operating the procedure, the sanction is confined to specific performance of that method; and those employing fewer than 21 workers[139] are excluded. Employers can also avoid the procedure altogether if they voluntarily recognise any other union, regardless of its level of support among the workforce and (usually) even if it lacks a certificate of independence. Moreover, even where there is recognition (voluntarily or otherwise) the capacity of individual employers and workers to negotiate terms and conditions of employment which differ from those collectively agreed has been explicitly affirmed, although, following the ECtHR decision in *Wilson* and *Palmer*, discussed in para 7.9, the Employment Relations Act 2004 contains a right not to be induced to abjure collective standards.

There are other indications that, while there is greater acknowledgement of the legitimacy of collective bargaining than under the Conservatives, its promotion is very far from being a central plank of labour market policy. The statutory recognition procedure is paralleled by a mechanism for compulsory derecognition of unions which have been recognised by the statutory procedure,

---

134 See Creighton, 1994; Ewing, 1994a; Mills, 1997.
135 Creighton, 1994.
136 See *Fairness at Work*, Cm 2968, 1998, and generally W Brown, 2000.
137 See generally Ewing, 1999a; Wedderburn, 2000; G Morris and T Archer, 2000; Novitz and Skidmore, 2001; L Dickens and M Hall, 2003; Fredman, 2004a.
138 For an assessment of the new procedure and comparison, variously, with its predecessors and with US and Canadian procedures, see S Wood and J Godard, 1999; McCarthy, 1999; Towers, 1999; Adams, 1999; Hepple 2000a; Dubinsky, 2000; S Wood *et al*, 2002, 2003. For discussion of various other strategies for structuring a recognition procedure, see Simpson, 1991; Townley, 1987; Ewing, 1990a and Ewing, 1996: ch 7; Bercusson *et al*, 1998.
139 Including those employed by any associated employer (see para 3.98).

and the CAC is required to assist the parties to agree, *inter alia*, to end the bargaining arrangements in the same way as it assists a recognition application. The pre-1993 statutory duty upon ACAS to extend collective bargaining has not been reinstated (although arguably its general duty 'to promote the improvement of industrial relations' can accommodate this).[140] Finally, the prohibition against requiring contractors to recognise trade unions (but not against requiring them not to do so), introduced by the Conservative Government, remains intact, although there is greater emphasis on consultation with trade unions in areas of the public sector, and the list of prohibited 'non-commercial matters' to which local authorities and other public bodies may not have regard when awarding and operating contracts has been shortened.[141]

Other important aspects of the Conservative legacy have remained substantially untouched. The reform of the law relating to the internal affairs of trade unions has stayed in place in its essentials, although the symbolically significant (but under-used) office of the Commissioner for the Rights of Trade Union Members has been abolished and greater powers granted to the Certification Officer. This means that the UK continues to violate ILO standards in a number of important areas.[142] However some changes have been forced on the government by external pressures. In 2001 the government reluctantly accepted the Information and Consultation Directive, having secured a longer transposition period for its full implementation, after other EU Member States which had previously also opposed the mandatory national level information and consultation it requires indicated their willingness to compromise. In addition, the Employment Relations Act 2004 has extended the scope of protection against anti-union discrimination in the light of the *Wilson* and *Palmer* judgment, although there remain questions as to whether the law, even after these amendments, is fully in compliance with international standards. The advent of a Labour Government has undoubtedly brought a more hospitable approach to collective organisation than its predecessor, but there remain evident limits to that hospitality.

BASIC DEFINITIONS AND CONCEPTS

7.19 In this section we examine the various legal categories into which collective organisations are divided and summarise the legal implications of such categorisation. We begin by analysing the legal definition of a 'trade union'. In Britain important legal consequences follow if an organisation falls within this definition. Some are beneficial, others onerous. On the one hand trade unions are protected against the application of some common law doctrines; their rules and purposes are protected against the doctrine of restraint of trade and their liability for damages in tort (with some exceptions) is subject to statutory limits. On the other, only trade unions are subject to the intricate statutory requirements regulating the selection of their executive committees; restrictions upon those whom they admit to, and expel from, membership; and the grounds upon which they discipline their members. We also outline here the definition of an 'employers' association'. Such bodies share some of the legal attributes of trade unions and a few, but by no means all, of their burdens.

---

140 Hepple, 2000a: p 153.
141 See generally G Morris, 2004a: pp 170–172.
142 See Novitz, 2000; G Morris, 2001b.

Trade unions themselves are sub-divided into categories which also have significant implications. First, they may be listed or unlisted. 'Listed' unions are those that appear on the Certification Officer's list of unions; while not compulsory, listing brings significant advantages. Second, they may be independent or non-independent. One important consequence of a union being independent is that its 'worker' members have the right not to be discriminated against on the grounds of their union membership or activities. Another is that only independent unions may invoke the statutory recognition procedure. Third, unions may be recognised or unrecognised. Unlike independence or, indeed, trade union status itself, 'recognition' is relevant only to the status of the union in relation to a particular employer; a union may be recognised by one employer but not by another. Being recognised entitles unions to a variety of statutory rights. We examine each of these concepts in turn. We then summarise the legal status and attributes of 'trade unions' and of 'employers' associations'.

The definition of a 'trade union' and an 'employers' association' and the concept of 'listing'

7.20   A 'trade union' means an organisation (whether temporary or permanent) which consists wholly or mainly of workers of one or more descriptions and whose principal purposes include the regulation of relations between workers of that description or those descriptions and employers or employers' associations.[143] As we saw in para 3.51 *et seq* the definition of 'worker' goes beyond those who work under a contract of employment to include any other contract whereby a person 'undertakes to do or perform personally any work or services for another party to the contract who is not a professional client of his'.[144] It also covers those who seek to work under such arrangements; thus an organisation composed solely of the unemployed could, in theory, constitute a trade union although it may have difficulty satisfying other elements of the definition. The exclusion of those who work for 'professional clients' means that the Law Society is not a trade union,[145] although it is not clear whether an organisation of *employed* solicitors could be.[146] The requirement for 'an organisation' may mean that a body that is no more than a part of the employer's consultative procedures does not satisfy the test.[147] 'Similarly, a body may not "consist" wholly or mainly of workers within the definition if it merely deems all employees of a particular employer to be its members, without individual employees having indicated any wish to join'.[148]

The need to engage in the 'regulation of relations' probably requires the organisation directly to regulate relations between employers and workers rather than simply engaging in political activities which may influence industrial

---

143 TULRCA 1992, s 1(a).
144 TULRCA 1992, s 296(1). The police and armed forces are specifically excluded from the definition: ss 280, 274. Otherwise, with limited exceptions, TULRCA 1992 has effect in relation to persons in Crown employment as in relation to other workers: s 273.
145 *Carter v Law Society* [1973] ICR 113. See generally *R (on the application of the BBC) v CAC* [2003] IRLR 460.
146 Specified health service practitioners are specifically included within the definition: s 279.
147 *Frost v Clark and Smith* [1973] IRLR 216: a works committee is unlikely to satisfy the definition of a 'trade union' because it will probably lack the attributes of an 'organisation'.
148 *Annual Report of the Certification Officer 2003–2004*: p 2.

relations or eschewing collective bargaining in favour of statutory regulation of terms and conditions. It has been suggested that the organisation must at least have sought recognition from employers. In *Midland Cold Storage Ltd v Turner*[149] the issue arose as to the status of a shop stewards' committee whose apparent activity was to recommend the taking or abandonment of industrial action in the London docks and organising any action which might be decided upon. There was no evidence that it sought recognition from the employers; rather, it left the conduct of negotiations to the established union machinery. The court held that no body whose principal purposes included the regulation of relations between workers and employers could fail at least to seek recognition from employers.

The organisation need not be of a minimum size or demonstrate any particular effectiveness or frequency of intervention in regulating relations, however; the crucial point is that its principal purpose includes such regulation.[150] This purpose need not be stated expressly in its constitution provided that it can be inferred from all the circumstances. Thus the British Association of Advisers and Lecturers in Physical Education was found to be a 'trade union' despite the fact that its constitution merely stated that it should be 'concerned with the professional interests of its members' since in practice it concerned itself with the pay and working conditions of its employed members through national negotiating machinery.[151] However there are strong grounds for concluding that, regardless of its constitution, an organisation cannot regulate the relations of a group of workers if it has no such workers in membership.[152] On the basis of existing authorities an organisation of workers which sought only to be consulted by employers would not qualify as a trade union; to extend the definition to such organisations would require taking a much broader view of the concept of 'regulation' than heretofore. In the light of the current emphasis upon consultation, it is arguable that such an extension should be considered, subject to the other elements of the definition of being satisfied. Although the existing definition focuses upon the traditional role of unions in engaging and seeking to engage in collective bargaining, there is nothing to prevent a union having other lawful objects, including political objects.[153] However, as we describe in chapter 10, where a union wishes to spend money on 'political objects' as statutorily defined it must establish a separate 'political fund' in accordance with a specified procedure.

Organisations which themselves consist wholly or mainly of trade unions or representatives of trade unions, and whose principal purposes include the regulation of relations between workers and employers or employers' associations, or the regulation of relations between their constituent or affiliated organisations, are also regarded as 'trade unions'.[154] Thus the TUC, for example, is a 'trade

---

149 [1972] ICR 230. See also *Midland Cold Storage v Steer* [1972] ICR 435, on the same set of facts.
150 *BAALPE v NUT* [1986] IRLR 497.
151 *BAALPE v NUT* [1986] IRLR 497.
152 See the CAC decision in *BECTU v City Screen Ltd* TURI/309/2003, 10 December 2003, para 32.
153 This has been the case since the TUA 1913; before that the objects of a union were stated exhaustively and in *ASRS v Osborne* [1910] AC 87 the House of Lords held that funding the candidature of prospective Labour MPs was not within the statutory object of the regulation of relations between workers and employers.
154 TULRCA 1992, s 1(b). Note that some provisions which apply to trade unions as defined in s 1(a) do not apply to these organisations or apply with modifications: see s 118.

union'.[155] From the opposite end of the scale the courts have held that a branch or division of a trade union can itself constitute a 'trade union' where it satisfies the statutory criteria, despite the fact that members of the branch are also members of the main trade union.[156] This may be significant in relation to the statutory limits on damages payable by a trade union in tort, for example.[157]

7.21   Unlike in some systems, there is no requirement for trade unions to be registered in order legally to exist. However, the Certification Officer maintains a list of trade unions and any union which complies with specified formalities is entitled to have its name entered on the list.[158] Being listed has a number of advantages for a union. It is evidence (although not conclusive evidence)[159] that the organisation is, indeed, a trade union;[160] it entitles the union to tax relief on income tax, corporation tax and chargeable gains applied for the purpose of 'provident benefits';[161] and there is a simplified procedure for vesting union property in newly appointed trustees.[162] Moreover, inclusion on the list is an essential preliminary to an application for a certificate of independence, described below. Thus, although listing is theoretically voluntary, a union is highly likely to seek entry to the list. It is irrelevant to a union's application that there may be other organisations which already recruit members in the same area of work, although if the organisation's name is the same as that of a listed union, or so closely resembles it as to be likely to deceive the public, listing will be refused.[163] The Certification Officer may remove a union from the list if he or she considers that it is not a union (after allowing the organisation to make representations) or if the organisation requests removal, or he is she is satisfied that it has ceased to exist (for example, as a result of merger with another union).[164] There is a right of appeal to the EAT on a question of law against the Certification Officer's decision not to list a union, or to remove it from the list.[165] At the end of March 2004 there were 195 listed trade unions and a further 20 which had not sought to be listed (although they submitted annual returns to the Certification Officer, as required by law).[166]

The Certification Officer also maintains a list of employers' associations, and at the end of March 2004 there were 85 on this list.[167] Again listing is not

---

155 Another example is the Iron and Steel Trades Confederation.
156 *BAALPE v NUT* [1986] IRLR 497; *News Group Newspapers Ltd v SOGAT '82 (No 2)* [1986] IRLR 337.
157 See para 11.47 below.
158 TULRCA 1992, ss 2, 3. Unions listed under the Trade Union and Labour Relations Act 1974 (now repealed) were automatically entered on the list; this statute, in turn, automatically listed organisations registered under the provisions of the TUA 1871 (or organisations formed by an amalgamation of such organisations) and those affiliated to the TUC.
159 This may be important in the context of the recognition procedure, for example: see the CAC decision in *BECTU v City Screen Ltd* TUR1/309/2003, 10 December 2003.
160 TULRCA 1992, s 2(4).
161 ICTA 1988, s 467, as amended. For the definition of 'provident benefits' see ICTA 1988, s 467(2).
162 TULRCA 1992, ss 13, 14.
163 TULRCA 1992, s 3(4).
164 TULRCA 1992, s 4.
165 TULRCA 1992, s 9, as amended by ERelA 2004, s 51, which removed the right of appeal on questions of fact.
166 *Annual Report of the Certification Officer for 2003–2004*, paras 1.9 and 1.14; App 1 and Schedule to App 1. Being unlisted does not limit an organisation's statutory responsibilities (although 'federated' trade unions, whether listed or unlisted, are exempted from several statutory obligations).
167 *Annual Report of the Certification Officer for 2003–2004*, para 1.9; App 2.

mandatory (and 80 which were not listed submitted returns to the Certification Officer as of March 2004[168]), but it constitutes evidence that the organisation falls within the legal definition.[169] An 'employers' association' means an organisation (whether temporary or permanent) which consists wholly or mainly of employers or individual owners of undertakings of one or more descriptions whose principal purposes include the regulation of relations between employers of that description or those descriptions and workers or trade unions.[170] There is no case law directly on the interpretation of this definition[171] but one would expect the same approach to be applied to phrases such as the 'regulation of relations' as apply in the context of trade unions. Organisations consisting wholly or mainly of constituent or affiliated organisations which themselves fulfil the definition of an employers' association or representatives of such organisations are also included provided, again, that their principal purposes include regulating relations with workers or trade unions or between their constituent or affiliated organisations.[172]

The concept and implications of trade union 'independence'

7.22   Once a union has been entered on the Certification Officer's list it is eligible to apply to him or her for a certificate of independence. Satisfying the test of 'independence' (which refers to independence from employers rather than the state) is essential for access to a number of statutory rights: only ('worker') members of independent unions are protected against subjection to a detriment by their employers on grounds of their union activities; only independent unions may invoke the statutory recognition procedure; and only independent recognised unions have certain rights to information and consultation and their members the right to claim time off to participate in union activities.[173] In broad terms the concept is intended to preclude access to these rights by employer-dominated 'house unions' or 'staff associations'. This was particularly significant when, in the past, employees could be fairly dismissed for refusing to join a union with which the employer had agreed a 'closed shop'. A certificate is not a prerequisite of independent status but it constitutes conclusive proof of such and if the question of the independence of a non-certificated union arises in any proceedings they must be stayed pending a decision by the Certification Officer on the matter.[174]

On receiving an application for a certificate, which is entered on a record open to public inspection for at least a month, the Certification Officer must make such inquiries as he or she thinks fit and take into account any relevant information submitted by any person.[175] If a certificate is refused the Certification

---

168   *Annual Report of the Certification Officer for 2003–2004*, para 1.14; Schedule to App 2.
169   TULRCA 1992, s 123. The procedure required to gain entry to the list, and provision for appeal against refusal, is set out in ss 123–126 and is the same, *mutatis mutandis*, as that applicable to trade unions.
170   TULRCA 1992, s 122.
171   Although see *National Federation of Self-Employed and Small Businesses v Philpott* [1997] IRLR 340, where the Federation was held to be an 'organisation of employers' for the purposes of the SDA 1975, s 12, notwithstanding that not all its members employed labour, given that the majority did.
172   TULRCA 1992, s 122.
173   See chs 8 and 9.
174   TULRCA 1992, ss 6(1), 8.
175   TULRCA 1992, s 6. See *Guidance for Trade Unions Wishing to Apply for a Certificate of Independence*, Certification Office, 2000, for further details about the procedure which is followed.

Officer must give reasons for this decision; he or she may also withdraw a certificate after following a procedure similar to that laid down for applications.[176] An appeal lies to the EAT on a question of law against the Certification Officer's decision to refuse, or withdraw, a certificate of independence.[177] A union which has been refused a certificate may reapply at a later stage, although it would be advised to scrutinise carefully its constitution, finances and conduct before doing this. There is no right of appeal for a third party which wishes to contest the granting of a certificate (which it may wish to do now, perhaps, for purposes relating to the statutory recognition procedure).[178] The only way in which such an third party could proceed would be to attempt to obtain an order for judicial review to overturn the Certification Officer's decision, but as this would require showing that the decision was vitiated by a procedural irregularity, illegality, or 'irrationality' it would probably be a difficult task.

7.23   A trade union is 'independent' if it is not under the domination or control of an employer or group of employers or one or more employers' associations and is not liable to interference by an employer or any such group or association (arising out of the provision of financial or material support or by any other means whatsoever) tending towards such control.[179] This test directs attention therefore both to whether the employer in fact exercises domination or control over the union and whether it is exposed to the risk of interference tending towards such control. 'Liability to interference' has been interpreted by the courts as 'vulnerable to interference'; thus there is no need to show that such interference is likely in the circumstances.[180]

Beyond this general test the statute does not specify the criteria relevant to independence, although further guidance is available from the decisions of the Certification Officer and the courts. Among the factors which the Certification Officer considers relevant are the extent of any assistance given by the employer in establishing and maintaining the organisation; whether the constitution allows for interference by the employer in the union's affairs; the scope of the union's membership base; the strength and sources of the union's finances; and its negotiating record.[181] These criteria were referred to with approval in the judgment of the EAT in *Blue Circle Staff Association v Certification Officer*,[182] a case where the decision of the Certification Officer

176 TULRCA 1992, ss 6, 7.
177 TULRCA 1992, s 9. as amended by ERelA 2004, s 51, which removed the right of appeal on questions of fact.
178 *GMWU v Certification Officer* [1977] ICR 183.
179 TULRCA 1992, s 5.
180 *Squibb UK Staff Association v Certification Officer* [1979] IRLR 75. After the ban on membership of national civil service unions, described in para 7.10, it became a condition of service for staff at GCHQ that they could only belong to a departmental staff association approved by the director of GCHQ, and industrial action could lead to disciplinary action. The EAT confirmed the decision of the Certification Officer that the association in question was 'vulnerable to interference': see *Government Communications Staff Federation v Certification Officer* [1993] IRLR 260. For the grounds of refusal of a subsequent application by the Federation to the Certification Officer, see *Annual Report of the Certification Officer for 1996*, para 2.9. In May 2001 the Certification Officer refused an application from NISA (the News International Staff Association) on the grounds that it was liable to interference from the employer.
181 *Guidance* from the Certification Office, note 175 above, para 16 *et seq*.
182 [1977] IRLR 20.

to refuse a certificate of independence was confirmed. The background to this case demonstrates the need for vigilance in this area. In 1971 the employer realised that its salaried staff (some 4,000 in number) wanted some form of collective voice. The employer was eager that any emerging body should represent only its own employees and, following a ballot, an organisation called a 'staff consultative organisation', dominated by the employer, was formed. The organisation had a central committee on which the employers had five representatives; the chairman of the committee was nominated by the employers, and there were area committees on which management had a right of representation. Members with less than three years' service with the employer were not eligible for election as representatives. The employer provided facilities and paid virtually all the expenses, although members had to pay a nominal subscription. Initially the organisation was empowered only to make recommendations to the employer but in 1974 it was given negotiating rights. Between 1975 and February 1976 further changes were made to its structure, including renaming it a staff association, in order to strengthen its independence.

The Certification Officer took the view that, given the degree of dependence to which the organisation had been subject in the first five years of its life, that history imposed a duty to look scrupulously at all the facts to see that it had changed its character. In this case, although the association had taken steps towards independence it had not gone far enough along this road and he thought that it should establish some record for itself which he expected to take some time.

The EAT, looking at the issue afresh,[183] agreed with the Certification Officer's decision. The rules still showed traces of the old dependence – for example, it was for the employer to appoint the chairman of the Joint Central Committee, those with less than three years' service were still excluded from office, irrespective of their negotiating experience, and the employer had the right to withdraw recognition of a representative regardless of the views of the association's central council. Moreover, the association was dependent on the goodwill of the employer for the bulk of its communications with its members and its very slender financial base gave rise to doubt as to its viability. The court found that it was 'difficult to identify any real sign that anything has changed in this Association except the formal documents that came into existence … when the management was helping the Staff Consultative Organisation to find new clothes to make it respectable for its introduction to the Certification Officer'. It was:

> … unlikely that the employer's dominant role would have been modified at all had it not been the view of the employer that it was in its interest to concert with the Association a constitution and negotiating machinery consistent with the end of the existing company control … When the matrix of the new constitution is regarded, it is found to be an organisation whereby the association of the salaried staff members was penetrated at every point by the interference and control of the management. There must be a heavy onus on such a body to show that it has shaken off the paternal control which brought it into existence and fostered its growth, and which finally joined in drafting the very rules by which the control appears to be relaxed.[184]

---

183 Prior to 6 April 2005, appeals could be made to the EAT on questions of fact as well as questions of law.
184 *Blue Circle Staff Association v Certification Officer* [1977] IRLR 20, 24.

The court concluded by warning the association that, although it was open to it at any time to make a fresh application for a certificate, 'they must recognise that the process of asserting genuine and effective independence after some years of such domination by management ... is likely to be protracted'.[185]

7.24   It is important to emphasise that the criteria listed by the Certification Officer are only guidelines whose relevance and weight may vary depending on the circumstances; thus, whilst single company unions, for example, are scrutinised more carefully because their membership base makes them more vulnerable to employer interference, they are not precluded altogether; the National Union of Railwaymen[186] and National Union of Mineworkers were not refused certificates during periods when virtually all their members were employed by single employers in the form of nationalised state corporations. Similarly, the provision of facilities by an employer is not of itself a bar to independence and, indeed, the ACAS Code of Practice on Time Off for Trade Union Duties and Activities recommends that employers should make available facilities such as notice boards, a telephone, accommodation for meetings and office space.[187] In an analysis of the management of unions' financial resources during the period 1980–89, Willman et al indicated the difficult passage which unions may need to steer in this respect, pointing out that:

> ... [d]ependence is ... to some extent, an indication of negotiating success, given the structure of British unions. Lay involvement, the key to cost control and perhaps to a wider range of union objectives, depends on employer support. But too much employer support may threaten independence and in fact usurp the union's role unless the employer is simultaneously dependent on the union. The issue, then, is one of managing this dependence, of making such dependence mutual.[188]

The crucial question would seem to be whether the union could survive if its facilities were suddenly withdrawn. As the Certification Officer's *Guidance for Trade Unions Wishing to Apply for a Certificate of Independence* explains:

> A distinction can properly be drawn between a broadly-based union which could continue to function even if an employer withdrew facilities from one or more of its branches and a single company union which might well find it difficult or even impossible to carry on at all if such action were taken by the company which employs its entire membership.[189]

A 'robust attitude in negotiation' and a good negotiating record are regarded as indicative of independence although, again, this varies with the circumstances; in the case of a 'good, tactful and sensitive employer' these could be difficult to demonstrate.[190] Willingness to take industrial action is not a criterion of independence and organisations whose rules forbid this have been granted certificates. In view of this it is interesting to note that legislation clarifying the position of prison officers, which also removed their freedom to take industrial action, provided that the Certification Officer should disregard

---

185   *Blue Circle Staff Association v Certification Officer* [1977] IRLR 20, 24.
186   Now the National Union of Rail, Maritime and Transport Workers.
187   Para 38; see further para 8.40.
188   Willman *et al*, 1993: p 207.
189   Certification Office, 2000, para 22. See also the *Annual Report of the Certification Officer for 1996*, para 2.9, regarding GCHQ, referred to in note 180 above.
190   *Blue Circle Staff Association v Certification Officer* [1977] IRLR 20, 23.

their inability lawfully to take industrial action in determining whether their unions are independent.[191]

7.25 The concept of independence is a crucial one in the context of freedom of association. ILO Convention No 98 emphasises the need for workers' (and employers') organisations to enjoy 'adequate protection against any acts of interference by each other or each other's agents or members in their establishment, functioning and administration'. In particular acts 'designed to promote the establishment of workers' organisations under the domination of employers or employers' organisations, or to support workers' organisations by financial or other means, with the object of placing ... [them] under the control of employers or employers' organisations' are deemed to constitute acts of interference.[192] The Freedom of Association Committee of the ILO Governing Body considers that legislation should make express provision for appeals and establish sufficiently dissuasive sanctions against acts of interference by employers.[193] In the United States, for example, it is an unfair labour practice for an employer to provide financial assistance to a labour organisation and it can be ordered to desist from doing so.[194] It is notable that under English law there is nothing to prevent an employer establishing and supporting a non-independent union. It is strongly arguable that the law should be changed in this respect; even though an employer cannot lawfully dismiss or otherwise discriminate against a worker, or deny employment to someone, because they refuse to join a non-independent union, nevertheless the social pressures to join may be strong and the very existence of such an organisation may discourage workers from joining independent unions. Moreover, the Employment Relations Act 1999 has given a further incentive to employers to establish non-independent unions; recognition of a non-independent union will (usually) bar a claim for recognition by an independent union under the statutory recognition procedure, a position which it can be argued violates ILO Convention 98.[195] Finally, it is inappropriate that an employer which does not recognise an independent union can fulfil its statutory obligations to inform and consult in a number of important areas, such as collective redundancies and matters covered by the Information and Consultation Regulations,[196] by informing and consulting worker representatives whose position may not comply in a number of respects with the criteria of independence outlined above, not least because it is a condition that they are employed by the employer at the time of their selection as such representatives.[197] This is another area in which the law is in urgent need of reform. Indeed, it may be thought desirable to consider extending the application of the concept of independence to enterprise worker representative bodies in general, even though they may be single employer organisations and may not seek to engage in collective bargaining, only consultation, and may not therefore fall within the current definition of a 'trade union'.

191 CJPOA 1994, s 127(7). See further G Morris, 1994b and 1994c.
192 Art 2.
193 ILO 1996, para 764.
194 29 USC para 158(a)(2), 160(c) (1976). There is considerable debate about how expansively this provision should be interpreted: see Gould, 1993: p 234 nn 15–17.
195 See further para 9.7 and Ewing, 2000a.
196 SI 2004/3426.
197 See further ch 9.

The concept and implications of union 'recognition'

7.26 An employer may elect to 'recognise' a trade union; it may also (if 21 or more workers are employed) be compelled to recognise an independent union in relation to pay, hours and holidays pursuant to a statutory procedure. Recognition of an independent trade union, voluntary or otherwise, has a number of important legal consequences. Recognition entitles the union to claim disclosure of information for collective bargaining purposes (see para 9.22); union representatives and members are entitled to time off work for specified activities (see para 8.33 *et seq*); and a variety of statutory consultation rights, which we describe in para 9.29 *et seq* apply. Recognised unions therefore have significant rights which are not available to those which are unrecognised. Furthermore, recognition has significant implications for the operation of the statutory recognition procedure: where an employer recognises an independent union for a particular group of workers, an application by another union in respect of a bargaining unit which overlaps to any extent with that group will not be accepted by the CAC; perhaps surprisingly, the same principle generally applies even where a non-independent union is recognised (see para 9.7). Finally, an employer must consult a recognised independent union on training matters where that union is recognised in accordance with the statutory procedure and a method for the conduct of collective bargaining has been specified by the CAC (see para 9.49).

7.27 'Recognition' in relation to a trade union means 'the recognition of the union by an employer, or two or more associated employers, to any extent, for the purposes of collective bargaining'.[198] 'Collective bargaining' means 'negotiations relating to or connected with' one or more of the matters specified in the Trade Union and Labour Relations (Consolidation) Act 1992, section 178(2).[199] These matters are:

(a) the terms and conditions of employment, or the physical conditions in which any workers[200] are required to work;
(b) engagement or non-engagement, or termination or suspension of employment or the duties of employment, of one or more workers;
(c) allocation of work or the duties of employment as between workers or groups of workers;
(d) matters of discipline;
(e) a worker's membership or non-membership of a trade union;
(f) facilities for officials of trade unions; and
(g) machinery for negotiation or consultation, and other procedures, relating to any of the above matters, including the recognition by employers or employers' associations of the right of a trade union to represent workers in such negotiation or consultation or in the carrying out of such procedures.

The phrase 'to any extent' in the definition of 'recognition' means that it is sufficient that the employer negotiates with a union on any one of these matters for the union to be recognised within the meaning of the statute, although the precise extent of recognition is relevant to the scope of the rights to disclosure of information and time off. Recognition may be the product of an express

---

198 TULRCA 1992, s 178(3).
199 TULRCA 1992, s 178(1).
200 Defined TULRCA, s 296; see para 3.51 *et seq* above.

agreement between the parties or implied from their conduct, probably only over a period of time.[201] We discuss in para 9.3 the considerations which are relevant in determining whether recognition can be implied. Even where express, voluntary recognition, granted wholly outside the statutory procedure, may be varied or withdrawn unilaterally by the employer although, as we outline again in 9.4, derecognition may have legal implications which employers need to take into account. By contrast, as we explain in para 9.20, where a union has been recognised pursuant to a request under the statutory procedure, it may not normally be derecognised within three years, and if recognition was granted pursuant to a finding that a majority of workers were members of the applicant union or consequent upon a ballot, the employer may derecognise only if the requisite support for this course of action has been demonstrated in a ballot.

Although the legislation does not prevent employers and unions negotiating on matters outside the definition of 'collective bargaining', the definition reflects a perception of the matters which are likely to be viewed as appropriate for joint regulation. Thus it does not extend to future investment strategy or product development, for example.[202] These matters are identical to those which constitute the subject-matter of a 'trade dispute' for the purpose of the statutory immunities relating to industrial action; the scope of 'legitimate' industrial action and that of 'collective bargaining' are therefore co-extensive. The case law relating to the interpretation of these matters (holding, for example, that in (a) 'terms of employment' extends beyond contractual terms and (b) can cover fear of future redundancies) has, in fact, issued from the industrial action context and we discuss it therefore in para 11.27.

The legal status and attributes of trade unions and of 'employers' associations'

7.28   At common law the legal nature of trade unions is based on an association of individuals bound together by a contract of membership which regulates the relationship between those members. Although this remains their legal basis, in reality they are subject to a complex overlay of statutory provisions which modify the common law position in most important areas.[203] Thus, for example, all property belonging to the union must be vested in trust for the union (not, notably, for its members)[204] and unions can only exclude individuals from membership on grounds specified by statute.[205] In this section we outline those provisions which relate to the legal status of unions and indicate in broad terms the scope of public accountability.[206] We analyse in greater detail in chapter 10 the extensive statutory constraints upon the conduct of internal trade union

---

201 *NUGSAT v Albury Bros Ltd* [1978] IRLR 504.

202 Cf the wider range of matters on which employers must inform and consult information and consultation representatives under the standard provisions in ICER 2004, reg 20: see further para 9.54.

203 We refer here only to the modern law. For further detail on the history of the law in this area see Elias and Ewing, 1987, and references therein.

204 TULRCA 1992, s 12 and see *Hughes v TGWU* [1985] IRLR 382 (individual members have no interest severable or in common in union property); cf the puzzling wording of s 23(2)(b) which refers to 'property belonging to any member of the union otherwise than jointly or in common with the other members'.

205 See para 10.9 below.

206 For a more detailed consideration of these matters see G Morris and T Archer, 2000: paras 2.8–2.11.

affairs, enforceable by union members. Their intricacy and complexity casts doubt on whether unions can in any sense now be regarded as voluntary autonomous bodies.

The significant features of the legal status of trade unions fall into three broad categories. First, although they cannot be incorporated,[207] they have been accorded by statute many of the attributes of incorporated bodies. Thus, they are capable of making contracts; they can sue[208] and be sued, and are amenable to criminal prosecution, in their own name; and judgments, awards and orders may be enforced against any property held in trust for the union (although certain property is protected against the enforcement of any award of damages, costs or expenses).[209] Second, they have statutory protection against the common law doctrine of restraint of trade, without which it would be impossible for most unions to function lawfully;[210] the purposes of a trade union are not, by reason only that they are in restraint of trade, unlawful so as to make any members liable to criminal proceedings or so as to make any agreement or trust void or voidable, nor is any union rule unlawful or unenforceable on that ground.[211] Finally, although trade unions have been potentially liable in tort since the Employment Act 1982, there are statutory limits on the amount of damages which may be awarded against a union in any proceedings in tort (with specified exceptions).[212] We discuss further in para 11.47 the nature and importance of these limits in relation to liability for organising industrial action which is the context in which, in practice, they are likely to be most relevant.

Unlike trade unions, employers' associations may be either incorporated or unincorporated.[213] Where unincorporated, they have the same attributes of incorporated bodies as do trade unions.[214] Again, all the property must be vested in trust for the association.[215]

---

207 TULRCA 1992, s 10(1), (2) (cf the Industrial Relations Act 1971, s 74, which accorded registered trade unions corporate status). There is an exception in the case of the 13 (as at the end of March 2004) 'special register bodies' which are companies registered under the Companies Act 1985 or incorporated by charter or letters patent whose names appeared on a special register maintained under the Industrial Relations Act 1971, s 84: TULRCA 1992, s 117. These organisations are bodies whose principal purposes are to maintain professional standards or training but which also became involved in negotiating terms and conditions of employment for their members. Most are in the public services; they include the Royal College of Nursing and the British Medical Association. Special register bodies whose principal purposes do not include employer-worker relations cannot be listed or seek a certificate of independence. There are various exceptions and modifications to the legislation governing trade unions which apply to these bodies: TULRCA 1992, s 117(3), (4).

208 There has been some doubt as to whether unions can sue in defamation: in *EETPU v Times Newspapers Ltd* [1980] 1 All ER 1097, it was held they could not, but cf *NUGMW v Gillian* [1946] KB 81, cited without adverse comment by the House of Lords in *Derbyshire County Council v Times Newspapers Ltd* [1993] 1 All ER 1011.

209 TULRCA 1992, s 12(2). See s 23 for the definition of protected property.

210 In *Hornby v Close* (1867) LR 2 QB 153 it was held that the purposes of a union whose rules enabled a majority to control the terms on which all members disposed of their labour were unlawful. The TUA 1871 granted protection as far as trade union purposes were concerned; this was extended to trade union rules by TULRA 1974 following the suggestion in *Edwards v SOGAT* [1971] Ch 354 that the 1871 Act did not protect rules in restraint of trade.

211 TULRCA 1992, s 11.

212 TULRCA 1992, s 22.

213 TULRCA 1992, s 127.

214 TULRCA 1992, s 127.

215 TULRCA 1992, s 129.

7.29 Both trade unions and employers' associations[216] (regardless of whether they are listed) are subject to detailed obligations in respect of their accounting practices.[217] They must also submit an annual return to the Certification Officer which includes audited revenue accounts and such other audited accounts as he or she requires, together with a balance sheet and a copy of the organisation's rules.[218] In relation to trade unions, details of the salary paid to, and other benefits provided to or in respect of, the president, general secretary and each member of the executive during that period must also be included.[219] Unions and employers' associations must supply any person on request with a copy of their most recent annual return and of their rules (either free or on payment of a reasonable charge) and the Certification Officer must keep copies of all returns available for public inspection.[220] In addition, union members must be supplied with a statement containing specified information, including the total income and expenditure for the period to which the return relates; how much income consisted of payments in respect of membership; the income and expenditure of the political fund, if relevant; and information as to the salary and benefits referred to above.[221] It should also include the auditor's report together with a prescribed statement which advises members of the action they may take should they consider that some irregularity may be occurring, or has occurred, in the conduct of the union's financial affairs.[222] It is a criminal offence for a union or employers' association to refuse or wilfully neglect to perform any of these duties, punishable by a fine of up to level 5 on the standard scale.[223] Where the organisation is guilty of such an offence it is deemed also to have been committed by any officer bound by the rules to discharge the relevant duty or, if none, every member of the general committee of management.[224] It is also an offence, punishable with up to six months' imprisonment as well as a fine, wilfully to alter a document required for the statutory purposes, to falsify it or to enable the organisation to evade any statutory requirements.[225] Unions have a duty to ensure that no person convicted of any of these offences holds any office in the union covered by the mandatory election requirements described in para 10.14.[226] The Certification Officer is responsible for enforcing the statutory requirements[227] and since 1993 has been granted extensive powers of investigation in relation to the financial affairs both of unions and employers' associations including the power, in specified circumstances, to appoint an inspector to conduct an investigation.[228]

---

216 Except those which consist wholly or mainly of representatives of constituent or affiliated organisations.
217 TULRCA 1992, ss 28 and 131.
218 TULRCA 1992, ss 32 and 131.
219 TULRCA 1992, s 32(3)(aa). See para 10.14 below for the definition of these posts.
220 TULRCA 1992, ss 27, 32, 131.
221 TULRCA 1992, s 32A(3).
222 TULRCA 1992, s 32A(5), (6).
223 TULRCA 1992, ss 45, 45A, 131. At the time of writing £5,000 is level 5 on the standard scale established by the Criminal Justice Act 1982, s 37(2), as amended.
224 TULRCA 1992, ss 45, 131.
225 TULRCA 1992, ss 45, 131.
226 TULRCA 1992, s 45B.
227 Note, however, that the Certification Officer does not generally undertake prosecutions for offences such as theft or fraud which would normally be dealt with by other prosecuting authorities: *Annual Report of the Certification Officer for 2003–2004*, para 3.13.
228 TULRCA 1992, s 37A–37E; s 131. Up to 31 March 2004 the Certification Officer had used his powers to appoint inspectors on two occasions: *Annual Report of the Certification Officer for 1997* para 3.19; and *Annual Report of the Certification Officer for 1998*, para 3.23.

THE ROLE OF TRADE UNIONS IN CONTEMPORARY INDUSTRIAL RELATIONS

7.30   Trade unions currently face an uncertain future.[229] First, and most fundamentally, the number of workers who are union members has fallen substantially, from a post-war peak of more than 13 million in 1979 to just over 7.7 million in 2002/3.[230] With two exceptions,[231] each year since 1979 has shown an annual fall in membership, although the decline in recent years has been relatively modest.[232] As well as being a decline in absolute numbers the statistics show a large fall in the proportion of the active labour force who are unionised; over half in 1979, 29.3% in 2003.[233] It is also notable that membership is concentrated in the public services, themselves vulnerable to workforce reduction; in 2003 union density in the public sector was 59.1% as compared with 18.2% in the private sector.[234] A particularly worrying feature for the unions is the low proportion of young workers in trade unions.[235]

Several reasons have been identified for the decline in union membership since 1979 although the weight of their respective contributions is more difficult to assess.[236] Key factors have been high levels of unemployment and major structural changes in the economy as a whole. The evidence suggests that in the first half of the 1980s the demise of large, highly-unionised manufacturing plants was an important factor.[237] Moreover, employment growth has been concentrated in areas in which unions have traditionally not been well represented – smaller

---

229 For recent surveys of the issues see the Report of the House of Commons Employment Committee, Session 1993–94, *The Future of the Trade Unions*, HC 676-I; Taylor, 1994; Fairbrother, 2000; Machin, 2000; J Waddington, 2003b; Gospel and Wood, 2003; Heery *et al*, 2003; Charlwood, 2004b; Metcalf, 2004; Ewing, 2005. Note that the challenges facing unions are not confined to the UK (see Hyman, 1994; W Brown *et al*, 1997: p 74; Crouch, 2000; Raday, 2002; Kochan, 2003), although the nature of these challenges may vary between countries.

230 *Annual Report of the Certification Officer for 2003–2004*, paras 4.5–4.6; App 4. The information is based on returns from unions that range in date from October 2002– September 2003. The Labour Force Survey shows a lower figure for autumn 2003 (7.38 million) but the two sources are not directly comparable because, unlike the Certification Officer's figures, the Labour Force Survey covers only those in employment: T Palmer *et al*, 2004, forward. The total number shown in the Certification Officer's figures includes all members, not only those paying contributions; the total number of contributing members was around 12% less than total membership: para 4.8.

231 See the *Annual Report of the Certification Officer for 1999–2000*, para 4.6 and for *2000–2001*, para 4.6

232 Around 0.2% and under 0.4% according to figures shown in para 4.6 of the *Annual Report of the Certification Officer* for 2003–2004 and 2002–2003 respectively.

233 T Palmer *et al*, 2004: p 1. The 2003 figure on union density is taken from the Labour Force Survey of the autumn of that year.

234 T Palmer *et al*, 2004: p 1.

235 In autumn 2003 union density was only 10.6% for employees aged 16–24: T Palmer *et al*, 2004: p 5. Freeman and Diamond, 2003, conclude that this is partly because unions do not recruit the young and have little contact with them.

236 See the Memorandum from Professor Brian Towers to the Employment Committee, Volume III, Appendices to the Minutes of Evidence, HC 676-III; Kessler and Bayliss, 1995; J Waddington and C Whitson, 1995; W Brown *et al*, 1997: p 74; Millward *et al*, 2000: pp 230–234; Crouch, 2000; Machin, 2000, 2003. It is important to note in this connection that the picture was not simply one of a withering of membership among a pool of former union members; the reality is much more 'fluid' and '[s]tudies have shown that new recruits to membership often form a substantial proportion of total union membership': Cully and Woodland, 1997: p 232.

237 Millward *et al*, 1992: pp 101–102.

enterprises and private sector services, where work is often offered on a part-time, casualised or self-employed basis; indeed, the failure to organise in establishments and firms set up since 1980 has been claimed to be the critical factor in union decline.[238] However, this alone does not provide a sufficient explanation, given that the decline in membership and density is a feature of all categories of employment.[239] More difficult to measure, but also influential, was the anti-union culture which, as we saw in para 7.17, it was the policy of the 1979–1997 Conservative Government to promote; in the words of Professor Brian Towers 'a climate in which employers ... increasingly adopted anti-union or union avoidance policies and public policy and legislation ... sought to weaken trade union authority and influence at the place of work and in political and economic institutions affecting policy'.[240] A further contributory factor in the decline of union influence was the reduction in the proportion of employers recognising trade unions and the consequent reduction in the coverage of collective bargaining. As we indicate in chapter 9, employers found alternative methods of communicating with their workers which may leave little room for trade union involvement.

Unions responded in a number of different ways to these various pressures. First, there has been a growing movement for individual unions to seek partners for mergers.[241] In 1962 there were 182 unions affiliated to the TUC,[242] in March 1998 only 73.[243] A prominent example of this process was the amalgamation between the National and Local Government Officers Association, the National Union of Public Employees and the Confederation of Health Service Employees to form UNISON – The Public Service Union in 1993 which, with over 1.5 million members at the time of merger, became the largest union in the country (although its membership has since decreased[244]). Another was the amalgamation of the Manufacturing Science and Finance Union with the Amalgamated Engineering and Electrical Union in 2002 to form Amicus, with more than a million members.[245] In 1999 the TUC leadership launched a programme to encourage union mergers, with the ultimate aim of only one 'industry union' for each key industrial sector, a structure which would avoid the risk of inter-union competition for recognition.[246] Unions embarking upon the merger strategy claim that the resulting economies of scale allow them to provide better services more effectively. It is also a development which some employers seem to favour because of its effect in simplifying bargaining structures. On the other hand, however, it carries the danger that such unions can become monolithic and remote from their members.[247] Moreover, far from simplifying the trade union structure, mergers have merely added to its complexity; because mergers have

238 Cully *et al*, 1999: pp 234–238; Machin, 2000
239 Cully and Woodland, 1997: p 232; see also Millward *et al*, 2000: pp 84–95.
240 Note 236 above.
241 See Kessler and Bayliss, 1995: pp 159–161; J Waddington and C Whitson, 1995: pp 176–186; Undy, 1999 (who notes that during the period 1978–1994, five 'aggressive' unions accounted for 79% of the 117 transfers to TUC unions).
242 Evidence of the TUC to the Employment Committee, Vol II, p 40.
243 In 2002/3 the 16 unions with over 100,000 members accounted for 84% of total union (TUC and non-TUC affiliated) membership: *Annual Report of the Certification Officer for 2003–2004*, para 4.5.
244 In 2002/3 it stood at 1,289,000: *Annual Report of the Certification Officer for 2003–2004*, App 4.
245 *Annual Report of the Certification Officer for 2003–2004*, App 4.
246 Labour Research, June 1999: pp 9–11.
247 House of Commons Employment Committee, above, note 229, paras 90–101.

taken place across industrial and occupational boundaries, unions have created complex forms of internal representation which have thus 'transformed traditional issues of inter-union relations into intra-union relations, with no obvious benefits in terms of strategic advantage'.[248]

Second, unions adopted a 'managerial servicing relationship' in which they sought 'to research members' needs and design and promote attractive servicing packages in response',[249] placing greater emphasis on benefits beyond collective bargaining, such as legal services, professional advice, cash benefits covering accident insurance and convalescence, representation at work or in employment tribunals, and advantageous deals on mortgages and loans, life assurance, credit cards, home and motor insurance and travel. Unions recognised that 'consumerist' benefits would not of themselves suffice to attract members,[250] and recent developments may bring more work-related services to the fore again, such as helplines on individual rights, representation at disciplinary and grievance hearings (now a statutory right),[251] and collective consultation and collective bargaining. Since the advent of the Labour Government, unions also have played a greater role in workplace training, with £8 million of public money being committed to a 'Union Learning Fund' and, since 2003, 'union learning representatives' having a right to paid time off from work.[252] In addition the TUC has established an 'Organising Academy' to which unions can send representatives to train as specialist membership recruiters.[253] The ERelA 2004 gave the Secretary of State authority to provide financial assistance to independent trade unions for, *inter alia*, improving the way they carry out their functions and increasing the range of services they offer to their members.[254] It is envisaged that the 'Union Modernisation Fund' will be in the region of £5–£10 million in total, with funding spread over several years, beginning in 2005/6, with the emphasis on supporting innovative projects which speed unions' adaptation to changing labour market trends and new ways of working, such as greater use of the internet and other new technologies.[255] There is a specific prohibition on funds being added to a union's political fund.[256]

In relation to employers, unions have sought to emphasise their ability to co-operate as partners, rather than as adversaries, in introducing greater flexibility and change whilst at the same time protecting the interests of employees.[257] 'Partnership' is a difficult concept to define, but in 1999 the TUC identified what it regarded as the principles underlying it: shared commitment to the organisation's business goals; recognition that the partners may have legitimate differences which needed to be heard; recognition that flexibility of employment should not be at the expense of employees' security, which should be protected by measures such as ensuring transferable skills and qualifications; the need to improve the personal development of employees; open and well informed consultation, involving genuine dialogue; and 'adding value' by raising employee

248 Heery *et al*, 2003: p 84; see also J Waddington, 2003: pp 222–224.
249 Heery, 1996: p 187; see also Ewing, 2005, for discussion of these developments.
250 Heery, 1996: p 190.
251 ERelA 1999, ss 10–15; see para 5.132 *et seq*.
252 TULRCA 1992, s 168A.
253 Heery *et al*, 2003.
254 TULRCA 1992, s 116A, inserted by ERelA 2004, s 55.
255 Gerry Sutcliffe, Parliamentary Under-Secretary of State for Employment Relations, Competition and Consumers, HC Debs col 1368W, 10 February 2004, (written answer).
256 TULRCA 1992, s 116A(4)–(7).
257 See Taylor, 1994: ch 5; Taylor, 2000: ch 8.

motivation.[258] In 2001 the TUC launched a Partnership Institute to help organisations improve industrial relations and develop partnerships between unions and employers.[259] The CBI also associated itself with this initiative, and partnership deals have been signed at a wide variety of workplaces, although their content varies significantly,[260] ranging from 'some that do indeed seek to nurture trade unions as genuinely representative and independent, albeit on a cooperative basis, through to some that are thinly veiled devices to limit and constrain union influence.'[261] Recent years have also been marked by an increase in the incidence of voluntary recognition agreements, reached in the shadow of the statutory recognition procedure,[262] and the legislation on information and consultation, which came into force in April 2005,[263] has encouraged the establishment of consultative bodies on a voluntary basis, although these are not confined to union representatives. Finally, the role of unions (and employers) as social partners has also been enhanced at European Union level, within the framework of the 'social dialogue', although there are unresolved issues of 'representativity' in this area, given that the TUC does not represent all workers nor even all trade unionists,[264] nor does the CBI represent all employers.

During the period of the 1979–97 Conservative Government trade unions became increasingly excluded from the political process, collective bargaining coverage contracted, and the decline in membership seemed irreversible. The picture now is very different. At the time of writing the future of trade unions continues to be unpredictable, but there are indications that the more hospitable political environment, as reflected in changes to the law relating to recognition, consultation and representation of workers, may lead to a revival of influence, albeit of a different nature than in the past, for the trade union movement.

258 *Partners for Progress: New Unionism at the Workplace*; see W Brown 2000: pp 305–306.
259 W Brown and S Oxenbridge, 2004: p 73.
260 W Brown 2000: p 306; Bacon and Storey, 2000; Guest and Peccei, 2001; Heery, 2002; Oxenbridge and Brown, 2004; Taylor, 2004; Stuart and Martinez-Lucio, 2005.
261 W Brown and S Oxenbridge, 2004: p 73.
262 Gall and McKay, 1999; Gall, 2004; S Wood *et al*, 2002; Moore *et al*, 2004.
263 See para 9.50.
264 The TUC told the House of Commons Employment Committee above, note 229, that 86% of trade unionists belonged to unions within the TUC: *Report*, para 12.

CHAPTER 8

Freedom of association and the right to organise

INTRODUCTION

8.1 As we saw in chapter 7, workers' freedom to associate and organise may potentially be subject to restriction by the state, by employers, or, arguably, by trade unions exercising power to admit, or expel from, membership. There we examined the history and current scope of restrictions on freedom of association imposed by the state. In this chapter we analyse workers' rights in relation to trade union membership and activities as regards employers. The rights which the law gives individuals in relation to trade unions are discussed in chapter 10.

The chapter begins by analysing the legal position of workers who are denied employment, or dismissed or otherwise disadvantaged, because of their trade union membership or activities. This includes consideration of the right not to be induced to move from terms of employment that have been collectively agreed. We also examine the remedies of those who are subject to disadvantageous treatment because they *refuse* to join a union, although whether the right not to join should be regarded as intrinsic to freedom of association in the employment context, and of equal status to the right to join, is a contentious issue which we address later in the chapter. We discuss this question within this framework because the development of the legislation which upholds the right to join cannot be properly understood in isolation from it. We also, in this connection, outline restrictions upon the operation of contract compliance policies relating to union membership or non-membership. We then consider the extent to which the law provides more positive support for union organisation by requiring employers to allow time off during working hours for union representatives and other union members. Unlike the provisions relating to anti-union discrimination, these rights are confined to members of unions which are recognised. Finally, we examine the legal restrictions which surround the practice of the 'check-off' whereby employers deduct union subscriptions from workers' pay and pass them directly to the union. As this summary demonstrates the chapter involves a heterogenous collection of rights whose fragmented nature can be properly understood only in the light of their legislative history.

PROTECTION OF TRADE UNION MEMBERSHIP AND ACTIVITIES IN RELATION TO EMPLOYERS

8.2 All workers other than the police[1] are now free to form and join trade unions.[2] However, this negative freedom from restraint means little if its exercise

---

1   Police Act 1996, s 64. See further para 7.13 above.
2   Members of the armed forces (as well as the police) are specifically excluded from the anti-union discrimination provisions: TULRCA 1992, ss 274, 280. Note also s 275 which permits particular groups of persons, or particular individuals, in Crown employment to be exempted from the application of the Act, and thus from the statutory protections against anti-union discrimination, for the purpose of safeguarding national security; this enables it to be made

can be thwarted by employers refusing to employ, or dismissing or otherwise discriminating against, trade union members. This point is emphasised by ILO Convention No 98 which states that '[w]orkers shall enjoy adequate protection against acts of anti-union discrimination in respect of their employment', more particularly in relation to acts 'calculated to (a) Make the employment of a worker subject to the condition that he shall not join a union or shall relinquish trade union membership; (b) Cause the dismissal or otherwise prejudice a worker by reason of union activities or because of participation in union activities outside working hours or, with the consent of the employer, within working hours'.[3]

As we saw in chapter 7, legal intervention in Britain in this area came late. Official encouragement of trade union membership and participation following the reports of the Whitley Committee[4] was manifested by the Government seeking to set an example to the private sector by its own employment practices rather than by introducing legislation upholding the right to organise.[5] However, exhorting public servants to join trade unions was not universally successful in persuading other employers, particularly in the white-collar sectors, to follow suit.[6] Employer strategies to discourage union organisation ranged from making it a term of the contract of employment that employees should not join trade unions, denying union members promotion and pay rises, and continuously transferring active unionists between departments, on the one hand, to establishing 'company unions' to ward off external organisations and offering rewards to 'loyal' employees on the other.[7] The 1946 version of the House of Commons Fair Wages Resolution (now rescinded) specified that government contracts with private employers should require contractors to recognise the freedom of their workers to be members of trade unions. However, although symbolically significant, the Resolution appears to have been of little practical effect in influencing employment practices due to inadequate monitoring and enforcement.[8]

8.3   The United Kingdom was the first country to ratify ILO Conventions 87 and 98 (in 1949 and 1950 respectively). However, the first statutory intervention to

---

a valid term of employment for members of the security and intelligence agencies that they will not join a trade union. See para 7.10 above on the withdrawal of the freedom of workers at Government Communications Headquarters to join national civil service trade unions (now reinstated). In addition, if on a complaint of unfair dismissal, or a complaint relating to an inducement or detriment under TULRCA 1992, ss 145A, 145B or 146, it is shown that the action complained of was taken for the purpose of safeguarding national security, the employment tribunal must dismiss the complaint: ETA 1996, s 10(1), as substituted by ERelA 1999 and amended by ERelA 2004.

3   Convention Concerning the Application of the Principles of the Right to Organise and to Bargain Collectively, 1949, Art 1.

4   For a summary of the Committee's recommendations, and references to interim reports, see Ministry of Reconstruction: Committee on Relations between Employers and Employed: *Final Report*, Cd 9153 (1918).

5   See generally Fredman and Morris, 1989: ch 4.

6   See the *Report of the Royal Commission on Trade Unions and Employers' Associations 1965–1968* (the Donovan Commission), Cmnd 3623, 1968, paras 213–224.

7   See Bain, 1970: pp 131–135, who divides such strategies into those of 'forceful opposition' and 'peaceful competition'.

8   See Bercusson, 1978: ch 17. The Local Government Act 1988 made it unlawful for local authorities and certain other bodies to stipulate such requirements; see now the Local Government Act 1999, s 19 and SI 2001/909, discussed at para 2.6; see also TULRCA, 1992, ss 144 and 145, discussed in para 8.32 below.

uphold freedom of association came only in 1971,[9] when the Industrial Relations Act extended protection to workers against discrimination by employers on grounds of trade union membership and participation in union activities (as well as bestowing correlative rights not to join). As these rights applied only to membership of unions which 'registered' under the Act, and it was TUC policy not to do this, they had little practical effect. They were maintained in an amended form in the 1974–1979 Labour Government's 'Social Contract' legislation and have continued in force, with important modifications, ever since. Their survival – and indeed, extension[10] – in a climate hostile to trade unions during the period of the 1979–1997 Conservative Government can be understood only by appreciating that the real target of that government's policy was the protection of the right not to join a union, a right to which these provisions were perceived as the corollary. Initially the Labour Government which succeeded it maintained the basic framework intact in its essentials. However the Employment Relations Act 2004 significantly extended the scope of protection, with effect from 1 October 2004, to give effect to the decision of the European Court of Human Rights in *Wilson and NUJ v UK, Palmer, Wyeth and RMT v UK* and *Doolan and others v UK*,[11] discussed in para 7.9 above. In these cases the employers had each refused a pay rise to employees who refused to transfer to personal contracts in place of collectively agreed terms and conditions of employment. These contracts also required those who signed them to forego the entitlement to be represented by a union in some or all of their dealings with the employer. The ECtHR held that the UK had failed in its positive obligation to secure the enjoyment of rights guaranteed by Article 11 of the ECHR by permitting employers to use financial incentives to induce employees to surrender important union rights. 'This failure amounted to a violation of Article 11, as regards both the applicant unions and the individual applicants.'[12] In response to the judgment, the government introduced a new right for a worker not to have an offer made to him or her by an employer where the employer's sole or main purpose is that workers' terms of employment, or any such term, will not be determined by collective agreement.[13] It is also now unlawful to offer a worker an inducement not to join an independent union, or to participate in its activities or use its services, or to join a union.[14] These provisions are in addition to the more long-standing remedies against discrimination by employers on trade union grounds. The government also introduced amendments to the pre-existing law to deal with matters it considered would have been regarded by the Court as contrary to Article 11 had they been at issue.[15]

---

9   The Donovan Commission (above, note 6) pointed out (para 243) that these Conventions were not drafted in terms which required legislation; 'successive British Governments' had taken the view that the trade union movement was sufficiently strong to make legislation unnecessary and the TUC had not pressed for it.

10   For example the introduction of enhanced compensation levels and protection against discriminatory hiring.

11   Judgment of 2 July 2002, [2002] IRLR 568. See Ewing, 2003.

12   Above, para 48.

13   TULRCA 1992, s 145B–145F, inserted by ERelA 2004, s 29.

14   TULRCA 1992, s 145A, 145C–145F, inserted by ERelA 2004, s 29.

15   Memorandum from the DTI in response to concerns raised by the Committee in its Third and Fourth Progress Report of Session 2003–2004, Joint Committee on Human Rights, Thirteenth Report, Session 2003–2004. Appendix 2a, para 44. Examples given of such additional matters include new TULRCA 1992, s 145A and the application of ss 145A, 145B, and 146 to 'workers' rather than 'employees'. ERelA 2004 also repealed the notorious 'Ullswater Amendment' contained in s 148(3)–(5) and ERelA 1999, s 17 (the latter was never brought into force). See G Morris and T Archer, 2000: paras 3.12 and 4.72 for an analysis of these repealed provisions.

In broad terms the legislation now provides access to remedies (which cannot be excluded by contract) in relation to three major forms of discrimination by employers,[16] although, as the more detailed analysis below reveals, their application is hedged around with restrictions. First, employees have the right not to be dismissed (or selected for redundancy[17]) on account of their membership of an independent trade union or participation in the activities of, or making use of the services of, such a union at an appropriate time.[18] Protection also extends to dismissal (or selection for redundancy) for failing to accept an inducement not to be a union member or engage in such activities or to move from terms of employment that have been collectively agreed. Second, workers (not only 'employees') have the right not to be subjected to any detriment by any act, or deliberate failure to act, to penalise or deter such membership or activities or because of the worker's failure to accept an inducement.[19] The detriment in question may amount to dismissal, but only for workers who are not 'employees'; those who are employees must rely upon the protection described above.[20] Last, it is unlawful to refuse a person employment because he or she is a member of a union.[21] Significantly, however, it is not unlawful to refuse employment because of participation in union activities, although the Employment Relations Act 1999 has accorded the Secretary of State a power – as yet unexercised – to make regulations prohibiting the compilation of lists of those who have taken part in union activities, as well as of union members, with a view to their use by employers or employment agencies to discriminate in relation to the recruitment or treatment of workers.[22]

8.4   We examine the scope of each of these rights in turn before assessing, from a broader perspective, their effectiveness in protecting the freedom to associate and organise. It should be noted that despite the changes introduced by ERelA 2004 there are still respects in which the legislation, and case law interpreting that legislation, does not fully comply with international standards. The Human

16   Certain categories of worker are excluded from these rights: see note 2 above. For the protections against prejudicial action for those involved in health and safety activities see para 5.104 above.

17   Here it must be shown that the circumstances constituting the redundancy (the principal reason for dismissal) applied equally to one or more other employees in the same undertaking who held positions similar to that held by the applicant and who have not been dismissed by the employer, and the reason or principal reason for selection was one of those specified in TULRCA 1992, s 152(1): TULRCA 1992, s 153. There is no requirement to find that employers were motivated by malice or the deliberate desire to be rid of a union activist: *Dundon v GPT Ltd* [1995] IRLR 403, EAT. In determining whether the dismissed employee and his or her comparator hold similar 'positions', regard should be paid only to their relative positions as employees; no account should be paid to what any of them did, or had a contractual right to do, in other capacities, such as a union official: *O'Dea v ISC Chemicals Ltd (t/a Rhône-Poulenc Chemicals)* [1995] IRLR 599, CA. Moreover, the way in which employees carry out their duties as union officials should not count either in their favour or against them: *Smiths Industries Aerospace and Defence Systems v Rawlings* [1996] IRLR 656 (a case concerning a health and safety representative).

18   TULRCA 1992, s 152, as amended by ERelA 2004, s 32. In *Driver v Cleveland Structural Engineering Co Ltd* [1994] IRLR 636 the EAT held that this section could also cover the situation where a redundant employee was not offered alternative employment within the organisation; if this was on grounds of trade union membership or activities it would be automatically unfair.

19   TULRCA 1992 s 146, as amended by ERelA 2004, ss 30, 31.

20   TULRCA 1992, s 146(5A), inserted by ERelA 2004, s 30(6).

21   TULRCA 1992, s 137.

22   S 3.

Rights Act 1998 may be invoked to persuade courts and tribunals towards a more expansive interpretation of some of these provisions, and may afford a free-standing right to individuals and unions discriminated against by public authorities (or, at least, 'pure' public authorities) who lie outside the ambit of the specific protections or whose particular activities are not protected:[23] Article 11 of the ECHR, which guarantees the right to join to trade unions, applies to '[e]veryone', as does Article 10, which guarantees the right to freedom of expression. In addition, as we saw in para 7.11, there is authority in European Community law to support the recognition of freedom of association as a fundamental right,[24] and the ECJ has derived from the right to join trade unions a right to participate in their activities. However, the details of these rights await clarification. From another perspective it should also be noted that recent legislation to implement Community law obligations, in particular new rights to information and consultation, which we discuss in chapter 9, may encourage the fragmentation of worker representation away from the single channel of trade unions, the traditional repository of this role in Britain, to a dual channel system which also incorporates the establishment of representative bodies existing separately from unions, although union members and officials may be elected to them. Those who serve on these representative bodies are protected against dismissal or other detriment for exercising their functions, as are employees who participate in activities related to their establishment, but there is no broader protection against discrimination of the kind that applies in relation to trade unions and their activities. The more frequent establishment of bodies of this nature prompts the question as to whether the scope of protection for freedom of association and the right to organise should expand commensurately to cover collective organisation and activity beyond the ambit of traditional trade unionism.

Protection for employees against dismissal: procedure and remedies

8.5 Protection for employees against dismissal for trade union membership and activities is secured through the unfair dismissal procedure described in chapter 5. It is thus confined at the time of writing to 'employees'.[25] However, since 1 October 2004, protection against subjection to a detriment has applied to the broader category of 'workers', and 'workers' who are not 'employees' may rely upon that protection, discussed in para 8.13 *et seq* below, in the event of dismissal.[26] However, as we discuss in para 3.51 *et seq*, this may still leave some categories of dependent labour, such as casual workers, unprotected[27] unless courts and tribunals can be persuaded, in accordance with the Human Rights Act 1998,[28] to construe the term more broadly than in other contexts in order to give effect to the protection afforded by Articles 10 and 11 of the ECHR

---

23   Ss 6, 7.
24   Note also Art 12 of the Charter of Fundamental Rights of the European Union, which affirms the right to form and join trade unions in similar terms to Art 11 of the ECHR. See para 2.43 for the status of the Charter.
25   See para 3.20 *et seq*. As with the general provisions Crown employment (other than the armed forces and those excluded under TULRCA 1992, s 275) is included.
26   TULRCA 1992, s 146, as amended by ERelA 2004, s 30. 'Employees' are excluded from that protection in relation to dismissal by s 146(5A). See s 151(1B) for the definition of 'worker' for the purposes of ss 146–150.
27   As a result of the insistence upon mutuality of obligation: see further para 3.56.
28   S 3.

to '[e]veryone'.[29] As we discuss in para 8.13 below, requiring 'employees' to rely upon the 'unfair dismissal' protection rather than the general protection against 'detriment' in this context can, in some respects, put them at a disadvantage, and may produce the unusual situation of individuals arguing that they are 'workers' other than 'employees'.

Subject to the constraint on its personal scope, the legislation accords some specific recognition of the position of trade unions in that dismissal,[30] and (with one exception[31]) selection for redundancy, on grounds of union membership and activities are subject to some special provisions (which also apply to dismissals on certain other grounds[32]).

First, once such a reason is found by the employment tribunal, the dismissal is automatically unfair; an employer cannot argue that it was reasonable in the circumstances.

Second, no minimum period of employment is required[33] and there is no maximum age limit.[34] The significance of this second category of exceptions is modified, however, by a Court of Appeal decision that where employees are claiming in circumstances where they would not otherwise qualify to claim, it is for them to prove the reason, or principal reason, for dismissal given that they are invoking a jurisdiction which the tribunal would otherwise not have.[35] This may be a difficult burden to satisfy, particularly as employers will generally take care to ensure that other reasons, such as poor work or a disciplinary offence, are attributed to such dismissals,[36] although the need since 1 October 2004 to institute the statutory dismissal and disciplinary procedure prior to dismissal may make it easier for an employee to refute a specious reason.[37] The treatment of employees who have not been dismissed is usually irrelevant to whether the dismissal of the applicant is unfair. In this context, however, it may be important for the employee to show that non-unionists in a similar position have not been dismissed in order to undermine the credibility of the employer's evidence.[38] The difficulty of the employee's task in discharging the burden of proof may be exacerbated if the decision was taken by a group of persons, as

---

29   See para 7.10 above for the exceptions to these guarantees. In cases where it is not possible for an individual to be deemed to be a 'worker', they will probably be denied a remedy unless they are employed by a 'public authority' against whom proceedings may be brought directly: HRA 1998, ss 6.7.

30   See para 5.62 *et seq.* for the definition of 'dismissal'. In this context, as in relation to complaints of unfair dismissal on other grounds, 'constructive dismissal' is included.

31   The remedy of 'interim relief' described below.

32   See para 5.95 *et seq* above.

33   TULRCA 1992, s 154, as substituted by ERelA 2004, s 35. The EAT has held that an employee can claim for unfair dismissal if her contract of employment is terminated for an 'anti-union' reason before she has taken up her duties: *Sarker v South Tees Acute Hospitals NHS Trust* [1997] IRLR 328.

34   TULRCA 1992, s 154, as substituted by ERelA 2004, s 35.

35   *Smith v Hayle Town Council* [1978] ICR 996; *Marley Tile Co Ltd v Shaw* [1980] ICR 72. Where an employee would otherwise qualify to claim, the employer must show that the reason for dismissal was one of those specified in ERA 1996, s 98(1), (2) in the usual way in order to defend the claim: *Maund v Penwith District Council* [1984] IRLR 24.

36   Evans and Lewis, 1987: p 95.

37   See further para 5.124 *et seq.* It is difficult to imagine circumstances in which an employer would be justified in relying on the 'modified' procedure in this situation: see para 5.126.

38   Employment Tribunals (Constitution and Rules of Procedure) Regulations 2004, SI 2004/1861, Sch 1, para 10. Note that there is no equivalent under TULRCA 1992 to the Sex Discrimination (Questions and Replies) Order 1975, SI 1975/2048 or other similar provisions in the areas of race, disability, religion or belief, or sexual orientation discrimination.

the facts of *Smith v Hayle Town Council* exemplify. The applicant was a town clerk who applied to join a union. He told two councillors that he had done this. Shortly afterwards he was dismissed at a council meeting by a vote of six to five. The evidence showed that at least one member of the council had voted for dismissal because of his application to join a union but there was no evidence to show why the remaining five had voted as they did. The Court of Appeal concluded that, although there was an 'element of [anti-union] prejudice', that had not been shown to be the principal reason behind the thinking of the 'corporate mind'.[39]

The final departure from the norm in relation to dismissals for 'anti-union' reasons lies in the area of remedies. Here there are two distinctive features. First, the dismissed employee may apply for 'interim relief' pending the outcome of the tribunal hearing, provided that the application is presented within seven days of the effective date of termination[40] and is supported by a certificate signed by an official[41] of the union authorised to act for this purpose.[42] If the tribunal finds that the employee's claim is 'likely'[43] to succeed at the full hearing it may order his or her reinstatement or re-engagement pending the determination or settlement of the complaint or, if the employer refuses this, order the continuation of the contract, thus continuing the other benefits of employment until that time.[44] This provision reduces the need for the employee to seek other employment pending the tribunal hearing. Second, if the unfair dismissal complaint succeeds a minimum basic award of £3,800 is payable.[45] Prior to the Employment Relations Act 1999 a complainant who sought reinstatement or re-engagement[46] was also entitled to a special award in addition to the basic and compensatory awards.[47] This has now been abolished, and, as in other cases where employers fail to comply with an order to reinstate or re-engage an

---

39 [1978] ICR 996, 1003 (Eveleigh LJ).

40 See para 5.83 *et seq* above.

41 Defined in TULRCA 1992, s 119. Note that this is wide enough to cover shop stewards. On authorisation see *Sulemany v Habib Bank Ltd* [1983] ICR 60, EAT. For the required content of the certificate see s 161(3) and *Barley v Amey Roadstone Corpn Ltd* [1977] IRLR 299, EAT; *Stone v Charrington and Co Ltd* [1977] ICR 248, EAT; *Bradley v Edward Ryde and Sons* [1979] ICR 488, EAT; *Sulemany v Habib Bank*, above; *London Borough of Camden v Maharaj* EAT/1323/00, 9 November 2000.

42 See generally TULRCA 1992, ss 161–166. Note that this remedy is also available where the applicant alleges that the dismissal is unfair on certain other grounds: see para 5.163 above. It does not apply to selection for redundancy on union grounds. See para 5.129 for the implications of the statutory dismissal and disciplinary procedures for an application for interim relief.

43 This has been interpreted as 'pretty good': *Taplin v C Shippam Ltd* [1978] ICR 1068.

44 *Quaere* whether, if a shop steward had a contractual right to be on the premises to exercise his or her functions (see *City and Hackney Health Authority v NUPE* [1985] IRLR 252, CA) this would be covered by TULRCA 1992, s 164(1), which includes 'any ... benefit derived from the employment ...' In practice such circumstances are likely to be rare. In *Dowling v ME Ilec Haulage and Berkeley Logistics Ltd* UKEAT/0836 it was held that liability under a continuation order did not transfer under TUPE.

45 TULRCA 1992, s 156; rate as of 1 February 2005 and at the time of writing. This also applies if an employee has been selected for redundancy on trade union grounds under TULRCA 1992, s 153. However, the award may be reduced on the same grounds as in other cases subject to s 156(2) in cases of unfair selection for redundancy.

46 See para 5.148 *et seq* above for the meaning of these terms and criteria for granting orders.

47 At the time of abolition, this stood at a minimum of £14,500 and a maximum of £29,000 if reinstatement or re-engagement was not ordered, and a minimum of £21,800 and a maximum of 156 weeks' pay if an order was made and not complied with.

unfairly dismissed employee, an additional award which is limited to 26–52 weeks' pay may be made unless the employer shows that it was not reasonably practicable to comply with the order. As we indicated in para 5.151, the Court of Appeal has adopted a broad view of the concept of practicability in this context.[48] The restricted level of compensation for dismissal for trade union reasons stands in marked contrast to dismissal for 'whistleblowing' and reasons relating to health and safety, where there is no limit on the compensatory award.[49] We discuss the adequacy of the remedies in general further in para 8.26.

The scope of protection

8.6   The provisions outlined above apply where the principal reason for dismissal falls into one of four categories:[50] first, if the employee was, or proposed to become, a member of an independent trade union;[51] second, if the employee had taken part, or proposed to take part, in the activities of an independent trade union at an appropriate time;[52] third, if the employee had made use, or proposed to make use, of trade union services at an appropriate time;[53] and fourth, if an employee had failed to accept an offer made for a specified unlawful purpose.[54]

(i) Membership of an independent trade union

8.7   Dismissal for membership of an independent trade union has been held to cover membership of a particular union as well as unions in general so employees are protected if they are dismissed for joining union X instead of union Y.[55] This prevents employers from inhibiting employees' freedom to join the union of their choice. However, as a result of restrictive judicial interpretation of this provision, the extent to which the concept of union membership goes beyond a bare right to hold a union card, and in particular whether it covers making use of union services, became unclear.[56] Prior to the introduction of extended protection

---

48   See *Port of London Authority v Payne* [1994] IRLR 9.
49   ERA 1996, s 124(1A).
50   Note that where the terms of TULRCA 1992, s 152 (or s 153) are not satisfied an anti-union dismissal may still be unfair under the ordinary unfair dismissal provisions.
51   TULRCA 1992, s 152(1)(a). See para 7.23 above for the definition of an 'independent' trade union. The restriction means that members of 'embryonic' unions may be excluded: Todd, 2000: p 579. The employee need not have decided which particular union he or she wishes to join: *Cotter v Lynch Bros* [1972] IRLR 20. Membership of a union includes membership of a particular branch or section of that union or one of a number of such branches or sections, and references to taking part in the activities of a union and to services made available by a union are to be similarly construed: s 152(4), (5).
52   TULRCA 1992, s 152(1)(b). Where the employee is dismissed for proposing to take part in union activities there is no requirement to identify the precise activities: see *Fitzpatrick v British Railways Board* [1991] IRLR 376.
53   TULRCA 1992, s 152(1)(ba).
54   TULRCA 1992, S 152(1)(bb). See further paras 8.17 *et seq* below.
55   *Ridgway and Fairbrother v National Coal Board* [1987] IRLR 80, CA. Although *Ridgway* was overruled in *Associated Newspapers Ltd v Wilson; Associated British Ports v Palmer* [1995] IRLR 258, this element of the reasoning in that case would appear to remain valid.
56   See *Discount Tobacco and Confectionery Ltd v Armitage* [1990] IRLR 15, EAT (membership extended to using the 'essential services' of the union); *Associated Newspapers Ltd v Wilson; Associated British Ports v Palmer* [1995] IRLR 258, HL (membership of a union and making use of its services could not be equated); *Speciality Care plc v Pachela* [1996] IRLR 248, EAT (observations in *Wilson* were *obiter*).

against dismissal by ERelA 2004, this constituted a serious limitation, given that employers are likely to object not to the mere act of joining a union but to its practical implications. The specific protection now accorded against dismissal for making use of trade union services has removed much of the practical significance of this debate, although the issue may still arise if the individual's act (clarifying terms of employment, for example) is not at an 'appropriate time'; there is no such limitation in relation to union membership.

(ii) Participation in the activities of an independent trade union at an appropriate time

8.8   Crucial to the second reason are the concepts of '*activities of an independent trade union*' and '*appropriate time*'. '*Activities*' are not defined in the legislation; they clearly include activities connected with internal union organisation and industrial relations and should, in theory, extend to any activities which a union may lawfully undertake (although, in applying this term within the time off provisions, certain political activities have been excluded).[57] The courts have held that, because it is dealt with elsewhere in the legislation,[58] participation in industrial action (as opposed to preparation for it)[59] is not within the scope of protected activities[60] although, as others have argued,[61] this conclusion does not necessarily follow from the structure of the legislation: this separate provision relates only to whether the tribunal has jurisdiction to hear a claim; where it does have such jurisdiction there seems no reason why industrial action should not be a union activity. Ultimately this debate is of little practical significance as, to be effective, industrial action is unlikely to be at an 'appropriate time' (see below).

8.9   More problematic is the decision as to when activities are those '*of the union*'. The courts have emphasised that it is not sufficient that a union member is taking part in the type of activities which his or her union pursues ('trade union' is not 'adjectival');[62] rather, it seems that the union must in some sense have 'authorised' the individual to act on its behalf. Such authorisation will usually derive from custom and practice rather than being direct and specific. Thus, union members will generally be protected while participating in internal union affairs, such as recruitment and other organisational activities,[63] attending

---

57   See *Luce v London Borough of Bexley* [1990] IRLR 422, EAT, discussed in para 8.39 below.

58   See paras 11.72 *et seq.*

59   *Britool Ltd v Roberts* [1993] IRLR 481, EAT.

60   *Drew v St Edmundsbury Borough Council* [1980] IRLR 459, EAT.

61   See, for example, P Davies and M Freedland, 1984: p 191; Harvey, 1972, as updated: Division N, para 517 *et seq.* The strength of this argument may be reduced by the creation of protection against dismissal for taking 'protected industrial action' (see para 11.78), which could be seen as demonstrating the intention of the legislature that protection against dismissal should be confined to participation only in a restricted form of industrial action.

62   *Dixon and Shaw v West Ella Developments Ltd* [1978] IRLR 151, 153 (Phillips J).

63   *Lyon v St James Press Ltd* [1976] IRLR 215. It is irrelevant that these activities are not disclosed to the management. The qualification in this case that 'wholly unreasonable, extraneous or malicious acts' done in support of union activities may not be protected is hard to justify. See, however, the dictum of Pill LJ in *Bass Taverns Ltd v Burgess* [1995] IRLR 596, at 599, where he opined that malicious, untruthful or irrelevant statements at a union recruitment meeting may not fall within the scope of trade union activities.

union meetings,[64] and discussing union matters.[65] Contacting a union official for advice in certain circumstances has also been included,[66] although since 1 October 2004 it would be preferable to rely on the specific protection for use of trade union services, discussed in para 8.11 below. On the basis of the case law, individual union members probably have little or no authority to act on behalf of the union in any dealings with the employer. In *Chant v Aquaboats Ltd*[67] a union member who organised a petition complaining about safety standards in the workplace was found not to have been taking part in the activities 'of the union' in presenting the petition to the employer, despite the fact that a union official had approved the petition before it was presented; this did not make it a communication of the union given that Mr Chant was not a shop steward and the petition had been signed by a majority of workers who were not union members. By contrast, union representatives, such as shop stewards,[68] would seem to be 'authorised' to perform a wider range of activities, such as taking up members' grievances with management, calling meetings of the workforce (regardless of whether they are critical of more senior officials),[69] and any other activities normally associated with officials of their grade, provided that they act in accordance with union practice.[70]

As well as differentiating between activities of individual trade unionists and those 'of the union' the courts have also, from the opposite perspective, distinguished between an employer's reactions to an individual employee's activities in a union context and activities of the union. In *Therm A Stor Ltd v Atkins and Carrington*[71] between 60 and 65 of the company's 70 employees had joined the Transport and General Workers Union, and representatives of those employees asked the union's district secretary to apply to the company for recognition. The company then instructed its chargehands to select 20 employees for dismissal. The employment tribunal found that, although the employers were strongly anti-union and the dismissals were in reaction to the union's letter seeking recognition, the chargehands had not taken account of the actual or proposed union membership of, or participation in union activities by, the employees concerned and therefore those employees could not show that this was the reason for their dismissal. The EAT allowed the appeal and said that failure to construe the legislation to cover dismissal of individuals by way of reprisal for the involvement of the union would render the legislation 'wholly inoperative' in many instances where it must have been intended to apply. The

---

64 *Rasool v Hepworth Pipe Co Ltd (No 2)* [1980] IRLR 137; *British Airways Engine Overhaul Ltd v Francis* [1981] IRLR 9.

65 *Zucker v Astrid Jewels Ltd* [1978] IRLR 385.

66 *Brennan and Ging v Ellward (Lancs) Ltd* [1976] IRLR 378, EAT; *Dixon and Shaw v West Ella Developments Ltd* [1978] IRLR 151 (but note the limitation suggested there – of questionable authority – that the union should take some action in response to this approach for the employee to be protected. There is no such limitation in TULRCA 1992, s 152(1)(ba)).

67 [1978] ICR 643.

68 Union representatives are often referred to as 'shop stewards', especially among blue-collar workers, but sometimes have other titles (eg. convenor, or Father or Mother of the Chapel): Cully *et al*, 1999: p 214, n 1. In this chapter we use the term 'union representative' to cover all lay union representatives.

69 *British Airways Engine Overhaul Ltd v Francis* [1981] IRLR 9.

70 See, for example, *British Airways Engine Overhaul Ltd v Francis* [1981] IRLR 9; *Marley Tile Co Ltd v Shaw* [1980] IRLR 25.

71 [1983] IRLR 78.

Court of Appeal, however, restored the decision of the employment tribunal, holding that the reason for dismissal was not related to anything which the employees personally had done. The Court rejected the argument of the applicants' counsel – that union activities were essentially collective and that where reasons for dismissal were the activities of the group (ie, the union) they were, therefore, those of individuals – as a 'valiant attempt at purposive construction' which went beyond permissible limits'.[72]

It is strongly arguable that this very narrow interpretation of the legislation does not take adequate account of the fact that the union was acting on behalf, and at the request, of individual members. More broadly, it highlights the limitations of locating the protection of collective activity wholly within a framework of individual rights, a theme to which we return in para 8.24. In relation to the decision itself the burden of proof may have been a crucial factor. The applicants in the case lacked the period of continuous employment needed to bring a general unfair dismissal claim and thus were required to prove that their dismissal was for union activities. Had they been qualified to bring such a claim it is difficult to see that the employers would have been able to demonstrate a potentially fair reason for dismissal.[73] The *Therm A Stor* decision now stands in marked contrast to the situation where a union has sought recognition pursuant to the statutory procedure, discussed in chapter 9; in that context workers have protection against dismissal or selection for redundancy (or subjection to other detriment) for specified acts relating to the recognition procedures, including acting with a view to obtaining, or indicating support for, recognition.[74] Given that it is government policy to encourage unions and employers to reach voluntary recognition agreements outside the statutory procedure, it is most unfortunate that these protections were not extended to situations where no request for recognition has been made pursuant to the statute.[75] It may be possible to derive such protection from the Human Rights Act 1998 in the light of the interpretation of Article 11 in *Wilson* and *Palmer*,[76] but it would be strongly preferable for such protection to be made explicit. As we explain in para 8.11 below, the applicants in *Therm A Stor* would not be regarded as making use of 'trade union services' under the provisions introduced by ERelA 2004.

---

72 Per Sir John Donaldson at 80.
73 See further para 5.115 *et seq* above.
74 TULRCA 1992, Sch A1, paras 156–165.
75 *Quaere* whether an employee who voiced support for voluntary recognition where it was official policy to seek it could be regarded as 'authorised' by the union.
76 Judgment of 2 July 2002, [2002] IRLR 568, para 46: 'The Court agrees with the Government that the essence of a voluntary system of collective bargaining is that it must be possible for a trade union which it not recognised by an employer to take steps including, if necessary, organising industrial action, with a view to persuading the employer to enter into collective bargaining with it on those issues which the union believes are important for its members' interests. Furthermore, it is of the essence of the right to join a trade union for the protection of their interests that employees should be free to instruct or permit the union to make representations to their employer or to take action in support of their interests on their behalf'. This argument may be more successfully located in the context of dismissal on the grounds of union membership rather than union activity, given that it starts from the perspective of the individual rather than the union. If a public authority (or at least a 'pure' public authority) interfered with the rights of its workers in this way, they could invoke this argument (and possibly, in some circumstances, an argument based upon interference with the right to freedom of expression) to pursue a free-standing claim against the authority: HRA 1998, ss 6, 7.

8.10   An '*appropriate time*' in relation to union activities means a time outside the employee's working hours, or a time within his or her working hours at which, in accordance with arrangements agreed with or consent given by the employer, participation in the activities of a union is permissible.[77] 'Working hours', in relation to an employee, means any time when, in accordance with his or her contract of employment, he or she is required to be 'at work'[78] and 'at work' has been held to mean when actually working.[79] This means that no permission is required for union activities during recognised breaks or before or after the working day, even if the employee is paid during these times. The House of Lords has inferred from this an entitlement for employees to take part in union activities on the employer's premises, using facilities normally available to the employer's workers, provided that this does not require the employer to incur expense or cause substantial inconvenience either to it or to fellow workers who are not union members.[80] In this respect employers 'must tolerate minor infringements of their strict legal rights which do them no real harm'.[81] Whether activities do cause 'substantial inconvenience' will be a question of fact; thus, a union meeting in the staff canteen at lunchtime may be permissible if all, or a significant majority, of staff are union members but not if only a minority are.[82]

Consent to union activities during working hours may be express (an agreement to hold union meetings during working hours, for example[83]) or implied from the circumstances, although consent cannot be implied purely from an employer's silence when the intention to conduct the activity is announced.[84] The principle of implied consent was invoked to mean that employees who were permitted to converse with fellow employees while working could discuss union, as well as other, matters.[85] In relation to union representatives, once an employer has accepted the appointment of an employee as such, or if it is custom and practice for a union to nominate a representative for a particular workgroup, the employer's consent to the employee carrying out the duties of a representative during working hours will probably be implied[86] unless there is an express agreement which limits this.[87]

---

77   TULRCA 1992, s 152(2).
78   TULRCA 1992, s 152(2).
79   *Post Office v Union of Post Office Workers* [1974] ICR 378 (decided under the equivalent provisions of the Industrial Relations Act 1971).
80   *Post Office v Union of Post Office Workers* [1974] ICR 378, applied in *Zucker v Astrid Jewels Ltd* [1978] ICR 1088. It may be possible to apply this reasoning to the use of e-mail and the internet for union activities: see generally G Morris, 2002a.
81   *Post Office v Union of Post Office Workers* [1974] ICR 378, 400 (Lord Reid). It is unlikely that this principle is open to challenge under the HRA 1998 as interfering with the peaceful enjoyment of possessions under Art 1 of Protocol 1 of the ECHR: see further para 9.16.
82   Cf, for example, the employment tribunal decision in *Carter v Wiltshire County Council* [1979] IRLR 331 (meeting in a social club where all but one employee a union member).
83   In *Bass Taverns Ltd v Burgess* [1995] IRLR 596 the Court of Appeal rejected the suggestion that the employer's consent to the applicant addressing trainee managers to recruit them to the union was subject to an implied limitation that he would not use the occasion to criticise the company. Pill LJ emphasised (at 598) that a consent to recruit 'must include a consent to underline the services which the union can provide. That may reasonably involve a submission to prospective members that in some respects the union will provide a service which the company does not'.
84   *Marley Tile Co Ltd v Shaw* [1980] IRLR 25.
85   *Zucker v Astrid Jewels Ltd* [1978] ICR 1088. Similar reasoning could be invoked in relation to access to notice boards or e-mail or the internet for matters not pertaining directly to the employment.
86   See *Marley Tile Co Ltd v Shaw* [1980] IRLR 25.
87   Cf *Robb v Leon Motor Services Ltd* [1978] ICR 506.

The definition of 'appropriate time' might appear to conflict with the extension of protection to those who 'propose' to take part in union activities. However the courts have avoided this result by adopting a purposive interpretation to the legislation in this context in holding that the precise activities need not be identified.[88] Moreover, although the 'activities' referred to are those in the employment from which the employee has been dismissed, this does not necessarily mean that past activities are irrelevant if a sufficient link with the current employment can be shown. In *Fitzpatrick v British Railways Board*[89] the applicant, when she obtained her job, deliberately failed to give full details of her previous employment or to disclose her former participation in union activities. She joined the National Union of Railwaymen and engaged in some union activity and intended to seek an official position in the union. In the meantime another British Railways employee read a newspaper article in which the applicant was referred to as a union activist with links with some ultra-left Trotskyite groups. When the employers learned of this they decided to dismiss her. The employment tribunal concluded that the principal reason for her dismissal was her previous union activities, which gave her a reputation for being a disruptive force and that she did not, therefore, fall within the legislation. The EAT dismissed her appeal. The Court of Appeal, however, held that the tribunal had failed to ask the critical question: *why* had the employers dismissed the employee because of her previous activities? The Court recognised that where an employer, having learnt of an employee's previous trade union activities, decides that it wishes to dismiss that employee, 'that is likely to be a situation where almost inevitably the employer is dismissing ... because ... [it] ... feels that the employee will indulge in industrial activities of a trade union nature in his [or her] current employment'. When the only 'rational explanation' for dismissal is the employer's fear that the employee will 'repeat those ... activities in [his or] her employment with them' the dismissal will be unfair.[90] However, if an employee obtains employment by deceit and such deceit was the principal reason for dismissal, then even though the deceit relates to previous union activities he or she will then be outside the scope of the statutory protection.[91] This approach invites employers to frame their reasons for dismissal with care. It may now be possible to argue, on the basis of the Human Rights Act 1998, that prospective employees have no obligation to admit to previous union activity if questioned prior to their appointment where this is likely to lead to the employer failing to offer them a job on the ground that this would constitute an interference with their freedom of association or the right to respect for private life,[92] and

---

88   *Fitzpatrick v British Railways Board* [1991] IRLR 376.
89   [1991] IRLR 376.
90   [1991] IRLR 376, 379 (Woolf LJ).
91   *Fitzpatrick v British Railways Board* [1991] IRLR 376, affirming this aspect of *Birmingham District Council v Beyer* [1977] IRLR 211, EAT.
92   In *NATFHE v UK* Application No 28910/95, the European Commission of Human Rights acknowledged that there may be circumstances where requiring an association to reveal the names of its members to a third party could constitute an unjustified interference with freedom of association; see also the DPA 1998, discussed in para 8.22. It is submitted that requiring an individual to reveal his or her associations may also be incompatible with Art 11, in addition to constituting an interference with the right to respect for private life under Art 8. In *Grande Oriente D'Italia di Palazzo Giustiniani v Italy*, judgment of 2 August 2001, the ECtHR held that a requirement for applicants for nomination and appointment to specified public offices to declare that they were not freemasons violated the Art 11 right of the applicant freemason association, which would suffer damage in terms of members and prestige, and that the interference could not be justified.

that failure to disclose such activity should not prejudice a claim for unfair dismissal (or subjection to a detriment). It is conceivable also that employees may be afforded a measure of protection if regulations are eventually issued prohibiting the compilation of 'blacklists'.[93] Ultimately, however, this matter, in common with other cases where individuals are asked to reveal information at the recruitment stage which, if used to penalise them once in employment, would constitute a violation of their fundamental rights, would be better dealt with by specific legislative protection against subjection to such questions.[94]

(iii) Using trade union services at an appropriate time

8.11 Protection against dismissal for making use, or proposing to make use, of trade union services at an appropriate time was introduced by ERelA 2004 in response to the decision of the ECtHR in *Wilson and NUJ v UK, Palmer, Wyeth and RMT v UK* and *Doolan and others v UK*,[95] discussed in para 7.9 above. The same definition of 'appropriate time' applies in this context as in relation to union activities.[96] 'Trade union services' are broadly defined as 'services made available to the employee by an independent trade union by virtue of his membership of the union'.[97] This definition is clearly broad enough to cover raising grievances and queries with employers and negotiating terms and conditions of employment for an individual employee, and could also extend to services outside the field of employment, such as legal and financial services. It is expressly stated that an employee's 'making use' of services includes 'his consenting to the raising of a matter on his behalf by an independent trade union of which he is a member'.[98] In addition, where the reason for dismissal is that such a union (with or without the employee's consent) raised a matter on behalf of the employee as one of its members, this is deemed to fall within the scope of the protection.[99]

This provision is subject to the reservation that '[h]aving terms of employment determined by collective agreement' does not constitute 'making use of a trade union service' in this context.[100] This is designed to ensure that matters relating to collective agreements and personal contracts are considered exclusively under one provision of the Act, that is, that affording protection against inducements to give up representation or the possibility of representation by a union through collective bargaining (see para 8.17 *et seq* below).[101] However, it appears to leave open a 'spectacular lacuna in the structure of protection'.[102] In para 8.9 we discussed the implications of the Court of Appeal decision in *Therm A Stor Ltd v Atkins and Carrington*,[103] which held that employees dismissed in reaction to a letter from the union to the employer seeking recognition had not been taking part in the activities of the union. In that case the relevant provision was held 'not [to be] concerned with an employer's reactions to a trade union's

---

93   ERelA 1999, s 3; see further para 8.2.
94   See further G Morris, 2001a.
95   Judgment of 2 July 2002, [2003] IRLR 568.
96   TULRCA 1992, s 152(2); see further para 8.10.
97   TULRCA 1992, s 152(2A)(a).
98   TULRCA 1992, s 152(2A)(b).
99   TULRCA 1992, s 152(2B).
100   TULRCA 1992, s 145B(4).
101   TULRCA 1992, s 145B, s 152(1)(bb); *Explanatory Notes to Employment Relations Act 2004*, 2004, para 203.
102   Bogg, 2005: p 74.
103   [1983] IRLR 80.

activities, but with his reactions to an individual employee's activities in a trade union context'.[104] It is hard to see how employees in this situation would be protected under the new provisions.[105] They would not have been dismissed for proposing to make use of trade union services because having terms of employment determined by collective agreement is specifically excluded from its scope. At the same time it would be difficult to argue that they had been made an 'offer' by the employer to avoid their terms of employment being so determined.

(iv) Failure to accept an offer made for an unlawful purpose relating to union membership, activities or services or collective bargaining

8.12   We discuss the circumstances in which an offer is deemed to be unlawful in paragraph 8.17 *et seq* below.

Protection against subjection to a detriment short of dismissal on grounds of trade union membership and activities

8.13   A 'worker'[106] has the right not to be subjected to any detriment as an individual by any act, or any deliberate failure to act, by his or her employer if the act or failure takes place for the sole or main purpose of preventing or deterring him or her from joining, or participating in the activities of, an independent trade union, or making use of the services of such a union, or penalising him or her for doing so.[107] In addition a worker has the right not to be subjected to any such detriment because he or she had failed to accept an offer made for an unlawful purpose relating to union membership, activities or services or collective bargaining.[108] In this context not conferring a benefit that, if the offer had been accepted by the worker, *would* have been conferred on him or her under the resulting agreement is taken to constitute subjection to a detriment and a deliberate failure to act.[109] This means that those who refuse such an offer should be no worse off than those who accept; the value of the offer should be reflected in the award of compensation.

In terms of the activities protected, this right parallels the protection afforded to employees against dismissal. Thus it is unlawful to take action against a worker for joining one union rather than another, for example, and in relation to 'activities' or 'services' of a union, identical criteria must be satisfied. Notably, however, protection now extends not only to 'employees' but to the wider category

---

104 [1983] IRLR 78, 80 (Sir John Donaldson MR).

105 Although, as we explain in para 8.9, it may be possible to derive such protection from HRA 1998, this is far from certain.

106 A 'worker' is an individual who works, or normally works, as mentioned in TULRCA 1992, s 296(1), s 151(1B); see further para 3.51 *et seq* above. A person who 'seeks to work' is not, therefore, covered, an exclusion that could create difficulties in the case of casual workers as they may lack the requisite mutuality of obligation: see further para 3.56. The same comments apply here as in relation to dismissal as regards the position under international treaties of those outside this definition: see para 8.5 above. The same groups are excluded from protection: see para 8.2 above. Once again there is no minimum period of employment or maximum age limit. However a 'worker' who is not an 'employee' is excluded where 'under his contract personally to do work or perform services [the] worker ... works outside Great Britain': TULRCA 1992, s 285(1A); see further para 2.51. Special provisions apply to employment on board a ship: s 285(2).

107 TULRCA 1992, s 146, as amended by ERelA 1999 and ERelA 2004.

108 TULRCA 1992, s 146, as amended; see further para 8.17 *et seq* below.

109 TULRCA 1992, s 146(2D).

of 'workers'[110] as a result of ERelA 2004, a long-overdue reform. Where the detriment takes the form of dismissal and the worker is an 'employee', however, he or she must complain under the provisions discussed in para 8.5 *et seq* above.[111] As we indicate below, this can have the anomalous consequence that compensation in respect of dismissal may be lower for employees than for workers as there is no statutory limit on the amount that can be awarded in the context of subjection to a detriment and compensation can be awarded for injury to feelings. It may also be more difficult for an employee to win a dismissal claim where he or she lacks the qualifying period necessary to bring an ordinary unfair dismissal complaint because of the burden of proof and the absence of any express requirement for an employer to show the purpose for which it acted.[112] In addition, only 'employees' fall under the general obligation to institute the appropriate statutory grievance procedure prior to presenting a complaint. This may produce the unusual consequence of some 'workers' attempting to maintain that they are outside the category of 'employee' in this context.

8.14　A worker may be subjected to a detriment 'by any act or any deliberate failure to act'.[113] It is clear that it both acts and omissions, such as failing to award a pay increase or promote a worker, for example. However the meaning of 'deliberate' in this context is obscure; a government spokesman indicated that it covered both 'conscious and unconscious failures'[114] which, if correct, would leave the term with little meaning. The notion of subjection to a 'detriment' has been interpreted by the courts in the context of the anti-discrimination legislation,[115] and it is likely that case law deriving from that context will be regarded as heavily persuasive in this. It is unclear whether workers who are *threatened* with deleterious consequences unless they cease their union membership or activities will be regarded as subjected to a detriment, but there are two grounds upon which it can be argued that it should be so regarded. First, threats of this nature have a serious psychological impact which can be deemed to constitute a detriment in itself.[116] Second, the Human Rights Act 1998 would also argue in favour of such an interpretation. The European Court of Human Rights has held in the context of the closed shop that the threat of dismissal involving loss of livelihood is a 'most serious form of compulsion',[117]

110　TULRCA 1992, s 146.

111　TULRCA 1992, s 146(5A). The definition of dismissal in ERA 1996, s 95 applies in this context: s 298. Note, however, the difficulties that may arise in drawing the line between damage caused by detriment short of dismissal, on the one hand, and dismissal on the other: see para 5.161 above and Bowers and Lewis, 2005: pp 86–89.

112　See para 8.5 above. The same applies if the employee exceeds the maximum age limit for a 'normal' unfair dismissal complaint.

113　Prior to ERelA 1999, protection was afforded against 'action short of dismissal', which was held by the House of Lords in 1995 (controversially) not to include omissions: *Associated Newspapers Ltd v Wilson; Associated British Ports v Palmer* [1995] IRLR 258. This rendered the protection almost useless.

114　Mr Michael Wills, Minister for Small Firms, Trade and Industry, Official Report of Standing Committee E, 18 March 1999, 2.30 pm (opposing an amendment to replace 'deliberate' with 'wilful').

115　See para 6.43. Note, in particular, *Shamoon v Chief Constable of the Royal Ulster Constabulary* [2003] IRLR 285.

116　Support for this view is provided by *Gloucester Working Men's Club and Institute v James* [1986] ICR 603, 606. S 146(1) speaks of the act or failure to act *taking place* for the specified purposes. It is submitted that this is not inconsistent with a 'threat' constituting an act. In *Brassington v Cauldon Wholesale Ltd* [1978] ICR 405, the EAT left open the question whether 'action' included threats.

117　*Young, James and Webster v UK* judgment of 13 August 1981, (1982) 4 EHRR 38, para 55.

and its other jurisprudence supports the view that the threat of lesser forms of disciplinary action should also of itself constitute an interference with the exercise of Convention rights, including the rights to join a trade union and freedom of expression.[118]

The worker must be subjected to a detriment *as an individual*. As we indicated in para 8.2, protection against subjection to a detriment (in a different guise) was originally introduced in the Industrial Relations Act 1971. Although aimed at the protection of individuals, that Act did not exclude this protection being used as a vehicle for collective rights and, indeed, it was held by the House of Lords in *Post Office v Union of Post Office Workers*[119] that a disparity in the facilities accorded to one union as compared with another could give rise to a complaint by a member of the latter. In order to avoid this result the equivalent provision in the subsequent 'Social Contract' legislation inserted the qualification that the action must be taken against the employee 'as an individual'. This meant that adverse action taken against a union as an organisation, such as non-recognition or derecognition, could not be treated as action against individual workers even though it was likely to impact upon individual union members. However, action against members of a particular union as a group, such as failing to accord them a pay increase, could be protected provided that it affected them as individuals.[120] Moreover, in *FW Farnsworth Ltd v McCoid* the Court of Appeal affirmed that the legislation is not confined to the protection of a worker in his or her capacity as such; thus, the derecognition of an employee as a shop steward could constitute an act against him 'as an individual', although it was open to the employers to establish that they had taken the action in order to remove an unsuitable individual from that role rather than to prevent or deter him from taking part in union activities.[121]

8.15 The qualification at the end of the paragraph above is based on the last condition; that where prevention or deterrence of union membership or activities or use of union services, is alleged, the employer's act or failure to act must have taken place *for the sole or main purpose* of such prevention or deterrence. It is for the employer to show the sole or main purpose for which it acted or failed to act,[122] but it remains for the worker to show that the employer's purpose breached the statute. This may not be an easy task. In certain situations, such as a failure to promote, disclosure of information concerning other workers may be important and, if necessary, an order for further particulars and disclosure of documents can be sought from the employment tribunal.[123] However, even if such information is available, the worker may face considerable difficulty in

---

118 *Dudgeon v UK* judgment of 22 October 1981, (1982) 4 EHRR 149, paras 40, 41; *Ahmed v UK* judgment of 2 September 1998, [1999] IRLR 188.
119 [1974] ICR 378.
120 *Ridgway and Fairbrother v National Coal Board* [1987] IRLR 80. See also *Marshall v The Hampshire Probation Service* EAT 1440/98, 29 September 1999 (unreported); *Howle v GEC Power Engineering Ltd* [1974] ICR 13; *Cheall v Vauxhall Motors Ltd* [1979] IRLR 253.
121 [1999] IRLR 626 (placing in context the dictum of Nicholls LJ in *Ridgway and Fairbrother*, above, at 88, that the action has to affect the employee other than merely *qua* member or officer of a union).
122 TULRCA 1992, s 148(1). No account is to be taken of any pressure exercised on the employer to act or fail to act by calling, organising, procuring or financing industrial action or threatening to do so: s 148(2).
123 Employment Tribunals (Constitution and Rules of Procedure) Regulations 2004, SI 2004/1861, Sch 1, para 10.

the light of the restrictive judicial approach to the interpretation of 'purpose' exemplified by the Court of Appeal decision in *Gallacher v Department of Transport*.[124] In this case a promotions board had recommended that the employee should not be promoted because it was four years since he had held an official job and doubts as to his managerial ability and attitude remained. His career development officer advised him that to achieve promotion, he would need to acquire more line management experience. This would necessitate reducing his union activities (which took up 80% or 100% of his time). The employment tribunal held that these comments were intended to deter the employee from continuing with his union activities. The EAT and Court of Appeal upheld the employer's appeal, the Court of Appeal on the basis that the recommendation was not made 'for the purpose of' deterring him from continuing with his union activities, even if this was its likely effect. Neill LJ averred that 'purpose' denoted an object which the employer desired or sought to achieve which was, on these facts, ensuring that only those with sufficient managerial experience and skill were promoted. In *Associated Newspapers Ltd v Wilson; Associated British Ports v Palmer* the House of Lords confirmed that the fact that union membership may become less attractive as a result of an employer's act did not thereby mean that deterring union membership became its purpose.[125] On this basis it seems difficult to distinguish *Gallacher* even though the course of action recommended by the employer would inevitably mean that the worker ceases his or her union activities, provided that the employer puts in credible evidence of another purpose. In *London Borough of Southwark v Whiller*[126] the employers failed to do this. Here, the employer offered the applicant, a union official, promotion to a higher grade on the basis that she would be paid at the higher rate of pay applicable to that grade only when she was able to undertake the duties of the post in question. The Court of Appeal held that the employment tribunal was entitled to conclude that the employer's purpose was to deter the applicant from taking part in the activities of her union, there being no evidence for holding that they had any other purpose than to oblige her to chose between promotion and retaining her union office.

Prior to ERelA 2004 it was sufficient that prevention or deterrence of union membership, etc, was the employer's 'purpose'; the legislation did not require it to be the 'sole or main' purpose. As we discuss in paras 8.18 and 8.19 below, the 'sole or main' purpose test is used in determining whether an employer's offer is unlawful and the Government claimed that the amendment to TULRCA 1992, s 146 was designed to ensure consistency between the relevant provisions and that, in any event, it reflected the approach that tribunals could be expected to adopt.[127] As we shall see, however, the use of that test in the context of inducements is highly controversial, and, arguably, has the result that UK law remains in breach of Article 11 of the ECHR. Clearly the change will not assist applicants who, as we have seen, as a result of *Gallacher* already face a difficult task. The problem may be compounded where the employer is a corporate

---

124 [1994] IRLR 231. See also *Smyth-Britt v Chubb Security Personnel* UKEAT/0620/03/DA, 24 February 2004.
125 [1995] IRLR 258, Lord Lloyd at 267.
126 [2001] ICR 1016.
127 Lord Triesman, HL Debs, GC 210, June 16 2004. In *Smyth-Britt v Chubb Security Personnel* UKEAT/0620/03/DA, 24 February 2004 the EAT considered that the legislation prior to the amendment invited 'consideration of the main or principal purpose of the employer' (para 25).

body where decision-makers may not share a common motivation.[128] Where the complaint of subjection to a detriment is based on a worker's failure to accept an offer made for an unlawful purpose it is sufficient that the employer's act or failure to act was 'because of' this.[129] Here, it may be possible to argue that it is enough to show that the failure to accept the offer was one of a number of reasons, rather than the predominant purpose, but the matter is not free from doubt.

8.16 A complaint of subjection to a detriment must be presented to an employment tribunal within three months beginning with the date of the act or failure to which the complaint relates or, where that act or failure is part of a series of similar acts or failures, the last of them.[130] A failure to act is treated as done when it was decided on;[131] in the absence of evidence to the contrary an employer is taken to have decided on a failure to act when it does an act inconsistent with such an act or, if no such inconsistent act was done, when the period expires when it might reasonably be expected to have done the failed act if it was to be done.[132] Where a complaint is upheld the tribunal makes a declaration to that effect and may also award such compensation as it considers 'just and equitable in all the circumstances having regard to the infringement complained of and to any loss sustained by the complainant which is attributable to the act or failure which infringed his [or her] right',[133] which may include non-pecuniary loss.[134] The EAT has indicated that there are no grounds for awarding lower levels of compensation for injury to feelings in this context than would be awarded in relation to other forms of discrimination, although the degree of distress caused in the instant case must be carefully examined.[135] Unlike the remedies for dismissal, there is no statutory limit on the amount of compensation, and unlike the discrimination legislation,[136] or, indeed, the provisions relating to refusal of employment on

---

128 *Smith v Hayle Town Council* [1978] ICR 996, discussed para 8.5 above. On the amendment to s 146 see Letter and Memorandum from Professor Lord Wedderburn of Charlton QC FBA, Joint Committee on Human Rights, Thirteenth Report, Session 2003–2004, Appendix 2c, paras 7.0–7.4.

129 TULRCA 1992, s 146(2C).

130 TULRCA 1992, s 147(1). Where the act extends over a period, the 'date of the act' refers to the last date of that period: s 147(2)(a): see also *Adlam v Salisbury and Wells Theological College* [1985] ICR 786 and *British Airways Board v Clark and Havill* [1982] IRLR 238. Where the tribunal is satisfied it was not 'reasonably practicable' for the complaint to be presented before the end of the three month period, it may be presented within such further period as it considers reasonable: see para 2.17 above. Note also EADRR 2004, reg 15, discussed in para 2.23 above, in relation to employees.

131 TULRCA 1992, s 147(2)(b).

132 TULRCA 1992, s 147(3). In the event that the employer can show that it decided on a course earlier than it might reasonably be expected to do but that decision was not communicated to the worker, the tribunal may be inclined to extend the time limit if the worker could not be expected to have known of the decision.

133 TULRCA 1992, s 149(2).

134 *Brassington v Cauldon Wholesale Ltd* [1978] ICR 405 (non-pecuniary loss could include injury to health or the frustration of a 'deep and sincere wish to join a union'); see also *Ridgway and Fairbrother v National Coal Board* [1987] IRLR 80, and *Cleveland Ambulance NHS Trust v Blane* [1997] IRLR 332. There is an obligation on complainants to mitigate loss and compensation may be reduced if the tribunal finds that they contributed to the action: TULRCA 1992, s 149(4), (6), although note also s 145E(6).

135 *London Borough of Hackney v Adams* [2003] IRLR 402, applied in *Saunders v Apcoa Parking UK Ltd* EAT/0526/02/RN, 18 March 2003.

136 See ch 6.

grounds of union membership discussed in para 8.21, tribunals have no power formally to recommend any course of action such as cessation of the unlawful treatment. Employees are required to institute the appropriate statutory grievance procedure prior to presenting a complaint of subjection to a detriment, and the provisions for increasing or reducing compensation apply in the event that the employer or the employee respectively fails to complete that procedure.[137] These provisions do not apply to a 'worker' who is not an employee.

Protection against inducements relating to union membership, activities or services and collective bargaining

8.17   Protection against inducements relating to union membership, activities or services, on the one hand, and to collective bargaining, on the other, was introduced by ERelA 2004 in response to the decision of the ECtHR in *Wilson and NUJ v UK, Palmer, Wyeth and RMT v UK* and *Doolan v UK*,[138] discussed in paras 7.9 and 8.3 above. These protections are available not only to 'employees' but to the wider category of 'workers' (both former and existing).[139] Complaints must be presented to an employment tribunal within three months beginning with the date when the offer was made by the employer or, where the offer is part of a series of similar offers to the complainant, the date when the last of them was made.[140] In either case, if the complaint is upheld, the tribunal must make a declaration to this effect and award the complainant the sum of £2,500,[141] although this sum may be reduced or increased, in the case of employees, for failure on their part, or that of their employer, respectively to complete an applicable statutory grievance procedure.[142] If an offer unlawfully made is accepted, and this results in the worker agreeing to vary his or her terms of employment at a later date, the employer cannot enforce this agreement, nor can it recover any sum paid or other asset transferred under the agreement to vary.[143] If, however, the terms of employment have already been varied, the variation remains enforceable even though there has been a breach of the statutory provision.[144]

The respective rights in relation to inducements apply independently of the right to complain of subjection to a detriment discussed above,[145] and

---

137   EA 2002, ss 31, 32, and Schs 3, 4 and 5, as amended by ERelA 2004, Sch 1, para 43.
138   Judgment of 2 July 2002, [2003] IRLR 568.
139   TULRCA 1992, ss 145A(5), 145B(5), 145F(3); see further para 8.13 and para 3.51 *et seq* above.
140   TULRCA 1992, s 145C. Where the tribunal is satisfied it was not 'reasonably practicable' for the complaint to be presented before the end of the three month period, it may be presented within such further period as it considers reasonable: see para 2.17 above. Note also EADRR 2004, reg 15, discussed in para 2.23 above, in relation to employees.
141   TULRCA 1992, s 145E(1)–(3). This sum was chosen as being about half the amount awarded by the ECtHR in *Wilson* and *Palmer* as compensation to individuals for non-pecuniary damages: Gerry Sutcliffe, Parliamentary Under-Secretary of State, Department of Trade and Industry, HC Standing Committee D, col 109, 5 February 2004. In determining whether the employer made the offer or the purpose for which it did so, no account is to be taken of any pressure by calling, organising, procuring or financing industrial action or threatening to do so: TULRCA 1992, s 145D(3).
142   EA 2002, ss 31, 32, and Schs 3, 4 and 5, as amended by ERelA 2004, Sch 1, para 43.
143   TULRCA 1992, s 145E(4)(a).
144   TULRCA 1992, s 145E(4)(b).
145   TULRCA 1992, s 145E(5).

compensation for the latter right is not be reduced by any award in respect of an inducement found to have been unlawfully offered.[146] Not conferring a benefit that, had an offer been accepted by a worker, would have been conferred on him or her constitutes subjecting him or her to a detriment,[147] so allowing those who refuse an offer to be no worse off than those who accept it.

The scope of the protection against inducements relating to collective bargaining, with which *Wilson* and *Palmer* was most directly concerned, attracted greatest controversy during the legislation's parliamentary passage. We discuss this first, before considering inducements relating to union membership and activity, to which the same points, *mutatis mutandis*, apply.

(i) Inducements relating to collective bargaining

8.18 A worker who is a member of an independent trade union which is recognised, or seeking to be recognised, by his or her employer has the right not to have an offer made to him or her by the employer if (a) acceptance of the offer, together with other workers' acceptance of offers which the employer also makes to them, would have 'the prohibited result' and (b) the employer's sole or main purpose in making the offers is to achieve that result.[148] The 'prohibited result' is 'that the workers' terms of employment, or any of those terms, will not (or will no longer) be determined by collective agreement negotiated by or on behalf of the union'.[149] There is no requirement that the offers be made to the workers simultaneously.[150]

This provision is designed to make it unlawful for an employer to offer a worker an inducement to give up representation, or the possibility of representation, by a union in relation to the negotiation of terms and conditions of employment. Initially the government sought to confine the protection to members of recognised unions,[151] but it finally accepted the view of the Joint Committee on Human Rights ('JCHR')[152] and others that this would not give full effect to the decision in *Wilson* and *Palmer*. It is notable, however, that the union in question must still be 'seeking recognition'. On this basis it would be advisable for unions with members in a workplace to write to the employer to indicate their desire for recognition, even if the membership level is relatively low. The legislation envisages that the offer will be made to more than one worker, but not necessarily simultaneously. In this context the requirement to present a complaint to a tribunal within three months of the offer being made to the complainant could present a difficulty to the first recipient of an offer if no further offer is made within the three month period. Although *Wilson* and *Palmer* arose in the context of a concerted campaign by the respective employers, it is not clear why the requirement for offers to be made to other workers was thought appropriate or necessary in this context given that the right not to be treated less favourably for refusing to renounce union representation rests in the individual worker.

146 TULRCA 1992, s 145E(6).
147 TULRCA 1992, s 146(2D).
148 TULRCA 1992, s 145B(1).
149 TULRCA 1992, s 145B(2).
150 TULRCA 1992, s 145B(3).
151 See Memorandum from the DTI in response to concerns raised by the Committee in its Third and Fourth Progress Reports of Session 2003–2004, JCHR, Thirteenth Report, Session 2003–2004, Appendix 2a, paras 40–48.
152 JCHR, Tenth Report, Session 2003–2004, para 1.8.

The employer must show what its sole or main purpose was in making the offers,[153] but it remains for the worker to show that this purpose was unlawful. As in the case of subjection to a detriment, this may not be easy where credible evidence of another purpose can be shown, particularly if tribunals and courts continue to distinguish between 'purpose' and 'effect'. In this context, however, tribunals are required to take into account any evidence relating to three specified matters. First, that when the offers were made, the employer had recently changed or sought to change, or did not wish to use, arrangements agreed with the union for collective bargaining. Second, that when the offers were made the employer did not wish to enter into arrangements proposed by the union for collective bargaining. Third, that the offers were made only to particular workers and were made with the sole or main purpose of rewarding those particular workers for their high level of performance or of retaining them because of their special value to the employer.[154]

8.19   It was strongly argued during the legislation's passage that the requirement that achievement of the 'prohibited result' must be the employer's 'sole or main' purpose in order for the offer to be unlawful, rather than merely its 'purpose', would fatally undermine the effectiveness of the protection and would fail to give effect to the judgment in *Wilson* and *Palmer*, where no such requirement is envisaged.[155] The government resisted exhortations to amend this provision, concluding that:

> The words 'sole or main' are an essential component of the regime that we are seeking to construct. They are necessary to ensure that employers have some flexibility in setting their reward systems. We do not consider that employers should be prevented from making offers for justifiable business purposes just because a by-product or incidental consequence of making such offers would be to deter a person's involvement with a trade union.[156]

However it did undertake to keep the matter under review.[157] The difficulty of permitting employers to maintain that their primary purpose is to 'reward and retain key staff'[158] and that withdrawing adherence to terms that have been collectively agreed is only a subsidiary purpose, is that 'key staff' may come to be identified precisely by their willingness to transfer to personal contracts. In this context much may depend on the preparedness of tribunals to probe employers' evidence that particular individuals merited special treatment on the grounds of their performance or importance to the organisation.

---

153 TULRCA 1992, s 145D(2).
154 TULRCA 1992, s 145D(4).
155 See, for example, Letter and Memorandum from Professor Lord Wedderburn of Charlton QC FBA, JCHR, Session 2003–2004, Appendix 2c, paras 6.0–7.4; Lord McCarthy HL Debs, GC 136, 15 June 2004. The JCHR at one stage recommended the omission of 'sole or main' (Tenth Report, Session 2003–2004, para 1.6) but accepted, in the light of a subsequent DTI Memorandum, that there was a case for retaining it and relying on tribunals sensibly to distinguish between cases where offers are made for the purpose, in effect, of achieving derecognition of a union and cases where they are made to retain or reward valuable staff, on the basis that amending legislation be introduced if the Art 11 right was not being protected in practice: JCHR, Thirteenth Report, Session 2003–2004, para 2.21.
156 Lord Sainsbury, Parliamentary Under-Secretary of State, Department of Trade and Industry, HL Debs GC 139, 15 June 2004.
157 Letter from Gerry Sutcliffe, JCHR, Seventeenth Report, Session 2003–2004, Appendix 2.
158 Gerry Sutcliffe, HC Standing Committee D, col 104, 5 February 2004.

A further criticism of the legislation is that it fails to accord a remedy to a union, as well as to the individual union member, despite the finding by the ECtHR in *Wilson* and *Palmer* that the rights of the applicant unions, as well as the individual applicants, had been violated[159] and the conclusion of the JCHR that the absence of such a remedy could leave the UK in continuing breach of Article 11.[160] The Government's defence of its position can be divided into three lines of argument. The first rests on the interpretation of the ECtHR judgment. Here it maintained that 'the infringement of the rights of the applicant unions simply resulted from and was consequential upon the infringement of the rights of their members rather than an infringement of a free standing right of the unions.[161] Moreover, 'the Article 11 right of the applicant unions to strive for the protection of their members' interests is not a right separate from and independent of the Article 11 right of their members to freedom to belong to a union for the protection of their interests ... [T]rade unions are voluntary associations consisting of their members; if adequate remedies are given to the members the rights of the union are also protected'.[162] These views were not accepted by the JCHR and, in our view, are not sustainable. Second, it asserted that '[w]hile the continuation of collective bargaining may be at issue, the objectionable conduct is done in relation to the individual members of the union.'[163] This fails to recognise the separate and legitimate interest of trade unions as collective organisations. Third, it argued that no other provisions in UK law that conferred individual rights in relation to union matters gave a separate means of redress to unions which could, in any event, actively support their members in making claims.[164] However this fails to accord adequate weight to the difficulties and risks that individuals may face in bringing a complaint, and, once again, overlooks the distinct position of unions as beneficiaries of freedom of association. We discuss this further in para 8.25 below.

Finally, the legislation extends protection only to those who are offered an inducement and not to those who are not recipients of such an offer. This means that if 'the employer accurately selects amongst the union members in his employ those who will succumb to the offer and he makes no offer of inducement to those who would refuse it ... there remain[s] no remedy for those subject to precisely the discrimination which the ... Court ... held was incompatible with Article 11'.[165] Initially the Joint Committee on Human Rights was sympathetic to this view,[166] but later accepted the Government's argument that the basis of the violation in *Wilson* and *Palmer* was that the offer *had* been made to union members to give up their rights and that there was currently no legal duty to

---

159 Judgment of 2 July 2002, [2002] IRLR 568, para 48.
160 Thirteenth Report, Session 2003–2004, para 2.19. As the Committee pointed out, if the employer were a 'public authority' for the purposes of HRA 1998, s 6 the union could bring proceedings under HRA 1998, s 7 in the event that its rights under Art 11 had been violated, but in relation to other employers it would be forced to seek redress before the ECtHR: Tenth Report, Session 2003–2004, para 1.4.
161 Memorandum from the DTI in response to concerns raised by the Committee in its Third and Fourth Progress Reports of Session 2003–2004, Thirteenth Report, Session 2003–2004, Appendix 2a, para 25.
162 Above, para 28.
163 Lord Sainsbury, HL Debs, GC 151, 15 June 2004.
164 Lord Sainsbury, HC Debs, GC 151–152, 15 June 2004.
165 Letter from John Hendy QC, JCHR, Session 2003–2004, Appendix 1.
166 JCHR, Tenth Report, Session 2003–2004, para 17.

change the law in relation to other possible violations, although it recommended that the issue be kept under review.[167]

(ii) Inducements relating to union membership or activities

8.20   The provision relating to union membership or activities is similarly structured to that relating to collective bargaining. A worker has the right not to have an offer made to him or her by his or her employer for the sole or main purpose of inducing the worker not to be or seek to become a member of an independent trade union; not to take part in the activities of such a union at an appropriate time; and not to make use, at an appropriate time, of union services.[168] 'Appropriate time', 'trade union services' and 'making use' of union services are defined in the same way as in the context of the protections against discrimination discussed above.[169] Once again the employer must show what its sole or main purpose was in making the offer,[170] although it remains for the worker to show that this purpose was unlawful. The comments that we made in para 8.19 above about this test apply equally in this context, as do our remarks about the failure to accord a remedy to unions as well as to individual applicants.

Refusal of access to employment

8.21   It is unlawful to refuse a person employment under a contract of service or apprenticeship because he or she is a member of a trade union or a particular union or is unwilling to agree to leave, or not to join, a union.[171] It is also unlawful for an employment agency to refuse a person any of its services for such a reason.[172] Unlike protection against dismissal and subjection to a detriment, the union in question need not be 'independent' although clearly breaches of the statute are more likely to arise in practice where it is.[173] 'Refusal' goes beyond not offering a job; it also extends to refusing to process an application or inquiry (for example failing to respond to telephone calls); causing an individual to withdraw an application (for example saying there are no vacancies); offering the job on terms which no employer who wished to fill the post would offer and which the applicant does not accept (a test which, contemptuous offers apart,

---

167 JCHR, Thirteenth Report, Session 2003–2004, para 2.24. The JCHR also accepted the government's argument that the reference to an 'offer' did not enable an employer to circumvent the legislation by inviting employees themselves to make the offer on the ground that, at some stage, the employer is likely to have to make a counter offer: para 2.23. Cf Letter from John Hendy QC, JCHR, Tenth Report, Session 2003–2004, Appendix 1; Letter and Memorandum from Professor Lord Wedderburn of Charlton QC, FBA, JCHR, Session 2003–2004, Appendix 2c, paras 8.0–8.6.
168 TULRCA 1992, s 145A.
169 See paras 8.10 and 8.11.
170 TULRCA 1992, s 145D(1).
171 TULRCA 1992, ss 137(1), 143, 295. As in the case of dismissal and subjection to a detriment Crown employment is included unless s 275 applies but the armed forces and police are not. The protection does not apply where, under the contract, the employee would ordinarily work outside Great Britain: s 285; see further para 2.51. However ETA 1996, s 10(1) does not apply to s 137; cf. para 8.2, note 2.
172 TULRCA 1992, s 138. An 'employment agency' means a person who, for profit or not, provides services for the purpose of finding employment for workers or supplying employers with workers: s 143(1). The definition of employment (see ss 143, 295) means that services in relation to those other than employees are not covered. Unions are not regarded as employment agencies by reason of services provided by them only for, or in relation to, their members.
173 Membership of a particular branch or section of a trade union is also covered: TULRCA 1992, s 143(3).

may be difficult to apply); and withdrawing an offer previously made.[174] Where employment is offered on condition that the applicant is not a union member, or leaves or agrees not to join a union, and the applicant does not accept the offer because he or she is unwilling to accept that requirement, this is treated as a refusal of employment for that reason.[175]

A person who is unlawfully refused employment on grounds of union membership may complain to an employment tribunal within three months of the conduct complained of or within such further period as the tribunal considers 'reasonable' where it is satisfied that compliance with the time limit was not 'reasonably practicable'.[176] The applicant must prove the reason for refusal; in doing so, as in the case of other forms of unlawful discrimination, discovery of information about successful candidates, if any, may be crucial (although there is no need to show that employment was offered to another person).[177] If an advertisement is published which might reasonably be understood as indicating that the employment is closed to those who do not satisfy the conditions relating to union membership (such as 'non-union members welcome') an applicant who does not satisfy such a condition is conclusively presumed to have been refused employment for that reason, regardless of his or her suitability for the job (although clear lack of suitability may affect compensation).[178] In the absence of such (improbable) evidence, asking questions about union membership should be sufficient to raise a *prima facie* case that this was relevant to the refusal, although it may be displaced by evidence to the contrary, for example that other members of the union are already employed by the employer. The remedies available are identical in form to those for sex and race discrimination except that in this case statutory limits on compensation remain:[179] they are a declaration; financial compensation (subject to the limit of the compensatory award for unfair dismissal);[180] and/or a recommendation that the applicant takes, within a specified period, action to obviate or reduce the adverse effect on the complainant of the unlawful conduct.[181] As in the case of other grounds of

---

174 TULRCA 1992, s 137(5). S 138(4) defines refusal of service by an employment agency.
175 TULRCA 1992, 137(6). Any pre-employment agreement not to join an independent trade union (or participate in its activities) would not, of course preclude access to protection against dismissal or subjection to a detriment if breached after the individual had been employed.
176 TULRCA 1992, ss 137(2), 138(2), 139. See para 2.17 for the meaning of not 'reasonably practicable'. The 'date' of the conduct to which the complaint relates depends upon the nature of that conduct: s 139(2). It is submitted that this date should not be earlier than that on which the complainant becomes aware of the refusal (cf *McMaster v Manchester Airport plc* [1998] IRLR 112). See ss 141 and 142 for provisions for joinder of another prospective respondent or third parties.
177 On discovery of documents, see Employment Tribunals (Constitution and Rules of Procedure) Regulations 2004, SI 2004/1861 Sch 1, para 10. On a complaint by the TUC to the ILO that British law and practice failed to meet the requirements of Art 1 of Convention No 98 in relation to recruitment the Committee of Experts concluded that workers 'faced many practical difficulties in proving the real nature of their ... denial of employment' and that in this respect the United Kingdom did not comply with the Convention: Case 1618, 287th Report, paras 224–267.
178 TULRCA 1992, ss 137(3), 138(3).
179 See para 6.66 *et seq* above.
180 From 1 February 2005 and at the time of writing, £56,800.
181 TULRCA 1992, s 140. Other analogies with sex and race discrimination are limited, however. There is, for example, no concept of indirect discrimination in this context (although if a requirement were clearly a smokescreen for excluding union members, for example by limiting recruitment to those who had previously worked for a notorious non-union employer, this could be viewed as direct). See generally Townshend-Smith, 1991 and see further para 8.31 below.

discrimination, compensation may be awarded for injury to feelings, and awards in those contexts may provide some guidance. Where it cannot be said that the complainant would have got the job but for the unlawful discrimination, for example if he or she was one of several rejected applicants, the difficulty of assessing loss does not mean that the award will thereby be purely nominal.[182] If the respondent fails without reasonable justification to comply with a recommendation, the tribunal may increase its award of compensation, subject to the overriding maximum limit or, if it has not made such an award, make one.[183]

8.22   The introduction of this protection against discriminatory hiring, which came only in 1990, was originally rooted in the Conservative Government's desire to prevent the lawful operation of pre-entry closed shops[184] where only union members could be considered for a job; this was the only aspect referred to in the Green Paper which preceded the legislation.[185] However, the legislation itself also covered discrimination against those wishing to be union members. Strikingly, by contrast to protection during employment, this protection does not cover participation in trade union activities. This was a deliberate omission; the government took the view that employers were entitled to protect themselves against 'troublemaker[s]'.[186] Currently, therefore, an employer may blatantly defend a claim before a tribunal by maintaining that employment was refused because of an applicant's record of union activities rather than his or her union membership. This makes particularly important the concept of 'membership' in this context; as Townshend-Smith points out, 'in many cases the fact of membership will be less significant both for the individual and the prospective employer than what has been done with that membership'.[187] As we indicated in para 8.7 above, the concept of 'membership' was given a narrow meaning by the House of Lords in *Associated Newspapers Ltd v Wilson; Associated British Ports v Palmer*[188] in the context of detriment once in employment, although other cases took a broader view. This issue has become less pressing in relation to workers in employment because of the specific protection now accorded to making use of trade union services,[189] in addition to taking part in union activities. However, it remains important in this context. It may be possible to rely on the Human Rights Act 1998 to argue for a more expansive interpretation of TULRCA 1992, s 137, both for ordinary members[190] and those who have acted in capacities

---

182 See *Chaplin v Hicks* [1911] 2 KB 786, CA, where it was held that substantial damages could be claimed for loss of a contractual right to belong to a limited class of competitors for a prize; *Allied Maples Group Ltd v Simmons and Simmons (a firm)* [1995] 4 All ER 907; and see further para 6.67 above.

183 TULRCA 1992, s 140(3).

184 See *Removing Barriers to Employment*, Cm 655, 1989: ch 2; see also para 8.30 below.

185 *Removing Barriers to Employment*, Cm 655, 1989: ch 2.

186 Patrick Nicholls, Parliamentary Under-Secretary of State for Employment, House of Commons, Official Report of Standing Committee D, col 27, 8 February 1990.

187 Townshend-Smith, 1991: p 107.

188 [1995] IRLR 258. In *Harrison v Kent County Council* [1995] ICR 434, discussed IRLB 519, 1995, p 6, the EAT held that if a person was refused employment because he or she was or had been a union activist it would be open to a tribunal to find that this was because of union membership. This reasoning cannot stand in the light of the House of Lords decision in *Associated Newspapers*.

189 Although note the exclusion of having terms of employment determined by collective agreement from this protection; see further para 8.11 above.

190 See *Wilson* and *Palmer*, discussed in para 7.9 above.

beyond that of the ordinary member. In *X v Ireland*[191] the European Commission of Human Rights considered that threats of dismissal or other actions intended to make an employee relinquish the office of shop steward could, in certain circumstances, seriously restrict or impede the lawful exercise of freedom of association under Article 11. Moreover the European Court of Human Rights has held that action taken in relation to participation in the activities of a political party, including holding party office, may violate Article 10, which guarantees freedom of expression, as well as Article 11.[192] It is conceivable that domestic courts and tribunals could be persuaded to interpret 'membership' in the light of these decisions. Alternatively, if the discriminatory employer is a 'public authority' (or at least if it is a 'pure' public authority) an individual may have a free-standing right of action, although this would depend upon acceptance of the argument that denial of employment constitutes an 'interference' with a Convention right.[193]

The confinement of the protection against discriminatory hiring to union membership is particularly anomalous in the light of the power accorded to the Secretary of State by the Employment Relations Act 1999 to issue regulations prohibiting the compilation of lists of persons who have taken part in the activities of unions, as well as union members, with a view to their being used by employers or employment agencies to discriminate in relation to recruitment or the treatment of workers.[194] Such regulations may prohibit both the use, and the sale or supply, of such 'blacklists'.[195] The Secretary of State has a wide range of possible remedies at his or her disposal, including the creation of criminal offences punishable by fines (but not imprisonment), compensatory remedies for individuals who have suffered loss as a result of blacklisting, and enforceable orders to require blacklisting organisations to stop disseminating lists. Interestingly, provision is made to enable unions to bring proceedings on behalf of their members in specified circumstances. At the time of writing no regulations in this area have yet been issued, and it seems that they may never be: in 2003 the DTI issued draft regulations for consultation but stated that, as there was no evidence of current blacklisting activity, it did not propose to implement them until there was evidence that the practice was returning.[196] The Data Protection Act 1998 offers a measure of protection in this context. Whether an individual is a union member constitutes 'sensitive personal data' which can be collected, held and disclosed to third parties only in a very limited range of circumstances;[197] although union activities are not explicitly included, it would

---

191 (1971) Application No 4125/69.
192 *Vogt v Germany* judgment of 26 September 1995, (1996) 21 EHRR 205; see also *Ahmed v UK* judgment of 2 September 1998, [1999] IRLR 188.
193 See G Morris 1999c: pp 497–501.
194 For further discussion of these provisions see Ewing, 1999: pp 284–286.
195 The most prominent 'blacklisting' organisation was the Economic League, established in 1919; however, this was reported to have gone into voluntary liquidation in 1993: Ewing, 1994a: para 6.7. Its records were kept on manual files and so were not subject to data protection legislation then in force (the Data Protection Act 1984; now repealed). See further Evidence by the TUC and the Economic League to the House of Commons Employment Committee Inquiry into Recruitment Practices: House of Commons, Session 1989–1990, HC 409-i and iii; Hollingsworth and Tremayne, 1989.
196 *Draft Regulations to Prohibit the Blacklisting of Trade Unionists – A Consultation Document* DTI, URN 03/648, February 2003.
197 DPA 1998, ss 2, 4(3), Sch 2 and 3. The full force of this Act does not apply to manually held data until 2007. On the Act generally see further Jay and Hamilton, 2003, and para 4.106.

not seem possible to disclose information about such activities without disclosing the fact of union membership. However the Government itself concluded in 2003 that the provisions of the Act were insufficient to outlaw blacklists and ensure that blacklisted individuals were appropriately compensated for any loss.[198] It is submitted that lack of evidence of organised blacklisting activities does not mean that individuals may not suffer discrimination as a result of their previous activities being made known to employer in other ways and, indeed, that the absence of legislation to regulate blacklisting strengthens the case for protection at the individual level.

The limits of protection

8.23   Analysis of the legislation upholding the rights to join, and participate in the activities of, trade unions reveals a number of deficiencies which raise doubts as to whether UK law affords adequate protection to comply with Article 11 of the ECHR even after the amendments made by ERelA 2004. In addition to these substantive deficiencies, there remain a number of other limitations relating to the procedures for the enforcement of these protections and the remedies available. In all these areas significant defects stem from the attempt artificially to separate individual and collective interests in a context in which the two are inextricably linked. We discuss these briefly and suggest some ways in which the problems which they present could be overcome.

8.24   In relation to the content of the rights, the difficulty of maintaining a boundary between individual and collective spheres is demonstrated by the volume of case law in which its location has been at issue. Its artificiality is perhaps most clearly exemplified in the requirement that a worker is only protected against subjection to a detriment 'as an individual'. As we have explained, this was inserted in 1975 into re-enacted provisions of the Industrial Relations Act 1971 which contained no such limitation and has been interpreted as excluding complaints relating to differential provision of trade union facilities of the kind which gave rise to a successful claim in *Post Office v Union of Post Office Workers*.[199] However, as Lord Reid explained in that case, 'discrimination against a man's [sic] trade union generally affects him personally'[200] and withdrawal of facilities such as notice boards, meeting rooms and office space has obvious implications for the individual. One concern about removing the existing limitation on individual claims is that this would enable members to seek a remedy if their union, unlike another, was unrecognised. However, there would be nothing to prevent recognition being specifically excluded.[201] Moreover, the House of Lords in the *Post Office* case emphasised that its decision did not entail the provision of identical facilities for recognised and unrecognised unions; indeed, where a union was unrecognised the disparity in facilities as compared with a recognised union would need to be 'substantial'.[202] The line between

---

198   *Draft Regulations to Prohibit the Blackslisting of Trade Unionists – A Consultation Document* DTI, URN 03/648, February 2003.
199   [1974] ICR 378. See, for example, *Ridgway and Fairbrother v National Coal Board* [1987] IRLR 80 at 88 (Nicholls LJ), 94 (Bingham LJ).
200   [1974] ICR 378, 399.
201   Although cf Hendy and Walton, 1997, who argue that there should be an *individual* right to be represented by a union; see also Hendy, 1998.
202   [1974] ICR 378, 412.

'organisational' and 'negotiating' activities which this approach implies is a much more logical and defensible line to draw than that between the individual and collective. A further exemplification of the anomalies which attempts to apply the existing divide have produced is the Court of Appeal decision in *Therm A Stor*, where the distinction drawn between an employer's reactions to the activities of individual members and those of their union again bears no relationship to industrial realities.

It is possible to frame legislation in a way which recognises the interplay between the individual and collective. In the United States, for example, the National Labor Relations Act 1935 provides that '[e]mployees shall have the right to self-organisation to form join or assist labor organisations to bargain collectively through representatives of their own choosing and to engage in other concerted activities for the purpose of collective bargaining or other mutual aid or protection'.[203] It is an unfair labour practice for employers to interfere with, restrain or coerce employees in the exercise of these rights.[204] This is not to imply that the US legislation does not have other defects[205] and, indeed, there is weighty evidence of employer opposition to trade unions in that country which the law in its existing form has been unable to counteract.[206] However, it remains the case that affirming general principles of the right to organise can provide a touchstone for a purposive interpretation of more specific provisions (those relating to discrimination against trade unionists, for example). In the British legislation, where no such general principles are enunciated, the courts have tended towards a narrow and technical approach, and decisions which attempt a more purposive interpretation by invoking the inferred policy of the legislation seem liable to be overturned.[207] Although the Human Rights Act 1998 may now encourage a purposive interpretation in some areas, it is no substitute for principles formulated specifically to apply to the employment context. The model of a statement affirming general principles followed by specified prohibited practices and remedies also communicates in a much clearer form the precise nature of both parties' respective rights and obligations. One example of where this would be particularly advantageous in British labour law would be an express prohibition on specifying non-membership of a union as a contractual term; although such a term is void,[208] it may nevertheless have an unwarranted deterrent effect upon an employee.

8.25   The second area where the legislation is deficient concerns the procedure for enforcement. Remedial action against an anti-union employer is entirely dependent upon an individual employee bringing a claim, with all its attendant difficulties and risks; there is no statutory acknowledgement that a union has a

---

203 S 7.
204 S 8(a)(1).
205 For example the exclusion of supervisors and managers from the definition of employee. For a useful summary of the law see Gould, 1993; see also Towers, 1997; S Wood and J Godard, 1999 and references therein.
206 Estimates of the proportion of union supporters dismissed by employers have ranged between one in twenty (Weiler, 1983) and one in sixty (LaLonde and Meltzer, 1991). Kochan states that 'in many organisations' a 'union avoidance ideology' is 'now a part of their publicly stated personnel policies': Kochan, 2003: p 169. Union density in the US is under 14% overall, and 9% in the private sector: Kochan, 2003: p 167.
207 See, for example, the EAT's decision in *Therm A Stor*, discussed in para 8.9, and the Court of Appeal's decision in *Associated Newspapers Ltd v Wilson* [1994] ICR 97.
208 TULRCA 1992, s 288.

legitimate interest either on its own behalf or that of its members in pursuing such an action. To maintain, as the government did, that giving unions the right to seek redress where employers have induced their members to cease union membership or activities or surrender representational rights would be inconsistent with the general pattern of protection is to turn the argument on its head; the more appropriate course is to extend the capacity of unions to bring complaints to other areas. Again an instructive comparison can be made with the United States, where anyone can report an unfair labour practice to the National Labor Relations Board which can then investigate and, if appropriate, issue an order which can be enforced through the courts. Although this is, in practice, a protracted process,[209] the concept of admitting complaints by unions and others is a helpful one and, indeed, with appropriate reforms to correct their current defects, the powers of investigation and enforcement bestowed upon the EOC, CRE and DRC in relation to the areas of discrimination for which they are responsible (discussed in chapter 6) could provide a model. A further current procedural difficulty is caused by the burden of proof lying upon the complainant (other than where he or she has been dismissed and would meet the general qualifications to claim unfair dismissal), particularly where a union reason needs to be the 'principal' reason or there is a need to establish an employer's 'sole or main purpose' in acting or failing to act. Unlike in the case of the discrimination legislation, there is no questionnaire procedure which forces the employer to commit itself in writing to a reason for its action which is admissible in subsequent proceedings and from which adverse conclusions can be drawn in the event of evasion or equivocation. Last, in relation to procedure, the difficulties an applicant faces may be enhanced by the lack of any specific protection against victimisation for those who provide information or otherwise assist in supporting another worker's claim (although admittedly such provisions in other contexts are in need of strengthening). Such acts may possibly amount to protected participation in union activities, but this may depend upon whether the union encouraged them; it is unclear whether the requisite 'authorisation' could be implied within the principles set out in para 8.9. Failing that, protection against dismissal would require the applicant to meet the general qualifications for claiming unfair dismissal.

8.26   The final general criticism concerns the inadequacy of the remedies. The tribunals and courts have no capacity to issue an order which forces an employer to change its practices; the most which can be sought, in the context of discriminatory hiring only, is a non-enforceable recommendation relating specifically to the complainant. In the context of dismissal there is no automatic right to reinstatement or re-engagement and, even if ordered, the non-practicability of compliance is assessed in the light of the circumstances of the business rather than giving paramount weight to the employee's rights. In any case it is open ultimately to an employer to 'buy out' an employee (and possibly all union presence at the workplace) at a price which is most unlikely to constitute adequate compensation for an employee who may never work again.[210] In this context the lack of status quo provisions pending a ruling on the justification for dismissal, which, it may be argued, should apply across

---

209 See Gould, 1993: pp 54–58 and 119–127.
210 Cf ILO, 1996: para 707.

the board, is particularly damaging. In the case of a shop steward or other union official[211] the argument for a status quo procedure is even stronger as their removal from the workplace has an impact upon union organisation generally, not only on the individual.[212] The remedy of interim relief, which may be perceived as partly meeting this requirement, necessitates employees taking the initiative rapidly to seek it following termination, does not apply to unfair selection for redundancy and, unless the employer consents, does not secure continued access to the workplace.[213] The remedies for subjection to a detriment are even more inadequate; there is no mechanism for inhibiting such action from continuing, and the lack of any 'penal' element in the compensation, combined with the potential difficulties of demonstrating quantifiable loss, mean that it is unlikely to serve as a deterrent to a determined anti-union employer, who may escape with virtual impunity in financial terms from a successful claim against it. In relation to discriminatory hiring the ceiling upon compensation stands in marked contrast to the lack of any limit on awards for other forms of discrimination, such as sex and race, and once again is unlikely to serve as a significant deterrent. In several respects, therefore, British legislation stands in need of reform if it is adequately to protect workers' rights of association and organisation in relation to employers.

Protection of the right not to join in relation to employers

8.27 It may appear anomalous that individuals should need to be protected against prejudicial action by employers for refusing union membership. The right not to join a union became significant in Britain because of the practice of the closed shop, 'a situation in which employees come to realise that a particular job is only to be obtained and retained if they become and remain members of one of a specified number of unions'.[214] Closed shops can, broadly speaking, take one of two forms: pre-entry, where an individual must be accepted into union membership before being considered for employment (historically important in the British merchant shipping, dockworking and printing industries, for example), and the more common post-entry closed shop (known in American parlance as the 'union shop') which requires employees to join a specified union shortly after taking up a job. By the early 1960s an estimated 3.75 million workers in Great Britain (16% of the total workforce) worked in a closed shop.[215] The common law placed no restriction on enforcing closed shops,[216] but legislative

---

211 See Millward *et al* 2000: pp 114–116 and 152–155 for the incidence of lay union representatives and Cully *et al* 1999: ch 4 for their role and activities.
212 And see ILO, 1996: para 724 *et seq.*
213 *Quaere* whether, if a shop steward had a contractual right to be on the premises to exercise his or her functions (see *City and Hackney Health Authority v NUPE* [1985] IRLR 252) this would be covered by TULRCA 1992, s 164(1) (which includes 'any ... benefit derived from the employment ...'). In practice such circumstances are likely to be rare.
214 McCarthy, 1964: p 9.
215 McCarthy, 1964: p 9. Coal-mining, iron and steel, engineering, shipbuilding and printing accounted for two-thirds of this number.
216 Union action to enforce a closed shop was ultimately accepted by the courts as a legitimate interest for the purpose of the tort of conspiracy: *White v Riley* [1921] 1 Ch 1; *Reynolds v Shipping Federation Ltd* [1924] 1 Ch 28; *Crofter Hand Woven Harris Tweed Co Ltd v Veitch* [1942] AC 435. See generally von Prondzynski, 1987: ch 8. Industrial action to enforce union membership is now excluded from the statutory immunities: see para 11.30 below.

intervention came with the Industrial Relations Act 1971[217] and the closed shop has been subject to varying kinds of statutory regulation ever since.

Debate about whether closed shops should be permitted has been highly polarised and founded, from each side, upon both pragmatism and principle. Supporters have argued that closed shops strengthen unions' bargaining power, remove a source of alternative labour during strikes, and avoid 'free riders' who take the benefits of collective bargaining without contributing to union funds. Opponents have cited their allegedly harmful economic consequences and their unwarranted interference with individual liberty.[218] The former have been said to include restricted output; resistance to change; maintenance of outdated skills differentials; and damaging strikes, leading to escalating production costs, uncompetitive pricing, depressed profit margins and closures. In the light of this catalogue it may seem surprising that not all employers shared the antagonistic view. The reasons why any given closed shop was negotiated and accepted by respective employers depended upon a number of variables including the particular sector or workplace and industrial relations climate of the time.[219] However, research shows that in the late 1970s, at least, closed shops were regarded by many managers as bringing advantages, such as greater stability in bargaining arrangements; greater likelihood of compliance with unpopular negotiating decisions, reinforced by the possibility of union discipline against dissenters; and a method of warding off the danger of inter-union competition.[220]

8.28   At international level legal policy towards forms of the closed shop at one time varied widely: some countries proscribed them, others permitted them, others still permitted modified arrangements such as making union membership (but not that of any particular union) compulsory, or allowing 'agency shops' whereby the non-member was required to pay a sum to a specified union or to charity. Recent years have seen more widespread legislative prohibition of such arrangements, but international treaties remain inconsistent on this issue. Whether there should be a right not to join a union and, if so, whether it has equal weight to the right to join has been dubbed 'one of the oldest set of issues in trade union law in most industrial democracies'.[221] Its complexity is reflected in the terms of relevant international treaties. After considerable debate on this issue[222] the ILO adopted a neutral stance; the Conference specifically endorsed the view that Convention No 87, which grants workers the right to join organisations of their own choosing, neither authorised nor prohibited union security arrangements,

---

217 Between 1927 and 1946 the Trade Disputes and Trade Unions Act 1927, s 6(1) made it unlawful for a local or other public authority to make it a condition of employment for any person that he or she should be a union member, or to impose any condition which subjected non-union members to any 'disability or disadvantage'.

218 Burton, 1979; Hanson *et al*, 1979; Robbins, 1978.

219 See generally McCarthy, 1964; Dunn and Gennard, 1984; Dunn and Wright, 1993.

220 See above. A survey of manufacturing industry found that three-quarters of employers with experience of closed shops saw advantages in the practice while only half saw disadvantages: M Hart, 1979. However, managers had few regrets that the law had changed: Dunn and Wright, 1993: p 22.

221 Leader, 1992: p 123.

222 Betten, 1993, records (at pp 76–77) that '[t]he question of whether or not the freedom of association includes also the freedom not to join, was one of the reasons why attempts failed in 1927 to get a freedom of association Convention adopted by the International Labour Conference ...'.

such matters being for regulation by national practice.[223] However, the supervisory bodies have concluded that where such arrangements are imposed by law, rather than by voluntary agreement, this constitutes a breach of the Convention (a distinction which may appear illogical given that in the latter case the decision to permit such arrangements equally involves an exercise of state power).[224] By contrast the Universal Declaration of Human Rights 1948, article 20(2) provides that no one may be compelled to belong to an association, although proposals to give legal effect to this principle in the International Covenant on Civil and Political Rights were rejected. There was 'no real discussion' of the matter during the drafting of the International Covenant on Economic Social and Cultural Rights, but the UN supervisory committee, in common with the Committee of Independent Experts (now the European Committee of Social Rights) under the European Social Charter, has inferred that the right to join a trade union implies the right not to join.[225]

8.29   The position under the ECHR is more opaque. In *Young, James and Webster v United Kingdom*[226] three British Rail employees complained that their dismissals for refusing to join a trade union pursuant to a closed shop agreement introduced after their employment had commenced breached Article 11 (see para 7.9 above). Two of the applicants had ideological objections to joining any of these unions; the third simply refused to join. Despite evidence from the *travaux préparatoires* that Article 11(1) did not incorporate a right not to join and that the closed shop was intended to be unaffected, the majority of the Court declined to rule directly on the question of whether it was included. Rather the Court concluded that on the facts of the particular case the threat of dismissal directed against persons engaged before there was any obligation to join a particular trade union struck at the 'very substance of the freedom guaranteed by Article 11', although it did not then explain the content of such substance (which on this analysis would clearly need to include non-membership).[227] It also held that, in the light of the protection of personal opinion afforded by Articles 9 and 10, it was a breach of the Convention to exert pressure of this kind to compel individuals to join an association contrary to their convictions.

The unwillingness of the majority of the Court to decide whether Article 11 embraced a right not to join was not shared by all its members. A number of those who concurred with the majority judgment placed on record their view that the negative aspect of freedom of association was a correlative of, and inseparable from, its positive aspect; obligatory membership of itself, even without the implementation of a sanction for non-membership, was irreconcilable with the freedom of choice inherent in freedom of association.[228] Judge Evrigenis, who also concurred with the majority in the result, took a less clear-cut view,

---

223   ILO, Record of Proceedings, ILC, 32nd Session, 1949, 468; ILO, 1994: para 205.
224   For a critique of the neutral position see Leader, 1992: pp 152–158.
225   Craven, 1998: pp 268–269.
226   Judgment of 13 August 1981, [1981] IRLR 408.
227   See Forde, 1982, for a trenchant critique of this decision. On the facts it was found that the restriction of the right was not 'necessary in a democratic society' within Art 11(2) because it could not be said that the railway unions would have been prevented from striving for the protection of their members' interests in the absence of legislation permitting the applicants' dismissal.
228   [1981] IRLR 408, 419 (Judges Ganshof van der Meersch, Bindschedler-Robert, Liesch, Matscher, Pinheiro Farinha and Pettiti).

affirming that trade union freedom was to a large extent determined by its character as a collective right and that in attempting to strike a fair balance, account had to be taken of the welfare of the public and of the collective interests of the union organisation that were at stake as well as the individual's freedom of association.[229] A third view was articulated by three dissenting members of the Court: that the positive and negative aspects of freedom of association were not two aspects of the same freedom.[230] The positive right concerned 'the individual as an active participant in social activities' and was in a sense 'a collective right in so far as it can only be exercised jointly by a plurality of individuals'. The negative freedom, by contrast, 'aims at protecting the individual against being grouped together with other individuals with whom he does not agree or for purposes which he does not approve ... However strongly such protection of the individual may sometimes be needed, it is neither in logic nor by necessary implication part of the positive freedom to associate'.[231] The drafting history of Article 11 showed that the parties to the Convention had not assumed any international obligation in relation to the right not to join but had deliberately reserved this as a matter for each national system to determine, and on that basis the closed shop was neither authorised nor prohibited by the Convention.

In a more recent decision the European Court of Human Rights – invoking the principle that the Convention is a 'living instrument which must be interpreted in the light of present-day conditions' – concluded that Article 11 does encompass a negative right, although it did not determine whether this should be considered on an equal footing with the positive.[232] It is notable that the Court drew for support on ILO principles which, as we indicate above, affect only union security arrangements imposed by law; the Court here made no such distinction and, although the case at issue concerned such an arrangement, its judgment appears to extend more widely.[233] The Court also cited the Community Charter of the Fundamental Social Rights of Workers, adopted by eleven Member States (excluding the UK) in Strasbourg in 1989, which includes a right to join or not to join trade unions without suffering any 'personal or occupational damage'.

Whether the 'common ground' referred to by the European Court of Human Rights will emerge remains in the area of speculation (notably the right not to join trade unions is not included in the 2000 Charter of Fundamental Rights of the European Union).[234] It seems clear that questions in this area can be addressed only against a backcloth of broader legal policy. This point is neatly illustrated by the Donovan Commission's conclusion that the right not to join is not the corollary of the right to join because inhibiting the latter is 'designed to frustrate

229 [1981] IRLR 408, 419.
230 Judge Sorensen, joined by Judges Thor Vilhjalmsson and Lagergren at 419–420.
231 For a critique of this position see Leader, 1992: pp 32–34 who argues, *inter alia*, that the 'conditions under which a right can be exercised tell you little about who possesses it' and it is 'quite possible for an individual to possess a right which can only be exercised collectively' (see pp 33–34).
232 *Sigurour A Sigurjonsson v Iceland* judgment of 30 June 1993, (1993) 16 EHRR 462: para 35. A closed shop would probably be difficult to justify under Art 11(2). See also *Chassagnou v France* judgment of 29 April 1999, (2000) 29 EHRR 615, paras 103–117. Cf *Sibson v UK* judgment of 20 April 1993, (1994) 17 EHRR 193, where the relocation of the applicant to another depot, as permitted by his contract, was found by the ECtHR not to strike at the substance of the freedom.
233 On this basis, individuals falling outside the definition of 'workers' who are subjected to a detriment for non-membership of a union would have a free-standing right of action under the HRA 1998 against a public authority (or at least a 'pure' public authority). In practice, this situation seems highly unlikely to arise.
234 See further para 2.43; Bercusson, 2000: pp 418–419.

the development of collective bargaining, which it is public policy to promote'.[235] During the period of the 1979–1997 Conservative administration a very different public policy would have been prayed in aid in addressing this issue.

8.30 Returning to the position under British legislation, the Industrial Relations Act 1971 attempted a concerted attack on the closed shop and created an individual right not to join a union. However, unions and employers co-operated to discourage individuals from exercising their new right and this provision had little impact on existing closed shops.[236] The succeeding Labour government's legislation, by contrast, marked a near-return to the previous non-interventionist position by removing restraints upon closed shops' enforcement; it was automatically fair for an employer to dismiss an employee who refused to join an independent trade union specified in a closed shop agreement except where the employee objected to the principle of union membership on grounds of religious belief.[237] Although the introduction of closed shops remained a matter of voluntary agreement it is notable that by mid-1978 at least 5.2 million workers in Great Britain (23%) were covered by such arrangements.[238]

The legal pendulum swung again with the election of the Thatcher government, whose hostility to union organisation we have described in chapter 7. Predictably the closed shop was regarded as complete anathema. Rather than attempting to outlaw the practice altogether, however, the government took incremental measures to reduce its effective operation. The first target was the post-entry closed shop, which became increasingly difficult to enforce; the range of exempted categories was expanded significantly and ballots requiring high majorities to start or continue closed shops were required. Finally, in 1988, the post-entry closed shop became completely unenforceable when the right of an individual not to join a union was given parallel protection to the right to join, with statutory protection against dismissal[239] and action short of dismissal for exercising that right.[240] This was followed by the death knell of the pre-entry closed shop in 1990, with the introduction of protection against refusal of employment for non-membership (and, as an afterthought, for membership as well).[241] The Labour Government which entered office in 1997 left the position unchanged in its essentials, beyond amendments that parallel those applicable to the right to join. Closed shops are not now illegal as such but they cannot be lawfully enforced and, although it seems that informal practices remained for a time in individual workplaces or among some types of employee, if they now exist at all they involve a fraction of those covered in 1978.[242] In practice,

---

235 *Royal Commission on Trade Unions and Employers' Associations 1965–1968*, Cmnd 3623, 1968; para 599.
236 Weekes *et al*, 1975: ch 2.
237 TULRA 1974, as amended by the Trade Union and Labour Relations (Amendment) Act 1976, para 6(5) of the Schedule.
238 Dunn and Gennard, 1984: p 15.
239 See now TULRCA 1992, s 152.
240 See now TULRCA 1992, s 146.
241 TULRCA 1992, s 137. In early 1989 the Department of Employment estimated that 1.3 million persons were in pre-entry closed shops: *Removing Barriers to Employment*, Cm 655 (1989), para 2.6–2.7, although others argued this figure was grossly exaggerated: see Lord McCarthy, HL Debs Vol 521, col 154, 10 July 1990; Dunn and Wright, 1993: pp 8–10.
242 See generally Dunn and Wright, 1993 and Wright, 1996. The 1998 Workplace Employee Relations Survey found that in 2% of workplaces managers said employees had to be union members to get or keep their jobs, but did not probe further the basis of this compulsion: Cully *et al*, 1999: p 89; Millward *et al*, 2000: pp 146–149.

therefore, contentious issues arising in relation to the right not to join may be more likely to emerge from the consequences of a single-union recognition deal which accords differential treatment to members and non-members of that union rather than from the closed shop as such.[243] Because the entitlement, procedure and remedies for the right not to join are, in most respects, identical to those relating to the right to join we identify only the distinctive features of this right in para 8.31 below.

The scope of protection, entitlement and remedies

8.31   There is a statutory right not to join (or to refuse or propose to refuse to join) any, or a particular, union(s).[244] Enforcement of the 'agency shop', requiring a payment equalling the union subscription to the union or to charity to counter the free-rider charge, is also precluded; there is a right not to comply with a requirement to make a payment, or allow a deduction from remuneration, as an alternative to union membership.[245] In addition, it is automatically unfair to select an employee for redundancy on these grounds where the circumstances described in para 8.3 apply.[246] As in the case of the right to join, an employee who is dismissed need not meet the usual qualifications for claiming unfair dismissal (although, where they are not met, the applicant will need to prove the reason for dismissal), and identical remedies apply, including provision for the dismissed employee to seek interim relief, although if this is sought there is no requirement to obtain a certificate from a union official.[247] 'Workers' (not only 'employees') are protected against subjection to a detriment by any act or failure to act by the employer whose sole or main purpose is to compel the worker to be or become a member of a union or a particular union.[248] The procedure for complaining of subjection to a detriment on grounds of non-membership, and the remedies available, are identical to those available for infringement of the right to join (see para 8.13 *et seq*). In addition, workers have a right not to have an offer made by the employer for the sole or main purpose of inducing the worker to be or become a member of a union or a particular union,[249] and are protected against subjection to a detriment for failing to accept such an offer.[250]

The provisions covering refusal of employment specifically prevent employers relying on unions to supply labour; it is unlawful for an employer (or employment agency) to refuse to employ non-members pursuant to an arrangement or practice whereby employment is offered only to persons put forward or approved by a

---

243 See para 8.2 above for further discussion of single-union deals.
244 TULRCA 1992, ss 137(1), 146(1)(c), 152(1)(c). This also includes membership of a particular branch or section of the union or one of a number of such branches or sections: ss 143(3), 151(1), 152(4). Note that this right is not confined to membership of an independent union.
245 TULRCA 1992, ss 137(1)(b)(ii), 146(3), 152(3). See Benedictus, 1979: pp 162–163 for discussion of the use of such practices in the 1970s.
246 TULRCA 1992, s 153. Note that where the terms of s 152 or 153 are not satisfied, a dismissal for non-membership may still be unfair under the ordinary unfair dismissal provisions.
247 TULRCA 1992, s 161(3).
248 TULRCA 1992, s 146. 'Employees' must use s 152 in the event of dismissal; see further para 8.13 for the implications of this.
249 TULRCA 1992, s 145A(1)(d); see further para 8.17.
250 TULRCA 1992, s 146(2C). Once again 'employees' must use s 152 in the event of dismissal.

union where the union does this only in respect of its members (although an affected individual would need to complain for the practice to be challenged).[251] In providing job-finding services, however, unions may legitimately discriminate between members and non-members; they are not regarded as 'employment agencies' by reason of services provided by them only for, or in relation to, their members.[252] Unions may also continue to demand that those applying for union office are members of that union[253] (but not of another union, even if that may be more appropriate to the job in question).

In relation to any proceedings relating to the right not to join, if either the complainant or respondent claims that the employer was induced to take the action in question by pressure from a union or other person calling, organising, procuring or organising a strike or other industrial action (or threatening to do so) because the complainant was not a union member, either party may request the tribunal to direct that such a person be joined as a party to the proceedings.[254] That third party may then be liable to pay all or a proportion of any compensation awarded to the complainant.[255]

Although the provisions governing the right not to join a union parallel those governing the right to join, in practice they are likely to be easier to enforce. An employer who takes prejudicial action against an employee for non-membership is likely to do so only against a background of universal or near-universal membership and it is, therefore, much more likely that an employee will be able to invoke circumstantial evidence to satisfy the employment tribunal that this was the reason for the action. To this extent, therefore, while the comments relating to the burden of proof in para 8.25 remain valid in formal terms, they are likely to present less of an obstacle to a successful claim. If one were to accept the principle of formal equality between these rights, the remarks made earlier as to the inadequacy of the remedies available are equally valid in this context. However, in practice it seems less likely that an employer will wish to buy its way into a closed shop than into a union-free environment; letting sleeping dogs lie or social sanctions by other workers are a more likely response to the presence of a non-member than dismissal.[256]

CONTRACT COMPLIANCE AND UNION MEMBERSHIP

8.32   We outlined contract compliance as a strategy for encouraging particular employment practices in chapter 2. In the context of union membership, as we indicated in para 8.2, the 1946 version of the House of Commons Fair Wages Resolution specified that government contracts with private employers should require contractors to recognise the freedom of their workers to be members of trade unions. Most local authorities also followed this example, although not required to do so, and some attempted to support trade unionism by requiring contractors to employ only union labour.[257] 1982 brought a complete

251   TULRCA 1992, s 137(4).
252   TULRCA 1992, s 143(2).
253   This covers 'officials' within s 119 or any other position to which the duty to hold elections applies: TULRCA 1992, s 137(7), (8).
254   TULRCA 1992, ss 142, 150, 160.
255   TULRCA 1992, ss 142, 150, 160.
256   Dunn and Wright, 1993: p 4 *et seq.*
257   In 1982 about one in eight imposed such requirements for manual workers: Ingham and Thompson, 1982: table 5A.

reversal of policy when the Conservative Government gave notice to rescind the Fair Wages Resolution and introduced legislation proscribing the implementation of contract compliance policies in this area.[258] A term or condition of any contract for the supply of goods or services (including one entered by individual householders) which requires that the work, or any part, is done only by members of a union, or a particular union, or by non-union members, is void, and there is a statutory duty not to exclude persons from a list of approved suppliers, or to terminate or refuse to consider entering contracts with them, if one of the grounds is that such a requirement is unlikely to be met. This duty is owed both to the potential contractor and to 'any other person who may be adversely affected by its contravention'.[259] Unlike the Local Government Act 1988, which prohibits local authorities and several other public bodies from making decisions relating to public supply and works contracts by reference to 'non-commercial matters',[260] there is no requirement for persons awarding contracts to give reasons for their decisions. The ban on non-union labour clauses was inserted to demonstrate formal equality between the rights to join and not to join rather than because non-union clauses were perceived as presenting any problem in practice.[261]

FACILITIES FOR TRADE UNION REPRESENTATIVES AND TRADE UNION ACTIVITIES

8.33   As we saw in chapter 7, trade unions conduct a multiplicity of functions on behalf of their members. At workplace level these may include negotiation and consultation with employers, dealing with individual and collective grievances, and representing members at disciplinary hearings.[262] These functions are often performed by lay representatives (or 'shop stewards').[263] Lay representatives began to play an increasingly important role in British industrial relations after the Second World War. By 1961 there were estimated to be about 90,000 shop stewards; research for the Donovan Commission later in the decade put the number at 175,000 and by the late 1970s the figure had reached between 250,000 and 300,000.[264] In 1998, 72% of establishments with recognised unions (33% of the total) had at least one representative.[265] This compared with 82% and 54% respectively in 1984, although the fall was concentrated in workplaces employing fewer than a hundred people and in the period 1984–1990; there was no further decrease between 1990 and 1998.[266]

---

258 See now TULRCA 1992, s 145.
259 TULRCA 1992, s 145(5).
260 Local Government Act 1988, s 17(1). The Local Government Act 1999, s 19, empowers the Secretary of State to remove by order specified matters from the category of non-commercial matters in relation to 'best value' authorities, such as local authorities; see SI 2001/909, discussed at para 2.6, for the exercise of this power.
261 See Evans and Lewis, 1988, for the background to these provisions.
262 Note now the statutory right for workers to be accompanied by the companion of their choice, who may be a union official, at disciplinary and grievance hearings: see ERelA 1999, ss 10–15 and para 5.132 *et seq*.
263 See para 8.9 above for discussion of this term.
264 Various research findings summarised in P Edwards *et al*, 1992: p 22.
265 Millward *et al*, 2000: pp 114–116 and 152–154. The figures refer to establishments with 25 or more employees. See generally Cully *et al*, 1999: ch 9 for the activities of lay representatives in 1998 and, for a broader discussion, Terry, 2003.
266 Millward *et al*, 2000: pp 114–116 and 152–154.

Lay representatives can carry out their functions much more effectively if employers make available appropriate facilities at the workplace to assist them. In many cases the most important single facility is likely to be time. In 1978 a survey estimated that in 12% of establishments with manual stewards (and 2% of non-manual) at least one was full-time,[267] and even in 1990, 4% of workplaces with recognised unions had one or more full-time representatives (a higher proportion than in 1984).[268] In 1975 the Labour Government's 'Social Contract' legislation introduced a statutory obligation on employers to grant officials of *recognised* independent trade unions a reasonable amount of paid time off during working hours for industrial relations duties and training relevant to those duties. In addition, members of such unions were entitled to reasonable time off (which need not be paid) to participate in union activities or represent the union. Perhaps surprisingly, these rights survived the legislative changes of the 1980s, albeit with significant amendment in 1989 when the Employment Act narrowed the duties for which officials could claim time off to those concerned with negotiations on matters for which the union was specifically recognised. The Employment Act 2002 added an obligation to give paid time off to a newly-created class of 'union learning representatives'.

Time off has always been conditional on the employer granting permission, with a right to complain to an employment tribunal in the event of it being refused. Although time rights apply to all employers without exception as to size and type of business or service, they have always been located within a framework which acknowledges the need to pay adequate regard both to the operational requirements of individual workplaces and to the difficulties of communicating with the specific workforce (for example, if part-time or shift work is common). The ACAS Code of Practice on Time Off for Trade Union Duties and Activities (revised most recently in 2003), applicable to all the time off rights discussed in this section,[269] strongly encourages local level agreements which can reflect these needs.[270] Such arrangements may be more generous than the legislation requires. Ultimately, however, only the denial of the statutory entitlement can be the subject of complaint to a tribunal.

We examine below the scope of the statutory rights, and the remedies for their infringement, before commenting upon their adequacy. At the time of writing these rights apply only to employees rather than the wider category of 'workers',[271] but require no minimum period of employment. We do not include in this discussion the specific rights of safety representatives to time off which are subject to separate legislative provision, outlined in para 9.46.

Time off rights of trade union officials

8.34 Union 'officials' (which include any lay representative elected or appointed in accordance with the union rules)[272] are entitled to paid time off for three

---

267 W Brown, 1981: pp 63–67.

268 Millward *et al*, 2000: p 153–154.

269 See para 2.4 for the status of ACAS Codes of Practice.

270 Paras 43–48. For the operation of time off in practice by way of agreement, see Cully *et al*, 1999: ch 9. See also *Time off for union duties*, Bargaining Report 198, Labour Research Department.

271 Note, however, ERelA 1999, s 23, discussed at para 3.72. Special provision is made for attendance by a member of a police force at specified meetings of the Police Federation: Police Regulations 2003, SI 2003/527, reg 23.

272 See TULRCA 1992, s 119.

purposes (although there is nothing to prevent the parties agreeing to such entitlement in a wider range of situations). The first is to carry out any of their duties, as such an official, concerned with negotiations with the employer related to or connected with any matters falling within the statutory definition of collective bargaining in relation to which the union is recognised by the employer.[273] To fall within this category, three conditions must be satisfied. First, the duties must relate to a matter for which the union is recognised by the employer in question; the fact that other employers in the same industry, or even an associated employer,[274] may have granted more extensive recognition is irrelevant. As we saw in para 7.27, recognition may be express or implied from conduct. Second, the matter must be listed in the Trade Union and Labour Relations (Consolidation) Act 1992, s 178(2), which specifies the matters constituting the subject-matter of 'collective bargaining'.[275] Last, the duties must be 'concerned with negotiations' with the employer. This condition was inserted by the Employment Act 1989 to require proximity to actual negotiations; attending meetings of bodies with no negotiating power to determine national union policies concerned with industrial relations matters, covered under previous legislation,[276] would no longer suffice.

Whether sufficient proximity exists will involve examining the facts in each case. In *Adlington v British Bakeries (Northern) Ltd*, decided during the legislative passage of the Employment Act 1989, branch officials of the Bakers, Food and Allied Workers' Union claimed paid time off to attend a union workshop concerning government proposals to repeal the Banking Industry (Hours of Work) Act 1954. The Court of Appeal upheld the claim on the basis that repeal would threaten the continued existence of the industry's National Working Agreement and was thus likely to lead to negotiations between the union and employers, Kerr LJ stressing the 'exceptionally close connection' between the repeal of the legislation and a specific bargaining matter that existed.[277] In drafting the 1989 Act the Government sought explicitly to incorporate the concept of proximity propounded in this case. *London Ambulance Service v Charlton*[278] was decided under the new provision. Union officials sought paid time off to attend a union committee to coordinate the activities of its district committee within the London Ambulance Service. The EAT affirmed that meetings which were called actively to prepare for negotiations in connection with collective bargaining were covered provided that there was 'sufficient nexus between the collective bargaining and the duty involving preparation for that particular issue'.[279] Moreover, officials of a union which was a member of a multi-union Joint Consultative Committee (JCC) might wish to have their own meeting in the absence of other unions, although the frequency and timing of these separate meetings in relation to those of the JCC might be relevant in considering the issue of reasonableness (discussed below).

The second purpose for which an employer should grant paid time off is to carry out duties concerned with the performance on behalf of its employees of functions related to or connected with 'collective bargaining' matters which the

---

273 TULRCA 1992, s 168(1).
274 See para 3.98.
275 See para 7.27. See the Code of Practice, para 11, for examples under each heading.
276 *Beal v Beacham Group Ltd* [1982] IRLR 192.
277 [1989] IRLR 218, 222.
278 [1992] IRLR 510.
279 [1992] IRLR 510, 513.

employer has specifically agreed may be performed by the union.[280] Thus, officials should be given time off to represent individuals in grievance proceedings in circumstances beyond those required by statute,[281] for example, where the employer has agreed to this. The ACAS Code of Practice emphasises that an official's duties must be connected with or related to negotiations or the performance of functions both in time and subject matter. It suggests that reasonable time off may be sought, for example, to prepare for negotiations; inform members of progress; explain outcomes to members; and prepare for meetings with the employer about matters for which the union has only representational rights,[282] although the latter is not, strictly speaking, within the terms of the legislation. Informing members about the outcome of industry-wide negotiations would seem not to be included,[283] although employers may wish to consider allowing time off for this purpose. The third purpose for which time off should be granted is to carry out duties concerned with the receipt of information from and consultation with the employer in relation to collective redundancies and a transfer of the undertaking. We discuss those provisions in detail in chapter 9.

8.35   In addition to the conduct of these duties, officials are also entitled to paid time off for training relevant to them.[284] Training courses must be approved by the Trades Union Congress or by the official's own union. The kind of training a particular official should have will depend upon the scope of any recognition or other agreement; the structure of the union; and the role of the official.[285] The relationship between training and the scope of recognition may put into question entitlement to attend courses which relate to several topics, not all of which may be covered by the individual recognition agreement.[286] However the EAT has indicated that the statute should not be given a narrow interpretation,[287] and many contemporary courses focus upon the development of skills required by officials, such as negotiating and representational skills, rather than substantive topics and so circumvent this problem. The Code of Practice recommends that employers should consider releasing officials for initial training in basic representational skills as soon as possible after their election or appointment, bearing in mind that suitable courses may be infrequent. It also recommends consideration of time off for further training, particularly where the official has special responsibilities; for training courses to develop representational and negotiating skills; where there are proposals to change the scope or nature of collective bargaining at the workplace, where significant changes in the organisation of work are being contemplated, or where legislation may affect the conduct of industrial relations at the place of work and may require the reconsideration of existing collective agreements.[288] The EAT relied

---

280 TULRCA 1992, s 168(1).
281 See ERelA 1999, s 10; see further para 5.132 *et seq*.
282 Para 12.
283 Representation on regional or national bodies negotiating with a range of employers would also not be covered, although officials would be entitled to unpaid time off for this purpose: see para 8.39.
284 TULRCA 1992, s 168(2).
285 Code of Practice, para 19.
286 *Menzies v Smith and McLaurin Ltd* [1980] IRLR 180. The identity of the personnel for whom the course is described as being designed may be a relevant factor: *Ministry of Defence v Crook and Irving* [1982] IRLR 488.
287 *STC Submarine Systems v Piper* (11 March 1993, unreported), EAT.
288 Para 21.

upon the concept of 'special responsibilities' in holding that a union branch secretary who had been elected to the Management Committee of a pension scheme to represent his members and others, to report back to shop stewards and to advise members in connection with their pensions, was entitled to paid time off to attend a course on pensions.[289]

The 1998 Workplace Industrial Relations Survey found that 70% of representatives had received some training for their role. However this varied according to size of workplace and length of time in office; those in small workplaces were less likely to be trained, and only 44% of those in office for a year or less had received training as compared with 91% of those in office for ten years or more.[290] From 1976 until 1996 the TUC and, latterly, non-affiliated independent unions also, received a government grant towards the cost of training lay and safety representatives, but this was withdrawn by the Conservative Government on the grounds that industrial relations had improved and the coverage of collective bargaining reduced, a step that overlooked the wide range of functions that representatives perform. In a reversal of its predecessor's policy, Labour Government has provided support for TUC Education, in addition to funding for 'partnership' projects, some of which included, *inter alia*, training union representatives.[291] In 2004 the Government announced the establishment of a Union Modernisation Fund of some £5–£10 million to provide assistance to independent unions and their federations to modernise their operations, including supporting innovative projects in such areas as training union representatives (for example, in the area of business and people management) in order to help promote the development of high performance workplaces.[292]

8.36 The amount of time off which an employer should permit an official to take, and the purposes for which, occasions on which, and conditions subject to which it may be taken, are those which are 'reasonable in all the circumstances'.[293] In determining what it reasonable, which is pre-eminently a question for the employment tribunal as 'industrial jury' to decide,[294] regard is to be had to the ACAS Code of Practice. Where the employer and union have concluded their own time off agreement, as the Code strongly recommends,[295] its provisions are likely to influence a tribunal considerably in determining

---

289 *STC Submarine Systems v Piper*, above, note 287. Although the pension scheme was not directly negotiable, the EAT held that the employment tribunal was justified in concluding that pension rights were relevant to any negotiations over pay and conditions in general, and involved at least in the preparation of matters relevant to collective bargaining.

290 Cully *et al*, 1999: pp 197–198.

291 A Partnership at Work Fund was established pursuant to a power granted to the Secretary of State by ERelA 1999, s 30 to provide money 'for the purpose of encouraging and helping employers (or their representatives) and employees (or their representatives) to improve the way they work together'. It is anomalous that this power is confined to 'employees', given that trade unions are organisations of 'workers': TULRCA 1992, s 1, discussed further para 7.20. An outline of successful projects is given at www.dti.gov.uk/partnershipfund.

292 Gerry Sutcliffe, Parliamentary Under-Secretary of State for Employment Relations, Competition and Consumers, HC Debs col 1368W, 10 February 2004 (written answer). Statutory authority for this expenditure is given by TULRCA 1992, s 116A, inserted by ERelA 2004, s 55.

293 TULRCA 1992, s 168(3).

294 *Thomas Scott & Sons (Bakers) Ltd v Allen* [1983] IRLR 329; *Wignall v British Gas Corpn* [1984] IRLR 493.

295 Para 43.

what is reasonable in the circumstances, although an agreement which is less favourable than the legislation ought not to prejudice an employee's position.[296] The nature, extent and purpose of time off already taken by the employee may be a relevant factor, as may adequate cover for safety, the production process or provision of service.[297] Officials should give management as much notice as possible when time off is sought, giving details of its purpose, the intended location, and its timing and duration.[298]

8.37   When time off is granted the employee should be paid as if he or she had worked.[299] The pre-Employment Act 1989 cases conflict on whether an employer can allow an official time off but argue that it was not reasonable for the official to be paid for that time.[300] Even then it was hard to reconcile such an argument with the statutory language[301] and the tighter definition of the duties for which paid time off is due would seem to diminish its chances of success. An employee who performs the relevant duties outside his or her own 'working hours'[302] (a night shift worker who attends meetings during the day, for example) has no statutory entitlement to compensating paid time off in lieu.[303] In practice unions and employers should attempt to reach an agreement to cater for circumstances of this kind.[304] Problems may also arise for employees who do not work full-time who may thereby be disadvantaged if the time they spend on union duties exceeds their working hours. The European Court of Justice has held that compensation received for loss of earnings due to attendance at training courses for staff committees in Germany falls within the definition of 'pay' for the purposes of Article 141 of the EC Treaty (ex Article 119) and the Equal Pay Directive 75/117 because it constitutes a benefit paid by reason of the existence of an employment relationship. Since the members of such committees who are employed part-time are generally women, a legislative provision which results in part-time workers being paid less than full-time workers for attending courses whose length exceeds the number of hours they work constitutes indirect discrimination against women.[305] In *Manor Bakeries v Nazir*[306] the EAT held that this principle did not apply to attendance at a British union conference on the basis that this was not a species of 'work'. However in the later case of *Davies v Neath Port Talbot County Borough Council*[307] a differently-constituted

---

296 TULRCA 1992, s 288 (cf the discussion in *Ashley v Ministry of Defence* [1984] IRLR 57, where the EAT distinguished between time off pursuant to an internal agreement, which may be in some respects more favourable and in others less favourable than the statute, and time off pursuant to the predecessor of s 168.)

297 Para 35; *Wignall v British Gas Corpn* above note 294.

298 Para 39.

299 TULRCA 1992, s 169. Where an employee's pay varies with the amount of work done, payment is to be calculated by reference to the average hourly earnings for the work the employee is employed to do.

300 In *Beecham Group Ltd v Beal (No 2)* [1983] IRLR 317 the EAT held that the right to payment followed automatically; cf *Thomas Scott & Sons (Bakers) Ltd v Allen* [1983] IRLR 329, where the EAT took a different view but did not explain the basis for this conclusion.

301 See Fitzpatrick, 1983: p 260 for further comment.

302 The same definition as in the context of 'appropriate time' (see para 8.10) applies: TULRCA 1992, s 173.

303 See *Hairsine v Kingston upon Hull City Council* [1992] IRLR 211.

304 See Code of Practice, para 45.

305 C-360/90 *Arbeiterwohlfahrt der Stadt Berlin e V v Bötel* [1992] IRLR 423, ECJ; Case 457/93 *Kuratorium für Dialyse und Nierentransplantion eV v Lewark* [1996] IRLR 637.

306 [1996] IRLR 604.

307 [1999] IRLR 769.

EAT held that *Nazir* should not be followed, affirming that attendance at a union training course, like that of German staff committees, was by reason of the existence of the employment relationship. The European Court of Justice had indicated that it was open to a Member State to justify legislation which limited part-time workers to compensation for their working hours by objective factors unrelated to any discrimination on grounds of sex.[308] In *Davies* the EAT took a robust approach to this issue, affirming that there could not be 'a justifiable policy or aim which maintains the inequality'.[309]

If an official is refused permission to take time off, the sole remedy is to complain to an employment tribunal;[310] there is a right to time off only with permission. (An employee who took time off without permission and was subsequently disciplined for doing so could not claim to have been taking part in a protected union activity because it would not have been at an appropriate time: see para 8.10.) An official can also complain if he or she was not paid in accordance with the legislation for time off which was granted.[311] Claims must be brought within three months of the failure to permit time off, or to make the requisite payment.[312] There is no obligation to institute the statutory grievance procedure before presenting a complaint. If it upholds the complaint, the tribunal must make a declaration and may award compensation, having regard to the employer's default and any loss sustained by the employee because of the failure.[313] By analogy with the provisions relating to subjection to a detriment it seems likely that 'loss' can include non-pecuniary loss such as injury to health (see para 8.16). Where the complaint concerns a failure to pay the official, the tribunal will order payment by the employer of the amount due. Tribunals have no power to impose conditions on the parties as to how time off should be granted in the future.[314]

Time off for union learning representatives

8.38 'Union learning representatives' (ULR) are a new type of lay union representative, whose main function is to advise union members about their

---

308 See *Lewark* note 305 above for consideration of the factors which may be relevant in this context.
309 Above note 307 at 772.
310 TULRCA 1992, ss 168(4), 173(2). Curiously, s 173(2) states that the sole remedy is by way of complaint to an employment tribunal under Part III of TULRCA 1992. However, ERA 1996 s 27(1)(e) includes payment for time off for union duties within the definition of 'wages', so allowing tribunals to treat non-payment as an unlawful deduction from 'wages' under ss 13–27 of that Act: see paras 4.68 and 4.69. Nothing would seem to turn on this in relation to a failure to pay on one occasion, but if the failure related to a series of non-payments the time limit under ERA 1996, s 23(3)(a) appears to be more generous.
311 TULRCA 1992, s 169(5).
312 TULRCA 1992, s 171. If the tribunal is satisfied that compliance with this time limit was not 'reasonably practicable' the complaint must be presented within such further period as the tribunal considers 'reasonable': see para 2.17. In *Young, Stewart and Morris v British Airways Board* unreported, EAT 175/83, it was held that the three-month period runs from the date when permission was refused.
313 TULRCA 1992, s 172. To establish a right to compensation an employee must establish, on the balance of probabilities, that a request was made for time off, that it came to the notice of the employer's appropriate representative, and that they either refused it, ignored it or failed to respond to it: *Ryford Ltd v Drinkwater* [1996] IRLR 16. In *Skiggs v South West Trains Ltd* [2005] IRLR 459 the EAT held that 'compensation' could include the concept of a cash reparation to the individual for the fact that a wrong had been done to him, independently of any special consequential loss.
314 *Corner v Buckinghamshire County Council* [1978] IRLR 320.

training, educational and developmental needs. Their advice is usually provided direct to union members at their place of work. Prior to EA 2002 there were estimated to be around 3000 ULRs in existence, but their activities were seen as being constrained by the limited abilities of unions to find, train and support suitable volunteers for this work.[315] Research conducted for the government suggested that ULRs had a significant impact in increasing motivation and enthusiasm for learning among both employers and employees,[316] and EA 2002 introduced a right to paid time off for ULRs to prepare for and conduct their activities.[317] Although the CBI, like the TUC, agreed that ULRs could play a valuable role, the CBI considered that ULRs should be appointed only with the employer's agreement. The TUC opposed employers having any right of veto, and the government concluded that unions should be free to decide on the identity and number of ULRs at the workplace, although their entitlement to time off, like that of union officials, is subject to the requirement of 'reasonableness'.[318]

An employee who is a member of a recognised independent union and a 'learning representative' of that union is entitled to paid time off during working hours for specified activities in relation to fellow employees who are members of the ULR's union and for whom the ULR has the function of acting as such ('qualifying members' of the union).[319] ULRs are not therefore entitled to time off to provide services to non-union members or members of other unions. The activities for which time off should be permitted are to analyse learning or training needs; provide information and advice about learning or training matters; arrange learning or training; and promote the value of learning or training in relation to 'qualifying members'.[320] Time off should also be given for the ULR to consult the employer about carrying on any such activities[321] and to prepare for any of the specified matters.[322] An employee constitutes a ULR if he or she has been appointed as such in accordance with the union rules,[323] but is entitled to time off only if the union has notified the employer in writing that he or she is a ULR and has met the 'training condition'.[324] The 'training condition' requires the employee to have undergone sufficient training to enable him or her to carry out the role either at the start of the appointment or within six months of it; in the latter case, if the union does not confirm to the employer within the six month period that the requisite training has been completed, entitlement to time off lapses.[325] In deciding what constitutes sufficient training, regard is to be had

---

315 *Regulatory Impact Assessment: Placing Union Learning Representatives (ULRs) on a Statutory Footing*, DTI. The Government stated that about a third of ULRs did not receive paid time off for training, and about half did not receive paid time off to carry out their workplace duties: John Healey, Parliamentary Under-Secretary of State for Education and Skills, HC Standing Committee F, col 491, 17 January 2002.
316 *Regulatory Impact Assessment: Placing Union Learning Representatives (ULRs) on a Statutory Footing*, DTI.
317 This provision came into force on 27 April 2003.
318 The TUC estimated that there would be more than 22,000 ULRs after the legislation had been in force for an eight-year period: note 315 above.
319 TULRCA 1992, s 168A(1),(2),(10).
320 TULRCA 1992, s 168A(2)(a).
321 The Code of Practice states that ULRs should liaise with their employers to ensure that their respective training activities complement each other and that the scope for duplication is minimised: para 14.
322 TULRCA 1992, s 168A(2)(b)(c).
323 TULRCA 1992, s 168A(11).
324 TULRCA 1992, s 168A(3).
325 TULRCA 1992, s 168A(4).

to the ACAS Code of Practice.[326] The union cannot extend the appointment of a 'probationary' ULR by giving a second notice of future training,[327] although the Code of Practice states that in the interests of good practice the six-month period can be extended by agreement to take into account any significant unforeseen circumstances such as prolonged absence from work due to ill health, pregnancy or bereavement.[328] Both 'probationary' and 'fully-fledged' ULRs are entitled to time off for training.[329]

Time off for ULRs, like that of union officials, is subject to a test of reasonableness and similar considerations to those indicated in para 8.36 apply. The remedies for wrongful refusal of time off are identical.

Time off for trade union activities

8.39   An employer must permit employees who are a members of an independent trade union which it recognises in respect of that description of employee to take reasonable time off during their working hours to take part in 'any activities' of the union and any other activities in relation to which they are acting as a representative of it.[330] The requirement of recognition for their description of employee means that if, for example, the employer recognises the X union exclusively for clerical staff, managerial grades who belong to the union will not be able to claim time off. There is no requirement that time off for these purposes should be paid, but employers and unions may nevertheless agree that it should be, and the Code of Practice suggests that employers should consider payment in certain circumstances, for example in order to ensure that workplace meetings are fully representative or that employees can make use of the services of a Union Learning Representative ('ULR').[331]

The scope of union 'activities' is a question of fact for the employment tribunal. The Code of Practice gives as examples: attending workplace meetings to discuss and vote on the outcome of negotiations with the employer; meeting full-time officials to discuss issues relevant to the workplace; and voting in union elections.[332] It is arguable that the right should extend to any activities which the union may lawfully undertake, including those of a political, social or educational nature. However, the EAT has said that 'in a broad sense the activity should be one which is in some way linked to [the] ... employment relationship'.[333] On that basis it upheld the decision of the tribunal that a teacher was not entitled to time off to attend a TUC lobby of Parliament intended to convey political or ideological objections to proposed legislation, although it emphasised that not all lobbying would be outside the entitlement. The EAT contrasted lobbying consisting of 'the presentation of arguments intended to persuade a Member of Parliament to vote in a particular way on a particular issue' with 'an approach which is in essence based upon mere protest',[334] a distinction

---

326 TULRCA 1992, s 168A(6). See the Code of Practice, paras 24–27.
327 TULRCA 1992, s 168A(5).
328 Para 23.
329 TULRCA 1992, s 168A(6).
330 TULRCA 1992, s 170.
331 Para 34; see para 8.38 above.
332 Para 30. Note that where union elections are governed by statute, at the time of writing voting must be fully postal: see para 10.16.
333 *Luce v Bexley London Borough Council* [1990] IRLR 422, 425.
334 *Luce v Bexley London Borough Council* [1990] IRLR 422, 425.

whose logic is hard to discern; even if (contrary to our view) one accepts such a limitation in principle, the subject-matter of the lobby would seem of greater relevance than the method of conducting it. Uncertainty as to whether accessing the services of a ULR constituted taking part in union 'activities' has been resolved by making specific provision for employees to have time off for this purpose.[335]

Activities where the employee is acting as a union 'representative' may include taking part in branch, area or regional meetings of the union, or meetings of official policy-making bodies such as the executive committee or annual conference, or meetings with full-time officials to discuss issues relevant to the workplace.[336] Thus union officials who are not entitled to paid time off for particular duties may qualify under this heading. The statute specifically excludes industrial action from the right to time off;[337] however, activities connected with its organisation or threat appear not to be excluded (although the matter is not free from doubt),[338] and the Code of Practice emphasises that officials should be given paid time off to represent members who are taking industrial action when they are not themselves so doing.[339] There is no definition of 'industrial action' in this context; the test of the purpose of the activity applied in the context of unfair dismissal (see para 11.73) would probably be applicable here.

Time off for union activities is again subject to a test of reasonableness and similar considerations to those indicated in para 8.36 apply. The remedies for wrongful refusal of time off are identical, except that in this context there is no requirement that the time off should be paid.

Assessment

8.40 The provisions relating to the provision of facilities for trade union representatives and members are subject to a number of limitations. The first is their confinement to the provision of time off; there is no statutory requirement to provide other facilities which may assist union organisation, such as office space. ILO Convention No 135 provides that such facilities shall be afforded to workers' representatives 'as may be appropriate in order to enable them to carry out their functions promptly and efficiently'.[340] However, although the British legislation is restricted, interestingly the Code of Practice goes further in recommending that employers should 'consider making available to officials

---

335 TULRCA 1992, s 170(2A)–(2C). The right applies only if the ULR would be entitled himself or herself to time off to provide services to such members. The right does not extend to undergoing any consequent training.

336 Code of Practice, para 31. Representing individual members at employment tribunals would probably also fall within this category. Note that time off for workers (not just employees) to accompany individuals at disciplinary and grievance proceedings pursuant to the statutory right to be accompanied must be paid, regardless of whether the companion is a union official: ERelA 1999, s 10.

337 TULRCA 1992, s 170(2).

338 See *Midland Plastics v Till* [1983] IRLR 9, where for the purposes of TULRCA 1992, s 238, as amended, the threat of industrial action was held not to amount to 'industrial action', but cf *Lewis and Britton v E Mason and Sons* [1994] IRLR 4, where the EAT refused to characterise as perverse the tribunal's finding that the threat of industrial action itself constituted 'industrial action'.

339 Para 49.

340 Art 2(1). See also the more specific provisions of Recommendation No 143 concerning Protection and Facilities to be Afforded to Workers' Representatives in the Undertaking.

the facilities necessary for them to perform their duties efficiently and communicate effectively with their members, colleague lay officials and full-time officers'. Where resources permit, such facilities could include accommodation for meetings; access to a telephone and other office equipment; and the use of notice boards which could include forms of electronic communications such as e-mail and intranet/internet; and, where the volume of the official's work justifies it, the use of dedicated office space.[341] In practice a high proportion of employers with recognised unions do provide other facilities[342] and it is arguable that this is a matter which it would be difficult to enforce through legislation, particularly given the need to ensure that a union's independent status is not prejudiced by dependence on employer-provided facilities (see para 7.24).

A more fundamental objection is the limitation of all time off provisions to members of recognised unions. Lay representatives of all unions may have an important part to play in representing members in disciplinary and grievance proceedings; although they have a separate statutory right to time off for these activities, this applies only if specified conditions are met[343] and does not include time off for training for this role. There is also no reason why time off to participate in union activities should be dependent upon recognition, particularly given the part that unions may come to play in information and consultation roles short of recognition, discussed in chapter 9. A further serious omission from the legislation is any right of access by paid officials of the union to the workplace to address meetings or investigate collective complaints, for example, which again we would argue should be independent of recognition.[344] In *Post Office v Union of Post Office Workers*[345] the House of Lords affirmed that employers should be required to accept minor infringements of their rights of property in relation to members' access to facilities on the premises, and in this context also employers' rights of property should be modified.

Turning to the more specific aspects of the existing time off provisions, the first limitation is that there is a right to time off only with permission. This would be unobjectionable if combined with a speedy method of redress where requests for time off were denied. Currently, however, the employee's only remedy is to complain to an employment tribunal which will hear the complaint long after the event for which time off was sought has passed. In this respect expedited access to a remedy along the lines of interim relief might be appropriate, with provision for a fuller hearing at a later date if one or other party wished to challenge the grounds of the decision. Furthermore, the remedies for a successful claim are totally inadequate. The tribunal has no power even to recommend a future course of conduct on the part of the employer, let alone enforce it. Financial

---

341 Para 38.

342 In 1998 two-fifths of representatives in workplaces with 25 or more employees had access to some form of office facilities and most had access to a telephone or photocopier: Cully *et al*, 1999: pp 205–207.

343 ERelA 1999, s 10; see further para 5.132 *et seq*.

344 Cf the right of access which 'appropriate representatives' have to employees who are threatened with 'collective' redundancy, for example (see para 9.36) or rights of access to workers in the bargaining unit on the part of unions seeking recognition under the statutory procedure (see para 9.16).

345 [1974] IRLR 22, discussed in para 8.10 above. See para 9.16 for discussion of compatibility of access provisions with the HRA 1998 in the context of the statutory recognition procedure.

compensation is not an adequate remedy particularly as, in many cases, any 'loss' suffered (which in any event may be very difficult to quantify) will be by the union or other members and not the individual concerned. It would be advantageous in appropriate cases for the tribunal to have the power to make recommendations for future conduct, if not enforceable orders.

UNION MEMBERSHIP AND DEDUCTIONS FROM WORKERS' PAY

8.41   An important method by which employers may show their support for union organisation is by facilitating the collection of union subscriptions. The practice of employers deducting subscriptions directly from workers' pay and passing them to the union concerned, known as the 'check-off', grew substantially from the 1960s onwards, and in 1998, two-thirds of unionised workplaces were found to have a check-off system in place.[346] The introduction and maintenance of check-off was not necessarily a totally altruistic gesture by employers; as well as assisting good industrial relations, it enabled them to keep track of the number and identities of union members and avoided the need for personal collection of subscriptions by union representatives who, in carrying out this function, had increased opportunity for contact with individual members.

The deduction of subscriptions was always subject to individual workers agreeing to this arrangement as a term of their contract with their employer, either directly or by virtue of a collective agreement incorporated into the contract.[347] In 1993, however, the Conservative Government introduced further restrictions requiring each worker[348] to provide specific written authorisation for a deduction and renewed written authorisation for such deduction at least every three years.[349] It also gave workers the right to withdraw authorisation for deductions at any time, and provided that where a deduction was made by an employer without due authorisation, or after the worker had given notice to withdraw it, the worker could complain to an employment tribunal which could order the employer to repay the amount deducted.[350] In addition, employers were also made responsible for giving workers written notification of any increase in the union subscription at least one month before making the deduction at the higher rate.

This procedure placed a considerable additional burden on employers and attracted considerable criticism from them, as well as, clearly, from trade unions. It was initially predicted that its effect on union membership and finances would be catastrophic. In the event this proved not to be the case on a general scale,

---

346 Cully *et al*, 1999: p 89. Millward *et al*, 2000, report (at 151) that three-quarters of workplaces with recognised unions had the check-off in place.

347 *Williams v Butlers Ltd* [1974] IRLR 253 and [1975] IRLR 120. Provided the worker had consented in writing the restrictions on deductions from pay now contained in ERA 1996 (see para 4.69 above) were not applicable: see ERA 1996, s 14(4).

348 See para 3.51 *et seq* above for the definition of this term.

349 TULRCA 1992, s 68, as substituted by TURERA 1993, s 15 (now further substituted by SI 1998/1529; see note 353 below).

350 Where the deduction also infringed other statutory rights (ERA 1996, ss 15 *et seq* (see para 4.68), the right to an itemised pay statement (para 4.69) and protection for non-contributors to a political fund (see para 10.19)) the amount ordered to be repaid could not exceed the greatest amount which could be awarded under any of them.

although many unions reported difficulties contacting all their members, and in September 1994 it was estimated that between 600,000 and 1.2 million trade unionists who formerly had paid their subscriptions though the check-off had not signed new instructions by the beginning of the previous month.[351] Many unions had already transferred to a system of direct debit for the payment of subscriptions, some as a result of appreciating their vulnerability to interruption during industrial disputes; others encouraged their members to do this following the introduction of the new provisions. It was notable that trade union membership services packages frequently included discounted banking to encourage members to establish the requisite facilities for direct debit to operate.[352]

With effect from 23 June 1998 the requirements for employers to seek fresh authorisations from workers for the check-off every three years and to notify workers of increases in subscriptions were repealed, although the need to give an initial consent, the right to withdraw from the arrangement, and the right to seek redress in an employment tribunal for an unauthorised deduction, remained.[353] This reform was welcomed by both the TUC and the CBI, and removed at least one source of difficulty for unions which were struggling to maintain their levels of membership.

351 Labour Research Department, reported *Financial Times*, 1 September 1994.
352 Willman *et al*, 1993: p 209.
353 The Deregulation (Deduction from Pay of Union Subscriptions) Order 1998, SI 1998/ 1529, made under the DCOA 1994.

CHAPTER 9

Collective representation and the law

INTRODUCTION

9.1   The distinctive voluntarist approach to the conduct of industrial relations in Britain has been emphasised at several points in this book. While this tradition still predominates, since 1971 legislation has played a role (albeit of diverse kinds) in regulating worker representation in relation to employers, and there is now a myriad of provisions in this area. Here, as in relation to freedom of association, the law is fragmented and incoherent and its distinctive features can properly be understood only in the light of the historical development of British legal policy outlined in chapter 7. During the 18 years of Conservative Government, beginning in 1979, the law in this area underwent radical transformation, reflecting government hostility towards collective organisation. Even at the end of that period, however, remnants of the previous order remained and obligations under EC law necessitated the retention of some measures which would undoubtedly otherwise have been repealed as incompatible with free market individualism. The entry into office of a Labour Government in 1997 heralded a more hospitable climate for worker representation and brought three important changes: the re-introduction of a statutory procedure for the mandatory recognition of trade unions by employers; the implementation of the EC Directive on European Works Councils following the UK 'opt-in' to the Agreement on Social Policy;[1] and, more recently, the introduction of information and consultation obligations at national level following agreement to the Information and Consultation Directive. However, the importance of the voluntarist tradition is reflected by the continuing absence of a legal obligation upon the employer to apply terms and conditions which have been collectively agreed, even when recognition has been imposed by law.

We begin the chapter by considering the relationship between collective bargaining and the law. We first consider the nature and legal effect of voluntary recognition outside the statutory procedure. We then analyse the statutory procedure, under which employers of 21 or more workers may be required to recognise an independent trade union in relation to pay, hours and holidays, and the mechanism by which recognition is enforced. This is followed by a discussion of other legal consequences of recognition, irrespective of whether it is voluntary or mandatory in nature. We then examine the areas in which legislation requires all employers to provide information to, and consult, worker representatives. These arise in four important areas: in the event of a proposed dismissal for 'redundancy' (which in this context has a much broader meaning than that governing statutory redundancy payments); on a transfer of the undertaking; in relation to health and safety;[2] and pensions. The latter two categories lie beyond the scope of this work, although we refer to them in

---

1   See para 2.42.
2   In this area, unlike the other three, employers also have the option of providing information to, and consulting, employees directly, although it is unclear whether this complies with EC obligations: see further para 9.46 below.

outline; the former are discussed in greater detail and assessed, where appropriate, against the requirements of the EC Directives which they are designed to implement. We then consider the obligation on some employers to consult on training. Finally we analyse the new obligations on larger employers to inform and consult on a wider range of matters,[3] with reference, once again, to the relevant Directive. This is followed by an overview of the regulations that implement the European Works Council Directive, applicable to transnational 'Community-scale undertakings' or groups of undertakings, and a brief discussion of the requirements of the European Company statute and its accompanying Directive on Employee Involvement.

Until 1995 all the existing consultation requirements in Britain were vested exclusively in trade unions which were recognised by the employer in question. In the absence of a mandatory recognition procedure, they were thus dependent solely upon a voluntary act of the employer, a position which was held by the European Court of Justice to infringe obligations imposed by the respective directives relating to redundancies and transfer of undertakings.[4] As a consequence of this decision, the legislation was amended to require employers to consult, at their choice, *either* a recognised union or elected representatives of the affected employees. This marked a dramatic break with the traditional pattern of workers' representation in this country, which had been based upon 'single channel' union representation, and led Davies to warn that, in insisting upon Community-required consultation of a specific kind, national collective bargaining could be undermined and worker-representation ultimately down-graded.[5] This has proved a prescient prediction.[6] Although the legislation was further amended in 1999 to permit consultation of 'employee representatives' only if no independent union was recognised,[7] the concept of alternative-channel representation remains, and, indeed, has been radically extended: first, by the introduction of 'workforce agreements' in the context of working time, parental leave, and fixed-term contracts;[8] latterly and very significantly, by provision for informing and consulting non-union representatives on a much wider basis.[9] The TUC has taken these developments on board in its own policy formation, and has shown itself prepared to countenance non-union channels of representation operating alongside trade union-based collective bargaining.[10] We discuss the implications of these developments at the end of the chapter in the context of a broader consideration of the purposes of, and challenges faced by, worker representation in the contemporary labour market.

We have used the term worker 'representation' in this chapter in preference to the term 'participation'. Although the latter is often used interchangeably with representation, the term participation is, in our view, more appropriate to

---

3   Here, again, it is open to employers to inform and consult directly in some circumstances: see further para 9.53.

4   Case C-382/92 *EC Commission v United Kingdom* [1994] IRLR 392 and Case C-383/92 [1994] IRLR 412, ECJ.

5   P Davies, 1994b: p 284.

6   See generally P Davies and C Kilpatrick, 2004.

7   The Collective Redundancies and Transfer of Undertakings (Protection of Employment) (Amendment) Regulations 1999, SI 1999/1925.

8   See paras 4.74, 6.104 and 3.86 respectively.

9   See para 9.50 *et seq*.

10   See the Joint Statement by the TUC and CBI on Statutory Trade Union Recognition, para 8, published 9 December 1997; *High Performing Workplaces – Informing and Consulting Employees: Consultation Document*, DTI, 2003: pp 5–23. See also Hall, 1996.

signify direct forms of worker involvement in the enterprise. Such direct involvement may take different forms. It may revolve around the organisation of the working process; examples include quality circles, where employees meet regularly to discuss solutions to work-related problems, and delegation of work by management to self-organising teams. However, participation may also have a wholly different meaning of financial involvement in the enterprise. This type of participation, as described in para 4.70, may be constituted in a variety of arrangements, ranging from share option schemes to profit-related pay. Direct forms of participation are predicated upon, and are generally designed to promote, a more individualistic view of the employment relationship than a representational model, together with a close identification on the part of workers with the employer's objectives. While such schemes do not preclude the co-existence of collective representation they may sometimes be perceived by employers and/or workers as incompatible with it, although it is important to note that the two serve very different functions. Financial participation, in particular, does not bring with it access to decision-making at any level; even share ownership empowers workers ultimately only if they hold a sufficient proportion of the total share equity, an unlikely eventuality in practice. Moreover, financial participation is not required by law, although as we indicated in para 4.70 tax incentives have been given to encourage certain models. We do not consider these forms of participation further in this work, although our concluding discussion of the future of worker representation takes place against a backcloth of developments of this nature.

COLLECTIVE BARGAINING AND THE LAW

9.2   As we have indicated in earlier chapters, the essential feature of collective bargaining is the concept of joint regulation by the collective parties of the employment relationship, with the sanction of industrial action or recourse to some form of agreed dispute resolution procedure, such as arbitration, in the event of a failure to agree. As such it stands in contrast to consultation, where the employer retains the discretion to impose its views unilaterally although, as we discuss below, the two processes may sometimes be difficult to separate in practice. As we saw in chapter 7, the right to engage in collective bargaining is regarded by the ILO as an essential element of freedom of association and an undertaking on the part of contracting states to promote and encourage collective bargaining machinery is also contained in the European Social Charter. However the European Court of Human Rights has refused as yet to derive from the right to join trade unions a right for union members that their union should be able to engage in collective bargaining, or even to be consulted by their employer; although there is a right that the trade union should be 'heard', the state has a free choice of the means to be used towards this end.[11]

In chapters 2 and 4 we emphasised the important role of collective agreements as a source of labour law in Britain even though they lack contractual status and there is no legal obligation to treat them as a source of norms for individual contracts. This remains the case today even though the reach of collective bargaining narrowed considerably during the 1980s due cumulatively to a reduction in the proportion of workplaces where trade unions were recognised

11   See para 7.9.

for at least some employees (from two-thirds in 1980[12] to just over half (53%) in 1990[13]) and in the proportion of employees covered by collective agreements (from 64% in 1984[14] to 47% in 1990[15]). It was estimated that in 1998 the number of employees covered by collective bargaining had fallen further, to 41% of all employees.[16] Moreover,

> ... [t]he range of issues over which bargaining took place shrunk massively. By the end of the 1990s, in workplaces where 20 years earlier it would have been normal for managers to negotiate with union activists over questions of manning, overtime, recruitment, and working practices, it had become a rarity. For one-third of workplaces with union recognition there were no longer even annual pay negotiations.[17]

However, there has been a growth in the number of recognition agreements in recent years, possibly in response to the alternative prospect of unions applying for recognition under the statutory procedure,[18] and this may, in turn, translate into a growth in collective bargaining coverage. We begin this section by exploring in greater detail the legal concept of 'recognition' outside the statutory procedure, and examine the legal implications of variation and withdrawal of recognition. We then analyse the statutory recognition procedure. This is followed by an account of the (limited) right of all recognised trade unions to information from employers for the purpose of collective bargaining; an examination of the statutory concept of a 'collective agreement'; and an analysis of the position as regards trade union recognition and existing collective agreements when an undertaking is transferred. Finally, we examine provisions which prohibit contract compliance strategies being used to promote collective bargaining and adherence to collectively-agreed terms.

Recognition and derecognition outside the statutory procedure

9.3   We outlined in para 7.27 when a trade union is 'recognised' for statutory purposes and the importance of this definition in terms of a union's access to a variety of statutory rights. It will be remembered that this means recognition by an employer, or two or more associated employers, 'to any extent, for the purposes of collective bargaining'.[19] In turn 'collective bargaining' is defined as 'negotiations relating to or connected with' one or more of the matters specified in TULRCA 1992, s 178(2).[20] We examine these matters, which are also material to the definition of a 'collective agreement' and of a 'trade dispute' for the purposes of immunity against liability for industrial action, more closely elsewhere.[21] Here, we are concerned primarily with the process of collective bargaining and, in particular, when the parties can be said to have engaged in 'negotiations', an issue which has been left to the tribunals and the courts to decide.

---

12   Daniel and Millward, 1983: p 20.
13   Millward and Stevens, 1992: p 70.
14   Millward and Stevens, 1986: p 94.
15   Millward and Stevens, 1992: p 70.
16   Cully *et al*, 1999: p 242.
17   W Brown and S Oxenbridge, 2004: p 70.
18   S Wood, S Moore and K Ewing, 2003; S Oxenbridge. W Brown, S Deakin and C Pratten, 2003; Gall, 2004.
19   TULRCA 1992, s 178(3).
20   TULRCA 1992, s 178(1).
21   See paras 7.27 above and 11.27 below.

The case law on what constitutes 'recognition' has developed mainly in the context of redundancy dismissals where the union has argued that it has been recognised by the employer and should therefore have been consulted before the dismissals were implemented. The cases turn on their own facts but a number of general principles have emerged. First, there must have been an agreement between the employer and the union to negotiate on one or more of the specified matters, although such agreement may be express or implied. An express agreement which specifies the range of bargainable issues has advantages for both parties; it puts the fact and extent of recognition beyond doubt and will assist in determining the scope of the rights to disclosure of information and time off for union officials. However, in the absence of such agreement the conduct of the parties may allow recognition to be implied, although the courts have taken a cautious approach to this issue in the light of the legal obligations to which employers are then subject.

In the leading case of *NUGSAT v Albury Bros Ltd*[22] the Court of Appeal specified the requirements to be met. The union, NUGSAT, wrote to the employers stating that their rates of pay did not appear to accord with those specified in the collective agreement between the union and the employers' federation and asking for a meeting to discuss the matter. The employers tried to see the district secretary, who was busy, and then wrote to the union offering a meeting. When the parties met they discussed whether the wages of one particular employee came within the general scale but did not come to any agreement. Later that day redundancy notices were issued to three employees. The employment tribunal and EAT both concluded that the contacts between the parties did not amount to recognition, and the Court of Appeal supported this conclusion. Eveleigh LJ emphasised the need for clear and distinct evidence that the employer had agreed to negotiate with a view to striking a bargain; a willingness merely to discuss would not suffice.[23] Sir David Cairns affirmed previous EAT decisions which had stressed that the acts relied upon 'must be clear and unequivocal and usually involve a course of conduct over a period of time'.[24] Here the matters relied upon were 'too limited in scope, too inconclusive in character, and of too brief a duration to have any such effect as would constitute recognition'.[25] Finally, the court affirmed that the fact that the employers' federation, of which the employer was a member, recognised the union did not constitute recognition by that employer.[26]

By contrast in the earlier decision of *Joshua Wilson & Bros Ltd v USDAW*[27] the EAT inferred recognition from the cumulative effect of contacts between the employer and the union over the period of a year: allowing the local union representative to put up a notice publicising an increase agreed by the joint industrial council for the industry; consulting him over changes to the allocation of duties; allowing him to collect union dues on the premises; and consulting with the area union organiser over security and discipline. 'Separately none [of

22   [1978] IRLR 504.
23   [1978] IRLR 504, 506.
24   [1978] IRLR 504, 506.
25   [1978] IRLR 504, 507.
26   See also *Cleveland County Council v Springett* [1985] IRLR 131 where the EAT affirmed that appointment by the Secretary of State to a committee which at one time negotiated teachers' pay at national level did not bring recognition by an individual local education authority employer.
27   [1978] IRLR 120.

these] might have been sufficient' but, taken together, they constituted 'clear and unequivocal evidence' of recognition.[28] By further contrast in *USDAW v Sketchley Ltd*[29] an agreement to provide 'recognition for representation' of members in grievance procedures, together with facilities for appointing shop stewards and collecting union subscriptions, did not amount to recognition for the purposes of negotiation.

One issue which remains unresolved is whether a disclaimer of recognition can prevent a union being 'recognised' in law. In *USDAW v Sketchley Ltd* the EAT, in assessing the implications of particular events, stated:

> ... [a]lthough during this period the union is plainly trying to gain wider recognition and the employers are getting very close to negotiating terms and conditions of employment with the union, the employers throughout make it clear by their express words that they have no intention of recognising the union. In such circumstances, it is impossible to draw any inference of a mutual intention contrary to Sketchley's expressed intention.[30]

However, this approach seems open to dispute; at the very least it could be argued that a concerted attempt by an employer to use the services of a union to secure agreements covering the workforce whilst disclaiming any intention to recognise could be challenged as an attempt to exclude entitlement to statutory rights.[31]

9.4   Where a union has been recognised outside the statutory procedure, there is no statutory constraint upon an employer varying the scope of recognition or withdrawing it altogether. A number of prominent employers derecognised trade unions during the 1990s,[32] although in numerical terms the incidence of wholesale derecognition, as opposed to an initial refusal to recognise, remained comparatively small.[33] Even where recognition is express a recognition agreement will constitute a 'collective agreement' in law and thus be covered by the statutory presumption of non-enforceability, displaceable only by a specific statement to the contrary of a kind which is rarely found. This is one area where the statutory imposition of legally enforceable collective agreements may have benefited trade unions in potentially requiring greater notice of intention to derecognise, although ultimately not preventing this development in the longer term. Moreover, it is most unlikely that a recognition agreement could be enforced through the individual contract; even if part of a wider collective agreement which is capable of incorporation into individual contracts of employment, terms relating to recognition will almost certainly be viewed by the courts as collective in their nature and thus not appropriate for such incorporation.[34] This does not mean that a decision to derecognise will never have legal implications, however. First, although a commitment to recognise a union is unlikely in itself to be a

---

28   [1978] IRLR 120, 121.
29   [1981] IRLR 291.
30   [1981] IRLR 291, 295.
31   TULRCA 1992, s 288. Cf, in the context of unfair dismissal, *Igbo v Johnson Matthey Chemicals Ltd* [1986] IRLR 215.
32   See Taylor, 1994: pp 48–54; Claydon, 1996.
33   Gall and McKay, 1994; Millward *et al*, 2000: pp 105, 232.
34   See para 4.29 *et seq*. Withdrawal of recognition of one's union does not, *per se*, amount to subjection to a detriment on grounds of trade union membership or activities: see para 8.14 above.

term of an individual contract, it is possible that some provisions which have been linked to recognition, such as time off rights for union members or individual representation in disciplinary and grievance proceedings which exceed the statutory rights, may have been incorporated into employees' contracts of employment. If so, any contractual term linked to recognition which the employer wishes to remove will require one of the procedures for contractual variation which we describe in para 4.34 to be followed. Second, derecognition cannot be used to avoid statutory duties which have already become binding: thus once a union has requested specific information for collective bargaining purposes, for example, the duty to disclose such information survives subsequent derecognition.[35] Last, in the case of employers which are potentially susceptible to judicial review a decision to derecognise may be open to challenge by this means, at least as regards the procedure which is followed. In *R v Educational Services Committee of Bradford City Metropolitan Council, ex p PAT*[36] the (no-strike) Professional Association of Teachers successfully sought judicial review of the (Labour) Council's decision to rescind a resolution made three months earlier (by its Conservative predecessor) on the ground that it should have been afforded the opportunity to make representations to ensure that the deprivation of the valuable rights thereby occasioned was not unfair. Even this procedure does not ultimately constitute a substantive constraint on the employer's decision to derecognise, however. This position contrasts sharply with the restrictions on derecognition where recognition follows from a union having invoked the statutory procedure, which we describe in para 9.20.

A further, and less commented upon, consequence of the voluntary nature of trade union recognition is that there is no mechanism to control the employer's choice of union. Thus there is nothing to prevent an employer recognising a union which may have only minimal support among the workforce. Although workers who are members of other unions would remain protected against discriminatory action by the employer on grounds of their union membership and participation in union activities, and use of union services, at an appropriate time, there would be nothing to prevent an employer allowing only the recognised union access to facilities on its premises[37] and, by definition, members of unrecognised unions lack access to the decision-making process. The 1980s saw some highly-publicised incidents of single-union deals, many on new sites in the 'high-tech' sectors, reached in some cases after a 'beauty contest' between unions before a single worker was employed.[38] The latter practice in particular makes a mockery of union recognition being the democratic representation of employee 'voice'. Moreover such deals have backfired on unions, many of which found that they 'do not guarantee high membership levels, because the employer selects the union, undermining employee choice, and the structures of bargaining are often restrictive rendering the union ineffectual'.[39]

35 *Ackrill Newspapers Ltd v NUJ* (CAC 14 February 1992, unreported).
36 (1986) Independent, 16 December.
37 A worker must be subjected to a detriment 'as an individual': TULRCA 1992, s 146; see further para 8.14 above. Note, however, the right of workers to be accompanied by the companion of their choice, who may be a union official: ERelA 1999, s 10; see further para 5.132 *et seq.*
38 Although highly-publicised, in numerical terms these deals were of negligible importance: Gall, 1993: p 72.
39 Gall, 1993: pp 73–74.

These arrangements, which caused bitter inter-union conflict, were partially reinforced by the operation of the TUC's Bridlington Principles which, as we saw in para 2.13, were formulated in 1939 (with subsequent amendments) to minimise disputes between unions over membership by regulating their organisational and recruitment activities. These have long provided that unions should not commence organising activities at any establishment or undertaking in respect of any group of workers in which another union has the majority of workers employed and negotiates terms and conditions[40] unless by arrangement with that union, and a fresh obligation was introduced in 1979 (and amended in 1985) to require prior consultation and agreement before a union made any form of agreement that would deprive another union of existing rights of negotiation and consultation. In 1988 these Principles were supplemented by a code of conduct on recognition which required prior notification of single union deals to the TUC for advice and guidance, a requirement extended by the current edition of the Principles to agreements sought under the statutory procedure.[41] However, the effectiveness of this code (now incorporated into Principle 3) is hard to judge.[42] In practice single union deals have undergone a sharp decline since 1988–89, although it is possible that the statutory procedure, which bars recognition applications when another union is recognised for any worker in the proposed bargaining unit, may encourage a revival.[43] Regardless of their numbers, they raise important issues in the wider debate as to the principles which should govern worker representation.

The statutory procedure for recognition and derecognition

9.5   The current statutory procedure enabling trade unions to obtain mandatory recognition by employers was introduced by ERelA 1999 and amended by ERelA 2004.[44] It takes effect as TULRCA 1992 Schedule A1. As we saw in para 7.18, this was the most controversial aspect of the 1999 legislation, with employer representatives opposed to the very concept of mandatory recognition, and aspects of the procedure continue to remain contentious.[45] However, to date its operation, which is in the hands of the CAC,[46] has not been undermined by successful judicial review applications of the kind that paralysed its 'Social Contract' predecessor.[47] This may be due to

---

40   The current version reads 'and/or' is recognised to negotiate terms and conditions.

41   *TUC Disputes Principles and Procedures*, TUC, 2000, notes on Principle 3.

42   Non-compliance with this code seems not to have been a decisive factor in disputes before the TUC Disputes Committee: Elgar and Simpson, 1994: pp 57–62.

43   For a notorious example, see the facts of *R (on the application of the NUJ) v CAC and MGN Ltd* [2005] IRLR 28. In this instance the union which concluded the recognition deal, the British Association of Journalists, although independent, is not a TUC-affiliate.

44   The ERelA 2004 amendments came into force on 6 April 2005, with the exception of s 9 (additional duties on employers) and ss 10 and 13 (unfair practices), which at the time of writing the Government intends to commence on 1 October 2005 following the adoption by Parliament of a Code of Practice on Access and Unfair Practices during Recognition and Derecognition Ballots.

45   See Simpson, 2000; Ewing, Moore and Wood, 2003; *Review of the Employment Relations Act 1999: Government Response*, DTI, 2003: ch 2.

46   See further para 2.37.

47   See Simpson, 1979; L Dickens and G Bain, 1986.

the detailed statutory criteria that inform the CAC's decision-making, in contrast to the more open-ended discretion accorded to ACAS under the earlier provision.

The procedure is complex and consists of several stages.[48] As we indicate below, there is generally a tight timetable for completion of each stage, although this can be extended by agreement of the parties and/or the CAC. There is a preference throughout for voluntary agreement between the parties (and the CAC is charged to assist this process at specified points), with a fall-back of determination by a tripartite panel in default of agreement, if necessary after a hearing at which the parties may (but need not be) legally represented. In addition to applying the specific tests applicable to a given stage of the procedure, the CAC has a general duty to 'have regard to the object of encouraging and promoting fair and efficient practices and arrangements in the workplace', in so far as that object is consistent with applying other provisions of the Schedule in the case concerned.[49] There is no general statutory requirement for the CAC to give reasons for its decisions in relation to the recognition procedure, but a failure to do so could be susceptible to challenge under general principles of judicial review and/or the HRA 1998,[50] and in practice reasons are provided. Recognition can be ordered only in relation to 'pay, hours and holidays', and the CAC may specify a 'method' of collective bargaining, enforceable by specific performance in the courts, only in relation to those matters, even if the parties, during the course of the statutory procedure, agree to recognition for a wider range of issues.[51] 'Pay, hours and holidays' are left undefined, and the meaning of 'pay', in particular, may prove contentious; although it probably covers pay systems, for example, it is less clear whether it extends to aspects of work organisation that affect pay, or job classification systems.[52] The issue has yet to come before the courts. The ERelA 2004 has made clear that 'pay' does not include any matters relating to a person's membership or rights under an occupational or personal pensions scheme or an employer's contribution to such a scheme,[53] but it empowers the Secretary of State by order to add matters relating to pensions to the 'core' bargaining topic of pay, hours and holidays should he or she choose to do so at some future date.[54] The Government has indicated that it intends to exercise this power when there is evidence that pensions are typically included as an item for negotiation in voluntary agreements.[55]

---

48   For a detailed technical analysis of the recognition and derecognition procedures prior to the ERelA 2004 amendments see G Morris and T Archer, 2000: paras 4.5–4.63; see also Simpson, 2000 and Bowers, Duggan and Reade, 2004. For comparison with, variously, earlier British legislation and with US and Canadian procedures, see S Wood and J Godard, 1999; McCarthy, 1999; Towers, 1999; Adams, 1999; Hepple 2000a and Dubinsky, 2000. Guidance as to the practice of the CAC, information on applications for recognition, and decisions may be found at www.cac.gov.uk.

49   TULRCA 1992, Sch A1, para 171.

50   See G Morris and T Archer, 2000: para 4.7.

51   The CAC may specify a 'method' of collective bargaining at the request of either party where recognition has been agreed pursuant to a statutory request: see further below.

52   Cf S Wood and J Godard, 1999: p 232.

53   TULRCA 1992, Sch A1, para 171A(1), inserted by ERelA 2004, s 20; cf *Unifi v Union Bank of Nigeria plc* [2001] IRLR 712, CAC, discussed Rideout, 2002: pp 30–31.

54   TULRCA 1992, Sch A1, para 171A(3)–(7).

55   Lord Davies, HL Debs GC65, 9 June 2004.

(i) The recognition procedure: outline and analysis

9.6   *A valid request to the employer and the implications of the employer's response to that request.*   To invoke the statutory recognition procedure, a union[56] must first make a written request to the employer for recognition in respect of a specified group of workers (a 'bargaining unit'), making clear that the request is made under TULRCA 1992, Schedule A1. The union must have a certificate of independence, and on the day of the request the employer, together with any associated employer, must employ at least 21 workers, or have employed an average of at least 21 workers in the 13 weeks ending with that day,[57] although the proposed bargaining unit may be smaller. There is no requirement that workers should have worked a minimum number of hours to be counted for qualifying purposes, and the inclusion of 'associated employers'[58] means that employers cannot attempt to circumvent the application of the procedure by dividing their business into separate companies, each employing fewer than 21 workers. Even then, however, the 21 worker threshold (which has no place in ILO jurisprudence)[59] was estimated by the government itself to exclude 31% of the workforce – located in small enterprises in which the incidence of recognition is generally low – from the recognition procedure.[60]

The next stage depends upon the employer's response to the request. If the employer and union agree a bargaining unit and recognition within ten working days starting with the day after the employer receives the request (the 'first period') no further steps are taken in relation to the application; the same applies if, within that period, the employer indicates a willingness to negotiate and the parties reach agreement on these matters within 20 working days, starting with the day after the first period ends or such longer period as the parties may from time to time agree. The parties may request ACAS to assist in conducting the negotiations.[61] Any agreement reached during the first or second periods (or, indeed, at any stage prior to recognition being ordered or a recognition ballot being arranged) is capable of constituting an 'agreement for recognition',[62] and as such is protected against unilateral termination by the employer for a minimum three-year period unless the parties otherwise agree,[63] although it can be

---

56   For simplicity we refer throughout to 'a union' applying for recognition, but unions may present a joint request, although the admissibility of such a request depends on compliance with specified conditions, discussed below.

57   See generally TULRCA 1992, Sch A1, paras 4–9. The request must be received by the employer. Para 7 stipulates how the average number of workers is to be calculated and the treatment of workers employed by associated companies outside Great Britain.

58   See, for example, *GMB and Sussex Grange Furniture Ltd* TUR1/208, CAC. Note that bargaining units cannot be comprised of workers from two or more associated employers, although cf *GPMU v Derry Print Ltd* [2002] IRLR 380, CAC.

59   Novitz, 2000: pp 388–389. For a broader critique of the 'small employer' exclusion see Ewing and Hock, 2003; cf *Review of the Employment Relations Act 1999: Government Response*, DTI, 2003: paras 2.3–2.8.

60   Simpson, 2000: p 196; Cully *et al*, 1999: pp 264–266.

61   TULRCA 1992, Sch A1, para 10.

62   Defined in TULRCA 1992, Sch A1, para 52. See *NUJ and Emap Healthcare* TUR2/1/02.

63   TULRCA 1992, Sch A1, para 56. No sanction is prescribed if an employer sought to terminate an agreement for recognition prematurely but the statutory language suggests that such an attempt would be void, so that the union would still be 'recognised' for the purposes of rights dependent on recognition, such as consultation rights, and could seek the assistance of the CAC in specifying a bargaining method or specific performance of a method already specified by the CAC.

terminated after that time without the additional constraints, described below, that apply when recognition has been ordered by the CAC. In the event that the employer fails to respond to the union's request, or no agreement is reached between the parties, the union may apply to the CAC to determine whether the proposed bargaining unit is appropriate, and whether the union has the support of a majority of workers constituting the appropriate bargaining unit. The application must be made in such form, and supported by such documents, as the CAC specifies.[64] The CAC must then decide, within ten working days starting with the day after that on which it receives the application, whether the application followed a valid request for recognition to the employer and whether it is admissible according to specified criteria.[65]

9.7 *Conditions of admissibility.* There are four substantive grounds on which an application will be inadmissible.[66] The first is if the CAC is satisfied that there is already in force a collective agreement under which a union is recognised as entitled to conduct collective bargaining on behalf of *any* workers falling within the proposed bargaining unit.[67] This reflects the priority given to existing voluntary bargaining arrangements. This priority applies regardless of the level of membership that the incumbent union has within the bargaining unit; thus it was sufficient to bar an application by a union which claimed to have more than half the workers in the proposed bargaining unit in membership that a union with at most one member had been recognised by the employer.[68] However the collective agreement relied upon must be *in* force, which may require examination of whether it is used in practice.[69] It is notable that it is sufficient to bar an application that recognition is accorded in respect of a matter to which the recognition procedure itself does not apply, such as discipline or the allocation of duties.[70] Moreover, it would seem to be sufficient that a worker in the bargaining unit is covered by a national agreement so that a union is recognised to conduct collective bargaining on his or her behalf, even if their own employer

---

64 TULRCA 1992, Sch A1, paras 11, 12, 33. If the parties have agreed the bargaining unit, the union may apply to the CAC to decide solely the question of support. Note that the union will be barred from applying to the CAC if it has rejected the employer's proposal, made within a specified period, that ACAS should be asked to assist in the negotiations: para 12(5).

65 TULRCA 1992, Sch A1, para 15.

66 An application is also inadmissible if the union fails to give the employer notice, and a copy, of the application and any documents supporting it: TULRCA 1992, Sch A1, para 34.

67 TULRCA 1992, Sch A1, para 35. There is no requirement for a formal agreement: see, for example, *NUM and RJB Mining (UK) Ltd* TUR1/32, CAC.

68 See *R (on the application of the NUJ) v CAC and MGN Ltd* [2005] IRLR 28, where the court rejected the argument that Art 11 of the ECHR imposed a positive obligation on the state to grant a union the right to conduct collective bargaining with any particular employer. Because the incumbent union, the British Association of Journalists, had a certificate of independence it was not open to the workers in the bargaining unit to apply for the union to be derecognised under the procedure we describe in para 9.20 below.

69 *POA and Wackenhut (UK) Ltd Escort Services* TUR1/108, CAC; *TSSA and Rail Europe Ltd* TUR1/154, CAC. In *R (on the application of the NUJ) v CAC and MGN Ltd* [2005] IRLR 28, however, the court emphasised that a recognition agreement did not need to be 'implemented' to be in force, although acknowledging that an agreement could be abandoned or fall into disuse.

70 This is because 'collective bargaining' in this context is defined by TULRCA 1992, s 178 (see para 7.27): Sch A1, para 3(6); *TGWU and Asda* [2004] IRLR 836, CAC.

does not recognise the union.[71] However, the bar does not apply if the pre-existing recognition agreement is with the applicant union, and that union is not recognised in respect of all of the 'core topics' (pay, hours and holidays).[72] This means that independent unions can extend the scope of their existing recognition if it does not cover all these topics. Perhaps surprisingly, although only independent unions can invoke the recognition procedure, there is no requirement for the pre-existing recognition agreement to be with an independent union, a position which, it can be argued, violates Articles 2 and 3 of ILO Convention No 98 in giving implicit encouragement to employers hostile to 'outside' union organisation to establish and recognise non-independent unions.[73] As we indicate below, the legislation affords a mechanism for workers to obtain mandatory derecognition of such bodies, which has the effect of clearing the way for an application by an independent union for a three year period,[74] but despite the protection afforded against employers subjecting workers to any detriment for bringing and supporting such applications, described below, workers may well feel fearful of pursuing such a course. An agreement with an organisation that does not satisfy the definition of a 'trade union' will not bar an application.[75]

9.8   The second ground of inadmissibility relates to the level of existing union membership and potential support for recognition. The CAC must find that members of the applicant union constitute a minimum of 10% of workers in the bargaining unit and that a majority of the workers in that unit would be 'likely' to favour recognition.[76] The first of these tests will be decided on the basis of factual evidence placed before the CAC. The admissibility requirement relating to potential support can often be particularly contentious. Evidence that a majority of workers in the bargaining unit are members of the applicant union is likely to be sufficient, in the absence of any evidence to the contrary; petitions from workers or surveys of the workforce, where available, may also be produced as evidence, as may statistics showing a growth in membership as a result of the recognition campaign. However, it cannot be assumed that workers who are not members of the union will not support recognition; indeed, the level of potential support may well be greater than actual membership. This is a matter for the CAC to decide in all the circumstances.

The CAC does not require the names and addresses of individuals to be disclosed, either in a union's application form or in supporting evidence. However, the union is required to specify the number of its members in the

---

71   This follows from the definition of a 'collective agreement' in TULRCA 1992, s 178, which includes agreements made by or on behalf of one or more employers or employers' associations: see para 9.26; see also *Offshore Industry Liaison Committee and Wood Group Engineering (North Sea) Ltd* TUR1/282, CAC.

72   TULRCA 1992, Sch A1, para 35(2)(b), as amended by ERelA 2004, s 11.

73   See Ewing, 2000a; *POA and Securicor Custodial Services Ltd* TURI 5/00, CAC. The Government was 'not attracted' to changing the position, and had seen 'no evidence of widespread recognition of non-independent unions ... as a device to avoid recognition claims by independent unions': *Review of the Employment Relations Act 1999: Government Response*, DTI, 2003: paras 2.95 and 2.98.

74   This is the effect of the tortuously-worded TULRCA 1992, Sch A1 para 35(4), which can also apply in a wider range of circumstances.

75   *TGWU and W Jordan (Cereals) Ltd* TUR1/258, CAC; *BECTU and City Screen Ltd* TUR1/309, CAC.

76   TULRCA 1992, Sch A1, para 36.

bargaining unit in its application, and if the employer challenges this there may be an independent check by CAC staff, subject to the agreement of both parties that the requisite information from each (petition evidence and membership and staff lists) may be provided in confidence for this purpose. If one or other party does not agree to such a course of action, ERelA 2004 empowers the CAC to require an employer and union to provide information relating to workers or union members in the bargaining unit, as appropriate, together with information concerning the level of potential support for collective bargaining, to a CAC case manager, with power for the CAC to 'draw an inference' against a party who fails to comply with this requirement.[77]

9.9　Third, an application will be inadmissible where more than one union makes an application, unless the unions show that they will co-operate with each other 'in a manner likely to secure and maintain stable and effective collective bargaining arrangements' and that, if the employer wishes, they will enter into arrangements under which collective bargaining is conducted by the unions acting together on behalf of the workers in the bargaining unit.[78] This means that the applicant unions would need to agree to single-table bargaining, for example, if the employer wished to conduct collective bargaining on that basis. It also means that competing applications are ruled out. If an application is received in respect of a bargaining unit that overlaps to any extent with the unit specified in another application, and neither has been accepted, the CAC must apply the '10% membership' test to each (or all): if only one application passes the test, its admissibility may be further considered; otherwise all must be rejected.[79] Moreover, even if the CAC has accepted an application, if the appropriate bargaining unit in respect of that application remains undetermined, either by the parties or the CAC, and the 10% test is passed in respect of the competing application, the original application will be cancelled and treated as if it had never been admissible.[80] This reduces the possibility that a union which may have less support than the union presenting the competing application will be recognised. The fact that the application is treated as never having been admissible means that the union party to the original application will not be barred from presenting a fresh application by the 'three-year rule' described in the paragraph below. Clearly, however, it would be desirable for the unions party to both the original and the competing applications to attempt to reach agreement on the appropriate demarcation line between their desired bargaining units or, if possible, present a joint application, as appropriate. The TUC provides assistance to unions applying to the CAC for recognition and will try to minimise inter-union problems and, where appropriate, facilitate joint applications. Unions preparing applications are required to notify the TUC General Secretary at least two weeks before they submit an application.[81]

9.10　Finally, an application will be inadmissible if the CAC had previously accepted an application relating to a bargaining unit and the application is

---

77　TULRCA 1992, s 170A, inserted by ERelA 2004, s 19.
78　TULRCA 1992, Sch A1, para 37.
79　TULRCA 1992, Sch A1, para 14. See, for example, *GMB and Faccenda Group Ltd* TUR1/209.
80　TULRCA 1992, Sch A1, paras 38, 51.
81　*TUC Disputes Principles and Procedures*, TUC, 2000.

made by a union or unions in respect of substantially the same unit within three years.[82] This provision is designed to deter premature applications. It does not prevent a different union making an application within three years; it is less clear whether, in the case of multi-union applications, the bar applies only if *all* such unions were party to the first application or if it is sufficient that any of them were. The three-year bar also applies where a union has been derecognised following a ballot of the workers in a bargaining unit (see below).[83]

9.11 ERelA 2004 introduced a new provision to afford a union (indirect) postal access to workers within the bargaining unit if its application for recognition has been accepted by the CAC.[84] A union that wishes to take advantage of this opportunity is likely to do so fairly quickly and, in any event, before the next stage of the statutory procedure, described in para 9.12 below. However, because it is easier to comprehend the details of the access provisions having understood that next stage, we discuss that first; we then examine the access provision in para 9.13 below.

9.12 *Determining the bargaining unit.* Provided that the criteria of admissibility are met, the next question for the CAC will be to determine whether the bargaining unit proposed by the union is appropriate (unless this issue has already been agreed by the parties, in which case the CAC proceeds to determine whether recognition should be granted). The CAC must first try to 'help' the parties to reach within the 'appropriate period' (20 working days starting with the day after that on which notice of acceptance of the application is given or longer if the CAC so decides) an agreement as to what the appropriate bargaining unit is, although this period may be curtailed at the request of the parties or if the CAC considers that there is no reasonable prospect of agreement.[85] 'Help' in this context may include suggesting that the assistance of ACAS is sought. To facilitate this process, the employer must provide the union and the CAC with a list of the categories of worker in the proposed bargaining unit, a list of the workplaces at which they work, and the number of workers the employer reasonably believes to be in each category at each workplace.[86] If the parties fail to reach agreement within the 'appropriate period' (or sooner, at the request of the union if the employer fails to supply the requisite information about workers in the bargaining unit)[87] the CAC itself will determine whether the proposed bargaining unit is appropriate.[88] If (and only if) it decides that the proposed bargaining unit is not appropriate, it must also decide a bargaining unit that is appropriate.[89] In taking an employer's views into account for the purpose of deciding whether the proposed bargaining unit is appropriate, the

---

82 TULRCA 1992, Sch A1, para 39; see also para 40.
83 TULRCA 1992, Sch A1, para 41.
84 TULRCA 1992, Sch A1, para 19C–19F, inserted by ERelA 2004, s 5.
85 TULRCA 1992, Sch A1, para 18, as amended by ERelA 2004, s 2.
86 TULRCA 1992, Sch A1, para 18A, inserted by ERelA 2004, s 3. 'Workplace' is defined in the same way as in TULRCA 1992, s 228(4), discussed in para 11.35.
87 TULRCA 1992, Sch A1, para 19A, inserted by ERelA 2004, s 4.
88 TULRCA 1992, Sch A1, paras 19 and 19A, inserted by ERelA 2004. This formulation reflects the Court of Appeal decision in *R v CAC, ex p Kwik-Fit (GB) Ltd* [2002] IRLR 395.
89 The amendment made by ERelA 2004 makes clear that the CAC cannot decide that there is *no* bargaining unit that is appropriate; cf *BECTU and BBC* TUR1/273, CAC.

CAC must take into account any view it has about any other bargaining unit that it considers would be appropriate.[90]

In deciding whether a bargaining unit is appropriate, the CAC must take into account 'the need for the unit to be compatible with effective management', together with five other matters 'so far as they do not conflict with that need'. These matters are the views of the employer and the union(s); existing national and local bargaining arrangements; the desirability of avoiding small fragmented bargaining units within an undertaking; the characteristics of workers falling within the bargaining unit under consideration and of any other employees (not workers) of the employer whom the CAC considers relevant; and the location of workers.[91] It is easy to imagine situations where these factors may not all point in one direction. If a plant, consists, say, of production, maintenance and managerial workers, each of which belong to separate unions, a 'worker characteristics' approach may suggest separate bargaining units for each group. However, this solution may conflict with the desirability of avoiding fragmented bargaining units, although much may depend upon the systems currently in place for determining the terms and conditions of employment for each group. In cases where the employer maintains that the bargaining unit should embrace more than one plant, the organisation of the personnel and finance functions may be significant; if, in practice, each plant operates autonomously in these respects it may be more difficult to sustain the argument that effective management requires a single unit. The parties are likely to argue tactically in this context; the union will wish to confine the bargaining unit to groups among which it has the greatest membership, employers will wish to broaden it to avoid the prospect of recognition being granted on the bases we describe below. The legislation does not prevent the CAC taking into consideration matters additional to those specified in the statute, although its decision could be challenged in judicial review proceedings if these matters were deemed to be irrelevant considerations or to further a purpose which was extraneous to that of the statute.[92]

If the bargaining unit agreed by the parties during the appropriate period, or decided by the CAC, differs from that proposed in the original application, the CAC must decide whether the application is 'invalid' by reference to the same tests that govern admissibility, described above.[93] If the union considers that it is unlikely to win recognition in respect of the revised bargaining unit it would be prudent for it to withdraw its application at this stage as it will otherwise be subject to the three-year bar on any later application in relation to the revised, as well as the original, unit in the event that the application is not regarded as invalid.[94]

9.13 We referred in para 9.11 above to the new right of access for a union to workers in the bargaining unit, introduced by ERelA 2004.[95] If the CAC accepts an application the union may apply to it to appoint a 'suitable independent person' to handle communications between the union and 'relevant workers' (those within the proposed bargaining unit, or appropriate bargaining unit once that has been

90   TULRCA 1992, Sch A1, para 19B(4), inserted by ERelA 2004, s 4.
91   TULRCA 1992, Sch A1, para 19.
92   *Associated Provincial Picture Houses v Wednesbury Corporation* [1948] 1 KB 223.
93   TULRCA 1992, Sch A1, paras 20, 43–50.
94   TULRCA 1992, Sch A1, para 39.
95   ERelA 2004, s 5, inserting TULRCA 1992, Sch A1, para 19C–19F. Prior to this amendment the legislation afforded access only during the balloting period; see para 9.15 below.

agreed or determined) during the 'initial period'.[96] The 'initial period' starts when the CAC informs the parties of the name and date of the appointment of the 'appointed person', and ends when either the CAC informs the union of a declaration of recognition without a ballot or of the name of a person appointed to conduct a ballot;[97] the application is withdrawn; or the application is regarded as 'invalid' (see para 9.12 above). The employer then has a duty to give to the CAC, within ten working days starting with the day after that on which it is informed about the 'appointed person', the names and home addresses of the relevant workers, and to update this information if the relevant workers change as a result of an agreement or decision on the appropriate bargaining unit or if workers join or leave the bargaining unit for some other reason.[98] The CAC must pass any such information to the 'appointed person' as soon as reasonably practicable; he or she must then, at the union's request, send on to any relevant worker information supplied to him or her by the union.[99] The union is liable to pay the costs of the appointed person.[100] If the CAC is satisfied that the employer has failed to fulfil any of its duties and the initial period has not yet ended, it may order the employer to take specified steps within a specified time to remedy the failure.[101] If the employer then fails to comply with such an order, and the parties have agreed or the CAC has decided an appropriate bargaining unit, the CAC may declare the union recognised.[102] This means that recognition may be granted even if a majority of the workforce is not in fact in favour of this, although the CAC will need to have been satisfied that the majority would be *likely* to favour recognition in order for the application to have been ruled admissible. Where the employer's failure to comply with a remedial order occurs before the agreement or decision on the appropriate bargaining unit, that will need to be agreed or decided prior to the CAC deciding whether recognition should be granted.

9.14 *The criteria and procedures for determining recognition.* Assuming that the application is not invalid (or withdrawn) following an agreement or decision on the appropriate bargaining unit, the CAC must then determine whether the union should be recognised. If it is satisfied that a majority of the workers in the bargaining unit are members of the applicant union, it must declare the union recognised; otherwise it must notify the parties that it intends to arrange for the holding of a secret ballot. Controversially, it may also order a ballot even if the union has a majority of the bargaining unit in membership if one of 'three qualifying conditions' is fulfilled.[103] The first is if the CAC is satisfied that this

---

96　TULRCA 1992, Sch A1, para 19C(1)–(4). A 'suitable independent person' is defined in the same way as a 'qualified independent person': para 19C(6) and para 9.15 below.

97　The union then has a separate right of communication during the balloting period under TULRCA 1992, Sch A1, para 26(6); see para 9.15 below.

98　TULRCA 1992, Sch A1, para 19D(1)–(3). The employer must comply with these duties 'so far as it is reasonable to expect him to do so': para 19D(1).

99　TULRCA 1992, Sch A1, para 19D(4), 19E(1).

100　TULRCA 1992, Sch A1, para 19E(2)–(7). See also para 165A, inserted by ERelA 2004, s 14, for the right of appeal against a demand for costs.

101　TULRCA 1992, Sch A1, para 19F(1).

102　TULRCA 1992, Sch A1, para 19F(2)–(5).

103　TULRCA 1992, Sch A1, paras 22, 23. Unusually, no time limit is laid down within which the CAC must decide if a ballot should be held. In *Fullerton Computer Industries Ltd v CAC* [2001] IRLR 752 the Court of Session held that since there was no obligation on the CAC Panel to give reasons for its decision under para 22(4), the fact that its reasoning was inadequate did not make its decision open to challenge given that there was no evidence of a flaw or irrationality in the reasoning.

should be done in the interests of 'good industrial relations'.[104] The second is if the CAC has evidence, which it considers to be credible, from a significant number of the union members within the bargaining unit (not merely their employer) that they do not want the union to conduct collective bargaining on their behalf.[105] The reference to evidence that the CAC considers 'credible' gives the CAC discretion to examine the quality of the evidence, including whether workers were pressurised by the employer to write letters to the CAC that did not reflect their true views.[106] What constitutes a 'significant' number of union members will probably vary according to the context; the total number of workers in the bargaining unit and the percentage of union members may be relevant factors, for example.[107] The third is if 'membership evidence' is produced which leads the CAC to conclude that there are doubts whether a significant number of the union members within the bargaining unit want the union to conduct collective bargaining on their behalf. 'Membership evidence' is exhaustively defined for this purpose as evidence about the circumstances in which union members became members, or evidence about the length of time for which they have been members in circumstances where the CAC is satisfied that such evidence should be taken into account. The first of these limbs is presumably designed to take account of allegations of undue pressure being placed on individuals. In relation to the second, the fact that a substantial number of workers have recently joined the union may be indicative of enthusiasm for recognition, and it is for the CAC to decide on the facts whether it constitutes grounds for the holding of a ballot. In this context, the terms on which workers joined – whether they were offered free or discounted membership, for example – may be material.[108]

Recognition through a ballot must be supported by a majority of the workers voting *and* at least 40% of the workers constituting the bargaining unit.[109] The second of these conditions, which 'represents a political compromise between employers' demands for a threshold of support by a majority of the ... bargaining unit ... and the trade union position that under normal principles applicable to ballots a majority of those voting should be sufficient',[110] is strongly opposed by the union movement.

9.15 Once the CAC has notified its intention to hold a ballot the union (or the parties jointly) may indicate within a specified period (the 'notification period')

---

104 See, for example, *GPMU and Red Letter Bradford Ltd* TUR1/12/00, CAC; *TGWU and Economic Skips Ltd* TUR1/121/01, CAC.

105 There is no definition of 'union' in the Schedule to confine the term to the union which has brought the request for recognition (cf the definition of 'employer' in TULRCA 1992, Sch A1, para 2(4)) but the reference to 'the' union suggests that this is intended in this context.

106 TULRCA 1992, Sch A1 para 22(4)(b), inserted by EReIA 2004, s 6; Gerry Sutcliffe Parliamentary Under-Secretary of State for Trade and Industry, HC Debs col 1471, 16 September 2004. In *R (on the application of Gatwick Express) v CAC* [2003] EWHC 2035 (Admin), decided prior to the amendment, the CAC had before it eight letters from union members of a bargaining unit of 38, all of which were in standard form, on company headed paper, and seven of which had been sent to the CAC by the employer's Human Resource Department. The court held that the CAC had erred in law in refusing to place evidential weight on the seven letters.

107 See, for example, *UNIFI and Turkiye Is Bankasi* TUR1/90, CAC.

108 See, for example, *AEEU and Huntley Healthcare Ltd* TUR1/19/00, CAC but cf *ISTC and Mission Foods* TUR1/256/03, CAC.

109 TULRCA 1992, Sch A1, para 29.

110 Simpson, 2000: p 212.

that it (or they) do not wish the ballot to take place.[111] The costs of the ballot are divided equally between the employer and union,[112] a provision justified by the government as an incentive to encouraging a party that knew its prospects of winning were remote to agree recognition or withdraw its application, as appropriate. The ballot must be conducted by a 'qualified independent person' ('QIP') appointed by the CAC, within 20 working days starting with the day after the 'QIP' is appointed or such longer period as the CAC decides, at a workplace or workplaces decided by the CAC; by post; or a combination of the two, depending upon the CAC's preference.[113] In reaching its decision the CAC must take into account the likelihood of the ballot being affected by unfairness or malpractice if it were conducted at a workplace; costs and practicality; and such other matters as it thinks appropriate (for example, which method is likely to secure a high participation rate). The CAC may not decide upon a combination ballot unless there are 'special factors' making this appropriate; these include factors arising from the location of workers or the nature of their employment, and those put to it by either party, but other matters, such as the absence on leave of members of the bargaining unit, may also be considered. However, if the CAC decides that the ballot should (in whole or in part) be conducted at a workplace, it may require arrangements to be made for workers who would be unable, for reasons relating to them as individuals, to cast their vote in the ballot to be given the opportunity to vote by post if they request this far enough in advance of the ballot for this to be practicable.[114] This allows special arrangements to be made for workers who are absent because of sickness or otherwise on leave without the ballot thereby becoming (and needing to fulfil the conditions for) a combination ballot.

Once the employer has been notified of the arrangements for the ballot, it is subject, at the time of writing, to three duties.[115] The first, and overriding duty, is 'to co-operate generally, in connection with the ballot, with the union ... and the person appointed to conduct the ballot'. The wording of this provision was left deliberately vague to allow the CAC (which decides whether the duties have been breached) maximum flexibility. The second duty is to give the union 'such access to the workers constituting the bargaining unit as is reasonable to enable the union ... to inform the workers of the object of the ballot and to seek their support and their opinions on the issues involved'. This duty is expanded upon in a detailed Code of Practice, whose provisions we discuss in the paragraph below.[116] Third, the employer

111 TULRCA 1992, Sch A1, para 24. The period may be extended by the CAC on joint application by the parties (for example, if they are discussing voluntary recognition): para 24(5)–(7), as amended by ERelA 2004, s 7.

112 TULRCA 1992, Sch A1, para 28. See also para 165A, inserted by ERelA 2004, s 14, for the right of appeal against a demand for costs.

113 TULRCA 1992, Sch A1, para 25. See the Recognition and Derecognition (Qualified Persons) Order 2000, SI 2000/1306, as amended.

114 TULRCA 1992, Sch A1, para 25(6A), inserted by ERelA 2004, s 8.

115 TULRCA 1992, Sch A1, para 26.

116 ERelA 2004, s 9(3), (4D), inserting sub-para (4D) into TULRCA 1992 Sch A1, para 26, provides that an employer is taken to have failed to comply with the duty to give the union access if he refuses a request for a meeting between the union and all or any of the workers in the bargaining unit to be held without him or a representative of his (other than one who has been invited to attend) being present and it is not reasonable in the circumstances for him to do so; if he or a representative of his attends such a meeting without an invitation; or if he seeks to record or otherwise to be informed of the proceedings at any such meeting, or refuses to give an undertaking that he will not seek to do either of these things, where to do the thing in question is not reasonable. At the time of writing the Government intends to bring this provision into force on 1 October 2005.

must give the CAC the names and home addresses of the workers constituting the bargaining unit, and update it on those who later join or leave the unit. This information is passed to the QIP, who is required to send to such workers, at the union's expense, any information the union requests. This enables the union to transmit information without workers' personal details being revealed.[117] In addition to these duties ERelA2004 provides for a further two, which at the time of writing the Government intends to commence on 1 October 2005. First, the employer must refrain from making any offer to any or all of the workers constituting the bargaining unit which has or is likely to have the effect of inducing any of them not to attend any 'relevant meeting' between the union and those workers and is not reasonable in the circumstances. This duty might be breached if, for example, the employer offered an additional payment to workers who failed to attend such a meeting or offered to allow them to go home early. Second, the employer must refrain from taking or threatening to take any action against a worker solely or mainly on the grounds that he or she attended or took part in any 'relevant meeting' between the union and workers in the bargaining unit or indicated his or her intention to attend or take part. A 'relevant meeting' for this purpose means a meeting that is organised in accordance with any agreement between the union and employer or as a result of a remedial order granted by the CAC and which the employer is required by such an agreement or order to permit the worker to attend.

If the CAC is satisfied that the employer has failed to fulfil any of these duties, and the ballot has not been held, it may order it to take specified steps to remedy the failure within a specified period.[118] If there is insufficient time for the request to be considered and any failure remedied prior to the ballot, the ballot may be rescheduled for a later date.[119] If the employer fails to comply with an order of the CAC, and the ballot has still not been held, the CAC has a discretion to declare the union recognised without a ballot.[120] This provision, like that we described in para 9.13 above, means that recognition may be granted even if a majority of the workforce is not in favour. However, it leaves a gap if the employer's non-compliance is not evident prior to the holding of the ballot or there is insufficient time before the ballot for a declaration to be issued; no account can be taken of any consequent disadvantage that the union may have suffered in the event that the result is opposed to recognition. This contrasts with the position where the employer has committed an 'unfair practice', introduced in relation to recognition ballots by ERelA 2004 (at the time of writing not yet in force). We discuss these, and the consequences if one or other party is found to have used such a practice, in para 9.17 below.

9.16 Workers are likely to be subjected to intensive campaigning by their employer in the period prior to the ballot. The degree of access to them that the

---

117 If the employer has already passed the relevant information to the CAC in relation to the union's communications with workers via an 'appointed person' (see para 9.13) it need not do this again: TULRCA 1992, Sch A1, para 26(4F), (4G).

118 TULRCA 1992, Sch A1, para 27(1).

119 Code of Practice on Access to Workers during Recognition and Derecognition Ballots 2000, para 48. The power to reschedule could probably be derived from TULRCA 1992, Sch A1, para 25(3). See *R (on the application of Ultraframe) v CAC* [2005] EWCA Civ 560 for the supervisory role of the CAC in relation to the conduct of ballots, including the power to order a re-run of a ballot which did not comply with the statutory requirements. On the powers of the CAC under ERelA 2004 where it finds an unfair practice has been committed (at the time of writing not yet in force), see para 9.17.

120 TULRCA 1992, Sch A1, para 27(2), (3).

union can secure to put its case is therefore crucial. The Code of Practice on Access to Workers during Recognition or Derecognition Ballots,[121] which deals only with access at the workplace and/or during working time, aims in the first instance to help the parties agree their own arrangements which can take full account of individual circumstances, a process which should be started during the 'notification period'. It assumes that initial proposals should be made by the union which, if rejected by the employer, should be matched by timely counter-proposals. Where the parties fail to reach agreement, either party, acting separately or together, may ask ACAS to conciliate; if the process remains deadlocked, the CAC may be asked to assist and, ultimately, adjudicate and make an order.[122] The Code affirms that employers should be prepared to give access to full-time union officials, as well as nominated individuals from the proposed bargaining unit and other workplaces, in numbers proportionate to the scale and nature of the activities or events occurring within the agreed access programme.[123] The employer's typical methods of communicating with the workforce should be used as a benchmark of communication with the union. Where practicable access should be granted at the workplace, and the employer should provide appropriate accommodation and ensure that the meeting is held in private.[124] If, 'exceptional[ly]', the nature of the business or space restrictions preclude large-scale meetings on site, the employer should assist in notifying workers in advance where such meetings will be held.[125] On-site access should usually be during normal working hours but at times which minimise disruption to the employer's business (once again, the employer's custom and practice in this regard will be material); off-site access will normally be outside such hours unless within reasonable walking distance of the workplace.[126] The Code proposes minimum standards for the frequency and duration of union activities, although what is reasonable for the union depends in part on the number of meetings held by the employer during working time. Interestingly, it is suggested that where 'appropriate' there should be union 'surgeries' at the workplace during working hours at which each worker, without losing pay, would have the opportunity to meet a union representative for fifteen minutes on an individual basis or in small groups.[127] However whether this is appropriate depends in part on whether the employer is holding similar meetings and whether it would 'lead to an unacceptable increase in tension at the workplace'. Employers are urged 'where practicable' to provide a notice board for the union's use in a prominent location, and workers should be permitted access to the union's web-page and to the employer's e-mail and intranet systems where this is generally allowed for non-job-related purposes and in any event if the employer uses such systems to circulate information hostile to the union's case. Finally, employers are urged

---

121 The current edition of the Code came into force on 6 June 2000. See para 2.4 for the legal effect of Codes of Practice generally. At the time of writing the Government intends a new Code of Practice on Access and Unfair Practices during Recognition and Derecognition Ballots to commence on 1 October 2005.

122 Code of Practice, paras 14–22. Note that the employer's statutory duty of co-operation and access take effect only when it has been informed that a ballot is to be arranged, ie, once the notification period has ended.

123 Para 26.

124 Paras 27, 46.

125 Para 28.

126 Para 29.

127 Paras 31–33. There is no provision in the *statute* for workers to be paid: for the implications of this, see G Morris and T Archer, 2000: para 4.27.

to be receptive to suggestions from unions for securing access to 'non-typical' workers such as those who work from home or on a part-time basis.[128]

Although these provisions, if implemented, go some way to redressing the imbalance of power between unions and employers during a recognition campaign, unions remain disadvantaged in that employers are not prevented from organising 'captive audience' meetings during working hours, and they have direct access to individuals whose identities are known to them, whereas unions must hope that workers pick up literature made available to them at the workplace or via the internet or QIP. As we indicated above, complaints that the employer has failed in its duty to permit reasonable access may be taken to the CAC,[129] although the Code suggests that efforts should first be made to resolve minor complaints internally. It has been argued that the access provisions are vulnerable to challenge by employers under the HRA 1998 as an interference with the employer's right to the peaceful enjoyment of its possessions, contrary to Article 1 of the First Protocol of the ECHR.[130] However the current Convention jurisprudence does not support this view. At one time it seemed that violation of the article required the economic value of a right or interest to be affected,[131] which clearly would not be the case here. However, in *Chassagnon v France*[132] the ECtHR found that the compulsory transfer of hunting rights over land belonging to landowners opposed to hunting constituted an interference with their rights as owners of the property, even though they were not deprived of their right to sell or use it and its market value did not seem to be reduced. It is submitted that the level of access required by the Code is of a very different nature and should be regarded as *de minimis* in this context; it may also be seen as relevant that the duty to afford it arises in the context of a process designed to establish the right of a union to be 'heard', an objective compatible with Article 11 of the ECHR.[133] Moreover, even if, contrary to this view, access were to be regarded as an 'interference', it would be open to the state to justify it as 'lawful' and striking a fair balance between the demands of the general interest of the community and the requirements of the protection of the individual's fundamental rights.[134]

9.17 *Unfair practices*   ERelA 2004 provides that once the parties have been informed by the CAC of the arrangements for the ballot they 'must refrain from using any unfair practice'.[135] At the time of writing the Government intends to commence this provision on 1 October 2005. Under the Act, a party uses an unfair practice if, with a view to influencing the result of the ballot, it:

(a)   offers to pay money or give 'money's worth' to a worker entitled to vote in the ballot in return for the worker's agreement to vote in a particular way or

---

128   Paras 34–39.
129   Note that there is no mechanism by which employers can complain about a union's conduct, but the Code indicates that this may be a factor in determining whether the employer has acted unreasonably: para 50.
130   D Brown and K Ewing, 2000: p 215.
131   *Rayner v UK* Application No 9310/81 47 DR 5 (1986); *S v France* Application No 13728/88 65 DR 250 (1990).
132   Judgment of 29 April 1999, (1999) 29 EHRR 615.
133   See *Van der Musselle v Belgium* judgment of 23 November 1983, (1984) 6 EHRR 163, para 49.
134   *James v UK* judgment of 21 February 1986, (1986) 8 EHRR 123; *Iatridis v Greece* judgment of March 25 1999 (1999) 30 EHRR 97; *Sporring and Lonnroth v Sweden* judgment of 23 September 1982, (1983) 5 EHRR 35, para 69.
135   ERelA 2004, s 10, inserting para 27A into TULRCA 1992, Sch A1. See Bogg, 2005.

to abstain from voting. 'Money's worth' is not a term that is used in any other area of employment law, although it is used in a variety of other contexts such as property and family law. Despite a voluminous body of case law, there is no settled meaning of the term. Although it is tolerably clear that free goods or services, on which a monetary value can be put, would be covered, it is less clear whether some forms of benefits, such as an additional day's paid holiday, would be: it could be argued that a worker's salary remains unchanged but that they are effectively being offered an extra day's non-work time on which no material value may be able to be put. The draft Code of Practice on Access and Unfair Practices during Recognition and Derecognition Ballots did not resolve the difficulty, stating only that offers to provide additional paid holiday or other paid leave are *likely* to constitute 'money's worth'.[136] At the time of writing it remains to be seen whether the final version of the Code will provide greater clarification.

(b)   makes an 'outcome-specific offer' to a worker entitled to vote in the ballot. An 'outcome-specific offer' is an offer to pay money or give money's worth which is conditional on the CAC issuing a declaration that the union is, or is not, recognised, as the case may be, and is not conditional on anything which is done or occurs as a result of the declaration. 'Such offers are not explicitly linked to a person's agreement to vote in a particular way or not to vote at all. Instead, they represent more general offers to make payments to the workforce or give them money's worth provided the outcome of the ballot goes a particular way.'[137] The exclusion of things done as a result of recognition means that an offer which is conditional on the outcome of collective bargaining resulting from an award of recognition, for example, is not included.

(c)   coerces or attempts to coerce a worker entitled to vote in the ballot to disclose whether he or she intends to vote, or how he or she has voted or intends to vote;

(d)   dismisses or threatens to dismiss a worker.[138] This may lead to difficulties where an employer intends to close or relocate its business, necessarily leading to dismissals, in the event of a vote in favour of recognition. The draft Code of Practice stated that such statements 'should be avoided',[139] so suggesting that in the event that the employer communicates such a message to the workforce this may lead to an adverse finding by the CAC. It is arguable that where a statement of this kind represents the employer's genuine intention, to impose a sanction for communicating it may be open to challenge under the HRA 1998 as an interference with the employer's freedom of expression which cannot be justified as 'necessary in a democratic society'. Again, it remains to be seen whether this provision will be included in the final version of the Code.

(e)   takes or threatens to take disciplinary action against a worker;

(f)   subjects or threatens to subject a worker to any other detriment; or

(g)   uses or attempts to use undue influence on a worker entitled to vote in the ballot. This term, borrowed from the Representation of the People Act 1983, is designed to be 'a general test that will catch all possible cases of intimidatory or similar behaviour'.[140]

---

136 Para 53.
137 Gerry Sutcliffe, HC Debs, col 1472, 16 September 2004.
138 Note that this, in common with (e) and (f) below, is not restricted to a worker entitled to vote in the ballot.
139 Para 66.
140 Lord Triesman, HL Debs, GC 48–49, 7 June 2004.

ERelA 2004 provides that one party may complain to the CAC that the other has committed an unfair practice.[141] The complaint must be made on or before the first working day after the date of the ballot or, if votes may be cast on more than one day, the last of those days. The CAC must decide whether the complaint is well-founded within ten working days starting with the day after that on which the complaint was received or such longer period as the CAC may specify (the 'decision period'), and may postpone the ballot if it has not begun at the beginning of the decision period. A complaint is 'well-founded' for this purpose if the CAC finds that the party complained against used an unfair practice *and* the CAC is satisfied that the use of that practice changed or was likely to change the voting intentions (in terms of how, or whether, he or she would vote) or voting behaviour (how he or she voted) of a worker entitled to vote in the ballot. In the event that the CAC so finds, it may issue a remedial order requiring the party concerned to take specified action within a specified period to mitigate the effect of the unfair practice.[142] However, if the unfair practice consisted of or included the use of violence or the dismissal of a union official,[143] the CAC may declare at this stage that the union is, or is not, entitled to be recognised, depending on the party in default.[144] It may also issue such a declaration in the event that a second complaint is upheld against one of the parties or the party concerned fails to comply with a remedial order. There seems nothing in the legislation to exclude the CAC from requiring an employer to reinstate a dismissed worker under a remedial order, although such an order would not confer rights on the individual worker.[145]

Where the CAC finds an 'unfair practice' complaint to be well founded, it may also (or alternatively) cancel the initial ballot or annul a completed ballot without disclosing the result, and give notice to the parties that it intends to arrange for the holding of another ballot.[146] Where the CAC orders a fresh ballot to be held in these circumstances, that ballot is subject to the same principles as the original ballot, described in para 9.15 above, with three main exceptions.[147] First, the notification period is five, not ten, working days; second, the employer need only inform the CAC of any changes in the names and home addresses of any workers in the bargaining unit rather than supplying a complete new list; and third, the costs of the ballot must be borne by such of the parties and in such proportions as the CAC may determine, rather than shared equally between them, so enabling the CAC, if it chooses, to require the party that committed the unfair practice to pay all or the majority of the costs. In addition, any remedial order made in relation to the holding of the original ballot, relating either to the breach of the employer's duties or an unfair practice, will have effect in relation to the fresh ballot to the extent the CAC specifies.

9.18 *Consequences of recognition.* If the CAC declares a union recognised, the parties have 30 days (or longer if they so decide) in which to agree a 'method'

---

141 ERelA 2004, s 10, inserting para 27B into TULRCA 1992, Sch A1.
142 ERelA 2004, s 10, inserting para 27C into TULRCA 1992, Sch A1.
143 Defined TULRCA 1992, s 119.
144 ERelA 2004, s 10, inserting para 27D into TULRCA 1992, Sch A1.
145 TULRCA 1992, Sch A1, para 27A(4).
146 TULRCA 1992, Sch A1, paras 27C(3)(b), 27E, 29(1A). This is at the CAC's discretion; it will not need to re-run a ballot if the victim of the unfair practice won the ballot: Gerry Sutcliffe, HC Debs col 472, 16 September 2004.
147 TULRCA 1992, Sch A1, para 27F.

by which they will conduct collective bargaining. If no agreement is made during this 'negotiation period' either party may apply to the CAC for assistance.[148] The CAC must first try to help the parties reach agreement, failing which it must itself specify a 'method', which has effect as if it were contained in a legally-enforceable contract unless the parties agree in writing otherwise. This does not prevent the parties replacing the method at a later stage; an agreement to effect such a replacement would also be legally enforceable but the replacement method itself, if appropriately drafted, need not be.[149] The term 'method' is not defined in the legislation; it is clear that it does not impose a substantive obligation to reach agreement, nor even to negotiate with a view to reaching an agreement (a requirement which is imposed on employers in order to fulfil their obligations to *consult* on transfers and collective redundancies); rather, it is a duty 'simply to meet and to talk'.[150] The government justified this limited obligation on the basis that statutory recognition should not deliver more than voluntary, where there are no constraints on bargaining conduct unless the parties otherwise agree. In specifying a 'method' the CAC must 'take ... into account' a detailed 'model' laid down by the Secretary of State, although it may depart from it as it thinks appropriate.[151] This model includes provision for a single Joint Negotiating Body, with exclusive bargaining rights over pay, hours and holidays; provision for paid time off for its union members employed by the employer to prepare the claim and attend the JNB, and access for other officials to the employer's premises for these purposes; the provision of accommodation and facilities for the union's private and exclusive use, where resources so permit; and a six-step bargaining procedure for dealing with the union's claims (presumptively presented annually), with specified actions and time limits attached to each stage. The employer is not permitted to vary the pay, hours, or holidays of workers in the bargaining unit unless it has first discussed its proposals with the union, although this restriction does not apply where a worker has agreed that his or her terms may be varied by direct negotiation with the employer.[152]

Although the 'method' specified by the CAC has effect as a contract, the remedy for non-compliance is confined to one of specific performance,[153] an equitable and discretionary remedy which may be refused if applicants cannot show that they themselves have performed their contractual obligations and are ready and willing to perform future ones.[154] At one time the courts adopted the

---

148 TULRCA 1992, Sch A1, para 30. Either party may also apply for assistance in the event of non-compliance with an existing agreement: para 32, as amended by ERelA 2004, Sch 1, para 7.

149 TULRCA 1992, Sch A1, para 31. Note also the obligation on employers to consult on training matters if a 'method' of collective bargaining has been specified by the CAC and the parties have not varied its legal effect or content: see para 9.49 below.

150 Lord McIntosh of Haringey, Deputy Chief Whip, HL Debs Vol 601, col 1275, 7 June 1999.

151 TULRCA 1992, Sch A1, para 168; The Trade Union Recognition (Method of Collective Bargaining) Order 2000, SI 2000/1300.

152 Note, now, however, TULRCA 1992, s 145B, inserted by ERelA 2004, s 29, discussed in para 8.18 *et seq.*

153 TULRCA 1992, Sch A1, para 31(6). Note that failure to comply with the terms of the 'method' may also be relevant to the exercise of judicial discretion to grant an interim injunction to halt industrial action (see para 11.49) and for the length of time for which it is automatically unfair to dismiss an employee for taking 'protected industrial action' (see para 11.78 *et seq*).

154 See generally Jones and Goodhart, 1996.

approach that there was no power to order specific performance of contracts which involved continuous or successive acts and which consequently required the continuous supervision of the court. In recent years, however, this position has been modified and greater emphasis has been placed on whether there is a sufficient definition of what it required to be done to comply with an order of the court.[155] The model procedure would seem capable of enforcement according to these criteria. Failure to comply with an order for specific performance constitutes contempt of court.[156] It remains uncertain whether an interim injunction could be available in this context;[157] in general, interim relief may be claimed in a specific performance action, and would be particularly useful to a union claimant in the event that an employer was attempting to vary terms and conditions of employment without going through the requisite procedure.

Both the nature of the obligation imposed on employers if recognition is ordered – the obligation merely to comply with a collective bargaining 'method' and the exclusive remedy of specific performance – have been heavily criticised by commentators, who contrast it unfavourably with the remedy of unilateral arbitration of substantive terms and conditions contained in the earlier procedure (and still applicable to claims for disclosure of information).[158] It is clear that the application of a 'method' does not of itself guarantee any material improvement for workers, and that even if collective agreements are reached, employers are not obliged to apply the norms they set to workers' individual contracts. However it is important not to overlook the collateral benefits, such as time off and consultation rights, that recognition brings, which we outline in para 7.26

The procedure came into operation on 6 June 2000. As of 28 February 2005, 434 applications had been presented to the CAC, 259 of which were accepted, 47 not accepted, and 117 withdrawn, with decisions pending on the remainder.[159] 71 were withdrawn at later stages of the procedure and 8 found to be invalid when the bargaining unit changed from that in the original application. Recognition was ordered in 114 cases, 69 following a ballot and 45 without. Of those 114, a collective bargaining 'method' had been agreed between the parties in 90 cases and specified in 9; the issue was outstanding in the remainder. These figures may appear to suggest that relatively little use is being made of the procedure. However, this would fail to appreciate the impetus that its existence gives for employers to agree to recognition on a voluntary basis. Moreover, even if employers grant recognition once the statutory procedure has started, they retain greater flexibility in varying or terminating it (and may have a prospect of better relations with the union) than if it is ordered by the CAC. To that extent, therefore, the comparatively low number of recognition awards could be seen as a measure of success.

155 *Posner v Scott-Lewis* [1987] Ch 25.
156 See para 11.51 for the consequences of being found in contempt of court.
157 The legislation, in stating that '[s]pecific performance shall be the only remedy available' would appear to exclude this, but the matter is not free from doubt. The government rejected an amendment to exclude interim proceedings in this context: see HL Debs Vol 601, cols 1234–1237, 7 June 1999. The government also rejected a proposed amendment to exclude liability in tort (in relation to trade disputes) in this context: see further Wedderburn, 2000: pp 40–41.
158 See, for example, Wedderburn, 2000: pp 37–42; Simpson, 2000: pp 212–216. See para 9.22 *et seq* on disclosure of information.
159 Figures supplied by the CAC.

(ii) Changes in the bargaining unit

9.19   As we have seen, recognition ordered by the CAC relates to a specific bargaining unit. It is possible, however, that a bargaining unit that was appropriate when recognition was being determined may cease to be so because of changes in the structure, organisation or nature of the business. In that event, the legislation makes provision for either party to apply to the CAC for the bargaining unit to be varied.[160] In order for the application to be admissible the CAC must decide that it is likely that the original unit is no longer appropriate by reference to statutory criteria. The parties then have the opportunity to agree a new bargaining unit, which will replace the old provided that it does not overlap with any pre-existing unit; in default of agreement, the CAC must decide upon the appropriate unit (which may turn out to be the existing one). An employer may also apply to the CAC for the bargaining arrangements to cease altogether if it believes that the unit covered by the declaration imposing recognition has ceased to exist, although this, too, may result in a revised bargaining unit (or maintenance of the old unit) if unsuccessful. There are complex provisions designed to ensure that there is no overlap between the new and any pre-existing bargaining unit. The CAC must then decide whether support for recognition in the new bargaining unit needs to be assessed; if so, it must determine whether there is the same level of actual and potential support required for an initial application to be admissible. If such support is found, whether recognition should be ordered is determined in an identical way to the initial application. At the time of writing, there have been two applications to the CAC under this procedure.

(iii) Derecognition

9.20   As we saw in para 9.4, there is no statutory constraint on an employer which has recognised a union outside the statutory procedure varying the scope of recognition or withdrawing it altogether. The position is wholly different where recognition follows from the union having invoked the statutory procedure. As we have already indicated, even if recognition is enshrined in an 'agreement for recognition' agreed voluntarily by the employer following a request under the statutory procedure, the employer may not terminate that agreement unilaterally within three years unless the parties have modified this restriction by consent.[161] However once that period (or any additional or lesser period that has been agreed) has passed, the employer is free to terminate recognition without union consent. By contrast, where recognition follows a declaration by the CAC it can be terminated by the CAC only in specified conditions, on application by the employer or worker a minimum of three years after the initial declaration.[162] The situations where recognition may be terminated mirror, in broad terms,

---

160   For a more detailed analysis of these highly complex provisions, which are contained in Part III of TULRCA 1992, Sch A1, see G Morris and T Archer, 2000: paras 4.35–4.42. See also *GMB and Ardengate Ltd* TUR3/2/03, CAC. Note that provisions relating to the collective bargaining method (whether derived from the parties' agreement or specified by the CAC) must apply in relation to the unit: para 64(1)(b).

161   TULRCA 1992, Sch A1, para 56.

162   There is an exception to the three-year rule if a union recognised pursuant to a request for recognition loses its certificate of independence; it is then immediately treated as being recognised on a voluntary basis unless there are other unions recognised for the unit that retain their certificates: TULRCA 1992, Sch A1, paras 149–154.

those applicable to the granting of recognition. They are, in outline, as follows. The first is where the employer, together with any associated employer, employs an average of fewer than 21 workers in any period of 13 weeks ending on or after the 'relevant date' – the expiry of the period of three years starting with the date of the CAC's declaration awarding recognition. Derecognition on this basis is invoked by a notice served by the employer on the union and the CAC, and may be adjudicated upon by the CAC if challenged by the union.[163] Second, the employer may begin the derecognition process by making a request to the union to end the bargaining arrangements. Third, a worker in the bargaining unit may apply to the CAC. In the second and third cases, where recognition was ordered following a ballot, the CAC must first decide that at least 10% of the workers in the bargaining unit favour an end to the bargaining arrangements and that a majority of the workers constituting the unit would favour this. It will then order derecognition, failing agreement between the parties, if the requisite support for the termination of the bargaining arrangements has been demonstrated in a ballot of the workers in the unit, conducted according to the principles that govern recognition ballots.[164] Where recognition was ordered without a ballot (on the basis of majority membership), however, and the application is made by an employer, it will be admissible if the CAC is satisfied that fewer than half the workers are members of the union.[165] In a parallel with the three-year bar on recognition applications, derecognition applications by employers and by workers may be considered only if there has been a three-year gap since the last application,[166] so ensuring an element of industrial relations stability.

It is conceivable that workers may wish their employer to change its bargaining partner from one union to another. For recognition agreements reached outside the statutory procedure there has traditionally been no legal mechanism for achieving this without the employer's consent. Moreover, even if a union has been the subject of a derecognition declaration, there is nothing to prevent an employer recognising it on a voluntary basis, so barring a claim for statutory recognition by another union. There is one exception to workers' inability to obtain recognition of a substitute union, which is where the employer recognises a union that lacks a certificate of independence. It is then open to any worker within the bargaining unit to apply to the CAC to have the bargaining arrangements ended, and the CAC will order this if it is supported in a ballot by a majority of the workers voting and at least 40% of the workers in the unit.[167] This is likely, in practice, to arise as the first step of an initiative by an independent union to gain recognition for the bargaining unit in question; even if the employer were to re-recognise the non-independent union, that recognition agreement, if made within

---

163 TULRCA 1992, Sch A1, paras 96–103, as amended by ERelA 2004.
164 TULRCA 1992 Sch A1, paras 104–121, as amended by ERelA 2004. As in the context of recognition, the additional duties on the employer and the provisions relating to unfair practices are not yet in force at the time of writing; the Government intends to commence them on 1 October 2005. Note the difference in sanction for a second unfair practice, breach of a CAC remedial order, dismissal of a union official or use of violence committed by an employer in relation to an application by a worker in para 119H (employer may be barred from further campaigning in relation to the ballot).
165 TULRCA 1992, Sch A1, paras 122–133.
166 In the case where the employer issues a notice stating that it employs fewer than 21 workers as above, the bar applies where the CAC accepts the earlier notice as complying with the requirements of TULRCA 1992, Sch A1, para 99(3): para 99A.
167 TULRCA 1992, Sch A1, paras 134–148.

three years of the previous recognition agreement ceasing, would not constitute a barrier to an application by an independent union to the CAC which, if successful, would mean that the bargaining arrangements with the non-independent union would cease.[168] Unlike other contexts in which derecognition may be sought, there is no requirement that the union should have been recognised for a minimum three-year period, nor is there any restriction on the frequency with which applications may be brought. However the efficacy of the procedure may be hindered in practice by the initial admissibility requirement that the CAC must find that at least 10% of the workers in the bargaining unit favour an end to the arrangements and that a majority of those in the bargaining unit would be likely to do so. Obtaining evidence of this may be difficult for workers in a situation where neither employer nor union are likely to co-operate

(iv) Protection of workers during recognition and derecognition campaigns

9.21   Workers are accorded protection against dismissal or subjection to other forms of detriment by their employer for specified acts relating to the recognition and derecognition procedures.[169] We discussed the concept of 'subjection to a detriment' in para 8.13 in relation to trade union membership and activities and the same comments apply, *mutatis mutandis*, in this context. Here, in particular, workers may be subject to threats of detrimental consequences if they lend their support to recognition; once again it is strongly arguable that workers have been 'subjected to a detriment' if they cease activities they wish to carry out because of intimidation. It is essential, however, that the employer's act can be attributed specifically to the action of the individual worker. Thus, a threat to the workforce in general that terms and conditions of employment will be less favourable, or that redundancies will follow, if a union is accorded recognition, whilst it may constitute an unfair practice once this provision has been brought into force,[170] will not suffice for the purpose of obtaining an individual remedy.[171] The grounds to which protection pertains are acting with a view to obtaining or preventing recognition or indicating support or lack of support for it; acting with a view to securing or preventing the ending of bargaining arrangements or indicating support or lack of support for this; voting in a ballot or influencing or seeking to influence other workers to vote or not to vote, or the way they cast their votes; or proposing, failing or proposing to decline to do any of these things. However an act is excluded from these grounds 'if it constitutes an unreasonable act or omission by the worker'.[172] Clearly there may be scope for argument as to when an act constitutes an 'unreasonable act or omission' – canvassing other workers during working hours rather than performing normal duties may be one example – so it may be prudent, where appropriate, to include an additional complaint in a tribunal application that the worker has been subjected to a detriment for taking part in union activities, where no such qualification applies.

---

168 TULRCA 1992, Sch A1, paras 35(4), 148.
169 TULRCA 1992, Sch A1, paras 156–165.
170 See para 9.17 above.
171 Under ERelA 2004, s 10, inserting para 27A(4) into TULRCA 1992, Sch A1, dismissal or the threat of dismissal can constitute an unfair practice; use of an unfair practice does not confer a right on an individual worker but does not affect any other right which he or she may have. At the time of writing the Government intends to bring this provision into force on 1 October 2005.
172 TULRCA 1992, Sch A1 paras 156(3), 161(3).

A worker who is subjected to a detriment on one of the specified grounds may complain to an employment tribunal; in the event that he or she is an employee, and the detriment amounts to dismissal, a remedy must be sought under the unfair dismissal legislation, which has the additional advantage of the possibility of interim relief.[173] In addition, where an employee's contract has been terminated by the employer,[174] the statutory disciplinary and dismissal procedure which we discussed in para 5.124 *et seq* must be followed, and complaints based on constructive dismissal and other forms of detriment are subject to the grievance procedures discussed in para 2.21 *et seq*.[175] The time limit, procedure for complaining, and remedies available are identical to those applicable to detriments on grounds of union activities. Thus, there is no limit on the compensation that may be awarded, although if the detriment consisted of termination of the contract of a 'worker' who was not an 'employee', it is restricted to the total of the basic and compensatory awards for unfair dismissal.[176] In theory, therefore, a worker could be awarded more for suffering a detriment short of dismissal than for dismissal itself. Where an employee has been dismissed (or, in a 'redundancy case' selected for dismissal) on one of the specified grounds, the dismissal will be automatically unfair. There is no qualifying period, or upper age limit, applicable to such dismissals, although where the employee would not otherwise qualify to claim he or she must prove the reason for dismissal. The remedy of interim relief may be particularly significant where the employer has dismissed employees prior to the ballot in the hope that they will thereby be excluded from participation in it.[177] It is a moot point, however, whether all the remedies available would secure participation. Reinstatement, which probably would, requires the consent of the employer, as does re-engagement (where the position is less clear). An order for continuation of the contract would allow participation only if it could be argued that this constitutes a 'benefit derived from the employment'. Even if this were to be the case, it may be otiose if the ballot had been held after the dismissal and prior to the tribunal's order. In these circumstances unions may wish to inform the CAC of any application for interim relief and request postponement of the ballot pending its outcome.

The conduct of collective bargaining: disclosure of information

9.22 As we saw in para 9.18, where a trade union is recognised pursuant to a statutory request for recognition, the CAC may specify, at the request of either party, the 'method' by which collective bargaining is to be conducted. Other than in these circumstances, the conduct of the collective bargaining process is left entirely to the discretion of the parties, with the exception of a limited statutory duty on employers to disclose certain information. Access to information about an undertaking, particularly its financial position, is crucial to the conduct of collective bargaining; in Kahn-Freund's striking phrase, 'recognition does not deserve its name if one of the negotiating partners is kept in the dark about matters within the exclusive knowledge of the other which are

---

173 TULRCA 1992, Sch A1, paras 156(4), 161; ERA 1996, ss 128(1)(b) and 129(1), as amended by ERelA 1999, s 6.
174 Or a limited-term contract expires without renewal.
175 EA 2002, Schs 3 and 4.
176 TULRCA 1992, Sch A1, para 160.
177 See further para 5.163.

relevant to an agreement'.[178] It may also be in an employer's interest that a union's case is not based upon false assumptions about the undertaking's state of health.[179] The need for adequate information is stressed in ILO Recommendation 163 concerning the Promotion of Collective Bargaining, Article 7 of which states that measures adapted to national conditions should be taken, if necessary, so that the parties have access to the information required for meaningful negotiations. Since 1977[180] employers have been required by legislation to disclose to representatives of recognised unions on request information about their undertaking for the purposes of all stages of collective bargaining about matters, and in relation to descriptions of workers, for which the union is recognised.[181] The information may be either in the employer's own possession or that of an associated employer. However, the utility of this requirement has been severely limited by its very restrictive scope.

9.23   The first restriction lies in the nature of the duty itself, which provides that the information must satisfy two tests. First, it must be information without which the union representatives would be to a 'material extent' impeded in carrying out collective bargaining with the employer. This test, in addressing the importance rather than the relevance of the information, 'focuses attention not on the nature of the bargaining that disclosure might facilitate but, rather, on whether bargaining can take place at all without disclosure'.[182] It may be difficult for a union to argue that bargaining is impossible if it has managed without such information in the past, and the difference which access to the information in question would have made can be a matter of speculation only. Research on the operation of the procedure has led to the conclusion that '[m]any employers have successfully objected that there was no impediment and unions are severely disadvantaged in arguing the need for information that they do not have'.[183] Second, it must be information which the employer should disclose in accordance with good industrial relations practice, on which regard should be had, *inter alia*, to the ACAS Code of Practice.[184]

---

178 P Davies and M Freedland, 1983: p 110.
179 See L Dickens, 1980.
180 When this provision of the EPA 1975 came into force. Provision for disclosure was made in the IRA 1971 but it was never implemented.
181 See now TULRCA 1992, s 181(1). 'Representative' means an official (defined TULRCA 1992, s 119) or other person authorised by the union to carry out such collective bargaining. For the definition of 'worker' see TULRCA 1992, s 296 and para 3.51 *et seq* above. Other rights of employee representatives to information are dealt with later in this chapter. Note that providing information which is confidential under the contract of employment to union representatives will be a breach of contract on the part of individual employees and seeking it may constitute the tort of inducing breach of contract: see *Bent's Brewery Co Ltd v Hogan* [1945] 2 All ER 570.
182 L Dickens and G Bain 1986: p 98. It is noteworthy, however, that the CAC has emphasised that 'collective bargaining must be looked at more widely than simply relating to a process in which two parties are clearly agreed that they are negotiating to reach a mutually acceptable solution. The term "collective bargaining" refers to the continuing relationship between an employer and a trade union, not simply the nature of the interaction on one particular occasion': *Annual Report*, 1995, para 2.17.
183 Gospel and Lockwood, 1999: p 244.
184 ACAS Code No 2: *Disclosure of Information to Trade Unions for Collective Bargaining Purposes* (1997). This Code, which came into force on 5 February 1998, replaces the original version published in 1977. The CAC Annual Reports are a more useful source of guidance on good practice in this area. The CAC has emphasised that the 'information' to be disclosed may include the basis upon which subjective or professional judgments are made: *Annual Report*, 1995, paras 2.16 and 2.18.

The Code is not particularly helpful on this matter, however (possibly because of the difficulty of reconciling the views of the two sides of industry in preparing it).[185] It does not attempt to provide a 'checklist' of items which should be disclosed on the basis that this will vary according to factors such as the subject-matter and level of negotiations and the size of the company and business in which it is engaged.[186] Rather, it confines itself to giving examples of information which it suggests could be relevant in certain situations which it divides into five broad headings: pay and benefits; conditions of service; manpower (sic); performance (eg, productivity and efficiency data, savings from increased productivity and output, return on capital invested, sales and state of the order book) and financial matters (eg, profits; assets; loans to parent or subsidiary companies; and liabilities).[187] This rudimentary list does, at least, make clear that subjects which are not themselves within the statutory definition of 'collective bargaining' are nevertheless potentially within the duty. Two further aspects have emerged from decisions of the CAC, which adjudicates on complaints of failure to comply with the duty to disclose: that its application to 'all stages' of collective bargaining means that there is no need for negotiations to have started before disclosure is sought,[188] and information about workers who are outside the union's sphere of recognition may nevertheless be relevant to bargaining about those who are within it.[189] However, it is clear that the information need be disclosed only for the purpose of collective bargaining and, depending upon its nature, it is conceivable that an employer could restrain its use in any other context on the basis that this would constitute a breach of confidence.[190]

As well as being narrowly defined, the duty to disclose is also subject to additional limitations. First, there is a list of six specific categories of information which need not be disclosed.[191] The most wide-ranging are any information 'which has been communicated to ... [the employer] in confidence'[192] and information whose disclosure 'would cause substantial injury to ... [the employer's] undertaking for reasons other than its effect on collective bargaining'. For the latter the Code gives as examples cost information on individual products, detailed analysis of proposed investment, marketing or pricing policies, and price quotas or the make-up of tender prices;[193] substantial injury may occur if, for example, certain customers would be lost to competitors, or suppliers would refuse to supply necessary materials, or the ability to raise funds to finance the company would be seriously impaired as a result of disclosing certain information.[194] A further

185 See Gospel, 1976.
186 ACAS Code No 2, paras 11, 12.
187 ACAS Code No 2, para 11.
188 This approach was approved by Forbes J in *R v CAC, ex p BTP Tioxide Ltd* [1982] IRLR 60, 67.
189 On the latter point see, for example, CAC *Annual Report* 1993, para 2.6, which recognises the interest of unions in knowing the level of pay increases, including those of senior managers, throughout a company.
190 IT Smith and GH Thomas, 2003: p 82.
191 TULRCA 1992, s 182(1).
192 In *CSU v CAC* [1980] IRLR 274, it was held that the Ministry of Defence could rely on this defence in refusing to disclose to the Civil Service Union information as to the number of cleaners and their hours of work supplied in a tender from private contractors. Several cases before the CAC in recent years have concerned market-testing and contracting-out, including the information given to potential bidders. The CAC has urged upon those conducting the process the benefits of involving staff and their representatives at an early stage: see, for example, *Annual Report*, 1996, para 2.8.
193 ACAS Code No 2, para 14.
194 ACAS Code No 2, para 15.

exempted category – information relating specifically to an individual without that individual's consent – has assumed greater practical significance with the spread of performance-related pay and management-only grading schemes. The CAC has acknowledged unions' interests in having the information necessary to monitor the operation of such schemes and has reconciled this with respect for individual confidentiality by awarding that particular breakdowns of annual salary increases should be provided, for example, by age groups, sex, and by functional area.[195] The second important limitation is that employers are not obliged to produce, or allow inspection of, any document,[196] a restriction which contrasts sharply with systems, most notably the Swedish,[197] which have allowed worker representatives, or their accountants, this right, and that requires a degree of trust on the part of unions which, if not present, risks merely fuelling cynicism and suspicion. Last, employers need not compile or assemble any information where this would involve an amount of work or expenditure 'out of reasonable proportion to the value of the information in the conduct of collective bargaining'.[198] This exception assumes both that the value of information can be objectively assessed and, moreover, that it can be assessed before disclosure. However, the Code goes beyond the statute in recommending that employers should present information in a form and style which recipients can reasonably be expected to understand,[199] and clearly it may be in the interests of employers to sustain any additional costs involved in doing this.

The general tenor of the Code is that the parties should try to reach their own understanding as to how the duty to disclose can best be fulfilled,[200] in contrast to the adversarial approach of the statute (which the CAC has attempted to minimise[201]) which seems to cast the employer in a role of 'reluctant divulger of secrets rather than active participant in information transmission'.[202] This is reinforced by the emphasis upon the confidentiality of information as a ground for withholding information. One method of circumventing this would be to allow privileged access to union representatives but to make this access subject to a duty of confidentiality: ILO Recommendation 163 states that 'where the disclosure of ... information could be prejudicial to the undertaking, its communication could be made conditional upon a commitment that it would be regarded as confidential to the extent required ...'.[203] This solution is adopted in ICER 2004 and TICER 1999.[204]Clearly, however, it runs the risk of placing union representatives, as bearers of knowledge denied to members, in an invidious position.[205]

9.24 Where an employer fails to disclose information the union may complain to the CAC which may refer the complaint to ACAS for conciliation if it considers

195 See, for example, *Annual Reports* for 1991, 1992, and 1993.
196 TULRCA 1992, s 182(2).
197 Joint Regulation of Working Life Act 1976.
198 TULRCA 1992, s 182(2).
199 ACAS Code No 2, para 21.
200 ACAS Code No 2, para 22.
201 See, for example, *Annual Report*, 1993, para 3.4 and 1994, para 2.3.
202 Gospel and Willman, 1981: p 22.
203 Art 7(2)(a).
204 See paras 9.56 and 9.63 below.
205 In its *Annual Report*, 1996, para 2.7 the CAC referred rather cryptically to the possiblity of an employer 'negotiating some understanding with a trade union officer over a wider release of confidential information' relating to a job evaluation exercise.

that this is reasonably likely to produce a settlement.[206] The CAC also seeks to encourage the parties to resolve their differences jointly, and generally holds an informal meeting involving a chairman, both parties and usually an ACAS conciliator as the first stage of the proceedings, although this may depend upon whether conciliation measures have already been attempted unsuccessfully prior to the presentation of the complaint. Failing a resolution of the complaint, the case proceeds to a full hearing, at which the parties are sometimes legally represented, following which the CAC makes a declaration on whether it finds the complaint well-founded, giving reasons. If the declaration requires the employer to disclose information and this is not done within the specified period, the union may present a further complaint to the CAC, and at the same time or subsequently present a claim that contracts of particular descriptions of employees should include specified terms and conditions.[207] The CAC, if it upholds the complaint, may, after hearing the parties, make an award (either in the terms sought by the union or otherwise) which takes effect as a term in the contracts of the employees affected, and may be superseded or varied only by a subsequent award under the same procedure, a collective agreement between the employer and the union representing those employees, or by express or implied agreement between the employer and individual employees if that agreement improves upon the terms specified in the award. This sanction thus constitutes a rare example of direct statutory intervention in the contract. However, as a remedy it contains significant weaknesses. First, it means that the duty to disclose cannot, ultimately, be enforced.[208] Second, although the duty is framed in terms of 'workers', only 'employees' may be the subject of a claim for improved terms and conditions. Third, although the duty covers information in the possession of an associated employer, there is no provision for a remedy against an associated employer who fails to comply. Fourth, there is no penal element allowed for in the award[209] and an employer whose terms and conditions compare favourably with those of others in the area may therefore have little to fear. Finally, the CAC is not empowered to prescribe the information which should be disclosed on future occasions,[210] although clearly the parties may be guided in their behaviour by the outcome of previous complaints. However, the fact that the CAC may adjudicate only upon a past failure to disclose means that 'the matter in dispute has to be capable of being pursued over a considerable length of time. Otherwise it will mean the employer can delay disclosure of the information until its usefulness is limited or has passed.'[211]

---

206 TULRCA 1992, s 183.

207 TULRCA 1992, ss 184, 185.

208 *Quaere* whether the CAC could award any of the information sought as part of the contracts of employment. In *Holokrome Ltd v ASTMS* (CAC, 6 August 1979, unreported) the CAC did not accept the employer's argument that it could not award any of the information sought; the test was whether what was claimed was appropriate as a term or condition of an individual contract. In its decision the CAC thought that individual contracts could contain a term requiring information about salary ranges and increments within the grade in which an employee fell. However the actual award does not appear to mention 'information'; the CAC awarded that the salary ranges and increments should have effect as part of the contracts of employment.

209 Another option would be a fixed sum payable to employees; cf, for example, the remedy for failure to provide an individual employee with a written statement of reasons for dismissal: see para 5.91 above.

210 *R v CAC, ex p BTP Tioxide Ltd* [1981] ICR 843 at 859.

211 Gospel and Lockwood, 1999: p 245.

9.25   In practice there has been only limited recourse to the enforcement provisions. Between February 1977 (when these provisions came into force) and the end of 2004, 518 complaints had been received of which only 13.13% went to a full hearing.[212] The majority of the balance were withdrawn after a settlement had been reached, a tribute to the success of the CAC's procedure which favours the avoidance of 'win/lose scenarios'.[213] The highest number of complaints in any year was 62 (in 1978) and in many there have been considerably fewer.[214] This does not of itself indicate that the disclosure provisions have had little impact; their existence may have encouraged voluntary disclosure, a view endorsed by the CAC itself.[215] Moreover, from another angle, unions may think twice about pursuing complaints in a climate where, if not in the instant claim,[216] recognition obtained outside the statutory procedure may be jeopardised by such a course of action. However, it seems to be generally accepted that the limited scope of the information of which disclosure may be ordered has contributed to the low level of recourse to this provision.[217] Its survival in a period of overt hostility to collective bargaining when the Conservative Government was in office could be regarded as a tribute to its ineffectual nature.[218] In its present form it perpetuates a view of workers as on 'the outside' of the enterprise, in comparison, for example, with shareholders, a view that ICER 2004, discussed in para 9.50 *et seq*, has the potential to ameliorate, although much will depend upon the nature of the agreements for information and consultation that employers reach and how these agreements operate in practice.

The legal effect of collective agreements

9.26   We discussed the role of collective agreements as a source of law in chapters 2 and 4. In those chapters we noted that collective agreements had become, and remained, an important source of norms despite their independence from the formal legal system. As we indicated, collective agreements are, in general, not legally enforceable between the collective parties nor do they automatically take effect as terms of individual employment contracts, the latter occurring only with the consent, express or implied, of the individual parties.

---

212   Information supplied by the CAC.

213   *Annual Report*, 1996, para 2.2. There have been only two cases to date where the CAC has had to issue a second award after an employer's failure to honour the first declaration.

214   Information supplied by the CAC. In the period 1 April 2003–31 March 2004, there were six complaints received: *Annual Report* 2003–2004: p 20.

215   *Annual Report* for 1993, para 3.4.

216   *Ackrill Newspapers Ltd v NUJ* (CAC, 14 February 1992, unreported): provided the union was recognised at the time of the request subsequent derecognition is irrelevant. See also *HM Prison Service v POA* (CAC, 27 March 1995, unreported) IRLB No 523, p 9: an employer cannot avoid the obligation to supply information by announcing in a given situation that it has decided not to negotiate.

217   For an analysis of the matters in relation to which information has been sought, and CAC decisions up to the time of their respective publication, see Gospel and Willman, 1981; L Dickens and G Bain, 1986: pp 94–101; Gospel and Lockwood, 1999. In recent years information has been sought on a wide range of issues, including staffing, grading and pay distribution; pensions; financial information; market-testing and contracting-out; and redundancy plans and selection procedures.

218   The Conservative Government's last White Paper in the area, *Industrial Action and Trade Unions*, Cm 3470, 1996, sought views on the abolition of the statutory procedure in favour of allowing disclosure of information to be the product of voluntary agreement between employers and unions: paras 3.4–3.5.

We also noted the lack of legal regulation of the content of collective agreements which, specific statutory exceptions aside, remains a matter for the negotiating parties. In this section we explore in greater detail the statutory concept of a 'collective agreement' and consider what is required if the collective parties wish to displace the statutory presumption of non-enforceability and to accord their agreements legal force.[219] We also discuss the status of those agreements which fall outside the statutory definition and are thereby not subject to the statutory presumption.

A 'collective agreement' generally means 'any agreement or arrangement made by or on behalf of one or more trade unions and one or more employers or employers' associations and relating to one or more of the matters specified' in TULRCA 1992, section 178(2).[220] These matters are, in brief, the terms and conditions of employment, or the physical conditions in which any workers are required to work; the engagement or non-engagement, or termination or suspension of employment or the duties of employment, of one or more workers; the allocation of work or duties as between workers; disciplinary matters; a worker's membership or non-membership of a trade union; facilities for union officials; and machinery for negotiation or consultation, and other procedures, relating to any of the above.[221] Such an agreement is conclusively presumed not to have been intended by the parties to be a legally enforceable contract unless the agreement is in writing and contains a provision which (however expressed) states that the parties intend the agreement to be a legally enforceable contract.[222] The courts have taken a strict approach to what is required to demonstrate this intention. A statement merely that the parties intend their agreement to be 'binding' will not suffice as this could equally mean 'binding in honour only'. In the words of Scott J, '[u]nless a collective agreement contains a statement in terms that show, at least, that the parties have directed their minds to the question of legal enforceability and have decided in favour of ... [it], there is, in my

219 Note that agreements made between 1 December 1971 and 16 December 1974 were, under the IRA 1971, conclusively presumed to be legally enforceable unless they contained an express exclusion clause. It was almost universal practice for them to contain such a clause: see para 2.9 above.
220 TULRCA 1992, s 178(1). For the purpose of excluding or modifying provisions of the WTR 1998, determining the terms upon which parental leave is taken, and modifying provisions relating to successive fixed-term contracts, however, the union parties are required to be 'independent': see paras 4.77, 6.104 and 5.78. For the purposes of s 178(1) it is irrelevant how an agreement was achieved, and the fact that it requires endorsement from another body makes no difference to its status: *Edinburgh Council v Brown* [1999] IRLR 208. In *Burke v Royal Liverpool University Hospital NHS Trust* [1997] ICR 730, the EAT, in holding that an exchange of letters between the employer and the union as to future terms of employment could constitute a 'collective agreement', stated at 738 that there needed to be 'a mutual intention on the part of employers and employees' bargaining agents to enter into a collective bargain, the effect of which will be to modify the contracts of employment between employer and employee'. The latter constitutes a gloss on the statute, and does not cater for procedural agreements or other agreements not dealing with substantive terms and conditions of employment. In *HM Prison Service v Bewley* [2004] ICR 422, the EAT held that where a collective agreement itself provides a mechanism for the final resolution of disputes (short of industrial action) in the form of binding pendulum arbitration, the arbitrator's award constitutes a 'collective agreement'.
221 These matters, which are analysed in greater detail in para 11.27 below, also constitute the subject matter of 'collective bargaining': see para 7.27 above.
222 TULRCA 1992, s 179(1), (2). Parts only of the agreement may be specified as intended to be enforceable; the presumption against enforceability will then apply to the remainder: s 179(3).

view, no sufficient statement of intention ...'[223] However, while such a statement is a prerequisite to enforceability it does not follow that an agreement which includes it will necessarily constitute a contract; it may, for example, use language which is insufficiently clear to be judicially interpreted, or void as in restraint of trade, or for some other reason not a contract. In practice it is very rare for the collective parties to attempt to make their agreements legally enforceable[224] (although, as we saw in chapter 4, this does not prevent them being a source of enforceable terms of individual employment contracts).

Agreements may be made between employers and unions which fall outside the statutory definition of 'collective agreements'. Examples would include those concerning union involvement in future investment decisions or product development relating to the undertaking. These agreements are governed by the common law, which offers no clear guidance. It would be open to the parties to stipulate that they intended their agreement to constitute a contract and provided that the terms were sufficiently certain to be capable of enforcement by the courts, there would seem to be no barrier to this. If the agreement were silent on the question of intention it seems probable, in the light of *Ford Motor Co Ltd v AEU*,[225] that a court would conclude that the parties had not intended to create legal relations although it is conceivable (if unlikely) that the 'climate of opinion' may change so as to provide a different answer to that given in that case.

The effect of a transfer of the undertaking

9.27   As we discussed in chapter 3, when an undertaking is transferred within the meaning of these terms in TUPE 1981 a variety of consequences follow. There are two which relate specifically to collective bargaining.

First, regulation 9 states that where the transferor employer recognised an independent trade union in respect of the employees transferred the transferee is deemed to recognise the union to the same extent provided that the undertaking or part transferred 'maintains an identity distinct from the remainder of the transferee's undertaking'. This means that all rights which are dependent upon recognition will apply in the transferred undertaking. However, the requirement that a distinct identity is maintained may be difficult to show when the transferee already operates an undertaking of its own; it is common in such circumstances for trading methods, etc, as well as employee terms and conditions to be harmonised.[226] The practical effect of this provision is further weakened by the fact that where the employer has recognised the union voluntarily (and not pursuant to a statutory request for recognition) there is nothing in the Regulations to prevent the transferee employer varying recognition or derecognising the union after the transfer, subject to the existence of contractual obligations consequent upon recognition (see para 9.4) and any obligations relating to

---

223 *NCB v NUM* [1986] IRLR 439, 449. See also *Monterosso Shipping Co Ltd v ITWF* [1982] IRLR 468.

224 The collective agreement to ensure staff relations are conducted peacefully and without disruption to operations at GCHQ, 3 September 1997, and the 2004 Joint Industrial Relations Procedural Agreement in the prison service (and its 2001 predecessor) are notable exceptions to this: see further para 11.14 below.

225 [1969] 2 QB 303; see para 2.9 above.

226 The precise meaning of 'distinct identity' has not, to date, been clarified: it could require a separate legal structure or merely a separate management structure.

disclosure of information (see para 9.22 *et seq*) or consultation (see para 9.29) which may already have arisen. However, if a transferor employer were to derecognise a union prior to the transfer at the insistence of the transferee it may be possible to argue, by analogy with *Litster v Forth Dry Dock and Engineering Co Ltd*[227] that recognition should nevertheless continue to the point of transfer. Where the transferor recognised the union pursuant to a CAC declaration or 'agreement for recognition' (see para 9.6), it would seem to be the case that the transferee employer will be bound by the same obligations as the transferor if the undertaking or part transferred maintains a distinct identity, given that the union is 'deemed to have been recognised by the transferee to the same extent' in respect of the employees for which it was recognised by the transferor. Thus the transferee would be unable, for example, unilaterally to terminate an agreement for recognition before three years had expired from the date of the agreement. However, the Regulations apply only to recognition in respect of 'employees', not, like the recognition procedure, 'workers'.[228] Thus, if the transferor's workers who comprised the bargaining unit were not employees, recognition would not transfer; if only some were employees and recognition were pursuant to a CAC declaration, the transferee employer would be able to invoke the statutory procedure applicable to changes in the bargaining unit outlined in para 9.19 above. ERelA 2004 empowers the Secretary of State to make provision by order for cases where, *inter alia*, an employer's identity has changed after a declaration of recognition.[229] At the time of writing no such regulations have yet been issued.

Second, regulation 6 provides that any 'collective agreement'[230] made by the transferor employer with a union recognised in respect of an employee whose contract is preserved by regulation 5(1) applies to that employee as if made by the transferee. In the light of the presumption that collective agreements are not intended by the parties to be legally enforceable contracts (a presumption expressly preserved by the regulation) this provision also is of limited significance, although it may be relevant in contexts where regard is paid to the terms of collective agreements in determining the scope of individual employees' rights, such as whether it was reasonable for a union official or member to claim time off for union duties or activities. Extra-contractual disciplinary and redundancy procedures may also be relevant to unfair dismissal claims.

Regulation 6 will also be important where employees have a contractual entitlement to have their terms and conditions of employment determined by reference to the collective agreement from time to time negotiated between the transferor employer and a specific union or unions. In *Whent v T Cartledge Ltd*[231] the applicant employees had been employed until 1994 by the London Borough of Brent, and their contracts specified that their terms of employment would be in accordance with the agreement made by a specific National Joint

---

227 [1989] IRLR 161. See further para 5.196 above.
228 See further para 3.19 *et seq* and 3.51 *et seq* for analysis of these terms.
229 TULRCA 1992, Sch A1, paras 169B, 169 C, inserted by ERelA 2004, s 18.
230 Defined as in TULRCA 1992, 178(1): see para 9.26 above.
231 [1997] IRLR 153. Cf *William West and Sons (Ilkeston) Ltd v Fairgieve and EXEL/BRS Ltd*, (2000) IRLB January 2000, Vol 632, p 15, EAT: on the proper construction of the contract of employment the name of the transferee had been substituted for that of the transferor; *Atkinclose v Gateshead MPC* [2005] IRLR 79, EAT: contract of employment made reference only to a specific agreement; successor agreement not incorporated. See also *Ralton v Havering College of Further Education* [2001] IRLR 738.

Council ('NJC'). In 1994 the activities of the Borough which the applicants were employed to fulfil were taken over by a private contractor which, after the transfer, wrote to their union withdrawing recognition and stating that any collective agreements which may have been in force covering the transferred employees no longer had effect. The applicants sued for the benefit of new pay rates subsequently agreed by the NJC, and the EAT held that their contracts of employment continued, by virtue of regulation 5 of TUPE, to provide that terms were determined by reference to the NJC agreement and it was irrelevant that their employer was not a party to that agreement.

Regulation 6 also states that 'anything done under or in connection with' the collective agreement by or in relation to the transferor before the transfer shall, after the transfer, be deemed to have been done by or in relation to the transferee. The meaning of this is obscure. It has been suggested that it includes commitments or offers made by the transferor during negotiations which have not yet been formalised in an agreement; if so, in the light of the opening words of the regulation, it can cover only changes to an existing agreement.[232]

It is debatable whether the UK currently complies with the Acquired Rights Directive in relation to collective agreements. The Directive provides that following a transfer 'the transferee shall continue to observe the terms and conditions agreed in any collective agreement on the same terms applicable to the transferor under that agreement, until the date of termination or expiry of the collective agreement or the entry into force or application of another collective agreement'.[233] Member States may limit the period for observing such terms and conditions, subject to a minimum period of a year. Although in the British context some terms of a collective agreement may be incorporated into individual contracts of employment, and may thus, as we described in para 3.110 (and in *Whent v T Cartledge Ltd*, above), be preserved under regulation 5, some terms are not appropriate for incorporation and there is, therefore, nothing to prevent the transferee departing from them.[234] In 1989 the European Commission gave notice to the UK government that it had failed to comply with its obligations under the Directive in a number of respects which we outline in para 9.31. Among these was the complaint that the legislation did not require a transferee to continue to observe the terms and conditions agreed in any collective agreement on the same terms applicable to the transferor. It did not, in the event, proceed with this complaint.

Contract compliance and collective bargaining

9.28   As we saw in chapter 7, it was an important feature of the policy of successive governments from early in the twentieth century until 1979 that the government should act as a model employer which set an example in its employment practices to the private sector, a strategy which served, in some respects, as a substitute for legislation.[235] As we explained this policy was partly promoted by the strategy of contract compliance, whereby government

---

232 Younson, 1989: p 115.

233 See now Council Directive 2001/23/EC, Art 3(3).

234 In the case of employers whose decisions are potentially subject to judicial review, it is conceivable that a public law remedy may be sought but the circumstances would probably need to be unusual and this is not a remedy of general application.

235 For a general discussion of this policy, and subsequent developments in the area, see Fredman and Morris, 1989: ch 12.

departments undertook, in furtherance of a succession of House of Commons Fair Wages Resolutions, to include in contracts with private sector employers a term that contractors should pay their workers the 'going rate' for the job. This was defined in the 1946 Resolution specifically by reference to collective agreements for the trade or industry in the district made by substantially representative organisations. Although not covered by the Resolution, local authorities and other public employers were encouraged by successive governments to follow suit and did so regardless of their political hue: a 1982 survey of local authorities in Britain showed that over 87% inserted a fair wages clause in their outside contracts.[236]

The advent of the Thatcher Conservative Government in 1979 heralded a very different concept of the model state employer. As we described in para 8.32, the government not only rescinded the Fair Wages Resolution in 1983, itself a radical break with tradition; it went further and took steps to prevent the operation of contract compliance policies. The 1982 legislation, as well as covering union membership, also rendered void in contracts for the supply of goods or services any term or condition which required a party to recognise a union for its workers or any class of worker or negotiate with or consult a union official.[237] In addition it created a statutory duty not to exclude a person from a list of approved suppliers, or to terminate or refuse to consider entering contracts with them, if one of the grounds was that such a requirement was unlikely to be met.[238] As in the case of union membership, this duty is owed both to the potential contractor and to 'any other person who may be adversely affected by its contravention'.[239] Organising or threatening industrial action to induce a person to include a term requiring recognition, etc, or to take a decision in relation to a contract with reference to one of these factors, also has no immunity in tort.[240] However, unlike the union membership provision, which covers insistence both on membership and non-membership, no reciprocal ban exists on taking decisions relating to contracts on the ground that a contractor recognises, rather than refuses to recognise, a union.

This legislation did not prevent the operation of fair wages clauses or insistence that contractors complied with the terms of collective agreements provided that this was not expressly linked to union recognition, and the practices of local authorities, for example, appear to have continued unchanged after it was introduced, despite government exhortations to follow its own example and abandon them. Such arrangements were finally prohibited altogether by the Local Government Act 1988 which forbids local authorities and several other public bodies from operating contracts by reference to 'non-commercial matters',[241] which, *inter alia*, cover fair wages clauses. The Act enables any person who has suffered loss or damage due to a breach of this provision to sue for damages and potential and former contractors are specifically empowered to bring judicial review proceedings.[242] The latter persons also have the right to written reasons for the decision in relation to a particular contract on request.[243]

---

236 Ingham and Thomson, 1982: table 5A.
237 See now TULRCA 1992, s 186.
238 TULRCA 1992, s 187.
239 TULRCA 1992, s 187(3).
240 TULRCA 1992, s 225.
241 LGA 1988, s 17.
242 LGA 1988, s 19(7).
243 LGA 1988, s 20.

There is no statutory restriction on organisations not covered by the 1988 Act from operating such clauses but in practice their use by such bodies is likely to be limited. To date, the advent of a Labour Government in 1997 has brought no material change to this area. The Local Government Act 1999 empowers the Secretary of State to provide by order in relation to local authorities and other 'best value' bodies that any matter should cease to be a 'non-commercial' matter.[244] At the time of writing three matters, including the terms and conditions of employment of workers, are no longer to be treated as 'non-commercial', but only so far as necessary or expedient to permit or facilitate compliance with the best value requirements of the Act or where there is a transfer of staff to which TUPE may apply.[245] The general prohibition on prescribing recognition or consultation has remained untouched, and there are no indications that it will be subject to amendment.

STATUTORY RIGHTS OF INFORMATION AND CONSULTATION

Overview

9.29   There are four distinct contexts in which all employers have a statutory duty to consult employee representatives: in relation to dismissals for redundancy; where there is a transfer of the undertaking; on health and safety matters;[246] and (where the employer recognises an independent trade union) before contracting-out of the state earnings related pensions scheme. In addition, employers must consult on training matters if they recognise a union in accordance with the statutory procedure and certain other conditions are met.[247] Finally, at domestic level, from 6 April 2005 undertakings employing at least 150 employees in the UK may be required to inform and consult representatives (or, in certain circumstances, employees themselves) on a wider range of matters, as may those employing a minimum of 100 employees on 6 April 2007 and a minimum of 50 a year later.[248] A further (limited) class of employers is subject to transnational consultation obligations; these are discussed separately in para 9.59 *et seq* below.

Collective bargaining and the current statutory forms of consultation are both based upon collective representation. However, there is a crucial difference between them; whereas, as we explained above, bargaining connotes joint regulation of a particular area, in the case of consultation the right to decide remains ultimately with the employer. However, this does not mean that the

---

244 LGA 1999, s 19. 'Best value' authorities are defined in s 1; see also s 2.

245 The Local Government Best Value (Exclusion of Non-Commercial Considerations) Order 2001, 2001/909; see further para 2.6 above. Note also the Local Government (Best Value) Performance Plans and Reviews Order 1999 (SI 1999/3251), as amended by SI 2003/662, which requires local authorities to consult recognised unions and organisations representing relevant staff, and staff themselves, in conducting best value reviews.

246 In this area, unlike the other three, employers also have the option of consulting employees individually: see further para 9.46 below.

247 If a method of collective bargaining has been specified by the CAC and the parties have not varied its content or legal effect.

248 Directive 2004/3426 requires implementation on 23 March of the respective years; however the Government has applied its general policy of bringing new employment law into force on two dates only, 1 October and 6 April.

consultation process is a mere formality; serious consequences may ensue if an employer fails to meet its obligations. Moreover, in legal terms 'consultation' may mean different things in different contexts; thus, in relation to redundancies, for example, the employer must undertake consultation 'with a view to reaching agreement', a requirement which takes it close to negotiation.

In Britain legislation relating to consultation is of relatively recent origin. Historically the concept was not unknown but it was a purely voluntary practice. As Davies and Freedland explain:

> There has always been in the UK during this century a commitment amongst some employers and trade unions to the notion of consultation, even if it has been overshadowed by the development of collective bargaining. In the inter-war period certain progressive employers ... developed systems of consultation with their employees, generally through structures in which trade unions were accorded no role, the employee representatives being elected by and from the whole body of workers. Such forms of consultation can act as much to keep trade unions at bay as to involve employees in determining matters affecting their working lives. In the Second World War and the immediate post-war period there was a great development of Joint Production Committees, a tangible expression of the commitment of both unions and employers to the war effort, which committees the trade unions backed and were involved in. That joint commitment was dissipated in the 1950s and, with the growth of plant-level structures for bargaining with employers through shop stewards, the machinery for consultation, the lesser form of participation, naturally underwent a demise.[249]

During the 1970s, joint consultative committees once again became more common, and in 1980 they were reported in around a third of workplaces with 25 or more employees, although by 1990 this figure had fallen to 29%[250] In 1998, just over half such workplaces had a committee which either operated in the workplace or elsewhere in the organisation, although this does not provide a direct comparison with earlier surveys because the latter counted higher level committees only if local representatives attended meetings.[251] A constant feature of the surveys, however, has been the higher incidence of committees in workplaces where unions are recognised. In 1998 the primary matters discussed by these committees were working practices, health and safety, welfare services and facilities, and future workplace plans.[252] It is notable that these issues clearly exceed the scope of matters traditionally viewed as suitable for collective bargaining.

9.30 Legal obligations in Britain in the area of information and consultation derive almost entirely from EC law. From the early 1970s worker representation and participation was a central feature of European Community social policy proposals and the European Commission drafted a range of legislative measures in this area[253] designed to influence practices both within Member States and at transnational level. For many years little of this prodigious output was translated into practice; successive drafts of the European company statute, requiring

---

249 P Davies and M Freedland, 1984: pp 230–231.
250 Millward *et al*, 1992: pp 151–155. See also MacInnes, 1985.
251 Cully *et al*, 1999: pp 98–112.
252 Cully *et al*: p 101.
253 See Hall, 1992; Cressey, 1993; Wedderburn, 1997; and Weiss, 2004 for a discussion of these initiatives.

European Companies or Societas Europeae (SE) to allow employees to participate in the supervision and strategic development of the company;[254] the fifth company law Directive; and the 'Vredeling' Directive on procedures for informing and consulting employees in multinational and multi-establishment enterprises via local management all failed to gain acceptance, and the only measures enacted by the Community were those requiring the provision of information to, and consultation with, worker representatives in the contexts of redundancies, transfers of undertakings and health and safety.[255] It will raise little surprise that the UK Conservative government was obdurately opposed to all these abortive initiatives although, in fairness, it was probably not alone in this; the Vredeling Directive, for example, attracted strong opposition from multinational business.[256] The difficulties of making any progress in this area were further compounded by the diversity of national systems of employee representation. However the Commission had greater success when, in the late 1980s, it focused more specifically upon the transnational dimension of employee information and consultation. This strategy was reflected in the Community Charter of the Fundamental Social Rights of Workers, concluded in 1989, which, in stating that '[i]nformation, consultation and participation for workers must be developed along appropriate lines, taking account of the practices in force in the various Member States',[257] affirmed that this was to apply especially in companies with establishments in several Member States. The Action Programme which accompanied the Charter eventually bore fruit in the shape of the European Works Council Directive, passed under the Agreement on Social Policy (from which the UK initially opted-out),[258] whose preamble stresses that national legislation is frequently not oriented to the transnational nature of the entity which takes decisions and emphasises the need to ensure that workers are informed and consulted about decisions taken in other Member States. Following the UK opt-in to the Agreement on Social Policy in 1997, the Directive was extended to the UK, with an implementation date of December 1999,[259] resulting in regulations which we discuss in para 9.60 *et seq* below. In December 2000 another important breakthrough for the Commission came when, thirty years after its first proposal, the Council of Ministers reached political agreement on a Regulation to establish a European Company Statute, allowing companies to form an SE which can operate under Community law throughout the EU, together with a related Directive concerning worker involvement in such companies. UK legislation to implement this provision came into force in October 2004.[260] Finally, in March 2002, agreement was reached on a Directive establishing an EU-wide framework of minimum standards of

---

254 See Wedderburn, 1990: ch 5.

255 The Merger Control Regulation 4064/89 (see Anderman, 1993) gave a limited right to recognised representatives of workforces affected by a merger to be heard by the Commission as part of the process of deciding whether or not to approve that merger. This, however, is a right to be heard by a public authority rather than an employer.

256 P Davies, 1992: p 333.

257 Art 17.

258 Council Directive 94/45 of 22 September 1994 on the establishment of a European Works Council or a procedure in Community-scale undertakings and Community-scale groups of undertakings for the purposes of informing and consulting employees. See Gold and Hall, 1994 for the background to this Directive; see also Colaianni, 1996. The Directive was extended to cover the three other Member States of the European Economic Area in June 1995.

259 See Barnard, 1997, for the procedure adopted in relation to the extension directive.

260 EPLLCR 2004; see further para 9.65.

information and consultation at national level in undertakings where 50 or more employees are employed covering, *inter alia*, the development of employment within the undertaking and decisions likely to lead to substantial changes in work organisation or in contractual relations.[261] This proposal was initially vehemently resisted by the UK Government, which preferred any such arrangements to be adopted on a purely voluntary basis, but after other countries previously opposed to it had indicated their willingness to compromise, the UK reluctantly agreed to it, having secured a longer transition period for its full implementation.[262] Thus, although Member States in general were required to implement the Directive by 23 March 2005, a state in which there was, at the date of the Directive's entry into force, no 'general, permanent and statutory system of information and consultation of employees', nor such a system of employee representation at the workplace, was permitted to limit the application of national provisions to undertakings employing at least 150 employees until 23 March 2007, and those employing at least 100 employees until the following year.[263] We discuss in greater detail the requirements of the Directive, and the extent to which UK law may fall short of its requirements, in para 9.50 *et seq* below.

9.31   It remains to be seen whether the newly-introduced UK legislation relating to information and consultation will lead to infringement proceedings before the ECJ. An earlier version of the legislation relating to redundancies and transfers of undertakings was subject to such proceedings, and it was amended in a number of respects, with significant implications for patterns of collective representation in general. The Directive on Collective Redundancies[264] and the Acquired Rights Directive[265] require the provision of information to, and consultation with, the 'worker' or 'employee' representatives respectively provided for by the law or practice of the Member States. The redundancy procedure was initially enacted as part of the Labour government's 'Social Contract' legislation in 1975 which it was likely would, in any event, have contained provisions on this subject although their shape was clearly influenced by the Directive.[266] By contrast, the transfer provisions were introduced in 1981 by the Conservative government only after the Commission had begun non-implementation proceedings in the ECJ, and even then it gave effect to the Directive with overt reluctance.[267] In both cases, the duty to consult arose only where the employer recognised a trade union for the category of employees affected.

From an early stage commentators had questioned whether either of the UK provisions in their initial form met the requirements of the respective Directives

---

261 Directive 2002/14/EC.

262 See Bercusson, 2002 for the background to the Directive; also useful is P Lorber, 2003.

263 Directive 2002/14/EC, Art 10. Alternatively, such states could limit the application of the Directive by reference to the number employed at establishments, but the UK chose the option in the text.

264 Council Directive 75/129 on the approximation of the laws of the Member States relating to collective redundancies. The Directive was amended in 1992 by Council Directive 92/56, and both Directives were consolidated in Council Directive 98/59/EC.

265 Council Directive 77/187 on the approximation of the laws of the Member States relating to the safeguarding of employees' rights in the event of transfers of undertakings, businesses or parts of businesses. The Directive was amended by Council Directive 98/50/EC, and both Directives were consolidated in Council Directive 2001/23/EC.

266 P Davies, 1992: p 328. For a more detailed discussion of the background to the Directive and to the 1975 Act see Freedland, 1976a.

267 P Davies and M Freedland, 1993: p 577.

and in 1992 the European Commission instigated infringement proceedings citing a number of deficiences.[268] Most of these had been admitted by the UK Government by the time the matter came before the ECJ, and important amendments were introduced in TURERA 1993 to correct them. (It is arguable, however, that other deficiencies, which were not grounds of complaint in those proceedings, still remain; we address these below.) The major outstanding issue from the infringement proceedings was the lack of any provision in UK law for the designation of worker representatives where the employer failed to recognise a union. The Commission argued that, for the obligations in the Directives to be effective, Member States must take all appropriate measures to ensure that representatives were designated; in UK law designation could be prevented where the employer was not in agreement. For its part, the UK contended that the Directives were not intended to amend existing laws or practices concerning designation. While accepting this argument the Court affirmed, on the basis of its previous decisions, that national legislation which made it possible to impede protection unconditionally guaranteed to workers was contrary to EC law.[269] The Directives left to Member States only the task of determining the arrangements for designating representatives; they could not be deprived of full effect by failing to have any system of designation whatsoever.

As a result of this decision, the Conservative Government introduced the Collective Redundancies and Transfer of Undertakings (Protection of Employment) (Amendment) Regulations 1995,[270] which required employers to consult, at their choice, *either* a recognised trade union or elected representatives of any of the employees who may be dismissed. The Regulations also made other significant amendments to the legislation.[271] Most notably, they provided that the duty to consult representatives on proposed redundancies arose only where the employer was proposing to dismiss 20 or more employees at one establishment within a period of 90 days or less. Although this threshold accords with the Directive,[272] prior to this the UK provisions had been more favourable, requiring consultation where only one employee was affected.[273] It was estimated

---

268 Case C-382/92 *EC Commission v United Kingdom* [1994] IRLR 392 (transfers) and Case C-383/92 [1994] IRLR 412 (collective redundancies).

269 See Case 61/81 *EC Commission v United Kingdom* [1982] IRLR 333.

270 SI 1995/2587.

271 For an overview of the Regulations, see Hall, 1996 and Wedderburn ,1997 and on their operation in practice see J Smith *et al*, 1999 and Hall and Edwards, 1999. Hall and Edwards report that hardly any employers which recognised trade unions took the 'non-union' option: pp 306–308. Cf Cully *et al*,1999: p 97.

272 Council Directive 75/129, Art 1(1)(a). The alternative threshold under the Directive is that the number of redundancies is, over a period of 30 days, at least 10 in establishments employing more than 20 and fewer than 100 workers; at least 10% of the number of workers in establishments normally employing at least 100 but fewer than 300; or at least 30 workers in establishments employing 300 or more. See Barnard, 2000: p 490 for a useful table summarising the definition of collective dismissals in the Member States.

273 In *R v Secretary of State for Trade and Industry, ex p Unison* [1996] IRLR 438 the Divisional Court rejected the argument that by effecting this amendment of TULRCA 1992, s 188(1) by secondary legislation under the ECA 1972, s 2(2)(b), the Secretary of State was acting *ultra vires*, holding that 'the obligation to consult a trade union in regard to one redundancy' was 'related to a Community obligation, and not distinct, separate, or divorced from it' (per Otton LJ at 443). The Court also rejected the argument that because statistical evidence showed that one-third of women were employed in workplaces with fewer than 20 employees as compared with one-quarter of men, the change constituted unlawful discrimination contrary to Art 119 (now 141) of the EC Treaty and the Equal Treatment Directive 76/207 because more women than men worked in workplaces where

by the Government that this amendment would remove the statutory obligation to consult from some 96% of UK businesses.[274]

Although the Employment Department claimed that the 1995 Regulations brought UK law into compliance with the Directives it is debatable whether was the case.[275] Further amending Regulations were introduced in 1999, following a fresh complaint by the European Commission to the UK Government that the Directives had not been properly implemented, questioning in particular the procedures for designating employee representatives and the effectiveness of the sanctions if employers failed to meet their obligations. Major changes introduced in 1999 included more detailed regulation of the election of employee representatives; the requirement that, if the employer recognised an independent trade union, its representatives should be consulted (so removing the employer's option to consult employee representatives in such circumstances); and, in relation to transfers, increased compensation for employees if an employer failed to meet its obligations. However, the 20-employee threshold introduced in 1995 remained, despite earlier indications that the Government was inclined to remove it.[276] Its maintenance does not mean that consultation becomes a purely voluntary act where fewer employees are dismissed, however; where those individuals qualify to claim unfair dismissal, employers must (unless particular circumstances apply)[277] follow the statutory dismissal and disciplinary procedure discussed in para 5.124 *et seq* which requires a meeting with the employee prior to dismissal.[278] Moreover,

20 or more employees could not be made redundant. The Court appears to have accepted the Government's argument that the impact of the measure could not be inferred from an analysis based on establishment size; it was necessary to look at the number of redundancies proposed at an establishment. Cf *R v Secretary of State for Employment, ex p Seymour-Smith and Perez (No 2)* [2000] IRLR 263, where the House of Lords was prepared to find prima facie indirect discrimination on the facts when presented with statistical evidence that women disproportionately had less than two years' service; it did not require evidence as to the incidence of dismissals relative to length of service: see further para 3.84 above.

274 DTI press notice, 5 October 1995.

275 A judicial review application in which it was argued, *inter alia*, that the arrangements for selecting employee representatives meant that employers could still impede the protection guaranteed to employees by the Directives was unsuccessful: *R v Secretary of State for Trade and Industry, ex p Unison* [1996] IRLR 438, QBD. See Skidmore, 1996b for a critique of this decision.

276 *Employees' Information and Consultation Rights on Transfers of Undertakings and Collective Redundancies*, Department of Trade and Industry, URN 97/988, February 1998, paras 37–40.

277 See EADRR 2004, reg 4(1)(a) (dismissal of all the employees of a description or in a category to which employee belongs, provided that all are offered re-engagement before or on termination of their contracts) and reg 4(1)(e) (the employer's business suddenly ceases to function, because of an event unforeseen by the employer, with the result that it is impractical for it to employ *any* employees).

278 EA 2002, Sch 2, paras 1–3. There is no requirement to follow the statutory dismissal and disciplinary procedure where a dismissal is one of a number in respect of which TULRCA 1992, s 188 applies. However general standards of procedural fairness, discussed in para 5.136 *et seq*, will continue to apply; *King v Eaton Ltd* [1996] IRLR 199 usefully illustrates the relationship between individual and collective consultation, although failure to follow procedures beyond the statutory minimum will now be subject to the 'no difference' rule under ERA 1996, s 98A(2); see further para 5.143 *et seq*. In the light of the current Regulations consultation with non-union representatives should suffice where no union is recognised. Note that in *King* it was emphasised that fair consultation required consultation 'when the proposals are still at a formative stage': see further the discussion in para 9.33 below.

recognised trade unions may have a right to information about prospective redundancies under the disclosure of information provisions, discussed in para 9.22 *et seq*, where no such qualifying threshold applies.[279] Finally, information and consultation representatives (or, in some circumstances, employees themselves) may have the right to be informed and consulted under ICER 2004 about 'decisions likely to lead to substantial changes in work organisation or in contractual relations' where fewer than 20 employees are involved.[280]

It is strongly arguable that, even after the amendments to the legislation governing collective redundancies and transfers of undertakings, the consultation provisions continue to fall short of the requirements of the respective Directives in important respects. If this is correct, it is conceivable that the *Francovich* principle could be invoked by those affected, although this requires proof that the Member State manifestly and gravely disregarded the limits on its discretion.[281] Moreover, in this context it may be difficult to prove that quantifiable loss was caused by the failure to comply. There has been no ruling as yet by the ECJ in whether the relevant provisions have direct effect, although in proceedings relating to redundancy consultation the High Court has held that, because the Collective Redundancies Directive gives the Member States such a wide discretion in the method of designating worker representatives, it is not unconditional and sufficiently precise to be directly effective.[282] We consider the compatibility of the current Regulations with EC law, as well as the desirability of other amendments, in greater detail in the analysis of the specific requirements of the current legislation which follows.

The duty to consult on redundancies

(i) Situations in which there is a duty to consult

9.32   An employer which is proposing to dismiss as redundant 20 or more employees at one establishment within a period of 90 days or less has a duty to consult about the dismissals 'all the persons who are appropriate representatives of any of the employees who may be affected by the proposed dismissals or may be affected by measures taken in connection with those dismissals'.[283] The duty applies regardless of whether the employees are entitled to a statutory redundancy payment (so can apply where they lack the requisite qualifying period of service or have waived the right to a payment, for example).[284] However the provisions do not apply to employment under a contract for a fixed term of three months

---

279   See, for example, the CAC *Annual Report* 1994, para 2.8.
280   ICER 2004, reg 20(1). Although the DTI Guidance states that this provision does not apply where 'a small number of employees' is to be made redundant, no lower limit is specified; this will depend on the circumstances of the case: *The Information and Consultation [of] Employees Regulations 2004: DTI Guidance*, January 2005: p 43.
281   Cases C-46/93 and C-48/93: *Brasserie du Pecheur SA v Federal Republic of Germany* and *R v Secretary of State for Transport, ex p Factortame Ltd* [1996] ECR I-1029.
282   *Griffin v South West Water Services Ltd* [1995] IRLR 15; cf Skidmore, 1995b. Note that this Directive (unlike the Acquired Rights Directive) does not apply to 'public administrative bodies'. The court in *Griffin* did not accept that such bodies were coincident with those subject to the concept of direct effect but clearly this exclusion would narrow the application of direct effect were it to apply.
283   TULRCA 1992, s 188(1).
284   Note, however, that Crown servants, the armed forces, the police, Parliamentary staff, and share fishermen are excluded from these provisions: TULRCA 1992, ss 273, 274, 277, 278, 280, 284. However the provisions for disclosure for collective bargaining purposes, which may be relevant in the context of redundancies, (see para 9.22 *et seq*), extend to

or less, or under a contract made in contemplation of the performance of a specific task which is not expected to last for more than three months, provided that the employee has not, in fact, been continuously employed for a period for more than three months.[285] This means that, as well as being excluded from the duty, such employees do not count towards the number of employees that triggers the obligation to consult. The Directive excludes collective redundancies effected under contracts of employment concluded for limited periods of time or for specific tasks except where such redundancies take place prior to the date of expiry or the completion of such contracts.[286] The UK exemption is wider in applying also where the redundancies take place prior to the date of expiry or completion, but the Government takes the view that this exclusion is objectively justified on the ground that the contracts in question would generally have terminated prior to the end of the consultation periods.[287]

In the context of the duty to consult, 'redundancy' goes beyond the definition applicable to statutory redundancy payments, extending to dismissal 'for a reason not related to the individual concerned or for a number of reasons all of which are not so related'.[288] It thus applies to dismissals arising from reorganisation or restructuring of a business as well as those arising from closure or slimming down the workforce, for example. Thus, if an employer dismisses employees and offers re-engagement on different terms and conditions it must comply with the duty to consult.[289] A potential difficulty with the definition of redundancy in this context is that it requires 'all' the reasons for dismissal not to relate to the individual concerned. Taken literally, this could narrow the application of the duty considerably, given that selection for redundancy, in the sense used in relation to individual payments, is usually based upon factors relating to the individual such as performance, attendance or, at the very least, length of service. Such an interpretation would not accord with the intention of the government department that introduced the legislation,[290] and would be an appropriate occasion for recourse to the less ambiguous wording of the Directive ('dismissals ... for one or more reasons not related to the individual workers concerned') which the legislation is designed to implement.[291] There is a statutory presumption that a dismissal is for 'redundancy' unless the contrary is proved.[292]

Crown employment, although they apply only where an independent union is recognised for the description of workers in question: see CAC *Annual Reports* for 1993 (para 2.3–2.5), 1994 (para 2.8), 1996 (para 2.9), and 1997 (para 2.13). See para 9.51 below for the application of ICER 2004 to public bodies.

285 TULRCA 1992, s 282(1).
286 Council Directive 98/59/EC, Art 1(2)(a).
287 *Government Response to the Final Consultation on the Draft Fixed Term Employees' (Prevention of Less Favourable Treatment) Regulations 2002.*
288 TULRCA 1992, s 195. Cf ERA 1996, s 139(1), discussed at para 5.165 *et seq*. The extended definition in this context was introduced in 1993 to comply with the requirements of the EC Directive.
289 See *GMB v Man Truck and Bus Ltd* [2000] IRLR 636; *Hardy v Tourism South East* [2005] IRLR 242 (applying *Hogg v Dover College* [1990] ICR 39 and *Alcan Extrusions v Yates* [1996] IRLR 327 in this context).
290 At that time the Employment Department, which in its summary of TURERA (press notice 2 July 1993, p 19) stated that the definition 'is now widened'.
291 Council Directive 98/59, Art 1(1)(a); on the principle of indirect effect see further Case C-14/83 *Von Colson and Kamann v Land Nordrhein-Westfalen* [1984] ECR 1891; Case C-106/89 *Marleasing SA v La Comercial Internacional de Alimentación SA* [1990] ECR I-4135; *Pickstone v Freemans plc* [1988] IRLR 357; *Litster v Forth Dry Dock and Engineering Co Ltd* [1989] IRLR 161.
292 TULRCA 1992, s 195(2).

In determining how many employees an employer is proposing to dismiss, no account is to be taken of any employees in respect of whom it has already begun consulting.[293] As Harvey points out, this can lead to apparently odd results:

> Suppose an employer declares 30 redundancies. Obviously he has to consult about all 30. On the other hand if he proposes 20 dismissals, begins consultations, and then decides that a further 10 dismissals are necessary, there is no duty to consult ... about those additional 10; the original 20 are discounted. Conversely if he begins with 10 (too few to attract the duty to consult) and subsequently adds 20 (within 90 days) then there is once more a duty to consult about all 30; the original 10 are *not* discounted unless the employer has begun consulting about them.[294]

Clearly employers may be tempted to try to avoid their statutory obligation by dividing a large group of redundancies into several successive small groups (although they would need to be aware of the implications of such a course of action as regards the application of the statutory dismissal and disciplinary procedures).[295] In situations where this may have happened, employment tribunals can be expected to scrutinise the evidence carefully to ensure that the employer acted in good faith.[296]

In calculating the number of employees the employer is proposing to dismiss, account is taken only of those working at one 'establishment'. Oddly, given its importance, there is no definition of 'establishment', a concept which exists in a variety of statutory contexts. Prior to a 1995 ECJ decision the courts had taken a fairly wide view of its meaning; although there was no comprehensive test, '[a]mong the relevant factors in determining the scope of an establishment may be the geographical separation of the premises from other premises owned by the employer, the separation of financial accounting, the separation of services, and the separation of profits'.[297] In addition, an establishment was said to require some degree of permanence or stability.[298] Thus it was possible that a number of different sites could together constitute an 'establishment': for example 14 building sites administered from a company's headquarters were not treated as separate establishments,[299] nor were 28 retail shops, a factory and a bakery.[300] In 1995, however, the ECJ ruled that for the purposes of the Directive the term 'establishment' should:

> ... be interpreted as designating, depending on the circumstances, the unit to which the workers made redundant are assigned to carry out their duties. It is not essential in order for there to be an 'establishment' for the unit in question to be endowed with a management which can independently effect collective redundancies.[301]

293 TULRCA 1992, s 188(3).
294 Harvey, 1972 (as updated), Division E, para 2505.
295 See further para 5.124 *et seq.*
296 Harvey, 1972 (as updated): Division E, para 2507, citing the tribunal decision in *TGWU v Nationwide Haulage Ltd* [1978] IRLR 143 as an example.
297 Hepple, 1981b: p 10. See generally *Barratt Developments (Bradford) Ltd v UCATT* [1978] ICR 319; *Bakers' Union v Clarks of Hove Ltd* [1977] IRLR 167 accepted on this point by the EAT [1977] IRLR 264 and CA [1978] IRLR 366.
298 *May and Robertson v Ministry of Labour* (1967) 2 ITR 607.
299 *Barratt Developments (Bradford) Ltd v UCATT* [1978] ICR 319; see also *Barley v Amey Roadstone Corpn Ltd (No 2)* [1978] ICR 190.
300 *Bakers' Union v Clarks of Hove Ltd*; see note 297 above. See also *Mills and Allen Ltd v Bulwich* (2000) IRLB 648, 13.
301 Case C-449/93 *Rockfon A/S v Specialarbejderforbundet i Danmark, acting for Nielsen* [1996] IRLR 168, 175, applied in *Mills and Allen Ltd v Bulwich* (2000) IRLB 648, 13; *MSF v Refuge Assurance plc* [2002] IRLR 324.

In the context in which this decision was given, the ECJ intended to maximise the application of the duty to consult.[302] However, when applied in the British context it may considerably reduce the occasions when the 20-employee threshold is crossed. The scope of protection is further narrowed by the fact that the duty to consult is confined to a single employer; thus even if associated employers operate from the same establishment each set of redundancies must be considered separately.[303]

(ii) When consultation must begin

9.33   The duty to consult arises as soon as the employer is 'proposing' to dismiss for redundancy. The term 'dismiss' is to be construed in accordance with Part X of ERA 1996,[304] a requirement which recently led the EAT to conclude that in the case of dismissal with notice, dismissal takes place on the expiry of that notice rather than when notice is given.[305] As we discuss in para 5.92 this is a defensible position in relation to the language of the statute. However in the context of collective redundancies the legislation must now be interpreted in the light of the landmark European Court of Justice decision in *Junk v Kuhnel*.[306] Here the ECJ affirmed that 'the event constituting redundancy consists in the declaration by an employer of *his intention* to terminate the contract of employment', not the actual cessation of the employment relationship on the expiry of the period of notice.[307] Such an interpretation was confirmed by the purpose of the directive, which is 'to avoid terminations of contracts of employment or to reduce the number of such terminations. The achievement of that purpose would be jeopardised if the consultation of workers' representatives were to be subsequent to the employer's decision'.[308] In addition the ECJ decided that a contract of employment could be terminated only after *the conclusion* of the consultation procedure.

> The effectiveness of ... an obligation [to negotiate] would be compromised if an employer was entitled to terminate contracts of employment during the course of the procedure or even at the beginning thereof. It would be significantly more difficult for workers' representatives to achieve the withdrawal of a decision that has been taken than to secure the abandonment of a decision that is being contemplated.[309]

302 Danish law had adopted the alternative 'threshold' formulation for the obligation to consult under the Directive which comes into play where, *inter alia*, redundancies affect at least 10% of workers in establishments employing at least 100 but fewer than 300 workers: Art 1(1)(a). According to this formulation, it benefits employees if 'the establishment' is defined as narrowly as possible.

303 *E Green & Son (Castings) Ltd; E Green & Son Ltd; E Green & Son (Site Services) Ltd v ASTMS* [1984] IRLR 135. *Quaere* whether the courts would ever 'lift the corporate veil' in this situation. Case law from the industrial action context suggests not (*Dimbleby and Sons Ltd v NUJ* [1984] IRLR 161, discussed at para 11.13 below) but cf the decision of the CAC in *GPMU v Derry Print Ltd* [2002] IRLR 380 in the context of the statutory recognition procedure.

304 TULRCA 1992, s 298. The definition in Part X is in ERA 1996, s 95.

305 *Middlesbrough Borough Council v TGWU* [2002] IRLR 332, paras 38–44, disapproving the dictum of Philips J in *NUT v Avon County Council* [1978] ICR 626.

306 Case C-188/03 [2005] IRLR 310.

307 Paras 39, 36.

308 Para 38.

309 Para 44. The Directive imposes an obligation to consult 'with a view to reaching an agreement'. The ECJ, somewhat controversially, characterised this as 'an obligation to negotiate': para 43.

One effect of *Junk v Kuhnel* may be to encourage employers to commence consultations at an early stage,[310] and so reduce the practical consequences of the discrepancy between the language of TULRCA 1992, under which the duty to consult arises when the employer is 'proposing' to dismiss, and the requirement in Art 2(1) of the Directive to commence consultations where an employer is 'contemplating' redundancies.[311] The courts have held that 'proposing' goes beyond the mere contemplation of a possible event or 'the diagnosis of a problem and appreciation that at least one way of dealing with it would be by declaring redundancies';[312] rather, it involves laying before others 'something which one offers to do or wishes to be done'.[313] In *R v British Coal Corpn, ex p Vardy*[314] Glidewell LJ highlighted the implications of the difference in wording between TULRCA 1992 and the Directive, pointing out that:

> ... [t]he verb 'proposes' in its ordinary usage relates to a state of mind which is much more certain and further along the decision-making process than the verb 'contemplate'; in other words, the Directive envisages consultation at an early stage when the employer is first envisaging the possibility that he may have to make employees redundant.

Although there is no ECJ decision directly on the point, the balance of opinion in British courts is that 'contemplation' is referring to an earlier stage in the decision-making process than 'proposing',[315] and that domestic legislation cannot be made to accord with the Directive 'without distortion'.[316] Assuming that this interpretation of 'contemplation' is correct, this means that in this respect UK law is not in conformity with the Directive, although, as we indicate above, employers now have an incentive to begin the consultation process earlier than they might otherwise have done. This will also be the case where dismissals arise in the context of reorganisation or restructuring, although this may work in opposition to the preferable course of attempting if possible to secure changes by agreement, with dismissals and re-employment only as a fall-back in the event that negotiations fail. However it may be difficult to determine when the duty starts if an employer, rather than dismissing, simply imposes changes to the contract and employees resign in response: constructive dismissal also constitutes 'dismissal' in this context.[317] Although, here, the employer may not have 'proposed' the dismissals it will have acted in a way

---

310 Note also the rights of information of recognised independent trade unions under the disclosure of information provisions, discussed in para 9.22 *et seq*, to information at an early stage; the CAC has held that union may have a right to information relating to the decision to reduce a level of activity, close a site or restructure an organisation: CAC *Annual Report* 1993, paras 2.3–2.5; CAC *Annual Reports* for 1994, para 2.8 and 1996, para 2.9. See also ICER 2004, Reg 20(1), discussed in para 9.54 below.

311 Directive 98/59, re-enacting Art 2(1) of Directive 75/129.

312 *Hough v Leyland DAF Ltd* [1991] IRLR 194, 198.

313 *MSF v Refuge Assurance plc* [2002] IRLR 324, para 44 (Lindsay P).

314 [1993] IRLR 104, 116; see also *MSF v Refuge Assurance Ltd* [2002] IRLR 324, para 42 (Lindsay P).

315 *R v British Coal Corpn, ex p Vardy* [1993] IRLR 104, 116; see also *MSF v Refuge Assurance Ltd* [2002] IRLR 324, para 42 (Lindsay P); cf *Griffin v South West Water Services Ltd* [1995] IRLR 15, 23 (Blackburn J).

316 *MSF v Refuge Assurance Ltd* [2002] IRLR 324, para 42 (Lindsay P); *Scotch Premier Meat Ltd v Burns* [2000] IRLR 639 (*obiter*).

317 TULRCA 1992, s 298; see also *Pearl Assurance plc v MSF* 26.2.97, EAT 1162/96, IRLB 572.

which risks provoking them and thus, again, could be said at the least to have them within its contemplation.[318]

Once the employer is 'proposing to dismiss', consultation with 'appropriate representatives' must begin 'in good time'[319] and in any event at least 90 days before the first dismissal takes effect where the employer plans to dismiss 100 or more employees at one establishment within a period of 90 days or less; otherwise at least 30 days before the first dismissal takes effect.[320] The fact that these periods are calculated back from the date when the first dismissal 'takes effect' may appear problematic in that this date may not be known at the time when the dismissals are initially proposed and, indeed, it is one of the purposes of the consultation procedures to avoid any dismissals whatsoever. The better view is that this means the requisite period before the date which the employer *proposes* for the first dismissal.[321] Where employees require periods of notice which exceed 30 or 90 days, employers may be tempted to issue notices before commencing consultation, but in the light of *Junk v Kuhnel* this would constitute a breach of the procedure. In circumstances where employee representatives need to be elected prior to the consultation process, it is sufficient for employers to comply with the statutory requirements as soon as reasonably practicable after the election provided that they have invited any of the affected employees to elect employee representatives long enough before consultation is required to begin to allow for an election to take place.[322] It is suggested in the DTI guidance on redundancy consultation that employers should also allow time for representatives to undertake appropriate training if necessary,[323] but, while this would be good practice, there is no provision for this in the legislation.

(iii) The persons who must be consulted

9.34 The employer must consult all 'appropriate representatives' of any of the employees who may be *affected* by the proposed dismissals or by measures taken in connection with those dismissals.[324] Before the 1999 amendments, the duty was confined to consultation with representatives of the employees whom it was proposed to dismiss. This wider formulation, which echoes the duty to consult in the event of a transfer of the undertaking,[325] would seem to cover all

---

318 Constructive dismissal seems not to be covered by Directive 98/59: Art 1(1) refers to terminations of an employment contract which occur 'on the employer's initiative', but it is questionable whether this is wide enough to extend to such dismissals. Case C-284/83 *Dansk Metalarbejderforbund and Specialarbejder-forbundet i Danmark v H Nielsen & Son Maskinfabrik A/S (in liquidation)* [1985] ECR 553, in which the ECJ held that termination by workers of their contracts following an announcement by the employer that he was suspending payment of his debts did not constitute dismissal, was decided prior to the amendment of the Directive in 1992.

319 Until the 1995 Regulations, this read 'at the earliest opportunity'. The new wording reflects Article 2(1) of the Directive.

320 TULRCA 1992, s 188(1A).

321 *TGWU v RA Lister & Co Ltd* (1986) IRLIB, 21 May 1989, p 11.

322 TULRCA 1992, s 188(7A).

323 *Redundancy Consultation and Notification* PL833 Rev 6, DTI: p 4.

324 TULRCA 1992, s 188(1).

325 See para 9.43. It is not clear that this amendment was required by the Directive; whereas Art 6 of the Acquired Rights Directive specifies consultation of employees affected by a transfer, the Collective Redundancies Directive merely requires an employer who is contemplating collective redundancies to begin consultation with the workers' representatives: Art 2(1).

those whose terms and conditions of employment or working conditions may be affected by the proposed dismissals, which could mean much, if not all, of the workforce. The change makes it easier to find employees to stand for election as employee representatives, and they may be less demoralised than those representing only those whose jobs are at risk. However, it may not always benefit those whom it is proposed to dismiss; representatives who are answerable to a broader, and possibly much more numerous, constituency may be less willing to fight hard for the interests of the target group for redundancy if, in return, they are given assurances regarding the remainder of the workforce.

There are three possible sources from which 'appropriate representatives' may be drawn. First, if the employees are of a description in respect of which an independent trade union is recognised by the employer, the employer must consult representatives of that union, irrespective of whether the affected employees are union members.[326] Where more than one union is recognised for a particular description of employees, it follows from the obligation to consult *all* the appropriate representatives that all such unions must be consulted about the dismissals of all employees in that group.[327] If there is no independent recognised union the employer must consult 'employee representatives'. It must also do this in respect of any employees who lie outside the scope of recognition; it cannot choose to consult union representatives in respect of such a group. In such cases, the employer may choose either to consult persons elected specifically for the purpose of the consultation exercise in question or persons appointed or elected by the affected employees for another purpose who (having regard to the purposes for and the method by which they were appointed or elected) have authority from those employees to receive information and to be consulted about the proposed dismissals on their behalf.[328] In either situation such representatives must be employed by the employer when they are elected or appointed,[329] although not necessarily thereafter, so excluding external professional advisers. No guidance is given about a minimum (or maximum) number of representatives to be consulted, but the use of the plural in the legislation strongly suggests that there must be more than one.

9.35   Where an employer chooses to consult specifically elected representatives, it must invite affected employees to hold an election.[330] Candidates for election must themselves be affected employees, and no affected employee may be

---

326 TULRCA 1992, s 188(1B)(a). 'Representatives of a trade union' in this context means 'officials or other persons authorised by the trade union to carry on collective bargaining with the employer'. See TULRCA 1992, s 119 for the definition of 'official' and s 178(1), (2) for the definition of collective bargaining.

327 This view, which seems clear from the wording of the legislation, was confirmed by the Northern Ireland Court of Appeal in *Governing Body of the Northern Ireland Hotel and Catering College and North Eastern Education and Library Board v NATFHE* [1995] IRLR 83.

328 TULRCA 1992, s 188(1B)(b). In Case C-382/92 *EC Commission v United Kingdom* [1994] IRLR 392 (transfers) and Case C-383/92 [1994] IRLR 412 (collective redundancies) the Advocate-General considered that the *ad hoc* designation of worker representatives would meet the requirements of the Directive. The ECJ was silent on the issue.

329 TULRCA 1992, s 196(1).

330 This is not directly stated in the legislation but is implicit from s 188(7A): see *Howard v Millrise Ltd t/a Colourflow (in liquidation)* [2005] IRLR 84 (on the equivalent provision in TUPE 1981); see also *R v Secretary of State for Trade and Industry, ex p Unison* [1996] IRLR 438.

'unreasonably excluded' from standing.[331] It is for the employer to determine the number of representatives, so that there they are sufficient to represent the interests of all affected employees having regard to their number and classes.[332] The employer may also decide if employees should be represented by representatives of all affected employees or of particular classes; in this context no criteria are prescribed to inform the employer's choice and, as under the earlier provisions, 'it would be open to employers to determine numbers of representatives ... [and] ... constituencies in ways which they thought might produce a desirable outcome'.[333] If the reference to 'sufficient' representatives is taken to impose a purely numerical requirement, it is conceivable that where both managerial staff and those below them are 'affected employees', representatives may be elected by the workforce as a whole who are derived from the managerial group. The more appropriate view, however, where both managerial and non-managerial groups are affected, is that 'anyone holding a significant managerial role is not properly independent from management',[334] and so would could not sufficiently represent the interests of other employees, even if this is not expressly stipulated in the legislation. The employer must, prior to the election, prescribe the employee representatives' term of office, ensuring that it is of sufficient length to enable the consultative process to be completed.[335] All affected employees must be entitled to vote in the election, which must be conducted so as to secure that, so far as is reasonably practicable, those voting do so in secret and the votes are accurately counted.[336] Although, unlike elections to union office, there is no requirement that the ballot be conducted by the marking of a voting paper, this would seem the most effective way of satisfying the statutory conditions. The employer has a general duty to 'make such arrangements as are reasonably practical to ensure that the election is fair'.[337] A purposive construction of this duty would suggest that the employer should give appropriate publicity to the election. It may also suggest that the election should be held over a number of days if the workforce is peripatetic, or if shift and part-time workers are employed, although the reference in the statute to 'the date of the election' presents a difficulty in this respect.[338] In these circumstances, as where the workforce is not based at the workplace, a postal ballot may be the better option. Unlike elections for a special negotiating body under TICER 1999 or under the 'standard' information and consultation provisions of ICER 2004,[339] there is no requirement for employers to employ an independent person to conduct the election, although they may consider this a

---

331 TULRCA 1992, s 188A(1)(e) and (f). The decisions of the Certification Officer on 'unreasonable' exclusion in relation to standing for union office, although of no precedent value, may be a useful source of guidance: see para 10.15.
332 TULRCA 1992, s 188A(1)(b).
333 *Consultation about Collective Redundancies and Business Transfers: TUC Response to Legislative Proposals*, para 12.
334 Hall and Edwards, 1999: p 310.
335 TULRCA 1992, s 188A(1)(d).
336 TULRCA 1992, s188A(1)(g),(h),(i).
337 TULRCA 1992, s 188A(1)(a).
338 See TULRCA 1992, s 188(1A)(e) and (g). Cf TULRCA 1992, s 246, in relation to industrial action ballots and TICER 1999, reg 13(3)(b) and ICER 2004, reg 2. In this context there is no explicit requirement that those entitled to vote be given the opportunity to do so (cf TICER 1999, reg 14(2)(c)(i)), but this can probably be implied from the duty to make arrangements to ensure that the election is fair.
339 See paras 9.61 and 9.54.

prudent course of action. In striking contrast to the provisions governing trade union elections and industrial action ballots,[340] the legislation does not prohibit the employer or third parties attempting to put pressure on employees to vote a certain way; it is questionable whether conduct of this nature would violate the duty to make 'arrangements' to ensure that the election is fair.[341] The statute does not expressly make compliance with the specific conditions relating to the ballot, such as voting entitlement and a secret ballot, the employer's direct responsibility. However, if the election does not satisfy all the statutory requirements listed, those elected will not be 'appropriate representatives' for consultation and it is therefore in an employer's interest to ensure compliance with them.

If the employer invites affected employees to elect representatives and they fail to do so, it will be treated as having satisfied its statutory obligation to consult provided that the invitation was issued long enough before the time when consultations were required to begin to enable the election to take place.[342] However if, pursuant to an invitation, the employees fail to elect representatives (for example, because no candidate comes forward) the employer must give each employee individually the information it is required to give to appropriate representatives,[343] although there is no commensurate obligation to consult them. The Collective Redundancies Directive appears to envisage consultation (and the associated provision of information) only through the medium of workers representatives,[344] although in *EC Commission v UK* the ECJ, in rather ambiguous terms, affirmed that the Directive required Member States to take 'all measures necessary to ensure that workers are informed, consulted and in a position to intervene through their representatives in the event of collective redundancies'.[345] If there are already potentially appropriate representatives in existence, such as a works council or other consultative body, it is strongly arguable that the employer should, in default of an election being held, consult those persons.

It is notable that although a union, in order to be consulted, must be independent of the employer, there is no explicit requirement that employee representatives should be; thus, they may be members of a body such as a staff council or consultative committee, which is dependent on the employer, financially or otherwise. In the consultation document that preceded the 1999 Regulations, the government claimed that independence would be secured if representatives were required to be properly elected, protected against dismissal or other detriment for acting as such, and with time off and the necessary training to fulfil their role (see iv below).[346] However this approach takes no account of other pressures, such as the threat to financial support of, or promise of future favours to, compliant representatives which may result from a relationship of dependence (and which also overlooks the fact that they may have obtained

340 See paras 10.16 and 11.37 below respectively.

341 Note that the protection against dismissal or subjection to a detriment extends only to taking part in an election and not to the way the employee votes: see (iv) below.

342 That is the implication of TULRCA 1992, s 188(7A), which treats the employer as complying with the requirements to inform and consult if this is done as soon as reasonably practicable after the representatives are elected. If no representatives are elected, the employer cannot take these steps.

343 TULRCA 1992, s 188(7B).

344 Cf Council Directive 89/391 on health and safety, discussed in para 9.46.

345 Case 383/92, [1994] IRLR 412, para 23.

346 *Employees' Information and Consultation Rights on Transfers of Undertakings and Collective Redundancies*, DTI, URN 97/988, February 1998.

their position by appointment rather than election). The lack of any requirement for representatives to be independent would appear to allow employers even now to frustrate the protection for workers provided by the Directive.[347] A redundant or affected employee may complain to an employment tribunal that any one of the employee representatives consulted was not 'appropriate', or that there has been a failure in relation to the election.[348] On a complaint relating to 'appropriateness', it is for the employer to show that the representative had the authority to represent the affected employees; where it relates to the election, it must show that the statutory requirements have been satisfied.[349] Where the employer consults a pre-existing body, it may be possible to argue that dependence on the employer means that it lacks the requisite implied authority to be consulted about the proposed dismissals on their behalf. However this may be more difficult if the body concerned includes within its terms of reference consultation relating to matters which include redundancies.[350] Unless representatives lack authority, or there is a defect in the electoral process, employees would seem to have no remedy in the event that they think their interests will not be properly represented by those elected or appointed.[351]

(iv) The rights of appropriate representatives

9.36 Employee representatives, and candidates for this position, are entitled to be permitted by the employer to take 'reasonable' paid time off during working hours to perform their functions and to undergo training to perform such functions (although the organisers of elections have no such right).[352] In its basic structure this provision is identical, *mutatis mutandis*, to that governing time off for union duties, discussed at para 8.34 *et seq*; thus, it is a right to time off only with the employer's permission, with recourse to an employment tribunal if time off or payment is unreasonably refused,[353] and payment need be made only for duties performed during working hours.[354] In contrast to time off for union duties, however, there is no reference to a Code of Practice to determine what is

---

347 Case C-383/92 *EC Commission v UK* [1994] IRLR 412, paras 16–27.
348 TULRCA 1992, s 189(1).
349 TULRCA 1992, s 189(1A), (1B).
350 In the case of representatives elected for another purpose, the DTI suggests that where redundancies are to take place among sales staff, for example, it would not be sufficient to consult a committee of managers set up to consider the operation of a staff canteen, but it may well be appropriate to consult a fairly elected or appointed committee of employees, such as a works council, that is regularly informed or consulted more generally about the business's financial position and personnel matters: *Redundancy Consultation and Notification* PL833 Rev 6, DTI.
351 Cf *Keane v Clerical Medical Investment Group Ltd*, IT Case No 2900491/97, IDS Brief 595, August 1997 where the Employment Tribunal held (in the context of consultation under TUPE) that once there are employee representatives and consultation has taken place with them, only those representatives can pursue a claim that the statutory duties have not been complied with. In *R v Secretary of State for Trade and Industry, ex p Unison* [1996] IRLR 438, Otton LJ emphasised at 446 that the expression 'appropriate representatives' must be 'an objective obligation or test and not subjective at the whim of the employer'. In the event of employees having been elected, however, it is difficult to see where the scope for challenge would be.
352 ERA 1996, s 61.
353 ERA 1996, s 63.
354 See ERA 1996, s 62 for the basis upon which payment is calculated. Note that these provisions are somewhat more detailed than those in TULRCA 1992, s 169 relating to payment for trade union duties.

reasonable, although the parties may find some assistance in referring to the ACAS Code governing that area. However, it is strongly arguable that in the context of redundancies, priority should be given to ensuring that employee representatives have the time off which they reasonably need to carry out their functions, so that considerations such as the amount of time off which the employee has had for other purposes, referred to in that Code,[355] should not be relevant in this context. The 'functions' for which time off must be permitted are not specified. The right to time off for training was added in 1999, but notably there is no right to training itself,[356] so that representatives who are not members of or otherwise associated with an independent union may find it difficult to get access to the requisite assistance, particularly as time is of the essence. Moreover, they are likely to be financially dependent on the employer for any training that they do receive. Employers may consider it good industrial relations practice to pay for representatives to have access to external professional advice, but, although the Collective Redundancies Directive permits Member States to provide for such assistance, there is no obligation so to do.[357] Where representatives of recognised trade unions are being consulted, their rights to time off for this purpose and for relevant training are governed by the provisions relating to trade union duties. Employers are required to allow appropriate representatives (union and 'employee') access to the affected employees and to afford them such accommodation and other facilities as may be appropriate; this would probably include meeting rooms and a telephone, for example.[358] The amount and timing of such access is not spelt out, but would probably be viewed by tribunals as subject to a test of reasonableness. The union or employee representatives may complain to an employment tribunal if reasonable access or appropriate facilities are denied; the remedies if the complaint is upheld, which may include a protective award of compensation to the employees dismissed as redundant or whose dismissal was proposed, are discussed in (vi) below. By contrast, if appropriate representatives are denied time off to perform their functions, which is potentially of equal, if not greater, significance for affected employees, the remedy is confined to a claim by individual representatives on their own behalf.

It is automatically unfair to dismiss, or to select for redundancy, an employee for performing or proposing to perform the functions or activities of an employee representative or of a candidate in an election for such a position, or for taking part in an election of employee representatives.[359] An employee who is dismissed on such a ground may apply for 'interim relief'.[360] The

---

355 ACAS Code of Practice on Time Off for Trade Union Duties and Activities, para 42.
356 Cf the Health and Safety (Consultation with Employees) Regulations 1996, SI 1996/1513, reg 7; see para 9.46.
357 Council Directive 98/59, Art 2(2).
358 TULRCA 1992, s 188(5A).
359 ERA 1996, ss 103, 105(1), (6). Where the principal reason for dismissal is redundancy it must be shown that the circumstances constituting the redundancy applied equally to one or more employees in the same undertaking who held similar positions and who were not dismissed: s 105(1)(b). See further para 5.95 above for the concept of automatically unfair reasons. Employees who are being consulted in their capacity as union officials will be covered by the protections afforded to those dismissed, or subjected to a detriment short of dismissal, for 'trade union' reasons. Whether the statutory dismissal and disciplinary procedure applies will depend upon whether the dismissal is one of those subject to the duty to consult: EADRR 2004, reg 4(1)(b); see further para 5.124 *et seq*.
360 ERA 1996, s 128; see further para 5.163.

minimum basic award applicable to dismissals for 'trade union' reasons applies in this context:[361] see further para 8.5. Such employees also have the right not to be subjected to any 'detriment' by any 'act' or 'deliberate failure to act' by the employer on these grounds;[362] where this right is infringed, an employment tribunal may award such compensation as it considers just and equitable in the circumstances, having regard to the infringement of the right and any loss attributable to the employer's act or failure.[363] There is nothing specific in the legislation to prevent employers from according employee representatives more favourable treatment than those whom they represent and where dismissals are selective and representatives are members of the 'target group', employers may err on the side of caution by not dismissing them. However this must be read in the light of the general principles governing dismissal for redundancy. Thus, if an employer selected employees according to specified criteria such as last in first out, or performance record, and did not apply those criteria to employee representatives, those dismissed in their stead may have a claim for unfair dismissal.

(v) The scope of the duty to consult

9.37 To comply with the duty to consult the employer must disclose in writing to the appropriate representatives a number of specified matters: the reasons for its proposals; the numbers and descriptions of employees it proposes to dismiss and the proposed method of selecting them; the total number of employees of such description(s) employed at the establishment in question; the proposed method of carrying out the dismissals, including the period over which they are to take effect; and the proposed method of calculating any redundancy payments, other than those required by statute.[364] However it has been suggested that it may not be essential for the employer to provide full and specific information under all these headings, or indeed any such information, before consultation can begin.[365]

The consultation must include ways of avoiding the dismissals, reducing the number of employees to be dismissed and mitigating the consequences of dismissals.[366] The first two categories may include consideration, for example, of alternative strategies such as reallocating work, reducing overtime or giving employees the opportunity to work more flexible hours or to job share. Where appropriate the possibility of redeployment elsewhere in the organisation, possibly after training, should also be explored. Where dismissals are inevitable

---

361 ERA 1996, s 120.

362 ERA 1996, s.47. 'Detriment' does not include dismissal in this context; in that event, the provisions relating to compensation for unfair dismissal apply.

363 TULRCA 1992, s 49; see further para 8.16. Loss includes any expenses reasonably incurred by the complainant in consequence of the act or failure to which the complaint relates and loss of any benefit which he or she may otherwise have had: s 49(3). There is a duty to mitigate loss (s 49(4)) and compensation may be reduced if the tribunal finds that the individual caused or contributed to the act or failure (s 49(5)).

364 TULRCA 1992, s 188(4).

365 *MSF v GEC Ferranti (Defence Systems) Ltd (No 2)* [1994] IRLR 113, 116; *Securicor Omega Express Ltd v GMB* [2004] IRLR 9 (noting that Directive 98/59, Art 2(3) states that information shall be supplied *during the course of the consultations*). Cf *E Green and Son (Casting) Ltd v ASTMS* [1984] IRLR 135, distinguished in *Securicor Omega Express*.

366 TULRCA 1992, s 188(2). It is mandatory to consult on all these matters; an employer cannot argue that consultation would, in the circumstances, be futile: *Middlesbrough Borough Council v TGWU* [2002] IRLR 332.

mitigating action may include providing counselling and outplacements for employees, and information about retraining elsewhere.[367]

The employer must undertake the consultation 'with a view to reaching agreement' with the appropriate representatives,[368] and must, therefore, be able to demonstrate that it took seriously the points which they put, and that it made reasonable efforts to reach an accommodation with them; the prudent employer will keep a written record of all meetings, with both parties signing them as accurate. While ultimately the employers retain the right to decide upon the implementation of redundancies, this procedure requires them to do more than go through the motions of listening to what representatives have to say.

(vi)   Remedies for failure to consult

9.38   If an employer fails to fulfil any of the statutory requirements a complaint may be made to an employment tribunal. If the failure relates to trade union or employee representatives, it may be made by the union or any of the employee representatives to whom the failure relates respectively; in any other case, including, specifically, a failure relating to the election of employee representatives, it may be made by any of the affected employees or any of the employees who have been dismissed as redundant.[369] However it seems that the scope for individual employees or ex-employees to complain about matters other than the conduct of an election may be confined to situations where the employer fails to issue an invitation to elect employee representatives; chooses to consult a body which does not have the authority of employees to consult on their behalf; or fails, in the event that there is no response to the invitation to elect employee representatives, to provide individual employees with the requisite information.[370] This is because, if appropriate representatives are in place, the employer's duty to provide information or engage in proper consultation is owed to them rather than to individual employees, and if such representatives are unwilling to complain to an employment tribunal there would seem nothing that individual employees could then do.[371]

The complaint to a tribunal must be presented before the date on which the last of the dismissals to which it relates takes effect or during the three-month period beginning with that date (with the usual exception where this was not 'reasonably practicable').[372]

9.39   The employer may defend the complaint by showing that there were 'special circumstances' which rendered it not reasonably practicable for it to

---

367 There is an obligation on employers to give employees who have been given notice of dismissal for redundancy time off work to look for new employment or to make arrangements for training for future employment: ERA 1996, ss 52–54.

368 TULRCA 1992, s 188(2).

369 TULRCA 1992, s 189(1).

370 See also paras (iii) and (iv) above.

371 In *Kerry Foods Ltd v Creber* [2000] IRLR 10, Morison P opined that in Case 383/92 *EC Commission v UK* [1994] IRLR 412, the ECJ had made clear that the Collective Redundancies Directive was designed to protect the rights of workers as individuals. On this view it may be possible to argue that workers should not be obstructed from pursuing an effective remedy. However we doubt whether the ECJ judgment gives sufficient support to that proposition.

372 TULRCA 1992, s 189(5); see further para 2.17 above.

comply with a particular requirement, and that it took all such steps to comply with that requirement as were reasonably practicable in the circumstances.[373] This defence (which does not appear in the Directive) has been construed narrowly by the courts: to be 'special', circumstances must be uncommon or out of the ordinary – a sudden and unexpected, rather than a predictable, disaster.[374] The fact that dismissals were triggered by the employer becoming insolvent is not of itself a special circumstance. As Geoffrey Lane LJ explained in *Clarks of Hove Ltd v Bakers' Union*:[375]

> It will depend entirely on the cause of the insolvency whether the circumstances can be described as special or not. If, for example, sudden disaster strikes a company, making it necessary to close the concern, then plainly that would be a matter which is capable of being a special circumstance; and that is so whether the disaster is physical or financial. If the insolvency, however, was merely due to a gradual run-down of the company, as it was in this case, then those are facts on which the ... [Employment] ... Tribunal can come to the conclusion that the circumstances were not special ...

In a later case the EAT applied this test to hold that shedding workers to make the purchase of a business more attractive to a potential buyer, and the fact that the business had no orders and could not be sold, were not special circumstances but rather common incidents of insolvencies.[376] Nor does the fact that a company is in administration and the administrator proposes the dismissals constitute a special circumstance *per se*.[377] By contrast, where a bank suddenly withdrew further credit facilities and appointed a receiver, this was capable of constituting a special circumstance,[378] as was a situation where the employer had continued trading despite adverse economic pointers in the reasonable expectation of avoiding redundancies (although shutting its eyes to the obvious would not have been).[379] At one time it was thought that a failure to consult prior to the public announcement of a merger could be justified on the basis that this was necessitated by Stock Exchange rules.[380] This is not the case, however. The DTI guidance on consultation states that:

> Stock Exchange rules do *not* preclude employee representatives being informed and consulted in advance where collective redundancies are planned in connection with a restructuring (eg a plant closure or a takeover) which may involve price sensitive information. Provision can be made for

---

373 TULRCA 1992, ss 188(7), 189(6).
374 *Clarks of Hove Ltd v Bakers' Union* [1978] IRLR 366.
375 [1978] IRLR 366, 369.
376 *GMB v Rankin and Harrison (as joint administrators of Lawtex plc and Lawtex Babywear Ltd)* [1992] IRLR 514. In *Middlesbrough Borough Council v TGWU* [2002] IRLR 332, the EAT held that it could not conceive of circumstances that would be 'special' where an employer had sufficient time to consult on some matters but had entered into none on another.
377 *Re Hartlebury Printers Ltd (in liquidation)* [1992] IRLR 516. Remuneration due under a protective award constitutes a preferential debt under the Insolvency Act 1986, Sched 6, para 13(2)(d).
378 *USDAW v Leancut Bacon Ltd (in liquidation)* [1981] IRLR 295. See also *Hamish Armour v ASTMS* [1979] IRLR 24 (application for a further government loan pending).
379 *Association of Pattern Makers and Allied Craftsmen v Kirvin Ltd* [1978] IRLR 318.
380 See the *Financial Times* 26/27 June 1999, reporting the employment tribunal decision in *MSF v Refuge Assurance* to this effect.

employee representatives to be subject to confidentiality constraints for a specified period, but at the same time be sufficiently informed to hold meaningful consultations with the employer.[381]

However, the position is uncertain if the union or employee representatives refused to accept the information subject to such confidentiality constraints which are not provided for in the legislation.[382] Moreover, the Listing Rules would not permit disclosure to all affected employees,[383] which the legislation requires in the event that they fail to respond to an invitation to elect employee representatives.[384] Finally, the statute provides that where the decision leading to the dismissals was taken by a person controlling the employer (directly or indirectly) rather than the employer itself, a failure by that person to provide information to the immediate employer cannot constitute the 'special circumstances' defence.[385] Thus a subsidiary of a transnational company, for example, cannot argue that it was unable to meet its obligations because its parent company, which took the decision to reduce the workforce, was unwilling to disclose the requisite information to it.

The 'special circumstances' defence does not appear in the Collective Redundancies Directive and it is curious that its presence in the legislation was not a ground of complaint by the European Commission in the infringement proceedings described in para 9.31. In the light of the principle that national legislation should be interpreted to conform with Community law, it would seem open to a complainant to argue that an employer should not be able to invoke it. Its presence in the legislation itself raises questions about the purpose of both the consultation procedure and the sanction for failure to comply with it, matters which we consider in further detail below.

9.40   If an employment tribunal upholds a complaint it must make a declaration and may also make a protective award in respect of employees in relation to whose dismissal or proposed dismissal the employer has failed to comply with a statutory

---

381   *Redundancy Consultation and Notification*, PL833 Rev 6, DTI: p 5. This reflects the terms of rules 9.4 and 9.5 of the Listing Rules issued by the Financial Services Authority. Note also that Art 6 of Directive 2004/25/EC on Takeover Bids provides that the boards of an offeree and offeror company come under a duty to inform the representatives of their respective employees, or, where thare are no such representatives, the employees themselves, of a relevant takeover bid, '[a]s soon as the bid has been made public'. On plans for the implementation of this Directive in the UK, see DTI *Company Law Implementation of the European Directive on Takeover Bids: A Consultative Document,* January 2005, and Takeover Panel, *Explanatory Paper. Implementation of the European Directive on Takeover Bids,* January 2005 (which, at p. 10, invites consultation on the inclusion, in the membership of the Panel, of a person 'with experience of employee relations issues from the employee's perspective').

382   Cf ICER 2004, reg 25 and TICER 1999, reg 23, discussed in paras 9.56 and 9.63 below.

383   Rule 9.5(c) refers to 'representatives of [the company's] employees or trades unions acting on their behalf'.

384   TULRCA 1992, s 188(7B); see para 9.35 above.

385   TULRCA 1992, s 188(7). In *GMB and Amicus v Beloit Walmsley Ltd* [2004] IRLR 18, the EAT held that information in s 188(7) was not defined exclusively by the information required to be disclosed by s 188(4), and meant 'information about the decision leading to the proposed dismissals', a phrase which connotes both the causal effect of the decision (some dismissals for redundancy) and contemplation of its consequences. Any period between the making of a decision by a parent company and the date on which the directors of the subsidiary were informed should be disregarded in considering the 'special circumstances' defence.

requirement.[386] The award entitles the employees subject to it to receive their normal pay for the period of the award (the 'protected period').[387] If the employer fails to pay the requisite remuneration to an employee he or she may present an individual complaint to an employment tribunal.[388] The length of the protected period is at the discretion of the tribunal, but may not exceed 90 days.[389] Its length is such as the tribunal considers 'just and equitable in all the circumstances, having regard to the seriousness of the employer's default in complying with any [statutory] requirement ...'.[390] The interpretation of this provision – and, in particular, deciding whether the award was designed to compensate the employees affected, penalise the employer, or both – caused considerable controversy for many years. In 2004 the Court of Appeal resolved the matter by affirming that the purpose of the award was to provide a sanction for breach of the obligations to consult, not to compensate employees for loss that they had suffered as a result of the breach.[391] Tribunals should focus on the seriousness of the employer's default, which may vary from the technical to a complete failure to comply; the deliberateness of the failure may also be relevant, as may the availability to the employer of legal advice about its obligations. A proper approach to assessing the length of the protected period in a case where there had been no consultation was to start with the maximum period and reduce it only if there are mitigating circumstances justifying a reduction to the extent that the tribunal considers appropriate. The EAT has since confirmed that the effectiveness of the sanction should be judged at the time that the employer's failure to consult occurs, not at a later stage when redundancies are implemented or a complaint is presented to a tribunal; the fact that an employer may be insolvent by the time of the proceedings is irrelevant.[392]

Deciding when the protected period should begin has also been a source of difficulty for the courts. The statute states that it begins with the date on which the first of the dismissals to which the complaint relates 'takes effect' or the date of the award, whichever is the earlier.[393] After conflicting decisions, the date on which the first of the dismissals 'takes effect' has most recently been interpreted by the EAT as the date on which it was *originally proposed* that the first of the dismissals should take effect rather than the *actual* date.[394]

---

386 TULRCA 1992 , s189(2), (3). In *Securicor Omega Express Ltd v GMB* [2004] IRLR 9, the EAT held (at 17) that 'proposed' dismissal referred to a claim before redundancies had been announced and did not cover those who ultimately remained in the employer's employment. *Quaere* if this interpretation is correct.

387 TULRCA 1992, ss 189(2), 190. The rate of remuneration is a week's pay (calculated according to ERA 1996, ss 220–229 (Chapter II of Part XIV): TULRCA 1992, s 190(5)) for each week of the award, with proportionate amounts for individual days. However the statutory maximum of a week's pay stipulated in s 227 does not appear to be applicable in this context: cf TULRCA 1992, s 70C(5B).

388 TULRCA 1992, s 192. On the approach to the time limit for presenting a complaint where the protective award is made after the protected period ends, see *Howlett Marine Services Ltd v Bowlam* [2001] IRLR 201.

389 TULRCA 1992, s 189(4).

390 TULRCA 1992, s 189(4).

391 *Susie Radin Ltd v GMB* [2004] IRLR 400, disapproving *Spillars-French (Holdings) Ltd v USDAW* [1979] IRLR 339.

392 *Smith v Cherry Lewis Ltd* [2005] IRLR 86.

393 TULRCA 1992, s 189(4).

394 *TGWU v Ledbury Preserves (1928) Ltd* [1986] IRLR 492, following *E Green & Son (Castings) Ltd v ASTMS* [1984] IRLR 135 on this point in preference to *GKN Sankey Ltd v NSMM* [1980] IRLR 8. The determination of this date was more significant before TURERA 1993 removed the provision requiring a protective award to be set off against payments under the contract of employment or damages for breach of contract.

The protective award is payable regardless of whether employees are working during the protected period. It is notable, however, that employees who are still employed during any part of the protected period will be entitled to payment under the protected award only if they would be entitled to payment under their contract of employment or under their statutory rights during a period of notice;[395] thus, employees who take unpaid leave, for example, will not be so entitled. Moreover, employees may lose the right to remuneration under a protective award if they are fairly dismissed for reasons other than redundancy[396] or unreasonably terminate the contract of employment when they would otherwise have been employed.[397] They also lose this right for the period when they would otherwise have been employed if, in circumstances where they are entitled to a statutory redundancy payment, they unreasonably refuse an offer of suitable employment from the employer (or new or renewed employment on the same terms), to take effect before or during the protective period.[398] If the purpose of the award is to provide a sanction for the failure to consult, it is not clear why any of these events should be relevant. Employees who are unemployed and in receipt of a protective award may not claim a Jobseeker's Allowance for this period; if they have already done so and a protective award is subsequently made in respect of the period in question, the employer must deduct that amount from the award and pay it to the DWP.[399]

We return to the question of the adequacy of the sanction for failure to consult, stated in the legislation to be the exclusive remedy,[400] in para 9.42 below. At this stage, however, we merely contrast it with the remedy which may lie where the employer is a body whose decisions are susceptible to judicial review and there are consultation procedures particular to the industry or service in question. In 1992 decisions by British Coal and the Secretary of State to close collieries without any consultation, in breach of obligations under the Coal Industry Nationalisation Act 1946 and machinery established thereunder, were deemed to be a matter of public law and a declaration was granted that no decision should be made as to the closure of any collieries until the stipulated procedure had been followed.[401] Where, however, there is no special procedure and such an employer has failed to consult in accordance merely with the general law the statutory provision for exclusivity presents obstacles to a claim for any

---

395 TULRCA 1992, s 190(4).

396 Note that in this context 'redundancy' has the wider meaning contained in TULRCA 1992, s 195(1).

397 TULRCA 1992, s 191.

398 TULRCA 1992, s 191. There is provision for a trial period where the terms and conditions of employment differ from the previous contract.

399 The Employment Protection (Recoupment of Jobseeker's Allowance and Income Support) Regulations 1996, SI 1996/2349, reg 8. Note also that in the context of business transfers, the Government is considering introducing joint and several liability of transferor and transferee for the protective award in respect of redundancy consultation: *TUPE Draft Revised Regulations Public Consultation Document*, DTI, March 2005, paras 81–85.

400 TULRCA 1992, s 188(8).

401 See *R v British Coal Corpn and Secretary of State for Trade and Industry, ex p Vardy* [1993] IRLR 104. Note that the concept of consultation in this context may not be identical to the statutory formulation: in *R v British Coal Corpn and the Secretary of State for Trade and Industry, ex p Price* [1994] IRLR 72, Glidewell LJ suggested (at 75) that it involved 'giving the body consulted a fair and proper opportunity to understand fully the matters about which it is being consulted, and to express its views on those subjects, with the consultor thereafter considering those views properly and genuinely'.

additional remedy.[402] Nevertheless, in principle, there seems no reason why, in an application for an interim injunction for breach of contract, the court cannot at least take into account an employer's breach of its statutory obligations to consult when exercising its discretion as to whether or not to make an order.[403] Equally, the fact that an employer has breached these obligations may render the dismissal unfair (although previous decisions on this point [404] must now be viewed in the light of ERA 1996, s 98A(2), discussed in para 5.143 above).

(viii) Notification requirements

9.41 In addition to the obligation to consult appropriate representatives, employers proposing to dismiss for redundancy 20 or more employees within a period of 90 days or less must notify the Department of Trade and Industry (DTI) within the same time limits applicable to consultation – ie, at least 90 days before the first dismissal takes effect where they propose to dismiss 100 or more employees at one establishment within 90 days or less; otherwise at least 30 days before.[405] In *Junk v Kuhnel*, discussed in para 9.33 above, the ECJ held that the obligation to notify, like that to consult, arises prior to any decision by the employer to terminate contracts of employment.[406] Thus, 'dismissal' in this context, too, should be interpreted as giving notice of dismissal.[407] However, the ECJ held that, in contrast to the consultation procedure, Directive 98/59 does not preclude termination of contracts of employment during the course of the notification procedure, provided that this occurs after the projected redundancies have been notified.[408] This decision was based on the wording of Article 4(1) of the Directive, which contemplates a period in which notice of termination has already been given. The notification must, *inter alia*, identify the appropriate representatives and state when consultation with them began[409] (although the general duty exists even if there were no 'appropriate representatives' because, for example, there were no candidates for an election). The employer must also supply any additional information which the DTI requires.[410] Employers who fail to comply with the obligation to notify risk criminal prosecution and a fine of up to level 5 on the standard scale (at the time of writing, £5,000)[411] and, where the employer is a limited company, specified officers may incur personal liability.[412] The same 'special circumstances'

---

402 See *Vardy*, above, at 116; *Griffin v South West Water Services Ltd* [1995] IRLR 15, where an application for an injunction restraining dismissals for redundancy pending conclusion of the consultation procedure was unsuccessful.

403 See further para 5.54 *et seq*.

404 See, for example, *King v Eaton Ltd* [1996] IRLR 199.

405 TULRCA 1992, s 193.

406 Case C-188/03, judgment of 27 January 2005.

407 Art 4(1) of Directive 98/59 requires that projected collective redundancies shall take effect not earlier than 30 days after notification, with a discretion for Member States to grant the competent public authority power to extend this to 60 days or longer in specified circumstances (Art 4(3)). The 90-day period is longer, therefore, than that required by the Directive.

408 Case C-188/03, judgment of 27 January 2005, para 53.

409 TULRCA 1992, s 193(4).

410 TULRCA 1992, s 193(5).

411 Criminal Justice Act 1982, s 37(2), as substituted by the Criminal Justice Act 1991, s 17(1).

412 TULRCA 1992, s 194.

defence as applies to the failure to consult applies also in this context.[413] Prosecutions may be instituted only by the Secretary of State or by an officer authorised for that purpose.[414] There is no record of any prosecutions for this offence.[415]

The duty to notify collective dismissals also appears in Directive 98/59. The draft form of its predecessor (Directive 75/129) contained power for public authorities to postpone or prohibit dismissals in certain circumstances, a provision reflecting the position in some Member States at that time. The UK was 'in the vanguard of the opposition to that part of the proposals'[416] and a compromise was eventually reached where it was agreed that the provision of veto powers would remain optional. It seems that a legal duty on employers to seek prior approval by public authorities for dismissals is now 'highly unusual', recent trends being to reduce the level of formal regulation.[417] In France, for example, a requirement for prior authorisation by the labour inspectorate in respect of redundancies was abolished in 1986. In contrast to the requirements of the Directive, the British legislation does not place a duty upon the state authorities with responsibility for employment placement to use the period after notification to seek solutions to the problems raised by the redundancies.

Assessment of the redundancy consultation legislation

9.42   Any assessment of the adequacy of the redundancy consultation legislation requires first a consideration of its purpose. It was initially introduced as part of the 'Social Contract' legislation[418] and was, as such, part of a package of measures aimed at promoting security of employment and strengthening collective bargaining although, because of the European Community dimension, its background and history were distinct from the remainder of those provisions.[419] At Community level, in the words of the European Court of Justice, '[b]y harmonising the rules applicable to collective redundancies, the Community legislature intended both to ensure comparable protection for workers' rights in the different Member States and to harmonise the costs which such protective rules entail for Community undertakings'[420] (although, as Davies has argued, it is notable that other costs, such as differing levels of severance or redundancy payments, were not addressed and the term 'harmonisation' may be inappropriate given that Member States remained free to set more demanding standards than the Directive[421]). In the previous section we referred to the difficulties caused by the current provisions and, in particular, the issue as to whether the capacity for employers to consult non-independent employee representatives constitutes a

---

413   TULRCA 1992, s 193(7).

414   TULRCA 1992, s 194(2).

415   Until EA 1989 a redundancy rebate was available from the Secretary of State and one sanction for breach of the notification requirements was that this rebate could be reduced. It seems that there may have been greater use of this sanction than that of prosecution: see *Secretary of State for Employment v Helitron Ltd* [1980] ICR 523.

416   Freedland, 1976a: p 27.

417   Hepple, 1998: paras 40, 39.

418   See para 7.16 above.

419   Freedland, 1976a: p 24.

420   See Case C-383/92 *EC Commission v United Kingdom* [1994] IRLR 412, 420.

421   P Davies 1992: p 330. Cf the notion of a 'floor of rights' in transnational labour law: see Deakin and Wilkinson, 1994.

continuing breach of the Directive. In this section we examine some more long-standing reasons which may account for the fact that, although the consultation process is potentially capable of averting redundancies (in the sense of job losses rather than reorganisation), it is far from clear that this has been achieved in practice.

First, the position of the representatives consulted may be undermined from the outset if employees volunteer for redundancy.[422] As we saw in chapter 5 the provision for statutory redundancy payments in the Redundancy Payments Act 1965 led to major changes in redundancy policies and practices including the introduction of voluntary severance schemes above the statutory minima. This had a dramatic impact upon the tactics which trade unions were able to deploy when redundancy dismissals were threatened. Whereas prior to this 'the characteristic trade union response had been to oppose and resist the need for redundancies', as Daniel explains 'trade unions soon found themselves to be powerless in the face of the growth of voluntary redundancy schemes':[423]

> If they tried to challenge and oppose the need for redundancies, they were undermined by individual members eager to accept voluntary redundancy terms. In consequence, caught in a pincer movement between managerial strategy and individualist opportunism upon the part of members, trade union representatives had no alternative but to adopt two stances in relation to redundancy. The first was to insist upon 'No redundancy other than voluntary redundancy'. The second was to bargain over the inducements to volunteer and, in particular, to try to bid up the size of the employer's supplement to the statutory minimum payments.[424]

Daniel found that in the light of these developments the consultation procedures, when introduced in 1975, 'had little impact': in workplaces where unions were strong the opportunities for protecting jobs had already been compromised, in schemes which left intact the power of management to decide on the level and categories of job reduction; where unions were weak there was little scope for them to have an influence.[425] Having said that, it seemed that the presence of recognised unions may, at least, have afforded greater protection against compulsory, as compared with voluntary, redundancies, and that consultation may, in some circumstances influence the way in which redundancies are handled.[426]

Second, from its inception in 1975 it has been a duty only to consult, and not to bargain over, the implementation of redundancies, a formulation which reflects the EC Directive.[427] It has been suggested that 'a major consideration [initially] in favour of a duty to consult rather than to bargain was that consultation ... [did] ... not commit the trade union to responsibility for approving the redundancy or selecting the employees to be made redundant to the degree that a joint agreement over these matters does'.[428] The duty which now exists to

---

422 In *R v British Coal Corpn and Secretary of State for Trade and Industry, ex p Price* [1994] IRLR 72, the court held that the payment of voluntary redundancy payments before the termination of the consultation process did not make that process a sham.

423 Daniel, 1985: p 74.

424 Daniel, 1985: p 74.

425 Daniel, 1985, pp 78–79; 81.

426 Millward *et al* 1992, pp 324–325; J Smith, P Edwards and M Hall, 1999.

427 The information and consultation model is also laid down as a minimum standard in ILO Convention No 158 of 1982, Art 13, and ILO Recommendation 166 of 1982, Art 20.

428 P Davies and M Freedland, 1984: p 237.

consult 'with a view to reaching agreement' with 'appropriate representatives' comes closer to the process of negotiation but ultimately leaves intact the managerial prerogative in this area.

Third, the duty does not extend to the policy decision which necessitated the redundancies (a decision to cease a particular area of operation, for example) only to the ways in which the consequences of that decision can best be dealt with. In this it once more echoes the Directive. The limitations of this may be particularly apparent when the employer is a subsidiary of another company and the initial decision has been taken elsewhere. Such a situation may also mean that, in practice, the discretion of the consulting employer to reach an agreement with the representatives which constitutes any significant modification of its original proposals may be limited.

Fourth, the sanction available against an employer which fails to fulfil its duty to consult is wholly inadequate. When the Collective Redundancies Directive was being revised it was proposed that redundancies implemented in breach should be null and void. This proposal was ultimately dropped but there are strong arguments for saying that it is the only appropriate penalty in the circumstances. It is certainly the case that when large number of employees are involved, the redundancy consultation provisions can be an effective method of bringing employers to the bargaining table, particularly where job losses are associated with a transfer of the undertaking.[429] However, a financial penalty allows an employer ultimately to buy its way out of its legal obligations and fails to take account of the fact that consultation may have prevented the job loss altogether. It will be remembered that under the legislation the protective award is stated to be the exclusive remedy.[430] In *Griffin v South West Water Services Ltd*[431] Blackburne J refused an injunction restraining dismissals for redundancy pending conclusion of the consultation procedure for, *inter alia*, this reason. In doing so he opined that:

> Even if it were open to me in appropriate circumstances to disregard the exclusive sanction which Parliament has provided and grant injunctive relief of the kind sought I am not persuaded that I would have any sufficient grounds for doing so. It seems to me that an order restraining an employer from effecting any redundancies unless he has 'consulted with' his employees' representatives 'with a view to reaching agreement', which is what the ... [claimants] ... seek, is one which is fraught with practical difficulties not the least of which would be the difficulty faced by the employer in knowing just what he would be obliged to do and over what period in order to achieve compliance with the order and avoid proceedings for contempt.

However, in *R v British Coal Corpn and Secretary of State for Trade and Industry, ex p Vardy*,[432] where, as we indicated above, a judicial review application was successful, the court granted a declaration that no decision should be made as to the closure of any collieries until the specified procedure had been followed. The employer then returned to the court at a later date to determine whether it had done what was necessary to comply. This is obviously a cumbersome and expensive method of proceeding. In this case, however, failure to follow the

---

429 See Armour and Deakin, 2000. *Kerry Foods Ltd v Creber* [2002] IRLR 10, discussed in para 9.45, is important in this context.
430 TULRCA 1992, s 188(8).
431 [1995] IRLR 15, 34–35.
432 [1993] IRLR 104.

procedure would have constituted a breach of an order of the court, a situation which the employers were no doubt anxious to avoid. If, by statute, dismissals implemented in breach of procedure were simply null and void the employer would be in no different a position from an employer which was implementing the procedure *ab initio*.

A final objection to the existing legislation of a rather different nature lies in the mechanism for enforcement of the duty. Although the sanction takes the form of a payment to the dismissed individual, once 'appropriate representatives' have been chosen he or she is dependent upon those representatives to take the matter to an employment tribunal in the first instance. Where the employer has voluntarily recognised a union it is possible to imagine circumstances where it may choose not to bring proceedings in order to safeguard its relationship with the employer, particularly if those dismissed are not union members. Even in the case of members there is no statutory mechanism by which an individual can force a union to bring proceedings on its behalf and it seems unlikely that this could be implied as a contractual term.[433] Where 'employee representatives' have the consultative role, they may lack the will, or the resources, to pursue a complaint on behalf of others. There is a strong argument for saying that an individual should have the right to seek a remedy either independently or if the 'appropriate representative' fails within a specified period to take action on his or her behalf.

Transfer of an undertaking

9.43   Where an undertaking is being transferred[434] both transferor and transferee employers have a duty to inform and consult 'appropriate representatives' of any 'affected employees'.[435] 'Affected employees' are defined as 'any employees[436] of the transferor or transferee (whether or not employed in the undertaking or the part of the undertaking to be transferred) who may be affected by the transfer or may be affected by measures taken in connection with it'.[437] In many cases this is likely to extend to many, if not all, of the employees of both transferor and transferee employer. Employees of 'associated employers' of the transferor or transferee are not included within the obligation, even though they may be affected by the transfer. However, unlike in the context of redundancies, there is no minimum number of employees which need to be affected by the transfer before the duty to inform and consult apply.

---

433 See *Iwanuszezak v GMBATU* [1988] IRLR 219, where it was held that there was no implied duty on a union to bring its collective strength to bear to safeguard an individual member's existing conditions of employment. Lloyd LJ stated (at 220) that 'where the collective interests of the union conflict with the interests of an individual member it only makes sense ... that the collective interests of the whole should prevail'.

434 See para 3.99 *et seq* above.

435 TUPE 1981, regs 10–11A.

436 Note that in this context the definition of 'employee' is wider than usual, extending to 'any individual who works for another person whether under a contract of service or apprenticeship *or otherwise* (our italics) but does not include anyone who provides services under a contract for services ...': reg 2(1). Note reg 13(1),(2) in relation to those who ordinarily work outside the UK (an exclusion removed by ERelA 1999, s 32, in relation to consultation on collective redundancies).

437 TUPE, reg 10(1). Although the text of this provision could be read to require employers to inform and consult with representatives other than those of its own employees, it seems highly unlikely that this effect was intended: see Elias and Bowers: pp 96–97.

'Appropriate representatives' are defined in the same way as in the redundancy consultation provisions, analysed in para 9.34, and the same comments which were made there apply, *mutatis mutandis*, in this context. Thus, if an employer recognises an independent trade union in respect of the employees affected, representatives of that union must be informed and consulted; alternatively the employer must inform and consult 'employee representatives'.[438] Such representatives (and candidates for this position) also have identical rights to time off and protection against detrimental treatment by the employer; union representatives are likewise subject to the same general protections. Unlike the redundancy provisions, however, the duties of information and consultation relating to transfers are separate. Whereas the duty to provide information applies in relation to representatives of all 'affected employees', the duty to consult applies only where the employer 'envisages that ... [it] will, in connection with the transfer, be taking measures' in relation to such employees.[439] 'Measures' are not defined, but would certainly include changes in working practices and working conditions.[440] Technically, therefore, the duty to inform is wider than the duty to consult, although, as Elias and Bowers point out:

> ... it is not altogether clear when employees may be said to be *affected* by a transfer without measures being taken. On a broad view virtually all workers will be affected by a transfer, if only because the merging of workforces is likely to have some further consequences – whether beneficial or not – for the workers of both transferor and transferee.[441]

The prescribed information must be conveyed '[l]ong enough before a relevant transfer to enable the employer of any affected employees to consult all those persons who are appropriate representatives of any of those affected employees'.[442] However, given that the duty arises only where an employer envisages 'taking measures', this formulation of the time limit would appear to allow an employer who envisages no measures to comply with the duty to inform by advising representatives immediately before the transfer.[443] Although the EAT has held that the duty to consult applies to a proposed transfer which does not, in the event, take place,[444] this does not overcome the difficulty because of the specific

---

438 Once again, if affected employees who have been invited to elect representatives fail to do so within a reasonable time, the employer must give specified information to each affected employee individually: TUPE 1981, reg 10(8A). On the employer's implied obligation to invite employees to elect representatives, see *Howard v Millrise Ltd t/a Colourflow* [2005] IRLR 84, discussed in para 9.35 above.

439 TUPE, 1981 reg 10(2), (5).

440 In *IPCS v Secretary of State for Defence* [1987] IRLR 373, at 376, Millett J considered that 'measures' included 'any action, step or arrangement' but did not include predictions which did not involve any positive steps being taken and that 'envisages' implied that the employer 'must have formulated some definite plan or proposal which it has in mind to implement'. It is suggested in Harvey that by transferring employees to the transferee the transferor thereby 'takes measures' in respect of them (Division E, para 281).

441 Elias and Bowers: p 93.

442 TUPE 1981, reg 10(2). It is unclear whether the 'relevant transfer' refers to the moment of exchange of contracts or completion. There is authority to support the latter (*IPCS v Secretary of State for Defence* [1987] IRLR 373, 377) although *BIFU v Barclays Bank plc* [1987] ICR 495 suggests otherwise.

443 See Hepple, 1982: p 32.

444 *BIFU v Barclays Bank plc* [1987] ICR 495. Cf the view of Millett J in *IPCS v Secretary of State for Defence* [1987] IRLR 373, 377 that 'transfer' means the date of actual transfer.

link which is made between the time limit for the transmission of information and the consultation – a link which is additionally confusing because the duty to inform covers a much wider spectrum of matters than the duty to consult.[445] It is to be hoped that a tribunal or court faced with the argument would take a purposive approach to the regulation. It has been suggested that an employer 'envisages' measures when it has 'formulated some definite plan or proposal which it has in mind to implement', so excluding mere hopes or possibilities.[446] The adoption of a wide interpretation of 'measures' does not solve the difficulty of estimating the appropriate time to be allowed for consultation, which may vary greatly depending upon the number of employees affected and the nature of the changes envisaged; at a minimum, employers should allow time for the representatives to present their views and for a reasoned response to be made to them.[447] The position is further complicated where the employer has invited any of the affected employees to elect employee representatives. Here, provided that the employer issued the invitation long enough before the time when information must be transmitted to representatives to allow employees to elect them, it is treated as complying with the regulations if it complies with those requirements as soon as reasonably practicable after the election.[448] Where an employer wishes to keep the transfer secret for as long as possible it may be tempted not to create suspicions by inviting an election but, rather, to consult with persons already elected for some other purpose at the latest possible time. ICER, discussed in para 9.50 *et seq*, makes it more likely than in the past that such representatives will be in place.

9.44　The information to be provided by transferor and transferee employers falls into four categories: the fact of the transfer, the approximate timing and the reasons for it; its legal, economic and social implications for the affected employees;[449] the 'measures' which each employer 'envisages' it will, in connection with the transfer, take in relation to its own affected employees (or, if none, that fact); and, in the case of the transferor, the measures which the transferee envisages it will take in connection with the transfer in relation to those employees who will transfer to its employment by virtue of the regulations (or, if none, that fact).[450] In relation to the final category of information the transferee must give the transferor the requisite information 'at such a time as will enable ... [it] ... to perform the duty imposed on' it.[451] On the wording of the legislation, this would seem to

---

445　In *IPCS v Secretary of State for Defence*, above, Millett J (at 376) reconciled the apparent inconsistency by stating that the opening words of (the equivalent of) reg 10(2) were referring to voluntary consultations 'which the unions [at that stage the only consultees provided for in the legislation] may seek on any topic once they have the requisite information, but which the transferring employer is not compelled to grant if it chooses not to do so'.

446　*IPCS v Secretary of State for Defence*, above.

447　See TUPE 1981, reg 10(6).

448　TUPE 1981, reg 10(8).

449　This phrase appeared in Art 6 of EC Directive 77/187; see now Art 7 of EC Directive 2001/23. 'Legal' implications would seem to cover employees' contractual and statutory rights; 'economic and social implications' are delphic phrases which may cover matters such as the economic prospects of employees and job security implications, but this awaits clarification from the courts.

450　TUPE 1981, reg 10(2).

451　TUPE 1981, reg 10(3). Information may not be supplied under the cloak of commercial confidentiality: *IPCS v Secretary of State for Defence* [1987] IRLR 373, 375.

imply that the information should be supplied in time for consultation to take place on those measures. However, in *IPCS v Ministry of Defence* Millett J pointed out that there was no obligation upon the transferee to envisage measures at any particular time, and, indeed, that 'measures' may be developed or changed once consultation with the transferee's own representatives has begun. He suggested that there was a duty for the transferee to supply the information 'as soon as measures are envisaged and if possible long enough before the transfer' for consultations to take place.[452] However the suggestion that consultations should take place if possible is not, in its unadulterated form, compatible with the statutory regime. The regulations do not lay down any means of enforcing this obligation directly but, as we discuss below, the transferor has the power to join the transferee to employment tribunal proceedings if it is unable to fulfil its duty because of the transferee's default.

The duty to consult applies only to measures which the employer itself envisages taking; thus the transferor does not have to consult representatives about measures which the transferee may envisage, (although it must inform them of those measures). As in the case of redundancy consultation the duty does not extend to measures which may be envisaged by an associated employer, thus excluding those of a parent company or another company in the same group.[453] In this context, however, the duty to consult is much less specifically defined: the regulations merely state that the employer must consider any representations made by the representatives, reply to them, and give reasons if those representations are rejected.[454] However, there is an analogous (but not identical) duty to enter the consultations with a view to seeking agreement.[455] Clearly there may be situations where, before or after the transfer of the undertaking, the transferor or transferee is proposing redundancy dismissals. In that situation the more extensive duty to consult on redundancies will apply contemporaneously.

9.45   If an employer fails to fulfil any of its statutory duties a complaint may be made to an employment tribunal.[456] If the failure relates to union or employee representatives, the complaint may be made by the union or employee representatives respectively; in any other case it may be made by any of the affected employees.[457] The remarks which we made about the limitations on the capacity of affected employees to complain of a failure in relation to redundancy consultation are equally applicable here. As in that context, the employer may

---

452 [1987] IRLR 373, 376.

453 Note, however, that a failure by a parent company to supply information to the employer cannot constitute the 'special circumstances' defence for the purposes of the redundancy consultation procedure.

454 TUPE 1981, reg 10(6). See also the definition of consultation propounded by Glidewell LJ in *R v British Coal Corpn and Secretary of State for Trade and Industry, ex p Price* [1994] IRLR 72, 75.

455 TUPE 1981, reg 10(5). In the context of collective redundancies, consultation must be undertaken with a view to *reaching* agreement: TULRCA 1992, s 188(2).

456 TUPE 1981, reg 11(1). The complaint must be presented before the end of the three-month period beginning with the date on which the relevant transfer was completed (with the usual exception where this was not 'reasonably practicable'): reg 11(8). This does not prevent a complaint being presented before the completion of the transfer: *BIFU v Barclays Bank plc* [1987] ICR 495; *South Durham Health Authority v UNISON* [1995] IRLR 407.

457 TUPE 1981, reg 11(1).

defend the complaint by showing that there were 'special circumstances which rendered it not reasonably practicable' for it to perform the duty in question and that it took all reasonable steps towards its performance as were reasonably practicable in the circumstances'.[458] The case law developed in that context will be relevant here, although it is possible that the defence will be applied more willingly in a transfer situation due to the speed with which a transfer can take place and because of the fact that, often, its occurrence is surrounded in secrecy.[459] Clearly, allowing secrecy *per se* as a defence could effectively nullify the duty. However, it is possible that if an exchange of contracts and completion took place on the same day, and a tribunal were persuaded that the sale would not otherwise have occurred, these may be regarded as 'special circumstances', although the defence is still subject to the requirement to take such steps as were reasonably practicable. As in the case of the redundancy consultation provisions the 'special circumstances' defence does not appear in the EC Directive and, once again, it would seem open to a complainant to argue that an employer should not be able to invoke it.

If a transferor wishes to defend a claim that it did not inform representatives of measures which the transferee envisaged taking because it was not supplied with the requisite information, it must give the transferee notice of that fact, whereupon the transferee becomes a party to the proceedings.[460] However, the complainant has no right to seek the joinder of the transferee on its own initiative. At one time this presented the possibility that employees could be left at risk of awards payable by an insolvent transferor,[461] but recent decisions of the EAT have held that liability for a failure to consult passes automatically, on a transfer, to the transferee under regulation 5 of TUPE.[462] This decision, however desirable from one perspective, is difficult to reconcile with the statutory regime, which clearly envisages claims being brought against either the transferor or transferee (although it could be argued that the statute is not left empty of purpose as it allows for claims where a proposed transfer does not proceed). However it has the capacity to act as an important incentive for compliance with the consultation provisions, particularly if redundancies are associated with the transfer so that the specific consultation requirements applicable to redundancies, as well as those relating to the transfer, apply.[463]

In proposals put forward in March 2005, the Government has suggested amending TUPE to make provision for joint and several liability of the transferor and transferee for failure to consult under the Regulations. The justification for this is that if liability for the protective award were to pass wholly to the transferee, 'there would arguably be little or no incentive for the transferor to comply with the relevant information and consultation requirements'.[464] Joint

---

458 TUPE 1981, reg 11(2).

459 Note, however, our discussion about the Listing Rules in para 9.39 above.

460 TUPE 1981, reg 11(3).

461 Although see Hepple and Byre, 1989: p 141, where it is argued that where a transferor fails to join the transferee, courts and tribunals may be persuaded to read into the regulation a right for the complainant to do so in order to ensure that employees are not deprived of compensation in these circumstances.

462 *Kerry Foods Ltd v Creber* [2000] IRLR 10, *Alamo Group (Europe) Ltd v Tucker* [2003] IRLR 266; cf *TGWU v James McKinnon, JR (Haulage) Ltd* [2001] IRLR 597.

463 See Armour and Deakin, 2000, 2003 for a case study of the operation of these provisions in the context of the Rover sale.

464 *TUPE Draft Revised Regulations Public Consultation Document*, DTI March 2005, at para 83; see generally paras 82–5.

and several liability, which is permitted by the Directive, would enable the employee representatives, or employees claiming the benefit of a protective award, to bring their claim against the party which in the best position to meet it. The same proposal invites consultation on the extension of the principle of joint and several liability to the protective award made in relation to a failure to consult in respect of collective redundancies under TULRCA 1992.[465]

If the complaint is upheld the tribunal will make a declaration and may also order the employer to pay 'appropriate compensation' to such descriptions of affected employees as are specified in the award.[466] 'Appropriate compensation' means such a sum not exceeding 13 weeks' pay for the employee in question 'as the tribunal considers just and equitable having regard to the seriousness of the failure of the employer to comply with [its] duty'.[467] Prior to the implementation of the 1999 amending regulations, compensation for breach of the duties in this context was limited to a maximum of four weeks' pay. It was strongly arguable that this did not meet the requirement under Community law for the penalty for infringements to be 'effective, proportionate and dissuasive'; it could still be argued, albeit with less force, that the revised figure fails to meet these conditions. An employee who does not receive the compensation due to him or her under an award may complain to a tribunal, which will order the employer to pay the amount awarded.[468]

A criticism relating to this procedure, which we also made in para 9.42, is that the decision to seek a remedy for non-compliance with the duties to inform and consult lies only with 'appropriate representatives' once they have been chosen. Where the representative is a union, then in relation to the transferee employer in particular it may not wish to risk prejudicing its future relationship and possibly voluntary recognition. Again it would seem desirable for an individual to have the right to seek a remedy either independently or if the union or employee representatives fail within a specified period to take action on his or her behalf, although the less well-defined nature of the obligations in this case as compared with those applicable to redundancy may present formidable obstacles to assembling the evidence necessary to bring a claim in the absence of union co-operation and assistance.

Health and safety

9.46   A full examination of the law relating to health and safety lies beyond the scope of this work.[469] However, in this section we outline very briefly the provisions relating to worker representation in this context because of the interesting contrasts they provide to the other areas we discuss.

Health and safety has 'always had a reputation as being particularly suitable for consultation and unsuitable for bargaining'[470] although the basis of this assumption – that there is a 'greater natural identity of interests'[471] in this area than in most others – is highly contentious and seems not to stand up to empirical

---

465 See above, para 9.40.

466 TUPE 1981, reg 11(4)(a).

467 TUPE 1981, reg, 11(11). There is little guidance in the case law on the appropriate amount to be awarded: see the discussion in para 9.40 relating to redundancy consultation. As in that context, the statutory maximum of a week's pay does not appear to be applicable in this context.

468 TUPE 1981, reg 11(5),(6).

469 See further Ford and Brown, 2003.

470 P Davies and M Freedland, 1983: p 231.

471 *Report of the Committee on Safety and Health at Work*, Cmnd 5034, 1972.

investigation.[472] However it is striking that the previous Conservative Government accepted proposals at European Community level furthering employee representation in health and safety, in marked contrast to its stance in other areas. The important provisions for information, consultation and worker participation contained in the Framework Directive on the working environment (Council Directive 89/391), which could have been adopted by a qualified majority under Article 137 EC (then Article 118a of the Treaty) were, in the event, approved unanimously.

Provision for employee representation in health and safety matters in domestic law was initially made in the Health and Safety at Work etc Act 1974. As originally formulated, this legislation envisaged the appointment of safety representatives either by trade union appointment or workforce election. However the latter option was quickly repealed by the 'Social Contract' legislation, partly on the ground that non-union representatives would lack the resources required to bring any effective pressure to bear on employers. Regulations were then promulgated under the Act giving recognised independent trade unions the right to appoint employees (who may, but need not be, union officials) as safety representatives, with the statutory functions, *inter alia*, of investigating potential hazards and employees' complaints and conducting regular inspections of the workplace.[473] Employers were also obliged to consult representatives on arrangements for co-operating with employees on promoting and developing health and safety measures and in checking their effectiveness[474] and to provide them with the information necessary to enable them to fulfil their functions (with specified exceptions).[475] Safety representatives were accorded the right to paid time off during working hours to perform their functions and to undergo reasonable training, with a right to complain to an employment tribunal if this was refused.[476] In addition, if at least two representatives so requested, employers were obliged to establish a 'safety committee' with the function of 'keeping under review the measures taken to ensure the health and safety at work of [the] employees and such other functions as may be prescribed'.[477] Beyond that their structure and remit was a matter for management and union(s) to decide.[478]

472 See James, 1992, and James and Walters, 1997, and references therein.
473 Safety Representatives and Safety Committee Regulations 1977, SI 1977/500; see also Health and Safety Commission Codes of Practice on Safety Representatives and Safety Committees (1978) and Time off for the Training of Safety Representatives (1978). The Police (Health and Safety) Regulations 1999, SI 1999/860 require police organisations to be treated as recognised unions in this context. In *Costain Building and Civil Engineering Ltd v Smith* [2000] ICR 215 the appointment of a safety representative was ineffective because at the time of the appointment he was not an employee.
474 HSWA 1974, s 2(6).
475 Safety Representatives and Safety Committees Regulations 1977, SI 1977/500, reg 7.
476 Safety Representatives and Safety Committees Regulations 1977, SI 1977/500, regs 4(2), 11 and Schedule. See also the Code of Practice issued by the Health and Safety Commission on Time Off for the Training of Safety Representatives (1978) and *Duthie v Bath and Somerset Council* [2003] ICR 1405.
477 HSWA 1974, s 2(7); SI 1977/500, reg 9.
478 It is automatically unfair for an employer to dismiss an employee in connection with being a safety representative or member of a safety committee (ERA 1996, s 100) and such employees have the right not to be subjected to 'any detriment': ERA 1996, s 44. There is no limit on the compensatory award for unfair dismissal if an employee is dismissed for health and safety reasons: s 124(1A). In *Shillito v Van Leer (UK) Ltd* [1997] IRLR 495, the EAT stated, *obiter*, that it was no defence to a complaint under s 44 that the safety representative intended to embarrass the employer in front of external safety authorities or that he performed these duties in an unreasonable way, unacceptable to the employer (see also *Bass Taverns Ltd v Burgess* [1995] IRLR 596, discussed at para 8.10).

Following the entry into force of Council Directive 89/391, a number of measures were introduced into UK law to comply with EC requirements, including a specific duty to consult safety representatives 'in good time' on specified matters including the introduction of any measures which may substantially affect the health and safety of the employees they represent and the consequences of introducing new technologies.[479] However voluntary recognition by the employer of a union remained a pre-condition for the obligations to inform and consult to be triggered. The Directive requires that 'information, dialogue and balanced participation[480] on safety and health at work must be developed between employers and workers and/or their representatives by means of appropriate procedures and instruments, in accordance with national laws and/or practices.[481] In the light of the decisions of the ECJ in 1994 that the UK was in breach of its obligations in relation to redundancies and transfers of undertakings because of dependence upon the will of the employer[482] it seemed tolerably clear that similar principles applied in this context. In response to this concern the Health and Safety (Consultation with Employees) Regulations 1996[483] were introduced. Like the current legislation relating to redundancies and transfers, these operate by way of a back-up to the pre-existing provisions, requiring employers to consult employees only where they are not covered by safety representatives appointed by recognised trade unions.[484] However, they differ from those provisions in that in this context employers may choose to consult employees directly *or*, in respect of any group of employees, to consult one or more persons in that group (referred to as 'representatives of employee safety'), who were elected by employees in the group at the time of the election, to represent them for the purposes of such consultation.[485] No procedures are stipulated for the conduct of such elections.[486] Employers have a duty to ensure that representatives of employee safety receive reasonable training for the performance of their statutory functions (unlike safety representatives, at the employers' expense)[487] and representatives have a right to paid time off during working hours for training and to perform their functions, and may complain to an employment tribunal if time off is not granted.[488]

479   SI 1977/500, reg 4A, inserted by the Management of Health and Safety at Work Regulations 1992, SI 1992/2051, reg 17, Schedule. The 1992 Regulations have now been replaced by SI 1999/3242 but the amendments made by the 1992 Regulations remain in force subject to a minor amendment made by the 1999 Regulations.
480   The meaning of 'balanced participation' is unclear: see Nielsen and Szyszczak, 1997: p 308; Neal, 1990: pp 97–98; Weiss, 1996: p 219.
481   Preamble, para 12. Cf the wording of Art 1(2) which refers to 'workers *and* their representatives'.
482   Case C-382/92 *EC Commission v United Kingdom* [1994] IRLR 392 (transfers) and Case C-383/92 [1994] IRLR 412 (collective redundancies); see further para 9.31 above.
483   SI 1996/1513. For a critique of the Regulations and discussion of the wider issues raised by them, see James and Walters, 1997.
484   SI 1996/1513, reg 3.
485   SI 1996/1513, reg 4.
486   Cf the provisions governing redundancies and transfers of undertakings, discussed in para 9.35.
487   Note, however, that the preface to the Code of Practice on Time Off for the Training of Safety Representatives suggests that the employer should provide training on hazards and arrangements specific to the workplace.
488   Reg 7. Candidates for election also have a right to reasonable paid time off. It is automatically unfair to dismiss an employee for taking part or proposing to take part in consultations under the Regulations or in the election of representatives of employee safety (with no limit on the compensatory award): ERA 1996, ss 100(ba), 124(1A), and such employees have the right not to be subjected to 'any detriment': s 44(ba).

Employers are required to provide 'representatives of employee safety' with such information as is necessary to enable them to participate fully and effectively in consultations on the matters specified in the legislation and to carry out their functions of making representations on various health and safety matters.[489] However, the functions of 'representatives of employee safety' are less extensive than those of safety representatives; thus they do not have the right to conduct workplace inspections or the investigation of employee complaints, nor are they entitled to require the establishment of safety committees.

9.47 The 1996 Regulations appear to have led to an increase in representative structures. Prior to their introduction, although initially the legislation led to a significant growth in worker representation (with some research suggesting that around 80% of all employees were employed in workplaces with safety representatives), by 1987 the number of workplaces with representatives had declined,[490] and the 1990 Workplace Industrial Relations Survey found that in 37% of workplaces with 25 or more employees, management engaged in no consultation over health and safety matters.[491] By 1998, however, managers reported that no steps were taken to consult in only 2% of workplaces, with 39% having joint health and safety committees, 29% consulting with safety representatives, and 30% consulting with employees directly. Having a committee in place was more common in workplaces with union recognition, but even in workplaces with no union members almost a third had a joint committee and over a quarter had elected safety representatives.[492] In the private sector, smaller workplaces and those without union recognition showed the clearest increases in health and safety representation.[493]

In the event that employers fail to comply with their duties to consult, health and safety inspectors are statutorily empowered to issue an 'improvement notice' which requires any person contravening the legislation to remedy the breach within a specified period; non-compliance with these regulations also constitutes a criminal offence. Initially the Health and Safety Commission resolved to try and avoid inspector involvement in industrial relations issues and stressed that enforcement action should not be considered unless inspectors were satisfied that all voluntary means of resolving a dispute, including resort to ACAS, had been exhausted.[494] Even in that eventuality the Commission suggested that the issuing of an improvement notice, rather than prosecution, would normally be the most appropriate first step. This reflects the emphasis of the Code of Practice which urges the employer, unions and safety representatives to make 'full and proper use of the existing agreed industrial relations machinery to reach the degree of agreement necessary to achieve the purpose of the Regulations and in order to resolve any differences'.[495] It was doubted by some commentators that a consensus-orientated approach of this nature could suffice,[496] and in 2000 the Commission consulted on a range of issues relating to employee consultation and involvement

---

489 SI 1996/1513, regs 5 and 6.
490 Walters, 1990: p 11.
491 Millward *et al*, 1992: pp 162–63 (and p 2).
492 Cully *et al*, 1999: pp 96–97.
493 Millward *et al*, 2000: pp 116–117.
494 HSC guidance issued October 1978.
495 Safety Representatives and Safety Committee (1978), para 3.
496 See James, 1992, for a discussion of possible reforms in this area; for discussion of the wider issues see James and Walters, 1997 and Gunningham and Johnstone, 1999; for useful background, see Beck and Woolfson, 2000.

in health and safety, including how greater publicity can be given to the statutory obligations and the possibility of greater use of enforcement action by inspectors.[497] At the time of writing no further steps have been taken in this area.

Pensions

9.48   If an employer wishes its employees to be contracted out of the state earnings-related pensions scheme it must give written notice to the Commissioners of Inland Revenue, having first consulted any independent trade union it recognises in respect of the earners concerned.[498] Where an employer has established a contracted-out scheme, unions also have the right to receive on request specified information relating to the scheme, including basic information about membership, contribution and benefits; the constitution of the scheme; and audited accounts and an actuarial statement.[499] These are purely domestic law requirements, and unlike the provisions relating to redundancies, transfers and health and safety, there is no provision for consultation of any other employees' representatives if no recognised union exists. At the time of writing the Government is consulting on the text of draft regulations to be made under the Pensions Act 2004, ss 259–261, requiring employers to consult on significant changes to occupational or personal pension schemes.

Training

9.49   An employer must consult an independent trade union about training matters where that union has been recognised in accordance with the statutory recognition procedure and a method for the conduct of collective bargaining has been specified by the CAC and neither its legal effect nor its content varied by the parties.[500] The employer must then 'from time to time' invite the union to send representatives to a meeting to consult on its training policy for workers within the bargaining unit and its training plans for the next six months, and to report on training since the previous meeting. The first meeting must be held within six months of the obligation coming into effect, with subsequent meetings at least every six months. Employers must provide the union with specified information, and must 'take account of any written representations about matters raised at a meeting' received from the union within four weeks of the meeting. It is unclear precisely what this duty entails; on one view it would suffice for the employer to take account of union views in its own mental deliberations, although a safer course would be to report its responses to the union in writing. If an employer fails to comply with its statutory obligations, a union may complain to an employment tribunal which, if it upholds the complaint, may award compensation of up to two weeks' pay to each member of the bargaining unit.[501]

---

497 *Employee Consultation and Involvement in Health and Safety*, Health and Safety Discussion Document, 2000: para 64. See James and Walters 2002, for a discussion of options for reform.

498 The Occupational Pension Schemes (Contracting Out) Regulations 1996, SI 1996/1172, reg 4, as amended.

499 See generally the Occupational Pension Schemes (Disclosure of Information) Regulations, SI 1996/1655 as amended. Any dispute about whether a union is an independent union recognised by the employer, or whether the employer has complied with the consultation requirements, may be referred to an employment tribunal.

500 TULRCA 1992, s 70B. See para 9.5 *et seq* for the statutory recognition procedure.

501 TULRCA 1992, s 70C. In this context the statutory maximum of a week's pay applies (£280 at 1 February 2005 and at the time of writing).

The Information and Consultation of Employees Regulations 2004

9.50 The Information and Consultation Directive, to which we referred in para 9.30, was implemented in Britain by ICER 2004,[502] which came into force on 6 April 2005. Undertakings employing at least 150 employees in the UK are currently covered by the Regulations; those employing at least 100 will be subject to them as from 6 April 2007, and those employing at least 50 as from 6 April 2008.[503] The Government was determined from the outset to avoid a 'one size fits all' approach to information and consultation; rather, the aim was to 'build on UK experience and create room for the wide diversity of practices that have built over the years, combining both representative and direct forms of participation. Individual organisations should be able to develop their own arrangements tailored to the particular circumstances, through voluntary agreements'.[504] The basic framework of the Regulations was agreed between the Government and the TUC and CBI. Important features of that framework are provision for the establishment of an information and consultation ('I and C') procedure under the Regulations either at the initiative of the employer or at the request of employees (but no requirement to do so otherwise); a requirement for a 40% majority to trigger the procedure where there is a 'pre-existing agreement' for I and C; the option for a negotiated agreement under the statutory procedure to provide that the employer informs and consults employees directly rather than through their representatives; and the operation of a 'standard' procedure, reflecting the terms of Article 4(2) of the Directive, in the event of a failure to agree. The Regulations are, in general, enforced by the CAC (with provision for reference to ACAS if the CAC considers that ACAS could assist),[505] with a right of appeal to the EAT on a point of law.[506] However, if an employer has concluded an I and C agreement prior to an employee request, such an agreement is not subject to enforcement under ICER 2004 nor will it be subject to other ICER provisions such as those governing disclosure of information or the terms on which information is disclosed; rather, its content, application and legal status will be entirely a matter for the parties to determine.[507] There are strong incentives, therefore, for employers to attempt to conclude such agreements with their employees. Unlike TICER 1999, which govern transnational I and C procedures, there is no requirement for such agreements to be concluded prior to the Regulations coming into force.

---

502 SI 2004/3426. See generally Hall, 2005.

503 ICER 2004, reg 3, Sch 1. The Regulations apply where the registered or head office of the undertaking or its principal place of business is in Britain; there are separate Regulations governing Northern Ireland. Where the registered office is in Britain but the head office or principal place of business is in Northern Ireland or vice versa, they apply only where the majority of employees are employed to work in Britain: reg 3.

504 *High Performance Workplaces – Informing and Consulting Employees: Consultation Document*, DTI, 2003: p 5.

505 ICER 2004, reg 38.

506 ICER 2004, reg 35(6). In this context the CAC is expressly required to give reasons for its decisions: reg 35(5). In reaching its decisions, the CAC may draw an adverse inference from a party's failure to comply with any reasonable request to provide information or documents relevant to a complaint presented to it or an application made to it: reg 35(3).

507 Whether such an agreement constitutes a 'collective agreement' within TULRCA 1992, s 178, and is thereby governed by the statutory presumption in s 179 will depend upon its content, as well as whether a trade union is a party to it: see further para 9.26. Non-applicability of ICER 2004 is without prejudice to the separate provisions governing disclosure of information for collective bargaining purposes, discussed in para 9.22.

The Regulations, which are complex, are supplemented by Guidance from the DTI which aims to provide a 'plain explanation' of them together with 'recommended good practice',[508] although, unlike a Code of Practice, it has no legal force. Space does not permit us to analyse in detail every aspect of ICER 2004. Rather, we examine below the general scheme prescribed by the Regulations before discussing those respects in which they may be regarded as falling short of the requirements of Directive 2002/14.

(i) Coverage

9.51   ICER 2004 apply to 'undertakings'. An 'undertaking' is defined as 'a public or private undertaking carrying out an economic activity' whether or not operating for gain'.[509] The DTI considers that this term covers a separately incorporated legal entity (a company), rather than an organisational entity (establishment, division etc). It also covers all other employers, such as partnerships and individuals, as long as they carry out an economic activity.[510] Decisions on the application of the Acquired Rights Directive, which also refers to 'economic activities' and which we discuss in para 3.101, are likely to be relevant here. The application of ICER 2004 to some areas of the public sector may be difficult to determine, particularly where they carry out a range of activities, only some of which may be 'economic' in nature. Government plans to draw up a code of practice that applies the principles of ICER to central government, and encouragement to local authorities to do likewise, if implemented, may reduce the incidence of cases on this point.[511]

In order to determine whether the undertaking has a sufficient number of employees to be covered by ICER 2004, it is necessary to calculate, according to specified criteria, the average number it has employed in the previous twelve months.[512] Employees on short-term contracts are included in this calculation, but certain part-time employees may be counted as half a person (in this context only) if the employer so decides.[513] Where an individual is employed in two or more undertakings he or she will be counted as an employee within each. There is no provision for adding the numbers employed by an 'associated employer' of the undertaking to determine whether the numerical threshold is met, in contrast to the statutory recognition procedure.[514] Whether an individual is an 'employee' of the undertaking, rather than being self-employed or working for an agency, for example, will be determined according to the principles that we discuss in chapter 3.

An employee or employees' representative (a term which under ICER 2004 is left undefined)[515] may request in writing data from an employer to determine the number of people employed by the undertaking.[516] This information may be

---

508 *The Information and Consultation [of] Employees Regulations 2004: DTI Guidance*, January 2005 (referred to below as 'DTI Guidance'): para 3.
509 ICER 2004, reg 2, enacting the definition in Directive 2004/14, Art 2(a).
510 DTI Guidance, 2005: pp 4–5.
511 DTI Guidance, 2005: p 5.
512 ICER 2004, reg 4(1), (2). If the undertaking has been in existence for less than twelve months, the number is to be calculated by reference to the number of months it has been in existence: reg 4(4).
513 ICER 2004, reg 4(3).
514 See para 9.6 above.
515 There seems to be no restriction on the person or body who may act in this capacity: DTI Guidance, 2005: p 9, n 9.
516 ICER 2004, reg 5.

required either to determine whether the undertaking is covered by ICER 2004; to calculate the number required to make a valid employee 'request', discussed below; or both. If, after a one-month period, the employer fails to provide this data, or it is false or incomplete in a material particular, the employee or representative who made the request may complain to the CAC, and if the complaint is upheld the CAC may order the employer to disclose specified data by a specified date.[517] Employers who do not consider that they are covered by ICER 2004 may themselves apply to the CAC for this to be determined, but only after an employee request has been made.[518]

(ii) Triggering the requirement to negotiate an information and consultation agreement

9.52 An employer is required to initiate negotiations with 'negotiating representatives' to reach a 'negotiated agreement' on I and C if it receives a 'valid employee request'.[519] A 'valid' request requires the support of at least 10% of employees in the undertaking, subject to a minimum of 15 and a maximum of 2,500 employees.[520] It may be made either in the form of a single request, or a number of separate requests, provided that these are made within a 'rolling' six-month period.[521] Requests (which must comply with certain formalities)[522] may be made directly to the employer or, alternatively, to the CAC, a route that employees may prefer to take if they do not wish to identify themselves to the employer. Where the CAC receives a request, it must notify the employer of this; request from the employer such information as it needs to verify the number and names of the employees who have made the request;[523] and, on the basis of this information inform the employer and the employees who have made the request how many employees have made it (but it will not name those employees).[524]

Special provision is made for the situation where a 'pre-existing agreement' is in place prior to the request being made. Here, if the request is made by fewer than 40% of the employees in the undertaking the employer has the option, instead of initiating negotiations, of holding a ballot of all employees in the undertaking to seek their endorsement of that request.[525] The employer must inform employees of its intention to hold such a ballot within one month of the

---

517 ICER 2004, reg 6. An order of the CAC may be relied on as if it were an order of the High Court: reg 35(4).

518 ICER 2004, reg 13.

519 An employer may also do this on its own initiative (ICER 2004, reg 11), but is much more likely to establish an agreement outside the statutory process where no prior request has been made (although note that where an employer has received a request in relation to one undertaking and wishes to negotiate an agreement covering both that undertaking and another undertaking where no request has been made it will need to notify the employees in the second undertaking of its intention to do this: reg 14(6), (7)). The same statutory framework applies where an employer initiates the statutory process *mutatis mutandis* as where it is initiated by employees. In this discussion we use the terminology applicable to the case in which the procedure has been initiated by employees.

520 ICER 2004, reg 7(1)–(3). The minimum figure will be relevant once ICER apply to undertakings employing at least 100 employees.

521 ICER 2004, reg 7(2).

522 ICER 2004, reg 7(4).

523 The employer must provide this information as soon as reasonably practicable: reg 7(6).

524 ICER 2004, reg 7(5).

525 ICER 2004, reg 8(1), (2).

employee request and arrange for the ballot to be held as soon as reasonably practicable thereafter (although not within 21 days of the ballot being announced).[526] A request is regarded as being 'endorsed' for this purpose if at least 40% of the employees employed in the undertaking *and* a majority of employees voting in the ballot have voted in favour: if this happens, the employer must then initiate negotiations;[527] otherwise a three-year 'moratorium' applies before another request can be made (subject to exceptions, discussed below).[528] The employer must make such arrangements as are reasonably practicable to ensure that the ballot is 'fair'; all employees must be given an entitlement to vote; and the ballot must be conducted so as to secure that votes are accurately counted and that, so far as is reasonably practicable, those voting do so in secret.[529] These conditions may best be achieved by employing an independent person to conduct the ballot, although this is not a statutory requirement. An employee or employees' representative may complain to the CAC if he or she considers that the statutory requirements governing such a ballot have not been met; if it upholds the complaint the CAC must then order the ballot to be re-run unless the employer has indicated, prior to this, that it would prefer to initiate negotiations.[530]

The high level of support required to trigger the obligation to negotiate an I and C agreement where there is a pre-existing agreement means that voluntary arrangements cannot be easily disturbed. The nature of the arrangements that will act as such a barrier is clearly a crucial issue for employers and, possibly, in some cases for trade unions particularly where they are effectively operating a 'single-channel' form of workplace representation. Although the obligation to initiate negotiations under the statutory procedure does not of itself displace the pre-existing agreement, that agreement will no longer of itself suffice to discharge the employer's statutory obligations. A requirement for a single pre-existing agreement to cover all employees would have presented practical difficulties where collective agreements gave unions consultation rights given that it is comparatively unusual for such agreements to extend to the entire workforce, including senior management. ICER 2004 deal with this by providing that the 40% barrier applies if, prior to the request being made, there are *one or more* pre-existing agreements which meet the specified criteria. Such agreements must: be in writing; cover all the employees of the undertaking; have been approved by the employees; and set out how the employer is to give information to the employees or their representatives and seek their views on such information.[531] This means that employers may, for example, have a collective agreement with a trade union or unions covering half the workforce and another agreement or set of agreements for the remainder. There are no restrictions on the method, frequency, timing or subject-matter of I and C arrangements established under pre-existing agreements.[532]

---

526 ICER 2004, ref 8(3). This gives an employee or employees' representative in the relevant undertaking the opportunity to complain to the CAC if he or she does not consider that there is a 'pre-existing agreement' complying with the statutory criteria in place: reg 10(1).
527 ICER 2004, reg 8(6), (5).
528 ICER 2004, reg 12(1)(c).
529 ICER 2004, reg 8(4).
530 ICER 2004, reg 10(2), (3). See also reg 8(7)–(9) for complaints relating to a failure to inform employees about the ballot or to hold the ballot.
531 ICER 2004, reg 8(1).
532 DTI Guidance, 2005: p 16. Annex 1 of the Guidance provides suggested contents.

Further flexibility is afforded by provision for the situation where a 'pre-existing agreement' in an undertaking also extends to employees in another undertaking or group of undertakings. Where a valid employee request is made by employees in an undertaking with a pre-existing agreement covering more than one undertaking, employers may choose to ballot all the employees in all the undertakings together to determine whether they endorse the request[533] as an alternative to balloting only the employees in the undertaking making the request.[534] If a combined ballot is held and the request is endorsed, the employer will be required to initiate negotiations in all the undertakings covered by the ballot; if it is not endorsed, the three-year moratorium on a further request will apply to all those undertakings.[535]

If an employee or an employees' representative disputes whether any of the statutory criteria for a 'pre-existing agreement' in either a single undertaking or group of undertakings is met, he or she may complain to the CAC which, if it upholds the complaint, may order the employer to initiate negotiations.[536] Whether an agreement has been 'approved by the employees' may be particularly contentious, particularly in the context of high labour turnover. Although no method of securing approval is prescribed, it would be prudent for employers to obtain evidence of such support in writing and to retain such evidence in the event of a complaint to the CAC.[537]

There are three situations in which an employee request to initiate negotiations is restricted. The first is where a negotiated agreement already applies; no valid request can be made within a period of three years from the date of the agreement or, where the agreement is terminated within that period, before the date when the termination takes effect unless the agreement has ceased to cover all the employees in the undertaking.[538] The second is where the 'standard' I and C provisions apply; here there is a three-year bar from the date on which they started to apply.[539] The third is where a pre-existing agreement or set of agreements was in place and employees failed to endorse an employee request in a ballot; no further request can be made within a period of three years from the date of that request.[540] However, the three-year bar does not apply where there are 'material changes in the undertaking during the applicable period' having the result that the pre-existing agreement or agreements no longer cover all the employees of the undertaking or have not been approved by all the employees.[541] This could include situations where the undertaking has been involved in a merger or acquisition or there had been an expansion in the business which resulted in significant numbers of additional employees who would not be covered by the agreement(s).[542] Employers may apply to the CAC

---

533 On the assumption that the request has been made by fewer than 40% of the employees in the undertakings covered by that agreement.
534 ICER 2004, reg 9.
535 ICER 2004, regs 9(2), 12(1)(c).
536 ICER 2004, reg 10(1),(3).
537 The DTI considers that employee approval could be demonstrated by the agreement of representatives of employees who represent a majority of the workforce, including officials of independent unions in workplaces with a recognised union: DTI Guidance, 2005: p 16. *Quaere* if this is correct.
538 ICER 2004, reg 12(1)(a), (2)(b).
539 ICER 2004, reg 12(1)(b).
540 ICER 2004, reg 12(1)(c).
541 ICER 2004, reg 12(2)(a).
542 DTI Guidance, 2005: p 26.

within one month of a request being made if they consider that the request is not valid because, for example, the requisite formalities were not observed; the requisite threshold has not been met; or it has been made during one of the restricted periods described above.[543]

(iii) Reaching a negotiated agreement

9.53   In order to initiate negotiations to reach an agreement, the employer must, as soon as reasonably practicable, make arrangements for the employees of the undertaking to elect or appoint negotiating representatives; inform employees in writing of their identity; and invite the representatives to enter into negotiations.[544] The number of negotiating representatives is not prescribed, but their election or appointment must be arranged in such a way that all employees are represented by one or more representatives and all are entitled to take part in the election or appointment.[545] An employee or employees' representative who considers that these conditions have not been met may complain to the CAC, which must order the process to be re-run if it upholds the complaint.[546] Negotiations may last no longer than six months (starting at the end of the period of three months beginning with the date on which the employee request was made)[547] unless the employer and a majority of the negotiating representatives agree that the period should be extended.[548] There is a general duty on the parties to work in a spirit of co-operation and with due regard for their reciprocal rights and obligations, a duty that applies also to the implementation of an I and C procedure.[549]

There is considerable flexibility in the form and content of a 'negotiated agreement'. The agreement must cover all employees of the undertaking, but it may consist either of a single agreement or of different parts (for example, covering different establishments) which, taken together, cover all the employees. The agreement or each part must, *inter alia*, set out the circumstances in which the employer must inform and consult the employees to which it relates; be in writing and dated; and either provide for the appointment or election of I and C representatives, or provide that the employer must provide information directly to the employees to whom it relates and consult them directly.[550] Beyond this, the contents of the agreement are not prescribed; the parties may agree on the method, frequency, timing and subject matter of I and C best suited to their circumstances. Where an agreement consists of different parts, these parts may

---

543   ICER 2004, reg 13.
544   ICER 2004, reg 14(1).
545   ICER 2004, reg 14(2).
546   ICER 2004, reg 15.
547   Where there is a pre-existing agreement or agreements and the employer holds a ballot to determine whether the request is endorsed, the period between the employer notifying its employees of the decision to hold a ballot and the date of the ballot does not count toward the three-month period: reg 14(3)(a)(i). Provision is also made for other periods not to count where a complaint has been made to the CAC: reg 14(3)(a)(ii)–(iv), (b), (c).
548   ICER 2004, reg 14(3), (5).
549   ICER 2004, reg 21.
550   ICER 2004, reg 16(1). 'Consultation' in this context means 'the exchange of views and establishment of a dialogue between' the I and C representatives or the employees and the employer, as appropriate: reg 2. See also *R v British Coal Corporation and the Secretary of State for Trade and Industry, ex p Price* [1994] IRLR 72, 75.

differ as to the terms and nature of I and C and with whom it occurs.[551] Agreements are required to be approved in accordance with statutory criteria. Where there is a single agreement, it must be signed by all the negotiating representatives or, alternatively, by a majority of those representatives and either approved in writing by at least 50% of employees in the undertaking or approved in a ballot of those employees in which at least 50% of those voting voted in favour.[552] The ballot must comply with the same conditions applicable to ballots to endorse an employee request, discussed in para 9.52 above, although in this instance only a negotiating representative, not an individual employee, may complain to the CAC about the conduct of the ballot.[553] Where the negotiated agreement consists of different parts, each part must be separately approved either by all the negotiating representatives involved in negotiating it or by a majority of those representatives and at least 50% of the employees to whom the part relates either in writing or in a ballot.[554] There is no requirement for each part of the agreement to be approved at the same time or in an identical way. However if any part of the agreement is not approved in accordance with these principles, there will not be a 'negotiated agreement' for the purposes of ICER 2004 and the standard I and C provisions, which we discuss below, will apply. Negotiated agreements are enforceable through the CAC.

(iv) The standard I and C provisions

9.54   The 'standard' I and C provisions apply where an employer fails to initiate negotiations for an I and C agreement when required to do so, or where negotiations have failed to lead to an agreement.[555] These provisions apply at undertaking level only; arrangements may not cover more than one undertaking, nor can there be different arrangements in different parts of the undertaking.

Where negotiations have taken place but failed to reach agreement, the employer has a further six months after the expiry of the specified negotiating period to arrange for the election of I and C representatives; they may also use this period to continue negotiations, but will be liable to a penalty if the period expires and there are no I and C representatives in place (see para 9.55 below).[556] Where the employer fails to initiate any negotiations, the standard provisions apply six months after the employee request (or sooner, if the I and C representatives are elected before that date).[557] I and C representatives must be elected in a ballot, which it is the responsibility of the employer to arrange and pay for;[558] an employee or employee's representative may complain to the CAC if the employer fails to make the requisite arrangements and the CAC may

---

551   ICER 2004, reg 16(2). It is also possible for agreements to cover more than one undertaking: see DTI Guidance, 2005: pp 33–34 for further details. As we indicate in para 9.52 above, where an employer has received a request in relation to one undertaking and wishes to negotiate an agreement covering both that undertaking and another undertaking where no request has been made it will need to notify the employees in the second undertaking of its intention to do this: reg 14(6), (7).
552   ICER 2004, reg 16(3).
553   ICER 2004, regs 16(5), 17.
554   ICER 2004, reg 16(4).
555   ICER 2004, reg 18(1).
556   ICER 2004, reg 18(2).
557   ICER 2004, reg 18(1).
558   ICER 2004, reg 19.

order it to do so.[559] There must be one representative per 50 employees or part thereof, subject to a minimum of two and a maximum of 25.[560] There can be separate ballots for separate parts of the workforce if the employer considers that this would better reflect the interests of employees as a whole. There are detailed statutory conditions governing the conduct of the ballot: *inter alia*, all employees in the undertaking must have the opportunity to stand as candidates; so far as reasonably practicable employees' representatives or, if none, employees must be consulted on the proposed arrangements for the ballot; the final arrangements must be published at least 21 days before the ballot is held; an employee or employees' representative who considers that the arrangements are defective may complain to the CAC; and the conduct of the ballot must be supervised by an 'independent ballot supervisor' who has a duty to ensure that all those who are entitled to vote have an opportunity to do so, an obligation which may require the ballot to be held over more than one day or take the form of a postal vote.[561] He or she must also ensure that those voting are able to do so in secret and that votes are fairly and accurately counted. If the independent ballot supervisor considers that any of the statutory requirements was not met, with the result that the outcome of the ballot would have been different, or that he or she could not form a proper judgment on this matter because of interference or lack of co-operation by management, an 'ineffective ballot report' must be issued which means that the ballot has no effect and another must be held.[562]

Where the standard I and C provisions apply, the employer must provide I and C representatives with information on the following matters:[563]

(a) the recent and probable development of the undertaking's activities and economic situation. The DTI Guidance suggests that this is information that will help I and C representatives understand the context in which decisions affecting employment, work organisation and contractual relations are made. It may include matters such as significant changes to products or services, takeovers and mergers, developments in production processes, reorganisations and changes in senior management.[564]

(b) the situation, structure and probable development of employment within the undertaking and on any anticipatory measures envisaged, in particular, where there is a threat to employment within the undertaking. In relation to 'anticipatory measures' where there is a threat to employment, recital 8 to the Directive refers to employee training and skill development' with a view to increasing the 'employability and adaptability' of employees likely to be affected.

(c) decisions likely to lead to substantial changes in work organisation or in contractual relations. The DTI Guidance suggests that 'contractual relations means an employer's contractual relations with its employees rather than with third parties', and would include a change of employer, a 'substantial change'

---

559 ICER 2004, reg 19(4), (5).
560 ICER 2004, reg 19(3).
561 A person is an 'independent ballot supervisor' for this purpose if the employer reasonably believes that he or she will carry out functions relating to the ballot competently and has no reasonable grounds for believing that his or her independence might reasonably be called into question: ICER 2004, Sch 2, para 6.
562 See generally ICER 2004, Sch 2.
563 ICER 2004, reg 20(1). The wording reflects Art 2(2) of Directive 2002/14.
564 DTI Guidance, 2005: pp 39–40.

in terms and conditions (excluding pay or benefits with a monetary value');[565] a change to the compulsory retiring age; changes to an occupational pension scheme where there is a contractual right to participate in the scheme; and changes in disciplinary or grievance procedures.[566] It considers that 'changes in work organisation' would include changes in the level or distribution of employment within the undertaking, including redundancies and relocation of posts; changes in policy on flexible working, part-time working and overtime; changes in work patterns; and the introduction of significant new technology or equipment and any training associated with it.[567]

Information must be given at such a time, in such fashion and with such content as are appropriate to enable, in particular, the I and C representatives to conduct an adequate study and, where necessary, to prepare for consultation.[568] The obligation to consult (defined as 'the exchange of views and establishment of a dialogue between' I and C representative and the employer[569]) applies only to categories (b) and (c) above.[570] Here, the employer must ensure that consultation is conducted in such a way as to ensure that its timing, method and content are appropriate; on the basis of the information supplied by the employer to the I and C representatives and of any opinion which they express to the employer; and so as to enable the I and C representatives to meet the employer at the relevant level of management depending on the subject under discussion[571] and to obtain a reasoned response from the employer to any opinions they express.[572] Failure on the part of a person who controls the employer to provide information to it is not a valid reason for the employer failing to inform and consult.[573] Neither the Directive nor ICER 2004 is specific about the timing or frequency of I and C – in particular, it is not spelt out whether consultation must take prior to decisions being made by the employer or only in relation to the implementation of such decisions – although the recitals to the Directive indicate that its objective is to preclude decisions being taken without prior consultation.[574] However the DTI Guidance indicates that the 'requirement to provide information on the probable development of the undertaking's activities and economic situation, and of employment, clearly means that some information must be provided in advance of these developments'.[575] It also suggests that the definition of consultation, and the subjects to be covered, 'imply that ... [I and C] ... should be on-going and regular, and not simply a one-off event when a problem arises'.[576]

565 The DTI justifies this exclusion on the ground that Directive 2002/14 is based on Art 137 of the EC Treaty, which excludes pay: DTI Guidance, 2005: p 43. We doubt whether exclusion on this basis is correct.
566 DTI Guidance, 2005: p 43.
567 DTI Guidance, 2005: p 42.
568 ICER 2004, reg 20(2).
569 ICER 2004, reg 2. See also *R v British Coal Corporation and the Secretary of State for Trade and Industry, ex p Price* [1994] IRLR 72, 75. The duty of co-operation, referred to in para 9.53 above, also applies in this context: reg 21.
570 ICER 2004, reg 20(3).
571 The DTI Guidance, 2005: p 45 regards this as the 'level of management with the authority to change the decision being consulted about'.
572 ICER 2004, reg 20(4)(a)–(c).
573 ICER 2004, reg 20(6).
574 See recitals 6 and 13 and the discussion in Bercusson, 2002: p 237–239.
575 DTI Guidance, 2005: p 46.
576 DTI Guidance, 2005: p 46.

In relation to matters falling within category (c) above, the employer must consult 'with a view to reaching agreement on decisions falling within the scope of the employer's powers'.[577] The points we made in para 9.37 above about what that requires apply equally in this context. It is made clear in the Regulations that decisions within category (c) include decisions covered by sections 188–192 of TULRCA 1992 (collective redundancies) and regulations 10–12 of TUPE 1981(transfers of undertakings),[578] which we discussed earlier in this chapter. However the duties to inform and consult under ICER 2004 cease to apply if the employer has become subject to one of these specific duties and has notified the I and C representatives in writing that it will be complying with it. This notification must be given on each occasion that the employer has become or is about to become subject to the duty.[579] Employers will need to ensure that they are, objectively speaking, under the statutory duty in question before giving notice; if the number of proposed redundancies is below the 20-employee threshold, for example, they will not be subject to the duty under TULRCA 1992. The DTI Guidance states that there is no requirement under ICER 2004 to inform and consult where 'a small number of employees' is to be made redundant, but does not specify a lower limit; 'this will depend on the circumstances of the individual case', including the proportion of employees in the undertaking.[580] Employers may be best advised to err on the side of caution in this regard. Consulting under ICER 2004 does not relieve the employer of its duties under TULRCA 1992 and TUPE 1981.

Where the standard provisions apply, it is open to the employer and elected representatives to come to a negotiated agreement. This must be a single agreement; cover all the employees in the undertaking; comply with other specified requirements relating to a 'negotiated agreement'; and be signed by a majority of the I and C representatives.[581] Although the three-year 'moratorium' on employee requests (or an employer notification) to initiate negotiations applies from the date of that agreement,[582] there seems no impediment to the parties mutually agreeing to terminate it before that date which they may wish to do if, for example, they agree it would be more desirable to have an agreement covering different parts of the undertaking.

(vi) Compliance and enforcement

9.55　Where a negotiated agreement has been signed or the standard I and C provisions apply, a complaint may be presented to the CAC by a 'relevant applicant' (an I and C representative or, if none, an employee or employees' representative) that the employer has failed to comply with the terms of the agreement or of the standard provisions, as appropriate.[583] Where the CAC upholds the complaint it must make a declaration to that effect and may make an order requiring the employer to take specified steps within a specified period.[584]

577　ICER 2004, reg 20(4)(d).
578　ICER 2004, reg 20(5).
579　ICER 2004, reg 20(5).
580　DTI Guidance, 2005: pp 43.
581　ICER 2004, reg 18(2), (3).
582　ICER 2004, regs 11, 12(1).
583　ICER 2004, reg 22(1)–(3). The complaint must be made within three months of the date of the alleged failure: reg 22(2).
584　ICER 2004, reg 22(4), (5).

Where a 'relevant applicant' obtains such a declaration, or where a complaint that the employer has failed to arrange for the election of I and C representatives for the purposes of the 'standard procedure' is upheld, the applicant may apply to the EAT for a penalty notice to be issued.[585] The EAT must issue such a notice, requiring payment of a penalty to the Secretary of State, unless satisfied, on hearing representations from the employer, that the failure 'resulted from a reason beyond the employer's control or that he has some other reasonable excuse for his failure'.[586] The penalty may be up to a maximum of £75,000.[587] Matters to be taken account by the EAT when setting the amount include the gravity of the failure and the number of employees affected by it; the period of time over which it occurred and the reason for it; and the number of employees employed by the undertaking or undertakings concerned.[588] In contrast to a failure to comply with the specific I and C requirements relating to collective redundancies and transfers of the undertaking (see paras 9.40 and 9.45), therefore, there is no provision for an award to the employees covered by the failure to inform and consult.[589] It is specifically provided that no CAC order can have the effect of suspending or altering the effect of any act done or agreement made by the employer, or of preventing or delaying any proposed act or agreement.[590]

(vii) Confidential information

9.56   The duties of employers under a negotiated agreement or the standard I and C procedure are subject to two significant qualifications.[591] First, they may require any information or document to be held in confidence, or on terms that restrict the extent of disclosure.[592] Employers may be obliged to impose an obligation of confidence on information that is price sensitive; employers are able, under UK Listing Rules, to provide information about 'impending developments or matters in the course of negotiation' that may be price sensitive to representatives of employees or unions acting on their behalf, but only if such information is given in confidence.[593] Unauthorised disclosure constitutes a breach

---

585 ICER 2004, reg 22(6), 19(6). The application must be made within three months of the declaration under reg 22(4). The time limit applicable to a complaint under reg 19(4) is unclear; *quaere* whether it is within three months of an order under reg 19(5).

586 ICER 2004, reg 22(7).

587 ICER 2004, reg 23(2).

588 ICER 2004, reg 23(3).

589 The legislation specifically provides that no other sanction can be imposed on the employer for infringement of the rights conferred by ICER 2004: reg 24. However as we explained in para 9.54 above, where there is a duty to consult under TULRCA 1992, ss 188–192 or TUPE 1981 regs 10–12, such a duty is not removed by any co-extensive duty under ICER 2004.

590 ICER 2004, reg 22(9). The Commission's original proposal that, in the case of a serious breach of the obligation to inform and consult employee representatives, a decision should have no legal effect on the contract of employment until adequate I and C had taken place was opposed by a number of countries, including the UK: see Bercusson, 2002: pp 239–240.

591 These reflect Directive 2002/14, Art 6.

592 ICER 2004, reg 25(1), (2).

593 Where a negotiated agreement provides for direct I and C, employers would not be able to share such information with the workforce as a whole. The DTI Guidance, 2005 encourages employers to take decisions that result in public announcements involving price-sensitive information during working hours so that details can be released to the stock market and to employees at the same time to avoid employees hearing about such developments in the media: see Annex 2.

of statutory duty owed to the employer, except where the recipient reasonably believes this to be a 'protected disclosure' under the 'whistleblowing' provisions of ERA 1996.[594] This is without prejudice to any other form of liability, such as breach of confidence, which the recipient may incur.[595] This provision contrasts sharply with other provisions in domestic law relating to disclosure of information discussed earlier in this chapter, where no statutory provision is made for information to be disclosed on confidential terms, although there is a similar provision in TICER 1999. A recipient to whom the employer has entrusted any information or document on a confidential basis may apply to the CAC to decide whether it was reasonable for the information to be impressed with confidence; if the CAC considers that disclosure would not, or would not be likely to, 'harm the legitimate interests of the undertaking' it will grant a declaration to that effect, whereupon the information is no longer subject to the confidentiality duty.[596] The second safeguard for employers is that there is no requirement to disclose any information or document where, 'according to objective criteria', this would 'seriously harm the functioning of, or would be prejudicial to, the undertaking.'[597] The fact that information is price sensitive would not, of itself, justify withholding information where there are I and C representatives to whom it can be disclosed on a confidential basis, but the DTI Guidance suggests that evidence of 'past leaks' may be relevant in assessing whether sensitive information should be disclosed.[598] A dispute between an employer and an I and C representative (if there is one) or an employee or employees' representative as to whether information falls within this category can be referred by either party to the CAC, which may order disclosure on specified terms if it does considers that disclosure would not be seriously harmful or prejudicial.[599]

(viii) Protection of individuals

9.57   Negotiating representatives and I and C representatives are entitled to be permitted to take reasonable paid time off during working hours in order to perform their functions, with recourse to an employment tribunal in the event that permission has been unreasonably refused or payment withheld.[600] However, in contrast to time off rights of officials of recognised trade unions,[601] there is no entitlement to time off for training. Representatives who are not members of or otherwise associated with an independent union may find it difficult to obtain the expertise required to act as an effective I and C representative; although it is not required by the legislation, it would be good industrial relations practice to afford employees access to external training to perform their roles. Such persons,

---

594 ICER 2004, reg 25(3), (5). See further para 4.103 on 'protected disclosures'. Technically an employer could still pursue other forms of action even if a disclosure were 'protected', but such an act would almost certainly fall within the public interest defence to breach of confidence (see generally Toulsen and Phipps, 1996: ch VI),and the standards set in ERA 1996 may themselves influence the courts in applying the public interest defence.
595 ICER 2004, reg 25(4).
596 ICER 2004, reg 25(6)–(8).
597 ICER 2004, reg 26. This reflects Art 6(2) of Directive 2002/14. 'It is not clear why, for some information to be banned, it must "seriously" harm functioning, but for other information it suffices to be merely "prejudicial" in order not to be disclosed': Bercusson, 2002: p 224.
598 DTI Guidance, 2005: p 54–55.
599 ICER 2004, reg 26(2)–(4).
600 ICER 2004, reg 27–29.
601 TULRCA 1992, s 168(2); see para 8.35.

together with candidates for such positions and employees' representatives, are protected against unfair dismissal and subjection to a detriment for the performance of their functions, or for requesting time off to perform them,[602] and employees generally are protected against such acts for a range of reasons relating to ICER 2004.[603]

(x) Compatibility with the Directive

9.58   ICER were introduced in order to implement the UK's obligations under Directive 2004/14. However it is strongly arguable that they fail to do this. First, there is provision for a negotiated agreement to allow for direct I and C of employees. The Directive, by contrast, envisages consultation through employees' representatives;[604] although it is 'without prejudice to those systems which provide for the direct involvement of employees' this is 'so long as they are always free to exercise the right to be informed and consulted through their representatives'.[605] Second, it can be argued that the provision for a 'trigger' in the form of a minimum level of support before employers are required to establish I and C constitutes an impediment to the exercise of rights under the Directive, particularly where there is a 'pre-existing agreement' (which can also provide for direct I and C) and a 40% majority of employees in the undertaking is required before the employer must initiate negotiations.[606] The fact that these provisions were agreed by the TUC and CBI reduces the risk in practice of a domestic judicial review application, but would not prevent infringement proceedings by the Commission. Third, concerns about the independence of I and C representatives which we articulated in the context of redundancies and transfers of the undertaking[607] apply equally in this context. Finally, it can be argued that the £75,000 penalty that can be imposed in the event of an employer's failure to meet its I and C obligations does not constitute an 'effective, proportionate and dissuasive' sanction,[608] particularly in the case of larger undertakings. At the time of writing it remains to be seen whether any action will be taken by the Commission in relation to any of these matters.

EMPLOYEE INVOLVEMENT AT TRANSNATIONAL LEVEL

9.59   As we indicated in para 9.30, there are two contexts in which European Community law requires employee involvement at transnational level: the European Works Council Directive and the Directive on Employee Involvement

---

602 The protections do not apply where the employee has disclosed confidential information in breach of a restriction imposed by the employer unless the employee reasonably believed the disclosure to be a 'protected disclosure': ICER 2004, regs 30(4), 32(4); see para 9.56 above.

603 ICER 2004, regs 30–33.

604 Art 1(3).

605 Recital 16.

606 There is no provision for a trigger in the Directive. Recital 15 states that the Directive is 'without prejudice to national systems regarding the exercise of this right in practice where those entitled to exercise it are required to indicate their wishes collectively. However, even if this permits some form of trigger, *quaere* whether the level of support required where there is a 'pre-existing agreement' is too high a hurdle.

607 See paras 9.35 and 9.43.

608 See Art 8(2) of Directive 2002/14.

in the European Company (SE). The European Works Council Directive was implemented in the UK by TICER 1999.[609] We outline the main provisions of TICER 1999 below. ICER 2004, which we discuss above, were modelled in certain respects on TICER 1999, although there are also significant differences between them. The Directive on Employee Involvement in the European Company was implemented by EPLLCR 2004,[610] which came into force on 8 October 2004. These Regulations can be properly understood only by reference to the European Company Statute, consideration of which lies beyond the scope of this work. We refer only briefly to the broad framework of the Statute and accompanying Directive in para 9.65 below.

European Works Councils

9.60   TICER 1999 require a European Works Council (EWC) or information and consultation procedure (ICP), to be established in every 'Community-scale undertaking', defined as any undertaking with at least 1,000 employees (not 'workers') within the Member States and at least 150 employees in each of at least two Member States,[611] and in every 'Community-scale group of undertakings.'[612] The rationale behind this dual threshold under the Directive

---

609 SI 1999/3323, issued under the ECA 1972, s 2(2) The Regulations can be taken to reflect the Directive unless otherwise indicated. For a more detailed analysis of TICER 1999 see G Morris and T Archer, 2000: paras 5.37–5.62.

610 SI 2004/2326 issued under the ECA 1972, s 2(2).

611 TICER 1999, reg 2(1); see reg 2(1) and para 3.19 *et seq* above for the definition of 'employee'. For UK employees, the number employed is determined by ascertaining the average number of employees employed during a two-year period, in accordance with specified criteria: reg 6. Certain part-time employees may be counted as half a person. The number of non-UK employees employed over a two-year period is to be calculated in accordance with the law and practice of the Member State in question. An employee or 'employees' representative' may request information from the management of an establishment or undertaking in the UK to determine whether it is part of a Community-scale undertaking or group of undertakings, with provision for complaint to the CAC if the recipient fails to provide accurate information as to the average number of employees employed by the undertaking or group in the UK and other Member States over the past two years: regs 7 and 8 (on which see *Haines and The British Council* EWC1/2004, CAC, 15 July 2004). There is no definition of 'establishment' in this context; see para 9.32 for the interpretation of this term in the context of collective redundancies. In Case C-62/99 *Betriebsrat der bofrost* Josef H Boquoi Deutschland West Gmbh & Co KG v bofrost* Josef H Boquoi Deutschland West Gmbh & Co KG* [2001] IRLR 403 the ECJ held that the communication of documents clarifying information provided for the purpose of determining whether employees or their representatives are entitled to request the opening of negotiations for establishing an EWC or ICP may be required. See also Case C-440/00 *Gesamtbetriebsrat der Kuhne & Nagel AG & Co KG v Kuhne & Nagel AG & Co KG* [2004] IRLR 332.

612 A group of undertakings with at least 1,000 employees within the Member States; at least two group undertakings in different Member States; and at least one group undertaking with at least 150 employees in one Member State and at least one other group undertaking with at least 150 employees in another Member State: TICER 1999, reg 2(1). See TICER 1999, reg 2(1) for the meaning of 'group of undertakings'. In *Bofrost* above, the ECJ confirmed the right of employees or their representatives to information enabling them to determine whether they have the right to demand the opening of negotiations for establishing an EWC or ICP even where it has not yet been established that the management to whom the request for information is addressed is that of a controlling undertaking within a group of undertakings.

was first, that small businesses should not be burdened with additional obligations which might be detrimental to their development, and second, that this proposal should have no effect on existing information and consultation procedures in Member States based on national legislation and practices.'[613] There is no definition of 'undertaking' in either TICER 1999 or the Directive,[614] but ECJ jurisprudence relating to Article 81 EC, which prohibits anti-competitive behaviour, has made clear that the term covers any natural or legal person carrying on activities of an economic or commercial nature,[615] including, for example, limited companies, partnerships, trade associations, sole traders, and state corporations. The fact that the body is engaged in non-profit making activities does not, of itself, deprive its activities of their economic character.[616] The Directive requires the 'central management' of the undertaking to create the conditions and means necessary for establishing an EWC or ICP.[617] Reflecting the terms of the Directive, TICER 1999 impose this obligation on the central management where it is located in the UK or treated as such: that is, where it is located outside a Member State (in the USA, for example) but its 'representative agent' is situated in the UK or, if none, there are more employees employed in an establishment or group undertaking in the UK than are employed in any other establishment in a Member State.[618] It is notable that in the latter situation the crucial issue is not the total number of employees employed in the UK but the total number employed *in an establishment* in the UK. Thus, if a Japanese group of companies owns fifty establishments in the UK, each employing 100 employees, and a single establishment in France employing 300, the central management will not be treated as situated in the UK.

9.61 Negotiations for establishing an EWC or ICP may be initiated by central management. Alternatively, they must be initiated if at least 100 employees, or employees' representatives who represent at least that number, in at least two undertakings or establishments in at least two Member States so request.[619] 'Employees' representatives' under TICER 1999 fall into two distinct categories.[620] First, if the employees are of a description for which an independent trade union is recognised, they are representatives of the union who normally take part in the collective bargaining process. Second, the term covers 'any other employee representatives elected or appointed by employees to positions in which they are expected to receive, on behalf of the employees, information (i) which is relevant to the terms and conditions of employment of the employees, or (ii) about the activities of the undertaking which may significantly affect the interests of the employees'. However, representatives who are expected to receive information relevant only to a specific aspect of the terms and conditions or interests of

---

613 Barnard, 2000: p 530.
614 Cf Directive 2002/14, art 2(1).
615 Case 170/83 *Hydrotherm Geratebau GmbH v Compact del Dott. Ing. Mario Andreoli and CSAS* [1984] ECR 2999, paras 10–12.
616 Case C-382/92 *Commission v UK* [1994] IRLR 392, 411. See further para 3.101 for the meaning of 'undertaking' in the context of TUPE and the Acquired Rights Directive.
617 Art 4(1).
618 TICER 1999, regs 4 and 5.
619 TICER 1999, reg 9. If the central management considers that the obligation to initiate negotiations did not apply to it on the relevant date it may apply to the CAC for a declaration: reg 10.
620 Cf ICER 2004, where the term 'employees' representative' is deliberately left undefined.

employees, such as health and safety, are excluded.[621] It is notable that in this context, unlike that of collective redundancies, health and safety and transfers of the undertaking, a trade union, where recognised, is not the exclusive channel; even where there is such a union other employees' representatives may act.

The scope, composition, functions and term of office of a EWC or the arrangements for implementing an ICP are determined by a 'special negotiating body' (SNB) in conjunction with central management.[622] This means that the management cannot unilaterally foist a procedure on its workforce. The composition of the SNB where the central management is situated in the UK is tightly specified in TICER 1999. It must contain at least one member representing each Member State in which the Community-scale undertaking has one or more establishments (or in which the Community-scale group of undertakings has its controlling undertaking or one or more controlled undertakings), with up to three additional members, the number determined according to the percentage of all employees employed in the Member States employed by the undertaking or group of undertakings in that Member State.[623] UK members of an SNB must be elected by a ballot of UK employees, supervised by an 'independent ballot supervisor', except where there is an elected 'consultative committee' representing the UK employees which may nominate SNB members from among its number.[624] These selection provisions apply regardless of whether the central management is in the UK. A 'consultative committee', broadly speaking, means a body whose normal functions include the carrying out of an information and consultation function in relation to all UK employees, which is able to carry out this function without interference from the UK management or from the central management, and which consists of persons elected by a ballot in which all the then UK employees were entitled to vote.[625] An election may be mandatory, therefore, even where there is a recognised independent union; whether it will be needed where there are I and C representatives in place will depend upon whether they were elected and satisfy the other elements of the definition of a 'consultative committee'. The conditions that must be satisfied where a ballot to elect members of the SNB is required are, broadly speaking, the same as those applicable to the election of I and C representatives for the purposes of the 'standard' provisions under ICER 2004.[626]

The central management of the undertaking or group of undertakings must convene a meeting with the SNB to reach a written agreement on the detailed arrangements for the information and consultation of employees.[627] 'Consultation' means 'the exchange of views and establishment of dialogue' between members of an EWC, or ICP representatives, and central management

---

621 TICER 1999, reg 2. There is no definition of 'recognition' or collective bargaining in this context; cf TULRCA 1992, s 178. Note that, unlike a trade union, 'employees' representatives' are defined in terms of their relationships with 'employees' and not 'workers'.

622 TICER 1999, regs 16 and 17.

623 TICER 1999, reg 12.

624 TICER 1999, reg 13.

625 TICER 1999, reg 15. There is provision for complaint to the CAC in the event that the UK management or an employee or employees' representative considers that the 'consultative committee' does not satisfy the statutory definition or any of the persons it nominates is not entitled to be nominated.

626 See para 9.54 above; TICER 1999, regs 13 and 14. An 'independent ballot supervisor' is defined in reg 13(7).

627 TICER 1999, reg 16(1).

or any more appropriate level of management;[628] notably this definition (which reflects that in the Directive) says nothing about the stage of any decision-making process at which consultation must take place, or even that it must take place before any decision is taken. For the purpose of its negotiations, the SNB may be assisted by experts of its choice; however, although the central management must pay for reasonable expenses incurred by the SNB that are necessary to enable it to carry out its functions, it is required to pay the expenses of one expert only.[629] The parties may decide to establish an ICP instead of an EWC; if so, the resulting agreement must specify a method by which the representatives are to enjoy the right to meet to discuss the information conveyed to them.[630] That information must relate in particular to transnational questions that affect the interests of employees; thus, the procedure is not designed to convey information relating to purely national or sub-national issues. If the parties decide to establish an EWC, their agreement must determine the undertakings or establishments covered by it; its composition, and the number and term of office of its members, and allocation of seats; the functions and procedure for informing and consulting it; the venue, frequency and duration of its meetings; the financial and material resources to be allocated to it; and the duration of the agreement and procedure for its renegotiation.[631] These provisions mean that the SNB has considerable discretion to negotiate arrangements which meet the particular circumstances of the individual enterprise. It is also free to decide, by a two-thirds majority, not to open, or to terminate such negotiations,[632] although it is difficult, prima facie, to imagine circumstances where it may wish to take this view.

9.62 As a fall-back to these provisions, the Regulations specify 'subsidiary requirements' which apply if the central management refuses to commence negotiations within six months of a valid request from employees or their representatives, or if the parties are unable to agree on information and consultation arrangements within three years of such a request.[633] In addition the parties may specifically decide to adopt all or any of the subsidiary requirements.[634] They provide, *inter alia*, for the composition of an EWC (between three and thirty members, determined according to the same formula applicable to an SNB); its competence; the appointment or election of its UK members; the frequency of its meetings; and its procedures.[635] If the EWC considers that its size so warrants, it must elect from its members a 'select committee' of up to three members to act on its behalf.[636] Notably, all UK members must be UK employees (in contrast to members of the SNB), so excluding union representatives who are not so employed.[637] Where all UK employees are represented by UK

---

628 TICER 1999, reg 2.
629 TICER 1999, reg 16(5), (6).
630 TICER 1999, reg 17.
631 TICER 1999, reg 17.
632 TICER 1999, reg 16. If this happens, a new request to establish an EWC or ICP less than two years after that date must be disregarded unless the SNB and central management agree otherwise.
633 TICER 1999, reg 18.
634 TICER 1999, reg 17(6), 18. For information on the forms of agreements which have been adopted throughout the EEA, see the *European Works Councils Bulletin*.
635 See generally TICER 1999, Schedule.
636 TICER 1999, Schedule, para 2.
637 TICER 1999, Schedule, para 3(1).

employees' representatives, those representatives choose the members of the EWC by whatever method they decide; otherwise UK members of the EWC must be elected by a ballot of employees which complies with the same conditions, *mutandis mutatis*, as apply to the election of members of the SNB, with identical provision for complaint to the CAC.[638] The competence of the EWC is limited to information and consultation on matters which concern the Community-scale undertaking or group of undertakings as a whole, or at least two of its establishments or group undertakings situated in different Member States.[639] Like an ICP, therefore, it cannot be used as a vehicle to deal with national or local concerns, although this is subject to the proviso that decisions taken in relation to employees in one Member State may impact on employees in another; in the area of redundancies, for example, job losses in one Member State may preserve jobs in another. The EWC has the right to meet with central management once a year to be informed and consulted, on the basis of a report drawn up by the central management, on the progress and prospects of the undertaking or group. This meeting must relate in particular to:

> ... the structure, economic and financial situation, the probable development of the business and of production and sales, the situation and probable trend of employment, investments, and substantial changes concerning organisation, introduction of new working methods or production processes, transfers of production, mergers, cut-backs or closures of undertakings, establishments or important parts thereof, and collective redundancies.[640]

In addition, whenever there are 'exceptional circumstances affecting the employees' interests to a considerable extent, particularly in the event of relocations, the closure of establishments or undertakings or collective redundancies', the select committee, or, where none exists, the EWC has the right to be informed and to meet, at its request, the central management or any other more appropriate level of management having its own power of decision, so as to be informed and consulted. If the meeting is held with the select committee, those EWC members elected or appointed by the establishments or undertakings directly concerned by the measures in question also have the right to participate in the meeting. However it is explicitly affirmed that an exceptional meeting of this nature does not affect the prerogatives of the central management.[641] Subject to the duty of confidentiality, discussed below, EWC members must inform employees' representatives in the relevant establishment or undertakings, or, if none, employees themselves, of the content and outcome of the information and consultation procedure.[642] Before either a routine or exceptional meeting the EWC or select committee is entitled to meet without the management concerned being present. The operating expenses of the EWC must be borne by central management; in common with an SNB, the EWC or select committee may be assisted by experts of its choice, but central management need only pay for one such expert. In addition, the central management must provide EWC members

---

638 TICER 1999, Schedule, paras 3–5. See para 3(2) for the definition of 'represented by UK employees' representatives'.

639 TICER 1999, Schedule, para 6(1).

640 TICER 1999, Schedule, para 7. Art 12 of the Directive specifies that this obligation operates without prejudice to the information and consultation requirements of the directives on collective redundancies and transfers of undertakings, and this is reflected in domestic law.

641 TICER 1999, Schedule, para 8.

642 TICER 1999, Schedule, para 9.

with the financial and material resources to enable them to perform their duties in an appropriate manner.[643] Four years after its establishment, an EWC constituted by reference to the subsidiary requirements must examine whether it wishes to continue operating on these principles or whether it wishes to open negotiations with central management for different arrangements, in which case it then assumes the role taken by an SNB in relation to any subsequent negotiations.[644] Research published in June 2000 indicated that, at the time of writing, there had been no known case in which a company in any Member State had been required to establish an EWC according to the subsidiary requirements (which are drawn from the Directive), but that these provisions had strongly influenced arrangements introduced by agreement.[645] Regardless of whether the EWC has been agreed or imposed, it and central management must work in a 'spirit of cooperation with due regard to their reciprocal rights and obligations'.[646]

If the parties agreed to establish an EWC or ICP, or the subsidiary requirements became applicable, but, due to a failure of central management, no EWC or ICP has been established, the SNB or, where none exists, a former SNB member or an employee or employees' representative may complain to the EAT, which may order central management to take specified steps to establish the EWC or ICP. It may also require the central management to pay a penalty to the Secretary of State on the same principles, and subject to the same maximum, as applicable under ICER 2004, discussed in para 9.55 above.[647] Employees have the right to paid time off to perform their functions in relation to membership of an SNB, EWC, or as an ICP representative, or as candidates for those positions.[648] Such persons also have protection against unfair dismissal and subjection to a detriment for the performance of their functions, or for requesting time off to perform them, and employees generally are protected against such acts for a range of reasons relating to the establishment or operation of an EWC or ICP.[649]

9.63 Regardless of whether information and consultation procedures are agreed or imposed they remain qualified by two very significant safeguards for

---

643 TICER 1999, Schedule, para 9.
644 TICER 1999, Schedule, para 10.
645 Carley and Hall, 2000: p 105. This remains the case in 2005: Hall, 2005: p 122.
646 TICER 1999, reg 19. The same duty is placed on ICP representatives.
647 TICER 1999, regs 20, 22. (cf ICER 2004, para 9.55 above, where provision is made for complaint in the first instance to the CAC). There is also provision in TICER 1999 for the central management, EWC or any ICP representative to complain to the EAT that the terms of the parties' agreement or the subsidiary requirements have not been complied with because of the failure of the other party: reg 21. £75,000 was chosen as a maximum penalty on the basis that the average estimated cost of holding an EWC was around £60,000: *Implementation in the UK of the European Works Council Directive*, URN 99/926, July 1999: p 37. The Directive merely requires Member States to 'provide for appropriate measures in the event of failure to comply with' the Directive, in particular adequate administrative or judicial procedures to enable the obligations it contains to be enforced: Art 11(3). It does not, therefore, specify the form of sanction.
648 TICER 1999, regs 25–27. These rights apply regardless of the location of central management. Controversially, there is no express provision for time off for training for any of these activities, despite the fact that new skills are likely to be needed (see D Miller and J Stirling, 1998). *Quaere* whether the subsidiary requirement for central management to provide EWC members with the material resources to enable them to perform their duties in an appropriate manner (Schedule, para 9(6)) could extend to training.
649 TICER 1999, regs 28, 29, 31.

management (which the Directive requires all Member States to put in place).[650] First, they provide that members of an SNB, EWC, ICP representatives or experts assisting them (collectively termed 'recipients') owe a permanent duty to the central management (UK or otherwise) not to disclose any information in their possession by virtue of their position as such which has been entrusted to them on confidential terms. As in the case of ICER 2004, disclosure constitutes a breach of a statutory duty, except where the recipient reasonably believes it to be a 'protected disclosure' under the 'whistleblowing' provisions of ERA 1996.[651] Again this is without prejudice to any other form of liability, such as breach of confidence, which the recipient may incur.[652] Where the central management is situated in the UK a recipient may apply to the CAC for a declaration as to whether it was reasonable for information to be impressed with confidence; if the CAC considers that disclosure would not be likely to prejudice or cause serious harm to the undertaking it grants a declaration to that effect, whereupon the information is no longer subject to the confidentiality duty.[653] Notably, however, the CAC will be powerless if the information reveals wrongdoing or a threat to the environment, for example, given that revelation of such information would almost certainly cause serious harm to the undertaking. In that event, the recipient would need to take the risk that he or she would be protected by ERA 1996 or the general 'public interest' defence, as appropriate, in the event of any ensuing detriment from the employer or legal action. The second safeguard for management is the exception from disclosure of any information where 'according to objective criteria' this would 'seriously harm the functioning of, or would be prejudicial to, the undertaking or group of undertakings concerned'. This applies only where central management is situated in the UK, but compliance with the Directive requires the same dispensation to be applied in other Member States. Again a dispute about whether information falls within the 'protected' category can be referred to the CAC, which may order disclosure on specified terms if it does not consider the criteria for protection to be met.[654] Logically, it would not seem reasonable for such terms to include a duty of confidentiality, given that the requisite criteria have not been satisfied, but the CAC could require information to be anonymised or particular sections to be removed from a document, for example.

9.64   The obligations laid down by the Directive did not apply if, by the deadline for its implementation by states other than the UK (22 September 1996) there was already an agreement, covering the entire workforce, providing for the transnational information and consultation of employees (although in the event of non-renewal of such an agreement the Directive became applicable).[655] It was estimated that around 450 such agreements were concluded.[656] The Directive

---

650 Art 8.
651 TICER 1999, reg 23; see para 9.56.
652 TICER 1999, reg 23(4).
653 TICER 1999, reg 23(7). Cf ICER 2004, reg 25(7) where the test is whether disclosure would be likely to 'harm the legitimate interests of the undertaking'.
654 TICER 1999, reg 24.
655 Art 13.
656 Carley and Hall, 2000: p 107. See Marginson *et al*, 1998, for the content of such agreements. As of 2004, fewer than half the undertakings covered by the Directive had established EWC agreements: an estimated 737 out of more than 2,100: see Hall and Marginson, 2004 (which also discusses the content and impact of EWCs). This figure includes the ten Member States that joined in May 2004, but even in 2002 more than 1800 undertakings were estimated to be covered.

that extended the original Directive to the UK afforded a similar exemption to companies which became subject to its terms solely as a result of the extension.[657] The facility to establish EWCs outside the regime of the Directive meant that 'the specific framework of each EWC derived from a complex bargaining process reflecting the relative power of employee representatives and employers'.[658] Research suggests that there is widespread dissatisfaction amongst EWC representatives with the current practices of EWCs, particularly regarding the quality of information and consultation.[659] More broadly, it remains to be seen whether the benefits of EWCs are more symbolic than real.[660]

Employee Involvement in the European Company (Societas Europaea)

9.65   The European Company statute[661] allows a European Company (SE) to be established in four different ways: the merger of two or more existing public limited companies from at least two Member States; the formation of a holding company promoted by public or private limited companies from at least two Member States; the formation of a subsidiary of companies from at least two Member States; and the transformation of an existing public limited company which has, for at least two years, had a subsidiary in another Member State.[662] The initial intention was to 'offer a uniform set of rules, separate from any national system, which companies merging across national borders could adopt',[663] but as the statute requires reference to the national law of the Member State where the SE is registered in a number of important areas this goal has been only partially achieved. The accompanying Directive on Employee Involvement in the European Company[664] is complex and can be properly understood only in relation to the European Company statute, which lies beyond the scope of this work. Space permits us to highlight only three important features.[665] First, no SE may be registered unless one of three conditions relating to employee involvement has been satisfied: management and employee representatives have reached an agreement on employee involvement; employee

---

657 Council Directive 97/74/EC, Art 3. Note that even during the period of the UK's opt-out from the Directive, it had important implications for multi-national companies based in this country: where they employed the threshold number of workers in two or more other Member States they fell within its terms. These companies appear to have extended EWC arrangements to their British operations, even though not legally obliged to do so: W Brown *et al*, 1997: p 74. Likewise, the vast majority of companies based elsewhere in the Community with an establishment in this country decided to include UK workers in their consultation arrangements, even though such workers had no legal right to require this: see Weber *et al*, 2000.
658 Royle, 1999: p 330; see also Wedderburn, 1997: pp 21–26.
659 J Waddington, 2003c; Hall and Marginson, 2004.
660 See further Villiers, 2000, and references therein. On 20 April 2004 the Commission initiated consultations with the EU-level cross-industry and sectoral social partners as part of a review of the Directive: see *European Works Councils Bulletin* Issue 51, May/June 2004: pp 10–14. For a useful discussion of desirable reforms, see P Lorber, 2004; see also Hall and Marginson, 2004.
661 Council Regulation (EC) No 2157/2001. We do not, in this very broad brush account, refer to numbered provisions of the Regulation or accompanying Directive.
662 Keller, 2002: p 428.
663 P Davies, 2003: p 77.
664 Directive 2001/86.
665 See P Davies, 2003: p 79 *et seq*.

representatives have decided that they do not wish to negotiate special involvement arrangements for the SE; or the Standard Rules on employee involvement, set out in the Annex to the Directive, have been triggered. Second, the I and C provisions in the Directive are based on a similar structure to the European Works Councils Directive, although applicable regardless of the size of the Company. Finally, and ostensibly more radically, there is provision for board-level participation where this was previously required under the national law governing a substantial proportion of the workforce to be employed by the SE after it is formed. However, this was a 'defensive, not proactive' policy, designed to prevent the SE being used as a vehicle for undermining existing national provisions on board-level participation rather than positively to promote board-level participation.[666] The Directive is implemented in the UK by the European Public Limited-Liability Company Regulations 2004.[667] It remains to be seen whether the establishment of SEs will prove an attractive option

COLLECTIVE REPRESENTATION: PROSPECTS FOR THE FUTURE

9.66   In this concluding section we discuss some of the broader issues raised by the subject-matter of this chapter.

The most basic question is whether, and on what ground, there should be *any* form of employee involvement, even consultation, in the decision-making processes of an enterprise. It could be argued that the employment relationship is purely a commercial one, based upon the exchange of wages for labour power, and that mutual satisfaction of that bargain is the sole legitimate interest of the worker. In reality, whatever their ideological stance, it is unlikely that many employers translate this view wholeheartedly into practice, although their channels of communication may be individualised rather than collective and information and consultative mechanisms may be merely cosmetic.

The arguments which proponents of worker involvement invoke divide broadly into three (overlapping) categories. The first can be labelled the 'democratic' argument – that workers have a right to participate in the decisions which affect their interests and working lives.[668] This may be viewed as an important element in a broader social consensus and cohesion; it is notable that the system of 'co-determination' introduced in Germany following the Second World War was seen as integral to the establishment of a democratic political order.[669] The second argument is economic: that although the representation of worker interests may delay the implementation of decisions, particularly in areas such as reorganisation and redundancies, ultimately it is likely to result in a much better reconciliation of interests between employers and workers which will be beneficial to the economic well-being of the enterprise. One commentator has

---

666 P Davies, 2003: p 84.

667 SI 2004/2326, which came into force on 8 October 2004.

668 See, for example, Towers, 1997.

669 For a useful analysis of the operation of 'co-determination' in Germany, see Streeck, 1992. The concept of 'co-determination' in Germany refers both to co-determination at the workplace, exercised through works councils, and in the enterprise, exercised through worker representatives on company boards. In the UK the inclusion of worker representatives on company boards has never been wholeheartedly supported by the labour movement: Roderick Martin, 1992: p 71.

concluded that in Germany, for example, co-determination 'has proven an effective mechanism to bring about an accommodation of interests at the level of the individual enterprise, resulting in a commitment of labour, in the form in which it is organised at the workplace, to competitiveness, productivity and profitability'.[670] The third argument relates to the well-being of the community. As Parkinson explains,[671] '[w]here employees have a say in investment or relocation decisions the economic well-being of the local community is likely to be better served than where these decisions are made entirely by distant boards or dispersed and remote investors. Similarly, employees might also be expected to show a greater sensitivity to the impact of commercial activity on the local physical environment, though there is no doubt scope here too for a conflict of interests between those who work in the enterprise and those who are otherwise affected by it'. The extent to which any of these three objectives underlying employee representation are realised in practice will depend upon a variety of factors including the form of worker involvement chosen and its relationship with other aspects of industrial relations, such as the structure of trade unions or other representative organisations, and with the broader political society.[672]

The second basic question posed is whether, and why, such representation should be collective rather than employees being informed and consulted by their employer on an individual basis. Recent years have seen a growing tendency by some employers to communicate directly with employees through methods such as newsletters.[673] Computer technology, in particular e-mail, has enhanced the possibility of interactive communications, sometimes to the top level of the organisation. In some cases this may be viewed and presented by management as a form of 'direct democracy' which circumvents the need for any collective representation. However, it is important to note that it is not a substitute. While individual employees may be well-informed about their own working environment and conditions they are unlikely to have the time, or possibly the resources and expertise, to be able to analyse from a broader perspective information about the enterprise as a whole. Moreover, their role in such procedures is likely ultimately to be a passive one of reacting to proposals emanating from management; even if they are invited to express their preferences the parameters of the discussion have been framed elsewhere. More fundamentally, the views of workers have considerably greater strength if they are presented as a collective voice rather than as a number of isolated individuals. Collectivism also minimises the possibility that individuals who challenge the status quo can be picked off silently as 'troublemakers': in this context solidarity (only) is power.

9.67 If one accepts the need for worker representation, this leads on to a question of its form. In accordance with the range of variables discussed above, there is no 'best' model of worker participation which can be readily transplanted between different societies and, indeed, there are wide discrepancies between individual countries. The problems of transplantation are compounded by the fact that

---

670 Streeck, 1992: p 166. See also Rogers and Streeck, 1995. It should not be overlooked, however, that this co-determination operates within a framework in which collective bargaining of a more adversarial nature takes place at sectoral level between trade unions and employers' associations.

671 Parkinson, 1993: p 398.

672 See Hyman, 1997.

673 Cully *et al*, 1999: pp 229–230.

'classificatory labels' which are 'apparently similar' such as 'works councils' are 'used to refer to different structures and even to completely divergent functions'.[674] Thus, while it may be beneficial to construct general criteria which it is desirable that a representative model should satisfy, which can then be incorporated into international standards, the precise structure needs to be considered in the light of national industrial relations culture and practice. Whether or not representation should continue to be channelled through trade unions has been, as we noted earlier in this chapter, an issue of debate in the UK in recent years in the light of reduced membership levels and of developments in European Community law. Enterprise-level representation and trade unionism are not mutually exclusive and, indeed, in this country consultative committees have traditionally co-existed with union recognition.[675] In recent years the TUC has recognised that non-union channels of representation can exist alongside trade union collective bargaining,[676] and this is likely to become an increasing pattern in the light of ICER 2004. One fundamental principle is clear, however – regardless of its form effective worker representation requires independence from the employer, with adequate resources for the organisation to function in the face of managerial hostility. As compared with enterprise-based organisations, trade unions – whose membership in Britain will usually cover a range of employers – are more likely to be able to satisfy these tests, having a separate organisational base and senior officials who are employed by the union rather than the employer of the members they represent. Moreover, in covering a range of employers, trade unions are likely to acquire a broader knowledge base of terms and conditions in a particular sector which can enable them to represent their members more effectively. Whether they act as reliable conduits of their members' views clearly depends upon the internal structures of the union which enable these views to be transmitted. In the context of this discussion, the significance of extra-union forms of representation in varying or determining labour standards in the important areas of working time, parental leave and successive fixed-term contracts are particular causes for concern.[677]

9.68   A subsequent question is the function of worker representation in relation to employers and, in particular, whether it should take the form of joint regulation or, rather, be purely consultative. The standards in this area promulgated by the ILO strongly urge collective bargaining as the primary method of determining terms and conditions of employment. Thus Convention No 98 provides, in Article 4, that '[m]easures appropriate to national conditions shall be taken, where necessary, to encourage and promote the full development and utilisation of machinery for voluntary negotiation between employers or employers' organisations and workers' organisations, with a view to the regulation of terms and conditions of employment by means of collective agreements'.[678] The arguments for collective bargaining as compared with consultation again rest

---

674   Biagi and Tiraboschi, 2004: para 2.

675   See Cully, *et al*, 1999: p 100.

676   Statutory Trade Union Recognition Joint Statement by TUC and CBI, December 1997, para 8; *High Performing Workplaces – Informing and Consulting Employees: Consultation Document*, DTI, 2003: pp 5–23.

677   See paras 4.74, 6.104 and 5.78.

678   See also Convention No 154 concerning the Promotion of Collective Bargaining (1981) (which the UK has not ratified); Recommendation No 163 concerning the Promotion of Collective Bargaining (1981).

on several grounds. Once more the democracy argument is at the forefront. In the much-quoted words of the Donovan Commission: 'Properly conducted, collective bargaining is the most effective means of giving workers the right to representation in decisions affecting their working lives, a right which is or should be the prerogative of every worker in a democratic society'.[679] One may add to this the need to ensure that collective bargaining is backed up by appropriate sanctions available to workers, such as access to industrial action or voluntarily agreed alternative dispute mechanisms such as arbitration, should negotiations break down. The other arguments in favour of collective bargaining are primarily those which are capable of benefiting employers, although whether they are so perceived is another matter. First, in the case of all but small employers, it is likely to be a more efficient method of determining terms and conditions than negotiating with employees on an individual basis.[680] The transparency of collectively-agreed terms is also more likely to avoid suspicion and attempts at 'bidding up' by individual employees. On a more specific note it may also help to protect employers against equal pay claims – at least those brought by recognised trade unions. Second, collective bargaining can assist employers in 'selling' unpopular decisions to the workforce; if the union is party to a low wage settlement, for example, because of information about the undertaking's financial situation made available to it by the employer, this may be more likely to diffuse discontent, or at least the blame. Third, effective collective bargaining helps to ensure that employers do not seek to gain a competitive advantage by depressing terms and conditions of employment. Such a strategy, while it may benefit a firm in the short run, carries long-term costs in terms of worker demotivation and a loss of quality in performance. Where collective bargaining entrenches basic labour standards, therefore, it not only protects employees' rights but may also contribute to the greater productivity of both labour and capital.[681] However, the structural challenges to collective bargaining, which have not been confined to the UK,[682] should not be underestimated. Collective bargaining in its traditional form is predicated on the model of a more or less stable workforce which works on harmonised, or comparable, terms and conditions. This model is under threat both externally and internally. Changes in the labour market, which have brought greater flexibility of labour, and a growth in short-term, temporary work and in self-employment, have eroded the bargaining power of those who remain in the 'core'. Within organisations, there has been a growth in individualised work arrangements, such as personal contracts and performance- related pay, which, while they do not preclude collective bargaining in theory, are, in the case of the former in particular, likely to do so in practice.[683] In the UK, the decline in

---

679 *Royal Commission on Trade Unions and Employers' Associations 1965–1968*, Cmnd 3623, 1968: para 212.

680 This is not to imply that collective bargaining is merely a collective version of individual bargaining, however. Such a view would overlook the rule-making function of collective agreements: see Flanders, 1970.

681 Streeck, 1992; Deakin and Wilkinson, 1994; see also W Brown *et al*, 1997: p 80 *et seq* and references therein; Davidov, 2004.

682 However, in no other western European country were there adverse changes in legal support for trade unionism of the type which occurred during the period of Conservative Government: see Terry, 1994: p 234; para 1.25 above.

683 For an analysis which emphasises the variety of ways in which individualism and collectivism may relate in this context, however, see Kessler and Purcell, 1995.

the coverage of collective bargaining did not of itself result in the development of alternative models of employee representation; on the contrary consultative committees tended to be confined to contexts where trade unions were recognised.[684] However, at the time of writing this seems likely to change; employers have a strong incentive to establish representative structures to avoid the more prescriptive provisions of ICER 2004, although this development could further threaten the hegemony of trade unions as worker representative bodies.

The future shape of employee representation in Britain has been unpredictable for some years.[685] The statutory recognition procedure is having an impact, not least in encouraging some employers to reach voluntary agreements. Nevertheless this procedure applies only in workplaces employing 21 or more workers, can be obstructed (at least temporarily) by employers recognising a non-independent trade union, and the requirement for at least 40% of the workers in the bargaining unit, as well as a majority of those voting, to support recognition in a ballot may prove a difficult hurdle to surmount. Moreover the procedure does not, ultimately require employers to reach agreement with a trade union (nor, even if they do, to apply the terms agreed to individual workers). These factors, coupled with the defects of specific performance as a sanction, have led to the suggestion that consultation laws may ultimately be more effective in promoting collective bargaining and genuine 'partnership' with employers than mandatory recognition,[686] although much depends on the powers of the consultative bodies established and the training and experience of those who serve on them.[687] Despite recent legal developments, it is still the case that the future nature and extent of collective representation, and its implications for the trade union movement, remains in the realm of speculation.

---

684 Cully *et al*, 1999: p 200.
685 See generally Hyman, 1997.
686 W Brown, S Deakin, M Hudson and C Pratten, 2001.
687 See P Davies and C Kilpatrick, 2004.

CHAPTER 10

Trade unions and their members

INTRODUCTION

10.1 In the preceding chapters we have examined the law governing the relationship between trade unions and the state and between trade unions and employers. In this chapter we examine the law which governs the relationship between trade unions and their members.[1] This derives both from common law and from statute. A trade union is constituted by an association of individuals bound together by a contract of membership and the courts have jurisdiction to enforce this contract at the suit of union members.[2] Before 1971 the common law was the primary means of controlling the conduct of union affairs,[3] statutory regulation being confined to the areas of union political activities and mergers. The Trade Union Act 1871, which granted trade union purposes protection against the doctrine of restraint of trade,[4] specifically endorsed the principle that unions were autonomous bodies which should be free to determine their own constitutions.[5] This did not, in the event, mean that the law took a wholly non-interventionist approach to the area of trade union government; on the contrary the courts imposed considerable fetters in the guise of interpreting the contract of membership and through their powers to imply in, and strike out, terms. In particular they took the opportunity, through these mechanisms, to impose on unions the duty to comply with public law standards of procedural fairness in exercising their decision-making powers. Nevertheless the degree of external regulation emanating from the common law was modest in comparison with the extensive legislative intervention which now exists.

The first radical break with the abstentionist framework of the 1871 Act came with the Industrial Relations Act 1971, although even then its provisions were largely concerned with requiring unions to have rules on particular matters rather than requiring them to take a specific form.[6] With the return of the Labour government in 1974 the principle of union autonomy was to a large extent restored, the major exception being the application of the sex and race

---

1 For a detailed analysis of this area up to the mid-1980s see Elias and Ewing, 1987. This text is particularly useful for the development of the common law which, in the light of the extensive scope of statutory intervention, we discuss only in outline in this chapter, although it still remains significant in some areas.

2 Note also the jurisdiction of the Certification Officer in this area since 1999: see further para 2.38 and 10.10.

3 Initially the courts viewed property rights as the basis of jurisdiction, the contract basis of jurisdiction being established only in *Lee v Showmen's Guild of Great Britain* [1952] 2 QB 329; Elias and Ewing, 1987: pp 23–25.

4 See para 7.12 above.

5 This Act required unions to have rules on a limited range of matters but the substance of those rules was for the union to decide. Section 4 of that Act (now repealed), which precluded any of their agreements from being directly enforceable or subject to damages for breach, was designed to exclude union rules from the purview of the courts but due to tortuous drafting it achieved only partial success in this endeavour: see Elias and Ewing, 1987: pp 6–12.

6 See Weekes *et al*, 1975, ch 3.

discrimination legislation to trade unions in their dealings with applicants and members. From 1980 onwards, however, the activities of unions were subjected to an increasing degree of statutory regulation. This process began slowly, starting with the introduction of protection for individuals against 'unreasonable' exclusion or expulsion from a union where a closed shop was in operation. The Trade Union Act 1984 brought much more extensive intervention with the introduction of statutory requirements to hold periodic elections for specified union offices, together with greater restrictions upon unions' political activities. In 1988 these requirements were extended and additional rights for union members were introduced, most notably restrictions on the type of conduct for which they could be disciplined by their unions. This Act also brought the creation of a Commissioner for the Rights of Trade Union Members (CROTUM), empowered to assist individuals wishing to bring proceedings against their unions. The Employment Act 1990 introduced additional restrictions on the conduct of ballots which were extended further in 1993. TURERA 1993 also prevented unions from excluding or expelling individuals except in circumstances permitted by the Act. In all cases the statutory provisions were deemed to prevail over anything to the contrary in the union rule book. The justifications for introducing individual statutory provisions varied. A central theme was the need for legislative imposition of democracy within trade unions, based on the assertion that union leaders did not adequately reflect the views of their members and that, in the light of the special 'privileges' and immunities which unions enjoyed, it was particularly important to ensure that the rights of individual members were adequately protected and that there was proper accountability for the use of union power.[7] We discuss the issues which are raised by these assumptions, and the approach to trade union government they exemplify, later in the chapter.

A number of the statutory constraints introduced by the Conservative Government (although not those pertaining to union elections) are regarded as incompatible with freedom of association principles by the ILO Committee of Experts on the Application of Conventions and Recommendations, and they have also attracted condemnation from the ECSR (formerly the CIE) of the European Social Charter. In addition, the European Commission of Human Rights has affirmed that the right to join a union guaranteed by Article 11 of the ECHR does not accord a general right to join the union of one's choice regardless of that union's rules.[8] Despite this, the incoming Labour Government has done very little to alter the substantive framework regulating union conduct inherited from its predecessors,[9] although the CROTUM has been abolished[10] and jurisdiction over specified contractual matters extended to the Certification Officer, providing an alternative (and speedier, cheaper and less formal) route

7   See, variously, the Green Papers *Democracy in Trade Unions*, Cmnd 8778, 1983; *Trade Unions and their Members*, Cm 95, 1987; *Industrial Relations in the 1990s*, Cm 1602, 1991. For a more detailed analysis, and powerful critique, of the assumptions upon which these statements rest see Fredman, 1992a. On the background to, and impact of, the balloting provisions, see P Smith *et al*, 1993; Undy *et al*, 1996.
8   *Cheall v UK* Application No 10550/83, (1986) EHRR 74.
9   As a result of ERelA 2004, s 33 unions are now expressly permitted to exclude or expel individuals as a result of their activities as a member of a political party; see further para 10.10.
10   In 1998, the CROTUM absorbed a budget of £247,328, and dealt with 94 calls and two applications, calculated by Mr John Healey to cost £2,600 per call and £20,000 per application: House of Commons, Official Report of Standing Committee E, 4 March 1999, 4.15pm.

to seeking redress to that afforded by the High Court.[11] This is not an area in which the Human Rights Act 1998 is likely to be of great assistance to unions in view of the very detailed nature of the legislation, which leaves little room for argument that it should be interpreted in accordance with general freedom of association principles,[12] although the Act may have some part to play in relation to common law regulation.

We begin the chapter by examining the contract of membership and the criteria which have informed the judicial approach towards its construction. We then provide an overview of the statutory rights which union members and applicants for membership are now accorded in relation to trade unions. There follows a more detailed analysis of the principles, both common law and statutory, which govern union conduct in three important areas: access to membership and the exercise of disciplinary powers; access to union office; and union political activities. Our aim here is not to provide an exhaustive technical account of these provisions; the legislation, in particular, is in many places intricate and complex.[13] Rather we aim to highlight their most important features and, where appropriate, to compare the scope of the common law and legislation. In the concluding section we ask whether, in the light of the extent of external regulation which currently exists, unions can continue to be viewed as voluntary, autonomous bodies and assess the implications of the current legal framework applicable to them.

THE CONTRACT OF MEMBERSHIP

General principles

10.2 The contract of membership which individuals enter when they join a union[14] serves as the 'constitution' of the union. As such it generally covers a wide variety of matters including the rights and obligations of individual union members; the powers and composition of various bodies within the union; the

---

11 See further para 2.38 for details of the Certification Officer's general jurisdiction, and para 10.5 below for a comparison of the remedies which may be sought from the respective avenues of redress for breach of union rules.

12 In *ASLEF v Lee* UKEAT/0625/03/RN it was argued that Art 11 of the ECHR was at issue but the matter was resolved on construction of the statute without reference to Art 11; see further para 10.10.

13 For a more detailed technical analysis see G Morris and T Archer, 2000: ch 2.

14 Before the IRA 1971 unregistered unions were incapable of contracting in their own right, while the judges were divided about whether registered unions had sufficient corporate status to contract or not. In *Bonsor v Musicians' Union* [1956] AC 104, the majority of the House of Lords considered that the contract of membership was a contract between the members *inter se* rather than between the member and the union. Under the IRA 1971 registered unions were incorporated bodies and so could contract; since that Act was repealed, all unions, listed and unlisted, can contract: see now TULRCA 1992, s 10(1)(a) and para 7.28 above. However, it does not necessarily follow from this that the contract is with the union. In practice, 'the courts may be tempted to adopt the view that every member is contractually bound to the union, unless there is a clear intention to the contrary. In order to reach this conclusion it would have to be agreed that not only were unions granted the capacity to contract, but in addition they have in fact exercised that power with those who were members when the capacity to contract was granted. However, even if the courts do not take this approach, *Bonsor* shows that the member will have no difficulty in enforcing the contract – even if it is with the members *inter se*': Elias and Ewing, 1987: p 46.

purposes for which union funds can be expended; and the powers of union officers. It is open to any member to challenge the validity of union conduct on the ground that it is not authorised by the union rules and thereby constitutes a breach of contract.[15] The primary source of this contract is the union rule book, which unions have a statutory obligation to supply to any person on request, either free or on payment of a reasonable charge.[16] The rule book is likely to be subject to amendment from time to time, either with the approval of the membership directly or that of their elected representatives, depending upon the procedure specified in the rules.

Rule books may vary considerably in the degree of detail they contain. Nevertheless, even if ostensibly comprehensive, they may also be supplemented by implied terms and by custom and practice within the union in question. The most notable judicial recognition of the role which custom and practice could play came from the House of Lords in *Heatons Transport (St Helens) Ltd v TGWU*[17] when Lord Wilberforce, giving the judgment of the court, affirmed that:

> ... it is not to be assumed, as in the case of a commercial contract which has been reduced into writing, that all the terms of the agreement are to be found in the rule book alone; particularly as regards the discretion conferred by the members upon committees or officials of the union as to the way in which they may act on the union's behalf. What the members understand as to the characteristics of the agreement into which they enter by joining a union is well stated in the section of the TUC handbook on the Industrial Relations Act which gives advice about the content and operation of unions' rules. Paragraph 99 reads as follows: 'Trade Union government does not ... rely solely on what is written down in the rule book. It also depends upon custom and practice, by (sic) procedures which have developed over the years and which, although well understood by those who operate them, are not formally set out in the rules. Custom and practice may operate either by modifying a union's rules as they operate in practice, or by compensating for the absence of formal rules. Furthermore, the procedures which custom and practice lays down very often vary from workplace to workplace within the same industry, and even within different branches of the same union.[18]

It is notable, however, that this statement was made in the context of industrial action proceedings where the court held the union liable for the acts of its shop stewards despite the lack of any authority for their actions in the rules. It has been observed that in other contexts the courts have shown much greater reluctance to take account of union practices, to the extent that 'the gap between the practical operation of the constitution and the way it works in theory, as reflected in the formal constitution, is effectively disregarded ...'.[19] Moreover,

---

15   Occasionally the rule in *Foss v Harbottle* (1843) 2 Hare 461 will deny the member a remedy in cases where the action is not totally outside the powers of the union, but has not been taken by the properly-constituted body as the rules require. See Elias and Ewing, 1984, ch 4. On expenditure of union finds without the authority of the rules, see *YMA v Howden* [1903] 1 KB 308, CA, [1905] AC 256, HL; *Taylor v NUM (Derbyshire Area) (No 3)* [1985] IRLR 99.

16   TULRCA 1992, s 27. Failure to supply a copy of the rules is a criminal offence, punishable by a fine not exceeding level 5 on the standard scale established by the Criminal Justice Act as substituted by the Criminal Justice Act 1991, s 17(1) (at the time of writing £5,000): s 45A.

17   [1972] ICR 308.

18   [1972] ICR 308, 393–394.

19   Elias and Ewing, 1987: p 33. For recent consideration by the Certification Officer of custom and practice see *Scobie v TGWU (No 2)*, 25 April 2005, CO.

in accordance with general contractual principles, while custom and practice may moderate the operation of a rule it cannot entitle a union to act in conflict with it.[20]

Terms may also be implied into the contract of membership according to other general contractual principles.[21] However, the courts have shown that they are most unlikely to imply terms which extend the duties of members as against those of the union. Thus, in *Radford v NATSOPA*,[22] for example, Plowman J refused to accept the argument that the applicant was in breach of an implied obligation he was alleged to owe to the union given the very specific circumstances indicated in the rules as to when expulsion could be justified. Again, in *Leigh v NUR*[23] Goff J rejected the contention that qualifications for nomination to the office of president specified in the union rules were subject to additional qualifications as a matter of implication. *Iwanuszezak v GMBATU*[24] constituted an unusual attempt by a member to argue that his union had an implied duty to bring its collective strength to bear to safeguard an individual member's existing conditions of employment. This argument was rejected by the Court of Appeal. The brief judgment in this case was given pursuant to a striking out application by the union and did not explore in detail the interesting issues to which such a claim could give rise.[25]

10.3 The implied term is one important mechanism by which the courts can shape the contract of membership. Others are the power to interpret the scope and application of union rules and the power to strike out terms on public policy grounds. The dicta differ in emphasis as to the approach which should be adopted where the terms of the rule book are ambiguous. In *Heatons* Lord Wilberforce pointed out that:

> ... [t]rade union rule books are not drafted by parliamentary draftsmen. Courts of law must resist the temptation to construe them as if they were; for that is not how they would be understood by the members who are the parties to the agreement of which the terms, or some of them, are set out in the rule book ...[26]

However in *British Actors' Equity Association v Goring* Viscount Dilhorne affirmed that the same canons of construction should be applied to rule books

---

20   *Porter v NUJ* [1980] IRLR 404, 410 (Viscount Dilhorne); *Taylor v NUM (Derbyshire Area)* [1985] IRLR 99.
21   See para 4.4 *et seq* for the nature of these tests; see also *AB v CD* [2001] IRLR 808.
22   [1972] ICR 484. See also *Spring v NASDS* [1956] 1 WLR 585. Cf, however, *McVitae v UNISON* [1996] IRLR 33, where Harrison J implied a power for the defendant union, created upon amalgamation of three existing unions, to discipline members for conduct prior to the amalgamation when such conduct was contrary to the rules both of the amalgamating union of which they were a member and of UNISON.
23   [1970] Ch 326.
24   [1988] IRLR 219.
25   Lloyd LJ opined at 220 that the [trial] 'judge put the matter well when he said that it is the primary function of a union to look after the collective interests of its members' ... and 'where the collective interests of the union conflict with the interests of an individual member it only makes sense ... that the collective interests of the members as a whole should prevail'. However, in view of the claimant's argument that this consideration was irrelevant it was put to one side by the court. There is authority to suggest that there may be scope to imply terms into the contract of membership requiring members' access to union services, particularly representation, to be decided in accordance with standards of substantive and procedural fairness: see further G Morris and T Archer, 2000: para 2.15.
26   [1972] ICR 308, 393.

as to any 'written documents. Our task is to construe them so as to give them a reasonable interpretation which accords with what in our opinion must have been intended'.[27] In *Jacques v AUEW (Engineering Section)* Warner J attempted to reconcile these approaches by stating that 'the rules of a trade union are not to be construed literally or like a statute, but so as to give them a reasonable interpretation which accords with what in the court's view they must have been intended to mean, bearing in mind their authorship, their purpose, and the readership to which they are addressed'.[28] This dictum has been cited frequently in subsequent cases. However, in the context of the exercise of disciplinary powers, where much of the case law has arisen, the courts have, in practice, tended towards an interpretation which protects the interests of the individual union member. In doing so, they have frequently referred to a dictum of Lord Denning MR that union rule books are:

> ... not so much a contract, ...but ... much more a legislative code laid down by some members of the union to be imposed on all members of the union. They are more like by-laws than a contract. In those circumstances the rules are to be construed not only against the makers of them, but further, if it should be found that if any of these rules is contrary to natural justice ... the courts would hold them to be invalid.[29]

This approach can be criticised as overlooking the role that members play in formulating and changing rules. It has nevertheless played an important part in shaping judicial attitudes towards unions as bodies against whom members are in need of protection. In an earlier judgment in *Lee v Showmen's Guild of Great Britain*, Denning LJ pointed out the differences between social clubs and those of certain other bodies of ostensibly identical legal status:

> In the case of social clubs the rules usually empower the committee to expel a member who, in their opinion, has been guilty of conduct detrimental to the club, and this is a matter of opinion and nothing else. The courts have no wish to sit on appeal from their decisions on such a matter any more than from the decisions of a family conference. They have nothing to do with social rights or social duties ... It is very different with domestic tribunals which sit in judgment on members of a trade or profession. They wield powers as great, if not greater, than any exercised by courts of law. They can deprive a man of his livelihood ... They are usually empowered to do this for any breach of their rules which ... are rules which they impose and which he has no real opportunity of accepting or rejecting. In theory their powers are based on contract. The man is supposed to have contracted to give them these great powers; but in practice he has no choice in the matter.[30]

This case also highlighted the degree to which unions could intervene in union decision-making through the mechanism of interpreting the contract of membership. Although a domestic union body may be regarded as the final arbiter of facts, Denning LJ pointed out that the application of the rules to the facts and the construction of the rules were often inextricably linked. Thus:

> ... the question whether the committee has acted within its jurisdiction depends ... on whether the facts adduced before them were reasonably capable of being

27　[1978] ICR 791, HL at 794–795.
28　[1986] ICR 683 at 692. This approach has been echoed by the Certification Officer: see, for example, *In the matter of complaints against BECTU*, 2 November 2000, CO; *Taylor v MU* 15 October 2002, CO.
29　*Bonsor v Musicians' Union* [1954] Ch 479, 485–486.
30　[1952] 2 QB 329, 343.

held to be a breach of the rules. If they were, then the proper inference is that the committee correctly construed the rules and have acted within their jurisdiction. If, however, the facts were not capable of being held to be a breach and yet the committee held them to be a breach, then the only inference is that the committee have misconstrued the rules and exceeded their jurisdiction.[31]

This approach has afforded the courts the opportunity to give their own interpretation of disciplinary offences such as conduct that renders an individual 'unfit for membership' or is 'detrimental to the interests of the union', so, effectively, pronouncing on what union interests require. One particularly striking example of this process, where the union did not even have the chance itself to consider whether the member's conduct breached a disciplinary rule, is *Esterman v NALGO*.[32] In pursuance of a dispute with local authority employers, NALGO instructed its members not to volunteer their assistance in forthcoming local elections and to withdraw any offers of assistance already made. The claimant refused to withdraw her offer of assistance, whereupon she was requested to attend a disciplinary meeting to consider whether her conduct merited expulsion from the union. The relevant disciplinary rule stated that '[a]ny member who disregards any regulation issued by the branch, or is guilty of conduct which, in the opinion of the executive committee, renders him unfit for membership, shall be liable to expulsion'. The claimant successfully sought an interim injunction against the union and members of the branch executive committee to restrain them from taking disciplinary action against her. Templeman J held that no committee, applying itself correctly to the law and obeying the principles of natural justice, could find that in these circumstances she had been guilty of conduct rendering her unfit to be a member of the union. It was not clear that the executive had the power to issue the order which they had and, even if they did, a member could well conclude that it was one to which it had no right to demand obedience and one which, as a loyal member of NALGO, acting in its best interests, he or she felt bound to disobey.[33]

The Human Rights Act 1998 has the capacity to serve as a brake on this form of interventionist approach to the interpretation of union rules. Article 11 of the ECHR guarantees the right to form and join trade unions.[34] In *Cheall v UK*[35] the European Commission on Human Rights took into account the terms of ILO Convention No 87, which affirms the right of unions to draw up their own rules and to organise their administration and activities, in concluding that unions should remain free to decide, in accordance with union rules, questions

---

31 [1952] 2 QB 329, 345.
32 [1974] ICR 625. In *Longley v NUJ* [1987] IRLR 109, the Court of Appeal emphasised that the courts should be slow to prevent domestic tribunals adjudicating upon a matter in the first instance and endorsed the view of the trial judge that this should be done only if there was persuasive evidence to suggest that the issues had been prejudged or that the prescribed procedures had not been complied with. However, cf *Porter v NUJ* [1980] IRLR 404, discussed in para 11.90 below.
33 As P Davies and M Freedland, 1984: p 606, point out 'although formally the test applied by the court was whether no reasonable tribunal could have come to the conclusion that the plaintiff was unfit to be a member of the union (which apparently gives the domestic tribunal some scope in its interpretation of the union's rules), in practice the test applied seemed to be more like whether a reasonable member might consider the call for industrial action a breach of the union's rules or even simply unwise (a very different test)'.
34 See further para 7.9.
35 Application No 10550/83, (1986) EHRR 74. See also *RSPCA v A-G* [2001] 3 All ER 530, para 37(b) (Lightman J).

concerning admission to and expulsion from the union, subject to the obligation on the State to protect individuals against abuse of a dominant position where rules were wholly unreasonable or arbitrary or where exclusion or expulsion resulted in exceptional hardship such as job loss. At the time of writing it still remains to be seen whether the principle of union autonomy reflected in *Cheall* informs the courts' (and Certification Officer's) approach towards the interpretation of union rules.[36]

10.4   A further means by which the courts may control the conduct of union affairs is by striking out rules that conflict with public policy. One area where this power has proved significant is in relation to terms which attempt to exclude the jurisdiction of the courts; a rule which provides that the decision of an internal body shall be final will be void as contrary to public policy.[37] In theory a rule that members should exhaust internal remedies before resorting to the courts could also be construed as an attempt to oust their jurisdiction, albeit temporarily. In practice at common law the courts took the view that where such a rule did exist, it was for the claimant to show cause why the contractual position should not be adhered to,[38] the protection afforded to the member pending the exhaustion of internal procedures being material here.[39] The position in this context is now subject to statutory provisions which we discuss in para 10.5. Another important area where the courts have exercised their discretion to strike out rules, although the basis of doing so is more controversial,[40] is where they provide for union bodies to act in conflict with the principles of natural justice. In the context of disciplinary hearings these principles, broadly speaking, require members to be given notice of the charge against them, an opportunity to be heard, and a fair hearing by an unbiased judge. In the past the courts have also sought to circumvent union rules governing admission to the union where these conflicted with the 'right to work', although the basis for this was questioned both by judges and by commentators. We discuss the application of this and other forms of control over union government further in later sections of the chapter.

Remedies

10.5   A union member who alleges that the union has acted or threatened to act in breach of the contract of membership may seek a remedy in the High Court or, with some exceptions, apply to the Certification Officer.[41] The remedies which may potentially be sought from the High Court, depending upon the context, are a declaration, an injunction and damages.[42] Where time is of the essence – an impending election allegedly involving unlawful expenditure, or

---

36   In *ASLEF v Lee* UKEAT/0625/03/RN para 20, the EAT opined, without deciding, that in the instant case the union's 'right of negative association' would seem likely to override the applicant's asserted right of freedom of association: see further para 10.10.
37   *Lee v Showmen's Guild of Great Britain* [1952] 2 QB 329 at 342 (Denning LJ); *Lawlor v UPW* [1965] Ch 712.
38   *Leigh v NUR* [1970] Ch 326 at 334; (cf *White v Kuzych* [1951] AC 585).
39   *Leigh v NUR*, above; see also *Hiles v ASW* [1968] Ch 440 at 453.
40   See Elias and Ewing, 1987: p 35–37.
41   Note that a complainant must choose between these avenues of redress: TULRCA 1992, s 108A.
42   For more detailed discussion of the issues raised by these remedies in relation to trade unions, and the basis on which unions may be liable for the acts of their officials, see Elias and Ewing, 1987: p 44–57.

expulsion from the union, for example – a claimant may seek an interim injunction to restrain the union from carrying out or continuing an allegedly unlawful act.[43] We discuss the procedure for applying for interim injunctions, the principles which govern the discretion to grant them, and the penalties for breaching them, in para 11.48 *et seq* below. Damages are most likely to be sought when a member is unlawfully expelled from a union. In practice there are very few reported cases dealing with this remedy,[44] and now that members cannot lawfully be deprived of their employment through loss of union membership,[45] quantifying such a claim may be difficult.[46]

As we discussed in para 10.4, where a union rule requires a member to exhaust internal remedies before resorting to the courts, the courts have considered that the claimant should show cause why the contractual position should not be followed. This rule is now subject to a statutory right not to be denied access to the courts.[47] Notwithstanding anything in the rules of the union or in the practice of any court, if a member or former member of a union brings proceedings in a court with respect to a matter to which this statutory right applies then, provided specified conditions are met, rules requiring or allowing the matter to be submitted for determination or conciliation, and the fact that any 'relevant steps'[48] remain to be taken under the rules, must be regarded as irrelevant to whether the legal proceedings should be dismissed or adjourned.[49] The right applies where:

> a matter is under the rules of a trade union required or allowed to be submitted for determination or conciliation in accordance with the rules of the union, but a provision of the rules purporting for that to be a person's only remedy has no effect (or would have no effect if there were one).[50]

The terms in which this right is framed are puzzling. The right clearly covers the situation where the rules attempt to oust the jurisdiction of the courts completely, and would also apply where the rules are silent; whether it applies where the rule merely provides for prior exhaustion of internal remedies is unclear, although it was the express intention of the Conservative Government that introduced the legislation that it should.[51] Two further conditions must be satisfied for the right to apply: the member or former member must have made a 'valid application' to

---

43   P Davies and M Freedland, 1984 highlight (at p 594) the contrast between the courts' willingness to grant injunctions to restrain unions from acting upon a member's unlawful expulsion and their reluctance to grant injunctions in the context of the contract of employment (see para 5.54 *et seq* above), the former not being viewed as a contract of personal service: see, for example, *Porter v NUJ* [1980] IRLR 404. In general the courts will not grant an interim declaration but for a rare example of such a case see *Clarke v Chadburn* [1984] IRLR 350, a case arising out of the 1984/85 miners' strike.

44   Elias and Ewing, 1987: p 55. The leading case is *Edwards v SOGAT* [1971] Ch 354, a case of expulsion in the context of a closed shop.

45   See para 8.31.

46   Note that the statutory limits on damages awards which apply to proceedings in tort do not apply in the context of contractual claims against unions: TULRCA 1992, s 22; see further para 11.47 below.

47   TULRCA 1992, s 63.

48   These include any steps falling to be taken in accordance with the rules for the purposes of, or in connection with, the determination or conciliation of the matter, or any appeal, review or reconsideration of any determination or award: TULRCA 1992, s 63(5)(b).

49   TULRCA 1992, s 63.

50   TULRCA 1992, s 63(1).

51   See, for example, Mr Patrick Nicholls, House of Commons, Official Report of Standing Committee F, col 62, 17 November 1987.

the union for the matter to be submitted for determination or conciliation in accordance with the union's rules,[52] and the court proceedings must not have been commenced sooner than six months after the union received the application.[53] Once this period has expired, the court has no discretion to dismiss or adjourn the proceedings on the ground that internal remedies have not been exhausted (unless there has been delay in furthering the proceedings caused by the unreasonable conduct of the member),[54] although its discretion to do so on other grounds remains unaffected. The discretion of the court on general common law principles to grant a remedy before the statutory time limit has expired also remains unaffected,[55] although it is possible that the courts may be guided by the statutory period and refuse to intervene before that period has expired.

The right of a member to apply to the Certification Officer where he or she alleges a breach or threatened breach of union rules was introduced by the Employment Relations Act 1999.[56] It applies where the breach or threatened breach relates to the appointment or election of a person to, or the removal of a person from, any office; disciplinary proceedings (including expulsion);[57] the balloting of members on any issue other than industrial action;[58] and the constitution or proceedings of any executive committee[59] or of any decision-making meeting.[60] The Secretary of State may add to this list by order.[61] As well as industrial action ballots, dismissal and disciplinary proceedings against an employee of the union are excluded as are, by implication, allegations relating to the misuse of funds.[62] In contrast to High Court proceedings, which may normally be brought up to six years after the breach, a tight time limit applies to applications to the Certification Officer: the application must be brought within a six-month period starting with the day on which the breach or threatened breach is alleged to have taken place, or, if within that period any internal union complaints procedure is invoked to resolve the claim, within a six-month period starting with the day on which the procedure is concluded or the last day of the period of one year beginning with the day on which the procedure is invoked, whichever is the earlier.[63] Interestingly, the legislation reflects a preference for the use of internal complaints procedures

52   TULRCA 1992, s 63(2)(a). An application is deemed to be valid unless the union informs the applicant, within 28 days of receipt, of the respects in which the application contravened the requirement of the rules: s 63(3).
53   TULRCA 1992, s 63(2)(b).
54   TULRCA 1992, s 63(4).
55   TULRCA 1992, s 63(6).
56   TULRCA 1992, ss 108A, 108B. On the broader jurisdiction of, procedure followed by, and appeal from the Certification Officer, see further para 2.38.
57   The Certification Officer has held that this covers the use made of a union's disciplinary procedure by a member (*Taylor v MU*, 15 October 2002, CO) and that his jurisdiction is not confined to considering only breaches of rules that deal expressly with disciplinary proceedings where, in substance, a disciplinary penalty (here, suspension of legal assistance) has been imposed: *Dennison v UNISON*, 15 April 2003, CO.
58   TULRCA 1992, s 108A(5). Industrial action ballots were excluded because they would draw the Certification Officer into deciding matters involving relations between unions and employers: Mr Michael Wills, Minister for Small Firms, Trade and Industry, Official Report of Standing Committee E, 4 March 1999, 4.15pm.
59   Note that this goes beyond the 'principal committee' as defined in TULRCA 1992. s 119; see s 108A(10),(12).
60   TULRCA 1992, s 108A(2), (11).
61   TULRCA 1992, s 108A(2)(e), (13).
62   Complaints relating to a failure to comply with political fund ballot rules must be brought under TULRCA 1992, s 80: s 108A(4).
63   TULRCA 1992, s 108A(6),(7). To rely on 108A(6)(b), the applicant must establish that the union has a complaints procedure: *Fradley v TSSA*, 23 October 2003, CO.

where these exist; the Certification Officer may refuse to accept an application unless he or she is satisfied that the applicant has taken reasonable steps to resolve the claim by these means.[64] If the complaint is upheld, the Certification Officer must make, unless it is considered inappropriate, an enforcement order requiring the union to take specified steps to remedy the breach or withdraw the threat of a breach within a specified period and/or to abstain from specified acts with a view to securing that a breach of the same or a similar kind does not occur in future.[65] Recourse to the Certification Officer is likely to prove a much speedier and cheaper option than the High Court, unless the applicant seeks interim relief or damages, in which case he or she will have no alternative but to commence High Court proceedings.

STATUTORY RIGHTS: AN OVERVIEW

10.6 The statutory rights which union members[66] may exercise in relation to their union, which apply regardless of the terms of union rules, can be divided into four broad categories. First, there are rights relating to union membership and discipline. Individuals who are excluded or expelled from a union other than in circumstances expressly permitted by the legislation,[67] or who are 'unjustifiably disciplined',[68] may seek a remedy from an employment tribunal and may be awarded substantial financial compensation. We examine these rights in greater detail in para 10.9 *et seq* below. In addition, the legislation implies into the contract of membership a right for members to terminate their membership on giving reasonable notice and complying with any reasonable conditions.[69] In relation to the latter, it has been accepted that resignation may be postponed until the completion of any pending disciplinary action and that a member can be required to make up any arrears of subscription,[70] but a union cannot require the member to provide a reason for resigning.[71]

The second category covers rights not to be discriminated against in relation to membership and the benefits of membership. First, where a union has a political fund, contribution to the fund cannot be made a condition of admission to the union, nor may non-contributors be placed at any disadvantage as compared with other members except in relation to the control or management of the fund.[72] We discuss this and other rights relating to political funds further

---

64   TULRCA 1992, s 108B(1).
65   TULRCA 1992, s 108B(3),(4).
66   It is not always easy to determine whether an individual is a union 'member', particularly where unions have different categories of membership, such as 'full', 'honorary', 'limited' and 'retired'. In *NUM (Yorkshire Area) v Millward* [1995] IRLR 411 the EAT affirmed that the provisions of the rule book may not always be determinative of membership for statutory purposes; in each case the relevant provision must be examined 'textually and contextually' (415).
67   TULRCA 1992, ss 174–177.
68   TULRCA 1992, ss 64–67.
69   TULRCA 1992, s 69. It has been suggested that where subscriptions are collected monthly, at least one month's notice should be given: *Ashford v ASTMS* [1973] ICR 296 (decided under the comparable provision of the IRA 1971). However, *quaere* whether, if subscriptions are collected on an annual basis, reasonable notice may be less than a year, albeit without a refund of subscription: Kidner, 1983: p 26, n 96.
70   *Ashford v ASTMS* [1973] ICR 296.
71   *Ashford v ASTMS* [1973] ICR 296.
72   TULRCA 1992, s 82(1)(c).

in para 10.19. Second, EC law requires that a worker who is a national of a Member State who is employed in the territory of another Member State shall enjoy equality of treatment as regards membership of unions and the exercise of rights attaching to membership, including the right to vote and to be eligible for the workers' representative bodies in the undertaking.[73] Last, the anti-discrimination legislation makes it unlawful for any 'organisation of workers'[74] to discriminate on grounds of sex, marital status, sexual orientation, religion or belief, or racial grounds, or against a disabled person, in admitting to membership; the terms on which membership is offered; access to benefits;[75] or by subjecting the member to 'any other detriment'.[76] There are exceptions to this general principle which enable the union to encourage persons of a particular sex or racial group to join, or to encourage or assist them to hold union office, where, respectively, they are significantly under-represented within the organisation or as holders of such posts,[77] and specified exceptions for positive action in relation to persons of a particular sexual orientation or religion or belief.[78] In addition, positions on elected bodies may be reserved for members of one sex where this is considered necessary to secure a reasonable lower limit to the number of members of that sex serving on them.[79] However, it is unlawful to discriminate in arrangements for determining entitlement to vote in an election to such a body or in membership of the organisation itself.

The third category concerns rights which may be exercised in the event of a union not complying with its statutory obligation to hold appropriately conducted ballots. These obligations arise in four situations: elections to specified offices; approval of the adoption by a union of 'political objects' and periodic reapproval of an existing political fund; industrial action; and union amalgamations and 'transfers of engagements'.[80] We discuss the first and second of these in paras

---

73   EC Regulation 1612/68, Article 8, as amended. 'Worker' has a 'Community meaning' and includes part-time workers: Case 75/63 *Hoekstra (née Unger)* [1964] ECR 177; Case 53/81 *Levin v Secretary of State for Justice* [1982] ECR 1035; Case 66/85 *Lawrie Blum v Land Baden-Wurttemberg* [1986] ECR 2121. Note that the definition varies according to the context in which it is to be applied: see, for example, Case C-256/01 *Allonby v Accrington and Rossendale College* [2004] IRLR 224, para 63.

74   This definition is wider than that of a 'trade union', discussed in para 7.20; in particular, no specific purposes are stipulated; the organisation need not be permanent; and those with a professional/client relationship are not excluded: see *Sadek v Medical Protection Society* [2005] IRLR 57. The organisation is liable for unlawful discriminatory acts committed by persons in the course of their employment with the union or its authorised agents, although in the case of employees it is a defence to prove that the union took all such steps as were reasonably practicable to prevent the employee committing any such act(s): SDA 1975, s 41; RRA 1976, s 32; DDA 1995, s 58; EE(RB)R 2003, reg 22; EE(SO)R 2003, reg 22; see further para 6.48 above.

75   The SDA 1975 and RRA 1976 also include access to facilities or services.

76   SDA 1975, s 12; RRA 1976, s 11, DDA 1995, ss 13–15; EE(RB)R 2003, reg 15; EE(SO)R 2003, reg 15. On the meaning of 'detriment' see now *Shamoon v Chief Constable of the Royal Ulster Constabulary* [2003] IRLR 285, discussed at para 6.43. See also *FTATU v Modgill* [1980 IRLR 142; *FBU v Fraser* [1998] IRLR 697. There is an exception under the SDA 1975 for provision made in relation to the death or retirement from work of a member: s 12(4). In *Diakou v Islington Union 'A' Branch* [1997] ICR 121, the EAT emphasised that RRA 1976, s 11 does not expressly cover constructively depriving an individual of membership. For a detailed analysis of the legislation, see ch 6.

77   SDA 1976, ss 48(2), (3); RRA 1976, s 38(3)–(5).

78   EE(SO)R 2003, reg 26; EE(RB)R 2003, reg 25.

79   SDA 1976, s 49.

80   Under a transfer of engagements, the transferor union loses its legal identity while the organisation to which it transfers continues in being with its legal identity unchanged. An amalgamation produces a new organisation replacing the amalgamating bodies, which then cease to exist.

10.17 and 10.19; the third in para 11.91. We do not consider further the highly specialist area of amalgamations and transfers of engagements which lies beyond the scope of this work.

Finally, members have a number of miscellaneous rights which enable them to supervise the conduct by unions of their statutory obligations. Unions are required to maintain a register of the names and addresses of their members and to secure, so far as possible, that the entries in that register are accurate and kept up-to-date.[81] Members are entitled to ascertain, free of charge and at any reasonable time, whether there is an entry on the register relating to them after giving the union reasonable notice.[82] Members also have the right to inspect, and take copies of, the union's accounting records or that of any of its branches or sections for the preceding six-year period within 28 days of so requesting.[83] They may be accompanied for this purpose by an accountant provided that he or she agrees to protect the confidentiality of the records.[84] A union member who claims that the union has failed to comply with its statutory duties relating to the register, or to comply with a request to inspect its records, may complain to the Certification Officer or the High Court (but not both).[85] A further set of provisions enables members to bring High Court proceedings on the union's behalf if the union unreasonably fails to recover payments unlawfully made to individuals who have committed, or may commit, an offence or contempt of court. They may also apply to the High Court for an order to prevent the union's trustees allowing unlawful application of its property or complying with an unlawful direction which has been given to them under the union rules. These rights are most likely to be exercised in the context of industrial action and we discuss them further in para 11.91 below.

RIGHTS RELATING TO UNION MEMBERSHIP AND DISCIPLINE

Common law

10.7   The power of a trade union to discipline its members is restricted by the Trade Union and Labour Relations (Consolidation) Act 1992, and the lawfulness of any disciplinary action should always be considered in the light of those restrictions, which we discuss in para 10.12 below. However these restrictions are in addition to, and not a substitute for, other rights,[86] and there may be situations where union action, although not contrary to the statute, constitutes a violation of its rules. Moreover, under statute the union cannot be required to halt disciplinary proceedings or to revoke a disciplinary penalty: the ultimate remedy is financial; by contrast, as we discuss in para 10.5, the courts and the Certification Officer may issue orders restraining a union from taking disciplinary action or from treating a disciplinary penalty as effective. The common law still remains important, therefore, in some contexts.

---

81   TULRCA 1992, s 24(1).
82   TULRCA 1992, s 24(3).
83   TULRCA 1992, s 30. On the meaning of 'accounting records', see *Mortimer v Amicus*, 14 February 2003, CO and *Foster v MU*, 22 May 2003, CO.
84   TULRCA 1992, s 30
85   TULRCA 1992, ss 24A(6), 31.
86   TULRCA 1992, s 64(5).

If members wish to challenge a decision to expel them from union membership, or to subject them to some other disciplinary penalty, at common law the first question to consider will be what the rule book states. The power to discipline the member for the conduct in question must (usually) be present in the rules and the penalty which may be imposed for that offence must be clearly expressed.[87] As we saw in paras 10.3 and 10.4, although the union rules may make the domestic body the final arbiter of the facts, the courts can inquire into the application of the rules to the facts and this has, in practice, afforded them considerable discretion to interpret union rules, even those which appear to give the union considerable discretion.[88]

As far as the procedure which is followed is concerned, any provision in the union rules must be followed to the letter.[89] In addition, regardless of the union rules, the courts will require the union to apply the rules of 'natural justice'.[90] These require a member to be given notice of the charge,[91] an opportunity to be heard, and a fair hearing by an unbiased judge.[92] If an initial hearing fails to comply with natural justice, it seems that this cannot be cured by a fair appeal within the union.[93]

10.8   The position of those who are refused entry to a union at common law is more complex given that they have no contractual relationship with the union; nor will the union have committed any tort against them provided that it is acting in what it perceives to be its own legitimate interests and no unlawful means are used.[94] In situations where membership of an organisation was necessary for access to, or retention of, employment the courts developed the concept of a 'right to work'[95] which meant that an application for membership should not be rejected arbitrarily or capriciously. In a departure from the existing principle,[96] in the landmark case of *Nagle v Feilden*[97] the Court of Appeal held

---

87   See, for example, *Spring v NASDS* [1956] 1WLR 585. Cf, however, *McVitae v UNISON* [1996] IRLR 33, discussed in para 10.2, although the circumstances of that case – an amalgamation of three existing unions – were unusual, and the court implied a power to discipline for pre-amalgamation conduct only where the conduct contravened the rules both of the individual's pre-existing union and of the amalgamated union.

88   See *Lee v Showmen's Guild of Great Britain* [1952] 2 QB 329; *Esterman v NALGO* [1974] ICR 625, discussed in para 10.3 above.

89   See, for example, *Bonsor v MU* [1956] AC 104; *Santer v NGA* [1973] ICR 60.

90   *Lee v Showmen's Guild of Great Britain* [1952] 2 QB 329; *Hiles v ASW* [1968] Ch 440; *Lawlor v UPW* [1965] Ch 712; *Roebuck v NUM* [1977] ICR 573. Cf *Maclean v Workers' Union* [1929] 1 Ch 602, 623–624.

91   *Annamunthodo v Oilfield Workers' Trade Union* [1961] AC 945.

92   *Maclean v WU* [1929] 1 Ch 602; *Taylor v NUS* [1967] 1 WLR 532; *Roebuck v NUM (Yorkshire Area)* [1977] ICR 573, and *Roebuck v NUM (Yorkshire Area) (No 2)* [1978] ICR 676.

93   *Leary v NUVB* [1971] Ch 34, 49. A more liberal approach has been supported by the Privy Council in *Calvin v Carr* [1979] 2 All ER 440 but the court indicated that the approach in *Leary* was probably appropriate for trade union cases. In *McKenzie v NUPE* [1991] ICR 155, it was held that in the context of disciplinary proceedings against one of its members it was an implied term of the contract that a tribunal which had once heard a disciplinary matter should be entitled to reopen or rehear it whenever, in all the circumstances, justice required it.

94   *Allen v Flood* [1898] AC 1. For liability in the economic torts see para 11.10 *et seq* below.

95   The basis of the 'right to work' has been questioned both by judges and by commentators: see *McInnes v Onslow Fane* [1978] 3 All ER 211, 217 (Megarry J); *Forbes v New South Wales Trotting Club Ltd* (1979) 25 ALR 1, 17 (Barwick CJ); Hepple, 1981a: pp 78–81.

96   Cf *Weinberger v Inglis (No 2)* [1919] AC 606.

97   [1966] 2 QB 633.

that the claimant female trainer had an arguable case for a declaration that the unwritten rule of the Jockey Club, which controls horseracing on the flat, that women should not be granted licences was void as being in restraint of trade. This concept was later applied to a trade union when in *Edwards v SOGAT*[98] Lord Denning declared that all union rules which imposed an unwarranted encroachment on the right to work were *ultra vires* and void. This decision ran counter to an earlier House of Lords decision.[99] It also raised questions about the relationship between the 'right to work' and the doctrine of restraint of trade, against which trade unions are protected by statute,[100] although if the right to work is 'more than simply a positive reformulation of the negative doctrine of restraint of trade'[101] this would not be problematic.

In the light of the statutory restrictions upon closed shops, which we discuss in para 8.27 *et seq*, the concept of the 'right to work' is probably now otiose in the context of trade union membership. However, it is possible that, even in the absence of a closed shop, unions may continue to be subject to the administrative law concept of the 'duty to act fairly', which requires a decision to be made honestly and without caprice in considering applications for membership.[102] However, as this concept does not require an applicant to be given reasons if admission is refused, its use is likely to be limited unless the decision is patently arbitrary. In practice the introduction of the statutory right not to be excluded from a union other than in specified circumstances is much more likely to be invoked, although the common law principles may remain relevant where the exclusion falls within a category permitted by the statute.

Statutory rights to membership

(i) General principles

10.9 The extensive statutory right not to be excluded or expelled from a trade union was introduced by TURERA 1993.[103] There are now only four situations in which exclusion or expulsion is permitted.[104]

---

98 [1971] Ch 354.
99 *Faramas v Film Artistes Association* [1964] AC 925.
100 See now TULRCA 1992, s 11. In *Faramas*, above, the court held that even if an arbitrary rule of exclusion was in restraint of trade at common law it would be protected by the statutory provision. The earlier statutory protection in the TUA 1871 only covered the 'purposes' of a trade union, and in *Edwards* Sachs LJ at 382 suggested that a rule which enabled 'capricious and despotic action' could not be proper to the 'purposes' of a union. This circumvention of the statutory protection was blocked by the inclusion of union rules as well as purposes in TULRA 1974 and subsequent legislation.
101 Hepple, 1981b: p 111. This was suggested by Slade J in *Greig v Insole* [1978] 3 All ER 449, 510.
102 See *McInnes v Onslow Fane* [1978] 3 All ER 211. In this case the application of the duty was based upon the fact that the body in question exercised monopoly control over boxing managers but it was suggested (at 216) that the duty may also apply to bodies which exercise control over activities which are important to many people both as a means of livelihood and for other reasons. *Quaere* whether the duty to act fairly could be extended to invalidate union rules themselves. For discussion of this case see Elias, 1979.
103 This was inserted into TULRCA 1992, s 174, which has itself been amended by ERelA 2004, s 33. See Simpson, 1993. Prior to this there was a right only not to be 'unreasonably' excluded or expelled from a union specified in a closed shop agreement: see K Miller, 1990.
104 In *NACODS v Gluckowski* [1996] IRLR 252, Maurice Kay J held that 'exclusion' refers to a refusal to admit and not to expulsion. He thought it unlikely that constructive expulsion would be covered by the legislation (and see *McGhee v TGWU* [1985] IRLR 198). Note TULRCA 1992, s 177(2)(a), which governs the position where a union fails to respond to an application for membership.

(i)   If the individual does not satisfy, or no longer satisfies, an 'enforceable membership requirement' contained in the union rules. A requirement is 'enforceable' if it restricts membership solely by reference to one or more of three sets of criteria: employment in a specified trade, industry or profession; occupational description (including grade, level or category of appointment); or the possession of specified trade, industrial or professional qualifications or work experience.

(ii) If the individual does not qualify, or no longer qualifies, for membership of the union because it operates only in a particular part or parts of Great Britain.

(iii) In the case of a union whose purpose is the regulation of relations between its members and one particular employer or a number of associated employers, if the individual is not, or is no longer, employed by a relevant employer. This enables 'house' unions to confine their membership to a single employer.

(iv) If the exclusion or expulsion is entirely attributable to the conduct of the individual (which includes statements, acts and omissions[105]), provided that it is not 'excluded conduct'. Conduct is 'excluded conduct' if it consists in the individual being or ceasing to be, or having been or ceased to be, a member of another trade union, or employed by a particular employer or at a particular place; or is conduct for which an individual has the statutory right not to be 'unjustifiably disciplined'.[106] Thus a union could not exclude an individual who expressed an intention never to take part in industrial action, for example. Membership of a political party, which was also included in TURERA 1993, is now subject to special provisions which we discuss in para 10.10 below.

A union cannot exclude an individual from membership purely on the ground that he or she has previously been expelled, but the EAT has held that exclusion does not breach the statute if it is entirely attributable to the conduct of the applicant which had led to the expulsion.[107] An individual is treated as expelled if under the union rules he or she ceases automatically to be a member on the occurrence of a specified event, such as non-payment of subscriptions.[108]

An individual who claims to have been excluded or expelled from a union in contravention of the legislation may complain to an employment tribunal.[109] Where the tribunal upholds the complaint it must make a declaration to this effect.[110] The applicant may then apply to a tribunal for an award of compensation from the union.[111] The award is to be such as the tribunal considers 'just and

---

105 TULRCA 1992, s 177(1)(b).
106 See further para 10.12 below. Where the disciplinary action which is 'unjustifiable' takes the form of expulsion the individual has a choice as to whether to pursue a remedy under TULRCA 1992, ss 64–65 or 174–177 but cannot proceed under both: ss 66(4), 177(4).
107 *Potter v UNISON* UKEAT/0626/03, 1 March 2004.
108 TULRCA 1992, s 177(2)(b). It seems likely that such a rule would now be seen as void at common law as being in breach of natural justice: see Elias and Ewing, 1987: pp 216–218.
109 TULRCA 1992, s 174(5). The complaint must be presented within six months of the date of the exclusion or expulsion or within such further period as the tribunal considers 'reasonable' where it is satisfied that it was not 'reasonably practicable' for the complaint to be presented within six months: s 175; see further para 2.17.
110 TULRCA 1992, s 176(1).
111 TULRCA 1992, s 176(2), as amended by ERelA 2004, s 34(7)-(11). Prior to 31 December 2004 applications were made directly to the EAT if the applicant had not by then been admitted or re-admitted to the union.

equitable in all the circumstances' subject to a maximum award of £65,200.[112] There is provision for a reduction of this award where the tribunal finds that the applicant has caused or contributed to the exclusion or expulsion.[113] However, if on the date of the application for compensation,[114] the applicant had not been admitted or re-admitted to the union, a minimum of £6,100 is to be awarded.[115] The statute does not, unlike the common law, afford a remedy that requires a union to retain the individual in membership, but he or she may bring proceedings for breach of contract, as well as a statutory complaint, if appropriate.[116]

(ii) Exclusion or expulsion for membership of a political party or activities as such a member

10.10 The right not to be excluded or expelled from a union, as initially introduced, expressly stated that an individual could not be excluded or expelled for being a member of a political party. It was unclear, however, whether a union could expel an individual for his or her political activities, an issue that became a pressing one for unions which discovered that they had in membership individuals who were active in the British National Party (BNP). The matter came before the courts in *ASLEF v Lee*,[117] where the union had expelled the complainant, who was an active member of the BNP, for bringing the union into disrepute. The complainant alleged that his expulsion breached TULRCA 1992, s 174. The EAT held that the tribunal was required to consider whether the expulsion was because of his membership of the BNP or whether it was entirely attributable to his conduct (whether as such a member or otherwise), and remitted the case to a different tribunal to decide this question on the facts.

   In response to this problem, the Government took the view that unions should be able to 'deal effectively with far-right political activists who infiltrate their ranks'.[118] ERelA 2004 was designed both to clarify the distinction between membership of a political party, on the one hand, and activities on the other, and to allow unions to expel or exclude individuals where membership of a political party was a relatively minor reason for the decision to do so.[119] Exclusion or expulsion from a union is now permitted if it is entirely attributable to the individual's conduct (other than 'excluded conduct') 'and the conduct to which it is *wholly or mainly attributable* is not protected conduct'.[120] 'Protected conduct' is conduct which consists in the individual's being or ceasing to be, or having been or ceased to be, a member of a political party.[121] Thus, if a union excludes or expels an individual from membership for a number of reasons, one of which is membership of a political party, the tribunal will be required to decide what was the main reason for its action: if it is conduct other than membership of a

---

112 TULRCA 1992, s 176(4), (6). Figures as of 1 February 2005 and at the time of writing.
113 TULRCA 1992, s 176(5).
114 Applications must be made no earlier than four weeks, and no later than six months, from the date of the declaration: s 176(3).
115 TULRCA 1992, s 176(6A), inserted by ERelA 2004, s 33(6).
116 TULRCA 1992, s 177(5).
117 UKEAT/0625/03/RN 24 February 2004. See D Mead, 2004.
118 Gerry Sutcliffe, Under-Secretary of State, Department of Trade and Industry, HC Standing Committee D, col 226, 2 March 2004.
119 These amendments, contained in ERelA 2004, s 33, came into force on 31 December 2004, but references to 'conduct' in ss 174 and 176 include conduct which took place before s 33 came into force: s 33 (7).
120 TULRCA 1992, s 174(2)(d). See s 174 (4) for the definition of 'excluded contract'.
121 TULRCA 1992, s 174(4A).

political party, it will not breach section 174 (provided that is not 'excluded conduct'). It is expressly provided that '[c]onduct which consists of activities undertaken by an individual as a member of a political party' is not protected conduct.[122] 'This means that a union will have acted lawfully if it expels a political activist principally on the grounds of their political activities where a subsidiary factor was the person's political party membership'.[123]

If a tribunal upholds a complaint and decides that exclusion or expulsion was mainly attributable to 'protected conduct' it must make an additional declaration to that effect.[124] If it does so, and it also considers that the *other* conduct to which the exclusion or expulsion was attributable consisted wholly or mainly of conduct which was contrary to a union rule or objective it must so declare, in which case the minimum award applicable where a union has not admitted or re-admitted the complainant does not apply.[125] For conduct to be found to be contrary to a union objective the union must show that, at the time of the complainant's conduct, it was reasonably practicable for that objective to be ascertained by a member of the general public (if the complainant was not then a member of the union) or by a member of the union (if he or she was a member).[126] The specification of union objectives, as well as rules, was 'a key issue for the TUC, which was worried by the fact that many unions do not refer to their equality or anti-racist policies in their rule books'.[127] However, this would seem to leave it open for a public sector union to argue, for example, that the minimum award should not apply in the event that it expels a member of a political party because he or she advocates privatisation of the health service.

There are sharply differing views as to whether the provisions introduced by ERelA 2004 are compatible with human rights. The Joint Committee on Human Rights (JCHR) concluded that they did not meet the requirements of Articles 10 and 11 of the ECHR because they allow individuals to be excluded or expelled from union membership for a reason related to their activities as a member of *any* political party, not only those that pursue racist and xenophobic policies, and therefore go beyond what is necessary to further a legitimate aim.[128] Others maintain that the reforms do not go far enough because trade unions remain liable to members of political parties that may be offensive to their aims, and, more fundamentally, that the legislation represents an infringement on trade union autonomy that conflicts with Article 11 and other international standards.[129] The DTI defended its position on the basis that it was necessary to balance the 'negative right' of the union and its members not to associate with those with whom they do not wish to associate against the Article 10 right of the excluded or expelled individual to freedom of expression, and that contracting states were accorded a wide margin of appreciation in doing this.[130] However this

---

122 TULRCA 1992, s 174 (4B).
123 Gerry Sutcliffe, above, note 118, col 228.
124 TULRCA 1992, s 176 (1A).
125 TULRCA1992, s 176(1B), (6B); see para 10.9 above.
126 TULRCA 1992, s 176(1D).
127 Gerry Sutcliffe, HC Debs, col 1478, 16 September 2004.
128 JCHR, Eighth Report, Session 2003-2004, paras 2.5–2.6; Thirteenth Report, Session 2003–2004, paras 2.15–2.17.
129 Institute of Employment Rights Submission on TULRCA 1992, s 174, prepared by Professor Keith Ewing and John Hendy QC, JCHR Thirteenth Report, Session 2003–2004, App 2b; see also App 2d.
130 Memorandum from the DTI in response to concerns raised by the Committee in its Third and Fourth Progress Report of Session 2003–2004, JCHR Thirteenth Report, Session 2003–2004, App 2a, paras 16–22.

argument gives inadequate weight to the decision in *Cheall v UK*[131] that Article 11 does not confer a general right to join the union of one's choice regardless of the union's rules, a view reflected in domestic case law.[132] Although it was suggested by the European Commission of Human Rights in *Cheall v UK*[133] that the state is required to protect an individual against a dominant position by unions, which could occur if there was a closed shop or union rules were wholly unreasonable or arbitrary, now that the closed shop cannot lawfully be enforced, the circumstances in which denial of union membership can be said in practice to constitute an interference with freedom of expression or another Convention right are likely to be very rare. The wide-ranging statutory constraints on union autonomy in British law have been found by ILO and ESC supervisory organs to infringe their respective treaties,[134] and for the reasons we discuss in greater detail in para 10.21, we concur with the view that the legislation should be urgently reviewed.

(iii) The 'Bridlington Principles'

10.11   The introduction of the right not to be excluded or expelled from a union necessitated revision of the TUC's Bridlington Principles, first promulgated in 1939 to minimise disputes between affiliated unions over membership issues. Although not intended to constitute a legally enforceable contract, they are 'accepted by all affiliated organisations as a binding commitment for their continued affiliation to the TUC'.[135] Before the 1993 revision these principles provided, *inter alia*, that the membership forms of all unions should inquire about the applicant's membership of other unions; that no union should accept as members applicants who were or had recently been members of any other affiliated union without inquiry of that union; that if that union objected, the applicant should not be accepted into membership; and that in the case of dispute the matter should be notified to the TUC and may be referred for adjudication by an internal Disputes Committee, composed of senior officials of affiliated unions. The Committee could award that individuals accepted into membership in breach of the Principles should be expelled, and advised to join or rejoin the appropriate union. Expulsions to give effect to decisions of the Disputes Committee were upheld at common law provided that the decision was properly one which fell under the terms of the Committee's remit under the procedures and the expulsion was authorised by the union rules.[136] In *Cheall v APEX*[137] the House of Lords rejected the argument that these arrangements contravened public policy in restricting the right of the individual to join and remain a member of the union of his choice. In giving the judgment of the court Lord Diplock affirmed that 'freedom of association can only be mutual; there can

---

131   Application No 10550/83, (1986) 8 EHRR 74; see para 10.3 above.
132   *Cheall v APEX* [1983] IRLR 215; *RSPCA v AG* [2001] 3 All ER 530, para 37(b) (Lightman J).
133   Above, note 131.
134   See the discussions in the references in note 131 above and para 10.21 below.
135   *TUC Disputes Principles and Procedures*, TUC, 2000; see further para 2.13 above for the status of these Principles.
136   Cf *Spring v NASDS* [1956] 1 WLR 585, which led to the TUC recommending unions to adopt a model rule permitting expulsions to comply with decisions of the Disputes Committee. See generally Simpson, 1993: pp 189–193 and Elgar and Simpson, 1994 for an evaluation of the operation of the Principles before revision.
137   [1983] IRLR 215.

be no right of an individual to associate with other individuals who are not willing to associate with him'.[138] He continued:

> ... I know of no existing rule of public policy that would prevent trade unions from entering into arrangements with one another which they consider to be in the interests of their members in promoting order in industrial relations and enhancing their members' bargaining power with their employers; nor do I think it a permissible exercise of your Lordships' judicial power to create a new rule of public policy to that effect. If this is to be done at all it must be done by Parliament.[139]

The argument that the expulsion breached Article 11 of the ECHR also failed, the European Commission of Human Rights affirming that the right to join a union did not confer a general right to join the union of one's choice, regardless of the union rules, and that the complaint was, therefore, inadmissible.[140]

Revised Principles were drafted to accommodate the statutory restriction on exclusion and expulsion; initially promulgated in 1993, these now appear in the 2000 edition of the Principles.[141] They affirm that all TUC affiliates accept 'that they will not knowingly and actively seek to take into membership existing or "recent" members of another union by making recruitment approaches, either directly or indirectly, without the agreement of that organisation'. Unions must continue to include in their membership application form questions regarding past or present membership of another union, and if that other union has cause to object to the recruitment of a current or former member it should request a meeting with the prospective recruiting union. The effort at resolution will include a moral obligation on the part of the respondent union to 'offer compensation to the complainant union for any loss of income that it has suffered as a consequence of any knowing and active recruitment of its members'. In case of continuing disagreement the issue will be referred to the TUC which, if other attempts at settlement fail, may refer it to the Disputes Committee. If it finds in its favour, the Committee may adjudicate on the financial compensation to be paid to the complainant union, up to a maximum of two years' loss of contributions, and/ or may censure the respondent union and require it to print the censure in a prominent place in its journal. However, the Committee no longer has power to require the expulsion of those admitted to unions in breach of the Principles. When the new statutory rights were being proposed, several employers' groups expressed disquiet that they may destabilise existing arrangements, particularly single union deals, by encouraging unions to commence recruitment activities in an enterprise where other unions were stronger.[142] In practice, unions in present circumstances seem more likely to favour concentrating their efforts in areas where they are able to build a significant membership body rather than spreading their resources more thinly.[143]

---

138 [1983] IRLR 215, 218.
139 [1983] IRLR 215, 218. The claimant's argument that the termination of his membership was void as being in breach of natural justice because he was not able to make representations to the Disputes Committee also failed.
140 *Cheall v UK* Application No 10550/83, (1986) 8 EHRR 74. Although the state was required to protect an individual against a dominant position by unions, which could occur if there was a closed shop or the union rules were wholly unreasonable or arbitrary, this was not the case here.
141 For an analysis of the 1993 changes to the Principles, see Simpson, 1994.
142 See Simpson, 1993: pp 187–189.
143 Simpson, 1993: p 188.

Statutory rights in relation to union discipline

10.12 In addition to the protection against expulsion, members have the broader right not to be 'unjustifiably disciplined' by their union.[144] Discipline is 'unjustified' if the actual or supposed conduct which constitutes the reason, or one of the reasons, for it is a form of conduct listed in the legislation or something believed by the union to amount to such conduct.[145] This right is in addition to any other rights which may be available to an individual,[146] so if disciplinary action were to infringe the union rules as well as the statute the member could also bring proceedings for breach of contract.[147] A member may also wish to bring common law proceedings if the challenge is based upon the procedure followed rather than the substantive reason for the action.

There are twelve types of conduct (which includes 'statements, acts and omissions')[148] for which disciplinary action is 'unjustified'.[149] Many relate to non-participation in, or opposition to, industrial action. In outline, they are as follows:

(i) failing to participate in or support any strike or other industrial action[150] or indicating opposition to or lack of support for such action;

(ii) failing to contravene, for a purpose connected with such a strike or other industrial action, a requirement imposed on the individual by or under a contract of employment;[151]

(iii) asserting (or encouraging or assisting another to make such an assertion) that the union, any official[152] or representative[153] of it or trustee of its property contravened, or is proposing to contravene, a requirement which is, or is thought to be, imposed by the union rules or any other agreement or by any enactment or rule of law. The protection does not apply, however, if the assertion was false and the individual believed that or was otherwise acting

---

144 TULRCA 1992, s 64(1). See further para 10.21 for discussion of the compatibility of these provisions with Article 11 of the ECHR and other international standards.

145 TULRCA 1992, s 65(1).

146 TULRCA 1992, s 64(5), although note s 66(4).

147 Note, however, the difference in remedies: see para 10.5 above. Note also that the statutory right arises only when a disciplinary 'determination' has been made; it does not allow the individual to forestall the disciplinary process, although if *Longley v NUJ* [1987] IRLR 109, para 10.3 above, is followed this may not make any practical difference.

148 TULRCA 1992, s 65(7).

149 TULRCA 1992, s 65(2)–(4). The statutory protection does not apply if it is shown that individuals would be disciplined by the union for such conduct irrespective of its connection with conduct for which discipline is unjustified: s 65(5). This provision was designed to protect unions, such as the Royal College of Nursing, which may discipline members in order to protect professional standards.

150 In *Knowles v FBU* [1996] IRLR 617, the Court of Appeal held that 'the question of what is industrial action for the purposes of s 65 ... is a mixed question of fact and law. In large measure it is a question of fact, but the facts have to be judged in the context of the Act which plainly contemplates that industrial action is a serious step'. It was 'necessary to look at all the circumstances ... [which] will include the contracts of employment of the employees and whether any breach of or departure from the terms of the contract are involved, the effect on the employer of what is done or omitted, and the object which the union or the employees seek to achieve' (621, Neill LJ). See generally para 11.73.

151 This includes any agreement between the individual and a person for whom he or she works or normally works: TULRCA 1992, s 65(7). Persons holding office or employment under the Crown are deemed to have contracts of employment for this purpose: TULRCA 1992, s 65(8).

152 Defined TULRCA 1992, s 119. Note that this definition is wide enough to cover shop stewards.

153 Defined TULRCA 1992, s 65(7).

in bad faith (although the member is not specifically required to have had reasonable grounds to believe that the assertion was true);

(iv) encouraging or assisting another to perform an obligation imposed by a contract of employment;[154]

(v) contravening a requirement imposed by or in consequence of a determination which infringes the individual's or another individual's right not to be unjustifiably disciplined;

(vi) failing to agree, or withdrawing agreement to, the check-off;[155]

(vii) resigning or proposing to resign from the union or from another union, becoming or proposing to become a member of another union, refusing to become a member of another union or being a member of another union;

(viii) working with, or proposing to work with, individuals who are not members of the union or who are or are not members of another union;

(ix) working for, or proposing to work for, an employer who employs or has employed individuals who are not members of the union or who are or are not members of another union;

(x) requiring the union to do an act which it is required under TULRCA 1992 to do at the requisition of a member;

(xi) consulting or asking advice from the Certification Officer on any matter or which involves consulting, or asking advice or assistance from, any other person with respect to a matter which forms, or might form, the subject of any assertion described in (iii) above;

(xii) proposing to engage in, or doing anything preparatory or incidental to, conduct falling within (i)-(xi) above.

A member is treated as 'disciplined' if a 'determination' is made, or purportedly made, under the union rules, or by a union official or persons including an official, that he or she should be expelled from the union or a branch or section of it; should make any payment or that subscriptions paid should be treated as unpaid or as paid for a different purpose; should be deprived to any extent of any benefits, services or facilities which would otherwise be available; that another union, or branch or section, should be encouraged not to accept him or her as a member; or that he or she should be subjected to 'some other detriment'.[156] In relation to the last 'catch-all' provision, the EAT has upheld the view that naming a member as a strike-breaker in a branch circular to cause her embarrassment could be described as a 'detriment'.[157] Banning a member from standing for, or holding, union office would almost certainly be included, as would preventing an individual from attending a branch meeting.

---

154 See note 151, above.
155 See para 8.41 above for rights against employers.
156 TULRCA 1992, s 64(2). The provision for union officials to bind the union means that the union may be held responsible even if the determination is made by persons who have no express or implied authority to act on its behalf in this regard. The EAT has held that 'determination' means a decision which disposes of the issue, so does not cover a recommendation that requires affirmation by another body: *TGWU v Webber* [1990] IRLR 462. However, as the EAT recognised, there may be more than one 'determination' within the expulsion process, eg suspension leading to deprivation of benefits prior to the decision to expel; if so, there will be a need to keep a careful eye on time limits.
157 *NALGO v Killorn* [1990] IRLR 464. In that case the EAT expressed the view (at 469) that 'whether or not a member suffered deprivation or detriment is the sort of question that … [Employment] … Tribunals, with their expertise on industrial matters, are peculiarly suited to answer'. See now *Shamoon v Chief Constable of the Royal Ulster Constabulary* [2003] UKHL 11, [2003] IRLR 285, discussed at para 6.43, applied to s 64(2)(f) in *Unifi v Massey* UKEAT/0223/04/MAA 3 August 2004.

An individual who claims to have been 'unjustifiably disciplined' may complain to an employment tribunal within three months of the date of the determination,[158] although this period may be extended, *inter alia*, where the tribunal is satisfied that any delay in making the complaint was due to a reasonable attempt to appeal against the determination or have it reconsidered or reviewed.[159] Where the tribunal upholds the complaint it must make a declaration to this effect, whereupon the applicant may apply for an award of compensation from the union.[160] The award is such as the tribunal considers 'just and equitable in all the circumstances', subject to a maximum award of £65,200.[161] An award may be reduced if the applicant has failed to mitigate his or her loss or where the tribunal finds that he or she has caused or contributed to the infringement.[162] However if, on the date of the application for compensation,[163] the determination infringing the applicant's right has not been revoked, or the union has failed to take all the steps necessary for securing the reversal of anything done for the purpose of giving effect to the determination,[164] a minimum of £6,100 is to be awarded.[165]

In common with the restriction on exclusion and expulsion from a union, this provision constitutes a considerable incursion on union autonomy. The provisions relevant to industrial action, which we discuss further in para 11.91, have been particularly controversial. It is a notable feature of these rights that they accord those who disagree with union policy a means of remaining in the union, enabling them, if they so choose, to bring legal proceedings in the event that the union does not comply with any element of the statutory requirements in their entirety. We return to a discussion of the compatibility of this situation with freedom of association principles later in the chapter.

TRADE UNION ELECTIONS

Common law

10.13 At common law the role of the courts has been largely confined to ensuring that the union rules are observed. Thus in *Leigh v NUR*,[166] for example,

---

158 TULRCA 1992, s 66(1), (2)(a).
159 TULRCA 1992, s 66(2)(b). An appeal need not be in any particular form and the EAT has said that tribunals should look at the reality and intention of a member's communication with the union rather than the use of specific wording: *NALGO v Killorn* [1990] IRLR 464. The period may also be extended where the tribunal is satisfied that it was not 'reasonably practicable' for the complaint to be presented in time: see para 2.17 above.
160 TULRCA 1992, ss 67(1), as amended by ERelA 2004, s 34.
161 TULRCA 1992, s 67(8) as amended; figure as of 1 February 2005 and at the time of writing.
162 TULRCA 1992, s 67(6), (7). Note that there is no duty to mitigate loss where the right not to be expelled or excluded from a union, discussed in para 10.9 has been infringed.
163 Applications must be made no earlier than four weeks and no later than six months from the date of the declaration: TULRCA 1992, s 67(3).
164 In *NALGO v Courteney-Dunn* [1992] IRLR 114, the EAT rejected the argument that 'necessary' meant 'requisite' or 'indispensable'; the union was required to put the member back into the same position he was in before the wrongful expulsion and the fact that the member himself could have done this (here, restored resumption of the check-off) was irrelevant. See also *Beaumont v Amicus MSF* UKEAT/0122/03/MAA, 12 February 2004.
165 TULRCA 1992, s 67(8A), inserted by ERelA 2004, s 34(6); figure as of 1 February 2005 and at the time of writing. Prior to 31 December 2004 applications were made directly to the EAT in such circumstances. Compensation may be awarded for injury to feelings: *Bradley v NALGO* [1991] IRLR 159; *Beaumont v Amicus MSF* 29 November 2004 (revised judgment).
166 [1970] Ch 326.

the claimant obtained an injunction to prevent an election taking place without his name being included on the list of candidates after he successfully argued that he met the qualifications for nomination specified in the rules. In two cases involving election to the office of shop steward, however, the concept of the duty to act fairly was successfully invoked by individuals who had been elected by their fellow workers but whose appointment was not given the requisite approval by higher bodies within the union.[167] As we describe in para 10.14, elections to the posts of union president, general secretary and member of the executive are now governed by detailed statutory procedures. However, if the rules impose restrictions which exceed, or do not conflict with, the statutory provisions, the common law will still be important. Thus in *Wise v USDAW*[168] for example, a decision by the executive council that a candidate for election to the office of general secretary must be nominated by not fewer than 25 union branches breached a rule that 'all branches shall have the right to make nominations' for the office of general secretary. Again in *Ecclestone v NUJ*[169] the union was found to have breached its rules in excluding the claimant from the shortlist for election to the post of deputy general secretary on the ground that he lacked the 'required qualifications' because he lacked the confidence of the union's national executive committee. Moreover, the common law will be the only avenue of redress in relation to offices not covered by the statutory provisions, such as that of shop steward. To date, however, there have been relatively few cases in the area of union elections pursued at common law.

The statutory requirements: the duty to conduct elections

10.14   Under statute, trade unions[170] must now ensure that their president,[171] general secretary[172] and every 'member of the executive'[173] hold office by virtue

---

167 *Breen v AEU* [1971] 2 QB 175; *Shotton v Hammond* (1976) 120 Sol Jo 780. Note the limitations of this doctrine, however: see para 10.8. In *Meacham v AEEU* [1994] IRLR 218, a union member who was not allowed for economic reasons to take up a full-time union post to which he had been elected was held to have only the same right to damages for breach of contract as any other prospective employee; the union was not obliged to act in accordance with natural justice in considering contracts of employment 'unless questions of vires arise, or the conduct or character of the member of the union was called into question' (at 226).

168 [1996] IRLR 609. See also *Douglas v GMPU* [1995] IRLR 426: no power in the union rules for the executive council to cancel an election after the candidate with the highest number of votes had been declared elected, although cf *AB v CD* [2001] IRLR 808, 812 (Sir Andrew Morritt,VC).

169 [1999] IRLR 166.

170 With the exception of unions of less than one year's standing, including those formed by amalgamation (TULRCA 1992, s 57), and those consisting wholly or mainly of constituent or affiliated organisations, or representatives of such organisations ('federated trade unions') and which either have no individual members, such as the TUC, or whose individual members are all merchant seamen and the majority are ordinarily resident outside the UK (s 118(6)), an exception asked for by the International Transport Workers' Federation. 'Special register bodies' need elect only voting members of their executive: ss 117(5), 46(5).

171 Where there is no such office, the holder of the equivalent or nearest equivalent: TULRCA 1992, s 119. There is a limited exception in TULRCA 1992, s 46(4A), inserted by ERelA 2004, s 52.

172 TULRCA 1992, s 119. Persons holding the position of president or general secretary on an honorary basis, with no voting rights, are not subject to election but this applies only where the holder changes on an annual basis and certain other conditions are satisfied: s 46(4),(5).

173 TULRCA 1992, s 119; see further below.

of an election conducted in accordance with complex statutory requirements.[174] These provisions apply notwithstanding anything to the contrary in the union's rules or practices,[175] although there is nothing to prevent a union adopting more stringent requirements in its rules. No officer who is subject to election may continue to hold office for more than five years without being re-elected.[176] Unless the election is uncontested the union must hold a fully postal ballot,[177] and in all cases[178] the election must be supervised by an independent 'scrutineer': either one of four specialist bodies specified in regulations or another appropriately qualified person (a solicitor or accountant qualified as an auditor, provided that their previous connections with the union do not disqualify them from this appointment).[179] These requirements alone mean that unions incur substantial costs in organising an election, particularly as the provision for refunding a proportion of the balloting costs, which was introduced in 1984, ceased for ballots after 31 March 1996.[180]

The term 'executive' means 'the principal executive committee of the union exercising executive functions, by whatever name it is called'.[181] This requires there to be one, but only one, such body;[182] other bodies which may exercise executive functions within the union which are subordinate to the 'executive' are not subject to the legislation. 'Members of the executive' clearly include those designated as such by the union's rules, either on an ordinary or an *ex officio* basis.[183] They also include:

> ... any person who, under the rules or practice of the union, may attend and speak at some or all of the meetings of the executive, otherwise than for the purpose of providing the committee with factual information or with technical or professional advice with respect to matters taken into account by the executive in carrying out its functions.[184]

This was intended to cover all those who 'act as though they are members of the ... [executive] and who participate in the decision-making process'.[185] This may not be an easy group to classify; it may vary according to the role of an individual

---

174 TULRCA 1992, ss 46–61. This requires direct elections to the office in question: *BECTU v Gates* EAT/1462/00 10 April 2001. We aim here to describe the framework for union elections. For a more detailed account see G Morris and T Archer, 2000: paras 2.33-2.45.

175 TULRCA 1992, s 46(6).

176 TULRCA 1992, s 46(1)(b). There is an exception in relation to persons within five years of retirement provided that complex conditions are met: s 58. See *Beaumont v Amicus*, 14 May 2004, CO.

177 TULRCA 1992, s 53.

178 *In the matter of a complaint against the Offshore Industry Liaison Committee*, 25 November 1994, CO, the Certification Officer held that an independent scrutineer must be appointed even in an uncontested election. He or she is required to report whether there were reasonable grounds to believe that any statutory requirement had been contravened, including whether a candidate had been unreasonably excluded from standing, which could apply equally to a contested and an uncontested election.

179 TULRCA 1992, s 49; The Trade Union Ballots and Elections (Independent Scrutineer Qualifications) Order 1993, SI 1993/1909, as amended.

180 TURERA 1993, s 7; the Funds for Trade Union Ballots Regulations (Revocation) Regulations 1993, SI 1993/233.

181 TULRCA 1992, s 119.

182 For a decision as to which of two union bodies should be designated the executive, see *Stone v NATFHE*, 30 June 1987, CO.

183 TULRCA 1992, s 46(2)(b).

184 TULRCA 1992, s 46(3).

185 Lord Trefgarne, Joint-Under-Secretary of State for Employment, HL Debs, vol 486, cols 484–485, 28 March 1988.

office holder within a union and possibly the behaviour of an individual incumbent; thus one cannot state that all national or regional officers, for example, need, or need not, be elected. The position is further complicated by the ambiguities of the statutory language. There are four major problems: the meaning of 'may attend and speak', which could mean 'may attend by entitlement', 'is not prohibited from attending' or 'it is theoretically possible may attend'; the meaning of 'practice', whose longevity or consistency is unspecified; the number of meetings which an individual may attend without attracting the requirements for election;[186] and whether attendance at only part of a meeting is sufficient. The exception of those providing information or advice was intended to exclude individuals who offer merely 'supporting advice' to the committee rather than participating in 'decision-taking' but the line between the two activities may be easily crossed.[187] Union legal officers who advise on the legal consequences of a course of action, or research or regional officers who give merely factual information, for example, would seem not to require election but their position may be jeopardised if they stray into a discussion of union policy based on their advice or report.

Individuals who fail to be re-elected can no longer continue to hold their positions, although the union may allow their membership of the committee to continue for a period of up to six months after the election in order to give effect to the result.[188] Any term or condition governing the official's employment with the union which conflicts with the obligation to leave office – for example, if or she is employed on a fixed term contract for a longer period – cannot affect this position.[189] This means that unions must ensure that the contracts of persons subject to election expire when the post falls due for election. It also means that unions are unable to offer any job security to individuals who may have been chosen for a particular office, in particular that of general secretary, for administrative rather than political skills.

The selection of candidates and election addresses

10.15   No union member may be 'unreasonably excluded' from standing as a candidate at an election.[190] Exclusion is not 'unreasonable' if it is because he or she belongs to a class all of whose members are excluded by the union rules.[191]

---

186 John Cope, Minister for Employment, considered that someone attending only occasionally was unlikely to require election (House of Commons, Official Report of Standing Committee F, col 366, 15 December 1987) but this is not made clear in the legislation.

187 In *Re a complaint against the GPMU*, 11 March 1993, CO, the Certification Officer accepted the General Secretary's assurance that particular individuals fell within the exception in the absence of any evidence from the applicant to the contrary. This case shows the importance of ensuring that the union rules do not describe such individuals as members of the executive: cf *Re a complaint against SOGAT '82*, 31 July 1991, CO.

188 TULRCA 1992, s 59. Note also that if an individual who holds a specific post is permitted by the union rules to remain on the executive for a period after leaving office then there may be no need to hold an election to the second office if they can be regarded as having been elected to both offices at the time of the initial election: *Paul v NALGO* [1987] IRLR 43, CO (immediate past president allowed to retain a voting position on the union's council for one year after holding the presidency for a year).

189 TULRCA 1992, s 46(6).

190 TULRCA 1992, s 47(1). See generally *GMB v Stokes* UKEAT/0769/03/ILB 23 January 2004.

191 TULRCA 1992, s 47(3). In *Ecclestone v NUJ* [1999] IRLR 166, Smith J held that the exclusion of those who did not have the confidence of the union's National Executive Council did not comply with s 47(3).

This means that unions may require a minimum number of years' membership of the union, or (at the time of writing) a maximum age limit, for example, although any such requirement must be stipulated in the rules; it cannot be a matter for the exercise of discretion on an ad hoc basis.[192] A further restriction is that no candidate may be required, directly or indirectly, to be a member of a political party.[193] Thus a union cannot require candidates to be a member of the Labour Party or to attend the Labour Party conference, which is open only to members. Notably, however, it does not prevent the exclusion of members of a particular party from standing; thus unions may lawfully exclude members of the Communist or the Conservative Party, for example. The Certification Officer has held that it is not unreasonable for a union to demand a certain level of support from fellow members as a pre-condition of standing, although the practical difficulties facing individuals seeking nomination will be relevant here.[194] All candidates must be given the opportunity to prepare an election address in their own words and to submit it to the union, which must distribute it with the voting papers to the electorate.[195] Any facilities and restrictions regarding the preparation or modification of an address must be applied equally to each candidate and the same method of producing copies (which must be done free of charge) must be applied to each.[196] Unions may set a maximum limit for the length of an address, subject to a minimum of 100 words.[197] They have no power to reject an address, regardless of its contents. They are protected against liability for defamation in the event that an address contains material which is libellous,[198] although if a union continues with an election where one candidate argues that he or she has been prejudiced by the circulation of such material it may find itself in difficulties. While the statutory provisions are clearly designed to ensure equality of treatment between candidates, there seems nothing to prevent a union from distributing additional material indicating, for example, those candidates whom the executive supports, a view echoed by the Certification Officer on a number of occasions.[199]

The balloting constituency and the conduct of the election

10.16 As a general rule entitlement to vote should be accorded equally to all members of the union.[200] This rules out any system of branch, block or delegate voting, or election to a body which then selects representatives to sit on the

---

192 TULRCA 1992, s 47(3).
193 TULRCA 1992, s 47(2). See para 10.20 for discussion of the meaning of 'political party'.
194 See *Paul v NALGO* [1987] IRLR 43, CO. Also relevant in this connection are *Re complaints against BETA*, 21 December 1990, CO; *Corti v TGWU*, 28 October 1986, CO; *Re a complaint against NATFHE*, 12 August 1988, CO; *Re complaints against ISTC*, 21 December 1990, CO; *In the matter of complaints against the MU*, 12 July 2000, CO.
195 TULRCA 1992, s 48(1).
196 TULRCA 1992, s 48(5)–(7). See generally *Beaumont v Amicus* 26 March 2003, CO.
197 TULRCA 1992, s 48(3). The union may also provide that addresses should incorporate only such matter as the union may determine as regards photographs and other matter not in words: s 48(3)(b). In *Re the matter of a complaint against the TGWU*, 19 June 1996, CO the Certification Officer held that the 'provision' did not need to be in writing; a long-established practice of not including photographs in addresses was sufficient, in the absence of any contrary indication.
198 TULRCA 1992, s 48(8).
199 See, for example, *Re a complaint against the CPSA*, 17 May 1995, CO.
200 TULRCA 1992, s 50(1). On the interpretation of 'member' see the EAT decision in *NUM (Yorkshire Area) v Millward* [1995] IRLR 411.

executive.[201] However, a union may lawfully restrict the balloting constituency in certain specified respects if it so chooses. First, provided that the union rules so provide, it may exclude all those who are unemployed, in arrears with their subscriptions or contributions, and apprentices, trainees, students or new members.[202] It may also decide, it seems on an ad hoc basis, whether overseas members are included.[203] Second, it may restrict entitlement to members falling within a class determined by reference to a trade or occupation; a geographical area; or one which is, under the union rules, treated as a separate section within the union, or one determined by any combination of these factors.[204] However these restrictions must, again, be specified in the union rules,[205] and should not have the effect of excluding any individual member from voting in all elections.[206] It is notable that there is no provision for determining balloting constituencies based upon the employers of members.

At the time of writing,[207] election ballots must be conducted entirely by 'post', which is defined in terms which exclude delivery by hand, internal mail or private courier.[208] Although the legislation recognises that it is unrealistic to expect a union to guarantee delivery to every member who is entitled to vote,[209] it is not necessary to show that the number of members who were not supplied with a ballot paper was sufficiently great to have affected the result of the ballot in order for a remedy to be granted.[210] There are various provisions designed to ensure the secrecy and security of the ballot.[211] Members must be entitled to vote at no direct cost to themselves; this has been seen as requiring the union to pay the cost of return postage.[212] Voters must be allowed to vote without interference from, or constraint imposed by, the union or any of its members, officials or employees.[213] To date the Certification Officer has generally interpreted this as excluding conduct which would 'intimidate or put a member generally

---

201   *BECTU v Gates* EAT/1462/00 10 April 2001. On the variety of voting methods before the statutory provisions were introduced, see Undy and Martin, 1984.
202   TULRCA 1992, s 50(2).
203   TULRCA 1992, s 60(1). 'Overseas members' are those (other than merchant seamen or offshore workers) who are outside Great Britain throughout the period during which votes may be cast (s 60(2)), thus allowing the exclusion of those on holiday.
204   TULRCA 1992, s 50(3).
205   TULRCA 1992, s 50(3). See *Ecclestone v NUJ* 2 July 2003, CO.
206   TULRCA 1992, s 50(4).
207   ERelA 2004, s 54 empowers the Secretary of State to make provision by order, in relation to any description of ballot or election authorised or required by TULRCA 1992, that it may be conducted by other means, subject to specified conditions, but at the time of writing no such orders have been made.
208   TULRCA 1992, s 298. However, the Certification Officer has accepted that where an employer provides a delivery service to and from employees internally within a building, that would not normally infringe s 51(4): *Re complaints against the POA*, 9 August 1996, CO.
209   See the concept of 'reasonable practicability' in TULRCA 1992, s 51(4).
210   In this context the Certification Officer has regarded as highly material the efforts made by the union to maintain an accurate register of members' addresses and other efforts to publicise the election, to inform members of what to do if they fail to receive a ballot paper, and to enable members to vote: *Re complaints against COHSE*, 17 August 1990, CO. He indicated here that a stricter approach may be appropriate for elections than industrial action ballots; in this context, unlike the latter, an order could relate to the procedure for future elections.
211   TULRCA 1992, s 51.
212   *Paul v NALGO* [1987] IRLR 43, CO.
213   TULRCA 1992, s 51(3)(a).

in fear of voting, or amount to physical interference',[214] but in 1996 an election was found to be inherently compromised because ballot papers before and after completion fell into the hands of union officials, even though there was no evidence of intimidation.[215] It is notable that the legislation does not prohibit employers or third parties from interfering with the conduct of the election or attempting to put pressure on individuals to vote in a particular way.

Votes must be fairly and accurately counted although any inaccuracy which is accidental and on a scale which could not affect the result of the ballot may be disregarded.[216] The union must ensure that the storage and distribution of voting papers, and the counting of votes cast, are undertaken by one or more independent persons appointed by the union.[217] This function may be performed either by the independent scrutineer or by some other person whose appointment is made subject, *mutatis mutandis*, to the same conditions.[218] The independent scrutineer engaged to supervise the conduct of the ballot must issue a report stating, *inter alia*, whether he or she is satisfied that the security arrangements for handling voting papers and counting votes were such as to minimise the risk of unfairness or malpractice, as well as commenting more broadly on whether any of the statutory requirements were contravened.[219] The union has a duty to comply with all reasonable requests by the scrutineer connected with the performance of his or her functions;[220] this probably entails, for example, allowing the scrutineer to look at records, obtain relevant information, and visit premises as appropriate. The union must not publish the result of the election until it has received the scrutineer's report.[221] Its contents should be made known to union members and be made available to them on request, either free or on payment of a reasonable fee.[222] While a critical report will not of itself invalidate the ballot it may serve to draw the attention of members to possible grounds for challenging it.

The result of the election must be ascertained solely by counting the number of votes cast directly for each candidate by those voting (although the use of the single transferable vote is expressly permitted).[223] However in *R v Certification Officer for Trade Unions and Employers' Associations, ex p EPEA* it was held by the House of Lords that this does not necessarily mean that a 'first past the post' system must be uniformly applied. The union's rules allowed a maximum of four members of any one of its nine geographical divisions to serve on the national executive committee. Nine members of the committee were elected in divisional ballots, the remaining fifteen in a national ballot. The rule meant that if there were more than three candidates from any one division in the national ballot, only the three who polled the greatest number of votes as between themselves could be elected, even if the fourth candidate in that division polled

---

214 *Paul v NALGO* [1987] IRLR 43, CO.
215 *Re complaints against the POA*, 9 August 1996, CO.
216 TULRCA 1992, s 51(5)(b).
217 TULRCA 1992, s 51A(1).
218 TULRCA 1992, s 51A(2)-(6).
219 TULRCA 1992, s 49(3); s 52.
220 TULRCA 1992, s 49(7).
221 TULRCA 1992, s 52(3). In *Douglas v GMPU* [1995] IRLR 426, Morison J thought it unlikely that a union could cancel a ballot once the scrutineer had expressed satisfaction under s 52, regardless of the terms of the union's rules. See also *Wise v USDAW* [1996] IRLR 609, but cf *AB v CD* [2001] IRLR 808, 812 (Sir Andrew Morritt, V-C).
222 TULRCA 1992, s 52(4)-(6).
223 TULRCA 1992, s 51(6), (7).

more than a successful candidate in another division. The court held that the
statutory provision was designed to secure that the only votes which would
determine the outcome of an election were those directly cast by individuals; it
did not mean that a bare count of votes determined the result of the election
without recourse to the union rules. Any other construction would have been an
'unreasonable result which the legislature could not sensibly have intended'.[224]

Remedies for breach of the statutory requirements

10.17   A trade union member, or a candidate in the election, who alleges that
the union has failed to comply with the statutory requirements may apply either
to the Certification Officer or to the High Court (but not both) for a declaration
to that effect.[225] Where either grants a declaration, an enforcement order should
also be granted, unless this is considered inappropriate.[226] This order should
require the union to secure the holding of an election in accordance with the
order; and/or to take any other specified steps to remedy the declared failure;
and/or to abstain from specified acts with a view to securing that the same or a
similar failure does not recur. The court may, additionally, grant interim relief,[227]
which may be appropriate if the applicant wishes to halt an election before it is
completed. In relation to an election which has taken place, non-compliance
with the legislation does not affect the validity of anything done by a person
improperly elected,[228] so any resolutions passed by the executive committee, for
example, remain in force.

TRADE UNION EXPENDITURE FOR POLITICAL PURPOSES

The statutory framework

10.18   In this area, unlike the others we have examined in this chapter, statutory
regulation dates back to early in the century.[229] As we saw in para 7.4, unions
were involved in the political process during the nineteenth century and gave
financial support to parliamentary candidates, initially to Liberals and
Independents then, in the first decade of the twentieth century, to those belonging
to the newly-formed Labour Party.[230] This practice was challenged in the famous
case of *ASRS v Osborne*,[231] in which a branch secretary of the railwaymen's
union sought a declaration that the compulsory political levy of his union was
unlawful, and an injunction to restrain the union from raising and distributing

---

224 [1990] IRLR 398, 400 (Lord Bridge).
225 TULRCA 1992, s 54(1), (2). See para 2.38 for the procedure followed by the Certification
 Officer and the effect of any orders made by him or her. Applications which relate to an
 election which has already been held must be made within one year of the union
 announcing the result: s 54(3). *Quaere* whether this precludes an application for breach
 of contract, which is not subject to this time limit, where the statutory requirements have
 been incorporated into the union rules: see *Veness and Chalkley v NUPE* [1991] IRLR
 76.
226 TULRCA 1992, ss 55(5A), 56(4).
227 TULRCA 1992, s 56(7).
228 TULRCA 1992, s 61(2).
229 See Ewing 1982b, 1984 for further discussion of this area.
230 Wedderburn, 1986: p 759.
231 [1910] AC 87.

money for political purposes. The House of Lords held that the definition of a trade union in the Trade Union Acts 1871–76, which made no reference to political action, was a limiting one and that it was therefore *ultra vires* the Act for the union to levy a contribution on members for this purpose.[232] This decision, which removed their only income from 16 Labour MPs,[233] put the whole future of the Labour Party at risk. The Liberal government of the day responded in two different ways. 'First, in 1911 public money was made available to provide salaries for the hitherto unpaid MPs ... Second, the government introduced a Bill to remove the legal restraints on trade union political spending, it being readily accepted that trade unions had a right to seek the realisation of their goals by representation in Parliament and that they should not be disabled from so doing by economic and legal barriers'.[234] The Trade Union Act 1913 effectively overruled *Osborne* by permitting a union to have objects additional to its statutory objects.[235] It did not leave unions completely unfettered in this area, however. Rather it required that those which wished to spend money on 'political objects' must first ballot their members on whether such objects should be adopted. If the majority of those voting were in favour, the union could then adopt rules to establish a separate political fund which alone could be used for the purpose of financing those objects. The rules were required to provide that every member had a right to be exempt from the contribution to the fund. Other than the period 1927–1946, which altered the scheme from one of contracting-out to contracting-in to payment of the political levy,[236] the framework of the 1913 Act remained in place until the Trade Union Act 1984. This Act introduced a requirement for periodic ballots and extended radically the definition of political objects. Subsequent legislation brought further constraints on the conduct of the balloting process.

10.19   As well as holding a ballot initially to approve political objects unions must now hold a fresh ballot at least once every ten years in order to retain an existing fund.[237] The rules governing each ballot must be approved by the Certification Officer;[238] they must reflect the complex requirements of the legislation which are in most material respects identical to those governing elections which we described in para 10.16. Again the ballot must be fully postal[239] and supervised by an independent scrutineer, so imposing substantial costs upon the union. In this context, however, the union may not exclude any groups from the balloting constituency, with the exception of overseas members where the ballot is to continue an existing fund.[240] Political fund rules must be

---

232 This decision involved the court treating the union as a corporate or, at least, a quasi-corporate entity, a highly questionable assumption: P Davies and M Freedland, 1984: p 685.
233 Wedderburn, 1986: p 760.
234 Elias and Ewing, 1987: p 168.
235 See para 7.20 above for discussion of the current definition of a 'trade union' contained in TULRCA 1992, s 1.
236 It seems that 'human apathy' plays a considerable role in this area; the contributions to political funds rose from 38% of members in TUC unions in 1945 to 60% in 1948: Wedderburn, 1986: p 762.
237 TULRCA 1992, s 73(3). For the issues which arise if a political fund resolution expires without being replaced, see G Morris and T Archer, 2000: para 2.52.
238 TULRCA 1992, s 74.
239 At the time of writing; see para 10.16 above.
240 TULRCA 1992, ss 76, 94.

approved by the Certification Officer and must stipulate that any payments in furtherance of 'political objects' are made only from the fund.[241] Payments for purposes outside this definition may be made from the general fund provided that the union's rules so permit. Property may be added to the political fund only from members' contributions or those of persons other than the union, and that which accrues to the fund in the course of administering its assets, such as interest.[242] Thus unions cannot add to their political fund income generated by the investment of other funds and the Act may also prevent them borrowing money for political activities.[243] No liability of the fund may be discharged out of any other union fund;[244] thus a creditor will be unable to secure payment of a political fund debt out of the general fund.

Members must be notified by the union of their right of exemption from contributing to the fund in a form specified by statute.[245] Those who exercise this right must then be relieved from the political fund element of the normal periodical contribution to the union.[246] The rules must provide that contribution to the fund is not a condition of admission to the union and that exempted members are not excluded from any union benefits, or placed directly or indirectly at any disadvantage as compared with other members, except in relation to the control or management of the political fund.[247] A union cannot exclude a non-contributor from holding union office by failing to separate control of the fund from other union activities.[248] In 1984, in return for the government agreeing not to attempt to re-introduce 'contracting-in', the TUC issued a 'statement of guidance on political fund arrangements' designed to ensure that union members are informed about and able to exercise their right to contract out from contributing. It is unlawful for employers who operate the 'check-off' to deduct an amount from the wages of non-contributors which includes the political levy, nor may they avoid the administrative inconvenience of making deductions at differential rates by withdrawing the check-off facility for non-contributors alone.[249] However, it seems that this difficulty may be circumvented if unions invite non-contributors to consent to deduction of the full subscription but give them a rebate for the political fund contribution in advance.

There are four major categories of complaint that may arise in relation to expenditure for political objects, all but one of which can be pursued by a member before either the Certification Officer or the High Court.[250] The first is a complaint relating to a breach of the union's political fund rules. In this context, unusually, any order made by the Certification Officer may be enforced

241 TULRCA 1992, s 82, as amended by ERelA 2004, Sch 1, para 6.
242 TULRCA 1992, s 83(1).
243 *ASTMS v Parkin* [1983] IRLR 448.
244 TULRCA 1992, s 83(3).
245 TULRCA 1992, s 84((1), (2).
246 TULRCA 1992, s 85(1). Where a member gives an exemption notice within one month of members being notified of their right to do so, and at the time of the political resolution ballot no political resolution is in force, the exemption takes immediate effect; in all other cases it takes effect from 1 January after the notice is given: s 84(4).
247 TULRCA 1992, s 82(1).
248 *Birch v NUR* [1950] Ch 602.
249 See TULRCA 1992, ss 86–88. On the regulation of the check-off, see para 8.41 above.
250 See para 2.38 for the procedure followed by the Certification Officer and the effect of an order made by him or her. The Political Parties, Elections and Referendums Act 2000 also has implications for union spending on political objects, as part of a wider regulation of spending in this area: see Ewing, 2001.

in the same way as an order of the county court rather than as an order of the High Court.[251] The second relates to a breach of the statutory provisions governing political funds, such as a complaint that money has been spent on 'political objects' without a political fund resolution being in force.[252] However it seems that if the political fund rules contain provisions that are permissible but not required by statute (the third category), complaints about breaches of those rules may be taken only to the High Court.[253] The final category is those relating to political resolution ballots.[254] In the case of a successful application, an 'enforcement order' requiring the union to remedy the defect will also normally be made.

The definition of 'political objects'

10.20 The 'political objects' which may be furthered exclusively by the expenditure of money from a union's political fund fall into six broad categories:[255]

(i) Any contribution to the funds of a political party, or on the payment of expenses incurred directly or indirectly by it. 'Contribution' includes affiliation or membership fees and loans[256] and also extends to investments made on a commercial basis.[257] 'Expenses' would cover such matters as salaries, rents and administration. There is no statutory definition of a 'political party' and the issue has not, to date, arisen for decision in this context.[258]

(ii) The provision of any service or property for use by or on behalf of any political party. 'Property' could include equipment, such as computers; 'service'; the provision of staff.[259]

(iii) Expenditure in connection with the registration of electors, the candidature of any person (including prospective candidature), the selection of any

---

251 TULRCA 1992, s 82(4A)(4B), inserted by ERelA 2004, Sched 1, para 6.
252 TULRCA 1992, s 72A. No specific provision is made in this context for the High Court to have jurisdiction, but s 72A(11) implies that it is intended to exist.
253 TULRCA 1992, s 82(2) applies only to rules *made in pursuance of this section*, and breach of rules relating to political funds is not covered by s 108A.
254 TULRCA 1992, s 79. Applications which relate to a ballot which has already been held must be made within one year of the union announcing the result: s 79(3).
255 TULRCA 1992, s 72(1), (2). In determining whether a union has incurred expenditure of this kind, no account is to be taken of the ordinary administrative expenses of the union: s 72(3). The union failed successfully to rely upon this exclusion in *Re a complaint against the ISTC*, 13 October 1994, CO.
256 TULRCA 1992, s 72(4).
257 *ASTMS v Parkin* [1983] IRLR 448.
258 The Political Parties, Elections and Referendums Act 2000 does not directly define a 'political party'; parties (which include 'any organisation or person': s 40) that intend to contest 'relevant elections' (parliamentary elections; elections to the European and Scottish Parliaments and the National Assembly for Wales and Northern Ireland Assembly; local government elections; and local elections in Northern Ireland) must register under the Act: ss 40; 22(5). See also the SDA 1975, s 33(1). On the meaning of 'political purpose' in the context of charity law see *McGovern v A-G* [1981] 3 All ER 493, 509 (Slade J); see also *R v Radio Authority, ex p Bull* [1997] 2 All ER 561, CA. On the basis of these latter decisions, it is conceivable that Amnesty, the League Against Cruel Sports, and Friends of the Earth could be regarded as political parties, although this goes beyond what would seem to be intended in this context.
259 Elias and Ewing, 1987: p 170.

candidate or the holding of any ballot by the union in connection with any election to a political office. 'Political office' covers members of the UK and European Parliament and of a local authority and also includes any position within a political party.[260] It therefore covers internal party elections, such as the nomination of parliamentary candidates or prospective candidates.

(iv) Expenditure on the maintenance of any holder of a political office. 'Maintenance' means the maintenance of a person as a politician and is not confined to expenses incurred to stay alive; it also covers expenses to facilitate the conduct of political functions, such as a grant for research, travel or secretarial expenses.[261]

(v) Expenditure on the holding of any conference or meeting by or on behalf of a political party or of any other meeting the main purpose of which is the transaction of business in connection with a political party.

(vi) Expenditure on the production, publication or distribution[262] of any literature, document, film, sound recording or advertisement, the main purpose of which is to persuade people to vote, or not to vote, for a political party or candidate.

The last category, first introduced by the TUA 1984, represented a particularly significant extension of the previous definition; under the TUA 1913, expenditure on political literature was required to be financed from a political fund only if it was directly and expressly in support of a political party.[263] In expanding the definition, the Conservative Government's primary target was 'the electoral expenditure of public sector unions concerned to protect their members' interests in the face of privatization and cuts'.[264] The government claimed that the 'main purpose' test would ensure that campaigns on matters such as jobs and other matters affecting members' interests could still be financed from unions' general funds; they would only need to be paid for out of political funds if their main purpose was to influence voting behaviour. The only case on this provision to date, *Paul v NALGO*,[265] lent some support to this view. NALGO, a public service union, issued leaflets during the run-up to local authority elections and in anticipation of a general election which drew attention to the impact of government cutbacks and privatisation policies on public services and pointed out that readers had a vote. The leaflets specifically disclaimed any intention of seeking or opposing the election of particular candidates but their distribution was concentrated in marginal Conservative constituencies. In finding that expenditure on the leaflets from the general fund was unlawful, the court dismissed the union's claim that this was a non-partisan campaign designed merely to persuade people that public services were a good thing; the only rational conclusion to be drawn from the literature was 'If you accept the message of this leaflet, vote against the Conservatives' and this being so the disclaimer was not effective to avoid liability. However, the court emphasised that it was the linkage of disapproval of Government

260 TULRCA 1992, s 72(4). 'Local authority' is defined in the Local Government Act 1972, s 270, as amended.
261 *ASTMS v Parkin* [1983] IRLR 448.
262 The Certification Officer has held that 'distribution' includes distribution to members and officials of the union, as well as to the general public, although limited circulation within a union office may not be covered: *McCarthy v APEX* [1980] IRLR 335.
263 *Coleman v POEU* [1981] IRLR 427, CO.
264 Elias and Ewing, 1987: p 172.
265 [1987] IRLR 413.

policies in a biased way with the invitation to vote at the time of an election which had made the campaign a 'political object' and stressed that:

> ... nothing in th[e] judgment should be taken as suggesting that a publicity campaign ... at times other than an election and therefore at a time when neither directly nor indirectly can the union be inviting anybody to exercise a vote at the time, is unlawful, merely because it expresses disapproval of the Government's policy.[266]

Despite this limitation, however, the provision ensures that unions which lack a political fund cannot promote campaigns which criticise government policies at a time when they may be most effective, that is, before an election.

In the event many public service unions established political funds for the first time in order to fend off the possibility of their campaigns being susceptible to legal challenge including, much to the government's chagrin, unions in the civil service.[267] In addition, contrary to expectations, all unions with existing political funds which were required to hold fresh ballots[268] returned a majority in favour of retaining them. The second wave of balloting in 1994/96 produced broadly similar results[269] although in 1997 members of the Civil and Public Services Association voted against a resolution to establish a new political fund,[270] a result echoed by the newly-formed Public and Commercial Services Union, of which the CPSA was a constituent part, in 1999.[271] At the end of March 2004 there were 32 political fund resolutions in force; returns for 2003/4 showed that more than 4.4 million trade unionists contributed to such funds, which contained a combined total of £15.9 million.[272]

ASSESSMENT

10.21 The law governing the relationship between trade unions and their members was transformed during the 1979-1997 Conservative Government from a relatively non-interventionist approach to one which is highly restrictive, limiting unions' scope for autonomous action. In analysing the significance of this development, it is important to note that the concept of trade union autonomy was not merely a product of the collective *laissez-faire* tradition in Britain; it is also regarded at international level as fundamental to the concept of freedom of association. Article 3 of ILO Convention No 87 concerning Freedom of Association and the Right to Organise (1948) declares that '[w]orkers' and employers' organisations shall have the right to draw up their constitutions and rules, to elect their representatives in full freedom, to organise their administration and activities and to formulate their programmes.[273] The public authorities shall refrain from any interference which would restrict this right or

---

266 [1987] IRLR 413, at 421.

267 See generally Fredman and Morris, 1989: pp 126–128.

268 Unions which had adopted political funds more than nine years before the relevant part of the TUA 1984 came into effect were deemed to have passed them nine years earlier and were therefore required to re-ballot within a year.

269 See Leopold, 1997. In 2003/4 Amicus and TGWU, respectively the second and third largest unions, held review ballots in which members voted to maintain their political funds.

270 *Annual Report of the Certification Officer for 1997*, para 7.10.

271 *Annual Report of the Certification Officer for 1999–2000*, para 7.10.

272 *Annual Report of the Certification Officer for 2003–2004*, paras 7.12–7.16; App 9.

273 Art 3(1).

impede the lawful exercise thereof'.[274] The current scope of external regulation of union government makes it particularly pertinent to consider the extent to which the law can and should legitimately intrude upon the principle of trade union autonomy. This raises a complex set of issues, only a few of which are outlined here.[275]

The most rudimentary level of legal intervention would be merely to ensure that unions obey the rules which they themselves have determined, with members having recourse to the courts if they are breached. This would entail treating unions in the same way as other bodies founded upon a contract of membership. In Britain, achieving this approach would require a reining in of the judicial inclination to treat unions distinctively from other private law organisations, which has led them to superimpose on the contract of membership public law standards of procedural fairness,[276] even, in some instances, at the cost of overriding substantive union rules. If the law is, on a principled and coherent basis, to take a more interventionist approach to union government than merely enforcing the contract of membership, the justifications for this need to be explored and clarified. In relation to access to union membership, in the past the closed shop has constituted the most powerful argument for constraining unions' capacity to act autonomously, given that denial of union membership could reduce or remove completely the access of the individual to the labour market. Now that the closed shop can no longer lawfully be enforced, the question arises as to whether other benefits of union membership justify constraining union discretion. It remains the case that, for most workers, union membership offers an important opportunity to participate in the regulation of their working life, particularly where their union is recognised. Other benefits of membership may include representation at disciplinary and grievance procedures[277] and legal representation. If one accepts the argument that these are benefits which should not be arbitrarily denied to workers, this leads to a discussion of the legitimate scope of any control. At a minimal level one may argue that the conditions of membership should be clearly articulated and that any discretionary powers which are left to unions should not be exercised in an arbitrary or capricious fashion. One may also wish to argue that fairness may demand that reasons should be given if membership is refused to an ostensibly qualified individual, as well as if an existing member is expelled. A further stage of interventionism is to exercise control over the substance of the rules themselves. If one is to exceed the principles which apply in other areas, such as those covered by the anti-discrimination legislation,[278] this involves much more complex inquiry as to the legitimate reach of legal policy. At present, unions cannot deny lawfully membership to, or expel from membership, individuals whose political views may be diametrically opposed to those of the membership as a whole unless those individuals undertake activities as members of the political party in question. In *Cheall v APEX* Lord Diplock affirmed that 'freedom of association

---

274 Art 3(2). The Committee of Experts has pointed out that legislative provisions which regulate in detail the internal functioning of workers' and employers' organisations pose a serious risk of interference by the public authorities. See the Report of the Committee of Experts on the Application of Conventions and Recommendations, Report III (Part 4A), ILO, Geneva, 1995: p 201.

275 For a more detailed discussion of these issues see Elias and Ewing, 1987: ch 8; Fredman, 1992a; Leader 1992; Wedderburn, 1995; Undy *et al*, 1996; Estreicher *et al*, 2001.

276 Although see D Oliver, 1997 for a justification of extending this approach to other bodies.

277 See now ERelA 1999, ss 10–15, discussed para 5.132 *et seq*.

278 See ch 6.

can only be mutual; there can be no right of an individual to associate with other individuals who are not willing to associate with him'.[279] Under the current law, an individual is accorded the choice of whether to associate with those whose aspirations he or she does not share; the remainder, collectively, have no such choice, a situation which would appear to be incompatible with Article 11 of the ECHR.[280] Although, ultimately, unions cannot be forced under statute to retain individuals in membership, the price of exclusion or expulsion can be a heavy one. The ILO Committee of Experts on the Application of Conventions and Recommendations considers that unions should have the right to determine whether or not it should be possible to discipline members who refuse to comply with democratic decisions to take lawful industrial action, and that the financial penalties imposed by the legislation infringe Article 3 of Convention No 87.[281] The ECSR, which supervises the ESC, has also concluded that the limitations on the right of unions to exclude or expel individuals, or to discipline their members, is incompatible with the right to organise.[282] Despite these findings, the Labour Government has refused to change the current legislation in this area.[283] To the extent, at least, that the law does not comply with international standards it is in urgent need of review.

10.22 The same issues as to the scope of union autonomy arise in relation to other aspects of union government, in particular the important area of access to union office. Is this an area where the role of the law, if any, should be confined to ensuring that unions comply with their own rules or is it one where a more interventionist approach is warranted: in short, should trade unions be obliged to behave according to some externally-imposed model of 'democracy'? One often-quoted answer to this question was given by VL Allen in 1954:

> Trade union organisation is not based on theoretical concepts prior to it, that is on some concept of democracy, but on the end it serves … the end of trade union activity is to protect and improve the general living standards of its members and not to provide workers with an exercise in self-government.[284]

The current legislation is predicated on the premise that, before statutory controls were introduced, unions were not sufficiently representative of and accountable to their members, although, as has been pointed out by many commentators, no evidence for this was provided.[285] On the basis of these assumptions, a uniform

---

279 [1983] IRLR 215, 218.
280 See Leader, 1991: pp 42–59 (where it is argued that the protection against expulsion of those who refuse to strike cannot be justified as 'necessary in a democratic society' under Art 11(2)) and the discussion in para 10.3 above. A challenge to the legislation on this ground would seem to require an application to the ECtHR; it seems difficult to envisage a remedy being available under the HRA 1998.
281 See Report of the Committee of Experts on the Application of Conventions and Recommendations, Report III (Part 4A), ILO, Geneva, 1999. See also para 11.91 below, where we discuss the ILO's condemnation of the response to the prohibition on unions indemnifying individuals for penalties for criminal offences or contempt of court.
282 For a more detailed analysis of ILO and ECSR conclusions on this area see Institute of Employment Rights Submission on TULRCA 1992, s 174, prepared by Professor Keith Ewing and John Hendy QC, JCHR Thirteenth Report, Session 2003-2004, App 2b; see also App 2d.
283 *Review of the Employment Relations Act 1999: Government Response*, DTI, 2003, para 6.17.
284 Allen 1954: p 122, quoted Wedderburn, 1995: p 180.
285 The issue of how 'democracy' in unions is to be measured is itself a highly complex one: see further Undy and Martin, 1984: p 189–210; Undy et al, 1996; Estreicher et al, 2001.

model of elections was imposed on unions, which previously operated according to a wide variety of practices.[286] One notable characteristic of the legislation is that it is based upon a model of union 'citizenship' which is highly individualistic. The introduction of these provisions led to substantial changes in union rules and practice.[287] To the extent that the Conservative Government's real agenda may have been not merely to change procedures but also to attempt to influence outcomes by creating the conditions in which a more 'moderate' leadership would prevail, the desired result did not materialise. Research has shown that, in its early years at least, the legislation 'singularly failed to initiate a transformation in the political complexion of union leadership or a reorientation of democracy in a 'moderate' direction ...'[288] Indeed, the suggestion has been made that in certain circumstances the need to ballot regularly can actively promote militancy.[289] Moreover, the Conservative Government's presumption that union members would display different political preferences when voting by secret ballot from when voting in a public forum was not borne out; voting patterns did not change in any consistent political direction.[290] This is not to suggest that compliance with these provisions has not had serious consequences for unions, including substantial financial costs. Given the additional obligation to employ an independent scrutineer, mandatory even in the case of uncontested elections, the price of the statutory concept of democracy for trade unions is now a very high one. Perhaps surprisingly, the regime of elections imposed upon unions has not been found by the ILO's Committee of Experts to breach Article 3, since it is seen as within the range of measures which are acceptable as 'intended to promote democratic principles within trade union organisations or to ensure that the electoral procedure is conducted in a normal manner and with due respect for the rights of members in order to avoid any dispute arising as to the result of the election'.[291]

10.23   A final major area of regulation which requires consideration is that of union political activities. It may be argued that the line between the industrial and political spheres of activity is impossible to draw and that unions should be entitled to decide whether, and to what extent, to use their resources to attempt to create a politically hospitable climate for their members. If one accepts that some limits should be imposed, it may be thought appropriate to view this question in the broader context of the funding of political parties and the constraints, if any, which are placed upon other organisations in this regard. Until recently, trade unions were treated wholly distinctively from other groups; companies, for example, were required to disclose their political donations[292] but there was no equivalent form of shareholder control. The Political Parties,

---

286 See generally Undy and Martin, 1984.
287 P Smith *et al*, 1993; Undy *et al*, 1996: ch 5.
288 P Smith *et al*, 1993: p 380.
289 P Smith *et al*: p 379.
290 Undy and Martin, 1996: ch 5. In unions which previously had used workplace ballots for the election of their executive committee, electoral participation declined: P Smith *et al*, 1993, p 179; thus, 'on the basis of the Conservatives' own limited model of representative democracy the introduction of postal ballots had the effect, in many unions, of reducing union democracy': p 242.
291 Report of the Committee of Experts on the Application of Conventions and Recommendations, Report III (Part 4A), ILO, Geneva, 1985: p 197.
292 Companies Act 1985, Sch 7. Note that paras 3–5 of that Schedule have been amended by the Political Parties, Elections and Referendums Act 2000, s 140.

Elections and Referendums Act 2000 now requires companies to obtain support in a general meeting for a donation to a registered political party or to any other EU political organisation, or to incur 'any EU political expenditure' which exceeds £5000 in aggregate over a specified period.[293] However, there are no equivalent rights to those of trade unionists for shareholders to contract out of such donations.

In 1984 Undy and Martin wrote that: '[t]o the extent that Conservative policy succeeds in reducing the unions to the status of other economic interest groups, the justification for external intervention in their internal decision-making procedures grows weaker'.[294] It is perhaps ironical that, during a period when the role of unions in the industrial and political spheres was marginalised, in relation to the regulation of internal union affairs it was government policy to accord unions a greatly enhanced 'public' status in legal terms. It may not be too cynical to suggest that, in the guise of individual rights, the Conservative Government promoted measures which were in reality 'highly restrictive of workers' rights and trade unionism'.[295] Acceptance of this view does not entail the argument that the interests of the individual, where these stand in opposition to those of the collective, should automatically be subordinate; rather that there is a need to construct a coherent framework which recognises the collective interest as legitimate and which attempts to give a principled justification for the appropriate balance to be struck between them. It also entails consideration of whether, if such a framework were to be formulated, it would be best operated by the courts or by some mechanism of self-regulation, possibly on the basis of a series of guidelines agreed between the government and the TUC, with these being embodied in a TUC Code of Practice and policed and enforced by the TUC. Proposals of this nature are far from new[296] and, indeed, a modest self-regulatory system was in operation to deal with admissions and expulsions for a number of years from 1976.[297] This may constitute a more appropriate method of resolving differences between trade unions and their members and prospective members than the highly adversarial means which is currently offered by the legal process.

293 Companies Act 1985, Part XA, inserted by the Political Parties, Elections and Referendums Act 2000, s 139; Sch 19.
294 Undy and Martin, 1984: p 218.
295 Fredman, 1992a: p 24.
296 See Elias and Ewing, 1987: pp 279–287; and see, in particular, the proposals of the Donovan Commission for a review body consisting of two trade unionists chosen from a panel appointed by the Secretary of State after consultation with the TUC, and a legally-qualified chairman: *Royal Commission on Trade Unions and Employers' Associations 1965–1968*, Cmnd 3623, paras 648–669.
297 In that year the TUC established an Independent Review Committee to consider appeals from individuals who had been dismissed or given notice of dismissal from their jobs as a result of being expelled from, or having been refused admission to, a union in a situation where union membership was a condition of employment. For an analysis of the work of the Committee, see Ewing and Rees, 1981.

CHAPTER 11

Industrial action

INTRODUCTION

11.1   In this chapter we examine the legal implications of organising and participating in industrial action. The concept of 'industrial action' generally connotes restrictions imposed collectively by workers against employers and most of our discussion concerns this. Such restrictions can take a variety of forms, ranging from a strike, which involves a complete withdrawal of labour, to a work-to-rule, go-slow, overtime ban or ban on particular duties. However employers, too, may take measures which disrupt the normal operation of the employment relationship, most notably by a 'lock-out' of workers from the workplace.

The right of workers to withdraw their labour is guaranteed by a number of international treaties and we begin by examining the nature of this right and its rationale. We then outline the development of legal policy in this country towards industrial action, knowledge of which is vital for any understanding of the labyrinthine structure of the current law. There follows an analysis of the common law liabilities which those who organise industrial action may incur and of the criteria which govern whether a trade union will be legally liable for their activities. We then examine the protection which statute affords against these liabilities. Where trade unions are legally responsible for industrial action any statutory protection is conditional upon a prior ballot and provision of specified information to relevant employers in addition to the usual restrictions. We discuss these highly complex requirements in the subsequent section. We then explain the remedies available against those who organise industrial action. This is followed by an overview of the liabilities, criminal as well as civil, which pickets may incur. Finally, in relation to the organisation of industrial action, we outline the restrictions on withdrawals of labour by particular categories of workers and indicate other methods, such as invoking emergency powers, by which the state may seek to lessen the impact of industrial disputes. The chapter then assesses the implications of industrial action for individual workers. It does so from three perspectives. The first, that of the employment relationship, involves analysing its impact both on contractual and on statutory rights, in particular protection against unfair dismissal. Second, we consider briefly the consequences of participation in industrial action for entitlement to a range of social security benefits. Although social security generally lies beyond the scope of this work it is particularly significant in this context because of its impact upon the financial capacity of workers to withstand disputes and, at a more theoretical level, as a product of the rhetoric of state neutrality. Lastly we indicate the rights which dissident union members can exercise against their unions when they wish to challenge the collective decision to take or support industrial action. In the concluding section we comment upon some of the major difficulties raised by the law in this area and outline those aspects which appear most in need of reform.

It will be rapidly apparent that the law in this area, even more than others which we examine in this work, is highly technical and even, at points, convoluted.

For this reason we re-emphasise that our aim, as expressed in the preface, is not to provide an encyclopaedic knowledge of the substantive law, but rather to explore the underlying themes and issues.

INDUSTRIAL ACTION: ROLE, RATIONALE AND INTERNATIONAL STANDARDS

11.2   In 1972, Kahn-Freund and Hepple introduced a study of laws against strikes with the following question:

> Why is it that in all democratic countries the 'freedom to strike' or, as it is sometimes put, the 'right to strike' is considered to be a fundamental freedom, alongside the freedom to organise, to assemble peacefully, to express one's opinion? Why is the strike, or, better perhaps, the potentiality of a strike, that is, of an event which of necessity entails a waste of resources, and damage to the economy, nevertheless by general consent an indispensable element of a democratic society?[1]

The freedom of workers to withdraw their labour has been justified on a number of grounds. It can be seen as a fundamental human right.[2] Thus one leading commentator describes it as complementary to freedom from slavery and forced labour given that (at its extreme) denial of the freedom involves being forced to work against one's better judgement.[3] Related to this is the 'democratic' argument; that such a freedom is intrinsic to the notion of a democracy, a view reinforced by the fact that, conversely, it is often banned in totalitarian societies. From a narrower perspective it may be viewed specifically within the context of industrial relations. Here there are two major (again associated) justifications. The 'equilibrium' argument maintains that the concentrated power of capital, expressed in the capacity of employers to hire and fire workers and close down an enterprise, can only be matched by workers acting in concert. Within this framework the collective withholding of labour is a vital weapon in an economic conflict which imposes costs on both the parties: disrupted production, on the one hand, lost wages on the other.[4] The 'autonomous sanctions' argument sees the right to have recourse to industrial action as integral to the concept of collective bargaining as an autonomous norm-making system. Thus 'those who have made the autonomous rules should also wield the sanctions ...',[5] a view acknowledged in 1942 by Lord Wright in describing the right to strike as 'an essential element in the principle of collective bargaining'.[6]

The context in which one locates the right may have fundamental implications for its scope and nature.[7] If it is regarded as a human – or even constitutional – right, for example, this may suggest that it inheres in all workers, regardless of whether their union approves the action or, indeed, regardless of whether they

1   Kahn-Freund and Hepple, 1972: p 4.
2   See Ben-Israel, 1988, ch 1; Ewing, 2004.
3   See Ben-Israel, 1988: p 25. However, as Kahn-Freund and Hepple point out, it is possible effectively to undermine the freedom to strike by imposing sanctions against the organisers rather than forcing individuals to go to work.
4   Ben-Israel, 1994: p 11.
5   Kahn-Freund and Hepple, 1972: p 7.
6   *Crofter Hand Woven Harris Tweed Co Ltd v Veitch* [1942] AC 435, 463.
7   See Novitz, 2003.

are members of a union.[8] Conversely, if it is viewed within the context of collective bargaining this may imply that it should be subject to the exclusive control of the collective bargaining agent.

11.3   At international level the right to strike is guaranteed explicitly only in treaties covering socio-economic, rather than civil and political, rights. Thus the International Covenant on Economic, Social and Cultural Rights guarantees the right to strike, although, because it is subject to the proviso that 'it is exercised in conformity with the laws of the particular country',[9] the substantive content of the right is limited.[10] At European level the European Social Charter requires contracting states to recognise 'the right of workers and employers to collective action in cases of conflict of interest, including the right to strike, subject to obligations that might arise out of collective agreements previously entered into'.[11] Curiously, perhaps, there is no reference to the right to strike in ILO Conventions Nos 87 on Freedom of Association and Protection of the Right to Organise or 98 on the Right to Organise and Collective Bargaining. The reasons for this omission are not wholly clear; they have been summarised as 'procedural difficulties, political differences, the feeling that specific elaboration was unnecessary, and workers' fears that specifying a right to strike would also lead to its restriction'.[12] In practice, however, the right has been derived by the supervisory bodies from general freedom of association principles; the Committee of Experts on the Application of Conventions and Recommendations has consistently affirmed that this is one of the essential and legitimate means by which workers and their organisations may promote and defend their economic and social interests and, as such, it is an integral part of the free exercise of the rights guaranteed by Conventions 87 and 98.[13] On the basis of this view they have developed an extensive jurisprudence as to what this right entails. As we shall see, UK law falls short of these standards in a number of significant respects. In contrast to the ILO, the supervisory organs of the European Convention on Human Rights have refused to imply a right to strike from the right to form and join trade unions, affirming that while the grant of such a right represents 'one of the most important' of the means by which the occupational interests of trade union members may be protected by trade union action, 'there are others'.[14]

---

8   Ewing, 2004: pp 48–50.

9   Art 8. See generally Craven, 1998: ch 7.

10   Ben-Israel, 1988: p 82. Cf Craven, 1998: p 281, where it is stated that it is 'arguably more appropriate to interpret the phrase "in conformity with the laws of the particular country" as legitimizing the imposition of certain procedural requirements, rather than allowing substantive limitations ...'. Note also that Art 8(3) affirms that for States that are party to ILO Convention No 87, Art 8 does not authorise measures that would prejudice the guarantees in that Convention (discussed below).

11   Art 6 (in both the 1961 Charter and the Revised Charter of 1996). Note that states which ratify the treaty can, in the case of certain articles, including Art 6, choose whether to be bound by them: see para 2.47. The reference to 'conflicts of interest' – conflicts over the terms of new collectively-agreed provisions – is in contradistinction to 'conflicts of right' over the interpretation or application of existing agreements, terms which have little meaning in the British context.

12   Ben-Israel, 1988: pp 45–46; see generally pp 35–46.

13   ILO, 1983: para 200; ILO, 1996, paras 475 *et seq*; Gernigon *et al*, 1998; Novitz, 2003: chs 5, 8, 11–15. In the case of public officials, however, recognition of the freedom to associate does not necessarily imply the right to strike: ILO, 1996: para 531.

14   *Schmidt and Dahlstrom v Sweden* judgment of 6 February 1976, (1979–80) 1 EHRR 632, para 36.

However, as we saw in para 7.9, in *UNISON v UK*,[15] the ECtHR, while reaffirming its traditional position, regarded restrictions on the right as falling within Art 11(1) in the case in question. It remains to be seen whether this marks the beginning of a more general willingness on the part of the ECtHR to view the right to strike as intrinsic to freedom of association.

11.4   Developed legal systems vary considerably in how they treat the right to strike. This is the case even within the European Union. As we saw in para 7.11, there is support for the view that there is a fundamental right in EC law for workers to take collective action, although issues as to the proper scope of such a right remain undetermined.[16] The Charter of Fundamental Rights of the European Union affirms the right of workers and employers, or their respective organisations, to take collective action, including strike action, in cases of conflicts of interest, but this is to be exercised 'in accordance with Community law and national law and practices.'[17] In practice there is no European standard,[18] let alone one on a more universal scale. Space does not permit us to describe the enormous diversity of provisions which can, in any case, be properly understood only within the broader framework of national legal and industrial relations systems.[19] We can, however, isolate some fundamental issues which all systems need to address. The first is the location of the right; does it lie with individuals (albeit exercised on a collective basis) – the 'individualist' right' – or only with trade unions (the 'organic')? If it is to be found in a national constitution, as in France or Italy, then it is likely to be individualist, although even then one should beware of oversimplifying the position; in the French public sector, for example, only a representative union can call a strike.[20] The second is the purpose for which the right exists. In general it is confined to 'industrial' or 'economic' matters and does not extend to the 'political' realm,[21] but systems can vary considerably in where they draw the line between the two, which can be a particularly fragile one where social and economic policies may have fundamental implications for wages and job security, for example. Whether the right is located solely within the framework of collective bargaining or whether it goes beyond it may be material here. A third issue is whether the right to strike can be restricted by agreement and, if so, by whom? In France, where it is an individual constitutional right it cannot be bargained away in relation to individual workers.[22] By contrast, in a number of systems where collective agreements are legally binding, industrial action over the terms of that agreement, or even over any issue during its currency ('relative' and 'absolute' peace obligations respectively) may be unlawful. This aspect is reflected in those international instruments which distinguish between conflicts of right, over the interpretation and application of existing collective agreements, and

---

15   Admissibility decision of 10 January 2002, [2002] IRLR 497. See further para 11.9 for the implications of the HRA 1998 for the right to strike.
16   Case C-67/96 *Albany International BV v Stichting Bedrijfspensioenfonds Textielindustrie* Opinion of Advocate General Jacobs, 28 January 1999, para 139; Council Regulation 2979/98, Art 2: see further para 7.11.
17   Art 28. The right affirmed by the EC Social Charter of 1989 was similarly qualified, being 'subject to the obligations arising out of national regulations and collective agreements'.
18   See Wedderburn, 1991b; A Jacobs, 2004.
19   See Ben-Israel, 1994.
20   The right is also guaranteed by the constitutions of Portugal, Spain, Greece and Sweden.
21   For an analysis of ILO principles see Ben-Israel, 1988, Pt III; see also ILO, 1996.
22   Rojot, 1994: p 61.

conflicts of interest over the terms of new collective rules. A fourth is the nature of the action which attracts the protection of the right. Some systems permit strikes but not certain lesser forms of action on the basis that the employer should not incur the expense of operating the enterprise if workers are in dispute. The fifth is the scope of the right: the legitimacy of secondary action by workers employed by other employers to further a dispute is also subject to wide discrepancies in treatment. In Germany, for example, it is lawful if the employer has compromised its neutrality with regard to the primary action by taking over production from the employer in dispute or if the economic relationship between the two employers is such that in economic terms they should be seen as one.[23] Sixth, some systems impose procedural limitations on the exercise of the right, requiring any withdrawal of labour to be preceded by the exhaustion of specified dispute settlement procedures, a ballot of the workers or the provision of a minimum period of notice to employers or the public authorities, for example. Seventh, there are a range of issues posed by the position of individual workers during disputes; should they be protected against dismissal or even temporary replacement, for example, and, if so, for how long? In many countries the contract of employment is suspended during a strike and workers are protected against discriminatory treatment due to their participation in it on resuming work.[24] Finally, a problem which every system faces is whether there are particular groups of workers which, because of the function they perform, should have no, or only limited, access to the right to strike. At one time it was common for all public servants to be denied this right on the ground that it was incompatible with their status as representatives of the sovereign power and, while comprehensive bans have generally been removed in western countries, it remains the case that the legal framework which governs public servants is usually more restrictive than for private sector workers,[25] although this is increasingly anachronistic in an environment in which identical tasks may be performed by workers in the public and the private sector. A more modern approach is to ask whether workers are performing an 'essential' service defined by reference to the function they perform rather than their legal status. The ILO, for example, considers that the right may be restricted in 'essential services', which it defines as those whose interruption 'would endanger the life, personal safety or health of the whole or part of the population'[26] provided that any restrictions are accompanied by reciprocal guarantees to safeguard workers' interests.[27] Unfortunately in this area, as in relation to freedom of association more generally, international standards are divergent;[28] the European Social Charter, for example, allows restrictions which are 'necessary in a democratic society for the protection of the rights and freedoms of others or for the protection of the public interest, national security, public health or morals',[29] a much broader test than the ILO's.

---

23 Weiss, 1994: p 71.
24 A Jacobs, 2004: para 59.
25 See Ozaki, 1993; A Jacobs, 2004: paras 42–46. The ILO considers that the right may be restricted in the case of public servants exercising authority in the name of the State: ILO, 1996: paras 534–535; Gernigon *et al*, 1998: pp 448–449.
26 ILO, 1996: paras 536, 540. The threat to 'life' etc must be 'clear and imminent'. See also Gernigon *et al*, 1998. Note that the police and armed forces are excluded altogether from the scope of these Conventions: see para 11.3 above.
27 ILO, 1996 paras 546–553.
28 See generally Novitz, 2003.
29 Art 31 (Art G in the Revised Charter of 1996). The police and the armed forces are excluded under both these treaties.

In the area of industrial action, as in many others, labour law in Britain is unusual in comparison to other systems in not addressing the majority of these issues in a coherent and systematic fashion. There is no principled concept of 'lawful' or 'unlawful' industrial action; at collective level whether industrial action attracts legal liability depends upon a complex and not always predictable interaction between the common law and statute; in relation to the individual worker industrial action generally constitutes a breach of the employment contract, and there is only limited statutory protection against dismissal.[30] Similarly the use of the lock-out weapon by employers, which in some systems is permitted only as a defensive measure in response to industrial action by workers, is not subject to clear regulation. As we shall see the legal framework in this country has developed in a ramshackle, ad hoc manner which is all but incomprehensible to those coming from outside Britain and little more easily accessible to those who are more familiar with its legal system.

LEGAL POLICY RELATING TO INDUSTRIAL ACTION: AN OVERVIEW[31]

11.5   In Britain those who organise industrial action have always been vulnerable to legal liability of some kind. Historically the most important source of constraint was the criminal law. Even when workers' combinations received limited protection against the doctrine of conspiracy this did not bring equivalent protection for industrial action; rather the 1825 Act specifically curtailed the freedom to strike and to picket against 'blacklegs' by creating vague offences of molestation, obstruction and intimidation. Moreover, it remained a criminal offence under the Master and Servant Acts to break a contract of employment. The Criminal Law Amendment Act 1871, in defining the offences laid down in the 1825 Act more precisely and adding those of 'persistently following a person' and 'watching and besetting premises', made virtually all picketing illegal and under this Act even posting-up a strike notice was held to constitute intimidation of employers.[32] In addition to the statutory liabilities industrial action could also offend the common law; in the notorious case of *R v Bunn*[33] London gas workers who threatened a strike unless a colleague dismissed for union activities was reinstated were convicted of a common law conspiracy by threatening to break their contracts and by their 'unjustifiable annoyance and interference with the masters in the conduct of their business'.

The decision in *Bunn*, together with the 1871 Act, provoked considerable protest, a campaign which peaked during the 1874 general election 'when newly enfranchised working men supported opposition Conservative candidates who appeared more responsive to trade union pressure than the Liberal Government responsible for the 1871 Act'.[34] In 1875 the incoming Conservative Government

---

30   The law of unfair dismissal makes some distinction between 'unofficial' and other industrial action, but even in the case of action which is not unofficial the protection afforded is limited and often dependent upon whether that action is protected by the statutory immunities.

31   In this section we aim merely to provide a framework for the more detailed analysis which follows. Full references are provided to the current law in later sections.

32   A Jacobs, 1986: p 212. The 1871 Act repealed the Molestation of Workmen Act 1859 which had protected certain forms of peaceful picketing.

33   (1872) 12 Cox CC 316.

34   A Jacobs, 1986: p 213.

led by Disraeli introduced the Conspiracy and Protection of Property Act. This Act repealed the Master and Servant Acts and the 1871 Act (although preserving some more specific offences) and also reversed the effect of *Bunn* in respect of acts 'in contemplation or furtherance of a trade dispute', the first appearance of the so-called 'golden formula'[35] protecting industrial action.

The 1875 Act marked the retreat of the criminal law from the area of industrial action. Since 1875, wartime apart, its role in this context has been largely confined to picketing.[36] For some groups of workers criminal liability remains potentially a threat. The 1875 Act made it an offence for a person 'wilfully and maliciously' to break a contract of service or of hiring, knowing or having reasonable cause to believe that the probable consequences, either alone or in combination with others, will be to endanger human life, cause serious bodily injury, or expose valuable property to destruction or serious injury. This offence is still on the statute book,[37] although there is no record of any prosecutions for it despite many disputes where there could have been. In addition, there are particular groups – the police, armed forces, merchant seamen and postal and, possibly, telecommunications workers – for whom industrial action is illegal.[38] However, with the possible exception of the police these provisions do not appear to have constituted a significant constraint (the armed forces not having threatened industrial action in recent times). Thus, even in essential services, the criminal law has not been invoked to restrict withdrawals of labour. Rather, unlike many countries, the traditional British strategy in these areas centred upon invoking emergency powers to lessen the impact of industrial action once it had been taken rather than attempting to forestall it in the first place. The Emergency Powers Act 1920 empowered the government, on proclaiming a state of emergency, to introduce measures to 'secure the essentials of life to the community' when the supply and distribution of specified commodities was interrupted or transport dislocated. It also legitimated the use of troops to replace striking workers, a practice which stretched back to the nineteenth century.[39] It did not, however, enable industrial action in essential services to be outlawed.

11.6 In the wake of the 1875 Act the legal focus in relation to industrial action shifted to the civil law. Between 1891 and 1906 the courts effectively outflanked the protections provided against the criminal law by expanding the scope of liability in tort. The new tort of conspiracy to injure was developed and the tort of inducing breach of contract applied to industrial action, for which the furtherance of union objectives was no defence. In 1901 the House of Lords decided, in the infamous *Taff Vale*[40] case, that a trade union registered under the Trade Union Act 1871, although not a corporate body, could nevertheless be sued for the torts of its officials, so exposing union funds to damages claims for losses caused by unlawful industrial action. This decision again provoked a

---

35 A phrase coined by Lord Wedderburn (P Davies and M Freedland, 1983: p 314, n 8) which has become common currency.

36 Note, however, its role in relation to incomes policies during the 1960s (P Davies and M Freedland, 1993: pp 177–181).

37 TULRCA 1992, s 240.

38 Criminal offences relating to industrial action in the gas and water industries, introduced in the 1875 Act, and extended to electricity in 1919, were repealed by the IRA 1971: see G Morris, 1986a: pp 21–22.

39 See G Morris, 1986a: pp 97 *et seq*. The Emergency Powers Act 1920 has now been replaced by the Civil Contingencies Act 2004; see further para 11.61.

40 *Taff Vale Rly Co v ASRS* [1901] AC 426.

powerful protest movement and, indeed, was one of the catalysts for the formation of the Labour Party. A Liberal government, having been elected with Labour support, pledged to change the law, and so the Trade Disputes Act 1906 was enacted. This Act accorded comprehensive immunity to trade unions against tortious liability. It also gave immunity to any person who 'in contemplation or furtherance of a trade dispute' committed the new tort of conspiracy, induced some other person to breach a contract of employment, or interfered with the trade, business or employment of another. In addition, it permitted peaceful picketing in trade disputes. A 'trade dispute' was defined as 'any dispute between employers and workmen, or between workmen and workmen, which is connected with the employment or non-employment, or the terms of the employment, or with the conditions of labour, of any person ...'[41]

The 1906 Act remained in force until 1971. With the exception of wartime restrictions on strikes and legislation passed in the wake of the General Strike, which were not in the event invoked,[42] it provided the bedrock of the freedom to organise industrial action for several decades.[43] It was also integral to the principle of collective *laissez-faire;* provided that the parties were acting peacefully and for 'industrial' objectives the law would not interfere in their disputes. This abstentionism was mirrored in the attitude of the state towards procedures for the settlement of industrial disputes.[44] Formal government responsibility in this area began with the Conciliation Act 1896 which gave the government the duty to encourage the development of joint machinery between employers and unions and powers to inquire into disputes and to initiate conciliation and arbitration. This process was strengthened in the aftermath of the Whitley Committee of 1916–1918; the Industrial Court (the forerunner of the CAC) was established as an arbitral body and the government itself was given power to inquire into trade disputes 'for the purpose of informing Parliament and the public of the facts' although it could not thereby impose a settlement. Crucially, therefore, dispute settlement within the private sector outside wartime[45] remained ultimately a matter for the collective parties who would be bound by the results of any procedures only if they so elected; only in certain minimum wage-fixing machinery was arbitration compulsory[46] and even then it was not linked to a ban on industrial action. As we saw in our account of ACAS and the CAC in chapter 2 this voluntary approach to the settlement of industrial disputes has continued to prevail up to the present day.

41 See para 11.25 below for the current definition.
42 The Trade Disputes and Trade Union Act 1927 declared illegal strikes and lock-outs having any object other than or in addition to the furtherance of a trade dispute within the strikers' trade or industry and 'designed or calculated to coerce the Government either directly or by inflicting hardship upon the community'. The Act was repealed in 1946.
43 See generally P Davies and M Freedland, 1993.
44 For a valuable survey see Sir John Wood, 1992. See also Wedderburn and Davies, 1969; Mumford, 1996.
45 During the two World Wars a system of compulsory arbitration was in force: see the Munitions of War Act 1915 and the Conditions of Employment and National Arbitration Order 1940 (SR&O 1940/1305). The latter continued in force until 1951, when it was replaced by the Industrial Disputes Order 1951, SI 1951/1376 which removed the ban on strikes contained in Order 1305: see further para 7.15 above. On developments in public services see Fredman and Morris, 1989: pp 417–422.
46 The machinery of the Fair Wages Resolution provided for determination by the Industrial Court.

11.7   Reliance upon an immunities approach to the legality of industrial action always carried risks, most notably that the courts would develop new forms of liability outside the scope of legislative protection, either in the context of industrial disputes or in other contexts where the 'economic torts' were at issue. As we shall see later in this chapter, judicial creativity in the industrial action forum was not wholly extinguished after 1906[47] but did not, in practice, threaten the basic framework of the law until the landmark House of Lords decision of *Rookes v Barnard*[48] in which the tort of 'intimidation' was applied to industrial action. At that time the Labour Government quickly introduced legislation in 1965 to extend immunity to this tort,[49] a response which has not been replicated in more recent years when new forms of liability have emerged. Individual dispute organisers also continued to remain vulnerable after 1906 because of the retention of the overriding discretion of the courts to grant injunctions to halt industrial action, the remedy which, in practice, is of most use to employers. Injunctions can be granted in interim proceedings, if necessary at short notice, to halt allegedly unlawful activity pending full trial of an action. Given that a case may take months or even years to come to trial, by which time the dispute is likely to have been settled, the interim proceedings effectively decide the issue in this context. The penalties for breaching an injunction, which constitutes a contempt of court, are severe: an unlimited fine; where appropriate, imprisonment; and possible sequestration of a defendant's assets. In impact, therefore, the ultimate penalties in civil law may differ little from those which may be imposed under the criminal law, with fewer procedural safeguards for respondents. Decisions made in interim proceedings have had fundamental consequences for the operation and development of industrial action law.

With certain well-publicised exceptions employers did not, before the 1980s, generally resort to the courts when faced with industrial action.[50] By the 1960s, however, there was growing concern about the number of unofficial strikes taking place in breach of (albeit unenforceable) procedures. The Donovan Commission which reported in 1968 emphasised the importance of attending to collective bargaining institutions and procedures rather than attempting to constrain industrial action by law.[51] The Heath Conservative Government thought differently and the Industrial Relations Act 1971 swept away the existing system of immunities and replaced it with a different framework which created new liabilities, dubbed 'unfair industrial practices', encouraged tighter control by unions of their shop stewards' activities and removed union immunity against liability in tort. In practice few employers relied on these provisions and research on the Act concluded that they had had relatively little impact on the conduct of industrial relations.[52] Novel emergency powers were similarly unsuccessful; inspired by the American Taft-

---

47   See in particular *DC Thomson & Co Ltd v Deakin* [1952] Ch 646, where the Court of Appeal developed the indirect form of the tort of inducing breach of a commercial contract at a time when inducing only contracts of employment was protected by the statutory immunities. For the rest of the decade, however, 'employers seemed little interested in exploiting the possibilities for injunctive relief that the decision had created': P Davies and M Freedland, 1993: p 131.

48   [1964] AC 1129.

49   TDA 1965. This Act also countered the effect of *JT Stratford & Son Ltd v Lindley* [1965] AC 269.

50   Evans, 1983: p 129.

51   *Royal Commission on Trade Unions and Employers' Associations 1965–1968*: Report, Cmnd 3623, 1968, ch VII.

52   Weekes *et al*, 1975: p 218.

Hartley Act 1947, they enabled the executive, with judicial sanction, to interfere directly in the conduct of 'emergency' disputes by imposing a 'cooling-off period' or compulsory ballot of the workforce but were used only once.[53] Even before its defeat in the 1974 General Election the government had accepted the need for substantial amendment of the industrial action provisions.[54]

The incoming Labour Government restored the structure established by the 1906 Act but made it 'stronger and clearer'[55] by extending the scope of protection against liability in tort and extending the definition of a trade dispute.[56] Some members of the judiciary did not conceal their distaste for this legislation, in particular the protection it afforded to secondary industrial action, and Lord Denning MR led the Court of Appeal into a series of decisions which sought to restrict the scope of the 'golden formula' by, *inter alia*, superimposing upon the concept of 'furthering' a trade dispute a remoteness and an 'objective' test.[57] Even when the House of Lords reminded lower courts of the principle of Parliamentary supremacy and the rule of law a senior judge did not feel constrained from describing the legislation as 'intrinsically repugnant to anyone who has spent his life in the practice of the law or the administration of justice'.[58] Perhaps surprisingly, however, the Labour Government did not seek to extend the protection afforded to dispute organisers to those participating in disputes. No immunity was accorded against individual liability for breach of contract, which industrial action, even if preceded by notice, almost invariably constitutes. Moreover, in continuing the protection against unfair dismissal introduced by the Industrial Relations Act it maintained the position that only in the event of selectivity between those dismissed while taking part in industrial action would employment tribunals have jurisdiction over their dismissals. The same principle was also extended to those locked-out. Although this avoided employment tribunals assessing the merits of disputes it left those taking industrial action in a highly vulnerable position. They also stood to lose access to other statutory rights, most notably redundancy payments. The only measure which could be said to protect participation in industrial action, although not confined to this situation, was the re-enactment (again from the Industrial Relations Act) of a statutory prohibition against individual employees being ordered to work by an order for specific performance, or an injunction restraining a breach or threatened breach, of the contract of employment.

11.8   In 1979 the Conservative Government was returned to office in the wake of a 'winter of discontent' of high-profile strikes in both the public and the private sectors. In 1980 it began a process of restriction and regulation which, by degrees, confined lawful industrial action by reference to its protected purposes and scope and the procedures which must precede it.[59] Thus, immunity

---

53   G Morris, 1986a: pp 82–87; Weekes *et al*, 1975: pp 213–216; Whelan, 1982.
54   See Weekes *et al*, 1975: pp 218–219.
55   *NWL Ltd v Woods* [1979] ICR 867, 886 (Lord Scarman).
56   TULRA 1974, as amended in 1976.
57   *Express Newspapers Ltd v McShane* [1979] ICR 210; *Associated Newspapers Group v Wade* [1979] ICR 664. See generally Ewing, 1979.
58   *Duport Steels Ltd v Sirs* [1980] IRLR 112, 117 (Lord Diplock); see also Lord Edmund Davies and Lord Keith, 121 and also *McShane and Ashton v Express Newspapers Ltd* [1980] IRLR 35.
59   For detailed analyses of the policy background to, and legislative history of, the relevant provisions up to their respective times of writing see Auerbach, 1990, and P Davies and M Freedland, 1993: ch 9 *et seq*.

was removed for secondary industrial action and secondary picketing (a technical exception apart); the concept of a 'trade dispute' was confined to disputes between workers and their own employer which related 'wholly or mainly' to a protected purpose; increasingly prescriptive and complex balloting (and, latterly, notification) requirements were imposed where liability for industrial action was attributable to a union; and unions lost their comprehensive immunity against liability in tort. As well as thereby extending the remedies available to employers faced by industrial action the legislation also made available to union members and, latterly, the wider public, mechanisms for encouraging challenges to the organisation of such campaigns, with the facility for affected members of the public to seek assistance to bring proceedings against a union to halt industrial action from a Commissioner for Protection Against Unlawful Industrial Action. In addition the already limited protection against dismissal while taking part in industrial action was further narrowed, and removed altogether for participants in 'unofficial' industrial action, so enabling selective dismissal of union activists. Union members were also given the right not to be 'unjustifiably disciplined' by their union for refusing to participate in industrial action, or seeking to persuade others not to do so, albeit the action had been approved by a majority in a ballot. This process of restriction occurred incrementally – the Conservative Government had not forgotten the experience of the Industrial Relations Act – and one should beware of viewing these reforms as the product of a preconceived agenda.[60] Nevertheless the cumulative result of a series of statutes through the 1980s and early 1990s was a radical reversal of the collective *laissez-faire* tradition which brought in general terms a much greater willingness on the part of employers to resort to legal sanctions when faced with disputes.[61] By the end of the 1980s the ILO Committee of Experts on the Application of Conventions and Recommendations was expressing concern as to the volume and complexity of legislative changes in industrial action law;[62] the 1990s saw both compounded. As a consequence, the organisation of industrial action became a very expensive process for trade unions, particularly given the growing need for detailed legal advice and (for all but small disputes) mandatory postal ballots. Between 1983 and March 1996 there were 204 separate legal actions against trade unions, of which 169 were applications for an injunction; of those 169 applications, 137 were successful.[63] In 1998 it was estimated that the costs to unions of defending legal actions since 1983 had been nearly £4 million.[64]

11.9 The entry into office of the Labour Government in 1997 brought few changes to this area. The law governing the organisation of industrial action remained intact in its essentials, although some minor but important changes were made to the pre-action balloting and notification requirements and the

---

60 See the texts referred to above.
61 Note, however, that this pattern varied between sectors and between individual years, and disputes where employers resorted to litigation still remained comparatively rare. See Gall and McKay, 1996; McKay, 1996; Undy *et al*, 1996: ch 6; W Brown *et al*, 1997: pp 77–78; *Labour Research* October 1998: pp 15–16.
62 See Report of the Committee of Experts on the Application of Conventions and Recommendations, Report III (Part 4A), ILO, Geneva, 1989: p 241.
63 Gall and McKay, 1996: pp 567 and 573.
64 *Labour Research*, October 1998, p 15.

(little-used) Commissioner for Protection Against Unlawful Industrial Action[65] was abolished. More significant are the changes to the position of employees who take industrial action. The Employment Relations Act 1999 broke with the traditional position by making it automatically unfair to dismiss an employee for taking 'protected' industrial action within eight weeks of that employee commencing it, or at a later date if either the employee had stopped taking industrial action within the eight-week period or the employer had failed to take such procedural steps as would have been reasonable to resolve the dispute. However, the scope of 'protected' industrial action is limited, being confined to action that an employee is induced to take by an act which is not actionable by virtue of the statutory immunities that protect dispute organisers. The Employment Relations Act 2004 lengthened the 'protected period' and reduced (but did not remove) the vulnerability to dismissal of those locked-out, but the position of those taking industrial action still remains precarious. Moreover, the status of industrial action as (generally) a breach of contract remains untouched. The fact that the law continues to remain more restrictive than in comparable systems is not regarded as a matter for apology; rather the Government has explicitly reaffirmed its commitment to maintain the essential features of the pre-1997 law.[66] It is improbable that the HRA 1998 will affect the way in which the courts approach the liability of dispute organisers or individual strikers other than (possibly) in the area of picketing;[67] as we indicated in para 11.3 above, the ECtHR has not implied a right to strike from the right to form and join trade unions. It is possible that domestic courts and tribunals may be willing to draw on the more expansive jurisprudence of the ILO, but it seems more likely that they will be cautious about deriving a right to strike given the attendant difficulties of defining its appropriate scope. Indeed, in some circumstances the HRA may add a further weapon to the armoury of employer claimants if industrial action interferes with the exercise of a Convention right such as freedom of expression or even, conceivably, the right to life.[68] The apparent recognition that the right to strike constitutes a fundamental right in EU law, which we discussed in para 7.11, may be invoked but its proper scope and relationship with other rights also remains, as yet, uncertain.[69]

The average number of disputes in the 1990s was 273, a sharp decline from the 1129 average of the 1980s.[70] This pattern has continued into the twenty-first century; the 2003 total of 133 stoppages was the lowest annual total on record.[71] It is difficult to state precisely the role that the law, as opposed to other social and economic factors, played in this; the changing structure and composition of the labour market and reduction in union membership were undoubtedly also

---

65   By 1998 the Commissioner had assisted only one applicant, which did not lead to a court case: *Fairness at Work* Cm 3968 (1998), para 4.31. In 1998 the Commissioner dealt with two applications, both of which were withdrawn, at a cost of £37,345 each: Ewing, 1999: p 296.

66   *Review of the Employment Relations Act 1999: Government Response*, DTI, 2003, para 3.19.

67   See further para 11.52 *et seq*.

68   HRA 1998, Sch 1, Arts 2, 10.

69   Note, however, that in Case C-67/96 *Albany International BV v Stichting Bedrijfspensioenfonds Textielindustrie* Advocate General Jacobs's Opinion suggests that any impairment of the substance of the right to strike, even if imposed in the 'public interest', might be unlawful: [1999] ECR I-5751, at paras 133, 162.

70   Monger, 2004: p 236.

71   As above.

relevant factors.[72] However, it seems unlikely that the highly restrictive nature of the law, which makes it virtually impossible to organise industrial action with confidence that it is free from legal liability, has not contributed at all to this process. At the time of writing there is little reason to suppose that the relatively minor recent changes to the law will, of themselves, give rise to an increase in the level of strike activity.

LIABILITY IN TORT

11.10 As we indicated in para 11.6, those who organise industrial action are highly likely to commit at least one of the 'economic torts'. The purpose of these torts is to protect interests in trade, business or livelihood. The principles which shape them were laid down in a series of decisions dating from the turn of the last century. One fundamental principle, laid down by the House of Lords in *Allen v Flood*[73] is that an intention to harm another will not of itself give rise to liability without some additional element of unlawfulness. Such unlawfulness may take the form either of an interference with a pre-existing right of the claimant, such as performance of a contract, or the use of some independently unlawful means. There is one well-established exception to this principle: the tort of conspiracy to injure, where the act of combination or association between the defendants, when coupled with an intention to harm the claimant, is sufficient for liability even though otherwise lawful means are used. In other respects the principle established by *Allen v Flood* remains essentially intact although, as we shall see, it has been subject to some partial erosion in recent years. Our framework for discussing these torts, which focuses in particular on their implications for industrial action,[74] reflects these principles in analysing first those torts which interfere with a pre-existing legal right; second, those which are based upon the use of unlawful means; and third, the torts of conspiracy. We also examine in this context the statutory right of individuals to seek an injunction to halt industrial action provided that certain conditions are met, a right which, in circumventing entirely the constraints upon the right to bring proceedings contained in the economic torts, expands considerably the range of potential claimants.

It is important to note at the outset that the boundaries of the economic torts and, in some cases, their very existence, remains unclear in crucial areas. What is the precise intention which the defendants is required to have in relation to the claimant to give rise to liability? Must the defendant's predominant purpose be injury to the claimant or will something less suffice? What kinds of action can constitute as 'unlawful means'? The judicial responses to these questions are not always consistent as between one tort and another. The difficulties of developing a coherent and principled framework of liability are exacerbated by the fact that many pivotal decisions have arisen out of applications for interim injunctions to prevent the commission or continuance of alleged torts when the

---

72 See P Edwards, 1995: ch 14, esp pp 446–447; J Waddington, 2003b: pp 244–251. See also Ben-Israel, 1994: pp 28–29, and ch 1 above.
73 [1898] AC 1.
74 For the most detailed consideration of the economic torts see Clerk and Lindsell, 2000, as updated, ch 24. See also Elias and Ewing, 1982; Wedderburn, 1986: ch 8; Carty, 1988; Weir, 1997; Carty, 2001; and Deakin, Johnston and Markesinis, 2003: ch 5.5.

court does not explore in detail the relevant legal principles and facts; it is sufficient for the claimant to show that there is a 'serious question to be tried'.[75] This has been a particular feature of industrial action cases because of the interest of employer claimants in arguing that wrongs have been committed which are outside the protection of the statutory immunities: inducing breach of statutory duty, for example. Convincing the court that such a wrong may exist can be sufficient, whereupon it can be added to the legal armoury of employers even though questions may remain as to its elements. The problems for dispute organisers are compounded by the fact that a decision in a wholly different context – litigation between two companies for example – may have fundamental (and unconsidered) implications for the scope of lawful industrial action. Thus labour lawyers must be constantly alert to developments in other areas. With these considerations in mind we now examine the current application of these torts to industrial action.

Torts based upon interference with the claimant's pre-existing rights

11.11   The most important tort to fall within this heading for the purposes of industrial action is that of inducing breach of contract. This tort can take two forms: direct and indirect.[76]

(i) The direct form of the tort

11.12   Direct inducement occurs if A intentionally induces B to breach a contract between B and C to the damage of C; C may then sue A. This tort originated in the decision of *Lumley v Gye*,[77] in which the claimant successfully argued that the defendant had acted tortiously in persuading a Miss Wagner, who was under contract to sing exclusively at the claimant's theatre for three months, to sing instead at his theatre for a higher fee. The defendant was aware of the terms of the contract between the claimant and Miss Wagner. It was applied by the House of Lords in *South Wales Miners' Federation v Glamorgan Coal Co Ltd*[78] in which the Miners' Federation had ordered workers employed by the claimants not to work on certain days in order to maintain the price of coal to which wage levels were linked. In later cases the courts affirmed that, although the defendant must intend to interfere with the claimant's contractual rights, he or she need not intend to cause the claimant harm.[79] A defendant cannot intend to induce the breach of a contract of which he or she is unaware.[80] However there is also authority to the effect that a defendant may, in some circumstances, be deemed

---

75   *American Cyanamid Co v Ethicon Ltd* [1975] 1 All ER 504. Whether or not the injunction will be granted will then depend upon the 'balance of convenience': see further para 11.49 below.

76   For the argument that the appropriate classification is between inducing breach of contract by persuasion, on the one hand, and prevention, on the other see Simester and Chan, 2004.

77   (1853) 2 E & B 216. For a wide-ranging critique of this decision, see Howarth, 2005.

78   [1905] AC 239.

79   *Smithies v NATSOPA* [1909] 1 KB 310, 316; *DC Thomson and Co v Deakin* [1952] Ch 646, Jenkins LJ at 696–697 and Morris LJ at 702; *Edwin Hill and Partners (a firm) v First National Finance Corporation Plc* [1988] 3 All ER 801. On the requisite intention cf *Millar v Bassey* [1994] EMLR 44 (and Weir, 1997, App 1), criticised Weir, 1997: pp 18–19 and 38–39.

80   See *Timeplan Education Group Ltd v NUT* [1997] IRLR 457.

to have knowledge of the almost certain existence of contracts,[81] although the court will not invent hypothetical contracts which might be breached were they to exist.[82] It is clear that the defendant need not know the precise terms of the contract provided that the requisite intent is present, and it seems that mere recklessness as to whether or not a breach occurs will suffice.[83] Despite a suggestion to the contrary by Lord Denning[84] it seems that for the *direct* form of the tort (in contrast to the indirect) bare interference with the contract which does not amount to a breach (where there is a *force majeure* clause in operation, for example) will not suffice.[85]

In the context of this tort a broad interpretation has been given to the notion of 'inducement'. Usually it will consist of a direct approach, but less direct methods may also constitute 'inducement', including passing on information that a given company is being boycotted by a union, which leads the recipient to act in breach of contract with it,[86] and 'direct prevention' of performance, such as hiding an employee's tools.[87] In *Union Traffic Ltd v TGWU*[88] the Court of Appeal took the concept of inducement even wider in holding that the mere presence of pickets may be sufficient if it is clear that their presence is intended to, and is successful in its object of, inducing breach of a contract.[89]

It is crucial for the direct form of the tort that the persuasion is directed at one of the parties to the contract, a requirement which was emphasised by the Court of Appeal in *Middlebrook Mushrooms Ltd v TGWU*.[90] The claimant mushroom growers and the union failed to agree on the employer's proposal to alter overtime arrangements. This led to industrial action followed by the dismissal of 89 workers who participated in it. The union's regional officer announced that union members would attend at supermarkets supplied by the employers and distribute leaflets to prospective customers to inform them of the situation. The leaflet asked customers to support the dismissed strikers by refusing to buy the claimant's mushrooms when shopping at the store. The first instance judge granted an interim injunction restraining the union and three of its officials from organising picketing 'for the purpose of causing or procuring breach or

---

81 See *Merkur Island Shipping Corpn v Laughton* [1983] 2 AC 570 (dictum of Sir John Donaldson MR approved); *Union Traffic Ltd v TGWU* [1989] IRLR 127.
82 *Middlebrook Mushrooms Ltd v TGWU* [1993] IRLR 232.
83 *JT Stratford & Son Ltd v Lindley* [1965] AC 269; *Emerald Construction Co Ltd v Lothian* [1966] 1 WLR 691; see also *Greig v Insole* [1978] 3 All ER 449, 488; *Metropolitan Borough of Solihull v NUT* [1985] IRLR 211.
84 In *Torquay Hotel Co Ltd v Cousins* [1969] 2 Ch 106, 137–138.
85 See Clerk and Lindsell, 2000, as updated, paras 24-31–24-35. See also Lord Diplock in *Merkur Island Shipping Corpn v Laughton* [1983] 2 AC 570: it is unclear whether he was referring to the direct as well as the indirect form of the tort in this opinion. *Falconer v ASLEF and NUR* [1986] IRLR 331, which we discuss below, appears to be a case of indirect and not direct interference.
86 *JT Stratford & Son Ltd v Lindley* [1965] AC 269, 333. Note that in *DC Thomson and Co Ltd v Deakin* [1952] 2 All ER 361, discussed below, the communication was found to fall short of an inducement.
87 *DC Thomson and Co v Deakin* above, Jenkins LJ at 696.
88 [1989] IRLR 127. Cf the stricter approach to inducement to procure the infringement of copyright by Lord Templeman in *CBS Songs Ltd v Amstrad Consumer Electronics plc* [1988] 2 All ER 484, 496–497: '[g]enerally speaking, inducement, incitement or persuasion to infringe must be by a defendant to an individual infringer and must identifiably procure a particular infringement in order to make the defendant liable as a joint infringer'.
89 Note that this decision may require reconsideration in the light of the HRA 1998: see paras 11.52 *et seq.*
90 [1993] IRLR 232.

breaches by customers of the ... [claimant] ... company of contracts made now or hereafter between the ... [claimant] ... company and such customers for the supply of mushrooms by the ... [claimant] ... or of interfering with the performance of any such contract'. On appeal to the Court of Appeal it was common ground that the employer's case depended upon showing direct interference with the employer's contracts. The court discharged the injunction. The leaflet in question was directed to the customers of the supermarket not to the managers and did not therefore fall within the principle of *Lumley v Gye* which required persuasion to be directed at one of the parties to the contract. In this case, by contrast, the suggested influence was exercised, if at all, through the actions or anticipated actions of third parties (the prospective customers) who were free to make up their own minds as to whether to buy the mushrooms.

Given that participation in industrial action, even when preceded by notice, will nearly always constitute a breach of contract (unless, unusually, notice of termination is given) dispute organisers will generally commit the direct form of the tort in persuading workers to take industrial action.[91] It may also be committed if, for example, a dispute organiser approaches a supplier of the employer in dispute and persuades it not to deliver supplies in breach of an existing contract.[92] There is a defence of justification available for this tort but it has been very narrowly construed. In the *South Wales Miners' Federation*[93] case the House of Lords rejected an argument to the effect that a union could be justified in organising industrial action where it was in the economic interests of its members. This means that the defence is virtually meaningless in the context of industrial action.[94] Indeed, it has succeeded only once in this context in highly unusual circumstances where it was argued that there was a duty to prevent the payment of insufficient wages to chorus girls because this led them to resort to prostitution.[95] It is strongly arguable that inducing employees to stop work for health and safety reasons should be covered given that there is a statutory right for individuals to stop work in these circumstances (see para 5.104)[96] but the caution of the courts in this

91 Note that where there is an element of doubt as to whether the action does constitute a breach of contract this, in itself, may give rise to a 'serious question to be tried': *Solihull Metropolitan Borough v NUT* [1985] IRLR 211. TULRCA 1992, s 245 provides that where any person 'holds any office or employment under the Crown on terms which do not constitute a contract of employment', those terms shall nevertheless be deemed to constitute such a contract for the purposes of the torts based upon inducing breach of, or interference with, a contract.

92 It remains lawful to persuade a person not to make a contract: *Midland Cold Storage Ltd v Steer* [1972] Ch 630. However, the courts have been prepared to countenance granting injunctions (formerly known as *quia timet* injunctions) to prevent respondents from inducing breach of a future contract: see *JT Stratford & Son Ltd v Lindley* [1965] AC 269 at 339 (Lord Upjohn); *Union Traffic Ltd v TGWU* [1989] IRLR 127; see further para 11.48 below.

93 [1905] AC 239. Cf the New Zealand case of *Pete's Towing Services v Northern Industrial Union of Workers* [1970] NZLR 32 where the defence was allowed when a union defendant was putting forward 'fair conditions' and the inducement was 'not being used as a sword to procure financial betterment but as a shield to avoid involvement in industrial discord' (Speight J at 51).

94 It may be easier, however, to establish in other contexts: see *Edwin Hill & Partners (a firm) v First National Finance Corpn plc* [1989] 1 WLR 225, and for a useful discussion see O'Dair, 1991.

95 *Brimelow v Casson* [1924] 1 Ch 302, approved in *Pritchard v Briggs* [1980] 1 All ER 294. See also *SOS Kinderdorf International v Bittaye* [1996] 1 WLR 987.

96 It may also be possible to argue that there is no breach of contract in these (or, indeed, a wider range of) circumstances if the approach in *Barber v RJB Mining (UK) Ltd* [1999] ICR 679 (see para 4.78) is applied: see A Edwards, 2000.

area makes it difficult to predict whether this would be accepted. Ultimately one can say with confidence only that the application of the statutory immunity is the sole reliable basis upon which there is any defence against liability for this tort.

(ii) The indirect form of the tort

11.13 Liability for the indirect form of inducing breach of contract may be a more complicated matter to determine. It occurs where, rather than directly inducing a breach of contract between B and C, A uses unlawful means which produce this result. In relation to industrial disputes a common situation is where A persuades B's employees to take industrial action in breach of their contracts of employment and by these unlawful means produces the result that B is unable to fulfil a commercial contract with C. This form of liability was first recognised in *DC Thomson & Co Ltd v Deakin*.[97] Here the claimants, a firm of printers and publishers, maintained a non-union shop. After they dismissed a worker belonging to a union, a number of unions organised a boycott of the company. Drivers and loaders employed by Bowaters, who supplied paper to the claimants, expressed reluctance to load or deliver paper to them and Bowaters, not wishing to become involved in the dispute, refrained from ordering any of their employees to do this. Bowaters then wrote to the claimants informing them that they had been prevented from performing their contract to supply paper by union action. The claimants sought an injunction to restrain the defendant union officials from procuring any breach of Bowaters' contract with the claimants.

The Court of Appeal held that liability in tort could arise where the interference, though indirect, came about through unlawful means, although on the facts of the case the action failed because Bowaters' employees, not having been required to undertake the necessary deliveries, had not broken their contracts of employment. In the case Jenkins LJ stated that the elements of the tort were as follows:

> .... first that the person charged with actionable interference knew of the existence of the contract and intended to procure its breach; secondly, that the person so charged did definitely and unequivocally persuade, induce or procure the employees concerned to break their contracts of employment with the intent I have mentioned; thirdly, that the employees so persuaded, induced or procured did in fact break their contracts of employment; and, fourthly, that breach of the contract forming the alleged subject of the interference ensued as a necessary consequence of the breaches by the employees concerned of their contracts of employment.[98]

The indirect form of the tort, unlike the direct, has been extended to cover the situation where the interference with the contract falls short of actual breach, although it may be argued that this conflicts with the principle laid down in *Allen v Flood*[99] that no liability should lie in the absence of independent unlawfulness. This first occurred in *Torquay Hotel Co Ltd v Cousins*.[100] Here

---

97 [1952] Ch 646. See also *JT Stratford and Son Ltd v Lindley* [1965] AC 269. For a discussion of the distinction between the direct and indirect form of the tort see *Middlebrook Mushrooms Ltd v TGWU* [1993] IRLR 232.
98 [1952] Ch 646, 697.
99 [1898] AC 1.
100 [1969] 2 Ch 106.

the contract for the supply of oil between Esso and the hotel provided that Esso was not to be liable for any failure to fulfil the agreement if it was prevented from doing so by labour disputes. Although, strictly speaking, there was no breach of contract when industrial action prevented deliveries, Lord Denning MR held that there could nevertheless be liability for preventing or hindering performance of the contract. Of the other members of the court, Russell LJ preferred to ground his decision on the basis that the clause was 'an exception from liability for non-performance rather than an exception from obligation to perform';[101] Winn LJ said that there was a cause of action if the normal course of dealing between the parties had led them to expect performance.[102] In 1983 the House of Lords approved this extension of the tort, Lord Diplock stating that in the elements articulated by Jenkins LJ the term 'interference with performance' should be substituted for breach (except in relation to the breaking by employees of their own contracts of employment).[103] He denied that this involved any extension of the decision in *Thomson v Deakin*; although Jenkins LJ had confined himself to breach of contractual rights because that was the form of interference in that case, '[a]ll prevention of due performance of a primary obligation under a contract was intended to be included even though no secondary obligation to make monetary compensation thereupon came into existence, because the second obligation was excluded by some form of force majeure clause'.[104] The consequence of this form of reasoning is that, even though the parties to the contract have specifically considered and allocated the risk of any losses incurred by industrial action, a third party to the contract can nevertheless incur liability for interfering with it. Logically it would appear to remove any impediment to finding that interference with performance is sufficient also for the direct form of the tort.

In *Dimbleby & Sons Ltd v NUJ*[105] the indirect form of the tort was again invoked, although in rather different circumstances. The NUJ was conducting a boycott of a third-party company, TBF Ltd, in pursuance of a trade dispute. Dimbleby had a contract for some printing to be carried out by another company in the TBF group, TBF Printers Ltd. The union called on its members employed by Dimbleby to refuse to provide copy to Dimbleby for printing by TBF. Dimbleby sought an injunction against the union on the basis that it had thereby interfered by unlawful means with the contract between Dimbleby and TBF Printers. The Court of Appeal upheld this argument and granted Dimbleby an injunction even though it had, in the event, managed to produce newspapers by finding copy from other sources. Sir John Donaldson MR affirmed that 'interference' meant 'hindrance as well as prevention'; the 'loss of services of staff journalists was quite clearly a hindrance to the performance by the ... [claimants] ... of their contractual obligations towards TBF Printers Ltd'.[106] It was a notable feature of this case that the claimant, Dimbleby, invoked this tort

---

101 [1969] 2 Ch 106, 143.
102 [1969] 2 Ch 106, 147.
103 *Merkur Island Shipping Corpn v Laughton* [1983] ICR 490, 506.
104 [1983] ICR 490, 506. This reasoning was developed in Lord Diplock's own judgment in *Photo Production Ltd v Securicor Transport Ltd* [1980] AC 827. In *OBG Ltd v Allan* [2005] EWCA Civ 106 the Court of Appeal refused to extend the tort to circumstances where the alleged tortfeasor was not intending to prevent the performance of any primary obligation of the contract: Peter Gibson LJ at para 47, Carnwath LJ at para 117.
105 [1984] IRLR 67. The point relating to the scope of interference with contract was not an issue on the subsequent appeal to the House of Lords.
106 [1984] IRLR 67, 73.

as the party whose performance was being interfered with not, as in *Torquay Hotel*, the party to whom performance was owed.

The nature of the intent required by the defendant for liability in this tort is not entirely clear. In *DC Thomson v Deakin* Jenkins LJ made clear that the defendant must have intended to procure the breach of contract by the use of unlawful means. On one view, this can be equated with an intention by the defendant to harm the claimant,[107] and in *Barratts & Baird (Wholesale) Ltd v IPCS*, Henry J stated that the defendant's predominant purpose must be injury to the claimant rather than acting out of his or her own self-interest.[108] However, it seems that liability is not confined to situations where the defendant intended this; rather, the courts have permitted proceedings to be brought by claimants who are not the direct target of the defendant's action.[109] An indication of the implications of widening the tort in this fashion is given by the county court decision of *Falconer v ASLEF and NUR*.[110] Industrial action by British Rail employees prevented the claimant from using his return train ticket from London to the north of England on the day he had intended, and he stayed in a hotel in London for a further two days. He successfully sued the rail unions for damages representing his expenses on the basis that they had interfered with the contractual obligation of British Rail to provide carriage by train. The court allowed this claim despite a clause in the Conditions of Carriage enabling British Rail to withdraw all services on any day or suspend the running of trains without being liable for any loss thereby occasioned. The judge held that this did not remove or exclude the primary obligation of British Rail to provide carriage, but merely limited its liability and, moreover, the unions could not rely on an exclusion clause when their own actions had caused the breach. He also accepted the claimant's argument that it was sufficient to show that the defendants knew that there were existing contracts between the Board and the group or class of persons (passengers) of which the claimant was one; it was irrelevant that his actual name and description were unknown to them at the time. He rejected the unions' argument that the claimant was not the object of the action when the strike was called. To suggest that harm to passengers was merely a consequence of, rather than an intended object of, their action was 'naive and divorced from reality'.[111] In any event, he was willing to hold that the 'reckless' imposition of harm was sufficient for the tort.

The decision in *Falconer* has not been tested in a higher court; were it to be upheld the extensive liability to which unions could be exposed in damages for action outside the protection of the statutory immunities is clearly evident. For the statutory right of action, which we discuss in para 11.19, no element of intention whatsoever need be proved against the applicant but in that situation, at least, the remedy is limited to an injunction.

(iii) Liability for inducements other than to breach a contract

11.14 In *Quinn v Leatham* Lord Macnaghten made clear that liability for inducing breach of contract rested upon the ground that 'a violation of a legal right committed knowingly is a cause of action'.[112] In recent years this form of

107 Sales and Stilitz, 1999: p 434.
108 [1987] IRLR 3, 11.
109 *Dimbleby and Sons Ltd v NUJ* [1984] IRLR 67.
110 [1986] IRLR 331.
111 [1986] IRLR 331, 334.
112 [1901] AC 495 at 510.

liability has been extended to inducement to breach an equitable obligation[113] and inducement to breach a statutory duty. These were particularly worrying developments for unions because neither of these wrongs is protected by the statutory immunities. Inducement to breach a statutory duty is a particular concern in public services, where many workers perform duties which their employer is obliged by statute to fulfil. The potential for this form of liability was first suggested by the Court of Appeal in *Meade v Haringey London Borough Council*.[114] Here the claimant parents argued that, by closing its schools during a strike by school caretakers, the authority was breaching its statutory duty to provide education. The majority of the court refused to decide this issue conclusively in interim proceedings but it was suggested that if the authority were in breach the unions, by calling on the employer to close the schools, could be inducing the authority to breach its statutory duty. The application of this tort in its direct form is circumscribed by the general principle that the statutory duty which is obstructed must be independently actionable at the suit of the claimant (a point not addressed in *Meade*).[115] Whether or not it will be independently actionable depends entirely upon the language and purpose of the statute in question; usually it involves showing that the duty was imposed for the benefit of a particular class of persons to which the claimant belongs[116] but whether this requirement will be met is often unpredictable.[117] However, it has been suggested that a non-actionable breach of statutory duty may constitute the requisite 'unlawful means' for the purpose of the tort of interference with trade or business by unlawful means.[118] We explore this possibility further below. Where the inducement to breach a statutory duty is indirect rather than direct then analogy with the indirect form of inducing breach of contract suggests that unlawful means should be required, although this has yet to be decided.[119] Were unlawful means not to be required there would be little scope for any form of industrial action in the public sector.[120]

Far from extending immunity to inducement to breach a statutory duty when the potential for this form of liability was shown, the Conservative Government specifically incorporated it in statute. This was first made explicit in the Telecommunications Act 1984,[121] now repealed and replaced by the

---

113   *Prudential Assurance Co Ltd v Lorenz* (1971) 11 KIR 78; *Boulting v ACTT* [1963] 2 QB 606, CA (breach of fiduciary duty); although cf *Metall und Rohstoff AG v Donaldson Lufkin Jenrette Inc* [1990] 1 QB 391. Whether there was a tort of procuring a breach of trust was left open in the Court of Appeal in *Crawley Borough Council v Ure* [1996] QB 13. In *Wilson v Housing Corpn* [1997] IRLR 346, Dyson J held that the tort of inducing unfair dismissal did not exist.

114   [1979] ICR 494. See also *Associated Newspapers Group Ltd v Wade* [1979] IRLR 201; *Associated British Ports v TGWU* [1989] IRLR 305 (the Court of Appeal decision was reversed by the House of Lords at [1989] IRLR 399 on the point that there was no statutory duty in those circumstances).

115   *Associated British Ports v TGWU* [1989] IRLR 305.

116   The other circumstance is where the statute creates a public right and a particular member of the public suffers special damage peculiar to himself or herself: see *Lonrho Ltd v Shell Petroleum Co Ltd (No 2)* [1981] 2 All ER 456, 461–462 (Lord Diplock).

117   See generally Clerk and Lindsell, 2000, as updated: ch 11; Stanton *et al*, 2002. Note also in this context *Barratts & Baird (Wholesale) Ltd v IPCS* [1987] IRLR 3, discussed Fredman, 1987, Simpson, 1987, where the scope of the statutory duty was at issue.

118   See *Associated British Ports v TGWU* [1989] IRLR 305; see also *Surzor Overseas Ltd v Koros* [1999] 2 Lloyd's Rep 611, 616–617 (Waller LJ).

119   In *Barratts & Baird (Wholesale) Ltd v IPCS* [1987] IRLR 3, Henry J was sympathetic to this argument.

120   Napier, 1987.

121   S 18.

Communications Act 2003.[122] It is also possible that such a right of action may, in certain circumstances, be available in the event of disruption to supply in the gas, electricity and water industries.[123] A prominent example of this form of liability is the Criminal Justice and Public Order Act 1994 which created a new statutory duty, owed to the Secretary of State, not to induce a prison officer (including a private sector 'prisoner custody officer' and 'custody officer'[124]) to withhold his services as such an officer or to commit a breach of discipline.[125] As well as being actionable by the Secretary of State, breach of this provision could also give rise to an application by a person exercising the statutory right to apply for an injunction to halt industrial action. At the time of writing the Home Secretary has announced that this provision will be withdrawn in relation to prison officers in the light of a new legally-enforceable Joint Industrial Relations Procedural Agreement between the Prison Service and the Prison Officers' Association which aims to ensure that 'all collective disputes or grievances ... are dealt with effectively and differences are resolved without affecting the normal working of the Prison Service'[126] However the statutory restriction will remain in force for 'prisoner custody officers' and 'custody officers' unless and until any similar collective agreement is reached in relation to these groups.

Interference with trade or business by unlawful means

11.15 The tort of interference with trade or business by unlawful means occurs where A intentionally uses unlawful means with the purpose and effect of causing damage to B in B's trade or business. This 'genus' tort is of potentially very wide application. There are two crucial questions in relation to it: first, what acts are capable of constituting unlawful means and second, given that the unlawful act must be directed against the claimant or intended to harm him or her, whether this needs to be the defendant's predominant purpose?[127] In addition, there may also be a prior question as to whether the claimant has a 'business' which is entitled to protection. In *Nottingham City Council v Unison*[128] the claimant local authority failed to obtain an injunction against the defendant union in relation to industrial action by its Approved Social Worker members on the ground that, although some of the authority's activities could be described as a 'business', its powers and duties in relation to mental health provision could not. In practice it is exceptional for this point to be at issue and we do not explore it further here.

(i) What acts may constitute unlawful means

11.16 The 'genus' tort of interference with trade or business by unlawful means embraces the 'species' tort of *intimidation*, which is particularly significant in the context of industrial action.[129] This tort is committed when A threatens B that he or she will commit an act or use means which are unlawful as against B

---

122 See s 104(3) for the equivalent provision to s 18 of the 1984 Act.
123 Gas Act 1986, s 30; Water Industry Act 1991, s 22; Electricity Act 1989, s 27.
124 CJPOA, s 127(4).
125 CJPOA, s 127(1), (2). See further G Morris, 1994b: pp 328–329.
126 This agreement replaces the 2001 Voluntary Agreement, on which see Corby, 2002.
127 See further Carty, 1988; Sales and Stilitz, 1999.
128 [2004] EWHC 893 (QB).
129 See *Hadmor Productions Ltd v Hamilton* [1982] IRLR 102, 109 (Lord Diplock); *Merkur Island Shipping Corpn v Laughton* [1983] IRLR 218, 222–223 (Lord Diplock).

with the intention of causing B to do or refrain from doing something which B is at liberty not to do or to do, so causing damage either to B (two-party intimidation) or C (three-party intimidation). It is almost certainly the case that the claimant must be a person whom A intended to injure.[130] For the purposes of this tort it has long been clear that the application of physical force or violence or the threat of such violence constitutes unlawful means.[131] Thus, a threat of violence by a picket against a worker who crossed a picket-line would fall within this category, for example.[132]

In the landmark case of *Rookes v Barnard*[133] the implications of this tort for industrial action were made apparent when the House of Lords accepted that a threat to break a contract could suffice. Here two shop stewards and a union official threatened an employer, BOAC, with a strike unless a non-unionist, Rookes, was dismissed. The employers terminated Rookes' contract lawfully and with due notice. Rookes then sued the union officers. It was conceded (most unusually) that a no-strike clause was incorporated as a term in the employees' contracts of employment.[134] The court held that, even though Rookes could not have sued BOAC for breach of contract this did not rule out his claim for the tort of intimidation given that BOAC had responded to pressure of an unlawful kind from the union officials who were intending to injure Rookes.[135] The threat to breach the contract of employment constituted intimidation; in Lord Reid's words, Rookes was suing for 'loss caused to him by the use of an unlawful weapon against him – intimidation of another person by unlawful means'.[136] In this respect a threat of a breach of contract was as much unlawful means as a threat of physical harm. As Lord Devlin put it, '[a]ll that matters to the ... [claimant] ... is that, metaphorically speaking, a club has been used. It does not matter to the ... [claimant] ... what the club is made of – whether it is a physical club or an economic club, a tortious club or an otherwise illegal club. If an intermediate party is improperly coerced, it does not matter to the ... [claimant] ... how he is coerced'.[137]

The tort of intimidation is likely to be committed whenever industrial action is threatened provided that the action constitutes a breach of contract and it is therefore crucial for potential defendants to ensure that they are protected by the statutory immunities. Although it has been suggested that the breach of contract should be more than a minor one,[138] it is improbable, even if that argument were to be accepted, that in interim proceedings the nature of the breach would be investigated unless it were possible to argue that it may be too

---

130 See Clerk and Lindsell, 2000: para 24-65, n 18.
131 *Tarleton v McGawley* (1793) Peake 270.
132 See *Messenger Newspapers Group Ltd v NGA* [1984] ICR 345.
133 [1964] AC 1129.
134 See para 11.66 for discussion of the current position.
135 The basis of liability of one of the union officials has always been puzzling given that he was not employed by the employers and therefore had no contract he could threaten to break. In *Morgan v Fry* [1968] 2 QB 710 Lord Denning suggested that he not only threatened to induce a breach of contracts of employment (which would have been within the immunities as they then existed) but was also party to the conspiracy of the others to break contracts. However, as Kidner, 1983: p 133, n 85 states, '[t]his explanation is not entirely satisfactory as he would not have been directly liable for conspiracy to injure by unlawful means, but could only be liable for conspiring with others to use the unlawful means of the others'.
136 [1964] AC 1129, 1168.
137 [1964] AC 1129, 1209.
138 *Morgan v Fry* [1968] 2 QB 710, 737–739.

minor to cause damage.[139] It seems unlikely that there is a defence of justification to this tort; if there is, the circumstances where it could apply would probably be rare.[140]

It has been argued that where a breach of contract constitutes the threat it would be inappropriate to extend the doctrine of *Rookes v Barnard* (a case of three-party intimidation) to two-party intimidation, where both claimant and defendant are parties to the same contract, on the ground that this would enable circumvention of rules of contract law, such as remoteness and mitigation, which limit the extent of contract damages in comparison with tort.[141] In practice this may be a less important issue in the light of the development of the doctrine of *economic duress*[142] which, if found to apply, enables a party to a transaction to claim later that the transaction is invalid because he or she did not truly consent to it and to recover any money paid to the other party. To establish economic duress it must be shown that the victim has been placed in a situation where he or she is deemed to have no practical alternative to agreeing to the demand made by the other party by pressure which the law does not regard as legitimate. The form of the duress may constitute intimidation (or some other tort), but its scope may also go wider in that the action threatened need not always be unlawful.[143] The doctrine was applied to industrial disputes in *Universe Tankships Inc of Monrovia v ITWF*[144] where the owners of a ship flying a 'flag of convenience' were able to recover from the International Transport Workers' Federation payments of back pay to the crew and a contribution to the Seafarers' Welfare Fund which they had previously agreed to make under threat of blacking. On appeal to the House of Lords it was conceded by the ITWF that the consequences to the shipowners of the blacking continuing were sufficiently catastrophic to constitute economic duress. It was also conceded that guidance could be found as to the boundary between legitimate and illegitimate pressure from examining whether or not the action was within the statutory immunities as being 'in contemplation or furtherance of a trade dispute'. This meant that the court did not hear argument on either of these points, leaving open the possibility that a remedy based on 'economic duress' may be granted even if the action would be granted immunity in tort,[145] although there are highly persuasive dicta that such an approach would be contrary to legislative policy.[146]

---

139 See Howarth and O'Sullivan, 2000: p 911 n 4.

140 The possibility of a justification defence was rejected by the House of Lords in *Rookes v Barnard*, above note 133; see also Lord Denning in *Cory Lighterage Ltd v TGWU* [1973] ICR 339, 357. Deakin *et al*, 2003 suggest that there may be a limited justification defence that the defendant was asserting a pre-existing legal right which was at least the equal of the right he or she was interfering with (p 525).

141 See Carty, 1988: pp 260–262; cf Sales and Stilitz, 1999, pp 422–425.

142 For discussion of the doctrine see J Beatson, 1991: ch 5; Birks and Yin, 1995, and see generally G Jones, 2002, as updated. Note that the statutory limits which govern trade union liability in tort (see para 11.47) do not apply in this context.

143 In *Universe Tankships Inc of Monrovia v ITWF* [1982] IRLR 200, 212, Lord Scarman seemed to suggest that economic duress could be actionable as a tort *per se*. If this were to be the case the principle of *Allen v Flood* requiring independent unlawfulness would be further undermined.

144 [1983] 1 AC 366. See also *Dimskal Shipping Co SA v ITWF* [1992] IRLR 78.

145 [1982] IRLR 200, 205 (Lord Diplock), 214 (Lord Brandon). Cf Lord Scarman at 212 who considered that it would be 'inconsistent with legislative policy' to say that acts which were protected by statute from liability in tort could nevertheless amount to duress. See also *Dimskal Shipping Co SA v ITWF* [1992] IRLR 78, 82 (Lord Goff).

146 See Lords Scarman and Goff, above.

In relation to the wider tort of interference with trade or business by unlawful means, the requirement of 'unlawful means' delimits what conduct by the defendant will be regarded as illegitimate; the dividing line is between 'doing what you have a legal right to do and doing what you have no legal right to do ...'[147] The categories of unlawful means are now very wide[148] (although acts which are afforded immunity under the 'golden formula' cannot constitute unlawful means).[149] Threats of unlawful action, as well as constituting the tort of intimidation, may also constitute 'unlawful means' for the purposes of the wider tort.[150] It seems that the torts of *nuisance* (for example, blocking the entrance to an employer's premises) or *trespass* may suffice.[151] In *Associated British Ports v TGWU* the majority of the Court of Appeal considered that inducing breach of a statutory duty may also constitute unlawful means, regardless of whether the duty is independently actionable by the claimant,[152] in contrast to the direct form of the tort where independent actionability is required. If this view prevails, it is capable of having widespread implications for industrial action in public services whose provision is subject to statutory duties, particularly if, as has been suggested,[153] an employer upon whom the statutory duty has been placed could invoke the tort. It could also have implications if the unlawful means which it is sought to invoke consists of breach of a penal statute, although there is weighty authority to the effect that breach of a penal statute should not amount to unlawful means for the purposes of this tort.[154] Finally it has been suggested that breach of contract *per se* may constitute unlawful means for the purposes of the wider tort as it may for the tort of intimidation.[155] If accepted, this view would mean that individual participants in industrial action could be personally liable in tort to third parties whose businesses were interfered with by the action merely by breaching

---

147   See *Rookes v Barnard* [1964] AC 1129, Lord Reid at 1168–1169; see also Lord Pearce at 1234; Lord Devlin at 1207, 1209; *DC Thomson and Co Ltd v Deakin* [1952] Ch 646, Lord Evershed MR at 679–682; *Torquay Hotel Co Ltd v Cousins* [1969] 2 Ch 106, Lord Denning MR at 139.

148   Here we mention only those most material to industrial action. For a wider discussion, see Sales and Stilitz, 1999; Carty, 2000; Deakin, Markesinis and Johnston, 2003: pp 519–524.

149   *Hadmor Productions Ltd v Hamilton* [1982] IRLR 102.

150   [1982] IRLR 102.

151   See *Norbrook Laboratories Ltd v King* [1984] IRLR 200; *Messenger Newspapers Group Ltd v NGA* [1984] IRLR 397.

152   [1989] IRLR 305; Butler-Sloss LJ at 314; Stuart-Smith LJ at 316; cf the reservations expressed by Neill LJ at 311. Cf also *Michaels v Taylor Woodrow Developments Ltd* [2000] 4 All ER 645, Laddie J. The issue was also discussed (but not resolved) in *Nottingham City Council v Unison* [2004] EWHC 893, QB, paras 33–37. The House of Lords reversed the Court of Appeal decision in *Associated British Ports* on the ground that the obligation of a registered dock worker to work for his employer was essentially a contractual obligation, and the statutory scheme did not impose a statutory obligation to work independent of, and additional to, this obligation. The case was therefore one of inducing dock workers to break their contracts of employment: [1989] IRLR 399.

153   Deakin, Johnston and Markesinis 2003: p 523. This is by analogy with *Dimbleby and Sons v NUJ* [1984] IRLR 67.

154   *Lonrho Ltd v Shell Petroleum Co Ltd* (No 2 [1981] 2 All ER 456; *RCA Corporation v Pollard* [1982] 3 All ER 771; *Lonrho Plc v Fayed* [1989] 2 All ER 65. Cf Sales and Stilitz 1999 p: 416, and authorities therein, where it is argued that this should not be a barrier if the requisite intention is shown.

155   *Barratts & Baird (Wholesale) Ltd v IPCS* [1987] IRLR 3, 10. See further Fredman, 1987; Simpson, 1987: p 506.

their own contracts of employment.[156] This would be particularly significant in view of the fact that there is no statutory immunity against breach of contract *simpliciter* and claimants would be able to claim damages from individual workers in circumstances where the dispute organisers were immune from liability, a consequence which would undermine entirely the already narrow freedom to withdraw labour.

(ii) The requisite intention for the tort

11.17 The potentially wide application of the tort of interference with trade or business by unlawful means makes the nature of the intention which must be proved against the defendant particularly important. It is generally accepted that it needs to be shown that the unlawful act was directed against the claimant or intended to harm him or her.[157] There is also authority for the view that this need not be the defendant's predominant purpose.[158] However, at the time of writing there is no clear line of authority on the requisite mental element,[159] a matter which awaits clarification by the House of Lords.

Conspiracy

11.18 There are two forms of conspiracy: *conspiracy to injure*, which does not require an element of independent unlawfulness, and *conspiracy to commit an unlawful act or use unlawful means*.

For the tort of *conspiracy to injure*, the combination of two or more persons is the gist of the wrong, although damage is necessary to complete the cause of action.[160] Thus action which would not be unlawful if taken by one person can become so by virtue of the element of combination. However, it must be shown that the predominant purpose of the conspirators is to injure a third party rather than to serve their own bona fide and legitimate interests (itself an exception to the general principle that motive is irrelevant in relation to the lawful act of an individual).[161] This tort is now of little importance in the context of industrial disputes since the House of Lords decision in *Crofter Hand Woven Harris Tweed Co v Veitch* where the legitimacy of trade union interests (in this case to achieve 100% union membership) was recognised. Officials of the Transport and General

---

156 Note that in view of TULRCA 1992, s 236, which prohibits a court from compelling an employee to do any work by way of an order for specific performance of the contract of employment or injunction restraining a breach or threatened breach, the claimant's remedy in such a case would probably be limited to damages.

157 *Allen v Flood* [1898] AC 1, Lord Watson at 96, 98. Cf *Lonrho plc v Fayed* [1989] 2 All ER 65, Woolf LJ at 73, who considered that the tort could be committed if a defendant deliberately embarked upon a course of conduct appreciating the probable consequence for the claimant (but cf again *Associated British Ports v TGWU* [1989] IRLR 305, where intent to injure was treated as the essence of the tort, although without fully explaining the nature of the requisite intent).

158 *Lonrho v Fayed*, above. The ingredients of the tort of interference with trade or business by unlawful means were not discussed in the opinions on appeal to the House of Lords [1991] 3 All ER 303 (although see Lord Bridge at 312).

159 See further Clerk and Lindsell, 2000, as updated para 24–88 *et seq*; Sales and Stilitz, 1999: pp 425–430.

160 *Quinn v Leathem* [1901] AC 495.

161 This requirement was emphasised in *Crofter Hand Woven Harris Tweed Co Ltd v Veitch* [1942] 1 All ER 142; *Lonrho Ltd v Shell Petroleum Ltd (No 2)* [1981] 2 All ER 456, *Lonrho plc v Fayed* [1991] 3 All ER 303.

Workers' Union and a group of employers with whom the union operated a 'closed shop' agreed to 'black' the supplies of the claimant and other employers on the island of Harris who were outside the closed-shop agreement. The union had members both in the mills and in the docks at Stornoway, the island's main port. The claimant's claim in conspiracy was rejected on the ground that the predominant purpose of the defendants was to protect their own economic interests not to injure the claimant. Moreover, it was emphasised that the court would not make its own assessment of whether the action was, in objective terms, likely to achieve the combiners' goal. In the words of Lord Wright, 'The true contrast is ... between the case where the object is the legitimate benefit of the combiners and the case where the object is deliberate damage without any such just cause. The courts have repudiated the idea that it is for them to determine whether the object of the combiners is reasonably calculated to achieve their benefit'.[162] In a later decision it was held that the 'lawful interest' of a union extended beyond those which could be exchanged for cash when a boycott by the Musicians' Union of the claimant's ballroom in protest against a 'colour bar' was found to be legitimate.[163] However, the concept does not extend to personal reasons, and members of a union district committee which treated the claimant as expelled from the union (although he was not) and prevented him from getting jobs was found to be based not on the interests of the union but on the 'ruffled dignity' of the defendants.[164]

The 'anomalous' nature of the tort has been acknowledged in a number of cases, particularly given the establishment of large corporations which, although legally single individuals, may wield extensive power.[165] Despite this the House of Lords has affirmed that it is 'too well-established' to be discarded.[166]

In the case of *conspiracy to commit an unlawful act or use unlawful means* the predominant purpose test does not apply. However, the precise nature of the intent required is not clear although logic would suggest that it should be consistent with that required for interfering with business by unlawful means.[167] As in the case of the latter, acts which are afforded statutory immunity cannot constitute the requisite 'unlawful act' or 'unlawful means' for the purposes of the tort.[168]

Conspiracy to commit an unlawful act or use unlawful means remains important because those who cannot commit the tort directly may nevertheless be co-conspirators to its commission.[169] It is unclear whether the unlawful means need to be actionable at the suit of the claimant.[170] It is also unclear whether the

162 [1942] AC 435.
163 *Scala Ballroom (Wolverhampton) Ltd v Ratcliffe* [1958] 3 All ER 220.
164 *Huntley v Thornton* [1957] 1 All ER 234, 249.
165 *Crofter Hand Woven Harris Tweed Co Ltd v Veitch* [1942] 1 All ER 142, 161 (Lord Wright); *Lonrho Ltd v Shell Petroleum Ltd (No 2)* [1981] 2 All ER 456; *Lonrho plc v Fayed* [1991] 3 All ER 303.
166 *Lonrho Ltd v Shell Petroleum Ltd (No 2)* [1981] 2 All ER 456, 464 (Lord Diplock).
167 In *Lonrho plc v Fayed* [1991] 3 All ER 303 the House of Lords affirmed that the two causes of action should stand or fall together. See also *Kuwait Oil Tanker Co Sak v Abdul Fattah Sulaiman Khalad Al Badar* [2001] 2 All ER (Comm) 271, para 118; *Michaels v Taylor Woodrow Developments Ltd* [2000] 4 All ER 645.
168 *Hadmor Productions Ltd v Hamilton* [1982] IRLR 102.
169 See *Rookes v Barnard* [1964] AC 1129, discussed in para 11.16 above.
170 For suggestions that it might not be, see *Surzur Overseas Ltd v Koros* [1999] 2 Lloyd's Rep 611, 616–617 (Waller LJ); *Kuwait Oil Tanker Co Sak v Abdul Fattah Sulaiman Khalad Al Badar* [2001] 2 All ER (Comm) 271; cf *Credit Lyonnais Bank Nederland NV v Export Guarantee Department* [1998] 1 Lloyds Rep 19, 22 (Stuart-Smith LJ); *The*

tort extends beyond combinations to commit a tort[171] and, in particular, whether there can be an actionable conspiracy to break contracts *simpliciter*[172] (an open question, as we saw in para 11.16, in relation to the tort of interference with trade by unlawful means). If the latter argument were to be upheld this would mean that any two or more workers who agreed to take industrial action in breach of contract could be liable for conspiracy and would not be protected by the statutory immunities.

The statutory right of action

11.19 TURERA 1993 introduced a new statutory right of action which is notable in circumventing entirely the restrictions on the category of potential claimants erected by the courts at common law.[173] It enables any 'individual' who claims that a 'trade union or other person has done, or is likely to do, an unlawful act to induce any person to take part, or to continue to take part, in industrial action' where 'an effect, or a likely effect ... is or will be to prevent or delay the supply of goods or services', or to reduce the quality of those supplied, to him or her to apply to the High Court for an order.[174] The right applies irrespective of whether the individual is entitled to be supplied with the goods or services in question; although, in theory, in the absence of a contract or other document specifying standards it may be hard to measure precisely the reduction in quality which may occur the courts will probably not scrutinise this question too closely.[175] There is no requirement to demonstrate that material loss or damage, or even inconvenience, has been, or would be, suffered as a result of the disruption so that non-collection of rubbish on a particular day, for example, would suffice.[176]

An act to induce any person to take part, or to continue to take part, in industrial action is 'unlawful' for this purpose in two contexts. The first is where it is actionable in tort *by any person*. Thus even if, at common law, the only claimant would be the employer in dispute, any 'individual' who meets the statutory test may apply; there is no requirement to show any intent towards him or her. Moreover, the individual is able to bring proceedings even if the protection of the statutory immunities in relation to the act in question is otherwise lost only in relation to the employer in dispute because the union has failed to

Rialto (No 2) [1998] 1 Lloyd's Rep 332, 334 (Toulson J). In *Michaels v Taylor Woodrow Developments Ltd* [2000] 4 All ER 645 Laddie J affirmed that the means must be actionable in their own right against at least some of the conspirators, and that where the wrongful act consists of the breach of the provisions of a statute or subordinate legislation, it will only support an action for conspiracy by unlawful means if it is the intention of the legislature that such causes of action should be available to enforce the provisions of the legislation.

171 In *Lonrho Ltd v Shell Petroleum Co Ltd* [1981] 2 All ER 456 the House of Lords held that there could not be liability based upon the commission of criminal acts which did not also constitute torts.

172 This point was left open in *Rookes v Barnard* [1964] AC 1129. In *Barratts & Baird (Wholesale) Ltd v IPCS* [1987] IRLR 3, Henry J thought that there was an arguable case that a breach of contract was unlawful means for the purposes of the tort of interference with business.

173 For a detailed discussion of this right see G Morris, 1993.

174 TULRCA 1992, s 235A. The normal statutory principles apply in determining whether an act of inducement is done by a union.

175 In *P v NAS/UWT* [2003] IRLR 307, discussed para 11.27 below, Morison J was willing to assume in favour of P that the industrial action was in breach of contract and that it reduced the quality of teaching that he received (Lord Hoffman, para 18).

176 Baroness Denton, HL Debs Vol 543, col 494, 25 March 1993.

comply with the requisite information and notification requirements.[177] The second context in which an act is 'unlawful' is if it is attributed by statute to a trade union and could form the basis of an application by a union member under TULRCA 1992, section 62 that he or she has been, or is likely to be, induced by the union to take part in industrial action which is not supported by a valid ballot. This second category will normally overlap with the first, but its inclusion means that there may be an individual right to bring proceedings in relation to industrial action which does not constitute a breach of contract by those participating in it and which may not, therefore, attract liability in tort. Where the argument is based upon a defect in the ballot this second category of unlawfulness will be the simplest line of argument as there will be no need to demonstrate that any tort has been committed.

Where the court finds the claim 'well-founded' it must make an order requiring the person committing the inducement to take steps to ensure that no (or no further) act is done by him or her to induce any persons to take (or continue to take) part in the industrial action and that no person takes industrial action as a result of any prior inducement. Interim relief may be granted for this purpose and in practice most applications will be dealt with in this way. Until 1999 where the actual or prospective defendant was a trade union, the individual could seek assistance to bring proceedings from the Commissioner for Protection Against Unlawful Industrial Action, but this office was abolished by the ERelA 1999.[178]

This right of action dramatically extends the range of persons who may apply for an injunction to halt industrial action. In doing so it raises fundamental questions about the autonomy of the parties to the employment relationship (a factor which provoked widespread opposition by employers to its introduction[179]). Modern drafting practice treats 'individual' as excluding corporations, so a corporate claimant will need to rely upon the common law, as will any person seeking damages. However, there is nothing to prevent an individual member of an employer company, including a director, exercising the right *qua* individual. Perhaps surprisingly, at the time of writing little use has been made of this right.[180]

THE LIABILITY OF TRADE UNIONS IN TORT

11.20   As we explained in chapter 10, a trade union can act only through its members or officials. Whether and on what basis a union is fixed with legal liability for their tortious acts depends upon the tort in question. TULRCA 1992, section 20 governs union liability for the torts of inducing breach of contract, interfering with performance of a contract, intimidation, or conspiracy to commit one of these torts, and for proceedings for failure to comply with an injunction imposed to restrain further commission of these torts. As we have seen in para 11.10 *et seq*, those who organise industrial action will generally commit at least one of these torts so the statutory formula is likely to apply in this context.

---

177 See para 11.32.
178 S 28. See further para 11.9.
179 See G Morris, 1993.
180 It was relied upon, however, in *P v NAS/UWT* [2003] UKHL 8, [2003] IRLR 307, discussed in para 11.27 below.

It is important to know in advance of any dispute whether the union will be liable because in that event the action must be preceded by a ballot; if it is not, then statutory immunity will automatically be lost (unless the union takes advantage of the limited opportunity to repudiate the act in question). In the case of torts not within the statutory formula, such as nuisance, liability is determined by principles derived from the common law. Fixing liability to the union does not absolve individuals from personal liability,[181] but proceedings are likely to be brought against the union where this is possible, although individuals may be joined as a co-defendants.

(i) The statutory scheme of liability

11.21   TULRCA 1992 attributes liability to a union where an act was 'authorised' or 'endorsed' by one of three categories of persons.[182] The first is any person empowered by the union rules to do, authorise or endorse such acts. The term 'rules' is defined to mean both the written rules of the union and any other written provision forming part of the contract of membership.[183] Custom and practice in the union which has not been reduced to writing is therefore excluded in this context.[184] Second, regardless of the union rules, there is liability for the 'principal executive committee', president or general secretary of the union.[185] Last, again regardless of the rules, there is liability for any other 'committee' of the union[186] or any other official, whether employed by it or not. The definition of 'official' means that shop stewards and other lay officials fall within its scope provided that their election or appointment is in accordance with the union rules.[187] This means that the union is potentially liable for the acts of a very wide range of individuals irrespective of any limitations in its rules; action which would be viewed internally as 'unofficial' is nevertheless deemed to be its responsibility, the underlying purpose being to encourage greater control by unions over their officials' actions.[188] Moreover, the legislation attributes to an official any act done, authorised or endorsed by any 'group' (ad hoc or otherwise) of which he or she was at the material time a member whose purposes included organising or coordinating industrial action or an act by any member of such a group. This means that the official need not personally have been involved in taking the decision to take industrial action – it is sufficient that he or she was a member of the group at the 'material time' – and, indeed, he or she may conceivably have participated in the activity of the 'group' in order to discourage this decision.[189] There have been no cases on this point to date.

---

181 This is made explicit in TULRCA 1992, s 20(5).
182 TULRCA 1992, s 20(1)–(4). 'Authorised' and 'endorsed' are not defined in the statute; the term 'authorisation' is generally used when industrial action is approved before it commences; endorsement when it is authorised at a later stage.
183 TULRCA 1992, s 20(7).
184 *British Railways Board v RMT* (QBD, 17 September 1992, unreported).
185 See para 10.14 above for definitions of these terms.
186 Any group of persons constituted in accordance with the union rules is a 'committee': TULRCA 1992, s 20(3).
187 TULRCA 1992, s 119.
188 Research showed that unions were exercising a greater degree of centralised control over members' actions even before EA 1990 widened the scope of potential liability: see Martin *et al*, 1991. See also Undy *et al*, 1996: ch 6.
189 Although the Conservative Government denied that liability would attach in this situation (see Lord Strathclyde HL Debs, Vol 521, col 1250, 23 July 1990) this is not precluded by the statute.

In relation to an act by the third category of persons only, the union can avoid liability if the act in question is repudiated by the executive, president or general secretary as soon as reasonably practicable after coming to the knowledge of any of them.[190] Whether this happens 'as soon as reasonably practicable' will be a question of fact; in practice many disputes organised at local level begin and end very rapidly and may be over before repudiation has an opportunity to take place. 'Repudiation' involves an 'open disavowal and disowning of the acts of the officials concerned'.[191] The union must follow a rigid procedure to effect this. First, written notice of repudiation must be given 'without delay' to the committee or official whose act is attributable to the union.[192] Second, the union must 'do its best' to give individual written notice of the fact and date of repudiation, without delay, to every member who the union has reason to believe is taking part, or 'might' otherwise take part, in the action as a result of this act and to the employer of every such individual.[193] Trying to decide which individuals 'might' participate in the action, particularly where the call comes from a relatively junior or maverick official, may be highly problematic. The notice given to members must include the following words:

> Your union has repudiated the call (or calls) for industrial action to which this notice relates and will give no support to unofficial industrial action taken in response to it (or them). If you are dismissed while taking unofficial industrial action, you will have no right to complain of unfair dismissal.[194]

As well as ensuring that they comply with this initial procedure, unions must also be vigilant about their subsequent activities; repudiation may be rendered ineffective if, at any time in the future, the executive, president or general secretary behave in a manner inconsistent with the purported repudiation.[195] If this were to happen it seems that this would expose the union to liability at the instance of any person who would have had a claim against it had repudiation not occurred.

The effect of a union repudiating liability is to make the industrial action 'unofficial' as from the end of the next working day after the day on which repudiation takes place.[196] As we describe in para 11.84 below, employees participating in unofficial industrial action are denied the possibility of protection against even selective dismissals unless it is shown that they were dismissed for one of a narrow range of reasons. In any given situation, therefore, a union will have to consider carefully the consequences before embarking on repudiation which, while it may save union funds, puts members' jobs at risk and may create damaging splits among the membership, particularly if the grievance is thought justified or has implications for other workers. It is, of course, open to

190 TULRCA 1992, s 21(1).
191 *Express and Star Ltd v NGA* [1985] IRLR 455, 459.
192 TULRCA 1992, s 21(2)(a).
193 TULRCA 1992, s 21(2)(b).
194 TULRCA 1992, s 21(3).
195 TULRCA 1992, s 21(5). They will be treated as so behaving if they fail to confirm the repudiation in writing 'forthwith' on a request made within three months of the purported repudiation by a party to a commercial contract whose performance was at risk of interference from the act in question who has not already received written notice of it: s 21(6).
196 TULRCA 1992, s 237(4). In *Balfour Kilpatrick Ltd v Acheson* [2003] IRLR 683 the EAT held that 'the end of the next working day' meant midnight on the following working day, not the end of the period which constitutes the normal working hours for the day in question. That case also illustrates the fact that industrial action may be 'official' in relation to some employees but 'unofficial' in relation to others.

the union to repudiate but immediately call a ballot on the issue, although it would be advisable in that event for it to broaden the scope of the dispute, so rendering it a different dispute, to avoid the difficulty that immunity could be lost because it had 'called' the action before the date of the ballot, albeit that the call had subsequently been repudiated (see para 11.43). Where a purported repudiation by a union is deemed subsequently to be ineffective by a tribunal, it seems that the industrial action will remain 'non-unofficial' for unfair dismissal purposes and employees will retain the protection against selective dismissal.[197]

(ii) Liability at common law

11.22   For torts not specified in the statute, such as nuisance, union liability is determined according to principles established by the common law. These dictate that the union is liable for the acts of individuals acting with its express or implied authorisation, regardless of whether they are its employees. The concept of authorisation in this context was interpreted broadly in the leading case of *Heatons Transport (St Helens) Ltd v TGWU*.[198] The defendant union had a policy that the loading and unloading of containers carried at sea should be reserved for dock workers registered under the statutory National Dock Labour Scheme then in operation and that lorries of firms refusing to honour this policy should be 'blacked'. Shop stewards at Liverpool and Hull established unofficial committees at their own initiative to direct the blacking although such committees were not provided for in the union rule book. The union argued that it could not be liable for the shop stewards' acts. The House of Lords rejected this argument on the ground that the stewards had general implied authority and discretion to act on the union's behalf in protecting members' wages and working conditions in the circumstances in question and they were promoting general union policy in doing this. The court emphasised that in determining the scope of the authority of an official to bind the union regard must be had both to the written rule book and to custom and practice, which could have the effect of modifying the union's rules as they operated in practice or compensating for the absence of formal rules. To avoid liability in this situation the union would have needed to withdraw the authority of the stewards to continue organising the industrial action 'in terms which would be reasonably understood by them as forbidding them to continue',[199] possibly by withdrawing their credentials and, if necessary, taking disciplinary action.

The approach to liability in *Heatons*, to the extent that it pays regard to the wider circumstances, and in particular whether officials are acting in accordance with union policy,[200] accords greater respect to internal union practices than the statutory approach. Nevertheless, it may require unions to go to extreme lengths to disassociate themselves from the actions of their members. The measures which the courts may require to avoid liability for the acts of members and officials who commit a tort in the course of picketing were considered by Stuart-Smith J in *News Group Newspapers Ltd v SOGAT '82 (No 2)*[201] where the liability of unions for, *inter alia*, the torts of public and private nuisance was at

---

197 *Balfour Kilpatrick Ltd v Acheson* [2003] IRLR 683.
198 [1972] ICR 308.
199 [1972] ICR 308, 404 (Lord Wilberforce).
200 On the importance of this element, see *General Aviation Services (UK) Ltd v TGWU* [1976] IRLR 224.
201 [1986] IRLR 337.

issue. The court accepted that unions were not liable merely by organising a march or picketing during the course of which tortious acts are committed by third parties even though such acts can be foreseen. However, he held that unions may be taken to have authorised the commission of a nuisance or other tort or to have continued a nuisance[202] where they continue to organise events which in the light of experience constitute a tort, in the knowledge or presumed knowledge that such torts are being committed by those whom they organise. In this case the conduct of the pickets had been repeated regularly and must have been well known to the unions. The court rejected the argument that the union lacked sufficient control over its members to restrain commission of the torts in question; they had failed to discipline or threaten to discipline those who persistently flouted union instructions that picketing was to be peaceful, nor had they forbidden them to act as official pickets. If the union could not exercise sufficient control they might have to desist from picketing altogether or organise it elsewhere. On the basis of this reasoning unions need to curtail or abandon picketing altogether to avoid liability for their members' acts.

THE SCOPE OF STATUTORY IMMUNITY

11.23   As we saw in para 11.10 *et seq*, the organisation of industrial action will almost invariably give rise to civil liability at common law. It then becomes necessary to ask whether that liability is removed because the tortious act in question is protected by the statutory immunities. This requires two elements to be satisfied. First, there must be statutory immunity for the tortious acts in question. We list the torts which are accorded immunity in para 11.24 below. Second, the act must fall within the formula which sets the perimeter of legitimate industrial action: it must have been done 'in contemplation or furtherance of a trade dispute'. We analyse this formula in para 11.25 *et seq*. Even if the act satisfies these two requirements, however, it may still be excluded from the statutory protection for one of several reasons. We examine these in para 11.30 *et seq*. They are, in outline: if the action constitutes unlawful secondary action or unlawful picketing; if its purpose is to enforce trade union membership or to require the employer to pursue a 'union-only' or 'recognition-only' practice in supply contracts; if it is related to the dismissal of employees in connection with unofficial industrial action; or, if a union is legally responsible for the action, if the statutory balloting requirements have not been followed. In addition, protection is excluded in relation to the employer in respect of whom the default occurs (and in relation to an individual exercising the statutory right of action) when a union fails to provide specified pre-ballot information, notify it of the ballot result, or give notice before industrial action starts. It is readily apparent from this list that unions have to steer a careful course in order to remain within the statutory protection.

Torts which are granted statutory immunity

11.24   The legislation states that an act done by a person in contemplation or furtherance of a trade dispute is not actionable in tort on the ground only (a)

---

202   The concept of 'continuing' a nuisance, developed in the context of private nuisance in *Sedleigh-Denfield v O'Callaghan* [1940] AC 880, was applied by Stuart-Smith J also to public nuisance.

that it induces another person to break a contract or interferes or induces another person to interfere with its performance; or (b) that it consists in his or her threatening that a contract (whether one to which he or she is a party or not) will be broken or its performance interfered with, or that he or she will induce another person to break a contract or to interfere with its performance.[203] In addition, an agreement or combination by two or more persons to do or procure the doing of an act in contemplation or furtherance of a trade dispute is not actionable in tort if the act is one which, if done without any such agreement or combination, would not be actionable in tort.[204] This means that there is statutory immunity for the torts of inducing breach of contract, 'simple' conspiracy and intimidation based upon the threat to break (or induce the breach of) a contract. In *Hadmor Productions Ltd v Hamilton*[205] the House of Lords affirmed that an act which was not actionable in itself by virtue of the legislation may not constitute the requisite 'unlawful' means for torts such as interfering with business by unlawful means or conspiracy to use unlawful means.[206]

This method of listing torts, rather than of giving a comprehensive immunity against civil liability, means that those organising industrial action have always been vulnerable to new nominate torts being created. As we saw in para 11.10, it is a sufficient argument on an interim application that there is a serious issue to be tried; if the claimant can convince the court that a wrong has been committed which lies outside the scope of the immunity the issue shifts to the balance of convenience. Following *Rookes v Barnard*,[207] where, as we saw, the House of Lords accepted that a threat to breach a contract could be sufficient to constitute the tort of intimidation, the legislature extended protection to this tort.[208] Since 1979, however, an equivalent response to other extensions of the common law has not been forthcoming. Thus there is no statutory protection afforded against torts based upon breach of statutory duty, for example; nor is there any longer any immunity against breach of contract *simpliciter*,[209] an omission which would be highly significant if it were to be accepted as constituting the requisite unlawful means for the tort of interference with business by unlawful means.[210] We discuss the scope of any immunity which may apply to torts committed in the course of picketing, such as nuisance, in para 11.55 below.

The concept of a 'trade dispute'

11.25 A 'trade dispute' is defined as 'a dispute between workers and their employer which relates wholly or mainly' to one or more of the matters which now constitute the statutory subject-matter of 'collective bargaining'.[211] This definition requires consideration both of the parties to the dispute and its purpose.

---

203 TULRCA 1992, s 219(1).
204 TULRCA 1992, s 219(2).
205 [1982] IRLR 102.
206 Before 1980 this was specifically stated in the legislation (Trade Union and Labour Relations Act 1974, s 13(3), repealed by the Employment Act 1980).
207 [1964] AC 1129.
208 TDA 1965.
209 TULRA 1974, s 13(3) declared '[f]or the avoidance of doubt' that a breach of contract in contemplation or furtherance of a trade dispute shall not be regarded as the doing of an unlawful act or use of unlawful means for the purpose of establishing liability in tort. This provision was repealed by EA 1980.
210 See *Barretts & Baird (Wholesale) Ltd v IPCS* [1987] IRLR 3, and the discussion in para 11.16 above.
211 TULRCA 1992, s 244(1).

(i)   The parties to a 'trade dispute'

11.26   It is consistent with the definition of a trade union that 'workers',[212] not merely 'employees', may be party to a trade dispute (although at the time of writing only employees have any chance of being protected against dismissal). Moreover, in this context the term 'worker' extends beyond those employed at the time of the dispute to former workers if their employment was terminated in connection with the dispute or where the termination was one of the circumstances giving rise to it.[213] At one time there was statutory provision that a dispute involving a union should be treated as one to which workers were a party; although now repealed it is probably the case that a union can be party to a dispute along with its members as long as it is representing them (but not if it is acting independently or has no members in that employment).[214]

The need for a dispute to be between 'workers and their employer' imposes five important limitations. First, it excludes cases where workers are employed through an intermediary company which is not their true 'employer'. To date the courts have refused to 'lift the corporate veil' and look at where power is centred in reality in the context of industrial action.[215] Second, it excludes situations where the employer's own workers are not in dispute with it, for example if picketing is organised at an employer's premises because it employs low-paid foreign workers who are not themselves objecting to their conditions.[216] Third, it excludes disputes between workers, such as demarcation or inter-union disputes, although circumstances where this does not spill into a dispute with the employer may be rare. Fourth, it excludes disputes which are characterised as being with an employer to whom workers may at some future date transfer. In *University College London NHS Trust v UNISON*[217] Trust employees threatened strike action because the Trust refused to guarantee that those of its employees transferred to a private sector consortium, and new employees engaged by the consortium, would have equivalent terms and conditions to those not transferred. The Court of Appeal rejected the argument that this could be regarded as a dispute between the employees and their current, rather than their so-far-unidentified new, employer. This conclusion was reached despite the fact that the current employer had the power to specify in a contract with the consortium the terms and conditions which would apply to the employees when employed by their new employer.[218] Last, it excludes industrial action against the government with three exceptions: where the government is the direct employer; if a settlement requires a minister to exercise a statutory power (such as the powers of the Secretary of State to make orders relating to teachers' pay and

---

212   See para 3.51 *et seq* above.
213   TULRCA 1992, s 244(5).
214   See *NALGO v Bolton Corpn* [1943] AC 166, (Lord Wright); *Associated British Ports v TGWU* [1989] IRLR 291, 300 (Millett J).
215   *Dimbleby and Sons Ltd v NUJ* [1984] IRLR 161.
216   Cf *NWL Ltd v Woods* [1979] IRLR 478. Before 1982 defendants could claim immunity in disputes between workers and any employer.
217   [1999] IRLR 31. An application to the ECtHR that British law violated Art 11 of the ECHR was declared inadmissible; the prohibition on the union's ability to strike could in the circumstances regarded as 'necessary in a democratic society' for the protection of the rights of their current employer under Art 11(2).
218   As R Davies, 2004 states at pp 101–102, UNISON achieved many of its objectives when the government introduced the 'Retention of Employment Model' in the NHS and the Code of Practice on Workplace Matters in Local Authority Service Contracts; see also G Morris, 2004a: pp 170–172.

conditions of employment);[219] or the dispute relates to matters which have been referred to a joint body on which there is statutory provision for a minister to be represented.[220] These circumstances aside, in the light of the close relationship between the industry and the labour market, on the one hand, and government economic policies on the other, the line between action against the government and against an individual employer may sometimes be difficult to draw. As Kahn-Freund asked some years ago:

> Is it not true that, not only in publicly owned industries, governmental decisions on wages policies – whether statutory or not – on credits and on subsidies, on the distribution of industry ... and on a thousand other things, affect the terms and conditions of employment at least as much as the decisions of individual firms? Where is the line between a strike to induce an employer to raise, or not to reduce, wages and a strike to press the government for measures which would enable the employer to do so?[221]

To date the courts have not been faced with this argument in this form[222] although, as we indicate below, related problems may arise in determining a dispute's predominant purpose.

(ii) The purpose of a 'trade dispute'

11.27   The purposes of a 'trade dispute' are now co-extensive with the definition of the objects of 'collective bargaining' as statutorily defined (although originally no such link was made and even now the immunity is not linked to the practice of collective bargaining[223]). As we indicated in para 7.27, it is in the context of industrial action that the courts have been called upon to clarify the scope of some of these objects. They fall into seven categories:

(i) *Terms and conditions of employment, or the physical conditions in which any workers are required to work.* It has long been clear that the expression 'terms of employment' is not confined to contractual terms,[224] and in the recent case of *P v NAS/UWT* the House of Lords affirmed that the 'composite' phrase 'terms and conditions of employment' ('chosen to avoid arguments as to whether something should properly be described' as a 'term' or 'condition') should be given a 'broad meaning'.[225] Here, the court held that a dispute about whether teachers should be required to comply with the head teacher's direction to teach P, an allegedly disruptive pupil, was about their 'terms and conditions of employment'. In reaching this conclusion the court rejected the claimant's argument that this was a dispute about the application of a rule rather than the rule itself and was not, therefore, about terms and conditions; Parliament could

---

219 These powers are now contained in the Education Act 2002, s 122; see *Wandsworth London Borough Council v NAS/UWT* [1993] IRLR 344.

220 TULRCA 1992, s 244(2).

221 P Davies and M Freedland, 1983: p 317.

222 However, see *Associated British Ports v TGWU* [1989] IRLR 291 for a related discussion.

223 Auerbach, 1990.

224 In *British Broadcasting Corpn v Hearn* [1977] IRLR 273 Lord Denning MR stated (at 275) that it could also cover those terms used and applied by the parties in practice or habitually or by common consent without ever being incorporated into the contract, and this was approved by Lord Diplock in *Hadmor Productions Ltd v Hamilton* [1982] IRLR 102, 108.

225 [2003] IRLR 307, para 24 (Lord Hoffman, with whose opinion Lords Hobhouse, Scott and Walker agreed).

not have intended the immunities to turn upon such fine distinctions which were, in any event, impossible to make. 'A dispute about what the workers are obliged to do or how the employer is obliged to remunerate them, at any level of generality or particularity, is about terms and conditions of employment.'[226] Moreover, the fact that not all of those taking action are personally affected by the subject-matter of the dispute does not take the dispute outside the immunities:[227] '... the representative function of trade unions would be set at nought if it were the case that employees could not take industrial action in relation to an attempt to change terms and conditions of employment of only some of them'.[228] However, 'terms and conditions of employment' does not cover terms which regulate a relationship between an employer and a third party acting as principal (rather than as agent for the employee) and for which no provision is made in the terms under which the employee works for the employer, such as the clauses of a collective agreement which relate solely to the relationship between a trade union and employer.[229] Moreover, in *University College London Hospital NHS Trust v UNISON*, discussed above, the Court of Appeal held that 'terms and conditions' were confined to those under which employees worked for their existing employer, and refused to characterise the dispute as one with the existing employer over future employment conditions; rather, it was with the new, to-date-unidentified, employer.[230]

(ii) *Engagement or non-engagement, or termination or suspension of employment or the duties of employment, of one or more workers.* As well as dismissals which have already taken place the courts have held that this includes fear of future dismissals, including redundancies; there is no need for dismissal notices to have been issued.[231]

(iii) *Allocation of work or the duties of employment as between workers or groups of workers.* This is limited to demarcation disputes between workers or groups of workers employed by the same employer.[232] Thus, if an employer's business is divided into separate companies, which may be operating on the same premises (a manufacturing and a distribution division, for example), a dispute over the allocation of work between those companies would not be a 'trade dispute'.

(iv) *Matters of discipline.*

(v) *A worker's membership or non-membership of a trade union* (although see now para 11.30 below).

---

226 Lord Hoffman, para 28
227 *British Telecommunications plc v CMU* [2004] IRLR 58.
228 Above, para 18 (Stanley Burnton J).
229 *Universe Tankships Inc of Monrovia v ITWF* [1982] IRLR 200, 206 (Lord Diplock).
230 [1999] IRLR 31; see also note 217 above. Hendy, 2000 argues (p 58) that this decision may require industrial action to be confined to existing terms and conditions, as well as being with an existing employer, so removing immunity from any worker seeking to change those terms, for example by pursuing a wage claim. However, it is far from clear that the decision does have this consequence, and in any event a dispute over higher wages could be regarded as a dispute over the unsatisfactory nature of the existing terms; the fact that it may lead to increased pay does not prevent the current pay level being the issue in dispute.
231 *Hadmor Productions Ltd v Hamilton* [1982] IRLR 102; *General Aviation Services (UK) Ltd v TGWU* [1975] ICR 276; *Health Computing Ltd v Meek* [1980] IRLR 437.
232 *Dimbleby & Sons Ltd v NUJ* [1984] IRLR 161.

(vi) *Facilities for officials*[233] *of trade unions.*

(vii) *Machinery for negotiation or consultation, and other procedures, relating to any of the above.* This includes the recognition by employers or employers' associations of the right of a trade union to represent workers in such negotiation or consultation or in the carrying out of such procedures.

11.28 The statute requires the dispute to relate 'wholly or mainly' to one of these matters. This requires a court to examine its predominant purpose.[234] Disputes which are judged to be furthering a 'political' or other non-industrial purpose, such as a personal feud or grudge,[235] will have no immunity. In this context, as in relation to determining the parties to a dispute, the line between the 'political' and the industrial may be difficult to draw. Particular problems may arise in public services; for example, disputes over matters such as wages or job cuts, which are clearly within the definition of a trade dispute, often involve challenging broader government policies, such as incomes policies, reductions in public spending or privatisation. At the time the predominant purpose test was introduced,[236] ministers maintained that they did not intend to jeopardise the lawfulness of public sector disputes concerning pay, conditions or jobs, even if they did challenge government policies. However, in interim proceedings, doubt about the predominant purpose of a dispute may be sufficient to persuade a court to grant an interim injunction. To date there have been five decisions where the predominant purpose of a dispute has been at issue.[237]

Mercury Communications Ltd v Scott-Garner and the POEU[238] took place against the background of the breaking of the monopoly over the operation of telecommunications. The POEU instructed its members employed by the existing monopoly supplier, British Telecommunications (BT), not to connect Mercury, a private company, to the BT network. The union argued that it had issued this instruction in furtherance of a dispute with BT over employees' job security which, it claimed, would be put at risk if Mercury was connected. The Court of Appeal rejected this argument and held that the dispute was primarily concerned with the union's opposition to government policies of liberalisation and privatisation of the telecommunications industry. In reaching its decision the court was influenced heavily by evidence of a Job Security Agreement between the union and the employer which the union had not sought to invoke, a fact which pointed away from the union having a genuine concern about jobs.

The decision in *Mercury* does not mean that all industrial action relating to the consequences of privatisation will be unlawful, but unions need to be careful to ensure that it is linked sufficiently closely with one of the matters that characterise a trade dispute; had the union invoked the Job Security Agreement

---

233 Defined TULRCA 1992, s 119.
234 *Mercury Communications Ltd v Scott-Garner and the POEU* [1983] IRLR 494, CA.
235 See, for example, *Huntley v Thornton* [1957] 1 WLR 321.
236 EA 1982 amended TULRA 1974 (now repealed) which provided that the dispute had only to be 'connected with' a collective bargaining matter; a court had only to be satisfied that a collective bargaining matter was genuinely at issue: see *NWL Ltd v Woods* [1979] IRLR 478.
237 In 1987 the Department of Employment secured an injunction against an officer of the Civil and Public Services Association who organised a strike in opposition to an ethnic monitoring exercise in unemployment benefit offices on the ground that this was a 'political' issue but no full judgment was given.
238 [1983] IRLR 494.

it might have been able to sustain the argument that, while the dispute took place against the background of privatisation, its predominant purpose was concern about the risk to jobs. *Mercury* can be contrasted with *Associated British Ports v TGWU*,[239] where the union called a strike in furtherance of its demand from port employers for new national conditions in the docks after the government had announced the introduction of legislation to abolish the statutory National Dock Labour Scheme which provided that only registered dock workers could be employed in the docks, a measure which directly affected their terms and conditions of employment. Millett J rejected the employers' argument that this was not a 'trade dispute'; whereas in *Mercury* the matters of genuine industrial concern were only aspects of a 'wider political dispute', in this case 'the union's concern for the future employment conditions of former registered dock workers' could not be so characterised.[240] He also roundly rejected the contention that the dispute with the employers was manufactured as a spurious pretext for a dispute with the government; this was a 'serious calumny', 'wholly without substance'.[241] The link between legislation abolishing the scheme and dockers' terms and conditions of employment was inextricable, and given that the employers had made clear their intention to deprive dockers of valued features of their employment relationship which the scheme had bestowed, there was a genuine dispute between them. Although this case demonstrates that linkage with government policies need not preclude a 'trade dispute', it was pointed out by one commentator that the unions' success was 'secured only by very deliberate action' to ensure that there was the necessary evidence to substantiate its case.[242]

Third, in *Wandsworth London Borough Council v NAS/UWT* the union had instructed its members to boycott 'all the unreasonable and unnecessary elements of assessment connected with the national curriculum'. The Court of Appeal dismissed the employers' argument that this was a dispute about the content of work which the national curriculum required teachers to undertake; rather it was about teachers' working time, and therefore mainly related to terms and conditions of employment. In reaching this conclusion the court attached 'considerable importance' to the wording of the question put to members in the ballot which preceded the industrial action, which asked them whether they were willing to take action 'to protest against the excessive workload and unreasonable imposition made upon teachers, as a consequence of national curriculum assessment and testing'.[243]

Fourth, in *University College London Hospital NHS Trust v UNISON*[244] the employer sought to argue that the threatened industrial action over its refusal to guarantee that staff transferred to a private consortium, and those subsequently employed by the consortium, would be employed on terms at least as favourable as those applicable to staff it continued to employ, had a political objective. This argument was rejected by the Court of Appeal, although the more limited objective ascribed to the union of alleviating the consequences of the Private Finance Initiative was found, on the facts, not to fall within the terms of TULRCA 1992, s 244(1).

---

239 [1989] IRLR 291, Ch D.
240 [1989] IRLR 291, 301.
241 [1989] IRLR 291, 299. The employers did not seek to raise this argument on appeal: [1989] IRLR 305, CA; revsd [1989] IRLR 399, HL.
242 Simpson, 1989: p 237.
243 [1993] IRLR 344, 350.
244 [1999] IRLR 31.

Finally, in *The Lord Mayor and Citizens of Westminster City Council v UNISON*[245] the employer maintained (successfully at first instance) that a dispute over the compulsory transfer of staff to the employment of a private company was in reality a dispute about public policy. The Court of Appeal dismissed the argument, finding that the judge had drawn unwarranted inferences from the evidence, and that the dispute concerning the identity of the union members' employer related to their terms and conditions of employment.

Last in this context, a dispute relating to matters occurring outside the United Kingdom is capable of constituting a 'trade dispute,' but only if the person(s) whose actions in the UK are said to be in contemplation or furtherance of a dispute relating to such matters are likely to be affected by the outcome of the dispute in respect of one or more of the matters specified in TULRCA 1992, s 244(1).[246] This prevents the organisation of any form of solidarity action with workers overseas where there is no immediate connection between the outcome of that dispute and UK workers. It also overlooks the fact that transnational companies may now be organised in such a way that decisions taken in relation to workers in another country (for example, in relation to working conditions or redundancies) may have significant repercussions in the UK.[247]

'In contemplation or furtherance of a trade dispute'

11.29 Once a 'trade dispute' has been established it is necessary to show that the defendant was acting 'in contemplation or furtherance' of it. Here both the *timing* of the action and its *purpose* are relevant. As far as *timing* is concerned:

> ... either a dispute is imminent and the act is done in expectation of and with a view to it, or ... the dispute is already existing and the act is done in support of one side to it.[248]

When a dispute is not in existence whether it is sufficiently imminent will be a question of degree. In *Bent's Brewery Co Ltd v Hogan*[249] the union sought certain information from its pub-manager members, including their takings, trade, and total wages bill, prior to formulating a wage claim. Giving the union this information would have involved these members breaking their contracts of employment. On an application for a declaration by the employers that their employees were not entitled to provide this information the court rejected the argument that the union was acting in contemplation of a trade dispute; such a dispute was neither in being nor imminent. No demand had been made for better conditions or increased wages by any of the managers or by the union on their behalf. The most that could be said was that the union had sent out documents which, after consideration of the information obtained, might lead to a request which, if not granted, might lead to a dispute. By contrast, in *Health Computing Ltd v Meek*[250] the union was held to be acting in contemplation of a trade dispute in sending out a circular instructing its members not to co-operate with the claimants, a private contractor which specialised in

---

245 [2001] IRLR 524.
246 TULRCA 1992, s 244(3).
247 See Wedderburn, 2000: pp 28–33; Germanotta and Novitz, 2002.
248 Lord Loreburn in *Conway v Wade* [1909] AC 506 at 512. See also *JT Stratford & Son Ltd v Lindley* [1965] AC 269 (emphasising the need for a 'live' dispute).
249 [1945] 2 All ER 570.
250 [1980] IRLR 437.

computer systems for medical services and which was seeking to do business with health authorities. The purpose of the circular, according to the union general secretary, was to pre-empt the disputes which would inevitably arise if the health authorities did do business with them. The evidence showed that some health authorities, at least, would be likely to say that they reserved the right to use the contractor's services and it was reasonable to foresee that the enforcement of the union's policy of banning the claimants from the NHS might lead to disputes with those authorities, the disputes being motivated by fear of future redundancies. Thus the court concluded that the circular had been distributed in contemplation of those disputes.

From the other end of the spectrum, there may be scope for argument as to whether a dispute has ended or still remains in being. This question is particularly significant because, where a union is organising the action, the requisite ballot must relate to the dispute it covers. Again, it will be a question of scrutinising the facts to establish whether the original dispute remains 'real or live'.[251]

Finally on this point, it is possible that a dispute may never come into existence at all if an employer submits to workers' demands under threat of industrial action. Such a threat, as we saw in para 11.16, can constitute the tort of intimidation. To cover such a situation the legislation provides that an act, threat or demand which, if resisted, would have led to a trade dispute shall be treated as having been done in contemplation of it even though no dispute arises because the other first submits.[252] It is essential, however, in this situation that the union ensures that the demand is sufficiently closely related to one of the matters listed in the statute. In *BBC v Hearn*[253] the union asked its members not to transmit the (football) Cup Final after the BBC refused to take steps to ensure that the broadcast would not be transmitted to South Africa where the policy of apartheid, to which the union was opposed, was still in force. The Court of Appeal held that there was no trade dispute in existence. However, Lord Denning MR suggested that it could have become one had the union asked the BBC to insert a clause in its members' contracts, or for a condition to be understood, that they would not be asked to participate in any broadcasts to South Africa while there was a policy of apartheid. This suggestion received support from Lord Diplock in a later case.[254] However its possibilities are not unlimited. In a subsequent decision Lord Cross emphasised that a union could not turn a dispute which in reality had no connection with terms and conditions of employment (in that case a demand that the employer made a payment to the union welfare fund) into a trade dispute merely by insisting that the employer inserted appropriate terms into contracts of employment.[255] This approach allows the courts discretion to decide whether the dispute has the appropriate connection.[256]

---

251 See *Newham London Borough Council v NALGO* [1993] IRLR 83, 87. The suggestion made that for a dispute to continue it is sufficient if the side which still regards itself as being in dispute 'honestly and genuinely believes this is the position' is contrary to authority and indeed the court went on to affirm the need for the dispute to be 'real or live'. See also *Re South West Trains* (25 October 1999, Turner J), IRLB 647: pp 12–14.

252 TULRCA 1992, s 244(4).

253 [1977] IRLR 273, CA.

254 *NWL Ltd v Woods* [1979] IRLR 478, 483, HL.

255 *Universe Tankships Inc of Monrovia v ITWF* [1982] IRLR 200, 208.

256 See, for example, Griffiths LJ at 71, Lord Donaldson MR at 73 in *Dimbleby & Sons Ltd v NUJ* [1984] IRLR 67 (decision affirmed [1984] IRLR 161, HL).

The test of the dispute organiser's *purpose* in acting is a subjective one; it is sufficient that he or she honestly thinks at the time that the action may help one of the parties to the trade dispute to achieve its objective and it is done for that reason.[257] It is therefore immaterial that this belief may be unreasonable; that the action did not, in fact, assist the dispute, or that the action taken was disproportionate to the grievance to be settled. However, evidence that no reasonable person could have thought the action may have this result may be relevant to the credibility of the defendant's evidence that the belief was honestly held.[258] In practice, now that the legislation outlaws virtually all forms of secondary industrial action this issue is unlikely to be contentious other than in the context of picketing, where, as we describe in para 11.55 below, a narrow form of secondary action is permitted.[259]

Situations where the statutory protection does not apply

11.30 Having established that the tortious acts alleged are covered by the statutory immunities and that the defendant is acting in contemplation or furtherance of a trade dispute it is then necessary to examine whether protection is excluded for any reason. The grounds for exclusion can be divided into four main categories: where the requisite balloting and information procedures are not followed in relation to action organised by a union; where the action constitutes unlawful picketing; where the action is taken for a proscribed purpose; and where it constitutes unlawful 'secondary action'. The first and second are discussed in paras 11.32 *et seq* and 11.52 *et seq* respectively; the remainder we discuss below.

The 'forbidden' reasons for industrial action, which need not be the primary but only one motivating factor, fall into two categories. The first category concerns action relating to union membership and to recognition and collective consultation; initially introduced as a reflection of the Conservative Government's anti-collectivist stance, it has survived unscathed under Labour. There is no protection for action motivated by the belief that an employer is employing, has employed, or might employ a non-union member (or a person who is not a member of a particular union) or may fail to accord more favourable treatment to union members or members of a particular union.[260] Thus, as well as preventing the imposition of a closed shop by these means, a union cannot take industrial action to enforce a demand that only union members should benefit from a wage increase secured by collective bargaining or that union members should be given preference when jobs are allocated. However, it would be open to a union to take action where an employer was favouring non-unionists provided that it was arguing only for equal treatment for its members. Acts to induce an employer to stipulate in a contract for the supply of goods or services that the work should be done only by union (or non-union) labour (or by members of a particular union) or to induce the employer to refuse to deal with another party who does not comply with these requirements are also unprotected. Any stipulation that the other party to a contract should recognise a union or consult

---

257 *Express Newspapers Ltd v McShane and Ashton* [1980] IRLR 35. Note, however, that the 'trade dispute' itself must exist or be imminent as an objective fact: Lord Diplock at 39.
258 *Express Newspapers*, above; see also *Duport Steels Ltd v Sirs* [1980] IRLR 116.
259 TULRCA 1992, s 224(1), (4).
260 TULRCA 1992, ss 219(4), 222.

with a union official is similarly treated. This means that industrial action cannot be used as a means of helping workers employed by another employer to gain recognition, or even consultation, rights from their employer. It is also unlawful for a union to organise industrial action by employees to persuade their employer's supplier to recognise the union. Second, industrial action is unprotected if one of the reasons for it is the fact or belief that an employer has dismissed one or more employees who have no right to complain of unfair dismissal because they were taking part in 'unofficial' industrial action at the time.[261] The fact that this need not be the primary reason means that if industrial action is taken for other reasons against an employer who has recently dismissed employees in such circumstances the union will have to ensure that the action is dissociated completely from the dismissal.

11.31   The exclusion of 'secondary action' from the statutory immunities is the culmination of the process of 'enterprise confinement';[262] the idea that collective organisation is legitimate, if at all, only at the level of the enterprise. 'Secondary action' occurs when there is inducement to breach, or interference with the performance of, a contract of employment (or the threat of such inducement or interference) and the employer under the contract is not party to the trade dispute.[263] By contrast, 'primary action' is where there is action of this nature and the employer under the contract is party to the trade dispute.[264] Exclusion of secondary action means, for example, that if employees of employer X are in dispute with X then if the union calls on employees of employer Y, who supplies goods to X, not to deliver those supplies, it will thereby have induced them to breach their contracts of employment, an act for which it will have no immunity in tort. An employer may not be treated as party to a dispute between another employer and its workers, and where more than one employer is in dispute with its workers each dispute is to be treated separately.[265] This means that it is impossible to organise national industrial action against more than one employer unless a dispute with each individual employer can be shown; a dispute with an employer as a member of an employers' association with which the union is in dispute, for example, will not suffice. However, an act in contemplation or furtherance of a trade dispute which is primary action in relation to that dispute may not be relied upon as secondary action in relation to another.[266] Thus, even if industrial action taken against one employer assists workers in dispute with another employer, it does not thereby constitute secondary action (unless it could not be said, in reality, to have been taken to further a dispute with the first employer). Thus, if a number of disputes are conducted contemporaneously and each reinforces the effectiveness of the other (in the National Health Service, for example, where individual locally-based trusts are autonomous employers) they are not thereby rendered unlawful.

The only exception to the ban on 'secondary action' is where there is an inducement, or threatened inducement, to breach a contract of an employee of another employer, such as a customer or supplier, in the course of otherwise

---

261   TULRCA 1992, ss 219(4), 223. In *British Railways Board v RMT* (17 September 1992, unreported, QBD) industrial action had no immunity on this basis.
262   Wedderburn 1989: pp 27–30.
263   TULRCA 1992, s 224(2).
264   TULRCA 1992, s 224(5).
265   TULRCA 1992, s 224(4).
266   TULRCA 1992, s 224(5).

lawful picketing. This means that if a picket peacefully persuades a lorry driver employed by a supplier not to cross the picket line and thereby induces a breach of his or her contract of employment immunity will not be lost on that ground. We explain this exception further in para 11.55.

The withdrawal of immunity for secondary action applies even where the employers have parallel shareholdings; the courts refuse to 'lift the corporate veil' to take account of the financial realities of the situation and there is no exception for 'associated employers'.[267] This means that the scope of lawful industrial action is defined entirely by the legal scope of the employment unit; even if a dispute between one company and its employees in a group directly affects workers in another company in the same group, possibly operating from the same premises, the workers in the second company cannot take supportive industrial action. The same point applies if workers are employed by a subsidiary company which is legally their employer but which lacks the decision-making power to resolve the issues in dispute. Equally workers cannot organise industrial action against another employer to whom the manufacture or supply of goods or services have been diverted by the employer in dispute, even if that employer is 'associated' with the same employer. It is conceivable that workers employed by the second employer could take industrial action against their own employer as a result of the transfer of work if they could bring it within the scope of matters covered by a 'trade dispute', possibly by asking for a clause in their contract that they should not be required to handle such work (a 'hot cargo' clause).[268] However, such action, if official, would need to be supported by a ballot and the organisers would need to ensure that its predominant purpose was to further that dispute and not, in reality, the first.

The ban on secondary action represents a serious constraint on the organisation of industrial action. It is unclear whether employers would seek to structure their companies with the sole aim of circumventing disruption of this nature although it is unlikely that, in reorganising areas of the public sector, such as water, electricity and the NHS, into smaller employer units during the 1980s and 1990s the Conservative Government was unaware of these implications.[269] The restriction contravenes ILO standards on freedom of association; the Committee of Experts has held that action against an employer not directly involved in a given dispute should be regarded as a legitimate exercise of the right to strike where it 'relates directly to the social and economic interests of the workers involved in either or both of the original dispute and the secondary action', provided that the original dispute and the secondary action are not unlawful in themselves.[270] The fact that unions cannot take action against a company which is the 'true' employer but which may hire workers through an intermediary company has also been criticised by the Committee of Independent Experts (now the European Committee of Social Rights) that supervises

---

267 *Dimbleby and Sons Ltd v NUJ* [1984] IRLR 161. See para 3.98 above.
268 See further para 11.29 above.
269 See G Morris, 1993: pp 91–93. Note also in relation to education the Education (Modification of Enactments Relating to Employment) (England) Order 2003, SI 2003/1964 Art 5, which renders industrial action by teachers in schools with delegated budgets in support of colleagues in other schools actionable in tort in certain circumstances, notwithstanding that those employees may share a common employer: see Freedland, 1989 on a predecessor of the current Order.
270 Report of the Committe of Experts on the Application of Conventions and Recommendations, 1989, REport 111 (Part 4A), ILO, Geneva, para 238. For a critique of the ILO standards in this area see Germanotta, 2002.

compliance with the European Social Charter.[271] Nevertheless it is clear that the Labour Government has no intention of changing the position.[272]

INDUSTRIAL ACTION BALLOTS AND NOTICE TO EMPLOYERS

11.32   Industrial action for which a trade union is legally liable is protected by the statutory immunities only if it has the support of a majority of those voting in a ballot. This applies both to industrial action by employees and those working under 'any contract under which one person personally does work or performs services for another', so covering contracts for services.[273] This requirement applies irrespective of whether the action constitutes a breach of contract on the part of those participating (although, as we have seen, it generally will).[274] Industrial action must generally start within four weeks of the ballot unless the parties agree to a longer period not exceeding eight weeks; once this period has expired a fresh ballot will be required.

The requirements governing the conduct of the ballot are extremely complex, technical and, in parts, ambiguous, thus leaving unions vulnerable to potential challenge in the courts on several counts. In addition, unions are required to give employers of members covered by the ballot specified information both before and after the ballot takes place, and employers of proposed participants must receive a minimum of seven days' notice before it starts. The consequences of failing to comply with these requirements vary. In general, if industrial action lacks the support of a ballot the union has no immunity against liability in tort, regardless of the identity of the claimant. However, where the union fails to comply with its obligations to provide pre-ballot information, notify a relevant employer of the ballot result, or give notice before industrial action starts, protection is excluded only in relation to the employer in respect of whom the default occurs and, anomalously, individuals exercising the statutory right of action described in para 11.19. In addition, failure to comply with either the balloting or notification requirements means that an employment tribunal will be unable to determine a claim for unfair dismissal by any employee who is dismissed for taking part in the unprotected action, even during the first twelve weeks of his or her participation, unless that dismissal is 'selective' within the terms of the legislation.[275] The statutory requirements in this area are

---

271 See, for example, comments on the UK's compliance with Article 6(4) in the XIV-I supervision cycle.

272 *Review of the Employment Relations Act 1999: Government Response*, DTI, 2003, para 3.19.

273 TULRCA 1992, s 235, as amended. Ballots must also be held in respect of industrial action by civil servants and others holding 'any office or employment under the Crown': s 245.

274 Where the action does not constitute a breach of contract, it may not attract liability in tort, but for applications by union members, and those exercising the statutory right to seek injunctive relief, 'industrial action' is defined as 'any strike or other industrial action by persons employed under contracts of employment' (in the extended sense applicable in this context): TULRCA 1992, s 62(6).

275 See para 11.71 *et seq*. The definition of 'protected' industrial action in terms of an act 'which is not actionable in tort' (TULRCA 1992, s 238A(1)) suggests that action is outside the definition if immunity is lost in relation to only one of a number of employers involved in the dispute.

supplemented by a Code of Practice issued by the Secretary of State for Trade and Industry. Its stated purpose is to provide 'practical guidance to trade unions and employers to promote the improvement of industrial relations and good practice in the conduct of trade union industrial action ballots'.[276] As we discuss in para 11.45, it does not forbear from making recommendations which exceed the limits of the legislation. Although, like other Codes, its contents are not strictly speaking legally enforceable as such, non-compliance with its provisions may be influential when a court is deciding whether or not to grant an interim injunction to halt the action.

An exhaustive account of the intricacies of the balloting and notification requirements would occupy many more pages of this work than space permits. We have confined ourselves, therefore, to highlighting the essential elements and their implications. Even engaging in such a process at this level rapidly reveals the legal minefield which unions enter when embarking upon industrial action; despite greater clarity in some areas as a result of amendments made by the Employment Relations Acts of 1999[277] and 2004[278] many points of uncertainty remain. It is also an extremely costly process: at the time of writing ballots must be fully postal,[279] and, since 1 April 1996 there has been no state subsidy for the costs of holding them.[280] In addition, a union is unlikely to navigate the statutory channels without expert legal advice. Moreover, where more than 50 people are balloted the union must appoint (and pay for) an 'independent scrutineer' to supervise the conduct of the ballot; this must be either one of four specialist bodies specified in regulations or another appropriately qualified person (a solicitor or accountant qualified as an auditor, provided that their previous connections with the union do not disqualify them from this appointment).[281] When consideration is given also to the possibility of challenge in the courts, with the attendant costs this brings, it is readily apparent that organising industrial action can be a very expensive undertaking for any union.

Determining the balloting constituency

11.33 The statutory principles governing the determination of the balloting constituency are in themselves extremely complex. They involve consideration of two interlocking questions: which union members should be given a vote, and how should the general scope of the balloting constituency be defined?

---

276 Para 1.
277 ERelA 1999, s 4; Sch 3.
278 ERelA 2004, s 22–25; Schs 1 and 2. These amendments came into force on 6 April 2005, with the exception of the provisions relating to information about employees to be balloted on industrial action and information about employees to be contained in notice of industrial action: ERelA 2004, ss 22 and 25 respectively. At the time of writing the Government intends to bring these sections into force on 1 October 2005.
279 ERelA 2004, s 54 empowers the Secretary of State to make provision by order, in relation to any description of ballot authorised or required by TULRCA 1992, that it may be conducted by other means, subject to specified conditions, but at the time of writing no such orders have been made.
280 The Funds for Trade Union Ballots (Revocation) Regulations 1993, SI 1993/233. When mandatory balloting before industrial action was initially introduced the Certification Officer was empowered to refund certain costs associated with holding secret postal ballots.
281 TULRCA 1992, s 226B; the Trade Union Ballots and Elections (Independent Scrutineer Qualifications) Order 1993, SI 1993/1909, as amended.

(i) Entitlement to vote

11.34 The legislation states that entitlement to vote in the ballot must be accorded equally to all union members whom it is reasonable 'at the time of the ballot' *for the union* to believe will be induced by the union to take part or to continue to take part in the industrial action in question, and to no others.[282] The words 'for the union' were inserted by ERelA 2004 to put beyond doubt that the union does not have to give such an entitlement to members who might take part even though not induced to do so by the union itself.[283] In addition, ERelA 1999 has established by implication that industrial action is not regarded as failing to have the support of a ballot because individuals who take up employment or join the union after the ballot has been held participate in it, (giving statutory force to an earlier Court of Appeal decision[284] to this effect).[285] However, unions still need to ensure that if they call members out in rotation (for example, where there is a need to ensure a minimum level of service) all participants, and no non-participants, are included in the ballot.[286] In *P v NAS/ UWT* the House of Lords held that an omission to send a ballot paper to a person entitled to vote did not of itself amount to a denial of entitlement to vote;[287] otherwise the requirement elsewhere in the legislation that 'so far as is reasonably practicable' every person who is entitled to vote must be sent a ballot paper[288] would be rendered otiose.

    An accidental failure to comply with the requirement relating to entitlement to vote which is on a scale which is unlikely to affect the ballot result can be disregarded.[289] This may be a particularly useful provision where some of those voting are workers under contracts for services, whose whereabouts may not always be known or who may be difficult to contact.

(ii) Geographical scope of the balloting constituency

11.35 In general the constituency for a ballot is a 'workplace'. Where intended participants have separate workplaces, there must be a separate ballot for each, and entitlement to vote must be accorded equally to, and restricted to, union members who have that workplace.[290] A separate majority must be obtained in each workplace and all the other statutory requirements must be satisfied for industrial action therein to be lawful.[291] 'Workplace' in relation to a person

---

282 TULRCA 1992, s 227(1), as amended by ERelA 2004, s 23. 'Time of the ballot' is not defined. In *P v NAS/UWT* [2003] IRLR 307 the House of Lords took the view that, in the light of its interpretation of the balloting provisions as a whole, it did not matter which particular time was meant; the question was whether 'looking at the balloting process as a whole' individuals had been denied entitlement to vote: para 49 (Lord Hoffmann).
283 Cf the approach to this issue in *RMT v Midland Mainline Ltd* [2001] IRLR 813, para 16 (Schiemann LJ).
284 *London Underground Ltd v RMT* [1995] IRLR 636.
285 TULRCA 1992, s 232A. This interpretation was approved by the House of Lords in *P v NAS/UWT* [2003] IRLR 307, para 47 (Lord Hoffmann).
286 In *P v NAS/UWT* [2001] IRLR 532 the Court of Appeal held that workers can take part in industrial action by making it clear that they fully support it and would participate in it if asked, a dictum which assists unions with members in essential services. See para 11.74 below for discussion of this concept in the context of dismissal.
287 [2003] IRLR 307, para 41 (Lord Hoffmann).
288 TULRCA 1992, s 230(2).
289 TULRCA 1992 s 232B, as amended by ERelA 2004, s 24(1), confirming the position reached by the House of Lords in *P v NAS/UWT* [2003] IRLR 307.
290 TULRCA 1992, s 228.
291 TULRCA 1992, s 226(3).

who is employed means '(a) if the person works at or from a single set of premises, those premises, and (b) in any other case, the premises with which the person's employment has the closest connection'.[292] The 'closest connection' means that everyone has a 'place of work'; for delivery drivers, for example, it will be the depot from which they set out, for homeworkers probably the administrative office of the employer with which they deal. 'Premises' are not defined.[293] It seems clear that different sites of the same undertaking would require a separate ballot; for a single site containing a number of buildings (such as a university) it is possible that a separate ballot may be required for each building: this would seem an undesirable consequence, but the matter is not free from doubt.[294] The 'workplace' of a worker who is employed to work in one place but temporarily moved to another is also unclear. However, the requirement to hold a separate ballot for each workplace does not apply if the union reasonably believes that the members accorded entitlement to vote have the same workplace,[295] so even if a court subsequently decides that the union was incorrect in its conclusion the ballot remains valid provided that the union's belief was 'reasonable'.

The restriction of ballots to a 'place of work' was originally designed to ensure that unions could not achieve a majority in favour of industrial action by aggregating votes at 'militant' and 'moderate' workplaces.[296] Votes could be aggregated in specified circumstances, but the statutory language governing these bordered on the incomprehensible. The Labour Government considered that there was little or no evidence that unions had attempted to obtain majorities by illegitimate means,[297] and the Employment Relations Act 1999 introduced a simplified (although still complex) provision which allows aggregate ballots instead of separate workplace ballots in three sets of circumstances, based, loosely speaking, on a common interest in the subject-matter of the dispute; common occupation(s); or a common employer or employers.[298] Aggregation is permitted on the basis of *common interest* where the workplace of each member of the union entitled to vote is the workplace of at least one member who is affected by the dispute. Those 'affected' fall into four categories, depending on the subject matter of the dispute. In relation to terms and conditions of employment, termination of employment, allocation of duties or matters of discipline, for example, 'affected' means members whom the decision directly affects. The fact that only one member at each workplace needs to be affected reflects the recognition that '[w]here one or more workers are directly involved, it will normally be the case that others at the same workplace, sometimes many others, will rightly feel themselves to be indirectly involved by an employer's handling of an issue ... [which] may set a precedent in relation to other workers'.[299] It may not always be clear when workers are 'directly affected'

292 TULRCA 1992, s 228(4). Cf the position prior to ERelA 1999, when the equivalent definition required the premises to be 'occupied' by the employer.
293 Cf the HSWA 1974, s 53.
294 A government spokesman at the time of the original legislation's parliamentary passage considered that for the most part the term 'premises' implied a building: Patrick Nicholls, Parliamentary Under-Secretary of State for Employment, House of Commons, Official Report of Standing Committee F, col 523, 19 January 1988.
295 TULRCA 1992, 228(2)
296 Mr Patrick Nicholls, above, note 294, col 494, 14 January 1988.
297 Lord McIntosh of Haringey, Deputy Chief Whip, HL Debs Vol 604, col 576, 15 July 1999.
298 TULRCA 1992, s 228A(1).
299 Lord McIntosh of Haringey, above, note 297.

however;[300] it is not sufficient that the union reasonably believes them to be so, and in cases where this is unclear unions may prefer to hold separate workplace ballots. Where a dispute relates to facilities for union officials, only those officials who would use the facilities concerned are 'affected members', so precluding aggregation in the case of full-time officials who are not attached to any particular workplace. Aggregation is permitted on the basis that members share a *common occupation or a number of specific kinds of occupation* provided that the union is not selective in according entitlement to vote. Here, aggregation may be across a number of employers with which the union is in dispute. The meaning of 'occupation' is unclear; it could be seen in terms of broad job specification of function, grade, qualifications, or a combination of those factors.[301] In this context it is sufficient that the union has a 'reasonable belief' that members have an occupation of a particular kind. Finally, aggregation is permitted where entitlement to vote is accorded, and limited, to all the members of the union who are employed by *a particular employer, or any number of employers*, with which the union is in dispute. Again it is crucial that the union is not selective in according entitlement to vote.

Of the three tests allowing aggregation, the 'common interest' test gives unions the greatest flexibility in that it does not require the inclusion of *all* workplaces at which the common interest applies. This means that a union may choose to exclude particular workplaces from the aggregated ballot, even if they are part of the same bargaining unit as those which are balloted together. Conversely, it means that if responsibility for industrial relations matters is devolved to regional management or regional centres of operation, those workplaces within the region may be balloted together. The need to ballot on a non-selective basis where a ballot is aggregated on the common occupation and common employer tests may create difficulties for unions which wish to maintain emergency cover during disputes. They may ballot only those whom they reasonably believe will be called upon to participate in the action, which suggests that members involved in maintaining emergency cover should not be balloted. However the union cannot exclude them if it wishes to aggregate the ballot (unless it is aggregated on the basis of a common occupation and all those furnishing emergency cover fall within a distinctive occupation). In this situation a union will probably have to try to ballot all the workers in dispute and then rotate those who provide emergency cover so that all those balloted are called upon at some stage to participate in the industrial action.[302]

The content of the voting paper

11.36   The statute prescribes in detail the content of the voting paper for the ballot. It must state, *inter alia*, the name of the independent scrutineer, where

---

300   Cf the interpretation of 'directly interested' in TULRCA 1992, 238(3)(a) as those whose terms of employment are likely to be immediately and automatically affected by the outcome of the dispute: see para 11.75. This does not cater for forms of trade dispute, such as those motivated by fear of future redundancies, where employees are potentially, but not automatically, at risk.

301   Cf TULRCA 1992, s 174(3)(b), where 'occupational description' is said to include 'grade, level or category of appointment'.

302   The dictum in *P v NAS/UWT* [2001] IRLR 532 as to when workers are regarded as taking part in industrial action, discussed in para 11.34 above, may be useful to essential service unions here. The House of Lords did not refer to this point.

applicable, and must specify, either individually or by description (members of the executive or regional officers for example), who in the event of a vote in favour of industrial action is authorised to call upon members to participate in it.[303] The member must be asked to indicate, by answering 'yes' or 'no', whether he or she is prepared to take part, or to continue to take part, in a strike or industrial action short of a strike, as the case may be. If the union wishes to obtain approval for both these forms of action the questions for each must be asked separately; it cannot be assumed that those who voted for a strike would necessarily approve of industrial action short of a strike.[304] However, it is sufficient for the union to obtain a majority on an individual question, and not the voting process as a whole, in order for that action to be approved.[305] Given the tendency by the courts to scrutinise voting papers closely, unions are best advised not to specify the form of industrial action they may take any more than the statute requires; otherwise they risk unnecessarily restricting the ballot mandate.[306] The need to obtain separate approval may necessitate the union holding more than one ballot during the course of a dispute; because the mandate provided by a ballot lapses after four weeks (unless extended by agreement between the union and the employer) a union cannot rely upon strike action as a 'fall-back' beyond that time if the more limited sanctions fail to produce a satisfactory settlement. Finally, it is mandatory for the voting paper to contain the statement:

> If you take part in a strike or other industrial action, you may be in breach of your contract of employment. However, if you are dismissed for taking part in strike (sic) or other industrial action which is called officially[307] and is otherwise lawful, the dismissal will be unfair if it takes place fewer than twelve weeks after you started taking part in the action, and depending on the circumstances may be unfair if it takes place later.[308]

This statement must not be 'qualified or commented upon by anything else on the voting paper'. Thus, even if industrial action, such as a ban on voluntary overtime,[309] is (probably) not a breach of contract, the union can indicate this only in a separate document, preferably, to be completely safe, to be sent out under separate cover.

---

303 TULRCA 1992, s 229.
304 *Post Office v UCW* [1990] IRLR 143. In the context of the balloting provisions in general, a 'strike' means 'any concerted stoppage of work': TULRCA 1992, s 246. ERelA 1999 amended this section to make clear that an overtime ban and call-out ban constitute industrial action short of a strike (see TULRCA 1992, s 229(2A)), to overrule *Connex South Eastern Ltd v RMT* [1999] IRLR 249. However, this continues to leave unclear the status of other forms of action which may involve stoppages for specific periods, such as a ban on lunch-time cover or on duties that take place only at specified times of day. In *British Telecommunications plc v CMU* [2004] IRLR 58 the court held that it was highly unlikely that the employers would succeed at trial in arguing that a strike was not supported by a ballot because of the outdated information given to members that a vote for strike action would also authorise industrial action short of a strike.
305 *West Midlands Travel Ltd v TGWU* [1994] IRLR 578.
306 *Blue Circle v TGWU* (7 July 1989, Alliott J, unreported) (support requested for one 24-hour strike per week did not permit action which went beyond that).
307 Note than this term is not used elsewhere in the legislation: see para 11.71 *et seq.*
308 TULRCA 1992, s 229(4). ERelA 2004, s 57(1), Sch 1, para 13 substituted 'twelve' for 'eight' with effect from 6 April 2005.
309 See para 11.65 below.

Despite the highly prescriptive nature of these provisions judicial creativity has still crept into this area. In *London Underground Ltd v NUR*[310] Simon Brown J suggested that the legislation would not be satisfied where the ballot posed a question which, either wholly or in part, asked whether members were prepared to participate in a strike by reference to matters which were not existing matters in dispute. In that case the ballot asked: '[d]o you agree to support the executive committee in their fight to maintain the current agreement on seniority and to resist the imposition of organisational changes [unsatisfactory attendance procedures and competitive tendering] by taking strike action?' The employers argued that, at the time of the ballot, there was no 'genuine, definite, substantial dispute' between the parties on any of the issues other than seniority, and the court considered that there were 'powerful arguments' to support this contention.[311] This approach has been criticised as confusing 'the conditions for a valid ballot with the need for a union to prove that it was acting in contemplation or furtherance of a trade dispute ... a separate prerequisite for the protection of the immunities.[312] Nevertheless, the same approach was adopted by the Court of Appeal in *University College London Hospital NHS Trust v UNISON*.[313] Here the ballot asked members whether they were prepared to take strike action, *inter alia*, because the employer had failed to guarantee that staff who were employed by a private sector consortium in the future (and who had never been employed by the Trust) would receive the same terms and conditions of employment as those whom the Trust continued to employ. Having held that this demand could not constitute the subject-matter of a 'trade dispute', the court went on to hold that it was therefore 'an impermissible subject for the ballot' and, although it was only one of the issues identified on the ballot paper, nullified the ballot which had taken place.[314] A first instance court has held that there is no requirement for a union to define or describe every issue with which a dispute is concerned in the information supplied to members taking part in the ballot; it is sufficient that there was evidence to identify the strike which had been approved in the ballot.[315] Where there are a number of different issues, not all of which fall squarely within the 'trade dispute' definition, a union would be well advised not to detail those over which there is uncertainty. However, where there is some contention as to whether the central issue constitutes a 'trade dispute', spelling it out on the ballot paper in appropriately-drafted terms may help to substantiate the union's case.[316] In *London Borough of Wandsworth v NAS/UWT*,[317] where it was argued for the employers that the dispute in question was about the content of the work which the national curriculum required schoolteachers to undertake, the Court of Appeal attached 'considerable importance'[318] to the wording on the ballot paper which asked teachers whether they were willing to take action '[i]n order to protest against the excessive workload and unreasonable imposition made upon teachers, as a consequence of national curriculum assessment and testing ...'.[319]

---

310 [1989] IRLR 341.
311 [1989] IRLR 341, 342.
312 Simpson, 1989: p 235.
313 [1999] IRLR 31.
314 [1999] IRLR 31, 35 (Lord Woolf MR).
315 *Associated British Ports v TGWU* [1989] IRLR 291.
316 *Wandsworth London Borough Council v NAS/UWT* [1993] IRLR 344.
317 [1993] IRLR 344.
318 [1993] IRLR 344, 350.
319 [1993] IRLR 344, 348.

The conduct of the ballot

11.37 At the time of writing industrial action ballots must be conducted entirely by 'post',[320] which is defined in terms which exclude delivery by hand, internal mail or private courier.[321] 'So far as is reasonably practicable' every person who is entitled to vote in the ballot must have a voting paper sent to his or her home address[322] and be given a convenient opportunity to vote by post.[323] Members must be entitled to vote at no direct cost to themselves. The Code of Practice interprets this to mean that pre-paid reply envelopes should be included with the voting paper.[324] Ballots must be conducted so as to ensure that, so far as reasonably practicable, voting is in secret and there must be no interference from, or constraint imposed by, the union or any of its members, officials or employees.[325] However, in *Newham London Borough Council v NALGO*[326] the Court of Appeal affirmed that the union was 'perfectly entitled to be partisan'[327] and campaign for a 'yes' vote; when such campaigning will cross the line into unlawful interference is not readily apparent.[328] It is notable that no mention is made of interference by employers and, indeed, the requirement to give a pre-ballot notice to employers, which we describe in para 11.39, is designed, *inter alia,* to facilitate the case against industrial action being put to workers. Votes must be fairly and accurately counted although any inaccuracy which is accidental and on a scale which could not affect the result of the ballot may be disregarded.[329] As soon as reasonably practicable the union must take steps to ensure that voters are informed of the number of votes cast and the result of the ballot.[330] In addition the independent scrutineer engaged to supervise the conduct of the ballot must issue a report within four weeks of the ballot, stating, *inter alia*, whether he or she is satisfied that the security arrangements for handling voting papers and counting votes were such as to minimise the risk of unfairness or malpractice as well as commenting more broadly on whether any of the statutory requirements were contravened.[331] The union has a duty to comply

---

320 TULRCA 1992, s 230(2). ERelA 2004, s 54 empowers the Secretary of State to make provision by order, in relation to any description of ballot authorised or required by TULRCA 1992, that it may be conducted by other means, subject to specified conditions, but at the time of writing no such orders have been made.

321 TULRCA 1992, s 298.

322 Or any other address he or she has requested the union in writing to treat as his or her postal address: s 230(2)(a). In *RMT v Midland Mainline Ltd* [2001] IRLR 813, the Court of Appeal considered that where a ballot paper was sent to an address from which a member had moved without informing the union, the union would probably have done all that was reasonably practicable if it had a system of reminding members of the need to notify a change of address and the member had not done this.

323 See *P v NAS/UWT* [2003] IRLR 307. Note also TULRCA 1992, s 232B.

324 Para 26. See also *Paul v NALGO* [1987] IRLR 43.

325 TULRCA 1992, s 230(1)(a).

326 [1993] IRLR 83.

327 [1993] IRLR 83, 86.

328 In relation to union elections the Certification Officer has held that this excludes 'such conduct as would intimidate or put a member in fear of voting, or amount to physical interference': *Rey v Film Artistes' Association* (11 April 1986, unreported).

329 TULRCA 1992, s 230(4).

330 TULRCA 1992, s 231.

331 TULRCA 1992, ss 226B(1); 231B. Given that the ballot ceases to be effective at the end of a period of four weeks beginning with the date of the ballot (unless otherwise agreed between the union and employer) the industrial action may begin before the scrutineer's report has been received. To that extent the advice in the Code of Practice that unions may wish to delay any call until receiving the scrutineer's report (para 49) seems unrealistic.

with all reasonable requests by the scrutineer connected with the performance of his or her functions;[332] this probably entails giving him or her access to look at records, obtain relevant information, and visit premises as appropriate. The scrutineer's report must be made available on request to any person entitled to vote in the ballot and the employer of any such person, either free or on payment of a reasonable fee. While a critical report will not of itself invalidate the ballot it may serve to draw the attention of employers and union members to possible grounds for challenging it.

Information and notice to employers

11.38   The information that unions must give to employers falls into three broad categories: information to be provided before the ballot; the result of the ballot; and information prior to the commencement of industrial action. ERelA 2004 contains significant amendments regarding the information required to be given about the employees to be balloted and the employees who will take part in the industrial action.[333] At the time of writing the Government intends to bring these provisions into force on 1 October 2005. In the account which follows, we outline the legislation in force at the time of writing before explaining the significance of the amendments.

(i) Information to be provided before the ballot

11.39   Under the legislation in force at the time of writing, the union must take such steps as are 'reasonably necessary' to ensure that, not later than the seventh day before the opening day of the ballot,[334] written notice of intent to hold it is received by all the employers of those to be balloted, and not later than the third day before the opening day of the ballot, a sample of the form of voting paper to be sent to its own employees is received.[335] This will enable the employer to learn whether a strike and/or industrial action short of a strike is contemplated. The pre-ballot notice must contain specified information, including 'such information in the union's possession as would help the employer to make plans and bring information to the attention of those of his employees' who it is reasonable for the union to believe would be entitled to vote in the ballot.[336] If the union possesses information as to the number, category

---

332   TULRCA 1992, s 226B(4).

333   See ERelA 2004, ss 22 and 25. At the time of writing the Government is consulting on the text of a revised Code of Practice on Industrial Action Ballots and Notice to Employers, designed to reflect these amendments: see DTI, *Industrial Action Ballots and Notice to Employers: Revised Code of Practice: Consultation Document* 11 March 2005.

334   The first day when a voting paper is sent to any person entitled to vote: TULRCA 1992, s 226A(4).

335   TULRCA 1992, s 226A.

336   Prior to the amendments made to this provision by ERelA 1999, a union was required to describe, so that the employer could 'readily ascertain them', the employees covered by the ballot, a requirement that the Court of Appeal held, on the facts, could be satisfied only if the union named individual staff: *Blackpool and Fylde College v NATFHE* [1994] IRLR 227. The Committee of Independent Experts (now the European Committee of Social Rights) that supervises the ESC considered that this was a threat to the right to organise as guaranteed by Art 5: Conclusions XIII-3, 109; Conclusions XIV-I. However, an application alleging that the requirement to reveal names violated Art 11 of the ECHR was ruled inadmissible by the European Commission of Human Rights: *NATFHE v UK* Application No 28910/95.

or workplace of the employees concerned, the notice is required to contain that information (at least). It is expressly stated that it cannot be a ground of non-compliance that the notice does not name any employees. However, the requirement to provide information that would help the employers to 'make plans' is a vague one which could arguably, in some circumstances, necessitate the provision of information that is so specific that it is tantamount to naming individuals.

ERelA 2004 contains a more precise definition of the information that the union must provide.[337] As noted in para 11.38 above, at the time of writing the Government intends to bring this provision into force on 1 October 2005. First, it requires the notice to list the categories of employee to which the employees concerned belong and the workplaces at which they work, and to state the total number of employees concerned; the number in each category listed; and the number who work at each workplace listed.[338] 'Workplace' has the same definition as in the context of the balloting constituency,[339] and the comments we made in para 11.35 apply equally in this context. Second, the union must supply an explanation of how those figures were arrived at.[340] If some or all of the employees concerned are employees in relation to whom the employer operates the 'check-off', the union may, alternatively, supply other information that will enable the employer readily to deduce the total number of employees concerned; the categories to which they belong and the number in each category; and the workplaces at which they work and the number who work at each.[341] In either case the lists and figures, or information, supplied must be as accurate as is reasonably practicable in the light of the information in the possession of the union at the time when it complies with the obligation to ensure it is received by the employer(s) concerned.[342] Information is 'in the possession of the union' for these purposes if it is held, for union purposes, in a document (whether in electronic or any other form) and 'in the possession or under the control of an officer or employee of the union'.[343] This means that information held only by branch officials or other lay representatives of the union is not in the union's possession for this purpose.[344] It is, again, expressly provided that nothing requires a union to supply an employer with the names of the employees concerned.[345] Whether these amended provisions will afford employees greater protection than their predecessor, however, may turn on how the term 'category' of employee is interpreted by the courts. In *Westminster City Council v Unison* the Court of Appeal rejected the employer's argument that it was insufficient for the union to refer to the 45 workers in the council's 'advice and assessment office' who paid their subscriptions by check-off; there was no requirement to distinguish between managers and other staff or to identify the various sub-units of the unit in

---

337 ERelA 2004, s 22, amending TULRCA 1992, s 226A.
338 TULRCA 1992, s 226A(2(c),(2A),(2B).
339 TULRCA 1992, s 226A(2I).
340 TULRCA 1992, s 226A(2)(c)(i).
341 TULRCA 1992, s 226A(2)(c)(ii).
342 TULRCA 1992, s 226A(2D).
343 TULRCA 1992, s 226A(2E). 'Officer' is defined in s 119 as including (a) any member of the governing body of the union, and (b) any trustee of any fund applicable for the purposes of the union.
344 Explanatory Notes to the ERelA 2004, para 149. Cf the position before the amendment, as applied in *RMT v London Underground Ltd* [2001] IRLR 228 and *Willerby Holiday Homes Ltd v UCATT* [2003] EWHC 2608 (QB).
345 TULRCA 1992, s 226A(2G).

question.[346] However even this broad-brush approach may not offer employees protection against identification by implication in small workplaces or where there are only a small number of individuals in a particular category. There is no specific protection against dismissal or other forms of detriment for taking part in an industrial action ballot (in contrast, for example, to ballots relating to recognition or derecognition).[347] It is arguable that were an employer to take measures, or, possibly, threaten them, this would infringe the protection against taking part in union activities at an appropriate time,[348] but it would be preferable for protection to be expressly accorded.

(ii) The result of the ballot

11.40   After the ballot, the union must take reasonable steps to ensure that every employer of persons entitled to vote in the ballot is informed of the result of the ballot.[349]

(iii) Information prior to the commencement of industrial action

11.41   Under the legislation in force at the time of writing, the union must ensure that, before it induces any person to take part in industrial action, his or her employer receives a notice which, *inter alia*, gives such information as would enable the employer to make plans and bring information to the attention of those of its employees whom the union intends to induce to take part in the industrial action (the 'affected employees'), and states whether the action is intended to be continuous or 'discontinuous'.[350] The notice must be received by the employer at least seven days before the action will begin (but this period cannot start before relevant employers have been informed about the ballot result). Industrial action is 'discontinuous' where the union intends it to take place only on some days where there is an opportunity to take it (for example, Mondays and Fridays); otherwise it is continuous. For continuous action the notice must specify when any of the affected employees will begin to take part in it; for discontinuous, the intended dates for any of the affected employees to take part. When continuous industrial action is called off or suspended, a fresh notice must be given if industrial action (whether continuous or discontinuous) is resumed at a later date. This is subject to two exceptions. The first is where the action is called off or suspended pursuant to a court order or undertaking to the court; this could occur if action were the subject of an interim injunction at first instance which was then lifted on appeal. The second (an exception introduced by ERelA 1999) is where the union agrees with the employer, prior to the action being suspended, that suspension will occur with effect from a specified date and that the action may be resumed from another specified date; this may encourage unions to allow a breathing space for negotiations. In the case of discontinuous industrial action there is no obligation for the union to take the action on any of the days it has previously notified, and the tactic of failing to take action on notified days could be highly

---

346 [2001] IRLR 524, paras 57, 61. See also Buxton LJ at para 78: 'Category' is 'a very broad word and not to be either exclusively or narrowly defined. It means no more than a reference to the general type of workers'.

347 See para 9.21.

348 See para 8.8 *et seq* and 8.13 *et seq*.

349 TULRCA 1992, s 231A. It would seem to be the case that where separate workplace ballots are required, results must be notified for each ballot; otherwise, employers should receive notification of the overall result.

350 TULRCA 1992, s 234A.

effective (although an employer could probably refuse to pay for the days unexpectedly worked, or prevent workers from working, on the basis of an anticipatory breach of contract).[351]

As in the case of pre-ballot notices, ERelA 2004 replaces the requirement to give such information as would help the employer to make plans, etc, with an obligation to give information about the number and categories of employees, framed in similar terms, *mutatis mutandis*, to those discussed in para 11.39 above.[352] At the time of writing the Government intends to bring this provision into force on 1 October 2005. The comments that we made in para 11.39 about the continued risk that employees in some workplaces may be identified under these provisions apply equally in this context. There is a strong case for such individuals to be accorded specific protection against being put under pressure by their employers not to participate in the industrial action; although there is protection against dismissal in specified circumstances for those who take part in industrial action,[353] there is no protection for those threatened with a detriment were they to do so.[354]

11.42 As we indicated in para 11.32, in the event of a failure to comply with the obligations to give pre-ballot information, notify a relevant employer of the ballot result, or give notice before industrial action starts, the protection of the immunities is lost only in relation to the employer in respect of whom the default occurs and for the purposes of the statutory right of action. In the case of failure to provide the requisite pre-ballot information it is unclear at what stage a remedy could be sought. The general principles governing injunctions would suggest that it would be inappropriate to grant an injunction until, at the earliest, it is known that there is a majority in favour of industrial action on the basis that an unlawful act is not, before then, sufficiently likely.[355] Experience suggests, however, that the courts may be willing to grant a remedy at an earlier stage; during a seafarers' dispute in 1988 employers obtained an injunction restraining the union from conducting a ballot of the workforce (a lawful activity) on the basis that the proposed action would be unlawful secondary action.[356] While it may be argued that, if action is to be injuncted, unions would benefit from saving the costs involved in holding a ballot for action which never takes place, a majority in a ballot can be an important negotiating tactic for a union;[357] indeed, it was suggested early in the 1990s that balloting had been incorporated into bargaining processes by management and unions and that their results had often 'come to be seen as a useful indicator of the strength of employee feeling which clarifies positions, rather than one which commits parties to a definite course of action'.[358] Since then this has become an expensive method of ascertaining views, given that ballots must now be fully postal and supervised by an independent scrutineer, with no provision for recovery of costs. Despite

---

351 See further para 11.67 *et seq.*
352 ERelA 2004, s 25, amending TULRCA 1992, s 234A.
353 See further para 11.71 *et seq.*
354 See para 8.8 and 8.13.
355 See Spry, 2001: pp 377–382 and 468–470 on the principles governing injunctions formerly known as *quia timet* injunctions. As Auerbach (1988: p 229) points out, at the most there can only be a 'conditional' inducement of industrial action at the point when the ballot is proposed. For the statutory right of action an individual must claim that the unlawful act was, at the very least, 'likely': TULRCA 1992, s 235A(1).
356 Auerbach, 1988.
357 See Martin *et al*, 1991; Elgar and Simpson, 1992 and 1996; Undy *et al*, 1996: ch 6.
358 ACAS Annual Report 1993: p 16.

this, nearly a thousand ballots were conducted by TUC-affiliated unions in 1999.[359] The Code of Practice states that unions should hold a ballot only if it is contemplating the organisation of industrial action.[360] However, it may be seen as objectionable that an organisation should be prevented from seeking the views of its members on any issue it chooses, regardless of whether it is then able to put those views fully into practice.

Call by a specified person

11.43   Industrial action may be validly called only by a person specified (either individually or by description) on the voting paper.[361] Curiously, such a person need not be authorised under the union rules to call industrial action; it is sufficient that he or she is within the range of persons for whose actions the union is responsible in the absence of any valid repudiation (see para 11.21). In *Tanks and Drums Ltd v TGWU*[362] the Court of Appeal allowed some flexibility in holding that it was permissible for a specified person to authorise a subordinate union official to call a strike should further negotiations with the employer prove unsuccessful, although it emphasised that a very close link in time between the strike and the event precipitating the final action, such as an unsuccessful meeting, would be required, such closeness to be a question of fact and degree. The court also recognised in that case that it would be impractical to leave matters so that no discretion could be exercised by local officials as to how a call for industrial action was to be put into operation.

It is essential to the lawfulness of industrial action approved in a ballot that there should have been no call by the union to take part in it (or any authorisation or endorsement of such action) before the date of the ballot. The meaning of 'call' here is obscure, but appears to refer to a specific event rather than a prevailing attitude towards prospective action; in *Newham London Borough Council v NALGO*[363] the Court of Appeal affirmed that the union was not required to take a neutral stance before that time on whether industrial action should be taken; rather, it was 'perfectly entitled to be partisan'.[364] In the event that a 'call' for action is made before the date of the ballot the union will either need to repudiate it (where this is possible) or accept liability. The implications of a non-specified person whose actions are attributable to the union making a call depend upon the timing. A call made before the date of the ballot cannot be endorsed; the union will then have to choose between repudiation (where this is possible) or accepting liability. If a non-specified person makes a call after the date of the ballot it is possible that the union will not be liable provided that a specified person endorses it, although this is not free from doubt, nor is it clear whether the union can repudiate the unauthorised call (where it is open to it to do so) and still rely on the ballot to make a valid call thereafter, although the Code of Practice suggests that it can.[365] If an unauthorised call is made after a call by a specified person, the unauthorised call will be irrelevant.

---

359   Nicholls and Bradley, 2000: p 5 It should be noted that more than 400 of these were held by one union, the Communication Workers Union, in relation to disputes over call centres.
360   Para 6.
361   TULRCA 1992, s 233.
362   [1991] IRLR 372.
363   [1993] IRLR 383.
364   [1993] IRLR 83, 86 (Woolf LJ).
365   See footnote 10 in the Code.

The expiry date on the ballot mandate

11.44 A ballot in favour of industrial action ceases to be effective at the end of a period of four weeks beginning with the date of the ballot or a period 'of such longer duration not exceeding eight weeks as is agreed between the union and the members' employer'.[366] The provision for extension, introduced by ERelAct 1999, means that a union is not obliged to commence industrial action within the four-week period where, for example, the parties consider that a settlement could be achieved by negotiation. It is possible that industrial action may start and then be suspended for further negotiations to take place, only to be followed by the re-imposition of industrial action if these negotiations are not successful. As we indicated in para 11.41, the legislation now provides that where this is done by agreement between the parties no fresh notice need be issued in respect of resumed industrial action. However there is also the additional question whether or not a further ballot is required for the second period of industrial action. This depends upon whether it can be viewed as sufficiently connected with the first to be regarded as a continuation of it, or whether the first was deemed to have terminated, in which case a fresh ballot will be required. In *Monsanto plc v TGWU*[367] union members voted in favour of industrial action 'in pursuit of a settlement of the dispute with Monsanto Ltd over the employment of Temporary Labour'. The company responded with counter-sanctions, including the suspension of sick pay, guaranteed week and early retirement schemes. The union suspended the industrial action pending further negotiations but re-imposed it two weeks later after negotiations broke down over these counter-sanctions. The Court of Appeal held that there was no need for a further ballot; the industrial action had not been discontinued but merely suspended temporarily for the purposes of negotiation with the intention that it would be resumed should negotiations fail. The court also rejected the employer's argument that the re-imposed action fell outside the terms of the ballot; these terms were sufficiently wide to encompass any matters within the scope of settlement of the original dispute.

This case was distinguished in *Post Office v UCW*.[368] In September 1988 postal officers and assistants voted in favour of industrial action in support of the union's opposition to the Post Office's plans to close up to 750 post offices, and between October and December there was a series of selective 24-hour strikes, culminating in a national one-day strike on 12 December. Between January and April 1989 there was no industrial action, although the union mounted a public relations campaign in opposition to the Post Office's policy, but in May the union's Assistant General Secretary told the annual conference that industrial action would continue. There were two brief local strikes in the autumn and in January 1990 the union gave instructions for a 24-hour strike in London and the South-East. The Post Office successfully applied for an interim injunction to halt this strike. The ground for the decision was that the form of question on the ballot paper did not meet the statutory requirements (having been presented in the rolled-up form 'are you willing to take industrial action

---

366 TULRCA 1992, s 234. The period of four weeks ends at the stroke of midnight on the last day of the fourth week, so where a ballot ceased to be effective on 12 June at the stroke of midnight, action called for 13 June was outside the period of the ballot mandate: *RJB Mining (UK) Ltd v NUM* [1995] IRLR 556.
367 [1986] IRLR 406.
368 [1990] IRLR 143.

up to and including strike action?'). However the Court of Appeal also held that the campaign of industrial action authorised by the ballot had terminated with the national strike in December 1988 and industrial action subsequent to that required the support of a fresh ballot. According to Lord Donaldson MR, it was implicit that industrial action, once begun, should continue without 'substantial interruption' if reliance were to continue to be placed upon the verdict of the initial ballot. This was a question of fact and degree but 'the question which the Court has to ask itself is whether the average reasonable trade union member, looking at the matter at or shortly after any interruption in the industrial action, would say to himself "the industrial action has now come to an end" even if he might also say "the union may want to call us out again if the dispute continues"'.[369]

For unions these cases contain two major lessons. First, where industrial action is suspended, they should make clear to their members that this suspension is contingent upon a successful outcome to negotiations, and they should not delay its resumption for an extended period.[370] Second, as *Monsanto* demonstrates, it is important to ensure that the terms of the questions on the ballot paper are sufficiently wide to cover any matters which might arise out of the dispute at issue (although bearing in mind the dangers of going beyond the central matter in dispute).

Originally the legislation made no provision for the situation where industrial action was halted temporarily by legal proceedings and during a docks dispute in 1989 the ballot mandate expired by the time that an interim injunction granted by the Court of Appeal was discharged by the House of Lords. The unfairness of this situation was appreciated by the Conservative Government. The legislation was amended to provide that where for any part of the four-week period the calling of industrial action was prohibited by a court order or by an undertaking to the court which subsequently ceases to apply, the union may apply to the court for an order that the period during which the prohibition took effect should not count towards the four-week limit, although no ballot may be regarded as effective more than twelve weeks after it took place.[371] Granting this extension is entirely at the discretion of the court, from which there is no appeal, but the extension must not be granted if the court considers that the ballot result no longer represents the views of the members concerned or that an event is likely to occur as a result of which those members would vote against industrial action were another ballot to be held. The speculative nature of this latter requirement, in particular, may present difficulties for a union, especially as one may argue that, given that most disputes end in compromise at some stage, such an 'event' will almost inevitably occur. Where an extension is refused a union will have to incur all the trouble and expense of a fresh ballot, even though its actions may have been fully vindicated in the legal proceedings which temporarily halted the industrial action.

369 [1990[IRLR 143, 147; see also Butler-Sloss LJ at 147–148. It is unclear why the test should depend on the views of a trade union member (or, indeed, an employer) rather than a court's objective assessment of the facts before it.

370 See also *London Underground Ltd v RMT* (22 December 1998, unreported, QBD). In the case of continuous industrial action, due regard must also be paid to the provisions governing notice, discussed in para 11.41.

371 TULRCA 1992, s 234. The period between the making of an application and its determination does not count towards the four-week period.

The Code of Practice on Industrial Action Ballots and Notice to Employers

11.45 As we indicated in para 11.32, the Code of Practice, now in its fourth version, includes provisions which exceed the requirements of the legislation.[372] Particularly significant is the statement that a ballot should not take place until any agreed procedures, whether formal or otherwise, which might lead to a resolution of the dispute without the need for industrial action have been completed and consideration has been given to resolving the dispute by other means, including seeking assistance from ACAS.[373] This seems somewhat anomalous in the light of the fact that collective agreements are not, in general, legally enforceable and there is no equivalent exhortation where employers break agreements. There could also be scope for argument as to whether procedures have been exhausted in any given case. Another notable provision is that unions should consider delaying any call for industrial action following a ballot until the scrutineer's report has been received, which could create considerable difficulties given the tight time limits which apply.[374] Although neither these nor other provisions of the Code are directly enforceable it is conceivable that non-observance of them, particularly the first, may be influential when a court is deciding whether to grant an interim injunction to halt the action.

CIVIL LAW REMEDIES

11.46 There are two primary remedies which those affected by unlawful industrial action may seek in the courts: an injunction and damages. As we discussed in para 11.16, claims in restitution for 'economic duress' are also possible, but as these claims can be brought only in limited circumstances we do not discuss them further here.

Damages

11.47 Damages are awarded according to the general principles applicable to the law of tort, aiming to put the claimant in the position he or she would have been in had the tort not been committed.[375] It is conceivable that exemplary or aggravated, as well as compensatory, damages may be awarded if the court considers that the defendant's conduct warrants this,[376] although the circumstances when exemplary (punitive) damages may be awarded have been restricted by the courts.[377] As usual it is necessary to prove that the defendant's act caused the

---

372 This was also a feature of earlier Codes: see Simpson, 1995. On the 2000 Code, see Simpson, 2001. At the time of writing the Government is consulting on the text of a revised Code, incorporating guidance on ERelA 2004, ss 22 and 25, which it intends to bring into force on 1 October 2005: DTI, *Industrial Action Ballots and Notice to Employers: Revised Code of Practice: Consultation Document*, 11 March 2005. The Consultation Document proposes the retention of the provisions referred to in this paragraph.
373 Para 6.
374 Para 49.
375 See generally McGregor, 2003, as updated.
376 See *Messenger Newspapers Group Ltd v NGA* [1984] IRLR 397.
377 See *Kuddus v Chief Constable of Leicestershire Constabulary* [2001] 3 All ER 193.

damage in question, a requirement which may create difficulties where a defendant has committed various torts, all of which contributed to the claimant's loss but some of which are protected by the statutory immunities.[378] There have been no reported cases on this point as yet in English law, but the Northern Ireland Court of Appeal has held that damages must be limited to loss attributable to the non-protected torts.[379]

Before 1982 it was rare for employers to sue for damages, one reason doubtless being that such claims could be brought only against union officers and not against trade unions. This immunity was removed in 1982, although the implications for unions of unlimited liability were partially recognised in that the amount of damages which could be awarded in any proceedings in tort was subject to statutory maxima (with specified exceptions not relevant in the industrial action context).[380] The limit depends upon the size of the union: there is a maximum of £10,000 if the union has fewer than 5,000 members; £50,000 if it has between 5,000 and 24,999; £125,000 if it has between 25,000 and 99,999; and £250,000 if it has 100,000 or more.[381] However, this protection is less extensive than it may appear; it does not include any interest which may be awarded on the damages, which may be substantial,[382] and it applies only in respect of a single set of proceedings, so that if there are multiple claimants suing in relation to a single act, each may claim to the limit, although if a single claimant issued several claim forms for different torts, or in respect of different acts, the union could ask for the proceedings to be consolidated. Moreover, the limits do not apply to actions outside the law of tort, such as restitution, nor to fines for contempt of court or to legal costs which unions may be required to pay.

The threat to sue for damages is a powerful weapon in the armoury of employers although it carries the disadvantage that the hearing is likely to take place long after the dispute is settled and proceedings are unlikely to promote good industrial relations.

Interim injunctions: introduction

11.48   Given the disadvantages of a damages claim referred to above, the remedy which is much more commonly sought in practice is an interim injunction to prevent the action starting or continuing, issued under the discretionary power of the High Court to make such orders pending the full trial of an action. Injunctions may order the defendant to desist from specified conduct, such as restraining a union from inducing breach of contract, or to take positive steps to undo a wrong, for example to withdraw instructions to take industrial action. It is also possible to grant an injunction (formerly known as a *quia timet* injunction) to prevent an apprehended legal wrong where an applicant can provide adequate

---

378 Wedderburn, 1986: p 682.
379 *Norbrook Laboratories Ltd v King* [1984] IRLR 200.
380 Damages for personal injury resulting from negligence, nuisance or breach of duty, or a breach of duty in connection with the ownership, occupation, possession, control or use of property or proceedings relating to product liability: TULRCA 1992, s 22(1).
381 TULRCA 1992, s 22(2). The Secretary of State may vary these sums by order: ss 22(3), (4). As Wedderburn points out (1986: p 682) the relevant time for counting numbers is not specified: is it the date of the commission of the tort, the date of the claim form or the date of judgment?
382 See *Boxfoldia Ltd v NGA* [1988] IRLR 383 (£90,000 interest awarded).

evidence of the fear that a wrong is likely otherwise to be committed.[383] The courts have granted such an injunction to prevent a respondent from inducing the breach of a future contract,[384] and in 1988 such an order was even granted against the National Union of Seamen to prevent it from conducting a (lawful) ballot on the basis that the proposed industrial action would be unlawful.[385] However, injunctions cannot be used to force individual employees to return to work; by statute, no court may compel an employee to work or attend at any place to work by way of an injunction restraining a breach or threatened breach of a contract of employment.[386]

The normal purpose of an interim injunction is to preserve the status quo pending the full trial of an action. This may be necessary where, for example, the subject-matter may be destroyed without such an order. In the context of industrial action, however, the granting of an interim injunction effectively decides the matter. This makes the grounds upon which such injunctions may be granted particularly crucial; indeed, it may be said that the very freedom to take industrial action hinges upon this issue. For this reason we examine both the grounds and the procedure in some detail below.

Interim injunctions: the courts' approach

11.49 The granting of an interim injunction, which is an equitable remedy, is always at the discretion of the court.[387] In general, however, as a first step the court must be satisfied that there is a '*serious question to be tried*', a test which, in the House of Lords decision in *American Cyanamid Co v Ethicon Ltd*,[388] replaced the more stringent pre-existing requirement to show a *prima facie* case. To demonstrate a 'serious issue' may not be a difficult test to satisfy in industrial action cases, where the facts may be complex and disputed and the applicant may allege the commission of several torts, the boundaries and, indeed, the very existence of which may be debatable. If an applicant suggests a novel head of liability, the courts may be reluctant to dismiss the suggestion out of hand. In general the evidence before the court will be in written form – although there is power to cross-examine the deponent of a witness statement this is rarely done at interim stage [389] – and where the evidence before the court is

---

383 See Spry, 2001: pp 377–382, 468–470 for the principles governing such injunctions.

384 *JT Stratford & Son Ltd v Lindley* [1965] AC 269, 339 (Lord Upjohn); *Union Traffic Ltd v TGWU* [1989] IRLR 127. As Auerbach argues (1989: p 170), given that it remains lawful to persuade a person not to make a contract (*Midland Cold Storage Ltd v Steer* [1972] Ch 630) and if in fact the applicant has no long-term contract, this comes 'perilously close' to protecting the applicant's expectations, and not merely rights.

385 See Auerbach, 1988: p 229.

386 TULRCA 1992, s 236.

387 For the statutory right of action an order to halt industrial action is the only form of relief available and, where a claim is well-founded, the statute states that the court 'shall' grant an order: TULRCA 1992, s 235A. However, it also indicates that interim relief may be granted for this purpose and we would argue that at the interim stage the decision as to whether to grant a remedy remains one for the discretion of the court.

388 [1975] 1 All ER 504. Although some decisions in other contexts have shown a willingness to recognise the importance of a test of merits (*Lansing Linde Ltd v Kerr* [1991] 1 All ER 418; *Cambridge Nutrition Ltd v BBC* [1990] 3 All ER 523) this approach has yet to appear in the context of industrial action.

389 For a rare example see the cross-examination of Ron Todd, General Secretary of the TGWU, and other TGWU officials in *Associated British Ports v TGWU* [1989] IRLR 291.

insufficient to decide a disputed matter the court is likely to conclude that there is a 'serious question'. In *Solihull Metropolitan Borough v NUT* there was a direct conflict of evidence as to whether teachers were contractually obliged to perform a particular task. The court affirmed that this was 'not the sort of conflict one can resolve on motion, on affidavit [written] evidence, without cross-examination, and before discovery ...'.[390] On this basis it could not be said that there was no serious question to be tried.

Once a claimant has crossed this preliminary hurdle the court decides whether or not to grant an injunction according to the '*balance of convenience*' (although, as we indicate below, the statutory immunities, where applicable, will also need to be considered). This test requires the court to consider whether damages would be an adequate remedy for either side if its position were vindicated at the trial; if so, an injunction should be refused. Damages will rarely be viewed as adequate if the respondent is unable or unlikely to pay them and may not be sufficient if the alleged wrong is regarded by the court as irreparable, incapable of pecuniary compensation or if damages would be very difficult to assess.[391] If damages are not regarded as a sufficient remedy, the court will then consider whether more harm will be done by granting or refusing the injunction. As Lord Diplock expressed the position in *American Cyanamid*:[392]

> The object of the ... [interim] ... injunction is to protect the ... [applicant] ... against injury by violation of his right for which he could not be adequately compensated in damages recoverable in the action if the uncertainty were resolved in his favour at the trial; but the ... [applicant's] ... need for such protection must be weighed against the corresponding need of the ... [respondent] ... to be protected against injury resulting from his having been prevented from exercising his own legal rights for which he could not be adequately compensated under the ... [applicant's] ... undertaking in damages if the uncertainty were resolved in the ... [respondent's] ... favour at the trial. The court must weigh one need against another ...[393]

In *American Cyanamid* the House of Lords warned against attempts to specify exhaustively the matters which the courts should take into account in assessing the 'balance of convenience'. With that warning in mind, some factors can be isolated which have proved influential in the industrial action context. One consistently weighty factor is the extent of the loss which the employer would suffer if the action went ahead. This was a particularly powerful argument before 1982, when trade unions could not themselves be sued in tort, leaving employers with a remedy only against individual dispute organisers who were unlikely to have the means to pay substantial damages and costs. In 1984 the House of Lords stated that the repeal of this immunity by EA 1982 meant that there was no reason for judges to assume that a case would never come to trial where the respondent was the union itself.[394] In practice, however, this change does not seem to have made judges less willing to grant interim injunctions, although it has made employers more willing to apply for them.[395] Moreover,

---

390 [1985] IRLR 211, 214.
391 *Merchant Adventurers Ltd v Grew and Co Ltd* [1972] Ch 242.
392 [1975] 1 All ER 504.
393 [1975] 1 All ER 504, 509.
394 *Dimbleby & Sons Ltd v NUJ* [1984] IRLR 161.
395 For an early survey see Evans, 1987; for later statistics see Gall and McKay, 1996; *Labour Research* October 1998: pp 15–16; TUC, *Focus on Balloting and Industrial Action: Trade Union Trends Survey*, 2001.

the statutory limit upon the amount which may be claimed in damages against a union, introduced to protect union funds, has been used against them in some cases, where the court has found that the losses which the employer would incur were the action not injuncted would exceed this sum.[396]

It has proved much more difficult for unions to persuade the courts that they and/or their members will suffer irrecoverable losses if an injunction is imposed; admittedly the losses which may arise from the inability lawfully to pursue industrial action are less tangible and less easy to quantify.[397] However the difficulty of qualifying loss, which on occasion has swayed the issue in favour of an employer,[398] has traditionally met with less success when used by unions, and the courts have tended not to accord great weight to the argument that industrial action, once postponed, may not be easily revived.[399] However, in the light of the statutory requirements for a postal ballot and (usually) independent scrutiny of industrial action ballots, both of which impose considerable costs on unions, the position may be different: these costs are quantifiable and, where claimed, will need to be taken into account by the court in exercising its discretion whether the injunction should be granted. Where an interim injunction has been granted, unions may be more inclined to take a case to full trial to recover these amounts. A further factor, whose weight remains untested, is that of damage to the 'public interest', which was propounded by the Court of Appeal has a factor for consideration during the 1989 docks dispute.[400] In 1998 a court took into account in granting an interim injunction to restrain strikes on the London underground the public disruption which the strikes would occasion, particularly if they were to take place on New Year's Eve, when large numbers of people wishing to travel into London would also raise questions of public safety.[401] The concept of the 'public interest' is undefined and malleable, and has the potential to justify injuncting industrial action in a wide variety of situations; indeed, '[i]n major disputes it could turn the balance of convenience into a mere formality'.[402] Another consideration of uncertain significance and scope is non-compliance with the extra-statutory requirements of the Code of Practice, such as those affirming that industrial action should be taken only after all other avenues have been explored.[403] Under the HRA 1998, the fact that industrial action will interfere with a 'Convention right', such as freedom of expression

---

396 See, for example, *Mercury Communications Ltd v Scott-Garner* [1983] IRLR 494, CA; *News Group Newspapers Ltd v SOGAT '82 (No 2)* [1986] IRLR 337.

397 For an example of judicial acknowledgement of this see *Barretts & Baird (Wholesale) Ltd v IPCS* [1987] IRLR 3, 11 (Henry J).

398 See *News Group Newspapers Ltd v SOGAT '82 (No 2)* [1986] IRLR 337 (value of loss of key staff could not be quantified).

399 See, for example, *Mercury Communications Ltd v Scott-Garner* [1983] IRLR 494, 504 (May LJ); *Metropolitan Borough of Solihull v NUT* [1985] IRLR 211; *Associated British Ports v TGWU* [1989] IRLR 305. Cf recognition by Lord Diplock in *NWL v Woods* [1979] IRLR 478, 484 of the need for unions to 'strike while the iron is still hot', and *Cambridge Nutrition Ltd v BBC* [1990] 3 All ER 523: damages would not be an adequate remedy for the BBC if an action to restrain the broadcast of a TV programme failed at full trial because it would have been deprived of the opportunity to broadcast on a matter of public interest in the form and manner of its choice. See also the HRA 1998, s 12.

400 *Associated British Ports v TGWU* [1989] IRLR 305, above. The relevance and significance of this factor was not discussed by the House of Lords: [1989] IRLR 399.

401 *London Underground Ltd v RMT* (22 December 1998, unreported, QBD).

402 Simpson, 1989: p 240.

403 See para 11.45.

or, possibly, the right to life, may also influence a court in favour of granting an injunction and, indeed, in relation to some of the Convention rights at least, there may be a positive obligation on the court to grant the order. Finally, where the balance of convenience does not weigh decisively one way or the other, the court has regard to the desirability of preserving the status quo[404] which, where industrial action has not yet started, means preventing it occurring.[405]

Taken alone the criteria by which the courts decide whether or not to grant interim injunctions could undermine entirely the protection afforded by the statutory immunities. In an attempt to avoid this situation TULRCA 1992, s 221(2) (re-enacting a provision introduced shortly after the decision in *American Cyanamid*) states that where a respondent claims to have acted in contemplation or furtherance of a trade dispute:

> ... the court shall, in exercising its discretion whether or not to grant the injunction, have regard to the likelihood of that party's succeeding at the trial of the action in establishing any matter which would afford a defence to the action under section 219 (protection from certain tort liabilities) or section 220 (peaceful picketing).

In *NWL v Woods*[406] the House of Lords stated that this provision required the courts to put into the balance of convenience the degree of likelihood of the defence succeeding; the greater the degree of likelihood the greater the weight to be accorded to it. On this approach, where the immunities seem likely to apply the injunction should be refused. However, the impact of this provision is restricted in three different ways. First, it does not apply to situations where the applicant suggests heads of liability which are not within the scope of the immunities, such as breach of statutory duty; these will be decided on the basis of the *American Cyanamid* test alone. Second, as we have seen, considerable uncertainty surrounds elements of the statutory immunity defence, particularly the balloting requirements, and in cases of doubt, other factors are likely to sway the balance of convenience towards an injunction. In *London Underground Ltd v NUR*[407] for example, Simon Brown J acknowledged that he was reaching a decision about whether the immunities applied 'after insufficient argument and certainly insufficient consideration'[408] but nevertheless granted the injunction. Third, the courts have continued to affirm their residual discretion to grant an injunction irrespective of the likelihood of the immunities applying where the consequences of disruptive action for the employer or the public may be particularly 'disastrous'.[409] According to Lord Fraser, 'if the probable result of the threatened act would be to cause immediate serious danger to public safety or health and if no other means seemed to be available for averting the danger in time' then it would not be wrong to grant an injunction.[410] This position means that even industrial action which is clearly protected by the statutory immunities may nevertheless be enjoined by an injunction if the court considers that the circumstances warrant it. There have been no cases as yet where this has occurred.

---

404 *American Cyanamid Co v Ethicon Ltd* [1975] 1 All ER 504, 511.
405 See, for example, *Associated British Ports v TGWU* [1989] IRLR 305; *London Underground Ltd v NUR* [1989] IRLR 341.
406 [1979] IRLR 478.
407 [1989] IRLR 341.
408 [1989] IRLR 341, 342.
409 Lord Diplock in *NWL Ltd v Woods* [1979] IRLR 478 (as amended [1980] ICR 167).
410 *Duport Steels Ltd v Sirs* [1980] ICR 161, 187.

Interim injunctions: procedure

11.50   The true significance of interim injunctions in the industrial action context can be appreciated only with knowledge of the procedure by which they may be sought. Normally applicants should serve on the respondent the application notice, together with evidence in support, not less than three days before the court is due to hear the application, and the hearing will then take place with all the parties to the proceedings being present before the court.[411] However, where a matter is sufficiently urgent the application may be made to the court even more speedily, even before a claim form is issued, without notice to the respondent. Due to the fact that imminent industrial action will generally be deemed sufficiently urgent to justify an application without notice, TULRCA 1992 attempts to provide some rudimentary protection for respondents. It states that when a party against whom an injunction without notice is sought claims, or in the opinion of the court would be likely to claim, that he or she acted in contemplation or furtherance of a trade dispute the court shall not grant the injunction unless satisfied that all steps which in the circumstances were reasonable have been taken with a view to securing that notice of the application and an opportunity of being heard with respect to it has been given to him or her.[412] There is an important obligation on an applicant to give full and frank disclosure of all material facts to the court, but nevertheless the absent respondent may still be at risk of losing the benefit afforded by the legislation since it will be for the applicant to explain to the court why better notice could not have been given, an explanation which, by definition, the respondent cannot challenge. It should be noted that only the steps, not the notice itself, need to be reasonable; the union which receives notice which is inadequate but nevertheless sufficient to enable it to appear in court, albeit unprepared, may be unable to rely on the statutory protection.[413] The requirement to take 'reasonable steps' to give the respondent notice has been liberally interpreted, covering telex, fax, or telegram and sometimes even a telephone call to the union headquarters (although it is strongly arguable that with the extensive use of fax machines and e-mail, an abortive communication by telephone should no longer be regarded as 'reasonable steps' save in exceptional circumstances). In *Barratts & Baird (Wholesale) Ltd v IPCS*[414] the appliants left a message on the union's answering machine after 5pm on a Friday afternoon. They then obtained an injunction without notice over the telephone the following Sunday afternoon. This decision seems at odds with the intention of the statute. The difficulties for unions are compounded by the fact that, once the injunction has been granted, it is very difficult to get it lifted. Although normally the terms of the injunction will grant the respondent the right to apply to the court to discharge or vary it on giving notice to the applicant of a specified number of hours or days (often 24 or 48 hours), such applications are not always afforded the expeditious treatment received by the original application and the court may be reluctant to disturb the status quo. In *Barratts & Baird*, for example, the hearing of the respondent's

---

411 CPR Practice Direction 25 – Interim Injunctions.
412 TULRCA 1992, s 221(1).
413 Although note the approach of Turner J in *Post Office v UCW* [1990] IRLR 143, who refused to grant an injunction on the ground, *inter alia*, that TULRCA 1992, s 221(1) had not been complied with, despite the attendance of the union, which had refused the offer of an adjournment, at the hearing.
414 See [1987] IRLR 3 for the discharge of the injunction.

application for a discharge of the injunction made two days after it was granted was adjourned for a week because of pressure of business and a further two days passed before judgment was given and the injunction discharged. One may well imagine circumstances where these days may be vital to a union; indeed, delay of this length may mean that a union loses the protection provided by a ballot if the industrial action has not already started (see para 11.44).

An appeal can be made only with permission against the decision of a judge to grant or refuse an interim injunction.[415] Many appeals in the industrial action context proceed to the Court of Appeal and even to the House of Lords very swiftly under an expedited procedure. An appeal court will only allow an appeal where the decision of the lower court was wrong, or where it was unjust because of a serious procedural or other irregularity in the proceedings.[416] Following the introduction of the Civil Procedure Rules in 1999, every appeal is now limited to a review of the decision of the lower court unless the Court considers that in the circumstances of an individual appeal it would be in the interests of justice to hold a re-hearing.[417] A decision of a lower court may, however, be set aside on the grounds that there has been a change of circumstances since the judge made the order that would have justified his or her acceding to an application to vary it.[418] There may be greater scope for appeal under the HRA 1998; failure to take appropriate account of the requirements of that Act will constitute a misunderstanding of the law.

The legal consequences of breaching an injunction

11.51   Breach of an interim injunction constitutes a contempt of court.[419] Where a union is a named respondent it will be liable for the acts of its members or officials according to the principles discussed in para 11.20 *et seq*. This means that where the injunction covers the torts specified in TULRCA 1992, s 20 the statutory principles will apply,[420] otherwise the situation is governed by common law principles of vicarious liability, so that the union will be liable for persons acting within the scope of their express or implied authority. If a union knows that breaches of the law are occurring it must take active steps to secure compliance;[421] in the case of union officers this may entail the union withdrawing their credentials.[422] Even if a union is not named in the interim order, it may be

---

415 CPR, r 52.3.
416 CPR, r 52.11(3). See also *Tanfern Ltd v Cameron-MacDonald* [2000] 2 All ER 801.
417 CPR, r 52.11(1). A Practice Direction may also make different provision for a particular category of appeal.
418 *Union Traffic Ltd v TGWU* [1989] IRLR 127. For an example of important new evidence being introduced at the appeal stage see *Mercury Communications Ltd v Scott-Garner and the POEU* [1983] IRLR 494.
419 Committal for a civil contempt is at the behest of the applicant, although it is possible that the court may also act of its own motion: CPR Sch 1 RSC Ord 52, r 5; see also *Re Supply of Ready Mixed Concrete* [1992] ICR 229, 248 (Lord Donaldson MR); for a critique see Wedderburn, 1992b. For a detailed account of the law of contempt see Arlidge *et al*, 1999. For the operation of contempt during the 1984–1985 miners' strike see Lightman, 1987; also useful is O'Regan, 1991.
420 TULRCA 1992, s 20(6).
421 *UKAPE and Newall v AUEW (Technical and Supervisory Section)* [1972] ICR 151; *Heatons Transport (St Helens) Ltd v TGWU* [1972] IRLR 25; *Richard Read Transport Ltd v NUM (South Wales Area)* [1985] IRLR 67.
422 *Heatons Transport (St Helens) Ltd v TGWU* [1972] IRLR 25; see also *Re Supply of Ready Mixed Concrete* [1992] ICR 229, 258 (Lord Donaldson MR).

in contempt if it knowingly acts in breach of its terms or knowingly 'aids and abets' a respondent to commit a breach (as indeed may any third party).[423]

The penalties for contempt are designed to force the contemnors to purge their contempt and accept the authority of the court. This may mean imprisonment, although in the industrial action context the courts are now unlikely to risk the martyrdom this can create; thus in 1984 when the president of the National Union of Mineworkers, Arthur Scargill, was judged guilty of 'wilful and repeated disobedience' of an order the penalty was a £1,000 fine. Where a union is in contempt the statutory limits applicable to awards of damages do not apply and in serious cases fines well in excess of these limits have been imposed; in 1983, for example, the NGA was fined over £525,000. However, the courts recognise that contempt may take various forms, ranging from 'flat defiance' at the top end of the scale to a 'half-hearted or perhaps colourable attempt' to comply with the court's order, down to a 'genuine whole-hearted' use of best endeavours to comply which has nevertheless been unsuccessful.[424] 'Flat defiance' is likely to attract a greater fine than a more minor or technical breach, when the penalty may be low or even waived altogether.[425] Where an individual union member or officer for whom the union is not legally liable is found to be in contempt, it is unlawful for union property to be used to pay the fine; if this were to happen it would be open to any union member, as well as the union itself, to recover from the individual the amount applied for this purpose.[426]

A further possible consequence of being found in contempt is sequestration of the union's assets, which will be returned only when the contemnor is released from the contempt, minus any fines, which may be deducted from the property, or costs incurred, which are likely to be large.[427] Third parties have a duty not to obstruct the sequestrators in carrying out their duties and a union's banks and auditors must co-operate in identifying the whereabouts of union property.[428] In *Clarke v Heathfield*,[429] the court even ordered the removal of the union's trustees and appointment of a receiver of its assets and income after 16 members brought an action claiming that the assets were in jeopardy since the union had already been fined for contempt and was likely to incur further fines. Thus a union may

---

423 *Seaward v Paterson* [1897] 1 Ch 545. See also *A-G v Punch Ltd* [2002] UKHL 50, [2003] 1 All ER 289, discussed Devonshire, 2003.

424 *Howitt Transport Ltd and Howitt Bros Ltd v TGWU* [1973] IRLR 25. On the requisite intention which needs to be shown, see *Re Supply of Ready Mixed Concrete* [1992] QB 213; *P v P* [1999] 3 FCR 547.

425 In *Austin Rover Group Ltd v AUEW (Technical and Supervisory Section)* [1985] IRLR 162 no penalty was imposed because the contempt was not serious and the union might have taken sufficiently vigorous steps to dissociate itself from the industrial action had it taken legal advice at an early stage. Cf *Richard Read (Transport) Ltd v NUM (South Wales Area)* [1985] IRLR 67 (deliberate defiance); *Kent Free Press v NGA* [1987] IRLR 267 (union taking as long as possible to withdraw instructions).

426 TULRCA 1992, s 15. This restriction does not cover payment of the expenses of defending the contempt proceedings. It is a moot point whether a union could organise a voluntary collection to indemnify a member who had been required to pay a fine; this would depend upon whether the money collected could be deemed to be the 'property' of the union.

427 For the use of sequestration orders during the 1984–1985 miners' strike see Lightman, 1987. In a seafarers' dispute in 1988 the National Union of Seamen incurred sequestration costs of £0.5 million: Auerbach, 1990: p 99, n 118.

428 *Eckman v Midland Bank Ltd* [1973] 1 All ER 609; *Messenger Newspapers Group Ltd v SOGAT '82* [1984] ICR 345.

429 [1985] ICR 203; *Clarke v Heathfield (No 2)* [1985] ICR 606.

lose completely the ability to control its assets.[430] What is sufficient to purge contempt depends upon the attitude of the judge; in some cases rigorous action by the union to repudiate the unlawful action, coupled with an apology in open court, has been required; in others the judge has not insisted upon a formal apology if satisfied that the union has otherwise accepted the authority of the court.[431] The discretionary nature of this matter can make the process appear even more of a lottery.

PICKETING

11.52   Workers who are involved in a dispute will generally wish to publicise, and mobilise support for, their campaign. One traditional way of doing this has been by picketing. This is not a legal 'term of art' but it is commonly understood to mean persons, either singly or in groups, attending at or near premises connected with an industrial dispute.[432] Pickets may have several objects; the most usual are to persuade non-strikers or substitute workers not to continue working or to persuade suppliers not to furnish goods or services to the employer in dispute. However, as Bercusson has pointed out a wide range of activities may be covered:

> The pickets may limit themselves to merely observing scabs; they may attempt to communicate information to them as to the existence of a strike; they may go beyond this and attempt to persuade them not to aid the employer by working for him (or in the case of customers, doing business with him) – using placards, speaking, shouting ... They may go beyond persuasion to where their behaviour amounts to a threat – through their mere presence, by physical violence, social ostracism or economic boycott; or they may engage in actual assaults, destruction of property or the physical blocking of entrances and interference with traffic. Picketing activity may range from one extreme to the other on this spectrum.[433]

Pickets have commonly been at risk of incurring civil liability; at the very least they are likely to commit the tort of inducing breach of contract and possibly also other torts both within and beyond the statutory immunities. They may also incur criminal liability, even if acting peacefully. In addition to restrictions the general law imposes, guidance as to the conduct of picketing is provided by a Code of Practice, initially issued by the Secretary of State for Employment in 1980 and revised in 1992. Like its counterpart in the area of ballots this Code contains provisions which exceed the requirements of the legislation. One provision which has proved very influential is the statement that the number of pickets at any entrance to or exit from a workplace should not generally exceed six.[434] This figure has to date been reflected in the terms of injunctions ordered by the court to restrict the conduct of future picketing[435] and in the use of police discretion in this area. However this and other aspects of the legal framework governing picketing

---

430   There are now also extensive statutory provisions in this connection: see TULRCA 1992, s 16 and para 11.91 below.
431   *Richard Read (Transport) Ltd v NUM (South Wales Area)* [1985] IRLR 67.
432   Hepple, 1981b: para 89.
433   Bercusson, 1977: pp 271–272.
434   Para 51.
435   See *Thomas v NUM (South Wales Area)* [1985] IRLR 136 and *News Group Newspapers Ltd v SOGAT '82 (No 2)* [1986] IRLR 337.

require reconsideration in the light of the HRA 1998, which has the potential to have much greater implications for the rights of pickets than for those who organise or participate in industrial action generally. Both Article 11 of the ECHR, which guarantees the right to freedom of peaceful assembly, and Article 10, which guarantees the right to freedom of expression, are material in this context. The jurisprudence on this aspect of Article 11 is relatively meagre, but the European Court of Human Rights has affirmed that Article 11 must be considered in the light of Article 10, given that '[t]he protection of personal opinions, secured by Article 10, is one of the objectives of freedom of peaceful assembly as enshrined in Article 11'.[436] In practice, therefore, the principles governing Article 10 are relevant in this context, even if the case appears more directly concerned with freedom of assembly. The concept of 'expression' has been interpreted widely by the Court, which has extended it to protests which take the form of impeding activities of which demonstrators disapprove.[437] Cases therefore generally turn on whether an interference with the exercise of the right can be justified under Article 10(2), which provides that its exercise:

> ... since it carries with it duties and responsibilities, may be subject to such formalities, conditions, restrictions or penalties as are prescribed by law and are necessary in a democratic society, in the interests of national security, territorial integrity or public safety, for the prevention of disorder or crime, for the protection of health or morals, for the protection of the reputation or rights of others, for preventing the disclosure of information received in confidence, or for maintaining the authority and impartiality of the judiciary.

In this context, the scope of the margin of appreciation accorded to the state when the Court is deciding whether a restriction is 'necessary in a democratic society' has varied, with a wide margin being accorded in relation to 'commercial' expression,[438] a much narrower to that which is regarded as contributing to the democratic process or 'public' or 'general' interest.[439] At the time of writing the Court has not been required to decide where picketing lies on this spectrum (whose nature is, in any event, controversial),[440] but where an interference with freedom of expression has taken the form of an injunction the categorisation approach appears, in any case, to be less prevalent.[441] It is strongly arguable that in the case of the provision of information, in particular, (for

---

436 *Ezelin v France* judgment of 26 April 1991, (1992) 14 EHRR 362, para 37. For a discussion of the issues raised by Arts 10 and 11 in relation to the broader freedom to demonstrate, see Fenwick, 1999.

437 *Steel v UK* judgment of 23 September 1998, (1999) 28 EHRR 603, para 92; *Hashman and Harrap v UK* judgment of 25 November 1999, (2000) 30 EHRR 241, para 28.

438 *Markt Intern Verlag GmbH v FRG* judgment of 20 November 1989, (1990) 12 EHRR 161, although cf *Hertel v Switzerland* judgment of 25 August 1998, (1999) 28 EHRR 534.

439 See, for example, *Lingens v Austria* judgment of 8 July 1986, (1986) 8 EHRR 103; *Castells v Spain* judgment of 23 April 1992, (1992) 14 EHRR 445; *Thorgeir Thorgeirson v Iceland* judgment of 25 June 1992, (1992) 14 EHRR 843.

440 See Tierney, 1998; Lester, 1998a.

441 *Observer and Guardian v UK* judgment of 26 November 1991, (1992) 14 EHRR 153; *Open Door Counselling and Well Women v Ireland* judgment of 29 October 1992, (1993) 15 EHRR 244; *Hertel v Switzerland*, above, note 438; cf *Markt Intern Verlag GmbH v Germany*, above. In the United States, picketing has been regarded as protected speech on the ground that discussion of conditions in industry and the causes of labour disputes is indispensable to popular government; however, it has been argued by Hogg, 1997 that it should best be regarded as commercial expression, 'since its main purpose is to encourage employees not to work and consumers not to buy': see Hepple, 2000b: p 191.

example, to other workers, or to customers) domestic courts should be 'exceedingly slow to make interim restraint orders where the applicant has not satisfied the court he [or she] will probably ... succeed at the trial.[442] Regardless of the form that picketing takes, the principle of proportionality requires the courts to look more carefully at the terms in which interim injunctions are framed than heretofore to ensure that restrictions are not excessive in the light of individual circumstances, and to play closer attention to the exigencies of the situation rather than merely adopting the six-picket guideline in the Code of Practice (a provision which itself now requires amendment in the light of the HRA 1998). Indeed, the courts may also be required to consider the implications of Convention rights in deciding whether a tort has even been committed. We consider the implications of the HRA 1998 further in our discussion of the civil and criminal liabilities that pickets may incur.[443]

Civil liability

11.53   As with industrial action generally, the primary remedy sought by employers faced with picketing is an interim injunction to halt the action. The same general principles apply to the granting of injunctions in this context as those outlined in para 11.48 *et seq*. In the past, showing a serious issue to be tried has been unlikely to be difficult and the statutory immunities, which we discuss below, apply only when stringent conditions as to the conduct of the picketing are met. However, as we indicate in para 11.52 above, the courts will now additionally need to consider, in deciding whether an injunction should be granted (and possibly as a prior question, whether the defendant's action constitutes a tort), whether the interference with the respondents' rights to freedom of expression and/or freedom of assembly can be justified.

Pickets may commit any of the torts discussed in para 11.10 *et seq*. In particular they frequently commit the tort of inducing breach of contract, the contracts being either the employment contracts of the workers they seek to persuade to stop working or commercial contracts between an employer and its customers or suppliers. As we indicated in para 11.12, in *Union Traffic Ltd v TGWU*[444] the Court of Appeal held that the mere presence of pickets may be deemed sufficient to constitute an 'inducement' if it is clear that their presence is intended to induce breach of a contract and is successful in this object, although this may require reconsideration in the light of the HRA 1998. However, it is important to note that persuasion must be directed at one of the parties to the contract for the direct form of the tort. In *Middlebrook Mushrooms Ltd v TGWU*[445] the

---

442   *Cream Holdings Ltd v Banerjee* [2005] 1 AC 253, para 22 (Lord Nicholls, giving the opinion of the Court). HRA s 12(3) provides that no relief which, if granted, might affect the exercise of the Convention right to freedom of expression, is to be granted so as to restrain publication before trial 'unless the court is satisfied that the applicant is likely to establish that publication should not be allowed'. In *Cream Holdings* the House of Lords affirmed that the degree of likelihood of success needed to satisfy s 12(3) must depend on the circumstances, but the statement in the text should be the 'general approach'.

443   Note also that state action which has an impact upon the free movement of goods when this process is disrupted by the activities of pickets may raise issues under EU law: see Case C-265/95 *Commission v France* [1997] ECR I-6959; *R v Chief Constable of Sussex, ex parte International Trader's Ferry Ltd* [1999] 1 All ER 129; Case C112/00 *Eugen Schmidberger Internationale Tranporte Planzuge v Austria* [2003] 2 CMLR 34. See generally Barnard and Hare, 2000; Facenna, 2004.

444   [1989] IRLR 127.

445   [1993] IRLR 232.

claimants failed to obtain an injunction to prevent union members handing out leaflets to customers of a supermarket to which they supplied their produce, one ground being that, even assuming the existence of a contract between the supermarket and the claimants, there was no direct pressure on the supermarket to breach it.

11.54 In addition to liability in the economic torts, there are four other forms of tortious liability to which picketing may give rise: trespass to the highway, private nuisance, public nuisance and liability under the Protection from Harassment Act 1997. Until recently it appeared that trespass to the highway was committed by using the highway for purposes not reasonably incidental to passage.[446] However, in *Jones v DPP*[447] the House of Lords held that this view was unduly narrow, and that reasonable user of the highway could potentially extend to peaceful and non-obstructive assembly, although whether it did so would depend on the facts of the case. In practice this tort has been a dead letter in the context of industrial action because only the owner of the subsoil – normally the highway authority – may sue for it, and a highway authority is most unlikely to seek an injunction and any damages it could obtain would almost certainly be nominal. More frequently invoked is the tort of private nuisance, which consists of an unlawful interference with a person's use or enjoyment of land, or some right over or in connection with it.[448] There has been judicial controversy as to whether picketing *per se* can constitute private nuisance. In 1899 the Court of Appeal considered that it could simply because of the attempt to persuade and regardless of any obstruction caused.[449] Seven years later, however, a different Court of Appeal reached the opposite conclusion[450] and this latter view was echoed by Lord Denning in a widely-quoted dissenting judgment in *Hubbard v Pitt* when he stated that:

> ... [p]icketing is not a nuisance in itself. Nor is it a nuisance for a group of people to attend at or near the ... [claimant's] ... premises in order to obtain or to communicate information or in order peacefully to persuade. It does not become a nuisance unless it is associated with obstruction, violence, intimidation, molestation or threats.[451]

In *Mersey Docks and Harbour Co v Verrinder*, however, the High Court held that putting what was perceived as improper pressure on employers could constitute a nuisance, thus relating liability to the motive for the pickets' action rather than the nature of that action. The aim of the pickets, who stood at the entrance to two container terminals, was to protest at the use of 'cowboy' haulage contractors who undercut established operators. They brought the terminals to a virtual standstill because drivers refused to cross the picket line but there was no allegation of violence. Judge McHugh found that the intention of the pickets was to ensure that only established operators were employed to the exclusion of others not acceptable to them, not merely to obtain or communicate information.

---

446 *Harrison v Duke of Rutland* [1893] 1 QB 142, CA; *Hickman v Maisey* [1900] 1 QB 752, CA; *Hubbard v Pitt* [1975] ICR 77; 308.
447 [1999] 2 All ER 257, 263, 265 (Lord Irvine LC), 287 (Lord Clyde), 297 (Lord Hutton).
448 In *Hunter v Canary Wharf Ltd* [1997] 2 All ER 426 the House of Lords affirmed the need for the claimant to have a right to the land affected. Ordinarily this requires a right to exclusive possession of the land. A mere licensee on the land has no right to sue.
449 *J Lyons & Sons Ltd v Wilkins* [1899] 1 Ch 255.
450 *Ward, Lock & Co Ltd v OPAS* (1906) 22 TLR 327.
451 [1975] ICR 308, 318.

'In other words, the intention is to force the company to take some action against shipowners who employ "cowboys" or "scalliwags". It is tantamount ... to an attempt on the part of the defendants to regulate and control the container traffic to and from the company's terminals. If that is right, the conduct of the pickets is ... capable of constituting a private nuisance'.[452] This approach may now require reconsideration in the light of the HRA 1998; it is strongly arguable that conduct which does not obstruct others from crossing a picket line should not be regarded as a tort.[453]

In *Thomas v NUM (South Wales Area)* Scott J sought to extend the application of the tort of private nuisance in a number of respects. As well as affirming that mass picketing was in itself an actionable nuisance, a view supported by authority, he also considered that regular picketing outside the home of an individual non-striker would constitute the tort regardless of the number of those involved and however peaceful their conduct.[454] Even more controversially he also held that unreasonable interference by way of harassment of workers who wished to use the highway to go to work could constitute a tort, which could be described as a species of private nuisance, despite the absence of any interference with the enjoyment of land. On this basis he held that the daily presence of between 50 and 70 men hurling abuse in circumstances requiring a police presence and the use of vehicles to transport the workers into work, was sufficient to constitute this wrong.

This decision provides a further instance of the judicial creativity which we saw to be a feature of the economic torts. In *News Group Newspapers Ltd v SOGAT '82 (No 2)*[455] Stuart-Smith J acknowledged the substance of the defendant's criticisms of such an extension of the tort, especially given that it did not appear that damage was a necessary ingredient. In the light of the House of Lords decision in *Hunter v Canary Wharf Ltd*[456] affirming the nature of private nuisance as a tort based upon the enjoyment of land, it would be difficult to argue that harassment *per se* can constitute a nuisance. However, the wider question whether there was a separate tort of harassment was not considered,[457] although this is now a less pressing question in the light of the Protection from Harassment Act 1997.

The tort of public nuisance is less commonly relied upon by claimants. It consists of an act or omission which obstructs or causes inconvenience or damage to the public in the exercise of rights common to all Her Majesty's subjects. To sue for public nuisance an individual must show particular damage greater than that suffered by the public at large,[458] although this loss need not be of a pecuniary nature; inconvenience or delay may be sufficient.[459] Obstruction of the highway can constitute public nuisance provided that the defendant's use of the highway is 'unreasonable'.[460] In

---

452 [1982] IRLR 152, 155.
453 See, *mutatis mutandis*, *Steel v UK* judgment of 23 September 1998, (1999) 28 EHRR 603.
454 [1985] IRLR 136, 153, 149. See now the Protection from Harassment Act 1997, discussed below.
455 [1986] IRLR 337, 348.
456 [1997] 2 All ER 426.
457 See *Khorasandjian v Bush* [1993] 3 All ER 669; Hepple, 2000b: p 180, n 22.
458 The meaning of particular damage in this context is obscure; see generally Spencer, 1989: especially pp 74–75.
459 See for example *Halsey v Esso Petroleum Co Ltd* [1961] 2 All ER 145.
460 See *DPP v Jones* [1999] 2 All ER 257, discussed above, on reasonable user.

News Group Newspapers Ltd v SOGAT '82[461] the conduct of pickets and daily demonstrators was found by Stuart-Smith J to constitute unreasonable use, and various claimants were found to have suffered special damage, including the Times Newspaper which had lost journalists because of the demonstrations and an individual worker who could not leave the plant during the day and felt drained by the constant pressure of having to come to work through the picket line.

Finally, the Protection from Harassment Act 1997 also introduced a new statutory tort which, although aimed at stalkers, pickets may also commit.[462] The Act makes it an offence to pursue a 'course of conduct' (defined as involving conduct 'on at least two occasions'[463]) which amounts to harassment of another and which the defendant knows or ought to know amounts to harassment of the other (the latter element to be tested by reference to whether a reasonable person in possession of the same information would think this).[464] 'Conduct' in this context includes speech.[465] In addition, a person who is or may be the victim of such conduct may seek an injunction to restrain it, and it is an offence, punishable by up to five years' imprisonment, to breach that injunction without reasonable excuse.[466] Damages may also be awarded in respect of harassment, including for any anxiety caused by it.[467] References to harassing a person include 'alarming the person or causing the person distress',[468] but the concept is not confined to this. The wrong is not committed, *inter alia*, if the person who pursued the conduct shows that 'in the particular circumstances the pursuit of the course of conduct was reasonable'.[469] Previous judicial attitudes do not suggest that pickets are likely to be able successfully to invoke this defence, although once again the HRA 1998 may be relevant in this context. It has been held that it is difficult, if not impossible, to imagine circumstances in which the pursuit of a course of conduct amounting to harassment in breach of an injunction could be 'reasonable', although an isolated act in exceptional circumstances, such as rescuing someone in danger, may be defended on that basis.[470]

---

461 [1986] IRLR 337.
462 See Finch, 2002.
463 S 7(3).
464 S 1(1), (2). Note also liability for aiding, abetting, counselling or procuring such conduct by any person: s 7(3A). Harassment may also constitute a criminal offence: s 2; see further para 11.59. A person also commits an offence under the Act if he or she knows or ought to know that their course of conduct will cause another to fear, on at least two occasions, that violence will be used against them: s 4. In the case of both offences a court sentencing or otherwise dealing with a defendant may make an order prohibiting specified behaviour in order to protect the victim or any other person mentioned in the order from the offending conduct: s 5. In *DPP v Dunn* [2001] 1 Cr App Rep 352, QBD, it was held that 'another' and 'the other' included the plural and that in certain circumstances charges could be brought in relation to harassment of a 'close knit definable group' even though only one might have been present during any one incident of harassment; see also *DPP v Dziurzynski* [2002] EWHC 1380.
465 S 7(4).
466 S 3. A corporate entity cannot be a victim of harassment under the Act, but claimants may, where they have the same interest in the proceedings, bring proceedings both on their own behalf and on behalf of employees of a company under CPR 19.6: *Daiichi UK Ltd v SHAC* [2003] EWHC 2337 (QB).
467 S 3(2).
468 S 7(2).
469 S 1(3)(c).
470 *R v DPP, ex p Moseley*, (QBD, 9 June 1999, unreported).

The scope of statutory immunity

11.55   The scheme of statutory immunity applicable in the context of picketing is complex. First, there is a specific (but limited) immunity contained in TULRCA 1992, s 220. Second, the general immunities which we outlined in para 11.23 *et seq*, affording protection against certain of the economic torts, may also be applicable. However this itself depends upon two requirements being met. First the usual conditions for their application must be satisfied (if the action is attributable to a union a ballot must be held, and so on), and the general exclusions from their scope apply (see para 11.30). Second, the conduct of the pickets must stay within the boundaries of s 220; s 219(3) provides that nothing in s 219(1) or (2) prevents an act done in the course of picketing from being actionable in tort unless it is done in the course of attendance declared lawful by s 220.[471]

Section 220(1) provides that it is 'lawful for a person in contemplation or furtherance of a trade dispute' to attend at or near his own place of work 'for the purpose only of peacefully obtaining or communicating information, or peacefully persuading any person to work or abstain from working'. A union official may also attend for that purpose at or near the place of work of a member of that union whom he is accompanying and whom he represents. The term 'official' includes shop stewards, provided that their election or appointment is in accordance with the union rules, as well as branch and other union officers, but a person who has been elected or appointed to represent only a portion of the membership (eg those in an individual workplace or region) may attend to represent those particular members only.[472]

There is no statutory definition of 'place of work' for the purposes of s 220, in comparison with the provisions governing industrial action ballots where the equivalent term 'workplace' is defined.[473] The Code of Practice indicates that the 'place of work' restriction means that 'lawful picketing must be limited to attendance at, or near, an entrance to or exit from the factory, site or office at which the picket works'.[474] On this basis the immunity would not cover those picketing other premises of their own employer in a multi-plant group. If the picket works at an establishment composed of a large number of buildings on a single site (a university or a hospital, for example), on a narrow view this restriction could imply that the immunity extends only to the individual building in which the worker's office is located. However this would seem an unduly restrictive interpretation, which would not reflect the understanding of either the worker or the employer as to the location of the employment.

Union officials apart there are two further qualifications to the 'place of work' restriction. First, a worker who is 'not in employment' whose last employment was terminated in connection with a trade dispute, or the termination of whose employment was one of the circumstances giving rise to a trade dispute, can attend at or near his or her former place of work.[475] However, the exclusion of those 'not in employment' means that a worker who had found even a part-time job elsewhere would not qualify under this provision. Second, where a person does not normally work at any one place, or the location of the place

---

471   Note that the immunity is displaced *by an act done in the course of picketing*, not, for example, an act inducing a union to organise picketing in breach of its rules: see *Thomas v NUM (South Wales Area)* [1985] IRLR 136, 155.

472   TULRCA 1992, ss 119, 220(4).

473   See para 11.35.

474   Para 17.

475   TULRCA 1992, s 220(3).

makes it impracticable to attend there for the protected purposes, the place of work is 'any premises of his employer from which he works or from which his work is administered'.[476] A lorry driver or a travelling service engineer would come into the first category, an oil-rig worker into the second. Notably, however, there is no express provision for picketing by dismissed workers whose former place of work has closed down. In *News Group Newspapers Ltd v SOGAT '82 (No 2)*[477] the court held that dismissed workers who had formerly worked in central London were outside the immunity when they picketed the employer's new premises in Wapping, given that they had never worked there. A similar result was reached in *Union Traffic Ltd v TGWU*[478] where the claimants had decided to close down one of their transport depots in Liverpool and make a number of drivers redundant. The drivers picketed another depot in Liverpool, where the employers carried on a container repair business, and a transport depot 13 miles away. The Court of Appeal found that, although these places had been ports of call, neither had been the 'base' from which the defendants worked and so could not be deemed their 'place of work'. This reasoning leaves workers in this situation with no premises which they can effectively picket.[479] It may be possible to argue that attendance at the empty site at which the pickets previously worked is 'impracticable' and that they should therefore be able to picket the new premises of the employer, but this approach has yet to be accepted by the courts.[480]

The Court of Appeal has interpreted the phrase 'at or near' in a more purposive fashion, however. In *Rayware Ltd v TGWU*[481] the claimant's factory was on a private trading estate on a private road some seven-tenths of a mile away from the entrance to the estate from the highway. The employees in dispute had established a picket at a gate leading from the highway on to the estate as being the nearest practicable point at which to picket without committing a trespass. The Court of Appeal held that they were within s 220. The court considered that the phrase 'at or near' had to be considered in a geographical sense in the light of the purpose of the legislation, which was to grant a freedom peacefully to persuade, and that 'near' should be seen as an 'expanding' word. Whether a particular spot will be deemed 'near' is a question of fact but two members of the court indicated that if their decision 'establish[ed] a precedent for other comparable industrial and commercial developments' they would 'not flinch from that result in an area of the law where it is especially desirable that rights and duties should be certain'.[482]

---

476 TULRCA 1992, s 220(2). 'Any' in this context would appear not to limit the worker to one set of premises although cf Lloyd LJ in *Union Traffic Ltd v TGWU* [1989] IRLR 127, 133, who limited 'place of work' to the worker's 'principal place or work' or 'base'. By definition, however, this interpretation cannot apply in the case of those for whom picketing their place of work is impracticable.

477 [1986] IRLR 337, 350.

478 [1989] IRLR 127.

479 Lloyd LJ assumed that a person could only have one 'place of work', his 'principal place of work' or 'base' (at 133) and Bingham LJ too spoke of the 'base' (at 131). However there is nothing in the section to prevent a person within s 220(2) having both a place 'at' which and a place 'from which' he works; the lorry drivers in *Union Traffic Ltd v TGWU*, above, note 476, may have come into this category.

480 Auerbach 1989: pp 168–169. This involves arguing that s 220(2) and (3) may apply simultaneously, a proposition not ruled out by the statute. Lloyd LJ left the point open in *Union Traffic Ltd v TGWU* [1989] IRLR 127, above.

481 [1989] IRLR 134.

482 [1989] IRLR 134, 137.

In other respects the ambit of s 220(1) and its predecessors[483] has been interpreted very restrictively by the courts. In particular the courts have been ready to infer that the conduct of pickets has gone beyond that of communicating information or peacefully persuading. In *Tynan v Balmer*[484] the Divisional Court held that 40 pickets who were walking in a circle which spilt onto the public highway at the entrance to a factory had no immunity because one of their objects was to seal off the highway. In *Broome v DPP*[485] Lord Reid suggested that if pickets assembled in 'unreasonably large numbers' it would not be difficult to infer that they were doing this to prevent the passage of others. In more recent cases the courts have been influenced by the six-picket limit suggested by the Code of Practice.[486] Thus, in *Thomas v NUM (South Wales Area)*[487] Scott J considered that the 50–70 pickets at the entrance to a workplace were outside the protection, suggesting that mere attendance in sufficient numbers could be sufficient to exceed its scope.

> It may be that the six persons who are selected to stand close to the gates could bring themselves within the provision, but the many others who are present cannot do so. What is their purpose in attending? It is obviously not to obtain or communicate information. Is it peacefully to persuade the working miners to abstain from working? If that is the case what is the need for vehicles to bring the working miners safely into the collieries?[488]

On the basis of these dicta it seems that mere attendance in sufficient numbers may, without more, take pickets outside s 220. However the HRA 1998, whose application to picketing we explained in para 11.52, will now be relevant in this context; in interpreting the application of s 220,[489] it is submitted that the courts will henceforth need to pay much closer regard to the exigencies of the situation rather than relying upon the provisions of the Code.

Even if pickets manage to remain within s 220(1), however, the protection it affords is very limited. It does not give a right to picket, merely a limited immunity to attend for the specified purposes;[490] *a fortiori*, pickets have no right to require others to listen to their case.[491] This lack of any positive right has been particularly significant in the light of the broad discretionary powers of the police to control picketing, which we outline below, although once again the HRA 1998 will now be material to the scope of these powers. Section 220 does not give any right to attend on land against the wishes of the owner (or the person to whom the owner has granted exclusive occupation), nor does it affect the operation of any byelaws by which the use and operation of land may be regulated.[492] It may afford protection against the torts of trespass to the highway

---

483   TDA 1906, s 2, continued in a modified form by the IRA 1971, s 134, substantially re-enacted by the TULRA 1974, s 15 and amended significantly by the EA 1980.
484   [1967] 1 QB 91.
485   [1974] ICR 84, 90.
486   Para 51.
487   [1985] IRLR 136.
488   [1985] IRLR 136, 148. See also *News Group Newspapers Ltd v SOGAT '82 (No 2)* [1986] IRLR 337.
489   HRA 1998, s 3.
490   *Broome v DPP* [1974] ICR 84, HL; *Kavanagh v Hiscock* [1974] ICR 282, DC.
491   [1974] ICR 84, 89–90 (Lord Reid).
492   *British Airports Authority v Ashton* [1983] IRLR 287. On the issues posed by the use of 'quasi-public' spaces, see Gray and Gray, 1999 and the ECtHR decision in *Appleby v UK* judgment of 6 May 2003 (no breach of Arts 10 and 11 when applicants banned from distributing leaflets by a private company that owned a shopping centre although there may be circumstances, such as a 'corporate town', where a different approach may be taken.)

and private nuisance,[493] but this is of little real importance; the former is irrelevant in practice, and where there is an actionable nuisance it is unlikely that the conduct will fall within the section, particularly if nuisance is henceforth interpreted more restrictively in the picketing context. Its major significance is in relation to the application of s 219(1) of TULRCA 1992; as we indicated earlier, straying outside the terms of that section will of itself remove any protection against the torts it covers such as inducing breach of contract. Moreover, it is possible that liability for conspiracy to use unlawful means may arise if pickets who are 'lawfully' attending actively associate with others from whom the protection of the immunities has been removed.

The general withdrawal of immunity for secondary industrial action is particularly significant in this context.[494] It applies equally to pickets with one narrow exception: where secondary action occurs in the course of attendance which is lawful under s 220 by a worker employed[495] by the employer party to the dispute, or by a union official lawfully in attendance.[496] This means that protection will not automatically be lost if pickets interfere with the contract of employment of a worker employed by another employer, such as a lorry driver delivering goods from a supplier.

Picketing and the criminal law

11.56 Picketing is one area of industrial action where the criminal, as well as the civil, law may be important. There is a multiplicity of criminal offences which pickets may commit. In this section we merely outline the major ones in order to give an indication of the range of liabilities which pickets may incur.[497] It should be noted that, unlike liability under the civil law, criminal liability falls wholly on the individuals concerned. It is unlawful for union property to be used to pay a fine; nor may individuals be indemnified by the union for any liability they may incur,[498] although this restriction does not extend to the payment of the expenses of defending a prosecution if the union rules permit this.[499] The immunity afforded by TULRCA 1992, s 220 is negligible in this context.[500]

11.57 First, there is an offence specifically enacted to deal with picketing, originally contained in the Conspiracy and Protection of Property Act 1875 and

---

493 The Code of Practice oversimplifies the position in para 5 by stating that the immunities afford no protection in relation to any civil wrong not specified in s 219; the examples given in para 27 of the Code are more appropriate.

494 In the USA and Canada restrictions on this type of industrial action have usually been regarded as legitimate in order to prevent the spread of action to so-called neutrals, and it seems unlikely that domestic courts will be inclined to take a different view under the HRA 1998: see Hepple, 2000b: pp 191–192. Cf the ILO jurisprudence on secondary action, discussed in para 11.31.

495 In the case of a worker not in employment, last employed.

496 TULRCA 1992, s 224(1), (3).

497 For further details on the offences which pickets may commit see Sir John Smith, 2002: ch 27; Card, 2000. For more detailed analyses of the policing of industrial disputes see Kahn *et al*, 1983; Geary, 1985; McCabe and Wallington, 1988.

498 TULRCA 1992, s 15. At common law it was not unlawful for a union to authorise payment of fines for picketing offences by members after the offences were committed: *Drake v Morgan* [1978] ICR 56.

499 TULRCA 1992, s 15.

500 At most it may support the argument that picketing within its terms is not an 'unreasonable user' of the highway under the Highways Act 1980, nor without 'legal authority' for the purposes of TULRCA 1992, s 241.

now contained in an updated version in TULRCA 1992. Section 241 of that Act makes it an offence to do one of five acts 'wrongfully and without legal authority' 'with a view to compelling'[501] another person 'to abstain from doing or to do any act which that person has a legal right to do or abstain from doing'. These acts are:

(a)   using violence to or intimidating that person or his wife (sic) or children or injuring his property;
(b)   persistently following that person about from place to place;
(c)   hiding any tools, clothes, or other property owned or used by that person, or depriving him of or hindering him in the use thereof;
(d)   watching or besetting the house or other place where that person resides, works, carries on business or happens to be, or the approach to any such house or place; or
(e)   following that person with two or more other persons in a disorderly manner in or through any street or road.

It seems now to be accepted that the term 'wrongfully and without legal authority' requires an activity to constitute at least a tort before it can give rise to liability under this section;[502] without this requirement many forms of picketing would immediately be illegal as involving 'watching and besetting'. It is also arguable that picketing within the terms of s 220 is not 'without legal authority'. However, the protection afforded by the requirement that the activity should be tortious would be undermined almost entirely if the view of a Scottish court were accepted, to the effect that economic torts protected by the statutory immunities can nevertheless constitute the requisite 'wrongful' act because s 219 expressly applies only to proceedings in tort.[503] On the basis of this reasoning any picketing which involved an inducement to breach a contract could lead to a criminal charge, however few persons were involved. Given a maximum penalty of six months' imprisonment and a fine which currently stands at a maximum of £5,000[504] this would be an unfortunate result. However, it has been suggested that an interpretation of s 241 which means that peaceful picketing can become a criminal offence merely because it involves the torts of inducing breach of contract or nuisance would be incompatible with Articles 10 and 11 of the ECHR as it would not be proportionate to the aim of protecting the 'rights of others'.[505]

11.58   Other lesser charges to which pickets may be subject are obstruction of the highway under the Highways Act 1980, s 137 and obstruction of a constable in the execution of his duty under the Police Act 1996, s 89(2). The former makes it an offence 'in any way' to 'wilfully obstruct the free passage along a highway' without 'lawful authority or excuse'.[506] The requirement that the obstruction should be 'without lawful authority or excuse' allows consideration of whether the user was 'reasonable', which depends on factors such as the length of time the obstruction continues, its location, purpose, and whether

---

501   Persuasion is not compulsion for this purpose: *DPP v Fidler* [1992] 1 WLR 91. Note also the Criminal Justice and Public Order Act 2001, s 42.
502   *Ward, Lock & Co Ltd v OPAS* (1906) 22 TLR 327; *Thomas v NUM (South Wales Area)* [1985] IRLR 136; cf *J Lyons & Sons v Wilkins* [1896] 1 Ch 811.
503   *Galt (Procurator Fiscal) v Philp* [1984] IRLR 156.
504   Level 5 on the standard scale established by the Criminal Justice Act 1982, s 37(2), as substituted by the Criminal Justice Act 1991.
505   Hepple, 2000b: p 191.
506   There is a maximum fine of level 3 on the standard scale (at the time of writing £1,000).

there was an actual or only a potential obstruction.[507] It is arguable that picketing within the statutory immunity would be considered 'reasonable' but anything beyond that may not, although once again the HRA 1998 will be material here. The offence of obstructing a constable most frequently arises in the picketing context if pickets refuse to obey police instructions designed to prevent a breach of the peace.[508] The police and, indeed, all citizens, have a common law power to take any steps necessary to prevent a breach of the peace[509] on either public or private property[510] which may include restricting the number of pickets present, ordering them to move away or, where appropriate, arresting them.[511] The police may also be empowered to prevent pickets approaching picket lines from some distance away provided that the risk to the peace is sufficiently proximate 'both in place and time'. *Moss v McLachlan*[512] arose out of the 1984 miners' strike during which the police used road blocks to prevent intending pickets assembling at working collieries, in some cases many miles away. In *Moss* a road block had been set up on a motorway junction which was stationed between one-and-a-half to two miles from two collieries and between four to five miles from two more. The police believed that strikers from outside the county intended to form a mass picket at one or more of these collieries and wanted to prevent this. The four appellants, together with a number of others, attempted to force their way through a police cordon which had been established to stop the miners proceeding and were charged under the predecessor of s 89(2). The Divisional Court upheld the magistrates' finding that there was ample evidence to support the belief of the police that there would be a breach of the peace if a mass picket were to gather at one of the collieries. In reaching this conclusion the police were entitled to take into account all they had read and heard about disturbances at collieries in the area in previous weeks as well as events taking place in front of them. Anyone with knowledge of the strike would have realised that there was a substantial risk of violence and the mere presence of a body of striking miners at the junction justified the police taking preventative measures. The court emphasised, however, that the police must honestly and reasonably believe that the risk to the peace was real in the sense that it was 'in close proximity both in place and time'.[513] The imminence or immediacy of the threat determined what action was reasonable. Here the risk to the peace was sufficiently proximate to justify the police preventing a convoy of cars whose occupants demonstrated hostility towards working miners from proceeding further. This decision has recently been endorsed by the Court of Appeal,[514] where the court also explained that, whereas in some situations it will be possible to identify the 'likely

---

507 *Nagy v Weston* [1965] 1 All ER 78; see also *Hirst and Agu v Chief Constable of the West Yorkshire Police* (1986) 85 Cr App Rep 143. In *Jones v DPP* [1999] 2 All ER 257, Lord Irvine LC (at 266) and Lord Hutton (at 293) drew on these authorities in determining the boundaries of the tort of trespass to the highway.

508 This carries a maximum penalty of 51 weeks' imprisonment and/or a maximum fine of level 3 on the standard scale.

509 For consideration of this concept see *R v Howell* [1982] QB 416.

510 *Thomas v Sawkins* [1935] 2 KB 249; power preserved by the Police and Criminal Evidence Act 1984, s 17(6).

511 See, for example, *Piddington v Bates* [1960] 3 All ER 660; see also *Albert v Lavin* [1982] AC 546 at 565.

512 [1985] IRLR 76. See G Morris, 1985a, and see also the Police and Criminal Evidence Act 1984, s 4.

513 [1985] IRLR 76, 78.

514 *R (on the application of Jane Laporte) v Chief Constable of Gloucestershire Constabulary* [2004] EWCA Civ 1639.

troublemakers', in others 'preventing a breach of the peace will only be possible if action is taken which risks affecting a wholly innocent individual'.[515]

The power to prevent a breach of the peace has, in the past, accorded the police a broad discretion to control picketing behaviour. However, although the concept of a breach of the peace is centuries old, its precise definition has been the subject of judicial controversy,[516] focusing, in particular, on whether there must be a risk of violence[517] and whether, if so, that violence needs to be perpetrated by the defendant or whether it is sufficient that others may be provoked to violence.[518] In *Nicol v DPP* Simon Brown LJ affirmed that:

> the court would surely not find a [breach of the peace] proved if any violence likely to have been provoked on the part of others would be not merely unlawful but wholly unreasonable – as, of course, it would be if the defendant's conduct was not merely lawful but such as in no material way interfered with the other's rights. *A fortiori* if the defendant was properly exercising his own basic rights, whether of assembly, demonstration or free speech.[519]

The entry into force of the HRA 1998 strengthens support for this approach, although even before that time the courts were prepared to give weight to the exercise by defendants of their Convention rights in deciding whether a police officer was justified in perceiving a breach of the peace.[520] In particular the courts may (and, in our view, should) be more sceptical of the adoption by the police of the six-picket guideline suggested by the Code of Practice where their apprehension of a breach of the peace is derived solely from the numbers present. A constable who interfered with the exercise of freedom of expression or freedom of assembly which could not be justified would have acted unlawfully[521] and would not, therefore, be acting in the execution of his duty.

11.59   More specific preventive measures are laid down in the Public Order Act 1986, which gives the police extensive powers to control 'public processions' and 'public assemblies'[522] and makes it an offence to organise, take part in, or incite others to take part in, such assemblies or processions and knowingly fail to comply with conditions imposed by the police.[523] These conditions may be imposed either in advance or on the spot where the 'senior police officer' reasonably believes that an assembly or procession may result in serious public

---

515   Above, para 48.
516   See Fenwick, 1999: pp 506–511.
517   See *R v Howell* [1981] 3 All ER 383, 389 (Watkins LJ); cf *R v Chief Constable of Devon and Cornwall, ex p Central Electricity Board* [1982] QB 458, 471 (Lord Denning MR).
518   See *Percy v DPP* [1995] 1 WLR 1382, where the latter view was adopted.
519   *Nicol and Selvanayagam v DPP* [1996] JP 155, 163.
520   *Redmond-Bate v DPP* [1999] 163 JP 789. Notably, however, the jurisprudence of the ECtHR has shown less tolerance of peaceful direct action than the stance in *Nicol*, above; in *Steel v UK* judgment of 23 September 1998, (1999) 28 EHRR 603 the Court required only an interference with the rights of others and the possibility of disorder in order to be satisfied that interference with the right to freedom of expression was proportionate; no added requirement to find that the defendant rather than the other party was acting unreasonably was proposed: see Fenwick, 1999: p 510. This decision sits uneasily with the judgment in *Plattform 'Arzte fur das Leben' v Austria* judgment of 21 June 1988, (1991) 13 EHRR 204, para 34.
521   HRA 1998, s 6.
522   Assemblies (which require two or more persons) or processions are 'public' where they are on the highway or any other place to which at the material time any section of the public has access as of right or by express or implied permission: Public Order Act 1986, s 16, as amended by the Anti-social Behaviour Act 2003, s 57.
523   Public Order Act 1986, ss 12, 14.

disorder, serious damage to property, or serious disruption to the life of the community, or that the purpose of the organisers is the intimidation of others with a view to compelling them not to do an act which they have a right to do or to do an act which they have a right not to do. Such conditions as to the place, size and maximum duration of the assembly or procession may then be imposed as appear to the officer to be necessary to prevent these consequences occurring. In the case of pickets this may involve moving them away from a workplace entrance to avoid contact with those going into it or restricting them to times when other workers are not using the entrance, as well as restricting their number,[524] although in this context, once again, relying automatically on the six-picket limitation contained in the Code of Practice may be susceptible to challenge under the HRA 1998.[525] The Act also lays down a requirement to give the police advance notice of 'public processions'.[526] The Act introduced five new statutory offences which may be relevant to the conduct of picketing: in declining order of seriousness these are riot, violent disorder, affray, causing fear of violence or provoking it, and causing harassment, alarm or distress.[527] All may be committed in both public and private places. In addition, the Criminal Justice and Public Order Act 1994 inserted into the Public Order Act 1986 a new offence of intentional harassment which, unlike the pre-existing offence, does not require a prior warning to cease the offending conduct.[528] Punishable by up to six months' imprisonment and a fine of £5,000, this may constitute a considerable threat to those who participate in picketing. Finally, the Protection from Harassment Act 1997 created the offences of harassment and putting another in fear of violence, which we described in para 11.54 in the context of the civil liability to which such conduct also may give rise. Harassment is punishable by a minimum of six months' imprisonment and/or a fine of up to level 5 on the standard scale; putting a person in fear of violence a maximum of five years' imprisonment, an unlimited fine, or both.[529]

'ESSENTIAL SERVICES' AND EMERGENCY POWERS[530]

11.60 In many countries workers in 'essential services', or in the public sector, have been subject to additional restrictions in relation to their capacity lawfully

---

524 See also s 14A of the Public Order Act 1986, inserted by CJPOA 1994, which permits a chief officer of police to apply to the council of a district where he reasonably believes that an assembly is intended to be held on land to which the public has no, or only a limited, right of access and, *inter alia*, may result in serious disruption to the life of the community. The council may make an order with the consent of the Secretary of State. See *Jones v DPP* [1999] 2 All ER 257.

525 See also the police powers of dispersal under the Anti-social Behaviour Act 2003, s 30, although directions to disperse may not be given in respect of persons who are engaged in conduct which is lawful under TULRCA 1992, s 220: s 30(5).

526 Public Order Act 1986, s 11.

527 Public Order Act 1986, ss 1–5.

528 Public Order Act 1986, s 4A.

529 Protection from Harassment Act 1997, ss 2, 4. See *R v Liddle* [1999] 3 All ER 816 for guidelines on sentencing.

530 For a detailed analysis of the law and practice in this area see G Morris, 1986a and 1991 from which the material in this section is drawn. As we indicated in para 11.4 above, there is no consensus as to the meaning of 'essential' in this context; here we adopt the ILO criterion of services whose disruption would threaten the life, personal safety or health of the whole or part of the population. For a summary of ILO standards in this area see Gernigon *et al*, 1998: pp 448–453; see also Novitz, ch 13.

to take industrial action.[531] Restrictions on the former are determined by reference to the importance of the service to the community; the latter are based upon the notion of the state as 'sovereign employer'.[532] Labour law in Britain has never followed either of these approaches; there are particular groups of workers for whom distinctive restrictions apply but these restrictions were introduced at differing times for different reasons; they are not the product of an integrated strategy towards public or essential services. The only criminal offence affecting such groups[533] which was introduced with the specific purpose of curbing industrial action was the Police Act 1919, which also prohibited the police from joining trade unions.[534] Now contained in the Police Act 1996, it provides that:

> ... [a]ny person who causes, or attempts to cause, or does any act calculated to cause, disaffection amongst the members of any police force, or induces or attempts to induce, or does any act calculated to induce, any member of a police force to withhold his services

is liable to a maximum of two years' imprisonment, an unlimited fine, or both.[535] Those organising industrial action among the police would clearly commit this offence and it could probably be argued that participants would do so too by doing an act 'calculated to induce' other members of the force to do the same.[536] In fact no member of a police force has ever been charged with this offence.[537] An analogous provision relating to the armed forces, the Incitement to Disaffection Act 1934, also penalises the incitement of unrest, and could be applied to industrial action although it was enacted with wider purposes in mind.[538] For many years postal workers were subject to restrictions, derived from measures enacted in the early eighteenth century to deter individual acts of interference with the Royal Mail, although no charges were ever brought despite several campaigns of industrial action. The current legislation on postal services, unlike its predecessor,[539] exempts from the offence of intentionally delaying a postal packet in the course of its transmission delays as a result of industrial action in contemplation or furtherance of a trade dispute.[540] It is possible that postal workers could be prosecuted for intentionally intercepting a communication in the course of its transmission under the Regulation of

---

531 See Pankert, 1980; Cordova, 1985; Bernier, 1994; A Jacobs, 2004.
532 For a useful discussion of the traditional position see Aaron and Wedderburn, 1972. For a critique of the 'sovereign employer' argument see G Morris and S Fredman, 1993; see also G Morris, 2000.
533 Industrial action by merchant seamen is also restricted but this is to protect the safety of ships and the interests of employers rather than the public at large: Merchant Shipping Act 1995, s 59. This provision (and its predecessor) has been condemned as violating the prohibition on forced labour in Art 1(2) of the European Social Charter by the Committee of Independent Experts (now the European Committee of Social Rights) that supervises the Charter: see, for example, Conclusions XIV-I.
534 Note also TULRCA 1992, s 240.
535 Police Act 1996, s 91.
536 Participation in industrial action would also infringe the statutory Code of Conduct in the Police (Conduct) Regulations 2004, SI 2004/645.
537 The only recorded prosecutions involved persons connected with the National Unemployed Workers' Movement between 1921 and 1932.
538 In 1931 the printer of the Daily Worker was convicted under the Incitement to Mutiny Act 1797 (now repealed) after the paper had exhorted sailors to join a fight against pay cuts: Young, 1976. Participation in industrial action would infringe military law.
539 Post Office Act 1953, ss 58, 68.
540 Postal Services Act 2000, s 83. 'Trade dispute' has the same meaning as in TULRCA 1992, s 244, and 'industrial action' is to construed in accordance with that Act: s 83(5). As we discuss in para 11.73, the latter may not be a straightforward process.

Investigatory Powers Act 2000, which contains no such exemption, but this would require the consent of the DPP.[541] Telecommunications workers, too, could incur liability under that Act in certain circumstances.[542] As we discussed in para 11.14, in relation to certain groups of workers liability may lie for inducement to breach a statutory duty, a wrong against which there is no statutory immunity. As we have seen, it is not difficult for applicants to obtain an interim injunction to halt industrial action in any dispute, and in relation to disputes in essential services the nature of the disruption is likely to give them additional ammunition. Given the severe penalties for breaching an injunction, this may be a more powerful constraint than the criminal law.[543]

11.61   More important historically than restrictions on individual categories of workers have been the extensive powers available to the government to introduce alternative labour and take other emergency measures, such as rationing resources, when essential services and supplies are threatened by industrial action. Until recently these powers generally derived from the Emergency Powers Act 1920, which enabled the government, on proclaiming a state of emergency, to take extensive measures 'to secure the essentials of life to the community' when the supply and distribution of food, water, fuel or light, or the means of locomotion, were put at risk, although the Act could not be used to impose compulsory military service or to make it an offence to strike or peacefully persuade others to do so. There were twelve separate states of emergency under the Act, most recently in 1973–1974.[544] The enactment of this legislation was accompanied by administrative contingency planning to counter the impact of disruption, a process which became increasingly elaborate after the miners' strike of 1972. This Act was repealed by the Civil Contingencies Act 2004, which contains more extensive powers to prepare for and deal with disruption in a much wider range of circumstances, including industrial action, at both national and local level. Once again, however, emergency regulations may not impose compulsory military service or 'prohibit or enable the prohibition of participation in, or any activity in connection with, a strike or other industrial action'.[545]

Integral to contingency planning in the industrial sphere has been the use of troops to replace striking workers, a strategy dating back to the nineteenth century. Since 1939 the government has had a standing power, now contained in the Emergency Powers Act 1964, to deploy troops on 'urgent work of national importance' without a proclamation of emergency. Troops have been used to replace workers in dispute on over 30 occasions since 1945, most recently during a firefighters' dispute in 2002/2003. On some occasions (in 1979, 1981, 1982

---

541 S 1.
542 Note, however, the restricted definition of 'intercept' in relation to communications in the course of transmission by means of a telecommunications system, which requires that the contents of the communication be made available to a person other than the sender or intended recipient of the communication: RIPA 2000, s 2(2). For potential liability for inducing a breach of statutory duty, discussed in para 11.14 above, see the Communications Act 2003, s 104(3).
543 It is also conceivable that industrial action in essential services could fall within the definition of 'terrorism' under s 1 of the Terrorism Act 2000. The government denied that the definition was intended to cover lawfully organised industrial action in connection with a legitimate trade dispute, but refused to create an explicit exemption: see J Rowe, 2001: pp 531–532.
544 See generally G Morris, 1986a: ch 3.
545 Civil Contingencies Act 2004, s 23(3).

and 1989–1990) the police have been used to replace ambulance workers in dispute, although their deployment for this purpose is of dubious legal and constitutional propriety.[546]

As well as these general provisions there is also legislation of a more specific nature. When the electricity and water industries were privatised in 1989 government ministers were granted extensive powers to issue confidential directions, both general and specific, to relevant operators for purposes which include mitigating the effect of any 'civil emergency' which may occur, 'civil emergency' being defined in terms which are sufficiently wide to cover disruption caused by industrial action.[547] The powers under this legislation may be exercised without parliamentary approval or even knowledge.

11.62   The 'emergency powers' approach to disputes has limitations in relation to services that cannot be stored or rationed and where a workforce has special skills and cannot easily be replaced. These limitations were shown during the disputes of the 1970s when many public service workers, including health service staff, civil servants and local authority manual workers, took national industrial action for the first time and there were also forceful campaigns by other groups such as coalminers, electricity power workers and firefighters. In general during these disputes trade unions exercised self-restraint in their choice of sanctions and commonly formulated Codes of Conduct which indicated those services which members should seek always to maintain. This approach was formalised by the TUC in 1979 when it issued a Guide to Affiliated Unions on the Conduct of Industrial Disputes which advised unions to:

> ... make arrangements in advance and with due notice, in consultation and preferably by agreement with the employer, for the maintenance by their members of supplies and services essential to the health or safety of the community or otherwise required to avoid causing exceptional hardship or serious pollution.

This 'self-restraint' approach on the part of employees was usually expressly or impliedly conditional on employers exercising reciprocal self-restraint and not seeking to undermine the unions' campaign in ways which were considered unacceptable; reaching an 'understanding' that certain services should not be provided during the dispute, for example, or agreeing to pay workers who maintained emergency cover their full wages even though they were not performing all their duties.[548]

The 'winter of discontent' disputes of 1978–1979, which involved a number of public service groups, put on the political agenda the argument that industrial action in essential services should be restricted and the election manifesto of the incoming Conservative Government undertook to do this. In the event no specific legislation was introduced in this area, despite a further manifesto commitment in 1983. It is sometimes concluded from this that the Conservative Government did nothing about essential services.[549] However, it is strongly arguable that, on

---

546 See G Morris, 1980 and 1986a: pp 106–108.

547 Electricity Act 1989, s 96; Water Industry Act 1991, s 208.

548 For a case study of this approach in the NHS see G Morris with S Rydzkowski, 1984.

549 In 1996 the Conservative Government issued proposals which included removing immunity for industrial action which would have 'disproportionate or excessive effects': *Industrial Action and Trade Unions* DTI, Cm 3470, 1996, The Stationery Office. This proposal was not well received even by employers, and no further steps were taken before the Conservatives left office in May 1997.

the contrary, it achieved the goal of inhibiting industrial action in this sector without having to pay either a political or financial price in the form of access to arbitration, index-linking or some other method of compensating those denied recourse to industrial action.[550] A number of these services, including electricity, water and the NHS, were divided into smaller employer units (there are now, for example, 26 water companies in England and Wales alone) and this, combined with changes in the general law, particularly the removal of protection from secondary action, made the organisation of effective industrial action much more difficult. Wide-ranging competitive tendering programmes in the civil service, NHS and local government also reduced the scope for coordinated action. Moreover, confirmation by the courts of the legitimacy of making deductions from the pay of workers who do not perform their full range of duties, an area we explore in para 11.68 *et seq* below, placed a further significant weapon in the hands of employers. Combined with the availability of the statutory right of individuals to seek injunctions to halt industrial action, which undermines the autonomy of the parties to manage their dispute, there is now very little incentive for unions to co-operate with employers in minimising the damage which may be caused by industrial action in essential services.[551] At the time of writing there is no indication that the Labour Government will reform the law in this area in any material way.

INDUSTRIAL ACTION AND CONTRACTUAL RIGHTS

11.63 In assessing the implications of taking industrial action on contractual rights the first question to consider is whether the action constitutes a breach of the contract of employment. If it does the employer has three remedies at its disposal: to sue individual workers in damages for the loss the industrial action causes; to withhold their pay; and, where the breach is sufficiently serious to repudiate the contract, to dismiss them without notice (although depending upon the circumstances, employees may then be able to claim unfair dismissal). These are powerful sanctions which, if threatened, may intimidate workers into abandoning their action. However, the employer cannot obtain a legal order to force employees back to normal work; by statute a court is prohibited from ordering an employee to work by way of an order for specific performance of the contract or an injunction restraining a breach or threatened breach.[552]

The common law does not recognise industrial action as any kind of 'special case' but in some circumstances the courts have sought to mitigate what they perceive to be the injustice for one or other party of applying contractual doctrines, on occasion leading to some fine distinctions and anomalous results. It is notable that, although the Labour Government accorded more extensive (albeit still heavily circumscribed) protection to participants in industrial action against

---

550 This argument is developed in G Morris, 1991.
551 In 1997 a collective agreement between management and unions at Government Communications Headquarters (GCHQ) committed the unions not to induce or authorise any form of industrial action by GCHQ staff if this would disrupt GCHQ operations, such a question to be determined by the Secretary of State. This agreement, unusually, is contractually binding. Entry into an agreement of this nature was the price the unions paid for a restoration of staff rights to join national civil service unions: see further para 7.18 above. See also para 11.14 above for the collective agreement in the Prison Service.
552 TULRCA 1992, s 236.

unfair dismissal (see para 11.71 *et seq*), the Employment Relations Acts of 1999 and 2004 made no change to their contractual position. As we discussed in para 7.9, the HRA 1998 will probably not affect this situation if the current ECHR jurisprudence on the scope of the right to join trade unions under Article 11 is followed. However, it is widely thought that the HRA 1998 requires the courts to interpret the employer's managerial prerogative and the corresponding duty on employees to obey lawful and reasonable orders in a way which is compatible with the 'Convention rights'.[553] This may be material in assessing whether employers are entitled to issue a particular instruction to their workers (to submit to intimate body searches, for example), and whether workers have a correlative obligation to obey; a collective refusal to comply may not be regarded as a breach of contract if the employer had no contractual authority to issue this instruction in the first place.[554] These circumstances apart, however, the position as set out below will apply.

Strikes and the contract of employment

11.64   The courts have generally assumed that a strike, as a total cessation of work, will always constitute a breach of the contract of employment, regardless of the circumstances which provoked it.[555] Whether or not giving notice of a strike changes the position depends upon the terms of the notice given. The notice may explicitly evince an intention to break the contract, so enabling the employer to treat it as an anticipatory breach. Conversely, it may express an intention to terminate the contract. In that event, provided that a period of notice of sufficient length in relation to the individual participant has been given, and that notice has expired before strike action begins, there will be no breach because the contract will have ended (provided that there are no additional constraints on termination).[556] However, it is rare for this to happen and for good reason; collective resignation would be a very unwise course for workers to take, given that they would thereby forfeit even those limited statutory employment protection rights which they would otherwise have.

Commonly strike notices merely express an intention 'to strike', thereby leaving their legal effect for determination by the courts. In these circumstances there are powerful dicta to support the view that they should be interpreted as notices of intended breach of contract rather than of termination on the ground that strikers do not, in reality, wish to leave their employment but, rather, to remain on terms other than those on offer by the employer. Thus in *Rookes v Barnard* Lord Devlin stated that the object of the strike was to 'break the contract by withholding labour but keeping the contract alive for as long as the employers

---

553   See G Morris, 2001a.

554   In the case of public authorities (or 'pure' public authorities at least), issuing an order to violate the Convention rights of others could be regarded as an unlawful act for the purposes of HRA 1998, s 6, and the order could be regarded as one which an employee is entitled not to obey: see *Gregory v Ford* [1951] 1 All ER 121; *Lister v Romford Ice and Cold Storage Co Ltd* [1957] AC 555 (Viscount Simonds); *Morrish v Henlys (Folkstone) Ltd* [1973] ICR 482.

555   See, for example, Ewing, 1991. For a contrary argument, see Elias, 1994, summarised below.

556   It is conceivable that a 'no-strike' agreement may restrict the right of workers collectively to terminate their contracts during a dispute but this restriction would need to have been incorporated into the contract of employment: see TULRCA 1992, s 180, discussed further below.

would tolerate the breach without exercising their right of rescission'.[557] However, in *Boxfoldia Ltd v NGA*,[558] Saville J asserted that the meaning and effect of the words used in a strike notice should be examined in their context, with no preference for any particular construction. However, the details of his judgment indicate that even on this view the court is unlikely to find that notice of collective termination has been given without clear evidence of this. The union had given the employers by letter '14 days' notice of withdrawal of all NGA members' labour from the company'. The company claimed that the union had induced the employees to breach their contracts of employment and that, as this had not been preceded by a ballot, the union was liable in tort for damages. The union argued that the letter gave contractual notice of termination on behalf of all the NGA's members. Saville J was not persuaded that there was a rule of law that strike notices should be regarded as notice of intended breach, a view which presupposed 'that the party giving the notice wishes the contracts of employment to continue'. He developed this point by stating that:

> ... [t]o my mind this is not necessarily so, for in any given case the employees (or their union) may consider that by actually terminating the contracts on due notice, greater or more effective pressure can be put upon the employers, though, of course, by doing this the employees would ... lose certain unfair dismissal rights which would otherwise exist. Furthermore ... there is a distinction to be drawn between wanting to continue with the existing but improved contracts of employment and wanting to continue (but with new contracts) the relationship of employer and employee ... In addition there is something to be said for the proposition that it should not too readily be assumed that a party is acting unlawfully when his actions could equally well be construed as lawful'.[559]

In this case Saville J considered that 'withdrawal of labour' was capable of referring to notice of termination but on the facts found that this was not the case: the letter did not purport to be written by the union on behalf of or as agent for the employees, it did not communicate any decision by them to terminate their contracts, nor give on their behalf the appropriate termination notice stipulated in their contracts. This finding suggests that, despite his earlier remarks, Saville J too in practice required clear evidence in order to find that notice to terminate had been given. He also observed that there was nothing in the union's rules which gave it the requisite authority to terminate contracts on its members' behalf and he refused to imply such authority from the union's power to instruct members to take industrial action and to publicise that instruction.

On the reasoning adopted in *Boxfoldia*, in the absence of express authority for a union to terminate its members' contracts, each striker would need to give notice of termination of employment on an individual basis or expressly authorise the union to give such notice on his or her behalf.[560] Where employees are

---

557 [1964] AC 1129, 1204. See also *JT Stratford & Son Ltd v Lindley* [1965] AC 269 at 285 (Lord Denning). To date the courts have not treated showing an intention to participate in a threatened or rolling strike if and when called upon to do so as a breach of contract: see *Ticehurst and Thompson v British Telecommunications plc* [1992] IRLR 219.

558 [1988] IRLR 383.

559 [1988] IRLR 383, 385.

560 See also *Ideal Casements Ltd v Shamsi* [1972] ICR 408, where the need for authorisation by the rules for the giving of any form of strike notice by union officials was made clear. It is possible that custom and practice may also provide sufficient authority: *Heaton's Transport (St Helens) Ltd v TGWU* [1972] ICR 308, although it is suggested that the courts should require very clear evidence before finding this.

required to give notice of differing lengths either of these procedures would be a complex organisational exercise. In view of the serious consequences for individuals of collective resignation, it is desirable that such obstacles exist to unions purporting to terminate their contracts of employment, especially given that, as *Boxfoldia* demonstrates, unions may be tempted to safeguard their own legal position by arguing that the form of the notice – one of termination – means that no tort has been committed.

In a number of systems industrial action suspends, rather than breaches, the contract of employment. In *Morgan v Fry*[561] Lord Denning made a preliminary attempt to introduce this concept into English law, stating that:

> The truth is that neither employer nor workmen wish to take the drastic action of termination if it can be avoided. The men do not wish to leave their work for ever. The employers do not wish to scatter their labour force to the four winds. Each side is, therefore, content to accept a 'strike notice' of proper length as lawful. It is an implication read into the contract by the modern law as to trade disputes. If a strike takes place, the contract of employment is not terminated. It is suspended during the strike: and revives again when the strike is over.[562]

As Ewing points out[563] Lord Denning's approach would not, itself, protect employees without employers being additionally constrained from terminating their contracts with due notice. In the event this approach was never taken further by the courts[564] and, as we discuss in para 11.92, could almost certainly take root only within a broader framework of reform of industrial action law. As the law now stands a strike would be viewed as suspensory only if there was a contractual term which specifically granted employees the right to suspend in these circumstances. It has been argued that if the terms of a collective agreement which forbids industrial action until a disputes procedure has been exhausted are incorporated into individual contracts then, on exhaustion of this procedure, a right to strike could be implied.[565] However, there is no authority to support this proposition and, in any event, incorporation of this kind of clause has been rare.[566]

It has been argued extra-judicially by Patrick Elias QC (now Elias J) that a defensive strike in response to a continuing repudiatory breach of contract by an employer should not be treated as a breach of contract by employees.[567] Elias justifies this contention on two separate grounds. The first is that employees can lawfully initiate the strike by 'concerted constructive dismissals' which, provided that it is made clear that they are resigning in response to the employer's repudiatory breach, need not require any period of notice.[568] He argues that this would then allow employees to claim wrongful dismissal if not subsequently

---

561 [1968] 2 QB 710.

562 [1968] 2 QB 710, 728.

563 Ewing, 1991: pp 5–6.

564 See *Simmons v Hoover Ltd* [1977] ICR 61.

565 Hepple, 1981b: para 495.

566 See para 11.66 below.

567 Elias, 1994.

568 Elias, 1994: p 259. In *Wilkins v Cantrell and Cochrane (GB) Ltd* [1978] IRLR 483, the EAT held that going on strike in response to a repudiatory breach of contract by the employer should not be regarded as a termination of the contract. To the extent that the judgment may be taken to imply that employees are not in law entitled as part of a concerted campaign to terminate their contracts in response to a repudiatory breach Elias argues that it is erroneous.

reinstated and, more tentatively, that they would not at this point be 'taking part' in industrial action and so would not thereby jeopardise their unfair dismissal rights. As it stands, this argument is open to the objection which we discuss above as to the inadvisability of employees terminating their contracts of employment. However, it could be invoked for the purposes of unfair dismissal to support the argument that the employees have been constructively dismissed because their existing contracts of employment have terminated prior to the industrial action starting, even though they remain in the employment.[569] Elias's second argument is based upon the proposition that, by analogy with the position of employees, if the employer is not prepared to provide the whole of the consideration which is due to the employee under the contract of employment (for example, by cutting wages) the employee has the right to refuse to work.[570] At the time of writing there is no judicial authority which supports these arguments directly and, indeed, such authority as exists is to the contrary.[571]

Industrial action short of a strike and the contract of employment

11.65 The effect of industrial action short of a strike on the contract of employment depends upon its nature. In this area the implied duty of co-operation which employees owe to their employer, which, as we saw in para 4.86 *et seq* above has been extensively interpreted by the courts, has been particularly crucial. Sometimes a refusal to perform a particular duty, or to handle particular goods, as instructed by the employer will clearly constitute a breach. Where it is not apparent that it does constitute a breach, the duty of co-operation may lead the courts to conclude that the employee should nevertheless obey the instruction to perform the task, even if the task in question constitutes the very subject-matter of the dispute.[572] The same point applies to the operation of new working methods; provided that they can be viewed as different methods of performing the same task, rather than as a wholly different job, refusal to comply with the instruction to change will be a breach of contract.[573] The courts have leant towards an interpretation which favours flexibility and where workers dispute the employers' right to force the change upon them their only safe recourse is to the courts.[574] However, even then their chances of an interim injunction to restrain the alleged variation may not be great, and if the case went to full trial, which may be some years later, it is difficult to predict what damages, if any, could be obtained.

Where industrial action takes the form of a 'work-to-rule' this is likely to be viewed as a breach of the implied duty of co-operation or fidelity, at least where the rule book is construed as containing the lawful instructions of the employer

569 See *Hogg v Dover College* [1990] ICR 39; *Alcan Extrusions v Yates* [1996] IRLR 327, discussed in para 5.71.

570 Authority for this is drawn from Lord Templeman's dictum in *Miles v Wakefield Metropolitan District Council* [1987] IRLR 193 at 198 that '[i]f the employer declines to pay, the worker need not work' which Elias extends to the whole of the consideration.

571 In *Simmons v Hoover Ltd* [1977] ICR 61 it was suggested that strikes in opposition to changes imposed by the employer in breach of contract should not be treated as *repudiatory* breaches of the contract but other judges have refused to accept even this view: *Wilkins v Cantrell and Cochrane (GB) Ltd* [1978] IRLR 483; *Marsden v Fairey Stainless Ltd* [1979] IRLR 103.

572 *Sim v Rotherham Metropolitan Borough Council* [1986] IRLR 391; *Solihull Metropolitan Borough v NUT* [1985] IRLR 211. See generally Fredman and Morris, 1987b.

573 See, for example, *Cresswell v Board of Inland Revenue* [1984] IRLR 190.

574 *MacPherson v London Borough of Lambeth* [1988] IRLR 470.

to its workers as to how they are to work. Authority for this view is provided by the Court of Appeal decision in *Secretary of State for Employment v ASLEF (No 2)*[575] which we discussed in para 4.87 above. It will be remembered that in this case a number of grounds were offered for the view that working to the letter of this rule book (which contained 239 rules) in the context of industrial action constituted a breach of contract.[576] For Lord Denning the breach consisted of taking steps wilfully to disrupt the undertaking, 'to produce chaos so that it will not run as it should'.[577] Thus it was the motive or object with which the act was done which rendered it unlawful. For Roskill LJ it lay in an implied term that the employee would not seek to obey lawful instructions in a wholly unreasonable way which 'has the effect of disrupting the system, the efficient running of which he is employed to ensure',[578] an approach which focuses upon the impact of the action. Buckley LJ based his decision upon an implied term that the employee would serve the employer faithfully with a view to promoting those commercial interests for which he is employed.[579] This decision does not mean that every work-to-rule will automatically be viewed as a breach of contract but the range of dicta in the case provide ample ammunition for the argument that it will. A 'go-slow' is likely to be similarly viewed; in *General Engineering Services Ltd v Kingston and St Andrew Corpn*[580] this form of action by firemen was classified by the Privy Council as a 'wrongful repudiation of an essential element of their contract of employment'.[581]

As we pointed out in para 4.87, Lord Denning's approach in *Secretary of State for Employment v Associated Society of Locomotive Engineers and Firemen (No 2)* conflicts with the general principle of English law that a bad motive does not render an otherwise lawful act unlawful. Despite this the courts have invoked an analogous approach in relation to a withdrawal of 'goodwill' or 'co-operation'. In *Ticehurst and Thompson v British Telecommunications Ltd*[582] the employee, a manager in charge of 40 staff, had participated in her union's campaign of industrial action which consisted of a withdrawal of goodwill, followed by a series of one-day strikes. After participating in three of these strikes Mrs Ticehurst was asked by the employer to sign a document undertaking 'to work normally in accordance with the terms of my contract with BT from now on'. When she refused to sign she was asked to leave the premises and was not paid for the day in question. The same thing occurred on subsequent working days until the dispute was settled. The Court of Appeal found that the withdrawal of goodwill constituted a breach of the implied term of her contract identified by Buckley LJ in *ASLEF*; the duty to serve the employer faithfully within the requirements of the contract. The court rejected the argument that this term could not be breached unless the intended disruption of BT's undertaking was achieved in practice. Rather the term was breached 'when the employee does an act, or omits to do an act, which would be within her contract and the discretion allowed to her not to do, or to do, as the case may be, and the

575 [1972] 2 QB 455.
576 See Napier, 1972, for a discussion of the principles underlying the judgment in this case.
577 [1972] 2 QB 455, 492.
578 [1972] 2 QB 455, 509.
579 [1972] 2 QB 455, 498.
580 [1988] 3 All ER 867.
581 [1988] 3 All ER 867, 869 (Lord Ackner). The court concluded from this that the firemen were not acting in the course of their employment and the employer was not vicariously liable for the damage caused by their default.
582 [1992] IRLR 219.

employee so acts or omits to do the act, not in honest exercise of choice or discretion for the faithful performance of her work but in order to disrupt the employer's business or to cause the most inconvenience that can be caused'.[583]

Although *Ticehurst* concerned a managerial employee this dictum seems likely to be applied, *mutatis mutandis*, to all categories of worker. The court left open the position 'if the ill-intentioned course of conduct is shown to have had no significant consequences adverse to the employer and to be incapable of causing any such adverse consequences in future',[584] but the emphasis upon intent suggests that even this is likely to be regarded as a breach. The logic of this approach is that even a ban on voluntary overtime could constitute a breach of the contract of employment if employees' refusal to provide it was deliberately designed to cause disruption. In *Burgess v Stevedoring Services Ltd*, however, the Privy Council distinguished between employees performing duties in a deliberately obstructive way and 'refusing to do things altogether outside their contractual obligations (like going to work on Sunday) merely because they do not have a bona fide reason for refusal. They do not have to have any reason at all.'[585] In this case, employees were contractually obliged to report for overtime duty when so assigned by the union. The union, in breach of its obligations under the collective agreement with the employer, refused to make up overtime gangs. The Privy Council considered that had employees been assigned work and said that they were unavailable as part of a concerted action the *ASLEF* case might have had some relevance, but this was not the case here.

Finally, it should be noted that for industrial action short of a strike, giving notice cannot change its legal consequences; if the action itself breaches the contract, notice merely constitutes notice of intended breach, regardless of the circumstances.

The effect of 'no-strike agreements' on the contract of employment

11.66   In some areas of the private-sector collective agreements have been concluded which prohibit or restrict resort to industrial action.[586] Prominent examples were those agreed in the context of 'single-union' deals in high-tech industries. Although these agreements provoked considerable controversy within the union movement because of the symbolic significance of 'giving up' the freedom to take industrial action, in reality their legal implications have been minimal. At collective level the parties have not inserted the explicit statement of enforceability which would be necessary to render them enforceable contracts.[587] In relation to the individual worker, given that industrial action is generally treated as a breach of contract, they would appear to add nothing to the general position. The only additional constraint which such an agreement might impose is if it were to restrict the right of workers collectively to terminate their contracts during a strike. However, there have been no test cases on this point.

---

583 [1992] IRLR 219, Ralph Gibson LJ at 225, with whom the other members of the court agreed.
584 [1992] IRLR 219, 225.
585 [2002] IRLR 810, para 27 (Lord Hoffmann).
586 For an analysis of these 'deals' see R Lewis, 1990; Bassett, 1986. Note also the agreement concluded at GCHQ in 1997: see para 11.10 above.
587 R Lewis, 1990: p 38. Cf the agreements at GCHQ and in the Prison Service which, unusually, do provide a legally enforceable contract.

If the parties were to attempt to incorporate a 'no-strike' agreement into individual contracts, possibly to serve as a 'reminder' of their obligations, a specific procedure must be followed. As we saw in para 4.29, not all the terms of a collective agreement are appropriate for incorporation into individual contracts and it would be necessary to ensure that the restriction was in a suitable form. A clause which merely stated, for example, 'there shall be no strikes or lock-outs until the procedure for the settlement of disputes has been exhausted' would seem not to be appropriate; it is unclear what the nature of the obligation on the individual would be and there is the additional problem that disputes procedures can usually only be invoked by the collective parties. More likely to be effective is a clause which attempts directly to translate the obligation into individual terms, for example a clause stating that:

> ... [t]here shall be expressly incorporated into the contract of each employee a provision that during the course of any negotiations, conciliation or arbitration, he [or she] will not participate in any strike or other forms of industrial action.[588]

However, by statute,[589] a clause which restricts the right of workers to engage in a strike or other industrial action may only form part of the individual contract if the collective agreement is in writing; contains a provision stating that the terms may be incorporated; is reasonably accessible at their place of work to the workers to whom it applies and available for them to consult during working hours; and each union party to the agreement is 'independent'. In practice it has been rare for the collective parties to attempt this.[590]

On occasion employers have attempted to require employees to sign undertakings that they will not participate, or take any further part in, existing disputes as a condition of being allowed to return to work. The courts have held that a refusal to give such an undertaking does not, of itself, constitute a breach of the contract of employment.[591]

Employer responses to industrial action in breach of contract

11.67   Where industrial action constitutes a breach of the contract of employment employers have a range of responses available to them. First, if the breach is sufficiently serious to constitute a repudiation of the contract the employer may decide summarily to dismiss the worker. Whether the breach will constitute a repudiation depends upon the facts. In general, strikes have been regarded as repudiatory.[592] It has been suggested that strikes in opposition to changes made by the employer which breach the contract would not be repudiatory,[593] but other judges have refused to accept this view.[594] It is arguable that a strike of very short duration (for example, for a day or less) should not be

---

588   R Lewis, 1990: p 51.
589   TULRCA 1992, s 180(3).
590   R Lewis, 1990: pp 37–38.
591   See *Ticehurst and Thompson v British Telecommunications plc* [1992] IRLR 219, 228. *Chappell v Times Newspapers Ltd* [1975] ICR 145 also lends support to this view.
592   See *Simmons v Hoover Ltd* [1977] ICR 61, 76.
593   *Simmons v Hoover Ltd* [1977] ICR 61. See also *Thompson v Eaton Ltd* [1976] ICR 336, 342.
594   *Wilkins v Cantrell and Cochrane (GB) Ltd* [1978] IRLR 483; *Marsden v Fairley Stainless Ltd* [1979] IRLR 103. Cf the position under the HRA 1998 where the employer's instruction interferes with the exercise of a Convention right, discussed at para 11.63.

seen as such, but such authority as there is on this point suggests the contrary.[595] For industrial action short of a strike a refusal to perform only a minor part of the employees' total duties should not, in principle, be seen as repudiatory but it is difficult to predict how a court will view such action. In *Wiluszynski v London Borough of Tower Hamlets* the claimant, an estates officer in the council's housing directorate, as part of a campaign of industrial action, refused to answer enquiries from council members as he was contractually obliged to do. When the campaign ended five weeks later it took him about three hours to deal with the backlog of inquiries. Despite the limited proportion of working time this occupied, two members of the Court of Appeal considered, obiter, that this was a repudiatory breach.[596]

Where a breach is not repudiatory an employer wishing to dismiss would need to give the contractual period of notice and comply with any other restrictions on termination contained in the contract. Where the employer fails to do this, however, the remedy would almost certainly be confined to damages; as we have seen the courts exercise their discretionary power to grant injunctive relief against dismissal only in exceptional circumstances and are unlikely to do so in a context where employees cannot show that they are ready and willing to perform their side of the contract[597] (see our discussion in para 5.54 *et seq*).

11.68 In theory employers who suffer loss as a result of industrial action in breach of contract could sue each individual worker for the damages flowing from that breach, regardless of whether the breach is repudiatory. However, each worker may be sued in contract only for the loss for which he is she was personally responsible.[598] In the case of assembly-line workers, for example, this would be the value of the lost production minus the costs which the employer would have had to incur as part of the process of production.[599] Where the worker is a supervisor or a managerial worker, on the other hand, it may be harder to establish direct loss; the most likely measure is the extra cost to the employer of providing a replacement if this was necessary.[600] This creates the somewhat paradoxical result that 'the damages assessed against a production worker will be greater than those assessed against a supervisory worker, even though the actual loss to the employers may ... be far greater where the industrial action is taken by members of the latter group because it causes a total closure of the enterprise'.[601] In practice it has been very rare for employers to sue

---

595 *Rasool v Hepworth Pipe Co Ltd* [1980] IRLR 88 (one-hour mass meeting during working hours without employer's consent a repudiatory breach of contract).

596 [1989] IRLR 259; see Nicholls LJ at 264 with whom Mann LJ agreed.

597 In *Chappell v Times Newspapers Ltd* [1975] ICR 145 the Court of Appeal refused to grant an injunction to restrain employers from treating workers as having terminated their contracts of employment where the workers had been instructed by their union to take industrial action, although they had not yet breached their contracts as individuals, on the basis, *inter alia*, that in the light of union instructions they would not undertake to perform their part of the contract.

598 *National Coal Board v Galley* [1958] 1 WLR 16. However, proof of inducing fellow workers to break their contracts, or of conspiracy among workers to induce a breach, may give rise to liability in tort, and see also *Barretts & Baird (Wholesale) Ltd v IPCS* [1987] IRLR 3, discussed in para 11.16 above, which suggests that breach of contract *per se* could constitute unlawful means for the tort of interference with trade by unlawful means.

599 *Ebbw Vale Steel, Iron and Coal Co v Tew* (1935) 79 Sol Jo 593.

600 *National Coal Board v Galley* [1958] 1 WLR 16.

601 Ewing, 1991: p 19.

individual workers; in general they prefer to pursue a remedy in tort against those organising the industrial action. However, employers have become much more willing in recent years to invoke the 'self-help' remedy of making deductions from workers' wages and in this context the existence of a right to sue for damages, even if it is not exercised as such, is significant.

As we saw in para 4.59 *et seq*, the principles governing the right to payment, and the right of employers to make deductions, are complex. A number of the cases have been decided in the context of industrial action and the resulting principles are not completely clear. It is clear that workers who go on strike have no right to be paid for this period. In addition, workers who refuse to perform their full range of contractual obligations may be sent home without pay unless the contract places some restriction on this.[602] It also seems that if partial working is imposed for only a proportion of the working week employers may state that they are not prepared to accept less than the full range of duties and 'send the worker home' without pay for that proportion of the week. This was the situation in the leading case of *Miles v Wakefield Metropolitan District Council*.[603] Mr Miles, a superintendent registrar of births, marriages and deaths, had refused to perform marriages on Saturday mornings for 14 months as part of a campaign for higher pay. He normally worked a 37-hour week, of which 3 hours were on Saturdays. The council told him that unless he was prepared to perform his full range of duties he would not be required to attend work on Saturdays and would not be paid for doing so. Mr Miles nevertheless continued to do other work on Saturday mornings and when the council withheld 3/37ths of his pay he sued for the unpaid salary. The House of Lords held that the council was entitled to refuse his offer of reduced working on Saturdays and his position was then the same as if he had withdrawn his labour completely for that period; he had no right to be paid for the work he had carried out on Saturdays.[604]

11.69   Where an employer allows workers to continue working on a restricted basis the legal position as regards the employee's right to payment is confused. In *Royle v Trafford Borough Council*[605] Park J refused to allow the council to deprive a teacher working restrictively of his entire wage; having accepted imperfect performance it could not then refuse to pay him anything for this. Another line of authority, however, holds that workers are not entitled under their contracts to any payment whatsoever. This view received support from Lords Templeman and Brightman, obiter, in *Miles*, although they considered that employees could claim payment on a *quantum meruit* basis for the amount and value of the work they had performed,[606] a view which was contested by

---

602   *Cresswell v Board of Inland Revenue* [1984] IRLR 190; see also *MacPherson v London Borough of Lambeth* [1988] IRLR 470; *Ticehurst and Thompson v British Telecommunications plc* [1992] IRLR 219 (although in *Ticehurst* it was stated that evincing an intention to respond to a strike call by the union, if and when made, would not have itself have entitled the employers to refuse to permit the employees to work in a situation where the value of the services received would not be reduced by the risk that at some future date the employee might refuse to perform her contract).

603   [1987] IRLR 193. See also *Jakeman v South West Thames Regional Health Authority and London Ambulance Service* [1990] IRLR 62, QBD, where pay was withheld for periods for which the employer had refused to accept partial performance of duties. Mandatory interim relief was sought by the claimant employees and refused.

604   On the issue of whether the pay period in question should properly have been treated as divisible, see para 4.65 above.

605   [1984] IRLR 184.

606   [1987] IRLR 193, 199 (Lord Templeman), 195 (Lord Brightman).

Lord Bridge who questioned whether entitlement to a *quantum meruit* could replace entitlement to remuneration at the contractual rate.[607] It also accords with the principle upheld by the Court of Appeal in *Henthorn and Taylor v Central Electricity Generating Board*.[608] Here the employers had refused to pay manual workers any wages for days when they were working to rule. A claim for unpaid wages by two employees was rejected by the courts on the basis that in order to claim money due under the contract they had first to prove that they themselves were willing to perform their contracts. Because they could not do this they had no remedy.[609] This view has been criticised on the ground, *inter alia*, that willingness to perform the contract is not relevant to a claim for money due in debt[610] (although it would not preclude an employer's counterclaim).

Argument may sometimes arise as to whether the employer has, indeed, accepted imperfect performance. This was the case in *Wiluszynski*.[611] The council responded to the employees' industrial action – refusing to answer council members' inquiries – by informing them that their presence on the premises was not required until they were prepared to resume normal working, and were they to attend for work and undertake limited working this would be regarded as unauthorised and voluntary in nature. Mr Wiluszynski continued to attend work during the five weeks the action lasted, performing all his other duties. On resuming his normal duties it took him about three hours to deal with the backlog of inquiries. When he sued for his unpaid salary the Court of Appeal rejected the argument that the council had acquiesced in his work and taken the benefit of it; it had not given him any directions to work so as to contradict the statement that it would regard any work as voluntary, and he could not have been misled as to the genuineness of the employer's pronouncement. The council could not be expected physically to prevent the relevant staff from entering the premises. Mr Wiluszynski had failed to discharge a material part of his contractual duties and the council was entitled to withhold his entire salary for the period.

The reasoning in this case is open to question. The court relied upon the principle that employees who sue for remuneration must show that they are ready and willing to discharge their own obligations, which it took to be the principle upheld in *Miles*. However, if this were to be the case there would seem to be nothing to prevent an employer accepting imperfect performance and still refusing to pay, making discussion of whether there had been acceptance of such performance irrelevant. The combined effect of *Miles* and *Wiluszynski* may suggest that those organising industrial action short of a strike would be best advised to restrict sanctions to limited quantifiable periods of time with full performance in between. If employers wish to maintain services, whilst also making some deduction, this may satisfy honour on both sides.[612] Even then, however, the reasoning in *Wiluszynski* indicates that employers may still be within their rights to withhold the entire salary on the basis that employees were not willing to perform the contract in its entirety. There is a fundamental and unresolved conflict here. *Wiluszynski*, in particular, presents considerable

---

607 [1987] IRLR 193, 195. See also Burrows, 1993: p 280 who considers that the strength of the dicta by Lords Templeman and Brightman is weakened because it was not made clear that a restitutionary analysis could only come into play once the employer had elected to terminate the contract.
608 [1980] IRLR 361.
609 See also *MacPherson v London Borough of Lambeth* [1988] IRLR 470.
610 See Napier, 1986.
611 [1989] IRLR 259.
612 See McLean, 1990.

problems for unions with members in essential services who may wish to maintain an emergency service yet would be unwilling to do this for no renumeration whatsoever. One approach to this difficulty may be to argue that by accepting partial performance employers have thereby waived their right to claim non-performance of the contract, without prejudice to a claim in damages for loss caused by the employees' breach.

In *Royle*, as we have seen, the employee successfully challenged the employer's right to withhold the entire wage where it had accepted restricted working. There have been other cases where employees have challenged the employer's right to make even a partial deduction from wages. This argument has not met with success. However, the only attempt to provide a principled justification for deductions in this context has come from Scott J in *Sim v Rotherham Metropolitan Borough Council*.[613] Here the defendant education authority had deducted a sum from the claimant teacher's salary to represent her failure to provide cover for an absent colleague for a 35-minute period during a campaign of industrial action. She sued to recover this amount claiming, first, that she owed no contractual obligation to provide cover and, second, that even if she had, the employer's remedy lay only in damages. Scott J, having held that her failure to provide cover was a breach of contract,[614] affirmed that, given that she had been allowed to continue working, the contractual obligations on both sides remained on foot and she was entitled to her salary. However, her claim to payment in full was subject to the employer's cross-claim for damages for the loss flowing from the breach. Applying the doctrine of 'equitable set-off' Scott J held that it would be unjust to allow the claimant to proceed without taking account of the loss to the employer, which in this case it was agreed was no less than the sum the employers had deducted.

This decision allows employers to decide what sums reflect the damages to which they are entitled and puts the onus on employees to challenge this. The reluctance of the courts to grant interim relief during disputes to order the employer to make withheld payments compounds the difficulties for employees who may suffer hardship as a result.[615] Moreover, because the restrictions on deductions imposed by the ERA 1996 do not apply to those made on account of industrial action,[616] employees who are dismissed for instituting legal proceedings on this matter who lack the requisite period of continuous employment will not qualify for protection against unfair dismissal (see para 5.101 above). The difficulties of quantifying loss in the case of clerical, managerial or professional workers[617] has not prevented this being a significant threat in the education

---

613 [1986] IRLR 391.

614 See Fredman and Morris, 1987b, for a critique of this reasoning.

615 See *Jakeman v South West Thames Regional Health Authority and London Ambulance Service* [1990] IRLR 62.

616 Section 14(5). In *Gill v Ford Motor Company Ltd* [2004] IRLR 840, the EAT held that an employment tribunal must make a finding of fact as to whether a worker who has suffered a deduction has taken part in industrial action. However, if the worker has taken part in industrial action, a tribunal has no jurisdiction to examine whether the deduction was authorised by the contract: *Sunderland Polytechnic v Evans* [1993] IRLR 196; *Scott v Strathclyde Fire Board* EATS/0050/03 26 April 2004.

617 In *Royle v Trafford Borough Council* [1984] IRLR 184, a teacher had refused to admit an additional five pupils into his class of 31. A reduction of 5/36ths was said to represent the 'notional value' of the services he had failed to perform. See also G Morris with S Rydzkowski, 1984: pp 160–161 on deductions in the NHS during the 1982 dispute. In *Jakeman v South West Thames Health Authority and London Ambulance Service* [1990] IRLR 62, the employer was seeking to rely on the losses it would otherwise incur in calling upon other agencies, such as the police and army, to help it out.

sector and in white-collar areas of the civil service and local government where industrial action has traditionally taken the form of industrial action short of a strike.[618] It should be noted that all the time during which a worker is 'engaged in taking industrial action' is excluded in respect of the time for which the national minimum wage is payable.[619] Thus workers such as Wiluszynski would have had no minimum wage entitlement in relation to the work which they actually did.[620] There is no definition of 'industrial action' in this context, and on the basis of the interpretation of this concept in relation to unfair dismissal even a ban on non-contractual duties could fall within it (see para 11.73). By analogy with the unfair dismissal provisions, disputes may also arise as to when a worker is 'engaged in taking' industrial action; it would seem to be confined to times when the worker individually is working restrictively (going-slow, for example), but it could conceivably be argued to extend to any period during which the worker has evinced an intention to participate in industrial action (such as a programme of rolling strikes) if called upon to do so.

Lock-outs and the contract of employment

11.70 Unlike some systems, English law does not formally distinguish between 'offensive' and 'defensive' lock-outs of workers by employers. However, as we have seen, where employees refuse to perform their full range of normal duties an employer is legally entitled to send them home without pay, the functional equivalent of one form of 'defensive' lock-out.[621] Where there is no preceding industrial action, or the threat of it, by employees a lock-out is likely to constitute a breach of contract on the part of the employer unless (exceptionally) there is provision for suspension of the contract during a lock-out or notice of appropriate length to terminate the contract is given. Merely giving notice to 'lock-out' may not be sufficient as this, like strike notice, can be seen as notice of intended breach.[622] Provided that employees can show that they were ready and willing to work during this period they would be able to sue for any losses to them resulting from the breach. Whether or not the breach will be serious enough to amount to repudiation of the contract will depend upon the facts;[623] the duration of the lock-out may be material here. Even if a lock-out is repudiatory, however, employees would be ill-advised to resign in response without careful consideration of the circumstances; although they would have a wrongful dismissal claim, there is no protection against unfair dismissal for employees dismissed during a lock-out unless the employer discriminates between those 'directly interested';[624] dismisses for a limited range of automatically unfair reasons; or dismisses the employee for taking protected industrial action once the 'protected period' has commenced.[625] Moreover, for the purposes of a statutory redundancy payment,

---

618 Elgar and Simpson, 1992: p 50.
619 NMWR 1999, SI 1999/584, regs 15(6), 17(2), 18(2) and 21(4).
620 Simpson, 1999a: pp 17–18; see also Simpson, 1999b.
621 'Defensive' lock-outs take a variety of forms within different systems: see Ben-Israel, 1994: pp 14–19.
622 In *Sanders v Ernest A Neale* [1974] ICR 565, the court assumed for the purposes of argument that a lock-out was a breach of contract by the employer; similarly in *Chappell v Times Newspapers Ltd* [1975] ICR 145. However, the Court of Appeal decision in *Express and Star Ltd v Bunday* [1987] IRLR 422, discussed in para 11.73 below, assumes that a lock-out will not necessarily constitute a breach.
623 *Cummings v Charles Connell & Co (Shipbuilders) Ltd* 1969 SLT 25.
624 TULRCA 1992, s 238.
625 See para 11.71 *et seq* below.

an employee who leaves during a lock-out cannot claim to have been constructively dismissed.[626] This leaves the extraordinary situation that an employer may be able to impose new terms and conditions upon its workforce and then lock out and dismiss with relative impunity those who do not accept them.[627] As we shall see in para 11.73, the position is further complicated by the fact that the line between a strike and a lock-out may, on occasion, be hard to draw.

Further difficulties arise if only a proportion of an employer's workforce is taking industrial action and it wishes to lock out the remainder. The limited authority which exists on this point suggests that, in the absence of a contractual right to suspend employees in these circumstances, the lock-out will constitute a breach of contract unless the employees have evinced a definite intention of participating in the action. In *Ticehurst v British Telecommunications plc*[628] the Court of Appeal rejected the employers' argument that the employee's evinced intention of future participation in a campaign of rolling strikes would alone be sufficient ground for them to refuse to allow her to work during the dispute unless it could be argued that the present value of her services would be reduced by such a risk. As Ralph Gibson LJ, giving the judgment of the court, explained:

> If in this case the only intention evinced by Mrs Ticehurst was to continue to respond to a strike call if and when called upon by her union to strike then ... she would in effect have been saying to BT that she was intending ... to perform the full range of her contractual duties until some time in the future, which might not happen at all, when she would break her contract by going on strike ... If, during that time that her services would be rendered, BT would receive full value for those services, I can see no reason why BT should not perform their part of the contract which they had chosen to keep in existence.[629]

Similarly a refusal to give an undertaking not to participate in any further action will not, of itself, justify a lock-out.[630] However, the effectiveness of the remedy which may be available to an employee in this situation may be limited. In *Chappell v Times Newspapers Ltd*[631] the Court of Appeal refused to grant an injunction to restrain an employer from treating workers as having terminated their contracts of employment on the basis that they could be called upon to take industrial action, the grounds being that, even if the employers' action was not lawful, these workers could not affirm that they were ready and willing to perform their side of the contract. In such a case the employees' sole contractual remedy would be a claim for unpaid wages or damages for breach of contract.

If the contract of employment does permit an employer to lay off employees whose workload is reduced due to industrial action by other workers they may forfeit their right to a statutory guarantee payment. The legislation provides that this right is excluded where the failure to provide work occurs in consequence of a strike, lock-out or other industrial action involving fellow employees or those of an associated employer.[632]

---

626 ERA 1996, s 136(1), (2).
627 See K Miller and C Woolfson, 1994, for a description of the use of this tactic by Timex in 1993.
628 [1992] IRLR 219.
629 [1992] IRLR 219, 227.
630 [1992] IRLR 219, 228.
631 [1975] ICR 145.
632 ERA 1996, s 29(3). Note that there is no statutory definition of strike, industrial action or lock-out in this context; see further para 11.71 below.

INDUSTRIAL ACTION AND STATUTORY RIGHTS

11.71 As the previous section makes clear the common law is ill-equipped to deal with the issues raised by industrial action. Perhaps more surprisingly, legislation, too, has not until recently accorded employees any additional protection; indeed, those taking industrial action have risked prejudicing a number of their statutory rights. In relation to unfair dismissal, the prevailing philosophy of all governments has been to exclude dismissals taking place during industrial disputes from the purview of employment tribunals. However, there has been a limited measure of protection against victimisation of particular employees in the case of 'non-unofficial' action only.[633] More recently, tribunals have been afforded jurisdiction where the employee was dismissed (or, in a redundancy case, selected for dismissal) for specified reasons, which render the dismissal automatically unfair. The most wide ranging of these reasons, introduced by the Employment Relations Act 1999, and applicable only to 'non-unofficial' action, is because the employee took industrial action (termed 'protected industrial action') that he or she was induced to take by an act which, by virtue of TULRCA 1992, s 219, is not actionable in tort; it is then automatically unfair to dismiss the employee during the first twelve weeks of his or her participation in the action,[634] or at a later date in specified circumstances. Although, as we discuss in para 11.78 *et seq*, this provision affords far from comprehensive protection to those who take industrial action, it marks a considerable extension of the previous position. Other statutory rights remain more vulnerable, however: participants in industrial action risk losing all or part of a statutory redundancy payment to which they may otherwise be entitled, and statutory rights to payment during statutory minimum notice periods are also put in jeopardy; if the employer gives notice but then terminates the contract in response to a repudiatory breach of contract by the employee (which can include industrial action) during the notice period, no payment will be due for the balance of the original notice period.[635] Furthermore, those who suffer financial loss against a background of industrial action may be denied access to payments to which they may be entitled in other contexts. We indicated the position in relation to statutory guarantee payments in para 11.70 above. Employees are also disqualified from receiving statutory sick pay if there is a stoppage of work due to a trade dispute at their place of employment unless they can prove no 'direct interest' in the dispute.[636] Entitlements to social security benefits, which we discuss in para 11.86 *et seq*, are also curtailed. Dismissal rights apart, only the continuity provisions provide a measure of protection to strikers. A week during any part of which an employee takes part in a 'strike', however short, does not count for the purpose of calculating his or her period of continuous employment but, in contrast to the usual position when a week

---

633 We use the inelegant term 'non-unofficial' for two reasons: first, because there is no statutory definition (or use in this context) of the term 'official' industrial action; and second, because 'unofficial' as defined in the Act does not correspond to the commonly understood meaning of that term.

634 From 6 April 2005, the basic 'protected period' is twelve weeks but this period is lengthened if the employee is locked-out by the employer once he or she has started protected industrial action: TULRCA 1992, s 238A(7A)–(7D), inserted by ERelA 2004, s 26(3).

635 ERA 1996, s 91(4). The right to payment is also excluded if the employee gives notice but participates in a strike as defined in s 235(5) before the notice expires: s 91(2).

636 SSCBA 1992, 153(3), Sch 11.

cannot be credited, continuity remains unbroken so that the periods of employment before and after the strike can be aggregated.[637] This applies even if the employee is dismissed during the strike and subsequently re-employed.[638] Identical provision is made for weeks during any part of which the employee is locked-out from work where the contract does not remain in existence;[639] if it does so remain then the week of the lock-out counts for continuity purposes in the normal way.

The continuity provisions are unusual in being accorded a definition of 'strike' and 'lock-out'. 'Strike' in this context means:

(a) the cessation of work by a body of employed persons acting in combination, or

(b) a concerted refusal, or a refusal under a common understanding, of any number of employed persons to continue to work for an employer in consequence of a dispute,

done as a means of compelling their employer or any employed person or body of employed persons, or to aid other employees in compelling their employer or any employed person or body of employed persons, to accept or not to accept terms or conditions of or affecting employment.[640]

This definition covers strikes in support of other employees but does not extend to political or other stoppages whose purpose is not related to compelling acceptance of terms of or affecting employment. 'Lock-out' is defined in analogous terms and means:

(a) the closing of a place of employment, or

(b) the suspension of work, or

(c) the refusal by an employer to continue to employ any number of persons employed by him in consequence of a dispute,

done with a view to compelling persons employed by the employer, or to aid another employer in compelling persons employed by him, to accept terms or conditions of or affecting employment.[641]

These definitions apply also to the provisions governing notice rights and redundancy payments. They are not applied by statute to other contexts, however, although in the absence of any other definition, they may be seen as having some persuasive authority.[642] There is no meaningful definition of the term 'industrial action' in any part of the legislation.[643]

We devote most of this section to a consideration of the rights under the unfair dismissal legislation of employees dismissed while taking industrial action or locked out, which is one of the most crucial areas in practice. In this context it is necessary to distinguish between 'unofficial' disputes, whose participants generally have no protection in any circumstances, and action which is not

637 ERA 1996, s 216(1), (2).
638 *Hanson v Fashion Industries (Hartlepool) Ltd* [1980] IRLR 393.
639 ERA 1996, s 216(3).
640 ERA 1996, s 235(5).
641 ERA 1996, s 235(4).
642 Until TULRCA 1992 there was no definition of 'strike' or 'lock-out' for unfair dismissal purposes and the courts drew some guidance from these definitions. 'Strike' is now defined in this context (rather unhelpfully) as a 'concerted stoppage of work': s 246.
643 The definition in TULRCA 1992, s 62(6) (rights of union members in relation to industrial action ballots) is tautologous.

'unofficial', where there is some protection. Because the distinction between the two was introduced only by the Employment Act 1990 the preponderance of the case law concerns non-unofficial disputes, and we therefore discuss these first, although much of the case law formulated in that context is relevant also to unofficial action. We then examine the effect of taking industrial action upon the right to a redundancy payment. It is notable that protection against dismissal during disputes is confined to 'employees' whereas the immunities against liability in tort apply where there is a 'trade dispute', defined as a dispute between 'workers' and their employer.[644] The obligation to hold a ballot also covers disputes involving those who work under contracts for services. In so restricting the protection, as in several other respects, the law falls short of the protection required by the freedom of association principles of the ILO.[645]

Unfair dismissal during 'non-unofficial' industrial action and lock-outs

11.72 Until recently, the fundamental policy of the unfair dismissal legislation has been to exclude dismissals during industrial disputes from the purview of employment tribunals. This also remains the starting-point of the current law, which affirms that tribunals have no jurisdiction to determine fairness where at the date of dismissal the complainant was taking part in a strike or other industrial action or the employer was conducting or instituting a lock-out.[646] There is no requirement to invoke the statutory dismissal or disciplinary procedures, which we discuss in para 5.124 *et seq*, prior to such dismissals.[647] However, in the case of industrial action which is not 'unofficial' within the meaning of the statute jurisdiction is restored in two broad sets of circumstances. The first is where it is shown that the employer discriminated between those defined as 'relevant employees' and a dismissed employee would otherwise qualify to claim;[648] the employer may then defend the claim in the normal way.[649] The second applies where the employee was dismissed (or, in a redundancy case, selected for dismissal) on one of a number of specified grounds: taking 'protected industrial action' during the first twelve weeks of participation in that action (or longer in some circumstances); specified activities relating to health and safety; acting, or standing for election, as an employee representative or representative of the workforce; on the grounds of pregnancy or childbirth; reasons relating to leave for family reasons or flexible working; or reasons related to jury service. In these cases the dismissal is automatically unfair.[650]

The justification offered for excluding the jurisdiction of tribunals during industrial disputes was the desire to avoid them becoming embroiled in the merits of such disputes, although it has been argued that, in their initial form in the Industrial Relations Act 1971, the real purpose was to preserve the employer's sanction of dismissal.[651] This latter rationale was at the forefront of the judgment of the National

---

644 See para 11.25 above for the definition of a 'trade dispute' and paras 3.19 *et seq* and 3.51 *et seq* above for the definition of 'employee' and 'worker' respectively.
645 See further para 11.92.
646 TULRCA 1992, s 238(1).
647 EADRR 2004, reg 4(1)(c).
648 TULRCA 1992 s 238(2).
649 In this situation there is an obligation to use the appropriate statutory dismissal and disciplinary procedure: EADRR 2004, reg 4(1)(c)(ii); see further para 5.124 *et seq*.
650 TULRCA 1992, s 238(2A), (2B); s 238(2A); see further para 5.95 *et seq* above.
651 See P Davies and M Freedland, 1993: pp 323–327; 375–376; Ewing, 1991: pp 41–44.

Industrial Relations Court in *Heath and Hammersey v JF Longman (Meat Salesman) Ltd*[652] where it was held that in the context of the excluding provision 'date of dismissal' meant 'time', so preventing employers from dismissing employees who have indicated that their action is at an end.[653] Sir Hugh Griffiths stated:

> It appears to this court that the manifest overall purpose of ... [the section] ... is to give a measure of protection to an employer if his business is faced with ruin by a strike. It enables him in those circumstances, if he cannot carry on the business without a labour force, to dismiss the labour force on strike; to take on another labour force without the stigma of its being an unfair dismissal. That being the overall purpose it would appear to be manifestly wrong, when an employer has been told that strike action has been called off, that he should nevertheless still be free to dismiss those who took part in the strike, without any risk of a finding that he was acting unfairly.[654]

The continuation of this position in 1974 was a mark of the Labour Government's adherence in this area to the principle of collective *laissez-faire*; as Davies and Freedland point out, '[a] confident labour movement in 1975 may have felt few qualms about foregoing a protection it had never previously had – since before 1971 the issue could not have arisen'.[655] Even during the latter part of the 1970s, however, the weakness of this approach was highlighted by the sacking of strikers during the Grunwick dispute[656] and further emphasised by similar events in the Wapping dispute during the 1980s.[657] Although the protection afforded to participants in 'protected industrial action' ameliorates the position, the general principle of exclusion remains significant, not least because of the restricted scope of the new provision. Moreover, much of the case law which has developed in the context of the exclusionary principle is relevant to the discussion of 'protected industrial action'. For both these reasons, we discuss this principle first before considering 'protected industrial action'.

(i) The scope of the exclusion of jurisdiction

11.73   The language in which the general exclusion is drafted, as interpreted by the courts, has resulted in even narrower protection than might at first appear. First, jurisdiction is excluded if, judged objectively, employees were taking part in industrial action or locked out at the time of their dismissal; this need not be the reason for dismissal.[658] It follows that it is irrelevant whether the employers knew or acted properly in attempting to decide whether the dismissed employees were participating in a particular campaign. Second, under current case law there is no room to argue that the action was engineered or provoked by the unreasonable or even the unlawful conduct of the employer. In *Wilkins v Cantrell and Cochrane (GB) Ltd*[659] there had been a number of occasions in which lorries

---

652   [1973] IRLR 214.
653   'Date of dismissal' is defined in the statute as, where the employee's contract of employment was terminated by notice, the date on which the employer's notice was given and in any other case the effective date of termination: TULRCA 1992, s 238(5).
654   [1973] IRLR 214, 215.
655   P Davies and M Freedland, 1993: p 375.
656   See Rogaly, 1977: pp 136–140.
657   See Ewing and Napier, 1986.
658   *Faust v Power Packing Casemakers Ltd* [1983] IRLR 117 at 121 (Stephenson LJ); *Bolton Roadways Ltd v Edwards* [1987] IRLR 392; *Manifold Industries Ltd v Sims* [1991] IRLR 242; *Jenkins v P & O European Ferries (Dover) Ltd* [1991] ICR 652.
659   [1978] IRLR 483.

had been sent out from the employers' depot in an overloaded condition. Ultimately the lorry drivers felt compelled to take strike action and were dismissed. It was argued for the three applicants that the employers were in breach of the law in sending out the lorries in this condition; that in requiring the drivers to go out with them they were putting the drivers at risk because they might find themselves charged with aiding and abetting the employers; and that in these circumstances the employers were in breach of the contract of employment. The employment tribunal concluded that at the worst these instances 'indicated negligence not amounting to deliberate breaches of the law' which did not constitute a fundamental breach of contract. The EAT, although expressing sympathy with the men, endorsed this view.[660] This approach may require modification in some circumstances in the light of the HRA 1998, which we discuss below.

Third, whether or not there is a 'strike', 'lock-out' or 'industrial action' taking place is a question of fact for the tribunal, acting as an industrial jury, to decide. Until TULRCA 1992 there was no statutory definition of 'strike' in this context; it is now (rather unhelpfully) defined as a 'concerted stoppage of work'.[661] For 'lock-out' and 'industrial action' there is no statutory definition whatsoever. The Court of Appeal has instructed tribunals to give the words 'industrial action' 'their natural and ordinary meaning'.[662] Thus one tribunal may decide that there is 'industrial action', another the opposite, on the same set of facts, with the scope for appeal being confined to the argument that the tribunal has given the term a meaning it could not reasonably bear (or that there is no evidence to support the finding of fact).[663]

In relation to a 'lock-out' and, before the 1992 Act, 'strike' the courts have had regard to the definitions provided for continuity purposes,[664] whilst emphasising that these definitions should not be applied exclusively and, indeed, it may be difficult to predict into which of these categories a particular situation falls. The difficulty in distinguishing between a strike and a lock-out is a particularly serious matter given that the definition of 'relevant employee' differs in each case and there is no protection afforded to employees who are dismissed while locked-out before 'protected industrial action' has started. In *Express and Star Ltd v Bunday*[665] the Court of Appeal rejected the argument that a lock-out required a breach of contract on the part of the employer; although in some cases this might be critical, its materiality would depend upon the facts. Thus if an employer unilaterally introduces new technology which employees refuse to use and they are then told not to return to work until they are so willing, this

---

660 See also *Marsden v Fairey Stainless Ltd* [1979] IRLR 103. The view expressed by Elias, 1994 (see para 11.64) would produce a different result but this has yet to be tested in the courts.

661 TULRCA 1992, s 246. In *Connex South Eastern Ltd v RMT* [1999] IRLR 249, a ban on overtime and rest-day working was said to constitute a strike for the purposes of deciding whether the action was authorised in a ballot. This definition of 'strike' has been excluded for the purposes (only) of the question on the voting paper.

662 *Faust v Power Packing Casemakers Ltd* [1983] IRLR 117 at 121 (Stephenson LJ). See also *Knowles v Fire Brigades Union* [1996] IRLR 617, discussed in para 10.12 above.

663 *Express and Star Ltd v Bunday* [1987] IRLR 422; *Faust v Power Packing Casemakers Ltd* [1983] IRLR 117.

664 See, for example, *Express and Star*, above. In relation to a strike some cases also refer to the definition offered by Lord Denning MR in *Tramp Shipping Corpn v Greenwich Marine Inc* [1975] ICR 261, 266.

665 [1987] IRLR 422.

may equally be perceived as a strike or a lock-out. How it is perceived may be crucial for employees' rights.

It is perhaps even more anomalous that industrial action need not constitute a breach of the contract of employment. In *Faust v Power Packing Casemakers Ltd*[666] the Court of Appeal affirmed that a refusal to work overtime because of a wage dispute could constitute 'industrial action', notwithstanding that there was no contractual obligation for employees to do this work. This could be distinguished from a refusal to perform work for other reasons, such as personal reasons or the desire to attend a football match, by reference to its purpose – to put pressure on the employer. This emphasis on motive had been applied by the Court of Appeal in *Rasool v Hepworth Pipe Co Ltd (No 2)*[667] in finding that attendance at an unauthorised mass meeting convened to consider employees' views about impending wage negotiations was a union activity rather than industrial action because the intention was not that of putting pressure on the employer.[668]

The emphasis upon putting pressure on the employer as the hallmark may be appropriate in some cases but is probably unduly narrow in excluding disruptive action in protest at government policies or as a demonstration of solidarity which would almost certainly be viewed in practice as 'industrial action'. From another perspective, the interpretation of 'industrial action' may now require reconsideration in the light of the HRA 1998. As we discussed in para 11.63, the employer's managerial prerogative and the employee's correlative duty to obey lawful and reasonable orders must be interpreted by the courts and tribunals in the light of Convention rights. It is strongly arguable that the duty under HRA 1998, s 3 to give effect to legislation 'so far as it is possible to do so' in a way that is compatible with Convention rights requires courts and tribunals not to regard as 'industrial action' a refusal by workers to obey an order which interferes with the exercise of a Convention right and which will not as such constitute a breach of the contract of employment. The statutory exception where employees stop work for safety reasons should also be noted. As we indicated in para 5.104, it is automatically unfair to dismiss employees who leave, propose to leave or refuse to return to their place of work or any dangerous part thereof in circumstances of danger which they reasonably believe to be serious and imminent and which they could not reasonably have been expected to avert.[669] However, employees who stop work in order to exert pressure on an employer to improve safety conditions outside this specific situation,[670] or to support other workers whose safety is at risk, will not be protected by the statute and are likely to be viewed as taking part in industrial action. Moreover, the statute does not deal directly with the contractual position of the employee who

---

666 [1983] IRLR 117.
667 [1980] IRLR 137. See also, however, *Knowles v Fire Brigades Union* [1996] IRLR 617, discussed in para 10.12 above, where Neill LJ, giving the judgment of the Court of Appeal in a case concerning TULRCA 1992, s 65, opined that in determining what was industrial action it was 'necessary to look at' all the circumstances, including the employees' contracts of employment and whether any breach of or departure from the terms of the contract are involved; the effect on the employer of what is done or omitted; and the object which the union or employees seek to achieve (at 621).
668 Note that the EAT has held that TULRCA 1992, ss 146 and 152, on the one hand, and s 238 on the other are mutually exclusive: *Drew v St Edmundsbury Borough Council* [1980] IRLR 459.
669 ERA 1996, s 100(1)(d).
670 See *Balfour Kilpatrick Ltd v Acheson* [2003] IRLR 683, discussed in para 5.104; see also D Lewis, 2004.

stops work,[671] nor the position in tort of any individual who induces employees to stop work, although these may now be regarded as subject to the employer's statutory duty to give effect to appropriate procedures to be followed in the event of serious and imminent danger to persons at work, including enabling them to stop work and to require them to be prevented from resuming work.[672]

Until recently it was regarded as clear that 'industrial action' is a collective activity which cannot be taken by one employee alone, a view which corresponds both with the emphasis upon combination and concert in the statutory definitions of a strike and with industrial reality.[673] In *Lewis and Britton v E Mason & Sons*,[674] however, the EAT found that it was open to a tribunal to find that a single employee could be taking part in 'industrial action', thus potentially exposing an employee who refuses on one occasion to carry out an instruction by the employer to dismissal without statutory redress.[675] Although we would regard this decision as erroneous it demonstrates the serious implications of a non-interventionist approach by the legislature and judiciary to this matter. In that case also the EAT refused to characterise as perverse the tribunal's finding that the threat of industrial action itself was 'industrial action' on the basis that there was no further prospect of negotiation before the following day, despite earlier (and we would argue correct) authority to the contrary.[676]

11.74   The courts have held that the issue of whether an employee was 'taking part' in industrial action is also primarily a question for the tribunal, with scope to appeal only if the words are given a meaning of which they are not 'reasonably capable'.[677] With that reservation in mind, the cases offer guidance on some of the issues which this term raises. First, when do employees begin to 'take part' in industrial action? There is authority to suggest that this may be before the contractual obligation to work arises if they have made clear that they will withdraw their labour at that point. In *Winnett v Seamarks Bros Ltd*[678] the EAT upheld the decision of the employment tribunal that the applicant coach driver was 'taking part' in industrial action even though he was not due to work until the following morning given that he had intimated to the employers that he would not work then.[679] Second, when does participation cease? What if

---

671   However see A Edwards, 2000, for the argument, based on *Barber v RJB Mining (UK) Lrd* [1999] ICR 679, that there may be a right for employees to refuse to comply with instructions which are harmful to their health, including circumstances beyond those within the terms of ERA 1996, s 100(1)(d).

672   The Management of Health and Safety at Work Regulations 1999, SI 1999/3242, reg 8. Note also the implied term that employees will take reasonable care to safeguard the health and safety of their employees: see para 4.81. *Quaere* whether in relation to inducing breach of contract the defence of justification would be accepted: see para 11.12.

673   *Bowater Containers Ltd v Blake* (27 May 1982, unreported); see also *Coates and Venables v Modern Methods and Materials Ltd* [1982] IRLR 318, 323 (Eveleigh LJ). Cf *McCormick v Horsepower Ltd* [1981] IRLR 217 (individual employee could be said to be on strike but not the same strike as other workers because community of purpose lacking).

674   [1994] IRLR 4. See Dolding, 1994.

675   This is highly unlikely to constitute 'protected industrial action'; see below.

676   See *Midland Plastics v Till* [1983] IRLR 9.

677   *Coates and Venables v Modern Methods and Materials Ltd* [1982] IRLR 318.

678   [1978] IRLR 387.

679   Cf *Naylor v Orton and Smith Ltd; Naylor v D Twedell Engineering Ltd* [1983] IRLR 233, where the EAT upheld the employment tribunal's decision that a resolution to impose an immediate overtime ban did not constitute industrial action; this decision presents the problem of defining when the action does begin (when the first employee refuses to work overtime?) and whether other employees are taking part in the action as from that moment or only when they in turn refuse such a request.

the employee falls sick, for example? In *Williams v Western Mail and Echo Ltd*[680] it was held that 'once men (sic) have stated that they will apply sanctions and do so they may be regarded as applying the sanctions either until they are discontinued or until they indicate an intention of stopping them'. However, there is no authority as to the position in relation to 'rolling strikes', whereby one group of employees comes out on one day, another the next. Should all employees who may be called upon to strike at some point be treated as 'taking part' from the outset? Conversely, should those who have already been on strike be treated as 'taking part' throughout because they intend to strike again should they be called upon to do so? Third, what of employees who fail to cross a picket line, perhaps for fear of abuse by strikers? In *Coates and Venables v Modern Methods and Materials Ltd*[681] the Court of Appeal supported an objective approach to this question; an employer is entitled to assume that any employee who does not come to work during a strike is taking part in it. Stephenson LJ appeared to consider that expressing disagreement with the strike may alter the position;[682] for Kerr LJ it was actions only which were material, although he suggested that if an employee was absent at the beginning of a strike for reasons unconnected with it, such as sickness or holidays, he would not be 'taking part'.[683] However, in *Bolton Roadways Ltd v Edwards*[684] the EAT held that employees who were lawfully absent when the action started would be capable of 'taking part' if they associated themselves with the strike, attended at the picket line, or took part in the other activities of the strikers with a view to furthering their aims; taking part in a strike did not require a breach of the contractual obligation to work.

(ii) Jurisdiction on the basis of victimisation

11.75   The employer's protection against unfair dismissal claims by employees dismissed while taking part in industrial action or locked out is lost in two situations (in addition to those where 'protected industrial action' or another specified reason is the reason for dismissal). The first is where it is shown that one or more 'relevant employees' of the same employer have not been dismissed.[685] The second is where it is shown that any 'relevant employee' has 'before the expiry of the period of three months beginning with the date of his dismissal been offered re-engagement and ... the complainant has not been offered re-engagement'.[686] Where a tribunal has jurisdiction to determine whether a dismissal is fair because the employer has dismissed the employee in one of these two situations the statutory dismissal and disciplinary procedures, which we described in paras 5.124 *et seq*, apply.[687]

---

680 [1980] IRLR 222, 224.
681 [1982] IRLR 318.
682 [1982] IRLR 318, 323.
683 [1982] IRLR 318, 325.
684 [1987] IRLR 392. This approach is consistent with *Winnett v Seamarks Brothers Ltd*, above. See also *Rogers v Chloride Systems Ltd* [1992] ICR 198 where the EAT considered that had the applicant, who was on sick leave throughout the dispute, answered 'no' on being asked if she would have returned to work on a specific date had she not been sick, or whether she would have undertaken to work normally as soon as she was able, that would have been sufficient to constitute 'taking part'. Cf *Hindle Gears Ltd v McGinty* [1984] IRLR 477, 480.
685 TULRCA 1992, s 238(2)(a).
686 TULRCA 1992, s 238(2)(b).
687 EADRR 2004, reg 4(1)(c)(ii).

In relation to a strike or other industrial action, 'relevant employees' are 'those employees at the establishment of the employer at or from which the complainant works who at the date of his dismissal were taking part in the action'.[688] By analogy with the interpretation of this phrase in relation to the exclusion of jurisdiction,[689] 'date of dismissal' in this context is likely to be interpreted as 'time' of dismissal, so if a number of employees returned to work on the morning of a particular day the employer could probably safely dismiss those who had not done so later that day. There is no requirement that employees should receive any warning that they will be dismissed unless they return. There is no definition of 'establishment' nor has this issue to date arisen in the case law in this context; it is likely that the criteria applied by the British courts in relation to redundancy consultation, which we discussed in para 9.32, would be applied here as well.

For a lock-out, the concept of 'relevant employees' is more widely drawn to mean those who were 'directly interested in the dispute in contemplation or furtherance of which the lock-out occurred',[690] with no requirement that they should work at or from the complainant's establishment. 'Direct interest' is a concept borrowed from social security law and covers anyone whose terms of employment are likely to be immediately and automatically affected by the outcome of the dispute.[691] Whether or not employees were 'directly interested' is to be assessed on the date on which the lock-out occurred.[692] The scope of 'relevant employees' in the context of a lock-out was considered by the EAT in *Fisher v York Trailer Co Ltd*.[693] The employers were concerned that the employees who worked on the main container line at one of their factories were 'going slow'. They sent a letter to each of the 34 employees concerned which required them to give an undertaking that they would work at a normal incentive pace under the existing bonus scheme, failing which they would be suspended from the start of the next shift. On the next day no production occurred and the men held meetings. Subsequent to those meetings all but seven of the employees signed the document. The seven were eventually dismissed. The EAT upheld the tribunal's finding that they had been dismissed while the employer was conducting a lock-out. It also held that employees who are 'directly interested' in a dispute are not limited to those who remained locked out until the end of the dispute and, indeed, could extend to those who were not locked out at all. In this case all 34 employees were 'relevant employees'. This decision shows that an employer who wishes to retain the immunity may need to dismiss a much wider range of employees in a lock-out than a strike. In practice, a well-advised employer is more likely now to argue that employees were taking part in industrial action, thus enabling a smaller pool to be at issue, unless this would mean that the dismissals would then be automatically unfair because they were due to the employees taking part in 'protected industrial action' or for some other specified automatically unfair reason.

---

688 TULRCA 1992, s 238(3)(b). Where the action is 'unofficial' for some employees taking part in it but not others, the 'unofficial' participants remain 'relevant employees': s 238(3).
689 See *Heath and Hammersey v JF Longman (Meat Salesman) Ltd* [1973] IRLR 214.
690 TULRCA 1992, s 238(3)(a).
691 *Presho v Department of Health and Social Security (Insurance Officer)* [1984] IRLR 74.
692 *H Campey & Sons Ltd v Bellwood* [1987] ICR 311.
693 [1979] IRLR 385.

11.76   For the discriminatory treatment to take the form of offering re-engagement, this means:

> ... an offer (made either by the original employer or by a successor of that employer or an associated employer) to re-engage an employee, either in the job which he held immediately before the date of dismissal or in a different job which would be reasonably suitable in his case.[694]

The offer must be made specifically to the individual; a press advertisement inviting applications from the public at large constitutes merely an offer to treat for re-engagement,[695] in contrast to a communication which indicates that should individuals apply they will be re-engaged.[696] The offer need not be in writing and, indeed, may be constituted by tacit acceptance that the employment is continuing.[697] Although the employer must know about the first job from which the employee had been dismissed, this knowledge may be constructive (in the sense that it has the means of obtaining it) as well as actual, thus putting the onus on the employer to make adequate enquiries about the worker's position before re-engaging him or her.[698]

There is no definition of 'job' in TULRCA but under EPCA 1978, applicable before the entry into force of the 1992 Act, it was defined as 'the nature of the work which [the employee] ... is employed to do in accordance with his contract and the capacity and place in which he is so employed', and this definition, which now appears in ERA 1996, s 235(1), also applies in this context.[699] The term was examined by the Court of Appeal in *Williams v National Theatre Board Ltd.*[700] Thirty strikers were offered re-engagement on the basis that they were on second warning as regards their general conduct; one had an offer with no such conditions. The Court of Appeal held that if an employee was offered re-engagement in the same capacity as before there was no requirement that the terms and conditions should be identical, although Lord Denning MR opined that if the terms were unreasonable – half-pay or half-time, for example, to a former full-time worker – that might not constitute the same 'job'.[701] In this case, however, the condition of second warning did not prevent it being the same job. This decision means that employers may discriminate between employees to whom 're-engagement' is offered both in relation to their position under the disciplinary procedures and, at least in minor ways, substantive terms and conditions. Moreover, the terms offered to employees, on either a uniform or differential basis, may be the very ones which were the subject-matter of the original dispute.[702] Where an employee is offered a different job whether it is 'reasonably suitable' will probably depend, by analogy with cases relating to redundancy payments, upon factors such as status, use of skill, and pay and benefits.

---

694   TULRCA 1992, s 238(4). For a claim based on selective re-engagement the complainant must present the claim to an employment tribunal within six months of his or her own dismissal (with the usual provision for extension where the tribunal is satisfied that this was not 'reasonably practicable'): s 239(2).
695   *Crosville Wales Ltd v Tracey* [1993] IRLR 60.
696   *Williams v National Theatre Board Ltd* [1982] IRLR 377.
697   *Bolton Roadways Ltd v Edwards* [1987] IRLR 392.
698   *Bigham and Keogh v GKN Kwikform Ltd* [1992] IRLR 4.
699   TULRCA 1992, s 239(1) originally stated that s 238 shall be construed as one with Part V of EPCA 1978, and now states that it shall be construed as one with ERA 1996, Part X, to which the definition in ERA 1996, s 235(1) applies.
700   [1982] IRLR 377.
701   [1982] IRLR 377, 379.
702   Ewing, 1991: p 59.

11.77   The claim that the employer has selectively dismissed or offered re-engagement within the meaning of the legislation must be established before an employment tribunal has jurisdiction to hear the claim. The date upon which discrimination between 'relevant employees' must be shown is the time when the tribunal either determines the substantive issue (involving determination of the jurisdiction point as well) or the jurisdiction point on a preliminary hearing.[703] This means that an employer who dismisses selectively and then learns during the course of the hearing that one relevant employee was not dismissed can defeat the claim by dismissing that employee before the hearing ends. Even though the employee so dismissed may then have a claim for unfair dismissal, this may be the cheaper option for the employer. Moreover, in *P & O European Ferries (Dover) Ltd v Byrne*[704] the Court of Appeal held that where the identity of an alleged 'relevant employee' is unknown to the employers, the tribunal may order the name of that person to be disclosed by the complainant(s) either before or at the hearing in order to enable the employer to know the case it has to meet, even though this may enable the employer to take action which would defeat the claim. Less objectionably, an employer may defeat a claim based on selective re-engagement by offering the complainant 're-engagement' before the end of the tribunal hearing.[705]

It is important to emphasise that proving selectivity merely gives the tribunal jurisdiction to hear the unfair dismissal claim, which will be determined according to general principles. Thus, if the employee has been dismissed , or selected for dismissal, for reasons which constitute an automatically unfair dismissal, such as participation in union activities, the dismissal will be automatically unfair; otherwise it will be potentially fair if the employer can show that it is for a 'substantial' reason under section 98(1)(b) or 98(2) of ERA 1996.[706] In cases of selective re-engagement references to the principal reason for dismissal are to be read as references to the reason or principal reason for which he or she has not been offered re-engagement.[707] The relevant question then is 'not whether the initial dismissal was justified but whether the refusal to re-engage the applicants was justified when some employees have been taken back'.[708] Acts of gross misconduct during the dispute (such as damaging or stealing the employer's property) may justify selection for dismissal or failure to re-engage; an employee's conduct prior to the dispute may also be material. Thus in one case an employer implemented the next appropriate stage of the disciplinary code against employees who had participated in a strike and it was held that it was not unfair to dismiss those who were on final warning.[709] Participation in industrial action may also, in some circumstances, be a ground for selecting employees for redundancy. In *Cruikshank v Hobbs*[710] the EAT suggested three circumstances where this may be a fair ground for selection: if the strike had 'caused or aggravated the redundancy'; after a long strike, the difficulties of reintroducing strikers due to

---

703 *P & O European Ferries (Dover) Ltd v Byrne* [1989] IRLR 254.
704 [1989] IRLR 254.
705 See, for example, *Highlands Fabricators Ltd v McLaughlin* [1984] IRLR 482.
706 See para 5.115 *et seq* above.
707 TULRCA 1992, s 239(3).
708 *Edwards v Cardiff City Council* [1979] IRLR 303, 305. In *Laffin and Callaghan v Fashion Industries (Hartlepool) Ltd* [1978] IRLR 448 it was held that if a reason would not justify dismissal, it would not justify a refusal to re-engage.
709 *Bernard Matthews plc v Rowland* (24 May 1982, unreported).
710 [1977] ICR 725. Cf *Laffin and Callaghan v Fashion Industries (Hartlepool) Ltd* [1978] IRLR 448, where it was held unfair to select on the basis solely of a 'loyalty' test.

technical or administrative changes during their absence; and if the friction which would arise from dismissing non-strikers and replacing them with strikers would impair morale and efficiency.

(iii) 'Protected industrial action'

11.78   The Employment Relations Act 1999 accorded tribunals jurisdiction to examine whether an employee has been dismissed for taking 'protected industrial action'; if this is found to be the case, and specified conditions are met, the dismissal is automatically unfair.[711] No minimum period of employment is required and there is no upper age limit barring claims.[712] The statutory dismissal and disciplinary procedures, which we described in para 5.124 *et seq*, do not apply to such dismissals.[713] However, the scope of this protection is heavily circumscribed. First, an employee takes 'protected industrial action' only if he or she commits an act which, *by virtue of section 219 of TULRCA 1992*, is not actionable in tort.[714] The restriction to acts not actionable by virtue of section 219 means that industrial action which is not actionable in tort at common law (for example, a ban on voluntary overtime, which may not constitute a breach of contract by those participating in it) is excluded. More importantly in practice, as we saw in para 11.24, section 219 does not afford protection against all the torts that those who induce employees to take part in industrial action may commit; thus, for example, it does not cover torts based upon a breach of a statutory duty. Finally protection under section 219 is conditional upon the union having met all the requirements relating to ballots and notices to employers (see para 11.32 *et seq*). The statutory language (an act 'which is not actionable in tort') suggests that it will be sufficient that immunity is lost in relation only to one of a number of employers involved in the dispute. Thus, if a union fails to give only one employer the requisite notice of the action to be taken, all employees who have been induced by a call made by the union to take industrial action will lose any protection against dismissal. Framing the definition of 'protected industrial action' in terms of immunity in tort also means that employment tribunals may be required, for the first time, to decide complex issues relating to the scope of the economic torts, a difficulty compounded by the fact that many of the decisions relating to the existence and ambit of these torts have been reached in interim proceedings only. Where proceedings in tort are being brought in the High Court against the union that organised the industrial action, it would seem sensible for tribunals to adjourn the unfair dismissal hearing pending judgment on that claim. Notably, however, tribunals are specifically empowered to adjourn unfair dismissal proceedings only until the conclusion of any *interim* proceedings,[715] although strictly speaking only a full trial on the merits would give an authoritative ruling on whether action was 'protected'. Where proceedings have not been brought in tort, there seems no basis on which a tribunal could refer the matter to the courts.

---

711 TULRCA 1992, s 238A. Note that this provision does not apply to 'unofficial' action, defined in s 237(2); see further para 11.84.
712 TULRCA 1992 s 239(1).
713 EADRR 2004, reg 4(1)(d).
714 TULRCA 1992, s 238A(1).
715 The Employment Tribunals (Constitution and Rules of Procedure) Regulations 2004, SI 2004/1861, Sch 1, para 55.

11.79 The second important limitation is that it is not sufficient to attract protection that the employee was dismissed while protected industrial action was being taken; the fact that the employee took such action must be the *reason* or principal reason for dismissal (or, in a 'redundancy case', for selection for dismissal).[716] Moreover, the burden to show the reason will lie on the employee, given that the tribunal would not otherwise have jurisdiction. As cases in the context of 'trade union' dismissals show, this may not be an easy test to satisfy, particularly where the decision is taken by a group of persons.[717] Moreover, employers may well be tempted to use the occasion of the industrial action to dismiss those whom it has been wishing to dismiss for other reasons, such as their poor performance or absence records, without going through the requisite disciplinary or performance procedures. Provided that they do not displace their immunity by discriminating between 'relevant employees', or by dismissing for a limited range of other automatically unfair reasons, they will be able to do this with impunity. The restriction of protection to situations where the industrial action is the reason for dismissal stands in marked contrast to the general exclusion of jurisdiction, which applies where the employee is *taking part* in such action. It is also notable that the protection applies only if the employee 'took' such action; it does not appear to cover threatening to take it. Although participation in activities prior to a strike can constitute protected trade union activities,[718] it is unclear whether threatening to take industrial action would be covered by such protection in the light of the finding (in our view, mistaken) in *Lewis and Britton v E Mason and Sons*,[719] discussed above, that this could, of itself, constitute industrial action.

11.80 Third, the protection against dismissal for having taken protected industrial action applies only in three sets of circumstances. The first is where the date of dismissal[720] is 'within the protected period'.[721] Originally this was a period of eight weeks. Since the ERelA 2004 amendments came into force,[722] the 'protected period. in relation to the dismissal of an employee, is the sum of the basic period and any extension period in relation to that employee'.[723] The 'basic period' is twelve weeks 'beginning with the first day of protected industrial action', which is defined as 'the day on which the employee starts to take protected industrial action'.[724] Framing the protection in terms of the employee's own participation makes it crucial to determine when the employee individually started to take such action, a matter which, as we discussed above, may not be easy to determine, particularly in relation to rolling strikes and overtime bans. The initial legislation made no allowance for the situation where employees were locked-out by their employer, so allowing employers to 'sit-out' the period

716 TULRCA 1992, s 238A(2); ERA 1996, s 105(7C). See ERA 1996, s 105(1),(9) for the definition of 'redundancy case'.
717 *Smith v Hayle Town Council* [1978] ICR 996; see further para 8.5.
718 *Britool Ltd v Roberts* [1993] IRLR 481. Industrial action itself has been held not to be within this protection: *Drew v St Edmundsbury Borough Council* [1980] IRLR 459.
719 [1994] IRLR 4; cf *Midland Plastics v Till* [1983] IRLR 9.
720 As defined in TULRCA 1992, s 238(5), s 238A(9). Under s 238(5) where notice of termination is given by the employer the 'date of dismissal' is the date when notice is given, not the date when it expires: see para 11.72 above.
721 TULRCA 1992, s 238A, as amended by ERelA 2004, s 26(2).
722 On 6 April 2005.
723 TULRCA 1992, s 238A(7A).
724 TULRCA 1992, s 238A(7B),(7D), as inserted by ERelA 2004, s 26(3).

of automatic protection by preventing any return to work by employees taking industrial action (possibly also employing temporary workers in their stead). The Government recognised that this was an undesirable position and ERelA 2004 introduced provision for an 'extension period', which is 'a period equal to the number of days falling on or after the first day of protected industrial action (but before the protected period ends) during the whole or any part of which the employee is locked out by his employer'.[725] Thus, if the employer locks out employees who are working-to-rule or banning specific duties, for example, for a ten-day period, those ten days will be added on to the twelve-week 'basic' period, and protection against dismissal for taking 'protected industrial action' during those ten days will continue to apply. In theory the period of protection could be extended indefinitely if workers remain locked out. However the protected period does not start until the employee himself or herself has started taking industrial action. Although this can be a day on which he or she is locked-out,[726] there is no unfair dismissal protection (other than for selective dismissals or the narrow range of other automatically unfair reasons) prior to that.

The second circumstance in which protection applies is if the dismissal takes place after the end of the protected period and the employee had stopped taking protected industrial action before the end of that period,[727] so preventing subsequent victimisation. Once again this is linked to the employee's own participation. An employee who wishes to cease to take protected industrial action and who is absent from work for other reasons, such as illness or holiday, would be well advised to ensure that he or she informs the employer in writing that his or her participation has ceased. The third is where the dismissal takes place after the end of the protected period; the employee had not stopped taking protected industrial action before the end of that period; and 'the employer had not taken such procedural steps as would have been reasonable for the purpose of resolving the dispute to which the protected industrial action relates'.[728] In determining whether an employer has taken such steps, tribunals are directed to have regard in particular to whether the employer or union complied with the procedures established by any applicable collective or other agreement; whether either party offered or agreed to commence or resume negotiations after the start of the protected industrial action; and whether either party unreasonably refused, after the start of the protected industrial action, a request that conciliation services be used, or mediation services be used in relation to procedures to be adopted for the purposes of resolving the dispute.[729] In addition, where there was agreement to use conciliation or mediation services, regard is to be had to the participation, co-operation and other specified conduct of the respective parties in the process,[730] a measure introduced by ERelA 2004 to give the parties a 'clearer indication' of their responsibilities 'to take reasonable procedural actions to resolve the dispute'.[731] However, no regard may be paid to the merits

---

725 TULRCA 1992, s 238A(7A),(7C), inserted by ERelA 2004,s 26(3). 'Lock-out' is not defined, the Government having decided that this should be left to courts and tribunals to decide on the facts: Lord Triesman, HL Debs GC 122, 9 June 2004.
726 TULRCA 1992, s 238A(7D), inserted by ERelA 2004, s 26(3).
727 TULRCA 1992, s 238A(4), as amended by ERelA 2004, S 27.
728 TULRCA 1992, s 238A(5), as amended by ERelA 2004, s 27.
729 TULRCA 1992, s 238A(6)(a)–(d).
730 TULRCA 1992, s 238A(6)(e), 238B, inserted by ERelA 2004, s 28.
731 *Review of the Employment Relations Act 1999: Government Response*, DTI, 2003, para 3.39.

of the dispute.[732] Claims that rest upon this third ground are likely to be particularly contentious.

11.81   The extension of the protected period introduced by ERelA 2004, and provision for periods of lock-out, were welcome amendments to the original legislation.[733] However there remains no protection for those who are dismissed when locked-out by the employer (possibly in breach of contract) prior to 'protected industrial action' commencing, although the justification for a 'breathing space' for negotiations applies equally in this context. The Government's justification for this was that lock-outs themselves were 'rare, and '[p]re-emptive lock-outs are much rarer still and there is less need to reshape the law to deal with this unlikely possibility'.[734] The fact that it is 'unlikely' does not mean that it may not occur, however, and indeed, the new provision for periods of lock-out in calculating the protected period may encourage such pre-emptive action. Moreover, as we discussed above, the dividing-line between a strike and a lock-out may be difficult to draw and the opportunities for appeal are limited. A further weakness of the legislation is that, in contrast to other automatically unfair reasons for dismissal, there is no accompanying protection against subjection to a detriment short of dismissal. However, it may be possible to circumvent this gap if the detriment constitutes a fundamental breach of contract, such as a unilateral cut in wages or breach of the implied term of trust and confidence; in that event, the employee may be able to claim that he or she has been constructively dismissed, while remaining in the employer's employment.[735]

(iv) Other automatically unfair reasons for dismissal

11.82   There are other reasons, in addition to taking 'protected industrial action', that render the dismissal (or, in a 'redundancy case', selection for dismissal) of those taking part in industrial action automatically unfair. These reasons also extend to those dismissed while locked-out. The specified reasons are, in brief, specified activities relating to health and safety;[736] acting, or standing for election, as an employee representative or representative of the workforce; on the grounds of pregnancy or childbirth; reasons relating to leave for family reasons or flexible working; or reasons related to jury service.[737] Once again, there is no minimum period of employment required to qualify to claim, nor is there an upper age limit barring claims, but the burden of proof lies on the applicant to show the reason for dismissal.[738] In practice, it may be difficult (but not impossible) to envisage circumstances where an individual would be able to show that he or she had been dismissed for any of the unfair reasons where all those participating in the action have been dismissed. It is notable that dismissal on grounds of

---

732 TULRCA 1992, s 238A(7).
733 That there is any time limit 'imposes a threshold not contemplated by international labour standards', however: Novitz, 2000: p 387.
734 *Review of the Employment Relations Act 1999: Government Response*, DTI, 2003, para 3.38.
735 *Hogg v Dover College* [1990] ICR 39; *Alcan Extrusions v Yates* [1996] IRLR 327. See further para 5.74.
736 Note, however, the limited scope of the protection afforded to employees who stop work for health and safety reasons: see *Balfour Kilpatrick Ltd v Axheson* [2003] IRLR 683, discussed in para 5.104; see also para 11.73 above.
737 TULRCA 1992, s 238(2A).
738 ERA 1996, ss 108, 109.

trade union membership or participation in union activities is not specified as a reason that restores the tribunal's jurisdiction in this context.

(v) Remedies

11.83   Employees who are found to have been unfairly dismissed while taking industrial action have the usual remedies, discussed in paras 5.148 *et seq*, available to them. The weakness of reinstatement, arguably the only satisfactory remedy to counter the absence of a doctrine of suspension of the contract during industrial action,[739] should be borne in mind here. If the employer has recruited replacement labour during the course of the dispute then, in reality, regardless of the circumstances, it may be impossible for dismissed workers to regain their jobs.[740] The position may be exacerbated when employees have been unfairly dismissed for taking 'protected industrial action', where no order for reinstatement or re-engagement may be made until *all* employees have ceased to take industrial action in relation to the relevant dispute, given that more time may then have passed since the applicant's dismissal.[741] Until recently it was unclear whether participation in a strike or other industrial action could constitute contributory fault which can bring a reduction in the basic and/or compensatory award under ERA 1996, ss 122(2) and 123(6)(see paras 5.154 and 5.160). In *TNT Express (UK) Ltd v Downes*[742] the EAT held that employers should be able to invoke such arguments where the industrial action was wholly unmerited, an approach which conflicted with one objective of the legislation, to keep the merits of disputes away from employment tribunals. By contrast, in *Crosville Wales Ltd v Tracey (No 2)*[743] the House of Lords affirmed that any compensation due to the complainants in respect of their unfair dismissals, which arose from the employers' selective re-engagement of those dismissed while taking part in industrial action, did not fall to be reduced because of their conduct in participating in industrial action because of the difficulty of allocating blame for the industrial action to any individual complainant.[744] However, their Lordships stated obiter that individual blameworthy conduct additional to or separate from the mere act of participation in industrial action was in principle capable of amounting to contributory fault.[745] This means that individuals whose behaviour is perceived by a tribunal as 'over-hasty and inflammatory' may still be subject to a reduction in their compensation even if their dismissals are found to be unfair.[746]

---

739 See para 11.64. On ILO standards in this area see Gernigon *et al* 1998: pp 461–467.
740 See *Port of London Authority v Payne* [1994] IRLR 9, discussed at para 5.151 above.
741 TULRCA 1992, s 239(4)(a). This was justified by the Government on the dual grounds that it would 'make no sense' for tribunals to issue re-employment orders when 'the employees are unwilling to work', and that the terms of settlement of the dispute may include reinstatement of those dismissed: Mr Ian McCartney, Minister of State, Department of Trade and Industry, Official Report of Standing Committee E, 9 March 1999, 6.45 pm.
742 [1993] IRLR 432, not following *Courtaulds Northern Spinning Co v Moosa* [1984] IRLR 43 on this point.
743 [1997] IRLR 691.
744 It was agreed between the parties that, even though the claim only came into existence because of the selective re-engagement, the wording of the legislation meant that the relevant question in the context of the compensation provisions was whether an employee had contributed to his or her dismissal, not to the failure to be re-engaged, following *Moosa* and *Downes* on this point.
745 [1997] IRLR 691, 698.
746 Lord Nolan expressly endorsed, at 698, the judgment of Waite LJ in this case relating to contributory fault: see [1996] IRLR 91, 98.

Unfair dismissal and 'unofficial' industrial action

11.84 Where an employee is dismissed while taking part in 'unofficial' industrial action an employment tribunal has no jurisdiction to hear a claim for unfair dismissal,[747] the sole exceptions being where the reason for dismissal, or selection for redundancy, is one of those specified in para 11.82 above or, additionally, that the employee made a 'protected disclosure' within the terms of ERA 1996, ss 43A-43L (see para 4.103).[748] Notably, once again, there is no protection for those chosen on grounds of their union activities, thus enabling employers to dismiss with impunity the 'ringleaders' behind industrial action. The same provision for stoppages in circumstances of serious and imminent danger applies in this context and, indeed, may be particularly significant here if the circumstances are such that no union official is involved and it may otherwise be deemed 'unofficial'. Our remarks relating to the HRA 1998 are also relevant.

As we stated in para 11.8, the policy which underlies this provision was to ensure that industrial action is either 'unofficial', or it is action for which a trade union is legally liable, in which case a ballot and prior notices to employers are required in order for immunity to be retained. There is a presumption that industrial action is 'unofficial' in relation to a particular employee[749] unless one of three conditions applies.[750] First, if he or she is a union member and the action is authorised or endorsed by that union. Second, if he or she is not a union member but participants in the action include members of a union which has authorised or endorsed the action.[751] Last, if none of the participants is a union member. Whether an employee is a member of a union is determined at the time he or she begins to take part in the action.[752] This means that employees cannot resign from the union after that point in order to protect their union against legal liability on the one hand and themselves against selective dismissal on the other.

Whether action has been authorised or endorsed by a union is determined according to the principles discussed in para 11.20 *et seq*. If the union is *prima facie* liable but is able, and elects, to repudiate the action, participants in the industrial action have a short period within which to end their action before being liable to selective dismissal; it is not to be treated as unofficial 'before the end of the next working day after the day on which the repudiation

---

747 TULRCA 1992, s 237(1). The exclusion applies when the employee was taking part in the action 'at the time of dismissal' (defined in (s237(5)), which makes it explicit that once an employer knows that industrial action has ended, it cannot dismiss employees later that day.

748 TULRCA, s 237(1A); see further para 5.95 *et seq*. The statutory dismissal and disciplinary procedures, which we discuss in paras 5.124 *et seq*, do not apply where at the time of an employee's dismissal he or she is taking part in an unofficial strike or other unofficial industrial action: EADRR 2004, reg 4(1)(c)(i).

749 Action may be 'unofficial' in relation to some employees and not others; an individual may be a member of a union which has not authorised or endorsed the action even though another union has and thus not fall within either of the first two categories. See, for example, *Balfour Kilpatrick Ltd v Acheson* [2003] IRLR 683.

750 TULRCA 1992, s 237(2).

751 There is no requirement that these other participants should be 'employees' rather than 'workers'.

752 TULRCA 1992, s 237(6). However, membership of a union 'for purposes unconnected with the employment in question' should be disregarded: ibid. This would cover, for example, a 'resting actor' who is a member of Equity, the actors' union, but temporarily engaged in different employment.

takes place'.[753] 'Working days' are days other than Saturdays, Sundays, Christmas Day, Good Friday and bank holidays.[754] The definition does not, therefore, allow for any variation according to the working patterns of the individual enterprise or individual employees. Thus, if a participant in unofficial action is not due to work the day following a repudiation by the union, or is unable to attend work due to illness, he or she will have to ensure that the employer is aware that his or her participation in the industrial action has come to an end; failure to do this will entitle the employer to assume continued participation and will therefore expose the employee to dismissal.[755] Employees who are unaware of the repudiation, whatever the reason, have no special protection; although unions are required to notify every member who they have reason to believe is taking part in the action for a repudiation to be effective in removing liability from the union, there is no requirement for members to receive such notice before their protection against selective dismissal is removed.

In *Balfour Kilpatrick Ltd v Acheson*[756] the EAT indicated that a repudiation which is treated as ineffective for the purposes of union liability is also ineffective in the context of protection against unfair dismissal, thus rendering the action 'non-unofficial' and removing the employer's ability to dismiss selectively with impunity.[757] This case also shows the danger for the employer of dismissing an employee before the time when the action is treated as 'unofficial'.

Industrial action and redundancy

11.85   The effect of taking industrial action upon the right to receive a redundancy payment is complex. As we saw in para 5.180, section 140(1) of ERA 1996 deprives employees of a payment where the employer is entitled to terminate the contract without notice due to the employee's conduct provided that specified procedures are followed. This provision will apply to employees who take industrial action short of a strike provided that this constitutes a repudiatory breach of contract. In *Simmons v Hoover Ltd*[758] the EAT affirmed that this was the case both where there is a 'single' dismissal (ie a dismissal for redundancy, not explicitly for misconduct) as well as a 'double' dismissal (dismissal for redundancy followed by dismissal for misconduct); thus, an employer who gives insufficient notice of redundancy but then discovers misconduct on the part of the employee is relieved of liability.[759] Where the employer follows the section 140(1) procedure and the dismissal takes place within the 'obligatory period', the tribunal has discretion to award all or part of

---

753 TULRCA 1992, s 237(4). In *Balfour Kilpatrick Ltd v Acheson* [2003] IRLR 683 the EAT held that 'the end of the next working day' meant midnight on the following working day and not the end of the period which constitutes the normal working hours for the day in question.

754 TULRCA 1992, s 237(5).

755 See *Williams v Western Mail and Echo Ltd* [1980] IRLR 222, discussed in para 11.74. The case for individual notification is stronger for unofficial action because it may not be clear when the action has ended.

756 [2003] IRLR 683.

757 Note also TULRCA 1992, s 237(4) which states that the question whether industrial action is taken to have been authorised or endorsed by a union is to be determined by reference to the facts at the time of dismissal.

758 [1976] IRLR 266.

759 *X v Y Ltd* (1969) 4 ITR 204.

the redundancy payment if it thinks this just and equitable.[760] However, in *Simmons v Hoover* the court considered that this applied only where there are two dismissals, a view which benefits employers who act wrongfully by giving insufficient notice on a single dismissal.

Section 140(1) is modified in the case of strikes (for which the definition provided for continuity purposes applies).[761] An employee who has been dismissed who then takes part in a strike will retain the right to payment provided that the strike occurs during the obligatory period of the employer's notice.[762] In *Simmons* the EAT considered that this applied only where there was a 'double' dismissal and the strike followed the redundancy notice; where the redundancy followed the strike, section 140(1) remained the governing provision. Where an employee takes strike action following notice of redundancy, the employer can serve written notice requesting the employee to agree to extend the contract by the number of days the strike lasts.[763] Employees who refuse to agree to this lose the right to a redundancy payment unless they can show that they were unable to comply or it was reasonable not to, in which case the tribunal has a discretion to award some or all of the payment.[764] Finally, if an employee terminates his or her contract of employment without notice in response to a lock-out which constitutes a repudiatory breach of contract by the employer, this is excluded from the definition of 'constructive dismissal',[765] so denying the employee any form of statutory redundancy payment. There is a clear danger that employees who lack appropriate advice may be manipulated into resigning by employers who may initiate a lock-out by proposing terms which they can predict will be unacceptable to the workforce, knowing that redundancies would in any case be imminent. It is difficult to understand the policy justification for this position.

INDUSTRIAL ACTION AND SOCIAL SECURITY BENEFITS

11.86 An individual who participates in or who, in certain circumstances, is affected by a strike or industrial action, thereby loses the right to receive the jobseeker's allowance for the period while he or she is out of work as a consequence of the relevant stoppage.[766] A claim may be made for income support in respect of other members of the claimant's family for the relevant period, but any such payment will be subject to a number of deductions, including an amount in respect of strike pay from the claimant's trade union whether or not such strike pay is actually received. These rules go back to the beginnings of the modern social security system. The National Insurance Act 1911 excluded the right to unemployment benefit where the claimant was out of work 'by reason of a stoppage which was due to a trade dispute at the factory, workshop or other premises at which he was employed'.[767] This was justified, above all, by the

---

760 ERA 1996, s 140(5), (3). See s 136(4) for the definition of 'obligatory period'.
761 ERA 1996, s 235(5).
762 ERA 1996, s 140(2), (5).
763 ERA 1996, ss 143, 144. The notice must contain specified information.
764 ERA 1996, s 143(5).
765 ERA 1996, s 136(2).
766 Jobseekers Act 1995, s 14. The Jobseekers Act 1995 replaced earlier measures with broadly equivalent provisions. See Wikeley, 2002: pp 379–381 and 505–514 for a fuller treatment of this subject; see also Ewing, 1991: chs 5–8; and Mesher and Sutcliffe, 1986.
767 NIA 1911, s 87(1).

principle of state neutrality. In evidence given to the Royal Commission on Unemployment Insurance in 1931,[768] the Ministry of Labour argued that it would have been inappropriate for the national insurance fund to be seen to support either side to the dispute. As a general justification, the argument of neutrality is very flimsy. In *Lascaris v Wyman* the New York Court of Appeal referred to the same argument as a 'fiction' in the context of a constitutional challenge to the state's practice of paying social assistance to destitute strikers: 'although, on the one hand, the State may not be acting in a strictly neutral fashion if it allows strikers to obtain public assistance, it may not, on the other hand, be seriously maintained that the State adopts a neutral policy if it renders strikers helpless by denying them public assistance or welfare benefits to which they would otherwise be entitled'.[769] A more specific reason for the approach taken in the UK, which is consistent with general attitudes towards the role of the courts in this area, is that social security tribunals and officials should not be drawn into judging the merits of particular industrial disputes. In addition, concern has been expressed at various times that the payment of benefits prolongs disputes,[770] and that the potentially large number of claims arising out of industrial action would disrupt the administration of the social security system.

The exclusionary rule in respect of means-tested benefits may be traced to the decision of the Court of Appeal in *A-G v Merthyr Tydfil Union*[771] in 1900. There the court held that the Poor Law Guardians had no power to make payments to the strikers themselves, but that it was not necessarily unlawful for them to give outdoor relief to members of their families, nor to other workers laid off as a result of the dispute. In this last respect, the position under the poor law was more favourable than that taken by the National Insurance Acts, which excluded both those taking part in a strike and others who were the incidental victims of the stoppage. However, later legislation in the area of social assistance adopted the wider exclusion contained in the national insurance legislation, ostensibly on the same ground of state neutrality.[772]

Unemployment-related benefits and the trade dispute disqualification

11.87   Under section 14 of the Jobseekers Act 1995, a person is not entitled to a jobseeker's allowance for any week which includes a day where there is a stoppage of work which is due to a trade dispute at his or her place of work and which causes them not to be employed on that day, unless they can show that they were 'not directly interested in the dispute'. For this purpose, the legislation retains the substance of the definition of trade dispute taken from the Trade Disputes Act 1906, namely 'any dispute between employers and employees, or between employees and employees, which is connected with the employment or non-employment or the terms of employment or the conditions of employment of any persons, whether employees in the employment of the employer with whom the dispute arises, or not'.[773] It is significant that the narrowing of the

768 Royal Commission on Unemployment Insurance, Minutes of Evidence 10.7.31, Q 9779, cited in Ewing, 1991: p 65.
769 292 NE 2d 667 (1972), discussed by Ewing, 1991: p 160.
770 For discussion, see Durcan and McCarthy, 1974; Gennard and Lasko, 1974.
771 [1900] 1 Ch 516; Ewing, 1991: pp 91–94.
772 Ewing, 1991: pp 97–98.
773 Jobseekers Act 1995, s 35(1).

trade dispute formula for collective purposes[774] after 1982 did not take place as well in the area of social security. The social security definition is now considerably broader: as a result, the jobseeker's allowance may be lost even in a situation where the organisers and union involved are not protected from liability in tort. Moreover, the social security exclusion applies even if there are good grounds, objectively speaking, for the stoppage: claimants have been disqualified for taking part in strikes over their employer's infringement of health and safety regulations[775] and after being dismissed for refusing to accept cuts in pay.[776]

The disqualification applies even to those affected by a stoppage in which they are not directly participating if it occurs at their 'place of work'. This means, 'in relation to any person, ... the premises or place at which he was employed'.[777] This is limited by the important proviso that the claimant must have been 'directly interested' in the dispute. At one stage the claimant also had to show that he or she was neither participating in nor financing the dispute, *and* that he or she was not a member of a 'grade or class' whose members were either participating in, financing or directly interested in the dispute. The Donovan Commission[778] recommended the removal of these provisions on the grounds that there need be no necessary assumption of a common interest from the membership of a 'group or class'; the reference to finance, in particular, was capable of producing unfairness since it would exclude many individuals simply on the grounds that their trade union was paying strike pay to those immediately involved. This recommendation was implemented in the SSA 1975.

The meaning of 'directly interested' was considered by the House of Lords in *Presho v Insurance Officer*.[779] Their Lordships rejected an argument that only those whose own pay and conditions of employment were in dispute could be 'directly interested', in favour of a two-stage test formulated by Lord Brandon. First, it had to be shown that the result of the dispute would be applied to groups of employees other than those participating in the strike or industrial action and, second, that this wider application would take place automatically by virtue either of a collective agreement (whether legally binding or not) or custom and practice in the workplace concerned.

The denial of unemployment benefit to those directly involved in the dispute can be seen as putting pressure on them to break the strike, notwithstanding the official claims that state neutrality is the basis for the rule; the employees' need for income will often be much more immediately pressing than the employer's need for their services.[780] But even if the trade dispute disqualification could be justified on the slightly different ground that it is important to avoid placing social security officers and tribunals in a position of adjudicating on the rights

---

774 TULRCA 1992, s 244; see above, para 11.25 *et seq.*
775 *R v National Insurance Comr, ex p Thompson*, appendix to *R(U) 5/77*; *R(U) 4/65*; *R(U) 3/71*.
776 *R(U) 27/56*.
777 Jobseekers Act 1995, s 14(4). On the need for a causal link between the stoppage and the loss of employment, see Wikeley, 2002: pp 508–511.
778 *Royal Commission on Trade Unions and Employers' Associations 1965–1968* Cmnd 3623, 1968, paras 975–976.
779 [1984] AC 310.
780 The supply of agency labour by an employment business in substitution for workers taking part in industrial action is prohibited by the Conduct of Employment Agencies and Employment Businesses Regulations 2003, SI 2003/3319, reg 7. However this prohibition does not apply if the industrial action in question is 'unofficial' for the purposes of TULRCA 1992, s 237.

and wrongs of industrial action, this would hardly justify the disqualification of those who are not taking part but may in some way be affected by the outcome of the dispute. As Ewing has pointed out, claimants disqualified under this heading could include those who might be *prejudiced* by the outcome of the dispute.[781] This group in particular might be expected to respond to disqualification by putting extra pressure on the strikers to end their dispute.

The second category of disqualification relates to claimants who withdraw their labour in furtherance of a trade dispute.[782] This provision, which was introduced by the SSA 1986, catches those who take part in a trade dispute which is not connected with a stoppage at their own place of work.

The loss of entitlement may continue as long as the stoppage or the withdrawal of labour, as the case may be. However, it comes to an end if the claimant has, in the meantime, become bona fide employed elsewhere (the assumption being that he or she then lost this second employment while the original stoppage was still continuing); is dismissed by reason of redundancy; or bona fide resumes his or her employment with the employer and then leaves for a reason unconnected with the dispute.[783]

Loss of income support

11.88   An individual who would be disqualified from the jobseeker's allowance under the provisions which we have just considered is also disqualified from claiming income support unless, during the same period, he or she is incapable of work by reason of disease or disablement, or she is pregnant, in which case a claim may be made for the 'maternity period' either side of the expected week of confinement.[784] In other cases, after a period of seven days the claimant is able to make a claim in respect of other members of his or her family. The benefit payable is calculated by reference to the normal allowances, or their equivalents, for dependent members of the claimant's family. The sums payable are subject, however, to a deduction in respect of any strike pay received from the claimant's trade union, or any sum of strike pay which the claimant was entitled to receive, but did not, up to a maximum sum which from 11 April 2005 and at the time of writing is £30.50.[785] This provision was introduced in 1980 on the grounds that the full payment of social assistance amounted to subsidising strikes and prolonging their duration.[786] It is arguable that in addition to being a potential cause of hardship for families, it contradicts the official position of state neutrality in industrial disputes.

781 Ewing, 1991: p 87.
782 Jobseekers Act 1995, s 14(2). In addition, where the partner of a person in receipt of the jobseeker's allowance becomes involved in a trade dispute, a deduction from the allowance may be made in respect of the partner: s 15.
783 Jobseekers Act 1995, s 14(3); see Wikeley 2002: pp 513–514. Note also that the claimant's loss of entitlement may affect a claim for the jobseeker's allowance by his or her partner, even where the latter is not involved in any trade dispute. See Jobseekers Allowance Regulations 1996, SI 1996/207, reg 52(2).
784 SSCBA 1992, s 126.
785 This is the effect of SSCBA 1992, s 126(5)–(7) and the Income Support (General) Regulations 1987, SI 1987/1967, Sch 9, para 34. Certain other special rules apply for the calculation of income which have the effect of reducing entitlements: see Wikeley, 2002: p 333.
786 SSA 1980, s 6(1); see Mesher, 1985, for a discussion of its impact in the 1985 miners' strike.

INDUSTRIAL ACTION AND THE RIGHTS OF UNION MEMBERS

11.89   As we saw in chapter 10, union members have rights against their union which may derive either (or concurrently) from the common law or statute. In this section we summarise the rights which are most relevant to industrial action, although some also have a wider application. In doing so we shall assume that readers are familiar with the general principles of union government outlined in chapter 10.

Rights at common law

11.90   Union members may challenge the decision of their union to support industrial action in three major ways.[787] First, they may wish to restrain the union from organising the industrial action in question. Second, they may seek to restrain the unauthorised expenditure of money, such as strike pay, in support of it. Last, they may refuse to participate in the action and attempt to forestall or challenge disciplinary action against them for this refusal. In the context of industrial action, where time is of the essence, plaintiffs commonly seek an interim injunction to halt the allegedly unlawful activity. In deciding applications the criteria set out in para 11.49 *et seq*, *mutatis mutandis*, will be applied by the court and the penalties described in para 11.51 will be relevant if an order is granted and breached. In this context the power to order sequestration of a union's assets in the event that it acts in contempt of court, or to appoint a receiver to manage and control its assets, may be particularly important.[788]

The grounds for challenging the union's actions are various. Most straightforward are the arguments that the union's rules do not permit industrial action in the circumstances in question or, more likely, that the procedure stipulated in the rules has not been followed. Despite the comprehensive statutory procedures the common law may remain relevant here if, for example, the rules require the support of a two-thirds majority in a ballot, rather than a simple majority, before industrial action can be called. Even if the rules do ostensibly permit the action, there is some authority that it is beyond the powers of a union deliberately to embark upon activities, including industrial action, which would be bound to involve offences against the criminal law; this could be relevant to certain kinds of picketing and also industrial action by specific groups of workers.[789] It has also been argued on occasion, with less success, that union rules cannot authorise industrial action which would lead to a commission of a tort; in *Thomas v NUM*[790] the court refused to hold that picketing was outside the union's powers merely because it was 'almost certain' that the union had

---

787 Elias and Ewing, 1987: p 236. The case law concerning the 1984–1985 miners' strike illustrates all three of these processes in operation: see Ewing, 1985. For a more detailed analysis, see G Morris and T Archer, 2000: paras 6.109–6.117.
788 See *Clarke v Heathfield* [1985] ICR 203.
789 See *Thomas v NUM (South Wales Area)* [1985] IRLR 136, 153. See Ewing, 1985: pp 164–165; 174–175; Elias and Ewing, 1987: pp 237–240. On picketing see para 11.52 *et seq* above; on special groups para 11.60 above.
790 [1985] IRLR 136, 154. See also *Sherard v AUEW* [1973] ICR 421, 433 (Lord Denning MR). Cf *National Sailors' and Fireman's Union of Great Britain and Northern Ireland v Reed* [1926] Ch 536, 539–540, where it was held unlawful for a union to call a strike where there was no trade dispute.

exposed itself to liability for interference with contract, although the question whether action which was bound to constitute any other tort would be similarly treated was left open.[791] Clearly if this argument were ever to be accepted if would expose a very high proportion of campaigns to challenge. However, a direct instruction to commit a tort would be unlawful;[792] this would be the situation, for example, if the union were to instruct its members to 'sit-in', so committing a trespass. Other grounds upon which it may arguably be unlawful to discipline a member, although they rest on only tenuous authority, are failure to strike in breach of a procedure agreement[793] and where the member was justified in concluding that the order was one to which the union had no right to demand obedience.[794] However, neither of these have been applied other than in the particular case in which they were suggested.

Disciplinary action against members is, in practice, most likely to be challenged under the statutory protection against 'unjustifiable discipline' outlined below. The common law, however, may remain relevant for two reasons: first, because, it offers the possibility of injunctive relief, whereas the statute provides only for financial compensation; and second, because the statute requires a disciplinary 'determination' to have been made, whereas on occasion the courts have been prepared to grant a remedy at an earlier stage, sometimes restraining the union from holding even an initial inquiry as to whether there has been a breach of the union rules. Thus in *Esterman v NALGO*[795] Templeman J considered that no reasonable tribunal could *bona fide* conclude that disobedience to the strike call in question demonstrated unfitness to be a member of the union as charged and granted an interim injunction to restrain any disciplinary action (although emphasising that this should be done only in 'exceptional circumstances'[796]). In *Porter v NUJ*[797] the House of Lords also took a highly interventionist approach, holding that since there were serious issues of disputed fact as to the lawfulness of the strike call and as to whether the union was entitled to take disciplinary proceedings against the claimants the balance of convenience lay in favour of maintaining the status quo, by which the claimants remained members of the union, until the trial. However, in the later case of *Longley v NUJ*[798] the Court of Appeal emphasised that the courts should be slow to prevent domestic tribunals adjudicating upon a matter in the first instance and endorsed the view of the trial judge that this should be done only if there was persuasive evidence to suggest that the issues had been prejudged or that the prescribed procedures would not be complied with. This latter approach accords with that of the legislation and, if followed, would make it more difficult for claimants to forestall the disciplinary process. In view of the fact that an interim injunction forces the union to undertake potentially lengthy litigation if it wishes to proceed with a disciplinary matter it seems the preferable approach to take, particularly now that with the demise of the closed shop, loss of union membership no longer carries the threat of exclusion from employment.

791 At 153–154.
792 See Treitel, 2003: ch 11.
793 *Partington v NALGO* [1981] IRLR 537, 542 (Lord Allanbridge); see also *Porter v NUJ* [1979] IRLR 404, 407 (Lord Denning MR) (decision upheld by the House of Lords [1980] IRLR 404 without reference to this point).
794 *Esterman v NALGO* [1974] ICR 625.
795 [1974] ICR 625.
796 [1974] ICR 625, 632.
797 [1980] IRLR 404; see Lord Diplock at 406.
798 [1987] IRLR 109.

Statutory rights

11.91 The statutory rights most relevant to industrial action can be divided into four broad categories. The first is the right to a ballot. A member who claims that members of the union (of which he or she is one) are likely to be, or have been, induced by the union to take part in industrial action which lacks the support of a properly-conducted ballot may apply to the High Court for an injunction restraining such inducment.[799] The second is the highly controversial right not to be 'unjustifiably disciplined', with substantial financial compensation available if this right is infringed.[800] Debate about this right, which we discussed in para 10.12, focused in particular upon its relevance to industrial action. It accords absolute supremacy to the individual over the collective by providing that an individual may not be disciplined for failing to participate in or support any industrial action, notwithstanding that it is lawful and may have achieved a high level of support in a ballot. The introduction of this provision attracted considerable criticism from the right, as well as the left, of the political spectrum, one argument from the former being that it would undermine the representativity of the ballot by discouraging those opposed to the action from expressing their views at that stage if they knew they would be protected against retaliatory action for non-participation.[801] It has been found by the ILO Committee of Experts to infringe Article 3 of Convention 87 on the ground that this requires that union members should be permitted when drawing up their constitutions and rules to determine whether or not it should be possible to discipline members who refuse to participate in lawful strikes or other industrial action. It has also been regarded by the Committee of Independent Experts (now the European Committee of Social Rights) as incompatible with the right to organise guaranteed by Article 5 of the European Social Charter.[802] However, despite these findings, the Labour Government has taken no steps to date to remove these restrictions and shows no intention of doing so; rather it has specifically defended them as providing 'necessary protections for individual workers in their relationship with their unions'.[803] The Conservative Government's justification for their introduction was that 'every union member should be free to decide for himself whether or not he wishes to break his contract of employment and run the risk of dismissal without compensation',[804] although this was inadequate to explain the extension of protection to those who attempted to persuade others to continue working. Their retention now that there is at least limited protection against dismissal for participating in 'protected industrial action' is even more difficult to justify.

The third statutory intervention in this area is the prohibition upon unions indemnifying individuals for penalties for criminal offences or for contempt of

---

799 TULRCA 1992, s 62. The 'inducement' need not be effective: s 62(6). A member may also apply if the union has called on its members to take part in the action before the date of the ballot or if the call is made by someone other than a specified person: s 62(2).
800 TULRCA 1992, ss 64–67.
801 See Leader, 1991, where it is also argued that the measure impinges on trade unionists' right to freedom of association under Art 11(1) of the ECHR in forcing them to keep within their ranks individuals who refuse to take part in industrial action.
802 See, for example, Conclusions XIV-I.
803 See, for example, the 2002 Report of the ILO Committee of Experts on the Application of Conventions and Recommendations on the UK's compliance with ILO Convention No 87.
804 *Trade Unions and their Members* Cm 95, 1987: pp 7–8.

court.[805] At one time several unions made provision in their rules for indemnifying members, in particular officials, for specified unlawful acts. At common law, provided that their rules so permitted, unions were free to resolve to make payments in respect of offences already committed, but not future offences.[806] This practice is now prohibited and any payments made are recoverable from the recipient at the suit of the union or an individual member on behalf of the union where he or she claims the union's failure to act is 'unreasonable'.[807] This, too, was condemned by the ILO Committee of Experts in its 1989 report in the following terms:

> The Committee has consistently taken the view that legislative provisions which are intended to ensure sound administration and the honest and efficient management of union funds and other funds and assets are not incompatible with the Convention ... However such provisions should not be of such a character as to deprive unions of the right to draw up their constitutions or rules and to organise their administration and activities free of interference by the public authorities – nor should they deny trade unions the right to utilise their funds as they wish for normal and lawful trade union purposes. [This provision] appears to do both of these things ...[808]

In more recent reports, however, the Committee took a less confident tone, appearing to acknowledge the Conservative Government's case which included the argument that where penalties were imposed on an individual, rather than a union, this would 'imply a clear finding of wilful and unlawful action by that individual'.[809] However, it has maintained the view that indemnification in respect of legal liabilities incurred on behalf of the union should be possible. The European Committee of Social Rights also takes the view that in principle unions should be free to use their property as they consider appropriate.

The final statutory right allows members to apply to the High Court if they claim that the union's trustees are carrying out, or proposing to carry out, their functions so as to 'cause or permit' any unlawful application of the union's property, or that they have complied or are proposing to comply with an unlawful direction which has or may be given under the union rules.[810] The latter provision means that even if the trustees are specifically empowered by the rules or trust instrument to act in a particular way, or are obliged to obey the instructions of the union's executive, the member may have a remedy.[811] If the court upholds the complaint it may make such order as it considers appropriate including requiring the trustees to take specified steps to protect or recover union property; to appoint a receiver; and to remove one or more trustees.[812] If union property

---

805 TULRCA 1992, s 15. The Secretary of State may by order designate offences in relation to which the section does not apply (s 15(5)) but at the time of writing no such order has been made.

806 *Drake v Morgan* [1978] ICR 56; cf *Thomas v NUM (South Wales Area)* [1985] IRLR 136.

807 TULRCA 1992, s 15(2), (3).

808 Report of the Committee of Experts on the Application of Conventions and Recommendations, Report III (Part 4A), ILO, Geneva 1989: p 237.

809 Report of the Committee of Experts on the Application of Conventions and Recommendations, Report III (Part 4A), ILO, Geneva, 1992: p 245.

810 TULRCA 1992, s 16(1). As union property is held on trust for the union, members would seem not to be direct beneficiaries of the trust so their *locus standi* to bring an action for breach of trust, other than where there has been a breach of the union rule book, is uncertain: cf *Hughes v TGWU* [1985] IRLR 382.

811 Under the general law trustees are bound to obey only the lawful instructions of the union's executive committee: *Clarke v Heathfield (No 2)* [1985] ICR 606, 614.

812 TULRCA 1992, s 16(3).

has been applied in contravention of a court order, or the trustees were proposing such action, all the trustees must be removed except any who can convince the court there is 'good reason' to allow him or her to remain.[813] This may lead to the appointment of new trustees by the court[814] or the appointment of a receiver. The power of members to intervene when they claim that trustees are 'proposing' to act in one of these ways gives them a wide preventative power, particularly as the court is empowered to grant relief on an interim basis. They are protected against being disciplined for exercising this right.[815] The existence of powers of this nature may throw greater light on the legislative strategy of the former Conservative Government of making it prohibitively expensive for unions to remove dissident members, who may be opposed to every aspect of union policy, from their midst.

ASSESSMENT

11.92 Our analysis of the law relating to industrial action reveals that it is fragmented, complex, often unpredictable and sometimes unprincipled in nature. These characteristics alone are cause for concern. In substance it breaches international standards in a number of important respects, in particular those determined by the ILO. This is the case both in relation to the position of individual workers and that of their organisations.

These conclusions are not difficult to reach. Much more contentious is the direction which any reform of the law should take. In para 11.4 we outlined some fundamental questions which any legal system needs to address in relation to industrial action. We do not attempt to address all those issues here but merely isolate those areas which in our view are most in need of scrutiny by policy makers.[816]

(i) One issue which is often raised is whether withdrawing labour should be expressed as a freedom or a right. If one accepts the view that it is necessary to define the scope of the capacity of workers lawfully to withdraw their labour, and the conditions under which this may be done, the existence of a positive right has advantages. It accords the withdrawal of labour a status among competing rights, such as rights of property and, once established, may make it more difficult to curtail than an immunity, which carries the danger of being presented as a 'privilege'. However, even a positive right is not immune from creative interpretation by the courts[817] and may, indeed, be as vulnerable to circumvention as an immunity in the hands of an adjudicating body which is attuned more to the individualistic tradition of the common law rather than collective values. Thus, of itself, there is no guarantee that a system of positive rights would confer greater legal freedom to strike.[818] The crucial question is the substance of the 'right' or 'freedom', not its form.[819]

813 TULRCA 1992, s 16(4).
814 Trustee Act 1925, s 41.
815 TULRCA 1992, s 65(2)(c).
816 For more detailed discussions see Ewing, 1991 and Wedderburn, 1991b; for a useful international perspective see Ben-Israel, 1994 and for a study of international standards, Novitz, 2003.
817 See Wedderburn, 1991b: pp 314–316.
818 P Davies and M Freedland, 1984: pp 786–787.
819 On the merits of recognising a right to strike as a human right, see Ewing, 2004.

(ii) UK law has traditionally focused upon protecting the organisers of industrial action from legal liability, overlooking the vulnerability of the individual worker for whom there is no regime of 'statutory immunity', however rudimentary. However, the freedom to take industrial action is undermined completely if individual workers thereby jeopardise the continuation of their employment or are otherwise vulnerable to discriminatory treatment. Despite the introduction of protection for employees (only) against dismissal for taking 'protected industrial action', a welcome but still unduly limited reform, there remain a number of features of the present law which require reconsideration here. One is the position whereby industrial action generally constitutes a breach of the contract of employment. In 1968 the Donovan Commission pointed to the technical problems raised by the introduction of a doctrine of suspension of the contract. These included how to define the forms of industrial action to which it would apply; whether an employer would be able to dismiss an employee for gross misconduct during the course of the dispute; whether strikers would be free to take up other employment while the contract of employment was suspended; and if efforts to end the strike failed, upon what event would the suspension of the contract cease and be replaced by termination?[820] None of these difficulties is insuperable, however, and indeed the legal systems of many other European countries, including France, Italy and Germany, incorporate a doctrine of suspension, albeit that the conditions under which it operates may vary.[821] A further question is the issue of effective protection for workers (not just employees) participating in lawful disputes against dismissal and other prejudicial action, which suspension of the contract alone would not achieve. The requirement that protection be effective leads in turn to the issue of remedies for infringing workers' rights. Should there be automatic reinstatement for dismissed employees regardless of the circumstances, for example? What of the position of any replacement labour which the employer may have hired during the dispute? Should such persons be subject to a statutory presumption that their dismissal is for a fair reason, by analogy with replacements for those on maternity leave, on the basis that they were aware of the position when they took the job? A final important issue in relation to the rights of individual workers is that of payment if the employer accepts partial performance of contractual duties. Although this form of industrial action is not protected in some legal systems it has advantages, particularly in essential services where a total withdrawal of labour can present serious difficulties. If it is to be permitted, consideration should be given as to whether there should be prior approval of any deduction from wages by an external body rather than maintaining the current position which allows the employer unilaterally to set the level of wages to be paid, with the onus upon workers to challenge this amount.

(iii) At the collective level a fundamental question is whether a new framework of protected action, with corresponding liabilities for action beyond it, should be enacted. If the organisation of industrial action could be insulated against the common law this would avoid it being prey to developments which can radically affect its lawfulness, such as the application of the wrong of inducing breach of a statutory duty and that of economic duress. If the doctrine of

820 *Royal Commission on Trade Unions and Employers' Associations 1965–1968*, Cmnd 3623, 1968, para 943.
821 See A Jacobs, 2004: para 59.

suspension of the contract of employment, which would remove liability for inducing breach of such a contract, were to be accepted this would necessitate constructing a new framework. Consideration would also need to be given to the permissible limits of secondary action, particularly in view of the lack of limitation on employers transferring work between companies and the reluctance of the courts to 'lift the corporate veil'. Pre-industrial action procedures also require attention, albeit that the Employment Relations Acts 1999 and 2004 made some reforms; thought should be given to reducing the complexity and cost to unions of holding ballots with a view to the creation of a climate more conducive to a settlement of the underlying issues rather than focusing attention upon complying with the technicalities of the legal process.[822] Any reform would also need to consider whether it would be possible to minimise the possibility of the statutory framework being undermined by the availability of interim injunctions. In Ireland once the requisite pre-strike procedures have been followed the employer is prohibited from obtaining an injunction without the respondent being present before the court, and the court 'shall not grant an injunction restraining the strike or other industrial action where the respondent establishes a fair case that he was acting in contemplation or furtherance of a trade dispute'.[823] Although this provision (which operates within a continued system of immunities) has been criticised as inadequate (it does not extend to applications by third parties, for example) it provides one example of how the present position could be modified.[824] A more radical solution might be possible if the area of industrial action was removed from the purview of the common law courts altogether.

(iv) In line with the review of industrial action by workers there is a need to examine the circumstances in which an employer may lawfully institute a lock-out and the impact of such action upon the employment relationship, including protecting affected workers against dismissal.

(v) In relation to trade unions the restrictions on discipline of members who seek to retain their membership whilst refusing to accept collective decisions should be subject to review, as should restrictions on expenditure to indemnify members who incur penalties in the course of complying with union policy.

(vi) Consideration should be given as to whether there should be separate provision for industrial action in 'essential services' and if so, of what nature and subject to what conditions.[825] In this context the 'statutory right of action' available to consumers of goods of services is particularly pertinent in threatening to remove control over the management of disputes from the parties.[826]

In reforming the law, the overriding aim should be to construct a coherent legal framework which incorporates ILO standards and makes a genuine attempt to balance the legitimate interests of the parties and, where appropriate, of the wider public. British law still has some considerable way to go before this aim can be said to have been achieved.

---

822 See further Elgar and Simpson, 1996.
823 Irish Industrial Relations Act 1990, s 19.
824 For a trenchant critique of this Act see B Wilkinson, 1991.
825 See further G Morris, 1991.
826 See further G Morris, 1993.

Bibliography

Aaron, Benjamin and KW Wedderburn (1972) *Industrial Conflict: a comparative legal survey* (Longman, Harlow).

Adams, Roy J (1999) Why Statutory Recognition is Bad Labour Policy: the North American Experience *Industrial Relations Journal* 30, 96-100.

Addison, John T (1986) Job Security in the United States: Law, Collective Bargaining, Policy and Practice *British Journal of Industrial Relations* 24, 381-418.

Addison, John T and Alberto Castro (1987) The Importance of Life-Time Jobs: Differences between Union and Non-Union Workers *Industrial and Labor Relations Review* 40, 393-405.

Addison, John T and W Stanley Siebert (1991) The Social Charter of the European Community: Evolution and Controversies *Industrial and Labor Relations Review* 44, 597-625.

Addison, John T and W Stanley Siebert (1992) The Social Charter: Whatever Next? *British Journal of Industrial Relations* 30, 495-513.

Alcock, A (1971) *History of the International Labour Organisation* (Macmillan, London).

Allen, V L (1954) *Power in Trade Unions: a study of their organisation in Great Britain* (Longman, London).

Anderman, Steven D (1986) Unfair Dismissal and Redundancy, in *Labour Law in Britain* ed Roy Lewis (Basil Blackwell, Oxford).

Anderman, Steven D (1993) European Community Merger and Social Policy *Industrial Law Journal* 22, 318-321.

Anderman, Steven D (2000) The Interpretation of Protective Employment Statutes and Contracts of Employment *Industrial Law Journal* 29, 223-242.

Anderman, Steven D (2004) Termination of Employment: Whose Property Rights? in *The Future of Labour Law: Liber Amicorum Sir Bob Hepple QC* ed Catherine Barnard, Simon Deakin and Gillian S Morris (Hart Publishing, Oxford).

Anderson, Gordon (1991) The Employment Contracts Act 1991: An Employer's Charter? *New Zealand Journal of Industrial Relations* 16, 147-162.

Anderson, Lucy (2003) Sound Bite Legislation: The Employment Act 2002 and New Flexible Working 'Rights' for Parents *Industrial Law Journal* 32, 37-42.

Arlidge, Anthony, David Eady and ATH Smith (1999) *Arlidge, Eady and Smith on Contempt* (Sweet and Maxwell, London).

Armour, John and Simon Deakin (2000) The Rover Case (2): Bargaining in the Shadow of TUPE *Industrial Law Journal*, 29: 395-402.

Armour, John and Simon Deakin (2003) Insolvency and employment protection: the mixed effects of the Acquired Rights Directive *International Review of Law and Economics* 23, 1-23.

Armour, John and Sandra Frisby (2001) Rethinking Receivership *Oxford Journal of Legal Studies* 21, 73-102.

Arrowsmith, S (1995) Public Procurement as an Instrument of Policy and the Impact of Market Liberalisation *Law Quarterly Review* 111, 235-284.

Arthurs, Harry (2002) Private Ordering and Workers' Rights, in the Global Economy: Corporate Codes of Conduct as a Regime of Labour Market Regulation in *Labour Law in an Era of Globalization: Transformative Practices and Possibilities* ed Joanne Conaghan, Richard Michael Fischl and Karl Klare (Oxford University Press, Oxford).

Ashburner, Walter (1933) *Principles of Equity* 2nd edn by Dennis Browne (Butterworths, London).

Ashiagbor, Diamond (2000) Flexibility and Adaptability in the EU Employment Strategy in *Legal Regulation of the Employment Relation* eds Hugh Collins, Paul Davies and Roger Rideout (Kluwer, Deventer).

Atkinson, John (1985) *Flexibility, Uncertainty and Manpower Management* IMS Report No 89 (Institute of Manpower Studies, Brighton).

Atleson, James B (1983) *Values and Assumptions in American Labor Law* (University of Massachusetts Press, Amherst).

Auerbach, Simon (1988) Injunction Procedure in the Seafarers' Dispute *Industrial Law Journal* 17, 227-238.

Auerbach, Simon (1989) Injunctions against Picketing *Industrial Law Journal* 18, 166-170.

Auerbach, Simon (1990) *Legislating for Conflict* (Clarendon Press, Oxford).

Auerbach, Simon (1993) *Derecognition and Personal Contracts: Fighting Tactics and the Law* (Institute of Employment Rights, London).

Auvergnon, Philippe and José-Luis Gil y Gil (1994) La Réforme du Droit du Travail en Espagne *Droit Social*, 199-208.

Ayres, Ian and Robert Gertner (1989) Filling Gaps in Incomplete Contracts: a Theory of Default Rules (1989) *Yale Law Journal* 99, 87-130.

Bacon, Nicholas and John Storey (2000) New Employee Relations Strategies in Britain: Towards Individualism or Partnership? *British Journal of Industrial Relations* 38, 404-427.

Bailey, Ruth, and John Kelly (1990) An Index Measure of British Trade Union Density *British Journal of Industrial Relations* 28, 267-270.

Bailey, Suzanne (1989) Equal Treatment/Special Treatment: the Dilemma of the Dismissed Pregnant Employee *Journal of Social Welfare Law* 85-100.

Bain, George Sayers (1970) *The Growth of White-Collar Unionism* (Clarendon Press, Oxford).

Bain, George Sayers and Robert Price (1983) Union Growth: Dimensions, Determinants, and Destiny, in *Industrial Relations in Britain* ed George Sayers Bain (Basil Blackwell, Oxford).

Bainbridge, D (1990) *Computers and the Law* (Pitman, London).

Bamber, GJ and P Sheldon (2004), Collective Bargaining: Towards Decentralisation? in *Comparative Labour Law and Industrial Relations in Industrialised Market Economies* 8th edn, ed Roger Blanpain (Kluwer Law International, The Hague).

Bamforth, Nicholas (1994) Sexual Orientation and Dismissal *New Law Journal* 144, 1402-1419.

Bamforth, Nicholas (1997) *Sexuality, Morals and Justice: A Theory of Lesbian and Gay Rights Law* (Cassell, London).

Bamforth, Nicholas (1999) The Application of the Human Rights Act 1998 to Public Authorities and Private Bodies *Cambridge Law Journal* 58, 159-170.

Bamforth, Nicholas (2000) Sexual Orientation Discrimination after *Grant v South West Trains Modern Law Review* 63, 694-720.

Barbagelata, H (1986) Categories of Workers and Labour Contracts, in *Comparative Labour Law and Industrial Relations in Industrialised Market Economies Vol 1* ed R Blanpain (Kluwer, Deventer-Boston).

Barmes, Lizzie (2003) Promoting Diversity and the Definition of Direct Discrimination *Industrial Law Journal* 32, 200-213.

Barmes, Lizzie (2004) The Continuing Conceptual Crisis in the Common Law of the Contract of Employment *Modern Law Review* 67, 435-464.

Barnard, Catherine (1992) A Social Policy for Europe: Politicians 1, Lawyers 0 *International Journal of Comparative Labour Law and Industrial Relations* 8, 15-31.

Barnard, Catherine (1994) Sunday Trading: a Drama in Five Acts *Modern Law Review* 57, 449-60.

Barnard, Catherine (1997a) The United Kingdom, the 'Social Chapter' and the Amsterdam Treaty *Industrial Law Journal* 26, 275-282.

Barnard, Catherine (1997b) *P v S*: Kite Flying or a New Constitutional Approach? in eds A Dashwood and S O'Leary *The Principle of Equal Treatment in EC Law* (Sweet and Maxwell, London).

Barnard, Catherine (1998) The Principle of Equality in the Community Context: *P, Grant, Kalanke* and *Marschall*: Four Uneasy Bedfellows? *Cambridge Law Journal* 57, 352-373.

Barnard, Catherine (1999) The Working Time Regulations 1998 *Industrial Law Journal* 28, 61-75.

Barnard, Catherine (2000a) *EC Employment Law* 2nd edn (Oxford University Press, Oxford).

Barnard, Catherine (2000b) The Working Time Regulations 1999 *Industrial Law Journal* 29, 167-171.

Barnard, Catherine and Simon Deakin (2000) In Search of Coherence: Social Policy, the Single Market and Fundamental Rights *Industrial Relations Journal* 31, 331-345.

Barnard, Catherine and Ivan Hare (2000) Police Discretion and the Rule of Law: Economic Community Rights versus Civil Rights *Modern Law Review* 63, 581-595.

Barnard, Catherine, and Bob Hepple (1999) Indirect Discrimination: Interpreting *Seymour-Smith, Cambridge Law Journal* 58, 399-412.

Barnard, Catherine, and Bob Hepple (2000) Substantive Equality *Cambridge Law Journal* 59, 562-585.

Barnard, Catherine, and Tamara Hervey (1998) European Union Employment and Social Policy Survey 1996 and 1997 *Yearbook of European Law*, 18, 613-657.

Barrett, Brenda (1995) Work-induced Stress *Industrial Law Journal* 24, 343-352.

Barrett, Brenda (1996) Stress and the Public Liability of Employers *Industrial Law Journal* 25, 45-55.

Barrett, Brenda (1997) Employers' Criminal Liability Under HSWA 1974 *Industrial Law Journal* 26, 149-158.

Barrett, Brenda (1998) Renaissance of Civil Liability for Breach of Statutory Duty? *Industrial Law Journal* 27, 59-63.

Barrett, Brenda (1999) Compensation for Psychiatric Injury: Have their Lordships Righted a Wrong? *Industrial Law Journal* 28, 263-268.

Barrett, Brenda (2000) Harassment at Work: A Matter of Health and Safety *Journal of Business Law* 214-231.

Barrett, Brenda (2001) Policy Issues Concerning Compensation for Psychiatric Injury *Industrial Law Journal* 30, 110-115.

Barrett, Brenda (2004) Employers' Liability for Stress at the Work Place: Neither Tort nor Breach of Contract? *Industrial Law Journal* 33, 343-349.

Barrett, Brenda (2005) Employers' Liability after *Hatton v Sutherland, Industrial Law Journal* 34, 182-189.

Bartolomei de to Cruz, Hector G, Geraldo von Potobsky, and Lee Swepston (1996) *The International Labour Organisation: The International Standards System and Basic Human Rights* (Westview Press, Boulder).

Bassett, Philip (1986) *Strike Free: New Industrial Relations in Britain* (Macmillan, London).

Bayliss, F J (1962) *British Wages Councils* (Basil Blackwell, Oxford).

Beatson, J (1991) *The Use and Abuse of Unjust Enrichment: Essays on the Law of Restitution* (Clarendon Press, Oxford).

Beatson, J (1997) Has the Common Law a Future? *Cambridge Law Journal* 56, 291-314.

Beatson, Mark (1995) Progress towards a Flexible Labour Market *Employment Gazette* 103, 55-66.

Beaumont, PB and RID Harris (1991) Trade Union Recognition and Employment Contraction in Britain 1980-84 *British Journal of Industrial Relations* 29, 49-73.

Beck, Matthias and Charles Woolfson (2000) The Regulation of Health and Safety in Britain: from Old Labour to New Labour, *Industrial Relations Journal* 31, 35-49.

Becker, Gary S (1971) *The Economics of Discrimination* 2nd edn (University of Chicago Press, Chicago).

Becker, Gary S (1975) *Human Capital: A Theoretical and Empirical Analysis, with Special Reference to Education* 2nd edn (University of Chicago Press, Chicago).

Belcher, Alice (1997) *Corporate Rescue* (Sweet & Maxwell, London).

Bell, Derrick (1992) An Allegorical Critique of the United States Civil Rights Model, in *Discrimination: the Limits of the Law* eds B A Hepple and Erika Szyszczak (Mansell, London).

Bell, DW and CG Hanson (1987) *Profit-Sharing and Profitability* (Kogan Page, London).

Bell, Mark (2000) Article 13 EC: The European Commission's Anti-discrimination Proposals *Industrial Law Journal* 29, 79-84.

Bellace, Janice R (2001) The ILO Declaration of Fundamental Principles and Rights at Work *The International Journal of Comparative Labor Law and Industrial Relations* 17, 269-287.

Benedictus, Roger (1979) Closed Shop Exemptions and Their Wording *Industrial Law Journal* 8, 160-171.

Ben-Israel, Ruth (1988) *International Labour Standards: The Case of Freedom to Strike* (Kluwer, Deventer).

Ben-Israel, Ruth (ed) (1994) *Strikes and Lock-outs in Industrialized Market Economies* (Kluwer, Deventer-Boston).

Bennett, Michael (1994) Practicability of Reinstatement and Re-engagement Orders *Industrial Law Journal* 23, 164-166.

Bercusson, Brian (1976) The New Fair Wages Policy: Schedule 11 to the Employment Protection Act *Industrial Law Journal* 5, 129-147.

Bercusson, Brian (1977) One Hundred Years of Conspiracy and Protection of Property: Time for a Change *Modern Law Review* 40, 268-292.

Bercusson, Brian (1978) *Fair Wages Resolutions* (Mansell, London).

Bercusson, Brian (1986) Workers, Corporate Enterprise and the Law, in *Labour Law in Britain* ed Roy Lewis (Basil Blackwell, Oxford).

Bercusson, Brian (1990) The European Community's Charter of Fundamental Social Rights *Modern Law Review* 53, 624-642.

Bercusson, Brian (1992) Maastricht: a Fundamental Change in European Labour Law *Industrial Relations Journal* 23, 177-191.

Bercusson, Brian (1994a) The Dynamic of European Labour Law after Maastricht *Industrial Law Journal* 23, 1-31.

Bercusson, Brian (1994b) *Working Time in Britain: Towards a European Model Part I: The European Union Directive* (Institute of Employment Rights, London).

Bercusson, Brian (1994c) *Working Time in Britain: Towards a European Model Part II: Collective Bargaining in Europe and the UK* (Institute of Employment Rights, London).

Bercusson, Brian (1994d) Collective Bargaining and the Protection of Social Rights in Europe, in *Human Rights and Labour Law* eds KD Ewing, CA Gearty and BA Hepple (Mansell, London).

Bercusson, Brian (1996) *European Labour Law* (Butterworths, London).

Bercusson, Brian (2000) Transnational Trade Union Rights, in *Legal Regulation of the Employment Relation* eds Hugh Collins, Paul Davies and Roger Rideout (Kluwer, London).

Bercusson, Brian (2001) A European Agenda?, in *Employment Rights at Work* ed KD Ewing (Institute of Employment Rights, London).

Bercusson, Brian (2002) The European Social Model Comes to Britain *Industrial Law Journal* 31, 209-244.

Bercusson, Brian (2004) Episodes on the Path Towards the European Social Model: The EU Charter of Fundamental Rights and the Convention on the Future of Europe in *The Future of Labour Law: Liber Amicorum Sir Bob Hepple QC* ed Catherine Barnard, Simon Deakin and Gillian S Morris (Hart Publishing, Oxford).

Bercusson, Brian, Ulrich Mückenberger and Alain Supiot (1992) *Application du Droit du Travail et Diversité Culturelle en Europe* Etude réalisée pour le Ministère du Travail, de l'Emploi et de la Formation Professionelle (Nantes, ARSH).

Bercusson, Brian, Mike Clancy, Keith Ewing, John Foster, Sandy Fredman, Aileen McColgan, Rod Robertson and Stephen Wood (1998) *Need to be Heard at Work?: Recognition Laws – Lessons From Abroad* (Institute of Employment Rights, London).

Bercusson, Brian, Simon Deakin, Pertti Koistinen, Yota Kravaritou, Ulrich Mückenberger, Alain Supiot and Bruno Veneziani (1997) *A Manifesto for Social Europe* (European Trade Union Institute, Brussels).

Bernier, Jean (1994) *Strikes and Essential Services* (Les Presses de l'Université Laval, Quebec).

Betten, Lammy (1993) *International Labour Law* (Kluwer, Deventer-Boston).

Betten, Lammy, and Vivienne Shrubshall (1998) The Concept of Positive Sex Discrimination in Community Law – Before and After the Treaty of Amsterdam *International Journal of Comparative Labour Law and Industrial Relations* 14, 65-80.

Biagi, Marco (1998b) The Implementation of the Amsterdam Treaty with regard to Employment: Co-ordination or Convergence? *International Journal of Comparative Labour Law and Industrial Relations* 14, 325-337.

Biagi, M and M Tiraboschi (2004) Forms of Employee Representational Participation, in *Comparative Labour Law and Industrial Relations in Industrialised Market Economies* 8th edn ed R Blanpain (Kluwer Law International, The Hague).

Bird, D (1991) Industrial Stoppages in 1990 *Employment Gazette* 99, 379-390.

Bird, D, M Stevens and A Yates (1991) Membership of Trade Unions in 1989 *Employment Gazette* 99, 347-353.

Birks, Peter and Chin Nyuk Yin (1995) On the Nature of Undue Influence in Good Faith and Fault in Contract Law in *Good Faith and Fault in Contract Law*, ed Jack Beatson and Daniel Friedmann (Clarendon Press, Oxford).

Bishop, William, and John Kay (1987) Taxation and the Rule in *Gourley's* Case *Law Quarterly Review* 193, 211-233.

Black, Ole, Ian Richardson and Rhys Herbert (2004) Jobs in the Public Sector mid-2003 *Labour Market Trends* (July), 271-281.

Blair, Tony (1998) *The Third Way: New Politics for a New Century* (Fabian Society, London).

Blake, Leslie (1991) 'Compensation for Child Care Costs' *New Law Journal* 141, 1734-1743.

Blake, Nicholas and Raza Husain (2003) *Immigration, Asylum and Human Rights* (OUP, Oxford).

Blanchflower, David, Neil Millward and Andrew Oswald (1988) *Unionisation and Employment Behaviour* Centre for Labour Economics Discussion Paper 339 (London School of Economics, London).

Blank, Rebecca (1994) Does a Larger Social Safety Net Mean Less Economic Flexibility?, in *Working Under Different Rules* ed Richard B Freeman (Russell Sage Foundation, New York).

Blanpain, Roger (ed) (1988) *Legal and Contractual Limitations on Working Time in the European Community* European Foundation for the Improvement of Living and Working Conditions (OOPEC, Luxembourg).

Blanpain, Roger (ed) (1999) *Private Employment Agencies* Bulletin of Comparative Labour Relations No 36 (Kluwer, The Hague).

Blanpain, Roger (ed) (2001) *The Council of Europe and the Social Challenges of the XX1st Century* (Kluwer, The Hague).

Blanpain, Roger, and Chris Engels (1993) *European Labour Law* (Kluwer, Deventer-Boston).

Blanpain, Roger and Ronnie Graham (eds) (2004) *Temporary Agency Work and the Information Society* (Kluwer Law International, The Hague).

Bogg, Alan L (2005) Employment Relations Act 2004: Another False Dawn for Collectivism? *Industrial Law Journal* 34, 72-82.

Bond, Abigail (1995) The Young Persons Directive *Industrial Law Journal* 24, 377-382.

Bourn, Colin (1992) *Sex Discrimination Law: A Review* (Institute of Employment Rights, London).

Bowers, John, and Andrew Clarke (1981) Unfair Dismissal and Managerial Prerogative: a study of 'Some other Substantial Reason' *Industrial Law Journal* 10, 34-44.

Bowers, John and Jeremy Lewis (2005) Non-Economic Damage in Unfair Dismissal Cases: What's Left after *Dunnachie?* in *Industrial Law Journal* 34, 83-95.

Bowers, John, and Elena Moran (2002) Justification in Direct Sex Discrimination: Breaking the Taboo *Industrial Law Journal* 31, 307-320.

Bowers, John, Michael Duggan and David Reade (2004) *The Law of Industrial Action and Trade Union Recognition* (Oxford University Press, Oxford).

Bowers, John, Jack Mitchell and Jeremy Lewis (1999) *Whistleblowing: The New Law* (Sweet & Maxwell, London).

Bowers, John, Elena Moran and Simon Honeyball (2003) Justification in Direct Sex Discrimination: A Reply *Industrial Law Journal* 32, 185-187.

Braverman, Harry (1974) *Labour and Monopoly Capital* (Monthly Review Press, New York).

Brillat, Regis (1996) A New Protocol to the European Social Charter Providing for Collective Complaints *European Human Rights Law Review*, 52-62.

Brodie, Douglas (1996) The Heart of the Matter: Mutual Trust and Confidence *Industrial Law Journal* 25, 121-136.

Brodie, Douglas (1998a) Specific Performance and Employment Contracts *Industrial Law Journal* 27, 37-48.

Brodie, Douglas (1998b) Beyond Exchange: the New Contract of Employment *Industrial Law Journal*, 27, 79-102.

Brodie, Douglas (1999a) A Fair Deal at Work *Oxford Journal of Legal Studies* 19, 83-98.

Brodie, Douglas (1999b) Wrongful Dismissal and Mutual Trust *Industrial Law Journal* 28, 260-262.

Brodie, Douglas (2001a) Mutual Trust and the Values of the Employment Contract *Industrial Law Journal* 30, 84-100.

Brodie, Douglas, (2001b) Legal Coherence and the Employment Revolution *Law Quarterly Review* 117, 604- 625.

Brodie, Douglas (2002) Fair Dealing and the Disciplinary Process *Industrial Law Journal* 31, 294-297.

Brodie, Douglas (2003) *A History of British Labour Law 1867-1945* (Hart Publishing, Oxford).

Brodie, Douglas (2004) Protecting Dignity in the Workplace: the Vitality of Mutual Trust and Confidence *Industrial Law Journal* 33, 349-354.

Brodin, Emma (1996) The Employment Status of Ministers of Religion *Industrial Law Journal* 25, 211-224.

Brodin, Emma (1997) *Sex Discrimination in Employment within the Church of England*, Ph D, University of Huddersfield, 1997.

Brown, Damian (1994) Remedies for Breach of Employment Contracts *Industrial Law Journal* 23, 331-333.

Brown, Damien and Keith Ewing (2000) Human Rights at Work: Possibilities and Problems, in *Human Rights at Work* ed Keith Ewing (Institute of Employment Rights, London).

Brown, Damian and Aileen McColgan (1992) UK Employment Law and the International Labour Organisation: The Spirit of Cooperation? *Industrial Law Journal*, 21, 265-279.

Brown, William (1972) A Consideration of Custom and Practice *British Journal of Industrial Relations* 10, 42-61.

Brown, William (1973) *Piecework Bargaining* (Basil Blackwell, Oxford).

Brown, William (ed) (1981) *The Changing Contours of British Industrial Relations: A Survey of Manufacturing Industry* (Blackwell, Oxford).

Brown, William (1992) Bargaining Structure and the Impact of Law, in *Legal Intervention in Industrial Relations: Gains and Losses* ed William McCarthy (Blackwell, Oxford).

Brown, William (1993) The Contraction of Collective Bargaining in Britain *British Journal of Industrial Relations* 31, 189-200.

Brown, William (2000) Putting Partnership into Practice in Britain *British Journal of Industrial Relations* 38, 299-316.

Brown, William and Sarah Oxenbridge (2004) Trade Unions and Collective Bargaining: Law and the Future of Collectivism, in *The Future of Labour Law: Liber Amicorum Sir Bob Hepple QC* ed Catherine Barnard, Simon Deakin and Gillian S Morris (Hart Publishing, Oxford).

Brown, William, and Sushil Wadwhani (1990) The Economic Effects of Industrial Relations Legislation since 1979 *National Institute Economic Review*, 57-70.

Brown, William, and Janet Walsh (1990) Pay Determination in Britain in the 1980s: the Anatomy of Decentralisation *Oxford Review of Economic Policy* 7, 44-59.

Brown, William, Simon Deakin and Paul Ryan (1997) The Effects of British Industrial Relations Legislation 1979-1997 *National Institute Economic Review* 161, 69-83.

Brown, William, Paul Marginson and Janet Walsh (2003) The Management of Pay as the Influence of Collective Bargaining Diminishes in *Industrial Relations: Theory and Practice* 2nd edn ed Paul Edwards (Blackwell Publishing, Oxford).

Brown, William, Simon Deakin, Maria Hudson and Cliff Pratten (2001) The Limits of Statutory Trade Union Recognition *Industrial Relations Journal* 32, 180-194.

Brown, William, Simon Deakin, David Nash, and Sarah Oxenbridge (2000) The Employment Contract: from Collective Procedures to Individual Rights *British Journal of Industrial Relations* 38, 611-629.

Browne-Wilkinson, The Hon Mr Justice (1982) The Role of the Employment Appeal Tribunal in the 1980s *Industrial Law Journal* 11, 69-77.

Büchtemann, Christoph (1990) More Jobs through Less Employment Protection? Evidence for West Germany *Labour* 3, 23-56.

Büchtemann, Christoph (1993) Introduction: Employment Security and Labor Markets, in *Employment Security and Labor Market Behavior. Inter-Disciplinary Approaches and International Evidence* ed Christoph Büchtemann (Cornell University Press, Ithaca NY).

Büchtemann, Christoph, and Sigrid Quack (1989) 'Bridges' or 'traps'? Non-standard Employment, in the Federal Republic of Germany, in *Precarious Jobs in Labour Market Regulation* eds Gerry and Janine Rodgers (International Institute for Labour Studies, Geneva).

Burchell, Brendan, Simon Deakin and Sheila Honey (1999) *The Employment Status of Workers in Non-standard Employment*. EMAR research series 6 (Department of Trade and Industry, London).

Burton, J (1979) *The Trojan Horse: Union Power in British Politics* (Adam Smith Institute, London).

Caraciollo di Tirella, Eugenia (1999) Recent Developments in Pregnancy and Maternity Rights *Industrial Law Journal* 28, 276-282.

Card, Richard (2000) *Public Order Law* (Jordans, Bristol).

Carley, Mark and Mark Hall (2000) The Implementation of the European Works Councils Directive *Industrial Law Journal* 29, 103-124.

Carty, Hazel (1988) Intentional Violation of Economic Interests: The Limits of Common Law Liability *Law Quarterly Review* 104, 250-285.

Carty, Hazel (2001) *An Analysis of the Economic Torts* (Oxford University Press, Oxford).

Casey, Bernard (1988) *Temporary Employment in Britain* (Policy Studies Institute, London).

Casey, Bernard, Hilary Metcalf and Neil Millward (1997) *Employers' Use of Flexible Labour* (Policy Studies Institute, London).

Charlwood, Andy (2003) Willingness to unionize amongst non-union workers in *Representing Workers: Trade Union Recognition and Membership in Britain* ed Howard Gospel and Stephen Wood (Routledge, London).

Charlwood, Andy (2004a) Influences on Trade Union Organising Effectiveness in Britain *British Journal of Industrial Relations* 42, 69-93.

Charlwood, Andy (2004b) The New Generation of Trade Union Leaders and Prospects for Union Revitalization *British Journal of Industrial Relations* 42, 379-397.

Christian, TJ and KD Ewing (1987) Labouring under the Canadian Constitution *Industrial Law Journal* 17, 73-91.

Churchill, Robin R and Urfan Khaliq (2004) The Collective Complaints System of the European Social Charter: An Effective Mechanism for Ensuring Compliance with Economic and Social Rights? *European Journal of International Law* 15, 417-456.

Clancy, Mike and Roger Seifert (2000) *Fairness at Work? The Disciplinary and Grievance Provisions of the 1999 Employment Relations Act* (Institute of Employment Rights, London).

Clark, Jon (1999) Adversarial and Investigative Approaches to the Arbitral Resolution of Dismissal Disputes: A Comparison of South Africa and the UK *Industrial Law Journal* 28, 319-335.

Clark, Jon and Mark Hall (1992) The Cinderella Directive? Employee Rights to Information about Conditions applicable to their Contract or Employment Relationship *Industrial Law Journal* 21, 106-118.

Clark, Jon, and Lord Wedderburn (1983) Modern Labour Law: Problems, Functions and Policies, in *Labour Law and Industrial Relations: Building on Kahn-Freund* eds Lord Wedderburn, Roy Lewis and Jonathan Clark (Clarendon Press, Oxford).

Clark, Jon, and Lord Wedderburn (1987) Juridification – A Universal Trend?, in *Juridification of Social Spheres* ed Gunther Teubner (Walter de Gruyter, Berlin).

Clarke, Linda (1999) Mutual Trust and Confidence, Fiduciary Relationships and the Duty of Disclosure *Industrial Law Journal* 28, 348-360.

Claydon, Tim (1996) Union De-Recognition: a Re-Examination in *Contemporary Industrial Relations*, ed Ian J. Beardwell (Oxford University Press, Oxford).

Clayton, Gina (2004) *Textbook on Immigration and Asylum Law* (OUP, Oxford).

Clegg, Hugh (1985) *A History of British Trade Unions since 1889 Volume II: 1911-1933* (Clarendon Press, Oxford).

Clements, Luke, Nuala Mole and Alan Simmons (1999) *European Human Rights: Taking a Case under the Convention* 2nd edn (Sweet and Maxwell, London).

Clerk and Lindsell (2000) *Clerk and Lindsell on Torts*, 18th edn (Sweet and Maxwell, London).

Cockburn, David (1995) Changes to the Industrial Relations System *Industrial Law Journal* 24, 285-291.

Colaianni, Tia (1996) *European Works Councils* (Sweet and Maxwell, London).

Collard, R and B Dale (1989) Quality Circles, in *Personnel Management in Britain* ed Keith Sisson (Basil Blackwell, Oxford).

Collins, Hugh (1982) Capitalist Discipline and Corporatist Law *Industrial Law Journal* 11, 78-93, 170-177.

Collins, Hugh (1986) Market Power, Bureaucratic Power and the Contract of Employment *Industrial Law Journal* 15, 1-15.

Collins, Hugh (1989a) Employee Share Option Schemes *Industrial Law Journal* 18, 54-59.

Collins, Hugh (1989b) Transfer of Undertakings and Insolvency *Industrial Law Journal* 18, 144-158.

Collins, Hugh (1989c) Labour Law as a Vocation *Law Quarterly Review* 105, 468-484.

Collins, Hugh (1990a) Ascription of Legal Responsibility to Groups in Complex Patterns of Economic Integration *Modern Law Review* 53, 731-744.

Collins, Hugh (1990b) Independent Contractors and the Challenge of Vertical Disintegration to Employment Protection Laws *Oxford Journal of Legal Studies* 10, 353-380.

Collins, Hugh (1993) *Justice in Dismissal* (Clarendon Press, Oxford).

Collins, Hugh (1994) CCT, Equal Pay and Market Forces *Industrial Law Journal* 23, 341-345.

Collins, Hugh (1997) The Productive Disintegration of Labour Law *Industrial Law Journal* 26, 295-309.

Collins, Hugh (2000a) Justifications and Techniques of Legal Regulation of the Employment Relation, in *Legal Regulation of the Employment Relation* eds Hugh Collins, Paul Davies and Roger Rideout (Kluwer, London).

Collins, Hugh (2000b) Employment Rights of Casual Workers *Industrial Law Journal* 29, 73-78.

Collins, Hugh (2000c) Finding the Right Direction for the 'Industrial Jury' *Industrial Law Journal* 29, 293-296.

Collins, Hugh (2001a) Is there a Third Way in Labour Law?, in *Labour Law in an Era of Globalisation: Transformative Practices and Possibilities* eds. Joanne Conaghan, Michael Fischl and Karl Klare (OUP, Oxford).

Collins, Hugh (2001b) Regulating the Employment Relation for Competitiveness *Industrial Law Journal* 30, 1-31.

Collins, Hugh (2001c) Claim for Unfair Dismissal *Industrial Law Journal* 30, 305-309.

Collins, Hugh (2003) *Employment Law* (OUP, Oxford).

Collins, Hugh (2004) *Nine Proposals for the Reform of the Law on Unfair Dismissal* (Institute of Employment Rights, London).

Collins, Hugh, Paul Davies and Roger Rideout (eds) (2000) *Legal Regulation of the Employment Relation* (Kluwer, London).

Collins, Lawrence, with specialist editors (2000) *Dicey and Morris on the Conflict of Laws* 13th edn (Sweet and Maxwell, London).

Conaghan, Joanne (1996) Gendered Harms and the Law of Tort: Remedying Sexual Harassment *Oxford Journal of Legal Studies* 16, 407-431.

Conaghan, Joanne, and Louise Chudleigh (1987) Women in Confinement: Can Labour Law Deliver the Goods? *Journal of Law and Society* 14, 133-147.

Connolly, Michael (1998) Discrimination Law: Requirements and Preferences *Industrial Law Journal* 27, 133-142.

Connolly, Michael (2000) Discrimination Law: Victimisation *Industrial Law Journal* 29, 305-311.

Coppel, Jason (1997) Horizontal Effect of Directives *Industrial Law Journal* 26, 69-73.

Coppel, Jason (1998) *The Human Rights Act 1998: Enforcing the European Convention in the Domestic Courts* (Wiley, Chichester).

Corby, Susan (2002) On Parole: Prison Service Industrial Relations *Industrial Relations Journal* 33, 286-297.

Cordova, Efren (1985) Strikes in the Public Service: Some Determinants and Trends *International Labour Review* 124, 163-179.

Cornford, Tom and Maurice Sunkin (2001) The Bowman Report, Access and the Recent Reforms of the Judicial Review Procedure *Public Law*,11-20.

Cousins, Christine (1994) A Comparison of the Labour Market Position of Women in Spain and the UK with Reference to the 'Flexible' Labour Debate *Work, Employment and Society* 8, 45-67.

Coutts, Ken, and Robert Rowthorn (1995) *Employment in the United Kingdom: Trends and Prospects* ESRC Centre for Business Research, University of Cambridge, Working Paper No 3.

Couturier, Gérard (1988) *Droit du Travail I: Les Relations Individuels de Travail* (PUF, Paris).

Craig, Christine, Jill Rubery, Roger Tarling and Frank Wilkinson (1982) *Labour Market Structure, Industrial Organisation and Low Pay* (CUP, Cambridge).

Craig, Christine, Jill Rubery, Roger Tarling and Frank Wilkinson (1985) Economic, Social and Political Factors in the Operation of the Labour Market in *New Approaches to Economic Life* eds Bryan Roberts, Ruth Finnegan and Duncan Gallie (MUP, Manchester).

Craig, John DR and Hazel D Oliver (1998) The Right to Privacy in the Workplace: Should the Private Sector be Concerned? *Industrial Law Journal* 27, 49-59.

Craig, PP (1996) Proceeding Outside Order 53: A Modified Test? *Law Quarterly Review* 112, 531-535.

Craven, Matthew (1998) *The International Covenant on Economic, Social and Cultural Rights* (Clarendon Press, Oxford).

Creigh, Stephen, Ceridwen Roberts, Andrea Gorman and Paul Sawyer (1986) Self-employment in Britain. Results from the Labour Force Surveys 1981-1984 *Employment Gazette* 94, 193-194.

Creighton, Breen (1994) The ILO and Protection of Freedom of Association in the United Kingdom, in *Human Rights and Labour Law: Essays for Paul O'Higgins* eds KD Ewing, CA Gearty and BA Hepple (Mansell, London).

Creighton, Breen (2004a) Freedom of Association in *Comparative Labour Law and Industrial Relations in Industrialised Market Economies* 8th edn, ed Roger Blanpain (Kluwer Law International, The Hague).

Creighton, Breen (2004b) The Future of Labour Law: Is there a Role for International Labour Standards? in *The Future of Labour Law: Liber Amicorum Sir Bob Hepple QC* ed Catherine Barnard, Simon Deakin and Gillian S Morris (Hart Publishing, Oxford).

Cressy, P (1993) Employee Participation in *The Social Dimension: Employment Policy in the United Kingdom* ed M Gold (Macmillan, London).

Cripps, Yvonne (1995) *The Legal Implications of Disclosure in the Public Interest* 2nd edn (Sweet and Maxwell, London).

Cripps, Yvonne (2000) The Public Interest Disclosure Act 1998, in *Freedom of Expression and Freedom of Information* ed Jack Beatson and Yvonne Cripps (Oxford University Press, Oxford).

Crouch, Colin (2000) The Snakes and Ladders of Twenty-First-Century Trade Unionism *Oxford Review of Economic Policy* 16, 70-83.

Cullen, Holly (2000a) The Collective Complaints Mechanism of the European Social Charter *European Law Review* 25, HR 18-29.

Cullen , Holly (2000b) The Interaction of Forms of Regulation in International Labour Law, in *Legal Regulation of the Employment Relation* ed Hugh Collins, Paul Davies and Roger Rideout (Kluwer, London).

Cully, Mark and Stephen Woodland (1997) Trade Union Membership and Recognition *Labour Market Trends*, June, 231-239.

Cully, Mark, Stephen Woodland, Andrew O'Reilly and Gill Dix (1999) *Britain at Work. As depicted by the 1998 Workplace Employment Relations Survey* (Routledge, London).

Cunningham, Naomi (1995) Sex Discrimination: Equal but Different? *Industrial Law Journal* 24, 177-181.

Curran, Simon (1994) Unfairly Dismissed though still Employed? *Hogg v Dover College* Revisited *Industrial Law Journal* 23, 166-169.

Curtin, Deirdre (1992) State Liability under Community Law: A New Remedy for Private Parties *Industrial Law Journal* 21, 74-81.

Daniel, WW (1985) United Kingdom, in *Managing Workforce Reduction* ed M Cross (Croom Helm, London).

Daniel, WW (1987) *Workplace Industrial Relations and Technical Change* (Frances Pinter/PSI, London).

Daniel, WW (1990) *The Unemployed Flow* (Policy Studies Institute, London).

Daniel, WW and Neil Millward (1983) *Workplace Industrial Relations in Britain: The DE/PSI/SSRC Survey* (Heinemann Educational Books, London).

Daniel, WW and Elizabeth Stilgoe (1978) *The Impact of Employment Protection Laws* (Policy Studies Institute, London).

Daübler, Wolfgang (1991) *Das Arbeitsrecht* (Rowohlt, Reinbek).

Daübler, Wolfgang, and Martine le Friant (1985) Un récent exemple de flexibilisation législative: la loi allemande pour la promotion de l'emploi du 26 avril 1986 *Droit Social*, 715-720.

Davidov, Guy (2004) Collective Bargaining Laws: Purpose and Scope *International Journal of Comparative Labour Law and Industrial Relations* 20, 81-106.

Davies, Anne CL (2004) *Perspectives on Labour Law* (CUP, Cambridge).

Davies, Paul (1989) Acquired Rights, Creditors' Rights, Freedom of Contract, and Industrial Democracy *Yearbook of European Law* 9, 21-53.

Davies, Paul (1992) The Emergence of European Labour Law, in *Legal Intervention in Industrial Relations: Gains and Losses* ed William McCarthy (Blackwell, Oxford).

Davies, Paul (1994a) Employee Claims in Insolvency: Corporate Rescues and Preferential Claims *Industrial Law Journal* 23, 141-151.

Davies, Paul (1994b) A Challenge to Single Channel *Industrial Law Journal* 23, 272-285.

Davies, Paul (1995) Market Integration and Social Policy in the Court of Justice *Industrial Law Journal* 24, 49-77.

Davies, Paul (1996) The European Court of Justice, National Courts and the Member States, in *European Community Labour Law: Principles and Perspectives. Liber Amicorum Lord Wedderburn* eds Paul Davies, Antoine Lyon-Caen, Silvana Sciarra and Spiros Simitis (Clarendon Press, Oxford).

Davies, Paul (1997) Posted Workers: Single Market or Protection of National Labour Law Systems? *Common Market Law Review* 34, 571-602.

Davies, Paul (1998) Amendments to the Acquired Rights Directive *Industrial Law Journal* 27, 365-375.

Davies, Paul (2001) Transfers – the UK Will Have to Make Up Its Own Mind *Industrial Law Journal* 30, 231-235.

Davies, Paul (2003) Workers on the Board of the European Company? *Industrial Law Journal* 32, 75-96.

Davies, Paul and Mark Freedland (1983) *Kahn-Freund's Labour and the Law* (Stevens and Sons, London).

Davies, Paul and Mark Freedland (1984) *Labour Law: Text and Materials* 2nd edn (Weidenfeld and Nicolson, London).

Davies, Paul and Mark Freedland (1993) *Labour Legislation and Public Policy* (Clarendon Press, Oxford).

Davies, Paul and Mark Freedland (1997) The Impact of Public Law on Labour Law 1972-1997 *Industrial Law Journal*, 26, 311-335.

Davies, Paul and Mark Freedland (2000) Employees, Workers and the Autonomy of Labour Law, in *Legal Regulation of the Employment Relation* eds Hugh Collins, Paul Davies and Roger Rideout (Kluwer, London).

Davies, Paul and Mark Freedland (2004) Changing Perspectives on the Employment Relationship in British Labour Law, in *The Future of Labour Law: Liber Amicorum Sir Bob Hepple QC* eds Catherine Barnard, Simon Deakin and Gillian S Morris (Hart Publishing, Oxford).

Davies, Paul and Claire Kilpatrick (2004) UK Worker Representation After Single Channel *Industrial Law Journal* 33, 121-151.

Davies, Paul, Antoine Lyon-Caen, Silvana Sciarra and Spiros Simitis (eds) *European Community Labour Law: Principles and Perspectives. Liber Amicorum Lord Wedderburn* (Clarendon Press, Oxford).

Davies, Robert (2004) Contracting Out and the Retention of Employment Model in the National Health Service *Industrial Law Journal* 33, 95-120.

Davis, JE (1868) *The Master and Servant Act 1867* (Butterworths, London).

Dawson, Sandra, Paul Willman, Alan Clinton and Martin Bamford (1988) *Safety at Work: the limits of self-regulation* (Cambridge University Press, Cambridge).

De Búrca, Gráinne (2001 The Drafting of the European Union Charter of Human Rights *European Law Review* 26, 126-138.

De Schutter, Olivier and Simon Deakin (2005) *Social Rights and Market Forces: Is Open Coordination the Future for European Employment and Social Policy?* (Bruylant, Brussels).

De Smith, Stanley, Lord Woolf and Jeffrey Jowell (1995) *Judicial Review of Administrative Action* (Sweet and Maxwell, London).

Deakin, Simon (1986) Labour Law and the Developing Employment Relationship in the UK *Cambridge Journal of Economics* 10, 225-246.

Deakin, Simon (1989) *Contract, Labour Law and the Developing Employment Relationship* PhD Thesis, University of Cambridge.

Deakin, Simon (1990a) Equality under a Market Order: the Employment Act 1989 *Industrial Law Journal* 19, 1-23.

Deakin, Simon (1990b) The Floor of Rights in European Labour Law *New Zealand Journal of Industrial Relations* 15, 219-240.

Deakin, Simon (1991) Legal Change and Labour Market Restructuring in Western Europe and the US *New Zealand Journal of Industrial Relations* 16, 109-125.

Deakin, Simon (1992) Logical Deductions? Wages Law before and after *Delaney v Staples Modern Law Review* 55, 848-857.

Deakin, Simon (1994a) Part-time Employment, Qualifying Thresholds and Economic Justification *Industrial Law Journal* 23, 151-155.

Deakin, Simon (1994b) Open for Business *Industrial Law Journal* 23, 333-337.

Deakin, Simon (1995) Levelling Down Employee Benefits *Cambridge Law Journal* 54, 35-37.

Deakin, Simon (1996a) The Utility of Rights Talk: Employees' Personal Rights, in *Understanding Human Rights* eds Conor Gearty and Adam Tomkins (Mansell, London).

Deakin, Simon (1996b) Labour Law as Market Regulation, in *European Community Labour Law: Principles and Perspectives. Liber Amicorum Lord Wedderburn* eds. Paul Davies, Antoine Lyon-Caen, Silvana Sciarra and Spiros Simitis (Clarendon Press, Oxford).

Deakin, Simon (1996c) Law and Economics, in *Legal Frontiers* ed Philip A Thomas (Dartmouth, Aldershot).

Deakin, Simon (1998) The Evolution of the Contract of Employment 1900-1950: the Influence of the Welfare State, in *Governance, Industry and Labour Markets in Britain and France. The modernising state in the mid-twentieth century* eds Noel Whiteside and Robert Salais (Routledge, London).

Deakin, Simon (1999) Organisational Change, Labour Flexibility and the Contract of Employment in Great Britain, in *Employment Relations, Individualisation and Union Exclusion. An International Study* eds. Stephen Deery and Richard Mitchell (Federation Press, Annandale, NSW).

Deakin, Simon (2000) Legal Origins of Wage Labour: the Evolution of the Contract of Employment from Industrialisation to the Welfare State in *The Dynamics of Wage Relations in the New Europe* eds Linda Clarke, Peter de Gijsel and Jörn Janssen (Kluwer, Deventer).

Deakin, Simon (2001a) The Changing Concept of the Employer in Labour Law *Industrial Law Journal* 30, 72-84.

Deakin, Simon (2001b) Employment Protection and the Employment Relationship: Adapting the Traditional Model?, in *Employment Rights at Work: Reviewing the Employment Relations Act 1999* ed Keith Ewing (Institute of Employment Rights, London).

Deakin, Simon (2001c) The Many Futures of the Contract of Employment, in *Labour Law in an Era of Globalisation: Transformative Practices and Possibilities* eds Joanne Conaghan, Michael Fischl and Karl Klare (OUP, Oxford).

Deakin, Simon (2002) Equality, Non-Discrimination, and the Labour Market: a Commentary on Richard Epstein's Critique of Anti-Discrimination laws, in *Equal Opportunity or More Opportunity? The Good Thing about Discrimination* ed. Richard Esptein (Institute for the Study of Civil Society, London).

Deakin, Simon (2003) Interpreting Employment Contracts: Judges, Employers and Workers, in *Commercial Law and Commercial Practice* ed Sarah Worthington (Hart Publishing, Oxford).

Deakin, Simon (2004) Workers, Finance and Democracy, in *The Future of Labour Law: Liber Amicorum Sir Bob Hepple QC* eds Catherine Barnard, Simon Deakin and Gillian S. Morris (Hart Publishing, Oxford).

Deakin, Simon and Alan Hughes (1999) Economic Efficiency and the Proceduralisation of Company Law *Company, Financial and Insolvency Law Review* 3, 169-189.

Deakin, Simon and Hannah Reed (2000a) The Contested Meaning of Labour Market Flexibility: Economic Theory and the Discourse of European Integration in *Social Law and Policy in an Evolving European Union* ed Jo Shaw (Hart Publishing, Oxford).

Deakin, Simon and Hannah Reed (2000b) River Crossing or Cold Bath? Deregulation and Employment in Britain in the 1980s and 1990s in *Why Deregulate Labour Markets?* eds Gosta Esping-Andersen and Marino Regini (OUP, Oxford).

Deakin, Simon, and Frank Wilkinson (1991) Labour Law, Social Security and Economic Inequality *Cambridge Journal of Economics* 15, 125-148.

Deakin, Simon, and Frank Wilkinson (1992) The Law and Economics of the Minimum Wage *Journal of Law and Society*, 19, 279-392.

Deakin, Simon, and Frank Wilkinson (1994) Rights vs Efficiency? The Economic Case for Transnational Labour Standards *Industrial Law Journal* 23, 289-310.

Deakin, Simon, and Frank Wilkinson (1996) Contracts, Cooperation and Trust: the Role of the Institutional Framework, in *Contract and Economic Organisation: Socio-Legal Initiatives* eds David Campbell and Peter Vincent-Jones (Dartmouth, Aldershot).

Deakin, Simon and Frank Wilkinson (1999) The Management of Redundancies in Europe – the Case of Great Britain *Labour* 13, 41-89.

Deakin, Simon and Frank Wilkinson (2000a) Labour Law and Economic Theory: A Reappraisal, *Legal Regulation of the Employment Relation* eds Hugh Collins, Paul Davies and Roger Rideout (Kluwer, London).

Deakin, Simon and Frank Wilkinson (2000b) 'Capabilities', ordineo spontaneo del mercato e diritti sociali *Il diritto del mercato del lavoro*, 2, 313-344; also published in English as ESRC Centre for Business Research Working Paper No. 174.

Deakin, Simon and Frank Wilkinson (2005) *The Law of the Labour Market: Industrialization, Employment and Legal Evolution* (OUP, Oxford).

Deakin, Simon, Sara Horrell and Jill Rubery (1989) *Working Time and Plant Operating Times in the EEC Internal Market: the UK Report*, Report for the European Commission (Department of Applied Economics, University of Cambridge).

Deakin, Simon, Angus Johnston and Basil Markesinis (2003) *Markesinis and Deakin's Tort Law*, 5th edn (Clarendon Press, Oxford).

Deakin, Simon, Jonathan Michie and Frank Wilkinson (1992) *Inflation, Employment, Wage-bargaining and the Law* (Institute of Employment Rights, London).

Del Rey Guanter, Salvador (1992) Contrato de Trabajo y Derechos Fundamentales en la Doctrina Constitucional, in *Constitucion y Derecho del Trabajo: 1981-1991 Análasis de Diez Años de Jurisprudencia Constitucional* ed RM Alarcón Caracuel (Marcial Pons, Madrid).

Denning, AT (1939) Wages during Sickness *Law Quarterly Review* 54, 353-357.

Desmond, Helen (2000) Research and Reports, *Winning the Generation Game* etc. *Industrial Law Journal* 29, 403-406.

Desmond, Helen (2003) The Generation Game: Pensions and Retirement *Industrial Law Journal* 32, 218-222.

Devonshire, Peter (2003) *Spycatcher* Returns to the House of Lords *Law Quarterly Review* 119, 384-387.

Diamond, Paul (1991) Dishonourable Defences: the Use of Injunctions and the EEC Treaty – Case Study of the Shops Act 1950 *Modern Law Review* 54, 72-87.

Dicey, AV [1908] (1979) *An Introduction to the Study of the Law of the Constitution* 7th edn reprinted with an introduction by ECS Wade (Macmillan, London).

Dickens, Linda (1980) What are Companies Disclosing for the 1980s? *Personnel Management*, April, 28-30, 48.

Dickens, Linda (1988) Justice in the Industrial Tribunal System *Industrial Law Journal* 17, 58-61.

Dickens, Linda (1992a) *Whose Flexibility?* (Institute of Employment Rights, London).

Dickens, Linda (1992b) Maintaining a Collective Interest *Industrial Law Journal* 21, 305-6.

Dickens, Linda (2000) Doing More with Less, in *Employment Relations in Britain: 25 Years of the Advisory Conciliation and Arbitration Service* ed Brian Towers and William Brown (Blackwell, Oxford)

Dickens, Linda and George Sayers Bain (1986) A Duty to Bargain? Union Recognition and Information Disclosure, in *Labour Law in Britain*, ed Roy Lewis (Blackwell, Oxford).

Dickens, Linda and Mark Hall (2003) Labour Law and Industrial Relations: A New Settlement? in *Industrial Relations: Theory and Practice* 2nd edn ed Paul Edwards (Blackwell Publishing, Oxford).

Dickens, Linda, Michael Jones, Brian Weekes and Moira Hart (1985) *Dismissed: A Study of Unfair Dismissal and the Industrial Tribunal System* (Blackwell, Oxford).

Dickens, Richard and Alan Manning (2003) Minimum Wage, Minimum Impact, in *The Labour Market under New Labour: The State of Working Britain 2003* eds Richard Dickens, Paul Gregg and Jonathan Wadsworth (Palgrave, Basingstoke).

Dickens, Richard, Paul Gregg, Stephen Machin, Alan Manning and Jonathan Wadsworth (1993) Wages Councils: Was There a Case for Abolition? *British Journal of Industrial Relations* 31, 516-529.

Dicks, M and N Hatch (1989) *The Relationship between Employment and Unemployment*, Bank of England Working Paper (London).

Dilnot, Andrew and Richard Disney (1989) Pension Schemes after the 1989 Budget *Fiscal Studies*, 10/3, 34-49.

Disney, Richard (1990) Explanations of the Decline in Trade Union Density in Britain: an Appraisal *British Journal of Industrial Relations* 28, 165-177.

Disney, Richard, and Erika Szyszczak (1984) Part-Time Employment and Sex Discrimination in Great Britain *British Journal of Industrial Relations* 22, 78-100.

Disney, Richard, and Erika Szyszczak (1989) Reply to Catherine Hakim *Industrial Law Journal* 18, 223-228.

Dix, Gill (2000) Operating with Style: the Work of the ACAS Conciliator in Individual Employment Rights Cases in *Employment Relations in Britain: 25 Years of the Advisory Conciliation and Arbitration Service* ed Brian Towers and William Brown (Blackwell, Oxford)

Dix, Gill and Sarah Oxenbridge (2004) *Coming to the Table: The role of Acas in collective disputes and improving workplace relations* (ACAS, London).

Dolding, Lesley (1994) Unfair Dismissal and Industrial Action *Industrial Law Journal* 23, 243-246.

Donaldson, Sir John (1975) The Role of Labour Courts *Industrial Law Journal* 4, 63-68.

Dore, Ronald (1987) *Taking Japan Seriously: A Confucian Perspective on Leading Economic Issues* (Stanford University Press, Stanford).

Douglas Scott, Sionaidh (1998) In Search of Union Citizenship *Yearbook of European Law* 18, 29-65.

Doyle, Brian (1994) *New Directions Towards Disabled Workers' Rights* (Institute of Employment Rights, London).

Doyle, Brian (1995) *Disability, Discrimination and Equal Opportunities* (Mansell, London).

Doyle, Brian (1997) Enabling Legislation or Dissembling Law? The Disability Discrimination Act 1995 *Modern Law Review*, 60, 64-78.

Doyle, Brian (2000) *Disability Discrimination: Law and Practice* 3rd edn (Jordans, Bristol).

Dubinsky, Laura (2000) *Resisting Union-Busting Techniques: Lessons from Quebec* (Institute of Employment Rights, London).

Dunn, Stephen and John Gennard (1984) *The Closed Shop in British Industry* (Macmillan, London).

Dunn, Stephen and Martyn Wright (1993) *Managing Without the Closed Shop* (Centre for Economic Performance Discussion Paper No 118, London School of Economics).

Durcan, JW and WE J McCarthy (1974) The State Subsidy Theory of Strikes: An Examination of Statistical Data for the Period 1956-1970 *British Journal of Industrial Relations*, 12, 26-47.

Eady, Jennifer (1994) Collective Dismissals, Consultation and Remedies *Industrial Law Journal* 23, 350-354.

Earnshaw, Jill and Stephen Hardy (2001) Assessing an Arbitral Route for Unfair Dismissal *Industrial Law Journal* 30, 289-304.

Earnshaw, Jill, and David Pace (1991) Homosexuals and Transsexuals at Work: Legal Issues, in *Vulnerable Workers: Psychosocial and Legal Issues* eds Marilyn J Davidson and Jill Earnshaw (Wiley, Chichester).

Earnshaw, Jill, John Goodman, Robin Harrison and Mick Marchington (1998) *Industrial Tribunals, Workplace Disciplinary Procedures and Employment Practice* EMAR Research Paper No 2 (Department of Trade and Industry, London).

Edwards, Anna (2000) *Barber v RJB Mining* in the Wider Context of Health and Safety *Industrial Law Journal* 29, 280-287.

Edwards, Paul (1995) Strikes and Industrial Conflict in *Industrial Relations: Theory and Practice in Britain*, ed Paul Edwards (Blackwell, Oxford).

Edwards, Paul, Mark Hall, Richard Hyman, Paul Marginson, Keith Sisson, Jeremy Waddington and David Winchester (1992) Great Britain: Still Muddling Through, in *Industrial Relations in the New Europe* eds Anthony Ferner and Richard Hyman (Blackwell, Oxford).

Edwards, Paul, Mark Hall, Richard Hyman, Paul Marginson, Keith Sisson, Jeremy Waddington and David Winchester (1998) Great Britain: From Partial Collectivism to Neo-liberalism to Where?, in *Changing Industrial Relations in Europe* ed Anthony Ferner and Richard Hyman, 2nd edn (Blackwell, Oxford).

Elgar, Jane and Bob Simpson (1992) *The Impact of the Law on Industrial Disputes in the 1980s* (Centre for Economic Performance, London School of Economics).

Elgar, Jane and Bob Simpson (1994) A Final Appraisal of 'Bridlington'? An Evaluation of TUC Disputes Committee Decisions 1974-1991 *British Journal of Industrial Relations* 32, 47-66.

Elgar, Jane and Bob Simpson (1996) *Industrial Action Ballots and the Law* (Institute of Employment Rights, London).

Elias, Patrick (1978) Unravelling the Concept of Dismissal *Industrial Law Journal* 7, 16-29.

Elias, Patrick (1979) Admission to Trade Unions *Industrial Law Journal* 8, 111-113.

Elias, Patrick (1981) Fairness in Unfair Dismissal: Trends and Tensions *Industrial Law Journal* 10, 201-217.

Elias, Patrick (1982) The Structure of the Employment Contract *Current Legal Problems* 35, 95-116.

Elias, Patrick (1994) The Strike and Breach of Contract: A Reassessment in *Human Rights and Labour Law: Essays for Paul O'Higgins* eds KD Ewing, CA Gearty and BA Hepple (Mansell, London).

Elias, Patrick and John Bowers (no date given) *Transfer of Undertakings: The Legal Pitfalls* (FT Law and Tax, London).

Elias, Patrick and Keith Ewing (1987) *Trade Union Democracy, Members' Rights and the Law* (Mansell, London).

Elias, Patrick, Brian Napier and Peter Wallington (1980) *Labour Law: Cases and Materials* (Butterworths, London).

Ellis, Evelyn (1991) *European Community Sex Equality Law* (Clarendon Press, Oxford).

Ellis, Evelyn (1994) The Definition of Discrimination in European Sex Equality Law *European Law Review* 19, 563-580.

Ellison, Robin (1987 as updated) *Pensions Law and Practice* (Longman, London).

Elvin, Jesse (2003) Can an Employer be under a Duty to Dismiss an Employee for his Own Good in Order to Protect his Health? *Cambridge Law Journal* 62, 20-23.

Emerson, Michael (1988) Regulation or Deregulation of the Labour Market: Policy Regimes for the Recruitment and Dismissal of Employees in Industrialised Countries *European Economic Review* 32, 775-817.

Enonchong, Nelson (1996) Contract Damages for Injury to Reputation *Modern Law Review* 59, 592.

Epstein, Richard (1983) A Common Law for Labour Relations: a Critique of the New Deal Labor Legislation *Yale Law Journal* 92, 1357-1408.

Epstein, Richard (1984) In Defense of the Contract at Will *University of Chicago Law Review* 51, 947-982.

Epstein, Richard (ed) (2002) *Equal Opportunity or More Opportunity? The Good Thing About Discrimination* (Institute for the Study of Civil Society, London).

Estlund, Cynthia L (2002) An American Perspective on Fundamental Labour Rights in *Social and Labour Rights in a Global Context* ed Bob Hepple (Cambridge University Press, Cambridge).

Estreicher, Samuel, Harry C Katz and Bruce E Kaufman eds (2001) *The Internal Governance and Organisational Effectiveness of Labor Unions: Essays in Honor of George Brooks* (Kluwer Law International, New York).

Evans, Stephen (1983) The Labour Injunction Revisited: Picketing, Employers and the Employment Act 1980 *Industrial Law Journal* 12, 129-147.

Evans, Stephen (1987) The Use of Injunctions in Industrial Disputes *British Journal of Industrial Relations* 25, 419-435.

Evans, Stephen (1990) Free Labour Markets and Economic Performance: Evidence from the Construction Industry *Work, Employment and Society*, 4, 239-252.

Evans, Stephen and Roy Lewis (1987) Anti-Union Discrimination: Practice, Law and Policy *Industrial Law Journal* 16, 88-106.

Evans, Stephen and Roy Lewis (1988) Labour Clauses: From Voluntarism to Regulation *Industrial Law Journal*, 17, 209-226.

Evans, Stephen, John Goodman and Leslie Hargreaves (1985) *Unfair Dismissal Law and Employment Practice in the 1980s* Research Paper No 53 (Department of Employment, London).

Evju, Stein (2001a) The European Social Charter in *The Council of Europe and the Social Challenges of the XX1st Century* ed R Blanpain (Kluwer, The Hague).

Evju, Stein (2001b) Collective Agreements and Competition Law: The *Albany* Puzzle and *van der Woude International Journal of Comparative Labour Law and Industrial Relations* 17, 165-184.

Ewing, Keith (1979) The Golden Formula: Some Recent Developments *Industrial Law Journal* 8, 133-146.

Ewing, Keith (1982a) Homeworking: A Framework for Reform *Industrial Law Journal* 11, 94-110.

Ewing, Keith (1982b) *Trade Unions, the Labour Party and the Law. A Study of the Trade Union Act 1913* (Edinburgh University Press, Edinburgh).

Ewing, Keith (1984) Trade Union Political Funds: The 1913 Act Revisited *Industrial Law Journal* 13, 227-242.

Ewing, Keith (1985) The Strike, the Courts and the Rule-Books *Industrial Law Journal*, 14, 160-175.

Ewing, Keith (1986) The Right to Strike *Industrial Law Journal* 15, 143-160.

Ewing, Keith (1988) Il diritto del lavoro negli anni '20: l'esperienza inglese, in *Diritto del lavoro e corporativismi in Europa: ieri e oggi* ed G Vardaro (Franco Angeli, Milan).

Ewing, Keith (1989) Job Security and the Contract of Employment *Industrial Law Journal* 18, 217-222.

Ewing, Keith (1990a) Trade Union Recognition – A Framework for Discussion *Industrial Law Journal*, 19, 209-227.

Ewing, Keith (1990b) Economics and Labour Law in Britain: Thatcher's Radical Experiment *Alberta Law Review* 28, 632-651.

Ewing, Keith (1991) *The Right to Strike* (Clarendon Press, Oxford).

Ewing, Keith (1993a) Swimming with the Tide: Employment Protection and the Implementation of European Labour Law *Industrial Law Journal* 22, 165-180.

Ewing, Keith (1993b) Remedies for Breach of the Contract of Employment *Cambridge Law Journal* 52, 405-436.

Ewing, Keith (1994a) *Britain and the ILO*, 2nd edn (Institute of Employment Rights, London).

Ewing, Keith (1994b) The Bill of Rights Debate: Democracy or Juristocracy in Britain? in *Human Rights and Labour Law: Essays for Paul O'Higgins* eds KD Ewing, CA Gearty and BA Hepple (Mansell, London).

Ewing, Keith (ed)(1996) *Working Life: A New Perspective of Labour Law* (The Institute of Employment Rights, Lawrence and Wishart, London).

Ewing, Keith (1998a) Australian and British Labour Law: Differences of Form or Substance? *Australian Journal of Labour Law* 11, 44-68.

Ewing, Keith (1998b) The Human Rights Act and Labour Law *Industrial Law Journal* 27, 275-292.

Ewing, Keith (1999) Freedom of Association and the Employment Relations Act *Industrial Law Journal* 28, 283-298.

Ewing, Keith (2000a) Trade Union Recognition and Staff Associations – A Breach of International Labour Standards? *Industrial Law Journal* 29, 267-273.

Ewing, Keith (ed) (2000b) *Human Rights at Work* (Institute of Employment Rights, London).

Ewing, Keith (2001) The Political Parties, Elections and Referendums Act 2000 – Implications for Trade Unions *Industrial Law Journal* 30, 199-205.

Ewing, Keith (2003) The Implications of *Wilson and Palmer Industrial Law Journal* 32, 1-22.

Ewing, Keith (2004) Laws Against Strikes Revisited, in *The Future of Labour Law: Liber Amicorum Sir Bob Hepple QC* ed Catherine Barnard, Simon Deakin and Gillian S Morris (Hart Publishing, Oxford).

Ewing, Keith (2005) The Function of Trade Unions *Industrial Law Journal* 34, 1-22.

Ewing, Keith and Andrew Grubb (1987) The Emergence of a New Labour Injunction *Industrial Law Journal* 16, 145-163.

Ewing, Keith and Anne Hock (2003) Trade Union Recognition in Small Enterprises (Popularis Ltd, Kingston upon Thames).

Ewing, Keith and Gillian Morris (2000) Labour Law, in *Law's Future(s)* ed David Hayton (Hart Publishing, Oxford).

Ewing, Keith and Brian Napier (1986) The Wapping Dispute and Labour Law *Cambridge Law Journal* 45, 285-304.

Ewing, Keith and William Rees (1981) The TUC Independent Review Committee and the Closed Shop *Industrial Law Journal* 10, 84-100.

Ewing, Keith and Tom Sibley (2000) *International Trade Union Rights for the New Millenium* (Institute of Employment Rights, London).

Ewing, Keith, CA Gearty and BA Hepple (eds) (1994) *Human Rights and Labour Law: Essays for Paul O'Higgins* (Mansell, London).

Facenna, Gerry (2004) *Eugen Schmidberger Internationale Transporte Planzuge v Austria*: Freedom of Expression and Association versus Free Movement of Goods *European Human Rights Law Review* 73-80.

Fairbrother, Peter (2000) *Trade Unions at the Crossroads* (Mansell, London).

Fairgrieve, Duncan (2001) The Human Rights Act 1998, Damages and Tort Law *Public Law*, 695-716.

Farrington, DJ (1998) *The Law of Education* 2nd edn (Butterworths, London).

Felstead, Alan and Nick Jewson (1995) Working at Home: Estimates from the 1991 Census *Employment Gazette* 104, 95-99.

Fenwick, Helen (1999) The Right to Protest, the Human Rights Act and the Margin of Appreciation *Modern Law Review* 62, 491-514.

Finch, Emily (2002) Stalking the Perfect Stalking Law: An Evaluation of the Efficacy of the Protection from Harassment Act 1997 *Criminal Law Review* 703-718.

Finkin, Matthew W (ed) (1994) *The Legal Future of Employee Representation* (ILR Press, Ithaca, NY).

Finley, Lucinda (1986) Transcending Equality Theory: A Way Out of the Maternity and the Workplace Debate *Columbia Law Review* 86, 1118-1182.

Fischel, Daniel and Edward Lazear (1986) Comparable Worth and Discrimination in Labor Markets *University of Chicago Law Review* 53, 901-909.

Fitzpatrick, Barry (1983) Time Off: Recent Developments in the Court of Appeal *Industrial Law Journal* 12, 258-61.

Fitzpatrick, Barry (1992) Community Social Law after Maastricht *Industrial Law Journal* 21, 199-213.

Fitzpatrick, Barry (1994) Equality in Occupational Pension Schemes: Still Waiting for *Coloroll, Industrial Law Journal* 23, 155-163.

Fitzpatrick, Barry (1997) Straining the Definition of Health and Safety *Industrial Law Journal*, 26, 115-135.

Fitzpatrick, Barry (1999) The Fair Employment and Equal Treatment (Northern Ireland) Order 1998 *Industrial Law Journal* 28, 336-347.

Flanders, Allan (1970) *Management and Unions: The Theory and Reform of Industrial Relations* (Faber and Faber, London).

Flynn, Leo (1995) Gender Equality Law and Employers' Dress Codes *Industrial Law Journal* 24, 255-272.

Fodder, Martin and Gary Freer (2001) The Effect of Contractual Provision for Payment in Lieu of Notice *Industrial Law Journal* 30, 215-224.

Ford, Michael (1998a) Rethinking the Notice Rule *Industrial Law Journal* 27, 220-233.

Ford, Michael (1998b) *Surveillance and Privacy at Work* (Institute of Employment Rights, London)

Ford, Michael (1999) The Data Protection Act 1998 *Industrial Law Journal* 28, 57-60.

Ford, Michael (2000) Article 8 and the Right to Privacy at the Workplace, in *Human Rights at Work*, ed Keith Ewing (Institute of Employment Rights, London).

Ford, Michael (2002) Two Conceptions of Worker Privacy *Industrial Law Journal* 31,135-155.

Ford, Michael and Eric Brown eds (2003) *Redgrave's Health and Safety* (Butterworths, London).

Forde, Michael (1982) The 'Closed Shop' Case *Industrial Law Journal*, 11, 1-15.

Fordham, Michael (2001) Judicial Review: the New Rules *Public Law*, 4-10.

Forshaw, Simon and Marcus Pilgerstorfer (2005) Illegally Formed Contracts of Employment and Equal Treatment at Work *Industrial Law Journal* 34, 158-177.

Foster, Ken (1983) The Legal Form of Work in the Nineteenth Century: The Myth of Contract? Paper presented to the conference on *The History of Law, Labour and Crime*, University of Warwick.

Fox, Alan (1974) *Beyond Contract: Work, Power and Trust Relations* (Faber, London).

Fox, Alan (1985) *History and Heritage* (Allen & Unwin, London).

Fredman, Sandra (1985) Crown Employment, Prerogative Powers, Consultation and National Security *Industrial Law Journal* 14, 42-46.

Fredman, Sandra (1987) The Right to Strike: Policy and Principle *Law Quarterly Review* 103, 176-182.

Fredman, Sandra (1992a) The New Rights: Labour Law and Ideology in the Thatcher Years *Oxford Journal of Legal Studies*, 12, 24-44.

Fredman, Sandra (1992b) European Community Sex Discrimination Law: A Critique *Industrial Law Journal* 21, 119-134.

Fredman, Sandra (1994a) Equal Pay and Justification *Industrial Law Journal* 23, 37-41.

Fredman, Sandra (1994b) A Difference with Distinction: Pregnancy and Parenthood Reassessed *Law Quarterly Review* 110, 106-123.

Fredman, Sandra (1997a) Reversing Discrimination *Law Quarterly Review* 113, 575-600.

Fredman, Sandra (1997b) Labour Law in Flux: The Changing Composition of the Workforce *Industrial Law Journal* 26, 337-352.

Fredman, Sandra (1997c) *Women and the Law* (Clarendon Press, Oxford).

Fredman, Sandra (2001) Equality: A New Generation? *Industrial Law Journal* 30, 145-168.

Fredman, Sandra (2004a) The Ideology of New Labour Law, in *The Future of Labour Law: Liber Amicorum Sir Bob Hepple QC* eds Catherine Barnard, Simon Deakin and Gillian S. Morris (Hart Publishing, Oxford).

Fredman, Sandra (2004b) Women at Work: The Broken Promise of Flexicurity *Industrial Law Journal* 33, 299-313.

Fredman, Sandra (2004c) Marginalising Equal Pay Laws *Industrial Law Journal* 33, 281-285.

Fredman, Sandra, and Simon Lee (1987) Natural Justice for Employees: the Unacceptable Face of Proceduralism *Industrial Law Journal* 25, 15-31.

Fredman, Sandra and Gillian S Morris (1987a) Teachers' Pay and Conditions Act *Industrial Law Journal* 16, 107-110.

Fredman, Sandra and Gillian S Morris (1987b) The Teachers' Lesson: Collective Bargaining and the Courts *Industrial Law Journal* 16, 215-226.

Fredman, Sandra and Gillian S Morris (1988) Union Membership at GCHQ *Industrial Law Journal* 17, 105-108.

Fredman, Sandra and Gillian S Morris (1989) *The State as Employer: Labour Law in the Public Services* (Mansell, London).

Fredman, Sandra and Gillian S Morris (1991a) Public or Private? State Employees and Judicial Review *Law Quarterly Review* 107, 298-316.

Fredman, Sandra and Gillian S Morris (1991b) Judicial Review and Civil Servants: Contracts of Employment Declared to Exist *Public Law*, 485-490.

Fredman, Sandra and Gillian S Morris (1992) School Teachers' Pay and Conditions Act 1991 *Industrial Law Journal* 21, 44-47.

Fredman Sandra and Gillian S Morris (1994) The Costs of Exclusivity: Public and Private Re-examined *Public Law*, 69-85.

Fredman, Sandra and Sarah Spencer (eds) *Age as an Equality Issue: Legal and Policy Perspectives* (Hart Publishing, Oxford).

Freedland, Mark (1976a) Employment Protection: Redundancy Procedures and the EEC *Industrial Law Journal* 5, 24-34.

Freedland, Mark (1976b) *The Contract of Employment* (Clarendon Press, Oxford).

Freedland, Mark (1980) Leaflet Law: the Temporary Short-Time Working Compensation Scheme *Industrial Law Journal* 9, 254-258.

Freedland, Mark (1983) Labour Law and Leaflet Law: the Youth Training Scheme of 1983 *Industrial Law Journal* 12, 220-235.

Freedland, Mark (1984) High Trust, Pensions and the Contract of Employment *Industrial Law Journal* 13, 25-39.

Freedland, Mark (1989) The Education (Modification of Enactments Relating to Employment) Order 1989 *Industrial Law Journal* 18, 231-234.

Freedland, Mark (1992) The Role of the Department of Employment – Twenty Years of Institutional Change in *Legal Intervention in Industrial Relations: Gains and Losses* ed William McCarthy (Blackwell, Oxford).

Freedland, Mark (1994) Equal Treatment, Judicial Review and Delegated Legislation *Industrial Law Journal* 23, 338-341.

Freedland, Mark (1995) Contracting the Employment of Civil Servants – A Transparent Exercise? *Public Law*, 224-233.

Freedland, Mark (1996a) Employment Policy, in *European Community Labour Law: Principles and Perspectives: Liber Amicorum Lord Wedderburn* eds Paul Davies, Antoine Lyon-Caen, Silvana Sciarra and Spiros Simitis (Clarendon Press, Oxford).

Freedland, Mark (1996b) The Rule against Delegation and the *Carltona* Doctrine in an Agency Context *Public Law* 19-30.

Freedland, Mark (1999) Deductions, Red Herrings and the Wage-Work Bargain *Industrial Law Journal* 28, 255-259.

Freedland, Mark (2000) Finding the Right Direction for the 'Industrial Jury' *Industrial Law Journal* 29, 288-293.

Freedland, Mark (2001) Claim for Unfair Dismissal *Industrial Law Journal* 30, 309-311.

Freedland, Mark (2003) *The Personal Employment Contract* (Oxford University Press, Oxford).

Freeman, Richard and Wayne Diamond (2003) Young Workers and Trade Unions in *Representing Workers: Trade Union Recognition and Membership in Britain* ed Howard Gospel and Stephen Wood (Routledge, London).

Freeman, Richard B and Jeremy Pelletier (1990) The Impact of Industrial Relations Legislation on British Union Density *British Journal of Industrial Relations* 28, 141-164.

Frisby, Sandra (2000) TUPE or not TUPE? Employee Protection, Corporate Rescue and 'One Unholy Mess' *Company, Financial and Insolvency Law Review* 4, 249-271.

Fryer, Robert (1973) The Myths of the Redundancy Payments Act *Industrial Law Journal* 2, 1-16.

Gall, Gregor (1993) What Happened to Single Union Deals? – a Research Note *Industrial Relations Journal* 24, 71-75.

Gall, Gregor (2004) Trade Union recognition in Britain 1995-2002: turning a corner? *Industrial Relations Journal* 35, 249-270.

Gall, Gregor and Sonia McKay (1994) Trade Union Derecognition in Britain *British Journal of Industrial Relations* 32, 433-448.

Gall, Gregor and Sonia McKay (1996) Research Note: Injunctions as a Legal Weapon in Industrial Disputes *British Journal of Industrial Relations* 34, 567-582.

Gall, Gregor and Sonia McKay (1999) Developments in Union Recognition and Derecognition in Britain 1994-1998 *British Journal of Industrial Relations* 37, 601-614.

Geary, Roger (1985) *Policing Industrial Disputes: 1893-1985* (Cambridge University Press, Cambridge).

Genn, Hazel and Yvette Genn (1989) *The Effectiveness of Representation at Tribunals* (Faculty of Law, Queen Mary College, University of London).

Gennard, J and R Lasko (1974) Supplementary Benefits and Strikers *British Journal of Industrial Relations* 12, 1-25.

Germanotta, Paul (2002) *Protecting Worker Solidarity Action: A Critique of International Labour Law* (Institute of Employment Rights, London).

Germanotta, Paul and Tonia Novitz (2002) Globalisation and the Right to Strike: The Case for European-Level Protection of Secondary Action *International Journal of Comparative Labour Law and Industrial Relations* 18, 67-82.

Gernigon, Bernard, Alberto Odero and Horacio Guido (1998) ILO Principles Concerning the Right to Strike *International Labour Review* 137, 441-481.

Gernigon, Bernard, Alberto Odero and Horacio Guido (2000) ILO Principles concerning Collective Bargaining *International Labour Review* 139, 33-55.

Gibbons, Steve (2004) *Decoding Some New Developments in Labour Standards Enforcement* (Institute of Employment Rights, London).

Giddens, Anthony (1998) *The Third Way: The Renewal of Social Democracy* (Polity Press, Cambridge)

Gill, Tess and Karon Monaghan (2003) Justification in Direct Sex Discrimination Law: Taboo Upheld *Industrial Law Journal* 32, 115-122.

Gladstone, A (2004) Settlement of Disputes over Rights in *Comparative Labour Law and Industrial Relations in Industrialised Market Economies* 8th edn, ed Roger Blanpain (Kluwer Law International, The Hague).

Glasbeek, Harry (1984) The Utility of Model Building: Collins' Capitalist Discipline and Corporatist Law *Industrial Law Journal* 13, 133-152.

Gobert, James and Maurice Punch (2000) Whistleblowers, the Public Interest, and the Public Interest Disclosure Act 1998 *Modern Law Review* 63, 25-54.

Gold, Michael and Mark Hall (1994) Statutory European Works Councils: the Final Countdown? *Industrial Relations Journal* 25, 177-186.

Gooding, Caroline (1996) *Disability Discrimination Act 1995* (Blackstone Press, London).

Goodman, Alissa and Steven Webb (1994) For Richer, for Poorer: the Changing Distribution of Income in the UK, 1961-1991 *Fiscal Studies* 15/4, 28-62.

Goodman, John (2000) Building Bridges and Settling Differences: Collective Conciliation and Arbitration under ACAS, in *Employment Relations in Britain: 25 Years of the Advisory Conciliation and Arbitration Service* ed Brian Towers and William Brown (Blackwell, Oxford)

Goodman, Michael J (ed) (1978 as updated) *Encyclopaedia of Health and Safety at Work, Law and Practice* (Sweet & Maxwell, London).

Gordon, A (1984) *Redundancy in the 1980s* (Institute of Manpower Studies, Brighton).

Gosling, Amanda and Stephen Machin (1995) Trade Unions and the Dispersion of Earnings in British Establishments, 1980-1990 *Oxford Bulletin of Economics and Statistics* 57, 167-84.

Gospel, Howard (1976) Disclosure of Information to Trade Unions *Industrial Law Journal*, 5, 223-236.

Gospel, Howard and Graeme Lockwood (1999) Disclosure of Information for Collective Bargaining: The CAC Approach Revisited *Industrial Law Journal* 28, 233-248.

Gospel, Howard and Paul Willman (1981) Disclosure of Information: the CAC Approach *Industrial Law Journal* 10, 10-22.

Gospel, Howard and Stephen Wood (2003) Representing Workers in Modern Britain in *Representing Workers: Trade Union Recognition and Membership in Britain* eds Howard Gospel and Stephen Wood (Routledge, London).

Gould, William B IV (1993) *A Primer on American Labor Law*, 3rd edn (MIT Press, Cambridge, Mass).

Gouldner, Alvin W (1954) *Wildcat Strike* (Antioch Press, New York).

Graham, Cosmo and Norman Lewis (1985) *The Role of ACAS Conciliation in Equal Pay and Sex Discrimination Cases* (Equal Opportunities Commission, Manchester).

Grahl, John, and Paul Teague (1992) Integration Theory and European Labour Markets *British Journal of Industrial Relations* 30, 515-529.

Gray, Kevin and Susan Francis Gray (1999) Civil Rights, Civil Wrongs and Quasi-Public Space *European Human Rights Law Review*, 46-102.

Grief, Nicholas (1991) The Domestic Impact of the European Community on Human Rights as Mediated through Community Law *Public Law* 555-567.

Griffith, JAG and Michael Ryle (1989) *Parliament: Functions, Practice and Procedures* (Sweet and Maxwell, London).

Grosz, Stephen, Jack Beatson and Peter Duffy (2000) *Human Rights: the 1998 Act and the European Convention* (Sweet and Maxwell, London).

Guest, David (1990) Personnel Management: the End of Orthodoxy? *British Journal of Industrial Relations* 29, 149-175.

Guest, David E and Riccardo Peccei (2001) Partnership at Work: Mutuality and the Balance of Advantage *British Journal of Industrial Relations* 39, 207-236.

Gunningham, Neil, and Richard Johnstone (1999) *Regulating Workplace Safety: Systems and Sanctions* (Oxford University Press, Oxford).

Hakim, Catherine (1985) *Employers' Use of Outwork* Research Paper 44 (Department of Employment, London).

Hakim, Catherine (1987) Trends in the Flexible Workforce *Employment Gazette* 95, 594-560.

Hakim, Catherine (1989a) Employment Rights: a Comparison of Full-Time and Part-Time Employees *Industrial Law Journal* 18, 69-83.

Hakim, Catherine (1989b) Workforce Restructuring, Social Insurance Coverage and the Black Economy *Journal of Social Policy* 18, 471-583.

Hakim, Catherine (1990) Core and Periphery in Employers' Workforce Strategies: Evidence from the 1987 ELUS Survey *Work, Employment and Society* 4, 157-188.

Hakim, Catherine (1993) The Myth of Rising Female Employment *Work, Employment and Society* 7, 97-120.

Hall, M (1992) Behind the European Works Council Directive: The European Commission's Legislative Strategy *British Journal of Industrial Relations*, 30, 547-566.

Hall, Mark (1996) Beyond Recognition? Employee Representation and EU Law *Industrial Law Journal* 25, 15-27.

Hall, Mark (2005) Assessing the Information and Consultation of Employees Regulations *Industrial Law Journal* 34, 103-126.

Hall, Mark and Paul Edwards (1999) Reforming the Statutory Redundancy Consultation Procedure *Industrial Law Journal* 28, 299-318.

Hall, Mark and Paul Marginson (2004) *Developments in European Works Councils* (European Foundation for the Improvement of Living and Working Conditions, Dublin)

Hanson, Charles and Graham Mather (1988) *Striking Out Strikes* (Institute of Economic Affairs, London).

Hanson, CS, S Jackson and D Miller (1979) *The Closed Shop* (Gower Press, Aldershot).

Hardy, Stephen, and Richard Painter (1999) The New Acquired Rights Directive and its Implications for European Employee Relations in the Twenty-First Century *Employee Relations* 21, 378-388.

Hare, Ivan (1991) Pregnancy and Sex Discrimination *Industrial Law Journal* 20, 124-130.

Harpum, Charles (1986) The Stranger as Constructive Trustee *Law Quarterly Review* 102, 114-162, 267-291.

Harpum, Charles (1994) Knowing Assistance and Receipt as the Basis of Equitable Liability, in *The Frontiers of Liability* ed PBH Birks (Clarendon Press, Oxford).

Harris, DJ (1984) *The European Social Charter* (University Press of Virginia, Charlottesville).

Harris, DJ, M O'Boyle and C Warbrick (1995) *Law of the European Convention on Human Rights* (Butterworths, London).

Harris, Neville (2000) *Social Security Law in Context* (OUP, Oxford).

Hart, Moira (1979) Why Bosses Love the Closed Shop *New Society*, 15 February.

Hart, Oliver (1989) Incomplete Contracts, in *Allocation, Information and Markets* eds John Eatwell, Murray Milgate and Gianfranco de Vivo (Macmillan, London).

Hartley, Trevor (1998) *The Foundations of European Community Law*, 4th edn (Clarendon Press, Oxford).

Harvey (1972 as updated) *Harvey on Industrial Relations and Employment Law* (Butterworths, London).

Harvey, Mark (1995) *The Tax Trap of Self-Employment: Towards the Insecurity Society* (Institute of Employment Rights, London).

Hay, Douglas and Paul Craven (eds) (2004) *Masters, Servants and Magistrates in Britain and the Empire, 1562-1955* (University of North Carolina Press, Chapel Hill and London).

Hayek, FA (1960) *The Constitution of Liberty* (Routledge, London).

Hayek, FA (1973) *Law, Legislation and Liberty Volume 1: Rules and Order* (Routledge, London).

Hayek, FA (1980) *1980s Unemployment and the Unions* (Institute of Economic Affairs, London).

Hayward, Bruce, Mark Peters, Nicola Rousseau and Ken Seeds (2004) *Findings from the Survey of Employment Tribunal Applications 2003*, Employment Relations Research Series No 33 (DTI, London)

Heap, Daniel (2004) Redundancies in the UK *Labour Market Trends* (May)

Heather, Pauline, Jo Rick, John Atkinson and Stephen Morris (1996) Employers' Use of Temporary Workers *Labour Market Trends* September 1996, 403-411.

Heery, Edmund (1996) The New New Unionism in *Contemporary Industrial Relations: A Critical Analysis*, ed. Ian J. Beardwell (Oxford University Press, Oxford).

Heery, Edmund (2002) Partnership versus Organising: Alternative Futures for British Trade Unionism *Industrial Relations Journal* 33, 20-35.

Heery, Edmund, John Kelly and Jeremy Waddington (2003) Union Revitalization in Britain *European Journal of Industrial Relations* 9, 79-97.

Heldman, D, J Bennett and M Johnson (1981) *Deregulating Labor Relations* (Fisher Institute, Dallas).

Hendrickx, Frank (2001) Privacy and Employment Law: General Principles and Application to Electronic Monitoring, in *On-line Rights for Employees in the Information Society* ed Roger Blanpain (Kluwer Law International, The Hague).

Hendy, John (1998) *Every Worker Shall Have the Right to be Represented by a Trade Union* (Institute of Employment Rights, London).

Hendy, John (2000) Caught in a Fork, *Industrial Law Journal* 29, 53-60.

Hendy, John, and Jeremy McMullen (1987) Injunctions in Contracts of Employment: the New Growth (Part 1) *Law Society Gazette*, 3568-3576.

Hendy, John, and Jeremy McMullen (1988) Injunctions in Contracts of Employment: the New Growth (Part 2) *Law Society Gazette*, 28-31.

Hendy, John and Michael Walton (1997) An Individual Right to Union Representation in International Law *Industrial Law Journal* 26, 205-223.

Hepple, Bob (1968) *Race, Jobs and the Law* (Penguin, Harmondsworth).

Hepple, Bob (1974) Conflicting Collective Agreements; Effect of Signed Receipt of Employment Terms *Industrial Law Journal* 3, 164-166.

Hepple, Bob (1978) Conflict of Laws on Employment Relationships in the EEC, in *Harmonisation of Private International Law by the EEC* ed K Lipstein (Institute of Advanced Legal Studies, London).

Hepple, Bob (1981a) A Right to Work? *Industrial Law Journal* 10, 65-83.

Hepple, Bob (1981b) *Hepple and O'Higgins: Employment Law* 4th edn (Sweet and Maxwell, London).

Hepple, Bob (1982) The Transfer of Undertakings (Protection of Employment) Regulations *Industrial Law Journal* 10, 29-40.

Hepple, Bob (1983) Individual Labour Law, in *Industrial Relations in Britain* ed George Sayers Bain (Basil Blackwell, Oxford).

Hepple, Bob (1986a) Introduction, in *The Making of Labour Law in Europe* ed BA Hepple (Mansell, London).

Hepple, Bob (1986b) Restructuring Employment Rights *Industrial Law Journal* 15, 69-89.

Hepple, Bob (1987) The Crisis in EEC Labour Law *Industrial Law Journal* 16, 77-87.

Hepple, Bob (1990a) *Working Time A New Legal Framework?* Employment Paper No 3 (Institute for Public Policy Research, London).

Hepple, Bob (1990b) The Implementation of the Community Charter of Fundamental Social Rights *Modern Law Review* 53, 643-654.

Hepple, Bob (1992a) The Fall and Rise of Unfair Dismissal in *Legal Intervention in Industrial Relations: Gains and Losses*, ed William McCarthy (Blackwell, Oxford).

Hepple, Bob (1992b) Have Twenty-Five Years of the Race Relations Acts in Britain been a Failure?, in *Discrimination: the Limits of the Law* eds BA Hepple and Erika Szyszczak (Mansell, London).

Hepple, Bob (1993) *European Social Dialogue – Alibi or Opportunity?* (Institute of Employment Rights, London).

Hepple, Bob (1995) The Future of Labour Law *Industrial Law Journal* 24, 303-322.

Hepple, Bob (1996) Equality and Discrimination, in *European Community Labour Law: Principles and Perspectives Liber Amicorum Lord Wedderburn* eds. Paul Davies, Antoine Lyon-Caen, Silvana Sciarra and Spiros Simitis (Clarendon Press, Oxford).

Hepple, Bob (1997a) New Approaches to International Labour Regulation *Industrial Law Journal*, 26, 353-366.

Hepple, Bob (1997b) European Rules on Dismissal Law *Comparative Labor Law* 18, 204-228.

Hepple, Bob (1998a) Flexibility and Security of Employment, in *Comparative Labour Law and Industrial Relations in Industrialized Market Economies* 6th edn, eds R Blanpain and C Engels (Kluwer, Deventer-Boston).

Hepple, Bob (1998b) The Impact on Labour Law in *The Impact of the Human Rights Bill on English Law*, ed B Markesinis (Oxford University Press, Oxford).

Hepple, Bob (1999a) Employee Loyalty in English Law *Comparative Labor Law and Policy Journal* 20, 204-224.

Hepple, Bob (1999b) A Race to the Top? International Investment Guidelines and Corporate Codes of Conduct *Comparative Labor Law and Policy Journal* 20, 347-363.

Hepple, Bob (1999c) UK in *Private Employment Agencies* Bulletin of Comparative Labour Relations No 36 ed Roger Blanpain (Kluwer, The Hague).

Hepple, Bob (2000a) Supporting Collective Bargaining: Some Comparative Reflections, in *Employment Relations in Britain: 25 Years of the Advisory Conciliation and Arbitration Service* ed Brian Towers and William Brown (Blackwell, Oxford)

Hepple, Bob (2000b) Freedom of Expression and the Problem of Harassment, in *Freedom of Expression and Freedom of Information* ed Jack Beatson and Yvonne Cripps (OUP, Oxford).

Hepple, Bob (2001a) *Human Rights and the Contract of Employment* (Employment Lawyers' Association, London).

Hepple, Bob (2001b) The EU Charter of Fundamental Rights *Industrial Law Journal* 30, 225-231.

Hepple, Sir Bob (2005a) *Rights at Work: Global, European and British Perspectives* (Sweet and Maxwell, London).

Hepple, Sir Bob (2005b) *Labour Laws and Global Trade* (Hart Publishing, Oxford).

Hepple, Bob and Angela Byre (1989) EEC Labour Law in the United Kingdom – A New Approach *Industrial Law Journal* 18, 129-143.

Hepple, Bob and Sandra Fredman (1992) *Labour Law and Industrial Relations in Great Britain*, 2nd edn (Kluwer, Deventer-Boston).

Hepple, Bob and Gillian S Morris (2002) The Employment Act 2002 and the Crisis of Individual Employment Rights *Industrial Law Journal* 31, 245-269.

Hepple, Bob and Karen Mumgaard (1998) Pension Rights in Business Transfers *Industrial Law Journal* 27, 309-324.

Hepple, Bob and Brian Napier (1978) Temporary Workers and the Law *Industrial Law Journal* 7, 84-99.

Hepple, Bob and Paul O'Higgins (1971) *Public Employee Trade Unionism in the United Kingdom: The Legal Framework* (Institute of Labor and Industrial Relations, The University of Michigan – Wayne State University, Ann Arbor).

Hepple, Bob and Erika Szyszczak (eds) (1992) *Discrimination: the Limits of the Law* (Mansell, London).

Hepple, Bob, Mary Coussey and Toufyal Choudhury (2000) *Equality: A New Framework. Report of the Independent Review of the Enforcement of UK Anti-Discrimination Legislation* (Hart Publishing, Oxford).

Hepple, Bob, TM Partington and Bob Simpson (1977) The Employment Protection Act and Unemployment Benefit: Protection for Whom? *Industrial Law Journal* 6, 54-58.

Hervey, Tamara (1997) *Francovich* Liability Simplified *Industrial Law Journal* 26, 74-79.

Hervey, Tamara (1998) *European Social Law and Policy* (Longmans, London).

Hervey, Tamara and Jeff Kenner (eds) (2003) *Economic and Social Rights under the European Charter of Fundamental Rights: A Legal Perspective* (Hart Publishing, Oxford).

Hervey, Tamara and David O'Keeffe (1996) *Sex Equality Law in the European Union* , (John Wiley and Sons, Chichester).

Hills, John (1988) *Changing Tax* (Child Poverty Action Group, London).

Hills, John (1993) *The Future of Welfare. A Guide to the Debate* (Joseph Rowntree Foundation, York).

Hobbs, Richard and Wanjiru Njoya (2005) Regulating the European Labour Market: Recent Developments *British Journal of Industrial Relations* 43, 297-319.

Hodges-Aeberhard J and A Odero de Dios (1987) Principles of the Committee on Freedom of Association concerning Strikes *International Labour Review* 126, 543-563.

Hogg, Peter W (1997) *Constitutional Law of Canada* 4th edn (Carswell, Scarborough, Ontario).

Holland, James and Adrian Chandler (1988) Implied Mobility Clauses *Industrial Law Journal* 17, 253-256.

Hollingsworth, Mark and Charles Tremayne (1989) *The Economic League: The Silent McCarthyism* (National Council for Civil Liberties, London).

Honeyball, Simon (1988) Employment Law and the Primacy of Contract *Industrial Law Journal* 17, 97-108.

Honeyball, Simon (2000) Pregnancy and Sex Discrimination *Industrial Law Journal* 29, 43-52.

Horrell, Sara and Jill Rubery (1991a) *Employers' Working Time Policies and Women's Employment* EOC Research Series (HMSO, London).

Horrell, Sara and Jill Rubery (1991b) Gender and Working Time: an Analysis of Employers' Working Time Policies *Cambridge Journal of Economics* 15, 373-391.

Horrell, Sara, Jill Rubery and Brendan Burchell (1989) Unequal Jobs or Unequal Pay? *Industrial Relations Journal* 20, 176-191.

Howarth, David (1988) The Autonomy of Labour Law: A Response to Professor Wedderburn *Industrial Law Journal* 17, 11-25.

Howarth, David (2005) Against *Lumley* v *Gye Modern Law Review* 68, 195-232.

Howarth, David and Janet O'Sullivan (2000) *Hepple, Howarth and Matthews' Tort: Cases and Materials* 5th edn (Butterworths, London).

Howe, John and Richard Mitchell (1999) The Evolution of the Contract of Employment in Australia: a Discussion *Australian Journal of Labour Law* 12, 113-130.

Hunt, Jo (1999) Success at Last? The Amendment of the Acquired Rights Directive *European Law Review* 24, 215-230.

Hunt, Murray (1997) *Using Human Rights Law in English Courts* (Hart Publishing, Oxford).

Hunt, Murray (1998) The 'Horizontal' Effect of the Human Rights Act *Public Law*, 423-443.

Hutchins, B and A Harrison (1926) *The History of Factory Legislation* (Routledge, London).

Hydén, Haken (1992) Working Environment, in *The Nordic Labour Relations Model* eds Niklas Bruun, Boel Flodgren, Marit Halverson, Haken Hydén and Ruth Nielsen (Dartmouth, Aldershot).

Hyman, Richard (1994) Changing Trade Union Identities and Strategies, in *New Frontiers in European Industrial Relations* eds Richard Hyman and Anthony Ferner (Blackwell, Oxford).

Hyman, Richard (1997) The Future of Employee Representation *British Journal of Industrial Relations* 35, 309-331.

IFS (1995) *Pensions Policy in the UK: An Economic Analysis* (Institute of Fiscal Studies, London).

Ingham, Mike and Andrew Thomson (1982) *Dimensions of Industrial Relations in Local Authorities* (University of Glasgow, Glasgow).

Inglis-Jones, Nigel (1989 as updated) *The Law of Occupational Pension Schemes* (Sweet & Maxwell, London).

Ingram, Peter (1991) Changes in Working Practices in British Manufacturing Industry in the 1980s: a Study of Employee Concessions Made during Wage Negotiations *British Journal of Industrial Relations* 29, 1-13.

Institute of Personnel Management (1987) *Contract Compliance: The UK Experience* (IPM, London).

International Labour Office (ILO) (1956) Social Aspects of European Economic Cooperation *International Labour Review* 74, 99-123.

International Labour Office (ILO) (1994) *Freedom of Association and Collective Bargaining: General Survey by the Committee of Experts on the Application of Conventions and Recommendations* (International Labour Office, Geneva).

International Labour Office (ILO) (1996) *Freedom of Association: Digest of decisions and principles of the Freedom of Association Committee of the Governing Body of the ILO* 4th ed. (International Labour Office, Geneva).

Jackson, David (1999) *Immigration: Law and Practice* (Sweet & Maxwell, London).

Jackson, David and George Warr (2001) *Immigration Law and Practice* (Sweet and Maxwell, London).

Jacobs, Antoine (1986) Collective Self-Regulation, in *The Making of Labour Law in Europe* ed Bob Hepple (Mansell, London).

Jacobs, A (2004), The Law of Strikes and Lockouts in *Comparative Labour Law and Industrial Relations in Industrialised Market Economies* 8th edn, ed Roger Blanpain (Kluwer Law International, The Hague).

Jacobs, Francis G and Robin CA White (1996) *The European Convention on Human Rights,* 2nd edn (Clarendon, Oxford).

Jacoby, Sanford M (1982) The Duration of Indefinite Employment Contracts in the United States and England: an Historical Analysis *Comparative Labor Law,* 85-128.

James, Phil (1992) Reforming British Health and Safety Law: A Framework for Discussion *Industrial Law Journal* 21, 83-105.

James, Phil (1993) *The European Community: A Positive Force in UK Health and Safety Law?* (Institute of Employment Rights, London).

James, Phil and David Lewis (1986) Health and Safety at Work, in *Labour Law in Britain* ed Roy Lewis (Basil Blackwell, Oxford).

James, Philip and David Walters (1997) Non-Union Rights of Involvement: The Case of Health and Safety at Work *Industrial Law Journal* 26, 35-50.

James, Phil and David Walters (2002) Worker Representation in Health and Safety: Options for Regulatory Reform *Industrial Relations Journal* 33, 141-156.

Jay, Rosemary and Angus Hamilton (2003) *Data Protection Law and Practice* 2nd edn (Sweet and Maxwell, London).

Jefferson, Michael (1997) Restraint of Trade: Dismissal and Drafting *Industrial Law Journal* 26, 62-68.

Jenkins, G and M Poole (1990) *New Forms of Ownership* (Routledge, London).

Jenkins, Richard (1988) Discrimination and Equal Opportunity in Employment: Ethnicity and 'Race' in the United Kingdom, in *Employment in Britain* ed Duncan Gallie (Basil Blackwell, Oxford).

Johansen, Atle Sonsteli (2004) The '*Albany*-Test' Compared with the 'EFTA Guidelines' *Industrial Law Journal* 33, 73-80.

Jones, Gareth (2002) *The Law of Restitution* 6th edn (Sweet and Maxwell, London).

Jones, Gareth and William Goodhart (1996) *Specific Performance* 2nd edn (Butterworths, London).

Justice (1987) *Industrial Tribunals* (Justice, London).

Kahn, Peggy, Norman Lewis, Rowland Livock and Paul Wiles (1983) *Picketing: Industrial Disputes, Tactics and the Law* (Routledge and Kegan Paul, London).

Kahn-Freund, Otto (1949) The Tangle of the Truck Acts *Industrial Law Review* 4, 2-9.

Kahn-Freund, Otto (1951) Servants and Independent Contractors, *Modern Law Review* 14, 504-509.

Kahn-Freund, Otto (1954a) Intergroup Conflicts and their Settlement *British Journal of Sociology* 5, 193-227.

Kahn-Freund, Otto (1954b) Legal Framework, in *The System of Industrial Relations in Britain* eds Allan Flanders and Hugh Clegg (Basil Blackwell, Oxford).

Kahn-Freund, Otto (1959) Labour Law, in *Law and Public Opinion in Britain in the Twentieth Century* ed M Ginsberg (Stevens, London).

Kahn-Freund, Otto (1967) A Note on Status and Contract in Modern Labour Law *Modern Law Review* 30, 635-644.

Kahn-Freund, Otto (1972) On Uses and Misuses of Comparative Law *Modern Law Review* 37, 1-27.

Kahn-Freund, Otto (1978a) Notes on the Conflict of Laws in Relation to Employment Contracts in English and Scottish courts, in *Selected Writings* (Stevens, London).

Kahn-Freund, Otto (1978b) Blackstone's Neglected Child: the Contract of Employment *Law Quarterly Review* 93, 508-528.

Kahn-Freund, Otto and BA Hepple (1972) *Laws Against Strikes* (Fabian Research Series 302, London).

Keep, Ewan (1990) Training for the Low Paid, in *Improving Incentives for the Low-Paid* eds Alex Bowen and Ken Mayhew (Macmillan/NEDO, London).

Keller, Berndt (2002) The European Company Statute: Employee Involvement – and Beyond *Industrial Relations Journal* 33, 424-445.

Kelly, John (1990) British Trade Unionism 1979-1989: Changes, Continuity and Contradictions *Work, Employment and Society*, Special Issue May 1990, 35-45.

Kelly, John, and Rachel Bailey (1989) British Trade Union Membership, Density and Decline in the 1980s *Industrial Relations Journal* 20, 54-61.

Kenner, Jeff (1999a) The EC Employment Title and the Third Way: Making Soft Law Work? *International Journal of Comparative Labour Law and Industrial Relations* 15, 33-60.

Kenner, Jeff (1999b) Statement or Contract? – Some Reflections on the EC Employee Information (Contract or Employment Relationship) Directive after *Kampelmann Industrial Law Journal* 28, 205-231.

Kenner, Jeff (2003) *EU Employment Law* (Hart Publishing, Oxford)

Kerr, Tony (1984) Contract Doesn't Live Here Any More? *Modern Law Review* 47, 30-47.

Kessler, Ian and John Purcell (1995) Individualism and Collectivism in Theory and Practice: Management Style and the Design of Pay Systems, in *Industrial Relations: Theory and Practice in Britain*, ed. Paul Edwards (Blackwell Business, Oxford).

Kidner, Richard (1983) *Trade Union Law* 2nd edn (Stevens, London).

Kidner, Richard (1991) Unjustified Discipline by a Trade Union *Industrial Law Journal*, 20, 284-291.

Kidner, Richard (1998) Jurisdiction in European Contracts of Employment *Industrial Law Journal* 27, 103-120.

Kilpatrick, Claire (1994) Deciding When Jobs of Equal Value Can be Paid Unequally: an Examination of s 1(3) of the Equal Pay Act 1970 *Industrial Law Journal* 23, 311-325.

Kilpatrick, Claire (2004) Has New Labour Reconfigured Employment Legislation? *Industrial Law Journal* 32, 135-163.

Knight, KG and Paul L Latreille (2000) Discipline, Dismissals and Complaints to Employment Tribunals *British Journal of Industrial Relations* 38, 533-555.

Kochan, Thomas A (2003) A US Perspective on the Future of Trade Unions in Britain, in *Representing Workers: Trade Union Recognition and Membership in Britain* eds Howard Gospel and Stephen Wood (Routledge, London).

Labour Research Department (1986) The Growing Army of the Self-Employed *Labour Research* February.

Lacey, Nicola (1986) Dismissed by Reason of Pregnancy *Industrial Law Journal* 15, 43-46.

Lacey, Nicola (1992) From Individual to Group?, in *Discrimination: the Limits of the Law* eds BA Hepple and Erika Szyszczak (Mansell, London).

LaLonde, Robert J and Bernard D Meltzer (1991) Hard Times for Unions: Another Look at the Significance of Employer Illegalities *University of Chicago Law Review*, 58, 1006-1014.

Langrish, Sally (1998) The Treaty of Amsterdam: Selected Highlights *European Law Review* 23, 3-19.

Larkin, Philip (2000) Compensation for Repetitive Strain Injury *Industrial Law Journal* 29, 88-95

Laws, The Hon Sir John (1993) Is the High Court the Guardian of Fundamental Constitutional Rights? *Public Law*, 59-79.

Laws, The Hon, Sir John (1997) Public Law and Employment Law: Abuse of Power *Public Law*, 455-466.

Le Sueur, Andrew (2005) The Rise and Rise of Unreasonableness? *Judicial Review* 10, 32-51.

Leader, Sheldon (1991) The European Convention on Human Rights, The Employment Act 1988 and the Right to Refuse to Strike *Industrial Law Journal* 20, 39-59.

Leader, Sheldon (1992) *Freedom of Association* (Yale University Press, New Haven and London).

Leigh, Ian (1999) Horizontal Rights: The Human Rights Act and Privacy: Lessons from the Commonwealth *International and Comparative Law Quarterly* 48, 57-87.

Leigh, Ian and Laurence Lustgarten (1991) Employment, Justice and Detente: the Reform of Vetting *Modern Law Review* 54, 613-642.

Leigh, Ian and Laurence Lustgarten (1999) Making Rights Real: The Courts, Remedies and the Human Rights Act *Cambridge Law Journal* 58, 509-543.

Leighton, Patricia (1982) Employment Status and the 'Casual' Worker *Industrial Law Journal* 13, 62-66.

Leighton, Patricia (1986) Marginal Workers, in *Labour Law in Britain* ed Roy Lewis (Basil Blackwell, Oxford).

Leighton, Patricia, and Stephen Dunville (1977) From Statement to Contract: Some Effects of the Contracts of Employment Act 1972 *Industrial Law Journal* 16, 133-148.

Lenaerts, Koen (2000) Fundamental Rights in the European Union *European Law Review* 25, 575-600.

Lenaerts, Koen and Eddy Eddy de Smijter (2001) A 'Bill of Rights' for the European Union *Common Market Law Review* 38, 273-300.

Leonard, Alice (1986) *The First Eight Years: a profile of applications to the industrial tribunals under the Sex Discrimination Act 1975 and the Equal Pay Act 1970* (Equal Opportunities Commission, Manchester).

Leonard, Alice (1987) *Pyrrhic Victories: Winning Sex Discrimination and Equal Pay Cases in the Industrial Tribunals 1980-1984* EOC Research Series (HMSO, London).

Leopold, John W (1997) Trade Unions, Political Fund Ballots and the Labour Party *British Journal of Industrial Relations* 35, 23-38.

Lester, Lord (1994) Discrimination: What can Lawyers Learn from History? *Public Law*, 224-237.

Lester, Lord (1998a) Universality versus Subsidiarity: A Reply, *European Human Rights Law Review*, 73-81.

Lester, Lord (1998b) Opinion: The Art of the Possible – Interpreting Statutes under the Human Rights Act *European Human Rights Law Review*, 665-675.

Lester, Lord and David Pannick (2000) The Impact of the Human Rights Act on Private Law: The Knight's Move *Law Quarterly Review* 116, 380-385.

Levie, H, D Gregory and C Callender (1984) Redundancy Pay: Trick or Treat? in *Fighting Closures* eds H Levie, D Gregory and N Lorentzen (Spokesman, Nottingham).

Lewis, Clive (2004) *Judicial Remedies in Public Law* 3rd edn (Sweet and Maxwell, London).

Lewis, Clive and Sarah Moore (1993) Duties, Directives and Damages in European Community Law *Public Law*, 151-170.

Lewis, David (1995) Whistleblowers and Job Security *Modern Law Review* 58, 208-221.

Lewis, David (1998) The Public Interest Disclosure Act 1998 *Industrial law Journal* 27, 325-330.

Lewis, David (1999) Re-Employment as a Remedy for Unfair Dismissal: How Can the Culture be Changed? *Industrial Law Journal* 28, 183-185.

Lewis, David (2001) Whistleblowing at Work: On what Principles Should Legislation be Based? *Industrial Law Journal* 30, 169-193.

Lewis, David (2004) How Should Safety Concerns be Handled? *Industrial Law Journal* 33, 42-45.

Lewis, Paul (2000) Pregnant Workers and Sex Discrimination: the Limits of Purposive, Non-comparative Methodology *International Journal of Comparative Labour Law and Industrial Relations* 16, 55-69.

Lewis, Roy (1979) Collective Agreements: The Kahn-Freund Legacy *Modern Law Review* 42, 613-622.

Lewis, Roy (1986) The Role of the Law in Employment Relations, in *Labour Law in Britain* ed Roy Lewis (Basil Blackwell, Oxford).

Lewis, Roy (1990) Strike-free Deals and Pendulum Arbitration *British Journal of Industrial Relations*, 28, 32-56.

Lewis, Roy (1998) The Employment Rights (Dispute Resolution) Act 1998 *Industrial Law Journal* 27, 214-219.

Lewis, Roy and Jon Clark (1993) *Employment Rights, Industrial Tribunals and Arbitration: The Case for Alternative Dispute Resolution* (Institute of Employment Rights, London).

Lightman, Gavin (1987) A Trade Union in Chains: Scargill Unbound - The Legal Constraints of Receivership and Sequestration *Current Legal Problems* 40, 25-54.

Lightman, Sir Gavin and John Bowers (1998) Incorporation of the ECHR and its Impact on Employment Law *European Human Rights Law Review* 560-581.

Lindbeck, Assar, and Dennis J Snower (1989) *The Insider-Outsider Theory of Employment and Unemployment* (MIT Press, Boston).

Lindley, RM (1983) Active Employment Policy, in *Industrial Relations in Britain* ed George Sayers Bain (Basil Blackwell, Oxford).

Lindsay, Craig and Claire Macauley (2004) Growth in Self-Employment in the UK *Labour Market Trends* 112, 399-404.

Lindsay, Hon Mr Justice (2001) The Implied Term of Trust and Confidence *Industrial Law Journal* 30, 1-16.

Lock, GF (1983) Labour Law, Parliamentary Staff and Parliamentary Privilege *Industrial Law Journal* 12, 28-37.

Lorber, Pascale (1999) Regulating Fixed-Term Work in the United Kingdom: A Positive Step towards Workers' Protection? *International Journal of Comparative Labour Law and Industrial Relations* 15, 121-135.

Lorber, Pascale (2003) National Works Councils: Opening the Door on a Whole New Era in United Kingdom Employment Relations? *International Journal of Comparative Labour Law and Industrial Relations* 19, 297- 319.

Lorber, Pascale (2004) Reviewing the European Works Council Directive: European Progress and United Kingdom Perspective *Industrial Law Journal* 33,191-199.

Lorber, Stephen (2004) Data Protection and Subject Access Requests *Industrial Law Journal* 33, 179-190.

Low Pay Unit (1988) Escaping the Clutches of the Poverty Trap *Low Pay Review*, Spring.

Low Pay Unit (1992) NES 1991: Pay-Gap Yawns as Low-Paid Left Behind *New Review of the Low Pay Unit*, 13, 8-12.

Lupton, T and A Bowey (1974) *Wages and Salaries* (Penguin, Harmondsworth).

Lustgarten, Laurence (1986) *The Governance of Police* (Sweet and Maxwell, London).

Lyon-Caen, Gérard, Jean Pélissier and Alain Supiot (1996) *Droit du Travail* 18th edn (Dalloz, Paris).

MacDonald, Elizabeth (1992) Exclusion Clauses: the ambit of s 13(1) of the Unfair Contract Terms Act *Legal Studies* 12, 277-301.

Macdonald, Ian and Nicholas Blake (1995) *Immigration Law and Practice in the United Kingdom* (Butterworths, London).

Machin, Stephen (1996) Wage Inequality in the UK *Oxford Review of Economic Policy* 12, 47-64

Machin, Stephen (2000) Union Decline in Britain *British Journal of Industrial Relations* 38, 631-645

Machin, Stephen (2003) Trade Union Decline, New Workplaces and New Workers, in *Representing Workers: Trade Union Recognition and Membership in Britain* ed Howard Gospel and Stephen Wood (Routledge, London).

Machin, Stephen, and Andrew Manning (1992) *Minimum Wages, Wage Dispersion and Employment: Evidence from UK Wages Councils* Discussion Paper 80 Centre for Economic Performance (London School of Economics).

MacInnes, John (1985) Conjuring Up Consultation: The Role and Extent of Joint Consultation in Post-War Private Manufacturing Industry *British Journal of Industrial Relations* 23, 93-113.

MacMillan, John K (1999) Employment Tribunals: Philosophies and Practicalities *Industrial Law Journal* 28, 33-56.

Maine, Sir Henry [1861] (1927) *Ancient Law: its connection with the early history of society, and its relation to modern ideas* ed Sir Frederick Pollock (Murray, London).

Marchington, Mick (1992) *New Developments in Employee Involvement* Employment Department Research Series No 2 (Employment Department, London).

Marginson, Paul, Mark Gilman, Otto Jacobi and Hubert Kreiger (1998) *Negotiating European Works Councils: an Analysis of Agreements under Article 13* (European Foundation for the Improvement of Living and Working Conditions).

Marginson, Paul, PK Edwards, Rod Martin, John Purcell and Keith Sisson (1988) *Beyond the Workplace: Managing industrial relations in the multi-establishment enterprise* (Basil Blackwell, Oxford).

Markesinis, Basil S (1990) Our Patchy Law of Privacy – Time to Do Something About It *Modern Law Review* 53, 802-809.

Markesinis, Basil S (1994) A Matter of Style *Law Quarterly Review* 110, 607-627.

Markesinis, Basil (1999) Privacy, Freedom of Expression and the Human Rights Bill: Lessons from Germany *Law Quarterly Review* 115, 47-88.

Marsden, David, and Marc Thompson (1990) Flexibility Agreements in Practice *Work, Employment and Society* 4, 83-104.

Marsh, Catherine (1991) *Hours of Work of Women and Men in Great Britain.*

Marsh, Catherine, Rosemary McAuley and Sian Penlington (1990) The Road to Recovery? Some Evidence from Vacancies in One Labour Market *Work, Employment and Society* 4, 31-58.

Martin, Roderick (1992) *Bargaining Power* (Clarendon Press, Oxford).

Martin, Roderick, Patricia Fosh, Huw Morris, Paul Smith and Roger Undy (1991) The Decollectivisation of Trade Unions? Ballots and Collective Bargaining in the 1980s *Industrial Relations Journal* 22, 197-208.

Martin, Ross M (1980) *TUC: The Growth of a Pressure Group 1868-1976* (Clarendon Press, Oxford).

Marx, Irene (1999) Low Pay and Poverty in OECD Countries *Employment Audit* 10, 17-21.

Matthews, Paul (1982) Salaries in the Apportionment Act 1870 *Legal Studies* 2, 302-312.

Mayhew, Ken and John T Addison (1983) Discrimination in the Labour Market, in *Industrial Relations in Britain* ed George Sayers Bain (Basil Blackwell, Oxford).

McCabe, Sarah and Peter Wallington (1988) *The Police, Public Order and Civil Liberties* (Routledge, London).

McCallum, Ronald (1989) Exploring the Common Law: Lay-off, Suspension and the Contract of Employment *Australian Journal of Labour Law* 2, 211-233.

McCarthy, Lord (1999) *Fairness at Work and Trade Union Recognition: Past Comparisons and Future Problems* (Institute of Employment Rights, London).

McCarthy, WEJ (1964) *The Closed Shop in Britain* (University of California Press, Berkeley and Los Angeles).

McCarthy, WEJ (1992) The Rise and Fall of Collective Laissez-Faire in *Legal Intervention in Industrial Relations: Gains and Losses* ed WEJ McCarthy (Basil Blackwell, Oxford).

McCarthy, WEJ (2000) Representative Consultations with Specified Employees – or the Future of Rung Two, in *Legal Regulation of the Employment Relation* eds Hugh Collins, Paul Davies and Roger Rideout (Kluwer, London).

McColgan, Aileen (1994) *Pay Equity – Just Wages for Women?* (Institute of Employment Rights, London).

McColgan, Aileen (1997) *Just Wages for Women* (Clarendon Press, Oxford).

McColgan, Aileen (2000a) Missing the Point? The Part-time Workers (Prevention of Less Favourable Treatment) Regulations 2000 (SI 2000, No 1551) *Industrial Law Journal* 29, 260-267.

McColgan, Aileen (2000b) Family Friendly Frolics? The Maternity and Parental Leave etc. Regulations 1999 *Industrial Law Journal* 29, 125-144.

McColgan, Aileen (2000c) *Discrimination Law. Text, Cases and Materials* (Hart Publishing, Oxford).

McColgan, Aileen (2000d) Article 10 and the Right to Freedom of Expression: Workers Ungagged? in *Human Rights at Work* ed Keith Ewing (Institute of Employment Rights, London).

McCrudden, Christopher (1983) Equal Pay for Work of Equal Value: the Equal Pay (Amendment) Regulations 1983 *Industrial Law Journal* 12, 197-219.

McCrudden, Christopher (1985) Institutional Discrimination *Oxford Journal of Legal Studies* 4, 303-367.

McCrudden, Christopher (1988) The Northern Ireland Fair Employment White Paper: a Critical Assessment *Industrial Law Journal* 17, 162-181.

McCrudden, Christopher (1996) Third Time Lucky? The Pensions Act 1995 and Equal Treatment in Occupational Pensions *Industrial Law Journal* 25, 28-42.

McCrudden, Christopher, David Smith, Colin Brown and Jim Knox (1991) *Racial Justice at Work* (Policy Studies Institute, London).

McGregor, Harvey (2003) *McGregor on Damages* 17th edn (Sweet and Maxwell, London).

McHale, Jean (1992) Whistleblowing in the NHS *Journal of Social Welfare Law*, 363-371.

McHale, Jean (1993) Whistleblowing in the NHS Revisited *Journal of Social Welfare and Family Law*, 52-57.

McKay, Sonia (1996) *The Law on Industrial Action under the Conservatives* (Institute of Employment Rights, London).

McKay, Sir William (ed) (2004) *Erskine May's Treatise on the Law, Privileges, Proceedings and Usage of Parliament* 23rd edn (LexisNexis UK, London).

McKendrick, Ewan (1988) The Rights of Trade Union Members – Part I of the Employment Act 1988 *Industrial Law Journal* 17, 141-161.

McKendrick, Ewan (1990) Vicarious Liability and Independent Contractors – a Reassessment *Modern Law Review* 53, 770-784.

McKinnon, Catherine (1979) *Sexual Harassment of Working Women* (Yale UP, New Haven).

McLaughlin, Eithne, Jane Millar and Kenneth Cooke (1989) *Work and Welfare Benefits* (Avebury, Aldershot).

McLean, Hazel (1990) Contract of Employment - Negative Covenants and No Work, No Pay *Cambridge Law Journal*, 49, 28-31.

McLean, Hazel (1992) An Employer's Right to be Unreasonable *Cambridge Law Journal* 51, 23-26.

McLean, Hazel (1994) *Fair Shares – The Future of Employee Financial Participation in the UK* (Institute of Employment Rights, London).

McMullen, Jeremy, and Philippa Kaufman (1991) *Labour Law Review* (Institute of Employment Rights, London).

McMullen, John (1982) A Synthesis of the Mode of Termination of Contracts of Employment *Cambridge Law Journal* 41, 110-141.

McMullen, John (1992) *Business Transfers and Employee Rights* 2nd edn (Butterworths, London).

McMullen, John (1994) Contracting-out and Market Testing – the Uncertainty Ends? *Industrial Law Journal* 23, 230-240.

McMullen, John (1995) Enforcing Contracts of Employment – 'Going Back to Basics' in the Resolution of Employment Disputes *Industrial Law Journal* 24, 353-363.

McMullen, John (1996) Enforcing Contracts of Employment – A Postscript *Industrial Law Journal* 25, 140-144.

McMullen John (1997) Extending Remedies for Breach of the Employment Contract *Industrial Law Journal* 26, 245-247.

McMullen, John (1999a) TUPE: Waiver of Employment Rights & Contract Changes after *Wilson Industrial Law Journal* 28, 76-84.

McMullen, John (1999b) TUPE – Sidestepping *Süzen*, *Industrial Law Journal* 28, 360-364.

Mead, David (2004) To BNP or Not to BNP: Union Exclusion on Ground of Political Activity – A Commentary on *ASLEF* v *Lee*, *Industrial Law Journal* 33, 267-277.

Mead, Geoffrey (1990) The Role of Intention in Direct Discrimination *Industrial Law Journal* 19, 250-252.

Mead, Geoffrey (1991) Restitution within Contract? *Legal Studies* 11, 172-188.

Meager, Nigel (1986) Temporary Work in Britain *Employment Gazette* 94, 7-15.

Meehan, Elizabeth (1985) *Rights at Work: Campaigns and Policy in Britain and the United States* (Macmillan, Basingstoke).

Merritt, Adrian (1982a) 'Control' v 'Economic Reality': Defining the Contract of Employment *Australian Business Law Review*, 105-124.

Merritt, Adrian (1982b) The Historical Role of the Law in the Regulation of Employment – Abstentionist or Interventionist? *Australian Journal of Law and Society* 1, 56-86.

Mesher, John (1985) Social Security in the Coal Dispute *Industrial Law Journal* 14, 191-202.

Mesher, John (1993) Social Security for Occupational Pensions: Is the Law of Trusts Superannuated? *Current Legal Problems* 46, 96-112.

Mesher, John and Frank Sutcliffe (1986) Industrial Action and the Individual, in *Labour Law in Britain* ed Roy Lewis (Blackwell, Oxford).

Metcalf, David (1986) *Labour Market Flexibility and Jobs: a survey of evidence from OECD countries with special reference to Great Britain and Europe* Discussion paper No 254 (Centre for Labour Economics, London School of Economics).

Metcalf, David (1989) Water Notes Dry Up: the Impact of the Donovan Reform Proposals and Thatcherism at Work on Labour Productivity in British Manufacturing *British Journal of Industrial Relations* 27, 1-31.

Metcalf, David (1993) Industrial Relations and Economic Performance *British Journal of Industrial Relations* 31, 255-284.

Metcalf, David (1999) The British National Minimum Wage *British Journal of Industrial Relations* 37, 171-201.

Metcalf, David (2004) British Unions: Resurgence or Perdition? http://cep.lse.ac.uk/people/cv/david_metcalf.pdf.

Meyers, Frederic (1964) *Ownership of Jobs: A Comparative Study* (University of California Press, Los Angeles).

Middlemiss, Sam (2004) The Truth and Nothing but the Truth: The Legal Liability of Employers for Employee References *Industrial Law Journal* 33, 59-67.

Miller, D and J Stirling (1998) European Works Council Training: An Opportunity Missed? *European Journal of Industrial Relations* 4, 35-49.

Miller, Kenneth (1990) Reasonableness and Section 4 of the Employment Act 1980 *British Journal of Industrial Relations* 28, 69-83.

Miller, Kenneth and Charles Woolfson (1994) Timex: Industrial Relations and the Use of the Law in the 1990s *Industrial Law Journal* 23, 209-225.

Mills, Shaun (1997) The International Labour Organisation, the United Kingdom and Freedom of Association: An Annual Cycle of Condemnation *European Human Rights Law Review* 1, 35-53.

Millward, Neil and Mark Stevens (1986) *British Workplace Industrial Relations 1980-1984: the DE/ESRC/PSI/ACAS Surveys* (Gower, Aldershot).

Millward, Neil, Alex Bryson and John Forth (2000) *All Change at Work?* (Routledge, London).

Millward, Neil, Mark Stevens, David Smart and WR Hawes (1992) *Workplace Industrial Relations in Transition: The ED/ESRC/PSI/ACAS Surveys* (Dartmouth, Aldershot).

Minford, Patrick, with Paul Ashton, Michael Peel, David Davies and Alison Sprague (1986) *Unemployment: Cause and Cure* (Basil Blackwell, Oxford).

Mirza, Qudsia (1994) *Race Relations in the Workplace* (Institute of Employment Rights, London).

Mitchell, Richard (ed.) (1995) *Redefining Labour Law* (Centre for Employment and Labour Relations Law, University of Melbourne).

Moffat, Graham and Sue Ward (1986) Occupational Pensions, in *Labour Law in Britain* ed Roy Lewis (Basil Blackwell, Oxford).

Mogridge, Christine (1981) Illegal Contracts of Employment: Loss of Statutory Protection *Industrial Law Journal* 20, 23-33.

Moher, Jim (1989) *The London Millwrights and Engineers 1755-1825* PhD Thesis, University of London.

Moher, Jim (1995) *Trade Unions and the Law – The Politics of Change* (Institute of Employment Rights, London).

Monaghan, Karon (2000) *Challenging Race Discrimination at Work* (Institute of Employment Rights, London)

Monger, Joanne (2004) Labour Disputes in 2003 *Labour Market Trends* (June).

Moore, Sian, Sonia McKay and Helen Bewley (2004) *The Content of New Voluntary Trade Union Recognition Agreements, 1998-2002: Volume One – An Analysis of New Agreements and Case Studies* (DTI, London).

Moore, Sian, Stephen Wood, and Paul Davies (2000) Recognition of Trade Unions – Consultation over the Access Code and Method of Bargaining *Industrial Law Journal* 29, 406-415.

Morris, Debra (1993a) The Commissioner for the Rights of Trade Union Members – A Framework for the Future? *Industrial Law Journal* 22, 104-118.

Morris, Debra (1993b) 'Trade Union Members Are My Prime Concern' *Industrial Law Journal*, 22, 307-309.

Morris, Debra (1999) Volunteering and Employment Status *Industrial Law Journal* 28, 249-255.

Morris, Gillian S (1980) The Police and Industrial Emergencies *Industrial Law Journal* 9, 1-12.

Morris, Gillian S (1985a) Road Blocks and Bail Conditions *Industrial Law Journal* 14, 109-111.

Morris, Gillian S (1985b) The Ban on Trade Unions at Government Communications Headquarters *Public Law*, 177-186.

Morris, Gillian S (1986a) *Strikes in Essential Services* (Mansell, London).

Morris, Gillian S (1986b) Employment Rights and Public Law Remedies *Industrial Law Journal*, 15, 194-196.

Morris, Gillian S (1991) Industrial Action in Essential Services: The New Law *Industrial Law Journal* 20, 89-101.

Morris, Gillian S (1993) Industrial Action: Public and Private Interests *Industrial Law Journal* 22, 194-210.

Morris, Gillian S (1994a) Freedom of Association and the Interests of the State, in *Human Rights and Labour Law: Essays for Paul O'Higgins*, eds KD Ewing, CA Gearty and BA Hepple (Mansell, London).

Morris, Gillian S (1994b) Employment in the Prison Service: Whither Public Service Regulation? *Public Law*, 535-39.

Morris, Gillian S (1994c) The New Legal Regime for Prison Officers *Industrial Law Journal* 23, 326-331.

Morris, Gillian S (1998a) Local government workers and rights of political participation: time for a change *Public Law*, 25-33.

Morris, Gillian S (1998b) Political Activities of Public Servants and Freedom of Expression in *Importing the First Amendment*, ed Ian Loveland (Hart Publishing, Oxford).

Morris, Gillian S (1998c) The Human Rights Act and the Public/Private Divide in Employment Law *Industrial Law Journal* 27, 293-308.

Morris, Gillian S (1999a) Fragmenting the State: Implications for Accountability for Employment Practices in Public Services *Public Law*, 64-83.

Morris, Gillian S (1999b) The Political Activities of Local Government Workers and the European Convention on Human Rights *Public Law*, 211-218

Morris, Gillian S (1999c) The European Convention on Human Rights and Employment: To Which Acts Does it Apply? *European Human Rights Law Review*, 496-511.

Morris, Gillian S (1999d) The Role of Local Education Authorities as Employers *Journal of Local Government Law* 2, 54-57.

Morris, Gillian S (2000) Employment in Public Services: The Case for Special Treatment *Oxford Journal of Legal Studies* 20, 167-183.

Morris, Gillian S (2001a) Fundamental Rights: Exclusion by Agreement? *Industrial Law Journal* 30, 49-71.

Morris, Gillian S (2001b) The Employment Relations Act 1999 and Collective Labour Standards *International Journal of Comparative Labour Law and Industrial Relations* 17, 63-77.

Morris, Gillian S (2002a) The Use of E-Mail and the Internet at Work in English Law in *Online Rights of Employees* ed R Blanpain (Kluwer, The Hague).

Morris, Gillian S (2002b) Extending the Police Family: Issues and Anomalies *Public Law* 670-677.

Morris, Gillian S (2004a) The Future of the Public/Private Labour Law Divide, in *The Future of Labour Law: Liber Amicorum Sir Bob Hepple QC* ed Catherine Barnard, Simon Deakin and Gillian S Morris (Hart Publishing, Oxford).

Morris, Gillian S (2004b) England, in *Temporary Agency Work and the Information Society* ed Roger Blanpain and Ronnie Graham (Kluwer Law International, The Hague).

Morris, Gillian S (2005) Britain's New Statutory Procedures; Routes to Resolution or Barriers to Justice? *Comparative Labor Law and Policy Journal*, forthcoming.

Morris, Gillian S and Timothy J Archer (2000) *Collective Labour Law* (Hart Publishing, Oxford).

Morris, Gillian S and Sandra Fredman (1993) Is there a Public/Private Labour Law Divide? *Comparative Labor Law Journal* 14, 115-137.

Morris, Gillian S with Stephen Rydzkowski (1984) Approaches to Industrial Action in the National Health Service *Industrial Law Journal* 13, 153-164.

Morris, Jenny (1985) *Women Workers and the Sweated Trades* (Gower, Aldershot).

Morse, CJG (1982) Contracts of Employment and the EEC Contractual Obligations Convention, in *Contract Conflicts* ed PM North (North Holland, Amsterdam).

Mosley, Hugh (1990) The Social Dimension of European Integration *International Labour Review* 129, 147-163.

Mowbray, Alastair (1997) The European Court of Human Rights' Approach to Just Satisfaction *Public Law*, 647-659.

Mückenberger, Ulrich, and Simon Deakin (1989) From Deregulation to a European Floor of Rights: Labour Law, Flexibilisation and the European Single Market *Zeitschrift für ausländisches und internationales Arbeits- und Sozialrecht* 3, 157-206.

Mumford, Karen (1996) Arbitration and ACAS in Britain: a Historical Perspective *British Journal of Industrial Relations*, 34, 287-305.

Munday, Roderick (1981) Tribunal Lore: Legalism and the Industrial Tribunals *Industrial Law Journal* 10, 146-159.

Murray, Jill (1999) Normalising Temporary Work *Industrial Law Journal* 28, 269-275.

Murray, Jill (2001) A New Phase in the Regulation of Multinational Enterprises: The Role of the OECD *Industrial Law Journal* 30, 255-270.

NACAB (1990) *Hard Labour* (National Association of Citizens' Advice Bureaux, London).

Napier, Brian (1972) Working to Rule – A Breach of the Contract of Employment? *Industrial Law Journal*, 1, 125-134.

Napier, Brian (1983) Dismissals: the New ILO Standards *Industrial Law Journal* 12, 17-27.

Napier, Brian (1986) The Contract of Employment, in *Labour Law in Britain* ed Roy Lewis (Basil Blackwell, Oxford).

Napier, Brian (1987) Breach of Statutory Duty and Unlawful Means in Strike Law *Cambridge Law Journal* 46, 222-224.

Napier, Brian (1989) AIDS, Discrimination and Employment Law *Industrial Law Journal*, 18, 84-96.

Napier, Brian (1992) Computerisation and Employment Rights *Industrial Law Journal* 21, 1-14.

Napier, Brian (1993) *CCT, Market Testing and Employment Rights. The effects of TUPE and the Acquired Rights Directive* (Institute of Employment Rights, London).

Naylor, Kate (1994) Part-time Working in Britain: an Historical Analysis *Employment Gazette*, 102, 473-484.

Neal, Alan C (1990) The European Framework Directive on the Health and Safety of Workers: Challenges for the United Kingdom? *International Journal of Comparative Labour Law and Industrial Relations* 6, 80-117.

Neal, Alan C (1998) Regulating Health and Safety at Work: Developing European Union Policy for the Millenium *International Journal of Comparative Labour Law and Industrial Relations* 14, 217-236.

Nicholls, Paul and David Bradley (2000) It's Good to Talk: The Eighth Annual Industrial Relations Survey (Gee Publishing, London).

Nickell, Stephen (1997) Unemployment and Labour Market Rigidities: Europe versus North America *Journal of Economic Perspectives* 11, 55-74.

Nickell, Stephen (1999) Unemployment in Britain, in Paul Gregg and Jonathan Wadsworth (eds) *The State of Working Britain* (Manchester University Press, Manchester).

Nielsen, Ruth and Erica Szyszczak (1997) *The Social Dimension of the European Community*, 3rd edn (Handelshojskolens Forlag, Copenhagen).

Njoya, Wanjiru (2004) Employee Ownership and Efficiency: An Evolutionary Perspective *Industrial Law Journal* 30, 211-241.

Nobles, Richard (1986) Pensions: the New Framework *Modern Law Review* 49, 42-67.

Nobles, Richard (1993) *Pensions, Employment and the Law* (Clarendon Press, Oxford).

Nobles, Richard (1996) Pensions Act 1995 *Modern Law Review* 59, 241-260.

Nobles, Richard (1998) The Death of Deferred Pay? *Industrial Law Journal* 27, 142-146.

Nobles, Richard (2000a) Access to the Law of Pensions: the Lessons from *National Grid v Laws, Industrial Law Journal* 29, 172-175.

Nobles, Richard (2000b) Enforcing Employees' Pension Rights – the Courts' Hostility to the Pensions Ombudsman *Industrial Law Journal* 29, 243-259.

Nobles, Richard (2001) Pension Scheme Surpluses: *National Grid* in the House of Lords *Industrial Law Journal* 30, 318-324.

Nolan, Donal (1995) Recovering Damages for Psychiatric Injury at Work *Industrial Law Journal* 24, 280-284.

Nolan, Peter (1989) Walking on Water? Economic Performance and Industrial Relations under Thatcher *Industrial Relations Journal* 20, 81-92.

Nolan, Peter, and Paul Marginson (1990) Skating on Thin Ice? David Metcalf on Trade Unions and Productivity *British Journal of Industrial Relations* 28, 227-247.

Novitz, Tonia (1997) Negative Freedom of Association *Industrial Law Journal* 26, 79-87.

Novitz, Tonia (1998) Freedom of Association and "Fairness at Work" – An Assessment of the Impact and Relevance of ILO Convention No 87 on its Fiftieth Anniversary *Industrial Law Journal* 27, 169-191.

Novitz, Tonia (2000) International Promises and Domestic Pragmatism: To What Extent will the Employment Relations Act 1999 Implement International Labour Standards Relating to Freedom of Association *Modern Law Review* 63, 379-393.

Novitz, Tonia (2003) *International and European Protection of the Right to Strike* (OUP, Oxford).

Novitz, Tonia and Paul Skidmore (2001) *Fairness at Work. A Critical Analysis of the Employment Relations Act 1999 and its Treatment of Collective Rights* (Hart Publishing, Oxford).

O'Cinneide, Colm (2001) The Race Relations (Amendment) Act 2000 *Public Law*, 220-232.

O'Dair, Richard (1991) Justifying an Interference with Contractual Rights *Oxford Journal of Legal Studies* 11, 227-246.

O'Higgins, Paul (1991) The European Social Charter in *Human Rights for the 1990s* eds Robert Blackburn and John Taylor (Mansell, London).

O'Higgins, Paul (2002) The interaction of the ILO, the Council of Europe and European Union Labour Standards in *Social and Labour Rights in a Global Context* ed Bob Hepple (Cambridge University Press, Cambridge).

O'Regan, Catherine (1991) Contempt of Court and the Enforcement of Labour Injunctions *Modern Law Review*, 53, 385-407.

Oakley, Ann (1972) *Sex, Gender and Society* (Temple Smith, London).

OECD (1986a) *Labour Market Flexibility: a report by a high level group of experts to the Secretary-General* (Organisation for Economic Cooperation and Development, Paris).

OECD (1986b) *Flexibility in the Labour Market* (Organisation for Economic Cooperation and Development, Paris).

OECD (1991) *Employment Outlook* (Organisation for Economic Cooperation and Development, Paris).

OECD (1994) *Employment Outlook* (Organisation for Economic Cooperation and Development, Paris).

Oliver, Dawn (1993) *Pepper v Hart*: a Suitable Case for Reference to *Hansard*? *Public Law*, 5-13.

Oliver, Dawn (1997) Common Values in Public and Private Law and the Public/ Private Divide *Public Law* 630-646.

Oliver, Hazel (2002) Email and Internet Monitoring in the Workplace: Information, Privacy and Contracting-Out *Industrial Law Journal* 31, 321-352.

Oliver, Hazel (2004) Sexual Orientation Discrimination: Perceptions, Definitions and Genuine Occupational Requirements *Industrial Law Journal* 33, 1-21.

Orth, John V (1991) *Combination and Conspiracy: A Legal History of Trade Unionism 1721-1906* (Clarendon Press, Oxford).

Oxenbridge, Sarah and William Brown (2004) Achieving a New Equilibrium? The stability of cooperative employer-union relationships *Industrial Relations Journal* 35, 388-402.

Oxenbridge, Sarah, William Brown, Simon Deakin and Cliff Pratten (2003) Initial Reponses to the Statutory Recognition Provisions of the Employment Relations Act 1999 *British Journal of Industrial Relations* 41, 315-334.

Ozaki, M (1993) Labour Relations in the Public Service, in *Comparative Labour Law and Industrial Relations in Industrialised Market Economies* 5th edn, eds R Blanpain and C Engels (Kluwer, Deventer-Boston).

Palmer, Stephanie (2000) Human Rights: Implications for Labour Law *Cambridge Law Journal* 59, 168-200.

Palmer, Tom, Heidi Grainger and Grant Fitzner (2004) *Trade Union Membership 2003* (DTI, London).

Panitch, Leo (1976) *Social Democracy and Industrial Militancy* (CUP, Cambridge).

Pankert, A (1980) Settlement of Labour Disputes in Essential Services *International Labour Review*, 119, 723-37.

Pankhurst, Kate (1988) Work Effort under the Incomplete Contract of Employment (Mimeo, New Hall, Cambridge).

Pannick, David (1985) *Sex Discrimination Law* (Clarendon Press, Oxford).

Pannick, David (1998) Principles of Interpretation of Convention Rights under the Human Rights Act and the Discretionary Area of Judgment *Public Law*, 545-551.

Parker, Kenneth (1992) State Liability in Damages for Breach of Community Law *Law Quarterly Review* 108, 181-6.

Parker, S, C Thomas, N Ellis and WEJ McCarthy (1971) *Effects of the Redundancy Payments Act* (HMSO, London).

Parkinson, JE (1993) *Corporate Power and Responsibility: Issues in the Theory of Company Law* (Clarendon Press, Oxford).

Pedrazzoli, Marcello (ed) (1989) *Lavoro Subordinato e Dintorni: Comparazione e Prospettive* (Il Mulino, Bologna).

Pélissier, Jean, Alain Supiot and Antoine Jeaummaud (2004) *Droit du Travail* 22nd ed (Dalloz, Paris).

Pendleton, Andrew, Nicholas Wilson and Mike Wright (1998) The Perception and Effects of Share Ownership: Empirical Evidence from Employee Buy-Outs *British Journal of Industrial Relations* 36, 99-123.

Phillips, The Hon Mr Justice (1978) Some Notes on the Employment Appeal Tribunal *Industrial Law Journal* 7, 137-142.

Pitt, Gwyneth (1989) Dismissal at Common Law: the Relevance in Britain of American Developments *Modern Law Review* 52, 22-41.

Pitt, Gwyneth (1992) Can Reverse Discrimination be Justified?, in *Discrimination: the Limits of the Law* eds BA Hepple and Erika Szyszczak (Mansell, London).

Pitt, Gwyneth (1993) Justice in Dismissal: a Reply to Hugh Collins *Industrial Law Journal* 22, 251-268.

Pollard, David (1996) Insolvent Companies and TUPE *Industrial Law Journal*, 25, 191-210.

Pollard, David (2005) Pensions and TUPE *Industrial Law Journal* 34, 127-157.

Pollert, Anna (1991) *Farewell to Flexibility?* (Basil Blackwell, Oxford).

Pollock, Sir Frederick (1908) *Law of Torts* 8th edn (Stevens & Sons, London).

Pond, Chris, and Anna Searl (1991) *The Hidden Army: Children at Work in the 1990s* (Low Pay Unit, London).

Poole, Michael (1989) *The Origins of Economic Democracy* (Routledge, London).

Poole, Thomas (2000) Judicial Review and Public Employment: Decision-Making on the Public-Private Divide *Industrial Law Journal* 29, 61-67.

Popplewell, Sir Oliver (1987) Random Thoughts from the President's Chair *Industrial Law Journal* 16, 209-214.

Prechal, S (1996) Case note on Case C-450/93 *Kalanke v. Freie Hansestadt Bremen* [1995] ECR I-3051 *Common Market Law Review* 33, 1245-1259.

Price, Robert and George Sayers Bain (1976) Union Growth Revisited: 1948-1974 in Perspective *British Journal of Industrial Relations* 14, 339-355.

Puttick, Keith (1999) 2020: A Welfare Odyssey – A Commentary on Principles into Practice and the Reform Programme *Industrial Law Journal* 28, 190-196.

Raday, Frances (1997) Trials and Tribulations of *Associated Newspapers* in Foreign Forums *Industrial Law Journal* 26, 235-245.

Raday, Frances (2002) The Decline of Union Power – Structural Inevitability or Policy Choice? in *Labour Law in an Era of Glabalization: Transformative Practices and Possibilities* ed Joanne Conaghan, Richard Michael Fischl, and Karl Klare (Oxford University Press, Oxford).

Reynold, Frederic and Anya Palmer (2005) Proving Constructive Dismissal: Should One be Concerned With What Was in the Employer's Mind? *Industrial Law Journal* 34, 96-102.

Richardson, JH (1938) *Industrial Relations in Great Britain* 3rd edn (PS King, London).

Rideout, RW (2002) What shall we do with the CAC? *Industrial Law Journal* 31, 1-34.

Robbins, L (ed) (1978) *Trade Unions: Public Goods or Public 'Bads'* (Institute of Economic Affairs, London).

Rodgers, Gerry, and Janine Rodgers (eds) (1989) *Precarious Jobs in Labour Market Regulation The growth of atypical employment in Western Europe* (International Institute for Labour Studies, Geneva).

Rogaly, Joe (1977) *Grunwick* (Penguin, Harmondsworth).

Rogers, Joel, and Wolfgang Streeck (eds) (1995) *Works Councils: Consultation, Representation, and Cooperation in Industrial Relations* (University of Chicago Press, Chicago).

Rogowski, Ralf (1994) Industrial Relations, Labour Conflict Resolution and Reflexive Labour Law, in *Reflexive Labour Law* eds Ralf Rogowski and Ton Wilthagen (Kluwer, Deventer-Boston).

Rogowski, Ralf and Ton Wilthagen (1994) Reflexive Labour Law An Introduction, in *Reflexive Labour Law* eds Ralf Rogowski and Ton Wilthagen (Kluwer, Deventer-Boston).

Rojot, Jacques (1994) France, in *Strikes and Lock-outs in Industrialised Market Economies*, ed Ruth Ben-Israel (Kluwer, Deventer-Boston).

Rowe, JJ (2001) The Terrorism Act 2000 *Criminal Law Review* 527- 542.

Rowe, Nicola and Volker Schlette (1998) The Protection of Human Rights in Europe after the Eleventh Protocol to the ECHR *European Law Review* 23 HR, 3-16.

Royle, Tony (1999) Where's the Beef? McDonald's and its European Works Council *European Journal of Industrial Relations* 5, 327-347.

Rubery, Jill (1989) Precarious Forms of Work in the United Kingdom, in *Precarious Jobs in Labour Market Regulation* eds Gerry and Janine Rodgers (International Institute for Labour Studies, Geneva).

Rubery, Jill and Frank Wilkinson (1981) Outwork and Segmented Labour Markets, in *The Dynamics of Labour Market Segmentation* ed Frank Wilkinson (Academic Press, London).

Rubery, Jill, Simon Deakin and Sara Horrell (1994) United Kingdom, in *Times are Changing: Working Time in 14 Industrialised Countries* eds Gerhard Bosch, Peter Dawkins and Francois Michon (International Institute for Labour Studies, Geneva).

Rubery Jill, Roger Tarling and Frank Wilkinson (1987) Flexibility, Marketing and the Organisation of Production *Labour and Society* 12, 131-151.

Rubin, Gerry (1987) *War, Law and Labour* (Clarendon Press, Oxford).

Rubin, Gerry R (2000) The Historical Development of Collective Labour Law: The United Kingdom in *The Rise and Development of Collective Labour Law* ed Marcel van der Linden and Richard Price (Peter Lang, Bern).

Rubinstein, Michael (1988) *The Dignity of Women at Work* (Commmission of the European Communities, Brussels).

Ryan, Bernard (1997) Employer Enforcement of Immigration Law after Section Eight of the Asylum and Immigration Act *Industrial Law Journal*, 26, 136-148.

Sales, Philip (1990) Covenants Restricting Recruitment of Employees and the Doctrine of Restraint of Trade *Law Quarterly Review* 104, 600-616.

Sales, Philip and Daniel Stilitz (1999) Intentional Infliction of Harm by Unlawful Means *Law Quarterly Review* 115, 411-437.

Samuel, Lenia (1997) *Fundamental Social Rights: Case Law of the European Social Charter* (Council of Europe Publishing, Strasbourg).

Sargeant, Malcolm (1999) *Age Discrimination in Employment* (Institute of Employment Rights, London).

Sargeant, Malcolm (2003) Protecting Employees with Insolvent Employers *Industrial Law Journal* 32, 53-59.

Schiek, Dagmar (1996) Positive Action in Community Law *Industrial Law Journal* 25, 239-246.

Schiek, Dagmar (2000) Positive Action before the European Court of Justice – New Conceptions of Equality in Community Law? From *Kalanke* and *Marschall* to *Badeck, International Journal of Comparative Labour Law and Industrial Relations* 16, 251-275.

Schoer, Karl (1987) Part-time Employment: Britain and West Germany *Cambridge Journal of Economics* 11, 83-94.

Schumacher, Robert (1994) Business Transfers and Insolvency. Case-law of the German Federal Labour Court *Industrial Law Journal* 22, 101-107.

Scrutton, TE (1923) The Work of the Commercial Courts *Cambridge Law Journal* 1, 6-20.

Sedley, Stephen (1994) Public Law and Contractual Employment *Industrial Law Journal* 23, 201-208.

Selznick, Philip (1980) *Law, Society and Industrial Justice* (Transaction Books, New Brunswick).

Sengenberger, Werner (1994) Labour Standards: an Institutional Framework for Restructuring and Development, in *Creating Economic Opportunities: The Role of Labour Standards in Industrial Restructuring* eds Werner Sengenberger and Duncan Campbell (International Institute for Labour Studies, Geneva).

Sewerynski, Michal (ed) (2003) *Collective Agreements and Individual Contracts of Employment* (Kluwer Law International, The Hague)

Shaw, Jo (ed) (2000) *Social Law and Policy in an Evolving European Union* (Hart Publishing, Oxford).

Simester, AP and Winnie Chan (2004) Inducing Breach of Contract: One Tort or Two? *Cambridge Law Journal* 63, 132-165.

Simitis, Spiros (1987) Juridification of Labor Relations, in *Juridification of Social Spheres* ed Gunther Teubner (Walter de Gruyter, Berlin).

Simitis, Spiros (1991) Developments in the Protection of Workers' Personal Data *ILO Conditions of Work Digest* 10/2, 7-24.

Simitis, Spiros (1994) The Rediscovery of the Individual in Labour Law, in *Reflexive Labour Law* eds Ralf Rogowski and Ton Wilthagen (Kluwer, Deventer-Boston).

Simitis, Spiros (1998) From the General Rules on Data Protection to a Specific Regulation of the Use of Employee Data: Policies and Constraints of the European Union *Comparative Labor Law and Policy Journal* 19, 351-371.

Simon, Daphne (1954) Master and Servant, in *Democracy and the Labour Movement* ed J Saville (Lawrence and Wishart, London).

Simpson, Bob (1979) Judicial Review of ACAS *Industrial Law Journal* 8, 420-426.

Simpson, Bob (1987) The Labour Injunction, Unlawful Means and the Right to Strike *Modern Law Review* 50, 506-516.

Simpson, Bob (1989) The Summer of Discontent and the Law *Industrial Law Journal* 18, 234-241.

Simpson, Bob (1990) Code of Practice on Trade Union Ballots on Industrial Action *Industrial Law Journal* 19, 29-32.

Simpson, Bob (1991) *Trade Union Recognition and the Law* (Institute of Employment Rights, London).

Simpson, Bob (1993) Individualism versus Collectivism: an Evaluation of Section 14 of the Trade Union Reform and Employment Rights Act 1993 *Industrial Law Journal* 22, 181-193.

Simpson, Bob (1994) Bridlington '2' *Industrial Law Journal* 23, 170-174.

Simpson, Bob (1995) Code of Practice on Industrial Action Ballots and Notice to Employers *Industrial Law Journal* 24, 337-342.

Simpson, Bob (1999a) A Milestone in the Legal Regulation of Pay: The National Minimum Wage Act 1998 *Industrial Law Journal* 28, 1-32.

Simpson, Bob (1999b) Implementing the National Minimum Wage – The 1999 Regulations *Industrial Law Journal* 28, 171-182.

Simpson, Bob (2000) Trade Union Recognition and the Law, a New Approach – Parts I and II of Schedule A1 to the Trade Union and Labour Relations (Consolidation) Act 1992, *Industrial Law Journal* 29, 193-222.

Simpson, Bob (2001) Code of Practice on Industrial Action Ballots and Notice to Employers 2000 *Industrial Law Journal* 30, 194-198.

Simpson, Bob (2004) The National Minimum Wage Five Years On: Reflections on Some General Issues *Industrial Law Journal* 33, 22-41.

Sims, Vanessa (2001) Is Employment a Fiduciary Relationship? *Industrial Law Journal* 30, 101-110.

Singh, Rabinder, Murray Hunt and Marie Demetriou (1999) Is there a Role for the "Margin of Appreciation" in National Law after the Human Rights Act? *European Human Rights Law Review*, 15-22.

Sinzheimer, Hugo (1910-11) Die Fortentwicklung des Arbeitsrechts und die Aufgabe der Rechtslehre *Soziale Praxis* 20, 1237.

Skidmore, Paul (1995a) No Gays in the Military – Lawrence of Arabia Need Not Apply *Industrial Law Journal* 24, 363-368.

Skidmore, Paul (1995b) Enforcement of Rights to Worker Representation in Community Law *Modern Law Review* 58, 744-751.

Skidmore, Paul (1996a) Homosexuals have Human Rights Too *Industrial Law Journal* 25, 63-65.

Skidmore, Paul (1996b) Worker Rights – A Euro-litigation strategy? *Industrial Law Journal* 25, 225-230.

Skidmore, Paul (1999) Dress to Impress: Employer Regulation of Gay and Lesbian Appearance *Social and Legal Studies* 8, 509-29.

Skidmore, Paul (2001) EC Framework Directive on Equal Treatment in Employment: Toward a Comprehensive Community Anti-Discrimination Policy? *Industrial Law Journal* 30, 126-32.

Sly, Frances and Darren Stillwell (1997) Temporary Workers in Great Britain *Labour Market Trends* September, 347-354.

Smith, Adam [1776] (1886) *An Inquiry into the Nature and Causes of the Wealth of Nations* With an Introductory Essay and Notes by Joseph S Nicholson (Nelson, London).

Smith, ATH (1987) *The Offences against Public Order* (Sweet and Maxwell, London).

Smith, Graham (1989) Part Work, No Pay? The Obligation to Pay Wages for Part Performance of Contracts of Employment *Australian Journal of Labour Law* 2, 91-106.

Smith, IT and GH Thomas (2003) *Smith and Wood's Industrial Law*, 8th edn (LexisNexis UK, London).

Smith, J, P Edwards and M Hall (1999) *Redundancy Consultation: A Study of Current Practice and the Effects of the 1999 Regulations* (DTI, Employment Relations Research Series No 5, London).

Smith, Sir John (2002) *Smith and Hogan Criminal Law* 10th edn (LexisNexis UK, London).

Smith, Paul and Gary Morton (2001) New Labour's Reform of Britain's Employment Law: The Devil's Not Only in the Detail but in the Values and Policy Too *British Journal of Industrial Relations* 39, 119-138.

Smith, Paul, Patricia Fosh, Roderick Martin, Huw Morris and Roger Undy (1993) Ballots and Union Government in the 1980s *British Journal of Industrial Relations* 31, 365-382.

Smith, Raymond, and Valerie Cromack (1993) International Employment Contracts – the Applicable Law *Industrial Law Journal* 22, 1-13.

Smith, Stephen (1986) *Britain's Shadow Economy* (Clarendon Press, Oxford).

Sooben, Philip A (1990) *The Origins of the Race Relations Act 1976* Research Papers in Ethnic Relations No 12 (Centre for Research in Ethnic Studies, University of Warwick).

Spaak (1956) *Rapport des chefs de délégation aux ministres des affaires étrangères* (Comité Intergouvernmental créé par la Conférence de Messine, Brussels).

Spain, Jonathan (1991) Trade Unionists, Gladstonian Liberals, and the Labour Law Reforms of 1875, in *Currents of Radicalism Popular Radicalism, Organised Labour and Party Politics in Britain 1850-1914* eds Eugenio F Biagini and Alistair J Reid (CUP, Cambridge).

Spencer, John (1973) Signature, Consent and the Rule in *L'Estrange v Graucob, Cambridge Law Journal* 32, 104-122.

Spencer, JR (1989) Public Nuisance – A Critical Examination *Cambridge Law Journal* 48, 55-84.

Spry, ICF (2001) *The Principles of Equitable Remedies* 6th edn (Sweet and Maxwell, London).

Stacey, Mary, and Andrew Short (2000) *Challenging Disability Discrimination at Work* (Institute of Employment Rights, London)

Stanton, Keith, Paul Skidmore and Michael Harris (2002) *Statutory Torts* (Sweet and Maxwell, London).

Stanworth, J and Stanworth, C (1989) Hometruths about Teleworking *Personnel Management*, November.

Steinfeld, Robert (2001) *Coercion, Contract and Free Labor in the Nineteenth Century* (CUP, Cambridge).

Stewart, Margaret (1969) *Britain and the ILO: The Story of Fifty Years* (HMSO, London).

Streeck, Wolfgang (1988) Comment on 'Rigidities in the Labour Market' *Government and Opposition* 23, 413-23.

Streeck, Wolfgang (1992) *Social Institutions and Economic Performance: Studies of Industrial Relations in Advanced Capitalist Economies* (Sage, London).

Streeck, Wolfgang (1995) Neo-Voluntarism: A New European Social Policy Régime *European Law Journal* 1, 31-59.

Street, Harry, Geoffrey Howe and Geoffrey Bindman (1967) *Report on Anti-Discrimination Legislation* (Political and Economic Planning, London).

Streit, Manfred, and Werner Mussler (1995) The Economic Constitution of the European Community: From 'Rome' to 'Maastricht' *European Law Journal* 1, 5-30.

Stuart, Mark and Miguel Martinez-Lucio (eds) (2005) *Partnership and Modernisation in Employment Relations* (Routledge, London).

Summers, Clyde (1969) Collective Agreements and the Law of Contracts *Yale Law Journal* 90, 537-575.

Supiot, Alain (1994) *Critique du Droit du Travail* (PUF, Paris).

Supiot, Alain (ed) (1999) *Au-delà de l'emploi: Transformations du travail et l'avenir du droit du travail en Europe. Rapport pour la Commission Europeénne* (Flammarion, Paris).

Supiot, Alain (2001) The Dogmatic Foundations of the Market *Industrial Law Journal* 29, 321-345.

Supiot, Alain (2005) *Homo juridicus: Essai sur la fonction anthropologique du droit* (Seuil, Paris).

Supperstone, Michael (1997) The Ambit of Judicial Review, in *Judicial Review* ed Michael Supperstone and James Goudie, 2nd edn (Butterworths, London).

Sweeney, Kate (1997) Labour disputes in 1996 *Labour Market Trends* June, 217-229.

Sweet and Maxwell's Encyclopaedia of Employment Law, 1992, as updated (Sweet and Maxwell, London).

Swepston, Lee (1997) Supervision of ILO Standards *International Journal of Comparative Labour Law and Industrial Relations* 13, 327-344.

Swepston, Lee (2004) International Labour Law, in *Comparative Labour Law and Industrial Relations in Industrialised Market Economies* 8th edn, ed Roger Blanpain (Kluwer Law International, The Hague).

Szyszczak, Erika (1985) Pay Inequalities and Equal Value Claims *Modern Law Review* 48, 139-157.

Szyszczak, Erika (1986) Employment Protection and Social Security, in *Labour Law in Britain* (Basil Blackwell, Oxford).

Szyszczak, Erika (1990) *Partial Unemployment The Regulation of Short-Time Working in Britain* (Mansell, London).

Szyszczak, Erika (1999) The Working Environment v. Internal Market *European Law Review* 24, 196-201.

Szyszczak, Erika (2000a) *EC Labour Law* (Longman, Harlow).

Szyszczak, Erika (2000b) The Evolving European Employment Strategy, in *Social Law and Policy in an Evolving European Union* ed Jo Shaw (Oxford, Hart).

Tarling, Roger, and Frank Wilkinson (1977) The Social Contract: Post-war Incomes Policies and their Inflationary Impact *Cambridge Journal of Economics* 1, 395-414.

Tarling, Roger, and Frank Wilkinson (1982) The Movement of Real Wages and the Development of Collective Bargaining in the UK: 1855-1920 *Contributions to Political Economy* 1, 1-35.

Taylor, Robert (1994) *The Future of the Trade Unions* (Andre Deutsch, London).

Taylor, Robert (2000) *The TUC: From the General Strike to New Unionism* (Palgrave, Basingstoke).

Taylor, Robert (no date given) *Britain's World of Work – Myths and Realities* (ESRC, Swindon).

Taylor, Robert (2004) *Partnerships at Work: The Way to Corporate Renewal?* (ESRC, Swindon).

Terry, Michael (1994) Workplace Unionism: Redefining Structures and Objectives, in *New Frontiers in European Industrial Relations*, eds Richard Hyman and Anthony Ferner (Blackwell, Oxford).

Terry, Michael (2003) Employee Representation: Shop Stewards and the New Legal Framework, in *Industrial Relations: Theory and Practice* 2nd edn, ed Paul Edwards (Blackwell, Oxford).

Tether, Melanie (1995) Sex Equality and Occupational Pension Schemes *Industrial Law Journal* 24, 194-203.

Thomas, Melanie (2000) Equal Pay and Redundancy Schemes *Industrial Law Journal* 29, 68-72.

Thurman, J and G Trah (1990) Part-time Work in International Perspective *International Labour Review* 129, 23-40.

Tierney, Stephen (1998) Press Freedom and Public Interest *European Human Rights Law Review*, 419-429.

Tillyard, FW (1928) *Industrial Law* 2nd edn (A & C Black, London).

Tiraboschi, Michele (1999) Glancing at the Past: An Agreement for the Markets of the XXIst Century *International Journal of Comparative Labour Law and Industrial Relations* 15, 105-119.

Todd, Paul (2000) Action Short of Dismissal, in *Legal Regulation of the Employment Relation* eds Hugh Collins, Paul Davies and Roger Rideout (Kluwer, London).

Tomlins, Christopher L (1993) *Law, Labour and Ideology in the Early American Republic* (CUP, Cambridge).

Toulson, RG and CM Phipps (1996) *Confidentiality* (Sweet and Maxwell, London).

Towers, Brian (1997) *The Representation Gap: Change and Reform in the British and American Workplace* (Oxford University Press, Oxford).

Towers, Brian (1999) *Developing Recognition and Representation in the UK: How Useful is the US Model?* (Institute of Employment Rights, London).

Towers, Brian and William Brown (2000) *Employment Relations in Britain: 25 Years of the Advisory, Conciliation and Arbitration Service* (Blackwell, Oxford).

Townley, Barbara (1987) Union Recognition: A Comparative Analysis of the Pros and Cons of a Legal Procedure *British Journal of Industrial Relations* 25, 177-199.

Townshend-Smith, Richard (1991) Refusal of Employment on Grounds of Trade Union Membership or Non-Membership: The Employment Act 1990 *Industrial Law Journal*, 20, 102-112.

Townshend-Smith, Richard (2000) Seymour-Smith: the Closing Stages *Industrial Law Journal* 29, 296-304.

Trades Union Congress (1993) *TUC Disputes: Principles and Procedures* (TUC, London).

Trades Union Congress (1995) *Your Voice at Work* (TUC, London).

Treitel, GH (2003) *The Law of Contract* 11th edn (Sweet & Maxwell/Stevens and Sons, London).

Tsogas, George (2000) Labour Standards in the Generalised Systems of Preferences of the European Union & the United States *European Journal of Industrial Relations* 6, 349-370.

Turnbull, Peter (1991) Labour Market Deregulation and Economic Performance: the Case of Britain's Docks *Work, Employment and Society* 5, 17-35.

Turner, Adair (2001) *Just Capital* (Macmillan, London).

Turner, HA (1962) *Trade Union Growth, Structure and Policy* (Allen and Unwin, London).

Undy, Roger (1999) The British Merger Movement: the Importance of the "Aggressive" Unions *Industrial Relations Journal* 30, 464-481.

Undy, Roger and Roderick Martin (1984) *Ballots and Trade Union Democracy* (Basil Blackwell, Oxford).

Undy, Roger, Patricia Fosh, Huw Morris, Paul Smith and Roderick Martin (1996) *Managing the Unions: The Impact of Legislation on Trade Unions' Behaviour* (Clarendon Press, Oxford).

Upex, Robert (1999) The Acquired Rights Directive and its Effect Upon Consensual Variation of Employees Contracts *European Law Review* 24, 293-299.

Upex, Robert (2001) *The Law of Termination of Employment* 6th edn (Sweet and Maxwell, London).

Valticos, Nicolas and Geraldo von Potobsky (1995) *International Labour Law* (Kluwer, Deventer-Boston).

Van Dijk, Pieter and GJH Van Hoof (1998) *Theory and Practice of the European Convention on Human Rights*, 3rd edn (Kluwer, The Hague).

Vickers, Lucy (1995) *Protecting Whistleblowers at Work* (Institute of Employment Rights, London).

Vickers, Lucy (2002) *Freedom of Speech and Employment* (OUP, Oxford).

Vickers, Lucy (2003) The Employment Equality (Religion or Belief) Regulations 2003 *Industrial Law Journal* 32, 188-193.

Villiars, Charlotte (2000) The Rover Case (1) – The Sale of Rover Cars by BMW – The Role of the Works Council *Industrial Law Journal* 29, 386-394.

Vogel-Polsky, Eliane (1986) The Problem of Unemployment, in *The Making of Labour Law in Europe* ed BA Hepple (Mansell, London).

Vogel-Polsky, Eliane (1990) What Future is there for a Social Europe following the Strasbourg Summit? *Industrial Law Journal* 19, 65-80.

Von Prondzynski, Ferdinand (1987) *Freedom of Association and Industrial Relations: A Comparative Study* (Mansell, London).

Vousden, Stephen (2000) Albany, Market Law and Social Exclusion *Industrial Law Journal* 29, 181-191.

Waddington, Jeremy (2003a) Heightening Tension in Relations between Trade Unions and the Labour Government in 2002 *British Journal of Industrial Relations* 41, 335-358.

Waddington, Jeremy (2003b) Trade Union Organization, in *Industrial Relations: Theory and Practice* 2nd edn ed Paul Edwards (Blackwell Publishing, Oxford).

Waddington, Jeremy (2003c) What do Representatives Think of the Practices of European Works Councils? Views from Six Countries *European Journal of Industrial Relations* 9, 303-325.

Waddington, Jeremy and Colin Whitson (1995) Trade Unions: Growth, Structure and Policy in *Industrial Relations: Theory and Practice in Britain*, ed. Paul Edwards (Blackwell Business, Oxford).

Waddington, Lisa (1999) Testing the Limits of the EC Treaty Article on Non-Discrimination *Industrial Law Journal* 28, 133-151.

Waddington, Lisa (2000) Article 13 EC: Setting Priorities in the Proposal for a Horizontal Employment Directive *Industrial Law Journal* 29, 176-181.

Wade, HWR (1993) Visitors and Errors of Law *Law Quarterly Review* 109, 155-159.

Wade, HWR (2000) Horizons of Horizontality *Law Quarterly Review* 116, 217-224.

Wade, HWR, and Christopher Forsyth (2004) *Administrative Law* 9th edn (Clarendon Press, Oxford).

Waite, Sir John (1986) Lawyers and Laymen as Judges in Industry *Industrial Law Journal* 15, 32-41.

Walsh, Janet and William Brown (1990) *Regional Earnings and Pay Flexibility* Department of Applied Economics Working Paper 9008 (University of Cambridge).

Walters, David R (1990) *Worker Participation in Health and Safety: A European Comparison* (Institute of Employment Rights, London).

Wareing, M (1992) Working Arrangements and Patterns of Working Hours in Britain *Employment Gazette* 100, 88-100.

Watson, Loraine (1995) Employees and the Unfair Contract Terms Act *Industrial Law Journal* 24, 323-336.

Watt, Robert A (1992) HIV, Discrimination, Unfair Dismissal and Pressure to Dismiss *Industrial Law Journal* 23, 280-292.

Watt, Robert A (1998) Goodbye 'But-for', Hello 'But-Why?' *Industrial Law Journal* 27, 121-132.

Weatherill, Stephen (2001) Breach of Directives and Breach of Contract *European Law Review* 26, 177-186.

Webb, Sidney and Beatrice Webb (1920) *The History of Trade Unionism* New edition (Longmans, Green and Co, London).

Webb, Sidney and Beatrice Webb [1898] (1920) *Industrial Democracy* (Longmans, Green and Co, London).

Weber, Tina, Peter Foster, and Kursat Levent Egriboz (2000) *Costs and Benefits of the European Works Councils Directive* (DTI Employment Relations Research Series No 9, London).

Wedderburn, Lord (1980) Industrial Relations and the Courts *Industrial Law Journal* 9, 65-94.

Wedderburn, Lord (1983) Otto Kahn-Freund and British Labour Law, in *Labour Law and Industrial Relations: Building on Kahn-Freund* eds Lord Wedderburn, Roy Lewis and Jonathan Clark (Basil Blackwell, Oxford).

Wedderburn, Lord (1984) Labour Law Now – a Hold and a Nudge *Industrial Law Journal* 13, 73-85.

Wedderburn, Lord (1985) The New Politics of Labour Law, in *Trade Unions* 2nd edn, ed WEJ McCarthy (Penguin, Harmondsworth).

Wedderburn, Lord (1986) *The Worker and the Law* 3rd edn (Penguin, Harmondsworth).

Wedderburn, Lord (1987a) Labour Law: From Here to Autonomy? *Industrial Law Journal* 16, 1-29.

Wedderburn, Lord (1987b) Freedom of Association or Right to Organise? *Industrial Relations Journal* 18, 244-254.

Wedderburn, Lord (1989) Freedom of Association and Philosophies of Labour Law *Industrial Law Journal* 18, 1-38.

Wedderburn, Lord (1990) *The Social Charter, European Company and employment rights: An outline agenda* (Institute of Employment Rights, London).

Wedderburn, Lord (1991a) The Social Charter in Britain – Labour Law and Labour Courts *Modern Law Review* 54, 1-47.

Wedderburn, Lord (1991b) *Employment Rights in Britain and Europe: Selected Papers in Labour Law* (Lawrence and Wishart, London).

Wedderburn, Lord (1992a) European Community Law and Workers' Rights after 1992: Fact or Fake? *Dublin University Law Journal* 13, 1-25.

Wedderburn, Lord (1992b) Contempt of Court: Vicarious Liability of Companies and Unions *Industrial Law Journal* 21, 51-58.

Wedderburn, Lord (1992c) Inderogability, Collective Agreements, and Community Law *Industrial Law Journal* 21, 245-264.

Wedderburn, Lord (1993) Companies and Employees: Common Law or Social Dimension? *Law Quarterly Review* 109, 220-262.

Wedderburn Lord (1995) *Labour Law and Freedom: Further Essays in Labour Law*, (Lawrence and Wishart, London).

Wedderburn, Lord (1997) Consultation and Collective Bargaining in Europe: Success or Ideology? *Industrial Law Journal* 26, 1-34.

Wedderburn, Lord (2000) Collective Bargaining or Legal Enactment? The 1999 Act and Union Recognition *Industrial Law Journal* 29, 1-42

Wedderburn, Lord (2001) Underground Labour Injunctions *Industrial Law Journal* 30, 206-214.

Wedderburn, Lord (2004) *The Future of Company Law: Fat Cats, Corporate Governance and Workers* (Institute of Employment Rights, London)

Wedderburn, KW (Lord) and PL Davies (1969) *Employment Grievances and Disputes Procedures in Britain* (University of California Press, Berkeley and Los Angeles).

Wedderburn, Lord, and Silvana Sciarra (1988) Collective Bargaining as Agreement and as Law: Neo-Contractualist and Neo-Corporative Tendencies of our Age, in *Law in the Making* ed A Pizzorusso (Springer, Berlin).

Weekes, Brian, Michael Mellish, Linda Dickens and John Lloyd (1975) *Industrial Relations and the Limits of Law; The Industrial Effects of the Industrial Relations Act 1971* (Blackwell, Oxford).

Weiler, Paul (1983) Promises to Keep: Securing Workers' Rights to Self-Organization under the NLRA *Harvard Law Review* 96, 1769-1827.

Weir, Tony (1991) Physician – Kill Thyself! *Cambridge Law Journal* 50, 397-399.

Weir, Tony (1997) *Economic Torts* (Clarendon Press, Oxford).

Weiss, Manfred (1992) *European Employment and Industrial Relations Glossary – Germany* European Foundation for the Improvement of Living and Working Conditions (Sweet & Maxwell, London/OOPEC, Luxembourg).

Weiss, Manfred (1994) Germany, in *Strikes and Lock-outs in Industrialised Market Economies* ed R Ben Israel (Kluwer, Deventer-Boston).

Weiss, Manfred (2004) The Future of Workers' Participation in the EU, in *The Future of Labour Law: Liber Amicorum Sir Bob Hepple QC* ed Catherine Barnard, Simon Deakin and Gillian S Morris (Hart Publishing, Oxford).

Weitzman, Martin (1983) *The Share Economy. Conquering Stagflation* (Harvard University Press, Cambridge MA).

Wheeler, Sally (1997) Works Council: Towards Stakeholding? *Journal of Law and Society* 24, 44-64.

Whelan, Christopher J (1982) On Uses and Misuses of Comparative Labour Law: A Case Study *Modern Law Review* 45, 285-300.

White, M and J Lakey (1992) *The Restart Effect: Does Active Labour Market Policy Reduce Unemployment?* (Policy Studies Institute, London).

White, Richard (1997) Repudiatory Breach and the Definition of Dismissal *Industrial Law Journal* 26, 252-258.

White, Richard (1998) Waiver of Statutory Rights in Fixed Term Contracts *Industrial Law Journal*, 27, 238-244.

White, Stuart (1999) Rights and Responsibilities: A Social Democratic Perspective, *Political Quarterly* 70, 166-186.

Whiteford, Elaine (1993) Social Policy after Maastricht *European Law Review*, 202-222.

Wikeley, NJ (1989a) Migrant Workers and Unemployment Benefit in the European Community *Journal of Social Welfare Law*, 300-315.

Wikeley, NJ (1989b) Unemployment Benefit, the State and the Labour Market *Journal of Law and Society* 16, 291-309.

Wikeley, NJ (1990) Training for Employment in the 1990s *Modern Law Review* 53, 354-368.

Wikeley, NJ (2002) *Wikeley, Ogus and Barendt's The Law of Social Security* 5th edn (Butterworths, London).

Wilkinson, Brian (1991) The Irish Industrial Relations Act 1990 – Corporatism and Conflict Control *Industrial Law Journal* 20, 21-37.

Wilkinson, Frank (1987) Deregulation, Structured Labour Markets and Unemployment, in *Unemployment: Theory, Policy and Structure* eds P Pedersen and R Lund (Walter de Gruyter, Berlin).

Wilkinson, Frank (1991) *Why Britain Needs a Minimum Wage* (Institute of Public Policy Research, London).

Wilkinson, Frank (1995) Changing Notions of Unemployment and what they Mean for the Poor. Paper presented to the Annual Conference of the International Working Party on Labour Market Segmentation, University of Siena.

Williams, David W (1982) *Social Security Taxation* (Sweet and Maxwell, London).

Williams, Glanville (1941) Partial Performance of Entire Contracts *Law Quarterly Review*, 57, 373-389, 490-511.

Williams, Glanville (1960) The Effect of Penal Legislation in the Law of Tort *Modern Law Review*, 23, 233-259.

Williams, Kevin (1983) Unfair Dismissal: Myths and Statistics *Industrial Law Journal* 12, 157-165.

Williams, Kevin and David Lewis (1981) The Aftermath of Tribunal Reinstatement and Re-engagement, Department of Employment Research Paper No 23.

Willman, Paul, Tim Morris, and Beverly Aston (1993) *Union Business* (Cambridge University Press, Cambridge).

Wintemute, Robert (1997a) Recognising New Kinds of Direct Sex Discrimination: Transsexualism, Sexual Orientation and Dress Codes *Modern Law Review* 60, 334-359.

Wintemute, Robert (1997b) *Sexual Orientation and Human Rights: the United States Constitution, the European Convention and the Canadian Charter* (Clarendon Press, Oxford).

Wintemute, Robert (1998) When is Pregnancy Discrimination Indirect Discrimination? *Industrial Law Journal* 27, 23-36.

Wood, Penny (1978) The Central Arbitration Committee's Approach to Schedule 11 to the Employment Protection Act 1975 and the Fair Wages Resolution 1946 *Industrial Law Journal* 7, 65-83.

Wood, Sir John (1990) The Employment Appeal Tribunal as it Enters the 1990s *Industrial Law Journal* 19, 133-141.

Wood, Sir John (1992) Dispute Resolution – Conciliation, Mediation and Arbitration in *Legal Intervention in Industrial Relations: Gains and Losses,* ed William McCarthy (Blackwell, Oxford).

Wood, Stephen and John Godard (1999) The Statutory Union Recognition Procedure in the Employment Relations Bill: A Comparative Analysis *British Journal of Industrial Relations* 37, 203-244.

Wood, Stephen, Sian Moore and Keith Ewing (2003) The impact of the trade union recognition procedure under the Employment Relations Act, 2000-2 in *Representing Workers: Trade Union Recognition and Membership in Britain* ed Howard Gospel and Stephen Wood (Routledge, London).

Wood, Stephen, Sian Moore and Paul Willman (2002) Third Time Lucky for Statutory Union Recognition in the UK? *Industrial Relations Journal* 33, 215-233.

Woods, DC (1982) The Operation of the Master and Servant Acts in the Black Country *Midland History* 7, 93-115.

Woolf, The Rt Hon Lord Justice (1986) Public Law – Private Law: Why the Divide? A Personal View *Public Law*, 220-238.

Woolf, The Rt Hon Lord Woolf of Barnes (1995) Droit Public – English Style *Public Law*, 57-71.

Wright, Martyn (1996) The Collapse of Compulsory Unionism? Collective Organisation in Highly Unionised British Companies 1979-1991 *British Journal of Industrial Relations* 34, 497-513.

Wynn, Michael (1999) Pregnancy Discrimination: Equality, Protection or Reconciliation? *Modern Law Review* 62, 435-447.

Wynn-Evans, Charles (2005) Self Incrimination in English Employment Law *Industrial Law Journal* 178-182.

Young, Thom (1976) *Incitement to Disaffection* (The Cobden Trust, London).

Younson, F (1989) *Employment Law and Business Transfers A Practical Guide* (Sweet and Maxwell, London).

Zabalza, A and Z Tzannatos (1985) *Women and Equal Pay. The effects of legislation on female employment and wages in Britain* (CUP, Cambridge).

Index

Terms of employment–*contd*
  implied–*contd*
    trade usage, 4.32
    transactions, giving effect to, 4.6
  incorporation, 4.12
  job classification clause, 4.34
  job security clauses
    benefits of, 5.31
    damages for breach of, 5.31
    enforcement of, 5.32
    guarantee, as, 5.31
    incorporation into contract, 5.34
    legal effect, 5.33-5.40, 5.47
    notice rule, relation to, 5.41-5.43
    obstacle to effectiveness of, 5.41
    restriction on employer's right to give
      notice, as, 5.43
    specific relief for, 5.46
    whether intended to have legal
      effect, 5.34
  minimum standards, 4.10
  minimum wage, as to, 4.9
  mobility clause, 4.34
  new, dismissal and re-employment on,
    4.39
  notice periods, as to, 4.9
  protective rights taking effect as, 4.10
  refusal to abide by, 4.38
  restrictive covenants, 4.96
  sources of, 4.2
  statute and collective bargaining,
    regulation by, 4.9-4.12
  variation
    agreement, by, 4.34
    collective agreement, by, 4.36-4.38
    expiry of contractual notice, after,
      5.43
    reservation of right, 4.34
    unfair dismissal legislation, challenge
      by, 5.71
    unilateral, 4.34
    written statement, by reference to,
      4.35
  wages and salaries *see* Wages
  works rules, 4.33
  written statement of
    calculation of pay, methods of, 4.32
    change of particulars, for, 4.20
    company handbooks, 4.33
    contract distinguished, 4.24
    contract terms, as strong prima facie
      evidence of, 4.24
    declaratory, being, 4.24
    disciplinary and grievance
      procedures, rules concerning,
      4.18
    evidence of terms, as, 4.24
    failure to comply with requirements,
      4.21
    holidays, particulars of, 4.22
    issue of, 4.19
    limited normative effect of
      provisions, 4.22, 4.23

Terms of employment–*contd*
  written statement of–*contd*
    mandatory and non-mandatory
      terms, 4.22
    new, offer of, 4.24
    normative effect of, 4.24
    reasonable accessible document,
      information in, 4.17
    reference document, right to invoke,
      4.14, 4.33
    requirement of, 1.19
    right to, 4.13
    scope of, 4.14-4.21
    separate document, information in,
      4.16
    single document, information in,
      4.15, 4.33
    statutory provisions, 4.14
    timing of notification, 4.19
    variation of terms by reference to,
      4.35
Tort
  breach of contract, inducing, 1.8
  conspiracy, of, 1.5, 1.8
  economic, expansion of, 1.8
  industrial action, liability for *see*
    Industrial action
  intimidation, of, 1.8
  trade union, liability of *see* Trade unions
Trade boards
  establishment of, 4.41, 7.15
  expansion of system, 1.14
  setting up, 1.12
  Wages Councils, becoming, 4.41
Trade dispute
  act in contemplation or furtherance of
    immunity from action in tort, 11.24
    purpose in acting, test of, 11.29
    submission to demands, 11.29
    timing, 11.29
  arbitration, 1.12
  concept of, 11.25—11.28
  conciliation, 1.12
  definition, 1.8, 11.6, 11.25
    extension of, 11.7
  formula, narrowing, 1.25
  furthering, 11.7
  immunity in tort, 11.6
    economic torts, covering, 1.8
    formula for, 1.7
    judicial outflanking, 1.8
    legislative restrictions on, 1.8
    literal construction of, 1.8
  matters occurring outside UK, as to,
    11.28
  national curriculum, as to elements of,
    11.28
  objects to which relating 11.27
  parties to, 11.26
  political objective, 11.28
  purposes of, 11.27, 11.28
  restrictive legal intervention, removal
    of, 1.8